INDUSTRIES OTHER THAN FINANCIAL SERVICES

FINANCIAL SERVICE INDUSTRIES

THE PROFESSION AND ITS ENVIRONMENT

HANDBOOK OF ACCOUNTING AND AUDITING

SECOND EDITION

Editors

ROBERT S. KAY, CPA
Senior Partner
Touche Ross & Co.

D. GERALD SEARFOSS, DBA, CPA
Director, Accounting Standards
Touche Ross & Co.

with

BRUCE N. WILLIS, CPA
ALFRED M. YATES, CPA

WG
&
L

WARREN, GORHAM & LAMONT
Boston • New York

HF
5635
H22
1989

This publication is designed to provide accurate and authoritative information in regard to the subject matter covered. In publishing this book, neither the authors nor the publisher is engaged in rendering legal, accounting, or other professional service. If legal, accounting, or other expert assistance is required, the services of a competent professional should be sought.

Preface

Purpose of the *Handbook*

The original edition of the *Handbook* was written at the beginning of this decade as a resource for the financial executive and professional auditor in coping with a multiplicity of sources affecting their day-to-day problems; and it was written for those less intimately involved in the profession, who faced an even greater barrier in penetrating the tangle of accounting, auditing, and regulatory agency requirements.

We think the first edition served that need well by providing a comprehensive, understandable reference source—practical and authoritative, with ample references to the professional literature. This was accomplished by using the resources of Touche Ross & Co. in combination with outside experts. The result was the best possible contemporary coverage in a comprehensive and cross-referenced work, reworked and edited over a period of two years into a consistent style and depth.

The first edition contained seven major sections into which forty-nine chapters of complementary content were grouped. This second edition continues that approach, but the sections have been modified to reflect major shifts in the profession and the economy in the past eight years, a large part of which was covered in annual *Updates*. This volume contains fifty chapters in the following six sections:

- **Part I** deals with general issues of accounting measurement and disclosure.
- **Part II** provides an overview of auditing concepts and procedures.
- **Part III** covers the major areas of financial accounting, reporting, and auditing in general, as they exist today (and often with a prognosis about the future). This section includes chapters on the components of financial statements organized as much as possible according to the typical business-transaction flow. Also included are chapters on financial instruments and transactions, future-oriented information, and bankruptcy, reorganization, and restructuring.
- **Part IV** deals with accounting and auditing in eleven specialized industries—including smaller and emerging businesses—reflecting the accounting profession's greatly increased emphasis on industry practice. The original *Handbook* had only four chapters.
- **Part V** provides a comprehensive one-source coverage of the financial service industries—perhaps the most important development in the United States economy in recent years. Banks, thrifts, securities, commodities, insurance, mutual funds, venture capital, real estate investment trusts, finance companies, and credit unions are all covered in these five chapters. The first edition had only one chapter.

• **Part VI** discusses and analyzes the profession's institutions and its environment. Covered are the profession itself, as well as the FASB, SEC, and IRS. In addition, a legal environment chapter makes for sober reading. The *Handbook* closes with a discussion of the research process in the practice arm of the profession.

Why This *Handbook* Is So Large

When designing the second edition coverage, we were confronted with the fact that accounting and auditing information has exponentially expanded in the past seven years; indeed, the continually increasing size of the annual *Updates* has provided clear proof. Since publication of the first edition, there have been 58 additional statements issued by the FASB, 28 statements issued by the Auditing Standards Board, and numerous interpretations and bulletins to explain the new pronouncements. The SEC also has been most active, recodifying its ASRs into two new series, and issuing over 60 new releases and staff accounting bulletins. Last but certainly not least, the Emerging Issues Task Force—new since the first edition—has addressed nearly 200 specific issues. This deluge has been daunting for the professional practitioner regularly immersed in these subjects; for others, especially persons outside the public accounting profession, the onslaught may seem entrancing (literally) and some of the pronouncements inscrutable.

Although the availability of the cumulative *Update* eased the effort of identifying current *Handbook* topics, the velocity of change in our profession necessitated that we adopt a clean slate approach in all but a few chapters. This has resulted in the truncation, elimination, or recombination of much of the content of the first edition. In particular, the second edition emphasizes industries; and new and novel financial instruments, hardly visible in the first edition, occupy an entire chapter in this edition, with prominent mention in many more.

Constant change now seems to be the norm. Although this *Handbook* has been updated to within 120 days of publication additional changes will have occurred by the time it is published. To provide readers with the most up-to-date reference book possible, we will continue our practice of preparing a periodic *Update*, containing a cumulative index that is integrated with the index in this *Handbook*.

Where Credit Is Due

Without the efforts of many experts, there would be no *Handbook of Accounting and Auditing*. The initial recognition must, of course, go to Sandy Burton for conceptualizing the first edition of the *Handbook* in 1978, and to Russ Palmer for his willingness to commit Touche Ross resources to a project that took many times longer than original estimates. In addition, Sandy and Russ enlisted a stellar group of outside authors to augment the many Touche Ross partners and staff who spent more than 17,000 hours on the project. The first edition outside authors are listed below.

A. Rashad abdel-Khalik
University of Florida

Bipin B. Ajinkya
University of Florida

Michael O. Alexander
Gordon Capital Corp.

Marshall S. Armstrong
Former Chairman, FASB

Victor H. Brown
Member, FASB

John C. Burton
Columbia University

Edward B. Deakin III
University of Texas

Patricia Fairfield
*Baruch College,
City University of New York*

Oscar S. Gellein
Former Member, FASB

R. James Gormlet
Bell, Boyd & Lloyd

Ronald D. Greenberg
Columbia University

David D. Hale
Kemper Financial Services, Inc.

Emerson O. Henke
Baylor University

Gerald W. Hepp
Plante & Moran

Arthur L. Litke
Former Member, FASB

James K. Loebbecke
University of Utah

Harvey L. Pitt
Freid, Frank, Harris, Shriver & Jacobson

Jack C. Robertson
University of Texas

Leonard M. Savoie
University of Notre Dame

James H. Schropp
Freid, Frank, Harris, Shriver & Jacobson

Gordon Shillinglaw
Columbia University

David Solomons
University of Pennsylvania

Miklos A. Vasarhelyi
AT&T Bell Laboratories

This second edition has been prepared entirely by Touche Ross partners and staff (and an alumnus), building on the foundation of the first edition. In many chapters, the principal work was performed by the "editor group" consisting of the undersigned, Bruce Willis (recently of the FASB staff and previously of Touche Ross), and Al Yates, Client Service Manager at Touche Ross. As noted earlier, a very large part of this edition covers new topics, or gives in-depth coverage to areas that required only brief mention in the first edition. This expansion and refocus also required the extensive efforts of the many persons named below (all of Touche Ross except as noted); we express our sincere appreciation to them, and to all the others not listed who also helped.

Chapter

7   PERFORMING THE AUDIT
      John F. Mullarkey

9   AUDIT SAMPLING
      Ann M. Thornton

10   AUDITING IN AN EDP ENVIRONMENT
      Kent F. Yarnall

In addition to those who directed their efforts to specific chapters, several Touche Ross people deserve special mention: to Edwin H. Ruzinsky for getting this project on track with our publisher; and for review and advice ranging across many chapters, Raymond E. Perry for financial institutions, Morton Poloway and R. Eugene Marion, Jr. for SEC matters, John F. Mullarkey for auditing procedural matters, and Andrew P. Gale for database searches. Also deserving of special thanks is Eugene Simonoff, our publisher, who was convinced despite our great delays that we could actually finish the project.

The final manuscript for the second edition of the *Handbook* fills over 4,300 pages. The word processing effort was headed up by Burton C. Alho and Rose M. Backus, who had to see each chapter through six or more drafts. Their "can do" attitude made manageable a seemingly insurmountable problem, and we express our sincere appreciation for their dedication and effort. Several offices also put up with more than their share of administrative burden; our specific thanks go to the National Office, Financial Services Center, and the Stamford Office.

Al Yates and Bruce Willis wrote many chapters and segments, and Al shouldered most of the production process coordination with the publisher. Al and Bruce were tireless and unsinkable, and we are most grateful to them. Finally, thanks to our managing partner, Ed Kangas, and to our national director of accounting and auditing, Jerry Daily, for allowing us to preempt over 15,000 hours of Touche Ross time for this second edition.

ROBERT S. KAY
D. GERALD SEARFOSS

September 1988

References

Throughout the *Handbook* there are countless references included directly in the text, minimizing the clutter of footnotes. In addition, certain features have been designed to provide readers with easy access to their topics of interest.

Acronyms

Certain acronyms commonly used in the *Handbook* should be recognized:

AAER	SEC Accounting and Auditing Enforcement Release
AcSEC	AICPA Accounting Standards Executive Committee
AICPA	American Institute of Certified Public Accountants
APB	Accounting Principles Board; predecessor of the FASB
ARB	Accounting Research Bulletin
ARS	Accounting Research Study
ASB	Auditing Standards Board (successor to AudSEC, the AICPA Auditing Standards Executive Committee)
ASR	Accounting Series Release; issued by the SEC before May 1982
EITF	FASB Emerging Issues Task Force
FASB	Financial Accounting Standards Board
FIN	FASB Interpretation
FRR	SEC Financial Reporting Release
GAAP	Generally accepted accounting principles
GAAS	Generally accepted auditing standards
GASB	Governmental Accounting Standards Board
IAS	International Accounting Standard
SAB	SEC Staff Accounting Bulletin; issued by the chief accountant without the formal Commission action required for FRRs and AAERs
SAP	Statement on Auditing Procedure
SAS	Statement on Auditing Standards (replaces SAPs)
SEC	Securities and Exchange Commission

SFAC   Statement of Financial Accounting Concepts
SFAS   Statement of Financial Accounting Standards
SOP   Statement of Position; issued by AICPA Accounting Standards
        Division or Auditing Standards Division
SSARS   Statement on Standards for Accounting and Review Services
TB   FASB Technical Bulletin

There are, of course, many more acronyms that apply in specific chapters; these are explained when first encountered.

Bibliography

The *Handbook* contains a consolidated bibliography near the end of the book, permitting use within the text of "telescope" citations consisting only of the author, year of publication, and page or paragraph numbers where applicable. For example: (Jones, 1984, pp. 19–26) or (AICPA, 1987c). The letter accompanying the year of publication is used to identify a particular item where the author has more than one publication in a specific year.

Index

A very conscious effort has been made to prepare the most comprehensive index possible. The choice of index terms was made in light of available major indexes, but scaled down from the extremes taken by the AICPA and FASB in sheer number of terms, levels, and cross-references to focus on what is most likely to be searched by readers. To assist in interpreting the index entries, chapter numbers and titles are printed inside the back cover; thus the searcher can tell whether a page reference among many to a given topic relates to the area of interest.

Professional Literature Access

Professional Practice Pronouncements Listing. The *Handbook* also contains a separate back-end section in which all major professional pronouncements are listed, along with an indication of the chapter or chapters in which the pronouncement is discussed. Using this list will permit the reader who knows which pronouncement he wishes to access to locate all the chapters in which it is discussed, including the principal chapter, where applicable.

Because this list of professional practice pronouncements is so comprehensive, the pronouncements are not listed by number in the index. Of course their topical content is indexed.

AICPA Professional Standards. Reference to AICPA professional pronouncements codified in *AICPA Professional Standards* is accomplished through citation of section and paragraph number. Alphabetical prefixes that refer to a particular section of the AICPA codification are:

AC International Accounting Standards
AR Accounting and Review Services
AU Auditing Standards
BL AICPA Bylaws
ET Professional Ethics
MS Management Advisory Services
QC Quality Control Standards
TP AICPA Statements of Position and Practice Bulletins
TX Responsibilities in Tax Practice

For example, AU 625.02 refers to the applicability provisions of SAS 50, *Reports on the Application of Accounting Principles.*

FASB Current Text. References to FASB pronouncements codified in the *Current Text* are similar to the AICPA method (above); that is, citations are made to alphanumeric sections and paragraph numbers.

For example, Section A10 deals with Accounting Policies. (Note that the A in the reference relates to the first letter of the topic. The numeric portion of the reference essentially is an arbitrary assignment made in the initial development of the referencing system.) Within section A10, source references are provided to indicate the relationship of the section in the *Current Text* to the location in the original document; for example, Section A10.102 is referenced to [APB 22, ¶ 8].

The FASB also issues a *Current Text* on industry standards in which the letters in the reference relate to the first two letters of the industry name; for example, Oi5 relates to accounting standards that impact only oil and gas producing activities.

Financial Reporting Releases. In June 1982, the SEC codified all Accounting Series Releases (ASRs) into two groups—Financial Reporting Releases (FRRs) and Accounting and Auditing Enforcement Releases (AAERs). All outdated ASRs were rescinded and those covered in other regulations were deemed obsolete. The FRRs have been codified in a numerical system.

SEC Staff Accounting Bulletins. The SEC codified Staff Accounting Bulletins (SABs) 1 through 38 (39 was rescinded) into SAB 40. SAB numbers are usually shown with a topic number assigned in the SEC codification. For example, SAB 54 will also be identified as Topic 5.J.

Contents

PART IV
INDUSTRIES OTHER THAN FINANCIAL SERVICES

PART I

Financial Accounting

1

The Role of Financial Information

NATURE OF FINANCIAL INFORMATION

Monetary Unit Representations

Gathering and disseminating financial information is an evolving social process responding to the need for communication of economic events. Our present structure of financial statements was originally created by Renaissance merchants who found that to communicate economic events in an understandable way, a common denominator for presentation was necessary—the monetary unit came to be that common denominator.

Since the owners of economic resources are primarily interested in keeping track of their ventures and measuring the success of their investments, and because the input and the output of the investment process is cash, the monetary unit was a logical choice. People are able to comprehend cash measurements because prices expressed in monetary terms are the means by which they make the resource allocation decisions in their daily lives between current consumption and deferred consumption (i.e., savings or investment). The system of economic measurement expressed in monetary terms is described as financial accounting and reporting.

While the advantages of measuring and reporting economic events in financial terms are substantial, there are also many weaknesses. Economic events themselves are inherently not financial. Goods, services, physical facilities, and human resources are tangible, multidimensional phenomena. While they may be exchanged for cash, they are not cash. Expressing them in monetary terms therefore requires a transformation function that is artificial.

The danger of any accounting transformation used for purposes of reporting is that some users of the reports begin to believe that the transformation designed to achieve communication actually transforms a variety of economic assets into cash. The early users of financial accounts were often intimately involved with the operations of the enterprise and had little difficulty distinguishing between representations on the balance sheet and the physical resources under their control. However, the financial statements prepared in our society are often read by persons having no direct connection with any of the physical resources of the enterprise. Generally, since most persons confront measurements expressed in cash primarily when their bank accounts are involved, people tend to think of monetary units in terms of dollar bills that can easily be converted into other goods and services. Thus, many present-day users of financial reporting may view the accountant as an alchemist who converts base metals into precious metals, even though the user has been told time and again that the accountant is a communicator using a humanly devised arbitrary system of measurement and presentation intended to *assist* users in making economic decisions. Said differently, there is a strong behavioral tendency in humans to equate the symbol for the monetary unit with money itself, particularly when the physical resources symbolized by the dollars are not under the direct control of the individual. When such a misperception occurs, the user is misled rather than assisted in making economic decisions.

A system based on some other more arbitrary unit such as "utils," or on physical units, or a specially designed index of output or input, might avoid many of the problems inherent in using the accounting transformation model in a society characterized by complex systems of ownership. Nevertheless, because the difficulties in developing the multiple transformations required to create a new model are staggering, it seems likely that financial accounting and reporting will continue to be the cornerstone of our economic measurement system.

Objectivity vs. Relevance

An additional problem created by the financial reporting process is the difficulty of establishing measures that are considered objective. The extent to which a measurement can be repeated with the same result is considered to be of paramount importance to the accountant, for obvious reasons. If the figures on a financial report are dependent entirely on who is doing the measuring, then the numbers are invalid for external use.

However, the emphasis placed on objectivity in financial statements has also led to a situation in which subjective types of financial information (e.g., interpretive analysis, forecasting) which are potentially most useful to investors have been resisted by accountants.

More attention is being given to the trade-off between relevance and reliability in financial statements—between information that is fundamentally sound, but of limited value, and information that is central, but less reliable. The traditional bias has been toward the former, but changing economic and social circumstances are shifting that bias toward accepting more relevant information.

Complexity of the Social Environment

While the limitations of financial accounting and reporting are significant in the case of profit-seeking enterprises—those that have the ultimate objective of producing a cash outflow to the owner—the problems become more acute when dealing with the reporting problems of nonprofit and governmental enterprises, so prevalent in our society. Here the objective of the enterprise cannot be expressed in terms of ultimate cash flows to the owner or to the enterprise itself. Rather, the objective lies in a broader social goal, and a more segmented approach of measuring inputs and outputs in different units must be developed.

Problems also result from the nature of our social and capital structures, particularly with respect to the widespread separation of ownership and control and to the vast increase in public-sector responsibilities. As social structures evolve to encompass evermore complex and interdependent relationships between people and institutions, society's perspective on the financial reporting process must keep pace.

It is thus necessary to continually reexamine the answers to the following questions that form the foundation of the financial accounting and reporting process:

1. How should the *objectives* of financial reporting be developed and articulated to correspond to the conditions and ideals of society?
2. Who are the *participants* in the financial reporting process, and what are their information requirements and responsibilities?
3. What are the requirements for success of a *standard-setting body* in a complex environment, and are they understood by those responsible for the standards?
4. How do the characteristics of the *environment* in which financial information is used affect the parameters of the communication process?

5. Finally, how do the preceding concerns determine the *form* in which financial information is to be presented so that it may best serve its social purpose?

The sections that follow look at each of these problems, and explore ramifications of decisions that are shaping the communication of financial information in our society.

In addition, the final sections of this chapter examine the issues in earnings measurement (which seems to be the focus of most contemporary users of financial information) and in the timing of recognition (that is, at what point is an event or transaction sufficiently complete to merit recording in the financial statements?). These issues are the bridge to much of the specifics that appear throughout the *Handbook*.

OBJECTIVES OF FINANCIAL ACCOUNTING AND REPORTING

If financial reporting is to be successful, its objectives must be understood. It is not sufficient simply to say that the purpose is to communicate economic facts and events. To become operational in any sense, objectives must specify *by whom, for whom,* and *for what purpose* financial reporting is to take place.

The different characteristics of commercial (including nonprofit) and governmental organizations necessitate the development of two sets of objectives, each reflecting the spirit of the underlying enterprise. The FASB inherited the responsibility for articulating the objectives of financial reporting in business enterprises and has assumed responsibility for defining objectives in nongovernmental nonprofit reporting. Governmental enterprise objectives and standards have become the domain of the GASB. As the demarcation between commercial, nonprofit, and governmental is imprecise, conflicts between FASB and GASB will occur.

Business Enterprises

The objectives of reporting by business enterprises have been expressed by the FASB in SFAC 1 (FASB, 1978c) in relatively simple terms, given the complexity of the relationships that characterize a modern business organization. Financial reporting is aimed at investors and creditors and is designed to assist them in predicting the amount, timing, and uncertainty of future cash flows *to them*—which can best be assessed by predicting the amount, timing, and uncertainty of future cash flows *to the firm*. The current objectives of business financial reporting are the result of an evolutionary process, which is described in the next chapter.

The original purpose of financial reporting was to account for the disposition of assets by managers in the interest of owners. This objective, described as stewardship accounting, is derived from the English feudal system under which the owner of an estate turned over his property to the supervision of a manager. The fundamental characteristic of this relationship was ownership retention—the owner was not likely to sell his property if he found the performance of the steward unsatisfactory; the more rational choice would be to hire a new manager for the estate.

In current contrast stands the development of increasingly sophisticated capital markets allowing for easy liquidation of traded investments, which represent much of the economic resources of our country. Thus it has become equally rational in today's society for an investor to elect to sell his property in the event of poor performance by his "managers." It is not that he no longer holds management responsible for supervision of the assets, but he now considers other criteria in deciding whether to maintain his current ownership status.

The contrast between stewardship accounting and user-oriented accounting depends on one important distinction: the parameters of the owner's investment choice. Thus, in the case of stewardship accounting, a fair historical representation of the managers' actions is adequate to support a decision to keep those managers; the question the owner is seeking to answer is whether another manager could care for his property in a more responsible way. On the other hand, the modern stockholder is seeking an answer to a second question as well: would a different investment yield a higher return for the same risk? The property holdings (e.g., shares of stock) are no longer assumed to be stable, and therefore the investor seeks to predict not only future behavior of the managers but also future economic performance of his company. Stewardship accounting is insufficient for this purpose, and some information useful in predicting the future performance of the company must be provided.

The philosophy underlying the federal securities laws also suggests this kind of user orientation. It is broadly recognized that potential investors in publicly held companies have as much right to financial information as do current stockholders, and a heavy obligation rests on management to avoid prejudicing those rights in either direction.

While the progression from stewardship to user-oriented financial reporting is a reasonable response to changing ownership characteristics, the evolution of financial reporting certainly is not complete; users still lack some information that management could provide them for making rational economic decisions.

Nonbusiness Enterprises

Postulating nonbusiness enterprise financial reporting objectives is more complex; it involves more users and more purposes. Statement of Financial Accounting Concepts No. 4, *Objectives of Financial Reporting by Nonbusiness Organizations* (FASB, 1980c), therefore expands on SFAC 1. It suggests that resource providers, constituents, governing and oversight bodies, and managers are all primary users of financial reporting and that the uses to which they put the reports are numerous:

1. Resource allocation decisions,
2. Assessment of services and the ability to continue to provide them,
3. Assessment of management stewardship and performance,
4. Information about economic resources and obligations and changes therein, and
5. Information about service efforts and accomplishments.

Considering that our society supports increasing numbers of public organizations, the problems of financial reporting in nonbusiness organizations are now receiving the kind of attention they warrant. The accounting practices in governmental units

(Chapter 31) and not-for-profit organizations (Chapter 32) have not been consistent among reporting entities, or have even been internally inconsistent, and in too many cases have not provided useful financial information. Some improvements are now evident.

Gaining the confidence of managers of nonbusiness organizations has not been easy. Despite the acceptance of the FASB in the private sector, there are many in the nonprofit and public sectors who have been hesitant to expose themselves to a rigorous standard-setting mechanism. Because of strong opposition to the FASB's intervention, an alternative structure featuring a GASB was adopted in 1983. Nongovernmental nonprofit organizations, however, have remained within the FASB jurisdiction.

Beyond the question of jurisdiction, most of the substantive issues revolve around the fact that the purposes of nonprofit and governmental entities cannot be described by a "bottom line." A statement of operations may reflect the cost of operations and the methods of funding those costs, but it does not reflect success or failure.

Shaping Objectives

The objectives of financial reporting are shaped by the values and characteristics of the society, and thus must be periodically reexamined. One of the most ambitious attempts to establish a set of objectives for the profession culminated in the Trueblood Report in 1973.

The conclusions, contained in this report formally known as the *Report of the Study Group on Objectives of Financial Statements* (AICPA, 1973d), attest to the social role of financial accounting. The focus is on the needs of financial statement users, and particularly on the needs of those who have limited access to alternative sources of information. The goals of users were determined to be predicting, comparing, and evaluating potential cash flows – the product of an enterprise's earning power. Recognizing a user orientation, the study group attempted to modify the accountant's traditional bias toward objectivity; it recommended that current values be reported when these are significantly different from historical cost, although the emphasis continued to be reporting on factual aspects of enterprise transactions.

What may be the most significant points of the report, however, are two observations that still point the way toward the future – that earnings forecasts are useful for the predictive process, and that companies may be expected to report on aspects of their business that affect the goals of society. The definition of user groups would be broadened considerably beyond the FASB's "present and potential investors and creditors" if and when this view becomes an accepted objective.

FASB Objectives

The FASB's statement on *Objectives of Financial Reporting by Business Enterprises* (SFAC 1) does not diverge in most respects from the Trueblood Report although two significant differences do exist. The first is that management forecasts are downplayed in favor of estimates and judgmental information. While the future orientation remains, an explicit recommendation that forecasts be presented as information that would assist investors in determining earning power thus has been omitted.

More noticeable may be the fact that SFAC 1 omits all references to accounting for social goals.

Thus, the objectives identified by the FASB, while reasonable in themselves, may still be broadened.

A Broader View

Further attestation to the social nature of the financial reporting process and to the role that society's values play in determining the objectives of financial reporting can be found in contrasting reporting environments in other countries. The FASB's emphasis on investors and creditors as the primary focus of financial reporting is not the primary objective in many countries of the world, even some of those in which businesses have similar capital structures. There is general acceptance in many countries of the proposition that numerous constituencies with diverse interests have a legitimate interest in financial reporting.

In the Common Market, for example, labor representatives have been trying to shape common reporting requirements with an employee orientation. The interest shown by the United Nations in reporting practices of multinational enterprises has emphasized the perspective of host countries, particularly developing countries, in the financial reporting process.

Even in the United States a developing school of thought holds that the responsibility of corporations to their stockholders represents only one of the numerous obligations the modern company accepts in this society. Many proponents of this viewpoint believe that the accounting profession must prepare for, and encourage, the development of *social accounting*. Broadly speaking, social accounting encompasses reporting on those activities of the firm that have an impact on the society at large but that are not necessarily represented in its traditional financial report.

One of the most articulate positions on the broader reporting responsibilities of business organizations is contained in *The Corporate Report,* prepared by the Accounting Standards Committee of the Institute of Chartered Accountants in England and Wales in 1975. This publication has not received the attention it deserves, either in the United States or in the United Kingdom, where it is "on the shelf" while other issues preoccupy the standards-setters.

The Corporate Report takes what can be considered a very radical position on the objectives of financial reporting. It would expand the definition of user groups, the types of enterprises required to report, and the nature of their communication.

Regarding users, *The Corporate Report* defines any group that has a "reasonable right" to information as a legitimate user group. Identified as being among these users are stockholders, creditors, employees, customers and suppliers, financial analysts, government, and the public in certain respects.

Any economically significant organization is considered responsible to the identified user groups. A size test is recommended for determining economic significance, but reporting enterprises would be expected to include private partnerships, government agencies, professional associations, and nonprofit organizations.

The kinds of additional information presented would include:

1. Employment report, possibly in the form of human resource accounting;
2. Statement of corporate objectives;
3. Statement of value added;
4. Report on foreign currency transactions revealing balance of payments position;
5. Forecast of future earnings, employment, and investment levels; and
6. Accounting for various social objectives.

It is interesting that much of the information proposed in *The Corporate Report* is required by various government agencies, but frequently is not publicly available, nor is it timely when available. Though *The Corporate Report* has not resulted in reporting changes, it remains a valuable source of ideas for the future.

PARTICIPANTS IN THE REPORTING PROCESS

The process of communicating financial information not only requires a clear statement of objectives, but also demands that the participants in the process be identified and that their particular contributions and needs be incorporated into the standards of reporting. Managers, auditors, the government, investors, and creditors all play an important part in the reporting process, and each has significant responsibilities and concerns attached to his role.

Management

Most observers of the financial reporting process would agree that management has a primary responsibility to keep investors and creditors informed of the financial condition and results of operations of the corporation and at the same time seek to maximize the wealth of stockholders. Unfortunately, however, fulfilling both these responsibilities suggests a conflict of interest.

On the one hand, management will wish to disclose enough information to investors and creditors to maintain their support and to cultivate potential new sources of capital. For a company in an unstable or unusual financial condition, disclosure of too much information could result in precisely the opposite: withdrawal of investor support and closing off of capital sources. At the same time, management must also be sensitive to the costs of disclosure—the direct costs of collecting, affirming, and distributing information, and the indirect costs of competitive disadvantages resulting from disclosure.

There is controversy about both types of disclosure costs. Estimates about the direct costs of providing certain types of information vary widely depending on the source of the estimates. There is even greater disagreement about the extent of the competitive disadvantage produced by certain disclosures, and the propriety of mandating such disclosures nationally, in an environment in which companies must compete on an international scale with others not subject to similar disclosure requirements.

It would be a mistake to cast this argument in terms of the stockholders' interests versus management's interests. Not only is it possible that certain competitively disadvantageous disclosures will ultimately reduce the value of the total stockholders' investment, but there is also a question whether all stockholders, including potential investors, can be viewed as a homogenous group. Investors are likely to have different risk preferences and thus favor different amounts of disclosure at different costs; they also have varying investment horizons and thus react to the timing of disclosures as well as to their content.

A more reasoned approach to the question of management's responsibility in financial reporting is to consider the needs of various user groups in the context of the overriding economic objective — efficient allocation of resources throughout society. This macroeconomic goal will serve to check the demand for information where more or costlier resources are used to produce it than can be justified by the resulting values. However, the mechanism for efficient resource allocation operates within wide tolerances and over long time periods and thus cannot be counted on to make prompt fine tuning adjustments.

Auditors

The usefulness of financial information in society is dependent as much on the faith with which users accept the information as on the information itself. The user of a financial report must be satisfied that the auditor has understood and evaluated the information in the statements and that his testimony is a fair one. Therefore, the auditor has an initial responsibility to bring to his task a comprehensive knowledge of the accounting model, a familiarity with the complexities of information systems, and an understanding of the economic substance of the transactions of the enterprise.

The auditor has another responsibility, often overlooked: not only must his performance and commitment be entirely professional, it must also appear so to the users of his information. Regardless of the degree of expertise and integrity he brings to his work, unless he can convince outsiders of the reliability of his work, it remains valueless to them.

Unfortunately, the auditor cannot simply perform his particular task and present the results to users. He must instead assume the initiative of educating users about the nature and function of an audit, and demand that the profession continually reaffirm, publicly and privately, its allegiance to the highest standards of accounting measurement and financial reporting.

The fee relationship between auditor and client makes the accountant's responsibility for the professional appearance of his role particularly problematic. While this relationship contributes to the conduct of an audit that is both economic and thorough and emphasizes the joint responsibility of management and auditor for the audit, it necessarily introduces doubt in the mind of the public about the independence of the accountant.

In theory, the most reliable way of guaranteeing auditor independence would be to establish a public authority, vest it with the responsibility for conducting audits, and charge all publicly held firms an annual fee for the service. However, the disadvantages of such a system would ultimately outweigh the benefits of guaranteeing auditor independence. In particular, economic pressure for audit efficiency would be reduced for both parties if the company were not paying directly for services rendered. The removal of the economic incentive for efficiency, and the presumed weakening of communication links between the assigned auditor and client, would likely contribute to more expensive and less thorough, albeit more independent, financial reports.

Another problem that might be encountered were a third-party audit agency to be established is the loss of information currently obtained by the auditor from nonaudit services to a company. This information has usually served to enhance the quality of an audit rather than compromise it. A public audit agency, offering no other client services, also might fail to attract the most qualified individuals to the profession.

If the option of a third-party auditor is compared with the current system, the advantages of the latter become clearer. Absolute independence may be sacrificed when the audit fee is introduced, but the economic incentives for producing an efficient and fair report remain high. For example, the huge cost of litigation against auditors has served to bolster the auditor's insistence on quality control in the audit process, since his firm's reputation and profits depend on it.

At the present time it should be emphasized that the auditor has extensive responsibilities in the reporting process, and thus the term *auditor independence* technically is a misnomer. It is only through acknowledging his necessary ties to management, and by insisting on their joint responsibilities in the reporting process as well as his primary professional commitment to proper financial reporting, that the auditor could fully justify the absence of independence in the present fee arrangement relationship.

Much more on the role of the auditor and his profession is provided in Chapters 5 and 45.

Government

Among the many users whose demands determine the type of financial information gathered, the government—especially federal—figures significantly. A variety of regulatory agencies trying to implement social goals is the cause of much of the accounting information disseminated by all kinds of enterprises, at a significant cost.

When considering the social desirability of government regulation, it is important to address not only the issue of the cost-benefit trade-off of the government's demands for disclosure, but also the behavioral impacts of the monitoring and reporting process. It is axiomatic that how you keep score will determine how you play the game. Thus results can be achieved directly through the coercive power of the federal government and through the more subtle method of changing the reporting rules.

While society should recognize and take advantage of the possibilities for furthering its goals through legislation mandating certain disclosures, or through stipulation of the methods of reporting certain economic facts, an even higher priority of all parties should be the maintenance of a measurement system that does not obscure or debase the reported transactions. The integrity of the capitalistic procedure for resource allocation requires a reliable reporting process; to jeopardize that process is to endanger the economic system on which it depends.

Investors and Creditors

While there may be some dispute as to the primacy of investors and creditors as users of information, there is no dispute that in a capitalist country they represent a very important category. Since so much has been done to tailor the reporting systems to the investor group of users (including creditors for this purpose), a closer look at who they are is warranted.

In the first place, investors are not a monolithic category. There are those with major interests and those with small interests, those who make their own decisions and those who rely on others, direct and indirect investors possessing a wide range of risk/return preferences.

Nearly ten and a half million adults in households with income under $25,000 owned 25% of the shares in public companies held by individuals, both on the NYSE and elsewhere. Retired, unemployed, or nonemployed persons were listed as owners of over 27% of the personally held stock; two-thirds of the portfolios held in 1985 by individuals were worth less than $10,000.

The New York Stock Exchange (NYSE) periodically sponsors a survey of stockholders; the most recent was completed in 1985 (reported in the *New York Stock Exchange Fact Book,* 1987). The figures are a convincing testimonial to the existence of a shareholder democracy.

Information on NYSE holdings indicates a very interesting shareholder demography. In 1985 over 25 million Americans, or 1 in 4 adults, owned stock in companies traded on the NYSE. The median age of these stockholders was 44, the average income $37,000 per household.

In discussions of the responsibilities of financial reporting, one of the repeated refrains is the need to protect the "unsophisticated investor." Statistics on ownership cannot really identify the numbers of unsophisticated investors nor the extent of their naiveté. It is possible that the 45% of investors who have college degrees have no more sophisticated an understanding of the accountants' reports than the 7% who lack high school diplomas. However, in making commonsense hypotheses about the ability of different investor groups to make informed investment judgments, one encouraging fact does stand out. Pension fund holdings constitute a substantial part of all institutional holdings; presumably administered by trained financial managers, these investments are likely made on behalf of relatively naive investor groups. Thus the potential to protect even the most uninformed investor is there through the agency of the financial manager.

STANDARD SETTING IN A COMPLEX ENVIRONMENT

The process of developing reporting standards in a society characterized by complex economic and social organizations is necessarily a matter of interest to many groups. The accounting profession has accepted the role of the standard-setting body, but its efforts to fill this role have had uneven success. Occasionally, there has been a failure of the profession's standard-setters to recognize the political nature of their function, and a reluctance to initiate changes in the reporting process in response to a changed environment.

Early Efforts

In 1917, in response to a suggestion from the Federal Trade Commission that regulatory powers be vested in the government and that a uniform code of accounting principles be drawn up to guide the profession, the AIA (American Institute of Accountants, forerunner of the AICPA) appointed a committee to study the problem. Led by George O. May, the committee succeeded in demonstrating to the federal authorities that the newly formed professional organization would serve as a control for audit practice. Furthermore, the committee shifted emphasis from the development of a uniform code of accounting, which was likely to have turned into a list of rules, to the promulgation of standard audit requirements and procedures. This bold move set the profession on an independent course directed away from government authority.

The second important development in the professionalization of audit practices in America was motivated by the 1929 stock market crash. The origins of GAAP can be traced to this period, when the U.S. accounting profession showed its first signs of professional maturity. After the 1929 crash, pressures on the AIA to take the initiative in formulating general principles for accounting began to arise. At the time of the enactment of the Securities Act of 1933, George O. May was serving as chairman of a committee of the AIA that was engaged in discussions on cooperation with members of the New York Stock Exchange. He considered the creation of the SEC (by the Securities Exchange Act of 1934) to be a clear mandate for definition of audit responsibilities, and in 1934 the institute published the results of the committee's negotiations.

The resulting document, *Audits of Corporate Accounts* (AIA, 1934a) was actually the text of correspondence between the Stock Exchange and the AIA committee, along with a proposal for generalized accounting principles. The correspondence stressed the significance of professional judgment in determining audit procedures and focused on the importance of the income statement over the balance sheet. The most important characteristic of the document, however, was its discretion in limiting the principles of accounting to five very general statements (still applicable through ARB 43, Chapter 1A, "Prior Opinions").

Committee on Accounting Procedure

In 1936 the AIA initiated a more formal attempt to delineate a set of accounting principles. A seven-member Committee on Accounting Procedure (CAP) was formed (later expanded in size and discretionary powers at the urging of May) and immediately began to provoke controversy in the profession and the financial community. Its first publication, *A Statement of Accounting Principles* (Sanders, Hatfield, and Moore, 1938) was decried in the academic community as being little more than a codification of current accounting practice.

Those early criticisms of the CAP set the tone for two decades of commentary on the committee's endeavors. Because the committee was conceived in an atmosphere of threatened government regulation of financial reporting, many of its pronouncements were inspired by political considerations, which dictated that the committee's decisions be practical and quick as opposed to theoretical and slow.

Accountants review the CAP's history with varying degrees of disappointment or scorn. It is widely agreed that, lacking a theoretical framework to guide the formulation of GAAP, the committee left itself vulnerable to charges of inconsistency or to accusations that it was an apologist for prevailing corporate preferences. Chief among its benefits is that it accomplished the primary task of establishing an independent standard-setting body in the private sector, maintaining the essential support of the SEC and the private financial community. To have succeeded in establishing its professional authority during a period of rampant government regulation was no small task, and to view its record out of this context is to judge it unfairly.

During the decades following the Second World War, the American Accounting Association sponsored attempts to provide a conceptual framework for the standard-setting function. Among the most important of these was the monograph *An Introduction to Corporate Accounting Standards* (Paton and Littleton, 1940).

Accounting Principles Board

Pressure on the CAP to develop a theoretical basis for its pronouncements increased in the 1950s, but the attempts to develop a comprehensive framework were short-lived. Criticism of the standard-setting body increased and was publicized through the efforts of some particularly dissatisfied academics and practitioners. Finally, in 1957, the president of the AICPA, Alvin Jennings, proposed that a new research body be organized to study the theoretical assumptions of different accounting practices and to propose alternatives when deemed appropriate.

The APB, although fundamentally committed to a research orientation as the foundation of its pronouncements, was nonetheless subject to many of the same pressures that had troubled the CAP. Its first attempt to identify fundamental accounting postulates (ARS 1; Moonitz, 1962) and principles (ARS 3; Sprouse and Moonitz, 1962) was not well received, although critics did not necessarily concur in their dissent.

The APB quickly adopted a more conservative stance toward the development of an accounting framework, and proceeded to examine prevailing practices with the objective of selecting appropriate principles from among those already in use. Needless to say, the board was not overwhelmingly successful in this task, a fact which contributed to its ultimate demise.

Financial Accounting Standards Board

The *Wheat Committee* was appointed in 1971 to examine the problems of the APB and to recommend solutions to them. Its findings (AICPA, 1972b) led to the formation of the FASB in 1973. The new standard-setting body, composed of both accountants and nonaccountants, reflects the profession's increased recognition of the changing environment of financial reporting. Although not free from controversy, the FASB's statements demonstrate its commitment to ascertaining and adequately addressing the needs of users of financial statements. Furthermore, the SEC's formal recognition in ASR 150 (FRR § 101) of GAAP as constituting "substantial authoritative support" under the securities acts has contributed to the authority of the

FASB, and with a few notable exceptions the two organizations appear to be capable of maintaining a partnership, strengthened by open dialogue.

International Accounting Standards

While this *Handbook* is devoted primarily to accounting and auditing in the United States, substantial professional activities in these areas have been going on elsewhere in the world as well. In most of the English-speaking world, standard-setting bodies of the accounting profession have been at work for many years developing accounting, reporting, and auditing standards. It is fair to say that the United States has taken the lead in this respect, and its standards have had a substantial effect on international practice both because of its head start in the area and because U.S. business enterprises have played a leading role in international business.

In the early years of standard setting in the United Kingdom, Canada, Australia, and elsewhere, there was a strong tendency to follow the pronouncements of the American standard-setting bodies. In recent years, however, divergencies have become greater. In addition, as Western Europe has developed into a more unified economic unit, it also has devoted more attention to accounting and reporting standards. Historically, the accounting professions in continental Europe had not been strong, and accounting standards to the extent that they existed were largely embodied in the companies' acts of each country rather than in professional pronouncements. Stronger economies, stronger capital markets, and the development of the Common Market all led to the need for improved and harmonized reporting standards in Europe. After several years of negotiation, the fourth directive of the European Economic Community (EEC) was adopted in 1979, and it spells out basic financial reporting requirements. The member countries have now essentially conformed their laws to this directive. The EEC, meanwhile, is at work on additional accounting directives. The seventh directive, dealing with consolidation practices, is now in the process of being legislated by the member countries, to become effective in 1990.

In addition to this legally based effort at international harmonization in Europe, the worldwide accounting profession has also undertaken a major project to encourage voluntary harmonization. The first part of this effort focused on accounting standards and grew out of meetings following the International Congress of Accountants in Sydney, Australia in 1972. At that time, under the leadership of Sir Henry Benson of the United Kingdom, the professional groups in the leading industrial countries of the world formed the International Accounting Standards Committee (IASC) and charged it with responsibility for articulating international standards. All of the member countries' professional organizations agreed to use their best efforts to ensure compliance with the standards adopted or at least disclosure of deviations.

Since its inception in 1973, IASC has issued 26 international accounting standards. In addition, four exposure drafts were outstanding at the end of 1987. In general, international standards have been less proscriptive than those adopted by national bodies, and have permitted alternative practices (though efforts are now beginning to narrow the permitted alternatives). Thus, conflicts with standards adopted in the United States and the United Kingdom have been minimized so far. While international standards have therefore not broken major new ground, they have been a major step in the direction of international harmonization and have served as a useful articulation of standards in countries where no national body with standard-setting authority exists.

The relative success of voluntary association of international bodies in accounting standard setting encouraged further efforts at coordination between national professional bodies. At the International Congress in Munich in 1977, the national organizations in most leading nations agreed to the formation of a federation of accountancy bodies around the world. This federation, called the International Federation of Accountants (IFAC), has assisted in international communication and has also created an International Auditing Practices Committee, which is developing standards with international application.

ENVIRONMENTAL FACTORS

The characteristics of the environment in which financial information is used are an important factor in the reporting process. In this society, the market for securities is the focus of most efforts to determine those environmental characteristics, since the allocation of a substantial portion of investors' resources is achieved through public trading.

Disclosure as a Check on Business Behavior

While the objectives of financial reporting in the United States are generally expressed in terms of users' needs and the impact of the data on their behavior, the legitimacy of an additional factor of disclosure policy must also be considered — the impact of the disclosure requirements on those obligated to make the disclosure.

It is widely recognized that certain disclosure requirements have been established by regulatory bodies primarily because they represent a check on the behavior of managers. In 1913 Justice Brandeis noted in an oft-quoted opinion that "sunlight is said to be the best of disinfectants." The philosophy implicit in this statement has been extensively applied, sometimes to the point that managers have been known to growl that too much sunlight causes cancer.

The SEC, for example, requires disclosure of auditor changes, and such disclosure must state whether there were disagreements over accounting principles, auditing procedures, or financial statement disclosure. In its enforcement activities, the SEC also uses the obligation for disclosure as the means for enforcing a code of corporate behavior. For example, in the mid-1970s, the effort to curtail the practice of illegal or improper corporate payments was based on registrants' failure to have disclosed such practices, rather than on any direct attack on the legality of the payments themselves.

If questionable business practices can be minimized through disclosure requirements, the public will benefit both by the elimination of such practices and by saving the cost of investigations and litigation concerning them. However, certain detailed disclosures may have an anticompetitive impact or may cause management to avoid certain actions that might be to the benefit of both the firm and society, simply because management is unwilling to devote the time and emotional effort to deal with the questions that might result.

Care must be exercised to avoid indiscriminate use of a well-developed disclosure system for purposes other than to meet the needs of investors and creditors. There is always the danger that such expropriation will reduce the usefulness of the system for investors by burying significant data among a mass of information designed for other purposes.

Usefulness of Financial Information[1]

In a 1987 second edition of a research report published by the FASB in 1982, Professor Paul Griffin has examined and summarized a prodigious amount of empirical research about how investors, creditors, and others use financial reporting information.

Griffin first discusses empirical accounting research and the standard-setting process, suggesting ways in which research can affect the FASB's standard-setting methodology. For example, research on the informational efficiency of capital markets can shape Board members' perceptions of the accounting and reporting environment; and research on the ability of accounting information to predict cash flows can affect the assumptions used by the Board in developing SFASs.

Griffin then segregates the research into six categories (Griffin, 1987, Chapter 2):

1. Accounting and reporting environment – the context in which investors and creditors make decisions and use information in securities markets.
2. Properties of reported accounting numbers – statistical properties of amounts and ratios provided by financial reports and the use of this information for earnings forecasts.
3. Behavioral research, reporting standards, and the usefulness of information – traditional psychological research methods (e.g., questionnaires, interviews, and controlled experiments) now beginning to focus on human information processing, with computer based interactive experiments.
4. Predictive value of accounting information – the ability to predict matters such as business failure, bond ratings, and a modified auditor's report, with the possibility that, in reality, investors base their decisions on other than accounting information that happens to be correlated.
5. Use of information in capital markets – the efficient market hypothesis, that is, whether at the time accounting information is disclosed publicly there is an effect on security price in the right direction, of the right size.
6. Agency theory research in accounting – shareholders and creditors "contracting" with management to increase the wealth of the enterprise, and the influence of accounting information thereon.

---

[1] In the first edition of this *Handbook,* two complete chapters were devoted to "Accounting Information and Efficient Markets" and "The Financial Analyst's Role." With the availability of Professor Griffin's current research study, which encompasses efficient market research and financial analysis, this *Handbook* omits much of those earlier chapters in favor of more current information. A digest is first given herein of the role of security analysis as an environmental factor. Thereafter, certain summarized excerpts about the efficient market that seem to have continuing relevance, and which are also cited by Griffin, are included in the sections that follow.

Financial Analysts' Role

Security Analysis. The basic objective of security analysis is to determine a value for a company's securities through investigation of all the available information. There has been considerable evolution in how this objective is achieved in terms of the volume of information reviewed by analysts, the methods they use to interpret it, and the integration of their analysis into the investment decision-making process.

Because security analysts operate across the multiplicity of disciplines that affect information about a company, they must understand specific industry trends and broad economic changes and have a general comprehension of financial statements. Analysts often feel overwhelmed by the need to absorb an ever-increasing volume of nonfinancial information and to acquire a much broader general knowledge. They must keep generally informed about regulatory developments affecting specific industries and about public policy matters; and analysts frequently seek research advice on the potential business implications of corporate litigation long before a final verdict is handed down or a settlement reached.

Using low-cost, high-performance computer software, analysts link a company's sales and profit forecasts to larger models of industry sectors, the U.S. economy, and the world economy. Analysts have long since stopped relying solely on intuitive judgments about the potential impact of different economic scenarios for a particular company or industry. The ubiquitous computer facilitates intensive analysis, comparison, and display of large volumes of security valuation data.

Analysts still supply fundamental research opinions about earnings and dividends to their organization's portfolio managers, but the process by which these managers integrate the analysts' conclusions into actual stock selection is much more systematized and quantitative than intuitive. Analysts' estimates of earnings and dividend growth for individual stocks are fed into *valuation models,* which compare their expected rate of return to the market as a whole. These expected rates of return are then risk-adjusted quantitatively by the use of either historical measures of the stock's volatility or by *regression models,* which predict risk on the basis of changes in the company's financial condition and earning power.

In organizations that assign a high priority to formal valuation models, the role of portfolio managers has become progressively less important. They have lost much of their traditional freedom to develop a personal investment style and are now often forced to rely on either their firm's official valuation model or strike out on their own.

While this trend can only go so far before investment strategy becomes totally rigid, it still has important implications for the structure of power and careers in many investment organizations.

Financial Analysis. While the mosaic of information used by investors today is probably broader and more diverse than ever, financial statements continue to play a preeminent role.[2] In no other single place can the investor obtain so much detailed

---

[2] The mosaic theory holds that there is no single piece of information used by investors to the exclusion of all other information. Financial statement analysis requires using all the bits—hence mosaic—of information to form an overall assessment.

information about a company's sales, earning power, liquidity, assets, and capital structure.

Analysts do not read financial statements exactly the way accountants prepare them to be read; they always adjust reported income for items they do not regard as significant to the sustainable trend of profitability, distributable income, or free cash flow.

Earning Power Analysis. Economists use a concept of income that measures the increase in a company's wealth, before dividend distributions, from one year to another. The concept was described by Hicks (1946, p. 172):

> The purpose of income calculations in practical affairs is to give people an indication of the amount they can consume without impoverishing themselves. Following out this idea it would seem that we ought to define a man's income as the maximum value which he can consume during a week and still expect to be as well off at the end of the week as he was at the beginning.

The net income reported by companies in their financial statements is supposed to serve this purpose, but practical considerations and accounting conventions have heavily diluted its economic significance.

Analysts typically arrive at an earning power falling somewhere between reported income and cash flow. Their objective is to find an earnings figure that captures normal recurring income stripped of unusual gains and losses. The analyst does not want pure cash-flow accounting, since it would obscure the relationship between a firm's profitability and liquidity, and would be impractical for industries with legitimate timing gaps between revenues and collections. What concerns analysts is the *noise* in conventional accounting, that is, generally accepted financial accounting and reporting practices that produce income figures frequently exceeding sustainable cash-flow earnings. The stock market perceives such earnings to have low "quality" and usually assigns a below-average capitalization (low P/E ratio) to them.

Distributable Income Analysis. Measuring distributable income combines analysis of profitability with analysis of a company's liquidity, capital needs, and external fund-raising capacity. It requires a model for forecasting a company's sources and uses of funds. Analysts have traditionally tried to forecast dividends by comparing projected capital spending with cash flows plus whatever amount the company could borrow from outside sources. Cash flow from operations is adjusted for replacement cost depreciation[3] and the replacement cost of goods sold to produce an estimate of the funds available.

Capital spending forecasts and borrowing capacity also require subjective evaluation. Deducting such amounts from operating cash flows determines ranges for dividend growth. Although distributable income analysis requires a complete review of a

---

[3] Depreciation calculated on a replacement cost basis is appropriate for the portion of a company's productive facilities that its managers would choose to replace. But managers redeploy capital, including productive facilities, from low-profit investments to those offering a higher return. Depreciation on facilities such as these should be calculated on a current price level rather than replacement cost basis to determine distributable income.

company's income and growth characteristics, segment information often plays an important role (see Chapter 4). Many firms have one or two divisions that are essentially mature, and provide the other operations with cash. If the earnings performance of these "cash cows" were to change substantially, the impact on dividend policy would be pronounced.

Forecasting distributable income not only allows the analyst to project dividends, it also provides a good check on the consistency of management's growth strategy considering its wherewithal.

Income Statement Analysis. Income statement analysis has three primary objectives: (1) to isolate the different components of profit change in a particular year; (2) to identify the underlying trend of profitability; and (3) to determine the sensitivity of profits to various operating and economic factors.

Analysts break down the sources of earnings change because it is impossible to evaluate the quality of earnings without knowing the individual components; for example, the contributions that came from sales volume changes, price increases, productivity improvement, control of administrative and marketing expenses, or nonoperating factors such as interest cost and income taxes.

The trend of profits is very important, because the stock market values companies relatively on the basis of long-term earning power, not short-term fluctuations of income. A modest deterioration or improvement in a company's perceived earning power will have a far greater impact on the share rating than larger one-time income adjustments caused by nonrecurring events.

The variability of profit growth differs with each industry, and analysts evaluate trends accordingly. Large changes in profitability from one year to the next will not by themselves influence market perceptions of a company if analysts expect them. What matters is the magnitude of profit change relative to the profit growth normal standard deviation.[4]

Identifying the sensitivity of profits to operating, financial, and economic variables requires far more information than the income statement by itself provides. However, the income statement and balance sheet together provide enough data for the analyst to qualitatively and quantitatively review many aspects of a company's profitability; and with other financial information provided, they are also the raw material for ratios that can give the analyst useful insights into a company's operating and profit characteristics.

Liquidity Analysis. Analysts measure liquidity largely by monitoring changes in working capital and a variety of balance sheet ratios, including:

---

[4] Normal standard deviation refers to the usual variation in corporate profits over the course of business cycle expansions and contractions. Analysts typically expect profits to rise and fall over the course of a business cycle; their expectations of by how much are based on the past (i.e., normal) standard deviation of profits from their trend growth rate. Thus, in a recession, analysts will not be surprised if steel industry profits decline. What will concern them is whether profits fall by the usual 20-25% or whether they fall by significantly more or less. If they fall by more, steel company shares could decline. If they fall by less, steel company shares could increase despite weak profits. For companies in volatile or cyclical industries, it is the standard deviation of profit performance, not just absolute gains or losses in profits over the short-term, that determines stock market valuation.

• Current assets to current liabilities (the *current ratio*),
• Cost of goods sold to inventory *(inventory turnover),*
• Accounts receivable to sales *(accounts receivable turnover),*
• Cash, cash equivalents, and accounts receivable to current liabilities (the *quick ratio),* and
• Cash and cash equivalents to current liabilities (the *cash ratio*).

These and other ratios are discussed in Chapter 7.

Liquidity analysis also involves considerable cash-flow analysis. The statement of source and application of funds also plays a role in liquidity analysis, but until changing to a cash-flow orientation in 1987 it was thought to have too strong a working-capital orientation to fully satisfy analysts' needs.

Asset Analysis. The most important categories of noncurrent assets on company balance sheets are long-term marketable investments, intangible assets, and tangible plant assets.

Companies must publish information about the market value of their marketable securities, so the analytical problems posed by differing accounting treatments of long-term investments are not great. But balance sheet ratios can be distorted when there is a large gap between market value and balance sheet carrying amount, as can occur in specialized industries or with respect to nonequity portfolios.

Analysts generally deduct goodwill and deferred charges from shareholders' equity. Intangible assets such as patents, licenses, or other commercial rights are potentially of much greater importance. The problem for the analyst is putting a value on such assets.

Analysts are very interested in the current value of assets. SFAS 33, *Financial Reporting and Changing Prices,* had required supplementary footnote information about the effects of inflation, and had been helpful in this regard. However, with the change for 1987 making the disclosures voluntary (SFAS 89; C28), many companies have omitted these disclosures, reducing the input available to financial analysts.[5] The major problem with current value disclosure as prescribed by the FASB is the *nonstatic nature* of the current value concept. Current value is ultimately a function of enterprise profitability, which will fluctuate with the business cycle, industry trends, and the company's own management quality. Estimating the current or replacement cost of assets is a useful starting point, but no investor or takeover bidder has ever bought a company solely on the basis of replacement cost information. Buyers are attracted to assets by expectation of future cash flow, not by estimates of their replacement cost.

Liability and Capital Structure Analysis. Liability analysis usually focuses on the suitability of a company's *capital structure,* given its asset mix, to its *long-term*

---

[5] Paul Griffin (1987, p. 171) summarizes numerous research studies on the impact of changing prices disclosures on security returns, pointing out that, overall, the impact was not significant. Griffin cautions, however, that changing prices data should not therefore be considered irrelevant, but rather that much of the information is available or developed by analysts who have approximated such adjustments well before SFAS 33 was issued. Given SFAS 89's reprieve, analysts presumably will still make their own computations.

solvency. The single most important balance sheet ratio is debt to equity (either long-term debt or all debt). The lower the ratio of debt to equity, the less vulnerable a company will be to financial problems. This vulnerability is aggravated, for example, in the multitude of leveraged buyouts occurring in 1986 and 1987.

In addition to the overall relationship between equity and debt, analysts pay careful attention to how the debt/equity mix compares with a company's asset mix. Among the ratios commonly used for this purpose are:

* Fixed assets to equity
* Fixed assets to equity and long-term debt
* Current liabilities to total liabilities
* Bank loans to total liabilities
* Current assets to total debt

As with liquidity, cash-flow ratios are also used to monitor long-term solvency. They include:

* Cash flow to long-term debt
* Cash flow to interest expense
* Net income before interest expense to interest expense (times interest earned)
* Cash flow to fixed charges

Which particular cash-flow ratio analysts emphasize depends on the purpose of their research. Equity analysts are typically interested only in general coverage trends and their implications for new borrowing capacity. Credit analysts, by contrast, are also concerned with specific earnings and cash-flow coverage of particular categories of debt—long-term bonds, senior notes, preferred stock, bank loans, and so on.

Investment Risk. Investment valuation models have long attempted to adjust the expected rate of return on individual stocks for investment risk through "beta coefficients." Beta relates the volatility of individual stock to the volatility of the stock market as a whole. A beta of 1.0 means that a stock should move with the market. A beta above 1.0 indicates more volatility, while a beta below 1.0 suggests less volatility.

Traditionally, beta has been computed on the basis of a stock's actual performance over a number of market cycles. Analysts also employ a concept of beta aimed at predicting stock volatility on the basis of changes in a company's profitability and financial condition. Risk quantification through mathematical models also creates pressure for accounting information to be more economically meaningful and to provide comparable figures that can be used in models linking dozens of financial relationships among hundreds of companies.

Efficient Market Hypothesis (EMH)

Succinctly stated, the EMH holds that if there are enough analysts at work in the marketplace to absorb the information currently available and to assure by their own competition that the information is reflected in the price of the security, then all investors are protected by the fact that the security is fairly priced based on all facts and expectations that are then publicly known. If the market for securities is such an "efficient" market, developing disclosure rules and practices designed to simplify financial reporting may not be in the best interests of the "average investor." Greater summarization of complex data aimed at improving the comprehensibility of the information for the "average investor" is likely to result in a diminution of the data available to the sophisticated analyst. If such a diminution occurs, the "average investor" will be damaged rather than helped, since even the most efficient market cannot absorb data that is unavailable.[6]

Over time, a result of efficient market research has been to push standard setters and government regulators in the direction of requiring more data aimed at the sophisticated analyst, even at a cost of diminished understandability to the layman. While summaries and explanations of complex data are encouraged and in some cases required, the thrust of disclosure, discussed in Chapter 4, has been in the direction of increased detail and complexity.

Overview. There are three main variants of the EMH – the strong, semistrong, and weak forms. These forms are functions of information categories identified as private and public. The market is considered efficient if it processes information instantaneously and reflects it in security prices. Under these conditions, a trading strategy based on information publicly available to the market could not be used to consistently earn above-average returns.

The form of the informational efficiency of the market depends on the category, private or public, of the information being processed. Public information is available to every interested person, and some of it is embedded in past security prices while some is not. According to this classification, the securities market is said to be informationally efficient if it processes the information in such a manner that no market trader can use the information to consistently earn above-normal returns:

1. If the information consists only of the historical pattern of prices, the efficiency is said to be of the *weak form*;
2. If the information consists of all publicly available information, the efficiency is said to be of the *semistrong form;* and
3. If the information consists of all information, public and private, the efficiency is said to be of the *strong form.*

The model underlying most of the EMH studies is the capital asset pricing model (CAPM). Under this model, the expected rate of return of a single security or a portfolio is equal to the risk-free rate plus a risk premium. Other linear models have been used as CAPM surrogates, using data generated by security prices in the market. The objectives of using linear models to estimate the expected rates of return are to observe significant deviations in average returns from those expected, and to evaluate changes in the relative risk, or beta. Griffin (1987) describes beta as expressing

---

[6] Knowledge of actual "inside information" (i.e., not in the public domain) may allow those who possess it to earn above-normal returns; hence the market is not efficient with regard to such undisclosed data.

the riskiness of a security relative to the return on the market portfolio; it is calculated based on its estimated return versus the market return (p. 187).

Accounting Changes. While EMH research has proceeded in numerous areas such as earnings announcements, soft data, and various disclosure rules, of most interest to accountants may be the research performed on the relationship of accounting changes to market efficiency.

The conventional inference emerging from early studies suggested that the market understands and reacts only to "real" accounting changes, not to "cosmetic" changes. In this context, cosmetic accounting changes refer to changes in accounting methods, principles, or estimates that do not entail obvious cash-flow consequences and that merely reflect a book transformation of accounting measurements. Real accounting changes, on the other hand, embody obvious real economic effects. For example, the change in depreciation methods for accounting purposes alone is a cosmetic change, whereas the change in depreciation methods for both accounting and tax purposes is an accounting change with real cash-flow consequences. ("Obvious" is used here as a qualifier because almost all accounting changes entail some real, although indirect, consequences.)

One of the first studies dealing with the effect of accounting changes on security prices was reported by Archibald (1967), who evaluated the reaction of the stock market to the change in depreciation methods from accelerated to straight-line for accounting purposes only. For a sample of 55 firms, Archibald evaluated changes in security prices around the announcement of the depreciation change. He did not state his conclusions in 1967, but in a 1972 report on the study, Archibald stated that abnormal returns after the switch did not show any systematic pattern, suggesting that the change had no significant effect on stock prices. While there may be a temporary, but not a significant, improvement in market returns for a few weeks following announcement of a cosmetic change, investors in the market will not behave as if the change in reported earnings represented a real economic happening. However, as to real changes, e.g., first-in, first-out (FIFO) to last-in, first-out (LIFO), the savings of cash flow from reduced taxes increase the present (economic) value of the firm, and the stock market sees through the artificially lowered accounting earnings.

Studies show that nondiscretionary (e.g., FASB-mandated) accounting changes increasing reported income have an impact on stock prices that is significantly greater than if the change is discretionary. However, changes decreasing earnings, whether or not mandated, have had little effect on stock prices.

Implications for Policy Making. Reading research on the association between accounting numbers or events and security prices leaves many accountants perplexed. It would be wrong to claim that prices of stocks are independent of accounting methods used. On the other end of the spectrum, however, there is little support for the claim that the market anticipates all accounting information prior to its release (the strong form of the EMH).

Similarly, until factors and constraints (market "frictions") such as taxes, transaction costs, government regulations, imperfect competition, and incomplete markets become a part of the empirical research methodology and their effects become known, the reported evidence and conclusions must be presumed colored by assumptions made about them.

The evidence has been focused on changes in stock prices, not determinants of their levels. Abdel-khalik (1972), in an early "point of view" statement, observed that there was nothing in the concept of efficient markets that would warrant making any implication as to the quality of accounting systems and products. He wrote:

> Efficiency (in the context of efficient markets) is a property of the market, not of accounting numbers, and, therefore, other things being equal, the reaction of the market will not be any less efficient (had an alternative accounting method been used) but it might be quite different. Accordingly, drawing implications from the efficient market hypothesis to accounting numbers *does not* shed light on the nature of the accounting process or its alternatives. . . . One ought not to confuse the two issues: the quality of the market and the quality of accounting numbers. [p. 793]

Market Gyrations. What is now referred to as the "Crash of 1987," the 500+ point drop in the Dow Jones industrial average on October 19, 1987, has puzzled EMH proponents. Some would tentatively attribute the volatility to chaotic trading conditions in the market (such as futures trading and program trading). Further, restrictions on trading commencing the following day may have exacerbated the problem.

The EMH critics, however, point out that perhaps the theory did not hold because the market in reality was not efficient. It seems clear that EMH proponents have a great deal of work to do in examining what happened. The EMH will, at least for a time, receive some scorn.

The Shrinking Role of Financial Statements

One of the most significant changes in financial reporting is the erosion of the relative importance of financial statements. SFAC 1, *Objectives of Financial Reporting by Business Enterprises* (FASB, 1978c), is evidence that financial statements are becoming less important; it puts the emphasis on financial *reporting* rather than on financial *statements*. Reporting was the thrust of the *Trueblood Report* (AICPA, 1973d) and this thrust has become the basis for most FASB conclusions. In 1977, the SEC's Advisory Committee on Corporate Disclosure emphasized the need for interpretation and analysis of results, and the SEC-mandated MD&A in annual reports is steadily increasing in importance.

This trend in the broader area of financial reporting might, if not checked, ultimately make the financial statements a well-defined ritual where objective data are arrayed without great regard for their relevance. One indicator of this trend is the interest companies are beginning to show in summary annual reports. These contain highlights of the year's operations and year-end financial position, but omit GAAP financial statements, MD&A, and much of the explanatory detail that ordinarily goes into glossy annual reports. Of course, the full financial report with all the trimmings appears in the company's Form 10-K filed with the SEC; this is all that is mandated for public companies. While summary annual reports are initially being justified as a cost saving (by eliminating reporting duplication), at least part of the reason has been the increasing volume of required disclosures that seize space in expensive published annual reports.

Thus the impact of this trend is slowly unfolding. The FASB spends most of its time on issues directly related to the financial statements. The Conceptual Framework has been expected to help the FASB sort out the issues and provide a matrix for decision-making, but its usefulness for this purpose so far is debatable. While no one with reasonable expectations believes that the framework can resolve all specific issues, it has the potential for providing decision guidelines to the Board that should enhance (but certainly not ensure) the consistency and neutrality of its standard-setting efforts. From this, the role of financial statements and other financial reporting may emerge with greater clarity.

FORMS OF FINANCIAL REPORTING

The reporting model is constantly evolving in response to changes in and complexity of business enterprises. Both the requirements of an efficient market for information production and the needs of different types of users are being considered in modifications of the reporting process.

The original reporting model was designed to describe a simple trading enterprise and was frequently created for a single project. As business became continuous and encompassed manufacturing, more and more conventions were required to squeeze a more complex reality into the simple model. Today's world of corporate interrelationships—conglomerate and multinational enterprises utilizing a wide variety of operating and financial techniques—is beyond the descriptive capacity of any simple measurement and disclosure model. Thus the model must be allowed to become more complex to reflect the business reality. At the same time, the information-gathering costs of certain preparer groups, and the need of investors for more future-oriented information, are forces for further change in the reporting process.

Differentiation in Reporting Requirements

Preparation requirements drafted with the circumstances of a complex multinational enterprise in mind may prove burdensome and perhaps irrelevant when applied to a small and relatively simple concern. Similarly, the demands of a particular industry situation may lead to specialized requirements that have no applicability elsewhere.

The SEC has adopted industry-specific disclosure rules, developed disclosure exemptions for small companies, and applied certain of its rules only to very large enterprises.

The AICPA membership includes many practitioners who deal primarily or exclusively with small nonpublic companies and thus has been particularly concerned about the tendency of GAAP to address the problems of large public companies while imposing requirements on all. In 1974 a Committee on GAAP for Smaller and/or Closely Held Businesses was appointed. The resulting Werner Report (*Report of the Committee on Generally Accepted Accounting Principles for Smaller and/or Closely Held Businesses*, AICPA, 1976) cited as a major problem the cost burden imposed on small businesses by requirements that they comply with all GAAP, necessitating the preparation of some information not relevant to their financial statement users.

The Werner Report concluded that the needs of the public investor and financial analyst, which have dictated many of the GAAP disclosure requirements, are very different from the needs of owners, owner/managers, and creditors in small or closely held businesses.

Rather than make wide-ranging proposals for the development of different accounting principles for different entities, the committee upheld the belief that standard measurement principles enhance the usefulness of all financial statements. Its more conservative recommendation, to differentiate between disclosures that provide additional or analytical data for some users and disclosures that should be reported by all organizations, thus would preserve the integrity of the measurement process. At the same time it would relieve some of the disclosure burden that has fallen on smaller and closely held companies.

Largely in response to the Werner Report, the FASB suspended the effectiveness of segment reporting requirements and earnings per share requirements for nonpublic companies. In addition, size characteristics have been used in different situations to differentiate among disclosure requirements.

Financial Statements and Financial Reporting

The once slow evolution of the communication of financial information is accelerating to respond to the wide-ranging implications of changes that have taken place in our society.

Role of Supplementary Information. One of the most significant developments is the diminishing role of financial statements in financial reporting; instead, supplemental information is becoming a prime ingredient in meeting the reporting objectives.

Financial statements were once the totality of financial reporting. The typical annual report of the first half of the twentieth century was a set of financial statements with a brief, uninformative transmittal letter from the chief executive. While consumer products companies sometimes used the annual report as a marketing device, seldom was much (if any) financial data presented outside the financial statements. Even footnotes to the statements were generally brief, and the need to present more than a few was considered something of a sign of weakness in the statements themselves. GAAP focused almost exclusively on the methods of presenting numbers in the statements.

There has been a steady erosion, however, in the perceived validity of financial statement numbers that are not explained and augmented. Both regulators and private-sector standard-setting bodies continue to expand disclosure requirements outside the basic financial statements, both in the notes (though defined as an integral part of the statements, notes are primarily narrative rather than tabular) and in other supplemental information.

Although the FASB regularly addresses the question of what supplemental statement disclosure is needed and to whom such requirements should apply, there has been little activity in this arena since the flurries surrounding Changing Prices (SFAS

33) and Oil and Gas reserve information disclosures peaked in 1982. (See Chapter 4 for a further discussion of supplementary information.) Mandatory adherence to SFAS 33 has been suspended by SFAS 89 (C28); and while Oil and Gas disclosures are still required under SFAS 69 (Oi5.157), the SEC has begun to show some signs of disenchantment with the operation of the full cost method, which could have repercussions on the usefulness of the supplemental data. (See Chapter 34 regarding Oil and Gas developments.)

Future-Oriented Information. In SFAC 1, *Objectives of Financial Reporting by Business Enterprises*, the Board was quite explicit (in direct contrast to the Trueblood Report (AICPA, 1973d)) that it was unwilling to conclude that forecasts were data that would assist investors in predicting future cash flows. But the FASB clearly reemphasized the basic future orientation of financial reporting. Thus, both in supplemental disclosures and in the financial statements, there has been substantial movement in the direction of data with predictive implications, in recognition of the business continuum being described. It seems likely that this direction will continue and that ultimately, explicit forecasts could be part of the reporting package for external purposes.

Effects of Information Technology. The SEC is experimenting with a pilot program for Electronic Data Gathering, Analysis and Retrieval (EDGAR). The proposed system will allow registrants to file their corporate reports with the SEC electronically, and users, in turn, to access this data by computer. EDGAR does not propose to alter the basic information available but only the medium for filing and retrieval. (EDGAR is further described in Chapter 47.)

Beaver and Rappaport (1984) have pointed out that information technology can change not only the way financial information is delivered but also its essential character and usefulness:

> Information technology makes it possible to accommodate [a] data-base approach to corporate financial reporting. An electronic financial data base containing the data needed to produce conventional financial statements as well as alternative forms of analysis can be developed. Such a data base could make users less dependent on the companies' financial statements. With the data base and a variety of software, users could prepare financial statements under a variety of accounting assumptions. They could compute any number of income figures, or none at all. By merging the data about a specific company with industry and macro-economic data bases, users could develop better and more comprehensive evaluations.
>
> Regulators are concerned that the lack of uniformity in accounting methods impairs the credibility of financial reporting. This problem could be minimized with the data base approach because users could choose the methods they prefer.
>
> A shift would occur in the role of accounting standards. Instead of deciding which inventory or depreciation method to permit, the issue for policymakers would be which data to include in the data base and how consistency should be maintained across companies and over time. In brief, there would be less concern with how to calculate the bottom line and more concern with the adequacy and relevance of disclosure. . . .
>
> The cost of implementing this approach will be one problem, of course. But the major obstacle is likely to be resistance to change. Because the "let the user choose" approach

would alter the present corporate reporting system, it no doubt will be vigorously debated. It is already technically feasible. If it does not come to pass, the reason probably will be political, not technological.

THE IMPORTANCE OF EARNINGS

Earning power is defined in the Trueblood Report as "the enterprise's ability to be better off, to generate more cash, and to have earnings convertible into cash at some future date" (AICPA, 1973d, p. 23). The ability to generate cash is clearly a prerequisite to dividend and interest payments, and cash generation expectations are also one of the primary determinants of securities prices in the marketplace. It is the ability to generate cash and to pay dividends (periodic or liquidating) that must be present for common stocks to have value. Dividend payments need not be actually expected, but the ability to pay dividends at some time must be. An enterprise's earnings can affect market prices of equity securities that participate in those earnings simply by implying increasing or decreasing cash-generating and payout ability.

The income (or earnings) statement is an attempt to measure the results of the earning process that took place in a given period. As discussed earlier, the analyst generally uses these statements over time as the principal means of evaluating the earning power, or long-run cash-generating capacity, of the enterprise. Any particular period's result as expressed in its earnings statement therefore provides the basis for an estimate of the long-run cash-generating capacity of the enterprise at its operating level during that period. This in essence is the result of the accrual accounting process: revenue recognition estimates the long-run average cash flow at the current level of activity, while recognition of expenses is an estimate of the long-run average cash outflows needed to generate such inflows.

It must be recognized, however, that this conceptual construct must be made operational so as to be applied to the multiplicity of circumstances that are found in business activity. Problems of uncertainty, measurability, and abuse avoidance often lead to rules that supplement and sometimes vary from this theoretical approach.

Nevertheless, this basic concept of earnings is probably the one most closely related to the FASB's objective for financial reporting, which provides that financial reporting should supply information helpful to the investor in predicting the amount, timing, and uncertainty of future cash flows to the firm (see SFAC 1, ¶ 48). An enterprise with a record of stable or increasing earnings will generally be thought to have substantial earning power (assuming there is a consensus on the continued need for the enterprise's products or services). It will therefore attract investment, or at least make investment units already in the hands of owners transferable to others who may wish to participate in the process. The essential element of the earnings measurement—revenue and expense recognition—is thus extremely important.

Economist's View

Hicks's view of economic income, cited earlier under "Earning Power Analysis," is a very comprehensive view of income, but it could be broadened beyond its quantitative intent to include all monetary, nonmonetary, and personal satisfactions, whether related to a transaction or to an external event that simply had some effect on "well-offness." It is thus consumption- and utility-based rather than business-oriented in the above formulation.

Certain accounting measurements aim for the economist's quantitative view of income, but it is impossible to measure all of the qualitative ingredients, at least in a way that will generally satisfy a variety of users. Not the least of the problems is the absence of standards to measure and recognize the values of the human asset or to recognize synergies in business enterprises.

The ultimate conclusion might be that each company would have a value represented by the discounted cash flow of *all* of its net future cash inflows. Of course, this is not accurately measurable, though in some simple businesses a reasonable approximation could be made.

The uncertainties involved in predicting the future cause obvious problems for government economists who provide advice to the administration. Likewise, uncertainties about the future cause severe problems for the accountant, who can expect to be sued for failure to accurately foresee the future.

Taxation View

Keeping the economist's definition in mind, it is interesting to note that the federal government in its taxation policies has never been much bothered by economics. As discussed more fully in Chapter 48, the income tax is a levy on income determined according to any method of accounting that clearly reflects income. However, by evolution this now means simply that the IRS may apply its judgment against that of a taxpayer concerning a particular issue for which there is vague specification (if any) in the tax regulations.

In general, the tax law's view of income has been more closely related to short-run cash flows than is normal accounting practice, based on the recognition that tax cannot be paid until the cash is available to do so. More recently, however, the IRS and Congress have taken a view of taxable income that more closely aligns with financial reporting, and thus perhaps to some extent with economics. Examples are the taxability of imputed interest and the Corporate Alternative Minimum Tax based on the difference between taxable income and financial reporting income.

In some cases the income tax is used as a means of administering social benefits — that is, to redistribute income in a certain way, to stimulate certain areas of economic growth, to penalize certain transactions considered less desirable for the common good, and for other reasons.

Accountant's View

Accountants have been accused of being especially unappreciative of economic reality in financial accounting and reporting. The traditional accounting view of earnings is based on the premise that: (1) the value of the medium of exchange (cash or currency) is stable and (2) all business transactions eventually devolve to cash. Thus, what comes in is some kind of investment or revenue, what goes out is some kind of return of capital or expense, and what is left after deducting expenses from revenues (all measured in static currency units) is earnings. This approach fails to recognize changing prices and values and perhaps was never intended to be anything other than pragmatic. Surely the problems with historical cost-basis accounting (mentioned later in this chapter) must have been recognized at the dawn of commercial record-keeping.

The historical cost model for businesses usually operates on the accrual basis — that is, resources and obligations are recognized when they have reached a "degree" of measurability and irreversibility. As is well known, however, the degree is very subjective, depending on the area.

For companies that operate worldwide, currencies have values in relation to each other that depend in substantial measure on the perceptions of the fiscal condition of the country. There have been times when the value of the U.S. dollar has steadily risen in relation to major world currencies, but these may be periods of fond memory, since this has not happened in the recent past. Thus, the declining value of the measurement unit in terms of the goods and services it can command is a problem of worldwide scope.

For a brief period, 1979 through 1986, some recognition was given to the instability of the monetary unit through supplemental disclosures required by SFAS 33, *Financial Reporting and Changing Prices*. However, inflation in recent times has been relatively low in the United States resulting in the FASB's suspension in SFAS 89 (C28) of the mandatory application of SFAS 33. While the SFAS 33 methodology is on hold and ready to be reactivated at a moment's notice, it is worth observing that neither SFAS 33 nor any other accounting convention has grappled with the continuous erosion of the value of the U.S. dollar in relation to other major currencies, which of course confounds interpretation of financial statements of U.S. based multinational enterprises.

Even apart from the changing value of the monetary unit, accountants do not agree on how earnings are to be measured assuming its stability and tend to gravitate into two groups.

The asset/liability group holds that the difference between owners' equity (assets less liabilities) at two points in time, adjusted for transactions with owners, constitutes "results of operations," whether that is called net earnings or something else. The balance sheet and income statement *articulate* — a net change in one has a corresponding change in the other.

Under the asset/liability view, a cost that does not meet the definition of an asset cannot temporarily rest in the balance sheet and must be charged against current operations. This approach results in a balance sheet that usually contains harder rather than softer (e.g., exchangeable versus nonexchangeable) assets and liabilities and generally avoids deferral of soft costs for matching against future revenues.

The revenue/expense group holds that the most important goal of financial accounting is the measurement of earnings, and therefore amounts received in advance of "being earned" and costs incurred that will benefit future periods regardless of their lack of hardness or exchangeability should not enter the income statement at the time of the transaction, but should be deferred until they are properly matched with applicable costs and revenues.

Although practicing CPAs would more likely choose the asset/liability basis because it is less subjective, there are perhaps other ways of looking at the problem. Many of the proponents of the revenue/expense view might come to accept the asset/liability view if earnings were defined as something other than the difference between net assets at two points in time (as adjusted for transactions with owners).

This is indeed what the FASB did in its postulation of a *comprehensive income* concept (SFAC 6, ¶ 70) of which net earnings would only be a part, albeit the most incisive. This may be the substance of the economist's view as given by Hicks (1946). With comprehensive income, the asset/liability proponents achieve their desired articulation, while the revenue/expense proponents retain their "net earnings."

Whether comprehensive income could encompass all variable factors is debatable. An astute management will take measures to enhance, preserve, hedge, or adjust the mix of net assets that are exposed to valuation declines due to events not within its direct control. Thus, a management that constantly readjusts to the environment will usually do a reasonable job of predicting the future as it affects the company's net assets. Some other managements may not operate this way, and thus will obtain different results in the area of events not within management's control. Further research is needed to see if the distinction can be sharpened.

Accrual Method

Under the accrual method of accounting, many elements of financial statements are recognized prior to their being settled in cash transactions. This is done on the basis of "sufficient" achievement of the applicable recognition criteria and a probability of irreversibility (i.e., the transaction will "stick"). For example, the sale of a tried and true product to a continuing customer who has never had a credit-rating problem results in recognition of revenue and a receivable at the time of the transaction, even though the transaction in the broad sense is not finally complete until the customer pays the amount owed. On the seller's side, he may not have paid obligations incurred in obtaining or manufacturing the goods, but they were nevertheless recorded as inventory and subsequently as cost of sales. It is readily agreed that accrual basis accounting is more reflective of the economics of a tranaction than a cash-only basis.

Time Segments

When accrual basis accounting is combined with the need to report at specified intervals on the progress and condition of the business, problems multiply. Under the accrual method, numerous transactions at any given reporting date are not complete in that they have not had their ultimate cash consequences. A longer-term example is the investment in plant, which is intended to be realized by allocations to product costs for a period of up to 50 years.

Of course, if no report were required by a business entity until it had totally completed its operations and liquidated itself through distributions to its owners, an accurate determination of earnings in terms of the unadjusted monetary unit could then be made. A separate computation, however, would still be required to approximate the unrecorded ingredient in the enterprise's lifetime earnings – the change in the value of the unit of measure. The value of the dollars invested by owners simply is not the same as the value of the dollars returned.

Periodic reporting, despite the problems it presents, is necessary and required. Public companies must report annually and quarterly and must file current reports about significant transactions, financial or otherwise, affecting the enterprise. And

	Temporality	Entry/Exit Value	Factuality
Historical cost	Past	Entry	Actual
Current cost	Present	Entry	Hypothetical
Current exit (or "market") value	Present	Exit	Hypothetical
Expected exit (or "net realizable") value	Future	Exit	Expected
Discounted cash flows	Future	Exit	Expected

FIG. 1.1   Classification of Measurement Bases

the trend is toward even more discreteness in reporting; some proponents of *continuous reporting* believe an enterprise should be able to report, given today's computer technology and measurement systems, on a daily basis if it is deemed useful for them to do so (some financial institutions have long done this internally). However, doing this may not be based on improvements in reporting ability; it may manifest the type of reporting now done on an annual basis, but simply done much faster. It may not improve the quality of the information reported, which could deteriorate because insufficient time might be available for the judgmental aspects of accounting measurement. And continuous reporting would certainly aggravate the problem of earnings measurement by requiring that those measurements be made for shorter and shorter periods. What must be recognized in any reporting system is that each period is part of a business continuum, and the allocation methodology used must be helpful in allowing a user to understand that continuum and its economic implications.

Measurement Approaches

Earnings measurement cannot be fully accomplished without deciding on the scale of measurement to be used. In the accounting area, there are five basic approaches (each having many possible permutations and which may be intermixed) that have been commonly acknowledged and are now incorporated in SFAC 5 (¶ 67):

1. *Historical cost*
2. *Current cost*
3. *Current exit value in orderly liquidation*
4. *Expected exit value in due course of business*
5. *Discounted cash flows*

These five bases can be classified in the various ways shown in Figure 1.1.

Constant Dollars. It is interesting that *constant dollars* do not make the list of measurement bases. This approach represents a basically mechanical translation of initial entry (historical) costs into hypothetical amounts computed in terms of the purchasing power of today's dollars. Nothing more than a change in the valuation of currency is involved. But the cost of various items does not rise symmetrically; purchasing power changes affect one item differently than another. Thus, constant dollar accounting is a grand averaging scheme that, in restating the entire financial statements, provides information of questionable usefulness that has generally been found by analysts to be unrevealing and distracting.

However, none of the measurement methods discussed hereafter directly concern themselves with the changing value of the dollar. Thus, a second calculation is sometimes needed to separate this ingredient from other specific value changes.

Capital Maintenance. A decision needs to be made on how a business enterprise should maintain its capital and on whether there should be a charge against operations for doing so. *Physical capital* is determined in units of productivity; those who take a physical capital approach maintain capital at whatever amount of current cost is necessary to sustain the productive capacity or service potential of the enterprise. The *financial capital* approach, which the FASB favors, would require maintaining the total dollars of capital, adjusted for changes in the value of those dollars. Should financial capital not be so maintained, a partial liquidation of the business would be occurring. Thus the question is: does the undistributed retained earnings account become simply the repository for the net effect of changes in values (however measured) during the year, or should stockholders' equity first be "maintained" by a charge deducted from earnings (and hence from retained earnings) and credited to invested capital?

The FASB almost dealt with the capital maintenance charge issue when it considered capitalization of interest. The Discussion Memorandum on *Accounting for Interest Costs* (FASB, 1977) contained several advisory issues along these lines. If interest is a cost of a certain kind of capital (debt) and is deemed capitalizable in the development of certain assets (up to the time they are ready to produce in a normal way), then why not treat the other kind of capital (equity) in the same manner? Does it not have a cost as well, which should be charged against earnings or capitalized and deferred?

Historical Cost. This is defined as the amount of cash, or its equivalent, paid to acquire an asset (less subsequent amortization) or the amount received when a liability was incurred (SFAC 5, ¶ 67a). It should be noted that, even though current basic financial statements are said to be prepared on the historical cost basis, there are several kinds of adjustments based on some other method, such as inventories written down to lower of cost or market or assets fair valued in nonmonetary exchanges. By and large, however, current financial statement amounts can be pinned to a previous inflow or outflow of cash or monetary assets. Historical cost is often referred to as *initial entry value* or *original entry value*, thus signifying that these are the amounts at which the transactions entered the financial statements.

The main advantage of the historical cost method is its objectivity; its major defect is that it often lacks relevance because (1) it does not track changes in the value of the measurement unit; (2) it does not recognize that the value of those constant dollars changes irregularly in relation to different kinds of assets and liabilities; and (3) it does not account for many external events (as contrasted with transactions directly entering the financial statements) having an effect on the value of enterprise net assets and thus on the measurement of its earnings.

Current Cost. Also sometimes called the *replacement cost* or *current entry value* method, this approach restates the assets and liabilities of an enterprise at the number of monetary units (dollars) it would take to acquire or incur them today. There has been some dispute over whether replacement cost of assets should be figured in terms of productive capacity (new assets of equivalent operating capacity) or service potential (identical assets, generally), with the FASB choosing the latter, in the now-superseded SFAS 33.

Replacement cost data is viewed by many as an improvement over the historical cost basis and the constant dollar approach because it gives recognition to specific changes (relative to each asset and liability) in the value of the measurement unit. Hence, inflation is presumably recognized in the specific circumstances of the enterprise.

A major drawback, however, is that it is quite hypothetical. An enterprise would not normally replace many or all of its assets and refund all of its liabilities at once. The fact that it owns and uses certain assets means that the benefits from continuing to own them are estimated to exceed the cash inflow that realistically could be achieved from selling them. This assessment by management does not mean that the assets currently provide a good return on investment; there currently may be other limiting factors that make replacement unrealistic, such as the complexity of a major restructuring or the availability of funds.

Nonetheless, current cost data would seem desirable for financial analysts and other serious users of financial statements because of the reasonably sharper picture provided of the specific effects of inflation.

Current Exit Value. A substitute name more familiar to accountants may be *current market value*—the amount of cash that could be obtained by selling an asset in orderly liquidation, or the amount required currently to eliminate an obligation (SFAC 5, ¶ 67c). For example, marketable equity securities (SFAS 12, I89) and inventories are already evaluated on a lower-of-cost-or-market basis.

The problem, of course, is that not every asset or liability in a balance sheet has an exit value, much less such a value in orderly liquidation. The going concern concept that underlies GAAP does not reasonably accommodate the orderly liquidation approach.

Expected Exit Value. The major difference between this basis and the preceding one is that due course of business is substituted for orderly liquidation. The expected exit value approach would tolerate the normal length of time, even years, it might take for an asset to be converted to, or a liability liquidated by, cash. This presents particular problems in case of long-term captial assets, which, of course, the enterprise does not hold for liquidation except indirectly through the allocation of cost in some rational and systematic manner to the cost of products or services; in a way, this results in an exit value in the due course of business.

The inability to disaggregate or separate a group of assets doing one thing (e.g., a plant complex) creates major problems in attempting to value individual assets at expected exit values. The method, of course, is also hampered by the fact that not all separable assets will have an exit value or can be expected to have an exit value anywhere near as high as the value in use to the business.

Discounted Cash Flow. This is also called present value of expected cash flows, and the FASB describes it as the discounted amount of net cash inflows pertaining to an asset, or the discounted amount of net cash outflows required to eliminate a liability (SFAC 5, ¶ 67e). GAAP already requires that long-term receivables and payables be discounted at an appropriate rate of interest, and that the discount be accreted on the interest method (I69.108) over the period between initiation and realization. A good example of discounted cash flow accounting (for capital leases) can be found in SFAS 13 (L10).

In its fullest measure, discounted cash flow provides the overall value of the business currently, discounted at an appropriate rate of return. However, there are major uncertainties involved in arriving at discounted cash flow:

1. What discount rate should be used?
2. How are future cash flows from present nonmonetary assets to be dealt with?
3. Is disaggregation of assets possible or even necessary?

The discount rate selected should vary according to some indication of return relative to the risk in a particular situation. Assigning a risk factor is problematic, of course, since risk in an investor's assessment is dependent on numerous factors and changes over time, as discussed earlier.

A further assumption needs to be made that as nonmonetary assets are converted into cash, the net inflows are either returned to the shareholders or reinvested in the business, or that some combination of the two occurs. Apart from short-term forecasts, it may not be possible to predict what management will do with the net cash inflow, since future alternative uses will be speculative. Therefore, the simple (and unrealistic) assumption is often made that such cash flow is invested in U.S. government treasury securities.

As with expected exit value in the due course of business, it is not realistic to disaggregate an individual asset from an integrated operation for the purpose of determining its future cash flow. Thus, large segments of the business—in some cases virtually the entire enterprise—will have to be forecast as to future operations, and the cash flows resulting from the aggregation of the segment's assets then subjected to discounting.[7]

RECOGNITION PROBLEMS

Authoritative Rules

How does an acknowledged element of financial statements, measured in accordance with the foregoing bases, merit recognition in financial statements? The authoritative accounting literature is sparse in the area of recognition criteria for income statement elements—those that affect earnings measurement. The basic premise is contained in

---

[7] For an excursion into an advanced form of discounted-cash-flow-based accounting, see "Relevant Accounting" (Ronen and Sorter, 1972). This article contains proposals dealing with disaggregation problems, and incorporates the market's valuation of the enterprise. While its outputs seem attractive, little effort has gone into its further development perhaps because of its complexity.

ARB 43, Chapter 1A (R75.101), which states, "Profit is deemed to be realized when a sale in the ordinary course of business is effected, unless the circumstances are such that the collection of the sale price is not reasonably assured."

This basic specification has been built into numerous accounting guides, AcSEC SOPs, SEC Financial Reporting Releases, and some FASB Statements and Interpretations. With so little articulation, it is no wonder that revenue and expense recognition rules have been eclectic.

In December 1984, the FASB released its Statement of Financial Accounting Concepts on *Recognition and Measurement in Financial Statements of Business Enterprises* (SFAC 5). As with the other SFACs, it is a roadmap by which the FASB plans to arrive at consistent solutions to analogous problems.[8]

Recognition Scales

As a way of visualizing revenue recognition (as well as the concomitant expense recognition), imagine a scale of 1 to 100 whereby it takes a rating of 60 for an executory transaction (that is, one that is not yet fully performed by either or both parties) to be recognized as recordable in financial statements. However, if uncertainties arise after recognition but before final cash realization, perhaps the scale has to drop to 50 in order to reverse the prior recognition. As another illustration, when an item achieves 20 on the scale, it is time for disclosure as financial information outside the financial statements, and when 40 is reached, it moves into the disclosures in financial statement notes. The scale idea is clumsy, of course, and does not begin to consider countless variations. Still, its simplicity should make it easy to keep in mind as recognition criteria are considered in the following sections, though undoubtedly numerical demarcations are not plausible.

Recognition by Disclosure

It can be readily argued that disclosure is not an issue relevant to recognition criteria. However, the FASB already realizes that some threshold has to be set for information to enter the financial statements (or to enter supplementary information required to accompany the financial statements). The FASB might as well deal with the broader rather than the narrower subject. Even if recording in the financial statements were the major focus, the Board would inevitably have to deal with whether items that do not meet the recognition criteria should at some point be disclosed; so it is merely a question of which end of the problem will be the starting point.

Uncertainties

Another way of visualizing the measurement scale is in terms of a spectrum of certainty/uncertainty. The Trueblood study group (AICPA, 1973d, p.33) pointed out

---

[8] In concluding this SFAC (the "last leg" of the conceptual framework) the FASB commissioned a research report by Professor Henry Jaenicke (1981), who cataloged concepts and practices. A perusal of this report will amply demonstrate the difficulty of achieving harmony in recognition criteria.

that information in financial statements should be segregated, to the extent possible, according to factual data and interpretive data, which are akin to certainty and uncertainty. Factual data is objectively measurable, and recognition is made easier by facts. Interpretive data is subjective and hard to quantify. But there are infinite gradations; there may be a mixture of fact and interpretation in a given transaction. Thus, even in what is considered "hard" information – a characteristic of most financial statement amounts – there are significant variations in tensility. Classifying financial statement amounts as to mostly factual or mostly interpretive may seem impossible, but it is worthy of further research because of the communications improvements that could result.

Criteria for revenue recognition might be grouped in a similar manner: broad criteria (uncertain) and specific criteria (certain). Another issue has to do with how strong each chosen criterion must be: convincing (very factual), persuasive (moderately factual), or suggestive (substantially uncertain, but contributing some value in the recognition process).

An important issue is the association of costs with revenues. The so-called matching concept (SFAC 6, ¶ 146) is uncertain in many applications, and as a result has been dealt a number of significant blows by the FASB. For example, SFAS 2 recognized that expenditures for research and development (R&D) were clearly aimed at matching with future revenues to be derived from the results of such R&D; but the Board chose to require write-off of those expenditures in view of the larger issue: the inability to demonstrate with any degree of consistency that positive and beneficial results would be obtained (SFAS 2, ¶ 49).

Criteria for Earnings Recognition

Transactions and Events. A decision needs to be made whether only transactions, or both transactions and events (and which ones), are to be admitted to financial statements. Present GAAP is substantially transaction oriented, although some events are used to modify the amounts resulting from recording transactions at historical cost.

Transactions include exchanges of assets or services. A transaction arising as a result of relations with an outsider is an *external* transaction; one resulting from the expiration of cost, or by an accrual, transfer, or allocation of income or expense, is an *internal* transaction (see Kohler, 1983, p. 283). The distinction between internal and external transactions is somewhat dependent on one's perception of the boundaries of the business enterprise.

Events, on the other hand, do not require, and mostly will not involve, any direct participation by the affected business enterprise; they occur outside the enterprise. Events currently used to modify transactions recorded at historical cost include the lower of cost or market value for inventories where some external event reduces its value.

Qualitative Characteristics. By referring to SFAC 2, *Qualitative Charateristics of Accounting Information* (FASB, 1980d), there are several characteristics of financial information that significantly affect earnings recognition criteria, specifically:

1. Relevance
2. Reliability
3. Verifiability
4. Representational faithfulness (validity)
5. Neutrality

Transactions usually have a larger measure of the foregoing qualitative characteristics than do external events.

Monetary and Nonmonetary Transactions

A major variable in revenue recognition is the extent, if any, to which a transaction is nonmonetary. For example, a machine purchased for cash is a monetary transaction to the purchaser as well as to the seller; one gives cash and the other gets cash. Adding a trade-in to that transaction may make it partly nonmonetary. Swapping one machine for another similar machine with little or no cash involved is an entirely nonmonetary transaction, and special accounting rules govern such transactions.

Determining the extent to which the earning process is complete or substantially complete would seem to require the selection of some critical event in the earning process to permit any revenue to be recognized, and in current practice this largely depends on whether the transaction is monetary or nonmonetary.

A PROGNOSIS ON FINANCIAL REPORTING

The traditional accounting model cannot cope with the demands placed on it if financial statements are to be viewed as the core of financial reporting. At one level there is a demand for greater definitional precision and certaintly in financial statements—to meet preparers' and auditors' concerns about liability, and users' wishes for comparability of reported financial results and absence of undue bias by the statement issuers. The FASB's efforts in setting standards have operated in this direction generally, and statements have therefore become more objective.

At the same time there is increased demand for an orientation toward the future. This orientation is inevitably subjective and cannot be achieved within an objective model. Even in the presentation of historical data the multiple complexities and uncertainties of a business enterprise make it increasingly difficult to utilize a well-defined, single-valued, consolidated model to describe results in a meaningful way. Thus there is dual movement in financial reporting: in the direction of a better-defined, more circumscribed, and more objective (but also less useful) set of financial statements; and toward a more future-oriented, subjective, and expansive set of supplementary disclosures. Both thrusts seem likely to continue.

The result should be a reporting package that no longer forces the same degree of trade-off between reliability and relevance in a single set of financial statements but rather permits reliability to be the dominant concern in one part of the reporting framework while relevance is the primary element in the other. This approach inevitably implies increased complexity and hence greater responsibility being placed on preparers, auditors, and users of financial reporting. The natural human longing of users for a simple "handle," like earnings per share, to describe a complex reality must be put aside and replaced by a recognition that an analyst's role must necessarily include the construction of a complicated mosaic in order to achieve an understanding of an enterprise.

2

Conceptual Framework for Accounting and Reporting

THE QUEST FOR CONCEPTS

A conceptual framework is intended to contribute order and thereby discipline. Engineering concepts, for example, permit construction of a bridge that will meet perceived standards of safety. Public expectation that those standards have been met underlies confidence that the bridge will stand, even against exceptional stresses – although occasionally it doesn't. Similarly, belief that coordinated concepts underlie accounting standards bolsters confidence that the reporting is neutral and conforms with those standards – although on occasion it might not.

Investors and lenders are concerned about amount, timing, and risk associated with return *on* investment and return *of* investment. The unique role of financial reporting is to furnish some of the information useful in the assessment of risk and return and thereby contribute to maintenance of healthy capital markets, both public and private. Fulfilling that role requires identification of purposes and bounds of competence of financial reporting as well as compatible accounting concepts that further public understanding and public confidence.

Historical Perspective

The progress of record-keeping has been reasonably well documented for about 500 years. Only during the past 60 years have formal efforts been made in the United States to search for an underlying conceptual structure. Since the early 1900s, accountants and others have written "around" the subject of accounting concepts. In 1929, John B. Canning, an economist, questioned the imprecision with which accountants approached conceptual matters such as the then confusing array of definitions of terms as basic as "assets." Since that time, persons interested in financial reporting — such as Paton, Littleton, Gilman, Hendrickson, Moonitz, Sprouse, Chambers, and Sterling — have written varied and instructive views on the subject of accounting concepts. However, none of those writers developed what might be considered a conceptual framework. That development awaited the creation of the FASB and its work on the conceptual framework project. Not surprisingly, many people today believe that the FASB's conclusions in its concepts statements are incomplete. Future accounting historians may simply add the FASB to the long list of progenitors.

Progress Toward a Structure

New York Stock Exchange. Early evidence of attention to broad principles is contained in correspondence between the American Institute of Accountants (now the AICPA) and the New York Stock Exchange, starting in 1932. From that correspondence, five "broad principles" surfaced (AIA, 1934a).

One "broad principle" recognizes the sale, with some exceptions, as the point of profit realization and admonishes against recognition of unrealized profit. Another proscribes charges to capital surplus that should instead be made to income. A third deals with subsidiary earned surplus accumulated before acquisition and dividends declared from that earned surplus. The fourth principle acknowledges that treasury stock in some circumstances may be shown as an asset, but holds that dividends declared on treasury stock should not be included in income. The fifth, more a "rule" than a broad principle, requires receivables from officers, employees, and affiliates to be shown separately. Although far short of a conceptual framework, it was a beginning.

Committee on Accounting Procedure. During the period that the Committee on Accounting Procedure (CAP) of the AICPA was in operation from 1938 to 1957, no formal attention was devoted to conceptual framework issues. In part, it was that omission that led to the creation in 1958 of the AICPA Accounting Principles Board (APB) and the Accounting Research Division to conduct independent research of pertinent accounting subjects including conceptual matters. Two conceptual research projects were sponsored.

The first study, conducted by Maurice Moonitz, who had been named Director of Accounting Research of the AICPA, resulted in the publication in 1962 of Accounting Research Study No. 1, *The Basic Postulates of Accounting*. In that same year, Accounting Research Study No. 3, *A Tentative Set of Broad Accounting Principles for Business Enterprises*, by Robert Sprouse and Moonitz, was also published.

The *postulates study* focused on the kinds of problems in the economic or political environment with which accountants are concerned. Moonitz concluded, however, that

> relatively heavy reliance must be placed on deductive reasoning in the development of accounting postulates and principles. We must first recognize and define problems to be solved, then move to their solution by careful attention to what ought to be the case, not what "is" the case. Hopefully, the two, "ought" and "is," will not be too far apart, but we have no reason to expect them to be identical [Moonitz, 1962, p. 6].

Moonitz identified three levels of postulates:

1. Those deriving from analysis of the environment:
   - quantification
   - exchange
   - entities
   - time period
   - unit of measure
2. Those concerning aspects of accounting itself:
   - financial statements
   - market prices
   - entities
   - tentativeness
3. Imperatives:
   - continuity
   - objectivity
   - consistency
   - stable unit
   - disclosure

The *broad accounting principles study* sought compatibility with the postulates identified in the earlier study and noted that accounting's proper functions "derive from the measurement of the resources of specific entities and of changes in those resources" (Sprouse and Moonitz, 1962, p. 23). The study went on to define financial statements, assets, costs, depreciation, liabilities, owners' equity, invested capital, retained earnings, net profit, net loss, revenue, expense, gains, and losses, thus comprehending elements of financial statements as then constituted.

Accounting Principles Board. The studies on postulates and principles were addressed by the APB, which concluded in APB Statement 1, *Statement by the Accounting Principles Board* (AICPA, 1962):

> While these studies are a valuable contribution to accounting thinking, they are too radically different from present generally accepted accounting principles for acceptance at this time.

The APB added, almost plaintively, that

> There is ample room for improvement in present generally accepted accounting principles and a need to narrow or eliminate areas of difference which now exist. Some of the specific recommendations in these studies may prove acceptable to the Board while others may not.

Not surprisingly, the APB found it necessary to follow the path marked by the CAP. No significant further conceptual research was commissioned by the APB.

The APB remained mindful of the need for a broad conceptual basis for discharging its responsibilities and occasionally found itself arguing basic issues. However, significant resources were devoted to existing GAAP. An APB-commissioned study, Accounting Research Study No. 7, *Inventory of Generally Accepted Accounting Principles for Business Enterprises* (1965), by Paul Grady, at the time Director of Accounting Research for the AICPA, surveyed the then generally accepted practices. Grady's study dealt both with practices common to all industries and with specialized industries. Further, he summarized the status of accounting principles deemed to have reached accepted status in the United States in terms of broad objectives, standards of accounting performance and measurement, and standards of disclosure.

With Grady's work as a starting point, the APB issued Statement 4, *Basic Concepts and Accounting Principles Underlying Financial Statements of Business Enterprises* (AICPA, 1970). That Statement dealt with the environment of financial accounting, uses of the information resulting from financial accounting, its objectives, and its basic elements.

Somewhat like Canning's analysis over 40 years earlier, APB Statement 4 deduced the fundamentals underlying GAAP from what was discerned in the practices of the times. If there were gaps or holes in the discernible concepts, they would show up, and they did. For example, in connection with perhaps the most fundamental of all notions, the nature of assets, the study recursively reasoned that assets shown in balance sheets consisted of

1. Economic resources that are recognized and measured in conformity with generally accepted accounting principles.
2. Certain deferred charges that are not resources but that are recognized in conformity with generally accepted accounting principles (¶ 132).

Other basic financial statement elements, including liabilities, revenues, and expenses, were also defined in part in terms of what was generally accepted at the time.

Financial Accounting Standards Board. By 1970, 11 years after the formation of the APB and the Accounting Research Division, discontent with the state of corporate financial reporting and the effectiveness of standard setting had reached a level of considerable concern within the accounting profession. The profession itself responded by initiating a fresh look. The outcome was the naming of two task forces in 1971: one to consider the structure for standard setting, the other to study objectives of financial reporting.

The report on the first of those studies, *Establishing Financial Accounting Standards* (AICPA, 1972b), also called the *Wheat Study* after Francis Wheat, the chairman of the study group, was issued in 1972. The AICPA quickly adopted the recommendation to replace the APB with the FASB under the auspices of the newly formed Financial Accounting Foundation. The particulars of this restructuring are discussed in Chapter 46. The second study is discussed in the next major section.

Political Equilibrium

Standard setting for financial accounting is accomplished within an environment of shifting, swirling, conflicting forces, commonly characterized as a political climate. If the process is to be successful over the long term, those forces must be kept in balance. An implied consequence of the process is that some enterprises, perhaps many, will be required to change or modify their financial reporting practices. And each requirement to change will meet resistance, if only because resistance to change is an abiding human condition.

A conceptual framework that will effectively guide reporting, then, must take account of attitudes and should attempt both to influence and to accommodate them, but not to get too far ahead of them; above all, it must be, and be perceived as, evenhanded. Further, the results must be attainable at reasonable cost.

FASB CONCEPTUAL FRAMEWORK PROJECT

At the very outset, the FASB took care to tell its constituents that financial statements cannot fully satisfy the needs of users interested in making investment, credit, and similar decisions. Indeed, there is a spectrum of financial information of which financial statements are only a part. In its *Invitation to Comment on Financial Statements and Other Means of Financial Reporting* (1980b), the FASB presented a graphic depiction of this seminal issue, to establish what part of financial reporting would be covered in the planned concepts statements and, of course, in the FASB standards issued. This information spectrum is shown in Figure 2.1. (The FASB did not include this illustration in its initial concepts statements, although its import was discussed; Figure 2.1 is taken from SFAC 5, and is similar to the initial spectrum chart.)

After "staking out its turf," the FASB started with objectives determined from preexisting conventions. Analysis of those objectives, and ways to fulfill them, led to the conclusion that many long-standing conventions are both compatible and useful. Basic to the reporting of business activities are a balance sheet, an earnings statement, a statement of cash flows, articulation of assets and liabilities, and changes in those elements manifested in revenues, expenses, gains, losses, and capital adjustments. In other words, conventions are more than assumptions – they grow out of efforts to meet initially perceived objectives.

A conspicuous FASB "given" is that a proprietary view, rather than an entity view, will continue.[1] Perhaps the most significant implications of that assumption

---

[1] Under the proprietary theory, all entities in a consolidated enterprise are viewed as owned by the shareholders of the parent company. Therefore, minority interests in these subsidiaries are not part of the capital structure, but are a simple, mathematical by-product of the consolidation process. Under the entity theory, the consolidated enterprise is seen as a single entity, with no separation among its components. Thus, there are no minority interests, but only different kinds of shareholders.

concern the nature of payments to creditors and of distributions to owners. An entity view might lead to the conclusion that by nature those payments and distributions are alike, that in both instances they are either a cost or a distribution of earnings. That matter should be reexamined at some point, but there is no pressing need to do so now.

The Hierarchy

Desirable as it may be to treat coordinated concepts together, some partitioning is necessary; otherwise, the issues cannot be kept in focus by the diverse interests entitled to have a role in bringing about changes in financial reporting. The FASB necessarily identified a hierarchy of conceptual considerations. At the peak are *objectives* — purposes to be served by financial reporting. Then there are the *elements* — the financial statement representations of the things (assets, liabilities, revenues, expenses, gains, losses, capital) for which accounting accounts. In addition, there are the *measurements* of the elements — the scales to be used and the attributes to be scaled — and the events or conditions giving rise to the *recognition* of the elements. Finally, there are the *qualitative characteristics* of financial accounting, which are the qualities of data entitled to be included in financial statements and the characteristics sought to be satisfied. These conceptual considerations are fundamental, but there of course are other factors: the way things are displayed, concern about cash flows, and the scope of financial reporting, that is, reporting beyond the formal financial statements. The FASB did not finalize its concepts statements in the order mentioned; nevertheless, they will be discussed in that logical order.

The Board states that these concepts statements will provide conceptual guidance on matters of recognition, measurement, *and display*, and that further development of those matters may occur as these concepts are applied *at the standards level*. This suggests that the FASB considers the conceptual framework complete, at least for the present.

Business Enterprises

Objectives. The objectives of financial reporting necessarily derive from the role of financial reporting in a society. That role in American society concerns allocation of economic resources (goods and services) to enterprises, both those seeking a monetary return on investment and those not so concerned. For some business enterprises, this allocation process is facilitated by a public capital market, in which investors and creditors can, in effect, exchange holdings; for many others, mainly small enterprises, the capital allocation process results from direct negotiation of enterprises with investors and creditors. In either situation, the role of financial reporting concerns the use of financial data about enterprises as part of the basis for investing and lending choices.

In 1978 the FASB issued SFAC 1, *Objectives of Financial Reporting by Business Enterprises*, the first in a series of Statements of Financial Accounting Concepts. It builds on the 1973 *Report of the Study Group on Objectives of Financial Statements*

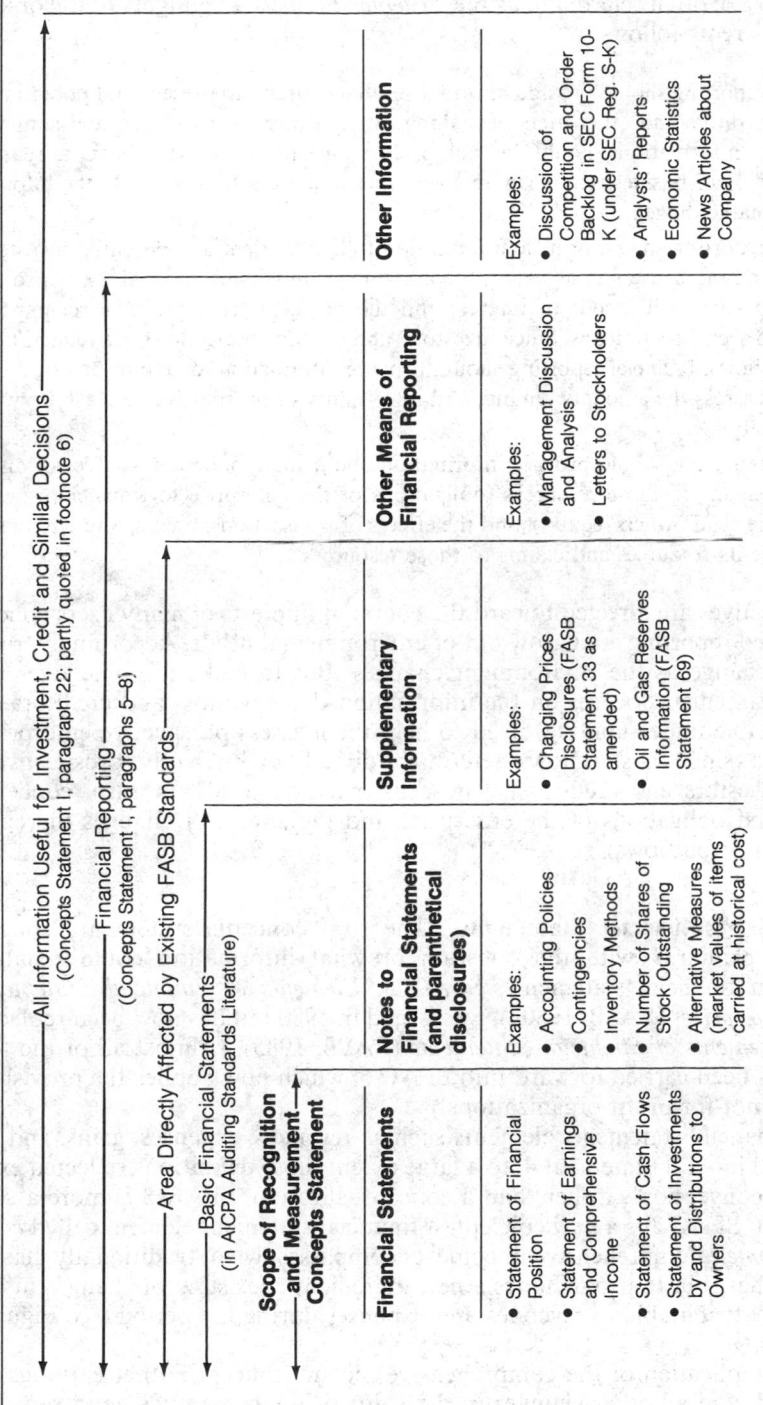

FIG. 2.1 Information Spectrum

Source: SFAC 5, ¶ 8.

(AICPA, 1973), often referred to as the *Trueblood Report*. Highlights of the objectives in SFAC 1 are as follows:

- Financial reporting should provide information that is useful to present and potential investors and creditors and other users in making rational investment, credit, and similar decisions. The information should be comprehensible to those who have a reasonable understanding of business and economic activities and are willing to study the information with reasonable diligence.
- Financial reporting should provide information to help present and potential investors and creditors and other users in assessing the amounts, timing, and uncertainty of prospective cash receipts from dividends or interest and the proceeds from the sale, redemption, or maturity of securities or loans. Since investors' and creditors' cash flows are related to enterprise cash flows, financial reporting should provide information to help investors, creditors, and others assess the amounts, timing, and uncertainty of prospective net cash flows to the related enterprise.
- Financial reporting should provide information about the economic resources of an enterprise, the claims to those resources (obligations of the enterprise to transfer resources to other entities and owners' equity), and the effects of transactions, events, and circumstances that change its resources and claims to those resources.

The objectives are directed toward the common interests of many users concerned with financial reporting, and grow out of environmental needs. Accordingly, they are subject to change as the environment changes. But to make the objectives operational, the statement focuses on the information that investors and creditors (those with reasonable understanding) need to help them assess prospective enterprise net cash inflows (since those inflows determine, directly or indirectly, prospective cash flows to investors and creditors). Those information needs, in turn, concern the resources and obligations of the enterprise and the effects of changes therein (i.e., cash inflows or outflows).

Elements of Financial Statements. The first concepts statements concerned themselves primarily with the question of what information could reliably be displayed in financial statements. SFAC 3, *Elements of Financial Statements of Business Enterprises* (FASB, 1980a), was issued in 1980 but has now been replaced by SFAC 6, *Elements of Financial Statements* (FASB, 1985). (Almost all of the text of SFAC 3 has been carried forward into SFAC 6, which now applies the provisions of SFAC 3 to not-for-profit organizations.)

When financial statements elements such as revenues, expenses, gains, and losses were defined in APB Statement 4, to a large extent those definitions reflected existing accounting conventions, rather than a conceptualization. SFAC 3 is more assertive.

Central to SFAC 3 is a new concept: a financial statement element called *comprehensive income*. Comprehensive income encompasses what traditionally has been called earnings; but it also includes a new ingredient consisting of changes in equity not directly attributable to revenues and expenses during the period (see Figure 2.2, item B.1.b.).

A clear implication of the comprehensive income concept is that earnings, however defined, and all other changes in the value of the company's net assets, essen-

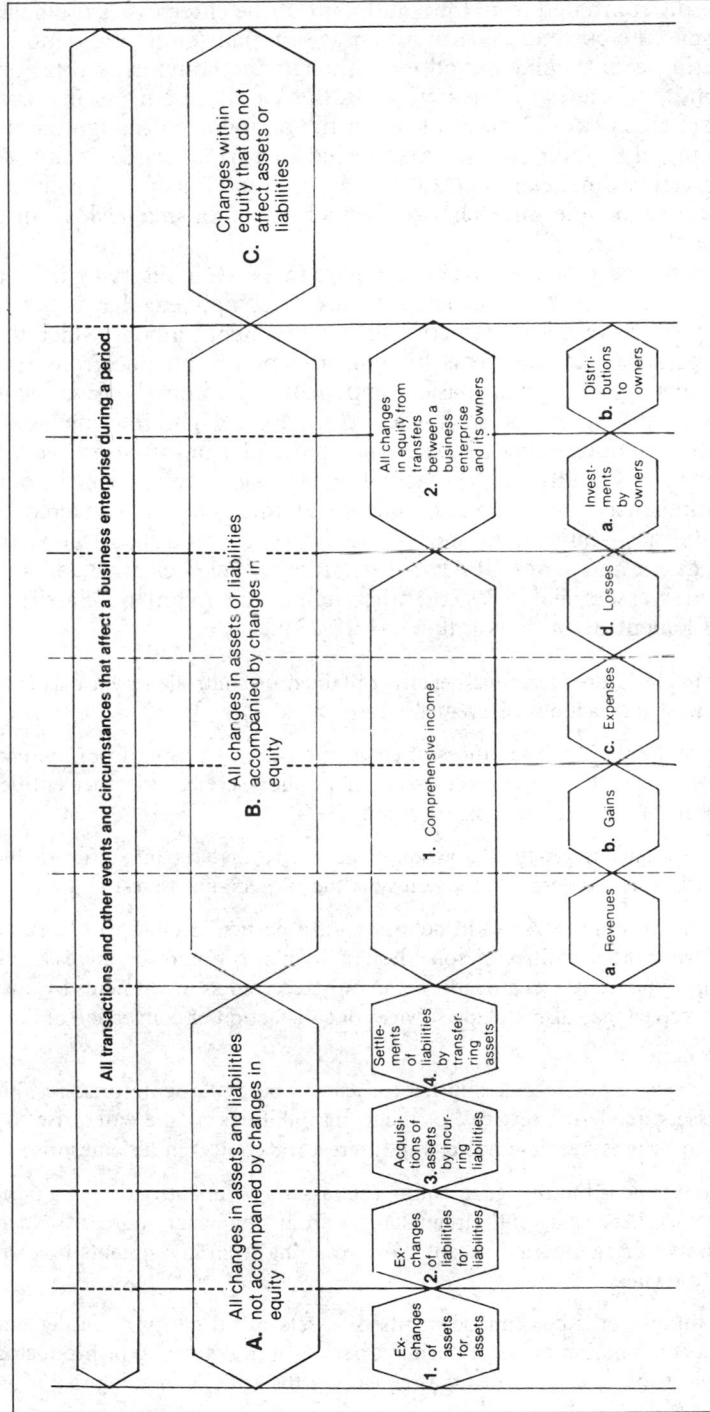

FIG. 2.2 Interrelationship of Financial Statement Elements

Source: SFAC 6, ¶ 65.

tially cannot be differentiated from the standpoint of the enterprise's financial condition. For example, the current value of a mining company's mineral deposits might be doubled during a particular period even though the company's total operating expenses outrun its revenues for the period. In this case, the current historical cost-based income statement would show a loss for the period even though the increased value of the company's total assets, as expressed in current values, may offset the loss. But presumably financial reporting built on the concept of comprehensive income, if it were to include value changes, would display a smaller loss (or perhaps even a gain) for the period.

The FASB chose not to define the term *earnings* in SFAC 3, reserving it for possible future designation of some "intermediate measure or component that is part of comprehensive income" (p. xiii). Those intermediate components, among which the FASB also includes operating income, gross margin, and pretax income from continuing operations, are distinguished from basic components of comprehensive income (the revenues/expenses and gains/losses shown in Figure 2.2). The intermediate components are only aggregations intended to supply a particular information need, whereas the basic components broadly describe actual increases or decreases in income.

Besides comprehensive income, the financial statement elements covered in SFAC 3 are assets, liabilities, equity investments by owners, distributions to owners, revenues, expenses, gains, and losses. SFAC 3 discusses these elements broadly instead of defining particular assets, liabilities, or other items that might be classified under each of them. Element definitions follow (¶¶ 18-73):

Assets are probable future economic benefits obtained or controlled by a particular entity as a result of past transactions or events.

Liabilities are probable future sacrifices of economic benefits arising from present obligations of a particular entity to transfer assets or provide services to other entities in the future as a result of past transactions or events.

Equity is the residual interest in the assets of an entity that remains after deducting its liabilities. In a business enterprise, the equity is the ownership interest.

Investments by owners are increases in net assets of a particular enterprise, resulting from transfer to it from other entities of something valuable to obtain or increase ownership interests (or equity) in it. Assets are most commonly received as investments by owners, but that which is received may also include services or satisfaction or conversion of liabilities of the enterprise.

Distributions to owners are decreases in net assets of a particular enterprise resulting from transferring assets, rendering services, or incurring liabilities by the enterprise to owners. Distributions to owners decrease ownership interest (or equity) in an enterprise.

Comprehensive income is the change in equity (net assets) of an entity during a period from transactions and other events and circumstances from nonowner sources. It includes all changes in equity during a period except those resulting from investments by owners and distributions to owners.

Revenues are inflows or other enhancements of assets of an entity or settlements of its liabilities (or a combination of both) during a period from delivering or producing goods, rendering services, or other activities that constitute the entity's ongoing major or central operations.

Expenses are outflows or other using up of assets or incurrences of liabilities (or a combination of both) during a period from delivering or producing goods, rendering services, or carrying out other activities that constitute the entity's ongoing major or central operations.

Gains are increases in equity (net assets) from peripheral or incidental transactions of an entity and from all other transactions and other events and circumstances affecting the entity during a period except those that result from revenues or investments by owners.

Losses are decreases in equity (net assets) from peripheral or incidental transactions of an entity and from all other transactions and other events and circumstances affecting the entity during a period, except those that result from expenses or distributions to owners.

Assets, liabilities, and equity differ from the other seven elements in that these three describe levels or amounts of resources, or claims thereto, as of a given moment. The other elements describe the effects of other events and circumstances affecting assets, liabilities, and equity. This interconnection (or articulation) of changes results in financial statements that are fundamentally interrelated.

The FASB does not expect that SFAC 3 alone will have a significant impact on current practice. This is because the SFAC 3 does not do much beyond defining the basic financial statement elements. However, these definitions are a significant first step in determining what should be included in financial statements, since the definitions screen out items that lack one or more of the requisite characteristics.

Recognition and Measurement. In 1984, the FASB issued SFAC 5, *Recognition and Measurement in Financial Statements of Business Enterprises* (FASB, 1984c).

The Statement represents the recognition, measurement, and display concepts on which six Board members were able to agree. Because their individual views range over a broad spectrum, most of the agreed-upon matters are either so basic as to be indisputable or so abstract and general that they can accommodate a wide range of specific practices. SFAC 5 is more pragmatic than conceptual; it is more an inventory of existing practices than a consensus on future direction.

SFAC 5 describes recognition as

the process of formally recording or incorporating an item into the financial statements of an entity as an asset, liability, revenue, expense, or the like. Recognition includes depiction of an item in both words and numbers, with the amount included in the totals of the financial statements. For an asset or liability, recognition involves recording not only acquisition or incurrence of the item but also later changes, including those that result in removal from the financial statements. [¶ 6]

An item should be recognized in the financial statements, according to SFAC 5, when it meets the following four criteria, (¶ 63), subject to a cost-benefit constraint and materiality threshold:

1. *Definitions* – the item meets the definition of an element of financial statements.
2. *Measurability* – it has a relevant attribute measurable with sufficient reliability.
3. *Relevance* – the information about it is capable of making a difference in user decisions.
4. *Reliability* – the information is representationally faithful, verifiable, and neutral.

The FASB combined into SFAC 5 the previously separate projects on recognition and measurement because they were so interdependent. Though SFAC 5 offers little guidance for recognition, it offers even less for measurement.

Generally, a measurement decision consists of two parts: (1) the choice of a unit (or scale) of measurement and (2) the choice of the attribute of an item to be measured. The Board expects that nominal units of money will continue as the unit of measure, even though a stable unit would be ideal. SFAC 5 acknowledges that elements in financial statements are presently measured by different attributes (such as historical cost, current cost, current market value, net realizable value, or present value of future cash flows). Further, the Statement indicates that the use of different attributes will continue, and relevance and reliability (qualitative characteristics that will be discussed later) are overriding considerations in the measurement decision. That is the extent of the guidance on measurement.

Nevertheless, SFAC 5 (pp. vii–viii) includes some important observations about financial statements. For example:

1. For items that meet the criteria for recognition, disclosure is not a substitute for recognition in the financial statements.
2. A full set of financial statements for a period should show:
   a. Financial position at the end of the period;
   b. Earnings for the period;
   c. Comprehensive income for the period;
   d. Cash flows during the period; and
   e. Investments by and distribution to owners during the period.
3. Financial statements result from simplifying, condensing, and aggregating masses of data. As a result, they convey information that would be obscured if great detail were provided. Although those simplifications, condensations, and aggregations are both necessary and useful, the Board believes that it is important to avoid focusing attention almost exclusively on "the bottom line," earnings per share, or other highly simplified condensations.
4. A statement of financial position does not purport to show the value of a business enterprise but, together with the other financial statements and other information, should provide information that is useful to those who desire to make their own estimates of the enterprise's value. Those estimates are part of financial analysis, not financial reporting, but financial accounting assists financial analysis.
5. Statements of earnings and of comprehensive income together reflect the extent to which, and the ways in which, the equity of an entity increased or decreased from all sources other than transactions with owners during a period.

Although SFAC 5 does not define *earnings* in any precise way, it describes earnings as a measure of entity performance during a period. It also acknowledges that comprehensive income is a broader measure of performance than earnings and describes two classes of gains and losses that are included in comprehensive income, but excluded from earnings. Those classes are (p. ix):

1. Effects of accounting adjustments of earlier period estimates that are recognized in the current period;

2. Certain other changes in net assets (principally, certain holding gains and losses). Examples in current practice are some changes in market value of investments (SFAS 12, *Accounting for Certain Marketable Securities* (189)) and foreign currency translation adjustments (SFAS 52, *Foreign Currency translation* (F60)).

Thus, the FASB has formally legitimized those adjustments as components of comprehensive income. This may remove some of the confusion that accompanied the introduction of those adjustments in SFAS 12 and 52, along with charges of "dirty surplus."

Although SFAC 5 does little more than bless and clarify current practice, it does not foreclose the possibility of future change. But it establishes a tight screen through which such changes must pass. That screen is summarized in the last sentence of the Statement:

> When evidence indicates that information about an item that is more useful (relevant and reliable) than information currently reported is available at a justifiable cost, it should be included in financial statements. [¶ 91]

Recognition and measurement are further discussed in Chapter 1.

Nonbusiness Organizations

Objectives. The FASB's fourth concepts statement (SFAC 4), *Objectives of Financial Reporting by Nonbusiness Organizations* (FASB, 1980c), is essentially a modification of SFAC 1. In Statement 1, the FASB announced it would develop a set of basic concepts applicable to all entities, and that particular differences among different types of enterprises would be given appropriate consideration only when and where the specific need arose. As between business and nonbusiness organizations, a separate statement of reporting objectives was merited on the strength of three fundamental differences between business and nonbusiness entities (SFAC 4, ¶ 6):

1. "Investors" in nonbusiness organizations do not expect to recover what they put in;
2. Nonbusiness operations do not aim for a profit; and
3. There are no ownership interests that can be sold or transferred, or that carry rights to a share of the entity's net assets should the organization be liquidated.

Probably the most obvious of those differences is the second. That nonbusiness organizations do not aim for a profit raises the issue of whether their service efforts and accomplishments should be reported in a manner similar to that used in the external profit-oriented reporting of business organizations. Certainly "investors" (meaning effectively, resource providers) in not-for-profit organizations have an interest in seeing information that shows how well their company has achieved its goals. Presently, however, this sort of information is generally unavailable.

The fundamental conceptual question about nonbusiness organizations is whether useful nonfinancial measures are feasible; that is, can nonbusiness performance indicators be developed to serve the function performed by measures of profits in financial reports for business enterprises? According to SFAC 4, nonbusiness organizations should provide information that is useful (1) to present and potential resource providers in making decisions about allocation of resources; (2) in assessing the services that a nonbusiness organization provides, and its ability to continue to provide those services; and (3) in assessing how managers of an organization have discharged stewardship responsibilities. Such information, properly measured and reported, would be most helpful to users of their financial statements.

Nongovernmental not-for-profit organizations are discussed in Chapter 32.

Elements of Financial Statements. In 1985, the FASB issued SFAC 6, *Elements of Financial Statements* (FASB, 1985) (1) replacing SFAC 3, (2) expanding its scope to include not-for-profit organizations, and (3) amending SFAC 2 (discussed later in this chapter) to apply it to financial reporting by not-for-profit organizations. Most of the text of SFAC 3 is carried forward.

The statement defines three classes of net assets of not-for-profit organizations and the changes in those classes during a period:

1. *Permanent restricted net assets* are those whose use by the organization is limited by donor-imposed stipulations that neither expire by passage of time nor can be fulfilled or otherwise removed by actions of the organization.
2. *Temporarily restricted net assets* are those whose use by the organization is limited by donor-imposed stipulations that either expire by passage of time or can be fulfilled and removed by actions of the organization pursuant to those stipulations.
3. *Unrestricted net assets* are those whose use is not limited by donor-imposed stipulations.

SFAC 6 does not preclude the classification of assets and liabilities into fund groups. It merely points out that such a classification is not a necessary part of general purpose external financial reporting. Presumably, if an entity chose to use fund accounting, it would have to use the three groupings of net assets within each fund where applicable.

In SFAC 6, the FASB indicated that temporarily restricted contributions do not fit the definition of a liability and are thus revenue items, as opposed to deferred revenues, that increase temporarily restricted net assets. When the restrictions are satisfied, the assets are reclassified (added) to unrestricted net assets. So far, however, this approach appears to affect only temporarily restricted contributions. It does not apply to temporarily restricted grants for which the grantor expects to receive commensurate value. These types of grants would not be gifts. Presumably, such grants and advance payments, such as membership dues, would continue to be classified as deferred revenue.

Further, SFAC 6 adopts the financial capital maintenance concept (see Chapter 3) and, consistent with that concept, advocates depreciation for assets of not-for-profit organizations (required by SFAS 93, *Recognition of Depreciation of Not-for-Profit Organizations* (D40), but suspended pending resolution of jurisdiction with GASB).

Qualitative Characteristics

In 1980, the FASB issued SFAC 2, *Qualitative Characteristics of Accounting Information,* to describe the criteria the FASB uses in developing standards. SFAC 2 states

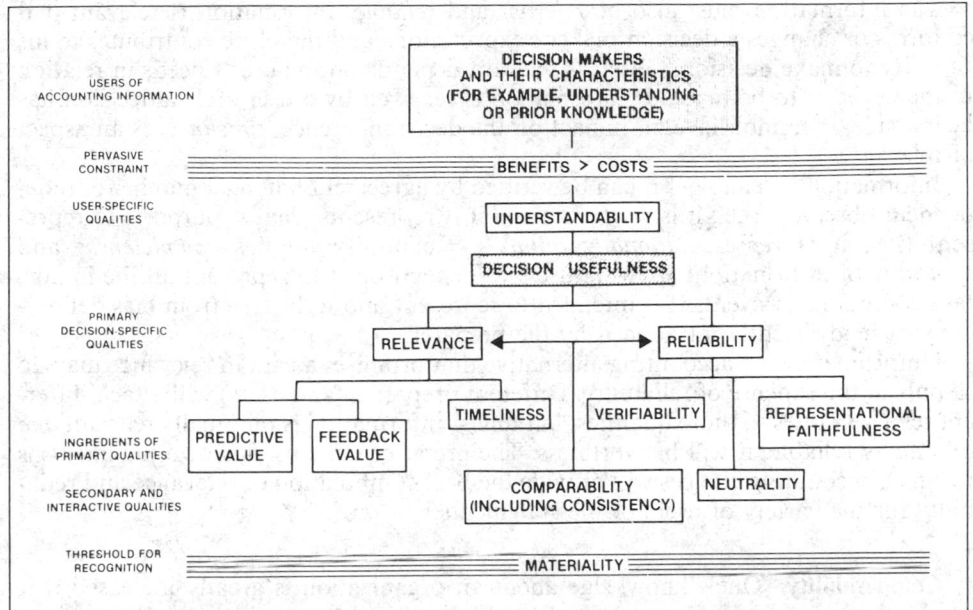

FIG. 2.3 A Hierarchy of Accounting Qualities
Source: SFAC 2, ¶ 32.

that those same criteria should be used by preparers and users of financial statements in selecting and evaluating alternative accounting and reporting methods or disclosures. In 1985, SFAC 6 specified that these qualitative characteristics applied both to business and nonbusiness entities.

Examples of accounting alternatives include methods of cost allocation (e.g., alternative depreciation or inventory-costing methods) and recognition of revenue (e.g., alternative treatment of long-term construction contracts). Examples of reporting alternatives include showing more detail or less, aggregating or disaggregating accounting items, and showing related revenues gross or net.

The actual selection of accounting alternatives has to confront conflicting interests and needs. Judgment is required to balance these conflicts to provide the most useful information in a way that is meaningful to users. SFAC 2 presents a hierarchy of qualities of accounting information with *usefulness for decision making* as the primary criterion of choice. Figure 2.3 reproduces the chart used by the FASB to frame its commentary; it is also the focus of the explanatory remarks that follow.

Relevance and Reliability. Information useful for decision making must be *understandable.* If the information is so complex or fragmented that it cannot be comprehended, it is of no use. But information that cannot be understood by one user may be understood by another. Thus, whether information is understandable depends on both the nature of the information and the understanding of the user.

The information must also be *relevant* and *reliable.* Information is relevant if it confirms or changes a decision maker's expectations and therefore contributes to his capacity to make decisions. What is relevant depends on the user's needs in relation to the decision to be made. If information is received by a user after a decision has been made, it cannot have an impact on the decision. Hence, *timeliness* is an aspect of relevance.

Information is reliable if it can be verified by agreement among a number of independent observers (i.e., it is *verifiable*) *and* if it represents what it purports to represent (i.e., it is *representationally faithful*). Reliability implies *completeness* and *neutrality* of information, allowing users to depend on it to represent all the important conditions or events it is intended to represent and to be free from bias deliberately or inadvertently introduced by the preparer.

Unfortunately, an accounting alternative that promises a gain in relevance may do so only at the expense of reliability. Different preparers (and users) will attach different relative values to those qualities, but unless information is minimally relevant *and* minimally reliable, it will be worthless. The preparer must use his own judgment as to which accounting choices will provide the best combination of relevance and reliability for the variety of users of the statements.

Comparability. One's knowledge about an organization is greatly increased if it can be compared in significant respects with other similar organizations. Comparison of the financial statements of two or more similar enterprises is one of the most widely used and most effective ways of gaining insights into the strengths and weaknesses of the enterprises. This can be achieved if the enterprises being compared are using uniform accounting methods or if disclosure is adequate to allow the user to make adjustments to a common basis. It would be useless to compare, without adjustment, the current ratios of two manufacturing enterprises if one carried its inventory on a FIFO basis and the other on a LIFO basis.

Within a diversified organization, comparisons can be made between divisions or other segments, and the same considerations apply. In addition, if accounting methods are applied consistently over time, new insights may be gained from interperiod comparisons without looking for external benchmarks. From such comparisons, it may be possible to detect significant trends or to interpret important fluctuations in operating results or in financial position. Thus, both *uniformity* in accounting methods and *consistency* in their application over time are essential to comparability.

But uniformity of method alone is not sufficient. Valid comparisons can be made only if the accounting methods used reflect, with reasonable completeness, the underlying economic activity being reported. To cite one of the FASB's examples, a comparison of the performance of two investment managers on the basis of their realized gains during a year could be carried out using completely uniform accounting methods, and yet, by ignoring unrealized gains made by one of them and not by the other, the comparison could fail altogether to reflect their relative success (SFAS 2, ¶ 118).

Likewise, consistency of method alone may not bring true comparability between two measurements if the measurements do not truly represent what they purport to represent. This can be exemplified by a series of sales figures prepared consistently and showing considerable growth from period to period. When price level changes are taken into account, however, the growth could be largely illusory.

Costs and Benefits. A pervasive constraint overriding all these qualitative characteristics is the relative *cost and benefits* resulting from providing the accounting information. Information is costly to gather, process, report on, audit, interpret, and use. As with other commodities or services, new financial information should be supplied only if its benefits exceed its costs. Even though identification and measurement of these costs and benefits is extremely complex and subjective, their consideration is essential in selecting and evaluating accounting and reporting policies.

Materiality. Another pervasive factor is *materiality*. This concept is discussed extensively in SFAC 2, ¶¶ 123–132 and ¶¶ 161–170. It is defined as

> the magnitude of [an omission or misstatement of accounting information that, in the light of surrounding circumstances, makes it] probable that the judgment of a reasonable person relying [on the information] would have been changed or influenced by the inclusion or correction of the item. [¶ 132]

An item of information can be relevant and yet be too small to matter. To be material, an item or a misstatement of an item must be of sufficient magnitude to make a difference to a decision maker. For that reason, materiality is shown in Figure 2.3 as the "threshold for recognition." Whether an item is material will depend on the circumstances surrounding it, and judgments must therefore be made on a case-by-case basis. The professional literature recognizes that in applying accounting standards, common sense demands a *de minimis* rule. Thus, each FASB statement bears this legend: "The provisions of this Statement need not be applied to immaterial items."

An item that may be immaterial in one set of circumstances may be material in another. Thus, an otherwise immaterial item may become material because it may result in a breach of covenant, or because it arises out of a related party transaction, or because a taint of illegality attaches to it, or because it reverses an earnings trend. These are only a few examples of the kinds of circumstances that may lower a materiality threshold; many others could be cited.

Materiality has many legal connotations, and a definition by the U.S. Supreme Court in *TSC Industries Inc. v. Northway Inc.* [2] is in fact referred to in SFAC 2 (¶ 165) as "the most authoritative judicial definition of what constitutes a material omitted fact":

> An omitted fact *is* material if there is a substantial likelihood that a reasonable shareholder would consider it important in deciding how to vote. This standard is fully consistent with the general description of materiality as a requirement that "the defect have a significant *propensity* to affect the voting process." It does not require proof of a substantial likelihood that disclosure of the omitted fact would have caused the reasonable investor to change his vote. What the standard does contemplate is a showing of a substantial likelihood that, under all the circumstances, the omitted fact would have assumed actual significance in the deliberations of the reasonable shareholder. Put another way, there must be a substantial

---

[2] TSC Indus. Inc. v. Northway Inc., Fed. Sec. L. Rep. (CCH) ¶ 95,615 (US 1976).

likelihood that the disclosure of the omitted fact would have been viewed by the reasonable investor as having significantly altered the "total mix" of information made available. [¶ 164]

Other judicial interpretations of materiality will be found in Chapter 49, dealing with the legal environment.

It is easier for an accountant to learn formal accounting rules than to learn how to form judgments about the degree of precision with which they should be applied or the rigor with which an audit test should be followed up. Research has thrown light on the way that materiality judgments have been made in practice in several different situations, and some success has been achieved in modeling these decisions' relation to materiality. Yet human judgment must still play an indispensible part in making such decisions, and the FASB has declined to promulgate general quantitative guidelines for determining questions of materiality, while recognizing that there may be specific situations where such guidance is appropriate. Indeed, the Board, in a small number of instances, has already specified materiality thresholds, and in other cases the SEC has done so. Some of the quantitative guidelines presently in force are set out in Appendix C of SFAC 2, ¶ 166.

Governmental Accounting Concepts

In 1984, the Board of Trustees of the Financial Accounting Foundation organized a separate GASB under its auspices. The GASB is responsible for establishing concepts and standards for accounting for the activities and transactions of state and local government entities. The FASB will continue to establish concepts and standards for all other entities. In the absence of a GASB pronouncement for a particular activity or transaction, government entities will be expected to look to the FASB for guidance. See Chapter 31 for a more comprehensive discussion of GASB's work on concepts.

APPLYING CONCEPTS

How do the FASB concepts statements discussed in this chapter help the FASB and other standard-setting groups? Concepts, being neither rules nor standards, give no pat answers. They do, however, furnish guidelines in deliberating standards, limiting the issues being argued, and providing a better chance for order and fulfillment of financial reporting objectives.

Where asset considerations are involved, the steps in an analytical process might be described this way:

1. Is there an asset, that is, is there (a) an expected future benefit (or service) that the enterprise can (b) exclusively claim as a result of (c) a transaction or an event that has occurred?
2. What measure of the asset should be used?
3. What is the event that triggers recording?
4. Is the uncertainty about the benefit or its measure so significant that the asset should not be recorded in financial statements?

Look for the *future benefit*; be sure there is an exclusive claim on the benefit; identify the *event* that gave rise to the exclusive claim; assess the *uncertainty* of realizing the benefit, and then decide on all those bases whether to record.

Where liability considerations are present, the steps could be described thus:

1. Is there a liability, that is, is there (a) an obligation (equitable or otherwise) to others not acting as owners to (b) transfer assets as (c) a result of a past transaction, event, or circumstance?
2. What measure of the liability should be used?
3. What is the event triggering the recording?
4. Is the uncertainty about the obligation or its measure so great that the obligation should not be reported as an obligation?

Look for the *obligation* (but do not be too legalistic, because economic considerations may override) to *transfer* assets; identify the *event* that gave rise to the obligation; assess the *probability* and *estimability* of having to transfer assets, and then decide on all these bases whether to record.

For an indication of how sharper concepts aid specific standard setting, consider three brief examples: leases, casualty insurance catastrophe reserves, and costs as assets.

Leases

Accounting for leases has captured the attention of standard-setters for a long period. The APB first focused on lessee accounting in 1964 and later dealt separately with lessor accounting. The FASB issued a statement on accounting by both lessors and lessees in 1976. First, the focus was on lessee liabilities and, incidentally, expenses; then, it switched to lessor assets, mainly revenues. Finally, the focus reached all of the financial statement elements of the two principal parties – lessee and lessor – on a coordinated basis.

Would accounting for leases today have been different if asset and liability concepts had been applied earlier? It might be for reasons to be noted later, but one thing is certain: Resolution of the problem would have suffered fewer false starts if those concepts had been recognized and applied as the matter was being considered.

Two views of leases are noted in SFAS 13, *Accounting for Leases* (L10). The first is that "a lease that transfers substantially all of the benefits and risks incident to ownership of property should be accounted for as the acquisition of an asset and the incurrence of an obligation by the lessee and as a sale or financing by the lessor" (L10.103). The second view states that "regardless of whether substantially all the benefits and risks of ownership are transferred, a lease, in transferring for its term the right to use property, gives rise to the acquisition of an asset and the incurrence of an obligation by the lessee" (SFAS 13, ¶ 63).

The first of those views emphasizes the physical property as the asset; the second emphasizes the services provided by the property, the benefits from use. Both views are compatible with the proposed concepts of assets and liabilities, the first by reference to substantially all the benefits and risks inherent in ownership, the second by reference to the right to use property. The second view focuses on services from use and recognizes that the total services of, or benefits produced by, a physical resource can be divided among several parties, a lease being one way of so dividing. The first view, however, is an all-or-nothing view—a physical asset is an asset because of its wholeness; it is an asset to one party, not several. Early on, the concepts would have settled the arguments about assets and liabilities with respect to leases. The standard of accounting for leases would then have been developed on the basis of relevance of information, reliability of measurement, and cost of assembling or compiling data.

Once accounting for leases had been developed this far, if a line were needed between leases to be capitalized and those to be treated as operating leases, it would have been drawn on grounds of practicality, not on ever-elusive concepts aimed at distinguishing the two.

The psuedoconceptual approach used in SFAS 13 has given rise to many, many interpretations, amendments, technical bulletins, and SEC releases. Indeed, the FASB has stated several times that lease accounting needs to be reexamined; and if that were to be done, there is a likelihood that all leases would result in some capitalization as an asset by lessees. Business enterprises are not encouraging this reevaluation, because SFAS 13 may be a "better deal" for most. But the day will come, and the conceptual framework will play a large role.

Catastrophe Reserves

The liability concept came into play in resolving the accounting for catastrophe reserves of casualty insurance companies. In SFAS 5 (C59) the FASB met head on a long-standing, simmering issue that by mid-1975 had resulted in charges to income for "future losses" of various kinds. Potential losses from catastrophes of the type covered by casualty insurance (hurricanes, floods, etc.) had come to be recognized as liabilities by a number of insurance companies. The FASB saw no conceptual problem with loss provisions for catastrophes that might occur within the terms of effective insurance policies, but concluded that the uncertainty of timing and amount of losses would not justify their recognition; the loss prospects did not appear to pass necessary tests of probability and estimability.

The substantive conceptual issue that the FASB faced concerned catastrophes that might occur after the end of the term of existing policies—catastrophes not covered by existing contracts. The FASB concluded that the characteristics of a liability were not present: there was no obligation to an outside party stemming from a past event or transaction; no outside party or class of parties could be identified that, based on existing relations, would have a reasonable basis for sustaining a claim against the insurance company. A new policy would have to be written (or an old one renewed) before a party could be identified who could sustain a claim. The liability tests were not met and, accordingly, the provision did not qualify for admission to financial statements.

Costs as Assets

Perhaps one of the most difficult classes of assets to analyze conceptually is that of costs of developing new business, training employees, moving, and similar activities for which no separable economic resource can be identified. The difficulty relates to the notion of an asset as a resource, a potential service, or a future benefit with cash-flow prospects. The discussion here focuses on concepts; the state of the art in accounting for "near-assets," and the SEC's general resistance to asset classification, are covered in Chapter 15.

Moving, training, and business generation are activities not ordinarily perceived as resources and accordingly, their costs are not deferrable simply on the plausibility that a company would not incur them without perceiving a benefit. Surely a cost is not per se an asset, although the presumption is not unreasonable that a cost is willingly incurred only if an asset (perhaps of very short life) is received in return. But a cost incurred to obviate a future cash outflow otherwise required or to obtain benefits from other assets surely is a benefit even though a separable resource cannot be identified. With that thought in mind, the question of accounting for a cost incurred to move a plant to another location becomes one of identifying the asset, if any, to which the moving cost should be attached.

The reasons for the move need analysis. Consider three possibilities: (1) a move made primarily because of a local subsidy in the form of either a bargain purchase of a facility or reduced taxes for a specified period; (2) a move made to take advantage of a labor supply that, after adequate training, would result in relatively low wage rates, even after considering the cost of the move and training; (3) a move made to escape onerous local laws concerning environmental restraints.

One helpful way to view the accounting for the cost of moving is to test the results against the accounting for an enterprise that enjoys the same benefits but did not have to move to realize them. If one has an asset, surely the other one has; if one incurred a moving cost to acquire the asset and the other did not, one may have an amount to record, the other may not. For the three cases:

1. *As to the move made to take advantage of a local subsidy,* the asset is either the facility acquired at a bargain price or prepayment of an item in lieu of taxes. There is nothing in the asset concept that rules out recognition of moving costs as an asset in these situations.

2. *As to the move made to obtain access to certain labor skills,* the asset is a labor skill. The cost of the move and of training may well be part of the cost, paid in advance, of the service to the enterprise. A right to the benefits deriving from the talent or skill of people surely qualifies as an asset, and it ordinarily has a cost. There is nothing in the asset concept that proscribes recognition of these costs as an asset.

3. *As to the move to escape an onerous local law,* escaping a bad situation is not in itself an asset, despite its advantage. There is nothing in the asset concept that views relief from a bad situation as an asset, unless it obviates obligations otherwise requiring cash outflows.

In the above cases, especially the first two, considerations other than the asset concept would determine whether the asset is recordable. Without being definitive, some of these moves will give rise to recordable assets; some moving costs, therefore, are part of asset acquisition cost; and some labor training costs for a short duration may qualify as assets. However, both moving and training costs may be the types of activities for which uncertainty as to the amount and timing of enhanced benefits rules out recognition on grounds of measurement unreliability.

The question of whether costs are assets is left with this methodology:

1. Determine the reason for incurring the cost.

2. Determine whether the cost can be identified with a previously recorded asset or with a recordable asset of any kind. The three asset tests should be applied in making this determination.

3. Assess the uncertainty of future benefits and their measurability to determine whether an asset identifiable from the first two steps meets the test for recording.

As a general observation, the word *cost* is often in the reporting caption of assets that are not exchangeable, or for which there is not a separable resource. Not very much has been done to describe assets that are not exchangeable individually but that enhance benefits obtainable from other assets; too often these assets have been characterized as if the cost itself were the asset.

3

Basic Financial Statements

COMMUNICATING FINANCIAL INFORMATION

Though an enterprise can communicate financial information by means other than its basic financial statements, those statements are the most widely used and the most comprehensive means of conveying such information externally. Whether the organization in question is a sole proprietorship, a partnership, a corporation, an association, a charitable group, or a governmental unit, whether it has profit-seeking or not-for-profit objectives, whether it is regulated or unregulated, it is primarily through its financial statements that it will report on its financial affairs. The nature and circumstances of the enterprise determine to whom it will report. It must always report to its owners, but it may also need to report to its employees, to certain creditors, to regulatory agencies, to taxation authorities, or to other constituents.

Different users of financial statements have different needs, and the selection of the information to be presented and the form of presentation must be adapted to meet those needs as fully as possible. Ideally, several different forms of financial statements would be helpful to users with quite disparate needs, but such a system would likely be unwieldly and costly. As a result, *general purpose* financial statements have been developed and are widely used. General purpose financial statements are addressed primarily to the needs of investors and creditors, who are the principal users of financial statements, but such statements are highly useful in meeting the needs of others as well. This chapter describes those general purpose statements, referred to as *basic financial statements*, and reviews the important variations, including special considerations applicable to interim statements – usually quarterly reports.

The typical accounting entity is a profit-seeking enterprise, with its owners organized as a corporation; therefore, the illustrations used in this chapter apply particularly to corporations – in particular, commercial and industrial corporations. However, other kinds of organizations have peculiar reporting problems and reflect them in the form and content of their statements. Other chapters in this *Handbook* are concerned with many of those organizations. Since most accounting problems are common to a wide spectrum of enterprises, most of the following discussion should be relevant as well to enterprises with special reporting considerations.

Before discussing the basic financial statements presently in use, it bears mention that (1) the underlying form of presentation, i.e., a summary of financial position and of operating results, has not changed much over time and (2) changes in the composition and details of those financial statements have occurred slowly.

Basic Financial Statements

Basic financial statements comprise four distinct but interrelated statements:

1. Statement of financial position or balance sheet;
2. Income statement or statement of earnings;
3. Statement of capital changes (or shareholders' equity); and
4. Statement of cash flows.

The purpose of the *financial position statement* or *balance sheet* (Figure 3.1) is to present an enterprise's financial position at a particular moment in time in terms of economic resources (assets), economic obligations (liabilities), and the residual claims of owners (the owners' equity). Assets and liabilities are usually shown in the order of their liquidity, with the most current shown first. By definition the total

BALANCE SHEETS

The Mead Corporation and Consolidated Subsidiaries

Assets

December 31	1987	1986
	(All dollar amounts in millions)	
Current assets:		
Cash and temporary cash investments	$ 45.3	$ 18.6
Accounts receivable, less allowance for doubtful accounts of		
$20.5 in 1987 and $19.3 in 1986 (Note G)	543.4	422.9
Inventories (Note B)	331.5	339.4
Prepaid expenses	38.5	40.0
Total current assets	958.7	820.9
Investments and other assets:		
Investments in and advances to jointly-owned companies (Note C)	116.1	293.0
Other assets (Note D)	255.4	225.9
	371.5	518.9
Property, plant and equipment, at cost (Notes G and N):		
Land	88.3	77.2
Timber and timberlands, net of timber depletion	201.7	106.2
Buildings	429.1	403.2
Machinery and equipment	1,907.3	1,612.7
Construction in progress	41.0	56.6
	2,667.4	2,255.9
Less accumulated depreciation on buildings and machinery and equipment	1,080.3	874.5
	1,587.1	1,381.4
Total assets	$2,917.3	$2,721.2

Liabilities and Share Owners' Equity

December 31	1987	1986
	(All dollar amounts in millions)	
Current liabilities:		
Accounts payable:		
Trade	$ 201.8	$ 206.1
Affiliated companies	68.8	160.4
Outstanding checks	62.5	23.3
Accrued liabilities (Note F)	246.5	217.6
Income taxes	15.7	6.7
Current maturities of long-term debt	32.5	21.0
Total current liabilities	627.8	635.1
Long-term debt (Note G)	764.6	803.7
Deferred items:		
Income taxes	231.6	179.8
Other	47.3	43.7
	278.9	223.5
Share owners' equity (Notes H and I):		
Common shares	187.2	186.8
Additional paid-in capital	107.3	106.8
Foreign currency translation adjustment	(3.9)	(13.9)
Retained earnings	955.4	779.2
	1,246.0	1,058.9
Total liabilities and share owners' equity	$2,917.3	$2,721.2

See notes to financial statements.

FIG. 3.1 Sample Balance Sheet

Source: The Mead Corporation, 1987 Annual Report (notes excluded).

STATEMENTS OF EARNINGS
The Mead Corporation and Consolidated Subsidiaries

Year Ended December 31	1987	1986	1985
	(All dollar amounts in millions except per share amounts)		
Net sales	$4,208.8	$3,217.7	$2,740.4
Cost of products sold	3,362.7	2,608.9	2,257.5
Gross profit	846.1	608.8	482.9
Selling, administrative and research expenses	510.7	367.6	305.2
Earnings from vertically integrated operations	335.4	241.2	177.7
Equity in earnings before taxes of jointly-owned companies (Note C)	43.5	22.0	15.8
Earnings from operations	378.9	263.2	193.5
Other revenues – net (Note L)	86.4	31.7	18.6
Interest and debt expense (Note E)	(80.4)	(69.1)	(66.9)
Earnings from continuing operations before income taxes	384.9	225.8	145.2
Income taxes (Note M)	166.7	116.5	48.5
Earnings from continuing operations	218.2	109.3	96.7
Loss from discontinued operations (Note P)		(65.9)	(3.2)
Extraordinary loss due to retirement of debt (Note G)	(1.5)	(7.1)	
Net earnings	$ 216.7	$ 36.3	$ 93.5
Per common share:			
Earnings from continuing operations	$ 3.47	$ 1.75	$ 1.56
Loss from discontinued operations		(1.06)	(.05)
Extraordinary loss	(.02)	(.11)	
Net earnings	$ 3.45	$ .58	$ 1.51

See notes to financial statements

FIG. 3.2 Sample Income Statement
Source: The Mead Corporation, 1987 Annual Report (notes excluded).

amount of owners' equity equals the total amount of assets less the total amount of liabilities.

The purpose of the *income statement* (Figure 3.2) is to show the results of operations for a given period of time. The significant categories of income and expense are shown. The difference between income and expense, measured on the accrual basis of accounting, is the amount by which owners' equity changes as a result of the enterprise's operations.

The *statement of capital changes* or *shareholders' equity* shows the increases and decreases in earnings retained by the company over a given period of time, along with changes in other capital accounts. The retained earnings segment of this statement is comprised principally of the accumulated net income from operations less dividends declared or paid; when there is no other activity in retained earnings, this statement is sometimes appended to the income statement. A sample *statement of capital changes* is shown in Figure 3.3.

The purpose of the *statement of cash flows* (Figure 3.4) is to reflect in one statement the changes in cash flows of the enterprise over a given period of time. (This

STATEMENTS OF SHARE OWNERS' EQUITY

The Mead Corporation and Consolidated Subsidiaries

	Common Shares		Additional Paid-In Capital	Foreign Currency Translation Adjustment	Retained Earnings
	Shares	Amount			
	(All dollar amounts in millions except per share amounts; all share amounts in thousands)				
January 1, 1985	61,736	$184.1	$ 95.0	$ (32.8)	$724.1
Net earnings					93.5
Stock option activity – net	410	1.2	4.9		
Common cash dividends – $.60 a share					(37.2)
Foreign currency translation adjustment				.8	
December 31, 1985	62,146	185.3	99.9	(32.0)	780.4
Net earnings					36.3
Stock option activity – net	468	1.5	6.9		
Common cash dividends – $.60 a share					(37.5)
Foreign currency translation adjustment (includes $12.8 million resulting from sale of a jointly-owned company)				18.1	
December 31, 1986	62,614	186.8	106.8	(13.9)	779.2
Net earnings					216.7
Common shares purchased	(282)	(.9)	(6.5)		
Stock option activity – net	446	1.3	7.0		
Common cash dividends – $.645 a share					(40.5)
Foreign currency translation adjustment				10.0	
December 31, 1987	**62,778**	**$187.2**	**$107.3**	**$ (3.9)**	**$955.4**

See notes to financial statements.

FIG. 3.3 Sample Statement of Capital Changes
Source: The Mead Corporation, 1987 Annual Report (notes excluded).

statement is required by SFAS 95, *Statement of Cash Flows* (C25), which superseded APB 19, *Reporting Changes in Financial Position*.) A discussion of the changes and samples of the revised cash flows statement are presented later under "FASB Statement No. 95" and in Figures 3.10 and 3.11.

Because three of the basic statements describe financial activity for the same period — i.e., the period of time between the dates of two balance sheets — key figures reported in one statement correspond to balances included in the others. The four basic financial statements *articulate*. For example, in Figure 3.2, the net earnings reported in the 1987 statement of earnings ($216,700,000) equal the amount of change in retained earnings from the enterprise's operations, as shown in the last column of the statement of capital changes (Figure 3.3). The beginning and ending balances in the statement of capital changes equal the corresponding balances in the stockholders' equity section in the balance sheets. Each of these basic financial statements is further described later in this chapter.

The notes and other supplementary information applicable to the statements in Figures 3.1, 3.2, and 3.3 have not been reproduced here. However, the *notes* are an integral part of a complete set of financial statements. The notes are commonly also

CONSOLIDATED STATEMENTS OF CASH FLOWS

Super Valu Stores, Inc. and Subsidiaries

	February 27, 1988 (52 Weeks)	February 28, 1987 (53 Weeks)	February 22, 1986 (52 Weeks)
Cash flows from operating activities:			
Net earnings	$111,780,000	$ 89,301,000	$ 91,247,000
Adjustments to reconcile net earnings to net cash provided by operating activities:			
Depreciation and amortization of property and intangibles	103,268,000	86,215,000	72,769,000
Amortization of capital leases	6,970,000	6,959,000	4,692,000
Provision for losses on receivables	4,855,000	2,368,000	3,168,000
Loss (gain) on sale of property, plant and equipment	240,000	(2,496,000)	(6,234,000)
Deferred income taxes	9,317,000	(5,620,000)	14,735,000
Minority interest		(3,785,000)	
Change in assets and liabilities net of effects from acquired companies:			
Increase in receivables	(31,662,000)	(382,000)	(1,448,000)
Increase in inventory	(43,375,000)	(51,173,000)	(103,295,000)
Decrease (increase) in prepaid supplies and expenses	(907,000)	7,805,000	(14,049,000)
Increase in direct finance leases	(5,467,000)	(3,542,000)	(208,000)
Increase (decrease) in checks outstanding, net	(26,934,000)	(19,395,000)	8,409,000
Increase in accounts payable and accrued expenses	28,739,000	53,931,000	59,999,000
Increase (decrease) in income taxes payable	(8,444,000)	15,580,000	(16,441,000)
Increase (decrease) in other liabilities	(1,981,000)	2,624,000	780,000
Net cash provided by operating activities	146,399,000	178,390,000	114,124,000
Cash flows from investing activities:			
Additions to long-term notes receivable	(46,612,000)	(36,247,000)	(35,412,000)
Payments on long-term notes receivable	34,294,000	42,030,000	42,088,000
Proceeds from sale of property, plant and equipment	14,575,000	26,571,000	19,234,000
Property, plant and equipment additions	(193,745,000)	(191,732,000)	(176,646,000)
Disposals of leased assets	13,292,000	15,239,000	3,360,000
Leased asset additions	(20,174,000)	(3,411,000)	(7,051,000)
Net assets of acquired companies, net of cash acquired	(19,065,000)	(65,081,000)	(92,216,000)
Other assets	(12,952,000)	(4,161,000)	(1,507,000)
Net cash used in investing activities	(230,387,000)	(216,792,000)	(248,150,000)
Cash flows from financing activities:			
Issuance (reduction) of short-term notes payable	16,564,000	104,134,000	(25,947,000)
Proceeds from issuance of long-term debt	100,100,000	3,792,000	209,694,000
Repayment of long-term debt	(9,657,000)	(19,719,000)	(24,293,000)
Additions to obligations under capital leases	20,174,000	3,411,000	7,051,000
Reduction of obligations under capital leases	(13,888,000)	(22,912,000)	(6,761,000)
Sale of common stock under option plans and ESOP	1,910,000	2,596,000	1,875,000
Cash dividends declared	(32,477,000)	(30,511,000)	(27,462,000)
Net cash provided by financing activities	82,726,000	40,791,000	134,157,000
Net increase (decrease) in cash	(1,262,000)	2,389,000	131,000
Cash at beginning of year	3,432,000	1,043,000	912,000
Cash at end of year	$ 2,170,000	$ 3,432,000	$ 1,043,000
Supplemental cash flow information:			
Cash paid during the year for:			
Interest (net of amount capitalized)	$ 59,450,000	$ 50,767,000	$ 37,657,000
Income taxes	83,665,000	84,742,000	81,344,000

See notes to consolidated financial statements.

FIG. 3.4   Statement of Cash Flows
Source: Super Valu Stores, Inc., 1988 Annual Report (notes excluded).

called footnotes, though their usual multipage length would not allow them to be shown at the foot of any one or all of the statements.

Certain information may be presented in either the main body of a statement or in the related notes. An example is accumulated depreciation, which is commonly shown in the balance sheet as a deduction from the cost of property assets. An equally acceptable presentation is to show on the balance sheet only a net carrying amount for property, plant, and equipment and to disclose accumulated depreciation in the footnotes. (Chapter 4 discusses the use of financial disclosures in the notes and elsewhere outside the tabular financial statements.)

Another integral part of annual published financial statements is the *auditor's report*, which ordinarily states the auditor's opinion that the statements are fairly presented in all material respects in conformity with GAAP. See Chapter 11 for a complete discussion of the auditor's report.

Regulatory agencies such as the SEC may require disclosure of summarized financial information, or such information may be provided because it is useful to readers in interpreting financial statements (e.g., a ten-year summary of key figures in an annual report). This information is rarely presented as part of the basic financial statements.

FINANCIAL STATEMENT PRESENTATION CONCEPTS

APB Statement 4

APB Statement 4, *Basic Concepts and Accounting Principles Underlying Financial Statements of Business Enterprises* (AICPA, 1970), initially set forth (¶¶ 191–201) eleven principles of financial statement presentation. Subsequently, APB 19, *Reporting Changes in Financial Position,* required a statement of changes in financial position for profit-oriented business enterprises; this increased the number of principles to twelve. (APB 19 was superseded in late 1987 by SFAS 95, *Statement of Cash Flows* (C25), discussed later in this chapter in "Statement of Cash Flows.") These twelve early principles encompassed

1. Basic financial statement designations (as mentioned previously)
2. Balance sheet
3. Income statement
4. Statement of changes in financial position (i.e., cash flows)
5. Accounting period (one year, or segments thereof – usually quarters)
6. Consolidated financial statements (presumed more meaningful)
7. Equity method (for less than 50% owned companies and unconsolidated subsidiaries)
8. Translation of foreign balances
9. Classification and segregation (into informative categories, including working capital, gains and losses other than normal activities, extraordinary items, and net income; and an admonition against offsetting assets and liabilities)
10. Other disclosures (i.e., all information that is needed)

11. Presentation format (no particular style mandated)
12. Earnings per share (on the face of the income statement)

Although APB Statement 4 was issued in 1970, it still is designated by the FASB as a pronouncement that continues to serve its intended purpose of explaining the objectives and concepts underlying accounting standards and practices existing when such standards and practices were issued or adopted. As further discussed in Chapter 2, APB Statement 4 was criticized as simply being a recitation of what existed (based as it was on ARS No. 7, *Inventory of Generally Accepted Accounting Principles for Business Enterprises* (Grady, 1965)), rather than a taxonomy of concepts whose logic was compelling. Viewed in the perspective of what has been achieved in the ensuing 18 years, Statement 4 has been useful in maintaining a general sense of direction; and it has contributed substantially to the FASB's conceptual framework project.

FASB Concepts

FASB Concepts Statements 1 through 6 have readdressed much of the material covered by APB Statement 4 and divide the financial reporting process differently. Some of the labels have changed and a broader approach is recommended, but in substance the flavor remains the same.

SFAC 5, *Recognition and Measurement in Financial Statements of Business Enterprises* (FASB, 1984), describes financial statements in relation to the objectives of financial reporting stated in SFAC 1. A synopsis of the SFAC 5 approach follows.

Full Set of Financial Statements. A full set of financial statements comprises statements that show (1) financial position at the period end, (2) net income for the period, (3) cash flows during the period, and (4) investments by and distributions to owners during the period (SFAC 5, ¶ 13). SFAC 5 discusses each of these financial statements individually, as does this chapter in later sections.

The FASB also included an avant-garde statement, comprehensive income, intended to encompass net income plus or minus all changes in equity other than investments by and distributions to owners. (The comprehensive income concept was first introduced in SFAC 3 (now in SFAC 6, ¶ 70), which did not deal with how statements would be presented.)

This would allow for the possibility that value changes, for example, can be presented in a way that does not affect the present concept of net income. (One such situation, value changes in marketable equity security investments carried as noncurrent assets, is presently sequestered as an element of shareholders' equity, with changes not flowing through net income (I89.105)). Thus far, the FASB has not tried to implement this idea en masse; changes will come item by item.

Classification and Aggregation. Reasonably homogenous groupings are needed to condense masses of data; otherwise too much detail will obscure the communication (SFAC 5, ¶ 20–22). On the other hand, condensation and simplification can go too far, resulting in users focusing only on specific summary indicators (e.g., earnings per share) as the key information and overlooking the fact that the component items may contain more useful and relevant data.

Complementary Nature. The basic financial statements articulate; changes in financial position are also reflected in the income statement or shareholders' equity statement; and the cash flow statement correlates with the other three basic statements (SFAC 5, ¶ 24). This occurs by design, because it would be possible to have nonarticulating financial statements; indeed, the FASB would create this situation if value changes not presently recorded under GAAP became required in the statement of financial position, but not in the net income statement. This prospect has been considered, and as previously indicated, the FASB opted for a statement of comprehensive income that would preserve articulation without necessarily changing the definition of net income. (Articulation is also discussed in SFAC 6, ¶ 21.)

Financial Capital Maintenance. Financial statements are based on the premise that the financial capital of the enterprise is the measure of whether a return on or of investment has occurred. The owners' equity is reckoned in financial rather than physical terms (SFAC 5, ¶ 45–48). For example, if shareholders' equity rises due to recorded net income, financial capital has been both maintained and enhanced. However, if the productive capacity of the company has decreased substantially from what it was at the previous reporting date, the physical capital may have been impaired by an amount greater than the enhancement arising from net income, resulting in a negative return on investment. A good example of an attempt at reckoning physical capital maintenance is SFAS 33, *Financial Reporting and Changing Prices* (now superseded), which required presentation of the current cost of major nonmonetary assets as supplementary information.

The financial capital maintenance concept (also discussed in SFAC 6, ¶ 71) appears firmly cemented into present GAAP. The fate of SFAS 33 is evidence on point: Originally mandated in 1979, application became voluntary in 1987 (SFAS 89, C28); SFAS 33 didn't run as long as some Broadway plays.

STATEMENT OF FINANCIAL POSITION

A statement of financial position (which will probably more commonly be called a balance sheet for years to come notwithstanding SFAC 5's terminology) is a listing of assets, liabilities, and ownership interests. This may seem straightforward, but determining what those terms cover is hardly simple. Only when the term *asset* has been defined can a logical distinction be made between expenditures to be called assets in the balance sheet and those to be written off in the income statement. Only when a *liability* has been defined can a distinction be made between those future outlays that must be accrued in the balance sheet by current charges to income, and those planned discretionary expenditures that should not.

For a conceptual discussion of assets and liabilities see Chapter 2; for purposes of this chapter, the definitions given in SFAC 6, *Elements of Financial Statements* (FASB, 1985), are appropriate:

> *Assets* are probable future economic benefits obtained or controlled by a particular entity as a result of past transactions or events [¶ 25].

Liabilities are probable future sacrifices of economic benefits arising from present obligations of a particular entity to transfer assets or provide services to other entities in the future as a result of past transactions or events [¶ 35].

Cutoff Date

The balance sheet presents financial position as of a given moment in time. Therefore, in accordance with the part of the definitions of assets and liabilities related to "past transactions or events," assets and liabilities (and the resulting owners' equity) are reflected in the balance sheet only if the event that gives rise to the asset or the liability has already occurred as of the balance sheet date. For instance, if an uninsured factory is completely destroyed by fire after the balance sheet date, the amount at which the factory is shown in the balance sheet would remain unchanged. If material, the amount of the loss would be disclosed in the footnote narrative or in pro forma statements. This reduction in assets would be first reflected in the balance sheet only upon its presentation *as of* a date after the fire. Likewise, anticipated capital expenditures, although already authorized by management or board action, would not be recorded as a liability in the balance sheet until the event that gave rise to the expenditure (e.g., receipt of building materials or design and labor services) had occurred.

Classification of Assets and Liabilities

The usefulness of a balance sheet is enhanced if the assets and liabilities in it are classified in a meaningful way as to current and noncurrent items. A number of relationships useful for financial analysis can then be obtained. The classification of assets has additional significance because GAAP sometimes requires different bases of measurement to be applied to different classes of assets.

One key problem for all enterprises is being able to meet their obligations as they arise. To provide information in this regard, a broad distinction has been made between current and noncurrent assets and liabilities; and current assets less current liabilities results in working capital, one measure of ability to meet its near-term obligations. (Another indicator is the cash flow statement in the format newly required by the FASB for years ending after July 15, 1988, as discussed later under "FASB Statement No. 95.")

Operating Cycle. The *operating cycle* refers to the period of time needed to convert cash first into materials and services, then into products, then by sale into receivables, and finally back into cash when collected. In some businesses in which products have to mature or age (e.g., distilleries or forest products), the cycle goes well beyond a year. In most businesses, however, there will be more than one cycle per year; in other businesses (e.g., many service establishments) there is no recognizable operating cycle.

When an operating cycle does not exist or is shorter than a year, a one-year convention is used for classifying both assets and liabilities. If the operating cycle exceeds a year, the longer period should be used; in practice it is common to use the longer period for current asset classification but to apply the one-year convention to liabilities not directly related to the longer-cycle assets. This is done because extremely long cycles (e.g., shipbuilding) make it implausible to evaluate the extent to which general liabilities, such as long-term debt service, will be paid out of funds generated from the specific assets included in current assets.

Current Assets. Current assets include cash and other assets that are reasonably expected to be realized in cash or sold or consumed during one year, or within the normal operating cycle of the business if the operating cycle is longer than one year (B05.105). Thus, current assets normally include

1. Cash, unless it is not available for current operations because it is restricted for some special purpose (e.g., the liquidation of a long-term debt);
2. Marketable securities, available to be converted to cash as needed and not held for control of or affiliation with another business;
3. Receivables, unless they arise from unusual circumstances such as transactions with affiliates or officers of the company and are not expected to be collected within 12 months of the balance sheet date;
4. Inventories of raw materials, work in process, finished goods, and operating and maintenance supplies; and
5. Prepaid expenses (e.g., insurance, rent, or advertising) that, though not realizable in cash, would involve an outlay of cash during the operating cycle if not prepaid.

Current Liabilities. Current liabilities are "obligations whose liquidation is reasonably expected to require the use of . . . current assets, or the creation of other current liabilities" (B05.108). They include short-term obligations for items that have entered into the operating cycle, such as payables for materials and supplies, wages, expenses and taxes, and amounts collected in advance of the delivery of goods or services. As mentioned above, 12 months is the most common period of time for classifying a liability as current or noncurrent, but the operating cycle, if longer, is sometimes used for liabilities specifically related to that cycle. Current liabilities also include other obligations expected to be liquidated within 12 months, such as the short-term portion of long-term debt.

In SFAS 6, *Classification of Short-Term Obligations Expected to be Refinanced* (B05), the FASB considered the classification of short-term obligations expected to be refinanced. If refinanced when it becomes due, an obligation does not require the use of cash. Accordingly, SFAS 6 provides that short-term obligations may be excluded from current liabilities if two conditions are met. The enterprise (1) must intend to refinance the obligation on a long-term basis and (2) must be able to do so (B05.113). Some complicated situations have arisen in evaluating whether those conditions have been met, and they are discussed further in Chapter 18.

Effect of Classification on Measurement Methods. The significance of the distinction between current and noncurrent assets goes beyond the estimation of an enterprise's liquidity, because under GAAP different bases of measurement may apply to the two categories of assets. Broadly speaking, noncurrent assets are carried at cost, with a proportionate deduction for amortization of intangibles (and for depreciation in the case of depreciable assets) and with a reduction (to "new cost") for any permanent diminution in value. Some current assets, such as receivables, are carried at their expected realizable value, the face value of the receivables being reduced by the deduction of allowances for uncollectible amounts and for discounts. Other current assets, such as inventories and certain marketable securities, are carried at the lower of cost or market value. The effect of the current/noncurrent classification on the carrying amounts of specific types of assets is discussed primarily in Chapters 12 through 15.

Asset contra accounts are used in reporting the carrying value of certain types of assets. In the balance sheet in Figure 3.1, accumulated depreciation (of $1,080.3 million and $874.5 million in 1987 and 1986, respectively) is offset against the capitalized cost of plant and equipment, and the allowance for doubtful accounts (of $20.5 million and $19.3 million in 1987 and 1986, respectively) is offset against related receivables.

Owners' Equity

The excess of assets over liabilities in a balance sheet represents the owners' equity. This is the claim of the owners to their share in the entity's assets after its obligations have been met.

The claims of owners who are either sole proprietors or partners may be satisfied by withdrawals of cash or other assets. The claims of stockholders in corporations are met through dividend payments and/or realization of the market value of the shares of the corporation's stock, for which cash proceeds may be obtained by sale of the shares. Also, from time to time, corporations buy back their own stock and hold it as treasury stock (pending possible reissue) or cancel it (thereby reducing the total number of owners' shares issued).

Not all of the owners' equity represents an indivisible residual claim to the net assets (and earnings) of the enterprise. A corporation may have preferred stockholders, who have a higher priority to the receipt of dividends or in liquidation but limited rights to share in net income. Common stockholders in a corporation are entitled to the residual assets of the enterprise after all prior claims have been met. The various classes of stock are shown separately in the balance sheet, along with accumulated retained earnings. (Equity capital is discussed further in Chapter 20.)

INCOME STATEMENT

The primary purpose of an income statement is to display an enterprise's operating performance, i.e., its net income (or loss). This statement shows whether the net worth (the owners' interests) in the enterprise has increased or decreased, apart from dividends and other transactions with owners, over the reporting period.

Format

The format of an income statement should show the significant components of net income, usually in their order of importance. For profit-seeking businesses, the principal elements of its operations are the revenues from the sales of its products or services and the costs at which those products or services are provided. Other factors that enter into the results of current operations are general and administrative expenses, debt financing costs, taxes, and realized gains and losses on the disposal of assets.

The specific presentation of an income statement depends on the nature of the enterprise's operations. In selecting the most meaningful display, the preparer should consider the usefulness of the presentation for decision making purposes. Figure 3.2 is a typical income statement in that earnings from continuing businesses are shown separately as part of net earnings. Reporting the effects on net income of discontinued operations is one of the special items for which APB 30, *Reporting the Results of Operations* (I13), prescribes the treatment. Other items for which treatment is prescribed are extraordinary items (I13), prior-period adjustments (A35), and accounting changes (A06), discussed later.

Figure 3.2 also shows earnings per share (EPS) data on the face of the statement of earnings, a requirement of APB 15 (E09.103), discussed in Chapter 20. APB 15 also requires EPS data to be presented for various subcategories of earnings, including income before extraordinary items, continuing and discontinued operations, effects of accounting changes and pro forma computations of EPS assuming dilution from exercise of options, convertible securities, and similar items.

Aid in Assessing Cash Flows

One of the principal objectives of financial reporting, according to SFAC 1, *Objectives of Financial Reporting by Business Enterprises* (FASB, 1978c), is to help the users of financial reports assess the amounts, timing, and uncertainty of future cash flows to an enterprise, an intermediate step toward helping them to assess either or both (1) the cash distributions that the enterprise will make to its creditors and owners and (2) the cash that may be received upon disposition of their investments. A statement of cash receipts and disbursements alone is not a useful indicator of future cash flows because it does not allow for relating current costs to the future revenues they may produce. Accrual accounting makes allowances for the uneven timing of the actual payments and receipts of cash, and better enables financial statement users to judge the future earning power of the enterprise.

Net earnings determined using accrual accounting under GAAP do not reflect two factors affecting the future cash-flow potential of the owners' interests. One factor is the unrealized changes occurring during the reporting period in the value of assets and liabilities. The second is the change in the market's expectations regarding the enterprise's future cash flows; those expectations, more than any other factor, determine what an enterprise is worth. But financial statements are largely the reflection of *past* transactions and events representing past acquisitions of assets, issues of capital, actual sales transactions, and expirations of costs. Even if important future developments are known with a considerable degree of certainty at a financial statement date, those developments will not be directly reflected in the financial statements.

For example, assume that two companies have incurred identical amounts of expenditures on research and development during the past year. One company knows that its efforts to develop a new product have been unsuccessful to date and are not likely to succeed in the future. The other company knows that it has achieved

PHILLIPS PETROLEUM COMPANY
Consolidated Statement of Income
Years Ended December 31
(Millions of dollars)

	1986	1985	1984
Revenues			
Sales and other operating revenues	$9,786	$15,636	$15,527
Equity in earnings of affiliated companies	64	37	42
Other revenues	165	127	177
Total revenues	10,015	15,800	15,746
Costs and expenses			
Purchased crude oil and products	5,313	9,041	9,057
Production and operating expenses	1,626	1,829	1,898
Exploration expenses	457	449	573
Selling, general and administrative expenses	308	412	476
Depreciation, depletion, amortization and retirements	1,097	1,044	905
Taxes other than income taxes	210	406	405
Interest and expense on indebtedness	685	846	314
Unusual items	(373)	(180)	
Total costs and expenses	9,323	13,847	13,628
Income from continuing operations before income taxes	692	1,953	2,118
Provision for income taxes	458	1,357	1,281
Income from continuing operations	234	596	837
Discontinued operations (net of income taxes)			
Loss from operations		(7)	(27)
Loss on disposal	(6)	(171)	
Net income	$ 228	418	810
Net income applicable to common stock	$ 202	401	810
Income per share of common stock			
Continuing operations	$ .91	*2.07	*1.81
Net income	$ .89	*1.44	*1.75
Average common shares outstanding (in thousands)	227,546	*278,916	*462,247

*Adjusted for three-for-one stock split in the form of a 200-percent common stock dividend effective May 31, 1985.

See accounting policies and notes to financial statements.

FIG. 3.5   Income Statement with Unusual Items
Source: Phillips Petroleum Company, 1986 Annual Report (notes excluded).

a breakthrough and that substantial profitable sales of the new product are highly probable during the next few years. Nevertheless, in conformity with GAAP, research and development expenditures will be expensed in both companies' income statements. Though the future profits will not be indicated in its current year financial statements, the successful company will (and probably must under the federal securities laws) find ways to communicate its success to stockholders and the public. This could be done through press releases, management's letter to shareholders in the annual report, or in the management discussion and analysis comments required in SEC filings as discussed in Chapter 4.

Extraordinary and Unusual Items

The usefulness of an earnings statement for predictive purposes is greatly enhanced if normal and recurrent items are distinguished from unusual and nonrecurrent items. The guiding standards to achieve these purposes are contained in APB 9, *Reporting the Results of Operations*, APB 30 and SFAS 16, *Prior-Period Adjustments*, as amended by SFAS 96, *Accounting for Income Taxes*. Those pronouncements require that all items of profit and loss recognized during a period (except prior-period adjustments for error corrections) should be reflected in currently reported net income, and that extraordinary items (less related income taxes) should be shown separately as an element in arriving at net income.

Where applicable, income from discontinued operations, along with any gain or loss on the sale or disposal of related facilities, less income taxes, should be reported separately, after income from continuing operations. The statement of earnings in Figure 3.2 illustrates an income statement with both discontinued operations and an extraordinary item. Figure 3.5 displays both unusual items and discontinued operations. (Note that the loss from discontinued operations in Figure 3.5 is shown separately from the loss on their disposal, both being shown net of applicable income tax benefits.)

Extraordinary Items. The criteria provided by the APB to identify extraordinary items (I17.107-.110 and .117) are quite restrictive. The presumption is that an event or transaction is ordinary and usual unless there is clear evidence to the contrary. To be classified as extraordinary, an event or transaction must be material (in relation to reported earnings or the trend of earnings, or for other reasons); and it must be both unusual in nature and infrequent in occurrence.

Whether an event or transaction is unusual will depend in part on the nature of an enterprise and the environment in which it operates. The event or transaction must be abnormal and significantly different from the ordinary activities of the enterprise, and what is abnormal for one enterprise may be normal for another. An event or transaction is to be regarded as infrequent in occurrence only if it is not reasonably expected to recur in the foreseeable future. Again, what is infrequent for one enterprise may not be infrequent for another.

This definition is sufficiently restrictive so that extraordinary items comprise little besides losses suffered through expropriation, revolutions, natural disasters, and exceptional legal actions. Some apparent exceptions to the definition have been made if the standard-setting body at the time felt that the impact of a particular event or transaction should be reported separately. These exceptions include gains and losses resulting from the extinguishment of debt, whether at scheduled maturity date or before (SFAS 4, I17.113), material write-offs of interstate operating rights subject to the Motor Carriers Act of 1980 (SFAS 44; I17.114), and significant asset disposals after a pooling-of-interests (APB 16; I17.117).

Unusual Items. The income statement can usually be made more informative if items that are either unusual or infrequent in occurrence (but not both) are shown separately from continuing operations as a component of income; this is required for material items, but unlike items shown below operating income, they may *not* be reduced for applicable income taxes (I22.101). This presentation allows users to better assess a company's past performance and thus better evaluate its future performance potential.

An example of unusual item presentation is shown in Figure 3.5. Note 1 indicates that unusual costs comprising (1) special separation programs, (2) retirement plan restructuring, and (3) an asset disposition program were incurred in 1985 and 1986.

Restructuring Charges. One incident that demonstrates the difficulty of categorization in practice may be found in the SEC and EITF actions regarding restructuring charges commonly representing the cost of consolidation and/or relocation of operations, abandonment of specific plants and operations, impairment of operating assets, and relocation and/or termination of employees (the EITF considered this subject first in Issue 86-22, *Display of Business Restructuring Provisions in the Income Statement*, but did not reach a consensus). Prior to issuance of SAB 67, *Interpretations Regarding Restructuring Charges* (Topic 5.P), some SEC registrants presented those charges as a separate item after income from continuing operations but before the provision for income taxes. The SEC staff has stated that restructuring charges do not meet the criteria for classification as extraordinary items and therefore should be reported as a component of income from continuing operations, separately disclosed as an unusual item if material.

The staff also stated that the proper classification of a restructuring charge depends on the assets and operations to which the charge relates. Therefore, the charge may be part of operations, or may be part of other income and expense. Further, it would be inappropriate to describe the restructuring in such a way as to suggest that earnings before those charges are more meaningful.

In January 1987, the EITF considered Issue 87-4, *Restructuring of Operations: Implications of SEC Staff Accounting Bulletin No. 67,* and reached a consensus that the provisions of SAB 67 are not required for a fair presentation of the results of operations in accordance with GAAP and, therefore, do not apply to nonpublic companies.

Operating Versus Nonoperating Activities. Recurrent gains and losses from sources other than normal manufacturing or merchandising operations should preferably be shown separately, if amounts are material. In Figure 3.6 this is accomplished by categorizing operating and nonoperating activities. Typically,

TRIANGLE INDUSTRIES, INC. AND SUBSIDIARIES
Consolidated Statements of Income
Years Ended December 31
(Dollars in thousands except per share data)

	1986	1985	1984
Net sales	$2,667,912	$1,645,721	$169,509
Cost of products sold	2,326,185	1,407,728	144,280
Gross profit	341,727	237,993	25,229
Selling, general and administrative expenses	169,975	106,489	18,700
Operating income	171,752	131,504	6,529
Other income (expenses)			
Investment income—Note L	39,981	25,764	9,533
Gain on sale of investment—Note B		12,518	
Interest expense	(124,390)	(96,939)	(20,421)
Minority interest—Note H		(8,807)	
Other income (expense), net—Note E	15,426	7,642	(40)
Income (loss) from continuing operations before taxes and extraordinary charge	102,769	71,682	(4,399)
Provision (benefit) for taxes on income—Notes A and K	55,211	40,706	(3,785)
Income (loss) from continuing operations before extraordinary charge	47,558	30,976	(614)
Discontinued operation, net of taxes—Note C			
Income from operation		1,443	3,850
Gain (loss) on sale of operation	(647)	4,404	
	(647)	5,847	3,850
Income before extraordinary charge	46,911	36,823	3,236
Extraordinary charge—Note G	(33,983)		
Net income	$ 12,928	$ 36,823	$ 3,236
Earnings per share—Note A			
Primary			
Continuing operations	$2.61	$2.75	$(.04)
Discontinued operation	(.04)	.60	.35
Extraordinary charge	(2.12)		
Net income	$ .45	$3.35	$ .31
Fully diluted			
Continuing operations	$2.05	$2.66	$(.04)
Discontinued operation	(.03)	.58	.35
Extraordinary charge	(1.39)		
Net income	$ .63	$3.24	$ .31

See notes to consolidated financial statements.

FIG. 3.6 Separation of Operating and Nonoperating Activities
Source: Triangle Industries, Inc., 1986 Annual Report (notes excluded).

income from investments, gains or losses on the sale of property, interest expense, and interest earned are examples of income or loss from nonoperating activities. However, an operating activity for one enterprise may not be the same for another. For example, interest income and expense are operating activities for a bank but not for most manufacturing companies. Likewise, gains or losses on securities are operating activities for a securities broker but not for most manufacturers.

Prior Period Adjustments and Errors

Under SFAS 16, *Prior Period Adjustments* (A35), every item of profit or loss that is recognized in a period, including changes in estimates that had entered into the determination of the income of an earlier period, is included in the current-period results with only one exception now permitted (A35.103). That exception is the correction of an error in the financial statements of a prior period. Error corrections are to be shown as additions to, or deductions from, the opening balance of retained earnings unless the financial statements of the prior period are presented together with those of the current period, in which case the earlier statements should be adjusted appropriately.

The distinction between an error and a change in accounting estimate is explained in APB 20, *Accounting Changes* (A35.104):

> Errors in financial statements result from mathematical mistakes, mistakes in the application of accounting principles, or oversight or misuse of facts that existed at the time the financial statements were prepared. In contrast, a change in accounting estimate results from new information or subsequent developments and accordingly from better insight or improved judgment. Thus an error is distinguishable from a change in estimate. A change from an accounting principle that is not generally accepted to one that is generally accepted is a correction of an error for purposes of applying this opinion.

Thus the information necessary for the correction of an error was available during the prior period, whereas the information necessary to revise an accounting estimate, such as the estimate of the life of an asset or the result of an income tax settlement relating to a prior year, was not available when the financial statements of the earlier period were originally issued.

Accounting Changes

Considerable importance is attached to the consistent use of accounting procedures from period to period, for without consistency, interpretation of financial statements by comparing them over time would be useless. Therefore, a change from one accounting method to another can only be justified if management believes that the newly adopted principle is preferable. Examples include a change in the method of inventory pricing, of depreciation, or of accounting for long-term contracts. The treatment of accounting changes is prescribed in APB 20 (A06).

Changes Without Restatement. When a change in an accounting principle is adopted, the nature of the change and management's justification for it must be disclosed in the financial statements of the period in which the change is made

Consolidated Statements of Results of Operations
Fairchild Industries, Inc. and Consolidated Subsidiaries

In thousands, except per share amounts	Year Ended Dec. 31		
	1987	1986	1985
Revenue:			
Sales	$453,832	$448,834	$407,294
Other income (expense)—net	20,758	(334)	4,454
Interest income	7,703	3,871	1,978
	482,293	452,371	413,726
Cost and expenses:			
Cost of sales	340,442	331,614	299,067
Selling, general and administrative	81,833	90,023	83,170
Research and development	10,161	9,427	6,885
Interest expense	26,924	23,904	33,089
	459,360	454,968	422,211
Earnings (Loss) from Continuing Operations before Income Taxes and Cumulative Effect of Accounting Changes	22,933	(2,597)	(8,485)
Income Tax Provision (Benefit)	11,442	1,531	(3,404)
Earnings (Loss) from Continuing Operations	11,491	(4,128)	(5,081)
Discontinued operations:			
Income (loss) from discontinued operations, net of related income tax provision (benefit) of $2,518, $(16,484) and $(104,362), respectively	2,525	5,040	(180,205)
Gain (loss) on disposal of discontinued operations, net of related income tax provision of $2,941 in 1987	(6,897)	(55,823)	18,191
Loss from Discontinued Operations	(4,372)	(50,783)	(162,014)
Extraordinary Credit—Utilization of Net Operating Loss Carryforward	13,199	—	—
Cumulative Effect of Accounting Changes, Net of Related Income Tax Provision of $2,157 in 1987	2,753	44,949	—
Net earnings (Loss)	$ 23,071	$ (9,962)	$(167,095)
Preferred Dividends	$ 11,018	$ 12,370	$ 12,370
Net Earnings (Loss) Applicable to Common Stock	$ 12,053	$ (22,332)	$(179,465)
Earnings (Loss) Per Common Share:			
Continuing operations	$ .03	$ (1.17)	$ (1.28)
Discontinued operations	(.30)	(3.58)	(11.89)
Extraordinary credit	.92	—	—
Cumulative effect of accounting changes	.19	3.17	—
Net earnings (loss)	$ .84	$ (1.58)	$ (13.17)

1986 and 1985 have been restated to reflect discontinued operations. See Notes to Financial Statements.

FIG. 3.7 Income Statement with Cumulative Effect of an Accounting Change
Source: Fairchild Industries, 1987 Annual Report (notes excluded).

(unless it represents the adoption of a new FASB statement). The justification must explain why the new principle is thought to be preferable to the prior one. (For SEC registrants, the auditor is also required to concur in the preferability justification, as discussed in Chapter 11.)

In general, the cumulative effect of the change on retained earnings at the beginning of the period in which the change is made (including the income tax effect) should be shown between the captions "extraordinary items" and "net income" in the income statement for the period of the change. The effect on net income of the period of the change should also be disclosed, and per share information for the cumulative effect of the accounting change is required. When comparative financial statements for prior periods are shown, they should appear as originally reported (A06.115–.116).

A *pro forma statement* – that is, what the effects would have been if the accounting change had been made retroactively must also be shown for each year presented (A06.117). This pro forma disclosure must present the effect on income before extraordinary items and on net income, and must include both the direct effect of the change and "non-discretionary adjustments of items based on income before taxes or net income," such as profit-based incentives or royalties; the related income tax effects must also be recognized (A06.115(d), fn.2).

The statement of income in Figure 3.7 presents the cumulative effect of changes identified in Notes 2 and 5 (not presented) to Fairchild Industries' financial statements for 1987 and 1986 in the method of accounting for inventory costs and from adopting SFAS 88, *Employers Accounting for Settlements and Curtailments of Defined Benefit Pension Plans and for Termination Benefits* (P16), respectively. The entire cumulative amount is included in net income of the period of change.

Changes With Restatement. Though financial statements for prior periods are generally not to be restated for accounting changes, the APB accorded special treatment in APB 20 to three types of accounting changes (A06.123):

1. A change from the LIFO method of inventory pricing to another method,
2. A change in the method of accounting for long-term construction-type contracts, and
3. A change to or from the full cost method of accounting that is used in the extractive industries.

The APB concluded that for those changes the financial statements of all periods presented should be restated. The nature and justification for the change, and the effect of the change on income before extraordinary items, net income, and the related per share amounts for all periods presented, must be disclosed either on the face of the income statement or in the notes (A35.114).

The FASB added a fourth type to those provided by the APB. In SFAS 73, *Reporting a Change in Accounting for Railroad Track Structures* (A06.123), a change from retirement–replacement–betterment accounting to depreciation accounting was included as another accounting change that, if made, would require restatement.

APB 20 recognizes that in some instances a future pronouncement mandating a change in accounting principles might require retroactive application, and thus provides that any such pronouncement takes precedence over APB 20. There have been numerous FASB statements issued since APB 20 that require retroactive application.

Consolidated Balance Sheets as of December 31, 1986 and 1985

	1986 Historic	1986 Pro Forma (Note 2) Unaudited	1985
ASSETS		*(in thousands)*	
Current Assets:			
Cash, including temporary cash investments (Note 3)	$ 1,386	$ 2,386	$ 8,808
Accounts receivable:			
Oil and gas sales	4,267	4,267	5,711
Joint owners, net of allowance for dobtful accounts of $200,000 in 1986 and $350,000 in 1985	1,188	1,188	1,174
Oil and gas programs	1,309	1,309	1,213
Federal income tax refund	5	5	230
Prepaid expenses and other current assets	121	121	941
Total Current Assets	8,276	9,276	18,077
Property and Equipment (Notes 1, 2, 3, 4 & 8):			
Oil and gas properties, at cost, using the successful efforts method of accounting	161,311	138,171	157,390
Office furniture, fixtures and equipment	2,090	2,090	2,087
	163,401	140,261	159,477
Less: Accumulated depletion, depreciation and impairment	(91,906)	(91,906)	(61,671)
Net property and equipment	71,495	48,355	97,806
Other noncurrent assets (Note 3)	2,282	2,282	414
Total Assets	$ 82,053	$ 59,913	$116,297
LIABLITIES AND PARTNERS' CAPITAL			
Current Liabilties:			
Accounts payable and accrued liabilities	$ 559	$ 559	$ 2,921
Oil and gas proceeds payable	3,524	3,524	4,087
Distribution payable	–	–	5,387
Due to associated corporations (Note 1)	2,302	2,302	370
Notes payable (Note 1)	–	–	5,000
Total Current Liabilities	6,385	6,385	17,765
Long-term Debt (Note 3)	60,873	40,895	55,438
Long-term Advance from Associated Corporation (Note 1)	3,620	3,620	7,595
Amounts Payable Under Gas Balancing Arrangements	5,480	3,318	3,637
Deferred Income Taxes (Note 5)	95	95	575
Partners' Capital (Note 1)			
Limited Partners and General Partners of Partnership	5,489	5,489	30,893
General Partners of Operating Partnership	111	111	394
	5,600	5,600	31,287
Total Liabilities and Partners' Capital	$ 82,053	$ 59,913	$116,297

The accompanying notes are an integral part of these consolidated financial statements.

FIG. 3.8 Pro Forma Presentation of Subsequent Events
Source: Graham McCormick Oil and Gas Partnership, 1986 Annual Report (notes excluded).

(In addition, in 1977, AICPA Statements of Position were granted the right to specify their manner of application (A06.127).)

When financial statements are issued prior to the effective date of an FASB statement, disclosure of pro forma financial data for application of the new provisions may be necessary if the effects of application will be material. Pro forma statements are also used for a variety of other purposes, including the accounting change disclosures discussed earlier. Their purpose is to present the effects of a major transaction occurring after the financial statement date, or the effects of a transaction that may or may not take place, for example, a proposed merger of two or more companies. Pro forma disclosures normally include only pertinent key elements, such as sales, income, and EPS.

Occasionally, the effects of a transaction subsequent to year-end may be so significant that disclosure can best be made by pro forma presentation of an entire statement. Figure 3.8 shows a pro forma balance sheet for a year ended December 31, 1986. In March 1987, the company sold a significant portion of its operations. The pro forma December 31 balance sheet gives effect to the sale as if it had been consummated on December 31, 1986. See Chapter 27 for a further discussion of pro forma statements.

Discontinued Operations

Another category of current-period results required to be set out separately between income from continuing operations and net income is discontinued operations resulting from the sale or abandonment of a segment of the business (I13). A segment is defined narrowly, thus precluding eclectic disposals from being given this special treatment. The determination that an operation has become discontinued is made as of a measurement date generally defined as the date on which management, having the requisite authority, decides to sell, offers to sell, or abandons the segment. Once this decision is made, if a loss will be incurred on disposal, an estimate of that loss is required to be charged against operations at that time; and if a gain is anticipated, it is not to be recognized until realized, usually on the disposal date. In either case, when the next financial statements are prepared, the historical financial statements will show the operations of the discontinued segment below income from continuing operations.

The objective of this income statement stratification is to allow users to assess earning power, that is amounts that are supported by ongoing activities. This assessment is facilitated by segregating major activities that no longer are part of the company. The segregation is easy when a decision is made on one day to sell a segment on the same day for cash. Nothing is that simple, however. There will always be some delay between the measurement date and the disposal date, sometimes months and even years. Operations will ordinarily continue during that hiatus, resulting in gains or losses in addition to those that are expected to result from the difference between the recorded investment in the discontinued segment plus estimated costs associated with disposal, and the proceeds expected to be received therefor.

Thus the APB provided that earnings expected to be achieved during the temporary continuance period could be offset against the estimated disposal loss, but any greater amount would have to await recognition until realized. If a gain was also expected on disposal, both that gain and the earnings during the interim would be recognized only as realized.

The matter becomes more complex, however, when the interim period operations are expected to result in losses. The APB provided that such losses were to be anticipated and recorded as part of the loss on discontinuance; or if a gain was expected on disposal the losses could be deferred up to the amount of the gain. It is this last proviso that became the focus of an EITF debate that again points up the difficulty of reaching conclusions in gray areas.

In EITF Issue 85-36, *Discontinued Operations with Expected Gain and Interim Operating Losses*, the discussion centered on whether losses from operations during the interim period should be recognized as incurred or deferred until the disposal date and reported as part of the net gain. The EITF concluded that estimated losses from operations should be deferred assuming there is reasonable assurance that a net gain would occur. The EITF specifically noted that APB 30 requires the ability to make projections with reasonable accuracy, and a usual expectation that the plan of disposal would be carried out within one year.

Additional discussion centered on (1) whether the above conclusion would apply to a disposal that is not deemed to be a "disposal of a segment of a business" but satisfies all other related requirements of APB 30 and (2) whether the anticipated combined net gain from the disposal of two separate segments should be netted if one involves a net gain and the other involves a net loss.

On the first additional issue, the Task Force reached the same conclusion, consistent with AICPA Accounting Interpretation 1 of APB 30 (I13.501). On the second issue, the EITF agreed with netting if the multiple dispositions are part of the same formal plan and satisfy all other related requirements in APB 30. This conclusion would *not* apply to disposals of unrelated assets unless they are segments as defined in APB 30.

STATEMENT OF CAPITAL CHANGES

The statement of capital changes presents the changes that have taken place in owners' equity during a period.

Retained earnings are normally increased by the addition of net income and reduced by a net loss and the payment of dividends. Less frequently, changes in retained earnings may arise from restatement of prior years' statements because of retroactive application of a new FASB standard. The statement of retained earnings in Figure 3.9 shows changes caused by restatement for an accounting change from LIFO to FIFO. When the changes in retained earnings are simple and straightforward, the statements of income and retained earnings are often combined.

APB 12 (C08.102) requires "disclosure of changes in the separate accounts comprising stockholders' equity (in addition to retained earnings). . . . Disclosure of such changes may take the form of separate statements or may be made in the basic financial statements or notes thereto." When there are changes in several of the capital accounts, a separate statement of owners' equity or capital changes (which usually includes retained earnings) is often presented. An example of a separate statement of capital changes is shown in Figure 3.3.

Consolidated Statements of Retained Earnings

For the three years ended January 31, 1987

	1987	1986	1985
Balance at beginning of year as previously reported	$72,786,913	$80,064,702	$75,391,236
Cumulative effect of applying retroactively the change in the method of accounting for inventories (see Note 2)	3,235,002	2,314,877	2,247,207
Balance at beginning of year, restated	76,021,915	82,379,579	77,638,443
Net income (loss)	517,736	(4,161,736)	7,011,614
Cash dividends on common stock, $1.40 per share	(2,195,928)	(2,195,928)	(2,270,478)
Balance at end of year	$74,343,723	$76,021,915	$82,379,579

*Restated, see Note 2

The accompanying notes are an integral part of the consolidated financial statements.

Note 2. Accounting Change

In the fourth quarter of fiscal 1987, the Company changed the method of valuing its inventories to the FIFO method from the LIFO method which was used in prior years. This change was made due to continual fluctuations in the worldwide market for ferrous and non-ferrous scrap metal, the depressed economic environment in the United States steel industry, the Company's principal market, and to more accurately reflect results of operations and financial condition during periods of declining prices.

The change has been applied by retroactively restating the financial statements for prior years. As a result of adopting the FIFO method, net income for the year ended January 31, 1987 is approximately $1,200,000 or $.77 per share less than it would have been on the LIFO method.

FIG. 3.9 Restated Retained Earnings
Source: Proler International Corp., 1987 Annual Report.

STATEMENT OF CASH FLOWS

General

Changes in the financial position of an enterprise during a period can be determined by comparing the enterprise's balance sheet at the beginning and end of the period. Sometimes intelligent guesses can be made about the causes of the changes, but guesses are a poor substitute for reliable information about the transactions that have caused the changes to occur. An income statement covering the period between the two balance sheet dates shows the impact of those transactions relating to the enterprise's revenue-producing activities, but it will not show the impact of other kinds of transactions that materially affect liquidity, such as acquisitions of plant assets. It is the purpose of the statement of cash flows to summarize all the transactions, revenue-earning and others, that have changed the financial position shown in the balance sheet at the beginning of the period to the position shown in the balance sheet at the end of the period.

In a profitable business, the primary source of net cash inflows is usually the enterprise's net income. However, some costs that do not involve an expenditure are nevertheless expensed during a financial period, thereby reducing income. The most prominent of these costs is depreciation. Here, the outflow of cash occurs when the assets are first acquired, so that no further outflows need be recognized as they are systematically expensed. Therefore, in calculating the amount of cash derived from operations, those expenses not requiring the use of cash must be added back to net profit.

Though depreciation is the most important noncash expense, it is not the only one. Like depreciation, amortization of intangible assets does not give rise to an outflow of cash. Another noncash expense is the provision for deferred income tax. Temporary differences between the accounting treatment of certain expenses and their tax treatment cause accounting profits and taxable profits to diverge, so that during a given financial period more is charged against income for taxes than needs to be paid. Because the eventual liability is systematically expensed, profits are diminished, but no cash payment is made and no current tax liability is created.

In addition to cash generated by operations, the main sources of cash are disposals of plant and equipment and issuance of debt and equity securities. The principal uses of cash are expenditures for the acquisition of plant and equipment, purchases of long-term investments (e.g., investments in affiliates), retirement of debt, purchases of treasury stock, and the payment of dividends.

From 1971 to 1987, APB 19, *Reporting Changes in Financial Position*, specified the form and content of a statement of changes in financial position that was required as one of the basic financial statements whenever an income statement and balance sheet were presented. APB 19 improved on earlier practice by requiring certain transactions that did not have direct funds flows (e.g., purchase of real estate by issuance of securities) to be included "broad," that is, as both a source and a use of funds. However, the main defect of APB 19 practice was that funds were permitted to be defined as "working capital," thus allowing companies to avoid reporting significant cash flows within current assets and current liabilities.

From late 1980 through 1984, the FASB considered the concept and nature of funds and cash flow reporting in a series of Board documents. In December 1984 the Board issued SFAC 5, *Recognition and Measurement in Financial Statements of Business Enterprises* (FASB, 1984c), which included general guidance on a statement of cash flows and concluded that, from a conceptual view, a cash flow statement should be part of a full set of financial statements. In addition, in 1984 the Financial Executives Research Foundation of the Financial Executives Institute published a research study that solicited and analyzed the views of both preparers and users on issues pertaining to funds flow reporting. That study describes areas of diversity in practice in presenting cash flow information. Issues identified in practice included comparability difficulties arising from wide diversity in the focus of statements of changes in financial position (e.g., cash or working capital) and the definition of funds (e.g., cash flows) from operations. Also there was concern that funds statements in financial statements of banks and other financial institutions were not useful. The FASB therefore placed the cash flow reporting project on its agenda in April 1985.

FASB Statement No. 95

Scope and Definitions. In October 1987 the FASB issued SFAS 95, *Statement of Cash Flows* (C25), superseding APB Opinion 19. SFAS 95 identifies as the primary purpose of a cash flow statement the presentation of information about the cash receipts and cash payments during a period. A secondary purpose is to disclose the entity's financing and investing activities. Along with information in the other financial statements, a cash flow statement should help investors, creditors, and others to assess:

1. The entity's ability to generate positive future net cash flows;
2. The entity's ability to pay dividends and to meet its obligations and needs for external financing;
3. The reasons for differences between earnings and comprehensive income and operating cash receipts and payments; and
4. Both the cash and noncash aspects of the entity's investing and financing transactions during the period.

For purposes of the cash flow statement, cash also includes short-term highly liquid investments (cash equivalents). In addition to currency on hand, cash is interpreted to include

> demand deposits with banks or other financial institutions. All charges and credits to [a demand deposit account] are cash receipts or payments to both the entity owning the account and the bank holding it. For example, a bank's granting of a loan by crediting the proceeds to a customer's demand deposit account is a cash payment by the bank and a cash receipt of the customer when the entry is made. [C25.105]

Cash equivalents are short-term, extremely liquid investments that are both "readily convertible to known amounts of cash" and so near their maturity that they present a small "risk of changes in value because of changes in interest rates." Generally, only investments with maturities of three months or less qualify under the definition. Treasury bills, commercial paper, money market funds, and federal funds sold (for banks) are examples.

Companies are encouraged to provide gross amounts of operating cash receipts and payments. However, the FASB believes that providing the net amounts of related cash receipts and disbursements is sufficient in certain circumstances. Netting is acceptable:

1. For cash equivalents (deemed to be "cash" for purposes of this statement);
2. For items with quick turnover, when the amounts are large and maturities are short (e.g., accounts payable of a broker-dealer or investments, loans receivable, and debt if the original maturity is three months or less); and
3. For companies not selecting the direct method (see "Direct Method" in this chapter) of reporting cash receipts and disbursements.

Classification. A statement of cash flows must classify cash receipts and disbursements into three categories: investing, financing, and operating activities. *Investing activities* comprise the making and collecting of loans, and the acquisition and disposition of debt or equity issues and of property, plant, and equipment (including certain other productive assets). *Financing activities* comprise the obtaining of capital from owners, returns on and of such capital, and securing and repaying loans or other long-term credit. *Operating activities* comprise all transactions and events other than those for investing and financing and generally include the production and delivery of goods and services. Cash receipts and disbursements that have aspects of more than one of the above-described activities should be classified based on the predominant source of cash flows for the item.

A company with foreign currency transactions should "report the reporting currency equivalent of foreign currency cash flows using the exchange rates in effect at the time of the cash flows" (C25.123).

Direct Method. Companies are encouraged to report major classes of gross cash receipts and disbursements for operating activities; this is called the *direct method.* Such reporting should include at least the following classes of receipts and payments:

- Cash collected from customers, including lessees, licensees, and the like
- Interest and dividends received
- Other operating cash receipts, if any
- Cash paid to employees and other suppliers of goods or services, including suppliers of insurance, advertising, and the like
- Interest paid
- Income taxes paid
- Other operating cash payments, if any

An example of the direct method is illustrated in Figure 3.10.

Indirect Method. If the direct method is not used, then net cash flows must be reported indirectly by adjusting net income to reconcile it to net cash flows from operating activities. The reconciliation provides for adjustment of net income by deducting:

1. All deferrals of past operating cash receipts and disbursements, for example, changes in inventory and deferred income;
2. All accruals of expected future operating cash receipts and disbursements, for example, changes in receivables and payables; and
3. The effects of items for which the cash effects relate to investing or financing cash flows, for example, depreciation, goodwill amortization, gains or losses on sales of capital equipment, gains or losses from discontinued operations, and gains or losses on extinguishment of debt.

An example of the indirect method is illustrated in Figure 3.11.

COMPANY M
Consolidated Statement Of Cash Flows
for the Year Ended December 31, 19X1

Increase (Decrease) in Cash and Cash Equivalents

Cash flows from operating activities:

Cash received from customers	$13,850	
Cash paid to suppliers and employees	(12,000)	
Dividend received from affiliate	20	
Interest received	55	
Interest paid (net of amount capitalized)	(220)	
Income taxes paid	(325)	
Insurance proceeds received	15	
Cash paid to settle lawsuit for patent infringement	(30)	
Net cash provided by operating activities		$1,365

Cash flows from investing activities:

Proceeds from sale of facility	600	
Payment received on note for sale of plant	150	
Capital expenditures	(1,000)	
Payment for purchase of Company S, net of cash acquired	(925)	
Net cash used in investing activities		(1,175)

Cash flows from financing activities:

Net borrowings under line-of-credit agreement	300	
Principal payments under capital lease obligation	(125)	
Proceeds from issuance of long-term debt	400	
Proceeds from issuance of common stock	500	
Dividends paid	(200)	
Net cash provided by financing activities		875
Net increase in cash and cash equivalents		1,065
Cash and cash equivalents at beginning of year		600
Cash and cash equivalents at end of year		$1,665

Reconciliation of net income to net cash provided by operating activities:

Net income		$ 760
Adjustments to reconcile net income to net cash provided by operating activities:		
Depreciation and amortization	$ 445	
Provision for losses on accounts receivable	200	
Gain on sale of facility	(80)	
Undistributed earnings of affiliate	(25)	
Payment received on installment note receivable for sale of inventory	100	
Change in assets and liabilities net of effects from purchase of Company S:		
Increase in accounts receivable	(215)	
Decrease in inventory	205	
Increase in prepaid expenses	(25)	
Decrease in accounts payable and accrued expenses	(250)	
Increase in interest and income taxes payable	50	
Increase in deferred taxes	150	
Increase in other liabilities	50	
Total adjustments		605
Net cash provided by operating activities		$1,365

FIG. 3.10   Statement of Cash Flows—Direct Method
Source: SFAS 95 (C25.137).

Supplemental schedule of noncash investing and financing activities:

The Company purchased all of the capital stock of Company S for $950. In conjunction with the acquisition, liabilities were assumed as follows:

Fair value of assets acquired	$1,580
Cash paid for the capital stock	(950)
Liabilities assumed	$ 630

A capital lease obligation of $850 was incurred when the Company entered into a lease for new equipment.

Additional common stock was issued upon the conversion of $500 of long-term debt.

Disclosure of accounting policy:

For purposes of the statement of cash flows, the Company considers all highly liquid debt instruments purchased with a maturity of three months or less to be cash equivalents.

Reconciliation. Regardless of whether the direct or indirect method of reporting cash flows is used, companies are required to provide a reconciliation of net cash flows from operating activities to net income. For companies using the direct method, the reconciliation must be provided in a separate schedule. For companies using the indirect method, the reconciliation may be provided either in the statement of cash flows or in a separate schedule.

Other Provisions. Generally, both investing and financing cash inflows and outflows are to be reported separately in a statement of cash flows. In addition, factors relating to investing and financing activities that affect assets and liabilities but do not affect cash receipts and disbursements must be reported in related disclosures. Those disclosures may be either in narrative form or summarized in a schedule. Examples are converting debt to equity, acquiring assets by assumption of liabilities and assets acquired though capital leases.

Financial statements shall *not* report cash flow per share. SFAS 95 is effective for annual financial statements issued for years ending after July 15, 1988, with early application encouraged.

INTERIM FINANCIAL STATEMENTS

Precise financial information cannot be determined until a business has terminated and all its transactions are complete, but reporting at annual intervals has become accepted by custom and law because the users of financial information have been willing to sacrifice some precision for the sake of currentness. Reporting at less than annual intervals, *interim financial reporting*, has also become common since decisions based on financial data are made daily and require current financial information. Interim reporting could someday evolve to continuous reporting.

COMPANY M

**Consolidated Statement Of Cash Flows
for the Year Ended December 31, 19X1**

Increase (Decrease) in Cash and Cash Equivalents

Cash flows from operating activities:		
Net income		$ 760
Adjustments to reconcile net income to net cash provided by operating activities:		
Depreciation and amortization	$ 445	
Provision for losses on accounts receivable	200	
Gain on sale of facility	(80)	
Undistributed earnings of affiliate	(25)	
Payment received on installment note receivable for sale of inventory	100	
Change in assets and liabilities net of effects from purchase of Company S:		
Increase in accounts receivable	(215)	
Decrease in inventory	205	
Increase in prepaid expenses	(25)	
Decrease in accounts payable and accrued expenses	(250)	
Increase in interest and income taxes payable	50	
Increase in deferred taxes	150	
Increase in other liabilities	50	
Total adjustments		605
Net cash provided by operating activities		1,365
Cash flows from investing activities:		
Proceeds from sale of facility	600	
Payment received on note for sale of plant	150	
Capital expenditures	(1,000)	
Payment for purchase of Company S, net of cash acquired	(925)	
Net cash used in investing activities		(1,175)
Cash flows from financing activities:		
Net borrowings under line-of-credit agreement	300	
Principal payments under capital lease obligation	(125)	
Proceeds from issuance of long-term debt	400	
Proceeds from issuance of common stock	500	
Dividends paid	(200)	
Net cash provided by financing activities		875
Net increase in cash and cash equivalents		1,065
Cash and cash equivalents at beginning of year		600
Cash and cash equivalents at end of year		$1,665

Supplemental disclosures of cash flow information:

Cash paid during the year for:	
Interest (net of amount capitalized)	$220
Income taxes	325

Supplemental schedule of noncash investing and financing activities:

The Company purchased all of the capital stock of Company S for $950. In conjunction with the acquisition, liabilities were assumed as follows:

Fair value of assets acquired	$1,580
Cash paid for the capital stock	(950)
Liabilities assumed	$ 630

FIG. 3.11 Statement of Cash Flows—Indirect Method
Source: SFAS 95 (C25.138).

A capital lease obligation of $850 was incurred when the Company entered into a lease for new equipment.

Additional common stock was issued upon the conversion of $500 of long-term debt.

Disclosure of accounting policy:

For purposes of the statement of cash flows, the Company considers all highly liquid debt instruments purchased with a maturity of three months or less to be cash equivalents.

The preceding portion of this chapter implicitly emphasized annual financial statements. This section focuses on interim financial statements, especially those of publicly held companies because that has been the focus of professional standard-setting bodies and the SEC.

Evolution

Public interim financial reporting began in 1902, when the United States Steel Corporation first published quarterly financial information. In 1910, the New York Stock Exchange added quarterly financial reporting to its listing requirements. The SEC established formal interim reporting requirements in the 1970 issuance of Form 10-Q, which requires summarized quarterly information on operations and financial position.

In 1973, the APB reacted to the need for interim information by issuing APB 28, *Interim Financial Reporting* (I73). Also in 1973 the SEC introduced Form 8-K, covering the reporting of unusual charges and credits to income. This form was designed to achieve more timely reporting than quarterly, and to assure the involvement of the independent auditor in the disclosure of these items (see FRR § 216).

FRR §§ 301, 303, and 304 (ASR 177, subsequently amended) increased the disclosure requirements for quarterly reporting by publicly held companies, and in addition auditors began to be publicly associated with the review of interim financial statements of public companies through optional identification in Form 10-Q. Auditor involvement with interim financial reporting is covered by SAS 36, *Review of Interim Financial Information* (AU 722). For further discussion of this subject, see Chapter 11. Interim financial reporting for private companies is covered by Statements on Standards of Accounting and Review Services, *Compilation and Review of Financial Statements* (AR 100) (see Chapter 39).

Though these basic documents — Forms 10-Q and 8-K, APB 28, SAS 36, and the SSARS — continue to be amended and interpreted by the AICPA, the FASB, and the SEC, many issues still cloud interim reporting. These issues center on the objectives and uses of interim financial data, on whether there is a need for greater precision in this data, on the extent of financial disclosures, and on the relative costs and benefits.

FASB Discussion Memorandum

In 1978, the FASB issued a discussion memorandum, *An Analysis of Issues Related to Interim Financial Accounting and Reporting* (FASB, 1978) that examines five possible objectives of and uses for interim reporting:

* To estimate annual earnings
* To make projections
* To identify turning points
* To evaluate management performance
* To supplement the annual report

The discussion memorandum explores methods of determining net income for an interim period, including the integral and discrete approaches (described in the next section). In addition, the question of how much information interim period reports should disclose is considered. Finally, the discussion memorandum asks whether some companies should be exempt from interim disclosure standards.

Less than a year after releasing the discussion memorandum, the FASB indefinitely deferred further consideration of the issues surrounding interim reporting (and that deferral continues today). A conceptual framework for assets and liabilities in annual reporting was being developed in 1979, and the FASB concluded that the issues in interim reporting hinged on resolution of those in annual reporting.

Accounting Issues

Estimates and judgments are required for determining results of operations for any period, even a whole year. Normally, though, the shorter the period, the less precise the results, because the relative importance of estimates and judgments increases as the materiality base (e.g., the reported amounts) decreases. Further, to speed the release of interim results, companies simply must rely more on estimates.

For example, it is almost invariably considered impractical to count and price the inventory every quarter or every month; as an alternative, estimates of gross profit must be used to determine cost of goods sold. Even if the company has perpetual inventory records integrated with the accounting records, allowing direct determination of cost of goods sold, the perpetual records may not have been verified by cycle counts, and some interim allowance will be needed for annual physical inventory adjustments.

The inventory problem is further complicated for companies on LIFO, since these companies must estimate not only the gross profit on their sales but also the year-end inventory quantity and price level. Interim LIFO computations are described in detail in Chapter 14.

Companies fortunate enough to escape inventory problems are likely to encounter similar interim problems in other areas, such as income taxes—a complex area requiring considerable estimation. In order to calculate interim income taxes, a company must estimate such items as the annual pretax income and book/tax differences for the full year. (See Chapter 17 for a detailed discussion of interim income taxes.) Interim accruals for various selling expenses, general and administrative expenses, allowances for doubtful accounts, and deferrals and contingencies are further illustrations of items that normally require companies to rely heavily on estimates.

Because investors have a tendency to project a full year's results on the basis of data given for the short period, random fluctuations (a one-time significant sale), or seasonal business (the Christmas sales quarter) that occur in short periods, if not recognized, would lead to erroneous projections. Seasonal business also leads to questions about matching revenues and expenses during the year.

The APB had to develop a transitional definition of the objective of interim information in order to release APB 28, *Interim Financial Reporting* (I73), and concluded that "interim financial information is essential to provide investors and others with timely information as to the progress of the enterprise. The usefulness of such information rests on the relationship that it has to the annual results of operations" (¶ 9). In other words, the APB concluded that the objective of interim reports is to convey information on the financial progress of the company between annual reports.

With this objective, APB 28 adopted the *integral view:* "each interim period should be viewed primarily as an integral part of an annual period" (I73.103). Thus, the APB recognized that the *discrete view* — using accounting principles and practices followed for annual reporting purposes giving no recognition to the fact that a period shorter than a year is involved — had to be modified for reporting at interim dates. However, the Board also recognized that the integral view does not always provide for the proper matching of revenues and expenses at interim dates. The result is that GAAP requires interim financial statements to be prepared basically according to annual accounting policies, with certain noteworthy exceptions, described later in this chapter.

Revenues

Revenue from products sold or services rendered should be recognized as earned during an interim period on the same basis as that followed for the full year. For example, when the percentage-of-completion method is used in accounting for contracts, that method should be used for interim periods as well as for the full year.

Costs and Expenses

Costs Associated With Revenues. Costs and expenses associated with revenue should be charged against income in those interim periods in which the revenue is recognized. Examples are materials, wages and salaries and related fringe benefits, manufacturing overhead, and provision for warranties on products sold during the period.

Although APB 28 states that costs and expenses associated with revenue for an interim period should be similar to those for an annual period (I73.106), the method used to determine the cost of inventory may be different at the interim date. For example (I73.107):

1. An estimated gross profit rate may be used to determine cost of goods sold during interim periods, and a physical inventory may be used at year end.
2. When LIFO base inventories liquidated at an interim date are expected to be replaced by year end, cost of goods sold for the interim period should include the cost of replacement.

3. Inventory losses from market declines should not be deferred beyond the interim period in which the decline occurs, unless the decline is temporary and no loss is expected to be incurred in the fiscal year.

4. Companies that use standard cost accounting systems for determining inventory and product costs generally should account for interim variances in the same manner as annual ones. Thus, planned variances at interim periods that are expected to be absorbed by year end should ordinarily be deferred.

Seasonal businesses often have interpreted the last requirement in APB 28 as a justification for the capitalization of costs and expenses associated with revenue during slack off-season periods. This practice is discussed later under "Seasonal Businesses."

Costs Not Associated With Revenues. Costs and expenses other than product costs should be charged against income in interim periods as incurred, or be allocated among interim periods on some empirical basis (I73.108a). These costs and expenses include selling and general and administrative expenses.

In applying the required accounting treatment to other costs and expenses, the APB viewed the interim period as an integral part of the annual period. Thus, a specific item benefiting more than one interim period, though normally charged to expense in an annual period, may be allocated among those interim periods; but this allocation should not be made arbitrarily. Instead it should be based on an estimate of time expired, of benefit received, or of other activity associated with the period.

When costs and expenses are based on minimum levels (contingent rentals or quantity discounts), the accrual should be figured on the total estimated expense for the year. When costs and expenses incurred in a particular interim period cannot readily be identified with the activities of other interim periods, they should be charged off as incurred. Interim gains and losses should not be deferred to later interim periods within the same fiscal year if they would not qualify for deferral at year end.

APB 28 illustrates these points with examples of quantity discounts, property taxes, interest, rent, and advertising costs (I73.150). An additional example is research and development expenses.

Costs and expenses other than product costs normally require estimation at the interim financial date, either for the timely release of interim data or because the benefit of greater accuracy is not worth the cost. Also, uncertainty of amount (such as pension expense, which is determined only once a year) is often a factor.

Additional guidance on interim accounting for income taxes, discontinued operations, extraordinary items, and contingencies is given in the following subsections.

Income taxes. In a manner consistent with its conclusions on the accounting for other costs, the APB in APB 28 (I73.111 and .122) and later the FASB in FIN 18, *Accounting for Income Taxes in Interim Periods* (I73.111), required income taxes for each interim period to be viewed as an integral part of the taxes due for the annual period. SFAS 16, *Prior Period Adjustments* (A35), had required the restatement of prior interim periods of the current fiscal year for adjustments or settlements of litigation, income taxes, and utility revenues in rate-making proceedings that meet certain criteria. However, in TB 86-1, *Accounting for Certain Effects of The Tax*

Reform Act of 1986 (I24.547), the FASB staff stated that the tax effects of any retroactive provisions of the Tax Reform Act on interim prior periods before the date the law became effective should be recognized as a component of income tax expense in the interim period during which the Act became effective. As a result, SFAS 96, *Accounting for Income Taxes,* amends SFAS 16 to exclude the effects of retroactive tax legislation from being treated as "an adjustment related to prior interim periods of the current fiscal year" (I73.143).

In addition, SFAS 96 amends APB 28 by confirming the above, i.e., that new tax legislation should not be recognized prior to enactment of the law. That amendment also states:

> The tax effect of a change in tax law or rates on taxes currently payable or refundable for the current year shall be reflected after the effective dates prescribed in the statutes in the computation of the annual effective tax rate beginning no earlier than the first interim period that includes the enactment date of the new legislation. The effect of a change in tax law or rates on a deferred tax liability or asset shall not be apportioned among interim periods through an adjustment of the annual effective tax rate. The tax effect of a change in tax law or rates on taxes payable or refundable for a prior year shall be recognized as of the enactment date of the change as tax expense (benefit) for the current year. [I73.122]

Chapter 17 details the requirements of accounting for income taxes in interim financial statements.

Discontinued operations and extraordinary items. APB 28 (I73.124) requires that gains and losses from disposition of a business, discontinued operations, and extraordinary items should be disclosed separately in the income statement for the period in which they occur; they should not be prorated over the balance of the fiscal year. In determining materiality, extraordinary items should be related to the estimated income for the full year.

Contingencies. Contingencies and other uncertainties that could be expected to affect the fairness of presentation of financial data at an interim date should be accrued and/or disclosed in interim reports in the same manner required for annual reports by APB 28 (I73.125) and SFAS 5, *Accounting for Contingencies* (C59). Again, the determination of significance should be judged in relation to annual financial statements.

Accounting Changes

Estimates. Since estimates provide much of the information presented in interim financial reporting, changes in estimates are common. The effect of any such change should be accounted for in the period in which the change is made, and the previously reported interim information should not be restated (I73.133). Disclosure as to the nature and amounts of such changes, if material in relation to the interim amounts, should be made to avoid misleading comparisons. This conforms with the requirements of APB 20, *Accounting Changes* (A06.132), for reporting estimate changes in year-end financial statements.

Cumulative Effect. SFAS 3, *Reporting Accounting Changes in Interim Financial Statements* (I73.135–.137), requires the cumulative effect (to the beginning of the fiscal year) of an accounting change made during the first interim period of a fiscal year to be included in net income of that period. However, if such an accounting change is made in a period other than the first interim period, the cumulative effect should not be included in the net income of the period of the change; instead, financial statements for interim periods before the change should be retroactively restated. The cumulative effect of the change on retained earnings at the beginning of the fiscal year should be included in the net income for the year-to-date amounts. Whenever financial information is given for interim periods earlier than the period of the change (but within the same fiscal year or trailing 12 months), it should be presented on the restated basis, as if the new accounting principle had been in effect during those periods. Prior years' interim income statements presented for comparative purposes should be restated on a pro forma basis. SFAS 3 (I73.137) also calls for extensive disclosure of the effect of the change in all interim period reports for the fiscal year in which the change is made.

Figure 3.12 illustrates the requirements for reporting an accounting change that has a cumulative effect. APB 20 indicates there are some rare situations, principally a change to LIFO, in which the cumulative effect is not determinable, and it is therefore not possible to compute pro forma amounts (A06.122). If this type of change is made in the first interim period, the disclosures required by SFAS 3 for accounting changes that have a cumulative effect should be made (I73.140); but if the change is made in a later interim period, restatement of the interim periods before the change is also required (I73.141).

Correction of Error. Previously issued interim financial statements must be restated for the correction of a material error. (See the earlier discussion under "Prior-Period Adjustments and Errors.") Materiality, again, is based on the estimated income for the full fiscal year and the trend of earnings.

Summarized Information

Certain minimum disclosures are required by APB 28 (I73.146–.149) when publicly traded companies report summarized interim financial information to their shareholders. There are no similar requirements for summarized interim information of privately held companies, but it is advisable that they follow the same guidelines as public companies. (Private companies may, however, issue unaudited financial statements that omit substantially all disclosures required under GAAP (AR 100.19–.21). This is discussed further in Chapter 39.)

According to APB 28 (I73.146), public companies that report summarized financial information to their shareholders at an interim date must disclose at least the data indicated in Figure 3.13. When summarized financial data are regularly reported every quarter, the information in Figure 3.13 should be furnished for the current quarter and the current year to date (the last 12 months, or *trailing 12 months*, may be given), together with comparable data for the preceding year.

ASSUMPTIONS

ABC Company has 1,000,000 shares of common stock issued and outstanding, and no dilutive securities, in both 19X4 and 19X5. In 19X5, the company decided to adopt the straight-line method of depreciation for manufacturing equipment. The amounts applicable to each quarter are shown below:

Period	Net income on the basis of old accounting principle (accelerated depreciation)	Gross effect of change to straight-line depreciation	Gross effect less income taxes (50%)	Net effect after incentive compensation and related income taxes
Before first quarter 19X4		$ 20,000	$10,000	$ 9,000
First quarter 19X4	$1,000,000	30,000	15,000	13,500
Second quarter 19X4	1,200,000	70,000	35,000	31,500
Third quarter 19X4	1,100,000	50,000	25,000	22,500
Fourth quarter 19X4	1,100,000	80,000	40,000	36,000
Total at beginning of 19X5	$4,400,000	$250,000	$125,000	$112,500
First quarter 19X5	$1,059,500	$ 90,000	$ 45,000	$ 40,500
Second quarter 19X5	1,255,000	100,000	50,000	45,000
Third quarter 19X5	1,150,500	110,000	55,000	49,500
Fourth quarter 19X5	1,146,000	120,000	60,000	54,000
Total at beginning of 19X6	$4,611,000	$420,000	$210,000	$189,000

FIRST QUARTER CHANGE

If the change in the depreciation method was made in the first quarter of 19X5, the manner of reporting the change is as follows:

	Three months ended March 31	
	19X5	19X4
Income before cumulative effect of a change in accounting principle	$1,100,000	$1,000,000
Cumulative effect of depreciation method change on prior years	125,000	–
Net income	$1,225,000	$1,000,000
Amounts per common share:		
Income before cumulative effect of a change in accounting principle	$1.10	$1.00
Cumulative effect of depreciation method change on prior years	.13	–
Net income	$1.23	$1.00
Pro forma amounts assuming the new depreciation method is applied retroactively:		
Net income	$1,100,000	$1,013,500
Net income per common share	$1.10	$1.01

(continued)

FIG. 3.12 Interim Reporting of Accounting Changes
Source: Adapted from Appendix A of SFAS 3 (I73.151-.155).

THIRD QUARTER CHANGE

If the change had been made in the third quarter, the manner of reporting the change in the third quarter and year-to-date financial statements is as follows:

	Three months ended September 30		Nine months ended September 30	
	19X5	19X4	19X5	19X4
Income before cumulative effect of a change in accounting principle	$1,200,000	$1,100,000	$3,600,000	$3,300,000
Cumulative effect of depreciation method change on prior years	–	–	125,000	–
Net income	$1,200,000	$1,100,000	$3,725,000	$3,300,000
Amounts per common share:				
Income before cumulative effect of a change in accounting principle	$1.20	$1.10	$3.60	$3.30
Cumulative effect of depreciation method change on prior years	–	–	.13	–
Net income	$1.20	$1.10	$3.73	$3.30
Pro forma amounts assuming the new depreciation method is applied retroactively:				
Net income	$1,200,000	$1,125,000	$3,600,000	$3,375,000
Net income per common share	$1.20	$1.13	$3.60	$3.38

FIG. 3.12 *(continued)*

These minimum disclosures required by the APB do not meet the SEC requirements for quarterly reporting on Form 10-Q (discussed later) nor do they constitute a fair presentation in conformity with GAAP. However, users of summarized interim financial data are presumed to have read the latest annual report, including the financial statements and related disclosures, and the management commentary concerning the annual financial results. These disclosure requirements for summarized interim information should be viewed in that context.

1. Sales or gross revenues, provision for income taxes, extraordinary items (including related income tax effects), cumulative effect of a change in accounting principles or practices, and net income
2. Primary and fully diluted earnings per share data for each period presented
3. Seasonal revenues, costs, or expenses
4. Significant changes in provisions for income taxes
5. Disposal of a segment of a business and extraordinary, unusual, or infrequently occurring items
6. Contingent items
7. Changes in accounting principles or estimates
8. Significant changes in financial position

FIG. 3.13   Summarized Interim Information for Disclosure to Shareholders of Public Companies

Special Disclosure Problems

Segment Information. SFAS 18, *Financial Reporting For Segments of a Business Enterprise—Interim Financial Statements* (S20.105), requires that if any segment information is presented in interim financial statements it must be consistent with the requirements of SFAS 14 (S20). However, the segment information originally called for by SFAS 14 for interim periods is not required as a result of the SFAS 18 amendment.

Fourth Quarter Adjustments. In the absence of a separate fourth quarter report or the disclosure of that information in the annual report, disposals of segments of a business and extraordinary, unusual, or infrequently occurring items, as well as adjustments material to the results of that quarter, are required by APB 28 to be disclosed in a note to the annual financial statements (I73.147).

Seasonal Businesses. To avoid the possibility that interim results with material seasonal variations may be used to extrapolate the results for a full year, businesses should disclose the seasonal nature of their activities. These companies should also consider supplementing their interim reports with information for the trailing twelve months for both the current and preceding years.

There is no authoritative guidance for seasonal businesses to follow in deciding whether to defer slack-period costs and expenses. Each set of circumstances must be viewed on its own merits, and industry practices often will govern. Seasonal businesses that do defer such costs and expenses should disclose their accounting policies and the nature of their activities in their interim financial statements. An example of such a disclosure might be:

> The interim results of ABC Baseball Team, Inc. are not necessarily indicative of the annual results of operations. Substantially all of the Company's revenue is earned during the regular baseball season, which, except for postseason games, extends from the middle of April to the beginning of October. Expenses such as players' and coaches' salaries, stadium and game expenses, and broadcasting expenses, which are directly related to the playing of baseball, are deferred and will be amortized to expense on the basis of the number of games played. Expenses such as general and administrative expenses, public relations, scouting, player development, and spring training have been expensed as incurred.

Earnings Per Share. Each interim period stands alone for the calculation of earnings per share. Thus, total earnings per share for the combined interim periods will not necessarily equal the annual or year-to-date calculation. For example, because of changes in the market price of the stock, an option may be antidilutive in the calculation for the third quarter but dilutive in the calculation for the nine months then ended. Market price changes are probably the main cause of the four quarters' earnings per share not equaling the annual total; other changes, some applied retroactively, are summarized in the earnings per share interpretations (E09.525–.526).

SEC Requirements for Quarterly Reports

Public companies are required to report, on Form 10-Q, quarterly information on operations and financial position within forty-five days of the end of each of the first three fiscal quarters. Also, registration statements filed with the SEC generally are required to contain financial information as current as the most recent Form 10-Q. Larger public companies are required by Item 302(a) of Regulation S-K to include selected quarterly financial data in their annual reports; and many other companies have also decided to publish this information in their annual reports, although they are not required to do so.

Public companies have the option of using their annual and quarterly reports to shareholders to satisfy Exchange Act requirements for all, or any part, of the information required to be filed. When a report to shareholders contains some or all of the required information, appropriate portions of that report may be simply incorporated by reference into the Form 10-Q.

Periods to be Covered. Condensed balance sheets at the end of the most recent quarter and at the preceding year-end are required. However, a balance sheet at the end of the corresponding quarter of the preceding year should also be provided if it is necessary to understand the impact of seasonal fluctuations on financial condition. Obviously, the preceding year-end balance sheet is audited, but in the context of a Form 10-Q filing, this balance sheet will usually be condensed, with footnotes omitted. Accordingly, this year-end balance sheet will be described as having been taken from the audited financial statements; it will not be labeled "unaudited."

Change in Method of Accounting. When a registrant changes a method of accounting, Regulation S-X requires that the following information be included in Form 10-Q:

1. The date of any material accounting change;
2. The reasons for the change;
3. A letter from the independent accountants, to be filed as an exhibit in the first Form 10-Q after the date of an accounting change, stating whether the change is to an alternative principle which is preferable under the circumstances. If the change occurs in the fourth quarter, the *preferability letter* may be included in either Form 10-K or in the subsequent first quarter's Form 10-Q.

These data are in addition to the disclosure requirements of APB 28, SFAS 3, and FIN 18 (I73.131–.142).

A preferability letter need not be filed when the change is made in response to a standard adopted by the FASB that creates a new principle, expresses a preference for a principle, or rejects a specific principle.

The SEC has seven interpretations on the subject of preferability in SAB Topic 6.G.2.b (SAB 40, as amended), summarized as follows:

1. Where no authoritative body has specified criteria for determining the preferability of one alternative accounting principle over another, preferability should be based on the particular circumstances described and discussed by the registrant.

2. Management's business judgment and planning may be major considerations in determining that the change is to a preferable method.

3. Business judgment and planning may be accepted by the independent accountant as justification for the change as long as the judgments and plans do not seem to be unreasonable.

4. Justification for a change in accounting is not nullified if business judgments must be changed later as a result of changed economic factors.

5. A registrant may revert to an original accounting principle if the principle can be justified as preferable under the circumstances as they currently exist.

6. Registrants in apparently similar circumstances may make changes in opposition directions if each registrant and its independent accountant determine that the change is preferable under the circumstances of each and because it results in improved financial reporting. The emphasis here relates to registrants in apparently similar circumstances, even if they have the same firm as independent accountants.

7. When a registrant changes from an unacceptable method to one of two methods specifically approved by the FASB in an SFAS, no letter is required. When the registrant changes from one specifically approved method to another specifically approved method, a letter is required.

These detailed prescriptions underscore the seriousness with which the SEC staff views the integrity of the basic financial statements, even interim unaudited statements.

SPECIAL REPORTS

In certain circumstances, a financial statement is prepared in accordance with a comprehensive but non-GAAP basis of accounting, for example, an income tax basis, cash basis, or regulatory agency statutory basis. In those cases the titles of the statements and the classification of individual elements in the statements should reflect the basis being used. As stated in SAS 14, *Special Reports*, "a cash basis financial statement might be titled *Statement of Assets and Liabilities Arising From Cash Transactions* or *Statement of Increases or Decreases in Funds Arising From Cash Transactions*, and a financial statement prepared on a statutory or regulatory basis might be titled *Statement of Income—Statutory Basis*" (AU 621.07). This subject is further covered in Chapter 11.

For a discussion of special financial presentations that address voluntary liquidations and bankrupt companies, see Chapter 28; for development stage companies, see Chapter 39; and for personal financial statements, see Chapter 39.

4

Financial Disclosure

DISCLOSURE EVOLUTION

In establishing objectives of financial reporting rather than objectives of financial statements, the FASB indicated that its concern extends to financial reporting beyond the statements themselves. In SFAC 1, *Objectives of Financial Reporting by Business Enterprises* (FASB, 1978c), the Board concluded (¶ 5):

Although financial reporting and financial statements have essentially the same objectives, some useful information is better provided by financial statements and some is better provided, or can only be provided, by means of financial reporting other than financial statements.

Accordingly, a distinction is made between financial statements and financial reporting. The previous chapter dealt with the *basic* financial statements, excluding footnotes and supplementary data. The basic financial statements including footnotes are generally referred to as *financial statements*; these plus other financially oriented disclosures make up *financial reporting*. The role of this chapter is to explore the footnote portion of financial statements and the supplementary portion of financial reporting apart from the basic financial statements, tying together the disclosure discussions contained in most of the other chapters in this *Handbook* in an attempt to portray the overall logic of the disclosure structure.

Expanding the Boundaries

The quantity and variety of financial information made available to investors and creditors by business entities seems to continually flow, though there are a few ebbs. The increasing complexity of business, the continuing refinement of accounting principles, and public demands for additional information are among the causes. The business community has voluntarily implemented many changes in reporting and disclosure practices, while standard-setting bodies and the SEC have established numerous additional requirements. Those changes in the business and regulatory environment have led to evolution – some corporate managements say revolution – in the disclosure area.

At an early stage the basic financial statements, particularly the balance sheet, were the first to become more detailed. More information was provided in caption form, and information that was previously included in highly condensed form (e.g., property, plant, and equipment) was subdivided and given separate display within the statements. Eventually, however, it became apparent that the basic statements alone could not accommodate all the added detail. Consequently, much of the information began to appear first in footnotes, then moved into other supplementary and narrative forms.

The terms *footnotes, supplementary*, and *narrative* as used in this chapter encompass financially related information that is part of or an adjunct to the basic financial statements, both in annual reports to shareholders and in filings with the SEC. In the broadest sense, this is often referred to as financial disclosure. Footnotes are part of the basic financial statements presented in conformity with GAAP and, with occasional exception for an unaudited subsequent event, are covered by an auditor's opinion. Supplementary and narrative information, appearing in almost any form, including but not limited to condensed financial statements, tabular data, or extensive prose, are generally *not* audited and *not* covered by the auditor's opinion.[1] Regardless of the form of the data, its placement, or whether it is subjected to audit, such data represents what is characterized as the disclosure process.

---

[1] However, auditors are often associated with such data, as discussed in Chapter 11.

As previously suggested, financial disclosures were first used primarily to provide expanded detail on financial statement captions. For example, the total of long-term debt shown in the balance sheet would be detailed by issue in a footnote or schedule (which is, in effect, also a footnote). Along with the expansion of historical information in recent years, footnotes have also begun to exhibit new dimensions – in particular, a trend toward disclosures intended to enable users to better interpret and assess the historical information contained in the financial statements. The required footnote disclosure of major accounting policies is an obvious example.

More recently, a new emphasis has become apparent. Many believe that the disclosure process should, in addition to merely expanding on historical data and assisting in their interpretation, provide greater assistance to investors and creditors in predicting future financial performance. Accordingly, disclosures of an analytical nature have become increasingly significant. For example, requirements for segment reporting, discussed later in this chapter, and for the inclusion of a management discussion and analysis of financial condition and results of operations (MD&A), are intended to provide investors with a better appreciation of the composition of business assets and underlying trends in enterprise profitability. This movement in turn has extended naturally to the question of disclosing more future-oriented information, such as forecasts and projections, although their desirability and utility are continuously debated.

There are no signs that the expanding disclosure movement will halt or reverse. Rather, the quantity and type of information disclosed are likely to continue to expand and evolve. Accordingly, financial statement preparers, auditors, and users must be well informed about the disclosure requirements of applicable professional organizations and the SEC; and financial information must be summarized and presented in a manner that will provide users with a base of data to facilitate informed decisions. As more soft, judgmental information is provided, there is an increasing need to exercise care in presentation so as to minimize the risk that a user will misunderstand it.

Disclosure in the Context of Financial Reporting

SFAC 1, *Objectives of Financial Reporting by Business Enterprises* (FASB, 1978c), discusses the distinctions between financial statements and financial reporting:

> Financial statements are a central feature of financial reporting. They are a principal means of communicating accounting information to those outside an enterprise. Although financial statements may also contain information from sources other than accounting records, accounting systems are generally organized on the basis of the elements of financial statements (assets, liabilities, revenues, expenses, etc.) and provide the bulk of the information for financial statements. [¶ 6, in part.]

> Financial reporting includes not only financial statements but also other means of communicating information that relates, directly or indirectly, to the information provided by the accounting system – that is, information about an enterprise's resources, obligations, earnings, etc. Management may communicate information to those outside an enterprise by means of financial reporting other than financial statements either because the information is required to be disclosed by authoritative pronouncement, regulatory rule, or custom or because management considers it useful to those outside the enterprise and discloses it

voluntarily. Information communicated by means of financial reporting other than financial statements may take various forms and relate to various matters. Corporate annual reports, prospectuses, and annual reports filed with the Securities and Exchange Commission are common examples of reports that include financial statements, other financial information, and nonfinancial information. News releases, management's forecasts or other descriptions of its plans or expectations, and descriptions of an enterprise's social or environmental impact are examples of reports giving financial information other than financial statements or giving only nonfinancial information. [¶ 7]

SEC Influence in Disclosure

The SEC has the statutory authority to establish GAAP for publicly held companies. Generally, the SEC relies on the private sector, principally the FASB, to establish GAAP. However, in the area of adequacy of disclosure, the SEC's principal objective, a number of SEC releases require disclosures in addition to those promulgated in the private sector.

SEC disclosure requirements are specified principally in Regulation S-X, Articles 3 (Rules of General Application) and 5 (Commercial and Industrial Companies), and Regulation S-K. Although the SEC's initial disclosure release contained in FRR § 101 (ASR 4) suggests brevity, the rules issued to date are anything but brief. Further, the original ASR stated a very significant general rule: Disclosure is not a substitute for proper accounting. This means, for example, that the use of an improper measurement standard coupled with disclosure of the effect of the difference between the use of the improper and proper measurement standard is not an acceptable substitute for use of the proper measurement standard. A general discussion of the content of Regulation S-X and S-K is contained in Chapter 47 of the *Handbook*. Numerous references to those regulations also are provided throughout the *Handbook*.

SEC filings include primary financial statements, footnotes, MD&A, and a great deal of other supplementary information. The information required by Regulation S-X to be included with the financial statements should be audited. However, certain information required by Regulation S-K (e.g., selected quarterly financial data and disclosures of oil and gas reserve data) are supplemental, that is, outside the financial statements, and are unaudited.

All the disclosure requirements in Regulation S-X, other than supplementary schedules, are to be included in the annual report to shareholders. Although certain of those items are not specifically GAAP disclosures, by custom they are frequently presented in annual reports. Those disclosures include:

1. Restrictions on the payment of dividends.
2. Domestic and foreign components of income before taxes.
3. Warrants and rights.
4. Separate presentation of and disclosures regarding redeemable preferred stock.
5. Excess of replacement or current cost over the stated LIFO value of inventories.
6. Five-year maturities of long term-debt.

Certain information is deemed to be important to financial analysts but not of prime importance to shareholders. The following are examples of this information, to be included in schedules:

1. Detailed information regarding marketable securities.
2. Details of certain borrowings by related parties and others, including employees.
3. Investments in and amounts due to or from affiliates.
4. Components of property, plant, and equipment.
5. Details of valuation accounts.
6. Information on short-term borrowings.
7. Supplementary income information.

Form 10-K is the basic annual reporting form for commercial and industrial companies, and because the disclosure requirements of S-X exceed GAAP requirements, most companies in the past filed a 10-K that was separate, and in some ways different, from an annual report for shareholders. Under the SEC's 1980 Integrated Disclosure System revisions, Form 10-K requirements are quite close to normal GAAP reporting. (For a discussion of Form 10-K, see Chapter 47.)

In an SEC filing—for example, a prospectus or proxy statement—important disclosures that are customarily presented as footnotes to the financial statements or in selected financial information are occasionally presented in the forepart or text of the filing document. To avoid repetition of such data, the SEC permits cross-referencing from the financial statements section of the filing to such separately presented information. When such cross-referencing is used, it should be very explicit in identifying the nature and location of the information. Referencing from the forepart or text to the financial statements also is often appropriate.

Location of Financial Disclosure

Approaching disclosure from a location viewpoint facilitates definition of the general area to be addressed, but it also tends to overlook the practical problem of distinguishing information that might be better contained in the basic financial statements. This distinction is frequently blurred, and few rules for making it are available. For example, the preparer of a financial report has rather wide discretion as to whether details of authorized and outstanding capital stock should be displayed as part of the caption on the face of the balance sheet or in a separate schedule as part of the footnotes.

In general, it is desirable to present summarized information in the basic statements and details elsewhere, since this should enable the user to gain a broad overview of the financial position, results of operations, and cash flows. The user's comprehension can then be enlarged by studying supporting schedules and narrative disclosures. Moreover, many users desire only general knowledge, and presenting relatively uncluttered basic statements should help them while not detracting from the ability of more analytical users to gain a detailed understanding.

Once a decision has been reached about what should be contained in the basic financial statements, the issue of location of other disclosures must be addressed. Again, few explicit rules exist. In distinguishing information to be presented in the footnotes from that disclosed in other locations apart from the basic financial statements, the qualitative characteristics of the data to be disclosed are important. Generally, information presented in the footnotes tends to be precise, objective, verifiable, and historical (frequently termed *hard data*). Conversely, information reported other than in the basic financial statements and footnotes, is often judgmental, predictive, experimental, imprecise, uncertain, or unverifiable (frequently termed *soft data*).

In the FASB Invitation to Comment, *Financial Statements and Other Means of Financial Reporting* (1980b), the FASB made a distinction in location based on a *complete* perspective versus a *different* perspective (p. 21). In the Board's tentative view the basic statements and footnotes should be complete, covering all the elements of financial statements from a single perspective—for example, historical costs measured in nominal units of currency. This definition would then classify as supplementary any information giving a different perspective, such as voluntary information about effects of changing prices. SFAC 5, *Recognition and Measurement in Financial Statements of Business Enterprises*, provides a similar definition (FASB, 1984a, ¶ 7c).

This approach may be useful to the FASB in making decisions on what supplementary information to require, but does not seem sufficiently clear for determining whether required supplementary information should accompany the financial statements and notes or should be available on request. These decisions should be made on the basis of optimizing relevance, reliability, and costliness—the three essential considerations applicable to all financial information.

Differential Disclosures

Among users of financial reports are those who have knowledge of economics, business, and reporting practices and who, as a result, are able to interpret and assess detailed quantitative data. Such users include professional analysts who desire to develop an in-depth understanding of corporate activity and operating results. On the other hand, some users have only a very limited understanding of information in financial reports. Such users generally do not have the time to study, or the training necessary to fully understand, such quantitative information. Degrees of understanding exist between these two extremes.

Information users also vary widely in how they utilize financial statements in the decision-making processes. Some rely extensively on the analysis of quantitative data, while others base their conclusions on more subjective factors. Accordingly, whether information is of primary importance is a matter of how it is used and the extent of its usage.

Industry has generally attempted to meet the needs of all users by issuing a single set of general purpose financial statements and supplementary narrative disclosures in annual reports to shareholders. However, the arrangement of financial information within annual reports suggests that many companies are aware of the varying levels of interest among users and attempt to accommodate these interests by careful presentation.

For example, many annual reports now include a highlights section that contains only a few key data series such as net income, earnings per share, capital expenditures, and so on (a very basic level of detail). A second level consists of a compendium of trends in significant financial and operating data. Such summaries frequently extend to several pages and include information for five or ten years. A third level of detail comprises the actual financial statements for the period. Although presentation practice varies, many companies prefer to keep the three primary statements relatively undetailed and to provide supplementary detail either in the footnotes or in a related financial review.

Interim Reporting

Certain minimum disclosures are required by APB 28, *Interim Financial Reporting* (I73.146–.149) when publicly traded companies report summarized interim financial information to their shareholders. There are no similar requirements for summarized interim information of privately held companies, but generally it is advisable that they follow the same guidelines as public companies. Chapter 3 contains a discussion of interim disclosures.

Future Trends

Narrative disclosures have expanded significantly in recent years and there is every indication that their role will continue to increase. The growing complexity of business and the environment within which it operates, the continuing refinement of accounting principles, and public demands for additional information all have contributed to this trend.

The character of narrative disclosures has also displayed a significant change in emphasis. Not only has there been a great increase in the disclosure of hard, quantitative information extracted from the historical accounting system, but attention has focused on providing users with assistance in interpreting available information and, in some cases, providing forward projections and other soft or judgmental data. This changing emphasis in part reflects a belief that the greater relevance of soft information more than outweighs its reduced reliability.

Another area of potential increase in disclosure is risks and uncertainties, mostly for items that are not readily quantifiable. The AICPA has issued a report prepared by the Task Force on Risks and Uncertainties that recommends additional disclosures related to these two subjects. In addition, the FASB project on financial instruments includes the subject of disclosure about risks and uncertainties. The Board has issued an Exposure Draft, *Disclosures About Financial Instruments* (FASB, 1987a) that covers part of the AICPA report recommendations. For further discussion about this subject, see Chapter 21.

NOTES TO FINANCIAL STATEMENTS

The FASB has suggested that footnote disclosures be used essentially as an extension of the basic financial statements and could be used to present items such as (FASB, 1980b, p. 18):

a. Qualitative information about recognized elements (of financial statements) in general.
b. Qualitative information about particular recognized elements.
c. Quantitative information about particular recognized elements.
d. Information about unrecognized elements (oil and gas reserves, possible contingencies).

While it may be possible to think in these abstract terms in building a financial disclosure model, it is difficult to translate them into current practice. The FASB created confusion by requiring some supplemental data in notes (e.g., segment reporting) and some outside (e.g., oil and gas reserves). However, it should be remembered that the FASB has not reached a conclusion about the content of financial reporting versus financial statements in any of the concepts statements issued to date. In SFAC 1, *Objectives of Financial Reporting by Business Enterprises* (FASB, 1978c, ¶¶ 5–8), the Board discusses some differences between financial reporting and financial statements but by way of example only; no clear distinction is drawn between the two. Without guidelines, it is not surprising that inconsistencies surface.

Characteristics of GAAP Note Disclosures

Information appearing in financial statements, including footnotes, tends to (but does not always) have certain characteristics. Among these are:

* Information entering the accounting processing system and included in the financial statements must be quantifiable in units of money. Data that cannot be quantified generally is not included within the body of the basic financial statements.
* The accounting process collects and reports information of a historical nature—the results of transactions that have occurred in the past. These transactions are denominated in terms of the exchange prices in effect at the date the transactions were consummated.
* The information must be of a type susceptible to objective verification by independent accountants (though sometimes, as with contingencies, it may be extremely difficult to verify).
* The elements of information should be similar to permit reasonable aggregation.

In addition, footnotes should also possess the general characteristics of readability, understandability, and relevance. Future-oriented information, subjective analyses, and disclosures of an experimental nature are typically not presented in the footnotes.

Determining the Content of Notes

Although it is reasonable as a general guideline to limit footnote disclosure to hard data, additional factors may need to be considered; differences in management judgment and in company circumstances will necessarily result in variations in presentation.

Information directly related to amounts reported in the basic financial statements will typically be presented in the footnotes. General information relating to the activities of the reporting entity, economic conditions affecting operations, statistical data, descriptions of environmental impact matters, and other items that are not

	Number of Companies			
	1986	1985	1984	1983
Consolidation basis	579	584	581	580
Depreciation methods	579	580	580	582
Inventory pricing	554	557	556	560
Interperiod tax allocation	510	532	530	533
Property	493	496	497	481
Earnings per share calculation	400	393	375	376
Amortization of intangibles	309	304	294	292
Employee benefits	243	274	281	308
Translation of foreign currency	235	236	261	268
Research and development costs	113	124	145	142
Capitalization of interest	61	78	86	93

FIG. 4.1 Disclosure of Accounting Policies
Source: AICPA, Accounting Trends and Techniques, *1987b, p. 37.*

closely related to the basic financial statements are usually disclosed outside the footnotes.

Since data appearing in the footnotes are covered by the independent accountant's report unless marked unaudited, the susceptibility of information to audit is a consideration in determining where a particular element of information should be disclosed. Presentation in the footnotes conveys a greater sense of reliability and may lend additional emphasis to the information.

Authoritative standards or regulations sometimes provide for soft information to be presented in the footnotes. If the FASB has not recognized these disclosures as GAAP, the SEC does not require that they be audited by public accountants.

Types of Information in Notes

To a significant extent, footnote disclosures are made to comply with specified GAAP, the rules and regulations of the SEC, industry accounting and audit guides issued by the AICPA, and other semiauthoritative pronouncements, such as AcSEC SOPs. Thus footnote disclosures may be characterized as oriented toward compliance to a considerable degree. Disclosures required by GAAP and other semiauthoritative pronouncements are discussed in the relevant chapters throughout the *Handbook*.

Regardless of the compliance orientation, the specific information disclosed in the footnotes, and the manner in which it is presented, still depend heavily on management's judgment, the unique characteristics of the enterprise and the industry, and other matters that may be significant to users of the statements. A good illustration of this variety is provided by Figure 4.1, which shows the type of information frequently disclosed in a summary of accounting policies and the number of surveyed companies (out of a total of 600) disclosing such information.

Figure 4.1 indicates remarkable stability in the number of companies—in fact, most of those surveyed—reporting on the first six categories. Predominant majorities considered each of these areas as deserving coverage in all years.

Note Preparation Considerations

Several factors to be considered in the preparation of footnotes follow.

* The notes should be grouped together in a separate section of the annual report adjacent to the financial statements of which they are an integral part.
* The notes should be individually numbered or clearly titled because this is ordinarily necessary to facilitate cross-referencing to appropriate items in the financial statements.
* The section containing the notes should be identified as *Notes to Financial Statements* or something similar, to distinguish it from other sections in the report.[2]
* The notes should be legible and, for SEC filings, the minimum type size utilized must meet specified criteria.

The order in which the notes are presented varies greatly, but the notes should be in a logical sequence. Frequently they appear in the same order in which they are referred to in the financial statements. Sometimes they are in order of importance as perceived by the company. Also, the description of accounting policies, as required in APB 22 (A10), generally appears as either the first note or as a separate statement immediately preceding the footnotes or basic financial statements. Footnotes not required under GAAP, covering such items as quarterly financial data and soft information, may be located at the end of the footnote section and clearly identified as unaudited.

In instances in which financial statements for two or more fiscal years are presented, appropriate disclosures should be included for each year. This does not mean that all of the same disclosures are required for each year. Rather, judgment should be exercised in determining which disclosures relating to a prior year (if not mandatory for all years presented) remain meaningful and which are no longer relevant.

EXPANDED DISCLOSURES

Publication of detailed business segment information and MD&A were the first major steps in expansion of supplementary disclosures. Equipped with such details, investors are supposedly better able to understand the character and composition of a given business, to isolate unusual elements affecting the profitability of its components, and, accordingly, to develop an understanding of underlying trends that may have predictive value.

Essentially, this approach provides users with an enhanced ability to formulate their own projections, but the demand continues for additional analytical data—for example, communication of forecasts and other future-oriented information directly

[2] A few companies intersperse footnote data in an annual report financial review section, without specific cross-referencing from the financial statements.

to users – to further improve those capabilities. The SEC permits such future-oriented disclosures and has encouraged publication through provision of a safe harbor for information issued in good faith and with a reasonable basis. (In some cases, e.g., leveraged buy-out transactions, the SEC may in fact require presentation; see Chapter 23.)

By its power to approve or disapprove the registration of securities and the acceptance of other filings and through its responsibility to oversee the operation of the securities markets, the SEC can and unquestionably does exert a major influence on the nature and extent of narrative disclosures. Traditionally, the SEC has encouraged the expansion of disclosure information, whether outside or within the footnotes, operating on the basic premise that if competitive markets are to function efficiently, they require full disclosure of all material facts.

Management's Discussion and Analysis

The importance of management's analysis and interpretation of reported financial information is summarized in SFAC 1, *Objectives of Financial Reporting by Business Enterprises* (¶ 54, in part):

> Management knows more about the enterprise and its affairs than investors, creditors, or other "outsiders" and can often increase the usefulness of financial information by identifying certain transactions, other events, and circumstances that affect the enterprise and explaining their financial impact. Moreover, financial reporting often provides information that depends on, or is affected by, management's estimates and judgment. Investors, creditors, and others are aided in evaluating estimates and judgmental information by explanations of underlying assumptions or methods used, including disclosure of significant uncertainties about principal underlying assumptions or estimates.

Clearly, there is an increasing awareness of the need to more fully communicate management's perceptions of operating results to investors. This approach involves the use of opinions, analytical data, and other soft information; however, a consensus seems to have been reached that the potential utility of the information is sufficient to overcome its inherently imprecise nature.

Historical Developments. A major step toward using narrative disclosures to aid financial statement users in dentifying underlying trends in profitability occurred in 1974 with the issuance of ASR 159 (now substantively incorporated in Reg. S-K) by the SEC. That release required that reports filed with the Commission contain a separate section entitled "Management's Discussion and Analysis of the Summary of Operations," and although the ASR did not specify the subjects that should be covered, a list of recommended topics was provided.

Subsequent to ASR 159, the Advisory Committee on Corporate Disclosure (SEC, 1977) recommended that (1) corporate managements be given broader latitude in making analytical disclosures, (2) better direction should be provided to identify the nature of quantitative analysis and what the results of such analysis mean, and (3) any analysis should include disclosure of factors that would tend to indicate that historical operations may not be indicative of future operations.

Results of Operations

Net sales of $284 million in 1987 represented an increase of 18% over 1986 and a 30% increase over 1985. The sales increase in 1987 was primarily due to increased demand for electronic connectors, including new products, and the foreign exchange effects of the weakening United States dollar, particularly in Europe.

Cost of sales as a percentage of sales decreased to 65% in 1987 from 67% in 1986 and 71% in 1985. The decrease from 1985 reflected the increased sales as well as reduced inventory and production costs resulting from improved inventory controls.

Selling, general and administrative expenses as a percentage of sales were 26% for 1987, 25% for 1986 and 31% for 1985. The decrease from 1985 was due primarily to the increased sales volume, cost control programs, and nonrecurrence of 1985 severance payments, primarily in France.

Interest expense was $9.3 million in 1987, as compared to $6.8 million in 1986 and $9.7 million in 1985. The increase in 1987 over 1986 was due primarily to borrowing in Brazil which had increased interest costs of $2.5 million over 1986. This was the only significant effect of inflation on the Company in 1987. The higher costs in 1985 were due primarily to higher interest rates and higher average debt outstanding.

Other earnings are $2.1 million in 1987, $5.4 million in 1986 and $4.8 million in 1985. The reduction in 1987 is primarily due to the loss on the sale of the Grillet subsidiary in France. For further explanation see Note 10 in the Notes to Consolidated Financial Statements.

The effective income tax rate decreased to 35% of pretax income in 1987 from 50% in 1986. The Company recorded minimal taxes in 1985 due to its net loss of $9.1 million. The lower tax rate in 1987 resulted primarily from the decrease in the U.S. statutory rate and resolution of certain tax matters. For further explanation of the various items affecting taxes, see Note 6 in the Notes to Consolidated Financial Statements.

The Company had increased net earnings to $11.6 million in 1987 compared to net earnings of $9.5 million in 1986 primarily due to improved operating earnings and a lower effective tax rate which more than offset its losses from the operation and disposition of its Grillet subsidiary in France.

Liquidity and Capital Resources

The Company attempts to maintain a balance between total liabilities and shareowners' equity which is both prudent and manageable, and consistent with strategic plans. This balance is affected by its needs for funds for working capital to support sales growth, its capital expenditure program, and any payment of dividends to its shareowners. The terms in certain of the loan agreements also require that certain ratios relating to these accounts must be maintained.

The Company has maintained the following percentages of total liabilities to shareowners' equity: 68% in 1987, 75% in 1986 and 80% in 1985.

The Company entered into no new major long-term loans in 1987 but continues to maintain a $50 million revolving credit agreement to accommodate future growth. Long-term debt, as a percentage of shareowners' equity, decreased to 20% at the end of 1987 compared to 25% at the end of 1986 and 30% for 1985.

In 1987, operating cash flow increased $1.9 million from 1986 which is primarily the result of increased net income. The increase in 1986 over 1985 of $14.0 million was due primarily to the net earnings, the omission of cash dividend payments, and lower capital expenditures which more than offset the increase in accounts receivable.

The working capital ratio has remained constant at 2.7 to 1 for each of 1987, 1986 and 1985.

FIG. 4.2 Management Discussion and Analysis—Trends Section
Source: Burndy Corp., 1987 Annual Report.

In ASR 279 (FRR § 501) issued in 1980, the SEC restructured the MD&A portion of Form 10-K. These rules have been incorporated into Regulation S-K, Item 303, and form the present requirements.

Current Requirements. FRR § 501 focuses the MD&A coverage on the financial statements as opposed to the prior requirement that emphasized the summary of operations. The current requirements follow:

1. Discussion should include three financial aspects of the registrant's business – liquidity, capital resources, and results of operations.
2. Favorable or unfavorable trends should be emphasized, and significant events or uncertainties identified. An MD&A excerpt that discusses trends is presented in Figure 4.2.
3. Management discussion of segment information is required only if, in the registrant's judgment, it would be appropriate to an understanding of the business. Segment disclosure information contained in MD&A is presented in Figure 4.3.
4. Information concerning the effects of inflation and changing prices is required only if such effects are material to financial statement trends. No specific numerical data is prescribed. With the issuance of SFAS 89, *Financial Reporting and Changing Prices* (C28), presentation of changing prices data is no longer a GAAP requirement, but may be given voluntarily. Therefore, the SEC's admonition is the only remaining disclosure requirement. Few companies are expected to continue any disclosure especially if inflation remains at relatively low levels.
5. The causes for material changes in line items should be discussed. The previous percentage tests and line-by-line analyses are eliminated. A portion of a line item discussion in MD&A is presented in Figure 4.4.
6. Although projections or other forward-looking information are not specifically required, presentation on a voluntary basis is encouraged. An example of the types of forward-looking information that might be included in MD&A is shown in Figure 4.5.
7. There are no specific provisions with respect to the location of management's discussion, except for the general requirement that the discussion should be included within the annual shareholders' report.

In 1981, the Commission issued an interpretive release, FRR § 501 (ASR 299) giving the staff's evaluation of disclosures made in response to the MD&A requirements adopted in 1980. This release focused on areas where further improvements were needed. For instance, it stresses the MD&A requirement to discuss known trends and matters that have had an impact on past operations but are not expected to continue to do so, as well as matters expected to affect future operations even though they have not had an impact in the past.

Liquidity and Capital Resources. A number of guidelines are given by ASR 299 for the presentation of liquidity information: the release also cautions that discussion of working capital only may not necessarily describe a company's liquidity. The release emphasizes that:

(continued on page 4-17)

Electrical Equipment Segment

The Company's continued growth in the international marketplace and increased market share for the domestic electrical business contributed to the current year increase in sales of the electrical equipment segment of the business. In addition, 1987 sales benefited from increased inventory-stocking purchases by domestic electrical distributors protecting against possible production delays during the Company's labor negotiations. Sales of the United States operations within this segment increased $40.3 million in 1987 and $30.5 million in 1986. These increases in sales were due to volume increases of approximately $45.0 million in 1987 and $46.0 million in 1986, offset by a net decrease in selling prices in each of the two years.

International sales within this segment increased $22.5 million, or 13.1 percent, in 1987 and $18.3 million, or 11.9 percent, in 1986. Realized price increases primarily attributable to the Latin American operations, contributed approximately $12.9 million to the increase in 1987 sales. Volume decreases reduced 1987 sales by approximately $4.0 million. Volume increases of approximately $4.0 million and net price increases of approximately $1.5 million contributed to the increased sales level in 1986. Generally higher exchange rates used to translate foreign currency amounts into U.S. dollars, particularly European currencies, increased international sales within this segment by $13.6 million in 1987 and $12.8 million in 1986. In addition, effective management of foreign currency exposure for the Latin American operations contributed favorably to international results in 1987.

Despite a fourth quarter restructuring charge of $8.4 million, current year operating earnings of $199.2 million for the electrical equipment segment improved significantly over 1986 operating earnings of $190.7 million and surpassed 1985 operating earnings of $198.9 million. The increased sales level in 1987 and improved operating efficiencies resulting from major cost reduction and efficiency-improvement programs contributed significantly to the current year increase in operating earnings. Competitive pressures within the marketplace had an adverse effect on operating earnings in 1986. Increased sales volume and product cost reductions were more than offset by increased selling, administrative, and general expenses in 1986. These additional costs, primarily marketing expenses, were incurred to aggressively meet competitive challenges within the electrical industry.

Electronic Products Segment

For the electronic products segment of the business, 1987 was a year of transition. An economic recovery from the severe recession within the electronics industry, which began in 1985, was the most significant factor contributing to the improved performance of this segment. Net sales of the electronic products segment reached their highest level, as sales increased 7.1 percent in 1987 to a record $270.5 million from $252.6 million in 1986. Sales of this segment were $246.0 million in 1985. Increased sales volume, particularly for the copper foil operations, contributed approximately $9.4 million to the increase in 1987 sales. The translation of foreign currency amounts into U.S. dollars at higher exchange rates in 1987 accounted for approximately $11.4 million of the current year increase in sales. However, net price decreases due to continued price competition reduced 1987 sales by approximately $2.9 million. Higher exchange rates increased sales of the electronic products segment by approximately $14.2 million in 1986. Sales in 1986 were reduced by a net price decrease of approximately $4.1 million due to intense price competition and decreased sales volume of approximately $9.2 million resulting from the depressed electronics markets. The Company's 1986 acquisition accounted for $5.7 million of 1986 sales. The electronic products segment accounted for 18.2 percent of consolidated sales in the current year compared to 18.0 percent and 18.2 percent in 1986 and 1985, respectively.

FIG. 4.3   Management Discussion and Analysis—Segment Discussion Section
Source: Square D Co., 1987 Annual Report.

The electronic products segment achieved significant gains during 1987 through cost reductions and improved operating efficiencies. Selling, administrative, and general expenses decreased $1.9 million from 1986. However, this segment reported an operating loss of $6.6 million, which included a restructuring charge of $13.3 million. Without the restructuring charge, operating earnings would have been $6.7 million in 1987. The restructuring charge was incurred to divest unprofitable operations within this segment and to further improve operating efficiencies. Due to an improved market and cost reductions, the power systems and conditioning equipment business reported improved operating earnings in 1987; however, in 1986 reduced sales of power conditioners and uninterruptible power systems adversely affected operating earnings in that year. The electronic products segment reported operating losses of $6.4 million in 1986 and $4.3 million in 1985. The 1985 recession in the electronics industry resulted in lower sales and production volume, which contributed heavily to the 1985 operating loss.

Interest Income and Expense—Interest expense, net of interest income, dropped substantially from $31.1 million in 1985 to $20.0 million in 1986 due to a reduction in borrowings and increase in short-term investments during 1986. The net borrowings and short-term investment position improved dramatically in 1987, but the decrease in net interest expense to $19.2 million was less pronounced because 1987 included $5.3 million of accrued interest expense for post-retirement health care and other long-term liabilities, recorded at net present value. The decrease in net interest expense in 1987 was also limited because the improvements in cash and borrowings occurred primarily in the second half of the year.

Corporate Administrative Expense—After a sharp rise in 1985, following the company's move to new corporate headquarters in late 1984, administrative expense has declined the last two years as a result of cost-cutting measures, including reductions in corporate staff. This decline is partially offset in 1987 by a non-recurring charge of $.6 million related to corporate staff reductions made early in the year.

Corporate administrative expense has not generally been allocated to discontinued operations. However, because of the significant impact of the closing of Fairchild Republic Company, corporate administrative expense for prior years has been reduced by amounts allocated to discontinued operations of $6.3 million in 1986 and $5.3 million in 1985. No such costs were allocated to discontinued operations in 1987.

Other Corporate Income (Expense)—In 1987, the company recorded a $14.7 million pretax gain for the sale of excess land in Germantown, Maryland, and a $10.5 million pretax gain from pension annuity contracts. In 1986, the company recognized a charge of $4.0 million related to excess capacity at the corporate headquarters. As a result of further downsizing of the corporate staff in 1987, an additional $6.0 million charge was recognized to reflect lease obligations associated with the headquarters building through 1991.

Royalty income was $.6 million in 1987, $1.8 million in 1986, and $2.1 million in 1985. The reduction in royalty income in 1987 is due to the suspension of royalty payments by a licensee pending resolution of a government contract issue.

Income Taxes—The 1985 net tax benefit represents the carryback of losses to offset taxable income in prior years and the recovery of taxes previously paid. The 1986 net tax benefit is the result of a change in the estimate of required tax accruals of $14.0 million plus additional state tax refunds of $3.7 million, offset by state and foreign tax provisions.

In 1987, the Federal tax provisions for continuing and discontinued operations were substantially offset by utilization of net operating loss (NOL) carryforwards. The effective rate of 49.9 percent on continuing operations was greater than the Federal statutory rate as a result of state and foreign income taxes of $2.7 million and non-deductible items amounting to $1.0 million. See Note 7 to the Financial Statements on page 24.

Loss from Discontinued Operations—During 1987, the company disposed of several businesses, including the remainder of its airframe manufacturing operations. The loss from discontinued operations in 1987 reflects operating income, the net result of completed transactions, and an estimate of losses to be incurred to complete the planned divestitures, including provisions for future aircraft products liability and post-retirement health care benefits. The substantial losses in 1986 and 1985 were due primarily to losses on two major aircraft programs that have been terminated. See Note 8 to the Financial Statements on page 25.

Cumulative Effect of Accounting Changes—The accounting change in 1987 represents a more preferable method of accounting for certain costs in inventory at several of the company's manufacturing operations. See Note 2 to the Financial Statements on page 20.

The 1986 accounting change represents the income resulting from the effect of changes in pension

(continued)

FIG. 4.4 Management Discussion and Analysis—Material Changes in Selected Line Items
Source: Fairchild Industries Inc., 1987 Annual Report.

accounting rules relating to excess assets recovered from pension plans terminated in 1985. See Note 5 to the Financial Statements on page 22.

Earnings (Loss) Per Share—For discussion of earnings (loss) per share see Note 1 to the Financial Statements on page 20.

Cash Dividends—Dividends declared per common share in 1987 and 1986 were five cents per quarter. Quarterly dividends were reduced from 20 cents to five cents in the second quarter of 1985. The regular annual dividend of $3.60 per share on the Series A Convertible Preferred Stock (Series A Preferred) was declared quarterly in each of the last three years.

FIG. 4.4 (continued)

Future Prospects

Continuing Operations—A strong order backlog supports the growth prospects in the space & defense electronics segment. New satellite contracts, won in 1987 by Fairchild Space, are generating dramatic sales increases which should continue for at least the next two years. Sales are also expected to increase substantially at Fairchild Communications & Electronics as several avionics programs enter the production phase and as the company meets the demand for higher production rates on mature programs. In addition, initial orders for new products such as MAPS should expand this division's sales volume through 1989. Higher sales and improved manufacturing performance at both Fairchild Communications & Electronics and Fairchild Control Systems led to better profit margins in the last quarter of 1987. Continued improvement is expected.

Moderate growth is expected in the aerospace fasteners business based on the current backlog for new commercial aircraft production and the company's strong position in supplying the overhaul, repair and maintenance market. No major change in profit margins is anticipated given a reasonably stable economic situation, although changes in the general business outlook can have a significant effect in this industry.

Sales in the industrial products segment are anticipated to be relatively unchanged in 1988. Continued increases in sales at D-M-E, particularly due to the effect of the lower U.S. dollar, is expected to be offset by reduced sales of communications equipment by Fairchild Data. Profit margins should show improvement as Fairchild Data operates near a break-even level compared to an unprofitable performance in 1987.

Sales in communications services are expected to almost double in 1988 as the existing customer base is penetrated and new service locations are added. Positive profit contributions from the maturing projects should further reduce the operating loss of this segment in 1988 and the business could reach an overall profitable level in 1989.

Corporate administrative expenses should be lower in 1988 as a result of staff reductions and other cost-saving measures taken in 1987 and 1986.

Net interest expense should decline from the 1987 level as a result of the sharp reduction in high-rate senior debt, the introduction of lower-rate subordinated debt, and the increased level of short-term investments. These savings will be partially offset by interest accrued on the higher level of long-term post-retirement health care liabilities.

The tax provision in 1988 may be partially offset by the utilization of book NOL carryforwards of $23 million. The recognition of these carryforwards may depend upon the timing of other future tax events, the resolution of the proposed adjustments with the Internal Revenue Service, and the effect of application of the new tax accounting rules recently issued by the Financial Accounting Standards Board.

Discontinued Operations—Completion of the sale of the Farmingdale, New York, property and equipment and several smaller discontinued operations is expected in 1988. Sales proceeds are anticipated to be approximately $65 million. Timing of the sale of the New York real estate is dependent on a number of factors including completion of the environmental closure plan. Much of the proceeds will be offset by the projected costs to complete the closing of the Fairchild Republic facility. The financial impact of these activities was estimated and included in the results of discontinued operations in 1987 and 1986.

Cash Flow, Liquidity and Capital Resources—The continuing operations are generally expected to fund required growth in working capital and capital expenditures out of operating income. Capital expenditures are expected to be near the 1987 level.

The company plans to continue to restructure its capitalization, to cut the after-tax cost of borrowed funds, and to improve the relationship of current and projected sales volumes to total capital employed.

Management believes that the company's anticipated cash flows and current cash balances are more than sufficient to meet its capital requirements. These resources, together with the $75 million bank line of credit, will provide the financial flexibility required to complete the restructuring plan and to support continued strategic investments.

FIG. 4.5   Management Discussion and Analysis—Forward-Looking Information Section
Source: Fairchild Industries Inc., 1987 Annual Report.

1. Liquidity information should help users in evaluating a company's ability to generate cash to meet its needs both currently and in the future.
2. Existing sources of liquidity include cash balances, assets readily convertible to cash, current operating cash flows, and noncurrent assets convertible to cash.
3. MD&A should describe internal and external sources, current conditions as well as future commitments and trends in liquidity, changes in circumstances, and uncertainties or significant events to the extent these may impact operating cash flows.
4. Companies should identify those balance sheet, income statement, and cash flow items believed to be indicators of liquidity.
5. The liquidity discussion should compare assured available resources to expected requirements, both short- and long-term, discuss any identified deficiencies and the remedial action the company intends to take to meet such deficiencies.

An example of a portion of MD&A commentary on liquidity and capital resources is presented in Figure 4.6.

For discussion of the approach to providing liquidity disclosures, refer to the Chapter 3 commentary on SFAS 95, *Statement of Cash Flows* (C25), issued in November 1987. SFAS 95 will undoubtedly bear on future SEC disclosure requirements.

Foreign Currency Translation Effects. In FRR 6 (§ 501.06), issued in 1982, the SEC discusses the philosophy underlying SFAS 52, *Foreign Currency Translation* (F60), the complexities of applying the functional currency approach, the danger that comparability could be lost, and the need for experimentation concerning disclosures for items such as the functional currencies used for significant foreign operations and commentary on the degree of exposure to exchange rate risks that exists in all foreign operations.

Because of the complex approach in SFAS 52, the SEC does not specify the location (MD&A is suggested) or content of such disclosures. However, companies are encouraged to disclose information regarding two areas. These areas are:

1. Significant foreign operations reported in a functional currency other than the reporting currency. A company should consider whether the cash flows of such operations are generally available to meet the short-term cash needs of other operations of the company. If not, the company might separately discuss those operations. Intercompany financing practices and the extent, if any, to which the cash flows of the foreign operations are available to meet the needs of other company operations are appropriate discussion topics.
2. Significant foreign operations considered to be in highly inflationary economies. Although such operations are treated as if their functional currency is that of the reporting company and the effects of all exchange rate changes are included in net income, those operations may be self-contained or their cash flows restricted. In those cases, companies should consider separately discussing the liquidity and capital resource aspects of such foreign operations.

Repurchase and Reverse Repurchase Agreements. In 1986, FRR 24 (§ 501.07) expressed the Commission's view that companies have an obligation to disclose in MD&A any material impact on liquidity and operations, or material risk, due to

New Fruehauf—Liquidity and Capital Resources

Our sources of liquidity have been substantially limited by the Company's leveraged buyout debt structure and the high interest rates that the debt carries. Our primary sources of liquidity for working capital requirements have been and will continue to be cash provided by operations and borrowings under a bank credit agreement. The non-cash depreciation and amortization charges of $113 million were charges against earnings which had no cash impact. Cash used by continuing operations aggregated $37 million in 1987. However, as a result of the disposition of certain assets held for sale at December 31, 1986, cash flow before principal payments on long-term debt was a positive $600 million in 1987.

The Corporation has a credit agreement with a consortium of twenty-one banks that provided for a $425 million term loan facility which was repaid in August, 1987; a $425 million Revolving Credit Facility that was reduced to $230 million at December 31, 1987; and a $132 million Letter of Credit Facility which provides standby letters of credit until December 1989. The credit agreement also provides for an additional $50 million in revolving credit for foreign currency and international borrowings. Borrowings under the domestic Revolving Credit Facility totaled $128 million at December 31, 1987.

In 1987, the Corporation accomplished early retirement of its bank term loan and reduction of its long-term debt through the sale of various operations previously identified for divestiture. We were able to complete these divestitures in a relatively short time frame reducing short and long-term debt from $1.4 billion at December 31, 1986 to $786 million at December 31, 1987, and to approximately $700 million by the end of the first quarter of 1988. The aggregate selling price of the operations divested during 1987 and January 1988 was $840 million. We received an additional $54 million from the sale of a fleet of leased equipment.

By utilizing proceeds from the initial group of divestitures, the term loan was repaid by August 1987. Proceeds from subsequent divestitures have been used largely to reduce bank revolving credit borrowings. The divestitures resulted in approximately $120 million of debt of operations classified as assets held for sale either being repaid or assumed by the purchasers, including $52 million related to divestitures completed early in 1988. We further reduced our revolving credit borrowings in February 1988, through the application of proceeds of $56 million from the sale of 60% of the European trailer operations and $38 million from termination of a pension plan. This resulted in the reduction of long-term debt to approximately $700 million and the domestic borrowing capacity under the Revolving Credit Facility to $162 million. Proceeds of $36 million from the termination of a second pension plan are expected in the second quarter of 1988.

The Corporation entered into an agreement with Associates Corporation of North America ("Associates") in connection with the sale of Fruehauf Finance Company whereby Associates will continue to provide financing and leasing services to our customers throughout the United States. This arrangement has been very effective for the Corporation. However, under this agreement, certain trailer service and parts receivables and maritime receivables previously purchased by Fruehauf Finance Company are not being sold to Associates, resulting in higher trade receivables at December 31, 1987 and increased borrowings.

Capital expenditures in 1987 for property, plant and equipment totaled $43 million. Major capital projects included expansion of automotive capacity for aluminum wheels and steel wheels, expansion of rear wheel anti-lock capacity, equipment for more efficient trailer production and the relocation of a dump trailer production line. We expect capital spending to approximate $45 million in 1988.

We had working capital of $298 million at December 31, 1987, compared with $403 million at December 21, 1986, the decline being due primarily to a reduction in assets held for sale result-

FIG. 4.6 Management Discussion and Analysis—Liquidity and Capital Resources Section
Source: Fruehauf Corp., 1987 Annual Report.

ing from the completion of most of the divestitures. The ratio of current assets to current liabilities rose to 1.75 to 1 at December 31, 1987 from 1.44 to 1 at December 31, 1986.

The Class B Common Stock and the preferred stock are publicly traded, principally on the New York Stock Exchange, under the symbols FTRB and FTRPrA, respectively; by its terms there cannot be an established public market for the Class A Common Stock. The bank credit agreement imposes restrictions on the payment of cash dividends on the preferred stock and any dividends on the common stock. No dividends have been paid on the common stock and none are anticipated in the foreseeable future. Through December 31, 1991, dividends on the preferred stock are payable, at the option of the Corporation, either in cash or additional shares of preferred stock at a quarterly rate of 3.68 shares for each hundred shares of preferred stock held. During 1987, quarterly dividends on the preferred stock were "paid in kind" by issuing additional shares of preferred stock. We anticipate continuing to pay preferred dividends in this manner through 1991.

---

significant exposure as a result of repurchase and reverse repurchase agreements. In addressing the impact on operations for any given period, companies would, of course, have to consider all transactions during the period, not only those existing at the balance sheet date. The FRR notes that failure to take possession of assets under reverse repurchase agreements is required to be disclosed, as are provisions designed to ensure that the market value of the underlying assets remains sufficient to protect the company in the event of counterparty default.

Effects of the Tax Reform Act of 1986. In FRR 26 (§ 501.08) issued in 1986, the SEC added a transitional provision for information to be presented outside the financial statements that addresses the effects of the Tax Reform Act of 1986 in combination with expected changes in accounting standards. The Act provides an overall reduction in corporate income tax rates, eliminates the investment tax credit, reduces investment tax credit carryforwards, changes depreciation lives and rates for property, plant and equipment, and invokes other provisions for special industries. For many publicly held companies, future payments of deferred tax amounts will be less than the amounts that were originally provided under old rules. The SEC specified that disclosure in MD&A should discuss the potential effects on future liquidity resulting from the reversal of book/tax differences, and discuss the nature and potential effects of the repeal of the investment tax credit and changes in the depreciation rules and foreign tax credit.

Companies were told in FRR 26 to apply the provisions of the then-outstanding FASB exposure draft on income tax accounting (FASB, 1986a) for 1986 MD&A disclosures. If quantified disclosures are presented, they should be displayed either in narrative form, by presentation of pro forma selected data, or in complete (condensed or full) financial statements; and there should be a discussion of the purpose of the disclosures and the assumptions used.

An example of a paragraph in MD&A that discusses the effects of the Tax Reform Act of 1986 is presented in Figure 4.7. This type of disclosure will also appear in annual reports for 1987 and 1988, because application of the new FASB rules on income taxes (SFAS 96, issued in December 1987), becomes mandatory for fiscal

The effective tax rate was 42.8 percent in 1987 compared to 43.5 percent in 1986 and 43.9 percent in 1985. The variances in rates between 1987 and the prior two years are primarily due to federal income tax law changes resulting from the Tax Reform Act of 1986. The most significant federal tax law change was the reduction in the U.S. Federal statutory tax rate from 46.0 percent in 1986 and 1985 to 40.0 percent in 1987.

In December 1987, the Financial Accounting Standards Board issued the Statement of Financial Accounting Standards No. 96, "Accounting for Income Taxes." This standard requires an asset and liability approach for financial accounting and reporting for income taxes. Management anticipates that when implemented, this statement will have an overall favorable effect on the Company's future earnings and financial position. Implementation is required for fiscal years beginning after December 15, 1988.

FIG. 4.7   Management Discussion and Analysis—Discussion of the Tax Reform Act of 1986
Source: Square D Co. and Subsidiaries, 1987 Annual Report.

years beginning after December 15, 1988. Thus companies holding out until the end will have to comply with FRR 26. (See also the following section regarding SAB 74.)

Delayed Adoption of New Accounting Standards. Usually the FASB allows some grace period prior to the date a company is required to adopt a major change made by the FASB in an accounting standard. In SAB 74 (Topic 11.M), issued at the end of 1987, the SEC staff requires current disclosure of the impact that a recently issued accounting standard is expected to have on financial position and results of operation when the standard is to be adopted in a future period. Such disclosures are to be provided in MD&A (and in the notes to the financial statements, if appropriate) and should generally include:

1. A brief description of the new standard, the date the adoption is required, and the date that the company plans to adopt, if earlier.
2. A discussion of the methods of adoption allowed by the standard and the method expected to be utilized by the company, if determined.
3. A discussion of the impact that adoption of the standard is expected to have on the financial statements of the company, unless not known or reasonably estimable.
4. Disclosure of the potential impact of other significant matters that the company believes might result from the adoption of the standard (such as technical violations of debt covenant agreements, planned or intended changes in business practices, etc.) is encouraged.

Disclosure is also encouraged when future adoption of a new standard is not expected to have a material effect on the financial statements.

SEC Proposal to Revise MD&A. In early 1987, the SEC issued a Concept Release on MD&A (Release 33-6711) requesting comments on the need for more specific disclosure requirements. In addition, the release proposes some specific changes relating to: (1) risk analysis, perhaps similar to that required in a prospectus; (2) auditing of the MD&A data, and the possible effects of such audit; (3) the adequacy of current requirements for disclosure of forward-looking information; (4) the impact, if any, on the incidence of litigation and how liability might be allocated among auditors, company board members, and others if a broader spectrum of disclosures were to be required; and (5) how to assess the cost/benefit relationship. (The ASB also has in process a proposed statement on attestation standards dealing with the "audit" of MD&A, but is holding off action until the SEC's decision has been made. See later discussion herein under "Auditor Association With MD&A.")

Segment Reporting

Historical Perspective. Useful segment information enhances a reader's ability to understand a diversified company. For example, a portion of a company's operations may be in an industry whose products will soon be in great demand; as a result, investors and creditors might conclude that the future bodes well for increased cash flows to the company. On the other hand, a company might derive a significant portion of its consolidated income from operations in a politically unstable part of the world; as a result, investors and creditors would conclude that their expectation of future cash flows would be riskier than it otherwise might have been.

Segment information gives investors and creditors the opportunity to make these types of evaluations. Financial analysts, for example, have advocated segment reporting because this information improves their ability to forecast earnings and dividends. Analysts recognize that growth cycles, profit characteristics, and capital requirements differ among a company's business segments and that an adequate forecast comprehends the variability of these factors. Segment information may also identify a company's strengths and weaknesses, which helps other users understand its operations.

Prior to SFAS 14, *Financial Reporting for Segments of a Business Enterprise* (S20), presentation of selected business segment information in financial statements had not been required by GAAP and regulatory agencies such as the SEC, although the Federal Trade Commission had certain line-of-business reporting requirements. The need for more extensive segment disclosure has been the result of many factors, the most important of which follow.

The business environment of the 1960s was characterized by aggressive merger and acquisition activity. Frequently, takeover candidates were not selected on the basis of common or linked products and markets; rather, they were chosen because the accounting results of complex business combinations maximized earnings per share at the time the merger was effected. More often than not, the subsequent operating results of the resulting conglomerates disappointed investors, who also complained they were unable to understand the complexities of the companies' operations.

As the U.S. economy matured in this same period, many companies found that the growth prospects of foreign economies offered more opportunities to realize a higher rate of return on their investment than was available domestically. Increased rates of overseas marketing activity and direct foreign investment followed. Investors and creditors required information about a company's foreign markets to analyze its future prospects and to evaluate the risk of the company's doing business in less stable political climates.

The end of the conglomerate era has not meant an end to ongoing merger activity. Current business combinations are stimulated largely by the availability of companies at prices substantially less than the cost of acquiring equivalent operating assets individually. Also, many companies have added to their traditional lines of business to benefit from higher rates of return or to reduce undue concentration in a single industry. The recent popularity of leveraged buy-outs has further compounded the user's problem of understanding the mix of businesses in general purpose financial statements.

In short, many modern corporations are large, complex, heterogeneous structures. Segment reporting enables investors to evaluate the building blocks of the structure as a basis for their assessment of its future prospects.

In 1967, the APB urged companies to voluntarily disclose supplemental financial information about their industry segments. APB Statement 2, *Disclosure of Supplemental Financial Information By Diversified Companies* (AICPA, 1967a), did not specify the type of information required; instead, it urged companies to experiment with segment disclosure so that the APB would have a sound basis for ultimately issuing a definitive pronouncement. Few companies complied with the APB's request, and not until almost a decade later did the APB's successor, the FASB, finally mandate segment reporting.

Limited segment information was required by GAAP even before release of SFAS 14. Those elements, required by pronouncements still in effect, are as follows:

1. ARB 43, Chapter 12, (F65) requires adequate disclosure of foreign operations by U.S. companies.
2. APB 18 (I82.110) requires companies to disclose various information about their significant investments carried on the equity method, including summarized assets, liabilities, and results of operations.
3. APB 30 (I13.105, and I13.107–.109) requires companies to disclose various types of information about discontinued business segments, including operating profit or loss and data about assets and liabilities. (Note, however, that SFAS 14 defines business segments differently than does APB 30.)

SFAS 14 Overview. In December 1976, the FASB issued SFAS 14, *Financial Reporting For Segments of a Business Enterprise* (S20), establishing the appropriate basis for segment information presented in accordance with GAAP and requiring extensive disclosures about a company's segment operations. After its release many companies objected to the high cost of following its rules. The FASB considered these objections and subsequently issued several amendments.

When originally issued, SFAS 14 applied to annual financial statements prepared in conformity with GAAP and to those interim statements "expressly described" as being in conformity with GAAP. The rules covered virtually all businesses, and many companies objected to these broad requirements. The meaning of "expressly described" was questioned; the usefulness of the disclosures for certain types of companies, especially parent companies and consolidated subsidiaries, was challenged; and the burden of compliance for smaller privately held companies was said to be especially onerous. As a result, the FASB issued three amendments to the original standard, narrowing its applicability. The requirement to include segment data in interim financial statements was suspended by SFAS 18, *Financial Reporting for Segments of a Business Enterprise—Interim Financial Statements* (S20.105); and applicability was restricted by SFAS 24, *Reporting Segment Information in Financial Statements That Are Presented in Another Enterprise's Financial Report* (S20.109–.110), to:

1. Consolidated financial statements of publicly held companies.
2. Separately issued financial statements of publicly held company investees if they themselves are publicly held (subsidiaries, corporate joint ventures, and 50% or less owned investees).
3. Financial statements of a significant publicly held investee accounted for by the cost or equity method that are included in the financial report of another publicly held entity.

According to the FASB, a *public company* is one: "(a) whose debt or equity securities trade in a public market on a foreign or domestic stock exchange or in the over-the-counter market (including securities quoted only locally or regionally) or (b) that is required to file financial statements with the Securities and Exchange Commission" (E09.417). If a company's financial statements are issued in preparation for the sale of securities in a public market, it is also public.

Separately issued refers to the manner in which financial statements arc released by a company. Consolidated financial statements may be accompanied in the same publication by the financial statements of subsidiaries or other investees. If these financial statements are also published apart from the consolidated financial statements, they are said to be separately issued.

In addition to the two standards discussed above, SFAS 21, *Suspension of the Reporting of Earnings Per Share and Segment Information by Nonpublic Enterprises* (S20.101), suspends application of the segment reporting requirements to nonpublic companies. A fourth amendment, SFAS 30 (S20.145), modifies certain disclosure requirements rather than the scope of SFAS 14 and is discussed later in this chapter.

Under SFAS 14, as amended, companies must disclose a great deal of information about their operations in different industries, foreign operations, export sales, and major customers. However, the most complicated task companies face is determining how to group their operations into segments. SFAS 14 permits considerable judgment in the critical area of determining segments.

Companies may present segment information as part of their basic financial statements, with explanatory footnotes; entirely in the footnotes; or in a separate schedule that is clearly referenced to and incorporated in the financial statements.

Objectives and Accounting Principles. The purpose of SFAS 14 is "to assist financial statement users in analyzing and understanding the enterprise's financial statements by permitting better assessment of the enterprise's past performance and future prospects" (S20.106).

Differences in companies' operations and their accounting systems prevented the Board from developing the highly specific rules that would be necessary if different companies were expected to report comparable information. In SFAS 14, paragraph 76, the Board warns users that segment information "may be of limited usefulness" in comparing similar segments of two companies.

SFAS 14 does not introduce new accounting principles to be applied to individual transactions. Instead, the consolidated financial information is "disaggregated" into segments of similar products and services and, if appropriate, among geographic

S. Industry Segments

The company operates in a number of industry segments. The Paper segment includes the manufacture and sale of printing, writing, carbonless copy, publishing and specialty paper. The Packaging and Paperboard segment includes the manufacture and marketing of beverage and food packaging materials, corrugated shipping containers, paperboard and other paperboard products. The Pulp segment includes the manufacture and sale of pulp. The Distribution and School and Office Products segment includes the distribution of a full line of paper products and the manufacture and distribution of school and office products. Corporate and other includes electronic publishing.

(All dollar amounts in millions)	Sales[1]						Earnings from Continuing Operations Before Income Taxes		
	1987		1986		1985		1987	1986	1985
	Unaffiliated	Intersegment	Unaffiliated	Intersegment	Unaffiliated	Intersegment			
Industry segments:									
Paper	$1,048.5	$ 135.9	$ 987.7	$ 115.9	$ 947.4	$ 100.3	$176.5	$172.4	$155.6
Packaging and Paperboard	991.6	18.5	912.8	12.1	832.9	11.3	133.2	62.2	27.2
Pulp	81.9	15.4	57.2	14.9	35.4	11.7	28.8	2.5	(5.2)
Distribution and School and Office Products	1,863.7	4.6	1,072.5	3.8	771.0	3.6	56.4	36.1	34.7
Intersegment elimination		$(174.4)		$(146.7)		$(126.9)			
Equity in earnings before taxes of jointly-owned and non-consolidated companies[2]							80.3	51.9	39.5
Corporate and other	231.1		187.5		153.7		(90.3)	(99.3)	(106.6)
Total	$4,208.8		$3,217.7		$2,740.4		$384.9	$225.8	$145.2

	Identifiable Assets[3]			Capital Expenditures			Depreciation and Timber Depletion		
	1987	1986	1985	1987	1986	1985	1987	1986	1985
Industry segments:									
Paper	$1,100.1	$1,071.3	$1,029.0	$ 71.1	$ 66.1	$185.1	$ 68.8	$ 66.9	$ 64.4
Packaging and Paperboard	654.6	372.8	347.6	27.4	28.9	40.1	25.7	24.7	23.8
Pulp	83.2	57.2	41.1	5.5	6.4	6.2	6.9	6.2	6.4
Distribution and School and Office Products	638.3	676.3	204.4	10.5	8.5	9.7	15.4	6.0	4.5
Intersegment elimination	(17.6)	(15.8)	(17.4)						
Investments in and advances to jointly-owned and non-consolidated companies[4]	121.7	303.6	425.6						
Corporate and other	337.0	255.8	214.7	60.8	67.1	57.7	24.9	19.6	11.9
Total	$2,917.3	$2,721.2	$2,245.0	$175.3	$177.0	$298.8	$141.7	$123.4	$111.0

(1) Intersegment sales are made at substantially the same prices and on the same terms as to unaffiliated customers.

(2) Amounts applicable to vertically integrated jointly-owned companies are (Packaging and Paperboard) $16.5 million - 1987, $23.3 million - 1986, $26.9 million - 1985; and (Pulp) $18.5 million - 1987, $6.5 million - 1986, ($4.9) million - 1985. Operations of these companies are conducted within the United States except for those of Northwood, which operates in Canada. These amounts are included as a part of cost of products sold.

(3) The assets of "Corporate and other" consist primarily of cash and temporary cash investments, receivables, terminal equipment and property, plant and equipment. In 1987, the company completed the allocation of the purchase price for the 1986 acquisitions. Accordingly, identifiable assets for 1986 have been restated to conform to the 1987 classification.

(4) Amounts applicable to vertically integrated jointly-owned companies are (Packaging and Paperboard) $16.7 million - 1987, $222.8 million - 1986, $220.6 million - 1985; and (Pulp) $49.4 million - 1987, $36.6 million - 1986, $41.3 million - 1985.

FIG. 4.8   Example of SFAS 14 Segment Disclosures
Source: Mead Corporation, 1987 Annual Report.

areas. To disaggregate is not to deconsolidate; the latter would suggest an allocation on the basis of companies legally constituted as subsidiaries. Because segment data are a disaggregation of consolidated financial information, they should reflect the same accounting principles the company used in preparing its basic financial statements, with one exception – significant intercompany transactions are eliminated in the consolidated financial statements, but transactions between segments are included in the information required by SFAS 14.

An example of the segment disclosures required by SFAS 14 is shown in Figure 4.8. The company shown has four significant or reportable segments: paper, packaging and paperboard, pulp, and distribution and school and office products. Electronic publishing is included in corporate and other. Sales to unaffiliated customers are shown separately, and other adjustments are made so that the segment information in total agrees with the company's consolidated balance sheet and income statement.

Determining how to disaggregate operations into industry segments requires considerable judgment; determining which of these industry segments qualify as reportable involves the application of numerical tests. Both of these matters are described in the following text.

Reportable Industry Segments

Grouping products and services. A company first analyzes the goods and services produced by each of its *profit centers*, defined by the FASB as "components of an enterprise that sell primarily to outside markets and for which information about revenue and profitability is accumulated" (S20.409). But profit centers may cross industry lines. For example, a company might operate a division that manufactures small metal consumer appliances and also fabricates metal automotive parts. Even if the company does not maintain separate accounting records for each operation, it should nonetheless develop the financial information through special analysis in order to disaggregate the profit center along both industry lines for purposes of determining segments.

After the company has identified the various industries in which it operates, it groups related industry lines into segments. No hard-and-fast rules apply to this step; as a result, companies have considerable flexibility and must exercise careful judgment to make the reported information meaningful. Although no rules are given to guide companies in this judgment, the FASB suggests the following factors should be among those considered by a company in determining which of its products and services are related (S20.115):

a. *The nature of the product.* Related products or services have similar purposes or end uses. Thus, they may be expected to have similar rates of profitability, similar degrees of risk, and similar opportunities for growth.

b. *The nature of the production process.* Sharing of common or interchangeable production or sales facilities, equipment, labor force, or service group or use of the same or similar basic raw materials may suggest that products or services are related. Likewise, similar degrees of labor intensiveness or similar degrees of capital intensiveness may indicate a relationship among products or services.

c. *Markets and marketing methods.* Similarity of geographic marketing areas, types of customers, or marketing methods may indicate a relationship among products or services. For instance, the use of a common or interchangeable sales force may suggest a relationship among products or services. The sensitivity of the market to price changes and to changes in general economic conditions may also indicate whether products or services are related or unrelated.

A company may use an existing *business classification system* such as Standard Industrial Classification (SIC) or Enterprise Standard Industrial Classification (ESIC) to help group its products and services. However, such classification systems, designed to gather national economic data, have important limitations: Their narrowest classifications include a wide variety of products, and alternatively, similar products are often included under different classifications. The use of business classification systems alone will usually not result in business segments that fulfill the objectives of SFAS 14.

Selecting reportable segments. After a company has grouped its related products and services into segments, it must select which of these segments are important enough to be included separately in the information reported. Some segments may not be of interest to investors and creditors because they historically have not had or are not expected to have a significant impact on the company's operations.

SFAS 14 (S20.119) provides the following tests to determine if a segment is reportable:

a. Its revenue (including both sales to unaffiliated customers and intersegment sales or transfers) is 10 percent or more of the combined revenue (sales to unaffiliated customers and intersegment sales or transfers) of all of the enterprise's industry segments.

b. The absolute amount of its operating profit or operating loss is 10 percent or more of the greater, in absolute amount, of:

   i. the combined operating profit of all industry segments that did not incur an operating loss, or

   ii. The combined operating loss of all industry segments that did incur an operating loss.

c. Its identifiable assets are 10 percent or more of the combined identifiable assets of all industry segments.

In general, if a segment meets any of these tests, it is reportable. However, a company should also evaluate the results of these tests for aberrations. For example, if a company reports abnormally low combined operating profits in a given year, a historically insignificant segment may qualify as reportable because the segment's results satisfy the arithmetical operating profit or loss test. If it is unlikely that the segment will meet one of the significance tests in the forseeable future, the company may choose not to consider that segment reportable, although the company must explain these circumstances in its segment disclosures. Conversely, a historically significant segment expected to so continue should be considered reportable even if, in an aberrant year, it happens to fail the three tests.

Reportable segments must explain a significant part of a company's operations without confusing the reader with overly detailed information. Guidelines to achieve this include the following:

1. Until the combined sales to unaffiliated customers of all reportable segments equal or exceed 75% of the combined sales to unaffiliated customers of all segments, additional segments must be reported.

2. If the segment information is too detailed, it may not be useful. The FASB suggests that this point may be reached when a company has more than 10 reportable segments. If this occurs, a company might consider combining the most closely related reportable segments, although the 75% test must still be met.

3. Many companies are not diversified or are only diversified to a very limited extent. A company has a dominant industry segment if a single segment's revenue, operating profit or loss, and identifiable assets are more than 90% of these items totaled for all the company's segments and no other segment would qualify in its own right as reportable. The financial statements must identify the dominant industry, but segment reporting of revenue, profitability, identifiable assets, and certain other information is not required in this situation.

SEC view on reportable segments. The SEC tends to lean heavily on the qualitative characteristics of an industry segment in guiding registrants in determining reportable segments. While not ignoring the quantitative considerations incorporated from SFAS 14, Item 101 of Regulation S-K identifies the general qualitative factors of significance, pervasiveness, and impact that should be considered. The SEC concludes (in the Instructions to Item 101) that "situations may arise when information should be disclosed about a segment, although the information in quantitative terms may not appear significant to the registrant's business taken as a whole."

Operations in Different Industries. SFAS 14 requires information about the revenue, profitability, and identifiable assets of a company's operations in different industries.

Revenue. Sales of products and services to unaffiliated customers and intersegment sales (sales to other segments) consisting of products and services similar to those sold to unaffiliated customers should be separately presented for each segment. The disclosure in Figure 4.8 (note 1) indicates that "intersegment sales are made at substantially the same prices and terms as to unaffiliated customers." Frequently, however, a company prices such sales on a different basis than it uses for pricing sales to outside customers; yet SFAS 14 requires companies to report intersegment sales or transfers on the actual basis the company used in recording the transaction. Financial statement users should therefore be wary of equating non-arm's-length intersegment sales with arm's-length outsider transactions. Interest earned by the segment, except on loans to other segments, is generally included in revenue. (Note that special rules apply to segments in financial service industries such as banking, insurance, or leasing.)

Operating profit or loss. Operating profit or loss, which is revenue less all operating expenses and is reported for each segment, is computed before any provision for income taxes. It also excludes general corporate expenses, interest expense, income or loss from unconsolidated subsidiaries, and other items. A segment's operating profit or loss may reflect revenue from intersegment sales or costs from intersegment purchases. (Again, special rules apply in certain financial service industries.)

A company often incurs expenses that benefit the operations of two or more segments. For example, a company may operate a computer facility that processes records for different segments. SFAS 14 requires that companies allocate common operating expenses on a reasonable basis to those segments that derive benefits. One problem is distinguishing general corporate expenses from common operating expenses; the nature of the expense rather than the location incurred is the determining factor. A more significant problem is that financial data that incorporate judgmental allocations are usually less reliable than financial data based solely on arm's-length market transactions.

Most diversified companies have, over the years, allocated common operating expenses for internal financial reports and have developed a wide variety of allocation methods. Some methods are sophisticated, involving the use of formulas and narrow categories of common expense; others are simpler – common expenses are pooled and allocated on a single-factor basis (such as sales). Because of the diversity of methods employed, cross-company comparisons of similar segments could be misleading, and the reliability of segment operating results varies depending on how closely the basis of allocation approximates results that would have been produced by market transactions. Figure 4.9 illustrates four different bases (revenue, operating profit before allocation of common operating expenses, tangible assets, and number of employees) that a company might use for allocating common operating expenses among segments. As the figure shows, each segment reports a different operating profit or loss depending on the basis used to allocate operating expenses. Furthermore, the difference between each segment's resulting highest and lowest operating profit can be a significant percentage of consolidated income.

Companies must disclose the methods used for allocating common operating expenses. The methods should be consistent from period to period; however, if they are changed, companies must indicate the nature of the change and the effect on segment operating results in the period the change occurred.

An example of disclosure of operating profit and loss data by segment is contained in Figure 4.10.

Identifiable assets. Each segment must disclose the carrying amount of its tangible and intangible assets, including an allocated portion of assets used jointly with other segments. Goodwill is included in identifiable assets, but general corporate assets not used in the operations of any industry segment are excluded. Also excluded are loans to other segments of the company. (Special rules apply in certain financial service industries.)

Other information. Other information required about operations in different industries includes:

	Segment 1	Segment 2	Segment 3	Total
	(All amounts are in thousands, except employees and percentages)			
Selected financial and operating data				
Revenue	$ 825	$1,000	$1,000	$2,825
Operating profit before allocation of common operating expenses	$ 250	$ 75	$ 175	$ 500
Tangible assets	$1,250	$1,500	$1,000	$3,750
Number of employees	75	82	78	235
Common operating expenses*				
Centralized research and development				$ 75
EDP operation				100
Noncorporate legal and accounting				50
Other				50
Total				$ 275
Operating profit (loss) after allocation of common expenses; allocation based on				
Revenue	$ 170	$ (22)	$ 77	$ 225
Operating profit before allocation of common expenses	$ 112	$ 34	$ 79	$ 225
Tangible assets	$ 158	$ (35)	$ 102	$ 225
Number of employees	163	(22)	84	225
Range of segment income as a percentage of consolidated operating income depending on allocation method used	50%–76%	(16%)–15%	34%–45%	

* All segments derive benefits from listed operating expenses.

FIG. 4.9 Effect on Segment Operating Profit of Various Bases Used to Allocate Common Operating Expenses

1. Basis of intersegment sales or transfers and nature of change in basis, if any, and its effect on the segment's operating profit or loss in period of change.
2. Nature and amount of any unusual or infrequently occurring items included in operating profit.
3. Types of products and services for each reportable segment.

SEC views on operations in different industries. As noted in the discussion of reportable segments above, the SEC generally adopts a more qualitative approach to segment disclosures. While the revenue, operating profit (or loss), and identifiable asset information are required by GAAP to be disclosed in the financial statements

13. Segment Reporting:
In addition to its interest in URS (note 3), the Company operates principally in three segments: Convenience Food Stores, Import Stores, and Craft Stores. The Convenience Food Stores operate retail grocery units, some of which sell self-service gasoline. The Import Stores operate and franchise retail stores specializing in imported gift and home furnishing items. The Craft Stores operate retail stores specializing in craft and hobby items.

Operating earnings (loss) by segment is total revenue less operating expenses. In computing operating earnings (loss), gain on disposals of assets, interest income and expense, and income taxes have been excluded.

The following information relates to the Company's operation in different segments (in thousands):

| | Year Ended December 31, 1987 | | | | | |
	Convenience Food Stores	Import Stores	Craft Stores	Corporate and Other	Elimi-nation	Total
Net sales and other revenue	$309,604	$74,870	$73,721			$458,195
Operating earnings (loss)	$ 711	$(7,235)	$ 3,118	$(1,750)		$ (5,156)
Identifiable assets	$ 54,560	$55,076	$31,566	$36,646	$(1,249)	$176,599
Depreciation and amortization	$ 3,892	$ 2,028	$ 1,533	$ 1,089		$ 8,542
Capital expenditures	$ 4,849	$ 1,283	$ 3,861	$ 91		$ 10,084

| | Year Ended January 1, 1987 | | | | | |
	Convenience Food Stores	Import Stores	Craft Stores	Corporate and Other	Elimi-nation	Total
Net sales and other revenue	$328,170	$70,003	$61,328			$459,501
Operating earnings (loss)	$ 11,224	$(7,915)	$ 2,275	$(1,845)		$ 3,739
Identifiable assets	$ 58,305	$50,939	$25,127	$30,060	$(1,249)	$163,182
Depreciation and amortization	$ 3,995	$ 1,850	$ 1,455	$ 1,157		$ 8,457
Capital expenditures	$ 5,364	$ 1,776	$ 1,574	$ 762		$ 9,476

| | Year Ended January 2, 1986 | | | | | |
	Convenience Food Stores	Import Stores	Craft Stores	Corporate and Other	Elimi-nation	Total
Net sales and other revenues	$358,478	$71,354	$26,730			$456,562
Operating earnings (loss)	$ 9,809	$ (198)	$ 2,061	$(2,174)		$ 9,498
Identifiable assets	$ 58,678	$59,667	$27,992	$26,884	$(1,459)	$171,762
Depreciation and amortization	$ 3,952	$ 1,800	$ 587	$ 1,217		$ 7,556
Capital expenditures	$ 4,432	$ 2,304	$ 712	$ 124		$ 7,572

FIG. 4.10   Example of Segmented Operating Income Reporting
Source: Munford Inc., 1987 Annual Report.

for each separately identified industry segment, Regulation S-K, Item 101, requires narrative disclosure of: (1) the principal products produced and services rendered; (2) the principal markets; (3) methods of distribution; (4) the status of a product or segment; (5) the sources and availability of raw materials; (6) the importance, duration, and effect of patents and trademarks; (7) the practices relating to working capital items; (8) seasonal characteristics; (9) comparative backlog information; (10) a description of any material portion of the business which may be subject to renegotiation of profits or termination at the election of the government; and (11) competitive conditions.

In addition, disclosures are required about the registrant's business in general, including research and development, effects of compliance with environmental regulations or laws, and the number of persons employed.

FRR § 503 provides a number of examples of segmentation for selected industries in which there had been some debate as to the number of segments; in some cases the company argued that it operated in a single industry segment. FRR § 503.03.b. covers the following industries:

* Electrical and electronic products
* Forest products
* Chemicals
* Drugs
* Property/casualty insurance

Foreign Operations and Export Sales. The information about industry segments helps financial statement readers evaluate a company's prospects based on the types of products and services it provides. To further their understanding, readers may also be interested in knowing the extent of a company's foreign operations. For this reason, SFAS 14 contains another set of requirements that stipulates the presentation of segment information based on the geographic areas in which a company operates. Thus, a manufacturer producing a variety of products in locations around the world would report two disaggregations of its consolidated operations, one on the basis of related products and one on the basis of geographic areas. A company with significant foreign operations would disaggregate its consolidated operations on the basis of geographic area even if all locations produced an identical product or service.

SFAS 14 requires companies to separate foreign operations from domestic operations. Figure 4.11 contains an example of geographic area information, with a further separation of foreign operations into geographic areas: Europe and the rest of the world.

The information about, and the identification of, significant foreign operations required by SFAS 14 is similar to the information a company provides on its industry operations. Important differences are explained hereafter.

Profitability. A company may present operating profit or loss (as defined earlier) for each geographic area, or it may elect to report net income or another measure of profitability between these two. The same measure must be used for all geographic areas, although the company at its option may report additional profitability information for some or all of its geographic areas. In Figure 4.11, only "operating income" (operating profit) is shown for each geographic area.

Export sales. Export sales are those made by a company's domestic operations to unaffiliated customers in foreign countries. If export sales exceed 10% of the company's consolidated revenues from sales to unaffiliated customers, the amount of export sales in total and by geographic area (as appropriate) must be reported. A company must report export sales meeting this test regardless of whether it is necessary to provide the other information required by SFAS 14. Export sales are not

NOTES TO FINANCIAL STATEMENTS
Industry Segments and Geographic Areas
In Millions Except for Share Amounts

The Company conducts its worldwide operations through separate geographic area organizations which represent major markets or combinations of related markets. Transfers between areas are valued at cost plus a markup. There were no direct sales to foreign customers from domestic operations.

☐ Aggregation of products is generally made on the basis of process technology, end-use markets and channels of distribution. The Basic Chemicals segment embodies inorganic chemicals, organic chemicals and hydrocarbons and energy. The Basic Plastics segment is comprised of plastic materials. Industrial Specialties encompasses functional chemicals, polymeric materials and fabricated products. Consumer Specialties includes agricultural chemicals, pharmaceuticals, and food protection, cleaning, and personal care products.

☐ The Unallocated segment includes activities of the insurance companies, the banking operations (in 1985 and first half of 1986), and unallocated overhead cost variances beginning in 1987.

☐ Transfers between industry segments are generally valued at standard cost. Depreciation related to industry segments includes costs associated with the restructuring charges.

Industry Segment Results (Restated)	Basic Chemicals	Basic Plastics	Industrial Specialties	Consumer Specialties	Unallo- cated	Corporate and Elim.	Consoli- dated
1987							
Sales to unaffiliated customers	$4,676	$2,318	$3,853	$2,530			$13,377
Intersegment transfers	1,440	131	35	9		$(1,615)	
Operating income (loss)	925	592	413	399	$ (37)		2,292
Identifiable assets	4,748	1,547	3,084	2,175	591	2,211	14,356
Depreciation	414	86	232	72	10		814
Capital expenditures	456	113	286	140			995
1986							
Sales to unaffiliated customers	$3,903	$1,621	$3,339	$2,250			$11,113
Intersegment transfers	1,267	118	35	2	$ 1	$(1,423)	
Operating income	399	226	353	311	50		1,339
Identifiable assets	4,481	1,120	2,538	2,000	311	2,103	12,553
Depreciation	369	71	219	30	5		744
Capital expenditures	417	57	294	122			890

FIG. 4.11   Example of Geographic Segmentation
Source: The Dow Chemical Company, 1987 Annual Report.

Industry Segment Results (Restated)	Basic Chemicals	Basic Plastics	Industrial Specialties	Consumer Specialties	Unallo-cated	Corporate and Elim.	Consoli-dated
1985							
Sales to unaffiliated customers	$4,224	$1,506	$2,816	$1,954			$10,500
Intersegment transfers	1,416	120	26	6		$(1,568)	
Restructuring charge	379	31	27	17	$ 138		592
Operating income (loss) (after restructuring)	(214)	29	145	223	(85)		98
Identifiable assets	4,762	1,079	2,267	1,584	2,575	2,138	14,405
Depreciation	619	92	186	72	8		977
Capital expenditures	372	55	271	108			806

Geographic Area Results (Restated)	United States	Europe	Rest of World	Corporate and Elim.	Consoli-dated
1987					
Sales to unaffiliated customers	$5,946	$4,307	$3,124		$13,377
Transfers between areas	978	249	289	$(1,516)	
Operating income	1,037	717	561	(23)	2,292
Identifiable assets	6,728	4,200	2,837	591	14,356
Gross plant properties	7,508	3,473	2,521		13,502
Capital expenditures	617	260	118		995
1986					
Sales to unaffiliated customers	$5,165	$3,357	$2,591		$11,113
Transfers between areas	904	206	264	$(1,374)	
Operating income	601	412	272	54	1,339
Identifiable assets	6,193	3,395	2,654	311	12,553
Gross plant properties	7,162	3,152	2,401		12,715
Capital expenditures	520	248	122		890
1985					
Sales to unaffiliated customers	$5,153	$3,121	$2,226		$10,500
Transfers between areas	908	216	229	$(1,353)	
Restructuring charge	360	99	133		592
Operating income (loss) (after restructuring)	(105)	187	(37)	53	98
Identifiable assets	6,197	2,939	2,570	2,699	14,405
Gross plant properties	6,803	2,770	2,302		11,875
Capital expenditures	506	168	132		806

to be combined with foreign operations located in the foreign countries in which export sales are made.

Identification of foreign operations. The basic distinction a company must make is between *foreign and domestic operations.* Foreign operations are located outside the company's home country and generate revenue either from sales to unaffiliated customers or from intra-enterprise sales or transfers between geographic areas.

At first glance this appears straightforward. But in applying the requirements of SFAS 14, companies with *mobile assets* (offshore drilling rigs, ships, cargo containers leased out for ocean transport, etc.) have experienced difficulties. To determine whether operations using mobile assets are foreign or domestic, a company should consider the area with which the assets are normally associated.

However, TB 79-4 (S20.502) states that because of the political, social and economic interrelationship between the United States and Puerto Rico (as well as non-self-governing U.S. territories such as the Virgin Islands and American Samoa), Puerto Rican operations of U.S. enterprises are to be considered domestic operations.

A company presents information about foreign operations only when its foreign operations are significant. According to SFAS 14 (S20.138), this occurs when either of the following conditions is met:

a. Revenue generated by the enterprise's foreign operations from sales to unaffiliated customers is 10 percent or more of consolidated revenue as reported in the enterprise's income statement.

b. Identifiable assets of the enterprise's foreign operations are 10 percent or more of consolidated total assets as reported in the enterprise's balance sheet.

Unlike the tests for determining reportable segments, there is no operating profit or loss test for determining significant foreign operations.

Determination of geographic areas. A company may be required to further segregate its foreign operations into *geographic areas* – countries or groups of countries – if any area alone meets the significance tests in the preceding paragraph. Each company must evaluate its own unique circumstances to determine appropriate geographic areas; the FASB suggests consideration of the following factors:

proximity, economic affinity, similarity in business environments, and the nature, scale, and degree of interrelationship of the enterprise's operations in the various countries [S20.140].

In addition to the revenue, profitability, and identifiable asset information called for by SFAS 14, Regulation S-K requires that any risks attendant to the foreign operations and of any dependence of one or more of the registrant's industry segments upon such foreign operations be described, although not necessarily as part of the financial statements.

Major Customers. SFAS 14 requires information about significant customers so users of financial statements can assess a company's degree of dependency on these customers. For example, if an aerospace contractor derives a significant portion of its business from sales to the federal government, a user is alerted that the company's near-term future performance will largely depend on factors affecting governmental spending. These factors may be complex and difficult to assess, but they cannot be ignored in considering the company's prospects.

SFAS 14 defines a *major customer* as one who provides 10% or more of a company's revenues from sales to nonaffiliates and states that several customers under common control should be treated as a single customer. SFAS 14 originally required companies to aggregate sales to domestic government agencies and to aggregate sales to foreign governments for purposes of the 10% test. The Board reconsidered this point and concluded, in SFAS 30, that the definition of a major customer should be revised: "Thus, the federal government, a state government, a local government (for example, a county or municipality), or a foreign government shall each be considered a single customer" (S20.145). If sales are concentrated in a particular government agency, however, SFAS 30 encourages companies to disclose that fact and the amount of revenue derived.

A company subject to SFAS 14 rules must report information about major customers even if it is required neither to disclose industry segments (for lack of diversification) nor to provide information about foreign operations (for lack of nondomestic activities). The FASB allayed fears of disclosing competitively damaging information by not requiring companies to identify by name their major customers (including domestic government agencies or foreign governments).

While applying the same 10% threshold to major customers, Regulation S-K requires that both the name and relationship of such customers to the registrant be disclosed (but not necessarily in the financial statements).

Equity Method Investees. Companies that have nonsubsidiary investees and joint ventures carried on the equity method of accounting do not have to include these operations or assets in their segment information. However, the investor company must identify the industry and the geographic area in which the equity method investee or joint venture operates. SFAS 14 encourages disaggregation of equity investee financial information if this would help a user better understand the investor's overall operations.

Special rules apply to *vertically integrated investees*, which are those whose products or services are sold primarily to other components of the company. Rules requiring disclosures for vertically integrated investees are as follows:

1. For each reportable segment, disclose equity in net income from, and investment in net assets of, equity method investees and joint ventures whose operations are vertically integrated with the operations of the segment.

2. Disclose geographic areas in which such vertically integrated investees and joint ventures operate.

Notes (4) and (5) in Figure 4.8 illustrate the rules for vertically integrated investees.

Regulation S-K contains no specific requirement to disclose the information on equity method investees. However, the SEC's emphasis on qualitative characteristics could cause such disclosure.

Other Required Disclosures. In addition to the broader areas already described, other required disclosures include:

• Accounting policies relevant to segment information to the extent not adequately explained in the accounting policies footnote;

• Aggregate depreciation, depletion, and amortization expense for each reportable segment;

• Capital expenditures for each reportable segment;

• Effect on operating profits of reportable segments of a change in accounting, for the period of change; and

• Retroactive restatement of prior-period information and disclosure of effect and nature of restatement when

  − Financial statements of the company have been retroactively restated, for example, because of a change in accounting principle or a pooling of interests or

  − A company decides to change the method of grouping industry segments or geographic areas. If reported industry groups or geographic areas change due to a change in the underlying nature of a company's operations or because of the results of segment percentage tests, no retroactive restatement is required.

SEC Requirements. Regulation S-K provides that financial information about industry segments, foreign operations, and export sales disclosed in response to Item 101, if it complies with GAAP, may be included in the financial statements by a cross reference to the Item 101 data, in lieu of presenting duplicate information about its segments in the financial statements (in practice, seldom done). Conversely, a registrant may cross reference the Item 101 narrative data to the financial statements (in practice, more commonly done), to incorporate financial statement disclosures that comply with both Item 101 and SFAS 14.

Regulation S-K also requires, as supplementary financial information, the disclosure of certain effects of any disposal of segments of a business.

As to financial information about industry segments, foreign operations, and export sales, Regulation S-K provides that if a registrant is required to include interim financial statements, it is to discuss any facts relating to the performance of any of the segments during the interim period that in the opinion of management suggest the three-year segment financial data may not be indicative of current or future operations of the segment. Comparative financial information is to be included to the extent necessary to the discussion.

The SEC had once proposed that segment information should be given in complete detail in quarterly reports; this was in recognition of the needs stated by financial analysts. This proposal was never finalized, although it may some day be raised again if the analyst community can better organize its appeal.

International Status. In 1981, the International Accounting Standards Committee issued IAS 14, *Reporting Financial Information by Segment* (AC 9014). The Standard applies to enterprises whose securities are publicly traded and to other economically significant entities, including subsidiaries. When both parent company and consolidated financial statements are presented, segment information need be presented only on the basis of the consolidated financial statements.

IAS 14 is more general than SFAS 14 in establishing guidelines for identifying and reporting segments of a business enterprise. For example, it concludes that:

• The 10% guideline contained in SFAS 14, while useful in identifying reportable segments, is not the only quantitative measure that might be used.

• The "segment result" under IAS 14 is generally the same as under SFAS 14 (i.e., operating profit is the difference between segment revenue and segment expense). However, IAS 14 permits alternative measures for segment profitability.

IAS 14 became effective for financial statements covering periods beginning on or after January 1, 1983, except that, for subsidiaries whose securities are not publicly traded, it becomes effective when its requirements become, in all material respects, accepted practice for economically significant domestic entities in the country.

Changing Prices and Values

One of the basic assumptions applied to historical cost accounting is that financial statement amounts are based on a constant monetary unit. Since the end of World War II that assumption has been in error, dramatically so in some periods, such as the inflationary years 1973 through 1985. It is the lack of a constant monetary unit that some critics suggest causes historical cost financial statements to be inadequate for users during periods of rapidly increasing prices.

If the role of financial reporting is to provide relevant information so that investors, creditors, labor, government, and the public can make decisions affecting individual enterprises and, ultimately, the allocation of resources within the economy, then price changes that affect financial statements are important.

Considerable research and experimentation in recent years have developed a system that captures and displays the effects of increasing prices, most notably the efforts of the FASB that resulted in a requirement for supplementary disclosure (discussed in the following subsections), that was in effect for six years.

Ways of Looking at Inflation. There are two ways of looking at inflation. In one view it is seen as an erosion in the value of the monetary unit, a decline in the currency's purchasing power. In the other view it is seen as individual changes in the specific prices affecting a firm's operations, its capital, and its cash flow. These are the changes in price of the specific items and services a firm buys, makes, or sells. The aggregate of these individual changes for a specific firm is not necessarily equal to the general inflation rate for the total economy.

The accounting solution to the problem of inflation when it is seen as a decline in the currency's purchasing power is usually called *general price level accounting, current purchasing power accounting*, or in the terminology of the FASB, *constant purchasing power accounting*. The method used in this solution is to adjust the monetary unit for the general inflation rate while continuing to use historical cost as a basis for valuation of assets and liabilities and related revenues and expenses. Historical costs are translated into units of current purchasing power or constant dollars.

The accounting solution to the problem of inflation when it is seen as specific price changes is known as *current cost accounting*. There are many methods for determining current cost, but all depart in some way from the historical cost basis employed to value assets and liabilities under conventional GAAP. Current cost methods employ various approaches to measuring the cost of currently reproducing or replacing existing assets with identical or equivalent assets and are sometimes referred to as *entry values*. Conversely, current value methods employ various approaches to determining the amounts obtainable or expected to be obtained on disposing of assets (including their consumption in the company's production process); these are sometimes referred to as *exit values* and include *net realizable value* and *present value of future cash flows. Current value* is sometimes used generically to refer to current cost as discussed above.

A third accounting solution is a combination approach that recognizes both general inflation in terms of constant dollars as measured by a broad price index, and specific price changes as measured by a current cost method. The FASB's voluntary current cost approach in SFAS 89 (C28), discussed in the section "Voluntary Disclosure System," is one example of such a combination approach.

Existing guidance does not preclude the use of a current value approach to the determination of current cost. Technically, current cost is described as being derived from a method of indexation or direct pricing. However, the use of recoverable amounts, which could be derived by applying various current value techniques including discounted cash flow, is permissible under certain circumstances. As a practical matter, companies generally use a form of specific price indexation to develop the changing prices disclosures.

Recent History. The arrival of double-digit inflation in the late 1960s led to action by the APB and the SEC. In 1969, the APB issued Statement 3, *Financial Statements Restated for General Price-Level Changes*. And in 1977, the SEC issued ASR 190 (now rescinded) on replacement cost. This action eventually prompted the FASB to issue SFAS 33, *Financial Reporting and Changing Prices* and subsequent amendments. That statement, which replaced APB Statement 3 and ASR 190:

- Retained the basic financial statements based on historical cost.
- Required supplemental disclosure in financial reports of the effects of both specific and general price changes on income from continuing operations, as well as other selected data such as purchasing power gain or loss and holding gains or losses on property, plant and equipment, and inventory.
- Covered only large publicly owned companies, but encouraged other companies and organizations to present such supplemental disclosure.
- Recognized the need for experimentation with reporting the effects of changing prices.
- Provided for the different treatment of certain assets in special industries, for example, oil and gas reserves, timberlands, mining properties, and income-producing real estate.

FASB Evaluation of SFAS 33. The Board commented at the time of its issuance that SFAS 33 would be reviewed after five years to evaluate the experience gained in its application. Part of the review encompassed research projects concerning the utility of the data. One such project resulted in publication of an FASB research report, *Incremental Information Content of Statement 33 Disclosures*, by Professors William Beaver and Wayne Landsman of Stanford University (1983). The authors studied the relationship between stock prices and SFAS 33 adjusted earnings reported for the years 1979 through 1981. The authors concluded that "Statement 33 earning variables provide no incremental information over and above that already provided by historical cost earnings" (p. 15).

Later that year, the FASB issued an Invitation to Comment, *Supplementary Disclosures About the Effects of Changing Prices* (FASB, 1983d), to solicit input from users, preparers, and auditors regarding the SFAS 33 disclosures.

Also as part of this FASB evaluation process the Board issued SFAS 82 in 1984. That standard eliminated the requirement for historical cost/constant purchasing power information for those companies that also reported current cost/constant purchasing power information.

Although a substantial majority of respondents to the invitation to comment were highly critical of the changing prices disclosures, in 1984 the Board issued an Exposure Draft, *Financial Reporting and Changing Prices: Current Cost Information* (FASB, 1984b). Effectively, that draft would have continued the current cost/constant purchasing power requirements of SFAS 33, as amended, and reaction was extremely negative. A substantial majority of respondents recommended that the Board discontinue any changing prices disclosure requirement. Many commented that the data was not used by the institutional investment community, bankers, or investors in general. Almost all preparers indicated that the data were not used internally. Many reasons were cited for the lack of use but, in summary, the key failure was reviewed as the negligible benefit from the disclosures as contrasted with the cost of preparation.

Voluntary Disclosure System—SFAS 89. During 1985 and 1986 the FASB considered alternative approaches to disclosure of changing prices information. The Board then decided to eliminate disclosure of supplementary information about changing prices as a GAAP requirement but to encourage voluntary continuance of the disclosures, as covered in SFAS 89, *Financial Reporting and Changing Prices* (C28). SFAS 89 became effective for financial reports issued after December 2, 1986.

SFAS 89 contains an appendix that includes the provisions of Statement 33, as amended, as guidance for any company that elects voluntarily to continue the changing prices disclosures. However, companies need not follow the guidance in SFAS 89 if they determine that other methods are preferable. A summary of the basic provisions of SFAS 89 follows:

1. A company that "prepares its financial statements in U.S. dollars and in accordance with U.S. generally accepted accounting principles is encouraged, but not required, to disclose supplementary information on the effects of changing prices" (C28.101).

2. A company is encouraged to disclose the following data for each of the five most recent years:

   a. "Net sales and other operating revenues" (C28.103).

   b. "Income from continuing operations on a current cost basis" (C28.103). This is computed by adjusting the historical cost amounts by the difference between the historical cost and current cost of (1) depreciation and (2) inventory cost in cost of goods sold.

   c. "Purchasing power gain or loss on net monetary items" (C28.103). This is the net gain or loss determined by "restating in units of constant purchasing power the opening and closing balances of, and transactions in, monetary assets and monetary liabilities" (C28.136).

d. Increase or decrease in the current cost or lower recoverable amount of inventory and property, plant, and equipment, net of inflation (C28.103). Current cost amounts of inventory and property, plant, and equipment are measured as follows:

- Inventory at current cost or lower recoverable amount at the measurement date.

- Property, plant, and equipment at the current cost or lower recoverable amount of the assets' remaining service potential at the measurement date.

- Resources used on a partly completed contract at current cost or lower recoverable amount at the date of use on or commitment to the contract" (C28.112).

- "Recoverable amount is the current worth of the net amount of cash expected to be recoverable from the use or sale of an asset. It may be measured by considering the value in use or current market value of the asset concerned. Value in use establishes the recoverable amount of an asset if immediate sale of the asset is not intended. Current market value is used to determine recoverable amount only if the asset is about to be sold" (C28.125).

e. "The aggregate foreign currency translation adjustment on a current cost basis, if applicable" (C28.103).

- "If current cost information for operations measured in functional currencies other than the dollar is based on the translate-restate[3] method, the aggregate translation adjustment on the current cost basis is stated net of any income taxes allocated to the aggregate translation adjustment in the primary financial statements (C28.134).

- "If current cost information for operations measured in functional currencies other than the dollar is based on the restate-translate method, the aggregate translation adjustment on the current cost basis is stated net of both any income taxes allocated to the aggregate translation adjustment in the primary financial statements and the aggregate parity adjustment. The parity adjustment is the amount needed to measure end-of-year net assets in average-for-the-year dollars, if income from continuing operations is measured in average-for-the-year functional currency units; or end-of-year dollars, if income from continuing operations is measured in end-of-year functional currency units (C28.135).

f. "Net assets at year-end on a current cost basis (C28.103). If the company presents the minimum information recommended by this statement. [the shareholders' equity] is the amount of net assets reported in the primary financial statements, adjusted for the difference between the historical cost amounts and the current cost or lower recoverable amounts of inventory and property, plant, and equipment" (C28.123).

g. "Income per common share from continuing operations on a current cost basis" (C28.103).

---

[3] Under the *translate-restate method,* the accounts of the foreign operation are first translated at the appropriate foreign exchange rate to U.S. dollars. The U.S. dollar accounts are then restated by the U.S. inflation rate. Under the *restate-translate method,* the accounts of the foreign operation are first restated by the foreign inflation rate. The inflation adjusted foreign currency amounts are then translated at the appropriate forcign exchange rate to U.S. dollars. [In practice, the restate-translate method was rarely used when SFAS 33 was effective.] [Footnote not in original.]

h. "Cash dividends declared per common share" (C28.103).

i. "Market price per common share at year end" (C28.103).

The data listed above is to be adjusted to units of constant purchasing power using the Consumer Price Index—All Urban Consumers (CPI-U) (C28.104).

In addition to the information to be disclosed as previously listed, SFAS 89 encourages companies to disclose the following for the current year:

1. Sufficient information in a statement format or reconciliation format to determine the difference between the amounts in the primary statements and the current cost amounts of (a) cost of goods sold and (b) depreciation, depletion, and amortization expense (C28.108).

2. The current cost or lower recoverable amount at the end of the year of inventory and property, plant, and equipment, as well as the changes in current cost or lower recoverable amount before and after adjusting for the effects of inflation on inventory and property, plant, and equipment (C28.109).

3. The approach and information used to calculate the current cost of inventory; property, plant, and equipment; cost of goods sold; and depreciation, depletion, and amortization expense (C28.109).

4. Any differences between (a) the depreciation methods, estimates of useful lives, and salvage values of assets used for determining the current cost/constant purchasing power depreciation and (b) the methods and estimates used for calculations of depreciation on a historical cost basis (C28.109).

As mentioned previously, the SFAS 89 disclosures are provided as guidance only. Companies that voluntarily present changing prices information may select that information believed to be the most informative. In Figure 4.12, the company chose to disclose only selected items adjusted to a constant dollar basis. Many companies believe that this approach is reliable and inexpensive, and serves as an adequate indicator of the general effects of inflation on historical cost-based financial statements. Such limited information will probably be common, at least until or unless high inflation returns.

SEC Acceptance. During the period that SFAS 33, as amended, was effective, the SEC also required supplementary disclosure of changing prices information in many registration forms required by the Securities Act of 1933, in Forms 10 and 10-K under the Securities Exchange Act of 1934, and in proxy statements (FRR § 505, ASR 287).

That supplementary information was not an SEC requirement in published interim reports, in financial statements of companies not meeting the FASB size criteria, or for certain foreign private issuers. However, the SEC required, for all companies, management discussion and analysis of the effects of changing prices if such effects were significant.

Because SFAS 89 has downgraded changing prices disclosure from a requirement to an option, the SEC followed suit in FRR 30, *Disclosure of the Effects of Inflation and Other Changes in Prices.* However, Regulation S-K continues to require commentary in MD&A about the effects of general and specific price changes on a

SUPPLEMENTARY FINANCIAL STATEMENT INFORMATION
(UNAUDITED)

THE EFFECT OF CHANGES IN THE GENERAL PRICE LEVEL

The Company is voluntarily presenting certain historical cost/constant dollar information to indicate the impact of changes in the general price level on certain items that are shown in the primary financial statements based on dollar values determined as of the varying historical dates when the transactions occurred.

The Financial Accounting Standards Board encourages experimentation with presenting disclosures on the effects of changing prices on the financial statements. The Company wishes to participate in this experimentation by presenting the historical cost/constant dollar information below.

Revenues for 1987 are assumed to have occurred ratably in relation to the change in the Consumer Price Index during the year and are, therefore, already expressed in average 1987 dollars. The presentation also shows the decline in purchasing power as a result of holding more monetary assets than monetary liabilities during a period of rising prices. All information shown is in terms of average 1987 dollars as measured by the Consumer Price Index for all Urban Consumers (CPI-U).

The preparation of these numbers requires the use of certain assumptions and estimates and these disclosures should, therefore, be viewed in that context and not necessarily as a precise indicator of the specific effect of changing prices on the Company's operating results or its financial position. In addition, the company's costs may not change in proportion to changes in the Consumer Price Index.

Five Year Comparison of Selected Supplementary Financial Data Adjusted for the Effect of Changes in the General Price Level

	Year Ended December 31				
	1987	1986	1985	1984	1983
Revenues (in thousands):					
Historical	$564,611	$519,394	$466,839	$422,655	$388,956
Constant Dollar Basis	$564,611	$538,373	$493,209	$462,313	$443,702
Loss from Decline in Purchasing Power of Net Monetary Assets Held (in thousands)	$8,364	$2,095	$6,155	$5,834	$5,184
Cash Dividends Declared per share*:					
Historical	$1.28	$1.20	$1.06	$0.91	$0.86
Constant Dollar Basis	$1.28	$1.24	$1.12	$1.00	$0.98
Market Price per share (at December 31)*:					
Historical	$61.50	$61.00	$49.25	$33.25	$30.00
Constant Dollar Basis	$61.50	$62.71	$51.21	$35.87	$33.65
Average Consumer Price Index (CPI-U)	340.4	328.4	322.2	311.2	298.4

*Reflecting two-for-one stock split in 1986.

FIG. 4.12   Voluntary Disclosure of Changing Prices Information
Source: Commerce Clearing House Inc., 1987 Annual Report

company's financial statements if such effects are material. Materiality is to be viewed on a cumulative rather than a year-to-year basis. No specific numerical data is required.

International Status

IAS 15—changing prices. IAS 15, *Information Reflecting the Effects of Changing Prices* (AC 9015), supersedes IAS 6, *Accounting Responses to Changing Prices* (AC 9006), and applies to enterprises whose levels of revenues, profit, assets, or employment are significant in the economic environment in which they operate.

The revised IAS, effective beginning in 1983, presents various methods to reflect the effects of changing prices in financial statements, from general purchasing power to various current cost methods and combinations of both. The basic methodologies are described as follows:

1. General purchasing power – the recognition of income after the general purchasing power of shareholders' equity has been maintained.
2. Current cost approach – the recognition of income after operating capacity has been maintained, with or without an adjustment for changes in general purchasing power.

IAS 15 makes clear, however, that an international consensus on the subject does not currently exist and that experimentation is necessary before a final position can be developed.

The standard requires the following minimum disclosures, usually on a supplementary basis, about the effects of changing prices (without requiring a specific method to be employed) on enterprises whose levels of revenues, profit, assets, or employment are significant (term not defined) in the economic environment in which they operate:

1. a. The amount of the adjustment to or the adjusted amount of depreciation of property, plant, and equipment.
   b. The amount of the adjustment to or the adjusted amount of cost of sales.
   c. The adjustments relating to monetary items, the effect of borrowing, or equity interests when such adjustments have been taken into account in determining income under the accounting method adopted.
   d. The overall effect on results of the adjustments described in (a) and (b) and, where appropriate, (c), as well as any other items reflecting the effects of changing prices that are reported under the accounting method adopted.
2. When a current cost method is adopted the current cost of property, plant, and equipment, and of inventories, should be disclosed.
3. Enterprises should describe the methods adopted to compute the aforementioned information, including the nature of any indices used.

Other Disclosures

Oil and Gas Information. In November 1982, the FASB issued SFAS 69, *Disclosures About Oil and Gas Producing Activities* (Oi5), establishing a comprehensive set of supplementary disclosures for oil and gas producing activities of publicly held companies and replacing requirements of several earlier SFASs. Concurrently, the SEC withdrew its requirements, in Regulation S-X, for certain supplementary disclosures about oil and gas producing activities, as these are now covered by SFAS 69. See Chapter 34 of the *Handbook* for a detailed discussion about oil and gas accounting and auditing, including auditor review of information furnished to comply with SFAS 69.

Financial Reviews. In addition to the financial statements section and management's discussion and analysis of earnings, annual reports to stockholders generally include a wide variety of other voluntary financial data, often presented in a financial review section. Some financial reviews contain only limited data, while in other cases mandatory footnote information has been integrated into a large volume of statistical and operating data with an extended narrative description of operations and results.

The financial review section can also accommodate a great variety of both general and industry-specific information pursuant to requirements established by the SEC, stock exchanges, and other regulatory bodies. Common disclosures include such items as comments by management on significant aspects of operations during the period, a description of major changes in productive facilities or assets, and data regarding changes in key members of management of the board of directors. Examples of mandatory industry-specific disclosures include reserve information for oil and gas producing companies, methods utilized in the determination of policy reserves for life insurance companies, and purchase order backlogs for government contractors.

Almost every industry has unique characteristics on which managements may wish to elaborate in their annual reports. Examples include discussion of geographic regions served and quantities of aircraft, vehicles, or track mileage for transportation companies; timber resources for forest products companies; and acreage owned by land developers. Factors that may influence the extent of voluntary disclosures include:

* Management's view that certain data is important to the understanding of the company's affairs and the business environment in which it operates.

* The extent to which competitors disclose voluntary information, together with the extent to which management may desire to adopt a progressive or leading disclosure role within its industry.

* The extent to which the general public is perceived to want additional information with respect to a particular industry's activities.

* Pressures from financial analysts for expanded operating and financial data.

* The extent to which disclosures made on a voluntary basis may preempt the establishment of more onerous reporting requirements by regulatory bodies.

* The potential that exists to inform the public concering industry problems, with the objective of improving consumer attitudes and the political climate in which business operates.

Clearly, not all of these factors are likely to be present for any single company at any given time. And given the variety of motivations behind voluntary disclosures, such disclosures are themselves extremely varied in practice. For example:

- Business has shown concern over the costs of government regulation. Some companies have included information on such costs.
- Discussion of the effects of foreign exchange translation often extends well beyond the requirements imposed by SFAS 52 (F60), particularly in the case of companies subject to large exposures.
- Oil and gas producing companies have published very detailed operating and financial statistics for many years, in response to interest expressed by security analysts and the general public in their industry's activities.
- With the change in the requirement for supplementary information on changing prices to a voluntary basis, such disclosure becomes another matter for the financial review section.

The financial review section offers several clear advantages, but some possible drawbacks also exist. Care must be exercised to ensure that data included beyond that required by GAAP is not in any way contradictory to the mandatory disclosures. Further, the additional data will usually be subjected to testing and review by the independent accountants—especially if the financial review is used in lieu of some footnotes—and this may result in some additional audit costs. Also, the auditors may not be in a position to evaluate some of the financial review disclosures, causing some physical rearrangement of the information so that only parts of it will be specifically incorporated into the financial statements (usually by listing the applicable page numbers).

AUDITING AND REVIEW OF SUPPLEMENTAL DISCLOSURES

Auditor's Perspective

Adequacy of disclosure is a primary concern to the auditor under the third generally accepted auditing standard of reporting, which states: "Informative disclosures in the financial statements are to be regarded as reasonably adequate unless otherwise stated in the report" (AU 150.02). This was further articulated in SAS 32, *Adequacy of Disclosure in Financial Statements:*

> The presentation of financial statements in conformity with generally accepted accounting principles includes adequate disclosure of material matters. These matters relate to the form, arrangement, and content of the financial statements and their appended notes including, for example, the terminology used, the amount of detail given, the classification of items in the statements, and the bases of amounts set forth. [AU 431.02]

Whether disclosure of a particular matter is required is for the independent auditor to consider in light of the circumstances and facts of which he is aware at that time.

The most significant part of the auditor's involvement always has been with "hard" objective information. When the ten GAAS were approved in 1948 it had not been contemplated that any of the material with which the auditor would be associated would be less than objectively verifiable. To compensate for increasing subjectivity in disclosures, the ASB issues, as needed, specific SASs to deal with soft data.

Audit Implications of Soft Disclosures

The auditor is required by SAS 8, *Other Information in Documents Containing Audited Financial Statements* (AU 550), to read other information in documents containing audited financial statements, such as the annual report, for reasonableness and consistency with that included in the financial statements; but such additional data are not mentioned in the auditor's report unless there is something negative to say. However, the large amount of soft disclosures has caused some change in this approach. SAS 8 is discussed further in the section of this chapter covering reviews of voluntary changing prices information.

Existing professional standards require that there be sufficient competent evidence available to afford a reasonable basis for the auditor's opinion on the financial statements. Thus, soft disclosures must be examined on a case-by-case basis to assess the extent to which such evidence can be obtained.

Auditor Association With MD&A

Profession's Proposals

ASB attest proposal. One of the many recent initiatives by the AICPA, in response to criticisms of the accounting profession, was the issuance of an Exposure Draft of a proposed Statement on Standards for Attestation Engagements, *Examination of Management's Discussion and Analysis* (AICPA, 1987i). This proposed statement would provide performance and reporting guidance for engagements covering management discussion and analysis. If approved, the proposed Statement would:

* Apply to engagements to examine and report on MD&A included in a report on audited financial statements for either a public or private company. (For a public company, that report might be, for example, a registration statement filed pursuant to the requirements of the Securities Act of 1933 or a Form 10-K. For a public company, an independent public accountant would not undertake to report on the MD&A unless that report addresses the three-year period covered by the MD&A requirements.)

* Require an independent public accountant to address a number of procedural matters. Those matters include, but are not limited to: (1) the completeness, veracity, and mathematical accuracy of the data; (2) an assessment of any representations concerning the data by management or outside experts such as attorneys; (3) an analysis of data trends; (4) an assessment of uncertainties, commitments, and unusual transactions, if any, described in the data; and (5) a determination that any forward-looking information presented contains the data required by SEC regulations.

* Require the independent public accountant's report to (1) identify the engagement and period covered, (2) state that the examination was performed in accordance with AICPA standards, (3) refer to the report of another or predecessor accountant if appropriate, (4) express or disclaim an opinion, and (5) contain a caveat that management's assessment of future operations, capital resources, and liquidity may differ materially from actual results.

In addition, the report should be dated on or after the date of the report on the GAAP financial statements. For a closely held company, a middle paragraph should

We have examined management's discussion and analysis of the financial condition and results of operations of XYZ Company for the three-year period ended December 31, 19XX, appearing on pages . . . of this 19XX annual report to shareholders. Our examination was made in accordance with standards established by the American Institute of Certified Public Accountants and, accordingly, included such procedures as we considered necessary in the circumstances.[1]

In our opinion[2] management's discussion and analysis, referred to above, when considered in conjunction with the financial statements, is presented in conformity with the rules and regulations of the Securities and Exchange Commission. While management's discussion and analysis presents information with respect to expected sources of liquidity and capital resources, operating trends, commitments, and uncertainties, actual results may differ materially from management's present assessment of these matters because events and circumstances frequently do not occur as expected.

---

1 If predecessor accountants examined and reported in the MD&A for a prior period included in the current MD&A and their report is *not* included in the document, add: "Management's discussion and analysis for the *(insert period covered)* was examined by other accountants whose report dated March 25, 19XX, expressed an unqualified opinion on the discussion and analysis."

  If other accountants have examined and reported on the MD&A of a component, the following should be added to the scope paragraph: "We did not examine management's discussion and analysis of ABC Company, a wholly owned subsidiary of XYZ. ABC Company's management discussion and analysis was examined by other accountants whose report was furnished to us, and our opinion expressed herein, insofar as it relates to ABC Company, is based solely on the report of other accountants."

2 Add the following when applicable: "Based on our examination and the report of other accountants."

FIG. 4.13 Sample Auditors' Report on Management Discussion and Analysis
Source: AICPA Exposure Draft of a proposed Statement for Attestation Engagements, Examination of Management's Discussion and Analysis *(AICPA, 1987i).*

be included in the proposed report on MD&A, indicating that the company is not subject to but has voluntarily followed the requirements of the SEC.

The Exposure Draft contains the report illustration presented in Figure 4.13. The report could be presented separately or included in the report on the GAAP financial statements following the opinion paragraph.

A final statement was planned for 1988, after the SEC decided what action it would take on its outstanding proposal regarding the content and auditability of MD&A, discussed in the earlier MD&A section of this chapter. In March 1988, the SEC staff, without withdrawing the concept release, stated its decision that changes to the MD&A rules were not needed at this time. The staff noted that in reviewing disclosure made by more than 200 companies in 12 industries, deficiencies were noted in about 90% of the cases. The staff plans to review more companies' disclosures and eventually publish an interpretive release about frequently observed deficiencies. In view of this SEC development, the ASB has now placed its proposal in abeyance.

In April 1986 seven of the Big 8 public accounting firms (excluding Price Waterhouse which took its own initiative earlier) proposed a set of recommendations to the AICPA entitled *The Future Relevance, Reliability, and Credibility of Financial Information.* The purpose of the report was to encourage the AICPA to take steps to implement the recommendations that, in the opinion of the seven firms, would resolve many of the issues raised in recent criticisms of the profession. One of those recommendations encouraged that disclosures of risks and uncertainties should be subject to audit. Until such a requirement became enacted they recommended that the MD&A be subject to audit coverage. However, the ASB's proposal aims to provide guidance for the auditor *when* he is engaged by the client to audit the MD&A, as opposed to developing a requirement that MD&A be audited.

Price Waterhouse did not specifically address the MD&A matter, but Coopers & Lybrand (which also joined in the seven firms' proposal) had made certain recommendations to the SEC in 1986 (referenced in the SEC concept release on MD&A (33-6711)). Coopers had recommended a more focused disclosure of business risks, review and approval by the directors, and determination of "reasonableness" by the auditors.

Auditing Segment Disclosures

As mentioned earlier in this chapter, a company may report segment information directly in the financial statements with explanatory footnotes, entirely in the footnotes, or in a separate schedule incorporated into the financial statements. Whichever option is chosen, segment disclosures are an integral part of the financial statements. If auditors are examining the financial statements with the objective of expressing an unqualified opinion, they must also consider the reasonableness of the segment information reported by their client.

Segment disclosures present auditors with two major problems. First, because SFAS 14 permits companies to exercise considerable judgment, the grouping a company selects as a basis for segmenting its operations probably is not the only one possible. Therefore, to what extent should an auditor investigate a company's methods for grouping related industries and to what extent should the auditor explore alternatives? Second, consolidated revenues, profits, and assets are now addressed as segmented amounts. In his tests, therefore, should the auditor incorporate a smaller materiality level appropriate to the smaller segment amounts or retain a materiality level appropriate for the consolidated financial statements? Because of these and other problems, the Auditing Standards Division of the AICPA issued SAS 21, *Segment Information* (AU 435), in 1977. The following is a discussion of the auditor's objectives, audit procedures, and reporting considerations presented in SAS 21.

Objectives and Materiality. The auditor reviews segment information with the objective of obtaining "a reasonable basis for concluding whether the information is presented in conformity with FASB Statement No. 14... *in relation to the financial statements taken as a whole*" (AU 435.03; emphasis added). Auditors should treat segment information like other informative disclosures. That is, they do not apply audit procedures to the extent required if they were to issue an opinion on the segment information alone.

Materiality is critical in determining the extent of an auditor's procedures. According to SAS 21, the auditor must make quantitative judgments primarily, and qualitative judgments secondarily, in determining the materiality of segment information.

Quantitative judgments. The auditor's quantitative judgments relate the dollar magnitude of the segment information to the consolidated financial statements taken as a whole. For example, if during an audit the auditor concludes that 5% of consolidated operating income is an appropriate cumulative materiality level, he does not have to apportion this amount to segments. In a ten-segment company, a 5% consolidated materiality does not become 5% at the segment level.

Qualitative judgments. Though quantitative materiality considerations are useful to the auditor as rules of thumb, the auditor must also consider *qualitative factors.* A misstatement of the segment information may cause a company's financial statements taken as a whole to be misleading even if the magnitude of the misstatement is below the dollar materialitiy level the auditor judges is appropriate for the consolidated statements. The auditor should insist that the segment information be corrected to eliminate the misstatement or appropriately modify his report.

For example, consider a segment of a company whose operating profit has grown at an exceptional rate in recent years. The auditor is aware through analysts' reports that present and potential investors believe the growth rate will continue in the future and that the market price of the company's stock incorporates the investors' evaluation. During his examination the auditor discovers that the current year's joint operating expenses have been misallocated and understated for the segment in question; as a result, the reported trend in earnings continues. Athough the consolidated income is correct (a misallocation would not affect total expense), the auditor must assess whether the segment's misstated profit, in light of the probable importance of the trend, makes the financial statements taken as a whole misleading. If in his judgment the statements are misleading, the misstatement in segment information is material even though the dollar impact on consolidated income is zero.

SAS 21 requires auditors to consider the following when evaluating whether a qualitative segment matter is material to the financial statements taken as a whole:

1. The significance of a matter to a particular entity,
2. The pervasiveness of a matter, and
3. The impact of a matter.

Audit Procedures. Because the profession has decided that segment information does not require a different quantitative materiality standard, an auditor theoretically does not have to increase the overall level of auditing procedures during his examination. As a practical matter, however, segment information will require additional effort on the auditor's part. In general, segment information affects the audit plan and must be considered throughout the engagement.

Auditors should consider segment information when planning the audit. For example, in the absence of segment information, an auditor might plan to have staff persons observe physical inventory counts of items representing 50% of the dollar value of the consolidated inventory balance. If the same company is reporting segment information, the auditor would probably still plan to cover 50% of the inventory, but might locate his observations on the basis of the company's segments. He may emphasize a reportable segment encompassing several divisions over another segment with a single operation and a single accounting system.

SAS 21 indicates that segment information may cause the auditor to "modify or redirect selected audit tests to be applied to the financial statements taken as a whole." The auditor considers the following when deciding whether to redirect or modify his tests (AU 435.06):

a. Internal accounting control and the degree of integration, centralization, and uniformity of the accounting records.

b. The nature, number, and relative size of industry segments and geographic areas.

c. The nature and number of subsidiaries or divisions in each industry segment and geographic area.

d. The accounting principles used for the industry segments and geographic areas.

Auditors should also consider segment information when performing their normal tests of the underlying accounting records. Auditors should challenge whether revenue, operating expenses, and identifiable assets are properly classified among industry segments and geographic areas.

SAS 21 lists a number of specific procedures auditors should perform to determine if a company's segment information is presented in conformity with SFAS 14. These procedures, (summarized below from AU 435.07) cover the segmenting procedures followed by the company when grouping related products and industries, the bases used for intersegment sales and transfers, the disaggregation of the company's financial statements, and other matters. The auditor should:

1. Inquire concerning the company's method of determining segment information. Evaluate the reasonableness of the method in relation to SFAS 14 guidelines.

2. Inquire as to the basis for sales and transfers between segments and areas. Test whether the basis conforms to recorded transactions.

3. Test the disaggregation of the financial statements into segment information.

   a. Evaluate the application of SFAS 14 percentage tests. Check if the data are properly summarized and recompute as necessary.

   b. Analytically review the segment data and inquire if items or relationships appear unusual.

      • Compare current-year data to prior-year and current-year budgeted data.

      • Consider the interrelationship of elements that should correlate based on the company's experience.

      • Consider matters that have required adjustment to segment information in the past.

4. Inquire about, evaluate reasonableness, and mathematically test as necessary the allocation of operating expenses and jointly used assets.

5. Determine whether segment information has been consistently presented. If not, determine that appropriate disclosures, and restatements if appropriate, are being made.

Auditors' Reports. Although segment information rarely affects the auditor's report, in some situations (if material) the report should be modified. A brief description of those situations follows.

Misstatement or omission of segment information. The auditor should issue either a qualified or an adverse opinion if there has been a misstatement or omission of segment information. The auditor should describe the effects of the misstatement, but he is not required to provide omitted information regarding segments. An auditor will rarely encounter omitted segment information in situations for which it is required. However, Japanese companies, such as Sony Corporation, Pioneer Electronics Corporation, Canon Inc., Matsushita Electric Industrial Co., Ltd., Makita Electric Works Ltd., Kubota Ltd., NEC Corporation, TDK Corporation, and Hitachi Ltd., whose securities trade in the United States, omit segment information in their annual reports presented in accordance with U.S. GAAP. Those companies are subject to SEC annual reporting requirements under Form 20F. The instructions to Form 20F make specific reference to SFAS 14 and permit companies filing that form to omit presentation of segment information. Interestingly, the omission is not permitted for foreign private issuers under the 1933 Act.

The 1934 Act's exclusion of segment information resulted from agitation by Japanese companies and *Keidanren,* a prestigious Japanese association of businesses. However, this type of special exclusion is rare for the SEC. (In another instance, the SEC has repeatedly refused permission for a Japanese bank that will not file the Guide 3 (bank holding company) information to sell securities in the United States.)

All auditors' reports for Japanese companies not providing the segment data are qualified. The opinion paragraph of each company indicates that the financial statements are presented in accordance with U.S. GAAP except for the omission of the segment information. Figure 4.14 presents an example of the auditors' qualified opinion (in the reporting format used prior to SAS 58).

Scope limitation. A scope limitation occurs when a company requests that the auditor not examine its segment information. SAS 21 also discusses the situation of an auditor not being sure which provisions of SFAS 14 (existence of reportable segments, export sales, major customers, etc.) apply to his client. If the company refuses to develop information to this end, the auditor also faces a scope limitation. It is difficult to imagine an auditor not being sufficiently familiar with his client's operations to conclude that he faced an omission of segment information rather than a scope limitation. Conceivably, the SAS includes this situation in order to help auditors convince reluctant clients that it is the clients' responsibility to assemble the information required by SFAS 14. The auditor should explain a scope limitation and qualify his opinion.

Separate reports. Occasionally an auditor will be asked to issue a separate report on his review of financial information prepared in accordance with SFAS 14 for one or more of the diversified company's segments. The auditor's procedures will be more extensive than the procedures he would direct to those same segments in an examination of the company's financial statements, because the auditor must base materiality on the particular segment information itself.

SAS 21 refers the auditor to AU 621.10–.13 (special reports expressing an opinion on one or more specified elements, accounts, or items of a financial statement) for guidance in this type of examination and also instructs the auditor to state in his separate report whether segment information is presented fairly in accordance with GAAP (if the segment constitutes a separable entity whose complete financial state-

Report of Independent Public Accountants
Touche Ross & Co.
Tohmatsu Awoki & Sanwa

Shareholders and Board of Directors
Kubota, Ltd.
Osaka, Japan

We have examined the consolidated balance sheets of Kubota, Ltd. and consolidated subsidiaries as of April 15, 1987 and 1986, and the related consolidated statements of income, shareholders' equity and changes in financial position for each of the three years in the period ended April 15, 1987, all expressed in Japanese yen. Our examinations were made in accordance with generally accepted auditing standards and, accordingly, included such tests of the accounting records and such other auditing procedures as we considered necessary in the circumstances.

Certain information required by Statement of Financial Accounting Standards No. 14 has not been presented in the accompanying consolidated financial statements. In our opinion, presentation of segment information concerning the Company's operations is required for a complete presentation of the Company's consolidated financial statements in accordance with generally accepted accounting principles in the United States.

In our opinion, except for the omission of information discussed in the preceding paragraph, the consolidated financial statements referred to above present fairly the financial position of Kubota, Ltd. and consolidated subsidiaries as of April 15, 1987 and 1986, and the results of their operations and the changes in their financial position for each of the three years in the period ended April 15, 1987, in conformity with generally accepted accounting principles prevailing in the United States on a consistent basis.

The United States dollar amounts shown in the accompanying consolidated financial statements have been translated solely for convenience. We have reviewed this translation and, in our opinion, the consolidated financial statements expressed in yen have been translated into dollars on the basis described in Note 2 to the consolidated financial statements.

TOUCHE ROSS & CO.
TOHMATSU AWOKI & SANWA
Tokyo, Japan
June 12, 1987

FIG. 4.14 Auditors' Report—Omission of Segment Data
Source: Kubota Ltd., 1987 Annual Report.

ments are presented in conformity with GAAP, usual audit considerations apply, not the guidance in this section).

The separate reporting requirements of SAS 21 are ambiguous. When the auditor reports that segment information is presented fairly in accordance with GAAP, does this mean that only the disclosures required by SFAS 14, no more or no less, have been made? Or does it mean that the auditor should consider whether additional informative disclosures required by GAAP other than SFAS 14 are necessary so that the segment information is not misleading?

The auditing literature does not resolve the dilemma. But because segment information provides a broad view of one or more components of a diversified company (information about revenue, profitability, assets, etc.) the auditor must seriously consider whether potential users might view the information as misleading unless accompanied by disclosures beyond those required in SFAS 14. For example, when the enterprise as a whole is faced with a material uncertainty, the auditor might conclude that the disclosures required by SFAS 5, *Accounting for Contingencies* (C59), are also necessary for a fair presentation of the segment information.

Consistency. A company may change an accounting practice that in turn affects the way segment information is prepared or presented. According to SFAS 14, a company must disclose the nature and effect of a change in the period the change occurs, and for certain changes the segment information must be retroactively restated.

If an auditor is reporting on the consoslidated financial statements taken as a whole, the effect of the change on the segment information would not cause him to modify his report. Certain changes, such as a change in the basis of pricing intersegment sales, affect only the segment information, and the auditor would not mention such changes in his report. On the other hand, if a company changes accounting principles as discussed in APB 20 (A06), the change also affects the consolidated financial statements, and for that reason the auditor would mention the change in his report.

However, if a company does not disclose the nature and effect of a change affecting the segment data or make the retroactive restatements as required by SFAS 14, the auditor would issue a qualified (in rare instances an adverse) opinion, because the company's failure to provide this information constitutes a departure from GAAP. The auditor may also consider including the nature and effect of a change in an explanatory paragraph in his report. Unlike segment information that is omitted in its entirety, the nature and effect of a change may be readily ascertainable and compactly presented.

If an auditor is reporting separately on segment information, he should mention any of the following if changed:

1. The basis for recording intersegment sales.
2. The method of allocating common operating expenses or identifiable assets among segments.
3. The method of determining or presenting segment profitability.
4. An accounting principle as discussed in APB 20.
5. Retroactive restatement of the company's financial statements as a whole.
6. The method of grouping industry segments or geographic areas.

Reviewing Changing Prices Disclosures

For changes described in the last two items above, prior-period segment information must be retroactively restated.

With changing prices disclosures now made on a voluntary basis, the ASB has issued SAS 52, *Omnibus Statement on Auditing Standards—1987,* to rescind or revise the numerous prior SASs that had dealt with required supplementary information.

The auditor's review of voluntarily provided information included in a document that contains audited financial statements is governed by SAS 8 (AU 550).

SAS 8 indicates that the auditor's responsibility does not extend beyond the financial information described in his report. He has no obligation to audit other information, for example, voluntarily disclosed changing prices information. However, the SAS does require that the auditor read the other information to determine whether it is inconsistent with any financial statement information that has been audited.

If the auditor concludes that the other information is inconsistent with the audited financial statements or results in a material misstatement of fact, he should take appropriate action. Such action might include:

1. Assessing the validity of (or requesting the company to secure outside expertise to assess the validity of) the inconsistent information. If such a procedure does not result in resolving the inconsistency, the auditor should consider (a) a revision in his report to discuss the matter, or (b) withholding his report and withdrawing from the engagement.

2. Assessing the nature and effect of any material misstatement and if the matter cannot be resolved by the company and the auditor, he should consider further steps such as (a) notifying the company in writing of his views and (b) consulting his legal counsel.

For a further discussion, see Chapter 11.

PART **II**

Auditing

5

The Role of Auditors and Auditing Standards

OVERVIEW

Origins

The word "audit" comes from the Latin *audire,* which means "to hear"; literally, an "auditor" is a person who hears or listens. When we say that a student audits a class, we still use the word in its oldest sense; the auditor merely listens to the lectures without responsibility for the required classwork. As a tool of social and commercial control, however, auditing has concentrated on verifying the fulfillment of responsibility.

For centuries, audits were oral hearings in which people entrusted with fiscal responsibility justified their stewardship, a word that occurs frequently in any discussion of auditing. Two New Testament parables, for example, center around such events. In the parable of the unjust steward, a "certain rich man" learns that his steward has wasted the goods entrusted to him. Summoning the steward, the rich man demands an oral accounting. In the parable of the talents, the "man travelling into a far country" brings his servants together on his return to determine how they managed the wealth he had placed in their care.

Similarly, medieval audits took on the nature of ritual, attempting to prove the "personal integrity of stewards, not the quality of their accounts" (Chatfield, 1977, p. 112). In medieval England, audits were oral verifications of estate, manorial, and even royal accounts. The Chancellor of the Exchequer held oral audits twice a year around a table covered by a checkered cloth.

But audits do more than help to keep people honest. In the most general sense, they provide assurance in a wide variety of human endeavors. Hospitals carry out audits of their various services. Social programs are audited for compliance and effectiveness. And while most audits are no longer oral examinations, they remain public hearings in spirit. They are formal examinations systematically and objectively carried out by people expert in the subject under scrutiny.

Development of Auditing in the United States

Even a cursory glance at the events of the past 80 years will show that the profession's history is characterized by the assumption of increasing responsibility and by growing public demands and expectations.

As organized professional activities, auditing and accounting are relative newcomers. The development of auditing began in Great Britain during the nineteenth century, largely as a result of the industrial revolution, the growth of capital, and the attendant chaos in financial reporting. These British roots have profoundly influenced the evolution of the profession in the United States.

Rudimentary audits were carried out in the United States during the nineteenth century, mainly to satisfy bankers' needs for information about companies seeking loans. But as American business experienced phenomenal expansion later in that century, investors and lenders began to demand greater assurance that a company's financial statements provided reliable information for making economic decisions.

Many of the developments in auditing practices and standards grew out of specific economic problems. Credit problems of the early 1900s, for example, led to bankers' demands for certification of corporate balance sheets. In 1917, a rash of business failures and the lack of uniformity in financial statements prompted the Federal Reserve Board to issue the first audit guidelines. The stock market crash of 1929, and the Great Depression, led to the Securities Act of 1933 and the Securities Exchange Act of 1934, which created the SEC, opening the way for governmental regulation of the securities markets and the financial information used in those markets. The Depression also resulted in the New York Stock Exchange requirement for audits of listed corporations.

In the 1970s and 1980s, major business failures and scandals prompted congressional investigations of the public accounting profession and the appropriateness and effectiveness of auditing standards. These investigations, other studies, and actions by the accounting profession resulted in increased responsibilities for independent auditors and a new Code of Professional Conduct for the accounting profession. These matters are discussed at length in Chapter 45 and later in this chapter.

Other developments can also be traced to initiatives taken by the accounting profession itself. The formation of the American Institute of Accountants in 1916 – the forerunner of today's AICPA – was an important first step in creating a national professional body to develop uniform goals and standards. The profession developed the uniform CPA examination, which is used throughout the United States as the principal means to determine admission to the profession. The profession was and is instrumental in developing curricula to assure that prospective CPAs obtain an educational foundation appropriate to perform their responsibilities. The Committee on Accounting Procedure (CAP), the APB, the AcSEC, and currently, the FASB, the GASB, and the ASB – all private, profession-sponsored organizations – have provided the standards of accounting and auditing through the years.

Auditing of Business Enterprises

There are two general categories of auditing that relate to business enterprises: financial auditing and operational auditing.

Financial Auditing. In financial auditing, attention is focused on the financial statements, management's primary communication with its various publics. In the United States, audits of financial statements are performed by independent, outside auditors. Independent verification provides a degree of assurance as required by shareholders, creditors, government agencies, suppliers, and others. Depending on the circumstances, financial statements may be subject as well to audits by regulatory auditors, bank examiners, state auditors, U.S. General Accounting Office (GAO) auditors, and others.

It might be useful at this point to distinguish between two separate but intimately related activities: accounting and auditing. Strictly speaking, the discipline of auditing includes accounting. Yet the tasks of auditor and accountant differ. Accountants prepare financial information; auditors check it. Put more formally, auditors perform independent examinations to evaluate the propriety of accounting procedures, measurements, and communications.

A financial audit requires a substantial input of professional time and talent to enable the auditor to develop the necessary understanding of the business and its systems and to express an opinion on its financial reports. Such professional inputs should generally create audit outputs which can go beyond the report on financial statements. The financial audit, therefore, will generally result in recommendations to the client regarding possible improvements in business systems, information presentation, internal control, and tax savings. Some of these recommendations are summarized in the management letter which the auditor normally submits at the conclusion of an audit, but more may emerge from the day-to-day contacts between audit personnel and client management during an engagement. And, of course, the audit inputs place the independent accountant in a position to perform special engagements in the various areas where recommendations for improvement are made based on the audit. While the primary objective of the financial audit must always remain the professional evaluation of financial reports by an expert third party, the other outputs of the service may substantially enhance its economic usefulness.

Thus, the audit services that independent CPAs provide to business are not restricted to the examination of financial statements. Examples of other related services include:

1. Reviews and compilations of financial statements;
2. Reviews of financial records, business practices, and other aspects of companies under consideration for acquisition;
3. Various special reports;
4. Review and evaluation of the company's internal controls beyond that required for the examination of financial statements;
5. Examinations or compilations of forecasts or projections;
6. Performance of feasibility studies;
7. Examinations of financial statements of employee benefit plans; and
8. Assistance in development of an internal audit function.

The list is long, and these and many other service areas are mentioned throughout this *Handbook.*

Independent CPAs are not the only professionals involved in financial auditing. For example, internal auditors may examine and evaluate their company's internal accounting controls, often carrying out various testing procedures in determining the effectiveness of control systems (see Chapter 7). Regulatory auditors furnish another example; they carry out a variety of financial audit services, often to verify compliance with specific regulations that affect financial statements.

Operational Auditing. Auditors in the private sector and in government may also carry out operational audits, reviewing such matters as the efficiency of an organization's operations. Outside auditors are not directly involved in operational auditing while they carry out the audits of a company's financial statements. Because of their familiarity with the organization, however, they can and usually do offer useful recommendations. Beyond this, independent CPA firms that maintain the necessary skills can be engaged to assist in developing and improving production planning, scheduling, and inventory management policies. They can advise an enterprise about improving the control and efficiency of its operations.

Internal auditors usually play a more prominent role than outside auditors in operational auditing. Management will often use internal auditors primarily to study an organization's operating practices to increase efficiency and to search for errors and irregularities.

Finally, governmental auditing such as that performed by the GAO is usually oriented strongly toward operational auditing (see Chapter 31).

AUDITOR'S ROLE IN FINANCIAL REPORTING

Accountability

The profession has its roots in the broad issue of *accountability*. Without accountability, society cannot function. "Whoever has a responsibility to others for his actions and their consequences is accountable to them" the Trueblood Committee reported in 1973. "That responsibility may derive from law, contract, organization policy or moral obligation" (AICPA, 1973d, p. 25). Efforts to measure the degree to which that "responsibility to others" – that accountability – has been met have become a necessary social endeavor.

In business, accountability takes on crucial dimensions. Business is accountable to shareholders, creditors, suppliers, government, and other interested "publics." Corporate financial statements, prepared by management accountants, serve as reports of fiscal accountability. Independent audits of these reports are needed to assure that management has not biased economic information in its favor. The auditor, who enforces standards for the presentation of financial information and evaluates management's judgment in applying these standards, thus exerts a restraining influence. Although a CPA engages in many activities also performed by non-CPAs, when he performs an independent audit of financial statements he is acting in a capacity legally reserved for his profession.

Audited Financial Statements

An independent auditor performs an audit with the objective of issuing a report containing his opinion on his client's financial statements. Although the audit may take months – at some large corporations the audit is spread throughout the year – the standard report is brief. An analysis of the contents of a typical auditor's report makes one wonder about its brevity; according to standards established by the profession, the auditor must communicate specific information to readers, generally by using prescribed terminology. An example of an auditor's standard report, with special terms italicized and explained, follows: [1]

---

[1] This new form of auditor's report prescribed by SAS 58 is effective for reports issued on or after January 1, 1989. The prior two-paragraph form of standard report, effective for over forty years, was worded as follows:

We have examined the accompanying balance sheets of X Company as of December 31, 19X2 and 19X1, and the related statements of income, retained earnings, and cash flows for the years then ended. Our examinations were made in accordance with generally accepted auditing standards and, accordingly,

INDEPENDENT AUDITOR'S REPORT

We have audited the accompanying balance sheets of X Company as of December 31, 1988 and 1987, and the related statements of income, retained earnings, and cash flows for the years then ended. These financial statements are the responsibility of the Company's management. Our responsibility is to express an opinion on these financial statements based on our audits.

We conducted our audits *in accordance with generally accepted auditing standards.* Those standards require that we plan and perform the audit to obtain reasonable assurance about whether the financial statements are free of material misstatement. An audit includes examining, on a test basis, evidence supporting the amounts and disclosures in the financial statements. An audit also includes assessing the accounting principles used and significant estimates made by management, as well as evaluating the overall financial statement presentation. We believe that our audits provide a reasonable basis for our opinion.

In our opinion, the financial statements referred to above *present fairly, in all material respects,* the financial position of X Company at December 31, 1988 and 1987, and the results of its operations and its cash flows for the years then ended *in conformity with generally accepted accounting principles.*

New York, New York   Touche Ross & Co.
February 3, 1989   Certified Public Accountants

In Accordance With GAAS. In this phrase the auditor is reporting that he has complied with GAAS—those standards adopted by the AICPA to ensure the quality of the performance by CPAs who are engaged in an independent examination of financial statements.

Ten standards form the foundation of GAAS. These 10 standards are expressed in fewer than 350 words. The standards are not audit procedures; they do not instruct auditors how to conduct a financial statement examination. The AICPA draws the following distinction:

Auditing standards differ from auditing procedures in that "procedures" relate to acts to be performed, whereas "standards" deal with measures of the quality of the performance of those acts and the objectives to be attained by the use of the procedures undertaken. *Auditing standards* as distinct from *auditing procedures* concern themselves not only with the auditor's professional qualities but also with the judgment exercised by him in the performance of his audit and in his report. [AU 150.01]

The ASB, a senior technical committee of the AICPA, issues pronouncements known as SASs, which amplify the 10 basic standards and guide the auditor in certain significant areas of the examination. Although the guidance given by SASs is

---

included such tests of the accounting records and such other auditing procedures as we considered necessary in the circumstances.

In our opinion, the financial statements referred to above present fairly the financial position of X Company at December 31, 19X2 and 19X1, and the results of its operations and its cash flows for the years then ended in conformity with generally accepted accounting principles applied on a consistent basis.

more concrete than the broad principles of the basic standards, taken together as GAAS they form only a framework and set of objectives the auditor must satisfy in his audit and report. The auditor selects the myriad steps and procedures necessary to plan and conduct an audit using his professional judgment within the confines of this broad framework.

In Conformity With GAAP. In this phrase the independent auditor is reporting that the financial statements prepared by his client comply with GAAP, the accepted conventions of financial accounting and reporting. The FASB is the independent organization responsible for promulgating GAAP in its pronouncements (see Chapter 46). The GASB performs this function as to state and local governmental units (see Chapter 31).

GAAP is a much misunderstood term; there are no immutable accounting truths, because accounting principles are conventions that depend on acceptance. As conventions, accounting principles do not necessarily parallel economic reality. For example, the balance sheet representation of a factory's historical cost (reduced by periodic depreciation charges) usually differs significantly from the market value of the structure or the cost the company would incur if it were to replace the structure. For the most part, accounting principles have been oriented toward the financial effects of actual transactions that have occurred in the past.

The FASB's conceptual framework for financial accounting and reporting serves as a theoretical construct against which proposed accounting standards are compared and preexisting standards evaluated (see Chapter 2). Over time, a closer synthesis of accounting principles and economic reality should occur as the FASB concepts statements are built into more accounting standards.

Present Fairly. The auditor is reporting several pieces of information in this phrase. First he is reporting that while the financial statements capture the underlying events within an acceptable range of approximation, they remain summaries of innumerable transactions that cannot be exactly portrayed. Beyond this acceptable range, an error or misstatement is deemed to be *material*. The profession has not precisely articulated the boundary that separates material from immaterial items, because this is so dependent on the specific circumstances. As a result, the exact criteria—within accepted ranges—used by different accountants are based on individual judgments that critics have labeled as inconsistent or arbitrary. Nonetheless, materiality is so integral to the financial reporting process, that the new auditor's report (in 1988) appends the phrase "in all material respects" to the "present fairly" assertion.

"Present fairly" means that the accounting principles selected by the company are generally accepted and appropriate in the circumstances. "Present fairly" always is coupled with "in conformity with GAAP" in an auditor's report on an examination of financial statements. GAAP is the standard by which to measure fairness. "Fairness" in the abstract could mean all manner of beneficence conceivable by financial statement users, and litigation against accountants often focuses on plaintiffs' broad assertions of "unfairness."

Although general purpose financial statements should be "fair" in the sense of being free from bias, the process of financial accounting involves continuous judgments and estimates on the part of those who prepare and audit financial statements. The process is inherently subjective, and critics maintain that the auditor's report should emphasize – not obscure – this fact.

Significance of the Audit – Added Assurance. Investors and creditors risk funds based on their assessment of an enterprise's future. Financial statements serve two purposes in this assessment: existing financial statements provide some (though far from all) of the data needed for users to make the prediction; and financial statements will confirm or correct aspects of the prediction as the future unfolds. An audit and the auditor's report increase the user's confidence in the information contained in financial statements. But users of financial statements should understand that the auditor plans his examination economically and cannot, and should not, check all transactions. Although the auditor plans his examination to locate problems, his conclusion could be wrong because of the sampling nature of an audit, procedural faults, or most devastatingly (but infrequently), the lack of integrity by management. Such erroneous conclusions by auditors are uncommon, but when they occur and involve large public companies, they receive widespread attention in the financial press, the courts, and even in Congress.

Audit sampling. An auditor comes to his conclusions based on a sampling of the transactions related to the period under examination (see Chapter 9). To do otherwise – that is, to examine every transaction – would mitigate the usefulness of audits because the cost of such examinations would radically exceed the total benefits to investors, creditors, and others.[2] But, by virtue of examining only a portion of the transactions, the auditor and those who read his report must accept an element of uncertainty about the auditor's conclusions. By understanding the types of transactions a company enters, by specializing in assessing systems of internal control, and by using a variety of sophisticated audit procedures and audit tools where appropriate, auditors are generally able to minimize risks associated with their sampling approach and are able to design an audit plan that balances the costs and benefits of an audit.

Procedural and performance errors. An auditor may mistakenly use an audit procedure inappropriate for discovering the error or misstatement, fail to properly perform a procedure through misunderstanding of instructions, fail to accurately evaluate the results of a procedure, or fail to recognize that his subordinates on the audit team have made these mistakes. To minimize these occurrences, the profession has established requirements for entry and continued practice, and accounting firms utilize a hierarchical structure so that persons with the appropriate experience are designing, performing, and reviewing all phases of the audit. Nonetheless, audits are conducted by people, and errors may occur in isolated cases regardless of the complex safeguards designed to prevent them.

---

[2] It is also a fallacy that an examination of every transaction would assure the correctness of the auditor's conclusion. The estimates and judgments involved in financial statement presentation, and the intentions and integrity of management, are substantially non-transaction-based.

Management integrity. To many laymen, it is incomprehensible that auditors occasionally fail to detect a major fraud. But collusive fraud by management lacking integrity is extremely difficult (often impossible) to detect. Fictitious receivables may pose as assets, and the auditor's confirmation procedures count for naught if the parties circularized cooperate with the fraud perpetrators; underlying documents may be forged, and cash receipts from unexpected sources may not be recorded. In SAS 16, the AICPA had defined the auditor's responsibility for detecting irregularities as a passive obligation: unless his audit found evidence to the contrary, his reliance on the truthfulness of management's representations and on the genuineness of records and documents was deemed to be reasonable.

As discussed at the end of this chapter, under "The Auditor's Role and Society's Expectations," society has not been satisfied with this limitation of an auditor's responsibilities. In early 1988, the ASB enacted SAS 53, under which the auditor is required to take an affirmative, active approach to the discovery of management fraud and other irregularities; he must plan his audit to provide reasonable assurance of detecting material misstatements.

Need for Audit Services

Generally, one or more of the following characteristics will exist when a company engages a CPA to perform an audit:

1. *Public companies* almost without exception require an annual audit of their financial statements. A public company is defined by the AICPA as one whose securities trade in a public market or one that has filed with a regulatory agency in preparation for the sale of securities in a public market (I73.101, fn.1).
2. *Users' needs* often include the added assurance of an audit for financial statements of non-public companies as well as public ones. Instances when users often need such added assurance are:
   a. The company has entered into a significant contractual arrangement with a bank or other creditor, a joint venture partner, a large vendor, a lessor, or the like.
   b. The company has a fiduciary responsibility to the public or others. For example, mutual savings and loan associations, mutual life insurance companies, health maintenance organizations, charities, country clubs, and many other not-for-profit organizations have such a responsibility.
3. *Owner's needs* sometimes call for an audit; for example, the owner may have infrequent contact with the actual managers and thus desire added audit assurance. More frequently, the owner believes that the benefits of an audit, including recommendations for improved internal control and operating efficiencies, outweigh the added expense of an audit.

Unaudited Financial Statements

Many companies require the expertise of the independent CPA in preparing periodic financial statements but do not need the added assurance of a report based on an audit. To provide standards for auditor's reports on unaudited financial statements of *nonpublic* companies, the Accounting and Review Services Committee, a senior

committee of the AICPA, issues SSARS. The basic services are summarized in the
following subsections and are discussed more fully in Chapter 39.

Compilation. A compilation is presenting, in financial statement form,
information that is the representation of management. The CPA must have or gain a
general understanding of his client's industry and business, but he is not required to
"make inquiries or perform other procedures to verify, corroborate, or review
information" supplied by his client (AR 100.12). His report mentions that a
compilation has been performed, describes a compilation, and states that no opinion
or other form of assurance is expressed on the financial statements.

Review. The CPA must have or gain familiarity with his client's industry and
business. He also makes inquiries and performs certain analytical and other
procedures so that he has a reasonable basis for expressing limited assurance on the
financial statements. If, in performing any of these procedures, the auditor becomes
aware that any information is "incorrect, incomplete, or otherwise unsatisfactory, he
should perform the additional procedures he deems necessary . . ." (AR 100.29).

The accountant's review report states that a review was performed in accordance
with AICPA standards and that the information in the financial statements is the
representation of management, and it describes the nature of a review as distinct
from an audit. The report gives the limited assurance that, based on the review, the
CPA is not aware of any material modifications that should be made to the financial
statements in order for them to be in conformity with GAAP.

Other Services. Throughout this *Handbook* other unaudited services are
mentioned, for example, interim financial statement reviews (Chapter 11), unaudited
data appearing in public company annual reports (Chapter 11), letters for
underwriters (Chapter 20), and forecasts and projections (Chapter 27). Although
these services do not provide the same degree of assurance as an audit, they are
nevertheless useful in their specific circumstances.

Other Independent Auditor Activities

The CPA's qualifications and knowledge of his client's business enable him to provide significant accounting and audit-related services in addition to reporting on
financial statements. The accountant may provide additional services when he is
engaged to report on financial statements, or he may provide these services independently of an audit, review, or compilation.

Letter of Recommendations. According to GAAS, the auditor must make a study
and evaluation of his client's system of internal control when he performs an audit.
As a result, he is in a position to recommend that the company modify or install
elements of internal control that will strengthen management's ability to safeguard
company assets or improve the reliability of the company's financial records (see
Chapter 8). Normally the auditor communicates his suggestions in a letter of
recommendations (also known as a *management letter*).

Often the letter will contain suggestions related to the efficiency of a company's operations. For example, an auditor experienced in retailing may suggest that his client consider physically redesigning its warehouse distribution center to provide a more efficient flow of goods, or an auditor of a geographically diverse fast-food chain might recommend the installation of a cash management system to increase average daily balances.

In addition to suggestions for improvements in operations and controls, the auditor must communicate to the client internal control-structure related matters noted in an audit. Once limited to "material weaknesses," these have now been expanded to include "reportable conditions" under SAS 60, as discussed in Chapter 8.

Special Reviews. A company will frequently engage an independent CPA to perform an in-depth review of all or a portion of its internal control system, or to originate or evaluate proposals designed to increase operating efficiency. These studies often stem from suggestions contained in the auditor's letter of recommendations.

Many other types of special reviews are performed in the management consulting area, but this area is not extensively covered in this *Handbook*.

Special Reports. The independent CPA may be engaged to perform appropriate procedures aimed at the issuance of a seemingly endless variety of special reports. Under guidelines issued by the AICPA in SAS 14 (AU 621), special reports have been grouped into four categories as listed below (and discussed more fully in Chapter 11):

1. Reports on financial statements prepared in accordance with a comprehensive basis of accounting other than GAAP.
2. Reports on specified elements, accounts, or items of a financial statement.
3. Reports on compliance with aspects of a contractual agreement related to audited financial statements.
4. Reports on information presented in prescribed forms or schedules that require a prescribed form of auditor's report.

To assist the auditor in dealing with the burgeoning special reporting situations not clearly falling within these criteria, in 1986 the AICPA released standards for attestation engagements, discussed under "Attestation and Other Standards" in this chapter.

Income Taxes. Based on the knowledge of his client's business and his familiarity with tax regulations and rulings, the independent CPA will frequently be able to suggest ways his client can lawfully reduce or defer payment of income taxes. He may also be asked to prepare tax returns, and if he is conducting an audit, he will review the adequacy of the financial statement provision for income taxes (see Chapters 17 and 48). Because tax matters can be very complex, accounting firms usually have a separate department consisting of tax specialists, and the auditors and tax personnel work jointly to serve clients' income tax needs.

AUDITING STANDARDS

Importance of Auditing Standards

The theory of auditing includes basic concepts, fundamental principles, and a set of guiding standards. In everyday practice the standards are paramount, because they contain the criteria governing the overall quality of audit performance.

Auditing standards remain the same for all audits. Auditing procedures, on the other hand, consist of detailed steps that vary depending on the complexity of an engagement, the nature of an accounting system, the type of business under audit, and other features of a particular job. Auditors conform to auditing standards by performing auditing procedures necessary in the circumstances.

The auditing standards, known as GAAS, were approved by vote of the membership of the AICPA in the late 1940s and early 1950s. Interpretations of these standards are issued in the form of binding SASs, which are promulgated by the ASB. Somewhat different standards are recognized in other major areas of auditing practice. For example, government auditors operate under GAO *Standards for Audit of Governmental Organizations, Programs, Activities and Functions,* (the *Yellow Book*) issued by the Comptroller General of the United States (see Chapter 31). And internal auditors, discussed in a separate section later in this chapter, operate under *Standards for the Professional Practice of Internal Auditing,* approved by the membership of the Institute of Internal Auditors (IIA).

GAAS is not the only source of qualitative criteria for independent auditors. The AICPA has adopted a code of professional conduct, and several of the rules in this code pertain directly to auditing practice. The AICPA also publishes auditing interpretations and audit and accounting guides. The interpretations, which are issued by the ASB, are specific responses to questions and problems that arise in the practical application of GAAS. The audit and accounting guides are books dealing with the application of GAAS to special industry situations. Some typical guides are *Audits of Banks, Audits of Investment Companies,* and *Audits of Savings and Loan Associations.*

Attestation and Other Standards

CPAs in public practice perform attestation services other than audits of financial statements. In recent years, the auditor has increasingly been called upon to provide reports on such matters as descriptions of systems of internal accounting control; descriptions of computer software; compliance with statutory, regulatory, and contractual requirements; investment performance statistics; and information supplementary to financial statements.

While the auditor has generally been able to apply the concepts underlying GAAS in performing these engagements, it has become increasingly difficult to do so. GAAS, after all, was developed to provide standards for basically one service: an examination of historical financial statements.

To address this situation, the ASB and the Accounting and Review Services Committee of the AICPA issued *Statement on Standards for Attestation Engagements* (AU 2000) in 1986. This pronouncement introduced a new set of standards to all members of the AICPA. The main objective of the attestation standards is to provide a general framework and set reasonable boundaries for the attest function. These standards are discussed later in this chapter under "Attestation Engagements."

In addition, other areas of practice (taxation, management advisory services, financial statement compilation and review services, and prospective financial information services) are governed by other statements of practice standards. Senior technical committees of the AICPA periodically issue Statements on Responsibilities in Tax Practice, Statements on Management Advisory Services, Statements on Standards for Accounting and Review Services, Statements on Quality Control Standards, and other special statements on standards, which apply to broad areas of practice and are discussed elsewhere in this *Handbook*.

Genesis of Auditing Standards

AICPA Prominence. The AICPA has been setting auditing standards for a long time. The CAP was formed in 1939 and functioned under that name until 1972, by which time it had issued 54 SAPs plus several codifications and special reports. When the FASB came into existence as an organization independent of the AICPA in the early 1970s, the AICPA reorganized its own auditing area and created an Auditing Standards Division. The AudSEC took over the work of the CAP. Turning its attention from procedures to standards, AudSEC and its successor, the ASB, issued 61 SASs from 1973 through early 1988. SAS 1, issued in 1973, is a compilation (with few changes of substance) of all prior SAPs; a regularly updated codification of SASs is available with topics arranged by section number rather than by SAS number.

Throughout this 50-year period, and especially in the last two decades, the SEC has been actively commenting on the direction of auditing standards, sometimes imposing a very significant influence on particular standards. (See Chapter 45.)

AudSEC was born in a reorganization movement stemming from a need to meet the problems of establishing auditing standards. At that time, AudSEC consisted of 21 professionals appointed by the AICPA chairman. The members, who received no compensation for serving on the committee, gave part-time attention to committee duties while they were engaged in their own practices. It died from external pressures exerted on two fronts. In 1977, a congressional staff study entitled *The Accounting Establishment* was published by the Subcommittee on Reports, Accounting and Management, chaired by the late Senator Lee Metcalf (U.S. Congress, 1976). The *Metcalf Report* severely criticized the organization of the accounting profession and its mechanism for setting auditing standards and recommended governmental intervention in the establishment of auditing standards.

Cohen Commission. The Commission on Auditors' Responsibilities (CAR) was an independent study group appointed and funded by the AICPA in 1974 to consider whether there was any gap between what the public expected of or needed from auditors and what auditors could and should reasonably expect to accomplish (and if there was such a gap, how to close it). It released its final statement in 1978. The commission, chaired by the late Manuel F. Cohen, former chairman of the SEC, fully demonstrated its independence of the AICPA by the nature of many of its recommendations. In *Report, Conclusions and Recommendations* (CAR, 1978), the

Cohen Commission called for several specific changes in the institutional structure for establishing auditing standards. In summary, it concluded (in Section 10):

1. A standard-setting organization separate from the AICPA would create great economic and organizational problems.
2. AudSEC should be replaced by a smaller, full-time committee compensated by the AICPA.
3. A full-time committee would require a larger and highly qualified staff. Within a budget allocated by the AICPA, the committee should select its own staff and make all personnel decisions.
4. Participation in the setting of auditing standards by people outside the profession should be encouraged. Formal procedures for this outside participation in the process should be provided.

The AICPA did not adopt all of the Cohen Commission's recommendations, but in late 1978 it created the ASB to replace AudSEC. The ASB has 21 part-time members appointed by the AICPA chairman. All board members must be AICPA members. Most portions of the board meetings are now open to the public. The board issued its first statement, SAS 24, *Review of Interim Financial Information* (AU 722), in March 1979, and by early 1988 was up to SAS 61.

Hardly a step was missed between the death of AudSEC and the birth of the ASB, largely because 11 members of AudSEC, including the chairman, carried over to the board and continued their work on projects started earlier.

Treadway Commission. The occurrence of major business failures and scandals involving banks, savings and loans, and government securities dealers in the mid-1980s resurrected the "expectation gap" between what the public and other users of financial statements believe the auditor is responsible for, and what the auditor believes his responsibilities are. As a result, there are more-or-less continuing congressional investigations; and a National Commission on Fraudulent Financial Reporting (the *Treadway Commission*), was established. Nine SASs were issued in early 1988 addressing expectation gap issues and many recommendations were made in 1987 by the Treadway Commission in its final report. (See Chapter 45.)

One of the Treadway Commission's recommendations concerned the ASB and the audit standard-setting process. The Commission recommended in its *Report of the National Commission on Fraudulent Financial Reporting* (NCFFR, 1987) that the AICPA reorganize the ASB "to afford a full participatory role in the standard-setting process to knowledgeable persons who are affected by and interested in auditing standards but who either are not CPAs or are CPAs no longer in public practice" (p. 60). In its recommendation, the Commission was most concerned with the timely recognition and resolution of emerging issues, and believed a smaller, more diverse group would be most effective.

The Commission offered the following suggestions for implementing this recommendation (NCFFR, pp. 60–62):

1. The ASB should continue to be under the auspices of, and to be supported by, the AICPA.
2. The ASB should be significantly smaller (8–12 members) than the present board and have an even number of members. One half should be practicing public accountants; the other

half should be composed of persons who are not engaged in public accounting practice but are qualified and knowledgeable about auditing.

3. The AICPA Board of Directors should select the ASB members. Selection should be based on personal expertise and qualifications, not on the basis of constituencies.

4. The chairman and vice-chairman of the ASB should both serve full time. One should be from current professional auditing practice; the other should be from the ranks of knowledgeable persons not engaged in that practice. To attract qualified members, the ASB should sufficiently compensate all members, both full- and part-time.

5. The reorganized ASB, in setting auditing standards, should perform a management role: (1) setting the agenda, priorities, and policy direction and (2) considering, approving, disapproving, or changing technical auditing standards.

6. The AICPA should ensure that the ASB has an adequate, technically qualified senior staff.

7. In addition to using the services of AICPA staff and rotating practice fellows, the ASB also should be able to continue to draw on the technical expertise of partners currently engaged in auditing practice who now serve the ASB on a part-time basis for difficult, technical matters that demand the partner's level of experience and judgment.

Other recommendations of the Treadway Commission are concerned with the responsibility for detection of fraud, audit quality, and auditor communications. Many of these recommendations were addressed in the nine expectation gap SASs previously mentioned.

GENERAL STANDARDS

GAAS comprises 10 standards in three categories: general standards, standards of fieldwork, and reporting standards. The numbered SASs are interpretations of one or more of these standards and have the same binding force and effect. Thus, the SASs themselves are often called GAAS. The 10 GAAS (AU 150.02) are shown in Figure 5.1.

The second general standard, independence in mental attitude, is the place to begin an analysis of GAAS. The other nine standards will then be covered in order.

Independence

Independence is a central concept for CPAs engaged in auditing practice. The credibility conferred on a financial report when it is independently audited can be completely destroyed by any compromise of the auditor's independence, for an audit has value to recipients of financial statements only insofar as the auditor is perceived as independent of the control of management, objectively reviewing and reporting on management's representations contained in the statements.

Independence may be defined as an auditor's ability to act with integrity and objectivity. *Integrity* is an individual's ability to make difficult ethical decisions of right and wrong by correctly applying categorical rules for behavior to particular cases and by weighing the costs and benefits of alternative actions from the viewpoint of all persons who may be affected. This is the same integrity that all professionals must possess. *Objectivity* is an auditor's ability to be impartial. In

---

General Standards

1. The examination is to be performed by a person or persons having adequate technical training and proficiency as an auditor.
2. In all matters relating to the assignment, an independence in mental attitude is to be maintained by the auditor or auditors.
3. Due professional care is to be exercised in the performance of the examination and the preparation of the report.

Standards of Field Work

1. The work is to be adequately planned and assistants, if any, are to be properly supervised.
2. There is to be a proper study and evaluation of the existing internal control as a basis for reliance thereon and for the determination of the resultant extent of the tests to which auditing procedures are to be restricted.
3. Sufficient competent evidential matter is to be obtained through inspection, observation, inquiries, and confirmations to afford a reasonable basis for an opinion regarding the financial statements under examination.

Standards of Reporting

1. The report shall state whether the financial statements are presented in accordance with generally accepted accounting principles.
2. The report shall identify those circumstances in which such principles have not been consistently observed in the current period in relation to the preceding period.
3. Informative disclosures in the financial statements are to be regarded as reasonably adequate unless otherwise stated in the report.
4. The report shall either contain an expression of opinion regarding the financial statements, taken as a whole, or an assertion to the effect that an opinion cannot be expressed. When an overall opinion cannot be expressed, the reasons therefor should be stated. In all cases where an auditor's name is associated with financial statements, the report should contain a clear-cut indication of the character of the auditor's examination, if any, and the degree of responsibility he is taking.

FIG. 5.1   Generally Accepted Auditing Standards
Source: AU 150.02.

performance of an audit, a CPA should act exclusively in the capacity of an auditor or reviewer, not as a business consultant bent on giving management advice (although helpful control and efficiency advice may be a by-product), not as a business partner, and not as an advocate of any special interest. Throughout the duration of the audit – often almost continuously – the CPA may also operate in a consulting role or an advocacy role (as in tax practice), but in the audit itself these roles are set aside. Of course, knowledge gained by the auditor in the course of performing nonaudit services must be taken into account during performance of the audit. These concepts underlie the straightforward dictum of the second AICPA general standard: "In all matters relating to the assignment, an independence in mental attitude is to be maintained by the auditor or auditors" (AU 220.01).

Two Aspects of Independence. Auditing standards further recognize two aspects of independence: (1) an auditor must be intellectually honest, acting with integrity and objectivity, and (2) an auditor must be *recognized* as independent, free from any obligation to or interest in the audit client, the company under audit, its management, or its owners. The first of these aspects is often called independence in *fact* (a mental attitude that only the auditor himself possesses), and the second is often called independence *in appearance* (the absence of connections that can more easily be seen by others). The appearance of independence is important to maintaining public respect for the auditing profession.

AICPA Rules of Professional Conduct. Specific AICPA Rules of the Code of Professional Conduct reinforce the independence auditing standard. Rule 101 requires: "A member [of the AICPA] in public practice shall be independent in the performance of professional services as required by standards promulgated by bodies designated by council" (ET 101.01). The rule gives examples of impairment of the appearance of the auditor's independence, such as having a direct financial interest or material indirect financial interest in the client, having served as a trustee, officer, underwriter, or promoter of the enterprise, or having other associations that would enable observers to wonder about his ability to be objective.[3] Additional interpretations of this rule cover many details, including the effect of family relationships, litigation involving auditor and client, and other problem areas that have needed clarification from time to time. The SEC has laid down a similar rule and issued a series of examples and interpretations over the years for the guidance of auditors.[4]

Auditors can be penalized for failing to observe the spirit of independence rules. To the credit of the profession, however, there have been few cases in which auditors were specifically accused of lack of independence.[5]

Independence Criticism. The profession as a whole, however, has continuously been criticized for maintaining relationships that some see as impairing audit independence.

Scope of services. Some critics contend that when CPA firms perform a wide variety of management advisory services for an audit client, the consultancy bond is so close as to make the auditor's objectivity improbable. The Cohen Commission reviewed this criticism and concluded that it was generally unfounded (CAR, 1978, pp. 1–17). Nevertheless, certain services have been prohibited by rules of the SEC Practice Section of the AICPA as to publicly held companies.

---

[3] It is interesting to note that many years ago an auditor's direct financial interest was thought to be desirable, on the theory that he would operate in the best interests of all owners if he himself were one.

[4] In FRR 4 (§ 600) the Commission set a policy that letters on accountants' independence received by the Commission's Office of the Chief Accountant, as well as the staff's responses, are available for public inspection and copying. Since the letters set forth particular sets of circumstances, the staff's responses are not to be regarded as precedents binding on the Commission.

[5] SEC Accounting and Auditing Enforcement Releases (AAERs) as well as FRRs are a source of information on independence problems of specifically identified CPAs associated with SEC filings. The AICPA semimonthly newsletter, *The CPA Letter,* publishes disciplinary notices that cover other subjects and other CPAs as well.

One notable exception to the profession's good record is found in AAER 118, which describes an independent auditor's direct involvement in a significant fraud perpetrated by the management of ESM Government Securities, Inc. AAER 118 asserts that Jose L. Gomez, an audit partner with a national CPA firm and in charge of the ESM engagement, accepted money from ESM principals after becoming aware of ESM's fraudulent acts, which he did not reveal to members of his firm.

The profession's Public Oversight Board (POB) thoroughly examined suggestions for more general prohibitions of advisory services and concluded that only a few other services, not extensively provided in practice, should be proscribed until compelling objective evidence is produced proving that the services are indeed incompatible with the independent auditing role (POB, 1979). A later study by the POB, however, indicated a perception among key public groups that certain other types of consulting services might impair auditor independence (POB, 1986).

The scope-of-services issue is explored in depth in Chapter 45, but it is interesting to note here that the perceptions of independence vary and are the subject of extended debate.

Client fee dependence. Some critics ask how an auditor can truly be independent when his fee is paid by the client he audits. However, no one has suggested any preferable payment method that would be workable. Critics can be comforted in knowing that the penalties of exposure, litigation, and monetary loss that befall an auditor are far more severe than loss of an audit fee. One mitigating arrangement is for the engagement of the auditor to be approved by an audit committee composed of outside members of the client's board of directors, or by the board as a whole. This practice is now virtually standard for publicly held companies. The audit committee arrangement, including a periodic review of audit fees to evaluate whether they are proper given the company's situation, is widely perceived as enhancing the auditor's insulation from pressures that might be exerted by the client's management. The New York Stock Exchange requires listed companies to have audit committees composed of outside directors, and the SEC requires disclosure of the existence or nonexistence of audit committees and certain information about the committee's activities. (See Chapter 6.)

Independence Monitoring. Auditing firms are required to have quality control procedures that monitor compliance with the independence standards and rules. Authoritative AICPA pronouncements known as Statements on Quality Control Standards (SQCS), discussed later in this chapter under "Quality Control for a CPA Firm," give general guidance, and firms are expected to formulate specific policies and procedures. Many firms conduct regular briefings for new professional employees, require annual "independence sign-offs" in which partners and employees attest to the absence of any conditions that might impair independence, distribute notifications of new clients with directions for divestiture of financial interests, and provide counseling on independence problems. Firms often have policies that are more restrictive than AICPA rules.

Technical Training and Proficiency

For all auditors, competence is as important a key to independence as integrity. Great difficulties arise in trying to remain impartial and objective when faced with a complex task beyond one's capabilities. Thus, independence is not a separate standard but goes hand in hand with other auditing standards, particularly those of technical proficiency and professional care.

Competence is indispensable for a quality audit, because the auditor who does not understand the significant aspects of his client's business or its complex transactions puts himself in jeopardy of error that could have serious repercussions. Thus, the AICPA's first general standard requires: "The examination is to be performed by a person or persons having adequate technical training and proficiency as an auditor" (AU 210.01).

Academic and On-the-Job Training. Auditing standards recognize that technical training and proficiency are obtained through a combination of formal education and on-the-job training, with emphasis on the latter. Auditors must first be very competent accountants who know the principles of accounting and how to apply them. They must also have a grasp of economics in order to perceive the elusive economic substance represented by, or sometimes disguised in, transactions and balances. In some situations, the accounting rules may produce results that fail to reflect this substance; the auditor is expected to recognize these situations if they are material. Another level of education involves general business awareness of such fields as finance, marketing, management, law, statistics, and electronic data processing. Last but far from least, an auditor must know how to audit.

A typical university course in auditing combines auditing theory, professional ethics, and legal liability with technical material on the use of statistics and computers, reporting the results of auditing work, and procedures for audit planning and evidence gathering. With this technical material the student can begin to learn how to recognize problems, gather evidence about them, evaluate this evidence, and make a decision. Proficiency as an auditor finally comes down to one's ability to make decisions based on evidence. Although formal education provides a valuable introduction, it can never cover the wide variety of problems found outside the classroom. Practical experience in facing many unique situations is an absolute necessity if an auditor is eventually to be considered truly proficient. Explanations of this auditing standard therefore contain admonitions that neophyte auditors ought to be well supervised in their initial practical experience in order to gain the most benefit from it.

After some period of experience, depending on the kind of exposure obtained, an auditor may be sufficiently experienced to supervise the progress of newly hired auditors.

It should be noted that the complexity of contemporary accounting and auditing practice motivated the membership of the AICPA in 1987 to vote to increase the education requirements to five years of study (effectively, 30 credit hours of post-graduate work) to become a member of the AICPA. This requirement will take effect in the year 2000.

Continuing Professional Education. Along with on-the-job experience, continuing professional education (CPE) in formal modes is required of most auditors. Nearly 90% of the state CPA licensing boards require auditors to obtain an average of forty hours of CPE credit a year to retain their license to practice. Almost all of the remaining jurisdictions have voluntary CPE programs. The AICPA's Division for Firms requires professional staff in member firms to obtain a minimum of 120 hours of CPE credit over three years—effectively 40 hours each year.

In 1987, the membership of the AICPA approved a far-reaching and significant restructuring of professional standards (see Chapter 45). The new professional standards require *all* AICPA members (not only members of the Division for Firms) except those in retirement to obtain a specified number of CPE hours over a three-year period. Members in public practice will be required to take 120 hours over three years beginning in 1989, while members not in public practice will be required to take 60 hours over the same period beginning in 1989, increasing to 90 hours for subsequent three-year periods.

The AICPA and state CPA societies offer hundreds of courses, ranging in length from four hours to several days and covering a variety of topics that would make most business college deans envious. In addition, all the larger CPA firms spend a great deal of money on their own in-house training programs.

The AICPA quality control standards require firms to establish policies and procedures assuring that persons hired possess characteristics that will enable them to perform competently. Typical procedures for screening candidates include interviews with recruiting personnel, checks of references and college transcripts, and orientation briefings. For professional staff too, the standards call for policies and procedures to assure that members of a firm will have the knowledge they need to fulfill their assigned responsibilities. Most CPA firms monitor each professional's CPE time, including specialized industry training, and take measures to provide varied on-the-job experience. New accounting and auditing pronouncements are distributed to professional staff, along with instructions on applying those pronouncements in the context of the firm's quality control system. A firm is also required to have policies and procedures assuring that promotion is based on qualification to assume more responsible duties, not simply on tenure. Staff performance evaluations, published promotion guidelines, and advancement counseling are considered good practices for quality control in promotion.

Due Professional Care

Due professional care concerns what an auditor does on an engagement and how well he does it. The third general standard declares: "Due professional care is to be exercised in the performance of the examination and the preparation of the report" (AU 230.01). Other passages in the professional literature further explain that this standard is discharged in part by full observance of the field work and reporting standards (discussed in later sections of this chapter).

Whether due care has been exercised depends on all the facts and circumstances of a particular audit situation. Due care cannot be defined so precisely that its application to every case is clear. Indeed, in most large, complex audits its achievement is based on many, many factors. The concept is well understood nevertheless. It is the opposite of negligence in the law, which is described by this classic passage from *Cooley on Torts* (cited in AU 230.03):

Every man who offers his service to another and is employed assumes the duty to exercise in the employment such skill as he possesses with reasonable care and diligence. In all these employments where peculiar skill is prerequisite, if one offers his service, he is understood as holding himself out to the public as possessing the degree of skill commonly possessed by others in the same employment, and, if his pretentions are unfounded, he commits a species of fraud upon every man who employs him in reliance on his public profession. But no man, whether skilled or unskilled, undertakes that the task he assumes shall be performed successfully, and without fault or error. He undertakes for good faith and integrity, but not for infallibility, and he is liable to his employer for negligence, bad faith, or dishonesty, but not for losses consequent upon pure errors of judgment.

Auditors are expected to have keen auditing perceptions and the ability to make decisions or judgments that would escape the attention of others, but the *degree* of skill and diligence required of auditors (i.e., whether due professional care has been exercised) always comes into question when financial statements are disputed and audited businesses encounter serious financial difficulties. Mautz and Sharaf (1961) have elaborated the concept with these specific notions:

1. A prudent practitioner is presumed to
   a. Have a knowledge of the philosophy and practice of auditing,
   b. Have the degree of training, experience, and skill common to the average independent auditor,
   c. Have the ability to recognize indications of irregularities, and
   d. Keep abreast of developments in the perpetration and detection of irregularities.
2. Due audit care requires that the auditor
   a. Acquaint himself with the company under examination,
   b. Review the method of internal control operating in the company,
   c. Obtain any knowledge readily available that is pertinent to the accounting and financial problems of the company,
   d. Be responsive to unusual events and unusual circumstances,
   e. Persist until he has eliminated from his own mind any reasonable doubts he may have about the existence of material irregularities, and
   f. Exercise caution in instructing his assistants and reviewing their work.

SQCSs contribute to fulfillment of the due care standard by requiring that firms establish policies and procedures for assigning personnel to engagements, providing consultation resources on audit problems, and performing effective supervision and inspection. No single auditor acting individually can solve every conceivable problem, so firms must have policies for providing consultation with persons of knowledge, experience, and authority who can contribute to a solution. Larger CPA firms operate their own technical research services in national or regional offices, which receive inquiries from the field. All AICPA members can avail themselves of the technical information service at the AICPA in New York. Consultation can take many forms, but every firm needs to keep lines of communication open so that the expertise available from professional personnel can be shared.

Policies and procedures for effective supervision and inspection augment those for consultation. At the highest level of supervision, firms provide for the involvement of a concurring partner to review the audit report and the performance of the audit. This procedure is required for publicly held companies under the AICPA's SEC Practice Section rules; so also is the procedure of periodic quality control review (inspection) of audit working papers on a test basis. Supervision at other levels is carried out in the field in observance of the field work standards (described later in this chapter), and all these activities performed diligently synthesize into the accomplishment of due professional care.

Errors, Irregularities, and Illegal Acts. The concept of due professional care has a specific application in the search for errors (mistakes), irregularities (fraud), and illegal acts in a clients' records and financial statements. The auditor's responsibilities in performing this function have undergone upheaval in recent years. But due care is inevitably the contested issue and thus deserves a brief review in this context.

In 1961, Mautz and Sharaf (pp. 44–46) reflected the times by expressing one of the basic auditing assumptions: "There is no necessary conflict of interest between the auditor and the management of the enterprise under audit." They explained that both management and the auditor are interested in the long-run prosperity and progress of the enterprise. If auditors are unable to accept this assumption, they went on, audits would have to be so detailed and extensive as to become uneconomical, especially if managements are assumed at the outset to be untrustworthy. This view was to change following the dramatic events of the 1970s and 1980s. These events included corporate failures, massive frauds, and disclosures of illegal payoffs that caused strenuous public criticism of the business community and the accounting profession.

During this period, the U.S. Supreme Court cast the independent auditor as the "public watchdog."[6] (See Chapter 49.) This label was again applied during the Dingell Committee[7] congressional hearings of the mid-1980s. The public's perception of the auditor's responsibilities with respect to the detection of errors, irregularities, and illegal acts was significantly different from that of the independent auditor, resulting in what has become known as the "expectation gap."

The ASB addressed these expectation gap issues in several 1988 SASs setting forth the auditor's responsibilities for various misstatements in financial statements, that is, how he should exercise due care in specific areas. The following subsections briefly review the standards relating to errors and irregularities and illegal acts. (The additional 1988 SASs are mentioned at the conclusion of this chapter.)

Detection of errors and irregularities. Errors are usually defined as unintentional mistakes; *irregularities* are intentional distortions of financial statements. Persons who rely on financial statements look to an entity's internal controls and to independent audits for reasonable assurance that financial statements are not materially misstated as a result of errors or irregularities. SAS 16 (AU 327) gave the independent auditor the responsibility, within the inherent limitations of the auditing process: (1) to plan the examination to search for errors or irregularities that would have a material effect on the financial statements; and (2) to exercise due skill and care in the conduct of that examination. SAS 16 went on to say that the auditor's standard report implicitly indicates a belief that the financial statements taken as a whole are not materially misstated as a result of errors or irregularities.

---

[6] United States v. Arthur Young & Co. *et al.* 465 U.S. 805, 79 L. Ed. 2d 826, 104 S. Ct. 1495 (1984).

[7] Subcommittee on Oversight and Investigation of the Committee on Energy and Commerce, U.S. House of Representatives.

Many critics asserted that SAS 16 did not go far enough in establishing the responsibility of the independent auditor to detect material errors and irregularities. For example, the *Report of the National Commission on Fraudulent Financial Reporting* states (1987, p. 51):

Notwithstanding its specific requirement that the auditor has the obligation to plan his examination to search for irregularities, SAS No. 16 does not specify how such a search is to be conducted. Accordingly, the Commission recommends that the independent public accountant's responsibility for the detection of fraudulent financial reporting be restated. The auditing standards should include requirements to (1) assess the risk of fraudulent financial reporting and (2) design tests to provide reasonable assurance of detection.

The Commission appreciates the limitations inherent in the audit process. The auditor cannot and should not be held responsible for detecting all material frauds, particularly those involving careful concealment through forgery or collusion by members of management or management and third parties. Auditors nonetheless should be responsible for actively considering the potential for fraudulent financial reporting in a given audit engagement and for designing specific audit tests to recognize these risks.

Existing literature emphasizes the auditor's responsibility to assess the risk of error or irregularity at the specific account level. The existing literature does not require auditors to evaluate the control environment, and it allows the auditor to assume management integrity unless his examination reveals evidence to the contrary. The auditor's procedures thus do not focus at a sufficiently high level. Moreover, because the Commission has found that the majority of fraudulent financial reporting cases involve top management, the auditor should not assume management integrity but should apply professional skepticism to this determination.

SAS 53, *The Auditor's Responsibility to Detect and Report Errors and Irregularities* (AU 316), issued in 1988, was well along before the Treadway Commission first publicized its recommendation. SAS 53 addresses the Commission's concerns by requiring, in audits of financial statements for years beginning on or after January 1, 1989, that auditors assess the risk that material errors and irregularities exist. The auditor is then required to design the audit, based on the risk assessment, to provide reasonable assurance that material errors and irregularities are detected.

SAS 53 further instructs the auditor to plan and perform his audit with an attitude of professional skepticism, and assume neither that management is dishonest nor that it is totally forthright.

Illegal acts by clients. Many of the corporate disclosures of the mid-1970s involved illegal or questionable payments. SAS 17 (AU 328) explained the auditor's need to consider whether illegal acts may have occurred and to report them. Although an auditor is neither a legal expert nor an administrative enforcement agent, he should be generally familiar with business law and be able to recognize a possibly illegal act in the area of financially related transactions (those that enter into the accounting system, for example, income tax transactions and selling prices controlled by legislation or administrative rules). Actions that exist outside the accounting system, such as violation of health and safety laws and environmental control laws, are much less likely to be recognized by the auditor.

SAS 17 described some procedures to help the auditor identify possibly illegal acts by clients and directed him to seek legal counsel. If an illegal act was discovered, the auditor was directed to assess its materiality, with due regard to possible ramifications. For example, public disclosure of a relatively small bribe (say $100,000 in a billion dollar company) might endanger a large contract, a business license, or the right to operate in a foreign country. Findings were to be reported to a high level in the client organization, up to and including the audit committee, for appropriate action.

SAS 54, *Illegal Acts by Clients* (AU 317), was issued in 1988, and carries over much of the SAS 17 guidance. But it goes on to indicate that the auditor's responsibility to detect and report illegal acts having a material effect on the financial statements is the same as that described previously in SAS 53 for errors and irregularities. SAS 54 is also effective for audits of financial statements for years beginning on or after January 1, 1989.

STANDARDS OF FIELD WORK

All audits are different, except that any audit of financial statements is generally understood to involve unrestricted access to all the client's accounting information pertaining to the financial statements. Independent auditors are engaged to express opinions on these financial statements, and GAAS applies to these engagements. If the engagement is an audit but not an audit of financial statements presented in conformity with GAAP, GAAS nevertheless applies (AU 621.02).

Planning and Supervision

The auditing standards on planning and supervision are an extension of due professional care. The first field work standard declares: "The work is to be adequately planned and assistants, if any, are to be properly supervised" (AU 310.01).

Auditing standards point out that early appointment of the auditor is beneficial, so that time is available to plan the engagement in advance. Particularly helpful is the ability to perform some of the audit work before the fiscal year end and to plan for early confirmation of receivables and observation of inventories. Auditors may accept late appointments near or after year end, but auditing standards suggest particular attention in such cases to the problem of completing the audit satisfactorily. *Interim* audit work, which is performed before the client's fiscal year end, is also encouraged as a means of spreading the firm's workload more evenly over the year and of making planning and supervision more effective.

SAS 22, *Planning and Supervision* (AU 311), contains many suggestions for effective field work and establishes three definitive requirements:

1. A written audit program should be prepared.
2. The auditor should obtain a knowledge of the entity's business, its organization, and its operating characteristics.

3. Assistants should be informed of their responsibilities, the objectives of the procedures they are to perform, and the method by which they should document disagreements with the auditor in charge if they believe it necessary to be dissociated from the resolution of a disputed issue.

Consideration of the Internal Control Structure

An entity's internal control structure consists of the control environment, the accounting system, and control procedures. The auditor is to obtain an understanding of each of these elements to assess *control risk* — the risk that a material misstatement could occur and not be prevented or detected on a timely basis by the internal control structure.

After obtaining the understanding and assessing control risk, the auditor decides whether it is efficient and appropriate to obtain additional evidence to support the effectiveness of the entity's control structure. If so, this will influence the nature, timing, and extent of substantive tests in the audit.

Knowledge of the internal control structure is indispensable for planning the audit, and the testing of controls is essential in determining the degree of reliance an auditor can place on the control structure (see Chapters 7 and 8). When an internal control structure is found to be effective, auditing standards allow the auditor to limit or restrict substantive auditing procedures but not to eliminate them altogether. Consequently, regardless of the assessed level of control risk, substantive tests should be performed for significant account balances and transactions.

On the other hand, after obtaining an understanding of the internal control structure and assessing control risk, the auditor may decide not to place reliance on the internal control structure because he believes effective policies and procedures are not in place or because it would not be cost-efficient to evaluate their effectiveness.

Sufficient, Competent Evidence

Auditing is a *problem solving process* that can be viewed in four steps:

1. Formulate the problem so that evidence concerning it will permit a decision, either positive or negative.
2. Specify and perform procedures to collect such evidence.
3. Evaluate the sufficiency and competence of the evidence and determine whether its weight is positive or negative.
4. Make the decision.

The first step in this process is crucial. Auditors must be able to formulate all the problems that are implied in management's statements of financial transactions and events. For example, the balance sheet caption "Buildings—net of $130,000 accumulated depreciation . . . $70,000" actually contains several assertions, among them that the buildings exist, are owned by the company, are useful in the business, that they cost $200,000, and that the depreciation is computed properly. Each assertion is taken as a hypothesis and thus presents the problem of whether it should be accepted or rejected.

Auditors can expect to find empirical evidence supporting or denying a hypothesis in only a limited number of cases. The hypothesis that certain buildings exist, for example, can be tested empirically by going to see the buildings. In other cases, auditors can decide whether management's assertions are *warranted*, that is, supportable by evidence and by reference to generally accepted criteria for the type of assertion under audit. For the depreciation of a building, for example, auditors can read the contract or purchase agreement stating the cost and review the useful-life and depreciation figures to decide whether management's figure is appropriate. Auditors will then consider whether the utility of the building is impaired, based on evidence from other procedures such as analytical review. These procedures only produce evidence that can be used to decide whether the assertion must be rejected, as it would be if it were not in conformity with GAAP for historical cost basis accounting and for calculating depreciation. This simple example makes the point that evidence is the crux of performing the audit.

The decision-making methodology described above forms the basis for the third field work standard in GAAS: "Sufficient, competent evidential matter is to be obtained through inspection, observation, inquiries, and confirmations to afford a reasonable basis for an opinion regarding the financial statements under examination" (AU 326.01).

Evidence is considered *sufficient* when an auditor has enough of it to make a decision. How much is enough is a matter of professional judgment. Evidence is *competent* when it is relevant to the decision problem, reasonably objective, and free from bias. Whether it meets these criteria is also a matter of professional judgment. The auditor's professional judgment, in turn, depends on his independence, due professional care, training and proficiency, planning and supervision, and knowledge of the internal control system. Thus, the AICPA general and fieldwork standards constitute a coordinated system of theory that finds application in decision-making based on evidence.

Consultation With Others

Auditors often call on others for aid in the evidence gathering process, and several SASs provide guidance for this consultation. The standards briefly described in the following subsections set forth considerations for using the work of internal auditors and specialists, for inquiry of the client's lawyers, and for representations from the client's managers.

Internal Auditors. SAS 9 (AU 322) states that independent auditors cannot substitute the work of internal auditors for their own. In fact, they are not even required to consult with a client's internal auditors. When internal auditors are involved in the client's internal control structure, however, the independent auditor should acquire an understanding of the internal audit function. Going somewhat further, if the independent auditor decides that the internal auditors' work may have a bearing on his own procedures, he should (1) consider the competence and objectivity of the internal auditors and (2) evaluate their work. This coordination is explored in Chapter 7.

Internal audit personnel may perform procedures that would otherwise be performed by persons on the independent auditor's staff, but the independent auditor should supervise and test their work. All important judgments in an independent auditor's financial statement audit must be made by the independent auditor, and not delegated to internal auditors.

Specialists. A *specialist* is a person or firm possessing special skills or knowledge in a field other than accounting or auditing. Auditors frequently consult actuaries, appraisers, attorneys, engineers, and geologists for such services as the valuation of art works, estimation of mineral resources, actuarial determination of life insurance reserves, and interpretation of laws and regulations. SAS 11 (AU 336) states that when using a specialist the auditor should conduct inquiries or otherwise obtain satisfaction as to the specialist's professional qualifications and reputation. The auditor should also gain a general understanding of the methods and assumptions used by the specialist, be sure that the data the specialist is considering are the same data the auditor wants assessed (i.e., they tie in to the books), and know enough about the work to determine what bearing the specialist's findings have on financial statement information. Some testing and review of the specialist's work may be appropriate. In general, specialists should be independent of the client, but this is not always possible. Other chapters discuss specialists frequently used in the accounting and auditing process.

Lawyers. Auditors are required to obtain written responses from clients' lawyers concerning litigation in progress and other matters that might be accounted for and disclosed as contingencies in accordance with SFAS 5, *Accounting for Contingencies* (C59). SAS 12 (AU 337) sets forth procedures for obtaining representations from management and corroboration from the lawyers, and contains an illustrative inquiry letter and the American Bar Association's Statement of Policy regarding lawyers' responses. (See Chapter 26.)

Management. Auditors are required to obtain written representations from management, not as substitutes for evidence obtainable through other procedures, but to complement other audit evidence. In a few cases, management representations may be the primary source of information, for example, concerning related-party transactions and intentions to refinance short-term obligations on a long-term basis. SAS 19 (AU 333.04) gives an illustrative list of 20 points of information about which representations may be obtained. Representation letters are to be signed by responsible, informed members of management, normally the chief executive officer, the chief financial officer, and the chief accounting officer. The formality of this process is intended to impress upon management its primary responsibility for the financial statements and related disclosures.

STANDARDS OF REPORTING

Independent auditors' reports are of several types and have several variations, as explained in Chapter 11. The auditor's standard report was presented under "Audited Financial Statements" earlier in this chapter.

There are four summary reporting standards in GAAS. The first three are:

1. The report shall state whether the financial statements are presented in accordance with GAAP (AU 410.01).
2. The report shall identify those circumstances in which such principles have not been consistently observed in the current period in relation to the preceding period (AU 420.01).
3. Informative disclosures in the financial statements are to be regarded as reasonably accurate unless otherwise stated in the report (AU 430.01).

A major conceptual theme underlies these standards: the notion of *fair presentation* in financial reporting. Current practice reflects the auditor's assumption that application of GAAP results in the fair presentation of financial position and the results of operations. As Mautz and Sharaf (1961, pp. 47–48) have pointed out, this assumption is necessary if auditors are to have the benefit of *any* criteria for appropriate accounting.

Management has important prerogatives in selecting the accounting principles, procedures, and methods that in their opinion best reflect the effect of financial transactions and economic events on their business. Indeed, management bears primary responsibility for the financial statements and the decisions that go into preparing them. The troublesome decisions for auditors revolve around whether management's financial statements are presented fairly, in all material respects, in conformity with GAAP.

Fair Presentation

SAS 5, *The Meaning of "Present Fairly in Conformity with Generally Accepted Accounting Principles" in the Independent Auditor's Report* (AU 411), explains that the auditor's decision is based on his professional judgment as to whether:

1. The accounting principles selected and applied have general acceptance.
2. The accounting principles are appropriate in the circumstances.
3. The financial statements are sufficiently informative.
4. The financial statement information is classified and summarized in a manner that is neither too detailed nor too condensed.
5. The financial statements are presented within a range of acceptable limits that are reasonable and practicable to obtain.

"General acceptance" of accounting principles is established through *authoritative support*, which is automatically attributed to FASB statements and interpretations, to pronouncements issued by FASB predecessors (the APB and the CAP), and to GASB statements and interpretations. If no official pronouncement exists, SAS 5 (as amended by SAS 52) identifies numerous other formal sources that may provide guidance. But no amount of accounting pronouncements can cover every real-world condition properly, so auditors are allowed in very narrow circumstances to "break the rules." Rule 203 of the AICPA rules of conduct, quoted below, strongly acknowledges the role of officially pronounced accounting principles, but leaves some latitude for deviation, as the passage in italics indicates. The fact that only a few Rule 203 opinions have been issued on publicly held companies underscores the credence auditors place in GAAP.

A member [of the AICPA] shall not (1) express an opinion or state affirmatively that the financial statements or other financial data of any entity are presented in conformity with generally accepted accounting principles or (2) state that he or she is not aware of any material modifications that should be made to such statements or data in order for them to be in conformity with generally accepted accounting principles, if such statements or data contain any departure from an accounting principle promulgated by bodies designated by Council to establish such principles that has a material effect on the statements or data taken as a whole. *If, however, the statements or data contain such a departure and the member can demonstrate that due to unusual circumstances the financial statements or data would otherwise have been misleading, the member can comply with the rule by describing the departure, its approximate effects, if practicable, and the reasons why compliance with the principle would result in a misleading statement.* [ET 203.01; emphasis added]

To help auditors decide whether accounting principles are "appropriate in the circumstances," the standards provide that consideration should be given to whether the substance of transactions differs materially from their form, because reporting economic substance is recognized as paramount. However, the standards also state that individual auditors should not be expected to rule on the appropriateness of principles where alternatives exist (such as depreciation methods) and the FASB has not specified criteria for matching methods with circumstances. This area is a constant problem for auditors, because, as the Cohen Commission observed (CAR, 1978, p. 13), users of audited statements expect auditors to "evaluate the disclosures made by management and determine whether financial statements are misleading, even if they technically conform with authoritative accounting pronouncements."

Auditor's Report

The last three considerations set forth in SAS 5 need little explanation. All of them enable auditors to cope with the fourth AICPA reporting standard, which consists of two basic requirements (AU 150.02).

The first requirement is: "The report shall either contain an expression of opinion on the financial statements, taken as a whole, or an assertion to the effect that an opinion cannot be expressed. When an overall opinion cannot be expressed, the reasons therefor should be stated." This requirement divides opinion statements into two classes: opinions on statements taken as a whole, and disclaimers of opinion. An "overall opinion" in the context of this standard is an unmodified opinion. Thus, when an unmodified opinion is not given, all the substantive reasons must be explained.

The second requirement states: "In all cases where an auditor's name is associated with financial statements, the report should contain a clear-cut indication of the character of the auditor's examination, if any, and the degree of responsibility he is taking."

"In all cases" means precisely what it says. Every time auditors are associated by name or action with financial statements, they must report on their audit or other relationship and on their responsibility; detailed specifications are given in SAS 26 (AU 504). The character of an audit is usually described in the auditor's standard report as an audit conducted in accordance with GAAS. However, if the audit was restricted in some way, or if the statements were not audited, the independent accountant must say so in the scope paragraph.

The "degree of responsibility" is indicated by the form of the opinion. Auditors take full responsibility for their belief that the financial statements are (or are not) fairly presented in all material respects in conformity with GAAP when they give a standard (or an adverse) opinion. They take no such responsibility when giving the disclaimer of opinion. The various forms of opinions – standard (or unmodified), modified, qualified, adverse, and disclaimer – are explained more fully in Chapter 11.

INTERNAL AUDITING STANDARDS

The IIA went through a somewhat more elaborate process in formulating its *Standards for the Professional Practice of Internal Auditing.* A professional standards and responsibilities committee was formed in 1974 to develop these standards. Over the three years of its work, the committee included members from industry, banking, government, insurance, and academia, along with several experienced consultants. After some exposure of several drafts and publication of a tentative set of standards, the IIA board of directors adopted the final version in 1978.

While the original standards remain unchanged thus far, the Professional Standards and Responsibilities Committee (PSRC) of the IIA has issued several authoritative Statements on Internal Auditing Standards (SIAS), as follows:

* SIAS 1 – *Control: Concepts and Responsibilities,* provides guidance on the nature of control and the roles of participants in its establishment, maintenance, and evaluation (July 1983).
* SIAS 2 – *Communicating Results,* is an interpretation of an original standard and deals with report types, content, and attributes; discussion of findings and conclusions; and report approval and distribution (July 1983).
* SIAS 3 – *Deterrence, Detection, Investigation, and Reporting of Fraud,* interprets the original standards on due professional care and scope of work (May 1985).
* SIAS 4 – *Quality Assurance,* provides guidance for implementing a quality assurance program in an internal auditing department. It covers supervision, internal reviews by the director, and external quality reviews at least every three years (November 1986).
* SIAS 5 – *Internal Auditors' Relationships with Independent Outside Auditors,* deals with maximizing coordination, mutual access to working papers, and mutual understanding of audit technologies (June 1987).
* SIAS 6 – *Audit Working Papers,* covers objectives and preparation of working papers, and restrictions on access by other than the independent outside auditor (December 1987).

In addition, nonauthoritative guidance is presented in Professional Standards Bulletins (PSBs) prepared by the Standards Information Service Subcommittee of the PSRC. These are in question-and-answer form, with a series for each year beginning in 1981. While not codified, a topical index to the standards, SIASs, and PSBs adequately directs internal auditors to relevant coverage. In addition, tables of coverage by topics are available.

Independence

Internal auditors are required to "be objective in performing audits." This means that auditors should not subordinate their judgment to that of others; they should have an honest belief in their work product; they should not audit activities for which they had recent operating line authority or responsibility; and they should not design, install, or operate information systems that they will later be assigned to audit. IIA standards do not, however, expressly prohibit financial and business interests.

Technical Training and Proficiency

The IIA has four standards that deal directly with technical training and proficiency. Two focus on the internal auditing department as a whole and require that the department provide assurance that its collective technical proficiency, educational background, knowledge, skill, and discipline are adequate to its responsibilities. The other two standards focus on individual auditors and require that they possess the requisite knowledge, skills, and disciplines and can communicate with people effectively.

The IIA standards include one stating: "Internal auditors should maintain their technical competence through continuing education." This standard recognizes that maintaining proficiency and keeping abreast of current developments can be satisfied by attending conferences, seminars, college courses, and in-house training programs, and by participating in research projects. Note that if an internal auditor is a member of the AICPA he must abide by the AICPA Rules of the Code of Professional Conduct, and must also meet the AICPA's CPE requirements beginning in 1989.

Due Care

Internal auditors have a standard that is almost identical to the AICPA "due care" standard; and the IIA explanation parallels that of the AICPA standard. In addition IIA has a standard that states: ". . . internal auditors should follow up to ascertain that appropriate action is taken on reported audit findings."

Errors, Irregularities, and Illegal Acts

Internal auditing standards contain two statements concerning errors, irregularities, and illegal acts. The first, made in explanation of the IIA due professional care standard, states: ". . . internal auditors should be alert to the possibility of intentional wrongdoing, errors and omissions, inefficiency, waste, ineffectiveness, and conflicts of interest [and] to those conditions and activities where irregularities are most likely to occur." The second statement requires internal auditors to "review the systems established to ensure compliance with those policies, plans, procedures, laws, and regulations which could have a significant impact on operations and reports, and [to] determine whether the organization is in compliance."

Field Work Standards

Planning and Supervision. IIA standards covering planning and supervision are essentially the same as AICPA standards, but call on the director of internal auditing to coordinate internal audit efforts with those of the independent CPA firm.

The AICPA standards are not as explicit as the IIA's about requiring coordination of efforts with other auditors, but they do provide guidance on (1) where other independent auditors are involved in parts of the examination and (2) how to use the work and assistance of internal auditors. In practice, independent CPAs regularly coordinate their audit efforts with those of the client's internal auditors (see Chapter 7) and those of government auditors, to the extent possible.

Internal Control Evaluation. IIA standards also provide guidance for the study and evaluation of internal control. Since the scope of IIA audits may include more than financial statements, the standards specifically deal more with goals or objectives of internal control than with ensuring the reliability of financial statements. IIA standards require the internal auditor to evaluate the ability of systems to meet objectives of

- Reliability and integrity of information.
- Compliance with policies, plans, procedures, laws, and regulations.
- Safeguarding of assets.
- Economical and efficient use of resources.
- Accomplishment of established objectives and goals for operations or programs.

Other Standards

The IIA summary reporting standard is brief: "Internal auditors should report the results of their audit work." However, this has been considerably amplified by SIAS 2. Internal auditors need broad reporting standards because their wide range of assignments is simply not amenable to a standard report. Finally, IIA standards for evidence parallel the AICPA standards.

QUALITY CONTROL FOR A CPA FIRM

SQCSs and some of their particular features were mentioned earlier in this chapter. These standards, issued by the Quality Control Standards Committee (a senior technical committee of the AICPA), were inaugurated to separate professional quality control requirements from the basic SASs, which focus on individual engagement quality but not on quality assurance per se. Prior to the establishment of the Quality Control Standards Committee, the AudSEC had issued SAS 4 (subsequently superseded by SAS 25), *Quality Control Considerations for a Firm of Independent Auditors* (AU 161, December 1974); and the SAS 4 elements were subsumed into the first SQCS as the starting point.

SQCS 1, *System of Quality Control for a CPA Firm* (QC 10), applies to all members of the AICPA's Division for Firms (both SEC and Private Practice Sections) and requires that a CPA firm shall have a system of quality control that includes, in a manner suitable to its organizational structure, the following elements (QC 10.07):

a. *Independence.* Policies and procedures should be established to provide the firm with reasonable assurance that persons at all organizational levels maintain independence to the extent required by the Rules of the Code of Professional Conduct of the AICPA.

b. *Assigning Personnel to Engagements.* Policies and procedures for assigning personnel to engagements should be established to provide the firm with reasonable assurance that work will be performed by persons having the degree of technical training and proficiency required in the circumstances.

c. *Consultation.* Policies and procedures for consultation should be established to provide the firm with reasonable assurance that personnel will seek assistance, to the extent required, from persons having appropriate levels of knowledge, competence, judgment, and authority.

d. *Supervision.* Policies and procedures for the conduct and supervision of work at all organizational levels should be established to provide the firm with reasonable assurance that the work performed meets the firm's standards of quality.

e. *Hiring.* Policies and procedures for hiring should be established to provide the firm with reasonable assurance that those employed possess the appropriate characteristics to enable them to perform competently.

f. *Professional Development.* Policies and procedures for professional development should be established to provide the firm with reasonable assurance that personnel will have the knowledge required to enable them to fulfill responsibilities assigned.

g. *Advancement.* Policies and procedures for advancing personnel should be established to provide the firm with reasonable assurance that the people selected will have the qualifications necessary for fulfillment of the responsibilities they will be called on to assume.

h. *Acceptance and Continuance of Clients.* Policies and procedures should be established for deciding whether to accept or continue a client in order to minimize the likelihood of association with a client whose management lacks integrity.

i. *Inspection.* Policies and procedures for inspection should be established to provide the firm with reasonable assurance that the procedures relating to the other elements of quality control are being effectively applied.

In addition, SQCS 1 requires (1) assignment of responsibilities to personnel to provide for effective implementation, (2) effective communication of the policies and procedures throughout the firm, and (3) monitoring so that the system retains its effectiveness.

On the basis of having such a system in place and described in a quality control document, a firm is able to undergo a peer review (see Chapter 45) as required by the rules of the AICPA.

Although this chapter has focused on the ten basic GAAS and the continual binding interpretations thereof through SASs, it is clear that audits are not performed in a vacuum; most are performed by firms of all sizes and kinds. The SQCSs have assisted in standardizing firm practices that each firm previously had to invent on its own.

ATTESTATION ENGAGEMENTS

As mentioned earlier in this chapter, auditors in recent years have been requested to provide a variety of reports on other than historical financial statements (e.g., reports on descriptions of systems of internal control and computer software; compliance with statutory, regulatory, and contractual requirements; investment performance statistics; and supplemental information to financial statements).

GAAS has been increasingly difficult to apply to these types of engagements. Accordingly, in 1986 the ASB and the Accounting and Review Services Committee of the AICPA issued its first Statement on Standards for Attestation Engagements (AU 2000). This release, entitled *Attestation Standards*, does not supersede any of the existing standards in SASs or SSARs, or the *Statement on Standards for Accountants' Services on Prospective Financial Information* (AU 2100). See Figure 5.2 for a comparison of the attestation standards with GAAS. Specifically, the attestation standards address the following issues:

- An attest engagement is defined as one in which a CPA is engaged to issue or issues a written communication that expresses a conclusion about the reliability of a written assertion that is the responsibility of another party.
- For all attest engagements, standards are provided that are a natural extension of (but do not supersede) the ten GAAS.
- Five preconditions exist for the performance of attest services:
  - The practitioner has adequate training and proficiency in the attest function.
  - The practitioner has adequate knowledge of the subject matter.
  - There are reasonable measurement and disclosure criteria concerning the subject matter.
  - The assertions are capable of reasonably consistent estimation or measurement using such criteria.
  - The practitioner is independent.
- Two levels of attest assurance are available for general distribution reporting:
  - Positive assurance, in reports that express conclusions on the basis of an "examination."
  - Negative assurance, in reports that express conclusions on the basis of a "review."
- Attest services may be based on agreed-upon procedures or agreed-upon criteria, as long as the report is restricted to the parties who agreed to those procedures or criteria.

Attestation Standards	Generally Accepted Auditing Standards
GENERAL STANDARDS	
1. The engagement shall be performed by a practitioner or practitioners having adequate technical training and proficiency in the attest function.	1. The examination is to be performed by a person or persons having adequate technical training and proficiency as an auditor.
2. The engagement shall be performed by a practitioner or practitioners having adequate knowledge in the subject matter of the assertion.	
3. The practitioner shall perform an engagement only if he or she has reason to believe that the following two conditions exist: • The assertion is capable of evaluation against reasonable criteria that either have been established by a recognized body or are stated in the presentation of the assertion in a sufficiently clear and comprehensive manner for a knowledgeable reader to be able to understand them. • The assertion is capable of reasonably consistent estimation or measurement using such criteria.	
4. In all matters relating to the engagement, an independence in mental attitude shall be maintained by the practitioners.	2. In all matters relating to the assignment, an independence in mental attitude is to be maintained by the auditor or auditors.
5. Due professional care shall be exercised in the performance of the engagement.	3. Due professional care is to be exercised in the performance of the examination and the preparation of the report.
STANDARDS OF FIELDWORK	
1. The work shall be adequately planned and assistants, if any, shall be properly supervised.	1. The work is to be adequately planned and assistants, if any, are to be properly supervised.
	2. There is to be a proper study and evaluation of the existing internal control as a basis for reliance thereon and for the determination of the resultant extent of the tests to which auditing procedures are to be restricted.
2. Sufficient evidence shall be obtained to provide a reasonable basis for the conclusion that is expressed in the report.	3. Sufficient competent evidential matter is to be obtained through inspection, observation, inquiries, and confirmations to afford a reasonable basis for an opinion regarding the financial statements under examination.

(continued)

FIG. 5.2 Comparison of Attestation Standards With Generally Accepted Auditing Standards
Source: Attestation Standards (AU 2010.77).

Attestation Standards	Generally Accepted Auditing Standards
STANDARDS OF REPORTING	
1. The report shall identify the assertion being reported on and state the character of the engagement.	
2. The report shall state the practitioner's conclusion about whether the assertion is presented in conformity with the established or stated criteria against which it was measured.	1. The report shall state whether the financial statements are presented in accordance with generally accepted accounting principles.
	2. The report shall identify those circumstances in which such principles have not been consistently observed in the current period in relation to the preceding period.
	3. Informative disclosures in the financial statements are to be regarded as reasonably adequate unless otherwise stated in the report.
3. The report shall state all of the practitioner's significant reservations about the engagement and the presentation of the assertion.	4. The report shall either contain an expression of opinion regarding the financial statements, taken as a whole, or an assertion to the effect that an opinion cannot be expressed. When an overall opinion cannot be expressed, the reasons therefore should be stated. In all cases where an auditor's name is associated with financial statements, the report should contain a clear-cut indication of the character of the auditor's examination, if any, and the degree of responsibility he is taking.
4. The report on an engagement to evaluate an assertion that has been prepared in conformity with agreed-upon criteria or on an engagement to apply agreed-upon procedures should contain a statement limiting its use to the parties who have agreed upon such criteria or procedures.	

FIG. 5.2 (continued)

Examples of professional services typically provided by a practitioner that would *not* be considered attest engagements include:

• Providing advice or recommendations to a client as a part of a management consulting engagement (however, this does not apply to attest portions of consulting engagements as discussed later).

• Advocating a client's position (e.g., tax matters being reviewed by the IRS).

• Preparing tax returns or providing tax advice.

• Compiling financial statements (because the practitioner is not required to examine or review any evidence supporting the information furnished by the client and does not express any conclusion on its reliability).

• Solely to assist the client (e.g., acting as the company accountant in preparing information other than financial statements).

• Testifying as an expert witness in accounting, auditing, taxation, or other matters, given certain stipulated facts.

• Providing an expert opinion on certain points of principle, such as the application of tax laws or accounting standards given specific facts provided by another party, so long as the expert opinion does not express a conclusion about the reliability of the facts provided by the other party.

As Figure 5.2 shows, many of the attestation standards are similar to GAAS, especially with respect to training and proficiency, independence, due professional care, planning and supervision, and the gathering of evidence. Significant differences exist, however, with respect to (1) the measurement and disclosure criteria against which an assertion is to be evaluated, and (2) reporting on the engagement.

Assertion Criteria

Under GAAS, the measurement and disclosure benchmark against which assertions in historical financial statements are evaluated is GAAP. In attestation engagements, such criteria may come not only from GAAP but also from pronouncements by regulatory agencies and other bodies composed of experts following due process procedures.

Criteria established by industry associations or similar groups that do not follow due process procedures should be carefully considered. Such criteria lack authoritative support and may not be reasonable for the purpose of the assertion. The criteria should, above all, yield information that is useful, that is, relevant to the purpose of the assertion and reliable as to measurement.

In this regard, the staff of the AICPA's Auditing Standards Division issued an interpretation of *Attestation Standards* in early 1988 that precludes CPAs from providing any form of assurance, through examination, review, or agreed-upon procedures engagements, that an entity:

• Is not insolvent at the time debt is incurred or would not be rendered insolvent thereby;
• Does not have unreasonably small capital;
• Has the ability to pay its debts as they mature.

Providing such assurance is precluded because these matters are concepts subject to definition and interpretation that are not clearly defined in a legal or accounting sense. Consequently, they do not provide the CPA with the reasonable criteria required to evaluate assertions about solvency under the attestation standards. (See Chapter 23 for a further discussion.)

Reporting

In a report on assertions, the practitioner refers to a separate presentation of the assertions. This is analogous to referring to the audited financial statements in an auditor's report. As is the case in an audit engagement, the assertions and their presentation are the responsibility on the asserter.

The practitioner's report describes the nature and scope of the work performed (examination, review, or agreed-upon procedures), and either refers to the professional standards governing the engagement (e.g., GAAS) when they have been formally promulgated or to "standards established by the AICPA" when they have not.

We have examined the accompanying [*identify the presentation of assertions — for example, Statement of Investment Performance Statistics of XYZ Fund for the year ended December 31, 19X1*]. Our examination was made in accordance with standards established by the American Institute of Certified Public Accountants and, accordingly, included such procedures as we considered necessary in the circumstances.

[*Additional paragraph(s) may be added to emphasize certain matters relating to the attest engagement or the presentation of assertions.*]

In our opinion, the [*identify the presentation of assertions — for example, Statement of Investment Performance Statistics*] referred to above presents [*identify the assertion — for example, the investment performance of XYZ Fund for the year ended December 31, 19X1*] in conformity with [*identify established or stated criteria — for example, the measurement and disclosure criteria set forth in Note 1*].

FIG. 5.3 Example of Unmodified Report on Examination of the Presentation of an Assertion
Source: Attestation Engagements (AU 2010.54).

We have reviewed the accompanying [*identify the presentation of assertions — for example, Statement of Investment Performance Statistics of XYZ Fund for the year ended December 31, 19X1*]. Our review was conducted in accordance with standards established by the American Institute of Certified Public Accountants.

A review is substantially less in scope than an examination, the objective of which is the expression of an opinion on the [*identify the presentation of assertions — for example, Statement of Investment Performance Statistics*]. Accordingly, we do not express such an opinion.

[*Additional paragraph(s) may be added to emphasize certain matters relating to the attest engagement or the presentation of assertions.*]

Based on our review, nothing came to our attention that caused us to believe that the accompanying [*identify the presentation of assertions — for example, Statement of Investment Performance Statistics*] is not presented in conformity with [*identify the established or stated criteria — for example, the measurement and disclosure criteria set forth in Note 1*].

FIG. 5.4 Example of Unmodified Review Report on the Presentation of an Assertion
Source: Attestation Engagements (AU 2010.58).

For agreed-upon procedures the report will refer to conformity of such procedures with the arrangements agreed to by the specific users of the assertion. Examples of each type of report are presented in Figure 5.3 (examination), Figure 5.4 (review), and Figure 5.5 (agreed-upon procedures). These examples illustrate unqualified opinions on the presentation of the assertions. As with auditor's reports, however, reports on assertions may be similarly qualified or modified.

When the presentation of assertions is in conformity with criteria that have been specified and agreed upon by the asserter and the user, the practitioner's report should state that use of the report is limited to the specified parties (as required by the fourth reporting standard) and, when applicable, indicate that the presentation differs materially from that which would have been presented if intended for general distribution. (For example, financial statements prepared in accordance with criteria

---

To ABC Inc. and XYZ Fund

We have applied the procedures enumerated below to the accompanying [*identify the presentation of assertions – for example, Statement of Investment Performance Statistics of XYZ Fund for the year ended December 31, 19X1*]. These procedures, which were agreed to by ABC Inc. and XYZ Fund, were performed solely to assist you in evaluating [*identify the assertion – for example, the investment performance of XYZ Fund*]. This report is intended solely for your information and should not be used by those who did not participate in determining the procedures.

[*Include paragraph to enumerate procedures and findings.*]

These agreed-upon procedures are substantially less in scope than an examination, the objective of which is the expression of an opinion on the [*identify the presentation of assertions – for example, Statement of Investment Performance Statistics*]. Accordingly, we do not express such an opinion.

Based on the application of the procedures referred to above, nothing came to our attention that caused us to believe that the accompanying [*identify the presentation of assertions – for example, Statement of Investment Performance Statistics*] is not presented in conformity with [*identify the established, stated, or agreed-upon criteria – for example, the measurement and disclosure criteria set forth in Note 1*]. Had we performed additional procedures or had we made an examination of the [*identify the presentation of assertions – for example, Statement of Investment Performance Statistics*], other matters might have come to our attention that would have been reported to you.

FIG. 5.5 Example of Agreed-Upon Procedures Report on the Presentation of an Assertion
Source: Attestation Engagements (AU 2010.62).

specified in a contract may differ materially from statements prepared in conformity with GAAP.)

Consulting Engagements Involving Attest Services

In December 1987 the Management Advisory Services Executive Committee of the AICPA issued an amendment to the Attestation Standards (AU 2010.71–.76), which states that when a practitioner provides an attest service as part of a consulting engagement, the Statements on Standards for Attestation Engagements apply, but only to the engagement portion involving the attest service. The Statements on Standards for Management Advisory Services apply to the balance of the consulting engagement. Thus the practitioner should issue separate reports on the attest and consulting portions of the engagement.

Proposal to Report on MD&A

In early 1987, the AICPA issued an exposure draft of a proposed Statement on Standards for Attestation Engagements, *Examination of Management's Discussion and Analysis* (AICPA, 1987i). The proposed statement, if approved, would add another attestation standard to those discussed previously. The AICPA has tabled this proposal pending a decision by the SEC on its own proposal for MD&A reporting and disclosure. See Chapter 4 for a discussion of this matter.

THE AUDITOR'S ROLE AND SOCIETY'S EXPECTATIONS

In the past, CPAs have relied almost solely on the accounting and auditing standards (GAAP and GAAS) to define their responsibilities to preparers and users of financial information. But the harsh criticism of the profession in the 1970s and 1980s has given the CPA a new perspective—he now understands that professional standards must reach beyond his own view of the auditor's role and consider as well society's expectations of what it is the independent CPA should do.

The profession has attempted to respond to these concerns with the adoption in 1988 of a new Code of Professional Conduct and the issuance of nine "expectation gap" SASs as follows:

* *The Auditor's Responsibility to Detect and Report Errors and Irregularities* (SAS 53). This SAS supersedes SAS 16, *The Independent Auditor's Responsibility for the Detection of Errors or Irregularities,* and requires the auditor to design the audit to provide reasonable assurance of detecting material misstatements.

* *Illegal Acts by Clients* (SAS 54). This SAS supersedes SAS 17 of the same title. It defines the auditor's responsibility for detecting illegal acts that could have a direct and material effect on financial statement amounts as being equal to that for detecting errors and irregularities.

* *Consideration of the Internal Control Structure in a Financial Statement Audit* (SAS 55). This SAS supersedes AU 320, *The Auditor's Study and Evaluation of Internal Control.* SAS 55 broadens the auditor's responsibility to study and evaluate internal control when planning an audit and incorporates the concepts of audit evidence and audit risk.

* *Analytical Procedures* (SAS 56). This SAS supersedes SAS 23, *Analytical Review Procedures,* and requires the use of analytical procedures in the planning and the final review stages of all audit engagements. It also provides guidance on the development and use of analytical procedures, and on their effectiveness and efficiency in detecting errors and irregularities.

* *Auditing Accounting Estimates* (SAS 57). This SAS describes procedures an auditor may consider in evaluating the reasonableness of accounting estimates. It also identifies internal control structure elements that may reduce the likelihood of material misstatements of estimates.

* *Reports on Audited Financial Statements* (SAS 58). This SAS is intended to help financial statement users better understand the auditor's role. It requires the auditor's standard report to explicitly address the responsibility assumed by auditors, the procedures they perform, and the assurances they provide. This SAS also eliminates the use of opinions qualified for uncertainties and revises the second standard of reporting by requiring the auditor's report to address consistency only when accounting principles have not been consistently applied.

* *The Auditor's Consideration of an Entity's Ability to Continue as a Going Concern* (SAS 59). This SAS supersedes SAS 34, *The Auditor's Consideration When a Question Arises About an Entity's Continued Existence,* and requires the auditor to consider, in *all* engagements, the continued existence of the entity. Furthermore, although SAS 58 eliminates the "subject to" opinion qualification for "going concern" uncertainties, SAS 59 requires the auditor to modify his report with an explanatory final paragraph when substantial doubt exists about an entity's ability to continue in existence.

* *Communication of Internal Control Structure Related Matters Noted in an Audit* (SAS 60). This SAS supersedes SAS 20, *Required Communication of Material Weaknesses in Internal Accounting Control,* and sections of SAS 30, *Reporting on Internal Accounting Control.* SAS

60 requires auditors to report "reportable conditions" – a concept that is broader than material weaknesses. This SAS also prescribes a form of written communication of reportable conditions that is more intelligible than the report on internal control presented in SAS 30.

- *Communication with Audit Committees* (SAS 61). This SAS requires auditors to ensure that persons responsible for oversight of auditing and financial reporting (such as audit committees) are informed about certain matters related to the conduct of an audit.

Whether these actions by the profession will ultimately satisfy the needs of our society remains to be seen. However, the accounting profession's responsiveness to those needs and expectations, and its ability to change and adapt over time, are very significant.

All the attention focused on auditors during the last two decades emphasizes their crucial role in today's world – adding assurance and credibility to the information that serves as our commercial life's blood. Ultimately, auditors are public servants in the best sense of the phrase. Today's risks and challenges, then, should be looked on as opportunities for personal and professional growth and an open invitation to employ professional skills in solving numerous vexing problems. Taking advantage of these many opportunities, however, requires creativity, imagination, leadership, hard work, and sacrifice. In the past, the profession has demonstrated its willingness to step up to its responsibilities. It will do so in the future.

6

The Audit Committee

OVERVIEW

As the issues affecting directors' responsibilities expand, requiring more knowledge
and decision making in a diminishing time frame, the importance of directors' effectiveness and efficiency is rising. A major factor contributing to board effectiveness
and efficiency is the board committee structure.

Committees are formed to fulfill, not expand, the board's responsibilities. In
essence, they allow directors to increase their scrutiny of specific issues by assigning
these matters to committees. Over the past decade, the audit committee has become a
focus of corporate accountability and governance. It plays an integral role for the
board, especially with respect to the integrity of the company's financial information

and controls, and the legal and ethical conduct of company representatives. Active audit committees now operate on the boards of most large buinesses and many non-profit organizations.[1]

Advocates of audit committees include the New York and American Stock Exchanges, the SEC, the AICPA, and virtually all CPA firms.

Membership on the audit committee offers the director a broad overview of the company's financial operations. This insight provides a valuable basis for shaping the company's future. To contribute successfully, most committee members find that the quality and focus of information is what is important – not its volume.

This chapter covers the audit committee's principal responsibilities and meetings, as well as the relationships that exist among the board of directors, audit committee, management, internal auditors, and independent accountants. In addition, numerous proposals affecting the audit committee, made in 1987 by the National Commission on Fraudulent Financial Reporting (Treadway Commission), are discussed in the following section.

The origin of audit committees is obscure. Boards of banks and other financial institutions are among the earliest known to have had audit committees, perhaps because these companies were required by statute to conduct audits. The Prudential Insurance Company of America, for instance, has had an audit committee for over 75 years.

Audit committees first received public attention when the New York Stock Exchange report on the infamous *McKesson and Robbins* case (New York Stock Exchange, 1939) strongly endorsed audit committees as a means of assuring auditor independence: "Where practicable, the selection of the auditors by a special committee of the board composed of directors who are not officers of the company appears desirable." The SEC expressed a similar opinion about the case in 1940 (ASR 19, now in AAER 1).

Initially, these early endorsements of audit committees by the New York Stock Exchange and the SEC had very little effect. In 1967 the AICPA recommended that publicly owned companies establish audit committees composed of outside directors (AICPA, 1967b), but by 1970 not much progress had been made; survey research indicated that the audit committee concept was not being widely used (Mautz and Neumann, 1970, p. 15). In 1977 the AICPA repeated its recommendation (AICPA, 1979d, p. 1) and urged its members to encourage their clients to establish audit committees, but the impetus was primarily in response to congressional pressures (see Chapter 45) aimed at laxities in corporate governance.

In addition to requiring audit committees as part of specific consent settlements, the SEC has used its rule-making authority to encourage audit committee formation generally. It first required disclosure of the existence or nonexistence of audit committees in 1974 (ASR 165, now in FRR §§ 601 and 603), and it strengthened those reporting requirements in its corporate governance rules released in late 1978

---

[1] This chapter is written in the context of the audit committee of a publicly held company, because the preponderance of discussion, proposals, and rules deal with public business enterprises. However, the chapter is equally applicable to fiduciary institutions that are not publicly traded: numerous kinds of nonbusiness enterprises, such as eleemosynary institutions or nonproprietary hospitals, and larger privately held businesses, especially if there are major outside lenders. Though the chapter encourages separate audit committees, if this is not feasible or desirable, many of the guidelines and suggestions can be used directly by a board of directors or board of trustees.

(Release 34-15384). This Release amended Item 7 of Schedule 14A of the proxy rules, but a more persuasive force for creating audit committees has been the prospect that the SEC would adopt even more requirements. The SEC has been vocal about the idea that audit committees should be *required* if an audit is to be performed in accordance with GAAS.

THE TREADWAY COMMISSION

In October 1987, the National Commission on Fraudulent Financial Reporting (the Treadway Commission) issued its finalized recommendations (NCFFR, 1987), aimed at reducing the incidence of fraudulent reporting. The Commission was an independent private sector initiative, jointly sponsored by the AICPA, American Accounting Association, Financial Executives Institute, Institute of Internal Auditors, and National Association of Accountants.

The Treadway Commission's objectives were threefold:

1. Determine what causes fraudulent reporting, and what environmental factors are involved.
2. Define the auditor's role in preventing, detecting, and reporting fraud.
3. Identify those corporate structures and attitudes that contribute to the problem.

The Treadway Commission's concentration on audit committees is apparent throughout its report. In addition, its report presents (in Appendix I) "Good Practice Guidelines for the Audit Committee," tying together the numerous applicable recommendations. Because of the contemporary significance of the Commission's Report, the complete "Guidelines" are reproduced as Appendix 6.

Not explored here but undoubtedly of interest to audit committee members is the Commission's recommendation that the SEC should reconsider its long-standing position that it is contrary to public policy for independent directors to be indemnified by the company for liabilities under the Securities Act of 1933. Recognizing the difficulty in attracting qualified independent directors due to liability concerns, the Commission has taken note of certain state-level actions that minimize the risks involved in normal directorship pursuits, and has asked the SEC to follow suit.

The Treadway Commission's recommendations will have an effect on all audit committees. In some cases, the AICPA or the SEC may require auditors to take certain steps that necessarily involve the audit committee (see the "Audit Committee Relationships" section of this chapter for certain AICPA actions); in other cases, regulators may make rules that directly affect the committee. The effects will be felt in the near term, and all audit committees should review their mode of operations and scope of coverage to assure that they, and management and the auditors, meet the spirit of the recommendations as well as the specific requirements, now and as they become promulgated.

A summary listing of the Commission's forty-nine recommendations for public companies, independent accountants, regulators and educators is contained in the Appendix to Chapter 45. In this chapter the focus is on recommendations directly or indirectly affecting audit committees, discussed immediately below and as appropriate throughout this chapter.

Corporate Environment

The Commission begins with the "tone at the top" – the environment established by management, within which corporate financial reporting occurs. Invariably, the views of the audit committee underlie this environment. The specific recommendations (paraphrased) for management are:

- Oversee the financial reporting process; identify, understand, and assess the factors that may cause the company's financial statements to be fraudulently misstated.
- Maintain internal controls to provide reasonable assurance that fraudulent financial reporting will be prevented or subject to early detection.
- Develop and enforce written codes of corporate conduct.
- Maintain accounting functions that are designed to meet the company's financial reporting obligations.

Internal Auditing

The Commission especially focuses on internal auditors in this series of recommendations, in recognition of the fact that in more than a few situations the internal audit function has not been given the significant role it ought to occupy. The audit committee can assure that the internal auditors provide the full measure of their potential. The recommendations relating to internal auditing (paraphrased) are:

- Maintain an effective internal audit function staffed with an adequate number of qualified personnel appropriate to the size and the nature of the company.
- Ensure that internal audit functions are objective.
- Consider the implications of their nonfinancial audit findings for the company's financial statements.
- Be involved in the audit of the entire financial reporting process and properly coordinated with the independent public accountant.

Audit Committee Activities and Responsibilities

The majority of the Treadway Commission's recommendations for public companies specifically mention the audit committee, leaving little doubt as to the Commission's belief that this is the seat of corporate financial governance. The recommendations relating to the audit committee's role (paraphrased) are:

- Be required by SEC rule to exist and be comprised solely of independent directors.
- Be informed, vigilant, and effective overseers of the financial reporting process and the company's internal controls.
- Develop a written charter setting forth the duties and responsibilities of the committee.
- Have adequate resources and authority to discharge the committee's responsibilities.

- Review management's evaluation of factors related to the independence of the company's public accountant.
- Before the beginning of each year, review management's plans for engaging the company's auditor to perform management advisory services during the coming year, considering both the types of services that may be rendered and the projected fees.
- Oversee the quarterly reporting process, including approving financial results prior to public release.

Management and Audit Committee Reports

More extensive communication with financial statement users is also a goal of the Treadway Commission. It seems axiomatic that if management and the audit committee are required to publish a report on their activities and responsibilities, they will give thorough consideration to whether they have diligently performed them. In addition, one recommendation is made regarding "shopping" for accounting answers. The recommendations for reporting (paraphrased) are:

- All public companies should be required by SEC rule to include in their annual reports to stockholders management reports signed by the chief executive officer and the chief accounting officer and/or the chief financial officer. The management report should acknowledge management's responsibilities for the financial statements and internal control, discuss how these responsibilities were fulfilled, and provide management's assessment of the effectiveness of the company's internal controls.
- All public companies should be required by SEC rule to disclose publicly the nature of any material accounting or auditing issue discussed with its old and new auditor during the three-year period preceding a change in auditors.
- All public companies should be required by SEC rule to include in the annual reports to stockholders a letter signed by the chairman of the audit committee describing the committee's responsibilities and activities during the year.
- The audit committee should be advised when management seeks a second opinion on a significant accounting issue.

ESTABLISHING THE AUDIT COMMITTEE

There are no prescribed rules for the establishment and operation of an audit committee. The New York Stock Exchange is the only exchange to *require* audit committees for certain companies. But its policy (Figure 6.1) does not define the responsibilities to be discharged. Though the SEC has used its rule-making authority to encourage the formation of audit committees and the AICPA has considered whether they are necessary for the accomplishment of an audit, neither organization has actually made them a requirement. The SEC has indicated its support for the Treadway Committee recommendation that would mandate audit committees (NCFFR, 1987, p. 40), but would prefer that some other body issue the rule. This may be wishful thinking because the SEC seems to be the only access to *all* public companies. However as of mid-1988 no specific implementation steps had been taken.

Exchange Policy

Each domestic company with common stock listed on the Exchange, as a condition of listing and continued listing of its securities on the Exchange, shall establish no later than June 30, 1978 and maintain thereafter an Audit Committee comprised solely of directors independent of management and free from any relationship that, in the opinion of its Board of Directors, would interfere with the exercise of independent judgment as a committee member. Directors who are affiliates of the company, or officers or employees of the company or its subsidiaries, would not be qualified for Audit Committee membership.

A director who was formerly an officer of the company or any of its subsidiaries may qualify for membership even though he may be receiving pension or deferred compensation payments from the company if, in the opinion of the Board of Directors, such person will exercise independent judgment and will materially assist the function of the committee. However, a majority of the Audit Committee shall be directors who were not formerly officers of the company or any of its subsidiaries.

Supplementary Material

In order to deal with the complex relationships that may arise, the following guidelines are provided to assist the Board of Directors to observe the spirit of the policy in selecting members of the Audit Committee.

A director who has been or is a partner, officer or director of an organization that has customary commercial, industrial, banking, or underwriting relationships with the company which are carried on in the ordinary course of business on an arm's length basis may qualify for membership unless, in the opinion of the Board of Directors, such director is not independent of management or the relationship would interfere with the exercise of independent judgment as a committee member.

A director who, in addition to fulfilling the customary director's role, also provides additional services directly for the Board of Directors and is separately compensated therefor, would nonetheless qualify for membership on the Audit Committee. However, a director who, in addition to his director's role, also acts on a regular basis as an individual or representative of an organization serving as a professional advisor, legal counsel or consultant to management, would not qualify if, in the opinion of the Board of Directors, such relationship is material to the company, the organization represented or the director.

A director who represents or is a close relative of a person who would not qualify as a member of the Audit Committee in the light of the policy would likewise not qualify for the committee. However, if the director is a close relative of an employee who is not an executive officer or if there are valid countervailing reasons, the Board of Directors' decision as to eligibility shall govern.

While Rule 405 under the Securities Act of 1933 may be helpful to the Board of Directors in determining whether a particular director is an affiliate or a close relative for purposes of this policy, it is not intended to be so technically applied as to go beyond the spirit of this policy.

FIG. 6.1   New York Stock Exchange Policy on Audit Committees
Source: New York Stock Exchange Listed Company Manual.

The functions assigned to audit committees will vary with the structure and phi-losophy of each board of directors—factors that must be articulated by the board. Generally, audit committee responsibilities are grounded in

* *A broad understanding* of the relationships between the company's operations and its finan-cial position and performance,
* An *awareness* of the company's major financial, economic, and operating risks,
* An *informed view* of the effectiveness of the company's internal control structure.

The existence of an audit committee does not diminish management's primary responsibility for the financial statements and for operating the business, nor the outside auditor's responsibility for independently attesting to the fair presentation of the financial statements in conformity with GAAP. Rather, the audit committee needs to be satisfied that both management's and the outside auditor's responsibili-ties are appropriately carried out.

Committees operate most effectively when there is a clear, preferably written, delineation of their responsibilities and authority. This often takes the form of a charter, resolved by the entire board, stating the committee's purpose, composition, duties, and, in broad terms, its agenda. Figure 6.2 is a sample of an audit committee charter.

Committee Membership

Normally, boards of directors establish audit committees with at least three mem-bers, limit membership terms, and stagger the terms to ensure continuity. In a survey of 50 corporate audit committees compiled by *Directors & Boards* (1984) from proxy documents, committee membership ranged from 3 to 9, with 82 percent of the com-mittees consisting of 3 to 5 members. Generally, one director is appointed by the board chairman to head the committee; some committees may elect their own chairmen.

An audit committee member's knowledge of accounting and auditing matters needs to be extensive in breadth, but not necessarily in depth. Financial accounting and reporting cover a vast area and are governed by GAAP, regulatory requirements, and industry practices. Audit performance and reporting standards—generally accepted auditing standards (GAAS)—are important to audit committee members. Although members are not expected to be expert in all these areas or to understand the fine details, a working knowledge of the basics is necessary. Of course, as is the case for all directors, an understanding of the company's industry is required for members to recognize what is significant and to focus their knowledge on effective and efficient committee action.

Independence

Independence has been the most debated issue surrounding audit committees. The practice of barring otherwise qualified board members from the audit committee because they lack independence, whether apparent or real, is a debatable issue. Should only outside directors be audit committee members? The only definitive

The board of directors of XYZ Corporation hereby constitutes and establishes an audit committee with authority, responsibility, and specific duties as described in the following text.

Composition

The committee shall be comprised of three directors who are independent of management and operating executives. Their terms shall be staggered so that the committee annually includes a new member, and members with one and two years' service. One of the members shall be appointed committee chairman by the chairman of the board of directors.

Authority

The audit committee is granted the authority to investigate any activity of the company, and all employees are directed to cooperate as requested by members of the committee. The committee is empowered to retain persons having special competence as necessary to assist the committee in fulfilling its responsibility.

Responsibility

The audit committee is to serve as a focal point for communication among noncommittee directors, the independent accountants, internal audit, and XYZ's management, as their duties relate to financial accounting, reporting, and controls. The audit committee is to assist the board of directors in fulfilling its fiduciary responsibilities as to accounting policies and reporting practices of XYZ and all subsidiaries and the sufficiency of auditing relative thereto. It is to be the board's principal agent in assuring the independence of the corporation's independent accountants, the integrity of management, and the adequacy of disclosures to stockholders. The opportunity for the independent accountants to meet with the entire board of directors as needed is not to be restricted.

Meetings

The audit committee is to meet at least three times per year, and as many times as that committee deems necessary.

Attendance

Members of the audit committee are to be present at all meetings. As necessary or desirable, the chairman may request that members of management, the director of internal audit, and representatives of the independent accountants be present at meetings of the committee.

Minutes

Minutes of each meeting are to be prepared and sent to committee members and the XYZ directors who are not members of the committee.

Specific Duties

The audit committee is to

1. Inform the independent accountants and management that the independent accountants and the committee may communicate with each other at all times; and the committee chairman may call a meeting whenever he deems it necessary.
2. Review with the company's management, independent accountants, and director of internal audit the company's policies and procedures to reasonably assure the adequacy of internal accounting and financial reporting controls.

FIG. 6.2   Sample Audit Committee Charter

3. Have familiarity, through the individual efforts of its members, with the accounting and reporting principles and practices applied by the company in preparing its financial statements. Further, the committee is to make, or cause to be made, all necessary inquiries of management and the independent accountants concerning established standards of corporate conduct and performance, and deviations therefrom.

4. Review, prior to the annual audit, the scope and general extent of the independent accountant's audit examination, including the engagement letter. The auditor's fees are to be arranged with management and annually summarized for committee review. The committee's review should entail an understanding from the independent accountant of the factors considered by the accountant in determining the audit scope, including

- Industry and business risk characteristics of the company
- External reporting requirements
- Materiality of the various segments of the company's consolidated and nonconsolidated activities
- Quality of internal controls
- Extent of involvement of internal audit in the audit examination
- Other areas to be covered during the audit engagement

5. Review with management the extent of nonaudit services planned to be provided by the independent accountants, in relation to the objectivity needed in the audit.

6. Review with management and the independent accountants instances where management has obtained "second opinions" from other accountants.

7. Review with management and the independent accountants, upon completion of their audit, financial results for the year, prior to their release to the public. This review is to encompass

- The company's annual report to shareholders and Form 10-K, including the financial statements, and financial statement and supplemental disclosures required by generally accepted accounting principles and the Securities and Exchange Commission
- Significant transactions not a normal part of the company's operations
- Changes, if any, during the year in the company's accounting principles or their application
- Significant adjustments proposed by the independent accountants

8. Arrange for receipt from the independent accountants of their reports on review of the company's quarterly financial statements on Form 10-Q. These reports should be reviewed with management and the independent accountants at committee meetings if timely; otherwise, the independent accountants should be instructed to communicate with the committee if there is a probability that any quarterly review report will be other than standard.

9. Evaluate the cooperation received by the independent accountants during their audit examination, including their access to all requested records, data, and information. Also, elicit the comments of management regarding the responsiveness of the independent accountants to the company's needs. Inquire of the independent accountants whether there have been any disagreements with management which if not satisfactorily resolved would have caused them to modify their report on the company's financial statements.

10. Discuss with the independent accountants the quality of the company's financial and accounting personnel, and any relevant recommendations which the independent accountants may have (including those in their "letter of comments and

(continued)

recommendations"). Topics to be considered during this discussion include improving internal financial controls, the selection of accounting principles, and management reporting systems. Review written responses of management to "letter of comments and recommendations" from the independent accountants.

11. Discuss with company management the scope and quality of internal accounting and financial reporting controls in effect.

12. Apprise the board of directors, through minutes and special presentations as necessary, or significant developments in the course of performing the above duties.

13. Recommend to the board of directors any appropriate extensions or changes in the duties of the committee.

14. Recommend to the board of directors the retention or replacement of the independent accountants, and provide a written summary of the basis for the recommendations.

FIG. 6.2 (continued)

statement on this is the NYSE policy (Figure 6.1) requiring that all listed companies have only "independent" directors on the committee. The American Stock Exchange *recommends* that audit committee members be "free of any relationship that would interfere with the exercise of independent judgment." While stopping short of a requirement, its policy recognizes that even where management directors comprise a part of the audit committee, independence and objectivity are paramount.[2]

The position of the exchanges notwithstanding, a certain degree of independence is essential. To function effectively, a director serving on any board committee has to be independent in spirit and judgment in order to ask the right questions, get the necessary facts, and act accordingly.

SEC Involvement. Independence has been scrutinized extensively by the SEC, with emphasis on its relevance to audit committee membership. Accounting Series Release 165 (FRR §§ 601 and 603) ushered in an era of escalating SEC concern because it required disclosure of the existence or nonexistence of audit committees and the names of committee members (this requirement is now found in Item 7(e)(1) of Schedule 14A). In 1978, the SEC's tentative release on corporate governance (Release 33-5868) included a proposed requirement that directors be identified as management, affiliated nonmanagement, or independent. Later, this proposal was withdrawn (Release 34-15384); in fact, the SEC did an about-face and urged registrants not to label their directors.

To further its efforts in directing policy on board independence, the SEC has incorporated suggestive comments in its formal releases, and, through speeches and

---

[2] The American Stock Exchange board adopted a policy recommending that the audit committees of all listed companies entirely comprise (rather than have a majority of) independent directors. The board also expanded its definition of independent director to include directors who "are free of any relationship that would interfere with the exercise of independent judgment" as well as nonofficers who are neither related to the company's officers nor represent concentrated family shareholdings. Most of the companies whose stock is traded on the American Exchange have audit committees, but these are not required to exclude management directors from committee membership.

articles, it has informally expressed its continuing interest. In short, the SEC strongly favors audit committees.

AICPA Interest. The other participant in the independence dialogue, the AICPA, also considered whether audit committees were needed for public companies to fulfill the auditing standard calling for outside auditor independence. Although the AICPA has no authority to require audit committees, it has stated that it will support such a requirement imposed by the proper authorities, if there is a reasonable cost-benefit relationship (AICPA, 1979d).

Delegation and Support

The director is an overseer, challenging management's establishment and execution of broad strategies. In carrying out this role, the director has to rely on management and others to carry out charges and to measure success. The Model Business Corporation Act, as amended in 1974, addresses limitations on what and on whom directors may rely in delegating matters necessary to the efficient conduct of their responsibilities. It provides that directors may rely on information, opinions, reports, or statements by corporate and outside experts, unless they have knowledge that refutes such reliance.

An audit committee might delegate to staff the tasks of communicating with corporate counsel, the company's accounting and financial managers, outside and internal auditors, and specialists. Generally, such staff assistance would not be extensive. It is simply a prudent means of satisfying the committee's charge, in much the same way that delegation by the board of specified responsibilities to committees enhances its own effectiveness and efficiency.

Directors with diverse backgrounds and expertise can expand the board's capacity to cope with expanding and complex responsibilities. Because outside directors have other time constraints, boards have developed various means, discussed in the following section, to limit the time commitments required.

Coping With an Expanded Role

Three factors seem to contribute the most to board time-efficiency gains: well-qualified members, improved board-support functions, and an expanded board committee structure.

Boards have aggressively sought qualified members by frequently engaging executive search firms and increasing directors' fees. In some cases, persons having particular backgrounds are sought; specialists can help the board to focus on the most important issues more quickly.

Greater support for board activities has sometimes resulted in more effective use of the board members' time. Information pertaining to matters under consideration by the board and its committees is routinely prepared and distributed. The internal audit function and members of operating management often undertake board-directed fact-finding tasks. One example of a report prepared especially for the board, that of the outside auditor's report for audit committee meetings, is discussed later in this chapter under "Audit Scope Meeting."

Committee Structure

More and more board activities are conducted through committees. The board is able to increase its scrutiny of specific matters by assigning them to the committees. This increases the board's overall effectiveness, because the full board is able in a limited time to focus directly on the issues the committees identify as important. Effectiveness is also increased by placing members having specialized skills on committees where those skills are needed.

The committee structure also enables the board to take a more active role in supervising certain activities between board meetings. For example, audit committees often monitor adherence to company codes of conduct.

Committee Authority

The formation of committees does not relieve other board members of responsibility for matters considered by those committees. In most jurisdictions there are legal restrictions on what can be delegated to committees. Ministerial or routine functions can be delegated, and so can some of the board's discretionary or judgmental powers. Usually the full board is responsible for areas such as amending or proposing amendments to bylaws; appointing or removing officers, directors, and committee members; determining to whom specific board powers can be delegated; and controlling possible abuse by committees of powers delegated to them.

PRINCIPAL AUDIT COMMITTEE ACTIVITIES

Company management—not the audit committee or the outside auditor—is responsible for the company's financial statements and its operating results. Outside auditors are responsible for attesting to the fairness of presentation of the financial statements in accordance with GAAP. The audit committee's task is to be satisfied that *both* effectively discharge these responsibilities.

Traditionally, audit committees recommend the outside auditors; approve the overall audit scope; review the adequacy of internal control systems, including internal audit activities; review the interim financial statements and the annual financial statements and audit report thereon; and direct special investigations for the board. These traditional duties remain relevant; if anything, the diligence with which they must be pursued has taken on a new imperative, based on the Treadway Commission Report (discussed at the beginning of this chapter and in Appendix 6).

In the following discussion of principal audit committee activities, the focus is on interaction with the outside auditor, whose foresight in anticipating the strengths and needs of the committee and its members and in fulfilling those needs can make the committee a vital force rather than an organizational formality. Recognize, however, that the audit committee should also interact as appropriate with management and the internal audit function in the areas described below. The degree of the committee's involvement with the internal audit function will vary more from company to company than its involvement with management and the outside auditors.

In developing an overall course of action, an audit committee might consider the methodology of the outside auditor—who documents, tests, and evaluates the com-

The Board of Directors, on the recommendation of the Audit Committee, has appointed Touche Ross & Co. as independent certified public accountants to examine the financial statements of the Company for the year ending December 31, 1988. Touche Ross & Co. has audited the Company's financial statements since 1972, and is considered to be well qualified. If the selection is not approved, the Board of Directors will reconsider its appointment.

FIG. 6.3   Typical Ratification Proposal Explanation

pany's control systems to establish the extent of their reliability. Similarly, an audit committee must meet its responsibilities, in part, by establishing a basis for reliance on the knowledge, expertise, and work of others—most often that of company management, internal auditors, and outside auditors.

Selection of Independent Accountants

The audit committee may be empowered by the board to nominate or select the outside auditors or, as is more often the case, to recommend an audit firm to the full board, which formally approves selection. In addition, many boards seek ratification of the selection by shareholders, with some companies providing for shareholder ratification in their bylaws. (Figure 6.3 illustrates a typical ratification proposal explanation in a proxy statement.)

When an audit committee is considering a change in outside auditors, it may screen a number of firms, often requesting several to submit formal written proposals. In its evaluation, the audit committee will consider a firm's

- Independence
- Reputation (including litigation involving the firm)
- Range of services
- Persons who would be responsible for the services provided to the company
- Levels of industry and other technical expertise
- Ability to serve all the company's geographic locations
- Quality control standards, including reports on recent peer reviews
- Fee estimates

Each year, the audit committee should evaluate the performance of the outside auditors, considering: (1) the quality of services rendered; (2) the efficiency and effectiveness achieved in the audit and other services; (3) their knowledge of and expertise in the company's industry; (4) benefits obtained from their recommendations for improvements; (5) independence factors, including the extent of nonaudit services (see Chapter 45 for an in-depth discussion of nonaudit services and auditor's independence); and (6) the overall strength of the relationship. The evaluation is based partly on the interaction between the outside auditors and the committee (mostly at meetings), but it is principally dependent on an assessment by management. In making its evaluation, the audit committee must remain cognizant of the

Questions Addressed to Auditors

1. Is your firm a member of the SEC Practice Section of the AICPA Division for Firms? When was the last time your firm received a peer review, and what was the nature of the report rendered?[a]

2. Does your firm meet all SEC Practice Section membership requirements?[b]

3. Is your firm independent of the company?

4. What is your firm's policy on rotation of audit partners? Of other personnel?

5. What are the qualifications of your firm in our industry/locale and of the partner who would be in charge of our engagement?

6. Do you have offices in particular locations where the company has significant operations?

7. What type of support services, such as newsletters, industry programs, and information, can your firm provide?

8. Do you regularly furnish suggestions for improvements in controls and operational efficiencies?

9. What is the range of tax, management consulting, and other services you can offer?

10. How are your fees determined, and how do you achieve efficiencies and still maintain your quality standards?

11. What would be the advantages and disadvantages of our retaining (or changing to) your audit firm?

12. How do you coordinate performance of the work of other offices, including international, and to what extent does the engagement partner participate in a review of their work?

Questions Addressed to Management

1. Have the auditors been responsive on a timely basis to requests for assistance, and have they met preestablished deadlines?

2. Are the auditors sensitive to your organizational structure, and do they communicate their observations, findings, recommendations, and criticisms at the appropriate management levels?

3. What is your assessment of the level of the auditors' understanding of the company's industry and business, and technical quality of the auditors' services?

4. Do the auditors appear to manage their work effectively to avoid unnecessary time charges?

5. Does the audit partner devote sufficient time to the engagement?

(a) SEC Practice Section member firms must submit to a peer review once every three years. On completion of the review, the review team submits (1) a report containing its evaluation of whether or not the reviewed firm's quality control system and the compliance therewith is consistent with professional standards and (2) written communication of matters the review team believes require correction action.

(b) SEC Practice Section members must adhere to AICPA quality control standards, ensure that all professionals meet continuing professional education requirements, assign a new audit partner to each SEC engagement on which another partner was in charge for seven consecutive years, and have a partner other than the one in charge perform a preissuance review of the audit report on each SEC engagement.

FIG. 6.4   Questions an Audit Committee Might Ask in Assessing an Auditor's Qualifications

SEC requirements specifically dealing with auditors' independence on an ongoing basis, not just in conjunction with an initial appointment. In addition to determining that the firm and its members have no direct or material indirect interest in the company, the audit committee must evaluate whether the firm's independence has been impaired by other relationships.

Figure 6.4 lists questions an audit committee might ask in assessing the qualifications of independent accountants. The questions in Figure 6.4, as well as those in Figures 6.5–6.9, are illustrative rather than exhaustive.

Audit Scope Assessment

Although the audit committee normally assesses the audit scope, committee members need not have a detailed understanding of the decisions the auditor makes or how the auditor performs the audit. Instead, the audit committee may evaluate the adequacy of the auditor's conclusions about the reliability of the financial statements and systems of internal control, as well as the basis for those conclusions, such as the overall results of audit tests and procedures.

Usually, the audit committee considers the overall audit plan and scope before the outside auditor performs any significant portion of the audit for the year. But it also can meet its responsibility by evaluating whether the audit was appropriately performed after the fact and, where relevant, by focusing on areas of special interest.

Audit Scope Determinants. Some determinants of audit scope include key areas of business and financial risk, the adequacy of the company's system of internal control, and the financial reporting requirements. Committee members may want to discuss

- The allocation of audit procedures among the company's units
- Significant transaction cycles
- Individual financial statement balances or disclosures
- The nature of audit tests
- The extent of reliance on internal controls
- Materiality levels
- Levels of assurance obtained

Viewing the audit in terms of a conceptual model is often helpful to the audit committee. In reviewing the audit scope, the audit committee typicaly considers

- The company's external financial reporting requirements
- The company's accounting policies
- Organizational, operational, and industry-related considerations (including their impact on processing and interpreting accounting information)
- The requirements and needs of financial information users (investors and creditors, the SEC, and other regulatory bodies)

During the review, the audit commitee may need input from counsel, management, and the outside auditors, on whose assurances the committee primarily relies.

The objective is the audit committee's satisfaction that the scope of the audit contemplated by the outside auditors adequately considers all important reporting needs and questions.

Committee Evaluation. The audit committee should consider whether the audit plan covers all areas with which it is concerned. For example, the committee may want the plan to cover selected areas in greater depth than required under generally accepted auditing standards, such as a review of officers' expense accounts or corporate aircraft usage.

The committee also may request the outside auditors to perform special or supplementary reviews of certain control areas not required for audit purposes. Such reviews help monitor compliance with specific corporate policies and objectives. Outside auditors might, for example, review responses to corporate conflict-of-interest questionnaires. Ordinarily, additional reviews are considered along with the audit requirements in order to efficiently integrate them into the audit logistics.

Audit Results Review

Understanding the Issues. Ordinarily, audit committees acquire the knowledge they need to review the results of the audit by reading the financial statements, the forepart of the annual report on Form 10-K, and other data, and by briefings from management and the independent auditors on the impact of accounting principles especially important to the company. Additional sources of information are the financial press, directors' publications, and the newsletters prepared by large accounting firms that summarize new accounting, auditing, and regulatory developments and analyze their features. An audit committee need not probe all areas in depth, but each member should know factors influencing asset valuations, the recording of contingencies, or disclosure in the financial statements.

Once they understand the issues, audit committee members can define what specific information they need and obtain it from management, the independent auditors, and the internal auditors; they can also isolate the sensitive areas requiring in-depth attention. They can then devote time to obtaining a more thorough understanding of the issues in sensitive or important areas and to advising management on the way these issues should be handled. For example, the audit committee can question the auditors and management on matters such as whether the company's accounting practices are consistent with those of others in the company's industry, the basis for major judgments such as estimating inventory obsolescence or receivables collectibility, changes in accounting principles, and auditor-perceived pressures by management to contrive desired results.

Annual Report. A primary responsibility of the audit committee is to review the annual report and the underlying audit results with management and the outside auditors. This review considers

• Reasons for a nonstandard audit opinion
• Changes in accounting policies or principles during the year, and their reasons

- Important differences in financial accounting and reporting from those of other companies in the industry
- Significant areas of judgment in the financial statements, such as receivables collectibility, inventory obsolescence, or warranty reserves
- Unusual or significant commitments or contingencies
- Significant accounting and auditing problems encountered during the audit, including differences of opinion between management and the auditors
- Unexpected adjustments or additional disclosures proposed by the outside auditors
- Changes in report format or the nature of footnote disclosures from the prior year's financial statements

Many committees schedule a review of preliminary audit results before the audit is finalized. This enables the committee to address significant issues before the annual financial statements and operating results are ready for release to the public.

Interim Reports. Another audit committee role is to review the interim financial statements included in Form 10-Q and in the quarterly shareholder reports. While interim statements are not audited, SEC regulations and SAS 36, *Review of Interim Financial Information* (AU 722), are relevant to the performance of such reviews by outside auditors. The auditor will have, or if newly appointed will obtain, an "audit base," a knowledge of the company's financial reporting practices and internal controls, to enable him to make the interim review. Most audit committees review interim information every quarter; others perform their review along with the review of the annual financial statements. In either case, the audit committee needs to be assured that GAAP, including disclosure requirements, has been properly and consistently followed.

Internal Control Review

Although oversight of a company's internal control system has traditionally been part of the audit committee's function, the Foreign Corrupt Practices Act of 1977 (FCPA) accentuated the board's responsibility for internal control matters. In addition, the Treadway Commission Report (discussed at the beginning of this chapter and in Appendix 6) makes it clear that internal control should be a major audit committee agenda item; and the Auditing Standards board has issued two SASs in late 1987 that affect the committee's internal controls agenda (discussed later under "Comments and Recommendations Meetings").

Legal Requirements. As its name suggests, the FCPA considers certain corporate acts to be criminal if they are intended to induce foreign officials, and specific others, to help obtain or retain business.

Actually, the law is much broader. It requires any company registered with the SEC to keep accurate and reasonably detailed records of its transactions, and to maintain internal controls that ensure compliance with the following objectives:

- Transactions are to be executed in accordance with management's authorization.
- Records are to be sufficient to permit preparation of appropriate financial statements.

* Access to assets is to be limited to authorized persons.
* Periodic checks are to be made to verify the existence of recorded assets and to resolve any differences.

The FCPA underscores the audit committee's obligation to ensure that management maintains an appropriate internal control system. Therefore the committee should

* Inform itself about how the internal control objectives are achieved within the company.
* Consider whether the control environment and specific control procedures could reasonably be expected to accomplish their specific objectives.
* Be satisfied that appropriate monitoring devices are in place to detect dysfunctions.

To carry out this responsibility, the audit committee must understand how decision-making authority is delegated between management and supervisory personnel. It should also consider whether management measures the adequacy of the control system to identify and correct exceptions or out-of-pattern items. The committee should be satisfied that management continually challenges its control system and organization structure to ensure proper alignment with board-established policies and assignments of authority. To those involved in control evaluation efforts, including internal auditors, the committee may ask how their scope was determined and findings documented, and how identified problems were dealt with. The committee also may ask the outside auditors to review this management process and report the findings to them.

As part of its overall corporate governance role, the audit committee should also oversee the control structure that encompasses broader controls concerning management's authorization of transactions aimed at achieving the company's objectives. For example, tracking the development of laws and regulations and ensuring compliance with them is an administrative control, as is the continual measurement of the effectiveness of present controls and consideration of changes to improve them.

Other Activities. The board of directors may assign special projects to the audit committee to ensure that the company's disclosure obligations are satisfied; indeed, many of these projects are deemed by the Treadway Commission to belong on the audit committee's agenda (see Appendix 6). These projects may include:

* Investigating questionable payments or lapses of internal control,
* Monitoring compliance with the company's code of conduct,
* Evaluating acquisition candidates or divestiture plans and their effects on the company,
* Assessing the adequacy of internal control over electronic data processing (EDP) operations or certain computer-accessible data (especially important with the proliferation of microcomputers),
* Measuring the likely impact on the company of changes in accounting standards proposed by the FASB or other regulatory bodies.

Most audit committees devote some of their meeting time to their own education, and select certain subjects to study in depth each year, such as the company's internal control systems and accounting principles employed, other financial reporting requirements, and generally accepted auditing standards. The educational efforts may also focus on legal considerations and the impact of new nonfinancial laws and litigation matters. The audit committee's educational efforts may reveal areas and issues that should receive greater attention from them and from the board as a whole.

AUDIT COMMITTEE MEETINGS

In a survey of 50 corporate audit committees compiled by *Directors and Boards* (1984) from proxy documents, the number of meetings per year ranged from 1 to 11, with 62% of the committees meeting either three or four times per year. The meetings normally cover audit scope (early in the year), financial statements (prior to public release of financial results), internal controls, and preparation for the annual share-holders' meeting. The committee's oversight is continuous. Factors that determine the number of times the committee meets and the specific issues to be discussed at each meeting include: the preparation, knowledge, and experience of the committee members; the nature of the committee's specific responsibilities; and characteristics of the company, such as the complexity and size of operations and the quality of the control environment.

Committee Agenda

One of the most important topics for the audit committee to consider is its own agenda in light of evolving public expectations. The committee may make recommendations to the board as to matters that should come within its purview, be transferred to other board committees, or be dealt with by the board as a whole.

The outside auditors' knowledge and experience give them a unique perspective and an obligation to advise their client's directors concerning oversight of corporate financial matters. To do this well, the auditor must know the audit committee's current activities and future agendas. Also, the auditor may suggest topics for the committee's agenda from current developments that affect their duties or responsibilities. Advance materials and reports on significant agenda matters may be provided by management and the outside and internal auditors to assist committee members in preparing for their meetings.

Audit Scope Meeting

The principal purpose of the audit scope meeting, which normally occurs before significant audit work has begun, is the approval of the planned audit scope. The meeting usually addresses the outside auditor's planned approach to the annual audit and may include a summary of critical dates and plans for engagement timing and staffing. Important aspects of staffing are the continuity of staff members from year to year and the competence and relevant expertise of individual members, such as in taxes or in EDP auditing. Other aspects of the plan are usually discussed, including the auditor's engagement to perform a limited review of interim financial statements or other audit-related work known at the outset. Timing considerations include the scheduling of subsequent audit committee meetings, plus the establishment of procedures for reporting unexpected events to the audit committee between meetings.

In order to focus on important phases of the audit, it is helpful to have the auditor's engagement letter on hand during the meeting. The engagement letter summarizes the outside auditor's understanding of the terms and objectives of the engagement, including the estimated fees and the basis on which they are determined; if the committee requires greater detail than is provided by the engagement letter, a separate letter or report to the committee from the outside auditors may serve as an agenda for the meeting. Topics covered in the letter might include:

• General issues affecting the planned scope for the examination, considering the financial and business risks as they relate to the company and the industry.

• Basis for determining audit scope, covering such matters as the conceptual audit process, financial reporting requirements, the established materiality level, and the adequacy of internal control.

• Audit scope for the current year, including the identification of significant segments and subsidiaries, the basis for selecting certain subsidiaries for full audits or limited reviews, regulatory requirements, financial arrangements, foreign statutory requirements, the general areas subject to audit testing, and how sampling is employed to arrive at a satisfactory level of confidence about the overall financial statements.

• Coordination of the audit work with the internal auditors' activities.

• Review of interim financial statements.

• Other areas to be covered during the engagement, such as an audit of employee benefit plans.

• Issues of the prior year's engagement that bear on the current year's audit scope.

• Nonaudit services to be performed, such as tax or management consulting services.

Time will not permit the outside auditor to explain, or the committee to ask about, all details of the engagement, especially when the company's operations are complex. Instead, some audit committees explore one phase of the audit in depth each year, most commonly by having the auditor explain the approach to auditing transactions processed through one of the major accounting cycles or systems. This in-depth review allows committee members to understand more fully the major internal control systems and the audit methodology used. Figure 6.5 is a list of questions about the audit scope that an audit committee might ask auditors.

Another topic often discussed at this meeting is an overview of new developments in accounting and auditing. New standards that have been issued or proposed and that would affect the company, either currently or prospectively, should be identified by the outside auditors or management and their impact determined.

Financial Statements Meeting

The purpose of this meeting, usually held near the conclusion of the audit, is for the audit committee to formally approve the draft financial statements on behalf of the board or, as is more commonly the case, to recommend their approval to the board. Once again, the committee must conclude that the responsibilities of management for the financial statements and financial results and of the outside auditors for

---

1. Have all of the company's consolidated and unconsolidated units been considered in formulating your planned audit scope? If not, which ones were excluded, and why? Where you rely on the work of other firms, have you participated in scoping their work? How will you satisfy yourselves as to its adequacy?

2. Has management restricted, or attempted to restrict, your audit scope in any way?

3. Do you plan an audit scope significantly different than last year's? Do you plan significant modifications this year in the nature and extent of procedures to be performed in any major locations?

4. Have you identified possible changes in the character of our business? How have they affected your audit approach or scope?

5. To what extent will you rely on the company's systems of internal controls in conducting your examination?

6. What techniques and approach do you plan to employ with respect to our EDP systems?

7. How do you plan to collaborate with the internal audit department in your audit approach?

8. Is there any area in which additional company assistance could significantly reduce the planned extent of your work?

9. How have expected changes in particular accounting principles and auditing standards affected your audit approach or scope?

10. Explain how your audit would uncover any material (and, perhaps, less-than-material) defalcations or fraudulent financial reporting, questionable payments, or violations of laws or regulations?

11. What areas of the audit deserve special attention by the audit committee, and why?

FIG. 6.5   Questions an Audit Committee Might Ask Auditors About Audit Scope

attesting to the fair presentation of the financial statements in accordance with GAAP are effectively discharged.

Financial management usually presents the draft financial statements. Their discussion will center around the most significant matters disclosed in the statements and/or any areas where management judgment could significantly affect the financial statements, such as allowances for doubtful accounts or for warranty costs. Questions may arise about trends or changing patterns apparent or implicit in the financial statements. Also, important changes in the format of or account classifications in the financial statements from those of the prior year may be identified and the reasons for them discussed. Figures 6.6, 6.7, 6.8, and 6.9 illustrate questions an audit committee might ask both management and the auditors about the financial statements, and might ask auditors about audit results.

Financial Statement Disclosures. The audit committee will devote attention to the disclosures in the footnotes to the financial statements and significant changes in them from the prior year. The discussion usually will begin with the company's accounting policies; the committee should understand the reasons for a change in accounting principles or in methods of their application and assure itself of the concurrence of the outside auditors. It may also ask for a comparison of the company's accounting methods with those of other companies in the industry.

1. How do the company's reporting practices and disclosures compare with those of other companies in our industry? Are the formats of the income statement and the statement of cash flows consistent with industry practice and appropriate for the company?

2. Have there been any significant changes in the company's accounting practices during the year? Do all of the company's accounting practices fall within generally accepted accounting principles? Where alternative principles are available, which ones are being used by the company? What would be the impact of using the other available choices? Are the company's accounting practices appropriate for its specific needs? Are they consistent with industry practice?

3. Were there any unusual items that significantly affected operating results for the year? Are any of our operations incurring a loss?

4. Were there any important transactions with nonsubsidiary affiliated or related companies?

5. Are there any new or proposed FASB statements or SEC requirements that will materially affect the company's accounting methods or reported results of operations and financial position in the near future? Has there been full compliance with existing statements and requirements?

6. Does the company follow any accounting principles that conflict with the recommendations contained in the AICPA's audit and accounting guides and statements of position?

7. Were there any disagreements between management and the auditors about accounting, auditing, and reporting matters?

8. Are there any changes in the financial statements from those of the prior year regarding their format or the nature of the disclosures in the footnotes? What are the reasons for any changes?

FIG. 6.6 Questions an Audit Committee Might Ask About Financial Statements in General

Disclosure of commitments and contingencies also is an area of significant interest. Committee members may wish to challenge the disclosure of a particular contingency by asking if it is sufficiently predictable to warrant its recording in the accounts; if not, they will be concerned that the disclosure conveys the appropriate level of uncertainty.

Supplemental Disclosures. The committee will review management's discussion and analysis (MD&A) of the company's financial condition and its results of operations. The MD&A must include discussion of capital resources and liquidity, in addition to analyses of financial condition and operating results, with emphasis on the company's ability to meet future operating needs and to execute its strategies.

Other matters that might be considered by the committee include required supplemental disclosures, such as quarterly financial information, data on changing prices, the chairman's and president's letters, and other disclosures and analyses normally included in the annual report or in the 10-K. Committee members will focus on whether the supplemental disclosures are consistent with their own knowledge and understanding and are a reasonable portrayal of the company's operations and prospects.

1. For what periods are the company's time deposits committed? What are the company's compensating balance requirements?

2. Has the quoted market of the company's short-term investments changed significantly since year-end?

3. How does the relationship between the allowance for doubtful receivables and receivables compare with last year? What is the average age of accounts compared with a year ago, and how is the change explained? Is the company following an appropriate credit policy? Are there large individual amounts where collectibility is in question? Have receivables been discounted or pledged? Are there receivables from officers or other management employees?

4. Are there adequate physical controls over inventory? Is the method of inventory valuation (LIFO or FIFO) appropriate?

5. What steps have the independent public accountants taken regarding inventories at outside locations?

6. How does the company monitor inventories so that timely action is taken concerning possible obsolescence? Were any significant write-downs incurred? Generally, how do the outside auditors satisfy themselves that the inventory does not contain obsolete or excess stock?

7. What is the basis of valuation of long-term investments? Is the valuation more or less than quoted market?

8. How does the company's equity in foreign companies compare with cost? What is the total amount at risk when intercompany receivables and temporary advances are considered? How does the company effectively hedge its exposure?

9. Are the company's methods of depreciation for book purposes consistent and appropriate for all assets? Is the company's policy regarding the differentiation between capital and expense items responsive to its needs?

10. Is the company policy regarding amortization of intangible assets realistic? Should the company consider amortization of goodwill arising from acquisitions before November 1, 1970?

11. Are there nonoperating properties or idle facilities? Why have they been retained? How are they valued?

FIG. 6.7 Questions an Audit Committee Might Ask About Assets

Report by Management on Internal Control. In 1979, the SEC proposed that management provide a statement in the annual report on whether the internal control systems in place during the year provided reasonable assurance that the related control objectives specified in the FCPA were met. Later, the SEC withdrew this proposal, finally announcing in early 1982 that it was satisfied with the extent of voluntary reporting and that it no longer intended to prescribe rules in this area. The Treadway Commission has recommended that all annual reports to stockholders be required by the SEC to include a management report (1) acknowledging management's responsibilities for the financial statements, (2) describing how these responsibilities were fulfilled, and (3) assessing the effectiveness of the company's internal controls. The Commission's concept of a comprehensive report by management is illustrated in Figure 6.10; this approach was endorsed by the SEC, which proposed (in Release 34-25925, July 19, 1988) that all public companies include such a report in their 10-K filings and annual shareholder reports.

1. What is the status of federal income taxes, such as open years and items in dispute? Does the accrural for federal income taxes appear to be adequate to cover possible assessments resulting from subsequent examinations by the IRS?
2. Has the company complied with financially related debt indenture covenants, or have waivers been required? Have all significant restrictions been disclosed?
3. Are there any restrictions pertaining to senior stock issues that effectively limit company activities? Has the company purchased any treasury stock during the year? If so, for what purposes?
4. Are there any contingencies of a legal or other nature in which the appropriate treatment is in doubt or which might significantly affect the company's financial position?
5. Has the company made any unusual commitments, such as the purchase of inventories or the acquisition or construction of property assets? Is the company's capital budgeting system adequate?
6. What is the relationship between the company's funding of pension plans and the accounting provisions charged against operations? Has the company's funding policy changed? Can the funding policy be changed under the provisions of ERISA?

FIG. 6.8 Questions an Audit Committee Might Ask About Liabilities and Stockholders' Equity

1. Did management attempt to or actually restrict your work in any way?
2. Were company personnel cooperative?
3. Why and in what specific ways was your audit approach modified from the plan you discussed with us?
4. Will your report be nonstandard in any respect?
5. Did any improprieties come to your attention during the course of your examination? If so, how were they resolved?
6. What work did you do concerning acquired businesses?
7. What is your opinion about the quality of the accounting and financial staffs?
8. Were any important internal control deficiencies encountered after our meeting concerning internal controls?
9. At any time during the year were errors found that required previously reported quarterly results to be corrected?
10. What was the nature and scope of your review of information that was outside the basic financial statements but that was included in the annual report or Form 10-K?

FIG. 6.9 Questions an Audit Committee Might Ask Auditors About Audit Results

The audit committee will want to review management's report to ensure that it is factual.

Auditor's Participation. At the meeting dealing with financial statements, the committee ordinarily will ask the auditors about the effects of new accounting and auditing standards (if this has not been addressed at other meetings throughout the year) and what matters they consider most sensitive in the financial statements, including areas where management's estimates and judgment are significant.

MANAGEMENT REPORT ON RESPONSIBILITY FOR FINANCIAL REPORTING

The management of ABC Corporation and its subsidiaries has the responsibility for preparing the accompanying financial statements and for their integrity and objectivity. The statements were prepared in accordance with generally accepted accounting principles applied on a consistent basis and are not misstated due to material fraud or error. The financial statements include amounts that are based on management's best estimates and judgments. Management also prepared the other information in the annual report and is responsible for its accuracy and consistency with the financial statements.

The corporation's financial statements have been audited by XYZ Co., independent certified public accountants, elected by the shareholders. Management has made available to XYZ Co. all the corporation's financial records and related data, as well as the minutes of stockholders' and directors' meetings. Furthermore, management believes that all representations made to XYZ Co. during its audit were valid and appropriate.

Management of the corporation has established and maintains a system of internal control that provides reasonable assurance as to the integrity and reliability of the financial statements, the protection of assets from unauthorized use or disposition, and the prevention and detection of fraudulent financial reporting. The system of internal control provides for appropriate division of responsibility and is documented by written policies and procedures that are communicated to employees with significant roles in the financial reporting process and updated as necessary. Management continually monitors the system of internal control for compliance. The corporation maintains a strong internal auditing program that independently assesses the effectiveness of the internal controls and recommends possible improvements thereto. In addition, as part of its audit of the corporation's financial statements, XYZ Co. completed a study and evaluation of selected internal accounting controls to establish a basis for reliance thereon in determining the nature, timing, and extent of audit tests to be applied. Management has considered the internal auditor's and XYZ Co.'s recommendations concerning the corporation's system of internal control and has taken actions that we believe are cost-effective in the circumstances to respond appropriately to these recommendations. Management believes that, as of [date], the corporation's system of internal control is adequate to accomplish the objectives discussed herein.

Management also recognizes its responsibility for fostering a strong ethical climate so that the corporation's affairs are conducted according to the highest standards of personal and corporate conduct. This responsibility is characterized and reflected in the corporation's code of corporate conduct, which is publicized throughout the corporation. The code of conduct addresses, among other things, the necessity of ensuring open communication within the corporation; potential conflicts of interests; compliance with all domestic and foreign laws, including those relating to financial disclosure; and the confidentiality of proprietary information. The corporation maintains a systematic program to assess compliance with these policies.

Chief Executive Officer

Chief Financial Officer
(and/or)
Controller

FIG. 6.10   Sample Report by Management
Source: NCFFR, 1987, pp. 184–185.

The auditors will explain the nature of their report and the basis for any modifications or qualifications, which, if unanticipated at the outset, should have been communicated to the committee in advance of this meeting. The auditors also will discuss unexpected conditions that caused them to modify their audit approach and any other matters they believe the audit committee should know about the audit, the financial statements and their footnotes, and supplementary disclosures.

The outside auditor's candor and comprehensiveness are vital to the audit committee's effectiveness. To conserve time, prior to the meeting the auditors and management should discuss the matters to be presented. This will eliminate any redundancy and identify any differences of opinion so they can be resolved before the meeting. Where differences cannot be resolved and they are significant to the financial statements and might affect the auditor's report on them, the auditor should notify the chairman of the audit committee promptly if a committee meeting is not imminent.

Comments and Recommendations Meeting

The purpose of this meeting is to present to the audit committee the outside auditor's comments and recommendations concerning the company's internal control. Relatively minor deficiencies are not usually discussed with the audit committee, although they may be provided to the committee through a letter from the auditors in which they report summary findings on internal control. At the same time, management would normally submit a letter to the audit committee containing its plan of action to correct these control deficiencies. Management also may want to inform the committee of its plans concerning internal control system objectives for the next year, including:

* Planned systems changes.
* Reassessment of cost/benefit relationships in particular areas or the criteria for making assessments.
* Internal control implications of organizational changes.
* EDP-related projects, such as microcomputer control policies and procedures.
* Implementation of planned corrective action in response to the internal and outside auditors' findings and recommendations.

Figure 6.11 is a list of questions an audit committee might ask auditors about internal control.

Independent auditors have been required for the past decade to report to the board or its audit committee material internal control weaknesses that come to their attention during the examination of the financial statements. Such weaknesses constitute a condition in which the auditor believes the specific control procedures, or the degree of compliance with them, are not sufficient to ensure a relatively low risk that material errors or irregularities would be prevented or detected within a timely period by employees in the normal course of performing their assigned functions.

In late 1987, the ASB issued SAS 60, *The Communication of Internal Control Structure Related Matters Noted in an Audit.* This SAS makes a distinction between

1. Have you found any material weaknesses or reportable conditions in internal control?
2. Have you found other matters in the system of internal control that call for corrective action?
3. Has management taken appropriate action in response to comments and recommendations you have made in the past?
4. Has the company documented its system of internal controls to adequately support representations made about it in the management's published report on its responsibility for the financial statements and the internal controls?
5. Have you modified your planned audit approach based on the results of your tests of the internal control system?
6. Is the internal audit function adequately staffed and organized?
7. What activities would you recommend the audit committee undertake in connection with its oversight of internal control?
8. In your judgment, has the company succeeded in creating an environment conducive to achieve the objectives of internal control?
9. Does the system in place provide reasonable assurance that errors and conditions contrary to policy are reported?
10. Does management do an adequate job of monitoring reported exceptions as possible indications of needed improvement?
11. During the course of your examination, did any conditions come to your attention that may warrant in-depth investigation by management, the internal auditors, or the audit committee?
12. What are the critical internal control areas that warrant the attention of the audit committee? Why are they important?
13. What is your impression of the quality of the long-range planning and budgetary controls employed by the company?
14. Does the company control its electronic data processing operations effectively, especially regarding microcomputer use and access? Are controls adequate to ensure the integrity of computer-accessible data?
15. Is the company's policies and procedures manual adequate? Is it maintained on a current basis?
16. Are company policies and procedures regarding conflicts of interest adequate?
17. Are you aware of any instances where management has exceeded its authority in any matters prescribed by the directors or failed to comply with any resolution passed by the directors?

FIG. 6.11 Questions an Audit Committee Might Ask Auditors About Internal Control

internal control matters noted during an audit and "material weaknesses" disclosed as part of a special review of internal controls. Because audits are expected to touch upon the design and functioning of the company's control structure (which broadly encompasses the control environment, accounting system, and control procedures) that could adversely affect the integrity of the financial statements, the ASB concluded that a material weakness concept was too narrow for the purpose of communicating the auditor's concerns. Therefore, for audits, the concept of *reportable conditions* has been developed, defined as

Matters coming to the auditor's attention that in his judgment represent significant deficiencies in the design or functioning of the control structure, that could adversely affect the organization's ability to record, process, summarize, and report financial data consistent with the assertions of management in the financial statements.

This revision, though perhaps subtle, should expand the discussions at audit committee meetings regarding the control system, as contrasted with only specific weaknesses.

In addition, the auditor is responsible for informing the audit committee about material errors and irregularities (AU 316) and about illegal acts (AU 317), if these involve senior management. Also in late 1987, the Auditing Standards Board issued SAS 61, *Communication With Audit Committees*. This SAS retains and endorses the foregoing requirements, and further establishes a list of matters that must be communicated by the auditor to the audit committee, either orally or in writing (discussed later under "Audit Committee Relationships").

Annual Shareholders' Meeting

Since many of the key issues addressed at shareholders' meetings are financial, the audit committee may be involved in the preparations for such meetings. The committee is in an excellent position to benefit from the experience gained by the audit firm which attends the annual meetings of many other companies. Each year, many large CPA firms prepare booklets containing questions that are likely to be asked at the annual shareholders' meetings. These questions can help corporate executives and directors identify questions that they should be prepared to answer. Before the meeting, it is good practice to decide who should answer which questions—management, the board (or audit committee), or outside auditors.

Annual meeting planning should be done after the financial statements have been approved and the comments and recommendations meeting has been held. The financial statements, internal controls, and auditors' recommendations can generate numerous shareholders' questions. Proxy statements, other materials sent to shareholders, recent press releases, and SEC filings are likely to have caught some shareholder's eye, so these also are normally reviewed in advance of the annual meeting.

Other Meeting Topics

Additional audit committee meetings may be held to deal with any of the committee's functions and activities. At one of the meetings—usually the one that "closes out" the previous audit year—the audit committee will decide whether to retain the incumbent outside auditors for another year and will take that recommendation to the full board. In many instances, the decision to retain the auditors will be ratified by the shareholders. If the auditors will not be retained, the schedule for ratification will change.

Meetings are sometimes held when a prospectus is in preparation for the sale of securities or when there are to be other major releases to the public on important developments or activities. Still other meetings may be held to consider

• Merger or acquisition prospects, including tender offers or takeover bids
• Major lawsuits filed against the company
• Significant changes in new accounting and auditing standards, SEC rules, or other regulatory requirements

- Major organizational changes within the company
- The audits of financial statements of related entities, such as pension plans and investees accounted for on the equity method
- Events that raise questions about the integrity of a member of top management

Executive Sessions

Many audit committees arrange to meet with the outside auditors without management present. This is usually done during regular audit committee meetings and is referred to as an executive session. In such a session, the committee may raise questions it does not feel comfortable asking in the presence of management, for example, "What do you think of the financial vice-president?" or "How cooperative was the controller?" The auditors can then respond to such sensitive issues in a less formal manner. Similarly, the committee may meet separately with the directors of the internal audit and with senior financial management, to help it assess the competence and qualities of the outside auditors.

An audit committee meeting with the outside auditors in closed session by no means indicates that management's credibility is in doubt or that management is not meeting its responsibilities. To conduct their examination, the outside auditors must maintain an open and candid relationship with management; their obligation to discuss sensitive matters with the board need not override this. Auditors must use good judgment and tact to avoid misunderstandings.

AUDIT COMMITTEE RELATIONSHIPS

Because the role and responsibilities of the audit committee, management, internal auditors, and outside auditors are so interrelated, open lines of communication are important. Each must understand and be sensitive to the concerns of the others. Careful planning and coordination are characteristics of an effective audit committee.

Interaction With Outside Auditors

Independent accountants are required to bring certain matters to the attention of a client's board of directors. Where an audit commmitee exists, it is normally the appropriate vehicle for auditor-board communications. Audit committees, therefore, may properly view the outside auditors as a fact-finding arm and as surrogates in making evaluations requiring accounting and auditing expertise.

In an attempt to improve the flow of information to audit committees or owner-managers, the ASB in late 1987 issued SAS 61, *Communication With Audit Committees*. This SAS requires auditors to be assured that audit committees or owner-managers are informed about certain important matters. Those matters may be communicated either orally or in writing. If information is communicated orally, the auditor must document the communication in writing in the audit workpapers. The communication need not occur before issuance of the audit report; however, the auditor should consider whether any part of the information should be communicated earlier.

The matters about which information should be communicated to audit committees include the following:

* The initial selection of significant accounting policies and their application.
* The process management uses to prepare accounting estimates and the basis for the auditor's conclusions about the reasonableness of those estimates.
* The implications of adjustments arising from the audit—both those that have been reflected in the financial statements and those that have not.
* The auditor's responsibility for unaudited information in documents containing audited financial statements, the procedures performed, and the conclusions reached.
* The level of responsibility the auditor assumes for an audit performed in accordance with generally accepted auditing standards and the nature of the assurance an audit provides.
* All instances, including those that have been satisfactorily resolved, in which the auditor and management disagreed about matters that, individually or in the aggregate, could be significant to the entity's financial statements or the auditor's report.
* Any major issues that management discussed with the auditor in connection with the retention of the auditor, including the application of accounting principles and auditing standards.
* Any serious difficulties encountered that the auditor considered detrimental to the effective completion of the audit and indicative of conditions that could impair the financial reporting process.

This SAS is in fact somewhat belated, because in December 1986 the AICPA's SEC Practice Section Executive Committee agreed that members will be required to communicate with audit committees about many of the subjects described in the SAS, for audits of fiscal years ending on or after June 30, 1987.

SEC Practice Section members are required to communicate with audit committees about the following:

* Material errors, irregularities, or illegal acts.
* Material weaknesses in internal accounting control.
* Opinions on accounting and financial reporting obtained by management from other accountants.
* Accounting and disclosure considerations associated with material contingencies or unusual transactions.
* Adoption of or change in an accounting principle.

This list is added to earlier requirements to communicate with audit committees regarding disagreements and management advisory services fees and activities. With the exception of the MAS fee and activity disclosure requirement, the SEC Practice Session will rescind its existing membership requirements applicable to audit committee communications when SAS 61 becomes effective (audits of financial statements for periods beginning on or after January 1, 1989).

The obligation of the outside auditor is to be sensitive and alert to the needs of the audit committee, even when issues arise that are not listed in the foregoing requirements. The importance of issues varies from company to company, and auditors should guard against the tendency to provide the committee with a comprehensive and detailed analysis of all the technical factors pertinent to a particular accounting or auditing issue. Since most committee members are not experts in acccounting and auditing matters, such presentations could add more confusion than enlightenment. In cases where committee discussion is necessary, the issue should be simplified to its essence.

As a matter of good practice, the auditors should prepare a written report to the audit committee highlighting the subjects to be raised at any meeting, and this report should be distributed beforehand. It may be as formal or as informal as the topics require. In addition, presentations on complex issues are often made simpler with visual aids; however, overpresentation may wrest control of the meeting from the audit committee chairman and interfere with the committee's functioning.

Interaction With Internal Auditors

Most audit committees regularly review the internal audit function as a part of their consideration of internal control and operational efficiency, anticipating that the internal auditors will cover areas not included in the outside auditors' scope. Among the issues within the committee's charge is whether the director of internal audit should report directly to the audit committee chairman and serve as the committee's fact-finding arm.

The committee may have the director of internal audit report to a senior financial officer on a day-to-day basis, yet still maintain a separate, independent reporting role with the audit committee. The independence of the director of internal audit can be assured through several ways, such as requiring audit committee approval or participation in the evaluation and compensation review or hiring of the director of internal audit. In practice, some companies are able to combine management efficiencies and reporting independence to achieve an effective and valuable internal audit department. Proponents of the traditional structure, in which the internal auditor reports to senior management, point out the availability of the outside auditor as the audit committee's resource for fact finding. Audit committees regularly engage outside auditors for special reviews or investigations; or the outside and internal auditors work together as a team. Structural preferences notwithstanding, virtually everyone agrees that both management and the committee need access to both internal and outside auditors, and vice versa.

Nonetheless, many companies have taken steps to ensure that (1) the director of internal audit has access to the board through its audit committee on both a scheduled and as-needed basis, and that (2) management hierarchy does not hamper internal audit effectiveness. Ordinarily, much of this liaison is achievable by having the director of internal audit present at all regular audit committee meetings and by having a report on internal audit activities and scope presented at those meetings.

Interaction With Management

By defining the respective roles of management, the board, and the audit committee from the beginning, unnecessary strains may be prevented. Because management deals with the daily conduct of business and should foresee problems, the reasonable approach would be to let management "propose" and let the audit committee, and full board, reserve the right to "dispose."

Where a difference of opinion exists, the audit committee should inform management and the board of its position, and if management still disagrees, the full board could act as a forum for discussion. In short, keeping communication lines open among management, the board, and the committee is good practice. Otherwise, an adversary relationship could develop, which could hamper productivity.

For management to perform efficiently, the committee should not be part of either the operational or managerial decision-making process. It should, of course, be free to challenge management decisions about internal controls and other matters within its scope. But when it becomes part of the decision-making process, it intrudes into the area of management and loses its value. In its role as overseer, the audit committee is especially valued for its objectivity and independence.

Auditor, Management, and Committee Relations

Earlier in this chapter, executive sessions were mentioned as a desirable forum for audit committees to discuss potentially sensitive issues with outside and internal auditors, and with management. To reduce the likelihood of misunderstandings among them, auditors should be guided primarily by common sense and discretion. There are various techniques that can be employed.

First, the auditors should make certain that they have the relevant facts. For example, indications that an irregularity may exist or that an officer may have acted illegally do not automatically indict management or impugn its integrity. But such indications do require a thorough examination by the auditors, and also a discussion with the audit committee or full board when their concurrence is an important audit procedure.

Similarly, an expressed preference by management to adopt an accounting method that appears inappropriate to the auditors does not become a formal disagreement until the auditors and management agree on all the facts. But when a formal disagreement occurs on a material accounting, auditing, or reporting issue, the auditors are obliged to bring this to the attention of the audit committee.

In view of their potentially sensitive nature, such disagreements should be clarified as to the facts and the positions of both management and the outside auditors. These matters, along with other topics the auditors expect will arise in executive session, should be discussed with management in advance of meeting with the committee to enable management and the auditors to consider the issues fully. While such discussions do not compel the auditors to change their views, they can prevent damage to the mutual trust and candor essential between the auditors and management. Certain matters that the auditors feel should be brought to the attention of the audit committee fall squarely within the province of management, and it may be better that management raises the topic with the audit committee.

Representatives of the audit firm and management should discuss in advance all the items on the audit committee's meeting agenda, including the general thrust of the comments that both the auditors and management plan to make, the questions the committee is expected to raise, and the intended responses. Also the factors considered in the planning meeting between the auditor and management should not be restricted to agenda items, if it is anticipated that nonagenda subjects will arise.

Another outcome of the planning session might be an agreement about who is to prepare advance distribution materials on particular topics and who is to present them at the meeting. Some topics lend themselves well to joint presentation.

Audit Committee Chairman's Letter

With the audit committee having fulfilled its responsibilities as discussed in this chapter, the users of financial statements need to be informed of this accomplishment. The Treadway Commission recommends that a separate report by the chairman of the audit committee be placed in the annual shareholders' report. To this time, companies have included relevant comments in management's letter; and the Treadway Commission has bisected that letter to more clearly communicate the audit committee's focal role. An example of a chairman's letter is shown in Figure 6.12.

AUDIT COMMITTEE CHAIRMAN'S LETTER

The audit committee of the board of directors is composed of _____ independent directors. The members of the audit committee are: John Doe, Chairman, _____, and _____. The committee held _____ meetings during fiscal year _____.

The audit committee oversees the company's financial reporting process on behalf of the board of directors. In fulfilling its responsibility, the committee recommended to the board of directors, subject to shareholder approval, the selection of the company's independent public accountant. The audit committee discussed with the internal auditor and the independent public accountant the overall scope and specific plans for their respective audits. The committee also discussed the company's consolidated financial statements and the adequacy of the company's internal controls. The committee met regularly with the company's internal auditor and independent public accountant, without management present, to discuss the results of their examinations, their evaluations of the company's internal controls, and the overall quality of the company's financial reporting. The meetings also were designed to facilitate any private communication with the committee desired by the internal auditor or independent public accountant.

John Doe, Chairman
Audit Committee

FIG. 6.12 Audit Committee Chairman's Letter
Source: NCFFR, 1987, p. 187.

Appendix 6
GOOD PRACTICE GUIDELINES FOR THE AUDIT COMMITTEE

Introduction

Primary responsibility for the company's financial reporting lies with top management, overseen by the board of directors. To help boards of directors carry out this oversight responsibility, the Commission recommends that all public companies establish audit committees consisting of independent directors. Establishment of such committees, of course, does not relieve the other directors of their responsibility with respect to the financial reporting process. The Commission therefore reinforces its general recommendation with more specific recommendations for audit committee duties and responsibilities.

First, specific recommendations directed to audit committees highlight the need for the audit committee (1) to be informed and vigilant, (2) to have its duties and responsibilities set forth in a written charter, and (3) to be given resources and authority adequate to discharge its responsibilities. Among other things, the audit committee should review mangement's evaluation of factors related to the independence of the company's public accountant, help preserve that independence and review management's plans for engaging the company's independent public accountant to perform management advisory services during the coming year, considering the types of services that may be rendered and the amount budgeted for such services.

In addition, the Commission highlights other important audit committee functions throughout Chapter Two [of the NCFR report—ed.]. The audit committee should review the company's process of assessing the risk of fraudulent financial reporting and the program that management establishes to monitor compliance with the code of corporate conduct. The audit committee should have open lines of communication with the chief accounting officer and the chief internal auditor. In fact, the chief internal auditor's direct and unrestricted access to the audit committee is vital to his objectivity. Management should advise the audit committee when it seeks a second opinion on a significant accounting issue. Audit committees should oversee the quarterly reporting process. Finally, the chairman of the audit committee should write a letter describing the committee's activities and responsibilities for inclusion in the annual report to stockholders.

The Commission developed this set of recommended audit committee duties and responsibilities from a review and consideration of the practices many well-managed companies follow today, of the extensive guidance the public accounting and legal professions have published on the subject, and of practices suggested by the results of the Commission's research projects, and by presentations made to the Commission.

The Commission believes that more detailed delineation and description of responsibilities is best left to the discretion of management and the board of directors to tailor to the needs and circumstances of each company. In the course of its research and deliberations, however, the Commission has identified additional, more specific practices and procedures that can help audit committees perform their oversight role effectively. The Commission is not prescribing these additional measures, and therefore has not included them as recommendations, but offers this guidance in the form of the following Good Practice Guidelines, which companies can consider within the exercise of their judgment. To companies that already have audit committees, the guidelines will serve as a standard for review and assessment. Other companies—those just establishing audit committees or those seeking to improve their committees' effectiveness—may find them to be helpful in suggesting practical ways for audit committees to discharge their responsibilities.

General Guidelines

* *Size and Term of Appointment.* An audit committee normally should consist of not fewer than three independent directors. The maximum size may vary, but the committee should be small enough so that each member is an active participant. The term of appointment is at the discretion of the board of

directors, but it is desirable to have terms arranged to maintain continuity while bringing fresh perspectives to the work of the committee.

- *Meetings.* The committee should meet on a regular basis and special meetings should be called as circumstances require. The committee should meet privately with the internal auditor and the independent public accountant.
- *Reporting to the Board of Directors.* The committee should report its activities to the full board on a regular basis, such as after each meeting, so that the board is kept informed of its activities on a current basis.
- *Expand Knowledge of Company Operations.* A systematic and continuing learning process for audit committee members will increase their effectiveness. One way is to review various financial aspects of the company on a planned basis.
- *Company Counsel.* The committee should meet regularly with the company's general counsel, and outside counsel when appropriate, to discuss legal matters that may have a significant impact on the company's financial statements. In a number of companies the general counsel and/or outside counsel attend meetings.
- *Audit Plans.* The committee should review with the chief internal auditor and the independent public accountant their annual audit plans, including the degree of coordination of the respective plans. The committee should inquire as to the extent to which the planned audit scope can be relied upon to detect fraud or weaknesses in internal controls.
- *Electronic Data Processing.* The committee should discuss with the internal auditor and the independent public accountant what steps are planned for a review of the company's electronic data processing procedures and controls, and inquire as to the specific security programs to protect against computer fraud or misuse from both within and outside the company.
- *Other Auditors.* The committee should inquire as to the extent to which independent public accountants other than the principal auditor are to be used and understand the rationale for using them. The committee should request that their work be coordinated and that an appropriate review of their work be performed by the principal auditor.
- *Officer Expenses and Perquisites.* The committee should review in-house policies and procedures for regular review of officers' expenses and perquisites, including any use of corporate assets, inquire as to the results of the review, and, if appropriate, review a summarization of the expenses and perquisites of the period under review.
- *Areas Requiring Special Attention.* The committee should instruct the independent public accountant and the internal auditor that the committee expects to be advised if there are any areas that require its special attention.

Selection of an Independent Public Accountant

A primary responsibility of the audit committee should be the selection of an independent public accountant for the company. The actual selection generally is proposed by management, with the audit committee confirming management's selection, and is ratified by the stockholders. Suggested below are a number of considerations that may enter into the decision. There will be variations, of course, including those that depend upon whether the committee is considering management's proposal to retain the present independent public accountants or management's proposal to appoint a new public accounting firm.

Issues related to this audit:

- Opinions on the performance of the public accounting firm by appropriate management and the chief internal auditor
- The proposed audit fee and the independent public accountant's engagement letter; explanations for fee changes
- The expected level of participation by the partner and other management personnel in the audit examination, the mix of skills and experience of the staff, and staff rotation policy

- If a new public accounting firm is being considered, the steps planned to ensure a smooth and effective transition.

Issues related to the firm generally:

- The report of the public accounting firm's latest peer review conducted pursuant to a professional quality control program
- Any significant litigation problems or disciplinary actions by the SEC or others
- The public accounting firm's credentials, capabilities, and reputation and a list of clients in the same industry and geographical area.

Post-Audit Review

- The committee should obtain from management explanations for all significant variances in the financial statements between years. (This review may be performed at a meeting of the entire board.) The committee should consider whether the data are consistent with the Management's Discussion and Analysis (MD&A) section of the annual report.
- The committee should request an explanation from financial management and the independent public accountant of changes in accounting standards or rules promulgated by the Financial Accounting Standards Board, Securities and Exchange Commission or other regulatory bodies, that have an effect on the financial statements.
- The committee should inquire about the existence and substance of any significant accounting accruals, reserves, or estimates made by management that had a material impact on the financial statements.
- The committee should inquire of management and the independent public accountant if there were any significant financial reporting issues discussed during the accounting period and if so how they were resolved.
- The committee should meet privately with the independent public accountant, to request his opinion on various matters including the quality of financial and accounting personnel and the internal audit staff.
- The committee should ask the independent public accountant what his greatest concerns were and if he believes anything else should be discussed with the committee that has not been raised or covered elsewhere.
- The committee should review the letter of management representations given to the independent public accountant and inquire whether he encountered any difficulties in obtaining the letter or any specific representations therein.
- The committee should discuss with management and the independent public accountant the substance of any significant issues raised by in-house and outside counsel concerning litigation, contingencies, claims or assessments. The committee should understand how such matters are reflected in the company's financial statements.
- The committee should determine the open years on federal income tax returns and whether there are any significant items that have been or might be disputed by the IRS, and inquire as to the status of the related tax reserves.
- The committee should review with management the MD&A section of the annual report and ask the extent to which the independent public accountant reviewed the MD&A section. The committee should inquire of the independent public accountant if the other sections of the annual report to stockholders are consistent with the information reflected in the financial statements.
- The committee and the board of directors should consider whether the independent public accountant should meet with the full board to discuss any matters relative to the financial statements and to answer any questions that other directors may have.

Source: NCFFR, *1987,* pp. 179–181.

7

Performing the Audit

THE AUDIT PRACTICE

Although much of the profession's literature discusses auditing in terms of the *auditor*, audit examinations are in fact generally performed by audit *teams* who are partners and employees of auditing *firms*. Three important aspects of the audit practice are the team approach, the auditing firm's resources, and quality control.

The Audit Team

Auditing firms have several levels of experienced professionals. On an audit examination, the audit team comprises one or more persons from each level. The leader of the team is the audit partner. Since large auditing firms are almost invariably partnerships, the partner is an owner; and even when the firm takes the form of a professional corporation, the actual operation is the same. The partner in charge of the audit engagement has ultimate authority and responsibility for all important decisions and judgments made during the audit, including the nature of the audit opinion reached. The partner is also responsible for business matters with the client, such as fee determination. The partner and the engagement team will act in accord with specific policies of their firm, to the extent that such policies have been articulated in more detail than provided in professional standards and pronouncements.

On a day-to-day basis, the audit engagement is managed by an experienced auditor who is one to five years below the partner level. In many larger firms there are people at two staff designations who may exercise this responsibility: senior manager and manager, and on large audits, both will be assigned responsibilities for various elements of the engagement. More than one partner may also be on the team.

The managers usually concern themselves with specific problem areas and management tasks. The performance of detailed procedures is usually under the direct control of audit seniors, who perform the more complex tasks and supervise staff assistants – team members with less than two or three years' experience – in performing less complex tasks.

This hierarchical structure provides several advantages. First, all work performed is reviewed by the performer's superior, assuring that work is done properly and that the team members receive on-the-job training. Second, each member's capabilities are matched to the requirements of his task. More difficult tasks and judgments are reserved for more experienced auditors, and more routine activities are performed by those less experienced. Third, costs are minimized. Most of the time billed in the engagement is that of auditors who are lower in the hierarchy, because their tasks tend to be time-consuming by nature. Since these persons are newer to the firm and earn lower salaries, their billing rates are lower.

A major challenge for such a team, especially when some of its members are in different cities or even countries, is communication. To meet this challenge, the auditing firm must have a sound system of working paper documentation, so that as work is performed by individual auditors, it can be made available to and understood by other members of the team. Most audit firms prescribe the format for such documentation. For example, detailed procedures and other relevant information are presented in a program of examination. As work is performed, detailed working papers are prepared that summarize what was accomplished. Steps are usually signed off in the program as well. Finally, key matters – problems, judgments, findings – are often summarized in memoranda.

In addition, the audit involves a significant administrative operation, which is documented by time summaries and budgets, coordination and timing schedules, and correspondence.

Often, a client's internal auditing department will provide assistance to the audit team in performing portions of the audit. In addition, internal audit is usually an important aspect of the internal control structure. An example of a firm policy statement on the appropriate utilization of the internal audit function is contained in Appendix 7; and a review of internal audit standards is contained in Chapter 5.

Firm Resources

Most auditing firms provide important resources to support the audit team both in performing a particular engagement and in developing their professional competence as individuals.

Training Programs. Most firms have in-house training programs as well as access to the excellent programs offered by outside organizations. Because accounting and auditing is a field with a large and expanding body of rules, interpretations, and technology, continuing professional education (CPE) is an essential part of every professional's development. Indeed, most states have CPE requirements for licensing. The AICPA's SEC Practice Section, whose membership comprises firms that audit publicly held companies, goes further: every professional in a member firm is required to devote 120 hours to accredited CPE over three years. In a 1987 AICPA referendum, a requirement was passed that all members in public practice (not only SEC Practice Section members) must achieve this level of CPE credit beginning in 1989.

Manuals, Information Releases, and Forms. Auditing firms, like most organizations, set forth many of their policies and practices in firm manuals. This format facilitates training, implementation, and communication. Firms often have manuals covering administrative and operational matters as well as technical matters. With so much that is new or in the process of change in areas affecting accountants and auditors, information releases such as technical newsletters or topical narratives are commonplace in audit firms. Firms that do not maintain in-house information release systems obtain the material from the AICPA and voluntary associations of firms.

In addition to (and often as part of) manuals, many firms prescribe specific forms to standardize and control certain audit activities. These include administrative forms, examples of typical audit correspondence, internal control structure questionnaires, and generalized audit procedure lists.

Computer Tools. In today's audits, much company information is usually in the form of computer readable files. On-line systems present a particularly formidable challenge to the auditor in planning his procedures, because he must address company data in computer form during the limited time it is available. To meet these challenges, the auditor often has at his disposal computer software programs that are used to process this data in performing audit steps. The problems that computers raise in the audit, and their solutions, are discussed in Chapter 10.

In addition to special audit software tools, many auditors use computer programs for such purposes as selecting random samples, evaluating sample results, making financial analyses, and performing lease computations. Computer applications involving sampling are highlighted in Chapter 9.

Research Materials and Sources. As in most disciplines, auditing involves knowing how to find and apply the right answer. Because the body of accounting and auditing knowledge is so large, many problems encountered during the audit must be researched. Audit firms provide such research facilities as libraries, topical information files, and data search and retrieval systems, often including microfiche, the National Automated Accounting Research Systems (NAARS), and micro-search capabilities. Consultation with research staff members is another important resource. In larger firms these persons may be found at the local, regional, and national levels. Chapter 50 discusses professional research in detail.

Specialists. Specialists in certain areas are often called on to participate in audit engagements. Industry and SEC specialists, technical specialists in areas such as data processing and statistics, tax specialists, and management consultants are among those frequently consulted. Some firms also have actuaries, appraisers, and other specialists on staff to assist the audit team in performing tests and making judgments in the complex areas of the specialists' expertise.

Quality Control

This chapter focuses on the individual audit engagement and, by inference, the individual auditor. But most audits are performed by firms. The AICPA has given special consideration to the problems of managing an audit practice and its effect on the quality of audit engagements. Statements on Quality Control Standards present standards that cover a firm's entire professional auditing practice. These are listed and discussed in Chapter 5.

AUDIT CONCEPTS

This chapter presents a highly simplified approach to performing an audit of financial statements. In a way, this is the conceptual framework on which much of the auditing material in the other chapters of this *Handbook* is built.

An audit is basically a problem-solving process. The subject of the problem is an enterprise that conducts financial activities and reports the results of those activities to interested parties in the form of financial statements. The broad purpose of the audit is to determine whether these financial statements fairly present, in all material respects, the enterprise's actual activities in conformity with the accounting standards established for the type of entity and the circumstances involved. The result of the audit is the auditor's report, adding credibility to the financial statements. In following professional standards during performance of the audit, the auditor considers appropriate evidence addressing the risks that the financial statements could be materially misstated.

The fundamental concepts involved in the audit process are audit evidence, materiality, audit tests including sampling, and assessment of internal control structure; an additional dimension is introduced when electronic data processing (EDP) records are involved. These are discussed later in the "Enterprise Attributes" section of this chapter. (Chapters immediately following this one are devoted specifically to internal control structure, sampling, and EDP auditing.)

Audit Objectives

The overall objective of the audit is to form a correct opinion as to whether the financial statements are fairly presented, in all material respects, in conformity with GAAP. This broad objective is satisfied by meeting a series of detailed audit objectives, through performance of specific procedures in which the auditor obtains and evaluates evidential matter. These specific audit objectives are related to the five fundamental assertions, whether explicit or implicit, embodied in all components of financial statements. As discussed in SAS 31, *Evidential Matter* (AU 326.03), management's assertions underlying financial statements are as follows:

* The assets and liabilities *exist*, and the transactions have *occurred*;
* The accounts and transactions that should be included are included, making the financial statement *complete*;
* The assets are *rights* of the entity, and the liabilties are its *obligations*;
* Assets, liabilities, revenues, and expenses are appropriately *valued*, and are appropriately *allocated* to accounting periods; and
* Amounts shown in the financial statements are properly *presented* and *disclosed*.

In the audit process, these general objectives arc made more specific. Management's assertions are assessed in a materiality context; material matters are then used as the focal point for accumulation of sufficient competent cvidence on which the auditor forms a professional opinion on the client's financial statements. When the audit is complete, the auditor will have formed an opinion on the following:

1. All assets are owned and all liabilities owed (existence of rights and obligations).
2. All recorded transactions actually took place (i.e., are valid occurrences), and all actual transactions are recorded (occurrence and completeness).
3. All recorded amounts are reasonably accurate, and changes in economic circumstances that affect recorded amounts are reflected in the financial statements (valuation).
4. Amounts are recorded in the proper period (allocation).
5. Amounts are correctly posted to and summarized in the financial statements, and are recorded in the correct financial statement classification (presentation).
6. Adequate pertinent information is set forth in the financial statements so that the statements are not misleading and are a fair presentation in all material respects (disclosure).

Structured Approach to the Audit

Many auditors will use a structured approach, based on a framework of concepts, to design a program for each specific audit engagement. This approach is based on two major assumptions:

* No two audits are alike, and major differences will have to be dealt with in each audit.
* A methodology that assesses risk and focuses on the company's transactions is adaptable for application to all audits.

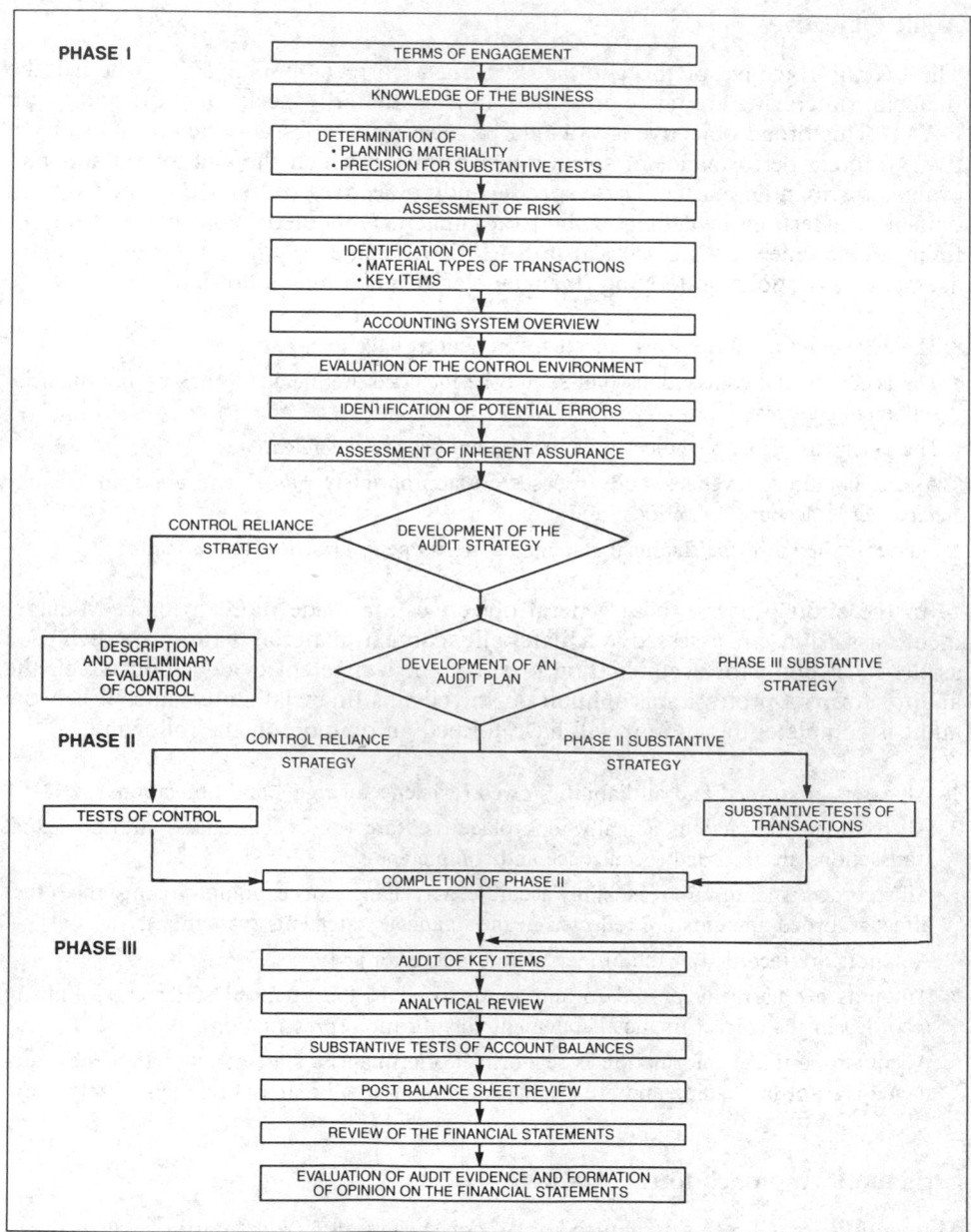

FIG. 7.1 Schematic of a Structured Audit Approach

Under the structural approach, the process is neither overly rigid nor flexible; it provides a disciplined approach, based on risk assessment, to determine the audit effort required. By recognizing that no two companies operate in the same way, the process focuses on the company's transactions, unifying the audit effort. The auditor thus approaches the audit in the following manner:

1. Understanding the company's business because that understanding is vital to a focused audit.
2. Understanding the company's operating transactions because they are tangible evidence of business activity and the unifying ingredient in every company's internal control structure.
3. Focusing these understandings on
   a. The potential errors in transactions or in their recording during the period under audit;
   b. Judgments about probable future transactions or events and their potential effect on the company's financial statements.

The structured audit approach is graphically illustrated in Figure 7.1 and consists of three phases:

- *Phase I—Planning and Evaluation.* In this phase, the central issue concerns where audit attention should be concentrated and how the auditor should satisfy his audit objectives. This depends, of course, on what the company does, its location, size, control systems, and many other factors. Using his knowledge of the industry, the auditor broadly considers information about the client's business, identifies areas of significance and risk, documents major accounting systems, develops an understanding of the internal control structure, and develops the overall audit plan.

- *Phase II—Systems Testing.* If the auditor intends to significantly rely on the satisfactory functioning of the internal control structure, he tests and evaluates the control systems in this phase. The reliance decision is based on perceived audit efficiency and effectiveness, and therefore must be based on the apparent reliability of the system and the probable costs of a reliance-based audit versus other choices. Ordinarily, the larger the company, the more significant the need for a well-developed control system that sorts and processes a large number of transactions. The smaller the company, the more necessary it may become to directly test transactions and balances rather than "prove-up" the internal control structure. In either case, both kinds of tests are significant. The audit process ordinarily uses a combination of both approaches to transaction testing to achieve the auditor's objectives.

- *Phase III—Completion of the Audit.* The nature and extent of the work in this phase depends on the auditor's assessment of the likelihood of errors in the financial statements, giving consideration to his conclusions from Phases I and II. Phase III procedures are analytical and detailed, and all are correlated with specific audit objectives.

The structured audit approach is far more than a recognition that different industries may require different approaches; it also addresses such issues as whether the audit should be conducted substantially at year end, or whether significant work can be performed at interim dates.

All levels of staff can understand a structured approach, use it in determining what work needs to be done, and interrelate the work performed to achieve the audit objectives. Furthermore, the staff can understand their assigned audit objectives, design effective approaches, and indeed even challenge the approach in a logical and informed way. A structured approach enables the auditor to focus his audit effort—and obtain results—in areas where audit risks and significance are greatest.

Auditors are not required by professional standards to use a structured approach; what is required is that the auditor reach a reasonably based conclusion that the financial statements are not materially misstated. Another common approach is the use of standard programs for various client groupings (e.g., industries), with customizing performed during execution based on conditions encountered. The choice is commonly made based on research performed by each firm, resulting in a decision as to what is deemed best in the circumstances given the nature of its practice and clientele.

Audit Environment

Contemporary auditing practice is very competitive. Consequently, some emphasis must be placed on how audit objectives can be achieved in a cost-beneficial way. Additionally, to retain good auditors, whose audit experience makes excellent credentials for financial and management positions outside the profession, the nature and level of work assignments must be challenging, pertinent, and build useful skills.

Rapid, significant changes in the United States and world economies present unprecedented challenge. For example, the United States has moved from essentially a manufacturing-based to a service-based economy in fewer than 20 years; moreover, what had been some of the most stable sectors are now much more fluid (e.g., the entire financial services sector, discussed in Chapters 40 through 44). All these factors have a major impact on designing and executing audit activities in a competitive environment. Given these major environmental shifts, serious attention needs to be given to the nature of services the audit team will be expected to provide in the future.

Auditing is also a demanding profession. It encompasses a significant range of activities from the specific (e.g., determining how many items to test) to the complex and subjective (e.g., assessing the acceptability of an accounting estimate). Auditing will become even more demanding as the business community takes on expanded reporting prerogatives, such as assurances on prospective financial information or on differently measured information, such as human resource accounting information, which may be a natural part of evolution in a service-based economy.

Financial Information Continuum

A useful way to address the audit is to consider the nature of the financial information subject to audit, segmented to illustrate the procedures and the levels of auditors involved (staff, in-charge, and engagement management).

Financial information can be roughly segmented as shown in Figure 7.2. Some information is mostly factual (lower left) and thus can be examined to ascertain its existence and condition. Moving right along the arc, information begins to require more interpretation (top); and at the lower right, it is almost entirely predictive. Of course, not many matters are precisely classifiable into the three broad categories depicted, but are matters of degree; hence this schematic is called a continuum. Using inventory to illustrate these broad categories, questions that may be asked are:

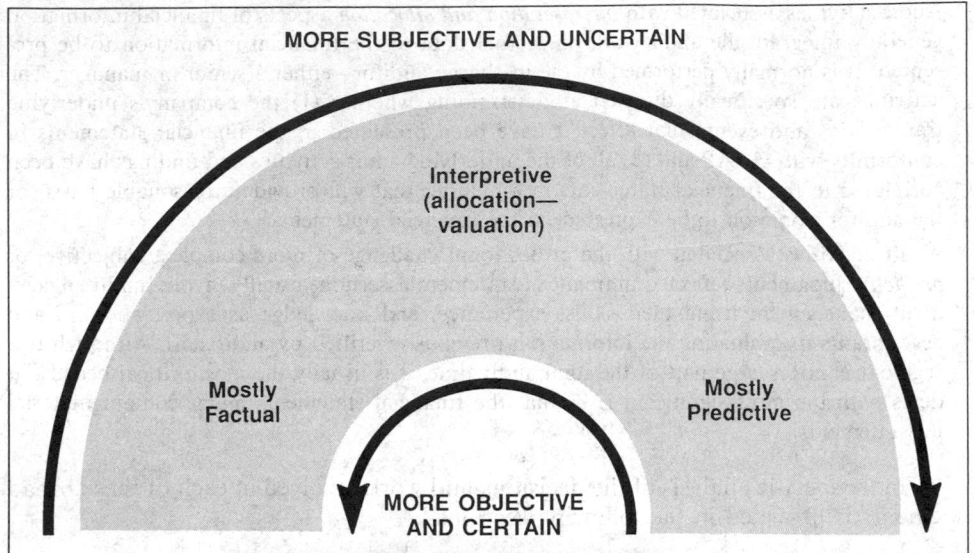

FIG 7.2 Financial Information Continuum

- *Mostly fact.* How many and what types of inventory items are there? (One related audit decision is: how many items should the auditor count?)
- *Interpretation and allocation.* How should the cost of material and labor be related to each inventory unit? (One related audit decision is how consistent with prior years is the method used this year to allocate these costs, and has the allocation resulted in a reasonable cost amount for each inventory item?)
- *Mostly prediction.* Should the inventory be valued at cost or market? (One related audit issue is what is the likelihood that the probable sales price of the item will be greater than its cost?)

Audit activities should be directly correlated with the level of the knowledge, skill, and experience of the audit team, and should focus directly on the conclusions that each audit team member is qualified to make. Audit team members performing the activities must have sufficient ability to understand their findings and the interrelationship of these findings with other parts of the audit.

A broad analysis of audit activities and consideration of who should perform them follows:

- Audit activities associated with the verification of *mostly factual* information involve staff from the initial to senior category (usually less than four years' experience). This area usually makes up the largest part of the time spent on each audit. These activities are critical to the audit because they provide the fact basis on which many financial statement items are stated. Equally critical, they provide the evidence necessary for more experienced audit team members to challenge assertions in the financial statements that require subjective or more complex judgments, especially those involving consideration of future probabilities.

- Audit activities associated with *interpretation and allocation* aspects of financial information generally integrate the audit work on factual data to the financial information to be presented. It is normally performed by the in-charge auditor—either a senior or manager. The activities are specifically directed at determining whether (1) the company's underlying transactions and events that affect it have been presented in the financial statements in conformity with GAAP and (2) all of the underlying audit activities and findings have been correlated to the financial statements in a manner that will provide a reasonable basis for the auditor's opinion to be expressed on the financial statements.

- Audit activities associated with the professional challenge of more complex, subjective, or *predictive* judgments reflected in financial statement assertions usually involve audit engagement management using their skills, experience, and knowledge as expert auditors and accountants in evaluating the information previously verified by audit staff. Although this segment is not a large part of the total audit time, it is usually the most critical because it deals with the most significant risks that the financial statements might contain material misstatements.

A more specific analysis of the decisions and work involved in each of these broad segments is provided in the following sections.

Factual Information. The work associated with the audit verification of the mostly factual information is a large part of most audits and is performed by the less experienced members of the audit team. It involves a wide range of possible audit approaches, for example, an audit involving a degree of reliance on the internal control structure ranging from minor to extensive, or a mix of reliance in some parts of the audit and little or no reliance in other parts of the audit.

This stage also involves a number of "generic" audit procedures, including assessments of whether specific controls are working, and the application of substantive tests. The actual procedures will depend on how the company authorizes, executes, records, and summarizes transactions and events, and how it maintains accountability for its resources. As with all audit work, the objective of the auditor's verification activities is to search for errors or irregularities that would have a material effect on the financial statements, and to exercise due skill and care in the conduct of that examination. According to SAS 53, *The Auditor's Responsibility to Detect and Report Errors and Irregularities*:

> The auditor should assess the risk that errors and irregularities may cause the financial statements to contain a material misstatement. Based on that assessment, the auditor should design the audit to provide reasonable assurance of detecting errors and irregularities that are material to the financial statements. [AU 316.05] . . . The auditor's objective is to reach a conclusion on whether the financial statements, taken as a whole are materially misstated. [AU 316.23]

To accomplish this objective, it is necessary for the auditor to determine the conditions under which material misstatement risks could exist. Using a structured transaction and risk approach, the significance of the asset or liability is determined, and the specific risk of possible material errors or irregularities is assessed by category (high, moderate, low; or by use of a mathematical expression such as the precision and accuracy parameters used in statistical sampling). Moreover, because transactions tie together most of the major activities of the company, following a transaction under audit from initiation to its final location in the company's records enables the auditor to articulate the relationship of this work to other audit work.

The interrelationships for just a single transaction will illustrate the complexity. If the auditor believes that a significant risk could exist, he must consider a number of possible things that can go wrong. For example, some of the errors that could occur in a sales transaction are:

- Sales can be recorded but goods are not shipped
- Goods can be shipped but not recorded
- Sales can be recorded incorrectly
- Goods can be shipped to a bad credit risk
- Sales can be misclassified
- Sales can be improperly costed
- Sales can be recorded in the wrong period
- Sales can be summarized or posted incorrectly

Even this degree of articulation may not provide a sufficiently specific focus for the audit, and a more detailed assessment at the specific cause level is needed (frequently done when significant accounting applications involve complex EDP processing, as described in Chapter 10.)

To prevent or detect these possible errors, many different controls may appear to exist. A decision therefore has to be made as to which controls – manual or EDP-based – to test in relation to one or more potential errors. Alternatively, tests of controls may not be a significant part of the audit plan. If substantive tests will be used without placing any reliance on controls, it will be necessary to test controls only to the extent required to determine that the company is auditable and that the controls are sufficient to enable substantive audit tests to be performed. (See Chapter 8.)

Some auditing procedures may pertain to more than one potential error; conversely a combination of auditing procedures and related assurances may be needed to deal with a single potential error type.

The interrelationships with which the auditor must deal often are quite complex. A single transaction (and related potential errors) will affect at least two financial statement account balances because of double-entry bookkeeping. Further, the related potential errors in one transaction can affect other parts of a related transaction stream (e.g., the relationship between the sales system and the sales costing system).

Interpretive and Allocative Information. In this segment the auditor addresses whether all the underlying events and transactions have been presented in conformity with GAAP, *before* consideration of valuation decisions. In other words, the auditor will ascertain that all of the underlying audit activities up through this segment have been correlated in a manner that provides a reasonable basis for an audit opinion, subject to the evaluation that must be performed in the next segment.

The work performed is arranged in relation to major transactions (from transaction initiation to account balance at the reporting date) or in relation to balances (working in reverse order back to the transaction base). This work provides an indication of risks, considers their significance, and demonstrates how the audit work leads to the specific assessments and conclusions by the auditor.

The structured audit approach provides a framework of the major transactions or balances and the assessment of the nature of the risk in relation to the possibility that material errors or irregularities may exist. This approach in the interpretative and allocative segment is quite different from the approach used in other audit planning and performance methods (i.e., use of standard programs for various client groupings, with customizing performed during execution based on conditions encountered). The structured approach requires that the auditor study the company and *think* through the audit process in relation to the specific risks under consideration; it encourages him to be intensive and specific in deciding how those risks are to be dealt with. When this is accomplished, the auditor performing a task is much more aware of why the task is performed and what the results of the work signify. Although the structured approach places the responsibility for actual involvement in audit strategy much closer to those who perform the procedures than do other commonly used audit approaches, it does require a clear understanding by, and proper development of the skills and knowledge of, the specific auditors who will perform the tasks.

The structured approach also requires that firms using it provide comprehensive training in audit techinques, theory, and audit interrelationships, in the context of the audit tasks that each staff member will be authorized to perform. Thus a significant investment in training and on-the-job supervision is required. For a staff engaged mostly in audit-type activities, it is cost-effective. On the other hand, if auditing work is incidental to a firm's practice, it is doubtful that the investment will be warranted since planning time ordinarily will be greater than is the case in other approaches.

Predictive Information. Complex, subjective, or predictive judgments reflected in financial statement assertions usually involve consideration by audit engagement management of information that has been verified by the audit staff, in the context of the management group's skills, experience, and knowledge as expert auditors and accountants. The structured approach provides an integrated presentation to engagement management of: (1) specific major transaction streams and all financial statement balances interrelated to the specifically identified risks (potential errors); (2) how these risks were addressed by the audit work (including why more work was done than planned), and the results of that work; and (3) the related conclusions. In effect, an integrated view of the whole audit is segmented into major interrelated groups of transactions and financial statement balances.

Although not a large part of the time is spent on mostly predictive information in most audits, it is usually the most critical in that it deals with the most significant risks that the financial statements might contain a material misstatement.

Materiality

Management is responsible for preparing the financial statements of the reporting enterprise. These statements must be *reasonably* accurate. In practice it is virtually impossible for them to be precisely accurate, but they must be sufficiently accurate so as not to be misleading to users who have a reasonable understanding of business and economic activities and who are willing to study the information with reasonable diligence. The degree to which financial statements may be imprecise but not misleading is known as *materiality*. When a misstatement or omission is so great as to lead an informed user of the financial statements to make a different economic decision than he would have made if the defect had not existed, the deficiency is said to be material. The materiality of an item depends, therefore, not only on its size, but also on qualitative aspects such as whether it involves related parties or conflicts of interest, or whether it appears irregular or even illegal.

The concept of materiality is important to management because it allows the preparation of acceptable financial statements without incurring inordinately high accounting and preparation costs in a vain effort to be exact. This concept is also applied by the auditor to control auditing costs, for it allows him to gather only enough competent evidence to provide reasonable assurance that the financial statements are not materially affected by errors or irregularities. Total certainty by the auditor is not economically feasible, and it is not required by professional standards, nor even by the severest informed critics of the auditing profession.

Internal Control Structure

The financial statements are based on the enterprise's accounting process. This process consists of systems and controls designed to provide a level of discipline and reliability adequate to assure management that (1) the financial statements are appropriately prepared, (2) the assets are safeguarded and their existence is periodically verified, and (3) transactions are executed only as authorized and are recorded in a manner that maintains accountability for the assets.

The existence of systems and controls, commonly termed the *internal control structure*, provides the auditor with numerous auditing options. In effect, the auditor can audit the results of processing (the financial statements), he can audit the process itself (the internal control structure), or he can do some of both. These two approaches are termed the *substantive approach* and the *reliance approach*, respectively. In practice, a combination approach is commonly used. The auditor seeks to design an optimal combination for any given audit, depending on the quality of the internal control structure, the relative effectiveness of available procedures, the adequacy of evidence, and the economies offered by various alternatives. Internal control structure is fully covered by Chapter 8.

Enterprise Attributes

Certain characteristics of the audited enterprises affect the auditing process. Among the most important are size, ownership, processing systems, and industry.

The size of the entity will often affect the audit approach. Small companies are likely to have less sophisticated and less developed internal control structures than large companies, but audits of large companies require more logistics because of their complexity and transaction volume. Because of these differences, auditors tend to adopt a predominantly substantive approach in audits of small companies and a predominantly reliance approach in audits of large companies. The substantive approach minimizes the uncertainties about appropriate presentation of the financial statements that could arise from potentially weak controls; the reliance approach allows work to be performed over a longer period of time and prior to the close of the company's fiscal year.

Publicly held companies are subject to the provisions of the 1933 and 1934 securities acts (and in some cases other acts administered by the SEC), which place formidable reporting requirements on the companies and audit reporting burdens on their auditors. Many other companies with a fiduciary responsibility to the public, such as financial institutions (Chapters 40–44), are regulated and audited in much the same way. The seriousness of these responsibilities is emphasized by the legal sanctions contained in the securities acts and interpreted by the courts (Chapter 49) and by the regulations administered by the SEC (Chapter 47).

Because of the broad regulatory reach, auditors must be knowledgeable about the applicable laws and regulations and must perform numerous additional steps in conducting audits of publicly held companies.

The great majority of business enterprises of any size use EDP equipment, either in-house or through service bureaus, for processing at least some of their financial information. And constantly decreasing per-unit processing costs have brought the computer within the reach of even the smallest enterprises. The computer presents the auditor with both an opportunity and a challenge. The opportunity is to use this powerful tool to assist in performing a more effective and efficient audit, as discussed in the next section. The challenge is to be adept with the complex technology used in EDP information, and to evaluate its impact on the audited company's internal control structure. These matters are discussed in detail in Chapter 10.

In discussions of auditing such as in this chapter, the typical application is to commercial or manufacturing companies, but many audits are of companies in industries with special characteristics. Banks, insurance companies, construction companies, health care organizations, securities broker/dealers, and the extractive industries are a few examples of industries with special business characteristics that the auditor must understand because they usually require specific recognition in audit planning and performance. As specialized industries are discussed in this *Handbook,* unique auditing aspects are emphasized.

Use of Microcomputers

Microcomputers are found everywhere in the business environment, with continuous growth in number and in application sophistication. Auditors were quick to recognize that microcomputers can increase audit efficiency and effectiveness, and can use them to support the audit in a variety of ways. There are three broad levels of sophistication in microcomputer use by auditors:

* Automation of record-keeping and reporting activities
* Assistance in basic audit routines
* Assistance in complex audit functions

The optimal automated record-keeping and reporting applications are those that involve the single capture of information for multiple use. In a system to control audit time and budget, for example, the initial capture of the time information also can be used in budgets, estimates of overall costs, and scheduling of staff time. Such automated applications reduce manual processing time and increase the amount of information available for audit decisions.

In basic audit routines, the power of the microcomputer permits efficient integration, analysis, comparison, and communication of data, and performance of "what if" scenarios. Specific applications ordinarily include spreadsheet analysis of transaction cycles and balances, audit risk analysis, simple analytical review, planning of statistical sampling applications, and evaluation of sampling results. Microcomputers can also help perform a variety of procedures related to specific account balances, such as:

* Depreciation recalculation
* Accounts receivable confirmation control
* Tax accrual recalculation
* Interest expense recalculation
* Inventory observation and valuation control

At the complex level, the microcomputer can be used by engagement management to test decisions, for example, accounting estimates, asset valuations, and risk and scope assessments at subsidiary and division levels as well as in the aggregate. These applications typically involve sophisticated analytical review techniques, forecasting and model-building, accessing of information data bases to enable industry-related analysis of client operations, and micro-based accounting research.

An auditing procedure study, *Auditors' Use of Microcomputers* (AICPA, 1986d) was issued to familiarize practitioners with ways in which microcomputers are being used on audit engagements. The study concludes:

> We can expect the auditor to evaluate more client data with microcomputers and in different ways. The microcomputer can be used to directly access data stored on the client's mainframe or microcomputer so that this information can be processed on the auditor's microcomputer. In addition, the microcomputer may be used as an on-site data-collection device recording client data as it is processed by the client's computer—either for a limited period or in a monitoring mode, recording only those transactions that the auditor has instructed the computer to record. Specially designed microcomputer software would then analyze the data.
>
> We will no doubt see more and higher-level decision-making capabilities included in audit software. Referred to as expert systems, artificial intelligence, or decision support or processing systems, these audit support systems exist and other systems are currently in the research and development stage. Although the more complex generally require computers larger than the present microcomputers, these capabilities may soon be available on the microcomputer.

THE AUDIT PROCESS

With the conceptual background covered in the preceding portions of this chapter, the audit phases depicted in Figure 7.1 can now be addressed in more detail.

Phase I: Planning

Understanding the Business. The auditor is auditing a *business*, not just a set of books and records. Therefore, he must understand its operations in terms of its industry, products, markets, production processes, distribution systems, facilities, personnel, financing, and other aspects relevant to the audit.

There are several specific reasons this understanding should be kept in mind as information is obtained:

- To identify the degree of professional risk
- To identify the need for special expertise in problem areas
- To provide information about the client's systems
- To provide a basis for assessment of accounting policies
- To provide the best possible client service

These reasons are discussed in the subsections that follow.

Degree of professional risk. When investors or creditors lose money, it is common for them to seek recovery through claims against auditors. The usual allegations in these cases, discussed in detail in Chapter 49, are that the investors and creditors relied on audited financial statements that failed to provide them with information that would have influenced their decisions and enabled them to avoid their losses. Such claims may or may not be sustained, but the auditor must recognize that they present a significant professional risk. Since a client's economic downturn increases that risk, the auditor should identify early warning signs of potential economic downturns. Conventional forms of financial analysis (discussed under the section entitled "Analytical Review" later herein) are often used for this purpose.

A weak management organization or poor managerial performance or control can also result in "hard times" for the client, or may lead to defensive business decisions that are not in the company's best overall interest. Thus, in addition to using conventional financial analysis, including bankruptcy predictors, the auditor should consider conditions pointing to weaknesses in management performance or control.

Finally, the auditor must recognize that the integrity of management and its good faith in providing audit information are fundamental to the performance of an adequate audit. If members of management lack integrity and good faith in their dealings with the auditor, they could circumvent controls established for the proper recording of transactions, and the resulting financial statements could be misstated. It is essential, therefore, that the auditor attempt to understand the motives of management and to identify conditions that might lead it to act without integrity or good faith. (Lack of integrity is often manifested through concealed related party transactions, discussed in Chapter 25.)

The auditor's appraisal of his own professional risk is made on a continuing basis for existing clients and before an engagement is accepted with a new client. If the professional risk is high, the auditor will adjust his audit to compensate for it. In some cases, the auditor may decline to perform the audit. Several examples of prominent factors that the auditor should consider in appraising professional risk are the complexity of the client's business and the nature of the industry, as well as are the likelihood of fraud, bankruptcy, takeover or merger, or sudden collapse. SAS 47,

Audit Risk and Materiality in Conducting an Audit (AU 312) discusses the essential ingredients at length.

Special expertise in problem areas. Auditing is normally a team effort. One reason for this is the sheer size of most audits, coupled with the need to perform all the required tasks by a deadline. Another reason is that certain tasks require special skills that not all auditors possess. When these skills are required, they must be identified, and the person able to provide them must usually be arranged for in advance. The areas most commonly requiring special skills are:

• Industry expertise;

• EDP expertise;

• Advanced auditing methodology; and

• Expertise in other professional disciplines, such as geology or actuarial science.

When the client is in an industry with unique accounting and auditing problems, a person with a knowledge of that industry should be involved. If this knowledge is not possessed by the engagement team, a consultant may be required on a part-time basis. When the client is a publicly held company, there is a need for an auditor with SEC experience.

As discussed in Chapters 9 and 10, auditing firms have various philosophies about and approaches to the use of auditing methods such as statistical sampling, computer audit techniques, and expert systems. Some firms use persons designated as specialists who perform these tasks on several engagements with which they are not otherwise associated. Other firms train all their auditors to a sufficient level of expertise so that the advanced methods can be applied by members of the engagement team, with consultation from a technical expert required only where necessary. Whatever the approach, persons with the requisite skills to properly apply these techniques must be brought into the engagement.

Outside experts or specialists are often needed on an engagement, for example:

• Actuaries, to review pension provision and funding computations;

• Engineers, to measure bulk inventories or mineral reserves;

• Gemologists, to determine the value of precious stones;

• Appraisers, to value real estate; and

• Lawyers, to interpret contracts and agreements.

Whenever such specialists are used, the auditor must have a basic understanding of the special expertise being applied and must consider whether the specialist's findings support the related representations in the financial statements. The auditor must also make appropriate tests of accounting data provided by the client to the specialist (SAS 11; AU 336).

Information about the client's systems. A major portion of Phase I of the audit involves developing an understanding of the client, business, industry, and the internal control structure. Knowledge of the business will lead to the identification of elements of the client's internal control structure and their relative significance to the audit examination. To identify the most important systems, the auditor first identifies the material types of transactions that take place in the business – the major economic events that are processed by the company's systems and that affect the financial statements. Those systems that process material types of transactions are very significant to the audit. Other systems are of interest, but need not be described in the detail necessary to support a critical evaluation by the auditor.

Whenever a transaction – material individually or as a type – is not processed by a formal system or by one of appropriate strength, it usually requires greater audit scrutiny than if it were subject to appropriate systems and controls. The auditor should always consider whether a control-related "reportable condition" exists that needs to be communicated to the client (SAS 60, AU 325).

Assessment of accounting policies. An understanding of the business provides an important context for the judgments the auditor must make throughout his examination. The appropriateness of the accounting policies followed and their effect on and presentation in the financial statements, the need for and wording of specific financial statement disclosures, the reasonableness of client representations and explanations, and the broad implications of financial results as they are to be reported, must all be viewed in terms of the client's business.

Providing the best possible client service. Although the auditor's primary objective is to express an opinion on the financial statements, a strong secondary objective is to provide helpful advice in the form of recommendations to management. In gaining an understanding of the client's business, the auditor will have an opportunity to recognize particular problems and suggest solutions to them. Based on the auditor's objectivity and broad business experience gained by auditing many companies, these recommendations may fall in operations areas as well as the financial area.

Information about the client's business is available to members of the audit team from a number of sources, including:

1. Audit working paper files from prior years.
2. Visits to the client's locations and tours of facilities.
3. Discussions with client management and employees.
4. Industry publications, the business press, libraries, firm publications, professional institute publications, and annual reports of other companies in the same business.
5. Client publications such as annual reports, prospectuses, advertising literature, interim financial reports, and policy manuals.
6. Management's financial reports, budgets and forecasts, and directors' minutes.

Since this information is gathered by all the members of the audit team over a period of time, it is important that it be properly communicated within the team. To accomplish this, it should be assembled with forethought and made accessible to team members as needed. Much of the external data in this listing is also available through databases (see Chapter 50).

The auditor's documented understanding of the business should include a summary of the following types of information (each type is accompanied by a few examples):

- Long-range company plans—corporate objectives, targets for products or market share, financial goals in terms of profits or share price.
- Organization structure—operating divisions, diversification, management organization, departmentalization, decentralization.
- Marketing—customer characteristics, major markets, potential markets, marketing strategy, future products.
- Production—product lines, facilities and locations, purchasing, labor relations and policies, physical flow of materials, inventories and warehousing.
- Sales—sales force, distribution system, commission policies, selling techniques.
- Financial matters—banking relationships, financial resources, plans for future financing, profitability of the industry, stock trading performance.
- Ownership and management—principal stockholders, principal debt holders, directors and officers, key management personnel.
- Special relationships with other parties—common ownership or management, franchisers or franchisees, government relationships.

Evaluation of Internal Control Structure. As a part of every audit, the auditor is required to understand an entity's internal control structure.

If a reliance approach is planned, the process of evaluating the internal control structure often comprises a significant portion of the audit. The nature of the internal control structure, the steps in evaluation, the various purposes of evaluation, and related matters are discussed in depth in Chapter 8.

Objective of the evaluation. For purposes of understanding the audit process, the objective of the evaluation of the internal control structure is to assess the likelihood of errors in the financial statements. If the auditor concludes that there is little likelihood that material errors exist, he can perform a satisfactory audit of the financial statement balances with less effort than if he strongly suspects the presence of such errors; in that case his procedures must be extensive enough to provide an approximation (within tolerances of materiality) of their amounts, thus enabling the client to record the adjustments proposed by the auditor.

Evaluation steps. Briefly, the steps in evaluating the internal control structure are:

- *Identify the accounting systems* that process transactions having a material effect on the financial statements.
- *Describe the systems.* This is normally done in a way that highlights the accounting controls contained in the systems and facilitates analysis. Many auditors use flowcharting for this purpose.
- *Verify the systems descriptions.* Because systems descriptions usually come from secondary sources—procedures manuals, interviews with client's supervisory personnel—it is important to assure their validity by reference to actual client data. This is done by selecting one or a few transactions of each type being processed and "walking" them through the system.
- *Identify the applicable objectives of control procedures*—or their converse, error types—in detail. An analysis of each material transaction type is made to hypothesize what the internal control structure must deal with to achieve the objectives or, alternatively, what kinds of

errors could occur that should be prevented, or detected and corrected, by the control procedures.

• *Identify the existing controls* for these objectives or error types. The systems descriptions are now analyzed to determine the characteristics and procedures that constitute effective controls – that is, the conditions and activities that the auditor believes will prevent, detect, and correct errors on a timely basis, thus reducing the likelihood of their affecting the financial statements.

• *Assess the likelihood of errors.* From the previous step, the auditor will know the set of controls for each specific error type. Based on this knowledge, the auditor can make a judgment on the likelihood that each error will occur. Together, these likelihoods constitute the auditor's evaluation of the internal control structure, although the evaluation remains detailed in terms of each individual error type rather than aggregated in terms of the structure as a whole. This is important because it allows the three phases of the audit to mesh effectively.

The form of the assessment has not been established by any predominant practice, and varies among auditors. One approach is to assess the likelihood of error either through quantification or use of agreed terms such as *low, moderate,* or *high,* defined as follows:

• *Low.* The auditor expects few, if any, errors.
• *Moderate.* The auditor expects errors, but believes they are not likely to be material.
• *High.* The auditor expects errors and believes they may be material.

Using the evaluation. The auditor uses the evaluation to set the approach for the overall audit plan. When control is not good and the likelihood of errors is high, the auditor must perform substantive tests to an extent sufficient to measure the errors in the financial statement balances within reasonable tolerances of materiality. If the internal control structure is so poor that evidence for these substantive tests is not available, the entity is not auditable.

When control is moderate, the auditor can rely on the controls, but not as heavily as when control is good. Often, the systems test in Phase II will be designed to look for errors in transactions as well as for indications of the application of control procedures. These substantive tests of transactions often allow the auditor to accomplish a portion of his substantive procedures more efficiently than if he performed them in Phase III after year end.

When control is good and the likelihood of errors is low, the auditor is entitled to take a reliance approach. He will include tests of the controls being relied on in Phase II and reduce the substantive procedures performed in Phase III accordingly. Of course, he can take a substantive approach even when control is good, if he decides this will be more efficient.

Because the evaluation made at this step in the audit process is subject to later verification through audit procedures, it is called the initial evaluation.

Internal auditors. An important aspect of the internal control structure is often provided by the client's internal audit department. This is further discussed in Appendix 7. Chapter 5 discusses standards applicable to the practice of internal auditing.

Preparing an Overall Audit Plan. An overall audit plan is prepared as a basis for designing detailed audit procedures to be performed in Phases II and III. As procedures are performed and results obtained, the plan, along with the auditor's understanding of the client's business, provides a framework for making audit judgments. When the results obtained are as anticipated, the plan is validated, and the auditor proceeds on that basis. When unexpected results are obtained, the plan is used to determine the necessary changes in detailed procedures and approach.

Preparing the audit plan requires careful consideration of how to allocate materiality tolerances among the multitude of audit steps and procedures so that tests designed to identify material errors in a certain area do not overlook immaterial errors if there is a possibility that undetected immaterial errors in all audit areas could be material in total. The auditor's judgment is the primary ingredient in this decision; his experience, knowledge of transaction cycles and account interrelationships, and tendency to set test parameters conservatively, all contribute to the judgment.

The audit plan should be written in such a way that it communicates the audit approach to the audit team. It is often the nucleus of the formal audit program, containing the detailed procedures to be performed during the audit. A comprehensive audit plan consists of three main elements:

1. An identification of the major accounting systems and related transaction types, accompanied by a summary of the auditor's evaluation of the internal control structure and likelihood of errors. As previously explained, this information will suggest the available alternative audit approaches. Transaction cycles are the basic organizational framework for audit scope consideration. These cycles are described in Chapter 8; and Chapters 12 through 15 are built around the transaction cycle approach.

2. An identification of important financial statement accounts, indicating approximate balances expected to exist at year end and the relative audit significance or risk associated with each account. Since the auditor cannot perform a 100% examination of all details of all accounts, an allocation of effort is required. It is important to assign the greatest audit effort to the areas where the greatest payoff is expected. The evaluation of internal control structure will give information about the likelihood of errors from a transaction perspective. Further analysis will indicate the financial statement areas where those and other errors in significant amounts are likely to show up.

3. A statement of the planned approach, indicating for each account:
   • The planned degree of reliance on the internal control structure.
   • The planned extent of substantive procedures in both Phase II and Phase III.
   • The timing of Phase II procedures.
   • The timing of Phase III procedures.
   • For larger clients, the allocation of audit work among enterprise components.
   • Other major planning decisions, for example, use of computer audit techniques or outside specialists.

Phase II: Systems Testing

All systems tests have one objective: to reach a formal assessment, supported by audit evidence, of the likelihood of errors in the accounts. One of the two basic types of systems tests is the *control test*. In this procedure, the auditor obtains evidence supporting his understanding of the way internal controls work. Such evidence is gathered by making observations of internal control procedures in operation and by examining documents for specific indication of properly applied internal controls. Control tests have the effect of converting the initial evaluation of the internal control structure into a firmer evaluation.

The second basic type of systems test is the *substantive test of transactions*. By this procedure the auditor gains evidence about the correctness of the amounts resulting from transactions processed by the accounting systems and entered in the accounts. These tests can be performed at year end just as well as during the second phase of the audit process. However, it is often efficient to combine a large proportion of the substantive tests with compliance tests, thereby broadening the results of the systems testing phase. Note that both types of tests are dual purpose, to an extent. Control tests often identify monetary errors, and substantive tests provide compliance evidence.

Although both types of tests contribute to an assessment of the likelihood of errors in the financial statements, control tests generally do this indirectly, and substantive tests of transactions do it directly. Control tests confirm or modify the auditor's understanding of internal control structure, which he then uses to assess the likelihood of errors, whereas substantive tests of transactions measure the actual incidence of error. Of course, monetary errors found in control tests will be corrected as well, if other than trivial.

The assessment of likelihood of errors may be in the same form as that previously described for evaluation of internal control structure, either through quantification or use of terms such as low, moderate, or high. When such an assessment has been made as part of the initial evaluation and that evaluation is supported by control tests, the auditor's assessment for the third phase remains the same. When control tests yield other results, the assessment will change accordingly. For error types addressed by substantive tests, the assessment will be the direct result of these tests. Generally, there will also be some error types identified but not assessed by systems tests. The assessment for these error types must remain unknown even if they have been considered in the initial evaluation, for the auditor cannot rely on controls (i.e., evaluate the control risk at less than maximum (AU 319.39)) unless they are tested.

In practice, the lines between the phases in some transaction cycles are often not very distinct, especially between the second and third phases. This is so because a decision to use substantive procedures in Phase II is quite similar to using substantive procedures in Phase III.

Phase III: Verification of Financial Statement Balances

Designing Tests. The procedure for designing tests of financial statement balances consists of the following six steps:

1. For each important account, identify the set of transaction types that affect it.
2. For each transaction type affecting an account, identify the set of possible errors. Since each transaction type should affect two or more accounts, satisfactorily auditing one type of transaction usually contributes to the evidence supporting more than one account.

3. Recognize that each account has a set of audit objectives that must be supported by audit evidence.

4. Construct a matrix for each account in which the transaction error types form the columns and the audit procedures form the rows.

5. Enter information on the likelihood that the account will contain the error types assessed in Phase II.

6. Select audit procedures to accomplish the applicable audit objectives, taking the likelihood of errors into consideration. Generally, when the likelihood is low or moderate, fewer or less extensive procedures will be required; when the likelihood is high or unknown, more procedures, or more extensive ones, will be required.

The matrix referred to in step 4 can take various forms, but the purpose is to correlate transaction error types—what can go wrong in the particular audit area— with the audit objectives applicable in the specific circumstances. Using accounts receivable and sales as an example, Figure 7.3 identifies the detailed objectives in terms of potential error types interrelated to applicable client controls in a hypothetical situation. Figure 7.4 identifies in summary form how the substantive tests, both analytical and detailed, are correlated with each potential error. Note that often a single procedure accomplishes several objectives; it is important that the auditor consciously plan these steps to avoid both omitting procedures and performing redundant procedures.

This analysis is a key part of the audit process. It connects the Phase II systems tests with the Phase III tests of financial statement balances. Without this analysis as part of preparing the audit program, the auditor runs the risk of omitting important procedures, misallocating audit effort, or overauditing and incurring unnecessary costs.

The possible audit procedures that may be performed on a given account are almost infinite. Each yields a certain type and quality of evidence, and each has its own cost characteristics. The selection of specific procedures is a matter of audit judgment and depends on the accounts and objectives involved, the nature and effectiveness of the evidence to be obtained, and the costs of the alternative tests that will produce the necessary level of auditor satisfaction. There is no standard audit program that can be used without the need for exceptions and modifications. It is up to the auditor to develop the optimal program for each audit examination.

Once the procedures are selected, their timing and extent must be decided as well. Although many Phase III procedures are performed as of the balance sheet date, many others are performed as of a date prior to year end. This is pragmatic in terms of scheduling workloads and meeting completion dates, and is appropriate as long as procedures are performed to support the carryforward of the interim-date balances to year end.

Phase III procedures are of two general types, *analytical procedures* and *detailed tests of balances*. Analytical review procedures substantiate the reasonableness of account balances by use of comparisons with balances between years, with other accounts, and with industry data. Often the comparisons are in the form of ratios and trends. In some cases, mathematical techniques such as *models, regression estimation,* or *discriminant analysis* are used for such tests. Analytical tests do not provide precise results, but are very helpful in two other ways: (1) when they indicate plausible relationships, they corroborate that the balance of an account is reason-

Controls - A/R & Sales

Client: ABC Distribution Co.   Year Ending: Dec., 1988

Prep'd: D. Jones   9-15-88   Rev'd: N. Franklin   9-21-88

Sales Potential Errors

Sales Recorded, Goods Not Shipped

Goods Shipped, Sale Not Recorded

Sales Amount Recorded Incorrectly

Goods Shipped to a Bad Credit Risk

Sales Misclassified

Sales Recorded in the Wrong Period

Sales Summarization or Posting Error

1	2	3	4	5	6	7	Controls
		X					1 - Sales order approved for credit
X	X	X					2 - Shipping doc quantity checked in warehouse
X	X						3 - Shipping doc matched to sales invoice
	X						4 - Sales invoice matched to sales order
X	X						5 - Shipping docs checked for serial continuity
		X					6 - Sales invoice price/discount checked
		X					7 - Sales invoice additions/extensions checked
			X				8 - G/L code checked on sales invoice
		X					9 - Sales invoice qty agreed to shipping doc
X	X	X					10 - Sales invoices balanced to daily sales jnl
0		0					11 - Daily sales jnl recon to A/R ledger posting
						X	12 - Mthly sales jnl agreed to sum of daily jnls
			X				13 - Mthly sales jnl reviewed for reasonableness
					X	X	14 - Adequate written cut-off instructions
					X	X	15 - Personnel adequately instructed re cut-off
					X	X	16 - Achievement of cut-off reviewed
X		X	X				17 - Overdue A/R independently investigated
						X	18 - Mthly sales jnl agreed to G/L posting
X	X	X		X		X	19 - A/R account in G/L reconciled to A/R ledger

Assessments

1	2	3	4	5	6	7	
70	70	70	30	0	50	70	Control Assurance - Accounts Receivable
70	70	70	0	70	50	70	Control Assurance - Sales

Key: X = an effective control   0 = NOT an effective control

FIG. 7.3   Sample Matrix for Correlating Error Types with Applicable Client Controls

Cycle Summary - Accounts Receivable

Client: ABC Distribution Co.   Year Ending: Dec., 1988

Prep'd: D. Jones   9-15-88   Rev'd: N. Franklin   9-21-88

Sales Potential Errors

Sales Recorded, Goods Not Shipped
- Goods Shipped, Sale Not Recorded
- Sales Amount Recorded Incorrectly
- Goods Shipped to a Bad Credit Risk
- Sales Misclassified
- Sales Recorded in the Wrong Period
- Sales Summarization or Posting Error

1	2	3	4	5	6	7	Procedure Group Description
30	10	50					Total - Inherent Assurance
70	70	70	30		50	70	Total - Tests of Controls
5		5	5				Analytical Review - A/R Aging Analysis
5		5	5				Analytical Review - Days Sales in A/R Analysis
65		65			30	65	Phase III Test - Accounts Receivable Confirmations
30		10	70				Phase III Test - Allowance for Doubtful Accounts
					70		Phase III Test - Cut - off
70	70						Assessment of Assurance from Inventory Cycle
99	92	96	81		90	90	COMBINED ASSURANCE

FIG. 7.4 Illustration of Correlation of Substantive Tests With Potential Errors

able; and (2) when they indicate a possibly misstated balance, they provide direction for focusing detailed tests. Analytical review is discussed in detail in a subsequent section of this chapter.

Detailed tests of balances are the most widely used procedures in auditing. They generally involve sampling. In designing samples, the number of items to test is only one important audit decision. Sampling is discussed in detail in Chapter 9.

Performing Tests and Evaluating Results. After all the audit procedures and tests are properly planned, they must be performed by properly trained and supervised personnel, in accordance with GAAS. Supervision includes reviewing subordinates' work as well as giving direction.

A proper working paper record of work performed is essential, and is required under SAS 41 (AU 339). The media used for this purpose include audit programs, working paper schedules, copies of client documents, computer printouts, and memoranda. These working papers document the auditor's work and conclusions and are not to be confused with the client's documentation of its transactions, although the two often overlap, as when copies of client records are incorporated into the auditor's documentation. Some working papers are of a permanent nature, useful from one audit to the next, and are usually kept in separate files.

Audit procedures performed, and the results obtained, are indicated in the auditor's working papers using tick marks, footnote notations, narratives, and so forth. As documentation is prepared, it is initialled and dated by the preparer and later by the reviewer.

In performing individual tests of details of financial statement balances it is critical that:

1. The objectives of the test are clearly stated.
2. The documentation developed is in a form that relates the evidence gathered to the objectives.
3. A conclusion is achieved in terms relevant to the objectives.

When no errors are found through these tests, it is usually concluded that the objectives set for the tests have been met. When errors are found, the auditor must determine what they mean in relation to three auditing aspects:

1. What weaknesses in the internal control structure allowed the errors to occur?
2. What is the estimated magnitude of all such errors (found and not found), and is the aggregate material?
3. How should the audit approach be modified in view of these systems weaknesses and the materiality of error?

An approach taken by many auditors in answer to the magnitude question is to classify known and estimated error amounts into these categories:

1. *Negligible amounts.* These errors are considered insignificant and require no further consideration, except that the company would be expected to correct known errors as a matter of good business practice.

2. *Individually immaterial amounts.* These errors are accumulated throughout the audit to determine whether they are material in the aggregate. Again, a client's correction of its records for known immaterial errors is advisable, even if these corrections are not worked into the financial statements.

3. *Material amounts.* These errors require an adjustment by the client in order that the auditor may express an opinion as to the conformity of the financial statements with GAAP.

In addition to procedures and tests concerning the amounts in the financial statements, the auditor is responsible for performing a review of the period from the balance sheet date to the date of his audit report (usually upon completion of virtually all audit procedures that could have an effect on the nature of the auditor's report). This step is termed a *post-balance sheet review*, and is designed to assess whether any significant events have occurred after the balance sheet date that should be disclosed in or cause revision of the financial statements.

Phase III procedures are complete when sufficient competent evidential matter has been obtained in support of all audit objectives for all accounts, when the post-balance-sheet review has been completed, and when appropriate written representations have been obtained from management.

In addition, the auditor will review and corroborate footnote and supplementary disclosure data at this time if not accomplished as part of other procedures. Often such data is not incorporated in the formal accounting systems. Mention of the more prominent disclosures and their related audit approaches is provided throughout this *Handbook.*

The matters to be covered in the *letter of representations* are dictated by professional standards (SAS 19; AU 333). The letter is intended to assure that management accepts its responsibilities regarding the financial statements in general and the specific factual statements it has made to the auditors, and that it understands the nature of the auditor's examination.

Issuing the Audit Report. The distillation of all the audit evidence gathered is the auditor's judgment as to whether, within the bounds of materiality, the financial statement amounts are fairly presented and the necessary disclosures are made in conformity with GAAP. This judgment will determine the nature of the auditor's report. The auditor's unmodified report is the hoped for result, but in some cases the auditor will have to depart from the standard form. The most common types of departures (based on SAS 58, (AU 508) effective January 1, 1989) are listed below:

1. *A qualified opinion* indicates that the auditor believes the financial statements are incorrect in a particular material respect.

2. *An adverse opinion* indicates that the financial statements are so materially misstated or misleading overall that they do *not* present fairly the financial position or results of operations in conformity with GAAP.

3. *A disclaimer of opinion* is used when the auditor is unable to obtain adequate evidence to support the client's presentation of financial position or results of operations. This may arise because of a significant limitation on the scope of the auditor's examination, the existence of unusual uncertainties of great magnitude, or for other reasons.

Auditors' reports are covered extensively in Chapter 11.

ANALYTICAL REVIEW

Analytical Procedures as an Audit Tool

SAS 56, *Analytical Procedures* (AU 329), issued in 1988, amended the auditing literature by formally recognizing analytical review procedures as a major ingredient of
"sufficient competent evidential matter" (AU 326.20). Auditors are now required to
use analytical procedures in the planning and completion phases of the audit. In
actuality, auditors have always intuitively analyzed data, and many auditors and
audit firms have used analytical procedure systems of their own design or that were
created as software by the audit firms or commercial vendors. The analytical procedures should be designed to:

* Enhance and maintain the auditor's understanding of the client's business and industry.
* Assist the auditor in penetrating the form of financial statements to reach their substance.
* Alert him to potential risk situations.
* Help him see his client as others see them (e.g., present and potential owners and creditors).

Analytical procedures are an important part of the audit process and consist of
evaluations of financial information made by a study of plausible relationships
among both financial and nonfinancial data. Analytical procedures range from simple comparisons to the use of complex models involving many relationships and elements of data. A basic premise underlying the application of analytical procedures is
that plausible relationships among data may reasonably be expected to exist and
continue in the absence of known conditions to the contrary.

The expected effectiveness and efficiency of an analytical procedure in identifying
potential misstatements depends on, among other things:

* The nature of the assertion,
* The plausibility and predictability of the relationship,
* The availability and reliability of the data used to develop the expectation, and
* The precision of the expectation.

Analytical procedures involve comparisons of recorded amounts, or ratios developed from recorded amounts, to expectations developed by the auditor. The auditor
develops such expectations by identifying and using plausible relationships that are
reasonably expected to exist based on the auditor's understanding of the client and
of the industry in which the client operates. Examples of sources of information for
developing expectations include:

* Financial information for comparable prior period(s), giving consideration to known
  changes.
* Anticipated results, for example, budgets or forecasts including extrapolations from interim
  or annual data.
* Relationships among elements of financial information within the period.
* Information regarding the industry in which the client operates, for example, gross margin
  information.
* Relationships of financial information with relevant nonfinancial information.

Information for industry comparisons is available from many sources. Management often regularly obtains annual reports of competitors and industry leaders for the purpose of ratio comparison. Trade associations and security analysts publish extensive industry reports giving data on specific companies and the industry as a whole. Financial journals, such as *Barron's*, also publish this kind of data.

Substantive Tests. The auditor's reliance on substantive tests to achieve an audit objective related to a particular assertion may be derived from tests of details, from analytical procedures, or from a combination of both. The decision about which procedure or procedures to use to achieve a particular audit objective is based on the auditor's judgment.

The auditor considers the level of assurance needed from substantive testing for a particular audit objective and decides, among other things, which procedure or combination of procedures can provide that level of assurance.

Trend Comparisons. The use of analytical review procedures for comparisons of related account balances, ratios, trends, and the like provides useful evidence of the reasonableness of account balances or transaction streams, or of their conformity with an expected trend, as in a seasonal business. An example of this form of evidence is a comparison of the current period's repair expense with that of the previous year; if the comparison suggests that the repair expense is unexpectedly high or low, the auditor will then investigate the cause. If the area is not material to the financial statements, the auditor may request the client to investigate and explain.

Methodology

The most obvious sources of financial information are the balance sheet and the income statement. The balance sheet provides a beginning basis for assessing profitability, liquidity, and leverage; the income statement provides additional information for profitability analysis.

No definitive answers emerge from analyzing the balance sheet or income statement. However, analysis of relatively few ratios and trends can provide an insight into the client's business and its results, and assist the auditor in achieving the level of knowledge required by the audit process in Phase I. It may also raise questions about, and focus attention on, certain financial items which the auditor can pursue during the audit using company information or other sources of available data. For example, financial budgets, sales forecasts, and related operating results may provide more detailed information; and comparison between budgets, actual and forecast, can be revealing. Data regarding the client's industry and its key competitors may also be accessed.

Trend analysis considers changes in financial statement numbers over time. It tends to be more useful if the numbers being compared over time are put on a common basis, using percentages or indexing. For example, whether operating expenses

Questions	Component items
PROFITABILITY	
How profitable?	
Gross profit margin	Sales
Profit margin (operating income)	Gross profit
Net return on sales	Operating income
	Income before tax
How efficiently are resources used?	
Sales to total assets	Sales
Return on average total assets	Income before tax
Return on average tangible net worth	Total assets
	Tangible net worth
What is the profitability trend?	
Percentage sales change	Sales
Percentage gross profit change	Gross profit
Percentage income change	Income before tax
LIQUIDITY	
What is the short-term debt paying ability?	
Current ratio	Current assets
Quick ratio	Current liabilities
Cash ratio	Quick assets
How efficiently are resources used?	
Accounts receivable turnover	Accounts receivable (net)
Average days in receivables	Inventory
Inventory turnover	Working capital
Average days in inventory	
Working capital turnover	
Can future charges be met?	
Interest coverage	Net income
Interest to long-term debt	Interest expense
Long-term debt	
LEVERAGE	
How strong is debt coverage?	
Long-term debt to tangible net worth	Long-term debt
Total debt to tangible net worth	Total debt
Cash flow to total debt	Tangible net worth
	Operating cash flow
How high is debt leverage?	
Long-term debt to total assets	Long-term debt
Total debt to total assets	Total debt
Equity and preferred stock to total assets	Equity and preferred stock
	Total assets
How liquid are current assets?	
Ratio of each component of current assets to total current assets	Individual current asset components
	Total current assets

FIG. 7.5 Commonly Used Analytical Review Ratios

have increased or decreased may be less helpful than whether operating expenses as a percentage of sales have increased or decreased.

Trend analysis is most likely to be useful in analyzing profitability, selected liquidity measures, and cash flow. It is usually supplemented by ratio analysis, which compares the ratio of selected financial statement numbers with similar ratios for that company from prior periods (time series analysis) or with similar ratios derived from other entities within the same industry (cross-sectional analysis).

Some ratios are stable over time (e.g., the ratio of cost of sales to sales), and tend to be similar for different companies within the same industry group. This may allow a meaningful comparison over a period of years or between a number of companies, regardless of growth or size.

Ratio analysis is most often used to highlight changes over time in profitability, liquidity, and leverage. Cross-sectional analysis is used less frequently since variability within an industry group often reduces its usefulness.

Several studies of how ratio analysis might be used to predict potential bankruptcy have been published. The most extensive and well known is Altman's development of the *Z-Score* model.

The Z-Score is computed by adding the results of multiplying five ratios, derived from the company's financial statements, by specified weightings. The score is then compared to an upper and lower bound. If above the upper bound, the company is unlikely to go bankrupt. If below the lower bound, the company is in danger of bankruptcy. If in between the two bounds, no prediction is possible. For a detailed explanation of the Z-Score approach, see Altman, 1983.

To obtain an overview of the three key factors—profitability, liquidity, and leverage—a set of financial ratios has been derived from the balance sheet and income statement items. The ratios most commonly used by auditors, independent analysts, and creditors are included; Figure 7.5 lists questions related to these three areas, names the ratios, and identifies the financial statement components used to calculate the ratios listed under each question grouping. A computer spreadsheet is used to compute the ratios and display their components graphically over time. A printout report includes the ratios, their components, and a percentage change analysis of the ratios and their components. It also includes the Z-Score.

Key Issues in Performing Analytical Review

While it is tempting to measure the success of a business in terms of absolute increases in sales or profits over a series of years, a client's financial strengths or weaknesses are determined by factors that require a deeper analysis. For example, if analysis indicates the business is healthy and growing, the auditor must challenge whether his judgment and the evidence he has gathered support that indication. The client can, in fact, be going bankrupt despite apparent signs of sales and profit growth.

Before getting buried in which financial figures to analyze, where to find them, and how to analyze their meaning, an auditor should review some of the fundamental questions to be asked about any client's financial condition. These questions, although simple in appearance, are profound for the added insights the answers will provide.

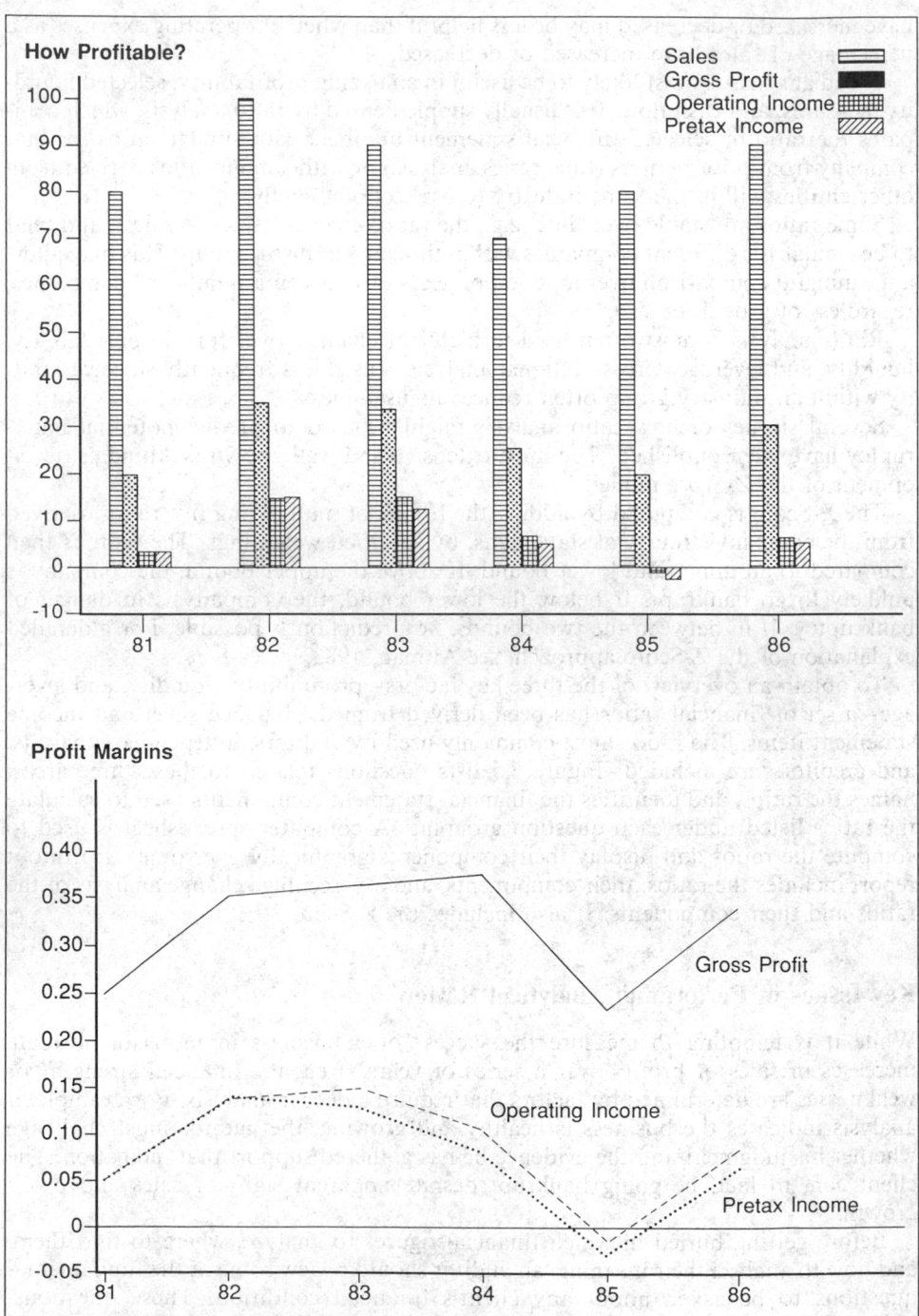

FIG. 7.6   Graphic Representation of Profitability Ratios

The questions and issues described in the following sections stem from four key factors: profitability, liquidity, leverage, and financial competence of management. Analysis of the financial statements can provide information regarding profitability, liquidity, and leverage (see Figure 7.5).

Management's financial competence must be determined by observation and interviews. In the extreme, incompetence may throw doubt on the financial statements and invalidate the basis for analysis.

Profitability. Without a clear understanding of how a company generates its profits, there is little ability to actually understand its key operations. The perceptive auditor may discover that the client's true source of profitability is different from that believed by top management. If the chief executive officer has a financial background, he may attribute profitability to shrewd debt management, when in reality the source is a "mad scientist" in R&D with an aptitude for new product discoveries!

Questions to be asked include:

- How does the company make money?
  - Through one key product (despite, perhaps, several losers)?
  - By high sales volume on low margin products?
  - By high quality products with a high mark up?
  - With advanced products that lead the competition?
- What does the company do with the money it makes?
  - Does it pay out high dividends to the owners or large bonuses to employees and managers?
  - Does it reinvest earnings in research and development or in reserves for future plant and equipment expansion?
- Has the way in which the company makes money changed substantially in the past few years?

Figure 7.6 illustrates in bar chart and line graph form the profitability history of a hypothetical company, based on information contained in a computer spreadsheet used for computation of key ratios. Figure 7.7 illustrates the return on assets and tangible net worth. Profitability may be analyzed in terms of historic trend or comparison with peers, but should always take into account external economic conditions. Consider the wisdom of companies who proudly proclaim a 5% return on equity as out-performing the competition, even when the cost of money is much higher. Numerous manufacturers have faded over the years because their capital was eroded by inflation and poor returns from outmoded product lines. They could have earned more by placing their net assets in a money market instrument.

Liquidity. Managing liquid resources can be critical. There are two facets to liquidity: achieving a targeted level of net cash flow and utilizing cash properly. A client may recognize that cash flow can be increased through lengthening the settlement period of accounts payable, but fail to utilize the additional cash in a profitable manner.

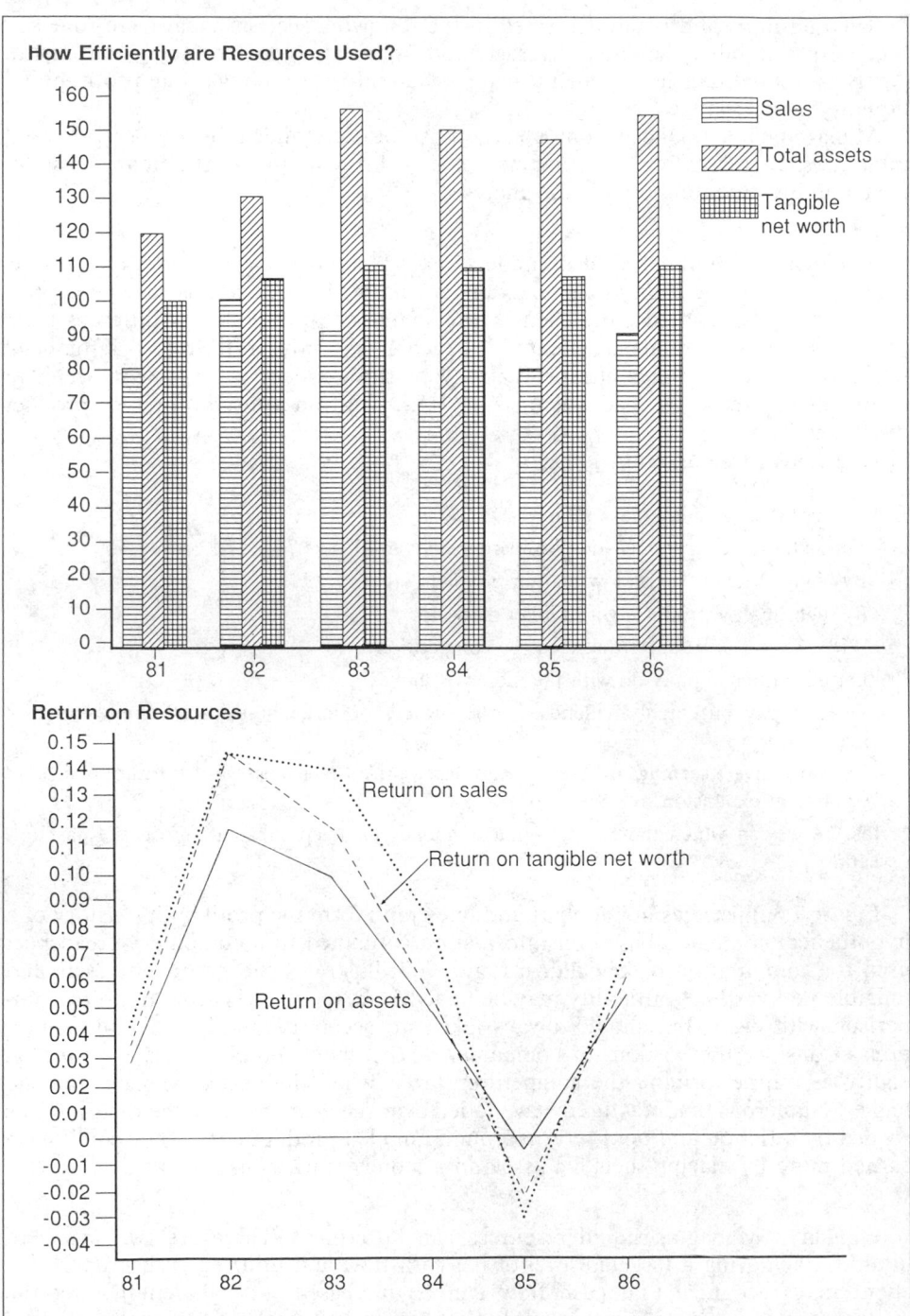

FIG. 7.7   Graphic Representation of Return on Assets and Tangible Net Worth

Key considerations are:

* How efficiently does the company use its resources?
  - Does it collect its receivables on time?
  - Is excess cash deposited in an interest bearing account?
* What risks does the company face as a result of its financial management strategies?
  - Is cash flow and capital adequate to meet future demands?
  - If sales dropped 20%, could current liabilities be paid?
  - Are there reserve sources of credit?

Relationships with and attitude toward banks is important. Does the company deal with only one bank "because we've always used them," or has the financial officer investigated the rates and services offered by competing banks?

Figure 7.8 illustrates in bar chart and line graph form the short-term liquidity ratios for a hypothetical company, trended using information contained in a computer spreadsheet used for computation of key ratios.

Leverage. A critical review of how the company allocates its economic resources is essential. This includes reviewing the company's opportunities for capital deployment and asset leveraging versus the payback anticipated; reviewing the efficiencies of current asset and liability usage; and comparing these results with the stated objectives of the company.

Questions to be considered are:

* How efficiently does the company allocate its resources?
  - Does it have too much short-term debt when it should have long-term debt at a lower cost?
  - Is each capital investment scrutinized carefully for its expected return?
* What risks does the company face as a result of its financial management strategies?
  - What is the client's actual risk position versus management's philosophy toward risk?
* How is leverage in the present debt structure being used?
  - Is the company highly leveraged or does it pride itself on never having to borrow?
  - Is money being drained off to cover short-term expenses without creating added value through long-term investments?
  - Would it be cheaper to arrange bank loans or to seek equity financing for future growth?
* If a company is leveraged aggressively:
  - What would be the effect on net earnings if the cost of debt service were lowered?
  - Would equity financing be more economical or would it endanger control of the company?

The auditor must assess the degree of risk in the client's present financial condition, and also whether management's plans for the future will overextend the company's resources.

Figure 7.9 illustrates in bar chart and line graph form the trend in leveraging ratios for a hypothetical company based on information contained in a computer spreadsheet used for computation of key ratios.

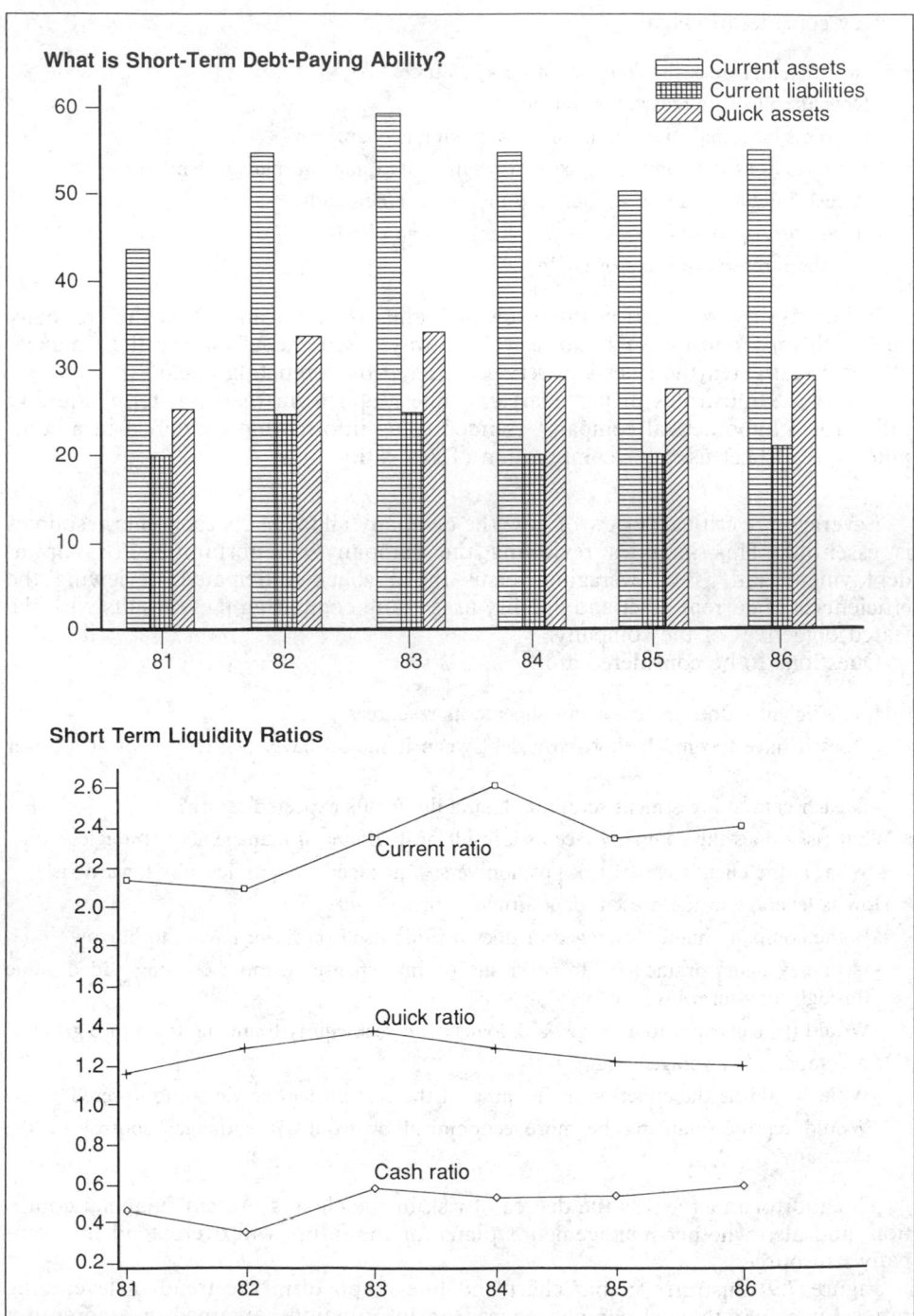

FIG. 7.8   Graphic Representation of Liquidity Ratios

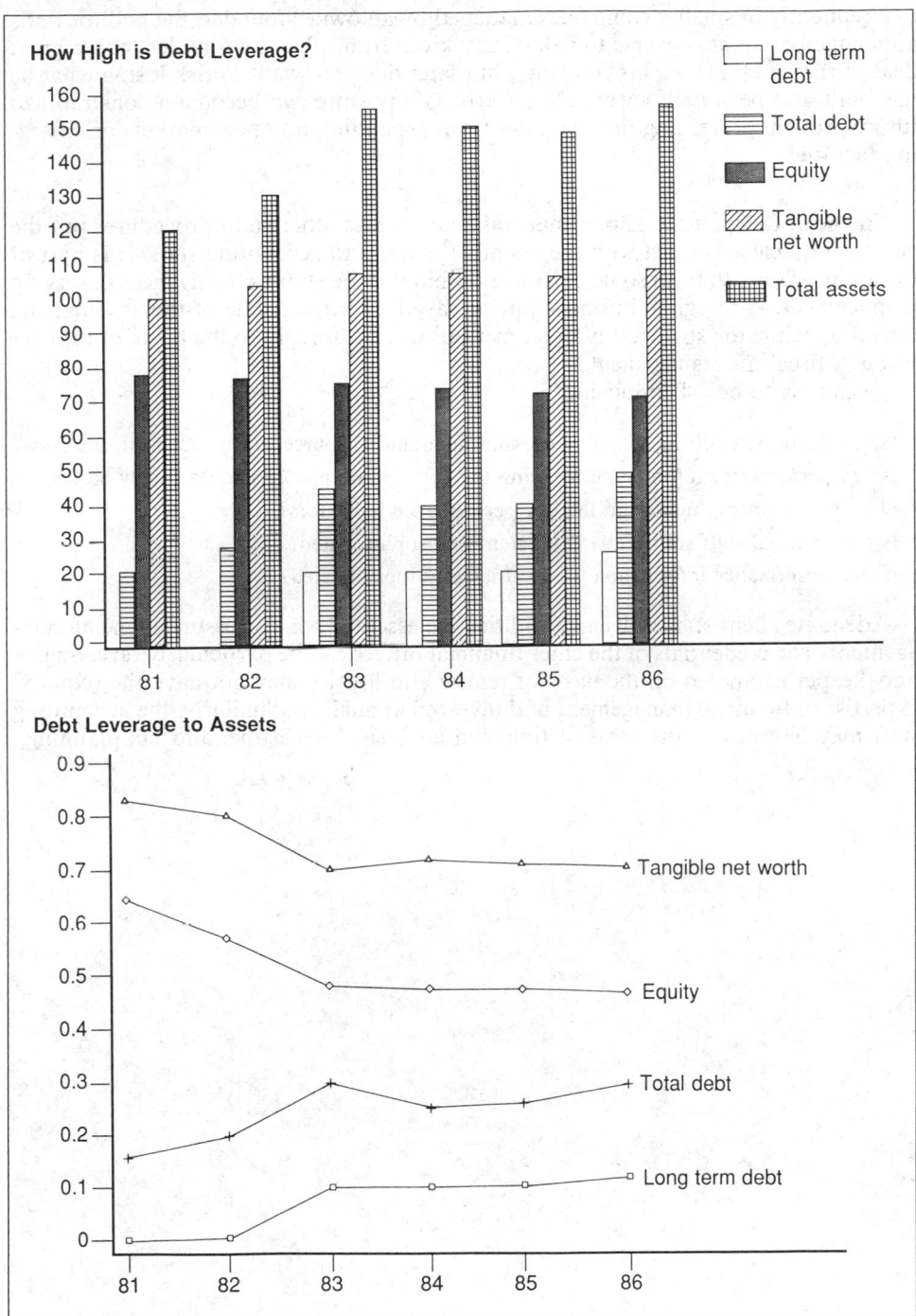

FIG. 7.9   Graphic Representation of Leverage Ratios

Frequently in smaller companies managed by an owner-founder, the auditor finds a management that is averse to risk of any kind. Ironically, the founder took a great deal of risk in launching his company, but later does not want to risk losing what he has built and personally owns. This overly safe posture can become a constraint to future growth, preventing the company from expanding into new markets or enlarging facilities.

Financial Competence. Both financial analysis and other audit procedures put the auditor into close contact with the client's finance and accounting staff. It is part of the audit process to form some objective opinion of the staff's effectiveness in serving management. A marginal business can be saved by bright, state-of-the-art financial direction, while the strongest of organizations can be brought to the brink of disaster through fiscal mismanagement.

Questions to be asked include:

- How effectively does the company use and maintain its sources of financial information?
- Is key performance information reaching the appropriate managers on a timely basis?
- Does management understand the key performance indicators?
- Is the financial staff sufficiently competent and sophisticated?
- Is the performance information used sufficiently sophisticated?

Adequate client staff skills and abilities are essential for successful financial management. The credentials of the chief financial officer can be particularly revealing. A bookkeeper promoted on the basis of tenure and loyalty may not have the required expertise in financial management and investment analysis. Similarly, the accounting staff may be weak in the areas of financial analysis, forecasting, and tax planning.

Appendix 7   UTILIZATION OF THE INTERNAL AUDIT FUNCTION

Policy

This section covers a CPA firm's policy on two aspects of the internal audit function and its role in the audit process:

A. The internal audit function as a part of the internal control structure,

B. The internal audit function in providing assistance to us as independent auditors in performing our audit of the financial statements.

It serves to reinforce and clarify the requirements of SAS 9, *The Effect of an Internal Audit Function on the Scope of the Independent Auditor's Examination* (AU 322).[1]

When either or both of these aspects are present in a particular audit engagement, we must make an evaluation of the internal audit function.

A. This evaluation should begin as part of the planning process.

B. It must be supported by appropriate audit procedures. (Possible procedures are outlined below.)

C. It will specifically include the competence and objectivity of internal audit personnel, as well as their level of performance.

D. The results of the evaluation along with other factors will determine the degree to which we rely on the internal audit function as part of the control structure or use internal audit to assist us in our examination.

Internal Audit as Part of Internal Control Structure

Internal audit is part of a class of controls that operate across the basic units and accounting systems of a company to determine that the procedure level controls are operating effectively. In other words, they are, in a real sense, controls of controls. Other common corporate-level controls are management budgeting, reporting and follow-up systems, and standard procedures manuals. Often, internal audit will relate to these other corporate-level controls, such as in performing follow-up of variances from budget or in determining that standard procedures manuals are in use. In other instances, internal audit will review the efficiency, effectiveness, and degree of compliance with procedural controls as a direct objective, or indirectly by examining data processed by the systems for errors. This is extremely important in large systems where no single person oversees both the initiation and completion of transactions, so that unreasonable processing results are observed and corrected (e.g., where EDP is used extensively).

The form of reliance on internal audit will depend on the types of internal control structure activities performed. In many companies, internal audit will review the performance of others performing control functions. For example, they will review processed transactions for correctness, observe segregation of duties, and investigate accounting problem areas. If we are satisfied that this entire internal control structure — including the procedural controls and internal audit — is functioning effectively, we can rely on it to a greater extent in designing substantive procedures than we could on the procedural controls alone.

In companies with multiple units or several locations, internal audit is frequently used to visit individual locations to evaluate whether the prescribed policies and procedures issued by the home office are being followed and whether accurate information is being reported to the home office by the individual locations. In this situation, particularly where other corporate-level controls are in effect, internal audit can provide very effective control.

Although reliance on internal audit and other corporate-level controls often allows us to reduce significantly the number of locations we visit and the amount of detailed work we perform, it is important to understand that once we determine the extent of such work necessary for our purposes, we cannot

---

[1] In 1988, an ASB Task Force, working with the Canadian Institute of Chartered Accountants, expects to release nonauthoritative guidance regarding the independent auditor's use of the work of the internal auditor. This report may result in a revision of SAS 9.

then improperly delegate it to the internal auditors to perform on our behalf; however, as discussed below, they can provide us with assistance.

Assistance in Performing Auditing Procedures

The nature, timing, and extent of year-end-oriented substantive procedures are determined by the outside auditor's appraisal of the likelihood of various types of errors in the financial statements after completion of the control testing phase of the examination. Internal audit as a control may or may not have been a factor in that appraisal. In either case, the appraisal reached is a fixed point of reference for determining the remaining amount of work to be completed by the independent auditor.

Thus, the independent auditor is responsible for performing and evaluating several types of procedures at levels established by his audit plan. These are control tests (observations and tests of the operation of controls and of transactions) relating to controls being relied on, and substantive procedures (test of transactions, year-end-oriented substantive tests of details and analytical procedures) relating to financial statement amounts. Where internal audit is being relied on as a control, tests will be applied to the internal audit function by the independent auditor. In testing other controls and substantive procedures, internal audit assistance may be appropriate.

Although it may be appropriate for internal auditors to assist in performing these procedures, as indicated above the independent auditor retains the final responsibility for them. The independent auditor will fulfill this responsibility by several means, including:

- Assuring the competence and objectivity of internal audit personnel relative to the assistance provided;
- Restricting internal audit assistance to areas where there is less chance of significant error;
- Adequately supervising and reviewing the work performed by the internal auditors in providing assistance; and
- In some cases reperforming a portion of the work done by internal auditors in providing assistance, particularly for larger and more complex items.

Competence and Objectivity

As indicated above, a significant portion of our evaluation of the internal audit function will focus on the competence and objectivity of its members.

Competence relates to the internal auditor's skill (i.e., knowledge and experience) in performing an assigned task. As will be seen below, a person may approach a task objectively, but if he does not have the skill to perform it, the job may not get done as intended.

Competence can be viewed at two levels: general competence and specific-task-related skill. General competence relates to a person's basic intelligence, problem-solving capabilities, and communication skills. Specific-task-related skill relates to finding and matching appropriate people to the tasks to be performed. In internal auditing, the following are examples of tasks that require specific skills:

- Management of the internal audit function — requires extensive general audit experience; knowledge of current developments; extensive knowledge of the company and its business; strong communication skills; and personnel and behavioral skills.
- Review of data processing — requires understanding of EDP fundamentals; understanding of EDP controls; understanding of computer auditing and control evaluation techniques; and working knowledge of EDP data access and testing techniques, including audit software.
- Inventory observation — requires understanding of auditing principles underlying inventory observation; understanding the nature of inventory-taking and the function of instructions, second counts, tag control, etc.; and knowledge of the plant or warehouse location, the people involved, the products, and the underlying manufacturing process.

Objectivity relates to the internal auditor's ability to make an unbiased judgment, in terms of seeking necessary information, evaluating the information properly, and taking appropriate actions based on the results. Objectivity is a function of two factors: the basic attitude of the person involved and the environmental influences in the circumstances surrounding a particular judgment. A desirable basic attitude would be one formed where the person involved understands the purpose of this function and wants to fulfill his function in an unbiased fashion (i.e., he understands the nature and value of objectivity and internalizes it).

The environmental influences affecting the objectivity of internal audit judgments are primarily organizational in nature, that is, the internal auditor is likely to be biased in the following situations:

- He is judging the performance of a direct superior.
- He is judging the results of systems and procedures he personally participated in developing.
- He is not knowledgeable in the area and must rely on the persons responsible for the area for extended guidance.
- The internal audit function is organizationally weak (e.g., small, does not have management support, or is "under-resourced") and subject to second guessing by those criticized in its reports.
- Because of the attitude of management, internal audit operates under significant pressure to justify its existence by identifying cost savings or by covering an excessive range of projects during the year.

Competence and objectivity are matters of degree relative to the circumstances. The external auditor has the responsibility to establish and support with evidence that both these characteristics are present to the degree the external auditor believes is necessary for the particular use he intends to make of the internal audit function—that is, to rely on (as an element of the internal control structure) to some planned extent, or to assist in performing specific tasks.

The general procedures for evaluating competence and objectivity of internal audit are inquiry, analysis, observation and review, and testing of work performed.

Tests for Internal Audit Evaluation

In this section is a general set of test procedures that can be used in obtaining evidence to support our evaluation of internal audit. The inclusion and extent of application of any one or combination of these procedures will depend on the circumstances of the engagement and the degree to which we rely on internal audit as a control or use them to assist us in our examination. The general procedures are as follows:

- Gather descriptive information about the internal audit function.
- Evaluate the competence of internal audit personnel.
- Evaluate the objectivity of internal audit personnel.
- Plan the degree to which we will rely on internal audit as part of the internal control structure. Where reliance exists, evaluate the performance of internal audit during the year.
- Plan the extent to which internal audit will provide assistance to us in our examination:
  - The extent to which they will be available will usually be at the discretion of client management.
  - Where they will provide assistance, identify the specific tasks they will peform and the procedures we will follow to evidence their competence and objectivity and to control their activities in assisting us.
- Provide for proper documentation in our working papers of the planning and completion of the above procedures.

Other Considerations

We will generally review internal audit reports issued during the year in connection with review and evaluation of internal audit activities. Where we do this and note that significant control problems were encountered by internal audit, the corrective follow-up measures taken and an evaluation of how these control problems affected our year-end procedures should be discussed in our audit working papers.

We must always structure our approach to internal audit to recognize that it is an ongoing function. Although the bulk of our procedures regarding internal audit will come at particular points in time, our evaluation must be of a continuous nature. We should become aware of significant changes that take place in internal audit and include the impact of such changes in our audit design.

8

Internal Control

OVERVIEW

Perhaps no auditing topic has been more written about and discussed than internal control. It has been the subject of many studies since the AICPA released the first study in 1949,[1] as well as numerous SASs refining the concepts.

---

[1] *Internal Control—Elements of a Coordinated Systems and Its Importance to Management and the Independent Public Accountant.*

In early 1988, the ASB released SAS 55, *Consideration of the Internal Control Structure in a Financial Statement Audit* (AU 319). In many respects, SAS 55 is similar to the 1949 study: both recognize that a system of internal control extends beyond the accounting and financial functions of an entity—a thought that had lost some of its import over the years—as articulated in SAS 55 (AU 319.06):

> Although the internal control structure may include a wide variety of objectives and related policies and procedures, only some of these may be relevant to an audit of the entity's financial statements. Generally, the policies and procedures that are relevant to an audit pertain to the entity's ability to record, process, summarize, and report financial data consistent with the assertions embodied in the financial statements.

This restoration of comprehensiveness should relieve auditors' long-standing confusion about how to segment internal controls for audit study and evaluation. To enable auditors to focus on the SAS 55 concepts, the ASB chose to revise key terminology; in the longer run, these new terms should become accepted as being more precise than the old wording, but in the near term no doubt there will be some confusion over these changes:

New	Old
Internal control structure	Internal accounting control system
Assessing control risk	Study and evaluation of internal control
Control risk assessment procedures	Review of system and compliance tests
Tests of financial statement balances	Substantive tests
Conclusion about the level of control risk/assessment of control risk	Reliance on internal control
Control structure elements relevant to financial statement assertions	Accounting controls and administrative controls

SAS 55 defines internal control structure as being composed of three elements: control environment, accounting system, and control procedures. The auditor is required to obtain an understanding of the structure even if he does not plan to place reliance on it in performing his audit. Under prior requirements, the auditor could generally bypass this first step if he planned to do an entirely substantive audit. SAS 55 thus offers some response to criticism of the profession for failure to have known about serious weaknesses that cause a business to collapse even though the last audited financial statements were proper at the date of the financial statements.

The auditor aims to evaluate the risk that the financial statements could contain a material misstatement. This risk has three facets:

1. *Inherent risk*—that a financial statement assertion (i.e., certain attributes of balances, transactions, or disclosures) could be materially misstated.
2. *Control risk*—that the inherent risk will not be prevented or detected on a timely basis by the internal control structure.
3. *Detection risk*—that the auditor will not detect a material misstatement.

In planning the audit, the inherent risk is first identified, and the control structure and accounting system are then examined as necessary to understand the degree to which the system is designed to guard against the inherent risks. In this phase, generalized procedures to be used by the auditor in obtaining an understanding are provided in SAS 55.

After obtaining an understanding, the auditor must assess the control risk. If he chooses to do an entirely substantive audit, he must assume that control risk is at the maximum level (i.e., the system cannot be relied on to catch any material misstatements), and the auditor will achieve the level of assurance he needs as to detection risk solely by substantive procedures. If, however, the auditor wishes to restrict his substantive testing, he can perform procedures to provide him with evidence about the degree of reliance he may place on the control system (i.e., the control risk in the specific area may be assessed at something less than maximum). The auditor may use various quantification methods (as discussed in Chapter 7) to state the degree of control risk, but there is no requirement to quantify.

Finally, because the essence of studying the internal control system is to determine the extent, if any, to which substantive procedures may be restricted under the second standard of fieldwork (AU 150.02), the auditor must correlate the level of control risk (that the financial statements could contain an undetected material misstatement) with the level of detection risk (that the auditor might not catch it). SAS 55 addresses this matter more clearly than prior guidance, but this still is the "black box" of auditing, requiring additional specifications by audit firms and hard thinking by individual auditors.

SAS 55 provides several appendices, including a discussion of numerous factors that affect an entity's control environment, a commentary on what management's control objectives ought to encompass, and definitions of the more important terminology used in the statement. In particular, a flow chart of the control consideration process is provided, shown in abridged form in Figure 8.1. It may be helpful to refer to this chart to place the various sections of this chapter in context.

Because SAS 55 is new and its exposition is more logical than prior auditing standards' coverage of internal controls, this chapter basically follows the organization of the SAS, with several excursions into important related topics.[2]

INTERNAL CONTROL STRUCTURE

The three elements of the internal control structure — *control environment, accounting system,* and *control procedures* — are highly dependent on management properly exercising its responsibilities and on the organization style adopted. Dividing the internal control structure into these three elements facilitates discussion of the nature of controls and how the auditor considers them in an audit. The auditor's primary consid-

---

[2] SAS 55, issued in 1988, is effective beginning with calendar year 1990 audits, but earlier application is permitted. The most incisive new requirement under SAS 55 is that of obtaining an understanding of the internal control structure even where the auditor does not intend to place any reliance on it. Presumably, auditors will adopt SAS 55 terminology and concepts as audits are performed over time and into 1991. To apply the concepts in this chapter to preadoption audits, the reader should refer to the terminology cross-reference table at the beginning of this section.

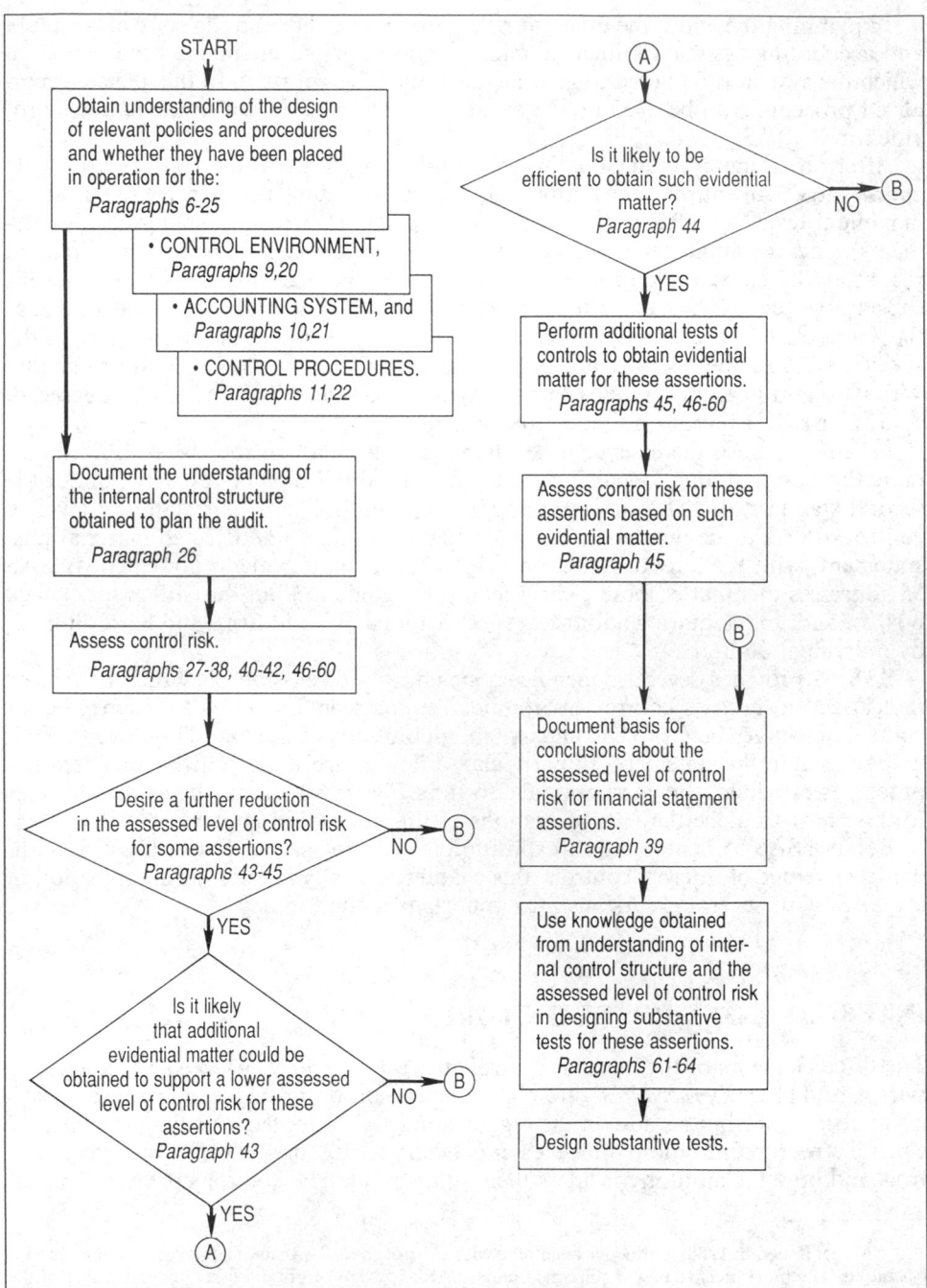

FIG. 8.1 Flowchart for Consideration of the Internal Control Structure in a Financial Statement Audit (Note: paragraph numbers are references to SAS 55)
Source: SAS 55, Appendix C (Abridged) (AU 319.68).

eration, however, is whether a policy or procedure affects financial statement assertions,[3] rather than in which of the three elements it may be classified.

There are several structure matters that can have a pervasive effect on the control environment, accounting systems, and control procedures, and hence on the risk that a material misstatement could be present in the financial statements. The auditor should take into consideration the entity's:

* Size
* Organization and ownership characteristics
* Nature of business
* Diversity and complexity of operations
* Methods of processing data
* Legal or regulatory requirements

Further, the cost of an entity's internal control structure should not exceed the benefits expected to be derived; and it is a proper management prerogative to assume certain risks if the cost of controls is assessed to be disproportionate to benefits.

Control Environment

The combination of all the factors that affect an entity's policies and procedures is referred to as the control environment. These factors can be involved in setting up controls, making them stronger, or perhaps weakening them. Such factors include AU 319.09:

* Management's philosophy and operating style;
* The entity's organizational structure;
* The functioning of the board of directors and its committees, particularly the audit committee;
* Methods of assigning authority and responsibility;
* Management's control methods for monitoring and following up on performance, including internal auditing;
* Personnel policies and practices; and
* Various external influences that affect an entity's operations and practices, such as examinations by bank regulatory agencies.

The quality of the control environment is an indication of whether controls are important to the board and management (and owners in a private company).

---

[3] *Financial statements assertions* is an all-inclusive notation for the presentation of account balances, classification of transactions, and disclosures in the financial stratements, which are the representations of management. As further discussed in Chapter 7, there are five categories of management assertions (AU 326.03): (1) existence or occurrence; (2) completeness; (3) rights and obligations; (4) valuation or allocation; and (5) presentation and disclosure.

Management Philosophy and Operating Style. SAS 55 points out that establishing and maintaining an internal control structure is an important management responsibility; thus it should be under ongoing supervision by management to determine that it is operating as intended and that it is modified as appropriate for changes in conditions (AU 319.13).

Although certainly part of the control environment, the integrity of management is fundamental to an ability to perform an audit. In identifying possible material errors, auditors must focus on the motives of management and recognize conditions that might cause management to act without integrity or good faith. Conditions that increase concern, aside from questionable reputation and a compulsion to take unnecessary risks, relate to inordinate or unreasonable management desires for:

* Favorable earnings (e.g., because of the need to support the price of the company's stock or because of management profit-sharing agreements).
* Low taxable income.
* Power ("empire building").

Some signals that should increase the auditor's concern about possible material errors and the effectiveness of the control environment are:

* High turnover in management positions, especially financial management.
* Failure to develop managerial talent in relation to growth of the business.
* Decentralized operations and record-keeping, with a centralized management.
* Diversified activities, each with its own acccounting system.
* Heavy dependence on computer processing for decision-making, without adequate knowledge of computer operations.
* Inadequate internal audit.

Other visible characteristics of management's philosophy may include (AU 319.66):

* Management's approach to taking and monitoring business risks;
* Management's attitudes and actions toward financial reporting;
* Management's emphasis on meeting budget, profit, and other financial and operating goals.

All of the foregoing factors can significantly affect the control environment. They are of special concern if management is dominated by one or a few individuals (or conversely by a lack of strong leadership), in which case other control environment factors might be manipulable regardless of how strong they may be by design.

Organizational Structure. There are various forms of organization structure, a few of which are mentioned here. The organizational form defines how authority and responsibility are assigned.

Development stage, level of technological use, and external environment can have significant effects on the choice of an appropriate organizational structure. Entities with a complex technology and a rapidly changing environment require an organization and human relations structure built around teams, delegation, and participation.

But entities with a relatively simple technology, in a stable development stage and marketplace, can be managed better through a hierarchical structure. For example, entities in high-tech or rapidly changing industries (e.g., computers, financial institutions) are more likely to require a decentralized and free-flowing organizational design, whereas a wholesaler or manufacturer can use a type of pyramid design.

It is also true that different parts of an organization may be best served by different organizational structures. For example, an entity with a standarized production process can use structured procedures to schedule its work and personnel. However, the company's research and development effort will probably do better in a more participative environment that is sensitive to the creative process.

Differentiation in Roles. The board of directors, officers, internal auditors, and outside auditors all have strong interests in the company's internal control structure but for different reasons. The internal control structure exists for and is created by management; it is designed and maintained to meet the basic objectives of safeguarding assets and providing a basis for management decisions as well as for external financial reporting. By contrast, the outside auditor's interest is utilitarian when viewed solely in an audit framework; it concerns the reliability of the systems for his purpose of formulating an opinion on management's financial statements.

Board of directors. The board has ultimate responsibility for the adequacy of the internal control structure, and must assure that the necessary resources are available to support adequate control procedures. While not responsible for detailed specification and enforcement, the board or its audit committee must be responsible for basic policies and compliance oversight, as discussed more fully in Chapter 6.

To meet these responsibilities, the audit committee (or if there is no audit committee, its equivalent or the full board) should:

- Understand in broad outline how the internal control structure functions, and judge its sufficiency.
- Broadly monitor compliance, and suggest improvements as needed.
- Review existing policies and whether they are adequately communicated, and consider changes as needed.
- See that appropriate actions are taken to remedy possible deficiencies in the system, or possible violations of policy.

Operating management. Although the board of directors has overall responsibility, tactics are the responsibility of operating management, which must install effective control procedures and create an accounting control environment in which those control procedures can operate. Operating management must also (1) systematically document the controls, (2) analyze the costs and benefits of possible control revisions, and (3) constantly review the adequacy of controls in light of changing circumstances, to assure their proper operation.

Internal auditors. Management relies heavily on feedback from the internal auditors to assure the continued effective operation of the internal control structure. The internal auditors also have a responsibility to the board of directors, which needs assurance that operating management is responsive to control structure requirements.

Independent auditors. The outside auditor, unlike the internal auditor, is not a part of the company's internal control structure. He has a unique objective in an audit – to form an opinion on the fairness of presentation of the financial statements in conformity with GAAP. To meet this objective under GAAS, the independent auditor plans his examination to obtain a reasonable basis for an opinion that the financial statements taken as a whole are not materially misstated as a result of errors or irregularities. The nature and quality of the internal control structure can have a significant effect on the nature, timing, and extent of the outside auditor's examination.

The outside auditor must decide the extent to which he will rely on the internal control structure when carrying out his examination (the reliance approach). This reliance depends both on control adequacy and auditing cost-effectiveness. Performing direct and extensive tests of financial statement balances (the substantive approach) by auditing the documentation underlying the amounts in the financial statements may be a more direct approach. In most cases the auditor will use a combination of the two approaches. (This is discussed in detail in Chapter 7.)

Professional standards require that the independent auditor gain an understanding of the systems and the operative controls in the flow of transactions through the business, to the extent that these systems and controls provide and validate the data from which the financial statements are prepared. Should he decide to rely on the internal control structure, the auditor's understanding of it must be thorough; and he must test and evaluate whether those systems serve as intended and can be relied on to produce reasonably accurate data. One area where reliance is virtually inevitable is that of controls over the completeness of information. It is not possible to carry out direct testing on information that is not available.

Authority and Responsibility. The auditor needs to understand the entity's internal relationships and responsibilities. Methods for communicating assigned authority and responsibilities (AU 319.66) include:

- Entity policy regarding such matters as acceptable business practices, conflicts of interest, and codes of conduct;
- Assignment of responsibility and delegation of authority to deal with such matters as organizational goals and objectives, operating functions, and regulatory requirements;
- Employee job descriptions delineating specific duties, reporting relationships, and constraints; and
- Computer systems documentation indicating the procedures for authorizing transactions and approving systems changes.

Management Control Methods. The auditor needs to consider how management controls the exercise of authority delegated to others and effectively supervises overall company activities. Management control methods (AU 319.66) include:

- Establishing planning and reporting systems that set forth management's plans and the results of actual performance. Such systems may include business planning; budgeting, forecasting, and profit planning; and responsibility accounting.
- Establishing methods that identify the status of actual performance and exceptions from planned performance, as well as communicating them to the appropriate levels of management.
- Using such methods at appropriate management levels to investigate variances from expectations and to take appropriate and timely corrective action.
- Establishing and monitoring policies for developing and modifying accounting systems and control procedures, including the development, modification, and use of any related computer programs and data files.

After setting budgets (a passive element), three active monitoring elements are employed:

1. Comparing performance to budget. To be effective as a monitoring tool, actual performance must be promptly and regularly scrutinized, variances from budget identified, and explanations sought and questioned.
2. Proper supervision. A well-structured organization assures that employees are adequately supervised at all levels.
3. Internal audit function.

The internal auditor's role, as enunciated in *Standards for the Professional Practice of Internal Auditing* (IIA, 1978), covers the following objectives:

- Assuring the reliability and integrity of information.
- Assuring compliance with policies, plans, procedures, laws, and regulations.
- Safeguarding assets.
- Assuring the economical and efficient use of resources.
- Assuring the accomplishment of established objectives and goals for operations or programs.

The role of the internal auditor can be variable: he operates simultaneously at the specific control level and as part of the control environment, as explained in Chapter 7.

Unless the control environment includes monitoring of performance, the effectiveness of the other elements and of the specific controls is greatly reduced. The knowledge that an organization effectively monitors control performance is a potent spur to obtaining conformity and achieving goals. Monitoring is also an essential part of management's continuing responsibility to assure that the established systems and controls continue to serve the changing needs of the organization effectively.

Personnel Policies and Practices. Personnel management methods include an entity's policies and procedures for hiring, training, evaluating, promoting, and compensating competent employees. To properly execute their assigned responsibilities, they have to be given the necessary resources.

A control structure is only as effective as the people who operate it. Thus, even a theoretically perfect control structure can be rendered ineffective by an inadequate staff. Proper motivation of competent personnel is fundamental and requires that they understand what they have to do, appreciate why they have to do it, and agree that it should be done. Proper motivation usually requires that, whenever possible, people be allowed to use their own initiative; this will increase job satisfaction through the overall feeling of being an important, thinking part of the control structure. However, unstructured initiative tends toward chaos; a balance has to be struck between those matters where the control structure is more important than individual initiative and those where it is not.

Controls in Smaller Enterprises. In smaller businesses, the operating procedures and methods of recording and processing transactions often differ significantly from those used by large enterprises. Indeed, many of the controls relevant to the larger enterprise are not possible or even appropriate or necessary. The focus is changed because most small entities are more comprehensible and controllable, and therefore direct management overview is possible and likely. Because there are fewer people, there is less segregation of duties. Management delegates less authority, relies less on environmental controls, and plays a far more direct role in assuring that its objectives are being met. Therefore, in smaller entities, control revolves more around individual management and less around systematized approaches. However, the close involvement of management in the details of running the business adds risks, particularly as to overriding controls and manipulating financial statements — although control *by* management may be strong, control *over* management may be weak.

External Influences. Influence by parties and events outside an entity can also have a significant effect. For example, requirements imposed by legislative and regulatory bodies, such as examinations by bank regulatory agencies, could make management take many actions they otherwise might not take. Although external influences are ordinarily outside an entity's control, they may cause management to establish specific policies or procedures to assure that these outside requirements are observed.

Accounting System

SAS 55 describes an accounting system, in the context of the internal control environment, as the various methods and records an entity uses to "identify, assemble, analyze, classify, record and report [its] transactions and to maintain accountability for the related assets and liabilities" (AU 319.10). A properly operating accounting system will accomplish the following:

* Identify and record all valid transactions.
* Describe on a timely basis the transactions in sufficient detail to permit their proper classification for financial reporting.
* Measure the value of transactions in a manner that permits recording their proper monetary value in the financial statements.

- Determine the time period in which transactions occurred to permit recording them in the proper accounting period.
- Present properly the transactions and related disclosures in the financial statements.

Control Procedures

Control procedures are the third leg of the control structure, and they can be of all kinds, applied throughout the entity. Control procedures generally pertain to (AU 319.11)

- Proper authorization of transactions and activities;
- Segregation of duties that reduce the opportunities to allow any person to be in a position to both perpetrate and conceal errors or irregularities in the normal course of his duties— assigning different people the responsibilities of authorizing transactions, recording transactions, and maintaining custody of assets;
- Design and use of adequate documents and records to help ensure the proper recording of transactions and events, such as monitoring the use of prenumbered shipping documents;
- Adequate safeguards over access to and use of assets and records, such as secured facilities and authorization for access to computer programs and data files; and
- Independent checks on performance and proper valuation of recorded amounts, such as clerical checks, reconciliations, comparison of assets with recorded accountability, computer-programmed edit controls, management review of reports that summarize the detail of account balances such as an aged trial balance of accounts receivable, and user review of computer generated reports.

   As to segregation of duties, in the least desirable accounting system one employee records a transaction from its origin to its ultimate posting to the general ledger, maximizing the likelihood that unintentional errors will remain undetected and increasing the opportunity for irregularities. Simply segregating the recording in original entry journals from the recording in the related subsidiary ledgers provides many automatic cross-checks. As a business becomes larger, it is possible to make many logical separations, and in most cases the simple fact that each person performs his work independently results in a substantial increase in segregation and control without any overall duplication of effort.

   In an electronic data proccessing (EDP) system, segregation of duties is of a different nature than in manual systems, but it is of equal importance. Frequent cross-checking is unnecessary because of the computer's ability to perform consistently and uniformly. The emphasis should be on the separation of responsibility for processing of data by computer operators, for custody of transaction and library files, and for programming, all as discussed in Chapter 10.

EFFECT OF CONTROL STRUCTURE ON AUDIT PLANNING

Auditing, particularly for larger entities, relies heavily on the study and evaluation of internal control structures as a basis for reducing the volume of substantive tests of transactions and balances. Although auditors have studied and used evaluations of internal control structures for many years, the professionals still debate the best and most effective way to do so.

Two sets of objectives must be kept in mind: (1) the basic objectives of internal control structures as to safeguarding assets and controlling transactions; and (2) the auditor's objective to provide reasonable assurance, through his opinion report, that there are no material misstatements in the financial statements. The auditor seeks to reach his opinion in the most efficient and reliable way, and he looks to internal control structures to aid in achieving this goal.

Although the auditor has the alternative of placing his audit emphasis on substantive testing of the financial statement balances and transactions, it becomes almost essential for audit efficiency in any large organization to review, evaluate, and test the internal control structure, to establish the acceptable degree of reliance. Reliance on control systems reduces the extent of substantive testing.

Identifying Material Misstatement Risks

Risk gets at the heart of any consideration of the internal control structure because it identifies how assests can be lost or abused and how transactions can be improperly processed. Obviously, the larger the risk the more important the controls that protect against it, and the greater the need to assess their effectiveness. Risk also is useful in determining who should be involved; larger risks require greater reviewer expertise.

The auditor should consider what could materially go wrong, either intentionally or unintentionally. This consideration encompasses both general and specific factors.

Based on his knowledge of the business, the auditor should consider whether general factors could result in possible material errors. These factors are considered in the three sections that follow.

Economic and Financial Conditions. The auditor must consider whether the company is under more strain than normal because of general economic or financial conditions, since this will usually increase the possibilty of material errors. Examples of factors and conditions that indicate increased strain include:

- Insufficient working capital or credit lines to operate at a profitable capacity.
- Significantly lower profitability than other companies in the industry.
- Demands for new capital in excess of availability.
- Dependence on a single (or relatively few) products, customers, or transactions,
- Violations, or possible violations, of debt restrictions or other convenants.
- A depressed industry, perhaps characterized by a large number of business failures.
- Excess capacity and high fixed costs.
- Significant litigation, especially between shareholders and management.
- Rapid expansion of business or product lines.
- Numerous acquisitions, particularly as a diversification move into new and unfamiliar activities.
- A long-term operating cycle for a company's products.
- Overly optimistic sales projections.

* Inadquate funds generated for capital investment.
* Intervention of government agencies.
* Inadquate supplies of labor, materials, or energy.

Personnel Attributes. A company with a positive commitment to good control usually can achieve the objectives of those controls. Evidence of such a commitment is found, to a large extent, in the quality of the control environment. Without this commitment, even well-designed systems will ultimately fail. Thus the auditor should focus his attention on the environment in identifying possible exposures to material errors.

Because the key to the control environment is people—both those who establish policy and those who follow it—a significant part of the auditor's evaluation of the effectiveness of an internal accounting control system lies in assessing the competence and motivation of personnel, their propensity to commit errors, and their ability to prevent or detect errors by others.

When performing tests of controls, the auditor will ascertain whether the controls seem to be operating. This involves identifying actual errors and judging whether potential errors—those that might have occurred—would have been detected and corrected. The auditor's evaluation process therefore considers whether, if an error is presented, an employee will actually isolate, correct, and resubmit the transaction into the processing stream, as intended by the system.

Analytical Procedures. SAS 56, *Analytical Procedures* (AU 329), requires the use of analytical procedures in the planning and completion phases of the audit. This requires that the auditor have a general knowledge of the client and the industry or industries in which the client operates; he must also understand the purposes and limitations of analytical procedures.

Analytical review of financial and operating data can include the relationships among past, present, and anticipated activity and comparisons with similar companies in the same industry; the results show whether account balances and relationships are plausible and reasonable. Analytical procedures are used for various purposes:

* To assist the auditor in planning the nature, timing, and extent of other auditing procedures (Phase I).
* As a substantive test to obtain evidential matter about particular assertions related to account balances or classes of transactions (Phase II).
* As an overall review of the financial information in the final review phase of the audit (Phase III).

Use of analytical procedures in Phase I may identify improbable relationships pointing to areas where material misstatement risks might be present. In Phase II there is some element of identifying risks as well as the objective of seeking out possibly material misstatements. In Phase III analytical procedures are used as substantive tests in pursuit of misstatements.

Available analytical procedures are, of course, extensive. While they vary between industries, most can be classified into the five distinct types shown in Figure 8.2. In all analytical procedures, the most useful and valid results are obtained when the analysis is done at a detailed level, for example, by product line or catagory of expense.

For a more extensive discussion of analytical review, refer to Chapter 7, which focuses on the use of computer software to develop significant ratios.

Understanding the Internal Control Structure

SAS 55 requires the auditor to obtain an understanding of the internal control structure.[4] In this phase of planning the audit, the auditor should consider:

* The knowledge obtained from previous audits.
* The industry in which the entity operates.
* Assessments of inherent risk.
* Judgments about materiality.
* Complexity and sophistication of the entity's transactions, operations, and systems.

Sufficient understanding of the *control environment* should be obtained in the context of planning the audit to understand the attitude, awareness, and actions of management and the board of directors. The auditor needs to carefully probe this area to assure that the substance of prescribed policies, procedures, and related actions are being followed. For example, management may establish appropraite policies and procedures but not act on them.

In planning the audit, the auditor needs to obtain knowledge of the *accounting system* sufficient to understand:

* Classes of significant transactions.
* How those transactions are initiated.
* Accounting records, supporting documents, and specific accounts involved in the processing and financial statement reporting of transactions.
* Accounting processing flow, from the initiation of a transaction to its inclusion in the financial statements.
* Financial reporting process used to prepare the entity's financial statements.

Finally, the auditor should consider the presence or absence of *control procedures* based on his understanding of the control environment and accounting system, in determining whether it is necessary to devote additional attention to the control procedures. In the audit planning phase, the auditor does not need to have a detailed understanding of the control procedures related to each account balance, transaction

---

[4] Understanding the internal control structure is discussed in this chapter prior to assessing control risk. However, these steps may be performed concurrently during the audit (AU 319.40).

Procedure	Example
1. Comparison of actual results or balances to predicted results or balances	Comparison of actual to budgeted figures and investigation of variances for such activitites as sales, costs, cash flow
2. Comparison of actual results and balances prior results and balances	Comparison of quantitative data, such as sales, purchases, overhead, receivables, payables, inventory Comparison of qualitative data, such as principal customers and suppliers
3. Examination of the consistency between interrelated results and balances.	Calculating accounts receivable based on sales and receipts; interest expense based on average borrowings; rental income based on rental units; payroll based on number of employees
4. Comparison of changes in interrelationships between accounts in comparable periods	Examining the ratio of sales to accounts receivable and comparing it to prior-period ratios; examining inventory turnover from period to period
5. Comparison of interrelationships between accounts in other comparable companies.	Ratio analysis as above, but comparing results internally (between like branches) or externally (as between similar businesses in the same industry)

FIG. 8.2   Types of Analytical Review Procedures

class, and disclosure component in the financial statements or to all of the assertions relevant to those components. Nevertheless, this step is necessary to achieve an effective audit, regardless of whether the subsequent audit plan will place reliance on controls.

Obtaining an Understanding. The methods used to obtain an understanding of the interrelationship and flow of transactions through the processing system are:

• Referring to available documentation, including last year's working papers.
• Making knowledgeable inquiries of appropriate management, supervisory, and staff personnel.
• Observing job assignments and operating procedures.
• Tracing transactions through the system.

The nature and extent of the procedures performed will vary from entity to entity. such procedures are influenced by:

• The size and complexity of the entity.
• The auditor's previous experience with the entity.
• The nature of the particular policy or procedure.
• The nature of the entity's documentation of specific policies and procedures.

Available data. Normally, the development of the understanding begins with a review of available system write-ups, including the client's flowcharts, narrative descriptions, procedural manuals, organization charts, and the like; also, the auditor's prior working papers will show significant information gathered in previous audits.

Inquiry. Usually the auditor will have to supplement the available documentation by the use of questionnaires or checklists and through interviews and discussions with appropriate management, supervisors, and personnel doing the work.

Observations. The auditor can learn a great deal by watching. For example, observation of the accounting department during processing can produce valuable information about the flow of transactions and how individuals interrelate. In fact, the auditor should, whenever possible, take a familiarization tour of the company's major facilities to obtain a general understanding of the business, its processes, and the interrelationships between departments and activities. Although observation helps, it does not, however, constitute a full assessment of performance.

Walk-through. This step, often referred to as tracing transactions, involves following a transaction as it moves from one point to another in the processing stream. This is usually done by tracing a transaction from its origin to its final account, or from an account to its source, and is a good way to relate the flow of transactions to control functions and individuals. It can also assure that the auditor's previous understanding of the system remains correct.

When portions of an accounting system involve EDP, the review of significant EDP activities is part of the overall understanding of internal control structure. The use of EDP typically results in increased concentration of data and increased integration of processing. This may require new controls to deal with new risks resulting from loss of traditional segregation of duties. As the extent of human involvement declines, new controls may have to be built into the EDP portions of systems to maintain satisfactory levels of control. For a more extensive discussion of how EDP affects the internal control structure, refer to Chapter 10.

Documentation of Understanding. The auditor must document his understanding of the control structure. This can be done as either a brief narrative or an overview flowchart. Either method is suitable for demonstrating the basic flow of documentation and information through the system and the key controls within that system. This documented understanding allows the next decision to be addressed: whether more detailed reviews of internal control structure should be undertaken in areas where reliance on them seems proper for audit efficiency and, if so, how the reviews should be structured. Even if it is decided not to place any reliance on controls, the understanding gained should be sufficient for the auditor to design effective substantive tests of transactions and account balance details.

Assessing Control Risk

The auditor is now able to determine whether additional study of the internal control structure is warranted.[5] Although the system has not yet been tested, there should be a sufficient understanding to decide between combinations of the following alternatives:

* Does reliance on parts of the internal control structure appear to be warranted for some or all of the potential error types?
* Can the audit objectives be accomplished in a more efficient and effective manner without reliance on the internal control structure?

In any case, if potential weaknesses have been isolated based on the review of controls, their possible impact on financial reporting must be assessed. If the weakness is a "material weakness" or "reportable condition" it must be communicated to senior management and directors (see section entitled "Reporting on Internal Control").

Substantive Approach. The auditor may decide that the internal accounting control structure does not provide a satisfactory basis for reliance; or he may decide not to rely on the structure as a basis for designing the nature, scope, and timing of audit tests, because reliance would not be efficient or cost effective. Accordingly, no further evaluation or testing of a system would be performed[6] and the emphasis would shift to tests of the results of the transaction flow on amounts and balances in the financial statements. These are called substantive tests because they aim to directly *substantiate* the reasonableness of individual transactions and balances, and to determine the presence or absence of monetary errors.

Reliance Approach. Since no testing has been done, any decision is preliminary; however, if reliance appears both warranted and efficient, the auditor must decide what controls to test and how the testing and evaluation of those controls should be performed. Thus a more formal study and evaluation is necessary. This involves:

* Describing the details of the processing system and the related controls.
* Verifying the system description.
* Testing the controls on which reliance will be placed.
* Reevaluating the controls actually relied upon.

This process is described in the next section.

---

[5] Ibid.

[6] There may be other valid reasons why the auditor would proceed with testing a system even though it would be more efficient to use a substantive approach. For example, the company may want a detailed assessment of controls in a department that has had problems; or the auditor may select a certain area or areas to study in depth on a rotating annual basis, as a means of providing incisive comments to management for improvements in controls in order to more efficiently operate the business.

EVALUATING CONTROL PROCEDURES

The review of an entity's internal control structure should be planned and carried out in a logical and systematic way, to assure adequate consideration of all important matters. While control system evaluations are often expressed in generalized terms, systems are made up of a series of interrelated and interdependent controls. Consequently, the evaluation is actually an accumulation of individual determinations ordinarily derived from the following steps:

- Identification of material transactions
- Allocation of transactions among cycles
- Determination of transaction characteristics
- Identification of material error possibilities
- Correlation of inherent risk with control risk
- Correlation of control risk with detection risk
- Completion of control evaluation
- Control testing

Identifying Material Transactions

Because transactions are the basic components of enterprise operations, they are the primary subject matter and the organizing framework for evaluation purposes. Only transactions that are material individually or in the aggregate, and those that are material because of qualitative factors, can materially affect the financial statements, and these must be the focus of the auditor's attention. The initial step, based on the auditor's knowledge of the business and of the industry as a whole, is to determine transaction sources, to assure that no material types are overlooked. The material transaction types are not subjected to detailed audit procedures at this point; they are simply identified and documented, usually in the form of a list that is organized by transaction cycle. In doing so, it is necessary to consider two levels of transactions:

- Flow of resources with others
- Flow of information or assets internally

External Transactions. Resources flow in and out of an enterprise, for example, through the purchase of raw materials and supplies (payments to vendors), the processing of that material into a product (wages and salaries), and the sale of the product to others (sales proceeds). Business cycles contain a series of interrelated steps that can be used as a framework for determining how transactions are controlled, processed, and summarized. For a large proportion of businesses there are three business cycles that encompass the vast majority of all material transactions related to the flow of resources, as shown in Figure 8.3

Internal Transactions. The business cycles involving flow of resources with outsiders result in an internal information cycle – books and records – that provides

Transaction cycle	Examples of types of transactions

1. Sales, Billings, Receivables, and Collections	Sales of:
	  Merchandise
	  Scrap or excess material
	  Investments
	  Fixed assets
	
	Cash received for:
	  Cash sales
	  Collection of accounts receivable
	  Return on investments
	  Borrowings
	  Investments
	  Cash Transfers

2. Purchases, Payables, and Payments	Purchases of:
	  Inventory
	  Fixed assets
	  Recurring services and supplies
	  Nonrecurring services and supplies
	  Investments
	
	Payments for:
	  Accounts payable
	  Other accrued liabilities
	  Borrowings
	  Investments
	  Dividends
	  Cash transfers

3. Wages and Salaries	Work performed:
	  Accrue salaries
	  Accrue wages
	  Accrue payroll taxes and benefits
	
	Payments made:
	  Salaries, wages, and
	    benefit plan contributions
	  Payroll and tax returns

FIG. 8.3 Basic External Transaction Cycles

information useful in accounting for or safeguarding the company's resources. And if the entity is a manufacturing business, an additional internal cycle will exist—cost, inventory, and warehouse records—to track assets moving to different locations or categories during processing. For example, raw materials in a manufacturing company will be transferred to work in process and ultimately to inventory for sale.

The books and records cycle is concerned with the functions involved in transferring financial data from the books of original entry to the general or subsidiary ledgers, and with the transfer of financial data within those ledgers. It also deals with the recording of such items as allowance for bad debts; adjustments to the carrying value of property, plant, and equipment (via depreciation); and investments (via reduction to the lower of cost or market). It begins where the external cycles leave off.

Documentation of the books and records cycle should indicate how original entries are summarized, classified, and posted to the general ledger and by whom these processes are carried out. The write-up should detail the types of posting media used, the frequency of posting, the levels of authorization, and the review of such postings. And it should disclose the presence in the system of checks such as the maintenance and reconciliation of control accounts and the regular extraction and review of trial balances.

For a description of the inventory and cost of sales cycle, see Chapter 14.

Allocating Transactions by Cycles

Virtually all of a company's transaction types can be allocated among several major business or transaction cycles. The identification of material types of transactions should be done continuously throughout the evaluation of internal control structure; as the evaluation proceeds, previously unconsidered types of transactions may be identified.

Although the cycles outlined in Figure 8.3 will normally suffice for commercial and industrial companies, different kinds of cycles may be observed in other companies such as financial institutions. The cycle concept, however, is normally effective no matter what type of business is under consideration. The AICPA Special Advisory Committee on Internal Accounting Control stated:

> The cycle approach transcends the difference in the ways companies are organized and results in an overview of all the effects of a transaction that frequently cross functional lines in a company. [AICPA, 1979c, p. 21]

Determining Transaction Characteristics

Once all transactions, both external and internal, have been correlated with the basic business cycles, a decision must be made as to the extent of attention different transactions or groupings of transactions should receive. Three key tests are:

- Is it an *individually material* transaction?
- Is it a *key* transaction, that is, material from a qualitative standpoint (e.g., policy, image, legal) although not from a quantitative standpoint (i.e., financial statement amount)?
- Is it a *cycle* transaction?

Individually Material Transactions. Auditing concentrates attention on matters that can affect the auditor's report, and hence materiality guidelines apply. As summarized in SAS 47, *Audit Risk and Materiality in Conducting an Audit*:

> The auditor's consideration of materiality is a matter of professional judgment and is influenced by his perception of the needs of a reasonable person who will rely on the financial statements. The perceived needs of a reasonable person are recognized in the discussion of materiality in Financial Accounting Standards Board Statement of Financial Accounting Concepts No. 2, *Qualitiative Characteristics of Accounting Information*, which defines materiality as "the magnitude of an omission or misstatement of accounting information that, in the light of surrounding circumstances, makes it probable that the judgment of a reasonable person relying on the information would have been changed or influenced by the omission or misstatement." [AU 312.06]

Quantitative materiality guidelines could include determination of the appropriate measurement base (e.g., total revenue, net profit before tax, total stockholders' equity, total assets, or individual components of the financial statements, as appropriate in a specific situation), tempered by consideration of the problems inherent in certain situations (e.g., breakeven or low-margin companies). But material transactions must receive individual attention because of their significance.

Also in this category are transactions or balances that may not meet quantitative materiality guidelines but are significiant in relation to the matter under review. This requires sifting to determine whether a significant portion of an account balance is made up of a few large transactions. Concentration on those few transactions provides a high degree of audit satisfaction about the account for a relatively low effort.

Key Transactions. Auditors devote particular attention to certain transactions not monetarily significant that may nonetheless represent high error opportunities or involve unusual relationships. Characteristics often used to isolate such key transactions are shown in Figure 8.4.

Although it is not possible for an auditor to isolate every key transaction, increased audit attention is always appropriate once it is identified. The auditor should also be particularly concerned with transactions having both significant financial impact and opportune timing (e.g., occurring very near the end of a reporting period).

When individually material or key transactions are subject to a separate internal control structure, this structure should be documented. However, all material and key transactions must be individually audited using the substantive approach.

Cycle Transactions. All transaction types other than individually material or key transactions should be cycle transactions—a logically interrelated series of transactions that flow from source to related asset, liability, revenue, or expense. Cycle transactions need not be tested individually but can be covered within the context of the overall cycle. In other words, the auditor can use the total cycle as the basis for evaluating whether the processing properly achieves its objectives.

Sales, receivables, and collections. The majority of transactions affecting this cycle will arise from the sale of the company's regular products or services, and the systems will be designed primarily to process such transactions. Documentation of the sales cycle, discussed in Chapter 13, should tell how the following basic activities are performed and controlled:

* Recording and invoicing all goods shipped.
* Updating inventory quantity records (when perpetual records are kept) and inventory cost records to reflect goods shipped to or returned by customers.
* Approving credit and following up on overdue accounts.
* Handling, recording, and depositing cash received for credit sales and cash sales.
* Issuing credit memos for goods returned, adjustments, invoice errors, and so forth.
* Recording miscellaneous income (when significant).

- An unusual degree of management involvement in authorization, execution, recording, or accountability
- Direct or indirect economic benefit to management
- Dealings with related parties
- Activities apparently not in the ordinary course of business
- Valuation of transaction or balances that is based to a great degree on judgment
- Risk or probability of involving questionable or illegal matters

FIG. 8.4 Sample Characteristics of Key Transactions

Other transactions may also result in revenue, receivables, and cash receipts, and these transactions, being of an unusual or infrequent nature, may not be subject to the same systems. These miscellaneous sources of income could include such items as the sale of fixed assets or scrap, and, if material, the subsystems that process these transactions should be documented.

Purchases, payables, and payments. In this cycle the majority of transactions will be purchases of goods and services, setting up payables due to the related creditors and making payments. However, less frequent transactions will include the purchase or construction of fixed assets and the purchase of miscellaneous items such as investments. The documentation of this cycle should address the following basic activities:

- Authorizing the acquisition of goods or services.
- Recording liabilities for all goods or services received.
- Allocating purchases to the appropriate accounts.
- Updating inventory quantity and cost records to reflect purchases from or returns to suppliers.
- Checking, approving, and recording payments.

Cash and payables are discussed in Chapter 12.

Salaries and wages. Documentation required for this cycle concerns the following activities:

- Controlling the authorization for and hiring of new employees.
- Controlling the authorization for and implementation of changes in employment conditions.
- Controlling the authorization for and preparation, calculation, and payment of wages and salaries.
- Allocating wage and salary costs to the appropriate accounts.
- Controlling executive and management payroll.

Inventory costs and records. This transaction cycle will be encountered whenever the company's costing and inventory records are sufficiently complicated that they cannot be adequately described as part of other systems. The cycle, discussed in

Chapter 14, is concerned with the recording of inventory movement and changes through labor and overhead in arriving at finished goods.

Correlating Risk With Structure Understanding

"Audit risk is the risk that the auditor may unknowingly fail to appropriately modify his opinion on financial statements that are materially misstated" (AU 312.02). The auditor needs to consider audit risk at the individual account-balance of class-of-transactions level because such consideration directly assists him in determining the scope of auditing procedures for the balance or class. The auditor should seek to restrict audit risk at the individual balance or class level in such a way that will enable him, at the completion of his examination, to express an opinion on the financial statements taken as a whole at an appropriately low level of audit risk.

At the account-balance or class-of-transaction level, audit risk consists of:

- The risks (consisting of inherent risk and control risk) that the balance or class contains error that could be material to the financial statements when aggregated with error in other balances or classes, and
- The risk (detection risk) that the auditor will not detect such error.

The risk of material misstatement in financial statements consists of three separate risks (AU 319.28).

- *Inherent risk* is the susceptibility of an assertion to a material misstatement assuming there are no related internal control structure policies or procedures.
- *Control risk* is the risk that a material misstatement that could occur in an assertion will not be prevented or detected on a timely basis by the entity's internal control structure.
- *Detection risk* is the risk that the auditor will not detect a material misstatement that exists in an assertion.

The magnitude and the type of risk differ depending on the asset exposed. For example, different risks are involved when cash and equipment are compared. Cash and items readily convertible into cash are more easily conscripted for personal use and the controls over cash should therefore reflect this. Other assets and transactions usually have a lower degree of risk and their controls should be tailored accordingly.

Error Types and Sources. Up to this point, the auditor has developed an understanding of the nature, source, and characteristics of transactions to the extent needed to provide a focus for his assessment of the significance of the internal control structure in the audit plan. He has also reviewed and assessed the general factors that contribute to material error types. Now he must identify, for each material transaction cycle, those potential error types that could result in a material error in the financial statements. There are two steps:

1. Applying general potential error types to transaction cycles.
2. Identifying the possible causes of those potential error types.

General potential error types	Basic types of control
Transactions are not properly *authorized*	Policy on specific or general authorization at key points (e.g., granting credit) Procedures for approvals consistent with policy and requiring documentation (e.g., signatures or attaching supporting documents)
Recorded transactions are not *valid*	Segregation of duties Use of prenumbered documents that are accounted for Cancellation of documents to prevent reuse Monthly reconciliation of subsidiary records and follow-up by an independent person
Existing transactions are not *recorded*	Use of prenumbered documents that are accounted for Segregation of duties Monthly reconciliation of subsidiary records and follow-up by an independent person
Transactions are improperly *valued*	Internal verification of details and calculations and posting by an independent person Reconciliation of details to control totals (e.g., bank reconciliation) by an independent person
Transactions are improperly *classified*	Use of an adequate chart of accounts Internal review and verification
Transactions are recorded at the improper *time*	Procedures to assure prompt recording of all transactions Internal review and verification
Transactions are improperly included in the subsidiary records and incorrectly *summarized*	Segregation of duties Monthly reconciliation of subsidiary records by an independent person Internal review and verification

FIG. 8.5   General Error Types and Basic Remedies

The general error types imply a failure to achieve the basic objectives of the control structure. A summary of these errors and basic remedies is shown in Figure 8.5.

Once the specific potential error types for the transaction cycle are defined, the auditor should consider the circumstances under which those errors could occur. At the most detailed level, the possibilities are almost limitless, arising whenever a document is prepared, processed, passed from one person to another, or transcribed. There are, however, general causes to keep in mind when assessing whether a system appears to control a specific potential error type:

• Failure to prepare documents
• Loss of documents

- Duplication of documents
- Inaccurate recording
- Inaccurate processing
- Incomplete processing
- Untimely processing and recording
- Failure to follow authorization procedures

Applying general potential error types to specific transaction cycles will identify potential error types in the context of transactions within that cycle—that is, the "points in the processing of transactions and the handling of assets where errors or irregularities could occur" (AU 642.21). For example, the potential error types relating to the sales element of the sales, billings, receivables, and collection cycle (discussed in Chapter 13) are as follows:

- Sales recorded but goods not shipped (existence-validity).
- Goods shipped but not invoiced (existence-recording).
- Goods shipped to bad credit risk (valuation).
- Sales invoiced but not recorded (recording).
- Sales amount recorded incorrectly (accuracy-valuation).
- Sales invoiced but not properly costed (accuracy-valuation).
- Sales recorded in wrong period (timing).
- Sales misclassified (classification).
- Sales journal incorrectly added (accuracy-summarization).

Assessing Error Probability. The assessment of any risk requires a consideration of *probability* of loss as distinct from *possibility*. Many risks are possible; fewer are probable. Controls can reduce the probability, but rarely eliminate the possibility. A control system should take into account the possible risks that could materially affect the financial statements. But at the same time the degree of probability must also be considered when deciding on the extent of controls that are necessary and cost-justifiable.

Management's asset-safeguarding responsibilities require that there be adequate protection and control, but management's operating performance responsibilities require that controls always be weighed to see if they will hamper the productivity of any asset. Attempts to increase productivity usually involve elements of risk. And usually the extent of potential reward and risk rises concurrently. Specifically the auditor would (AU 319.30).

- [Identify] specific internal control structure policies and procedures relevant to specific assertions that are likely to prevent or detect material misstatements in those assertions.
- [Perform] tests of controls to evaluate the effectiveness of such policies and procedures.

The auditor has to assess which policies and procedures can have what kinds of effects on the financial statements. For example, the control environment and the accounting system will affect almost all important financial statement items, and therefore the auditor will pay closer attention to these aspects (to the extent they are relevant) when deciding whether to perform certain procedures at interim dates, or in deciding how many locations to audit. The auditor can make this assessment even though at this point he has not considered every financial statement assertion that could be affected by his decisions. Some control procedures are far less pervasive, however. For example, those related to physical inventory counting are only in effect when the count is performed.

Control structure procedures can be direct or indirect. The more they tend to the latter, the less effective they will be in reducing control risk. Using the example given in SAS 55 (AU 319.33), a review of a sales activity summary by a sales manager indirectly relates to whether all sales are recorded; a more direct control procedure would be matching shipping and billing documents.

Designing an Internal Control Structure Review

To test the design or operation of the internal control policies or procedures, the auditor employs tests of controls. These tests assess how well the control is matched with the risk of misstatement it is designed to prevent or detect. In performing tests of controls, the auditor may use the basic types of evidence, including inquiry, inspection, observation, flowcharts, questionnaires, and decision tables.

To conclude that the control risk is less than maximum requires that the auditor look at evidence; he cannot intuit this result. How much evidence he must examine to provide him with proper support for the degree of assurance he is allowing for a given control procedure or set of procedures is, however, a matter of judgment. It would not be possible to set specifications for the infinite variety of circumstances the auditor encounters.

Types of Evidence. There are several basic types of evidence-gathering techniques employed by the auditor, including inquiry, observation, inspection, and reperformance. Which to use depends on the matter under study: systems write-ups by the company would likely be inspected if they exist, but observation may be needed for such matters as assignment of authority and responsibility, and reperformance may be needed for certain computer-related controls.

If the performance of a control procedure leaves no documentary evidence, the only method of testing is by observation. Although observation can provide evidence of performance for a wide variety of controls, the reviewer must always consider that the control may not be in operation when he is not there to observe it. Observation tests, therefore, should be supplemented by other evidence, such as inquiry as to the operation of controls at other times.

Examples of controls that usually leave no documentary evidence and must be tested by observation include those over:

- Distribution of wages
- Opening of mail
- Punching of timecards
- Inventory
- Segregation of duties

In addition, observation supplements tests of documentation by providing evidence of the apparent thoroughness and competence of the person doing the job.

Sources of Evidence. The type of evidence has varying degrees of persuasiveness in the circumstances under which it is used. For example, observing how processing is done counts more than merely asking how it is done, or looking at employee initials, or asking about the person doing the work (AU 319.50). Concommitantly, observation at a point in time does not give assurance that the process will continuously be performed in the manner observed. SAS 55 draws the line on one technique, however (AU 319.51):

> Inquiry alone will not provide sufficient evidential matter to support a conclusion about the effectiveness of design or operation of a specific control procedure. When the auditor determines that a specific control procedure may have a significant effect in reducing control risk to a low level for a specific assertion, he ordinarily needs to perform additional tests to obtain sufficient evidential matter to support the conclusion about the effectiveness of the design or operation of that control procedure.

When the performance of a control procedure is documented, records can be examined for compliance. Tests should be designed to detect compliance deviations or failures to perform as prescribed.

For example, a test for evidence that all good shipped have been billed may require comparing sales invoices to shipping documents. Here, the definition of a compliance deviation should include an unmatched shipping document, a shipping document matched to the wrong sales invoice, incorrect recording of quantities shipped, arithmetical errors in extensions and footings, and any other matters important in the specific control situation.

When a control is evaluated as reliable, it is because the auditor is persuaded that (1) the control is effective in achieving its purpose, and (2) the persons performing the control are competent and will properly and consistently perform the control. Evidence of the performance of the control is evidence of compliance. If, on the other hand, a negative finding results, the control may not meet the need, and this fact has to be considered in determining other audit procedures to be performed to minimize the likelihood of errors in the financial statements.

Timeliness of Evidence. Evidence is perishable as well as limited by how probatory it is in relation to the matter under audit consideration. For example, observing a process informs the auditor how it was done that one time. A computer program is a good example: By running the program, the auditor may prove to his satisfaction that it properly executed a control procedure; however, he will have to employ other forms of evidence to become reasonably assured that the program was unmodified and consistently employed during the audit period.

Documented evidence obtained in prior audits may also be used, but it may need to be updated. In deciding how much weight to place on systems write-ups obtained and tests thereof made in prior audits (e.g., through a cycle approach to testing controls in various areas), the auditor should consider how old the data is, and (AU 319.53):

- The significance of the assertion involved;
- The specific internal control structure policies and procedures evaluated during the prior audits;
- The degree to which the effective design and operation of those policies and procedures were evaluated;
- The results of the tests of controls used to make those evaluations; and
- Evidential matter about design or operation that may result from substantive tests performed in the current audit.

A similar problem arises when tests of controls are performed during interim periods. Deciding on the validity of the results for the rest of the audit period is dependent on:

- The significance of the assertion involved.
- The specific internal control structure policies and procedures evaluated during the interim period.
- The degree to which the effective design and operation of those policies and procedures were evaluated.
- The results of the tests of controls used to make that evaluation.
- The length of the remaining period.
- The responses to inquiries for the remaining period.
- The nature and amount of transactions or balances occurring subsequent to interim testing.
- The results of analytical reviews.
- The evidential matter about design or operation that may result from substantive tests performed in the remaining period.
- Nature and extent of any significant changes in the internal control structure, including changes in policies, procedures, and personnel that occur subsequent to the interim period.

Interrelationships. Auditing is a cumulative process; evidence continues to be examined until the auditor is satisfied that he has reduced his detection risk to an acceptable level. The auditor therefore recognizes that different types of evidence are likely to be needed to support a single assertion in the financial statements; indeed, the degree of assurance provided by evidence is multiplied when different forms all support the same conclusion.

As discussed in Chapter 7, many account interrelationships exist from which the auditor can derive additional corroboration. Testing "one side" of a transaction flow provides evidence as to the contra side. So too with internal controls; a control over recording of sales will have some value with respect to controls over accounts receivable.

If the auditor uses various types of evidence aimed at a specific financial statement assertion and the support is not uniform, the level of assurance drops. In fact, this should raise questions about whether a professed control procedure is operating effectively, if at all. Upon investigation, the auditor will appropriately revise his substantive scope, or may decide to perform more tests of control procedures to establish whether the indications to date are confirmed.

Achieving Reasonable Assurance

The balancing act outlined in the preceding section is solved in the concept of reasonable assurance, based on the premise that the cost of control should not exceed the anticipated benefits. The direct cost of a specific control generally can be estimated; it usually involves known factors such as extra equipment or additional people. However, effectiveness is more difficult to determine: if an error or risk situation arises, will the control under consideration actually prevent or detect that occurrence in a timely manner? Most difficult is weighing the indirect costs and benefits: has the new control restricted operations to the extent that profit reductions are greater than the assets at risk prior to installing the control? And some benefits cannot be assigned a monetary value, for example, a company's image resulting from having (or not having) controls over otherwise minor exposures to off-book accounts.

Thus the evaluation of the net benefit arising from increased controls necessarily involves considerable estimation and judgment. This assessment, however, is valuable to management because it helps emphasize the range of alternative controls and strategies available.

When the auditor is considering the effectiveness of internal accounting controls, some inherent limitations must be recognized:

1. *Personnel.* People are essential to, and form the major limitation in, any system of internal accounting control, because people operate the systems, whether manually or via computers. The competence and fallibility of the pesonnel operating a system must always be a consideration when evaluating that system. Personal performance can be faulty because of a misunderstanding of instructions, a mistake in judgment, distraction, fatigue, or carelessness.

2. *Circumvention or collusion.* Whenever the internal control structure relies on the work of one person being checked by the work of another, there is always a risk that circumvention or collusion can reduce or destroy the effectiveness of those procedures. Circumstances that increase the possibility of collusion, such as the formation of personal relationships within the organization, or the presence of dominant personalities who can exert their will, should be considered.

3. *Control override.* Procedures may be overridden in certain circumstances. The most notable examples are bypasses (by senior management or by subordinates under orders) of controls that would otherwise monitor the occurrence of errors or irregularities.

4. *Changing circumstances.* The environment in which internal accounting controls operate is constantly changing. Factors external to the organization, such as commercial and political forces, are always in flux, and internal factors such as changes in operations, systems, or the people involved can occur without conscious or complete planning. Thus the effectiveness of controls may be constantly changing, and projecting past evaluations of the internal control structure to future periods is subject to the risks arising from these changes.

SAS 55 (AU 319.36) refers to the auditor's assessment conclusion as the "assessed level of control risk." The auditor combines this risk with his assessment of inherent risk to reach a conclusion as to the level of detection risk – all such risks relating, of course, to whether the financial statements could contain a material misstatement. This blending procedure is easy to assert, but hard to do. Equally hard is the auditor's determination of what level of detection risk he is prepared to accept in his audit, which in turn depends on how he views materiality (see SAS 47, AU 312).

If the auditor has little tolerance for detection risk, or does not assess the level of control risk to be much less than maximum, he will perform a substantial portion of his audit using substantive procedures. He may also look for more effective procedures (those that provide greater assurance, like independent confirmations), do less at interim dates in favor of year-end procedures, and use larger substantive sample sizes.

In the end, the auditor endeavors to provide reasonable assurance that the financial statements are presented without material misstatement. He cannot provide absolute assurance, and thus there is some level of detection risk he must accept. The auditor's evaluation of inherent risk and control risk leads him to conclude what level of detection risk exists before the performance of substantive tests.

Documenting the Assessment. Auditing is a complex subject, and it has never been legally advisable for an auditor to take the position that he simply "used his professional judgment" in deciding (for purposes of reliance) on the strength of the internal control system. Under SAS 55 (AU 319.39) it is not permissible professionally either; the auditor must document both his understanding of the control structure and his conclusion as to the level of control risk involved in that structure. The type and amount of assessment documentation is not specified in SAS 55, which states that this is dependent on how low the assessment is and how well the company has documented its systems.

However, SAS 55 also allows the auditor to briefly document an assessment of maximum control risk without stating his reasons; this is logical because in such an assessment the auditor will not rely on the control structure in designing his substantive audit approach.

Verifying the Systems Descriptions. Having completed the description of a specific system, the auditor must trace each type of transaction through the system to satisfy himself that it is correct. This involves tracing transactions from initiation to final recording, or vice versa. While doing this, the auditor should observe whether permanent and temporary records appear to be up to date and balanced regularly or whether they contain old or irregular items, and whether the continuity of documents in the files is complete.

Once the auditor is satisfied that all systems descriptions are complete and accurate, he should proceed to test those controls on which he plans to rely. In those instances, he arrives at a conclusion as to what reliance he may place on those controls, and uses this level in determining the effect on his detection risk. He may not give the controls much credit, in which case he will still do mostly substantive work; or he may alter the nature, timing, and extent of substantive tests based on a stronger assessment.

In performing substantive tests of transactions and balances as well as analytical procedures, the auditor may also design such tests to provide him with information on the effectiveness with which control procedures are operating. This type of test is called a *dual-purpose test;* properly planned, it can result in improvements in audit efficiency. It must be noted, however, that such tests are best designed for application during the Phase II review of the internal control structure, at which time their value as substantive tests can be factored into the Phase III design. It is possible to work backwards from Phase III to Phase II, but doing so is more complex, the results are less predictable, and timing constraints are likely to diminish their value as tests of control procedures.

Summary of the Evaluation Process. The conclusion of the evaluation process is an assessment of the likelihood of a material error occurring and being included in the financial statements. This assessment involves a series of subjective judgments and recognition of the inherent limitations of any internal control structure. Essentially, this represents a probability analysis for errors as well as controls. It requires a determination of how much reliance can be placed on the internal control structure and an assessment of other auditing procedures, and it is expressed as a matter of degree rather than an absolute.

The auditor can express his judgment concerning the liklihood of risk in general terms – high, moderate, or low – rather than by attempting to assign a monetary value. Four possible levels of risk are frequently identified:

1. *High.* The auditor expects errors and believes they may be material in relation to the financial statements.
2. *Unknown.* The auditor has not proceeded beyond his preliminary evaluation of the reliability of internal accounting controls and is not relying on these controls. (In this case, the internal accounting controls have not affected the structure of substantive audit procedures, except for dealing with apparent weaknesses noted in the preliminary review.)
3. *Moderate.* The auditor expects errors but has reason to believe they are not likely to be material in relation to the financial statements.
4. *Low.* The auditor expects few, if any, errors.

Risk assessments, whether words or numbers, relate specifically to individual potential error types. If the concept of evaluating internal accounting controls based on potential error types is being used, all the steps in the review revolve around assessments about specific error types. The conclusions relating to these error types cause additional substantive audit work to assure that potential errors, either singly or in the aggregate, have not resulted in actual material errors in the financial statements.

High risk. This evaluation indicates that the operation of the systems could cause the financial statements to be materially in error. Because the system is weak the auditor must resolve his uncertainty through substantive tests of transactions and balances. He must seek the most convincing audit evidence available – evidence from physical inspection or outside verification and from a detailed analysis of financial statement amounts.

The timing of the substantive audit procedures would be as of year end, to directly support the formulation of an opinion on the financial statements. Because the internal accounting control system is considered unreliable, substantive tests at interim dates should only address accumulating balances, that is, income statement accounts. The substantive procedures used would be extensive and would be directed at obtaining evidence about a significant part of the accounts making up the financial statements. This testing could be done on either a judgmental or a statistical sampling basis and could involve the segmentation of different strata within accounts.

Therefore, for a *high-risk* assessment, the audit strategy can be summarized as follows (also applicable when risk is unknown because controls were not evaluated):

Nature   To establish existence and amount:
- Physical inspection
- Confirmation
- Review of documents from outside the organization
- Recalculations

Timing   Basically year end

Extent   Extensive, and concentrated on testing significant parts of affected accounts

Moderate risk. Here, the auditor would use a combination of physical evidence procedures (the most persuasive form of audit evidence) and corroborative procedures, such as analytical review and inquiry, to augment his reliance on the system. The timing, nature, and extent of the tests are interdependent and reflect the nature of the available audit evidence and the practicality of performing substantive tests at different times. If physical audit evidence can be obtained at or near year end, it will provide a high degree of assurance about the validity of the year-end account balances and reduce the requirements for additional evidence needed to support the audit opinion. This can be summarized as follows:

Nature   Mixed, including:
- Tests to establish existence and valuation
- Corroborative tests

Timing   Interim and year end

Extent   Mixed, depending on audit evidence available:
- If physical existence tests are possible and applied, less overall testing
- If only corroborative procedures possible, more testing

Low risk. When the quality of the internal accounting control system is such that there is a low risk of material errors in the financial statements, the internal control structure carries the major burden of reducing audit uncertainty. Thus the additional work required need only seek essentially corroborative evidence, which is less extensive and can be spread throughout the year.

In low-risk situations, substantive evidence is gathered to determine whether the evaluation of the internal control structure is contradicted or materially altered. Analytical review, interrelationship with other audit evidence, and limited tests of transactions and balances would be applied.

REPORTING ON INTERNAL CONTROL

Auditing Standards Overview

Nonpublic reporting on internal controls – that is, to the company and to regulatory agencies – has been with the profession for many years. Although various ground rules existed in the early professional standards, these were first codified into specific standards relating to reporting in the early 1970s (SAP 49 and SAP 52, both superseded). This codification resulted in a standard reporting style for public use that contained a lengthy explanation of the objectives and inherent limitations of internal controls. The form of report was much criticized because of its many caveats and its failure to address the adequacy of the company's systems. In 1980, the ASB issued SAS 30, *Reporting on Internal Accounting Control* (AU 642), superseding the earlier SAPs. SAS 30 discusses:

- Public reporting by auditors, with expression of an opinion, based on an examination of the system of internal controls either at a specified date or for a period of time.
- Nonpublic reporting to management or specified third parties, without expression of an opinion, based solely on the review and evaluation of the system performed as part of the audit.
- Reporting on controls to regulatory agencies or management, based on the regulatory agencies' established criteria.
- Issuance of special purpose nonpublic reports.

SAS 30 continued the long-standing definition of material weakness (discussed in the next section) as the focus of the auditor's responsibility to report to senior management, the board and the audit committee.

In response to a hot issue at the time, SAS 30 did not allow auditors to report on the company's compliance with the internal control requirements of the Foreign Corrupt Practices Act of 1977 (FCPA). SAS 30 makes the following observation (AU 642.12):

> Whether a company is in compliance with those provisions of the FCPA is a legal determination. An independent accountant's opinion does not indicate whether the company is in compliance with those provisions but may be helpful to management in evaluating the company's compliance.

Subsequently, to deal with the proliferation of service bureaus (EDP and other types) in the U.S. economy, the ASB released SAS 44, *Special-Purpose Reports on Internal Accounting Control at Service Organizations* (AU 324).

In 1988, the ASB issued SAS 60, *Communication of Internal Control Structure Related Matters Noted in an Audit* (AU 325), superseding only that portion of SAS 30 that dealt with reporting based solely on an audit. SAS 60 added a new term, *reportable condition,* to the internal control lexicon. Additionally, the definition of internal control system was revamped in SAS 55, *Consideration of the Internal Control Structure in a Financial Statement Audit* (AU 319), also issued in 1988.

Material Weaknesses vs. Reportable Conditions

Until the release of SAS 60 (effective for 1989 calendar year audits, with early application permissible), the auditor has been concerned with how to deal with a material
weakness in internal accounting control. As revised by SAS 60, a material weakness
is defined as (AU 325.15):

> a . . . condition in which the design or operation of the specific internal control structure
> elements do not reduce to a relatively low level the risk that errors or irregularities in
> amounts that would be material in relation to the financial statements being audited may
> occur and not be detected within a timely period by employees in the normal course of
> performing their assigned functions.

Under SAS 30, the auditor was required to communicate such matters to the client, if any were found during the audit. In engagements to report on internal controls, the auditor also focused on material weaknesses.

The material weakness concept was difficult to apply in practice, in part because
of definitional problems now presumably rectified by SAS 55, *Consideration of the
Internal Control Structure in a Financial Statement Audit* (AU 319). Because the profession has been under fire in the mid-1980s for a number of alleged shortcomings
including failure to be more assertive with respect to internal controls, the auditor's
responsibility was broadened by requiring him to communicate with the audit committee regarding reportable conditions, defined as (AU 325.02):

> matters coming to the auditor's attention that, in his judgment, should be communicated to
> the audit committee because they represent significant deficiencies in the design or opera-
> tion of the internal control structure, which could adversely affect the organization's ability
> to record, process, summarize and report financial data consistent with the assertions of
> management in the financial statements.

SAS 60 maintains a distinction between the two concepts, pointing out that "A
reportable condition may be of such a magnitude as to be considered a material
weakness" (AU 325.15). In reporting to the audit committee, the auditor is not
required to distinguish between reportable conditions and material weaknesses.
However, if the auditor reports matters that are of lesser concern than reportable
conditions, these should be distinguished. Finally, in contrast to SAS 30, the auditor
is not required under SAS 60 (but is permitted) to describe the limited purpose of his
study and the inherent limitations of the control structure; and under SAS 60 he is
not expected to express a disclaimer of opinion on the internal control structure as a
whole.

As of mid-1988, the ASB had not determined whether reportable conditions
should become the basis for reporting when the auditor is specifically engaged to
report on internal control. SAS 60 recognizes that this new basis may be used, however, in audit-based reports that are required to be furnished to governmental and
regulatory authorities (AU 325.10).

In the sections that follow, the focus of reporting will be on reportable conditions
for audit-based communications and on material weaknesses for specific
engagements.

Types of Auditor's Reports

In addition to communications based on audits, auditors may be specifically engaged to study and evaluate an entity's internal control structure and to issue a report thereon for public or private distribution, for distribution to government agencies based on specified criteria, and for use by other auditors.

Audit Basis. SAS 60, *Communication of Internal Control Structure Related Matters Noted in an Audit* (AU 325), requires that auditors communicate with the audit committee regarding reportable conditions. Such a report must contain the following elements (AU 325.11):

* An indication that the purpose of the audit was to report on the financial statements and not to provide assurance on the internal control structure.
* Definition of reportable conditions.
* Restriction on distribution solely to the audit committee, management, and others in the organization (including governmental agencies where required).

An illustration of a report that meets these conditions is shown in Figure 8.6. If the auditor wishes, or has been requested, to differentiate between reportable conditions and material weaknesses, the report would contain also a definition of the latter, an indication of which (if any) of the reportable conditions is a material weakness, and a paragraph stating (AU 325.16):

Our consideration of the internal control structure would not necessarily disclose all matters in the internal control structure that might be reportable conditions and, accordingly, would not necessarily disclose all reportable conditions that are also considered to be material weaknesses as defined above.

If no reportable conditions were deemed material weaknesses, the final sentence would read, "However, none of the reportable conditions described above is believed to be a material weakness."

The auditor is required to communicate reportable conditions coming to his attention even if he does not test the control structure (in the relevant area) for purposes of reliance thereon (because he will follow a fully substantive audit approach in the area).

The auditor does not need to report in writing, but oral communications should be documented in his audit files. He also does not have to communicate a reportable condition previously reported, if the audit committee has acknowledged the existence of the condition and has decided to accept the related risks as a matter of cost/benefit considerations or for other reasons.

The auditor is not permitted to issue a report stating that no reportable conditions were noted during the audit because of the potential for misunderstanding as a "clean bill of health." Further, interim communications are encouraged, especially if corrective action may be urgently needed. SAS 60 also contains an appendix that lists possible reportable conditions.

In planning and performing our audit of the financial statements of the ABC Corporation for the year ended December 31, 19XX, we considered its internal control structure in order to determine our auditing procedures for the purpose of expressing our opinion on the financial statements and not to provide assurance on the internal control structure. However, we noted certain matters involving the internal control structure and its operation that we consider to be reportable conditions under standards established by the American Institute of Certified Public Accountants. Reportable conditions involve matters coming to our attention relating to significant deficiencies in the design or operation of the internal control structure that, in our judgment, could adversely affect the organization's ability to record, process, summarize, and report financial data consistent with the assertions of management in the financial statements.

[Include paragraphs to describe the reportable conditions noted.]

This report is intended solely for the information and use of the audit committee (board of directors, board of trustees, or owners in owner-managed enterprises), management, and other within the organization (or specified regulatory agency or other specified third party).

FIG. 8.6   Sample Report on Internal Control Structure Based on an Audit
Source: SAS 60 (AU 325.12).

Specific Study and Evaluation Basis. SAS 60 only addresses reporting on internal control based on an audit. Although the ASB has a project in the works that will correct this, as of mid-1988 the public reporting guidelines of SAS 30 remain in effect.

When reporting on the results of a specific study and evaluation of the internal control structure that includes all the significant systems of an entity (i.e., not as the result of an audit of the financial statements), the report should include the following items:

• Description of the engagement scope.
• Date to which the opinion relates.
• Statement that the establishment and maintenance of the system is management's responsibility.
• Brief explanation of the broad objectives and inherent limitations of internal accounting control.
• Accountants' opinion on whether the system, taken as a whole, was sufficient to meet the broad objectives of internal accounting control as they relate to the prevention of detection of errors or irregularities which would be material in amount in relation to financial statements.

This report need not be restricted to internal use. The standard form of a point-in-time report is illustrated in Figure 8.7.

When the study and evaluation disclose conditions which, individually or in combination, result in material weaknesses, they should be enumerated in the opinion paragraph of the auditor's report. The report should describe the material weakness, state whether it results from the absence of controls or failure to adhere to controls, and state the general nature of the potential error or irregularities which may occur as a result of the weakness.

We have made a study and evaluation of the system of internal accounting control of XYZ Company and subsidiaries in effect at (date). Our study and evaluation was conducted in accordance with standards established by the American Institute of Certified Public Accountants.

The management of XYZ Company is responsible for establishing and maintaining a system of internal accounting control. In fulfilling this responsibility, estimates and judgments by management are required to assess the expected benefits and related costs of control procedures. The objectives of a system are to provide management with reasonable, but not absolute, assurance that assets are safeguarded against loss from unauthorized use or disposition, and that transactions are executed in accordance with management's authorization and are recorded properly to permit the preparation of financial statements in accordance with generally accepted accounting principles.

Because of inherent limitations in any system of internal accounting control, errors or irregularities may occur and not be detected. Also, projection of any evaluation of the system to future periods is subject to the risk that procedures may become inadequate because of changes in conditions, or that the degree of compliance with the procedures may deteriorate.

In our opinion, the system of internal accounting control of XYZ Company and subsidiaries in effect at (date), taken as a whole, was sufficient to meet the objectives stated above insofar as those objectives pertain to the prevention or detection of errors or irregularities in amounts that would be material in relation to the consolidated financial statements.

FIG. 8.7 Sample Report on Internal Control Structure Based on a Specific Study and Evaluation
Source: AU 642.39.

An illustration of the opinion paragraph to be used in Figure 8.7 when reporting a material weakness is:

Our study and evaluation disclosed the following conditions in the system of internal accounting control of XYZ Company and subsidiaries in effect at (date), which, in our opinion, result in more than a relatively low risk that errors or irregularities in amounts that would be material in relation to the consolidated financial statements may occur and not be detected within a timely period. (Describe material weaknesses.)

If the document that contains an auditor's opinion identifying a material weakness also includes management's assertion that corrective action is not practicable due to cost-benefit considerations, the auditor should not express any opinion as to management's statement. However, the auditor is not precluded from disclaiming an opinion on any such statement or from separately advising the client privately on the practicability or likely benefits of specific control procedures.

When the auditor is reporting on reportable conditions which are not material weaknesses, they should clearly be distinguished from those relating to material weaknesses. If the auditor wishes to report to the client on other matters that are not reportable conditions, a separate letter (see "Letters of Recommendations" later herein) should address these matters and should be clearly distinguishable from reportable conditions or material weaknesses.

Where the report includes comments on other matters (e.g., comments to a regulatory agency on specific aspects of control or on compliance with contract provisions or regulations), the report should be modified to clearly identify these other matters and describe in reasonable detail the scope of the review, tests, and conclusions reached.

When the opinion on the specific engagement to study and evaluate the internal control structure is issued in conjunction with an examination of the entity's financial statements, a sentence should be added to the paragraph that describes a material weaknesses stating that: (1) such weaknesses were taken into account when determining the nature, timing, and extent of audit tests; and (2) that the report on the internal control structure does not affect the auditor's report on the financial statements.

The auditor can express an opinion on an entity's overall internal control structure only if he has been able to apply all the procedures he considers necessary. Restrictions on the scope of the engagement, whether imposed by the client or by circumstances, require the auditor to disclaim an opinion on the internal accounting control structure.

Government Agency Criteria Basis. Many government agencies require reporting on internal control, particularly for organizations receiving federal grants. The auditor's scope will be based on criteria published by the grantor agency as set forth in audit guides, questionnaires, or other releases, and may encompass specified aspects of the control structure and references to statutes.

Although the auditor does not accept any responsibility for the comprehensiveness of the agency's criteria, he must report any matter coming to his attention that would be a material weakness even though it is not covered by the specified criteria. For government agency internal control reporting, the definitions of material weakness is modified to relate to the applicable grant or program rather than to the overall financial statements, and has the following additional descriptor (AU 642.57):

> A condition in which the lack of conformity with the agency's criteria is material in accordance with any guidelines for determining materiality that are included in such criteria.

The U.S. General Accounting Office (GAO) requires a report on the study and evaluation of internal controls made as part of the financial and compliance audit performed in accordance with *The Yellow Book* (see Chapter 31). However, the GAO requires the auditor to identify in his report the entity's significant controls, with identification of those controls that were not evaluated. Furthermore, if the auditor decides not to place any reliance on, and therefore does not assess the control procedures in, the internal control structure, he must state to the GAO why this was omitted.

These matters are discussed at length in AU 642.54 –.59 and in numerous interpretations released by the ASB, contained is AU 9642.

Service Organizations. The ASB issued SAS 44, *Special-Purpose Reports on Internal Accounting Control at Service Organizations* (AU 324), in December 1982. This SAS provides guidance on how, under certain circumstances, one independent auditor (the user auditor) might use a special-purpose report issued by another independent auditor (the service auditor) on an accounting or custodial services organization. Such reports might be useful in examining the financial statements of a client that uses accounting or custodial services provided by the following types of organizations:

- Service centers that provide data processing functions for other organizations.
- Reinsurers that handle accounting for ceded policies.
- Security depositories or clearing organizations that perform services such as the execution and clearance of trades for another broker or dealer.
- Bank trust departments or similar entities that provide services such as administering pension plans.
- Mortgage bankers or savings and loan associations that service loans for others.
- Banks or trust companies acting as registrar or transfer agent for a corporation.

The AICPA issued an auditing interpretation, *Definition of a Service Organization* (AU 9324.01–.05), to clarify that, for purposes of AU 324, an organization is considered to be a service organization if it provides either or both of the following services:

- Executing transactions as an agent or in a fiduciary capacity for another entity and maintaining the related accountability.
- Recording transactions executed entirely by the user organization and processing the related data.

The Interpretation provides examples of service organizations that provide these services. These examples are similar to the types of organizations previously listed.

The service auditor may issue the following types of special-purpose reports, examples of which are included in SAS 44:

- Reports on the design of the system.
- Reports on both the design of the system and compliance tests that are directed to specific objectives of internal accounting control.
- Reports on the system of a segment of the service organization.

SAS 44 includes a discussion of the factors affecting the decision to obtain a service auditor's report and of the circumstances when each type of special-purpose report might be appropriate. If the special-purpose report is not adequate and the user auditor plans to rely on controls at the service organization, the user auditor may perform his own compliance tests at the service organization or arrange to have the service auditor apply agreed-upon procedures to test the controls on which he intends to rely.

In using a service auditor's report, the user auditor should inquire about the service auditor's competence and consider the timing of the service auditor's report relative to the period of the financial statements he is examining. In reporting on the examination of his client's financial statements, the user auditor should not make reference to the service auditor's report as a basis, in part, for his own opinion, because the service auditor has not examined any portion of the client's financial statements.

The Company prepared, and is responsible for, its consolidated financial statements and the other information appearing in this annual report. The Company believes that the consolidated financial statements fairly present its financial position in conformity with generally accepted accounting principles. In preparing its consolidated financial statements, the Company includes amounts that are based on estimates and judgments which the Company believes are reasonable under the circumstances.

The Company maintains a system of internal accounting control which it believes is sufficient to provide reasonable assurance that the Company meets its responsibilities in the preparation of its consolidated financial statements and maintains a reasonable accountability for its assets. In establishing and maintaiing any system of internal accounting control, estimates and judgments are required to assess the relative costs and expected benefits. Also, the Company maintains an internal auditing program that assesses the effectiveness of the internal accounting control system and performs other internal audit functions.

The independent accountants provide an objective, independent review of reported operating results and financial position.

The Audit Committee of the Board of Directors, composed entirely of non-employee directors, oversees the Company's financial reporting process on behalf of the Board of Directors. Its functions include: reviewing and recommending to the Board the selection of the independent accountants, and reviewing the scope and discharge of the responsibilities of management, internal auditing and the independent accountants during periodic meetings with representatives of these groups.

On behalf of the Company,

s/J.C. Jacobsen
Vice President and
Chief Financial Officer

FIG. 8.8   Company Report on Responsibility for Financial Reporting
Source: Shell Oil Company, 1987 Annual Report.

Other Reports. The auditor may be engaged to provide other special purpose reports for the restricted use of named parties. Examples include a report on the design of a control structure or control procedures in advance of implementation, or a report on the application of agreed-upon procedures to specific aspects of the control structure.

Letters of Recommendations

Under SAS 60 (AU 325.03), the auditor is advised that matters not constituting reportable conditions may also be communicated to the client and others. As a matter of good practice, most auditors will issue a letter of recommendations (or management letter), usually as a separate letter (not combined in a letter communicating material weaknesses or reportable conditions), even though combining these matters is not precluded under SAS 60 (which only requires that they be differentiated). Recommendations letters will also often include suggestions for improvements in operating matters and for efficiencies that have little relationship to the internal control structure.

Management Reports

Although not required in annual reports to shareholders, management reporting on its responsibility for the financial statements and for the system of internal controls is now commonplace, and is encouraged by the Financial Executives Institute. A sample management report is shown in Figure 8.8. However, a mandate for the inclusion of such a report may be coming soon. Based on the recommendations of the Treadway Commission (NCFFR, 1987), the SEC has proposed (in Release 34-25925, July 19, 1988) that all public companies include a separate report on management's responsibilities in both their Form 10-K filings and annual reports to shareholders. This would go beyond the example shown in Figure 8.8 in that management would be required to explicitly state (1) its assessment of the effectiveness of the system as to material matters, and (2) how it responded to recommendations made by internal and outside auditors regarding controls.

Under SAS 8, *Other Information in Documents Containing Audited Financial Statements* (AU 550), the auditor is required to read management's report to evaluate that it does not contradict other assertions in the financial statements. Further, if the auditor is aware of a material misstatement in management's report, he should notify the management and the board of directors (audit committee) in writing. For example, the auditor may have communicated the existence of a material weakness, but no reference thereto has been made in management's report. While this apparent omission may be explainable by a prudent management decision to accept the risk because of cost-benefit considerations, the auditor should be convinced that this rationale is sound. If in doubt, he should consult his own legal counsel. Note that the SEC proposal would require the outside auditor to address the appropriateness of the management report content.

9

Audit Sampling

SAMPLING PROCEDURE

Any procedure that leads to a conclusion about a complete set of data on the basis of information obtained from only a portion of the set is a *sampling procedure*.

This chapter focuses on the independent auditor's use of sampling, but of course it applies with equal measure to internal or government auditors and corporate financial management seeking adequate answers without looking at every item in a set of data. Facing up to sampling as a useful method for assessing controls has become critical, especially with the Foreign Corrupt Practices Act requiring publicly held companies to maintain systems meeting the Act's specified objectives of internal accounting control, and with the Treadway Commission Report (NCFFR, 1987) concluding that management, audit committees, and auditors must have a higher level of assurance about the adequacy of controls.

In the early days of the independent audit, it was not unusual for an auditor to examine 100% of the entries and records of the company audited. But companies soon grew so large that complete examination of the tremendous volume of entries and supporting documentation became uneconomical. It also came to be recognized as unwarranted, for a 100% examination does not guarantee 100% accuracy; the possibility of not having all factors available for evaluation, of human error in evaluating an item, or of a less than fully effective procedure inevitably leaves some element of uncertainty in any audit conclusion. In practice, an audit undertakes to provide reasonable, not absolute, assurance of its conclusions. Reasonable assurance can be achieved through examining only a portion of the entries or records subject to audit. Thus, the practice of audit sampling has become widely used and accepted.

Necessarily, sampling introduces an element of uncertainty about the audit conclusion, called the *sampling risk*. The element of uncertainty arising from the possibility of less than fully effective performance or procedures is called the *nonsampling risk*.

Sampling risk depends on *sample size*: the larger the sample, the lower the sampling risk. In designing an audit test, the auditor must determine the acceptable degree of sampling risk by considering the length of time (and thus the cost) required to examine the data, the consequences of not detecting an error, and the degree of assurance that he is seeking. When these factors permit the acceptance of only a minimal sampling risk, a relatively larger sample must be examined.

There are two types of sampling: *judgmental* or *nonstatistical sampling*, based on the auditor's judgment, and *statistical sampling*, based on mathematical probabilities in addition to the auditor's judgment. In statistical sampling, it is possible to measure the sampling risk in quantitative terms; in judgmental sampling, the sampling risk can only be evaluated subjectively.

Auditing Standard—SAS 39

In June 1981, the Auditing Standards Board (ASB) issued SAS 39, *Audit Sampling* (AU 350), superseding SAS 1, Sections 320A, *Relationship of Statistical Sampling to Generally Accepted Auditing Standards*, and 320B, *Precision and Reliability for Statistical Sampling in Auditing*. An Audit and Accounting Guide entitled *Audit Sampling* (AICPA, 1983b) has also been issued.

Applicability. The guidance in the SAS applies equally to nonstatistical and statistical sampling and states that either approach, when properly applied, can provide sufficient evidential matter. The choice between these two approaches depends on relative cost and effectiveness in the circumstances.

After brief coverage of fundamental concepts and terms, the SAS deals specifically with sampling in substantive tests of details, and in compliance tests of internal accounting controls. An appendix considers the sufficiency of sample sizes for substantive tests of detail in relation to other sources of audit reliance (e.g., reliance on internal controls and analytical review procedures).

SAS 39 does not address how to reckon materiality for audit purposes or how sampling actually integrates with other audit evidence. It also intentionally avoids giving specific guidance regarding sample sizes or methods of sample selection other than stating: "Sample items should be selected in such a way that the sample can be expected to be representative of the population" (AU 350.24).

Additional Guidance—AICPA Guide. As does the SAS, the guide covers both nonstatistical and statistical approaches to substantive and compliance testing and emphasizes that either approach involves audit judgment in planning and performing a sampling procedure and evaluating the results of the sample. The guide specifically covers one statistical technique for compliance tests of internal accounting control procedures, *attribute sampling*. The substantive statistical techniques explicitly covered are *probability–proportional-to-size* (PPS) sampling and *classical variables* sampling. The section on PPS sampling includes sufficient guidance, formulas, and tables to enable an auditor to perform a PPS application. The section on variables sampling overviews the different techniques and describes the judgmental decisions to be made, but expects the auditor to use computer or timesharing programs to determine sample size and evaluate sample results.

The sampling guide elaborates on most of the major points included in the SAS with regard to substantive tests of detail and compliance testing. Items not addressed are how to reckon materiality for audit purposes, and how to combine projected error results from different sampling applications.

Key Sampling Terms

It is important to have in mind certain key terms prior to addressing methodologies.

* *Sampling.* Any procedure that leads to a conclusion about a complete set of data on the basis of information obtained from only a portion of the set.
* *Nonstatistical sampling.* A sampling procedure whereby the sample is not selected and evaluated using mathematical theorems of probability. Selection of the sample is based on the auditor's knowledge of the population, which enables him to select items that he believes will fairly represent the whole. By definition, sampling risk in nonstatistical sampling cannot be statistically measured.
* *Statistical sampling.* A sampling procedure whereby the sample is selected and evaluated in accordance with specific rules based on the mathematical theorems of probability. In a statistical sample, it must be possible to determine the mathematical probability that any particular population item will be included in the sample and that any possible combination of items will be selected to constitute the entire sample.
* *Statistical statement.* A statement that includes an estimated range of the population characteristic being examined, which may be a value characteristic or a frequency characteristic, and the reliability of the estimate.

- *Confidence interval.* The estimated range within which the true value of the population characteristic is contained, so named because it is associated with a specific confidence (or reliability) level. The confidence interval may have both a lower and an upper bound for a *two-sided* estimate, or only one bound, upper or lower, for a *one-sided* estimate.
- *Reliability level.* The mathematical probability, usually expressed as a percentage, that the true value of the population characteristic being tested is contained within the confidence interval.
- *Sampling risk.* The probability that the true value of the population characteristic is not contained within the confidence interval. Thus it represents the risk that the auditor's conclusions based on a sample may be incorrect. Sampling risk is the complement of reliability.
- *Precision.* The measurement of the width of the confidence interval; the width between the lower and upper bounds of a two-sided confidence interval equals twice precision.
- *Tolerable error.* A planning concept related to preliminary estimates of materiality levels. Specifically, the amount of monetary error in a balance or class of transactions that may exist without causing the financial statements to be materially misstated.
- *Nonsampling risk.* The risk that an audit procedure may be improperly applied or may be incapable of detecting an error.

BASIC SAMPLE DESIGN CONSIDERATIONS

In designing any sampling procedure, the basic considerations are to define or assess the

1. Audit objectives
2. Required sampling statement
3. Population
4. Sampling unit
5. Sampling risk
6. Tolerable error
7. Nonsampling risk
8. Expectation of errors

These form the basis for determining the sampling method, and hence sample size, sample selection, and sample evaluation.

Audit Objectives

The most important factor in designing a sampling procedure is defining the objectives of the audit. For each detailed objective there are usually several interchangeable types of procedure that may be performed to achieve it. The procedure selected, its timing, and its extent should be the most effective and economical of all the procedures available for meeting the audit objectives, not merely adequate. Effectiveness is paramount, for no matter how large a sample is, it cannot compensate for an ineffective procedure.

Required Sampling Statement

When statistical sampling is used and evaluated, a statistical statement is incorporated in the auditor's conclusion regarding the achievement of the audit objectives. This statement includes an estimated range of the population characteristic being examined, which may be a value characteristic (e.g., total population dollar value) or a frequency characteristic (e.g., total population error rate), and the reliability of that estimate.

For example, if an estimate of total dollar value comprises a confidence interval of $150,000 to $180,000 and an associated reliability level of 90%, there is a 90% probability that the true value will lie between $150,000 and $180,000; and there is a 10% risk that the value is less than $150,000 or more than $180,000. All other things being equal, the wider the confidence interval, the higher the probability that it contains the true population characteristic. As an interval widens, however, its value in meeting audit objectives will most likely decrease.

The smaller the precision, the narrower the confidence interval. At a fixed level of reliability, precision is a function of sample size; specifically, it is inversely proportional to the square root of sample size. By increasing the sample size, the auditor obtains more information about the population, narrowing the confidence interval.

When nonstatistical sampling is used, the sampling statement is based solely on the auditor's judgment (as mathematical theorems of probability are not available). However, the statement should acknowledge sampling risk; and if it includes an estimated value, the statement should consider the allowance for error above or below the estimate. (This is similar to precision in a statistical estimate.)

Population

The results of a sampling procedure are projected upon the whole set of items from which the sample is drawn. This *population*, as the whole set is called, must be carefully defined in a manner consistent with the audit objectives.

When an auditor plans any audit sampling application, he generally identifies items or groups of items that have special significance with respect to the audit objective. SAS 39 requires the auditor to determine if there are items for which sampling risk is not justified, and such items should be examined on a 100% basis (AU 350.21). For example, an auditor planning to use audit sampling as part of his tests of an inventory balance in conjunction with an observation of the physical inventory would generally identify those items that have significant balances or those items that might have other special characteristics (such as higher susceptibility to obsolescence or damage). In testing accounts receivable, an auditor might identify accounts with large balances, unusual balances, or unusual patterns of activity as individually significant items. The auditor considers all such special knowledge about the items comprising the balance or class before designing audit sampling procedures. These considerations should not be influenced by the auditor's intentions to use either nonstatistical or statistical sampling on remaining items.

If the intention is to test population item values, the auditor may also treat, as separate populations, negative and zero-value items (e.g., credit or zero balances in the accounts receivable listing). This decision will depend primarily on whether the negative and zero-value items are significant enough to require equal audit consideration with the positive values and whether these items can be audited effectively under a procedure designed for positive values. For example, a confirmation test of accounts receivable balances to determine whether the total is correct may be restricted to positive balances if it is known that there are many zero balances pertaining to closed accounts; those would be tested with a different procedure.

Sampling Unit

The population consists of a set of items from which the sample is to be selected. These items are called *sampling units*. Each sampling unit must be definitely distinguishable, must be individually accessible for sample selection, and must be of such a nature that the selected audit procedure can be applied to it. All the sampling units together must add up to the defined population.

Sampling Risk

With regard to a particular account balance or class of transactions, sampling risk is the risk that there is monetary error equal to or greater than tolerable error in the balance or class, that the auditor fails to detect. The auditor should use his professional judgment in determining the acceptable sampling risk for a particular test after he considers such factors as the risk of material misstatement in the financial statements, the cost to reduce the risk, and the effect of the potential misstatement on the use and understanding of the financial statements.

As recognized by SAS 39 (AU 350.19) and the second standard of field work, the extent of reliance the auditor requires from a substantive test of details varies according to the level of sampling risk he deems acceptable and the extent of reliance he can place on internal accounting control and other substantive tests, such as analytical review, directed toward the same specific audit objective. The greater the reliance he requires from the substantive test, the smaller the planned allowable sampling risk. The appendix to SAS 39 (AU 350.47) provides a model expressing the general relationship of sampling risk to the sources of assurance obtained from tests directed toward the same audit objective.

The greater the reliance on internal accounting control or on other substantive tests directed toward the same specific audit objective, the greater the allowable sampling risk for the substantive test of details being planned and, thus, the smaller the required sample size for the substantive test of details. For example, if the auditor relies neither on internal accounting control nor on other substantive tests directed toward the same specific audit objective, he should specify a low sampling risk for the substantive test of details. Thus, the auditor would select a larger sample.

Samples taken for compliance tests are intended to provide a basis for the auditor to conclude whether internal accounting control procedures are being applied as prescribed. Since the compliance test is the primary source of evidence, the auditor generally wishes to obtain a high degree of assurance that his conclusions about the application of the control procedure, based on a sample of transactions, are appropriate for the population of transactions. Therefore he should allow for a low level of risk.

Tolerable Error

When planning a sample for a substantive test of details, the auditor should consider how much monetary error in the related account balance or class of transactions may exist without causing the financial statements to be materially misstated. This maximum monetary error for the balance or class is called tolerable error for the sample. Tolerable error is related to the auditor's preliminary estimates of materiality levels in such a way that tolerable error, combined for the entire audit plan, does not exceed those estimates.

For a given account balance or class of transactions, the sample size required to achieve the auditor's objective at a given sampling risk increases as the auditor's assessment of tolerable error for that balance or class decreases.

When planning a sample for a compliance test, the auditor should consider that, while deviations from pertinent control procedures increase the risk of material errors in the accounting records, such deviations do not necessarily result in errors. A recorded disbursement that does not show evidence of required approval may nevertheless be a transaction that is properly authorized and recorded. Therefore, a tolerable rate of 5% does not imply that 5% of the dollars are in error. Auditors usually select a tolerable deviation rate for compliance tests greater than the tolerable rate of dollars in error. This conclusion is based on the fact that deviations would result in errors in the accounting records only if the deviations and the errors occurred on the same transactions. Consequently, deviations from pertinent control procedures of a given rate ordinarily would be expected to result in errors at a lower rate.

Nonsampling Risk

The audit procedure must also be designed to reduce nonsampling risk to a minimum. The two types of nonsampling risk are: (1) *procedural risk* (the possibility of inherent ineffectiveness of the audit procedures used), which can be minimized by substituting other procedures to achieve the same audit objectives; and (2) *performance risk* (the possibility of human errors in executing and evaluating the test), which can be controlled through adequate training, supervision, and review.

Expectation of Errors

If errors are known to exist in a population, the objective of the sampling procedure will probably be to estimate the total monetary amount or quantity of error in the population; but if the population is believed to contain no errors, the objective will probably be to confirm the nonexistence of errors. It is important to make this distinction during planning, because it generally takes less audit effort to confirm the nonexistence of errors than to measure or estimate the total amount of error. In deciding whether to expect errors, the auditor should evaluate internal control and consider (1) the results of related audit procedures, (2) the results of previous audits in the same area, (3) the size and makeup of the population, and (4) the materiality to the financial statements of transactions or balances to be examined.

Determining Sample Size

Sample size depends on both the objectives and the design of the sample. In general, for a given objective, careful design can produce more efficient samples. SAS 39 requires that, when determining the size of samples, the auditor should consider the tolerable error, the allowable sampling risk, and the characteristics of the population; and he should apply professional judgment to relate these factors in determining the appropriate sample size (AU 350.37). These factors are described as follows:

- *Tolerable error and error expectation.* As the tolerable error increases for a particular test (at a given sampling risk), the sample size decreases. As the size or frequency of expected errors in the population increases, the sample size, for a fixed tolerable error, increases.
- *Sampling risk.* The greater the reliance on other procedures directed toward the same audit objective, the greater the allowable level of sampling risk, and the smaller the required sample size.
- *Variation within the population.* For a substantive test, when the values of individual items in a population vary significantly, a larger sample size is required to achieve a representative sample. Stratifying the population (separating the population into subpopulations with like values) can reduce sample size.
- *Expected population deviation rate.* For a compliance test, as the expected population deviation rate increases and approaches the tolerable rate, sample size increases, for a fixed allowable risk. In general, compliance tests are only applied to populations where very few deviations are expected.

Sample size for a statistical test is usually based on the above planning decisions, which are quantified and combined using a statistical formula. Sample size for a nonstatistical sampling application should be based on the same planning decisions, but these need not be quantified.

Sample Selection

SAS 39 requires that sample items should be selected in such a way that the sample can be expected to be representative of the population. Therefore, all items in the population should have an opportunity to be selected. (AU 350.38.)

Sample Evaluation

Sample evaluation includes both projection of the sampling results to the population, and consideration of the qualitative aspects of errors. For a substantive test SAS 39 (AU 350.26–.30) requires that

1. The auditor should project the error results of a sample to the items from which the sample was selected and add that projection to errors discovered in any items examined on a 100% basis. This total projected error should be compared with the tolerable error.
2. In addition, consideration should be given to the qualitative aspects of errors; and the auditor should relate the evaluation of a sample to other relevant audit evidence.
3. Projected error results for all sampling applications and all known errors from nonsampling applications should be considered in the aggregate along with other relevant audit evidence

when the auditor evaluates whether the financial statements taken as a whole may be materially misstated.

For a compliance test SAS 39 (AU 350.40–.42) requires that

1. The deviation rate in the sample should be compared to the tolerable rate of deviations to determine if there is an unacceptably high rate of deviations in the population.
2. In addition, consideration should be given to the qualitative aspects of deviations, including the nature and causes of deviations and possible relationships of deviations to other phases of the audit.
3. If the auditor concludes that sampling results do not support the planned degree of reliance on a control procedure, planned substantive tests should be altered to provide additional coverage.

Projecting Sample Results. The sample results should be used to estimate the maximum possible error or rate of deviation in the specific population tested.

In general, if the estimated upper limit on error is less than and not close to tolerable error, the sample results would support the conclusion that the population is not misstated by more than tolerable error at the specified sampling risk.

If the upper limit of error exceeds tolerable error, this negative result may have been obtained because the sample results do not reflect the auditor's expectation of error. In designing a sampling application, the auditor makes an assumption about the amount of error in the population. If the sample results do not support the auditor's expectation of errors because more error exists in the population than was anticipated, the precision of the estimate will not be adequately limited. If this is the case the auditor can

*   Examine an additional representative sample from the population, or
*   Perform additional substantive tests, such as analytical review, directed toward the same audit objective.
*   If the negative result is obtained from a compliance test, modify the extent of planned reliance on internal accounting control.

Qualitative Evaluation. In addition to his evaluation of the frequency and amount of errors, the auditor should consider their qualitative aspects. These include: (1) the nature and cause of misstatements, such as whether they are (a) differences in principle or in application, (b) errors or irregularities, or (c) the result of misunderstanding of instructions or of carelessness; and (2) the possible relationship of the misstatements to other phases of the audit. The discovery of an irregularity ordinarily requires a broader consideration of possible implications than does the discovery of an error.

If the sample results suggest that the auditor's planning assumptions were in error, he should take appropriate action. For example, if errors are discovered in a substantive test of details in amounts or frequency greater than that implied by the degree of reliance initially placed on internal accounting control, the auditor should consider whether the planned reliance is still appropriate.

NONSTATISTICAL SAMPLING

In nonstatistical sampling, the criteria for coverage determine the sample size. Selection of the sample is based on the auditor's knowledge of the population, and evaluation of the sample is done using audit judgment.

Sample Design

Four factors that affect sample design are:

1. The nature of related audit procedures.
2. The nature of the population. This factor includes the diversity of types of items in the population and the diversity of magnitudes. (Unless it is very small, the size of the population generally has no direct effect on sample design.
3. The expectation of error, both in terms of frequency and magnitude.
4. Materiality. As a general rule, the smaller the minimum amount that is considered material, the larger the sample must be to provide a sufficiently precise result on which to base audit judgments.

   Determining Sample Size. The foregoing sample design factors must be considered whether using nonstatistical or statistical sampling since they affect choice of sampling method and sample size. When using statistical sampling the impact on sample size is determined objectively using mathematical formulas. When using nonstatistical sampling the impact on sample size must be determined judgmentally. The chart in Figure 9.1 illustrates this relationship. It identifies the components of each factor and shows the effect on sample size of opposing degrees for each component. When designing a compliance test, for example, the lower the planned reliance on internal control, the smaller the sample need be. Conversely, the higher the planned reliance on internal control, the larger the sample should be.
   Although neither SAS 39 nor the related guide requires the auditor to compare the sample size for a nonstatistical sampling application with a corresponding sample size calculated using statistical theory, an auditor may find familiarity with sample sizes based on statistical theory helpful when he applies professional judgment and experience in considering the effect of various planning considerations on sample size. The guide includes an illustrative sample size table and an illustrative model for determining statistical sample sizes solely to illustrate the relative effects of different planning considerations on sample size. These tools are not intended as substitutes for professional judgment as appropriate in the circumstances.
   The auditor using a statistical sample size in planning a nonstatistical application will need to apply professional judgment in

- Quantifying risk level
- Determining the appropriate sample size that would reflect any difference in efficiency between his nonstatistical approach and the statistical sampling approach underlying the illustrative table. For example, the auditor should consider the extent of stratification used in the nonstatistical sampling plan.

	Quality tending to	
	Decrease sample size	**Increase sample size**
1. Nature of related audit procedures		
For compliance tests		
Planned reliance on internal control	Low	High
Planned substantive procedures		
Implicit effectiveness	Very effective	Less effective
Coverage	Large	Small
Timing with respect to balance sheet date	Near	More distant
For substantive tests		
Results of evaluation of internal control	Good	Less than good
Effectiveness of other substantive procedures	Very effective	Less effective
2. Nature of population		
For compliance tests		
Diversity of types of items	Homogeneous	Diverse
Diversity of magnitude of items	Generally no direct effect	
For substantive tests		
Diversity of types of items	Homogeneous	Diverse
Diversity of magnitude of items	Homogeneous	Diverse
3. Expectation of error		
For compliance tests		
Frequency	None	Some
For substantive tests		
Frequency	Low	High
Magnitude	Small	Large
4. Materiality		
For compliance tests	No direct effect	
For substantive tests		
Minimum materiality amount apportioned to the specific area being sampled	Large	Small

FIG. 9.1 Factors Affecting Sample Size

Sample Selection. In nonstatistical sampling, the selection of items to be tested is based on the auditor's knowledge of the population, which enables him to select the items that he believes will yield an accurate conclusion about the whole. Although the sampling risk cannot be mathematically measured, the auditor judges that it will not be excessive.

Sample Evaluation

If a nonstatistical approach is used, the projection of the sample errors to the population may be done in several different ways, but the appropriate allowance for sampling risk cannot be accurately measured; it must be assessed based on the auditor's judgment.

Two acceptable methods of projecting the results of a nonstatistical substantive test sample are described in the SAS 39 guide:

* Divide the amount of error in the sample by the fraction of total book dollars from the population included in the sample; or
* Estimate the average difference between the audited and the book values of the sample items (the amount of error in the sample divided by the sample size), and multiply it by the total number of items in the population.

When a nonstatistical approach is used for a compliance test, calculating the deviation rate in the sample (by dividing the number of deviations by the sample size) gives the best estimate of the deviation rate in the population. This estimate contains no allowance for sampling risk. If the estimated deviation is close to the tolerable rate, the auditor will need to use considerable judgment in deciding whether the level of risk is acceptable.

When to Use Nonstatistical Sampling

The decision to use nonstatistical sampling should be reached by answering two questions:

1. Is nonstatistical sampling feasible? It is if the auditor's knowledge of the population is sufficient to justify his belief that the items selected for testing will reflect a reasonably accurate conclusion about the population as a whole.
2. Is nonstatistical sampling more appropriate than statistical sampling? In general, it is if:
   a. A sample that can be evaluated statistically is impossible or very difficult to obtain. This may be the case, for example, when the population is a filing cabinet of unnumbered invoices and there is no obvious way of referencing an individual invoice.
   b. A sample of material balances or transactions is both sufficient to meet the audit objectives and considered more economical than a statistical sample. Whether or not this is the case is a matter of judgment.
   c. The auditor's knowledge of the population allows him to subjectively select a sample that gives him more audit assurance than a sample selected according to the theorems of probability. This may be the case, for instance, when the population contains diverse types of items and specific types are known to be particularly error prone.

Nonstatistical sampling is *not* appropriate when it is possible to obtain a sample that can be evaluated statistically and either (1) a mathematical determination of sampling risk is required or (2) the auditor has little knowledge of the items in the population.

Illustration

Audit objective: To confirm that the total accounts receivable balance due from 200 customers is materially correct.

Sampling plan: The auditor decides to use nonstatistical sampling, based on his knowledge that approximately 20 accounts cover 80% of the total value. He samples these accounts 100%, performs separate tests of zero and negative balances, and examines only a few of the remaining accounts on the judgmental grounds that the remaining population is not sufficently large or material in total value to warrant statistical sampling.

Sample evaluation: One large customer disputes his account. After checking the account, the auditor suggests an adjustment, although the amount does not exceed materiality. No other errors are found.

Audit conclusion: The (adjusted) balance is confirmed as being materially correct.

STATISTICAL SAMPLING

When using statistical sampling, the sample is selected and evaluated in accordance with specific rules based on the mathematical theorems of probability, in addition to the auditor's judgment.

Sample Design

In statistical sampling, evaluation and selection methods must be chosen before sample size can be computed or sample items selected. The choice of evaluation method, in turn, depends on the type of statistical statement required. The choice of selection method may be affected by the population's physical characteristics and must be compatible with the evaluation method. Sample size is primarily affected by two judgmental factors: (1) the desired reliability (or its complement, sampling risk) and (2) the desired precision of the statistical estimate at the chosen reliability level.

The practical steps to follow in an application of statistical sampling are to

1. Translate the audit objectives into sampling objectives;
2. Establish the required statistical statement format, that is, establish the type of estimate required;
3. Determine sampling criteria, that is, reliability (or risk) and precision;
4. Choose sampling evaluation and selection methods;
5. Determine sample size;
6. Select a sample and perform auditing procedures;
7. Statistically evaluate the evidence obtained;
8. Judgmentally review the statistical statement to ensure that it meets the original sampling (and hence audit) objectives; and
9. Arrive at an audit conclusion based on the statistical evaluation plus the results of any related audit procedures.

Translating Audit Objectives Into Sampling Objectives. In this first step, the following factors must be defined:

• Sampling unit and population.

• Population characteristic of interest. (Is it a value or a frequency?)
• How to measure or determine the characteristic in each sampling unit. (This will usually require an exact definition of what constitutes an error.)
• Expectation of errors. (Is the objective to confirm the nonexistence of errors or to estimate the total population error rate or amount?)

Establishing the Statistical Statement Format. In establishing the type of estimate required, the statistical statement sampling objectives should recognize not only whether the estimate is of dollar magnitude or occurrence rate, but also whether a confidence interval with both a lower and an upper bound is required (a two-sided estimate) or only one of those bounds is important (a one-sided estimate). For example, if a FIFO inventory valuation is being audited and an audit adjustment is likely, the auditor will want to estimate the probable minimum and maximum amount of error in the book value. In other words, he will want to estimate a two-sided interval. A resulting conclusion (statistical statement) might be: We estimate with 95% reliability that an accurate FIFO valuation of inventory is between $950,000 and $1,030,000. For most compliance tests, on the other hand, an auditor is concerned only with the probable maximum error rate in the population; that is, he will be satisfied with a one-sided interval estimate. Then the statement might be: We estimate with 90% reliability that no more than 5% of the purchase orders issued during the year lack evidence of proper approval. The one-sided versus two-sided decision is important because, all other things being equal, a substantially larger sample size is required to produce a two-sided estimate than a one-sided estimate.

Determining Sampling Criteria. The auditor must now judgmentally determine the level of reliability he requires for his estimate (or conversely, the maximum amount of risk he feels is acceptable in the context of the audit objectives and any related audit tests), and the least rigorous precision (i.e., the maximum width of the confidence interval) he can tolerate. If the test is for substantive purposes, precision in terms of dollars will be based on materiality. For compliance purposes, precision in terms of a maximum occurrence rate will depend on the importance of the test relative to the associated substantive tests to be performed in the same audit area.

Choosing Sampling Methods. Besides indicating which type of statistical evaluation method is most suitable, the sampling objectives should also indicate which modes of sample selection are permissible. The most commonly used evaluation methods for each objective and the corresponding methods of sample selection are shown in Figure 9.2.

Attribute sampling. Attribute sampling is a method of evaluating a probability sample to obtain an estimate of the proportion of population items containing some specified characteristic. Attribute sampling can apply to a single random sample of physical units or to a systematic sample (defined later in this chapter under Statistical Sampling Techniques) that approximates a simple random sample. Each

Sampling objective	Evaluation method*	Sample selection method
To estimate an error or occurrence rate	Attribute sampling	Simple (unrestricted) random sample of physical units†
To estimate maximum dollar error amount	Dollar-unit sampling: Simple attribute Combined attribute-variables Multinominal-bound	Simple random sample of dollar units†
To estimate total dollar value or dollar error amount	Variables sampling: Mean-per-unit‡ Difference Ratio	Simple random sample or stratified random sample of physical units
	Mean-per-unit difference	Simple random sample of physical units

* All the listed evaluation methods are estimation methods. Two other methods commonly used in compliance tests are *acceptance sampling* and *discovery sampling,* both forms of attribute sampling that do not provide a confidence interval. Acceptance sampling provides a simple accept-reject decision based on the reliability level and the maximum tolerable error rate specified by the user. Discovery sampling assures, at a specified reliability, the discovery of one error if the true error rate exceeds a specified maximum. These are discussed later under Statistical Sampling Techniques.

† A systematic sample may be used where it approximates a random sample.

‡ The mean-per-unit method can also be used to evaluate a simple random sample of dollar units. (See Statistical Sampling Techniques.)

FIG. 9.2 Common Statistical Evaluation and Selection Methods

sample item either has or lacks the characteristic; magnitude of the characteristic is not considered. The resulting statistical statements are of the form: The true occurrence rate in the population is not greater than Y% [or is between X% and Y%] stated at a specified reliability level.

Illustration

Audit objective: To test shipping documents for the year to evaluate the extent to which goods shipped may not have been invoiced.

Sampling plan: The objectives are to test the population of 5,000 consecutively numbered shipping documents to ascertain whether each document has corresponding sales invoices. No errors are expected, and the required statistical statement, to be made with 90% reliability, is: No more than 4% of the documents lack corresponding invoices. Therefore, attribute sampling with a simple random selection of documents is the sampling method chosen. The sample size, ascertained from tables, is 60, based on a reliability of 90% and precision of 4%.

Sample evaluation: No errors are found.

Audit conclusion: The auditor is 90% confident that no more than 4% of the shipping documents do not have corresponding sales invoices.

Dollar-unit sampling. This approach is also known as monetary-unit sampling or sampling with probability proportional to size, and is based on attribute sampling. In this method, sample units of one dollar are tested to see whether each one is or is not in error. Hence it can only be used to evaluate random samples of monetary units rather than physical units, and only provides estimates of the *maximum* proportion or amount of dollars in error in the population. (Of course, any currency unit other than a dollar may be sampled by this method, but dollars will be used here for convenience.)

Separate evaluations must be made for overstatement errors and for understatement errors. When sample errors are found, various evaluation methods such as *combined attribute-variables* or *multinomial-bound* (in which more than the two outcomes, right or wrong, are possible for any sampling unit) can be used to modify the simple attribute result, which otherwise would not recognize the magnitude of the errors. However, the estimates become overly conservative, and hence less useful, as more errors are found; dollar-unit sampling thus should be restricted to situations where no or few errors are expected. The statistical statements that result from this method are of the form: There are overstatement errors of no more than $200,000 in the population – or the population is overstated by no more than $100,000 and understated by no more than $80,000 – stated at a specified reliability level.

Illustration

Audit objective: To confirm that the total accounts receivable balance of $980,000 is materially correct.

Sampling plan: The auditor's apportionment of audit materiality to this area requires a statistical statement at 90% reliability that the total overstatement does not exceed $30,000. To achieve this objective he chooses the dollar-unit sampling method. A simple attribute sample size of 95 is computed from tables, based on 90% reliability and a one-sided upper precision of 2.5% (a conservative precision level, since a precision of $30,000 in a population of 980,000 dollar units corresponds to a precision of 30/980, or 3%). He selects a random sample of 95 dollar units from the population of $980,000, resulting in a selection of 89 balances (a single customer balance may contain more than one sample dollar). Since dollar-unit sampling biases selection in favor of high dollar balances, a 100% sample of such balances is judged unnecessary.

Sample evaluation: No errors are found in completing the confirmation procedures.

Audit conclusion: The auditor is 90% confident that the total balance is overstated by no more than $24,500 (2.5% of $980,000), and the balance is concluded to be materially correct.

Variables sampling. Variables sampling methods estimate total dollar amounts from samples of physical units (e.g., samples of detail balances). The estimate may be of population total dollar value or of population total dollar error. Unlike dollar-unit sampling estimates, variables sampling can provide a one- or two-sided interval. The resulting statistical statement (two-sided) could be of the form: The true population value is between $1,500,000 and $1,650,000 stated at a specified reliability level. Such estimates are suitable for audit adjustments, but dollar-unit sampling estimates, which provide only an upper bound, are not.

Method	Estimated population characteristics	Sample characteristic
Mean-per-unit	X	x_j
Difference	$D = X - Y$	$d_j = x_j - y_j$
Ratio	$R = X / Y$	$r_j = x_j / y_j$

where X = estimate of true population value
Y = population book value
D = estimate of true population error (difference between X and Y)
R = estimate of true population ratio of X to Y
x_j = jth sample item audited value
y_j = jth sample item book value
d_j = jth sample item difference between x_j and y_j
r_j = jth sample item ratio of x_j to y_j

FIG. 9.3 Symbolic Representation of Statistical Sampling Methods

The several variables sampling evaluation methods shown in Figure 9.2 are based on different value characteristics. The *mean-per-unit* method is based on sample item values alone; *difference estimation* is based on the difference between sample item audit value and book value (or on that between any other two defined values relating to one sample item); *ratio estimation* is based on the ratio of two defined values per sample item; and *mean-per-unit difference* is a weighted combination of the first two methods.

For example, consider a population of balances of which a sample has been audited. The mean-per-unit method can be used to estimate the total value of the balances based on the audited values of the sample. The difference method can be used to estimate the total error in the population (where the error equals the difference between the true population value and the book value) based on the differences (audit minus book values) found in the sample balances. The ratio method can be used to estimate the ratio of the true total population value to the book value based on the ratios (audit over book values) of the sample balances. The functions of these three methods can be represented symbolically as shown in Figure 9.3. Note that the difference and ratio estimates can both be manipulated to estimate the true population value, X (i.e., $X = D + Y$; $X = R \times Y$).

Sample selection for variables sampling may be unrestricted or stratified and in general must be of physical units. (The exception is that the mean-per-unit method can be applied to a dollar-unit sample.) In *stratified sampling* the population is first formally divided into subpopulations (strata), and then a simple random sample is selected from each stratum. The results for each stratum can be mathematically combined to yield an estimate of the whole population. Stratification is usually done for reasons of sample size efficiency. Other, more sophisticated modes of sample selection include *multistage sample selection* and *cluster sampling*; these are discussed later under Statistical Sampling Techniques.

Illustration

Audit objective: To confirm whether or not the total accounts receivable balance of $980,000 is materially correct.

Sampling plan: The auditor knows that balances exceeding $5,000 total $140,000 but has little knowledge of the rest of the population. Therefore, he decides on 100% confirmation of balances over $5,000 and on statistical sampling to confirm the other balances. He expects errors, so his sampling objective is to estimate whether or not the total dollar error is a material amount ($20,000 is judged material). He therefore requires a statistical statement at a high reliability (say 95%) that the total error amount is between $X and $Y where the range $X to $Y is less than $20,000 (say $15,000). To achieve this objective he chooses the variables sampling method, based on audit differences, with unrestricted random sample selection. Using a microcomputer program, the auditor computes a sample size of 118 based on a reliability of 95% and a precision of ± $7,500 (for a two-sided interval estimate the width of the interval is twice the precision amount, in this case $15,000). The auditor then judgmentally increases the sample size to 130 because his assessment of the expected distribution of errors may be incorrect, which would affect the precision of his estimate; and he cannot expand the sample later. He selects a random sample of 130 balances less than $5,000 plus all the balances over $5,000 and performs appropriate confirmation procedures.

Sample evaluation: The resulting statistical conclusion based on the 130 balances is: We are 95% certain that the total overstatement is between $15,600 and $31,800. The 100% confirmation of high dollar-value balances shows a total overstatement of $9,000.

Audit conclusion: The combined results confirm that the total balance is materially overstated. An audit adjustment of $9,000 (to correct the high dollar balances) plus $23,700 (the midpoint of the estimated overstatement interval) is proposed.

Determining Sample Size. Sample size can be computed mathematically and depends on the specified sampling criteria. In practice, it is usually derived from tables or microcomputer programs. However, the computed sample size may need to be increased judgmentally because of special considerations. These considerations include:

- The importance of the test in the overall audit context.
- The accuracy of the estimate of expected error rate when attribute sampling or dollar-unit sampling is being used. The sample sizes required to achieve a fixed reliability and precision must be much larger when the error rate is high.
- The accuracy of the estimate of error rate and magnitude when using variables sampling. (The effectiveness of the evaluation methods differs according to error rate and error magnitude.)
- The possibility of unreliable statistical results when using variables estimation with a small sample size. (A minimum sample of 100 items is considered advisable.)

A general rule whenever variables sampling is used is to cut off all the high dollar-value items from the rest of the population and to sample them 100%. This often improves the efficiency of the sample required from the rest of the population (i.e., it permits the use of a small sample size for fixed criteria) and gives extra audit assurance by confining sampling risk to smaller dollar value items.

Sample Selection. A statistical sample, or *probability sample,* is selected in accordance with specific rules based on the mathematical theorems of probability. In a probability sample, it must be possible to determine the mathematical probability that any particular population item will be included in the sample and that any possible combination of items will be selected to constitute the entire sample.

There are many different types of probability sample, but most of them require the random selection of items from the population. This is done with the use of random number tables or microcomputer random number generator programs.

Sample Evaluation

When statistical sampling is used, the sample is evaluated mathematically, usually with the assistance of tables or microcomputer programs. The estimated range may be stated with a measurable level of sampling risk corresponding to the precision of the estimate.

Selection of the statistical method to be used is determined in part by estimates of error conditions and other factors. Whenever the actual results obtained are found to differ from expectations, the statistical results will also differ. In fact, they may turn out to be unusable for achieving the audit objectives. Therefore fallback plans should be arranged in case of unexpected results. Three basic types of fallback plans can be distinguished, though they are not mutually exclusive. The first is the use of other preconceived audit procedures; this is nearly always applicable. The second is sample expansion; this is not always possible or advisable, in that a larger sample may not rectify an inappropriate sampling technique. The third is statistical evaluation using another method; this is particularly useful if the estimated error rate was incorrect.

A single probability sample can be evaluated by any method compatible with the method of sample selection used. For example, a simple random sample of physical units can be evaluated using any attribute or variables sampling method but not a dollar-unit sampling method, as Figure 9.2 shows. Evaluation by a different method may even improve the precision of the statistical estimate at a fixed reliability level (i.e., it may reduce the width of the confidence interval). For example, difference estimation results in a narrower confidence interval than does mean-per-unit when errors (differences) are found in a sample. Similarly, multinomial-bound evaluation of a dollar-unit sample produces a narrower estimate of maximum dollar error than does combined attribute-variables evaluation when more than a few errors are found.

When to Use Statistical Sampling

Whether to use statistical sampling should be decided by answering two questions:

1. Is statistical sampling feasible? It is whenever a probability sample can be obtained. This is generally easy, in that random numbers can be generated using microcomputer programs. However, factors weighing against statistical sampling exist when the correspondence between a group of random numbers and the population is difficult to establish, thus making random selection difficult. Or, there may be practical difficulties in selecting a stratified sample; manual stratification by value, for example, may be excessively time-consuming.

2. Is statistical sampling more appropriate than judgmental sampling? In general, it is if:

   a. Objective results (results that can be defended mathematically) are desired. The size of a statistical sample, its selection, and its evaluation all have a mathematical basis and therefore are objectively defensible before other auditors, client personnel, and a court of law.

   b. The auditor has insufficient knowledge of the population to judgmentally select a sample that will provide a reliable basis for his audit conclusion without that sample being significantly larger than an equally adequate statistical sample.

   c. A representative selection from a population of similar physical units is required, implying use of a probability sample. As a general rule, whenever a probability sample is selected, it should be evaluated statistically, even when it is also evaluated judgmentally. This eliminates the risk of overlooking a statistical conclusion that contradicts the judgmental conclusion.

Statistical sampling is *not* appropriate when a judgmentally selected sample provides a greater degree of assurance for the audit conclusion, or involves less sampling, or is easier to select than a statistical sample giving equal audit assurance.

Statistical sampling has some inherent advantages. Nonstatistical sampling can encourage a vague and indefinite approach; there may be little or no attempt to define the population or the basis for selection specifically, and it may be difficult to prove a relationship between the sample results and the whole population. Statistical sampling, on the other hand, forces the auditor to plan his sampling approach carefully and gives him an objective foundation on which to build his audit judgments.

But statistical sampling does not eliminate the need for audit judgment. Judgment is at least as important in planning and evaluating a statistical sample as it is in judgmental sampling. With statistical samples, however, it is usually applied discretely to decision factors such as reliability, precision, and expected error conditions, thus simplifying an otherwise aggregate judgment.

Another advantage of statistical sampling is that it reveals past instances of excessive sampling stemming from an overconservative intuition that adequate assurance could be provided only by sampling, say, 5% or 10% of the population.

STATISTICAL SAMPLING TECHNIQUES

Sample Selection

Selection of a probability sample is the essential ingredient of statistical sampling. The three most common methods of sample selection are

1. Unrestricted or simple random selection,
2. Stratified random selection, and
3. Systematic selection when it approximates random selection.

The first two methods may be used with or without replacement of an item already selected, since audit populations are usually large enough to negate the impact of replacement on selection. Two more-sophisticated methods are

1. Multistage sample selection, and
2. Cluster sample selection.

The choice of statistical evaluation method largely determines which of these five sample selection methods to use. Figure 9.2 lists the most common choices. Basically, attribute sampling requires an unrestricted random sample of physical units, dollar-unit sampling requires an unrestricted random sample of dollar units, and variables sampling requires a random sample of physical units, either unrestricted or stratified.

Unrestricted Random Sampling. In this method, each sampling unit has an equal chance of being selected as each selection is made, and every possible combination of sampling units has an equal chance of constituting the sample. The sample is usually selected in three steps:

1. Establishing a correspondence between a set of identifying numbers (or letters) and the sampling units in the population, so that each unit is uniquely identified,
2. Using random-number tables or a random-number generator to obtain a random selection, equal to the required sample size, of numbers (letters) from the complete set of identifying numbers (letters) and
3. Selecting the population units corresponding to the selected identifiers.

The sampling unit may be a physical unit or a dollar (monetary) unit. Physical units can often be identified by using the same means the company uses (e.g., voucher number or check number) or by physical location (e.g., warehouse row and bin, or page number and line number on a computer listing). Dollar units are identified by the cumulative values of the population. That is, whatever the order of physical units containing the dollars, their values are accumulated in dollar increments, and the cumulative value at any point represents the last dollar unit included.

Selection of a dollar-unit sample necessarily implies selecting physical units containing the randomly selected dollars. The probability of selecting a physical unit increases in direct proportion to its dollar value; in other words, the sampling probabilities are proportional to size. Also, one physical unit may contain more than one randomly selected dollar. For example, selection of the 21st and 29th dollar units from three invoices, the totals of which are $12, $8, and $10, results in selection of the third invoice (cumulative value $30) twice.

Stratified Random Sampling. In this method, the population is formally divided into subpopulations, or strata, and then an unrestricted random sample is selected from each stratum. Each sampling unit, therefore, has an equal probability of selection within its own stratum, but across the whole population its chances are weighted by the relationship of sample size and stratum size to the total size of the population. Stratification cannot be used for sampling dollar units. There are three main reasons for using stratified random sampling:

1. It can give special attention to a particular subpopulation (e.g., old items),
2. It is sometimes the only practical approach to sample selection (e.g., if units must be sampled at a series of different goegraphic locations), and

3. It produces subpopulations that are individually more homogeneous, thus decreasing the sample size required to accomplish given statistical objectives (e.g., stratification by value produces subpopulations of similarly valued items).

The key step is the identification of the strata. Any criteria can be used, but each item in the population must fit the criteria for one, and only one, stratum. Then, before sampling, the number of items in each stratum must be determined.

Systematic Selection. This approach is only valid when it approximates a random selection, and therefore requires a relatively homogeneous population, the absence of any correlation (i.e., a built-in bias) between the order of the population units and the sampling objectives, and a fairly uniform error pattern. Since this third constraint is difficult to prove, systematic selection is chiefly recommended when no errors are expected.

To obtain a systematic sample of either physical or dollar units:

1. Determine the selection interval (I) by dividing the total number of units in the population by the required sample size.
2. Select a random number between 1 and I as a starting point.
3. Select units from the population according to their physical sequence in the population, starting with the unit located at the random start position and then selecting every Ith unit following that. For instance, to select 100 units from a total of 1,200, the selection interval (I) will be 12; and if a random start of 7 is determined, then the 7th, the 19th (7 + 12), the 31st (19 + 12), and so forth, units will be selected, counted in the order with which they physically exist in the population.

To guard against unwarranted correlation between the population sequence and the sampling objectives, more than one random start may be used. This results in as many systematic samples as there are random starts, and the required sample size must be equally divided between them before determining the common interval I.

Multistage and Cluster Sampling. These techniques are generally restricted to samples of physical units where a dollar-value estimate is required. *Multistage sampling* involves sample selection at several levels. For example, the auditor may require a selection of locations, with a further selection of inventory items at each of the selected locations. (The selections at each level can be achieved using any of the methods discussed above.) *Cluster sampling* involves selecting groups of items, rather than individual units, at randomly selected points in the population. For example, it might be a selection of 20 groups of 5 consecutively numbered invoices, starting with each of 20 randomly selected invoices. Both of these methods are used to overcome practical selection difficulties, such as those that occur when a population is dispersed widely over a large geographic area and coverage of the entire area is not economically feasible. These methods usually require larger sample sizes and involve more complex evaluation formulas than do simple or stratified random selection techniques.

How to Obtain Random Numbers. Selection of a probability sample usually involves random numbers. These can be obtained manually, using random number tables (Arkin, 1974, provides a table of 105,000 random digits), or by using a generalized computer or microcomputer program that will create random numbers according to user specifications. Use of a microcomputer program is highly preferable to manual determination of random numbers because manual determination is a tedious and time-consuming process. The output from a typical microcomputer random number generator is shown in Figure 9.4.

Attribute Sampling

Attribute sampling is based on the binomial distribution. It can be used to estimate the probable occurrence rates of specified characteristics in a population where each characteristic has two, and only two, mutually exclusive outcomes (hence the name binomial). Attribute sampling of physical units cannot be used to estimate the total of a variable characteristic such as value.

Techniques Available. *Simple attribute estimation* provides a one- or two-sided estimate of occurrence rate, resulting in one-sided and two-sided statements, respectively, such as: We are 95% certain that the error rate in the population does not exceed 5%. We are 95% certain that the error rate in the population is between 1% and 5%. Two related forms of sampling, which do *not* provide an interval estimate, are *acceptance sampling* and *discovery sampling. Acceptance sampling* is generally more useful for testing internal control over errors on an ongoing basis than for auditors' test purposes since it provides only an accept-reject decision and requires a precise advance decision as to the rate of error at which rejection is necessary. For example, a reject decision resulting from an ongoing test check of internal control procedures indicates a weakening of the system and instigates an investigation of the system. A reject decision resulting from an external audit test, on the other hand, generally gives insufficient basis for an audit judgment. Alternative procedures, probably including an attribute estimate, have to be used.

Discovery sampling is commonly used in auditing, particularly when the auditor's first interest is whether or not an acceptable population error rate is exceeded. If the error rate is not exceeded, the objective of his test is met and no further work is required. If it is exceeded, he will then apply alternative procedures, possibly including an attribute estimate. Discovery sampling is based on the minimum sample size that would include at least one error if the population errors exceed a specified rate. Thus, discovery of an error in the sample immediately resolves the test: the error rate is exceeded. Since discovery sampling is based on the minimum sample size necessary to detect only one error, the sample usually must be expanded if a useful attribute estimate (i.e., of the true error rate in the population) is desired.

How to Apply Attribute Sampling. Whichever method is used, the appropriate sample size can be determined from tables, which are available in the AICPA Guide. For attribute estimation, the interval estimate can also be obtained using attribute

```
=================================    RANDOM NUMBERS-SELECTION ORDER
            TOUCHE ROSS & CO.         --------------------------------

        M I C R O - S A N G E N                        01-2729
        - - - - - - - - - - -                          03-1537
                                                       03-0411
                                                       04-2190
=================================                      03-0582
                                                       04-0630
                                                       03-3338
NUMBER OF RANDOM NUMBERS                                03-3926
 GENERATED                      20                     04-1213
SET GENERATION MODE:            1                      03-0994
  1 - INDIVIDUAL SET MODE                              03-0068
  2 - ENTIRE NUMBER MODE                               04-2383
HIGHEST NUMBER OF DIGITS USED   6                      10-8077
NUMBER OF SETS                  2                      01-1209
NUMBER OF RANGES                3                      01-1512
RANDOM NUMBER SEED (-32768 TO                          04-0696
 32767)                         -9963                  10-8796
                                                       03-1716
                                                       03-3443
THE FOLLOWING RANGES HAVE BEEN                         04-1813
SELECTED

------------------------------------    RANDOM NUMBERS-NUMERICAL ORDER
RANGE                                   ------------------------------
 -----
  1 - LOW   1-1
        HIGH 1-3072                     SEQUENCE
                                        SELECTED    RANDOM NUMBERS
  2 - LOW   3-1                         --------    --------------
        HIGH 4-4099                        14         01-1209
                                           15         01-1512
                                            1         01-2729
  3 - LOW   10-7002                        11         03-0068
        HIGH 10-9116                         3         03-0411
                                            5         03-0582
                                           10         03-0994
                                            2         03-1537
SUMMARY OF NUMBERS SELECTED                18         03-1716
------------------------------------        7         03-3338
                                           19         03-3443
                                            8         03-3926
          TOTAL NUMBER   QUANTITY           6         04-0630
RANGE NO. OF ITEMS       SELECTED          16         04-0696
--------- -------------  --------           9         04-1213
   1         3,072          3              20         04-1813
   2         8,198         15               4         04-2190
   3         2,115          2              12         04-2383
          -------------  --------          13         10-8077
TOTALS      13,385         20              17         10-8796
          =============  ========
```

FIG. 9.4   User Entries To and Output From Random-Number-Generating Program

tables. An alternative method of sample size determination or evaluation is to use microcomputer programs.

Figure 9.5 illustrates the use of attribute estimation tables. It is an extract from a table of one-sided upper precision limits at 95% reliability for an infinite population.

To determine the sample size required for an attribute estimate at 95% reliability:

1. Determine the rate at which the attribute is expected to occur in the population (or sample).
2. Determine the desired precision of the interval estimate. Add this to the attribute occurrence rate to determine the desired upper limit of the estimate (the upper precision limit).
3. Find the column for the expected occurrence rate and go down to the line corresponding to the upper precision limit (interpolation may be required).
4. On the left axis opposite the upper precision limit, find the sample size.

Evaluation of an attribute sample employs the reverse process, starting with sample size and sample occurrence rate to determine the upper precision limit of the interval estimate. For example, a 1% expected occurrence rate and 3.7% precision (or 4.7% [1% + 3.7%] upper precision limit) implies a sample size of 100. Conversely, a sample size of 100 with one error (1% error rate) gives an upper precision limit of 4.7%; that is, we are 95% certain that there are no more than 4.7% errors in the population.

Obviously, the tables cannot provide exact results for every combination of criteria. Microcomputer programs are much more flexible and in general allow entry of most combinations of reliability, occurrence rate, precision, and sample size used in auditing. They also adjust results to recognize that populations are finite in size.

Dollar-Unit Sampling

This technique has been described earlier in this chapter. It is generally used when the sampling objective is to confirm that a population value is materially correct, since estimates are of upper bounds only and are unsuitable for audit adjustments.

Techniques Available. The most common evaluation method is *simple attribute estimation* applied to samples of dollar units so as to provide an upper precision limit of the error rate. Assuming that the maximum amount of error (either overstatement or understatement) in any dollar unit is $1.00, this upper precision limit can be directly translated into a dollar amount. For example, an upper precision limit (maximum error rate) of 3% in a population of 120,000 dollars implies a maximum error amount of $3,600 (.03 × $120,000). However, if there is positive indication that the assumption of $1.00 maximum error amount is wrong, the population estimate of the maximum error amount may be amended. For example, assuming the maximum understatement error per dollar unit is $1.50 (e.g., a debt with a book value of $100 may be understated by $150), a 3% error rate in a population of 120,000 dollars implies a maximum understatement error amount of $5,400 (.03 × $120,000 × $1.50). Note that both the assumed error amount per dollar and the error rate are maximums. This results in more conservative upper precision limits than those produced by variables sampling. That is, at a fixed reliability, the stated upper precision

Sample Size	Occurrence Rate																				
	0.0	.5	1.0	2.0	3.0	4.0	5.0	6.0	7.0	8.0	9.0	10.0	12.0	14.0	16.0	18.0	20.0	25.0	30.0	40.0	50
50	5.8			9.1		12.1		14.8		17.4		19.9	22.3	25.1	27.0	29.6	31.6		42.4	52.6	62.4
100	3.0		4.7	6.2	7.6	8.9	10.2	11.5	13.0	14.0	15.4	16.4	18.7	21.2	23.3	25.6	27.7	33.1	38.4	48.7	58.6
150	2.0			5.1		7.7		10.2		12.6		15.0	17.3	19.6	21.7	24.0	26.1		36.7	47.0	56.8
200	1.5	2.4	3.1	4.5	5.8	7.1	8.3	9.5	10.8	11.9	13.1	14.2	16.4	18.7	20.9	23.1	25.2	30.5	35.7	45.7	55.6
250	1.2			4.2		6.7		9.1		11.4		13.7	15.9	18.1	20.3	22.4	24.6		34.8	44.8	54.7
300	1.0		2.6	3.9	5.2	6.4	7.6	8.8	10.0	11.1	12.2	13.3	15.5	17.7	19.8	22.0	24.1	29.1	34.1	44.1	54.1
350	.9			3.7		6.2		8.5		10.8		13.0	15.2	17.4	19.5	21.7	23.6		33.6	43.6	53.6
400	.7	1.6	2.3	3.6	4.8	6.0	7.2	8.3	9.5	10.6	11.7	12.8	15.0	17.2	19.2	21.2	23.2	28.2	33.2	43.2	53.2
450	.7			3.5		5.9		8.2		10.4		12.6	14.8	16.8	18.9	20.9	22.9		32.9	42.9	52.9
500	.6		2.1	3.4	4.6	5.8	6.9	8.0	9.2	10.3	11.4	12.5	14.6	16.7	18.6	20.7	22.6	27.6	32.6	42.6	52.6
550	.5			3.3		5.7		7.9		10.1		12.3	14.4	16.4	18.4	20.4	22.4		32.4	42.4	52.4
600	.5	1.3	2.0	3.2	4.4	5.6	6.7	7.8	9.0	10.0	11.2	12.2	14.2	16.2	18.2	20.2	22.2	27.2	32.2	42.2	52.2
650	.5			3.2		5.5		7.7		10.0		12.1	14.1	16.1	18.1	20.1	22.1		32.1	42.1	52.1
700	.4		1.9	3.1	4.3	5.4	6.6	7.7	8.8	9.9	10.8	11.9	13.9	15.9	17.9	19.9	21.9	26.9	31.9	41.9	51.9
750	.4			3.1		5.4		7.6		9.8		11.8	13.8	15.8	17.8	19.8	21.8		31.8	41.8	51.8
800	.4	1.1	1.8	3.0	4.2	5.3	6.4	7.5	8.7	9.7	10.7	11.7	13.7	15.7	17.7	19.7	21.7	26.7	31.7	41.7	51.7
850	.4			3.0		5.3		7.5		9.6		11.6	13.6	15.6	17.6	19.6	21.6		31.6	41.6	51.6
900	.3		1.7	3.0	4.1	5.2	6.3	7.5	8.5	9.5	10.5	11.5	13.5	15.5	17.5	19.5	21.5	26.5	31.5	41.5	51.5
950	.3			2.9		5.2		7.4		9.4		11.4	13.4	15.4	17.4	19.4	21.4		31.4	41.4	51.4
1000	.3	1.0	1.7	2.9	4.0	5.2	6.3	7.4	8.4	9.4	10.1	11.4	13.4	15.4	17.4	19.4	21.4	26.4	31.4	41.4	51.4
1500	.2		1.5	2.7	3.8	4.9	5.9	6.9	7.9	8.9	9.9	10.9	12.9	14.9	16.9	18.9	20.9	25.9	30.9	40.9	50.9
2000	.1	.8	1.4	2.6	3.7	4.7	5.7	6.7	7.7	8.7	9.7	10.7	12.7	14.7	16.7	18.7	20.7	25.7	30.7	40.7	50.7
2500	.1	.8	1.4	2.6	3.6	4.6	5.6	6.6	7.6	8.6	9.6	10.6	12.6	14.6	16.6	18.6	20.6	25.6	30.6	40.6	50.6
3000	.1		1.4	2.5	3.5	4.5	5.5	6.5	7.5	8.5	9.5	10.5	12.5	14.5	16.5	18.5	20.5	25.5	30.5	40.5	50.5
4000	.1	.7	1.3	2.4	3.4	4.4	5.4	6.4	7.4	8.4	9.4	10.4	12.4	14.4	16.4	18.4	20.4	25.4	30.4	40.4	50.4
5000	.1	.7	1.3	2.3	3.3	4.3	5.3	6.3	7.3	8.3	9.3	10.3	12.3	14.3	16.3	18.3	20.3	25.3	30.3	40.3	50.3

FIG. 9.5　Attribute Estimation Table (95% Reliability)

Source: Arens and Loebbecke, Auditing: An Integrated Approach (1976), p. 293. Reprinted with permission of Prentice-Hall, Inc.

limit tends to be higher than the true, but unknown, upper limit. To emphasize this, the estimated maximum error amounts are termed *error bounds*.

The simple attribute estimation method is always applicable, but its usefulness diminishes as errors are found. Other evaluation techniques have been designed to modify the simple attribute estimate on the basis of the error amounts actually found. Most of these methods are based on empirical rather than theoretical research, and one such method is called *combined attribute-variables estimation* (CAV). Instead of assuming that all population dollars in error are misstated by the estimated maximum amount, CAV reasons that the portions of the maximum error rate applicable to the errors found are misstated by the actual amounts of error found in the sample dollar units. This can be illustrated as follows:

A dollar-unit sample of 100 is extracted from a population of $120,000. Two dollar units are found to be in error by $.10 and $.20, respectively. Simple attribute estimates of the upper precision limits at 95% reliability for a sample size of 100 with zero, one, and two errors are 3%, 4.7%, and 6.2%, respectively, as shown in Figure 9.5. The simple attribute approach thus results in an error bound of $7,440 (.062 × $120,000), assuming a $1.00 maximum error amount per sample unit.

CAV reasons, on the other hand, that the error rate of 6.2% can be split into three portions: 3% errors of assumed maximum amount $1.00; 1.7% (4.7% − 3.0%) errors of maximum amount $.20; 1.5% (6.2% − 4.7%) errors of maximum amount $.10. (The error amounts are taken in descending order to be conservative.) Thus, the CAV upper error bound (at 95% reliability) is $4,188 ([.03 × $120,000 × $1.00] + [.017 × $120,000 × $.20] + [.015 × $120,000 × $.10])

For a more complete explanation of this bound, see Goodfellow, Loebbecke, and Neter (1974).

The simple attribute method and the combined attribute-variables method are both based on the binomial distribution, which assumes no more than two outcomes for any sampling unit. A different and more complex technique known as *multino-mial-bound evaluation* assumes a broader set of possibilities, based on the error information obtained. It often provides tighter precision bounds than CAV, particularly when there are more than a few errors, but the calculations are so complex that it requires computer assistance.

Dollar-unit sampling is designed for use with populations with low error rates. When a dollar-unit sample is found to contain more than a few errors, none of the above methods are likely to give useful results because the upper error bounds will be too high. In this case, it may be appropriate to evaluate the dollar-unit sample using the mean-per-unit variables estimation method, which will result in a confidence interval estimate of the total dollar error (and thus a statement that the error is between $X and $Y at a certain reliability). Note that mean-per-unit is the only variables sampling method that can be applied to a sample of dollar units.

How to Apply Dollar-Unit Sampling. Sample size for dollar-unit sampling should be determined on the basis of the simple attribute approach. This will involve using attribute tables or an attribute microcomputer program, translating the required dollar precision amount into a percentage of population value, and following the steps described above for attribute sampling. When no errors are found in the sample, evaluation can be done in a similar fashion. When errors are found, manual modification of the simple attribute upper precision limit is usually required. To apply combined attribute-variables estimation:

1. Determine the error amount per dollar unit by prorating the error per physical unit, (i.e., divide the amount of the error by the number of dollar units represented in the physical unit).
2. Segregate the overstatement errors from the understatement errors, so that separate evaluations can be made. (Overstatement errors do not affect understatement estimates, and vice versa.)

Then, for overstatement and understatement estimates separately:

3. Rank errors in descending order of magnitude.
4. For each error, determine the appropriate portion of the upper precision limit for the total error rate. (That is, for the first error, ascertain the upper precision limit relating to one error and subtract the upper precision limit relating to zero errors; for the second error, ascertain the upper precision limit for two errors and subtract the portion of this precision equal to the upper precision limit for one error; for the third error, ascertain the upper precision limit for three errors and subtract that for two errors; etc. This will require the use of attribute tables or an attribute microcomputer program.)
5. Multiply each error amount (determined in Step 1) by its corresponding error-rate portion (determined in Step 4), including the assumed maximum error amount by the zero error-rate portion (the upper precision limit for zero errors).
6. Add the multiplication products.
7. Multiply this sum by the total population value to give the modified upper bound of the total error amount.

As an illustration, take the previously described case of a sample of 100 dollar-units from a population of $120,000, but suppose that three dollar-units are found to be in error: two are overstated by $.10 and $.20, and one is understated by $1.50. The maximum overstatement per dollar unit is assumed to be $1.00, and the maximum understatement, $2.00. The CAV upper error bound for *overstatement* errors at 95% reliability is $4,188, computed as in the previous example; the CAV upper error bound for *understatement* errors at 95% reliability is [($2.00 × .03) + ($1.50 × .017)] × $120,000 = $10,260.

Variables Sampling

Variables sampling, also discussed earlier in this chapter, is based on the normal distribution and the related central limit theorem, and provides confidence interval estimates of total population dollar amounts. For an introduction to variables sampling and normal distributions see Arens and Loebbecke (1984).

Techniques Available. The most common variables sampling methods are mean-per-unit, difference, and ratio. They are all based on the same theory, but use different value characteristics to make estimates, as shown in Figure 9.3.

The confidence intervals in variables sampling are based on an estimate of the total population amount and a precision factor that varies according to the reliability required of the confidence interval. For example, for a two-sided confidence interval, the estimate of the population total value will be the midpoint of the interval.

The midpoint estimate is calculated using the average of the sample item characteristic values. For example, using the mean-per-unit method, the population value is estimated from the average of the sample item audited values (x_j). The precision amount is calculated using three factors: reliability, the standard deviation of the sample item characteristic values, and sample size (precision = reliability normal coefficient $\times$ standard deviation/square root of sample size). For details of the calculations, including formulae, see Roberts (1978), Chapters 5 and 6, and Appendix 2. In practice, microcomputer programs can be used to perform all the calculations.

In selecting the most appropriate variables sampling method in any given audit situation, the following guidelines have been suggested by Neter and Loebbecke (1975):

1. When only one value per sample item is available (e.g., when no book value exists) the mean-per-unit method must be used.

2. If the purpose of the estimate is to compare *two* values per sample item, either to estimate the total difference or the overall ratio, either the difference, ratio, or mean-per-unit method may be used. Difference and ratio methods are preferable when more than a few errors are expected (say 10% or more) in that these methods tend to require much smaller sample sizes than mean-per-unit (for fixed precision and reliability). However, difference and ratio methods are likely to be unreliable when few differences exist in the population, that is, the true reliability level of the estimate will tend to be lower than the stated reliability.

3. When few or no differences are expected, mean-per-unit (or the combined method, mean-per-unit difference) may be used. Mean-per-unit usually has large sample size requirements unless stratification can be used to break the population into more homogeneous subgroups. For instance, stratification by book value will usually result in a much smaller sample size, but stratification is often impractical unless a computer program is available and the population is maintained on a computer file. When these conditions exist, the computer program can also calculate an optimal stratification plan. The mean-per-unit difference method is the alternative when stratification is not feasible. It combines the two methods, so that sample sizes are smaller than for mean-per-unit; yet estimates are still reliable even though few errors are found.

When two values per sample item are available and differences *are* expected, an alternative to the difference or ratio method is *regression estimation*, based on the linear relationship between two values. It can be more efficient in terms of sample size than difference or ratio methods, but the calculations are slightly more complex. For a brief description of regression estimation, including formulae, see Roberts (1978), pp. 86–92.

How to Apply Variables Sampling. Whichever method is used, sample size can be determined mathematically, based on the sampling criteria. The calculations are tedious if performed manually, so a microcomputer program is preferable. The sampling criteria needed are the required reliability level and the precision amount, the population size, and an estimate of the population standard deviation.

The *standard deviation* of the sample item characteristic values is a mathematical measure of their dispersion about their average value. Estimation of standard deviation is often difficult, but is important because sample size increases in proportion to its square. When practical, a preliminary or advance sample may be drawn to estimate the standard deviation. Otherwise, prior sampling experience or judgmental knowledge of the population may be used.

The following four rules should always be observed in sample size determination for a variables estimate:

1. When applicable, pull out all the high-value items and test them 100% to reduce variability of the sampling population.
2. Avoid small sample sizes (less than 100) because they tend to give unreliable results.
3. Consider whether the sample size is large enough to be useful if unexpected results are obtained. (For example, what sample size would be required if an alternative evaluation method had to be used?)
4. Consider whether the sample size seems judgmentally acceptable in the context of the specified audit objectives.

When the sample has been drawn, evaluating it by a variables method is also done with the use of mathematical formulas, most easily using a microcomputer program. The required reliability must be specified and the sample data details must be entered. Figure 9.6 shows the output of a typical microcomputer program using difference estimation to evaluate the total error amount in a population of 8,900 items from an audited sample of 160.

Hypothesis Testing

Variables sampling provides support for the statement that, at a specific reliability level, the estimated value is contained within a specific confidence interval. When the value being estimated is the population audit value, it may be used in hypothesis testing.

There are two possible approaches to hypothesis testing: the positive approach, which hypothesizes that the book value is materially correct, and the negative approach, which hypothesizes that the book value is incorrect by a material amount. Statistical results are then used to support or reject the hypothesis. (See Roberts, 1978, pp. 40–48, for a description of each approach.) Although the two approaches are equivalent, the negative approach is used here.

When variables sampling provides a two-sided estimate of a population audit value, a hypothesis test applies two main rules to determine whether the book value is materially incorrect;

1. If the book value is less than a material amount away from both confidence limits of the interval, accept it as not being materially incorrect.
2. If the book value is a material amount away from the farthest confidence limit, reject it. Either an audit adjustment is required or further audit work must be done.

```
                              ESTIMATION SAMPLING
                MASTER DATA
                -----------

        FILENAME                           EXAMPLE


   1.   CLIENT                             ABC Co.


   2.   AUDIT AREA & YEAR END              A/cs Receivable Dec 31 1988


   3.   SAMPLING METHOD (D, M OR R)        D
          Difference, MUS-Variables or Ratio


   4.   SAMPLING POPULATION SIZE (D, M OR R)          8,900


   5.   SAMPLING POPULATION BOOK VALUE (M OR R)


   6.   SAMPLING POP. DENOMINATOR VALUE (R only)




              SAMPLE TOTALS
              -------------------
   1.   SAMPLE SIZE               160
   2.   SUM X
   3.   SUM X SQD
   4.   SUM Y
   5.   SUM Y SQD
   6.   SUM X * Y


   7.   SUM D                     -33
   8.   SUM D SQD                 484


        NOTE: DIFFERENCE = X - Y
                              ESTIMATION SAMPLING
                        SAMPLE EVALUATION CRITERIA ENTRY
   1.   1 OR 2 SIDED INTERVAL             2


   2.   CONFIDENCE LEVEL                  90
          1 to 99 if 2 sided interval
          51 to 99 if 1 sided interval


   3.   IF 100% ITEMS ARE TO BE INCLUDED:
                   NUMBER OF 100% ITEMS    5 ...
                        TOTAL X VALUE      21015 ...
                        TOTAL Y VALUE      21015 ...


           NOTE: DIFFERENCE = X - Y
```

(continued)

FIG. 9.6 User Entries to and Output From a Program to Evaluate Error Amount by the Variables Method

```
                    ESTIMATION SAMPLING
                 SAMPLE EVALUATION RESULTS


              USING DIFFERENCE ESTIMATION

   FOR A 2 SIDED INTERVAL
   AT A CONFIDENCE LEVEL OF                        90 PERC

   BASED ON: TOTAL SAMPLE SIZE =                   160
   PLUS 100% ITEMS: NUMBER OF  =                     5
   DIFFERENCE IN               =                     0

   ESTIMATES OF THE TOTAL DIFFERENCE ARE:
        MAXIMUM                                    151
        MINIMUM                                 -3,823
        POINT ESTIMATE                          -1,836
        PRECISION OF ESTIMATE                    1,987


   (STANDARD DEVIATION OF DIFFERENCE 1.73)
```

FIG. 9.6 (continued)

These rules are illustrated in Figure 9.7.

For both the accept decision and the reject decision, there is a risk that it is wrong. The risk of accepting a materially incorrect book value, known as the *beta risk*, is directly related to the reliability level of the confidence interval. The risk of rejecting a correct book value, known as the *alpha risk*, is a function of the precision of the confidence interval compared to the materiality amount. (For precise definitions of the relationships, see Roberts, 1978, p. 41.)

Thus, when the auditor expects the book value to be accepted, a hypothesis test is the logical way to reach the decision, since this method provides a simple acceptance decision with a judgmentally acceptable risk level.

How to Apply Hypothesis Testing. Sample size for hypothesis testing can be determined mathematically, either manually or by using a microcomputer program, in the same way as for variables sampling. Instead of depending on reliability and precision, it is based on the beta and alpha risks deemed acceptable and on the amount deemed material. Evaluation is also based on these risks rather than on reliability.

SUPERVISORY REVIEW OF AUDIT SAMPLING APPLICATIONS

The AICPA Guide, *Audit Sampling (AICPA*, 1983b), offers the following advice on what a reviewer of audit work might consider in reviewing audit sampling, whether compliance or substantive, nonstatistical or statistical:

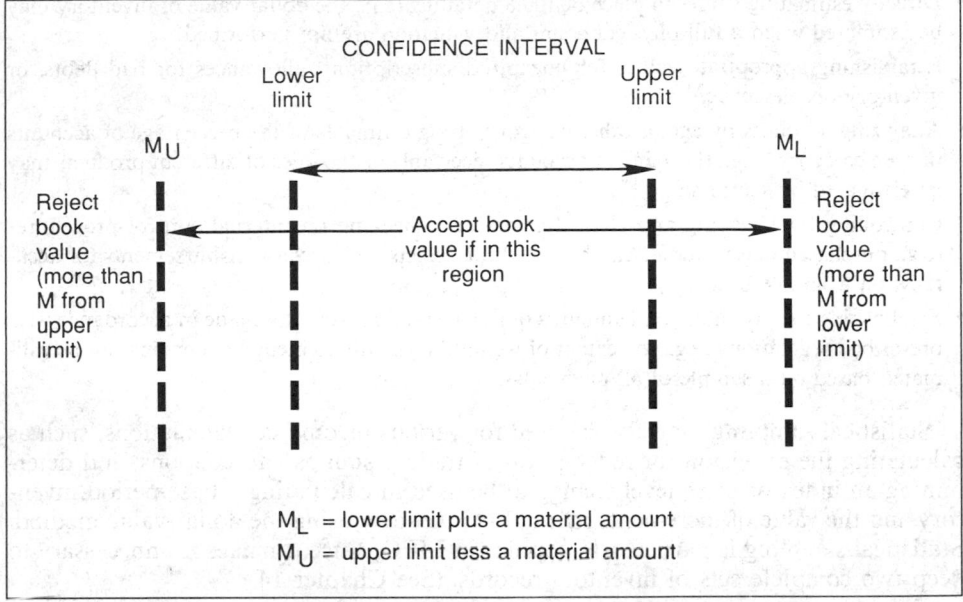

FIG. 9.7 Hypothesis Test Rules—Two-Sided Estimate of Population Audit Value

- Were the population and sampling unit defined appropriately for the test objectives?
- Were tests performed to provide reasonable assurance that the sample was selected from the correct population?
- Did the design of the sampling application provide for an appropriate risk level? For example, did the design reflect planned reliance on related internal accounting controls or additional related substantive tests?
- If additional audit tests were planned in designing the sampling procedure, did these tests support the book value of the account being tested?
- Were planned procedures applied to all sample items? If not, how were those unexamined items in the sample considered in the evaluation?
- Were all errors discovered in the test properly evaluated?
- If the test was a compliance test, did it support the planned reliance on the internal accounting control procedure? If not, were related substantive tests appropriately modified?
- Was the audit objective of the test met?

COMMON USES OF STATISTICAL SAMPLING IN ACCOUNTING AND TAXATION

There are many opportunities to use statistical sampling to assist in accounting activities. The more popular uses are:

- Directly estimating values in place of 100% detailing (e.g., the dollar value of inventory may be estimated when a full physical count and valuation are not performed).
- Establishing appropriate values for unexpired subscriptions, allowances for bad debts, or inventory obsolescence.
- Analyzing accounts by age or other category, using estimates of the percentage of accounts in each category. (e.g., the aging of accounts receivable or the sales of different products may be estimated by sampling).
- Controlling bookkeeping and clerical errors and checking on internal control procedures (e.g., purchased raw materials can be tested for defects, or purchase disbursements for accuracy, on a sample basis).
- Establishing the probable total amounts of payments that were not made in accordance with prescribed regulations (e.g., the extent of welfare payments to ineligible persons can be estimated based on a sample of all payments).

Statistical sampling may also be used for various income tax calculations, such as calculating the provision for redemption of trading stamps and coupons, and determining an index of price level change to be used in calculating a base-period inventory and the value of increments in a LIFO inventory using the dollar-value method. Statistical sampling is particularly popular in LIFO, since it makes it unnecessary to keep two complete sets of inventory records. (See Chapter 14.)

10

Auditing In An EDP Environment

AUDITORS AND COMPUTERS

The principal groups involved in electronic data processing (EDP) auditing are internal auditors employed by the organization being audited and independent external auditors. Internal audit emphasis varies with the characteristics and special concerns of a particular company or industry, and independent audits also vary widely in emphasis and approach. However, the maturation of EDP auditing has brought with it an increased awareness that there is no one best approach, and that every audit must be designed to consider specific engagement risks and requirements.

This chapter discusses the audit in an environment that includes EDP. The audit of EDP as performed by the independent auditor is emphasized, but the coverage should also be of interest to management personnel and internal auditors who are responsible for or dependent on EDP. The total audit process used by independent auditors and the related internal control concepts are covered in detail in Chapters 7 and 8; this chapter builds on those basics with a minimum of repetition.

Beyond the primary purpose of an independent auditor – expression of an opinion on the financial statements – the external audit may include a wide range of computer-related services. These services might include operational audits of data processing operations, or the review of exposures not directly related to the financial statements, such as invasion of privacy or data center disaster prevention and recovery. Many organizations consider these expanded scope services to be an essential supplement to their overall program of computer control.

Background

EDP has been characterized by constantly changing technology. During the late 1950s and the 1960s, the predominant method of EDP was *batch processing* at a centralized location. Initially, batch applications were designed with few controls, but in time the degree of batch system control reached reasonably high levels. Advances in EDP technology from the late 1960s through the 1970s resulted in a trend toward on-line, terminal-oriented systems. Since many batch control techniques were not suitable for on-line applications, the development of new systems once again preceded that of control methodology. In the late 1970s and early 1980s, the trend was toward *distributed processing* using terminals linked by telecommunications to a central computer, or small computers operating independently at remote locations. The direction today, in the late 1980s, is toward linking these small remote computers to central computers or to other small remote computers. Appropriate control concepts for distributed processing are only now envolving.

Future Trends

Several themes are likely to dominate future EDP trends: decreasing costs, especially for the hardware (the equipment) used for on-line and distributed processing; an exponential growth in the number of small but very powerful computers; a propensity to develop all new applications (the programs, or software) with on-line terminals; increasingly sophisticated file structures; and a growing awareness of the need for computer controls. For the foreseeable future, EDP will include a mixture of batch, on-line, and distributed processing; and the degree of internal control in any specific EDP situation will probably vary widely.

These trends are resulting in increased concentrations of data, increased integration of processing and controls, and changes in the responsibilities for control. Data, rather than being stored in manual files throughout an organization, are now being physically concentrated in EDP systems. However, with increased concentration of data comes a new sharing of responsibilities. Originally, a single organizational unit had been responsible for creating its own transactions, maintaining its own files, and monitoring its own processing; in many current EDP systems, the responsibilities for these functions involve several departments. The department using the processed data frequently relies extensively on processing performed by others and even on transactions entered by others. Similarly, files once maintained and controlled by a single department are now frequently used and changed by others.

The concentration and sharing of data has been accompanied by the concentration and integration of processing functions. In many EDP systems, a series of functions are automatically performed with nominal human supervision. Some of these functions include initiation, authorization, and execution of transactions; processing of documents that authorize the use or disposition of assets; performance of accounting controls; and the reporting of processing results.

Accounting Impact

Obviously, EDP systems can have significant impact on accounting controls.

- The traditional segregation of duties may be impaired, because a single individual is able to perform incompatible functions, such as making and concealing an error.
- The number of persons who handle a transaction is typically reduced, often to just the individual who enters the data into the computer. As the number of persons involved declines, a consistent level of control can be maintained only if additional controls are included in the EDP system.
- It is frequently difficult to identify the requirements for coordination and control. In a simple environment, a single manager was typically responsible for gathering, processing, and using data; that manager could informally assure the quality of the results. In EDP systems, an individual manager is increasingly only responsible for a portion of the processing and the associated controls. This sharing of responsibility can result in the loss of control, unless control requirements and responsibilities are clearly and formally defined and effectively communicated, monitored, and enforced.

In addition, computer-related exposures and related controls are not dependent on the size of the computer involved. Highly sophisticated systems can be implemented on small, relatively inexpensive computers. The degree of control needed for any system should be determined by the value and sensitivity of the data and the processing, not by a computer's size or its cost. Accordingly, this chapter applies to all EDP systems, without regard to size or cost.

EDP EXPOSURES AND CONTROLS

Effective auditing in an EDP environment requires a knowledge of EDP techniques, what can go wrong with these techniques, and what controls can be used to prevent, detect, and correct unintentional errors or deliberate irregularities.

Exposures

EDP techniques vary considerably, depending on the purpose of the processing, the design of the EDP system, and the type of computer used. Nevertheless, most processing includes

* Conversion of data to machine-readable or electronic media
* Transmission of data to the computer
* Initial processing
* Data retention on magnetic tape or disk files
* Subsequent processing to produce output reports or output replies in response to terminal inquiries

In batch applications, the processing phases are relatively discrete; in on-line applications, two or more phases frequently overlap. For example, in a batch environment, documents might be mailed to a central location, converted to electronic media, and read by a computer. In an on-line application, documents are converted to electronic media using a remote terminal and transmitted directly to the central computer.

In both batch and on-line applications, there are similar exposures:

* Unauthorized transactions may be processed;
* Authorized transactions may be unrecorded, lost, or duplicated;
* Transaction elements (e.g., account number or amount) may be incorrectly converted;
* Files may be lost;
* The wrong file may be used for processing; or
* Processing may be inaccurate or incomplete.

Major EDP application steps and major opportunities for EDP errors at each step are illustrated in Figure 10.1.

EDP exposures may either be specific to an application or apply generally to all applications. For example, an undetected logic error in a computer program will result in errors in only one application, whereas a fire in the data center can destroy files related to all applications. Certain exposures, like fraud, have to be considered in both specific and general terms. For example, a fraud may occur in the user department through the unauthorized submission of an otherwise routine application transaction, or in the data center through the manipulation of data files using unauthorized programs unrelated to the specific application.

Processing Steps \ What Can Go Wrong	Unauthorized transactions	Transactions unrecorded, lost or duplicated	Incorrect values or classification	File lost or wrong file used	Processing inaccurate or incomplete	Output inaccurate or incomplete
Convert data to electronic media	•	•	•			
Transmit data to the computer	•	•	•			
Initial processing	•	•	•	•	•	•
Data retention	•	•		•		
Output processing	•			•	•	•

FIG. 10.1 Opportunities for EDP Errors

Nature of EDP Controls

Numerous controls can be used to prevent, detect, or correct errors in EDP. For example, transaction counts, control totals, telecommunication controls, and computer hardware and software controls can all be used to prevent or detect the loss of transactions entered at a remote terminal.

Specific controls can be understood best in the context of general types of EDP controls. EDP controls usually relate to a specific processing phase. There are, for example:

- Input controls to prevent or detect lost, inaccurate, or unauthorized transactions.
- Processing controls to assure that processing was performed as intended and that no unauthorized processing was performed.
- Output controls to assure the accuracy of processing results.

In any processing phase, EDP controls may be specific or general. A specific control, frequently referred to as an application control, relates only to a specific EDP application. General controls, or information processing facility (IPF) controls, relate to more than one application. For example, keystroke ver-

What Can Go Wrong / Controls	Unauthorized transactions	Transactions unrecorded, lost or duplicated	Incorrect values or classification	File lost or wrong file used	Processing inaccurate or incomplete	Output inaccurate or incomplete
GENERAL CONTROLS						
Corporate level						
• EDP segregated from users	•					
• Internal audit of EDP	•					
User department						
• Physical security over terminals	•					
• Compare EDP results to budgets				•	•	•
EDP Organization						
• Segregation of duties	•					
• Supervision	•	•	•	•	•	•
• Hardware controls		•	•			
• Operating system controls				•	•	•
• Pre-implementation testing					•	•
• Passwords	•					
APPLICATION CONTROLS						
• Programmed edits and reasonableness tests		•	•			
• Keystroke verification			•			
• Batching and batch totals	•	•	•			
• Run-to-run totals				•	•	•
• Input to output balancing	•	•	•	•	•	•
• Review output for reasonableness	•	•	•	•	•	•

FIG. 10.2 Examples of EDP Controls

ification procedures can specifically detect transaction conversion errors, whereas data center file library procedures can prevent unauthorized access to all data center files.

Figure 10.2 includes examples of general and application controls that may affect a particular EDP application. As illustrated, controls may be technical or nontechnical and may be implemented at the corporate level, in the user department, in the EDP department, within computer programs, or within computer hardware.

Figure 10.2 also presents the layers of redundant preventive and detective controls that typically exist. For example, key verification to detect data conversion errors, hardware controls to detect an error caused by a hardware failure, batch controls, run-to-run controls, and input-to-output balancing procedures will each prevent or detect inaccurate transaction values. Balancing procedures alone may provide adequate detective control, but EDP operational considerations require preventive controls during early phases of processing. Without such early controls, errors would not be detected until the end of processing, and extensive reprocessing and delay would result.

In addition, controls may be characterized by the span of their effect. For example, both batch controls and overall system-balancing controls detect lost transactions, but batch controls typically monitor fewer than 50 transactions whereas system balancing may control all the transactions for a day, a month, or a year.

EDP AUDITING STANDARDS

Effects of EDP on Internal Accounting Control

EDP can have a significant effect on the characteristics of accounting controls. The general structure for a review of internal controls is discussed in Chapter 8, but new types of errors may be caused by EDP. For example, inappropriate accounting or authorization procedures may be included within computer programs, or irregularities may result from routines deliberately included in computer programs. New types of controls may be required to prevent and detect these EDP-related errors and irregularities. In addition, certain types of EDP controls involve sources of information and evidence that cannot easily be reviewed, and segregation of functions within EDP is different and sometimes difficult. Finally, unfamiliarity with EDP and EDP controls may impede management's ability to establish and supervise internal controls.

Frequently, control weaknesses related to the segregation of functions within EDP are not readily apparent. For example, a computer program that processes purchase orders, receiving reports, vendor invoices, and vendor payments typically verifies prices, quantities, and that the goods have in fact been received. If control weaknesses permit a person to make unauthorized changes to the computer programs or to the purchase order and receiving document files, the program may then be used to process unapproved vendor invoices. In certain situations, complete segregation of incompatible EDP functions may be impossible, impractical, or simply not cost justified. In such cases compensating controls may be required, including supervision, rotation of personnel, an independent EDP control group, user department controls, and periodic internal audit review.

SAS 48—An Overview

SAS 48, *The Effects of Computer Processing on the Examination of Financial Statements*, issued in July 1984, integrates prior professional guidance (into AU Sections 311, 318, 320, and 326) so that computer processing is considered in the same manner as other factors that may affect an examination in conformity with GAAS. The extent to which EDP is used in significant accounting applications (i.e., an accounting application that can materially affect the financial statements being examined), as well as the complexity of such processing, may also influence the nature, timing, and extent of audit procedures.

Four earlier SASs were amended to include SAS 48 guidance on the effects and use of computers (and two of these amendments were further changed in 1988). A summary of these amendments follows.

• SAS 22 (AU 311) *Planning and Supervision.* An additional category of considerations – the methods used by the entity to process significant accounting information (including the use of service centers) – has been added. In an elaboration of the considerations, the auditor should have, in relation to the entity's computer processing, a knowledge of:

   – The extent to which computer processing is used in each significant accounting application.
   – The complexity of the entity's computer operations (including the use of an outside service center).
   – The organizational structure of the computer processing activities.
   – The availability of data required by the auditor – particularly, information that may be available for only a short period of time or is computer generated.
   – The use of computer-assisted audit techniques to increase the efficiency of performing audit techniques.

   In making these considerations, the auditor also needs to determine whether specialized skills are necessary to understand the flow of transactions and the nature of internal accounting control procedures, or to design or perform audit procedures. If specialized skills are required, the auditor should have sufficient computer-related knowledge to communicate the objectives of the work to be performed, as well as to evaluate the procedures to be applied and the results of the procedures as they relate to the nature, timing, and extent of other planned audit procedures.

• SAS 56 (AU 329) *Analytical Procedures.* Added to the list of factors the auditor should consider when planning and performing analytical review procedures is the effect, if any, that the increased availability of computer-generated data may have on the auditor's decision to perform analytical review procedures (originally in SAS 23).

• SAS 55 (AU 319) *Consideration of the Internal Control Structure in a Financial Statement Audit.* SAS 48 amended SAS 1 (AU 320) and superseded SAS 3, *The Effect of EDP on the Auditor's Study and Evaluation of Internal Control;* these pronouncements had previously treated EDP auditing separately, and SAS 48 integrated them directly into auditing literature dealing with factors that affect most audit examinations. SAS 55 supersedes AU 320 and further reinforces the mainstream notion of EDP auditing.

   Continuing the focus established in planning the audit, the guidance emphasizes how the method the entity uses to process significant accounting applications and its complexity may influence the control procedures used to achieve the objectives of internal control and the nature, timing, and extent of audit procedures.

   The guidance also identifies the characteristics that distinguish computer processing from manual processing. The characteristics considered are transaction trails, uniform processing of transactions, segregation of duties, potential for errors or irregularities, increased management supervision, initiation or subsequent management execution of transactions by computer, and the dependence of other controls over computer processing. By distinguishing these characteristics, the SAS focuses on the key decisions an auditor would have to make when significant accounting applications are involved.

These characteristics also assist in considering whether the related control procedures either achieve or contribute to the achievement of one or more specific control objectives. While the SAS maintains the distinction of SAS 3 between general and application controls, the orientation of the auditor's consideration of these types of controls has been appropriately sharpened to a determination of whether one, the other, or both "provide reasonable, but not absolute, assurance that assets are safeguarded from unauthorized use or disposition and financial records are reliable to permit the preparation of financial statements." This reemphasizes the audit objective rather than the nature of the control.

• SAS 31 (AU 326) *Evidential Matter.* This amendment emphasizes that audit evidence is not affected by the entity's use of computer processing, only the methods that the auditor uses to gather that evidence. In some cases, it may be difficult or impossible to perform certain audit procedures without computer assistance.

Other Guidance

To further assist the auditor in conducting an examination of financial statements in an EDP environment, the AICPA has issued a series of Computer Services Guidelines addressing specific areas. Two of these Guidelines are: *Audit and Control Considerations in a Minicomputer Enviroment* (AICPA, 1981a) and *Audit and Control Considerations in an On-Line Environment* (AICPA, 1983a). While these Guidelines do not represent official positions of the AICPA, they are useful to the auditor in understanding the control considerations in an EDP environment and their effect on the nature, timing, and extent of audit procedures.

Computer Services Guidelines are intended for use by an auditor who has a basic understanding of EDP accounting controls and EDP concepts and is familiar with SAS 48. The two Guidelines previously mentioned are discussed in the following sections.

MINICOMPUTERS

The Computer Services Guideline, *Audit and Control Considerations in a Minicomputer Environment*, provides useful information to assist the auditor in planning and conducting an audit in an environment where a minicomputer is used to process significant accounting data. The publication considers:

• Control-related characteristics of the minicomputer environment,
• Risks and controls used to reduce risks, and
• Audit considerations including substantive audit techniques.

Also, an appendix to the publication describes a typical small computer and its control features.

Characteristics, Risks, and Controls

The Guideline identifies several characteristics of a minicomputer environment, the risks attendant to these characteristics, and possible controls to mitigate the identified risks.

Lack of Segregation of Accounting Functions. In a minicomputer environment, the auditor may find that personnel in the user department initiate and authorize source documents, enter data into the system, operate the computer, and use the output reports. The risks of a lack of segregation of duties in a minicomputer environment are much the same as, for example, in an accounting department that only has one or two employees. Controls that would help alleviate this risk include an effective system of transaction logs and batch controls, rotation of personnel, and effective supervision.

Lack of Segregation of EDP Functions. The functions of programming and operating the minicomputer are normally not segregated in a separate EDP department, because of limited personnel. In addition, programs and data files are frequently resident on the system at all times and accessible by any operator. Software with access restriction capabilities is often used to control access, sometimes in concert with manual controls.

Location of the Computer. The computer is often located in the same area as the user department rather than in a separate data processing department. Further, management may not be inclined to locate the minicomputer in a physically secure area since the minicomputer is not very sensitive to temperature, humidity, and so forth. Also, in many installations the minicomputer is not secured so as to prevent improper use or manipulation of data, programs, or computer resources. Software with access restriction capabilities is probably the best mechanism to control access.

Limited EDP Knowledge. In many minicomputer installations, the individuals responsible for data processing sometimes have a limited knowledge of EDP. In practice, for example, the minicomputer location, not personnel qualifications, often determines the assignment of supervisory responsibility. To reduce the possibility that inexperience may affect the quality of use and output of a minicomputer, use of a third party to assist in monitoring new applications is often helpful.

Auditor Qualifications

The Guideline booklet identifies the following desirable characteristics an auditor should possess in auditing in a minicomputer-based environment:

• A general understanding of computer systems and software;
• Familiarity with file processing techniques, data structures, and program and systems documentation;
• Working knowledge of EDP accounting controls;

• Familiarity with the process of developing and modifying programs; and
• A general understanding of the risks inherent in using computers to process significant financial information.

ON-LINE ENVIRONMENTS

The Computer Services Guideline *Audit and Control Considerations in an On-Line Environment* is designed to help auditors understand the variety of environments included in the classification "on-line," and identify the impact an on-line environment may have on the nature, timing, and extent of audit procedures.

The Guideline specifically describes the following:

• Common characteristics of on-line environments that distinguish them from other types of computer-processing.
• The effect of on-line processing on the identification of potential errors or irregularities and related control procedures.
• Possible audit strategies that might be applied in an on-line environment.
• The effect of on-line systems on other auditor concerns that are outside the study and evaluation of the internal control process.

Characteristics of an On-Line System

A major characteristic of an on-line system is the existence in user departments of terminals that permit direct access to data and programs. Such terminals may enable the user to continuously update these data or programs. Accordingly, the Guideline classifies on-line systems into groups, based on the type of data entry and the time of file updating:

• Single transaction input and immediate master file update
• Single transaction input and delayed master file update
• Batch transaction input and delayed master file update
• Remote job entry
• On-line processing at a service center

The Guideline discusses the characteristics of each type and provides an illustrative example of a system of single transaction input and immediate master file update. It also describes the input, processing, and output of data in this system, and the controls that exist over each process.

Potential Errors and Irregularities

Audit Considerations. While on-line technology does not change the types of errors and irregularities that could occur in processing transactions, the Guideline suggests several areas the auditor should consider. These include changes in the:

- Likelihood of occurrence of certain types of errors and irregularities,
- Nature and extent of controls, and
- Nature of the audit trail and the sources of audit evidence.

The Guideline discusses specific circumstances in which each of the above considerations might be affected.

Audit Approach. Changes in the likelihood of error, the extent of controls, and the nature of the audit trail may create a need to also change the approach to the audit. The Guideline presents specific changes that might occur as a result of the use of on-line processing (e.g., need to use audit software, need for staff with special EDP skills, timing of audit tasks based on the availability of evidence retained in temporary files, use of substantive tests because controls are too difficult or too time consuming to test, etc.).

Internal Control. An evaluation of internal accounting controls within the on-line portion of a system should be included as part of the overall evaluation of controls. The Guideline refers to "general controls" and "application controls." General controls are those which apply to more than one EDP application or processing function, such as passwords and other controls over access to data. Application controls, on the other hand, are intended to meet a specific objective or detect a specific error. Application controls include the use of balancing and batching. The Guideline includes a table of control objectives and related control procedures as well as descriptions for each control procedure and examples of tests of each control.

Audit Strategies

The audit strategies section of the Guideline illustrates how an auditor's evaluation of an on-line system affects the planning and extent of subsequent work over a three-year period. The emphasis is on planning the audit work, based on the auditor's findings made during his review of internal accounting control.

EDP AUDIT TECHNIQUES AND TOOLS

The auditor can use a variety of techniques and tools to understand a client's EDP activity, evaluate EDP controls, and evaluate the results of EDP. Figure 10.3 provides a *partial* list of audit techniques and tools related to particular EDP audit tasks, some of which are discussed in this section. Many of these techniques are nontechnical (e.g., checklists and questionnaires) and are useful to auditors who have a general understanding of EDP, its exposures, and its controls. Use of many other EDP tools requires a higher degree of technical expertise. Flowcharting is another tool commonly employed by auditors to analyze transaction cycles, and its use seems especially applicable to EDP. Of course, these are generalizations, with reality dependent on the specific engagement and the experience level – general and EDP – of the members of the audit team.

Audit Task	Techniques	Tools
Gather and verify application and data center information	Inquiries and observations	Application and data center questionnaires and checklists
	Flowchart transaction flow and controls	
	Review program code and logic	Logic flowcharting software
Test and evaluate controls	Observe controls or control evidence	
	Use test data to test controls	Test decks, audit software, test data generators
	Control analysis	Control evaluation tables
Test transactions for evidence of weak controls	Trace valid and invalid transactions	
	Reasonableness tests	Audit software
Verify processing routines	Manual recalculation	
	Test data, parallel simulation	Test decks, audit software, test data generators
Test transactions and balances for monetary errors	Confirmations, random or key item selection, parallel simulation	Audit software, statistical sampling software
	Analytical review	Analytical software

FIG. 10.3   EDP Audit Techniques and Related EDP Audit Tools

Risk Analysis

Although informal risk analysis has always been part of auditing, the complexity of EDP auditing has caused innovative auditors to experiment with formally analyzing EDP-related risks. The results of this analysis are then used to arrange audit work-schedule priorities. Risk analysis is characterized by an initial survey to gather only the information used in a risk analysis formula. Values are then calculated that represent the degree of risk for specific applications or for all applications serviced by a particular data processing operation. Factors frequently included in the various risk analysis methods are:

* Organizational considerations
* Dollar amount of individual transactions and resulting balances
* Normal error rates in the various processing phases
* Susceptibility of assets to theft or fraud
* Need for confidentiality or privacy
* Potential for EDP-related business interruption
* Probable impact of EDP interruptions on income and service levels
* Stability of the EDP operations (e.g., the number of new or modified applications)
* Complexity of processing

• Previous audit findings
• Perceived competency of the EDP and user departments
• Preliminary assessments of EDP controls

For example, one risk analysis methodology uses six major categories to analyze EDP application risk. These categories, with their assigned relative weights, are (1) impact of system failure, with a relative weight of 15; (2) impact on management decisions, with a relative weight of 10; (3) system status, (4) impact on other systems, (5) application controls, each with a relative weight of 5; and (6) technical complexity, with a relative weight of 2.

Within each of the six categories, scores related to specific application characteristics are assigned.

For example, in the system failure category, scores are assigned as follows: 10 if a failure has customer impact; 8 if the failure has company-wide impact; 4 if the application has user impact; and 1 if the failure also affects the management information system.

In the management decisions category, different scores are assigned for operational systems, financial systems, operational research systems, and statistical systems. In the systems status category, a new system may be assigned a score from 6 to 10, whereas an existing system may be assigned a score from 1 to 5 depending on the extent of recent modifications. In the impact-on-other-systems category, assigned scores depend on the degree of system independence or integration with other systems.

Scoring in the application control category is based on the need for various types of application controls. In the system scope category, local applications are assigned a score of 1 to 4, and divisional or corporate systems may be assigned a score up to 6 or 8, respectively. The technical complexity category considers such characteristics as processing mode (sequential, batch, on-line, and so forth), the programming language used, the developmental approach used, file data management techniques (sequential, indexed, data base, and so forth), and the application recovery mode.

To use this risk evaluation method, each category score is multiplied by the relative weight assigned to the category. The sum of these values represents the degree of risk for the application.

Control Analysis

Although the effectiveness of controls will always be very judgmental, the use of control evaluation tables to perform a more systematic analysis is gaining increased acceptance. Control evaluation tables used to evaluate application and general (IPF) controls are given in Appendixes 10A and 10B of this chapter, and are extracted from *Computer Control and Audit* by Mair, Wood, And Davis (1976). These tables indicate the relationship of potential errors to controls and suggest the probable strength of each type of control. For example, in an application control, document control counts will typically be a reliable control against lost or duplicated input and, in combination with other controls, may control the risk of processing the wrong file.

The exposure, cause, and control entries of the tables are extensive, and the numeric values have been developed with considerable thought based on actual practice. However, in applying these tables to specific situations, it is the technique that is important, not the specific entries or values. In particular, the effectiveness of a control in dealing with a particular cause can vary significantly according to circumstances. For example, training may be so necessary in complex or technical areas that several years of combined formal and on-the-job training are essential to assure adequate quality of results. Conversely, in simple functions, the usefulness of training may be limited, and other controls thus become much more important.

Test Data

Test data are sets of input transactions and master file records that can be used to verify the accuracy of computer routines or the adequacy of computer controls. Test data are a popular technique used by EDP professionals to test new and modified EDP applications and by auditors to test critical routines and controls. Theoretically, test data may be used to test all possible combinations of input and processing. However, in an EDP application of any complexity, such a comprehensive test might require hundreds of sets of test data. Although such a comprehensive approach may be required to test a new EDP application, audit testing is typically restricted to critical routines, perhaps with other routines tested on a sample basis. Two examples of how an auditor might use test data follow.

In a payroll program that includes a gross pay calculation based on regular hours, overtime hours, and production quotas, test data representing the various combinations of input may be used to test the accuracy of the payroll calculation. In a payroll-check-writing program that has a programmed control to prevent the printing of a check greater than $2,000, test data representing a payment over $2,000 may be used to test the control. The steps involved in the use of test data are:

1. Define the objectives of the test and identify the specific computer routines to be tested.
2. Prepare test data, including master file records if required.
3. Manually calculate the anticipated processing result.
4. If the system to be tested is already operational, establish test versions of the application computer programs and necessary files.
5. Process the test data through the application computer programs.
6. Compare manually prepared anticipated results to the results of actual computer processing.
7. Resolve differences between anticipated and actual results.

In most cases, the results of processing will be available on regularly produced computer reports. However, the processing result to be reviewed may only be available within a record in a computer file. In this case, audit software may have to be used to review the processing result.

The use of test data is not technically complex, but the technique does require a thorough understanding of the EDP application to be tested. This understanding is necessary so the auditor can limit testing to only critical routines, develop the necessary test and master-file records, and accurately calculate anticipated results.

When an operational system is to be tested, the auditor must be certain that the results of testing do not become intermingled with the results of actual processing. This is usually achieved by establishing, then testing, nonproduction copies of the application programs and the related files. Extensive cooperation and coordination with the data center staff is necessary to establish copies of computer programs and files and to guard against the accidental inclusion of test data within actual operation files. When this approach is used, the auditor must be certain that the copies of the programs tested are identical to the production versions of the programs.

The risk of introducing test data into actual production results may also be eliminated by using live transactions as test data. This alternative is practical if the required testing involves input transactions and master-file records that are typically found in regular production processing. The approach is similar to using regular test data: test objectives are defined, anticipated results are calculated, and the characteristics of required input and master-file test data are established. However, rather than develop test data, regular production transactions with the required characteristics are identified and the actual results of processing these transactions are compared to anticipated processing results.

Integrated Test Facility

The *integrated test facility*, or ITF, is a refinement of the test data approach that may be used to test operational applications directly. Use of ITF involves the establishment of records that represent "dummy" entities against which test data may be processed. These fictitious entities may be employees, customers, or an entire department or division. The technique is "integrated" because the test transactions are processed with regular production transactions and test master-file records reside on the same files with production master records. Since processing is integrated, the method of separating test transactions from live transactions is critical. Separation may be achieved either by journal or other reversing entries or by the use of production programs that have been designed or modified to automatically perform the separation.

Using ITF involves steps similar to those previously outlined for the use of test data – define objectives, prepare test data, calculate anticipated results, process test data through the system, and compare anticipated and actual results. However, since the ITF approach uses the operational version of programs and files, the auditor must at the end of the test reverse or otherwise eliminate the results of test processing.

Parallel Simulation

Parallel simulation, a powerful and popular EDP audit technique, uses computer programs prepared by auditors to reperform the functions initially performed by an actual computer application. The simulation program reads the same input and the master-file data, and then produces results for comparison with original application processing results. Matching results substantiate the accuracy of the application processing. The auditor may simulate processing for transactions that represent a single processing cycle only or an entire reporting period.

Parallel simulation is most frequently used as an alternative to manual recomputation performed on a sample basis. For example, if a complex depreciation method is used, the auditor might be required to recalculate depreciation on a sample basis;

however, by using parallel simulation, the auditor could recalculate complex depreciation for all items.

Parallel simulation requires the use of computer programs written in conventional programming languages, such as COBOL, or the use of generalized computer audit software, which is by far more popular.

Generalized Computer Audit Software

Generalized computer audit software (GCAS) may be used to perform a wide range of audit tasks, and permits the auditor to use the computer as an audit tool. GCAS consists of a series of computer program routines that can read computer files, select desired information, perform calculations, and print reports in an auditor-specified format. GCAS enables the auditor to have direct access to computerized records and to deal effectively with large quantities of data. Since GCAS can quickly scan, test, and summarize all the data on a computer file, many procedures traditionally performed on a sample basis can be extended to the entire population. In addition, the use of GCAS typically leads to a better understanding of automated systems and EDP operations, can make auditing more interesting and challenging, and is an excellent way to introduce the auditor to EDP.

GCAS can accomplish these six basic types of audit tasks:

1. Examine records for quality, completeness, consistency, and correctness (e.g., review bank demand deposit files for unusually large deposits and withdrawals).
2. Verify calculations and make computations (e.g., recompute interest).
3. Compare data on separate files (e.g., compare current and prior-period inventory files for obsolete and slow-moving items).
4. Select and print audit samples (e.g., accounts receivable confirmations).
5. Summarize, resequence, and analyze data (e.g., resequence inventory items by location to facilitate physical observations).
6. Compare data obtained through other audit procedures with company records (e.g., compare creditor statements with accounts payable files).

The steps in using GCAS parallel those involved in using a conventional programming language. The auditor establishes specific GCAS application objectives, reviews the data files for specific information to be accessed, designs the format of required reports, and develops the logic required to extract, manipulate, and print the required data. Specification sheets that define processing requirements are then prepared and submitted for computer processing. The specifications cause the GCAS to perform the required audit tasks.

GCAS is much easier to learn and to use than conventional programming languages. Most GCAS systems require only one week of training, and proficiency may be achieved after several weeks of use. In addition, GCAS specification coding typically requires only a fraction of the coding entries required for conventional programming languages, which permits faster coding and minimizes the opportunity for coding errors.

Statistical Sampling

Computer-assisted audit techniques have a two-edged impact on the use of *statistical sampling* by auditors. The availability of a computer for the auditor's use in analyzing masses of data frequently eliminates the need to audit on a sample basis. By preparing an audit software application that implements the logic of his audit analysis, the auditor can quickly examine every transaction and every record. In such situations, sampling may be unnecessary.

On the other hand, the computer is a tremendous aid in the selection of random samples and the evaluation of their results (see Chapter 9). Computers may be programmed to select a statistical sample of transactions or records, and thereby eliminate the cumbersome task of manual sample selection. Many of the general-purpose audit software languages provide simple user specifications that result in complex selection calculations. These computer-assisted techniques permit auditors to use statistical evaluation techniques that are virtually impossible on a manual basis.

Auditing Around or Through

There is a long-standing debate as to the merits of two techniques referred to as *auditing around the computer* and *auditing through the computer*. The differences of opinion, to a large extent, arise from imprecise definitions.

"Audit around" can be defined as the use of manual techniques to verify the accuracy of computer processing, without direct auditor involvement in the processing within the computer. Using this definition, audit around would include techniques such as observation of controls, system walk-through, documentation review, transaction tracing, review of processing results, and manual recalculation of processing results. "Audit through" requires auditor involvement in computer processing and may include techniques such as computer code review, the use of program logic flowcharting software, and processing of test data.

A third category of audit procedure, which could be called *automated audit around*, does not fit conveniently into either category. This procedure uses audit software—for parallel simulation, for selection and testing of transactions, or for reasonableness tests of transactions or balances—to detect theoretically impossible values that indicate control weaknesses or processing errors.

There is little to be gained by more precise definitions of audit around and audit through, since communication is more effective when specific audit techniques are identified and explained in the context of their planned use.

Selecting EDP Audit Techniques

The extent and availability of audit evidence frequently affects the audit approach and the selection of the appropriate EDP audit techniques. Certain techniques can only be used if an application or a control produces evidence that can be subjected to manual audit tests. This type of evidence includes documents that initiate automated transactions, documents that indicate that controls are effective, and transaction listings and computer reports that permit manual tracing and manual tests of processing. If this type of evidence is partially or totally unavailable, the auditor may have to test program processing or use the computer to test computer files that contain the results of processing. In practice it is unusual to find a system totally lacking in sources of evidence that can be manually audited. However, systems characterized by high transaction volumes, remote-terminal data entry, complex processing, and limited hard-copy reports may be difficult to audit exclusively by manual techniques.

COMPUTER ABUSE AND CATASTROPHE

General Concerns

Computer abuse includes fraud, embezzlement, theft of assets, invasion of privacy and malicious destruction of computer hardware, programs, or files. Computer catastrophes include natural disasters, like fire or flood, and the accidental destruction of computer programs or computer files due to operator error, hardware failures, or program errors.

Several factors related to EDP abuse and catastrophe deserve special attention:

1. EDP typically results in great concentrations of data and, correspondingly, great exposures.
2. Manipulation of a computer program or file is much less obvious than corresponding manipulations involving manual procedures and manual records.
3. Data processing professionals, frequently preoccupied with the technical aspects of EDP, may not appreciate the impact of potential EDP abuses or catastrophes.
4. Management outside the data processing organization may not understand or appreciate the risks related to the use of EDP.
5. As EDP becomes increasingly vital to operations, interruptions in service may cripple the overall organization.

The types and estimated frequencies of computer errors, abuse, and catastrophe are included in Figure 10.4. Estimates of the impact of abuse or catastrophe are, however, probably more important. The potential impact of abuse and catastrophe should be considered both for individual applications and for the entire data processing operation. For example, what is the probable impact of the accidental destruction of a payroll program or an accounts receivable file? What is the maximum dollar loss that may result from a theft or fraud related to a purchasing and payables application? What is the impact on profitability and service levels if the entire data center is destroyed by fire?

Controls related to destruction of hardware, programs, and files include conventional physical security controls (e.g., fire detectors) and general controls to prevent or correct the accidental destruction of programs and files (e.g., programmed label checks prior to all processing). Corrective controls typically include offsite storage of duplicate programs, files, and related operating procedures and a stand-by arrangement to use a second processing facility if the entire data center is destroyed.

Computer Fraud

Computer-related frauds generally receive dramatic attention whenever discovered; however, most organizations have not addressed these threats in a serious and sys-

Human Carelessness

Single record modified	10 times a day
Single record lost	once in 10 days
Wrong file used	once in 4 years
Wrong program used	once in 4 years
Entire file lost	once in 4 years
File damaged	once in 4 years

Hardware and Software Failures

Single records modified	once in 10 days
Single records lost	once in 100 days
Entire file lost	once in 4 years

Computer Abuse

Invasion of privacy	once in 100 days
Theft of data	once in 4 years
Embezzlement	once in 4 years
Industrial espionage	once in 4 years
Malicious destruction of files	once in 40 years

Acts of God

Fire	once in 40 years
Flood	once in 40 years

FIG. 10.4   Estimated Frequency of Various EDP Application Exposures
Source: Adapted from Martin, James. Security, Accuracy, and Privacy in Computer Systems. *Englewood Cliffs, N.J.: Prentice-Hall, Inc., 1973, pp. 12 and 13.* (The author cautions that the table values are only examples and would have to be evaluated anew for any specific application.)

tematized fashion. This lack of concern and action is usually based on assumptions that the odds of something happening are low, that the people involved are trustworthy, and that effective controls cost too much or are impossible to implement. There is some truth in all these statements. For example, available statistics indicate that losses related to fire, flood, and routine operational EDP errors far exceed those due to EDP-related fraud or theft, and that most EDP frauds that are discovered (many undoubtedly are not) are discovered by accident, not by controls designed to detect fraud.

Nevertheless, the use of computers frequently involves new and additional risks; and when EDP involves assets that can be manipulated or stolen, the possibility of fraud or theft cannot be ignored. Increased threats may, however, be offset by the increased levels of control that are possible in EDP systems and by techniques that actually use the computer to detect fraud.

The traditional reluctance to discuss computer-related frauds and to conduct aggressive programs of prevention and detection resulted from fears that such efforts might actually provide lessons in how to commit fraud. Recently, however, both popular and professional publications have discussed the details of specific cases. At this point it can safely be assumed that an active program of prevention and detection will not substantially add to the knowledge level of potential perpetrators. The entire issue, to some extent, may be irrelevant, since available statistics indicate that most acts of computer-related fraud and theft that have been uncovered were committed by first-time offenders who, as part of their routine duties, had or could acquire all the knowledge necessary to commit their fraudulent acts.

The computer may also process fraudulent records that result from a fraud or theft occurring exclusively outside the computer system. Although this situation is not really a computer-related fraud, controls within the computer system may detect this type of fraud.

Types of Fraud. In general terms, fraudulent activity has occurred in situations in which:

• The computer was used as an instrument to commit the act;
• The computer was used to conceal the act;
• The computer contributed to an environment that fostered and concealed the act; and
• Computer hardware, programs, or files were the object of the act.

Computer-related fraudulent acts might include, for example, theft of cash, negotiable securities, property, information, or computing resources; inflation of reported earnings or assets; or unauthorized reductions of financial obligations.

Representative Cases. Actual computer-related theft and fraud cases are summarized as follows:

• A computer operator copied, then sold, the customer name and address file.
• A programmer of one company penetrated a competitor's telecommunications system and stole a proprietary computer program.
• A bank programmer modified the daily overdraft report program to exclude his own account.
• An individual, not an employee of the company involved, penetrated the company's computerized inventory system, entered unauthorized orders for the delivery of equipment, then stole and sold the equipment.
• An EDP department employee inflated payroll totals, then forged checks equal to the inflated amount on blank check forms.
• A manager of a data center made unauthorized changes to a program, thereby issuing credits to his own account.
• A head teller, using an error correction routine from a computer terminal, manipulated hundreds of customer accounts; one of the techniques used was to reduce the amounts of large deposits so that cash could be withdrawn without detection.
• The management of a company inflated sales by creating unauthorized transactions that were then processed on a computer; the computer printouts, representing to a large extent fictitious transactions, were then used to shield the fraud.

In these cases, indeed in most known cases, collusion and high levels of EDP technical expertise were not involved.

Vulnerable Employment Positions. Computer abuse experts have tried without success to develop a personality profile that might be used to identify the potential perpetrator. However, it is becoming clear that persons in certain positions are more likely to be involved in computer abuse. Individuals who have committed acts of computer theft or fraud frequently occupied positions with the following characteristics:

• A degree of trust and, therefore, exclusion from routine supervision and review.
• The opportunity to understand the total scope of EDP and non-EDP, especially the overall structure of controls.
• The opportunity to initiate transactions, especially adjustments and corrections, without a second-party authorization or review.
• Involvement in the direct flow of a high volume of asset-related transactions.
• The opportunity to both initiate and conceal invalid and unauthorized transactions.
• The opportunity for unsupervised use of the computer.

Corporate Characteristics. Certain corporate characteristics also appear to be conducive to computer-related theft and fraud. For example:

• Senior management does not maintain high general standards of internal control.
• Record keeping is sloppy.
• Management outside the EDP department is not knowledgeable in EDP and EDP control.
• There are no EDP-qualified internal auditors.
• User departments are neither knowledgeable in EDP nor responsible for the accuracy and integrity of EDP related to their department.
• User-oriented application controls are weak.
• General controls within the EDP department are weak. ("Open shops," i.e., EDP departments with unrestricted access to the computer and to computer files, present an especially high risk.)
• The organization exhibits a high tolerance for computer errors, late processing, EDP reruns, and computer-related confusion and mystique.

Controls. A program to review and improve fraud and theft controls should consider two areas: (1) the general level of implementation of those controls known to prevent or detect computer irregularities; and (2) a comprehensive program of threat analysis to identify critical risk areas that should be subjected to a detailed analysis.

Controls that deserve special consideration in both general and specific reviews were identified in an analysis of the relationship between exposures and related preventive or detective controls (Blish, 1978). This analysis first considered the characteristics of 15 representative cases, then identified specific controls that might have prevented or detected the illegal acts. These controls, ranked by the

Percentage of cases	Controls that might have prevented or detected the activity
93	Source document authorization
80	Review by independent control group
66	Segregation of functions within EDP
66	Reconciliation of processing totals to input
66	Reconciliation of output to processing totals
60	Reconciliation of output to authorized users
53	Review of input for proper authorization
46	Control of document flow between departments
40	Run-to-run processing controls
40	Scan of output for reasonableness
40	Restricted access to files and programs
33	Programmed limit and reasonableness checks
33	Segregation between EDP and users
33	Internal audit review
26	Control over program changes
26	Hardware and operating system controls
26	Restricted access to documentation

FIG. 10.5   Controls Related to Computer Fraud and Theft
Source: Blish, Eugene. "Computer Abuse: A Practical Use of the AICPA Guide." EDPACS, September, 1978, pp. 6-12.

percentage of cases in which the control might have been effective, are included in Figure 10.5.

Industry Studies. Excellent information on the nature of actual EDP frauds is included in the AICPA *Report on the Study of EDP-Related Fraud in the Banking and Insurance Industries* (AICPA, 1984h). The report is an analysis of 85 EDP frauds in the banking industry and 34 frauds in the insurance industry. During the survey that produced this report, questionnaires were sent to 9,405 banks and 1,232 insurance companies. Over half the banks and two thirds of the insurance companies responded. Major findings are as follows:

• In almost all cases, the fraud occurred during normal processing.
• The type of computer system was not significant.
• Relatively few perpetrators used sophisticated techniques.
• Most frauds occurred in the input area.
• The range of perpetrators included most corporate positions.
• Rarely was an accomplice necessary.
• Only one third of the cases were detected by controls or routine internal or external audits.

The frequency of the methods, procedures, and positions involved, and the frequency of various sources of detection are included in Figure 10.6.

Table 1—Method Used

Transaction manipulation to:
Create original items	29%
Divert or capture items	19%
Force or divert rejects	12%

File maintenance changes to:
Nonfinancial fields	30%
Financial fields	1%
Direct file changes	6%
Other	3%

Table 2—Procedure

Prepared document improperly	44%
Unauthorized input or access	22%
Prepared EDP-media improperly	20%
Altered an authorized document	6%
Manipulated EDP-media	5%
Unauthorized program alteration	3%
Manipulated EDP output	1%

Table 3—Perpetrators

	Fraud under $100,000	Fraud over $100,000
Clerical	48%	2%
Managers and Supervisors	13%	9%
Data processors	9%	2%
Tellers	6%	1%
Other	8%	3%

Table 4—How Detected

Customer complaint or inquiry	24%
Accident, tip-off, unusual perpetrator activity	22%
Controls	18%
Routine audit	18%
Non-routine study	8%
Changes in operations, EDP, financial statements	6%
Unidentified	5%

FIG. 10.6   Tabulation (as percentages) of EDP-Related Fraud in the Banking and Insurance Businesses

Source: AICPA, 1984h. Report on the Study of EDP-Related Fraud in the Banking and Insurance Industries.

AUDIT IMPLICATIONS OF SYSTEM DEVELOPMENT AND MAINTENANCE

The development of computer applications begins with the definition of new user processing requirements and ends with a new computer system or application. Typically, the process only involves new application programs that run on an existing computer. However, certain types of new systems, such as a new telecommunications network, may involve new computer hardware as well.

System maintenance refers to changes to operational computer programs. Such changes may be necessary to add new program functions, modify existing functions, correct design or coding errors, or permit programs to operate on new computer hardware.

Auditor Concerns

The internal and external auditor share similar concerns related to control over both system development and maintenance. If the system development process is uncontrolled, the new programs may include routines that result in errors or irregularities. If system maintenance is uncontrolled, changes may accidentally modify previously correct routines or may introduce new routines that result in errors or irregularities. In addition, errors may result from inadequate control over conversion from an old to a new system or from the misunderstandings and confusion that frequently accompany the introduction of a new application.

The introduction of a new or modified application may require additional audit procedures or revisions to existing audit procedures. New systems descriptions may have to be developed and verified, new exposures and controls may have to be evaluated, new controls may have to be tested, and the degree of reliance on controls may change. If a new or substantially modified application is introduced other than at fiscal year-end, the independent auditor's review may have to include the features and controls of the old system, the conversion process, and the new system.

If computer program changes are frequent and uncontrolled, the auditor has no assurance that the findings of previous control reviews still apply to the most recent version of the application. In the extreme, the auditor may not know what version of the system was tested or what version is currently being used. Accordingly, the degree of control over maintenance may influence the auditor's approach and the selection of audit procedures.

System Development and Maintenance Processes

The system development process is similar to the process used to design and build a new automobile in that problems can occur either because of poor design or poor construction. In system development, poor application design (e.g., missing reports or control features) or developmental deficiencies (e.g., incorrect logic introduced by programmer error) may cause EDP problems. Phases in computer system development projects typically include:

1. Initial investigation to determine the nature of a proposed application,
2. Evaluation of technical and economic feasibililty,

3. Management review and a decision to continue,

4. Definition of user and technical processing requirements,

5. Definition of control requirements,

6. System design,

7. Development of technical EDP specifications,

8. Development of application program specifications (and perhaps prototyping),

9. Programming,

10. Program testing,

11. Development of user procedures,

12. User training, and

13. Conversion from the old to the new system.

Although the phases are generally similar, system development methodologies vary considerably among organizations and among project managers within the same organization. Phases are sometimes consolidated or eliminated, and the developmental effort may proceed in a very formal or informal manner.

Exposures and Controls

System Development. During system development, many things can go wrong. Required functions may be overlooked; the characteristics of required functions may be poorly communicated to the designer; or accounting, privacy, fraud, and disaster controls may be ignored or poorly designed. Even if system requirements and design are adequate, unauthorized features may be intentionally introduced while the system is being built; logic and computational errors may be accidentally introduced; and transactions and files may be lost or incorrectly processed during the conversion period. In addition, schedule dates may be missed and developmental cost estimates exceeded. If the new programs are obscure and poorly documented, they may be difficult to understand and expensive to maintain.

Figure 10.7 identifies major system development exposures and related major controls. Although many of these controls, such as project schedules and budgets, are conventional management controls, others, such as technical review for unauthorized codes, require a high degree of EDP technical expertise.

System Maintenance. In most respects, the phases, exposures, and controls in system maintenance are similar to those in system development. The inclusion of new or modified program functions may introduce processing errors, accidentally modify routines that were not to be changed, or bypass existing application controls. System maintenance activities also provide an opportunity for the deliberate circumvention of controls or the introduction of unauthorized processing routines.

If maintenance results in major application modifications, all the controls applicable to system development can be used to control system maintenance. If a specific maintenance effort is limited, applicable controls may only include a formal request for the change, a brief narrative description of the change, limited testing, limited technical review, and management's authorization to use the modified program for regular processing.

What Can Go Wrong / Controls	Design Errors and Omissions						Implementation Errors				Other Errors	
	User functions	Accounting controls	Privacy Controls	Fraud controls	Error correction controls	Recovery controls	Unauthorized changes	Unauthorized code	Coding errors	Start-up errors	Schedule errors	Cost estimate errors
Management Controls												
• Corporate steering committee	•	•	•	•	•	•					•	•
• Feasibility study	•										•	•
• Appropriate methodology	•	•	•	•	•	•	•		•	•	•	•
• Experienced project management	•	•	•	•	•	•	•	•	•	•	•	•
• Budget and schedules							•			•		•
• Periodic status reviews							•				•	•
• Change authorization procedure							•				•	•
Standards												
• Requirements standards	•	•	•	•	•	•					•	•
• Design standards	•	•	•	•	•	•					•	•
• Control standards		•	•	•	•	•					•	•
• Specification standards							•		•		•	•
• Documentation standards	•	•	•	•	•	•			•		•	•
• Programming standards							•	•	•			
Sign Offs												
• User requirements sign off	•	•	•	•	•	•					•	
• User design sign off	•	•	•	•	•	•					•	
• Auditor design sign off		•	•	•	•	•					•	
Ongoing Reviews												
• Periodic user review	•	•	•	•	•	•						
• Periodic auditor review		•	•	•	•	•						
• Periodic technical review			•	•	•	•	•	•	•			
Implementation Controls												
• System testing	•	•	•	•	•	•	•	•	•			
• Conversion plan										•		
• Conversion monitoring										•		
• Pilot or parallel operation	•	•	•	•	•	•	•		•	•		
• Post-implementation monitoring	•	•	•	•	•	•	•			•		

FIG. 10.7 System Development Exposures and Controls

PLANNING THE EDP PORTION OF THE AUDIT

Relationship of EDP to the Overall Audit

Auditing in an EDP environment frequently requires approaches and skills different from those for audits of entirely manual systems.

As more fully discussed in Chapter 7, the independent auditor's examination may be conducted in three phases.

In Phase I, the auditor gathers information and makes a series of assessments and determinations that will result in an audit plan. Specifically, the auditor

- Acquires a knowledge of the business to be audited;
- Appraises auditability;
- Establishes guidelines for materiality;
- Identifies material types of transactions;
- Assesses conditions that may require extension or modification of audit tests (i.e., related parties);
- Identifies the methods used to process significant accounting information, including whether a service center is used;
- Identifies potential sources of material errors;
- Identifies sources of audit evidence;
- Develops and verifies accounting system descriptions;
- Develops an initial understanding of internal accounting control; and
- Designs the audit approach and supporting audit procedures.

In Phase II, the auditor assesses the likelihood of material errors in the financial statements. The auditor may also test those controls identified in Phase I that appear to prevent or detect material errors. However, if controls appear weak or if the control-testing effort would exceed the expected reduction in Phase III effort, the auditor may proceed to Phase III without testing controls.

In Phase III, the auditor performs substantive procedures that lead to the issuance of the auditor's report. These procedures typically include analytical review of account balances, verification of key items, verification of account balances, a post-balance-sheet review, and a final review of the financial statements.

As recognized in SAS 48 (AU 311.09), the EDP aspects are an integral part of each phase of the overall audit and cannot be considered or performed independently. The overall audit approach and overall materiality guidelines determine the scope and extent of EDP-related procedures. To some degree, the overall audit approach is determined by the extent and complexity of EDP, the degree of control over EDP, and the ease with which EDP-related audit evidence may be obtained. EDP applications without good controls or readily available sources of audit evidence may, in extreme cases, raise questions of auditability. At best, poorly controlled applications will require more extensive audit procedures. In addition, client requests for EDP reviews beyond the scope of GAAS may affect the audit approach and the procedures to be performed.

Developing an Effective and Efficient Approach

Although coordinating and balancing procedures performed in the three audit phases is the key to an optimal audit approach, numerous factors in the EDP audit environment make this difficult. Many EDP applications are well controlled and relatively easy to audit, but certain situations require staff personnel with special technical skills and the use of technically complex audit procedures. The actual degree of audit complexity may not be immediately obvious, yet staff assignments and work plans must frequently be developed based on preliminary assessments of audit complexity. In addition, the trade-off between control testing and expected reductions in Phase III substantive procedures is frequently difficult to determine.

The EDP aspects the auditor would focus on in Phase I in determining the effect on the nature, timing, and extent of the auditor's work to be done are:

* The extent of computer processing in each significant accounting application;[1]
* Organizational considerations;
* The dollar amount of individual transactions and resulting balances;
* Normal error rates in the various processing phases;
* The susceptibility of assets to theft or fraud;
* The need for confidentiality or privacy;
* The potential for EDP-related business interruption;
* The probable impact of EDP interruptions on income and service levels;
* The stability of the EDP operations (e.g., the number of new or modified applications);
* The complexity of processing;
* Previous audit findings;
* Perceived competency of the EDP and user departments;
* Initial assessments of EDP controls; and
* The likelihood that computer-assisted audit techniques might be used.

The auditor is now able to determine the relative effect of EDP on the audit and whether additional study of the internal accounting control system is warranted. The specific client circumstances determine whether reliance is justified and efficient.

Once these factors and characteristics have been assessed, the initial phase of the evaluation of internal accounting control should begin. It should be designed to provide an understanding of the transaction flow and, for each significant accounting application, the basic structure of accounting controls. This preliminary understanding is necessary to achieve an effective audit whether or not the subsequent audit plan will place reliance on controls.

The initial understanding can be documented as either a brief narrative or an overview flowchart. Either method is suitable for demonstrating the basic flow of information through the system and the key controls within that system. This initial understanding allows the first-level decision to be addressed: whether more detailed reviews of internal accounting controls should be undertaken in areas where reliance

---

[1] "Significant accounting applications are those that relate to accounting information that can materially affect the financial statements the auditor is examining." (SAS 48, AU 311.09)

seems proper for audit efficiency, and if so, how the reviews should be structured. Even if it is decided not to place any reliance on controls, the initial understanding should be sufficient for the auditor to design effective substantive tests of transactions and account balance details.

For the portions of an accounting system that involve EDP, the review of significant EDP applications is part of the overall evaluation of internal control. The use of EDP typically results in more concentration of data and increased integration of processing. This may require new controls to deal with new risks resulting from loss of traditional segregation of duties. As the extent of human involvement declines, new controls may have to be built into the EDP portions of systems to maintain satisfactory levels of control.

In designing Phase II procedures, the auditor must consider the effort required to test controls relative to the expected reduction in Phase III procedures. In addition, the auditor should consider whether testing the results of computer processing might be better than testing controls. For example, the auditor might use generalized computer audit software to test transactions for invalid data, rather than test the controls to prevent the entry of invalid data.

In Phase III, the auditor should consider whether the use of the computer could make the audit more effective or economical. For example, the computer might be used for simple but time-consuming tasks such as footing files or for more complex tasks such as the recomputation of interest.

In all three phases, the auditor's appropriate level of EDP audit expertise must be considered. In certain situations, the degree of audit complexity will require the participation of auditors with more advanced EDP audit skills; however, in many situations, participation by auditors with knowledge of traditional manual procedures and less technically complex EDP audit procedures may be sufficient.

Performing Reviews of EDP Internal Controls

Until actual testing begins, any decision is preliminary; however, if EDP-related controls appear significant to the system of internal accounting control and reliance appears both warranted and efficient, an internal control review will be performed. During such an internal control review, the auditor typically performs the following steps:

1. Conducts an initial review of the application to determine the flow of transactions, the extent of EDP use, and the basic structure of internal accounting control.
2. Assesses the significance of internal accounting control within EDP in relation to the entire system of internal accounting control.
3. Conducts a review of general EDP controls to determine whether weak general controls might affect application controls, or whether environmental controls might complement the overall control of the application under review.
4. Completes the control review for the specific controls to be relied on, if reliance on application or general controls is planned.
5. Performs tests of controls, if controls still appear reliable.

6. Evaluates internal control, identifying errors and irregularities that could occur, controls that would prevent or detect these errors, and potential errors and irregularities not covered by existing controls.
7. Determines the effect of potential errors and EDP control strengths and weaknesses on the nature, timing and extent of subsequent audit procedures.

The initial review inquiries and observations (for example, Do there appear to be controls to prevent lost transactions?) typically result in yes-or-no findings. If the review continues into the completion phase, additional inquiries and observations seek specific information on controls and possible sources of audit evidence (for example, What are the specific features of the control procedures that prevent or detect lost transactions? What evidence will demonstrate that these controls are in use and effective?) The purpose of the initial phase is to understand the transaction flow and the extent of EDP use, and to determine if controls over EDP appear to be present. The purpose of the completion phase is to identify the control characteristics and related sources of evidence for specific controls in anticipation of control testing and reliance on specific tested controls.

During the initial phase of the review, the auditor gathers information through discussions with data center and user-department staff; through observations; or through the review of system documentation, flowcharts, job descriptions, organization charts, policy statements, operating procedures, or control procedures. The accuracy of this information is typically verified by tracing the flow of a limited number of sample transactions through both the EDP and non-EDP segments of an application. This tracing procedure is often called a *system walk-through*. During the completion phase of the review, the auditor expands the extent of the discussions and observations, and specifically observes controls that might be tested and relied on.

Both the initial and completion phases of an EDP application control review occur in Phase I of the overall audit process. In Phase II, the auditor may or may not perform tests of controls over EDP. During Phase II the auditor may also use audit software or manual techniques to test transactions for evidence of control weaknesses. In Phase III, EDP-related audit procedures shift from control evaluation to the use of the computer as an audit tool. For example, audit software may be used to analyze the accounts receivable file and to select items for confirmation.

Factors That Affect Audit Complexity

Understanding EDP audit complexity and the related levels of skill and effort required to accomplish various EDP audit procedures is critical to the planning process. It is usually not practical to classify EDP audit procedure complexity only in terms of EDP complexity, such as computer size or type of processing. Using this classification approach, an on-line application that operates on a large computer would always be a complex audit situation, but this may not be true. The degree of audit complexity is influenced by many factors, discussed in the following subsections.

EDP complexity. If an application involves complex telecommunications hardware and software, a very large computer and complex data-base software, an auditor with advanced EDP skills may be required just to understand and verify transaction flow and the content of data files.

Application complexity. If applications involve multiple transaction types, complex calculations, and updates using master files, significant effort may be required to understand the accounting implications of the application.

Decentralization. If source data originate at a variety of remote locations, the auditor is concerned that all data arrive at the processing location. If data conversion is performed at remote locations, the review of conversion procedures and related source documents may be difficult and time-consuming. If processing occurs at multiple locations, the auditor must consider whether the processing and controls are identical.

Nature of application controls. If an application is characterized by strong user-oriented application controls, control testing and reliance is typically not technically difficult. For example, in a telecommunications application, lost transactions may be prevented by complex hardware and software controls that are difficult to understand and test. However, lost transactions may be detected by simple user-department control totals that are easy to understand and test.

Strength of general EDP controls. Even if general EDP controls are excellent, auditors typically will not rely exclusively on them. However, if they are weak, auditors must consider whether they reduce the effectiveness of otherwise strong application controls.

Nature of compensating controls. The influence of compensating controls varies considerably. Controls such as supervision and rotation of duties have a positive but general effect. Certain other compensating controls, such as detailed internal audit reviews, can be used to control more specific exposures.

Availability of audit evidence. An EDP application can usually be audited by traditional manual procedures if the application is characterized by transaction listings, detailed reports, and documented user-oriented controls. However, if this type of audit evidence is not available, technically complex procedures may be required.

Stability. If there are no new EDP applications and old applications have not been modified, audit procedures used in prior years are probably still effective. However, in a dynamic EDP environment, auditors must always review the extent of change; and they may also have to review system development and maintenance controls, system conversion controls, and, possibly, new applications while they are still under development.

Audit objectives. Specific audit objectives can have a substantial impact on overall audit effort. For example, it is easier to identify and test controls that detect the loss of a transaction than those that should prevent the processing of an unauthorized transaction.

Applications Processed by Computer Service Centers

Many organizations use independent computer service centers to process their accounting data. These service centers may be other organizations with surplus computing capacity, subsidiaries of banks, or organizations exclusively devoted to this type of activity.

Neither the nature of EDP nor how the auditor audits is changed if an organization uses a service center. The same EDP errors may occur, and the same types of controls may be used to prevent, detect, and correct errors. The auditor must develop the same level of understanding of the processing, and he has the same option to rely or not rely on EDP controls.

There are, however, practical differences. Generally, the computer user has less influence over the extent of EDP controls to be employed. If a particular application is designed specifically for the user, the user can and should insist on controls that will address all significant application exposures. Frequently, however, users are only offered existing application packages and do not have the option to add controls. This does not, of course, preclude the implementation of user-oriented controls such as system balancing and reasonableness reviews of processing results. In either case, the user typically cannot influence the degree or type of general controls used within the data center.

Use of a computer service center does not change the independent auditor's responsibilities (AU 311.09). Consequently, the auditor must understand the flow of transactions, the extent of EDP use, and the basic structure of accounting control. The appropriate extent of the auditor's review of processing and controls depends upon application complexity and the auditor's intention to rely or not rely on controls. In certain cases, an extensive review of service center processing and controls may be required. In most cases, however, processing is not complex, and the auditor does not need to place heavy reliance on service center controls; therefore, extensive reviews at the service center are typically not performed.

When a service center processes applications for many different users, it is inconvenient and expensive for every user's auditor to conduct reviews at the data center. In this situation, the service center may retain an independent auditor to review the service center or specific applications and to issue a report that includes the scope and conclusions of this review. This type of review is frequently called a *third-party review*. The requirements for conducting and using third-party reviews are included in the AICPA Audit and Accounting Guide, *Audits of Service-Center-Produced Records* (1987). When auditors are conducting a regular audit for a client who uses a service center and a third-party audit report is available, the auditors must decide whether the contents of the third-party report complement their intended audit approach and to what extent they can rely on the third-party audit report.

Specifically, SAS 44 Special-Purpose Reports on Internal Control states:

> When a service organization records transactions and provides related data processing services for a client organization, the user auditor should identify significant classes of transactions that are processed by the service organization and obtain an understanding of the flow of transactions through the entire accounting systems including the portion maintained by the service organization. (AU324.08)

Appendix 10A APPLICATION CONTROL EVALUATION TABLES

		APPLICATION CAUSES OF EXPOSURES																								
		INPUT							PROCESSING									OUTPUT						OTHER		
PREVENTION CONTROLS	REFERENCE	LOST	DUPLICATED	INACCURATE	MISSING DATA	TRANSACTIONS NEVER RECORDED	BLANKET AUTHORIZE	INITIATED INTERNALLY	WRONG FILE	WRONG RECORD	INCOMPLETE	INCORRECT	UNTIMELY	INAPPROPRIATE	FILE LOST	PROGRAM LOST	PEOPLE LOST	IMPROPERLY DISTRIBUTED	LATE OR LOST	ERRONEOUS BUT PLAUSIBLE	OBVIOUSLY ERRONEOUS	EXCESSIVE ERROR CORRECTION	UNSUPPORTABLE	SHADOW SYSTEM	UNLIMITED ACCESS	MANAGEMENT OVERRIDE
Definition of responsibilities		1	2	2	2	2	2	2	1	1	2	2	2	1	1	1	1	1	2	1	1	1	2	2	2	
Reliability of personnel		1	1	1	1	1			1	1	2	2	2	1	2	1	2	2	1	1	2	2	2	2	2	1
Training		1	1	1	2	2			1	1	2	2	2	2	1	1		2	1	2	2	2	2	2		1
Competence		1	1	1	2	2			2	1	1	2	2	2	1	1	1	2	1	2	2	2	2	1	2	1
Mechanization		2	2			1		3	1	2	2	2	3	2						1	1	2	1		1	2
Segregation of duties									1							1		1		1	1	1		1	2	2
Rotation of duties																									2	
Standardization		1	2	1	2				1	1	2	2	1	1	1	1		2	2		1	1		2		1
Authorization		1	2	1	1	2			1	1	1			2	2	2		1	1	1	2	1	1	1	2	1
Secure custody		2							2						2	2		2	1				1		3	
Dual custody		1							2						2	2		2	1				1		3	
Forms design				2	2	1																	1			
Prenumbered		2	2								2	2														
Preprinted				2	2							2	2									1				
Simultaneous preparation		2										2	2									1				
Turnaround document			3	2	2	3						2	2													
Drum card				2	1																					
Endorsement		2									2	2		2												
Cancellation			2																							
Documentation		2		2		2		2	2			1	1	2	2	2		2	2	1	2	2	3	1		2
Exception input											2															
Default option											2															
Passwords									1	1				2											3	
EXPOSURES																										
Erroneous record keeping		3	3	3	3	3	2	2	3	3	3	3	3	3	3		2	2	2	3	2	2	1	1	1	1
Unacceptable accounting							2	2				2	2	3			2			2			2			1
Business interruption		1	1	1	1		1				1	1	1	1	2	2	2	2	2	2	1	2	1		2	1
Erroneous management decisions		2	2	2	2	2	1	1	2	1	2	2	2	2	2	2	2	2	2	3	1	2	1	1		1
Fraud			1	1	1	1	1	1		1	1	1		1			1	2	1	1	1	1	2	1	2	1
Statutory sanctions		2		1	1	1	1			1	1	1	1	1	1		1	1	1	1	1	1	3		1	1
Excessive costs/deficient revenues		2	2	2	2			1	2	2	2	2	1	2	2	3	3	2	2	2	2	3		3	1	1
Loss or destruction of assets							1	1	2	2		2		2	2		1	1	1						2	1
Competitive disadvantage		1	1	1	1	1				1	1	1	1	1	1	1	1	1	1	1	1	1			1	1

RELIANCE ON CONTROLS
3 — Reliably controls applicable cause
2 — Controls cause but should be accompanied by additional controls
1 — Useful but not especially effective
Blank — No significant contribution

(Exposures)
3 — Very likely to occur
2 — Likely to occur
1 — May occur
Blank — Generally little effect

Warning: Reliance and impact relationships must be tailored to individual circumstances.

© Touche Ross & Co.

Page 1

APPLICATION CAUSES OF EXPOSURES

RELIANCE ON CONTROLS
3 — Reliably controls applicable cause
2 — Controls cause but should be accompanied by additional controls
1 — Useful but not especially effective
Blank — No significant contribution

DETECTION CONTROLS	REFERENCE	LOST	DUPLICATED	INACCURATE	MISSING DATA	NEVER RECORDED	BLANKET AUTHORIZE	INITIATED INTERNALLY	WRONG FILE	WRONG RECORD	INCOMPLETE	INCORRECT	UNTIMELY	INAPPROPRIATE	FILE LOST	PROGRAM LOST	PEOPLE LOST	IMPROPERLY DISTRIBUTED	LATE OR LOST	ERRONEOUS BUT PLAUSIBLE	OBVIOUSLY ERRONEOUS	EXCESSIVE ERROR CORRECTION	UNSUPPORTABLE	SHADOW SYSTEM	UNLIMITED ACCESS	MANAGEMENT OVERRIDE
Anticipation		3				3					3			2	2	2	3	3							
Transmittal document		2	2	2*					2		2	2	1		3			2							
Batch serial numbers		3	3	2					2	1		1			2										
Control register		2	2	2	2				2	2	2	2		1				2							
Amount control totals		3	3	2	2				3	3	3	2		2											
Document control count		3	3						2	2	2	1													
Line control count		3	3	2					2	2	2	2		2											
Hash totals		3	3	2					3	2	2	2		2											
Batch totals		3	3						3	2	1	1		2											
Batch balancing		3	1	1					2		2	2		1				2							
Visual verification		2	2	1	2	2								2	1										
Sequence check				2																					
Overflow check				1																					
Format check				2	2				2		2	2		2											
Completeness check									2	1	2	2	1						1	3					
Check digit			2	3					2	2	2	2		2											
Reasonableness		1		2	2			2	2	2	2	2	1	2				1		2					
Limit check				2				2	1		2		1	2						2	2				
Validity check				2	2				1		2			2				2		2	2				
Readback		2		3		2			2					2	1			2							
Dating			1										2						1						
Expiration			2		2								2												
Keystroke verification				2	2	2	2		2					2				2							
Approval		2	1	2	2		2		3	2	3	2	1	2				2	2		2	3	2	3	1
Run-to-run totals		3	3	3	3	3	2	2	3	3	3	3	3	3	3	3	2	2	2		3	2	2	3	1

EXPOSURES

EXPOSURES	LOST	DUPLICATED	INACCURATE	MISSING DATA	NEVER RECORDED	BLANKET AUTHORIZE	INITIATED INTERNALLY	WRONG FILE	WRONG RECORD	INCOMPLETE	INCORRECT	UNTIMELY	INAPPROPRIATE	FILE LOST	PROGRAM LOST	PEOPLE LOST	IMPROPERLY DISTRIBUTED	LATE OR LOST	ERRONEOUS BUT PLAUSIBLE	OBVIOUSLY ERRONEOUS	EXCESSIVE ERROR CORRECTION	UNSUPPORTABLE	SHADOW SYSTEM	UNLIMITED ACCESS	MANAGEMENT OVERRIDE
Erroneous record keeping	3	3	3	3	3	2	2	3	3	3	3	3	3	3	2	2	2	2	3	3	2	3	2	3	1
Unacceptable accounting	1	1	1	1	2	2	2	3	2	3	2	2	3	3	2	2	2	2	2	2	2	2	1	1	1
Business interruption	2	1	1	1	2	1	1	2	1	1	1	1	2	2	2	2	2	2	3	1	2	2	1	2	1
Erroneous management decisions	2	2	2	2	2	1	1	2	2	2	2	2	2	2	2	2	2	2	3	1	1	1	1	1	1
Fraud	2	1	1	1	1	1	1	2	1	1	1	1	1	1	1	1	1	1	1	1	1	2	1	2	1
Statutory sanctions	1	1	1	1	1	1	1	2	2	2	2	1	2	2	2	3	2	2	1	1	1	3	1	2	1
Excessive costs/deficient revenues	2	2	2	2	2	1	1	2	2	2	2	1	2	2	2	2	2	2	2	2	3	2	3	2	1
Loss or destruction of assets	2	2	2	2	2	1	1	2	2	2	2	2	2	2	2	2	2	1	1	1	1	2	3	1	1
Competitive disadvantage	1	1	1	1	1	1	1	2	1	1	1	1	1	1	1	1	1	1	1	1	1	1	2	1	1

IMPACT OF CAUSES
3 — Very likely to occur
2 — Likely to occur
1 — May occur
Blank — Generally little effect

Warning: Reliance and impact relationships must be tailored to individual circumstances.

© Touche Ross & Co.

Page 2

APPLICATION CAUSES OF EXPOSURES

RELIANCE ON CONTROLS
3 — Reliably controls applicable cause
2 — Controls cause but should be accompanied by additional controls
1 — Useful but not especially effective
Blank — No significant contribution

EXPOSURES
- Erroneous record keeping
- Unacceptable accounting
- Business interruption
- Erroneous management decisions
- Fraud
- Statutory sanctions
- Excessive costs/deficient revenues
- Loss or destruction of assets
- Competitive disadvantage

	INPUT							PROCESSING										OUTPUT					OTHER		
REFERENCE	LOST	DUPLICATED	INACCURATE	MISSING DATA	NEVER RECORDED	BLANKET AUTHORIZE	INITIATED INTERNALLY	WRONG FILE	WRONG RECORD	INCOMPLETE	INCORRECT	UNTIMELY	INAPPROPRIATE	FILE LOST	PROGRAM LOST	PEOPLE LOST	IMPROPERLY DISTRIBUTED	LATE OR LOST	ERRONEOUS BUT PLAUSIBLE	OBVIOUSLY ERRONEOUS	EXCESSIVE ERROR CORRECTION	UNSUPPORTABLE	SHADOW SYSTEM	UNLIMITED ACCESS	MANGEMENT OVERRIDE
DETECTION CONTROLS (continued)																									
Balancing	2	2	2	1				3	3	3	2								2	3		2			1
Reconciliation	2	2	2	2	2			3	3	3	3		1									1			
Aging	2	2	1	2	2					2	2		1								2				
Suspense file	2	2								2	2	2	1								2				
Suspense account	2		3		2			3	2	2	2	2	1									1			
Matching	3	3	3	2					2	2	2	2	1									2			
Clearing account	2	2	2	2	1			3	3	2	2	2													
Tickler file	2	2										2	1												
Periodic audit							3	3	2	2	1	2	2	2	2	2	2	2	2	3		3	2	3	1
Redundant process										3	1		2	2	2		2				3				
Summary process			2	2	2	2							2	2	2		2								
Label	1	1	2					2		3				2										1	
Trailer record	2	2	1	1				3		3				2											

CORRECTION CONTROLS

	INPUT							PROCESSING										OUTPUT					OTHER		
REFERENCE	LOST	DUPLICATED	INACCURATE	MISSING DATA	NEVER RECORDED	BLANKET AUTHORIZE	INITIATED INTERNALLY	WRONG FILE	WRONG RECORD	INCOMPLETE	INCORRECT	UNTIMELY	INAPPROPRIATE	FILE LOST	PROGRAM LOST	PEOPLE LOST	IMPROPERLY DISTRIBUTED	LATE OR LOST	ERRONEOUS BUT PLAUSIBLE	OBVIOUSLY ERRONEOUS	EXCESSIVE ERROR CORRECTION	UNSUPPORTABLE	SHADOW SYSTEM	UNLIMITED ACCESS	MANGEMENT OVERRIDE
Discrepancy reports	2	2	3	2	2		2	3	3	3	3	3	2	3	3	3	2	3	3	2		2			1
Transaction trail		3	3	2			2		3	2	3	2	2	2	3	2	2	2	3	2		2		1	1
Error source statistics	2	2	2	2	2		1	2	2	2	2		2	2	2	2	2	2	2	1	3	2		2	1
Automated error correction			2	2						1			2					2	3	1	3	1	1		
Upstream resubmission		1	2		1		1	2		2		1	2	2	2	2	1	2	2	1		3	1	2	
Backup and recovery	3	2						3	2	1	1	1	1	3	3	2	1	3	2	2		1	3	1	1

EXPOSURES

3 — Very likely to occur
2 — Likely to occur
1 — May occur
Blank — Generally little effect

Warning: Reliance and impact relationships must be tailored to individual circumstances.

Page 3

Explanation of Application Controls

Preventive controls	Explanations
Definition of Responsibilities	Descriptions of tasks for each job function within an information processing system that indicate clear beginning and termination points for each job function and cover the relationship of job functions to each other.
Reliability of Personnel	Personnel performing the processing can be relied on to treat data in a consistent manner.
Training	Personnel are provided explicit instructions and tested for their understanding before being assigned new duties.
Competence of Personnel	Persons assigned to processing or supervisory roles within information systems have the technical knowledge necessary to perform their functions.
Mechanization	Consistency is provided by mechanical or electronic processing.
Segregation of Duties	Responsibility for custody and accountability for handling and processing of data are separated.
Rotation of Duties	Jobs assigned to people are rotated periodically at irregularly scheduled times, if possible, for key processing functions.
Standardization	Uniform, structured, and consistent procedures are developed for all processing.
Authorization	Limits the initiation of a transaction or performance of a process to the selected individuals.
Secure Custody	Information assets are provided security similar to tangible assets such as cash, negotiable securities, and so forth.
Dual Custody	Two independent, simultaneous actions or conditions are required before processing is permitted.
Forms Design	Forms are self-explanatory, understandable, concise, and gather all necessary information with a minimum of effort.
Prenumbered Forms	Sequential numbers on individual forms printed in advance so as to allow subsequent detection of loss or misplacement.
Preprinted Forms	Fixed elements of information are entered on forms in advance and sometimes in a format that permits direct machine processing so as to prevent errors in entry of repetitive data.
Simultaneous Preparation	The one-time recording of a transaction for all further processing, using multiple-copies, as appropriate, to prevent transcription errors.
Turnaround Document	A computer-produced document that is intended for resubmission into the system.
Drum Card	Automatic spacing and format shifting of data fields on a keypunch machine.
Endorsement	The marking of a form or document so as to direct or restrict its further use in processing.
Cancellation	Identifies transaction documents to prevent further or repeated use after they have performed their function.
Documentation	Written records for the purpose of providing communication.
Exception Input	Internally initiated processing in a predefined manner unless specifically input transactions are received that specify processing with different values or in a different manner.
Default Option	The automatic utilization of a predefined value in situations where input transactions have certain values left blank.
Passwords	The authorization to allow access to data or processes by providing a signal or "password" known only to authorized individuals.

Detective controls	Explanations
Anticipation	The expectation of a given transaction or event at a particular time.
Transmittal Document	The medium for communicating control totals over movement of data, particularly from source to processing point or between processing points.
Batch Serial Numbers	Batches of transaction documents are numbered consecutively and accounted for.
Control Register	A log or register indicating the disposition and control values of batches of transactions.
Amount Control Total	Totals of homogeneous amounts for a group of transactions or records, usually dollars or quantities.
Document Control Count	A count of the number of individual documents.
Line Control Count	A count of the individual line items on one or more documents.
Hash Total	A meaningless, but useful, total developed from the accumulated numerical amounts of nonmonetary information.
Batch Totals	Any type of control total or count applied to a specific number of transaction documents or to the transaction documents that arrive within a specific period of time.
Batch Balancing	A comparison of the items or documents actually processed against a predetermined control total.
Visual Verification	The visual scanning of documents for general reasonableness and propriety.
Sequence Checking	A verification of the alphanumeric sequence of the "key" field in items to be processed.
Overflow Checks	A limit check based on the capacity of a memory or file area to accept data.
Format Checks	Determination that data are entered in the proper mode — numeric or alphanumeric — within designated fields of information.
Completeness Check	A test that data entries are made in fields that cannot be processed in a blank state.
Check Digit	One digit, usually the last, of an identifying field is a mathematical function of all of the other digits in the field. This value can be calculated from the other digits in the field and compared with the check digit to verify validity of the whole field.
Reasonableness	Tests applied to various fields of data through comparison with other information available within the transaction or master records.
Limit Check	Tests of specified amount fields against stipulated high or low limits of acceptability. When both high and low values are used, the test may be called a "range check."
Validity Check	The characters in a coded field are either matched to an acceptable set of values in a table or examined for a defined pattern or format, legitimate subcodes, or character values, using logic and arithmetic rather than tables.
Read Back	Immediate return of input information to the sender for comparison and approval.
Dating	The recording of calendar dates for purposes of later comparison or expiration testing.
Expiration	A limit check based on a comparison of current date with the date recorded on a transaction, record, or file.

Detective controls	Explanations
Keystroke Verification	The redundant entry of data into keyboards so as to verify the accuracy of a prior entry. Differences between the data previously recorded and the data entered in verification will cause a mechanical signal.
Approval	The acceptance of a transaction for processing after it has been initiated.
Run-to-Run Totals	The utilization of output control totals resulting from one process as input control totals over subsequent processing. The control totals are used as links in a chain to tie one process to another in a sequence of processes or one cycle to another over a period of time.
Balancing	A test for equality between the values of two equivalent sets of items or one set of items and a control total. Any difference indicates an error.
Reconciliation	An identification and analysis of differences between the values contained in two substantially identical files or between a detail file and a control total. Errors are identified according to the nature of the reconciling items rather than the existence of a difference between the balances.
Aging	Identification of unprocessed or retained items in files according to their date, usually transaction date. The aging classifies items according to various ranges of dates.
Suspense File	A file containing unprocessed or partially processed items awaiting further action.
Suspense Account	A control total for items awaiting further processing.
Matching	Matching of items from the processing stream of an application with others developed independently so as to identify items unprocessed through either of the parallel systems.
Clearing Account	An amount that results from the processing of independent items of equivalent value. Net control value should equal zero.
Tickler File	A control file consisting of items sequenced by age for follow-up purposes. Such files are usually manual.
Periodic Audit	A verification of a file or a phase of processing intended to check for problems and encourage future compliance with control procedures.
Redundant Processing	A repetition of processing and an accompanying comparison of individual results for equality.
Summary Processing	A redundant process using a summarized amount. This is compared for equality with a control total from the processing of the detailed items.
Label	The external or internal identification of transaction batches or files according to source, application, date, or other identifying characteristics.
Trailer Record	A record providing a control total for comparison with accumulated counts or values of records processed.
Discrepancy Reports	A listing of items that have violated some detective control and require further investigation.
Transaction Trail	The availability of a manual or machine-readable means for tracing the status and contents of an individual transaction record backward or forward, among output, processing, and source.
Error-Source Statistics	Accumulation of information on type of error and origin. This is used to determine the nature of remedial training needed to reduce the number of errors.
Automated Error Correction	Automatic error correction of transactions or records which violate a detective control.
Upstream Resubmission	The resubmission of corrected error transactions so that they pass through all or more of the detective controls than are exercised over normal transactions (e.g., before input editing).
Backup and Recovery	The ability to recreate current master files using appropriate prior master records and transactions.

Appendix 10B   IPF CONTROL EVALUATION TABLES

RELIANCE ON CONTROLS
3 — Reliably controls applicable cause
2 — Controls cause but should be accompanied by additional controls
1 — Useful but not especially effective
Blank — No significant contribution

EXPOSURES
Erroneous record keeping
Unacceptable accounting
Business interruption
Erroneous management decisions
Fraud
Statutory sanctions
Excessive costs
Loss or destruction of assets
Competitive disadvantage

IMPACT OF CAUSES
3 — Very likely to occur
2 — Likely to occur
1 — May occur
Blank — Generally little effect

CAUSES OF IPF EXPOSURES

PREVENTION CONTROLS	Data Entry	Console Entry	Wrong File or Program	File Damaged	Interrupt Operation	Loss of Data	Logic Error	Theft	Embezzlement	Fraud	Espionage	Invasion of Privacy	Maliciousness	Mischievousness	Fire	Water	Wind	Civil Disorder
Definition of duties	1	1	1					1	1		1	2						
Segregation of duties	2	2	2	2				2	2	2	2	2						
Reliable personnel	2	2	1	1											1	1		
Competent personnel	2	2							2		2				1			
Job rotation			1	1				1			1	1			1			
Housekeeping		1			2	2	3						1	2				
Equipment maintenance					1	1	1				1	1	1					3
Air conditioning			2															
Scheduling								1	2	2	2	2	2	2				2
Limited physical access		2		1				1	2	2	2	2	2	2	2	2		
Restricted knowledge		2					2	2	2	2	2	1	1					
File custodian		2		1		1									2	2		1
Physical security		2					1	2			1	1	1		2	1		
External labels	1							1	1	1	1	1	1	1		1	1	
Internal labels	2				1	1									1	1	2	1
Protect rings	2			1											1	1	3	1
Disk enable	2											2	1	1				
Containerized operations				2			3	2	2	2	2	2	1	1	2	3	3	2
Training	2	2	2			2		1			2		2	1	2	3	2	1
Authorization		1	1		3	2	3	1	3	3		2	3	1	3	3	3	
Manufacturer design	2		1	2	2	2		2	3		2		2	1	2	2	2	2
Physical structure	1		2	2	2	2	2	2	3	2	1		3	1	3	3	2	3
Physical location	2	2	2	2	1	2	1	2	3	2	2	1	1	1	2	2	2	2

Warning: Reliance and impact relationships must be tailored to individual circumstances.   Page 1

© Touche Ross & Co.

CAUSES OF IPF EXPOSURES

RELIANCE ON CONTROLS
3 — Reliably controls applicable cause
2 — Controls cause but should be accompanied by additional controls
1 — Useful but not especially effective
Blank — No significant contribution

EXPOSURES
Erroneous record keeping
Unacceptable accounting
Business interruption
Erroneous management decisions
Fraud
Statutory sanctions
Excessive costs
Loss or destruction of assets
Competitive disadvantage

IMPACT OF CAUSES
3 — Very likely to occur
2 — Likely to occur
1 — May occur
Blank — Generally little effect

	HUMAN ERRORS				HARDWARE/SOFTWARE FAILURES			COMPUTER ABUSE							CATASTROPHE			
REFERENCE	DATA ENTRY	CONSOLE ENTRY	WRONG FILE OR PROGRAM	FILE DAMAGED	INTERRUPT OPERATION	LOSS OF DATA	LOGIC ERROR	THEFT	EMBEZZLEMENT	FRAUD	ESPIONAGE	INVASION OF PRIVACY	MALICIOUSNESS	MISCHIEVOUSNESS	FIRE	WATER	WIND	CIVIL DISORDER
DETECTION CONTROLS																		
Supervision	2	2	2	2				2	2	2	1	1	2	2				
Budgets	2	2	1					2		2	1		2	1				
Management reporting	2	2	2	2	1	2			1	1		2	1	1				
Operator logs				2	1	2	1											
Console logs (job journal)	1	2	2		2	1	2	1	2	1	2	2	2	2				
Library logs	2	2	2	2		2	1	1	1	1	1		1	1				
Control logs	2	2	3	2														
Keystroke verification	2		1															
Hardware checks	1	2	2	2	1	1												
Operating system checks	1	1	1	2	2	1	2	1										
Scan output	1							1										
Fire detectors															3			
Application controls	3	2	3	2		3	2	2	2	2			2	2	2	2	2	2
CORRECTION CONTROLS																		
Recovery plan			2	2	2	2	1	1		2			2	2	2	2	2	2
File histories				1	1	1	1	1					2	2				
Error statistics	2	1		1				1	2	2			2	2	2			
Fire extinguishers															2			
On-premises backup	2	3	3	3	2	3		2			1		2	2	3	3	3	3
Off-premises backup								2	2	2		1	2	2	2	2	2	2
Discharge personnel	1							2	2	2			2	1				
Insurance					2										3	3	3	3
Uninterruptable power	2				1	2	1	1					1	1		2	2	2

Warning: Reliance and impact relationships must be tailored to individual circumstances.
© Touche Ross & Co.

Explanation of IPF Controls

Preventive controls	Explanations
Definition of Duties	Description of tasks of each job function identifying the responsibilities, functions and relationships of all duties.
Segregation of Duties	Assignment of job responsibilities designed to separate and avoid incompatible duties and conflicts of interest.
Reliable Personnel	Personnel performing their assigned duties can be relied on to complete their daily tasks in a consistent quality manner.
Competent Personnel	Personnel assigned to operate the computer and control the processing have the technical knowledge necessary to perform their functions.
Job Rotation	Jobs assigned to people are rotated periodically at irregular intervals, if possible, for the processing of sensitive systems.
Housekeeping	Keeping the production areas of a data center neat, tidy, and organized to minimize hazards and the likelihood of confusion.
Equipment Maintenance	Computer hardware is kept in workable condition by qualified personnel on a regular (preventive) and as required (remedial) basis.
Air-Conditioning	The air in the computer room is maintained within limited temperature and humidity ranges as recommended by the computer manufacturer.
Scheduling	Jobs to be run on the computer are identified and placed on a log in priority order.
Limited Physical Access	Avenues of access to the computer room and file library are limited by design and by security measures that prevent unauthorized access.
Restricted Knowledge	Only qualified personnel within the technical data center functions possess knowledge on a need to know basis of run procedure, security, file access, and so forth.
File Custody	Computer files are maintained in a library and accounted for when they are not scheduled for processing.
Physical Security	The security of the building is sufficient to prevent environmental events that could occur in that location.
External Labels	Visual identification of a file includes file number, volume number, file name, creation date, purge date, and storage location.
Internal Labels	The external label information is also kept on the electronic media itself to be programmatically checked and verified by the application program.
Protect Rings	Write rings are placed into tapes so that the tape drive can copy information onto the tape. Without the ring, the hardware is prohibited by design from the writing function.
Disk Enable	A device on some disk drives that inhibits the write function.
Containerized Operations	The computer room is bounded by sturdy and resistant walls that limit the spread of fire, access, and so forth.
Training	Personnel are provided explicit instructions and tested for their understanding before being assigned the responsibilities of their positions.
Authorization	Only those persons with a need to know are permitted physical access, file access, or knowledge about operation activities.
Manufacturer Design	Manufacturer controls such as equipment testing that produce a reliable product.
Physical Structure	The computer room and library areas are constucted of durable quality in keeping with the value of the equipment and data that are being protected.
Physical Location	The data center is situated in a geographical location to minimize natural disasters.

Detective controls	Explanations
Supervision	Responsibilities of supervising the computer operations area include approving the schedules, monitoring daily operations, observing the activities of initiating and shutting down the equipment, reviewing the daily operations reports (manual and automated), and following up on all problem areas until resolved.
Budgets	Establishment of cost accountabilities for the production aspects of a data center.
Management Reporting	Reporting of accomplishments, activity completed, projected tasks, and outstanding problems to each level of the organizational structure.
Operator Logs	Computer operators complete a log indicating the programs that have been run and any abnormal occurrences.
Console Log	A log of computer console messages is maintained in sequential order for review and analysis.
Library Logs	A recording of data file information includes present location of file, file name, volume identification, date created, audit trail to prior data file version, date available for scratching, and serial number.
Control Logs	The input/output control clerk records all items given to and received from the production area. Also control logs state the anticipated and received batches of input from user areas.
Keystroke Verification	A second keypunch operation done by a separate person that checks the keypunched record against the keyed information.
Hardware Checks	Hardware features that identify abnormal occurrences to the operator.
Operating System Checks	System software features that identify abnormal occurrences to the operator.
Scan Output	Visual review of output to catch any gross error in form or content.
Fire Detectors	Devices that provide early recognition of smoke, fire, or heat.
Application Controls	A multitude of control techniques that are specifically incorporated into individual application systems to prevent or detect and correct IPF causes of exposure.
Recovery Plan	A contingency plan that outlines the fallback processing at various levels of disaster. The plan should be formal, modular, and tested.
File Histories	A record of uses of tape files and cleanings to schedule recleaning and certification.
Error Statistics	Records classifying detected errors according to their origin, usually an individual or equipment item for performance measurement.
Fire Extinguishers	Devices to extinguish fire.
On-Premises Backup	File backup (disc, tape, or cards) that is immediately available to reconstruct a file if a data file is unusable.
Off-Premises Backup	File backup (usually tape) that could produce current or near-current data files without using the files available in the computer room.
Discharge Personnel	Removal of a person from his or her assigned duties.
Insurance	A policy that provides recovery of monies lost due to destruction or the theft of computer assets.
Uninterruptible Power	Provision of a backup electrical supply to prevent loss of power on a temporary or continuous basis.

11

Auditor's Reports

SIGNIFICANCE

The product of nearly every audit engagement is the auditor's report, signed in the name of a certified public accounting firm, or personally by an individual practitioner. In Chapter 5, the auditor's role is explored and its importance established in the functioning of our capital-based economic system. This chapter discusses the form in which the auditor reports on an audit, as well as on the more prevalent engagement variations, and what users should understand about the reliance they can place on these reports.

It has been popularly assumed that any CPA's signature on almost any kind of report signifies a "certification" or an "O.K." Because the mere presence of the CPA's signature is so significant, and because a very large proportion of services provided by the accounting profession is in areas other than the auditing of historical financial statements prepared in conformity with GAAP, this chapter includes reports on some other types of unaudited information. Such reports are aptly referred to as accountant's reports instead of auditor's reports. In particular, this chapter covers standards for both performance of, and reporting on, reviews of interim financial information released by publicly held companies because the review procedures are so intertwined with what the accountant's report states.

Much of what the auditor does is related to forming a conclusion on the conformity of an accounting principle with GAAP. For that reason, this chapter devotes an entire section to "'Shopping' for Accounting Principles." Although perhaps overstated in the press, much concern continues to exist about whether a company should be required to disclose all instances of consultation with other accountants. The ASB has taken steps to formalize the consultation process, resulting in SAS 50, *Reports on the Application of Accounting Principles* (AU 625).

There are numerous specialized areas in which reports are also issued, for example, accountants' reports on compilation and review services, covered in Chapter 39. Other chapters in this *Handbook* that discuss these separate areas also describe the related reports. It would not be possible to prepare an exhaustive list of the instances in which a CPA might issue a formal report. Indeed, recognizing the futility of attempting to do so, the AICPA released an initial *Statement on Standards for Attestation Engagements* (AU 2000), creating a conceptual framework of sorts (discussed in Chapter 5) to provide guidance when no specific pronouncement existed. An attestation engagement is defined as

> one in which a CPA is engaged to issue or issues a written communication that expresses a conclusion about the reliability of a written assertion that is the responsibility of another party.

The attest may provide assurance (on the basis of an examination) or negative assurance (on the basis of a review), virtually doubling the imaginable reports.

Whatever the degree of responsibility the auditor or accountant assumes, it is clear that users of his product—whether the client or third parties—expect enhanced reliability through the association of an independent accountant's professional expertise and judgment. But users of financial information must evaulate carefully what the auditor or accountant says in his report; though many reports use formula wording, the possible variations are endless.

A persistent public perception seems to charge auditors with finding all fraud and financial statement errors, but auditors themselves have resisted accepting the asserted degree of responsibility. This gulf – between what the public perceives and what the auditor believes – has been addressed by Congress, the AICPA, and the SEC from time to time since 1975; but in the late 1980s, in an environment of Congressional hearings about potentially imposing on auditors statutory responsibilities for detection of fraud, error, and other illegal acts by clients, the accounting profession acted to close what by then came to be called the "expectation gap." (See Chapter 45 for a chronology.)

In February 1987, the AICPA's ASB released 10 proposals aimed at closing the "expectation gap," and issued the final standards in April 1988. Among the new standards are four that are aimed at both sharpening the auditor's focus and adjusting the public's perception of the meaning of the auditor's report:

1. SAS 58, *Reports on Audited Financial Statements* – the first significant change in 40 years in the composition of what had become a two-paragraph symbol. This chapter concentrates on this SAS.
2. SAS 53, *The Auditor's Responsibility to Detect and Report Errors and Irregularities* – the need for the audit approach to be designed to provide reasonable assurance that material instances of inadvertent or deliberate error are detected.
3. SAS 54, *Illegal Acts by Clients* – clarification of the auditor's responsibility to detect and communicate to others regarding such acts.
4. SAS 59, *The Auditor's Consideration of an Entity's Ability To Continue as a Going Concern* – imposition of an affirmative obligation on auditors to consider viability for the ensuing fiscal year.

These additional performance and reporting standards should provide additional credibility to audited financial statements. But increased responsibilities for auditors will have a cost, certainly in increased fees, and perhaps in the relationship between clients and auditors whose renewed mandate for "professional skepticism" might be overzealously applied.

REPORTS ON AUDITED FINANCIAL STATEMENTS

Standards of Reporting

Audits of financial statements are made in accordance with GAAS. Of the ten standards (AU 150.02), six are concerned with the qualifications of auditors, the quality of their work, and the performance of the audit itself, and are covered in other chapters. The other four standards are concerned with the nature of the report issued by the auditors.

Reporting standards require the auditor to comment in his report on whether: (1) the financial statements are presented in conformity with GAAP in all material respects; (2) the accounting principles have been consistently applied (now meaning that consistency is presumed unless a comment is made to the contrary); and (3) the disclosures in the financial statements are reasonably adequate. The standards then require the auditor to provide his opinion regarding the financial statements – an

Accountant's Report

Shareholders and Board of Directors
Nordstrom Inc.

We have examined the consolidated balance sheets of Nordstrom, Inc. and subsidiaries as of January 31, 1987 and 1986, and the related consolidated statements of earnings, shareholders' equity and changes in financial position for each of the three years in the period ended January 31, 1987. Our examinations were made in accordance with generally accepted auditing standards and, accordingly, included such tests of the accounting records and such other auditing procedures as we considered necessary in the circumstances.

In our opinion, the consolidated financial statements referred to above present fairly the financial position of Nordstrom, Inc. and subsidiaries as of January 31, 1987 and 1986, and the results of their operations and the changes in their financial position for each of the three years in the period ended January 31, 1987, in conformity with generally accepted accounting principles applied on a consistent basis.

Certified Public Accountants

Seattle, Washington
March 20, 1987

FIG. 11.1   Example of Auditor's Standard Report—Old Form
Source: Nordstrom, Inc. Annual Report, 1987.

unqualified, qualified, or adverse opinion, or a statement that he cannot express an opinion (a *disclaimer*).

Auditor's Standard Report

Until 1988, the auditor's standard report was based on a form of opinion recommended by the AICPA in the mid-1930s; an example is shown in Figure 11.1. Many financial statement users believed the AICPA guidance had turned into an inflexible dogma, preventing auditors from expressing their professional judgments about circumstances worthy of comment. Critics of the old standard report believed auditors should be given more flexibility in reporting and some even questioned the authority of the AICPA, as a voluntary membership organization, to require auditors to use a prescribed form of report.

After several attempts over many years, the ASB of the AICPA adopted a new form of report in SAS 58, *Reports on Audited Financial Statements,* to rectify many of the perceived deficiencies. The new report includes three basic paragraphs emphasizing that:

1. The financial statements are the responsibility of management.
2. The financial statements have been audited in a manner that provides reasonable assurance that they are free of material misstatement.
3. The auditor expresses an opinion as to whether the financial statements are fairly presented, in all material respects, in conformity with GAAP.

Independent Auditor's Report

We have audited the accompanying balance sheets of X Company as of December 31, 19X2 and 19X1 and the related statements of income, retained earnings, and cash flows for the years then ended. These financial statements are the responsibility of the Company's management. Our responsibility is to express an opinion on these financial statements based on our audits.

We conducted our audits in accordance with generally accepted auditing standards. Those standards require that we plan and perform the audit to obtain reasonable assurance about whether the financial statements are free of material misstatement. An audit includes examining, on a test basis, evidence supporting the amounts and disclosures in the financial statements. An audit also includes assessing the accounting principles used and significant estimates made by management, as well as evaluating the overall financial statement presentation. We believe that our audits provide a reasonable basis for our opinion.

In our opinion, the financial statements referred to above present fairly, in all material respects, the financial position of X Company as of December 31, 19X2 and 19X1, and the results of its operations and its cash flows for the years then ended in conformity with generally accepted accounting principles.

Auditor signature/name

Date

FIG. 11.2   Independent Auditor's Standard Report—New Form

Specifically, the new report, which must include the word "independent" in its title, contains the following principal assertions by the auditor:

1. The financial statements were audited.
2. Company's management is responsible for the financial statements and the auditor is responsible for expressing an opinion based on his audit.
3. The audit was conducted in accordance with GAAS.
4. GAAS requires planning and performance of the audit so as to provide reasonable assurance that the financial statements are free of material misstatement.
5. An audit includes:
   a. Examining, on a test basis, evidence supporting the amounts and disclosures in the financial statements.
   b. Assessing the accounting principles used and significant estimates made by management.
   c. Evaluating the overall financial statement presentation.
6. A belief that the audit provides a reasonable basis for his opinion.
7. An opinion as to whether the financial statements present fairly, in all material respects, the financial position of the company as of the balance sheet date audited and the results of its operations and its cash flows for the period then ended, in conformity with GAAP.

The standard report format for comparative financial statements is shown in Figure 11.2.

Cause of variation	Type of opinion			
	Qualified	Disclaimer	Adverse	Modifications not affecting opinion
Departures from GAAP (unjustified)	•		•	
Departures from GAAP* (Rule 203-justified)				•
Uncertainties*		•		•
Scope limitation*	•	•		
Change in accounting principle				•
Use of other auditors				•
Emphasis comments				•

*Degree of materiality determines the nature of auditor's report.

FIG. 11.3   Variations From the Auditor's Standard Report

Omitted from the new report format is the previously required reference to consistency in the application of accounting principles in all cases – even when no material accounting changes had been made. The ASB initially decided to eliminate this reference in all cases, because APB 20 (A06) requires financial statement recognition of the effects of changes. However, the SEC insisted that disclosure in the auditor's report was useful; and the compromise result is that a statement in the auditor's report is required when a change has occurred.

The auditor's standard report represents a professional judgment based on the results of applying audit procedures that are in accord with broad GAAS. It is not a guarantee or "insurance policy" that the financial statements are correct or that the audited enterprise should be entrusted with the funds of owners, investors, or creditors. As stated in SAS 53, "Since the auditor's opinion on the financial statements is based on the concept of reasonable assurance, the auditor is not an insurer and his report does not constitute a guarantee" (AU 316.08). (This kind of declaration also had been made in the past, but the level of protection it may afford has not been consistently high; see Chapter 49.)

Standard Report Modifications

Sometimes a "clean" (i.e., unmodified) auditor's standard report is not appropriate. Ordinarily, some modifications are required where, if material: (1) the financial statements improperly depart from GAAP, (2) there is a GAAP departure justified under Rule 203 (discussed in a later section entitled "Rule 203 Opinions"), (3) uncertainties exist as to the effects of contingencies on the financial statements, (4) there are limitations – sometimes client-imposed – on the scope of the audit, (5) accounting principles have not been consistently applied, (6) other auditors have performed a part of the audit, and (7) the auditor wants to explain or emphasize a particular matter.

A modified auditor's standard report will have four or more paragraphs instead of three. An explanatory paragraph (or paragraphs) inserted before or after the opinion paragraph explains the reason for the variation from the standard report. Four broad modifications of the auditor's standard report responsive to the previously described situations are qualified opinions, disclaimers of opinion, and adverse opinions and modifications not affecting an unqualified opinion. Figure 11.3 provides a matrix of causes and effects. In an audit engagement, the distinction between an unqualified opinion, a qualified opinion, a disclaimer of opinion, and an adverse opinion is a matter of degree. Auditor assessment of materiality determines whether the auditor will issue (1) an unqualified opinion because the matter is immaterial, (2) a qualified opinion because the matter is material, (3) a disclaimer of opinion because an uncertainty is so material that its potential effect on the financial statements is pervasive, or (4) an adverse opinion because a deliberate disregard of GAAP in a major area obviates the fairness of presentation.

Qualified Opinion. This form of modification of the auditor's standard report was common under the prior reporting format because uncertainties and accounting changes were covered. Now, however, qualified opinions relate only to nonpervasive (but nevertheless unjustified) departures from GAAP and to nonpervasive scope limitations; accordingly their incidence will be significantly reduced.

Disclaimer. When a material uncertainty exists and the auditor believes that it is so pervasive as to not be adequately communicable by the use of an explanatory emphasis paragraph, the auditor will issue a disclaimer, stating that he is unable to form an opinion on the financial statements. He will also issue a disclaimer if there is a significant restriction on his audit scope, whether or not client-imposed.

Adverse Opinion. This modification form is used when there is an unjustified departure from GAAP, and the effect is major. The auditor usually will be able to quantify departures from GAAP measurement standards, thus enabling an objective decision to be reached regarding their pervasiveness. However, it is also conceivable that failure to comply with disclosure standards (not affecting the amounts reported in the financial statements) could be sufficiently serious as to warrant an adverse opinion.

Modification Not Affecting Opinion. The auditor may comment on any other matter he feels is important to an understanding of the financial statements or his audit; however, he is not to make gratuitous remarks (e.g., thanking the management for its cooperation, as sometimes has been seen in private company audit reports.) There are four matters on which the auditor specifically must comment, if applicable:

1. Departures from GAAP justified under Rule 203
2. Significant (but not pervasive) uncertainties
3. Changes in accounting principles
4. Division of responsibility with other auditors

Causes of Modifications

Departures From GAAP. Nonconformity with GAAP, the most clear-cut reason for the auditor to depart from the standard report, involves (1) the misapplication or violation of GAAP in the recognition or measurement of amounts in the financial statements or (2) inadequate disclosure in the financial statements of important matters. Examples of measurement departures are noncapitalization of capital leases, use of prime costs for pricing inventories, and capitalization of research and development costs. In these situations, the auditor will determine the effects on the financial statements and disclose those effects in his report. The following is an example of an explanatory paragraph relating to noncapitalization of capital leases (AU 508.53):

> The Company has excluded from property and debt in the accompanying balance sheets certain lease obligations, that, in our opinion, should be capitalized in order to conform with generally accepted accounting principles. If these lease obligations were capitalized, property would be increased by $____ and $____, long-term debt by $____ and $____, and retained earnings by $____ and $____ as of December 31, 19X2 and 19X1, respectively. Additionally, net income would be increased (decreased) by $____ and $____ and earnings per share would be increased (decreased) by $____ and $____, respectively, for the years then ended.

The opinion paragraph then begins with a modification:

> In our opinion, except for the effects of not capitalizing certain lease obligations as discussed in the preceding paragraph, the financial statements referred to above present fairly, in all material respects . . .

The information in the explanatory paragraph(s) can be truncated if the details are given in a note to the financial statements, cross-referenced from the auditor's report.

If the departure from GAAP is deemed by the auditor to be so pervasive that the financial statements as a whole are not fairly stated, the auditor will issue an adverse opinion, such as:

> In our opinion, because of the effects of not capitalizing certain lease obligations as discussed in the preceding paragraph, the financial statements referred to above do not present fairly, in conformity with generally accepted accounting principles, the financial position of XYZ Company as of December 31, 19X2 and 19X1, or the results of its operations or its cash flows for the years then ended.

The third standard of reporting requires the auditor to comment in his report if the financial statements do not contain adequate disclosures involving material matters. In these circumstances, the auditor typically explains and quantifies the omitted information if readily available, in an explanatory paragraph(s) of his report. An example of the applicable portion of a report qualified because of a lack of adequate disclosure follows:

> Certain information with respect to long-term debt of $400,000 at December 31, 19X2, has been omitted from the accompanying financial statements. This debt consisted of bank

notes payable due December 31, 19X5, which bear interest at an 8% minimum rate or 1.5% over the prime rate. All the stock of Sub Corp., a wholly owned subsidiary having net assets of $1,000,000, is pledged as collateral under the terms of the note agreement.

In our opinion, except for the omission of the information discussed in the preceding paragraph, the financial statements referred to above present fairly, in all material respects. . . .

A key element in an auditor's report modified because of a departure from GAAP is the disclosure of the effect of the departure if it is known or readily determinable. While measurement departures are usually quantifiable, disclosure omissions are sometimes not readily determinable. In particular, if segment information or a statement of cash flows is omitted from financial statements, the auditor is not required to include such omitted data in his reports (AU 435.09–.10 and AU 508.55–.58).

To avoid a qualified or adverse opinion caused by a departure from GAAP, clients simply need to change the financial statements to properly apply the accounting principles or include the missing disclosure; publicly held companies *must* do so, because the SEC will not accept an auditor's report containing a correctible exception. In practice, unless there is truly a difference of opinion between the auditor and the client or the client does not care to incur the cost of developing the data for correction, changing the financial statements to eliminate the departure is the usual resolution.

Rule 203 Opinions. Rule 203 of the AICPA Code of Professional Conduct requires compliance with the pronouncements of the FASB and its predecessors (and also GASB). Therefore, an auditor must almost invariably issue a qualified or adverse opinion if the financial statements depart from GAAP in a material way. In rare cases, however, when the auditor "can demonstrate that due to unusual circumstances the financial statements or data would otherwise have been misleading" (ET 203.01), promulgated GAAP will not be followed. Such an auditor's report is called a Rule 203 opinion. A Rule 203 opinion must

* Describe the departure from GAAP;
* State the effects of the departure, if practicable; and
* State why compliance with GAAP would result in a misleading statement.

In ASR 150 (FRR § 101), the SEC refers to Rule 203 using language stronger than the AICPA intended: ". . . it is necessary to depart from accounting principles . . . if, due to unusual circumstances, failure to do so would result in misleading financial statements." The SEC may accept or require other principles in these cases. Auditors have issued Rule 203 opinions in only a few cases, because there is rarely a need to do so and because they assume a heavy burden of demonstrating that adhering to GAAP is not appropriate. An example of a Rule 203 opinion following reporting standards prior to SAS 58 is shown in Figure 11.4.

Uncertainties. Uncertainties (or *contingencies*) involve matters such as litigation, valuation or realization of assets, the ability of an entity to continue in existence, and tax liabilities (see Chapter 26). By their very nature, the probable outcome of material uncertainties cannot be assessed by the auditor or the client.

Uncertainties sometimes are chameleon-like. Many can be characterized as externally imposed scope limitations (e.g., the auditor could not get enough evidence), or perhaps client-imposed (e.g., the client would not let the auditor probe this matter). Or they can be seen as departures from GAAP (e.g., it is unrealistic for the client to maintain that the minimum probable result is undeterminable). Or they can be totally uncertain, with no ulterior qualifiers. The auditor must carefully consider each material uncertainty to judge whether it should be reported as such, or as something else.

Prior to 1988, auditors generally issued a qualified opinion regarding a material uncertainty. The auditor's opinion in those circumstances generally read: "In our opinion, subject to the effects on the financial statements of such adjustments, if any, as might have been required had the outcome of the uncertainty referred to in the preceding paragraph been known, the financial statements referred to above present fairly. . . ." Under the new standard, an auditor has three choices: (1) issue a standard report with modified wording, (2) disclaim an opinion, or (3) issue a standard report without modified wording. Which of these is chosen depends on the auditor's assessment of the materiality or pervasiveness of the uncertainties.

When the auditor believes an uncertainty is not so material as to require the issuance of a disclaimer of opinion, the auditor's standard report nevertheless may be modified to include a separate paragraph (usually following the opinion paragraph). No reference to the uncertainty should be made in the introductory, scope, or opinion paragraphs. An example of a separate paragraph describing a material uncertainty is as follows:

> As discussed in Note X to the financial statements, the Company is a defendant in a lawsuit alleging infringement of certain patent rights and claiming royalties and punitive damages. The Company has filed a counteraction, and preliminary hearings and discovery proceedings on both actions are in progress. The ultimate outcome of the litigation cannot presently be determined. Accordingly, no provision for any liability that may result upon adjudication has been made in the accompanying financial statements.

When the auditor concludes that a modified standard report does not adequately inform users of the pervasive magnitude of the uncertainty, the auditor should disclaim an opinion. The auditor's report should include explanatory paragraphs that describe the uncertainty and a final disclaimer paragraph such as:

> Because of the possible material effects on the financial statements referred to above of the matters described in the preceding paragraphs, we are unable to, and do not, express an opinion on these financial statements.

GAAP requires adequate disclosure, and this of course encompasses disclosures of uncertainties. With the footnotes containing adequate coverage, the auditor could decide that no mention is required in his report; and he would then issue an unmodified standard report. This new choice creates a dilemma for the auditor: prior to SAS 58, he had to conclude that an uncertainty was sufficiently consequential to cause the issuance of a qualified, "subject to" opinion; and to express such an opinion the auditor had to mention the uncertainty in a separate report paragraph.

With SAS 58 allowing only two forms of opinion paragraph–standard and a disclaimer – in the case of uncertainties, it is conceivable that fewer uncertainty explana-

---

Auditors' Report

Board of Directors and Shareholders
M.D.C. Corporation
Denver, Colorado

We have examined the consolidated balance sheets of M.D.C. Corporation and subsidiaries as of December 31, 1984 and 1983, and the related statements of income, shareholders' equity and changes in financial position for each of the three years in the period ended December 31, 1984. Our examinations were made in accordance with generally accepted auditing standards and, accordingly, included such tests of the accounting records and such other auditing procedures as we considered necessary in the circumstances.

As described in Notes G and I, in connection with the conversion of debentures in March 1983, the Company issued a warrant. As further stated in Note I, the accounting staff of the Securities and Exchange Commission commented that the accounting treatment afforded the conversion should be that normally given to any extinguishment of debt, as set forth in Accounting Principles Board Opinion No. 26, Early Extinguishment of Debt (APB 26). Following substantial discussions with the SEC staff, the Company decided to restate its 1983 financial statements to include, as an extraordinary item, a charge of $962,000 ($.08 per common share) to income for the value of the warrant issued in the extinguishment of the debentures and a credit to additional paid-in capital. Literal application of APB 26 would require measuring this transaction in a manner which would result in a further charge to income and a credit to additional paid-in capital of approximately $11,500,000. It is the opinion of the Company's management, an opinion with which we agree, that such a literal application of APB 26 would result in financial statements which do not reasonably and properly portray the economic consequences of the transaction and which would thus be misleading.

In our opinion, the consolidated financial statements referred to above present fairly the financial position of M.D.C. Corporation and subsidiaries at December 31, 1984 and 1983, and the results of their operations and the changes in their financial position for each of the three years in the period ended December 31, 1984, in conformity with generally accepted accounting principles applied on a consistent basis after the restatement described in the preceding paragraph.

Touche Ross & Co.
Certified Public Accountants

Denver, Colorado
March 5, 1985

FIG. 11.4 Example of a Rule 203 Opinion
Source: M.D.C. Corporation, 1984 Annual Report.

tory paragraphs will appear in auditors' reports that give a "clean" opinion. It remains to be seen whether auditors will regard the explanatory paragraph as a quasi-qualification, in which case they would follow traditional "subject to" reasoning to decide when the explanatory modification is required. Some clients, believing that any extra verbiage in the auditor's report is undesirable, will attempt to persuade the auditor that GAAP has been amply met in footnotes, and that therefore an additional "red flag" in the auditor's report is overkill.

It is reasonable to assume that this tug-of-war will not end in a draw, as audit firms will always strive to standardize practice in a highly sensitive area. Over time, either uncertainties will be uniformly and perhaps innocuously mentioned in the auditor's report with reference to the ubiquitous "contingencies" footnote; or auditors' reports will remain silent about virtually all uncertainties, except in those relatively few instances in which a disclaimer will be issued. The former seems more likely, given the auditor's instinct to avert, as much as possible, accusations of having given inadequate warning in advance of a company's demise or distress.

Scope Limitations. A limitation on the auditor's ability to perform all the procedures he believes necessary to complete the audit is broadly referred to as a *scope limitation*. Clients may impose some limitations, (e.g., restricting access to information or withholding permission to confirm certain accounts receivable or to observe physical inventories). External circumstances often impose others; for example, the auditor may not have been able to observe the physical inventory count at the beginning of the year because he was engaged later, or the financial statements may include an unaudited investee carried on the equity method. The auditor cannot report that his scope was limited and then say that he satisfied himself by other means. If he does not complete his normal procedures but uses other procedures to accomplish the same objectives, there is no scope limitation.

Scope limitations are akin to uncertainties in that the auditor cannot evaluate their possible effects on his audit results; as discussed in the preceding section, care should be taken to describe a scope limitation as such, and not as an uncertainty. When the maximum effect of misstatement in the area of the limitation can be quantified and is not pervasive, a qualified opinion is indicated; otherwise, a disclaimer of opinion is appropriate.

The auditor should always give a client-imposed scope limitation careful attention. In particular, he should be certain to understand the client's reasons for it and should evaluate all of its possible effects on his ability to express any opinion on the financial statements. Usually the auditor will disclaim an opinion; however, depending on the plausibility of the reason for the limitation, he must also evaluate whether continued association with such a client is in his best interest.

A report on an initial engagement where the auditor was engaged to audit the balance sheet only, as might be the case when opening inventories were not observed, is expressed in the following example:

INDEPENDENT AUDITOR'S REPORT

We have audited the accompanying balance sheet of X Company as of December 31, 19XX. This financial statement is the responsibility of the Company's management. Our responsibility is to express an opinion on this financial statement based on our audit.

We conducted our audit in accordance with generally accepted auditing standards. Those standards require that we plan and perform the audit to obtain reasonable assurance about whether the balance sheet is free of material misstatement. An audit includes examining, on a test basis, evidence supporting the amounts and disclosures in the balance sheet. An audit also includes assessing the accounting principles used and significant estimates made by management, as well as evaluating the overall financial statement presentation. We believe that our audit of the balance sheet provides a reasonable basis for our opinion.

Because we were not engaged to audit the related statements of income, retained earnings, and cash flows, we did not extend our auditing procedures to enable us to express, and accordingly we do not express, an opinion on those financial statements.

In our opinion, the balance sheet referred to above presents fairly, in all material respects, the financial position of X Company as of December 31, 19XX, in conformity with generally accepted accounting principles.

If the auditor had been engaged to audit all of the financial statements in this case, but was unable to observe opening inventories as required under GAAS (AU 331), and could not satisfy himself by other procedures, the report would be similar. However, it would identify all the financial statements included in the audit, describe the scope limitation in the explanatory paragraph, and append to the opinion paragraph a disclaimer on financial statements other than the balance sheet.

Changes in Accounting Principles. GAAP requires that the accounting principles used in the preparation of the financial statements be consistently applied within the periods reported on and in relation to the immediately preceding period. A change in accounting principles, such as from the straight-line to the declining-balance method of depreciation (if the effect is material) impairs the comparability of the financial statements and is therefore important to the reader. Many other matters, such as changes in estimates used in the application of accounting principles (e.g., the depreciable lives of fixed assets), may also affect comparability, and therefore require disclosure in financial statements. Under rules prior to SAS 58, the auditor would have commented in his report (i.e., taken a consistency exception) on material changes in principles, but not on changes in estimates. If there were no material changes in principles, the auditor's report would have explicitly affirmed that GAAP had been applied on a consistent basis.

Under SAS 58, the auditor's report is not to mention that GAAP has been consistently applied; but if a change in principles has occurred and it has a material impact on the comparability of the current financial statements with prior statements, the auditor must add a consistency comment (as a paragraph following the final opinion paragraph) describing the change (or referring to a note that describes the change). SAS 58 does not change prior rules that exempt changes in accounting estimates from required commentary in the auditor's report.

When making a change in accounting principle, the client must justify that the new principle is preferable. The auditor must evaluate whether (1) the new accounting principle is part of GAAP, (2) the manner of accounting for the change is as prescribed by GAAP, and (3) management's justification of preferability is reasonable. Most changes in accounting principles result from promulgations of the FASB (and GASB, for governmental entities). FASB and GASB accounting principles are preferable by definition. For other changes, if the auditor cannot satisfy himself as to any of the above matters, he would issue a qualified or adverse opinion.

Use of Other Auditors. Reference to other auditors is neither a qualification of the principal auditor's opinion nor a signal that the report is inferior to one that makes no such reference; rather, it is an indication to the reader of the divided responsibility between the principal auditor and the other auditors.

We have audited the consolidated balance sheets of ABC Company as of December 31, 19X2 and 19X1, and the related consolidated statements of income, retained earnings, and cash flows for the years then ended. These financial statements are the responsibility of the Company's management. Our responsibility is to express an opinion on these financial statements based on our audits. We did not audit the financial statements of B Company, a wholly-owned subsidiary, which statements reflect total assets of $____ and $____ as of December 31, 19X2 and 19X1, respectively, and total revenues of $____ and $____ for the years then ended. Those statements were audited by other auditors whose report has been furnished to us and our opinion, insofar as it relates to the amounts included for B Company, is based solely on the report of the other auditors.

We conducted our audits in accordance with generally accepted auditing standards. Those standards require that we plan and perform the audit to obtain reasonable assurance about whether the financial statements are free of material misstatement. An audit includes examining, on a test basis, evidence supporting the amounts and disclosures in the financial statements. An audit also includes assessing the accounting principles used and significant estimates made by management, as well as evaluating the overall financial statement presentation. We believe that our audits and the report of other auditors provide a reasonable basis for our opinion.

In our opinion, based on our audits and the report of other auditors, the consolidated financial statements referred to above present fairly, in all material respects, the financial position of ABC Company as of December 31, 19X2 and 19X1, and the results of its operations and its cash flows for the years then ended in conformity with generally accepted accounting principles.

FIG. 11.5   Example of Reliance on Other Auditors

If other auditors are examining certain divisions or subsidiaries included in the financial statements, the principal auditor—that is, the auditor who is examining the parent enterprise, auditing the consolidation, and issuing the auditor's report—must decide whether to refer in his report to the work of the other auditors. This decision requires an evaluation of the independence, professional reputation, and competence of the other auditors, and an inquiry into the other auditors' examination. Full details are given in the codified standards (AU 543); in brief, the principal auditor should consider both discussing with the other auditors the audit procedures followed and reviewing the audit program and working papers.

If he decides not to refer to the other auditors, the principal auditor assumes full responsibility for the auditor's report on the financial statements. Even if the principal auditor has little to do with the decision of which firm audits what piece, the use of other auditors without modification of the principal auditor's report becomes the equivalent of an audit procedure chosen and implemented by the principal auditor. Should a dispute later arise, the principal auditor will have to defend the auditor's report as solely his own. And if there is financial culpability, and the other auditor not mentioned may be the cause, the principal auditor will have to seek restitution or contribution from the other auditor. The other auditor performing an audit of a portion of an enterprise and issuing a standard auditor's report thereon is fully responsible to the shareholders/owners of the portion audited, despite the fact that his report is not presented in the annual shareholders' report of the consolidated enterprise.

Frequently, the principal auditor will decide to refer to the examination by other auditors, primarily because: (1) he is unable to review the other auditor's examination; (2) he is unable to apply sufficient procedures to otherwise be satisfied as to the other auditor's work; or (3) regardless of other considerations, the part of the financial statements examined by the other auditors is significant to the total. When the principal auditor makes this reference, he should do so clearly in both the scope and opinion paragraphs of the report. The introductory paragraph must specify the magnitude of the part of the examination performed by other auditors by including the dollar amounts or percentages of total assets, total revenues, net income, or other appropriate criteria. Figure 11.5 is an example of a principal auditor's report that refers to a division of responsibility with other auditors.

While there is no professional rule that an auditor must cover a minimum proportion of the financial statement amounts in order to be the principal auditor, the SEC has informally taken the position that a majority coverage of the total assets, revenues, or net income, as appropriate, is presumed necessary. There are, however, situations where such coverage cannot be achieved. For example, there may not be a principal auditor because one or more auditors' proportion is very large, but another auditor issues the report on the consolidated financial statements. In this case the auditor issuing the consolidated report may issue a *compilation-only* report; that is, after expressing an opinion on the portions he examined, he adds a paragraph explaining that the portions audited by others have been properly incorporated. The SEC will not accept a compilation-only report in lieu of a required certification since none of the auditors is taking responsibility for the sum of the parts.

The SEC's requirements for the submission of the separate reports of other auditors or predecessor auditors are given in Rule 2-05 of Regulation S-X and Rule 14a-3. Separate reports of other auditors must be included as exhibits in filings with the SEC, even though not required in annual reports to shareholders. Thus, if the annual shareholder report does not contain such other auditor's reports and is incorporated by reference in the Form 10-K, the other auditor's report must be filed in Part II and Part IV of that Form.

Emphasis Comments. In some situations the auditor, without qualifying his opinion, wants to emphasize an important matter regarding the financial statements, such as that: (1) the company is a part of a larger company, (2) the company has had significant related party transactions, (3) there has been a significant subsequent event, or (4) there is an accounting matter that affects comparability of the financial statements with those of prior periods (AU 508.37). Though such matters are not intended under SAS 58 (and were not, under prior rules) to affect the meaning of the introductory, scope or opinion paragraphs, their inclusion in the auditor's report may be misunderstood to be a qualification by the auditor. As a result, such auditor's reports have not been frequently issued.

Following is an example of an emphasis comment, which should be presented as a separate paragraph of the auditor's report.

As discussed in Note A, the company changed the estimated useful lives of its equipment for purposes of computing depreciation from 10 to 15 years, effective January 1, 19X2. This change had the effect of reducing depreciation expense in 19X2 by $500,000.

With SAS 58 having eliminated the possibility of a qualified auditor's report for uncertainties (still allowing disclaimers, however), an explanatory paragraph regard-

In our opinion, the financial statements referred to above present fairly, in all material respects, the financial position of Y Company as of December 31, 19X2, and the results of its operations and its cash flows for the year then ended, in conformity with generally accepted accounting principles.

The accompanying financial statements have been prepared assuming that the Company will continue as a going concern. As discussed in Note X to the financial statements, the Company has suffered recurring losses from operations and has a net capital deficiency that raises substantial doubt about its ability to continue as a going concern. Management's plans in regard to these matters are also described in Note X. The financial statements do not include any adjustments that might result from the outcome of this uncertainty.

FIG. 11.6   Example of Going Concern Uncertainty With a Standard Opinion

ing uncertainties, appended to the auditor's report, is an emphasis comment, strictly construed. As discussed in the earlier section "Uncertainties," there is a distinct possibility that uncertainty reporting could degenerate to a "stock paragraph." It is also possible that auditors will consider the need for an uncertainties paragraph as carefully as they have considered the need to impose a qualification.

Going Concern Uncertainties

Under SAS 59, *The Auditor's Consideration of an Entity's Ability to Continue as a Going Concern*, the auditor must specifically consider whether there are circumstances that could prevent the entity from remaining a going concern, at least until the next annual financial statement date. (Under prior standards, the auditor needed only to consider information coming to his attention that might contradict a going concern assumption.)

When the continuation of the business is in serious doubt, it is likely that several major uncertainties are interdependent and therefore not readily or individually quantifiable. Such pervasive uncertainties will necessarily be fully disclosed in the footnotes; and it is most probable that the auditor also will mention the going concern uncertainty in his report.

Even with massive uncertainties, the auditor is permitted to treat this mention as an emphasis comment following a standard opinion paragraph, on the premise that the reader is adequately informed of the problem. However, SAS 59 specifically notes that the auditor is not precluded from issuing a disclaimer of opinion in such cases. An example of a disclaimer (and further discussion regarding troubled companies) is given in Figure 28.10. An example of a standard opinion paragraph followed by a going concern paragraph is shown in Figure 11.6.

SEC Restriction on Offerings.   ASR 115 (issued in 1970) effectively precluded companies with pressing financial problems from raising funds by offering securities for public sale because the SEC would not consider financial statements to be certified for purposes of the 1933 Act if the auditor's report was so qualified as to indicate serious doubt about the status of the registrant.

FRR 16 (§ 607.02) repealed this restriction in 1984. The SEC now permits registrants to offer securities, notwithstanding an auditor's report that refers to uncertainties about an entity's continued existence, provided the full and fair disclosure is made of the registrant's financial difficulties and plans to overcome such difficulties. Financial statements will continue to be considered defective, however, if those statements are prepared on the assumption of liquidation or if the amounts and classifications of assets and liabilities in the statements should be otherwise adjusted.

The SEC's position thus emphasizes the importance to the auditor of evaluating management's plans for recovery and assessing the adequacy of disclosures whenever going concern uncertainties exist. An auditor's responsibilities in evaluating such issues are not fulfilled merely by appending an explanatory emphasis paragraph to the report. The auditor must have substantive reasons for concluding that the basis of financial statement presentation is appropriate.

FRR 16 does not change the unacceptability of disclaimers of opinion in 1933 Act filings. Accordingly, only a standard opinion paragraph (the only other choice under SAS 58) is acceptable in such filings.

SEC Preferability Requirements

For SEC registrants that make accounting changes, the auditor has been required since 1975 to go beyond GAAP and GAAS (as previously discussed) and state his own conclusion of preferability in a letter filed by the client with the SEC. Although a company's business judgment and planning may be considered by an auditor in forming his conclusion of preferability, he must still evaluate the

1. Acceptability of the change among the alternatives in GAAP, and
2. Preferability of the new principle in the client's particular circumstances.

Because criteria have not been established by the FASB for selecting among alternatives within GAAP, similar clients of the same auditor may use different methods or variations within methods. However, with the emphasis placed on each company's circumstances, this apparent inconsistency so far has not caused undue difficulty for auditors.

An example of a letter (which should be addressed to the client, not the SEC) to be included as an exhibit to Form 10-Q (or 10-K, if the change occurs in the last quarter) and stating the auditor's conclusion of preferability follows.

As stated in Note X to the financial statements for the three months ended March 31, 19X2, the company changed its method of accounting for (describe the nature of the accounting change) and states that the newly adopted accounting principle is preferable in the circumstances (state the circumstances and elements of business judgment and planning given by the company in the note). At your request, we have reviewed and discussed with you the circumstances and the business judgment and planning that formulated your basis to make this change in accounting principle.

It should be understood that criteria have not been established by the Financial Accounting Standards Board for selecting from among the alternative accounting principles that exist in this area. Further, the American Institute of Certified Public Accountants has not established the standards by which an auditor can evaluate the preferability of one accounting principle among a series of alternatives. However, for purposes of the company's compliance with the requirements of the Securities and Exchange Commission, we are furnishing this letter.

Based on our review and discussion, we concur in management's judgment that the newly adopted accounting principle described in Note X is preferable in the circumstances. In formulating this position, we are relying on management's business planning and judgment, which we do not find to be unreasonable. Because we have not audited any financial statements of the company as of any date or for any period subsequent to December 31, 19X1, we express no opinion on the financial statements for the three months ended March 31, 19X2.

Discovery of Omitted Audit Procedures

An auditor may determine subsequent to the date of his auditor's report that he has failed to apply one or more auditing procedures considered necessary in the circumstances; yet there is no indication that the audited financial statements are not presented in conformity with GAAP. These situations arise infrequently, most often in a subsequent peer review called for by the inspection standard forming a part of the *System of Quality Control for a CPA Firm* (QC 10.07i).

The auditor must assess the importance of the omitted procedure to his present ability to support the previously expressed opinion (SAS 46, AU 390.04). Where the omission materially affects his ability to support the opinion, the auditor should promptly perform the omitted procedure or alternate procedures. If, upon performing the procedures, the auditor becomes aware of facts that would have affected the audit report had he been aware of them earlier, the auditor should refer to the auditing standards regarding *Subsequent Discovery of Facts Existing at the Date of the Auditor's Report* (AU 561). When the auditor is unable to apply the necessary procedures, he should consult with his attorney concerning his responsibility to notify those who may be relying on the report.

LONG-FORM REPORTS AND ADDITIONAL INFORMATION

Purpose of Long-Form Reports

A long-form report consists of the basic conventional financial statements and footnotes plus other financial information. This other information is varied and might include consolidating or combining financial statements, condensed financial statements, schedules or analyses containing explanatory comments, or details of particular financial statement elements. A company may want such additional information because, for example, creditors require it, it may be useful in IRS examinations, or simply as a formal, permanent record. The auditor must take care that none of the additional information is required in the basic financial statements or in any way modifies them.

In the sections that follow, three types of additional information are covered: (1) additional information not required by FASB or GASB, (2) required supplemental information, and (3) information required for certain entities that is voluntarily presented by an entity not required to provide it. A matrix is provided in Figure 11.7 to

Possible permutations	Refer to notes indicated for supplementary data that is		
	Nonrequired (Note 11)	Required by FASB/GASB	Voluntary (Note 11)
Auditor submitted document, with the data			
Accompanying audited financial statements:			
Supplementary information —			
SAS 52 procedures applied	(1)	(6)	(6)
Supplementary information —			
SAS 52 procedures not applied	(1)	(7)	(11)
Not accompanying audited financial statements:			
Supplementary information —			
SAS 52 procedures applied	(2)	(8)	(10)
Supplementary information —			
SAS 52 procedures not applied	(2)	(8)	(11)
Client prepared document, with the data			
Accompanying audited financial statements:			
Supplementary information —			
SAS 52 procedures applied	(3)	(6)(9)	(6)
Supplementary information —			
SAS 52 procedures not applied	(4)	(7)(9)	(11)
Not accompanying audited financial statements:			
Supplementary information —			
SAS 52 procedures applied	(5)	(8)	(10)
Supplementary information —			
SAS 52 procedures not applied	(4)	(8)	(11)

(1) Since this is not data required of anyone by FASB or GASB, it should not be included as part of the basic financial statements, but should be appended thereto as a separate section. It is governed by SAS 29 (AU 551), which covers both audited and unaudited data.

(2) The auditor ordinarily is not expected to present supplementary financial data apart from the basic financial statements, and thus there is no specifically relevant provision in the SASs. However, if this separation should occur, the auditor's separate report on the data should clearly refer to the auditor's report on the basic financial statements, and reporting should follow SAS 29 (AU 551).

(3) Although the location is a client-prepared document (e.g., a brochure for presentation to the company's credit grantors), SAS 29(AU 551) applies if procedures are applied to this data. Presumably the data will be appended to the audited financial statements, but even if placed elsewhere in the client-prepared document, the auditor should cover it in his auditor's report or in an appropriate separate report.

(4) Nonrequired unaudited data in a client-prepared document does not require any consideration unless the data is contained in specified types of annual reports (AU 550.02), or the client asks the auditor to devote attention to the data. If the requirement for auditor consideration is met, SAS 8 (AU 550) applies.

(5) Supplementary financial data to which SAS 52 procedures have been applied ordinarily is not expected to be presented separate from the basic financial statement. If it is, however, follow note 2 guidance.

(continued)

FIG. 11.7   Matrix for Auditor Consideration of Supplemental Financial Data

---

(6) Appropriate procedures will be included in the regular audit scope; and the data may be included as part of the financial statements (clearly marked unaudited) or presented separately. If there are no departures from requirements for presentation of this material, the auditor will remain silent in his standard auditor's report. If there are departures, SAS 52 (AU 553) prescribes the commentary that should be given in the auditor's report.

(7) SAS 52 (AU 553) provides guidance for such situations.

(8) Since the information is required it will always accompany the basic financial statements. If for some reason it is also shown separated from those financial statements, it should be dealt with generally following SAS 52 (AU 553).

(9) Even though included in a client-prepared document, if the data accompanies the audited financial statements it should be treated as though it is an auditor-submitted document.

(10) Since the information is not required it need not accompany the basic financial statements. When presented separately either in an auditor-submitted or client-prepared document, it should be dealt with as nonrequired information, following SAS 29 (AU 551), but should be measured against the criteria in SAS 52 (AU 553).

(11) SAS 8 (AU 550) also applies when the data is contained in certain annual reports and in other documents to which the auditor, at the client's request, devotes attention.

FIG. 11.7 (continued)

help the reader keep track of the permutations caused by whether the auditor has been engaged to audit the data and whether it is located in an auditor-submitted document or in a client-prepared report.

Nonrequired Additional Information

Extent of Auditor's Association. SAS 29, *Reporting on Information Accompanying the Basic Financial Statements in Auditor-Submitted Documents* (AU 551), states that an auditor has the responsibility to report on all the information included in a long-form report when he submits to his client a document containing audited financial statements as well as other financial information (AU 551.04). However, if the auditor's report on audited financial statements is included in a client-prepared document along with other financial information and the auditor has not been engaged to report on the other information, the auditor's involvement is governed by SAS 8, *Other Information in Documents Containing Audited Financial Statements* (AU 550), and SAS 52, *Required Supplementary Information* (AU 558).

The reason for this bifurcation is that the auditor is presumed to have dealt with the additional information when it is presented by him bound in with the audited financial statements; thus he must make mention of the level of responsibility he is taking with respect to that material. When the audited financial statements are part of a client-prepared document (e.g., the rest of the annual report) there is no presumption that the auditor submitted the additional information. In this situation, the auditor will read the rest of the data to be sure that none of it appears to conflict with or contradict the audited financial statements.

Auditor's Report. When other financial information is contained in a document the auditor submits to his client or if the auditor has been engaged to report on such information contained in a client-prepared report, the auditor must issue a report. AU 551.06 outlines the content and form of this report.

a. The report should state that the examination has been made for the purpose of forming an opinion on the basic financial statements taken as a whole.

b. The report should identify the accompanying information. (Identification may be by descriptive title or page number of the document.)

c. The report should state that the accompanying information is presented for purposes of additional analysis and is not a required part of the basic financial statements. (The auditor may refer to any regulatory agency requirements applicable to the information presented.)

d. The report should include either an opinion on whether the accompanying information is fairly stated in all material respects in relation to the basic financial statements taken as a whole or a disclaimer of opinion, depending on whether the information has been subjected to the auditing procedures applied in the examination of the basic statements. The auditor may express an opinion on a portion of the accompanying information and disclaim an opinion on the remainder.

e. The report on the accompanying information may be added to the auditor's standard report on the basic financial statements or may appear separately in the auditor-submitted document.

Following are the standard forms of reporting when the auditor has examined the additional information, as well as several other reporting formats.

Standard Report (AU 551.12)
Our audit was made for the purpose of forming an opinion on the basic financial statements taken as a whole. The (identify accompanying information) is presented for purposes of additional analysis and is not a required part of the basic financial statements. Such information has been subjected to the auditing procedures applied in the audit of the basic financial statements and, in our opinion, is fairly stated in all material respects in relation to the basic financial statements taken as a whole.

Disclaimer on All of the Information (AU 551.13)
Our audit was made for the purpose of forming an opinion on the basic financial statements taken as a whole. The (identify accompanying information) is presented for purposes of additional analysis and is not a required part of the basic financial statements. Such information has not been subjected to the auditing procedures applied in the audit of the basic financial statements, and, accordingly, we express no opinion on it.

Disclaimer on Part of the Information (AU 551.13)
Our audit was made for the purpose of forming an opinion on the basic financial statements taken as a whole. The information on pages XX–YY is presented for purposes of additional analysis and is not a required part of the basic financial statements. Such information, except for that portion marked "unaudited," on which we express no opinion, has been subjected to the auditing procedures applied in the audit of the basic financial statements; and, in our opinion, the information is fairly stated in all material respects in relation to the basic financial statements taken as a whole.

Report When Opinion on Basic Financial Statements is Qualified (AU 551.14)
Our audit was made for the purpose of forming an opinion on the basic financial statements taken as a whole. The schedules of investments . . . , property . . . , and other assets . . . , as of December 31, 19XX, are presented for purposes of additional analysis and are not a required part of the basic financial statements. The information in such schedules has been subjected to the auditing procedures applied in the audit of the basic financial statements; and, in our opinion, except for the effects on the schedule of investments of not accounting for the investments in certain companies by the equity method as explained in the second preceding paragraph [i.e., a paragraph in the auditor's report], such information is fairly stated in all material respects in relation to the basic financial statements taken as a whole.

Report on Consolidating Information Not Separately Examined (AU 551.18)
Our audit was made for the purpose of forming an opinion on the consolidated financial statements taken as a whole. The consolidating information is presented for purposes of additional analysis of the consolidated financial statements rather than to present the financial position, results of operations, and cash flow of the individual companies. The consolidating information has been subjected to the auditing procedures applied in the audit of the consolidated financial statements and, in our opinion, is fairly stated in all material respects in relation to the consolidated financial statements taken as a whole.

Required Supplementary Information

FASB had required, from 1980 through 1985, larger public companies to present supplemental information on changing prices (under SFAS 33) as an accompaniment to the basic financial statements. Under SFAS 89 (C28), this requirement was changed to an option beginning with 1986 reports. As discussed in Chapter 4, all the instructions exist in SFAS 89 that would permit the FASB to again require this information should the level of inflation increase. At present, the only FASB-required supplemental disclosure relates to oil and gas reserve information (Oi5.157–.184; specifically covered in SAS 45 (AU 557)); and GASB requires governmental entities to present supplementary 10-year trend data regarding pension activities.

When FASB had first begun requiring supplemental data, the ASB released SAS 27, *Supplementary Information Required by the Financial Accounting Standards Board.* This has now been superseded by SAS 52, *Omnibus Statement on Auditing Standards—1987,* with the topic renamed *Required Supplementary Information* (AU 558). The amendment was made to recognize the change in status of the changing prices data, as well as to reword the text so that it will generically cover data that may become required in the future. It also now covers situations where information is given voluntarily in conformity with FASB and GASB specifications.

The procedures to be followed with respect to required supplementary data are specified in SAS 52 (AU 558). The auditor should not expand his report on the companion audited financial statements unless one of the following situations exists:

1. The supplementary information required by FASB or GASB is omitted.
2. The auditor concludes that the measurement or presentation materially departs from FASB or GASB guidelines.
3. The auditor is unable to complete the prescribed procedures.

4. The auditor is unable to remove substantial doubts about whether the supplementary information conforms to prescribed guidelines.

Ordinarily, supplementary information is presented outside the audited financial statements. Management, however, may choose to present this information in a footnote. In this circumstance, the footnote should be clearly marked unaudited, or the auditor's report should be expanded to include a disclaimer on the supplementary information.

Voluntarily Provided Information

If the auditor has been engaged to apply the SAS 52 procedures to a voluntary presentation of supplemental information that is required of certain other entities, he will report in the same manner. If, however, the auditor has not been so engaged, and the information is included as a supplement, or in a footnote to the basic financial statements, the data must be clearly marked to indicate that the auditor did not apply the SAS 52 procedures.

Alternatively, the auditor may expand his report on the audited financial statements to include a disclaimer on the information. Even with this disclaimer, the auditor's relationship nevertheless is governed by SAS 8, *Other Information in Documents Containing Audited Financial Statements* (AU 550); and thus the auditor would read the information to ascertain that it does not conflict with or contradict the basic financial statements.

If an entity provides changing prices data under SFAS 89 (C28), the requirements of SAS 52 (AU 558) do not apply because this data is, by definition, not required for any entity. Accordingly, the auditor's relationship is governed by SAS 8, as in the preceding paragraph.

UNAUDITED FINANCIAL STATEMENTS OF PUBLICLY HELD COMPANIES

Condensed Financial Statements and Selected Data

SAS 42, *Reporting on Condensed Financial Statements and Selected Financial Data* (AU 552), provides guidance on reporting in a client-prepared document on condensed financial statements that are derived from audited financial statements of a public entity that is required to file, at least annually, complete financial statements with a regulatory agency (for example, the condensed financial information contained in the annual shareholders' report).

Because condensed financial statements do not constitute a fair presentation of financial position, results of operations, and cash flows in conformity with GAAP, more limited auditor reporting is prescribed. When the auditor does report on such information, his report should indicate:

• That the auditor examined and expressed an opinion on the complete financial statements.

• The date of the auditor's report on the complete financial statements.

• The type of opinion expressed.

• Whether, in the auditor's opinion, the information set forth in the condensed financial statements is fairly stated in all material respects in relation to the complete financial statements
from which it has been derived.

Guidance is provided elsewhere (in SAS 29 (AU 551)) for reporting on selected
financial data that are derived from audited financial statements of either a public or
nonpublic entity and are presented in a document that includes (or with respect to a
public entity incorporates by reference) audited financial statements.

The auditor's report on selected financial data should be limited to data derived
from the audited financial statements. If the data include other information (such as
number of employees), the auditor's report should specifically identify the data on
which he is reporting.

A statement in a client-prepared document that identifies the auditor and states
that condensed financial statements or selected financial data have been derived
from audited financial statements does not, in and of itself, require the auditor to
report on such information provided it is included in a document that contains (or
incorporates by reference) audited financial statements. However, if such a statement
is made in a client-prepared document of a public entity that does not include (or
does not incorporate by reference) audited financial statements, the auditor should
request that the client either not include the auditor's name in the document or
include the auditor's report on the condensed financial statements. Where the client
refuses to do either, the auditor should advise the client that he does not consent to
either the use of his name or the reference to him, and should consider what other
actions might be appropriate.

Association With Interim Financial Information

Although annual financial statements are the usual focus, interim reports are prepared in almost all enterprises. In privately held companies, they are used principally
as information for management and lenders. Publicly held companies issue certain
interim information to shareholders and are required to provide condensed quarterly
financial statements (which are virtually complete except as to details of account
balances and notes) in filings with the SEC.

The highest level of auditor association is to perform audits of all interim financial
information. This is usually impractical, because a complete audit most likely would
take more time than is available for 1934 Act reporting; and interim information
would not be timely and thus would have limited usefulness. Also, the cost of an
interim audit is not likely to be commensurate with the related benefits. However, if
the client desires a complete audit of interim financial statements (or needs one, as is
common in a first public offering), the auditor can perform it just as he would any
annual audit.

Auditor association with unaudited interim financial information of publicly held
companies is covered by Item 302(a)(4) of Regulation S-K. There is no current
requirement that auditors must report on interim financial information. If such a
report is issued, SAS 36, *Review of Interim Financial Information* (AU 722), governs.

SAS 36 applies to reviews of interim financial information presented alone, as well
as to interim financial statements and summarized interim financial data that purport to conform with the provisions of APB 28, as amended, and are contained in

reports issued by a public entity to stockholders, boards of directors, or others, or filed with regulatory agencies. The procedures for a limited review set forth in the SAS constitute the appropriate professional standards and procedures for an accountant's review of interim financial information for the purpose of including in Form 10-Q a representation that the accountant has made such a review. If such a representation is made, a report in accordance with SAS 36 must be included with the filing.

Interim Financial Information Review Standards

The objective of an accountant's review of interim financial information is to provide him with a reasonable basis for evaluating whether material modifications to such information are necessary to place it in conformity with GAAP. A review is not an audit – far from it – and thus there is no assurance the accountant will find problems even if they exist. SAS 36 (AU 722) provides suggested review procedures, consisting of inquiries, analytical review, and reading, to the exclusion of the verification procedures and review of internal controls necessary in an audit. SAS 36 also guides the accountant in the extent of review procedures and the use of engagement letters and client representation letters.

Concept and Timing. The accountant[1] performs a review of interim financial information by applying his knowledge of the company's financial reporting practices and internal control procedures to those significant accounting matters of which he has become aware through inquiry and analytical review procedures. The core of his ability to perform a review is his knowledge of the company's financial reporting practices and internal controls. This knowledge, commonly referred to as the *audit base*, is almost invariably needed to facilitate an interim review (AU 722.09, fn. 4).

The review can be performed either on a timely basis (directed to quarterly reports as released) or in conjunction with the annual audit (directed to the footnote or other presentation containing the comparative four quarters' data). SAS 36 seems to lean toward performance of the reviews on a timely basis, because it permits the early consideration of significant accounting matters.

Review Process. If the accountant has obtained the requisite knowledge through having an audit base, he would need only to identify the differences between the company's reporting practices and internal controls for annual financial statements and those for interim statements (AU 722.10). However, there are situations (e.g., an auditor is newly engaged to audit the next completed fiscal year) in which it is not possible to complete an annual audit before conducting a review. In that case, the accountant needs to consider whether, under the circumstances, he can acquire an adequate knowledge of the company's reporting practices and internal controls for a review of interim financial information. Although SAS 36 does not say how he might do this, many accountants believe that an audit base can be obtained only through

---

[1] Use of the word "accountant" in nonaudit activities is meant to emphasize that the nature of the association is not that of an auditor.

the performance of a review and evaluation of the company's internal control structure and tests of the degree of compliance with the control procedures.

A possible problem implied in SAS 36 is that many companies use accounting and reporting procedures in determining interim data that significantly differ from the procedures used for annual data. A common example is the extent of the closing of the books and records. Some accountants believe a company must complete a reasonably formal closing to prepare an interim financial statement even if only summaries are to be reported to the public; but it might not be necessary to apply the breadth and depth of procedures used for an annual closing. The accountant, however, would usually require the books of original entry to be up-to-date and posted on a timely basis. All significant accounts and subsidiary ledgers would have to be reconciled, and certain complex accounts would have to be analyzed.

Just as he is required to understand the company's systems and procedures in an audit of financial statements, the accountant must also understand them when he performs a review of interim financial statements. Significant weaknesses in internal accounting controls or in the financial reporting processes in an interim period may preclude the accountant from performing the review.

After the audit base (or equivalent) has been obtained, procedures for reviewing interim financial statements consist primarily of inquiries about and analyses of significant accounting matters affecting the financial information to be reported. SAS 36 suggests that the following procedures be performed (summarized from AU 722.06):

a. Inquiry concerning (1) the accounting system, to obtain an understanding of the manner in which transactions are recorded, classified, and summarized, and (2) any significant changes in the internal control structure that might affect the interim financial information.

b. Application of analytical review procedures to identify and provide a basis for inquiry about relationships and individual items that appear to be unusual, including (1) comparison of the information with comparable information for preceding and corresponding previous period(s), (2) comparison of the financial information with anticipated results, and (3) study of the relationships of elements of financial information. In applying these procedures, the accountant should consider the types of matters that in the preceding year or quarters have required accounting adjustments.

c. Reading the minutes of meetings of stockholders, board of directors, and committees of the board of directors.

d. Reading the interim financial information to consider whether the information conforms with generally accepted accounting principles.

e. Obtaining reports from other accountants, if any, who have reviewed the interim financial information of significant components, subsidiaries, or other investees.

f. Inquiry of officers and other executives concerning (1) whether the interim financial information has been prepared in conformity with generally accepted accounting principles consistently applied, (2) changes in the entity's business activities or accounting practices, (3) questions that have arisen in the course of applying the foregoing procedures, and (4) events subsequent to the date of the interim financial information.

g. Obtaining written representations from management concerning its responsibility for the financial information, completeness of minutes, subsequent events, and other matters for which the accountant believes written representations are appropriate in the circumstances.

The issue of which company locations the accountant should visit is ordinarily decided by considerations similar to those in an audit of the annual financial statements. For auditors to be able to perform timely reviews of interim financial information for clients whose operations consist of numerous and widely dispersed subsidiaries or divisions, a detailed coordination plan prepared in advance is essential. A postreview of the unaudited footnote to the annual statements may be a practical solution in circumstances where constraints are such that timely performance of the interim review is not feasible.

Documentation. Although SAS 36 does not specify the form or content of the working papers, ordinarily the accountant should document the performance and results of the review procedures. This documentation is normally in the form of a review program, account analyses, memoranda that summarize the inquiries and the responses, and client correspondence.

An *engagement letter* is advisable to establish a clear understanding of the nature of the services to be performed and the responsibilities to be assumed. The letter should include: (1) a general description of the procedures to be performed, (2) an explanation that these procedures are substantially narrower in scope than an audit made in accordance with GAAS, and (3) a description of the form of the report.

At the completion of the timely review, *a letter of representations* must be obtained. Representations pertaining to retrospective reviews (of interim data in an annual report footnote) are ordinarily included in the year-end audit letter. A sample letter of representations for a timely review is shown below.

(Addressed to the independent accountants):

In connection with your review of the interim financial information to be included in the quarterly report to shareholders and in Form 10-Q for the quarter ended June 30, 19X1, we represent that, to the best of our knowledge and belief, the financial information included in the aforementioned documents is fairly presented in conformity with generally accepted accounting principles applied on a consistent basis with that of the interim report for the quarter ended June 30, 19X0, and substantially consistent with the audited financial statements as of and for the year ended December 31, 19X0. In preparing these interim financial statements, we believe we have complied with applicable generally accepted accounting principles.

Insert here any specific representations which seem to be required by the particular engagement.

Further, we have made available to you:

1. Financial records and related data.
2. Minutes of the meetings of stockholders, directors, and committees of directors, or summaries of actions of recent meetings for which minutes have not yet been prepared.

No matters have been discovered and no events have occurred since June 30, 19X1 which we believe would require adjustments to or additional disclosure in the financial information as of that date.

We understand that your review was not an audit in accordance with generally accepted auditing standards, and therefore cannot be relied on to disclose matters of significance with respect to the interim financial information.

Other Issues

Other accountants. On engagements involving secondary accountants on whom the primary accountant expresses reliance in his annual audit report, the primary accountant would also normally require reports from the secondary accountants as a partial basis for his own report on the interim financial statements (AU 722.06e, fn. 3).

Reference in the principal accountant's review report to another accountant is made in a manner similar to that followed for reports on audited financial statements. Even if the principal accountant does not express reliance in his report, he still would normally request participation from the secondary accountant unless the segment is immaterial. When the amounts involved are not material, the principal accountant may be able to perform sufficient inquiry and analysis at the company's corporate level to dispense with the involvement of the secondary accountant.

Internal auditors. As in audit engagements, the accountant should consider work performed by the company's internal audit staff. Although he cannot substitute that work for his own interim review work, the internal auditor's activity may affect the scope of his review because of its relationship to internal controls. Both the scope of the internal audit staff's work and the extent of the independent accountant's review of it should be documented in the working papers. Authoritative guidance on the effect of an internal audit function on the scope of the independent auditor's examination is provided in AU 322.

Estimates. Since estimates are usually a critical factor in the preparation of interim financial statements, the accountant should understand the basis for the important estimates used, and he should review the company's methods of allocating costs to the various interim periods. The estimates and projections used should be both logical and reasonable. In reviewing the allowance for doubtful accounts, for example, the accountant should understand the process or method used to arrive at the amount, the degree of accuracy achieved by the company in its previous allowance estimates, and the company's plans for the remaining interim periods.

To review the provision for income taxes, the accountant must understand the calculation of the prior year's provision, the company's effective tax rate for the entire fiscal year, the actual results to date, and the specific rules on this matter contained in APB 28, SFAS 96 and FIN 18 (I73.111–.130). After he has grasped the mechanics of the tax provision calculation, he must challenge the variables for reasonableness.

Subsequent Events. Some period of time elapses between the date of an interim statement and the completion of the accountant's review. The accountant is generally required to perform a subsequent events review for this period. SAS 36 limits this to inquiry and written representations; but an accountant may also decide to perform some other subsequent events review procedures as set forth in AU 560.10–.12 to evaluate whether postclosing transactions affect the reviewed financial statements or their disclosures. SAS 36 does not cover the accountant's procedures concerning a review of events subsequent to the date of his report on the interim financial statements included in an SEC registration statement. Such "bring-up" procedures to the effective date of 1933 Act filings are discussed in SAS 37 (AU 711).

Reporting on Interim Financial Statement Reviews

A company may wish to include the accountant's review report in its reports on Form 10-Q. The company may also request the accountant to render a report solely for its board of directors or audit committee. If reference is made to the accountant's review in any public document, his report should be included in the document. The report may be addressed to the company, its board of directors, or its stockholders. Generally, the report should be dated as of the date of completion of the review. In addition, each page of the interim financial information should be clearly marked "unaudited."

SAS 36 provides guidance on the type of review report, but there are numerous variations and tangential issues to be considered. The categories, covered in the following sections, are:

1. Timely reporting:
   a. Accountant's basic report on a review of interim financial information,
   b. Modifications of accountant's review report, and
   c. Nonavailability of accountant's review report to underwriters.
2. Reporting on interim financial information presented in a note to audited financial statements.

Accountant's Basic Report. The report on an interim review contains five elements: (1) a statement that a review was conducted in accordance with professional standards for these reviews; (2) the specific interim information reviewed; (3) a description of the review procedures (this can contain variable wording but is likely in practice to be formalistic, as in the example below); (4) a statement that a reveiw is less than an audit and that therefore no opinion is expressed; and (5) a statement as to whether the accountant is aware of material modifications that should be made to the financial statements. This report assures users of the interim financial information that the accountant has applied procedures under the guidance of the professional literature. The form of the report, given in AU 722.18, follows:

> We have made a review of (describe the information or statements reviewed) of ABC Company and consolidated subsidiaries as of September 30, 19X1, and for the three-month and nine-month periods then ended, in accordance with standards established by the American Institute of Certified Public Accountants.
>
> A review of interim financial information consists principally of obtaining an understanding of the system for the preparation of interim financial information, applying analytical review procedures to financial data, and making inquiries of persons responsible for

financial and accounting matters. It is substantially less in scope than an audit in accordance with generally accepted auditing standards, the objective of which is the expression of an opinion regarding the financial statements taken as a whole. Accordingly, we do not express such an opinion.

Based on our review, we are not aware of any material modifications that should be made to the accompanying financial (information or statements) for them to be in conformity with generally accepted accounting principles.

Modification of Basic Report. The accountant is required to modify his report on an interim review only for departures from GAAP. Modification is not required for otherwise adequately disclosed uncertainties or lack of consistency in applying GAAP, because the accountant's report itself is not an expression of opinion. The following are sample third and fourth paragraphs for the report form above for a company that did not record capital leases (AU 722.21):

Based on information furnished us by management, we believe that the company has excluded from property and debt in the accompanying balance sheet certain lease obligations that should be capitalized in order to conform with generally accepted accounting principles. This information indicates that if these obligations were capitalized at September 30, 19X1, property would be increased by $____, and long-term debt by $____, and net income and earnings per share would be increased (decreased) by $____, $____, $____, and $____ respectively, for the three-month and nine-month periods then ended.

Based on our review, with the exception of the matter described in the preceding paragraph, we are not aware of any material modifications that should be made to the accompanying financial (information or statements) for them to be in conformity with generally accepted accounting principles.

Nonavailability to Underwriters. In SAS 49, *Letters for Underwriters* (AU 634), the accountant is given guidance on what information he may provide to underwriters in a comfort letter in connection with underwriters' due-diligence procedures in 1933 Act securities offerings. Because underwriters are required to specify the procedures they wish the accountant to perform on their behalf, it is not proper to address an SAS 36-type report to them; the review procedures followed in an SAS 36 review are the accountant's choice, not the underwriter's. However, reference can be made in the introductory paragraph of the comfort letter that a review of interim financial information has been made; no further mention of or conclusions from such review should be included.

Interim Financial Information in an Annual Report Note. When any company, whether required by SEC Regulation S-K or voluntarily, includes a note on interim financial information in its annual financial statements or other financial report, the accountant should perform a limited review following SAS 36; but the procedures need not be done at the time quarterly information is issued. The interim information in an annual footnote is not deemed to be required for a fair presentation of the financial statements, is accordingly not audited, and is labeled unaudited. The accountant should not modify his opinion on the basic financial statements or include a report on a limited review in these circumstances unless the required interim financial information (1) has been omitted, or (2) has not been reviewed. An example of a final paragraph in an auditor's report on the annual financial statements for which there was a restriction on the scope of the limited review of interim financial information is (AU 722.29):

> The selected quarterly financial data on page xx contain information that we did not audit, and accordingly, we do not express an opinion on that data. We attempted to review the quarterly data in accordance with standards established by the American Institute of Certified Public Accountants but were unable to do so because we believe that the company's system for preparing interim financial information does not provide an adequate basis to enable us to complete such a review.

The auditor's report should also contain similar modifications when (AU 722.30):

1. Interim financial information is not marked as unaudited;
2. Information voluntarily presented has not been reviewed and it is not marked as unaudited;
3. Interim financial information does not appear to be presented in conformity with GAAP;
4. An indication is made that the interim financial information has been reviewed but fails to state that a review is substantially less than an audit and that no opinion is expressed.

The third and fourth situations are not applicable if the separate report on review of the interim financial information is also presented.

Safe Harbor Under Securities Act of 1933. SAS 37, *Filings Under Federal Securities Statutes* (AU 711), provides guidance for the independent accountant whose report, based on a review of interim financial information, is presented or incorporated by reference in a filing under the 1933 Act.

ASR 274 (FRR § 605) insulates independent accountants issuing reports on reviews of interim financial information under SAS 36 from liability under Section 11(a) of the 1933 Securities Act, when such reports are incorporated by reference in 1933 Act filings. The SEC amended the definition of a "report" for the purposes of Sections 7 and 11(a) of the 1933 Act so that a report on unaudited interim financial information is not considered a part of the registration statement prepared or certified by an accountant. In addition, a prospectus that includes a discussion concerning the accountant's involvement in interim financial data should also clarify that the accountant's report does not fall within the meaning of Sections 7 and 11(a) of the 1933 Act.

SPECIAL REPORTS

Auditors are often called on to issue reports on matters that are not financial statements prepared in conformity with GAAP. Four broad areas are discussed in detail in SAS 14, *Special Reports* (AU 621), and SAS 35, *Special Reports—Applying Agreed-Upon Procedures to Specified Elements, Accounts, or Items of a Financial Statement* (AU 622):

1. Financial statements prepared on a comprehensive basis of accounting other than GAAP.
2. Specified elements, accounts, or items of a financial statement.
3. Compliance with aspects of contractual agreements or regulatory requirements.
4. Financial information presented in prescribed forms or schedules.

A further type of special report is covered in SAS 50, *Reports on the Application of Accounting Principles* (AU 625).

Other Comprehensive Bases of Accounting

Commonly used comprehensive accounting bases other than GAAP include income tax basis, cash basis, prescribed regulatory basis, and bases having substantial support such as price level or current value. These bases may be audited in accordance with GAAS, and the auditor's report (AU 621.05 as modified to reflect SAS 58) on such an examination should include four paragraphs:

1. A paragraph identifying the financial statements audited, and a statement that they are the responsibility of management.
2. A scope paragraph stating that the audit was conducted in accordance with GAAS.
3. An explanatory paragraph stating (or referring to a note that explains) the comprehensive basis of accounting and how it differs from GAAP, and stating that the financial statements are not intended to be presented in conformity with GAAP.
4. An opinion paragraph stating whether the financial statements are presented fairly, in all material respects, in conformity with the comprehensive basis of accounting.

An example of a report on financial statements prepared on another comprehensive basis of accounting, the cash basis, is as follows (AU 621.08 as modified to reflect SAS 58).

INDEPENDENT AUDITOR'S REPORT

We have audited the statement of assets and liabilities arising from cash transactions of XYZ Company as of December 31, 19XX, and the related statement of revenue collected and expenses paid for the year then ended. These financial statements are the responsibility of the Company's management. Our responsibility is to express an opinion on these financial statements based on our audit.

We conducted our audit in accordance with generally accepted auditing standards. Those standards require that we plan and perform the audit to obtain reasonable assurance about whether the financial statements are free from material misstatement. An audit includes examining, on a test basis, evidence supporting the amounts and disclosures in the financial statements. An audit also includes assessing the accounting principles used and significant estimates made by management as well as evaluating the overall financial statement presentation. We believe our audit provides a reasonable basis for our opinion.

As described in Note X, the Company's policy is to prepare its financial statements on the basis of cash receipts and disbursements and they are not intended to be a presentation in conformity with generally accepted accounting principles.

In our opinion, the financial statements referred to above present fairly, in all material respects, the assets and liabilities arising from cash transactions of XYZ Company as of December 31, 19XX, and the revenue collected and expenses paid during the year then ended, on the basis of accounting described in Note X.

Specified Elements, Accounts, or Items

GAAS-Based Reports. This category includes reports on matters such as rentals, royalties, a profit participation, or a provision for income taxes. It may be an adjunct to an audit of the basic financial statements or a stand-alone engagement. Either way, the auditor must take into account the fact that the GAAS must be followed, although there may be variations in the application of the reporting standards concerning conformity with GAAP and the consistency of its application.

The GAAP standard relates to financial statements and specified elements. Individual financial statement accounts or items are not, per se, financial statements. The reporting format follows the usual guidelines for reporting on audited financial statements. The auditor should not express an opinion on specified elements, accounts, or items if he has either expressed an adverse opinion or denied an opinion on the basic financial statements if such a special report would be equivalent to a prohibited piecemeal opinion (AU 508.73). Further, the consistency standard applies only if the specified element, account, or item is presented in conformity with GAAP specifically applicable to it. An example of a report expressing an opinion on a specified financial statement item follows (AU 621.14 as modified to reflect SAS 58):

We have audited the schedule of gross sales (as defined in the lease agreement dated March 4, 19X1, between ABC Company, as lessor, and XYZ Stores Corporation, as lessee) of XYZ Stores Corporation at its Main Street store, (City), (State), for the year ended December 31, 19X2. The information contained in this schedule is the responsibility of the Company's management. Our responsibility is to express an opinion on this schedule based on our audit.

We conducted our audit in accordance with generally accepted auditing standards. Those standards require that we plan and perform the audit to obtain reasonable assurance about whether the accompanying schedule is free of material misstatement. An audit includes examining, on a test basis, evidence supporting the amounts and disclosures in the schedule. An audit also includes assessing the accounting principles used and significant estimates made by management, as well as evaluating the overall presentation of the schedule. We believe our audit provides a reasonable basis for our opinion.

In our opinion, the schedule of gross sales referred to above presents fairly, in all material respects, the gross sales of XYZ Corporation at its Main Street store (City), (State), for the year ended December 31, 19X2, on the basis specified in the lease agreement referred to above.

If appropriate, the distribution of the report should be restricted to the parties involved.

Agreed-Upon-Procedures Reports. A client may ask an auditor to undertake an engagement to render a report based on applying agreed-upon procedures that are not a sufficient basis for expressing an audit opinion. The auditor should accept such an engagement only if he and the client have a clear understanding of the procedures to be performed, and if distribution of the report is restricted to named parties. If the financial statements of the client (or another enterprise, such as a company being evaluated for possible acquisition) accompany the report, the accountant is associated with those financial statements, and will therefore state his relationship to them (e.g., disclaimer, auditor's standard report, compilation report, or review report as called for by AU 504 or AR 100). The auditor's report should specify the elements, accounts, or items; enumerate the procedures performed; state the findings; disclaim an opinion with respect to the specified elements, accounts or items; state that the report does not extend to the client's financial statements taken as a whole; and identify who is intended to receive the report.

SAS 35 specifies procedures that the independent accountant can apply when the application of agreed-upon procedures is not sufficient for the expression of an opinion on specified elements, accounts, or items of a financial statement, and the independent accountant is unable to discuss the procedures directly with all parties who will receive the report. Such a dialogue was previously required under SAS 14, but was modified by SAS 35 to permit one of the following when such communication cannot be accomplished (AU 622.02):

a. Discussing the procedures to be applied with legal counsel or other appropriate representatives of the parties involved, such as a trustee, a receiver, or a creditors' committee.

b. Reviewing relevant correspondence from the parties.

c. Comparing the procedures to be applied to written requirements of a supervisory agency, such as a bank regulatory agency that receives a report in connection with a bank directors' examination.

d. Distributing a draft of the report or a copy of the client's engagement letter to the parties involved, with a request for their comments before the report is issued.

An example of a special report in connection with claims of creditors, based on the results of applying agreed-upon procedures, follows (AU 622.06):

Trustee
XYZ Company

At your request, we have performed the procedures enumerated below with respect to the claims of creditors of XYZ Company as of May 31, 19X1, set forth in the accompanying schedules. Our review was made solely to assist you in evaluating the reasonableness of those claims, and our report is not to be used for any other purpose. The procedures we performed are summarized as follows:

a. We compared the total of the trial balance of accounts payable at May 31, 19X1, prepared by the company, to the balance in the company's related general ledger account.

b. We compared the claims received from creditors to the trial balance of accounts payable.

c. We examined documentation submitted by the creditors in support of their claims and compared it to documentation in the company's files, including invoices, receiving records, and other evidence of receipt of goods or services.

Our findings are presented in the accompanying schedules. Schedule A lists claims that are in agreement with the company's records. Schedule B lists claims that are not in agreement with the company's records and sets forth the differences in amounts.

Because the above procedures do not constitute an audit made in accordance with generally accepted auditing standards, we do not express an opinion on the accounts payable balance as of May 31, 19X1. In connection with the procedures referred to above, except as set forth in Schedule B, no matters came to our attention that caused us to believe that the accounts payable balance might require adjustment. Had we performed additional procedures or had we audited the financial statements in accordance with generally accepted auditing standards, other matters might have come to our attention that would have been reported to you. This report relates only to the accounts and items specified above and does not extend to any financial statements of XYZ Company, taken as a whole.

Contractual or Regulatory Compliance

The auditor may furnish reports concerning compliance with aspects of contractual agreements such as loan agreements, or with aspects of regulatory requirements of government agencies. This may be done – only in connection with his audit of the client's financial statements – by giving negative assurance. The auditor will state that in performing his examination nothing came to his attention to cause him to believe the client was not in compliance with the specified aspects of the contractual agreement (or regulatory requirement). If, as is common, the negative assurance is given in a report separate from the basic audit report, the fact that an audit of the basic financial statements (in accordance with GAAS) was performed, and the date of the auditor's report thereon, must be stated in the compliance report. The distribution of the report should be restricted to the parties involved.

An example of a report based on compliance with a contractual agreement follows (AU 621.19 as modified to reflect SAS 58):

We have audited, in accordance with generally accepted auditing standards, the balance sheet of XYZ Company as of December 31, 19X1, and the related statements of income, retained earnings, and cash flows for the year then ended, and have issued our report thereon dated February 16, 19X2.

In connection with our audit, nothing came to our attention that caused us to believe that the Company was not in compliance with any of the terms, covenants, provisions, or conditions or section XX to XX, inclusive, of the Indenture dated July 21, 19X0, with ABC Bank. However, it should be noted that our audit was not directed primarily toward obtaining knowledge of such noncompliance.

Prescribed Forms

Printed forms designated by the party with which they are to be filed often prescribe the wording of the auditor's report. Such forms commonly call for assertions that the auditor cannot properly make; or the auditor may not have done everything he deems would be necessary to express the prescribed opinion. In such situations, he should either reword the prescribed form or attach a separate report (AU 621.20–.21). However, see Chapter 39 for SSARS 3 engagements.

"SHOPPING" FOR ACCOUNTING PRINCIPLES

SAS 50, *Reports on the Application of Accounting Principles* (AU 625), was issued in July 1986 to provide guidance to accountants who respond to requests from other than their own audit clients for information regarding accounting principles and auditors' reports. More specifically, SAS 50 was designed to address the issue of "shopping" for accounting principles, a negative factor in the public's perception of the profession. In this regard the SEC issued FRR 31 (§ 603.07) in April 1988 to require the disclosure by public companies of accounting and/or auditing issues discussed with a newly engaged auditor prior to their engagement that resulted in an SAS 50 report. See Chapter 45 for details.

In addition to SAS 50, the AICPA SEC Practice Section (AICPA, 1986i) has two relevant membership requirements, under which a member firm must:

- Establish policies and procedures concerning the rendering of opinions on the application of generally accepted accounting principles (other than those relating to the financial statements of an ongoing audit client); such policies and procedures should include a discussion of the circumstances in which consultation with others in the firm is required and the nature, timing, and extent thereof, and the procedures that should be followed in communicating with a predecessor or continuing accountant.

- Communicate through a written statement to all professional firm personnel the broad principles that influence the firm's quality control and operating policies and procedures on, as a minimum, matters related to the recommendation and approval of accounting principles, present and potential client relationships, and the types of services provided, and inform professional firm personnel periodically that compliance with those principles is mandatory.

AICPA Ethics Interpretation 201-3, which had required consultation with the continuing accountants before responding to a request from their client (usually interpreted in practice to mean before giving a definitive response), has been rescinded because of the issuance of SAS 50.

SAS 50 Applicability

An accountant in public practice (reporting accountant), either in connection with a proposal to obtain a new client or otherwise, must follow SAS 50 (AU 625.02):

a. When preparing a written report on the application of accounting principles to specified transactions, either completed or proposed (*specific transactions*).

b. When requested to provide a written report on the type of opinion that may be rendered on a specific entity's financial statements.

c. When preparing a written report to intermediaries (defined as parties who may advise principals to a transaction, including attorneys and investment, merchant, and commercial bankers) on the application of accounting principles not involving facts or circumstances of a particular principal (*hypothetical transactions*).

SAS 50 also applies to oral advice on:

a. The application of accounting principles to a specific transaction, or

b. The type of opinion that may be rendered on an entity's financial statements,

when the reporting accountant concludes the advice is intended to be used by a principal to the transaction as an "important factor" considered in reaching a decision.

Further, SAS 50 must be followed if certain communications (e.g., position papers, newsletters, and so forth) are intended to provide guidance on the application of accounting principles to a specific transaction, or on the type of opinion that may be rendered on a specific entity's financial statements.

SAS 50 does not apply to advice given to audit and compilation/review clients, nor does it apply to litigation support work or advice given to other accountants in public practice.

SAS 50 Performance Standards

A summary (derived from AU 625.05–.07) of what the reporting accountant must do is listed below; the initial five items essentially repeat the relevant standards among the basic ten GAAS (AU 150.02):

1. Exercise due professional care.

2. Have adequate technical training and proficiency.

3. Plan the engagement adequately.

4. Supervise the work of assistants, if any.

5. Accumulate sufficient information to provide a reasonable basis for the professional judgment described in the report.

6. Consider who is the requester of the report, the circumstances under which the request is made, the purpose of the request, and the requester's intended use of the report.

7. Obtain an understanding of the form and substance of the transaction(s).

8. Review applicable GAAP.

9. If appropriate, consult with other professionals or experts.

10. If appropriate, perform research or other procedures to ascertain and consider the existence of creditable precedents or analogies.

In addition, when evaluating, at the request of a principal or an intermediary acting for a principal, accounting principles that relate to a specific transaction, or when determining the type of opinion that may be rendered on a specific entity's financial statements, the reporting accountant should consult with the principal's continuing accountant to ascertain all the available facts relevant to forming a professional judgment.

Reports on Application of Accounting Principles

The accountant's written report should be addressed to the principal or to the intermediary, and should ordinarily include (AU 625.08):

a. A brief description of the nature of the engagement and a statement that the engagement was performed in accordance with applicable AICPA standards.

b. A description of the transaction(s), a statement of the relevant facts, circumstances, and assumptions, and a statement about the source of information. Principals to specific transactions should be identified, and hypothetical transactions should be described as involving nonspecific principals (e.g., Company A, Company B).

c. A statement describing the appropriate accounting principle(s) to be applied, or type of opinion that may be rendered on the entity's financial statements, and, if appropriate, a description of the reasons for the reporting accountant's conclusion.

d. A statement that the responsibility for the proper accounting treatment rests with the preparers of the financial statements, who should consult with their continuing accountants.

e. A statement that any difference in the facts, circumstances, or assumptions presented may change the report.

An example of a report on the application of GAAP to a hypothethical transaction is shown in Figure 11.8.

FUTURE TRENDS IN AUDITORS' REPORTS

The National Commission on Fraudulent Financial Reporting (NCFFR, often called the "Treadway Commission") issued its final report in late 1987. The Treadway Report, discussed in Chapter 45, makes two recommendations concerning the auditor's communication with users of financial statements, described hereafter.

Degree of Reliance

NCFFR recommends that the auditor's report should be revised by the ASB to explicitly state that an audit provides reasonable but not absolute assurance that the audited financial statements are free from material misstatements resulting from fraud or error. The new standard report adopted in early 1988 (see Figure 11.2) essentially accomplishes this, with a few less words.

Of course, how the new form will be interpreted by plaintiffs and the courts cannot be determined yet; but if improvements are not forthcoming, it is conceivable that even stronger language could be placed in later revisions. (See also the discussion under "Uncertainties" in this chapter, for an analysis of the auditor's conundrum now that a qualified opinion may no longer be issued based on uncertainties.)

Internal Controls

NCFFR also wants the auditor's report to describe the extent to which the auditor has reviewed the internal control structure. This recommendation is aimed at informing readers of the fact that in at least some audits, not much of a review was done, and excessive reliance should therefore not be placed on the auditor. This recommendation has not been included in the new standard report (Figure 11.2).

Introduction

We have been engaged to report on the appropriate application of generally accepted accounting principles to the hypothetical transaction described below. This report is being issued to the XYZ Investment Bankers for assistance in evaluating accounting principles for the described hypothetical transaction. Our engagement has been conducted in accordance with standards established by the American Institute of Certified Public Accountants.

Description of Transaction

The facts, circumstances, and assumptions relevant to the hypothetical transaction as provided to us by XYZ Investment Bankers are as follows:

Appropriate Accounting Principles

[*Text discussing principles*]

Concluding Comments

The ultimate responsibility for the decision on the appropriate application of generally accepted accounting principles for an actual transaction rests with the preparers of financial statements, who should consult with their continuing accountants. Our judgment on the appropriate application of generally accepted accounting principles for the described hypothetical transaction is based solely on the facts provided to us as described above; should these facts and circumstances differ, our conclusion may change.

FIG. 11.8   Example of Report on Application of Accounting Principles for a Hypothetical Transaction

The Treadway Report also recognizes that the auditor could disagree with management's assessment of the company's internal controls, as stated in Management and Audit Committee Reports (see Chapter 6). At present there is no specific guidance on what the auditor should do in this event. The Treadway Commission recommends that the ASB provide explicit guidance—reporting or otherwise. This will undoubtedly be a topic for future discussion by the ASB.

PART III

Specific Areas of Financial Accounting and Auditing

12

Cash, Investments, and Payables

THE LIQUID ASSET CYCLE

Liquid assets consist of cash, temporary cash-equivalent investments, and marketable securities, and their proper management is essential to the viability of every business organization. The ultimate objective of liquid asset management is to have cash available when and where it is needed. To maximize earnings, cash needs should be satisfied by borrowing at the lowest possible interest cost and excess cash should be invested until needed in operation of the business. Liquid asset management is significantly affected by the demands placed on the enterprise by its creditors.

In many businesses, the cash account is affected by more transactions than any other account because cash is an integral part of the major transaction cycles and because most business activities begin or end with cash. The accounting concepts for cash and accounts payable are relatively simple, while those for marketable securities are more complex. Interestingly, this relationship is reversed for the auditing aspects of these accounts.

The importance of cash flows is underscored by SFAS 95, *Statement of Cash Flows* (C25), issued in late 1987. The FASB has concluded that, because cash generation ability of an enterprise is of central importance to financial statement users in predicting the cash flows that may ultimately be achieved from investing in or lending to the enterprise, more detailed information on cash flows is desirable. Accordingly, SFAS 95 calls for segregation of cash flows into operating, investing, and financing activities, as contrasted with the prior practice of presenting a hodgepodge of sources and uses. The cash flow statement is discussed in Chapter 3.

Investing Excess Funds

Excess funds can be temporarily invested in a number of different securities, depending on the length of time that the cash is expected to be available. Many companies will put money to work temporarily in short-term paper such as certificates of deposit (CDs), commercial paper, or treasury bills. If money is going to be available for a longer period of time, other security investment options are available, as discussed later in this chapter. Usually, such transactions are under the control of the senior company management and require the approval of the board of directors for other than routine purchases and sales of high-quality short-term investments.

Cash Sources

The primary source for cash receipts is the revenue cycle—selling merchandise or providing services to a customer and converting the sale or service into a receivable and ultimately into cash. See Chapter 13 for a complete discussion of this cycle, including the important controls.

Other major sources of cash are the sale of an equity interest in the enterprise and borrowings (see Chapters 20 and 18, respectively). These sources of cash can be very large, but for most companies other than financial institutions they are not part of a recurring stream of transactions processed in a major cycle. Cash received in this manner is generally subject to adequate internal control in most enterprises. Larger companies achieve control in these major business transactions through the active participation of the board of directors and top executive officers. Smaller companies generally achieve control through the involvement of the owners.

Less significant sources of cash include the sale of fixed assets and scrap, sale or discounting of receivables, and receipt of investment income. The extent to which such sources fall within a major transaction cycle or are under the control of the company's management is determined by the frequency of receipts and their significance to the enterprise.

Cash Use

The predominant use of cash is to pay for purchases of goods and services, such as raw materials, salaries and wages, supplies, utilities, repairs and maintenance, and research and development. The purchases/payables cycle discussion in this chapter does not include payrolls (see Chapter 14), nor does it include disbursements for capital asset acquisitions, repayment of borrowings and interest, and dividends (see Chapters 15, 18, and 20, respectively).

CASH AND CASH EQUIVALENTS

Cash Management

Objectives. The primary objective of cash management is to ensure that the company has sufficient cash to carry on its operations. Collecting receivables and paying bills have always been functions of cash management; however, because interest can be a significant additional cost, the ability to accelerate cash inflows, slow cash outflows, and invest excess funds or reduce costly borrowings is very important.

Budgeting. Effective cash forecasting, or budgeting, is the backbone of good cash management. Detailed planning of receipts and disbursements enables a company to schedule its expected borrowings and cash investments advantageously.

Most short-term cash budgets are designed to indicate the high and low points in a company's cash cycle. Identifying the low points alerts management not to schedule large discretionary payments at these times and can thus preclude the necessity of borrowing. Identifying the high points allows management to plan the company's short-term investment strategy.

The longer-term budget shows significant changes caused by acquisitions, the introduction of new products, and the planned growth of the company. It is used in determining whether to raise funds on a short- or long-term basis and how this decision will affect the company's capital structure. The long-term budget also assists in securing funds, since it shows potential lenders a comprehensive cash forecast of both capital needs and means of repayment.

The nature of the firm's business, overall company strategies, and the purpose of the budget all are factors that determine the length of the period the budget covers. Companies whose operations fluctuate widely generally prepare shorter-term cash budgets than companies with more stable operations.

Determining Size of Cash Balances. A sufficient cash balance must be maintained to meet payments arising in the ordinary course of business (e.g., purchases, payroll, taxes, and dividends). A precautionary cushion is also needed to meet unexpected contingencies. The more predictable the cash flows of the business and the more borrowing power available, the less need for a cushion. Not all of the company's funds need be held in cash to meet these requirements; a portion may be held in short-term investments as well. Also, the cash balance may actually be negative on the company's records if float (discussed later in this chapter) is used effectively.

Compensating Balances. Compensating balances are a part of a company's cash balances. These are amounts a company must maintain pursuant to an informal or formal agreement with a bank that has loaned funds or has made a line of credit available. They also effectively pay for bank services rendered to the company for which there is no direct fee, for instance, check processing and lockbox management. By requiring a compensating balance, the bank achieves a higher effective rate on a loan than the stated rate.

The compensating balance requirement can be either an absolute minimum balance below which the cash on deposit according to the bank's records should not fall, or a minimum average balance over some period of time, often a month. The former requirement is more restrictive because the company receives no benefit from its actual balance fluctuating above the required minimum. Funds on deposit to meet a minimum compensating balance are effectively unusable for other purposes. Before entering a compensating balance arrangement, a company should evaluate its true cost and compare it with bank charges that might be paid directly for services covered by the balances.

Concentration Banking. For large companies operating in multiple locations, the location of bank accounts is important. The establishment of strategic collection centers will accelerate the flow of funds into the firm by shortening the time between a customer's mailing of a payment and the company's having the use of the funds. The selection of collection centers is based on the geographic areas the company serves and the volume of billings in each area, and the costs to be charged by and benefits to be received from specific banks interested in having the company's business.

Customers are instructed to remit their payments to a designated collection center. Deposits are made into the collection center's local bank, thus reducing the time required to process checks, because the customers' banks are generally within the area of the collection center bank. The local bank deposits are then transferred to a major company account in a concentration bank. This is generally accomplished through a wire transfer, which makes the funds immediately available in the concentration account. However, if the amounts to be transferred from the regional account are small, it might be more economical to transfer them by drawing a check on that account.

Concentration banking reduces the size of a company's *collection float*, which is the difference between the amount on deposit according to the company's records and the amount of collected funds according to the bank records. By using regional accounts, amounts deposited clear through the Federal Reserve System more quickly and thus can be accessed sooner.

Although the operations of many companies are decentralized, cash control works best when centralized under direct corporate management, since less cash is required to support operations, fewer banks are used, balances required to serve as precautionary cushions are reduced, and overall compensating balance requirements may also be reduced.

Types of Bank Accounts. Cash management today has been expanded to a sophisticated financial function, but its original custodial function – cash control and safekeeping – remains significant. A company can vary the types of bank accounts it uses to obtain desired control objectives. The general cash account is the principal bank account in most companies and the only account in many small companies. Funds are received and cash is disbursed as part of the major transaction cycles through this account; also, deposits from and disbursements to all other bank accounts are made through it.

Imprest accounts. An imprest bank account makes a specific amount of cash available for a limited purpose. For example, it can be used at outlying locations, thus facilitating the disbursement of funds for minor local needs. Authorized personnel disburse these funds at their own discretion, as long as the payments are consistent with company policy. Funds in an imprest account are periodically reimbursed from the general cash account upon receipt of vouchers supporting disbursements made. No other deposits are made into an imprest account.

Imprest bank accounts are often used for disbursing payroll checks. Prior to the disbursement of the payroll checks, the total payroll amount is transferred to the imprest payroll account, whose balance is normally kept at zero or a nominal amount. The account thus acts as a clearing account for a large volume of checks. Separating payroll disbursement from other functions in this manner improves internal control and reduces the time needed to reconcile bank accounts.

The imprest approach is often also used to provide petty cash funds for expenditures that are most conveniently paid in cash. The fund should be sufficiently large to meet the normal need for small payments for a period of two to three weeks.

Branch accounts. A branch account allows a company operating in multiple locations greater local autonomy, since the business branch can deposit and withdraw from an account under its control. A branch account used in this manner functions very much like a general cash account but on a local level. Excesses or deficiencies in cash are periodically adjusted by transfers to or from the company's general cash account. Centralized control over branch accounts requires daily or weekly cash reports and careful monitoring of balances.

Branch accounts can also be used in a slightly different manner, by maintaining separate accounts for receipts and disbursements. As with concentration banking, a collection account can be established to receive all deposits, which are subsequently transferred to the general cash account. The disbursement account is set up on an imprest basis with a fixed balance.

Lockbox accounts. With a lockbox, payments can be collected and deposited quickly, making the money available for company use in the shortest amount of time. Large, multilocation companies will usually locate lockboxes in cities within regions of heaviest billing. The company rents a local post office box and authorizes its bank in each of these cities to pick up customers' remittances. The bank checks the box several times a day and immediately deposits the checks into the company account. The speed of collection and deposit into the account, which thus accelerates the availability of collected funds, is the greatest advantage of this approach.

The bank performs many services in connection with the lockbox: The checks are microfilmed for record purposes and cleared for collection; the company is sent a deposit slip and a list of payments, together with any other material mailed by the customer. Although the lockbox procedure frees the company from handling and depositing the checks, there could be a considerable cost for these banking services.

Because the cost of a lockbox system is almost directly proportional to the number of checks deposited, such arrangements may not be profitable for a company if the average remittance is small. If the income generated from accelerating the receipt of funds exceeds the cost of the system by a large enough amount, it is then considered profitable and worth undertaking. The main factors affecting the degree of profitability are the geographic dispersion of customers, the size of the typical remittances, and the earnings rate on the accelerated funds. Important considerations are whether internal control over cash is improved by a lockbox or whether its use results in a reduction of company personnel otherwise needed to process the receipts.

Electronic Funds Transfer. Electronic technology has made possible another method of transferring funds—electronic funds transfer (EFT). This process uses private wire or telephone rather than paper to request a bank to transfer some of the depositor's funds to someone else or to another bank account. EFT makes possible the instantaneous and inexpensive transfers of funds for both large and small companies.

EFT involves both debit and credit systems. In a debit EFT system, the payee has his bank charge the payor's bank account based on a preauthorized payment instruction the payor has given to his bank; examples include preauthorized payments made by a policyholder to an insurance company, or a customer's authorization to a power company to bill his bank account directly for monthly charges. In a credit EFT system, the payor instructs his bank to transfer funds to the payee's bank account; for example, an employer's automated payroll system generates data in electronic form, containing instructions for the employer's bank to transfer funds from the employer's account to the employees' accounts.

EFT, despite its widespread uses, is not without drawbacks. Safeguards have been built into EFT systems, but the exposure to fraud is increased because of the reliance on computer technology, which transfers funds without personal intervention. See

Chapter 10 for a commentary on these exposures and some of the controls used to guard against them.

Float. Another aspect in the control of bank balances is the use of float. There are two types of float, both of which involve a difference between the company's record of cash in the bank account and the bank's record of unrestricted cash in that account.[1]

In the first type of float, the company records the cash as soon as it is received and deposited, but cannot draw the funds until the bank has collected them from the banks on which the deposited checks are drawn. Until collected, the deposited checks represent a kind of float. If a company can accurately estimate the size of this float, that is, the time when funds credited to its bank account will be usable, it can significantly reduce excess cash balances that would otherwise be kept to meet its normal transaction needs.

The second type of float occurs when a company writes a check against its bank balance but the bank has not yet received and paid the check and deducted it from their record of the company's balance. The float is the total amount of such outstanding checks. The company's records can thus show a negative cash balance; however, when the outstanding checks are added to the company's balance, the balance reflected by the bank's records may be positive. By accurately estimating the amount of outstanding checks at a given time, the company can reduce its bank balance to a minimum and keep available only those funds necessary to meet the clearing checks; in some cases the company will maintain a very low balance in an account, with the bank informing the company of the dollar amount of checks presented. The company is then obligated to transfer funds from another account at the same bank to cover the checks. This method is commonly used for drafts, which look like checks but are not; the draft issuer must be informed by the bank that drafts have been presented, and the company must then transfer funds to cover them before the presenter receives credit.

Float is eliminated when EFT is used, because the movement of funds is instantaneously recorded.

Bank Relationships. A company's financial officer's primary concern is to develop adequate banking relationships to handle present and future financial requirements. The number and distribution of accounts depends largely on the size of the operating balances required, the geographical location of a company's facilities, and the amount of bank credit it may require. In most instances, it is wise for a firm to concentrate its bank accounts in a few banks, thus enabling it to maximize its importance to a particular bank. For one thing, banks are generally more inclined to

---

[1] Caution, however, must be exercised in any cash management program involving float. The distinction between aggressive cash management and illegal cash management practices was pointed out in 1985 during the U.S. government's proceedings against E.F. Hutton & Co. Hutton subsequently pleaded guilty to 2,000 counts of wire and mail fraud and paid the maximum penalty of $2,000,000 plus $750,000 for the government's cost of the investigation. In addition, Hutton was required to make restitution to financial institutions for lost interest because of the illegal scheme involving float. The core of the government's case focused on Hutton's intent to deceive the financial institutions, rather than on the program methodology itself.

accommodate larger customers; also, if several types of accounts are within one bank, the firm might incur smaller service charges than if the accounts were dispersed among several banks. The company's role in the community, payroll check services for employees, business relationships, and directorships also play important roles in the development of banking relations.

Temporary Investments

In temporarily investing available cash, a firm will have to make decisions regarding the amount of cash to be invested, the types of securities to be purchased, and the timing of security purchases and sales. Most nonfinancial companies do not have elaborate systems for handling marketable securities or short-term paper purchases and sales because the transactions usually are infrequent and uncomplicated.

Collection and recording of income from dividends and interest is another part of the temporary investments and marketable securities transaction cycle. Checks received as investment income are usually processed as a normal part of the cash receipts system. Companies periodically need to ascertain that all interest and dividend income due has been received and recorded.

Short-Term Paper. A wide range of short-term paper is available for investment. *Certificates of deposit* (CDs) represent formal evidence of indebtedness, issued by a bank, subject to withdrawal under the specific terms of the instrument. CDs are frequently negotiable or transferable. Negotiable CDs pay interest at maturity, are usually issued in $100,000 denominations (occasionally a smaller amount), and mature in 30 days to one year. Nonnegotiable CDs (savings certificates) pay interest at maturity, are typically issued in almost any denomination, usually with a lower limit of $500, and vary as to maturity from six months to two and one-half years. Many banks also issue such certificates for periods of up to 10 years.

As discussed in Chapter 44, *mutual fund* investment companies provide a service for their stockholders by directly investing in a variety of securities that are compatible with the funds' stated investment objectives. *Open-end funds* have no limit to the number of subscribers. An investment in an open-end fund is made at the fair market value of the fund's assets, determined on a unit basis and having fees ranging from none to 6% or more. An investment in an open-end fund is disposed of by redeeming the unit at fair market value. Investments in *closed-end funds* are similar to investments in corporate stock, and shares are bought and sold in the over-the-counter market.

In *money market funds*, the yield is determined by the mix of treasury bills and commercial paper making up the fund's investments. Some money funds require as little as a $500 initial minimum investment. Many allow withdrawal by checks or through wire transfers. The former can be advantageous to the investor, since the mutual fund account earns interest until the check clears and is charged against it.

Treasury bills are sold on a discount basis in $10,000 denominations at weekly auctions held by the government. These U.S. government obligations are generally sold with 91- and 182-day maturities; occasionally, nine-month and one-year maturities are available. *Treasury notes* mature in one to 10 years. *Treasury bonds* are issued for periods in excess of ten years. Both notes and bonds bear interest at a stated rate.

Commercial paper is a short-term debt (one day to 270 days) issued by large corporations with superior credit ratings. These interest-bearing obligations are usually issued in $100,000 denominations (occasionally in smaller amounts), and generally yield a higher rate than treasury bills.

A *repurchase agreement*, commonly referred to as a "repo," is a short-term sale of securities by a dealer in government securities whereby the dealer agrees to repurchase the securities from the investor at a specified time. The underlying instrument usually is a U.S. government or government-backed security. The holding period is tailored to the needs of the investor and can be established for very short periods, even a few days (usually one day to 30 days, occasionally more). Interest rates on repurchase agreements are tied to the rate on treasury bills, federal funds, and loans to government securities dealers by commercial banks.

There are many other types of short-term investments available, with varying degrees of risk. Many of these additional instruments are described in Chapter 21.

Financial Accounting and Reporting

In financial statements, the heading "cash" includes currency on hand and on deposit, demand deposits, and checks drawn prior to the balance sheet date but not released. SFAS 95, *Statement of Cash Flows*, provides more details on the definition of cash (C25.105, n.2). When certificates of deposit, time deposits, or savings accounts are included in the cash caption, the amount thereof is customarily given either parenthetically on the balance sheet or in a note to the financial statements. In addition, certain other items (cash equivalents) are frequently combined with the above cash items. Cash equivalents are discussed later in this chapter. Cash should not include funds received after the end of the fiscal period, even though the cash may have been in transit over the company's year end.

As mentioned earlier, some companies issue drafts in payment of purchase obligations; this is frequently done in paying farms for on-the-spot purchases of agricultural products. The issuing company should ordinarily deduct the amount of such outstanding drafts from cash rather than show them as a liability.

Cash Equivalents. SFAS 95, *Statement of Cash Flows* (C25) defines cash equivalents as short-term, highly liquid investments that are both readily convertible to known amounts of cash and so near maturity that they present insignificant risk of change in value. Examples of such items are Treasury bills, commercial paper, money market funds, and federal funds (for an enterprise with banking operations). Purchases and sales of these items are considered to be part of an enterprise's cash management activities rather than part of its operating, investing, and financing activities (C25.106-.107).

In this regard, SFAS 95 requires that the totals of cash and cash equivalents at the beginning and end of a period as shown in the statement of cash flows is to equal similarly titled line items or subtotals in the statements of financial position (balance sheet) as of those dates (C25.105).

Temporary Investments. Temporary or short-term investments that are not cash equivalents—such as certain commercial paper, bankers acceptances, U.S. Treasury notes, and reverse repurchase agreements—should not be combined with the cash caption on the balance sheet.

With respect to reverse repurchase agreements, Regulation S-X in Rule 4-08(m)(2) requires a public company, if the amount of its reverse repurchase agreements exceeds 10% of its total assets, to (1) disclose the amount of these agreements on the balance sheet, and (2) disclose in an appropriately captioned footnote the company's policy with regard to taking possession of the underlying securities or other assets, and whether there are any provisions to protect the company in the event of default by the counterparty.

Additionally, if the amount at risk (basically the carrying value in excess of the market value of the underlying assets) under reverse repurchase agreements with any individual counterparty exceeds 10% of stockholders' equity, the name of each such counterparty, the amount at risk with each counterparty, and the weighted average maturity of the agreements with each counterparty are to be disclosed.

See Chapter 21 for a further discussion of repurchase agreements.

Bank Overdrafts. A book cash balance may sometimes show an overdraft condition. An overdraft can occur by design (as part of a formal cash management program with a financial institution) or out of error (a lack of funds in the account on which checks have been drawn). As mentioned previously, cash management programs attempt to use an enterprise's excess cash most efficiently, and yet ensure that such cash is available when needed to pay checks, drafts, and so forth. As a result, the enterprise's outstanding (unpaid) checks may put the enterprise into a book overdraft condition. When these checks are presented for payment at the bank, the bank will notify the enterprise, which will then transfer funds from other sources, such as short-term or temporary investments (basically cash equivalents), or use available lines of credit or other borrowing arrangements to cover these claims on its cash.

In practice, cash overdrafts are normally classified as accounts payable or accrued liabilities on the balance sheet. (In fact, the SEC will insist on it.) However, GAAP is silent on this matter and practice does vary. If the overdrafts are combined with accounts payable or accrued expenses, they must be disclosed (on the face of the balance sheet or in a footnote), if they are material in relation to those balances.

It is permissible, however, to offset an overdraft in one bank account with *available* funds in other accounts in the same bank or in other banks. "Available" is defined in this context to require the existence of positive cash balances in other accounts unencumbered by any arrangements (such as compensating balance requirements or similar restrictions on the use of the cash). Offset is mandatory when there is available cash in another account in the same bank in which the overdraft exists and there is a formal offset arrangement. Overdrafts are not to be offset against certificates of deposit, commercial paper, or other cash equivalents, or temporary investments.

Restricted Cash. Cash available for general operations should be distinguished from cash restricted for special purposes. For instance, cash deposited with a trustee for the payment of mortgage interest and taxes should not be included with general cash (although it may be a current asset if the related liabilities are current).

Restricted cash funds not available for general operations, such as (1) a sinking fund for payment of long-term debt or retirement of preferred stock, (2) the proceeds of a construction mortgage that is restricted for use only for construction costs, and (3) funds allocated for special purposes by action of the company's board of directors should not be shown as unrestricted cash, nor should they be included under current assets, except for any portion to be used to satisfy current liabilities. For example, cash that has been earmarked for additions to properties should be included under the "Property, Plant, and Equipment" or "Other Assets" heading.

Compensating Balances. Contractual obligations to maintain compensating balances must be disclosed. When it can be specifically determined, the amount of the restricted cash should be segregated. It should be shown as a noncurrent asset to the extent that it relates to the long-term portion of the related debt (B05.107). A balance sheet caption such as "Cash on deposit maintained as compensating balance" would be appropriate. Footnote disclosure should include the terms of the requirement and details of withdrawal restrictions; if the amount restricted was raised substantially during the year, the average amount restricted during the year and the largest amount so restricted should be disclosed.

Other compensating balances should be disclosed by footnote as follows:

• Where there is a contractual agreement to maintain a compensating balance, but the amount is determined only as an average over a period, the terms of the agreement and the approximate dollar amount affected should be disclosed.

• Where the compensating balance is an acknowledged informal agreement, the footnote should again describe the terms of the agreement and, if determinable, the pattern of voluntary restrictions during the year.

Most of the disclosure rules for compensating balances originated with the SEC. Under FRR § 203.03 (ASR 148), restricted deposits held as compensating balances against short-term borrowing arrangements must be segregated and appropriately described in the balance sheet of an SEC registrant. The rule also requires footnote disclosure of

1. Compensating balances maintained to assure future credit availability, along with the amount and terms of the agreement, and

2. Unrestricted compensating balance arrangements, that is, those that do not restrict the use of cash shown on the balance sheet.

FRR § 203.02.a defines a compensating balance as

that portion of any demand deposit (or any time deposit or certificate of deposit) maintained by a corporation (or by any other person on behalf of the corporation) which constitutes support for existing borrowing arrangements of the corporation (or any other person) with a lending institution. Such arrangements would include both outstanding borrowings and the assurance of future credit availability.

Factors to be considered in deciding whether segregation and disclosure are required are suggested in the FRR and include the relationship of the compensating balance to

1. Total cash,
2. Total net liquid assets,
3. Net working capital, and
4. The impact of compensating balances on the effective cost of financing.

The FRR defines 15% of liquid assets (current cash balances, whether restricted or not, plus marketable securities) as usually being material.

Compensating balance arrangements with banks usually are expressed in terms of the collected bank ledger balance. The difference between the cash balance reflected in the financial statements and the collected bank ledger balance is *float* (outstanding checks less uncollected funds). Float can be negative if the amount of uncollected funds exceeds the amount of outstanding checks. If the compensating balance arrangement is expressed in terms of the collected bank ledger balance, an adjustment for a float is necessary to state the amount of the balance in book terms. If the compensating balance is fixed or determinable at a given time, the adjustment should be based on actual or estimated float at the date of the balance sheet. If the arrangement calls for an average compensating balance, average float must be used.

Banks customarily credit customer deposits on the date of deposit, not when the funds are collected, so precise information on uncollected funds is seldom readily available. Thus, it will ordinarily be necessary to estimate float. The basis of the estimate should be the method used by the bank in estimating uncollected items; however, a reasonable approximation of that method will suffice. Usually, a company official should discuss the estimation of uncollected items with the banker before calculating the compensating balance. The float adjustment, together with a short statement of criteria used to make the adjustment, is a required disclosure under the FRR.

The guidelines and interpretations section of the FRR states that it is not permissible to reduce compensating balance amounts by amounts maintained as minimum balances for operations. However, deposits maintained as compensation for services – bank reconciliations, lockbox arrangements, and so forth – need not be considered as compensating balances unless the funds also serve as compensating balances under borrowing arrangements.

FRR § 203 recognizes that lines of credit may be offered by financial institutions as a marketing device and that many companies accept them but do not intend to use them. These lines generally need not be disclosed.

When compensating balances under line of credit arrangements relate to both used and unused portions of the line, the FRR requires disclosure of the compensating balance maintained for each purpose. Nonenforceable compensating balance arrangements present the most disclosure difficulty, particularly if the company has not complied. In nonenforceable arrangements there is some uncertainty: the bank may not renew the loan; it may raise the interest; and, generally, noncompliance may negatively affect the relationship with the bank. There is obvious reluctance to detail such problems in writing, by both companies and banks. Nonetheless, the SEC requires disclosure of such arrangements and of any material sanctions.

Note D — Short-Term Debt and Compensating Balances

Greyhound satisfies its short-term financing requirements with bank lines of credit and by the issuance of commercial paper and promissory notes.

Greyhound's short-term bank lines in various currencies, amounting to approximately $35,686,000 at December 31, 1987, are subject to annual renewal and in most instances can be withdrawn at any time at the option of the banks. On $12,000,000 of these lines, compensating balances are required in an amount equal to five percent of the commitments. Cash balances required for operating purposes, float and specifically provided funds are utilized as compensating balances, with no restrictions on the use of these funds.

It is Greyhound's policy to support commercial paper and promissory notes outstanding with unused portions of $12,000,000 of committed short-term lines of credit and $775,000,000 of long-term revolving bank credit. In addition, Greyhound allocates unused portions of long-term bank credits under an agreement with a consolidated subsidiary to support its demand advances (up to $35,000,000) to Greyhound when outstanding ($35,000,000 at December 31, 1987).

The following information pertains to Greyhound's short-term debt (including short-term obligations classified as long-term debt):

(000 omitted)	1987	1986	1985
Maximum amount of short-term debt outstanding during year	$675,544	$497,020	$453,792
Average daily short-term debt outstanding during year	$393,004	$361,933	$293,604
Average short-term interest rate at end of year*	7.8%	6.7%	8.4%
Weighted average interest rate on short-term debt outstanding during year*	7.2%	7.1%	8.5%

*Exclusive of the cost of maintaining compensating balances and payment of commitment fees on long-term revolving bank credit agreements used to support such borrowings. Also, interest rate swap agreements, as discussed in Note E, have effectively fixed future interest rates on $150,000,000 of short-term obligations at 8.1%.

FIG. 12.1 Example of Compensating Balance Disclosure
Source: The Greyhound Corporation, *1987 Annual Report.*

SAB Topic 6.H (SAB 1) includes interpretations of FRR § 203 by the SEC staff; Figure 12.1 illustrates a compensating balance disclosure in a published annual report.

Auditing Cash

General Concepts. The overall audit philosophy for cash that is assumed in this section is explained in Chapters 7 through 10. The audit objective is to determine that cash and cash equivalents are fairly presented in the context of the financial statements as a whole.

To choose between a systems reliance approach and a substantive procedures approach, or to determine how much of each approach should be blended, the auditor must gain an understanding of the activities of the company that affect its accounting for cash and the potential seriousness of errors. An auditor must also understand the company's internal controls established to both prevent and detect the misuse of funds.

In assessing the inherent risk in cash and cash equivalent balances, the susceptibility to theft is considered. Of all the areas in the audit, the concern about theft is highest here; consequently, particular attention is given to the effectiveness of the client's segregation of duties and safeguarding procedures related to cash transactions.

Historically, it has been common for cash to be overaudited, both because it comforts the novice auditor who enjoys precision and because cash is the asset most susceptible to theft. It is important that the objective of the audit be kept in mind so as to avoid the use of excessive audit time in this area. At the same time, however, it must be recognized that nearly all transactions affecting the business pass through the cash account at some time, and the alert auditor can, from an unusual cash item, frequently start a chain of questioning that leads to important audit findings. This is particularly true in the case of smaller clients with limited accounting sophistication who may not understand the implications of transactions for financial reporting.

Transaction Types. The audit focuses on the primary transactions that affect cash and cash equivalents. These are the following:

1. The receipt of cash from the normal liquidation of receivables as well as from sources such as the cash sale of inventory and scrap; the sale of property, plant, and equipment; the sale or discounting of other assets such as receivables; the issuance of debt and equity securities; and the receipt of investment income. The auditor must be familiar with the company's procedures to control the receipt of cash from the varying sources, including controls over incoming mail, the handling of cash at the point of sale, the processing of cash receipts in the organization, and the depositing of cash into bank accounts.

2. The payment of cash for such items as the purchase of raw materials and property, plant, and equipment; the payment of expenses, including payroll expenses; the purchase of investments; and the payments on indebtedness. The auditor must be familiar with the client's controls over the cash payments system that ensure payments are authorized and are for valid and approved purchases of raw materials, assets, or services, or are in connection with authorized investment and financing decisions.

Audit Approach. The overall design of cash audit procedures for large companies normally involves extensive reliance on the client's internal control structure, assuming that a preliminary evaluation assesses the controls as good. The reason for this is the large volume of transactions flowing through the cash accounts and the interrelationship of cash with major transaction cycles.

Since most of the objectives of the audit of cash can be met through compliance testing procedures, favorable results obtained from such procedures can normally reduce the amount of substantive audit work on the cash and cash equivalent balances. Additionally, some of the substantive audit procedures can be performed prior to year end.

Much of the transaction testing for the cash component of the financial statements is performed as part of the tests for the sales/receivables cycle, the purchases/payables cycle, and payrolls. The internal control aspects and systems testing for these activities is discussed later in this chapter and in Chapters 13 and 14.

Analytical Review. Cash and cash-equivalent accounts do not usually have a direct or predictable interrelationship with other accounts. They are essentially the unexpended funds or reserves to pay anticipated bills, for expansion or for investment. Consequently, except for the identification of significant fluctuations, analytical procedures are usually limited to comparisons of interrelated balances and review of records for unusual entries. If the company prepares cash budgets they should be reviewed and compared with actual expenditures.

Objectives and Procedures. Figure 12.2 is a very condensed listing of the interim and year-end audit procedures that are commonly used to achieve these objectives. The procedures shown may be used to satisfy more than one audit objective, but are listed alongside the objective that they most typically satisfy, providing an overview of how the audit objectives are met.

Probably the most common audit procedures in the cash area are (1) obtaining bank confirmations of balances and liabilities using the standard form agreed to by the banking industry and (2) performing *proofs of cash.*

The ASB is considering a revision to the standard bank confirmation form that has been in use since 1966. Features of the proposed revision include restricting the confirmation request to information on deposit and loan balances. Guidance on requesting other information of interest to auditors, such as the existence of loan guarantees and other contingencies, is to be the subject of a future auditing interpretation.

In performing a proof of cash, the auditor reconciles deposits and disbursements according to one or more bank statements with the receipts and disbursements shown in the company's books. Also, the auditor may directly obtain *cut-off bank statements* for some accounts; these are bank statements for a short period, say ten days, after period-end, which the auditor receives directly to check the correctness of the company's period-end bank reconciliation.

Note that for cash equivalents, the audit procedures for marketable securities, discussed later in this chapter, are often applicable.

Audit objective	Sample year-end procedures*	Sample interim procedures
Existence. Determine whether there are cash and cash equivalent balances supporting the dollar amount shown in the balance sheet and whether all such balances have been properly included.	• Count or confirm petty cash funds. • Obtain directly from each bank with which the company had transactions during the period confirmation of the bank balances, loans, securities held, guarantees given, collateral held and any unused lines of credit available.	• Review bank reconciliations for independent approval. • Test the company's system for controlling payments. • Trace selected daily receipt listings to bank deposit slips and bank statements.
Ownership. Determine whether the cash and cash equivalent balances are owned by the company and whether they are subject to any lien or restrictions.	• Obtain confirmation of each balance direct from each bank together with details of any collateral held or restrictions or liens over the accounts. • Confirm with employees any cash balances held by them.	• Review the company's procedures for establishing and pledging bank accounts.
Mechanical Accuracy. Determine whether the basic mathematical calculations and clerical compilation procedures have been accurately carried out.	• Review reconciliations of bank balances and investigate reconciling items.	• Test the company's procedures for checking the mechanical accuracy of transactions being recorded or posted. • Test the addition and postings of the cash receipts and cash payments records.
Valuation. Determine whether cash and cash equivalent balances are fairly valued in conformity with generally accepted accounting principles.	• Review reconciliation of bank balances and investigate reconciling items. • Check exchange rate and translation calculation of foreign currency balances.	
Disclosure. Determine whether cash and cash equivalent balances disclosure in the financial statements is adequate.	• Agree financial statement disclosures to information noted in performance of the examination, including compensating balances and significant restrictions, if any, on availability (e.g. time certificates of deposit). • Review bank confirmations for details of collateral and liens.	

FIG. 12.2   Audit Objectives and Sample Procedures for Cash and Cash Equivalents

Audit objective	Sample year-end procedures*	Sample interim procedures
Classification. Determine whether cash and cash equivalent balances are properly classified as an asset or liability and as to liquidity.	• Review bank balances to determine whether there is any set-off of debit (overdraft) and credit balances. • Confirm with banks the terms (including maturity) of any time deposit.	
Cut-Off. Determine whether all payments or receipts before and after the year-end are appropriately treated.	• Review cash transactions shortly before and after the balance sheet date. • Review any interbank and intercompany transfers shortly before and after the year-end date. • Note numbers of last checks drawn at year-end and trace to cut-off bank statements to ascertain that no subsequent checks cleared before year end.	

*May also be performed at an interim date in some situations.

The use of EFT makes it more difficult to accomplish the cash audit objectives. With EFT, less paperwork (hard copy) is created to document transactions that have taken place. Computers can now communicate with one another, but unless they are programmed with specific instructions to print out a hard copy of the transactions, a visible audit trail may not be created. Companies should review plans with their internal and external auditors before installing major EFT applications, to ensure that ultimately there is adequate evidence available for required audits.

INVESTMENTS IN SECURITIES

Very broadly, all assets employed in the pursuit of profit are investments. This generalization is not very helpful; in fact, there is a host of definitions and interpretations that characterize the accounting for investments. There are many kinds of debt instruments and preferred and common stocks, and numerous combinations of warrants, voting rights, convertibility, and other special conditions. All of these complicate the accounting.

Investments can be passive or can bring a measure of influence over the investee. Generally, significant influence is deemed to exist with equity method investments of 20% to 50% ownership; at more than 50%, control is presumptively established and the rules change. (Equity investments of 20% or greater are discussed in Chapter 24.)

Security Types

Equity securities represent the underlying ownership interest in a business. They encompass common, preferred, and other capital stock and the right to acquire (e.g., warrants, rights, and call options) or dispose of (e.g., put options) ownership shares in an enterprise at fixed or determinable prices. To receive income while holding a stock investment, the equity owner is dependent on the declaration of dividends by the board of directors of the business. The capital invested in an equity security is normally regained by selling the security. Since the sale price is dependent on the fluctuations in the marketplace or in what a private buyer is willing to pay, there is no guarantee that the investor's original cost will be recovered.

Debt securities, such as bonds and notes, are promissory obligations to repay a certain sum (principal) plus interest at a specified rate. Individual certificates state the dates for payment of principal and interest. The rights and obligations of both parties are generally governed by an indenture that places restrictions on the issuing firm for the protection of investors.

Hybrid securities possess both debt and equity characteristics. Convertible debt securities are hybrids because they allow the investor to exchange one type of security (debt) for another (equity). Some preferred stocks are hybrids because by their terms they must be redeemed by the issuing enterprise, thus giving them characteristics of debt.

Accounting and Reporting—General

Cost. Like other assets acquired by a firm, securities must initially be recorded at their cost. Cost is considered to be the cash or fair market value of other assets given in exchange for the securities acquired; however, for readily marketable securities, quoted market price may be the proper initial valuation, with gain or loss recorded in an exchange of nonmonetary assets for the security. Cost includes all disbursements incident to the acquisition. Incidental disbursements commonly include brokerage fees, taxes, legal fees, and other expenditures necessary to complete the transaction.

Bonds and notes acquired between interest coupon dates are traded on the basis of the market price plus interest accrued since the most recent interest payment. The accrued interest is a separate asset—interest receivable—purchased simultaneously with the bond.

A new cost basis is established when a security is written down for an other-than-temporary decline in value or when there is a transfer between current and noncurrent portfolios which is recorded at the lower of cost or market, as discussed in the section on SFAS 12, *Accounting for Certain Marketable Equity Securities* (I87).

Nonmarketable investments are recorded at their acquisition cost, which includes commissions, transfer fees, and legal fees. Premium or discount on the acquisition of debt investments is a part of the security cost and is amortized on the interest method (I69.108).

Stock Dividends and Splits. When an equity owner in a corporation receives additional shares of the same class of stock in the form of either a stock dividend or a stock split, the investor's proportionate stockholding in the issuing company remains unchanged. Therefore, no dividend income should be recognized. The cost basis of the original investment should be allocated among the new shares received and the old shares held.

The same rule applies to dividends distributed in the form of preferred stock, warrants, or rights to purchase common or preferred stock. Again, the original cost is reallocated among the total holdings according to the proportionate relationship of their fair market value at the time the new securities are issued.

Relieving Cost Upon Disposition of Securities. If only a part of an investment in a security is disposed of and the original investment was acquired in two or more purchases, a problem of cost identification arises. In such situations four possible methods can be used to relieve cost: (1) specific identification, (2) first-in, first-out (FIFO), (3) last-in, first-out (LIFO), and (4) average cost.

Critics of the specific identification method point out that the use of that method permits considerable choice in the amount of gain or loss to be recognized if different lots of a security have been purchased at different prices. Advocates of the average cost method believe that once the different lots are purchased they are really fungible in character and that average cost recognizes this fungibility. Since the average cost method for security sales is not recognized by the Internal Revenue Service as an acceptable method, those companies that use it create a deferred tax temporary difference. The IRS recognizes only the specific identification and FIFO methods for general use. It will allow the use of the LIFO method for entities whose holdings of securities are considered to be equivalent to inventory, such as stockbrokers.

Investment Income. When cash dividends are declared by the investee's board of directors, income is recognized because the investor has a legal right to the dividend. For convenience, companies may record dividends on the ex-dividend date or as received, but at the end of a fiscal period an accrual should be made for dividends receivable, if material. Dividends in kind should be recorded at fair market value; stock dividends and splits are not recorded as income, as stated earlier.

Interest income accrues with the passage of time. The income recognized is adjusted for the amortization or accretion of bond premium or discount (the difference between the cost and face value of the debt security) over its remaining life to maturity. The amortization of premium or accretion of discount using the interest method prescribed by APB 21 (I69.109) results in the recognition of income or expense at the effective interest rate over the remaining period to maturity.

Often the premium or discount on short-term debt investments will not be amortized or accreted, because the holding period is uncertain or will be so short as to make the effect immaterial.

Accounting and Reporting—Marketable Equity Securities

Requirements of SFAS 12. In accordance with SFAS 12, *Accounting for Certain Marketable Securities* (I89), *marketable equity* securities represent any equity security (common or nonredeemable preferred stock) for which a quotation is available from a national or over-the-counter market (I89.404). *Nonmarketable*, as applied in this section, means any security—equity, debt, or hybrid—that does not meet the FASB's definition of marketable. This includes stock that is restricted from sale by governmental or contractual requirements for longer than one year from the financial reporting date. And of course it includes securities changing classification from marketable to nonmarketable as discussed later.

SFAS 12 requires that marketable equity securities be accounted for by using the lower of aggregate cost or aggregate market value. To do this a company must first group its securities into separate portfolios according to the current or noncurrent classification; when the balance sheet is unclassified, the marketable equity securities are treated as noncurrent assets. Next, the aggregate acquisition cost of each of the portfolios is determined; unless a security has been assigned a new carrying amount because of an other than temporary diminution in value or because of a transfer between current and noncurrent classifications, cost is the original cost.

Aggregate market value is the sum of the market price times the number of shares or units of each security in the portfolio. If the company has taken positions involving short sales, sales of calls, or purchase of puts in the same securities as those in the portfolio, these contracts are to be considered in determining market value.

These two aggregates are computed separately for current and noncurrent portfolios. If the aggregate market is less than the aggregate cost for a portfolio, a *valuation allowance* must be established. Note that under this approach a valuation allowance is required by the depressed market value of a portfolio, not a specific security.

When the valuation allowance for a current portfolio changes, the investor recognizes a gain or loss to be included in net income of the current period. The valuation allowance for a noncurrent portfolio is included in the equity section of the balance sheet as a so-called *dangling debit*; it is presented separately and not deducted from retained earnings or netted against any other category of net worth.

Classification. Nonmarketable securities, even though considered a current asset, should not be classified with marketable securities and should be carried at cost, subject to a net realizable value test applied to any asset held for sale. Debt securities are not covered under SFAS 12; however, they would be classified as current assets if they mature or are intended to be sold within a year.

Investments that management specifically intends, and evidences an ability, to hold for a year or more from the date of the financial statements should be classified as noncurrent assets. The propriety of classification as noncurrent will take into account the investor's financial position, working capital requirements, debt agreements, and other contractual obligations that bear upon the feasibility of holding the security for at least one year. If a marketable equity or debt security is expected to be converted to cash within the next 12 months, a current asset classification is appropriate.

Changes in current/noncurrent classification. One of the problems with the accounting promulgated by SFAS 12 is its manipulability based on the classification of securities as current or noncurrent. For example, if a company has the ability to hold securities on a long-term basis and can demonstrate that ability, the classification of the securities then depends on the company's representation as to its intentions. If a company represents that it will hold a security with a depressed market value on a long-term basis, the changes in the valuation reserve do not affect net income.

If the current or noncurrent classification of a marketable security changes, the security must be transferred between the two portfolios at the lower of its cost or market value. If market value is less than cost, the market value becomes the new cost basis. The difference between the old and new cost basis must be reflected as a loss in the determination of current net income.

Transfers between current and noncurrent classification are not accounting changes; however, such transfers, if material, may affect the comparability of the financial statements and should be disclosed (AU 9332.12).

Changes in marketable/nonmarketable classification. FIN 16 (I89) states that if the change in the status of an equity security between marketable and nonmarketable is coincident with the change in the classification between current and noncurrent and market value is less than cost, a new cost basis is established. For securities becoming marketable, market value is the first available market price; for securities becoming nonmarketable, market value is the last available market price. Since the accounting for a nonmarketable security is outside the scope of SFAS 12, it should be excluded from the portfolio of marketable equity securities of which it was a part for purposes of applying the statement. Conversely, when a nonmarketable equity security becomes marketable, it should be included in the portfolio at its cost.

Affiliated Entities. In determining carrying amount, SFAS 12 (I89.103) requires the current portfolios of entities that are consolidated in the financial statements, excluding those that follow specialized industry accounting practices, to be treated as a single consolidated portfolio with a comparison of aggregate cost and market value. Also, noncurrent and unclassified portfolios of consolidated entities should be combined in the same manner. The portfolios of marketable equity securities owned by entities accounted for by the equity method are not to be combined with the portfolios of any other entity included in the financial statements. However, such an entity must individually apply the rules of SFAS 12.

Additionally, an investor in an equity investee that has a valuation allowance carried in its shareholders' equity must effectively consolidate its proportionate share of that allowance; this is done by reducing the investor's investment account and increasing the investor's valuation allowance, as called for by TB 79-19.

FIN 13, *Consolidation of a Parent and Its Subsidiaries Having Different Balance Sheet Dates* (I89), clarifies the application of SFAS 12 when the financial statements of a subsidiary are as of a date different from that of its parent but are consolidated with the financial statements of its parent: to compute the amount of a valuation allowance in consolidated financial statements, aggregate cost and aggregate market value of the portfolio shall be determined for each consolidated subsidiary "as of the date of each subsidiary's balance sheet, and those aggregates shall be combined with aggregate cost and aggregate market value of the parent's portfolio determined as of the parent's balance sheet date" (I89.103). Disclosure should be made of the effect of intervening events that materially affect the financial position or results of operations of a subsidiary, including net realized gains or losses and net unrealized gains or losses applicable to marketable securities arising after the subsidiary's balance sheet date but prior to the parent's financial statement date. However, the subsidiary's financial statements should not be adjusted for such changes.

Market Value Changes After Balance Sheet Date. FIN 11 (I89) clarifies the accounting necessary when there is a change in the market price with respect to marketable equity securities after the date of the financial statements but prior to their issuance. The interpretation indicates that the subsequent disposition of a security or a change in its market price after the end of the year should be taken into consideration, along with other factors, in making the determination of whether there was an other-than-temporary diminution in value of any of the securities held at the balance sheet date. Any loss to be recorded in financial statements is limited to the excess of cost over market value at the balance sheet date; further declines in value should be reported as a loss in the following accounting period.

This FASB interpretation, of course, only affects those noncurrent or unclassified marketable securities for which the effect of a change in the carrying amount is included in stockholder's equity rather than in net income. It would seem that a recordable loss exists prima facie when a security is sold just after year end at an amount that realizes the deferred loss at year end, since this sale negates the noncurrent classification.

Other-Than-Temporary Diminution in Value. Regardless of balance sheet classification, each investment should be evaluated to determine if there are significant factors other than current market conditions that affect the realizability of the carrying amount (I89.115). For example, specific adverse conditions, such as a known liquidity crisis, may affect a particular company's securities, resulting in an other-than-temporary diminution in value; a bankrupt investee clearly reflects such a condition, as might a "going concern" commentary in the auditor's report on the investee's most recent financial statements. Securities valuations should reflect these conditions by a charge against current operations to reduce the carrying amount to estimated current realizable value. In such case, current realizable value becomes the new cost basis and is not adjusted for subsequent market recovery.

Keep in mind that the write-down to market of a noncurrent security simply results in a dangling debit (the valuation reserve) in the equity section of the balance sheet; whether an other-than-temporary diminution in value, chargeable against income, has taken place still needs to be assessed.

In most cases current market quotations may already reflect specific adverse conditions. It is by no means certain, however, that the other-than-temporary diminution is the amount of the deficiency of market under cost. Among the relevant factors are the investor's ability to continue holding the security, the percentage of current market to cost, and the length of time the market for the security has been depressed. Thus the same security, written down to reflect a decline that is other than temporary, could carry a different valuation for different investors.

SEC Rule on Assessment of Impairment. In September 1985, the SEC issued SAB 59 (Topic 5.M) that addresses the accounting for noncurrent marketable equity securities. SAB 59 sets forth the staff's interpretation of the phrase "other than temporary" as used in the discussion of impairment in SFAS 12, which specifies that a company must determine if a decline below cost in the market value of a security is other than temporary.

The SEC staff does not believe that "other than temporary" should be interpreted to mean permanent. SAB 59 states that if a decline in market value occurs, management should determine whether a write-down will be required, considering also the context of the investor's situation. In evaluating the realizable value of the investment, numerous factors should be considered, including:

- The length of time and the extent to which the market value has been less than cost;
- The financial condition and near-term prospects of the issuer, including any specific events that may influence its operations; and
- The intent and ability of the holder to retain its investment to allow for any anticipated recovery in market value.

Unless evidence exists to support a realizable value equal to or greater than the carrying value of the investment, a write-down accounted for as a realized loss should be recorded. Lack of evidence that the decline is other than temporary is not sufficient of itself.

SAB 59 raised questions about the adequacy of SFAS 12 and gave rise to EITF issue 85-39, *Implications of SEC Staff Accounting Bulletin No. 59 on Accounting for Noncurrent Marketable Equity Securities.* No consensus was attempted, but the Task Force felt that SAB 59 went beyond GAAP. The SEC Observer viewed SAB 59 more as an admonition to consider the need for a write-down, and would readily meet with registrants having difficulty with the SAB.

Sales of Marketable Equity Securities With Puts. EITF Issue 85-40, *Comprehensive Review of Sales of Marketable Securities With Put Arrangements*, was considered in November 1985, culminating a series of issues addressed by the Task Force on this subject (see, e.g., Issues 84-05, 85-25, and 85-30). Typically these transactions involve the granting of a put option by a seller to a buyer, allowing the buyer to sell the securities back to the seller at a fixed price in the future. The issues relate to (1) profit or loss recognition and (2) balance sheet classification of the securities involved. The consensus achieved at prior EITF meetings centered on the assessment of the probability of the put being exercised to determine whether sale or financing accounting is appropriate.

The Task Force position for transactions involving sales of marketable securities with put arrangements (developed over the period from September 1984 through November 1985) is as follows:

1. The accounting should be based on an assessment of the probability that the put will be exercised. If exercise is probable, the transaction should be accounted for as a borrowing. (Any difference between the sales proceeds and the put price would be accrued as interest expense, and any impairment of the underlying security would generally not be recognized.) If exercise is not probable, the transaction should be accounted for as a sale. If accounted for as a borrowing, there should be a continual reevaluation of the probability of exercise, with a change in the accounting treatment if appropriate. (This position assumes that if the probability assessment would result in sales accounting, the asset should be removed from the balance sheet.)

2. If accounted for as a sale but exercise of the put later becomes probable, the company should (1) immediately accrue any losses expected upon exercise of the put, (2) periodically

adjust the estimated loss accrual, and (3) ultimately record the repurchased security at the lower of cost or market.

3. The probability assessment would be affected by the length of the put period. A transfer of a security with a put that extends beyond 50% of the expected remaining life of the security should be recognized as a sale.

4. If a transaction is accounted for as a borrowing, the difference between the original sale price and the put price should be amortized over a period less than the expected remaining life of the security.

In addition, in the case of transactions involving gains when reported as sales, the Task Force concluded that the assets should be removed from the balance sheet but that the gain should be deferred because it represents a gain contingency under SFAS 5, *Accounting for Contingencies* (C59), that should not be recognized until the contingency is resolved by expiration of the put without exercise.

Income Tax Allocation. Unrealized gains and losses on marketable securities, whether recognized in net income or included in the equity section of the balance sheet, are temporary differences as described in SFAS 96 (I25). (See Chapter 17).

Specialized Industry Practices. Certain industries, including investment companies, brokers and dealers in securities, stock life insurance companies, and fire and casualty insurance companies, apply specialized accounting practices to marketable securities (I89.108–.111). SFAS 12 does not alter previous accounting practices in these specialized industries, except that entities that previously carried marketable equity securities at cost must carry them at the lower of their aggregate cost or market value. This does not preclude the use of the market value basis where the industry had formerly permitted either the cost basis or the market basis. The specialized industry practices for reporting gains and losses, whether realized or unrealized, remain unchanged. Specific reporting requirements are given for enterprises that include entities whose accepted accounting practices differ with respect to marketable securities (I89.112). (See Chapters 42, 43, and 44.)

Accounting and Reporting—Debt and Nonmarketable Securities

Current. SFAS 12 does not apply to marketable debt or similar securities. Nevertheless, there is little conceptual difference between accounting for current debt instruments and accounting for current equity securities, as discussed in preceding sections. Current asset classification connotes an ability or intention to liquidate the investment within 12 months. Thus, if the valuation concept of lower of cost or market has validity for marketable equity securities, then for the sake of consistency, the concept should have validity for current marketable debt securities. As a result, currently classified marketable securities, whether debt or equity, should be stated at the lower of cost or market; the cumulative amount needed to reduce aggregate cost to aggregate market is considered a securities valuation reserve (valuation allowance); increases or decreases in the allowance are included in current income.

In a lower-of-cost-or-market-basis comparison for debt securities, cost should be amortized cost; therefore, amortization would be recorded prior to making the market comparison.

The computation of the valuation allowance for current marketable nonequity securities should be based on market prices (or, infrequently, on other lower estimates of net realizable value) at the date of the financial statements. In determining aggregate cost and aggregate market for the current portfolio, marketable debt and equity securities could be combined.

Noncurrent. Because security investments appropriately classified as long-term carry with them a representation of a later realization date, current market quotations for such securities do not have the earnings impact of those classified as current assets. It is appropriate to classify, as part of noncurrent assets, investments in debt securities and in other securities with fixed maturity amounts at amortized cost, even when such amounts are in excess of quoted market, if

• There is no indication of other-than-temporary diminution in value,
• It is management's intent to hold such securities until maturity, and
• There is sufficient evidence that such retention is feasible.

Preferred stocks that by their terms are subject to mandatory redemption should be evaluated in the same manner as debt instruments.

Assessment of Value. When value falls significantly below cost, an evaluation of whether the impairment is temporary is necessary. If the investment is scheduled for redemption at a fixed date and price, if the security holder intends and is financially able to hold to maturity, and if there are no reservations regarding the ability of the debtor to pay, the temporary impairment is ignored, and there is no write-down. Otherwise it is necessary to examine clues from the performance of similar securities, through information obtained from analyzing the investee's financial statements, cash flow potential, security market conditions, industry conditions, economic conditions, and other relevant factors.

If the security holder determines that impairment is not temporary, a write-down will be reflected in the financial statements, and a new cost (i.e., carrying amount) established for the investment.

Good Faith Valuations. In the case of nonmarketable investments, it is often necessary for value to be determined by the investor or by a specialist engaged by the investor. The goal is to arrive at the amount that a willing buyer would pay a willing seller, for purposes of determining whether a write-down is needed and, if so, how much.

While no single standard has been established, factors that should be considered can be drawn from FRR § 404.03 (ASR 118), *Accounting for Investment Securities by Registered Investment Companies* (1970). The main factors include: (1) analytical data relating to the investment, such as earnings multiples, market value of a similar freely traded security, and yield to maturity; (2) the nature and duration of restrictions (if any) on disposition of the security; and (3) the forces that influence the market where the securities would be purchased and sold. Other considerations might include the type of security, financial standing of the issuer, availability of current financial statements, size and period of holding, discount from market value of similar but unrestricted securities at the time of purchase, special analysts' reports, and any transactions or offers with respect to such restricted or nontraded securities.

FRR § 404 was aimed at Small Business Investment Companies (SBICs), which are licensed by the Small Business Administration and generally used to provide venture capital to small businesses. The investments of SBICs are in small, start-up situations (often involving combinations of debt, convertibles, warrants, and preferred and common shares with special rights), and usually involve active participation by the SBIC in the investee's operations.

Such investments are generally carried at cost until there is evidence that value is other than cost. The investor in an SBIC generally encounters the same situation as the SBIC itself in valuing the investment and likewise carries it at cost until there is evidence that value is other than cost. Evidence is thus a matter of good faith valuation.

Valuation problems are discussed in Chapter 44 and in the industry audit guide, *Audits of Investment Companies* (AICPA, 1987d), which should be referred to for a more detailed discussion of the valuation process.

Other Valuation Approaches. For investments in securities based on future cash flows, such as real estate, it may also be necessary to obtain the opinion of independent experts. When real estate is an operating property leased to others, a common approach is to determine the present value of the future rent amounts and adjust the aggregate so determined by the estimated residual value, if any, at the end of the lease term.

With respect to "trade relation" investments (e.g., major customer or vendor) in securities not accounted for under the equity method, in addition to the evaluations discussed above there must be a current assessment by management of the value of any intangible benefits asserted to support the excess of cost over market or other indicator of current value.

Disclosures

Marketable Debt Securities. Specific disclosure requirements for marketable equity securities are given in SFAS 12 (I89.106), and similar disclosures make sense for marketable debt securities as well. The following information, which summarizes SFAS 12 requirements and incorporates nonequity securities, should be disclosed in the body of the financial statements or in the notes thereto:

• Aggregate cost and market value, segregated by current and noncurrent portfolios and between equity and debt securities, with an identification of the carrying amount, for each balance sheet presented;

• Gross unrealized gains and gross unrealized losses, segregated by portfolio, for the latest balance sheet presented;

• The net realized gain or loss included in income along with the basis used to determine cost (i.e., specific identification, average cost, etc.) for each income statement presented;

- The impact of market value changes (realized and unrealized) occurring after the balance sheet date on marketable debt securities held as of the reporting date.

  Other required disclosures, if material, are:

- The amount of marketable debt securities pledged as collateral for borrowings,
- The amount of securities reclassified between current and noncurrent,
- The amount of loss provisions, and
- Information concerning specific material investments.

Nonmarketable Securities. Nonmarketable securities carried at cost should be separately identified among Other Assets if amounts are material, with an indication that cost is the basis used. If premium or discount is being amortized, that fact may be disclosed by a caption phrase such as "at cost adjusted for amortization of premium and discount."

International Accounting Standard

In March 1986, the International Accounting Standards Committee (IASC) issued IAS 25, *Accounting for Investments* (AC 9025). The statement, which became effective January 1, 1987, is broader in scope than SFAS 12 and differs in many particulars. It addresses investments in all forms of securities, securities interests, and property investments, but not in subsidiaries, associates, or joint ventures. An investment is defined as

> an asset held by an enterprise for the accretion of wealth through distribution (such as interest, royalties, dividends and rentals), for capital appreciation or for other benefits to the investing enterprise such as those obtained through trading relationships.

The Statement contains the following requirements:

- Companies that present classified balance sheets should present separately current and long-term investments.
- Current investments should be carried at either (1) market value or (2) the lower of cost or market value (determined on an aggregate, category of investment, or individual investment basis).
- Long-term investments should be carried at (1) cost, (2) revalued amounts, or (3) in the case of marketable equity securities, the lower of cost or market value (on a portfolio basis).
- Revaluation increases of long-term investments should be credited to equity as "revaluation surplus." If no revaluation credit exists, decreases should be charged to income.
- Increases or decreases in current investments carried at market value should be consistently (1) included in or deducted from income or (2) treated like revaluations.
- Investment disposal gains or losses should be credited or charged to income. The Statement indicates that if the investment was a current asset carried on a portfolio basis at the lower of cost or market value, the profit or loss on sale should be based on cost; if the investment was previously revalued, or was carried at market value and an increase in carrying amount transferred to revaluation surplus, the company should adopt a policy either of crediting the

amount of any remaining related revaluation surplus to income or of transferring it to retained earnings.

• Long-term investments reclassified as current should be recorded at (1) the lower of cost and carrying amount, if current investments are carried at the lower of cost or market value. If the investment was previously revalued, any remaining related revaluation surplus should be reversed on the transfer; and (2) carrying amount if current investments are carried at market value. If changes in market value of current investments are included in income, any remaining related revaluation surplus should be transferred to income.

• Current investments reclassified as long-term should each be transferred at the lower of cost or market value, or at market value if they were previously stated at that value.

A provision is included for specialized investment companies that carry investments at market. In addition, various disclosures are required.

Auditing

General Concepts. The audit of investments is based on the same concepts that apply to cash and cash equivalents, as discussed earlier in this chapter. The auditor's purpose in applying procedures to investments is to obtain evidential matter to corroborate the amounts at which the investments are stated, whether at cost, realizable value, or equity in net assets.

To accomplish these audit objectives, the auditor must be satisfied as to existence, ownership, classification, cost or carrying amount of investments, periodic income or loss attributable to the investments, and the adequacy of any related disclosures. In assessing the inherent risk in investments, the auditor considers those risks (e.g., valuation of securities, susceptibility to theft, and high unit value of each investment that may be significant to the overall audit) in relation to the potential errors listed in "Audit Approach" below.

Transaction Types. The primary transactions affecting investments are

1. The purchase of investments, including authorization, execution, recording, controlling, and monitoring to ensure receipt and safeguarding of these investments.
2. The sale of investments, including the authorization, collection, recording of the resulting profit or loss, and the controls over the transfer of the investment or the funds received.
3. The valuation of marketable equity securities that, because of SFAS 12, are influenced by changes in the market values.
4. The receipt of investment income, including dividends, interest, and the entitlement to rights issues, stock options, warrants, and so forth.

Audit Approach. The nature of security investments is such that this segment is not greatly affected by the major transaction cycles. Unlike cash and accounts payable, for which much of the auditing can be performed through tests of compliance, it is generally much more efficient to confine the audit of investment securities to year-end substantive procedures. An exception to this general rule exists for enterprises that hold large portfolios of marketable securities.

Potential errors	Inherent risks
1. Investment purchased but not recorded. Risks a, b, c, d.	a. Value of balance or group of transactions typically large relative to materiality.
2. Investment recorded but not purchased. Risks a, b, c, d, e.	b. High value items typically present in balance sheet amount.
3. Investment purchase amount recorded incorrectly. Risks a, b, c.	c. Errors are not self-detecting.
4. Investment sold but not recorded. Risks a, b, c, d, e.	d. Errors tend to be 100%.
	e. There is a high susceptibility to fraud.
5. Investment recorded as sold but not sold. Risks a, b, c, d.	f. Errors have a direct impact on earnings.
6. Investment sale amount recorded incorrectly. Risks a, b, c.	g. Accounting judgments and estimates are involved.
7. Investment valued incorrectly. Risks a, b, c, e, f, g.	

FIG. 12.3   Potential Errors and Risks in Investment Transactions

Segmenting the broad objectives of an audit (existence, occurrence, completeness, ownership, valuation, allocation, presentation, or disclosure) as well as the broad objectives of internal control (authorization, execution, recording, and accountability) into account balances (or classes of transactions) and specific risks provides an effective and efficient method for planning a specific aspect of an audit. Potential errors (including those that might intentionally be made—irregularities) provide the "architecture" for the audit plan and provide a focus for assessing the magnitude and likelihood of the related exposure. The potential errors and related inherent risks for most types of nonaffiliate investments are shown in Figure 12.3.

A major issue is whether it is sufficient to merely confirm securities held by independent custodians as opposed to physically inspecting and counting them. With respect to the audit of an investment company, the auditor is required to describe in his report how he satisfied himself as to the existence of the securities, because of their relatively high value in relation to the total assets. The issue has been addressed in SAS 44, *Special-Purpose Reports on Internal Accounting Control of Service Organizations* (AU 324). This SAS provides the context for consideration of whether it is necessary to consider accounting control procedures at the depository or whether confirmation is ordinarily sufficient. The major factor in the decision is the nature of the work done at the depository. If those activities are limited to recording client transactions and processing related data and the client retains control over the flow of transactions (e.g., authorization and accountability), the client's controls are ordinarily the focus of the audit approach. On the other hand, if the depository's activities also include determining what securities to buy or sell and the related accountability, the audit focus shifts to the despository. This SAS addresses the nature of the work and types of reports that the depository and its auditors could provide to the client's auditor in such a case.

Audit objective	Sample year-end procedures*	Sample interim procedures
Existence. Determine whether there are investments supporting the amount shown in the balance sheet and whether all such securities have been properly included.	• Inspect securities and investments or obtain direct confirmation where they are held by independent custodians. If loans or advances are involved confirm with debtor or trustee for bondholders. • Determine reputation of custodian and the need for a special report on internal accounting control from that organizaton.	• Vouch additions to and disposals of investments to authorization, contract notes and other supporting documentation. Assure that the transaction was at an arm's-length price and that income was correctly accounted for.
Ownership. Determine whether the investments are owned by the company and whether they are subject to any lien or restrictions.	• Review and inquire as to whether any investments are pledged as collateral. Confirm details.	• Review brokers' advices.
Mechanical Accuracy. Determine whether the basic mathematical calculations and clerical compilation procedures have been accurately carried out.	• Obtain a schedule of investments at balance sheet date and trace totals to general ledger, agree opening balances to prior period financial statements and add and cross-add schedule. • Reconcile the general ledger control account with the detailed investment records.	• For selected periods test the accuracy of the detailed investment transactions by recomputing aggregate sales or market price and commissions based on units sold and per unit prices.
Valuation. Determine whether investments are properly valued in accordance with generally accepted accounting principles.	• Determine basis for valuing investments and verify market by reference to published quotations. If applicable obtain information on non-marketable investments. • Challenge for other-than-temporary diminution in value where cost exceeds market value substantially. • Verify dates and values of transfers between current and noncurrent portfolios.	• For selected purchases and sales agree cost and sale proceeds to independent sources of market price for reasonableness. • Test investment income to determine that interest and dividends are received based on stated rates and published data on dividends.

FIG. 12.4   Audit Objectives and Sample Procedures for Investments

Audit objective	Sample year-end procedures*	Sample interim procedures
Disclosure. Determine whether investment disclosure in the financial statements is adequate.	• Review and inquire as to whether any investments are pledged as collateral. Confirm details in conjunction with liabilities confirmation procedures.	
Classification. Determine whether investments are properly classified as to class of security and liquidity.	• Review and inquire as to the proper classification of investments for nonmarketable securities in addition to representations from management. Review minutes of board of directors and if applicable investment committee meetings to determine management's investment objectives.	• Review classification of individual purchases based on supporting detail.
Cut-Off. Determine whether all investment transactions before and after the year end are appropriately treated.	• Assure that purchases and sales are recorded in the correct period by reviewing purchases and sales immediately before and after the year end to confirm the actual date of the transaction.	• Review timeliness of recording interim transactions.

*May also be performed at an interim date in some situations.

Where the controls at the depository are the focus of the audit and a report of the depository and its independent auditor (or another independent auditor) is either not available or not sufficient for the client's auditor, additional work at the depository is necessary. Depending on the circumstances, that work can be performed either by the depositor's auditor, the client's auditor, or both.

To focus on possible problem areas, the auditor should initially perform these analytical procedures:

1. Review changes in balances and value of marketable securities and other investments during the period in light of the company's investment policy (considered in relation to management of cash), and
2. Compare interest and dividend income to prior years and as they relate to levels of marketable security and other investments.

Objectives and Procedures. In addition to carrying out analytical review procedures the auditor must devise other procedures, primarily substantive, to achieve the objectives of the audit of investments. Figure 12.4 is a very condensed listing of the interim and year-end audit procedures that are commonly used to achieve these objectives. Each procedure shown may be used to satisfy more than one audit objective, but to provide an overview of how the audit objectives are met, it is listed alongside the objective that it most typically satisfies.

Auditor's Report—Valuation Uncertainties. In the case of securities for which market quotations cannot be obtained, current values would ordinarily be determined by management or the board of directors. The independent auditor does not function as an appraiser and is not expected to substitute his judgment for that of management; rather, he is to review all information considered by management and ascertain that the procedures followed appear to be reasonable and adequate.

If the independent auditor is unable to satisfy himself as to the reasonableness of the amounts at which such investments are stated, appropriate qualification of the auditor's opinion should be made. This situation most commonly occurs in investment companies, discussed in Chapter 44.

ACCOUNTS PAYABLE AND ACCRUALS

Functions in the Purchases/Payables Cycle

The purchases/payables cycle involves the decisions and processes for obtaining goods and services to operate a business. The audit approach, objectives, and procedures are addressed later in this section. There are five primary functions in the purchases/payables cycle:

1. The internal requisition for goods or services is the starting point for the cycle. The exact form of the request and the required approval depends on the nature of the goods and services and the company policy.

2. The next step is the placement of a purchase order with a vendor for goods or services. The order is often in writing and may become a legal commitment for a specified item at the stated price when it is accepted by the seller.

3. The receipt by the company of goods or services ordinarily establishes a legal liability. Upon receipt the company examines the goods for quantity, condition, and conformity with the specifications of the original order.

4. The company next records its liability in accounts payable, charging the related expense or asset. This recording usually awaits the receipt of an invoice and its matchup with the related purchase order and receiving documents.

5. The final step in the cycle is the extinguishment of the liability through the disbursement of cash.

Financial Accounting and Reporting

In SFAC 6, *Elements of Financial Statements* (1985), the FASB defines liabilities as follows (¶ 35):

Liabilities are probable future sacrifices of economic benefits arising from present obligations of a particular entity to transfer assets or provide services to other entities in the future as a result of past transactions or events.

SFAC 6, ¶ 36, describes the three essential characteristics of a liability:

(a) it embodies a present duty or responsibility to one or more other entities that entails settlement by probable future transfer or use of assets at a specified or determinable date, on occurrence of a specified event, or on demand;

(b) the duty or responsibility obligates a particular entity, leaving it little or no discretion to avoid the future sacrifice; and

(c) the transaction or other event obligating the entity has already happened.

Some liabilities can be definitely determined as to existence and amount. Other liabilities definitely exist but their amounts must be estimated. Still other liabilities are contingent as to both existence and amount.

Current and Long-Term Classification. Current liabilities include: (1) all obligations for which payment will require the use of existing current assets or the creation of other current liabilities, and (2) all other obligations that will probably be paid from current assets within the period of one full operating cycle. ARB 43, Chapter 3A (B05.108), contains a more detailed description of current liabilities. (See also Chapter 18.)

Most companies have an operating cycle of one year or less, and thus it has become common practice to use a 12-month time period to distinguish between current and long-term liabilities. A company may operate on a longer cycle (e.g., several years for long-term construction contractors) and may use that cycle for classification of assets and for certain contract-related liabilities; but most liabilities in such a situation will be classified on the 12-month basis. (See Chapter 36.)

Present Valuing. The amount of a liability is the present value of the stream or sum of money or value of goods or services that must be paid to discharge the obligation. However, current liabilities are usually recorded at their face amount, because the difference between the present value of the liability and the face amount is generally not significant for the short time period involved. The slight overstatement of current liabilities that results from stating them at face amount seems a justifiable compromise with precision.

Specifically exempted from present-value techniques are those payables arising from transactions with customers or suppliers in the normal course of business that are due in accordance with customary trade terms not exceeding approximately one year (I69.102).

Extent of Disclosure. The details of disclosure vary with the circumstances of the business, but broad categories are generally used. Individual accounts or grouped captions may be shown, such as:

* Notes payable to banks
* Notes payable to trade creditors
* Accounts payable
* Income taxes payable
* Accrued expenses
* Dividends payable
* Other liabilities
* Current maturities of long-term debt

Notes payable are segregated because of their legal status as negotiable instruments and should be identified in the balance sheet or footnotes by type of payee. Collateralized notes should be segregated from noncollateralized notes and cross-referenced to the assets pledged as collateral; alternatively, this information can be given in the footnotes. Generally, accounts payable represent normal recurring trade obligations for which creditors' invoices are received. Income taxes are traditionally segregated, both because of their materiality and because of disclosure rules in SFAS 96.

Accrued expenses represent provisions for expenses incurred (but ordinarily not yet billed by the seller) during the period as a result of past contractual agreements, past services received, or tax laws. Because there is very little real difference between accounts payable and accrued expenses, the distinction between them has blurred. For SEC filings, any item in excess of 5% of total current liabilities is to be disclosed separately.

At the balance sheet date all trade payables arising from the purchase of goods and services that have been received or that are in transit should be recorded. Trade accounts payable may be recorded net of discounts if the company normally takes cash discounts and has the means of continuing the practice. The company's policy must be followed consistently. Material debit balances due from vendors that are collectible in cash should be reclassified as receivables; amounts that will be applied to future purchases should be reclassified as deposits, which for practical purposes can be combined in receivables.

As a rule of thumb, any single material liability should be separately reported in the current liability section of the balance sheet if it arises from an unusual source, is uncertain in amount, is contingent on a future event, is secured by assets of the business, or is to be paid from an unusual source. The unusual circumstances should be described either in a footnote or parenthetically. Unless they are minor in amount, accounts payable to subsidiaries and other affiliates, officers, directors, and principal stockholders should be shown as separate items.

A uniform, generally accepted ordering of current liabilities does not exist, and uniformity of classification from year to year is often affected by changes in the nature of a company's liabilities. Although current assets can be ordered in relation to their liquidity, a comparable ordering is not as easily made for current liabilities, because the various categories of current liabilities can have many different maturities. Bank overdrafts, which do not appear often, are usually listed first in deference to their priority of maturity.

Vacation Pay. The right to a paid vacation is normally contingent on the employee having worked for a specified length of time, or it may accrue ratably, such as one day per month worked. The length of vacation often increases after an employee has worked for a specified number of years.

SFAS 43, *Accounting for Compensated Absences* (C44), indicates that an employer should accrue a liability for an employees' right to receive pay for future absences, such as a vacation. The conditions that trigger accrual are based on the following:

1. The employee has a right to receive compensation for future absences that is based on service already performed.
2. The obligation represents a right that will eventually vest or accumulate.
3. Payment of the obligation is probable.
4. The amount of the obligation can be reasonably estimated.

Taxes Other Than Income Taxes. Real estate, personal property, franchise, and excise taxes should be grouped together under a caption such as "Taxes other than taxes on income." State franchise and excise taxes based on income should be included in the "Income taxes payable" caption.

In practice, real estate and personal property taxes have been accrued on several different bases, including:

1. Year in which payable (cash basis),
2. Fiscal year of governing body levying the tax, and
3. Year for which the tax is levied, as shown on the tax bill.

Generally, the most acceptable basis of providing for property taxes is monthly accrual during the fiscal year for which the taxes are levied. However, barring significant changes in the level of taxes, consistency is probably more important than technical accuracy.

Other Accruals. There are numerous accrued liabilities that can be applicable in a given company. Among the more common are

- Interest
- Payroll taxes
- Pension expense
- Professional fees
- Rent
- Repairs
- Royalties
- Travel
- Unpaid wages, salaries, and commissions
- Utilities
- Warranties

Ordinarily the appropriate amounts for a company's usual list of accruals are determined at each period-end and recorded by standard journal entry, which reverses the amount set up at the previous period-end. Under this approach, as actual disbursements are made they are charged to the appropriate asset or expense account, not to the accrual account.

If accruals as a group are material in amount (more than 10% of current liabilities), they are ordinarily shown separately in the financial statements; otherwise, one or more items are separately broken out so as to reduce the remainder to a small amount combinable with accounts payable.

Auditing Payables and Accruals

General Concepts. The overall objective of the audit of accounts payable and accruals is to determine whether they are fairly presented in the context of the financial statements taken as a whole. The broad objectives of an audit are discussed in Chapter 7 and the basic nature of the internal control structure in Chapter 8. This discussion assumes familiarity with those chapters.

Transaction Types. The primary transaction types that affect accounts payable and accruals consist of

1. The purchase of raw materials, supplies, capital assets, and services. The auditor must be familiar with the client's controls over the ordering, receipt, and return of goods and services.
2. The payments of liabilities arising from the above purchases. The auditor must be familiar with the client's controls over cash payments as outlined in the earlier section in this chapter on auditing cash and cash equivalents.

Audit Approach. Accounts payable is usually an area of considerable audit interest. To develop the appropriate program the auditor needs to consider:

- Inherent risks
- Potential errors
- Nature and effectiveness of the related controls
- Procedures that accomplish more than one purpose
- Effective use of analytical review
- The interrelationship of these transactions and balances to other transactions and the effect on audit work

Inherent Risks. In assessing the inherent risks (susceptibility of an account balance or class of transactions to errors that could be material) in accounts payable, the auditor will consider a number of interrelated factors. Specifically, in almost all audits the accounts payable amount is significant and a number of high value (or key items) are present. Further, in relation to most of the potential errors (see next section), the error could be a 100% error and thus would have a low probability of self-detection. Finally, a number of specific potential errors could raise concern as to fraud. See Figures 12.5 and 12.6 for a more specific analysis.

Potential Errors. Segmenting the broad objectives of an audit (existence, occurrence, completeness, ownership, valuation, allocation, presentation or disclosure) as well as the broad objectives of internal control (authorization, execution, recording, and accountability) into account balances (or classes of transactions) and specific risks provides an effective and efficient method for planning a specific aspect of an audit. Potential errors (including those that might intentionally be made—irregularities) provide the "architecture" for the audit and provide a focus for assessing the magnitude and likelihood of the related exposure. To better understand each potential error, its related cause is presented in Figures 12.5 and 12.6. The potential errors for all types of purchases and payables are:

Purchases

Purchase not authorized

Purchase recorded, goods/services not received

Liability incurred but not recorded

Purchase amount recorded incorrectly

Purchase charged to wrong account

Purchase recorded in wrong period

Purchase summarization and posting errors

Payables

Payment not authorized

Payment recorded, not made

Payment made, not recorded

Payment amount recorded incorrectly

Payment recorded in wrong period

Payment charged to wrong account

Payment summarization and posting errors

Depending on the specific circumstances and the significance of the amounts involved, the auditor might also develop additional specific audit approaches related to this cycle, for example:

* Significant purchase retruns
* Significant purchases in foreign currencies
* Related party purchases
* Key item purchases
* Royalty payments expected
* Intercompany purchases

Objective	Potential errors	Causes of errors	Inherent risk factors	Types of controls	Examples of controls
Existence — validity	Purchase not authorized	• Goods ordered without proper authorization • Unordered goods received • Services ordered without proper authorization • Unordered services received	• Value of transactions typically significant • High value items typically present • Errors are not self detecting • Errors tend to be 100% • High susceptibility to fraud	• Independent approval, review, check, or recalculation • Comparison with independent third party information • Matching of independent control totals	• Purchase order authorized prior to issuance • Receiving document quantity agreed to purchase order • Purchased services reviewed and approved • Checks reviewed and approved prior to issue
Existence — validity	Purchase recorded, goods/services not received	• Supplier invoice processed without receiving document • Invalid service supplier invoice processed • EDP entry without valid supplier invoice • Supplier invoice recorded/paid twice • Supplier invoice records duplicated in EDP • Receiving document posted twice • Receiving document records duplicated in EDP	• Value of transactions typically significant • High value items typically present • Errors have a direct impact on earnings • Errors are not self detecting • Errors tend to be 100% • High susceptibility to fraud	• Segregation of personnel, operations, and assets • Matching of independently generated documents • Prenumbering and sequence checking of key documents • Maintenance of independent control total • Cancellation of documentation • Timeliness of operations	• Receiving counts approved by supervisor • Receiving document matched to authorized purchase order • Supplier invoice matched to receiving document • Purchased services reviewed and approved • Supplier invoice cancelled upon recording/payment • Unmatched receiving documents periodically reviewed • Supplier invoice balanced to daily purchase journal • Accounts payable account in general ledger reconciled to accounts payable ledger • Supplier statement independently reviewed and reconciled • Receiving document cancelled upon posting • Receiving documents balanced to daily accruals journal • Checks reviewed and approved prior to issue

Objective	Potential errors	Risk factors	General controls	Specific controls
Existence – recording	Liability incurred but not recorded	• Receiving document not prepared • Receiving document lost before matching • Supplier invoice never received • Supplier invoice lost • Supplier invoice not recorded/paid • Supplier invoice records lost in EDP • Receiving document not posted • Receiving document records lost in EDP	• Value of transactions typically significant • High value items typically present • Errors have a direct impact on earnings • Errors tend to be 100% • High susceptibility to fraud	• Prenumbering and sequence checking of key documents • Independent approval, review, check, or recalculation • Timeliness of operations • Maintenance of independent control totals • Segregation of personnel, operations, and assets	• Receiving documents checked for serial continuity • Unmatched supply invoices periodically reviewed • Supplier invoice balanced to daily purchase journal • Accounts payable account in general ledger reconciled to accounts payable ledger • Supplier statement independently reviewed and reconciled • Receiving documents balanced to daily accruals journal
Valuation – accuracy	Purchase amount recorded incorrectly	• Supplier invoice quantity incorrect • Supplier invoice price incorrect • Supplier invoice incorrectly calculated or added • Supplier invoice amount recorded incorrectly • Supplier invoice amount processed incorrectly in EDP	• Value of transactions typically significant • High value item typically present • Errors have a direct impact on earnings	• Segregation of personnel, operations, and assets • Independent approval, review, checking, or recalculation • Matching of independent control totals • Timeliness of operations	• Receiving counts approved by supervisor • Supplier invoice additions/extensions checked • Receiving document quantity agreed to purchase order • Supplier invoice quantity agreed to receiving document • Supplier invoice price agreed to purchase order • Supplier invoice balanced to daily purchase journal • Accounts payable account in general ledger reconciled to accounts payable ledger • Supplier statement independently reviewed and reconciled • Monthly purchase price variance reviewed for reasonableness

(continued)

FIG. 12.5 **Purchasing and Accounts Payable Audit Planning Matrix (purchasing activity)**

Objective	Potential errors	Causes of errors	Inherent risk factors	Types of controls	Examples of controls
Classification	Purchase charged to wrong account	• Incorrect account code • Account code recorded incorrectly • Account code processed incorrectly in EDP	• Value of transactions typically significant • High value item typically present • Errors have a direct impact on earnings • Errors are not self detecting • Errors tend to be 100%	• Independent approval, review checking, or recalculation • Matching of independent control totals	• General ledger codes checked on supplier invoice • Monthly purchase journal reviewed for reasonableness • Accounts payable account in general ledger reconciled to accounts payable ledger
Cut-off	Purchase recorded in wrong period	• Receiving document dated in wrong period • Supplier invoice recorded/paid in wrong period • Supplier invoice processed in wrong period in EDP • End-of-period inventory accrual incorrect • End-of-period inventory accrual processed in wrong period • Prior period inventory accrual not reversed • End-of-period services accrual incorrect • End-of-period services accrual processed in wrong period • Prior period services accrual not reversed • Receiving document converted in wrong period in EDP • Receiving document posted in wrong period in EDP	• Value of transactions typically significant • High value items typically present • Errors have a direct impact on earnings • Errors are not self detecting • Errors tend to be 100%	• Independent approval, review, checking, or recalculation • Timeliness of operation	• Adequate written cut-off procedures • Personnel adequately instructed regarding cut-off

FIG. 12.5 (continued)

Objective	Potential errors	Causes of errors	Inherent risk factors	Types of controls	Examples of controls
Existence – validity	Payment not authorized	• Unauthorized signature on check • Amount on check higher than invoice amount • Invalid check produced • Payment made without valid supplier invoices • Payment made to other than beneficiary	• Value of transactions typically significant • High value items typically present • Errors are not self detecting • Errors tend to be 100%	• Independent approval, review, check, or recalculation • Segregation of personnel, operations, and assets	• Unissued checks controlled • Check signature plate physically secured • Checks reviewed and approved prior to issue • Checks issued agreed to cash request report
Existence – validity	Payment recorded, not made	• Check not printed by EDP • Check lost or stolen prior to mailing • Payment held for later issue • Payment record duplicated in EDP	• Value of transactions typically significant • High value items present • Errors tend to be 100%	• Maintenance of independent control totals • Matching of independently generated documents • Comparison with independent third party information • Timeliness of operations	• Accounts payable account in general ledger reconciled to accounts payable ledger • Supplier statement independently reviewed and reconciled • Checks issued balanced to daily payments journal • Monthly bank reconciliation prepared • Independent review of monthly bank reconciliation
Existence – recording	Payment made, not recorded	• Check printed, but payment record lost in EDP	• Value of transactions typically significant • High value items typically present • Errors are not self detecting • Errors tend to be 100% • High susceptibility to fraud	• Maintenance of independent control totals • Matching of independent control totals • Comparison with independent third party information • Timeliness of operations	• Accounts payable account in general ledger reconciled to accounts payable ledger • Checks issued balanced to daily payments journal • Monthly bank reconciliation prepared • Independent review of monthly bank reconciliation

(continued)

FIG. 12.6 Purchasing and Accounts Payable Audit Planning Matrix (accounts payable activity)

Objective	Potential errors	Causes of errors	Inherent risk factors	Types of controls	Examples of controls
Valuation – accuracy	Payment amount recorded incorrectly	• Payment amount processed incorrectly in EDP	• Value of transactions typically significant • High value items typically present	• Segregation of personnel, operations, and assets • Independent approval, review, checking, or reconciliation • Maintenance of independent third party information • Timeliness of operations	• Accounts payable account in general ledger reconciled to accounts payable ledger • Supplier statement independently reviewed and reconciled • Checks issued balanced to daily payments journal • Monthly bank reconciliation prepared • Independent review of monthly bank reconciliation
Cut-off	Payment recorded in wrong period	• Check issued, payment record processed in wrong period in EDP	• Value of transactions typically significant • High value items typically present • Errors are not self detecting • Errors tend to be 100%	• Independent approval, review, checking, or recalculation • Matching of independently generated documents • Comparison with independent third party information • Timeliness of operations	• Supplier statement independently reviewed and reconciled • Checks issued balanced to daily payments journal • Monthly bank reconciliation prepared • Independent review of monthly bank reconciliation
Classification	Payment charged to wrong account	• Incorrect code assigned • Account code recorded incorrectly • Account code processed incorrectly	• Value of transactions typically significant • High value items typically present • Errors have a direct impact on earnings	• Maintenance of independent control totals • Independent approval, review, checking, or recalculation	• Accounts payable account in general ledger reconciled to accounts payable ledger • General ledger account code checked on request for payment • Monthly payments journal reviewed for reasonableness

| Mechanical accuracy | Payment summarization and posting errors | • Daily payments journal incorrectly summarized to monthly payments journal
• Monthly payments journal posted twice
• Monthly payments journal not posted
• Monthly payments journal amount posted incorrectly to general ledger
• Monthly payments posted to wrong account
• Monthly payments journal posted to wrong period | • Value of transactions typically significant
• High value items typically present
• Errors are not self detecting
• Errors tend to be 100% | • Maintenance of independent control totals
• Independent approval, review, checking, or recalculation
• Matching of independently generated documents
• Timeliness of operations | • Accounts payable account in general ledger reconciled to accounts payable ledger
• Monthly payments journal reviewed for reasonableness
• Monthly payments journal agreed to general ledger posting
• Monthly bank reconciliation prepared
• Independent review of monthly bank reconciliation |

FIG. 12.6 (continued)

Nature and Effectiveness of the Related Controls. As described in Chapter 8, the audit process requires that the auditor obtain an understanding of the client's internal control structure, document his understanding, and analyze the internal controls to ascertain (1) the control points on which he chooses to rely and (2) the effect of systems weaknesses on his audit plan. The auditor must then develop specific audit procedures to test those areas of internal control on which he will rely.

To effectively determine whether the existing controls provide an adequate basis for an efficient reliance-based audit, they need to be specifically interrelated to the nature and extent of risk present. This can most effectively be done by comparing each potential error to the related controls ordinarily expected to be present. These controls are correlated with the inherent risk and potential error characteristics as shown in Figures 12.5 and 12.6.

It is possible for auditors to rely solely on substantive tests when auditing accounts payable and accruals. This approach is used when the auditor deems it more economical and efficient, such as in the audit of a small company whose internal control procedures are not especially sophisticated or in the audit of a company whose control procedures are not deemed effective or reliable. In most cases, however, the auditor will rely heavily on internal controls for the purchases/payables cycle. In doing so, the auditor will apply compliance tests to the system of internal control and, if the results of such tests are favorable, will reduce the amount of substantive tests applied to accounts payable and accrued expense balances.

Once the auditor is satisfied that the system is operating in the manner originally contemplated, or he has responsively modified that understanding, the extent of substantive audit procedures can be determined. Examples of year-end and interim procedures are provided in Figure 12.7.

Most audit procedures deal with more than one type of potential error. A selection of these more powerful procedures will usually result in a more efficient audit program.

Effective Use of Analytical Review. At its current stage of development, analytical review provides either a challenge to or a confirmation of the auditor's understanding of the client's environment and its accounting and control systems. Such analysis helps identify areas where more work appears warranted. The usefulness of analytical review is enhanced where detailed information and other complementing systems exist (e.g., well-designed budget or statistical operational data — such as units produced, backlog, or scrap reports — or industry data and competitor information). In such circumstances analytical review can provide a modicum of direct audit assurance that material errors (individually or in the aggregate) are not present. However, because the data available is so varied among companies, generalizations on the effectiveness of analytical review are not useful.

Fundamental analytical procedures generally applied in the audit of accounts payable and accrued liabilities include the following:

1. Compare the current listing of accounts payable and accruals with that of the previous audit date and note any significant changes — for example, changes in major suppliers, in the number of overdue accounts, or in the proportion of debit balances.
2. Determine whether there are any balances with related companies or with shareholders, directors, or officers. If so, how do these balances compare to similar balances at the last

Audit objective	Sample year-end procedures*	Sample interim procedures
Existence. Determine whether the liabilities recorded in the balance sheet exist and whether all such liabilities have been properly included.	• Obtain selected supplier's statements directly and reconcile to accounts. • Review accounts payable control account for the period and investigate any large or unusual entries or any significant increases or decreases in purchases toward the year-end. • Search for unrecorded liabilities by inquiry and examination of post-balance sheet transactions and confirmation as appropriate. • Check validity and accuracy of accruals by reference to supporting documents.	• Check numerical sequence of receiving documents and trace selected receiving documents to supplier's invoices and to purchase journal.
Ownership. Determine whether the liabilities recorded in the balance sheet are valid charges against the company.	• For selected items agree to supplier's invoice, goods receipt advices, copy of purchase orders, and other supporting documents.	• Vouch selected items from the purchase journal and the cash disbursements journal to supporting documentation, orders, and receiving documentation.
Mechanical accuracy. Determine whether the basic mathematical calculations and clerical compilation procedures have been accurately carried out.	• Obtain schedule of accounts payable and accruals. Add schedule, agree total to general ledger and agree selected items to subsidiary records or supporting documentation.	• Recompute details on vendor invoices. • Test footings of purchase journal.
Valuation. Determine whether accounts payable and accruals are fairly valued in accordance with generally accepted accounting principles.	• Reconcile supplier's statements to accounts. • Determine that liabilities payable in a foreign currency have been valued at the proper exchange rates. • Determine which liabilities are affected by discounts and ensure that they have been properly handled. • Ascertain basis of provisions made, check calculations and determine reasonableness.	• Review accounts payable control account for the period and investigate any large or unusual entries or increases or decreases in purchases.

(continued)

FIG. 12.7　Audit Objectives and Sample Procedures for Accounts Payable and Accruals

Audit objective	Sample year-end procedures*	Sample interim procedures
Disclosure. Determine whether disclosures included in the financial statements are adequate.	• Review accounts payable balances and accruals for amounts due to (or from) group and related companies, debit balances and unusual items.	• Review agreements underlying various liabilities and accruals (e.g., vendor supply contracts and union agreements).
Classification. Determine whether accounts payable and accruals are properly classified in the balance sheet.	• Review nature and magnitude of items which are combined for financial reporting purposes.	• Review account classification of initial recording of transactions.
Cut-Off. Determine whether the liabilities for goods or services received before and after the year-end have been recorded in the correct period.	• Determine that proper cutoff procedures were applied to assure that purchases and supplier debit memos have been recorded at the balance sheet date in the correct accounting period. • Where there is a lack of substantial internal evidence obtain direct confirmation of account balances from third parties.	• Test period of recording interim transactions.

*May also be performed at interim date in some situations.

FIG. 12.7 *(continued)*

audit date? These types of balances may or may not represent genuine trade accounts — possibly they should be excluded from the calculation of ratios and other statistics for trade accounts if they are large enough to be distortive. They may also pose particular verification problems (see Chapter 25).

3. Review such statistics as the relationship of accounts payable to purchases (or other meaningful volume relationships), compare to previous periods, and obtain satisfactory explanations for variations in the current figures. It is not sufficient merely to establish that there has been no significant change from the previous period; the important question is, should there be a change, and if so, how much?

For a more extensive discussion of analytical review, see Chapter 7 and SAS 56, *Analytical Procedures* (AU 329).

Effect of Interrelationships on Other Audit Procedures. The accounts payable audit work is directly related to the cash, cash equivalents, and investments audit work discussed earlier in this chapter. The audit work done in assessing an organization's inventory (see Chapter 14) is also directly related to work in accounts payable and purchases. A well-planned audit will recognize and take advantage of this interrelationship in the design of the audit work.

13

Revenue and Receivables

REVENUE RECOGNITION CONCEPTS AND STANDARDS

Revenue Transaction Cycle

This chapter discusses revenue cycle accounting, reporting and auditing for profit-oriented enterprises, and service transaction revenues. Expense recognition is also discussed because it is so interrelated with revenue recognition concepts and practices. Revenue recognition in specific industries is discussed in other chapters as applicable.

The revenue cycle encompasses a broad range of activities including credit granting, processing requests for and delivering goods or services, billing and collecting, and processing sales returns, bad debts, and other adjustments. This cycle can cover a very short period of time or extend over a number of years; and often the length of this period affects the accounting treatment for a revenue transaction.

Over the life of an enterprise, total revenues are not difficult to quantify. If all revenues and costs were to be recorded only when cash was received or disbursed, there would be no problem in identifying them with accounting periods. However, as accounting is segmented into fiscal years, quarters, and even months, the allocation of revenues to time segments through accrual basis accounting becomes increasingly difficult.

A revenue transaction can consist of selling products, rendering services, or permitting others to use enterprise resources. Revenue transactions do not include those related to the equity accounts of the business. FASB Concepts Statement (SFAC) 6, *Elements of Financial Statements* (FASB, 1985), defines revenues as follows (¶ 78):

> Revenues are in flows or other enhancements of assets of an entity or settlements of its liabilities (or a combination of both) from delivering or producing goods, rendering services, or other activities that constitute the entity's ongoing major or central operations.

Revenues are thus differentiated from "gain" transactions which are attributed to "peripheral or incidental transactions" of an entity.

SFAC 5—Recognition and Measurement

Revenue recognition is addressed in SFAC 5, *Recognition and Measurement in Financial Statements of Business Enterprises* (FASB, 1984c). While general recognition concepts, discussed in Chapter 2 of this *Handbook*, are the main subject of SFAC 5, some specific guidance is also provided by SFAC 5 (¶¶ 83–84) concerning revenue and gain recognition. SFAC 5 also states that before revenue is recognized in financial statements, the conditions of being earned and being realized (or realizable) must be met.

Earned. Revenues are earned when an entity has substantially accomplished what it must do in its ongoing major or central operations (i.e., its earning process) to be entitled to the benefits represented by the revenues. Gains, on the other hand, commonly result from transactions and other events that involve no "earning process." Thus for gain recognition, being earned is generally less significant than being realized or realizable.

Realized or Realizable. Revenues and gains are realized or realizable when products (goods or services), merchandise, or other assets are exchanged for cash, or for claims to cash or other assets that are readily convertible into known amounts of cash or claims thereto. Readily convertible assets are those that have interchangeable or fungible units, quoted prices, and are available in an active market that can rapidly absorb the quantity held by the entity without significantly affecting the price.

Recognition Guidelines. SFAC 5 also provides the following guidelines for recognizing revenues and gains (¶ 84):

a. The two conditions (being realized or realizable and being earned) are usually met by the time product or merchandise is delivered or services are rendered to customers, and revenues from manufacturing and selling activities and gains and losses from sales of other assets are commonly recognized at time of sale (usually meaning delivery).

b. If sale or cash receipt (or both) precedes production and delivery (for example, magazine subscriptions), revenues may be recognized as earned by production and delivery.

c. If product is contracted for before production, revenues may be recognized by a percentage-of-completion method as earned – as production takes place – provided reasonable estimates of results at completion and reliable measures of progress are available. (If production is long in relation to reporting periods, such as for long-term, construction-type contracts, recognizing revenues as earned has often been deemed to result in information that is significantly more relevant and representationally faithful than information based on waiting for delivery, although at the sacrifice of some verifiability.)

d. If sevices are rendered or rights to use assets extend continuously over time (for example, interest or rent), reliable measures based on contractual prices established in advance are commonly available, and revenues may be recognized as earned as time passes.

e. If products or other assets are readily realizable because they are salable at reliably determinable prices without significant effort (for example, certain agricultural products, precious metals, and marketable securities), revenues and some gains or losses may be recognized at completion of production or when prices of the assets change.

f. If product, services, or other assets are exchanged for nonmonetary assets that are not readily convertible into cash, revenues or gains or losses may be recognized on the basis that they have been earned and the transaction is completed. Gains or losses may also be recognized if nonmonetary assets are received or distributed in nonreciprocal transactions. Recognition in both kinds of transactions depends on the provision that the fair values involved can be determined within reasonable limits as described in APB 29, *Accounting for Nonmonetary Transactions* (N35).

g. If collectibility of assets received for product, services, or other assets is doubtful, revenues and gains may be recognized on the basis of cash received.

SFAC 5 concludes by stating that most aspects of current practice are consistent with the recognition criteria and guidance expressed in the Statement.

Research Reports. In developing SFAC 5, the FASB commissioned three Research Reports: *Recognition of Contractual Rights and Obligations: An Exploratory Study of Conceptual Issues* (Ijiri, 1980); *Survey of Present Practices in Recognizing Revenues, Expenses, Gains, and Losses* (Jaenicke, 1981); and *Recognition in Financial Statements: Underlying Concepts and Practical Conventions* (Johnson and Storey, 1982).

These Research Reports, especially the latter two, provide some interesting background material on current practices for recognizing revenues including their similarities, differences, and inconsistencies.

The 1982 Research Report notes that the most significant difference among the various bases of revenue recognition is in periodic income measurement. In other words, while the revenue recognized for a particular transaction would be the same under each of the various bases over time, the distribution of the revenue among accounting periods could vary considerably. In this regard, the report states (pages 179 and 180):

> Because each recognition procedure used in practice is a means for coping with uncertainty, their effects on the reliabilility of the resulting information is of primary importance. Accordingly, comparing those procedures involves comparing (a) the relative faithfulness with which they portray the economic things and events that they purport to represent and (b) the relative verifiability of the results of each procedure.
>
> Adoption of particular procedures depends not only on their relative reliability but also on their relative cost. Some methods are more costly to apply than others and some provide more reliable information than others. How the trade-off between costs and reliability is effected is a matter that ultimately can be decided only at the level of setting and applying standards.

Recognition Standards

It is interesting to note that the accounting standards covered by Rule 203 of the AICPA Rules of the Code of Professional Conduct (ARBs and APB, FASB, and GASB pronouncements) addressing revenue recognition in general are limited to three pronouncements: ARB 43, Chapter 1A (R75); APB 10, ¶ 12 (R75); and SFAS 48, *Revenue Recognition When Right of Return Exists* (R75). ARB 43, Chapter 1A states:

> Profit is deemed to be realized when a sale in the ordinary course of business is effected, unless the circumstances are such that the collection of the sale price is not reasonably assured. An exception to the general rule may be made in respect of inventories in industries (such as packing-house industry) in which owing to the impossibility of determining costs it is a trade custom to take inventories at net selling prices, which may exceed cost.

APB 10 states that revenues should be recognized at the time a transaction is completed, with appropriate provision for uncollectible accounts. Accordingly, APB 10 concludes that in the absence of exceptional circumstances concerning the collection of the sale price, the installment method of recognizing revenue is not acceptable.

Other specific revenue recognition guidance is provided in the authoritative literature regarding accounting for profits on contracts (see Chapters 36 and 37), franchise revenue recognition (discussed later in this chapter), and loan fee revenue (see Chapters 40 and 41).

International Accounting Standard

In December 1982, the International Accounting Standards Committee released IAS 18, *Revenue Recognition* (AC 9018), concerning the recognition of revenue arising from the sale of goods, the rendering of services, and the use by others of enterprise resources yielding interest, royalties, and dividends. While IASs are not binding under U.S. GAAP, enterprises are encouraged to comply with their provisions. In most respects IAS 18 provides a condensation of the U.S. GAAP standards discussed in this chapter.

With respect to the sale of goods, revenue should be recognized when:

* The risks and rewards of ownership have passed to the buyer and the seller retains no significant involvement to the degree usually associated with ownership.
* No significant uncertainty exists as to
  - The consideration to be received
  - The costs to be incurred
  - The extent to which goods may be returned.

In transactions involving the rendering of services, revenue should be determined by the completed contract method or percentage-of-completion method, whichever more clearly relates the revenue to the work accomplished. Revenue should be recognized when no significant uncertainty exists as to the consideration to be received, or as to the costs to be incurred.

An enterprise that earns interest, dividends, or royalties as a result of another enterprise using its resources would recognize such revenue when no significant uncertainty exists as to measurability or collectibility.

If at the time of sale or rendering of sevice it is unreasonable to expect ultimate collection, revenue recognition should be postponed. An enterprise should disclose the circumstances in which revenue recognition has been postponed pending the outcome of an uncertainty.

REVENUE RECOGNITION FOR MONETARY TRANSACTIONS

As will be seen in the discussion in this section, the critical event or significant act is not always recognized in current accrual-basis GAAP, since reliability often overshadows relevance. The critical event in a product sale may be its manufacture; in a service transaction it may be the performance of the most difficult action. In percentage-of-completion recognition, the critical event is even more elusive and indeed may not exist until the project is accepted by the customer as meeting the specifications. This gives rise to a variety of revenue recognition methods that may be applied to monetary transactions:

- Product sale
- Service performance
- Percentage-of-completion
- Passage of time
- Recognition prior to sale
- Installment
- Cost recovery
- Collection

Product Sales

Revenue is ordinarily recognized at the time the purchaser of the product is vested with ownership rights. For convenience, and historically for legal reasons, this point is deemed to be when title passes. Most manufacturers ship their products FOB factory, and thus a sale is ordinarily recorded at the time of shipment of merchandise. However, there can be many other timing arrangements. For example, the customer can have the merchandise placed aside in a segregated area, such as a bonded warehouse in the producer's factory, and if there are no other unusual uncertainties about whether a sale has been consummated, the transfer of specified goods into the segregated area will result in sale recording. Or goods may be shipped FOB destination or sold "on the high seas," as in the case of oil in tankers already en route to a particular port but without a specific customer having purchased the oil at the time of the tanker's departure.

Likewise, if goods are shipped on consignment, the goods are considered inventory of the seller because the recipient has the complete right to return them. Similarly, if there is a right of return, an assessment must be made of the extent to which returns are likely, and the enterprise must have a track record to indicate that the amounts are not material or are appropriately provided for as revenue reductions. (See futher discussion later in this chapter under "Sales With Right of Return.")

Examples of product transaction types discussed in this chapter that are different from a simple over-the-counter product transaction, in addition to those mentioned above, include:

1. Involuntary conversions;
2. Franchising, to the extent that services are required to be purchased by the franchisee from the franchisor; and
3. Sales of receivables with recourse.

Transaction types that differ from simple product sales and are discussed in other chapters include:

1. Some product financing arrangements, in whole or in part (see Chapter 21);
2. Rental of premises under operating leases (see Chapter 19);
3. Sales-type leases (see Chapter 19);
4. Construction industry activities, as to the items constructed (however, many activities in the construction industry involve services) (see Chapter 36);
5. Extractive industry sales, such as oil and gas products, hard minerals, and forest products (see Chapter 34);
6. Sales of real estate (see Chapter 35);
7. Sale-leaseback transactions (see Chapters 19 and 35).

The recognition issue becomes particularly complicated when a transaction consists of a mixture of products and services and occurs over a period of time. In such cases, the issue of what proportion of the transaction may be considered completed at a given interim point must be dealt with.

Consider, for example, a lease. To the extent that the lessor conveys to the lessee the use of the property for virtually its entire useful life and will recover his cost plus a reasonable rate of return, the transaction is considered a product sale. However, if the lease term is short and the lessor will have to re-lease or otherwise dispose of the product at the end of the primary lease term, the transaction with the original lessee is then considered a service transaction, that is, an operating lease; it is also deemed to result in the recognition of revenue by prorating the gross rental over the lease term.

When the lease qualifies as a sales-type (or direct financing) lease, there is an element of service income involved, that is, the financial income that will be earned by the lessor at a constant rate applied against the diminishing unpaid balance. An operating lease, of course, contains this same factor, but under SFAS 13 it is accounted for differently.

Real estate sales are mostly sales of products and, apart from an outright cash sale (not common), various earnings recognition methods will be found in practice. Because there are so many divisible rights in real estate, nonresidential transactions do not always transfer all of the rights of complete ownership. An entire hierarchy of rules has been created to deal with this problem, as discussed in Chapter 35.

Service Performance

Because of the intangibility of services, it has been exceedingly difficult to ascertain, in many situations, when a service consisting of more than a single act has been satisfactorily performed so as to warrant recognition of revenue. AcSEC undertook a lengthy project in this area, resulting in a proposed SOP that was taken up by the FASB and reissued as its first Invitation to Comment (FASB, 1978a). The large number of negative reponses sent to the FASB resulted in the entire project being deferred, and it was incorporated into the recognition phase of the conceptual framework resulting in SFAC 5. (Accounting for service transactions is discussed later herein.)

The most important ingredient in determining when a service transaction has been completed is whether *substantial performance* has occurred. Performance as defined by the invitation to comment is "the execution of a defined act or acts or occurs with the passage of time" (FASB, 1978a, p. 11). Because there are so many different kinds of service transactions, four possible groupings were suggested to account for them:

1. Specific performance method
2. Proportional performance method
3. Completed performance method
4. Collection method

This spectrum encompasses the percentage-of-completion method of accounting as well as the installment and collection methods.

Percentage-of-Completion

As discussed in Chapters 36 and 37 this method is mostly used in the construction industry and requires an estimation of total costs and total revenues in those longer-term transactions that afford adequate evidence for measuring progress toward completion. Progress may be based on physical evaluations, but perhaps more commonly is based on cost inputs to date versus the current estimate of total cost of the project (the *cost-to-cost* method). In the service area, AcSEC had described this approach as the *proportional performance method*.

Authoritative accounting literature deals very generally with the application of this accounting method in ARB 45 (Co4.103):

> The percentage-of-completion method recognizes income as work on a contract progresses. The recognized income shall be that percentage of estimated total income, either:
>
> (a) that incurred costs to date bear to estimated total costs after giving effect to estimates of costs to complete based upon most recent information, or
> (b) that may be indicated by such other measure of progress toward completion as may be appropriate having due regard to work performed.

The percentage-of-completion method should be used only when: (1) there is an enforceable agreement between parties who can fulfill their obligations and (2) there are reasonably reliable estimates of total revenue, total cost, and the progress toward completion. If these two criteria cannot be met, usually the completed contract method or some other approach that will result in recognition of the minimum assured revenue will provide the proper accounting treatment.

Percentage-of-completion accounting recognizes the economic substance of a transaction by allocating revenue to periods of performance of the work, so that revenue is recognized as it is earned. This conceptual view of percentage-of-completion accounting, however, oversimplifies its problems. Often enough, the revenue allocation is based on cost incurred, rather than on a physical measure of progress. The ultimate revenue can depend on a multitude of factors, and contracts can contain a variety of incentive and penalty clauses. These circumstances affect the timing and amount of revenue recognized, and uncertainties increase in complexity as the duration of the contract and the provisions in the agreement expand.

Cost incurred method. Utilizing the incurred costs as an indicator of progress toward completion is the most common technique and generally the simplest to apply. Under this technique, total contract costs and total contract revenue must be estimated. As costs are incurred, revenue is recognized according to a simple formula: current cost as a percentage of expected total costs equals current revenue as a fraction of total revenue (referred to as the *cost-to-cost method*).

The costs and revenue utilized in the formula must be based on current information. Costs to complete should be analyzed periodically to provide assurance that the estimate of total cost is reasonable. Furthermore, current costs must be adjusted for items that do not reflect a measure of work performed. For example, the cost of materials purchased but not yet utilized should normally be excluded; advances to subcontractors for future work should also be excluded because they would otherwise distort the estimate of progress.

Other methods. In many contracts, incurred costs bear little relationship to the progress toward completion. For example, most of the costs of installing a telephone system may rest in the telephone hardware in a particular situation, and the hardware may not be acquired by the contractor until the contract is nearly complete. In many contracts, costs incurred to date are not known, especially if a number of subcontractors are involved. In both situations it is inappropriate to base the amount of revenue to be recognized on incurred costs. Alternative techniques include such measures as figuring current labor hours as a percentage of the projected total (labor hours method), and using architectural or engineering estimates which measure progress by physical output. Regardless of the method chosen, it should base the actual progress made toward completion on rational criteria consistently applied.

Revision of estimates. Any changes resulting from revisions of estimates based on current information should be accounted for under the change in estimate provisions of APB 20 (A06.130). If these revisions indicate that there will be a loss on the contract, the entire loss must be recognized currently.

Program method. The program method of accounting is rationalized by analogy to the operation of the percentage-of-completion method. Under the program method, a company that expends considerable resources in developing a product believed to have a broad market will sometimes, in the process of costing the sale of individual units of production, defer certain costs even though there is not a contract in hand assuring their recovery. This method, discussed further in Chapter 37, is rarely used in practice, and is not considered appropriate for *government* contracts or subcontracts.

Passage of Time

When enterprise resources are provided for use by others for a specific term, revenue recording often is measured by the passage of time. This is the proportional performance method of accounting in its simplest form. Interest, rents under operating leases, and some royalties are earned and recognized by the passage of time, and sometimes in conjunction with a measure of relative asset usage. This approach is discussed further in the service transactions portion of this chapter.

Recognition Prior to Sale

For certain precious metals and agricultural products, revenue is sometimes recognized at the completion of production. This method results from practical considerations: the products are immediately marketable (at an assured price) with unit interchangeability (fungibility). Often, the difficulty in ascertaining unit cost is a contributing factor in the selection of this method.

Other Practices

As mentioned earlier, the installment method and cost recovery method are sanctioned as exceptions to the basic realization principle in APB 10 (R75.103, n.1):

> The Board recognizes that there are exceptional cases where receivables are collectible over an extended period of time and, because of the terms of the transactions or other conditions, there is no reasonable basis for estimating the degree of collectibility. When such circumstances exist, and as long as they exist, either the installment method or the cost recovery method of accounting may be used. (Under the cost recovery method, equal amounts of revenue and expense are recognized as collections are made until all costs have been recovered, postponing any recognition of profit until that time.)

Installment Method. Under the installment method the purchaser is obligated to make specified payments over a period of time. This approach is used when there is some uncertainty about whether the entire amount of revenue will be realized. To the extent there is an excess of total proceeds over cost, each installment is deemed to bear the same proportion of profit and that profit is recognized when the cash payment is received.

Cost Recovery Method. Under this method all proceeds received are deemed to apply to the carrying amount of the asset being conveyed to the buyer until the carrying amount has been recovered; thereafter, all proceeds are considered profit. This method is to be used when there is substantial uncertainty about whether the sale proceeds will be realized or whether there indeed will be any profit.

Collection Method. This is akin to the cost recovery method, except that a single payment is expected. Thus, if a product or service is "sold" to someone and there is no way of estimating to what extent payment will be received, revenue should then be recorded only when collection occurs. Although the result may be the same, it is not the cash method: it merely signifies that the uncertainty is so great as to warrant not recording a receivable.

Measurement of Revenue and Receivables

Measurement represents the calculation and recording of revenue and related receivables, once all other revenue recognition criteria have been fulfilled. Certain events occurring after the recognition of revenue can leave the seller with a different realizable amount from that originally anticipated. Most of these measurement differences are revenue reductions.

Discounts. The most common cause of revenue and receivable reduction is sales discounts—incentives offered by the seller to the buyer. They can be trade discounts, cash discounts, or quantity discounts.

Trade discounts are known at the time of sale and thus should be recognized at that point through a reduction in the amount of revenue and receivable recorded.

Cash discounts typically are allowed within a certain period of time after the sale is consummated. The seller could record such discounts as a reduction in revenue at the time the receivable is recorded and then increase the recorded revenue if the discount is not taken; or the seller may record them as sales and receivable reductions when they are taken in the customer's remittance.

Quantity discounts are allowances given to purchasers based on the aggregate purchases made during a specified period of time. The allowance may be paid to the purchaser in cash; or the purchaser may be given merchandise equal to the allowance amount; or the seller may simply reduce the buyer's accounts receivable balance. Because these allowances represent revenue transactions occurring over a period of time, a company may need to estimate the amount of volume discounts to be granted in order to properly record current revenues. A quantity discount usually is a revenue reduction, but companies that offer them in more than one form often record them as a sales promotion expense.

Sales With Right of Return. Accounting for sales with a right of return is the subject of SFAS 48, *Revenue Recognition When Right of Return Exists* (R75.106–.109). SFAS 48 is essentially an extraction from SOP 75-1 (carrying the same title), which addressed the diversity in practice that existed in the early 1970s.

SFAS 48 does not apply to (1) accounting for revenue in service industries if part or all of the service revenue may be returned under cancellation privileges granted to the buyer; (2) transactions involving real estate or leases; or (3) sales transactions in which a customer may return defective goods, such as under warranty provisions, discussed in Chapter 14.

If an enterprise sells its product but gives the buyer the right to return the product, revenue from the sales transaction is to be recognized at time of sale only if all of the following conditions are met (R75.107):

a. The price is substantially fixed or determinable at the date of sale.

b. The buyer has paid the seller or is obligated to pay the seller, and payment is not contingent on resale of the product.

c. The obligation to the seller would not be changed in the event of theft or physical destruction or damage of the product.

d. The buyer acquiring the product for resale has economic substance apart from that provided by the seller.

e. The seller does not have significant obligations for future performance to directly bring about resale of the product.

f. The amount of future returns can be reasonably estimated.

Sales revenue and costs of sales that are not recognized at time of sale because the foregoing conditions are not met shall be recognized either when the return privilege has substantially expired or the above conditions are subsequently met, whichever occurs first. Often the critical condition is the last one listed, especially when a company markets a low volume, high dollar product or lacks sufficient experience with a new product to know what level of returns to expect.

If sales revenue is recognized because all of the conditions described above are met, any costs or losses that may be expected in connection with any returns shall be accrued in accordance with SFAS 5, *Accounting for Contingencies* (C59). Sales revenue and cost of sales reported in the income statement are to be reduced to reflect returns—both actual and an estimate for future returns.

Allowances. Another type of revenue and receivables reduction results from sales allowances or credits, often connected with customer dissatisfaction. These adjustments, normally offered to accommodate customers and maintain goodwill, represent the reversal of a sale and thus should be recorded as a reduction of revenue. Since these revenue reductions cannot be identified at the point in time the receivable is recorded, an estimated amount should be recorded to anticipate them, if experience shows the amounts could be large. As a practical matter these reductions are not material in many organizations and thus they are recognized when they occur.

Price Reductions. The final category of revenue and receivables reduction occurs in contracts in which revenue is a function of costs incurred (cost plus fee contracts). As an example, a contractor may have to reduce current revenue in order to offset certain disallowed costs incurred earlier. These price reductions should, if possible, be estimated at the time revenue is initially recorded. A major expenditure likely to be challenged may need to have some initial reserve provided.

Present Valuing. One other measurement issue pertains to receivables which are not collectible within approximately one year. As stated in APB 21, *Interest on Receivables and Payables* (I69), there is a presumption that such a receivable has two components: an exchange price for the goods or services, and an interest factor to compensate the seller for the use of funds. The interest component is deemed to be a function of prevailing market rates. Accordingly, when recording receivables to which APB 21 applies (I69.101–.103), the seller must analyze the components of that receivable to determine both the revenue earned in the current transaction (the sale of goods or services) and the interest component to be earned as time passes.

Thus, a receivable to be collected over a number of years would be recorded at its discounted present value, and interest income would be accreted (on the interest method) periodically by the amortization of the discount, until the receivable is ultimately collected.

Involuntary Conversions. An involuntary conversion of a nonmonetary asset, even where the proceeds are reinvested in replacement property, is a monetary transaction because the recipient is *not obligated* to reinvest the proceeds in other nonmonetary assets. Despite the fact that APB 29 (discussed in the following section) is quite clear about the monetary nature of involuntary conversions, the FASB had to release FIN 30, *Accounting for Involuntary Conversions of Nonmonetary Assets to Monetary Assets* (N35.114–.119), because in practice some companies insisted on nonrecognition of gain or loss, accounting for the difference between carrying amount and the proceeds from insurance or eminent domain proceedings as an adjustment to the cost basis of the replacement property. (See also Chapter 15.)

REVENUE RECOGNITION FOR NONMONETARY TRANSACTIONS

APB 29, *Accounting for Nonmonetary Transactions* (N35), governs the accounting for transactions that are entirely or partly nonmonetary, that is, where the assets exchanged between the buyer and seller are for the most part other than monetary. It is to the APB's credit that near the end of its term as standard setter it dealt with the long-standing and difficult problem of nonmonetary transaction accounting. As it turned out, APB 29 concepts are in harmony with those espoused in SFAC 5.

Definitions

Monetary assets and liabilities are defined in APB 29 as

those assets and liabilities whose amounts are fixed in terms of units of currency by contract or otherwise. Examples are cash, short- or long-term accounts and notes receivable that will result in the receipt of cash, short- or long-term accounts and notes payable to be satisfied with cash; nonmonetary assets are anything else. [N35.402–.403]

A note to N35.402 refers the reader to C28.191–.203 for a listing of monetary and nonmonetary items. Of interest is the fact that marketable securities are considered nonmonetary, even though, as explained in Chapter 12, the line between certain kinds of marketable securities and cash is a thin one.

There are several additional definitions that must be kept in mind when considering nonmonetary transactions.

Productive Assets. These are assets held for or used in the production of goods or services by the enterprise. An investment in another entity is a productive asset if it is accounted for by the equity method. *Similar productive assets* are productive assets that are of the same general type, that perform the same function, or that are employed in the same line of business (N35.106–.107).

Exchange. Also referred to as a *reciprocal transfer*, this is a transaction that occurs between an enterprise and another entity that results in the enterprise acquiring assets or services, or satisfying liabilities by surrendering other assets or services, or by incurring other obligations (N35.401).

Examples of reciprocal nonmonetary transactions (exchanges) include: barter, accommodation transactions (whereby two parties holding fungible inventory such as crude oil, but in different places, swap so that each has the inventory where it needs it), and exchanges of similar productive assets (such as an interest in one oil property for an interest in another, or one parcel of real estate for another parcel of real estate).

Nonreciprocal Transfer. This is a transfer of assets or services in one direction, either from an enterprise to its owners (whether or not to acquire their ownership interests) or to another entity, or from owners or another entity to the enterprise. An example of a monetary nonreciprocal transfer to owners is an entity's reacquistion of its outstanding stock for cash (N35.405); it is nonreciprocal because no asset is received or liability liquidated in the transaction.

Examples of nonmonetary nonreciprocal transfers with owners might be marketable securities held as an investment by a corporation and issued as a dividend in kind to shareholders, or marketable securities issued for treasury stock acquisitions. Also in this category are spin-offs (distribution of stock of a subsidiary corporation to the shareholders of a parent) and rescissions of business combinations (whereby some or all of the stock issued in an earlier business combination is received in exchange for returning the previously acquired business to its original owners).

Examples of nonmonetary nonreciprocal transfers with nonowners would include a donation of a building to a charity or, going the other way, receipt of land from a government unit as an inducement for the company to locate a plant thereon.

Accounting Requirements

Applicability. APB 29 applies to most nonmonetary transactions, including those that are partly in cash. The only exceptions to its application are (N35.101):

1. Business combinations,
2. Transactions between a parent and subsidiary or between companies under common control,
3. Issuance of capital stock for the acquisition of nonmonetary assets or services, and
4. Stock dividends or stock splits.

Basic Rules. Prior to the passage of APB 29 in 1973, nonreciprocal transfers with owners were recorded at the carrying amount of assets given. Nonreciprocal transfers *from* nonowners were recorded at the fair value of the asset received, and *to* nonowners at the cost or other carrying amount of the asset given. Nonmonetary exchanges (reciprocal transfers) had been accounted for either way.

APB 29 states the basic principle that "in general, accounting for nonmonetary transactions should be based on the fair values of the assets (or services) involved, which is the same basis as that used in monetary transactions" (N35.105).

Fair value of a nonmonetary asset should be determined by referring to estimated realizable values in cash transactions involving the same or similar assets, quoted market prices, independent appraisals, estimated fair values of assets or services received in exchange, and other available evidence (N35.111). In offers to shareholders, the shareholder sometimes is given the choices of receiving a nonmonetary asset or cash. In those cases, the amount of cash that could have been received may be evidence of the fair value of the nonmonetary asset exchanged. (Where one of the shareholder's choices is biased to encourage its selection, the two choices should of course not be considered equivalent.) To determine fair value, it is not necessary that the parties be totally at arm's length. That is, they need not have essentially opposing interests.

In the subsections that follow, the specific fair valuing rules of APB 29 are described. Where fair values cannot be determined, the transaction should be based on recorded amounts.

Exchanges.   Where the asset received is not a similar productive asset, the exchange is considered the culmination of the earnings process, and gain or loss should be recognized by comparing the fair value of the asset given with its cost or other carrying amount. Where the fair value of the asset received is more clearly evident, that fair value should be used. On the other side of the transaction, presumably the other party will do the same, and thus the two parties are not likely to use the same values.

For example, if an excess plant carried on the books for $500,000 is exchanged for a desired office building site, and the party owning the plant has a reliable appraisal indicating that it is worth $1 million, that party would record a gain of $500,000 on the transaction and record the cost of the new office building site at $1 million. The party holding the office building site may have a reliable appraisal indicating it is worth $1.2 million, though it is carried at $1.3 million. Impairment in the value of the asset relinquished should be recorded prior to bringing the new asset onto the books; thus a loss of $100,000 will be recorded, and the plant will be recorded at $1.2 million. Symmetry can only be achieved if each party arrives at fair values in exactly the same way, and that is not often likely, because of value differentials caused by the use an owner may have for a particular nonmonetary asset.

If a reciprocal transfer does not culminate the earnings process, the enterprise should value the asset received at the carrying amount of the asset relinquished, also subject to impairment considerations. The APB specified two types of nonmonetary exchange transactions that do not culminate the earnings process (N35.108):

a. An exchange of a product or property held for sale in the ordinary course of business for a product or property to be sold in the same line of business to facilitate sales to customers other than the parties to the exchange [such as swaps of crude oil in two different locations]; and

b. An exchange of a productive asset not held for sale in the ordinary course of business for a similar productive asset or an equivalent interest in the same or similar productive asset.

There will be close calls on whether an asset is a similar productive asset. In the preceding example the company desiring the office building site for its own use may sustain the point that the developable property remaining after the previous plant construction is sufficiently dissimilar. There may be mixed views by accountants in such a case, and the closer a party is to being in the real estate development business, the more likely this transaction would be deemed an exchange of similar productive assets.

The EITF addressed this matter in Issue 86-29. A consensus was reached that the accounting should be based on a "same line of business" test. That is, a similar productive asset is one that is received in exchange for another productive asset and will be used in the same line of business as the productive asset given up.

In Issue 86-29 the EITF also addressed certain other related nonmonetary transactions and reached the following consensus:

- The exchange of a product or property held for sale for a productive asset (even if they are in the same line of business) should be recorded at fair value under APB 29.

- On the other hand, a company should account for an exchange of securities accounted for by consolidation (or by the equity method) for an investment in which it does not acquire control but will account for by the equity method, as a nonmonetary transaction under APB 29, valuing the new investment at the carrying amount of the old investment.

- A company should account for an exchange of securities in which it, in substance, acquires control of another company, as a business combination in accordance with APB 16 (B50).

Nonreciprocal Transfers. These transfers are often treated differently depending on whether owners or nonowners are involved.

Transfers to and from owners. Spin-offs and rescissions of business combinations are to be reflected at the carrying amount of the assets relinquished. In a business combination previously accounted for by the purchase method, the carrying amount includes the unamortized portion of the goodwill generated in the business combination.

In EITF Issue 87-17, a company distributed loans receivable to its owners by forming a subsidiary, transferring those loans receivable to the subsidiary, and distributing the stock of that subsidiary to shareholders of the parent. The book value of the distributed loans was in excess of their fair value. The EITF reached a consensus that this transaction was not a spin-off because the subsidiary was not an operating company. The transaction was, in substance, a dividend-in-kind that should be accounted for at fair value.

The preceding pseudospin-off and other nonreciprocal transfers of nonmonetary assets to owners are to be accounted for at fair value, if the fair value of the nonmonetary asset distributed is objectively measurable and clearly would have been realizable to the distributing entity in an outright sale at or near the time of distribution. This would cover such transactions as issuing marketable securities or other nonmonetary assets as a dividend or to acquire treasury stock. However, where the value of the treasury stock is more clearly evident than the value of the asset given, that more clearly evident value should be used to record the transaction.

Where an owner makes a nonreciprocal transfer to the enterprise (e.g., donating a parcel of land without receiving any stock or asset therefor), the accounting presents a challenge. If the owner owns all or substantially all of the enterprise, the fact that stock is not physically issued seems irrelevant; consistent with the exclusion of the issuance of stock for nonmonetary assets from APB 29 (N35.101(c)), such a donation should be recorded as donated capital (no gain recognized) at the lower of fair value or the contributor's carrying amount (EITF Issue 85-21). Fair value is often unknown in such cases, and the company's board of directors (if they can be objective under the circumstances) may have to resolve the valuation issue.

However, if in the preceding example the transaction involved a minority owner (say, under 20%), the transaction is covered by APB 29, and the asset received is recorded (again, as donated capital—no gain recognized) at fair value even if higher than the donor's carrying amount (N35.105).

What to do when the owenership level falls between "substantially all ownership" and "no significant influence" cannot be specified; each transaction needs to be examined individually, and the objectivity of the value weighed against the relationship of the parties.

Transfers to and from nonowners. In the case of a donation to a nonowner by the enterprise, the fair value of the asset given shall be charged as a donation expense. If fair value differs from carrying amount, a gain or loss would be recognized and classified in the income statement separate from the donation.

In the case of nonreciprocal transfers from nonowners, such as land received from a government unit, gain should be recognized, in concept, based on the fair value of the asset received. In practice, though, it is sometimes considered donated capital.

Impairments in Asset Values. In fair-valued exchanges, if the asset relinquished has a value less than its recorded amount, a loss on the exchange will be recognized. Underlying this accounting is the premise that the cost of the new asset acquired is the fair value of the old asset given up (N35.105). By the same token, if the fair value of the asset given up is greater than the recorded amount, a gain will be recognized.

Accounting literature is inconclusive on the issue of recording impairment on assets held for longer-term use, such as a plant operating with a chronic loss even though the company overall is in a satisfactory profit-making position. SFAS 5, *Accounting for Contingencies* (C59), states:

> In some cases, the carrying amount of an operating asset not intended for disposal may exceed the amount expected to be recoverable through future use of that asset even though there has been no physical loss or damage of the asset or threat of such loss or damage. For example, changed economic conditions may have made recovery of the carrying amount of a productive facility doubtful. The question of whether, in those cases, it is appropriate to write down the carrying amount of the asset to an amount expected to be recoverable through future operations is not covered by this Statement. [C59.137]

Although GAAP for impairment of retained assets is still under development (see Chapter 15 for a further discussion), in nonmonetary transactions (even those required to be recorded using the previous carrying amounts of the assets) losses for impairment are nonetheless to be recorded as a separate provision. This is required because it is illogical to bring the new asset in at the old carrying amount when a serious question exists about the appropriateness of that value. The APB's intent is clear from a reading of requirements where cash is involved (see N35.109 and the following subsection).

The problem becomes acute when an exchange transaction, in which a loss at fair value is indicated, is aborted. What should be done with the asset still retained, since it "almost" resulted in a loss? Different accountants might treat it differently, but the answer would seem to depend on the following:

1. How certain it is that the loss is inherent.
2. The nature of the asset—whether it is an extraneous or integral part of the owner's business.
3. The likelihood that the asset will again be offered for sale.

If the asset remains available for sale, then under GAAP it should be carried at net realizable value, and a loss should be recorded currently.

Partial Monetary Consideration. Sometimes cash, or *boot* (an income tax term), is given in nonmonetary exchange transactions. Boot occasionally is a relatively large amount, even though the general discussion by the APB prior to the passage of APB 29 suggested that boot would be small.

In a nonmonetary transaction accounted for at fair value, the fact that boot is received does not affect the recognition of gain or loss on the transaction. If anything, it makes the fair-valuing process easier. For example, if land costing $500,000 and worth $1 million is exchanged for marketable securities having an aggregate quoted market value of $750,000, and cash of $300,000, the fair value of the assets received undoubtedly would be considered more clearly evident than the fair value of the asset relinquished; thus the new assets would be recorded at $1,050,000, and gain on the exchange would be recorded at $550,000. However, where the land was exchanged for an interest in an oil lease plus $200,000 in cash, the oil lease would probably be recorded at $800,000, assuming the fair value of the asset given (the land at $1 million) were deemed to be more clearly evident.

Where nonmonetary exchanges that include boot are required to be recorded at the carrying amounts of the assets exchanged, gain or loss is still recognized, as indicated in the following subsection. In this regard, the EITF reached a consensus in Issue 86-29, discussed in the earlier section "Exchanges," that if the boot is 25% or more of the fair value of the exchange, the transaction should be considered monetary and fair values recorded. In the examples presented in the following subsections the boot received is less than 25% of the fair value of the exchanges.

Gains. In a transaction where the accounting would normally be based on recorded amounts (e.g., land exchanged for similar land plus cash), the cost-of-sales portion of the asset given up is determined by the ratio of cash to the total value received (including cash). The cash received minus the cost-of-sales portion equals the gain. A hypothetical calculation is shown below:

Cost of land to be exchanged for similar land	$500,000
Cash received	100,000
Fair value of similar land	700,000
Total fair value received	800,000
Cost of sales ($100,000/$800,000 × $500,000)	62,500
Gain ($100,000 − $62,500)	37,500
Carrying amount of new land ($500,000 − $62,500)	$437,500

On the other hand, the fair value of the asset given may be more readily determinable. In such case, the proportion of cash received to the fair value of asset given, multiplied by the recorded amount, equals the cost portion of the asset sold; the cash received minus that portion equals the gain. For example:

Cost of land to be exchanged for similar land	$500,000
Cash received	100,000
Fair value of asset given	600,000
Cost of sales for cash portion ($100,000/$600,000 × $500,000)	83,333
Gain ($100,000 − $83,333)	16,667
Carrying amount of new land ($500,000 − $83,333)	$416,667

Logic would suggest that the entire $100,000 cash receipt should be considered gain, because the fair value of the asset given less the cash received equals the previous carrying amount of the asset given. What takes precedence, however, is the fact that exchanges of similar productive assets are not intended to be fair valued.

As to the company giving up the cash, it records the asset received at the amount of cash paid, plus the recorded amount of the nonmonetary asset surrendered.

Losses. APB 29 states: "If a loss is indicated by the terms of a transaction described in this paragraph [boot transactions] or in N35.108 [which describes exchanges that do not culminate an earnings process], the entire indicated loss on the exchange should be recognized" (N35.109).

Relying on the information in the gains example, assume that the cash received is less than the cost portion allocable thereto, indicating a loss. What should be done? Record only the loss indicated by the cash proportion of the transaction or extrapolate this loss to the entire transaction? For example, if $100,000 cash is received along with land having a fair value of $400,000, and the carrying amount of the asset relinquished is $600,000, this would suggest that one fifth of the carrying amount has been sold for cash. There is clearly a loss indicated of $20,000 on the cash portion. If that is all that is recorded, however, the new asset will be carried at $480,000 (old carrying amount of $600,000 less $120,000 cost allocated to cash portion), when it is already known that the new asset received has a fair value of $400,000. In these circumstances, the entire loss, namely $100,000, should be recognized. This is an anomalous situation, since in boot transactions when losses are involved fair values are used but when gains are involved, recorded amounts are used if the transaction is not the culmination of an earnings process.

REVENUE RECOGNITION FOR SERVICE TRANSACTIONS

Service transactions can be as simple as a car wash, or as complex as a contract to provide the plans for a colony on the moon. In recent years, the number of businesses providing services or combining services with their products has increased dramatically, pointing to a need for more definitive GAAP, especially in the area of revenue recognition.

Service transactions are usually labor intensive and therefore the most significant attendant costs to be accounted for are labor costs and appropriate allocations of overhead. In the performance of certain service transactions, small amounts of material may be utilized (maintenance contracts). If such materials are incidental to rendering the service and are not separately charged to the customer in such a way as would vary the total transaction price, the transaction is a service transaction. If, however, a product and service are combined, and the service is incidental to the product and provided to all product purchasers (e.g., a warranty not separately charged for), the transaction is a product transaction.

Very little authoritative accounting literature is devoted to the subject of accounting for service revenues and costs, although some aspects are addressed by various industry specific SFASs, ARBs, and AICPA industry audit and accounting guides. Because of the paucity of guidance for most service industries, diverse accounting approaches have developed.

Some practices seem conservative, delaying revenue recognition until every aspect of the service is performed and deferring only costs directly incurred in providing the specific service. Other practices seem very liberal, recognizing all estimated revenues at the inception of the transaction. In the middle are accounting practices that recognize income periodically as the related service is provided and that defer costs associated with the services to be provided and related revenues to be recognized in the future. All approaches are premised on the idea of matching costs and revenues; the debate centers around determining the appropriate period for revenue recognition and identifying the appropriate costs to be deferred or accrued.

In 1978, the FASB issued an *Invitation to Comment—Accounting for Certain Service Transactions* based on a draft of an AcSEC SOP (published as Section II of the FASB release). The *Invitation to Comment* was not finalized by the FASB but was incorporated into the recognition phase of the conceptual framework project that resulted in SFAC 5 in 1984. The following discussion is based, to a large extent, on the provisions of the draft SOP, as it was the profession's first attempt at dealing conceptually with accounting in the broad area of service transactions. The draft SOP concludes:

> Revenue from service transactions should be recognized based on performance, because performance determines the extent to which the earnings process is complete or virtually complete. Performance is the execution of a defined act or acts or occurs with the passage of time. [¶ 10]

This conclusion results in four general revenue recognition methods: specific performance, completed performance, proportional performance, and collection. In applying these conclusions, in particular the proportional performance method, AcSEC confirmed the conceptual soundness of the percentage-of-completion method. A fifth possibility, immediate recognition, is discussed first and essentially dismissed.

Recognition Methods

Immediate Recognition. Some service industries might utilize an immediate recognition method, under which the entire service fee is recognized as revenue at the time the buyer purchases the service even though the service has not yet been rendered. In this method, ordinarily there would be a deferral of at least enough revenue to cover expected future direct costs or, as an alternative, an accrual of those costs. This method might be used where customers are irrevocably committed to, or had at the inception of the contract paid, the full purchase price and future direct costs to be incurred by the seller were minimal. In essence, the seller is allocating revenue to the selling effort, rather than to the service. It is unlikely that any company using its financial statements to obtain public debt or equity financing would use the immediate recognition method unless immaterial.

Specific Performance. Revenue is recognized when the specific significant act is performed. For example, a real estate sale commission is earned when the real estate sale is consummated.

Completed Performance. Where there is an indeterminate number of acts to be performed over an indeterminate period of time, or where the final act is so significant in the overall service transaction, revenue is recognized when that final act is performed. For example, a freight transportation company's significant act is delivery to the consignee. The application of this method could be difficult in accounting systems that maintain data primarily based on transaction origination; but most often these are short-term transactions within a single reporting period, and to solve the problem a provision for unearned revenues is estimated and accrued at period end.

Proportional Performance. Revenue is recognized in various ways depending on the nature of the various acts:

1. If the acts are a series of identical or similar acts, each act should be assigned an equal part of the revenue.
2. If the acts are specifically identified, but are not identical or similar, the revenue should be allocated to each specific act on the basis of its direct cost (see the section "Expense Recognition" later in this chapter) if determinable. Otherwise, some other systematic and rational allocation basis, such as using sales values if objectively determinable, should be used. The straight-line method is applicable if direct costs or sales values are indeterminable.
3. When there is an unspecified number of similar acts (e.g., use of health spa facilities), and even if the acts are contingent (e.g., an equipment maintenance contract), revenue should be recognized on a straight-line basis over the term of the contract. There is an exception, however: When the pattern of performance can be shown to differ from that assumed by straight-line amortization (e.g., seasonality or a pattern of usage considerably shorter than the duration of an agreement permitting use of enterprise facilities), the revenue recognition pattern should be modified accordingly.

Collection Method. Many services, especially personal services, have a significant degree of uncertainty of ultimate realization. Revenue should therefore be recognized upon collection.

Other Service Transaction Matters. Contracts that combine initiation fees and continuing service fees, or relate equipment to services, create some problems:

1. In the first situation, some objective value must be determined for initiation rights; if none are discernible, those rights should be considered an integral part of the continuing service transaction.
2. In transactions involving equipment installation combined with continuing maintenance, if the customer is able to purchase the installation separately from the service contract, the installation fee is not a service transaction but is a component of the equipment purchase transaction.

Franchise Fee Revenue

Between 1973 and 1980, accounting for franchise fee revenue and operations was governed by the AICPA Accounting Guide, *Accounting for Franchise Fee Revenue* (AICPA, 1973a). In March 1981, following its stated approach of reviewing and adopting appropriate accounting standards from existing AICPA SOPs and Guides, the FASB adopted SFAS 45, *Accounting for Franchise Fee Revenue* (Fr3), affirming the previous standards.

Franchising has been and continues to be a popular form of merchandising products and services, especially in the fast-food business. The primary advantage of a franchise operation to the franchisor is the ability to create a selling function without the normal capital requirements, while usually maintaining some control over the practices of the franchisee and quality of the franchised products or services. The advantage to the franchisee is, of course, the general ability to operate his own business.

Franchise Agreement. The agreement between the franchisor and franchisee usually meets the following principal criteria:

1. The relationship between the franchisor and franchisee is contractual, and an agreement confirming the rights and responsibilities for each party is in force for a specified period.
2. The continuing relationship has as its purpose the distribution of a product or service, or an entire business concept, within a particular market area.
3. Both the franchisor and the franchisee contribute resources for establishing and maintaining the franchise. The franchisor's contribution may be a trademark, a company reputation, products, procedures, manpower, equipment, or a process. The franchisee usually contributes operating capital, as well as the managerial and operational resources required for opening and continuing the franchised outlet.
4. The franchise agreement outlines and describes the specific marketing practices to be followed, specifies the contribution of each party to the operation of the business, and sets forth certain operating procedures that both parties agree to comply with.

5. The establishment of the franchised outlet creates a business entity that will, in most cases, require and support the full-time business activity of the franchisee. (There are numerous other contractual distribution arrangements in which a local business person becomes the non-exclusive "authorized distributor" or "representative" for the sale of a particular good or service, but such a sale usually represents only a portion of the person's total business.)

6. Both the franchisee and the franchisor have a common public identity. This identity is achieved most often through the use of common tradenames and is frequently reinforced through advertising programs designed to promote the recognition and acceptance of the common identity within the franchisee's market area.

Substantial Performance. Franchise fee revenue from an individual franchise sale usually should be recognized by the franchisor with an appropriate provision for estimated uncollectible amounts, when all material services for conditions relating to the sale have been "substantially performed" or satisfied by the franchisor. Substantial performance means that (Fr3.101):

• The franchisor has no remaining obligation or intent – by agreement, trade practice, or law – to refund any cash received or forgive any unpaid notes for receivables.

• Substantially all the initial services of the franchisor required by the franchise agreement have been performed.

• No other material conditions or obligations related to the determination of substantial performance exist.

If the franchise agreement does not require the franchisor to perform initial services, but a practice of voluntarily rendering initial services exists (or is likely to exist) because of business or regulatory circumstances, substantial performance shall not be assumed until either the initial services have been substantially performed or reasonable assurance exists that the services will not be performed.

Other Requirements. Conservatism justifies the presumption that the franchisee's commencement of operations is the earliest point at which substantial performance can occur; earlier recognition of revenue carries with it a burden of overcoming the presumption.

For area franchise fees, when initial services must be performed that relate to a number of area outlets, it may be necessary to view the franchise agreement as a divisible contract, either by estimating the number of outlets to be opened in a given time period, or by reference to maximum or minimum numbers of outlets specified by contract. In such cases, the initial franchise fee would be recognized ratably as such units are opened.

The installment or cost recovery method for recognizing revenue, as discussed previously, is an exception to normal accrual accounting and is to be used only when no reasonable basis exists for estimating the degree of collectibility of notes receivable from franchises. If continuing fees are inadequate to cover continuing costs, a portion or all of the initial fee should be deferred and amortized over the life of the franchise.

Reacquired franchises are accounted for either as contract terminations or as business combinations:

1. "Contract terminations" occur when the consideration is refunded; they are treated as sales cancellations in the current period. Recorded revenue in prior years is not adjusted retroactively. If the consideration is not refundable, usually under a breach of performance by the franchisee, previously recorded revenue is permitted to stand.
2. "Business combinations" sometimes occur, usually represented by the acquisition of profitably operating franchises in arm's-length transactions. Such an acquisition should be accounted for in accordance with the provisions of APB 16.

Revenue from initial franchise fees should be separately disclosed, and, insofar as possible, revenues and costs from company-owned and franchised outlets should be separately disclosed.

EXPENSE RECOGNITION

While the focus of this chapter has been on revenue and gain aspects of earnings measurement, many of the same considerations apply to the question of reflecting expenses.

SFAC 6, *Elements of Financial Statements*, defines expenses as follows:

> Expenses are outflows or other using up of assets or incurrences of liabilities (or a combination of both) from delivering or producing goods, rendering services, or carrying out other activities that constitute the entity's ongoing major or central operations. [¶ 80]
>
> Expenses represent actual or expected cash outflows (or the equivalent) that have occurred or will eventuate as a result of the entity's ongoing major or central operations. The assets that flow out or are used or the liabilities that are incurred may be of various kinds—for example, units of product delivered or produced, employees' services used, kilowatt hours of electricity used to light an office building, or taxes on current income. Similarly, the transactions and events from which expenses arise and the expenses themselves are in many forms and are called by various names—for example, cost of goods sold, cost of services provided, depreciation, interest, rent, and salaries and wages—depending on the kinds of operations involved and the way expenses are recognized. [¶ 81]

Expense recognition is addressed in SFAC 5, *Recognition and Measurement in Financial Statements of Business Enterprises*, as follows (¶¶ 85–87):

> Expenses and losses are generally recognized when an entity's economic benefits are used up in delivering or producing goods, rendering services, or other activities that constitute its ongoing major or central operations or when previously recognized assets are expected to provide reduced or no further benefits.
>
> Consumption of economic benefits during a period may be recognized either directly or by relating it to revenues recognized during the period:

a. Some expenses, such as cost of goods sold, are matched with revenues – they are recognized upon recogniton of revenues that result directly and jointly from the same transactions or other events as the expenses.

b. Many expenses, such as selling and administrative salaries, are recognized during the period in which cash is spent or liabilities are incurred for goods and services that are used up either simultaneously with acquisition or soon after.

c. Some expenses, such as depreciation and insurance, are allocated by systematic and rational procedures to the periods during which the related assets are expected to provide benefits.

An expense or loss is recognized if it becomes evident that previously recognized future economic benefits of an asset have been reduced or eliminated, or that a liability has been incurred or increased, without associated economic benefits.

Classification of Costs

Accounting literature recognizes two basic kinds of costs, direct and indirect. Direct costs are those that are clearly associated with the production of revenue during a period or with the production of assets held for future sale (such as inventories, discussed in Chapter 14). Indirect costs are all other costs.

These two categories can be further divided. Costs directly related to revenues of the period are considered expenses of the period, in that they arise in the same transaction or event in which revenue is recognized. These are usually thought of as *product costs*, but there are others, such as sales commissions and allocated costs.

Costs such as salaries and rent not related directly to particular revenues but related to a period on the basis of transactions or events occurring in that period, or costs providing no discernible future benefits, are considered *period costs* and are also recognized as expenses when incurred.

Finally, there are those costs that jointly benefit several periods and require systematic and rational allocation. Some of these costs intuitively seem to benefit several periods, but there is no way to be sure of the amount of the benefit, if any, or the timing of its arrival. A good example is research and development, which accordingly is recognized as an expense when incurred.

Three Tiers of Costs

In the Invitation to Comment on service transactions (FASB, 1978a), a three-tiered classification of costs was suggested. This classification is paraphrased below so as to not refer exclusively to service transactions:

1. *Initial direct costs* are costs incurred that are directly associated with negotiating and consummating revenue transactions. They include, but are not necessarily limited to, commissions, legal fees, cost of credit investigations, and installment paper processing fees. In addition, the portion of salespersons' compensation, other than commissions, and of the compensation of other employees that is applicable to the time spent in the activities described above with respect to revenue transactions are also included in initial direct costs. The portion of salespersons' compensation and of the compensation of other employees that is applicable to the time spent in negotiating revenue transactions that are not consum-

mated are not included in initial direct costs. No portion of supervisory and administrative expenses or other indirect expense, such as rent and facilities costs, is included in initial direct costs.

2. *Direct costs* are costs that have a clearly identifiable beneficial or causal relationship (a) to the product produced for inventory or sold or to the services performed, or (b) to the level of services performed for a group of customers (e.g., servicemen's labor, repair parts included as part of a service agreement).

3. *Indirect costs* are all costs other than initial direct costs and direct costs. They include provisions for uncollectible accounts, general and administrative expenses, advertising expenses, and general selling expenses. Indirect costs also include the portion of salespersons' compensation and of the compensation of other employees that is applicable to the time spent in negotiating transactions that are not consummated, as well as all allocations of facility costs (depreciation, rentals, maintenance, and other occupancy costs).

There is a problem in segregating initial direct costs from all other direct costs. Where an enforceable contract (oral or written) exists, it may be possible to observe whether the estimated future benefit is sufficient to permit deferral of the initial direct costs (or to advance the recognition of a portion of income on the contract) in an amount equal to the initial direct costs. To do otherwise would result in a loss, with the "remainder" of the transaction perhaps yielding a substantial profit. However, this approach does not solve the problem of how to account for costs during lengthy precontract negotiations.

Accounting literature is generally consistent in stating that indirect costs should be charged against operations as incurred if they have no arguable cause-and-effect relationship with future revenues (such as the salary of a mailroom clerk). However, many allocations of indirect costs affect future periods; an example is the allocation of factory overhead to units of inventory produced during a period and remaining on hand at period-end. Thus, the most difficult problem about indirect costs is that many of them consist of allocations of long-term assets (e.g., depreciation of plant and equipment, discussed in the following section).

Allocation Process

Depreciation, depletion, amortization of intangibles, and similar internal transactions are allocation processes designed to spread the cost of an asset in a *systematic and rational manner* over the period of its usefulness or over the number of units expected to be achieved. For example, if a machine costs $1,000, is expected to last for 10 years, will have no salvage value, and will produce 1,000 units over its life, the most common accounting approach would charge one-tenth of the asset cost against operations per year; in other approaches the pattern of allocation may not be level, or a provision for obsolescence or a shortening of life may be reflected. Some approaches might charge $1 per unit produced, with continual reevaluation of the remaining number of units to be produced for the purpose of allocating the remaining undepreciated cost.

Since there is no objective definition of systematic and rational allocation, some form of exit value may be the best approach in determining what proportion of the carrying amount of long-term assets should be charged against operations during a particular reporting period. The differential between such valuation of plant assets at the beginning and at the end of the period would be the amount charged against operations. That amount could be subdivided in several ways, to reflect changing prices, physical deterioration, enhancement due to scarcity, or other identifiable features. This approach has not been used in practice.

Future Benefits

The idea of matching costs with revenues has led, in the past, to treating some costs as assets, even though the resultant asset lacked attributes such as exchangeability or tangibility. Deferrals of such costs are based on the idea that future revenue is expected to be derived from current expenditures. In the defintion of assets in SFAC 6, exchangeability is not proposed as an essential criterion of an asset (¶¶ 25, 26).

Thus, if a cost has a demonstrably high probability of resulting in an identifiable and direct future benefit greater than the cost, it may qualify for deferral (except for research and development for which deferral is specifically prohibited by SFAS 2 (R50)). For example, under SFAS 86 (Co2) certain computer software costs are to be deferred. Alernatively, it may be preferable to recognize as revenue that portion of the future revenues equal to the current costs. This would substitute acceleration of revenues for making a cost into an asset and thus may be preferable conceptually. (See chapters 2 and 15 for further commentary.) Some would go further and allow a profit to be recognized on the currently deferred costs, just as a profit is earned on the mainstream activity, although this is rarely done in practice.

Initial direct costs are a prominent example of matching. In leasing transactions, the FASB until late 1986 required that initial direct costs on direct finance leases be charged to expense, with an equal amount of lease revenue recorded at inception of the lease. The FASB had initially proposed deferral of initial direct costs, but changed to "front-ending" because that was the practice in use in the leasing industry. Leasing companies complained that deferral and amortization was cumbersome and would require a great deal of systems rework. Nonetheless, the FASB subsequently adopted deferral accounting in SFAS 91, *Accounting for Nonrefundable Fees and Costs Associated with Originating or Acquiring Loans and Initial Direct Costs of Leases* (L20), issued in December 1986.

Interdependence of Cost and Revenue Recognition

Some revenue transactions are deemed to earn revenue over a period of time. In construction accounting, this has been called the *percentage-of-completion method* (as contrasted with the *completed contract method*); and in service transactions, AcSEC referred to this as the *proportional performance method*.

Where a proportional method of recognizing revenues is based on the extent of direct costs incurred, all costs should be charged against operations as incurred. However, where performance is measured in some other way, it may then be appropriate to defer some proportion of the costs, or accrue additional costs, so as to maintain a ratable gross margin (the profit percentage) throughout the period of performance or production. This is further discussed in Chapters 36 and 37 as to long-term construction or production-type contracts. Thus, costs do become assets in transactions that "earn" over a period of time, depending on the revenue recognition measurement method in use.

However, costs in excess of estimated related revenues are not to be deferred but should be recognized as an expense in the period incurred. In addition, if the total estimated future costs combined with the costs incurred to date exceed the total estimated revenue, the estimated loss should be recorded at the earliest date this determination can be made—first reducing the deferred costs already recorded, and then recording an accrual for additional loss in excess of the deferral.

ACCOUNTS RECEIVABLE—ACCOUNTING AND REPORTING CONSIDERATIONS

Valuation

With revenue having been properly measured and the related costs and expenses recorded, the corresponding receivable is recorded, and the valuation of that receivable must be considered. Valuation describes the process of estimating the cash to be realized on the receivables. This requires a provision for uncollectible accounts, or bad debts—a customer's default on a legitimate obligation.

Providing for bad debts is not part of the revenue recognition process, but as a consequence of granting credit it is an element of the revenue cycle. Estimates of bad debts should be periodically recorded among costs and expenses (not as revenue reductions) at the time revenue is recognized, with appropriate adjustments based on ongoing evaluations of accounts outstanding.

In determining the allowance for uncollectible accounts in large volume situations, a method may be developed to combine historical experience and current economic considerations in order to generate a future expectation. This may result in reflecting the average experience of the enterprise over time, thus averaging the effect of bad debts into the income statement. Such a method is not useful, however, where a company's receivables comprise a small number of relatively large balances. In these situations, the reserve should reflect the expected loss in the specific receivables at the financial statement presentation date. This loss allowance could be zero, or it could be large if a default by one major customer is expected.

Averaging Bad Debts

In an attempt to partly resolve the question of whether "averaging" was appropriate, the FASB in 1975 issued SFAS 5, *Accounting for Contingencies*, which recognizes collectibility of receivables as a loss contingency (C59.122a). SFAS 5 provides the following general guidelines (C59.105):

An estimated loss from a loss contingency ... shall be accrued by a charge to income if both of the following conditions are met:

(a) Information available prior to the issuance of the financial statements indicates that it is probable that an asset has been impaired or a liability has been incurred at the date of the financial statements. It is implicit in this condition that it must be probable that one or more future events will occur confirming the fact of the loss.

(b) The amount of loss can be reasonably estimated.

The above conditions seem to suggest an account-by-account evaluation, but the FASB put the matter straight in Appendix A (C59.128):

> Those conditions may be considered in relation to individual receivables or in relation to groups of similar receivables. If the conditions are met, accrual [of a loss provision] shall be made even though the particular receivables that are uncollectible may not be identifiable.

If a conclusion can be drawn from the FASB remarks, averaging in the sense of "smoothing" income is prohibited, but broad estimations for large numbers of homogeneous accounts are proper.

Selling or Transferring Interests in Receivables

Individual accounts or groups of accounts receivable may be sold or transferred to unrelated parties under a variety of agreements that may allow recourse against the seller for those accounts ultimately not collected by the purchaser. Additionally, certain types of longer-term receivables, for example, mortgage loans and automobile and other lease receivables may be sold or transferred to other parties who are interested in participating in, or obtaining the future economic benefits of, those receivables.

The FASB has attempted to deal specifically with these types of arrangements in two pronouncements, SFAS 77, *Reporting by Transferors for Transfers of Receivables with Recourse* (R20) and TB 85-2, *Accounting for Collateralized Mortgage Obligations* (C30).

Transfers of Receivables With Recourse. SFAS 77 applies to transfers of receivables with recourse that purport to be sales of receivables. Such transfers are to be recognized as sales if all of the following conditions are met (R20.105):

- The transferor surrenders control of the future economic benefits embodied in the receivables. Control has not been surrendered if the transferor has an option to repurchase the receivables.
- The transferor's obligation under the recourse provisions can be reasonably estimated. A sale is not to be recorded if collectibility of the receivables and related costs of collection and repossession are not subject to reasonable estimation.
- The transferee cannot require the transferor to repurchase the receivables except pursuant to the recourse provisions.

If all of these conditions are met, the transfer qualifies as a sale and all probable adjustments in connection with the recourse provisions are accrued. The difference between the sales price (less the accrual for probable adjustments) and the net carrying value of the receivables is to be recognized as gain or loss (R20.106).

If the transfer does not qualify as a sale, the proceeds from the transfer are to be reported as a financing (R20.108).

Collateralized Mortgage Obligations. Collateralized mortgage obligations (CMOs) funnel payments from underlying mortgages or mortgage-backed securities into two or more classes (tranches) of debt securities. The structure essentially converts one-class mortgage securities into a series of mortgage-backed bonds, each with different and more predictable maturities than the underlying securities. CMOs are often referred to as structured receivable financings. The concept has been extended to other types of receivables, including automobile and other lease receivables. (CMOs and progeny are further discussed in Chapters 21 and 40.)

Under TB 85-2, CMOs should be presumed to be borrowings that are reported as liabilities in the financial statements of the issuer unless all but a *nominal* portion of the future economic benefits inherent in the associated collateral have been irrevocably passed to the investor and no affiliate of the issuer can be required to make future payments with respect to the obligation.

TB 85-2 provides for consolidation of a majority-owned issuer's financial statements with the sponsor's because the issuer is acting as a conduit for the sponsor.[1] However, CMOs are often issued by a special-purpose nonsubsidiary corporation that is minimally capitalized; therefore, the collateral represents substantially all of the assets of the issuer. The special-purpose corporation is set up by a sponsoring parent corporation. The sponsor or an affiliate may or may not guarantee the collateralized debt.

To overcome the borrowing presumption, and thereby permit the issuer to remove the collateral from its financial statements and recognize gain or loss, the TB lists several conditions that must be met, as follows (C30.502):

- The issuer surrenders future economic benefits of the collateral.
  - The issuer cannot substitute collateral or call the obligation.
  - The expected residual interest in the collateral is nominal.
- No affiliates of the issuer can be required to make payments on the obligation.
  - The investors can only look to the issuer's assets or third-party guarantors.
  - The issuer or its affiliates cannot be required to redeem the obligation before maturity.

Reporting Requirements

Reporting receivables in a company's financial statements is affected by the nature of the originating transactions, the industry involved, and several practical considerations. As a general rule, significant balances should be segregated by type (e.g., lease receivables, trade accounts receivable). Related party receivables, even if originating in the ordinary course of business, should be classified by source (e.g., officers and directors, affiliates, and employees).

If an enterprise presents a classified balance sheet (current assets segregated from noncurrent assets), receivables should be segregated based on whether they will be collected within the next operating cycle (generally one year). There is, however, an exception to this general rule: In enterprises having an operating cycle of more than one year (e.g., distilleries, construction, tobacco, or lumber), accounts collectible within the operating cycle should be considered as current assets (B05.106). Also, if there is collateral for a receivable, that should be disclosed if material.

---

[1] Under SFAS 94, a majority-owned CMO subsidiary will be consolidated beginning in 1988 in any event. Thus TB 85-2 anticipated the eventual outcome.

Enterprises often receive revenues from sources other than their primary business activities. These sources may be tangentially related to the main business or earning process, for example, revenues from sales of fixed assets or scrap; or they may be totally unrelated, as with the receipt of dividends or interest on investment of temporarily available funds. Where these receipts are not significant they should be included in the financial statements in whatever manner is most expeditious. Otherwise there are two approaches for financial reporting of other revenues: a separately reported total, or a recovery of cost. The first method aggregates all such miscellaneous items and reports them as one total, for example, other income, simply as a practical expedient. The other method recognizes that many receipts actually represent the recovery of a previous expense and should be portrayed as such by deducting them from the related expense. The sale of scrap recovers some of the inventory cost previously charged to cost of sales; sublease income actually offsets or recovers rent expense. The reporting method chosen should take such economic realities into account.

Occasionally, an item of other revenue is very significant to the operations of an enterprise; ordinarily this would be referred to as a gain or loss transaction. If the item fulfills the criteria of being unusual in nature and infrequent in occurrence, as stated in APB 30, *Reporting Results of Operations* (I17), the gain or loss on the transaction should be presented as an extraordinary item, net of the related income tax effect. If only one of the two criteria is met, the gain or loss may be reported as a separate component of income from continuing operations; however, the related income tax effect may not be netted (I22).

Other Matters

Consignments. Merchandise shipped on a consignment or trial basis should not be considered as a sale and a receivable, because the consignee is not obligated until he has resold the merchandise or otherwise accepted it. The legal title still rests with the consignor, who has merely relinquished possession of the merchandise. For accounting purposes, the merchandise should remain classified as inventory, separately delineated if the amount is large.

Prepayments, Advance Billings, Deposits, and Unearned Revenue. Occasionally, funds are advanced by the customer. These can be in the form of contractual prepayments or advance billings, or they may simply be deposits. If the advance was made to secure performance under an agreement (e.g., of future rents) and is legally refundable, it should be classified as a deposit. As future revenues are recognized, the deposit is not reduced because it must utimately be refunded. If, on the other hand, the advance is to be applied as payment (either partial or complete), it should be classified as unearned revenue and credited to revenue when earned within the terms of the agreement.

Differentiation of a deposit from unearned revenue is normally based on the legal provisions of the agreement, as there may be little difference in substance in a particular transaction.

Careful description and disclosure of unearned or deferred revenue is advisable. There have been more than a few instances where amounts in the balance sheet labeled as "deferred profit" have been misunderstood as being assured of inclusion in future income. In fact, many such items are deferred for the reason that future events may cause the originating transaction to be undone and the deferred profit simply to be reversed.

Progress Payments. Progress payments may be made as contract performance proceeds. The proper accounting depends on the revenue recognition method being applied to the contract itself. Since the seller receives progress payments to fund his current costs on the customer's order, normally he should record them as an offset to those costs.

Under the completed contract method the contractor accumulates his costs in inventory, and thus credits progress payments to inventory accounts. To the extent that progress payments exceed costs, the excess should be classified as a liability.

When the contract is accounted for on the percentage-of-completion method, costs are accumulated in three categories: billed accounts receivable, unbilled accounts receivable, and inventory. Progress payments, especially under fixed price contracts, are usually applied first to amounts carried in billed and unbilled receivables, and then to accumulated costs classified as inventory. Excess payments should be classified as a liability.

REVENUES AND RECEIVABLES – AUDITING CONSIDERATIONS

Objectives and Error Types

The overall objective of the audit of revenue and receivables is to determine whether they are fairly presented in the context of the financial statements as a whole. To meet this objective, the audit must ad dress seven basic areas regarding revenue and receivables: existence, ownership, valuation, cutoff, mechanical accuracy, classification, and disclosure. The broad objectives of an audit and these seven basic areas are explained in Chapter 7, with related internal control matters discussed in Chapter 8. The audit philosophy in this chapter assumes that these earlier explanations are understood.

Transaction Types

The primary transaction types that affect revenue and receivables consist of:

- The shipment of goods or the provision of services to customers for cash or credit,
- Receipt of cash from customers, and
- Return of goods by customers and the issuance of credit notes.

Processing and Control Characteristics

Revenue systems vary significantly from industry to industry. Certain steps and basic documentation, however, are nearly universal. Most revenue and receivables systems possess the following types of documents (which are referred to in the figures later in the chapter):

- Customer sales orders
- Customer acceptance documents
- Credit approval forms
- Shipping documents
- Sales invoices
- Customer statements
- Credit memos
- Remittance advices
- Write-off authorization forms

These documents are generated in several steps. The first step in a revenue transaction—initiation—results in generation of customer sales orders or contracts, along with pertinent credit information. These documents can be simple or complex depending on the nature of the product, the size of the order, and so on. In long-term transactions, contracts usually spell out the terms in considerable detail, and these often are key to identifying the appropriate revenue recognition method. In short-term transactions, initiation documents are usually simple preliminaries to feed basic information into the system. Control must be exercised at the initiation point to assure that all orders are accurately recognized by the system. Errors here can lead to filling orders with the wrong merchandise or providing the wrong service; such problems ultimately show up in wasted costs and sales returns.

Making goods or services available for transfer is particularly important in long-term proportional performance transactions. Where the accounting system is used to document progress toward completion, this is done through the accurate accumulation of cost data. Otherwise, regularly scheduled evaluations of physical progress are used. Although the form of documentation of progress can vary, control over it is critical. In short-term transactions, documentation of progress is less important for revenue recognition than for other internal accounting purposes.

The next step is the exchange of resources; the delivery of the product or service often is the significant act that triggers revenue recognition. Shipping documents, customer acceptances, and the like capture the information that, when combined with the original sales order or contract, provides the data to be recorded on the invoice. This invoice is the key document signifying that revenue can be recognized and that an account receivable exists.

The final step is the receipt of cash—either in payment of the receivable balance or as an advance—or it may be the return of goods by the customer and issuance of a credit note.

Audit Approach

To develop an effective and comprehensive approach, the auditing of revenue, receivables, and cash receipts should be integrated. To develop the appropriate program the auditor needs to consider:

- Interest risks.
- Potential errors.
- Nature and effectiveness of the related controls.
- Effective use of analytical review.
- The interrelationship of these transactions and balances to other transactions and the effect on audit work; and the use of procedures that accomplish more than one purpose.

Inherent Risks. In assessing the inherent risks (susceptibility of an account balance or class of transactions to errors that could be material) in revenues, receivables, and cash receipts, the auditor will consider a number of interrelated factors. Specifically, in almost all audits a number of high value (or key items) are present. Further, in relation to most types of potential errors, the error could be a 100% error and thus would have a low probability of self-detection. Finally, a number of specific potential errors could raise concern as to fraud.

Potential Errors. Segmenting the broad objectives of an audit (Chapter 7) and of internal accounting control (Chapter 8) into account balances (or classes of transactions) and specific risks provides an effective and efficient method for planning the audit. Potential errors (including those that might intentionally be made, i.e., irregularities) provide the "architecture" for the audit and a focus for assessing the magnitude and likelihood of the related exposures. To better understand each potential error, its related cause is presented in Figures 13.1 and 13.2.

Depending on the specific circumstances and the significance of the amount involved, the auditor might also develop additional specific audit approaches related to the revenue cycle, for example:

- Significant sales returns
- Significant sales and receivables in foreign currencies
- Significant scrap or bulk sales
- Related party sales and receivables
- Key item sales
- Intercompany sales and receivables

Nature and Effectiveness of Related Controls. As described in Chapter 8, the audit process requires that the auditor obtain an understanding of the client's internal controls, document his understanding, and analyze the internal control structure to ascertain (1) the control points on which he chooses to rely and (2) the effect of systems weaknesses on his audit plan. The auditor must then develop specific audit procedures to test those areas of internal control on which he will rely.

Having identified the potential error types, the auditor must consider the pertinent controls within the system. For the revenue and receivables system there are three general control features that form the basis of the system.

Objective	Potential Errors	Causes of Errors	Inherent Risk Factors	Types of Controls	Examples of Controls
Existence—validity	Sale recorded, goods not shipped	• Shipping document prepared, goods not shipped • Goods not received by intended customer • Shipping document prepared twice • Invoice prepared twice • Sales invoice prepared without supporting shipping document • EDP entry without supporting documents • Sales invoice recorded twice • Sales invoice records duplicated in EDP • Shipping document recorded twice	• Value of a balance or group of transactions, typically large relative to materiality • High value items typically present in balance or transactions • Errors have a direct impact on earnings • Errors tend to be 100%	• Independent approval, review, checking, or recalculation • Matching of independently generated documents • Prenumbering and sequence checking of key documents • Maintenance of independent control totals • Comparison with independent third-party information • Soliciting independent third-party information • Segregation of personnel, operations, and assets • Timeliness of operation	• Shipping document quantity checked in warehouse • Shipping documents checked for serial continuity • Sales invoices balanced to daily sales journal • Daily sales journal reconciled to accounts receivable ledger posting • Overdue accounts receivable independently investigated • Accounts receivable in general ledger reconciled to accounts receivable ledger
Existence—recording	Goods shipped, sale not recorded	• Goods shipped without shipping document • Shipping document prepared, but not invoiced • Sales invoice not recorded • Sales invoice records lost in EDP • Shipping document prepared but not recorded	• Value of a balance or group of transactions, typically large relative to materiality • High value items typically present in balance or transactions • Errors have a direct impact on earnings • Errors are not self-detecting • Errors tend to be 100%	• Independent approval, review, checking, or recalculation • Matching of independently generated documents • Prenumbering and sequence checking of key documents • Maintenance of independent control totals • Segregation of personnel, operations, and assets • Timeliness of operation	• Shipping document quantity checked in warehouse • Shipping document matched to sales invoice • Sales invoice matched to sales order • Shipping documents checked for serial continuity • Sales invoices balanced to daily sales journal • Accounts receivable in general ledger reconciled to accounts receivable ledger
Valuation—accuracy	Sale amount recorded incorrectly	• Quantity shipped exceeds quantity ordered • Shipping document quantity incorrect	• Value of a balance or group of transactions, typically large relative to materiality	• Independent approval, review, checking, recalculation	• Shipping document quantity checked in warehouse

(continued)

FIG. 13.1 Audit Planning Matrix—Revenues

Objective	Potential Errors	Causes of Errors	Inherent Risk Factors	Types of Controls	Examples of Controls
		• Sales invoice quantity incorrect • Sales invoice price incorrect • Sales invoice incorrectly calculated • Sales invoice amount recorded incorrectly • Sales invoice amount processed incorrectly in EDP • Shipping document quantity recorded incorrectly	• High value items typically present in balance or transactions • Errors have a direct impact on earnings • Complex calculations involved	• Matching of independently generated documents • Maintenance of independent control totals • Soliciting independent third-party confirmation • Segregation of personnel, operations, and assets • Timeliness of operation	• Sales invoice price and discount checked • Sales invoice additions and extensions checked • Sales invoice quantity agreed to shipping document • Sales invoice balanced to daily sales journal • Daily sales journal reconciled to accounts receivable ledger posting • Overdue accounts receivable investigated • Accounts receivable in general ledger reconciled to accounts receivable ledger
Valuation – change in circumstances	Goods shipped to a bad credit risk	• Goods shipped to bad credit risk	• High value items typically present in balance or transactions • Errors have a direct impact on earnings • Errors are not self-detecting • Errors tend to be 100% • High susceptibility to fraud • Accounting judgements involved	• Independent approval, review, checking, or recalculation • Soliciting independent third-party confirmation • Segregation of personnel, operations, and assets	• Sales order approved for credit • Overdue accounts receivable investigated
Classification	Sale misclassified	• Incorrect account code on sales invoice • Incorrect sales amount code on sales invoice • Account code recorded incorrectly • Account code processed incorrectly in EDP	• Value of a balance or group of transactions, typically large relative to materiality • High value items typically present in balance or transactions • Errors have a direct impact on earnings • Errors are not self-detecting • Errors tend to be 100%	• Independent approval, review, checking, or recalculation • Segregation of personnel, operations, and assets	• General ledger account code checked on sales invoice • Monthly sales journal reviewed for reasonableness • Accounts receivable in general ledger reconciled to accounts receivable ledger

Cut-Off	Sales recorded in wrong period	• Shipping document dated in wrong period • Sales invoice dated in wrong period • Sales invoice recorded in wrong period • Sales invoice processed in wrong period in EDP • Shipping date recorded incorrectly • Invoicing data recorded in wrong period	• Value of a balance or group of transactions, typically large relative to materiality • High value items typically present in balance or transactions • Errors have a direct impact on earnings • Errors are not self-detecting • Errors tend to be 100%	• Independent approval, review, checking, or recalculation • Timeliness of operation	• Adequate written cut-off instructions • Personnel adequately instructed regarding cut-off • Achievement of cut-off reviewed
Mechanical accuracy	Sales summarization and posting errors	• Sales journal not included in summarization and posting to general ledger • Sales journal included twice in summarization and posting to general ledger • Sales journal amount incorrectly summarized and posted to general ledger • Entry in general ledger not supported by sales journal • Sales journal summarized and posted to wrong general ledger account • Sales journal summarized and posted to general ledger in wrong period	• Value of a balance or group of transactions, typically large relative to materiality • High value items typically present in balance or transactions • Errors have a direct impact on earnings • Errors are not self-detecting • Errors tend to be 100%	• Independent approval, review, checking, or recalculation • Matching of independently generated documents • Comparison with independent third-party information • Timeliness of operation	• Sales invoices balanced to daily sales journal • Daily sales journal reconciled to accounts receivable ledger posting • Monthly sales journal reviewed for reasonableness • Overdue accounts receivable independently investigated • Accounts receivable in general ledger reconciled to accounts receivable ledger

FIG. 13.1 (continued)

Objective	Potential Errors	Causes of Errors	Inherent Risk Factors	Types of Controls	Examples of Controls
Existence— validity	Cash receipts recorded but not deposited	• Receipt form prepared twice • Receipt form or remittance advice recorded twice • Receipts records duplicated in EDP • EDP entry without supporting receipt form or remittance advice • Check lost or stolen after recording • Check deposited in nonclient bank account	• Value of a balance or group of transactions, typically large relative to materiality • High value items typically present in balance or transactions • Errors have a direct impact on earnings • Errors are not self-detecting	• Independent approval, review, checking, or recalculation • Matching of independently generated documents • Maintenance of independent control totals • Comparison with independent third-party information • Cancellation of documentation • Segregation of personnel, operations, and assets • Timeliness of operation	• Accounts receivable in general ledger reconciled to accounts receivable ledger • Received checks protectively stamped • Checks received list prepared • Checks received list balanced to daily receipts journal • Daily receipts journal reconciled to accounts receivable ledger posting • Monthly bank reconciliation prepared • Independent review of monthly bank reconciliation
Existence— recording	Cash receipt not recorded or deposited	• Check lost or stolen before recording	• Value of a balance or group of transactions typically large relative to materiality • High value items typically present in balance or transactions • Errors tend to be 100% • High susceptibility to fraud	• Independent approval, review, checking, or recalculation • Maintenance of independent control totals • Comparison with independent third-party information • Soliciting independent third-party confirmation • Segregation of personnel, operations, and assets • Timeliness of operation	• Overdue accounts receivable independently investigated • Received checks protectively stamped • Checks received list: prepared • Checks received list balanced to daily receipts journal • Monthly bank reconciliation prepared • Independent review of monthly bank reconciliation
Existence— recording	Cash receipt deposited but not recorded	• Receipt form not prepared • Receipt form or remittance advice not recorded • Receipts records lost in EDP	• Value of a balance or group of transactions, typically large relative to materiality • High value items typically present in balance or transactions	• Independent approval, review, checking, recalculation • Matching of independently generated documents	• Overdue accounts receivable independently investigated • Accounts receivable in general ledger reconciled to accounts receivable ledger

Assertion	Potential error	Inherent risk factors	Control categories	Specific control procedures
(continued)		• Errors tend to be 100%	• Maintenance of independent control totals • Comparison with independent third-party information • Timeliness of operation	• Checks received list balanced to daily receipts journal • Daily receipts journal reconciled to accounts receivable ledger posting • Monthly bank reconciliation prepared • Independent review of monthly bank reconciliation • Monthly bank reconciliation prepared • Independent review of monthly bank reconciliation
Valuation	Cash receipt amount recorded incorrectly • Wrong amount on receipt form or remittance advice • Receipt form or remittance advice amount recorded incorrectly • Receipt amount processed incorrectly in EDP	• Value of a balance or group of transactions, typically large relative to materiality • High value items typically present in balance or transactions • Errors are not self-detecting	• Independent approval, review, checking, or recalculation • Matching of independently generated documents • Maintenance of independent control totals • Comparison with independent third-party information • Timeliness of operation	• Overdue accounts receivable independently investigated • Accounts receivable in general ledger reconciled to accounts receivable ledger • Checks received list balanced to daily receipts journal • Daily receipts journal reconciled to accounts receivable ledger posting • Monthly bank reconciliation prepared • Independent review of monthly bank reconciliation
Classification	Cash receipt credited to wrong account • Incorrect account code on receipt form or remittance advice • Account code recorded incorrectly • Account code processed incorrectly in EDP	• Value of a balance or group of transactions, typically large relative to materiality • High value items typically present in balance or transactions • Errors are not self-detecting • Errors tend to be 100%	• Independent approval, review, checking, or recalculation • Maintenance of independent control totals • Timeliness of operation	• Accounts receivable in general ledger reconciled to accounts receivable ledger • Monthly receipts journal reviewed for reasonableness • Non-trade receipts general ledger code checked

(continued)

FIG. 13.2 Audit Planning Activity—Cash Receipts

Objective	Potential Errors	Causes of Errors	Inherent Risk Factors	Types of Controls	Examples of Controls
Cut-Off	Cash receipt recorded in wrong period	• Receipt form or remittance advice dated in wrong period • Receipt form or remittance advice recorded in wrong period • Receipts records processed in wrong period in EDP	• Value of a balance or group of transactions, typically large relative to materiality • High value items typically present in balance or transactions • Errors are not self-detecting • Errors tend to be 100%	• Independent approval, review, checking, or recalculation • Maintenance of independent control totals • Comparison with independent third-party information • Timeliness of operation	• Adequate written cut-off instructions • Personnel adequately instructed regarding cut-off • Achievement of cut-off reviewed • Checks received list balanced to daily receipts journal • Daily receipts journal reconciled to accounts receivable ledger posting • Monthly bank reconciliation prepared • Independent review of monthly bank reconciliation
Mechanical accuracy	Cash receipts summarization and posting errors	• Monthly journal posted twice to general ledger • Entry in general ledger not supported by monthly journal • Monthly journal records not posted to general ledger • Monthly journal record amount posted incorrectly to general ledger • Monthly journal record posted to wrong ledger account • Monthly journal posted to general ledger in wrong period	• Value of a balance or group of transactions, typically large relative to materiality • High value items typically present in balance or transactions • Errors are not self-detecting • Errors tend to be 100%	• Independent approval, review, checking, or recalculation • Maintenance of independent control totals • Timeliness of operation	• Adequate written cut-off instructions • Personnel adequately instructed regarding cut-off • Achievement of cut-off reviewed • Accounts receivable account in general ledger reconciled to accounts receivable ledger • Monthly receipts journal agreed to sum of daily journals • Monthly receipts journal agreed to general ledger posting

FIG. 13.2 (continued)

Authorization. Authorization can take a variety of forms ranging from direct approval of individual transactions – such as management approval of new contracts – to implied approval through policy guidelines, such as current price lists approved by management. The basic areas in the revenue and receivables cycle in which suitable authorization controls are needed are:

* Granting of credit
* Acceptance of orders
* Shipment of goods or performance of services
* Determination of price and terms
* Adjustments to sales-related balances

Segregation of duties. Segregation of duties may be the key element of internal control in the revenue cycle. At least two internal control objectives – safeguarding assets and providing reliable information – can be substantially achieved when individual tasks are segregated. The shipping function, for example, should be separated from the billing and invoice processing function. Invoice processing should be segregated from the recording of accounts receivable, which in turn should be separate from the cash receipts function. In short, asset access must be segregated from record-keeping to prevent both errors and irregularities.

Key elements in the revenue system are those controls that assure completeness of data, that is, that all goods and services sold are recorded. The controls necessary to assure completeness also draw upon another fundamental element – the use of prenumbered documents. Once the initial transfer of goods or services is recorded on a prenumbered document, it is then possible to account for all such documents to assure that all shipments have been billed and also that no billings are duplicated.

Independent verification. The means of independent verification will vary significantly from one organization to another. The use of internal auditors to check the accuracy of the recording and processing of sales transactions helps fulfill the stated internal control objectives. A periodic independent check can help ensure that company strictures within the revenue system (e.g., credit authorization policies, accounts receivable write-off policies, and sales return policies) are being appropriately followed.

Also under the heading of independent verification comes the mailing of statements to customers on a regular basis. This provides a key control to confirm both the existence of receivable balances and the recording of all cash receipts.

Based on the results of the analysis of transactions, potential error types, and controls, an approach will be devised for the audit of revenues and receivables. Selecting the appropriate audit approach requires both an analysis of the strength of applicable internal controls and an assessment of (1) the level of direct management surveillance of transactions and (2) the significance of individual transactions. Management's direct surveillance can be an invaluable control; the auditor must observe it in context to evaluate that it does not constitute management override of the system, which can destroy its reliability. And all other things being equal, an error carries a greater risk in a significant revenue transaction than in a small transaction;

thus the auditor will plan to devote more of his attention to the individually significant transactions.

The next two stages of the audit of revenue and receivables, indentifying and evaluating controls and testing the system, are discussed fully in Chapter 8 and therefore are not covered here.

To effectively determine whether the existing controls provide an adequate basis for an efficient reliance-based audit, the controls need to be specifically correlated with the nature and extent of the risk. This can be done most effectively by comparing each potential error to the related controls ordinarily expected to be present. These controls are then correlated with the inherent risk and potential error characteristics as shown in Figures 13.1 and 13.2.

It is possible for auditors to rely solely on substantive tests when auditing revenue, receivables, and cash receipts. This may be efficient, such as in the audit of a small company whose internal control systems are not especially sophisticated or in the audit of a company whose systems are not deemed effective or reliable. In most cases, however, the auditor will rely heavily on the systems of internal control for the sales, receivables, and cash receipts cycle. In doing so, the auditor will apply compliance tests to the system of internal accounting control and, if the results of such tests are favorable, will reduce the number of substantive tests applied.

Once the auditor is satisfied that the system is operating in the manner originally contemplated, or he has responsively modified that understanding, the extent of substantive audit procedures can be determined. Examples of year-end and interim procedures are provided in Figures 13.3 and 13.4

Effect of Interrelationships on Other Audit Procedures

The revenue, receivables, and cash receipts audit work is directly interrelated in this chapter. The audit work done in assessing an organization's inventory (see Chapter 14) is also directly related to work in revenue, receivables, and cash receipts. A well-planned audit will recognize and take advantage of this interrelationship in the design of the audit work. In addition, most audit procedures deal with more than one type of potential error. A selection of these more powerful procedures will usually result in a more efficient audit program.

Analytical Review. At its current state of development, analytical review either provides a challenge to, or confirmation of, the auditor's understanding of the client's environment and its accounting and control systems. Such analysis helps identify areas where more work appears warranted.

The usefulness of analytical review is enhanced where detailed information and other complementary systems exist (such as well-designed budget or statistical operating data or industry data and competitor information). In such circumstances analytical review can provide a modicum of direct audit assurance that material errors (individually or in the aggregate) are not present. However, because the data available is so varied among companies, generalizations on the effectiveness of analytical review are not useful.

Analytical reviews of related account balances, ratios, trends, and the like provide evidence of the reasonableness of account balances. For example, the allowance for

Audit objective	Sample year-end procedures*	Sample interim procedures
Existence. Determine whether there are valid transactions supporting the revenues recorded in the financial statements, and whether all such valid revenue transactions have been properly included.	• Review a reconciliation of beginning and ending accounts receivables. • Where appropriate, reconcile units shipped with sales, production, and inventory records. • Review sales and gross profit by product line by month and investigate unusual fluctuations.	• Trace selected entries on the sales journal to supporting evidence of shipment/delivery. • Trace selected shipping documents to billing records to determine that all shipments are billed.
Ownership. Determine whether the revenue shown in the financial statements represents sales of company products or services.	• Confirm sales information with customer. • Review reconciliation of confirmation exceptions and verify significant items.	• Review journal entries, and for unusual items, check against supporting documentation. • Review sales contracts and arrangements to determine if company is a commission agent or broker that should record only fee income and not total proceeds.
Mechanical Accuracy. Determine whether the basic mathematical calculations and clerical compilation procedures have been accurately carried out.	• Obtain analyses of sales revenue and sales deduction amounts for the period, check clerical accuracy and agree to general ledger and analyses of other related accounts.	• For selected periods test postings from the sales and sales returns journals to the general ledger. • Test footings of selected sales journals.
Valuation. Determine whether the revenue balances are fairly valued in conformity with GAAP.	• Review analysis of doubtful accounts and related documents. • Where sales are made with a right of return, evaluate the appropriateness of the revenue recognition policy. • Review price adjustments issued for period to determine if errors exist in recorded sales which may not have been corrected by year-end.	• Compare sales prices in selected transactions to price lists.
Disclosure. Determine whether revenue disclosure in the financial statements is adequate.	• Inquire about sales to related parties and test to assure that they are properly disclosed.	• Test selected sales transactions to determine that stated revenue recognition policy is followed.

* Also often performed at an interim date.

(continued)

FIG. 13.3   Sample Audit Procedures for Revenue

Audit objective	Sample year-end procedures*	Sample interim procedures
Classification. Determine whether revenues are properly classified.	• Ascertain that nonoperating revenues are not included in sales.	• Test input to sales accounts to determine by review of underlying data that entries are properly classified.
Cutoff. Determine whether all revenue transactions before and after the year-end have been appropriately treated.	• Investigate shipping records immediately before and after balance sheet date and agree to sales records. • Investigate credit notes issued after the balance sheet date. • Review reconciliation of confirmation exceptions and verify significant items. • Where appropriate reconcile units shipped with sales, production and inventory records.	• Test cutoff at interim dates to assure system is working.

* Also often performed at an interim date.

FIG. 13.3 *(continued)*

bad debts or sales returns may be essentially a projection that can be corroborated through comparison of historical write-off totals to sales and average receivables balances. However, care must be taken in the use of an analytical procedure that employs a historical trend, especially if the enterprise has recently changed an operational policy—less stringent credit-granting criteria, for example. In such an instance, the auditor should evaluate the effect of this change on the results to be expected from the analytical procedures.

General examples of analytical procedures to be applied to revenue include an assessment of the validity of reported sales. This is tested in part by the procedures applied to other accounts, particularly accounts receivable and inventory. Thus, an unusual relationship detected in the examination of inventory or receivables may reflect an accounting problem for the reported sales figure as well. For example, unrecorded sales could be reflected in unusually high inventory shrinkage figures or an unusually low receivables turnover ratio. Because of these interrelationships, the combined review of sales, receivables, and inventories is probably the most effective audit approach (see Chapter 14 for analytical procedures related to inventory).

Two procedures that address the validity of sales are:

1. *Examination of gross profit percentage.* This ratio is compared with that of recent years for each major product line or segment. Unexplained large differences could be an indication of unreported or nonexistent sales.

2. *Comparison of reported sales to budget.* If available, a sales budget provides a valuable benchmark for evaluating actual sales performance. For the comparison to be most useful,

Audit objective	Sample year-end procedures*	Sample interim procedures
Existence. Determine whether there are valid accounts receivable supporting the dollar amount shown in the balance sheet and whether all such accounts receivable balances have been properly included.	• Confirmation of selected receivable balances. • Review reconciliation of confirmation exceptions, verify significant items, and trace nonreplies to remittance advices. • Review the accounts receivable control account for the period and reconcile to aged list of receivables.	• For a sample of shipping records, trace details to sales invoices, sales journal and customer accounts in sales ledger. • For a sample of entries in the sales journal trace to supporting evidence of shipment or delivery.
Ownership. Determine whether the accounts receivable balances are owned by the company and whether they are subject to any lien or restrictions.	• Review receivables for any notation that they have been assigned or discounted. • Review bank confirmations for indications of liens on receivables.	• Review cash receipts journal for evidence of receipts from accounts receivable factors. • Review company minutes to see if board of directors has authorized hypothecation of receivables.
Mechanical Accuracy. Determine whether the basic mathematical calculations and clerical compilation procedures have been accurately carried out.	• Obtain aged lists of receivables, trace total to general ledger, agree selected items to and from subsidiary records and sales invoices, test aging and add and cross-add. • Obtain analyses of the allowance for doubtful accounts and schedule of bad debt expense and check additions, trace total to general ledger, trace individual items to subsidiary records and agree provisions to the earnings statement. • Review reconciliation of confirmation exceptions, verify significant items and trace nonreplies to remittance advice.	• For selected periods, test postings from the sales journal, sales return journal and cash receipts journal to the accounts receivable ledger. • Test footings of various journals.
Valuation. Determine whether the accounts receivable balances are fairly valued in conformity with GAAP.	• Review reconciliation of confirmation exceptions, verify significant items, and trace nonreplies to remittance advice.	• Test pricing of sales invoice by comparison to price lists and contracts.

* Also often performed at an interim date.

(continued)

FIG. 13.4 Sample Audit Procedures for Accounts Receivable

Audit objective	Sample year-end procedures*	Sample interim procedures
	• Review analysis of doubtful accounts and related documents. • If balances are receivable in foreign currency, determine the exchange rate for conversion and check the conversion calculation.	
Disclosure. Determine whether accounts receivable balance disclosure in the financial statements is adequate.	• Review the accounts receivable control account for the period and investigate any large or unusual entries or entries arising from unusual sources. • Inquire about related party receivables and assure that they are properly disclosed. • Review receivables for any that have been assigned or discounted, or that are with related parties.	• Test interim entries to receivables to determine that nature of transactions conforms to the description of the business.
Classification. Determine whether accounts receivable are properly classified.	• Review lists of balances for amounts due from group or related companies, employees etc., credit balances and unusual items.	• Test entries to receivables control account to determine they represent sales in the normal course of business.
Cutoff. Determine whether all sales and cash receipts before and after the year end have been appropriately treated.	• Review reconciliation of confirmation exceptions, verify significant items, and trace nonreplies to remittance advice. • Review sales and credit notes issued before and after year-end to test if recorded in the correct accounting period.	• Check serial continuity of shipping and delivery records and trace selected items to sales invoices for timeliness of recording transactions.

* Also often performed at an interim date.

FIG. 13.4 *(continued)*

the auditor must examine the reasonableness of the budget through knowledge of the company and its current market environment.

General examples of analytical procedures to be applied to receivables include:

• Collectibility of receivables
• Provision for doubtful accounts
• Discount policy
• Validity of receivables

The most commonly applied analytical review procedures for analyzing collectibility of receivables are:

• *Receivables turnover* (i.e., the ratio of credit sales to average net receivables). This ratio is a measure of a company's success in implementing a good credit policy. It can be compared with prior years' results or with relevant industry ratios – the higher the ratio, the better the performance.

   A ratio that is low relative to prior years or to the industry average might indicate an audit problem related to uncollectibility of certain receivables. A decrease in the turnover ratio might also reflect fictitious credit sales or improper cutoff to improve profitability; or employee fraud may exist if collections are not recorded properly to customer accounts.

   Therefore, a low ratio should be further investigated by having the client prepare a schedule for the aging of receivables, by reviewing the bad debt provisions, or by other pertinent procedures. In comparing receivables turnover to the industry average, the auditor should consider differences in the nature of the production process between industries. Industries in which the product is durable and has high unit value may be expected to extend credit more freely and for longer periods than industries in which the product is nondurable and of low unit value. This would be reflected in differences in average receivables turnover for these industries.

• *Aging schedule of accounts receivable.* This is frequently prepared by the client. Typical aging categories are thirty day intervals (e.g., 0 to 30 days, 31 to 60 days, and so forth). The lower the percentage of receivables in older categories the better. The percentages can be compared with prior years' results or industry data if available.

• *Individual balance analysis*, both of the average balance and the largest individual balance. A relatively high average balance per customer, compared with prior years and the industry average, could be an indication of uncollectible accounts. Similarly, an unduly high individual balance should focus attention on the collectibility of this account.

Provision for doubtful accounts and customer discounts or customer credits and returns are usually analyzed as a percentage of receivables or of credit sales:

• *The ratio of the provision for doubtful accounts to total receivables or to credit sales* is used to investigate the sufficiency of the provision for doubtful accounts. If this ratio is significantly smaller relative to prior years or the industry average, this might be an indication of an inadequate allowance for uncollectible accounts.

• *The ratio of customer discounts to total receivables or to credit sales* is used to investigate the discount policy. (Customer credits or returns may be analyzed similarly.) If a client has a policy of giving discounts to customers for early payment of their accounts, this ratio can be used to analyze the effect of the policy both over time and relative to the industry average. Unexpected differences here may reflect audit or management problems needing prompt attention. For example, this approach might detect discounts improperly allowed by a receivables clerk.

Two approaches might be used to test the validity of receivables:

1. *The ratio of the largest receivable account balance to total receivables.* This ratio, if unusual when compared over time and with the industry average, should cause the auditor to give special attention to analyzing the validity and collectibility of this critical account.
2. *Roll forward* of the beginning of year accounts receivable balance, plus credit sales less cash receipts during the year, may be used to estimate the end-of-year receivables balance.

In addition to analytical review procedures and the assessment of risks and related controls and procedures, the revenue and receivables cycle also includes one technique, the use of confirmations, discussed in the following section. While sometimes encountered in similar forms in other areas (e.g., bank confirmations), it is most prevalent in this area, where it forms a very powerful audit tool.

Confirmation of Receivables

Confirmation of receivables is a standard audit procedure, and the auditor who omits this procedure has the burden of justifying the deviation (AU 331.01). It is most often used primarily as a substantive procedure—to obtain direct evidence in support of the recorded receivables; but in large volume, small individual balance situations, it is frequently used primarily as a compliance test—to establish that the client's systems are operating properly.

Omission can be justified on the basis that the confirmation procedures are impractical or impossible, and that the fair presentation of the receivables balances can be substantiated through alternative procedures. From a practical standpoint, it is rare that a sample of receivables is not circularized for confirmation where receivables are material, as third party verification of a company's records provides greater audit assurance than evidence from within the company.

Scope and Timing. The confirmation methodology is left to the auditors' discretion, and requires judgment in the following areas:

- Confirmation date
- Form of confirmation request
- Number of accounts circularized

Confirmation date refers to the timing of the confirmation procedures. Whether confirmations are requested as of year end or as of some other date will depend on the overall design of the audit approach, with the aim of making the examination more efficient or meeting client deadlines. A confirmation date other than year end can be justified when the internal control system is sufficiently reliable to produce reasonably accurate revenue and collection data between the confirmation date and year end. Otherwise confirmation must be performed at or very near to the balance

Please examine the accompanying statement carefully and either confirm its correctness or report any differences to our auditors

[*Name and Address of Auditors*]

who are auditing our financial statements.

Your prompt attention to this request will be appreciated. An envelope is enclosed for your reply. Please do not send your payments to the auditors.

[*Name of Client*]

_____

Confirmation:

The balance receivable from us of [*amount*] as of [*date*] is correct except as noted below:

_____

_____

_____

[*Name of Customer*]

Date _____   By_____
                                         [Respondent's signature]

FIG. 13.5   Positive Confirmation Request

sheet date. If there is a gap between confirmation date and year end, some level of substantive procedures will be applied to intervening transactions.

In making judgments as to the form of confirmation and the number of accounts to be circularized, the auditor will consider the strength of the internal controls, the nature of the receivables population, and the results of the previous year's procedures. Statistical sampling selection and evaluation methods, described in Chapter 9, are frequently used.

The circularization of individual accounts can be accomplished by using a *positive request* or a *negative request,* or some of both. A positive request (see Figure 13.5) asks the debtor to respond and state whether the information is or is not correct. A negative request (see Figure 13.6) requires action only if the information is incorrect. The positive confirmation is considered more reliable because it requires affirmative action on the part of the debtor – but it does require considerable effort in following up on nonreplies. Negative requests, although perhaps less conclusive, serve a useful purpose given both reasonably reliable internal controls, and a relatively large number of homogeneous accounts. Due to the possibility of nonreply when the balance is incorrect and the lack of follow-up on nonreplies (since the presumption is that the balance is correct), negative confirmation procedures require more requests than positive confirmation procedures for the same degree of auditor assurance. Also they should not be used if the auditor feels that the debtor would for some reason ignore negative requests.

Please examine this statement carefully. If it does NOT agree with your records please report any exceptions directly to our auditors

[*Name and address of Auditors*]

who are auditing our financial statements. An addressed envelope is enclosed for your convenience in replying.

Do not send your payment to our auditors.

FIG. 13.6 Negative Confirmation Request

Generally, the existence of a reliable control system will tend to reduce the number of confirmation requests required. And these requests would usually be limited to positive confirmation of large accounts or (where there is a large number of small accounts) negative confirmation of a relatively small sample of accounts. When the auditor deems the system unreliable or chooses not to test related internal controls as a matter of audit efficiency, he must perform more extensive confirmation procedures.

The auditor must be alert to the uncertainties inherent in confirmation procedures. There is the possibility that the debtor might not be conscientious and thus might verify an incorrect balance. Furthermore, a confirmation is an acknowledgment of indebtedness but not an indication of a debtor's ability or inclination to pay; thus a satisfactory confirmation does not assure a properly valued receivable.

Follow-Up Procedures. The use of alternative procedures is required on significant positive confirmation requests for which the auditor receives no replies (AU 331.08). In addition to the use of second or third requests as appropriate, the alternative procedures could include:

- Examination of shipping documents
- Review of customer order documentation
- Review of duplicate copies of sales invoices
- Examination of subsequent cash receipts
- Confirmation of subsequent cash receipts

Each of these procedures carries a different level of significance and should be considered in light of the company's particular accounting procedures and system of internal control.

If a customer responds to a confirmation request and reports a difference, it is necessary to determine the nature of and the reason for the difference. Timing differences, for example, are a very common reason for respondent complaints of error; these result when a delay in recording transactions, through the mails or otherwise, affects balances in the customer's or the client's records. Examples of differences and some possible causes are shown in Figure 13.7.

Difference	Some possible causes
Payments not recorded on company records	Postal delays
	Payment applied to wrong account
	Fraud
Goods or services not received by customer	Delivery delays
	Service not completed
	Invoice sent to wrong customer
	Goods delivered to wrong customer
	Fictitious invoice
Goods returned by the customer for credit	Delivery delays
	Returned goods received, but credit note not yet issued
Clerical errors	Wrong quantity
	Wrong price
	Duplicate invoice recorded
	Discounts calculated incorrectly
	Errors in recording invoices, payments, or credits
Disputed amounts	Goods received in damaged condition
	Quality or price of goods or services disputed by customer

FIG. 13.7 Possible Causes of Confirmation Differences

When all confirmation procedures have been completed, the auditor evaluates the results in the context of the results of other relevant auditing procedures, including analytical procedures and tests of revenue transactions.

Allowances for Doubtful Accounts

Valuation is a key factor in the audit of receivables, and it is also one of the most subjective of audit judgments. The auditor uses a variety of approaches to evaluate collectibility of receivables, including:

• Historical experience
• State of the economy and its effect on the client's customers
• Aging of the receivables
• Financial stability of the company's customers
• Credit granting policies

Ultimately, the auditor must be satisfied that the amount presented as receivables, after deducting an allowance for uncollectible accounts, is a reasonable presentation, in the context of the financial statements taken as a whole, of future realizable amounts.

Additional Audit Issues

Due to the typically large volume of revenue transactions and related number of individual accounts, the system encompassing the revenue cycle is often the first to be computerized. The risks inherent in the use of electronic data processing in the revenue cycle can create an additional burden for the auditor; this subject is fully discussed in Chapter 10.

When a system problem exists, the great speed at which computers operate tends to compound simple problems at alarming rates. Accordingly, it is important that the auditor understand the computer system and evaluate the attendant controls where he plans to rely on them in limiting the extent of his substantive audit tests.

There are also legal considerations associated with granting credit. For example, an enterprise may find itself subject to various penalties resulting from violations of state or federal regulations barring discriminatory practices in credit granting. Further, individual customers are entitled to know the rates of interest being charged on outstanding balances. And the auditor should be alert to evidence of interest rate violations and should make appropriate inquiry of management and company counsel in this area. (See SAS 54, *Illegal Acts by Clients,* for additional guidance.)

14

Inventories and Cost of Sales

PRODUCTION CYCLE

Inventory Concepts

Inventory is defined in the authoritative accounting standards, ARB 43, Chapter 4, *Inventory Pricing* (I78.102), as

> those items of tangible personal property which (1) are held for sale in the ordinary course of business (2) are in process of production for such sale or (3) are to be currently consumed in the production of goods or services to be available for sale.

For financial statement purposes, a major objective of accounting for inventories is "the matching of appropriate costs against revenues in order that there may be a proper determination of realized income" (I78.104). To accomplish this matching in the existing accounting framework, inventories and costs of sales must be measured generally on the basis of historical cost. Historical cost is usually the price paid or consideration given to acquire an asset, including applicable expenditures and charges directly or indirectly incurred in bringing an article to its existing condition and location.

In addition to accomplishing this matching, the accountant and auditor must also be concerned with such questions as the following:

- Will the company be able to sell the product?
- Will the company be able to sell the product it has on hand for at least as much as it cost to make and to hold in inventory?
- What future purchase commitments has the company made?
- Will it be able to recover these amounts through subsequent sales?
- Did the company order everything it received?
- Did the company pay for something it did not receive?
- Did the company bill for what it shipped.

In general, financial accounting for inventory is concerned with flow and aggregation of inventory costs. This accounting process is accomplished by first accumulating in the inventory balance sheet account the costs to purchase and manufacture the product and then transferring these costs to the income statement as cost of sales or cost of products sold. This is the cost-of-inventory/sales cycle. An accounting entry need not be generated every time there is physical movement or change in the inventory: summary entries that cover aggregate changes in a period are often used instead. Financial accounting allocates costs either to the balance sheet (to associate them with the inventory units that are still on hand) or to the income statement (showing the cost of inventory sold or consumed during the period).

In the historical cost context, the primary results of the cost-of-inventory/sales cycle are shown in two of the basic financial statements:

1. *Balance sheet.* The objective here is to report inventories either at the cost to acquire them or at market, whichever is lower. In this way, inventories will be reported at an amount that does not exceed the estimated amount the company can expect to recover if the inventory units are disposed of in an orderly fashion, that is, other than in a forced liquidation sale.

2. *Income statement.* The objective here is to report the cost of products sold, as determined in accordance with the matching concept. This cost includes all the costs of acquiring and manufacturing the products and excludes costs that are allocable to the unsold inventory presented in the balance sheet. In other words, the cost of sales shows the excess of the sum of the inventory at the beginning of the period plus the costs to acquire and manufacture the products during the period over the amount of such costs allocated to the ending inventory. While accounting for the cost of products sold attempts to match the costs of acquiring and manufacturing a product with the revenue derived from its sale, the cost of sales is actually a residual amount. It includes in varying amounts the costs of pilferage. theft, damage to goods, and other losses affecting units that are not themselves sold.

There are two basic types of costs associated with inventory: prime (or direct) costs and indirect costs, discussed in the following sections.

Prime Costs

Prime costs are the costs of direct material and direct labor. Direct material cost includes: the invoice price less any discounts; vendor charges for design, tooling, and fabrication; and the costs incurred by the manufacturer in obtaining the product from the vendor (transportation, import duty, and so forth). Direct labor represents that portion of the payroll costs incurred for personnel who are directly involved in the manufacture of the product. For a company that does not manufacture or process inventory for sale (e.g., a retailer), its prime inventory valuation basis is direct material cost.

Payroll costs are allocated to the accounts based on the assignment of the individual employee. Generally, these costs are included in either production, sales, or administrative categories, although they are sometimes capitalized as part of property, plant, and equipment if the individual is involved in the construction of equipment for the company's own use.

Payroll costs in a manufacturing concern are first allocated to production and then to inventory, either as part of direct labor to the extent the individual works directly on the production of the product (e.g., an assembly line worker) or as part of manufacturing overhead (discussed in the following section) to the extent the individual works in the manufacturing area but not directly on the product (e.g., a plant maintenance worker).

In the case of manufacturing employees, timecards generally record not only the hours worked but the nature of the work performed, for use in allocating these costs to inventory. In the case of a standard cost system, engineering studies are used to determine the "normal" amount of time devoted to an operation and that time is priced out at the hourly pay rate of the employee doing the work to determine the standard cost. The accounting treatment of differences between standard labor costs and costs actually incurred is also discussed in the section "Standard Costs".

Indirect Costs

These costs are sometimes called manufacturing overhead or factory burden and are nonprime manufacturing costs. Some are fixed and some are variable. Fixed indirect manufacturing costs, such as certain salaries and wages, real estate taxes, and operating lease rentals on a manufacturing facility, are incurred regardless of the level of production. Variable indirect manufacturing costs vary with the level of productive activity; energy costs, for instance, increase as production increases.

A major phase of accounting for the cost-of-inventory/sales cycle is the assignment of direct and indirect manufacturing costs to particular inventory units. Prime costs are readily assigned on the basis of direct association with the unit. Indirect manufacturing costs, on the other hand, cannot be associated directly with the unit, and different methods of accounting for them are possible.

Indeed, the IRS has on several occasions issued detailed regulations as to what must be included or excluded from inventory amounts for tax return purposes. The latest thrust came in the 1986 tax legislation. While business enterprises are accustomed to having book/tax differences in many areas (adjusting for the effect through deferred taxes), many tax rules will effectively allow no such differences—or at least not many differences—in inventories because of the tremendous record-keeping detail required. Thus, tax rules have a GAAP effect in this area.

Allocating Indirect Costs. One way to allocate indirect manufacturing costs, *prime costing*, is to charge all indirect manufacturing costs to expense when incurred. But the treatment of *all* manufacturing overhead costs as a period expense is not in accordance with GAAP (I78.106). The opposite approach, known as *full absorption costing*, allocates such costs to units produced. A compromise method, known as *direct costing*, allocates *variable* indirect manufacturing costs to units of production and *fixed* indirect manufacturing costs as a period expense. IRS regulations include specific guidelines as to the allocation of indirect costs for income tax purposes based on the Tax Reform Act of 1986 (TRA 1986). These superabsorption rules are discussed further in the following section.

The formula selected for apportioning indirect costs to various production units will have the amount of the indirect costs to be allocated as the numerator and the allocation base as the denominator. All indirect costs do not have to be allocated on the same basis. For instance, vacation pay expense may be allocated on the basis of direct labor assigned to units of production, whereas maintenance expense might be allocated on the basis of machine time. Furthermore, overhead may be applied to production on a departmental basis or on a plant-wide basis.

In practice, direct labor is often used as the allocation basis because it provides a measure of productive effort per unit that is readily available in most companies' records. Another factor in determining this denominator is the level of utilization of the manufacturing facility in relation to its capacity.

If the dollar amount of direct labor is chosen as the denominator for allocating indirect manufacturing costs, the accountant must then determine how the direct labor dollar base is to be established. Some of the ways in which the direct labor dollar base is established in practice are:

• Actual—the direct labor dollars *incurred* during the same period that the indirect manufacturing costs were incurred.

• Expected—the direct labor dollars that the company *planned* to incur during the period in which the indirect manufacturing costs were incurred.

• Normal—the historical *norm* of direct labor dollars incurred during such a period.

- Practical capacity—the direct labor dollars that would be incurred during the period if the company sustained *maximum* manufacturing output with a given number of workshifts per day for an extended period.

IRS Allocation Requirements. Section 803 of TRA 1986, and Section 263A of the Internal Revenue Code, provide a uniform set of rules for capitalization (for income tax purposes) of costs incurred in the manufacture or construction of property and in the acquisition of property for resale. These capitalization rules are particularly significant to retailers who prior to TRA 1986 generally capitalized only merchandise invoice costs and freight-in for both financial reporting and tax purposes.

Categories one, two, and three. The previous full absorption rules divided indirect manufacturing costs into three categories:

- Category 1 costs—those included as inventoriable costs irrespective of treatment of such costs for financial statement purposes.
- Category 2 costs—those excluded from inventoriable costs irrespective of the treatment of such costs for financial statement purposes.
- Category 3 costs—those included or excluded from inventoriable costs consistent with the treatment of such costs for financial statement purposes under GAAP.

The rules specified which costs fell into each category. If a company had inventory-related costs that were not specified, those costs were first compared with cost types in categories one and two and included therein if similar. Dissimilar costs fell into category three.

Superabsorption. The rules for capitalization of indirect costs under TRA 1986, often called the superabsorption rules, are effective for inventory produced or sold in the first taxable year beginning after 1986. Figure 14.1 compares the treatment of indirect costs under the previous law and the new law. The figure shows that virtually all Category 3 costs that a company could have alternatively expensed or capitalized previously must now be capitalized.

Since the new rules apply to all inventory sold after the effective date, a company must also revalue beginning inventories to include similar additional costs.

Accounting implications. In addressing compliance with the provisions of TRA 1986, companies will review the elements of cost included in the inventory valuation for financial reporting purposes. While some companies already include some or all of the mandated costs in inventory values, many will find differences. Three results are possible for financial reporting purposes where such differences exist: (1) financial statement cost components would be made to conform to tax reporting, (2) only certain costs included for tax would be included for financial statement purposes; and (3) financial statement cost components would not change.

FIN 1 (AO6.108) states that any change in the elements of cost included in inventory is an accounting change under APB 20 requiring cumulative effect accounting treatment in the period of change. In addition, assuming amounts that are currently or prospectively material, the change must be justified as preferable (i.e., an improve-

	Categorization	
	Old	New
Indirect Costs Treated Differently Under Old and New Law		
Excess of accelerated tax depreciation/amortization over financial statement depreciation/amortization	2	1
Percentage depletion in excess of cost depletion	2	1
Other general and administrative costs – incident to taxpayer's activities as a whole (e.g., personnel department)	2	1
Distribution costs – finished goods	2	1*
Warehousing costs – finished goods	2	1
Interest	2	1**
Engineering and product development expenses	2	1
Taxes (except income taxes)	3	1
General and administrative costs – incident to and necessary to production or operations	3	1
Factory general and administrative costs – incident to and necessary to production or operations	3	1
Officer salaries – incident to production or operations	3	1
Insurance – attributable to production or operations	3	1
Rework labor, scrap, spoilage – incident to production or operations	3	1
Current service pension contributions	3	1
Current fringe benefit contributions	3	1
Financial statement depreciation amortization	3	1
Cost depletion	3	1
Strike costs	3	2
Indirect Costs Unaffected by New Law		
Repairs	1	
Maintenance	1	
Utilities	1	
Rent	1	
Supervisory wages	1	
Indirect materials and supplies	1	
Tools and equipment	1	
Quality control/inspection costs	1	
Marketing	2	
Advertising	2	
Selling expenses	2	
Research and experimental costs	2***	
Disaster, casualty, theft, worthless security losses	2	
Past service pension costs	1****	

Key: 1. Cost must be included in inventory
       2. Cost not required to be included in inventory
       3. Cost must follow treatment on financial statements if prepared in accordance with GAAP

---

* The definition and treatment of distribution costs is unclear given the conflicting language present in the various Committee Reports.
** Only for the construction or manufacture of (1) real property, (2) long-lived property, (3) property costing more than $1 million with a production period exceeding one year, and (4) property requiring two or more years to construct or manufacture. Does not apply to real estate or personal property acquired solely for resale.
*** Only research and experimental costs deductible under § 174 are unaffected.
**** A change in the tax law in 1987 requires that such costs be capitalized for years beginning after 12/31/87.

FIG. 14.1   Indirect Production Costs Under Full Absorption and Uniform Cost Capitalization
Source: Adapted from Tinsey, Frederick, 1987. "Production and Acquisition Inventory Costs No Longer Deductible Under New Rules." Taxation for Accountants, February, p. 76. Boston: Warren, Gorham & Lamont, Inc.

ment in financial reporting). Preferability justification can be determined under several bases: (1) individual company justification, (2) prevailing practice changes, in industries or otherwise, or (3) FASB requirements.

Justification based upon FASB requirements is not possible, as this matter has not been and is not expected to be on the FASB agenda. Prevailing practice changes are not appropriate because practice has varied and will continue to vary considerably. Therefore, preferability must be determined on the basis of individual facts and circumstances, using the accounting principles established in ARB 43, Chapter 4. This has been confirmed by a consensus of the EITF in Issue 86-46, *Uniform Capitalization Rules for Inventory under the Tax Reform Act of 1986.*

ARB 43 also states: "A major objective of accounting for inventories is the proper determination of income through the process of matching appropriate costs against revenues" (I78.104). Thus the matching objective should be the key justification in an accounting change. ARB 43 defines costs to mean acquisition or production costs, discusses eligible costs and their determination and application, and is the source of prohibitions against the inclusion of general and administrative costs in inventory, except for expenses that are clearly related to production (I78.106).

Some of the IRS-specified capitalizable costs seem very similar to costs classified by many companies as general and administrative. However, it may be that tradition underlies preexisting treatment, and companies may not have great difficulty acknowledging that the relationship of an IRS prescribed cost to inventory is acceptable, though perhaps unpleasant due to the need to pay taxes on the increased balance over a period not exceeding four years. Many companies have made changes in 1987 to include some or all of the IRS prescribed costs in inventory, meeting the preferability challenge. Some portion of this challenge no doubt has been met on the premise that it is preferable to conform rather than spend major amounts of time and money on duplicate record-keeping and EDP systems to track differences.

Inventory Cost Flows

Financial accounting is a cost accumulator that uses cost-flow assumptions and conventions to develop financial statement presentation of inventories and cost of products sold. A comprehensive example of the results that can be obtained by applying the various cost-flow assumptions and conventions is presented in the appendix to this chapter and should be referred to for illustrations of the methods described later in this chapter.

Assumptions. After costs have been determined for inventory purchased and produced during the current period, certain assumptions must be made about the flow of these costs, so that the company can allocate the cost of inventory available for sale (which is the total of the cost of beginning inventory plus the cost to acquire and produce new inventory during the period) between ending inventory and the cost of products sold during the period. Specifically, should cost of products sold be based on the cost of the actual units sold, the cost of the oldest units available for sale, or the cost of the most recently acquired units? Should the ending inventory reflect the actual cost of the units on hand, the most recent cost incurred in obtaining the quantity on hand, or the earliest cost incurred in obtaining and sustaining the quantity on hand? The selection of a cost-flow assumption is not easy, because it could be argued that any of the following approaches meet the requirement of matching costs with revenues.

Specific identification. Presenting the cost of products sold at the actual cost of the units sold is known as the specific identification method. Use of this method provides an exact match of cost to revenue when a unit is sold, because the cost of acquiring that very unit is known. But keeping records that identify individual units is impractical when the number of inventory transactions is large and when most inventory items are fungible, so this method is not widely used.

First-in, first-out. Presenting the cost of products sold as the cost of the oldest units available for sale during the period is known as the first-in, first-out (FIFO) cost-flow assumption. Under the FIFO assumption, inventory costs follow what typically is the physical movement of inventories; that is, the first goods purchased (oldest on hand) are the first goods to be sold, leaving the last goods purchased (newest) in inventory. This method provides a practical way of matching the cost of products sold to current revenues, but critics point out that it results in charging old costs against current revenues.

Last-in, first-out. Presenting the cost of products sold at the cost of the most recent inventory acquisitions is known as the last-in, first-out (LIFO) cost-flow assumption. LIFO produces dramatically different results from those obtained with FIFO when price levels are changing rapidly, because the cost of products on hand at the beginning of the period or purchased early during the period may differ considerably from the cost of products purchased late in the period. Supporters of LIFO argue that it provides a better measure of current profits because it matches current, not old, costs with current period revenues. LIFO is used not only for this reason, but also because it is an acceptable method for income tax purposes (provided it is also used for the financial statements). In periods of rising prices, LIFO produces substantially lower taxable income than does the FIFO method. Critics of LIFO point out, however, that it does not reflect the normal physical movement of inventory and that it presents inventories in the balance sheet at an amount that almost never approximates the current cost of the physical units on hand.

Because LIFO practices essentially have been formed to comply with tax regulations, and because (like any other method) its use is not required for all inventories held by a consolidated enterprise, complex issues often arise in LIFO implementation. These matters are covered in a later section of this chapter devoted exclusively to LIFO.

Conventions. Various conventions are used for assigning costs to inventory units when either the FIFO or the LIFO assumption is applied. Their objective is to assign to inventory amounts that approximate its historical cost. Applications of these conventions are described in the appendix to this chapter, and are summarized below.

Specific identification. Invoices and other specifically identifiable unit costs for the actual items of inventory on hand are the source of the prices assigned to the inventory.

Average cost. Average costs of inventory units for the period of time associated with the inventory on hand are used to price the inventory.

Retail method. The inventory first is valued in terms of its normal selling price. This amount is then reduced to cost amount by applying the ratio of the cost of inventory available for sale during the period (beginning inventory plus purchases) to the selling price of this inventory. This is discussed more fully in Chapter 29.

Standard cost. Costs are assigned to inventory on the basis of a predetermined norm or standard for each unit.

Market value. In certain cases inventories may be stated at their market value, even if this exceeds cost:

> For example, precious metals having a fixed monetary value with no substantial cost of marketing may be stated at such monetary value; any other exceptions must be justifiable by inability to determine appropriate approximate costs, immediate marketability at quoted market price, and the characteristic of unit interchangeability. Where goods are stated above cost, this fact should be fully disclosed. [I78.119]

Standard Costs

A standard cost system is a management tool that predetermines what unit costs are expected to be for inventory items. These costs are then used to account for the inventory transactions from inception through the time of sale.

Variances. Because the system predetermines the unit cost for a given period, standard cost usually varies from the actual cost. The difference for a given item is called a variance. An *unfavorable variance* results when actual cost exceeds standard cost; a *favorable variance* results when standard cost exceeds actual cost.

When the actual amount paid differs from the amount at standard, the variance is described as a *price, rate, or spending variance.* For direct material and direct labor, these variances are differences between the actual per-unit cost and the standard per-unit rate. For overhead, they are the difference between the actual overhead incurred and the expected aggregate overhead. When the actual input quantity required to produce a given unit differs from the input anticipated by the standard, *volume and yield variances* arise. For instance, the quantity of material, number of direct labor hours, or number of machine hours actually incurred to produce a given unit of product may differ from the predetermined standards for these inputs.

Since GAAP requires that inventories be stated at cost (unless cost exceeds market), the occurrence of a variance indicates that standard cost should be adjusted to approximate historical cost. The analysis of standard cost variances should look not only to the differences between unit prices and volumes but also to the combined impact of the two. Because variances indicate that standard costs may differ from historical costs, the variances, if material, must be allocated in an appropriate manner between inventory and cost of sales.

Allocating Variances to Inventory. The choice of a variance allocation approach depends in part on the cost flow assumption used by the company. For instance, if the company uses the FIFO or average cost assumption, it would be appropriate in allocating between inventory and cost of sales to consider the total of purchase price variances for a fiscal period approximating the number of months' inventory on hand. For example, it would be appropriate to allocate to inventory only the portion of the purchase price variance that is related to purchases near the end of the year, perhaps based on inventory turnover, to determine which variances should be allocated to ending inventory.

For LIFO inventories, the allocation of variances will follow whichever basic approach is used to price LIFO increments – order of acquisition, most recent acquisition, or average purchase price.

If it is necessary to allocate variances to inventory, care must be taken to ensure that, in making the lower-of-cost-or-market test, the cost figures used include not only the standard cost but also the allocated cost variance. Similarly, when making LIFO calculations using a standard cost system, the LIFO current-year cost should reflect not only the standard cost but also any variances properly allocable to inventory.

An immaterial ending balance in a variance account should not lead the accountant to conclude that the variance need not be considered for allocation to inventory. In some cases, variances early in the period when combined with variances later may net to an immaterial amount, but there may still be a need to allocate a portion of the variances incurred late in the period to inventory in order to adjust inventory from standard cost to historical cost.

Costing of Transactions. In addition to the variances derived from the inventory and cost-of-products-sold accounting system, the accountant must be concerned with whether the standard cost of a given item is used consistently. Improper costing of transactions may be caused by human error or by failure of the system to account for physical conversions, substitutions, or scrap. There may also be a failure to adjust the carrying amount of inventory to new standard costs at the time new standards are put into effect. Unreported differences between input and output standards, and failure to recognize the effect on the inventory of a change in standards, result in unreported variances that remain in the inventory account.

At the time a physical inventory is taken and costed at the old standard, the book-to-physical difference will reflect unreported physical shrinkage and the effects of failure to use the same standards consistently in reporting input, conversions, substitutions, and interim changes in standards. If the effect of these unrecorded factors in the book-to-physical difference cannot be reasonably estimated, a major financial reporting benefit of applying a standard cost system is lost: the company may not be able to perform its physical inventory count at an interim date and rely on the standard cost system to carry forward the inventory cost to year end in a reasonable and accurate manner. Thus, the physical inventory will have to be taken at or quite near the fiscal year end. Additionally, such failures in the standard cost system may cause interim financial reporting to be incorrect.

Changing Standard Costs. A company will often institute a change in its standard costs at the same time it takes its physical inventory. This enables the company to quantify the effect of the change by valuing inventories at both the old and new standards. When the new standard exceeds the old, the difference should be recorded as a separate inventory reserve. However, when the old standard exceeds the new, a downward adjustment of inventories valued at the old standard may be appropriate. After adjusting for the book-to-physical inventory difference, the financial statements will reflect an inventory balance comprising the inventory at the new standard less the reserve for the excess of the new standard over the old standard (this step effectively states the inventory at old standard) and adjusted for any other inventory provisions based on the old standard (this step adjusts the inventory from the old standard to the lower of historical cost or market).

In subsequent periods, as costs of sales are charged based on the new standard, the reserve for the excess of the new standard over the old is credited to earnings, usually on an estimated turnover basis.

FINANCIAL ACCOUNTING AND REPORTING CONSIDERATIONS

Inventory Existence and Valuation

Inventory Quantities. Inventories typically represent a significant asset to a manufacturing company. Thus it is important to periodically conduct accurate and documented physical counts of inventories to determine the quantities of goods on hand. The counts also assist management in determining how well the inventory control and reporting system is working by providing a comparison of the physical count to the company records, either on a unit basis or in terms of aggregate dollars.

As noted in the next subsection, the company may count inventories on a cyclical basis, performing counts at different locations on different dates; or it may count everything at the same time. Either way, adequate instructions should be prepared for the counting operation. These instructions may include many procedures; typical ones include the following (additional factors are covered in the auditing section later in this chapter):

* Counts are to be performed by personnel familiar with the inventory. (Total responsibility for a count, however, should not rest with those who are charged with safeguarding the inventory.)
* Counts should be adequately supervised.
* Individuals who will test the counting should be identified.
* Control should exist over inventory tags issued and used.
* Orderly arrangement of inventory will facilitate counting.
* Production and movement of inventory should be limited during the counting, and preferably there should be no movement at all.

- Accumulation and identification of inventory at outside locations or held for others (consignments) should be arranged.
- Obsolete or scrap items that are not to be included in the count should be clearly identified.
- Appropriate cutoff information should be obtained.
- Treatment of shipments (including orders on shipping dock but not yet picked up) and receipts (including items returned by customers) during the count should be understood.

In determining inventory quantities, the company should look not only to its own materials on hand, but also to any units it may have out on consignment, stored in outside warehouses, or left with outside processors. Goods being held on consignment from another entity, customer materials on hand for processing, and units being warehoused for others should be excluded from the company's inventory, but these units may also be counted to make sure there is adequate control over all materials on hand that belong to others.

Inventory Date. The amount presented as inventories in the balance sheet is in theory the aggregate historical cost (determined using the selected cost-flow assumptions and valuation conventions) of physical units on hand at the reporting date, adjusted for certain economic and physical factors such as market conditions and excess, damaged, and obsolete stock. There are two basic approaches to the determination of the physical units on hand:

1. The inventory quantities are determined as of the reporting date and are valued at their historical cost using the selected cost-flow assumptions and valuation conventions. The quantities are determined either by physical count as of the reporting date, or by reference to perpetual inventory records for each inventory item.
2. The inventory quantities are determined by physical count at a date other than the reporting date and valued at their historical cost using the selected cost-flow assumptions and valuation conventions. This amount is then updated to the reporting date by adjusting for the cost of interim transactions such as purchases, cost of goods sold, scrapped material, and estimated shrinkage.

A company's selection of an approach to determining quantities should be based on both feasibility and on the relative costs and benefits of the alternatives. A physical count at the close of the reporting period provides the most accurate determination of the number of units on hand at period end because it is not exposed to the updating errors that can result from interim determination. Although the period end approach obviates the need for a sophisticated system to account for intervening transactions, it often delays the release of financial statements because of the time required to compile the data.

Since, a company often must shut down its entire operation at one time to carry out the physical inventory, an interim date may be a more opportune time to conduct the inventory. It may also be possible to cycle physical inventory counting so that not all operations are shut down at the same time. Based on its systems and controls, a company may use either approach, or both, for different types of inventory.

Book-To-Physical Differences. When a company has an accounting system designed to adjust inventory and cost of sales for transactions throughout the year, a good indicator of the performance of this system is to compare the inventory balance shown in the general ledger to the physical inventory at the same date valued at the old standard costs (assuming standard costs, discussed previously, are in use). If the amounts are substantially the same, the system probably adequately reflects the application of the company's cost-flow assumptions and valuation conventions to the physical movements of inventory, although it is possible that there may be offsetting errors. If the amounts differ substantially, this could be caused by several factors; the common factors are discussed in the following subsections.

Inventory cutoff errors. The inventory general ledger balance may not reflect shipments that have been removed from the physical inventory, or may not reflect receipts of merchandise that are included in the physical inventory. The general ledger balance may also reflect receipts of merchandise that have been excluded from the physical inventory, or may reflect shipments of merchandise that have not yet been removed from the physical inventory.

Unreported standard cost variances and adjustments. A standard cost system may have failed to consistently use the same standard for reporting inventory transactions. This results in standard cost differences remaining in inventory and becoming part of the physical inventory adjustment. (See the preceding "Variances" Section.)

Unreported scrap. Units of inventory have been scrapped, but their cost has not been removed from the inventory accounts.

Pilferage and theft. Units of inventory have been stolen, but their cost has not been removed from the inventory accounts.

Failure to cost out sales properly. The cost used to reduce the inventory accounts for units sold is not the same as the cost at which these units are carried in the inventory accounts.

Improper reporting of production. Reporting production (the basis for inventory cost input) is not the same as actual production.

Updating the Interim Inventory Determination. Identifying the causes of inventory adjustments is always valuable to management because it provides information that can be used for operating control. But it is even more important for companies that take their physical inventory at an interim date and wish to rely on their system to update the inventory accounts for the amount to be presented in the period-end financial statements.

To the extent that the physical inventory difference can be traced to specific system flaws (e.g., improper costing of sales), the effect of each flaw on inventory transactions between the inventory date and period end can be quantified, and the period-end inventory adjusted. If the reasons for material differences cannot be identified and quantified, there is prima facie evidence that the inventory accounting system cannot be relied on to adequately update the inventory accounts and cost of products sold from the interim date to the reporting date, unless some form of modification is applied to allow for deficiencies in the system that have repeatedly given rise to physical inventory adjustments. The modification that is normally employed is a provision for inventory shrinkage based on the book-to-physical differences that occurred in the past. The amount of the provision is normally quantified as some measure of production volume.

For instance, the past relationship of inventory adjustments to direct labor input might provide a ratio that could then be applied to direct labor incurred between the interim inventory date and the reporting date. Using such an approach, the cost of sales for the interim period would be the standard cost of sales adjusted by reported variances and the estimated shrinkage factor. This factor would adjust the inventory and cost of sales figures generated by the accounting system for the applicable portion of adjustments expected at the next inventory date.

It it not always possible to make these types of adjustments with adequate confidence. Unless the reasons for book-to-physical differences are well understood and the interim provisions can be made with reasonable objectivity, the company may have little choice but to take the physical inventory close to or at year end.

Lower of Cost or Market. GAAP normally requires the use of historical cost, but a departure from the cost basis is required when the utility of the goods is no longer as great as its cost, because of deterioration, obsolescence, changes in price levels, or other causes. The difference should be recognized as a loss of the current period, accomplished by stating inventories at the lower of cost or market (I78.109). A layman would probably interpret the term *market* to mean the amount that could be realized if the unit were sold, but in a technical accounting sense, market is somewhat different. The authoritative literature (I78.110) defines it as follows:

> As used in the phrase *lower of cost or market* the term *market* means current replacement cost (by purchase or by reproduction, as the case may be) except that:
>
> (a) Market should not exceed the net realizable value (i.e., estimated selling price in the ordinary course of business less reasonably predictable costs of completion and disposal); and
>
> (b) Market should not be less than net realizable value reduced by an allowance for an approximately normal profit margin.

The upper and lower limits placed on replacement cost as an equivalent of market are intended to prevent the inventory from being stated at an amount above the net proceeds that can be expected from the disposition of the item or at an amount below the net proceeds less normal profit margin. From a practical standpoint, at least for finished goods, the accountant has generally looked to the upper limit of the test in defining market, both because that number is often more available than the replacement cost figure, and because that number must be determined even if a replacement cost figure is determined, since it is the upper limit of market.

The lower-of-cost-or-market determination can be made based on individual items or by inventory groupings. The authoritative pronouncement dealing with this subject (I78.113) states:

Depending on the character and composition of the inventory, the rule of *cost or market, whichever is lower* may properly be applied either directly to each item or to the total of the inventory (or, in some cases, to the total of the components of each major category). The method should be that which most clearly reflects periodic income.

Thus, the lower-of-cost-or-market test can be made based on some logical aggregation of inventory items (account groupings, product line, production location, or geographic location). The selection of an approach should take into consideration the nature of the inventory items in the grouping. For instance, refrigerators and high-fashion clothing would not be put in the same group for purposes of determining the lower-of-cost-or-market valuation. Whatever system the company adopts, it should be applied consistently from year to year. Once the inventory carrying amount is written down to market because it is less than cost, the new carrying amount becomes the cost from that point forward (I78.401)

Some latitude exists in interim financial statements, however. In Issue 86-13, *Recognition of Inventory Market Declines at Interim Reporting Dates,* the EITF reached a consensus that inventory should be written down at interim dates *unless* there is substantial evidence that prices will recover before the inventory is sold, or in the case of LIFO, that the inventory will be restored by year end.

Excess and Obsolete Inventory. In addition to comparing the carrying amount of inventory to its market, a comparison must also be made of the actual volume of inventory with the demand for it or for the products into which this inventory ultimately is to be converted. Inventory on hand may exceed future demand either because the product is now outdated (obsolete) or because the amount on hand, whether of materials or finished products, is more than can be used to meet future needs (excess). The excess or obsolete portion of the inventory should be reduced to an amount not less than its net realizable value.

Such reserves may be established on some formula basis (e.g., everything over two years' supply might be fully reserved) for financial statement purposes if justified by historical or present conditions.

The physical inventory listings should carefully identify units that are obsolete or have previously been written off. Although these units may have no operating value to the company for its current production requirements, the company should institute controls over them to prevent misuse. These controls should also ensure that these units are not carried at more than recoverable value or at an amount higher than that at which they were recorded in prior periods.

Thor Power Tool ruling. A formula-type approach, while often acceptable for GAAP purposes, is not acceptable for determination of excess stock provisions for income tax purposes. The carrying amount of inventory can be reduced for tax purposes only if supported by objective evidence, such as having the items scrapped or offered for sale at a reduced price.

In *Thor Power Tool Co. v. Commissioner,*[1] the company used the lower-of-cost-or-market method of valuing inventories for both financial and income tax purposes.

---

[1] *Thor Power Tool Co. v. Commissioner* 439, U.S. 522 (1979); Revenue Procedure 80-5, as amended by Internal Revenue News Release 80-48 (April 4, 1980); and Revenue Ruling 80-6.

Thor wrote down what it considered as excess inventory to its net realizable value, which, in most cases, was determined to be scrap value. The company concluded that these articles were scrap because they were held in excess of any reasonably forseeable future demand based on a formula aging schedule. The company held the items in inventory and continued to sell them at original prices; the inventory was not sold at reduced prices or actually scrapped. Thor maintained that by writing down excess inventory to scrap value it reduced the inventory to market (net realizable value), in accordance with its lower-of-cost-or-market method of accounting, and in accordance with GAAP. The IRS, while not disagreeing that the write-downs were consistent with GAAP, disallowed them for tax purposes. The courts supported the IRS's position. Note that the company also wrote down inventory that was either promptly scrapped or actually sold at prices below cost. The IRS allowed these write-downs.

When inventory is written down to (1) replacement cost, and the company does not have evidence (e.g., quotes from suppliers) to support replacement cost, or (2) net realizable value and the write-downs are not supported by actual offerings, actual sales, or scrapping, the company may face a Thor-type valuation change. If the write-down to market does not comply with IRS requirements but for accounting purposes is in accordance with GAAP, the company should account for the difference in financial and tax reporting as a temporary difference.

Other Inventory Issues

Balance Sheet Classification. Current assets are those assets that are reasonably expected to be realized in cash or sold or consumed during the normal operating cycle of the business, or within one year if the operating cycle is shorter than one year (B05.105). Since inventories are acquired for production or sale and the acquisitions should not often exceed the quantity of inventory needed for the company's current operating cycle, inventories are generally classified as current assets.

Inventory is usually subclassified in terms of its stage of completion (raw materials, manufacturing supplies, work in process, or finished goods), or in terms of the types of cost components of the inventory (raw materials, direct labor, or manufacturing overhead), or as a combination of both. GAAP does not address whether the various components of inventory need be disclosed. Regulation S-X, Rule 5-02.6, requires that the major classes of inventory be disclosed in terms of their stage of completion. In practice, this approach is applied by all public companies and many nonpublic ones. The disclosure is made either on the face of the balance sheet or in a note.

Inventory is often used as collateral for loans obtained by the company. Authoritative literature requires disclosure of assets pledged as security for loans (C59.120), and Regulation S-X, Rule 4-08 (b), requires that the carrying amount of inventories being used as security be disclosed in the notes to the financial statements.

Capitalization of Interest. SFAS 34, *Capitalization of Interest Cost* (I67), limits the capitalization of interest on inventories to discrete projects that are not part of the repetitive inventory production cycle. When interest is capitalized in inventory, the accountant must look not only to the basic cost of the inventory unit but must consider all cost factors included in the inventory account, including capitalized interest, in making the realizable value tests. (For a discussion of interest capitalization, see Chapter 18.)

Purchase and Sale Commitments. Purchase commitments are entered into primarily to secure the acquisition of needed materials and to protect against unfavorable price fluctuations. They represent contracts and agreements for the future purchase of specified quantities of materials at a specified price. In financial reporting, they should be evaluated in the same fashion as inventory on hand for the purpose of determining any lower-of-cost-or-market adjustment. GAAP for inventory purchase commitments is stated in ARB 43, Chapter 4 as follows:

> Accrued net losses on firm purchase commitments for goods for inventory, measured in the same way as are inventory losses, shall, if material, be recognized in the accounts and the amounts thereof separately disclosed in the income statement. [I78.121]

Similarly, agreements requiring the sale of goods in the future for a specified price should be used in making the lower-of-cost-or-market valuation for existing inventory and should be viewed in the context of whether the cost to acquire and produce the product will exceed the agreed selling price. If firm agreements have been made for future sales, that selling price should usually be used in establishing net realizable value for the product on hand subject to the sales commitment. If the carrying amount of the inventory on hand (or estimated cost to produce inventory) needed to meet the future sales agreements exceeds such net realizable value, losses should be recognized currently in the financial statements.

A futures contract is similar to a purchase or sale commitment but includes a regulated futures exchange as a party to the transaction. Commodity futures transactions are accounted for in accordance with SFAS 80 (F80), which requires a futures contract to be carried at market value unless the contract qualifies as a hedge. Futures contracts are discussed in detail in Chapter 21.

Product Financing Arrangements. Product financing arrangements are transactions in which a company sells a portion of its inventory to another entity with the intent to reacquire that inventory in the future at a purchase price equal to the original sale price plus carrying and financing costs. In SFAS 49, *Accounting for Product Financing Arrangements* (D18), inventory repurchase arrangements meeting certain criteria (primarily those in which the seller retains the risks and rewards of ownership) are viewed as financing transactions. SFAS 49 requires that the merchandise covered by the arrangement be included with the inventory of the company and valued in accordance with the cost-flow assumption and pricing convention employed by the company, with the proceeds from the sale treated as debt. Because the criteria are specific, it is possible to keep these arrangements off the balance sheet. (See Chapter 21 for further discussion of product financings.)

Changes in Accounting — Consistency. ARB 43, Chapter 4 (I78.120) indicates:

> The basis of stating inventories must be consistently applied and should be disclosed in the financial statements; whenever a significant change is made therein, there should be disclosure of the nature of the change and, if material, the effect on income.

APB 20 (A06) specifies that accounting changes for inventory should be reflected in the financial statements in a fashion similar to other accounting changes (cumulative catch-up approach at the beginning of the current period) that are adopted when alternatives exist (i.e., their application is not mandated by a new FASB pronouncement), except as follows:

- A change from another cost-flow assumption to LIFO does not result in a cumulative catch-up adjustment, because the company cannot determine what the inventory would be at the date of change on a LIFO basis as if LIFO had been adopted at the inception of the company (A06.122). The inventory at the beginning of the first period in which LIFO is adopted is considered its base-period LIFO inventory regardless of the prior cost-flow assumption and pricing convention.

- A change from LIFO to another cost-flow assumption is to be reflected in the financial statements by retroactive restatement for all periods presented, and the cumulative effect of the change at the beginning of the first period presented is included as an adjustment of retained earnings of that period (A06.123). The pervasiveness of the difference between the two methods makes such restatement necessary and the availability of information makes this restatement feasible.

An earlier section of this chapter discusses TRA 1986 and its uniform capitalization rules. These rules may precipitate changes in accounting for elements of inventory cost by many companies. Such a change is a change in accounting principle covered by FIN 1 (A06.108).

Product Warranty Costs. Additional accounting considerations arise when products are sold subject to product warranties. SFAS 5 defines a warranty as "an obligation incurred in connection with the sale of goods or services that may require further performance by the seller after the sale has taken place" (C59.130). A warranty may be explicit in the sales agreement or it may be implicit. It may be direct, such as when the manufacturer sells directly to the end user; or it may be indirect, such as when the sale is made by an automobile dealership. Examples include agreements to provide repair services or to furnish replacement parts for a given period of time after the sale of an automobile.

The objective of accounting for warranty costs is to match revenues with related costs. This matching is normally accomplished at the time of sale by accruing as an operating expense or as part of cost of sales the estimated future costs related to the warranty. Normally, there is not a separate source of revenue related to the warranty, but where a special fee is paid for such warranty, it would be appropriate to defer such income over the warranty period, as is done for service contracts. If the estimated warranty costs exceed the separate fee, the excess cost would be accrued at the time of the sale.

Because warranties involve uncertainties as to the amount of costs to be incurred, the accounting for warranty obligations is covered by SFAS 5, *Accounting for Contingencies* (C59). Under SFAS 5, contingencies are to be accrued if it is probable that a liability has been incurred at the date of the financial statements *and* the amount of the liability can be reasonably estimated.

The most common basis for estimating future warranty costs is past experience with the same or similar product or product line. Often a reasonable estimate of warranty costs can be obtained by applying a predetermined rate to a measure of sales volume. For instance, future warranty costs might be reasonably estimated as a percentage of sales or as a fixed dollar amount per unit sold.

The rate might be obtained by calculating the average of the actual rates for a given number of prior years, or if the historical rates indicate a definite trend, the appropriate rate might best be obtained by extrapolation. As an example, if the current year sales were $10 million and the estimated rate of warranty cost was 1.5% of sales, the warranty cost accrual would be $150,000. If the warranty period was one year, the entire accrual would be included in current liabilities. Otherwise, an allocation of the obligation would be made between current and noncurrent liabilities, based on estimates as to the timing of warranty claims. For tax purposes warranty costs are deductible only when paid, often by means of supplying repair services or replacement parts, so their accrual will give rise to temporary differences.

Where there is no directly related past experience, the experience of other companies in the industry or of other related product lines might be used as a guide. Results of preproduction tests, either in the laboratory or in the field, and review of quality control procedures might provide a basis on which warranty costs could be estimated. Where there is no way of obtaining a reasonable estimate of the warranty costs, no accrual can be made; the existence of a possibility of significant warranty costs may raise a question about whether a sale should be recorded prior to expiration of the warranty period or until sufficient experience has been gained to permit a reasonable estimate of the obligations" (C59.131). Where no accrual is made, the nature of the contingency and the range of potential loss or the fact that such an estimate cannot be made should be disclosed in the financial statements (C59.109). Given the inherent uncertainties, judgment is necessary in arriving at a reasonable estimate of future warranty costs.

LIFO METHOD

Overview

The LIFO cost method has been used with IRS approval for nearly 50 years, yet until 1984 virtually nothing in the authoritative accounting standards or other AICPA releases provided guidance on precisely how it should be applied. In contrast, the Internal Revenue Code and IRS rules and regulations have provided many specific LIFO implementation rules, including the basic requirement that companies using LIFO for income tax purposes must also use LIFO for financial reporting purposes (the *LIFO conformity requirement*). This situation resulted in the general approach that "whatever is good for tax is good for financial reporting."

In 1981, the IRS relaxed its interpretation of the LIFO conformity requirement. As a result, companies may now apply LIFO differently for financial reporting purposes than for tax purposes, as long as an acceptable form of LIFO is used, and may provide supplemental non-LIFO disclosures, as long as they are indicated as supplemental and not presented on the face of the income statement.

Also in 1981, the SEC issued ASR 293, *The Last-In, First-Out Method of Accounting for Inventories* (FRR § 205). This document expresses the SEC's views that the conceptual basis for the LIFO method is the proper matching of current costs with current revenues and that the use of LIFO tax regulations for financial reporting purposes may not always accomplish this result. The ASR states that "since LIFO may now be applied differently for book accounting and tax accounting, it is appropriate for the current practices used in the application of LIFO to be examined."

At a minimum, the SEC requires disclosure of the following information when supplemental data is given:

- A clear statement that LIFO results in a better matching of costs and revenues;
- The reason supplemental disclosures are being provided; and
- Information about the supplemental income calculation that will enable users to understand its value.

In addition the SEC requires that the disclosures avoid the implication that non-LIFO earnings are "real" earnings.

In 1984, AcSEC and its Task Force on LIFO Inventory Problems released an Issues Paper, *Identification and Discussion of Certain Financial Accounting and Reporting Issues Concerning LIFO Inventories* (AICPA, 1984f). For the first time, significant attention had been given by the accounting profession to complex LIFO problems, narrowing the diversity in practice. And in some instances, the Issues Paper recommended approaches that differed from IRS treatments also used for GAAP reporting purposes in the past.

The IRS, AICPA, and SEC positions are discussed in the sections that follow.

IRS Requirements

Basic LIFO Method. Historically, IRS regulations have required that if a company uses LIFO to measure earnings and profits for tax purposes, the company must also use LIFO for external financial reporting. Limited exceptions were provided in cases in which GAAP requires a non-LIFO disclosure or measurement (for example, disclosing the effect of an accounting change or measuring inventories at the time of a purchase business combination), and in cases in which there is a regulatory requirement for a non-LIFO disclosure (for example, SEC requirements to disclose the replacement cost of LIFO inventory and the effect of a LIFO inventory liquidation).

Supplemental Non-LIFO Disclosures. In January 1981, the IRS conformity rule was liberalized to permit LIFO users to present designated supplemental non-LIFO disclosures.

The liberalized conformity rule applies if the non-LIFO information is contained in:

- Audited financial statements (including footnotes and supplementary information)
- Reviewed or compiled financial statements (including footnotes)
- Additional information (in long-form reports)
- Other types of financial reports

While taxpayers using the LIFO method may now follow the conformity rule in a less rigid manner, the supplemental information presentation must be carefully analyzed to determine that it does not go beyond what is permitted. IRS regulations

(§ 1.472-2(e)) provide that the following disclosures of non-LIFO income information will not violate the LIFO conformity rule:

- The use of a non-LIFO method to provide information as a supplement to or explanation of the taxpayer's primary presentation of income in the financial statements.
- The use of a non-LIFO method to ascertain the value of inventory on the taxpayer's primary balance sheet.
- The use of a non-LIFO method to ascertain information including income disclosures contained in internal management reports.
- The use of a non-LIFO method under certain conditions to determine income for a single continuous period of operations that is less than the whole taxable year and less than 12 consecutive months.
- The use of market when it is lower than LIFO cost.
- The use of different (alternative) costing or accounting methods for book and tax purposes, as long as an acceptable form of LIFO is used in both cases (e.g., double-extension, index, or link-chain; or different pooling or layer pricing methods).
- Disclosures of certain book/tax differences in LIFO inventory values.

Note that the IRS regulations permit the use of divergent inventory accounting methods in the primary balance sheet and income statement (second item in the preceding list). The SEC and the FASB, however, will not accept this presentation in GAAP financial statements. Therefore, if a taxpayer elects to use an inconsistent approach in primary financial statements, an independent accountant would not be able to issue an unqualified opinion.

Simplified LIFO Method. The IRS has attempted to simplify LIFO computations in TD 7814, *Final IRS Regulations on Valuation of Dollar-Value LIFO Inventories,* issued March 15, 1982. The regulations amend IRC § 472 and may be used by any business that is required to maintain inventories and elects to use the LIFO method. Use of the amended regulations is optional. The IRS took this action because many taxpayers, especially small businesses, perceived the LIFO rules to be unduly complex and burdensome. These regulations have been amended by the TRA 1986.

Prior to 1982, taxpayers generally were not permitted to use an inventory price index to determine the base-year dollars in an inventory pool unless the index was based on the price change experienced for the particular inventory pool. This meant taxpayers generally could not use price indices such as the consumer and producer price indices prepared by the Bureau of Labor Statistics (BLS) because they could not show that the use of such indices was accurate, reliable, and suitable for their particular inventory.

The 1982 rules permitted taxpayers classified as "small businesses" to compute a price index for valuing an inventory pool by using the percentage change in selected BLS consumer and producer price indices. A small business was defined as any company whose average annual gross receipts did not exceed $2 million for a three-year period. This method, commonly referred to as simplified LIFO, was intended to be an alternative to computing an internal inventory price index based on the taxpayer's own inflation rate. If the taxpayer was not classified as a small business, the requirement was that only 80% of the percentage change could be applied.

As finalized in 1982, the index or indices used for valuing an inventory pool must be the most detailed BLS index that most closely resembles the type of goods contained in the inventory pool. For example, a company whose inventory consists of household appliances must use a separate index for refrigerators and home freezers and another index for laundry equipment, if separate inventory pools are maintained for these specific categories of goods; otherwise, the use of a general single-pool index for household appliances is appropriate.

TRA 1986 provides an election to businesses whose average annual gross receipts for the three preceding taxable years do not exceed $5 million to use a simplified dollar-value LIFO method in accounting for their inventories. The simplified dollar-value LIFO method *requires* inventories to be grouped into pools in accordance with the major categories of the producer prices indexes of the Consumer Price Index (CPI) Detailed Report. The change in inventory costs for the pool for the taxable year is determined by the change in the published index for the general category to which the pool relates. The computation of the ending LIFO value of the pool is then made using the dollar-value LIFO method. The indices necessary to compute the equivalent dollar values of prior years are to be developed using the link-chain method. Although TRA 1986 replaces the prior rules, any taxpayer who has a valid election to use the single pool method of IRC § 474 of the prior law may continue under it, assuming the requirements continue to be met.

The simplified dollar-value LIFO method under TRA 1986 requires the use of multiple pools in order to avoid the construction of a weighted index specific to the taxpayer. Rather than construct such an index, the annual change in costs for each pool is measured by the change in the published index for the general category applicable to each pool. The percentage change for the year in the published index for the general category determines the annual index for the pool.

AICPA Guidance — Basic LIFO Method

The AICPA Issues Paper, *Identification and Discussion of Certain Financial Accounting and Reporting Issues Concerning LIFO Inventories* (1984f), presents a most comprehensive exposition of LIFO matters. No doubt it is even referred to by tax professionals when confronted with a LIFO tax issue, for guidance on what is acceptable for GAAP purposes. In some (but certainly not all) aspects, the tables have been turned; what is good for GAAP financial reporting is now good for tax.

The 1984 Issues Paper omitted one important area — intercompany transfers of LIFO inventories — because the Task Force did not want to delay the initial paper until there was a resolution of this complex area. However, this omission was eliminated by AICPA Practice Bulletin 2 (TP 12,020) in 1987.

The key aspects of AICPA guidance are discussed in the following sections.

Establishing LIFO Pools. The objective of LIFO inventory pooling is to group inventory items to match most recently incurred costs to current revenues, after considering the manner in which the company operates its business. It is not feasible to formulate detailed financial accounting guidance for selecting pools that could apply to all enterprises; however, there should be valid business reasons for establishing LIFO pools. Establishing separate pools with the principal objective of facilitating inventory liquidations is unacceptable.

LIFO Approaches and Techniques. The three basic approaches used in practice to price LIFO inventory increments are:

1. Order of acquisition (first purchase price)
2. Most recent acquisition (latest purchase price)
3. Average purchase price

While the order of acquisition approach is generally most compatible with the LIFO objective, as a practical matter any of these approaches may be used for financial reporting purposes.

The two approaches and various computational techniques that have developed in practice in applying LIFO are:

1. Specific-goods approach
2. Dollar-value approach, with the following computational techniques used:
   • Double extension
   • Internal index
   • Link-chain
   • External index

Both the specific-goods and dollar-value approaches are generally compatible with the LIFO objective of matching current costs with current revenues, and either may be used for financial reporting purposes.

Specific goods approach. Under the specific goods approach, changes in the quantity of individual types of inventory are the bases for determining whether inventory levels have increased or whether a portion of the existing inventory has been liquidated.

Dollar value approach. Under the dollar value approach, inventory items are grouped by pools and are priced in terms of each pool's aggregate base year cost. The result is compared with each pool's aggregate base year cost as of the end of the prior year to determine whether the inventory level of each LIFO pool has increased or whether a portion of the inventory has been liquidated. Various computational techniques are used with the dollar value approach, including:

• *Double extension,* in which the current and base year costs of each item in inventory are multiplied, or extended, by the units on hand at the current year reporting date.
• *Internal index,* in which the base year cost of ending inventory is determined by applying an index (based on a sample of current year costs to base year costs of items in inventory) to the dollar value of the ending inventory at current year cost.
• *Link chain,* in which the base cost of ending inventory is determined by applying a cumulative index to the dollar value of the ending inventory. The cumulative index is the relationship of the current year prices to those of the prior year (based on either double extension or

internal index) multiplied by the prior year's cumulative index, causing each year's index to be characterized as a link in a chain of indices back to the base year.

• *External index,* in which the dollar value of ending inventory at current year prices is restated to approximate the base year prices using an index determined by an outside source, such as the Bureau of Labor Statistics index.

Addition of New Item to LIFO Inventory. If dollar-value LIFO is used and a new item is added to inventory, the pricing index can become distorted if the current cost of the item is used as the base-year cost. Such an approach would, in effect, retroactively reduce the cumulative LIFO index for the pool, thus changing the current year's LIFO adjustment for the pool.

In this regard, the SEC in FRR § 205 (discussed further in the "SEC Requirements" section of this chapter) comments on certain enforcement actions in which inventory items were designated as "new items" and recorded at current costs without reconstruction of the base-year cost. In the enforcement actions cited, the designation of the inventory items as new items were not appropriate because of "insignificant and sometimes arbitrary differences," such as slight differences in chemical composition, changes in manufacturing, production, and location, and differences in supply sources. The Task Force supported the use of the reconstructed cost method and the link-chain technique. Their use mitigates problems associated wih new items, as previously discussed.

If the double extension or an index technique is used, the objective of LIFO is achieved by reconstructing the base-year cost of new items added to existing pools. Reconstructed costs should be based on the most objectively determinable sources available, such as (in order of objectivity): published vendor price lists, vendor quotes, and general industry indices. The base-year cost of the new item should be estimated if it is not otherwise objectively determinable. If the link-chain technique is used, reconstruction of base-year costs is unnecessary because the link-chain technique produces approximately the same results as reconstruction (see ¶ 4–23 of the Issues Paper for an illustration).

Lower of LIFO Cost or Market. ARB 43 discusses the lower of cost or market rule for pricing inventories:

> Depending on the character and composition of the inventory, the rule of *cost or market, whichever is lower,* may properly be applied either directly to each item, or to the total of the inventory (or, in some cases, to the total of the components of each major category). The method should be that which most clearly reflects periodic income. [I78.113]

Determining the LIFO cost of an individual item (the item-by-item approach) may be difficult if a company uses other than the specific-goods approach for its inventories. In these circumstances, a company might decide it is more appropriate to apply the lower-of-cost-or-market rule to the total amount of a pool (the aggregate approach) or a combination of pools.

The most reasonable approach to applying the lower-of-cost-or-market provisions of ARB 43 to LIFO inventories is to base the determination on reasonable groupings of inventory items; in general, a pool constitutes a reasonable grouping. The Task

Force believed that the authoritative accounting literature *permits* the item-by-item approach, particularly for identified product obsolescence and discontinuance. AcSEC, on the other hand, believed that the item-by-item approach *should be* used for identified product obsolescence and product discontinuance.

If pools are similar (such as those involving an integrated product relationship or similar product lines), aggregating may be appropriate in applying the lower-of-cost-or-market test. If, however, the compositions of the pools are significantly dissimilar, aggregating is inappropriate.

LIFO Inventory Liquidations. A LIFO inventory liquidation causes an accounting anomaly in that prior year LIFO costs, rather than current costs, are matched against current revenues. Thus, the effects on income of LIFO inventory liquidations should be disclosed. Additional reasons for disclosure include the perception that inventory liquidations are infrequent in occurrence, and thus APB 30, *Reporting the Results of Operations—Reporting the Effects of Disposal of a Segment of a Business, and Extraordinary, Unusual and Infrequently Occurring Events and Transactions* (I17), requires disclosure. SAB topic 11F also requires such disclosure.

Various methods have been used to calculate the income statement effect of LIFO inventory liquidations. The *reinstatement approach,* which measures the income statement effect of a LIFO liquidation by calculating the difference between actual cost of sales and what cost of sales would have been had the inventory been reinstated under the method used to cost increments (i.e., first purchase price, latest purchase price, or average purchase price) is supported in the Issues Paper. (See Figure 14.2 for an illustration of the inventory reinstatement approach using the entity's normal pricing conventions.)

The disclosure of the effects on income of LIFO inventory liquidations should give effect only to pools with decrements. This is considered appropriate because the object of the disclosure is to present the effect on income of prior versus current costs being charged against current revenues. Accordingly, it is not appropriate to net pools with increments against pools with decrements.

A replacement reserve should not be provided if there is a LIFO inventory liquidation at year end, even if replacement is probable. A replacement reserve would inappropriately mix current-cost accounting into historical-cost financial statements. Further, such a reserve is conceptually inconsistent with the LIFO objective, because current revenues would not be matched with current costs.

Purchase Business Combinations. While APB 16, *Business Combinations* (B50), requires that inventory acquired in a business combination accounted for by the purchase method be recorded at its fair value as of the date of the combination, the acquired company may be able (dependent on the form of the transaction for tax purposes) to carry over its prior LIFO tax basis. APB 16 had provided that, in these circumstances, the estimated future tax effects of a difference between the tax basis and the fair value otherwise appropriate to assign to the asset was one of the variables in estimating fair value.

The Issues Paper states in this regard that an adjustment should be made for the difference in the tax and book bases of the LIFO inventory acquired if it is estimated that the inventory will be reduced below its level at the acquisition date (i.e., a liqui-

	FIFO			LIFO			LIFO Reserve
	Units	Item value	Total value	Units	Item value	Total value	
19X1							
Inventory 1/1	1,000	@ $3	$ 3,000	1,000	@ $3 (base)	$ 3,000	
Purchases	3,000	@ $4	12,000	3,000	@ $4	12,000	
Shipments		(1,000 @ $3)					
(cost of sales)	(2,000)	(1,000 @ $4)	(7,000)	(2,000)	@ $4	(8,000)	
					(1,000 @ $3)		
Inventory 12/31	2,000	@ $4	8,000	2,000	(1,000 @ $4)	7,000	$1,000
19X2							
Purchases	2,000	@ $5	10,000	2,000	@ $5	10,000	
Shipments					(200 @ $3)		
(cost of sales)		(2,000 @ $4)			(1,000 @ $4)		
	(3,200)	(1,200 @ $5)	(14,000)	(3,200)	(2,000 @ $5)	(14,600)	
Inventory 12/31	800		$ 4,000	800		$ 2,400	$1,600

Pretax effect of LIFO layer liquidation—normal pricing convention:

1,000 units @ ($5–$4)	$ 1,000	
200 units @ ($5–$3)	400	
	$ 1,400	

Since the liquidated units would have been stated at 19 X 2 cost of $5 if there had been an increment, the difference between $5 X 3,200 units ($16,000) and the actual carrying amount charged to cost of sales ($14,600), or $1,400, represents the effect of the liquidation.

FIG. 14.2   **Example of LIFO Inventory Liquidation—Inventory Reinstatement Method Using the Entity's Normal Pricing Convention.**
Source: Adapted from AICPA Issues Paper, 1984f, p.40.

dation is anticipated). If near-term liquidation is not probable, the Issues Paper indicates that such an adjustment is unnecessary because the income tax effects would be minimal if computed on a discounted basis.

This accounting approach and Issues Paper commentary, however, have been superseded by the FASB's major revision to the income tax accounting standards (SFAS 96), as described in Chapter 17. Differences between tax and book bases in a purchase business combination are now considered to be temporary differences having deferred tax consequences for which a liability or an asset is to be recognized.

In addition, if inventory or an entity acquired in a business combination accounted for by the purchase method is treated as a separate business unit or a separate LIFO pool, the acquired inventory should be considered the LIFO-base inventory. If, however, the acquired inventory is combined into an existing pool, the acquired inventory should be considered as part of the current year's purchases.

Interim LIFO Reporting. Using LIFO compounds interim reporting problems. For example, interim LIFO reporting requires an estimate to be made of the effect of the LIFO calculation at the future year end. If there has been a reduction in LIFO inventories at the interim date but it is expected that the reduction will be eliminated by year end, a provision must be made in cost of sales to offset what otherwise would be shown as a LIFO layer liquidation having a favorable effect on reported income. This is necessary because LIFO for tax purposes is computed only at year end, and this rule has also been accepted as a convention for financial reporting purposes. Matters become even more complicated when a LIFO user has divergent tax and financial reporting year ends.

Few if any companies are believed to make complete LIFO determinations quarterly. Thus most companies estimate the effect of LIFO for purposes of interim reporting. Estimates of the LIFO interim effect can be based on either (1) interim year-to-date LIFO calculations (except for liquidations expected to be reinstated or increments expected to be reversed by year end) or (2) an allocation of the projected year end LIFO calculation. Both approaches should be considered acceptable as long as the result is a reasonable matching of most recently incurred costs with revenues, and taking into consideration such things as the effects of significant changes in price levels and mix.

Intercompany Transfers of LIFO Inventories In November 1987, the AICPA issued Practice Bulletin 2, *Elimination of Profits from Intercompany Transfers of LIFO Inventories* (TP 12,020), to close off an issue that remained open in the earlier Issues Paper. This release discusses the accounting for intercompany transfers of LIFO inventories between corporate components. Thus if one component of the tax entity using LIFO transfers inventory to another component of the same tax entity that uses a non-LIFO method (e.g., FIFO), a "profit" would likely result merely from the restatement of the inventory from LIFO to FIFO. (The "profit" technically results from a liquidation of LIFO inventories.) Or, if two entities in a consolidated enterprise are separate taxable entities, even if both are using LIFO, a similar result can occur.

The Practice Bulletin reinforces the accounting guidance of ARB 51, *Consolidated Financial Statements* (C51), by recommending elimination of intercompany profit on such inventory transfers. The effect of LIFO inventory liquidations caused by such transfers should be included in the amount of intercompany profit to be eliminated.

AICPA Guidance—Supplemental Non-LIFO Disclosures

As discussed earlier, the IRS in 1981 softened its interpretation of the LIFO conformity requirement to permit certain supplemental disclosures in financial statements, because such disclosures are presumably useful in comparing companies using different inventory methods. Therefore, a company may present supplemental non-LIFO disclosures following an alternative inventory valuation method considered appropriate under GAAP (e.g., lower of FIFO cost or market).

Before presenting computation and disclosure examples, important measurement matters addressed by the AICPA Issues Paper (previously discussed) are covered. Concluding this section is a discussion of auditor reporting on the supplemental disclosures.

Measurement of Supplemental Disclosures. While the restatement of LIFO cost of sales to a non-LIFO basis is not conceptually complex, certain ancillary issues

	December 31	
	19X1	19X0
	(in thousands)	
Balance Sheet Adjustment		
Cumulative excess of FIFO basis over LIFO basis, which is the adjustment to inventory net of related profit-sharing obligation of $20,000 (19X1) and $15,000 (19X0)	$180,000	$135,000
Deferred taxes provided at the statutory rate (35% percent in both years)	63,000	47,250
Cumulative effect of LIFO/FIFO differential after tax – presented as an element of stockholders' equity	$117,000	$ 87,750
Income Statement Adjustment		
Effects of change from LIFO to FIFO:		
Decrease in cost of goods sold	$ 50,000	$ 40,000
Increase in profit-sharing expense	5,000	4,000
Increase in earnings before income tax	45,000	36,000
Complement of income tax rate	×.65	×.65
Increase in net earnings	$ 29,250	$ 23,400

FIG. 14.3   Calculation of LIFO to Non-LIFO Adjustment

could be overlooked. Therefore, the following measurement issues concerning the presentation of supplemental non-LIFO information are discussed in the AICPA Issues Paper:

- *Consideration of nondiscretionary variable expenses.* If it is probable that nondiscretionary variable expenses (e.g., profit sharing based on earnings) would have been different based on the supplemental information, the company should give effect to the changes in such nondiscretionary variable expenses. This conclusion is based on the presumption that nondiscretionary variable expenses are based on existing formulas, unless disclosure is made to the contrary.

- *Income tax measurement.* The same type of tax effect required by GAAP in the primary financial statements should be used in determining supplemental disclosures of the after-tax effect on pro forma net income and financial position.

- *Consideration of imputed interest.* The supplemental presentation should not reflect additional interest costs that might have been incurred due to the loss of the cash tax savings obtained from using LIFO.

- *Supplemental balance sheet presentation of tax effect.* The difference between the LIFO inventories used to determine net income and the non-LIFO inventories presented in the supplemental balance sheet is to be regarded as a temporary difference. The tax effect of the temporary difference should be classified in a manner similar to that required by GAAP in the primary financial statements.

Computation Example. The following assumptions were used in determining the supplemental non-LIFO information presented in the sample disclosures discussed in the next subsection. Figure 14.3 presents an example of how the FIFO-based supplemental non-LIFO disclosures should be calculated.

Assumptions (dollars in thousands):

1. The income tax rate is 35% in both years.
2. LIFO cost of sales exceeded FIFO cost of sales by $50,000 in 19X1 and $40,000 in 19X0. The cumulative cost of sales effect to December 31, 19X1 is $200,000.
3. A profit-sharing plan provides for total profit-sharing equal to 10% of eligible earnings as defined. Profit-sharing expense included in general and administrative expense on a LIFO basis was $5,000 in 19X1 and $11,000 in 19X0; on a FIFO basis profit-sharing expense was $10,000 in 19X1 and $15,000 in 19X0. The profit-sharing plan defines eligible earnings as net income exclusive of the profit-sharing provision, income tax expense, cumulative effect of accounting changes, extraordinary items, and discontinued items. On a FIFO basis, the cumulative profit-sharing obligation would be increased to $20,000 in 19X1 and 15,000 in 19X0.

Disclosure Examples. Non-LIFO disclosures are considered by the IRS as a supplement to or explanation of the primary presentation of income, if they are clearly labeled as such and if the specific item of information being explained or supplemented, such as net income, cost of goods sold, or earnings per share, ascertained by using the LIFO method, is also presented.

Non-LIFO disclosures may be included in the basic financial statements, in other information outside the basic financial statements, or separately as additional information. Sample disclosures in each situation follow.

For inclusion in the basic financial statements. Non-LIFO disclosure included in footnotes or in information reported in an appendix or supplement to the basic financial statements and accompanying the income statement in a single report is shown in the following paragraphs; this content is required for public companies and is recommended for nonpublic companies although earnings per share data need not be presented by nonpublic companies.

Inventories are valued at the lower of last-in, first-out (LIFO) cost or market. The LIFO method results in a better matching of costs and revenues. Information related to the first-in, first-out (FIFO) method may be useful in comparing operating results to those of companies not on LIFO. On a supplemental basis, if inventories had been valued at the lower of FIFO cost or market, they would have been increased by $200 million in 19X1 and $150 million in 19X0; and net income would have increased by $29.3 million ($1.49 per share) in 19X1 and $23.4 million ($1.17 per share) in 19X0.

IRS regulations would permit a broad presentation of inventories on the balance sheet, which would show the FIFO cost, the reduction for the LIFO reserve, and the inventories at LIFO. In this regard, there is no reason to object to the type of presentation portrayed below.

Inventories, lower of FIFO cost or market	$400,000
Less reserve to reduce inventories to LIFO	200,000
Inventories, lower of LIFO cost or market	$200,000

	December 31	
	19X1	19X0
	(in thousands)	
Assets		
Cash	$ 60,000	$ 50,000
Accounts receivable	120,000	110,000
Inventory (note 1) (See Fig. 14.6)	400,000	390,000
Current assets	580,000	550,000
Property, plant and equipment – net	900,000	900,000
Total Assets	$1,480,000	$1,450,000
Liabilities and Stockholders' Equity		
Accounts payable	$ 40,000	$ 35,000
Deferred income taxes	63,000	47,250
Accrued expenses	90,750	95,600
Current liabilities	193,750	177,850
Long-term debt	380,000	424,400
Stockholders' equity		
Captal stock	200,000	200,000
Retained earnings (LIFO basis)	589,250	560,000
Cumulative LIFO/FIFO differential after tax	117,000	87,750
	906,250	847,750
Total Liabilities and Stockholders' Equity	$1,480,000	$1,450,000

See basis of presentation and accountants' report on additional information.

FIG. 14.4   Sample Supplemental Non-LIFO Balance Sheet

	December 31	
	19X1	19X0
	(in thousands)	
Sales	$4,800,000	$4,500,000
Cost of goods sold (FIFO basis – note 1) [see Fig.14.6]	4,200,000	3,950,000
Gross margin	600,000	550,000
General and administrative expense	310,000	265,000
Selling expense	150,000	100,000
Interest expense	50,000	50,000
Total expense	510,000	415,000
Earnings before income tax	90,000	135,000
Income tax	31,500	47,250
Net earnings	$ 58,500	$ 87,750

See basis of presentation and accountants' report on additional information.

FIG. 14.5   Sample Supplemental Non-LIFO Income Statement

Other information outside the basic financial statements. Non-LIFO disclosures included in press releases, and sections of an annual report such as those labeled "President's Letter" or MD&A, all of which are outside the basic financial statements, are also considered by the IRS as an acceptable supplement to or explanation of the primary presentation of income. However, as discussed under "Acceptability of Supplemental Disclosures," the SEC assumes such disclosures will *not* be made in financial highlights, presidents' letters, or press releases of public companies.

When supplemental disclosure is given outside the financial statements, the disclosure shown in the following illustration is equally acceptable for public and nonpublic companies (nonpublic companies need not present earnings per share data).

> Net income for XYZ Co. was $29.2 million ($1.47 per share) in 19X1 and $64.3 million ($3.22 per share) in 19X0 and was calculated using the LIFO method of inventory valuation. The LIFO method results in a better matching of costs and revenues. Information related to the FIFO method may be useful in comparing operating results to those of companies not on LIFO. On a supplemental basis, if the FIFO method of inventory valuation had been used, net income would have been $58.5 million ($2.96 per share) in 19X1 and $87.7 million ($4.39 per share) in 19X0.

Additional information. Non-LIFO disclosures included in a long-form accountant's report as additional information that is outside the basic financial statements is also considered by the IRS as a supplement to or explanation of the primary presentation of income. Sample supplemental non-LIFO balance sheets, income statements, and footnote disclosures, designed for inclusion as additional information in a long-form report, are presented in Figures 14.4, 14.5, and 14.6 respectively. It is recommended that these additional information disclosures be issued only in conjunction with the basic financial statements and in one cover; issuing them separately could cause readers to think of them as the primary financial statements.

Auditors' Reports. Generally speaking, if non-LIFO disclosures are included in the basic financial statements, the disclosures are covered by the auditor's standard report thereon, generally without modification, as long as the nature of the information is properly described and determined.

Non-LIFO disclosures included in other reports, issued separately (not with the basic financial statement), are not required to be covered by any form of auditor's report. However, if non-LIFO disclosures are included in annual reports or other published documents (containing financial statements or other information that is otherwise required to be covered by some form of auditor's report), the auditor has a responsibility to consider whether such disclosure, or the manner of its presentation, is materially inconsistent with information appearing in the basic financial statements, with other information covered by his report, or with his general knowledge of the facts. (AU 550).

When an auditor submits a document to his client or to others which contains audited financial statements or information in addition to the client's basic financial

Note 1—Basis of Presentation

The financial statements presented as additional information have been prepared on the same basis as the basic financial statements, except that the inventories, and items affected by inventory measurement, have been presented using the the first-in, first-out (FIFO) method of inventory valuation, which differs substantially from the last-in, first-out (LIFO) method used for inventory measurement in the basic financial statements. Differences in the basis of presentation are as follows:

Balance Sheets

Inventories are presented at the lower of FIFO cost or market. The profit-sharing obligation and deferred taxes related to the LIFO/FIFO inventory valuation difference are presented among current liabilities. The excess of the LIFO/FIFO inventory valuation difference over the related profit-sharing obligation and deferred taxes is presented as a separate element of stockholders' equity, determined as follows:

	December 31	
	19X1	19X0
	(in thousands)	
Cumulative excess of FIFO basis over LIFO basis, net of related profit-sharing obligation of $20,000 (19X1) and $15,000 (19X0)	$180,000	$135,000
Less deferred taxes	63,000	47,250
Cumulative effects of LIFO/FIFO differential after tax	$117,000	$ 87,750

Income Statements

Cost of goods sold is measured on a FIFO basis, representing the LIFO basis adjusted for the LIFO/FIFO inventory valuation difference. The provisions for income taxes and for profit-sharing expense (which is based on a percentage of pretax accounting income) are adjusted for the impact of the LIFO/FIFO adjustment to cost of goods sold, determined as follows:

	December 31	
	19X1	19X0
	(in thousands)	
Effects of change from LIFO to FIFO:		
Decrease in cost of goods sold	$ 50,000	$ 40,000
Increase in profit-sharing expense	5,000	4,000
Net increase in earnings before income tax	45,000	36,000
Income taxes on net increase	15,750	12,600
Increase in net earnings	29,250	23,400
Net earnings on a LIFO basis	29,250	64,350
Net earnings on a FIFO basis	$ 58,500	$ 87,750

FIG. 14.6   Sample Supplemental Non-LIFO Footnote Disclosures

statements, he has a responsibility to report on all the information included in the document, including non-LIFO disclosures (AU 551). The auditor's report on information accompanying the basic financial statements in such a document has the same objective as an auditor's report on the basic financial statements: to clearly describe the character of the auditor's examination and the degree of responsibility, if any, he is taking.

Sample language for the auditor's report on information accompanying the basic financial statements in an auditor-submitted document, based on several different assumptions, is presented later herein.

Opinion—Supplemental non-LIFO only. This sample auditor's report assumes that: (1) the divergence of accompanying information from the basic financial statements is limited to supplemental non-LIFO disclosures, and (2) the accompanying information has been subjected to the auditing procedures applied in the audit of the basic financial statements:

> Our audit was made for the purpose of forming an opinion on the basic financial statements taken as a whole. The accompanying supplemental condensed balance sheets and statements of income are presented for purposes of additional analysis and are not a required part of the basic financial statements. Such information has been subjected to the auditing procedures applied in the audit of the basic financial statements and, in our opinion, is fairly stated in all materials respects in relation to the financial statements taken as a whole, except that the inventories, and items affected by inventory measurement have been presented using the first-in, first-out method of inventory valuation (Note A), which differs substantially from the last-in, first-out method used for inventory measurement in the basic financial statements.

Opinion—Supplemental non-LIFO and other data. This sample auditor's report assumes that: (1) the accompanying information includes supplemental non-LIFO disclosures along with other additional information, and (2) the accompanying information has been subjected to the auditing procedures applied in the audit of the basic financial statements:

> Our audit was made for the purpose of forming an opinion on the basic financial statements taken as a whole. The additional information listed on the accompanying index is presented for purposes of additional analysis and is not a required part of the basic financial statements. Such information has been subjected to the auditing procedures applied in the audit of the basic financial statements and, in our opinion, is fairly stated in all material respects in relation to the financial statements taken as a whole, except that the inventories, and items affected by inventory measurements, in the supplemental condensed balance sheets and statements of income appearing on pages 000 and 000, have been presented using the first-in, first-out method of inventory valuation (Note A thereto), which differs substantially from the last-in, first-out method used for inventory measurement in the basic financial statements.

Disclaimer—Supplemental non-LIFO only. This sample auditor's report assumes that: (1) the divergence of the accompanying information from the basic financial statements is limited to supplemental non-LIFO disclosures, and (2) the accompanying information has not been subjected to the auditing procedures applied in the audit of the basic financial statements and, therefore, a disclaimer of opinion is required. (AU 551 provides for a modified opinion to be rendered under certain conditions.)

Our audit was made for the purpose of forming an opinion on the basic financial statements taken as a whole. The additional information listed on the accompanying index is presented for purposes of additional analysis and is not a required part of the basic financial statements; further, the presentation of inventories and items affected by inventory measurement in the supplemental condensed balance sheets and statements of income appearing on pages 000 and 000 is based on the first-in, first-out method of inventory valuation (see Note A), which differs substantially from the last-in, first-out method used for inventory measurement in the basic financial statements. This additional information has not been subjected to the auditing procedures applied in the audit of the basic financial statement, and, accordingly, we express no opinion on it.

AICPA Guidance—Simplified LIFO Method

With respect to the use of the Simplified LIFO tax method, a 1982 AICPA Issues Paper, (AICPA, 1982a) supports the use of 100% of the percentage change in the price index for applying simplified LIFO for financial reporting. AcSEC felt that as long as the items on which the index is based are representative of the type of items included in the taxpayer's inventory pools, the method would be acceptable. AcSEC did *not*, however, support the use of the 80% approach for financial reporting purposes. AcSEC indicated, however, that using the 80% approach for tax purposes and the 100% approach for financial reporting purposes does not violate the LIFO conformity requirements. The effect of the temporary difference should be accounted for in accordance with income tax accounting standards. The FASB has not, as yet, dealt with this topic. Therefore, the only guidance on Simplified LIFO is the AcSEC Issues Paper.

SEC Requirements

LIFO Concept Reaffirmation. The SEC has indicated that, conceptually, the purpose of using the LIFO method of inventory valuation is the proper matching of current costs with current revenues. In the SEC's view, any action (i.e, a LIFO transaction) by a registrant that is contrary to this concept will be challenged (ASR 293; FRR § 205).

The SEC position acknowledges the final IRS regulations of January 1981, and considers two aspects thereof to be significant:

1. Companies may apply LIFO differently for financial reporting purposes than for tax purposes, as long as they use an acceptable form of LIFO for financial reporting purposes.
2. Companies may provide supplemental non-LIFO disclosures, but not on the face of the income statement.

In FRR § 205, the SEC provides examples involving new product designations and inventory transfers that are unacceptable for financial accounting and reporting purposes (although some may be acceptable tax approaches).

- When new products are introduced into dollar-value LIFO inventory, computed using the double-extension approach, the comparison should be against a reconstructed base-year cost.

- Preexisting inventory items are not new products and, for example, slight differences in chemical composition, changes in manufacturing or production line location, or differences in supply sources do not make them so.
- Neither inventory misclassifications nor book transfers of inventory that are not accompanied by physical transfers or other changes in economic substance are reasons for LIFO changes. The SEC considers such "paper" transactions misleading.

In March 1985, the SEC issued SAB 58 (topic 5L) to state the SEC Staff's position on the AICPA LIFO Issues Paper (AICPA, 1984f). The SAB states:

> In the absence of existing authoritative literature on LIFO accounting, the staff believes that registrants and their independent accountants should look to the paper for guidance in determining what constitutes acceptable LIFO accounting practice. In this connection, the staff considers the paper to be an accumulation of existing acceptable LIFO accounting practices which does not establish any new standards and does not diverge from generally accepted accounting principles.
>
> The staff therefore believes that a registrant and its independent accountants should re-examine previously adopted LIFO practices and compare them to the recommendations in the Issue Paper. In the event that the registrant and its independent accountants conclude that the registrant's LIFO practices are preferable in the circumstances, they should be prepared to justify their position in the event that a question is raised by the staff.

Additionally, SAB topic 11F requires disclosure of LIFO liquidations where the portion liquidated is substantial and a material amount of income results. Disclosure may be made in a footnote or parenthetically on the face of the income statement.

In Issue 84-24, *LIFO Accounting Issues*, the EITF discussed whether the SEC staff's views on the preferability of the LIFO Issues Paper had any implications for standard-setting. The Task Force members were perhaps concerned that an issues paper, expressing tentative views not sanctioned by either an SOP or FASB statement, could become GAAP by SEC fiat. The SEC Observer noted that the absence of authoritative literature on LIFO accounting necessitated staff action.

Acceptability of Supplemental Disclosures. In FRR § 205, the SEC formally stated what previously had been informal requirements. Because some registrants apparently use supplemental FIFO disclosures to imply that FIFO earnings are the "real" earnings, registrants are reminded that disclosures must be considered carefully so as not to result in misleading financial reporting. In the SEC's view, the most troublesome disclosures relate to pro forma income information based on the FIFO method. The reason most often given for these disclosures is that they are necessary to permit comparison of companies using LIFO with those using FIFO. However, the SEC does not believe that FIFO-based supplemental income disclosures are necessarily the best way to obtain comparable information; a better method might be the changing prices disclosures described in SFAS 33, *Financial Reporting and Changing Prices* (subsequently superseded by SFAS 89 (C28)).

If, however, a registrant provides supplementary FIFO disclosure, any risk of misinterpretation by users would be mitigated if the disclosure:

- States clearly that the use of LIFO results in a better matching of costs and revenues.
- Indicates the reason why supplemental income disclosures are being provided.

	Processing of purchase orders	Receipt of new materials	Storage of raw materials*	Processing the goods*	Storage of finished goods*	Shipment
Flow of material and goods	1. Purchase requested by production department 2. Order placed by purchasing department	1. Goods received and inspected by separate receiving department	1. Goods placed in stockroom	1. Material placed in production 2. Direct labor incurred in production 3. Overhead costs incurred	1. Finished goods transferred from production to stockroom	1. Goods removed from stockroom and shipped

Related documentation	1. Production department issues purchase requisition
	2. Purchasing department issues purchase order and sends copy to
	  a. Vendor
	  b. Receiving department
	  c. Production department
	  d. Accounting
		1. Receiving department sends receiving reports and inspection reports to
		  a. Perpetual inventory
		  b. Purchasing
		  c. Stockroom
		  d. Accounting
		2. Accounting matches receiving reports, purchase orders, and invoices and records purchase
			1. Quantities compared with receiving report (receiving reports may be sent to accounting at this point in some systems)
			2. Entries made in perpetual inventory records
				1. Material requisitions recorded by
				  a. Perpetual inventory
				  b. Cost accounting
				  c. General accounting
				2. Labor and overhead costs distributed to applicable jobs or processes in cost records and in total in the general ledger
					1. Production reports sent to
					  a. Perpetual inventory
					  b. Cost accounting
					2. Cost transferred from work in process to finished goods account
						1. Shipping documents sent to
						  a. Perpetual records
						  b. Accounting
						2. Cost of sales entry made based on quantities shipped

* Inventory counts are taken and compared with perpetual and book amounts at any stage of the cycle, being certain that cutoff for recording documents corresponds to the physical location of the items. A count must ordinarily be taken at least once a year.

FIG. 14.7 Basic Inventory and Warehousing Cycle

Source: Arens, Alvin and Loebbecke, James, 1976. Auditing: An Integrated Approach, p. 512. Reprinted with permission of Prentice-Hall, Inc.

- Presents essential information about the supplemental income calculation to enable users to understand its value.

Such disclosures should not be made in financial highlights, press releases, or presidents' letters, since analytical data in the required detail usually is not included in those places; rather, they are better placed in footnotes to financial statements or in MD&A.

AUDITING INVENTORY AND COST OF SALES

The overall audit objective is to evaluate whether inventory and cost of sales are fairly presented in the context of the financial statements taken as a whole. The broad objectives of an audit are discussed in Chapter 7 and the basic nature of internal accounting control in Chapter 8. The following discussion assumes familiarity with these chapters.

Inventory usually includes goods held for sale, items in production, and materials and supplies used to produce those goods. All three types are present in a manufacturing company. The complexity of the manufacturing process and related cost systems presents the auditor with commensurately complex audit issues. Indeed, the audit of inventory in a manufacturing, processing, or merchandising business is usually the most complex and time-consuming part of the audit. The focus in this chapter is on the manufacturing company inventory audit.

Transaction Types

The primary transaction types that affect inventory and cost of sales are:

- Acquisition of raw material, labor, and application of overhead costs; these activities involve the processing of purchase orders, receipt and storage of materials, and application of labor and overhead to production.
- Internal transfer of materials and costs that takes place within the inventory cycle when materials are processed and stored.
- Shipment of goods to customers.
- Protective controls over inventory storage.
- Pricing of inventory movement.

These transactions are illustrated in Figure 14.7.

Audit Approach

To develop the appropriate program the auditor needs to consider:

- Inherent risks
- Potential errors
- Nature and effectiveness of the related controls

- Procedures that accomplish more than one purpose
- Effective use of analytical review
- Effect of interrelationship to other audit work.

Inherent Risks and Potential Errors. In assessing the inherent risks (susceptibility of an account balance or class of transactions to errors that could be material) in inventory and cost of sales, the auditor will consider a number of interrelated factors. In most audits, the inventory balance and cost of sales amounts are generally major items and a number of high value (or key) items are present. Further, some potential errors could be 100% errors and thus have a low probability of self-detection.

The broad objectives of an audit, as stated in Chapter 7, are existence, occurrence, completeness, ownership, valuation, allocation, presentation, and disclosure; and the broad objectives of internal accounting control as stated in Chapter 8 are authorization, execution, recording, and accountability. Segmenting these objectives by account balances or (classes of transactions) and specific risks provides an effective and efficient method for audit planning. Potential errors (including irregularities, i.e., those that might intentionally be made) provide the "architecture" for the audit and provide a focus for assessing the magnitude and likelihood of the related exposure to error.

To better understand the potential errors, their related causes are presented in Figures 14.8, 14.9, and 14.10. The potential errors for inventory and cost of sales are:

- Inventory

  Raw Materials
  - Raw materials or work-in-process lost or stolen
  - Transfers from raw materials improperly recorded
  - Transfers from raw materials recorded in wrong period
  - Transfers from raw materials summarization and posting errors

  Work In Process and Finished Goods
  - Finished goods lost or stolen
  - Transfers from work in process improperly recorded
  - Transfers from work in process recorded in wrong period
  - Transfers from work in process summarization and posting errors

- *Cost of Sales*
  - Cost of sales recorded, goods not shipped
  - Goods shipped, cost of sales not recorded
  - Cost of sales amount recorded incorrectly
  - Cost of sales posted to wrong account
  - Cost of sales recorded in wrong period
  - Cost of sales summarization and posting errors

Objective	Potential Errors	Causes of Errors	Inherent Risk Factors	Types of Controls	Examples of Controls
Existence—recording	Raw materials or work in process lost or stolen	• Raw materials lost or stolen • Work in process lost or stolen	• Value of a balance or group of transactions typically large relative to materiality • High value items typically present in balance or transactions • Errors have a direct impact on earnings • Errors are not self-detecting • Errors tend to be 100%	• Independent approval, review, checking, or recalculation • Segregation of personnel, operations, and assets • Timeliness of operation	• Periodic cycle counts performed • Raw materials warehouse physically secure • Production area physically sound
Validity Mechanical Accuracy	Transfers from raw materials improperly recorded	• Invalid materials requisition recorded • EDP entry without supporting materials requisition • Materials requisition recorded twice • Goods transferred without materials requisition • Materials requisition not recorded • Materials requisition item number incorrect • Materials requisition quantity incorrect • Materials requisition item number recorded incorrectly	• Value of a balance or group of transactions typically large relative to materiality • High value items typically present in balance or transactions • Errors are not self-detecting • Errors tend to be 100%	• Independent approval, review, checking, or recalculation • Segregation of personnel, operations, and assets • Timeliness of operation	• Periodic cycle counts performed • Raw materials warehouse physically secure • Reconciliation of raw materials account in general ledger to stock reports • Reconciliation of work in process account in general ledger to stock reports • Investigation of materials usage variances

(continued)

FIG. 14.8 Planning Matrix for Raw Materials

Objective	Potential Errors	Causes of Errors	Inherent Risk Factors	Types of Controls	Examples of Controls
		• Materials requisition quantity recorded incorrectly • Wrong standard cost used in EDP • Materials requisition record processed incorrectly in EDP			
Cut-off	Transfers from raw materials recorded in wrong period	• Materials requisition dated in wrong period • Materials requisition recorded in wrong period • Materials requisition processed in wrong period in EDP	• Value of a balance or group of transactions typically large relative to materiality • High value items typically present in balance or requisitions • Errors have a direct impact on earnings • Errors are not self-detecting • Errors tend to be 100%	• Independent approval, review, checking, or recalculation • Segregation of personnel, operations, and assets • Timeliness of operation	• Adequate written cut-off procedures • Personnel adequately instructed regarding cut-off • Achievement of cut-off reviewed
Classification mechanical accuracy	Transfers from raw materials summarization and posting errors	• Materials requisition processed to wrong accounts in EDP • Daily journals incorrectly summarized to monthly journal • Monthly journal posted twice to general ledger	• Value of a balance or group of transactions typically large relative to materiality • High value items typically present in balance or transactions • Errors have a direct impact on earnings	• Independent approval, review, checking, or recalculation • Matching of independently generated documents • Maintenance of independent control totals	• Periodic cycle counts performed • Monthly raw material transfers journal agreed to general ledger posting • Reconciliation of raw materials account in general ledger to stock reports

- Entry in general ledger not supported by monthly journal
- Monthly journal not posted to general ledger
- Monthly journal amount incorrectly posted to general ledger account
- Monthly journal amount posted to wrong general ledger
- Monthly journal amount posted to general ledger in wrong period

- Errors are not self-detecting
- Errors tend to be 100%

- Segregation of personnel operations, and assets
- Timeliness of operation

- Reconciliation of work in process account in general ledger to stock reports
- Investigation of materials usage variances
- Adequate written cut-off procedues
- Personnel adequately instructed regarding cut-off
- Achievement of cut-off reviewed

FIG. 14.8 (continued)

Objective	Potential Errors	Causes of Errors	Inherent Risk Factors	Types of Controls	Examples of Controls
Existence— Recording	Finished goods lost or stolen	• Finished goods lost or stolen	• Value of a balance or group of transactions typically large relative to materiality • High value items typically present in balance or transactions • Errors have a direct impact on earnings • Errors are not self-detecting • Errors tend to be 100%	• Segregation of personnel, operations, and assets • Timeliness of operation	• Periodic cycle counts performed • Finished goods warehouse physically secure
Existence/ Validity/ Recording/ Accuracy	Transfers from work in process improperly recorded	• Invalid production document prepared • EDP entry without supporting production document • Production document recorded twice • Production document records duplicated in EDP • Work in process transferred without production document • Production document not recorded	• Value of a balance or group of transactions typically large relative to materiality • High value items typically present in balance or transactions • Errors are not self-detecting • Errors tend to be 100% • Complex calculations involved	• Independent approval, review, checking, or recalculation • Maintenance of independent control totals • Segregation of personnel, operations, and assets • Timeliness of operation	• Periodic cycle counts performed • Production area physically secure • Reconciliation of work in process account in general ledger to stock reports • Investigation of labor efficiency variances • Reconciliation of finished goods account in general ledger to stock reports • Investigation of materials usage variances

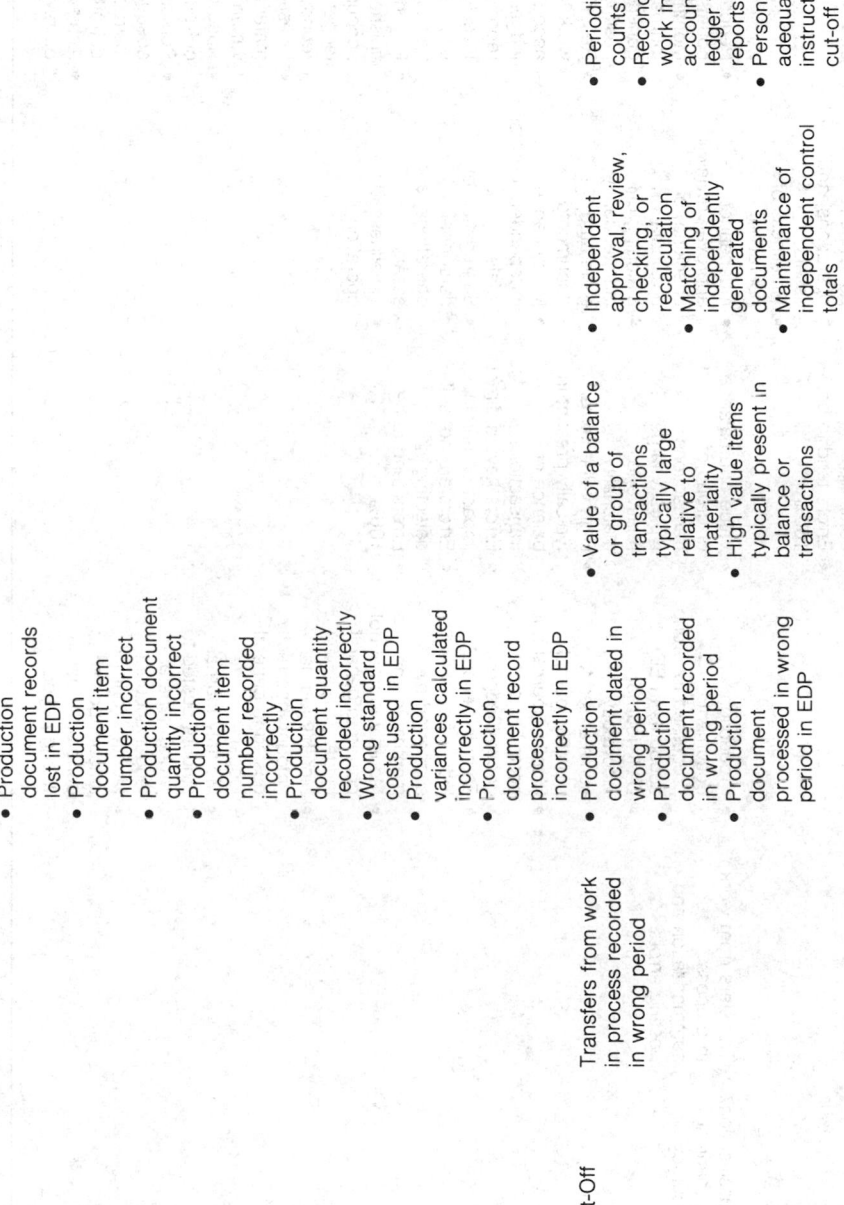

- Production document records lost in EDP
- Production document item number incorrect
- Production document quantity incorrect
- Production document item number recorded incorrectly
- Production document quantity recorded incorrectly
- Wrong standard costs used in EDP
- Production variances calculated incorrectly in EDP
- Production document record processed incorrectly in EDP

Cut-Off

- Transfers from work in process recorded in wrong period
- Production document dated in wrong period
- Production document recorded in wrong period
- Production document processed in wrong period in EDP

- Value of a balance or group of transactions typically large relative to materiality
- High value items typically present in balance or transactions

- Independent approval, review, checking, or recalculation
- Matching of independently generated documents
- Maintenance of independent control totals
- Periodic cycle counts performed
- Reconciliation of work in process account in general ledger to stock reports
- Personnel adequately instructed regarding cut-off

(continued)

FIG. 14.9 Planning Matrix for Work in Process and Finished Goods

Objective	Potential Errors	Causes of Errors	Inherent Risk Factors	Types of Controls	Examples of Controls
			• Errors are not self-detecting • Errors tend to be 100%	• Segregation of personnel, operations, and assets • Timeliness of operation	• Achievement of cut-off reviewed
Classification/ mechanical accuracy	Transfers from work in process summarization and posting errors	• Production document processed to wrong accounts in EDP • Daily journal incorrectly summarized to monthly journal • Monthly journal not posted twice to general ledger • Entry in general ledger not supported by monthly journal • Monthly journal not posted to general ledger • Monthly journal amount incorrectly posted to general ledger • Monthly journal amount posted to wrong general ledger account • Monthly journal amount posted to general ledger in wrong period	• Value of a balance or group of transactions typically large relative to materiality • High value items typically present in balance or transactions • Errors have a direct impact on earnings • Errors are not self-detecting • Errors tend to be 100%	• Independent approval, review, checking, or recalculation • Matching of independently generated documents • Maintenance of independent control totals • Segregation of personnel, operations, and assets • Timeliness of operation	• Periodic cycle counts performed • Monthly production journal agreed to general ledger posting • Reconciliation of work in process account in general ledger to stock reports • Investigation of labor efficiency variances • Reconciliation of finished goods account in general ledger to stock reports • Investigation of materials usage variances • Adequate written cut-off procedures • Personnel adequately instructed regarding cut-off • Achievement of cut-off reviewed

FIG. 14.9 (continued)

Objective	Potential Errors	Causes of Errors	Inherent Risk Factors	Types of Controls	Examples of Controls
Existence—Validity	Cost of sales recorded, goods not shipped	• Cost of sales record duplicated in EDP • Shipping document prepared, goods not shipped • Shipping document prepared twice • Shipping document invoiced twice • Sales invoice prepared without supporting shipping document • EDP entry without supporting invoice • Sales invoice recorded twice	• Value of a balance or group of transactions typically large relative to materiality • High value items typically present in balance or transactions • Errors have a direct impact on earnings • Errors are not self-detecting • Errors tend to be 100%	• Independent approval, review, checking, or recalculation • Maintenance of independent control totals • Segregation of personnel, operations, and assets • Timeliness of operation	• Periodic cycle counts performed • Shipping documents agreed to cost of sales journal • Invoices balanced to daily cost of sales journal
Existence/Recording	Goods shipped, cost of sales not recorded	• Cost of sales records lost in EDP • Goods shipped without shipping document • Shipping document prepared but not invoiced • Sales invoice not recorded • Sales invoice records lost in EDP	• Value of a balance or group of transactions typically large relative to materiality • High value items typically present in balance or transactions • Errors have a direct impact on earnings • Errors are not self-detecting • Errors tend to be 100%	• Independent approval, review, checking, or recalculation • Maintenance of independent control totals • Segregation of personnel, operations, and assets • Timeliness of operation	• Periodic cycle counts performed • Shipping documents agreed to cost of sales journal • Invoices balanced to daily cost of sales journal

(continued)

FIG. 14.10　Planning Matrix for Cost of Sales

Objective	Potential Errors	Causes of Errors	Inherent Risk Factors	Types of Controls	Examples of Controls
Valuation/ Accuracy	Cost of sales amount recorded incorrectly	• Shipping document item number incorrect • Sales invoice item number incorrect • Sales invoice item number recorded incorrectly • Sales invoice quantity recorded incorrectly • Wrong standard cost used in EDP • Cost of sales record processed incorrectly in EDP • Shipping document quantity incorrect • Sales invoice quantity incorrect	• Value of a balance or group of transactions typically large relative to materiality • High value items typically present in balance of transactions • Errors have a direct impact on earnings • Errors are not self-detecting	• Independent approval, review, checking, or recalculation • Maintenance of independent control totals • Segregation of personnel, operations, and assets • Timeliness of operation	• Periodic cycle counts performed • Invoices balanced to daily cost of sales journal • Reconciliation of finished goods account in general ledger to stock reports • Shipping document quantity checked in warehouse • Monthly cost of sales journal reviewed for reasonableness • Reconciliation of finished goods account in general ledger to stock reports
Classification	Cost of sales posted to wrong account	• Cost of sales record processed to wrong account in EDP • Incorrect general ledger account code on sales invoice • General ledger account code recorded incorrectly • General ledger account code processed incorrectly in EDP	• Value of a balance or group of transactions typically large relative to materiality • High value items typically present in balance or transactions • Errors have a direct impact on earnings • Errors are not self-detecting • Errors tend to be 100%	• Independent approval, checking, or recalculation • Timeliness of operation • Segregation of personnel	• Monthly cost of sales journal agreed to general ledger posting • Reconciliation of finished goods account in general ledger to stock reports
Cut-off	Cost of sales recorded in wrong period	• Cost of sales record processed in wrong period in EDP	• Value of a balance or group of transactions typically large relative to materiality	• Independent approval, review, checking, or recalculation • Timeliness of operation	• Adequate written cut-off procedures

		• Shipping document dated in wrong period • Sales invoice dated in wrong period • Sales invoice recorded in wrong period	• High value items typically present in balance or transactions • Errors have a direct impact on earnings • Errors are not self-detecting • Errors tend to be 100%		• Personnel adequately instructed regarding cut-off • Achievement of cut-off reviewed
Mechanical Accuracy	Cost of sales summarization and posting errors	• Daily journal incorrectly summarized to monthly journal • Monthly journal posted twice to general ledger • Entry in general ledger not supported by monthly journal • Monthly journal not posted to general ledger • Monthly journal amount incorrectly posted to general ledger • Monthly journal record posted to wrong general ledger account • Monthly journal record posted to general ledger in wrong period	• Value of a balance or group of transactions typically large relative to materiality • High value items typically present in balance or transactions • Errors have a direct impact on earnings • Errors are not self-detecting • Errors tend to be 100%	• Independent approval, review, checking, or recalculation • Maintenance of independent control totals • Timeliness of operation	• Monthly cost of sales journal agreed to sum of daily journal • Monthly cost of sales journal agreed to general ledger posting • Reconciliation of finished goods account in general ledger to stock reports • Adequate written cut-off procedures • Personnel adequately instructed regarding cut-off • Achievement of cut-off reviewed

FIG. 14.10 (continued)

Depending on the specific circumstances and the significance of the amounts involved, the auditor might also identify additional areas of potential error, for example:

• Customer returns
• Third-party inventory held by client
• Client inventory at third parties
• Scrap inventory
• Intercompany purchases

Nature and Effectiveness of Controls. As described in Chapter 8, the audit process requires that the auditor obtain an understanding of the client's internal control structure, document his understanding, and analyze the internal control structure to ascertain the control points on which he chooses to rely, and the effect of structure weaknesses on his audit plan. The auditor must then develop specific audit procedures to test those areas of internal control on which he will rely.

In assessing internal accounting control, the auditor would focus particularly on company activities that affect inventory and cost of sales most often and most heavily. These usually are:

• Purchasing and accounts payable activities for the acquisition of inventory materials and overhead items. The auditor must be familiar with the client's procedures that control the ordering, receipt, payment for, and returns of materials and overhead.
• Personnel-related activities that allocate labor costs to inventory (direct labor, indirect labor, and fringe benefits). The auditor must understand how employees are hired and terminated, payroll data is accumulated, payroll and fringe benefit costs are determined, and costs are allocated among periods and products.
• Capital asset activities that affect inventory. The auditor must understand how plant and equipment acquisitions, utilization, and disposals are controlled, and how the costs of these assets are allocated among periods and products.
• Inventory transfer activities within the company and scrap disposals. The auditor must understand how inventory movements are initiated, approved, effected, and recorded.
• Product sales activities. The auditor must understand the company's procedures to control order acceptance, shipment, recording of inventory relief, and customer returns.
• Inventory quantity and value determination procedures. The auditor must understand how and when the company physically determines the units of inventory it has on hand, what cost convention is used to assign a carrying amount to the units, how costs are methodically assigned to inventory, how market and economic considerations affect inventory values, and how inventory amounts (units or dollars) are updated from the date of the physical inventory to the reporting date if the dates differ.

To determine whether the existing controls provide an adequate basis for an efficient reliance-based audit, they need to be specifically correlated with the nature and extent of risk present. This can be done most effectively by comparing each potential error to the related controls ordinarily expected to be present. This correlation is shown for raw materials, work in process and finished goods, and cost of sales in Figures 14.8, 14.9, and 14.10, respectively.

It is possible for auditors to rely solely on substantive tests when auditing inventory and cost of sales. This approach is used when the auditor deems it more economical and efficient, such as in the audit of a small company whose internal control structure is not well developed, or when the structure otherwise is not deemed effective or reliable. In most cases, however, the auditor will rely extensively on the inventory systems of internal control. In doing so, the auditor will apply tests of controls to the systems, and if the results of such tests are favorable, will reduce the amount of the substantive tests applied to year-end balances.

Once the auditor is satisfied as to the manner in which the system is operating, the extent of substantive audit procedures can be determined. Because many audit procedures deal with more than one type of potential error, selection of more powerful procedures will usually result in a more efficient audit program.

Objectives and Procedures

Under either approach, the auditor needs to plan procedures to satisfy the inventory audit objectives. Figure 14.11 is a condensed listing of the interim and year-end audit procedures that are commonly used to achieve these objectives. The procedures shown may be used to satisfy more than one audit objective but are listed under the objective that they most typically satisfy to provide an overview of how the audit objectives are met. These procedures are discussed in more detail in the following sections.

Existence and Ownership. SAS 1 (AU 331.09–.13) indicates that the auditor should observe the physical inventory-taking and be satisfied with the effectiveness of the counting procedures used. The observation may take any combination of either of two forms:

1. In the systems reliance approach, the perpetual inventory records maintained by the client are tested. Companies that maintain perpetual inventory records may verify them in cycles continually throughout the year, never taking a complete shutdown physical inventory. The auditor should review the results of the company's cycle counts to make a preliminary assessment of the reliability of the system. If the system appears reliable, the auditor should test it himself. His tests will typically include a selection of items from the perpetual records for tracing to the inventory and a selection from the physical inventory items for tracing to the perpetual records. These tests can be performed either on an interim or a year-end basis. If the system does not appear reliable, the company may have to take a full physical inventory at year end.

2. The auditor observes and tests the count of the full physical inventory taken at an interim date or at year end. This observation can be used as a systems test at an interim date to assess the accuracy of the client's perpetual records or the aggregate inventory balance accumulated in the general ledger; or it can serve as a substantive procedure at year-end to test the company's determination of final inventory quantities. The timing of the inventory will be influenced by the company's operating cycle (a company generally prefers to count its inventory during low-production periods or when inventory quantities are at their lowest levels) and by the quality of internal controls.

Audit objective	Sample year-end procedures*	Sample interim procedures
Existence. Determine whether there are physical goods supporting the dollar amount of inventory in the balance sheet, and whether all such goods have been properly included.	• Observe inventory at year-end. • Review inventory instructions. • Tour facilities before count. • Tour completed areas for omissions or double counts. • Recount selected items. • Obtain count documents and related items. • Test control over inventory count tags and record for future testing. • Record test counts for subsequent tracing to the inventory compilation. • Agree quantity and type to inventory compilation. • Note items that appear to be slow-moving or obsolete.	• Observe inventory at an interim date. • Test perpetuals.
Ownership. Determine whether inventory owned by the company is included and whether inventories of others are properly identified and excluded from the inventory amounts.	• Confirm quantities and ownership of merchandise at outside locations. • Confirm with outsiders the merchandise identified as theirs. • Request vendor statements.	• Test company's system for controlling the receipt, movement, and shipment of merchandise belonging to others or shipped to others on consignment or for processing.
Mechanical accuracy. Determine whether the basic mathematical calculations of the physical inventory are proper, and whether data gathered during the observation are properly used.	• Agree test counts to quantities included in the compilation. • Test tag control. • Test mathematical accuracy of extensions and footings of inventory compilation. • Test company's method of accumulating unit costs and assigning them to physical inventory units.	• Select a sample of items and test extensions, footings, and postings of transactions between physical inventory date and period-end.

* Also often used at an interim date.

FIG. 14.11 Inventory Audit Objectives and Procedures

Audit objective	Sample year-end procedures*	Sample interim procedures
Valuation. Determine whether inventory quantities are fairly valued in conformity with generally accepted accounting standards.	• Obtain costed inventory compilation and for key raw material, work in process and finished good items and a sample of other items; — Discuss material and labor content with production personnel and overhead allocation with accounting personnel — Check material cost to purchase invoice — Check labor cost to labor rate listing — Assess reasonableness of overhead allocation • If applicable review update of interim inventory to year end and test it. • Review components of book to physical adjustment.	• Review and test the company's method for determining and adjusting for lower-of-cost-or-market situations and providing for allowances needed for obsolete or slow-moving items.
Disclosure. Determine whether disclosures included in the financial statements are adequate.	• Agree financial statement disclosures to information noted in performance of the examination.	• Test updating system to assure that inventory transactions after the physical inventory are recorded on same basis as physical inventory was valued.
Classification. Determine whether inventory is properly classified as raw materials, work in process, or finished goods.	• Review results of physical inventory testing to assess accuracy of classification. • Review inventory compilation for proper classification of inventory.	• Test the updating system to assure that interim inventory transactions are properly recorded by class of inventory.
Cutoff. Determine whether all inventory items received or shipped before and after the reporting date are appropriately considered.	• Obtain receiving or shipping cutoff documentation at time of inventory. • Test recording of purchases and sales for a period before and after the reporting date.	• Test recording of purchases and sales for a period of time before and after the inventory date and before and after the reporting date.

The auditor should be aware in advance about the location and identity of the major dollar items of inventory. As part of his observation of inventory-taking, the auditor should tour the plant, be familiar with the inventory instructions, be aware of any inventory not stored on the premises, and indicate to the company areas of concern before the count begins. Members of the audit team assigned to the inventory observation should be familiar with the type of inventory and the procedures to be followed in case difficulties arise that require immediate resolution. Even if members of the audit team have previously participated in an observation of the company's inventory, it is usually beneficial for them to tour the facilities and refamiliarize themselves with the critical locations (e.g., shipping, manufacturing, receiving).

Control of counting procedures. To facilitate an accurate count of the inventory, the auditor should ascertain that:

- The inventory is arranged to allow for easy access and counting.
- No production is scheduled. If production must go on, the departments should be segregated from other areas.
- No movement of goods occurs during the count. If movement is necessary, the auditor and the company personnel in charge of the inventory must be previously informed so as to control the goods and avoid double counting.
- The counting teams take a systematic approach, and do not skip around their assigned area.
- Inventory tags (which often are electronic data processing (EDP) cards) are used sequentially and systematically in each department and throughout the inventory.
- Inventory tags are not removed (pulled) before the auditor observing the count or a designated employee gives clearance, area by area.
- All inventory tags are accounted for.
- Personnel are available to identify parts and units of work in process.

Although these procedures will not guarantee an accurate count, they will assure that the count is well organized.

Accuracy of counts. The auditor observes the company's count to determine whether the inventory instructions are being followed. Thus, the auditor need not record all test counts made to confirm that the physical count was accurate. To allow him to make subsequent tests of the compilation of the physical inventory, he should record some test counts made during the observation. Tying in these test counts enables the auditor to evaluate whether the physical counts have been properly included in the company's subsequent inventory compilation. The auditor should know which inventory items have a high value, because an error in the counting of these items is more likely to have a significant effect on the financial statements.

Condition of inventory. During the observation the auditor should be alert for merchandise that appears to be slow moving or of impaired value. An accumulation of rust or dust, for example, may indicate valueless or slow moving items, and a discussion with the counting teams may elicit the comment that the same items were counted in last year's inventory. While this is not conclusive evidence of diminished value, it may point to a need for follow-up work.

Stage of completion. Counts of raw materials and finished goods may be relatively easy to test, because their quantities and classification are readily ascertained; but work in process presents another problem. The last operation completed on the work in process inventory must be identified on the tags to assist in valuation after the count. If possible, the auditor should obtain a routing sheet or other document to confirm that the last operation performed is appropriately identified on the tag. To facilitate subsequent compilation procedures, some companies gather all the material necessary to complete the in-process inventory in one place. In such cases the last operation recorded applies only to the labor and overhead components of the work in process inventory.

Cutoff data. To assure an accurate physical inventory as well as the proper recording of purchases and sales, it is important that the company have satisfactory cutoff procedures. The shipping cutoff should assure that no order shipped after the inventory count is included as a sale in the period before the count, and that an item sold before the count has been removed from the inventory compilation. The auditor can test this during the observation by referring to sequentially numbered shipping documents and obtaining the number of the last shipping document before the count. He should also make sure that no orders preceding the last shipping advice number have yet to be shipped. This can be done by observing the shipping area, inquiring of the counting personnel, and later reviewing freight bills.

The receiving cutoff is equally important, so the auditor should test the appropriateness of the company's recording of receipts of merchandise to be included in the book inventory. The auditor should make sure that subsequent receipts have not been included in the inventory count or recorded as a purchase and related liability.

In addition to receiving and shipping cutoff numbers, the following information also should be obtained by the auditor at the physical inventory count:

- Goods returned by the company to the manufacturer
- Customer returns for rework or replacement
- Interplant shipments
- Goods on consignment or out for process

Inventories being held on consignment, being stored at outside locations, or being processed outside the plant should be confirmed. If significant, they should be observed in conjunction with the physical inventory.

Ownership. Although the physical inventory observation would tend to support the ownership of the inventory, it is possible that merchandise on hand includes inventory owned by others. Ownership of the inventory can be ascertained during the tests of the purchasing system, which will include a review of the documentation supporting the purchases. Response to requests for information from vendors regarding consigned goods will also support the ownership of inventory.

Use of specialists. If the auditor is unfamiliar with the identification or measurement of quantity or quality of the inventory (paintings, diamonds, drugs, coal piles, etc.), he may find it necessary to obtain the services of specialists in determining whether the inventory actually is as represented by the company. SAS

11 (AU 336) describes the appropriate procedures to be followed when using specialists.

Valuation. The main purpose of valuation procedures in the audit of inventory is to test the appropriateness of pricing of the physical inventory, or in the absence of a complete physical count to otherwise corroborate the recorded inventory balances. The alternative cost-flow assumptions and conventions for the valuation of inventory were discussed at the beginning of the chapter. While it is management's responsibility to decide which assumption the company will use, the auditor still must determine whether the method chosen is generally accepted and is properly and consistently applied.

Compilation—quantities. A significant portion of the audit of inventory involves a determination of whether the compilation of the physical inventory quantities is reasonably accurate and whether these quantities are properly priced. The information gathered during the physical inventory observation is used to check the accuracy of the recording of the physical counts. This is done by means of test counts and tag controls.

Some (or all, if the controls seem weak) of the *test counts* taken during the observation should be agreed to the inventory compilation, and any adjustments or differences should be satisfactorily reconciled.

In recording test counts for tracing to the compilation, the auditor makes his own record of the data on the inventory tag. In tracing the amounts to the compilation, the auditor must take particular care to make sure that the unit of measure used in the compilation is the same as that recorded in the inventory test count; for instance, counts based on numbers of units should not be recorded as pounds without appropriate conversions.

The auditor must satisfy himself concerning *tag control* (that is, the inventory compilation includes only tags actually used to record the inventory unit counts). He must be alert that no additional tags were written and that none of the tags used were omitted. This is done by comparing the tags included in the physical inventory compilation to the tag control prepared by the company and checked by the auditor at the time of the physical inventory. He should obtain satisfactory explanations for any differences between the control established during inventory taking and the tags used in the compilation.

Similar procedures should be applied if the company uses count sheets or their equivalent instead of tags or EDP cards.

Compilation—dollars. Probably the most time-consuming phase of the inventory audit involves testing clerical accuracy and the accuracy of unit costs used in pricing the inventory quantities. The test of clerical accuracy is a mechanical test of the various multiplications (e.g., units times price) and additions (e.g., summation of dollar amounts of the individual items) made to arrive at a total inventory figure, and is often done using computer software applied to a client's EDP-prepared compilation. The procedures for testing unit valuation, on the other hand, depend on the type of cost records maintained by the company—that is, on whether the company uses a standard cost system, the retail inventory method, or actual costs.

A *standard cost system* probably allows for the easiest testing of unit cost. When the company has standard costs for all units at all stages of production, it is a simple clerical task to trace these costs from the company's records to the inventory compilation. The audit scope for agreement of standard costs to those used in the inventory compilation should concentrate on large dollar items and include a selected number of smaller items. This selective scope will enable the auditor to cover a large dollar portion of the inventory with a relatively small sample size.

To substantiate that the standard costs approximate actual costs will require more work, for it involves a test of the company's standard cost system. The method of testing and the scope of items to be tested must be determined by the auditor, but these tests should include a review of cost buildups—material costs, labor costs, and manufacturing overhead—for a representative number of standards.

1. The *material* component of the inventory item is tested by a review of the engineering bill of materials (see Figure 14.12 for an example). Inspection of the inventory item at some point in the manufacturing process is necessary to determine that all components included on the standard cost card (see Figure 14.13 for an example) are used during production. Agreement of the material cost to suppliers' invoices will determine the relationship of the material costs used in the standards to actual cost. (If the company takes cash discounts, they should be regarded as a reduction of inventory standard costs. If freight costs are invoiced separately, they should be added to unit costs.)

2. The *labor* component is tested by a review of industrial engineering estimates, timecards, and pay rates. When labor represents a significant portion of the inventory cost, the auditor must review the payroll system and test the development of payroll data. Companies ordinarily use some type of individual timecard to account for each employee's time according to activity performed. After these timecards are completed, the total hours worked are paid for at an authorized wage rate. The total payroll is then apportioned to the inventory based on data collected from timecards, production records, and engineering time studies. The auditor should test the company's method of accumulating time by employee and by activity performed. He must also test the labor rates used and the method of allocating the total payroll (i.e., inventory-direct, inventory-overhead, and administrative).

3. *Manufacturing overhead* (burden) is tested by a review of the company's method of overhead allocation, to satisfy the auditor of its reasonableness and its consistency with the method used in prior periods. The auditor should also determine whether the components of overhead are appropriate and consistent with those of prior periods.

The degree of adequacy of the company's inventory control system will influence the auditor in deciding whether the review of the standard costs should be performed at an interim date or at period end. Although detailed tests of the standard cost components may indicate that the standard cost approximates actual cost, the auditor should review variances generated throughout the period, as well as those generated after the physical inventory, to determine whether to consider some of the variances for adjustment of the inventory and, if so, the proper method of applying the variances (to individual products or to the total inventory).

The *retail inventory method* depends heavily on properly accounting for the relationship of cost to retail selling price at acquisition and for subsequent adjustments of the retail selling price. The auditor should review the company's system for calculating the markup percentage and cost complement, and recompute these percent-

Part no.	Quantity	Description
1-123	2	½″ diameter rod–8″ long
2-234	3	½ horsepower motor
3-345	6	Electrical assemblies
4-456	2	Clamps

FIG. 14.12   Sample Bill of Materials for Motor Assembly

Part no.	Quantity	Unit material cost	Total cost
1-123	2	$1.50	$3.00
2-234	3	3.00	9.00
3-345	6	9.00	54.00
4-456	2	.50	1.00
Total material			67.00
Assembly labor			5.00
Burden application (200% of assembly labor dollars)			10.00
Standard cost			$82.00

FIG. 14.13   Sample Standard Cost Buildup for Motor Assembly

ages for major categories of inventory. The auditor should also perform tests to ascertain that the retail selling price used in the cost complement calculations is the actual selling price; this can be done be reference to company catalogs, sales slips, and prices shown on the merchandise. (See Chapter 29 for a further discussion of the retail method).

When a company uses *FIFO actual cost* for its compilation, the auditor must refer to current period invoices for the purchase of inventory materials and verify that actual costs have been properly applied. The review should also determine that current period invoices contain sufficient quantities to be compared with the quantities and prices used in the inventory compilation; if current purchase quantities are less than the quantities in inventory, the auditor must look to purchases in prior periods to determine whether the unit prices used in the inventory compilation reflect the actual cost of the inventoried quantities. (If ending inventory quantities for a given item exceed the aggregate quantity of that item purchased during the current year, this is a signal to the auditor that there may be excess or obsolete inventory on hand.)

To test labor and overhead costs, the audit procedures previously described for use with a standard cost system may be used with an actual cost system.

If the company uses *LIFO actual cost,* the auditor must review the application of prior period costs to inventory quantities and make sure that adjustments of LIFO layers resulting from inventory increments or decrements (liquidations) are properly done. If the company uses a unit cost LIFO approach and the quantities of individual items have not increased since the end of the preceding fiscal year, the auditor has no need to refer to current period invoices to review the application of historical costs; but he should examine these invoices as part of his lower-of-cost-or-market evaluation, and should test the company's supplemental disclosure of the inventory at FIFO or replacement cost. If the company uses some form of index approach for the determination of LIFO cost, the auditor must review the application of both current and prior-period unit costs, and test the mathematical accuracy and consistency of the approach used. (See the appendix to this chapter for illustrations of dollar value calculations.)

If a liquidation occurs under LIFO, the auditor must be satisfied that the most recent layer costs are the first ones removed in determining the aggregate LIFO cost of the ending inventory. Further, if a LIFO liquidation occurs and the company must disclose its income effect, the auditor should make sure it has been properly calculated.

Payroll and personnel. An auditor must rely heavily on the internal controls of a company in the area of payroll. There is generally a segregation of duties between the personnel function (hiring, maintenance of employee records, and terminations) and the payroll function (timekeeping, preparation of payroll, and payments). This segregation is imposed principally to guard against fictitious employees being added to the payroll. There often is a further segregation of duties within the payroll function between timekeeping, payroll preparation, and distribution of payroll checks, to avoid fictitious or erroneous payments.

The auditor should review hiring practices, concentrating on controls used to assure that only real employees are placed on the payroll. Audit procedures may include a search for "ghosts" (nonexistent employees) by observing the distribution of payroll checks and having employees present identification in order to receive their checks; a review of the control over timecards; and a determination that manufacturing department heads are aware of the identities of all employees who are charged to their departments.

These procedures, coupled with clerical tests of the mechanical accuracy of the payroll preparation, provide the auditor with a basis to evaluate the company's determination of payroll costs and its departmental allocation. For payroll costs charged to inventory, the auditor must review the cost allocation approach to determine that it is reasonable. This will include a review of the methods used to assign labor to inventory (e.g., engineering studies and job cost tickets) and a test of the manner in which the labor is valued (actual cost or standard cost).

For a thorough discussion of the audit of payroll and personnel, see Chapter 16 of *Auditing—An Integrated Approach* (Arens and Loebbecke, 1984).

Inventory Valuation Allowances. The auditor must make sure that the company has consistently followed an appropriate policy in establishing valuation allowances for inventories whose market is lower than cost and for obsolete or excess inventory quantities. Such allowances are more commonly used than direct reductions of unit values in a standard cost system, as this permits dollar controls to be maintained at regular standard cost. Sufficient tests must be performed to assure that the preestablished company policy is appropriate and is being applied accurately. Such tests include review of past product turnover, future engineering plans, and sales forecasts. (Note that most valuation allowances may not be tax deductible, as discussed in the earlier section "Excess and Obsolete Inventory.")

Reconciliation of Book Inventory to Physical Inventory. Typically, the physical inventory compilation total differs from the amount of inventory recorded on the general ledger. The company should find the reasons for this difference if it is more than negligible, and the auditor should review these reasons to assure that they make sense and that all the necessary adjustments are made to present the inventory in conformity with GAAP in the financial statements.

The auditor should review and understand the nature of differences in the adjustment of book inventory to physical inventory—transaction costing errors, actual shrinkage, and so on—to gain a better understanding of the inventory system. And if the inventory was taken as of a date other than year end, this review will assist in determining whether the client has made appropriate adjustments in the update period.

Inventory Update. The auditor should review the transactions recorded during the period from the count date to the reporting date, testing the standard costs to assure they are the same as those used to price the physical inventory. Otherwise the ending inventory will include unreported variances, and it will be difficult to determine the adjustment required so that the inventory approximates historical cost. If the auditor has performed tests of controls throughout the year and has established the reliability of the controls, he can review the updated inventory by agreeing the individual general ledger entries to books of original entry, and he may not need to perform other detailed tests of these items. If any material intervening items look unusual compared with similar items noted in prior periods, he should obtain satisfactory explanations for them.

If the adjustment of the book inventory to physical inventory at an interim date is attributed to physical shrinkage or to some problem in the accounting system that remains uncorrected (e.g., failure to report the use of substitute materials), the auditor must be satisfied that the company has made adequate provision for the probable recurrence of similar events between the date of the physical inventory and year end.

Typically, a company will change its standard costs at the time the physical inventory is counted, and the inventory is compiled using both the old and the new standard costs. The old standard cost is used to compare the compilation amount to the accumulated inventory totals in the general ledger; this comparison provides the basis for determining how well the standard cost system performed. When the standard costs are changed at the time of an interim inventory, the auditor should review the company's system to ascertain that all transactions after the change use the new standards rather than the old ones.

The auditor must also become satisfied that the aggregate difference between old and new standards is properly considered in determining whether standard costs at year end approximate historical costs. The audit approach is similar to that used to review the reallocation of variances to ending inventory valued at standard cost.

Effective Use of Analytical Review. At its current state of development, analytical review either provides a challenge to, or confirmation of, the auditor's understanding of the client's environment and its accounting and control systems. Such analysis helps identify areas where more work appears warranted. The usefulness of analytical review is enhanced where detailed information and complementary systems exist (such as well-designed budgets; statistical operating data, e.g., units produced, backlog, or scrap reports; or industry data and competitor information). In such circumstances, analytical review can provide a modicum of direct audit assurance that materials errors (individually or in the aggregate) are not present. However, because the available date is so varied among companies, it is not possbile to generalize on the effectiveness of analytical review.

Analytical review procedures applied to the inventory account are primarily used in testing inventory pricing, and in efforts to detect misclassification errors arising from improper inclusion of costs in or exclusion of costs from overhead. A secondary use of analytical review is to provide a focus to determine if more work is needed in relation to obsolete inventory, inventory shrinkage, and cutoff. Note that analytical review contributes little to the audit objectives related to existence and ownership; these objectives are achieved by other procedures described earlier.

The following procedures each target one or more of the primary or secondary uses of analytical review procedures. The procedures should be completed for each major group of related products, or on a product line basis if feasible.

Inventory turnover (i.e., the ratio of cost of goods sold to average inventory). This ratio measures the relationship between inventory and sales, on the premise that a given volume of sales requires a certain level of inventory. This relationship will differ across industries, and may differ owing to management policy as influenced by seasonal factors, the availability of supply, and so forth.

The turnover ratio can be compared over time or with the industry average. A high ratio is favorable since it should indicate efficient inventory policies. However, a high ratio might reflect unrecorded inventory. A low ratio might indicate an audit problem such as obsolete or otherwise unsaleable inventory, or an overstated inventory valuation.

Failure to make appropriate write-downs of obsolete and unsalable items could have the effect of reducing the ability of the turnover ratio to detect error or theft. In this case, the high inventory value, including obsolete and unsalable items, could mask shortages in the faster moving items. Thus, consideration of inventory write-down policy and a related analysis of shrinkage rates are a necessary adjunct to the proper analysis of inventory turnover.

Raw materials inventory turnover (i.e., the ratio of raw materials issued in production to average raw materials inventory). For a manufacturing company, this additional turnover ratio can be computed. If relatively low, it might indicate an overstocking or overvaluation of raw materials, or the presence of unusable materials.

Shrinkage ratio (i.e., the ratio of inventory write-downs to total inventory). This ratio is used to highlight unusual write-downs, and should be analyzed in conjunction with the turnover ratios as described earlier.

Cost of goods sold budget analysis. If available, the current year's budgeted cost of goods sold can be compared to book, and next year's budget can be used to anticipate the inventory turnover for the coming year. Large differences between budget and actual need explanation. The anticipated turnover for next year can be compared to this year's turnover and the industry average to determine its reasonableness.

Raw materials budgeted usage analysis. If available, the current year's budgeted raw materials usage can be compared to actual usage, and next year's budgeted usage can be used to anticipate the raw materials turnover for the coming year.

Analysis of the relationship between materials, labor, and overhead to total product cost. On either a unit cost or total manufacturing cost, these three ratios can be used to analyze the composition of product costs over time and relative to the industry average. This analysis can be used to spot the improper classification of cost items, especially in the overhead component. Costs such as selling and marketing expenses and "learning curve" costs may be improperly included in overhead. Two computational approaches might be used to check the reasonableness of the overall inventory value:

1. *Multiply average unit prices by inventory units on hand* at the end of year to estimate the end of year inventory value.
2. *Roll forward* of the beginning of year inventory balance plus purchases less cost of sales during the year to estimate the end of year inventory balance.

Comparison of the inventory turnover ratio and associated ratios described previously, over time or to industry averages, is subject to some important qualifications. Comparison may not be possible for one or more of the following reasons:

• Differences in accounting methods for valuation of inventory affect the comparability of ratios. All or some portion of inventories may be valued by different methods across an industry, or may change over time for a particular inventory. For this reason, the turnover ratios and industry averages must be evaluated carefully. Do they reflect one method, or some mix of methods, for the included inventories?

• Inventory turnover ratios differ substantially among industries. Significant differences in the nature of production processes lead naturally to different turnover ratios. Thus, the auditor must be confident that a turnover ratio is compared with the proper industry average.

• A properly conceived and implemented management policy may dictate inventory levels different from the past or from those levels reflected in average industry turnover figures. Such factors as the availability of supply, seasonal fluctuations in demand, temporary price fluctuations, and storage costs all may be involved in the management of inventory levels.

Interrelationship with Other Audit Work. The inventory audit work is directly related to work in cash, payables, and purchases; and the cost of sales work is likewise related to the audit of revenue and receivables. (See Chapters 12 and 13, respectively.) A well-planned audit will recognize and take advantage of these interrelationships in design of the audit procedures.

Auditor's Use of Computers. Most companies use EDP to control and compile their inventories. Thus, the auditor should consider using the computer himself to assist in the audit of numerous aspects of the inventory, for instance:

- Testing clerical accuracy
- Tracing in test counts
- Accounting for inventory tags used
- Identifying and aggregating dollar concentrations of inventory
- Aging the inventory (if the company uses stock numbers or codes that make this practical)
- Identifying overstock conditions
- Performing lower-of-cost-or-market tests
- Selecting perpetual inventory items for test counting

As with all audit procedures, the auditor must evaluate whether using the computer is the most cost-effective method. For example, while the company's inventory may be compiled on a computer, it may consist of so few items as to make automated testing more expensive than manual testing. On the other hand, use of the computer can often add to the efficiency of a large inventory audit. In fact, in some circumstances the auditor may decide that although the company did not use a computer to compile the inventory, the most efficient audit approach requires entering the inventory data onto a computer file for analysis and testing. (See Chapter 10 for a discussion of auditing in an EDP environment.)

Other Audit Areas

Inventory at Public Warehouses. The auditor is expected to physically observe at least a portion of the inventory, either when an annual physical inventory is taken or alternatively by making test counts at other times and comparing them to the perpetual records (AU 331.09–.13). As to inventories held at public warehouses, the auditing of such inventory quantities is most often handled through confirmation, with additional work where amounts are material (AU 331.14).

The additional work might include:

1. Review and test the client's control procedures for investigating the warehouseman and evaluating the warehouseman's performance.
2. Obtain an independent accountant's report on the warehouseman's control system over custody of goods and, if applicable, pledging of receipts.
3. Apply alternative procedures at the warehouse to gain reasonable assurance that system information received from the warehouseman is reliable.
4. Observe physical counts of the goods, if practicable and reasonable.
5. If warehouse receipts have been pledged as collateral, confirm with lenders pertinent details of the pledged receipts (on a test basis, if appropriate).

A 1966 AICPA special report, *Public Warehouses—Controls and Auditing Procedures for Goods Held* (AU 901), deals with the internal controls at the warehouse, how such businesses operate, and what the auditors of the warehouse and of the owner of the goods might do.

Outside Inventory Services. Many companies, especially retailers, engage outside inventory services to perform their physical inventory counts and compilation procedures. Many of these services do not use the typical inventory tag system, but instead use computers and tape recorders to accumulate the inventory values without identifying specific items. Typically, these services will submit an inventory certificate showing the amount of inventory by class. If there are no inventory tags for the auditor to test, he must understand the procedures followed by the service and must observe the actual taking of the counts. He may also have to accumulate totals of inventory for selected test areas and agree these to totals reported by the service.

Detailed tests of the compilation may prove difficult, but if the outside inventory service is an independent contractor, the auditor should recognize that probably fewer tests of its compilation are necessary than would be the case for a compilation done by the company itself. Of course, the auditor must determine that the service is truly independent of the company, just as he would in employing the services of a specialist (AU 336).

Both the auditor and the company should review adjustments of book inventory to physical inventory to see if the adjustment appears reasonable in view of current facts and historical inventory levels. Typically, a given retail unit has a known range of inventory capacity. Results that are out of line for the location or the industry in general should be challenged, and perhaps a recount of the inventory should be performed.

Alternative Procedures for Opening Inventories. On a new engagement, the auditor usually is engaged after the beginning of the year. To issue an unqualifed opinion on the income statement and statement of cash flows, he will need to be satisfied with the opening inventory balance.

If the prior year was reported on by another auditor, the successor auditor should discuss the results of the prior examination with the previous auditor and review his working papers to become satisfied with the opening inventory balance. If this is not feasible or if no other auditor observed the prior year's inventory, the current auditor will devise other procedures to test the opening inventory balance. The nature and the extent of these tests will depend on the company's inventory system. If the system proves to be reliable, the auditor may be able to work back from the results of the current year's observation to the end of the prior year.

If the company's internal control structure is not sufficiently reliable, the auditor may not be able to perform satisfactory alternative procedures and may have to disclaim an opinion on the current year's statements of income and cash flows. This type of scope limitation disclaimer is discussed in Chapter 11.

Nonsubstantive LIFO Transactions. LIFO presents some unique audit questions since it is possible for a company to influence its earnings significantly by managing its LIFO inventories. Maintaining its LIFO layers for tax purposes so as to forestall large tax payments on the earnings results of inventory liquidations may also be a reason for a company to manage its LIFO inventory. Consequently, significant purchases or sales of inventory may be consummated near the end of the fiscal year. By themselves, these transactions do not present any special problem for recording inventories or cost of sales (although they may require footnote disclosure), but the auditor should review them, along with transactions after year end, to assure that the purchases or sales were not accommodation transactions made only to be later reversed or rescinded.

The auditor must be concerned with substance, not form. Accommodation transactions predicated on buy-back or sell-back of the inventory after year end may in substance be a loan of the inventory and not a transfer of the ownership risks.

In some such transactions, the inventory never even moves, because the sole purpose of the transaction is simply to attempt to qualify the transaction for tax purposes by establishing that the buyer is "at risk," if even for a brief period.

Earlier in this chapter, it was noted that the SEC has come down hard on LIFO transactions that lack substance. The auditor should take special care, therefore, when encountering potential problems in this area.

Auditing Product Warranty Costs. The auditing of product warranties entails determining the existence of the warranty obligation, and obtaining satisfaction as to the valuation and recording of the estimated liability. Normally, existence is determined by reading sales agreements; however, implicit warranties are often determined by observation of common industry practice, company practice, or by legal opinion. Valuation of the estimated liability is governed by SFAS 5 (C59.130–.131), and is normally based on past history, which should be updated for the most recent experience and for any changes in current conditions.

Appendix 14   PRICING OF ENDING INVENTORY: A COMPREHENSIVE EXAMPLE

Inventory can be priced in various ways when different cost-flow assumptions and costing conventions are used. This appendix provides an example illustrating the results of applying the different approaches to the same set of facts.

Assumptions

The company was formed in December, 19X0.

The only inventory transaction in 19X0 was the acquisition of inventory on December 15, 19X0. None of it was sold by December 31, 19X0.

The company's fiscal year ends December 31.

Ending inventory units
December 31, 19X0		200
December 31, 19X1, by purchase date:		
March 5, 19X1	200	
June 4, 19X1	50	
October 9, 19X1	100	350

Standard cost
During 19X0	$ .90/unit
During 19X1	1.10/unit

Purchase history

Date of purchase	Units	Purchase cost/unit	Extended cost	Sales price/unit	Extended selling price
December 15, 19X0	200	$ .90	$ 180	$1.10	$ 220
February 26, 19X1	300	1.00	300	1.20	360
March 5, 19X1	400	1.10	440	1.30	520
June 4, 19X1	500	1.20	600	1.40	700
October 9, 19X1	100	1.30	130	1.50	150
For the year	1,300	1.131 Avg.	$1,470		$1,730
Available for sale	1,500	$1.10 Avg.	$1,650		
Less sales	1,150				
Ending inventory	350				

APPLICATION OF METHODS

Specific Identification

Date acquired	Units on hand	Purchase cost/unit	Inventory cost
March 5, 19X1	200	$1.10	$220
June 4, 19X1	50	1.20	60
October 9, 19X1	100	1.30	130
	350		$410

FIFO

Date acquired	Units on hand	Purchase cost/unit	Inventory cost
October 9, 19X1	100	$1.30	$130
June 4, 19X1	250	1.20	300
	350		$430

Average Cost for Year

		Inventory cost
350 Units at $1.131/ Unit		$396

Retail Method

	Cost	Retail	Cost/retail	Inventory cost
Beginning inventory	$ 180	$ 220		
Purchases	1,470	1,730		
	1,650	1,950		
Markups	—	45[2]		
Available for sale	$1,650	$1,995	.827	
Ending inventory at retail (350 units at $1.50)			$525	
Ratio of cost to retail			.827	$434

LIFO

Earliest Purchase Price on Layer Year

Date acquired	Units on hand	Purchase cost/unit	Inventory cost
December 15, 19X0	200	$ .90	$180
February 26, 19X1	150	1.00	150
	350		$330

Average Purchase Cost for Year

Year acquired	Units on hand	Purchase cost/unit	Inventory cost
19X0	200	$ .90	$180
19X1	150	1.131	170
	350		$350

Latest Purchase Price by Layer Year

The theoretical approach, in which cost is determined using the most recent acquisitions that total to the ending quantity, produces these results:

	Units on hand	Purchase cost/unit	Inventory cost
Base layer	200	$ .90	$180
Current-year increment in terms of latest acquisitions Acquired:			
October 9, 19X1	100	1.30	130
June 4, 19X1	50	1.20	60
	350		$370

---

[2] For purposes of this example, markups are presumed to have been made at year-end and represent an additional $.10 markup on the 50 units purchased June 4, 19X1, and an additional $.20 markup on the 200 units purchased March 5, 19X1, which are unsold at December 31, 19X1.

The approach used in practice, in which cost is determined using the last acquisition in the period, produces these results:

	Units on hand	Purchase cost/unit	Inventory cost
Base layer	200	$ .90	$180
Current-year increment based on last acquisition (October 9, 19X1 cost per unit)	150	1.30	195
	350		$375

Dollar Value LIFO

Earliest Purchase Price

		Inventory cost
Ending inventory December 31, 19X1, at earliest cost incurred in current year (350 units at $1.00)	$ 350	
Divide by ratio of current costs to base costs (350 × $1.00/350 × $.90)	1.111	
Inventory in base-year dollars	315	
Subtract base-year inventory	180	$ 180
Increment in base-year dollars	135	
Multiply by ratio of current costs to base-year costs	1.111	
Increment in current-year dollars		150
		$ 330

Average Purchase Price

		Inventory cost
Ending inventory December 31, 19X1, at average current cost incurred in current year (350 units at $1.131)	$ 396	
Divide by ratio of average current costs to base-year costs (350 × $1.131/350 × $.90)	1.257	
Inventory in base-year dollars	315	
Subtract base-year inventory	180	$ 180
Increment in base-year dollars	135	
Multiply by ratio of average current costs to base-year costs	1.257	170
		$ 350

Latest Purchase Price by Layer Year

In the theoretical approach, the current cost of ending inventory is determined on a FIFO basis using the most recent acquisition costs.

		Inventory cost
Ending inventory December 31, 19X1, at FIFO (see FIFO example)	$ 430	
Divide by ratio of inventory at FIFO cost to inventory at base-year costs $\left(\dfrac{\$430}{350 \text{ units} \times \$.90/\text{unit}}\right)$	1.365	
Inventory in base-year dollars	315	
Subtract base-year inventory	180	$ 180
Increment in base-year dollars	135	
Multiply by ratio of FIFO cost to base-year costs	1.365	184
		$ 364

In the practical approach, the current cost of ending inventory is determined on the basis of the last acquisition in the period.

		Inventory cost
Ending inventory December 31, 19X1, at latest purchase cost incurred in current year (350 units at $1.30)	$ 455	
Divide by ratio of latest current-year costs to base-year costs (350 × $1.30/350 × $.90)	1.444	
Inventory in base-year dollars	315	
Subtract base-year inventory	180	$ 180
Increment in base-year dollars	135	
Multiply by ratio of latest current-year costs to base-year costs	1.444	195
		$ 375

Retail LIFO

	Retail	Inventory cost
December 31, 19X1 inventory at retail (350 units at $1.50/unit)	$ 525	
Divide by index reflecting effect of inflation from beginning to end of year.[3]	1.364	
Inventory at base-year retail	385	
Subtract base-year inventory retail (200 units at $1.10/unit)	220	$ 180
Increment in base-year retail dollars	165	
Multiply by inflation index to convert to current-year retail	1.364	
	225	
Multiply by ratio of cost to selling price of aggregate of current-year purchases (adjusted for additional markups)	.828	186
		$ 366

Standard Cost

The analysis of purchase variances for the year is as follows:

		Cost		Variance—Standard Over or (Under) Actual	
Purchase date	Units purchased	Actual	Standard	Per unit	Aggregate
February 26, 19X1	300	$1.00	$1.10	.10	$ 30
March 5, 19X1	400	1.10	1.10	—	—
June 4, 19X1	500	1.20	1.10	(.10)	(50)
October 9, 19X1	100	1.30	1.10	(.20)	(20)
	1,300				$(40)

[3] For purposes of this example, the index is based on the ratio of the ending per-unit selling price to the beginning per-unit selling price, or $1.50/$1.10. In a typical situation the company will use an externally generated index, such as the Bureau of Labor Statistics Index.

Average cost, assuming variance allocated on the basis of inventory turnover, is computed as follows:

		Inventory cost
Ending inventory at standard cost (350 units at $1.10/unit)		$385
Adjust standard to actual to reflect the fact that for the year standard cost was less than actual:		
Unfavorable purchase price variance	$40	
Multiply by ratio of ending inventory at standard to purchases at standard		
$\left(\dfrac{\$385}{1{,}300\ \text{units} \times \$1.10/\text{unit}}\right)$	.269	11
		$396

The LIFO cost is computed as shown below, using average cost of purchases for the year determined by adjusting standard cost of purchases by purchase price variances. It would also be possible to use the earliest or latest purchase price election with a standard cost system. This would be done by allocating the variances on the basis of when they were generated and recalculating the ratio of current cost to base-year cost.

		Inventory cost
Ending inventory December 31, 19X1, at standard (350 units at $1.10/unit)	$385	
Adjust standard to actual (see average cost example above)	11	
Ending inventory at current-year cost	396	
Divide by ratio of current cost to base-year dollars		
$\left(\dfrac{\$396}{350\ \text{units} \times \$.90/\text{unit}}\right)$	1.257	
Inventory in base-year dollars	315	
Subtract base-year inventory	180	$180
Increment in base-year dollars	135	
Multiply by ratio of current cost to base-year dollars	1.257	170
		$350

15

Plant, Equipment, and Other Assets

CAPITAL ASSET CYCLE

Investments in property, plant, and equipment (PP&E)—those long-lived tangible assets used for the production of other goods and services—often are a substantial portion of the total assets of many companies. Acquisition, control, expiration of assigned carrying amounts, and disposal are the transactions that make up the capital asset cycle. These phases are highlighted briefly in the following sections and then discussed in greater detail in the accounting and auditing sections that constitute the remainder of the chapter.

The acquisition of PPE may require a major use of funds and may represent a commitment for a relatively long period of time. Accordingly, acquisition is generally the object of long-term decision making, and major acquisitions must be ratified by the board of directors in most larger companies.

Capital Budgeting

The planning, analysis, evaluation, and final decision regarding major expenditures for long-term investments and their financing are encompassed in *capital budgeting*. Major investments in PPE are typical examples, but major research and development or advertising programs may also call for similar budgeting approaches.

A decision to make a capital expenditure depends primarily on an assessment of the projected cash flows from additional revenues, cost savings, or a combination thereof from the asset that may be acquired.

Alternative means of achieving a business objective must be considered, and incremental cash flow calculations will have to be made sequentially rather than simply compared to the present condition. In addition, the attribution of cash inflows to particular decisions may be difficult, and the problem of uncertainty is great where cash flows over a period of several years must be estimated. In fact, future estimates can only accurately be described by probability distributions, while most of the techniques used in present value analysis are applied to single point estimates. Various approaches, called *return-on-investment techniques*, are used. They include the (1) *payback*, (2) *unadjusted rate of return*, and (3) *internal rate of return* methods.

The payback method is a simple calculation that discloses how long it will take to recoup the cash outlay on an after-tax basis. The unadjusted rate of return is determined by dividing the estimated annual cash flow by the average investment, that is, the cost plus salvage value divided by two. Neither of these two methods give recognition to the time value of money, and are therefore less useful than the internal rate of return (IRR), under which all estimated cash flows are time-valued in relation to the initial outlay. The result is a constant rate that considers both timing and amount of future cash flows. This is important, because as cash flows are estimated into the more distant future (when they will be less predictable), their effect on the IRR decreases in significance.

When doing rate-of-return computations, keep in mind that these are means of quantifying estimates (that by definition will not be precise) and necessarily include making assumptions regarding qualitative factors, such as whether the utility of the asset can be sustained under various economic scenarios.

Alternatives to Acquisition for Cash

While it is common to acquire PPE assets for cash, many alternatives exist and a few are mentioned below.

Lease Financing. An important alternative to buying and owning assets is leasing them, either by taking a lease from the original owner of the asset or by purchasing the asset, selling it, and leasing it back from the buyer. To choose between leasing or buying, company management must compare the cost and feasibility of leasing with the cost and feasibility of ownership. For further discussion of leasing of assets, see Chapter 19.

Self-Construction. Another possibility in the acquisition of a capital asset is for the company itself to build the asset. The costs assigned to self-constructed assets are handled in much the same way as those for purchased assets: all the costs of putting the asset into the condition and location for use are capitalized.

Purchase Business Combinations. Long-lived assets may also be acquired through a purchase business combination. Briefly, the carrying amount applied to the assets acquired through a purchase business combination depends on the allocation of the total cost of the purchased business to the individual assets and liabilities included in it. Chapter 24 provides a description of business combinations and discusses accounting for assets acquired in that way.

Depreciation

Because assets have limited lives it is necessary to allocate a portion of their costs to each period over their useful lives. The general approach to allocation is called depreciation, defined in ARB 43 as

> a system of accounting that aims to distribute the cost or other basic value of tangible capital assets, less salvage value (if any), over the estimated useful life of the unit (which may be a group of assets) in a systematic and rational manner. It is a process of allocation, not of valuation. [D40.401]
>
> *Depreciation for the year* is the portion of the total charge under such a system that is allocated to the year. Although the allocation may properly take into account occurrences

during the year, it is not intended to be a measurement of the effect of all such occurrences. [AICPA, 1953]

Although depreciation can be simply described, few topics in accounting have been as controversial. Some of the factors giving rise to dispute are the costs to be included in the depreciable amount, estimation of useful life and salvage value, assessment of obsolescence, varying methods of allocating depreciation to product costs, treatment of constant dollar and current cost changes, and appreciation of property values.

Since depreciation is not a means of asset valuation but a process of cost allocation, it is conceptually an unreliable indicator of asset expiration. The objective of this process of allocation is basically to distribute the cost, less salvage value, over the estimated useful life of the asset. However, to estimate the useful life and salvage value of an asset, management must predict the effects of numerous economic and physical factors.

Projections of future events always involve uncertainties. In some cases the estimated physical life can be based on past experience with similar assets, but in other cases there is no past history. Also, unforeseen events, such as the sudden obsolescence of an asset due to revolutionary changes in technology, unsalability of the goods being produced due to changes in fashion, losses resulting from governmental edict, or catastrophic destruction, may end an asset's usefulness long before the end of its originally estimated useful life. On the other hand, an asset may appreciate in value rather than depreciate. For example, a building may double in value simply because it stands in an area that has become a prime business location.

Management is responsible for estimating useful lives that reflect economic circumstances as closely as possible. Because of the uncertainties of estimation, many companies simply adopt the useful lives published by the IRS, since these guidelines purport to reflect the actual experience of taxpayers. But situations that make a particular guideline unrealistic should not be ignored. For example, if a machine is purchased to produce goods that will be obsolete in five years and the machine will have no other useful purpose after that time, it should have an estimated economic life of five years even though its physical life might well be ten years.

The estimation of salvage value gives rise to similar problems. Some companies ignore salvage value if it is considered immaterial to the cost of the asset. Others, for the sake of simplicity, assume it to be a certain percentage of the cost of the asset. Estimates of salvage value should be based on conditions at the time of the purchase of the asset. However, if such estimates change materially over time, adjustments to depreciation expense and accumulated depreciation should be made.

Disposal

The final transaction in the capital asset cycle is disposal. Ultimately, property assets will be retired, either by sale, exchange, abandonment, or scrapping. If detailed records of property, plant, and equipment have been maintained, the accounting treatment for disposals is well defined. Since depreciation is merely an allocation of the cost of the asset, and the system is not intended to establish "value," gain or loss on disposal of the asset will probably occur.

FINANCIAL ACCOUNTING AND REPORTING CONSIDERATIONS

The objective of accounting for PPE is to report these assets at cost less an allowance for depreciation and to allocate cost over the useful lives of the assets. An important quality for capitalization and depreciation criteria is consistency. Whatever methods are chosen, they should be consistently applied.

Acquisition

PPE may be acquired through purchase (with or without trade-ins), self-construction, leasing, donation, or a business combination. The accounting for each type of acquisition other than through lease is described below. Leasing is discussed in Chapter 19.

Criteria for Capitalization. An asset should be capitalized if it is expected to be useful for more than the current period. It is usually not difficult to determine whether a particular asset should be capitalized or expensed. For some items (e.g., portable tools), however, the decision may be less obvious, so a company should establish rules that define the capitalization criteria. One expedient guideline for many companies is the amount of the expenditure: assets costing less than a specified amount, say $500, are expensed; those costing more are capitalized.

In some cases it may not be advisable to capitalize an item, even if it meets these criteria, because it is difficult to control. With small tools, for example, it may be better practice simply to record the item as a current expense.

Purchase for Cash. Capital assets should be recorded at cost plus any expenditures necessary to place those assets in "a ready for use" condition. Costs of acquisition thus include not only the invoice price but also installation, freight, testing, legal fees to establish title, and any other costs of putting the asset in the condition and location for use. Purchase discounts, including any allowance in lieu of a trade-in, should be applied to reduce the cost. In the case of land, demolition costs of a preexisting structure may properly be included in the land acquisition cost.

Purchase on Contract. Costs of properties acquired under a conditional sale or other installment contract should include the same basic elements as those for cash purchases. However, interest charges included in the purchase payments are not part of the cost of the asset; they should be accrued as interest expense. If the installment contract does not state the interest and the principal separately, a determination of the two parts should be made.

Generally speaking, the cost of the asset should approximate the present value of the payments required, using the stated interest rate if that rate is reasonable, or the current interest rate used for similar borrowings if the stated rate is unreasonably high or low. The amount included in the face value of a note or installment payable that is in excess of the present value of the payments is interest and should be recorded in accordance with APB 21, *Interest on Receivables and Payables* (I69).

Basket Purchase. If assets are purchased in groups (frequently called a *basket purchase*), the total purchase cost should be allocated among the individual assets in the group on the basis of their respective fair values. If the aggregate of the fair values is greater than the total cost, the cost should be allocated proportionately.

For example, if three assets are purchased together for $56,000 and the fair value of the three assets at time of purchase is $16,560, $48,240, and $7,200, respectively, the cost would be allocated as follows:

	Fair value	Proportion	Cost allocation
Asset A	$16,560	23%	$12,880
Asset B	48,240	67%	37,520
Asset C	7,200	10%	5,600
	$72,000	100%	$56,000

Purchase for Equity Securities. If assets are acquired through a business combination that meets all the conditions for a pooling of interests, the recorded historical cost of the assets of the separate companies becomes the recorded amount in the combined corporation. If, however, the acquisition is treated as a purchase for accounting purposes, the recording of the acquisition would follow the rules in APB 16, *Business Combinations* (B50); that is, assets acquired by exchanging equity securities are still recorded at the purchaser's cost. Cost in this situation is usually defined as the fair value of the assets acquired. Business combinations are discussed in more detail in Chapter 23.

If a company's equity securities are used to pay for capital assets apart from a business combination, the amount that would have been obtained from a sale of the securities for cash should be determined. If that is not possible, the fair value of the asset should be used. Par or stated value of the security is not an acceptable valuation. Note, however, that the SEC requires that nonmonetary assets obtained from promoters or shareholders should be valued at the transferor's historical cost (SAB 48, Topic 5.G).

Trade-Ins. When certain types of depreciable assets (such as automobiles or machinery) are purchased, part of the consideration is frequently the fair value of a similar asset being traded in. The trade-in allowance granted by the seller usually differs from the net carrying amount of the old asset. If greater, it would appear that a profit is being realilzed on the exchange, but the seller may also have an inflated list price for the new asset. Therefore, other reasonably objective evidence of a profit is required to account for the trade-in as if it were an unrelated asset disposal.

Because it is often difficult to separately determine the reasonableness of the purchase price and the trade-in allowance, the cost of the new asset is commonly recorded at the amount of the monetary consideration paid plus the unexpired cost of the trade-in surrendered.

Suppose, for example, that a delivery van was acquired four years ago at a cost of $10,000 and depreciated on a straight-line basis over an estimated useful life of five years. Now the old van is traded in for a new model having a list price of $12,000, but the dealer allows a trade-in value of $2,400 for the old van. The cost of the new van would be computed as follows:

Cost of old van	$10,000
Less accumulated depreciation ($2,000 × 4)	8,000
Unexpired cost of trade-in	2,000
Monetary consideration paid for new van ($12,000 − $2,400)	9,600
Recorded cost of new van	$11,600

However, if a gain or loss is clearly indicated, the entire gain or loss on the exchange should be recognized. Thus, if independent appraisals determined that the net realizable value of the old van is $2,500, a gain of $500 (the difference between that value and the net carrying amount) should be recognized. The new van would then have a cost of $12,100 (cash paid of $9,600 plus market value of old van of $2,500).

The cost and accumulated depreciation of an asset traded in should be removed from the accounts in conjunction with recording the acquisition cost of the new asset.

Self-Construction. The principle for recording costs of self-constructed plant and equipment is similar to that for purchased assets: record the cost to place the assets in condition and location for use. The practical problems in determining self-construction costs, however, are more like those encountered in determining the cost of goods manufactured for sale. Costs of material and direct labor are usually readily identified, but the treatment of indirect overhead and its apportionment between construction activity and the enterprise's normal production operations are not so simple in companies that do not normally construct their own assets. Accordingly, the extent of deductibility of overhead costs for income tax purposes during a period of self-construction often has a considerable influence on the allocation approach used for financial accounting. See Chapter 14 for a discussion of the IRS capitalization rules for costs incurred in the manufacture or construction of property.

Capitalization of interest is another issue in accumulating costs of a self-constructed asset. Most companies (other than public utilities) have traditionally treated interest as a period expense. Other nonutility companies have capitalized interest but have limited it to interest incurred during the construction period on amounts borrowed specifically for construction purposes. (Utilities also capitalize an allowance for equity funds; see Chapter 33).

SFAS 34, *Capitalization of Interest Cost* (I67.105), requires capitalization of interest cost as part of the historical cost of "assets that are constructed or otherwise produced for an enterprise's own use (including assets constructed or produced for the enterprise by others for which deposits or progress payments have been made)." The rate to be used for capitalization may be ascertained in this order (I67.110): (1) the rate of specific borrowings associated with the asset and (2) if borrowings are not specific, for the asset, or the asset exceeds specific borrowings therefor, a weighted average of rates applicable to other appropriate borrowings. Alternatively, a company may use a weighted average of rates of all appropriate borrowings regardless of specific borrowings incurred to finance the asset. Interest capitalized may not exceed total interest costs for any period, nor is imputing interest cost to equity funds permitted for other than utilities. (See Chapter 18 for a further discussion of interest capitalization).

Additions and Betterments to Existing Assets. There are fine distinctions among additions, betterments, improvements, alterations, and rearrangements—just as there are between costs of assets and costs of repairs. Regardless of how they are described, expenditures that extend the useful life of capital assets or increase their productivity should be capitalized as an addition to the individual or composite asset account. If a related asset is retired, its cost and accumulated depreciation are removed from the appropriate individual accounts; if composite accounts (described later) are used, the cost of the retired asset should be charged to accumulated depreciation.

Donated Assets. Assets donated by unrelated parties should be recorded at fair value, using either the applicable market price or, in the absence of a readily determinable market value, an appraisal value. Guidance with respect to the offsetting credit is provided in a 1979 AICPA Issues Paper, *Accounting for Grants Received from Governments* (AICPA, 1979a).

This Issues Paper indicates that under present practice some grants are accounted for as reductions of the cost of the related assets, some as deferred credits to be amortized over the life of the assets, some as income when received and some as additions to contributed capital.

The Issues Paper contains "advisory conclusions" taking the position that grants related to depreciable fixed assets should be recognized as income over the useful lives of the assets, and grants related to land should be amortized into income over the life of the depreciable fixed assets built on the land. In addition, it was concluded that a grant received before the conditions of the grant are met should be recorded as liabilities or deferred credits. If it is probable that a grant will be refunded, the grant should be reported as a liability.

Depreciation

Depreciation is a systematic method of charging operations with the cost of a capitalized asset, less salvage value, over its estimated useful life; but estimates of the useful life of assets are seldom accurate. An asset may be capable of operating a long time, but obsolescence or other factors may abbreviate its usefulness to a company. Because of this uncertainty, the general lives promulgated for tax purposes by the IRS frequently have been used in financial accounting as well. However, with the frequent changes in tax laws, especially in the asset cost recovery area, conformity of tax and book lives and maintaining a reasonable degree of consistency has become increasingly more difficult to achieve.

Salvage value is also difficult to predict. Therefore, it is often ignored in depreciation computations if it is estimated to be less than 10% of the cost of the asset.

Generally, depreciation has been a phenomenon unique to profit-making enterprises. However, in SFAS 93, *Recognition of Depreciation by Not-for-Profit Organizations* (D40), the FASB has extended the requirement to provide for depreciation on long-lived tangible assets to all not-for-profit organizations in general purpose external financial statements. However, depreciation need not be recognized for works of art and historical treasures in very limited circumstances. SFAS 93 also extends to not-for-profit organizations the requirements of APB Opinion 12, *Omnibus Opinion—*

1967 (D40.105), to disclose information about depreciable assets and depreciation. (In June 1988 the FASB issued an exposure draft (1988a) that would delay the effective date of SFAS 93 to fiscal years beginning on or after January 1, 1990.) For further discussion about the accounting by not-for-profit organizations, see Chapter 32.

Depreciation Methods. There are several depreciation methods, as described in the following paragraphs.

Straight-line method. Under this method, the cost (less salvage value) of the capitalized asset is spread in equal periodic portions over its estimated useful life. Straight-line depreciation is calculated simply by deducting the estimated salvage value from the cost of the asset and then dividing the remaining depreciable cost by the estimated years of useful life. It is acceptable to record a half-year's depreciation in the year the asset is acquired and another half-year's depreciation in the year it is retired. Companies that calculate depreciation on a monthly basis generally begin depreciating at the beginning of the month closest to the acquisition date. Other practical variations are acceptable, provided the criteria adopted are consistently applied.

Declining-balance method. Under the declining-balance method of depreciation, relatively larger amounts of depreciation are recognized in the earlier years of the asset's use, smaller amounts in later years. The conceptual reasons for adopting such a method are that the utility derived from a productive asset will often be greater in the early years and that repairs and maintenance will often be more costly in the later years. Thus, the sum of depreciation and repairs and maintenance expenditures is more likely to be fairly constant over the asset's life. In this light, an accelerated method of depreciation seems more realistic than the straight-line method.

Declining-balance depreciation is computed by applying a constant rate (generally double the straight-line rate for new assets, one and one-half times for used assets) to the remaining undepreciated balance. In theory, there will always be a small balance remaining, since a constant rate is being applied to successively smaller amounts of undepreciated cost. Therefore, depreciation stops when the asset has been written down to salvage value, or, at an appropriate point, when depreciation is switched to the straight-line method.

For example, for a machine that has an estimated useful life of ten years, costs $8,000, and has an estimated salvage value of $1,500, the double declining-balance depreciation would be calculated as shown in Figure 15.1.

Sum-of-the-years'-digits method. Another method of allocating a larger portion of the cost of an asset to its early years of use is the sum-of-the-years'-digits method. Each year's depreciation is calculated by using the sum of the total years of life as a denominator of a fraction of the depreciable base (cost of the asset less estimated salvage value). Thus, for a machine with a ten-year useful life, the denominator would be 55 (10 + 9 + 8 + 7 + 6 + 5 + 4 + 3 + 2 + 1); the numerator is always the remaining years of life.

Year	Net undepreciated cost	Depreciation for the year
1	$8,000	$ 800*
2	7,200	1,440
3	5,760	1,152
4	4,608	922
5	3,686	737
6	2,949	590
7	2,359	472
8	1,887	377
9	1,510	10
10	1,500**	–

*Depreciation taken for a half-year in the year of
acquisition.

**The machine is depreciated to salvage value in a
little more than nine years.

FIG. 15.1 Double Declining-Balance Depreciation

A simple formula for determining the denominator for the sum of the years' digits for any useful life is

$$n\left(\frac{n + 1}{2}\right)$$

where n signifies the estimated useful life.

Using the same data as in the preceding example, yearly depreciation would be calculated on a depreciable base of $6,500 ($8,000 cost − $1,500 salvage value). Figure 15.2 shows the calculation of sum-of-the-years'-digits depreciation. (For simplicity, it ignores the half-year convention.)

Units-of-production method. The useful lives of some assets, such as machinery, can be estimated in terms of units produced or hours of operation rather than years, since this measure may provide a more equitable allocation of asset cost. In this case depreciation is computed as the ratio of the actual number of units produced or hours operated during the period to the total number of units or hours in the estimated useful life.

For example, if a machine with a depreciable cost of $8,000 is estimated to produce 200,000 units of a product over its estimated life, and 10,000 units have been produced during the period, depreciation would be calculated as follows:

$$\frac{10,000 \text{ units}}{200,000 \text{ units}} \times \$8,000 = \$400 \text{ depreciation}$$

| Year | Depreciation for the year | |
	Fraction	Amount
1	10/55	$1,182
2	9/55	1,064
3	8/55	945
4	7/55	827
5	6/55	709
6	5/55	591
7	4/55	473
8	3/55	355
9	2/55	236
10	1/55	118
Total depreciation for ten years		$6,500

FIG. 15.2 Sum-of-the-Years'-Digits Depreciation

The difficulties involved in estimating the hours of operation of units of production for a particular asset or in keeping track of actual utilization generally deter most companies from using this method.

Variations Within Methods. The methods described above can be used to compute depreciation on an individual asset basis or on a group basis. Since depreciation accounting depends on estimates and judgments, the differing results derived from the use of various methods and bases are acceptable as long as the methods chosen are applied consistently. Thus, a company can use different methods to depreciate different assets; also, some assets can be depreciated individually, others in groups.

Unit basis. On the unit basis, each asset is recorded, depreciated, and retired individually. Very often the individual assets are recorded on asset cards that show the cost of the asset, the depreciation expense for the period, the accumulated depreciation, and the net undepreciated cost, as well as any other necessary information. Whatever the recording form, the unit basis is helpful in arriving at the net undepreciated cost when the asset is sold or retired. It is also valuable for purposes of physical accountability of individual items. EDP systems reduce the effort required to maintain a unit record system.

Composite accounts. In composite accounts, assets of the same general class are grouped together even though their individual estimated useful lives are different. A single composite life, generally a weighted average of the lives of the individual assets in the group, must be applied to the entire group. Composite accounts work best when the assets are segregated into appropriate groups by classification or function. If the "mix" of the group changes substantially, the composite life should be redetermined.

Composite accounts have the advantage of being simple, since they eliminate the necessity for computing depreciation accruals for individual assets. But if the net undepreciated cost of an individual asset is needed, the depreciation applied to the asset would not be computed at the composite rate. Instead it must be computed as if the asset had been depreciated on an individual basis.

Lapse schedules. Lapse schedules are spreadsheets showing all the assets of a similar class and life that were acquired during a given period. Depreciation is calculated on a group basis and recorded to show the "lapsing" of the cost of each group over its assigned life.

Changes in Methods and Lives. APB 20, *Accounting Changes* (A06.111), states that:

> in the preparation of financial statements there is a presumption that an accounting principle once adopted should not be changed in accounting for events and transactions of a similar type. Consistent use of accounting principles from one accounting period to another enhances the utility of financial statements to users by facilitating analysis and understanding of comparative accounting data.

However, companies sometimes voluntarily change to a different generally accepted accounting principle to improve the matching of revenue and expense, to adopt a method prevailing in the industry, or for other reasons.

A change from one method of depreciation of previously acquired and depreciated assets to another equally acceptable method is a change in accounting principle that should be accounted for as any other nonretroactive change (A06.115); financial statements for prior periods should be presented as previously reported, and the cumulative effect (less tax) of the change to the new depreciation method on beginning retained earnings should be included in the net income of the period of the change. Related per share amounts should also be included. For all periods presented, income before extraordinary items and net income should be shown on a pro forma basis on the face of the income statements as if the newly adopted accounting principle had been retroactively applied.

Because changes in depreciation methods have proven to be complex calculations in practice, the APB singled them out for specific recitation of steps (A06.118) and included an extensive example in Appendix A of APB 20 (A06.135–.137). The "bottom end" of the APB's sample income statement is shown in Figure 15.3.

A company may decide to depreciate newly acquired assets by a different method than that used for old assets. For example, a company may continue to depreciate all old machinery by the straight-line method and depreciate all new machinery by the double declining-balance method. For this type of change there is no cumulative effect on beginning retained earnings, since all assets prior to the date of change continue to be depreciated on the old (straight-line) method (A06.120).

A determination that a change in the estimated life of an asset or a change in the estimated salvage value is proper constitutes a change in accounting estimate. If the change will affect several future periods, current-period disclosure of the effect of the change in estimate is required in relation to income before extraordinary items, net income, and related per share amounts (A06.132).

	19X8	19X7
Income before extraordinary item and cumulative effect of a change in accounting principle	$1,200,000	$1,100,000
Extraordinary item (description)	(35,000)	100,000
Cumulative effect on prior years (to December 31, 19X7) of changing to a different depreciation method (Note A)	125,000	—
Net Income	$1,290,000	$1,200,000
Per share amounts		
Earnings per common share assuming no dilution:		
Income before extraordinary item and cumulative effect of a change in accounting principle	$1.20	$1.10
Extraordinary item	(0.04)	0.10
Cumulative effect on prior years (to December 31, 19X8) of changing to a different depreciation method	0.13	—
Net income	$1.29	$1.20
Earnings per common share assuming full dilution		
Income before extraordinary item and cumulative effect of a change in accounting principle	$1.11	$1.02
Extraordinary item	(0.03)	0.09
Cumulative effect on prior years (to December 31, 19X7) of changing to a different depreciation method	0.11	—
Net income	$1.19	$1.11
Pro forma amounts assuming the new depreciation method is applied retroactively		
Income before extraordinary item	$1,200,000	$1,113,500
Earnings per common share assuming no dilution	$1.20	$1.11
Earnings per common share assuming full dilution	$1.11	$1.04
Net income	$1,165,00	$1,213,500
Earnings per common share assuming no dilution	$1.16	$1.21
Earnings per common share assuming full dilution	$1.08	$1.13

FIG. 15.3 Income Statement Presentation of Change in Depreciation Method
Source: APB 20 (A06.137).

Amortization of Leasehold Improvements. Leasehold improvements are additions or improvements made to a leased asset. Because they revert to the owner of the property on termination of the lease, they should be amortized by the lessee over the economic life of the improvement to the asset or the life of the lease, whichever is shorter. In determining the amortization period, the likelihood that renewal options will be exercised should be considered.

Income Tax Allocation. Companies often use one depreciation method (usually straight-line) for financial reporting and another (usually accelerated) for tax purposes. Other temporary differences, such as in the case of depreciable lives, also occur. The purpose of such arrangements is to increase the company's cash flow by minimizing taxes currently payable, deferring them to a future period. The difference between book and tax depreciation gives rise to deferred taxes, determined by calculating the tax on income both before and after the deduction of the depreciation temporary difference using the current tax rate. The difference between the two tax amounts is the deferred tax attributed to the temporary difference. Most often this calculation is made on a net change basis (I25.135), which combines prior temporary differences that reverse in the current period with temporary differences that originate in the current period. For further discussion of income tax allocation, see Chapter 17.

Obsolescence. Occasionally, an asset built or purchased for a particular purpose can no longer be used because of sudden style changes, improved technology, or unforeseen reduction of demand. When an asset suddenly becomes obsolete and has no remaining useful life, the undepreciated cost, less salvage value, should be charged to operations. Incipient obsolescence may be dealt with by shortening depreciation lives.

Disposals and Retirements

As units of plant and equipment wear out or become obsolete, they must be sold, scrapped, traded in, exchanged, or abandoned. When an asset is disposed of or retired from use, the cost and related accumulated depreciation should be removed from the accounts. Since depreciation expense charged over the estimated useful life of the asset was only an allocation of the cost based on an estimate, a gain or loss will probably be realized on disposal of the asset.

Those gains or losses, adjusted for the costs of removal or disposal, are recognized as income or expense in the period of the disposal, except when the asset disposed of was part of a composite account.

Sale. When a unit of property is sold, the cost should be removed from the appropriate asset account, and the related depreciation removed from the accumulated depreciation account. The difference between the net undepreciated cost and the proceeds received on the sale represents a gain or loss. If assets are recorded on lapse schedules, it is necessary to determine the acquisition-year group in which the asset is included on the lapse schedule, the original cost of the individual asset, and its accumulated depreciation based on the number of periods it has been depreciated as part of the group.

In composite account situations, the cost of the asset should be removed from the appropriate asset account and charged to the accumulated depreciation account. Proceeds received on disposal should be credited to the accumulated depreciation account. No profit or loss should be recognized on a composite account asset disposal unless it is abnormal or unusual; this makes it necessary to determine the accumulated depreciation based on the individual life of the asset. Gains or losses should then be recognized as if the assets were not composites, based on the proceeds received.

Trade-ins are sometimes accounted for as outright disposals but perhaps more frequently as a reduction of the cost of new assets acquired. Trade-in accounting is discussed earlier in this chapter.

Involuntary Conversion. Assets may be lost or destroyed through fire, casualty, condemnation, or other involuntary events. Generally, the gains or losses resulting from these events are measured by the difference between the insurance proceeds received and the net undepreciated cost of the asset.

Federal income tax rules may allow deferral of the gain resulting from an involuntary conversion if the owner of the asset uses the funds received to replace the asset. In other words, the cost of the newly acquired replacement asset, adjusted for the gain, becomes the recorded cost of the asset for future tax depreciation purposes.

FASB Interpretation 30, *Accounting for Involuntary Conversions of Nonmonetary Assets to Monetary Assets* (N35), requires that gain or loss must be recognized in all involuntary conversions of nonmonetary assets to monetary assets. This would be true even though an enterprise may have to reinvest in similar nonmonetary assets to continue its business.

Retirement. When a property asset has become fully depreciated and no salvage value has been assigned to it, the asset and the related accumulated depreciation should be removed from the accounts if the asset is being retired. If it remains in use, the asset and the accumulated depreciation accounts should, as a matter of control, continue to be carried on the balance sheet.

Abandonment. Most frequently, no consideration is received when an asset is abandoned except perhaps for its salvage value. Property abandoned is presumed to have no more usefulness to its present owners. Accounting for an abandoned asset is the same as accounting for a retirement: the cost and the related depreciation are removed from the accounts, and a loss (net of any salvage) is recognized if the asset has not been fully depreciated.

Transfer. When an asset is transferred from one unit of a company to another, its original cost and accumulated depreciation to date of transfer should be recorded in the accounts of the acquiring unit. Depreciation may continue on the same basis as was used by the transferor, or the new unit may treat a transfer as if a used asset has been acquired via purchase in the open market. If the method is changed, this is dealt with as described earlier under the section "Changes in Methods and Lives." Similarly, transfers of property assets between account classifications within the same company unit should be recorded "gross," that is, using original cost and accumulated depreciation to date of transfer rather than net undepreciated cost.

Other Matters

Appraisals. Property, plant, and equipment should not be written up to reflect appraised values, as GAAP does not permit the periodic accretion in values of assets to be recorded in historical cost-based financial statements. (In rare situations, usually for a donated asset, the recording of appraised value is appropriate since the appraised value represents an acceptable surrogate for "acquisition price.") However, appraisal valuations may be useful for other purposes, such as determining insurance values, salvage values, and tax assessment figures; allocating cost to a finished product for the establishment of a selling price (when specific cost identification is difficult); allocating costs of a group purchase of properties; and preparing voluntary supplementary financial statements to show the effects of changing prices and values (see Chapter 4).

If appraisal values are used in the preparation of the basic financial statements, accountants should be sure to disclose the fact that the financial statements are not presented in conformity with GAAP, and give the effect of the departure. Concomitantly, depreciation should be computed on the written-up amounts (D40.102) if appraisals are recorded in disregard of GAAP. However, it should be noted that it is acceptable to present appraisal information, for example, in supplemental disclosures outside the basic financial statements or on a comparative basis with the historical cost information. Appropriate qualifications should be made in the auditor's report regarding the fact that the appraisal-based (current value) information is not in accordance with GAAP.

Appraisals are especially important to companies that have interests in real estate assets. The AICPA Real Estate Committee has prepared an audit and accounting guide, *Guide for the Use of Real Estate Appraisal Information* (AICPA, 1987j), intended to help auditors to:

- Understand the real estate appraisal process, its valuation techniques and standards.
- Use appraisal information to assist in auditing financial statements.
- Apply SAS 11, *Using the Work of a Specialist* (AU 336), to the efforts of a real estate appraiser.

Investment Tax Credit. Prior to passage of the Tax Reform Act of 1986 (TRA 1986), an incentive to businesses to invest in certain types of productive assets was made available in the form of a tax credit equal to a specified percentage of the asset cost. The 1986 Act repealed the investment tax credit, and property, plant and equipment additions in 1986 and subsequent years do not qualify for the credit, except in certain restricted circumstances. In addition, the use of any investment tax credits carried forward from previous years is also severely restricted. Briefly, carryover credits that can be applied against current income taxes are reduced by 35% on or after July 1, 1987. For a more detailed discussion of the effects of the TRA 1986, see Chapter 17.

Tax Basis Differentials. If a company uses one accounting method for tax purposes and another for financial statements, differences may arise in the recording of assets and liabilities as a result of a purchase business combination. APB 16 requires that all identifiable assets acquired and liabilities assumed be assigned a portion of the cost of an acquired company equal to their fair values at date of acquisition (B50.145). However, the fair values of the individual assets and liabilities recorded on the books may differ from their income tax bases, which will not change in an acquisition of the stock of the purchased company.

The tax effect of these differences depends on numerous factors. SFAS 96 (I25.159) states that the differences between assigned amounts and the tax bases are temporary differences, and accordingly deferred tax accounts should be recorded at the date of acquisition. Prior to SFAS 96, such differences were deemed not to be timing differences, and the tax basis differentials were taken into account in determining the fair value to be assigned to the asset. This represented "net-of-tax" accounting; that is, the tax effects were deducted from (or, less frequently, added to) the unadjusted fair value amount. This matter is further discussed in Chapter 23.

Asset Impairment Write-Downs. When management decides on the disposal of some element of property, plant, and equipment, its net realizable value should be estimated. If this is less than the net carrying amount, a write-down should be recorded to place the asset on a realizable value basis. If the asset is expected to be sold within 12 months, the asset should be carried as a current asset.

A more difficult problem arises in considering whether a company has the ability to fully recover from future operations the carrying amount of long-lived assets continued in use. As indicated in APB Statement 4 (¶ 183):

> In unusual circumstances persuasive evidence may exist of impairment of the utility of productive facilities indicative of an inability to recover cost although the facilities have not become worthless. The amount at which those facilities are carried is sometimes reduced to recoverable cost and a loss recorded prior to disposition or expiration of the useful life of the facilities.

This problem, often referred to as *impairment of value*, is described this way in SFAS 5, *Accounting for Contingencies* (C59.137):

> In some cases, the carrying amount of an operating asset not intended for disposal may exceed the amount expected to be recoverable through future use of that asset even though there has been no physical loss or damage of the asset or threat of such loss or damage. For example, changed economic conditions may have made recovery of the carrying amount of a productive facility doubtful.

Although it defines the issue, SFAS 5 does not address the question of whether it is appropriate to write down the carrying amount of the asset to an amount expected to be recoverable through future operations. In practice, there have been numerous write-downs and disclosures of impairment in value of assets continued in use. Part of this problem is attributable to the difficulty of forecasting the future realizable value of an asset.

This matter was debated by AcSEC, which proffered certain advisory conclusions (AICPA, 1980b) to the FASB. AcSEC concluded that:

1. The inability to fully recover the carrying amount of long-lived assets should be reported in financial statements;

2. The concept of *permanent decline* (see, e.g., FIN 11 (I89.115)) is unsatisfactory, but the *probability test* in SFAS 5 (C59.105(a)) is a workable alternative;

3. Judgment is necessary in selecting the asset measurement that best predicts future economic benefits, and it is difficult to select one measurement that would be appropriate in all circumstances; and

4. If the inability to fully recover the carrying amounts of a long-lived asset is recorded in the accounts, future upward adjustments to the asset's historical cost should be permitted if evidence indicates a recovery.

Impairment has also been discussed by the EITF in Issue 84-28, *Impairment of Long-Lived Assets*; however, no consensus was reached as to GAAP for any write-downs. The Task Force made the following observations:

1. Write-downs from economic impairment are permissible.
2. Write-downs do not exceed a break-even point in practice.
3. Assets written down are not subsequently written up in practice.
4. The number of write-downs is increasing.

Interestingly, the SEC Observer commented that it is likely that the SEC would insist on a write-down if the estimated undiscounted future cash flows from a long-lived asset will be less than net book value.

In 1987, the FASB agreed to consider this issue and the FASB Staff is considering the accounting for the inability to recover fully the carrying amounts of long-lived assets. The FASB consideration also includes a review of the Financial Executives Institute's Committee on Corporate Reporting study, *Survey on Unusual Charges* (FEI, 1986), of companies reporting write-downs during 1985. The purpose of the survey was to determine under what circumstances write-downs of long-lived assets are currently being made and how the amount of write-down is determined.

The FASB staff analyzed the responses to the questionnaire, which indicated four principal reasons for write-downs:

1. Planned sale or abandonment of all or a part of a segment of a business.
2. Whole or partial write-down of fixed assets that were retained in the business (either idle or still in use) because of economic impairment (recovery of cost not anticipated).
3. Accrual of loss contingencies.
4. Special termination benefits.

Respondents to the survey indicated that there were four principal measurement bases used to estimate the new carrying amount of the assets written down. They included (1) net realizable value, (2) undiscounted expected future cash flows, (3) net present value of expected future cash flows, and (4) a combination of the above.

Most respondents indicated that the determination of the "new cost" was based on a break-even assumption, that is, capital recovery was based on an assumption that would provide no gain or loss. In addition, a large majority of respondents stated that it would be inappropriate to restore all or part of the written down amount should the net realizable value of the assets subsequently increase.

Most respondents commented that the written down amount should be displayed as: (1) a separate line item in income from continuing operations, perhaps as an "unusual item," presumably like those items in APB 30, *Reporting the Results of Operations* (117.111) or (2) discontinued operations.

Almost half of the respondents indicated that additional technical guidance is unnecessary, believing that preparers are able to cope with the question of impairment. This is a curious response since some critics believe that a major unresolved problem in financial reporting is the failure to apply and the misapplication of the permanent impairment concept. Although the determination of the fact and amount of permanent impairment is most difficult, financial reporting history is replete with examples of companies that seem to avoid write-downs for a long period and then, with a change in management, institute major write-downs, derisively referred to as the "big bath."

In 1987, the AICPA issued Financial Report Survey, *Illustrations of Accounting for the Inability to Fully Recover the Carrying Amounts of Long-Lived Assets* (AICPA, 1987k). The survey includes several examples of the following:

• Companies that disclose a possible inability to fully recover the carrying amount of an asset without writing down the carrying amount. The accountants' reports for those companies (all containing "subject to" qualifications) are also included.

• Companies that have written down the carrying amounts of long-lived assets to amounts that could be identified as specific kinds of measurements (e.g., value in use).

• Companies that have written down the carrying amounts of their long-lived assets to amounts that could not be identified as specific kinds of measurements such as those described in the 1980 AICPA Issues Paper (1980b, discussed earlier in this section).

• Companies that have written off (reduced to zero) the carrying amounts of long-lived assets in response to an inability to recover the carrying amounts.

The FASB staff has received two additional technical papers from the AICPA that relate to the subject of impairment of value.

The first paper is the *Report of the Task Force on Risks and Uncertainties* (AICPA 1987l). The Task Force Report recommends that expanded disclosures be made of important information about risks and uncertainties that stem from (1) the necessary use of estimates and (2) the existence of significant operating concentrations as those factors affect the preparation of financial statements. The assessment of the ability of a company to recover the cost of assets, especially operating plant, is affected significantly by the risks and uncertainties that are inherent in normal operations. As a result, the Task Force Report may provide insights for the FASB in its deliberations about impairment of value.

The second paper is Issues Paper 87-2, *The Use of Discounting in Financial Reporting for Monetary Items With Uncertain Terms Other Than Those Covered by Existing Authoritative Literature* (AICPA, 1987p). That Issues Paper addresses the use of the discounting process to reflect the time value of money in accounting for the specified areas. Generally, current accounting practice ignores discounting except in isolated instances, for example, APB Opinion 21, *Interest on Receivables and Payables* (I69). Although Issues Paper 87-2 presents the issues in a conceptual manner, AcSEC hopes that it can be applied to specific issues in future papers dealing with individual topics, such as impairment of value.

Previously, the FASB has been reticent about requiring the application of discounting in specific situations without a broad examination of the general applicability of discounting. Therefore, the Issues Paper may serve to assist the FASB in considering discounting as it specifically relates to a determination of impairment of value of monetary assets, and as it generally relates to the applicability of discounting to other areas of financial reporting.

Financial Statement Presentation

Balances of major classes of depreciable assets should be disclosed at cost at the balance sheet date (D40.105(b)). Nondepreciable property (e.g., land) should be presented separately from depreciable assets. Property not used in the business, idle equipment, assets held for resale, and construction in progress should also be segregated if material in amount.

Accumulated depreciation, either by major classes of depreciable assets or in total, should be disclosed either in the balance sheet or in a note to the financial statements; in addition, depreciation expense for the period and a general description of the methods used in computing depreciation for financial statement and tax purposes should also be disclosed (D40.105(a), (c), and (d)).

As discussed in Chapter 19, *lessors* should include leased property under operating leases as noncurrent assets within or near the property, plant, and equipment caption; and property leased under capital leases should be recorded by a *lessee* as an asset and an obligation in an amount equal to the present value of the minimum lease payments during the term of the lease.

SEC Requirements

Disclosure. The SEC disclosure requirements go beyond GAAP, in that detailed property, plant, and equipment schedules and the related schedules of accumulated depreciation, depletion, and amortization (Schedules V and VI) are required to be presented where property, plant, and equipment is highly significant. The schedules are required when property, plant, and equipment, net of accumulated depreciation, depletion, and amortization, is 25% or more of total assets at both the beginning and end of the latest year, and they must be included for each year for which an income statement is presented. The schedules are required for previous years if required for the current year; conversely, if the schedules are not required currently they are not needed for prior years. The beginning *and* end of the year are used in the test to deal with unusual fluctuations.

Some companies prefer to disclose depreciation as a separate item in the earnings statement. The SEC does not object to this, but as stated in SAB Topic 11.B (SAB 40), if cost of sales or operating expenses excludes depreciation, depletion, or amortization, the caption should include a phrase similar to the following:

- Cost of goods sold (exclusive of items shown separately below).
- Operating expenses (exclusive of depreciation shown separately).

In SAB Topic 11.B, the SEC Staff also states its objection to any presentation of depreciation, depletion, or amortization in the income statement in a manner that results in reporting a figure for income before depreciation, "to avoid placing undue emphases on 'cash flow.' "

Accounting Measurement. SAB Topic 5.B (SAB 40) indicates that gains and losses resulting from the disposition of revenue-producing equipment depreciated on a specific-item basis should not be treated as adjustments to the provision for depreciation but should be shown as separate items in the income statement. Gains or losses on disposition of assets depreciated on a composite or "pooled" basis, such as vehicle fleets, may be charged or credited to accumulated depreciation. The SEC Staff states that this latter method is not considered appropriate for an enterprise that replaces its fleet on an "episodic" basis, such as an airline, or an enterprise whose equipment is replaced after limited use, so that the equipment on hand is relatively new and the carrying amount is closely related to acquisition cost, such as an auto leasing company.

The SEC staff generally would favor write-down of plant and equipment to economic value where utility has materially declined and the carrying amount is not expected to be recoverable through future use. GAAP does not address the issue of diminished utility of plant facilities, and SFAS 5, *Accounting for Contingencies,* expressly excludes consideration of whether such assets should be written down to an amount expected to be recoverable. The SEC Staff will consider the matter of write-down on a case-by-case basis.

International Accounting Standard

The International Accounting Standards Committee has issued IAS 16, *Accounting for Property, Plant and Equipment* (AC 9016). The requirements of IAS 16 generally conform with GAAP, except that a revaluation of property, plant, and equipment is permitted and may be presented in the financial statements. The revaluation should be done on a systematic basis, such as by use of a qualified appraiser, indexation, or reference to current prices.

An increase in net carrying amount as a result of revaluation would be credited to a separate revaluation surplus account in shareholders' equity. If later the revaluation amount is deemed to be overstated, the reduction is charged against current operations. Later increases in the revaluation amount are also credited directly to shareholders' equity, unless there had previously been a charge to operations for a downward revaluation, in which case the credit would go to current operations up to the amount of accumulated net charges to operations. The net result of this exercise is that the balance in revaluation surplus at any given time never will have been credited to income in any period; but some increases and decreases may enter operations during intervening periods.

The IAS requires disclosure of the basis used for determining the carrying amount of property, plant, and equipment. When more than one basis is used, disclosure of the carrying amount for each basis in each category is required. Where the accounts include revalued amounts, the disclosures should also include the method adopted to compute the revalued amounts, including the frequency of revaluations, the nature of any indices used, the year appraisals were made, and whether an external valuer was involved.

AUDITING CONSIDERATIONS—PLANT AND EQUIPMENT

Objectives of the Audit

The overall objective of the audit of property, plant, and equipment and the related depreciation provision and accumulated depreciation accounts is to evaluate whether these accounts are fairly presented in the context of the financial statements taken as a whole.

Chapter 7 discusses the audit process and its implementation, and Chapter 8 discusses internal control and its impact on the audit. To obtain an understanding of the audit philosophy utilized in the following discussion of the audit of property, plant, and equipment, those chapters should be consulted.

Controls Over Capital Assets

Most larger firms have formal procedures for determining capital budgets and monitoring capital expenditures for property, plant, and equipment. The audit of property, plant, and equipment is ordinarily focused on reviewing and testing changes in the account balance. While change may result from renovation or modification to existing assets and disposal, ordinarily emphasis is placed on additions. This is because acquisitions are likely to be material and infrequent.

After the assets have been acquired, it sometimes seems that control over them receives little attention. One of the reasons for this may be that the bookkeeping required for these assets is not elaborate; thus management's attention may be focused on the capital asset accounts only a few times a year. Also, auditors do not often require periodic physical inventories to be taken of these assets. The accounting standards provisions of the Foreign Corrupt Practices Act of 1977 require publicly held companies to have adequate internal accounting controls over all assets; this law has caused an improvement in physical and accounting controls over long-lived assets in covered companies.

Proper control of capital assets provides many benefits, such as optimization of cash flow by claiming the maximum depreciation allowed for income tax purposes; appropriate determination of current cost, enabling product pricing to include full costs of production; accurate measurement of return on investment; ability to evaluate the reasonableness of property tax assessments; and accurate evaluation of losses for insurance purposes.

Control over long-lived assets involves (1) control over the physical asset itself and (2) control over each phase of the transaction cycle, from introduction in the capital budget through acquisition to expiration and, finally, disposal.

Existence Controls. A property record system should be maintained for all property, plant, and equipment. Control accounts should be established in convenient categories, supported by individual records maintained on cards or sheets (for manual systems) or on computerized records. Each asset should be assigned an identification number, and periodic physical counts of the assets should be made by personnel (such as internal auditors) not having responsibility for their acquisition, use, or disposition.

Cycle Controls. A company's policy governing property acquisitions should be well defined. The system of internal control should provide for the authorization of all capital expenditures, whether they consist of purchases from outside parties or of construction using the company's own materials and labor.

Routine or recurring purchases are normally processed through the purchasing department and are subject to the same controls as other purchases. Acquisitions of more technically specialized assets would probably be handled by engineers or other specialists, and major acquisitions might be handled by top management.

A written policy should be established for rates and methods of depreciation. Forms or schedules for manual systems or EDP software for computing entries for depreciation should be developed. Standardized procedures should be initiated for periodically reviewing depreciation calculations, estimated lives, estimated salvage values, and depreciation methods. Documentation of this review should be required.

Controls over the disposition of property, plant, and equipment should be established to preserve the accuracy of the accounting records and to safeguard the assets. For example, no property should be removed or released without a properly authorized order. Retirement orders should be reviewed by a management-level employee, who will evaluate the reason for the disposition and take steps to have the asset disposed of and removed from the accounting records.

Audit Approaches

Systems Tests. The basis for evaluation of internal control includes two phases: (1) a knowledge and understanding of the company's prescribed methods and procedures and (2) a reasonable degree of assurance that these controls are in use and operating as planned. These two phases are referred to as understanding the system and tests of compliance, respectively, as fully discussed in Chapter 8.

In its simplest form the system for the acquisition of capital assets can be reviewed in conjunction with the purchasing system, especially if there are a large number of homogeneous units (e.g., a fleet of automobiles). In most situations, however, an auditor will decide to test some of the controls over property, plant, and equipment, because acquisitions will not occur frequently enough to assure satisfactory audit coverage merely through auditing the purchasing system. The applicable controls would include:

- Authorization and approval of major purchases and the extent of capital-budgeting activities
- Purchase orders for major acquisitions
- Evidence of receipt
- Reviews to assure compliance with accounting policies for determining costs and capitalizing or expensing transactions
- A check on the regularity and accuracy of depreciation computations
- A work-order system for plant additions
- Controls over disposals and retirements
- Physical protection and accountability for assets owned

If a client's system does not include some of these controls, the auditor will locate alternative controls or he will expand his substantive testing of property, plant, and equipment transactions and balances. In addition, an auditor should review and test controls that may exist over reevaluation of useful lives, net realizable values, and salvage values.

Analytical Tests. The nature of analytical tests depends on the individual nature of each client's operations. Because of relatively infrequent transactions in the property, plant, and equipment accounts, it is usually most effective to audit the details directly. However, analytical review can be used to test the validity of related expense accounts. Analytical review is best employed where expenses have a predictable and stable relationship with the property, plant, and equipment account. These accounts are:

- *Depreciation.* The ratio of depreciation expense to the related property, plant, and equipment balance should be predictable and comparable over time unless there is a change in depreciation method, basis, or lives.
- *Repairs and Maintenance.* The ratio of repair and maintenance expense to the related property, plant, and equipment account may fluctuate in any one period because of differences in management's policies. Maintenance expenses can be postponed without immediate breakdowns or loss of productivity. The auditor should interpret an unexpected deviation with this consideration in mind.
- *Insurance.* The ratio of insurance expense to the related property, plant, and equipment account may or may not be comparable over time, since external factors may cause premium fluctuations.

Some suggested analytical review procedures are listed below:

1. Review capital budgets (if used), compare amounts spent with amounts authorized, and determine whether differences were properly approved.
2. Consider the likelihood of property, plant, and equipment becoming idle during the period. Has there been a significant drop in production at one of the plants? Has there been a change in product lines that might render some machinery idle?
3. Review repairs and maintenance expense accounts for the period and compare with the previous periods to ascertain whether there are any material items that should have been capitalized.
4. Compare the ratio of depreciation to categories of property, plant, and equipment (exclusive of land) for the period with that of previous periods to evaluate the adequacy of the annual depreciation expense and whether a uniform policy of recognizing depreciation is in effect. Obtain satisfactory explanations for any unusual items noted.
5. Compare the ratio of insurance to the related plant and equipment account. Obtain satisfactory explanation of any unusual relationships noted.

Substantive Procedures

An auditor reporting on a client's financial statements for the first time may find it necessary to extend the examination of property, plant, and equipment to prior periods. Since the long-lived assets are apt to constitute a substantial part of the assets of a company, verification of the authenticity of those assets could be an important part of a first audit. On subsequent audits, the auditor may simply agree the prior year's ending balances to the current year's beginning balances as a starting point. He would then audit current-year additions, which are important because of their long-term effect on the financial statements. Failure to record an asset properly can affect the balance sheet and the income statement (through depreciation) for the entire life of the asset.

Using the results of the analytical review procedures previously mentioned, the auditor should select the nature and extent of the remaining audit procedures required to satisfy the property, plant, and equipment audit objectives. Figure 15.4 identifies some interim and year-end procedures commonly used to achieve those audit objectives; no attempt has been made to provide an exhaustive list, since the procedures must be tailored for each engagement. The listed procedures may satisfy a number of the audit objectives, but each is shown alongside the objective it most directly satisfies.

Information on Changing Prices

Under SFAS 89, *Financial Reporting and Changing Prices* (C28), financial statements may optionally provide certain current cost and constant dollar supplementary information as discussed in Chapter 4.

Under SAS 52, *Omnibus Statement—1987* (AU 558.07), the auditor is required to inquire of management whether the supplementary information has been prepared and presented in accordance with FASB guidelines on a basis consistent with prior periods. This includes inquiring as to the significant assumptions or interpretations underlying the measurement and presentation. SAS 52 withdrew SAS 28 and with it a listing of specific items on which the auditor's inquiries should focus; these are listed herein as they continue to represent valid (but not mandatory) guidance:

1. The sources of information presented for the fiscal year and for the five most recent fiscal years, the factors considered in the selection of such sources, and the appropriateness of their application in the circumstances;
2. The assumptions and judgments made in calculating constant dollar and current cost amounts (such as the methods and timing of acquisition and retirement of assets and the classification of assets and liabilities as either monetary or nonmonetary); and
3. The need to reduce the measurements of inventory and of PP&E from (a) historical cost/ constant dollar amounts or (b) current cost amounts to lower recoverable amounts and, if reduction is necessary, the reason for selecting the method used to estimate the recoverable amount and the appropriateness of the application of that method.

In addition, a comparison should be made of the supplementary information for consistency with (1) the responses obtained from inquiries directed to management, (2) the audited financial statements, and (3) other knowledge obtained during the audit.

The auditor has no obligation to perform any procedures to corroborate management's responses concerning the unaudited supplementary information. Furthermore, the auditor need not expand his report on the audited financial statements to refer to the supplementary information.

Audit objective	Sample year-end procedures*	Sample interim procedures
Existence. Determine whether there is property, plant, and equipment to support the dollar amount shown in the balance sheet and whether all such property, plant, and equipment has been properly included.	• Check physical existence of property, plant, and equipment, or participate in client's cycle counts of assets and check reconciliation to detailed asset records. • Review leases and determine that the leased assets and the related lease obligations have been properly accounted for.	• Vouch additions and disposals to supporting documentation using summaries showing detailed movements.
Ownership. Determine whether the property, plant, and equipment, is owned by the company and whether it is subject to any lien or restrictions.	• Examine, or obtain direct confirmation of, deeds or documents of title where appropriate. • Ascertain whether any items are pledged as collateral.	
Mechanical accuracy. Determine whether the basic mathematical calculation and clerical compilation procedures involved in maintaining the records of property, plant, and equipment costs and related depreciation have been accurately carried out.	• Obtain schedule of property, plant, and equipment showing cost, depreciation, additions, and disposals. Check adds, cross-adds, and cross-references, and agree totals to general ledger and related subsidiary ledgers. • Test depreciation calculations.	• Test posting and clerical accuracy of general ledger accounts.
Valuation. Determine whether the property, plant, and equipment is fairly stated at cost less an allowance for depreciation in accordance with generally accepted accounting principles.	• Review capitalization policy to assure that all significant capital expenditures are properly capitalized. • Review depreciation policy.	• Vouch additions and disposals to supporting documentation.
Disclosure. Determine whether property, plant and equipment disclosure in the financial statements is adequate, including disclosure of any liens on the assets.	• Review leases and determine that the leased assets and the related lease obligations have been properly disclosed. • Ascertain whether any items are pledged as collateral.	

FIG. 15.4 Sample Audit Procedures for Property, Plant, and Equipment

Classification. Determine whether property, plant and equipment is properly classified.	• Vouch additions and disposals from summaries showing detailed movements. • When examining the closely-related accounts of repairs and maintenance, be alert to items that should have been capitalized. • Particularly examine transactions near year-end for nature of asset and classification assigned.	• For selected items in the purchase journal and in the cash disbursements journal vouch to suppliers' invoices and check that the account distribution is proper.
Cutoff. Determine whether all purchases and sales of property, plant and equipment before end after the year end have been appropriately treated.	• Investigate purchases and sales of assets immediately before and after balance sheet date and verify date actually purchased/sold by reference to supporting documentation.	• Test date of recording purchases to ensure that proper depreciation is taken.

*Also often performed at an interim date.

OTHER ASSETS

Introduction

Cash is cash, but money spent for a license to manufacture an exotic new product, money used for research and development of a possible new product, or money spent to advertise a new product's advent may be wasted—or it may be a fountain of new cash. It's often very unpredictable. Some assets are hard to quantify, like intangibles, and their worth may vanish. So the rules for their quantification are piecemeal, equivocal, and somewhat inconsistent. A great deal of judgment is required.

What can appear in financial statements under the rubric "other assets" is somewhat of a hodgepodge. It can include research and development being performed under contract and similar costs; such intangibles as patents, copyrights, trademarks, licenses, and franchises; various incurred costs and investments, some of which may pay out but are "nonmarketable"; and such items as start-up costs, deferred charges, and prepaid expenses. The intent of this section is to illustrate the variety of concepts and standards that apply in this area of accounting and auditing, in which there are numerous, and sometimes incongruent, acceptable methods.

Some items in the other assets category are sufficiently important in specific contexts to be best treated elsewhere; thus, noncurrent marketable securities are covered in Chapter 12; deferred tax charges in Chapter 17; investments in equity investees and subsidiaries in Chapter 24; operating rights in Chapter 33; and research and development costs in Chapter 39.

Costs being deferred so that they can be matched with known related benefits in future reporting periods and expenditures that are *expected* to benefit future periods fit into the classification of prepaid expenses and deferred charges. The known benefit items usually include such assets as the cash surrender value of life insurance, unexpired multiyear insurance premiums, and insurance and other deposits. The expected benefit items cover such areas as organization costs, debt issuance expenses, deferred tooling, salable software costs, and start-up and preoperating costs.

The subject of cost deferrals was initially discussed in the FASB's Discussion Memorandum, *Accounting for Research and Development and Similar Costs* (1973). The Board subsequently issued SFAS 2, *Accounting for Research and Development Costs* (R50), and SFAS 7, *Accounting and Reporting by Development Stage Enterprises* (De4), but it has not yet dealt with "similar costs," except on a specific application basis, such as in accounting for the costs of computer software (SFAS 86) (Co2) and costs associated with originating or acquiring loans (SFAS 91) (L20). Accordingly, when costs are deferred, the following three general considerations must be addressed:

1. Nature of the costs to be deferred,
2. How such costs are to be charged to future periods: method of amortization and period of benefit,
3. Initial challenge to deferral, based on assessment of recoverability and continuing challenge to deferral policy as well as to assessment of recoverability.

SFAC 6, *Elements of Financial Statements* (FASB, 1985) ¶¶ 174–176, discusses the broad concepts of whether a particular item constitutes an asset. Specifically, ¶ 175 states:

> The kinds of items that may be recognized as expenses or losses rather than as assets because of uncertainty are some in which management's intent in taking certain steps or initiating certain transactions is clearly to acquire or enhance future economic benefits available to the entity. . . . The uncertainty is not about the intent to increase future economic benefits, but about whether and, if so, to what extent they succeeded in doing so.

Paragraph 176 continues with the thought that it is often difficult to distinguish between the items previously described and assets such as prepaid insurance and prepaid rent because costs are incurred for both groups and they tend to shade into each other. It states, "Indeed, the distinction is not based on the definition of assets . . . but rather on the practical considerations of coping with the effects of uncertainty."

The segregation below into two groups is done on the basis of common practice, but it is often hard to distinguish whether a particular "other asset" is a prepaid expense or a deferred charge, nor does it usually make much difference except in balance sheet classification. It is common in financial reporting to classify most prepaid expenses as current assets and most deferred charges as noncurrent assets.

Prepaid Expenses

Officers' Life Insurance. Businesses often purchase life insurance policies on the lives of key officers and owners, naming the business as the beneficiary. The proceeds are expected to help absorb the extra expenses involved in replacing a key executive or in buying an owner's interest. If a business purchases permanent insurance, which not only insures against the loss of life but also generates cash surrender value, the traditional accounting approach is the *cash value method,* as required by TB 85-4,

Accounting for Purchases of Life Insurance (I50). This method charges the income statement with the difference between the premium paid each year and the increases in cash value that year; the cash value would thus be the only asset recorded.

Cash surrender value is sometimes of sufficient importance to require separate presentation in financial statements. If loans are outstanding against the cash value, common practice is to offset the loans, as illustrated in the following footnote disclosure example:

> Policies of $500,000 each are carried by the corporation on the lives of the Chairman of the Board, President and Executive Vice-President. Policy loans bearing interest at 5% per annum are payable by application against the proceeds of the insurance contract in the event of death or cancellation of the contract.

In Issue 87-28, *Provision for Deferred Taxes on Increases in Cash Surrender Value of Life Insurance,* the EITF could reach no consensus on whether deferred income taxes should be provided for the difference between the increase in cash surrender value of an insurance policy and the premiums paid. The FASB staff believes that such excess meets the definition of a temporary difference and that a provision for deferred income taxes would be appropriate.

In Issue 88-5, *Recognition of Insurance Death Benefits,* the EITF considered the income effects of a life insurance policy purchased by an enterprise covering employees with the enterprise named as beneficiary. The enterprise intends to use the death benefits from such policies and any loans against the cash values of the policies to protect against the loss of a key executive or fund obligations to employees, such as deferred retirement or compensation plans, or buyout arrangements. Two issues were discussed:

1. Income recognition for the death benefits on an actuarially expected basis (as opposed to the event of death of the insured employee).
2. If the actuarial approach is not acceptable, the valuation of the policies at their net loan value (the policies' borrowing power) if the enterprise intends to hold the policies until the death of the insureds and borrow against the policies to meet any cash requirements.

As to the first issue, the EITF concluded that the actuarial approach to income recognition is not appropriate. TB 85-4 is a cash surrender value approach and does not countenance recording income based on mortality projections.

No decision was reached on the second issue; however, a majority of the Task Force believed that a valuation based on net loan value is consistent with management's intent and presumably therefore would be acceptable. The FASB staff is considering the issue further.

Prepaid Insurance. Property and liability insurance premiums are usually paid annually in advance, and thus a pro rata part of the cost will be unexpired if the policy anniversary does not coincide with the financial reporting date. The unexpired amount is carried as an asset in prepaid expenses.

In addition, some policies are written for a longer term, say three to five years, and require a deposit, which may be recoverable at the end of the policy term or which, alternatively, may be applied against premiums determined to be due. To the extent that adequate provision has been made for retrospective rating adjustments, the premium deposits are classified as assets in prepaid expenses.

In some cases, the "purchase" of insurance is really a way of spreading losses, the cost of which will be borne totally by the insured. For example, a five-year noncancellable policy with annual premiums based on prior experience may be a self-insurance device, depending on the rights of the parties as to overaccrual or underaccrual of losses at the end of the policy term. Also, especially for employee health, accident, and disability insurance, some companies use the insurer as a claims administrator for a fee, perhaps purchasing only "umbrella" (high limits) coverage. Though refundable deposits and unexpired premiums in these situations should be shown as assets, there is obviously another major aspect to consider—the proper liability accrual.

Interest, Rents, and Royalties. A bank loan may be issued on a discount basis—that is, the total interest is withheld by the lender from the proceeds given to the borrower. This discount is not a prepaid expense, but is classified as a reduction of the note in financial statement presentation (I69.109). Where interest is actually paid in advance, the unexpired amount is classified as a prepaid expense, and is amortized using the interest method (I69.108).

Rent is often paid in advance. The future portion of the prepaid rental period as of the financial reporting date will determine the amount of prepaid rent to be classified, along with rent deposits, as an asset.

Royalties and license fees entitling the licensee to use an intangible for a future period of time or number of units produced should be carried to the extent of the unexpired time period (assuming the unexpired asset is expected to be recoverable from operations in the future) or in proportion to the number of units permitted or reasonably estimated to be produced in the future.

Taxes. Refundable income taxes arise from recognition of the tax effects of operating loss carrybacks or other claims for payments made under protest. Though these items are receivables, they are sometimes grouped in prepaid expenses if minor in amount.

Property, franchise, and similar taxes may also be prepaid, with the unexpired asset amount usually being based on the future portion of the period to which the tax is applicable.

Deferred Charges

The term *deferred charge* is not defined in the authoritative literature of the profession. GAAP presently recognizes certain costs such as relocation, repair, training, or advertising services as eligible for treatment as assets if they have a defined and measurable relationship to future economic benefits. In addition, the concept of an existence of a relationship to future economic benefit is discussed in SFAC 6, *Elements of Financial Statements* (FASB, 1985), but the term *deferred charge* is not defined. However, SFAC 6 comments (¶ 249):

Costs incurred for services such as research and development, relocation, repair, training, or advertising relate to future economic benefits in one of two ways. First, costs may represent rights to unperformed services yet to be received from other entities. For example, advertising cost incurred may be for a series of advertisements to appear in national news magazines over the next three months. Those kinds of costs incurred are similar to prepaid insurance or prepaid rent. They are payments in advance for services to be rendered to the entity by other entities in the future. Second, they may represent future benefit that is expected to be obtained within the entity by using assets or in future exchange transactions with other entities. For example, prerelease advertising of a motion picture may increase the future economic benefits of the product, or repairs may increase the future economic benefits of a piece of equipment. Those kinds of costs may be accounted for as assets either by being added to other assets or by being disclosed separately.

Organization Costs. Organization costs usually represent those costs incurred in forming a business: legal services, filing fees, and stock issuance record costs are representative. The costs are either expensed as incurred or deferred and amortized over a reasonably short period. Since organization costs are deductible for income tax purposes over a 60-month amortization period, this period is also used generally for convenience in financial reporting. Some contend that organization costs should be retained intact as long as the organization exists. However, this is not often done in practice, because the costs are rarely significant.

Generally, an accumulated amortization account is not maintained or presented in financial reporting, and the asset account is usually reduced directly by the periodic amortization.

Debt Issuance Costs. Debt issuance expenses are legal fees, commissions, printing, and other costs incurred in the process of issuing debt instruments. Commonly, these expenses are deferred and amortized, along with the premium or discount, if any, over the life of the debt issue. (Related aspects of debt issues are discussed in Chapters 18 and 23.)

Marketing Research. The FASB's R&D Discussion Memorandum (1973, p. 18) defines marketing research as an information gathering activity aimed at:

1. The acceptance by customers of a company's products,
2. The possibility of increasing sales of its products to existing or to new customers, and
3. The possibility of attracting customers for new products which will either replace its current products or lead to new areas of enterprise.

Even before 1973, it was rare to find a deferral of marketing research costs; where it did occur, it was usually based on the cost of research performed by an outside specialist organization. The fact that the FASB neglected to include it by name in the examples in SFAC 6 cited at the outset of this section reinforces the current practice of charging these costs to expense as incurred.

Advertising and Promotion. In this category are various sales promotion activities which disseminate information about a company's products in order to create a favorable emotional response. Most such activities are short-lived and thus as a practical matter are simply expensed. A major campaign, however, sometimes gives rise to questions whether the cost is deferrable, but in practice, deferral is infrequent. In the R&D Discussion Memorandum, the FASB implied that such costs would be subjected to whatever treatment might apply to R&D (FASB, 1973, p. 19). Thus the matter was left at rest by the FASB's conclusion to write off all R&D (R50.108). The FASB has again raised the question by listing advertising as a potential deferral candidate in SFAC 6.

Of course, unused advertising and promotional supplies, catalogs, and the like — tangible items to be used or already in use by customers — may be deferred if material. Also, advance payments for advertising yet to be run is not expensed until run. An example of a disclosure of deferred promotion costs is shown in Figure 15.5.

Start-Up Costs. Start-up costs are often included in financial statements of companies involved in major new undertakings that involve a *learning curve* which consists of the excess costs, especially of labor, in a new facility that is expected to produce similar or identical products over an extended period. The concept is that, based on engineering studies, the expected normal cost will stabilize at a lower figure than initial costs, which are increased abnormally by testing, "debugging," training, and so on. When a particularly large program is involved, the deferred costs are often called *program costs* and may be included in the inventory classification if the program will be completed within the business cycle of the contractor, even though that may be several years. (See Chapter 37 regarding program costs.)

Preopening Costs. Preopening costs are sometimes deferred by multi-unit companies such as retailers, loan companies, and restaurant chains. Costs incurred in advance of opening a new unit (and also sometimes during a brief initial period of operation) are deferred and amortized against subsequent operations where there is no uncertainty as to recoverability. The nature of the costs should be limited to direct costs, such as payroll, occupancy, training, and direct unit advertising.

The period of deferral is typically for a short term, such as a period of 6 to 24 months. The period selected should coincide with the period expected to receive the benefit. The method of amortization is generally straight line; however, recoverability must be continually challenged by comparing the operating results of the unit with the amount of deferred costs, considering comparable units in similar circumstances, as well as the plan for the individual unit.

The policy with respect to deferring preopening expenses should be carefully monitored for enterprises without the experience of a number of other operating units against which to judge the probability of economic benefit. Challenge should also be made when activities commence in new geographic areas that are unfamiliar to the enterprise.

The adoption of an accounting policy for deferral of preopening costs should be carefully considered. The FASB in SFAS 7 indicated that GAAP applicable to established operating enterprises applies equally to development stage enterprises, and it could be said to apply equally to expanding enterprises. As operations mature, companies sometimes reevaluate their continued use of deferral of preopening costs, especially when amortization expense and actual costs incurred would be approxi-

---

Promotion.* Promotion costs related to sales of book and record series and book clubs are amortized over a 12-month period. Other promotion costs are primarily expensed within the year incurred.

*Presented under Summary of Significant Accounting Policies.

FIG. 15.5   Financial Statement Disclosure Policy Related to Deferral of Promotional Costs
Source: Time Incorporated, 1986 Annual Report.

mately equal. Any change in policy should be carefully considered, with recognition given to comparability of operating results (among other factors) in determining the preferability of the accounting change.

Relocation and Rearrangement. The costs of changing the location of a plant or office or of rearranging production facilities in a plant—in all instances intended to significantly enhance future profitability and productivity—have occasionally been recognized as deferred charges and amortized against subsequent operations for a relatively short time period, say three to five years. The justification is the same as that used for deferring any kind of cost: there is a demonstrable and acceptably high probability of obtaining a future economic benefit against which the costs thereof should be matched.

In Issue 88-10, *Costs Associated With Lease Modification or Termination*, the EITF discussed moving costs (among other issues). While no consensus was reached, the Task Force members felt that expensing such costs is the predominant practice. Although this discussion is likely to virtually eliminate instances in which moving costs are deferred, expensing treatment may not be categorically applicable to other types of relocation and rearrangemeant costs.

Other Deferred Charges. It seems clear that if a current expenditure has an economic benefit obtainable in a future period and is quantifiable, the expenditure possibly will be deferred in some financial statement. There is no way to identify with certainty the various items that have been deferred from time to time, but the FASB mentioned several in SFAC 6 that were not described in the above discussion:

* Legal costs
* Repair
* Training

Such items are less visible in the financial statements of publicly held corporations, either because the deferral approach is not used, or because the amounts are not consequential and are therefore included within a broad caption such as "Other Assets," without delineation. The former reason is the more likely, given the SEC's traditional skepticism about the realizability of such "assets" from future operations. In mid-1988, the SEC staff stated that an SAB was in process regarding deferrals of "soft costs."

NOTE 1. SIGNIFICANT ACCOUNTING POLICIES
Principles of Consolidation and Basis of Presentation

Educational contract acquisition costs. The Company defers the costs, principally marketing and sales, associated with acquiring TTR Contracts [contracts for its educational products and services]. These acquisition costs ("Educational contract acquisition costs") are shown as a reduction of deferred educational contract revenues in the accompanying balance sheets and are recognized as an expense on a pro rata basis when the related revenue is recognized.

Educational program production costs. Costs incurred by the Company in the original production of, and improvement to, educational courses (including interest costs associated with the funding thereof) are capitalized and amortized by the straight-line method over the estimated useful lives of the respective courses. During the fourth quarter of 1986, the Company revised the estimated useful life of its educational courses from four to six years. The effect of changing the estimated useful life of these courses on a prospective basis, effective August 1, 1986, was not material to the 1986 financial statements.

FIG. 15.6   Financial Statement Disclosure Policy Related to Deferral of Educational Program Costs
Source: Advanced Systems Incorporated, 1986 Annual Report.

Also in 1988, the FASB considered whether to add a project to its agenda on these types of costs, but declined to do so in view of higher-priority projects.

Operating Assets Other Than PP&E

There are several types of business that use information bases as the operating asset enabling the performance of their primary activities. Though these are tangible, they usually have little intrinsic value but may have a substantial value if sold as a unit. One of the possible types is highlighted in the following paragraph.

Correspondence and residency schools dealing with technical, paraprofessional, self-improvement, and similar subjects have sometimes deferred the costs of course development, amortizing them over the expected useful life of the course program. Because of the SFAS 2 indication that "conceptual formulation and design of possible product or process alternatives" is an R&D activity (R50.111) to be expensed, it is probable that the current practice generally is to write off course development costs when the production costs are not material. (See Chapter 39 for a further discussion of R&D activities.) However, there are some companies that defer and amortize educational program production and related costs that are material. An example of a disclosure in this area is shown in Figure 15.6.

Another type of information base is a *title plant*, which contains indexed and catalogued data about parcels of land in a particular geographic area. The data base is used in operations for the purpose of writing insurance policies protecting landowners from claims challenging their ownership rights. SFAS 61, *Accounting for Title Plant* (Ti7), discusses capitalization of costs incurred to construct and maintain the plant, and how to account for sales of complete or partial interests therein. Note that title plant is not depreciated or amortized; but a writedown may be necessary if its value becomes impaired.

Computer Software Development Costs

SFAS 86, *Accounting for the Costs of Computer Software to Be Sold, Leased, or Otherwise Marketed* (Co2), supersedes portions of SFAS 2, *Accounting for Research and Development Costs,* and FIN 6 (R50). The Statement (which is further discussed in Chapter 39) applies to internally developed software products, enhancements, and purchased software to be sold, leased, or otherwise marketed. It also applies to software that is to be part of another product, process, or service. It does not apply to software for internal use or software created for others under a contractual arrangement.

The Statement requires capitalization of production costs (coding, testing, documentation, and preparation of training materials) incurred after technological feasibility under development has been established. Technological feasibility is established by completion of a detailed program design or, absent that, a working model of the product. Duplication costs are capitalized as inventory and expensed when related revenue is recognized.

Capitalization must end, and amortization must begin, when the product is available for general release. Amortization is the greater of a percentage based on the ratio of current gross revenues to estimated future gross revenues or as determined by use of the straight-line method. A net realizable value test is required for all periods after capitalization begins.

SFAS 86 also requires capitalization of purchased software that will be part of another product, process, or service, if technological feasibility of the end product has been established or if the software has an alternative future use. Otherwise, the cost must be expensed.

In addition, maintenance and customer support costs must be expensed as incurred or as related revenues are recognized, whichever comes first.

The FASB published staff guidance on applying SFAS 86 in its February 1986 issue of *Highlights of Financial Reporting Issues* (McCallion, 1986). That document addresses questions relating to the scope of SFAS 86: research and development, production costs, maintenance and customer support, purchased software, amortization, disclosure, transition, balance sheet presentation, modifications to the product, and enhancements.

Intangible Assets

Intangibles is a collective term useful to accountants, but the nature of intangibles makes them impossible to define in any categorical way; indeed, the preceding section on deferred charges and similar costs contains some items that could as readily have been discussed in this section. A generally satisfactory concept is that intangible assets lack physical substance and possess economic value. Their value depends on, and varies with, many circumstances. It may rise, fall, disappear, reappear, or be extinguished forever.

A list of assets that most accountants generally would characterize as intangibles includes the following:

Copyrights	Franchises
Trademarks	Goodwill
Trade names	Operating rights
Secret processes	Covenants not to compete
Licenses	Future interests
Patents	Record masters

APB 17, *Intangible Assets* (I60), addresses the accounting for intangibles. The opinion was issued in 1970 contemporaneously with APB 16, *Business Combinations* (B50), to resolve the accounting for goodwill resulting from a business combination (discussed in Chapter 23); however, the APB properly decided to cover all intangibles at the same time. Research and development costs, which were then being capitalized by some companies as intangibles, were specifically excluded from APB 17. The accounting for research and development cost was resolved in SFAS 2 and is discussed in Chapter 39.

Characteristics. A useful way of classifying intangibles is contained in APB 17, ¶ 10 and is presented below.

Identifiability. Some intangibles are specifically identifiable, perhaps represented by a legal title that may be used to defend against infringement or other unlawful usage by others. Other intangibles may not be specifically identifiable; goodwill is not, and a purchased business territory may not be (see, e.g., B50.158(c)).

Manner of acquisition. Intangibles may be purchased from others or may be developed internally. Purchased intangibles may or may not be specifically identifiable, whereas by definition internally developed intangibles will be specific.

Expected period of benefit. Some intangibles have a duration limited by law or contract; others have an indeterminate or indefinite life, at least in an accounting sense. For example, a copyright is valid for the life of the author plus 50 years.

Separability from the enterprise. An intangible with a legal title is separable and thus may be salable. The general goodwill of an enterprise is not separable, but it may be salable in a sense, for example, through franchising.

Capitalizable Costs. When intangibles are purchased from others, they are recorded at purchase cost. Costs of developing specific intangibles such as patents are also capitalized, but only out-of-pocket items such as legal fees and application and filing fees are included. The more basic costs of development, which are akin to research and development, are expensed as incurred. Of course, self-developed intangibles that are not specifically identifiable and are inherent in a continuing business as a whole are not capitalized (I60.105).

Amortization. APB 17 postulates that all intangibles eventually lose their value and thus must be reduced by systematic charges to income over the estimated benefit period. For specific intangibles, legal, regulatory, or contractual provisions may set a maximum useful life, but certain other factors also need to be taken into account (I60.108):

* Provisions for renewal or extension may alter a specified limit on useful life.
* Effects of obsolescence, demand, competition, and other economic factors may reduce a useful life.
* A useful life may parallel the service life expectancies of individuals or groups of employees.
* Expected actions of competitors and others may restrict present competitive advantages.
* An apparently unlimited useful life may in fact be indefinite, and benefits cannot be reasonably projected.
* An intangible asset may be a composite of many individual factors with varying effective lives.

To put a limit on the variety of answers obtainable under the above guidelines by different evaluators, APB 17 specifies that the maximum amortization period for any intangible acquired after October 1, 1970 is 40 years (I60.110). The straight-line method of amortization is generally required unless it is demonstrated that some other method is more appropriate (I60.111).

Refer to Chapters 40 and 41 for a discussion of intangibles amortization, usually over a somewhat shorter period than the 40-year maximum, in banking and thrift institutions; and see Chapter 23 for a discussion of goodwill and negative goodwill.

Periodic Reassessment. As with any asset, intangibles must be assessed periodically to ascertain whether any permanent diminution in value should be recognized in addition to normal amortization. Also, each intangible right must be assessed periodically by management to see if the amortization term continues to be reasonable. If not, adjustment of the term may be necessary based on the actual facts and circumstances. As a practical matter, diminution in value often is recognized through shortening the amortization term. Occasionally, an intangible balance may be completely written off based on the occurrence of a single event. (For example, see the problem with motor carrier operating rights in Chapter 33.)

AUDITING CONSIDERATIONS – OTHER ASSETS

Prepayments, Deferrals, and Similar Items

A systems approach to auditing prepaid expenses, deferred charges, and similar items generally is not practicable because the volume of transactions is small and control over the transactions is often limited, except as these amounts may arise from basic operating cycles such as purchasing and cash disbursements.

In general, the auditor must establish the reasonableness of the amounts and the likelihood that the costs are properly deferrable as benefits of future periods. It is difficult to obtain assurance that untried and unproven operations will be profitable when commenced, let alone that there will be sufficient margin to absorb such items as deferred start-up costs. In a similar vein, knowing that program costs are deferred on the basis that the learning curve will be achieved (causing unit costs to decline),

---

1. Obtain schedules of prepaid expenses and deferred charges showing, where applicable:

   - Description of item,
   - Asset balance at beginning and end of period,
   - Accumulated amortization at beginning and end of period,
   - Additions giving date of purchase or acquisition and identifying vendor,
   - Amounts amortized or written-off in period,
   - Sales proceeds and profit or loss on disposal,
   - Lapsed items, renewal fees and amounts written-off, and
   - Any other relevant information.

   a. Check accuracy of information on schedule.
   b. Add and cross-add schedules.
   c. Trace totals to the general ledger.
   d. Trace balances at beginning of period to prior period's working papers.
   e. Check calculations where appropriate.

2. Obtain direct confirmation of material account balances, if feasible given the nature of the item.

3. Examine underlying documents in support of account balances. Vouch selected items to evidence of authorization required by company policy.

4. Determine whether balances are collectible or otherwise realizable or, alternatively, whether expectations of future benefits are reasonable in relation to prepayments and deferrals.

   a. Ascertain that adequate provision has been made for any items that are overdue or appear doubtful.
   b. Where applicable, ensure all suspense accounts not cleared are fully analyzed and represent amounts which are properly carried as other assets.
   c. Consider management's policy with regard to prepayment and deferral of expenses to evaluate that only those costs attributable to future periods are being carried forward, and that there is reasonable support for retaining such amounts as assets (e.g., continuing value, no adverse change in conditions or expectations).
   d. Where deferred charges are being systematically amortized, ascertain that the method has been consistently applied and that no events have occurred which might lead to a reduction in the write-off period.

FIG. 15.7   Prepaid Expenses and Deferred Charges—Substantive Tests of Balances

the auditor must satisfy himself that the costs of the program have a high probability of realization. The auditor must test actual experience to see that unit costs do decrease. He may have to rely on experience with previous contracts or programs if the current program is in its early stages.

The audit of operating assets such as computer software, educational program costs, and title plant is similar to the audit of self-constructed plant and equipment discussed earlier in this chapter.

Analytical Procedures. The auditor will have to deduce the appropriate procedures to fit the specific asset, and will use certain analytical procedures as a guide to the area to be examined. Typical analytical procedures might be to:

1. Compare the account balances to similar items at the previous audit date and determine whether the figures seem reasonable in relation to other information (e.g., increase in level of expenses over the previous year, changes in operations);
2. Review the reasonableness of deferral of expenditure in relation to operating results, prevailing economic conditions, immediate industry prospects, client's going concern status, and so forth; and
3. Consider the appropriateness of deferral under GAAP; sometimes this requires searching for analogies and precedents and could include discussion with other accounting firms or specialists who have experience with the matter.

Substantive Procedures. Results from analytical procedures guide the auditor in selecting the nature and extent of other substantive procedures. Such other procedures should reflect in their design the likelihood of errors in the financial statements for each transaction/error type affecting the account balance. An interrelationship matrix as described in Chapter 7 is a useful tool for this purpose.

A sample of substantive procedures is given in Figure 15.7. Each procedure may serve more than one purpose in assuring the auditor that all error types are adequately covered.

It must be emphasized here that, as with the audit of cash, there is a tendency for less experienced audit assistants to overdo the substantive procedures in analyzing and obtaining evidence for items that are relatively minor in relation to the overall financial statements, such as prepaid insurance and prepaid rent. The accountant in charge should monitor this area to ensure that efforts are focused on the real issues, which invariably deal with the propriety of deferring a cost that is material.

Intangible Assets

The auditing problems with and procedures for intangibles are like those described earlier for prepaid expenses, deferred charges, and similar items. A systems approach is not practicable, because the volume of transactions invariably is small and internal control structures are not often specifically designed to embrace intangibles.

Sample procedures in addition to those discussed earlier might include the following:

1. For additions and disposals, vouch to
   a. Independent supporting evidence, and
   b. Appropriate authorizations or board minutes.
2. Scrutinize unusual items and obtain satisfactory explanations for them.
3. For disposals:
   a. Check calculation of profit or loss on disposal and trace to income statement accounts, and
   b. Determine that proper reductions of carrying amounts have been made.
4. For amounts amortized or written down, vouch to appropriate authority. Determine whether policy is consistent with prior year.

5. Confirm title or ownership rights:
   a. Inspect renewal receipts or payments as evidence of title at date of renewal, and
   b. Consider obtaining direct confirmation of title.
6. Consider, discuss with responsible personnel, and document in working papers the reasonableness of amounts at which intangibles are carried in the financial statements. Intangible rights that have been allowed to lapse or are no longer used should be considered for write-off. Where book amounts appear excessive, discuss with management and evaluate management's decision regarding the write-off of any excess amount.

16

Pensions and Other Employee Benefits

INTRODUCTION

The Changing Environment

Changes in the social and political environment are having a significant impact on the role of employee and retiree benefits and the related employer's obligation. The types of benefits provided by employers range from the most common, such as paid vacation and sick pay for active employees, to health care and life insurance benefits for retirees and their dependents. In that range we also find perquisites, health care for active employees, special termination benefits, and normal retirement benefits. The most significant accounting and auditing issues relate to health care benefits for active employees and the obligation and costs related to pension benefits and health care for retirees and dependents.

The single most critical change in our society today is a demographic one. Our population is aging at a rapid rate. The portion of our population that was born in the post World War II "baby boom" will be reaching retirement age over the next twenty to forty years. This group will constitute an increasing percentage of our population far beyond what most people realize. (See Figure 16.1.)

These facts, combined with the impact of a health care inflation rate that on a national basis exceeded the general inflation rate by 5%–6% in 1987 (in the past the difference has been much greater), are contributing to concerns expressed by politicians and accounting standard-setters over the past few years. Their concerns relate to the commitments made by employers and the adequacy of current accounting for and reporting of the liabilities and costs related to retirement and health care benefits.

Another issue of concern to regulators has been the recent and increasing trend of employers to terminate existing pension plans in order to recapture excess assets from overfunded plans and attempts to significantly reduce or terminate health care benefits for retirees. Some members of Congress ardently believe regulation may be necessary to protect retirees, possibly even by mandating a minimum level of health care coverage for them. Some speculate that Congress may even go so far as mandating a minimum health care coverage for *active* employees.

Age Group	Percent increase (decrease) compared with 1982	
	Year 2000	Year 2030
18–24	(16)	(3)
25–34	(9)	(2)
35–54	53	50
55–64	8	46
65–74	10	100
75–over	45	143

FIG. 16.1 Changing Age Demographics in the United States
Adapted from: Bureau of the Census, "True Level Population Projections" (1977), and Social Security Administration, "Social Security Area Population Projections" (1981).

Regulatory Environment

ERISA. Accounting, reporting, and auditing of employee benefit plans, particularly pension benefit plans, and of the related sponsor costs and obligations in the company's financial statements and footnotes have taken on increased significance, and much of the reason can be found in the Employee Retirement Income Security Act of 1974 (ERISA). ERISA is mentioned throughout this chapter, and a later section provides a more complete discussion of its technical aspects.

The stated purpose of ERISA is to protect employee benefit rights by

- Requiring reporting to participants and beneficiaries
- Establishing the obligations of and standards of conduct for fiduciaries
- Providing a means to enforce the provisions of the law

The law also establishes minimum standards for participation, vesting, and funding, and requires plan termination insurance. Important, too, is the requirement for the filing of an annual report with the Internal Revenue Service. The annual report for plans that have more than 100 participants but that are not fully insured must include the independent auditor's opinion on the financial statements of the plan for the year of the filing.

From the company's viewpoint, accounting for pension benefit plans is principally a matter of expensing currently, in the period in which the company receives the employee's services, retirement benefits that are to be paid in the future. The principal operating considerations to the company are the impact of expense on earnings and the impact of funding on cash flow. From the perspective of the employee benefit plan, accounting consists of the proper recording of funds received or receivable, valuation of investments at current value, and recording of benefits paid. The plan's operating considerations made more important by ERISA relate generally to administration and compliance.

Many issues concerning accounting, reporting, and auditing of employee benefits stem from actuarial considerations. Changes in the actuarial method or in actuarial assumptions about covered employees or return on investment assets, for example, can have a significant impact on the company's current expense and pension obligation and on the timing and manner of funding the plan.

Pension Benefit Guarantee Corporation (PBGC). The PBGC was formed as an insuring entity to provide pension benefits to retirees in situations where the employer was no longer able to meet its obligations. Employers are charged an annual premium per employee to maintain a fund from which the PBGC makes payments to retirees of defaulting employers.

With the substantial number of bankruptcies over the past few years in which the PBGC has had to assume responsibility for such payments, its resources have been strained. As a result, there has been discussion regarding the possibility of increasing the premiums and narrowing the conditions under which the PBGC must assume the employer's obligation. Additionally, PBGC approval must be obtained to terminate a pension plan.

TYPES OF EMPLOYEE BENEFITS

Retirement Related Benefits

From an accounting perspective, the commitments by employers to provide benefits to employees after retirement present very difficult conceptual and practical issues. Benefits provided to active employees, on the other hand, are not an issue since the related costs are typically expensed as incurred. However, the commitment for benefits to be provided after retirement represents an obligation to make future disbursements based on employment and service rendered currently or in the past.

There are three basic types of retirement benefits: pension, health care, and life insurance.

Pension Benefits. These benefits generally take the form of annuity payments to retirees for the remainder of their lives with, in some cases, a residual benefit to a surviving spouse or other dependents.

Health Care Benefits. These benefits can include full or partial coverage of medical, dental, eyecare, and prescription costs. They may apply to the retiree, the spouse, and even to dependent children. Typically, the retiree and spouse are covered for life while dependent children are covered up to a certain age. Most plans take into consideration Medicare coverage and reduce the employer's cost of coverage accordingly.

Life Insurance Benefits. In some instances an employer will pay for a life insurance policy on the retiree. The beneficiary of the policy would be the surviving spouse or other dependents.

Termination Benefits

To encourage employees to take early retirement or otherwise voluntarily leave the company, the employer may offer special inducements. For example, an employer may, for a limited period, offer enhanced retirement benefits, such as lump-sum payments, larger pension benefits than would have been received had the employees retired at their current ages under normal circumstances, or both.

Inducements to leave the company, other than by retirement, may include severance payments, relocation costs, or the use of a placement firm at no cost to the employee.

Other Employee Benefits

Employers provide a host of other benefits, for example, paid vacation, paid sick leave, health care coverage, free use of an automobile, and reimbursement of continuing education costs. Although the costs of such benefits can be substantial, the accounting and social issues are generally less difficult and controversial than those related to retirees. Therefore, the primary focus of this chapter is on commitments made regarding retirement benefits and the related employer costs.

PENSIONS

Types of Pension Plans

There are basically two types of pension plans: defined contribution and defined benefit plans. However, a recently developed hybrid known as a *floor plan* combines the attributes of both a defined contribution and a defined benefit plan.

Defined Contribution Plans. The *defined contribution plan* specifies the amount of periodic contribution to be paid by the sponsor, rather than the benefits to be received by the participant. A participant's benefits, when he becomes eligible to receive them, are usually based on the amount credited to his individual account. Sponsor contributions are determined by applying a specified rate against a variable such as labor hours worked or wages earned (in the case of retirement savings plans) or by a formula applied to defined earnings of the sponsor (in the case of profit-sharing plans).

Defined Benefit Plans. Plans that specify the benefit (or the method used to determine the benefit) to be received at retirement are referred to as *defined benefit plans*. The most common example is a pension plan that calculates benefits as a function of average or final salary or years of service. The sponsor's annual contribution to the plan is determined by an actuarial valuation. Many defined benefit plans are integrated with government social security (FICA) benefits, so that the total calculated benefit is reduced by FICA benefits received.

Floor Plans. This recently developed type of plan essentially is based on a defined contribution plan (such as a profit-sharing plan), but specifies a minimum level of benefit to be provided during retirement, as is typical of a defined benefit plan. However, to the extent that the value of the assets in the defined contribution plan is not sufficient to provide the minimum benefit, the employer has an obligation for the difference. These plans have raised some interesting conceptual and implementation questions regarding appropriate accounting, some of which have been dealt with by the EITF.

Characteristics of Plans

Sponsorship. Plans can fall into categories by sponsor – single-employer or multiemployer plans. A *single-employer plan* is usually established unilaterally because the employer desires to provide certain benefits for his employees, although some may be collectively bargained. The plan is normally administered by the employer, who may also act as trustee for the plan or who may arrange for a bank or insurance company to act as trustee.

Multiemployer plans are normally established within an industry and are collectively bargained. This type of plan is jointly administered by union and employer representatives. Generally, plan assets are maintained in a bank trust arrangement or an insurance company contract. Such a plan usually provides pension, health benefits, or both to the participants. Multiemployer pension plans often have characteristics of both defined benefit and defined contribution plans in that the specified contribution rate is expected to produce a promised benefit. Employer contributions to multiemployer pension plans are usually based on a formula such as a fixed rate times employee hours or employee wages paid. Benefits, however, are calculated in a manner similar to defined benefit plans. Multiemployer plans usually require the services of an actuary to value plan obligations and establish the contribution rate employers should use. In practice, the contribution rate is normally determined through union negotiations and may not be directly related to promised benefits.

Funding Provisions. Plans are identified as contributory or noncontributory, depending on whether participants do or do not contribute to the plan. *Noncontributory* plans receive contributions only from the employer or employers. *Contributory* plans also receive mandatory or voluntary contributions from the participants.

Vesting. Most pension plans stipulate that a plan participant must remain in service for a certain number of years to earn benefits under the plan. Usually vesting is incremental over the specified period of time and is expressed as a percentage, but in some plans a participant has no vested rights until a specified period has elapsed, at which point he is vested 100%. For example, the plan may specify that a participant is 50% vested at the end of eight years of participation and that vesting increases 10% for each year of participation beyond eight years until fully vested (100%); or it may specify that a participant has no vested rights until he has completed ten years of service, at which time he becomes fully vested.

Eligibility to Retire. All plans specify the required minimum period of service and the age at which the employee can first elect to retire. Once the minimum eligibility requirements are satisfied, the employee could choose to retire at any time. However, the level of benefits to be received upon retirement are generally contingent, in part, upon the total years of service rendered by the employee.

Actuarial Measurement of Pension Cost and Obligation

At retirement, employees with vested pension rights are entitled to receive a stream of benefit payments called an *annuity*. These rights have been accruing to the individual over his employment term. Under GAAP, the cost of this annuity should be expensed over the period of the individual's employment.

Actuarial valuation of the pension plan has two purposes. The first is to estimate the amount of contributions necessary to provide to each employee his pension annuity upon retirement. The second is to provide a basis for attributing pension cost to the period of the individual's employment. To accomplish these two purposes the actuary must (1) apply the appropriate actuarial method for the plan and (2) make relevant assumptions about the nature of the work force, the expected interest rate to be earned by the assets held by the plan, and the appropriate discount rate to be applied in measuring the pension obligation.

Prior to SFAS 87 (P16), the methods for recognition of pension expense varied widely. The effect of SFAS 87, which is discussed in a later section in this chapter, was to restrict the alternatives for recognition of pension expense and to improve comparability in reporting.

Actuarial Valuation. An actuarial valuation produces several kinds of information, including:

1. *Vested benefit obligation,* the present value of accrued vested benefits, under the plan.
2. *Accumulated benefit obligation,* the present value of benefits attributed to periods prior to the date of the actuarial valuation (not considering future salary increases).
3. *Projected benefit obligation,* the accumulated benefit obligation plus the effect of future salary increases.
4. *Service cost,* the annual cost of the plan assignable to years subsequent to the inception of the plan or subsequent to a particular valuation date.

An *actuarial method* is a technique for determining the obligation for future benefits under the plan and for attributing a cost to successive years. Examples of actuarial methods include the unit credit method, the entry age normal method, the frozen initial liability method, and the aggregate method. All of these methods except the last result in separate identification of the employer's contribution for pension obligation and service cost. The aggregate cost method calculates only a single cost amount that includes a portion of the unfunded accrued liability.

SFAS 87, *Employer's Accounting for Pensions* (P16), has mandated the use of a benefits-based actuarial approach for financial reporting purposes. Therefore, the unit credit or projected unit credit approaches are the only ones currently acceptable.

However, in determining which method to use for funding purposes, the actuary will consider, among other things, the company's growth potential and cash-flow expectations. If a company is in a period of growth when cash is scarce, a method that provides for smaller contributions currently and larger contributions in later years might be more appropriate. Conversely, for some companies it might be more appropriate to apply a method that results in relatively stable contributions.

Assumptions. *Actuarial assumptions* are estimates of the likelihood of occurrence of future events. Examples of assumptions include: mortality (the probability of death in each future year for each member of the employee population), salary scale or progression rate (the expected rate at which salaries will increase), employee turnover (the termination rate of the employee population), rate of return (the expected growth rate of investment assets resulting from appreciation and earnings on investments), and the discount rate. The actuary must exercise his professional judgment in making the proper assumptions for a particular plan.

Of the assumptions previously mentioned, probably the most important are the rate of return assumption, since this affects the expected growth rate of plan assets, and the discount rate used to calculate the present value of the benefits (benefit obligation) and the present value of vested benefits. Relatively small changes in the discount rate have a large inverse effect on the results of present value calculations and, therefore, will have a significant impact on the benefit obligation and the present value of vested benefits.

An additional complication is introduced by inflation. During periods of inflation, the interest rate is normally higher. If benefits are a function of pay rate or salary in later years of employment, the salary scale assumption may also need to be adjusted for inflation.

Therefore, changes in the inflation assumption can cause an increase in the future amount of benefits to be paid. Further, the direction of the net change (i.e., increase or decrease) of the present value of the benefit obligation and the present value of vested benefits is difficult to assess because the assumptions could be moving in opposite directions, unless the effect of inflation on benefits is assumed to be the same or smaller than the effect on rate of return.

When an assumption is made, it generally should be applied consistently. For example, it would typically be inappropriate to take inflation into consideration for rate of return purposes but not for salary scale purposes. However, each significant assumption should represent the best estimate on a stand-alone basis. That is, the decision about one assumption may not necessarily be contingent on the decision on another.

Gains and Losses. The only certainty about actuarial assumptions is that inevitably they will diverge from actual experience. These divergences, referred to as actuarial gains or losses, arise because the actual experience of the plan differs from the actuarial assumptions and because assumptions about future events may be changed periodically. Actuarial gains and losses are typically recognized over future periods.

One example of a circumstance in which an actuarial gain or loss might occur is a sudden change in turnover that is expected to persist. A gain may well result in this circumstance, because the previous turnover assumption for the plan would probably prove to be too low. A second example is actual mortality versus expected mortality. The plan's mortality experience might deviate from the expected mortality for many reasons. On a statistical basis, deviation from the population norm is expected since the randomly selected sample of employees used to estimate mortality only approximates the total population. Further, in some industries the work force may be exposed to environmental factors that impact mortality. As actuarial gains or losses from such events occur, they must be considered in the actuary's periodic valuation of the plan.

Funding Pension Obligations

Funding refers to the employer's contribution of assets, usually cash, to a pension plan. While ERISA established statutory rules providing for a minimum contribution level, tax rules for many years have provided a maximum deductible amount that effectively limits the company contribution. The tax rules also provide that in order for the contribution to be deductible, it must be paid by the filing date, including extensions, of the company's federal income tax return.

The actuarially calculated contribution the company must make is determined as of a certain date, often January 1. Normally, the company contributes to the plan at a subsequent date. When the contribution is made, it must be increased by the amount of interest that would have been earned if it had been contributed on the date used by the actuary to make his calculations. The proper interest rate to use is the assumed interest rate used by the actuary in his cost calculations.

The employer must consider such matters as cost of money to the company, the company's rate of return on assets, and tax deductibility in deciding when to fund the pension obligation.

Taxation and Qualified Pension Plans

Pension plan arrangements are attractive in part because of the favorable tax treatment that results when the plans are qualified as tax exempt. Plan activities, including investment earnings and contributions, are tax exempt. The company contribution is deductible by the company as an ordinary and necessary business expense; the participants receive deferred compensation and, accordingly, deferred taxation.

A plan is qualified as tax-exempt if it meets certain technical requirements and if it is nondiscriminatory in operation. Through a formal application, a plan may request a determination letter from the IRS stating that the plan document meets the requirements for qualification. The IRS reviews the plan document for technical compliance with participation, vesting, funding, and benefit standards. The process of securing IRS approval may be accelerated by adopting a model or pattern plan that the IRS has precleared as a qualified plan. Once the IRS is satisfied that the plan document meets technical requirements, a determination letter is issued. In the event that the plan does not qualify, the IRS provides explicit information concerning modifications needed to secure a favorable ruling for the plan.

Final determination of a plan's tax-exempt status, however, is based on actual operation of the plan. If the plan is found in practice to be discriminatory, for example, by excluding from participation individuals who should be included, it will be ruled not to be a qualified plan. Generally, the penalties for such unfavorable rulings on plans already in operation are brought against the employer rather than against the plan or the participants. This is done to avoid the depletion of plan assets and hence the loss of benefits to participants who cannot control operations.

FINANCIAL ACCOUNTING AND REPORTING

SFAS 87—*Employers' Accounting for Pensions*

In December 1985 the FASB issued SFAS 87, *Employers' Accounting for Pensions* (P16), superseding APB 8, SFAS 36, and FIN 3. The statement's requirements include

* Possible recognition of an additional liability on the balance sheet.
* Use of a single actuarial approach based on benefits.
* Measurement of plan assets at fair value for the balance sheet impact and a market-related value in making the computations of periodic pension cost.
* Use of a discount rate based on current rates for settling the employers' obligation.
* Use of a long-term expected rate of return for cost computations.
* Amortization of prior service costs by using the future period of service for each employee active at the date of a plan amendment.
* Amortization of a transition amount, asset or obligation, over the average remaining service period of the employee group in place at the date of transition to this standard.

   Additional Minimum Liability. Annually, the additional liability would be computed as follows:

Accumulated benefit obligation	$XXX
Less pension plan assets (fair value)	XXX
Unfunded accumulated benefit obligation	XXX
Plus prepaid pension cost	
or	
Less unfunded accrued pension cost	XXX
Additional liability	$XXX

If an additional liability exists it must be recognized, and an intangible asset would also be recognized up to the amount of unamortized prior service cost, with any excess being charged to equity.

   Periodic Pension Cost. Periodic pension cost consists of service cost, interest cost, expected return on assets, and an amortized portion of each of the following: unrecognized prior service cost, the amount of unrecognized gain or loss exceeding 10% of the greater of the pension benefit obligation or the market-related value of plan assets, and the unrecognized net asset or net obligation existing at initial application of the Statement (P16.114). (Further, the amortization period for prior service cost must be based on the period of expected benefit. Thus, if an employer grants plan amendments regularly, the amortization period may well be less than the contract period. The EITTF verified this conclusion in Issue 87-13.)

Disclosure. The Statement requires the following disclosures for defined benefit plans:

* A description of the plan.
* The amount of net periodic pension cost, showing separately service cost, interest cost, actual return on assets, and the net total of the other components.
* A schedule reconciling the funded status of the plan with balance sheet amounts.
* The weighted average discount rate, the rate of compensation increase used to measure the pension benefit obligation, and the weighted average long-term rate of return on plan assets.

Additional disclosures may be required, depending on the circumstances (P16.150).

Defined Contribution Plans. For defined contribution plans pension cost equals the contribution for the period. The Statement requires disclosure of the plan description and the amount of cost recognized. Those disclosures must be separate from defined benefit plan disclosures (P16.160).

Multiemployer Plans. For multiemployer plans (plans that involve contributions by two or more employers usually pursuant to collective bargaining agreements) pension cost equals the contribution to the plan. Employers must disclose, separately from disclosures on single-employer plans, a description of the plan and the amount of cost recognized (P16.164).

Business Combinations. SFAS 87 supersedes APB 16 (B50.146[j]) and requires that in accounting for purchase business combinations, the allocation of the purchase price include a liability (asset) for the amount of the *total* pension benefit obligation in excess of (less than) plan assets. APB 16 called for recording an obligation equal to only the excess of the vested benefit obligation over plan assets whereas the SFAS 87 requirement could result in recognizing a much larger obligation (B50.146).

Effective Date. The Statement was effective for fiscal years beginning after December 15, 1986, for cost computations and disclosures, and after December 15, 1988, for (1) recognition of the additional liability; (2) foreign plans; and (3) nonpublic companies with defined benefit plans that have fewer than 100 participants. Earlier application is encouraged, but restatement is not permitted.

FASB Implementation Guide. Accounting for pensions is very complex, as anyone who reads the 132-page standard is likely to conclude. That complexity became evident as the publication date of SFAS 87 neared. The FASB staff persons that dealt with the pensions project were inundated with questions about application of the Statement. Although the Board is generally not in the business of interpreting its literature, there is an ongoing, unofficial service provided to constituents of the FASB that does exactly that. Given the large number of questions that have been directed to the staff (many questions tend to be repeated), the Board decided to publish a question-and-answer booklet on Statement 87. In late 1986, a Special Report, *A Guide to Implementation of Statement 87 on Employers' Accounting for Pensions* (FASB, 1986b), was issued. The Guide is a useful aid in that it contains over

100 questions and answers on various subjects, including recognition of net periodic pension cost, recognition of liabilities and assets, measurement of cost and obligations, annuity contracts, and multiemployer plans.

Additionally, the EITF has discussed an implementation issue usually found in foreign plans. In Issue 88-1, the Task Force considered whether the projected benefit obligation should be the discounted present value of future benefits (as called for by SFAS 87) when the employee is entitled to a higher amount if terminated (essentially because such amount would have to be paid in a lump sum.) The Task Force concluded that either approach would be acceptable; the SEC Observer agreed, noting that the method used should be disclosed.

Financial Statement Disclosure Examples. In March 1987, the AICPA issued a Financial Reporting Survey, *Illustrations of Accounting for Pensions and for Settlements and Curtailments of Defined Benefit Pension Plans—A Survey of the Application of FASB Statement Nos. 87 and 88.* The publication includes the following examples:

• Companies that have applied SFAS 87 to all the operations included in the consolidated entity.
• Companies that applied SFAS 87 to domestic but not to foreign operations of the consolidated entity.
• Companies that have applied SFAS 87 for the recent year and who have also applied SFAS 88 to account for a settlement or curtailment that occurred in that year.

Figure 16.2 contains an example of the typical disclosures made in compliance with SFAS 87.

SFAS 88—Settlements, Curtailments, and Termination Benefits

Recently a substantial number of pension plans have been terminated by employers. Although ERISA places restrictions on a company's freedom to terminate a plan without obligation to employees, whether active or retired, an employer can, under certain conditions, terminate the plan and settle its obligation.

The market value increases in equity securities in the mid-1980s caused the value of plan assets in many pension plans to far exceed the plan obligations. In accord with ERISA an employer could terminate the plan, settle its obligation with active and retired employees through lump-sum payments to them, or by purchasing annuites for them. The excess amount of plan assets then reverts to the employer.

In part, the FASB's concern about the accounting for gains on these plan terminations led the Board to issue SFAS 88, *Employers' Accounting for Settlements and Curtailments of Defined Benefit Pension Plans and for Termination Benefits* (P16), which is a companion to SFAS 87, *Employers' Accounting for Pensions* (P16), and, in fact, could not be applied unless SFAS 87 has been applied.

The Statement requires current recognition of gains and losses on settlements and curtailments of defined benefit pension plans. Prior to SFAS 88, the SEC would not permit current recognition of a gain related to the settlement of a pension obligation when the predecessor plan was terminated and replaced with another defined benefit plan having essentially the same benefits covering the same employee group.

10. Retirement Plan

Substantially all employees who have met certain requirements of age, length of service and hours worked per year are covered by the Carson Pirie Scott & Company Employees' Retirement Plan. Benefits paid to retirees are based upon age at retirement, years of credited service and average earnings.

The assets of the plan are maintained in a master trust account. The Company's policy is to satisfy the minimum funding requirements of ERISA. There are restrictions on the use of excess pension plan assets in the event of a change of control of the Company. Included in the assets at January 30, 1988, are 301,852 shares of Company common stock.

During 1985 the Company changed its method of accounting for pension cost in order to conform with the requirements of Statement No. 87 of the Financial Accounting Standards Board. On January 30, 1988, and January 31, 1987, the assumed discount rate, the estimated rate at which the retirement plan could have settled its liabilities, was 9% and 8.5%, respectively. In both years the expected long term rate of return on plan assets was estimated to be 10% and future salary increases were estimated to be 6.5%.

Net pension credit consists of the following:

(In thousands)	Jan. 30, 1988	Jan. 31, 1987
Normal service cost	$ 1,240	$ 1,631
Interest cost on projected benefit obligation	3,685	3,406
Return on plan assets	889	(10,251)
Net amortization and deferral	(8,486)	4,536
Net pension credit	$(2,672)	$ (678)

The reconcilation of the funded status of the plan to the consolidated amount reported in the accompanying Balance Sheet is as follows:

(In thousands)	Jan. 30, 1988	Jan. 31, 1987
Actuarial present value of benefit obligations:		
Estimated present value of vested benefits	$(39,591)	$(39,934)
Estimated present value of nonvested benefits	(711)	(1,421)
Accumulated benefit obligation	(40,302)	(41,355)
Value of future pay increases	(3,561)	(3,784)
Projected benefit obligation	(43,863)	(45,139)
Estimated market value of plan assets	66,139	69,075
Plan assets in excess of projected benefit obligation	22,276	23,936
Unrecognized net gain	(3,505)	(6,510)
Unrecognized net transitional asset	(14,980)	(16,307)
Pension asset on the accompanying Balance Sheet	$ 3,791	$ 1,119

The net pension credit and reconcilation of the funded status of the plan have been restated to reflect the transfer of $20.4 million of pension assets and the related benefit obligations to Greyhound as a result of the Merger. The information presented above excludes the benefit obligations of the other discontinued operations and the respective assets required to satisfy such obligations.

Prior to 1985 the Company used the projected unit credit actuarial cost method. The effect of the change to FASB No. 87 was to increase net earnings and earnings per share by $.8 million and $.08, respectively for 1985. The pension credit in 1985 was $.8 million.

FIG. 16.2 Typical Disclosure Under SFAS 87
Source: Carson Pirie Scott & Company 1987 Annual Report, January 30, 1988.

Settlements. SFAS 88 defines a *settlement* as an irrevocable action that relieves the employer of primary responsibility for a pension obligation and eliminates significant risks related to both the obligation and the assets used to effect the settlement. The FASB has taken the position that for the settlement to qualify as an irrevocable action resulting in recognition of gain or loss on settlement the employer must either have distributed lump-sum payments to the employees or must have already acquired the annuities, in other words, cash must have changed hands.

The amount of gain or loss to be recognized is a percentage of the unrecognized gain or loss (including the SFAS 87 unrecognized net asset or net obligation from transition), the percentage being the relationship of the amount of obligation settled to the total obligation of the plan.

The reason for the proportional recognition is that the employer may choose to settle with a certain group of employees, for example, only retired employees or only salaried active employees. Or, because the employer is terminating the plan and immediately starting a new similar plan, not all of the projected benefit obligation is considered settled.

Curtailments. The FASB defines a *curtailment* as

> an event that significantly reduces the expected years of future service of present employees or eliminates for a significant number of employees the accrual of defined benefits for some or all of their future services.

Examples of a plan curtailment are termination of employees' services earlier than expected, or termination or suspension of a plan so that employees do not earn additional benefits for future service. A curtailment may result in a gain or loss for the employer. SFAS 88 requires that a loss be recognized in earnings when a curtailment is probable and its effects can be reasonably estimated. A gain is to be recognized in earnings when the curtailment is completed. A curtailment and a settlement could both occur as part of the same event.

Special Termination Benefits. Special benefits may be offered to employees for a short period of time as an inducement for the termination of their employment. In such a case, SFAS 88 calls for recognition of a liability and a loss when the employees accept the offer and the amount can be reasonably estimated. Also, if there is a contractual requirement to provide termination benefits under the terms of a defined benefit pension plan, the employer must recognize a liability and a loss when it is probable that employees will be entitled to benefits and the amount can be reasonably estimated.

Effective Date. The Statement is effective for events occurring in fiscal years beginning with the fiscal year in which SFAS 87 is first applied. Restatement of previously issued annual financial statements is not permitted.

FASB Implementation Guide. There have been situations, such as major corporate restructurings, in which a settlement, curtailment, and special termination benefits all have been involved. The interplay among these transactions can be rather complex. The FASB, as in the case of SFAS 87, has issued a guide on implementation of SFAS 88 that incorporates the more complex and pervasive questions and answers on accounting for pension settlements and curtailments, and termination benefits (FASB, 1988c).

Termination of a Defined Benefit Plan to Fund a Defined Contribution Plan. Recently, there have been a number of employers that terminated their pension plan, withdrew the excess assets, and used the entire amount to make a contribution to a defined contribution plan. The issues raised in this transaction relate to how to account for the amount of assets contributed to the plan which were significantly in excess of the required, initial contribution and when to recognize compensation expense. The EITF, in Issue 86-27, concluded that

- The excess assets, if securities other than employer securities, should be recorded as if they were part of the employer's investments, and are to be accounted for in accordance with SFAS 12.
- Compensation expense is to be recognized at the date that a portion of the excess is allocated to employee accounts.

Also in Issue 86-27, the EITF dealt with the case where the defined contribution plan was an employee stock ownership plan (ESOP). ESOPs are discussed in Chapter 20.

The EITF has dealt with various other termination issues as well. In Issue 84-6, the Task Force considered whether a termination and reversion of assets should result in a gain if a replacement plan is instituted. This discussion incorporated consideration of SAB 52, also dealing with terminations of overfunded plans. In Issue 84-44, the employee was given a choice of replacement plan, either defined benefit or defined contribution. In Issue 85-10, the reversion was contributed to an ESOP, raising questions about how to classify the gain and the contribution expense in the income statement. SFAS 87 and SFAS 88 now effectively answer all these issues.

Other Postemployment Benefits (FASB OPEB Project)

The FASB staff currently is studying the OPEB issues. The Board is in the process of considering staff recommendations on the recognition and measurement issues, the nature and content of potential disclosures, and the transition provisions of any proposed statement. An exposure draft of a statement is planned for late 1988 and a public hearing is planned for early 1989.

The Nature of OPEB. Many companies provide retirees with various benefits beyond their pensions. The typical benefits include medical coverage, prescriptions, dental coverage, eye care and life insurance. Many of those benefits extend to the retiree's spouse for the remaining lifetime and to the retiree's dependent children up to a specified age.

Generally, Medicare benefits are offset against the coverage by the employer thus reducing the cost. Another approach applied recently to reduce costs is to establish a maximum amount of cost to be covered by the plan. The extent of coverage may also vary according to whether the retiree was an hourly or salaried employee.

In order to qualify for these benefits the employee must generally satisfy specified eligibility requirements. For example, a company may require that a person be employed for ten years of continuous active service at the time he reaches the minimum age at which he can retire.

The vast majority of plans are not funded, primarily because there is no tax incentive to do so as there is with pensions. Therefore, the plans are on a pay-as-you-go basis, that is, the reported expense is essentially equal to the payments made for claims or premiums.

The cost of these benefits often represents the most significant portion of the total benefits to both active and retired employees because of the higher than general health care inflation rate and the aging of our population.

The Employer's Commitment. In the past most companies believed that they did not have a recognizable liability since they legally had the ability to reduce or eliminate these benefits at any time. Recent court cases, however, have upheld the position of retirees who contended that the employer had made a firm, noncancellable commitment to them that could not subsequently be rescinded. These concerns are shared by some legislators, who believe that a minimum level of health care for retirees should be required of all employers. If such legislation were passed, there is some indication that there would be concessions by Congress in the form of increased Medicare benefits. This would reduce the costs for many employers who currently provide more than minimum coverage while increasing costs to those that had been providing little or no benefits.

The Accounting Issues. The primary accounting issues are whether an obligation exists that should result in the recognition of a liability and, if so, how to measure and report the obligation.

Many people, as well as the FASB, believe that the commitment to provide OPEB satisfies the SFAC 6 definition of a liability. Therefore, they are satisfied that the future outlays are probable. One open issue is whether the amount of an obligation is estimable with a sufficient degree of reliability to warrant recognition. The types of information necessary to make such a measurement are, to a great extent, the same as the information necessary to estimate a pension obligation, with a few significant exceptions. In the case of OPEB many of these benefits extend to the spouse and dependent children. Therefore, the information base must be expanded to incorporate those demographics. The other exception is the lack of history and large actuarial data bases that are available when dealing with pensions. Therefore, the range of estimates for some of the critical assumptions can vary widely among actuaries, resulting in tremendous differences in computed obligations for essentially identical plans.

Another open issue is determining the point at which the employer has a reportable liability. The FASB staff initially took the position that the liability did not exist until the employee became eligible to retire. Their rationale was based on the fact that if the employee left the company any time prior to becoming eligible to retire there was no obligation on the part of the employer to provide these benefits upon eventual retirement. This differs from pension benefits which, when vested, will be provided to a former employee upon that individual's retirement. The Board rejected that view, instead taking the position that assessing the probability of an employee remaining with the company until retirement is commonly done by actuaries for estimating pension obligations. Therefore, an obligation for OPEB is measurable and reportable prior to the point of eligibility or retirement.

As of August, 1988, the Board has tentatively decided that the expected benefit obligation (EBO—the actuarial present value of benefits expected to be provided during retirement) should be measured at each balance sheet date. The EBO would be ratably allocated over the service period up to the date at which the employee is expected to retire.

Obviously, the FASB has numerous issues to deal with prior to the issuance of an exposure draft. However, they have taken the position that accounting for OPEB should be as consistent as possible with SFAS 87.

If the Board continues down this path, it will need to deal with the fact that since these OPEB plans generally are unfunded, the initial obligations will be huge. Many companies are concerned about the potential balance sheet impact because in some instances it is estimated that this could result in recognition of the largest liability on the company's balance sheet.

If the FASB uses an SFAS 87 approach for cost determination, the expense would be recognized over the service period of each employee and the transition amount would be spread over some future period.

Interim Pronouncements. After early deliberations in the OPEB project, the FASB issued SFAS 81, *Disclosure of Postretirement Health Care and Life Insurance Benefits* (P50). This statement is considered to be an interim step pending completion of the Board's study of the recognition and measurement issues relating to OPEB. SFAS 81 requires the following disclosures concerning postretirement health care and life insurance benefits:

1. A description of the benefits offered and the employee groups covered;
2. The cost of those benefits included in net income for the period;
3. A description of the current accounting and funding policies for those benefits; and
4. Any significant matters that may affect comparability among periods.

Concurrent with the work on the broad OPEB project, in April 1987 the FASB issued Technical Bulletin 87-1, *Accounting for a Change in Method of Accounting for Certain Postretirement Benefits* (P50). The Technical Bulletin indicates that an employer making a change in the method of accounting for (1) postretirement life insurance benefits (not provided through a pension plan) or (2) postretirement health care benefits, should account for the effect of the change either prospectively or on a "catch-up and prospective" basis. The catch-up and prospective approach requires the cumulative effect of a change on prior periods to be recorded in the net income of the period of change. (This matter was first discussed in EITF Issue 86-19, with no consensus reached; TB 87-1 resolved the problem.)

AUDITING OF PENSION COSTS

Objectives and Procedures

The audit objectives in examining a company's pension costs, obligations, and gains or losses related to settlements and/or curtailments are to ensure proper recognition, recording, and disclosure as required by SFAS 87, SFAS 88, and ERISA, and to determine that the company is meeting its obligations as defined in the plan document or the collective bargaining agreement.

Once the auditor has investigated and understood the nature and operation of the plan, the examination procedures may be categorized into four general parts:

1. Examination of the company's payroll and personnel systems that accumulate data;
2. Examination of the system for retrieval and transmission of that data to the actuary;
3. Investigation of the qualifications of the actuary and of the work he performs, in accordance with SAS 11 (AU 336); and
4. Determination that the contribution, accrual, and disclosure (including the disclosure of unfunded vested benefits) are in accordance with GAAP and in compliance with the plan document; that IRS requirements for tax deductibility have been met; and that ERISA requirements, including those related to the funding standard account, have been met.

Because the volume of data in the first two categories is usually very large, the typical audit approach when accounting controls appear to be reliable is to rely on internal controls. Tests of compliance to assure that controls are operating should be used. Alternatively, representative samples may be selected for substantive testing of pension provisions and balances.

Under either approach, the auditor develops an appropriate level of assurance in order to rely on the payroll and personnel data supplied to and used by the actuary.

The auditor's examination of work performed by the actuary is guided by SAS 11, *Using the Work of a Specialist* (AU 336), which requires the auditor to satisfy himself concerning the professional qualifications and reputation of the actuary. The auditor should also consider the independence of the specialist in relation to the company; the nature, objectives, and scope of the specialist's work; and the validity of the data used by the specialist to perform his calculations. These steps may best be performed by confirmation at the same time that the auditor requests a copy of the specialist's report.

Appropriate procedures include standard substantive tests such as recomputation, examination of the contribution payment, examination of board minutes approving the contribution, review of the funding standard account, and discussion or confirmation with plan and company attorneys concerning plan compliance with ERISA and related regulations.

Auditing Issues

The timing of the actuary's report can present a problem in financial reporting of the company. It is not unusual for the actuarial report to be based on information a year or more old at the time the auditor completes his examination. Consequently, the actuarial evaluation will not have considered events during the year under examination. It is normally necessary to request the actuary to estimate the impact of any important changes prior to year-end. Such a procedure is not unusually difficult; however, it may be considerably more difficult to estimate the pension obligation if significant amendments to the plan have altered benefits or vesting or if an event, such as a plant closing, has had a significant impact on the actuarial assumptions.

SFAS 87 requires that the obligation be as of the entity's year-end. However, it does allow that measurement to be made as of a specified measurement date within 90 days prior to year-end. That date is to be used consistently from year to year once it is established.

The AICPA Committee on Relations With Actuaries has issued a sample actuary confirmation letter that contains the information necessary to assist in determining compliance with existing accounting guidance. (See Figure 16.3.)

An additional complexity that the auditor must deal with in complying with SFAS 87 is assessing the reasonableness of the actuary's and client's assumptions regarding the discount rate, the expected rate of return on plan assets, and the salary progression rate. Relatively small changes in these variables can have a significant impact on the measurement of both the obligation and pension cost. The guidance in SFAS 87 and the FASB's related Implementation Guide is not definitive regarding determination of the appropriate rate. The auditor may need to engage a consulting actuary to advise him on the reasonableness of these particular assumptions.

PENSION PLANS

Operations

General Administration. Overall operational responsibility for pension plans usually falls to a board of trustees, board of directors, or administrative committee. Day-to-day operations are normally the responsibility of an administrator, who may be an employee of the sponsor. Plan assets are usually in the custody of an investment trustee, such as a bank trust department, an insurance company, or in some cases a named individual. Investment decisions are the responsibility of the trustee, but may be made with the assistance of a professional investment adviser under guidelines established by the board of trustees. Defined benefit plans require the services of an actuary to value the plan and determine the amount of the annual contribution. Frequently, the plan's record-keeping is divided between the administrator and the investment trustee, and in some cases the investment adviser is also included. Division of administrative authority has implications for internal accounting controls that will be discussed in the following paragraphs.

Trust Arrangements Offered by Banks. The least complex trust arrangement offered by banks is a simple trust in a bank trust department. In this arrangement, investment decisions may be made, within authorized limits, by the bank or by an independent investment counselor; or the board of trustees or its investment committee may retain the investment decision activity.

A second investment arrangement is a common trust fund maintained by a bank's trust department. This type of investment arrangement operated in conjunction with a simple trust offers the advantages of greater risk diversification and professional investment management, particularly to smaller trusts. Since such commingled trusts are graded by risk category, the investment decision becomes a relatively straightforward choice among risk categories.

A third investment arrangement offered by some bank trust departments is the master trust — a single trust that holds the assets of several plans, usually those of a

Pension plan actuarial information
(Prepared on client's letterhead)

(Date)

(Name of Actuary)

(Address)

Dear_____:

In connection with the examination of our financial statements for the period ending (fiscal year-end) by our independent accountants, (name, address), please furnish them the information described below as it pertains to the XYZ pension plan, which is a defined benefit plan. For your convenience in response to those requests, you may supply pertinent sections, properly signed and dated, of your actuarial report, or pension expense report, if they are available and if they contain the requested information.

A.   Please provide a brief description of the following:
     1. The employee group covered.
     2. The benefit provisions of the plan used in the calculation of the net periodic pension cost for the period and of the accumulated benefit obligation and the projected benefit obligation at the end of the period.

     Please identify any such benefit provisions that had not taken effect in the year. Please also provide the date of the most recent plan amendment included in your calculation. Please identify any participants or benefits excluded from the calculations, such as benefits guaranteed under an insurance or annuity contract.

     3. The plan sponsor's funding policy for the plan.
     4. Any significant liabilities other than for benefits, such as for legal or accounting fees.
     5. The method and the amortization period, if any, used for the following:
        a. Calculation of a market-related value of plan assets, if different from the fair value.
        b. Amortization of any transition asset or obligation.
        c. Amortization of unrecognized prior service cost.
        d. Amortization of unrecognized net gain or loss.
     6. Any substantive commitments for benefits that exceed the benefits defined by the written plan that are included in the calculations.
     7. Determination of the value of any insurance or annuity contracts included in the assets.
     8. Nature and effect of significant plan amendments and other significant matters affecting comparability of net periodic pension cost, funded status and other information for the current period with that for the prior period.
     9. The following information relating to the employee census data used in calculating the benefit obligations and pension cost:
        a. The source and nature of the data is _____ and the date as of which the census data was collected is _____.
        b. The following information concerning participants:

Participants	Number of persons	Compensation (if applicable)
Currently receiving payments	_____	_____
Active with vested benefits	_____	_____
Terminated with deferred vested benefits	_____	_____
Active without vested benefits	_____	_____
Other (describe)		

Note: If information is not available for all the above categories, please indicate the categories that have been grouped and describe any group or groups of participants excluded from the above information.

       c. Information for the following individuals contained in the census:

Participants' name or number	Age or birth date	Sex	Salary	Date hired or years of service

[Note to auditor: The auditor should select information from employer records to compare with the census data used by the actuary. In addition, the auditor may wish to have the actuary select certain census data from his files to compare with the employer's records.]

FIG. 16.3   Standard Actuary Confirmation (Prepared on client's letterhead)
Source: Journal of Accountancy, AICPA, October 1987, pp. 160, 162, and 164.

B. Please provide the following information on the net periodic pension cost for the period ending on _____:
    1. Service cost
    2. Interest cost
    3. Actual return on assets
    4. Other components
        a. Net asset gain or (loss) during the period deferred for later recognition
        b. Amortization of net loss or (gain) from earlier periods
        c. Amortization of unrecognized prior service cost
        d. Amortization of the remaining unrecognized net obligation or (asset) existing at the date of the initial application of FASB Statement no. 87—transition obligation or (asset)
        e. Net total of components (a + b + c + d) $_____
    5. Net periodic pension cost (1 + 2 − 3 + 4e) $_____
    6. The above measurement of the net periodic pension cost is based on the following assumptions:

        Weighted-average discount rate   _____%
        Weighted-average rate of compensation increase   _____%
        Weighted-average expected long-term rate of return on plan assets   _____%

        Please describe the basis on which the above rates were selected and whether the basis is consistent with the prior period.
        Please briefly describe the other assumptions used in the above measurement.

    7. The calculations of the items shown in B1 to B5 are based on the following:
        Asset information at   _____
        Census data at   _____
        Measurement date (must be not more than three months before the end of the last
        fiscal year)   _____

        Please describe any adjustments made to project the census data forward to the measurement date or to project the results calculated at an earlier date to those shown in B1 to B5.

C. Please provide the following information on the benefit obligations for disclosure in the financial statements for the period ending _____ .

                                                                                            Estimated

    1. Pension benefit obligation
        a. Accumulated benefit obligation
            —Vested
            —Nonvested
            —Total $_____
        b. Additional benefits based on estimated future salary levels   _____
        c. Projected benefit obligation (a + b)   _____
    2. Fair value of plan assets
    3. Unfunded projected benefit obligation:
        (1c − 2)
    4. Unrecognized prior service cost
    5. Unrecognized net loss or (gain)
    6. Unrecognized net transition liability or (asset)
    7. Additional liability
    8. Accrued or (prepaid) pension cost in the company financial statements   _____
        (3 − 4 − 5 − 6 + 7) $_____
    9. The above amount of the projected benefit obligation is measured based on the following assumptions:
        Weighted-average discount rate   _____%
        Weighted-average rate of compensation increase   _____%

        Please provide a brief description of the other assumptions used in the measurement.

    10. The calculation of the items shown in C1 to C8 is based on the following:
        Asset information at   _____
        Census data at   _____
        Measurement date (must be not more than three months before the current fiscal year-end)_____

        Please describe any adjustments made to project the census data forward to the measurement date or to project the results calculated at an earlier date to those shown in C1 to C8.

    11. Please describe any significant events noted subsequent to the current year's measurement date and as of the date of your reply to this request and the effects of those events, such as a large plant closing, which could materially affect the amounts shown in C1 to C8.

                                                                                            (continued)

D. Please provide an analysis for the period showing beginning amounts, additions, reductions and ending amounts of the
  1. Projected benefit obligation,
  2. Unrecognized prior service cost,
  3. Unrecognized net loss (gain) and
  4. Net transition obligation (asset).

E. Please provide our independent accountants with descriptions and the amounts of gains or losses from settlements, curtailments or termination benefits during the year, such as
  1. Purchases of annuity contracts,
  2. Lump-sum cash payments to plan participants,
  3. Other irrevocable actions that relieved the company or the plan of primary responsibility for a pension obligation and eliminates significant risks related to the obligation and assets,
  4. Any events that significantly reduced the expected years of future service of employees,
  5. Any events that eliminated for a significant number of employees the accrual of defined benefits for some or all of their future service or
  6. Any special or contractual termination benefits offered to employees.

F. Was all of the information above determined in accordance with FASB Statements nos. 87 and 88 (including the FASB's *Guides to Implementation of Statements 87 and 88* and the American Academy of Actuaries *An Actuary's Guide to Compliance with Statement of Financial Accounting Standards no. 87*) to the best of your knowledge? If not, please describe any differences.

G. Describe the nature of your relationship, if any, with the plan or the plan sponsor that may impair or appear to impair the objectivity of your work.

Very truly yours,

_____

FIG. 16.3 *(continued)*

common sponsor or related sponsors. The master trust maintains the accounting for each plan's share of trust assets. Master trusts provide not only the economies of investment scale offered by commingled trust funds, but also, for the administrator responsible for multiple plans, the advantage of simplified trust contract maintenance.

Insurance Contract Arrangements. Insurance contracts purchased as assets by a plan provide a means of accumulating assets and generating income based on the premium paid. The specific features of the contract determine the rate and method of calculating the income. The most significant feature in insurance company contract arrangements is whether funds are unallocated or allocated.

Under an *unallocated insurance arrangement* benefit payments are made directly from the contract, and the insurance carrier has recourse to the plan for experience ratings. Experience ratings are based on, for example, the participants' actual mortality rate versus the expected mortality rate for a standard population. The annual experience rating will result in either a premium increase or refund. The contract value of an unallocated insurance arrangement is included among the assets of the plan's financial statements because the plan carries the risk of gain or loss on benefit payments and is responsible to provide assets to pay benefits.

Under an *allocated insurance arrangement,* plan assets are used to purchase an annuity contract from the insurance carrier. The cost of the contract is determined by the value of the monthly pension payment and the number of years for which the payment is guaranteed or projected. Once the annuity has been purchased, all risk of gain or loss based on the actual life of the retiree passes to the insurance carrier. Plan assets that have been used to purchase allocated insurance contracts are no longer considered assets of the plan.

Often insurance contracts are written with both an unallocated and an allocated portion. Under such a contract, certain types of benefits other than retirement and permanent disability will ordinarily be paid out of the unallocated funds.

Accounting by Pension Plans

With the passage of ERISA in 1974 and the FASB's issuance of SFAS 35, *Accounting and Reporting by Defined Benefit Pension Plans* (Pe5), in 1980, the accounting and reporting by employee benefit plans has become more uniform. However, SFAS 35 covers only defined benefit plans, and leaves unaddressed the accounting and reporting by other types of plans. The standard does not require the preparation, distribution, or attestation of financial statements for any plan. An overview of SFAS 35 is presented below:

1. The plan's statement of net assets is to be prepared on the accrual basis, and the plan is to be the reporting entity.
2. Investment assets other than insurance contracts are to be carried at fair value. This means that assets should be valued at their market value under normal transaction conditions between willing parties. The purpose for requiring fair value is to enable the user of plan financial statements to evaluate the plan's ability to meet its obligation to pay benefits. When a ready market does not exist for plan assets, the FASB suggests that discounted cash flows may be used to determine the value of investment assets.
3. Insurance contracts are to be reported at contract value as determined by the insurance company.
4. Only unallocated insurance contracts are to be included as assets of the plan.
5. Operating assets are to be carried by the plan at cost net of depreciation.
6. Net appreciation or depreciation of investment assets during the year as reported in the statement of changes in net assets is to include realized gains and losses on investments bought and sold within the year.
7. All plans must include information on the actuarial present value of accumulated plan benefits and the change since the previous valuation. This may be either in statement format or in footnotes to the financial statements.
8. Generally, plan benefits are to be based on current plan provisions and employee history of pay and salary. Future years of service are to be considered only in calculating certain selected types of benefits, such as early retirement, death, or disability benefits.

Reporting and Disclosure. SFAS 35 states that the primary objective of the financial statements of a pension plan is to provide the reader with information useful to assess the present and future ability of the plan to pay benefits when due. The financial statements must therefore include the following:

1. A statement of net assets available to pay benefits.
2. A statement of changes in net assets.

3. The actuarial present value of accumulated plan benefits and changes in benefits. Accumulated plan benefits are to be in three categories: vested benefits of participants currently receiving payments, other vested benefits, and nonvested benefits. This information must be presented as of either the beginning or the end of the plan year. If it is presented as of the beginning of the plan year, the statement of net assets available to pay benefits and the statement of changes in net assets must be comparative—preceding year and current year.

4. Notes to the financial statements must include information about investment asset valuation; the assumptions and methods for valuation of accumulated plan benefits; a description of the plan and plan amendments during the year; the priority of participant claims in the event of termination; funding policies, including participant contributions, if any; information on insurance contracts excluded from assets; plan tax status; individual investments in excess of 5% of plan assets; transactions with related parties; and significant subsequent events.

Governmental Accounting Standards. In November 1986, the Governmental Accounting Standards Board (GASB) issued SGAS 5, *Disclosure of Pension Information by Public Employee Retirement Systems and State and Local Governmental Employers,* (Pe6 and P20), establishing standards for disclosure of pension information by public employee retirement systems (PERS) and state and local governmental employers in notes to financial statements and in required supplementary information. This Statement standardizes pension disclosure guidance by superseding the pension disclosure requirements of paragraph 9 of SGAS 1, *Authoritative Status of NCGA Pronouncements and AICPA Industry Audit Guide.* In addition, SGAS 5 fills the gap left by the issuance of SFAS 75, which indefinitely suspends the applicability of SFAS 35 (discussed in the preceding section) to governmental units (Pe5.102, n.1). This suspension was occasioned by the creation of GASB after issuance of SFAS 35, but before its mandatory effective date.

The disclosures required by SGAS 5 are intended to provide information needed to assess (1) funding status of a PERS on a going concern basis, (2) progress made in accumulating sufficient assets to pay benefits when due, and (3) whether employers are making actuarially determined contributions.

Disclosures are required both in financial reports issued by the PERS and in financial reports issued by employers, including those that do not fund their pension obligations. In addition to disclosures about plan provisions, actuarially determined contribution requirements, contributions actually made, and significant actuarial assumptions, SGAS 5 requires the computation and disclosure of a standardized measure of the pension obligation. That measure, which may differ from that produced by the actuarial funding method used to determine contribution requirements, is the actuarial present value (APV) of credited projected benefits prorated on service: it considers both salary progression and step-rate benefits. An actuarial valuation to calculate this measure should be made at least once every two years, with an update in years when a full valuation is not performed.

Ten-year trend information should also be presented as required supplementary information. This information includes comparisons of (1) net assets available for benefits to the pension benefit obligation, (2) unfunded pension benefit obligation to annual covered payroll, and (3) revenues by source to expenses by type. Employers may make reference to the availability of 10-year trend information in publicly available PERS reports or in their own comprehensive annual financial reports (CAFR) rather than present the information with their general purpose financial statements (GPFS).

Small PERS and small employers (as defined in this Statement) may disclose the actuarially determined accrued liability developed from certain specified actuarial funding methods instead of the standardized measure of the pension obligation required of larger entites. These smaller entities are also exempted from the requirement for actuarial updates.

Guidance is also provided on disclosure of information on defined contribution pension plans.

Auditing of Pension and Other Employee Benefit Plans

The audit of a defined benefit pension plan is similar in many respects to the audit of other entities; consequently the discussion that follows highlights only unusual matters that the auditor must consider. Auditors must follow GAAS and also be alert to situations of noncompliance with regulations of the Department of Labor and the IRS. Because record-keeping and internal control may be divided among several locations and individuals, the examination requires careful planning, particularly to ensure the proper study, evaluation, and testing of internal control. If auditors examine the sponsoring company as well as the plan, consideration should be given to integration of company and plan audit procedures in the examination of participant payroll data.

In addition to examining the participant payroll data, the plan auditor must also test the calculation of benefit payments for accuracy, propriety, and compliance with the plan's provisions.

AICPA Audit and Accounting Guide. In February 1983, the AICPA Employee Benefit Plans and ERISA Special Committee issued an Audit and Accounting Guide, *Audits of Employee Benefit Plans* (AICPA, 1983c). This Guide presents the recommendations of the Committee regarding the application of GAAS to audits of financial statements of employee benefit plans, such as defined benefit pension plans, defined contribution plans, and employee health and welfare benefit plans, and includes illustrated financial statements for these types of plans.

The accounting guidance for defined contribution plans and employee health and welfare benefit plans is designed to be consistent with the principles in SFAS 35, to the extent they are relevant.

Defined contribution plans. The Guide contains the following significant accounting and reporting guidance for defined contribution plans:

- *Financial statements.* The financial statements should include information regarding net assets available for plan benefits as of the financial statement date and a statement of changes in net assets available during the period.
- *Plan investments.* Plan investments should be presented at their fair value, except for contracts with insurance companies, which are to be reported on the same basis as in filings under ERISA.

- *Changes in net assets available for plan benefits.* Certain minimum disclosure is required, including:
  - Net appreciation/depreciation in the fair value of each significant class of investment
  - Investment income
  - Employer contributions
  - Participant contributions
  - Benefits paid to participants
  - Payments to insurance companies to purchase contracts that are excluded from plan assets
  - Administrative expenses
- *Additional financial statement disclosures.* These disclosures include:
  - Description of the plan's accounting policies and significant fair valuation assumptions
  - A brief, general description of the plan agreement, and any significant plan amendments
  - The basis for determining contributions by employers and participants (if applicable)
  - The policy regarding the purchase of contracts with insurance companies
  - The federal income tax status of the plan
  - Identification of certain significant and/or unusual transactions that represent 5% or more of the net assets available for benefits
  - Investments pledged
  - Guarantees of debt of the plan by others
  - The amount of unallocated assets, as well as the basis used to allocate units (if applicable) and asset values to participants' accounts, including amounts allocated to participants who have withdrawn
  - Unusual post-balance-sheet events

Employee health and welfare benefit plans. This section of the Guide replaces the accounting and reporting practices specified in the 1972 Audit Guide, *Audits of Employee Health and Welfare Benefits Funds* (AICPA, 1972a), by changing certain of those principles and practices regarding

- The valuation of plan investments (to fair value for all investments, except contracts with insurance companies)
- Minimum disclosures in the statement of changes in net assets (same as disclosures required for defined contribution plans)
- Additional financial statement disclosures (same as disclosures required for defined contribution plans)

Fair Value. Fair valuation of assets that do not have a public market may present difficulties. Some assets, real estate for example, may require the services of an appraiser; or closely held stock may be difficult to value. Reporting the assets at fair value in the financial statements of the plan is the responsibility of the plan's board of trustees. In these circumstances, the auditor should review the valuation criteria to appraise whether they are reasonable and properly applied and to ascertain that specialists are consulted where appropriate (AU 336). In September 1987, the

AICPA issued its *Guide for the Use of Real Estate Appraisal Information* (AICPA 1987j) for use by auditors in evaluating the reasonableness of real estate appraisals. If these kinds of assets are material, the auditor may find it necessary to qualify his opinion because of uncertainty concerning asset valuation.

Multiemployer Plans. Multiemployer plans normally involve contribution calculations and participant data maintained and supplied to the plan by a number of companies, raising additional audit considerations. The plan may either maintain records of participant data, contributions receivable, and contributions, or review and verify such data at the employer company. The plan auditors may be able to test and review this information to gain an appropriate level of audit satisfaction. If this is not possible, they must be satisfed that the sponsoring companies' auditors have performed appropriate procedures, or request that they perform them. Usually this entails some review of the other auditors' working papers. Otherwise, the plan auditors must make arrangements to perform procedures themselves at the sponsor companies.

Audit Approaches. Examinations of defined benefit pension plans are divided into two categories. The first, the full-scope audit, requires a study and evaluation of the internal accounting controls of the plan, including those carried out by the

* Plan administrator
* Bank trust department or the insurance carrier
* Employer's payroll department
* Investment trustee

The plan auditors must identify and test all controls on which they plan to rely, without regard to where those controls are located. When the plan auditors intend to rely on internal accounting controls at the bank trust department or the insurance carrier rather than test those controls, they may obtain, if available, a report from the independent auditors of the bank or the insurance carrier concerning the adequacy of internal accounting controls applicable to trusteed investment assets. Such a procedure is called the single-auditor approach. If such a report is not available or if the plan auditors believe that additional work must be performed, they may request that the independent auditors of the bank or insurance carrier perform the work, or they may perform additional work there themselves.

Several issues exist concerning the use of the single-auditor approach. At present, there is neither a standard single-auditor program for use by the auditors of the bank or insurance carrier nor a standardized single-auditor report. Further, it is not altogether clear whether the approach is appropriate with regard to insurance carriers, since invested assets are held under contract rather than in trust. Until these issues are resolved, use of the single-auditor approach may require additional procedures by the plan auditor, such as review of the nature and scope of the procedures performed by the independent auditor of the bank or the insurance carrier.

The second category of examination is a restricted-scope examination as permitted by Department of Labor regulations. A restricted-scope examination is permitted when the bank trust department or the insurance carrier certifies the completeness and accuracy of the financial information it supplies. In these circumstances, the independent auditor is instructed by the plan administrator not to perform any steps related to the certified information, other than to ensure that it is reflected without alteration in the financial statements of the plan. The auditors' procedures are restricted to the examination of participant data, benefit payments, data supplied to the actuary, contributions receivable, and any other data not certified by the bank or insurance carrier.

Auditor's Opinion. When a full-scope audit has been performed with satisfactory results, the auditor may issue the standard unqualified report. (See the AICPA Audit Guide for modification of defined benefit plans.) If the scope of the examination has been restricted as permitted by Department of Labor regulations, the auditor's report included in the Audit Guide should be used, as illustrated in the following example:

> We have examined the financial statements and schedules of XYZ Pension Plan as of December 31, 19X1 and for the year then ended, as listed in the accompanying index. Except as stated in the following paragraph, our examination was made in accordance with generally accepted auditing standards and, accordingly, included such tests of the accounting records and such other auditing procedures as we considered necessary in the circumstances.
>
> As permitted by Section 2520.103-8 of the Department of Labor Rules and Regulations for Reporting and Disclosure under the Employee Retirement Income Security Act of 1974, the plan administrator instructed us not to perform, and we did not perform, any auditing procedures with respect to the information summarized in Note X, which was certified by ABC Bank, the trustee of the Plan, except for comparing the information with the related information included in the 19X1 financial statements and supplemental schedules. We have been informed by the plan administrator that the trustee holds the Plan's investment assets and executes investment transactions. The plan administrator has obtained a certification from the trustee as of and for the year ended December 31, 19X1, that the information provided to the plan administrator by the trustee is complete and accurate.
>
> Because of the significance of the information that we did not audit, we are unable to, and do not, express an opinion on the accompanying financial statements and schedules taken as a whole. The form and content of the information included in the financial statements and schedules, other than that derived from the information certified by the trustee, have been examined by us and, in our opinion, are presented in compliance with the Department of Labor Rules and Regulations for Reporting and Disclosure under the Employee Retirement Income Security Act of 1974.

Relationship of Auditors and Actuaries. Much of the controversy related to the 1977 FASB exposure draft on defined benefit pension plans, which was eventually released as SFAS 35, grew out of the FASB's belief that actuarially determined benefit obligations must be presented in the financial statements of such plans. The position expressed in promulgated generally accepted auditing standards is that the auditor is responsible for examination of the plan financial statements and should not express reliance on the actuary in expressing his opinion, as this may give the appearance of a division of responsibilities (AU 336.11). Some actuaries believe that the actuarial valuations are inappropriately scrutinized by nonmembers of the actuarial profession (i.e., auditors). SAS 11 (AU 336) requires, in effect, that the auditor examine data input to the actuary, review the actuary's qualifications and independence, and review the consistency and reasonableness of actuarial assumptions and methods. What SAS 11 does not allow, ERISA does: the auditor may rely on the actuary (effectively dividing the responsibility) if this reliance is expressed in the auditor's report. Understandably, then, actuaries believe that the auditor should rely on the actuary and not reexamine actuarial matters.

Ethics committee. The auditor-actuary relationship is further complicated by the AICPA Ethics Committee's ruling that "even though the [auditor's] firm provides actuarial services (the results of which are incorporated in the client's financial statements), if all of the significant matters of judgment involved are determined or approved by the client and the client is in a position to have an informed judgment on the results, the member's independence would not be impaired by such activities" (ET 191.108). Although the auditor's professional independence may not be compromised in fact, many actuaries believe that there is an appearance of lack of independence.

Public oversight board. In 1979, the Public Oversight Board (POB) issued *Scope of Services by CPA Firms* (POB, 1979). This report concluded that accounting firms may render services as enrolled actuaries to an employee benefit plan and at the same time audit that plan and/or its sponsoring company. The POB's view is that although the enrolled actuary must form an opinion as to, and present his best estimates of, the reasonableness of experience and expectations, it nevertheless cannot be said that the actuary has "usurped management's role and is making management's decisions" in rendering a professional opinion (p. 52). The POB also stated that a member of a CPA firm rendering employee benefit consulting services must be limited in such a manner that he

1. Provides only technical assistance and advice;
2. Avoids continuous involvement, which implies the usurping of the management function; and
3. Satisfies himself that the client has adequate understanding of technical implications and alternatives to be able to assume responsibility for decisions.

And, of course, the POB expects that he would avoid other activities that are inappropriate under the accounting profession's code of ethics.

EMPLOYEE RETIREMENT INCOME SECURITY ACT OF 1974

Applicability and Administration

The primary purpose of ERISA is to strengthen and encourage the growth of private employee benefit systems in the United States. Congress intended to accomplish this by increasing the quality of employee benefit plans through establishing consistent minimum standards, securing participant benefits, increasing company and fiduciary responsibility, and setting minimum funding standards. ERISA applies generally to all types of employee benefit plans, including defined benefit plans, defined contribution plans, and health and welfare benefit plans. Plans not covered by the legislation are the following:

- Government plans;
- Church plans, unless they elect to be covered;
- Plans established solely for the purpose of complying with applicable workers' compensation laws;
- Plans maintained outside the United States for persons who are nonresident aliens; and
- Plans that are unfunded and are maintained solely for the purpose of providing benefits for certain employees in excess of the maximum benefit limitation imposed by the IRS.

Initially, ERISA was jointly administered by the Department of Labor and the IRS. Administrative difficulties caused by this joint administration led in late 1978 to a presidential reorganization under which the IRS is now assigned responsibility for minimum standards, including participation, vesting, and funding, and for annual reporting on employee benefit plans. The Department of Labor now administers regulations related to fiduciary responsibility and participant and beneficiary reporting requirements.

ERISA also established the PBGC which is responsible for ensuring payment of minimum benefits by defined benefit pension plans and for administering defined benefit pension plans that have been terminated. The sponsor liability for plan benefits in the event of termination is limited to 30% of the sponsor's net worth at the date of the plan termination. (Furthermore, although it is still a matter for future litigation, there is the possibility that directors of sponsors may be personally liable for unfunded minimum pension benefits.)

Because ERISA makes the sponsor or sponsors liable to fund minimum benefits in the event of plan termination, the PBGC was also to establish and administer *Contingent Employer Liability Insurance* (CELI), which was to remove some of that burden by providing insurance coverage for that liability. To date CELI has not been established, and the PBGC has indicated that it does not believe that CELI as proposed by ERISA is a workable concept.

Reporting Requirements Under ERISA

Two major categories of ERISA reporting requirements of particular importance are annual reporting by the plan to the IRS and annual reporting to participants and beneficiaries.

Annual Report Filed With the IRS. All plans covered by ERISA are required to file annual reports with the IRS on the appropriate series 5500 form. Plans with 100 or more participants at the beginning of the plan year (including retired and vested terminated employees) typically file Form 5500. Plans with fewer than 100 participants at the beginning of the plan year file a Form 5500C every third year and a Form 5500R the intervening two years. Plans covering sole proprietorships and partnerships file Form 5500C/R. Government plans and church plans that do not elect to be covered by ERISA are exempt from filing. The series 5500 forms include information that the IRS supplies to the Department of Labor and to the PBGC.

The forms include questions intended to provide information about plan characteristics, participation, and vesting; and on Forms 5500 and 5500C (in a condensed format), space for financial information, including plan assets and liabilities at the beginning and the end of the year and changes in plan assets during the year. Three supporting schedules, A, B, and SSA, must be included in the annual filing of Forms 5500, 5500C, and 5500R if they are applicable:

1. Schedule A, Insurance Information, generally must be filed for any plan that provides benefits through an insurance carrier.
2. Schedule B must be filed for all defined benefit plans subject to the minimum funding standards. It requires the reporting of accrued vested and nonvested benefits (if the plan has more than 100 participants), actuarial value of the plan assets, actuarial cost method and assumptions used, and a reconciliation of the funding standard account, including disclosure of all charges and credits to that account during the past year. This schedule is the responsibility of the plan's actuary, who must sign it.
3. Schedule SSA is used to report all separated participants who are entitled to deferred vested benefits.

Schedule P may optionally be completed by the Trustee of the plan and filed with the series 5500 form filing. This form serves to commence the statute of limitations time period for the trustee's liability.

Certain other schedules supplementing the financial information included in the annual report must be included if certain tests are met. These are

1. Assets held for investment,
2. Party-in-interest transactions,
3. Obligations in default,
4. Leases in default, and
5. Reportable transactions.

Generally, the financial statements of all employee benefit plans with more than 100 participants that are not fully insured[1] must be examined and reported on by an independent qualified public accountant. ERISA also provides that assets certified by a bank or an insurance company need not be examined by the accountant. This has resulted in two types of examinations, as discussed earlier in this chapter.

The law also provides that the auditor's opinion must cover other financial information contained in schedules separate from the financial statements. This information includes investments held at year-end, debt instruments and leases that are in default at the end of the year, and any party-in-interest transactions or reportable transactions as specified by the law and regulations.

---

[1] Fully insured plans place all assets in allocated insurance contracts that are guaranteed by the insurance company. (There are also other technical requirements that must be met to qualify as a fully insured plan.)

The financial statements of plans with fewer than 100 participants are not required to be examined by an independent qualified public accountant. Further, plans that are unfunded, that is, plans for which there are no segregated funds outside the company's direct control, need not be examined. Plans involving certain group insurance arrangements for welfare plans where no trust exists or where assets held in trust are paid out or returned to the sponsor within 90 days of their receipt by the trust, or plans that are fully insured, are also excluded from the audit requirement of ERISA. Rules regarding exemption from examination by an independent accountant can be complex, and a legal ruling may be appropriate when there is uncertainty.

Annual Reporting to Participants and Beneficiaries. ERISA requires the plan administrator to furnish a summary annual report of the plan to each plan participant and beneficiary receiving benefits under the plan. Regulations prescribe specific wording for the report, including selected financial information that must be given, such as net assets at the beginning and end of the plan year and change in net assets for the year. The plan administrator must also furnish on request a copy of the plan's financial statements at no charge and a copy of the annual report filed with the IRS at a nominal fee. ERISA also requires reporting to each participant his individual benefit entitlement and other basic information regarding his benefits from the plan upon request, termination, or a one year break in service. There is no prescribed format for this report. Regulations governing reporting matters may be found in DOL regulations 2520.104-1–.104-50.

Other Reporting Requirements. Among the other reports required by ERISA, two are of particular interest. The first requires the reporting of significant plan amendments and must be filed with the Secretary of Labor within 60 days after the change is adopted by the plan. The second requires annual reporting to the PBGC by all defined benefit plans. The purpose of the PBGC filing is to assess the annual insurance premium for benefits guaranteed by the corporation. The form requires identification of the sponsoring company, the plan, and the plan administration, as well as the number of participants and beneficiaries under the plan. The premium payment should be included with the filing.

LIFE INSURANCE FUNDING OF DEFERRED COMPENSATION

Nontransferable Arrangements

Some insurance and compensation consultants have been marketing an insurance package to fund deferred compensation plans. These generally provide for payments after retirement (often providing a guaranteed minimum number of payments) and the payment of a death benefit should the employee die before retirement. Under these plans, the company is the beneficiary of a death benefit which will be greater than the combined after-tax payments under the deferred compensation plan and the cost of the life insurance premiums (exclusive of the interest cost on policy loans). Those offering this package proposed that all debits for the premium payments and charges for deferred compensation (either as paid or as accrued) be made to an asset account, to be relieved when the inevitable death benefit is received. Thus, operations would not be charged for the insurance premiums or compensation, nor would operations include income from the death benefit proceeds of the policy.

The AICPA recommended and the FASB subsequently required that accounting for these two features (compensation and insurance) be kept separate. They decided that the proposal confused the funding aspects of the insurance plan with the compensation expense aspects of the deferred compensation plan; and, accordingly, the proposed accounting did not conform with GAAP.

The deferred compensation plan should be accounted for in accordance with the provisions of APB 12, *Omnibus Opinion 1967*, related to deferred compensation plans (C38), thereby accruing the deferred compensation over the period of active employment. The life insurance aspects should be accounted for according to FASB Technical Bulletin 85-4 discussed later in this chapter.

Transferable Arrangements

Some of the plans include a substitution or transferability feature. Such a feature essentially provides insurance on a stated position (e.g., Vice-President of Finance), and the coverage may be transferred to any person filling that position at little or no added cost. Subsequent to the change in the insured, the premiums would be those of the insurance class of the individual filling the position (basically determined by the age and sex of the individual). If the company has the ability and intent to fund insurance with the transferability feature until the individual's death, and the aggregate premiums for the first 10 years will exceed the cash surrender value at the end of the tenth year, some accountants have argued that an acceptable approach would be for the company to charge to life insurance expense not less than one-tenth of the excess each year. The 10-year approach, also known as the pro rata ratable charge method, has been rejected by the FASB in Technical Bulletin 85-4.

FASB Technical Bulletin

In November 1985, the FASB Staff issued Technical Bulletin 85-4, *Accounting for Purchases of Life Insurance* (I50). The bulletin was issued in response to an AcSEC Issues Paper, *Accounting for Key-Person Life Insurance* (AICPA, 1984a), in which AcSEC narrowly rejected the pro rata ratable charge method while the AICPA Insurance Companies Committee supported it. The FASB Staff unequivocally rejected the pro rata ratable charge method, stating in the TB that an entity should account for its investments in life insurance as follows:

> The amount that could be realized under the insurance contract as of the date of the statement of financial position should be reported as an asset. The change in cash surrender or contract value during the period is an adjustment of premiums paid in determining the expense or income to be recognized under the contract for the period (I50.508).

This TB applies to all entities that purchase life insurance where the enterprise is either the owner or beneficiary of the contract, without regard to the funding objective of the purchase (that is, those intended to fund deferred compensation plans, buy-sell agreements, and postemployment death benefits). Purchases of life insurance by retirement plans that are subject to SFAS 35, *Accounting and Reporting by Defined Benefit Pension Plans* (Pe5), are not addressed by this TB.

OTHER EMPLOYEE BENEFITS

The company's financial statements should reflect the costs of employee benefit plans and other employee benefits in accordance with SFAS 87 (P16). They should also disclose, where material, the annual expense provision for defined contribution plans and information describing the plan and the employee groups covered. If individual executive compensation arrangements taken together are equivalent to a pension plan, they are also covered by SFAS 87, and appropriate disclosure of their current expense provision and funding arrangements should be included in the financial statements.

Compensated Absences

In December 1980, the FASB issued SFAS 43, *Accounting for Compensated Absences* (C44), which

> requires an employer to accrue a liability for employees' rights to receive compensation for future absences when certain conditions are met. For example, this Statement requires a liability to be accrued for vacation benefits that employees have earned but have not yet taken; however, it generally does not require a liability to be accrued for future sick pay benefits, holidays, and similar compensated absences until employees are actually absent.

SFAS 43 does not apply to severance or termination pay, postretirement benefits, deferred compensation, stock or stock options, group insurance or other long-term fringe benefits, or the accounting (addressed in AICPA SOP 75-3) for compensated absences by state and local governments.

A company's liability should be a reasonable estimate of the payments it expects to make, due solely to the employees' work already performed, and should be accrued as employees earn the right to be paid for future absences. An employer should accrue a liability for employees' compensation for future absences if all of the following conditions are met:

- The employer's obligation relating to employees' rights to receive compensation for future absences is attributable to employees' services already rendered;
- The obligation relates to rights that vest or accumulate;
- Payment of the compensation is probable;
- The amount can be reasonably estimated.

Voluntary Employee Beneficiary Associations (VEBAs)

A typical VEBA is a trust formed to fund employee benefits (e.g., sickness, accident, vacation) provided by employee benefit plans. The VEBA receives employee and/or employer contributions and pays benefits to the employee.

The advantages of using a VEBA are:

1. The company can take a deduction in the current year for advance contributions to the VEBA for benefits earned by the employee in the current year that would not be paid until the following year. For example, if the VEBA is used for health care benefits the employer could pre-fund the current year's estimated incurred claims that would not be paid out until the following year. (Company payments made to a VEBA prior to year-end relating to employee benefits of future periods should be recorded on the company's financial statements as a prepaid expense.)
2. Generally, the funds held by the trust may be invested and allowed to earn income tax-free.
3. A company can self-insure some of these benefits and still get a tax deduction for advance funding.

"Employee welfare benefit plans" funded by VEBAs are subject to ERISA's fiduciary, disclosure, and reporting obligations.

The AICPA Audit and Accounting Guide, *Audits of Employee Benefit Plans,* is applicable to the auditing of funded VEBA plans.

Perquisites

Perquisites (perks) are another example of executive compensation. These are special privileges, usually in kind, received by the executive (e.g., use of a company automobile for private purposes).

Current SEC rules (Item 402;(c), Regulation S-K) require that for individuals and groups who are listed in the management remuneration disclosures included in 10-K reports and proxy statements, the following information concerning perquisites must be disclosed:

• Perquisites are to be valued at incremental cost to the company and included in compensation.
• Separate footnote disclosure is required whenever an individual's perquisites exceed the lesser of $25,000 or 10% of that individual's total cash compensation.
• Separate footnote disclosure is required whenever the perquisites for the group of executives for whom remuneration disclosures are required exceed the lesser of $25,000 multiplied by the number of individuals in that group or 10% of aggregate compensation for the group.

The IRS is interested in the potential taxability of perquisites to the receiving executive. Corporate costs associated with perquisites are usually included in expense categories other than compensation. Certain perquisites are clearly taxable to the executive, for example, a company that incurs the cost of all or a portion of the executive's personal use of a car, country club, vacation home, boat, or aircraft.

INTERNATIONAL ACCOUNTING STANDARDS

Accounting by Employers for Retirement Benefits

International Accounting Standard 19, *Accounting for Retirement Benefits in the Financial Statements of Employers* (AC 9019), became effective for fiscal years beginning after December 31, 1984. IAS 19 deals with accounting for retirement benefits in the financial statements of employers and does not deal with employment termination indemnities, deferred compensation arrangements, long-service leave benefits, health and welfare plans, and bonus plans. However, if such benefit plans are the same as those of retirement benefits, it would usually be appropriate to account for them in a manner similar to retirement benefit plans.

The Statement provides the following significant standards for a defined benefit plan:

• Retirement benefit costs should be determined by using appropriate assumptions and by consistently using an acceptable actuarial valuation method.

• Current service costs, past service costs, experience adjustments, and the results of changes in actuarial assumptions should be systematically charged to income over a period not exceeding the participants' expected remaining working lives.

For defined contribution plans, the employer contribution applicable to a particular accounting period should be charged against income in that period.

Accounting and Reporting by Retirement Plans

In January 1987, the International Accounting Standards Committee issued IAS 26, *Accounting and Reporting by Retirement Benefit Plans* (AC 9026), to take effect for periods beginning on or after January 1, 1988. The Statement deals with the accounting and disclosures by a retirement plan to all participants and contains the following requirements:

• The plan report should contain either
  − A statement showing net assets available for benefits, the actuarial present value of promised benefits, distinguished between vested and nonvested, and the resulting excess or deficit, or
  − A statement showing net assets available for benefits including either a note disclosing the actuarial present value of promised retirement benefits, distinguished between vested and nonvested, or a reference to this information in an accompanying actuarial report.

• The actuarial present value of promised retirement benefits should be based on the benefits promised under the terms of the plan on service rendered to date using either current salary levels or projected salary levels with disclosure of the basis used. The effect of any changes in actuarial assumptions that have had a significant effect on the actuarial present value of promised retirement benefits should also be disclosed.

• Plan investments should be carried at fair value (usually market). However, those securities that have a fixed redemption value and have been acquired to match the obligations of the plan may be carried at amounts based on their redemption values.

• Various statements or items should be presented or disclosed including
  − Statement of changes in net assets available for benefits,
  − Summary of significant accounting policies,
  − Description of and changes to the plan,
  − Description of the funding policy, and
  − Explanation of the relationship between the actuarial present value of promised retirement benefits and net assets available for plan benefits.

17

Income Taxes

PERSPECTIVE

Accounting for income taxes is one of the most complex aspects of financial accounting, in concept as well as in practice. It is also vitally important, because federal income tax rates for high-bracket corporations in recent times have ranged from 34% to more than 50% of reported pretax earnings. In addition to the federal income tax, most corporations pay state and local income taxes. Not surprisingly, therefore, accounting for income taxes has given rise to much contention in the profession and to numerous official pronouncements and interpretations. Many pronouncements dealing with other matters in financial accounting, such as leveraged leases, interim financial reporting, and translation of foreign currency transactions, also discuss the related income tax aspects.

Much of the controversy and complexity arises because certain important items of revenue and expense are reported in one period's financial statements and in another period's tax returns. Perhaps the most common example of these temporary differences is depreciation expense; many companies use the straightline method for financial reporting and an accelerated method for income tax purposes. There are also some items of revenue and expense that are reported for financial accounting purposes but never subjected to taxation. The best known example of these is interest earned on state and local government securities, which, depending upon when the securities are issued and their purpose, may be exempt from federal income taxation. Still other sources of complexity and controversy are the special items that reduce tax liability directly, such as the investment tax credit (ITC) (despite its repeal in 1986, situations remain where it is still available), foreign tax credits, and carryovers of operating losses. The alternative minimum tax (AMT) and the related AMT credit have added a new dimension to the meaning of complexity for both income taxation and accounting.

Financial reporting determines net earnings for a given period by matching expenses to revenue. Thus, different ways of matching income tax expense to revenue and other expenses for the period can result in significantly different determinations of net earnings reported in conformity with GAAP.

Historical Overview

Until the mid-1950's, the amount shown for income tax expense in an annual statement was almost always the amount of tax indicated as payable on the income tax returns for the year. The few exceptions were the result of material and nonrecurring expenses recognized in one year for financial purposes but not allowable as a tax deduction until a succeeding year. For example, if a company decided to dispose of a plant, its financial reports would show the estimated loss in the year the decision was made; but a tax deduction for the loss could not be claimed until the discontinued plant was actually sold. In these circumstances it was considered appropriate to reduce the income tax expense in the year the loss was recorded. Similar approaches were also occasionally applied to unusual revenue items recognized in one period for financial accounting purposes and in another as taxable income.

The first official pronouncement to deal with these unusual and nonrecurring differences was ARB 23, *Accounting for Income Taxes*. ARB 23 discussed the disclosures appropriate when operating loss carry-forwards arose or income tax refunds were realized as a result of the carry-back of current year's losses to an earlier profitable year.

Accelerated Depreciation. The Internal Revenue Code, adopted in 1954, allowed companies to use accelerated methods of tax depreciation even if the straightline method was used for financial reporting. (See Chapter 15 for a discussion of depreciation methods.) Some accountants argued that the use of accelerated depreciation methods for tax purposes should not result in timing differences because companies should also use the same accelerated method for financial reporting. However, the practice of using different methods for taxes and financial reporting gained wide acceptance as many companies took advantage of accelerated methods for tax purposes, and this resulted in recurring timing differences.

Hence, many accountants advocated that during the early years of the useful life of a depreciable asset, an amount equal to the taxes saved should be recorded as an expense, with an offsetting deferred credit. The deferred credit could then be amortized to income during the later years of useful life, when the timing difference reversed. This procedure was often called *normalization*, particularly in the public utility industry (see Chapter 33), since the result was to normalize net income – that is, to eliminate the variations in reported income resulting from depreciation timing differences.

The opponents of normalization advocated just as strongly that providing such deferred taxes was improper because most continuing or growing companies would make expenditures for depreciable assets each year. Thus, the excess of reported income over taxable income would never reverse, or would reverse only in the indefinite future – so many years hence that recognizing it currently would be misleading. The deferred tax liability that resulted from such accounting, they argued, was not a true liability, but a subdivision of retained earnings.

Simply taking the actual tax liability as it appears on the income tax return and recording it as the income tax expense for that year in financial reports is often called *flow-through accounting*. It may also be called *partial allocation* if it requires deferred income taxes for nonrecurring differences but does not provide them for recurring differences. A third approach – providing deferred income taxes in all cases of timing differences – is called *comprehensive tax allocation*. The AICPA Accounting Research Committee considered these rival views and issued ARB 44, *Declining Balance Depreciation*. That bulletin adopted the partial allocation method.

SEC Pressures. Accounting Research Bulletins did not constitute mandatory guidance; and some companies provided deferred income taxes for recurring timing differences while others, following ARB 44 recommendations, did not. The Chief Accountant of the SEC publicly expressed the view that failure to provide the deferred taxes could mislead investors by resulting in the reporting of inflated net earnings; in several cases, the SEC used its authority to require companies filing registration statements to provide deferred taxes. The most frequent targets of this action were companies with histories of large annual increases in net earnings that were going public for the first time.

In the public utility industry, the controversy involved the question of whether deferred tax provisions should be allowed as an expense in rate determination. As explained in Chapter 33, the traditional practice for public utility companies had become one of conforming deferred tax accounting for financial reporting purposes with that allowed or required for rate-making purposes, whatever method was followed.

To reduce the confusion resulting from the alternative accounting methods, and in response to pressure from the SEC, the Accounting Research Committee reconsidered the matter and issued a revision of ARB 44. It required the provision of deferred income taxes for depreciation timing differences, except for regulated companies whose regulatory authorities specified flow-through accounting for rate-making purposes. Since the SEC fully supported this revision and required all registrants to follow it, the practice became mandatory.

In the years that followed, many companies also provided deferred taxes on other recurring differences between financial reporting income and taxable income, but such practices varied. Even when companies chose to provide deferred taxes, the methods of computing them and the manner of their presentation in financial statements were diverse.

In 1967, the APB issued APB 11, *Accounting for Income Taxes*, which adopted the deferral method of accounting (although certain aspects of the liability method were implicit in provisions dealing with operating losses). Later pronouncements, in particular, APB 23 (special areas) and APB 24 (equity method investees), and interpretations generally used a liability approach in dealing with relatively narrow tax issues.

The *deferral method* under APB 11 focused on the effects on income for the period in which the tax timing differences originated. For financial accounting purposes, deferred taxes applicable to the timing differences were computed using the tax rates in effect at origination and were not adjusted for subsequent tax rate changes or for new taxes later imposed. Ignoring loss carry-back situations for the moment, the tax effects of transactions that reduced taxes currently payable were treated as deferred tax credits – although classified among liabilities in the balance sheet. Conversely, the tax effects of transactions that increased taxes currently payable were treated as deferred tax charges – although classified among assets in the balance sheet. Such deferred credits and charges were to be amortized to income tax expense in future years as the timing differences reversed.

Investment Tax Credit

The Revenue Act of 1962, which reduced income taxes through an ITC based on a percentage applied to expenditures for designated depreciable assets, gave rise to still more variations. The initial rate was 7% for items with a useful life of more than seven years, and lower rates for shorter-lived assets.

On the principle that income can be earned only by the profitable employment of depreciable assets and not simply by purchasing them, the APB decided that tax benefits from the ITC should be reflected over the life of the related assets. Called the *deferral method* of accounting for the ITC, this practice was specified in APB 2 (I32.104), issued in 1962. However, most companies believed the tax benefits should be reflected in income immediately in the year for which the ITC reduced income taxes, a practice called the *flow-through method*.

The SEC decided, perhaps as a result of pressures from the Treasury Department, to accept either the deferral method required by APB 2 or the flow-through method. The APB subsequently recognized this divergence of practice by amending its opinion. In APB 4 (I32.102) it expressed a preference for the deferral method but said that the flow-through method was also acceptable.

Then, in 1967, the APB sought to reduce variations in practice by again prohibiting the flow-through method. The SEC's Chief Accountant supported the exposure draft, but opposition from industry was so intense that the APB and the SEC reversed their positions and permitted the two alternatives to continue.

By 1971, the APB was again reconsidering the question of the ITC, and many companies brought their concerns to the attention of Congress. The result was an accounting provision in the Revenue Act of 1971 (Section 101(c)) stating:

> notwithstanding any other provision of law . . . no taxpayer shall be required to use, for purposes of financial reports subject to the jurisdiction of any Federal agency or reports made to any Federal agency, any particular method of accounting for the [investment] credit [and] shall disclose, in any such report, the method of accounting for such credit . . . and . . . shall use the same method of accounting . . . in all such reports made by him, unless the Secretary of the Treasury or his delegate consents to a change to anther method.

Many believe this debacle was a significant factor in the decline of confidence in the ability of the APB to deal effectively with financial accounting matters, and that it led to replacement of the APB by the Financial Accounting Standards Board in 1973.

The Tax Reform Act of 1986 (TRA 1986) may have finally ended the debate by completely repealing the ITC. Unused credits previously earned and certain other credits will still be allowed under transitional rules, as discussed under "Tax Credits."

FASB Project

In early 1982, the FASB officially placed income tax accounting on its project agenda. This reconsideration was brought about by the ever-increasing complexity of the deferred method of accounting for income taxes, exacerbated by the passage of the Economic Recovery Tax Act (ERTA) in 1981 and the Tax Equity and Fiscal Responsibility Act (TEFRA) in 1982. In August 1983, the FASB issued a Discussion Memorandum, *Accounting for Income Taxes* (FASB 1983a), discussing the pervasiveness of the problem and suggesting alternative solutions.

SFAC 3, *Elements of Financial Statements of Business Enterprises*, states that deferred tax balances resulting from the application of APB 11 do not fit the conceptual definition of assets and liabilities.[1] Essentially then, such deferred taxes were neither fish nor fowl – not an asset or liability and not equity – but rather, as many would say, a nondescript deferred item of suspect origin and relevance carried in the balance sheet.

With the added layers of income tax accounting issues brought about by ERTA and TEFRA, and the continuing diversity of interpretation of APB 11 in practice, questions about usefulness of the deferred method could only increase.

The FASB staff, in recommending addition of the project by the Board, discouraged the idea of new or modified disclosure requirements on the grounds that nothing short of a total reassessment would be useful. Among the questions raised by the FASB staff and addressed by the Board were:

- What is the nature of income taxes?
- Is allocation still appropriate?
- If allocation is appropriate, what method should be used – deferred, liability, net-of-tax, or some combination approach?
- Should measurements of tax effects of timing differences be based on current tax rates or expected future rates? Should they be discounted?
- Should allocation be applied to all timing differences (comprehensive) or only to some (partial)?
- How should net operating loss carry-backs and carry-forwards be accounted for?
- How should ITC's be accounted for?
- Should standards for private and small public companies be the same as for large companies?

The Board held public hearings in 1984 in Chicago, Dallas, and San Francisco to hear the views of interested parties.

An Exposure Draft, *Accounting for Income Taxes*, was issued by the FASB in September 1986, followed by still more public hearings in early 1987 and discussions at numerous Board meetings. The final result, SFAS 96, is discussed throughout the remainder of this chapter.

SFAS 96 – AN ASSET AND LIABILITY APPROACH

In December 1987, the FASB issued SFAS 96, *Accounting for Income Taxes* (I25), superseding 19 pronouncements and amending 28 others, causing a dramatic effect on financial reporting for most tax paying companies. Due to numerous, complex implementation issues, in October 1988 the FASB approved the issuance of an ED, which will probably be approved, that proposes deferring the effective date of SFAS 96 by one year. Therefore, SFAS 96 would be applied for fiscal years beginning after December 15, 1989.

The new rules:

- Continue adherence to the concept of comprehensive interperiod tax allocation (with exceptions for APB 23 items).

---

[1] SFAC 3 was replaced by SFAC 6 in December 1985, but the substance of SFAC 3 was continued.

- Adopt an undiscounted asset and liability approach (the liability method) for measurement.
- Place severe limits on deferred tax asset recognition.
- Amend APB 16, *Business Combinations* (B50), to be consistent with SFAS 96.
- Significantly change the accounting treatment by regulated utilities for deferred taxes (discussed in Chapter 33).
- Leave the interim accounting for income taxes largely unchanged.
- Are effective for fiscal years beginning after December 15, 1988 with earlier adoption encouraged.
- Allow for either retroactive restatement or cumulative catch-up adjustment.

Some of the more important conceptual differences and similarities between SFAS 96 and APB 11 are presented in Figure 17.1.

SFAS 96 Implementation Task Force

Recognizing the significance of the changes in accounting for income taxes brought about by SFAS 96 and the complexities that were going to be faced by reporting companies, the FASB established an implementation task force. The purpose of this group is to bring implementation issues to the FASB staff's attention and discuss proposed guidance developed by the staff.

The guidance provided by the task force will be captured in a question and answer booklet. This booklet will be prepared by the FASB staff and issued as an FASB Special Report.

At the time this *Handbook* went to press, the Task Force had met twice and had dealt with approximately 60 implementation questions. The staff has made it clear that the guidance is tentative and is subject to change. At this point the tentative guidance has been discussed with the Board as to only a few issues; however, all will be discussed prior to the issuance of the booklet.

Certain implementation guidance developed to date that is necessary to determine the intent of the standard is discussed in this chapter within the appropriate section and is clearly identified as "Implementation Guidance." Given the tentative nature of this guidance the reader is advised to refer to the FASB booklet, when published, to ascertain whether the guidance has been modified.

Comprehensive Interperiod Tax Allocation

Because of variations between tax laws and financial accounting standards, tax consequences can arise from differences in (I25.108):

- The amount of taxable income and pretax financial income for the year.
- The tax bases of assets or liabilities and their reported amounts in financial statements.

Such differences are referred to as temporary differences, defined as differences between the tax basis of an asset or a liability and its reported amount in the financial statements that will result in taxable or deductible amounts in future years if settled at the reported amount. Certain revenues are exempt from taxation and certain expenses are not deductible; events that do not have tax consequences do not give rise to temporary differences.

SFAS 96	APB 11
Method	
• Asset and liability method: A balance sheet approach that determines deferred tax assets or liabilities using rates or laws expected to apply to future periods in which differences between financial reported income and taxable income originate and reverse.	• Deferred method: An income statement approach that matches the income tax expense reported in an income statement for a specific period with the revenues and expenses reported for that period.
Comprehensive Allocation	
• All material tax effects are considered in the determination of deferred tax assets or liabilities and the tax effects are related to the periods in which transactions enter into the determination of future taxable income or loss.	• All material tax effects are given recognition in the determination of income tax expense, and the tax effects are related to the periods in which transactions enter into the determination of pretax accounting income.
• However, deferred taxes are not required for the differences discussed in APB 23, *Accounting for Income Taxes – Special Areas* and for deposits to statutory reserve funds by U.S. steamship companies.	• Identical to SFAS 96.
Changes in Tax Rates or Laws	
• Deferred taxes are adjusted each period to reflect enacted changes in tax law or rate.	• Deferred taxes are not adjusted to compensate for changes in tax law or rates until timing differences reverse completely.
Types of Differences Requiring Tax Allocation	
• Temporary differences – between the tax basis of an asset or liability and its reported amount in financial statements that will result in taxable or deductible amounts in future years.	• Timing differences – between the periods in which transactions affect taxable income and the periods in which they enter into the determination of pretax accounting income.
Recognition of Deferred Tax Assets	
• Recognition is limited to scheduled net deductible amounts that, based on the tax law, would be available to offset taxes paid in the current year or a prior year.	• Deferred tax assets may be established subject to a realizability test.
Recognition of Deferred Tax Liability	
• A deferred tax liability is recognized for the tax consequences of scheduled future net taxable amounts – essentially a balance sheet orientation.	• Deferred tax credits represent a residual amount that is a by-product of an income determination orientation.
Discounting	
• A deferred tax liability may not be discounted to present value.	• Identical to SFAS 96.

FIG. 17.1   SFAS 96 vs. APB 11—Conceptual Differences and Similarities

SFAS 96	APB 11

Net Operating Losses

- Carry-back of operating losses results in asset recognition if a refund is available. Operating loss carry-forwards reduce or eliminate temporary differences that will result in taxable amounts provided they occur during the carry-forward period.

- If realization is assured beyond any reasonable doubt, the tax benefit of a net operating loss is recognized as an asset — if not assured, such benefits should offset deferred tax credits.

Tax Credit Carry-forwards

- Carry-forwards are used to reduce future taxes if those taxes will occur during the carry-forward period.

- If realization is assured beyond any reasonable doubt, the tax benefit of a net operating loss is recognized as an asset — if not assured, such benefits should offset deferred tax credits.

Tax Planning Strategies

- Strategies that accelerate future recovery of assets or settlement of liabilities are allowed in certain instances.

- Tax strategies are not considered.

Business Combinations

- Differences in the tax basis and reporting basis of assets and liabilities in connection with a purchase business combination require tax allocation.

- Differences between tax basis and reporting basis are considered permanent differences and do not result in deferred taxes.

- Assets and liabilities in a purchase business combination are presented gross.

- Assets and liabilities in a purchase business combination are presented net-of-tax (with the tax sometimes discounted).

- Tax benefits realized subsequent to a business combination first reduce positive goodwill, then noncurrent intangible assets and finally income tax expense.

- Tax benefits of preexisting loss carry-forwards (and tax basis differentials if realized within one year) realized subsequent to a business combination are an adjustment of the purchase price.

Interperiod Allocation

- Emphasizes allocation of income tax expense to continuing operations.

- Tax allocation is applied to obtain an appropriate relationship between the various components in the income statement.

Balance Sheet Classification

- Current and noncurrent classification is based on the scheduled reversal of temporary differences. A current deferred tax liability results from taxable temporary differences related to an asset or liability classified as current because the operating cycle is longer than one year. A noncurrent deferred tax liability results from taxable temporary differences scheduled to reverse beyond the next succeeding year.

- Classification of current and noncurrent amounts are determined based on the classification of the underlying asset or liability that gave rise to the deferred tax.

Category	Example	Type of difference
Taxable Income Versus Financial Statement Income		
1. Revenue taxed after being reported in financial statements	Gross profit on installment sales accrued when sold in financial statements but taxed on installment method	Taxable
2. Expense deducted before being reported in financial statements	ACRS depreciation for taxes and straightline depreciation over useful life in financial statements	Taxable
3. Revenue taxed before being reported in financial statements	Advance rental taxed when collected but deferred in financial statements over rental period	Deductible
4. Expense deducted after being reported in financial statements	Provision for product warranty expensed in financial statements when product is sold but tax-deducted later when claims are paid	Deductible
Other Causes of Book/Tax Differences		
5. Reduction of tax basis of depreciable assets because of tax credits	1982 TEFRA allowed choice of full ACRS deduction and reduced ITC or reduced ACRS deduction and full ITC	Taxable
6. Increase in tax basis due to tax legislation	Fresh start adjustment for casualty insurance companies; increase in tax basis because of indexing for inflation	Deductible
7. Businss combinations accounted for by the purchase method	Differences arising from assigned values and the tax basis of assets acquired and liabilities assumed in a purchase business combination.	Taxable or deductible

FIG. 17.2   Categories of Temporary Differences

The required tax allocation is considered to be comprehensive since it applies to all rather than just some of the book tax differences. It is not completely comprehensive, however, because after initially deciding otherwise, the FASB relented and allowed the exceptions set forth in APB 23, *Accounting for Income Taxes—Special Areas* (I25.169–.183), to continue. Temporary differences are a more inclusive concept than *timing differences* under APB 11; the latter only included differences between taxable income and pretax financial income. Temporary differences also include *any* difference between the tax and book basis of assets and liabilities that will have tax effects in future years.[2]

Some of the more common categories of temporary differences are shown in Figure 17.2.

---

[2] For example, the "fresh start adjustment" given to casualty insurance companies on January 1, 1987 allowed them to deduct again certain losses that had previously been deducted for tax purposes; under APB 11, this is a permanent and not a timing difference because it did not arise from a book/tax difference on a tax return. Under SFAS 96, this book/tax basis difference created by tax legislation is a temporary difference.

Implementation Guidance. The FASB staff has developed the following tentative guidance.

Intercompany profit items. If the purchasing entity records the asset at a different amount than the tax basis, that entity must recognize the temporary difference. For example, if a U.S. parent sells inventory to its foreign subsidiary at an amount in excess of cost, it will recognize a book gain that will be eliminated in consolidation if the subsidiary is still holding the inventory at the balance sheet date. The elimination entry is presumed to be pushed down to the foreign entity; therefore, it has a higher tax than book basis for the inventory. This is assumed to be a deductible temporary difference in the first subsequent year on the schedule of temporary differences. Since the subsidiary is in a different taxing jurisdiction, it would have its own schedule of temporary differences and the deductible amount is useful only if it will result in a tax asset or the reduction of a tax liability. If the foreign company has a higher tax rate than the U.S. parent, then it appears that the consolidated entity receives a tax benefit from the profit transfer in the consolidated statements assuming the deduction can be used by the subsidiary.

Scheduling Temporary Differences

After a temporary difference is identified and measured, companies must determine the future year(s) in which it will reverse. This process is known as *scheduling* and is necessary because the amount of deferred taxes to be recognized may differ depending on when temporary differences will affect taxable income and what tax rates and laws are in place for those years.

For example, if enacted tax law provides for a lower or higher tax rate in a future year, a company's deferred taxes could increase or decrease depending on the year in which the difference is scheduled to reverse. Other provisions contained in the tax law, such as graduated tax rates, exemptions, phase-in provisions, tax credits, carrybacks and carry-forwards, and favorable rates for certain transactions, could also affect the determination of deferred taxes, depending on the year in which a temporary difference is scheduled to reverse.

Assume that at the beginning of Year 1, a company buys $5,000 of depreciable assets and, by using straightline depreciation for financial reporting and an accelerated method for tax purposes, the following pattern emerges:

Year	Deductions		Temporary Difference	
	Financial Reporting	*Tax*	*Annual*	*Cumulative*
1	$1,000	$1,250	$ 250	$ 250
2	1,000	1,900	900	1,150
3	1,000	1,850	850	2,000
4	1,000	–	(1,000)	1,000
5	1,000	–	(1,000)	–
	$5,000	$5,000	$ –	$ –

At the end of Year 1, the temporary difference is $250, but SFAS 96 does not treat this amount as reversing in any one year. Instead, it views the reversal as the sum of the annual differences over the remaining life of the asset. Thus, for scheduling purposes the following schedule of future taxable and (deductible) amounts results:

Year	Taxable (deductible)
2	$ (900)
3	(850)
4	1,000
5	1,000
	$ 250

As a practical matter the scheduling of most temporary differences is as straightfoward as the preceding example. However, in some cases scheduling temporary differences is not as simple because the determination of the particular future year(s) in which a temporary difference reverses may not be clearly evident. For instance, it is difficult enough to determine the accrual provisions for litigation settlements and warranty expenses, and it is even more difficult to estimate when such items will be paid and thus become deductible. Management must use its best estimates based on all available information at the time the financial statements are prepared. In the case of litigation settlements, it may be advisable for management to consult with their attorneys or other experts. For other items like warranty expenses, it may be sufficient to base estimates on the company's prior experience with similar products or services. In any event, estimates used in scheduling should be based on the facts and circumstances related to the transaction or event creating the temporary difference. A sample schedule of temporary differences is shown in Figure 17.3.

While some aggregating of the temporary differences is possible, it will be necessary to segregate them into appropriate categories and to know the pattern of reversals by year for each category. The tax laws may not permit the offset of certain types of revenue and expense items; for example, if capital losses are only offsettable by capital gains, a separate schedule should be prepared for those items. The year of reversal is important because tax rates may differ by year.

	Balance End of Year 1	Year 2	Year 3	Year 4	Years 5–10
		Taxable (Deductible)			
Depreciation	$ 250	$ (900)	$(850)	$1,000	$1,000
Warranty Expense	(1,000)	(500)	(350)	(150)	–
Litigation Settlement	(2,000)	–	–	–	(2,000)
Other	550	300	250	–	–
	$(2,200)	$(1,100)	$(950)	$850	$(1,000)

FIG. 17.3 Sample Schedule of Temporary Differences by Year of Reversal

The AMT adds more complexity to the scheduling process. A separate schedule is required to make the AMT calculations because certain items, including accelerated depreciation, are treated as preference or adjustment items and separate tracking of such temporary differences is therefore necessary. Still more schedules will be required for the adjusted current earnings (ACE) component of the AMT.

Implementation Guidance. The FASB staff has developed the following tentative guidance.

Inventory cost capitalization. Assume that inventory adjustments are made only for tax purposes and that the inventory is classified as a current asset. In this case, the company would assume that the inventory was sold in the first year subsequent to the transaction and thus the company would have a deduction for the excess amount capitalized for tax purposes. The company is entitled, under the tax rules, to spread the increase over four years beginning with 1987. It might be assumed that this is the way in which it should be scheduled as taxable amounts; however, because the tax rules would disallow further spreading if the inventory were completely liquidated, the company should put all of the remaining taxable amount (after the 1987 amortization) in the first subsequent year on the schedule of temporary differences. Some members of the FASB Implementation Group pointed out that it was inconsistent to assume the company would not replace the inventory sold if it was also assumed that the company would be able to recover the recorded amounts of assets related to inventory, such as delivery equipment and warehouse facilities. The FASB staff refused to acknowledge the inconsistency.

Recognition and Measurement

Liability Method. Although the FASB agreed with the APB about comprehensive allocation, they rejected the deferred method (previously required in APB 11) as being overly complex, difficult to understand, and yielding debits and credits that did not meet the definition of an asset or a liability. Predictably, the FASB adopted an asset and liability approach that is generally referred to as the liability method.

The liability method emphasizes the balance sheet. It focuses on the tax payable or recoverable without regard to the impact on the current income statement. The liability method applies the tax rates expected to be in effect when the temporary differences reverse. If rates change, the deferred tax asset or liability is adjusted appropriately in the period the change is enacted.

The Board felt that the liability method was consistent with SFAC 6 (a revision of SFAC 3) and produced the most useful and understandable information for the reader of the financial statements.

No Anticipation of the Future. In general, financial reporting is based on a historical cost model, the objective of which is to recognize only the events and transactions that have already occurred. No assumptions are made that future income will be earned or that future costs will be incurred. (Historical cost recognition nevertheless includes recorded estimates of the effects of current events, such as the decision to sell a business segment, even though the exact amount of the loss is not determinable until a future sale transaction occurs.)

In its deliberations, the FASB concluded that tax consequences of future events and transactions likewise should be recognized only in the future. Thus, the only future tax consequences that are measured under SFAS 96 are those relating to events and transactions that have already transpired at the measurement date (I25.113). For SFAS 96 purposes, there is an assumption that each asset is realized and liability settled at its recorded amount at the measurement date; the only future taxable income or loss, therefore, relates to the tax consequences of the temporary differences that exist at that time. For example, the temporary differences caused by using different depreciation patterns for depreciable assets on hand at the balance sheet date will cause future taxable and deductible amounts. But there can be no anticipation that the company will acquire additional depreciable assets in future years, and thus the potential temporary differences that might arise in the future will not be considered.

A key concept in SFAS 96 is that the company will have no pretax income or loss for financial reporting purposes in future years regardless of its prior operating history. By ignoring the probability of future operating income or loss, the standard limits the future assumed taxable income or loss to the future tax consequences of temporary differences in existence at the measurement date.

Deferred Tax Expense. The net change in the deferred tax asset or liability for the year is the deferred tax benefit or expense (I.25.115). This is combined with the income taxes currently paid and payable or receivable to equal the income tax expense or benefit for the year, as follows:

Net deferred tax liability:	
At end of period	$1,500
At beginning of period	1,000
Deferred tax expense	500
Income taxes paid or current payable	750
Income tax expense for the period	$1,250

Computation of Deferred Tax Balance

The following procedures are to be applied in computing the *annual* deferred tax liability or asset (I25.116):

* Schedule the temporary differences over the future years in which they will result in taxable or deductible amounts (see Figure 17.3).
* Determine the net taxable or deductible amount for each year.
* Carry-back or carry-forward losses (net deductible amounts) as permitted or required by law (current law generally provides for carrying back net operating losses 3 years and forward 15 years) against net taxable amounts.

In concept, the calculation should be made for each future year but SFAS 96 states that the amounts may be aggregated if the result will not be significantly dif-

	Prior two years	Current year	Schedule of temporary differences to future periods					
			1	2	3	4	5–20	Total
Taxable income	$ 400	$ 1,400	$ –	$ –	$ –	$ –	$ –	$ –
Temporary differences:								
Taxable	–	–	500	500	2,100	500	2,200	5,800
Deductible	–	–	(2,500)	–	–	(3,100)	–	(5,600)
			(2,000)	500	2,100	(2,600)	2,200	200
Loss carryback	(400)A	(1,400)A	1,800 A	(300)C	(2,100)C	2,400 C	–	1,800
Loss carryforward	–	–	200 B	(200)B	–	200 D	(200)D	–
Net taxable amounts	$ –	$ –	$ –	$ –	$ –	$ –	$2,000	$ 2,000

A Carry-back of year 1 net deductible difference (NDD) against current and prior two years
B Carry-forward of remaining NDD from year 1 to year 2, which has a net taxable difference (NTD)
C Carry-back of year 4 NDD against unused NTD in year 2 and year 3
D Carry-forward of remaining NDD from year 4 to years 5-20, which have a net taxable difference (NTD)

FIG. 17.4   Carry-back and Carry-forward of Net Temporary Differences

ferent. (This is an improbable oversimplification; the complexities in the tax laws virtually mandate separate year computations to be able to determine whether aggregation produces an insignificantly different amount.) Separate calculations must also be made for each income-taxing jurisdiction based on its own tax laws, which will often vary from federal income tax laws.

Application of Carry-Back to Scheduled Differences. Applying the tax rules for carry-back and carry-forward of net tax deductions summarized on the schedule of temporary differences, a benefit only is obtainable by offsetting amounts that are taxable (I25.132). Any benefit of a deductible amount that cannot offset future or prior (recoverable) taxable amounts is essentially lost as of the current measurement date (although it might return at a later date).

For example, if the schedule showed net taxable items for the ensuing year and a large deductible item five years hence, the later tax deduction would have no value at the current measurement date if the tax law were to provide that the loss could only be carried back three years.

An example illustrating how the benefit of loss carry-back and carry-forward is recognized is shown in Figure 17.4.

Deferred Tax Asset. An asset is recognized only to the extent that the carry-back theory would result in recovery of taxes paid in a current or prior year (I25.116). In Figure 17.4, there is a tax asset related to the $1,800 of tax deductions that can be used to offset taxable income of the current and two prior years. If there had been no taxable income in those years, the $1,800 of tax deduction would have been carried forward and the net result would have been taxable income of only $200 (instead of $2,000) arising in years 5–20 upon which to provide the related tax liability.

As structured, however, the example in Figure 17.4 provides for both a tax asset in the form of a receivable for recovery of taxes previously paid and a tax liability for the net taxable amount of $2,000 in years 5–20. The amount of the asset is the amount that would have actually been recovered if the loss had been incurred in year one and a tax return filed on that basis.

In making the computation in Figure 17.4, the company could elect to carry the loss forward rather than back if it would work to its advantage (i.e., a lower net tax expense) because this election is permitted by the tax law. (The company would not do so in this example, however, as explained in the next section.) And of course, when the time comes to make the actual tax election in filing the return for Year 1, the company need not follow the assumption made for purposes of preparing the schedule a year earlier.

Deferred Tax Liability. The steps in computing the tax liability are (I25.116): (1) calculate the amount of tax for each of the remaining net taxable amounts using presently enacted tax rates and laws for those years (discounting is not permitted to reflect the time value of money); (2) deduct any tax credit carry-forward as permitted or required by law; and (3) recognize a deferred tax liability for the sum of the individual undiscounted amounts for each of the years.

Using the data in Figure 17.4, the tax effect on the current year would be as follows:

	Prior two years	Current	1–4	5–20	Total
		Scheduled Differences			
Taxable amounts	$400	$1,400	$ –	$2,000	
Tax rate	50%	40%	34%	34%	
Tax	$200	$ 560	$ –	$ 680	
Tax currently payable	$ –	$ 560	$ –	$ –	$560
Tax recoverable	(200)	(560)			(760)
Deferred tax liability			–	680	680
Tax expense (Benefit)	(200)	–	–	680	480
The journal entry is:					
Tax recoverable			$760		
Tax expense			480		
Tax currently payable				$ 560	
Deferred tax liability				680	

Note that although the company would have had the option of treating all scheduled amounts as carry-forwards in this example, it would not so do as this would result in a $148 increase in tax expense, caused by "utilizing" the losses entirely at 34% rather than partly at 40% and partly at 50%.

In the preceding example and in the others throughout, we have found it expedient to ignore the impact of the graduated tax rate. This would be appropriate if all companies earned at least the minimum ($335,000 currently) to lose the benefit of graduated rates, but such is not the case. In any situation where the income (net taxable amounts) in any year on the schedule of temporary differences is subject to graduated rates, they should be used in the calculation. The rates currently in effect

	Prior three years	Temporary differences taxable (deductible)				
		Current	Years 1–15	After Year 15	Total	Tax at 34%
Pretax income (loss)	$7,000	($12,000)	$ –	$ –	$ –	$ –
Temporary differences	(2,000)	(1,000)	1,000	–	1,000	$ 340
Taxable income (loss)	$5,000	($13,000)	$1,000	$ –	$1,000	$ 340
Temporary differences:						
Beginning of current year			5,000	2,000	7,000	2,380
End of current year			$6,000	$2,000	$8,000	$2,720
Loss carry-back	(5,000)	5,000				
Loss carry-forward		6,000	(6,000)	–	6,000	2,040
	$ –	($ 2,000)	$ –	$2,000	$2,000	$ 680

FIG. 17.5 Computation of Operating Loss Tax Benefit

are 15% of the first $50,000, 25% on the next $25,000, and 34% on the remaining balance with a surcharge of 5% on taxable income in excess of $100,000, but not to exceed $11,750.

Operating Loss Tax Benefits. In a year in which a company suffers a net operating loss (NOL), it will record an asset equal to the recoverable amount of taxes previously paid; if there is an NOL remaining after the carry-back, it will be used to reduce the existing tax liability for the tax effects of net taxable temporary differences that will reverse during the carry-forward period (I25.142–.143). The tax benefit realized for the year will be the sum of the taxes recoverable and the decrease in the deferred tax liability. Any portion of the NOL that cannot be used to either recover previously paid taxes or reduce a future tax liability will not be recorded in the financial statements but will be disclosed in the footnotes.

Assume the following situation, as shown in Figure 17.5. The Company had $7,000 in pretax income and temporary differences amounting to $2000 in the past three years. In the current year, the Company had a loss for tax purposes of $13,000 including $1,000 of deductible temporary differences that will reverse as a taxable amount within the next 15 years. At the beginning of the current year, the Company had $7,000 of taxable temporary differences that increased to $8,000 at the end of the current year; of this amount, $2,000 will not be taxable until some date beyond 15 years hence.

To compute the tax provision for the current year, the first step is to carry back $5,000 of the loss to recover $2,000 of taxes paid (assuming a 40% rate). Next, carry the NOL forward to eliminate temporary differences becoming taxable in the 15 year carry-forward period; this amounts to $5,000 (established at 34% or $1,700) at the beginning of the year plus $1,000 arising during the year for which no liability has been accrued.

If the actual tax paid on income for the current and prior three years had been $2,000 ($5,000 at a 40% rate) then the tax benefit for the current year would be calculated as follows:

Recoverable tax		$2,000
Decrease in deferred tax liability:		
Beginning of current year	$2,380	
End of current year	680	1,700
		$3,700

The following journal entry recognizing the tax benefit would be prepared:

Recoverable tax	$2,000	
Deferred tax liability	1,700	
Tax expense		$3,700

Note that the company has an NOL carry-forward for financial reporting purposes of $2,000 that it cannot use to shelter taxable temporary differences that reverse beyond the 15 year carry-forward period. For tax purposes, the company has an NOL carry-forward of $8,000, assuming it elected to actually carry back the loss on the tax return when filed. SFAS 96 requires that the amounts and expiration dates of significant carry-forwards be disclosed in the notes to the financial statements.

Tax Planning Strategies

Companies have always engaged in tax planning strategies to minimize the amount of tax payments, taking into consideration the company's best estimate of its future taxable earnings. Thus, a company might take certain actions to alter its pattern of future earnings or loss to take advantage of a tax situation. For example, a company with a large NOL carry-forward may switch its investments from tax free municipal bonds to higher yielding but taxable corporate bonds because the NOL will shield the tax effects of the action.

The FASB has decided that companies must consider tax planning strategies in the determination of the deferred tax asset or liablity; but they may only alter the timing of realization of the temporary differences that will result in taxable or deductible amounts in future years. Because SFAS 96 adopts the theory of breakeven operations in future years, strategies that contemplate the tax consequences of generating profits or incurring losses in future years are not allowed. Under SFAS 96 a tax strategy must meet two criteria (I25.118):

1. It must be a prudent and feasible strategy over which management has discretion and control. Management must have both the ability and intent to implement the strategy, if necessary, to reduce taxes.

2. It cannot involve significant cost to the enterprise, that is, significant expenses to implement the underlying transactions or significant losses as a result of changing the particular future years in which an asset is recovered or a liability is settled. The tax benefit derived from the strategy shall not be viewed as a reduction of the cost of the strategy for the purpose of determining whether that transaction gives rise to a significant cost.

To reduce the amount of the deferred tax liability on their books, companies are required by SFAS 96 to devise tax strategies that may substantially diverge from the strategies they plan to actually use to lower future tax payments. Under this FASB-required game of "let's pretend," financial reporting tax strategies will require companies to ignore the reality of forecasted future operations and act as though the only future activity of the company will be the reversal of the temporary differences.

The particular future year in which a specific temporary difference is scheduled to originate or reverse may have deferred tax consequences. For example, if the tax law provides for a higher tax rate in a future year, a company's tax consequence related to a taxable temporary difference would decrease if the difference could be moved from a higher rate year to a lower rate year.

For some types of temporary differences it may be possible to choose the particular future year that will be impacted. This is accomplished by either accelerating or delaying the recovery of assets or the settlement of liabilities. For example, a company may decide to implement a tax strategy to utilize tax credits that expire within the next year by accelerating the timing of taxable amounts.

Some of the tax strategies that might qualify for use under SFAS 96 are (I25.148–.154):

1. Accelerate or postpone the remittance of subsidiary earnings (where earnings are recognized when earned for financial reporting but taxable only when remitted) to take advantage of expiring NOLs, more favorable tax rates, or tax credits that would otherwise expire.

2. Accelerate or delay the particular year in which a contract will become completed (where the completed contract method is used for tax purposes and the percentage of completion method is used for financial reporting) to change the year in which a temporary difference results in taxable income.

3. Disposal of obsolete inventory written down to net realizable amounts for financial reporting purposes to accelerate the particular year(s) in which deductions would affect future taxable income.

4. Sale of discontinued operations on which a loss was recognized for financial reporting purposes, to accelerate the year in which deductions would affect future taxable income.

5. Funding a pension plan on which pension costs were recognized for financial reporting purposes earlier than allowable for tax purposes, to accelerate the particular future year(s) in which deductions will affect future taxable income.

6. Accelerate or delay the receipt of advance fees or advance service income that is taxable when received but is recognized as income for financial reporting purposes only when earned.

7. Consummate a transaction that is a sale for tax purposes but a financing arrangement for financial reporting purposes. This would accelerate taxable income or a tax deductible loss for the difference between "sales" price and the carrying amount of the assets.

Figure 17.6 illustrates how a tax planning strategy could be used to reduce a company's deferred tax liability. Assume the following:

• At the end of the current year, the company writes down the carrying value of its obsolete inventory by $200 to net realizable value for financial reporting purposes. Tax deductions will not be available until the inventory is actually liquidated. The resulting temporary difference will result in $200 of net deductible amounts in future years.

• Management estimates that the company will liquidate 10% of the obsolete inventory in each of the next 10 years.

	Temporary differences					
	Year 1	Year 2	Year 3	Year 4	Year 5	Year 6–10
Before use of tax strategy						
Taxable amounts	$ 100	$ 100	$ 100	$ –	$ –	$ –
Deductible amount	(20)	(20)	(20)	(20)	(20)	(100)
Net taxable amount	$ 80	$ 80	$ 80	($ 20)	($ 20)	($100)
Loss carry-back	(20)	(20)	(20)	20	20	20
Net taxable amounts	$ 60	$ 60	$ 60	$ –	$ –	
Unrecognizable net deductible amount						($ 80)
After use of tax strategy						
Taxable amounts	$ 100	$ 100	$ 100	$ –	$ –	$ –
Deductible amount	(20)	(20)	(20)	(20)	(120)	
Net taxable amount	$ 80	$ 80	$ 80	($ 20)	$(120)	$ –
Loss carry-back	(20)	(80)	(40)	20	120	
Net taxable amounts	$ 60	$ –	$ 40	$ –	$ –	$ –

FIG. 17.6 Effect of Tax Strategy on Deferred Tax Liability

- Temporary differences that arise from the use of accelerated depreciation for tax purposes and straightline depreciation for financial reporting purposes result in net taxable amounts in years 1 through 3.
- Tax laws provide for a three year carry-back of operating losses. The tax rate for all years is 40%.

At the end of the current year, the company would record a deferred tax liability of $72 for the tax consequences of $180 at a 40% tax rate on the net taxable amounts that occur in years 1 through 3. Loss carry-back is limited to $60 because only net tax deductions scheduled to occur in years 4 to 6 are available to offset taxable amounts occurring in years 1 to 3.

Now assume the preceding facts except that the company will now use the tax strategy of accelerating the deductible amounts to an earlier future year. The company will plan to physically dispose of the remaining obsolete inventory (which management believes will be at a price equal to its then net carrying amount) at the end of year 5, triggering a deduction for tax purposes. Acceleration of the particular future year in which deductible amounts caused by the inventory writedowns are scheduled to occur is a tax strategy that meets both criteria in SFAS 96: (1) it is a prudent and feasible strategy over which management has discretion and control and (2) it does not involve significant costs to the enterprise. This strategy allows the company to offset a larger portion of net taxable amounts, thereby reducing the amount of deferred tax liability it must recognize.

As shown in the lower portion of Figure 17.6, there now are no unused deductible amounts and the deferred tax liability is only $40 ($100 × 40%); the reduction of $32 is due to the utilization of $80 of previously unused deductions.

Implementation Guidance. The FASB staff has developed the following tentative guidance.

Active search for strategies. SFAS 96 requires management to search for all viable strategies to avoid loss of deductible amounts and to shift future deductions to earlier years if this will result in a carry-back to recover taxes paid at a higher rate than could be realized by carrying the amounts forward to offset net taxable amounts.

Incurring a loss on sale and leaseback. Assuming the incurrence of such a loss from an asset whose current fair value is below its present carrying value but for which recovery of its carrying value is expected through use in operations is not an allowable strategy because incurring a loss invalidates a strategy. The staff rejected the argument that in fact there was no economic loss involved since the loss would be offset by lower future lease payments.

Hypothetical carry-backs. A company may have scheduled future deductible items that exceed its future scheduled taxable items in certain years. Under SFAS 96 this net deductible amount is treated as though it were a net operating loss. The NOL must be assumed even though it is probable that the company will be profitable in the future.

Assuming that the tax rates in the current and two prior years are higher than future tax rates, the SFAS 96 requirement would be to carry back any NOL from the first three scheduled years to recover taxes paid in preceding years, and thus to maximize deferred tax assets. However, in future years when the company is in fact profitable these deductions will be utilized at the lower rate in effect in those years.

The staff guidance indicates that although this anomaly is created in the current year it will be offset in future years because in those future years the company will no longer be able to carry back to years in which the rates were higher.

Leveraged Leases

The FASB realized that it could not conform accounting for leveraged leases with SFAS 96 without reopening lease accounting. Consequently, the Board did as little as possible to leveraged lease accounting, requiring integration of such related deferred taxes when all of the following exist (I25.128):

- The accounting for a leveraged lease requires recognition of related deferred tax credits.
- Application of the requirements of SFAS 96 before consideration of leveraged leases results in limiting the recognition of a tax benefit for temporary differences that result in net deductible amounts or for an operating loss or tax credit carry-forward.
- Such unrecognized tax benefits could offset taxable amounts that result from future recovery of the net investment in the leveraged lease.

Because the FASB decided not to change the accounting for leveraged leases, it decided that the conditional integration of SFAS 96 should not override any results that are unique to income tax accounting for leveraged leases, such as the manner for recognizing the tax effect of an enacted change in tax rates (L10.521–.524). Further, the Board decided that because deferred taxes for leveraged leases are calculated differently under SFAS 13 (L10.145) than under SFAS 96, the amount to be offset when integration is required is the amount as calculated under SFAS 96. The example given in SFAS 96 (I25.158) is deceptively simple.

ALTERNATIVE MINIMUM TAX

TRA 1986 created what is essentially a separate parallel tax system that will cause many corporations to pay a tax based on the AMT. A complete understanding of the AMT provisions of TRA 1986 is necessary to calculate a tax provision and to measure deferred tax consequences.

The determination of the AMT begins with corporate taxable income computed under the regular system. Added to or subtracted from this amount are numerous tax preference items, a $40,000 exemption is then deducted, and the resulting adjusted alternative minimum taxable income (AMTI) is multiplied by a flat 20% rate. The final step is to compare this result (the AMT) to the "regular" tax. The corporation pays the greater of the two taxes. It sounds straightfoward but in reality it is quite complex.

Apart from the added complexity of calculating the AMT, *accounting* for its effects presents a multitude of problems, especially for the unwary. Among the difficulties is the requirement that NOL carry-forwards and carry-backs, ITCs and foreign tax credits are to be calculated separately, and sometimes differently for regular tax and AMT.

The Advent of the AMT

Prior to enactment of TRA 1986, corporations had not faced an AMT, but were subject to an add-on minimum tax on certain tax preference items. This tax was in addition to the corporation's regular federal income tax. In a political reaction to the perception that too many corporations report high earnings but pay little or no federal income tax, the Act repealed the corporate add-on minimum tax for taxable years beginning in 1987 and replaced it with a new 20% flat rate AMT that is designed to ensure that a corporation will pay tax of at least 10% of its economic (book) income.[3]

This is accomplished by imposing the AMT on an expanded list of preferences including a new preference created for 1987, 1988 and 1989—50% of the difference between pretax financial statement income and regular taxable income adjusted by all other preference items. This *book income preference* is an item that all corporations will have to consider in determining whether AMT is applicable. *Thus, the tax law now links income as reported in the financial statements with taxable income.* This means that all differences (both temporary and permanent) between pretax accounting income reported to investors, creditors, or others and taxable income as determined by the tax law will enter into the AMT calculation.

---

[3] This assumes the company has more than $310,000 of alternative minimum taxable income and does not have NOL or pre-1986 ITC carry-forwards.

Thankfully, Congress did not create a new enforcement structure to regulate the composition of reported earnings. Thus, several rank-ordered sources are acceptable in determining book profits for purposes of this preference.

Sources of Pretax Income

The pretax income amount used to compute the AMT must come from one of the following sources, listed in order of the priority established by the law. Companies must always use the highest ranked source that is applicable.

1. Financial statements filed with the SEC.
2. Financial statements audited and certified by a CPA that have been used as a report or statement for credit purposes, issued to shareholders, or used for any other substantial non-tax purposes.
3. Financial statements provided to the federal government or its agencies.
4. Financial statements provided to a state government or its agencies (or a political subdivision).
5. A noncertified report or financial statement actually used for credit purposes, sent to shareholders, or used for any other substantial nontax purpose.

If a corporation has none of the first four preceding items, an election may be made to treat *earnings and profits*[4] for tax purposes as pretax financial income for AMT purposes.

After 1989, the tax concept of adjusted current earnings will replace pretax financial income as a basis for this preference, but at a higher 75% rate.

Consolidated Financial Statements

A complicating factor in arriving at pretax book income is the requirement that it include earnings only of the company or companies included in a single tax return. Where separate returns are filed for constituent companies but consolidated financial statements are prepared, the earnings statement will have to be deconsolidated to arrive at each taxpayer's pretax book income.

When a consolidated tax return is filed, however, the corporations included may vary from those included in the consolidated statements. A corporation that is owned less than 80% but more than 50% is not consolidated for tax purposes, although it would be for financial reporting. In some circumstances (e.g., ownership of a life insurance subsidiary), full tax consolidation is not permitted. Deconsolidation and reconsolidation become necesssary, therefore, to determine pretax book income includible for AMT purposes.

---

[4] At the risk of oversimplification, "earnings and profits" could be viewed as current retained earnings computed on a tax basis, although there are numerous exceptions and adjustments.

Differing Fiscal Periods

If differing fiscal periods are used for financial statements and tax reporting, financial statement income included in the AMT preference may be based on a pro rata allocation of adjusted book income for the part of the year that is included in the tax return. For example, with a calendar year return at a June 30 reporting year-end, a taxpayer calculating the AMT book income preference for calendar 1987 will have 50% of pretax book income for the two reporting years ended June 30, 1987 and 1988; this is accomplished by either estimating the 1988 results or extending the filing of the 1987 return until the later overlapped year is completed. If an estimate is used, an amended return may be necessary within 90 days after the financial statement is available. As an alternative, where the accounting year ends five or more months after the tax year, an election is permitted to use the financial statement for the year ending within the tax year. Thus, in the 1988 calendar year return, financial statements for the year ended June 30, 1988 could be used. If this election is made it must be used in succeeding years until permission is obtained to revoke the election.

AMT Credit

Because of concerns raised over the potential injustice of double taxation that could result from differences between tax accounting and financial reporting, the Senate Finance Committee provided an AMT credit. To the extent that AMT preferences reflected deferral rather than permanent avoidance of tax liability, the Committee believed an adjustment was justified for the years after the corporation was required to include an item as a preference and as a result incurred an AMT. Without the AMT credit, the corporation could lose the benefit of certain deductions altogether. Therefore, TRA 1986 permits an AMT credit that allows taxpayers a reduction of regular tax paid in a subsequent year to the extent of cumulative AMT (relating to deferral preferences) paid in all prior years less minimum tax credits claimed in those years. However, the AMT credit cannot reduce the regular tax liability below the corporation's AMT for that taxable year.

The AMT credit is limited to the amount of AMT that would have been computed using only deferral preferences rather than both deferral and exclusion preferences. Exclusion preferences include tax-exempt interest on nonessential function bonds, percentage depletion and the appreciated property charitable contributions. The book income adjustment is treated as a deferral preference even though some differences between AMTI and pretax financial reporting income may result from exclusion of nontaxable items such as tax exempt interest. The AMT credit can be carried forward indefinitely but may not be carried back.

AMT Computation

The corporation's regular taxable income is the starting point for calculating the corporate AMT. Regular taxable income is first adjusted to cancel or reduce some effects of available tax advantages, and next to take into account differences between tax and financial reporting (any NOL deduction claimed in the regular tax calculation would have to be revised in the AMT calculation regardless of preferences or adjustments that might otherwise be involved). The adjusted amount, AMTI,

Regular taxable income

  +   AMT preference items

  +   or - AMT adjustment items

  =   Subtotal

  +   The book income adjustment (50% of the difference between adjusted pretax book income over the subtotal)

+ / −   The adjusted current earnings (ACE) preference (75% of the difference between ACE and AMTI). (Beginning in 1990 ACE replaces the book income preference.)

+ / −   AMT NOL adjustment

  −   AMT exemption of $40,000 (subject to phaseout)

  =   AMTI

  ×   AMT 20% rate

  =   AMT before credits

  −   foreign tax credits

  −   investment tax credits (transitional and carryover)

  =   Alternative minimum tax

FIG. 17.7   Components of the Corporate AMT Calculation

is reduced by a $40,000 exemption amount (phased out at the rate of 25¢ per each dollar of AMTI between $150,000 and $310,000), and the remainder subject to a 20% tax. This tax is reduced by foreign tax credits and pre-1986 ITC carryover.

The resulting AMT is compared with the amount of tax computed under the regular tax system, and the higher of the two amounts becomes the tax payable. The AMT computation is summarized in Figure 17.7.

Tax Preferences/Adjustments. Under the AMT system, the redetermination of taxable income requires that a separate calculation be made for certain income or deduction items (designed as tax preference items) for which the tax law provides favorable treatment to corporations.

All items designated as tax preferences in determining the superseded add-on minimum tax continue under the current law, which refers to those items as *preferences*. However, some preferences are called *adjustment type items* (e.g., the completed contract preference), and these items can *either increase or decrease* AMTI. The nonadjustment type preference items (such as pre-1987 accelerated depreciation on real property) can *only increase* AMT income. (See Figure 17.8.) Other than political trade-offs, it is difficult to determine a rationale underlying the characterization of an item as either an adjustment type item or a preference item.

Preference Example. Beginning in 1987 the ACRS deduction in excess of straightline depreciation for pre-1987 depreciable real property is a preference item for calculating AMT. Assume that a company acquired depreciable real property prior to 1986, and elected ACRS depreciation for tax purposes. In 1987, the ACRS deduction exceeds the straightline amount by $3,333. In 1988, however,

Adjustment-type Items (increase or decrease)	Preference Items (increase only)
Items carried from add-on minimum tax	
• Amortization of pollution control facilities**	• Accelerated depreciation on pre-1987 real property
• Accelerated depreciation on leased personal property for personal holding companies*	• Percentage depletion*
Items of preference that are new or modified	
• Accelerated depreciation on post-1986 property**	• Post 1986 tax-exempt interest*
• Passive activity losses of closely-held or personal service corporations	• Charitable contributions of appreciated value*
• Mining exploration and development**	• Intangible drilling costs
• Completed contract method	• Excess bad debt reserves
• Installment method for dealer sales	
• Circulation expenditures for personal holding companies	
• Marine capital-construction funds	
• Special deduction for tax-exempt insurance providers	

*   AMT credit exclusion item (an AMT credit that is available to reduce future regular tax is calculated without exclusion preferences).

**   A gain or loss on the sale of such assets will be computed by reference to the basis as adjusted for depreciation and amortization allowed under the AMT. Thus, the amount of gain or loss will differ for purposes of the regular tax and the AMT.

FIG. 17.8   AMT Preference Items

the ACRS deduction is $6,667 less than straightline. When the company computes its AMT, the $3,333 excess ACRS depreciation in 1987 increases AMTI in 1987; however, when the ACRS amount is less than the straightline amount by $6,667 in 1988, AMTI *cannot* be reduced because depreciation on pre-1987 assets is not an adjustment type preference.

Adjustment Example. An 18-month construction contract that will generate $10,000 of gross profit began in 1987. For financial reporting purposes, the company uses the percentage of completion method to recognize income on long-term contracts. Forty percent of the contract is complete at the end of 1987. The corporation has used the completed contract method for regular tax purposes but now must use percentage of completion for 70% and completed contract for 30% of the contract. For 1987, the company will recognize in its tax return $2,800 of income from the contract. Under the AMT system in 1987, the company must add as a preference item to AMTI the portion of income—$1,200—that would have been recognized if only the percentage of completion method had been used.

In 1988, the $1,200 addition to AMTI for 1987 would reduce 1988 AMTI. Since the completed contract method is an *adjustment* item, it can increase or decrease AMTI.

AMT Credit Calculation

The amount of AMT credit that can be carried forward to reduce regular tax in a subsequent year is determined by recalculating AMT without exclusion preference items. *Exclusion preferences* include tax exempt interest on nonessential function bonds, percentage depletion, and the appreciated property charitable contributions.

The AMT credit is limited to the amount of AMT that would have been computed using only deferral preferences rather than both deferral and exclusion preferences. The book income adjustment is treated as a deferral preference even though some differences between AMTI and pretax financial reporting income may result from exclusion preferences such as tax exempt interest. The AMT credit can be carried forward indefinitely but may not be carried back.

The AMT credit is calculated in concept as shown below; an example is given in Figure 17.9.

$$
\begin{array}{rl}
 & \text{Regular taxable income} \\
+ & \text{All preferences} \\ \hline
= & \text{AMT income} \\
\times & \text{20\% AMT rate} \\ \hline
= & \text{Tentative AMT} \\
- & \text{Regular tax} \\ \hline
= & \text{(A) AMT with preferences}
\end{array}
$$

$$
\begin{array}{rl}
 & \text{Regular taxable income} \\
+ & \text{Exclusion preferences} \\ \hline
= & \text{AMT income} \\
\times & \text{20\% AMT rate} \\ \hline
= & \text{Tentative AMT} \\
- & \text{Regular tax} \\ \hline
= & \text{(B) AMT with exclusion preference only}
\end{array}
$$

$$\text{(A)} - \text{(B)} = \underline{\text{AMT credit}}$$

Adjusted Current Earnings

Congress recognized that the quality of reported earnings could deteriorate if companies changed their financial reporting principles to minimize the effects of the book-profits preference. As a result, beginning in 1990, the tax concept of ACE will be substituted for pretax book profits. The definition of ACE is complicated and Congress has directed the Secretary of the Treasury to study and report on any refinements that may be appropriate prior to the law going into effect in 1990.

For the time being, interest in ACE can be confined to its impact on the schedule of temporary differences that reverse in 1990 and later years. The principal adjustment between taxable income and ACE appears to be a different depreciation allowance; ACE requires that depreciation be computed on the slower of the method used for books or the straightline method over the remaining life of the property:

	1988	1989
Regular tax calculation		
Pretax book income	$30,000	$30,000
Tax-exempt interest		
Pre-8/86 bond issues	(3,000)	(2,000)
Post-8/86 bond issues*	(12,000)	(3,000)
Completed contract adjustment	(5,000)	5,000
Regular taxable income	10,000	30,000
Regular tax @ 34%	$ 3,400	10,200
Less AMT credit (from below)		(1,300)
Regular tax after AMT credit		$ 8,900 **
AMT calculation		
Regular taxable income	$10,000	$30,000
Exclusion preference:		
Post-8/86 bond issues interest	12,000	3,000
Nonexclusion preference:		
Completed contract adjustment	5,000	(5,000)
SUBTOTAL	27,000	28,000
Book income preference:		
($30,000 − $27,000) × 50%	1,500	
($30,000 − $28,000) × 50%		1,000
Alternative minimum taxable income	28,500	29,000
20% AMT rate	× .20	× .20
Tentative minimum tax (TMT)	5,700 **	$ 5,800
Excess of TMT over regular tax	$ 2,300	N/A
1988 AMT credit carry-forward calculation		
AMT with preferences ($5,700−$3,400)	$2,300	
AMT with exclusion preferences only:		
Regular taxable income	$10,000	
Exclusion preferences:		
Post-8/86 bond issue interest	12,000	
AMT income	$22,000	
× 20% AMT rate	× .20	
Tentative AMT	$ 4,400	
Regular tax	(3,400)	
AMT with exclusion preferences only	(1,000)	
AMT Credit***	$1,300	

----

  * Exclusion preferences

 ** Tax payable

*** The AMT credit is available to reduce future regular taxable income and in this example
     reduces 1989 tax.

FIGURE 17.9   Example of Calculation of AMT Credit

| | Basis of property as of close of last taxable year |
Date acquired	beginning before 1990
Prior to 1987	Regular tax basis
1987 to 1989	AMT basis

The ACE adjustment is calculated as 75% of the difference between ACE and regular taxable income adjusted for AMT preference and adjustment items; the difference can be negative as well as positive if there is a bank of prior positive ACE adjustments to draw down.

The ACE adjustment, calculated as shown in the following, fits into the AMT calculation in place of the book income adjustment shown in Figure 17.7.

	Regular taxable income
−	Excess of ACE depreciation
	over regular tax depreciation
=	ACE
−	Subtotal (AMTI before ACE)
=	Excess of ACE
×	75%
=	ACE adjustment

An example showing the interplay of ACE, AMT, and the AMT credit carryforward is given in Figure 17.10. The assumptions used are as follows:

1. The first year of operations is 1987. Tax rates are 40% for 1987 and 34% thereafter.
2. The temporary differences at the end of 1987 are $500 of warranty expense deductible in the future and $300 of depreciation taxable in the future.
3. Depreciation is straightline for books and accelerated for tax; the following pattern is for illustrative purposes only and does not conform to the tax law.

Year	Book	AMT	Tax	ACE
1987	$1,000	$1,250	$1,300	$N/A
1988	1,000	1,250	1,850	N/A
1989	1,000	1,250	1,850	N/A
1990	1,000	1,250		625
1991	1,000			625
	$5,000	$5,000	$5,000	$1,250

The results are shown in the notes to Figure 17.10. The journal entry to record taxes for 1987 (keyed alphabetically to Figure 17.10) is:

Deferred tax asset ($520(A) − $180(C))	$340	
Tax expense ($180(C) + $34(F) + $160(H))	374	
Current taxes payable (A)		$520
Deferred taxes payable ($34(F) + $160(H))		194

	1987		Schedule of temporary differences			
	Actual	Memo	1988	1989	1990	1991
Regular Tax						
Pretax book income	$ 1,100	$ 1,100	$ –	$ –	$ –	$ –
Excess tax depreciation	(300)	(300)	(850)	(850)	1,000	1,000
Warranty expense	500	500	(300)	(100)	(50)	(50)
Taxable income	1,300	1,300	(1,150)	(950)	950	950
Loss carry-back		(1,300)	1,150	150		
Loss carry-forward				800	(800)	
Taxable income	1,300	$ –C	$ –	$ –	150	950
Tax rate	40%				34%	34%
Tax before credits	$ 520A				51E	$ 323E
AMT credit carry-forward		$ 180D			(17)	(163)
Tax					$ 34F	$ 160H
Alternative Minimum Tax						
Taxable Income	$ 1,300	$ 1,300	($1,150)	($950)	$ 950	$ 950
Adjustment item:						
Excess of tax over AMT depreciation	50	50	600	600	(1,250)	–
AMTI before ACE	1,350	1,350	(550)	(350)	(300)	950
ACE adjustment:						
Taxable income					950	950
Less excess ACE over regular Tax depreciation					(625)	(625)
ACE					325	325
Excess of ACE over AMTI					625	(625)
ACE adjustment @ 75%					470	(470)I
Book preference adjustment	–	–	275	175		
	1,350	1,350	(275)	(175)	170	480
Loss carryback		(450)	275	175		
AMTI	1,350	900	$ –	$ –	170	480
Tax rate	20%	20%			20%	20%
AMT	$ 270B	$ 180C			$ 34F	$ 96G
AMT credit carryforward		$ 180D				

A, B The tax actually payable in 1987 is based on the higher regular tax of $520.

C On a recomputed basis, the regular tax would be eliminated but it triggers an AMT tax of $180.

D The entire AMT tax can be carried forward as a tax credit since there were no exclusion items.

E, F, G, H The regular tax for 1990 and 1991 is higher than the AMT so it can be reduced by the AMT credit but not below the AMT tax for those years.

I A negative ACE adjustment is permitted in 1991 to the extent of prior positive ACE adjustments.

FIG. 17.10   Example of Interplay of AMT, ACE, and AMT Credit

If a company following APB 11 for 1987 switched to SFAS 96 on January 1, 1988 using the cumulative catch-up adjustment, the amount of that adjustment would have been calculated as follows:

Net asset set up for the temporary differences at 1/1/88 under the liability method ($340 − $194, in journal entry above)	$146
Less asset set up at 12/31/87 under APB 11; net timing differences of $200 @ 40%	80
Cumulative catch-up adjustment	$ 66

The $66 is the benefit of moving $1,100 from a 40% tax rate to a 34% rate by using the loss carry-back provisions of scheduling.

INDEFINITE REVERSAL CRITERIA

Although SFAS 96 is the most comprehensive pronouncement ever issued on accounting for income taxes, it does not address the accounting for five specific differences between reported income and taxable income. These were also omitted from APB 11 and the first four are covered by APB 23 (I25.169–.183). The five special situations are:

1. Undistributed earnings of subsidiaries.
2. Investments in corporate joint ventures.
3. General reserves of stock savings and loan associations.
4. Amounts designated as policyholders' surplus by stock life insurance companies.
5. Deposits in statutory reserve funds by U.S. steamship companies.

A sixth area, U.K. stock relief, had been considered as an item falling within the indefinite reversal criteria, but this status was eliminated by SFAS 96.

All five areas remaining unchanged by SFAS 96 involve transactions in which a specific originating difference between reported income and taxable income may not reverse until an indefinite future period, or conceivably may never reverse.

The practical effect of the omission from SFAS 96 coverage is that alternative practices will continue for financial reporting purposes: (1) deferred taxes may be provided in the same manner as prescribed for temporary differences or (2) the transactions may be treated as permanent differences with no deferred taxes provided.

Undistributed Earnings of Subsidiaries and Corporate Joint Ventures

A parent company's share in the earnings of a subsidiary is included in consolidated earnings simply by inclusion of the subsidiary in consolidated financial statements; this is so even if the earnings are not distributed. Investments in corporate joint ventures are also included in the financial statements of the investor, by use of the equity method. (Consolidation and the equity method are described in Chapter 24.) For tax purposes, however, such undistributed earnings of subsidiaries and corporate joint ventures are usually taxable to the investor only when distributed.

APB 23 (I.25.170) establishes the presumption that investors' shares of undistributed earnings of these two classes of investees eventually will be subject to income tax. Accordingly, deferred income taxes should be provided at the time the earnings are recognized for financial reporting purposes, unless this presumption can be overcome. If deferred taxes are required to be provided at the time the income is recognized by the investor, these deferred taxes should be amortized during the period when the actual income taxes become payable.

APB 23 also recognizes that in some cases it may be possible for the investor to postpone the distribution of the earnings indefinitely, and with it the reversal of the timing difference. In cases where the presumption that such earnings will be distributed can be overcome, the investor need not provide deferred taxes but may treat the difference between taxable income and reported income as a permanent difference. The presumption can be overcome:

> if sufficient evidence shows that the subsidiary [or joint venture] has invested or will invest the undistributed earnings indefinitely or that the earnings will be remitted in a tax-free liquidation. [The investor] should have evidence of specific plans for reinvestment of undistributed earnings ... which demonstrate that remittance of the earnings will be postponed indefinitely. Experience of the companies and definite future programs of operations and remittances are examples of the types of evidence required to substantiate [an investor's] representation of indefinite postponement of remittances from [the investee]. [I25.172].

After a determination that the criteria for indefinite postponement have been met, circumstances may change so that it becomes evident that some or all of the undistributed earnings will be remitted and taxed to the investor in the foreseeable future. Under such circumstances, the investor must include such taxable income in its schedule of temporary differences and apply the tax rates expected to be in effect during the year the event is expected to be taxed. Similarly, if deferred taxes have been recorded on undistributed earnings and it subsequently becomes evident that payment of such taxes is indefinitely postponed, it is then appropriate to eliminate the temporary difference from the schedule.

Equity Method Common Stock Investments

Investors in the common stock of investees other than subsidiaries and joint ventures follow the equity method of accounting for their pro rata share of undistributed earnings of the investee if it can be presumed that the investor has substantial influence over the investee. This presumption is usually established by ownership of at least 20% but not more than 50% of the voting stock interests (see Chapter 24). Such earnings are usually not taxed to the investor until distributed. Recognizing undistributed earnings in these circumstances creates a taxable temporary difference because the carrying amount of the investment in the investee increases while the tax basis remains unchanged.

The reason for requiring interperiod tax allocation in this case, while allowing such procedures to be avoided in the case of subsidiaries or corporate joint ventures where the indefinite reversal criteria are met, is the assumption that the purpose of making such investments is to earn a return either in the form of cash distributions or from disposition. Also, such investees are presumed not to be under the control of the investor, although subsidiaries and corporate joint ventures are; therefore, it is not possible for the investor to arrange the affairs of the investee in such a way that taxes can be indefinitely postponed.

In determining the rate to use in computing the related deferred taxes, SFAS 96 indicates that the investor should consider whether the distribution will be in the form of dividends or by ultimate disposition of the investment – if the tax laws specify different effective rates. A capital gain could be taxed at 34% but a dividend, because of the 70% dividend received deduction, would be taxed at only 10.2%. If a special rate for capital gains were reinstated in the tax law, an additional rate would have to be considered.

Savings and Loan Association Reserves

Savings and loan associations, both stock and mutual, are permitted tax deductions for estimated bad debts as computed by various formulas based on percentages of taxable income or loans. Since in most cases these deductions are greater than the bad-debt reserves that are appropriate for financial reporting purposes, they reduce income taxes that would otherwise be payable. Generally, they will only reverse and become subject to tax if they are distributed to shareholders, and such distributions are not common. The amount and timing of such distributions, moreover, are normally under the control of the association.

Regulatory authorities require savings and loan associations to appropriate a portion of earnings to general reserves as a protection for depositors. Such general reserves are not the same as the allowance for bad debts recognized for federal income tax purposes. However, the restriction on the distribution of general reserves usually also prevents the distribution of excess bad-debt reserves for tax purposes.

Accordingly, APB 23 provides that differences between bad-debt reserves for financial reporting purposes and those for tax purposes are not to be regarded as temporary differences requiring interperiod tax allocation unless evidence indicates that a portion of them will actually reverse and be taxed.[5]

Policyholders' Surplus

Internal Revenue Service provisions allow stock life insurance companies to deduct from taxable income certain formula-based allocations of funds to a policyholders' surplus account until the surplus equals a specified maximum. Generally, these amounts are subject to taxation in only two cases: (1) if the amounts are distributed to policyholders as dividends or (2) if amounts are transferred from the policyholders' surplus account to a shareholders' surplus account available for other business purposes.

Since companies are able to control the taxability of these amounts, and in most cases they are never actually taxed, APB 23 states that the provision of deferred taxes

---

[5] TRA 1986 designates as an AMT preference item for thrifts 100% of the excess of the bad debt reserve provision over the provision that would have been allowable had actual bad-debt experience been used for all tax years. If this causes a tax to become payable, then it must be accrued notwithstanding the exclusion under APB 23.

is not required except in circumstances indicating that the insurance company is likely to take an action that will subject a portion of policyholders' surplus to taxation (I25.183).

Statutory Reserve Funds of U.S. Steamship Companies

U.S. steamship companies are permitted to deduct from taxable income cash amounts paid into segregated funds to be used for the purchase or construction of vessels qualifying under the provisions of the law. Assuming that such cash is subsequently invested in qualifying vessels and not used for other purposes, it never becomes subject to taxation. Furthermore, after the funds are invested in vessels, depreciation on the vessels may nonetheless be deducted for tax purposes. But such depreciation may be recaptured (i.e., become subject to taxation) if the vessel is disposed of before a specified period of time.

This special area has never been covered by an official pronouncement. In practice, it is acceptable for steamship companies to treat deposits in the statutory reserve fund as either temporary or permanent differences. The predominant practice is to treat them as permanent differences and not to provide deferred taxes at the time the amounts are deducted for tax purposes. However, if circumstances indicate that the company will take an action that will result in the amount being taxed, provision of deferred taxes is then required.[6]

Accounting for U.K. Stock Relief

Under United Kingdom tax law, "stock relief" provisions permitted enterprises to deduct, for purposes of determining taxable income, increases in the carrying amount of inventories, thus providing relief from taxes that would otherwise be payable. If inventories decreased in future years, taxable income would be increased, resulting in the recapture ("clawback" in U.K. terminology) of the tax benefits previously granted. For fiscal periods beginning after March 13, 1984 stock relief and the corresponding clawback charge were abolished.

Under legislation enacted in 1979, the potential recapture of tax benefits expired six years after the year of origin. Prior to the 1979 legislation there was no time limit on the recapture, and the tax benefit from stock relief was generally treated as a timing difference, resulting in deferred tax credits in financial statements prepared in conformity with U.S. GAAP. The FASB was asked to study the matter and, in SFAS 31, concluded that the 1979 U.K. stock relief tax provisions did not give rise to temporary differences. Because of the potential recapture of stock relief, however, SFAS 31 required that the related tax benefit should be deferred unless it was probable that recapture would not occur.

SFAS 96 has superseded SFAS 31; and commencing with the application of SFAS 96, any remaining U.K. stock relief benefits represent temporary differences.

---

[6] After 1986, deposits into such funds are, however, treated as an AMT preference item. If this causes a tax to become payable, then it must be accrued notwithstanding the exclusion under APB 23.

Applicability of Indefinite Reversal Criteria

After APB 23 was issued, some accountants believed that the indefinite reversal criteria cited in that opinion justified the omission of deferred taxes for differences between reported income and taxable income in other circumstances as well. One specific question arose in connection with the treatment of differences between reported and taxable income relating to the cost of railroad gradings and tunnel bores. In 1978, the FASB issued an interpretation (FIN 22) that settled this matter by saying that the indefinite reversal criteria applied only to the specific cases cited in APB 23 and could not be used with any other differences between reported and taxable income. SFAS 96 has reinforced that decision by allowing only an exclusion for the four APB 23 areas and for deposits in statutory reserve funds by U.S. steamship companies.

Thus, it is now clear that comprehensive income tax allocation procedures must be applied to all differences between the tax basis of assets and liabilities and their reported amounts, except for the five special cases not addressed by SFAS 96. Further, the only situations that can be described as permanent differences are those for which it is clear that, because of specific provisions in the tax law or regulations, particular revenue or expense transactions either are exempt from inclusion in taxable income or are not deductible for tax purposes.

TAX CREDITS

Investment Tax Credits

During most years from 1962 until 1986, the Internal Revenue Code provided a general ITC that could be claimed as a reduction of taxes otherwise payable. The credit was based on a specified percentage of certain depreciable assets placed in service during the year for which the credit was claimed. The credit has ranged from 7% to 10% for qualified assets with a useful life of seven years or longer; smaller percentages were allowed for assets with shorter lives.

TEFRA, the 1982 Tax Act, required a taxpayer to reduce the cost basis of certain assets by 50% of the ITC claimed. However, a company could elect to take a reduced ITC and avoid a reduction in basis. Noting a lack of guidance in existing accounting literature, the FASB issued TB 83-1, *Accounting for the Reduction in the Tax Basis of an Asset Caused by the Investment Tax Credit.* The Bulletin indicated that an enterprise that recognizes ITCs by the flow-through method should have provided deferred taxes on a reduction in the tax basis of an asset caused by the ITC.

Tax Reform Act of 1986. TRA 1986 completely repealed the regular ITC. Generally, property placed in service in 1986 does not qualify for the investment credit except under transition rules. The main transition rule provides relief for property constructed, reconstructed, or acquired under a commitment that was binding before 1986. There also are numerous special transition rules for specific properties such as equipped buildings, plant facilities, sale-leasebacks, multi-use urban projects, solid-waste disposal projects, and others.

ITCs to be carried over and applied against tax in years after 1986 are restricted. The amount of credit that can be applied against tax is reduced by 35% for taxable years beginning on or after July 1, 1987. For tax years straddling that date, the decrease is prorated. Furthermore, the depreciable basis of property qualifying for transitional investment credits will drop by the full amount of the credit claimed. Carryovers of the credit can be applied against 25% of the AMT.

As described at the outset of this chapter, there are two acceptable methods of accounting for the ITC: the flow-through method and the deferral method. Under the flow-through method, the credit was treated as a reduction in reported income tax expense for the year in which it arose. Under the deferral method, it was recorded as a deferred credit in the balance sheet for the year in which it arose and amortized to reported income over the productive life of the related property on some systematic basis. Although the official pronouncements designate the deferral method as preferable (I25.185), in practice the flow-through method has been used by almost all except capital leasing companies. Companies were permitted to change from deferral to flow-through or vice versa despite the need for justification of the new method as preferable (A06.112), because of the special provisions adopted in the Revenue Act of 1971 as discussed earlier in this chapter under "Historical Overview."

ITC Carryovers. With ITC virtually eliminated by TRA 1986, the accounting focus shifts to utilization of ITC carryovers (and their effect on the calculation of deferred taxes). Prior tax law limited the amount of investment credit that could be used in any one year. Generally, the limitations were that (1) the credit could not exceed the liability of taxes otherwise payable, and (2) if the tax liability for the year exceeded $25,000, the tax credit could not exceed $25,000 plus 90 percent of the tax liability in excess of $25,000.

Any amount unused after taking advantage of the usual carry-back provisions was permitted to be carried forward for 15 years. As mentioned earlier, carryovers were reduced by 35%, effective July 1, 1987. The remaining available credits can be used to reduce the regular tax liability to not less than 75% of the AMT. For example, a corporation that has, before ITC, regular tax of $10,000 and AMT of $4,000 can use $7,000 of ITC (assuming it has that much carryover); this would reduce the tax payable to 75% of AMT.

For financial reporting purposes, an unused ITC carry-forward is recognized as a reduction of the deferred tax liability for temporary differences that will result in taxable amounts during the carry-forward period. In computing the amounts of investment credit offset, the 75%-of-AMT limitation must be observed.

The 35% cut in ITC carry-forwards did not have an immediate effect on companies that had used them as a reduction of deferred taxes, odd as that may seem. Under APB 11 and related pronouncements, the deferred method provided that the computation of the deferred tax provision was made for a discrete period, and changes in rates and percentages of ITC that could be used were future events that could not be given retroactive effect in the period a tax law change is enacted. Thus, the effect of the cut on such companies will be seen in the initial adoption of SFAS 96, which requires the liability method. When scheduling future tax differences, ITC carryovers will become reinstated to their usable amounts, ignoring the amounts once calculated as usable under old law and APB 11.

Deferral Method Balances. For those companies using the deferral method of accounting, ITC should be amortized over the same life as used for depreciation of the related depreciable property. As a practical matter, however, in some cases a straightline method of amortization is in use even though an accelerated depreciation method is used for the related property, because the differences are not material.

Lessors of property under capital leases normally use the deferral method of accounting for the investment credit. In their case the usual procedure is to use the interest method of amortizing the deferred ITC, so that income is recognized in relation to the outstanding principal balance on the capital lease. However, when amounts are relatively immaterial, a straightline amortization method is often employed. A special variation of the deferral method must be used when leveraged lease accounting is followed (L10.143–.149). Should a company decline to use the deferral method, leveraged lease accounting treatment is not available.

If a company uses the deferral method, under SFAS 96 it will treat the deferred amount as if it were a reduction in the book basis of the assets, and thus a temporary difference that will be deductible in the future.

Other Tax Credits

In addition to the ITC, corporations are entitled to various other credits, the most significant being foreign tax credit (which is recalculated for AMT and only 90% of which can be credited against AMT), targeted-jobs tax credit, research and development credit, and AMT credit (discussed earlier in this chapter). Ordinarily, these credits are included in income for financial reporting purposes for the year in which the reduction in taxes is realized. However, if a credit is not fully realized in the year in which it arises, either because of lack of taxable income or because of other limitations, carry-back and carry-forward provisions are provided (except that the AMT credit can only be carried forward). Carry-forward and carry-back provisions are also available when certain deductible expenses such as capital losses and contributions exceed limitations.

In determining the effects of temporary differences that will reverse in the future, carry-back and carry-forward rules as allowable for the particular credit will be used to offset the net liability for taxes, to the extent the credit is available in years that otherwise produce a deferred tax liability.

FINANCIAL STATEMENT PRESENTATION

Income Statement

All taxes based on income, including foreign, state, and local, should be reflected in the captions for income tax expense in the earnings statement. All state and local taxes based solely on income, regardless of their title, are considered income taxes. (For example, some state franchise taxes are based on income). These taxes should be accrued in the year the earnings to which they relate are reported.

The separate amounts of income tax expense or benefit related to continuing operations, discontinued operations, extraordinary items and the cumulative effect of an accounting change shall be disclosed (I25.125). In addition, disclosure is required for taxes allocated to prior period adjustments, to gains or losses included in comprehensive income[7] but excluded from net income, and to capital transactions.

SFAS 96 prohibits companies from continuing the practice of including interest and penalties assessed on income tax deficiencies (underpayment or improper computation) in income tax expense (I25.126).

Taxes on continuing operations are computed (usually by adjusting taxes paid or payable by the change in the deferred tax liability) based on the pretax income or loss on such operations as if there were no other taxable activities such as discontinued operations or extraordinary items. The full impact of all changes in rates, tax laws, or tax status of the company will be allocated to continuing operations, including those related to comprehensive income and excluded from net income.

The tax effect of each of the other categories (discontinued operations, extraordinary items, and so forth) is computed separately but, because of limitations on the use of tax credits or similar items, they may not aggregate to the incremental tax computed on all the categories; in this situation, the procedures to allocate the incremental tax effects are as follows (I25.167):

a. Determine the incremental tax benefit of the total net loss for all net loss categories.
b. Apportion that incremental tax benefit ratably to each net loss category.
c. Apportion ratably to each net gain category the difference between (1) the incremental tax effect of all categories other than continuing operations and (2) the incremental tax benefit of the total net loss for all net loss categories.

The procedure for allocating income taxes to each item within each category of items is similar to the procedure described above.

The tax benefit associated with an NOL carry-forward or carry-back will be allocated to the source of income (or loss) in the current year without regard to its source in a prior year. For instance, the benefit from the realization of an operating loss carry-forward would be allocated to continuing operations if the income that enabled its usage was derived from continuing operations. An example of the income statement apportionment of tax-effects is shown in Figure 17.11.

Components of Income Tax Expense. The components of income tax expense related to continuing operations should be disclosed separately, either on the face of the earnings statement or in a note. The separate components to be disclosed are (I25.126):

1. Taxes estimated to be currently payable.
2. Tax effects of temporary differences (exclusive of rate changes).

---

[7] The FASB definition of comprehensive income is "the change in equity of a business enterprise during a period from transactions and other events and circumstances from nonowner sources. It includes all changes in equity during a period except those resulting from investments by owners and distribution to owners." (SFAC 6, ¶ 70). Items included in "comprehensive income other than net income" at the present time are foreign currency translation adjustments (Chapter 22), and the valuation allowance for marketable equity securities (Chapter 12).

Assumptions

- The tax rate is 40% for the current year and 34% for all future years. AMT is ignored.
- The company has $3,000 of investment tax credits available, subject to a limitation of 90% of taxes payable.
- Nonqualified stock options were exercised during the year. Tax law permits the company to deduct from taxable income the excess fair value over the exercise price. The deduction for the current year is $2,000. For financial reporting purposes, the benefit of the deduction is an addition to paid-in-capital.
- Accelerated depreciation is used for tax purposes and straight line depreciation is used for financial reporting.
- Tax deductions for losses on discontinued operations are not permitted until the costs are actually paid.
- Pretax financial income for the year is:

Income from continuing operations	$ 6,000
Loss on discontinued operations	(1,000)
Extraordinary gain	5,000
Income before tax provision/benefit	$10,000

- At the balance sheet date, the company has the following temporary differences, all of which arose during the current year:

		Future reversing temporary differences	
	Current year	19X1	19X2
Continuing operations:			
Depreciable assets	$ (4,000)	$1,500	$2,500
Discontinued operations:			
Loss on discontinued operations	1,000	(1,000)	
	$ (3,000)	$ 500	$2,500
Tax rate	40%	34%	34%

- Taxable income for the current year is composed of:

Income before tax provision/benefit	$10,000
Accelerated depreciation in excess of straight line	(4,000)
Nondeductible accrual on discontinued operations	1,000
Tax deduction from the exercise of executive stock options	(2,000)
	5,000

(continued)

FIG. 17.11   Allocation of Income Tax Expense Among Income Statement Components

Calculation of Incremental Taxes

	Continuing operations	Total
Pretax income	$ 6,000	$8,000
Temporary differences	(4,000)	(3,000)
Taxable income	2,000	5,000
Tax rate	40%	40%
Tax before credits	$ 800	$2,000
Tax credits (90% limitation) (a)	(720)	(1,800)
Current tax expense	80	200
Deferred tax expense		
($4,000 × 34%)	1,360	
($3,000 × 34%)		1,020
Less tax credits available for offset at 90% limitation (a)	(1,224)	(918)
Deferred tax expense	136	102
Total tax expense	$ 216	$ 302
Incremental Tax	$ 86	

	Sum of loss categories	Discontinued operations	Benefit from exercise of stock options
Taxable income	$ 5,000	$5,000	5,000
Loss category	2,000	–	2,000
Taxable income without loss category	7,000	5,000	7,000
Tax rate	40%	40%	40%
Tax before credits	2,800	2,000	2,800
Tax credits (90% limitation) (a)	(2,520)	(1,800)	(2,520)
Current tax expense without loss category	280	200	280
Deferred tax:			
Net taxable temporary differences	3,000	3,000	3,000
Loss category	1,000	1,000	–
Taxable without loss category	4,000	4,000	3,000
Tax rate	34%	34%	34%
Tax before credits	1,360	1,360	1,020
Less remaining tax credits (a)	(480)	(1,200)	(480)
Deferred tax without loss category	880	160	540
Total tax expense without loss categories	1,160	360	820
Total tax expense	302	302	302
Incremental tax effect	$ 858	$ 58	$ 518

a Not more than $3,000—the total amount available—can be applied.

FIG. 17.11 (continued)

Allocation of Incremental Tax Effect of Loss Category
(The $858 tax effect is apportioned ratably to each net loss category).

	Each loss amount	Category percent	Apportioned amounts
Discontinued operations	$ 58	10%	$ 86
Executive stock options deductions	518	90%	772
	$ 576	100%	$ 858

Summary

	Pretax	Tax (provision) benefit	Net
Income statement items:			
Income from continuing operations	$ 6,000	$ (216)	$5,784
Loss on discontinued operations	(1,000)	86	(914)
Extraordinary gain	5,000	(944)(b)	4,056
Total income statement effect	10,000	(1,074)	$8,926
Balance sheet item allocated to additional paid-in-capital:			
Tax benefit of executive stock option deduction	—	772	
Total	$10,000	$ (302)	

b The $944 of tax expense allocated to the single net gain category is the difference between the $86 of incremental tax expense above for all items other than continuing operations and the $858 tax benefit for both net loss categories.

   Income tax expense for the current year should not be allocated to (i) accounting changes adopted either by retroactive restatement of prior periods or cumulative effect adjustments as of the beginning of the period; and (ii) corrections of errors in prior years' financial statements. For these items, the tax effects to be recorded should be the effects that would have been recorded if the newly adopted accounting principle or the correct accounting had been used in the prior periods.

3. Tax effects of investment credits, whether on the deferral method or the flow-through method. (The Revenue Act of 1971 requires disclosure, regardless of amount, of the method used in accounting for the investment credit. The amounts of investment credits are required to be disclosed unless immaterial.)
4. Benefits of operating loss carry-forwards.
5. Adjustments of a deferred tax liability or asset for enacted changes in tax laws or rates.
6. Adjustments for the effect of a change in tax status of the company.

   Tax Rate Reconciliation. Companies are now required by SFAS 96 to reconcile the actual tax expense for continuing operations with the amount that would result from applying the federal statutory rates to the pretax income, and to give the estimated amount and nature of each significant reconciling item (I25.127). Nonpublic companies do not have to give a numerical reconciliation but do have to disclose the nature of the significant reconciling items.

   The SEC has long required such disclosures for companies subject to its jurisdiction. Disclosure of individual items is not required if there is no individual item in excess of 5% of the amount computed by multiplying the income before tax by the applicable statutory tax rate. Also, if no single item is greater than such 5% and the total of all items is less than such 5%, the reconciliation is not required. An illustration of the SEC-required disclosure appears in an exhibit to rule 4.08(h) of Regulation S-X. This exhibit will probably be revised to reflect the changes in SFAS 96. Presumably the SEC also will continue its percentage prescriptions as well as the requirement to separately disclose foreign taxes.

Tax Effects Allocated to Stockholders' Equity. Stockholders equity is charged or credited with the income tax effects of:

1. Adjustment of opening balance of retained earnings for a change in accounting principles or correction of an error.
2. Gains and losses included in comprehensive income (but not the effects on their cumulative amounts of changes in tax laws or rates).
3. Increase or decrease in contributed capital, that is, costs of selling stock in a public offering.
4. Exercise of options under stock compensation plans (at least until the FASB completes its project on stock compensation plans).

In certain situations, the company may receive a tax deduction for dividends paid to shareholders; such benefits are a reduction of income tax expense.

Deferred Taxes Related to Comprehensive Income. In the income tax exposure draft (FASB, 1986a), the FASB indicated that the deferred tax consequences of an enacted change in tax rates on gains and losses included in comprehensive income[8] should be included in comprehensive income as well. In the final standard, the Board reversed direction—and decided that the entire effect for adjusting the related deferred tax asset or liability should be included in income from continuing operations (I25.119). This change was made in the belief that it was a desirable simplification.

Unfortunately, this change will have a considerable impact on insurance companies. Investments in equity securities are carried by insurance companies at market value, with the increase or decrease (less deferred taxes) classified in the equity section of the balance sheet.

For example, if an insurance company had unrealized gains of $1,000 on October 21, 1986, when the capital gains tax rate was 28%, the accounting treatment would have been: (1) an increase of $1,000 in the investment in equity securities, with a credit to unrealized gains in the equity section of the balance sheet and (2) the set up a deferred tax liability of $280 with a charge of the same amount to unrealized gains. Then, on the next day, when the new tax law was signed by the president of the United States, the insurance company would have had to increase the liability for deferred taxes up to 34%, with a charge to tax expense related to continuing operations. This result is quite clearly incongruent, and will require attention by the EITF or FASB. At present, however, based on how the rules are written, the insurance company will remove the tax effects from the equity account when the security is sold.

---

[8] Ibid.

Quasi-Reorganizations. In some quasi-reorganizations (discussed in Chapter 28), assets and liabilities are adjusted to current fair values, with the difference (almost always a net writedown) debited to net worth. In others, there is only the reclassification of a deficit in retained earnings against the other capital accounts.

SFAS 96 (I25.147) provides that in the former case, the tax benefit of an operating loss or tax credit carry-forward, if recognized subsequently, is to be added directly to contributed capital. In deficit reclassifications, however, the benefit is recognized in current earnings, and concurrently there is a transfer from retained earnings to contributed capital. This treatment equalizes the income statement effect of both approaches. SFAS 96 also requires that these rules be applied to any situation in which losses may have been charged directly to capital, whether or not labeled a quasi-reorganization.

Balance Sheet

The four possible income tax classifications on the balance sheet are (1) refundable income taxes, (2) deferred income tax debits and credits, (3) prepaid income taxes, and (4) currently payable income taxes.

Refundable Income Taxes. Refunds of past taxes arising from recognition of the tax effects of operating loss or other carrybacks should be classified as current or noncurrent assets, not netted against other tax accounts. The current portion should be determined by the extent to which realization is expected to occur during the current operating cycle.

Claims for refunds of taxes that depend for their allowances on unsettled interpretations of the law, or have been filed as protective measures, should usually not be given effect in the financial statements. But if they are properly includable and are material, they should be classified as noncurrent assets, with adequate footnote disclosure of their nature.

Deferred Income Tax Debits and Credits. Deferred income tax debits or credits arising from temporary differences will be classified as current or noncurrent depending on whether the temporary differences to which they relate will be taxable or deductible within the next year (I25.166). For enterprises using an operating cycle that is longer than one year for purposes of balance sheet classification of nontax assets and liabilities, the current portion of a deferred tax liability or asset should be the net income tax consequence of:

* Temporary differences that will result in net taxable or deductible amounts during the next year
* Temporary differences related to an asset or liability that is classified for financial reporting as current because of an operating cycle that is longer than one year
* Temporary differences for which there is no related, identifiable asset or liability for financial reporting ... whenever *other* related assets and liabilities are classified as current because of an operating cycle that is longer than one year.

Prepaid and Currently Payable Income Taxes. Prepayments of income taxes normally result from situations where the estimated tax deposits at a certain date during the year exceed the provision for current taxes payable to date, and thus they are classified as current assets. Currently payable income taxes should be classified as current liabilities and should not be combined with deferred taxes.

Disclosures

The amounts and expiration dates of operating loss and tax credit carry-forwards for both financial statement reporting purposes and income tax reporting should be disclosed; this amount will include the amount of future tax deductions related to temporary differences not eligible for recognition in the financial statements (I25.128).

Separate disclosure should be given of the amounts of NOLs of acquired companies that, if realized, would be used to reduce goodwill.

Finally, for those companies that escape provisions for deferred taxes because of the four exclusions of APB 23 (plus steamship statutory reserve funds, all of which are discussed earlier herein), detailed disclosures are required (I25.124), more or less as the price for remaining "uncorrected" by SFAS 96.

Figure 17.12 presents the 1987 financial statement disclosures provided by Aydin Corporation regarding the application of SFAS 96.

INTERIM FINANCIAL ACCOUNTING AND REPORTING

Accounting for taxes in interim periods was excluded from the scope of SFAS 96. The Board did not wish to reopen the subject at the time SFAS 96 was issued, despite the inconsistency of an interim period being treated as an integral part of the annual period under APB 28, whereas under the liability concept in SFAS 96 each period, whether interim or annual, would be treated as discrete. This lack of conformity has the effect of *requiring* the anticipation of future operations for the remainder of the year, even though SFAS 96 prohibits such anticipation for annual periods.

Nevertheless, SFAS 96 (I25.119) amends accounting for taxes in interim periods in several significant ways. Prior interim periods within the fiscal year will no longer be restated for retroactive changes in the tax laws (as had been required under SFAS 16 and TB 79–9); and the effect of a change in tax rates will be recognized in the period in which it occurs rather than spread over the remainder of the year (which was done by adjusting the estimated annual tax rate).

Reporting of the utilization of NOL carry-forwards and carry-backs has also been changed to harmonize with SFAS 96. In addition, the allocation of income taxes to the various segments of the income statement will follow the same rules as for annual periods; in essence, income or loss from continuing operations is first computed as if there were no other taxable or deductible items, and then the incremental amount of the tax expense or benefit is allocated to other segments.

The allocation of annual income tax expense to several interim periods within a year creates special problems, because many of the elements are based on annual amounts that are usually not known when the interim financial statements are

Aydin Corporation and Subsidiaries
Notes to Consolidated Financial Statements (continued)

Note H—Taxes on Income

As required by generally accepted accounting principles, the Company provides for the deferred income tax effects of transactions that are reported in different periods for financial reporting and income tax return purposes. Through December 31, 1986, deferred tax effects were computed based on the tax rates in effect during the period such differences arose.

In December 1987, the Financial Accounting Standards Board issued Statement 96, "Accounting for Income Taxes," which the Company has adopted as of January 1, 1987. Statement 96 requires that the balance sheet amounts for deferred income taxes be computed at rates to be in effect when the underlying differences will be reported in the Company's income tax returns. The deferred income tax provision for the period is then the difference in the liabilities as of the beginning and end of the period.

The effect of adopting Statement 96 is to increase net income for 1987 by $7,033,000 ($1.86 per share), of which $6,003,000 is reported as a cumulative effect of a change in accounting principle, and $1,030,000 ($.27 per share) is reported as a reduction in the 1987 tax provision. The primary reason for these benefits is the reduction in corporate federal income tax rates of the Tax Reform Act of 1986.

The provision for taxes on income consists of the following:

	Federal	State	Total
1987			
Current	$6,409,000	$1,823,000	$8,232,000
Deferred	(3,580,000)	(1,065,000)	(4,645,000)
Charge equivalent to tax benefit related to shares acquired by employees under stock options	152,000	30,000	182,000
	$2,981,000	$ 788,000	$3,769,000
1986			
Current	$ 328,000	$ 189,000	$ 517,000
Deferred	4,263,000	418,000	4,681,000
Charge equivalent to tax benefit related to shares acquired by employees under stock options	13,000	1,000	14,000
	$4,604,000	$ 608,000	$5,212,000
1985			
Current (credit)	$ (336,000)	$ -0-	$ (336,000)
Deferred	1,212,000	159,000	1,371,000
Charge equivalent to tax benefit related to shares acquired by employees under stock options	37,000	6,000	43,000
	$ 913,000	$ 165,000	$1,078,000

FIG. 17.12   SFAS 96 Disclosure Example. Source: Aydin Corporation, 1987 Annual Report

The components of deferred income taxes are as follows:

	1987	1986	1985
Completed contract method of reporting revenue for tax purposes	$(8,103,000)	$2,452,000	$3,316,000
Inventory valuation	1,201,000	(200,000)	(207,000)
Excess tax over book depreciation	380,000	404,000	850,000
Benefit of tax net operating loss	1,953,000	2,105,000	(2,272,000)
Other, net	(76,000)	(80,000)	(316,000)
	$(4,645,000)	$4,681,000	$1,371,000

A reconciliation between the federal statutory rate and the effective income tax rate (computed by dividing the provision for taxes on income by income-before taxes on income) is as follows:

	1987	1986	1985
Federal statutory rate	40.0%	46.0%	46.0%
State income taxes net of federal tax benefit	3.8	2.7	1.8
Benefit from nontaxable FSC income	(1.9)	(4.5)	(10.3)
Investment credits	-0-	(.2)	(8.0)
Research and development credit	(3.4)	-0-	(6.2)
Effect on deferred provision due to rate change	(7.9)	-0-	-0-
Other, net	(.6)	(1.2)	(1.2)
Effective income tax rate	30.0%	42.8%	22.1%

Deferred income tax liabilities primarily relate to contract accounting, inventories, and depreciation. Investment credits amounted to $26,000 and $393,000 in 1986 and 1985, respectively.

FIG. 17.12 (continued)

prepared. The basic approach for determining interim income tax expense set forth in APB 28 [I73.111]) is:

> At the end of each interim period the company should make its best estimate of the effective tax rate expected to be applicable for the full fiscal year. The rate so determined should be used in providing for income taxes on a current year-to-date basis. The effective tax rate should reflect anticipated investment tax credits, foreign tax rates, percentage depletion, capital gains rates, and other available tax planning alternatives.

Effective Annual Tax Rate

APB 28 (as amplified by FIN 18 (I73)) also provides that the effective tax rate should exclude the tax effects of unusual or infrequently occurring items, extraordinary items, results of discontinued operations, gains or losses on disposition of discontinued operations, and the cumulative effects of changes in accounting principles. These exclusions from the effective annual rate are necessary because the transactions giving rise to their effects are reported as discrete items of the specified interim period in which they occur, not apportioned over the entire year. The specific tax effect associated with each of these excluded items is reported during the same interim period as the related transaction.

The computation of an effective annual rate and its application to interim reporting is illustrated in the following simplified examples. Assume the following facts:

- The company expects annual pretax income for financial reporting purposes of $1,000.
- The company anticipates various tax credits of $100.
- The statutory tax rate (federal and state rates combined) is 40%.

The effective annual tax rate would be computed as follows:

Expected annual pretax income for financial reporting purposes	$1,000
Expected annual income taxes before tax credit at 40%	$ 400
Tax credit	100
Expected annual income tax	$ 300
Estimated annual effective tax rate	30%

The company will pay income taxes, considering all credits available to it, at the rate of 30% of its reported pretax income. The 30% effective tax rate would then be applied to the interim period pretax income for financial reporting purposes. Accordingly, if in the first quarter the company had pretax income of $300, its interim financial statements would appear as follows:

Income before taxes	$300
Taxes on income (30% effective tax rate)	90
Net income	$210

Cumulative Calculation

Any changes in the estimated annual effective tax rate are accounted for on a prospective basis. To illustrate, assume that during the second quarter the company revised its estimate of its annual income from $1,000 to $1,250. Its new effective annual tax rate would be computed as follows:

Expected annual pretax income for financial reporting purposes	$1,250
Expected annual income taxes before tax credits at 40%	$ 500
Tax credits	100
Expected annual income taxes	$ 400
Revised estimated annual effective tax rate	32%

In the second quarter, the company would apply a revised effective annual tax rate of 32% to its cumulative pretax reported income for the first two quarters and subtract the income tax expense reported on the first quarter's earnings to determine the tax expense for the second quarter. To illustrate, assume that the company had cumulative pretax income for the first two quarters of $500 ($300 for the first quarter and $200 for the second quarter). At an effective tax rate of 32%, the income tax expense for the first six months would be $160. Since the company had already reported $90 of income tax expense in the first quarter, it would report the difference — $70 — on the $200 of pretax income of the second quarter. The interim financial statements would appear as follows:

	First two quarters combined	Second quarter	First quarter (as previously reported)
Income before income taxes	$500	$200	$300
Taxes on income	160	70	90
Net income	$340	$130	$210

The tax reported for the second quarter includes taxes at the new revised rate of 32% on second quarter pretax income of $200, which equals $64, plus an additional 2% on the first quarter pretax income of $300, or $6, for a total of $70. The difference between the 32% revised effective tax rate and the 30% original effective tax rate applied to first quarter income is reported in the second quarter.

Interim Losses

Losses during the year also complicate the determination of interim tax expense. It is appropriate to provide a tax benefit in an interim period with a loss if realization in subsequent interim periods of the current year is assured beyond any reasonable doubt, or if it can be offset against income in earlier periods of the year. For example, continuing the previous illustration, assume that in the third quarter the company had a $100 pretax loss. Also assume that the company anticipated this loss and took it into consideration in estimating the annual tax rate. In this case it would be appropriate to record a tax benefit in the third quarter using the 32% rate. The financial statements for the third quarter would appear as follows:

	First three quarters combined	Third quarter
Income (loss) before income taxes	$400	$(100)
Taxes on income (refundable taxes)	128	(32)
Net income (loss)	$272	$ (68)

If a loss is expected for the full year, or if a loss is experienced in an interim period and it is not known whether profits in other periods will offset it, refundable taxes may be recorded, provided the company can also carry back the loss to earlier profitable years. Should carry-backs not be available, SFAS 96 now specifies that a deferred tax asset cannot be recorded. There are numerous examples of accounting for income taxes in interim periods shown in FIN 18 (I73), but caution is advised considering the conforming changes required by SFAS 96.

BUSINESS COMBINATIONS

SFAS 96 made significant changes in accounting for business combinations. Essentially it requires that the expected tax benefits of the combination be taken into consideration at the date of the combination. The effects of SFAS 96 on business combinations are also discussed in Chapter 23.

Purchase Accounting

In a purchase business combination, APB 16 had required that, in allocating purchase price to the fair values of assets acquired and liabilities assumed, it was necessary to give effect to differences between such fair values and tax bases. In a purchase that does not involve a step-up in tax basis of the net assets of the acquiree, fair values of assets acquired are often greater than tax basis, resulting in a portion of the fair value being non-deductible for tax purposes when the expiration or other usage of the asset occurs. A typical example is found in plant and equipment of the acquiree; the excess of fair value over the tax basis, while depreciable for postacquisition financial reporting purposes, is not deductible for tax purposes. Thus, such an excess has a value less than its face amount.

It was also not unusual to have excess of tax bases over fair values, such as in the acquisition of a leasing portfolio having an impaired value but not having been reduced to that value for tax purposes.

APB 16 provided that in such cases, the fair valuing process should give effect to these differences, and this was done by providing a tax against the asset value (in the case of fair values in excess of tax basis). Effectively, the nondeductible portion was tax-effected, that is, carried net of tax. Also, because this tax effect was not deemed to be governed by APB 11, the prohibition against discounting of deferred taxes was deemed by many accountants to be inapplicable. Therefore the tax effect was often discounted back to present value in determining the amount to offset against the asset value. It was generally not deemed appropriate to increase an asset above its fair value to give tax effect to a tax basis that was greater than fair value, but to let such benefits flow into income as realized; however, in some cases writeups above fair value have been made if overall there was a net tax reduction in recording the combination.

SFAS 96 abolished net of tax accounting for purchase business combinations. For business combinations consummated after the date of adoption of SFAS 96, the tax basis differentials must be treated as temporary differences with deferred taxes set up in recording the acquisition. Further, these deferred taxes, like any others, may not be discounted. Of even greater significance is the provision that:

> Accounting for a business combination should reflect any provisions in the tax law that permit or restrict the use of either of the combining enterprises' operating loss or tax credit carryforwards to reduce taxable income or taxes payable attributable to the other enterprise subsequent to the business combination. [I25.161]

This will permit an acquired company's NOL to shelter not only its own temporary differences but also (if allowable under the law) to shelter temporary differences of the acquiring company; or an NOL of the acquiring company could shelter the temporary differences of the acquiree. In either case, this would reduce the goodwill (or increase the negative goodwill) generated by the acquisition accounting.

If the acquired entity has NOLs, tax credits, or net deductible temporary differences that cannot be recognized at date of acquisition, then their subsequent realization will first reduce goodwill and other noncurrent intangible assets to zero. Any remaining benefits will then be used to reduce income tax expense.

Additional amounts of NOLs or tax credit carry-forwards may arise subsequent to an acquisition. The determination of which is deemed to be used first in the financial statements will follow the relevant provisions of the tax laws or regulations.

Pooling of Interests

Under traditional APB 16 accounting, the income statements of the combined companies are added together and no benefit is given for the losses suffered by one company to reduce the tax expense of another pooled entity because it is impossible to retrogress and file consolidated returns.

SFAS 96 recognizes this fact but states that if the companies intend to file a consolidated return in the future

> one combining enterprise's operating loss carryforward in a prior period reduces the other enterprise's deferred tax liability in the loss and subsequent periods to the extent that (a) the temporary differences will result in taxable amounts subsequent to the combination date and (b) the loss carryforward can reduce those taxable amounts based on provisions of the tax law. That tax benefit is recognized as part of the adjustment to restate financial statements on a combined basis for prior periods. The same requirements pertain to tax credit carryforwards and to temporary differences that will result in net deductible amounts in future years. [I25.162]

This will have the effect of restating historical results for tax benefits previously not recognized in operations.

It is not possible to evade this requirement by failing to file consolidated returns immediately after combination; if the group initially files separate tax returns but later files a consolidated return, then the benefits expected to be achieved that are related to conditions existing at the date of combination would be reflected in prior years by restatement.

Taxable Poolings

For taxable poolings, in which there is a step-up in the tax basis of the assets, the recognizable benefits related thereto at acquisition date are to be credited to paid-in capital. However, any tax benefits attributable to the step-up in basis that are not recognizable until a later date are to be reported as a reduction in income tax expense when the relevant recognition criteria are met (I25.163).

TRANSITION ACCOUNTING

When SFAS 96 is first adopted either retroactive restatement or cumulative catch-up adjustment is permitted. The Board also decided to require a different accounting treatment for business combinations under each method. Under the restatement approach, all prior business combinations would be remeasured and all provisions of

SFAS 96 applied. However, if a company chooses the cumulative catch up approach, the prior purchase business combinations are not restated to eliminate net of tax accounting (see preceding text); the difference between the remaining net-of-tax financial statement amounts and the related tax bases is treated the same as a temporary difference, and deferred taxes must be provided as a part of the cumulative catch-up adjustment.

Implementation Guidance

The FASB staff has developed the following tentative guidance.

Restatement of discontinued entities. The situation may arise where a company wishes to retroactively adopt SFAS 96 but no longer has the records related to a subsidiary it has sold. The staff believes that in this situation the company could not use the restatement election if the information is not available to do so. This could have a material impact on the financial statements. There may be situations where it would be possible to decide that the results can be approximated closely enough so as not to have a material impact, but that would depend on the facts and circumstances of the particular situation.

Adoption of SFAS 96 late in the fiscal year. If this situation arises the company should not use hindsight in restating quarters; for example, assumptions should not be applied to past quarters that differ from those previously used in those quarters.

INTERCORPORATE TAX ALLOCATION

When a company files a consolidated tax return with its subsidiaries, and separate financial statements for the parent or a subsidiary are to be prepared, the consolidated tax expense must be allocated among the affiliated companies. Special procedures for intercorporate tax allocation are required, because the consolidated tax expense usually differs from the summation of what the tax expense for the companies would be on the basis of separate returns.

Internal Revenue Code Methods

The Internal Revenue Code (§ 1552) and related regulations provide specific methods of apportioning a consolidated tax among the affiliated companies for tax purposes. The first alternative method of intercorporate allocation provided in the Internal Revenue Code apportions the consolidated tax currently payable to profitable component corporations based on their respective taxable incomes. The second alternative apportions the consolidated tax currently payable to each component corporation on the basis of the aggregate of taxes payable on a separate return basis. A third method is set forth in the Internal Revenue Code, but is rarely used.

Consolidated groups can also devise any other method of apportionment, but only with the prior approval of the IRS. In the absence of authoritative financial accounting pronouncements, the methods of apportionment provided in the tax law are also acceptable for financial reporting purposes, provided full disclosure of the method used is made in a note to the separate financial statements of the parent or the subsidiary. Companies often use the same method of apportionment for financial reporting purposes as they use for tax purposes in order to minimize the number of allocations required, which can become quite complex.

Note, however, that the SEC requires the pro forma use of the separate return method in security offerings by subsidiaries included in consolidated returns.

Other Financial Reporting Methods

Variations of the methods of apportionment set forth in the Internal Revenue Code are also acceptable for financial reporting purposes. These are briefly described in the following sections.

Separate Return With Differences Allocated to Parent. Under this method, taxes are reported in the financial statements for each subsidiary as if it filed a separate return. The difference between the total taxes so reported for the subsidiaries and the consolidated expense is reported as part of the parent company's tax expense. The parent therefore receives the benefit of or charge for any difference between the consolidated tax provision and separate return provisions.

Ratio of Individual Company Income to Consolidated Income. Under this method, each member of the consolidated group obtains an income tax charge or credit based on the ratio of its pretax income or loss to the consolidated group's pretax income or loss. For example, if the consolidated pretax income is $1,000, consolidated taxes on income are $340, the parent company's income is $600, subsidiary A has income of $500, and subsidiary B has a loss of $(100), the tax provision would be allocated as follows:

	Consolidated	Parent	Sub. A	Sub. B
Income (loss) before income taxes	$1,000	$600	$500	$(100)
Taxes on income (refund of taxes)	340	204	170	(34)
Net income (loss)	$ 660	$396	$330	$ (66)

Since subsidiary B had a loss, it would have a negative tax provision.

Marginal Contribution. Under this method, the provision for income taxes is first computed for the consolidated group. Then the provision is computed with one member of the group excluded. This amount is subtracted from the consolidated tax provision, and the difference is taken as the tax provision for the excluded member. The tax provision for each remaining member is computed in the same way. If there is any difference between the total of the provisions for all the members and the consolidated provision, it is added to or subtracted from the parent company's provision.

Disclosures

SFAS 96 requires the following disclosures where an enterprise issues separate financial statements but is part of a group that files a consolidated tax return (I25.129)

a. The amount of current and deferred tax expense for each income statement presented and the amount of any tax-related balances due to or from affiliates as of the date of each balance sheet presented.

b. The principal provisions of the method by which the consolidated amount of current and deferred tax expense is allocated to members of the group and the nature and effect of any changes in that method (and in determining related balances due to or from affiliates) during the years for which the disclosures in (a) above are presented.

   The consolidated amount is the amount of current and deferred taxes reported in the consolidated financial statements for the group, or the amount that would be reported if such financial statements were prepared. The sum of the amounts allocated to members of the group, including the parent, shall equal the consolidated amount.

Allocation of Deferred Taxes

Deferred income taxes arising from temporary differences should be allocated to the component members of a consolidated group on a basis that is consistent with the allocation of income tax expense. Generally, the deferred tax attributable to a specific temporary difference should be allocated to the component in which the temporary difference occurs. The computational procedures are generally less involved when separate return methods of allocation are used, and such approaches will most often accomplish the objective of normalizing the total tax expense of an individual component with temporary differences.

The separate return method would, of course, complicate the scheduling of temporary differences as this would have to be done both on a consolidated and individual company basis.

AUDITING

Objectives

Conceptually, the auditing objectives for income taxes are the same as for other costs and liabilities: Auditors must evaluate the reasonableness of the reported amounts. Auditing income taxes, however, is often more challenging than other areas, both because the amounts involved are usually a significant portion of income and are significant to the balance sheet, and because a thorough knowledge is required of the many specific tax rules that apply to the company under audit. The auditing of income taxes has the following three objectives.

1. To conclude that the income tax amounts presented in the balance sheet fairly represent, in the context of the financial statements taken as a whole, the amounts that are currently

payable or receivable in accordance with SFAS 96. Also, income tax items would be properly classified in the balance sheet among current or noncurrent assets and liablities.

2. To conclude that the amounts of income tax expense (or credit) presented in the income statement are fairly stated, including the separation between amounts currently payable and amounts deferred, in the context of the financial statements taken as a whole.

3. To conclude that disclosures in the financial statements about income taxes are appropriate in context – that they adequately explain the important aspects of the company's income taxes, including significant amounts of deferred taxes, amounts of tax carry-forwards available, and differences between the reported amount of income tax allocated to continuing operations and the amount of income tax expense that would result from applying the statutory federal tax rates to pretax income from continuing operations.

Substantive Approach to Auditing

Before the auditor can be satisfied as to the reasonableness of the reported income tax amounts, he must understand in considerable detail the specific tax rules that apply to the company under audit. The approach to auditing income taxes is substantive, rather than one of reliance on the internal control structure. Thus the auditor will obtain and review (or prepare) an analysis of all transactions affecting the income tax accounts for the year. The auditor must evaluate the company's computations and calculations of income tax expense and the related balance sheet accrual and deferrals. This will include review of the schedules of temporary differences and a test to see if an alternative minimum tax is appropriate. Where there is the possibility of a material assessment of additional taxes, the auditor, with his tax adviser, will consider the adequacy of accrual and disclosure under the rules covering accounting for contingencies (see Chapter 26).

In addition to checking tax computations, the auditor should review tax returns and any correspondence between the company and tax authorities relating to questions or open items on the company's tax returns. The auditor must understand and evaluate the status of any examinations by taxing authorities that are in process. Often, the auditor will need to seek precedent to evaluate a particular tax question or to draw analogies between the company's tax problems and similar problems of other companies, and to obtain advice from tax specialists. (For a detailed discussion of the relationship between auditor and tax adviser, and the contributions of tax specialists to an audit, see Chapter 48).

In principle, there are no differences between the auditing approach for federal income taxes and that for state and local taxes. An important aspect of auditing state and local taxes is to consider whether the company is appropriately providing for taxes in all jurisdictions in which it is subject to income tax.

Difficult Audit Issues

Undistributed Earnings of Subsidiaries and Corporate Joint Ventures. A company is not required to provide deferred taxes on its share of the undistributed earnings of subsidiaries or corporate joint ventures if the presumption that such earnings will be distributed and subjected to taxation can be overcome. In practice, the provisions for overcoming the presumption of distribution have been generally interpreted to require a documented position that is reasonable in the light of both statutory requirements and prevailing economic circumstances. The auditor must be satisfied, through the advice of a tax expert if necessary, that the relevant provisions of the tax laws, regulations, rulings, and decided court cases have been studied, analyzed, and properly interpreted to support the company's planned course of action. Alternatively, the company may plan to overcome the presumption by reinvesting in new facilities all funds generated internally by the subsidiary or the corporate joint venture. In such a case, the auditor must be satisfied that the plans for reinvestment have actually been formulated and that they are reasonable in the light of the past practices and the potential of the organization. Also, he must be satisfied that there are sound business reasons for carrying out the reinvestment plans.

The presumption of distribution of earnings cannot be overcome with respect to investments in investees that are not subsidiaries or corporate joint ventures. This sometimes requires a judgment as to whether or not a particular investee qualifies as a subsidiary or corporate joint venture.

A common example of a corporate joint venture is one owned 50% by each of two investors and operated jointly for their common benefit. Obviously, a venture can have more than two holders, or have one venturer with more than a 50% interest, and still qualify as joint, provided it is clear that all the joint venturers are involved in the management of the operation at least at a policy-making level. However, as the number of joint venturers grows, a point is reached where the investee is simply a corporation with a large number of minority holders and no longer qualifies as a joint venture; it would then be necessary for the investor to record deferred taxes on undistributed earnings regardless of the ability to overcome a presumption that distribution will be made. This is an example of a borderline case in which the auditor must carefully accumulate and analyze evidence. A complete understanding of all the facts and exercise of professional judgment are necessary, because again, specific rules and guidelines are not yet available for determining when a corporation can be considered a joint venture. The FASB has a project underway which, in part, should clarify these issues (see Chapter 24).

Indefinite Reversal Criteria. Prior to the adoption of FIN 22 (I24) in 1978, companies and auditors had to determine if the indefinite reversal criteria described in APB 23 (I42) also applied to situations not explicitly mentioned in that opinion.

An example of such a situation not explicitly covered by GAAP is the extinguishment by a corporation of debt for less than its carrying amount. The result is reported as income for financial statement purposes, but for tax purposes the company may be able to postpone the recognition of the income by adjusting the tax basis of certain assets. However, SFAS 96 says that indefinite reversal criteria apply only to situations explicitly covered in APB 23.

Accordingly, at present the only areas that require judgments of this type relate to interpreting the provisions of the law to determine whether a specific revenue qualifies for exemption from taxation or whether a specific expense is never deductible. In such situations the auditor must be satisfied, through the advice of a tax expert if necessary, that a sufficiently thorough study has been made of the relevant tax law and regulations to determine if the company's position is appropriate.

Tax Strategies. Where the company has devised a tax strategy to shift taxable and deductible temporary differences between years, the auditor must challenge it to ascertain that it meets the criteria of SFAS 96. This situation is made more difficult because the company will most likely never intend to actually implement these strategies. The real tax strategies will be based on forecasted earnings rather than a breakeven assumption.

Tax Allocation of Consolidation Adjustments. In some cases the parent company and some or all subsidiaries in a consolidated enterprise file separate tax returns. Accordingly, taxable income of the various components may include gains or losses resulting from transactions with other components. Intercompany profits and losses are required to be eliminated in consolidated statements (see Chapter 24), and thus the tax effects, if any, of such eliminated transactions must also be determined. The staff of the FASB has taken the position that the elimination entry creates a temporary difference on the books of the receiving entity where different taxing jurisdictions are involved.

In any large consolidated group where transactions occur among the separate companies, the allocation of taxes on consolidating adjustments can become quite complex. Auditors are often required to spend a great deal of time in study and analysis to determine that all the allocations are properly handled.

THE FUTURE

Accounting for income taxes is an extremely complex subject that has given rise to a great deal of contention over the years. Many had hoped that when the APB intensively studied accounting for income taxes and issued APB 11 in 1967, dealing with the subject in practice would have been simplified because of the availability of comprehensive and universal guidelines. However, the adoption of the deferred method, with its emphasis on mechanical calculations rather than on concept, created numerous interpretation problems over the years.

Now that the FASB has issued a new standard, SFAS 96, adopting the liability method (exclusive of the APB 23 exceptions), a more conceptual approach is prescribed, but many will still find fault with it. Perhaps the most significant flaw in SFAS 96 is the failure to deal with discounting of tax liabilities; such consideration is necessary to meaningfully display the true effects of amounts that will not be paid for many years.

The presumption of breakeven future operations will strike some as absurd. Still others will howl for repeal when the tax rates increase and they are forced to recognize the impact of the change in current operations—*including* the impact on taxes associated with items floating in the equity section (i.e., comprehensive income items).

Accounting for taxes will continue to be a difficult area for accountants, and further pronouncements, interpretations, and EITF deliberations will be necessary to cope with new tax laws and new situations encountered that were not anticipated in SFAS 96.

18

Debt and Interest

OVERVIEW

Nature of Debt and Interest

Liabilities are discussed in numerous chapters throughout this *Handbook*. A particular class of liabilities referred to as debt—amounts evidenced by formal documents indicating a promise to pay over money or equivalent assets—is discussed in this chapter.

SFAC 6, *Elements of Financial Statements* (FASB, 1985), defines liabilities as "probable future sacrifices of economic benefits arising from present obligations of a particular entity to transfer assets or provide services to other entities in the future as a result of past transactions or events (¶ 35). While SFAC 6 also points out that "obligations" are much broader than legal obligations (n.22), this chapter focuses on legal obligations.

Interest virtually always accompanies a debt obligation; as stated in SFAC 6, "a common feature of liabilities is interest—the time value of money or the price of delay" in payment (n.23).

Distinguishing Debt From Equity

Notwithstanding the SFAC 6 definitions of debt and equity (¶ 49), often it is not easy to differentiate between them. Uncomplicated examples on the borderline are mandatorily redeemable preferred stock (discussed in Chapter 20) and subordinated debt of securities broker/dealers (discussed in Chapter 42). In a sense, all of an enterprise's capitalization is one form or another of prioritized interest in its assets, starting at the most senior and secured debt and ending at the lowest form of equity right—perhaps an unvested option or an out-of-the-money warrant. Nonetheless, the present accounting model requires that a distinction be made in the balance sheet between debt and equity. Thus, much time is devoted by the FASB, its Emerging Issues Task Force, AICPA committees, and the SEC in attempting to sort out the characteristics of instruments to decide whether the balance tips one way or the other.

Because of the difficult distinctions to be made, the FASB is in the process of studying financial instruments and off–balance sheet financing. The first phase will require fulsome disclosures of various risks involved from the standpoint of the issuer and holder; some rules are likely to be in force by 1989, unless the Board delays the timetable. Subsequent phases will attack measurement and recognition issues. The Board's approach seems adequately conceptual to overcome the usual problem of issuing standards that are not adaptable to future economic developments.

The disclosures proposed to be required of all entities include for the most part information that is already given by some companies in varying degrees. Among the disclosures that would affect debt are future cash payments and interest-bearing financial instruments that will mature or reprice, and their effective interest rates. All such information would have to be presented for amounts grouped into (1) within one year, (2) after one year through five years, and (3) over five years. In addition, specified aggregated information would be required as to debt denominated in foreign currencies.

This chapter will focus on the "simpler" aspects of debt and interest. Chapter 21 discusses the more esoteric financial instruments and transactions involving debt attributes and their assembly into hybrid securities.

Sources of Debt Funding

In the sense of legal obligations, debt can arise from any source by which an enterprise commits itself to make future transfers of money or assets, or otherwise has such a commitment imposed on it. Intermediate- and long-term debt is raised in specific ways, such as:

- Public debt offering through an underwriter.
- Private placements with banks, pension funds, insurance companies, private venture capital firms, or investment management companies.
- Financing with a small business investment company.
- Domestic and/or international project financings.
- Public sector financing (e.g., industrial revenue bonds, housing authority bonds, general obligation bonds, and special tax and revenue bonds).
- Mortgaging property.

Typical sources of short-term funds may be (1) commercial banks, (2) commercial paper, (3) factors and finance companies, and (4) customers and suppliers.

Classification of Debt

To accommodate the changing business environment over the years, debt instruments have been created with many combinations of characteristics. As a result, notes and bonds take various forms. Debentures, floating rate notes, convertible bonds, equipment trust certificates, income bonds, and participating bonds are only a few of the common types.

Some debt may be secured or collateralized and some may not (e.g., debentures). If secured, debt can be further classified by the types of assets pledged. Debt can be secured by a mortgage or by company-issued collateral trust bonds and notes, guaranteed bonds, or securitized assets.

Debt can also be categorized by the purpose of the issue and the issuing agency. For example, the purpose can be classified into debt with a prior lien, a refunding issue, or a purchase-money mortgage. The issuing agency may be a commercial enterprise, railroad, utility, municipality, or quasi-government agency (e.g., toll road, sewer and water district, and so forth).

Adding to the complexity of classifying debt are an enormous number of descriptive features such as denomination of the principal, interest rate, interest payment dates, repayment terms, whether issued with warrants, if subordinated, and many others.

For purposes of this chapter, debt will be considered from the balance sheet classification perspective—short-term (and therefore classified as a current liability in a classified balance sheet) and long-term (not classified as a current liability). This distinction is important to most businesses because various ratios used in financial analysis place greater emphasis on short-term debt in assessing a company's cash flow prospects.

Covenants

While all liabilities have certain aspects enforceable at law, an enterprise entering into a debt financing arrangement ordinarily will agree to certain covenants — conditions the borrower specifically promises to achieve and/or maintain. For example, a covenant might specify that the company will not declare or pay any dividend or make any distribution on its capital stock to its stockholders unless a stated amount of retained earnings would remain after doing so; or a company might be required to maintain a stated minimum working capital, shareholders' equity, or various operating and balance sheet ratios. Some covenants are not all that precise; they may call for "no adverse change" in operations or financial position, or may be susceptible to evaluation only at the discretion of the lender. These are referred to as *subjective acceleration clauses*.

Failure to comply with these undertakings constitutes a default, giving the lender certain rights or adding further restrictions on the borrower. A common lender's right in the event of default is acceleration of the due date of the debt to the current date; however, this is unlikely to happen the minute the *grace period* (time allowed to cure the default) expires. In the event of default on a particular debt, other debts may also go into default because of the existence of a *cross-covenant*, which specifies that an event of default on any other debt is also an event of default under the debt containing the cross-covenant clause. The parties might agree to a *waiver* of the default for a stipulated period or to a revision of the covenant, or might even perform a troubled-debt restructuring under SFAS 15 (D22).

SHORT-TERM DEBT

Current Liabilities

Most commercial and industrial enterprises present a classified balance sheet; that is, the assets and liabilities are segregated as current and noncurrent. This approach affords the financial statement user some information about the liquidity aspects of the business, but this is by no means very precise and numerous other sources of liquidity information must be accessed. Generally, current assets are cash and those expected to be converted into cash within 12 months from the balance sheet date; and current liabilities are those expected to be settled within 12 months. This time frame frequently is changed for businesses that have a natural operating cycle longer than 12 months, for example, construction contractors. In these cases, the classification cutoff for liabilities is often maintained at 12 months, except that those liabilities directly related to greater-than-12-month current assets would also have to be classified as current liabilities.

By contrast, some types of entities do not use a classified balance sheet because of the highly monetary nature of their assets and liabilities (e.g., most financial institutions discussed in Part V of this *Handbook*).

ARB 43, Chapter 3A, *"Current Assets and Current Liabilities"* (B05), defines current liabilities as those whose liquidation "is reasonably expected to require the use of existing resources properly classified as current assets, or the creation of other current liabilities" (B05.108). That paragraph goes on to say that the current liabilities classification "is intended to include obligations for items which have entered into the operating cycle . . . and debts which arise from operations directly related to the operating cycle. . . ."

In ASR 148, *Disclosure of Compensating Balances and Short-Term Borrowing Arrangements* (FRR § 203), however, the SEC says that commercial paper and other short-term debt should be classified as a current liability even though the issuer's intention is to roll over the debt at maturity, unless: (1) the borrower has a noncancelable binding agreement from a creditor to refinance the debt; (2) the refinancing extends the maturity date beyond one year (or current operating cycle, if longer); and (3) the borrower's intention is to exercise this right.

Obligations Expected to Be Refinanced

In 1975, SFAS 6, *Classification of Short-Term Obligations Expected to be Refinanced* (B05), was issued in response to inconsistencies between ARB 43 and ASR 148 (FRR § 203) and to resolve diverse accounting that was found in practice. Short-term obligations that were expected to be refinanced on a long-term basis were being presented in the balance sheet in some cases as current liabilities, and in other cases as long-term liabilities.

For purposes of understanding SFAS 6, certain definitions are in order (B05.111).

* *Short-term obligations* are those scheduled to mature within one year after the balance sheet date. For those enterprises that use the operating cycle concept of working capital, debt related to assets within an operating cycle that is longer than one year is considered short-term if the assets are classified as current.

* *Long-term obligations* are those scheduled to mature beyond one year (or the operating cycle, if applicable) from the balance sheet date.

* *Refinancing a short-term obligation on a long-term basis* means either replacing it with a long-term obligation or equity securities, or renewing, extending, or replacing it with short-term obligations for an uninterrupted period extending beyond one year (or the operating cycle, if applicable) from the balance sheet date. Thus, despite the fact that the short-term obligation is scheduled to mature during the ensuing fiscal year (or operating cycle), it will not require the use of working capital during that period.

SFAS 6 requires short-term obligations arising from transactions in the normal course of business and payable in accordance with customary trade terms to be included in current liabilities (B05.112). Examples are: accounts payable; collections received in advance of the delivery of goods or performance of services; accruals for wages, salaries, commissions, rentals, and royalties; and income and other taxes.

Short-term obligations such as commercial paper, construction loans, the currently maturing portion of long-term debt, obligations arising from the acquisition or construction of noncurrent assets, and notes given to a supplier to replace accounts payable that originally had arisen in the normal course of business and that had been due on customary terms may be excluded from current liabilities, but only on two conditions: (1) the entity must intend to refinance the obligation on a long-term basis (B05.113) and (2) the intent to refinance must be supported by an ability to consummate the refinancing (B05.114).

When long-term debt or equity securities are issued after the balance sheet date, the amount of short-term debt excluded from current liabilities must not exceed the proceeds of the debt or equity securities issued. When there is a financing agreement, the amount of short-term debt excluded from current liabilities must be reduced to the amount available for refinancing under the agreement (when this amount is less than the amount of the short-term obligation). The amount must be further reduced if there are restrictions (e.g., as to transferability of funds) or if the funds obtainable under the agreement will not be available to liquidate the short-term obligation.

If the amount obtainable under the agreement fluctuates in relation to the entity's needs or in proportion to the value of collateral, the amount excluded from current liabilities must be limited to a reasonable estimate of the minimum amount expected to be available at any date from the scheduled maturity of the short-term debt to the end of the fiscal year or operating cycle. If no reasonable estimate can be made, the entire outstanding short-term debt should be included in current liabilities.

FIN 8, *Classification of a Short-Term Obligation Repaid Prior to Being Replaced by a Long-Term Security* (B05.117), states that a short-term obligation would be classified as current if it is repaid after the balance sheet date by using current assets, even though long-term financing is subsequently obtained before the issuance of the balance sheet. Further, replacing a short-term debt with another short-term debt between the balance sheet date and the date the balance sheet is issued is not, by itself, evidence of the enterprise's ability to refinance a short-term debt on a long-term basis.

Ability to Refinance. The ability to consummate the refinancing can be demonstrated by (B05.113):

1. Issuing a long-term obligation or equity securities after the balance sheet date, but before the balance sheet is issued, for the purpose of refinancing the short-term obligation on a long-term basis or

2. Before the balance sheet is issued, entering into a financing arrangement that clearly permits the enterprise to refinance the short-term debt on a long-term basis on terms that are readily determinable. In this case, however, all the following conditions must also be met:

   a. The agreement does not expire within one year (or longer operating cycle) from the balance sheet date.

   b. The agreement is not cancelable by the lender, prospective lender, or investor, except for violation of a provision with which compliance is objectively determinable or measurable.

   c. The obligations incurred under the agreement are not callable within one year.

   d. No violation of any provision in the financing agreement exists at the balance sheet date.

   e. There is no information indicating that a violation has occurred between the balance sheet date and the date of issuance (or if one has occurred, it must have been cured or a waiver obtained).

f. The lender, prospective lender, or investor with whom the agreement has been made is expected to be financially capable of honoring the agreement.

Examples indicating an ability to refinance on a long-term basis are (1) a replacement of the short-term debt made under the terms of a revolving credit agreement that provides for renewal or extension of a short-term obligation for an uninterrupted period extending beyond one year from the balance sheet date and that meets the other ability-to-refinance conditions and (2) a replacement made by a roll-over of commercial paper accompanied by a standby credit agreement that meets the other ability-to-refinance conditions.

Subjective Acceleration Clauses. SFAS 6 prohibits the long-term classification of short-term debt that is in existence at the balance sheet date but is to be replaced under a long-term financing agreement entered into before the balance sheet is issued, if the agreement is "cancelable for violation of a provision that can be evaluated differently by the parties to the agreement" (B05.113, n.12). This statement does not, however, address the question of the classification of preexisting long-term debt, or debt initially issued as long-term, that is subject to similar cancelation provisions. Since some long-term agreements contain such subjective acceleration clauses (which could result in acceleration of principal payments), a question arises as to whether the full amount of such a loan must be classified as a current liability, notwithstanding long-term scheduled maturities.

This matter was discussed in TB 79–3, *Subjective Acceleration Clauses in Long-Term Debt Agreements* (B05.501–.503). While not categorical, the TB does provide some guidance:

• If circumstances such as recurring losses or liquidity problems exist, current liability classification is likely to be appropriate.

• If the likelihood of acceleration of the due date is deemed remote, no reclassification or disclosure is necessary.

• In between, disclosure is probably the right thing to do.

See Figure 18.1 for an example of a subjective acceleration clause disclosure.

Callable Obligations

The definition of current liabilities in Chapter 3A of ARB 43 (B05) does not discuss how obligations callable by a creditor are to be presented in a classified balance sheet. To address this issue, the FASB issued SFAS 78, *Classification of Obligations That Are Callable by the Creditor* (B05), in 1983.

SFAS 78 specifies the balance sheet classification of obligations that, by their terms, are or will become due on demand within one year (or the operating cycle, if longer) from the balance sheet date. It also specifies the classification of long-term obligations that are or will be callable by the creditor because of a violation of a covenant at the balance sheet date, if not cured within a specified grace period. Such callable obligations are to be classified as current liabilities unless one of the following conditions is met:

As discussed in Note 3, the Company's Amended and Restated Term and Revolving Credit Agreement (Credit Agreement) requires the Company to maintain certain financial covenants, restricts cash advances based on management's projected cash flow and requires the repayment of all Revolving Credit by November 30, 1988 and the Term Note by November 30, 1989. In addition, the Credit Agreement provides for accelerated repayment of the Revolving Credit Loans at the bank's discretion. Management's projections for fiscal year 1988 indicate that sufficient funds will be available to repay the outstanding Revolving Credit Loans and maintain compliance with the financial covenants. However, management's projections do not indicate that sufficient funds will be generated from operations to repay the outstanding Term Note when it becomes due in 1989.

The accompanying financial statements do not include any adjustment relating to recoverability of recorded asset amounts or the amount of liabilities that might be necessary should the Company become subject to accelerated repayment of the Revolving Credit Loans, or be unable to meet its operating and cash flow projections.

FIG. 18.1   Example of Subjective Acceleration Clause Disclosure
Source: Northwestern States Portland Cement Company, 1987 Annual Report.

1. The creditor has waived or subsequently lost the right to demand repayment for more than one year (or the operating cycle, if longer) from the balance sheet date.
2. For long-term obligations containing a grace period within which the debtor may cure the violation, it is probable that the violation will be cured within that period, thus preventing the obligation from becoming callable.

The Statement does not address long-term debt agreements containing subjective acceleration clauses, and therefore does not modify TB 79-3.

Demand Notes With Repayment Terms. In Issue 86-5, *Classifying Demand Notes with Repayment Terms*, the EITF considered the question of whether loans made under agreements that specified a payment schedule but were also due on demand (if demand is made) should be classified as current or as long-term liabilities. The Task Force consensus was that these loans are always short-term. The related question of how to present these loans in a long-term debt schedule is therefore moot.

The EITF noted that the demand provision is not a subjective acceleration clause, and therefore does not merit the favorable treatment provided in TB 79-3.

GAAP Disclosures

Short-term debt, notes, and loans payable are usually listed as the first item in the current liabilities section of the balance sheet. Current maturities of long-term obligations, although frequently the last item under current liabilities, are sometimes grouped with short-term notes under a suitable caption. Short-term notes payable may be itemized in the balance sheet (or footnotes) by type of payee—banks, finance companies, trade, affiliates, officers and directors, and so forth. They may also be itemized by their significant terms—demand loans, collateralized notes, and so forth.

Short-Term Borrowings

The Company and its subsidiaries establish lines of credit with major domestic and foreign banks to satisfy their needs for short-term borrowing. At December 31, 1987 available lines of credit totaled $149 million, including $22 million of unactivated seasonal committed bank lines. Commitment fees of 1/4 percent per annum are paid on applicable lines of credit.

At December 31, 1987, $117 million of commercial paper, supported by lines of credit, and $38 million of short-term bank borrowings were outstanding at weighted average interest rates of 7.89 percent and 8.04 percent, respectively. At December 31, 1986, $16.0 million of commercial paper and $64.0 million of short-term bank borrowings were outstanding at weighted average interest rates of 7.97 percent and 6.82 percent, respectively.

Bank cash balances average about $7 million and compensate for the costs of maintaining accounts and other banking services. Such demand balances may be withdrawn at any time.

FIG. 18.2   Disclosure of Short-Term Debt
Source: NICOR, Inc., 1987 Annual Report.

The balance sheet (or footnotes) should clearly indicate the nature and amount of collateral supporting notes or loans and the seniority/subordination status of the debts. Disclosure should be made of obligations endorsed or guaranteed by others, or collateralized by assets belonging to others (e.g., shareholders). An example of footnote disclosure of short-term debt appears in Figure 18.2.

If a short-term obligation is excluded from current liabilities, the notes to the financial statements must include a general description of the financing agreement and the terms of any new obligations incurred or expected to be incurred, or equity securities issued or expected to be issued, as a result of the refinancing.

SEC Disclosures

The SEC's disclosure requirements (for both accounts payable and short-term notes payable), found in Rule 5–02.19 of Regulation S-X, are essentially the same as GAAP, and are summarized as follows:

a. Disclose the amounts payable to (1) banks for borrowings; (2) factors or other financial institutions for borrowings; (3) holders of commercial paper; (4) trade creditors; (5) related parties; (6) underwriters, promoters, employees (other than related parties); and (7) others.

b. Footnote the amount and terms (including commitment fees and conditions under which lines may be withdrawn) of unused lines of credit for short-term financing. Identify the amount of these lines supporting commercial paper arrangements.

Under Rule 5-02.20, any item in excess of 5% of total current liabilities should be shown under a separate caption. This includes accounts payable, which is therefore ordinarily shown as a separate item and not combined.

Requirements relating to short-term debt also include Schedule IX, *Short-term borrowings* (Regulation S-X, Rules 5-04 and 12-10). Schedule IX requires the following information for each period for which an income statement is required to be filed:

1. Aggregate short-term borrowings (ASTB) at the balance sheet dates categorized by amounts payable to banks, factors or other financial institutions, and holders of commercial paper.

2. General terms of each category of ASTB (also formal provisions for the extension of the maturity).

3. Weighted average interest rate.

4. Maximum amount of ASTB outstanding at any month end during the period.

5. Average ASTB outstanding during the period.

6. The weighted average interest rate for such ASTB during the period.

7. The means used to compute the average ASTB outstanding and the average interest rate.

Credit lines and commitments that may be offered by financial institutions as a marketing device, and accepted by corporations without any intention to use them and not as part of their financial plan, do not require disclosure. Unused lines of credit disclosed as supporting commercial paper or other debt arrangements should include only usable lines. Usable lines are those used to support commercial paper less lines needed to meet clean-up provisions (i.e., provisions that require borrowers to retire credit extended at a bank at some specified interval, for a specified period). Total lines outstanding are, therefore, not necessarily a measure of the total credit available on a continuing basis. Similarly, if a corporation has lines arranged with several banks that in total exceed borrowing levels permitted under existing lending agreements, disclosure should be limited to the usable amounts.

Finally, the SEC requires certain disclosures regarding compensating balances and short-term borrowing arrangements under Regulation S-X, Rule 5–02.1, the details of which are explained in ASR 148 (FRR § 203). The disclosures may be given in either a schedule to the financial statements or in the MD&A section, whichever "results in a more meaningful presentation of the information." An example of a footnote on short-term debt is given in Figure 18.2. Compensating balances are discussed in Chapter 12.

LONG-TERM DEBT

Straight Debt

When an enterprise issues a bond or note, it promises future payments: the payment of principal and the payment of interest. In almost all cases, the dates on which the payment or payments are to be made is specified (the exception being debt that is contingent, e.g., on operating results or cash flows). The principal and interest payments may be discrete, or the two may be combined such as in a level-amortization loan or in a single payment zero coupon bond. In some cases, the interest rate may vary by period, for example, 10% for the first year, 11% for the second year, and so on, until the issuer redeems the debt.

Interest on bonds is usually expressed as a percentage of the face amount. This is known as the nominal or coupon rate. But the interest actually incurred on bonds is determined by the price at which the bonds are sold. This is known as the *effective interest rate* or *yield*, and it depends on the current market. If the going market yield is identical to the coupon rate, the bonds will sell at face amount. If the bonds are sold with a greater yield than the coupon rate, they will sell for less than face amount, or at a *discount*. Conversely, if the bonds are sold with a yield that is less than the coupon rate, they will sell for more than face amount, or at a *premium*.

For example, suppose an entity issues a $300,000 term bond due in 10 years. The coupon rate is 9%, paid annually, but under current market conditions, the bond must yield 12%. The selling price and discount are computed as follows:

Present value of $300,000 due in 10 years at 12%	$ 96,592
Present value of $27,000 per year for 10 years at 12%	$152,556
Bonds sold for	$249,148
Discount on bonds	$ 50,852

Serial Obligations. The bond discussed in the previous example had a single fixed maturity date. Another type of bond, the *serial bond*, provides for the repayment of principal in a series of periodic installments. As with term bonds, serial bonds may sell at a discount or a premium because of differences between the coupon rate and the yield demanded in the market. The proceeds of a serial bond issue are a little more difficult to compute, but the approach is essentially the same.

For example, suppose an entity issues a $300,000 serial bond to be repaid in the amount of $60,000 per year. The coupon rate is 9% paid annually, but the bond is sold to yield 12%. The selling price and discount are computed as follows:

End of Year	Principal and interest due		Present value of 1 (12% table)	
1	$60,000 + $27,000	×	0.892857	$ 77,679
2	$60,000 + $21,600	×	0.797194	65,051
3	$60,000 + $16,200	×	0.711780	54,238
4	$60,000 + $10,800	×	0.635518	44,994
5	$60,000 + $ 5,400	×	0.567427	37,110
	Bonds sold for			$279,072
	Discount on bonds			$ 20,928

Serial bonds may also be priced differently for each segment in the series, with longer term bonds carrying a different rate than those having a shorter term.

Sinking Fund Obligations. Some bond indentures require that a sinking fund be established for the retirement of the bonds through the periodic redemption of a fixed amount of principal. The price for all redemptions through the sinking fund is usually the principal amount of the bonds redeemed plus the interest accrued to the redemption date. Most companies have the privilege of purchasing bonds on the open market to cover their future sinking fund requirements. Bonds so purchased and held in treasury to satisfy future sinking fund requirements are deducted from the related long-term debt.

Equity-Related Debt

Convertibles. Simply put, a convertible debt is one that may be exchanged for a specified number of shares of stock. Suppose a company sells a 6.5% subordinated debenture that is convertible at the holder's option into common stock at $29 per share. No fractional shares will be delivered on conversion of each bond, but a cash payment will be made in lieu thereof. Thus, the holder of each bond with a $1,000 face value will receive 34 shares of common stock and $14 cash. Further, the debentures have a call provision—that is, they are redeemable at the company's option, in whole or in part, at an initial redemption price of 106.5% plus accrued interest, with declining premiums thereafter. In this example, the net proceeds (after underwriting spread and selling concessions) are 98.693%. The issuance is recorded as follows, based on a $100 million face amount:

	Debit	Credit
Cash	$98,693,000	
Deferred debt issue costs	1,307,000	
6.5% convertible subordinated debentures		$100,000,000

To record the sale of 25-year debentures at beginning of year one.

Assume further that after being outstanding for two years, $45 million face amount of the debt is converted. The entry to record the conversion is as follows:

	Debit	Credit
6.5% convertible subordinated debentures	$45,000,000	
Cash		$ 630,000
Deferred debt issue costs		541,098
Common stock, $1 par value		1,530,000
Additional paid-in capital		42,298,902

To record the conversion of debentures into 1,530,000 shares of common stock and write off 45% of unamortized debt issue costs at end of year two.

If the bonds are redeemed pursuant to a call provision, the accounting should follow that prescribed in APB 26 and SFAS 4, discussed later under "Debt Extinguishments."

The terms of convertible bonds generally include: (1) an interest rate that is lower than the issuer could establish for nonconvertible debt, (2) an initial conversion price that is greater than the market value (commonly by 20–25%) of the common stock at the time of issue, and (3) a conversion price that does not decrease, except to prevent dilution. In most cases the bonds are also callable at the option of the issuer, and are subordinated to nonconvertible debt.

Convertible debt offers a number of advantages to both the issuer and the purchaser. For the issuer, it provides a lower interest rate than nonconvertible debt.

Further, the issuer may view convertible debt as essentially a means of raising equity capital. If the market value of its common stock should increase sufficiently, the issuer can force conversion of the convertible bonds into common stock by calling the issue for redemption. Thus, the issuer can effectively terminate the conversion option and eliminate the debt. If the market value of its common stock does not increase sufficiently to make conversion of the debt attractive, the issuer will still have received the benefit of the cash proceeds to the scheduled maturity dates at a relatively lower interest cost. For the purchaser, convertible debt provides both the status of a creditor and the opportunity to gain from price appreciation of the common stock.

APB 14, *Accounting for Convertible Debt and Debt Issued With Stock Purchase Warrants* (D10), holds that "no portion of the proceeds from the issuance of . . . convertible debt securities . . . should be accounted for as attributable to the conversion feature [because of the] inseparability of the debt and the conversion option . . . [and] practical difficulties" (D10.103).

When convertible bonds are issued, a portion of the proceeds is logically attributable to the conversion feature; this factor is reflected in a lower coupon rate of interest. But unlike stock purchase warrants (discussed in the next section) for which a separate price can be determined, the value of the inseparable conversion feature arguably cannot be established.

This premise had been successfuly argued by the investment banking community after a "sleeper" slid past in the form of APB 10, *Omnibus Opinion—1966*, which contained a section on "Convertible Debt and Debt Issued With Stock Warrants." This provided that a portion of the proceeds of a convertible bond should be credited to paid-in capital, with a corresponding charge to debt discount (amortizable in the future as interest expense). Shortly after being assailed by the investment community, the APB suspended this requirement in APB 12, *Omnibus Opinion—1967*, and issued the revised rules in APB 14.

Interest accrued at time of debt conversion. An issue arose in 1985 regarding the proper accounting treatment of accrued interest at the time of conversion of a convertible debt. Because interest is the cost of using someone else's money, it would seem that interest accrues by the moment, regardless of when it is scheduled to be paid. As an indication, if a company were to call a nonconvertible debt between interest payment dates, it would have to pay accrued interest to date of settlement. However, when calling a convertible debt that is "in the money" with the expectation that holders will instead convert into stock to avoid receiving only the call price (plus accrued interest), issuers started to question whether it was necessary to accrue interest expense, if upon conversion the accrued interest is merely credited to paid-in capital as part of the conversion entry (see earlier journal entry example). They argued that as a practical matter the holder does not have the option to receive the interest, given the economics of the situation.

In Issue 85-17, *Accrued Interest Upon Conversion of Convertible Debt*, the EITF considered this issue, noting that the matter takes on special significance if zero-coupon convertible debt (see Chapter 21) is involved. The Task Force concluded that interest must be accrued by a charge to interest expense to date of conversion, net of related income tax effects if any, and the net amount is to be credited to capital.

Detachable Warrants. Unlike convertible debt, debt issued with detachable warrants to purchase stock is usually issued with the expectation that the debt will be repaid when it matures. The detachable warrants are separate from the debt itself, and are often traded. Thus, the two elements of the security exist independently and may be treated as separate securities. For example, a corporation may issue $50 million of 10.5% subordinated debentures with warrants to purchase 3,750,000 shares of common stock. Each $1,000 debenture might have 75 warrants attached, with the debentures and warrants being separately transferable. The warrants may entitle the holder to purchase one share of common stock by tendering cash and may be exercisable for a period of 10 years. If the market value of each common share at the time of issue is, say, $6.50, the warrant price for the share (strike price) might be around $10 (depending on market conditions and the identity of the issuer).

Under APB 14, the proceeds are required to be split into the amount applicable to the debt and the amount applicable to the warrant. Specifically:

> The portion of the proceeds of debt securities issued with detachable stock purchase warrants that is allocable to the warrants shall be accounted for as additional paid-in capital. The allocation should be based on the relative fair values of the two securities at the time of issuance [which is generally the date when an agreement as to terms has been reached and announced, even though there may be further actions, such as directors' or stockholders' approval]. [D10.105 and n.4]

When stock purchase warrants are not detachable and the debt security must be surrendered to exercise the warrant, the two securities taken together are considered substantially equivalent to convertible debt, and no portion of the proceeds is considered attributable to the nondetachable warrant feature.

Some corporations issue "units" composed of, for instance, a $1,000 principal amount of subordinated convertible debenture, 100 shares of common stock, and 20 warrants. Here, too, an allocation should be made to additional paid-in capital for the portion of the proceeds of the debenture issue attributable to the common stock and detachable stock purchase warrants (as well as to the common stock account).

When warrants are exercised, the consideration tendered (cash or the debt security) is considered as proceeds from the issuance of common stock. When warrants are repurchased, additional paid-in capital is charged for the full purchase price.

Synthetic Warrants. When debt is issued with detachable warrants that permit the holder to acquire the stock either by the payment of the strike price or by tendering an equal amount of debt at face value, such warrants are called "synthetic" and the optionally tenderable debt is called "scrip." Because the warrants are detachable, APB 14 requires that they be treated the same as nonsynthetic warrants, that is, a portion of the proceeds must be allocated to the warrants and credited to paid-in capital (D10.105).

The synthetic feature derives from the interplay of the bond and the warrant. If the market price of the common stock rises sufficiently, the market value of the bond will stay high notwithstanding increases in prevailing interest rates—just like any other convertible. If, however, the stock fails to rise in value and interest rates increase, the bond may be bought on the market at a discount, and used at face value to exercise the warrant. This effectively reduces the strike price on the stock. Other phenomena also can be built into a synthetic warrant.

Discount and Premium

Unamortized debt discount or premium, either imputed (see "Interest" later herein) or actual, should be shown as a direct deduction from or addition to the face amount of the debt on the balance sheet. Further, the payable or receivable must show the effective interest rate and the face amount of the note, either in the balance sheet or in footnotes. Under APB 12, *Omnibus Opinion—1967*, premium or discount must be amortized using the *interest method* (I69.108, n.4). This method includes the discount or premium in the computation of interest expense so as to achieve a level yield on the debt proceeds over the period the debt is scheduled to be outstanding. Thus, larger amounts are amortized in the earlier periods than in later periods.

Issue Costs

Various costs are incurred in preparing and selling a bond issue. They may include underwriting discounts, legal fees, accounting fees, other professional fees, engraving, printing, registration fees, and others. APB 21, *Interest on Receivables and Payables* (I69), says that issue costs should be reported in the balance sheet as a deferred charge. APB 21 does not say how issue costs should be amortized, but when such costs are material, some accountants believe the amount deferred should be amortized (along with premium or discount, if any) over the life of the debt using the *interest method* discussed previously. Where amounts involved are not large, the straight-line method is often used.

In SAB 77, *Allocation of Certain Debt Issue Costs* (Topic 2.A.6), the SEC staff discusses the appropriate accounting treatment of debt issue costs relative to bridge financing in purchase business combinations (discussed in Chapter 23). It should be noted that SAB 77 specifies the use of the interest method to amortize debt issue costs over the life of the related debt.

Covenant Violations

In EITF Issue 86-30, *Classification of Obligations When a Violation Is Waived by the Creditor*, the EITF addressed the balance sheet classification of a long-term obligation when there is a violation or a potential violation of a covenant. A borrower has a long-term loan that requires compliance with certain covenants, such as maintenance of a minimum current ratio, minimum debt-to-equity ratio, or minimum level of shareholders' equity. The borrower must meet the covenants on a quarterly or semi-annual basis. At one of the compliance dates, the borrower violates a covenant. As a result of the violation, the lender has the ability to call the debt. The lender waives the default for a period of greater than one year, but retains the future covenant requirements. The accounting issue is whether the waiver of the lender's rights resulting from the violation of the covenant with the retention of the periodic covenant tests represents, in substance, a grace period. If viewed as a grace period, the borrower must classify the debt as current under SFAS 78, *Classification of Obligations That Are Callable by the Creditor* (B05), unless it is probable that the borrower can cure the violation (comply with the covenant) within the grace period.

The Task Force considered the balance sheet classification for an obligation under the following scenarios. Under each scenario, assume it is probable that the borrower will violate the subsequent covenant test.

1. The debt covenants are applicable only subsequent to the balance sheet date.
2. The borrower meets the current covenant requirement and must meet the same covenant in the next quarter.
3. The borrower meets the current covenant requirement but must meet a more restrictive covenant in the next quarter.
4. The borrower meets the covenant requirement in the prior quarter but prior to the balance sheet date negotiates a modification of the loan agreement that eliminates the covenant requirements at the balance sheet date or modifies the requirement so that the borrower will comply. Absent the modification the borrower would have been in violation of the covenant. The same or a more restrictive covenant must be met in the next quarter.
5. At the balance sheet date, the enterprise violates the covenant, and subsequent to the balance sheet date, but prior to issuing financial statements, obtains a waiver. The borrower must meet the same or a more restrictive covenant in the next quarter.

The Task Force reached a consensus that, unless facts and circumstances would indicate otherwise, the borrower should classify the obligation as noncurrent unless (1) a covenant violation has occurred at the balance sheet date or would have occurred absent a loan modification and (2) it is probable that the borrower will not be able to cure the default (comply with the covenant) at measurement dates that are within the next 12 months.

Applying this consensus to the five situations previously described, in (1), (2), and (3) the debt would be classified as noncurrent; and in (4) and (5) the debt would be classified as current. If, however, the debt is expected to be refinanced on a long-term basis and the borrower meets the provisions of SFAS 6, *Classification of Short-Term Obligations Expected to Be Refinanced*, the debt would be classified as noncurrent. When debt is classified as noncurrent in situations (1), (2), and (3), the borrower is required to disclose the adverse consequences of its probable failure to satisfy future covenants.

GAAP Disclosures

Long-term debt is itemized by lender (or by groups when there are a number of similar lenders, e.g., "banks") in the same manner as indicated earlier for short-term debt. The important features and provisions of the debt should be disclosed, including: (1) interest rate; (2) due dates and amount of debt installments; (3) collateralized property; (4) important covenants; (5) dividend restrictions; (6) convertible features; (7) defaults; and (8) subordination. An example of a long-term debt footnote is shown in Figure 18.3.

Long-term debt should be segregated between the current and the long-term portions. Further, when there is a discount or premium, the description of the note should include the effective interest rate (I69.109). Treasury bonds held but not retired are not an asset, and should be deducted from bonds payable shown in the balance sheet.

In SFAS 47, *Disclosure of Long-Term Obligations* (C32), the FASB provides disclosure requirements for commitments under unconditional purchase obligations that are associated with suppliers' financing arrangements where such commitments

Note 7—Long-Term Debt

Long-term debt, net of current maturities, at December 31, is as follows:

	1987	1986
Notes due 1994, 13³/₈%	$ 75,000	$ 75,000
Notes due 1996, 9¹/₂%	75,000	75,000
Convertible subordinated debentures due 2009, 9¹/₄%	50,000	50,000
Sinking fund debentures due 2011, 10¹/₂%	75,000	75,000
Borrowings under revolving lines of credit	222,200	–
Installment notes—various rates ranging from 7³/₄% to 21¹/₄% secured by lease contracts	66,484	64,794
Notes and mortgages at rates from ⁷/₈% to 12⁷/₈% with maturities through 2196	74,591	79,281
Lease obligations—various rates ranging from 9% to 15¹/₄% with maturities to 1995	4,923	1,899
	$643,198	$420,974

Long-term debt maturing in each of the next five years is as follows: 1988, $58,881; 1989, $81,017; 1990, $77,176; 1991, $70,962; 1992, $66,635.

The company is a party to a credit agreement with various banks under which it may borrow up to $300,000 through June 30, 1988, after which date the balance of outstanding loans converts to a term loan repayable in eighteen equal quarterly installments. Interest on borrowings under this agreement will be at either the Citibank Base Rate plus ¹/₈ percent or at ¹/₂ percent over the applicable Eurodollar Rate, or ⁵/₈ percent over the DMM-Bid Rate, until June 30, 1988, with each rate increasing ¹/₄ percent thereater. Additionally, letter agreements between the company and each of the banks provide lines of credit totaling $200,000. There is a commitment fee associated only with the credit agreement of ¹/₄ percent per annum on the average daily unused portion.

Repayment of borrowings under all of the loan agreements is guaranteed by the company's principal subsidiary, Grumman Aerospace Corporation. The agreements contain, among other things, provisions regarding maintenance of working capital, net worth and the payment of cash dividends on common stock. The company's working capital and net worth are substantially in excess of the minimum requirements and the amount of retained earnings available for the payment of cash dividends at December 31, 1987, was $38,670.

The agreements also restrict the payment of dividends to the company by its principal subsidiary, Grumman Aerospace Corporation. All of the amount available for payment of such dividends has been paid at December 31, 1987. There is no restriction on the amount of loans or advancing of funds to the company by Grumman Aerospace Corporation and certain other subsidiaries.

The company is also required to maintain compensating balances, which are not legally restricted, averaging 5 percent of the credit available.

The 13³/₈% notes due August 15, 1994, and the 9¹/₂% notes due February 15, 1996, will be redeemable at any time on or after August 15, 1991, and February 15, 1993, respectively, at the option of the company, at 100 percent of face value, together with accrued interest. The indentures under which the notes were issued contain a restriction on the payment by the company of cash dividends on common stock. However, there is a greater dividend restriction under the credit agreements, noted previously.

(continued)

FIG. 18.3   Disclosure of Long-Term Debt
Source: Grumman Corp., 1987 Annual Report.

The 9¼% convertible subordinated debentures due August 15, 2009, are convertible at any time prior to maturity into common stock at $34.75 per share and require annual sinking fund payments beginning in 1995 sufficient to retire 5 percent of the principal amount of debentures outstanding on February 15, 1995. This issue of debentures may be called by the company at any time at prices decreasing from 106.475 percent of face value currently to 100 percent in 1994. The 10½% sinking fund debentures due February 15, 2011, require annual sinking fund payments beginning in 1997 sufficient to retire $5,000 principal amount of debentures. This issue of debentures may be called by the company at any time at prices decreasing from 110 percent of face value currently to 100 percent in 2007.

FIG. 18.3 *(continued)*

are not recorded as liabilities; this is discussed in Chapter 21. In addition, SFAS 47 recognizes that many long-term obligations are recorded as liabilities, and specifically disavows any intent to change that. For recorded obligations (and redeemable preferred stock) the obligor must disclose the aggregate amount of payments to be made in the future, generally the same as long-term debt maturities by year are presented; indeed, the maturity table may combine regular long-term debt and the purchase obligation.

SEC Disclosures

Certain long-term debt disclosures in addition to those mentioned above are specifically required by the SEC. The following may be used as a reference to the pertinent Regulation S-X rules and schedules:

1. Bonds, mortgages, and similar debt: Rule 5-02-22.
2. Significant changes in bonds, mortgages, and similar debt: Rule 4-08(f).
3. Reacquired indebtedness: Rule 4-06.
4. Indebtedness to related parties, non-current: Rule 5-02-23.
5. Schedules to be filed in support of most recent audited balance sheet and any subsequent unaudited balance sheet: Schedule XII (Rule 12-29)—mortgage loans on real estate.
6. Schedule to be filed for each period for which an income statement is filed: Schedule IV (Rule 12-05)—indebtedness of and to related parties.

The SEC, in Rule 4-08(c) of Regulation S-X, requires the disclosure of the facts and amounts concerning any default in principal, interest, sinking fund, or redemption provision, or any breach of covenant of an indenture or agreement, if the default or breach existed at the date of the most recent balance sheet filed and has not been subsequently cured. If a default or breach exists, but acceleration of the obligation has been waived for a stated period of time beyond the date of the most recent balance sheet being filed, disclosure is required of the amount of the obligation and the period of waiver.

DEBT EXTINGUISHMENTS

Nature of Extinguishment

What constitutes a debt extinguishment has eluded precise definition by accounting standard setters over the years. Nevertheless, the gray areas have diminished as a result of FASB actions, building on a foundation laid by the APB.

Change in Cost of Money. Using historical cost accounting, debt is carried at its net issue price, with amortization of discount or premium over its term. When prevailing interest rates change, the market value of the debt will change, making the cost of reacquiring it either more or less than the carrying amount on the books. Whether this difference is a gain or loss depends on a conceptual issue: The company may be no better off after recognizing a gain on buying back debt with a coupon lower than prevailing rates if it has to replace the funds with new higher-rate debt or even with equity money. But from a historical cost standpoint, once the extinguishment is consummated, the old carrying amounts have to be removed from the books and the difference has to be accounted for in some way. The APB decreed with finality that it is gain or loss, not deferrable as an adjustment of future refunding costs.

Equity Nature of Convertible Debt. The APB's view that "all extinguishments of debt are fundamentally alike" (D14.102) is based substantially on the premise that only the change in the general cost of money causes a gain or loss in a nontroubled extinguishment. This ignores the fact that convertible debt (APB 14 notwithstanding) has an equity element. Ignoring the equity element causes peculiar things to happen. For instance, if convertible debt is reacquired, the difference between the cash acquisition price and its net carrying amount is required to be recognized currently in income. When the debt is equity in substance (because the value of the securities into which it is convertible is higher than the conversion price), the acquisition of such debt is in reality an acquisition of treasury stock. However, an extinguishment of convertible debt is never considered an acquisition of treasury stock (D14.104). The rules therefore require the unnecessary process of first converting the debt to common shares and then reacquiring the shares in order to reflect the financial reality inherent in the transactions—the purchase of treasury stock.

For example, assume the following facts: $3 million of convertible debentures due 1995, convertible at the option of the holder into common stock at $10.75 per share, current fair market value $14 per share. If the holder converts, he will get 279,000 common shares; if he then sells those shares back to the company in an unrelated transaction, the company will recognize no gain or loss and will record the shares purchased as treasury shares. However, if the company extinguishes the $3 million of debentures, it would have to pay $3,906,750 and would reflect a $906,750 charge to operations for the difference between the conversion price and the fair market value ($3.25 × 279,000 shares). (See example in Figure 18.4.)

Applicability of Extinguishment Accounting. APB 26, *Early Extinguishment of Debt* (D14), focuses on timing: something happening before scheduled maturity.

During 1987, the 6⅞ percent convertible subordinated debentures were called for redemption and subsequently $112,978,000 of the principal amount was converted into 4,918,477 common shares at the conversion price of $22.97 per share. The related unamortized discount and issue cost of $3,089,000 and accrued interest expense of $992,000 were transferred to additional paid-in capital. The remaining $2,022,000 of principal was redeemed resulting in an extraordinary loss of $134,000 net of income tax benefit of $110,000.

FIG. 18.4 Disclosure of Extinguishment of Convertible Subordinated Debentures not Converting on Call
Source: Caesars World, Inc., 1987 Annual Report.

SFAS 76, *Extinguishment of Debt* (D14), focuses on what has happened, not when; it essentially ignores "earliness," stating that it "applies to all extinguishments of debt, whether early or not" (D14.101). This mandate in itself eliminated several issues; but SFAS 76 leaves some open questions.

APB 26 points out that "all extinguishments of debt are fundamentally alike; the accounting for such transactions shall be the same regardless of the means used to achieve the extinguishment" (D14.102). In brief, extinguishment always results in gain or loss recognition, except for the following situations:

• Troubled debt restructurings (SFAS 15 (D22), discussed in Chapter 28).
• Convertible debt inducements (SFAS 84 (D10), discussed below under "Debt Modifications").
• Convertible debt that is converted in accordance with its terms.
• Debt that is exchangeable at the company's option, in accordance with its original terms.

Not all extinguishments are as simple as paying cash to the debtholder in satisfaction of all claims. Transactions that are deemed to accomplish this result, without necessarily involving the debtholder, can become very complex. Direct and not-so-direct debt extinguishments are discussed in the sections that follow.

Direct Extinguishment

A debt that is paid off at maturity in accordance with its terms is not described as an extinguishment, but can be referred to as a redemption, liquidation, or settlement. In this chapter the term "extinguishment" is reserved for noncontractual payments of money, assets, or other securities to eliminate existing debt. Thus, payments made to a trustee to redeem outstanding debt in accordance with the terms of the debt indenture are not extinguishments, even if the trustee must determine by lottery which bonds to call. However, all purchases of debt on the market for current or future sinking fund requirements are extinguishments, because this manner of acquisition would not be called for by the indenture.

Accounting treatment for an extinguishment is governed by APB 26, *Early Extinguishment of Debt* (D14), and SFAS 4, *Reporting Gains and Losses from Extinguishment of Debt* (D14). The difference between (1) the price paid (or value of other assets or debt or equity securities given) to acquire the debt and (2) the net carrying amount of the debt is a gain or loss recognized in current income (D14.103). The net carrying amount is the amount due at maturity, adjusted for unamortized premium or discount and issue costs (D14.402). If the extinguishment involves the exchange of other rights or privileges (stated or unstated), the portion of the consideration exchanged should be allocated to those items and be treated as an asset or expensed as appropriate.

APB 26 has no special disclosure requirements; however, the disclosures required by SFAS 4 (I17.104) are: (1) description of extinguishment transaction, including source of funds; (2) income tax effect; and (3) per share amount of aggregate gain or loss, net of related income tax effect.

Gains and losses relating to debt repurchased for sinking fund requirements due within one year are classified as a part of income from operations, and separately identified.

Extraordinary Classification. Gains and losses from debt extinguishment are aggregated for the reporting period and classified as extraordinary if the amount is material (D14.105–.106). However, under SFAS 64, *Extinguishments of Debt Made to Satisfy Sinking-Fund Requirements* (D14), gains and losses from extinguishments of debt made to satisfy sinking-fund requirements that a company must meet within one year of the date of the extinguishment may not be classified as extraordinary items. Previous standards required a company to classify, as extraordinary items, gains and losses resulting from the satisfaction of sinking-fund requirements without regard to when in the future they must be met.

SFAS 64 also amends present accounting rules by specifying that the classification of gains and losses resulting from extinguishment of debt under sinking-fund requirements should be determined without regard to the means a company may use to achieve the extinguishment. Debt subject to sinking-fund requirements may be extinguished by cash purchase, by a stock-for-debt or a debt-for debt exchange, or by other means. The Board decided that, whatever the means, the resulting gains and losses should be classified similarly.

Some obligations to acquire debt have the essential characteristics of sinking fund requirements, for instance, debt that is required to be purchased before its scheduled maturity at a certain percentage of the total amount outstanding each year. Gains or losses on such transactions are not required to (but may) be classified as an extraordinary item if the obligations must be met within one year of the date of the extinguishments. However, debt maturing serially does not have the characteristics of a sinking fund, and any resulting gain or loss from the extinguishment of serial debt is to be presented as extraordinary (D14.105, n.3).

Noncash Extinguishments. In TB 80-1, *Early Extinguishment of Debt through Exchange for Common or Preferred Stock* (D14.501–.504), the FASB staff affirmed that the fair value of such equity securities is the proper measure of the amount paid on extinguishment. This does not apply, however, to debt that is exchangeable at the issuer's option based on the terms of the indenture.

APB 26 does not discuss using nonmonetary assets to extinguish debt; however, this question may be resolved by analogizing to SFAS 15, *Accounting by Debtors and Creditors for Troubled Debt Restructurings* (D22.109–.110), and to APB 29, *Account-*

ing for Nonmonetary Transactions (N35). Essentially, the asset should be first marked to fair value and the difference entered into current income as a gain or loss. The fair value is then compared to the carrying amount of the debt, and the difference is gain or loss on extinguishment. The classification of the gain or loss on the "sale" of the asset would rarely be extraordinary (based on the criteria for this classification); but the gain or loss on the extinguishment portion will be extraordinary, as indicated above.

Refunding

For reasons such as declining interest rates, a more favorable payment schedule, extended maturity dates, or the removal or modification of restrictive debt covenants, business and governmental enterprises undertake programs to replace old debt with new debt, usually called refunding. However, when the preexisting debt does not allow for immediate retirement, the debtor may incur additional new debt and use the proceeds to establish a fund to retire the old debt. The fund invests in risk-free securities until the old debt can legally be retired.

Prior to the issuance of SFAS 76, *Extinguishment of Debt* (D14), the only guidance available on this subject was SOP 78-5, *Accounting for Advance Refundings of Tax-Exempt Debt*. Tax-exempt debt includes direct obligations of state and local governmental units as well as debt and lease obligations that serve as collateral for tax-exempt debt. SOP 78-5 has been superseded for nongovernmental enterprises by the issuance of SFAS 76; however, it is still applicable to state and local governmental units, as discussed in Chapter 31.[1]

A typical *advance refunding* situation involves major capital improvements of a company financed by government agencies. These government agencies obtain funds by issuing tax-exempt bonds, use the proceeds to purchase the capital improvements, and then lease them (or sell them subject to mortgage) to the company. The company pays rent (or mortgage payments) sufficient to permit the government agency to service the underlying debt. Title to the capital improvements usually passes to the company when all the outstanding bonds have been paid. The key terms in advance refunding are:

1. *Advance refunding.* Refunding debt (new debt) to replace refunded debt (old debt) at a specified future date(s), with the proceeds placed in trust or otherwise restricted to replacing the refunded debt.

2. *Defeasance provision.* A provision in the old debt instrument that provides the terms by which the debt may be legally satisfied and the related lien released without the debt necessarily being retired.

3. *Crossover advance refunding.* An advance refunding in which the proceeds from the new debt, the additional cash deposits, if any, and the income on the related investments are sufficient to pay the principal and any call premium of the old debt and the interest on the new debt until the date of crossover. Crossover occurs when the proceeds from the new

---

[1] See also Chapter 19 regarding SFAS 22, *Changes in the Provisions of Lease Agreements Resulting From Refundings of Tax-Exempt Debt* (L10.109–.110 and .113).

debt are used to retire the old debt and the entity becomes obligated to service the new debt. In a crossover, the old debt is never defeased at the time of advance refunding.

4. *Qualifying securities.* Direct U.S. Treasury obligations, securities backed by the U.S. government, or securities collateralized by U.S. government obligations (risk-free securities).

Tax Exempt Debt. SOP 78-5 had provided that for issuers of tax exempt debt other than state and local governments, an advance refunding in which the refunded debt is defeased was viewed as an early extinguishment, with gains or losses to be recognized. A nondefeased advance refunding meeting all the following criteria would also have been accounted for as a defeased refunding:

1. The issuer has an irrevocable commitment to refund the old debt.
2. Funds used to complete the refunding are placed in an irrevocable trust to satisfy the old debt at a specified future date(s) and invested in "qualifying securities."
3. Invested funds are not subject to lien for any purpose other than in connection with the advance refunding.

An advance refunding that did not meet the above criteria was not an early extinguishment; therefore, two liabilities (both the old and new debt) were to be presented in the balance sheet.

In a crossover advance refunding, since by definition the defeasance never occurs, there was no in-substance defeasance, and no gain or loss was recognized.

Non-Tax-Exempt Debt. Not covered by SOP 78-5 were advance refunding transactions of non-tax-exempt debt involving leases. These were being accounted for in accordance with either the provisions of SFAS 13 (prospectively) or APB 26 (immediately). Some companies began to question why the debt extinguishment provisions under SOP 78-5 could not be applied to non-tax-exempt debt; and a few accounting firms decided that such application was merited. This gave rise to SFAS 76 provisions on in-substance defeasance, discussed next.

In-Substance Defeasance

During the early 1980s, the level of interest rates was high, causing outstanding debt issues carrying lower coupons to sell at substantial discounts from face. Because GAAP decreed that all extinguishments result in gain (or loss) recognition, it seemed attractive to corporate America to extinguish the debt and record the gains; however, in many cases it was not possible to reacquire the debt directly because it was not traded, or (if traded) because a tender offer might have driven up the price.

By mid-1982, some companies were engaged in transactions described as "in-substance defeasances" of non-tax-exempt debt, based on the provisions of SOP 78-5 for tax-exempt debt. In 1983, the SEC imposed a moratorium (FRR 3) on the use of extinguishment accounting treatment for such transactions pending FASB resolution. In late 1983, the FASB released SFAS 76, *Extinguishment of Debt* (D14). For a time there appeared to be some question regarding SEC agreement with SFAS 76, but eventually the SEC released FRR 15 (§ 217) to emphasize certain issues about the nature of trust investments and the irrevocability of the trust.

While SFAS 76 encompasses all extinguishments of debt, including legal satisfaction of the creditor, the focal point of this pronouncement is in-substance defeasance. Under this technique, even though the creditor does not relieve the debtor of its primary obligation, the debt is to be considered extinguished if a trust is invested in government obligations that are adequate to service the debt until it is legally satisfied, and if the possibility is remote that the debtor will be required to make any further payments.

Prior to SFAS 76, an extinguishment of debt had always amounted to a single, irreversible event; the creditor was somehow satisfied or the debtor was somehow relieved of the obligation, and the transaction was a "done deal." Literally, "extinguishment" connotes finality, and accountants had been accustomed to dealing with it in that sense. SFAS 76 still approaches the issue in this frame of reference, trying to define one more circumstance that meets the test for "finality." Accordingly, while SFAS 76 is not explicit on this point, its basic intention is that an in-substance defeasance, once consummated, is a "done deal," and any undoing of the transaction, even in relatively modest respects, should indicate that an extinguishment of debt initially did not occur.

General SFAS 76 Requirements. This statement covers all extinguishments of debt, both direct and in-substance. As to in-substance defeasances, the Board states that such a procedure can be applied only to debt (including capitalized lease obligations) with specified maturities and fixed payment schedules. Accordingly, in-substance defeasance accounting is not permissible for a debt with floating interest rates because of the uncertain amount of future debt service requirements.

To be comprehensive, SFAS 76 includes the obvious statement that paying the creditor directly or reacquiring the bonds on the public securities markets constitutes an extinquishment of debt.

When the debtor is legally released from being the primary obligor and it is probable that the debtor will not be required to make future payments, such debt is considered extinguished.

The Board has also concluded that a "legal release" is accomplished when there is a sale of assets that serve as sole collateral for a debt, even though the seller is not relieved from a primary obligation. When such debt is assumed by the buyer, the creditor has recourse only to the asset.

Defeasance Requirements. When an irrevocable trust is created solely for satisfying scheduled payments of interest and principal on a specified obligation and the possibility that the debtor will be required to make future payments is remote, an extinguishment of debt is deemed to have occurred even though the debtor legally remains primarily obligated. Figure 18.5 presents an example of a simple in-substance defeasance.

In-substance defeasance is permitted for a part of a debt issue so long as all interest and principal for such fraction are covered.

The use of the term "remote" establishes a high threshold for achievement of in-substance defeasance. Determining "rcmoteness" requires an assessment of any other circumstances of the debtor that could cause future payments, such as an acceleration of the maturity of the defeased debt due to a violation of its covenants or of cross-default provisions of other debt issues.

A. Bonds outstanding, 9.50% interest coupon payable
semiannually, originally issued at par with unamortized issue
costs of $1,000, due in 5 years, not callable $100,000

Future cash outflows:
Interest payments

1	$	4,750
2		4,750
3		4,750
4		4,750
5		4,750
6		4,750
7		4,750
8		4,750
9		4,750
10		4,750

Principal repayment 100,000

B. To be in-substance defeased by placing qualifying U.S.
government securities in irrevocable trust; 9.50% coupon
bought to yield 11.25%; interest payment and maturity dates
coinciding with timing on the bonds

Purchase price $ 93,444

Interest receipts

1	$	4,750
2		4,750
3		4,750
4		4,750
5		4,750
6		4,750
7		4,750
8		4,750
9		4,750
10		4,750

Principal receipt 100,000

C. Summary of transaction
   1. Cash requirements are exactly matched.
   2. Gain on defeasance is as follows:

Principal of debt	$100,000
Less: Cost of government securities	(93,444)
Unamortized issue costs	(1,000)
Trustees fees paid at outset	(750)
Gain on extinguishment	$ 4,806

FIG. 18.5 Example of Simple In-Substance Defeasance

Trust assets. The trust will be restricted to owning only monetary assets that are
essentially risk-free as to the amount, timing, and collection of interest and principal.
For U.S. dollar debt, the essentially risk-free monetary assets are limited to U.S.
government: direct obligations; guaranteed obligations (with no time lag if the
guarantor must pay); and backed obligations where the instrument is a pass-through.
(However, pass-throughs that do not fix the timing of collection of interest and
principal do not qualify.)

The timing and amount of the cash flows on the assets held by the trust must approximately coincide with the debt service requirements.

The monetary assets shall be denominated in the currency in which the debt is payable. Forward contracts cannot be used to change U.S. dollar assets into foreign denominated assets. Accordingly, foreign government securities in which the trust can be invested should be the equivalent of the permissible U.S. government securities categories.

Reacquisition or defeased debt. The Board specifically deals with whether additional gain or loss results from acquiring in the marketplace (and holding) debt that has previously been in-substance defeased ("double-dipping"). SFAS 76 prescribes that this is not the case; such reacquired debt should be carried by the company as an investment in the future cash flows from the trust, resulting in no additional gain or loss at the time of repurchase. However, the additional gain or loss will come into income over the remaining duration of the irrevocable trust, the result of being treated as either discount or premium on the company's investment in its own bonds. Such discount or premium will be amortized for accounting purposes using the level yield, or interest, method.

Trust costs. Expenses such as trustee's fees to be paid by the trust should be built in as part of the initial investment in the trust. This will have the effect of reducing the gain (or increasing the loss) just as if the company itself had acquired the obligations and present-valued them at the interest rate being earned in the trust. If the debtor company must pay the related costs, those costs should be accrued as a liability at the time of the in-substance defeasance.

Disclosure. Disclosure is required in the financial statements of the fact that an in-substance defeasance has been done, stating the amount of debt that is considered extinguished at the end of the period.

Instantaneous Defeasance. With SFAS 76 in place, investment bankers noted an opportunity that seemed to make good economic sense as well as accounting sense. Debt could be issued in countries having interest rates lower than in the United States, the proceeds used to acquire qualifying government securities denominated in the currency in which the debt was payable, and a defeasance trust established for less than the debt proceeds—hence the term "instantaneous." This maneuver took advantage of (i.e., arbitraged) rate differentials existing in major money markets. The few companies that accomplished this transaction had benefited their shareholders and had fully complied with the letter (and they believed the spirit) of SFAS 76.

The FASB did not see it this way. Admittedly, the Board had not thought about this kind of transaction, but in any event concluded that they had not intended to allow it under SFAS 76.

In October 1984, the FASB issued TB 84-4, *In-Substance Defeasance of Debt* (D14). The TB became effective for debt incurred on or after September 12, 1984 (thus not upsetting earlier transactions), with earlier application encouraged (which advice went unheeded) for transactions in fiscal years for which annual financial statements had not yet been issued. The TB indicates that debt may *not* be extinguished through an in-substance defeasance if the debtor irrevocably places in trust assets that were acquired at about the time the debt was incurred. These were considered "borrow and invest" transactions.

In addition, this TB addresses other questions that had arisen regarding the application of SFAS 76, and indicates that a debtor may in some circumstances (and may *not* in other circumstances) use an assessment of the remoteness of risk that the cash inflows to the trust from its assets are essentially risk-free in determining whether a transaction meets the in-substance defeasance requirements. Clearing away the excess verbiage, what the TB was driving at was the German Schuldschein, a kind of a Treasury bill, comprising the trust assets used in defeasance of Eurodollar debt denominated in Deutschemarks, payable through Netherlands Antilles companies. The Schuldschein was technically callable, although the German government had not called any for 50 years.

The TB flatly rejects any asset that is callable regardless of the remoteness of the call possibility, and closed the loop by stating that a noncallable government security such as a U.S. Treasury obligation could not be synthesized into a foreign currency asset by the use of forwards, on the premise that the forward might not be fulfillable for some unspecified reason.

TB 84-4 also clarified that debt callable by the debtor may be extinguished through an in-substance defeasance. However, the debtor had to make a determination in advance of defeasance when the call date (if any) would be. If a call date was selected, the trust funding would have to cover the cash flow needs to the chosen maturity (or to final maturity if no call date was selected).

Unconsolidated subsidiary debt defeasance. In Issue 84-41, *Consolidation of Subsidiary after Instantaneous In-Substance Defeasance*, the EITF considered how TB 84-4 might apply to a situation in which an unconsolidated subsidiary (e.g., a finance company) enters into an instantaneous defeasance (and therefore is not allowed to offset the trust and the debt on its balance sheet or to recognize the built-in arbitrage gain). The question raised was whether the transaction might somehow require the subsidiary to be consolidated.

The Task Force did not reach a consensus, but the general feeling was that if the subsidiary was bona fide and had been established for valid business purposes, TB 84-4 would not affect it, and the subsidiary would not be consolidated under then current practice. However, creating a subsidiary to do the deal would not be acceptable.

Because SFAS 94 requires consolidation of all majority-owned subsidiaries commencing in 1988, this transaction has become academic.

Special-Purpose Borrowings. In Issue 84-26, *Defeasance of Special-Purpose Borrowings*, the EITF considered (without reaching a consensus) those situations in which the debtor defeases debt that has a subsidized interest rate, such as industrial development bonds and maritime bonds. These kinds of obligations were not required to have a market rate of interest imputed under APB 21; thus they could profitably be defeased by using normal-rate government securities. Some companies did in-substance defeasances on such issues, recording immediate gains.

The FASB staff had planned on releasing a TB precluding such defeasances on the grounds that the asset acquired with the special-purpose borrowing was linked thereto. The SEC Observer stated that the SEC staff categorically would not accept gain recognition treatment by registrants; and the Board itself did not want to issue the TB because it was beginning to wonder if it should reconsider SFAS 76. Accordingly, there was no release, but as with similar situations the notoriety inherent in EITF discussions (and the SEC's attitude) made the transaction unattractive.

Invasion of a Defeasance Trust. In EITF Issue 86-36, *Invasion of a Defeasance Trust*, the Task Force considered an exception to the requirement in SFAS 76 that requires a debtor to *irrevocably* place assets in trust (only for scheduled interest and principal repayments) to warrant in-substance defeasance accounting.

Because of changes in the tax laws in 1986, some companies saw a "last-chance" opportunity to arbitrage the tax rate differential between capital gains and ordinary income by acquiring most of the debentures that were previously defeased. This would produce an ordinary loss. To offset this, the company would exchange the reacquired debentures with the trustee of the defeasance trust for a proportional amount of the assets in the trust. Once in possession of those assets, they could be liquidated at capital gains rates. The pretax loss on reacquisition and the gain on sale of the reverted trust assets would be about the same in amount, but the tax rate on the gain would be lower than the tax benefit rate on the loss.

The EITF continued its equanimity about defeasance by reaching a consensus that the transaction did not affect previous accounting for the in-substance defeasance, despite the Board's emphatic view that extinguishment is a "done deal" and tinkering is not allowed. After conferring with the Board members, the FASB staff conceded that in this unique situation, because the tax opportunity was short-lived, the consensus would not be overturned by a TB. In all other respects, the trust must remain inviolable—for example, any invasion to exercise a call privilege not originally planned and provided for would indicate that the trust was not irrevocable and that an error had been committed in the original extinguishment accounting.

DEBT MODIFICATIONS

Modification of Debt Terms

In EITF Issue 86-18, *Debtor's Accounting for a Modification of Debt Terms*, the EITF addressed the accounting by debtors for transactions in which the leverage of a call provision is used to reduce the interest rate on long-term debt. One way to accomplish this transaction would be to exchange new debt without a call provision for the old debt. The new debt would have a lower interest rate, but the rate would be somewhat above current market interest rates to compensate for higher interest, which would have otherwise been paid until the call date. In other proposed transactions, the lender would pay the borrower a fee in return for an agreement by the borrower not to exercise the call feature for the life of the debt, or for some shorter period. The accounting question focused on the circumstances in which the existing debt should be considered substantively extinguished and replaced by new debt, resulting in recognition of an extraordinary gain or loss.

The Task Force reached a consensus that if the parties exchange new debt instruments evidencing the removal of the call provisions, the transaction is an extinguishment. However, the Task Force could not reach a consensus on the accounting treatment if the parties, without exchanging new debt instruments, amended the existing indenture to eliminate the call provision in exchange for cash consideration. A majority of the Task Force felt that the appropriate way to measure whether a debt modification occurs is to compare cash flows under the revised and original agreements, appropriately present-valued, and if the present value changes by more than 3 to 5%, the transaction should be treated as an extinguishment regardless of the form used to accomplish it.

Figure 18.6 illustrates the method of computing a change in cash flows. The Task Force did not address the rate to be used for present valuing; thus two approaches are shown. The more logical one would seem to be the approach using the coupon rate, which is a more restrictive test.

Induced Conversions

Sweeteners. Inducements are offered when the issuer wants to obtain conversion of debt into equity, but the conversion privilege is not sufficiently "in the money" to impel the holders to convert if the debt is called. A typical inducement format might be an offer to holders providing that if they convert within a stipulated limited period, the conversion ratio will be increased by a stated amount. In effect, the inducement, called a "sweetener," puts the conversion privilege "in the money." The FASB was asked to determine the accounting when convertible debt is converted to equity securities pursuant to such an offer.

Ordinarily, the debtor is required to recognize a gain or loss equal to the difference between the carrying value of the debt and the aggregate fair value of all securities issued and assets paid when convertible debt is extinguished by any means other than via the conversion privileges included in the terms of the debt at issuance.

In Issuance 84-3, *Convertible Debt "Sweeteners,"* the EITF considered this issue and, after several discussions, reached the conclusion that the incremental value of the sweetener should be valued and expensed, but that the conversion portion should not be considered an extinguishment. Because GAAP required the transaction to be considered an extinguishment, the FASB issued SFAS 84, *Induced Conversions of Convertible Debt* (D10), to specify the method of accounting for certain conversions of convertible debt to equity securities when the debtor induces conversion of the debt.

SFAS 84 amends APB 26 by requiring recognition of an expense equal to the fair value of only the additional securities or other consideration issued to induce the conversion. Examples of applications of this statement are included in an Appendix to SFAS 84. A simple example is shown in Figure 18.7.

Other Inducements. SFAS 84 covers only straightforward inducements, and it has been interpreted very narrowly and precisely in practice. Therefore, it covers exactly what it covers, and no more.

Among the matters omitted that have the same effect as sweetener transactions are:

A. Debt issue due in five years, having a coupon of 10%, callable at par at any interest payment date. $100,000

B. Present market rate of interest has dropped to 8%.

C. Lender agrees to amend interest coupon to 9% in exchange for borrower relinquishing the call privilege.

D. Comparison of cash flows:

Original interest	Revised interest	Original principal	Revised principal
$5,000	$4,500	$ —	$ —
5,000	4,500		
5,000	4,500		
5,000	4,500		
5,000	4,500		
5,000	4,500		
5,000	4,500		
5,000	4,500		
5,000	4,500		
5,000	4,500	100,000	100,000

E. Discounting at coupon rate (10%):

Present value of original cash flows	$100,000
Present value of revised cash flows	96,139
Percentage change	3.86%

F. Discounting at current market rate (8%):

Present value of original cash flows	$108,111
Present value of revised cash flows	104,055
Percentage change	3.75%

FIG. 18.6   Example of Computation of Change in Cash Flows Related to a Debt Modification

1. Sweetening of synthetic warrants.
2. Sweetening of nonsynthetic warrants.
3. Giving new convertible debentures with more liberal conversion or other features.
4. Giving less than the shares to which the holder would have been entitled, plus other consideration.

In the synthetic warrant situation, a debt that is optionally tenderable with the warrant in exchange for stock may be selling at a price that is not sufficiently low to motivate holders of the warrants to acquire the debt on the market and exchange it with the warrant for the company's common stock. Thus, the company might offer, for a limited period, to accept the debt ("scrip") at, say, 110% of face amount, sufficient to place the warrant in the money.

Because detachable (even though synthetic) warrants are treated differently than convertibles under APB 14, revising the terms of warrants is a capital transaction. The net effect of sweetening the scrip in this situation is to lower the strike price of the warrant, thereby giving a discount on the capital stock issued. There have not been very many of these transactions, and accordingly the FASB has not seen a need to deal with them.

A. If converted pursuant to an inducement:

    1. Number of shares issuable on conversion of $1,000

        face amount of convertible debt, before inducement   20

    2. Inducement conversion rate — number of shares   25

    3. Market price of stock at conversion date $ 45

    4. Computation:

           Value of stock issued (25 shares × $45) $1,125

        Value of original privilege (20 shares × $45)   900

                                                           $ 225

B. If bought out for equivalent cash:

    Cash buyout price $1,125

    Carrying amount   1,000

    Loss on extinguishment $ 125

C. Effect on net worth:

    Inducement:

        Loss charged to operations $ (225)

        Additional credit to common stock   225

        Change in net worth $ —

    Extinguishment:

        Loss charged to operations $ (125)

        Credit to net worth   0

        Change in net worth $ (125)

FIG. 18.7 Comparison of Inducement Accounting With Extinguishment Accounting

In the case of nonsynthetic warrants, the strike price can be reduced directly; for instance, during a limited time period, the cash price is reduced by say 25% (in whatever form this might legally be done based on the laws of the state of incorporation).

Giving new convertible debentures that have more liberal features than the old debt would of course be treated as a debt extinguishment; however, this may be more desirable from the company's standpoint if the fair value of the new securities is not greater than the carrying amount of the existing convertibles, as might happen depending on interest rate levels and the company's stock performance record. With extinguishment accounting, there may be no loss to be recorded, whereas with inducement accounting, a charge to expense would be required, regardless of the economic reality of the situation. Some accountants feel that if the new exchanged convertibles are virtually assured of conversion, the transaction should be accounted for under SFAS 84 as an inducement transaction in substance.

It should also be noted that inducement accounting under SFAS 84 will commonly produce a larger charge to current operations than extinguishment accounting, as illustrated in Figure 18.7. However, most companies that employ the inducement technique are short of cash and cannot do a cash extinguishment. Further, the net worth of the company is not changed overall by an inducement, but is by an extinguishment, also as shown in Figure 18.7; this may be an important consideration to some companies that are short on both cash and net worth.

SFAS 84 applies only if all the shares issuable under the original conversion terms are actually issued. Thus, giving less shares (perhaps only a nominal reduction) and paying cash to make the transaction attractive to the holder is not covered by SFAS 84, but is instead an extinguishment transaction. For the reasons indicated in the preceding paragraphs, the company may nevertheless find this more attractive.

INTEREST

Imputation Requirements

Cash Transactions. When recording a transaction involving debt, the face amount and interest rate of a note should be realistically stated. If the coupon or stated rate is not realistic, the correct rate must be derived.

The process of making a determination of the proper interest rate is called *imputation*, and the interest factor determined in this way is known as the *imputed interest rate*. APB 21, *Interest on Receivables and Payables* (I69), points out that the imputation process is not a new accounting principle, and that the purpose of the opinion is to refine the manner of applying existing accounting principles.

A significant matter addressed by APB 21 (I69.105) is the appropriate accounting for the exchange of notes for noncash consideration (property, goods, or services) when the face of the note does not reasonably represent the present value of the consideration. This situation exists when the note is non-interest-bearing, or when its stated interest rate is materially different from the prevailing interest rate at the date of the transaction. In such a situation, if reasonable present values are not used in recording the notes given or received, the financial statements of both buyer and seller will, in part, be misstated, and the financial statements will not be in conformity with GAAP (assuming, of course, that material amounts are involved). It should be recognized that even a small difference in rate may significantly affect the financial statements if the note is large and long-term.

Imputation of the interest is required when the stated rate of the note is unreasonable (I69.105b). Determination of whether the stated interest rate of a note is unreasonable should be based on the effect of imputation on income before extraordinary items or on net income of the company, and on the trend of earnings.

The major items to which APB 21 does *not* apply are (I69.102–.103):

1. Receivables and payables arising from transactions with customers or suppliers in the normal course of business that are due in customary trade terms not exceeding approximately one year.
2. Receivables or payables to be paid in property, goods, or services.
3. Deposits, progress payments, or other amounts that do not require repayment in the future, but rather will be applied to the purchase price of the property, goods, or services involved.
4. Security deposits, retainages on contracts, or other amounts intended to provide security for one party to an agreement.
5. The customary cash lending activities (and demand or savings deposit activities) of financial institutions whose primary business is lending money.

6. Transactions in which interest rates are affected by the tax attributes or legal restrictions prescribed by a government agency.

7. Transactions between parent and subsidiary companies and between subsidiaries of a common parent. (The fact that the APB deferred consideration of transactions between related parties when it issued APB 21 should not be interpreted to mean that imputation in these circumstances is inappropriate. Transactions between affiliates should be evaluated to determine whether imputation is required for a fair presentation of the results of operations in the particular circumstances (e.g., subsidiaries with minority interests).)

8. Accounting for convertible debt.

9. Warranties for product performance or other estimates of contractual obligations assumed in connection with sale of property, goods, or services.

Noncash Transactions. When a note is issued for property, goods, or services in a noncash, arm's-length transaction, the note contains two elements: (1) a principal factor, which is equivalent to a bargained exchange price, and (2) an interest element, which is equivalent to the interest that would have been earned by the seller had he received cash instead of a note.

If a transaction is at arm's length, there is a presumption that the stated rate of interest is fair to the seller. To determine fairness, a "form versus economic substance" test is required: The interest rate is not appropriate or fair if (1) there is no stated interest, (2) stated interest is not reasonable, or (3) the stated face of the note is materially different from current cash sales price for the same or similar items or the market value of the note at the transaction date (I69.105).

In these circumstances, the implicit discount or premium should preferably be measured as follows:

1. Face of note;
2. Less the value of:
   a. Property, goods, or services at the established exchange price (or cash sale price) or
   b. The notes as determined by the market rates of interest and the market value of the notes (when the notes are traded in an open market), whichever is more clearly evident;
3. Equals the discount or premium, which will be amortized by using the effective interest rate.

The market value of a note will generally be equivalent to the proceeds the maker could have received had he issued a note payable to a bank with identical terms and collateral. This market value would also be equal to the amount the holder would have been entitled to had the note receivable been discounted without recourse at the time it was received.

If an established exchange price is not determinable and if the note has no ready market, the problem of determining present value is more difficult. In this case, an imputed interest rate based on prevailing interest rate levels must be used to determine the appropriate discount or premium.

The imputed interest rate should be determined at the time the note is issued, assumed, or acquired. Any subsequent changes in the prevailing interest rate should be ignored. This eliminates fluctuations in the cost of money that would, if recognized, result in future income or expense.

Amortization of Discount or Premium. The discount or premium should be amortized to interest expense or income over the term of the note under the *interest method.* The objective of this method is to arrive at a periodic interest cost that will result in a constant (level) effective rate on the face amount of the note, plus or minus the discount or premium, at the beginning of each period (I69.108). Other methods of amortization may be used if they produce results that are not materially different from those obtained from using the interest method. Some of the other methods of amortization (which do not result in a level effective rate) are the straight-line method, the bonds outstanding method, and the dollar-year method, none of which is used as a practical matter.

Capitalization of Interest

Qualifying Assets. Interest is to be capitalized on assets that are constructed or otherwise produced for an enterprise's own use, and on assets intended for sale or lease that are constructed or produced as discrete projects (such as ships or real estate developments). Specifically excluded are inventories produced routinely regardless of the production period length (e.g., whiskey), any assets in use or ready for use in earnings activities, and assets not in such use nor in preparation therefor (I67.106).

In FIN 33, *Applying FASB Statement No. 34 to Oil and Gas Producing Operations Accounted for by the Full Cost Method* (I67.108), the FASB pointed out that assets in use and currently being depreciated, depleted, or amortized do not qualify for interest capitalization; however, major unproved properties in the process of development would qualify.

Amount Capitalizable. Only "real" interest cost (actually incurred, or imputed on debt or capital leases) can be allocated to qualifying assets. The rate to be used for capitalization may be ascertained in this order (I67.110): (1) the rate of specific borrowings associated with the qualifying asset and (2) if borrowings are not specific for the qualifying asset, or the asset amount exceeds specific borrowings therefor, a weighted average of rates applicable to other appropriate borrowings. Alternatively, a company may use a weighted average of rates or all appropriate borrowings regardless of specific borrowings incurred to finance the qualifying asset. However, the amount capitalized in an accounting period (presumably one year) cannot exceed the total interest cost incurred (I67.112); otherwise this would amount to capitalization of an allowance for the use of equity funds. The "allowance for funds used during construction" (AFUDC), which includes equity costs, is not affected by SFAS 34 in the case of enterprises regulated for rate-making purposes (see Chapter 33 regarding AFUDC).

The expenditures to which the interest rate is applied are those, generally, that are normally capitalized in the asset cost, provided cash has been paid or an interest-bearing obligation incurred.

Time Parameters. Interest capitalization starts when money is spent, asset preparation activities are underway, and interest cost is being incurred (at least somewhere in the consolidated group). If activity is suspended more than briefly, capitalization of interest stops during the suspension. When the asset is ready for its intended use, or separable parts are ready, interest capitalization is concluded (I67.113–.114).

Since interest cost is considered an integral part of the total cost of acquiring a qualifying asset, its disposition must be the same as that of other components of asset cost, that is, as part of the charge to depreciation or to cost of sales.

Disclosures. SFAS 34 requires certain disclosures: (1) for an accounting period in which no interest cost is capitalized, the amount of interest charged to expense during the period; and (2) for an accounting period in which interest is capitalized, the total amount of interest incurred during the period, and the amount that has been capitalized (I67.118).

Materiality. In November 1980, the FASB issued SFAS 42, *Determining Materiality for Capitalization of Interest Cost* (I67), to delete language that some believe allows capitalization of interest to be avoided under certain circumstances and to make clear that SFAS 34 does not establish new tests of materiality.

Like all FASB statements, SFAS 34 bears the legend: "The provisions of this Statement need not be applied to immaterial items." In addition, however, it included a discussion of how to determine whether the effect of capitalizing interest compared to expensing it is material. Some companies construed that discussion as establishing new tests of materiality, which they used as justification for avoiding the interest capitalization requirement. By deleting that discussion, the FASB makes clear that SFAS 34 did not create any new tests of materiality and that the "usual tests" are to be used.

Equity Method Investees. SFAS 34, *Capitalization of Interest Cost* (I67), as originally issued, limited interest capitalization to consolidated subsidiaries. Thus, there was some inconsistency between SFAS 34 (I67.112) and the requirement in APB 18, *The Equity Method of Accounting for Investments in Common Stocks*, that normal consolidation rules should apply to the investor's accounting for equity method investees (I82.101).

Since differences in practice occurred, the Board issued SFAS 58, *Capitalization of Interest Cost in Financial Statements That Include Investments Accounted for by the Equity Method* (I67), which amends SFAS 34. The statement concludes that equity in and loans and advances to equity method investees are qualifying assets (assets on which interest should be capitalized) of an investor "while the investee has activities in progress necessary to commence its planned principal operations provided that the investee's activities include the use of funds to acquire qualifying assets for its operations" (I67.105c).

This provision allows an investor company to capitalize interest that the investee company cannot, because the investor's qualifying assets are its investments and advances, whereas the investee's qualifying assets are only those that directly qualify under SFAS 34. Thus, there will be a difference created between the investor's equity account and its share in the investee's underlying net assets; this contradicts the general thrust of APB 18, which states that the consolidation method and the equity method should give essentially the same net income results (I82.109). The Board was impelled to state that this provision of APB 18 "provides important general guidance but was not intended to be inviolable under the circumstances."

This exercise will no longer affect subsidiaries accounted for by the equity method, because SFAS 94, *Consolidation of All Majority Owned Subsidiaries* (C51), requires full consolidation of such investees commencing in 1988. Once consolidated, the requirements of SFAS 34 are directly applicable, and interest capitalization can occur only on directly qualifying assets, not on the investment in a subsidiary. However, nonsubsidiary investees will still have the difference created under SFAS 58.

Tax-Exempt Borrowings, Gifts, and Grants. SFAS 62, *Capitalization of Interest Cost in Situations Involving Certain Tax-Exempt Borrowings and Certain Gifts and Grants* (I67), amends SFAS 34 in two respects. First, the amount of interest cost capitalized on the portion of a qualifying asset acquired with proceeds of a restricted tax-exempt borrowing would be all interest cost of the tax-exempt borrowing less any interest earned on temporary investment of the proceeds from the date of borrowing until the date the asset is ready for its intended use. Interest cost of the tax-exempt borrowing would be eligible for capitalization on other qualifying assets of the entity when the specified qualifying asset is no longer eligible for interest capitalization. Second, no interest cost may be capitalized on the portion of a qualifying asset acquired using a gift or grant that is restricted by the donor or grantor to acquisition of the specified asset. Nonbusiness entities, such as nonproprietary hospitals, universities, and governmental agencies, would be most affected by this Statement.

This statement supersedes TB 81-5, which prohibited the offsetting of interest income against interest cost in applying the capitalization criteria of SFAS 34.

Allocation of Interest

In most cases, interest expense is shown in the financial statements as a separate line item, or as part of other expenses, in arriving at income from continuing operations.

In Issue 87-24, *Allocation of Interest to Discontinued Operations*, the EITF considered whether interest expense should be allocated to discontinued operations, and, if so, on what basis. The SEC staff had been strongly resisting such allocation, especially in leveraged buyout (LBO) situations in which the acquirer planned to sell a portion of the businesses acquired in the LBO.

The Task Force reached a consensus that allocation is permissible but not mandatory. The maximum allocable amount would be the total of (1) interest on debt to be assumed by a buyer of the discontinued operations and (2) other general corporate interest, based on the ratio of the net assets to be sold to the net assets of the consolidated enterprise (after removing the debt to be assumed by the buyer).

International Accounting Standard

In March 1984, the International Accounting Standards Committee issued IAS 23, *Capitalization of Borrowing Costs* (AC 9023.21). The requirements of IAS 23 are not as detailed as those of SFAS 34 (I67), but they generally conform to GAAP, except as indicated in the following paragraph.

This standard does not require capitalization of borrowing costs but requires each enterprise that has incurred borrowing costs to adopt and consistently apply a policy on capitalization or noncapitalization of borrowing costs for assets that require a substantial period of time to be made ready for their intended use or sale. The standard then sets forth the requirements for capitalization and the required disclosures.

Ratio of Earnings to Fixed Charges

Conceptually, a company's ability to pay interest on long-term debt should be demonstrated by a ratio that compares earnings to fixed charges; in fact, the SEC requires the inclusion of this ratio in its registration forms. Under Regulation S-K, Rule 503(d), if debt securities are being registered, the ratio of earnings to fixed charges is to be disclosed for each year, on a total enterprise basis. In addition, for the most recent year or 12 months, pro forma disclosure must be made of the ratio of earnings to fixed charges adjusted to give effect: to the issuance of securities being registered; to any issuance, retirement, or redemption of securities during the period; or to any issuance, retirement, or redemption of securities taking place or presently proposed to take place within one year after the current period.

Earnings must be computed after all operating and income deductions except fixed charges and income taxes, and after eliminating undistributed income of 50%-or-less-owned persons. Fixed charges include: interest and amortization of debt discount or premium on all indebtedness; a portion of rentals that can be demonstrated to be representative of the interest factor in the particular case; and preferred stock dividend requirements of subsidiaries, excluding items eliminated in consolidation.

If long-term debt or preferred stock is being registered, the annual interest requirements of the debt or the annual dividend requirements on the preferred stock must be disclosed. To the extent that an issue represents refunding or refinancing, only the additional annual interest or dividend requirements must be stated. If preferred stock is being registered, there must also be disclosure in tabular form, for each year or other period, of the ratio of earnings to combined fixed charges and preferred dividend requirements.

The registrant must file as an exhibit the computations of all the required ratios. When the interest rate has not yet been fixed, an assumed maximum interest rate on the securities may be used for the purpose of this exhibit and the pro forma ratio. If this is done, the assumed rate must be disclosed.

The SEC has indicated that for the purpose of computing the ratio, it is unacceptable to reduce fixed charges by (1) amounts representing investment income earned or interest (either actual or imputed) on funds raised or being raised that are in excess of the company's requirements for working capital and (2) gains on retirement of debt.

The SEC staff has stated that one-third of rentals in the fixed-charge component was allowed in the past because it was considered a reasonable approximation of the interest portion of rentals. Although they feel that this approximation may not be exact, they will not automatically disallow it simply because SFAS 13 (L10) provides a different answer; one-third is still acceptable if it represents a reasonable approximation of the interest factor. Also, if practical, the computations of the ratio for prior years should be revised retroactively when a new method of estimating interest costs in rentals is used in the current year's ratio. In this way, all years will be presented on a consistent basis.

AUDITING

The overall objective of the audit of debt and interest is to determine whether they are fairly presented in the context of the financial statements taken as a whole. The broad objectives of an audit are discussed in Chapter 7 and the basic nature of the internal control structure in Chapter 8. This discussion assumes familiarity with those chapters.

Audit Approach

For companies that engage in frequent financings, the auditor will assess the control structure to ascertain the extent to which he will place reliance thereon (see Chapter 8). However, in the usual case the auditor approaches debt and interest using substantive procedures, because the number of transactions is relatively small and the dollar amounts involved quite high. The objective when using a substantive approach is to directly support the financial statement amounts; therefore the auditor devises procedures that provide satisfactory evidence for this purpose. In auditing debt and interest, this includes reading new loan agreements, determining what changes if any have been made in prior loan agreements, and confirming with outside parties the significant factors and transactions that have occurred during the audit period.

The auditor's objectives for debt and interest include ascertaining that:

1. All debt has been recorded.
2. The debt has been properly valued and classified in the financial statements.
3. All required disclosures have been made.
4. Interest expense, including interest payable and amortization of premium or discount and issue costs, is properly stated and all significant disclosures related to interest expense have been made.
5. The company has met all the requirements and restrictions imposed by debt covenants.
6. Debt retirements and modifications have been properly accounted for, as extinguishments or otherwise.
7. Interest has been properly imputed on debt instruments if required under APB 21.
8. Interest capitalization has been performed in accordance with the requirements of SFAS 34 and related releases, and disclosures made as required.

Analytical procedures (see Chapter 7) are useful in auditing debt and interest because of the auditor's ability to make overall computations of what expected balances of debt should be based on scheduled repayment requirements, and how much interest expense should be, based on stated rates and known amounts outstanding. Similar computations might be made for interest capitalization based on average balances of qualifying assets. Other sample substantive procedures are shown in Figure 18.8.

1. Prepare or obtain an analysis of notes and/or bonds payable and accrued interest showing:

• Payee	• Additions
• Date made	• Payments
• Date due	• Ending balance
• Interest rate	• Interest accrued or prepaid at beginning
• Date interest paid to	• Interest accrued
• Original amount of note	• Interest paid
• Collateral	• Interest accrued or prepaid at end
• Opening balance	• Cross-reference to loan agreement and/or abstract

   If there are numerous transactions, consider preparing a schedule of only that debt with an unpaid balance at the end of the year. In this event the analysis spreadsheet above should be appropriately modified.
2. Verify mechanical accuracy of the analysis, and compare totals to general ledger.
3. Check interest calculations by recomputation.
4. Corroborate interest expense for the period by reference to the amount of debt outstanding during the period.
5. Verify computation of amortization of debt premium or discount and expense.
6. Examine supporting documentation (i.e., bond, note, and loan indentures and agreements) for all debt and related expenses; examine corporate minutes for authorizations.
7. Examine agreements for restrictive covenants.
8. Ascertain the receipt of funds from borrowings and account for their disposition.
9. Confirm balances and collateral by direct communications with creditors (see Chapter 12 on compensating balances); if an independent trustee is used, confirm transactions and balances. Watch for indications of loans on standard bank confirmation forms.
10. Examine cancelled or paid notes and/or bonds and uncancelled bonds purchased (treasury bonds).
11. Review notes paid or renewed since balance sheet date; determine whether there were any unrecorded liabilities at year-end.
12. Account for all unissued bonds.
13. Review sinking fund activity.
14. Determine that mortgages have been recorded, and confirm liens on property.

FIG. 18.8   Sample Substantive Procedures for Debt and Interest

Guarantees

When the client acts as guarantor for another party or endorses a negotiable instrument, the auditor may follow these procedures:

1. Inquire as to guarantees the client has made. Review bank confirmation replies and loan payable confirmations for evidence of guarantees.
2. Confirm terms of guarantees that are mentioned in agreements or are disclosed through inquiry.
3. Determine whether it is probable, reasonably possible, or remotely possible that the client will be called upon to perform under the guarantee.

4. Be alert to "concealed" guarantees and the possibility of a forbearance. (An example of a forbearance is the failure of a lender to foreclose on defaulted debts when there is some commonality of management between the debtor and lender. Another example is the failure to enforce a guarantee given by a company whose management also exercises management authority over the party who is the beneficiary of the guarantee.)

5. Determine that the client has included in its representation letter the fact that "related-party transactions and related amounts receivable or payable, including sales, purchases, loans, transfers, leasing arrangements, and guarantees," have been properly recorded or disclosed in the financial statements (see Chapter 25).

6. Determine that the financial statements contain the appropriate disclosures concerning guarantees.

SAS 45 (AU 334) requires that an auditor obtain an understanding of the nature of related-party relationships; accordingly, all identified related-party guarantees must be reviewed, and the auditor should obtain reasonable satisfaction that such guarantees do not lack substance and are properly disclosed (see C59.113 and Chapter 25).

Debt Covenants

The client should have procedures designed to detect events of default, to measure the effect of any proposed transactions on restrictive debt covenants, and to notify the lender about transactions and events as required. The auditor should obtain an understanding of the client's debt compliance determination procedures.

To evaluate the client's internal control structure and to be reasonably sure that all operative restrictions are footnoted or otherwise adequately disclosed in the financial statements, the auditor should gather certain documents into his working papers, including a conformed copy of the debt agreement and all amendments, a summary of the calculations supporting the compliance with restrictive covenants, correspondence with the lender, and waivers of any defaults.

The auditor should inspect the documentation produced by the client's procedures. He should review the calculations and compliance checklists and compare these checklists with the underlying debt agreements. He should also obtain from the lender (or the client's attorney) a written opinion as to the proper interpretation of subjective covenants.

If there are any events of default, they must be carefully assessed. If violations of the restrictive covenants are not waived by the lender and the loan is in default, it can be declared immediately due and payable. In this case, the auditor must consider what financial statement classification and disclosures will be required and how the default will affect his opinion.

Waivers and Cures. The auditor must exercise care in evaluating a waiver of default to be sure that the waiver is applicable. A single waiver may be sufficient for a specific event of default, but if the default is or may be of a continuing nature, a waiver should be obtained for at least 12 months from the balance sheet date. Otherwise it may be necessary to classify the debt as current, as discussed earlier in this chapter under "Covenant Violations."

When the client corrects a default, it may be considered "cured." In this case, the auditor should determine that either the terms of the debt agreement or the lender have specified the corrective action to be taken, and that the action taken to cure the default is complete and in accordance with the agreement. If the corrective action is not complete at the date of the auditor's opinion, the auditor may not be able to satisfy himself that the debt is properly classified as long-term; he may then have to modify his opinion (see Chapter 11).

Debt Compliance Letters. Many debt agreements require the auditor to provide the lender with assurance as to the existence or nonexistence of certain conditions. For example, the debt agreement may require the maintenance of a certain amount of working capital at specified points in time, a limitation on investments, and an accountant's letter as to compliance with these requirements.

SAS 14, *Special Reports* (AU 621.18–.19) says that the auditor may only be requested to furnish assurance that the borrower has complied with those covenants of the loan agreement that deal with accounting and auditing matters. The scope of this assurance should exclude legal matters, items beyond the expected expertise of the auditor, and those financial matters that are not covered in the normal scope of an audit. Covenants that may be considered unauditable include, for example, restrictions on business activities and uses of property; title to property; continuation of licenses or franchises; obtaining of all appropriate permits, licenses and other authorizations; commissions of acts of bankruptcy; obtaining of legal opinions; lack of defaults in other agreements; "compliance with loan restrictions to the extent feasible through examination of books and records (language too broad); and "review of loan agreement" (language too broad).

A timely discussion with the client, lender, and counsel before finalization as to exactly what the terms to be used in the loan agreement mean, and how the various covenants will be measured, is essential. Only then can the auditor be assured that the final debt agreement will be worded in a manner that recognizes the boundaries of his expertise as an auditor.

See Chapter 11 for examples of special reports by auditors on a client's compliance with contractual provisions of a debt agreement.

Uniform Commercial Code

In addition to confirming with lenders the amount of debt outstanding and the existence of any security interest in the company's properties, the audit of debt has the objective of ensuring that the financial statements contain adequate disclosure of all assets pledged as collateral. To determine the existence of security interests and become familiar with their details, the auditor can examine the client's copies of security agreements and financing statements.

If the audit plan suggests a need to look to outside sources to evaluate whether all debt is recorded, the search may be facilitated by the Uniform Commercial Code (UCC). Under Article 9 of the UCC, any lender, in order to establish his interest in collateral, must either take possession of the collateral or give public notice of his interest in it by filing a financing statement or a security agreement with the appropriate filing officer. The UCC applies to any transaction intended to create a security interest in personal property (tangible or intangible) or fixtures but not to transactions involving real property. Definitions of some of the key terms used in UCC are given below.

A secured interest is an interest in personal property or fixtures that secures the payment or performance of an obligation. A security interest cannot exist until three conditions are met: (1) there must be an agreement that a security interest attaches to the collateral, (2) value must be given by the creditor, and (3) the debtor must have rights to the collateral.

A security agreement is an agreement that creates or provides for a security interest. It must be signed by the debtor and must contain a description of the collateral. Article 9 provides that "any description of personal property . . . is sufficient whether or not it is specific if it reasonably identifies what is described." For example, the collateral may be broadly described as accounts receivable or inventory. The agreement can provide for a *future security interest*; this is a typical clause found in agreements when the debtor is using inventory or accounts receivable as collateral in a revolving loan agreement. A security agreement may also contain a *future advance clause*, and/or an *acceleration clause*.

A financing statement is the document used to perfect a security interest in property by giving public notice. It gives the secured party enforceable rights in the collateral against third parties.

In every first audit, in any audit where the client is in liquidation, and in any case where the client's financial condition or borrowing ability is seriously deteriorating, it may be advisable to search for public filings of security interests. Other situations in which a search should be considered occur when the client has recently completed a new or complex financing program, or when there is a possibility of concealed management involvement in material transactions.

It is not necessary for the auditor to go in person to the various filing offices to search for financing statements or recorded security agreements. Instead, he may mail a confirmation to the UCC Division of the Office of the Secretary of State of the state in which the pledged property is located (Accounts receivable are "located" where the applicable receivable records are kept.) The request to the secretary of state to search the files is made using the standard Form UCC-11.

While most filings are made with the secretary of state, filings for the following types of collateral are made with county offices: fixtures (personal property that is attached to real property); consumer goods (household items in the hands of the ultimate consumer); and farm-connected collateral (farming equipment, crops, and farmers' accounts receivable). Purchase-money contracts (e.g., installment sales) are generally excluded from the public filing provisions of the code, but are covered by all of the code's other provisions.

The UCC cannot be relied on to disclose certain transactions, notably those involving real property and those involving liens against goods purchased for purchase-money contracts. Also, Louisiana has not adopted the UCC. Therefore, the auditor should continue to rely on other audit procedures to search for liens against any assets located in this state, or against excluded assets in any state.

19

Leases

OVERVIEW

Leasing transactions can be as complex and diverse as the imaginations of the experts who create them. They range from simply leasing a car to the leasing of multi-purpose real estate projects.

A lease gives the leaseholder certain rights and obligations, but not all of the rights or obligations that would apply if the leaseholder were an outright purchaser of the leased property. This divisibility of rights and obligations in a lease causes major problems for preparers, auditors, and users of financial statements. Some quantum of rights and obligations creates a recordable property asset and liability for the leaseholder, and a receivable by the lessor; something less than that quantum results only in an executory contract for both lessee and lessor, to be accounted for as it is performed.

Leases that are not recorded as assets and liabilities in a lessee company's financial statements—and many, perhaps most, are not—are considered off-balance sheet financing. In these situations, only certain attributes of use (risks and rewards of ownership) are transferred in the lease, but not enough of them to cause the lease to be deemed the equivalent of a purchase.

In recent years, as debt has overshadowed equity as a major source of capital, financial institutions have increased their attention to the financial strength ratios and liquidity indicators in a borrower's balance sheet. Since a balance sheet looks stronger with fewer liabilities, transactions that do not create balance sheet liabilities are preferred; and buyers readily can become lessees. Another lessee advantage is that leasing typically provides the ability to finance 100%; the user can get his truck or factory without a downpayment.

The ability to lease the property gives an equipment manufacturer or dealer an added marketing dimension—he can offer his customer a choice of purchase or lease. Further, a lessor may be in a position to obtain significant tax benefits from depreciating the leased property. And if leased property appreciates, the residual value is often a bonus to the lessor or creditor or other parties with an interest in the leased property.

Parties in a Leasing Transaction

The parties to a leasing transaction are the beneficiary and the equity participant, and often will include a financier and an underwriter. The *beneficiary* is the consumer, or user, of the leased property. The *equity participant,* or owner, may be involved for tax benefits and residual value appreciation or possibly to generate additional sales of his product inventory and cash inflow. The *financier* assumes a moneylending role for interest. The *underwriter* is the broker who brings the parties together; he typically is compensated by fees.

A single party may fulfill more than one of these roles, and the typical attributes of each of these parties can be reshuffled in many ways. Equipment manufacturers, equipment dealers, real estate developers, and leasing companies usually serve as financiers and equity participants. Banks, insurance companies, pension funds, and other investors are significant in the financier role. And leasebrokers (or underwriters), investment bankers, and securities brokers play the deal-making role.

Historical Perspective

Early Pronouncements. The evolution of lease accounting principles began in October 1949 with the issuance of ARB 38 by the AICPA Committee on Accounting Procedures (CAP). ARB 38 was included, unchanged, in the ARB 43 Codification in 1953. The focus of this ARB was almost totally on disclosure, although the Committee did say: "Where it is clearly evident that the transaction involved is in substance a purchase, the 'leased' property should be included among the assets of the lessee with suitable accounting for the corresponding liabilities . . ." (ARB 43, Chapter 14, ¶ 7). As interpreted, leases were capitalized only if the term was very short in relation to the useful life of the property, *and* the lessee had the right to acquire the property for a pittance at the end of the lease term.

APB Efforts. The APB, perceiving shortcomings in the ARB 43 guidelines, superseded them by issuing APB 5, *Reporting of Leases in Financial Statements of Lessees* (1964), and APB 7 (1966), *Accounting for Leases in Financial Statements of Lessors.*

APB 5 tried to provide a better definition of when a lease was in substance a purchase. The notion persisted that only those leases that substantively were purchases should be capitalized. Of interest here is the ominous dissent of one APB member, who portended that "a liability (discounted to present value) should be recorded for all material amounts payable under noncancellable leases, which are in fact 'take or pay' contracts representing a present liability payable in the future."

APB 7 covered accounting by the lessor. It distinguished between an *operating lease* (where the lessor accounted for the leased assets in the same manner as fixed assets) and a *financing lease* (where the lessor accounted for the leased assets in two segments—a receivable for rental payments, and the residual value). The basic distinction between the two was whether the lessor's risks resided more in owning the property or in having granted credit. Even though several other APB opinions addressed leasing questions, APB 5 and APB 7 were the authoritative guidance on lease accounting until the issuance of SFAS 13.

FASB Action. In December 1976, the FASB tried to resolve the continuing problem of how to account for leases by issuing SFAS 13 (L10). This statement establishes an extensive set of criteria to evaluate lease transactions and to identify whether they should be accounted for as sales and purchases, or as operating leases (i.e., executory contracts). Despite a multitude of subsequent amendments, interpretations, and technical bulletins, there is still debate over how to account for the economic resources and property rights embodied in a lease.

Modifications to SFAS 13. Since 1979, the FASB has refrained from issuing substantive amendments to SFAS 13, choosing rather to fine-tune it. In 1980, the FASB published a single volume integrating the standards section of SFAS 13 with the various amendments and interpretations issued up to that time. This volume also includes in its appendices the original texts of all the authoritative lease accounting pronouncements. Modifications made to SFAS 13 through early 1988 have been integrated into related topics discussed in this chapter; unrelated pronouncements are discussed in the section entitled "Other Amendments and Interpretations."

Implementation of SFAS 13 changes. The accounting for preexisting leases is not affected by an amendment, interpretation, or technical bulletin prior to its stated effective date. A lease transaction having identical terms but occurring after the effective date would have to be reported in accordance with the new pronouncement. Although this prospective-only treatment results in some inconsistency in reporting, the FASB recognized that earlier leases might have been written differently if the new criteria had been in effect at the time.

Possibility of FASB reconsideration. Since SFAS 13 was issued in 1976, many modifications have been made. The FASB periodically considers whether to place the broad subject of accounting for leases on its agenda, and has indicated on several occasions that a broad reconsideration of leasing would probably result in a new standard requiring the capitalization of most property rights. It is, therefore, not surprising that there has been almost no impetus from the business community to reopen the subject. However, numerous lease accounting issues have surfaced at the EITF, continually tempting the FASB to put leasing on the agenda. (See the subsection "Structuring to Avoid Capitalization" in the Auditing section of this chapter.)

LEASE ACCOUNTING UNDER SFAS 13

SFAS 13 occupies a rather narrow universe; it covers only agreements that convey the right to use property, plant, and equipment, that is, land and depreciable assets. This coverage is far less inclusive than that previously used by many accountants, which often included agreements for the use of intangibles. Although it does include certain agreements that are not nominally leases (e.g., heat supply contracts), it excludes many other similar agreements (e.g., take-or-pay agreements). In a sense, the FASB's decision to employ a narrow scope in SFAS 13 chartered the "off-balance sheet financing" boom (see Chapter 21).

Classification of Leases

The primary objective of SFAS 13 is to classify leases into two kinds: capital and operating. *Capital leases* are leases that transfer substantially all the risks and rewards of ownership, and are accounted for as sales and financings by the lessor and as purchases by the lessee. From the lessor's perspective there are sales-type, direct financing, or leveraged leases. In a direct financing lease, the lessor's income is deemed to come from charges equivalent to interest for the use of funds. A sales-type lease is a capital lease that includes recognition of a profit on sale by a manufacturer- or dealer-lessor in addition to the interest equivalent for the use of funds. In either case, the lessor might also have income in the residual value of the property, depending on how the lease is structured. A leveraged lease is a direct financing lease that includes financing of the property by the lessor with a significant proportion of nonrecourse debt. *Operating leases* are leases that fail to meet any of the tests for a capital lease; these are accounted for as the rental of property, rather than as purchases, sales, or financings.

The conceptual basis for SFAS 13 lease accounting lies in evaluating which party has the risks and rewards of ownership (L10.103). If substantially all the risks and rewards of ownership of the property reside with the lessee, he has "purchased" that property. Based on this concept, four tests for distinguishing capital leases from operating leases were developed. If any one of these tests is satisifed, the lease is to be accounted for as a capital lease:

1. Does the lease transfer ownership of the property to the lessee, either during its term or at its end?
2. Does the lease have a bargain purchase option?
3. Does the lease term (including any bargain renewal periods) equal at least 75% of the estimated economic useful life of the property?
4. At the beginning of the lease term, does the present value of the minimum lease payments equal at least 90% of the fair value of the leased property to the lessor at the inception of the lease minus the lessor's investment tax credit (ITC), if any? (ITC was extensively available before 1986, but currently is available in only a few situations.)

If none of these tests is satisfied, the lease is classified as an operating lease.

The first test is a question of fact: the lease either does, or does not, transfer ownership.

Although the definition of a bargain purchase option in the second test is unclear, accountants have been applying this criterion since the late 1960s and have managed with it for the most part.

The third criterion is not applicable when the property is well-used at the beginning of the lease term (75% or more of its estimated economic life has expired). In this situation, the economic life rule and the present value rule should be ignored. Economic life (a term also used for tax purposes) is a matter of judgment and is distinguishable from depreciable life.

The fourth classification criterion—the 90% test—is the most complex and most difficult to apply. It is also the test that most often results in a capital lease classification, because a lessor that is essentially providing financing wants to recover, through lease payments, his investment plus an appropriate rate of return. The 90% criterion is purely arbitrary and has been interpreted very narrowly in practice. If this calculation results in a present value of 89.9% at the inception of the lease, the test simply is not satisfied. This test also is not applied to property in the last fourth of its economic life.

From the lessor's standpoint, there are two additional criteria that must be met before a lease can be called a capital lease (L10.104):

1. Collectibility must be reasonably predictable; that is, there cannot be unusual uncertainties about the credit risk.
2. Any unreimbursable costs yet to be incurred by the lessor must be estimable within reasonable limits.

Definitions

Capital Leases Types. A lessor has three possible ways to record capital leases: sales-type lease, direct financing lease, or leveraged lease. Lessees have only two possibilities: capital and operating.

A *sales-type lease* is a capital lease that gives rise to a manufacturer's or dealer's profit for the lessor. This profit is recognized immediately and is measured by the difference between the fair value of the property and its cost to (or other carrying amount by) the lessor.

A *direct financing lease* is a capital lease in which the lessor's cost is the fair value of the property. Typically, a direct financing lease results where the lessor is a financial institution purchasing the property specifically for the lessee's use; that is, the lessee has arranged for the lessor to buy the property.

A *leveraged lease* is generally intended to be a tax deferral vehicle, and has these characteristics (L10.144):

1. It would be a direct financing lease if it were not a leveraged lease.
2. It involves at least three parties: the lessee, a long-term creditor, and a lessor.
3. The long-term creditor provides financing that is nonrecourse as to the general credit of the lessor.
4. The amount of the financing is a significant percentage of the cost of the property. (This percentage is not defined, but is interpreted to mean more than 50%.)
5. The lessor's investment (net of ITC, if any, and benefits of tax deductions) in the property declines after the original investment has been made, often turns negative, and then increases during later years of the lease before it finally is realized.
6. The investment credit, if any, on the leased property is to be deferred and amortized along with the rest of the lease income.

Accounting for leveraged leases is very complex, typically requiring computer assistance for the necessary calculations, and follows two basic premises:

1. Leveraged lease accounting is an after-tax concept and is based only on the lessor's net equity in the property.
2. Income after tax from a leveraged lease should represent a constant rate of return on the lessor's net investment. During those periods when the net investment is below zero, no income is to be recognized.

Lease Accounting Terminology. The definitions in SFAS 13 often necessitate consultation with the FASB staff and have resulted in numerous SFAS 13 modifications and EITF discussions. The criteria used for lease classification rely on definitions of numerous terms, summarized here from the *FASB Current Text* (L10.401–.423).

* *Bargain purchase option* is an option price set so low at the inception of the lease that predictability of exercise is almost certain (L10.401). The definition is cast so that the presence of a bargain should be very obvious; if it is not apparent, there is no bargain.

- *Bargain renewal option* makes renewal rents so inexpensive in relation to fair rental value that exercise is reasonably assured at the inception of the lease (L10.402). Again, if the existence of the bargain is not clear, there is none.

- *Contingent rentals* are lease payments that result from changes occurring subsequent to the inception of the lease in the factors on which the payments are based (L10.404). For example, payments based on machine hours or sales volume are contingent rentals and are excluded from the determination of minimum lease payments. SFAS 29, *Determining Contingent Rentals,* states that even though SFAS 13 excludes contingent rentals from the calculation of minimum lease payments, certain contingent rentals that are tied to published variables such as interest rates or price levels should be included in the calculation.

- *Estimated economic life of leased property* means the period over which the property is expected to be economically beneficial to one or more users for the purpose originally intended (L10.406). This definition is quite broad and has resulted in some interpretation issues. For example, the lessor of a freestanding single-story building may view his property as usable by any number of tenants for any number of purposes, while a food retailer who initially leases that property may view it only as a supermarket. If the intended use follows the lessee's view, the useful life may be relatively short, perhaps no more than 15 or 20 years. On the other hand, if the intended use follows the lessor's view, the property may be usable as long as it stands. Neither of these extreme positions is really justifiable. The use of a retail property after the primary lease term should be considered in light of general retail businesses, not the particular retail business of the lessee.

- *Estimated residual value of leased property* is the expected fair value at the end of the lease term (L10.407). A question originally existed as to whether this value should be figured in dollars at the inception of the lease or in those dollars expected at the end of the lease term after factoring for inflation. This question was answered by SFAS 23, *Inception of the Lease,* which states that the amount "shall not exceed the amount estimated at the inception of the lease." This standard also pointed out that the residual value at lease inception should be based on future expected increases only if the lease agreement provides for escalation of lease payments to cover inflation or some other measure of cost or value increases.

  FIN 19, *Lessee Guarantee of the Residual Value of Leased Property* (L10.417), clarifies issues related principally to leased automobiles and trucks. FIN 19 states that a surcharge for excessive wear and tear or for damages does not constitute a guarantee of residual value. It also states that when the lessee guarantees only a portion of the residual value, the balance is unguaranteed and is not to be included in minimum lease payments for purposes of determining whether the capital lease criteria have been met. This "split residual" guarantee was invented specifically to cope with SFAS 13; previously, it was customary for the lessee to guarantee 100% of the residual realization shortfall. Under the split arrangement, however, the economic risk to the lessor is negligible because the lessee's guarantee covers the top layer of loss.

  TB 79-14, *Upward Adjustment of Guaranteed Residual Values* (L10.514), proscribes upward adjustment of residual values for any reason, including a guarantee.

- *Fair value of the leased property* is the price at which the property is (or could be) sold in an arm's-length sale. Cost is often used as an approximation of fair value if the property is reasonably new (L10.409).

- *Inception of the lease* is the date of the lease agreement or, if earlier, the date of the written commitment specifying the significant terms (L10.410).

SFAS 23, *Inception of the Lease,* redefined inception as it applies to property that must be constructed or manufactured or that otherwise involves a significant delay between negotiation of the lease and availability for the lessee's use. SFAS 23 indicates that the inception of the lease occurs when agreement is reached on its significant terms. This closed a "new construction" loophole, whereby parties would negotiate the terms of a lease based on the expected cost of a building or shopping center to be constructed; by the time the property was finished and ready for occupancy, the lessee could argue convincingly that the property's fair value had increased to an extent that the present value of rentals would now be less than the capitalization trigger of 90% of the new fair value. This had occurred even though the lease might have been negotiated on the basis of the lessor recovering all of his costs.

The SFAS 23 amendment solved one problem but gave rise to another: SFAS 13 requires that minimum lease payments be present valued at the beginning of the lease term (i.e., when occupancy or possession occurs) for purposes of making the 90% test. However, if the present value is taken back to the inception of the lease, that value will be lower, perhaps under 90%. The FASB staff has informally advised inquirers that discounting should not be taken back earlier than the beginning of the lease term.

- *Initial direct costs* are those incremental costs that the lessor has incurred in transactions with unrelated third parties in directly evaluating, negotiating, administering, and closing specific transactions (L10.411). This excludes any selling, general, and administrative expenses (e.g., advertising and occupancy costs). This definition includes costs directly associated with making and closing transactions, and encompasses costs that vary with specific leasing transactions. Further, initial direct costs are reduced for any nonrefundable fees received in connection with the transaction.

  SFAS 17, *Accounting for Leases—Initial Direct Costs* (1977), broadened the definition of initial direct costs to include those costs that are not necessarily incremental to a specific lease but are related to the general level of leasing activity. This was subsequently amended by SFAS 91, *Accounting for Nonrefundable Fees and Costs Associated With Originating or Acquiring Loans and Initial Direct Costs of Leases,* to indicate that lessors must account for initial indirect costs as part of the investment in a direct financing lease (L20.104–.106); the practice of recognizing a portion of the unearned lease income at inception to offset initial direct costs is no longer acceptable. (See also the later section entitled "Bad Debts as Initial Costs.")

- *Interest rate implicit in the lease* is the discount rate that causes the sum of the minimum lease payments and the unguaranteed residual value at the end of the lease term to have a present value equal to the fair value of the property at the beginning of the lease term (minus ITC, if any, that the lessor keeps and expects to realize) (L10.412).

  SFAS 13 (L10.103d) requires that the lessee use the rate implicit in the lease to make the 90% test for capital lease classification if (1) it is practicable for the lessee to determine it and (2) if it is lower than the lessee's incremental borrowing rate. When SFAS 13 was first released, the immediate reaction of lessors was not to disclose the rate and therefore the exact percentage was generally unavailable to lessees, although a very close estimate usually could be made. The FASB staff has consistently stated, however, that the lessee is not required to estimate the interest rate implicit in the lease.

  However, in proposed TB 88-b, Issues Relating to Accounting for Leases (FASB, 1988d), the FASB staff circumscribed this wide latitude on interest rates by requiring that if the terms of the lease are such (e.g., a fixed-price purchase option) that the lessee can compute the maximum implicit interest rate inherent in the lease, he must compute it. If the rate is lower than the lessee's incremental borrowing rate, the computed maximum implicit rate should be used for the 90% test.

• *Lease term* is the noncancellable period of the lease plus (L10.414):

  – Bargain renewal periods,

  – Periods during which failure to renew would cause a *penalty* high enough that renewal is reasonably assured,

  – Periods during which the lessee has guaranteed (directly or indirectly) the lessor's debt on the property,

  – Ordinary renewal periods up to the point of a bargain purchase option, and

  – Periods during which the lessor may enforce renewal.

The bargain purchase option and the lease term can affect each other. For example, suppose that a five-year lease has a five-year renewal option and that if the lessee exercises the renewal, he then has an option to buy the property for a dollar at the end of the tenth year. The dollar price might seem to be a bargain, but the option is available only if the renewal option is exercised. Some view this type of lease arrangement as the existence of a purchase option at the end of five years, because if the lessee concludes at the inception of the lease that he is likely to exercise the renewal option and the purchase option, the term of the lease is really 10 years with a bargain purchase option. If it is plausible that renewal is not reasonably assured, the term of the lease is five years, and there is no bargain purchase option.

This definition also specifies when a lease is *noncancelable*. Included in this category are leases that are cancelable only upon the occurrence of a remote contingency, or with the permission of the lessor, or with the lessee required to enter into a substitute lease with the same lessor, or only on payment of a prohibitive penalty.

Under SFAS 98, *Accounting for Leases: Sale-Leaseback Transactions Involving Real Estate, Sales-Type Leases of Real Estate, Definition of the Lease Term, and Initial Direct Costs of Direct Financing Leases,* the FASB has further defined "lease term" to include all renewal periods during which there will be a loan outstanding from the lessee to the lessor.

• *Lessee's incremental borrowing rate* is the going rate at which the lessee could conceivably borrow the funds to buy the leased property with repayment requirements that extend over the term of the lease (L10.415).

TB 79-12, *Interest Rate Used in Calculating the Present Value of Minimum Lease Payments* (L10.509), resolved the question of whether a lessee can use a secured rate to calculate the present value of minimum lease payments. Under the TB, a secured borrowing rate may be used if determinable, but such a rate must be reasonable, and must be consistent with financing that would have been used.

• *Minimum lease payments* (L10.417) are payments by the lessee required by contract, excluding executory costs (e.g., insurance, taxes, maintenance (L10.408)). The lessee eliminates executory costs in all cases, and if they are not separately stated and the lessee does not know what they are, they are to be estimated. Minimum lease payments include any guarantee by the lessee of the residual value and any amount that the lessee would have to pay if the lease is not renewed. A lessor's right to require the lessee to purchase the property at the end of the lease term for a fixed or determinable amount is treated the same as a lessee guarantee. If the lessee agrees to make good on a deficiency in residual value of the property below a stated amount, that stated amount should be included as part of the minimum lease payments. From the lessor's standpoint, minimum lease payments include all of the above plus any guarantee of the residual value made by a third party not related to the lessor.

• *Penalty* is any requirement, either stated in the lease or external to the lease, that could make the lessee disburse cash, assume a liability, forego an asset or a right, lose an economic benefit, or suffer an economic penalty. In practice, the penalty clause had been interpreted very narrowly. However, in TB 79-11, *Effect of a Penalty on the Term of a Lease* (L10.506–.508), the FASB staff indicated that an economic penalty not specified in the lease agreement could be relevant. For example, if a company signs a five-year lease for a major plant facility and the lease includes a series of five-year renewals, the economic penalty to the lessee of not renewing but instead moving to a new facility might be so high that renewal is essentially assured. This type of economic penalty must be considered at the inception of the lease when its existence is known and the amount would make renewal reasonably assured.

In a further clarification of the intent of this clause, SFAS 98 states that such factors as uniqueness of purpose or location, importance or significance of the property to the lessee, availability of replacement property, and ability or willingness of the lessee to incur moving costs and expenses or allow others (i.e., competitors) to use the property, should be considered in determining whether an economic penalty exists. While there is still room for judgment, the SFAS 98 "laundry list" of what could constitute a penalty will undoubtedly restrict a large measure of what might have been tolerated in the past.

• *Related parties,* for lease transaction purposes, have the ability to exercise significant influence over each other; or a third party can exercise significant influence over both (L10.419).

• *Unguaranteed residual value* of the leased property is all or that portion of the residual that is not guaranteed to the lessor, either by the lessee or by a third party such as a lease broker (L10.422).

Accounting by Lessees

Operating Leases. For the lessee, accounting for an operating lease is relatively straightforward. Rental payments are charged to operations when they are due. The only variation occurs when payments are irregular in amount but not contingent; then the rent must be expensed on an arithmetical straight-line basis without discounting over the term of the lease.

TB 85-3, *Accounting for Operating Leases With Scheduled Rent Increases* (L10.525), emphasizes that scheduled and specified rent increases should be recognized on a straight-line basis over the lease term, unless another basis is more representative of the time pattern in which the leased property is *physically employed.* This TB was issued to nullify the consensus reached by the EITF in Issue 84-12, *Operating Leases With Scheduled Rent Increases*; the Task Force had held that separate accounting for the interest element in operating leases was acceptable in practice. The TB also states that allocation of scheduled rent increases based on such factors as the time value of money, anticipated inflation, or expected future revenues is inappropriate. The FASB thought it had thus clarified the language in SFAS 13, emphasizing that physical use of the leased property provides the only basis for deviating from a straight-line allocation of rents, regardless of scheduled changes in cash payments.

This subject again has been visited in proposed TB 88-b to quash another narrow practice. In some cases the lessee will have possession of the entire property, but will have its rents increased in proportion to the usage actually made of the property on some preagreed basis. For example, an entire warehouse may be under lease, but rents increase as the lessee fills more and more space. The TB takes the position, again, that if the lessee has possession or control, the operating lease rent has to be straight-lined. Only if the lessee gains possession or control over more leased property with the passage of time should the rent incidence pattern be changed to other than straight-line; and even so, the physical use of the additional leased property, not the contracted payment increases, would be the determinant of how the additional rent is spread.

Proposed TB 88-b also has a related charge-pattern twist to deal with: lease incentives in an operating lease. A lessor will often grant an incentive to obtain a lessee; for example, with an up-front cash payment, a sublease of the lessee's present space for the remaining term of the old lease, or a rent-free period at the beginning of the lease. It had been unclear whether the cost to the lessor and the benefit to the lessee should be spread evenly over the new lease, or should be considered in current operations. For example, a current cash payment equal to an amount the lessee must pay to an existing landlord to break a lease might logically be income to the lessee, to offset the charge he has to take for the payment to the prior landlord. Proposed TB 88-b again holds the line: All these incentives are to be spread over the new operating lease term.

While it is economically indisputable that the series of lease payments in an operating lease, whether straight-line or irregular, have a present value to the lessor and the lessee, and thus incorporate a time-value-of-money concept, the FASB decided to remain true to the basis for bifurcation in SFAS 13 between capital and operating leases: If it is not a capital lease, then it is solely the use of property, and cannot be a financing.

Proposed TB 88-b omitted a further variation, which was discussed by the EITF in Issue 88-10, *Costs Associated With Lease Modification or Termination.* The Task Force reached a consensus that remaining rental costs on a vacated operating leasehold, along with related leasehold improvements, should be expensed currently, net of estimated sublease costs, if any. If the lease is terminated, the cost of doing so should also be expensed. These costs should not be carried over to the lease for replacement facilities. The EITF did not reach a consensus on whether moving costs and other charges relating to the new lease should be deferred, but felt that predominant practice was to charge off moving costs as incurred.

Capital Leases. Capital lease accounting by the lessee is considerably more complex than operating lease accounting. The lessee records the present value of the minimum lease payments (calculated when making the 90% test under the fourth classification rule), classifying this amount as an asset in property, plant, and equipment and as a liability under long-term debt.

If the discounted present value exceeds fair market value, only the fair market value is recorded in the accounts, and the discount rate for the liability is increased to compensate. As rental payments are made, a portion of each payment is applied against the obligation and a portion is charged as interest expense. The amount to be charged as interest is the amount determined by applying to the remaining unpaid liability the discount rate used in establishing the asset and liability accounts. The asset is depreciated over its estimated useful life, or is amortized over the term of the lease (if the lease term is shorter or if the property reverts to the lessor at the end of the lease term).

Accounting by Lessors

Operating Leases. From the lessor's standpoint, accounting for an operating lease is straightforward. As the rents are earned, they are credited to income. The property under lease is part of property and equipment and the cost less its estimated residual or salvage value is depreciated over its estimated useful life. If the rental payments are irregular, the total lease payments should be averaged over the period of the lease, with rentals receivable or payable temporarily holding differences from a straight-line pattern (L10.525). This is the same treatment required for lessees, as discussed earlier.

Sales-Type Capital Leases. A sales-type lease is one in which fair market value exceeds the cost of sales, indicating that a profit is earned on the sale. The lessor's accounting for sales-type leases involves calculating these elements:

- *Gross investment in the lease*—minimum rentals receivable (excluding executory costs) plus the unguaranteed residual value.
- *Sales price*—present value of the minimum lease payments (less executory costs included therein) discounted at lessor's interest rate implicit in the lease.
- *Cost of sales*—carrying amount of the property (usually cost), plus net initial direct costs, minus present value (at the implicit interest rate) of the unguaranteed residual.
- *Unearned income*—gross investment in the lease minus the sum of the present value (at the implicit interest rate) of the minimum lease payments and the unguaranteed residual value.

An example of accounting for a sales-type lease transaction is shown in Figure 19.1. For balance sheet presentation, note that (1) unearned income is classified as an offset to the gross investment in the lease and (2) the net amount is carried like a receivable. Because most leasing companies do not use classified balance sheets, the usual current/noncurrent classification criteria are generally inapplicable. The unearned income is amortized by the interest method, using the rate at which the present values were discounted. Initial direct costs are charged immediately to cost of sales.

The estimated residual value is reviewed at least annually, and if the new estimate is lower than the recorded residual value, an immediate write-down is required, unless the decline is deemed temporary. The write-down is calculated by present-valuing the new residual estimate at the interest rate implicit in the lease and comparing that to the carrying amount of the residual (which will have been increased since the beginning of the lease by accretion of the present-valuation discount). Write-ups of residual value are not permitted, regardless of the strength of the evidence supporting a higher value.

SFAS 26, *Profit Recognition of Sales-Type Leases of Real Estate* (1979), was issued to conform real estate lease accounting to the requirements of SFAS 66, *Accounting for Sales of Real Estate* (Re1). SFAS 13 sanctioned recognition of profit on sales of real estate even though the buyer made no down payments, as long as the parties structured the transaction in the form of a sales-type lease. SFAS 26, however, prohibited profit recognition unless the buyer, at the inception of the lease, has made an investment adequate to assure that he is economically bound to the acquisition. Per-

Assumptions

Minimum rental payments — gross	$5,400	
— present value	4,517	
Unguaranteed residual — gross	650	
— present value	483	
Equipment fair value	5,000	
Equipment cost	4,750	
Initial costs	100	

Computations

Sales, equal to present value of minimum rental payments and guaranteed residual		$4,517
Cost of sales		
Equipment cost	$4,750	
Less present value of unguaranteed residual	(483)	
Plus initial direct costs	100	4,367
Gross margin		$ 150
Net investment in sales-type lease, composed of:		
Minimum rental payments		$5,400
Plus residual		650
Gross investment		6,050
Less unearned income		(1,050)
Net investment		$5,000

FIG. 19.1   Example of Lessor Accounting for a Sales-Type Lease

centages of investments deemed adequate and therefore required are given in SFAS 66 (Rel.152).

SFAS 26 was superseded by SFAS 98, issued in mid-1988 to rectify inconsistencies that continued to occur in the application of lease accounting provisions to real estate sales-type leases and sale-leaseback transactions. (See the section entitled "Sale-Leaseback Transactions" later in this chapter for further discussion.)

Direct Financing Leases. For a direct financing lease, the lessor's accounting is similar to the foregoing treatment of a sales-type lease, with a few exceptions. First, there is no immediate profit to be recognized, so there are no entries for sales or cost of sales. Second, unearned income is calculated simply as the difference between gross investment in the lease and the carrying value of the leased property, which is usually its cost. Third, initial direct costs are capitalized separately, similar to loan-granting expenses. An example of accounting for a typical direct financing lease transaction is shown in Figure 19.2.

The unearned income of $1,050 in Figures 19.1 and 19.2 is amortized into earned income using the interest method; that is, the scheduled rental payments are deemed to consist of both principal and interest, with the interest factor ascertained by determining the rate that, when applied against the periodic unpaid balance of the receivable, will yield $1,050 over the duration of the scheduled payments. The classification of gross investment and unearned income, the amortization method, and the requirement for at least annual review of the residual value of a direct financing lease are the same as the methods used for sales-type leases.

Assumptions

Minimum rental payments — gross	$5,400
Unguaranteed residual — gross	650
Equipment cost and fair value	5,000
Initial direct costs	100

Computations

Net investment in direct financing lease, composed of:	
Minimum rental payments	$5,400
Plus residual	650
Unamortized initial direct costs	100
Less unearned income	(1,050)
Net investment	$5,100

FIG. 19.2   Example of Lessor Accounting for a Direct Financing Lease

Under both sales-type leases and direct financing leases, any contingent rentals are credited to revenue as they are earned. For example, contingent rentals might relate to levels of sales (for a retail store) or excess mileage (for an automobile or truck).

Leveraged Leases. A leveraged lease must have three parties: a lessor, a lessee, and a lender. The lender's funding provides significant leverage for the lessor.

The initial step in accounting for a leveraged lease is to calculate the cash flows over the term of the lease. These cash flows include the income tax effects of tax deductions to the lessor,[1] the investment credit (if any), the lessor's initial investment in the property, rental receipts net of debt service, and proceeds estimated to be obtained from the sale of the residual. The cumulative net cash inflow is the total income from the lease; this amount is allocated to periodic income in proportion to the lessor's *positive net investment* in the lease.

Once cash flows are scheduled, the rate to be used to allocate income must be calculated; if possible, a computer should be used. The rate to be found is the rate that, when applied to the net investment in the years in which that net investment is positive, will exactly distribute the net income to only those positive years. The rate is determined through trial and error, using successive iterations within the computer. No income is allocated to current profit and loss during periods when the net investment is negative.

Nonrecourse debt financing is not recorded as such in the balance sheet, but is offset against the leased asset. The investment in the leased asset thus consists of only the excess of the present value of rental payments and estimated residual value over the present value of debt service requirements. The unearned income credit will consist of the investment tax credit (if any) and the *pretax* component of the total income.

---

[1] TB 79-16 (Revised), *Effect of a Change in Income Tax Rate on the Accounting for Leveraged Leases* (L10.521–.524), states that, because of the importance of the lessor's tax rate in accounting for leveraged leases, the income effect of a change in the tax rate should be recognized in the accounting period in which the change has been enacted.

Appendix E of SFAS 13 (L10.154, Exhibits 154A to 154I) presents a detailed example of the steps required to account for a leveraged lease. That example is indispensable to anyone who has to deal with a leveraged lease. Figure 19.3 shows the cash flow analysis of a leveraged lease taken from Exhibit 154B. Figure 19.4 illustrates the allocation of the gross income over the periods of positive investment, taken from Exhibit 154C. While the assumptions contained in Exhibit 154A have been omitted (and the example is dated because of the use of a 50.4% income tax rate and an investment tax credit) the mechanical complexities of leveraged lease accounting should readily be apparent.

In Issue 85-16B, *Leveraged Leases: Delayed Equity Contributions by Lessors,* the EITF addressed leases that are structured as leveraged leases but that provide for net cash rental payments by the lessee to begin one or two years after lease inception. The lease (or a separate agreement) obligates the lessor to contribute additional funds that are used to service the nonrecourse debt during the period before the lessee begins to make lease payments. The lessor's obligation to contribute these additional funds, which are referred to as "delayed equity" investments in the lease, is a recourse obligation. The principal question is whether the lessor's delayed equity investment, which is recourse debt to the lessor, should preclude accounting for such leases as leveraged leases because SFAS 13 (L10.144c) mandates that debt shall be nonrecourse. If leveraged lease accounting is considered appropriate, a secondary issue is whether the lessor's obligation to make the delayed equity investment should be recorded as a liability at the inception of the lease.

The EITF reached a consensus that the type of recourse debt resulting from the delayed equity investment does not contradict the notion of nonrecourse under SFAS 13, and therefore does not preclude leveraged lease accounting as long as all the other requirements of leveraged lease accounting are met. The Task Force also agreed that the lessor's related obligation should be recorded as a liability at present value at the inception of the lease. This recognition of the liability increases the lessor's net investment on which the lessor bases its pattern of income recognition. It was noted that while the increase to the net investment results in an acceleration in the income recognition pattern, this tends to be offset by the interest expense on the lessor's liability.

The EITF conclusion was short-lived, however. Proposed TB 88-b simply says that the lease has to be treated as a direct financing lease because the leveraged lease criteria have been breached.

In Issue 86-43, *Effect of a Change in Tax Law or Rates on Leveraged Leases,* the EITF discussed the impact of the Tax Reform Act of 1986 (TRA 1986) on accounting by lessors under leveraged leases. The Task Force reached a consensus that all components of a leveraged lease should be recalculated from inception of the lease based on the revised after-tax cash flows arising from the revised tax rates for 1987 and future years. The difference between income previously recorded and the recalculated amount would be charged or credited to income of the current year; and the recalculated allocation of income would be used for future periods.

In proposed TB 88-b, the FASB staff addresses the question of whether property can be leverage-leased if the lessor has had it around for a while. The response is convoluted: If the book value exactly equals the fair value in the marketplace, the answer is yes; however, the text would make it appear that there is no case in which this rare coincidence could ever happen. Therefore leveraged lease treatment is not permitted — thereby disallowing the favored debt offset treatment for leveraged leases.

Cash Flow Analysis by Years

Year	Gross lease rentals and residual value (1)	Depreciation (for income tax purposes) (2)	Loan interest payments (3)	Taxable Income (loss) (col. 1-2-3) (4)	Income tax credits (charges) (col. 4 × 50.4%) (5)	Loan principal payments (6)	Investment tax credit realized (7)	Annual cash flow (col. 1-3 +5-6+7) (8)	Cumulative cash flow (9)
Initial investment	—	—	—	—	—	—	—	$(400,000)	$(400,000)
1	$90,000	$142,857	$54,000	$(106,857)	$53,856	$20,435	$100,000	169,421	(230,579)
2	90,000	244,898	52,161	(207,059)	104,358	22,274	—	119,923	(110,656)
3	90,000	187,075	50,156	(147,231)	74,204	24,729	—	89,769	(20,887)
4	90,000	153,061	47,971	(111,032)	55,960	26,464	—	71,525	50,638
5	90,000	119,048	45,589	(74,637)	37,617	28,846	—	53,182	103,820
6	90,000	53,061	42,993	(6,054)	3,051	31,442	—	18,616	122,436
7	90,000	—	40,163	49,837	(25,118)	34,272	—	(9,553)	112,883
8	90,000	—	37,079	52,921	(26,672)	37,357	—	(11,108)	101,775
9	90,000	—	33,717	56,283	(28,367)	40,719	—	(12,803)	88,972
10	90,000	—	30,052	59,948	(30,214)	44,383	—	(14,649)	74,323
11	90,000	—	26,058	63,942	(32,227)	48,378	—	(16,663)	57,660
12	90,000	—	21,704	68,296	(34,421)	52,732	—	(18,857)	38,803
13	90,000	—	16,957	73,043	(36,813)	57,478	—	(21,248)	17,555
14	90,000	—	11,785	78,215	(39,420)	62,651	—	(23,856)	(6,301)
15	90,000	—	6,145	83,855	(42,263)	68,290	—	(26,698)	(32,999)
16	200,000	100,000	—	100,000	(50,400)	—	—	149,600	116,601
Totals	$1,550,000	$1,000,000	$516,530	$ 33,470	$(16,869)	$600,000	$100,000	$ 116,601	

FIG. 19.3 Cash Flow Analysis of a Leveraged Lease

Source: SFAS 13 (L10.154, Exhibit 154B).

Allocation of Annual Cash Flow to Investment and Income

	1	2	3	4	5	6	7
			Annual Cash Flow		Components of Income(b)		
Year	Lessor's net investment at beginning of year	Total (from Exhibit 154B, col. 8)	Allocated to Investment	Allocated to Income(a)	Pretax Income	Tax effect of pretax income	Investment tax credit
1	$400,000	$169,421	$134,833	$34,588	$9,929	$(5,004)	$29,663
2	265,167	119,923	96,994	22,929	6,582	(3,317)	19,664
3	168,173	89,769	75,227	14,542	4,174	(2,104)	12,472
4	92,946	71,525	63,488	8,037	2,307	(1,163)	6,893
5	29,458	53,182	50,635	2,547	731	(368)	2,184
6	(21,177)	18,616	18,616	—	—	—	—
7	(39,793)	(9,553)	(9,553)	—	—	—	—
8	(30,240)	(11,108)	(11,108)	—	—	—	—
9	(19,132)	(12,803)	(12,803)	—	—	—	—
10	(6,329)	(14,649)	(14,649)	—	—	—	—
11	8,320	(16,663)	(17,382)	719	206	(104)	617
12	25,702	(18,857)	(21,079)	2,222	637	(321)	1,906
13	46,781	(21,248)	(25,293)	4,045	1,161	(585)	3,469
14	72,074	(23,856)	(30,088)	6,232	1,789	(902)	5,345
15	102,162	(26,698)	(35,532)	8,834	2,536	(1,278)	7,576
16	137,694	149,600	137,694	11,906	3,418	(1,723)	10,211
Totals		$516,601	$400,000	$116,601	$33,470	$(16,869)	$100,000

(a) Lease income is recognized as 8.647 percent of the unrecovered investment at the beginning of each year in which the net investment is positive. The rate is that rate which when applied to the net investment in the years in which the net investment is positive will distribute the net income (net cash flow) to those years. The rate for allocation used in this exhibit is calculated by a trial and error process. The allocation is calculated based upon an initial estimate of the rate as a starting point. If the total thus allocated to income (column 4) differs under the estimated rate from the net cash flow (Exhibit 154B, column 8) the estimated rate is increased or decreased, as appropriate, to derive a revised allocation. This process is repeated until a rate is selected which develops a total amount allocated to income that is precisely equal to the net cash flow. As a practical matter, a computer program is used to calculate Exhibit 154C under successive iterations until the correct rate is determined.

(b) Each component is allocated among the years of positive net investment in proportion to the allocation of net income in column 4.

FIG. 19.4 Allocation of Gross Income on a Leveraged Lease

Source: SFAS 13 (L10.154, Exhibit 154C).

Financial Statement Disclosures

SFAS 13 and its progeny specify in great detail the required disclosures to be made about leases in the financial statements or footnotes. The overall objective is to present a description of leasing activities, the flow of lease income or expense, and the future cash flows related to leasing.

A brief summary of disclosure requirements is given in the following sections.

Lessees. A general description of leasing arrangements is required, including the basis for contingent rental payments, renewal or purchase options and escalation clauses, and any restrictions that may be imposed on corporate actions (e.g., on dividends, new debt, or additional leases) (L10.112d). In addition, numerous specific disclosures are required for capital and operating leases as follows (L10.112a–c):

For capital leases:

• Gross amount of assets capitalized, by major classes of assets (e.g., land, buildings, equipment).
• Aggregate future minimum lease payments.
• Minimum lease payments for each of the next five years.
• Executory costs and imputed interest, each as included in the two preceding disclosures.
• Minimum sublease rentals receivable.
• Contingent rents incurred, as expensed in the income statements presented.
• Total assets recorded under capital leases, and the accumulated amortization thereon.
• Amortization expense, unless it is, and is stated to be, included in depreciation expense.
• Obligations under capital leases.

For operating leases written for longer than a year:

• Aggregate future minimum lease payments.
• Minimum lease payments for each of the next five years.
• Minimum sublease rentals receivable.

For all operating leases, the total rental expense included in income statements presented, classified into minimum rents, contingent rents, and sublease rentals, must be disclosed.

Lessors. A general description of leasing arrangements is required, with additional specific disclosures for sales-type and direct financing leases, as follows (L10.119a):

• Components of net investment:
  – Future minimum lease payments receivable.
  – Executory costs, including profit, included in lease receivables.
  – Accumulated allowance for uncollectible lease receivables.
  – Unguaranteed residual values.
  – Unearned income.

- Minimum lease payments for each of the next five years.
- Contingent rentals earned in each income statement presented.

For operating leases, these items must be disclosed (L10.119b):

- Asset and accumulated depreciation amount by major classes.
- Minimum future rentals in the aggregate and for each of the next five years.
- Contingent rentals earned in each income statement presented.

For leveraged leases, the lessor must provide the same information as is provided for other capital leases with the further proviso that the deferred income taxes shall be separated from the net investment and classified in deferred taxes in the balance sheet; in the income statement or notes, the pretax income, the tax effects, and the ITC (if any) should all be separately shown (L10.149).

Real Estate Leases

The most complex leases covered by SFAS 13 generally are those involving real estate (L10.120–.124). Real estate leases can involve huge sums of money, particularly in industries such as retailing and banking. SFAS 13 observes that if ownership of land (which is perpetual and therefore does not depreciate) does not pass to the lessee either directly or through a bargain purchase option, a land lease is always an operating lease. If a lease covers both *a building and the land* it occupies, it should be treated as two leases, one for the land and another for the building, based on the relative fair values of each. However, if the land element of the lease is small (i.e., less than 25% of the total value of the property), the total package is treated as a building lease and classified accordingly. If a real estate lease also involves *personal property,* that element must be carved out and treated as a separate lease regardless of its significance.

Covered in a later section entitled "Sale-Leaseback Transactions" are the FASB's difficulties with real estate included in such transactions.

A common situation in real estate leases is the lease of only *part of a building.* For example, a tenant may occupy a suite of offices, or a storeroom in a shopping center. The parties to the lease may not be able to determine the fair value of the property under lease; and the lessor may not be able to determine the cost. In these circumstances, the lessee is to look to the estimated useful life of the property, and if the lease covers 75% or more thereof, it is treated as a capital lease by the lessee. The lessor, however, classifies these leases as operating leases regardless of their term.

The FASB has found it necessary to interpret the part-of-a-building provisions of SFAS 13, as described in the following sections.

Government Property Leases. FIN 23, *Leases of Certain Property Owned by a Governmental Unit or Authority* (L10.124, n. 27), clarifies a narrow question caused by the declaration in SFAS 13 that

> special provisions [are] normally present in leases involving terminal space and other airport facilities owned by a governmental unit or authority, [and] the economic life ... is essentially indeterminate. Likewise, concept of fair value is not applicable to such leases ... [and] they shall be classified as operating leases. (L10.124)

This had been interpreted in practice to mean that all such leases were automatically operating leases. FIN 23 established a series of rules all of which must be met if a lease is to be eligible for automatic classification as an operating lease.

Partial-Building Leases. FIN 24, *Leases Involving Only Part of a Building* (L10.124, n. 26), resolves another wording problem by providing guidance on how to calculate the fair value of part of a building. SFAS 13 provides that if a lease covers only part of a building and the fair value of the premises is not *objectively determinable,* the lessee should look only to the useful life in order to classify the lease. This practice led retailers (particularly large retailers operating in numerous shopping centers) to conclude that their leases had to be operating leases. FIN 24 reaffirms that it is possible to establish fair value even if there are no sales of similar property; but it has had very little practical impact because it provides minimal guidance on how fair value may be established.

Related Party Leases

SFAS 13 states that in instances "where it is clear that the terms of the transaction have been significantly affected by the fact that the lessee and lessor are related," the treatment of the lease is to be altered to follow its substance rather than its form (L10.125). Otherwise, the lease classification is not affected, and follows the rules applicable to unrelated party leases.

Accounting for arm's-length equivalence can be a difficult process. In many instances, the owner of a company will buy property and lease it to his company on a short-term basis. If the company and the auditor conclude that similar property would not be available for lease from unrelated lessors on a short-term basis or that the company would not risk being deprived of the property by leasing from a person who was not also the company's owner, appropriate accounting may require altering the term of the lease to make it reasonable. One way to alter the term of the lease is to assume that the lease terms have been extended so that the present-valued rents equal the owner's cost.

In another commonly encountered situation, the owner of a company buys property and leases it to the company at a rental higher than the market rate. If the lease is an operating lease, rent expense could be overstated, and some other expense, or dividends, could be understated. If it is a capital lease, the problem is even more complex. The leased asset cannot be capitalized at more than fair value, which presumably is the cost to the owner, and the liability cannot be discounted at more than the incremental borrowing rate of the company. Therefore these leases should be altered to achieve a proper accounting.

Because there may be a strong resistance to such alterations, it may be preferable to adopt the technique of issuing combined financial statements, that is, combining the company's accounts with the leasing operation of the company's owners. This combination provides a relatively simple solution to a vexing problem, and it also makes sense because the combined financial statements then account for the economic impact of the company's use of the property.

SFAS 13 also retains a previous APB requirement that subsidiaries must be consolidated if their principal activity is to lease property to the parent or other affiliates (L10.127).

Sale-Leaseback Transactions

The sale and leaseback technique has become a very important financing vehicle for many companies. Often these arrangements are facilitated by lease brokers or underwriters whose role – and the accounting problems they generate – is discussed later in this chapter under "Leasebrokers."

The lease portion of a sale-leaseback transaction is treated the same as any other lease for accounting and classification purposes. However, SFAS 13 (L10.128) states that because the sale portion of the transaction cannot be separated from the lease portion, any gain or loss on the sale portion should be deferred and amortized to income, using the straight-line method if the lease is an operating lease, or in tandem with the depreciation or amortization of the leased asset if the lease is a capital lease (L10.129). Nonetheless, when the fair value of the asset is demonstrably less than its carrying value at the time of the sale and leaseback, the transaction is considered complete, and the loss is recognized currently.

Real Estate. The sale-leaseback of real estate presents special problems. SFAS 13 attempted to harmonize transactions that also invoke SFAS 66, *Accounting for Sales of Real Estate* (Re1), but these attempts actually created more questions. SFAS 26, *Profit Recognition on Sales-Type Leases of Real Estate*, tried to respond to these questions, but it left too many unanswered questions, resulting in the EITF dealing with numerous conflicts among SFAS 13, SFAS 28, and SFAS 66. In particular, in the discussion of EITF Issue 84-37, *Sale-Leaseback Transaction with Repurchase Option,* the SEC Observer stated his concern that public companies were not always recording sale and leaseback transactions based on their substance. Further, in the discussion of Issue 86-17, *Deferred Profit on Sale-Leaseback Transaction With Lessee Guarantee of Residual Value,* he reiterated his concern that sales recognition was often not proper, and that the staff would deal with transactions on a case-by-case basis.

In January 1987, the FASB considered and rejected staff recommendation to place this subject on its agenda. Instead, the staff was directed to develop a TB addressing sale-leaseback issues. However, when the FASB considered a staff draft of the proposed TB, they rejected it and decided to place a project addressing sale-leaseback transactions onto the formal FASB agenda.

SFAS 98, *Accounting for Leases: Sale-Leaseback Transactions Involving Real Estate, Sales-Type Leases of Real Estate, Definition of the Lease Term, and Initial Direct Costs of Direct Financing Leases* (L10.130A–.130M), issued in mid-1988, declares that in all real estate transactions SFAS 66 is the controlling document; thus certain technical amendments to SFAS 13 and 66 were required, and SFAS 26 and TB 79-11 had to be rescinded.

SFAS 98 appears to resolve the diversity in practice by categorically requiring *all* real estate sale-leaseback transactions to meet the requirements of SFAS 66 for sales recognition. This statement further indicates that *any* continuing involvement, in addition to the leaseback, would preclude sales recognition. Accordingly, in real estate sale-leaseback transactions:

1. The seller-lessee must occupy the property from the inception of the lease.

2. The buyer-lessor must meet the initial and continuing investment tests of SFAS 66 (R10.114–.115).

3. The agreements must transfer *all* the risks and rewards of ownership. This can be demonstrated by the absence of continuing involvement as defined in SFAS 98 and in SFAS 66 (R10.128–.146).

If the transaction does not qualify as a sale, it would be accounted for as a financing, or under the deposit method described in SFAS 66. These mandated conditions have been made more stringent than those in either of the two basic statements (SFAS 13 and SFAS 66), because the FASB felt that under a very literal reading of SFAS 66, sale-leaseback transactions involving real estate should have been precluded.

SFAS 98 responds to SEC concerns about "abuses" in which ordinary financings have been given off-balance sheet treatment under sale-leaseback rules as interpreted in practice to date. Of particular import are the requirements relating to continuing involvement and economic penalty: the first is categorical, that is, absolutely no continuing involvement is permitted; and the second is still left to be judged subjectively, but with more specification.

Now it is more important than ever that the terms and details of any real estate sale-leaseback transaction be scrutinized in view of these complex requirements.

Nonrecourse Financing. In Issue 87-07, *Sale of an Asset Subject to a Lease and Nonrecourse Financing: "Wrap Lease Transactions,"* the EITF dealt with transactions in which a lessor arranges nonrecourse financing on a lease and later sells the underlying asset, subject to the lease and nonrecourse financing, to the lessee under a sale-leaseback arrangement. These transactions are commonly called wrap leases.

Accounting practice has varied. Some companies have recorded these transactions as in-substance sales of the residual value and tax benefits associated with the leased asset. Others have treated them simply as sales-leasebacks, thereby deferring and amortizing income under SFAS 13 provisions. The EITF contemplated the income recognition and balance sheet implications of this transaction, but no consensus was reached.

Shortly before the EITF discussion, the SEC issued SAB 70 on accounting for non-recourse debt collateralized by lease receivables and/or leased assets (Topic 5.R). This SAB expressed the staff's views on accounting and balance sheet presentation, stating that a registrant who borrows on a nonrecourse basis and assigns to the lender a security interest in lease receivables and/or the related leased assets should not remove the lease receivables and non-recourse debt from the balance sheet either by accounting for this transaction as a sale or assignment of the lease receivables *or* by offsetting the lease receivables and non-recourse debt. The staff believes that under existing GAAP, this type of transaction should be accounted for as a borrowing and, as such, the resulting debt should be reflected in the registrant's balance sheet.

Under SFAS 13 (as amended by SFAS 77), "the sale or assignment of a lease or property subject to a lease accounted for as a sales-type or direct financing lease shall not negate the original accounting treatment accorded the lease" and "any profit or loss on the sale or assignment shall be recognized at the time of the transaction" (L10.116). However, SAB 70 declares that the FASB *intended* the term "assignment" as used in SFAS 13 to represent the transfer from one party to another of a *direct* interest in a contractual right or property, and not a *security* interest. Therefore, non-recourse borrowing arrangements that involve the assignment of a security interest in a lease and/or property subject to lease do not result in recognition as if a sale had occurred.

Further, the accounting literature generally does not allow non-recourse debt and lease receivables and/or the related leased assets to be offset in the balance sheet. This has been affirmed by the staff of the FASB in TB 86-2, *Accounting for an Interest in the Residual Value of a Leased Asset* (L10.537), which was issued in response to the EITF's failure to reach a consensus on Issue 84-25, *Offsetting Nonrecourse Debt With Sales-Type or Direct Financing Lease Receivables*; and it has been reaffirmed in proposed TB 88-a, *Definition of a Right of Setoff* (FASB, 1988b).

Minor Leasebacks. SFAS 28, *Accounting for Sales With Leasebacks* (L10.129a–c), provides that if a leaseback is minor, the profit on sale may be recognized. Even if a major part is leased back, profit can be recognized to the extent it exceeds the present value of the minimum leaseback payments. SFAS 13 had mandated complete deferral of sales profit, which could result in the ludicrous situation of negative future rental expense.

Subleases

SFAS 13 provisions for sublease accounting (L10.131) were initially taken to imply that future losses on lease-sublease transactions need not be currently recognized. For example, if a retailer were to close a store and sublease the premises for an amount short of the rent payable on the primary lease, he would often not record a loss provision upon entering into the sublease. FIN 27, *Accounting for a Loss on a Sublease* (L10.135), was issued in 1978 to correct that impression and states that the FASB does not intend to prohibit timely recognition of a loss on a sublease. The interpretation did not provide much guidance, and therefore debates continued about whether a sublease shortfall loss needed to be accrued.

In another effort, TB 79-15, *Accounting for Loss on a Sublease not Involving the Disposal of a Segment* (L10.518), indicates that the general principles of loss recognition are applicable to leasing transactions, even though this is not stated in SFAS 13. Thus, if a loss on a sublease (operating or direct financing) is expected, TB 79-15 states that it should be recognized currently.

As a rule of thumb, a sublease of property no longer usable in the business should result in loss accrual, and property set aside for future use through short-term subleases should not require loss accrual.

Other Amendments and Interpretations

SFAS 13 reigns as undisputed champion in the sheer volume of amendments, official interpretations, and TBs generated by the FASB and its staff; and it has warranted much EITF and SEC attention as well. The following sections provide a brief synopsis of matters not related to specific subjects discussed to this point.

Leases With Tax-Exempt Debt. SFAS 22, *Changes in the Provisions of Lease Agreements Resulting From Refundings of Tax-Exempt Debt* (L10.110, n. 12), deals with the narrow issue of advance refunding of municipal bonds underlying leased property. Often a municipal authority acts as a financing conduit for a company that wants to build a factory or other facility; or the authority may own a facility that it leases to the company.

Typically, these "see-through" leases are clearly tied to the outstanding bonds: the rent exactly equals the required debt service. When the bonds are paid the rent ceases, and the property belongs to the company. Prior to SFAS 13, these arrangements were almost universally accounted for by the company as property ownership, with a liability for the bonded debt. Under SFAS 13, these arrangements are accounted for as capital leases.

A problem arose in applying an SFAS 13 requirement that if a capital lease is changed so that the amount of rents changes, the asset and liability should be recalculated using the original interest rate. This conflicted with APB 26, *Early Extinguishment of Debt* (D14.103), which says that where debt is extinguished before its maturity, any difference between the extinguishment price and the carrying amount of the debt is current profit or loss. Because there is no substantive difference between a see-through lease by an industrial development authority and the direct debt of the company, SFAS 22 treats them the same; it requires recognition of profit or loss at the time of the advance refunding.

Renewals or Extensions. SFAS 27, *Classification of Renewals or Extensions of Existing Sales-Type or Direct Financing Leases* (L10.113f), permits classification of these renewals or extensions as sales-type leases if they meet the criteria in SFAS 13. Previously, sales-type classification and the attendant profit were precluded the second time around.

Sales of Lease Receivables or Leased Property. SFAS 77, *Reporting by Transferors for Transfers of Receivables With Recourse* (R20), applies the provisions of SFAS 77 to sales, or assignments with recourse, of capital leases or property subject to capital leases. SFAS 77 requires the recognition of profit or loss currently. Previously, the profit or loss on such transfers was deferred and recognized over the lease term.

Under SFAS 13, the sale by a lessor of property subject to an operating lease is not to be treated as a sale if the seller retains substantial risks of ownership in the leased property (L10.117–.118). The risks recited are rather straightforward, with one exception: If the seller provides a remarketing agreement to the buyer (that is, when the property comes off lease, the seller will endeavor to release or sell the property now owned by the buyer), this will not preclude sale treatment if the buyer will pay a reasonable fee for the remarketing service, and the seller is not required to give priority to the buyer's property over his own.

The meaning of "priority" had been variously interpreted in practice. In proposed TB 88-b, the FASB staff points out that if any of the buyer's property can be remarketed prior to the seller first remarketing all of his own off-lease property, the remarketing provision violates SFAS 13, and the transaction with the "buyer" must be treated as a borrowing by the lessor.

Leases Acquired in a Business Combination. FIN 21, *Accounting for Leases in a Business Combination* (L10.137–.142), states that leases acquired in a purchase business combination retain their original classification under SFAS 13. Thus, they are regarded as capital leases or operating leases based on the factors present at the inception of the lease. Even though the leases are fair valued as part of the purchase price allocation, they are not retested as new leases against the classification rules at the date of the business combination.

Leased Asset Purchased by Lessee. FIN 26, *Accounting for Purchase of a Leased Asset by the Lessee During the Term of the Lease* (L10.109, n. 11), requires that any difference between the purchase price and the remaining liability on the lease obligation be an adjustment of the basis of the asset.

Fiscal Funding Clause. TB 79-10, *Fiscal Funding Clauses in Lease Agreements* (L10.501), was issued to resolve questions regarding a fiscal funding clause of a governmental agency. In short, a fiscal funding clause is a provision in a lease agreement signed by a state or local government, as lessee, that allows the lessee to abrogate the lease later in its term if the legislature or other governing body does not appropriate funds for the continued lease payments. The question arose as to whether these clauses precluded capital lease classification by lessors. The FASB concluded that the probability of the lease being canceled must be assessed, and if remote, the capital lease classification is not affected.

Current Value Financial Statements. TB 79-13, *Applicability of FASB Statement No. 13 to Current Value Financial Statements* (L10.512), indicates that the SFAS criteria may well be applicable in the preparation of current value financial statements. This was aimed at a lessor's lease receivables, and at the time of issuance there was some experimentation with current value financial statements.

Interest in a Residual. TB 86-2, *Accounting for an Interest in the Residual Value of a Leased Asset* (L10.528–.529), discusses whether an increase (by accretion over the remaining lease term) in the value of a residual to its estimated final value should be allowed by a company that has acquired an interest in that residual, or by a lessor who has retained an interest in the residual after selling the related minimum lease rental payments.

The accounting for an interest in the residual value of a leased asset has varied in practice. Some companies have recorded the lease residual at its acquisition cost (or in the case of the lessor who retains an interest in the residual value of a leased asset, at its carrying amount at the date of the sale of the related lease) and have carried it at that amount until ultimate disposition. Others have accreted the carrying amount of the lease residual to its estimated value over the remaining term of the related lease.

Prior to the issuance of TB 86-2, the EITF addressed this question in Issue 85-32, *Purchased Lease Residuals,* but failed to reach a consensus except for those instances in which a creditworthy guarantee is present. In such cases, the EITF (and the SEC Observer) would have allowed an enterprise to recognize increases in the residual value of a leased asset over the remaining lease term, up to the guaranteed amount. TB 86-2 reversed the EITF conclusion and went even further:

* It prohibits an enterprise from increasing the value of an acquired or retained interest in the residual value of a leased asset to its estimated value over the remaining lease term, even if the residual interest is guaranteed.

* It applies to a residual received by a leasebroker as a fee for services rendered (thereby nullifying previously permitted practice for leasebrokers).

* It permits offsetting of the lease receivable with non-recourse debt only in those circumstances in which a legal right of setoff exists or when, at the inception of the lease, the lease meets all of the characteristics of, and is appropriately classified as, a leveraged lease. Otherwise, the guidance provided in paragraph 7 of APB 10, *Omnibus Opinion 1966: Offsetting Securities Against Taxes Payable* (I28) (as now about to be augmented by proposed TB 88-a, *Definition of Right of Setoff*), should be applied.

Tax Indemnifications. When Issue 86-33, *Tax Indemnifications in Lease Agreements,* was considered in October 1986, the EITF addressed accounting for leases that had anticipated the tax law changes imposed by the Tax Reform Act of 1986. The EITF discussed the appropriate accounting by a lessor and lessee for leases containing clauses that would indemnify lessors, on an after-tax basis, for the loss of tax benefits.

The EITF reached a consensus that although indemnification payments may appear to be contingent rents under SFAS 13, they are not the type normally expected under contingent rent provisions. Further, because of the close association of the payments to specific tax law provisions, the payments should be accounted for in a manner that recognizes this association; and the original lease classification should not be affected.

The EITF concluded that lessors receiving indemnification payments should allocate the payments into two parts: ITC lost and all other tax effects. The ITC portion should be accounted for following the lessor's usual accounting policy for ITC (i.e., recognized in the income statement in the same period as the ITC would have been recognized). The remaining part should be reflected in income consistent with the classification of the lease: as an adjustment of the asset basis if the lease is a capital lease, or recognized ratably over the lease term if an operating lease.

Tax Law Changes and Safe Harbor Leases. In Issue 86-44, the EITF considered the *Effect of a Change in Tax Law on Investments in Safe Harbor Leases.* Safe harbor leases were created as a tax methodology to allow enterprises that could not utilize the investment tax credit and accelerated cost recovery system benefits provided by the Economic Recovery Tax Act of 1981 to transfer them, for a price, to other parties having the ability to use them. Essentially, this was accomplished by the end-user selling the property (and its tax attributes) to a buyer (often a major corporation) who would then lease it back to the seller. These tax-benefit-transfer leases, or TBTs, were not even deemed to be leases under SFAS 13. The FASB issued two exposure drafts addressing the accounting for safe harbor leases (and issued TB 82-1 specifying disclosures for such leases), but never issued a final statement due to changes in the tax laws that eliminated the TBT advantages. As a result, investments in safe harbor leases are accounted for in a variety of ways. TRA 1986 affects the net income to be recognized by an investor in a safe harbor lease over its remaining life. The accounting issue involves how to calculate and report the effect of the change in tax law.

The first exposure draft, *Accounting for the Sale or Purchase of Tax Benefits Through Tax Leases* (FASB, 1981a), is silent as to the subsequent accounting if there is a change in the tax law or in other significant assumptions. The revised exposure draft, *Accounting for the Sale or Purchase of Tax Benefits Through Tax Leases* (FASB, 1982), however, states that the income recognition pattern in a safe harbor lease should be recalculated, similar to the requirements for leveraged leases (L10.148).

The EITF reached a consensus that: (1) it is appropriate to account for the effect of TRA 1986 on an investment in a safe harbor lease accounted for under the first exposure draft either prospectively, or by recalculating the safe harbor lease from its inception, similar to a leveraged lease, and recording a cumulative catch-up adjustment; or (2) if the investor accounted for the investment under the revised exposure draft, the lease should be recalculated from inception in conformity with that exposure draft. When the cumulative catch-up approach is used, the difference between the current carrying amount (based on the amounts originally recorded) and the currently recalculated amounts would be included in income of the current year.

OTHER LEASE ACCOUNTING MATTERS

Leasebrokers

A significant contemporary issue in the leasing industry is accounting for leasebrokers (also called lease underwriters), an industry group that burgeoned with the advent of SFAS 13. Leasebrokers bring lessors and lessees together with financiers and equity participants. The deals are often very complex: A leasebroker may buy a property, sell it to a third party, lease it back, and then sublease it to the user, with different lease durations and leveraging in the various stages. Regardless of the many layers of paper involved, a leasebroker's compensation typically consists of a fee up front and an interest in the residual value of the property. At the end of the lease term, the leasebroker takes possession of the property, selling or releasing it to the lessee or to someone else. The leasebroker keeps all or part of the proceeds. Because SFAS 13 does not deal directly with these transactions, accounting practices by leasebrokers for income recognition have taken three divergent routes:

1. There is no accounting for the residual value until the property is sold or released.
2. The discounted present value of the estimated residual is recognized, and the discount is accreted to income over the term of the lease.
3. The discounted present value of the estimated residual is recognized, but the discount is not accreted.

Each of these approaches can be justified conceptually. If the residual value can be reasonably estimated, it should be recorded; otherwise it should not. The rationale for not accreting the discount is the same as that specified in TB 86-2, that is, a residual value (i.e., a fixed asset) has been acquired for services rendered; therefore, no accretion is permitted as with any other fixed asset. Accretion could be justified under time-value-of-money concepts, especially if the residual is guaranteed or is viewed akin to a monetary asset.

Nothing authoritative has been published on the very complex subject of leasebroker accounting for fees, residuals, and subleases. However, an AICPA Issues Paper, *Accounting by Lease Brokers* (1980a), went into considerable depth, and has been generally adhered to by entities in this business. The FASB never took action on the issues paper, concluding at the time that there were only a few companies that would be affected, and thus the issues paper became de facto GAAP in this microcosm.

Because the advisory conclusions in the issues paper seemed to make conceptual sense, they began to carry over to other similar situations (e.g., accounting by real estate syndicators (see Chapter 35), who have operated much like leasebrokers in some types of transactions). During 1985, the SEC staff began to question the transferability of the leasebroker issues paper conclusions to other situations, and first stated that it must be limited only to equipment leases; real estate was not covered. This resulted in the economically inverted result that residuals (much of the leasebroker's income) could be accreted on equipment, but could not be accreted on real estate.

This conceptual collision was rectified by the issuance of TB 86-2, *Accounting for an Interest in the Residual Value of a Leased Asset* (L10.528–.529), which categorically precludes accretion of residual by anyone other than the original owner in a lease transaction accounted for as a capital lease.

The coup de grace may have been dealt to the leasebroker issues paper in proposed TB 88-b, in its consideration of money-over-money lease transactions. This type of lease was commonly employed by a leasebroker when he purchased an asset, obtained a lessee, and sold or assigned (on a non-recourse basis) his right to receive rentals for the leased asset to third party financiers for an amount that exceeded his investment. The leasebroker issues paper had allowed income recognition at the beginning of the lease term equal to the amount of the cash received in excess of the investment, if certain conditions were met. Proposed TB 88-b says that it is *never* proper to do this; instead the transaction should be treated conventionally: an asset purchase followed by a lease-out accounted for under SFAS 13, and a borrowing (shown broad in the balance sheet unless a legal right of setoff exists, or it meets the SFAS 13 leveraged leased criteria).

Thus, a question that could have been answered in 1980, when it was relatively contained, has now been dealt with by edict. Proposed TB 88-b also covers other lease issues, including "wrap leases," discussed in the next section, which will also affect leasebrokers. Indirectly but effectively, new leasebroker accounting is being formulated.

Wrap Leases

In proposed TB 88-b, the FASB staff describes a wrap lease transaction in the following manner:

> An enterprise purchases an asset, leases the asset to a lessee, obtains non-recourse financing using the lease rentals or the lease rentals and the asset as collateral, sells the asset subject

to the lease and the non-recourse debt to the third-party investor, and leases the asset back while remaining the substantive principal lessor under the original lease.

The TB concludes that it is *never* proper to recognize all of the profit on a wrap lease transaction at inception. Instead, it should follow SFAS 13 provisions for sale-leasebacks (as amended), with the end-user lease accounted for as a sublease. Effectively, any gain is deferred and amortized over the leaseback term. Further, the non-recourse debt cannot be offset against the asset unless a legal right of setoff exists.

Bad Debts as Initial Costs

Prior to SFAS 91, many finance-leasing companies had been using a method of bad debt accounting referred to as the "initial transfer method," based somewhat on traditional practices of finance companies dealing with a large number of small loans. Under the initial transfer method, the lessor's unearned income at the inception of a lease was reduced by the estimated percentage of bad debts inherent in the lease receivable portfolio (with the percentage being revised from time to time in light of experience and economic conditions); and the offsetting was credit made to the allowance for doubtful accounts. Over the life of the lease, the full amount of unearned income was transferred to earned income in accordance with SFAS 13, and the provision for bad debts was charged to profit and loss in the same manner, thus effectively amortizing the reduced amount of unearned income on two lines (earned income and bad debts expense) in the income statement. There were several other bookkeeping approaches that essentially provided the same net result. The bad debts provision was being treated, in effect, as a front-loaded initial direct cost, and amortized over the life of the lease in the same pattern as the unearned income.

In addition, as is conventional under SFAS 5, the leases in the portfolio were reviewed at each reporting date, and if the sum of the specifically and generally required bad debt allowances exceeded the existing allowance for doubtful accounts, an additional bad debt provision would be made at the time.

FASB meetings and staff comments related to the development of SFAS 91 made it clear the FASB strongly believed that (with the possible exception of truly uniform small-receivable portfolios such as revolving charge accounts, which most finance-leasing companies did not have) bad debts expense should not be homogenized, and that proper accounting was provided in SFAS 5 (i.e., consider each receivable on its own merits, at each reporting date). Accordingly, this accounting methodology ceased after the effective date of SFAS 91, with some companies choosing to eliminate the initial transfer method retroactively as part of the adoption of SFAS 91. The SEC staff has been watchful that in retroactive adoptions there has not been a change in the prior reserve for bad debts because, as the staff has pointed out, SFAS 91 does not deal with bad debts accounting.

International Accounting Standard

The International Accounting Standards Committee (IASC) issued IAS 17, *Accounting for Leases* (AC 9017), to establish accounting standards and disclosure requirements for lessors and lessees. The statement deals with accounting for both finance and operating leases, except for the following specialized types of leases:

- Lease agreements to explore for or use natural resources, such as oil, gas, timber, metals, and other mineral rights.

- Licensing agreements for such items as motion picture films, video recordings, plays, manuscripts, patents, and copyrights.

The statement adopts the major accounting provisions and disclosure requirements of SFAS 13 substantially without change.

IAS 17 focuses on the extent to which risks and rewards incident to ownership of a leased asset lie with the lessor or the lessee. In general, it requires that a lease be classified as a finance lease (capitalized) if it transfers substantially all of the risks and rewards.

AUDITING CONSIDERATIONS

Structuring to Avoid Capitalization

The existence of SFAS 13 and its satellites along with the emphasis on projecting financial strength in the balance sheet and the continuing reluctance by management to accelerate charges against income creates the challenge of avoiding capitalization for prospective lessees. These same factors have created a problem for lessors because, to accommodate their customers, they may have to forego the sales-type or direct financing accounting they prefer. In some cases, structuring close to the line results in operating leases for lessees and capital leases for lessors (e.g., auto and truck leases through lessee guarantee of the top layer of residual).

SFAS 13 provides any number of ways to avoid capitalization, although some are more expensive for the lessee because they require that the lessor assume risks for which he wants to receive payment. By laying down precise rules for capitalization of leases, SFAS 13 provides a detailed design for structuring leases that qualify as operating leases. Lessees and leasebrokers are imaginative and resourceful in creating sophisticated leasing arrangements that use the SFAS 13 rules to their advantage. The useful life provisions, the contingent rental provisions, and the residual value guarantee provisions have provided ample opportunity for people intent on avoiding capitalization of leases to do so.

As an extreme example, suppose a retailer leases a store building for 20 years (less than 75% of the useful life) with the rent stated in terms of sales, such as 100% of the first $250,000 annual sales. It is clear that as long as the store remains open, the sales will be met and the rent will be paid. However, because the lessee can close the store, the entire rent is contingent, so it is not included in minimum lease payments. Thus the lease becomes an operating lease. Although other considerations, such as investment in leasehold improvements, agreements with employee unions, or operating history, might make it unlikely that the lessee will close the store, that fact is of no consequence.

The FASB all along has grimaced at the endless variations propounded by lease structurers, but tentatively has decided not to reopen the entire issue of lease accounting.

The message to the auditor is that, although he may not be able to personally do much about the complexities of lease accounting and the structuring that occurs, he should be wary of extending the boundaries further and perhaps being viewed by the FASB and SEC as disingenuous. The only other possibility seems to be that the FASB will reopen lease accounting, and will undoubtedly make it short and simple to avoid a repetition of the current lease accounting morass.

Audit Objectives

To understand complex leasing arrangements, the auditor must be aware of their economic substance and know what risks and rewards his client will obtain in the transaction. In addition to obtaining information from the client's counsel and management, this process may involve communicating with parties to the lease transaction and outside parties, such as suppliers, to obtain the information necessary for audit judgments. When he understands the transaction, the auditor must determine that the accounting and disclosures reflect its substance. One of the more difficult aspects involves auditing assets and obligations recorded by nonclient parties to the transaction, when this is necessary to evaluate the propriety of the client's accounting treatment.

The auditor's primary objective in examining leasing transactions must be to ensure that the financial statements are in compliance with SFAS 13, as amended. The transactions must also make economic sense to the auditor. He must determine whether the transaction is really a lease in accordance with the SFAS 13 definition and not a transaction requiring a different accounting treatment. He also must be satisfied that strict compliance with the rules does not result in obfuscation.

Audit Procedures

The auditor must consider several procedural issues when planning and conducting his examination. The accounting requirements for leases imply that much evidence is needed to support the treatment of complex leases. Proper lease accounting also requires that the parties make a number of estimates, and GAAS requires that the auditor challenge these estimates and their underlying documentation.

Lessee. For the lessee, leases are often material transactions. Misclassification of a lease could have a material effect on the financial statements. The typical purchase, accounts payable, and cash disbursements control procedures do not encompass the lease transactions, so the auditor needs a substantive approach to search out their features.

The auditor should take the simple but nonetheless important step of asking whether leases exist. A review of expense accounts, including the rent account, for recurring periodic charges can uncover new leases. When reading the minutes of the meetings of the board of directors and other senior groups in the company, the auditor should remain alert to discussion of lease arrangements. Typically, auditors will scrutinize lawyers' invoices to become aware of legal matters, which also helps uncover leases. After he has become aware of their existence, the auditor should read the leases and understand the rights and obligations conveyed. He should consider requesting confirmation of the terms of the lease from the other party or parties.

Lessor. If he is auditing a lessor, the auditor has the same kinds of procedural concerns as with a lessee, plus some new ones. For example, he is concerned about the existence, effectiveness, and functioning of internal control procedures covering multilease transactions. If contingent rentals are involved in leases, the auditor must satisfy himself that the company has an effective means of determining and monitoring compliance with the terms of those contingent rental arrangements. Lessors' accounting for bad debts is also of concern to the auditor. He must be concerned not only with the propriety of the bad debt provision amount, but also with the timing of charges against income. Finally, the auditor must be concerned with the general area of revenue recognition. Lease classification is only one element of this problem. Continuing involvement by the lessor, costs to be incurred, and executory cost estimates are all problems with which the auditor must deal.

Potential Lessee Problem Areas

When dealing with lease classification by the lessee, the auditor needs to substantiate a number of estimates, including the fair value of property at the inception of the lease, the residual value at the end of the lease term, the interest rate implicit in the lease, and the economic useful life. The auditor is also confronted with some difficult judgmental decisions. For example, when is a purchase option or a renewal option a "bargain"?

Related Party Leases. Related party leases continue to provide potential audit problems, just like any other related party transactions. The obvious first problem is to determine whether there is related party involvement, which may not be easy because leases typically are outside the company's regular transaction cycles. Once a related party lease is identified, the auditor has the difficult task of evaluating whether the lease terms have been significantly affected (i.e., is the lease equivalent to what could have been arranged with an unrelated party?). If the terms have been affected significantly, the auditor must convince the company of the need to account for the lease differently than by its stated terms. And while the required disclosure of the related party nature of these transactions is often difficult for the client to accept, the auditor must insist on it.

Implicit Interest Rate. SFAS 13 requires that the lessee use the interest rate implicit in the lease if it is known and it is lower than the lessee's incremental borrowing rate. SFAS 13 implies that the only way for the lessee to determine that rate is to ask the lessor and be told by him. If the lessor will not tell, the auditor must then decide what his obligation is to encourage communication between the lessee and the lessor. And if the lessor announces an interest rate, the auditor is faced with the problem of evaluating that rate.

As discussed in the accounting section of this chapter under "Definitions," TB 88-2 now requires that the maximum interest rate that could be implicit in a lease be computed by the lessee, and if it is less than the lessee's incremental borrowing rate, it should be used in determining lease classification. The auditor will have to observe whether the client's leases fit the criteria of TB 88-2, as many clients may overlook this computation.

Potential Lessor Problem Areas

Profit on Sales-Type Leases. The existence, measurement, and accounting for potentially unreimbursable costs to the lessor over a long lease term can be a significant problem. Sometimes customers will tend to lease, rather than buy, innovative but untried products. This may imply a requirement on the part of the lessor to provide technical support, product maintenance, or other services on a continuing basis, and the costs must be identified, estimated, and considered for their accounting impact.

Residuals. Residual values present one of the biggest problems in auditing lessors. The economics of leasing are such that leasing companies' fortunes are significantly affected by the residuals. The residual is an asset of the leasing company. If the leveraged financing and the lease receivables are looked on as an offset, then the residuals are probably the most significant *real* asset of the leasing company. It is most difficult for the lessor to estimate at the beginning of the lease term what the property is going to be worth at the end of the term. And it is sometimes more problematic for the auditor to reach a satisfactory level of comfort with that estimate.

At least as difficult as the initial estimate of residual value is the not-less-than-annual evaluation and rechallenge thereof. The residual must be written down if its previously determined value has been impaired, but it may not be written up if the first estimate was too low, or if market factors have increased its value.

20

Equity Capital and Earnings Per Share

OVERVIEW

Most smaller businesses are initially capitalized with equity investments by the incorporator(s). However, when a business enterprise wants to raise additional funds it may borrow, or it may sell a part of itself; the result of the latter approach is commonly called *equity capital*.

Two basic categories of equity capital, *preferred stock* and *common stock,* are distinguished by their respective rights. Two additional categories usually appearing in the equity section of the balance sheet are *paid-in capital* and *retained earnings.*[1]

This categorization may sound simple enough, but in fact a company's capitalization can be extremely complex, because equity and debt attributes are often blended to achieve perceived advantages, such as (1) financing opportunities available for certain types of investments, (2) tax law incentives or "angles," and (3) reduced capital costs available through collateralization that achieves a better rating from rating agencies.

Beginning in the early 1980s, exotic financial instruments and transactions—many having some measure of equity ownership characteristics—began to flourish for these types of reasons, and their development continues to burgeon. The FASB's Emerging Issues Task Force devotes considerable attention to such matters, which ordinarily are not addressed (at least not directly) by any single accounting standard—although a given issue may be covered by several that do not mix well (i.e., that are in apparent conflict). This chapter will focus on the "simpler side" of equity capital, with more complex matters discussed in Chapter 21, "Financial Instruments and Transactions."

Shareholders' Equity Accounts

The rights of *preferred stock* usually consist of a preference in the distribution of earnings (dividends) and a preference in the distribution of assets upon liquidation, hence the term preferred. In addition, most preferred stocks have a fixed face value (par value) and the right to a fixed rate of dividend distribution, stated as either a percentage of par value or a fixed dollar amount (e.g., 8% preferred stock or $2.50 preferred stock). Individual preferred stocks often have various other rights determined at issuance. For example, preferred stocks that must receive dividend distribution payments for all years prior to any common stock dividend payment are described as cumulative; those without this right are noncumulative. Preferred stocks may have voting rights in the election of directors or for other specific matters; most preferred stocks are without this right and thus are nonvoting. Some are redeemable optionally, some have mandatory redemption features, some have no redemption features but may be called for redemption, and some can be converted into common stock. Because preferred stocks can vary widely in their terms, some business enterprises have several classes and series of preferred stock, each with distinct rights.

Common stock almost always includes voting rights as to directors and to major changes in the activities of the enterprise (such as sale of the whole enterprise or a major division). It may have either a par or stated value. Common stock does not

---

[1] This chapter does not discuss two additional categories contained in shareholders' equity, marketable equity securities valuation allowance and foreign currency translation adjustments, discussed in Chapters 12 and 22, respectively.

usually have a fixed dividend rate but receives dividends only as declared by the board of directors. Sometimes there are separate classes of common stock having differing rights.

When preferred or common stock is sold by an enterprise, it will often be at a price above par or stated value. This premium is known as *additional paid-in capital,* capital contributed in excess of par (or stated value), or something similar. Depending on individual state law (and in some cases regulatory requirements), dividends may be declared out of paid-in capital. Those dividends are sometimes called *liquidating dividends,* because they are a return of capital to the shareholders (although not necessarily to the same shareholders who originally invested the capital). Although most companies with no par stock have a paid-in capital account, they need not; the excess of sales proceeds over stated value may be carried in the capital stock account.

When net earnings of an enterprise are not distributed to its shareholders through dividends, they are retained by the enterprise; hence they are called *retained earnings.* (They are also known as accumulated earnings, earnings retained (or reinvested) in the business, or earned surplus (a term considered archaic).) Some enterprises organized for a profit may incur cumulative losses; the amount by which invested capital is diminished through losses is called a *deficit.* In those relatively infrequent cases where cumulative losses exceed the total of preferred and common stock and paid-in capital, resulting in an excess of liabilities over assets, the result is referred to as a *deficiency in assets.*

Earnings Per Share

In SFAC 1, *Objectives of Financial Reporting by Business Enterprises,* the FASB indicates that investors and creditors "may use earnings information to help them (a) evaluate management's performance, (b) estimate 'earning power' or other amounts they perceive as 'representative' of long-term earnings ability of an enterprise, (c) predict future earnings, or (d) assess the risk of investing in or lending to an enterprise" (¶ 47). Among the numerous financial ratios used in analyzing investment decisions, the most prominent is probably earnings per share (EPS). In its simplest form, EPS are the earnings for the period divided by the weighted average number of shares outstanding, but there are many variations discussed later in this chapter.

Underwriters' Involvement

Underwriters are almost always involved in a securities offering to the public, whether the securities are debt, equity, or a hybrid. They assess the marketability of the security, the price that should be expected, and the conditions under which a public offering can or could be made. Various arrangements can exist between an underwriter and a company regarding a particular offering (for example, a "firm" underwriting, in which all securities are taken by the underwriter and resold or retained as permitted by market conditions or as otherwise desired; or an "all-or-nothing best efforts" underwriting, in which failure to achieve the resale of the securities effectively aborts the offering).

Underwriters are considered to be experts in securities valuation, and their advice is often needed by accountants (e.g., in determining the allocation of proceeds of a hybrid security or the valuation of a warrant).

Section 11 of the Securities Act of 1933 (Securities Act) charges underwriters with a *due-diligence* responsibility for the appropriateness of information contained in the offering documents up to the effective date of the registration statement (the date on which the SEC permits securities sales to commence). Traditionally, an underwriter obtains a *comfort letter* from a company's independent public accountants to assist the underwriter in discharging his responsibility for due-diligence with respect to the financial data usually contained in an offering: that is, audited operating and cash flow financial statements for five years and balance sheets for three years, unaudited subsequent interim data, and supplementary data derived from the enterprise's accounts and records.

Although many securities offerings are not underwritten, this chapter also applies to them. (How underwriters create a securities syndicate is described in Chapter 42. In addition, there are various concessions made by the SEC to the needs of smaller businesses, as discussed in Chapter 39.)

A company's independent accountants invariably are requested to aid the underwriters in exercising their due-diligence requirements by issuing a comfort letter describing the performance of certain procedures. In requiring comfort letters from independent accountants as a condition to the underwriting agreement, underwriters are seeking assistance in performing a "reasonable investigation" of unaudited financial information and other data included in a registration statement that are not based on the authority of an expert (i.e., are not "expertised").

Exchange Listing Procedures

A publicly held enterprise may want to increase the transferability of its stock. The usual way to do so is to obtain listing on a *stock exchange*.

There are many exchanges in the United States, the most important of which are the New York Stock Exchange (NYSE) and American Stock Exchange (Amex). The National Association of Securities Dealers Automated Quotation (NASDAQ) system also operates effectively as an exchange. In addition, there are many important foreign exchanges on which the larger U.S. companies may list. It is important to note that U.S. exchange listing requirements are imposed by the exchanges themselves, not the SEC, although the Commission must approve all changes in such requirements.

The exchanges have a substantial number of requirements, but only those concerning independent accountants will be mentioned here. Both the NYSE and the Amex have manuals to guide and assist enterprises and their accountants in preparing both original and subsequent listing applications.

New York Stock Exchange

Financial statements—original and subsequent listing. The NYSE requires the following financial statements or data to be included in a listing application:

1. A summary of earnings for the last five years, prepared in conformity with GAAP.
2. Audited financial statements in conformity with GAAP and the related independent accountant's opinion.
3. Latest interim financial statements for the current fiscal year, prepared in conformity with GAAP. Such statements shall be certified by either the company's independent accountants or its principal accounting officer.
4. A pro forma balance sheet giving effect to a completed or contemplated recapitalization, acquisition, reorganization, or major financing.
5. Parent company financial statements, if appropriate.
6. If shares are to be issued in an acquisition, financial statements of the potential acquiree. In addition, pro forma financial statements may be appropriate.

If previous applications contain any of this data, they may be incorporated by reference in the current application.

Manual signatures by the independent public accountants and the chief accounting officer are required and should be affixed to their reports on one of the proof copies of the application.

The NYSE provides that the financial statement data required for original or subsequent listings may at the company's option be incorporated by reference to a Securities Act prospectus or to proxy statements or an annual report on Form 10-K issued under the Exchange Act. This is a commonly used approach.

Annual and interim financial statements. In the NYSE listing agreement, the company also agrees to:

1. At least once a year, publish consolidated financial statements of the enterprise for that year and submit them to shareholders at least 15 days in advance of the annual shareholders' meeting. These financial statements should disclose the details of certain data regarding unconsolidated subsidiaries (prior to mandatory application of SFAS 94) and the existence of any defaults by the company or any of its subsidiaries (consolidated or unconsolidated).
2. Submit the opinion of certified public accountants covering the financial statements previously described. (The NYSE must be notified of a change in accountants.)
3. Publish quarterly statements of earnings disclosing substantial items of an unusual or nonrecurring nature, net earnings, and either taxes or earnings before taxes.
4. Maintain an audit committee in accordance with NYSE requirements (see the NYSE *Listed Company Manual* and Chapter 6 for details).

Pooling letter. The NYSE requires a special letter from the outside accountants before it will process a listing application that authorizes shares to be issued in a pooling-of-interests transaction. This letter should set forth, in detail, compliance with the criteria specified in APB 16, *Business Combinations* (B50), and should be tailored to meet the individual circumstances of the transaction, rather than generalized. (See Chapter 23 for further discussion.)

American Stock Exchange

Financial statements—original listing. The Amex requirements are substantially the same as those of the NYSE. The following financial information (either provided directly or incorporated by reference) is required in an original listing:

1. Latest annual report on Form 10-K.
2. Form 10-Q quarterly report(s) for periods subsequent to the latest Form 10-K.
3. Form 8-K current report(s), if any, for periods subsequent to the latest Form 10-K.

As an alternative to these requirements, a company may submit a prospectus declared effective by the SEC that contains equivalent information. Also required is the latest annual report distributed to shareholders.

In certain circumstances, the Amex may also require other financial information as deemed appropriate on a case-by-case basis.

Financial statements—subsequent listings. Although not directly specified, it apears that Amex practice requires items 1 and 2 (below) in subsequent listing applications. Item 3 (below) is a specified Amex requirement.

1. Independently audited annual report to shareholders for the latest year.
2. Financial statements as of a date not more than six months prior to the date of the filing of the listing application, certified by independent accountants or by the chief accounting officer.
3. If shares are to be listed for an acquisition, the balance sheet of the acquired company as of a recent date and earnings statement and retained earnings analysis to that date—usually the latest annual financial statements and latest available interim statements. A report of the independent accountants should be included if available; if not, certification by the chief accounting officer of such acquired company may be acceptable.

The Amex also accepts the incorporation by reference of a prospectus under the Securities Act or proxy statements under the Exchange Act as appropriate to fulfill the financial statement requirements for subsequent listing applications.

Annual and interim financial statements. The requirements of as to annual and interim financial statement reporting the Amex are virtually identical to those of the NYSE. They differ in that the Amex requires submission to shareholders of the annual report only 10 days in advance of the shareholders' meeting.

NASDAQ System. The requirements for listing under the NASDAQ system are much simpler than the NYSE or the Amex requirements. An enterprise must be registered under the Exchange Act if it has at least 500 holders of record and total assets of $5 million. The NASDAQ system contains a large number of the over-the-counter stocks, warrants, rights, and convertibles, as well as bank securities that are registered with the FDIC, Federal Reserve, or the Office of the Comptroller of the Currency, but not with the SEC. Further, certain insurance company and closed-end investment company securities are included in the NASDAQ system.

There is no formal application for inclusion in the NASDAQ system; an informal letter to the National Association of Securities Dealers will suffice. The letter should be accompanied by the latest available financial information statements filed with the appropriate regulatory agency.

EQUITY CAPITAL CYCLE

The equity cycle starts with initial equity capital, is increased by further equity capital infusions or earnings, and is decreased by dividends, reacquisition of stock, or losses from operations. Other kinds of transactions, (such as poolings, transfers, and exchanges) also cause changes in equity capital directly. All the methods by which equity capital can increase involve the issuance of an equity security for some type of consideration; the increase arises from recording the consideration received. If the consideration is cash and the security is a simple stock, no particular problems arise. If stock is issued in exchange for property or services, however, valuation of consideration received is often complex. Expenses incurred in the issuance of stock are deducted from the related proceeds, and the net proceeds are recorded as equity capital.

Issuance for Cash

The amount of net cash proceeds determines the valuation for stock issued. Net proceeds in excess of par or stated value usually are split out and included in additional paid-in capital. If the net cash proceeds are less than the par or stated value, the stock may not be fully paid or may be assessable, matters requiring the attention of legal counsel.

In addition to the straightforward sale of capital stock for full cash payment, there are several other common forms of issuance. Stock options granted to officers and employees bring in cash upon exercise; there are so many complexities in options that these are described in a separate section later in this chapter.

Rights and Warrants. *Rights* are issued to existing shareholders and enable them to purchase additional common stock at a stipulated price for a stated time period. If issued along with common stock, the rights are usually separable from the stock ("detachable"). Some companies' rights are publicly traded.

Equity *warrants* are usually issued as part of a debt financing package (see Chapter 18) and entitle the holder to purchase equity securities for a stated duration and price. Some warrants are detachable and may be exercised by surrendering the warrant and the cash payment required for the common stock. For nondetachable warrants, the debt security must be surrendered if the warrants are exercised, effectively a conversion of debt into common stock. Some warrants are *synthetic,* giving the holder the option of either paying cash or tendering the related bonds at face value when exercising the warrant. Detachable and synthetic warrants may also be publicly traded.

Because equity warrants may also be issued separately from another security, it is often not possible to make a distinction between rights and warrants, except by the name given them on issuance.

Detachable or synthetic warrants issued in conjunction with debt have a separate fair value that must be measured. Accordingly, as stated in APB 14, *Accounting for Convertible Debt Issued With Stock Purchase Warrants* (D10.105), if debt is issued with such warrants, the proceeds should be allocated between warrants and debt based on relative fair values. The portion allocated to the warrants increases paid-in capital. (See Chapter 18.)

If rights or warrants are issued to shareholders as a dividend (no cash paid or received by the issuing company), there are no accounting entries made unless a value must be placed on the right or warrant (e.g., when there is a significant reduction in exercise price below market price at time of issuance of the right or warrant). In such cases, the accounting is similar to that for stock dividends or stock options. If the issuance is in an offering for cash, the net proceeds from sale of rights or warrants is credited to paid-in capital.

Because rights and warrants effectively constitute options to buy stock, they have no accounting significance upon exercise, except in the sense of setting the price. Cash received is credited to common stock (to the extent of the par or stated value) and paid-in capital (to the extent there is an excess over par or stated value).

Subscriptions. An investor can subscribe for the purchase of stock, but not be required to make payment until a later time. Such transactions are common in the formation of corporations and are often part of special transactions with officers, major shareholders, and other related parties (see Chapter 25). Recording a subscription involves setting up the receivable and crediting capital stock subscribed. For financial reporting, however, the amounts are offset, because capital not paid in (cash or other value received) is not deemed to be capital. This is clear for publicly held companies. In SAB Topic 4.E., *Receivables From Sale of Stock* (SAB 1), the SEC has specified that subscriptions receivable from officers and employees may be shown as an asset only if collected prior to the publication of the financial statements. Private companies should also now be adhering to the practice of offsetting unpaid subscriptions against the related capital account.

Issuance for Other Than Cash

Ordinarily, noncash (nonmonetary) transactions are to be valued at the fair value of the consideration received or of the consideration given, whichever is more clearly evident (N35.105). Although there is a specific exception stated in N35.101(c) to this general principle for noncash equity transactions (APB 29 does not apply to acquisition of nonmonetary assets or services on issuance of capital stock), it is nonetheless generally regarded as applicable to equity transactions unless more specific principles exist, as they do for business combinations and stock option plans. If the stock issued has a quoted market price, that is usually the more clearly evident value.

There are numerous purposes and methods involved in the issuance of stock for other than cash. Two of those are discussed in other chapters, for property (Chapter 15) and in business combinations (Chapter 23), and will be omitted here. Situations covered in the following text are (1) stock issued for services, (2) assets acquired from promoters or shareholders, (3) stock issued to acquire results of research and development arrangements, (4) notes receivable received for common stock, (5) stock dividends and splits, (6) conversions of other securities, and (7) contingent warrants.

Services. In the formative stages, smaller companies often will issue stock for services. The company may lack the cash with which to pay, or the provider of the services may desire the opportunity for capital growth instead of cash payment. Valuation is simple if the service is one readily available commercially at prices not widely varying. The general rule of establishing as basis the more clearly evident value, that is, the service value or the stock value, should be followed. But most stock-for-service transactions involve a unique or special service, whose value will be problematic, and stock that ordinarily has indefinable values. Thus, the usual resolution is establishment of valuation by the issuing company's board of directors or management at an amount that they consider fair and that is not controverted by available evidence.

When stock for services is issued to officers, directors, or employees, the valuation process is complicated further by the relationship of the parties (see Chapter 25).

Assets From Promoters or Shareholders. SAB 48, *Transfers of Nonmonetary Assets by Promoters or Shareholders* (Topic 5.G), reflects the SEC's long-standing position that assets acquired in exchange for stock prior to or at the time of the registrant's initial public offering should be recorded at the historical cost to the promoter or shareholder. Deviations from this policy have been rare, generally applying to situations in which the fair value of the stock issued or assets acquired is objectively determinable and the promoter's or shareholder's ownership following the transaction is not so significant that a substantial indirect interest exists in the assets. The SEC also points out that estimating the fair value of the stock is not appropriate if the stock is privately held or seldom traded.

Research and Development Arrangements. TB 84-1 (R55.501–.504) provides guidance on how a company should account for stock issued to acquire the results of a research and development (R&D) arrangement. Specifically, if a sponsoring company issues stock to acquire successful R&D results, the stock should be recorded at its fair value as of the acquisition date. (This is also discussed in Chapter 39.)

Notes Receivable. In Issue 85-1, *Classifying Notes Received for Capital Stock,* the EITF discussed the manner in which a company should report a note received as consideration for the issuance of the company's stock. As mentioned previously, the SEC requires that public companies report such notes as a deduction from shareholders' equity. The EITF members confirmed that the predominant practice is to offset such notes in the equity section. However, some EITF members stated that they were aware of a few cases in which nonpublic companies reported such notes as assets in circumstances in which the notes either were secured by irrevocable letters of credit or other liquid collateral or were discountable at a bank and included a stated maturity of reasonably short duration. The EITF reached a consensus that reporting the note as an asset is generally not appropriate except in very limited circumstances in which there is substantial evidence of ability and intent to pay within a reasonably short period of time. Some EITF members would require collateralization or payment of the note prior to issuance of the financial statements to permit asset recognition. The SEC Observer at the EITF stated that, for SEC registrants, exceptions to the general rule would be rare.

Stock Dividends and Splits. Stock dividends and stock splits are similar in that both involve issuance by an enterprise of common shares to its common shareholders without additional consideration. A *stock dividend* is usually intended to give the shareholders a distribution of earnings without expending cash. A *stock split* is usually intended to increase the number of outstanding shares and reduce the current market price per share to obtain wider distribution and improve marketability. Neither stock dividends nor splits result in an increase in total equity capital, but are treated as reclassifications within the equity section.

ARB 43, Chapter 7B (C20), uses "20% or 25%" of the previously outstanding shares in determining whether stock issued to shareholders should be accounted for as a dividend (requiring capitalization of retained earnings for the fair value of the additional shares issued) or a stock split. The ARB concludes that distributions of less than 20% or 25% of the previously outstanding shares should be accounted for as a dividend, the distributions in excess of 20% or 25% should be accounted for as splits.

Given the inexact percentages used in ARB 43, disparity may occur in practice with respect to distributions between 20 and 25%. However, for public companies, in ASR 124 (FRR § 214) the SEC has interpreted GAAP as saying that distributions of more than 25% of previously outstanding shares must be accounted for as stock splits. While not specifically mentioned, distributions of exactly 25% would be accounted for as stock splits. The NYSE and the Amex rules are substantially the same as the SEC position.

Stock dividends should be accounted for at fair value. The NYSE position is that the fair value of stock dividends may be computed by (1) multiplying the quoted market price of the underlying stock at the declaration date by the number of shares to be issued or (2) dividing the current market price by the aggregate of outstanding shares plus shares to be issued and multiplying the result by the number of shares to be issued. In either case, the fair value of the stock dividend should be charged to retained earnings and credited to common stock (as to par or stated value) and paid-in capital (as to the excess of fair value over par or stated value).

If rights or warrants are issued to shareholders without any consideration and they have a value attributable to a bargain price for future stock purchases, that value should be charged to retained earnings and credited to paid-in capital.

Convertible Securities. Convertible securities benefit both the holder and the issuer. The holder obtains some of the benefits of common stock, such as participation in the earnings growth of the company and possible gains from rising stock prices, and the issuing company usually obtains a lower rate of interest or dividend requirement than could be obtained on a nonconvertible security. Further, if the convertible security can be called at the option of the issuer, the company can, under rising market conditions, force conversion into common stock, thereby eliminating interest or preferred dividend payments.

Although there is an economic value to the conversion feature of a convertible debt security, no accounting recognition is given to the conversion feature because of its "inseparability" (D10.102). The choices of the holder of convertible debt are mutually exclusive. Either the security is converted into common stock or held until redeemed for cash.

A conversion of convertible preferred stock into common stock will not affect total shareholders' equity, although the elements thereof will change. The preferred stock classification is reduced for the par or stated value of the shares converted, common stock is increased for the new shares issued, and the difference is an adjustment to paid-in capital.

A conversion of a convertible debt security into common stock reduces the debt classification and increases shareholders' equity by the carrying amount of the converted debt, net of proportionate unamortized debt issue costs. Debt with nondetachable warrants is the equivalent of convertible debt and is treated identically.

Contingent Warrants. In 1984, the SEC issued SAB 57 (Topic 5.K) to explain the staff's view on accounting for contingent warrants issued to certain customers that could become exercisable at some future date provided the customers purchased the registrant's products in amounts specified in related sales agreements. If purchase quotas were not met the warrants would lapse.[2]

The staff stated that whether such purchases occur is dependent on various factors, such as the registrant's ability to deliver products under the sales agreements, the customer's need for the products, and possibly the market price of the registrant's common stock during the term of the sales agreement. Valuation of the contingent warrant shares prior to resolution of those uncertainties would not provide an appropriate measurement of the cost to the registrant of the inducement to the customers to enter into the sales agreement. Prior to such resolution, it is not even determinable whether there is such a cost. Once the warrants become exercisable because the requisite purchases have been made, the warrants have a cost that can be measured. That cost is the difference between the quoted market price of the registrant's stock at the date that the customer earns the warrants and the amount the customer is required to pay. Prior to that date, however, the registrant periodically must deterine whether it is "probable" (as that term is used in SFAS 5 (C50)) that the customers will make purchases sufficient to earn the warrants. Sales made subsequent to a determination that a probable cost will occur should be charged with a pro rata allocation of the estimated ultimate cost of the warrants based on the quoted market price of the stock at the end of each reporting period.

The SEC staff intends to reassess its position after the FASB completes its project to reconsider APB 25, *Accounting for Stock Issued to Employees* (C47) (discussed later in this chapter), relating to accounting for stock issued to employees.

---

[2] This topic was also raised in EITF Issue 84-8, *Variable Stock Purchase Warrants Given by Suppliers to Customers,* but was not discussed by the Task Force because SAB 57 was issued beforehand.

Decreases

Reacquisitions. The acquisition by a company of its own shares reduces its equity capital. This reacquired stock, which may be common or preferred, is called *treasury stock*. Management of the company may decide that it can increase the earning power of its remaining shares outstanding more by utilizing cash resources for a partial liquidation than by investing in operating assets or holding the cash in liquid investments. Often, this might be a sensible strategy if management does not wish to expand its business. Also, the enterprise may wish to use the treasury stock in the future, for example, in stock option plans or business combinations.

Treasury stock is carried at cost and is shown as a deduction from total shareholders' equity.[3] Retained earnings are usually restricted from payment of dividends by the cost of treasury stock on hand. Disclosure of this restriction is required, if material. Whether retained earnings are in fact restricted and by how much is primarily a legal question, and counsel should be consulted.

A purchase of treasury stock may, under the rules in ASRs 146 and 146A (FRR § 201), affect an enterprise's ability to enter into a pooling transaction. Depending on the materiality of the treasury stock acquisition, it may preclude entering into an otherwise valid pooling business combination.

A company is not allowed to record profits from trading in its own stock; therefore, any difference between cost and proceeds on subsequent resale of treasury stock adjusts paid-in capital.

Retirements. There are two types of retirements, actual and constructive. Cancellation of reacquired shares through formal application to the secretary of state's office in the state of incorporation is an actual retirement. Constructive retirement is effecting the retirement on the financial statements by the authorization of the board of directors without formal cancellation through the secretary of state. The accounting and presentation (C23.102–.103) are the same for constructive and actual retirements.

When the cost of the treasury stock to be retired is in excess of par or stated value of the stock, the excess should be allocated to paid-in capital and retained earnings or charged entirely to retained earnings. The allocation is made first to paid-in capital to the extent paid-in capital arose from that issue or to the extent paid-in capital is available (left-over) from that issue's previous retirements. Any remaining excess is then allocated between paid-in capital and retained earnings on a proportionate basis. Practically, it is much simpler to allocate the excess of cost over the par or stated value to paid-in capital based on the per share amount of paid-in capital for all shares, with the excess charged to retained earnings. The only method not sanctioned by GAAP or by the SEC is a charge solely to paid-in capital that does not

---

[3] An interesting issue not dealt with in accounting literature is the presentation by a subsidiary of the stock it holds in its parent company (i.e., a *reciprocal investment*). Some accountants believe that the parent's stock should be shown on the subsidiary's balance sheet as treasury stock at cost. Other accountants believe it should be shown as a long-term investment at cost or at equity in the parent's net assets. Intracorporate investments of this nature lead to complex reciprocal equations to calculate earnings, EPS, and equity ownership.

arise from that issue. However, if the purchase price is less than par or stated value, the excess must be credited to paid-in capital.

Cash Dividends. The declaration and payment of a dividend decreases a company's retained earnings. The dividend may be required by the terms of a preferred stock or simply represent the return to common shareholders of accumulated earnings. Dividends also may be paid as a method of preventing an unfriendly takeover; this reduces equity and assets and thus may make the target company less attractive, or it may make shareholders less susceptible to the blandishments of the proposed acquirer. Dividends from paid-in capital (if legal) are technically a partial liquidation.

Liquidation. The management of a company may decide to cease business, dispose of assets, and declare a liquidating dividend. A liquidation usually occurs over a span of years, because assets need to be disposed of in an orderly manner to realize the greatest proceeds. In this process, equity is reduced by each liquidating dividend and eventually disappears.

Sometimes, the decision to cease business is taken out of management's hands by creditors. When a creditor is concerned about recovery of its receivable because of a company's financial difficulties, the creditor may petition a court to appoint a trustee under the Federal Bankruptcy Code. (See Chapter 28.)

Dividends-In-Kind. Dividends need not be in cash. Tax or other benefits are often associated with dividends-in-kind. Assets such as marketable securities may be distributed to shareholders, the difference between carrying amount and market value charged or credited to earnings, and the dividend charged to retained earnings at market value.

Accounting for the distribution of nonmonetary assets to owners in a complete or partial spin-off (whether of a subsidiary or a division) or other form of reorganization, in a liquidating dividend, or in rescission of a business combination, is to be based on the recorded amount of the assets distributed (reduced if appropriate for an impairment in value).

Other kinds of nonmonetary assets distributed to shareholders should be valued at fair value if that is objectively measurable and clearly realizable; otherwise, the carrying amount is used (N35.110).

Other Equity Capital Transactions

Reorganizations. A company in its formative years or one experiencing operating and financial difficulties may have accumulated large losses and thus may decide to reorganize. One type of reorganization other than those under the Federal Bankruptcy Code is a *quasi-reorganization*. In essence, with shareholder approval, the management revalues assets and eliminates the deficit (increased by asset devaluations if any) by charging it to other equity accounts. Although a charge to paid-in capital may be all that is required, a reduction in par or stated value may also be required to absorb part of the charge. The general rules describing quasi-reorganizations are enumerated in ARB 43, Chapter 7A, "Quasi-Reorganizations" (Q15), and FRR § 210. The entire procedure must be made known to all persons entitled to vote on matters of general corporate policy, and their appropriate consents to the particular transactions obtained in advance, in accordance with the applicable law and charter provisions. With respect to the accounts, a quasi-reorganization accomplishes substantially what might be accomplished in a reorganization by legal proceeding. Retained earnings accumulated after a quasi-reorganization must be "dated" for a period of 10 years; that is, the fact that a deficit was eliminated through a quasi-reorganization must be stated (Q15.111). (This is further discussed in Chapter 28.)

Another transaction that might be considered a reorganization is a *reverse stock split*. Total outstanding shares are reduced by issuing a smaller number of new shares for existing shares (e.g., two new shares for three old shares). This does not affect total equity but may affect the balances of the individual equity accounts.

Transfers and Exchanges. A change in the par or stated value of stock may affect other equity accounts. For example, a change from $1 par value to $2 par value causes an increase in the stock account and a corresponding decrease in paid-in capital or, sometimes, retained earnings. Conversely, a decrease in par value from $2 to $1 may cause a decrease in the common stock account and an increase in paid-in capital.

Although a company may decide that a change in par value is not feasible, it can accomplish the same result through an exchange. An exchange among different classes of preferred stock and common stock does not increase or decrease total equity, but it does cause an adjustment of the respective equity accounts.

Mandatorily Redeemable Preferred Stock

A preferred stock with a sinking fund or a mandatory redemption requirement has traditionally been classified as an equity security under GAAP, although it has some aspects of debt. The FASB reinforced the debt concept in its statement on marketable securities (I89.401–.409), which indicates that a preferred stock that must be redeemed by the issuing company or is redeemable at the holder's option is not, from the standpoint of the holder, an equity security.

ASR 268 (FRR § 211) describes presentation and disclosure requirements for preferred stock subject to mandatory redemption requirements. In addition, the carrying amount at which redeemable preferred stock should be reported, and how changes in its carrying amount should be treated in calculations of earnings per share and the ratio of earnings to combined fixed charges and preferred stock dividends, are contained in SAB 64, *Redeemable Preferred Stock* (Topic 3.C), issued in 1986.

1. The initial carrying amount of redeemable preferred stock should be its fair value at date of issue. Where fair value at date of issue is less than the mandatory redemption amount, the carrying amount should be increased by periodic accretions, using the interest method, so that the carrying amount will equal the mandatory redemption amount at the mandatory redemption date. The carrying amount shall be further periodically increased by amounts representing dividends not currently declared or paid, but which will be payable under the mandatory redemption features, or for which ultimate pay-

ment is not solely within the control of the [company] (e.g., dividends that will be payable out of future earnings). Each type of increase in carrying amount shall be effected by charges against retained earnings or, in the absence of retained earnings, by charges against paid-in capital.

2. [In calculating] earnings per share and ratios of earnings to combined fixed charges and preferred stock dividends, each type of increase in carrying amount described [above] should be treated in the same manner as dividends on nonredeemable preferred stock.

Figure 20.1 presents an example of accretion to the redemption price.

Increasing Rate Preferred Stock

In SAB 68, *Increasing Rate Preferred Stock* (Topic 5.Q), issued in 1987, the SEC staff addressed the situation in which preferred stock pays no dividends or pays dividends at a low but constantly increasing rate for a period of years. In such cases, the SEC staff believes that the stock should be:

1. Recorded at its fair value on the date of issuance. Thereafter, the carrying amount should be increased periodically to recognize the imputed dividend cost resulting from a discounting process that reflects the difference between "normal" and actual dividend amounts. "Normal" means a dividend rate or amount that exists for a comparable preferred stock without the special dividend condition (from an investment standpoint).
2. Periodically adjusted to reflect the discount mentioned above. The discount should be amortized over the periods preceding achievement of a normal dividend payment by charging imputed dividend cost against retained earnings and crediting the carrying amount of the preferred stock.

If stated dividends on an increasing rate preferred stock are variable, calculations of initial discount and subsequent amortization should be based on the value of the index (if applicable) that is used initially to determine the dividend rate. For example, the fluctuating yield on a particular treasury security, at the date of issuance, should not be affected by subsequent changes in the index.

This matter initially arose in EITF Issue 86-45, *Imputation of Dividends on Preferred Stock Redeemable at the Issuer's Option With Initial Below-Market Dividend Rate.* The Task Force was unable to reach a consensus, specifically because the stock was not mandatorily redeemable; but the SEC staff believed that some action was necessary to prevent abuses by the fabrication of such securities.

STOCK OPTIONS AND SIMILAR PLANS

A stock option is the right granted to an employee to receive stock upon payment of a specified price (the *option price*). Although the primary purpose usually is not to raise equity capital, the payment of the option price (*exercise*) increases equity in the same way as a sale for cash. Instituting a stock option plan usually requires shareholder approval. Stock option grants, or *awards,* contain restrictions as to when the option may be exercised. Restrictions are designed to achieve the objectives of the

Consolidated Statements of Stockholders' Equity (Deficit)

| | Preferred stock | | | | Common stock | | Capital in excess of par value | Retained earnings (deficit) | Treasury stock | |
| | Series A | | Series B | | | | | | | |
	Shares	Value	Shares	Value	Shares	Par value			Shares	Cost
Balance at June 30, 1986		$ —		$ —	7,111	$1,777	$1,964	$(16,255)	366	$(1,020)
Exchange of $20,000,000 of 14.5% subordinated debentures due 1993 for preferred and common stocks	140	4,980	100	7,156	6,744	1,686	2,630			
Net earnings								6,769		
Preferred dividends declared								(255)		
Accretion of discount on preferred stock		208		293				(502)		
Balance at June 30, 1987	140	$5,188	100	$7,449	13,855	$3,463	$4,595	$(10,243)	366	$(1,020)

FIG. 20.1 Accretion of Mandatorily Redeemable Preferred Stock ($ in 000)

Source: La Barge, Inc., 1987 Annual Report.

enterprise—specifically, to retain and motivate the employee. When the restrictions placed on the exercise of any or all options awarded are met, the option is said to be *vested.* Restrictions may include a predetermined length of future service (e.g., five years), performance restrictions (e.g., the enterprise must achieve 5% compounded growth in EPS over a defined period, say five years), or a combination of both (e.g., vesting based 80% on length of service and 20% on EPS growth). If an employee leaves the employ of the enterprise, the unvested options are forfeited. Antidilution and merger/sale provisions are common.

There are certain tax ramifications attendant to stock options. Under the tax law in 1988, the recipient of the option award ordinarily is not required to report income until the option is exercised.

Stock options have been used for many years to motivate, retain, or attract desired officers and employees. In recent years many variations of the basic stock option have developed, and the more common ones are discussed in this section. The main accounting issue is whether a stock-based plan results in a compensation cost to the sponsor and, if so, how it is measured and what the measurement date is. The APB addressed those questions in APB 25, *Accounting for Stock Issued to Employees* (C47), in 1972.

In the conventional stock option and purchase plans, an employer grants employees the right to buy a fixed number of shares at a fixed price over a specified period. If the options are made exercisable in installments, the awards are usually contingent only on continued employment. More complex forms of option plans require a more detailed analysis, but a common characteristic in such plans is that they are variable: either the number of shares or the option price is not fixed. The accounting issues, compensation expense and its measurement, are fundamentally the same.

The basic requirement regarding compensation expense is that it should be measured at grant date, not date of exercise. Some accountants believe that current practice is inappropriate because options granted at current market price are not valued nor is compensation recorded, although the option intends to give officers and employees something of value. Both the recipient and the enterprise hope and expect the value of the stock to rise, and in theory at least a part of any value increase is attributable to favorable company results achieved with the help of the grantee/employee. Therefore, it can be said that an expense has been incurred that can only be measured by the excess (if any) of the market price at exercise date over the option price.

Measurement

There are four general criteria for measuring whether a plan is to be treated for accounting purposes as noncompensatory:

1. Substantially all full-time employees meeting limited employment qualifications may participate.
2. The stock is offered to eligible employees equally or as a uniform percentage of salary (although there may be a maximum number-of-shares restriction).
3. Exercise is limited to a reasonable period.

4. A discount from quoted market, if any, is no greater than would be expected in an offering to shareholders or others.

Plans not meeting these four criteria are considered compensatory. However, a compensatory plan does not necessarly require the recording of compensation, as discussed later under "Compensation."

Measurement Date. The measurement date is the first date on which both the number of shares granted and the option price are fixed. It is usually the grant date; however, in complex (variable) plans, it may be as late as the exercise date.

Renewal of an option arrangement establishes a new measurement date, but a reduction in the number of granted shares because of early termination does not affect this determination. For grants of convertible stock, the measurement date is normally the date the ratio of conversion is fixed. Compensation is measured using the higher of either the quoted market price of the convertible stock or the market price of the security obtainable upon conversion.

Measurement Principle. Compensation is measured as the difference between the option price and the quoted market price at the measurement date. Thus, if options are granted at market (and there are no other complicating features as mentioned later in this chapter), there is no compensation, even though the plan technically is a compensatory plan. If treasury stock is used to fulfill the share requirements, its cost may be used to measure the amount of compensation only if it is acquired during the fiscal period in which the awards are made and the awards are made shortly thereafter.

Cash paid to settle an earlier award of stock should measure compensation. This has, however, caused various problems. If the enterprise also grants the employee a "put" exercisable at quoted market price when the shares are issued (e.g., to avoid the costs of registration), does the exercise of the put qualify as "cash paid to settle an earlier award" and thereby cause compensation to be measured at the exercise date, presumably at a higher quoted market price? Some accountants believe that it does. Many others view the put as a mechanism to save costs of registration or to provide the employee with the sum necessary to pay the income taxes on the appreciation gain, not as cash paid to settle an option award, since presumably the employee could sell the shares on the open market and receive the same proceeds.

Compensation. Compensation expense related to stock options should be accrued and amortized over the periods the employee performs services. When the measurement date has not yet passed, compensation should be accrued by charges to expense based on the quoted market price at the end of a period. This estimation will cause adjustments of compensation expense in future periods through fluctuations in the quoted market price.

In Issue 87-33, *Stock Compensation Issues Related to Market Decline,* the EITF considered that a stock option plan may be changed to reflect the decline in market price of a security by (1) repricing, (2) cancelling and reissuing, or (3) repurchasing and issuing a new option. In such cases, the Task Force concluded that compensation expense should be measured by use of the current market price and any new exercise price, effectively a fresh-start approach.

In plans not resulting in the accrual of compensation expense, the enterprise usually receives a tax deduction for the appreciation gain when taxable to the employee deemed to have received the income. The tax benefit of the excess deduction, when realized, should be credited to paid-in capital, since it is similar to profits on treasury stock transactions. In those rare instances in which the tax deduction is less than the *recorded* compensation expense, the charge to paid-in capital is limited to the amount of previous credits for excess deductions, with any remainder included in income tax expense.

Variable Terms

There are plans in which events that may affect either the number of shares to be issued or the option price are not known or determinable at the grant date (e.g., market performance criteria or earnings level attainment). Accordingly, the measurement date has not yet arrived. In addition, there are combination or *tandem plans*; for example, alternative plans where the employee has a choice in exercising options under either plan but not both. One type of tandem plan may have a fixed number of shares at a fixed option price coupled with another option plan with variable terms; and it may also have a cash payment option. The compensation expense accrued should be based on the alternative the employee is most likely to choose at the date of accrual.

Stock-based plans are plans whose value is derived from the market price movement in the underlying security, although there may be no intent to issue a security or its issuance may be delayed, either at the discretion of the company or the option of the employee. Such plans are sometimes called *phantom* stock option plans. Common examples of those plans are stock appreciation rights (SARs) and employee stock ownership plans (ESOPs).

Incentive Stock Options. The Economic Recovery Tax Act of 1981 (ERTA) provided favorable tax treatment for individuals who own incentive stock options (ISOs). An individual could receive ISOs in two ways, by a corporation issuing new ISOs or by converting existing issued options to ISOs conforming with the requirements of ERTA. ISOs have since lost much of their allure because of the elimination of favorable capital gains tax rates and the classification of gains as tax preferences. The effects of the Tax Reform Act of 1986 (TRA 1986) on the design of option plans are mentioned in the next section.

A major ISO requirement is that the option price must equal or exceed the market value of the stock at the date of grant, or at the most recent date of a plan amendment, if later. Conversion to ISOs may have forced a company to increase the option price to meet this requirement (often referred to as "repricing"). To limit the amount of repricing, ERTA permits a company to cancel certain prior plan amendments, such as an amendment to provide a tandem SAR, and accordingly to utilize a previous date for determining the extent of repricing.

The accounting issues raised by the repricing and cancellation of prior plan amendments were addressed in TB 82-2, *Accounting for the Conversion of Stock*

Options as a Result of the Economic Recovery Tax Act of 1981 (C47.507–.516). If a company converted existing options to ISOs and was required to increase the option price to meet the repricing requirement, compensation expense recognized in previous periods (relating to the excess of market price of the stock at the measurement date over the option price) was recaptured as a reduction of compensation expense in the period in which the repricing occurred.

Tax-Law-Motivated Plan Changes. In Issue 87-6, *Adjustments Relating to Stock Compensation Plans,* the EITF addressed four issues generally related to the certain changes in treatment of stock plans under TRA 1986. The issues were discussed in early 1987 and a consensus reached, but it was found to be inadequate. The Task Force further discussed these matters at three ensuing meetings, and arrived at the conclusions discussed in the following four subsections.

Change from incentive stock options to nonqualified stock options. The Tax Reform Act of 1986 permits companies to disqualify outstanding ISOs and convert them to nonqualified stock options (NSOs) to obtain a tax deduction for the difference between the market price and exercise price at the date of exercise of the option by an employee. If the method used by a company to disqualify such options involves only minor technical changes, presumably only to force disqualification, such action does not create a new measurement date if the total effect on the value of the option to an employee is de minimis. That determination must be made on a case-by-case basis. Changes beyond the minimum for disqualification would presumptively lead to a new measurement date.

Tax-offset cash bonus. After a plan is changed into an NSO, the employee is required to pay tax on the excess of market value over exercise price at the date of grant. Some plans have therefore incorporated a cash bonus feature to reimburse employees for this outlay. (Note that the cash bonus feature would, in itself, change an ISO into an NSO.)

The EITF held that, only as to grants outstanding on April 7, 1987 (the date on which this consensus was reached), the accounting should be split: The cash portion (if it meets specified conditions) is treated as a variable plan with compensation expense measured at date of exercise (i.e., the cash bonus) and the option portion is treated as a fixed stock option plan (if the plan is an ISO plan that existed before February 26, 1987 (when the issue was first discussed), and has not had a subsequent increase in the number of authorized shares).

It seems apparent that the EITF did not relish tinkering with option plans merely because Congress changed the tax laws. For this reason the eye of the needle was made very small.

Extra shares to cover tax withholding. Some plans were amended to allow employees to use shares received upon exercise to cover the tax required to be withheld by the employer upon exercise. The EITF reached a consensus that the plan is still considered a fixed plan if it meets all the other APB 25 requirements and only the exact number of shares needed for the withholding were cashed.

Phantom stock-for-stock exercise. The EITF also dealt with a transaction in which an employee is pyramiding (see later herein), but does not actually give up presently owned shares; instead the employer merely issues certificates for the net shares that would have been obtainable had the shares been presented (hence, phantom exercise). The Task Force concluded that so long as the six month holding period is met (as discussed earlier), the plan remains a fixed plan.

Stock Appreciation Rights. SAR plans consist of awards of rights, usually granted in combination with compensatory stock option plans but sometimes granted separately. SARs entitle the recipient to receive cash, stock, or a combination of both in an amount equivalent to the increase in quoted market price over the option price for a fixed number of shares. The option price is usually the quoted market price at date of grant. When granted in combination with other stock option plans, the SARs usually provide that the rights of each are mutually exclusive; that is, employees may elect benefits under one plan or the other, but not both. Accounting for SARs is dealt with in FIN 28, *Accounting for Stock Appreciation Rights and Other Variable Stock Option or Award Plans* (C47), which contains computational illustrations.

For SARs and other variable option plans, compensation should be measured as the amount by which the current quoted market price of the underlying stock exceeds the option price, subject to maximum limitations, if any, in the plan. Accordingly, variations in the quoted market price change the measure of compensation. Compensation should be accrued, as in other plans, over the period of the employee's service. This accrual is adjusted in subsequent periods for changes in the quoted market price (either up or down).

For combination or tandem plans, the choice that the employee is most likely to make determines the manner of computing compensation expense for the period. However, if a company has been accruing compensation based on the SAR alternative and circumstances change, the compensation previously accrued is not adjusted to a lower amount.

Employee Stock Ownership Plans. Another stock compensation arrangement is an ESOP. In one ESOP form, the ESOP borrows money from a bank and purchases the enterprise's stock. The loan is frequently guaranteed, formally, or as a practical matter informally, by the enterprise, and thus should be shown as a loan in the sponsor enterprise's financial statements with a corresponding decrease in shareholders' equity. In SOP 76-3, *Accounting Practices for Certain Employee Stock Ownership Plans* (TP 10,130), the AICPA takes the position that since the ESOP has no substance independent of its sponsor's undertaking to make future cash contributions, the sponsoring enterprise should record the cash received from the ESOP for the stock purchase as a loan. Further, payments by the ESOP on its bank debt should be recognized by the sponsor to reduce the "loan," and the equity offset shown in its financial statements. All shares held by the ESOP are to be treated as outstanding and included in EPS calculations.

In Issue 86-27, *Measurement of Excess Contributions to a Defined Contribution Plan or Employee Stock Ownership Plan,* the EITF concluded that the unallocated shares of common stock contributed to an ESOP should be reported as a reduction of shareholders' equity, as if such shares were treasury stock. In addition, since dividends paid are to be invested in additional stock, the dividends on unallocated stock do not create income and should increase treasury stock, not reduce retained earnings. Compensation expense at the allocation date should be recognized and should be based on the market value of the stock at the allocation date. The difference between the purchase price and the current market price of such "treasury stock" should be recognized as an increase or decrease in shareholders' equity.

Junior Common Stock. Junior common stock plans were increasingly popular among the many new high technology companies that were a growing factor in financial markets during 1983 (see Chapter 39). Such plans have been used to defend against competing start-up companies by retaining key talent. Important employees are offered the junior common stock at a price significantly less than the company's regular common stock price. If certain performance goals are met (i.e., in levels of sales or earnings), the stock is immediately exchangeable for the company's regular common stock, which presumably would have appreciated greatly in value as a result of the achievement of the performance goals.

In late 1983, the SEC administratively concluded that all plans and issuances henceforth would have to be accounted for in a manner similar to that for SARs. The amount of compensation expense to be recognized is not determined at the inception of the plan, but rather is measured at the date the junior common stock is convertible to full common stock. In 1984, the FASB issued FIN 38, *Determining the Measurement Date for Stock Option, Purchase and Award Plans Involving Junior Common Stock* (C47.135A), that incorporated the SEC position into GAAP.

Permanent Discount Plans. Permanent discount restricted stock purchase plans involve stock sold to employees at a price below market value. If a holder of such stock subsequently wishes to sell it, the company has a right of first refusal to purchase the shares at the then current market value, less the original discount. At issue is whether and how APB 25 applies to such plans and how charges to earnings, if any, are to be determined.

This subject was discussed by the EITF in Issue 84-34, *Permanent Discount Restricted Stock Purchase Plans.* Although no consensus was reached, the majority of the EITF indicated that they viewed the plans as a bargain purchase or ("cheap stock," in the SEC vernacular) and believed that such plans were always compensatory. The principal question related to the method of measurement of compensation expense. Most EITF members supported a date-of-grant measurement. However, some believed an accounting treatment similar to that for an SAR might be required under APB 25 if it is likely that the company would exercise its right of first refusal or the employee has a put back to the company. The buyback could be viewed as cash paid to settle an earlier award under APB 25, in which case the cash paid should be used to measure compensation cost.

The FASB staff's preliminary view is that permanent discount plans are always compensatory because the employee enjoys all the rights of a shareholder, including the benefit of all subsequent market appreciation, while making an investment significantly below market. The SEC Observer also indicated there is a presumption that such plans are compensatory, and if reviewed by the SEC staff and found to be compensatory when the registrant had not accounted for them as such, retroactive application would be required. Some EITF members suggested that it might be prudent for companies to review their plans with the SEC until the FASB project reconsidering APB 25 is completed.

Book Value Plans. In Issue 87-23, *Book Value Stock Purchase Plans,* the EITF considered the accounting for book value stock purchase plans. In a private company situation, the EITF concluded that if an employee makes a substantive investment in such a plan and that amount is at some market risk for a significant period of time, no compensation expense should be recognized if the employee sells shares back to the company (or to an ESOP) at fixed or determinable dates or at retirement. In addition, no compensation expense is recognized at any interim point. However, if the company (either private or public) "sells" options to an employee and the employee can sell such options back to the company at fixed and determinable dates, at retirement, or upon leaving the company, compensation expense should be recognized amounting to the difference between the grant price and the "exercise" price.

In Issue 88-6, *Book Value Stock Plans in an Initial Public Offering,* the EITF considered the accounting for book value stock purchase and stock option plans in a company undergoing an initial public offering (IPO). The Task Force concluded that book value *purchase* plans of public companies should be considered to be performance plans and accounted for like SARs.

As to book value *option* plans that convert to market value stock options (i.e., changes in market value rather than book value would henceforth govern compensation expense measurement), the EITF concluded that compensation expense should be recognized upon successful completion of the IPO in an amount equal to the difference between the market value (i.e., IPO issue price) and the book value, because the IPO results in a new measurement date; however, after this adjustment there would be no more compensation expense assuming the plan is not further changed.

For *option* plans that remain pegged to book value after the IPO, the EITF consensus holds that they will continue to be accounted for like SARs; but these plans will also require a one-shot charge to compensation expense at the consummation of the IPO to reflect the increase in book value (negative dilution) resulting from the IPO.

For stock *purchase* plans in which book value stock converts to market value stock at the IPO date, no compensation expense is to be recognized, provided however that shares issued under the plan within one year prior to the IPO are presumed to have been issued in contemplation of the IPO; as to such shares, compensation expense would be based on fair value at date of issuance. The same is true for purchase plans in which book value remains the measurement basis. However, book value purchase plans would continue to have compensation expense after the IPO, while market value plans would not.

Because of the complexity of these discussions, the abstract of Issue 88-6 contains an appendix indicating whether Issue 87-23 or Issue 88-6 applies, and the consensus answers. The SEC Observer made various remonstrations during the extended discussions, to the effect that: (1) pro forma data is essential in IPO registrations; (2) the one-year presumption zone could be longer depending on the evidence; and (3) if a company effectively may be required to buy back the issued stock, it will have to be classified outside shareholders' equity.

Pyramiding

An option transaction in which an employee tenders appreciated shares already held as the consideration for exercise of additional options is called pyramiding. This transaction theoretically could be replicated until the optionee has acquired all the stock currently available under option.

Taken to its extreme, an employee would exercise an option by purchasing only one share whose market value exceeds the option price, then continuously exchange appreciated shares for "bargain" shares using a pyramiding approach. Since some shares must be given up as the consideration, the optionee ultimately holds fewer shares than would be obtainable had cash been paid for the entire option price of the option shares, but the shares obtained through the pyramiding technique have been obtained with a miniscule payment of cash.

In Issue 84-18, *Stock Option Pyramiding,* the EITF considered whether there should be a required holding period for the stock exchanged to avoid the conclusion that the award of the option is, in substance, a cash award (thereby requiring a compensation charge), and if so how long the holding period should be. The Task Force concluded that a holding period is necessary, but did not agree on its length; however, a majority felt that six months would be adequate. This issue will be addressed in the FASB's project to reconsider APB 25.

FASB Reconsideration of APB 25

In 1984, the FASB approved adding reconsideration of APB 25, *Accounting for Stock Issued to Employees* (C47), to its agenda. Thereafter, the staff issued an Invitation to Comment (FASB, 1984a), which is an extraction of the AcSEC Issues Paper on *Accounting for Employee Capital Accumulation Plans* (AICPA, 1982a).

During the term of this project, the FASB has reached a number of tentative decisions, only to reconsider and change them in subsequent deliberations. One of the revised tentative decisions would abandon the minimum value option pricing model in favor of a fair value approach. The current tentative decisions, although subject to further change, are summarized as follows:

- The measurement method for compensation cost is the fair value of the options with a rebuttable presumption that fair value is not less than the minimum value. Fair value is generally (and tentatively) defined as the sum of the intrinsic value of the option (market price of the underlying security less the exercise price of the option) plus the time value (the value associated with a fixed exercise price effective for a fixed period, net of the value of the effect of the restrictions placed on an employee option).

- Minimum value is computed as the difference between (1) the market price of a company's stock at grant and (2) the present value of the exercise price and estimated dividends during the option period. The discount rate used to arrive at present value is a risk-free rate corresponding to the length of the option period (such as a corresponding treasury rate); dividends are based on best estimates but subject to a rebuttable presumption that they would be an extension of the current dividend pattern.

- The final measurement date is the later of the vesting date or the first date on which certain measurement factors, including number of shares and purchase price, are known.
- The provision in some plans requiring exercise on or shortly after termination is not sufficiently material to delay final measurement of compensation cost beyond the date described above.
- The criteria for describing a noncompensatory plan contained in APB 25 should be abandoned.

The FASB staff continues to perform research as directed by the Board. When this is completed, the Board will readdress the schedule for issuing an exposure draft, holding a public hearing and issuing a final statement.

PRESENTATION AND DISCLOSURE

General Requirements

The disclosure requirements for equity accounts (C08.102) include a description of the changes in each account as well as the changes in the number of shares for at least the annual period(s) for which financial statements are presented. Thus, a two-year comparative statement would contain a two-year analysis of changes.

Regulation S-X, Rule 5-02.30, requires disclosure of: the title of each security; the number of shares authorized, issued, or outstanding; and the total dollar amount of issued or outstanding stock. In addition, the SEC requires (under Rule 4-08(d) of Regulation S-X) that the liquidation preference of preferred stock be shown on the face of the balance sheet, if it is different than par or stated value.

In practice, a statement of shareholders' equity is provided for each period for which an income statement is given. Although this is an SEC rule, most companies (including those not publicly held) comply, and such presentation has become generally accepted.

Figure 20.2 provides an example of the typical balance sheet equity section classifications that would be supplemented by presentation of activity for the period and by footnote disclosures.

To comply with the detailed disclosure requirements, many enterprises present a statement of shareholders' equity for each period (Figure 20.3) and incorporate share changes instead of cramming all the information into the balance sheet captions.

There are other variations of the preceding, all of which are acceptable as long as all necessary disclosure requirements are met either in tabular or narrative form.

Footnotes

Changes or activity in the equity accounts are frequently disclosed in footnotes. Typical disclosures are (1) shares issuable upon and/or reserved for conversion or exercise of convertible securities, options, warrants, and rights; (2) features of preferred stock (i.e., voting, cumulative, redeemable); (3) restrictions on retained earnings; and (4) dividends per share and in the aggregate.

	January 31,	
Stockholders' Equity	**1986**	**1987**
Convertible preferred stock, $1 par stated at preference in involuntary liquidation authorized 500,000 shares; issued and outstanding 31,936 and 42,586 shares	$ 422	$ 562
Common stock, $1 par authorized 10,000,000 shares; issued and outstanding 5,103,662 and 4,857,373 shares	5,104	4,857
Additional paid-in capital	50,992	47,926
Retained earnings	6,575	18,204
	$63,093	$71,549

FIG. 20.2   Typical Balance Sheet Equity Classifications ($ in 000)
Source: Manhattan Industries Inc., Annual Report for year ending January 31, 1987.

An example of footnote disclosure of equity account transactions, highlighting a stock dividend, a stock split, and a special conversion feature, is given in Figure 20.4.

Since the terms of stock-based option and purchase plans require disclosure, including number of shares, option prices, and number of shares exercisable, those types of footnotes appear regularly in annual reports (see Figure 20.5).

Mandatorily Redeemable Preferred Stock

ASR 268 (FRR § 211) requires that mandatorily redeemable preferred stock (or for that matter other redeemable equity-type securities discussed in Chapter 21) cannot be included under the caption "Shareholders' Equity," but must be shown separately in a preceding caption (referred to as the "mezzanine"). This rule does not apply to privately held companies, and therefore practice among non-SEC registrants is mixed.

In addition, ASR 268 requires footnote disclosure of redemption features, combined aggregate amount of redemption requirements for the ensuing five years, and changes in such stock for periods presented in the financial statements. This footnote requirement is in addition to any statement presentation that may incorporate some or all of the disclosure features. An example of ASR 268 compliance is presented in Figure 20.6.

In Issue 86-32, *Early Extinguishment of a Subsidiary's Mandatorily Redeemable Preferred Stock,* the EITF considered the accounting by a company for the reacquisition of outstanding mandatorily redeemable preferred stock (MRPS) issued by a wholly owned subsidiary. Such stock is, of course, carried in the consolidated financial statements as minority interest, as if a liability. Because of its liability-like characteristics when considered from the perspective of the consolidated financial statements, a question arose as to whether repurchasing the MRPS at a substantial premium had to be treated in the consolidated financial statements as a loss on extinguishment of debt. The Task Force reached a consensus that the reacquisition of such preferred stock should be accounted for as a capital stock transaction; accordingly, the consolidated entity would record neither gain nor loss.

	Preferred stock	Common stock	Additional paid-in capital	Retained earnings	Treasury stock	Notes receivable
Balance at June 30, 1984	$ 2	$6,689	$49,507	$36,355	$ (2,871)	$ (2,344)
Net earnings				15,509		
Cash dividends ($.36 per common share)				(7,463)		
5 for 4 stock split		1,672		(1,672)		
Issuance of 3,440,860 common shares to ESOP		1,434	37,766			(38,566)
Purchase of treasury stock, 8,663 shares					(145)	
Issuance of preferred stock, Series B, 243 shares			629			(629)
Repurchase of preferred stock, Series B, 186 shares			(407)			407
Other		20	223			
Balance at June 30, 1985	2	9,815	87,718	42,729	(3,016)	(41,132)
Net earnings				3,582		
Cash dividends ($.36 per common share)				(8,312)		
Purchase of treasury stock, 280,600 shares					(2,639)	
Repurchase of preferred stock, Series B, 161 shares			(215)			215
Conversion of preferred stock, Series B, 100 shares and Series A, 1,000 shares	(1)	86	(85)			636
Other		10	115		1	
Balance at June 30, 1986	1	9,911	87,533	37,999	(5,654)	(40,281)
Net earnings (loss)				(5,445)		
Cash dividends ($.36 per common share)				(8,183)		
Purchase of treasury stock, 664,912 shares					(5,801)	
Conversion of preferred stock, Series B, 600 shares		47	(46)			483
Reduction of ESOP note receivable						2,600
Other		5	342			
Balance at June 30, 1987	$ 1	$9,963	$87,829	$24,371	$(11,455)	$(37,198)

FIG. 20.3 Columnar Statement of Stockholders' Equity ($ in 000)
Source: National Convenience Stores Incorporated, 1987 Annual Report.

Note 10. Stockholders' Equity

The two classes of Company's Common Stock are identical in all respects except that (a) all voting rights are held by the owners of Class B Common Stock and (b) holders of Class A Common Stock are entitled to receive dividends, when, as and if declared by the Board of Directors whether or not dividends are declared in respect of the Class B Common Stock, but in the event of the declaration of a dividend in respect of the Class B Common Stock, a dividend of at least the same amount must be declared in respect of the Class A Common Stock. The Company's Certificate of Incorporation provides that upon an affirmative vote of the holders of two-thirds of the outstanding Class B Common Stock, all shares of Class A Common Stock will be converted into Class B Common Stock. The conversion terms are one share of Class A Common Stock for one share of Class B Common Stock subject to certain antidilutive or other capital reorganization provisions.

On October 28, 1986, the Company declared an increased cash dividend of $.135 on the Class A Common Stock and a Class A Common Stock dividend of 3% on both the Class A and Class B Common Stock payable on January 2, 1987 to stockholders of record as of December 1, 1986.

On November 13, 1985 the Company declared a 2 for 1 stock split effected in the form of a 100% stock dividend to shareholders of record on November 25, 1985, payable December 2, 1985. In conjunction with this 2 for 1 stock split, $488,000 and $477,000 have been transferred from retained earnings to Class A Common Stock and $385,000 and $374,000 have been transferred from retained earnings to Class B Common Stock, at March 31, 1985 and 1984, respectively. The Company utilized all of its treasury shares in the payment of the 100% stock dividend and such utilization was accounted for in the third quarter of fiscal 1986. In addition to a $.125 regular cash dividend on the Class A Common Stock paid on January 2, 1986 to shareholders of record on December 3, 1985, a 3% stock dividend of Class A Common Stock was declared for each share of Class A Common Stock and Class B Common Stock outstanding to shareholders of record on December 3, 1985. Net income per share of common stock has been restated to reflect the current and prior years stock dividends and the 2 for 1 stock split. The number of shares issued, the number of treasury shares, and the cash dividends per share have been restated to reflect the 2 for 1 stock split.

On October 31, 1984, the Company declared, in addition to $.125 regular cash dividend on the Class A Common Stock, an extra stock dividend of 3% on both the Class A and Class B Common Stock payable on January 2, 1985 to stockholders of record as of December 3, 1984.

Changes in Class A Common Stock, Class B Common Stock, and Capital in Excess of Par Value during 1987, 1986 and 1985 were as follows:

| | CLASS A COMMON STOCK | | | | CLASS B COMMON STOCK | | Capital in Excess of Par Value |
| | Issued | | Treasury | | Issued | | |
	Shares	Amount	Shares	Amount	Shares	Amount	
Balance, March 31, 1984	9,543,604	954,000	2,325,326	(13,381,000)	7,480,000	748,000	17,609,000
3% Stock Dividend	261,076	22,000			224,400	22,000	6,089,000
Balance, March 31, 1985	9,759,680	$976,000	2,325,326	$(13,381,000)	7,704,400	$770,000	$23,698,000
Cancellation	(2,315,346)	(231,000)	(2,315,346)	13,323,000			(13,092,000)
Savings Incentive Plan(1)	16,672	2,000	(9,980)	58,000			276,000
3% Stock Dividend	444,280	44,000					10,521,000
Registration Costs							(209,000)
Balance, March 31, 1986	7,905,286	$791,000	—	—	7,704,400	$770,000	$21,194,000
Savings Incentive Plan(1)	22,824	2,000					589,000
3% Stock Dividend	468,471	47,000					12,133,000
Balance, March 31, 1987	8,396,581	$840,000	—	—	7,704,400	$770,000	$33,916,000

1 The Company has a voluntary savings plan for eligible domestic employees. Company contributions to this 401(K) plan are made in the form of the Company's Class A common stock.

FIG. 20.4 Typical Equity Footnote
Source: Block Drug Company, Inc., 1987 Annual Report.

The Company has three stock option plans. Under a non-qualified plan adopted in 1985 (1985 Plan), there are 333,333 shares of common stock reserved for grant. Under the incentive stock option plan adopted in 1981 and restated in 1984 (1984 Plan), there are 583,333 shares of common stock reserved for grant. A qualified stock option plan adopted in 1974 (1974 Plan) expired in 1984. Unexercised options previously granted under this plan, less all forfeitures after the 1984 expiration date, remain outstanding.

Under the terms of the 1985 Plan, options are granted at a price not less than the fair market value of the Company's common stock at date of grant. The options are exercisable at the discretion of the Board of Directors.

Under the terms of the 1984 Plan and the 1974 Plan, options are granted at prices not less than the fair market value of the Company's common stock at date of grant. The options are exercisable at a rate of 20% per year, on a cumulative basis, beginning on the date of the grant.

Stock option transactions under the plans are summarized as follows:

	Number of Shares	Option Price Per Share
Outstanding at January 1, 1984	390,881	$3.45–$12.28
Granted	109,518	9.85– 13.13
Forfeited	(47,001)	3.45– 13.13
Exercised	(17,973)	3.45– 4.28
Outstanding at December 31, 1984	435,425	3.45– 12.28
Granted	274,363	7.38– 12.75
Forfeited	(47,654)	4.28– 12.28
Exercised	(52,013)	3.45– 9.84
Outstanding at December 31, 1985	610,121	3.45– 12.75
Granted	124,950	9.88– 11.75
Forfeited	(9,555)	4.28– 12.28
Exercised	(116,152)	3.45– 12.28
Outstanding at December 31, 1986	609,364	5.67–$12.75

Options exercisable at December 31, 1986, 1985 and 1984 were for 356,604, 371,935 and 98,071 shares of common stock, respectively. Options available for future grant at December 31, 1986, 1985 and 1984 were for 118,880, 234,275 and 127,655 shares of common stock respectively.

FIG. 20.5 Typical Stock Option Footnote
Source: Lamaur Inc., 1986 Annual Report.

	December 31	
	1987	1986
Redeemable Preferred Stock		
$3.60 cumulative series A convertible preferred stock, without par value, 3,590,983 shares authorized, 3,582,832 shares issued, and 2,421,437 and 3,436,037 shares outstanding at redemption value of $45.000 per share	108,964	154,622
Non-Redeemable Preferred Stock		
Convertible preferred stock, second series, without par value, 2,650,500 shares authorized, issued, and outstanding at liquidation value of $3.87 per share	10,260	–
Common Stockholders' Equity		
Common stock, par value of $0.01 in 1987 and $1.00 in 1986 per share, 75,000,000 shares authorized and 14,355,101 and 14,300,697 shares issued	144	18,218
Paid-in capital	74,726	51,494
Retained earnings (deficit)	(28,144)	(37,342)
Cumulative translation adjustment	1,991	(3,493)
	48,717	28,877
Less Treasury stock at cost (228,730 and 359 shares)	(2,095)	(4)
Total Common Stockholders' Equity	**46,622**	**28,873**

FIG. 20.6   Exclusion From Shareholders' Equity of Mandatory Redemption Preferred Stock ($ In 000)
Source: Fairchild Industries, Inc., 1987 Annual Report.

EARNINGS PER SHARE

EPS data are considered an important tool in making investment decisions and are required to be shown on the face of the income statements of publicly held companies for all periods presented. Non-public companies are excluded from the requirement (E09.101),[4] as are mutual enterprises that do not have outstanding common stock or equivalents (mutual savings banks, cooperatives, credit unions, and similar entities).

EPS computations are governed principally by APB 15, *Earnings Per Share,* and FIN 28 and FIN 31 dealing with stock compensation plans. The bulk of EPS interpretations come, however, from over 100 detailed cases considered by the AICPA staff, incorporated into FASB standards at E09.503–.916. In the discussion that follows, reference should be made to the basic requirements contained in E09.101–.161 except as otherwise indicated.

---

[4] A nonpublic company is defined as "an enterprise other than one (a) whose debt or equity securities trade in a public market on a foreign or domestic stock exchange or in the over-the-counter market (including securities quoted only locally or regionally) or (b) that is required to file financial statements with the Securities and Exchange Commission" (E09.417). However, when EPS data are presented for a nonpublic enterprise, the presentation must be in conformity with APB 15, *Earnings Per Share* (E09).

Capital Structures

The extent of required EPS data varies with the complexity of the capital structure and income statement items. For simple capital structures (no potentially dilutive securities), a single presentation expressed as EPS is required. For complex capital structures at least two presentations of EPS data are required on the income statement, *primary EPS* and *fully diluted EPS.*

Primary EPS consists of earnings divided by the aggregate of (1) weighted average shares outstanding during the period plus (2) common stock equivalents if the effect is dilutive. Fully diluted EPS is a pro forma presentation that reflects a "worst case" position as if all contingent issuances that reduce EPS had occurred at the beginning of the period. Common stock equivalents should not be included in primary or fully diluted EPS calculations if their inclusion would have the effect of increasing the EPS amount or decreasing the loss-per-share amount (antidilution). Dilution of 3% or less in the aggregate may be omitted for all calculations.

Primary EPS. Primary EPS is based on outstanding shares and common stock equivalents. The latter are securities that may, by their nature or terms, be converted into common stock (e.g., convertible debt or preferred stock; options and warrants; participating securities; and contingent shares). The determination of whether a convertible security is a common stock equivalent to be included in primary EPS is made only at the time of issuance and is not changed thereafter.[5] If a convertible security is not a common stock equivalent as defined, then it is included in the computation of fully diluted EPS.

There are four guidelines used to ascertain whether a security is a common stock equivalent:

1. If the effective yield on convertible debt or preferred stock at issuance is less than 66-2/3% of the average Aa corporate bond yield, the security is a common stock equivalent.[6]

2. Options and warrants (and similar securities) always are common stock equivalents.

3. If the features of participating securities enable them to share in earnings potential of enterprise, they are deemed to be common stock equivalents.

4. If contingent shares are issuable based on mere passage of time or conditions unrelated to earnings or market price, they are deemed to be common stock equivalents.

Fully Diluted EPS. Fully diluted EPS computations are required if (1) common stock was issued during the period upon conversion of convertible securities or exercise of options and warrants or (2) there were contingently issuable shares at the

---

[5] There is an exception to this rule, involving resale of convertible securities from the treasury; see "Basic Considerations."

[6] APB 15 originally based this test on the bank prime rate, which proved to be unworkable; SFAS 55, *Determining Whether a Convertible Security Is a Common Stock Equivalent,* thus changed it to the cash yield on Aa corporate bonds without the conversion feature. In Issue 84-16, *Earnings-Per-Share Cash-Yield Test for Zero Coupon Bonds,* the EITF discussed the fact that the APB 15 test automatically resulted in all zero coupon bonds being classified as common stock equivalents. The consensus of the Task Force was that the test should be revised. This revision was made in SFAS 85, *Yield Test for Determining Whether a Convertible Security Is a Common Stock Equivalent.*

period close. Those requirements are met if (1) there is a convertible security that is not a common stock equivalent, (2) options and warrants are outstanding, or (3) shares are issuable based on earnings or market price conditions. If primary EPS would have been reduced by more than 3% had the actual issuance of such shares been made at the beginning of the period, fully diluted EPS must be presented.

Supplementary EPS. In addition to primary and fully diluted EPS, supplementary EPS is required (preferably in a note) when:

1. Conversions of convertible securities that are not common stock equivalents occurred during the period covered by the financial statements (or shortly thereafter but before issuance of the financial statements).
2. A sale of common stock occurs during the period (or shortly thereafter, as above) and the proceeds are used to retire preferred stock or debt.

Supplementary EPS is essentially a pro forma calculation of what the primary EPS would have been had the conversions or issuances occurred at the beginning of the reporting period, and would have changed primary EPS by more than 3%.

Computation and Presentation

Because the computational guidelines required to calculate EPS are complex, a tome of unofficial interpretations has been assembled over time to assist accountants in applying them (E09.501–.916).

Treasury Stock Method. The amount of dilutive shares to be reflected in EPS data should be computed by applying the treasury stock method. This method assumes that the proceeds to be obtained upon exercise of an option will be used to purchase common stock at the average market price during the period for primary EPS, and at the higher of average market price or end-of-period price for fully diluted EPS.

For example, if a company had options for 100 shares outstanding at an exercise price of $10, the $1,000 proceeds would be presumed to have been spent to repurchase common stock at the average market price, for primary EPS purposes. If that average market price were $20, then 500 shares would have been repurchased, leaving 500 shares (1,000 issued upon presumed exercise less 500 repurchased) to be included as additional outstanding shares. As a practical matter, exercise is not assumed until the market price exceeds the option price for at least the last three months of the period for which the EPS computation is made.

In FIN 31, *Treatment of Stock Compensation Plans in EPS Computations* (E09.128–.131), the FASB resolved an apparent conflict between APB 15 and FIN 28, *Accounting for Stock Appreciation Rights and Other Variable Stock or Award Plans* (C47), as to the appropriate method of deriving proceeds under the treasury stock method. FIN 31 states that for certain stock options, including SARs and other variable award plans, the exercise proceeds are considered to be the sum of (1) the amount the employee must pay, (2) the amount of deferred compensation expense, and (3) the amount of any excess tax benefit that would be credited to paid-in capital.

The use of the treasury stock method should also be modified in certain other instances. For rights or warrants that require the tendering of debt in lieu of cash payment, or for any other convertible securities, the *if converted method* should be used (E09.126). This method assumes that the applicable debt or preferred stock was tendered and/or converted. The common shares issuable are considered outstanding, and earnings applicable to common stock are increased for any after-tax interest savings or through reduced preferred dividend requirements.

For rights or warrants that permit (but do not require) the tendering of debt or other securities (synthetics), the computation depends on the test met. Those tests are (E09.126):

(a) The market price of the related common stock exceeds the exercise price.

(b) The security that may be (or must be) tendered is selling at a price below that at which it may be tendered under the option or warrant agreement and the resulting discount is sufficient to establish an effective exercise price below the market price of the common stocks that can be obtained upon exercise.

If both tests are met, the computation depends on the alternatives available to the holder, with the one most beneficial to the holder deemed to be chosen. If the first test is met, the treasury stock method must be used. If the second test is met, the computations must follow the *if converted method* as described previously for warrants that require the tendering of debt or other securities. (There are other permutations in this genre depending on whether only one of the tests is met and the holder has more than one option. These matters are described in E09.767–.785.)

If the number of shares obtainable upon exercise of all outstanding options and warrants exceeds 20% of outstanding common stock at period end, a modification of the treasury stock method is required. In that case, all options and warrants (dilutive or antidilutive) are presumed exercised, and the proceeds are applied in steps. First, stock is assumed to be repurchased up to a maximum of 20% of outstanding shares. Second, the balance of the proceeds, if any, is assumed to be applied to reduce borrowings, and any excess remaining is assumed to be applied to the purchase of U.S. government securities with appropriate recognition of income tax effects. The result of this two-step approach is aggregated and, if dilutive, enters the EPS computations.

The application of the treasury stock method can be very difficult, and several unofficial interpretations (see E09.684–.760) should be read to understand it. It is also likely, because of the averaging methods used, that the total sum of the four individual quarters will not equal the EPS on an annual basis, as in Figure 20.7.

Basic Considerations. All EPS calculations should be based on the weighted average number of common and common equivalent shares outstanding. Reacquired shares should be excluded from date of acquisition.

Sometimes the dilutive effect of a common stock equivalent might not be obvious. If there are several EPS captions required to be presented, inclusion of a common stock equivalent may be dilutive as to some EPS amounts but antidilutive as to others. In that case, even if antidilutive as to one of the required per share amounts, the dilutive effect should be included for all other computations (E09.121, n.8).

A delay in the effective date of a conversion privilege may affect the computation of EPS. If there is a delay of 10 years or more in the effective date of the conversion

Earnings per share for any period is calculated on the basis of the weighted average number of shares and share equivalents outstanding during the period. Issuances of significant numbers of shares or shares equivalents during any period (such as the issuance of $50 million principal amount each of 7% Convertible Subordinated Debentures due 2011 and 7¼% Convertible Subordinated Debentures due 2011 in August, 1986) have less impact on earnings per share during that period than in subsequent periods when such shares or share equivalents have been outstanding for the full period. Furthermore, the sum of earnings per share of all quarters in any period may not equal the earnings per share for the period because of different market prices for shares and number of shares outstanding during each quarter in the period. Earnings per share have been adjusted to reflect the distribution of Series A Preferred Stock. For further information relating to earnings per share, see Note 1 of Notes of Consolidated Financial Statements.

FIG. 20.7 Four Quarters' EPS Different From Annual EPS
Source: Columbia Savings and Loan Association, 1986 Annual Report.

feature, the security does not enter either the primary or fully diluted computation. If the delay is between 5 and 10 years, the security is included only in the fully diluted computation.

A sale of convertible securities from the treasury may affect the classification of existing outstanding securities. If the sale of a convertible security would be considered a common stock equivalent under current market conditions, any outstanding convertible securities of that same issue would also have to change classification (see E09.631).

A schedule or note should explain the basis on which primary and fully diluted EPS are calculated. The note should describe all assumptions and any adjustments used in arriving at the EPS data. See Figure 20.8 for an example of typical footnote disclosures of EPS computations.

Two-Class and Participating Stocks. Under the two-class method, participating securities are treated as the equivalent of common stock with a different dividend rate. The computation requires that the current distributions on the common and participating security be deducted from net earnings; the remainder (undistributed earnings) is divided by the total shares of common and participating stock outstanding to arrive at a per-share amount. This computed per-share amount is added to the common distribution to arrive at primary EPS (for an example of this calculation, see E09.846).

Contingent Issuances. Contingent issuances are usually based on earnings or market price. As a general rule, contingent shares are included in EPS calculations when the conditions precedent to their issuance are currently being met. If attainment or maintenance of a higher earnings level is the condition required to issue additional shares, the additional shares would be included in EPS on a fully diluted basis (giving effect to a higher earnings level) only if dilution results.

Contingent shares based on market price usually fall into two categories: (1) those with future market price guarantees (e.g., market price on issued shares will increase

Primary earnings per share is computed based on the weighted average number of shares plus shares issuable under stock option plans, reduced by the shares which could be purchased with the assumed proceeds from such shares. The primary earnings per share calculation does not give effect to the conversion of convertible subordinated debentures when such securities are not considered common stock equivalents or have an antidilutive effect on earnings per share. Fully diluted earnings per share assumes conversion of all convertible securities unless antidilutive.

The financial statements and all share and per share data have been retroactively adjusted for the three-for-two stock splits effected by 50% stock dividends on December 18, 1986, June 27, 1985 and September 18, 1984. As described in Note D the December 18, 1986 stock dividend for the Class A common shareholders was effected by the issuance of shares of Class A Special Common Stock.

FIG. 20.8   Typical EPS Footnote
Source: Comcast Corporation, 1986 Annual Report.

$5 over the next three years, or market on issued shares will not be less than $10 per share) and (2) those using market price conditions to determine the additional number of shares to be issued (predetermined total price originally fixed divided by market price at a later specified date).

When contingent shares are issuable based on future market price criteria, EPS calculations are based on the current period-end price. If the number of shares contingently issuable on a market price guarantee changes from earlier estimates, prior EPS calculations should be retroactively adjusted to reflect the new estimate.

Earnings contingencies may be complex; some may be based on total shares (i.e., one share for each $100 earned); others may be based on a formula approach (i.e., 10 times average earnings for five years divided by market price); still others may be premised on a maintenance of earnings and increased earnings levels. Both market price and earnings level contingencies may have variations of all methods (a formula basis with a minimum and maximum number of shares). If shares are issuable based on the present earnings level, and that level is currently being attained, all shares issuable would be considered outstanding for both primary and fully diluted purposes.

Shares issuable for earnings contingencies, either the maintenance of a level or the attainment of an increased level, are not retroactively changed for decreases (a drop in earnings level giving fewer shares earned) until the agreement expires and the lower number of shares is actually issued. If a higher number of shares is issued than assumed in prior-period calculations, those EPS calculations are not restated.

EPS Captions. EPS amounts (primary, and fully diluted if applicable) are required to be given for certain captions in the income statement: income from continuing operations; discontinued operations; income before extraordinary items; effect of changes in accounting principle (cumulative and pro forma); and net income. In addition, per-share amounts of prior-period adjustments should be disclosed, and EPS restated if appropriate (A35.105). EPS data should be restated for stock dividends, splits, and reverse splits, even those occurring after a period closes but before financial statements are issued. EPS data on any other captions, such as unusual and infrequently occurring events, may be disclosed, but only in footnotes and not on the face of the income statement.

SEC Requirements

Earnings Applicable to Common Stock. In SAB 64, *Income or Loss Applicable to Common Stock* (Topic 6.B.1), the SEC added reporting requirements for income or loss applicable to common stock. Prior to issuance of the SAB, the SEC's general position was that the amount of net income or loss applicable to common stock did not have to be disclosed on the face of the income statement except in unusual situations. SAB 64 indicates that such income or loss should be reported on the face of the income statement if the amount is materially different (interpreted to be 10% or more) from reported net income or loss, or if the amount is indicative of some significant trend. The amount is calculated by deducting from reported net income or loss (1) dividends on preferred stock, including undeclared or unpaid dividends if cumulative, and (2) periodic accretion in the carrying amounts of redeemable preferred stocks.

Cheap Stock. If stock is issued to selected persons at prices substantially below an IPO price, the SEC staff requires that such stock be presented as outstanding for all periods reported, in a registration statement covering an IPO. The SEC staff believes that this departure from the computational guidelines of APB 15 is necessary because of the relatively small consideration typically received for cheap stock.

The SEC follows a similar position for stock options, warrants, or other potentially dilutive securities granted or issued during the period prior to IPO. When the exercise price is less than the proposed public offering price, the EPS should be calculated using the treasury stock method as if such securities had been outstanding for all reported periods.

According to SAB 64 (Topic 4.D), the SEC staff will not normally insist on treating these types of instruments as outstanding prior to their issuance if:

1. The company can demonstrate that the securities are issued for their estimated fair value on the dates issued (or, regarding shares issued upon exercise of warrants, that the respective warrants were issued for their estimated fair value on the dates issued), and
2. The securities are not issued in contemplation of a public offering. Regarding this criterion, the SEC staff will generally presume that stock and warrants issued within one year of an IPO are issued in contemplation of the offering.

Computational Exhibit. The SEC requires a computational exhibit on EPS to be included in most filings (including annual reports on Form 10-K), as shown in the example in Figure 20.9.

Per-Share Amounts Other Than EPS. In ASR 142 (FRR § 202), the SEC indicated that per share data on the face of the income statement should be limited to those EPS calculations required by GAAP. However, some enterprises believe that

	Year Ended June 30					
	1987		1986		1985	
	Primary	Fully diluted	Primary	Fully diluted	Primary	Fully diluted
Income						
Net earnings (loss)	$1,737,537	$1,737,537	$744,598	$744,598	($5,368,594)	($5,368,594)
Preferred dividends			(35,000)	(35,000)		
Interest (less tax) on convertible subordinated debentures				23,847		
	$1,737,537	$1,737,537	$709,598	$733,445	($5,368,594)	($5,368,594)
Number of shares						
Weighted average shares outstanding	9,072,195	9,072,195	6,106,102	6,106,102	5,413,526	5,413,526
Incremental shares for outstanding stock warrants	249,593	249,593	233,339	301,465		
Incremental shares for outstanding stock options	110,906	110,906	64,498	75,347		
Shares issued upon conversion of convertible subordinated debentures				269,206		
Underwriter's options	83,134	83,134	4,976	34,376		
	9,515,828	9,515,828	6,408,915	6,786,496	5,413,526	5,413,526

FIG. 20.9   SEC Computational Exhibit for Earnings per Share
Source: Pharmakinetics Laboratories Inc., 1987 Annual Report.

conventional financial statement data and presentation do not adequately reflect business economics, and in the past some gave presentations to highlight data such as cash flow per share. Presentation in a "Financial Highlights" section accentuated that disclosure. Some enterprises even presented sales per share data. The SEC has ruled that such presentations are not acceptable in that unsophisticated investors could misinterpret the data and be misled. Accordingly, only EPS data recognized by GAAP may be presented in SEC filings.

AUDITING

General Approach

The objectives of auditing equity accounts are: (1) verification that the securities exist (that they are valid and properly recorded); (2) that they are accurately valued and properly classified; and (3) primarily, that there is adequate presentation and disclosure. A substantive approach is most commonly used, since the number of equity transactions with outside parties is usually small. The EPS calculation is also audited on a substantive basis. In a few instances, a public company may act as its own registrar or transfer agent. Such a situation is not contemplated in the brief coverage of auditing in this chapter.

The basic substantive procedures applicable to the equity accounts are described in the sample skeleton audit program in Figure 20.10. The integration of this program into the overall audit is discussed in Chapter 7. Of course, the auditor will take into account the results of other procedures in the audit, including his evaluation of internal control structure, to the extent such procedures apply to the equity accounts. General internal control considerations are discussed in Chapter 8.

Comfort Letters

Various auditing pronouncements have been issued on comfort letters in an attempt to clarify the nature and scope of the accountants' procedures, the most recent and comprehensive being SAS 49, *Letters for Underwriters* (AU 634), which codifies earlier statements and focuses on the following additional areas:

* Shelf registration statements
* Independence
* Compliance with SEC requirements
* Accountants' reports
* Pro forma financial information
* Unaudited interim statements not included in the registration statement
* Subsequent changes and decreases
* Tables, statistics, and other financial information

Since the due-diligence criteria for underwriters have never been authoritatively established, independent accountants cannot give assurance as to whether the procedures performed at the request of the underwriters are sufficient for establishing such due diligence. The underwriter is therefore required to specify the steps he wants the accountant to perform. Those procedures traditionally encompass unaudited changes in financial statement items and a review of statistical and tabular data.

The desired procedures and conclusions to be expressed in the comfort letter are usually specified in the underwriting agreement. Therefore, the independent accountant must read the underwriting agreement prior to its finalization to ascertain whether the stipulations are within the scope of his services as defined by professional standards.

A comfort letter includes negative assurance as to fairness of presentation of unaudited financial data in conformity with GAAP. An audit in accordance with GAAS is required for a positive opinion (auditor's standard report); thus, because comfort letter procedures are limited, only negative assurance ("nothing came to our attention . . .") is permitted.

Basic Coverage. Model comfort letters (AU 634.48–.60) were developed by the accounting profession to help independent accountants comply with underwriters'

1. Obtain a schedule of all equity accounts, showing:

   a. Nominal unit values and authorized number of shares.

   b. Number of shares issued and balances at beginning and end of period.

   c. Changes during the period.

   d. Any other relevant information.

   e. Identification of distributable and nondistributable balances.

2. Ascertain by review of general ledger and register of shareholders (by examining the sequence of unissued shares) whether there have been any changes in capital stock during the period.

   a. Request confirmation of the issued stock from the registrar and transfer agent (if used) and reconcile reply to schedule of shares outstanding.

   b. Examine documents supporting treasury stock transactions during the period.

   • Ascertain propriety of their recording.

   • Account for and inspect treasury stock certificates, noting that they are in the name of the company or are properly endorsed.

3. Examine supporting documents for increases in issued shares.

   a. Agree to board/shareholder minutes.

   b. Ascertain that amounts issued do not exceed those authorized.

   c. Vouch receipt of proceeds of issue.

   d. For issuances other than for cash, inspect documents supporting the assets acquired or services received.

4. Review canceled stock certificates to determine that reuse is not possible.

5. Review agreements and contracts for effect on equity accounts.

6. Inquire as to the existence of any stock options, warrants, rights, or conversion privileges existing at the balance sheet date.

   a. Ascertain the number of shares required for options, warrants, rights, or conversions at year-end.

   b. Ascertain options granted, cancelled, lapsing, and exercised during the year. Vouch authorization to board minutes, option agreements, receipts, and similar support.

7. Determine that dividend payments/liabilities have been correctly recorded.

   a. Review extracts of board minutes for dividends declared and paid.

   b. Confirm calculation of total dividends and trace total dividends to retained earnings statement.

8. Examine all changes in paid-in capital, retained earnings, and other capital accounts.

   a. Vouch to appropriate authorizations and supporting evidence.

   b. Determine propriety.

9. Review computation of EPS.

FIG. 20.10   Sample Auditing Procedures for Equity Accounts

requests. However, not every situation could be illustrated, and some letters will have to be modified for specific situations. Comfort letters usually meet the following criteria:

1. *Dating.* The letter is ordinarily dated at or shortly before the date the sale of securities is consummated (closing date). Another important date is the one on which the procedures are to be concluded (the cutoff date). The letter should specify that no procedures were performed after the cutoff date. A letter may also be requested at the date the registration statement becomes effective.

2. *Addressee.* The letter is usually addressed to the underwriter or the client. A request to address the letter to any other person should cause the independent accountant to consult legal counsel.

3. *Independence.* The Securities Act requires that an expert (the accountant) disclose any interest in the client (which is, of course, prohibited). The underwriter usually requests confirmation of the accountant's independence.

4. *Compliance with SEC requirements.* A request to give an opinion concerning compliance as to conformity of the financial statements with the pertinent published rules and regulations of the SEC is usual.

5. *Unaudited financial statements, capsule information, and subsequent changes.* Comments with respect to unaudited financial statements, changes in capital stock and long-term debt, decreases in other specified financial statement items, and pro forma financial statements should be given with care. Comments should always be made in the form of negative assurance. AU 634.19–.24 should be consulted as to the matter of complying with a request for comments on unaudited data.

Subsequent changes in financial statement items should concern only increases or decreases. The use of the term "adverse change" is not acceptable, as it is not defined in authoritative accounting literature and is subject to misinterpretation. A detailed discussion of appropriate wording is contained in AU 634.25–.31.

SAS 49 provides that "the accountants should not give negative assurance with respect to unaudited condensed financial statements, capsule information, or changes or decreases unless they have obtained knowledge of the client's accounting and financial reporting practices and its system of internal accounting control relating to the preparation of financial statements" (AU 634.19f). Ordinarily that knowledge is gained through one or more annual audits. This paragraph further states:

> If for whatever reason the accountants have not conducted such an audit, the need for an understanding of the client's accounting and financial reporting practices and its system of internal accounting control is not diminished, and the accountants should consider whether, under the particular circumstances, they can acquire sufficient knowledge of these matters to perform the inquiries and procedures requested by the underwriter.

Providing comfort in situations in which there is no audit base is most often an issue when there is a change in accountants. Although it is more difficult to acquire the knowledge of a registrant's accounting and internal control structure in those circumstances, it is feasible through a concerted effort. No doubt the risk of making an "incorrect" judgment is greater when a first audit has not been completed, because the auditor's verification of the operation of the systems will not have been completed.

6. *Tables, statistics, and other financial information.* Independent accountants should not comment on matters to which their competence as accountants is not related. They should comment only with respect to information (a) expressed in dollars or percentages derived from dollar amounts that have been obtained from accounting records subject to the internal control procedures of the enterprise or (b) derived directly from the accounting records by analysis or computation. The independent accountant should not comment on matters concerning management's exercise of business judgment or dollar amounts not subject to internal control procedures. The information should be covered in precise language by page, paragraph, and sentence. Further discussion of this aspect of negative assurance is contained in AU 634.40–.45.

7. *Concluding paragraph.* This should contain a statement restricting use of the comfort letter to the underwriters and the client.

8. *Miscellaneous.* More than one independent accountant can be involved in the examination of the financial statements; subsidiaries, branches, or equity investees may be audited by other independent accountants. In such instances, the principal accountant should request a letter from the other accountant(s) on all significant units.

As the original beneficiaries of negative assurance, underwriters have been asking that the various forms of permitted negative assurance, based on procedures outlined in professional pronouncements, be given also to them. Thus far, the profession has sustained the premise that due-diligence procedures for an underwriter under the Securities Act are his choice; for example, if an underwriter requests performance of an SAS 36 (AU 722) interim review, comfort letter comments thereon cannot be directed to him unless he specifies significant criteria for all the procedures so that there is no implication that the responsibility for the sufficiency of the agreed-upon procedures has been assumed by the independent accountants.

For detailed information on auditors' procedures in a Securities Act offering, including procedures for underwriters' letters, see *Accountants SEC Practice Manual* (Poloway, 1988).

Interim Financial Statements. An interpretation, *Negative Assurance on Unaudited Condensed Interim Financial Statements Attached to Comfort Letters* (AU 9634.10–.12), of paragraph 24 (AU 634.24) clarifies the nature of the negative assurance provided by an independent accountant in a comfort letter to an underwriter on unaudited condensed interim financial statements. The interpretation states that the comfort letter is based on:

> negative assurance that unaudited condensed interim financial statements for a period ending after the latest financial statements included in the registration statement, including financial statements that underlie capsule information, are in conformity with generally accepted accounting principles or are stated on a basis substantially consistent with the audited financial statements included in the registration statement. The unaudited condensed interim financial statements referred to in these situations should be attached to the comfort letter.

Shelf Registrations. Rule 415 of the Securities Act permits a company to register a specified amount of securities (equity or debt) for continuous or delayed offerings by filing a single shelf registration statement. This rule permits the registrant to offer and sell securities within the two ensuing years, generally without the need to prepare and file a new prospectus and registration statement for each sale.

The registration statement can be updated after the original effective date by the (1) filing of a post-effective amendment, (2) incorporation by reference of a subsequently filed document, or (3) addition of a supplemental prospectus ("sticker").

Because the independent accountant's responsibility under Section 11 of the Securities Act with respect to information covered by his report and included in the registration statement extends to the effective date of the registration statement, questions have been raised as to the circumstances in which the independent accountant has a responsibility to perform subsequent events review procedures after the original effective date of the shelf registration statement, at which point an underwriter might not have been selected, obviating the auditor's issuance of a comfort letter to a specified underwriter.

The underwriter must determine the procedures that will be sufficient for his purposes to enable an accountant to issue a comfort letter; accordingly, the accountant should not furnish a comfort letter to a legal counsel or to a nonspecific addressee such as "any and all underwriters to be selected." However, a draft may be issued indicating the letter the accountant would have been prepared to issue at the effective date of the shelf registration statement had the underwriter been selected. But because procedures will not have been specified by the underwriter at this time, the draft must indicate that the procedures shown are those often requested, and that the issuance of an actual comfort letter will depend on the procedures selected by the eventual underwriter.

21

Financial Instruments and Transactions

OVERVIEW

Some time ago accountants were taught that all capitalization was divided into three parts—debt, preferred and common stock, and maybe leases. In the three preceding chapters on debt, leases, and equity, the coverage is relatively uncomplicated; the subjects are discussed in as traditional manner as possible. This chapter covers—necessarily too briefly—the alchemy of "rocket scientists" in the capital markets who mix debt, equity and off-book promises, contingencies, privileges, and other rights, into innovative financial instruments. Today, financial instruments are offered in endless variety; there are TIGRs, LYONs, CATS, CARs, CLEOs[1] and a veritable zoo of other offerings.

A comprehensive analysis of why such exotic financial instrumentation exists is beyond the scope of the chapter, but several significant reasons bear mention. When the SEC experimentally permitted, and later made permanent, a procedure under which registrants could prepare and file "shelf" registration statements without having to identify an underwriter (Rule 415), a very fundamental change began in the investment banking community. Slowly but surely, investment banking relationships weakened. A company could choose terms and features from among numerous proposals, and select an underwriter at the last moment when taking the registration "off the shelf" and into the market. Thus the investment banker on last year's issue might very well not be the one on this year's—unless of course that firm still had the "best" or "most innovative" ideas as viewed by the issurer, resulting in obtaining needed funds at the least cost. The cost of funds is not based simply on the coupon rate or the offering price, but may depend on a host of other features as well.

To many issuers, the ultimate financial instrument is one classified as debt for tax purposes (thereby enabling a deduction for interest expense), but classifiable as shareholders' equity for financial reporting purposes. U.S. income tax laws (and, increasingly, those of other countries) have been continually refined by annual "tax simplification" acts that close one door and open a dozen others, encouraging the creation of new instruments.

Corporate treasurers and investment bankers are acutely aware that selling debt or equity purveys a huge bundle of inherent rights and that other rights can be synthesized for the occasion. Each of these ingredients has a price. For example, a collateralized debt or preferred stock may be less expensive than a noncollateralized issue, simply because the collateral itself has a higher credit rating than the general credit rating of the issuer. Accordingly, issuers and their financial advisors have learned how to thin-slice the bundle of rights in a financial instrument. And the more these areas are probed, the thinner the slicing, the more exotic the result, and the lower the all-inclusive (all-in) financing cost.

Innovative financial instruments seem to have a very short life. Investment bankers surround the invention process with considerable secrecy lest someone else—perhaps with more resources or a more ready and eager client—beats the concept inventor to the market. It is not realistic to expect that much publicity will attend

---

[1] The financial markets suffuse acronyms. Those listed here are Treasury Instrument Growth Receipts, Liquid Yield Option Notes, Certificates of Accrual on Treasury Securities, Certificates for Automobile Receivables, and Collateralized Lease Equipment Obligations.

these inventions – and most certainly many of these transactions will not be discussed in FASB due process deliberations, which could last for months as an idea languishes. Thus, as more and more transactions became the subject of calls or visits by firms to the SEC or FASB staff, something else was needed, and the EITF came into being.

Manifest in the creation of the EITF was that everyone – the SEC, the FASB, and the practitioners – wearied of a one-transaction-at-a-time approach. Many of the issues placed on the EITF agenda have been driven by financial instruments and transactions, and some of these issues are reviewed in this chapter.

Economic Motivators

The role of capital markets is to facilitate the movement of savings into capital investment for beneficial purposes of society. While all uses of capital may not squarely fit this curbstone economic definition, by and large, better ideas are served; and a large dose of regulation (see Section V of this *Handbook*) is employed in organized capital markets to inhibit the flow of capital to lucrative purposes that may be detrimental to society.

Global Market Development. Limited varieties of capital funding existed prior to the 1970s. But with the rapid advancements in telecommunications technology that have since occurred, it is now possible to execute financial transactions at virtually any time on some market around the world. The global market enables locating investment funds at the lowest cost, and it also presents the need for new financial products, such as currency forwards, options, and swaps to cope with fluctuations in currency and interest rate differentials.

Creditworthiness. The cost of funds to an enterprise is dependent on how investors view the prospects for recovery of their investments in relation to the possible monetary rewards. The higher the risk, the greater the cost. Accordingly, when seeking funds an enterprise wants to merit the best possible credit rating.

The two best known rating agencies in the United States are Standard & Poor's (S&P) and Moody's, whose rating classifications are summarized in Figure 21.1. These ratings are applied to the financial instrument offering, rather than to the company itself. If a proposed issue receives a high rating, the cost will be commensurately low, and the issue will be easy to sell. Of course, in a debenture offering, because the company's general credit stands behind the issue, the rating necessarily applies to the entire enterprise. However, with increasing frequency an issue is backed by specific collateral, enabling an enterprise with weak overall creditworthiness to obtain a triple-A rating on an issue. A good example is found in securitized assets, discussed later in this chapter.

Also important to companies seeking equity funds is the view of professional financial analysts (see Chapter 1) who consider the company's operating results, financial condition, and prospects for the future. While much of this evaluation is an art, there is a significant quantitative aspect involving ratio analysis, in particular the debt-to-equity ratio; the higher the ratio, the riskier the investment. For this reason,

Classification[a]	Standard & Poor's[c]	Moody's[d]
Highest rating, extremely strong capacity[b]	AAA	Aaa
High rating, very strong capacity[b]	AA	Aa
Moderately high rating, strong capacity[b]	A	A
Medium rating, adequate capacity[b] in the near term	BBB	Baa
Exposure to major risks, least speculative	BB	Ba
Exposure to major risks, not a desirable investment	B	B
Poor standing, in or close to default	CCC	Caa
Highly speculative, in or close to default	CC	Ca
Exposure to major risks, most speculative	C	C

(a) The classification definitions are very abbreviated from the rating agencies' definitions.
(b) Capacity refers to the ability of the issuer to pay interest and principal.
(c) S&P uses plus (+) and minus (−) to indicate relative standing within categories AA through CCC.
(d) Moody's uses the numerical modifiers 1, 2 and 3 to indicate higher to lower standing within categories Aa through B.

FIG. 21.1   Summary of Standard & Poor's and Moody's Debt Ratings

it is generally more attractive for a company to obtain funds via off-balance sheet financing, and GAAP has enabled this to some degree.

Competition in the Market. Investment banking—facilitating the obtaining of capital funds from investors—is a lucrative field for successful participants. Years ago, success was founded on loyalty and steadfastness, but these virtues have faded in the face of innovation and the bankers' ability to bring private money to the transaction. Investment bankers look for opportunities to blend tax and GAAP considerations into innovative instruments that obtain funds at the least cost. And like merchant bankers, investment bankers are investing their own funds in transactions. Even commercial bankers, long stereotyped as unwilling to lend to any but the soundest businesses, are putting their money into investment and merchant banking-type endeavors.

In the course of this heated competition for lucrative profits calculated as a small percentage of megadollar transactions, the financial community in the 1980s has come to know that tax and accounting rules are obstacles to free-form innovation.[2] The innovator often wants to be at the edge of what's right, not over it, and therefore has a need to obtain advice on how tax and GAAP rules affect a transaction or an instrument under design. While accounting firms have traditionally advised clients directly on the related consequences of transactions under consideration, the investment banker as an *intermediary* now needs to know these consequences in advance of

---

[2] The legal aspects of financial instruments and transactions have always been very significant. For example, the legal hurdles in creating collateralized mortgage obligations (CMOs) were daunting, but in the end overcome. The fact that this chapter does not focus on legal aspects should not be viewed as diminishing their importance.

making a proposal to a client, or before closing on a transaction that may involve placing the investment banking firm's capital at risk.

Some accounting firms have noted this new opportunity for intermediary consultation and now provide it. The variety of innovative financial instruments and transactions encountered inevitably give rise to different views on the same or similar matters. To standardize the consultation approach, the ASB issued SAS 50, *Reports on the Application of Accounting Principles* (AU 625), discussed in Chapter 11; however, SAS 50 does not take any position on what is or is not GAAP. The EITF debates and concludes on many of the SAS 50-type issues, but even so, the SEC staff has shown considerable interest in their content, encouraging registrants to submit such letters to the staff for perusal when received from intermediaries.

Possible Solutions

With the securitization, and thus monetization, of many of the assets employed by businesses, the accounting model may be straining at the seams. Under the current, historical cost accounting model, elements of financial statements are mostly recorded at entry values, that is, what they cost the enterprise in measurable and recognizable units of money. The FASB is unlikely to discard this approach because of its objectivity and reliability, but some revisions are in order.

The accountant practicing in the global capital markets has a bewildering array of instruments and transactions to consider. He must usually take them apart to see what makes them tick; often what they are labeled is not what they are. Even accountants diligently doing this arrive at different answers. It is time that some benchmarks be provided by the FASB by which reasonably consistent answers can be obtained regardless of the novel admixtures of debt, equity, and other promises encountered.

Although "truth" about financial instruments and transactions presumably can be found by any well-conceived route, the fact is that the route selected will have an indelible effect on the shape of the truth, because accounting is a collection of conventions. It is fair to say that because the FASB's Conceptual Framework is in place, the latitude available for truth should be suitably narrow; but wide parameters nevertheless exist in that framework.

Disclosure is the easiest area for the FASB to attack. As discussed in the next section, the FASB has proposed extensive disclosures for financial instruments as a prelude to considering what they mean for recognition and measurement purposes. While there is a need for dispatch because of the rapid growth in financial instrument innovations, there is also a need for measured progress, because there may be major changes made by the FASB that will heavily tax the business community as well as the absorption powers of accountants.

Display issues are another target, if not preempted by a disclosure glut. The admixture of all sorts of ingredients in financial instruments suggests that it is not so important to classify them into debt or equity, but more useful to rank-order them in terms of their sequence in claims on the assets of the enterprise. Eliminating the dividing lines would, of course, be a major change, but may be worth considering.

FASB FINANCIAL INSTRUMENTS PROJECT

In 1986, the FASB added to its agenda a project dealing with financial instruments and off-balance sheet financing. The overall objective of the project is to develop broad standards for resolving the many issues arising on a regular basis in accounting and reporting for diverse financial instruments as they are created.

The FASB quickly determined that the complexity of the recognition and measurement issues would require lengthy research and deliberation. Therefore, a decision was made to deal first with disclosure of financial instruments, which would facilitate the education of both the staff and the Board. Knowledge thus gained would then support the second broad phase, dealing with the recognition and measurement issues.

FASB Disclosure Proposals (Phase 1)

In late 1987, the FASB issued an Exposure Draft, *Disclosures About Financial Instruments* (1987a), which calls for a comprehensive set of disclosures related to financial instruments as defined. The following sections summarize the proposed requirements.

Definitions. The exposure draft provides the following definitions in establishing its scope:

* A financial instrument is any contract that is both a (recognized or unrecognized) financial asset of one entity and a (recognized or unrecognized) financial liability or equity instrument of another entity (¶ 27).
* A financial asset is any asset that is (a) cash, (b) a contractual right to receive cash or another financial asset from another entity, (c) a contractual right to exchange other financial instruments on potentially favorable terms with another entity, or an equity instrument of another entity (¶ 28).
* A financial liability is any liability that is a contractual obligation (a) to deliver cash or another financial asset to another entity or (b) to exchange financial instruments on potentially unfavorable terms with another entity (¶ 29).
* An equity instrument is any evidence of ownership interest in an entity (¶ 30).

Credit Risk. The credit risk inherent in each class of financial instrument should be disclosed by presenting the following information:

* Maximum credit risk. For recognized financial instruments (e.g., loans, investments) no further disclosure is required; however, for unrecognized financial instruments some additional disclosure will be necessary (e.g., interest rate swaps, guarantees).
* Reasonably possible credit loss. For financial instruments subject to credit risk and for which no loss reserve has been established and the possibility of a loss is more than remote, disclosure shall be made of the loss contingency with an estimate of the possible loss or range of loss, or a statement made that such an estimate cannot be given.

- Probable credit loss. Disclosure of credit loss reserves must be provided, whether reflected as a reduction of an asset balance (e.g., a loan loss reserve) or reflected as a liability (e.g., reserve or guarantee).
- Concentration of credit risk. If total maximum credit risk of all financial instruments with any individual counterparty exceeds 20% of total equity and is at least 1% of total assets, or exceeds 10% of total assets, disclosure must be given as to:
  - The counterparty's identity or the counterparty's industry or region.
  - Maximum credit risk, reasonably possible credit loss, and probable credit loss.
- Group concentrations. Counterparties engaged in similar activities, or activities in the same region, that would cause their ability to meet contractual obligations to be similarly affected by changes in economic or other conditions, should be disclosed, including:
  - Information about the shared activity or region that identifies the group.
  - Information about maximum credit risk, reasonably possible credit loss, and probable credit loss.
- Disclosure of collateral or other security supporting financial instruments is encouraged but not required.

Maturities (Cash Flows). Information regarding the future cash receipts or payments for each class of financial instrument should be disclosed. However, if the instrument is to be sold or settled prior to maturity and is reported at market value, the disclosures need not be provided. The following information would be required:

- Contractual cash flows (e.g., interest, principal, preferred dividends) broken down into time frames of (a) within one year, (b) after one year through five years, and (c) after five years.
- If significant, foreign currency cash flows, aggregated into total recognized financial assets, total recognized financial liabilities, total equity instruments, and total unrecognized financial assets and liabilities.

If debtors have the option to prepay financial assets, or if the entity has the option to prepay liabilities, before their contractual maturity, that fact shall be disclosed. In addition, disclosure of expected versus contractual cash receipts and payments information is encouraged but not required.

Interest Rates. The following rate information for each class of instrument, other than those held for sale and reported at market value, must be disclosed:

- Carrying or effective amounts (e.g., notional amount for interest rate swaps) of financial instruments with interest rates that contractually reprice or mature (a) within one year, (b) after one year through five years, and (c) after five years.
- Information about interest rates of financial instruments denominated in foreign currencies, if they significantly affect the average reported interest rate for a class of financial instrument.

Disclosure of expected versus contractual repricing or maturity information is encouraged but not required.

Market Values. The market value for each class of financial instrument other than those already reported at that value should be disclosed. If the market value cannot be determined or estimated the following should be disclosed:

• An explanation of the reasons for the inability to measure or estimate the market value.
• The carrying amount, interest rate, maturity, and any other information relevant to assessing value.

Effective Date and Transition. The proposed statement would be applied to financial statements issued for periods ending after December 15, 1988 (although this is expected to be delayed). Disclosures of maximum and probable credit loss information and market values are not required to be included in the financial statements, presented on a comparative basis, of periods ending before the effective date.

Reaction to FASB Proposal. The overall reaction is that the requirements of the proposed statement represent overkill. Many preparers believe that if nothing else the disclosure volume alone will overwhelm and confuse users.
Specific concerns include:

• Scope of the definition of financial instruments is too broad. As written it could include trade and accounts receivable and payable and demand deposits of financial institutions.
• The assessment of "reasonably possible" is too subjective to be useful.
• The use of contractual cash flows is not meaningful. Many financial instruments prepay and the actual amounts and timing may not equal the contractual amounts and timing.
• The determination of market values of some instruments is either not possible or its estimation would be highly subjective and not comparable among preparers.
• Due to the complexity and extensive data gathering that will be necessary the effective date should be extended to December 15, 1989.

FASB Recognition and Measurement Consideration (Phase 2)

The Board has only recently begun deliberations on this phase, by attempting to identify the characteristics that may be common to various types of financial instruments. The objective is to attempt to develop an approach to classifying financial instruments based on those characteristics and then to resolve the accounting issues related to the common types.
Some questions being dealt with by the Board and staff include:

• Whether financial assets should be considered sold if there is recourse or other continuing involvement with them, whether financial liabilities should be considered settled when assets are dedicated to settle them, and other questions of derecognition, nonrecognition, or offsetting of related financial assets and liabilities.
• How to account for futures contracts, interest rate swaps, options, forward commitments, nonrecourse arrangements, financial guarantees, and others and for the underlying assets or liabilities to which those risk-transferring items are related.

* How financial instruments should be measured (e.g., at market value, amortized original cost, or the lower of cost or market).
* How issuers should account for securities with both debt and equity characteristics.

The FASB plans to issue a Discussion Memorandum in the fourth quarter of 1988 with the remainder of the project extending into 1989 and 1990.

ALTERING FINANCIAL INSTRUMENTS

As defined in Chapter 18, debt is a formalized liability, which in turn is an obligation to transfer assets or provide services to other parties as a result of past transactions or events. A debt instrument promises to pay (usually in cash, but sometimes in other ways) certain amounts (although sometimes they may not be certain) at specified future dates (although the timing may also be uncertain). Equity instruments as discussed in Chapter 20 traditionally are quite simple; they represent the residual interest in an entity that belongs to the equity holders after all liabilities and claims are settled. These attributes suggest uncertainty of timing and amount, but many ways have been developed to add certitude. The more features in a debt or equity instrument, the more complex it is to account for it.

In the sections that follow, numerous specific examples are given as to how financial instruments can be transmogrified by alteration of their principal attributes. Although interest is generally differentiated from principal in the following discussion, it must be recognized that the distinction is artificial; all that accountants are concerned with is the amount and timing of future cash flows, whatever these are called. This is not meant to suggest that there are no legal distinctions, especially when a debtor falls on hard times. Likewise the distinctions between debt and equity, and between senior equity and common equity, are often blurred in actual cases.

Altering Debt Interest Amounts

Irregular or Increasing Interest Rates. Interest may be payable only if earned, although usually this is cumulative and perhaps compounded. Bonds offering this type of contingent interest payment are called "income bonds" and depending on other rights may be only a shade above an equity instrument. Contingent interest is commonly found in debt issued in a troubled debt restructuring (see Chapter 28).

While conventional debt usually carries a level rate of interest, it is of course possible to set fixed rates in whatever way the parties agree. For example, in the high-yield environment of leveraged buy-out or takeover debt ("junk bonds"), the acquirer may intend to reduce acquisition debt by the sale of certain portions of the acquired business. The debt provisions may require that interest be increased by a stipulated amount at each interest payment date, until the debt is called and repaid.

In Issue 86-15, *Increasing Rate Debt*, the EITF dealt with a debt instrument that matures every three months but can be extended at an increased rate of interest for up to five years. The EITF addressed the method of determining interest cost, the period over which interest is to be determined, the amortization period of debt issue cost, and the debt classification.

The EITF concluded that interest expense should be calculated by use of the interest method based on the estimated term of the debt. Such estimation should consider the plans, ability, and intent to service the debt. As to debt issue cost, the Task Force concluded that the amortization period should be the same as the interest cost determination period. If the debt is paid earlier, any unpaid accrued interest is an adjustment of interest expense and is *not* extraordinary. The EITF also concluded that current versus noncurrent classification depends on the planned source of repayment (e.g., a new short-term debt borrowing versus a long-term arrangement). This determination need not be consistent with the period used to determine interest cost.

Payments Made in Common Stock. It is convenient to think of interest as cash, but there is no reason it cannot be any other objectively identifiable asset — or in this case equity instrument. To conserve cash, an issuer may have an option to issue common stock, the number of shares to be based on the market price at the date the interest payment is due. The issuer may also have a similar option to pay the principal in stock. Note that when the issuer (not the holder) has the option, the debt is *not* a convertible.

Additionally, some financial institutions use equity commitment notes, as to which principal can only be paid out of proceeds received from the sale of primary capital securities (see Chapter 40).

Interest Payable in Additional Debt. Occasionally an issuer will arrange to "pay" interest in additional bonds of the same type and interest rate as the original instrument. These "baby bonds" are attractive to investors who believe that interest rates will fall, and therefore they will have the opportunity to immediately "reinvest" their interest in a higher-than-market yield. Of course, they could also guess wrong. These instruments limit the time period during which the baby bonds will be issued, at which time they (along with the mother bonds) commence cash interest payments and eventual cash liquidation of principal.

Delayed Rate-Setting. In Issue 84-14, *Deferred Interest Rate Setting*, the EITF addressed an arrangement wherein a borrower who needs to raise funds currently through issuance of fixed-rate debt believes that interest rates will decline in the near future. Simultaneous with the current debt issuance, the borrower enters into a deferred interest-rate-setting arrangement with an investment banker, under which the borrower and the investment banker agree to "set" the interest rate based on prevailing market conditions within a specified period (generally six months). At the date selected by the borrower, if rates have declined, the investment banker pays the borrower a cash amount representing the present value of the interest rate differential over the term of the debt, as if the debt had been issued at the lower prevailing rate. If interest rates have increased, the borrower pays the investment banker a similarly computed amount. The issue is whether the cash receipt or payment should be recognized currently or amortized as an adjustment of interest expense on the debt. A consensus was reached that, if the deferred rate setting agreement is an integral part of the original issuance of the debt, any amounts received or paid should be accounted for on the same basis as original issue premium or discount (i.e., as an adjustment to interest expense recognized over the term of the debt).

In Issue 86-26, *Using Forward Commitments as a Surrogate for Deferred Rate Setting*, the EITF discussed how to account for a change in the value of a forward commitment entered into simultaneously with the issuance of fixed-rate debt. To be in a position to take advantage of a decline in long-term interest rates anticipated in the near future, a company issuing long-term, fixed-rate debt may enter into a short-term forward commitment to purchase Treasury bonds (with terms equivalent to those of the debt) from the same investment banker that underwrote the issuance of the debt.

A consensus was not reached on this issue. Although some EITF members acknowledged the similarities to Issue 84-14, the majority concluded that the forward commitment should be viewed as a separate transaction and accounted for separately. The SEC Observer stated that the SEC would *not* allow registrants to account for the change in value of the forward commitment as an adjustment of the interest expense over the life of the debt.

Altering Debt Principal Amounts

Indexing. Occasionally, a company issues debt with both a guaranteed and a contingent payment. The contingent payment may be related to the price of a commodity like oil or to a specific index like the S&P 500. Sometimes the rights to the contingent payment are separable from the debt instrument. In Issue 86-28, *Accounting Implications of Indexed Debt Instruments*, the EITF considered (1) whether the debt proceeds should be split between the debt and the right to receive the contingent payment and (2) the issuer's accounting for increases in the commodity or index values.

As to the first issue, the EITF concluded that if the contingent payment is separable from the debt repayment, the proceeds should be split between the two elements. Any premium or discount on the debt that results from such allocation should be accounted for following APB 21, *Interest on Receivables and Payables* (I69). If not separable, no conclusion was reached. On the second issue, the Task Force concluded that in an increasing index situation, a liability should be recognized equal to the amount by which the contingent payment exceeds the amount originally allocated to the contingency feature. If no allocation was originally made because of inseparability, the increase in value is an adjustment of the carrying amount of the debt.

There have been circumstances, however, where such bonds have been deemed a hedge by the issuer. For example, a gold mining company may issue bonds payable at the holder's option in cash or in a certain number of ounces of gold. If the issuer has proved reserves that are adequate to cover the gold option, and the reserves will be produced at the times needed to honor the payment commitment, some accountants have concluded that the debt should not be repriced.

Debt Repayable in Common Stock. In Issue 84-40, *Long-Term Debt Repayable by a Capital Stock Transaction*, the EITF considered a very complex issue involving an attempt to turn debt (on which interest is tax-deductible) into shareholders' equity for financial statement presentation purposes.

A corporation forms a subsidiary whose sole purpose is to hold the entire beneficial interest in a grantor trust it creates. The parent company issues its preferred stock to the subsidiary in exchange for cash, which the subsidiary obtains by selling the stock to the grantor trust for cash, which the grantor trust obtains by issuing debt to third party investors. The trust does not pay cash for 25% of the preferred stock, but issues a certificate of beneficial interest therefor. The collateral for the trust's debt is the preferred stock (which is 133% of the face amount of the debt and is the trust's only asset).

The interest on the trust's debt is payable from dividends received on its preferred stockholdings. At the time principal payments are due on the trust's debt, the trust converts the preferred stock into common stock at a rate that will yield the number of shares having a market value equal to the payment due; the trustee is required to sell the shares and pay the cash to the trust's debtholders.

The objective of this exercise was to obtain a tax deduction for the interest paid on the trust's debt to third parties (because grantor trusts are consolidated for income tax purposes), and yet to allow 75% of the preferred stock held by the trust (i.e., the entire issue, less 25% represented by the subsidiary's beneficial interest) to be classified as shareholders' equity because it would be paid in common stock (although the exact number of shares was unknown). A few companies executed this transaction before it caught the attention of the EITF and SEC. Two issues were considered by the EITF:

1. How should the trust be presented in the consolidated financial statements?
2. How should the parent's intercompany preferred stock be shown in the balance sheet?

On the first issue, the EITF concluded that the trust must be consolidated; this seems obvious because the parent is a 100% indirect owner. As to the second issue, the EITF could not reach a consensus; there was support for equity classification in limited circumstances depending on the certitude of the company's common stock being salable by the trustee.

The absence of a consensus was moot; the SEC Observer commented that the staff would not accept equity classification absent a pronouncement from the FASB (which would not consider an issue such as this). The SEC Observer expected debt classification, with "dividends" to be shown as interest expense.

Convertibility Into Equity. Chapter 18 covers conventional convertible debt, the accounting treatment upon conversion, and transactions designed to induce conversion when the strike price (cost of each share when converting the debt) is out of the money (higher than the current market price). A more exotic conversion feature is mentioned in the following paragraphs.

In Issue 85-29, *Convertible Debt With a "Premium Put,"* the EITF considered a convertible financial instrument issued at par and containing an option permitting the holder to put the bonds to the issuer at a premium. After a specified date the put expires. At time of issuance, the common stock obtainable on conversion naturally is less than the face amount of the debt; and the premium put becomes operative later. The objective of this instrument is to obtain a lower all-inclusive cost for the issuer by using a very low coupon but giving the investor an opportunity to recoup the interest via either the put or the conversion into common stock, whose value might grow to exceed the put before its expiration date.

The EITF saw this instrument basically as a redeemable debt with a redemption price greater than issue price, notwithstanding any probabilities that the market price of the stock would sufficiently rise to emasculate the put. Accordingly, the issuer would have to accrue the redemption price over the period until the put becomes exercisable, regardless of whether the excercise of the put is unlikely due to market price conditions. If the put is unexercised because conversion into stock occurs, the accrued put premium is credited to paid-in capital. If conversion does not occur and the put expires, the put premium is then amortized as a downward yield adjustment over the remainder of the debt term.

Call Options as Convertibles. In Issue 85-9, *Revenue Recognition on Options to Purchase Stock of Another Entity*, the EITF dealt with situations in which a company issues debt securities (either "convertible" or with detachable warrants) that permit the holder to acquire common stock of another company in which the issuer has an investment. In situations involving detachable warrants, the issue is whether the warrant amount should be amortized over its term or eliminated by a credit to income only when it is exercised or expires. As to the "convertible" debt, the issue is whether the debt should be treated the same as traditional convertibles described in APB 14, *Accounting for Convertible Debt and Debt Issued With Stock Purchase Warrants* (D10), or as a "warrant" transaction in which separate accounting for the conversion feature is required.

The EITF concluded that if the debt is issued with detachable warrants, a liability for the value of the warrant should be recorded. Income would not be recognized until the warrant expires or is exercised. No consensus was achieved on the second issue; however, the SEC Observer commented that APB 14 does not apply and separation of the debt amount from that of the conversion feature is required. In the view of the FASB staff, APB 14 does apply, and it has been so applied in practice. This issue is being considered in the FASB project on financial instruments.

Warrants. Chapter 18 discusses traditional equity warrants as well as synthetic warrants. But there are others.

Put warrants. In Issue 86-35, *Debentures With Detachable Stock Purchase Warrants*, the EITF considered a detachable warrant issued along with notes, in which the warrant entitled the holder to (1) obtain a specified number of shares at a fixed price, or (2) put the warrants back to the company at a specified price (much higher than the warrant value on issuance) shortly after the maturity of the notes. Here again, the issuer's objective was to obtain a lower coupon on the debt by giving the investor an option that would not be used if the warrant value went into the money at the put exercise date. The issues considered by the EITF were:

1. Should the debt proceeds be allocated to the debt and the warrant (the usual warrant treatment)?
2. Should the carrying amount of the warrant be accrued to the put price?

3. If accrual to put price is proper, is it interest expense or a charge to retained earnings related to an equity instrument redemption?

The EITF reached a consensus that the warrant should be separately valued at issuance and that the resulting debt discount should be conventionally amortized. Further, the warrant was deemed a debt rather than an equity instrument, and thus the carrying amount of the warrant should be accrued to the put price by charges to interest expense up to the put date, presumably using the interest method.

If the put expired because the warrant was exercised, it is assumed that the liability accrual would be credited to paid-in capital as additional proceeds, although this aspect was not discussed by the EITF.

In Issue 88-9, *Put Warrants*, the EITF discussed a similiar situation, focusing on balance sheet classification of the proceeds. The SEC Observer stated that the SEC staff's view required such proceeds to be treated as temporary capital, similar to mandatorily redeemable preferred stock. Thus the EITF concluded that as to accounting by SEC registrants, seeking a consensus was moot. Further EITF discussions will be required to reach a consensus as to put warrants issued by nonpublic companies.

Warrants to obtain additional debt. Investors concerned that future interest rates will fall are willing to accept a slightly lower coupon rate on a debt issue if they are given warrants to acquire specified amounts of the same debt at the same rate during a specified time period. Conversely, the issuer assesses that the decrease in future interest rate levels is likely to be less than the "all-in" cost saved by attaching this feature to the debt issue.

This transaction is analogous to selling an interest rate option. Some issuers gave no accounting recognition to this feature, and when issuing debt later simply recorded the new debt at its face amount. Others considered the fact that the investor would not exercise the debt warrant unless interest rate levels had decreased, and accordingly accrued an interest cost on the original debt that factored in a discount on the anticipated debt issuance. (Essentially, the warrant was marked to market.)

Altering Debt Timing

Put features mentioned in the preceding sections may modify the timing of principal payment, depending on the value of the put in relation to the holder's other options. Additional examples of timing modifications are described in the following sections.

Negative Amortization.[3] In Issue 85-38, *Negative Amortizing Loans*, the EITF came astride a very complex subject with many subissues, but did not reach a consensus on any of them.

Negative amortizing loans are loans for which the rate at which interest is contractually earned (contract rate) is greater than the rate at which interest must be paid by

---

[3] The information in this section is abstracted from the EITF Issues summary prepared by Touche Ross & Co. based on cases in its practice. Because of the complexity of the subject, the information available in *EITF Abstracts* is extremely abbreviated.

the borrower (pay rate). For such loans, the principal balance typically increases during the period of time that the contract rate exceeds the pay rate.

Usually there is an expectation that the appraised value of collateral will increase to cover the loan buildup. Although there are many varieties of negatively amortizing loans, most can be classified into three categories:

1. *Variable rate loans on single family dwellings* generally provide for a fixed monthly payment rate or a cap on the monthly payment rate regardless of the variable contract interest rate. The excess of contract interest over interest paid is added to the principal balance of the mortgage. The mortgage terms provide for payment of the incremental principal through future monthly payments at the same or higher levels or at the end of the mortgage term. Typically, the principal balance of the loan does not exceed 80 to 90% of the value of the underlying collateral at the inception of the loan, and it is not uncommon for the lending institution to require mortgage insurance on such loans.

2. *Traditional "bowtie" loans* are granted by a financial institution for a term of three to five years. The loan is collateralized by commercial or rental property with existing cash flows, commonly having a loan-to-value ratio from 70 to 95%. The pay rate is usually based on cash flows from underlying properties, and typically is substantially below the contract rate. There is an expectation that the entire principal balance, including that portion arising from the negative amortization feature of the loan, will be repaid from the proceeds of refinancing.

3. *ADC-type loans and construction loans* are typically granted for an intermediate term necessary for the development of the collateral properties. Typically there are no underlying cash flows from the properties and accordingly no principal or interest payments are made on these loans. Consequently, the full amount of the contract interest is added to the principal balance. (These loans are discussed in Chapter 41.)

Accounting issues. The EITF was presented with several difficult accounting questions with respect to negative amortizing loans.

1. Is it appropriate to accrue interest at the contract rate? If so, is there a limit (assuming there exists no known problems with respect to collectibility)?

2. Is it appropriate to record a gain on the sale of negative amortizing loans under the following circumstances?
   - The sale is on a nonrecourse basis.
   - The sale is on a recourse basis.
   - The sale is on a nonrecourse basis, but the seller guarantees the purchaser a stated rate of interest (usually somewhat less than the contract rate but substantially more than the pay rate).
   - The purchaser has the right to "put" the loans back to the seller for a specified period of time.
   - The seller has an option to "repurchase" the loans during a specified period of time.

The EITF was presented with an example of a negative amortizing loan acquired in a "flip" transaction that was subsequently sold to an independent party. The terms of the sale required the seller to pay to the purchaser interest at a rate substantially in excess of the pay rate but below the original contract rate. The question

Due at end of year	Principal	Interest	Total annual cash flow	Present value of annual payments
1	$ —	$1,000	$1,000	$ 909
2		1,000	1,000	826
3		1,000	1,000	752
4		1,000	1,000	683
5	10,000	1,000	11,000	6,830
Present value of two streams	$ 6,209	$3,791		$10,000

FIG. 21.2   Present-Valuing Interest and Principal Streams Without Regard to the Yield Curve

posed in this case was how much, if any, gain could be recognized at the time of the sale of the negative amortizing loan.

Although this matter was not settled in 1985, the essentials in resolving it are covered in SFAS 91, *Accounting for Nonrefundable Fees and Costs Associated With Originating or Acquiring Loans and Initial Direct Costs of Leases* (L20), and in SFAS 77, *Reporting by Transferors for Transfers of Receivables With Recourse* (R20).

SFAS 91 discusses how a loan originator (in this case the buyer of the participation) should account for the purchased loan; by analogy, the recipient of the funds (the seller) would follow similar accounting. Although SFAS 77 was available at the time, its applicability to the sale of a negative amortizing loan was not discussed by the EITF; since that time, it has been frequently applied to loans sold with and without recourse.

Stripped Coupons or Principal. Some years ago, because the carrying amount of loans was deemed applicable to principal, some entities sold coupons from loans and recorded the entire proceeds as income. Of course, they then had no interest income for the duration for which the coupons were sold. The next development phase occurred when accountants grouped all cash flows alike and discounted them at the face rate of the instrument. For example, a $10,000 loan with a 10% coupon payable annually, with principal due in five years could be viewed as shown in Figure 21.2. Thus when all the coupons were sold on day one, the "cost of sales" was $3,791, the present value of the interest stream. The seller also could have sold the principal and retained the coupons, with a $6,209 basis to be allocated to the sale.

Even this has turned out to be too simplistic, and, although once approved by the AcSEC, it has now been abrogated. In reality, the values of individual future payments differ both because of the time factor and the yield curve, that is, the nonlinear change in rates that is based on duration of the instrument. A good example is shown in the treasury yield curve, changing constantly and published daily, as seen in Figure 21.3. This curve is not affected by credit risk considerations simply because of the nature of the securities. In this typical example, note that as maturities lengthen, the yield rises.

In Issue 88-11, *Sale of Interest-Only or Principal-Only Cash Flows From Loans Receivable*, the EITF reached a consensus that the carrying amount should be allocated between those cash flows sold (referred to as IO and PO strips) and those

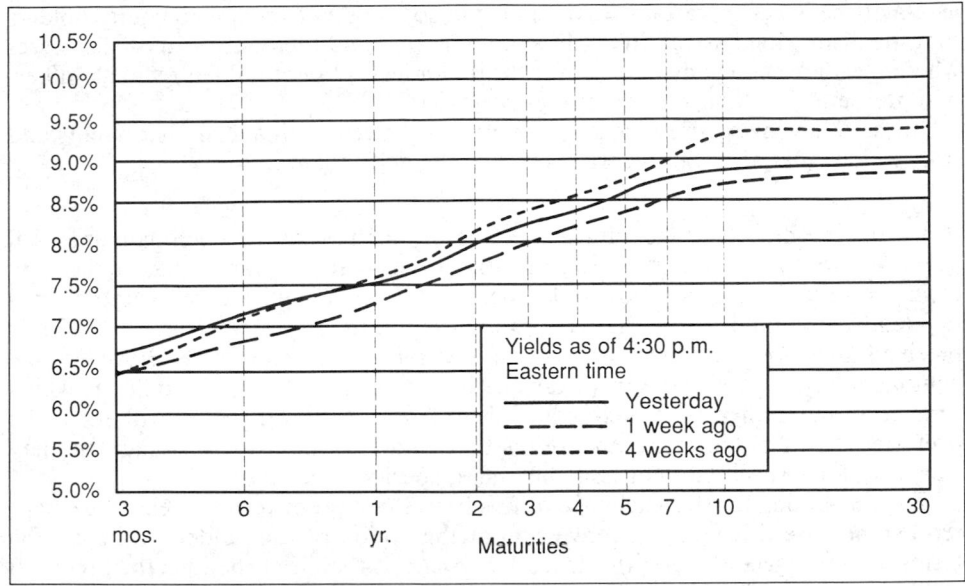

FIG. 21.3 Treasury Yield Curve
Source: Technical Data International, June 22, 1988.

retained on the basis of their respective fair values at the date the loan was acquired (the historical cost concept). If an acquisition date split is not feasible, the cost should be split on the basis of fair value proportions at the sale date. In most cases, using fair values based on the yield curve concept will produce different answers than the prior uniform cash flow discounting approach.

Generally, the EITF felt that gain recognition is not appropriate on the sale of a strip from an "underwater" receivable (one whose overall value is less than cost), even though a gain might be generated by the selection of specific cash flows to sell. This matter will be further discussed by the EITF.

In addition, CMO instruments have refined the idea of stripping in a situation where the cash flows are dependent on mortgagee prepayments, as further discussed in the "Securitized Assets" section later herein.

Perpetual Notes. These instruments have been used in the United Kingdom, but so far not in the U.S. markets. The quintessential ingredient of debt – a date at which the creditor is paid – is missing. Whether these are to be classified as debt or equity depends on a analysis of all the terms and conditions, especially any that may give the "creditors" a right to demand payment.

Altering Debt Collateral or Security

The traditional debt security has a claim on the issuer's assets that is prior to the participation of equity holders. While many debt issues are collateralized by specific assets of the issuer in various ways, some are so marginally senior to equity holders that the distinction has validity only in liquidation – and then only in those few cases where there are enough assets to cover the junior level of debt holders, who are otherwise no better off than the senior equity holders.

In the following sections, several examples are given of financial instruments and transactions that alter the secured status of the debt holder.

Exchangeability. To take advantage of its income tax status, a company may sell preferred stock when it is in a loss-generating or loss carryforward situation, because it has no need for the tax-deductible interest that accompanies debt. The preferred dividend rate will be less than the counterpart interest rate, because dividends received by corporate investors obtain favorable tax treatment. However, the company may project a return to taxable income status at a future date, at which time it would rather have tax-deductible interest. Accordingly, it will issue the preferred stock but include an option that under certain circumstances it may exchange for a specified debt issue bearing a specified interest rate.

The accounting for this exchange differs from that for convertible debt (see Chapter 18), because this is not a conversion at the option of the holder. Although the terms of exchangeables vary, the general approach is that, if at the time the preferred stock is issued the face amount of the debt that could be substituted for it is the same as the face amount of the preferred stock and the coupon rate is a market rate, the accounting for the actual exchange merely substitutes a debt in place of the equity amount in the balance sheet; the debt issue is not repriced at the time of exchange.

The reverse issuance is often done as well: a company will issue debt that it may exchange into preferred stock at its option. Other features also may accompany these issues. For example, the holder may not be required to accept the exchange security, but may retain his original security, which thereupon may enter into a redemption timetable. Or holders or issuers may have other options such as a choice of what the exchange medium may be (e.g., convertibles, cash, common stock, or even call options on stock held by the issuer in another company).

Because each unique situation must be examined to ascertain its substance for financial reporting purposes, the complexities have resulted in diverse answers.

Sureties and Guarantees. A company may need the assurance of a more creditworthy third party to sell its debt, or to reduce the cost of the debt from the level its unguaranteed rating would require in the market. In the latter case, the company will, of course, ascertain that the cost of the guarantee is less than the additional interest cost avoided.

Banks have traditionally offered letters of credit and other types of guarantees (see Chapter 40); but in recent years financial surety companies have sprung up, either as independents or as segments of insurance companies, to guarantee the payment of principal and interest, enabling the issue to obtain a very high S&P or Moody's rating.

Financial sureties. These enterprises evaluate the debt default probabilities on an applicant debt issue. If the risk is deemed acceptable by its underwriting standards, the surety will affix its guarantee and charge a premium. The substance of the guarantee is backed by the equity capital of the surety, which essentially operates on a zero-loss expectation based on its underwriting standards. Because each transaction is custom-tailored, the manner in which the surety's fees are charged may vary, presenting complex accounting issues in the timing of income recognition by the surety.

Indirect guarantees. Noninsurance enterprises also may issue guarantees. SFAS 5, *Accounting for Contingencies*, requires disclosure of guarantees in the financial statements of guarantors even though the possibility of loss may be remote (C59.113). In practice, this has been applied to direct guarantees of debt, but the FASB concluded that this was too narrow. Therefore, it issued FIN 34, *Disclosure of Indirect Guarantees of Indebtedness of Others*, defining an indirect guarantee in the following manner (C59.114):

> An indirect guarantee of the indebtedness of another arises under an agreement that obligates one entity to transfer funds to a second entity upon the occurrence of specified events, under conditions whereby (a) the funds are legally available to creditors of the second entity and (b) those creditors may enforce the second entity's claims against the first entity under the agreement. Examples of indirect guarantees include agreements to advance funds if a second entity's income, coverage of fixed charges, or working capital falls below a specified *minimum*.

SEC requirements. In 1985, the SEC issued FRR 23 (§ 104) describing its belief that certain oral guarantees are contingent liabilities requiring disclosure. The release directs auditors to make certain that their procedures are directed to this type of item. Subsequently, the planning subcommittee of the ASB stated that it had reviewed the literature and concluded that the existing guidance is appropriate and covers both oral and written guarantees.

The point made by these comments about indirect and oral guarantees is that if there is no apparent reason that a note should bear as low a rate of interest as it does, or that it has especially favorable terms, there may be an undisclosed guarantee. Accordingly, there may be situations in which an auditor will decide to supplement the wording of the standard bank confirmatin inquiry form, to make appropriate inquiries of the lending officer, or to consider an explicit reference to oral and written gurantees in the client representations letter.

Altering Senior Equity

Exchangeability. This feature was discussed in the preceding major section on debt. From the equity holders' perspective, a preferred stock can be made exchangeable at the issuer's option into debt under specified terms and conditions, presumably when the issuer is able to use the tax-deductibility of the interest payments.

Collateralization. Equity securities are commonly thought of as the residual interest in an enterprise, without collateralization, having only a prioritization in the event of liquidation. Several approaches involving the use of a separate legal entity have been used to evade this elementary concept.

For example, a company may create a subsidiary and transfer to it receivables having a face amount of, say, $150 million in exchange for a $100 million note and common stock of $50 million. The subsidiary sells preferred stock to outside investors at $100 million and uses the proceeds to pay off the parent's note. The preferred holders are collateralized because they have a prior claim on the receivables—the only asset—held by the subsidiary. This approach has been used when the parent company has an overall credit rating that is not as high as the credit rating that would be applicable to the assets sequestered in the subsidiary.

It should be noted that preferred stock of a subsidiary is classified in consolidated financial statements as a minority interest rather than as shareholders' equity; however, it is acceptable to display subsidiary preferred stock (so named) just above shareholders' equity (as if it were redeemable preferred stock). With this labeling and placement, it is not nearly so inscrutable as "minority interest," which some readers might take to be more like debt.

Tax-Deductible Preferred Stock. This topic was discussed earlier under "Debt Repayable in Common Stock." In brief, a company issuing preferred stock to a controlled grantor trust (which uses the stock as collateral for debt funds remitted to the parent) may try to classify the preferred stock as equity in the consolidated financial statements if the preferred stock is redeemable only by the issuance of common stock (number of shares dependent on common stock market value at redemption date). The SEC will not permit this presentation.

Auction Rate Preferred Stock. This type of preferred stock has a floating rate determined (after the initial setting) by a "Dutch auction" held every 49 days by the underwriter. At these intervals, the holders (and any other potential buyers) bid the dividend rate at which they would be willing to buy (or sell) the shares. Assuming enough buy bids are received, the issue is "resold" at a uniform revised dividend rate. If the auction fails, the issuer must pay another rate, usually the composite commercial paper rate. If there is a second consecutive auction failure, the issuer is required to redeem the shares. The objective of the auction is to obtain rock-bottom dividend rates through the bidding process, while maintaining the preferred stock price at or near par. The only accounting issue is whether the preferred stock should be classified as redeemable because of the redemption contingency; so far the classification has remained in shareholders' equity.

Unusual Dividends. In a few cases, preferred stock has been issued with a redemption amount substantially below issue price, but with "dividends" at a preposterous rate. Since redeemable preferred stock is not quite a debt instrument, imputation rules are not directly applicable. However, the substance of the transaction is the issuance of a liquidating of preferred stock interest with some of the dividends therefore being allocated on the interest method to reduce the preferred stock paid-in amount. For tax purposes, the parties generally have sought to treat the *megadividends* as eligible for the dividends received credit and the minuscule redemption price as generating a loss. It is not known if any of these transactions has succeeded in attaining these tax objectives. For financial accounting purposes, this transaction would be accounted for in accord with its substance; SEC registrants would apply the rules for mandatorily redeemable preferred stock.

The SEC also dealt with this type of matter in SAB 68, *Increasing Rate Preferred Stock* (Topic 5.Q), stating that a below-market rate dividend (or no dividend) should cause *nonredeemable* preferred stock to be discounted so as to achieve a "normal" dividend rate (see Chapter 20). Applying the "concepts" of SAB 68 to megadividends or any other situation in which the nominal dividend is materially *greater* than the normal rate, a "preferred stock premium" account should be established and the excess dividends charged thereto rather than to preferred dividend requirements (which reduces earnings applicable to common stock).

Dividend Strips. Similar to "Stripped Coupons or Principal" previously discussed, a holder of a preferred stock may sell a dividend strip consisting of all future dividends to be paid thereon for a specified period (e.g., to the first call date). A question arises as to whether the sale results in 100% income because dividends (unlike interest) are not obligations of the issuer until they are declared. Because the strip would not be salable unless the dividend stream were highly assured, the seller should reduce the carrying amount of the preferred stock and accrete the dividend income over time.

Altering Common Equity

Variations on Common Stock. It is not unusual that a company has more than one class or type of common stock, for example, Class A and Class B, or junior common stock (see Chapter 20). Often these arrangements are established to maintain voting control in a specific person or group, but sometimes they result in having no class of common stock that has voting control (causing pooling difficulties; see Chapter 23). Another reason for more than one class of common stock is to provide some kind of preferential right without, however, giving one class a priority in liquidation over another. In some respects these are like preferred stocks, but are distinguished on legal form.

Put-able Common Stock. A few issues of common stock have offered the buyers the right to put back the stock at purchase price if the market value did not increase to a specified level by a stipulated date; some have been based on other conditions. The SEC has insisted that such stock be classified in temporary equity in the "mezzanine" (below liabilities but above shareholders' equity, like redeemable preferred stock), until the put expires.

Income/Appreciation Split. Equity securities can be placed into a trust that will separate them into income and appreciation rights. An example is the Americus Trust, in which shares of AT&T and other companies are split in this manner. An investor may purchase either dividend interests ("primes") or appreciation interests ("scores"). The issuer, of course, has no control over this feature.

Put Options on Common Stock. In Issue 87-31, *Sale of Put Options on Issuer's Stock*, the EITF discussed a situation in which a company sells options on its own publicly traded stock, with each option enabling the holder to put one share of common stock to the company at a fixed price for two years. The EITF did not consider how a privately held company might account for this, but noted that ASR 268 (FRR § 211), which covers mandatorily redeemable preferred stock, would be applied. Essentially, the sales proceeds from the puts would be treated as a credit to paid-in capital, and a transfer of the put price times the number of put-able shares would be transferred from common equity to the "mezzanine" (referred to in this Issue as "temporary capital").

SPECIFIC TYPES OF INSTRUMENTS AND TRANSACTIONS

Off-Balance Sheet Financing

Financial accounting has been much criticized for "off-balance sheet financing," a mild pejorative for almost any source of funds (other than from issuances of bona fide equity or generated by operations) not shown as a borrowing in the financial statements. Said differently, an off-balance sheet financing is a financial instrument not required to be recorded under GAAP, at least so far.

Although this section covers off-balance sheet financing by name, it must be recognized that many situations not mentioned here are viewed by some accountants as improperly resulting in leaving something off the balance sheet; there is simply that uneasy feeling that all is not right. The SEC had proposed (Release 33-6514, 1984) to require a series of uniform disclosures regarding off-balance sheet financing, but withdrew the proposal in favor of the FASB's commencement of a major project on "Financial Instruments and Off Balance Sheet Financing," discussed earlier in this chapter. The FASB's initial thrust in proposing to require fulsome disclosures essentially would add specifications to what the SEC had in mind. Later phases regarding recognition will be more binding, as questions of offsetting assets and liabilities (a form of off-balance sheet accounting) and consolidation of sponsored entities will be addressed.

In addition, an FASB project on consolidation and the equity method will answer some of the unconsolidated entity issues. One step already taken appears in SFAS 94, *Consolidation of All Majority-Owned Subsidiaries,* (C51), which commencing in 1988 will no longer allow nonconsolidation of finance or any other subsidiaries (except when control is temporary or ineffectual). (See Chapter 24.)

Offsetting Assets and Liabilities. Many situations arise in which an asset is the only recourse for a debt. Thus a common assertion is that a right of offset exists, permitting crossover of the debt against the asset. APB 10, *Omnibus Opinion—1966* states:

> It is a general principle of accounting that the offsetting of assets and liabilities in the balance sheet is improper except where a right of setoff exists. [I25.190]

The problem centers around the meaning of "right of setoff." While it may be facile to set off a trade receivable from and payable to the same party when that is not the normal manner of settlement, it is not all that clear why a nonrecourse wraparound note should not be set off against an asset that is its only collateral, when the asset is no greater than the liability. However, the SEC has said "no offset" in this situation (SAB 70, Topic 5.R).

Two relevant EITF issues are mentioned in the following sections. Further, because the offsetting issue has recurred with such frequency, the FASB has proposed to issue TB 88-a, also described later in this chapter.

CDs offset against high-coupon debt. In Issue 87-20, *Offsetting Certificates of Deposit Against High-Coupon Debt,* the EITF considered a transaction structured to result in a debt extinguishment for tax but not for accounting purposes. In this transaction, the issuer of the debt purchases a certificate of deposit (current interest rate, same due date as the debt) from a bank in an amount equal to the par value of its debt security that has a high coupon rate of interest. At the same time, the bank purchases that debt security from holders at a premium. In addition to an arrangement fee, the issuer agrees to pay the bank for any unamortized premium should an early redemption occur. The debt would be redeemed by the issuer from the bank in exchange for the CD when it matures.

The objective of this structure was to achieve changes in cash flows that were below 3 to 5%, the range suggested in EITF Issue 86-18, *Debtor's Accounting for a Modification of Debt Terms,* as not resulting in a debt extinguishment (discussed in Chapter 18). The EITF avoided controversy over how to compute the change in cash flows (at current or at coupon interest rate) in this particular transaction, concluding that for other reasons offset was inappropriate and that the debt really was extinguished for GAAP purposes as well.

Note monetization. In Issue 84-11, *Offsetting Installment Note Receivables and Bank Debt ("Note Monetization"),* the EITF concluded that offsetting is not permissible for an installment note receivable accepted by a seller of property against a bank loan subsequently negotiated by the seller to obtain cash in an amount equal to the note receivable. Typically, the seller obtains an unconditional put option that permits delivery to the bank of the note receivable in full satisfaction of the loan, in effect making the bank loan a secured nonrecourse borrowing.

Subsequently, in SAB 70 (Topic 5.R), the SEC prohibited the offsetting of nonrecourse debt with a related lease receivable representing the collateral; and in TB 86-2, *Accounting for an Interest in the Residual Value of a Leased Asset* (L10.528–.539), the FASB restricted the offsetting of a lease receivable and related nonrecourse debt to situations in which (1) a legal right of offset exists and (2) a leveraged lease is involved.

Revised definition of setoff. In proposed TB 88-a, *Definition of a Right of Setoff,* the FASB staff restricts setoff to only those two-party situations in which the intent is to actually settle by offset. Further, the offset right has to be bankruptcy proof. It is hard to think of much that can pass these rigid tests. The original pronouncement (I25.190) said nothing like this.

TBs are intended to state the intent of the standard-setters when this is not clear in the pronouncement. It is perhaps a bit presumptuous to do this 22 years after the pronouncement was issued. This issue is part of the FASB's overall financial instruments project, discussed earlier, and the TB therefore may be viewed as a transitional device.

Unconditional Purchase Obligations

Nature of the obligation. An unconditional purchase obligation is defined in SFAS 47, *Disclosure of Long-Term Obligations* (C32), as an obligation to transfer funds in the future for fixed or minimum amounts or quantities of goods or services at fixed or minimum prices. Such obligations often are in the form of "take-or-pay contracts" or "throughput agreements," which generally require the buyer to pay specified amounts periodically, even if delivery of goods is not taken and/or the service is not used.

These arrangements are sometimes referred to as "project financings"—the project being funded is designed to generate cash flows sufficient to pay off the debt. They may be used to acquire and exploit natural resources or mining properties, for pipelines, power generation facilities, chemical plants, and the like.

An unconditional purchase obligation should be disclosed if it has all of the following characteristics (C32.101):

1. Noncancelable, or cancelable only:
   a. Upon the occurrence of some remote contingency;
   b. With the permission of the other party;
   c. If a replacement agreement is signed between the same parties; or
   d. Upon payment of a penalty in an amount such that continuation of the agreement appears reasonably assured.
2. Negotiated as part of arranging financing for the facilities that will provide the contracted goods or services, or for costs related to those goods or services (e.g., carrying costs for contracted goods).
3. Remaining term in excess of one year.

For most arrangements covered by this SFAS 47, financing considerations are an integral part of negotiating the terms of the unconditional purchase obligations. However, a purchaser is not required to investigate whether a supplier used an unconditional purchase obligation to help secure financing, if the purchaser would otherwise be unaware of that fact.

Disclosure requirements. The disclosure requirements of SFAS 47 distinguish between long-term obligations that are recorded in the purchasers' balance sheet and those that are not. The statement does not alter the accounting treatment for future unconditional purchase obligations that are substantially the same as those obligations already recorded as liabilities along with related assets, nor does it suggest that disclosure is an appropriate substitute for accounting recognition if the substance of an arrangement is the acquisition of an asset and incurrence of a liability.

To secure access to facilities to process chemical X, the company has signed a processing agreement with a chemical company allowing B Company to submit 100,000 tons for processing annually for 20 years. Under the terms of the agreement, B Company may be required to advance funds against future processing charges if the chemical company is unable to meet its financial obligations. The aggregate amount of required payments at December 31, 19X1 is as follows (in thousands):

19X2	$10,000
19X3	10,000
19X4	9,000
19X5	8,000
19X6	8,000
Later years	100,000
Total	145,000
Less: Amount representing interest	(45,000)
Total at present value	$100,000

In addition, the company is required to pay a proportional share of the variable operating expenses of the plant. The company's total processing charges under the agreement in each of the past three years have been $12 million.

FIG. 21.4   Example of Unconditional Purchase Obligation Disclosure
Source: SFAS 47 (C32.108).

The disclosures required for long-term unconditional purchase obligations associated with suppliers' financing that are not recognized on purchasers' balance sheets are:

1. Nature of the obligation;
2. Amount of the fixed and determinable obligation in the aggregate and for each of the next five years;
3. Description of any portion of the obligation that is variable; and
4. Purchases in each year for which an income statement is presented.

Appendix C of SFAS 47 contains several examples that clarify the types of arrangements intended to be covered. Figure 21.4 shows the footnote portion of Example 1.

Product Financing Agreements. SFAS 49, *Accounting for Product Financing Arrangements* (D18), extracts without much change the specialized principles and practices from SOP 78-8 (same title).

In product financing arrangements, an enterprise sells inventory and agrees to repurchase it with the repurchase price equal to the original sale price plus carrying and financing costs. Other similar transactions such as a guarantee of resale prices to third parties are also covered.

SFAS 49 specifies criteria for determining when an arrangement involving the sale of inventory is, in substance, a financing arrangement, and how it should be accounted for:

• If a sponsor (the enterprise seeking to finance the product pending its future use or resale) sells a product to another entity and, in a related transaction, agrees to repurchase the product (or a substantially identical product) or processed goods of which the product is a component, the sponsor should record a liability at the time the proceeds are received from the other entity. The sponsor should not record the transaction as a sale or remove the covered product from its balance sheet.

• If the sponsor participates in an arrangement whereby another entity purchases a product on the sponsor's behalf and, in a related transaction, the sponsor agrees to purchase from that entity the product or processed goods of which the product is a component, the sponsor should record the asset and the related liability when the product is purchased by the other entity.

Costs of the product, excluding processing costs, in excess of the sponsor's original production or purchase costs (or other entity's purchase costs) represent financing and holding costs. The sponsor should account for such costs, as they are incurred by the other entity, in accordance with its accounting policies applicable to financing and holding costs.

The approach in SFAS 49 seems inconsistent with that adopted in SFAS 47, *Disclosure of Long-Term Obligations* (C32), which differentiates between balance sheet recognition and disclosure of certain unconditional purchase obligations. The Board commented (SFAS 49, ¶¶ 21-22, partially contained in D18.105):

> There are similarities between a sponsor's rights and obligations under a product financing arrangement and a purchaser's rights and obligations under an unconditional purchase obligation. Both the sponsor and the purchaser obtain probable future economic benefits from the assured source of product. Both are obligated to make future cash payments to the other party to the agreement. Beyond those similarities, however, there is substantial difference in the related accounting issues.
>
> The accounting issue with respect to an unconditional purchase obligation is whether at the time the contract is entered into the purchaser should report rights to receive future product or services as a liability. Under a product financing arrangement, the product already exists and the other entity's purchase cost is known. The accounting issue addressed in this Statement is whether the sponsor should report the existing product currently held by the other entity as an asset and the obligation to pay the other entity as a liability. This Statement concludes that the sponsor is in substance the owner of the product and that the sponsor should, therefore, report the product as an asset and the related obligation as a liability. At the time a take-or-pay contract is entered into, by contrast, either the product does not yet exist (for example, electricity) or the product exists in a form unsuitable to the purchaser (for example, unmined coal); the purchaser has a right to receive future product but is not the substantive owner of existing product.

Securitized Assets

Securitized asset structures encompass a vast array of financing techniques. In general, investors in these structures look to the cash flow provided by a discrete pool of assets — rather than a company's overall creditworthiness — to recoup their investment and provide a positive return. Traditional *factoring*, when a finance company purchases a business' trade receivables, can be viewed as a securitized asset structure.

At the simplest level, securitized asset structures require the following:

- Cash generating assets. The assets should produce a steady and predictable stream of cash flows. Almost always, the assets are a type of receivable.
- Asset segregation. Usually, investors look only to the "securitized" assets for their return. An adequate mechanism to segregate these assets from others must exist.
- Sale of interests. Third parties invest by lending funds collateralized by the assets, by taking an equity stake, or by purchasing an ownership interest in the assets themselves.

The topic quickly becomes complex because each of these basic elements can be attained in a variety of ways.

Cash generating assets that produce a steady and predictable stream of cash flows include single family mortgages, mortgage-backed securities, leases, auto loans, and credit card receivable balances. Because each type of asset has unique payment characteristics, the structuring mechanisms will differ. Even within a single asset type, such as credit card receivables, different portfolios will generate cash flows at different rates and with differing reliability. Mortgage-backed securities and other forms of mortgage loans account for the preponderance of assets subject to structured financings.

The way in which *securitized asset segregation* is accomplished also can vary widely. The most basic method of segregation involves simply the separate identification of the securitized assets in a company's accounting records. Commonly, though, the *sponsor* establishes a *special-purpose entity* whose holdings, for the most part, consist of the securitized assets. Definitive asset segregation reassures investors; if the sponsor encounters financial difficulties, its creditors will not have access to the securitized assets if the special purpose entity is *bankruptcy-proof*.

Special purpose entities can take many forms: corporate subsidiaries, trusts, or partnerships. In fact, it is possible for a sponsor to cause an unrelated entity to serve as its special purpose entity. For example, managers and employees of a broker/dealer can serve as the shareholders of a special purpose entity whose assets were purchased from the broker/dealer. There are also businesses that specialize in creating their own subsidiaries to serve as an unrelated sponsor's special purpose entity, for a fee, of course, and with adequate indemnification.

Once again, diversity is the hallmark of how *sales of interests* are accomplished in securitized asset structures. An investor can lend funds to the special purpose entity by purchasing its debt. The investor can purchase stock or partnership interests in the special purpose entity or, in trust structures, buy the equivalent of stock by purchasing *certificates of beneficial interest*. Finally, investors can purchase *undivided interests* in the securitized assets themselves. To make matters even more complex, the special purpose entity can offer different types of interests in the same pool of assets.

The diversity does not end with the *form* of security that the investor purchases. By offering various classes of the same type of interest, such as different classes of debt, the sponsor can "re-sort" the cash flow generated by the assets, to satisfy investors with different investment horizons and different investment objectives. For example, a pension fund might be attracted to the relative interest rates that mortgage assets offer. However, the life of most mortgage rate investments might exceed the investment horizon of the fund. By investing in a short-lived CMO, the fund can satisfy both objectives.

From the sponsor's perspective, structured financings expand the range of potential investors or lenders. The greater supply of lenders translates into lower costs of funds – even when the expenses of arranging the structured financing are included in the "all-in" cost.

Collateralized Mortgage Obligations. CMOs best illustrate securitized asset structures with various investor classes. The securitized assets often are mortgage-backed securities, such as GNMA pass-through certificates. Each month, the special purpose entity will receive cash inflows consisting of scheduled mortgage interest, scheduled mortgage principal, and prepayments of mortgage principal.

Investors in the special purpose entity can be paid in exactly the same way: As the entity receives principal payments on its assets, all investors could receive a pro rata share of principal resulting in the issuer's obligations retiring in lock step with its mortgage assets. But commonly, the cash inflows are re-sorted among different classes of the special purpose entity's investors.

To illustrate, assume a special purpose entity owns pools of mortgage-backed securities.[4] The entity issues CMOs in three classes: Class A, Class B, and Class Z (the "Z" signifies zero). The terms of the CMOs call for the following "re-sort" of the *monthly* cash inflows the special purpose entity receives on the securitized mortgage assets:

- Class A. Quarterly, Class A holders are paid interest on the outstanding principal balance of the Class A obligations, at the contractual Class A interest rate. All principal payments the special purpose entity receives on the securitized mortgage assets during the quarter, including prepayments, are applied to reduce the principal balance of the outstanding Class A CMOs.

- Class B. Quarterly, Class B holders are paid interest on the outstanding principal balance of the Class B obligations, at the contractual Class B interest rate. However, none of the principal payments received by the special purpose entity is applied to the principal balance of the Class B CMOs until the Class A obligations have been paid in full.

- Class Z. Class Z holders receive no cash until both Class A and Class B have been satisfied entirely. Contractual interest on the Class Z notes accrues; once Class B obligations have been satisfied, Class Z holders will receive principal and interest payments quarterly.

Even though this might seem difficult to readers unfamiliar with structured financings, a three-class collateralized mortgage obligation with these terms is very basic. Frequently there are more classes, or the classes have even greater distinctions. For example, one class might provide a floating rate of interest to investors. As the interest rate index increases, investors in the floating class receive higher amounts of interest. To make the structure work, another class of collateralized mortgage obliga-

---

[4] The sponsor sells the mortgages to the special purpose entity in exchange for a note receivable. When the special purpose entity issues the collateralized mortgage obligations, it remits the debt proceeds to the sponsor to satisfy the note.

tions (the *inverse floater* class) would receive less interest as the interest rate index increases. *Superfloaters* and inverse superfloaters work in the same way except that the contractual interest rate on the CMO obligation varies as a multiple of the change in an interest rate index.

Accounting by Sponsors for CMOs. A fundamental question in accounting by sponsors and special purpose entities for securitized asset structures is whether the securitized assets remain in the consolidated balance sheet or whether the structure results in *off-balance sheet* treatment. Because the assets are almost always a type of receivable, accounting principles covering sales of receivables are important in answering this question.

The accounting analysis for a typical structure involves the following points:

1. The sponsor owns the assets to be securitized. It transfers them to the special purpose entity (the issuer) that sells interests to third party investors. Does the sponsor record this transfer as a sale or a financing?
2. When the issuer sells debt or equity interests to third party investors, does it account for the issuance of these securities as an economic sale of the securitized assets?
3. Should the sponsor consolidate the accounts of the issuer?

To summarize, accounting standards dealing with sales of receivables and consolidation as well as EITF deliberations need to be reviewed in determining the proper accounting treatment for securitized asset structures.

Conditions for sale treatment. SFAS 77, *Reporting by Transferors for Transfers of Receivables With Recourse* (R20), covers sales of receivables with recourse. Even though many structured financings do not involve recourse to the issuer or the sponsor, accountants have found these rules useful by analogy.

According to SFAS 77, a seller of receivables records a sale—removing the receivables from its balance sheet and recording a gain or loss—only when the transaction satisfies certain conditions. When the terms violate any of these conditions, the seller records the transaction as a financing. The proceeds of the offering are recorded as a liability in the seller's financial statements and the receivables remain as an asset. As the receivables are collected by the transferor, the seller records these amounts as payments of the liability and payments of interest.

SFAS 77 applies to transactions that *purport* to be sales. Thus, when the sponsor transfers securitized assets to the issuer, the terms should be compared to SFAS 77 conditions. If the issuer transfers to investors undivided interests in the securitized assets, the terms should also be compared to SFAS 77 requirements.

The conditions of SFAS 77, all of which must be satisfied to result in sale treatment, are as follows (R20.105).

1. *The transferor surrenders control of the future economic benefits embodied in the receivables.* The future economic benefits embodied in most receivables consist of the right to receive cash representing collections of the face amount of the receivable and often interest. This condition focuses on control; thus, a seller may retain the right to receive a portion of the cash flow from the receivables sold, so long as control is relinquished.

SFAS 77 points out that the seller has not surrendered control if he retains a repurchase option, even if the option price is equal to the prevailing fair market value of the receivables at the date of exercise.

2. *The transferor's obligation under the recourse provisions can be reasonably estimated.* Obviously this condition need not be satisfied if the terms of the sale do not involve recourse, defined by the FASB as the right of the receivables buyer to receive payment from the seller for (a) failure of the debtors to pay when due, (b) the effects of prepayments, or (c) adjustments resulting from defects in the eligibility of the transferred receivables (R20.404).

Many securitized asset structures do not involve recourse; for example, if GNMA mortgage-backed securities serve as the collateral for a CMO, the payment of principal is guaranteed by GNMA – obviating the need for further guarantees. In other situations, however, the sponsor will offer recourse if the cash flow from the collateral turns out to be less than expected.

Experience with similar types of receivables is usually the key to reasonably estimating a recourse obligation. (As to commercial properties, during 1988 the AICPA Savings and Loan Associations Committee began consideration of whether it is appropriate to permit the transfer of commercial mortgages (and securitized forms thereof) to be eligible for sale treatment, given the greater difficulty of reasonably determining obligations under recourse provisions. This matter has not yet been resolved by AcSEC.)

Sometimes, securitized asset structures involve *indirect recourse*. For example, a commercial bank unrelated to the sponsor or the issuer may issue a letter of credit in favor of the third party investors in the event the collateral turns out to be inadequate to provide the expected return. If the bank can look to the sponsor or its affiliates for reimbursement, the structure involves recourse. In other structures, the sponsor/issuer may sell a pro rata portion of the securitized assets to investors – for example, a 90% undivided interest in a pool of single-family home mortgages. If the sponsor/seller's rights to cash flows from the retained 10% interest is subordinate to the third party interests, most accountants would conclude that the subordination creates a recourse obligation.

3. *The transferee cannot require the transferor to repurchase the receivables except pursuant to recourse provisions.* Such a put requirement indicates that the sale transaction is incomplete and should not be accounted for as such until the put expires unexercised. A "nuisance" put or call (i.e., an obligation or an option to repurchase receivables when only minor amounts remain outstanding, to minimize administrative expenses), does not violate this provision.

Recording the sale. If the conditions of SFAS 77 are satisfied, a sale is recorded. The difference between the *adjusted sales price* and the seller's recorded investment in the receivables results in a gain or loss. The adjusted sales price takes into account loan servicing costs and the effects of any recourse obligation.

Typically, sellers of receivables continue to service loans sold on behalf of the buyer. For example, a savings and loan association may have originated a home mortgage and included the loan in a pool sold to investors in a securitized asset structure. Normally, this transaction is invisible to the homeowner; he continues to make payments to the savings and loan.

Collecting monthly mortgage payments, forwarding payments and related accounting reports to investors, collecting escrow deposits for the payment of mortgagor property taxes and insurance, and paying taxes and insurance from escrow funds when due, constitute the *loan servicing* activity (Mo4.411). Loan servicers are usually compensated for these services by retaining a portion of the monthly remittances collected on behalf of the owner of the receivables. The amount retained equals an agreed upon percentage of each receivable's outstanding principal balance.

The seller incurs costs to provide loan servicing; if the sale terms provide either too much or too little compensation for this activity the seller should adjust the sales price accordingly. If the sale terms do not provide for any servicing compensation or provide less than a current (normal) servicing fee rate,[5] a portion of the sale proceeds actually represents future servicing compensation. As a result, the seller should defer a portion of the sale proceeds, reducing the unadjusted gain or increasing the loss on the sale. The seller should recognize the deferred credit as servicing revenue in future periods as the activity is performed. Similarly, the sale terms may provide for servicing fee rates in excess of current or normal rates. The seller should include the present value of the excess servicing revenues as an element of the sale proceeds, increasing the unadjusted gain or decreasing the unadjusted loss on the sale.

In addition to properly assessing the servicing amounts, the seller should adjust the sales price for the effects of any *recourse obligation* by providing for expected losses and collection costs—calculated in accordance with SFAS 5 (C59.128). For example, a seller may agree to repurchase all defaulted receivables up to an aggregate of 10% of the receivable balances originally sold. If the seller's experience indicates that only 2.5% of the receivables will default, he would use the latter percentage in providing for the recourse obligation.

Retention of interest by seller. If the seller retains an interest in the securitized assets sold, he needs to properly allocate his recorded investment in the receivables between the portion retained and the portion sold. In Issue 88-11, *Sale of Interest-Only or Principal-Only Cash Flows From Loans Receivable*, the EITF reached a consensus that the allocation should be based on the relative fair values of each portion. (See earlier discussion of "Stripped Coupons or Principal.")

Debt obligations accounted for as sales. In securitized asset structures, a transaction purports to be a sale most often when third party investors purchase undivided interests in the assets of the issuer. If the form of the third party investors' interests is debt (i.e., the transaction does not purport to be a sale), almost always the issuer will account for the transfer of interests by recording a liability. TB 85-2, *Accounting for Collateralized Mortgage Obligations* (C30), provides for a single exception: If all but a nominal (trifling) amount of the economic benefits embodied in the collateral has irrevocably passed to the investors and if no affiliate of the issuer will ever be required to make payments on the debt, the issuer uses *like-a-sale* accounting for the transaction. The collateral is eliminated from the issuer's balance sheet and the issuer records a gain or loss by comparing the collateral carrying amount to the proceeds of the debt issue (effectively the unadjusted sale proceeds),

---

[5] Future servicing income is discussed in SFAS 65, *Accounting for Certain Mortgage Banking Activities* (Mo4). TB 87-3, *Accounting for Mortgage Servicing Fees and Rights* (Mo4), discusses the definition of a normal servicing rate for the sale of mortgage loans. See Chapter 41.

reduced by transaction costs and less-than-normal service fees. Unlike sale accounting, however, the issuer/seller would not include the present value of excess servicing fees or other expected residual interests in the collateral expected to remain after all of the obligations are satisfied.

Consolidating the issuer with the sponsor. If the securitized asset structure fails to result in sale accounting (or like-a-sale accounting under TB 85-2) the securitized assets and the proceeds of the third party investments will be included in the consolidated accounts of the sponsor—if the sponsor is required to consolidate the accounts of the issuer.

General consolidation principles (see Chapter 24) apply to the relationship between the sponsor and the issuer. If the issuer is a subsidiary of the sponsor, the accounts should be consolidated. TB 85-2 indicates that this same treatment should be followed if the issuer is a trust formed by the sponsor.

Sponsors can avoid consolidation by selling sufficient equity or residual interests to third party investors, using *vehicle companies.* The vehicle company is legally a subsidiary of or a trust formed by an entity unrelated to the sponsor. The legal parent of the vehicle has little at risk—the collateral will cover the cash flow requirements of the third party obligations and there may be credit enhancement such as seller recourse. The legal parent may also have little to enjoy if the structure is efficient and virtually all of the cash flows on the collateral revert to third party investors and the seller/sponsor.

The EITF has considered related issues on a number of occasions without reaching a consensus (see, for example, Issue 84-30, *Sales of Loans to Special-Purpose Entities,* and Issue 85-28, *Consolidation Issues Relating to Collateralized Mortgage Obligations*). However, when deliberating Issue 84-15, *Grantor Trusts Consolidation,* the EITF (while not reaching a consensus) identified broad considerations for deciding when consolidation may be appropriate by a sponsor of a legally unrelated vehicle company:

1. The extent to which related risks and rewards have been transferred to outside interests.
2. The amount of equity investment in the trust.
3. The extent of the company's influence on the operations of the trust.
4. The identity of the trust beneficiary.
5. The size of any residual interest in the trust.

In Issue 86-24, *Third-Party Establishment of Collateralized Mortgage Obligations,* the EITF considered whether a sale occurs if a financial institution "sells" mortgage loans to an outside party who then uses them as collateral for CMOs issued by a controlled entity. The financial institution:

1. Must replace mortgages that have eligibility defects;
2. Cannot repurchase any mortgages except those with eligibility defects;
3. Acquires the right to receive a residual interest in the periodic mortgage repayments in excess of servicing fees.

The outside party cannot put mortgages back to the financial institutions except for those that have eligibility defects.

The EITF concluded that the above transaction constitutes a sale and that any sale gain or loss, including the present value of the residual interest, if determinable, should be recorded at the time of sale.

Both the FASB staff and the SEC Observer expressed reservations about the conclusion. The SEC might challenge sale treatment on a case-by-case basis; the Board added this issue to the recognition phase of the financial instruments project.

Accounting by Sponsors for REMICs. In 1986, Congress enacted Internal Revenue Code §§ 860A–860G, which generally provide for REMICs (Real Estate Mortgage Investment Conduits). An entity that qualifies as a REMIC – usually a corporation, partnership, or trust – is not taxed on its income; the holders of REMIC interests are taxed directly.

To qualify as a REMIC, the entity's assets are limited to "qualified mortgages" and "permitted investments" as defined in the Internal Revenue Code. A further condition restricts the interests in the REMIC to regular classes and a single class of residual interests. Investors in regular interests are taxed as if their investments were debt instruments. Income or loss of a REMIC passes through to holders of the residual interest class.

The accounting issues for REMICs and investors in REMIC interests are the same as those for other securitized asset structures. The REMIC structure points out an anomoly in GAAP however. Because the regular interests are taxed as debt, investors are largely indifferent as to the form of the interests: actual debt or undivided interests in the securitized assets themselves. Yet the appropriate accounting principles apparently first look to the form of the transaction. If the interests are debt, the guidance in TB 85-2 applies. Yet if the regular class represents undivided interests in the collateral, most accountants would conclude that the provisions of SFAS 77 apply to the transaction.

Accounting by Investors

SFAS 91. If the third party investor acquires debt obligations of the issuer or purchases an undivided interest in the collateral, he has acquired loans. The accounting for acquired loans is covered in SFAS 91, *Accounting for Nonrefundable Fees and Costs Associated With Originating or Acquiring Loans and Initial Direct Costs of Leases* (L20).

Of concern is the investor's accounting for premium or discount on loans purchased. The premium or discount is the difference between the amount the investor pays to acquire the loan and its principal amount. Because securitized asset structures re-sort cash flows from the collateral, this commonly results in loan acquisitions at significant premiums or discounts.

This is dramatically illustrated in the following simplified two class CMO structure. The principal and interest payments on $10 million of mortgage assets serving as collateral are re-sorted as follows: the *interest-only (IO) class* is entitled to a token $1,000 of the total principal payments, plus all of the interest payments on the collateral. The *principal-only (PO) class* is entitled to all of the remaining principal ($9,999,000) and none of the interest payments.

An investor in the principal-only class will purchase the issuer's debt obligation at a significant discount. The price is the present value of the $9,999,000 principal amount. The investor/lender must make an assessment of when the principal amount will be returned to perform the present value calculation. The maximum period is the remaining contractual life of the underlying mortgages. No doubt that is too long because many of the mortgages serving as collateral will prepay.

An investor in the interest-only class will purchase the issuer's debt obligation at a significant premium. The purchase price represents the discounted present value of all expected interest payments and the token principal payment. Again, the estimated life of the collateral is key to the present value calculation.

According to SFAS 91, the premium or discount should be recognized as an adjustment of the loan yield (using the interest method) over the life of the loan. For most loans, SFAS 91 prohibits a lender from estimating prepayments. As actual prepayments are received, the lender makes a pro rata adjustment to unamortized loan premium or discount.

However, if the purchased loans consist of a large number of similar loans for which prepayments are probable and the timing and amount of prepayments can be reasonably estimated, SFAS 91 gives the lender the option of estimating prepayments in applying the interest method. If a lender chooses this option he should continually review his original estimate of prepayment rates and cumulatively correct the unamortized premium or discount in accordance with the method required in SFAS 91. While the collateral underlying a securitized asset structure would qualify for the optional SFAS 91 approach, this is not always true. Scheduled for future discussion at the EITF is Issue 88-20, *Difference Between Initial Investment and Principal Amount of Loans in a Purchased Credit Card Portfolio.*

The EITF considered the accounting for interest only certificates (Issue 86-38C, *Implications of Mortgage Prepayments on Amortization of Servicing Rights—Unanticipated Prepayments and Interest-Only Certificates).* The EITF concluded that SFAS 91 does apply to such an investment. But several members expressed concern that if the investor/lender did not estimate prepayments (because this is optional under SFAS 91), interest income may be unduly accelerated. Although the EITF did not reach a consensus on this point, the SEC Observer indicated that registrants are required to consider prepayments on IO certificates if the conditions of SFAS 91 are present.

Market value considerations. The market value of a long-term, fixed-interest-rate asset such as a mortgage is sensitive to interest rate changes in periods subsequent to acquisition. Obligations of securitized asset issuers are equally sensitive. If the structure results in re-sorted cash flows (fast-pay and slow-pay classes, superfloaters, interest-only obligations, and so forth), the market value of the issuer's obligations may be extremely volatile.

As a result, regulators of banks and savings and loan associations—frequent investors in securitized asset structures—are concerned that many financial institutions do not appreciate the economic risk of these investments. Financial institution investors should analyze regulatory requirements when considering an investment in a securitized asset structure.

Investments in residuals. If the investor acquires a residual interest—common shares of a corporate special-purpose issuer or certificates of beneficial interest in an issuer trust, for example—many accountants believe the investor should account for this investment as a loan. Economically, a residual interest in a securitized asset structure more closely resembles a receivable than it resembles a normal corporate investment. The issuer's business consists solely of collecting cash (from a defined collateral pool and from temporary cash investments) and distributing cash (to investors and to pay for administrative services). The timing and amount of cash flows that the residual interest holders will enjoy is based largely on the same factors affecting the timing and amount of cash flows that investors in senior obligations will enjoy. Thus some investors will use loan accounting.

Other investors will apply the principles of APB 18 (see Chapter 24) and account for the investment using the equity method of accounting (I82). Investors using the equity method will have to amortize the cost of the investment in the residuals over the expected life of the investment. Investors should consider using an accelerated method that relates the amortization of the cost to the benefit earned in each accounting period rather than a simple straight-line method of amortization. The interest method, producing a constant effective yield and producing a result similar to loan accounting, is conceptually preferable.

Repurchase and Reverse Repurchase Agreements

The failure of two unregulated government securities dealers in early 1985 generated a great deal of interest and controversy concerning the repurchase agreement ("repo") transactions that figured prominently in these failures. The collapse of these dealers had wide repercussions for thrift institutions, municipalities, and other participating investors.[6]

Description of Repos. Every repo transaction at origination involves two parties — a purchaser/lender, who, *in theory*, is disbursing cash and receiving title to securities, and a borrower/seller, who, *in theory,* is receiving cash and surrendering title to securities. At the same time, the two parties agree to a reversal of the transaction at a specified price at a specified or determinable future date.

The time interval between origination and reversal of a repo varies depending on the terms of the agreement. Common variations are as follows:

- *Overnight repo.* Repurchase date is the following day.
- *Term repo.* Repurchase date is a specified date in the future, normally within six months.

---

[6] In response, the AICPA Auditing Standards Board appointed a special Task Force to study the adequacy of then-current audit guidance. The Task Force conclusions are summarized as follows (AICPA, 1985d):

1. Existing SASs provide adequate general standards and standards of field work and reporting for auditing repo transactions.
2. Additional educational materials should be added to AICPA guides.
3. A separate task force should make a comprehensive study of all existing financial instruments and prepare a uniform audit guide.
4. The accounting standard-setting bodies should consider requiring certain disclosures (this has been effectively accomplished).

Other comments related to the possible need to obtain a third party auditor's report regarding custodians, the limited value of confirmation procedures, and the high-risk nature of related party transactions.

- *Open repo.* Indefinite repurchase date, in which borrower or lender typically has option to close at any time (an effective open repo may be achieved by continuously rolling over an overnight repo into another overnight repo). Open repos are sometimes referred to as floating rate repos, because the rate paid on them may vary from day to day.
- *Repo to maturity.* Repo in which term extends to maturity date of underlying security.

All repo transactions involve securities. The most common repos involve direct obligations of the U.S. government. However, repos can also involve negotiable certificates of deposit, bankers' acceptances, commercial paper, or mortgage-backed securities. A variation of repos, called dollar repos, involves an agreement to sell and repurchase substantially similar, but not identical, mortgage-backed securities of the same federal agency.

Thrift institutions, municipalities, and others who participate in repurchase agreements generally enter into these transactions with commercial banks or other government securities dealers either because they have excess funds to invest on a short-term basis or because they need to borrow funds on a short-term basis. There is no regulation of government securities dealers per se, but many of the dealers are subject to governmental regulation as a broker/dealer or bank because their activities extend beyond the government securities market. A dealer's financial position is of concern from an investor viewpoint. Dealers who operate with a very small capital base may not provide an adequate safety margin when difficulties occur.

It is important to understand that the same securities may be involved in many repo transactions at the same time. An entity executing a repo transaction as borrower/seller should not expect the dealer (purchaser/lender) to hold the securities in safekeeping for the term of the agreement. Most likely, the dealer will use these securities in other transactions. For example, the dealer may enter into a repo transaction with a bank using these securities as collateral, and the bank, in turn, may repo them out again, and so on. When the term of the original repo agreement expires, the dealer will either purchase the securities in the market or enter into another repo transaction as purchaser/lender to cover the agreement. If the dealer is not able to obtain the security needed to close the repo, he may try to extend it (roll it over) or he may suggest a substitution using comparable securities.

Pricing of Repos. The repurchase price is higher than the original purchase price, with the difference representing, in effect, interest. The "interest" rate specified in a repo or used to calculate the "repurchase" price is known as the repo rate. Generally, the repo rate is slightly lower than the federal funds rate for very short-term repos (e.g., overnight repos) and rises for longer-term repos.

Repos involving coupon securities should be priced with accrued interest. If accrued interest is not added on, the borrower/seller will be receiving less cash than the securities he has loaned/sold are worth.

Cash and Security Movement. Often no cash changes hands, or a net settlement may be made because two simultaneous transactions are linked. For example, an entity may purchase securities and at the same time enter into a repo transaction as a borrower/seller, and use the "proceeds" from the repo to pay for the purchase of the securities. Similarly, when a repo transaction matures and the borrower/seller would be required to disburse cash, such party may roll it over and merely make a net cash settlement.

The handling of the securities varies depending on the specific transaction involved. If the securities are delivered to the purchaser/lender or his custodian, the purchaser/lender has a perfected security interest. If they are held in safekeeping by an independent custodian for the benefit of the purchaser/lender, there should be a custodial agreement between the purchaser/lender and the independent custodian, as well as a confirmation from the custodian stating that the securities are being held in safekeeping for the purchaser/lender. However, if the securities are held in safekeeping by the borrower/seller "for the benefit of" the purchaser/lender, this is not a perfected security interest but essentially is an unsecured loan.

Accounting Requirements. Entities other than broker/dealers and commercial banks who enter into these transactions as purchaser/lender typically classify repos as short-term investments. Broker/dealers and banks acting as purchaser/lender generally treat repos as financings. However, it should be evident that the proper accounting for repo transactions will depend on the nature of the specific agreements. In many cases, it may be necessary for the investor to consult legal counsel. In governmental entities, it may be necessary for the purchaser/lender to obtain a further opinion as to the legality of the investment.

Entities that enter into repo transactions as borrower/seller typically account for repos as financing transactions (i.e., as collateralized loans). However, a repo to maturity by an investor other than a broker/dealer should usually be accounted for as a purchase and sale, assuming that title and possession of the securities has been transferred. Depending on the circumstances, a repo for a major portion of the term to maturity of the underlying securities may, in substance, be a purchase and sale with put and/or call options.

See Chapters 40 and 42 for additional comments regarding banks and broker/dealers. Dollar repos, discussed next, significantly affect savings and loans; in addition, other specific S&L requirements are covered in a following section.

Dollar repos. SOP 85-2, *Accounting for Dollar Repurchase—Dollar Reverse Repurchase Agreements by Sellers-Borrowers* (TP 10,380), addresses a type of repurchase agreement that involves similar, but not identical, mortgage-backed securities. This SOP was issued in the wake of a lengthy discussion regarding Issue 84-20, *GNMA Dollar Rolls,* spanning four EITF meetings in which a consensus was not achieved on three out of four types of transactions.

A dollar repurchase-dollar reverse repurchase agreement is "an agreement (contract) to sell and repurchase or to purchase and sell back certificates of the same agency but not the original certificates." Two variations of dollar repurchase-dollar reverse repurchase agreements are *fixed coupon* and *yield maintenance* agreements; the accounting treatment for each differs. In a fixed coupon dollar agreement, the seller and buyer agree that delivery will be made with certificates that have the same stated interest rate as the interest rate stated in the certificates sold. In a yield maintenance dollar agreement, the buyer and seller agree that delivery will be made with certificates providing the seller a yield specified in the agreement.

The SOP specifically applies to transactions involving only GNMA pass-through certificates and Federal Home Loan Mortgage Corporation (FHLMC) participation certificates (PCs), but it is applied to all mortgage-backed securities that have been owned and held in the portfolio of the seller-borrower for a reasonable period of time, and to the lending of certificates. Accounting and reporting by the purchaser/ lender in these transactions is not addressed in the SOP. Other types of repurchase-reverse repurchase transactions are not covered by the SOP, nor does the SOP affect the accounting described for those other agreements. The principal conclusions of SOP 85-2 are:

- *Fixed coupon dollar agreements* should be accounted for as collateralized borrowings, unless the agreement contains a "right of substitution clause," in which case it should be accounted for as a yield maintenance agreement.[7]
- *Yield maintenance dollar agreements* should be accounted for as sales and purchases of securities, in that they do *not* represent transactions involving substantially identical securities. Disclosure of the commitment to repurchase is required.
- *Rollovers and extensions* of dollar agreements should be accounted for based on the facts and circumstances at the time of the rollover or extension; if a rollover or extension is from one type of agreement to another, the nature of the new agreement governs the prospective accounting. (Note that rollovers generally must not extend the final maturity beyond one year; if this occurs, SOP 85-2 calls for recording the transactions as actual sales with gain or loss recognition, plus a commitment to purchase securities.)
- *Breakage* — the difference in principal amounts of the securities originally sold and subsequently repurchased under dollar agreements — presents a problem with respect to dollar agreements accounted for as collateralized borrowings. For such transactions, if the principal amount of the certificate repurchased is greater than that of those originally sold, the difference is recorded as an incremental purchase of securities. If the principal amount is less, gains and losses should be recorded upon relieving the investment account of the proportionate share of the certificates sold.[8]

SEC Requirements. The SEC issued FRR 24 (§ 501.07) to require disclosure regarding the nature and extent of registrants' repurchase and reverse repurchase agreements and the degree of risk involved in these transactions. The Executive Summary to the Release states:

Specifically, the amendments require that where the higher of carrying or market value of assets sold under repurchase agreements or the carrying value of reverse repurchase agreements exceeds 10 percent of total assets, the amounts involved should be disclosed as a separate line item in the balance sheet.

Where the higher of the carrying value or market value of assets sold under repurchase agreements exceeds 10 percent of total assets, footnote disclosures are required regarding the assets sold and the terms of the agreements. (Repurchase agreements that involve the

---

[7] This accounting is consistent with the treatment of reverse-repurchase agreements as discussed in the S&L Audit Guide (AICPA, 1987f) and the related SOP 86-1 (TP 10,400); the Broker/Dealer Audit Guide (AICPA, 1985a); and SFAS 65, *Accounting for Certain Mortgage Banking Activities* (Mo4).

[8] "Good delivery" was deemed under SOP 85-2 to be accomplished with a security whose breakage was not greater than 2.5%. The AICPA has issued an exposure draft of an SOP on *Definition of "Substantially the Same" for Debt Instruments* (1988e), which would require that breakage be within the accepted "good delivery" standards for the type of security involved, rather than a generous 2.5%.

sale of securities or other assets for which unrealized changes in market value are reported in current income, or which were obtained pursuant to reverse repurchase agreements, need not be considered for purposes of this requirement.)

Where the carrying value of reverse repurchase agreements exceeds 10 percent of total assets, footnote disclosures are required regarding the registrant's policies with respect to taking possession of the underlying assets and the existence and nature of provisions, if any, to ensure that the market value of the underlying assets remains sufficient to protect the registrant in the event of default by the counterparty.

S&L Requirements. SOP 86-1, *Reporting Repurchase—Reverse Repurchase Agreements and Mortgage-Backed Certificates by Savings and Loan Associations* (TP 10,400), specifies required disclosures for such transactions. For repos these include, as to end of period balances, a description of the securities, cost and market value, dollar amount of related resale agreements, and material concentrations. For reverse repos, the disclosures include similar data, plus maturity dates, accrued interest, and weighted-average interest rates. As to transactions during the period, disclosure is required of average outstandings and the maximum outstandings at any month end.

Interest Rate Swaps

Fixed/Floating Swaps. The mechanics of most interest rate swaps are easily understood. Two parties agree to exchange cash, at defined intervals, for a period of time. The amount of cash exchanged at each interval depends on the then prevailing level of an agreed upon interest rate index, such as six-month LIBOR (London Interbank Offered Rate).

The most common type of interest rate swap, known as a *fixed/floating swap*, is illustrated below. The *floating rate payer* agrees that at each interval payment date during the term of the swap, he will pay[9] the counterparty cash, equal to the product of the following formula:

$$\frac{\text{Notional}}{\text{amount}} \times \frac{\text{Prevailing}}{\text{interest rate}}_{\text{index}} = \frac{\text{Periodic}}{\text{floating}}_{\text{payment}}$$

where:

Notional amount = An agreed upon amount (such as $10, $25 or $100 million), that remains unchanged during the term of routine fixed/floating swaps.

Interest rate index = The variable in the formula, this equals the current level of an index interest rate, agreed to at the outset of the swap.

The periodic payment obligation of the *fixed rate payer* is established at the inception of the interest rate swap and remains unchanged during the term of the agreement. As a result, if the interest rate index increases during the term of the swap, the fixed rate payer will benefit by higher cash receipts at each interval payment date. Conversely, the floating rate payer will benefit if the interest rate index decreases.

---

[9] Most swaps call for a net settlement of the counterparties' respective obligations.

To illustrate, assume two parties agree to an interest rate swap calling for quarterly cash exchanges during a five year term. The notional amount of the swap is $25 million and the selected interest rate index is six-month LIBOR. Finally, the periodic payment obligation of the fixed rate payer is set at $437,500 at each interval payment date. The first cash exchange occurs at the end of three months. If the weighted average annual six-month LIBOR rate is 7.25% during this period, the following cash exchange occurs:

Obligation of the floating rate payer, computed as the notional amount ($25 million) multiplied by the weighted average index rate (7.25% / 4)	$453,125
Less obligation of the fixed rate payer	437,500
Net settlement in favor of the fixed rate payer	$ 15,625

If six-month LIBOR decreases during the next three months to a weighted annual average rate of 6.5%, the second cash exchange would be calculated as follows:

Obligation of the floating rate payer	$406,250
Less obligation of the fixed rate payer	437,500
Net settlement in favor of the floating rate payer	$(31,250)

Similar calculations are made at the end of each three-month period during the remaining term of the interest rate swap. When the final cash payment is made, the agreement expires and no further payments between the parties occur.

Although the calculation of the floating rate payer's obligation depends on prevailing levels of interest rates, an interest rate swap does not have the characteristics of a debt obligation. One party has not advanced funds to the other (interest rate swaps normally do not involve "principal" to be repaid) and neither counterparty is assured of aggregate positive cash inflows during the term of the interest rate swap. The net cash outcome depends on interest rates during the course of the swap.

Swap Parties. Parties to interest rate swap agreements can be categorized as *swap users* or *swap dealers*. Swap users span the spectrum of commercial enterprises and even include government agencies and entities such as the World Bank or the International Monetary Fund. Swap dealers usually are securities broker/dealers or commercial banks.

Swap users. Typically, swap users engage in interest rate swaps in conjunction with interest rate sensitive assets or liabilities (i.e., cash items). If the cash flows of the interest rate swap and the cash item are considered together, the swap can be viewed as *synthetically* changing the interest rate characteristics of the cash item.

	End of year		
	1	2	3
1 year CD rate	7.5%	8.4%	6.6%
Interest expense on $30 million of CDs	$ 2,250	$ 2,520	$ 1,980
Swap results:			
Thrift receives floating amount ($30 million notional amount, index rate equals 1 year CD rate)	$ 2,250	$ 2,520	$ 1,980
Thrift plan pays fixed amount of	(2,310)	(2,310)	(2,310)
Thrift inflow (outflow)	$ (60)	$ 210	$ (330)
Combined inflows (outflows):			
Interest on CDs	$(2,250)	$(2,520)	$(1,980)
Swap results	(60)	210	(330)
Combined outflow	$(2,310)	$(2,310)	$(2,310)

FIG. 21.5   Illustration of Fixed/Floating Rate Swap Creating Synthetic Fixed-Rate CDs

For example, the combined effects of a three-year interest rate swap and one-year certificates of deposit (deposits that will be rolled over for three years) of an S&L are depicted in the simplified illustration in Figure 21.5. The swap has had the effect of synthetically changing the interest rate characteristics of the one-year certificates of deposit; as interest rates climb in year two, the higher cost of the deposits is offset by the results of the interest rate swap; the opposite is true in year three. When the swap and a related amount of deposits are considered together, the combined result is similar to the thrift having issued fixed interest rate liabilities for the three-year term of the swap. This phenomenon is also referred to as synthetically *extending* the term of the one-year CDs to three years.

Instead of synthetically creating three-year fixed interest rate debt, the S&L might simply have issued three-year CDs. However, the combined net cost of the swap and the short-term liabilities ($2.31 million in the above illustration or 7.7% on $30 million of related deposits) often may be less than the going market rate for the longer term cash instrument. Second, swaps are *flexible* and easily understood; they can be quickly arranged and tailored to fit an entity's particular needs. Third, swaps with terms of ten years or longer are available; other instruments such as interest rate futures contracts offer interest rate management opportunities only for much shorter periods. Finally, swaps can be readily terminated if an entity changes its strategies for coping with interest rate volatility.

The illustration in Figure 21.5 depicts a *liability swap*; *asset swaps* are used, too. A portfolio of fixed rate government securities may synthetically be converted into floating rate by entering into a swap similar to the one previously illustrated. Alternatively, an investment in short-term commercial paper can be converted to a longer term, fixed-rate investment by the holder taking a position as the floating-rate payer in a rate swap (provided, of course, that the investor has the intent and ability to maintain a short-term commerical paper investment for the duration of the rate swap).

Swap dealers. Swap dealers are financial institutions that offer interest rate swaps to customers as a product line. In the early 1980s, as the interest rate swap market was developing, dealers most often acted as brokers. For a fee, the dealer would identify two entities with different interest rate management objectives and bring them together as counterparties in a rate swap. Although dealers avoided the risk of serving as a principal in swaps, the task of locating two parties with exactly opposite interest rate management objectives proved cumbersome given the strong user demand for swaps and the competition among dealers.

Brokered swaps are much less common today. Instead, dealers take a principal position by acting as the counterparty in a swap with a customer/user. Dealers cope with *credit risk* – the risk that the counterparty will default – by scrutinizing the creditworthiness of their customer and sometimes requiring collateral or letters of credit when they conclude the credit standing of the customer warrants additional security. Dealers cope with *market risk* – the possibility that swaps will decline in value due to changes in interest rates – by entering into swaps whose value will change in offsetting directions and by engaging in other hedging strategies involving the purchase and sale of interest rate futures contracts or other interest-sensitive assets and liabilities.

Swap dealers can simultaneously act as swap users. The treasury department of a commercial bank may use interest rate swaps for asset/liability management purposes while the capital markets department of the bank offers interest rate swaps as a product line to bank customers.

Other Types of Swaps. Dealers offer other than the ubiquitous fixed/floating swaps discussed in the preceding section.

Basis swaps, also known as *floating swaps*, feature variable payment obligations of both counterparties, each calculated with reference to a different interest rate index. A user may have invested in assets whose return varies with the prime rate of interest; a basis swap enables the user to synthetically convert the yield to a rate that better matches the cost of liabilities financing the investment.

The notional amount of an *amortizing swap* decreases during the swap's term according to a predetermined schedule. Such swaps are used to synthetically alter the interest rate characteristics of assets or liabilities whose principal balance declines over time.

The total obligation of the fixed-rate payer is known at the time the parties agree to the terms of a fixed/floating interest rate swap. In a *zero-coupon swap*, the fixed-rate payer remits the present value of his entire obligation to the counterparty at the date the swap is launched and makes no further payments. The recipient of the fixed payment eliminates credit risk in such swaps. Most often, these swaps are used as tools in sophisticated income tax strategies.

Users of *mortgage swaps* are generally S&Ls. Mortgage swaps are more complex than most other interest rate swaps; a mortgage swap provides the thrift with a cash flow for a period of time (five years is common) that replicates the net cash inflow or outflow of a long-term investment in a mortgage-backed security financed by short-term obligations. When the swap terminates, the thrift must purchase a similar mortgage-backed security from the dealer/counterparty at a price agreed to when the swap commenced. Alternatively, the thrift can pay (receive) cash to (from) the counterparty for a decline (increase) in the value of the mortgage-backed security.

In Issue 88-8, *Mortgage Swaps*, the EITF has had preliminary discussions regarding whether:

1. A mortgage swap should be off-balance sheet or recognized on the balance sheet.
2. Its value should be at market, cost, or lower of cost or market, if shown on the balance sheet.
3. Changes in market value should be recognized even if off-balance sheet.
4. Hedge accounting is appropriate, if it is used as a hedge.

While the Task Force had little difficulty in reaching a consensus that the mortgage swap should be treated as an off-balance sheet transaction (like an interest rate swap), the remaining issues were not resolved. The SEC Observer indicated that "naked" mortgage swaps (those not linked to or designated as a hedge of an asset or liability) should, in the view of the SEC staff, be marked to market, as would be the case with an interest rate swap that similarly is not a hedge.

   Cross-currency interest rate swaps are transactions that economically combine currency and interest rate swaps. One form of a cross-currency interest rate swap involves the following:

• At the swap initiation date, both counterparties exchange cash. For example, counterparty A receives yen and distributes U.S. dollars to counterparty B at the prevailing rate of exchange on the date the exchange occurs. All future cash exchanges feature a right of setoff between the parties.
• Periodically during the term of the swap, counterparty A pays yen to counterparty B at a fixed interest rate multiplied by the amount of yen A received. Counterparty B pays U.S. dollars to A at a variable interest rate multiplied by the amount of U.S. dollars received.
• At the termination date, both counterparties reexchange the same units of currency originally exchanged at the outset.

For example, if counterparty B has issued fixed rate, yen-denominated debt with terms symmetrical to the cross-currency interest rate swap; the swap has the effect of synthetically converting the yen debt to a floating rate U.S. dollar obligation. In some cross-currency interest rate swaps, the initial exchange of currencies does not occur although the periodic payments (akin to interest) and the exchange of the notional amount at maturity are as previously described.

   Cross-currency interest rate swaps cause a sticky accounting problem. Standard currency swaps are accounted for in accordance with SFAS 52, *Foreign Currency Translation* (F60), as a series of forward exchange contracts and all foreign currency amounts to be purchased are translated at prevailing exchange rates at the balance sheet date. Most interest rate swaps are accounted for off-balance sheet, however. In practice, counterparties that use cross-currency interest rate swaps to hedge other foreign currency transactions often translate the foreign currency notional principal amount of the swap at prevailing exchange rates at each balance sheet date. Periodic exchanges prior to maturity are accounted for like most interest rate swaps – off balance sheet until the period in which the related payment occurs.

   A *forward rate agreement* is contracted between two parties wishing to protect themselves against a future interest rate movement. The two parties agree to lock in an interest rate for a specified future settlement date based on an agreed principal amount. No commitment is made by either party to lend or borrow the principal amount; rather their exposure is only the interest difference between the agreed and actual rates at settlement.

Swaps are also structured in various ways. For example, a *cap* makes the swap operative only when the index rate is above a certain level; and a *floor* does the reverse. A *collar* or *corridor* works when the rate is above or below the agreed index rates. The various types of swap arrangements are interestingly discussed in "Interest Rate Swaps—Your Rate or Mine?" (Wishon and Chevalier, 1985).

Financial Accounting. Promulgated accounting literature does not discuss interest rate swaps. Except for some discussion by the EITF and an informational meeting hosted by the FASB staff, accounting methods have developed informally. Generally, parties use either a *market-adjusted method* or a *settlement method* to account for interest rate swaps and changes in their value. At any point in time, the economic value of a party's position in an interest rate swap mostly depends on interest rate movements since the date the swap was created.

An informal, although active, secondary market created by swap dealers exists for interest rate swaps.[10] An entity will agree to substitute for an original counterparty for the remaining term of an existing swap if it is compensated for any decline in the swap's value. However, if the original swap terms are favorable relative to existing market conditions, the substitute party will compensate the original party. For appropriate compensation, a dealer often will release the customer directly without finding a substitute.

Because of the demand for swaps and the active informal secondary market, it is relatively easy to obtain reliable information on increases or decreases in the value of most fixed/floating swaps.

Market adjusted methods. Swap users should use the *mark-to-market method* or the *lower-of-cost-or-market method* (LOCOM) for interest rate swaps in the following situations:

• The user enters the swap to achieve a profit if interest rates move in an anticipated direction (i.e., trading). The user does not intend the swap to synthetically alter the interest rate characteristics of other assets or liabilities.

• The user intends the swap to synthetically alter the interest characteristics of other assets or liabilities but the swap fails to qualify for settlement accounting (discussed in the next section).

• The underlying linked asset or liabililty is extinguished and the swap remains in place.

Under the *mark-to-market method*, at each balance sheet date the user records an asset or a liability to value its position. If the interest rate index has moved in favor of the user, the asset represents the amount of cash the user would receive if the swap were terminated at that date. A liability represents the user's cash obligation if he were to settle a swap in which the interest rate index has moved against him. The change in the asset or liability equals periodic income or expense; in its statement of operations, a user should classify gains or losses with the results of other speculative investment activities.

---

[10] The International Swap Dealers Association has been successful in encouraging dealers to standardize the language of swap contracts, facilitating the development of secondary market activity.

The *lower-of-cost-or-market method* is identical to the mark-to-market method, except that the user does not recognize *unrealized gains*. The user's maximum gain in any period is generally limited to the cash received from the counterparty for the periodic settlement payment. (If the settlement period coincides with a balance sheet date and the payment is determinable at that date, the user should accrue the expected receipt.) However, if the interest rate index has moved in favor of the user's counterparty, the user should record an obligation for the entire loss in value of the swap.

In deciding which method to use if a market-adjusted accounting approach applies, most users should apply LOCOM, especially if a swap has unusual terms or conditions that prevent the user from obtaining reasonably reliable information about a swap's value. Some accountants believe LOCOM is appropriate even if the swap is easily valued, because historical cost based accounting rarely permits the recognition of unrealized gains (except for dealers). Other accountants believe that mark-to-market accounting is acceptable if the swap can be reliably valued because this method better captures the economic results of the swap agreement. Although precedents seem to favor LOCOM, diversity in practice is likely to continue until the issue is tackled by standard-setters or regulators.

Settlement accounting. Settlement accounting is by far the most common method users employ to account for interest rate swaps, because most swaps are designed to and are sufficiently effective at synthetically changing the interest rate characteristics of other assets and liabilities. This approach was discussed by the EITF in Issue 84-36, *Interest Rate Swap Transactions.* The EITF agreed that if a company entering into a swap transaction has an underlying debt obligation on its balance sheet and the result of the swap is to change the nature of the debt, for example, from a fixed to a variable interest rate instrument, the swap should be accounted for as a hedge of the obligation. (However, this is not a hedge in the normal sense because the swap does not necessarily reduce rate risk.)

With settlement accounting, a user calculates the amount that would be due to or due from the counterparty as if the next periodic settlement date actually coincided with the balance sheet date. When the actual settlement payment occurs, the user adjusts the accrued amount to actual. Cash payments are charged or credited to the adjusted accrued amount.

As the user adjusts the accrued swap payable or receivable, he includes the offsetting entry in interest income or interest expense in the income statement. The classification depends on the cash item whose interest rate characteristics the swap is designed to synthetically alter. A thrift institution *extending* the maturity of short-term deposits with an interest rate swap (see Figure 21.5) would include the offsetting entry in interest expense. Similarly, the adjustment of a swap linked to interest-bearing assets would be included in interest income.

Using settlement accounting, only a minor piece of the swap (the accrued amount related to a forthcoming settlement payment) shows up in the financial statements. In market-adjusted accounting, however, the present value of the entire change in net amounts payable or receivable may be shown in the balance sheet. Because settlement accounting is *off-balance sheet*, it should be used only when an interest rate swap is *intended* to change and is *reasonably effective* at changing the interest rate characteristics of an asset or liability. To adequately document its intention, the user should create (no later than the time it commits to the swap) a formal record of the purpose of the swap that identifies the linked asset or liability. This record should be approved at an appropriate level within the organization.

To determine that a swap is reasonably effective at changing the interest rate characteristics of related assets and liabilities, the user first compares the notional amount of the swap to the expected balance of the related cash item during the term of the swap. For example, a user probably would not conclude that a five-year $100 million notional amount interest rate swap was effective at extending the term of $100 million of 60-day commercial paper if the user's financial plans called for refinancing the commercial paper with fixed-rate debt in the foreseeable future.

Additionally, if the swap is designed to convert variable-rate cash items to fixed-rate (or to extend the maturities of short-term cash items), the user needs to compare the interest rate indexes and the repricing dates of the swap to attributes of the cash item. A swap with quarterly settlement dates may not be effective at synthetically extending the terms of one-year CDs, for example, although in some cases it is feasible.

Note that reduction of *enterprise risk*, a condition for hedge accounting for financial futures contracts has not been mentioned as a condition for settlement accounting. A user can qualify for settlement accounting even if the interest rate swap increases its overall exposure to the risk of changing interest rates. This is so by analogy to a company's investment in fixed-rate assets or issuance of floating-rate debt, which might expand or reduce its overall exposure to changes in interest rates; generally, the accounting for these cash items is not affected by whether the item creates or reduces overall interest rate risk. Accordingly, the synthetic cash item created by the swap should not be treated differently.

Largely due to its off-balance sheet nature and its inconsistency with hedge accounting for futures contracts, the FASB might eventually reject the settlement approach when it studies the issue as part of its financial instruments project.

Disclosure. Users should adequately disclose interest rate swap information in the footnotes to the financial statements. SEC registrants should additionally cover swaps in MD&A. Footnote information should include the following:

• The nature of and effect on the cash items related to interest rate swaps.

• The method of accounting used.

• A description of assets or letter-of-credit arrangements collateralizing the swaps.

• The notional amount of swap positions or other information indicating the magnitude of an entity's swap position.

Some companies also disclose interest income and/or expense absent the effect of swap positions and the unrecorded unrealized gain or loss for swaps accounted for by the settlement method.

Other Accounting Considerations

Dealer accounting. While most dealers account for their interest rate swap portfolios using the mark-to-market method, the timing of *revenue recognition* is unsettled.

Some dealers recognize revenue when they enter a swap with a user; other dealers believe that revenue is appropriately recognized over the term of the swap.

Dealers also have varying approaches to measuring the amount of revenue earned at the outset of the swap. Alternatives include an amount not to exceed (1) an equivalent fee for brokering a swap, (2) the dealer's cost of arranging the swap, or (3) the present value of expected net cash inflows discounted at a credit-risk-adjusted rate of return.

Swap terminations by a user. When a user terminates a swap appropriately accounted for under the settlement method, any gain or loss should be deferred and amortized as a yield adjustment on the related cash instrument, but the amortization period should not extend beyond what had been the maturity date of the terminated swap.

In Issue 84-7, *Termination of Interest Rate Swaps*, the EITF concluded that gains or losses on a terminated swap that had been accounted for as a hedge must be deferred and amortized. When a swap hedges existing assets, liabilities, or firm commitments, the gain/loss from a swap termination is to be deferred and accounted for as an adjustment to the basis of (and yield on) the hedged item. When the swap hedges an anticipated transaction, the gain/loss from a swap termination is to be accounted for as a deferred credit/debit until the anticipated transaction occurs. The applicable portion of the deferred credit/debit should then be reclassified as an adjustment to the basis of the hedged item and should be amortized as a yield adjustment over the shorter of the life of the hedged item or the remaining swap period.

Elimination of the hedged item. A user may sell the asset or settle the obligation related to an interest rate swap appropriately accounted for under the settlement method. At the date the asset is sold or the obligation is settled, the interest rate swap should be marked to market and any gain or loss on the adjustment should be included in the gain or loss on the disposal of the asset. In subsequent periods, the user should account for the swap using a market-adjusted method of accounting.

Care should be taken that gains or losses are not inappropriately recognized, however. For example, a manufacturer may refinance existing variable-rate bank debt with short-term commercial paper. Depending on the terms of the bank debt and the commercial paper, the manufacturer may be in relatively the same position before and after the refinancing. In this case, it may not be appropriate to recognize a gain or loss on a swap linked to the original bank debt.

Financial Futures

A financial futures contract is a standardized contract, traded on a regulated exchange to buy or sell a specific type and amount of a debt security at a specified future date.[11] The futures exchange acts as the "other" side of the transaction, guar-

---

[11] Forward contracts differ from futures contracts in that forwards are negotiated between the contracting parties calling for delivery of a specified amount of a particular commodity or financial instrument at a fixed date in the future. Since forward contracts are negotiated the amount and maturity date of the contract is flexible; however, forwards cannot be closed without the consent of the other contracting party.

anteeing that every contract will be properly executed. The exchange marks futures contracts to market at the end of each day and the buyer and seller are notified about the change in the value of their futures contracts. Although the buyer-seller of a futures contract can technically take or make delivery of the debt security that underlies the futures contract, less than 5% of the underlying securities are delivered.

The most common use of financial futures contracts by financial institutions is to hedge the cost of money. Examples are a financial institution using futures to lock in the interest rate of a certificate of deposit that will reprice, or to lock in the cost of a non-fixed-rate future borrowing. Financial futures contracts are also used to protect the value of interest-bearing assets (securities and mortgage loans) and mortgage loans originated for sale.

This section of the chapter discusses financial accounting and reporting considerations relating to futures. Difficult tax accounting issues can arise when futures are encountered; a qualified tax expert may need to be consulted. Additionally, the auditing issues are significant, and the nature of the criteria necessary for hedge accounting suggest that the auditor's most important task will be a determination that all the criteria are met for the required durations.

Key Concepts. Like the underlying security, the value of the futures contract moves inversely with interest rates. Therefore, to hedge against rising interest rates, futures contracts are sold (short position). To hedge against falling interest rates, futures contracts are bought (long position).

Basis is the difference between the price of a cash security and the futures invoice price. Basis risk is the risk that the value of the cash security will not move exactly in concert with the value of the futures contract. If the movement in value of the cash security equals the movement in value of the futures contract, the basis is constant and the *correlation* of the hedge is perfect.

Correlation measures the stability of the basis relationship, and correlation is usually calculated as the change in the value of the futures contract divided by the change in the value of the cash item. If the security and futures contract move perfectly in unison, the correlation is 1, but this is rarely achieved. Many different types of regression analysis can be performed by futures traders to determine the historical strength of the basis relationship; the result is usually between 0 and 1. A numerical example of a correlation calculation is shown in Figure 21.6. When the correlation percentage is greater than 100%, it can be converted to a percentage between 1 and 100 by calculating its reciprocal. For example, if the correlation is 115%, it is converted to 87% (1/1.15).

Creating the Hedge. The first step in creating a hedge is to identify the interest rate risk to be managed. Hedging can be either very specific (protecting the market value of an investment security) or broadly based (hedging a repricing gap).

Interest rate risk can be identified by a variety of methods. The most common method is referred to as *gap analysis*. A gap analysis defines the repricing gaps between interest bearing assets and liabilities. Duration models are also used but are less common than gap models. Every interest bearing asset or liability has a duration, or the time-weighted average of the security's cash flow. When the duration of an asset and liability are not equal, interest rate risk exists.

Market value of hedged asset at inception of hedge	$300,000
Market value of hedged asset currently	(250,000)
Loss in cash market (change in market value of hedged item)	$ 50,000
Market value of futures contract at inception of hedge	$270,000
Market value of futures contract currently	(315,000)
Gain in futures market (change in market value of futures contract)	$ 45,000
Correlation ($45,000/$50,000)	90%

FIG. 21.6   Example of Futures Correlation Calculation

The interest rate risk analysis of a financial institution can be complex because interest bearing assets and liabilities have a myriad of repricing time periods and basis for repricing. Although hedging a gap is not possible theoretically because a gap is a combination of many components, an institution can effectively accomplish the same result by identifying assets or liabilities that make up the gap and hedging those items. In addition, some hedge strategies may be successful at hedging a gap as such, because the make-up of the hedge instrument parallels the components of the gap.

The next step is to determine the futures contract that has the best correlation and the number of contracts that will be necessary for the hedge. The number of contracts can be determined by several different methods, all having the same objective: to determine how much the price of the futures contract will change given a price change in the cash item.

Managing the Hedge.   Hedging is a dynamic, ongoing process. The hedge is structured based on an assessment of interest rate risk, correlation, and technical factors which must be monitored during the hedge. If the conditions that existed at the outset of the hedge change during the hedge, the hedge should be restructured.

An enterprise can use a static or a dynamic hedge management approach. Static management is used when a hedge is entered into with a specific target or objective and the hedge position does not change regardless of the movement of interest rates (except to adjust the hedge ratio). Dynamic management is used when a conscious effort is made to predict the direction of interest rates and adjust hedge positions accordingly. For example, if lower rates are forecast and there are short futures positions, the futures contacts are partially or completely lifted. If rates fall, the institution realizes opportunity profits and avoids losses on futures contracts. The dynamic trader takes much more risk than the static trader since forecasts of interest rate movements are frequently wrong. A hedge management program that is a blend of the static and dynamic methods is often used.

There is debate about the point at which a dynamic management approach becomes speculative. This is an important distinction because futures contracts must be carried at market value, and the change in value of speculative contracts during a period is entered into current operations. The objectives and targets that are set for the hedge program will help show whether a static or dynamic hedging program is used. Therefore, it is very important that hedge objectives and targets be clearly documented. Hedge objectives or targets might change during the hedge, necessitating a change in the hedge structure; these changes also should be clearly documented.

The number of contracts should be adjusted based on changes in two variables, interest rates and maturity. Even if interest rates remain constant, the decreasing maturity of the hedged cash item often results in a change in the number of futures contracts needed.

Financial Accounting. SFAS 80, *Accounting for Futures Contracts* (F 80), requires futures contracts to be carried at market value. If the futures contract qualifies as a hedge, the gain or loss can be deferred (F80.103).

To qualify for deferral accounting, a futures contract must meet the SFAS 80 hedge criteria (F80.104):

1. *Interest rate risk.* The hedged cash item exposes the enterprise to rate risk at the inception of the hedge. Rate risk is the potential gain or loss on a cash item that can result from a change in interest rates. Risk must be assessed on an overall, or enterprise, basis. Specifically:

   • The market value or yield of the cash item is affected by interest rate changes.

   • Such interest rate risk is not offset by other assets, liabilities, firm commitments, or anticipated transactions.

   • Financial futures contracts reduce enterprise risk if they reduce the rate risk of the cash items that cause enterprise risk.

   SFAS 80 does not specifically require that futures contracts continuously offset rate risk throughout the hedge. However, from a risk management standpoint, futures contacts that no longer offset rate risk should be lifted; if they are not, many accountants believe they should be carried at market value starting at the point in time the risk offset ceases.

2. *Correlation.* The futures contract, because of high correlation, reduces the rate risk. High correlation must be probable at the inception of the hedge and continue throughout the hedge. If high correlation disappears during the hedge, the futures contracts are deemed to be speculative, and changes in market value after that point are entered into current operations. In addition, any difference between the change in value of the hedge and the change in value of the hedged item should be recognized as a gain or loss at that point.

3. *Designation.* The futures contract is designated as a hedge of a specific cash item(s).

If the cash item is an anticipated transaction, the cash item must meet the following additional requirements (F80.109):

• The significant characteristics and expected terms of the anticipated transaction are identified.

• It is probable that the anticipated transaction will occur.

The general accounting rules for the gain or loss on futures contracts that qualify for deferral accounting are: (1) the gain or loss becomes part of the carrying value of the cash item; and (2) the gain or loss is matched against the income, expense, or sales price of the cash item. The following discussions illustrate how these rules are applied to different types of hedges.

Hedge of an existing cash item carried at cost. The futures gain or loss adjusts the basis of the cash item and is recognized the same way that other adjustments to the basis of the cash item are recognized (F80.106). Recognition of gain or loss theoretically should begin as soon as incurred, but this would mean that amortization would have to be adjusted daily. SFAS 80 allows postponing recognition of the futures gain or loss until the futures contract closes.

For example, assume a gain is realized on a futures contract that hedged a cash security not held for sale. The futures gain decreases the basis of the security and the gain is amortized to income by the level yield method over the life of the security (similar to a discount), commencing when the contract is closed.

Hedge of an existing cash item carried at fair value. For hedges of cash items carried at fair value, the change in the futures value is recognized in the financial statements in the same manner as the change in the cash item value (F80.105).

Hedge of an existing cash item carried at lower of cost or market. The basis of a cash item carried at the lower of cost or market is adjusted for the gain or loss on futures contracts. The gain on futures is deducted from the cash item to reflect the write-down of the cash item to market value. The loss on futures is added to the cash item and increases the basis of the cash item to its market value (if correlation is perfect). The basis of the item might need to be adjusted further to meet the lower of cost or market requirement since the correlation usually is imperfect. The futures gain or loss is not accreted to income.

Hedge of an anticipatory item or firm commitment. The futures gain or loss is deferred until the transaction occurs, at which time it adjusts the basis of the cash item. The gain or loss is amortized using the rules for existing cash items. When the anticipated item is a repricing of deposits, straight-line amortization of the futures gain or loss usually produces the same results as level yield amortization.

Financial Reporting

Financial statements. The change in value of futures contracts that are not accounted for as hedges is recorded currently in the statement of earnings. If the amount is material, it should be shown separately as gain or loss on financial futures contracts.

For futures contracts that qualify as a hedge, the gain or loss is deferred and is offset against the cash item, and the amortization is netted against the income, expense, or sales price of the cash item. When an anticipatory item or firm commitment is hedged, the deferred gain or loss is classified on the balance sheet as a deferred credit or charge until the transaction occurs.

The commodity futures margin deposit should be classified on the balance sheet as a receivable from broker.

Footnotes. SFAS 80 requires the following disclosures in footnotes (F80.112):

1. Nature of the hedged assets, liabilities, firm commitments, or anticipated transactions.

2. Method of accounting for futures contracts, including a description of the events or transactions that resulted in the change in value of the futures contracts being recognized in income.

SFAS 80 implementation issues. In Issue 85-06, *Futures Implementation Questions*, the EITF reviewed a number of implementation issues presented by the FASB staff, including enterprise risk, business unit risk, designation of a hedge, cross-hedging with financial futures, assessment of correlation, and termination of a hedge. No decisions were made. Subsequently, the staff's questions and answers were presented in *Highlights of Financial Reporting Issues*—Futures Contracts: Guidance on Applying Statement 80 (Wishon, 1985).

If futures contracts are used by a financial institution to hedge the risk inherent in the anticipated issuance (and long-term rollover) of a reverse repurchase agreement, or other short-term debt that finances fixed rate assets, three issues must be addressed. They are:

1. Can the futures contracts can be accounted for as hedges?
2. If so, is the accounting affected by a subsequent sale of fixed-rate assets?
3. Does the high correlation criterion in SFAS 80 continue to apply if a hedge is terminated prior to the future issuance of short-term debt?

In Issue 86-34, *Futures Contracts Used as Hedges of Anticipated Reverse Repurchase Transactions*, the EITF concluded (as to the first question above) that such transactions qualify for hedge accounting if the futures contract reduces interest rate risk and the following two criteria are met:

1. The characteristics and terms of the anticipated transaction are identified.
2. It is likely that the anticipated transaction will actually occur.

However, a subsequent sale of a fixed-rate asset (second question above) may change the original assumptions that the financial institution will continue to rollover short-term debt, or that any enterprise risk will exist.

As to the third question above, the EITF reconfirmed the FASB staff position in the *Highlights* paper (Wishon, 1985): the high correlation requirement is inapplicable if the hedge is discontinued.

In Issue 87-1, *Deferral Accounting for Cash Securities That Are Used to Hedge Rate/Price Risk*, the EITF addressed whether a cash security that is used to hedge rate/price risk qualifies for deferral accounting. Although the EITF did not reach a consensus, a large majority believes that current accounting standards require realized gains and losses on cash securities to be recognized currently. The SEC Observer and the FASB staff agreed with the EITF majority.

Questions regarding correlation continue to arise. Accordingly, the FASB staff has placed Issue 88-7, *Hedging Correlation Issues Under Statement 80,* on the forward EITF agenda.

Regulatory Reporting. Futures trading is regulated under the Commodity Exchange Act (CEA), enforced by the Commodity Futures Trading Commission (CFTC) (see Chapter 42). The CFTC is a five-member federal commission that has jurisdiction over all futures transactions and the exchanges on which the futures are traded. The CFTC approves all new futures instruments, can levy civil fines, and can issue cease and desist orders. However, the CFTC does not have jurisdiction over the operational and accounting rules that financial instruments must follow if they use futures. As discussed in Part V of this *Handbook,* a myriad of federal and state agencies issue regulations that the financial institutions must follow.

Internal Control Structure. Strong internal controls over futures contracts are important because futures are complex and their value changes daily. There can be large gains or losses on futures contracts with only a small amount of invested capital. There have been numerous publicized instances in which an institution incurred large unexpected losses on futures contracts. Because of these risks, the internal control structure must insure that management's policies are followed, that transactions are recorded promptly and accurately, and that management receives useful reports.

Internal controls for futures contracts will vary depending on the size of the institution, the sophistication and size of its futures department, and the function of its internal audit department.

Options

A purchased option represents a right to receive (call) or sell (put) a commodity or security at a set price for a specified period or on a specified date. A written option represents a commitment to sell or purchase the commodity or security to or from the purchaser (holder) of the option.

Regulatory Environment. Options trading, like futures trading, is regulated in accordance with the CEA, which created the CFTC. The Commission's responsibility for enforcing the requirements of the Act includes approving all new options instruments, levying civil fines for violations, and issuing cease and desist orders. The SEC, however, has the responsibility for regulating any options on publicly traded debt and equity securities.

Many financial institutions trade in options, primarily those options with underlying financial instruments. S&Ls must adhere to the specific regulations established by the Federal Home Loan Bank Board. These regulations affect the accounting for options and lay out specific responsibilities that must be met by the board of directors of an S&L in monitoring its trading in options. Banks are affected by Circular 79 and the related Federal Reserve and FDIC regulations. These regulations also affect accounting and the responsibilities of the board of directors. Insurance companies are not federally regulated but each state may establish its own regulations regarding option accounting and operational issues. Additionally, other various state regulations may affect the accounting for options.

Definitions.

Purchased option. The purchaser of an option pays a premium for the right to put or call the underlying commodity or security. If the option is purchased to provide a hedge against changes in price or interest rates this premium is, in essence, a payment for insurance against any downside risk related to the underlying commodity or security. On the other hand, the option could be purchased strictly for the purpose of speculating on future changes in rates or prices, which will increase or decrease the value of the underlying commodity or security while allowing the holder to put or call the item at a favorable spread.

Both futures (discussed in the preceding section of this chapter) and options can be used to hedge against price and interest risk. However, there is a significant difference in that the purchaser of an option contract attempting to hedge a risk does not lock in the price of the underlying item. For example, assume that a company acquires a put option for $200 allowing it to sell 1,000 units of a commodity for $4 per unit, and the price of the commodity increases to $5.50 per unit. The purchaser is protected against a price decrease by having the right to sell (put) at $4. However, when the price increases to $5.50 the purchaser of the put would decide not to exercise the option but rather to sell the commodity at $5.50 and recognize a gain of $1.50 per unit (less the option premium). The cost of the option, $200, is in essence the cost of insurance against a price decline. The only potential loss is the amount of the premium.

On the other hand, assume that a company enters a futures contract that commits it to deliver the commodity for $4. If the price drops the company would be guaranteed a $4 selling price; however, if the price increases to $5.50 they still would only receive $4. Therefore, the futures contract locks in the price of the commodity at $4, but the company has a two-sided risk: that the price will be higher or lower than the desired price. This protects the company from loss, but does not allow the company to take advantage of gains.

Written option. Essentially, written options have the opposite impact of purchased options. The potential gain to the seller (writer) of the option is limited to the amount of the premium received but has unlimited downside risk, that is, risk of loss. For example, if the company had written rather than purchased the put option on the commodity in the preceding example, it would suffer a loss if the value of the commodity decreases to $3 per unit but is committed to accept it at $4. On the other hand, if the price increases to $5.50 the holder of the option would not exercise the put and the gain to the writer is limited to the $200 premium received.

Value of an option. The intrinsic value of an option is dependent on whether the exercise (strike) price of the underlying asset is greater or less than its current market price. If the market price is equal to the exercise price the option is "at the money" and provides no advantage for the holder. However, in the case of a call, if the market price of the underlying asset is less than the exercise price, or in the case of a put the market price is greater than the exercise price, the option is "out of the money" and would not be exercised; the holder could purchase the underlying item for less or sell it for more by going to the market. An option is "in the money" when the opposite circumstances exist. When the exercise price is so substantially different from the current market price that the holder would have a significant advantage if he exercises the option, the option is considered to be "deep in the money."

If an option is in the money it will have an *intrinsic value* equal to the difference between the market price of the underlying asset and the exercise price of the option.

The *time value* is the difference between the current market value of the option and the current intrinsic value. In essence, it represents the cost of bearing the risk of loss over the exercise period.

Financial Accounting. An AcSEC Issues Paper, *Accounting for Options* (AICPA, 1986b), provides guidance on the accounting for options on both commodities and financial securities, specifically:

* Determining the carrying value of options.
* The appropriateness of hedge accounting and related application concerns.
* Accounting for non-exchange-traded options.

To a great extent the Issues Paper relies on the guidance provided in SFAS 52, *Foreign Currency Translation* (F60), as applicable to hedging foreign currencies. Additionally, it relies heavily on SFAS 80, *Accounting for Futures Contracts* (F80).

The primary issues of concern in the Issues Paper are whether an option can be considered a hedge and, if so, the related accounting for the option at the date of the transaction and during the period up to the point at which the option either expires or is exercised. All of the Issues Paper's 24 issues and sub-issues dealt with in the paper relate directly or indirectly to hedging questions. (Paragraph citations in the following discussion refer to the Issues Paper.)

Carrying value. The vast majority of AcSEC supported the use of mark-to-market accounting for options if they are not considered hedges (¶ 180). This method requires the current recognition of gains and losses due to changes in market value regardless of whether the option has expired or has been exercised. The basis for this conclusion is that options have many of the characteristics of futures contracts and foreign currency forward contracts, both of which are required to be reported at market value under SFAS 80 and SFAS 52 respectively. Additonally, the available information on the current market prices of options is considered reliable, is not difficult or costly to obtain, and options are quite liquid. (Note, however, that equity options and warrants are to be accounted for at the lower of cost or market under SFAS 12 (I89).)

Hedge accounting. A significant concern of AcSEC members who objected to hedge accounting for options is that options and futures contracts differ substantially, primarily in that options have only a one-sided risk and return and therefore do not lock in a price. For this reason the holder of the option has an unlimited gain potential and the transaction could have the appearance of a speculation rather than a hedge.

If the investment qualifies as a hedge, any gains and losses on the options generally would be deferred until gain or loss on the hedged item is recognized. However, if the hedged item is reported at market value, the option should also be accounted for in that manner.

The criteria that an option contract must meet to qualify for hedge accounting are (¶ 195):

• The option must reduce the rate or price risk of a transaction. This is achieved if a high correlation exists between the changes in market value of both the hedged item and the item underlying the option.

• There is a clear economic relationship between the prices of both items.

• The entity has designated the option as a hedge.

One of the issues dealt with in SFAS 80 is whether price or interest rate *risk* to the hedging entity has to be assessed on an enterprise basis or only on the basis of the risks inherent in each hedged transaction. SFAS 80 concludes that enterprise risk is to be considered; if risk is assessed for each transaction on a standalone basis, any given hedge could be counterproductive because the risk to the enterprise may be in the opposite direction. The Issues Paper nevertheless supports the use of transaction risk as a basis for determining whether an option qualifies as a hedge (¶ 196). Some accountants disagree with this conclusion and under certain circumstances continue to use enterprise risk rather than transaction risk.

Out-of-the-money purchased options. Some AcSEC members were concerned that an out-of-the-money option essentially provided no hedging benefit, because the underlying item could be sold or acquired in the market at a better price. Others felt that the out-of-the-money spread is often temporary and, even when it does exist, is equivalent to a deductible that would be used to offset a potentially larger loss. The Issues Paper concludes that an out-of-the-money option can be considered a hedge assuming that high correlation is still probable (¶ 202).

Time and intrinsic value. For purchased options, time value is viewed as an insurance premium paid for absorbing the risk of loss over the exercise period. Intrinsic value, however, is more directly related to the use of an option as a hedge because it represents the spread between the market price and the exercise price of the underlying item. Therefore, AcSEC concluded that hedge accounting should be applied only to changes in intrinsic value; the time value existing when the option is purchased should be amortized on a systematic and rational basis over the exercise period if the item being hedged is not carried at market. (This is also the case if the item being hedged is carried at market and any changes in the intrinsic value are separately recorded in stockholders' equity.) (See ¶¶ 218 and 278.) If the underlying item is carried at market and changes in intrinsic value are reported in income, the time value should not be treated differently than intrinsic value (i.e., the option should be stated at market).

When an option that qualifies for hedging is closed out, the unamortized portion of the time value should be recognized in income immediately (¶ 283).

Written options as hedges. Because written options provide unlimited potential for loss there is some question about whether they can qualify as a hedge. Therefore, AcSEC concluded that written options can only qualify as a hedge to the extent of the premium (¶ 242). Although the AcSEC conclusion implies that losses on the option could be deferred up to the amount of the premium, the illustration of the accounting in the appendix of the Issues Paper reflects an immediate recognition of loss (¶ 380). Some accountants believe that the illustration does not reflect AcSEC's intent, and therefore are deferring losses up to the amount of the premium. AcSEC also concluded that written options must meet the same criteria as purchased options to qualify for hedge accounting.

With respect to written options accounted for as hedges, AcSEC decided that the time and intrinsic values should not be split, because the purpose of the time value of a written option is to act as a hedge against rate or price risk (¶ 267).

Continuing high correlation. One of the most significant criteria that must be satisfied for an option to qualify as a hedge is a probable high correlation at the inception of the hedge between the market value of the item hedged and the item underlying the option. AcSEC concluded that such correlation must be reassessed periodically and must continue; otherwise hedge accounting must be terminated (¶ 290). This conclusion is consistent with the guidance in SFAS 80.

Fair value limitation. When an option qualifies for hedge accounting, the recognition of gains and losses on the option are deferred. It is possible that the effect of such loss deferrals could result in a carrying value of the hedged item that is greater than its market value. SFAS 80 did not impose a fair value limitation on the carrying amount of items being hedged with futures contracts. However, AcSEC concluded that there should be such a limitation for options (¶ 291). Some accountants believe that this conclusion is inappropriate, and follow the position in SFAS 80; in any event, if there is continuing high correlation it is not likely that market value and the carrying value will differ substantially.

Anticipated transactions. AcSEC agreed that options can be used to hedge anticipated transactions (¶ 297) but not possible transactions (¶ 326). An *anticipated* transaction is defined as one whose characteristics and terms are known and whose occurence is probable. A *possible* transaction is generally one that may happen and the necessity for the transaction is contingent on factors that have not yet occurred and are beyond the company's control. For example, a company bids on a project and, if awarded the contract, it would have to acquire a commodity that is subject to price fluctuations (¶ 315).

Exchange-traded vs. non-exchange-traded options. Often the market values of non-exchange-traded options are not published and such options may be very illiquid. Although some members of AcSEC were concerned about the ability to apply hedge accounting for these options, AcSEC concluded that sufficiently reliable value estimates can be obtained.

Options on Financial Futures Contracts. Options on financial futures contracts were developed as another tool to manage interest rate risk. Options on T-bond financial futures contracts were introduced in 1982 and options on T-note and Eurodollar financial futures contracts followed in 1985.

Options on financial futures can be used separately to manage rate risk, or in conjunction with other options on financial futures, or in conjunction with financial futures contracts. The primary difference between hedging with options and hedging with financial futures directly is that financial futures are a two-way hedge and options are a one-way hedge. The value of a financial futures contract will increase or decrease in value to offset the change in the value of the cash item. The value of a purchased option on a financial futures contract will also increase to offset a decrease in the value of the cash item; however, the purchased option will only decrease in value to zero.

For example, assume that a thrift purchased a put option on a T-bond financial futures contract for $1,500 to protect the value of a $100,000 T-bond in its portfolio. The value of the T-bond is protected against an increase in interest rates, since any decrease in the value of the T-bond would be offset by the increase in the value of the put option. However, if interest rates fall, the thrift will be able to retain the appreciation of the T-bond, less the $1,500 premium, because the value of the option can only decrease to zero. Permitting the purchaser of an option to hedge rate risk while still allowing for upside appreciation (less the premium paid) is the greatest advantage of options on financial futures contracts.

Written covered call programs have become a popular technique for thrifts that use options on financial futures contracts. In a written covered call program, an institution writes (sells) a call option on a financial futures contract, and the institution owns the security that underlies the financial futures contract.

When a call is written and interest rates stay flat or increase, the option expires worthless, and the option writer retains the premium received for writing the option. If the interest rates fall, the value of the option increases. The option writer can either deliver the covering security to the option holder or pay the option holder in cash. If the option is settled by cash payment, the option writer can recover the payment by selling the covering security and realizing the appreciation.

There are a variety of written covered call programs in the marketplace. Several of these programs change the number of option contracts outstanding as the value of the option changes. The complexity of these written covered call programs has been one of the reasons that the accounting profession has been unable to reach a consensus on how to account for written options.

22

Foreign Currency

OVERVIEW

Foreign operations encompass a wide variety of activities requiring the attention of accountants. Foreign currency translation and transactions are covered in this chapter, along with several issues concerning auditing of foreign activities of domestic enterprises and of multinational companies (MNCs). Other foreign-related areas in which accountants are generally involved are consolidated financial statements (Chapter 24), segment and geographical area reporting (Chapter 4), and financial disclosure (also Chapter 4).

Not covered in this *Handbook* are foreign taxes or U.S. taxation of foreign operations, although income tax accounting implications of foreign currency translation are briefly discussed. Likewise, accounting principles and practices in individual foreign countries, and how they are established, are omitted; there are specialized treatises on this subject, including an AICPA series on *Professional Accounting in Foreign Countries.*[1] However, this *Handbook* contains, in each applicable chapter, mention of international accounting standards developed by the International Accounting Standards Committee (IASC).

International Trade

The United States has always been an international trader, even in the eighteenth century before its independence. International trade has continued to be an important aspect of this nation's economic life despite interludes of isolationism, government intervention, currency value gyrations, and the fact that the United States has become a net importer of goods.

Interest in international accounting has grown, especially since the early 1960s when a significant general increase occurred in the rate of international investment, capital flow, and trade. That trend accelerated even more in the 1970s when U.S. dependency on imported oil became publicly evident through shortages and skyrocketing world oil prices. Oil producing nations collected and recycled massive amounts of "petrodollars," reinvesting them in the industrial nations and using them to purchase goods and services needed for their own international growth (Evans, Taylor and Holzmann, 1985).

In more recent times, with the "world oil glut," a large part of these invested petrodollars have been repatriated by oil producing nations; but funds available from export surpluses of Asian countries have taken their place. The net result of one cycle following another is that considerable foreign capital is invested in U.S. government securities, funding part of the continual and large federal budget deficits.

Figure 22.1 indicates that U.S. exports of goods and services are about 10% of Gross National Product (GNP) and have ranged from 8.9% to 12.9% over the last ten years. U.S. exports of goods and services in 1960 also were approximately 10% of GNP, excluding the effect of any price level changes during the period.

Except for 1987 (which is based on estimates), exports as a percentage of GNP have declined every year since 1980. The decline is small but persistent. Further, there has been a dramatic increase in imports over the same period: during the six years from 1980 through 1987, imports more than doubled. It is not surprising that the United States now incurs significant annual foreign trade deficits, estimated to be $118 billion in 1987 excluding net transfer payments ($15.7 billion) and interest paid to foreigners ($24.5 billion).

Regardless of the deficit, foreign trade continues to be a very important part of U.S. economic activity. Perhaps for this reason alone, significant interest by accountants in foreign operations and in foreign currency translation concepts continues. In addition, with a generally negative trade situation and a persistent decline in the

---

[1] Inaugurated in 1987, these booklets cover auditing, accounting principles and practices, and the business environment, with emphasis on comparison to those of the United States. As of mid-1988, booklets were available for the United Kingdom, Sweden, Canada, the Netherlands, Japan, Italy, and Hong Kong.

Year	Gross national product (billions)	Exports of goods and services (billions)			Percentage of total exports		Exports as a percentage of GNP		
		Total	Goods	Services	Goods	Services	Total	Goods	Services
1978	$2,128	$207	$141	$ 66	68%	32%	9.7%	6.6%	3.1%
1979	2,369	258	177	81	69	31	10.9	7.5	3.4
1980	2,633	339	220	119	65	35	12.9	8.4	4.5
1981	2,954	369	233	136	63	37	12.5	7.9	4.6
1982	3,073	348	209	139	60	40	11.3	6.8	4.5
1983	3,305	336	199	137	59	41	10.2	6.0	4.2
1984	3,663	364	219	145	60	40	9.9	6.0	3.9
1985	4,010	370	221	149	60	40	9.2	5.5	3.7
1986	4,235	376	225	151	60	40	8.9	5.3	3.6
1987[1]	4,445	417	248	169	59	41	9.4	5.6	3.8

1 Annual amount estimated based on second quarter 1987 actual data.

FIG. 22.1 U.S. Exports of Goods and Services

Source: Survey of Current Business, U.S. Department of Commerce Bureau of Economic Analysis, October 1980, 1982, 1983, 1985, and September 1987, U.S. Government Printing Office, Washington, D.C.

value of the U.S. dollar relative to Japanese and European currencies, hedging of foreign currency transactions and balances is virtually essential to those U.S. companies and MNCs involved in foreign trade. The FASB and EITF deliberations concerning foreign exchange contracts and hedging are the result of issues raised by the continuing attempts of U.S. companies to protect themselves in an uncertain foreign trade and currency environment.

Figure 22.1 also presents the percentage relationship of goods and services in U.S. annual exports from 1978 to 1987. The service element of total exports has grown steadily—perhaps dramatically—in relative terms. Service exports have increased 177% in actual dollars during the decade presented, while the export of goods has increased only 76%. Although annual differences seem insignificant, they continue to accumulate. Projecting the same growth, U.S. service exports will exceed exports of goods by 1997.

Presently, the United States is the primary world exporter of services (Evans et al., 1985). Whether it will remain in this position is unclear. U.S. business generally focuses on short-term profits, and concomitantly deemphasizes research and development. Whether an edge in the export of services—a substantial part of which is technology—can be increased, or even maintained, in the absence of significant research and development activities remains to be seen.

Historical Perspective on Translation Standards

As a company moves toward a significant commitment to foreign operations, its financial statements must properly reflect the related financial impact. The purpose of foreign currency translation is to convert the results of transactions involving foreign currencies into a common denominator for financial reporting purposes. Generally the denominator is the currency of the parent company. This process can be complex because of the impact of fluctuating exchange rates, transactions occurring worldwide, restrictions by foreign governments on the movement of financial resources out of their economies, and other factors.

Current/Noncurrent Approach. It is not surprising that practically no attention was given to formal accounting pronouncements on foreign operations until recent years. Prior to 1973 when the FASB issued SFAS 1, *Disclosure of Foreign Currency Translation Information* (now superseded), the only authoritative pronouncement that had been issued was a scant eight pages contained in ARB 4, *Foreign Operations and Foreign Exchange* (now mostly superseded), issued in 1939. That statement responded to the unsettled international conditions at the outbreak of World War II, not to any perceived need to develop accounting standards for dealing with the consequences of a growing volume of international trade.

ARB 4, subsequently codified in ARB 43, Chapter 12 (F65), adopted the current/noncurrent approach to foreign currency translation. Under that approach, all of a foreign subsidiary's current assets and current liabilities were translated at the exchange rate in effect at the balance sheet date, and all noncurrent assets and liabilities were translated at the exchange rates in effect when the assets were acquired or the debt incurred.

Unrealized translation losses were recognized immediately, but unrealized translation gains were deferred in a suspense account to be absorbed by future translation losses. Realized exchange gains and losses were recognized immediately. Although the accounting standards that sanctioned this approach were prepared at a time when there was general concern about the stability of foreign investments, there was also a feeling that the dollar would always appreciate in relation to other currencies. Therefore, it seemed prudent or conservative to maintain the lower exchange rate for those assets that would be realized over a longer term, but reasonable to use the current rate for those assets that were to be turned over promptly.

Monetary/Nonmonetary Approach. Some companies were following the monetary/nonmonetary approach, effectively approved in APB 6, *Status of Accounting Research Bulletins* (¶ 18). When reviewing ARB 43, the APB apparently decided that the distinction in Chapter 12 between current and noncurrent items was too simplistic. APB 6 was conceptually different because the translation rate to be used was to be determined by the characteristics of the item to be translated, not by its balance sheet placement. The APB concluded that monetary items, including long-term receivables and payables, were to be translated at current rates "in many circumstances" (which in practice meant virtually always). All nonmonetary items, including inventory, were to be translated at historic rates.

It should be noted that the dollar was still appreciating in the mid 1960s, and many companies with substantial foreign debt were happy to adopt the new method. The anticipated translation gain in their foreign long-term debt appeared to provide a significant cushion against potential foreign losses.

FASB Disclosure Standard. At the inception of the FASB, accounting for foreign currency translation was among the first group of seven topics selected for its agenda. The subject was deemed critically important for three reasons:

1. Existing accounting principles affected only translation of local currency financial statements of foreign entities and did not deal with the problems related to translating transactions of an importing or exporting company that were denominated in terms of foreign currency.

2. Except for slight modifications, the accounting principles for translation of financial statements of foreign companies were formulated in another era when the typical company was a domestic corporation with minor foreign operations, often in the form of branches selling goods produced in the United States. That approach was changed as a result of (1) World War II and the concomitant increase in the international activities of U.S. companies, especially the use of foreign currency borrowings to finance U.S. overseas operations; and (2) changes in the world monetary system (including U.S. dollar devaluations in 1971 and 1973) that changed the way U.S. companies operated in the foreign arena.

3. Significant variations in methods used to translate the financial statements of foreign companies had become established in practice.

During 1973, when an FASB Task Force and the Board were in the midst of considering the foreign currency translation problem, the Board issued SFAS 1, *Disclosure of Foreign Currency Translation Information* (now superseded), as an interim step prior to the issuance of SFAS 8, discussed in the section that follows. SFAS 1 required disclosures about (1) a company's translation policies; (2) the amounts of exchange adjustments that originated in a year and were either deferred or included in the determination of net income; (3) the amount by which long-term receivables and payables would change if translated at current rather than historical exchange rates; and (4) the amount of any gain or loss that was unrecognized on unperformed forward exchange contracts at the balance sheet date.

FASB Temporal Approach. In 1975, the FASB issued SFAS 8, *Accounting for the Translation of Foreign Currency Transactions and Foreign Currency Financial Statements* (also now superseded). SFAS 8 replaced the monetary/nonmonetary method with the temporal method, so called to emphasize an important new concept: the temporal method was concerned with the timing of acquisition or occurrence of the item to be translated, and not with the balance sheet placement of the item or the character of the item itself.

Translation of foreign financial statements. Accounts that a foreign subsidiary carried at prices in past exchanges (historical costs) were translated at the exchange rate in effect at the acquisition date. That originating exchange rate was used regardless of whether the asset (such as plant or inventories) was acquired for cash or for debt, and whether the settlement of the debt happened to be at the same exchange rate or at a vastly different one. For example, fixed assets were translated at the rates in effect at the acquisition date, not because fixed assets are monmonetary items, but because under GAAP they are intended to be carried in the financial statements at historical cost.

The foreign subsidiary's cash, cash-type items such as receivables and payables, and other assets or liabilities that were carried at current prices, were translated at the exchange rate in effect at the balance sheet date. Any change since the last reporting date in the difference between those translated balances and the translated balances as originally recorded was recognized as translation gain or loss and included in the current income statement.

All revenue and expense transactions were translated at the rates in effect when those transactions took place. As a practical matter, a weighted-average rate was used for transactions during the reporting period, to avoid the detail involved in recomputing U.S. dollars for each individual transaction.

Generally, it was not necessary to mention the company's translation policies in the accounting policies footnote. A company that prepared its financial statements in accordance with GAAP presumably was following SFAS 8 in its entirety. Because SFAS 8 left almost no room for interpretation or alternative application (for example, SFAS 8 specifically precluded the deferral of translation gains or losses both at year end and at interim reporting dates), there was nothing unique a company could say about its translation policy.

Foreign transactions. A domestic company's sale (or purchase) denominated in a foreign currency had to be viewed as two transactions. The first transaction was the sale itself, and was translated at the rate in effect at the date of the transaction. The collection of the related receivable (or the payment of the payable) was a separate transaction, and if the settlement produced (or required) more or fewer dollars than were anticipated in the original transaction, that difference was accounted for as an *exchange* gain or loss. The difference was not netted against (or combined with) the first part of the transaction.

Economic unreality. Soon after the issuance of SFAS 8, a consensus developed within industry and the accounting profession that deficiencies in financial reporting of foreign operations and currency transactions often resulted from applying its provisions. Specifically, some companies were reporting significant variations in periodic income due solely to short-term fluctuations in exchange rates when those rates were in fact being applied to long-term net investments denominated in foreign currencies. Such fluctuations resulted primarily in unrealized (but nevertheless recognized) gains and losses, tending to exaggerate the effects of changes in exchange rates when the foreign operations were reported in the parent's financial statements. Indeed, SFAS 8 often produced accounting results that were the opposite of the economic effects of an exchange rate change.

FOREIGN CURRENCY TRANSLATION – SFAS 52

In 1979, the FASB expanded its agenda to include a reconsideration of SFAS 8. An early step in the reconsideration process was to identify and deal with four basic alternatives:

1. *Change the accounting model to reflect currently the effects of all changing prices in the primary financial statements.* This concept was rejected.
2. *Defer recognition of currency changes on all foreign assets and liabilities until realized.* Because deferral does not recognize in financial statements the possibly significant economic effects of currency changes when they occur, this alternative was rejected.
3. *Currently recognize currency changes on the carrying amounts of designated foreign assets and liabilities.* This was the SFAS 8 approach. Some proposed simply modifying SFAS 8 to add or delete items from the list of foreign assets and liabilities subject to current rate translation. This was rejected because the FASB had not yet agreed on conceptual distinctions among balances and accounts to be translated. Therefore, adding a new item to the list, such as inventories, would have been arbitrary.
4. *Currently recognize exchange rate changes on all foreign assets and liabilities.* This is the approach adopted by SFAS 52, *Foreign Currency Translation* (F60), which superseded SFAS 8.

Overview

SFAS 52 (F60) is applicable to all investments in foreign enterprises including subsidiaries, divisions, branches, joint ventures, and equity investees, and to all foreign currency transactions. In this chapter, investments in foreign enterprises usually will be referred to simply as subsidiaries or equity investees, and the investing company usually will be referred to as the parent or the reporting company.

An enterprise can be involved with foreign currencies in various ways: It may have investments in foreign subsidiaries or investees; or it may make commitments to buy, sell, lease, or otherwise be obligated in transactions that are to be settled in a foreign currency; or it may directly acquire assets or incur obligations denominated in a foreign currency.

When an enterprise prepares financial statements in conformity with GAAP, it must restate all foreign currency balances and transactions into a common denominator, namely, the currency — called the reporting currency — that will be used in the presentation of the financial statements. Although this chapter assumes that the U.S. dollar is the reporting currency, the reporting currency can be any currency used in financial statements prepared in conformity with U.S. GAAP.

For example, a U.S. company's West German subsidiary that conducts operations throughout Europe in various currencies, and that has direct investments in subsidiaries in Italy and Sweden, will follow the provisions of SFAS 52 when preparing U.S. GAAP-basis financial statements denominated in Deutschemarks (DM).

Likewise, companies will enter into foreign-currency denominated commitments that will have a time span between initiation and consummation, for example, a firm purchase order for Japanese equipment, a direct investment in Swiss franc debt, or the issuance of parent company debt payable in pounds sterling.

SFAS 52 prescribes a methodology for translating foreign currency financial statements and transactions for inclusion in financial statements of a reporting company (e.g., a U.S. parent). Its principal objective is to report the effects (on a company's cash flows and shareholders' equity) of changes in *exchange rates* — the ratio between a unit of one currency and the amount of another currency for which it can be exchanged — in a manner that is consistent with expected economic consequences. To illustrate, if a company has an operating subsidiary in the United Kingdom with substantial net assets, and the U.S. dollar strengthens in relation to the pound sterling between financial reporting dates, the expected result (absent hedges) is that the U.S. dollar value of those net assets will have decreased. This was not necessarily the case under SFAS 8.

Translation Summary. Prior to translating foreign currency financial statements, SFAS 52 requires that the *functional currency* of the subsidiary or equity investee be determined. Most often this is the currency of the country in which the subsidiary is located and operates. If the foreign subsidiary's books are not kept in its functional currency, or if the subsidiary has transactions in a nonfunctional currency, those books or transactions need to be remeasured into the functional currency (F60.146-147).

All assets, liabilities, income, and expenses in the subsidiary's financial statements denominated in the functional currency are then translated into the *reporting currency* (e.g., the U.S. dollar) by applying the current exchange rate to the balance sheet and a weighted-average rate to the income statement. (The weighted averaging is aimed at approximating the translation that would have been achieved had the current rate at the time of each transaction been applied.) If the current rate changes after the end of the reporting period but before the financial statements are issued, the statements are not to be changed; if the change is significant, disclosure must be made. Pro forma financial statements also may be provided (see Chapter 27).

The exchange rate to be used for translation of foreign currency financial statements is the rate applicable to conversion of that currency for dividend remittances. In most developed countries, that rate is also the current *spot rate* for immediate delivery of the two currencies.

The translation of foreign financial statements at an exchange rate that differs from the rate used at the prior reporting date will result in a translation adjustment, classified in a separate component of shareholders' equity.

Transactions Summary. Like translation adjustments, balances resulting from transactions in foreign currencies are revalued at the rate at which the currencies could be exchanged (again, generally the spot rate) at the reporting date. For example, a U.S. company's debt denominated in DM is revalued to the product of the DM payable multiplied by the number of dollars to the DM at the reporting date. Unlike translations, however, the gain or loss is a part of current operations, unless it is a hedge of a foreign net investment or firm commitment. Transactions that are hedges are also revalued, but usually the gain or loss is deferred along with the hedged item.

If the transaction is a speculative forward exchange contract (F60.124-126), it is valued at the price available on the market for a forward having a duration equal to its remaining term. For example, a three-year forward purchased a year ago is valued currently at the price quoted for a two-year forward.

Forwards and hedges are discussed in separate sections later in this chapter.

Foreign Currency Financial Statements

The first step in the translation process is determination of the functional currency of the foreign unit whose financial statements are to be translated.

The *functional currency* is the currency of the primary economic environment in which a company operates, that is, the country in which the company normally generates and expends cash (F60.104). Judgment by management is the key to its determination, as long as that judgment is not contradicted by the facts.

Nature of Foreign Operations. There are two broad categories of foreign operations:

1. Those that are relatively self-contained and integrated within a particular country or economy. This means that those foreign operations:
   a. Are not dependent on a day-to-day basis on the parent company's environment;
   b. Primarily generate and expend foreign currency; and
   c. Can reinvest cash flows, or convert and distribute them to the parent.
   In this case, the foreign currency is the functional currency.
2. Those that are primarily a direct and integral component or extension of the parent's operations. This means that:
   a. Purchase or sale of significant assets between the foreign entity and its parent are generally made in dollars;
   b. Financing is generally from the parent or other dollar sources; and

c. Day-to-day operations are substantially dependent on the environment of the parent's currency, and changes in foreign assets and liabilities are presumed to affect the parent's cash flows in the parent's currency.

In this case, the parent's currency is the functional currency.

Factors in Functional Currency Determination. Factors to be considered in determining the functional currency are (F60.110):

- Cash flow
- Sales price
- Sales markets
- Expenses
- Financing
- Intercompany transactions and arrangements

The effects of these factors in deciding whether to consider the U.S. dollar or a foreign currency as the functional currency of a foreign subsidiary included in U.S. GAAP financial statements are presented in the following list. Examples of situations and typical transactions involving functional currency determination are presented in Figure 22.2.

1. The foreign subsidiary's currency is the functional currency when:
   a. Cash flows are primarily in the foreign currency and do not directly affect the parent's cash flows.
   b. Sales prices are not responsive to short-term changes in exchange rates but are determined more by local competition or local government regulation.
   c. There is an active local market for the foreign entity's products or services, although there may be significant exports as well.
   d. Labor, materials, and other costs for the foreign entity's products or services are primarily local costs.
   e. Financing is primarily denominated in a foreign currency, and funds generated by the foreign entity's operations are sufficient to service existing and normally expected debt obligations.
   f. There is a low volume of intercompany transactions and a limited interrelationship between the foreign entity and its parent. Use of or reliance on the parent's or an affiliate's competitive advantage (e.g., product reputation) is not a factor in this evaluation.
2. The parent's currency (U.S. dollar in this example) is the functional currency when:
   a. The foreign entity's cash flows affect the parent's current cash flows (e.g., by frequent remittances).
   b. Sales prices are responsive to short-term changes in exchange rates, with prices determined more by worldwide competition or by international prices than by local conditions.
   c. Sales are made mostly in the parent's country, *or* sales contracts written in foreign countries are denominated in the parent's currency.

Description of event	Functional currency
• A subsidiary assembles locally from materials purchased locally and from its U.S. parent, with its products generally sold locally.	• Probably the local currency inasmuch as purchases and sales are concentrated locally.
• A subsidiary functions principally as a foreign sales office, performing no manufacturing or assembly operations.	• Generally, the currency of the country in which the products are manufactured.
• A mining subsidiary transports raw materials to a processing plant owned by its parent or affiliate.	• The currency of the country in which the processing plant is located.
• A subsidiary manufactures subassemblies or performs subassembly work for products final-assembled by an affiliate in another country for final sale to yet another country.	• The currency of the country in which the products are final-assembled; the currency of the country in which the products are sold would likely be the functional currency of the affiliate.
• A subsidiary's sole function is to borrow local currency and lend the proceeds to its parent.	• The currency of the parent's country.
• A financial subsidiary borrows and lends funds in several countries and in several currencies and has locations in several countries.	• The currencies in the countries in which it transacts business. This is an example of the separate-entity concept advanced by the FASB, which allows designation of several currencies as the functional currency where operations are conducted in several countries and/or currencies.

FIG. 22.2   Examples of Situations and Transactions That Affect Functional Currency Selection

    d. Labor, materials, and other costs for the foreign entity's products or services, on a continuing basis, are primarily costs for components obtained from the country in which the parent is located.

    e. Financing is primarily from the parent or is otherwise arranged in dollar-denominated obligations; or the foreign entity cannot service existing or expected debt obligations without a dollar infusion.

    f. There is a high volume of intercompany transactions and an extensive interrelationship between parent and foreign entity.

    g. A foreign entity is used as a device or shell corporation for holding nonoperating assets and liabilities (e.g., marketable securities and intangible assets) that could readily be carried on the parent's books.

3. Other factors that bear on determination of the functional currency include the following:

    a. Separability of operations. If a foreign entity deals in more than one foreign currency, has operations involving both its parent and unrelated entities, or operates in two or more economic environments or countries, each operation may be considered as a separate entity for purposes of identifying the functional currency (F60.111).

b. Influence of parent. The fact that the parent exercises the control or significant influence necessary to permit consolidation or application of the equity method of accounting for foreign investments does not, per se, imply that the functional currency of the foreign investee is the parent's currency (F60.112).

Change in Functional Currency Designation. Once the functional currency has been established it should not change except for clearly evident and significant changes in economic facts or circumstances (F60.113–.114). A change in the functional currency from the foreign currency to the reporting currency does not affect previous translation adjustments, and restatement of previously issued financial statements is inappropriate. Translated amounts at the end of the prior period are established as the "new basis" in the reporting currency.

If the functional currency changes from the reporting currency to a foreign currency, the adjustment attributable to the current rate translation as of the date of change is included in comprehensive income and hence in the currency translation adjustment account in shareholders' equity, as described in the following section.

If a company's books of record are not maintained in its functional currency, remeasurement into the functional currency is required. The remeasurement process is intended to produce the same result as if the books had been maintained in the functional currency (F60.115).

Translation Method. By adopting the functional currency approach, SFAS 52 views the economic environment of a foreign company as the critical element in determining whether the company is in fact an extension of its parent or is self-contained. If dependency is not evident, a foreign subsidiary of a U.S. company is considered to have a functional currency other than the dollar, in which case the current exchange rate is used to translate foreign currency statements (F60.118). For assets and liabilities, this is the rate in effect at the balance sheet date; for revenue and expense items, it is generally a weighted-average rate during the period. Translation at the current or weighted-average exchange rate applies equally to accounting allocations such as depreciation, cost of sales, and amortization of deferred revenues and expenses. Those allocations are translated at rates in effect (or average rates) when they are reflected in the earnings statement, not when the related balances were first recorded in the balance sheet (F60.118). Similarly, when preparing consolidated financial statements, elimination of intercompany profits is based on exchange rates at the date of the sale or transfer giving rise to the profit (F60.135).

If a company's functional currency is a foreign currency, translation adjustments are not included in net income. These adjustments are, however, considered part of *comprehensive income* and are accumulated in a separate component of shareholders' equity called *foreign currency translation adjustments* (F60.119). These cumulative adjustments enter into the determination of net income only when the foreign investment is fully or partially sold or is liquidated by the parent (F60.120).[2]

---

[2] In FIN 37 (F60.120), the FASB concluded that when a partial interest in a foreign company is sold, a pro rata portion of the accumulated translation adjustment should be recognized in income.

In SFAC 6 (FASB, 1985), the FASB defines comprehensive income of business enterprises as "the change in equity ... during a period from transactions and other events and circumstances from nonowner sources. It includes all changes in equity during a period except those resulting from investments by owners and distributions to owners" (¶ 70). Thus, although current net income is a part of comprehensive income, some other items, including foreign currency translation adjustments, are classified directly in shareholders' equity.[3]

This treatment—marking foreign assets, liabilities, and current operations to the current rate for consolidation purposes (or for the use of the equity method for non-subsidiary foreign investees) but sequestering in shareholders' equity the effect of exchange rate changes on the net investment—generally will produce reported results that comport with expectations based on how the exchange rates moved during the reporting period. However, because cash flows are not currently affected by these fluctuations, the classification of the adjustment in shareholder's equity until cash flows are affected also comports with economic expectations.

As nonliquidating dividend remittances are made from the foreign subsidiary or investee, no portion of the translation adjustment is transferred to the income statement. However, in a substantially complete liquidation, or a sale of the equity ownership by the parent, the adjustment account is charged against the liquidation or sale proceeds.

Figure 22.3 shows an analysis of the separate component of shareholders' equity in which currency translation adjustments are accumulated. Note that the year-end balance is classified in the balance sheet among the equity accounts. Figure 22.3 also refers to hedges and income tax allocation, discussed later in this chapter.

As a further example, a portion of the accounting policies note of Marine Transport Lines Inc. for 1986 is presented in Figure 22.4. The note discusses the effects of foreign currency translation and transaction adjustments. The translation of Rowbotham Tankships Limited operations (denominated in a foreign functional currency) resulted in a translation gain recorded in shareholders' equity. In addition, for a second operation, International Oil and Bulk Trade Company, Ltd. (denominated in U.S. currency), translation losses were recorded in net income, because the U.S. dollar was deemed the functional currency.

Intercompany Accounts. It is important to determine whether intercompany accounts between the reporting company and its foreign subsidiaries are transaction accounts, or are part of the net investment. If the former, then gains and losses based on currency exchange fluctuations occurring between the transaction date and the settlement date are included in current operations because the reporting company's cash flows are affected. If the latter, as might be the case when a demand note is used as part of the foreign company's capitalization with payment not anticipated in the foreseeable future, it is treated as part of the net investment, and exchange

---

[3] As of mid-1988, the only other item specifically required to be "dangled" in shareholders' equity is the valuation reserve necessary to reduce marketable equity securities classified as noncurrent (or that are carried in an unclassified balance sheet) to the lower of cost or market. (See Chapter 12.) Additionally, in practice, receivables from shareholders for capital stock subscriptions are usually offset against shareholders' equity (see Chapter 20).

Balance sheet excerpt	1986	1985
	($ millions)	
Shareholders' Equity		
Capital Stock:		
Preferred stock, liquidation preference $2.3 million in 1986 and $2.9 million in 1985	$ .1	$ .2
Common stock, 91,824,968 shares issued in 1986 and 1985	229.6	229.6
Capital in excess of par value	147.6	151.5
Retained earnings	1,398.7	1,461.5
Currency translation adjustment	(54.4)	(85.0)
Investment valuation allowance	(39.2)	–
	1,682.4	1,757.8
Less treasury common stock, at cost	157.6	105.3
Total shareholders' equity	1,524.8	1,625.5

Note to Financial Statements

Currency Translation Adjustment:

Following is an analysis of the change in the currency translation adjustment for the years ended December 31:

	1986	1985	1984
	($ millions)		
Currency translation adjustment at January 1	$(85.0)	$(95.9)	$(67.0)
Current translation adjustments and net asset hedges	21.7	9.9	(27.8)
Amounts allocated to income tax liabilities	0.1	1.0	(1.1)
Amounts applicable to Air Conditioning*	8.8	–	–
Currency translation adjustment at December 31	$(54.4)	$(85.0)	$(95.9)

*Company spun off to shareholders.

FIG. 22.3 Example of Foreign Currency Translation Adjustment Account
Source: Borg-Warner Corporation, 1986 Annual Report.

differentials are accounted for in the same manner as the equity investment, that is, included in the translation adjustments account (F60.127b).

Determining whether an intercompany account with a foreign subsidiary meets the SFAS 52 criteria for deferral of related gains or losses is often difficult. The FASB requirements—that such transactions be of a long-term nature with no planned or anticipated settlement in the foreseeable future—is subject to considerable interpretation.

The intent of management of the investor and foreign investee entities and the ability of both entities to fulfill that intent are key factors. Another more controversial factor relates to changes in the components of intercompany foreign currency balances when there is no corresponding change in their total amount.

A "rolling balance" or "minimum balance" intercompany account is generally viewed as a transaction account, not a part of the net investment, and results in gains

---

Foreign Currency Gains and Losses: The assets and liabilities of Rowbotham were translated at the British pound sterling — U.S. dollar exchange rates in effect at December 31, 1986 and 1985, and the statements of operations were translated at the average prevailing exchange rates for the year 1986 and the period from October 18, 1985, date of acquisition, to December 31, 1985. The gains resulting from the translations of those financial statements, amounting to $310,000 and $117,000 in 1986 and 1985, respectively, were deferred and recorded as a separate component of consolidated shareholders' equity. Foreign currency gains and losses incurred in Rowbotham's day-to-day operations are recognized as incurred and reported in the statement of operations.

The Spanish peseta portion of the debt owed by International Oil and Bulk Trade Company, Ltd. ("IOBT") and Marine Renaissance (see Notes E and G*), was translated at the Spanish peseta-U.S. dollar exchange rates in effect at December 31, 1986 and 1985 and the losses resulting from the translations, amounting to $1,181,000 and $1,088,000, respectively, were recognized and reported as an expense in the statements of operations.

That portion of cash in banks, excluding cash of Rowbotham, which is denominated in currency other than U.S. dollars, was translated at the various exchange rates in effect at each year end and the gains or losses resulting therefrom also were recognized and reported in the statements of operations.

---

*Notes omitted

FIG. 22.4   Foreign Currency Translation and Transaction Adjustments
Source: Marine Transport Lines, Inc., 1986 Annual Report.

and losses that should be currently reflected in net income, as settled throughout the reporting period or as a result of revaluing at the current exchange rate at the balance sheet date if not yet settled.

Shortly after issuance, an SFAS 52 implementation task force reached the following conclusions with respect to intercompany transactions:

1. If a parent guarantees the dollar-denominated debt of a foreign subsidiary, the guarantee does *not* create the equivalent of a long-term intercompany transaction under SFAS 52. The opposite view, rejected by the FASB staff and the task force, would hold that the existence of the parent's guarantee is the equivalent of the parent having borrowed U.S. dollar-denominated debt and transferred it through an intercompany account to the foreign subsidiary, and thereby the parent should be allowed to treat it as a long-term intercompany investment.

2. Intercompany balances must be evaluated on a discrete transaction basis, rather than on a minimum balance basis. While there is a rationale for considering at least a portion of an intercompany balance akin to a long-term equity investment, the task force concluded that the discrete approach is more appropriate.

Highly Inflationary Economies. SFAS 52 recognizes that foreign companies may operate in highly inflationary economies. In such cases, the functional currency, if different from the reporting currency, has lost so much value and stability as to make it unusable for translation purposes. Consequently, when inflation exceeds

Note 12. Foreign Currency Translation

In accordance with the provisions of Statement of Financial Accounting Standards No. 52, "Foreign Currency Translation," (SFAS No. 52) the assets and liabilities of Erbamont's subsidiaries located outside Italy are generally translated into Italian lire at the rates of exchange in effect at the balance sheet dates. Income and expense items are translated at the average exchange rates prevailing during the period. Gains and losses resulting from foreign currency transactions are recognized currently in income and those resulting from translation of financial statements are, with the exception of entities operating in highly inflationary economies, accumulated in a separate component of shareholders' equity.

Certain of the Company's subsidiaries operate in highly inflationary economies (where cumulative inflation has exceeded 100% over a three-year period), particularly in Latin America. With respect to the financial statements of these entities, SFAS No. 52 requires the use of historical exchange rates to translate nonmonetary items (primarily fixed assets and inventories) and current exchange rates to translate monetary items. The effect of exchange rate changes is reflected in net income.

FIG. 22.5 Foreign Currency Adjustments in Highly Inflationary Economies
Source: Erbamont N.V., 1986 Annual Report.

approximately 100% over the most recent three-year period (F60.116), measured cumulatively over the period, historical rates are used to translate nonmonetary items and current rates are used to translate monetary items. SFAS 52 indicates that judgment must be used, because designation of an economy as highly inflationary is not always clear-cut.[4]

A consistent means of measurement and identification should be applied to the highly inflationary designation on a year-to-year basis; that is, an economy should not be considered highly inflationary one year but not the next, unless there is a marked change in inflationary circumstances. When a designation changes from highly inflationary to nonhighly inflationary, the accounting is the same as that applied when the functional currency changes from the reporting currency to the foreign currency; when the opposite occurs, the change should be accounted for prospectively as a change in estimate (F60.114). (See the earlier section "Change in Functional Currency Designation.")

Figure 22.5 presents a foreign currency translation note that discusses the accounting for operations in highly inflationary economies.

The SFAS 52 implementation task force reached the following conclusions about the highly inflationary designation:

1. A highly inflationary determination should generally be made on a quarterly basis, and if there is a change, it should be made without restatement of earlier quarters within a given year.

2. A change in designation from highly inflationary to nonhighly inflationary should be reflected by translating the historical dollar amounts at the date of change to the functional

---

[4] The consumer price indices of various countries published by the United Nations in its *Monthly Bulletin of Statistics* provides useful information in making this determination.

currency at current exchange rates, with the resulting amounts deemed to be the new functional currency accounting basis of the assets and liabilities. This approach avoids the problem of "disappearing assets" that would occur if an entity simply changed to the current rate approach using the historical foreign currency amounts.

Income Tax Consequences of Rate Changes. The income tax effects of translation adjustments are to be accounted for as temporary differences in accordance with SFAS 96, *Accounting for Income Taxes*, discussed in Chapter 17. As a result, deferred income taxes are provided for items of income, expense, gain, or loss for which the financial statement and income tax bases differ (F60.132). Deferred income taxes are calculated using the income tax rate in effect at the time of the transaction that gives rise to the difference, and are adjusted each time there is a change in the income tax law or rate.

Income taxes and deferred income taxes related to translation adjustments accumulated in the separate shareholders' equity account are to be allocated to such gains and losses (and not to ordinary income). (See Figure 22.3.)

In a decision intended to simplify the application of SFAS 96, the FASB decided that when there is a need to change the deferred income tax effects allocated to the cumulative translation adjustments account because of a change in rates or tax laws, the computed amount of the change should be charged or credited to current operations, rather than to shareholders' equity. This seems inconsistent with the concept underlying the establishment of the cumulative translation adjustments account; that is, absent remittances or hedges, the income tax effects also do not affect current cash flows. Although an intuitive reaction is that this is a small matter, it can be significant if a rate change is more than nominal.[5]

If a company does not provide for deferred income taxes on unremitted earnings of foreign subsidiaries (as permitted under APB 23 (I42.107)) deferred income taxes likewise are not provided on translation adjustments.

In a related matter, the EITF discussed *Income Tax Effects of Asset Revaluations in Certain Foreign Countries* (Issue 84-43). Under governmental programs in these countries, a company is periodically permitted to increase the tax basis of depreciable assets (usually by indexation, to reflect the effects of inflation), and to depreciate such increases over the remaining lives of the assets. If a company affected by this procedure has previously been providing for deferred taxes on an excess of tax depreciation over book depreciation, a question arises as to whether the indexing restored some or all the basis previously tax-depreciated, eliminating the need for the deferred taxes.

The EITF reached a consensus that the deferred taxes should not be eliminated because the deferred method under APB 11 did not allow this type of adjustment. This conclusion has now been obviated by SFAS 96, which requires that deferred taxes be recognized for all temporary differences. SFAS 96 gives as an example of a temporary difference an increase in the tax basis of assets because of indexing for inflation (I25.109).

---

[5] This FASB "simplification" is especially significant with respect to the other item "dangled" in shareholders' equity: the lower-of-cost-or-market valuation differential for noncurrent marketable equity securities. The income tax aspects are discussed in Chapter 17.

Foreign Currency Transactions

Transactions Included in Current Income. A foreign currency transaction is one that requires settlement in a currency other than an entity's functional currency. Such transactions affect the reporting company's cash flows because the denominations of the two currencies are different. Therefore, they result in transaction gains and losses.

Generally, transaction gains or losses are included in determining net income for the period in which the transaction is settled or when the exchange rate changes (if prior to settlement). For all foreign currency transactions except forward exchange contracts (see later section on such contracts), this is accomplished by measuring and recording each asset, liability, revenue, expense, gain, or loss arising from the transaction in the functional currency of the recording entity by use of the exchange rate in effect at the recognition date—that is, the rate at which the transaction could be settled at that date (F60.123a). Subsequently, at each balance sheet date, recorded balances that are denominated in a currency other than the functional currency of the recording entity are adjusted to reflect the then current exchange rate (F60.123b).

Examples of foreign currency transactions include a debt incurred by a U.S. company payable in Swiss francs or a debt payable in pounds sterling incurred by its German subsidiary whose functional currency is the DM. In the former case, determination of gain or loss is straightforward: simply determine the U.S. dollar equivalent of the Swiss francs at the reporting date, and record as a gain or loss the difference between that U.S. dollar amount and the amount at which the debt was carried at the last reporting date. In the latter case an intermediate step is required: first translate the pound debt into DM, recognizing gain or loss in the German subsidiary's results of operations in the current period. Upon translation of the German subsidiary's financial statements, the gain or loss will carry through into the U.S. dollar consolidated financial statements.

The remeasurement and valuation of marketable nondebt securities denominated in a currency other than the functional currency require special consideration if the securities are carried at market or lower of cost or market, for example, an investment by a U.S. company in a U.K. company's ordinary shares traded on the London Stock Exchange. In such cases, the carrying amount of the security should first be adjusted in the reporting currency to reflect the current exchange rate, and the resulting gain or loss should be recognized in the income statement. Second, the current market price stated in the functional currency should be translated and compared to the adjusted carrying amount, with additional adjustments to market or lower of cost or market recorded, if appropriate.

Transactions Excluded From Current Income. These are: (1) foreign currency transactions designated as, or effective as, economic hedges of a net investment in a foreign entity (discussed in the two following sections), commencing as of the designation date and (2) intercompany foreign currency transactions that are not planned or anticipated to be settled in the foreseeable future.

Generally, such transactions are accounted for in the same manner as translation adjustments, with net amounts included in the separate component of equity.

Forward Exchange Contracts

These contracts are agreements to exchange different currencies at specified future dates and rates (F60.124). Thus, a forward contract is a foreign currency transaction under SFAS 52. Forwards that are designated as a hedge of a net investment in a foreign investee or of a firm foreign currency commitment are deemed to be non-speculative forward contracts. All other forward contracts are speculative.

For hedged net investments in foreign investees, the forwards are marked to the current exchange rate at each reporting date, and the change since the last reporting date is included as part of the translation adjustment in shareholders' equity. If the forward hedges a foreign currency commitment not yet recorded in the financial statements (e.g., a firm order for the purchase of foreign equipment), the value change may also remain unbooked until the transaction is recorded (e.g., upon taking title to the equipment), and then included in the measurement of the transaction.

Gains or losses on speculative forward contracts (including currency swaps or other agreements which are, in substance, forward contracts) are included in the determination of net income in the same manner as other foreign currency transactions (F60.126).

At the inception of a forward contract, there will be a difference between the spot rate and the contracted forward rate, referred to as the *premium or discount* (F60.125). This differential is composed of two blended elements: (1) the traders' anticipations of how the currency ratios will move over the contract period and (2) a time-value-of-money factor.

To calculate gain or loss on a contract that is a nonspeculative forward contract, the foreign currency amount of the contract must be multiplied by the difference between the spot rates at the balance sheet date and at the date of inception of the contract or the date of last valuation, whichever is applicable. The premium or discount is accounted for separately from the gain or loss and is included in net income over the life of the contract.

SFAS 52 does not describe the method to be used to amortize the discount or premium over the contract life. While the interest method may be conceptually preferable, the straight-line method is often used in practice.

There are two other accounting treatments for discount or premium:

1. If a gain or loss is deferred on a foreign currency transaction that hedges a foreign currency commitment, the discount or premium related to the commitment period may be included in measurement of the transaction.

2. If the foreign currency transaction represents a hedge of a net investment and is accounted for as such, any discount or premium is to be included with translation adjustments in the separate component of shareholders' equity.

To calculate gain or loss on a speculative forward contract, the foreign currency amount of the contract should be multiplied by the difference between the forward rate available for the remaining duration of the contract, and the contracted (or most recently used) forward rate. No separate accounting recognition is given to the discount or premium on a speculative forward contract (F60.126).

Offsetting Currency Swaps. In Issue 86-25, *Offsetting Foreign Currency Swaps*, the EITF discussed the balance sheet treatment of the effects of a change in exchange rates on a foreign currency swap transaction. A company with debt denominated in a foreign currency will experience changes in the reporting currency value of the debt if the exchange rate changes. If the company, to hedge this debt, has entered into a currency swap contract that creates a foreign currency receivable and a reporting currency payable, and if the terms of the swap require settlement only for the amount of net change in the contract value, the company should record only the net change in the amount of the swap at each balance sheet date. From an economic standpoint, in effect, those two transactions substitute a reporting currency debt for the foreign currency debt.

The Task Force reached a consensus that the amount of the accrual related to the currency swap transaction cannot be offset against the foreign currency debt, which is a transaction legally distinct from the swap; therefore, the right of setoff does not exist. Thus, the debt is marked to the spot rate at the reporting date, and the net swap amount will be carried separately as an accrued liability or asset. The FASB staff is considering a TB covering several matters related to hedging, forwards, and swaps, and may revisit this matter.

Valuation Methodology for Speculative Forwards. In Issue 87-2, *Net Present Value Method of Valuing Speculative Foreign Exchange Contracts*, the EITF considered the method of determining the gain or loss on unsettled speculative foreign currency forward exchange contracts. As a simple example, a contract for forward delivery one year hence of a specified quantity of DMs at U.S. $.60 can be valued at $.60 per DM, or it can be discounted back to its present value of some lesser amount. Long-dated forwards of five to ten years, discussed by the EITF, make the example more complex. SFAS 52 is silent on whether discounting is permitted.

The Task Force reached a consensus that discounting is allowed (but not required) in applying SFAS 52 to this type of contract. The consensus is based on the belief that the intent of SFAS 52 is to mark speculative foreign exchange contracts to market, and that discounting more accurately reflects market value. The FASB has expressed concern over the increasing diversity in practice and has asked the FASB staff to propose a TB.

Hedging

As shown in the preceding section, SFAS 52 opts for an economic evaluation of forward contracts. If they are designated as, and act as, hedges of a foreign net investment (e.g., net assets of a foreign subsidiary) or a firm commitment (e.g., a purchase order for foreign machinery), then the accounting should reflect that fact (F60.127a). SFAS 52 does not permit hedge accounting for hedges of anticipated transactions, that is, transactions that probably will occur but are not evidenced by firm commitments.

With respect to hedging transactions, the following accounting treatment applies:

1. When hedging an identifiable foreign currency commitment, the gain or loss on measurement of the related foreign currency transaction is deferred, unless deferral of losses would lead to their recognition in later periods (in which case they are recognized currently)

(F60.130). For example, if it is anticipated that due to changes expected in the exchange rate, future sales volume would be insufficient to recover the cost of an operating asset (for which the purchase commitment was originally hedged), resulting in a loss (a recoverable amount notion), then any loss on the hedge may not be deferred as part of the cost of the operating asset. A firm agreement to purchase or sell equipment would qualify as a commitment that may be hedged by a designated foreign currency transaction.

2. Where the hedge exceeds the related commitment amount, the related gain or loss is (F60.130):

   a. Deferred, to the extent the transaction is intended to provide a hedge on an after-tax basis, and treated as an offset to the related tax effects in the period the tax effects are recognized; or

   b. Not deferred, to the extent the hedge on an after-tax basis exceeds the related commitment amount.

3. When hedging a net investment in a foreign investee, the gain or loss on the hedge is included in the cumulative translation adjustments account classified within shareholders' equity.

When a hedge is no longer a hedge (for example, it is terminated prior to the transaction date of the related commitment or it ceases to be designated as a hedge), any deferred gain or loss remains deferred and included in the measurement of the foreign currency transaction that occurs when the commitment is fulfilled, or in the currency translation adjustment account in shareholders' equity, as applicable.

The practical impact of applying the broader, more substantive guidance in SFAS 52 (as contrasted to the "cookbook" approach in SFAS 8) with respect to hedging transactions is that a company need only designate a foreign currency transaction as a hedge in applying SFAS 52, as long as the factual evidence surrounding the transaction indicates that it is, in substance, a hedge. To avoid later questions about intent, a formal written designation should be made that a specific foreign currency transaction is a hedge of a specific foreign net investment or currency commitment.

The SFAS 52 implementation task force reached the following supplemental conclusions:

1. SFAS 52 does not require that a commitment be "noncancellable" to be considered "firm." Accordingly, contractual amounts not yet legally receivable or payable may be hedged, provided execution of the commitment is probable and the amounts are reasonably estimable.

2. An intercompany account can be accounted for as a hedging transaction provided it meets the hedge criteria of SFAS 52, that is, it is designated and is effective as a hedge.

3. A foreign currency transaction of one entity in an enterprise generally may hedge a commitment of another entity in the same enterprise under SFAS 52, provided the hedged commitment is a foreign currency commitment to the entity that entered into it. For example, a U.S. parent generally may hedge a commitment of a subsidiary that is not denominated in the subsidiary's functional currency.

4. A transaction is "designated" as a hedge through an overt, documented action evidencing an intent to hedge. In practice, this would likely mean that failure to designate a hedge at its origination date precludes subsequent retroactive designation (assuming all documentation is accurately dated).

After-Tax Hedges. The many instruments that can be used to operate as a hedge will, of course, have tax consequences when they are settled. For example, a debt denominated in a foreign currency will not have tax consequences until debt service payments are made, even though adjustments continue to be made to its carrying amount for GAAP presentation purposes. Such tax differences are temporary differences under SFAS 96, as discussed earlier in the section "Income Tax Consequences of Rate Changes," and deferred taxes are to be appropriately provided.

In establishing a hedge relating to a fixed amount of foreign net investment or commitment, the actual tax consequences will effectively have reduced the hedge cover when the hedge is closed out. Thus, as permitted by SFAS 52 (F60.128 and .130), some companies may establish a hedge at an amount that is greater than the item being hedged, with the excess equal to the amount of expected taxes thereon. (Approximations may be used, as often it is not possible to know exactly what the tax consequences will be.)

Many factors relating to both the hedge and the hedged item will enter into the determination of an effective after-tax implementation strategy, including differing tax rates or treatments, timing of tax consequences, and whether withholding taxes are imposed on related cash flows. The tax laws are very complex in this area and proper hedging requires the involvement of appropriate tax experts.

Tandem Currencies. A difficult hedging issue revolves around the use of a currency other than that in which the net investment or commitment is designated. SFAS 52 provides that such an alternate currency may be used only if it is impractical to use the designated currency and there is a tandem movement of exchange rates of the two currencies (F60.129).

In Issue 87-26, *Hedging of Foreign Currency Exposure with a Tandem Currency,* the EITF concluded that a tandem currency cannot be used to hedge a net investment in a foreign subsidiary solely because it is less expensive to do so. In early 1988, this issue was under further consideration as part of an FASB staff project to prepare a TB addressing a number of hedge accounting issues.

A related issue is whether the European Currency Unit (ECU) may be used as a hedge of a net investment. The ECU is a synthetic currency comprising ten currencies in proportions established by the Council of the European Communities (EEC). As of early 1988, its composition was:

0.719	German marks
0.0878	United Kingdom pounds
1.31	French francs
140.00	Italian lire
0.256	Dutch guilders

3.71	Belgian francs
0.14	Luxembourg francs
0.219	Danish kroner
0.00871	Irish pounds
1.15	Greek drachmas

If a U.S. company makes a debt offering payable in ECUs, and if it has net investments in some or all of the foreign countries represented in the ECU basket, it may desire to designate the ECU borrowing as a hedge of such net investments.

The relative significance of each of the currencies in the ECU basket changes with the admission of new entrants in the common market and is subject to periodic realignment every five years (the last change having been made in September, 1984). The realignment introduces a form of *basis risk* (i.e., a mismatch between denomination of the item hedged and the hedging instrument) that does not exist if a specific currency transaction is used to hedge an exposure.

Notwithstanding this apparent obstacle, several approaches to determining whether the ECU is eligible for hedging have been proposed:

• Surrogate method. The ECU is viewed as a foreign currency. If the borrower can demonstrate that a reasonable correlation between the functional currency being hedged and the ECU has existed and is expected to continue, then unrealized gains or losses on the borrowing can be included in the cumulative translation account in equity.

• Composite borrowing method. An ECU borrowing is viewed as a composite borrowing. The borrower theoretically could have obtained the identical amount of proceeds by issuing various notes, each payable in a currency included in the ECU basket, whose relative principal amount equaled the percentage representation of the currency in the ECU basket (ignoring transaction costs and market constraints on certain currencies). Under the allocation method, only the borrowing's unrealized gain or loss attributable to the currencies in the basket that qualify as hedges of specific net investments qualify for hedge accounting. A similar result would obtain from a series of foreign currency borrowings—some of which would serve as hedges of net investments and the balance of which would simply be accounted for as foreign currency transactions.

• Tandem method. Same as composite method except the proponents of this view believe a valid business reason should exist for choosing an ECU borrowing over currency-specific transactions that would act as a hedge. For example, the company may have several European subsidiaries and the net investment in each may not be sufficiently large to justify a fixed-rate, long-term borrowing. Thus, proponents of this view would reject the use of an ECU borrowing if the borrower had a single net investment in a hard currency country such as the U.K. or West Germany—effectively, the decision reached by the EITF in the aforementioned Issue 87-26.

Although this issue was not dealt with formally by the FASB staff or relevant task forces, and the staff and the large firms had mixed views about which rationale, if any, is applicable, some large companies in fact have used the ECU as a hedging currency.

Disclosure

General. SFAS 52 (F60.140–.143) specifies a number of disclosures. In the financial statements or notes, disclosure should be made of aggregate transaction gains or losses affecting the income statement. This disclosure:

1. Includes gains or losses on forward contracts, except those that are hedges.
2. May include gains or losses of certain entities (primarily banks) that are dealers in foreign exchange; if excluded, they are identified separately as dealer gains or losses.

In the statement of changes in equity, in a separate statement, or in notes to the financial statements, the following minimum information concerning changes during the period in the translation adjustments component of shareholders' equity must be disclosed:

1. The beginning and ending amounts of cumulative translation adjustments.
2. The aggregate adjustments for the period.
3. The amount of income taxes allocated to translation adjustments for the period.
4. The amounts transferred from equity and included in net income for the period (that is, those resulting from the sale or liquidation of an investment in a foreign company).

All of this data is shown in the example in Figure 22.3.

If significant, the effect of rate changes subsequent to the balance sheet date and their effect on unsettled balances relating to foreign currency transactions may need to be disclosed.

SEC Recommendations. In 1982, the SEC issued FRR 6 (§ 501.06) expressing its view that more information concerning the nature of a company's foreign operations than is called for by SFAS 52 would be desirable. The SEC stated that in many cases the information obtained from implementing SFAS 52 could be used to develop improved disclosures relating to foreign operations and foreign currency translation effects. The improved disclosures suggested by the SEC include:

1. Information about the functional currencies used to measure significant foreign operations, or to measure the degree of exposure to exchange rate risks, such as the extent to which foreign operations are measured in local currencies versus the reporting currency.
2. Information about operations in highly inflationary economies, including a listing of specific countries.
3. Emphasis on the fact that the foreign currency translation adjustments do not affect current cash flow.
4. Information on how the strengthening or weakening of the dollar affects reported sales and operations, with a quantification of the effects if possible.
5. Discussion of foreign operating results as reflected in local currencies, with the effects of translation noted.

6. Analysis of the effect of exchange rate changes on items such as backlog, interest expense, wages, and cost of raw material purchased from a parent.

OTHER ACCOUNTING MATTERS

Inventories at Lower of Cost or Market

When the books of record are not maintained in the functional currency (as would be the case if the functional currency of a foreign subsidiary is the U.S. dollar but the books are kept in the local currency, here called LC for example purposes), problems can arise in determining lower of replacement cost or market of inventories. To make this computation, the investor carrying amount should be first restated into U.S. dollars, and then compared with market or replacement costs stated in U.S. dollars. This could cause a writedown to be made in the functional currency (U.S. dollar) financial statements even though making the same comparisons in LCs might not show any need for a writedown. Conversely, a writedown might be taken in the LC statements, but because the lower-of-cost-or-market comparison in U.S. dollars does not point to the need for such writedown, the provision in the LC statements would require reversal.

Although this problem usually is related to inventories imported by the foreign operation, locally produced or acquired inventories can be affected as well if the LC declines in relation to the U.S. dollar functional currency. However, the effect of such a decline could be erased by an increase in replacement costs or selling prices (expressed in LCs) that has the effect of causing the functional currency market price to exceed functional currency historical cost.

As with any other inventory writedown to market, the reduced valuation of inventories as stated in the functional currency remains as historical cost until sold or further written down.

Several examples of these convoluted computations are given in SFAS 52 (F60.150–.152).

Debt-for-Equity Swaps

In Issue 87-12, *Foreign Debt-for-Equity Swaps*, the EITF addressed the accounting for an exchange rate difference resulting from a transaction in which a domestic company purchases, at a discount, dollar-denominated debt that is payable by a foreign government or by a company operating in that country. Simultaneously, the domestic company exchanges that debt with the foreign government for foreign currency pegged at or near the official exchange rate. The foreign currency proceeds are then invested in the U.S. company's foreign subsidiary as required by the foreign country's program.

Because the dollar values of the two transactions are different, the EITF concluded that the excess of foreign currency proceeds (reinvested in capital of the foreign subsidiary at the official rate) over the purchase cost of the dollar denominated debt should reduce any long-term capital assets that might be constructed or acquired to comply with the agreement with the foreign government. Absent such an agreement, the excess should be first applied to reduce other long-term capital assets.

If all long-term capital assets are reduced to zero, the remaining excess should be credited to negative goodwill.[6]

In addition, the EITF also concluded that negative goodwill arises in a swap in which (1) a foreign branch has only nominal assets and liabilities other than local currency debt (resulting in an accumulated deficit) and (2) the proceeds from the swap are used to extinguish the local currency debt.

A similar matter involves foreign debt-for-debt swaps, that is, debt denominated in one currency exchanged for debt denominated in another currency, sometimes with additional cash consideration. This usually involves Lesser-Developed-Country (LDC) debt and principally affects commercial banks, as discussed in Chapter 40.

Another matter involves a so-called instantaneous in-substance defeasance, which actually is an arbitrage that takes advantage of interest rate differentials between two countries. This is discussed in Chapter 18.

Goodwill of Equity Investees

The SFAS 52 implementation task force discussed accounting for the goodwill of equity investees and reached the following conclusions. If a U.S. company purchases a foreign business in a purchase combination in which goodwill is generated, that goodwill is pushed down to the foreign subsidiary for purposes of applying SFAS 52. If the foreign currency is deemed to be the functional currency, then any translation effect of applying the current rate to the goodwill amount will be included as part of the cumulative translation adjustments classified in shareholders' equity. Some accountants would contend, however, that the provisions of SFAS 52 apply only to goodwill recorded when a foreign entity buys another foreign entity. This issue may be further reviewed in the FASB's work on consolidations (see Chapter 24).

SFAS 52 Research

Functional Currency. In 1986, the FASB published its first foreign currency research report, *Determining the Functional Currency Under Statement 52* (Evans and Doupnik, 1986a). The authors surveyed the functional currency determination process at U.S. based MNCs, to obtain insights into the approaches taken, the factors used, and the relative weights associated with each factor. In summary:

1. Differences in the functional currencies determined for specific foreign entities appear to reflect substantive differences in those foreign operations.
2. For the respondents as a group, the functional currency decisions in practice appear to be consistent with the guidelines presented in SFAS 52. Questions about situations in which different functional currencies were used for different foreign entities within the same country and in which one foreign entity was split into two or more different functional currencies elicited responses that indicate consistency with the objectives of SFAS 52.

---

[6] In May 1988 the AICPA issued Practice Bulletin 4, *Accounting for Foreign Debt/Equity Swaps*. This bulletin is directed primarily at financial institutions and specifies conditions under which a loss should be recognized. See Chapter 40.

3. The respondents reported using the "six salient economic factors" in determining the functional currencies for their foreign entities. The most heavily weighted factors were related to cash flows and expense and revenue aspects of their foreign operations. These factors appear to discriminate adequately between the foreign operations that are self-contained and those that are an extension of the parent company.

4. Only a small number of firms indicated that they have changed any of their functional currency determinations for reasons other than the classification of an economy as highly inflationary. For the large majority of the respondents, the functional currency determinations have been stable.

5. Almost three fourths of the respondents have a formal procedure (with either one person or a committee charged with the responsibility) to determine the functional currencies for their foreign operations. Generally, the functional currency decisions are centralized in domestic management. A majority of the firms have established a company-wide plan or policy to guide in the determination of functional currencies. More than two thirds of the respondents documented the functional currency decision.

6. For more than three fourths of the respondents, the external auditor specifically reviewed the functional currency determination process. In general, that review covered 100% of the determinations. In very few instances did the firms report any auditor challenges of their determinations.

Risk Management. In 1986, the FASB published a second research report, *Foreign Exchange Risk Management Under Statement 52*, by the same authors (Evans and Doupnik, 1986b). The authors found that although foreign exchange adjustments were treated differently between SFAS 8 and SFAS 52, foreign exchange risk management practices had changed little as a result of issuance of SFAS 52. Those changes that did occur appeared to result from economic factors. However, one accounting-related change in practice involved the use of foreign currency-denominated debt as a hedge of a foreign net investment. SFAS 52 relaxed the accounting criteria for hedging, significantly affecting the foreign financing decisions of a large number of companies. Another change noted by the research report was the increased use of forward contracts for short-term adjustments of foreign currency positions.

Equity Analysis. In early 1987, the FASB published a third research report, *Accounting for the Translation of Foreign Currencies: The Effects of Statement 52 on Equity Analysis* (Griffin and Castanias). The authors provide insights about the use by equity security analysts of financial information based on the effects of SFAS 52 exchange rate changes.

Significant among the authors' findings are:

1. Most analysts rely on relative valuation approaches, that is, approaches based on relative price-to-earnings ratios, to assess stock values.

2. Analysts appeared to have revised their earnings forecasts relatively more frequently when changes in accounting from SFAS 8 to SFAS 52 were occurring.

3. Analysts generally agree with the objectives of SFAS 52 and understand differences between whether the U.S. dollar or the local currency is used as the functional currency.

4. Analysts seldom adjust reported net income to incorporate translation adjustment amounts now deferred in shareholders' equity.

International Accounting Standard

The IASC issued IAS 21, *Accounting for the Effects of Changes in Foreign Exchange Rates* (AC 9021), effective for calendar year 1985. Like SFAS 52, the statement deals with both accounting for transactions in foreign currencies in the financial statements of an enterprise and with translation of financial statements of foreign operations for inclusion in the financial statements of the reporting enterprise.

IAS 21 provides that foreign currency transactions should be recorded using the exchange rate at the time of the transaction, and when reported in subsequent balance sheets, using the closing rate. Exchange differences arising upon settlement of monetary items, or upon reporting short-term monetary items using a different exchange rate, are to be recognized in income.

Exchange differences arising from reporting long-term foreign currency monetary items at a different exchange rate would normally be recognized in income. However, such exchange differences may be deferred and amortized over the remaining life of the related monetary items, except that an exchange loss may not be deferred if it is reasonable to expect that recurring exchange losses will arise on that item in the future.

Exchange differences related to intercompany monetary items that are, in effect, a part of the parent's net investment, and those that relate to loans and transactions that provide a hedge against a net investment, are to be recorded in shareholders' interests.

In dealing with the translation of financial statements, a distinction is made between a foreign company and a foreign operation that is integral to the operations of the parent. This distinction results in IAS 21 achieving essentially the same translation results as are achieved by the functional currency approach of SFAS 52. However, in translating the statements of a foreign company, the income statement may be translated at either the closing rate or the rates at the dates of the transactions. Differences resulting from translating the income statement at other than the closing rate (the balance sheet must always be translated at the closing rate) may be recorded in income or in shareholders' interests.

In translating the financial statements of a foreign operation, a monetary/non-monetary approach is used, with exchange differences included in income. Exceptions to this rule include deferral and amortization of exchange differences related to long-term monetary items, as discussed earlier, and the treatment of exchange differences arising from severe devaluation that affect liabilities arising from the recent acquisition of assets invoiced in a foreign currency. In the latter case, the exchange difference may be included in the carrying amount of the asset acquired.

AUDITING CONSIDERATIONS

Objectives

The objective of the audit of the translation process is to assure that the requirements of SFAS 52 have been met. To accomplish that objective, auditors must have a working familiarity with the requirements of the statement, and they also must have in-depth understanding of the nature of the company's business. They must know what is included in the foreign subsidiary's accounts so that they can be sure that the nuances of the SFAS 52 have been properly considered.

Approach

The audit of the translation process requires a substantive approach (see Chapter 7). Auditors will want to be satisfied that the appropriate exchange rate has been used, and they will verify that the proper rates have been applied to the foreign subsidiary balances.

In an MNC, different auditors may be responsible for different segments of the work—although commonly they will be part of the same firm or group of firms. Because the auditor must have a thorough understanding of the makeup of the subsidiary's accounts, it often makes more sense for the translation tests to be performed by the individual who is responsible for the audit of the subsidiary in the field.

Audit Reporting

Translated Financial Statements. When translating foreign financial statements for purposes of inclusion in consolidated financial statements, those foreign statements are effectively restated in units of the reporting currency (e.g., U.S. dollars). Sometimes the auditor is asked to issue a report on those translated amounts, or on a consolidating schedule containing those amounts.

Most auditors will refuse to give a "fairly presents" opinion on a subsidiary's translated financial statements because of the artificialities introduced by the translation process. They argue that they can only express a "fairly presents" opinion on the subsidiary's local currency financial statements, because that is the currency used by the subsidiary to transact its business and keep its records.

A possible way to deal with this problem is to present the subsidiary's statements in two columns—one in local currency and one translated into dollars. Thus, the subsidiary's auditors can express their opinion as to the fair presentation of the financial statements of the subsidiary expressed in local currency, and can add a paragraph to their report expressing an opinion as to whether the translation complies with the requirements of SFAS 52.

However, if the financial statements of a foreign company are to be presented separately, standing alone, they may be translated using the current rate for all balance sheet and income statement amounts. For example, a foreign company reporting to its shareholders in the United States may find that its financial statements will be more meaningful to readers in the United States if a version of the statements are shown in U.S. dollars. All years' statements shown should be translated at the exchange rate in effect at the date of the most current balance sheet. Such *translations for convenience* are specifically exempted from the requirements of SFAS 52 (F60.101).

Financial Statements Prepared for Use in Other Countries. Occasionally a U.S. auditor is asked to report on financial statements of a U.S. company prepared in conformity with accounting principles of another country. Such reports are usually for distribution outside the United States, but they also may receive limited U.S.

distribution. This situation is most frequently encountered in reporting on U.S. subsidiaries of foreign enterprises, and when a U.S. company decides to raise capital in a foreign country's public markets.

SAS 51, *Reporting on Financial Statements Prepared for Use in Other Countries* (AU 534), describes the applicable standards, including the need to be knowledgeable regarding the accounting principles in the foreign country and the need to expand U.S. GAAS to cover assertions to be made in the auditor's report that are not covered by U.S. GAAS.

The auditor may report using the U.S. form of auditor's report, appropriately modified; or he may issue the standard report form used in the foreign country if he is in a position to make the assertions contained therein. If the enterprise will issue financial statements both in the United States (in conformity with U.S. GAAP) and in a foreign country (conforming with that country's GAAP), a separate auditor's report should be used for each set of financial statements.

23

Business Combinations, Takeovers, and Buy-Outs

THE BUSINESS OF MERGING BUSINESSES

Businesses have combined as long as man has been involved in some form of organized commercial activity. One reason such transactions are the subject of keen interest is that their magnitude is generally much greater than that of most other transactions. In any particular industry, the sale of an entire company can have significant repercussions—on competition, on the market mechanism, and on industry practice.

In a purchase business combination, the purchaser is referred to as the *acquiring company* or the *acquirer*, while the seller is referred to as the *acquired company* or the *acquiree*. But when the business combination is accounted for as a pooling of interests, one company does not, in concept, *acquire* another, so different terms are used. A pooling of interests represents a *combining* of shareholder interests, the companies to be *pooled* are termed *combining companies*, the resulting entity is the *combined company*, and the formerly separate entities after the combination are the *combinee companies*.

Such specialized terminology is mostly a matter of semantics. Whether a business combination is a purchase or a pooling of interests is based on the precise circumstances attendant to the combination; the facts dictate the accounting method. This is so even when Goliath acquires David in a pooling. In this chapter, when a combination is discussed, it will often be in terms of a larger company acquiring a smaller one. Also, when discussing poolings, the company that issues the stock, or that is the initiator of the transaction, is often referred to for convenience as the acquirer, notwithstanding the semantics described above.

Background

The merger period that marked the introduction of the phrase *pooling of interests* started shortly after World War II and has been more or less continuous up to the present. The pooling notion first appeared in unofficial correspondence of the AICPA in late 1945 (Wyatt, 1963, p. 23), when a pooling of interests was considered to have occurred in a merger between two previously unrelated companies of comparable size. However, no accounting standard resulted. It was not until the latter part of 1950 that the AICPA Committee on Accounting Procedure (CAP), the forerunner of the APB, issued ARB 40. That bulletin distinguished between the accounting for (1) a purchase (involving enterprises disproportionate in size and in postmerger ownership interest, and having a discontinuity of management and dissimilarity in operations); and (2) a pooling of interests (involving a stock-for-stock exchange between two previously unrelated companies of comparable size). This distinction failed to be sufficiently definitive because numerous mergers did not fit easily into either category.

The CAP tried again in January 1957 with ARB 48. But this bulletin was really no more than a rewording of ARB 40.

A significant increase in merger activity occurred during the early 1960s, the so-called conglomerate era. During this period the size test criterion was so stretched that combinations of 100 to 1 were treated as poolings, and the practice of part-purchase, part-pooling accounting developed. This type of accounting was popularly applied to mergers using combined stock and cash (or other form of securities). Literally, part of the combination was accounted for as a purchase, and the balance as a pooling of interests.

Certain abuses also became evident. The successor of two pooled enterprises would occasionally sell off a significant operating asset of the smaller predecessor entity and obtain a dramatic boost in earnings. There is certainly nothing abusive about such a transaction normally, but when such sales occurred soon after a pooling was consummated and the profits from the sale sustained a continued earnings growth by the combined company, skepticism grew.

Earnings increases were also obtained by *retroactive pooling*, in which companies could merge after the year end of the principal company and retroactively pool their income before the combined annual report for the year was issued. In at least one such arrangement a June merger in the year subsequent to that being reported was treated as if the merger had occurred on or before the previous December 31, and financial statements were then issued for the combined enterprise. This practice provided an opportunity to locate a pooling partner after it was determined that the results of operations for the year were poor and needed augmentation. In the view of many, this was the most serious pooling abuse.

Still another procedure was to provide an earnings or market price contingency in the merger agreement, under which additional consideration would be received by the merged company's shareholders at a future date if certain earnings levels of the merged company, or market prices of the successor company's stock, were subsequently achieved. Some believed that this kind of transaction did not represent the marriage underlying a true pooling; it was more like a conditional dowry.

Accounting Concepts

Business combinations are normally complex transactions. Although there appears to be no conceptual difference between the purchase of an asset and the acquisition of a business (which some view as simply the purchase of a basket of assets), in practice the acquisition of a business creates a host of problems and decision points. Among the things acquired are operating or manufacturing processes; management, staff, and line employees; a marketing, manufacturing, and administrative structure; and a company and product names. One problem is that some of these assets are not recorded in the accounts of the acquired business. Further, some of these assets are not directly valued even when they specifically have been purchased. This aspect of GAAP frequently results in the creation of an intangible asset that accountants call *goodwill,* discussed in later sections under that name. These are some of the problems that attend a business combination when it is accounted for as a purchase.

But under certain circumstances, business combinations are accounted for as poolings of interests. Although there are many features that can be argued, most of the theoretical debate has focused on the medium of exchange and on the size of the companies.

Medium of Exchange. Some accountants argue that the medium of exchange used in a business combination affects the nature of the transaction. They contend that paying cash results in a net outflow of resources, since the cash goes to the shareholders of the acquired corporation and thus ends up outside the combined corporate entity. However, if the same combination is consummated by the issuance of common stock, no net resources are disbursed outside the combined corporate entity, and this would be a pooling of interests without a new basis of accounting.

This argument may put form over substance and is not particularly persuasive. Indeed, ARB 48 stated that the distinction between a purchase and a pooling rested on the circumstances of the combination, not its legal form. Nonetheless, when previously voting common shareowners exchange their stock for voting common stock of another entity, there is continuity of ownership by both sets of shareowners, and this notion is the theoretical justification for pooling-of-interests accounting.

Size of Companies. Some accountants believe the size of the components is critical in the purchase or pooling question. By one definition, a pooling of interests can only occur between entities of roughly equal size. The notion of pooling views the combining companies as if nothing had changed other than joining them; neither supposedly has become dominant in the combined company. If near equality of size were a criterion, the combining of General Motors with a small corporate parts supplier could hardly be considered a pooling of interests, since General Motors would obviously be the dominant company. Yet these kinds of combinations have been and still are accounted for as poolings of interests.

APB Action. With the pooling criteria of ARB 48 eroded, abuses occurring, and criticism coming from the SEC, investment analysts, and financial writers, the APB decided to act. Thus the present accounting rules, APB 16, *Business Combinations* (B50), and APB 17, *Intangible Assets* (I60), were issued in August 1970. By then, however, the conglomerate era, at which the opinions had been aimed, was practically over. In spite of criticisms, multiple interpretations, and some fine tuning by the APB, FASB, and SEC (see Appendix 23 for a listing of changes to these standards), APBs 16 and 17 remain the authoritative literature on business combinations.

The introductory text in APB 16 describes the nature and acceptance of two methods of accounting: purchase and pooling. In practice, if certain transactions qualified as poolings, anything else has to be a purchase. Thus, the problem APB 16 addresses is how to identify a pooling of interests. By making the definition rigorous, the APB also eliminated part-purchase, part-pooling accounting. But by failing to focus on purchase accounting, the APB neglected the possibility that companies might favor it because it could benefit subsequent results of operations in numerous situations.

POOLING-OF-INTERESTS ACCOUNTING

A business combination, to be accounted for as a pooling of interests, must meet all the conditions in APB 16 (B50.105–.107). Those conditions are grouped into (1) attributes of the combining companies, (2) manner of combining interests, and (3) absence of planned transactions. Each group is supported by two or more criteria.

Combining Company Attributes

A pooling of interests must bring about the combination of two or more unrelated groups of shareholder interests having separate operations. This condition is fulfilled by meeting two criteria: autonomy and independence.

Autonomy

Each of the combining companies is autonomous and each has not been a subsidiary or division of another corporation within two years before the plan of combination is initiated. [B50.105(a)]

A company newly incorporated within two years before initiation of a merger is poolable, provided its shareholders are not also major shareholders of the other combining company.

In addition, pooling accounting may be permissible for a subsidiary of a personal holding company. In a 1971 interpretation (B50.606), the AICPA stated that legal form may sometimes be ignored. Although the personal holding company is technically a parent corporation and in many cases a parent-subsidiary relationship does in fact exist, there are other cases in which the personal holding company is a convenience established for tax reasons, and the subsidiaries are in fact operated by the owners as if the personal holding company did not exist.

A wholly owned subsidiary may issue its parent company's voting common stock in a pooling, provided the parent itself meets all the pooling conditions as if it has issued stock directly. This approach is permitted because the parent company and its subsidiary are viewed as one autonomous group.

The initiation of a business combination is defined in B50.105(a) as that date when the major terms of the exchange offer are publicly announced or made known to at least one set of combining shareholders. The definition is important, since another criterion (B50.106), discussed in the section entitled "Single Transaction" below, places a time limit on an uncompleted business combination transaction.

Independence

Each of the combining companies is independent of the other combining companies. [B50.105(b)]

No combining company may have an investment in another combining company of more than 10% of its outstanding voting common stock. A corporation that engages in a step acquisition of another's outstanding common stock is precluded from using pooling-of-interests accounting if more than 10% and less than 90% of the other company's voting stock is acquired in any step. If a business combination is initiated and the acquiring company already holds more than 10% of the company to be acquired, pooling accounting may not be used even if some of the investment is sold prior to consummation. One purpose of this criterion was to stop part-purchase, part-pooling accounting.

Operating Company. APB 16 (B50.105(a)) does not require a combining company in a business combination to be an operating entity, but the SEC seems to have attached a third attribute criterion: Any company acquired must be an operating enterprise and have "significant operations (i.e., something other than nominal)." With respect to a large timber company acquiring another timber company having an extensive stand of maturing timber but only nominal sales and operations, the SEC staff deemed the acquiree other than an operating company and insisted on the use of purchase accounting, with substantially all the purchase cost being assigned the standing timber (*CPA Journal*, June 1974, p. 16). But the SEC staff failed to precisely define what constitutes significant operations, so care must be exercised in the acquisition of any nonoperating company for which pooling accounting is desired.

Manner of Combining Interests

The pooling method contemplates the merging of separate stockholder interests of two or more companies into one combined group of stockholders. This condition is fulfilled by meeting seven criteria: (1) single transaction, (2) exchange of shares, (3) change in equity interest, (4) treasury stock, (5) ratio of shareholders' interests, (6) proportionate voting rights, and (7) contingencies.

Single Transaction

The combination is effected in a single transaction or is completed in accordance with a specific plan within one year after the plan is initiated. [B50.106(a)]

A revision in a major term of the plan, such as the ratio of exchange, would create a new plan and initiate a new one-year period. If shares exchanged in accordance with the terms of the old agreement are not adjusted to the new terms and more than 10% of the shares of the company to be acquired have already been exchanged, pooling accounting simply may not be used. The acquiring company must obtain 90% of the *total shares* to be exchanged in a single transaction, in accordance with the new terms, to use pooling accounting.

If a delay in consummation beyond the one-year limit is caused by government proceedings, such as an antitrust suit or the need for regulatory agency merger approval, the time limit criterion is deemed not violated. Delays caused by the need for SEC registration of securities, on the other hand, are not an acceptable reason.

APB 16 does not clearly define what constitutes consummation. As a result, in late 1970 the AICPA issued an interpretation that states:

> A plan of combination is consummated on the date the combination is completed, that is, the date assets are transferred to the issuing corporation. The quantitative measurements specified in paragraphs .105(b) and .106(b) are, therefore, made on the date the combination is completed. If they and all of the other conditions specified in paragraphs .105–.107 are met on that date, the combination must be accounted for by the pooling-of-interests method. [B50.512]

There is no theoretical reason for the one-year criterion as a condition of pooling. The time limit was probably included because of the concern that consummation might be delayed until certain market conditions exist, in effect guaranteeing a market price. Such a guarantee, directly given, would invalidate a pooling.

Exchange of Shares

A corporation offers and issues only common stock with rights identical to those of the majority of its outstanding voting common stock in exchange for substantially all of the voting common stock interest of another company at the date the plan of combination is consummated. [B50.106(b)]

Voting common stock. Only common stock may be exchanged. Thus, pro rata distribution of warrants of the issuing corporation to stockholders of a combining company would ordinarily require the combination to be accounted for as a purchase.

In some circumstances, either the issuing company or the combinee company in a business combination to be accounted for as a pooling of interests does not have a majority class of common stock that has voting control as is required to meet this criterion. In such circumstances, the EITF has concluded (in Issue 87-27, *Poolings of Companies That Do Not Have a Controlling Class of Common Stock*) that pooling accounting may be used in the following circumstances:

1. If a *combinee* does not have a majority class of common stock that has voting control, the issuing company must exchange its common shares (of the class that has voting control) for substantially all (90%) of the voting common *and* other voting stock of that combinee.
2. If the *issuing* company does not have a majority class of common stock that has voting control, the issuing company must first exchange its common shares for sufficient shares of its other voting stock (so as to create a controlling class of common stock) prior to or at the date of the combination. The EITF has stated that such action does not violate the requirements of the condition in B50.106(c) relating to changes in equity interest in contemplation of a pooling (discussed later herein).

90% test. "Substantially all" means 90%. This 90% minimum must also take into account common stock investments in the acquiring company held by the acquired company. Depending on the relationship of the outstanding shares of the two companies and the exchange ratio, it is possible that an investment in less than 10%

	Company A	Company B
Shares outstanding	1,000,000	500,000

Assume company B holds 75,000 company shares. Assume company A is acquiring company B in a common-stock-for-common-stock exchange, one share of A for one share of B. For company B, the following computation must be made:

1. Company A shares held by company B in terms of company B shares (at ratio of 1 to 1) ... 75,000

2. Total company B shares ... 500,000
   Less: share equivalent above ... 75,000

   Number of shares of company B considered as exchanged ... 425,000

3. 90% of company B shares ... 450,000

The number of company B shares considered as exchanged must equal or exceed the number representing 90% of all company B shares outstanding. Because 90% is not attained, pooling accounting may not be used.

FIG. 23.1　Effect of Intercorporate Investment by Acquired Company in Acquiring Company

of the shares of the acquiring company could prohibit the use of pooling accounting. An example is shown in Figure 23.1.

When 90% or more of the voting common stock of the acquired corporation is obtained, the 10% or less not exchanged may remain outstanding as a minority interest, or these shareholders may be eliminated with cash or other securities. However, a single shareholder may not exchange shares for part of his interest and accept cash for the remainder (a *partial dissenter*) (B50.586).

This interpretation is aimed primarily at control group shareholders, as there will be no way of knowing whether a small shareholder contemplating a tender offer tenders only some of his shares. This kind of splitting ordinarily would not be significant enough to prevent attainment of the 90% threshold.

Prior to consummation, one shareholder may privately buy out another for cash or other consideration. As long as this agreement is separate from the merger contract and is not a condition of the merger, it will not upset a pooling. Such agreements have occasionally been negotiated to take care of a potential dissenter who holds more than 10% of the shares of the company to be acquired.

In making a tender offer for the voting common stock of another company, the tendering company frequently cannot be assured of obtaining 90% of the stock. As a result, the tendering of at least 90% of the shares is made a condition of the offer if the acquirer intends to achieve pooling accounting.

An unusual arrangement relating to a determination of the 10% test has been considered by the EITF in Issue 86-10, *Pooling With 10 Percent Cash Payout Determined by Lottery*. In the proposed transaction, the issuing company offers stock, but the acquisition agreement indicates that cash is to be paid to shareholders for fractional shares and to others electing to receive cash (dissenters) for not more than 10% of the total shares of the acquired company. If the sum of the fractional shares cashed out and other requests for cash exceed 10%, a lottery is to be held to reduce the cash paid to dissenters for no more than 10% of the shares.

The EITF reached a consensus that the 10% cash lottery feature would not preclude a pooling provided that all other pooling requirements were met, because an offer to issue stock for all or substantially all (defined as 90% in this criterion) of the common stock of the acquired company had been made.

More than two companies may be involved in a business combination, but if pooling accounting is contemplated, the 10% and 90% tests must be met by all companies. In applying the 90% test, all intercompany investments are treated as outstanding but not as exchanged (B50.641–.644).

In actual practice, it is not all that clear how the 90% test is met in multiple company combinations intended to be poolings, including cases where only two companies are combining but a third company is formed to effect the transaction. In Issue 87-16, *Whether the 90 Percent Test for a Pooling of Interests Is Applied Separately to Each Company or on a Combined Basis,* the EITF did not reach a consensus, noting that the choice of the issuer of the common stock in a pooling is supposedly a matter of convenience; but in reality there are legal differences, and the 90% test is not always met if it is hypothesized that a different combining company is the issuer. The main value of this discussion by the EITF was its reaffirmation of the method of computing tainted treasury stock by combining both the issuer's treasury stock and the combinee's equivalent shares (in the manner in which the SEC staff has interpreted ASR 146 (FRR § 201)).

Restricted shares. The acquiring company may issue shares that are not freely tradeable because they have not been registered with the SEC; and there cannot be a promise of future registration of such shares, only a best-efforts attempt, because the registration might not become effective. However, even though recipients of restricted shares can "dribble" the shares onto the market, it would be wise to provide them with an opportunity to "piggy-back" (i.e., be carried along) when the acquiring company subsequently registers and sells securities following the pooling. Any restriction other than SEC registration of common stock issued in a merger will most likely invalidate a pooling.

According to TB 85-5, *Issues Relating to Accounting for Business Combinations . . . Identical Common Shares for a Pooling of Interests* (B50.541A–.541B), if the issuer retains a right of first refusal to repurchase shares issued in a business combination, such shares do not have rights identical to those of the majority of its outstanding shares, and pooling accounting is prohibited. This subject had been discussed by the EITF in Issue 84-38, and the consensus was the opposite. The FASB staff and the SEC observer disapproved of this consensus, giving rise to coverage in TB 85-5.

APB 16 does not discuss the effect of restrictions on purchases of common stock of the acquiring company subsequent to consummation. Presumably, under the theory that shareholders cannot be restricted in their actions as part of the combination agreement (except that the SEC has imposed a holding period restriction, discussed later under "SEC No-Sell-off Rule"), any subsequent purchase restriction also would invalidate pooling-of-interests accounting. However, in Issue 87-15, *Effect of a Standstill Agreement on Pooling-of-Interests Accounting,* the EITF concluded that such an agreement (referred to as a "standstill agreement") with a minority shareholder, if not made in contemplation of the company entering into a pooling transaction, would not preclude pooling accounting. However, if the shareholder would own more than 10% of the combined company (post-merger), pooling is precluded because this would be a restriction that would violate the pooling criteria, and would be greater than the 10% allowed for pooling violations. Even if the shareholder has less than 10%, any other pooling violations could make the total violations exceed 10%, precluding pooling.

Other acquiree securities. The acquiring company has several choices for dealing with securities of the acquired company other than voting common stock. They may remain outstanding, they may be redeemed for cash, or they may be exchanged for similar or other equity or debt securities. In the normal case, they have no effect on a pooling transaction. However, when outstanding securities other than the majority class of voting common stock have features that permit their conversion into voting common stock and are essentially residual equity interests, the EITF (with the concurrence of the SEC staff) has stated in Issue 85-14, *Securities That Can Be Acquired for Cash in a Pooling of Interests,* that only the majority class of voting common stock may be exchanged therefor. The SEC staff believes that warrants and options must be exchanged for similar rights of the acquiree, and the EITF has gone along even though this is not specified by APB 16. APB 16 has been interpreted to allow warrants (or cash or debt) to be used to acquire up to 10% of the common stock of the combining company, as long as the other conditions for the 90% tests are met. Warrants may also be issued in exchange for warrants, but the issued warrants may not permit purchase of a greater number of shares than could be obtained if the original warrants were exercised and exchanged (B50.534–.538).

For convertible securities, a case-by-case assessment must be made as some such securities are not, in effect, residual equity interests. In addition, according to APB 16, if the acquired company had exchanged other equity or debt securities for its voting common stock within two years of initiation of the merger or between initiation and consummation dates, voting common stock also must be issued by the acquiring company for such other securities (B50.106(b)(7)).

Change in Equity Interest

None of the combining companies changes the equity interest of the voting common stock in contemplation of effecting the combination either within two years before the plan of combination is initiated or between the dates the combination is initiated and consummated; changes in contemplation of effecting the combination may include distributions to stockholders and additional issuances, exchanges, and retirements of securities. [B50.106(c)]

This criterion relates to voting common stock transactions and other net worth changes between the companies and their shareholders before consummation. This criterion is framed in terms that relate to capital stock companies. However, in practice there has been a general understanding that an entity in a legal form other than a capital stock company such as, for example, a cooperative or mutual company, could be a party to a business combination to be accounted for as a pooling of interests as long as all the applicable pooling criteria are met. Confirming this view and taking it one step further, in Technical Bulletin 85-5, *Issues Relating to Accounting for Business Combinations ... Poolings of Interests by Mutual and Cooperative Enterprises* (B50.653–.654), the FASB states that the conversion of a mutual or cooperative enterprise to stock ownership is not considered to be a prohibited change in equity interest and should not preclude a pooling of interests, even if it is done within two years prior to the combination.

A dividend paid in cash or other assets by any of the combining companies to shareholders before consummation will not invalidate a pooling as long as the dividend follows its own *normal* historical pattern. For example, a company to be acquired might determine *normal* by looking to the dividend equivalent that the acquiring company paid to its own shareholders before consummation. Extreme care must be used in applying this provision, since the APB could not have intended that a company, perhaps a closely held company that has never paid a dividend, could be allowed to disburse a large part of its assets to pay that dividend equivalent.

In a pooling, those assets used in the operation of the business would seem to be most important. Thus the liquidation into cash of the acquiree's significant portfolio of short-term investments representing excess funds would not preclude pooling treatment, nor would a provision in the merger agreement that the sole stockholder of a combining company may buy an insurance policy on his life for its cash surrender value.

This criterion (B50.106(c)) may originally have been included to prevent companies from adjusting their outstanding stock to meet a size test. Later the APB abandoned any size test, but it neglected to remove the criterion. Some have suggested that the criterion was retained to prevent acquired companies from "cashing out" dissenters before consummation, or to avoid a pro rata cash distribution instead of all stock.

Treasury Stock

Each of the combining companies reacquires shares of voting common stock only for purposes other than business combinations, and no company reacquires more than a normal number of shares between the dates the plan of combination is initiated and consummated. [B50.106(d)]

"For purposes other than business combinations" means for stock option and compensation plans and other recurring distributions, provided a systematic pattern of reacquisition has been established at least two years before the plan of combination is initiated. Treasury shares that do not meet this criterion are *tainted.* This criterion, which may be the most interpreted criterion in APB 16, was originally demanded by the SEC to govern situations in which the consideration paid is treasury stock, since the SEC tends to view such consideration as the equivalent of cash.

Treasury stock acquisitions by acquired companies to avert the need for buy-outs of potential dissenters to a merger transaction is another target of this rule. An AICPA interpretation (B50.562–.568) approved by the APB and the SEC permits a company to hold up to 10% tainted shares. The tainted shares are measured against the total shares to be issued in any combination to be accounted for as a pooling. The 10% test applies to all merger parties, and must cover all pooling violations. For the acquired company, the test is applied by restating treasury shares in terms of the acquiring company's stock using the combination ratio of exchange. If the merger parties individually have 10% or less tainted shares, but more than 10% in the aggregate, the merger may not be accounted for as a pooling.

Tainted shares held for two years or more become untainted. Other than by passage of time, a tainted share problem can only be cured by resale of the shares or the issuance or sale of an equivalent quantity of new shares. Formal retirement does not constitute a cure.

A systematic pattern is evidenced by the orderly, but not necessarily equal, acquisition of shares over a period of time. Such acquisition should relate in some manner to the anticipated requirements for an acceptable purpose, but this relationship need only exist at the date the shares are purchased. At a subsequent date there need only be a reasonable expectation that the shares will be issued eventually.

Acceptable purposes, according to the SEC, include purchases to meet share requirements for stock option plans, stock purchase plans, stock compensation plans, convertible debentures, convertible stock, and warrants. Another acceptable purpose for acquiring shares is to meet stock dividend requirements (paid, declared, or planned) considered to be a recurring distribution. A paid, declared, or planned stock dividend is considered *recurring* when at least one stock dividend similar in amount was paid in each of the two preceding years.

In addition, the SEC concluded that treasury stock purchased from a corporate "raider" is tainted, as it does not meet the "acceptable purposes" guidelines. Further, if a company reacquires warrants to purchase its common shares, such warrants would be viewed as "tainted treasury shares" for purposes of applying the 10% rule.

The SEC further states that it is not necessary to meet the systematic pattern test for purchase business combinations, or for existing contingent share agreements from a prior business combination, or to meet contractual obligations. To the extent reissued, such as in a purchase business combination, tainted treasury shares are cured in a last-in, first-out (LIFO) sequence. In addition, if tainted treasury shares on hand are less than 10% of the stock issued in a pooling they become untainted assuming there are no other violations to be covered by the "10% catch-all rule" discussed later.

Under certain conditions, tainted shares purchased subsequent to a pooling combination may upset the pooling. The number of shares that may be acquired increases as the pooling consummation date becomes more remote. For a detailed evaluation of this complex criterion, readers should refer to "Implementing SEC Rules on Effect of Treasury Stock Transactions on Accounting for Business Combinations—ASR Nos. 146 and 146A," issued by the SEC in conjunction with the AICPA (*Journal of Accountancy*, November 1974, pp. 76–82).

ASRs 146 and 146A (FRR § 201) and the unofficial AICPA/SEC interpretation services discuss in considerable detail the effect of treasury stock transactions on the pooling-of-interests criterion (B50.106(d)). The rules on the treasury stock criterion are almost pharisaical and in many respects extremely arbitrary.[1] If future pooling

---

[1] The rules on treasury stock acquisition, tainting, and untainting are very convoluted as a result of the SEC's issuance of FRR § 201. Arthur Andersen & Co. became so concerned over the SEC's adding rules to the professional literature that it filed suit against the SEC. The suit never came to trial, and the SEC issued the second release that retained the rigid requirements of the initial release, provided a few interpretations in sensitive areas, and passed the problem to the FASB, which has chosen to avoid further action.

After this skirmish with the accounting profession, the SEC thought it advisable to inform the world of its overall support of the FASB and issued ASR 150 (FRR § 101). ASR 150 stated, in effect, that the SEC regards promulgations of the FASB as GAAP. Instead of assuaging the profession's feelings, this brought another lawsuit from Arthur Andersen, alleging that the SEC was violating the Administrative Procedures

accounting is desired, all treasury stock transactions should be monitored. Orderly resale of tainted treasury shares, depending on their age, should be seriously considered.

Ratio of Shareholder Interests

The ratio of the interest of an individual common stockholder to those of other common stockholders in a combining company remains the same as a result of the exchange of stock to effect the combination. [B50.106(e)]

Each shareholder of the prospective merging companies must receive the same exchange terms. A problem occasionally arises when a control group exists in a publicly held company to be acquired. Normally, the control group will negotiate the merger agreement, and then a tender offer is made by the acquiring company to the noncontrolling group of shareholders. To encourage the noncontrolling group to tender, they may be offered a better ratio of exchange than is offered the control group. Although this is in no sense an abuse, it precludes the use of pooling accounting. To meet this criterion, all stockholders must be offered the same ratio of exchange. (For the meaning of "control group," see the discussion of the "SEC no-sell-off rule" later in this chapter.)

Proportionate Voting Rights

The voting rights to which the common stock ownership interests in the resulting combined corporation are entitled are exercisable by the stockholders; the stockholders are neither deprived of nor restricted in exercising those rights for a period. [B50.106(f)]

No special voting provisions, such as the transfer to a new voting trust of shares issued in a merger, are permitted. Each shareholder must have the same proportionate voting rights after the merger as before.

Contingencies

The combination is resolved at the date the plan is consummated and no provisions of the plan relating to the issue of securities or other considerations are pending. [B50.106(g)]

The contingencies criterion attempts to prevent the use of an *earn-out* in a pooling of interests (which was one of the more serious abuses of the period prior to APB 16), and it has been the subject of a considerable amount of interpretation.

Neither earnings contingencies nor market price contingencies or any combination of the two are permitted to exist at or after the consummation date. Contingency provisions in which shares issuable in a business combination are reserved or escrowed to back up *general management warranties* are acceptable. For example, a warranty by the management of an acquired company that the assets exist, that they

---

Act by the wholesale adoption of all FASB rules as SEC rules. That lawsuit failed to achieve the injunction sought, and FRR § 101 is still operative.

are carried on a specified basis, and that all liabilities have been accrued and/or otherwise disclosed, is a general representation.

An AICPA interpretation (B50.613–.619) permits up to 10% of the shares that are to be issued in a pooling to be held in escrow for a period not extending beyond the date of the first auditor's report following consummation. Such an escrow may include unspecified contingencies. Reservations of stock in addition to the 10% general provision are accepted in practice if specific asset valuation or potential liability problems exist. Examples are potential inventory obsolescence problems or additional income taxes that may be payable as a result of an IRS review of income tax returns. The additional percentage of shares reserved must relate to the amount of the asset valuation problem or the additional liability that may be incurred. Some contingencies, such as income tax or legal matters, may not be resolved for years. Thus the period for specific contingencies is permitted to extend beyond the date of the first subsequent auditor's report.

Although the rules regarding contingencies seem to have become more flexible in recent years, the SEC staff can be expected to scrutinize contingency provisions in specific transactions. The SEC staff has indicated that its criteria in evaluating the propriety of shares escrowed for a specific contingency follow the guidelines of SFAS 5, *Accounting for Contingencies* (C59.104). In the staff's view, such a contingency should, at as minimum, meet the "reasonably possible" test of SFAS 5. Literal compliance with B50.106(g) may be irrelevant if the provisions of SFAS 5 are not also met.

If shares are returned from escrow, they merely reduce consideration (stock) given; the expense remains as a charge to combined operations.

Employment contracts for acquired company personnel may be a condition in a merger to be accounted for as a pooling. If such plans are for stockholder employees who hold some nominal company position, they would probably be viewed as a form of earnings contingency and would likely invalidate a proposed pooling. Furthermore, bonus arrangements based on future results are not ruled out, as long as the compensation is not a camouflage for additional consideration under the plan of combination. Because fringe benefits are normally included in any compensation package, pension plans, profit-sharing plans, retirement plans, and other similar arrangements do not automatically rule out pooling accounting.

Employment agreements take many forms and are limited only by the imagination of those involved in the negotiations; thus precise rules cannot be given for determining whether they are genuine compensation or disguised additional consideration. Among the factors that will influence this determination are (1) compensation of other executives of the combined companies with similar responsibilities, (2) previous compensation, and (3) compensation of executives in other companies engaged in similar businesses. Note, however, that an employment agreement may not provide for an employee forfeiting his shares if he breaks the contract.

Absence of Planned Transactions

The third condition required for a pooling of interests is the absence of planned transactions. Holding that certain transactions after merger may raise doubts about whether a true combining of existing shareholder interests occurred, the APB specified three types of postcombination transactions that were presumed to proscribe pooling treatment. The SEC later added a fourth.

Reacquisition of Stock Issued

The combined corporation does not agree directly or indirectly to retire or reacquire all or part of the common stock issued to effect the combination. [B50.107(a)]

Any condition in a merger agreement that requires a shareholder of the combined company to sell or not sell shares is a violation of this criterion. Subject to restrictions inherent in the stock itself, such as a need for SEC registration, any shareholder should be able to arrange for the sale of his securities to another party after consummation, or hold them, as he wishes (subject to SEC sell-off limitations).

Other Financial Agreements

The combined corporation does not enter into other financial arrangements for the benefit of the former stockholders of a combining company, such as a guaranty of loans secured by stock issued in the combination, which in effect negates the exchange of equity securities. [B50.107(b)]

Under certain circumstances, an acquiring company may make a loan to an acquired company prior to consummation. Such a loan must be in accordance with normal commercial terms (i.e., not unusually liberal). Basically, any form of special benefit to a shareholder of a combining company is precluded, such as selective stock option or compensation plans, as previously noted.

Asset Dispositions

The combined corporation does not intend or plan to dispose of a significant part of the assets of the combining companies within two years after the combination other than disposals in the ordinary course of business of the formerly separate companies and to eliminate duplicate facilities or excess capacity. [B50.107(c)]

Asset dispositions to comply with orders of governmental or judicial bodies are acceptable. Some asset sales before consummation are also acceptable, but sale of an important subsidiary, division, or production process would probably violate the pooling, although no specific criterion in APB 16 can be cited. The reasoning is that such a sell-off would probably be viewed as changing the entity in contemplation of pooling.

Precombination Sale of Assets. Although APB 16 does not address the subject (in B50.106(c)), depending on the timing of the transaction, the SEC staff believes that the sale of significant assets of a combining company prior to consummation of a business combination is a pooling-of-interests violation, since it would be presumed that such action is in contemplation of the pooling. Such transactions are prohibited after consummation, and the SEC apparently believes companies should not be permitted to do before consummation what they cannot do after.

Dispositions of significant assets of a combining company occurring within three months are deemed to be in contemplation of the pooling and as such violate the pooling criterion. Dispositions between three and six months are presumed to be in contemplation of the pooling but the company may rebut the presumption with satisfactory evidence. Beyond six months and up to nine months prior to consummation, a disposition is not presumed to be in contemplation of the pooling if the companies will merely represent that fact in writing to the SEC staff.

10% Catch-All Rule

Because APB 16 was written in categorical terms, many questions were immediately raised about whether *any* deviation could be permitted while still achieving a pooling. For example, if an acquiring company makes a special arrangement for the benefit of a few shareholders of the acquired company (a prohibited transaction under B50.107(b)), does the transaction irretrievably fail to qualify as a pooling? Practice quickly settled into using the *10% catch-all rule* (and the SEC has also given its approval in FRR § 201), whereby any kind of transaction inimical to pooling has to be equated in terms of the number of shares of issuing company stock; the total of all such "negatives" cannot be more than 10% of the amount of stock the issuing company would issue to acquire 100% of the outstanding voting stock of the company to be acquired. The 10% comes, of course, from the fact that the APB required the issuing company to acquire 90% of the acquiree's voting common stock to have a pooling, so it seems obvious that whatever happens with the other 10%, whether it is unacquired or in some other way not supportive of pooling, seems of little concern. However, the 10% cushion generally cannot be used to cover partial special deals for shareholders. The creation of a situation that permits a *partial dissenter* (e.g., a 20% shareholder who tenders three-fourths of his stock like everyone else, but gets a special deal on the remainder) is not permitted for pooling accounting.

SEC No-Sell-Off Rule

Although APB 16 theoretically permits the sale of any shares immediately after consummation of a business combination (as long as the sell-off is not a condition of the merger), the SEC decided that under certain circumstances this condition is not acceptable for pooling accounting by a registrant. The Commission views this as a *bailout* if the selling shareholder is part of a *control group*. No SEC release defines *control group*. However, an *affiliate* as defined by Regulation S-X is considered a controlling shareholder. In general, the control group should be assumed to include officers, directors, and any direct or beneficial owner of 10% or more of the outstanding voting shares.

To clarify its views, the SEC issued ASRs 130 and 135 (FRR § 201.01). Under those rules, a pooling transaction can be made subject to filing a registration statement with the SEC of the issuable or issued shares, but the control group shareholders of the acquired company must nevertheless hold the stock they receive (be *at risk*) for a minimum holding period of 30 days of combined operations. Further, the results of combined operations must be published in a posteffective amendment to a registration statement, a Form 10-Q or 8-K, a quarterly earnings report, or any other public statement that includes combined sales and net income for at least the minimum period.

ASR 130 originally imposed the holding requirement on all shareholders of the acquired company. ASR 135, however, recognized the impracticality of that requirement and said only that *affiliates* of all combining companies would have to hold their new shares at risk for the holding period.

In late 1986, the SEC issued SAB 65, *Risk Sharing in Pooling of Interests* (Topic 2.E), expressing the staff's views regarding the meaning of FRR § 201, reaffirming that the restrictions apply to affiliates of all combining companies, including affiliates of the company that issues the shares. In addition, although APB 16 might be read to preclude it, the SEC generally will not object to pooling accounting if a preconsummation sell-off by an affiliate of a combining company occurs more than 30 days before consummation of the business combination. Conversely, such sales within 30 days by an affiliate probably will be deemed to be a "bailout," and pooling-of-interests accounting would be prohibited.

After the issuance of SAB 65, the SEC staff was asked whether de minimis sales by affiliates within the specified time period would preclude pooling accounting. In response, the staff issued SAB 76, *Effect of Certain De Minimis Sales by Affiliates on Compliance With the Requirements of ASR Nos. 130 and 135* (Topic 2.E), in early 1988. SAB 76 states that pooling will not be affected if the sales by an affiliate are not greater than 10% of the affiliate's shares, and the combined sales by affiliates do not exceed the equivalent of one percent of the company's precombination shares. Unexercised stock options may be included in the base depending on how closely they resemble outstanding stock. The SAB also allows charitable contributions and gifts, provided the donee holds the stock for the limits specified in the ASRs.

The fact that the stock ownership is widely spread over a large group does not necessarily mean that there are no affiliates. Other facts, such as relationships among some of the shareholders, would be considered. Clearly, though, the casual investor having a few hundred shares in a public company is not covered by the holding requirement.

Applying Pooling-of-Interests Accounting

If all of the pooling criteria are met, a business combination *must* be accounted for as a pooling of interests. Combining companies who want to account for a business combination as a purchase need only violate any pooling criterion. However, when the merger appears to require purchase accounting, it is usually impossible to restructure negotiations to meet the pooling criteria. Because APB 16 is designed to prevent pooling abuses, it provides no real way to prevent the arranged use of purchase accounting when the parties find it more advantageous.

Pooled Financial Statements. When companies combine in a pooling, the accounting basis for the assets and liabilities of all the combined companies remains virtually unchanged—previous balance sheets and statements of income are simply added together. There are a few exceptions to this:

1. The combined capital structure of the surviving company will not be the same as the components of the individual companies. This occurs because new capital shares are issued in exchange for the shares of one or more combining companies. Because it is necessary to show the new shares at their par or stated value, which is unlikely to be exactly the same as such amounts in the balance sheet of the acquired company, a different total for common stock will occur.

   As to the sequence of this capital combination accounting, all the retained earnings of the previously separate companies are added to form combined retained earnings. Then, if the total dollar amount at par or stated value of shares of stock outstanding after the pooling exceeds the total amount of capital stock of the separate combining companies, the excess should be deducted first from the combined additional paid-in capital, and if that is not sufficient, then from the combined retained earnings. If there is an excess of the individual companies' capital stock accounts over the par or stated value, that excess is credited to combined additional paid-in capital.

2. Any significant amount of purchases and sales of goods or services between the combining companies prior to the combination should be eliminated (along with the profits thereon) from the combined financial statements by the usual intercompany eliminations procedure performed in normal consolidation. To the extent the balance sheet is affected by intercompany profits in inventory or property, plant, and equipment, those should also be eliminated.

3. If the separate companies have recorded assets and liabilities using different methods (e.g., depreciation) and elect to conform them after the combination, they must be conformed retroactively (B50.111). However, they need not be conformed and very often are not. See Figure 23.2 for an example of a combining balance sheet in a pooling.

Tax Carry-Forward Benefits. In a business combination structured as a nontaxable transaction and accounted for as a pooling of interests, an operating loss or tax credit carry-forward of one combining company cannot offset retroactively any part of the taxable income of another combining company, simply because prior tax returns cannot be refiled on a pooled basis. On a prospective basis, if a consolidated tax return is to be prepared, a prior operating loss or tax credit carry-forward should be used to reduce the combined deferred tax liability if it can be offset (as provided by tax laws) against temporary differences that will result in subsequent taxable income that otherwise has not been offset by either combining company prior to the combination. The same treatment is applied to other temporary differences of either combining company that have not been offset by reversing differences.

Whenever the pooling results in the demonstrated ability to utilize otherwise unused benefits in reducing the deferred tax liability of either company once they are combined, a pooling adjustment is made when recording the pooling of the companies (i.e., net deductible temporary differences of one company offset net taxable temporary differences of the other). Further, the FASB staff has stated that even if the companies assert they do not intend to file a consolidated tax return in the future, and thus will not obtain the indicated benefits, the benefits must still be reflected in recording the pooling if a valid strategy (as defined in SFAS 96) would indicate that taxes can be reduced in this manner. This treatment was not pleasing to the merger

The following unaudited pro forma condensed balance sheet presents the combined financial position of May and ADG of August 2, 1986. This unaudited pro forma information gives effect to the proposed Merger using the pooling-of-interests method of accounting after giving effect to the pro forma adjustments described in the accompanying notes. This unaudited pro forma condensed balance sheet should be read in conjunction with the unaudited pro forma condensed statements of earnings notes to unaudited pro forma condensed financial information and the separate consolidated financial statements and notes thereto of May and ADG included elsewhere in this Joint Proxy Statement.

	Unaudited May	ADG	Unaudited pro forma adjustments increase (decrease)	Unaudited pro forma combined
			(dollars in millions)	
Cash	$ 47.3	$ 23.5	$ —	$ 70.8
Marketable securities	147.3	—	—	147.3
Accounts receivable, net	848.9	328.1	235.4(B)	1,412.4
Merchandise inventories	794.5	762.2	—	1,556.7
Other current assets	26.3	29.5	—	55.5
Total current assets	1,864.3	1,143.3	235.4	3,243.0
Property and equipment, net	1,546.0	993.3	—	2,539.3
Investment in ADG Credit Corp.	—	79.0	(79.0)(B)	—
Other assets	74.3	94.9	(16.0)(A)	153.2
Total Assets	$3,484.6	$2,310.5	$ 140.4	$5,935.5

Liabilities and Shareholders Equity

Notes payable	$ 15.0	$ 102.9	$ 147.4(B)	$ 265.3
Current maturities of long-term debt	21.5	18.4	—	39.9
Accounts payable and accrued liabilities	677.8	393.2	—	1,071.0
Income taxes	111.5	105.7	9.0(B)	226.2
Dividends payable	—	14.6	—	14.6
Total current liabilities	825.8	634.8	156.4	1,617.0
Long-term debt and capitalized lease obligations	720.8	509.8	—	1,230.6
Deferred income taxes and ITC	227.5	59.5	28.3(C)	315.3
Deferred compensation and other liabilities	67.7	78.1	—	145.8
Unrealized appreciation – real estate partnership	72.3	—	—	72.3
Redeemable preferred stock	102.8	—	—	102.8
Shareholders' equity	1,467.7	1,028.3	(44.3)(A)(C)	2,451.7
Total liabilities and shareholders' equity	$3,484.6	$2,310.5	$140.4	$5,935.5

(continued)

FIG. 23.2 Example of a Combining Balance Sheet in a Pooling
Source: Joint Proxy Statement – The May Department Stores Company and Associated Dry Goods Corporation – September 2, 1986.

Notes to Unaudited Pro Forma Condensed Financial Information

The pooling-of-interests method of accounting conforms the accounting policies followed by the combined entities. Certain differences in accounting policies exist between May and ADG. The following are those accounting policy differences and other items which were adjusted in the unaudited pro forma condensed balance sheet and unaudited pro forma condensed statements of earnings. There may be other differences in accounting policies which are not yet determinable.

(A) May and Holdings acquired in June 1986 330,400 shares of ADG Common Stock for approximately $16 million. These amounts are reflected as a pro forma reduction of shareholders' equity (i.e., treasury stock) as of August 2, 1986 in the Unaudited Pro Forma Condensed Balance Sheet. In addition, these shares are excluded in calculating the unaudited pro forma book value per share at August 2, 1986.

(B) May's consolidated financial statements include the accounts of all of its wholly-owned subsidiaries. ADG's consolidated financial statements include the accounts of all of its wholly-owned subsidiaries except ADG Credit Corporation. This adjustment consolidates ADG Credit Corporation to conform to May's accounting practice. Earnings before income taxes of ADG Credit Corporation are deducted from interest expense in ADG's consolidated statement of earnings with the provision for related taxes included in income taxes.

(C) For book purposes May's investment tax credits are deferred and amortized over the depreciable lives of the related property. ADG reduces federal income taxes by the investment tax credit in the year allowed. The adjustment to the unaudited pro forma condensed balance sheet as of August 2, 1986, reflects the estimated cumulative effect of this difference, assuming ADG's investment tax credits were deferred and amortized over a 10-year-period, which is the period used by May. The adjustments to the unaudited pro forma condensed statements of earnings for the three fiscal years in the period ended February 1, 1986, and for the 26 weeks ended August 2, 1986, and August 3, 1985, also reflect the estimated effect in such periods of ADG using the deferral method of accounting for investment tax credits.

FIG. 23.2 (continued)

and acquisition community, because prior to SFAS 96 such benefits had been included in post-pooling income.

In poolings that are treated as taxable transactions, differences between book and tax basis of net assets acquired in the taxable pooling are temporary differences under SFAS 96, and a deferred tax liability or asset is recorded as a pooling adjustment. Also, the tax benefits resulting from a step-up in basis that are recognizable (as defined in SFAS 96) at the date of the pooling are credited to paid-in capital; those not recognizible until later are treated as a reduction of income tax expense when recognizable.

For further discussion of the accounting for income taxes in a business combination, see Chapter 17.

Pooling Disclosures. The combined corporation should disclose in notes to the financial statements that a pooling of interests business combination has occurred during the period, and provide the following specific disclosures (summarized from B50.123):

- Names and descriptions of the combined companies.
- Type and number of shares issued in the combination.
- A summary of the results of operations of the combining companies prior to the combination.
- Adjustments to conform accounting methods (and combination tax benefits, as mentioned in the previous section) necessitated by the combination and their effects, if any, on net income of the previously separate companies.
- Details of an increase or decrease in retained earnings due to a change in fiscal year of a combining company.
- Reconciliation of revenues and earnings previously reported by the company issuing the shares with current reported amounts.

Retroactive poolings of interests, that is, recording in the previous year a business combination consumed shortly after a company's year end, are prohibited by APB 16 (B50.120). However, a business combination initiated after the date of the financial statements but consummated before the financial statements are issued, or incomplete at the date, must be disclosed in the notes to the financial statements (B50.124).

PURCHASE ACCOUNTING

This section deals with acquisition of a majority interest in an acquiree, usually in a single transaction. Chapter 24 also discusses step-by-step acquisitions, including those that start well below 50% ownership.

Any business combination that does not meet all the pooling criteria must be accounted for as a purchase. The consideration given can be any form—cash or any other kind of monetary assets, stock, debt, warrants, or nonmonetary assets. Determining fair values is quite easy when the consideration given is cash or readily marketable monetary assets. When other consideration is given, valuation problems will occur, as discussed in later paragraphs.

Takeovers vs. Purchases

Before delving into the accounting mechanics of purchase business combinations, a commentary on takeovers is in order. Recent years have seen an explosion of hostile takeover attempts, many of them successful despite all-out defensive efforts by the target. The environment has spawned an entire lexicon of quaint terminology, such as "shark" and "raider" (for the would-be acquirer), "white knight" (an interposed would-be acquirer that is more acceptable to the target company), "golden parachutes" (lucrative severance benefits for management of the target in the event of a takeover), and "poison pill" (a security issued by a target company to its shareholders that gives them, in the event a raider achieves a designated level of ownership, a disproportionately large number of voting shares or an expensively redeemable security).

Once the company has been "teed-up" (caused to become a target, when it otherwise might not have been) and it is "in play" (more than one bidder is in the auction), it might try many maneuvers to avoid takeover, such as "scorched earth" (any action that seriously dissipates the target's value to the raider) or sale of the "crown jewels" (those operations most desired by the raider). The target may also try a "pac-man" approach, making its own hostile tender offer for the raider company (some of these have been accomplished); or it may borrow to the hilt and declare a dividend to its shareholders so large that its net worth will be negative for a decade or more. The ways in which takeovers are pursued, and the defenses mounted, are as varied as the imaginations of the players, without much interference from the often-petitioned courts.

A common maneuver by a target company is a leveraged buy-out (LBO) offer by management, generally with the participation of outside parties such as investment bankers to help structure and fund the offer. LBOs are discussed in a separate secton of this chapter.

Clearing away all the mystique, a successful hostile takeover is still a purchase business combination. So are some but not all LBOs. An unsuccessful attempt can result in the raider holding a large block of stock in the target, and if this is bought back by the target at a price greater than its fair value, it is called "greenmail." It is also "tainted" treasury stock, as discussed earlier under "Treasury Stock".

In this regard, in 1985 the FASB issued TB 85-6, *Accounting for a Purchase of Treasury Shares at a Price Significantly in Excess of the Current Market Price of the Shares and the Income Statement Classification of Costs Incurred in Defending Against a Takeover Attempt* (C23, I17, I60). The TB, which nullified the EITF consensus in Issue 85–2, states that an agreement to purchase shares from a shareholder may also involve the receipt or payment of consideration in exchange for stated or unstated rights or privileges that should be identified to properly allocate the purchase price (greenmail). In addition, the TB requires that payments by an enterprise to a share-holder or former shareholder attributed, for example, to a "standstill" agreement or any agreement in which a shareholder or former shareholder agrees not to purchase additional shares, should be expensed rather than capitalized as incurred. Such costs do not meet the criteria for extraordinary classification.

A hostile takeover can never be a pooling, because the target easily can and cer-tainly will take some action that will fracture the pooling criteria. A friendly takeover bid can be a pooling, however, if the parties so structure it. Even so, once a friendly offer is announced, the company is in play and other bidders may appear. In friendly takeovers, therefore, the parties usually will try to arrange some type of advance "lock-up" (e.g., an option on the target's stock issued for no consideration and that is exercisable only if the proposed pooling does not occur, as might be the case if other bids are made). If the option expires unexercised (as it would if a pooling did occur), the SEC deems that the option never existed, and thus it would not affect pooling accounting treatment.

Most takeovers (and LBOs) are highly leveraged, that is, much of the cash used to buy out the target's shareholders (mostly arbitrageurs after the conflict is in progress) comes from many tiers of multiple-source borrowings. Indeed, the takeover and LBO business has been responsible for the creation of an entirely new segment of the investment industry—high-yield bonds (or so-called junk bonds), which are com-monly issued as the permanent financing debt.

The predominant manner by which the successful raider reduces the debt to man-ageable levels prior to seeking permanent financing is the sale of some of the acquiree's operating units or major assets. The seemingly astronomical expenses of raiders and targets in these contests, and the postacquisition debt refinancing and sell-off transactions have generated a host of new accounting issues, many of which are discussed in this section.

Identifying the Acquirer

APB 16 (B50.128) states that unless there is clear contrary evidence, the acquiring company in a purchase transaction is the company whose shareholders hold a majority of the voting stock after the purchase is consummated. In a specific case detailed in SAB 24, (Topic 2.A.2), the SEC identified what it considered to be convincing evidence that the smaller shareholder group was the acquirer. The SAB states that the decision as to which company was the acquirer was based on these considerations:

1. There would be restrictions on the ability of the former chairman of the board of the larger shareholder group company to solicit proxies or to participate in an election contest.
2. Top management and the board of directors of the combined corporation would be, for the most part, individuals currently holding such positions in the smaller shareholder group company.
3. The assets, revenues, net earnings, and current market value of the smaller shareholder group company significantly exceed those of the larger.
4. The market value of the securities (common and preferred) to be received by the former common shareholders of the smaller shareholder group company would significantly exceed the market value of the securities (common only) to be received by the former common shareholders of the larger.

The transaction in SAB 24 did not proceed; the choice of acquirer was critical because, as in any purchase, this drives the determination of how much goodwill is created. The company whose stock commands a greater price differential over book or fair value of identifiable net assets will, if it is the acquiree, cause more goodwill to be created, because its net assets upon revaluation will still fall far short of the value of the consideration paid.

The decision in SAB 24 is not obvious; and several major accounting firms did not agree with the SEC conclusion at the time. The SEC continues to question which company is the acquirer in purchase combinations accomplished substantially by the exchange of stock.

Establishing the Acquisition Date

The date of acquisition of a purchased company should ordinarily be the date the net assets are received and other assets (such as cash) are disbursed or securities are issued. For accounting convenience, the effective date may be at the end of an accounting period between initiation and consummation of the combination. In this case, however, the written agreement transferring control should contain no restrictions except those required to protect the stockholders of the acquired company, for example, permission to pay dividends equal to those regularly paid before the effective date.

An effective date other than the date assets or securities are transferred requires adjustment of the cost of the consideration and net income of the acquired company to compensate for the period between the actual acquisition date and the effective date of recording (B50.162). For example, if a purchase acquisition is consummated on May 5 and the parties agree to the convenience of effectively recording it as of the preceding April 1 (the beginning of a quarter), the income of the combined companies, which will include income of the acquired company from April 1, will have to be reduced by imputing interest at a current rate on the consideration given for the period April 1 to May 5.

Determination of Purchase Price

Costs of Acquisition. In a purchase business combination, the direct costs of the acquisition such as the expenses involved in the registration of debt or equity securities to be issued as consideration, including legal and accounting fees, are treated as part of the purchase cost. In addition, other costs that can be directly attributed to the combination are also treated as part of the purchase cost.

Indirect costs, such as the expenses of an acquisitions department that searches for potential acquisition opportunities and administers all successful acquisitions, are not part of any specific acquistion and may not be directly charged or allocated to the purchase cost of any combination. Such costs are chargeable to current income.

Costs of disposing of the duplicate facilities of the acquired company are treated as part of the purchase cost. If the disposal is incomplete at the date of consummation of the combination (which is almost always the case), all estimated costs of disposal should be accrued. (Of course, if a duplicate facility is held for sale as part of the disposal process, it should be recorded at the date of consummation at its estimated net realizable value.)

Costs of disposing of the duplicate facilities of the *acquiring* company cannot be treated as part of the purchase cost of a business combination. FASB Technical Bulletin 85-5, *Issues Relating to Accounting for Business Combinations, Including . . . Costs of Closing Duplicate Facilities of an Acquiree* (B50.651–.652), indicates that for such dispositions, any gain or loss should be charged to income. This TB was issued after the EITF addressed the matter in Issue 84-35, *Business Combinations: Sale of Duplicate Facilities and Accrual of Liabilities,* without achieving a clear consensus. Also discussed by the EITF, without a consensus reached, was a list of various liabilities that sometimes are, and other times are not, accrued in a purchase combination. The FASB felt that adequate guidance already exists in APB 16 (i.e., accrue all liabilities that exist at the acquisition date) and that a listing would be counterproductive. Among the issues thus bypassed were golden parachutes and adequacy of loan loss reserves of financial institutions. As to the golden parachutes, their existence as liabilities may or may not be dependent on whether the takeover occurs. Regardless, it would appear that they should be accrued as liabilities at the acquisition date (and charged to expense in the financial statements of the acquiree company). As to the loan reserve matter, the SEC staff dealt with it in SAB 61 (Topic 2.A.5). (See Chapter 40.)

Settlement of Stock Options. Often in a business combination to be accounted for by the purchase method, a target company has stock options or stock awards outstanding that the acquiring company wishes to eliminate. This raises a question about the accounting for cost incurred by the target company to settle the grant of options or to settle an earlier award of stock under varying circumstances: Does the timing or the fact that the settlement was made as part of the acquisition affect the accounting? Also at issue is the accounting for any reimbursements received by the target company from the acquiring company for settlement of the options.

The EITF reached a consensus in Issue 85-45, *Business Combinations: Settlement of Stock Options and Awards*, that APB 25, *Accounting for Stock Compensation Plans* (C47), requires a target company that settles stock options voluntarily at the direction of the acquiring company or as part of the plan of acquisition should account for the settlements as compensation expense in its separate financial statements. No consensus was reached on how the target company should account for any reimbursements received from the acquiring company.

Debt Issue Costs. In many purchase combinations, one or more investment bankers will act as advisers to the acquirer and the acquiree, and may also act as merchant bankers by providing and/or arranging for "bridge financing" covering some of the funds needed to complete an acquisition, pending the acquirer's arranging for long-term financing. The investment banker may also be designated to underwrite the planned permanent financing. For all the foregoing services the investment bankers may charge a lump sum (in addition to interest on the bridge financing), or they may specify the fees that are charged for each.

In a purchase business combination, fees paid by the acquirer for structuring advice are considered part of the purchase price. (Fees paid by the acquiree are expensed, except perhaps in some LBOs.) In SAB 77, *Debt Issue Costs* (Topic 2.A.6), the SEC staff addressed the need to properly allocate the investment bankers' fees to (1) advice given on structuring the acquisition, which is part of the purchase price; and (2) bridge loan fees, which are to be deferred as debt issue costs and amortized over the estimated life of the bridge loan. Presumably, if the anticipated underwriting charges were wholly or partly encompassed by an earlier fee charged, these would be also be set up as an asset pending the later transaction, at which time they would become amortizable debt issue costs as well.

Acquirers understandably try to avoid charges to postacquisition operations, and have argued that all or most of the investment bankers' fees should be charged to the purchase price, thereby effectively loading them into goodwill for an attenuated 40-year amortization. The rationale is that the transaction (usually a hostile takeover) is unitary: all parts run together, and the bridge financing in particular is the only way to successfully structure the transaction. Early indications from the SEC were that this logic was unacceptable, and that the bridge loan costs had to be segregated.

In the next iteration, acquirers took the position that the bridge loan and the permanent financing were two stages of a single financing transaction through the same source—the investment banker. Thus, even though bridge loan arrangement fees might be very high (reflecting the fees typically charged by outside parties because of the risk that the permanent financing might not occur or that the hostile takeover might not succeed), when the permanent financing was in place the unamortized fees from the bridge loan would be transferred to debt issue costs of the permanent financing, thus spreading them over a longer life. Not 40 years, of course, but 10 to 12 years is far better than six months to a year. SAB 77 squelched this combination treatment as well.

The SAB requires that appropriate fees be apportioned to each of the services rendered, based on the going prices in the marketplace. An itemized billing needs to be challenged in the same manner as a single-fee billing. Further, under SAB 77, the bridge loan fee is amortized over its estimated life, or shorter period if the permanent financing is in place earlier than planned. This treatment can result in an all-inclusive cost of bridge financing charged to postacquisition operations that is often as high as 25%.

Earnings and Market Price Contingencies. One of the determinants in the purchase price of a business combination may be an earnings contingency, or *earnout*. Such arrangements typically provide for the payment of additional consideration based on the acquired company maintaining or achieving a specified earnings level in future periods. If the level is achieved and the additional consideration becomes payable, the acquiring corporation must record the then current fair value of the additional consideration as additional purchase cost (B50.138). This additional cost must be spread among the affected assets acquired; because the identifiable assets would already have been fair-valued, the additional cost of the earnout is added to goodwill and amortized over its remaining life. If, however, there had been an excess of fair values of assets acquired over the purchase price, and such excess had been applied to reduce the carrying basis of noncurrent assets, the increase in purchase price as the result of the satisfaction of earnout provisions would be applied to restore some portion (or all) of that reduction. In effect, the purchase price is reallocated, but the adjustment is made prospectively from the date of redetermination.

A market price contingency (B50.139–.140) may also be part of a purchase agreement. It could result in the issuance of additional consideration by the acquiring company to the former shareholders of the acquired company if the market price of the security initially issued as consideration to the acquired company's shareholders does not at least equal a specified amount at a specified future date or dates. If this occurs, the acquiring company must record the then current value of the additional consideration, at the same time reducing the recorded amount of the consideration paid (the securities issued) when the combination was consummated. In this situation, the total cost of the purchase combination does not change; simply stated, more units of the security at the lower per-unit value are deemed to have been issued to accomplish the purchase acquisition. However, if the consideration originally issued is a debt security, a later reduction to a lower fair value results in a debt discount that must be recorded and amortized from the date additional consideration is issued.

Of course, there can be combination earnout and market price contingencies in a single deal; the effects of each should be segregated and then treated in accordance with the foregoing rules.

Valuation of Net Assets Purchased

In a purchase, the value of acquired assets and assumed liabilities is based on the consideration given or received, whichever is more clearly evident. Normally, the

Acquired Asset or Liability	Valuation
Marketable securities	Net realizable value
Receivables	Present value
Inventories	Finished goods: selling price less disposal costs and profit
	Work in process: estimated selling price less completion and disposal costs and profit
	Raw Materials: replacement cost
Property, plant, and equipment	To be used: replacement cost
	To be sold: net realizable value
	To be used temporarily: net realizable value less future depreciation
Intangible assets	Appraised value
Other assets	Appraised value
Accounts and notes payable, long-term debt	Present value (determined at current interest rates)
Other liabilities and accruals	Present value (determined at current interest rates)

FIG. 23.3   Asset and Liability Valuation Bases in a Purchase Business Combination (other than deferred taxes)

value of the consideration given (such as cash, common stock, preferred stock, or debentures) is more clearly evident; the consideration given becomes the new cost of the net assets in almost all cases. The acquisition of a group of assets and liabilities requires that the net cost be assigned to the individual assets and liabilities. General guidelines for the specific assignment of the purchase price are given in APB 16 (B50.146) and are summarized in Figure 23.3. In effect, all the assets and liabilities are to be recorded at their fair values as of the consummation date or a nearby accounting cutoff date. Certain of the items in Figure 23.3 are discussed in more detail in the paragraphs that follow.

Inventories.   For accounting purposes, the LIFO inventory valuation of an acquired company may not be carried forward after the purchase. Through its valuation guidelines, APB 16 (B50.146(c)) requires appropriate assignment of the purchase cost. The excess of cost assigned to LIFO inventories over the previous LIFO base in a purchase acquisition is added to inventories as if it were a discrete LIFO layer. Having such a difference does not violate the LIFO conformity rule, based on IRS pronouncements. (See Chapter 14 for further discussion of LIFO inventories in a purchase combination.)

As to the assignment of purchase price to inventories, APB 16 (B50.146(c)) takes the position that part of the profit derived from inventories is earned in the manufacturing process; not all of it comes from their sale. This method of valuation is also based on the belief that, should the same inventories, in exactly the same state of completion, be acquired in a bulk transaction, the least that the seller would expect is a profit for manufacturing efforts. Thus finished goods and work in process reflect this in the valuation; raw materials do not.

Identifiable Intangibles. Under APB 16, identifiable intangible assets should not be included in goodwill but should be separately recorded at fair value (B50.146). A common example is a favorable operating lease in which the facilities could presently be rented only at a higher cost. The intangible asset to be recorded in this example is the present value of rental expense differential, which would be written off over the remaining lease term. Note that as to leases capitalized by the acquired company, the fair valuing process must also be applied, but the value differential will adjust the capitalized asset balance rather than be classified as an intangible asset. (see L10.140, fn. 36.)

Any goodwill carried in the accounts of an acquired company before acquisition should not be carried forward, but if there is an excess of purchase price over fair values in the acquisition of a company that has goodwill on its books from prior acquisitions, the "old goodwill" may effectively become reestablished in whole or in part. This is caused simply by the mechanics of APB 16 in applying purchase accounting.

Research and Development. As stated in FIN 4, *Applicability of FASB Statement No. 2 to Business Combinations Accounted for by the Purchase Method* (B50.151–.152), any identifiable assets of the acquiree to be used in research and development (R&D) projects that do not also have an alternative future use should be first valued as part of the purchase price allocation, and then charged to expense of the combined companies simultaneous with consummation of acquisition.

The peculiar logic involved in FIN 4 was challenged in EITF Issue 86-14, *Purchased Research and Development Projects in a Business Combination.* The Task Force members pointed out the conundrum that if the amount has to be charged off immediately, then it has no assignable value under APB 16, and shouldn't be set up and knocked down all in the same maneuver. The FASB members gave this some thought but decided that neither FIN 4 nor SFAS 2, *Accounting for Research and Development Costs*, should be reconsidered.

Pensions. The valuation of pension plan obligations and assets is determined following the provisions of SFAS 87, *Employers' Accounting for Pensions* (B50.146(j)). That provision changed the requirement originally contained in APB 16. SFAS 87 requires that for a single-employer defined-benefit pension plan, the purchase price allocation process shall include a liability (or asset) for the amount that the projected benefit obligation is in excess of (or is less than) plan assets. This procedure eliminates any previously existing (1) unrecognized net gain or loss, (2) unrecognized prior service cost, or (3) unrecognized net obligation or net asset that would have existed at the time SFAS 87 became effective (generally, for fiscal years beginning after December 15, 1986). For a discussion of employer accounting for pension plans, see Chapter 16.

Other Postemployment Benefits. In Issue 86-20, *Accounting for Other Postemployment Benefits of an Acquired Company*, the EITF considered an issue in which the acquired company has an unfunded vested obligation for other postemployment benefits (OPEB). Until the FASB issues an expected pronouncement requiring that OPEB be accrued over the period earned by employees, most companies are not accruing for this liability, but are on a pay-as-you-go basis. Thus it would be common that an acquiree would have an obligation but not an accrual.

The Task Force concluded that it is preferable, but not mandatory, to recognize a liability in allocating the purchase price in the combination. Even if a liability is established, the acquired company would not be required to use the accrual method prospectively, nor would the acquiring company need to accrue a liability for similar benefits for its own employees. This peculiarity should disappear after FASB action on OPEB.

Assets to Be Divested. In Issue 87-11, *Allocation of Purchase Price to Assets to Be Sold*, the EITF considered the situation, most commonly encountered in hostile takeovers, in which an acquirer that has financed the acquisition with debt plans to sell operating units of the acquiree to obtain funds for debt reduction. Assuming that the proceeds of the sale and the timing of their receipt can be estimated with reasonable accuracy, some accountants would discount the estimated sales proceeds back to the acquisition date, thereby reducing the allocation of purchase price to those assets (and concomitantly increasing goodwill). In addition, to offset the interest expense being charged to postcombination operations, the carrying amount of the assets to be divested would be accreted to the expected amount of sales proceeds.

Assets held for sale are required by APB 16 (B50.146) to be stated at net realizable value in the purchase price allocation; however, APB 16 does not comment on whether discounting should be employed in this determination. While no consensus was reached, a majority of the Task Force believed that discounting was proper, and that in most cases so was accretion. The SEC observer stated that, while the SEC staff agrees with discounting,[2] they do not believe accretion is permissible unless a firm contract of sale exists at the acquisition date (not very likely).

Valuation Contingencies. A difficult and complex problem in purchase accounting has been the determination of the values to be placed on assets, liabilities, and contingencies of a purchased enterprise. Accrued liabilities and outstanding lawsuits may be easy to identify but difficult to value, and later actual settlement amounts can vary considerably.

Prior to 1977, if actual realization or settlement amounts varied substantially from estimates at the acquisition date, many companies retroactively restated the purchase price allocation, especially in the first year following acquisition, but often also in later years. Purchased goodwill was revised and current operations would not be affected.

---

[2] It bears mention that initially the SEC staff was very resistant to discounting because of the fact that goodwill was thereby increased; further, if discounting of accurately estimated sales proceeds was employed, then postcombination operations would be enhanced (either through a gain on sale, if not accreted, or by the accretion itself). In short, debit goodwill, credit income.

SFAS 16, *Prior Period Adjustments* (A35), issued in 1977, proscribes most prior period adjustments. As a result, the practice of holding open the valuation process in purchase business combinations and the retroactive adjustment of amounts assigned to assets and liabilities was curtailed. The significant remaining opportunity to adjust values retroactively was removed in September 1980 with the issuance of SFAS 38, *Accounting for Preacquisition Contingencies of Purchased Enterprises* (B50). That statement requires the estimation of preacquisition contingencies that will exist for a short period of time (generally, not exceeding one year) after the acquisition date. Later differences must be included in operations of the period of reestimation or settlement. This accounting is based on the theory that changes in estimates (which are not errors in the original estimation) should be current period events.

Income Tax Effects

Tax-Free Purchase. In a tax-free purchase, the tax basis of acquired assets carries over, and the purchase price allocated to the acquired assets and liabilities based on their fair values will usually differ from their tax bases. These are considered temporary differences under SFAS 96, *Accounting for Income Taxes* (I25), requiring that a deferred tax liability or asset be recognized for the difference between the fair values and tax bases of the net assets acquired (except for goodwill, unallocated negative goodwill, and leveraged leases). Figure 23.4 demonstrates how a liability for deferred taxes in the above situation is recognized and measured pursuant to the requirements of SFAS 96. In essence, the mechanics at acquisition date are similar to those required prior to SFAS 96 except that the tax effect sometimes had been discounted to present value and was offset against the asset or liability (i.e., carried net of tax). After acquisition date, the similarity stops: Under SFAS 96, the deferred taxes are treated like any others arising from current book-tax differences, and accordingly may be offset by the effects of reversing temporary differences. Under APB 11, the net-of-tax adjustment was considered a part of the valuation of the related asset or liability, and thus was run through operations before income taxes as the asset became used up and the liability settled.

Taxable Purchase. Quite often, a purchase business combination is a taxable transaction, dependent mostly on the type of consideration paid. In a taxable transaction, the fair values of the assets acquired usually become the new tax basis following the theory that, for tax purposes, the assets have been sold and have triggered tax consequences based on differences between selling price and tax basis. However, special provisions of the tax law sometimes permit the establishment of a new tax basis that is in excess of the fair value of a particular asset. For example, the tax law may allow the allocation of cost to an asset other than goodwill for tax purposes while for accounting purposes, the fair value of that acquired asset is less. Acquirers will strive to obtain this type of higher basis for assets that can be written off against future taxable income, because goodwill cannot be deducted for tax purposes. In such cases, SFAS 96 requires that the tax benefit of the difference between the fair values of the net assets acquired and their new tax bases should be applied to reduce goodwill; after exhausting goodwill, other noncurrent intangible assets are reduced down to zero. Any remaining tax benefit reduces current income tax expense. An example of this situation is presented in Figure 23.5

Assumptions

1. The enacted tax rate is 40% for all future years.

2. An enterprise is acquired for $20,000, and the enterprise has no leveraged leases.

3. The tax basis of the net assets acquired is $5,000, and the assigned value (other than goodwill) is $12,000. Future recovery of the assets and settlement of the liabilities at their assigned values will result in taxable and deductible amounts that can be offset against each other.

Amounts to Be Recorded

Assigned value of the net assets (other than goodwill) acquired	$12,000
Liability for deferred tax consequences (40% of the $7,000 net taxable amounts ($12,000 − $5,000) that will arise upon recovery of the assigned value of those net assets)	(2,800)
Goodwill	10,800
Purchase price of the acquired enterprise	$20,000

FIG. 23.4   Recognition and Measurement of Deferred Income Taxes in a Nontaxable Purchase
Source: Adapted from SFAS 96 (I25.159A).

Assumptions

1. The enacted tax rate is 40% for all future years.

2. An enterprise is acquired for $20,000, and the enterprise has no leveraged leases.

3. The net assets (other than goodwill) acquired have a tax basis of $20,000 and an assigned value of $12,000, that is, there are $8,000 of temporary differences that will result in deductible amounts in future years.

4. As of the acquisition date (1) the acquiring enterprise has a liability for the deferred tax consequences of temporary differences that will result in $30,000 of net taxable amounts in future years and (2) the acquired $8,000 of temporary differences ($20,000 − $12,000) will result in deductible amounts in the same future years.

Amounts to be Recorded

Assigned value of the net assets (other than goodwill) acquired	$12,000
Reduction of acquiring enterprise's deferred tax liability (40% of $8,000)	3,200
Goodwill	4,800
Purchase price of the acquired enterprise	$20,000

FIG. 23.5   Recognition and Measurement of Deferred Income Taxes in a Taxable Purchase
Source: Adapted from SFAS 96 (I25.160A).

Tax Carry-Forward Benefits.   If the tax benefits of an operating loss or tax credit carry-forward of either combining company are recognizable at the date of consummation of a purchase business combination, those benefits are applied to reduce any existing deferred tax liability of the other combining company. The result is either (1) to decrease goodwill (or noncurrent assets except long-term investments in marketable securities) of the acquired company or (2) to create or increase

Assumptions

1. The enacted tax rate is 40% for all future years.

2. The purchase price is $20,000. The tax basis of the identified net assets acquired is $5,000, and the assigned value is $12,000, that is, there are $7,000 of temporary differences that will result in taxable amounts in future years. The acquired enterprise also has a $16,000 operating loss carryforward which, under the tax law, may be used by the acquiring enterprise in the consolidated tax return.

3. The acquiring enterprise has a liability for the deferred tax consequences of temporary differences that will result in $30,000 of net taxable amounts in future years.

4. All temporary differences of the acquired and acquiring enterprises will result in taxable amounts before the end of the acquired enterprise's loss carryforward period.

Operating loss carry-forward offset

1. $7,000 of net taxable amounts that will result from future recovery of the assigned value of the acquired net assets.

2. Another $9,000 of net taxable amounts attributable to the acquiring enterprise's deferred tax liability.

Amounts to be Recorded

Assigned value of the identified net assets acquired	$12,000
Reduction of acquiring enterprise's deferred tax liability (40% of $9,000)	3,600
Goodwill	4,400
Purchase price of the acquired enterprise	$20,000

FIG. 23.6   Recognition of Loss Carry-Forward in a Nontaxable Purchase
Source: Adapted from SFAS 96 (I25.161).

negative goodwill in the combination. Figure 23.6 demonstrates how a loss carry-forward is recognized in a nontaxable purchase business combination pursuant to the requirements of SFAS 96.

If the tax benefits of an acquired operating loss or tax credit carry-forward are not recognized at the date of consummation but are recognizable at a later date, they should then (1) first be applied to reduce any goodwill and other intangible assets to zero and (2) after such reduction, any remaining amount of benefit should be recognized as a reduction of income tax expense. A lengthy example is provided in SFAS 96 (I25.164).

Tax Basis of Acquiree's Stock. In an acquisition in which the acquiree's tax bases for its net assets differs from the price paid by the acquirer (virtually always the case), and the acquiree is not liquidated and merged into the acquirer (or an acquirer's subsidiary), the acquirer's investment will be, and therefore its tax basis will apply to, the stock of the acquiree. If the acquiree has any APB 23 differences (I42) on which it had elected not to apply deferred tax accounting, then the acquirer is not permitted to consider the basis differential on the stock investment in the acquiree in calculating its deferred tax requirements. Instead, the potential tax benefit is used to reduce the footnoted amounts required to be shown as to deferred taxes omitted as result of opting to leave these APB 23 items out of the temporary difference computations. (This footnote disclosure requirement applies to all the APB 23 differences except undistributed earnings of subsidiaries, which are exempt from footnote disclosure under SFAS 96, (I25.124). Further, it only applies when the tax basis of the stock exceeds the tax basis of the net assets. See SFAS 96 (I25.165).

Transition Rules—SFAS 96. SFAS 96 may be adopted at any time after its issuance in December 1987, but in any event no later than fiscal years beginning after December 15, 1988. Thus some companies may wait until calendar year 1989 to adopt it. Further, two choices are given on implementation: SFAS 96 may be adopted prospectively only (affecting the year of adoption and later years), or retroactively (by restating all prior periods presented, with a cumulative catch-up adjustment in the earliest year).

The foregoing sections discuss the application of SFAS 96 to business combinations consummated after SFAS 96 has been adopted; however, if a company has not yet adopted it in 1988, the old rules under APB 11 are still applicable.

More significantly, if a company adopts SFAS 96 retroactively, prior business combinations are also remeasured to reflect the income tax effects according to SFAS 96. But if SFAS 96 is adopted prospectively, then the remaining balances of assets and liabilities that were fair-valued in a purchase and thus were carried net-of-tax should not be remeasured; and the differences between their present carrying amounts and tax bases are considered temporary differences at the date of SFAS 96 adoption, and are included in the adjustment that results from initial application of SFAS 96.

To illustrate the effect, if fixed assets to be depreciated straight-line over 10 years were acquired in a purchase five years ago, had a fair value of $1,000 and a tax basis of $500, and were recorded at $750 (giving undiscounted net-of-tax effect using a 50% tax rate), the current carrying amount would be $375, and the current tax basis (also assuming the same depreciation pattern) would be $250. If retroactive application of SFAS 96 is chosen, the asset would be restated to $500, and a temporary difference of $250 would be classified with other temporary differences in determining the SFAS 96 initial adoption adjustment.[3] If prospective adoption is chosen, however, the assets remain stated at $375, and the tax impact of a temporary difference of $125 is classified in the initial adjustment. The net result is that the initial "kicker" to equity experienced by most companies on adoption of SFAS 96 (generally as a result of reduction of prior deferred taxes because of reduced tax rates under the Tax Reform Act of 1986 (TRA 1986)) is lowered by prospective adoption. However, the prospective adopter will have a lower charge than the retroactive adopter against future operations for depreciation expense.

---

[3] Technically, the asset is restored to $1,000 as of the original acquisition date and is depreciated accordingly to the current balance of $500. Further, at acquisition date, a taxable temporary difference of $500 would be established, to be considered in the establishment of deferred taxes taking into account the other temporary differences existing at the time. The accounting is rolled forward to the beginning of the year of adoption of SFAS 96, to determine the adjustment to tax balances needed to bring the financial statements into conformity with SFAS 96 as if it had been applied all along. Ignoring these other temporary differences, there would be a $250 taxable difference at the current date.

Chapter 17 should be referred to for more details on SFAS 96, which is a very complex document.

Change in tax rates. In early 1987, the EITF discussed an issue that has possible continuing applicability to certain companies. In Issue 86-42, *Effect of a Change in Tax Rates on Assets and Liabilities Recorded Net-of-Tax in a Purchase Business Combination,* the EITF considered how the change in corporate tax rates from 46% to 34% under TRA 1986 should be treated.

For example, a liability fair valued at $1,000 and having a tax basis of $500 is recorded in the acquisition at $750 (tax-effecting at a 50% rate). With the rate change, the net-of-tax amount would now be $830, reflecting the fact that the nondeductibility of $500 excess of fair value over tax basis now represents only $170 ($500 × 34%) of taxes foregone. The issue related to whether the tax effects set up at older, higher rates, should be adjusted to the new, lower rates.

The consensus reached noted that the net-of-tax treatment was a valuation matter, not an income tax accounting matter, and that the original allocation was complete and should not be reopened. However, the current balances of such previously tax-effected items should be evaluated for recoverability or adequacy, just like any other balance, and if changes are needed, the adjustment flows through current operations. The SEC Observer noted that this evaluation cannot be made for the aggregate of net assets acquired in a purchase combination, as this would be tantamount to reopening the purchase price allocation. This matter has been resolved by SFAS 96, which precludes net-of-tax treatment, but the EITF consensus is still applicable to companies that have not yet adopted SFAS 96 (or will not adopt it retroactively).

Also on the matter of not disturbing the original allocation, the FASB staff has stated its tentative view that in a purchase business combination consummated just prior to a change in tax rates, SFAS 96 requires that the rates in effect at consummation date must be used to record deferred taxes. This has been objected to by the SFAS 96 Implementation Task Force as illogical, because the rate change would have been factored into the negotiations.

Purchase Presentation and Disclosure

The statement of income for the combined companies for the year in which the purchase acquisition occurs should include the operations of the acquired company commencing with the date of acquisition; specified footnote disclosures are required (B50.164–.165):

- Name and description of the acquired company.
- Identification that the purchase method of accounting was used.
- Results of operations for the acquired company from the date of acquisition to the end of the period.
- Cost of the acquired company and, if applicable, the number and value of shares issued.
- Goodwill amortization plan, method, and period.
- Proposed accounting treatment for contingencies specified in the acquisition agreement.
- Pro forma presentation of the results of operations as though the combination had been effected at the beginning of the period and, if comparative financial statements are pre-

sented, the same presentation for the preceding period. (Such pro forma data is not required for nonpublic companies (B50.165).)

Pro Forma Financial Data. For a purchase business combination, APB 16 requires the presentation of pro forma combined results of operations—revenue, income before extraordinary items, net income, and earnings per share of the acquiring company—for the current year and preceding year if comparative financial statements are presented (B50.165). The data should reflect the adjustments made to the acquiree company's net assets in allocating the purchase price, including the amortization of goodwill. In addition, in making the pro forma disclosures the SEC generally will allow adjustments in pro forma combined financial statements that reflect economies of scale, if auditable. In the SEC's view, auditability is demonstrated if:

• Cost savings resulting from the combination have been accomplished (e.g., employee terminations).

• Contracts or agreements from which a measurable savings will result (e.g., lease cancellations) have been executed by all parties.

• The evidence demonstrates that the savings will not be dissipated through other arrangements (e.g., replacement hiring, new leases).

The SEC also requires disclosure of the *contribution* to combined net sales and net income of material acquisitions in the year of acquisition.

Push Down Accounting. Although APB 16 requires the allocation of the purchase price based on the fair values of the net assets acquired (B50.145), it is silent as to the physical disposition of the excess over (or decrement under) the historical cost of the net assets acquired. The question then is whether the fair value increments (or decrements) should be held in consolidation or pushed down to the accounts of the acquired company. In a situation in which consolidated reporting is always the practice, the question is academic. But separate subsidiary financial statements are frequently presented. Even though all of an acquiree's voting common stock may be obtained, the subsidiary may have publicly held preferred stock or debt outstanding and thus have to publish financial statements. In addition, financial institutions dealing with the public will often publish separate statements aimed at showing financial soundness. An example of a purchase business combination in which push down accounting is used is presented in Figure 23.7.

Over the years, professional views on push down accounting have varied, and as a result, so has practice. To achieve consistency in the presentation of the separate financial statements of purchased subsidiaries, the SEC issued SAB 54, *Push Down Basis of Accounting Required in Certain Limited Circumstances* (Topic 5.J). The SAB indicates that:

• Push down accounting is required when the subsidiary is substantially wholly owned with no publicly held debt or preferred stock outstanding.

Acquisition by Ford: Prior to December 16, 1985, approximately 81.3% of the Company's issued and outstanding Common Stock was owned by NHC Corporation, a wholly owned subsidiary of National Intergroup, Inc ("NII"). The remaining 18.7% was held publicly and traded on the New York Stock Exchange. On December 16, 1985, Ford Motor Company completed the acquisition of the Company by means of a merger of Ford Affiliate Company, a wholly owned subsidiary of Ford, with and into the Company. As a result of the merger, all issued and outstanding shares of the Company's Common Stock were cancelled, with each former stockholder receiving $32.00 for each former share owned, and the Company became a wholly owned subsidiary of Ford.

The merger was accounted for as a purchase and "push down accounting" was applied, with the result that purchase accounting adjustments were reflected in the accounting of the Company, the Savings Bank and their subsidiaries.

Application of purchase accounting push down accounting resulted in adjustment of all outstanding assets and liabilities of the Company, the Savings Bank and their subsidiaries to their estimated "fair value" on the date of the merger. The following table reflects the changes made to the accounts of the Savings Bank and its subsidiaries as a result of applying push down accounting:

	Historical balances prior to merger	Purchase accounting adjustments	Fair value balances as of merger date
		(dollars in thousands)	
Assets			
Cash	$ 30,267	$ —	30,267
U.S. Government and other securities	997,751	(8,629)	989,122
Loans receivable, net	9,631,846	(93,934)	9,537,912
Premises and equipment, net	114,781	21,443	136,224
Other assets	744,652	(17,817)	726,835
Existing goodwill	29,466	(29,466)	
New goodwill		268,728	268,728
Total Assets	$11,548,763	$140,325	$11,689,088
Liabilities			
Deposit accounts	$ 8,551,155	$ 45,896	$ 8,597,051
Accrued interest on deposits	94,204		94,204
Notes, bonds and other obligations	2,129,459	26,591	2,156,050
Other liabilities	328,910	18,020	346,930
Deferred income	34,966	(34,996)	
Total Liabilities	11,138,694	55,541	11,194,235
Stockholder's Equity	410,069	84,784	494,853
Total liabilities and stockholder's equity	$11,548,763	$140,325	$11,689,088

FIG.23.7   Push Down Accounting

Source: Excerpt from Accounting Policies Note, First National Financial Corporation, 1986 Annual Report.

• Push down accounting is not required when (1) the subsidiary has publicly held debt or preferred stock that is outstanding when it becomes substantially wholly owned, and (2) there remains a large minority interest in the subsidiary.

SAB 54 applies to all SEC registration statements and periodic reports if the separate financial statements or summarized financial information for such purchased subsidiaries is presented.

SAB 54 left little doubt that push down of the parent's cost was deemed by the SEC to be "correct GAAP," required in cases where 90% or more of the ownership interest was held by the acquirer and there were few public preferred stockholders or debtholders. The SEC staff was concerned about the number of cases in which a wholly owned subsidiary, previously acquired at a considerable premium over book values, filed a registration statement offering a minority interest in its common stock, or in which the parent offered a portion of its own stockholdings in the subsidiary. (Either way, such an offering would create a so-called visible subsidiary of the parent.) In other cases, a majority interest, or even 100% of the previously acquired company, was offered to the public. By not employing push down accounting, the financial position and results of operations of the subsidiary company could appear substantially better on the old historical cost basis because of the absence of goodwill and other asset writeups, and the amortization and charge to expense thereof, respectively. This "better-looking" financial presentation was prized because the offered stock generally could be priced at a multiple of earnings, and the better the earnings the higher the offering proceeds.

The SEC staff has been vigilant in checking that push down accounting has been used in the maximum number of cases. And once a subsidiary that had publicly held preferred stock or debt retires those issues, it can no longer claim the exemption from push down if later it needs to present GAAP statements or summaries in SEC filings or periodic reports, even if an interest in it is not being offered to the public.

Push down accounting is included in the FASB's consolidations project-in-process; and based on reported progress through mid–1988, it would appear that push down accounting will be confirmed as GAAP. Unable to wait for FASB specifications, the SEC augmented SAB 54 by releasing SAB 73 (same Topic) at the end of 1987. SAB 73 deals with whether parent company debt (or mandatorily redeemable preferred stock) incurred in acquiring a subsidiary should be pushed down to that subsidiary's financial statements included in a public offering or other initial SEC registration. This situation is found in many leveraged buy-outs (discussed in the next major section) in which the leveraging is accomplished in a newly created parent that uses the cash to acquire a major proportion of the subsidiary's stock. While pushing down the parent's cost in these cases may also be required under SAB 54, the credit portion of the push down entry is usually paid-in capital, which under present GAAP does not carry a cost charged to operations.

The debt push down issue first arose in EITF issue 84-42, *Push-Down of Parent Company Debt to a Subsidiary*. The Task Force was unable to reach a consensus, and the resolution was left to depend on the circumstances of each case. These cases have turned up with increasing frequency, prompting the release of SEC guidelines.

SAB 73 requires that the debt (and related debt issue costs) be pushed down, and the interest expense and issue cost amortization be charged to the subsidiary's operations, if (1) the subsidiary will assume the debt at some point, (2) the proceeds of a subsidiary's debt or equity offering will be used to pay down the parent's debt, or (3) the subsidiary guarantees or pledges its assets as collateral for the parent's debt. Where none of these situations exists, but the parent has pledged the subsidiary's stock as collateral for the debt, push down is not required; but the arrangement must be fully disclosed in the subsidiary's financial statements so that readers can understand the probable impact on future cash flows. A typical impact might be that the subsidiary must pay substantial dividends (assuming they are earned) to the parent as the parent's wherewithal for debt service.

SAB 54 does not address one of the more important issues in push down accounting – whether 100% of fair value, or only that percentage of fair value that represents the percentage of the common stock acquired, should be pushed down. Because the SAB requirement applies to "substantially wholly owned" subsidiaries, it is likely that 100% is pushed down in most cases. Theoretically, however, because the parent company obviously did not purchase the minority interest, it should be maintained on its previous historical cost basis. The minority shareholders do not share in the additional capital resulting from the restatement, nor do they share in the depreciation, amortization, or any other charges or credits based on the differences between restated amounts and historical cost.

It should be noted that, unless and until the FASB issues a standard requiring push down accounting as part of GAAP, it need not be applied to companies that are not SEC registrants or whose separate financial statements or summarized information do not appear in a registrant's SEC filing or report. This point was reaffirmed in EITF Issue 86-9, *IRC Section 338 and Push Down Accounting*.

Goodwill

Positive Goodwill. Some of the intangible assets that an enterprise acquires in a business combination are clearly identifiable; but in most cases there remains a balance of purchase cost in excess of the fair values assigned to all identifiable net assets. This excess is *goodwill*, although it is often described in lengthier terms. In concept it is considered that portion of the purchase price paid for earning power in the future, but in reality it is the product of the bargaining process between parties to a business combination. The imponderables of merger negotiations make it nearly impossible to determine the worth of goodwill by direct valuation approaches.

In most cases, since a direct valuation process for goodwill cannot be used nor can the useful life of goodwill be determined, it is a reasonable compromise to define goodwill as the excess of purchase price over fair value of all identifiable net assets and assign it an arbitrary finite life. In constructing APB 17 (I60), the APB concluded that goodwill and other intangible assets have neither the "infinite" life of such assets as land nor the finite life of such assets as machinery (APB 17, ¶¶ 22–23). Goodwill must therefore be amortized systematically to income over the period estimated to be benefited, but not more than 40 years.

Although it is impossible to predict at the outset how long goodwill will last, it is sometimes possible to recognize that its value has diminished or expired. A company that reorganizes a purchased subsidiary and introduces substantially new product lines in place of previous lines, or a purchased subsidiary that has produced a string of operating losses, is generally demonstrating that the related purchased goodwill has significantly diminished in value and that part or all of the unamortized assets amount should be currently written off against income. The answer is not categorical, however. Many factors have to be considered, including what was expected of the purchased company at the date of purchase (e.g., realigning product lines or experiencing losses for a time may have been contemplated, with the goodwill still resulting through the arithmetic of the net asset valuation). Note that a company may not write off goodwill when the purchase combination is consummated (as is done in the United Kingdom and some other countries), even if it is not possible to identify attributes of the purchased company that would justify it as an asset; U.S. GAAP presumes no one would expend resources without receiving something of value.

In arriving at the position that all intangibles diminish in value, the APB suggested factors to be considered in estimating useful lives. Among them are (I60.108):

a. Legal, regulatory, or contractual provisions that may limit the maximum useful life;

b. Provisions for renewal or extension that may alter a specified limit on useful life;

c. Effects of obsolescence and other economic factors that may reduce a useful life;

d. Expected service life of individuals or groups of employees; and

e. Expected actions of competitors and other may restrict present competitive advantages.

In some circumstances, use of the maximum life of 40 years for goodwill is clearly incorrect. One such situation is identified in SFAS 72, *Accounting for Certain Acquisitions of Banking or Thrift Institutions* (Bt7). SFAS 72 specifies a different approach to goodwill arising from the acquisition of a banking or thrift institution with fair values of liabilities that are in excess of fair value of assets. Typically, those entities are in a troubled financial condition and are purchased or "absorbed" by other financial institutions, often with the assistance of regulatory authorities. See Chapters 40 and 41 for further discussion of this type of acquisition.

Negative Goodwill. When there is an excess of the fair value of net assets received in a purchase business combination over the fair value of the consideration paid (i.e., a *bargain purchase*), this excess must be allocated proportionately to reduce all noncurrent assets except marketable securities. After all such noncurrent assets are reduced to a zero value, any remaining amount should be separately classified as a deferred credit, usually referred to as *negative goodwill.* This negative goodwill should be amortized (as an addition to income) in a systematic manner. As a practical matter, the amortization period extends from three to approximately 15 years, depending on the nature of the business acquired and its operating record after acquisition.

There is a presumption in APB 16 (B50.160) that negative goodwill will rarely exist, and thus the net assets being valued in a purchase should have an inherently lower valuation close to the purchase price. However, there will still be some bargain purchases, such as the listed company whose stock is selling considerably below book value. In a purchase business combination brought about through an exchange of equity securities, when the acquired company has a low price/earnings ratio and the acquiring company has a high price/earnings ratio, a considerable amount of negative goodwill could arise. The amount would, or course, depend on whether the low price/earnings ratio represented market recognition of unrecorded impairment in net book values. If book values are in need of reduction to fair values, presumably little or no excess credit or negative goodwill should result.

APB 16 suggests that there may be cases where the quoted market price is not fair value of the stock issued, and that the net assets received should be estimated even though it would be difficult to measure their fair value directly (B50.133). One meaning attributed to this paragraph is that it was intended to cover a particularly significant purchase by issuing stock (e.g., one in which the issuing company doubles its stockholders' equity). There could be a drastic effect, perhaps upward, in the market value of the issuing company's stock after acquisition, and this possibility should be considered when valuing the shares issued. In such a case, most accountants would oppose recording negative goodwill when in fact positive goodwill may be involved.

LEVERAGED BUY-OUT ACCOUNTING

Background

An LBO is often described in the press in the following manner:

> In a leveraged buyout, a small group of investors acquires a company in a transaction financed largely by borrowing. Ultimately, the debt is paid with funds generated by the acquired company's operations or sale of its assets.

In fact, the transaction variations are endless, and the only part of the press definition that seems to apply in all LBOs is "leveraged."

The leveraging is not unique to LBOs; indeed many takeovers (both hostile and friendly) are extremely leveraged, because of the large amounts of cash needed to buy out the public shareholders. Also, many hostile takeovers are warded off by a management-led LBO, and the leveraging involved in doing so may be much the same as the debt load planned by the raider. Takeovers and LBOs have resulted in the issuance of so much debt by corporate America that high-yield bonds (also known as junk bonds), once reserved for companies with the poorest credit ratings, have become accepted by institutional and other reasonably conservative investors. In a highly leveraged business, there is, of course, a high risk that operations or postacquisition divestitures will not provide adequate funds for debt service; indeed, a number of such companies have had to restructure their junk bond debt not long after issuance, and a few have become bankrupt.

Nevertheless, the rewards to equity holders of buying a business with very little equity (say 3–10%) and a maximum debt load can be phenomenal. It has often been said that insiders have an unfair advantage in knowing the true value of their company's assets and operating units, and the public shareholder is mulcted even though he is (1) offered a price much greater than the highest market price ever attained by the stock, and (2) assured by an investment banker's formal opinion that the price is "fair." These criticisms are leveled when the buy-out group turns substantial profits on postacquisition sales of operating units, or after a brief hiatus as a private company, has a public offering of common stock at multiples of the earlier buy-out price. Whatever the frequency with which this bonanza occurs, there are more than enough fizzles and failures. Certainly, with high leveraging, success in the short term is often defined by a low-to-moderate level of interest rates.

In most LBOs, a public company "goes private"; but of course a nonpublic company can also be the subject of an LBO. There are many transaction formats, but commonly (1) a "Newco" is formed by a small group of investors, (2) it obtains equity contributions (usually modest) from these investors, and (3) it borrows the rest of the funds needed to pay the public shareholders the price offered (and accepted) for shares of the acquiree company, or "Oldco." A portion of Newco's equity injections can come from contribution of shares already owned by members of the investment group; or it may be that these investors will tender some or all of their shares for the cash offering price, reinvesting some or all of the cash as equity in Newco. The debt can be in many forms, but frequently it consists of bank and institutional term financing, private investor participation (both in equity and debt) arranged by the investment bankers, and an expensive bridge loan intended to be refinanced within a year (or two years at the most).

Because the private investors hold unregistered junk bonds that cannot be sold on the market, they invariably require registration within a stipulated time period to provide marketability. The bridge loan may be a term loan of up to 10 years; but it will have a high initial rate that is likely to increase at least annually. Consequently, registration and sale of permanent financing debt often follows shortly after the buyout, to obtain less expensive funds for the liquidation of the bridge loan. Although the company may be privately held from an equity point of view, publicly tradeable debt securities will keep the company's financial statements in full view.

Some LBOs are accomplished by issuance to the public shareholders of securities in addition to cash. A debenture, for example, or some warrants or convertible debt, may be used because it is not always possible for the company to raise 100% in cash. And to assuage the skeptical shareholder who feels that the insiders "are going to make a killing," numerous LBOs have included common stock of Newco in the offering package; the resulting minority public ownership (say 5–20%) is called a "stub" and it of course must be registered with the SEC to be publicly tradeable.

Finally, the investor group generally contemplates streamlining the operations, selling off unwanted or non-core businesses (the proceeds of which may be dedicated to the reduction of LBO debt), and taking the company public again within three to five years. Thus there is very little that is private about most LBOs, even though the company is "going private."

Forerunner Issues

There was some time lapse between the advent of megadollar LBOs and the admission by accountants that they posed a monumental accounting problem. Early on, the EITF addressed several tangential issues:

- 84-13 *Purchase of Stock Options and Stock Appreciation Rights in a Leveraged Buyout.* A consensus was reached that compensation expense of the acquiree company must be charged, rather than considering this payment a part of purchase price.

- 84-23 *Leveraged Buyout Holding Company Debt.* No consensus was reached as to the pushdown of debt into the separate financial statements of the acquiree.

- 85-11 *Use of an Employee Stock Ownership Plan in a Leveraged Buyout.* No consensus was reached on how an ESOP that is a major participant in an LBO should account for future compensation expense.
- 85-21 *Changes of Ownership Resulting in a New Basis of Accounting.* No consensus was reached as to what level of ownership change should result in a new basis. The SEC Observer admitted that there are inconsistencies in application perhaps caused by the fact that not all registrant filings are examined. This issue offered the opportunity to address LBOs nearly a year earlier than actually happened.

The identification of the real accounting issue that eluded the EITF in these earlier discussions is covered in the following sections.

Accounting Problem

The accounting problem with LBOs is easy to identify but hard to solve. In a purchase business combination, a new owner pays a price to acquire all (or a majority) of another enterprise; and the price paid is allocated to the acquired net assets and goodwill. In an LBO in which prior shareowners (often the management group) participate, the price paid to shareholders being bought out might not be a purchase price, but might be some type of capital transaction that should be charged to shareholder's equity, without the assets being fair-valued; or it may be some of both: a puchase mixed with a capital transaction. In other words, is the LBO to be regarded as a purchase business combination by new investors, or a step acquisition by existing owners, or a purchase of treasury stock by Oldco (variously called a redemption, distribution, or effective dividend)?

The genesis of this issue is found in APB 16, which defines a pooling and says that every other business combination, including the acquisition of a minority interest (and by inference a step acquisition), is a purchase. Thus a decision must be made as to whether an LBO is some kind of purchase business combination in the first place; if not, the only remaining choice under GAAP is some type of capital transaction.

GAAP is notoriously weak in defining "minority" versus "controlling" interests, as well as in discussing the appropriate treatment of capital transactions, and the FASB is working on this in its Consolidations project (see Chapter 24). Accountants left to their own devices (and the oversight of the SEC) have had to make decisions of overwhelming significance in post-LBO financial statements. If it is decided that some kind of purchase business combination has occurred, the net assets acquired are restated to their fair values and the remainder of the purchase price becomes goodwill—commonly the largest "asset" in the Newco financial statements. If it is decided that a business combination has not occurred, then consideration paid to Oldco shareholders is necessarily a reduction of net worth. Such a net worth reduction is approximately the same as the debit that would have gone to goodwill. In almost any of the major publicized LBOs the negative net worth would be massive if not accounted for using purchase accounting theory.

It is almost axiomatic that a company with a substantial negative net worth will find its securities not easily salable on the public market. At least investment bankers are not anxious to try. Therefore, having positive net worth and the concomitant 40-year goodwill even if immense is usually thought to be eminently preferable to negative net worth and minimal goodwill (despite the benefit of low goodwill on future earnings). While tangible net assets may be about the same in either case, what shows as equity in the audited financials contained in the registration statement is what seems to count!

SEC Concerns. The SEC staff, watching the LBO scene during 1985 and marveling at the variety of differing accounting treatments propounded with solemn belief by various accountants, finally decided that some action was required. The staff therefore began to insist that to the extent there was continuing ownership between the prior company (Oldco) and the newly formed company (Newco), such continuing interests had to be valued at "carry-over basis" — essentially the cost to these shareholders of their interest in Oldco plus equity in earnings since acquisition, adjusted for change in ownership percentage resulting from the LBO. This insistence was based on the concept that write-ups of assets (mostly goodwill) cannot occur unless an exchange transaction has taken place with an unrelated party.

The application of this SEC staff policy beginning in late 1985 left many questions unanswered, most significantly whether any and all Oldco shareholders continuing into Newco should have carry-over basis assigned, or whether the assignment should be made for only those who are part of a "control group."

Initial EITF Consenses. In April 1986, the SEC staff introduced the LBO accounting problem at the EITF (Issue 86-16, *Carryover of Predecessor Cost in Leveraged Buyout Transactions*). A consensus was reached in July 1986 on a half-dozen specified hypothetical cases. The consensus created two tests that, if met, would enable the post-LBO entity to treat the transaction as a full purchase, that is, to record 100% of the consideration paid as the purchase price of the acquired company:

- *50% test.* New investors must have obtained a controlling financial interest in the post-LBO entity. (The EITF did not define new investors or controlling financial interest. GAAP has traditionally defined control as holding more than a 50% voting equity interest.)
- *80% test.* Cash and other monetary consideration (such as debt, or similar instruments like redeemable preferred stock) must constitute at least 80% of the aggregate purchase price paid to the Oldco shareholders. Cash that is reinvested in Newco by these shareholders must be netted in making this test.

If the 50% new investor test was not met, the transaction was deemed to be a step acquisition or (step divestment) to the extent the continuing investors increase (or decrease) their ownership interest. If the 50% test was met but the 80% test was not, the carry-over basis (as defined below) of the Oldco shareholders (to the extent of their ownership interest in Newco) would have to be used in determining the amount of purchase price to be reflected in the postacquisition financial statements.

The EITF provided additional guidance to assist in implementing the two basic rules:

- The controlling financial interest had to be substantive, genuine, and not temporary.
- "De minimis passive interests" in Oldco were to be ignored; but note that officers and directors of Oldco were deemed not passive.

- Warrants and options were presumed the equivalent of voting financial interests. Convertible securities that were "equivalent" to a voting financial interest would also have to be taken into account in applying the 50% test.
- An unreasonable value assigned to the Newco ownership interest acquired by the Oldco shareholders could indicate a violation of the 80% test. This issue was important only when these shareholders contributed something other than cash, such as stock of Oldco.
- When carry-over basis was to be used because the 80% test was not met, it was to be valued at the amount the carry-over shareholders paid for their original ownership interest plus equity in undistributed Oldco earnings, less cash and other monetary consideration paid out to these shareholders.

Although the 1986 EITF consensus provided a minimum framework around which LBO transactions could be structured, there remained many important unanswered questions, among them:

1. GAAP usually requires that a voting equity ownership interest exceeding 50% demonstrates control. The actual controlling amount could be substantially less if the other shareholders are widely dispersed.
2. Many "new investors" in LBO transactions are institutional and similar investors that have no intention of being long-term shareholders. The investment horizon is probably only one to five years. Should this anticipated temporary stay as a private company be allowed to result in new basis accounting?
3. Warrants and options are presumed to be equivalent to voting financial interests. Supposedly this presumption can be overcome, but based on what kind of factors: strike price or date of exercise or something else?
4. Convertible securities "equivalent" to a voting financial interest also should be taken into account when applying the two tests. Factors such as voting rights, time until conversion, and remoteness of events triggering conversion are to be considered. No guidance was given on how to make this evaluation.
5. What is a de minimis passive interest? While an individual 1% owner may qualify as de minimis, what about 49 unrelated 1% owners aggregating 49%?
6. The EITF was silent as to the accounting for Newco when there is no controlling financial interest, for example, if the insiders' interest goes to 50% and new investors have the other 50%.

Finalized Accounting—Ownership Increases

The EITF's initial consensus on LBO accounting in July 1986 was difficult to apply and accountants did not uniformly follow it. After discussion at each subsequent EITF meeting, an extensively revised consensus was reached in July 1987.

The 1987 consensus contains a series of elements that should be present to warrant a change in basis of the acquired company, as follows:

1. A partial or complete change in accounting basis is appropriate only where there has been a change in control of voting interest, that is, a new controlling investor must be established.
2. To distinguish an LBO transaction from other business combinations, the LBO should be effected in a single, highly leveraged transaction (or a series of related and anticipated

transactions) that results in the acquisition by Newco of all previously outstanding voting equity interest of Oldco; that is, there can be no remaining minority interest in Oldco.

3. The form of a transaction by which a controlling investor obtains its interest in Newco does not change the accounting to be applied. If a controlling shareholder of Newco owned a voting interest in Oldco,[4] then the transaction must be accounted for as a step acquisition to the extent of that controlling shareholder's voting interest in Oldco.

4. The total consideration paid to noncontrolling shareholders of Newco to acquire the outstanding shares of Oldco should generally be measured at fair value; however, the fair value of any securities issued by Newco should be objectively determinable. To ensure that the fair value of Newco securities issued to acquire Oldco is objectively determinable, fair value should not be used, whether or not the Newco securities are publicly traded, unless at least 80% of the fair value of consideration paid to acquire Oldco equity interest from noncontrolling investors of Newco is comprised of monetary consideration.

Additional commentary on these elements is contained in the following sections.

New Control Group. The following factors must be considered when assessing whether a new controlling financial interest has been established:

- Controlling financial interest is defined as ownership of a majority of Oldco's voting securities. It may not be temporary in nature.
- Two or more shareholders acting in concert may join to form a control group. Evidence must suggest that their economic interests at the acquisition date are sufficiently compatible and that they will continue to collaborate to exert voting control over Newco after the LBO.
- If management participates in the LBO, there is a rebuttable presumption that they are a member of the control group. If this presumption is not overcome, only partial step-up to fair value is allowed.
- Convertible securities (e.g., convertible debt or convertible preferred stock), warrants, and options held by noncontrolling shareholders should be considered when determining whether a new controlling financial interest exists — especially if the new investor group does not have control on an if-converted basis.
- Warrants and options are presumed the equivalent of voting equity securities when determining whether control has changed. Factors to consider in overcoming this presumption include the relationship of the exercise price to the fair value of Newco equity securities and whether the ability to exercise is dependent on future events or passage of a significant period of time.

The consensus further provides that if a new control group is not identified, no step-up in basis is allowed and all of the purchase price is recorded as a charge against Newco's equity accounts (i.e., a recapitalization). When recapitalization accounting is employed, the usual result is negative net worth (i.e., a deficiency in assets).

---

[4] The EITF first discussed and eventually resolved the situation in which a noncontrolling shareholder in Oldco increases ownership in Newco. In 1988, an issue was raised as to the accounting treatment when such a shareholder's ownership percentage in Newco is less than the ownership percentage held in Oldco. This is discussed in "Ownership Decreases" later in this chapter.

Monetary Consideration. Newco may record nonmonetary consideration (e.g., Newco equity securities) paid to former Oldco shareholders who are not members of the Newco control group at fair value provided the "80% monetary consideration test" is met. This test provides that monetary consideration (e.g., cash, debt, or debt-type securities such as redeemable preferred stock), net of any required reinvestment in Newco, must constitute at least 80% of the total consideration paid to Oldco shareholders who are not members of the new control group. Therefore, to achieve full step-up, only 20% of the purchase price paid to non-controlling shareholders for their Oldco equity interests may be in the form of Newco equity securities.

If this test is not met, Newco would value the nonmonetary consideration paid the noncontrolling shareholders at the proportionate book value of Oldco. Newco would value the remaining Oldco interests acquired from the noncontrolling shareholders at the monetary consideration paid.

Partial Step-Up. Generally, Newco would reflect a partial step-up in basis when the following conditions exist:

- Members of the new control group in Newco had a voting equity interest in Oldco.
- Members of management, who are considered members of the control group, had a voting equity interest in Oldco.

The partial step-up refers to using a portion of the purchase price paid plus "predecessor cost" to value the LBO. Predecessor cost refers to a Newco shareholder's basis in a prior investment in Oldco. It is determined by adding the shareholder's portion of Oldco earnings since the date of acquisition to the original cost of the investment in Oldco less dividends and all payments received on Oldco voting stock. Figure 23.8 provides an illustration of this calculation. The assumptions are as follows:

1. Oldco has the following ownership interest before the LBO takes place.

	Shares	Net book value	Fair value
Management	10	$ 1,000	$ 1,500
Public	90	9,000	13,500
	100	$10,000	$15,000

2. Oldco has 100 common shares outstanding with a fair value of $150 per share. After the LBO, Newco will have 100 shares outstanding with a fair value of $10 per share.

3. Management's cost basis in its investment in Oldco (after adjustment for all dividends received since the stock was acquired) is $102 per share.

4. The LBO is effected as follows:
   - A new investor group forms Newco by contributing $450 in exchange for 45% of Newco common stock. The new investors plan to hold the stock for an extended period (e.g., not less than two to three years).
   - Management, acting in concert with the new investors, contributes some of its Oldco common stock to Newco in exchange for 30% of Newco common stock.

Analysis of Newco's Acquisition of Oldco Common Stock

| | Oldco Shares Acquired | |
	Number	Fair Value
From the public		
Cash	87.92	$13,250
Newco common stock (25 shares)	2.08	250
	90.00	$13,500
From management		
Cash	7.50	1,200
Newco common stock (30 shares)	2.50	300
	10.00	1,500
Total	100.00	$15,000

80% Monetary Consideration Test

Total monetary consideration to the public (not members of control group)	$13,250
Total consideration paid to the public	13,500
Percentage of consideration that is monetary	98%

Determination of Newco's purchase price

Oldco shares acquired from management (valued at predecessor cost)	$ (180)*
Oldco shares acquired for cash and stock	14,700
	$14,520

Valuation of Newco equity

Cash contributed by new investors	$ 450
Newco common stock issued to the public shareholders (valued at fair value)	250
Newco common stock issued to management (valued at predecessor cost)	(180)*
	$ 520

---

* Predecessor cost is determined as follows:

Management's basis in its Oldco investment ($102 × 10 shares)	$ 1,020
Less cash received	(1,200)
	$ (180)

FIG. 23.8   Illustration of Leveraged Buy-Out Accounting

- Newco acquires management's remaining outstanding Oldco shares for cash. Newco also acquires all other Oldco outstanding common shares for cash and 25% of Newco common stock.
- Newco issues debt totalling $14,000 and uses the proceeds to acquire Oldco common stock.

To determine whether Newco may use a new basis of accounting to value the LBO, Newco must determine whether a new control group has been established. In this example, the new investors and management are acting in concert to effect the transaction and together constitute a new control group.

Secondly, the 80% monetary consideration test will determine how much of a step-up is accorded to the Oldco equity acquired from the public. In Figure 23.8 this test is met, and Newco should record all of the Oldco shares acquired from the public at fair value. Also, because management is a member of the control group, Newco equity exchanged for management's Oldco common stock is valued at predecessor cost.

Ownership Decreases

In Issue 88-16, *Basis in Leveraged Buyout Transactions When the Previous Owner's Interest Declines*, the EITF considered the situation in which a shareholder in Oldco continued in Newco, but at a reduced percentage (also referred to as a "leveraged sell–off"). The preceding discussion (in Issue 86-16) focused on the reverse situation.

In mid–1988, the EITF reached a consensus that control has changed if a new investor (or group) can unilaterally (i.e., without participation of or interference from) control the carryover shareholder. However, if the selling stockholder retains an interest in Newco, carryover basis (as discussed in the preceding sections) would be required if the seller is deemed a member of the "control group." During August, 1988, the Task Force decided on criteria for determining whether the seller is part of the control group, adopting what was described as a "pragmatic position": For purposes of determining a change in control, a seller is presumed *not* to be a member of the control group if the seller's capital at risk is less than 20% of the total capital at risk in Newco, and the buy-out is essentially a cash deal. The presumption may be refuted by the facts and circumstances (although this will be very difficult).

OTHER ACCOUNTING MATTERS

Acquiring Assets or Stock

When a business combination is formed by acquiring all the stock of the acquiree company, generally all of its assets and liabilities are acquired; if there are particular assets or liabilities that are subject to future reevaluation, such as possible uncollectible receivables or lawsuit contingencies, those matters may be dealt with by an escrow arrangement and warranty (discussed in the earlier section "Contingencies"). However, business combinations (whether pooling or purchase) can also be performed by acquiring assets rather than stock. Of course, in a pooling, the assets tendered must be substantially all the operating net assets of the acquiree company, and this is accomplished by the acquiree company tendering assets and receiving the stock; it will then liquidate by distributing the stock to its shareholders. In a purchase business combination some of the assets may be held back, for example, the acquiring company may want only certain operations, or it may wish to leave the acquiree company with certain problem assets or liabilities instead of handling those through a warranty and escrow.

In this case, the consideration is distributed to the acquiree company in exchange for the agreed-upon net assets, and the acquiree company remains in existence pending liquidation of the assets not exchanged.

Entities Under Common Control

When parties to a combination are controlled by one entity, person, or group, the transaction is not a business combination under APB 16 and its rules do not apply (B50.101). For example, when the net assets of a wholly owned subsidiary are transferred to the parent company and the subsidiary is left holding treasury stock of the parent, only the legal organization is changed. But not all cases are as clear-cut. Two publicly held companies in which family interests directly own 60% of each is still probably clear enough; however, if smaller percentages are owned and that ownership is less direct, the classification becomes murky.

Historically, for publicly held companies, the SEC has insisted that such mergers be accounted for *like-a-pooling,* although technically they are not poolings of interest and do not meet the pooling criteria.

Much debate has occurred concerning the accounting for the acquisition by a wholly owned subsidiary of another subsidiary that is not wholly owned and vice versa. Some accountants believe that the first transaction represents the acquisition of a minority interest while the second should be accounted for as if it were a pooling of interests. Other accountants believe that both transactions should be accounted for like poolings. To put this debate to rest, the FASB issued Technical Bulletin 85-5, *Issues Relating to Accounting for Business Combinations ... Stock Transactions Between Companies Under Common Control* (B50.596A–.596D).

If, for example, a 100%-owned subsidiary acquires in exchange for its own stock all of the shares of an 80%-owned sister company, the transaction is accounted for as a purchase of the 20% minority interest. However, if the 80%-owned subsidiary is the acquirer, then the exchange is treated as a combination of companies under common control (like-a-pooling) solely because the minority shareholders do not have to exchange their present shares. The FASB thus clarified two apparently conflicting AICPA interpretations of APB 16 (B50.593–.596 and .645–.648), holding that "the accounting ... depends upon the nature of the exchange that takes place, not the apparent similarity of the results of different transactions."

Further, in a downstream merger in which a parent company is merged into a subsidiary, if the subsidiary is partially owned (i.e., less than 100%), the transaction is treated as if the minority interest in the subsidiary were being purchased for shares of the parent company (B50.596E–.596F).

The foregoing matters covered by TB 85-5 were raised in EITF issue 85-4, *Downstream Mergers and Other Stock Transactions Between Companies Under Common Control,* as to which the Task Force was not asked to reach any consensus. The FASB staff was "just checking" what was being done in practice, which as it developed varied somewhat from the staff's view. The TB came forth nine months later to memorialize the staff's view and thus to eliminate variations in practice.

TB 85-5 does not cover all possibilities, however. Master limited partnerships (MLPs), inspired by TRA 1986, are generally formed from assets in existing businesses, resulting in units that are publicly traded. Various forms of transactions in which MLPs are created are referred to as roll-ups, drop-downs, roll-outs, and reorganizations. MLPs are found principally in the oil and gas and real estate industries (as mentioned in Chapters 34 and 35 respectively). In Issue 87-21, *Change of Accounting Basis in Master Limited Partnership Transactions,* the EITF finally concluded in August, 1988 that carryover basis was appropriate for all forms of the transaction; that is, the basis of the assets should not be stepped up.

Sale of Subsidiary for Equity Interest in Buyer

In Issue 85-43, *Sale of Subsidiary for Equity Interest in Buyer*, the EITF struggled with the often encountered situation in which an enterprise sells a subsidiary for an equity interest (e.g., 20%) in the buyer. If the equity interest received is deemed a similar productive asset (as defined in N35.406–.407), then the ex-parent is not permitted to record a gain on the sale, but would merely assign the carrying basis of the subsidiary (written down if necessary to reflect impairment in value) to the buyer's stock received (regardless of the fair value of the stock).

The EITF did not reach a consensus, and essentially transferred this subject to the discussion under Issue 86-29, which deals with nonmonetary transactions more broadly. In the discussion under 86-29, the Task Force was divided on whether the fact that the buyer is in the same line of business makes the receipt of the 20% stock investment a similar productive asset. Further:

> The Task Force also discussed various exchanges involving investments accounted for by consolidation and by the equity method. The Task Force reached a consensus that an enterprise should account for an exchange of securities in which it acquires control of a subsidiary as a business combination in accordance with Opinion 16. An enterprise should account for an exchange of securities accounted for by consolidation or by the equity method for an investment in which it does not acquire control of a business but for which it will account by the equity method, as a nonmonetary transaction in accordance with Opinion 29. The Task Force noted that the provisions of this consensus were not intended to apply to exchanges involving joint ventures or the acquisition of a minority interest.

The SEC Observer expressed concern that literal application of the consensus (as quoted above) could result in a 100% write-up of an asset as to which the "seller" has not actually transferred control. For example, if an asset is sold for shares, and the seller thereby obtains control of the buyer, obviously the seller still has indirect control of the asset. The EITF decided that in such a case, gain could only be recognized to the extent of the minority interest percentage in the buyer. Further, intercompany profit elimination would be applicable on consolidation. The Task Force emphasized the need to exercise judgment and to avoid overriding APB 16 requirements.

SEC Requirements

Because of their importance, business combinations involving publicly held companies are subjected to a myriad of SEC regulations designed to protect the interests of existing and prospective shareholders. Many business combinations are accomplished by the issuance of additional securities, either unissued or treasury shares, and if the newly issued shares are to be unrestricted, they must be registered under the Securities Act of 1933.

Many combinatons involve the issuance of securities, requiring the preparation of a proxy solicitation under Section 14 of the Securities Exchange Act of 1934 to obtain shareholders' approval. If two publicly held companies are involved, each can use the same proxy with separate covers.

The SEC registration requirements for shares to be issued in a business combination are met by preparation of a 1933 Act Form S-4 (Form F-4 for foreign private issuers). The S-4 may incorporate by reference information from reports filed pursuant to the continuous reporting requirements of the 1934 Act. The extent of such incorporation, if any, is the same as would be permitted in a registration prepared not involving a business combination. If the requirements for Forms S-1, S-2, or S-3 would otherwise have to be met, then the Form S-4 submission also would have to meet those requirements. (Further information on these forms may be found in Chapter 47.)

A popular vehicle for accomplishing a business combination is the tender offer by one corporation inviting the shareholders of another corporation to tender or sell their shares for cash (or less frequently, for debt or equity securities or a combination thereof). SEC regulations controlling tender offers are contained in Sections 13 and 14 of the 1934 Act, and require substantial information about the tender offer and financial data about the tendering company to be filed with the SEC and sent to the target company shareholders.

Many publishers have services that describe in detail the ever-changing SEC requirements in the business combination area. (For an accounting and auditing viewpoint, as contrasted with the usual legal approach, see *Accountants SEC Practice Manual* (Poloway, 1988).

Generally, the SEC rigorously enforces the provisions of APBs 16 and 17. Over time, the SEC has interpreted and expanded those provisions, especially the ones related to the pooling-of-interests criteria. Some of the more important developments have been discussed previously in this chapter.

International Accounting Standard

In 1983, the International Accounting Standards Committee issued IAS 22, *Accounting for Business Combinations* (AC 9022). The requirements of IAS 22 are not as detailed as APB 16, but generally they conform to U.S. GAAP, except as noted in the following discussion.

Purchase Method. IAS 22 indicates that a business combination should be accounted for under the purchase method, except in the rare circumstance when it is deemed to be a uniting (pooling) of interests. Goodwill or negative goodwill can either be set up and amortized over its useful life (no maximum period given) or treated as an immediate adjustment of shareholders' equity. Under GAAP, this latter treatment would not be allowed.

Under GAAP, the realization of a net operating loss carry-forward of the acquired company would retroactively reduce the amount of goodwill; under IAS 22, the realization is recognized as income (unless the goodwill had been charged to the equity accounts, in which case the realized tax benefits would also be an equity adjustment). IAS 22 also requires a reassessment of the goodwill recorded so that any amount attributable to the realized tax benefits can be charged off to operations.

Pooling Method. The rules for pooling are much less detailed than under U.S. GAAP. A business combination is deemed to be a uniting of interests only if the shareholders of the combining enterprises achieve a continuing mutual sharing in the risks and benefits attaching to the combined enterprise. Further:

1. The basis of the transaction must be principally an exchange of voting common shares of the enterprises involved; and
2. Substantially all of the net assets and operations of the combining enterprises must be combined in one entity.

Although these are the only pooling criteria, the background information in the statement indicates that continuing participation by management of the combining enterprises in the combined entity would further demonstrate that pooling would be appropriate.

AUDITING CONSIDERATIONS

The companies involved in a business combination are most often audited by different CPA firms. Thus the first challenge faced by the auditors is to establish a working arrangement with each other. For the *lead* auditor who decides to express reliance on the auditor of the company to be acquired, a business combination presents no special problems other than the usual reliance considerations discussed in Chapter 11. Even if reliance is not expressed by the lead auditor, he should satisfy himself as to the financial statements and the *secondary* auditor following the guidance in AU 543.

The material that follows is written mostly from the perspective of the auditor for the acquiring company, but by reversing the focus, it is equally applicable to auditors of the acquiree.

Pooling vs. Purchase

The critical factor in the audit of a business combination is the degree of assurance the auditor achieves in determining that the proper accounting method has been used, either pooling-of-interests or purchase accounting. To confirm that all the criteria have been met for a pooling of interests, the auditor must assess the terms of the business combination agreement, the history of the capital structure of all combining companies, the financial transactions of all the companies (both prior transactions and those for a period of time after the combination is consummated), and the terms of any other possibly related contract, agreement, or arrangement coming to his attention that might affect the accounting for a combination. Once there is a breach of one pooling criterion, adherence to the other criteria is academic; purchase accounting must be applied. In a purchase, the auditor is no longer concerned with the pooling criteria, but instead faces a whole series of valuation problems.

When the pooling method has been used, the auditor must be particularly alert to the possibility that one of the combining companies, either inadvertently or intentionally, has performed some act after the combination was consummated that violates the criteria. If so, the combining companies theoretically could be faced with the very complex problem of unwinding the accounting, that is, a retroactive *depooling.*

As a practical matter, subsequent acts of this kind do not show up until quite some time after combination and are invariably justified on the basis of business developments occurring after the pooling date. Such "current events" do not result in retroactive depooling. This treatment is consistent with SFAS 16 (A35) proscribing prior-period adjustments, except that errors should be rolled back if material. Thus, if a preponderance of evidence demonstrates that a major violative act was contemplated at the pooling date but not disclosed to the auditor, this is an error (A35.104) requiring the auditor to follow SAS 1, *Subsequent Discovery of Facts Existing at the Date of the Auditor's Report* (AU 561); the treatment would be retroactive depooling or other accounting that currently accomplishes the same net result that would have been obtained if the transaction had been initially treated as a purchase.

Valuation of Consideration in a Purchase

The total purchase price is either the value of the consideration given or received, whichever is more clearly evident. In a combination in which all of the consideration given is cash, there is little question that this is the more clearly evident value and that it represents the fair value of the net assets received. Also reasonably clear, granting that there may be some blockage involved, is the issuance by the purchaser of a relatively small proportion (in relation to amounts outstanding) of freely traded, marketable equity or debt securities of the purchasing company. Generally, the value of such marketable securities also should represent the fair value of the assets received.

However, an audit challenge is necessary when the consideration given is an operating asset of the purchaser, thinly traded equity or debt securities of the purchaser, the equity securities of a closely held company, or a large block of securities whose issuance may alter market price. Often an investment banking concern is engaged to establish the value of a security to be issued in a purchase, but apart from actively traded public companies, the fair value of the consideration received may be the more clearly evident value. In this case, the appraised (or otherwise determined) fair values of the net assets received become crucially important. If the purchase price is determined in this way, the combination will not result in any goodwill. When the assets received are comprised substantially of natural resources (oil and gas reserves, hard minerals, or standing timber), generally their values are relatively more easily obtained and are readily usable as the fair value of the consideration received.

Negative Goodwill. In determining whether negative goodwill exists, the auditor should carefully consider whether stock being exchanged really has a value more readily determinable than the assets being acquired. The services of investment bankers could be used to evaluate the probable effect on the issuing company's stock as a result of making the offer, especially if the total amount of stock to be exchanged is larger than the preexisting outstanding stock of the issuing company.

The action in the market of both companies' stocks before and after the announcement of exchange would also be significant in setting valuation. Although that type of assessment is useful to the auditor in judging whether the valuation process is reasonable, that assessment is seldom used to adjust the valuation by the acquiring company in a purchase business combination. In any event, the auditor must be alert to the creation of negative goodwill, whereby the fair value of assets received is considerably in excess of the fair value of consideration given. If a credit exists, it is first applied, of course, to noncurrent assets (except marketable securities), and if those amounts should be offset, the future operations of the acquired company will not be burdened with charges such as depreciation. This is said to caution that there can indeed be abuses of purchase accounting, as there were in the late 1960s in pooling accounting.

Valuation and Appraisal Process. For other security valuations, the auditor should not act as an appraiser and does not substitute his judgment for that of management. However, he should review all information considered by management or other experts, read relevant minutes of directors' meetings, and ascertain the procedures followed in the valuation process. If the more evident value is a closely held security for which an investment banker's valuation has been secured, the auditor must also consider the investment banker's credentials.

The appraisal process is critical in any transaction, not only in the establishment of the purchase price (when the fair value of the consideration received may be more clearly evident than that given) but also in the establishment of the fair value of long-term assets such as plant and equipment. As with any other expert's advice and support, the auditor (adhering to AU 336) must assess the credentials of the appraiser, review the process by which the appraisals are calculated, and establish the reasonableness of both in relation to the intended use of the assets after acquisition.

Additional guidance is available regarding real estate in *Guide for the Use of Real Estate Appraisal Information* (AICPA, 1987j).

Assessment of Goodwill

Once the auditor is satisfied that the purchase price used is appropriate and that the purchase price allocation based on the fair value of the net assets acquired is reasonable, there will almost always be a net balance of purchase price in excess of, or less than, the fair value of the net assets acquired. The balance is goodwill or a deferred credit (negative goodwill), respectively.

On an ongoing basis both the amortization rate (i.e., amortizable life) and the periodic, ongoing value of goodwill are the subject of audit consideration (I60.111–.112). There is little possibility that goodwill will be amortized too rapidly; except for financial institution and high-technology acquirees, goodwill is almost universally amortized over the maximum permitted period of 40 years to minimize its effect on earnings. However, the auditor must periodically assess whether it has undergone a diminution in value, which would require a partial or complete write-off against income.

In the case of negative goodwill, it is unlikely that an auditor will find a long amortization period, since the nature of negative goodwill, and therefore its value, is nebulous. If anything, the negative goodwill will be considered a quasi-accrual of costs necessary to "turn around" the acquired business, and turnarounds should not take more than a few years if they are ever to occur. The amortization period for negative goodwill depends on the facts and circumstances of each case. Depending on the situation, the period might extend from as little as three years in a few cases to a maximum of 15 years.

Acquisition Audits and Reviews

The independent auditor is in an excellent position to assist a client in the review of an acquisition candidate. The scope of his assistance can vary considerably. In some engagements, the auditor will be part of the team involved in evaluating a merger opportunity for a client. In such a situation, his financial and investigative expertise will be drawn upon to point to areas of business vulnerability that may be present in the accounts, and to assist the client in reaching qualitative judgments about a potential acquisition candidate. In a more traditional role, an audit in accordance with GAAS could be performed, extended to include requested financial procedures if concerns exist that are not addressed in the normal audit work. Other situations may only necessitate a review of the working papers of the other party's auditor and discussions with financial personnel. Initial communication and understanding – obviously only one part of the overall acquisition evaluation process – is critical and may change during the course of the engagement. The importance of this cannot be overstressed, because many of the problems emanating from acquisitions stem from an inadequate understanding between the auditor and his client. The "Purchase Audits and Reviews" section in Chapter 49 is mandatory reading for any auditor about to be involved in a business combination. A more detailed exposition on the subject may be found in *Professional Risks in Purchase Audits and Reviews* (Gormley, 1980).

Scope of Involvement. Normally, an audit in accordance with GAAS would be performed if the acquisition candidate had not previously had an annual audit. For the auditor, such an assignment should be approached no differently than any first–time audit, with the exception of special attention to provisions of the acquisition agreement or other potentially sensitive areas.

But the acquisition can make the audit unusually stressful. The purchase price, or the acquisition itself, often depends on the results of the audit. In such circumstances, items normally of little significance or concern can become inordinately important. For example, if the purchase price is based on a specified multiple of earnings, minor items may have a measurable and substantial effect; or a book value amount required by the purchase agreement may represent a "go–no go" barrier. The auditor must be especially conscious of and plan his engagement around the possibility that the mergee's personnel will not volunteer negative information.

In many situations, a review rather than an audit may be warranted. For example, if the mergee has been audited by another auditor, a review of the working papers and discussions with the auditor and the proposed mergee's financial management personnel may be sufficient. This is most readily done when the assets and liabilities to be acquired are not significant, for example, a service company whose future revenue stream is the principal concern. In such instances, the current customer list and other "off-book" evidence of revenue potential are the more important items to evaluate in the acquisition review. But even if review of the other auditor's work and inquiries of financial management substantially comprise the acquisition review, the reviewing auditor must nonetheless acquire his own understanding of the business, the major risks, and the basic reasons for the acquisition, and know the probable form of the transaction.

When a review rather than an audit is sufficient, the auditor's inquiries are generally aimed at the accounting principles employed, and he will use various analytical procedures (see Chapter 7) to evaluate the reasonableness of the account balances. Typically, supporting documentation would be reviewed (e.g., accounts receivable agings, and excess and obsolete inventory analyses), but verifications of balances with outside parties would be omitted or not be extensive. SSARS 1, *Compilation and Review of Financial Statements* (AR 100), provides examples of inquiry and review procedures that are also appropriate ingredients in acquisition reviews.

Working With Attorneys. In an acquisition, attorneys for the parties perform a significant role in drafting the letter of intent, the actual or definitive agreement, and supporting documents. The acquirer's attorney will aim to reduce the risk of his client through requiring more of the sellers and their attorneys and auditors. Likewise, the attorney expects the acquiring company's auditor to help reduce the risks. Naturally, the other party's attorney has the same objectives for his client. It is therefore important that each client, its attorneys, and its auditors work together to properly assemble a feasible merger agreement and overall audit or review plan. The auditor must understand the timing sequence, which often will include a letter of intent, a definitive agreement, the signing of the definitive agreement, and the closing.

Unrealistic expectations of auditors by attorneys often result from an unclear understanding or communication of the audit or review process or of what work the auditor is actually performing. They can also result from the use of vague or imprecise language in the merger. Such terms as "sound accounting principles and practices," used in place of "generally accepted accounting principles," can subsequently be used to argue in court that an accounting principle may not be sound even though generally accepted. Indeed, it has been suggested that terminology is sometimes used with a private knowledge of its vagueness and imprecision, just so that all options are kept open. Therefore, let the auditor beware!

Other conditions of closing the agreement usually will be based on the receipt of acceptable reports from the auditor. Those may also involve qualitative aspects relating to one or both companies' financial statements discussed in the following section. Another common contingency relates to the accounting treatment of the merger, typically the acceptability of the pooling method.

Because the auditor obviously must stay within the boundaries of professional standards in determining both the scope of his work and the report that he may issue, he should ensure at the outset that his plan is acceptable to the parties. He may wish to draft the type of report he would expect to issue upon satisfactory completion, to make sure it is acceptable to the attorneys.

Qualitative Considerations. During the period between the date of signing the merger agreement and the closing, developments can occur that would make the acquisition substantially less desirable. Depending on the nature of the merger candidate's business, operations could perhaps decline markedly, or adverse government regulation or litigation could drastically affect the original evaluations. It is the client's responsibility to anticipate such possibilities.

Although the auditor may be requested to perform an update review covering the period from signing to closing, he should not permit the agreement to require that he report the occurrence of an unquantifiable development, such as a "material adverse change" compared with an earlier date. Such matters are rarely susceptible to subsequent agreement in the event of a dispute between the buyers and sellers, and the buyer's auditor is in an impossible situation if he in effect defines, by his report, what the parties did not adequately define in the merger agreement itself. The auditor must insist that any such report he would be expected to issue would address only quantitative standards, such as increases or decreases of recorded or otherwise readily determinable amounts.

Recognition of Business Risks. The auditor can be of considerable assistance to his client in recognizing exposure areas for which additional escrow may be warranted, as indicated in the following illustrative list:

• Uncollectible accounts receivable because of returns, allowance, or bad debts.
• Overvalued inventory because of mispricing or excess, obsolete, or nonexistent quantities.
• Obsolete or missing equipment or furnishings.
• Unrecorded liabilities to vendors, litigants, or tax authorities.

Subsequent operations and audits may disclose such matters; however, there is no assurance that all such matters that could affect the escrow, if any, would be noted by management or reported to the purchaser. This is particularly true if the former owners continue to manage the acquired company.

Large inventory adjustments subsequent to acquisition are particularly troublesome, because it is usually difficult if not impossible to establish when or why a loss occurred. Although this risk does not necessarily mean that a complete physical count and pricing must be made of all inventory and equipment in conjunction with the closing of the acquisition, the auditor should ensure that his client understands the potential for disputes that otherwise exists. The client must make those and other decisions (and compromises) based on materiality, available escrows, and effect on morale of the parties involved. Attempting to obtain absolute assurance is not practical.

Takeover Attempts

The auditor is often active in situations in which his client is a target in an unwanted takeover attempt, a frequent occurrence in recent years. He will work with his client in professionally acceptable ways to attack the insufficiency of the offer or the undesirability of the transaction at any price. The defensive efforts may encompass projections of an undervalued target company's operations (see Chapter 27) as well as analysis of the "unconservative" accounting principles of the proposed acquirer.

Auditor Communications

Comfort Letters. The acquiring company should attempt to obtain a "comfort letter" from the acquiree's auditor on any unaudited period subsequent to the last audit. Ordinarily, the auditor is able to issue a "negative assurance" letter comparable to that provided to underwriters in a 1933 Securities Act filing (see Chapter 20). For acquisitions, such letters are sanctioned by SAS 26 (AU 504.20). The acquiree's auditor is the proper party to issue the letter, because he undoubtedly has more audit experience with his client than is obtainable by the acquiring company's auditor during a typical acquisition review. At the same time, the acquirer's auditor may be asked to issue a comfort letter about his client's unaudited period, addressed to the acquiree company. When both auditors issue these letters they are called cross-comfort letters.

New York Stock Exchange Pooling Letters. Since the issuance of APB 16, the New York Stock Exchange has required that auditors provide a letter to the Exchange regarding the conformity of a particular business combination with the criteria for pooling-of-interests accounting. Auditors at first complained that this was "gilding the lily," since the auditor could not approve the transaction as a pooling unless it met all of the criteria of APB 16. However, the Exchange received its share of criticism from the public regarding high-flying stocks used for pooling prior to 1970, and therefore the NYSE felt it wanted to check the details to aid in preventing a recurrence of the problem.

After issuing the early NYSE pooling letters, auditors found that the Exchange asked many questions, particularly about escrows for future contingencies, and the result was a number of interpretations adopted by the AICPA. Thus the NYSE did have, and continues to have, an impact with respect to some of the fuzzy areas in APB 16. (An example of an NYSE pooling letter is shown in Poloway, 1988, ¶ 3570.)

Solvency Letters. In highly leveraged takeovers and LBOs, a practice had developed whereby auditors would issue a so-called solvency letter to lenders stating that, based on definitions provided by the borrower company and the lenders, the company was not insolvent at the time of taking down the debt. These letters are considered important by lenders, who want to obtain assurance from someone that the loans do not constitute a "fraudulent conveyance" under federal or state laws. Such a conveyance generally would occur if, by taking down the loan, the borrower is made insolvent, would have inadequate capital, or would be unable to pay its debts as they mature; if it occurred, the lender's priority claim may be set aside.

The question becomes crucial when a very major asset, perhaps the largest asset, of the posttransaction company will be the goodwill recorded in the transaction. Essentially, the company needs to be able to represent, usually with the support of its investment bankers, that the company parts are salable at an amount that would recover the goodwill, and/or that projected operations will be sufficient to amortize the goodwill and generate adequate cash flows to cover expected debts.

Auditor involvement in solvency letters was sanctioned by an ASB interpretation issued in late 1984 describing the process, and providing a sample report that concluded with negative assurance:

Nothing came to our attention as a result of the foregoing procedures, however, that caused us to believe that, as of [date], the borrower is not solvent, as that term is defined in the first paragraph of this letter.

Auditors began having second thoughts about the wisdom of issuing solvency letters when some early takeover and LBO debts could not be paid as scheduled and had to be restructured. Genuine alarm set in when the takeover debt began to regularly cross the billion-dollar threshold, with goodwill amounting to perhaps 80% thereof. Issuing these letters, while on the surface lucrative because high fees could be charged, could easily mean "betting the firm." The practice had been established, however, and lenders needed their letters; so when auditors decided with increasing frequency to decline to perform this service, investment bankers had to be engaged to do it.

To extricate the profession from this dilemma, in February 1988 the ASB rescinded the 1984 interpretation and replaced it with an integration of the attestation standards that absolutely bans anything resembling a solvency letter. The new interpretation precludes accountants from providing any form of assurance on matters relating to solvency or any financial presentation of matter relating to solvency. It describes other conventional services that may be provided, such as audits or reviews of historical financial statements, and association with prospective and pro forma information (see Chapter 27). Finally, if the accountant is requested to perform agreed-upon procedures, the attestation standards (see Chapter 5) are applicable, and the sample report is liberally laced with disclaimers and other exculpations. Specifically, a disclaimer stating that no assurance is provided on solvency, adequacy of capital, or ability to pay debts is required.

Appendix 23
SUMMARY OF AMENDMENTS, INTERPRETATIONS, AND TECHNICAL BULLETINS
APB OPINIONS 16 AND 17

The FASB has issued a number of amendments, interpretations, and technical bulletins dealing with accounting for business combinations. None of those pronouncements changes the basic thrust of that accounting in any significant way. The pronouncements include the following:

1. SFAS 10, *Extension of "Grandfather" Provisions for Business Combinations*, extends the "grandfather" provisions of APB 16. (The statement is still effective but no longer operative.)

2. SFAS 38, *Accounting for Preacquisition Contingencies of Purchased Enterprises*, deals with the postcombination accounting for preacquisition contingencies.

3. SFAS 72, *Accounting for Certain Acquisitions of Banking or Thrift Institutions*, provides for a shorter period of amortization of goodwill arising from an excess of the fair value of liabilities assumed over assets acquired in certain acquisitions of banks or thrift institutions.

4. SFAS 79, *Elimination of Certain Disclosures for Business Combinations by Nonpublic Enterprises*, deletes the pro forma presentation requirements for a purchase business combination by nonpublic companies.

5. SFAS 87, *Employers' Accounting for Pensions*, changes the pension liability (asset) recognition in a purchase business combination to the amount by which the projected benefit obligation is greater (less) than plan assets.

6. SFAS 96, *Accounting for Income Taxes,* changes the way the tax effects of differences between accounting and tax bases of assets and lliabilities acquired in a purchase business combination are treated. In addition, the SFAS also affects the accounting for poolings of interests in certain narrow circumstances.

7. FIN 4, *Applicability of FASB Statement No. 2 to Business Combinations Accounted for by the Purchase Method,* generally requires that the cost of research and development activities acquired in a purchase business combination shall be expensed at the date of consummation.

8. FIN 9, *Applying APB Opinions No. 16 and 17 When a Savings and Loan Association or a Similar Institution Is Acquired in a Business Combination Accounted for by the Purchase Method,* indicates that the net spread method is inappropriate for carrying forward the recorded values of assets and liabilities (basically book value) in a purchase business combination involving the acquisition of a banking or thrift institution.

9. TB 85-5, *Issues Relating to Accounting for Business Combinations . . . ,* addresses five very specific issues as follows:
   • Costs of Closing Duplicate Facilities of an Acquirer.
   • Stock Transactions Between Companies Under Common Control.
   • Downstream Mergers.
   • Identical Common Shares for a Pooling of Interests.
   • Pooling of Interests by Mutual and Cooperative Enterprises.

In addition to the changes described above, the AICPA issued over 100 unofficial interpretations of the Opinions between 1970 and 1973, contained in the FASB *Current Text,* B50.501 *et seq.* and I60.501 *et seq.* Some are discussed in this chapter, and all are regarded as reasonably "official."

24

Consolidation and the Equity Method

OVERVIEW

The purpose of consolidated statements is to present the results of operations and the financial position of a parent company and its subsidiaries as though they were a single company. ARB 51, *Consolidated Financial Statements* (C51), states that a consolidated presentation is presumptively more meaningful than presenting separate financial statements for the parent and each of its subsidiaries (C51.101).

Consolidation Theory

The theory behind the preparation of consolidated financial statements may be stated quite simply: when a company has the ability to exert control (through a majority financial interest in a subsidiary or by some other means), permitting it to direct the subsidiary's policies and its management, and to direct the subsidiary to pay a dividend, the assets, liabilities, and operations of the two companies should be presented in one set of consolidated financial statements as though they had operated as a single company. This general approach was articulated originally by the American Institute of Accountants (forerunner of the AICPA) in 1929, and 30 years later it was formally promulgated in ARB 51, which (as modified by SFAS 94, *Consolidation of All Majority-Owned Subsidiaries*) is still the authority for today's practice.

The theories espoused in ARB 51, however, are often difficult to apply because the parent-subsidiary relationship can be a complex one. For example, it is fair to question whether a parent should consolidate its wholly owned subsidiary when the creditors have de facto control as a result of restrictions in the subsidiary's lending agreements, or conversely whether a parent should deconsolidate an operationally integrated subsidiary just because it owns a shade less than a majority of the voting stock. These complexities make it difficult enough to apply the consolidation rules fairly, but other accounting standards add further complications.

For example, as leasing rules under SFAS 13 (L10) have tightened up, some companies have pushed otherwise capitalizable leases and other off balance sheet financing (discussed further in Chapters 19 and 21, respectively) into an independent financing company, nominally controlled by an outsider.[1] Also, because SFAS 2 (R50) requires expensing the costs of research and development activities, there have been numerous instances of those activities being performed as contract research by a company owned by literally unaffiliated parties but financed by the contract with the beneficiary company.[2]

No matter what the *form* of the association might be, the consolidation rules should be applied based on the *substance* of the relationship. The underlying consolidation theory requires consolidation of any company *substantively* controlled by its parent, but consolidation of companies not more than 50% owned is almost never permitted in practice.

---

[1] In the case of Avis Leasing Corporation in 1983, debt to acquire automobiles was incurred by a trust, which then leased the autos to Avis. Avis does not consolidate the trust. Lee, *Loose Ledgers*, Wall St. J., December 13, 1983, at 6.

[2] In 1982, the FASB issued SFAS 68, *Research and Development Arrangements* (R55), that establishes guidance for expense recognition by the parties with interests in separate R&D entities (see Chapter 39).

GAAP Definition of Control. There is no official definition of "control" in the authoritative acccounting literature, but the FASB has provided one in SFAS 57, *Related Party Disclosures,* closely following Regulation S-X, Rule 1-02 (g):

the possession, direct or indirect, of the power to direct or cause the direction of the management and policies of a specified party whether through ownership, by contract, or otherwise. [R36.402]

As a general rule, a parent may consolidate only those controlled subsidiaries in which it has a voting stock interest in excess of 50%. However, there are many other ways one company can exercise control over another. For all practical purposes, a company could find itself controlled by a major customer, a major supplier, or a major creditor. However, for consolidation purposes, the general definition of control is expressed in strict quantitative terms under ARB 51:

The usual condition for a controlling financial interest is ownership directly or indirectly of over fifty percent of the outstanding voting shares. [C51.102]

SEC Requirements. Even though the SEC definition of control was never limited to majority stock ownership, until recently the SEC staff virtually insisted on it as a condition precedent to consolidation. Rule 3A-02 of Regulation S-X, *Consolidated Financial Statements of the Registrant and Its Subsidiaries,* which deals with consolidation practices, had provided that "no subsidiary shall be consolidated which is not majority owned," and historically, there have been very few exceptions to the majority ownership rule. For example, a large multinational company had a 48% interest in a foreign subsidiary it clearly controlled. The parent provided all of the management and technical know-how and was assured a majority of the seats on the subsidiary's board of directors. Under local law, a majority of the subsidiary's voting stock had to be owned by nationals, and such stock was widely distributed. Consolidation of the subsidiary was justified by the substance of the parent's control and because of the unique circumstances that required an outside majority ownership. However, in other apparently similar situations the equity method (discussed later in this chapter) has been used, reflecting the diversity in practice when interpreting existing facts and circumstances.

In May 1986, the SEC amended Rule 3A-02 by issuing FRR 25 (§ 105). The amendment eliminated wording that suggested an absolute prohibition on consolidating any subsidary not majority-owned. In its commentary, the Commission states:

This [amendment] will eliminate any confusion about the overriding requirement of the rule which is that the registrant must adopt a consolidation policy that clearly exhibits the financial position and results of operations of the registrant and its subsidiaries.

The amendment to Rule 3A-02 also includes this statement:

In other situations, consolidation of an entity, notwithstanding the lack of technical majority ownership, is necessary to present fairly the financial position and results of operations of the registrant, because of the existence of a parent-subsidiary relationship by means other than record ownership of voting stock.

Total companies sampled	600
Companies consolidating all significant subsidiaries	434
Companies consolidating certain significant subsidiaries	159
Nature of subsidiaries not consolidated:	
Finance entities:	
Credit	104
Insurance	54
Leasing	21
Banks	7
Real estate	29
Foreign	10
Companies not presenting consolidated statements	7

FIG. 24.1   1986 Consolidation Practices
Source: AICPA. Accounting Trends and Techniques New York: 1987. (Adapted from Table 1–9.)

The need for this "technical amendment," as the SEC has characterized it, stems from earlier enforcement releases in which the SEC set forth its views concerning appropriate principles of consolidation. In the *Digilog* case (AAERs 34 and 45), the SEC announced actions against the registrant and the auditors, requiring the registrant to restate its financial statements for prior years to include an entity that effectively was totally controlled, but in which no stock, voting or otherwise, was held.

At one time the SEC had required parent-only financial statements, to make it clear that not all of the assets of the consolidated group were necessarily available to creditors and shareholders of the parent company. These rules were last advanced in ASR 302 (FRR § 213) in 1981 with implementation guidance given in SABs 43 and 44 (Topic 6.K), issued in early 1982. ASR 302 states that complete separate financial statements of the parent are no longer required; however, specified parent company disclosures are required, in footnotes and condensed financial information, when restrictions exist on the ability of subsidiaries to transfer funds to the parent. For more coverage of this topic, refer to Poloway (1988, ¶¶ 4012 and 4150).

Unconsolidated Subsidiaries

Historical Perspective. Prior to SFAS 94, *Consolidation of All Majority-Owned Subsidiaries* (C51), subsidiaries in a unique or specialized business usually were not consolidated with other subsidiaries in different businesses. (See Fig. 24.1 for statistics from *Accounting Trends and Techniques* (AICPA, 1987b).) That exclusionary practice had a practical basis: There was a concern that financial statements consolidating the activities of a manufacturing company and an insurance company, for example, might be a hodgepodge of significant numbers—inventories and investments, mortgage debt and insurance reserves—and that a consolidated presentation could obscure the true picture of the overall financial position and results of operations of an enterprise.

The idea that subsidiaries in fundamentally disparate businesses should be excluded from consolidation has long been part of the profession's thinking. The very first version of Regulation S-X in 1940 included rules prohibiting the consolidation of any subsidiary in insurance, banking, or the investment business. In addition to the concern about commingling different kinds of assets, there was apparently some feeling that the special legal status of those heavily regulated businesses should be a factor in the decision.

In 1974 the SEC amended its original position and repealed that part of Regulation S-X prohibiting the consolidation of finance-type subsidiaries. They concluded that such subsidiaries *could* be consolidated, provided their financial statements were also presented separately as footnotes to the consolidated statements. The requirement for presentation of the separate sudsidiary financial statements was eliminated in 1981, but this reprieve had little impact on practice. Many companies seemed reluctant to abandon tradition by extending their consolidation policies. Perhaps more importantly, many companies were reluctant to consolidate their finance-type subsidiaries because the consolidated statements would then include the normally large outstanding debt of those subsidiaries.

Real Estate and Credit Subsidiaries. Resistance by parent companies to reporting significant debt of subsidiaries in a consolidated balance sheet led to the issuance of APB 10, *Omnibus Opinion—1966.* This opinion required consolidation of any sudsidiary whose principal business is leasing real estate or other property to other members of the corporate group. Prior to APB 10 some companies had created separate real estate subsidiaries to hold the property required for the companies' businesses and to carry the related debt. They argued that their real estate subsidiaries were dissimilar businesses and therefore should not be consolidated. They were thus able to keep the property-related debt out of the consolidated statements. APB 10 maintained that the real estate subsidiaries were not in dissimilar businesses but were in fact integral components of the consolidated group, and that only consolidated statements could fairly present that integrated relationship.

Given the concept on which APB 10 was based, it would seem reasonable that captive credit companies should have also been consolidated, but this did not occur until SFAS 94 mandated it. Typically, a captive credit company borrows money in its own name, using long-term notes and short-term paper (sometimes guaranteed by the parent). The credit subsidiary may then use the proceeds of its borrowings to purchase its parent's trade accounts on a recourse basis. In other situations the credit subsidiary extends credit directly to the ultimate customer and assumes all credit risk.

In theory, consolidation practice should follow the substance of that risk. When the parent company remains responsible for the ultimate credit risk (because it has sold its accounts on a recourse basis or guaranteed the subsidiary's debt), it should consolidate its credit subsidiary. However, even when the parent has the ultimate credit risk, GAAP prior to SFAS 94 had permitted a parent to treat its credit subsidiary as a "dissimilar" business and to include the financial impact of its operations as a single-line item in the parent company's financial statements, using the equity method. If it was a material subsidiary, a summary of its financial statements would, in any event, be presented in a footnote or supplement to the consolidated financial statements.

Temporary or Ineffectual Control. ARB 51 previously indicated that a subsidiary should not be consolidated if there is some uncertainty as to the effectiveness or the permanency of the parent's control. For example, a parent should not consolidate a subsidiary's statements when the subsidiary is in bankruptcy, when a foreign subsidiary's funds are blocked because of currency exchange restrictions, or when the subsidiary's debt covenants prevent the parent from exercising its legal control.

Although the effect of this guidance for excluding subsidiaries was observed in practice, it was not invoked as often as one might have expected. For example, the ARB 51 foreign subsidiary exclusion and circumstances in which a subsidiary's loan agreement restricted the payment of dividends from the subsidiary to its parent did not in practice prior to SFAS 94, usually result in nonconsolidation.

Additionally, a parent might feel justified in consolidating a subsidiary even though there may be restrictions on its ability to exert control because the subsidiary is an important manufacturing facility or sales outlet or because it is significant to the enterprise as a whole in some other way. As long as the parent is in a position to significantly affect the deployment of the subsidiary's assets or its operating policies, the subsidiary's financial statements may (and probably should) be consolidated, even when there may be some restrictions on the parent's latitude. If the distribution of the subsidiary's earnings is blocked in some way, the existence of the blockage and the financial impact should be disclosed in the notes to the consolidated statements.

FASB Project

Background. In January 1982, the FASB added to its agenda a major project regarding the reporting entity, which includes consolidations, the equity method, joint ventures, and new basis of accounting. A task force was formed, and after some changes in direction, the project has evolved into three phases:

1. Development of a concept of reporting entity and consideration of related conceptual matters. The Board will then attempt to apply those concepts to the broad issue of consolidation policy, as well as to the numerous issues regarding consolidation techniques. A major, potentially contentious issue is the appropriateness of not consolidating partnerships, trusts, and other forms of organization used as off-balance sheet devices.
2. Application of the concept of the reporting entity and related conceptual matters to other accounting policy issues, such as equity method accounting and pushdown accounting.
3. Development of the concept of the reporting entity and related consolidation policy for not-for-profit organizations.

Because the underpinning of consolidation accounting in professional literature resides almost solely in ARB 51, issued 30 years ago and not significantly amended until recently, the FASB has extensive room to maneuver; by the same token, the number of issues that have built up over the years are voluminous, and this will take much time and effort to analyze and to resolve on a consistent basis.

Early in the project, in an FASB staff memorandum made available to the Financial Accounting Standards Advisory Council (FASAC), the staff noted the following issues, among others, relevant to this project:

• The problem is pervasive. Industry in general needs more guidance because the literature has become outdated. There is a lack of guidance for many types of joint undertakings, for example, oil and gas and real estate. The following Issues Papers prepared by AcSEC task forces are indicative of the problem:

—*Reporting Finance Subsidiaries in Consolidated Financial Statements* (1978)

—*Joint Venture Accounting* (1979)

—*Accounting by Investors for Distributions Received in Excess of Their Investment in a Joint Venture* (1979)

—*"Push Down" Accounting* (1979)

—*Accounting in Consolidation for Issuances of a Subsidiary's Stock* (1980)

—*Certain Issues That Affect Accounting for Minority Interest in Consolidated Financial Statements* (1981)

• Some aspects of this project are likely to be very controversial (e.g., the possibility of consolidation of finance subsidiaries and other noncorporate entities).

• If the area is left unattended indefinitely, further proliferation of a variety of approaches could encourage the SEC or Congress to address the problems.

The FASB staff memorandum to FASAC listed the issues being addressed by the Board, as follows:

1. What is the appropriate accounting entity?

2. ARB 51 provides guidance on the meaning of "controlling financial interest." (In general, ownership of over 50% of outstanding voting shares is the usual condition for a controlling financial interest.) Is controlling financial interest, however defined, the appropriate criterion?

3. ARB 51 presumes that in a "controlling financial interest situation," consolidated financial statements are more meaningful than separate statements. Should this presumption be reexamined? ARB 51 notes a number of exceptions to this presumption. Should the exceptions be altered?

4. Should there be a change in the APB 18 requirement that investments in corporate joint ventures be accounted for by the equity method?

5. Should the appropriateness of the equity method be reexamined?

6. Should the appropriateness of the criteria for applying the equity method for investments of 50% or less be reexamined?

7. Should the project address accounting for unincorporated joint ventures, partnerships, and other non-corporate forms of organization?

Reporting Entity Concept. Six years after the project was added to the FASB agenda, the Board, its staff, and the Task Force continue to consider a staff draft of a tentative conclusions document that conceptually identifies a reporting entity. The concept is based primarily on control rather than on the ownership of a majority of the voting interest of a company. Control may be difficult to define, but the draft indicates that: (1) the boundaries of a reporting company should be determined on the basis of a parent company's control of a subsidiary's operating and financing policies; and (2) all subsidiaries should be included in consolidation. The Board remains supportive of the general thrust of the staff draft but has reservations about some of its provisions.

Equity Method and Push Down Accounting. The project includes consideration of the equity method generally, as well as its specific application to joint ventures. Consideration of push down accounting (discussed in Chapter 23) will probably occur in late 1988 or 1989.

Not-For-Profit Organizations. Preliminary research suggests that both a control and legal entity approach are used presently for consolidation of not-for-profit organizations. With the FASB now requiring consolidation of most majority-owned subsidiaries, a similar approach is likely for not-for-profit organizations. This phase will probably not receive substantive attention until 1989.

CONSOLIDATED FINANCIAL STATEMENTS

Required Consolidation of All Subsidiaries

After protracted discussions with its staff on the reporting entity project, the FASB found that one of the very few issues on which the Board members were virtually unanimous was the consolidation of all majority-owned subsidiaries. Therefore, in 1986 the Board directed the staff to develop an exposure draft amending ARB 51 to require such consolidation. The exposure draft, was issued in late 1986.

In spite of significant resistance by virtually all reporting entities and many financial analysts in their comment letters and presentations at the public hearing, a final statement, SFAS 94, *Consolidation of All Majority-Owned Subsidiaries* (C51) was issued in late 1987. This statement requires the consolidation of all subsidiaries except when control is likely to be temporary or is not in the hands of the parent. The statement is effective for financial statements for fiscal years ending after December 15, 1988. Earlier application is encouraged, and restatement of earlier periods is required.

As a result of SFAS 94, the following exclusions from consolidation are no longer permitted:

1. Subsidiaries with nonhomogeneous operations (finance, insurance, real estate, and leasing).
2. Subsidiaries with large minority interests.
3. Foreign subsidiaries.

Subsidiaries over which control is temporary would continue to be accounted for using either the cost method or the equity method based on the guidance provided in existing authoritative pronouncements.

Information that was previously disclosed under APB 18, *The Equity Method of Accounting for Investments in Common Stock* (I82), about majority-owned subsidiaries that were unconsolidated for earlier fiscal years must still be disclosed (even though such subsidiaries would now have to be consolidated). Thus, summarized data about the assets, liabilities, and results of operations (or separate statements of those formerly unconsolidated subsidiaries) is still required.

The primary concern expressed by those who spoke against the issuance of the statement was the loss of substantial information through aggregation and the distortive impact on financial ratios. Many commentators recommended that if the FASB were to move ahead to a final standard it should develop guidance regarding disclosures. Most felt that the continuation of the APB 18 disclosures was a weak substitute for more expanded disclosures to overcome the problems resulting from aggregation. Additionally, there was concern about the lack of guidance and resulting lack of comparability that will result from various approaches to combining classified and unclassified balance sheets of the component entities.

In spite of these criticisms, the FASB declined to provide any such guidance and took the position that experimentation in financial reports would eventually lead to some degree of consistency in application among reporting entities. The Board expressed the view that SFAS 94 will result in improved comparability among enterprises, and will provide cash flow information that was not available when the equity method was used. They also believe that mandatory consolidation will, in part, resolve the "off-balance sheet" financing problem caused by not consolidating finance, insurance, real estate, and leasing subsidiaries.

It is also interesting to speculate on the effect of the FASB's final conclusions on SFAS 94. If the FASB eventually opts for a consolidation approach based on operating and financing control (in addition to legal control), presumably there would be a need to amend SFAS 94 to incorporate controlled but not majority-owned companies. The impact of such a position would be significant—for example, the effect of consolidating a large 30% owned company that is subject to the operating control of a "parent."

Consolidation Procedure

Conceptual Approaches. There are several ways of looking at a consolidated company, and each point of view suggests a different accounting. Some argue that the parent and subsidiaries as a consolidated group should be seen as a *single entity,* without any segregation of its components. Therefore, they would argue that there could never be a minority interest, only a separate subset of stockholder. However, those who look at a consolidated company from the viewpoint of the parent's shareholders have a *proprietary* perspective. They see the subsidiaries as separate legal companies and insist that a minority interest is not a part of the parent's capital structure but a simple, mathematical by-product of the consolidation process.

There are other accounting issues that separate the *entity theory* from the *proprietary theory,* and strong arguments abound on both sides. Unfortunately, current consolidation practice has evolved with mixed reliance on each of these theoretical arguments, and in fact without much regard for an overall conceptual basis. The remainder of this section, therefore, presents procedures as they exist today in practice, regardless of whether practice is logically consistent in all its aspects.

Formation of a Subsidiary. If the parent forms a subsidiary, its investment will be represented by the subsidiary's net assets. As long as transactions between the parent and the subsidiary are recorded at cost, the consolidation process will usually consist simply of replacing the parent's recorded investment on its balance sheet with the details of the subsidiary's assets and liabilities. Any intercompany advances or purchases and sales are offset and eliminated from the consolidated statements. Sales to third parties, and related costs and expenses, are combined with those of the parent.

Acquisition of a Subsidiary. A brief discussion of the accounting approaches to recording an acquisition of another company is provided in the following subsections. Chapter 23 deals in depth with the accounting for business combinations.

Pooling of interests. If a company acquires a subsidiary in a pooling transaction, the parent's investment is presumed to be equal to the subsidiary's net assets, based on its historical costs. Upon consolidation the intercompany accounts are eliminated and the details of the two companies' financial statements are simply combined.

Under APB 11, *Accounting for Income Taxes,* when the acquiring company restated prior years' financial statements on a consolidated basis, the hypothetical tax benefit of offsetting the prior years' tax losses of one entity against the taxable income of the other was ignored because of the impossibility of going back in time and filing consolidated returns. However, as discussed in Chapters 17 and 23, SFAS 96, *Accounting for Income Taxes* (I25) (which supersedes APB 11), significantly modifies the tax aspects of pooling accounting. The pronouncement now requires that the tax attributes of the combining entities be considered when the companies are initially pooled and also when restating prior years' financial statements on a consolidated basis.

For example, if consolidated tax returns are expected to be filed subsequent to the business combination and one of the entities had prior unrecognizable net operating loss carry-forwards, tax credits, or net deductible temporary differences, these benefits will now be recognized to the extent they will reduce taxable amounts of the other combining entity. Determination of whether tax benefits should be recognized is based on the tax law in effect during the periods for which the financial statements are restated.

Purchase. When one company acquires another in a purchase transaction, the accounting will be more complicated. At the date of the purchase, the subsidiary's identifiable assets and liabilities will be restated to reflect their fair values. However, in a nontaxable purchase, the tax basis of those assets remains the same. As a result of the restatement for financial reporting purposes, a temporary difference is created. SFAS 96 now requires that the tax consequences of the acquisition be recognized in the allocation of the purchase price. As a result, purchase price allocations must reflect the impact of any provisions in the tax law that permit or restrict the use of either entity's operating loss and tax credit carry-forwards or temporary differences that will reduce taxable income or taxes payable of the other entity subsequent to the business combination.

After the identifiable assets and liabilities are assigned a fair value and any deferred tax attributable to the purchase is computed, the net fair value is compared with the purchase price to determine the amount of any difference. The accounting treatment of the difference varies depending on whether the fair value of net assets is more or less than the purchase price.

- Where the parent's purchase price exceeds the fair value of the subsidiary's net assets, the difference is accounted for separately as goodwill. This intangible asset of the parent, attributable to the newly purchased subsidiary, is amortized over the period of its estimated benefit, not to exceed 40 years.

- If not recognized at the acquisition date, the tax benefits of an acquired operating loss, tax credit carry-forward or net deductible amounts that are recognized subsequently are first applied as a reduction of goodwill, and then noncurrent intangibles; and finally, any remaining benefit is recognized as a reduction of tax expense.

- When the parent's purchase price is less than the fair value of the subsidiary's net assets, that difference should be allocated first to the subsidiary's noncurrent assets (except marketable securities). Since any reduction in the carrying amount of a noncurrent asset will, in turn, cause a change in the magnitude of its related temporary differences, the determination of the ultimate amounts to be assigned to the assets and deferred tax accounts will require the use of a simultaneous equation. If noncurrent assets are completely eliminated, any remaining negative goodwill should be amortized to income over a period not in excess of 40 years. (In practice, this *negative goodwill* is amortized over 3 to 15 years.)

- When a parent acquires a majority, but not all, of the subsidiary's stock, the accounting can be more complicated. In allocating the purchase price, the buyer must first establish the fair value of 100% of the net assets acquired and then determine goodwill as the excess of purchase price over the proportion of fair-valued net assets actually acquired by the parent. It is not proper to assign 100% of the excess of fair values over carrying amounts of the subsidiary's assets to the parent's cost of purchasing less than a 100% interest, except where the effect would be immaterial (such as with a very small proportionate minority interest).

For example, if in a nontaxable transaction, Company A paid $100,000 for an 80% interest in Company B, which had net assets of $50,000 at previous tax basis and carrying amounts, and $80,000 at fair values assuming a 50% tax rate, the purchase price allocation would be determined as follows:

Fair value of net assets ($80,000 × 80%)	$ 64,000
Deferred tax [($80,000 − $50,000) × 80%] × 50%	(12,000)
Goodwill	48,000
Purchase price	$100,000

Intercompany Transactions and Balances. When viewed from a consolidated perspective, transactions between a parent and its subsidiaries are not considered completed transactions. Because such transactions and the resulting balances do not reflect arm's-length business dealings with third parties, the earnings process is not completed, and therefore the transactions and balances should be eliminated in consolidation. The consolidation process is facilitated when each component entity records intercompany amounts in separate, easily identified accounts.

Many companies record all intercompany transactions at cost. However, those companies that operate each component entity as a profit center will need to measure profitability for each entity and thus will record intercompany transactions at fair values. Sometimes the intercompany price is set at an arbitrary figure, perhaps to generate taxable profits in low rather than high tax-rate jurisdictions. In any event the intercompany profits not realized through transactions with third parties are to be eliminated upon consolidation; that is, if products are sold between a parent and a subsidiary at a price in excess of the cost of the transferor, the unrealized intercompany profit in the transferee's inventory must be eliminated upon consolidation.

Typically, the amount of intercompany profit included in inventory is determined from an analysis of inventory on hand at the end of the period. The parent must be able to determine how much and what items of intercompany inventory remain within the corporate system at the reporting date. It must then be able to calculate with reasonable accuracy the amount of intercompany profit included in the inventory, and eliminate it in consolidation.

If there are charges between a parent and subsidiary for management services or for interest on intercompany advances, those charges must also be eliminated in consolidation. However, an intercompany charge that is capitalized as part of fixed assets or included as overhead in inventory should not be eliminated if the charge is simply a pass-through of an item that would have been considered an asset in the accounts of the originating company.

Minority Interests. When a parent owns a majority (but less than 100%) of a subsidiary's stock, the consolidated financial statements must reflect the minority interest in the subsidiary. The minority interest will be equal to the proportionate share of the subsidiary's net assets not owned by the parent, based on the historical costs. When a parent purchases a controlling interest in a subsidiary, only the parent's proportionate interest should be fair valued in consolidation; the amount shown for minority interest must be based on the historical costs of the subsidiary.

The minority interest will be increased and decreased only for its share of the subsidiary's historical basis income and losses, and its share of the dividends paid out. Occasionally, a subsidiary will suffer losses to the extent that it incurs a deficiency in net assets. In most situations the minority interest will bear its share of losses only to the extent of its share of net assets. It is not appropriate to reflect a minority interest as a debit balance (in effect, a receivable) in the consolidated statements unless the minority owners have guaranteed the subsidiary's debt or have committed to provide additional capital. When a subsidiary's loss is sufficiently large as to completely eliminate the minority interest, only that portion of the loss sufficient to bring the minority interest to zero should be allocated to the minority (C51.116). The balance of the loss should be reflected as a part of the consolidated net loss attributable to the parent.

Balance sheet presentation. If the minority interest in the subsidiary's net assets is material to the consolidated statements, it should be presented in the consolidated balance sheet as a separate line item just above stockholders' equity. It should not be subtotaled with consolidated debt or with consolidated equity. The SEC, in Regulation S-X, Rule 5-02 (27), requires that when the minority interest is material the balance should be reported between long-term debt and stockholders' equity or mandatorily redeemable preferred stock, if any. Very often the minority interest is immaterial to the consolidated balance sheet and is simply aggregated within other long-term liabilities.

Income statement presentation. If the minority interest in the subsidiary's net earnings is material to the consolidated statements, it should be presented as a single line item just before net earnings and just after the deduction for income taxes. The subsidiary's income taxes on its total earnings will thus be included in the consolidated tax provision; the minority interest is presented after-tax.

If the minority interest in the earnings of the subsidiary is not material, it may be presented (after-tax) in the consolidated statements among the costs and expenses, either as a single line item or combined with other miscellaneous expenses.

Intercompany profit elimination against minority interest. Accountants have argued for many years about the elimination of intercompany profit on transactions within a corporate group when there is a significant minority interest. Some contend that the profit on an intercompany transaction that would accrue to the minority should not be eliminated, because that portion of the transaction is a third-party transaction. From the standpoint of the minority interest, that intercompany profit could be considered to have been realized. Others argue that the parent's control over the group makes it impossible for any intercompany transaction to be considered an arm's-length transaction, and accordingly they insist that all intercompany profit be eliminated. The latter view is required in practice. The total amount of intercompany profits is eliminated regardless of the size or the nature of a minority interest. However, the intercompany profit may be proportionally allocated to the parent and minority interest (C51.115).

Income Tax Allocation. Income taxes became a problem when some units of a consolidated group issue separate financial statements. In many situations the parent and its eligible domestic subsidiaries will file a single consolidated tax return, and the subsidiary will have tax expense only as the parent allocates the total consolidated tax liability among the components. If there is a minority interest in the subsidiary, or if the subsidiary enjoys a statutory tax benefit, that allocation of total tax expense should preferably be based on the taxable income of the individual components, computed as though they were filing separately.

There may be a difference between the aggregate "as if" tax computations of the individual components and the total tax liability, because some of the components may have tax credits that would be unusable if they were filing on their own. There are a number of ways of handling that difference—for example, it could be absorbed by the parent, allocated to the unit that benefits from the credit usage, or spread pro rata to the separate subsidiaries.

Whatever allocation method is used, it should be formalized and perhaps even documented by a resolution of the Boards of Directors of the respective companies. Where there is a minority interest in a subsidiary, the allocation decision should not disadvantage the cash flow of that subsidiary simply because it files with the consolidated group.

If the components in the consolidated group file separate tax returns, and if there are intercompany profits eliminated in the preparation of consolidated financial statements, there will be a difference between consolidated net income and the aggregate of the component entities' taxable incomes. That temporary difference should be tax-allocated, following the provisions of SFAS 96 (I25).

For example, when a parent and subsidiary file separate tax returns and the parent sold inventory to the subsidiary at a profit, it would ordinarily pay tax on the transaction. In consolidation, the profit would be eliminated and the inventory would be stated at the parent's original cost. Since the tax basis of the inventory has been increased to reflect the higher cost paid by the subsidiary, a temporary difference deductible in the future has been created. A benefit may be realized by the subsidiary by either a reduction of a taxable temporary difference or through establishment of a deferred tax asset by hypothetical carry-back of the deductible amount to reduce taxes paid in the current or prior years. If the criteria regarding tax asset recognition established by SFAS 96 cannot be satisfied at the subsidiary level, one alternative might be to consider a tax planning strategy that assumes consolidated tax returns will be filed in future years. Unofficially, the FASB staff has indicated that this strategy should be considered even if management does not intend to take this course of action. Their rationale for this position is that tax strategies are not elective and must be considered if they maximize a tax asset or minimize a tax liability. (See Chapter 17 for further discussion.)

In addition to the taxes that may be assessed against the individual components, the parent may be faced with taxes on the earnings of its subsidiaries, should they be distributed. It may or may not be necessary to provide for those taxes in the consolidated financial statements. (See APB 23, *Accounting for Income Taxes-Special Areas*, which contains a section on undistributed earnings of subsidiaries (I42.104–.109); and see Chapter 17.)

Differing Fiscal Years. There are situations where a subsidiary has a fiscal year different than that of its parent. For example, the subsidiary may be in a seasonal industry in which most of the companies use a specific fiscal year. Some parents have selected earlier fiscal year-end dates for their foreign subsidiaries to facilitate consolidation. For example, a calendar-year parent may have its foreign subsidiary use a November 30 year-end simply to assure that the foreign company's data is fully compiled and available to include with the parent's in a timely closing.

If the parent and the subsidiary have different fiscal years, the consolidation should use the best available data from the subsidiary. Timely, current information is generally preferred. Therefore, it would be better for consolidation purposes to use the subsidiary's data as of its interim date coinciding with the parent's balance sheet date. However, there are situations in which year-end data is better than interim data (e.g., where the subsidiary's system for producing interim data is not reliable).

If the parent concludes that the trade-off beween timeliness and reliability forces it to use the subsidiary's year-end data, the data for the subsidiary's 12 months should be combined with that of the parent, just as though they had the same year end. Significant transactions of the subsidiary between its year end and the date of the consolidated financial statements should be recorded or disclosed according to the professional guidelines regarding subsequent events (AU 560).

It should be noted that the SEC will not accept consolidated financial statements if the subsidiary's data is more than 93 days old. That SEC requirement has become broadly accepted in practice.

Current/noncurrent classification difficulties occasionally arise with diverse fiscal years. The EITF is scheduled to discuss this matter in Issue 88-15 later in 1988.

Unconsolidated Subsidiaries. Prior to SFAS 94, when it was determined that a subsidiary's financial statements should not be consolidated, the parent's investment ordinarily will have been accounted for using the equity method. Under SFAS 94, which is effective for 1988, there are only two reasons a majority-owned subsidiary should not be consolidated: temporary control;[3] or severe foreign exchange restrictions, controls, or governmentally imposed uncertainties. In these cases either the cost method or the equity method will be used, as appropriate in the circumstances.

When using the equity method, APB 18 explains that it should produce the same results as full consolidation, except for the level of detail presented (I82.109).

In consolidation, the subsidiary's assets, liabilities, revenue, and expenses are combined, line by line, with those of the remainder of the consolidated group. However, under equity accounting, the parent's investment in and advances to the subsidiary, increased or decreased by earnings, losses, and dividends, are combined and shown as a single-line item in its balance sheet. Similarly, the parent's share of the subsidiary's current net earnings or losses is shown as a single-line item in its income statement (except where the investee has, in amounts proportionately material to the investor, extraordinary items and cumulative effects of a change in accounting principle that should be specifically segregated (I82.109 d)).

All other aspects of consolidation accounting apply when accounting for a subsidiary using the equity method:

- Intercompany profit included in transactions between the parent and the subsidiary must be eliminated.
- Where the subsidiary is purchased, the fair values of its assets and liabilities must be determined and any resultant goodwill must be amortized.

A detailed description of the application of the equity method to *nonsubsidiary* investees is presented later in the section entitled "Nonsubsidiary Equity Investments."

Change in Reporting Entity. The decision to consolidate a subsidiary must be based on the facts existing at the end of each reporting period. If the status of the subsidiary changes, its status at the end of the period will determine the accounting treatment, and that accounting usually will be applied retroactively. The several situations discussed in the following subsections are illustrated in Figure 24.2. This chapter does not discuss accounting for a business combination accomplished in a single transaction (see Chapter 23). Note, however, that the accounting for a step acquisition *at such time as a majority voting equity position* is achieved is essentially the same as accounting for a single-transaction purchase business combination. Also,

---

[3] An example of nonconsolidation due to temporary control is given in EITF Issue 84-33, *Acquisition of a Tax Loss Carryforward—Temporary Parent-Subsidiary Relationship.* The EITF discussed an acquisition in which the former owners had an option to repurchase a 60% interest for a fixed price. This type of transaction was being done at the time to utilize the profitable operations of a temporary acquiree against an accumulated tax loss carry-forward of the acquirer. Although no consensus was reached, the Task Force agreed that the sensible thing for the "acquirer" to do was to carry the investment on the equity method but to recognize income only up to the amount of the fixed repurchase option.

Transaction[1]	Accounting treatment at time of transaction[2]	Accounting treatment in prior periods' financial statements
Purchase acquisitions, including step acquisitions		
1. Initial purchase of less than 20%	Cost Basis	Initial purchase; therefore none.
2. Purchase that results in owning 20% to 50% inclusive	Equity method	If initial purchase, none. If a step, restate on the equity method for the percentages owned in prior periods.
3. Purchase that results in owning over 50%	Consolidate from date of acquiring more than 50% ownership.[3]	If initial purchase, none. If a step and equity method was previously used, no change. If a step and cost method was previously used, restate to equity method for the percentages owned in prior periods.
Dispositions of subsidiaries, including step dispositions		
Segment of the business		
4. Retaining ownership of more than 50%	Set up (or increase) minority interest, continue to consolidate; gain or loss treated as part of continuing operations	No change, remains consolidated.
5. Retaining ownership of exactly 50%	Change to equity method, with gain or loss treated as part of continuing operations	Restate to equity method or leave as consolidated.[4]
6. Retaining ownership of 20% or more, but less than 50%	Change to equity method, with gain or loss treated as part of continuing operations or as discontinued operations, based on the facts	Restate to equity method and classify as discontinued or continuing operations, as appropriate
7. Retaining ownership of zero or less than 20%	Change to cost method for remaining investment if any, with gain or loss treated as discontinued operations.	Restate to equity method and treat as discontinued operations
Not a segment of the business		
8. Retaining ownership of more than 50%	Set up (or increase) minority interest, continue to consolidate; gain or loss treated as part of continuing operations.	No change, remains consolidated

FIG. 24.2   Accounting for Step Acquisitions and Dispositions

Transaction[1]	Accounting treatment at time of transaction[2]	Accounting treatment in prior periods' financial statements
9. Retaining ownership of 20% to 50% inclusive	Change to equity method, with gain or loss treated as part of continuing operations	Restate to equity method or leave as consolidated[4]
10. Retaining ownership of zero or less than 20%	Change to cost method for remaining investment if any, with gain or loss treated as part of continuing operations	Restate to equity method or leave as consolidated[4]

Dispositions of nonsubsidiary equity investees

Segment of the business

11. Retaining ownership of 20% or more, but less than 50%	Continue use of equity method, with gain or loss treated as part of continuing operations	No change, remains on the equity method
12. Retaining ownership of zero or less than 20%	Change to cost method for remaining investment if any, with gain or loss probably treated as part of discontinued operations	No change, but reclassify as discontinued operations

Not a segment of the business

13. Retaining ownership of 20% or more, but less than 50%	Continue use of equity method, with gain or loss treated as part of continuing operations	No change, remains on the equity method
14. Retaining ownership of zero or less than 20%	Change to cost method for remaining investment if any, with gain or loss treated as part of continuing operations	No change, remains on the equity method

[1] For presentation purposes it has been assumed that an ownership interest of (a) less than 20% requires the use of the cost method of accounting, (b) 20% through 50% inclusive requires the use of the equity method of accounting, and (c) over 50% requires consolidation as a subsidiary. In practice these percentages may vary depending on the circumstances; the equity method requires the ability to excercise a significant influence, and consolidation requires the ability to control.

[2] This figure has been prepared on the assumption that SFAS 94, *Consolidation of All Majority-Owned Subsidiaries*, has been applied. Under SFAS 94, which is effective for fiscal years ending after December 15, 1988, the only reasons for not consolidating a majority-owned subsidiary are that control (a) is likely to be temporary, or (b) does not rest with the majority owner.

[3] A step acquisition of a subsidiary within a single fiscal year preferably should be reported as an acquisition commencing at the date of the initial investment, with earnings applicable to percentages of ownership held by previous owners in various periods deducted, similar to treatment of a minority interest.

[4] If the ex-subsidiary is left consolidated in prior financial statements, footnote disclosure should be given as to the amounts included for the subsidiary that was later deconsolidated.

many of the situations shown in the figure will either require or would benefit from the presentation of pro forma statements, which are not discussed here. See Chapter 23 for pro forma statements in business combinations.

Step acquisitions. Assume, for example, that (1) a company acquires a 10% interest in another company during the first quarter, (2) during the second quarter it acquires an additional 5% interest, (3) during the third quarter it acquires an additional 10%, and (4) in the fourth quarter it acquries a 30% interest, giving it a 55% controlling interest in the subsidiary at year end. In its interim reports for the first two quarters, the parent would reflect its less-than-20% investment in the subsidiary at cost; the cost of the investment would be shown as an asset, and income would be recognized only to the extent of dividends received. In the third quarter when it has achieved a 25% total interest the parent would begin accounting for its investment on the equity method, reflecting its aggregate cost plus or minus its proportionate share of the earnings or losses in the prior quarters. It would reflect 10% of the subsidiary's earnings for the period when it owned 10%; 15% of the subsidiary's earnings for the period where it owned 15%; and 25% of the subsidiary's earnings for the period when it owned 25%.

ARB 51 (C51.112) states that the preferable method of reporting a step acquisition is to include the subsidiary's revenues and expenses in the consolidated income statement as though the subsidiary had been acquired at the beginning of the year and deduct out the preacquisition earnings separately at the bottom of the statement. This method facilitates future comparison of operations and provides a better indication of existing operations. Another method of reporting a step acquisition is to include in the consolidated income statement only the subsidiary's revenues and expenses subsequent to the acquisition dates. Both methods, of course, yield the same net results, but the former method provides a more meaningful presentation.

At year end the subsidiary's balance sheet would be consolidated with the parent's (as required by SFAS 94) because it now owns a majority interest. Prior financial statements usually would not be consolidated because of the absence of a majority interest at those dates; but pro forma statements of operations as if fully consolidated for the current and preceding year would be provided (B50.165). (See Chapter 27 for an in-depth discussion of pro forma financial information.)

Disposal of all or part of a subsidiary. When part of an investment in a subsidiary is sold during the reporting period, the status of the investee at the end of the period should determine the accounting followed:

1. If a parent sells a portion of its investment in a subsidiary but still retains a controlling interest, the consolidated financial statements at the end of the period should include the assets, liabilities, and operations of the subsidiary – and of course the new minority interest. The minority interest in results of operations would be calculated for the period from date of disposition of the interest to the reporting date.

2. If a parent sells a controlling interest in its subsidiary but still retains an investment of 20% or more, that remaining investment should be reflected in the balance sheet at the end of the period as a single line item, using the equity method; the subsequent results of opera-

tions should also be recast on a one-line basis (C51.113). In prior periods' comparative financial statements the subsidiary may be deconsolidated and restated using the equity method presentation; however those prior-period statements may also be left unchanged, and footnote disclosure given as to the later deconsolidation.

If the sale of a subsidiary qualifies as a disposition of a segment (I13.404), all its results of operations up to the date of sale are condensed and shown as a single-line item in the consolidated income statement as discontinued operations, following the subtotaling of after-tax income from continuing operations (I13.105). This treatment is required for any period income statement presented that includes any portion of that subsidiary's operations.

If the subsidiary that has been disposed of does not qualify as a segment, its operations need not be condensed into a single-line item. Its sales and expenses (up to the date of the sale) may be fully consolidated as they would have been had the disposition not taken place. When this is done, it is usually appropriate to include a footnote disclosing the sales and expenses and net results attributable to the subsidiary that are included in the consolidated income statements. It is also permissible to compress the subsidiary operations into a one-line equity presentation (C51.113), but when this is done, the equity in earnings of the subsidiary must be shown before arriving at income from continuing operations.

Subsidiaries With Specialized Accounting. In Issue 85-12, *Retention of Specialized Accounting for Investments in Consolidation,* the EITF considered whether specialized industry accounting practices applied by a subsidiary should be retained in consolidation when the parent did not apply such accounting. Specifically, they were dealing with a situation in which a subsidiary was a venture capital company that carried its investments at market. The EITF reached a conclusion that so long as the specialized accounting could be justified by the subsidiary it should be retained in consolidation.

Combined Financial Statements

Consolidated financial statements are prepared when there is a majority voting equity interest held by a parent in its subsidiaries. However, in some situations companies are economically linked because they are under common management or common control (such as brother-sister companies, i.e., subsidiaries of a common parent), but there is no controlling equity interest of one in another. In those situations, it may be appropriate to present combined statements.

Although ARB 51 attempts to distinguish between consolidated statements and combined statements (C51.121), the difference is mostly semantic. The principles and procedures used to prepare combined statements are virtually the same as those used to prepare consolidated statements: All intercompany transactions, balances, and profit must be eliminated in the combination (C51.122); to the extent there is any intercompany investment, it is offset against the related equity; and if there is no intercompany investment, the individual company equities are combined.

The combined statement approach is useful, for example, to present the financial statements of a group of subsidiaries that are all in a similar business. It is also commonly used to present the financial statements of separate companies controlled by one individual or a family.

Disclosures

Policies. APB 22, *Disclosure of Accounting Policies*, recommends a footnote comment with any set of consolidated financial statements, outlining the consolidation policies followed: "Examples of disclosures by a business entity commonly required with respect to accounting policies would include, among others, those relating to basis of consolidation ..." (A10.106). Practice follows that recommendation. The theory is that a company should disclose the accounting principles it applies in any situation in which there might be some confusion as to what principles were used.

Because the consolidation guidelines are generally well understood, it would not seem necessary for a company to comment specifically on its consolidation policy unless that policy deviates from the norm. This is especially so after the effective date of SFAS 94. Prior to SFAS 94, most companies that had a material subsidiary of any kind would have included a standard, innocuous consolidation policy statement in their accounting policies footnote.

Whenever a company follows a consolidation policy that is a little out of the ordinary or changes its policy, the details should be outlined in the policies footnote, as illustrated in Figures 24.3 and 24.4 (both pre-SFAS 94).

Details Regarding Subsidiaries. Prior to SFAS 94, the consolidated financial statements were not required to provide any details from the statements of the consolidated subsidiaries. Once the decision was made that a consolidated statement best presents the combined activities of the group, it would have been inconsistent to encumber the notes accompanying the consolidated statements with details from the statements of the component entities.

There have been some traditional exceptions to the general rule, however. When the assets of a subsidiary are not available for the use of the corporate group, either because of a government regulation, a business restriction, or a loan requirement, the details of the restricted assets should be spelled out in a footnote. The assets themselves should be classified in the consolidated balance sheet so as to properly reflect the restriction; in effect they may be noncurrent assets. Further, SFAS 14 (S20) requires disclosure of assets and earnings on a segment basis and on a geographic basis. (See Chapter 4 for a discussion of segment reporting.)

More significantly, as discussed earlier in this chapter, SFAS 94, *Consolidation of All Majority-Owned Subsidiaries*, requires continuation in consolidated financial statements of the APB 18 disclosures that were being made when the equity method was applied to subsidiaries; but SFAS 94 does not require such disclosures for subsidiaries that previously were consolidated.

Consolidation policy — The consolidated financial statements include the accounts of all majority-owned subsidiaries, either direct or indirect, except for finance subsidiaries of Northern Telecom Limited. These nonconsolidated finance subsidiaries and the investments in associated companies (20% to 50% owned) are accounted for by the equity method. The finance subsidiaries are not consolidated because their business is fundamentally different from that of the consolidated group.

FIG. 24.3 Disclosure of Exclusions From Consolidation (Pre-SFAS 94)
Source: Bell Canada Enterprise Incorporated, 1986 Annual Report.

The Company's other foreign subsidiaries have not been consolidated since they operate in relatively less developed countries. The investments therein are carried at cost reduced by declines in carrying value deemed to be other than temporary (primarily resulting from foreign exchange restrictions). To the extent intercompany inventory profits exceed the unrecorded equity in the nonconsolidated, foreign subsidiaries, those profits are deferred. Sales to foreign subsidiaries are recognized upon delivery, with goods-in-transit carried as inventory.

FIG. 24.4 Subsidiary Excluded Due to Economic Uncertainty (Pre-SFAS 94)
Source: Seaboard Corporation, 1986 Annual Report.

Changes in a Consolidated Group. When there is a material change in the makeup of the consolidated group, the effect of the change must be detailed in a footnote in the year of the change. APB 20 requires a footnote describing the nature, reason for, and effect of the change, if any, on income before extraordinary items, on net income, and on related per share amounts (A35.113). The footnote in Figure 24.5 illustrates a situation in which a previously unconsolidated operation is now consolidated (done voluntarily, pre-SFAS 94).

Changes in the makeup of a consolidated group resulting from acquisitions or dispositions also require certain disclosures. APB 20 specifically states that the disclosures required by the "change in entity rules" apply to subsidiaries acquired during the period that are accounted for as a pooling of interests (A35.112). But in fact APB 16 requires even more detailed disclosures for any change in the entity that occurs because of a pooling of interests (B50.122–124) or a purchase (B50.164–166). Similarly, APB 30 requires special disclosures in the notes whenever a segment of the business is disposed of during the period (I13.108).

Auditor reporting. From the viewpoint of the auditor reporting on financial statements, changes in the consolidated group constitute a change in the application of the consolidation accounting principle (AU 420.07). Therefore, in any of the following situations the auditor's report must include a statement calling attention to the lack of consistency (misnamed a *consistency exception*):

• Presenting consolidated or combined statements in place of statements of individual companies.

Consolidation policy and change in reporting entity – During the year ended August 31, 1986, the Company adopted the policy of including its previously unconsolidated foreign subsidiaries, all of which have a year end other than August 31, on a consolidated basis to better reflect financial position and operating results of the Company as a whole. The change in consolidation policy had the effect of increasing previously reported net sales by $33,079,000 and $27,804,000 for the years ended August 31, 1985 and 1984, respectively. This change had no effect on net income for the year ended August 31, 1986, or previously reported net income. All significant intercompany balances and transactions have been eliminated in consolidation.

FIG. 24.5   Disclosure of Change in Entity
Source: Pioneer Hi-Bred International, Inc. 1986 Annual Report

- Changing specific subsidiaries comprising the group of companies for which consolidated statements are presented.
- Changing the companies included in combined financial statements (discussed earlier in this chapter).
- Changing among the cost, equity, and consolidation methods of accounting for subsidiaries or other investments in common stock.

A consistency comment is not required when a consolidated group is changed because a subsidiary is created, purchased, dissolved, or sold (AU 420.09). A consistency comment is not to be used when pooling-of-interests accounting is properly applied in comparative statements, but is required when (1) comparative statements for prior years are not restated[4] for a pooling, or (2) comparative statements are not presented and the footnotes do not disclose specified comparative summary data (see AU 508.49).

In 1988, the ASB issued SAS 58, *Reports on Audited Financial Statements* (AU 508). This new SAS supersedes prior guidance that had required the inclusion in the auditor's report of a statement that the financial statements were prepared on a consistent basis. Effective for reports issued or reissued on or after January 1, 1989, a consistency comment is limited to circumstances in which accounting principles have not been consistently applied. Therefore, in the case of a change in reporting entity, which is considered a change in accounting, an explanatory paragraph would be included in the auditor's report. (For a more detailed discussion of SAS 58 see Chapter 11.)

SEC Releases

Continuing Involvement in a Sold Business. There are circumstances when disposal of a subsidiary should not be recognized as a sale. In SAB 30 (codified in SAB 40, Topic 5.E) the SEC specifies the accounting treatment when a company sells a subsidiary or other business operation but retains a continuing involvement in the business sold. Continuing involvement is retained if:

---

[4] This will also require a qualification in the auditor's report with respect to a departure from GAAP, unless immaterial.

- The seller has effective veto power over major contracts or customers.
- The seller has significant voting power on the company's board.
- The seller has continuing involvement in the company's affairs with risks and managerial authority similar to ownership.
- The buyer does not make a significant financial investment in the company (e.g., a minimal down payment).
- The buyer's repayment of debt that constitutes the principal consideration in the acquisition is dependent on future profitable operations.
- The seller continues to guarantee debt or contract performance.

In any of these instances the seller should not account for the transactions as a divestiture and may not recognize any gain – even a deferred gain. The seller should segregate on its balance sheet the assets and liabilities of the sold subsidiary or business operation under captions such as "assets of business transferred under contractual arrangements" and "liabilities of business transferred." If the seller's realization of the consideration is contingent on future profits, and if losses are incurred after the transaction, the seller should reflect these losses by recording a valuation allowance on its balance sheet with a corresponding loss on its earnings statement.

Sales of Stock by Subsidiaries Under promulgated GAAP (I82.109), gains are permitted only if the parent sells a portion of the stock it holds in the subsidiary; issuances by the subsidiary are considered to be capital transactions whose effect is to be recorded in the parent's equity accounts.

SAB 51, *Accounting for Sales of Stock by a Subsidiary* (Topic 5.H), states the SEC staff's position that it will accept, in consolidated financial statements, the accounting treatment for issuances of a subsidiary's stock specified in the AcSEC Issues Paper, *Accounting in Consolidation for Issuances of a Subsidiary's Stock* (AICPA, 1980c). As a result, a parent company will be able to record a gain[5] when a subsidiary issues shares of stock. SAB 51 is accepted as de facto GAAP; this disparity in requirements will be rectified in the FASB's consolidations project.

There are various implementation issues that arise from SAB 51:

- The SAB is permissive, not mandatory; accordingly, a subsidiary's issuances may be accounted for as capital transactions.
- If adopted by a company, the SAB would also apply to transactions of a less-than-majority-owned equity investee. Since the gains or losses from the sale of stock by the subsidiary must be disclosed as a line item, the SEC would require that the gain or loss arising from the

---

[5] In Issue 84-27, *Deferred Taxes on Subsidiary Stock Sales,* the EITF considered whether the gain had to be tax allocated. It seemed that, in reliance on the indefinite reversal criteria in APB 23, some companies were not tax-allocating, despite the fact that the APB 23 exclusions were intended to apply only to the items mentioned, and SAB 51 gains were not such an item. Under SFAS 96, such gains are temporary differences and therefore should be tax allocated. However, under U.S. tax law as of mid-1988, there is an election that permits a parent company in certain circumstances to recover its investment in an 80%-or-more-owned subsidiary tax-free. With respect to determining the tax effects of SAB 51 gains under SFAS 96, the FASB staff has tentatively concluded that if the parent company, by assuming that election, could recover its investment in the subsidiary without triggering a taxable amount for the temporary difference, the deferred tax consequences of that temporary difference are zero.

transactions of an equity investee be disclosed separately from the equity in the earnings of the investee.

- The SEC will look to current literature, primarily APB 23 and SFAS 96, to determine if tax allocation of the gain is required, rather than insisting on the advisory conclusions in the Issues Paper.

- SAB 51 applies to other situations described in the Issues Paper, for example, conversions of a subsidiary's debt or preferred stock into common shares, and exchanges of a subsidiary's shares for assets of another entity.

- Where a sale of shares by a subsidiary is part of a broader reorganization, SAB 51 requires the sale to be treated as a capital transaction. This is based on an actual case that involved a two-step transaction. In the first step a subsidiary issued shares and used the proceeds to settle a debt to the parent. The second step involved the spin-off of the parent's stock in the subsidiary at net book value to the parent shareholders in the form of a dividend. The SEC stated that no gain could be recognized in the first step.

Intercorporate Guarantees of Securities. SAB 53, *Financial Statement Requirements in Filings Involving the Guarantee of Securities by the Parent or by a Subsidiary* (Topics 1.G and H), presents the SEC staff position regarding required financial information where a subsidiary files a registration statement under the Securities Act of 1933 for the sale of debt guaranteed by its parent. Depending on whether the subsidiary is wholly owned, the subsidiary has independent operations, and the guarantee is full and unconditional, the disclosure required will be: (1) full separate financial statements of the subsidiary/issuer; (2) summarized financial information; or (3) no separate financial information of the subsidiary/issuer. In addition, full financial statements of the guarantor of a security, in this case the parent, are required. In 1934 Act filings, the same criteria would be applied.

SAB 53 also deals with the disclosure requirements in the "relatively infrequent" case of a parent's debt guaranteed by a subsidiary, and concludes that full financial statements for both the parent/issuer and the subsidiary/guarantor generally would be required.

Push Down Accounting. SAB 54, *Push Down Basis of Accounting Required in Certain Limited Circumstances* (Topic 5.J), expresses the SEC staff's opinion that push down accounting (as described in Chapter 23) should be used to present the financial position and results of operations of a substantially wholly owned subsidiary acquired by a company (or a company and related persons) in one or a series of purchase transactions. Since the form of ownership is within the control of the parent, the basis of accounting for purchased assets and liabilities should be the same whether the entity continues to exist or is merged into the parent's operations. Additionally, if less than substantially all the common stock is acquired or if the subsidiary has publicly held debt or preferred stock outstanding, the use of push down accounting may be permitted, but would generally not be required.

Allocation of Parent Expenses to Subsidiaries. SAB 55, *Allocation of Expenses and Related Disclosure in Financial Statements of Subsidiaries, Divisions or Lesser Business Components of Another Entity* (Topic 1.B), was issued as a result of a number of public sales of subsidiary stock by a parent, also called "carve-outs." It presents the SEC staff position that expenses incurred by the parent on behalf of a subsidiary becoming a registrant, such as officer and employee salaries, rent and depreciation, and other selling, general, and administration expenses, should be included in the historical financial statements of the subsidiary. Where specific identification of such expenses is not practicable, a reasonable allocation method must be selected and disclosed, along with management's assertion that the method used is reasonable.

As discussed in Chapter 17, neither SFAS 96, *Accounting for Income Taxes,* nor its predecessor, APB 11, specifies any particular method for allocating income taxes to individual members of the consolidated group. In situations involving "carve-outs" where a parent company retains sufficient ownership interest to permit the filing of a consolidated return, the SEC believes that investors should be aware of the effect on income had the subsidiary not been eligible to be included in the consolidated return. In practice, some of these subsidiaries have calculated their tax provision on the separate return basis, which the SEC believes is the preferable method. Others, however, have used different allocation methods. When the historical income statements in an SEC filing do not reflect the tax provision on the separate return basis, the SEC requires a pro forma income statement for the most recent year and interim period reflecting a tax provision calculated on the separate return basis.

As to interest on intercompany debt, financial statements of a subsidiary need not include such a charge if it had not been actually assessed. However, where interest has not been charged, disclosures relating to financing arrangements with the parent must also include an analysis of intercompany accounts, including a summary of transactions by major types and the average balance due to or from related parties for each period for which an income statement is required. To the extent the historical financial statements are not indicative of ongoing results (e.g., tax or other cost-sharing arrangements that will change), pro forma income statements should reflect such changes. Also, the subsidiary's historical earnings per share are not to be included; pro forma per share data should be presented only for the most recent year and interim period.

International Accounting Standard

Under IAS 3, *Consolidated Financial Statements* (AC 9003), a parent company should consolidate all subsidiaries except those where control is likely to be temporary; where it operates under severe long-term restrictions on transferability of funds to the parent (e.g., foreign government restrictions); or where subsidiary's activities are so dissimilar to the parent's that "better information" is provided by separate, unconsolidated financial statements.

"Associated companies" are nonsubsidiaries in which the investor has substantial voting power (no percentage specified) and the ability to exercise significant influence, and which the investor plans to hold long term. (The IAS has an exposure draft outstanding that would provide more detailed guidance for associated companies and joint ventures, described later at the end of the section on "Nonsubsidiary Equity Investments.")

Essentially, IAS 3 is consistent with U.S. GAAP as it stood before the issuance of SFAS 94, requiring the consolidation of all majority-owned subsidiaries.

IAS Exposure Draft. In September 1987, the International Accounting Standards Committee issued an exposure draft, *Consolidated Financial Statements and Accounting for Investments in Subsidiaries* (IASC, 1987), which if finalized, would supersede IAS 3. This Exposure Draft (ED) relies on a broader definition of control than that in either IAS 3 or in the guidance relied on in the United States. The ED indicates that although control normally results from majority ownership and voting rights it can also exist by agreement or the ability to appoint more than half of the members of the board of directors and implies that there may be other means by which control can be achieved.

The ED would require the consolidation of any controlled entity even if the entity is in a dissimilar business. Additionally, it also permits subsidiaries to be excluded from consolidation if control cannot be exercised. These provisions parallel SFAS 94; that is, consolidation is required unless control is temporary or there are significant, long-term restrictions that impair the parent's ability to exercise control over the subsidiaries' assets and operations.

NONSUBSIDIARY EQUITY INVESTMENTS

Other Than Joint Ventures

If an investment in voting stock gives the investor the power to exercise significant influence over operating and financial policies of the investee, the investment must be accounted for on the equity method. Under APB 18, *The Equity Method of Accounting for Investments in Common Stock* (I82), there is a presumption that ownership of 20% or more of the voting stock provides the ability to exert significant influence and that less does not. In each case, evidence may exist to support application of the equity method when less than 20% is owned, or to not support the equity method when more than 20% is owned.

Under the equity method broadly, the investment is initially recorded at cost; it is increased by the investor's share of the investee's net income, antidilutive capital transactions, and amortization of an excess of the proportionate share of the investee's net assets over purchase cost; and it is reduced by dividends, the investor's share of investee's net losses and dilutive capital transactions, and amortization of any excess of the purchase cost at acquisition over the proportionate share of the historical cost of the investee's net assets. Note that SAB 51, discussed in the earlier section "Sales of Stock by Subsidiaries," permits the recognition of gain (and presumably loss) if the subsidiary sells stock, generally if the transaction would have resulted in gain or loss had the same proportionate divestiture been accomplished by a sale of the parent's direct stockholdings. This SAB also applies to nonsubsidiary equity-method investees.

In the investor's income statement, the proportionate share of the investee's results of operations is shown as a single-line item (except where the investee has extraordinary items, prior period adjustments, or a cumulative effect of a change in

a. Intercompany profit and loss must be eliminated.

b. Where there is a difference between cost and underlying equity at acquisition, the fair valuing principles in APB 16 (B50.146) should be followed.

c. The investment is shown as a single amount in the investor's balance sheet; likewise for the income statement, except for extraordinary items, prior period adjustments, and cumulative effect of a change in accounting principle.

d. Extraordinary items, prior period adjustments, and cumulative effect of accounting changes of the investee that are material in the investor's income statement are shown by the investor separately.

e. Investee capital transactions are accounted for by the investor as he would account for them in a subsidiary — no gain or loss.*

f. Gain or loss on sale is based on carrying amount at the sale date.

g. The investor's share of earnings may be recorded based on the investee's most recent available financial statements; the time lag should be consistent from period to period.

h. A loss in value which is other than temporary should be recognized by the investor.

I. The investor should not reduce the investment account below zero as a result of losses of the investee unless he has an obligation to provide further financial support.

j. The investor should provide for income taxes on its share of investee net income based on whether distribution in the form of dividends or realization on disposal is a more likely means by which the investor will realize its investment. (However, if a tax planning strategy is available that reduces the investor's tax liability, it must be considered when determining any deferred tax consequence (I 25.154).

k. The investor's share of investee earnings is based on earnings less preferred dividend requirements.

l. When ownership falls below 20%, the investment account is carried forward as cost, without subsequent or retroactive adjustment.

m. When an investment first reaches 20%, the equity method is applied retroactively as in a step acquisition.

n. Goodwill or negative goodwill must be amortized based on APB 17 (I60.108–.110).

---

* However, see the SEC discussion of SAB 51 in the section "Sales of Stock by Subsidiaries."

FIG. 24.6 Equity Method—Summary of Implementation Issues
Source: I82.109.

accounting principles that would be material in the investor's income statement). Taxes must be provided by the investor as to his share of investee income, as discussed in the later section "Income Tax Allocation."

Figure 24.6 summarizes the implementation issues to consider in applying the equity method.

Applicability. APB 18 applies to investments in common stock of corporations and until the issuance of SFAS 94, *Consolidation of All Majority-Owned Subsidiaries* (C51), the requirements of APB 18 did not discriminate between subsidiaries and nonsubsidiaries. Because virtually all majority-owned subsidiaries must be consolidated commencing in 1988, the discussion in this section is primarily aimed at nonsubsidiary investees. It may be applicable to subsidiaries existing at the time SFAS 94 was promulgated that are not consolidated under the very narrow exclusions in SFAS 94. APB 18 will not apply to a newly acquired subsidiary, which almost invariably must be consolidated, or carried on the cost method if the SFAS 94 exclusions apply.

APB 18 does not expressly apply to investments in partnerships and unincorporated joint ventures; however, its provisions (except for income taxes) are applicable in accounting for investments in noncorporate investees (I82.508–.510).

Any tax consequence attributable to noncorporate investees should be recognized in accordance with the provisions of SFAS 96. For example, income taxes should be provided on the undistributed profits accrued by investor-partners. Deferred taxes should be recognized when the carrying amount of the investment in the investee differs from its tax basis. Investors should initially compute deferred tax effects based on the most likely circumstance in which they will ultimately realize their investment, that is, through distribution, liquidation, or sale of the investment. However, in measuring the deferred tax consequences, management must consider any prudent and feasible tax planning strategy to maximize tax assets or minimize tax liabilities (see Chapter 17).

The equity method should only be used by business enterprise investors, including those involved in leveraged buy-outs (see Chapter 23). This requirement excludes estates, trusts, individuals, and eleemosynary organizations.

Attributes of Significant Influence. Evidence of ability to exercise a significant influence (I82.104) includes representation on the board of directors, participation in policy-making processes, material intercompany transactions, interchange of managerial personnel, and technological dependency. The absence of concentration of other shareholdings is also a positive factor, but the use of the equity method is not negated simply because someone else has a substantial or majority interest in the investee.

APB 18 (I82.106–.109) states that there is a presumption that the investor has the *ability* to exercise significant influence *in the absence of evidence to the contrary* if he owns 20% or more of the investee. It should be emphasized that the opinion does not require the investor to actively exert significant influence but only to have the *ability* to exercise such influence. Examples of evidence to the contrary might be that

1. The investor is legally prohibited from exercising influence.
2. Hostile investee stockholders are effectively able to keep the investor from participating in investee decision-making.
3. The investee is a regulated company, and legal or practical problems make it impossible for the investor to affect the investee.
4. There are overriding exchange restrictions, controls, or other uncertainties with respect to foreign investees.

Examples of the ability to exercise significant influence where less than 20% ownership exists might include situations where the investor is also a primary creditor (or guarantor) or the principal customer and, as a result, effectively exercises influence much greater than is apparent from its stock ownership percentage.

The APB emphasized that "applying judgment is necessary to assess the status of each investment," but APB 18 did not provide any specific criteria for making such assessments. As a result, a number of businesses came to regard the percentage test as quite rigid, believing that achievement of 20% ownership requires use of the equity method to account for the investment regardless of circumstances. To remedy this problem, the FASB issued FIN 35, *Criteria for Applying the Equity Method of Accounting for Investments in Common Stock* (I82.106–.108), to reemphasize the need for judging each investment carefully. Interpretation 35 interprets the 20% test to be a "presumption that the investor has the ability to exercise significant influence over the investee's operating and financial policies"; the presumption "stands until overcome by predominant evidence to the contrary" (I82.107), such as that discussed in the following paragraphs.

It would be impossible to give a list of all factors that might prevent an investor from exercising significant influence, but FIN 35, issued essentially to clarify the use of the equity method by an investor that has signed a standstill agreement, offers a list of examples, noting that the list is only illustrative (I82.108):

* Opposition by the investee, such as litigation or complaints to governmental regulatory authorities, challenges the investor's ability to exercise significant influence.
* The investor and investee sign an agreement under which the investor surrenders significant rights as a shareholder.
* Majority ownership of the investee is concentrated among a small group of shareholders who operate the investee without regard to the views of the investor.
* The investor needs or wants more financial information to apply the equity method than is available to the investee's other shareholders (e.g., the investor wants quarterly financial information from an investee that publicly reports only annually), tries to obtain that information, and fails.
* The investor fails to obtain representation on the investee's board of directors.

Adjustment of Investment Carrying Amount. Investments that are appropriately valued on the equity method must be adjusted periodically to reflect the change in the investor's proportionate equity in net assets of the investee. Thus, the investment account is to be revised each reporting period to reflect the investor's equity in the results or operations of the investee, the dividends received from the investee, and any changes in the investee's capital structure that affect the investor's proportionate interest.

Any difference at the acquisition date between the cost of the investment and the equity in net assets of the investee is required to be accounted for as if the investee were a consolidated subsidiary. If the cost exceeds the investor's proportionate equity and is not attributable to specific accounts of the investee, APB 17 (I60) requires that the excess (goodwill) be amortized over a reasonable period not to exceed 40 years. An excess of equity over cost (negative goodwill) would generally be amortized over a lesser period, say 5 to 15 years.

The investor's share of an investee's losses may exceed the investor's cost. Ordinarily, the investor's financial statements would stop reflecting these losses when the investment account is reduced to zero. However, equity in losses would still be recognized if the investor is committed to provide further financial support to the investee, such as through legal obligations or assumption of liabilities. Also an investor should not provide for additional losses when the return to profitable investee operations seems assured. For example, a nonrecurring loss may reduce the investment below zero while the profitable operating pattern of the investee is unimpaired.

Income Tax Allocation. Interperiod tax allocation is necessary when the equity method of accounting for an investment in common stock is used.

Equity accounting results in an increase in the carrying amount of an equity investment when the investor recognizes its share of undistributed earnings. Assuming the investee has not elected S corporation status, the investor's tax basis in the investee will not change until those earnings are remitted. The higher book basis creates a taxable temporary difference that should be considered when an investor measures its deferred tax liabilities or assets.

Intercompany Profits and Losses. In applying the equity method, APB 18 requires intercompany profits and losses to be eliminated until realized by the investor or investee (I82.109 a.). Although ARB 51 (C51.115) provides for complete elimination of intercompany profits or losses in consolidation, it also states that the elimination of intercompany profit or loss may be allocated proportionately between the majority and minority interests.

From the perspective of the minority investor in a nonsubsidiary investee, it is not necessary to eliminate 100% of the profit. Instead, the investor must eliminate intercompany profit in relation to his proportionate common stock interest. The elimination is the same whether the transaction is "downstream" (i.e., a sale by the investor to the investee) or "upstream" (investee to investor). The following two examples illustrate how these eliminations might be made. Assume the following:

- An investor owns 30% of the common stock of an investee.
- The investment is accounted for under the equity method.
- The income tax rate for both investor and investee is 40%.
- Both have paid sufficient income tax in the current year to enable recognition of deferred tax assets for carry-backs of net deductible temporary differences.

Downstream. The investor sells inventory items to the investee. At the investee's balance sheet date, the investee holds inventory for which the investor has recorded a gross profit of $100,000. The investor's net income would be reduced $18,000 to reflect a $30,000 reduction in gross profit and a $12,000 reduction in income tax expense. A $12,000 deferred tax asset is recognized by the investor based on the investee's ability to carry back net deductible amounts.

Upstream. The investee sells inventory items to the investor. At the investor's balance sheet date, the investor holds inventory for which the investee has recorded a gross profit of $100,000. In computing the investor's equity in earnings, $60,000 ($100,000 less 40% of income tax) would be deducted from the investee's net income, and $18,000 (the investor's share of the intercompany gross profit after income tax) would thereby be eliminated from the investor's equity income. The investor would reduce the carrying amount of its inventory by $30,000 (the investor's share of the investee's gross profit) and recognize a deferred tax asset of $12,000 ($30,000 × 40%)

based on the carry back of the net deductible temporary difference created by the reduction.

Valuation of Equity Investees. In situations where an investment in a particular security of a nonsubsidiary is of such a magnitude that it is appropriately accounted for under the equity method, and it is also a marketable security, APB 18 requires:

> A loss in value of an investment which is other than a temporary decline should be recognized the same as a loss in value of other long-term assets. Evidence of a loss in value might include, but would not necessarily be limited to, absence of an ability to recover the carrying amount of the investment or inability of the investee to sustain an earnings capacity which would justify the carrying amount of the investment. A current fair value of an investment that is less than its carrying amount may indicate a loss in value of the investment. However, a decline in the quoted market price below the carrying amount or the existence of operating losses is not necessarily indicative of a loss in value that is other than temporary. All are factors to be evaluated. [I82.109 h.]

Thus, the investment should be specifically evaluated to determine whether particular adverse factors require a reduction in the carrying amount. The potential for maintaining the investment indefinitely, and the investor's holding intentions, should be considered.

In the case of public reporting entities, the investor must be aware of SAB 59, *Noncurrent Marketable Equity Securities* (Topic 5.M). In this SAB, the staff takes the position that an "other than temporary" decline in the value of an investment does not mean a "permanent" decline. Although it may be extremely difficult to determine that a decline is permanent, the staff believes that is is somewhat easier to determine whether a decline is "other than temporary." The SAB includes a listing of factors that could be used in making that determination. See Chapter 12 for additional discussion of this SAB.

Presentation of Equity in Earnings. There are several ways in which investors reflect their equity in earnings of 50%-or-less-owned companies. Where the investee has no extraordinary, unusual, or similar-type items that would be proportionately material in relation to the investor's financial statements, the investor's share of the investee's after-tax net income is most often shown after arriving at operating income (before taxes). For example, the investor's income statement might show:

Revenues (listed)	$ XXX
Less costs and expenses (listed)	XXX
Income from operations	XX
Equity in earnings of XYZ Co., 27% owned	XX
Income before taxes	XX
Provision for income taxes	X
Net earnings	$ X

It is also common for investors to include the equity amount as a separately delineated item within revenues. Where the equity investee exists solely to provide products or services to the investor, the equity in earnings may be offset (with parenthetical or footnote disclosure, if material) against the line item—grouped in costs and expenses—that contains the investee's product or service charges.

In all the above presentation approaches, the investor's income tax provision equals the sum of current and deferred tax expense, which is based in part on any tax consequences of its equity in earnings and temporary differences attributable to the investment. This provision should not be offset against the equity in earnings, because it is the investor's tax provision, not the investee's.

When the investee's financial statements contain extraordinary items (I17.106–.107), prior-period adjustments (A35.101–.103), or the cumulative effect of a change in accounting principles (A06.115), and the investor's proportionate share of any of these would be material in the financial statements of an investor, such amounts are to be similarly presented in the investor's financial statements. This situation creates complexities in the investor's income tax provision; unlike the approach in the preceding paragraph, the investor *would* apportion its income tax provision amount to the investee items that are reported below the after-tax income from operations.

Recognition of the investor's proportionate interest of both the items and their related tax consequences seems to be the most practical approach to apportioning any tax provision or benefit to be recognized in the investor's financial statements. According to the FASB staff, one alternative is for the investor to apply a method similar to the one illusrated in Paragraph 74 of SFAS 96 (I25.167). That method places primary emphasis on the allocation of tax expense to continuing operations. This may result in an effective tax rate applied by the investor for interperiod tax allocations on its proportionate share different than the rate used by the investee. See Chapter 17 for additional discussion of this SFAS 96 approach.

Another problem sometimes encountered is caused by the investee having an unusual item or an infrequently occurring item that is separately reported in its financial statements. Where the investor's proportionate share of this amount is material in the investor's financial statements, it may (but is not required to) be set out parenthetically in the investor's earnings statement. For example:

Equity in earnings of XYZ Co., 27% owned (including $25,000,000 pretax gain on disposal of certain oil producing properties)

Unusual items may not be shown net of tax on the face of the income statement. Thus it is especially problematic to set out a material proportionate share of an investee's unusual item in the investor's financial statements in any manner other than parenthetically. Of course, footnote discussion may be the best solution, because there are no proscriptions against disclosing the amounts net of tax in the notes.

It must be kept in mind in all of these presentational variations that the determination of what is extraordinary, unusual, or infrequently occurring is determined for each party—the investee and the investor—by reference to its own circumstances. Thus an item that qualifies as extraordinary for the investor, for example, might be ordinary for the investee, and vice versa. Conceivably, the result could be the same type of transaction showing up as ordinary and extraordinary in a single income statement, but there may be enough breadth in the definition of extraordinary, unusual, and infrequent to avoid this situation.

Disclosures. Required disclosures with respect to equity investees, if material, include (I82.110):

* The accounting policies of the investor with respect to investments in common stock.
* The name of each investee and the percentage ownership.
* The reasons any significant less-than-20% investment (to be named) is valued by the equity method.
* The reasons any significant 20%-or-more investment (to be named) is not valued by the equity method.
* The difference between the carrying amount of an investment and the underlying equity in net assets, and the accounting treatment of the difference.
* The aggregate quoted market price of the investment, if available.
* Summarized information as to investees' assets, liabilities, and operating results, if the investments are material in relation to the investor.
* Material effects of possible conversions, exercise, or contingent issuances of investees' securities.

Advances and loans are often made to equity method investees, and these are usually combined with the investment in the balance sheet under a caption such as "Investment in and Advances to XYZ Company." The footnote details conforming to the above list of required disclosures would provide the breakout of advances and loans for material investees.

Joint Ventures

An investment may be made in a particular situation in the form of a joint venture, which is defined as an entity that is owned, operated, and jointly controlled by a small group as a separate, specific business project for the mutual benefit of the ownership group (I82.401). Each venturer commonly participates in the overall management, and significant decisions commonly require the consent of each of the venturers (regardless of ownership percentage) so that no individual venturer has unilateral control. The venturers will not necessarily have equal ownership interests, and a venturer's share could be as low as 5% or 10%, or above 50%, or evenly split at 50%. These situations differ from what is encountered in the normal application of equity method or consolidation accounting, in that joint venturers have special rights and obligations assuring their significant influence even at ownership percentages less than 20%.

A joint venture may be organized as a corporation, partnership, or undivided interest. If organized as a corporation, APB 18 applies, and the investment in the corporate joint venture would be accounted for following the equity method. If the investment is in a joint venture organized as a partnership or some other unincorporated form, an AICPA staff interpretation of APB 18 says that many of the provisions of that opinion are appropriate in accounting for such investments (I82.508–512).

Until 1979, other than APB 18 and the unofficial interpretation, there was almost no other definitive guidance in the professional literature about accounting by investors for their investments in joint ventures. In that year an AcSEC task force prepared an Issues Paper entitled *Joint Venture Accounting* (AICPA, 1979b). The AICPA asked the FASB to consider a project on accounting and reporting for investments in joint ventures, and what basis of accounting should be used for a joint venture entity. In 1987, as part of its Reporting Entity project, the FASB also added joint ventures to its agenda.

The major problems identified in the issues paper, and AcSEC's advisory conclusion, are discussed in the following sections.

Defining a Joint Venture. If one looks beyond the authoritative definition given in APB 18 there are conflicting definitions of joint venture. Although the APB had a difficult time reaching a definition, the members no doubt felt compelled to reach some conclusion given the lack of any definition in the professional literature and the increasing use of joint ventures, including 50%-owned companies. The end result of the APB's effort, however, limited the definition to *corporate* joint ventures only, given the APB's primary focus on the equity method of accounting for investments in common stock.

AcSEC reached the advisory conclusion that joint venture should be defined very broadly to encompass all entities, regardless of legal form, that have certain characteristics — with the central distinguishing characteristic being joint control of major decisions. In its Issues Paper, AcSEC specifically recommended adoption of the definition used in the Canadian Institute of Chartered Accountants Handbook (Section 3055):

> A joint venture is an arrangement whereby two or more parties (the venturers) jointly control a specific business undertaking and contribute resources towards its accomplishment. The life of the joint venture is limited to that of the undertaking which may be of short or long-term duration depending on the circumstances. A distinctive feature of a joint venture is that the relationship between the venturers is governed by an agreement (usually in writing) which establishes joint control. Decisions in all areas essential to the accomplishment of a joint venture require the consent of the venturers, as provided by the agreement; none of the individual venturers is in a position to unilaterally control the venture. This feature of joint control distinguishes investments in joint ventures from investments in other enterprises where control of decisions is related to the proportion of voting interest held.

Accounting for Joint Venture Investments. AcSEC arrived at the following advisory conclusions in this area (AICPA, 1979b, ¶ 52):

a. The portion of APB 18 dealing with investments in joint ventures should be reexamined.

b. The one-line equity method as described in APB 18 should be required for investments (other than off-balance sheet financing arrangements) in joint venture entities (whether incorporated or unincorporated) that are subject to joint control, except that the cost method should be permitted for investments not material to the investor.

c. If an entity that otherwise meets the definition of a joint venture is, in fact, controlled by majority voting interest or otherwise, the entity should be required to be accounted for as a subsidiary of the controlling investor and to be fully consolidated by that investor.

d. If an entity that otherwise meets the definition of a joint venture is not subject to joint control, by reason of its liabilities being several rather than joint as in some undivided interests, investments in the entity should be required to be accounted for by the proportionate consolidation method.

e. The use of the same method in the balance sheet and income statement should be required.

f. Disclosure of supplementary information as to the assets, liabilities, and results of operations should be mandatory if the investments in the aggregate are material.

Although AcSEC did not conclude how an investor should account for a difference between carrying amount and valuation for assets contributed to a venture, it did conclude, by narrow majorities, that from the standpoint of the venture itself (¶ 53):

a. The creation of a joint venture establishes a reporting entity separate from its owners that requires a new basis of accounting for its assets and liabilities.

b. Assets contributed to the venture should be recorded at the amount agreed on by the parties, which is assumed to be determined by reference to fair market value, but not in excess of the assets' fair market value.

In an addendum to the Issues Paper, AcSEC pointed out the need for considering the problem of investor accounting when cash distributions from a venture exceed the investment carrying amount, but it could not reach an advisory conclusion.

Financial Statement Presentation. The AcSEC issues paper identifies seven possible approaches in displaying joint ventures in the investor's financial statements, as briefly described in the following subsections. While four of these approaches are considered acceptable in the AcSEC advisory conclusions, they are not interchangeable, and each is applied where the specified circumstances exist.

One-line equity method. This is the approach discussed in APB 18 (I82.109 c.) and described in the preceding investment section of this chapter. The issues paper took the position that this should remain the prevalent method (see advisory conclusion b).

Expanded equity method. Although there are several variations, the essence of this proposal is to include a proportionate share of the assets and liabilities in the venturer's statement, but without combining directly. This approach was not recommended by AcSEC.

Proportionate consolidation. Under this method the investor's proportionate share of the venture's assets, liabilities, income, and expenses is combined with the similar items in the investor's financial statements. This method has been in use for some time in the real estate and oil and gas industries, and has been supported in an unofficial AICPA staff interpretation (I82.512).

The issues paper contains a summary of a NAARS search of 4,071 annual reports for 1977, indicating that of 415 companies reporting investments in 50% owned companies, joint ventures, partnerships, or undivided interests, 65 companies used the proportionate consolidation method; these are enumerated in Appendix B of the issues paper (AICPA, 1979b, ¶¶ 57–63). This survey suggests that proportionate consolidation of joint ventures is used principally in the real estate and construction, oil and gas, and utilities industries. However, the SEC generally is not in favor of proportionate consolidation and therefore expansion of this practice to other industries is constrained. It should be noted that SOP 78-9, *Accounting for Investments in Real Estate Ventures* (TP 10,240), states that the usual full consolidation or equity accounting rules apply to *corporate* joint ventures in the real estate industry.

AcSEC recommended that proportionate consolidation be limited to those situations where the venture's liabilities are several, not joint (i.e., the investor is obligated for a specific portion of the venture's debt).

Full consolidation.   When a venturer has control, AcSEC concluded that the venture should be fully consolidated as if the venture were a subsidiary.

Cost method.   This approach is to be permitted only for immaterial investments in ventures.

Fair market value method.   This method is *not* recommened, because it would change the historical cost measurement basis underlying present GAAP. Essentially, it carries the investment (presumably on a one-line basis) at its fair market value; changes therein would be income or loss.

Combination of methods.   One method might be used in the investor's balance sheet and another in the income statement. For example, see Figure 24.7. As a practical matter, in the relatively few instances where this has been used, only two of the foregoing methods—one-line and proportional consolidation—are involved. AcSEC specifically recommended against this method.

Income Tax Allocation.   In APB 23, *Accounting for Income Taxes—Special Areas* (I42), the APB reached a conclusion that when ventures are essentially permanent in duration, the investor should not provide for income taxes on undistributed earnings when there is sufficient evidence that the venture has invested or will invest the undistributed earnings indefinitely, or that the earnings will be remitted in a tax free liquidation. This is the same rule used for subsidiaries.

For limited life ventures, the tax consequence of transactions or events giving rise to temporary differences should be recognized in the investor's financial statements. Measurement should be based on the most likely occurrence which will result in realization of the investment. If, for example, it is anticipated that realization will be in the form of dividends, the tax consequences to be recognized would consider dividend exclusions if they are permitted under the tax law. Of course the tax consequences would be different if management believed realization would occur through

Principles of consolidation—The consolidated financial statements include the accounts of Ashland and its majority-owned subsidiaries, except those engaged in insurance activities. Investments in engineering and construction joint ventures are accounted for on the equity method in the balance sheet and on the proportionate consolidation method in the income statement. Investments in other joint ventures, in 20% and 50% owned affiliates and in unconsolidated subsidiaries (including Integon Corporation prior to September 30, 1984) are accounted for on the equity method.

FIG. 24.7 Disclosures of Joint Venture Accounting—Equity Method in Balance Sheet, Pro Rata Consolidation in Income Statement
Source: Ashland Oil Inc., 1986 Annual Report.

sale. However, the FASB staff has indicated that tax planning strategies altering the manner in which management ultimately expects to realize an investment must be considered if they result in a lower tax.

International Accounting Standard

In July 1986 the IASC issued Exposure Draft No. 28, *Accounting for Investments in Associates and Joint Ventures* (IASC, 1986). This draft deals with the accounting by an investor for investments in associates and in joint ventures over which significant influence is exercised. An associate is defined as a company that is "neither a subsidiary nor a joint venture" and in which the investor has (1) significant influence and (2) no intention of disposing of his interest. According to the exposure draft:

Significant influence is the power to participate in the financial and operating policy decisions of the investee but is not control over those policies. An investor may exercise significant influence in several ways, usually by representation on the board of directors but also by participation in policy making processes, material intercompany transactions, interchange of managerial personnel, or provision of essential technical information. If the investor holds less than 20% of the voting power of the investee, it should be presumed that the investor does not have significant influence, unless such influence can be clearly demonstrated. Conversely, if the investor holds 20% or more of the voting power of the investee, it should be presumed that the investor does have significant influence, unless it can be clearly demonstrated that this is not the case.

The IASC exposure draft, if approved, would require that:

1. Investments in associates and in joint ventures over which significant influence is exercised should be accounted for in consolidation using the equity method, except in the following circumstances:

   a. An enterprise ceases to fall within the definition of an associate but is, either in whole or in part, retained; or

   b. An investor ceases to have significant influence in a joint venture but retains, either in whole or in part, its investment; or

c. The use of equity or proportionate consolidation methods is no longer appropriate because there is substantial doubt that the earnings of an associate or joint venture will flow through to the investor, in which case the investor should discontinue the use of the equity method or proportionate consolidation. The carrying amount of the investment at that date should be regarded as cost thereafter.

2. Permanent declines in investment values should be recognized.

3. Certain disclosures should be made:

a. An appropriate listing and description of significant associates and joint ventures, including the methods used to account for such investments.

b. A summary of the investor's share of the assets, liabilities, revenues, and expenses of associates and joint ventures, when such investments, or the income therefrom, represent a significant proportion of the assets or income of the investor. (If substantially all of the activities of an enterprise are carried out through joint ventures, and proportionate consolidation is used, then a statement to this effect is sufficient disclosure.)

c. The dates to which the financial statements of the investees have been prepared where such dates are different from those of the investor.

d. The amounts relating to any significant unadjusted transactions or events occurring between the dates of the investor's and associate's or joint venture's financial statements.

e. Where the investor does not publish consolidated financial statements and uses the cost method for investments in associates and joint ventures, the amounts that it would have included in its income statement and balance sheet had the equity method been used.

4. Investments should be classified as long-term assets, separately disclosed, along with the investor's share of income or loss and unusual items from such investments.

As of early 1988 the exposure draft was still under consideration by the IASC.

AUDITING CONSIDERATIONS

Audit Objectives

The audit of a client's consolidation process has several objectives. First and most importantly, the auditors must challenge the consolidation policy to be certain that it meets the requirements of ARB 51, SFAS 94, other good contemporary practice, and, where applicable, the SEC requirements. ARB 51 states that there is a presumption that consolidated financial statements are more meaningful than separate statements and are usually necessary for a fair presentation (C51.101).

The client's consolidation policy will be stated in the accounting policy footnote, although that note will not deal with procedures. Many companies include a more detailed statement in their internal policy manual; that policy statement should be a reference point for the auditors' challenge. Generally, the audit committee also will refer to such policy statements as it periodically challenges the company's various accounting policies.

A second audit objective, to ascertain that the consolidation policy is consistently and correctly applied, will obviously be critical when new subsidiaries are acquired or control is attained. In addition, there should be an ongoing challenge that subsidiaries excluded from the consolidated group in prior years still warrant that treatment.

As a third objective, the auditor must be concerned that the detailed consolidation eliminations, adjustments, and combinations of appropriate accounts have been properly made. The value of an audit of the individual components could be diminished if the final audit of the consolidation procedures is handled improperly or carelessly.

Finally, the auditors must be satisfied that the total consolidation presentation is appropriate. They must not only be satisfied that the detailed disclosures are adequate, but they must also be satisfied that the overall picture presented in the consolidated statements does not obscure significant information about individual units.

Audit Approach

Generally speaking, the audit approach will be substantive (see Chapter 7). A challenge to the consolidation policy requires an analysis of all the factors involved in the choice of the policy and in its application. Two substantive challenges warrant specific consideration here.

First, when evaluating the measure of control a company exercises over its investees, the substance of the intercompany arrangements must prevail. It will be important for the auditor to know the identity of the other owners, if any, to understand what relationships they might have to the corporate group. The auditors must be alert to relationships that provide indirect control by others as well as to those that result in direct control by the parent.

Second, while the auditors search for the nature of the intercompany relationships, they must be alert to legal or business restrictions which influence the substance of the parent-subsidiary relationship, especially the possibility that the assets, earnings, and funds of the subsidiary are not available to the corporate group even though the parent owns a majority of the voting stock. In those situations, the auditors should also consider whether the parent's investment in (and advances to) the subsidiary should be subjected to a net realizable value test.

In addition to substantively challenging the consolidation policy, the audit must cover the consolidation process itself. This aspect can follow a substantive approach or a systems reliance/compliance testing approach (see Chapter 7), depending on the strength of the company's system for performing the consolidation. As the auditor reviews and tests the system, he should determine that it properly:

1. Identifies intercompany transactions and balances for elimination purposes.
2. Calculates intercompany profit in inventory or fixed assets.
3. Combines the balances of appropriate accounts.
4. Accounts for changes in the consolidated group.

To allow the auditor to rely on the system, there must be sufficient controls to prevent or detect and correct errors in the above areas. If the auditor believes the substantive approach is more efficient, or if he is concerned about weaknesses in consolidation controls, he will adopt a substantive approach to the audit of the consolidation process and will extend his detailed testing accordingly.

Evaluating Carrying Amounts of Equity Investments

Evidential matter pertaining to the carrying amount of equity investments, income and losses attributable to the investments, and other transactions of the investee may be obtained from audited financial statements of the investee. If these are not available, unaudited financial statements, regulatory examination reports, and the like may be useful. However, the auditor for the investor may need to perform, or have performed by the investee's auditor, audit procedures to supplement the unaudited information (see AU 543). In some circumstances, as with real estate, mineral rights, and other natural resources, the auditor may need to use the work of a specialist (AU 336) in obtaining satisfaction.

The auditor must obtain information relating to intercompany transactions to determine that intercompany profit eliminations are properly made, and should obtain by inquiry and through other evidence an indication of management's intent with respect to holding, obtaining dividends from, or reinvesting earnings in an investee; this is necessary to determine the proper method for income tax allocation.

The auditor has a difficult task in being satisfied that the investor does or does not have the ability to exercise significant influence. The criteria for this determination have been problematic when a client asserts that it has overcome the presumption that the ability to exercise significant influence does not exist below 20% ownership. Problems also exist when there are signs that influence does not exist above 20%, such as litigation between the parties. The auditor must perform sufficient work to be satisfied that the basis for valuing the investment is supported and that appropriate disclosures as specified earlier are reflected in the investor's financial statements.

Differences in Year Ends

Differences in investor's and investee's year ends are often encountered. The condition often results in a time lag in reflecting equity by the investor. A time lag is acceptable but must be consistent from period to period. The auditor for the investor also needs to make inquiry as to events and transactions from the date of the investee's financial statements to the date of the auditor's report for the investor to see whether any material events or transactions have occurred that require presentation in the investor's financial statements or disclosure in the footnotes.

When unaudited interim financial statements of a material investee are used to coincide with the investor's year end, audit or review procedures will need to be applied by either the investor's or investee's auditor to corroborate the appropriateness of the amounts included in the investor's financial statements.

25

Related Party Transactions

PERSPECTIVE

In 1973, the New York Stock Exchange (NYSE) released a "white paper" reaffirming its long-standing policy of "precluding the continuation of conflict-of-interest situations" and suggesting that such situations could be eliminated through a policy of disclosure. Whenever a related party transaction was identified, the NYSE normally required the listed company (or the company applying for listing) to agree to eliminate the situation over a period of time, often two to five years. Traditionally, this has been the NYSE's response regardless of the nature of the transaction and whether or not it was believed by the company to benefit the enterprise and its shareholders.

The NYSE modified its policy in 1984 because of significant and positive developments in corporate governance, including:

• The NYSE's requirement that an audit committee composed of independent directors be established by each domestic listed company;

• The continuing and increasing participation of nonmanagement directors serving on corporate boards;

• The adoption by many companies of strict codes of corporate ethics; and

• Expanded disclosure of related party transactions in the company's annual report and proxy statements, as well as in other corporate filings.

Under the new policy, each related party transaction is to be reviewed and evaluated by an appropriate group within the listed company involved. While the new policy does not specify who should review related party transactions, the NYSE believes that the audit committee or another comparable body might be considered as an appropriate forum for this task. Following the review, the company should determine whether a particular relationship serves the best interests of the company and its shareholders and whether the relationship may be continued or should be eliminated.

The rules of the American Stock Exchange (AMEX) provide that the existence of material conflicts of interest between companies and their officers, directors, or substantial shareholders (or members of their families or concerns controlled by them) will be reviewed by AMEX on an individual basis in considering the eligibility of companies for original listing. In many cases, companies are able to eliminate conflict situations prior to listing or within a reasonable period after listing and may be asked to do so. Where a conflict cannot be resolved promptly for sound business reasons, AMEX will consider all pertinent factors. A company may be required to enter into a special agreement with AMEX, designed to reduce the possibility of abuse of a conflict situation that cannot be terminated immediately or that might arise in the future.

Both the NYSE and AMEX use the terms *transactions with insiders* and *conflict of interests*, and those terms convey a general message of what this chapter is all about. Though there are many different terms used to describe such transactions and situations, and there are many different types, they are all generically referred to as *related party transactions*. Their common characteristic is that one party (whether a person or an enterprise) is in a position to control the effect of a transaction or situation on another party; hence, a conflict of interests exists unless the two parties have identical beneficiaries.

For example, a parent company can control the results of its transactions with a wholly owned subsidiary. If consolidated financial statements are issued (assuming a consolidated income tax return and no other outside-party consequences), it is irrelevant for financial reporting purposes whether transactions between the two companies meet any kind of objective standards. For purposes of all investors and creditors, the financial statements of the two companies are looked on as one.

But if there is a reason to issue separate financial statements of either party, questions arise as to the objectivity of intercompany transactions. Even if special care is taken to base such transactions on verifiable external criteria, most users of the separate financial statements would, at the least, be justified in wondering whether the two companies could separately exist as is suggested by the appearance of separate reports. Of course, all these situations are a matter of degree, and very often the potential for concern is quite low (e.g., when a separately reporting subsidiary has no transactions with its holding company parent).

Concerns about ability to control the effect of transactions can also be seen in numerous similar situations, such as:

- An officer or director in relation to his responsibility to the company
- A principal stockholder in relation to the company in which he owns stock
- A partner or joint venturer in relation to the partnership or venture

Various kinds of related parties and transactions will be defined below. However, an initial review of the environment will be helpful in understanding why related party transactions have always been a hotly debated issue.

Nature of the Issues

Concealed relationships and hidden ownerships have been used by corporate managements to facilitate deceptions of the auditor and the public, usually to produce artificially inflated earnings reports and stock values. Related party transactions thus take on an odious flavor and consequently have been perceived by legislators and prosecutors from time to time as evils to be exposed, laid bare by punitive disclosure requirements, and finally eradicated.

The existence of business dealings between persons or parties who share some relationship or mutual economic interest is as old as commerce itself. Indeed major segments of legitimate commerce are dependent on transactions between related parties. But the focus of attention has led to an unfortunate misapprehension about the role that related party transactions play in commerce because they provide circumstances susceptible to at least two kinds of abuses:

1. In the absence of proper identification and disclosure that relationships exist between parties to a business transaction, the hidden relationships can be used to obscure the "true" financial condition and results of operations of one or more of the related parties.
2. The relationships may be used to improperly divert to one entity the economic benefit of a transaction from another entity to which it rightfully belongs. An example of such an abuse would be the sale of personally owned raw land by an officer of a corporate real estate developer to the corporate entity at inflated prices.

Related party transactions may be strongly criticized from time to time, but no one is seriously attempting to eradicate them. Underwriters have probably done more than anyone else, including the SEC and the public accounting profession, to discourage these transactions in public companies. They have done this by withholding support of new securities issues until high profile related party transactions, whether abusive or not, are stopped or profusely disclosed.

The obligation to preclude related party abuses falls primarily on corporate management and directors. The auditor is expected to remain alert for possible related party transactions, to make reasonable inquiry to ascertain that all material relationships are identified and disclosed, and to conclude that such relationships do not appear to have been used to violate fiduciary responsibilities.

In the understandable climate of public skepticism concerning related party transactions, managements are well advised to establish definitive policies and procedures governing such transactions.

Government Action

The Watergate investigations of 1973–1974 demonstrated a point of great interest to auditors. Though the investigators had unlimited powers of subpoena, unlimited financial resources, and no deadlines, they found it difficult and often impossible to disprove deceptive representations by high officials. Like the Watergate investigations, an audit is essentially a process of either supporting or disproving management's representations. An audit, however, operates under time pressures, financial limitations, and a total lack of subpoena power. Nevertheless, when certain kinds of deceptive representations by management, known in the vernacular as "cooking the books," escape exposure by the auditor, as can be arranged with a good deal of cleverness when all parties to a transaction are related, the auditor is often accused of an "audit failure."

Recognizing that a management lacking integrity can do a great deal to deceive the auditor, the SEC has supported legislation to prohibit such deception. In response to the SEC's efforts, and to the illegal payments and bribes brought to light by the post-Watergate investigations, Congress passed the Foreign Corrupt Practices Act of 1977 (the FCPA). This law requires publicly held companies to "make and keep books ... which, in reasonable detail, accurately and fairly reflect the transactions and dispositions of the assets of the [company]." To promote compliance, the SEC adopted rules that prohibit falsifying books and records of publicly held companies, making a false or misleading statement to the auditor, or omitting a statement of fact essential to the integrity of the financial statements.

The SEC has never adopted any regulation that would actually ban related party transactions. It has only required that transactions involving persons related to the management of a filing corporation be specifically disclosed to the Commission and to public investors and has noted that the presence of transactions between affiliates should raise broader questions about the reliability and completeness of the information provided. Other federal and state laws and regulations have, at various times, tried to curb abuses in transactions with related parties.

Definitions

Viewed from the perspective of the financial statements of an enterprise, a *related party* may be any of the following:

- Affiliates
- Principal owners and close kin
- Management and close kin
- Parents and subsidiaries
- Equity method investors and investees
- Trusts for the benefit of employees
- Any other party that has the ability to significantly influence the management or operating policies of the reporting enterprise, to the extent that it may be prevented from fully pursuing its own separate interests

This listing is based on SFAS 57, *Related Party Disclosures* (R36.406).

Affiliates. An affiliate is a party that directly or indirectly, through one or more intermediaries, controls, is controlled by, or is under common control with an enterprise; *control* means the possession, direct or indirect, of the power to direct or cause the direction of the management and policies of an enterprise through ownership, by contract, or otherwise (R36.401–.402). These definitions, though appearing in SFAS 57, are based on SEC definitions contained in Regulation S-X, Rule 1–02(b). This definition is cloaked in "fuzzy" words, such as *direct or indirect* and *otherwise*, prompting critics of related party transaction rules to interpret the definition as "you'll know 'em when you see 'em."

Principal Owners. SFAS 57 defines *principal owner* as the owner(s) of record or known beneficial owner(s) of more than 10% of the voting interests of the reporting enterprise (R36.405). This definition is also based on Regulation S-X, Rule 1–02(q), which contains the broader provision that determination is based on any class of equity securities, not only voting stock. At a minimum, this would encompass nonvoting convertible securities, where a determination should be made on an "if converted" basis.

By and large, this definition of principal owners also encompasses *promoters*, who are defined by Regulation S-X, Rule 1–02(r) as:

1. Any person who, acting alone or in conjunction with one or more other persons, directly or indirectly takes initiative in founding and organizing the business or enterprise of an issuer;
2. Any person who, in connection with the founding and organizing of the business or enterprise of an issuer, directly or indirectly receives in consideration of services or property, or both services and property, 10 percent or more of any class of securities of the issuer or 10 percent or more of the proceeds from the sale of any class of securities. . . .

Another situation that may fit the definition of principal owner may exist when two or more shareholders are known or presumed to operate in concert through a voting trust or informally (although it is often difficult to identify such situations in the absence of a representation so asserting). When these circumstances exist, the group may, in the aggregate, be a principal shareholder. If a group is able to control the policies of a company, it is considered a *control group*.

Management. Persons having responsibility for achieving the objectives of the organization, and the concomitant authority to establish the policies and make the decisions by which these objectives are to be pursued, are deemed to be management. This definition would normally include members of the board of directors, the president, secretary, treasurer, any vice-president in charge of a principal business function (such as sales, administration, or finance), and any other person who performs similar policy-making functions. Persons without formal titles also may be members of management (R36.404).

Close Kin. Members of the immediate families of principal owners and management are also to be considered, *ipso facto*, related parties. This has long been recognized for income tax purposes and also shows up as part of SEC definitions; for example, the definition of *associate* in Regulation 14A, Rule 14a–1(a), includes

> any relative or spouse of such person, or any relative of such spouse, who has the same home as such person or who is a director or officer of the registrant or any of its parents or subsidiaries.

As a practical matter, close kinships do not become an active audit concern unless circumstances or information become known that bring these relationships into question.

Parents and Subsidiaries. A parent company is one that controls a subsidiary directly, or indirectly through one or more intermediaries (based on Regulation S-X, Rule 1–02(o)). The GAAP definition of parent is a company that "directly or indirectly has a controlling financial interest" in a subsidiary company (C51.101). *Controlling financial interest* is defined as "ownership of a majority voting interest," that is, "ownership by one enterprise, directly or indirectly, of over fifty percent of the outstanding voting shares of another enterprise ..." (C51.102).

Equity Method Investors and Investees. Under APB 18 (discussed in Chapter 24), an investor who owns 20% or more of the voting stock in a company, but not more than 50%, is presumed, in the absence of evidence to the contrary, to have the ability to exercise significant influence over that investee and should therefore use the equity method of accounting (I82.104). Thus, a person or enterprise owning 20% to 50% of another company is deemed a related party of the investee company. Significant influence is described (I82.104) as

> representation on the board of directors, participation in policy making processes, material intercompany transactions, interchange of managerial personnel, or technological dependency. Another important consideration is the extent of ownership by an investor in relation to the concentration of other shareholdings, but substantial or majority ownership of

the voting stock of an investee by another investor does not necessarily preclude the ability to exercise significant influence by the investor.

The FASB has added to the above list in SFAS 13 (L10.419): guarantees of indebtedness, extensions of credit, ownership of warrants, debt obligations or other securities, and common officers or directors.

Other Parties. Significant influence can come from one party having a relationship with two or more otherwise separate transacting parties—that is, the transacting parties do not have a direct parent-subsidiary or investor-investee relationship. SFAS 57 concerns itself with this relationship "to the extent that one or more of the transacting parties might be prevented from fully pursuing its own separate interests" (R36.406).

SEC Definition. The SEC has not defined a related party in its own rules and regulations, but has incorporated the profession's definitions (first in SAS 6 (AU 334) and currently in SFAS 57 (R36.406)). The SEC's definition of affiliate can be interpreted quite broadly, since it recognizes the possesson of indirect power in ways other than through ownership or by contract. Thus, it is reasonable to conclude that the narrower term *affiliate* has expanded to become synonymous with *related party*.

Public vs. Private Companies

The SEC and some regulatory agencies have long required stringent accounting and disclosure standards for publicly held and otherwise regulated companies (e.g., banks), but these standards have not been automatically applied in reporting on privately held companies. That different accounting requirements might apply to privately held companies has also been acknowledged by the FASB. For example, in SFAS 21, the FASB exempts those companies from the requirement to report earnings per share and segment information.

Should the auditing of, accounting for, and disclosure of related party transactions also be different for privately held companies? No authoritative pronouncement has yet addressed this question. As discussed in Chapter 39, a major complaint of smaller and/or closely held companies has been the propensity of accounting and auditing standards to be written in reaction to the problems of larger, public companies, and this is also somewhat true with respect to SFAS 57 and SAS 6. Neither the FASB nor the Auditing Standards Board has offered any exceptions to applicability, and it can be easily argued that no conceptual basis exists in this area for a dual standard regarding large and small companies or privately held and publicly held companies.

Privately held companies may draw less attention for abuse of related party transactions than do publicly held companies: related party transactions are less likely to be questioned or attacked by shareholders or the general public in privately held companies. But privately held companies are often controlled by a few individuals, increasing the opportunities for such transactions. Thus, while readers may associate much of the discussion in this chapter with publicly held company situations, most is applicable to all companies and should be considered in the preparation, auditing, and review of all financial statements.

RELATIONSHIPS AND TRANSACTION TYPES

The preceding definition section might lead one to the conclusion that a related party is a chameleon; the same party can be defined variously depending on the relationship assumed in a specific situation. This is indeed so, and this chapter does not attempt to maintain any stringent distinctions among related parties, management, affiliates, or other terms of similar meaning.

The same may be true of attempts at specification of relationship and transaction types, because there are infinite gradations and overlaps. The SEC view is that related party transactions are not limited to any particular type or classification, but can take an infinite number of forms. However, some broad generalizations may be useful.

Overt/Covert Distinction

Most related party transactions are quite visible in relation to the financial statements of a reporting enterprise. Usually a parent-subsidiary relationship is obvious; or a material recorded transaction between an investor and equity method investee will at least become visible through inquiries. Management perquisites may be less observable, but for public companies the disclosure requirements are such that there is every likelihood the data will be complete. Further, the various SEC forms require information on remuneration of officers and directors, principal holders of equity securities, and material interest of management, directors and principal holders in the company's transactions, indebtedness of officers and directors to the company, and other similar items.

At the opposite end of the spectrum are the related party transactions of notoriety—those that have been deliberately concealed, often by collusion among the parties. Many cases involving management fraud have been based on concealed relationships, side deals, and gross misrepresentations of fact corroborated by conspirators who were allegedly independent.

Relationships

The introductory section of this chapter discussed a variety of situations that by broad definition qualify as related party relationships. Some of these relationships are easily identified. Others present greater challenge, either because they are difficult to distinguish from arm's-length dealings and other conventional business practices or because their nature makes them easily concealable.

Conflict of Interests. Webster defines the term *conflict of interest* as a conflict between private interests and the official responsibilities of a person in a position of trust. Today the term has a broader application, as if any interest not at arm's length were a conflict of interest. It need not be an actual conflict; the mere presence of the ability to bias a transaction seems an adequate basis for describing it as a conflict relationship.

An illustrative situation would be ownership of a supply company by an officer or employee of another company that purchases its supplies from the supply company.

Many companies have policies and internal controls aimed at identifying such situations; the conflict situation thus can be reviewed to ascertain that no special benefits resulted from it.

Of greater concern is an active conflict of interest in the form of bribes and kickbacks to officers, directors, stockholders, or employees. No record will exist on the payee side, since the payment will have gone directly to the individual. Thus, the likelihood of identification from that company's records is remote. The extent to which such payments are illegal is addressed in SAS 54, *Illegal Acts by Clients* (AU 317).

Although some reasonable chance of identification exists in the records of the company paying the bribe or kickback, note that a conflict of interest situation does not exist in that company, presuming the payoff was to obtain favorable treatment only for the company. If the paying company is publicly held, however, it may be in literal violation of the Foreign Corrupt Practices Act if such payments are not recorded as "bribery and kickbacks" in the company records.

For a conflict of interest to exist, a related party must be in a position to exercise a significant influence. All the related parties listed under "Definitions" earlier in this chapter have such an ability to a greater or lesser degree.

Absence of Transactions. In some cases the relationship among the parties is such that the person or entity having a conflict of interest causes transactions *not* to occur. Typical examples of nontransactions are:

- Loss of business opportunity. Where two or more businesses perform the same basic function under common management control, management has the choice of directing basically indistinguishable transactions to one company rather than another.
- Forebearances. A party does not foreclose on a defaulted debt, or fails to enforce a guarantee made by a related party of the debt of a third party.

Failure to enter into a transaction when the effects of that transaction rightfully or properly should inure to the related party can readily result in presenting a misleading picture in the financial statements of the related party. While a material transaction that did not occur cannot be recorded, disclosure of conditions under which this situation could occur, such as common ownership, is required under SFAS 57 (R36.104).

Components of a Business Enterprise. Components include identifiable segments, such as parent companies; majority-owned subsidiaries; divisions, branches, or other parts of a corporation; and brother-sister companies under common control. The status of a component as a member of a broader enterprise is in itself sufficient to deem it a related party, regardless of its apparent autonomy.

A component may be economically dependent on its parent or another component for its continued existence, or a company in a controlled group may operate independently of its parent with respect to products and customers but still be wholly dependent on its parent for financing. Although this dependence might not distort the balance sheet, its disclosure is vital to suppliers and vendors who could suffer losses if the parent company were to stop financing the subsidiary. Disclosure of these relationships is required in the financial statements and may need to be emphasized in the auditor's report, as discussed later. When the component is less intimately connected with the parent, simple disclosure of its controlled status should suffice.

Other Relationships. The one definition of significant influence, applicable to use of the equity method of accounting (I82.104), discusses several types of relationships that suggest an ability to exercise significant influence. These include:

* *Technological dependency*, such as a royalty arrangement with an otherwise unrelated party, when such arrangement is essential to a company's operation.
* *Common officers and directors*, for example, one director having significant influence on the boards of directors of two otherwise unrelated companies.

SFAS 57 (R36.104) states that such parties should not be considered related parties unless one of them clearly exercises significant management or ownership influence over the other. However, technological dependency and commonality of officers and directors may need to be disclosed in order to present a party's financial position in conformity with generally accepted accounting principles.

Transactions

Ordinary/Nonordinary Transactions. In this chapter, related party transactions fall into two categories—ordinary and nonordinary. The distinction is not official, but is made based on APB 30, *Reporting the Results of Operations—Reporting the Effects of Disposal of a Segment of a Business, and Extraordinary, Unusual and Infrequently Occurring Events or Transactions.*

Related party transactions made in the ordinary course of business are generally entered into because they offer some economic benefit to both parties involved, such as the retention of profits within the related group. For example, a petroleum refinery may sell gasoline and other products to a retail service station chain in which the refinery owns 50% of the stock, but it must do so at the same prices charged to all the refinery's other customers purchasing comparable volumes. These prices will also approximate those paid by the retail chain for products purchased from unrelated refiners.

Nonordinary related party transactions may or may not be made for the same reason. Often, instead of economic benefit to the group as a whole, the reason is to benefit only one of the parties. For example, a sale of real estate or investment securities may be made to a related party at or near year-end to increase the earnings of one of the parties. Or operating properties may be leased from a related party, such as a stockholder, mainly to increase the stockholder's compensation or improve his tax position. The less ordinary a related party transaction is, the more obscure the reason for it is likely to be. Sometimes the auditor, the SEC, the IRS, and the stockholders all have their own theories about the reason for such a transaction, and none of them believes the reason given by management.

Suppose, for example, that an executive buys a jet airplane and leases it to a corporation he manages. The official reason for this arrangement is to benefit the corporation, perhaps by keeping the debt for the airplane off the books or by supplementing the corporation's already strained borrowing capacity or by avoiding violation of a restrictive covenant in a debt agreement. Others may wonder, however, if the corporation benefits as much as the executive. Maybe he simply wants the "perk" of an airplane that the corporation may not need. Perhaps he will receive direct additional compensation by way of excess net rental income or indirect additional compensation by way of depreciation deductions.

Beneficial Transactions. Some related party transactions may appear to improve the reporting company's financial position. In these cases, some executives may also benefit personally, perhaps because their bonus participation is based on corporate earnings or because they own or have an option to acquire stock that is expected to rise in price when the improvement is reported. This is normal: good performance should result in proper rewards. Even when the transaction is of benefit to the reporting company exclusively, primarily, or mutually, the transaction must be disclosed if material.

Related party transactions are often used to obtain real benefits for the company through tax savings. Tax laws tend, more than accounting conventions, to follow the legal form of transactions, thus affording some opportunity to structure transactions that will produce tax savings. The use of foreign affiliates, for example, is a popular means of minimizing taxes; and the government encourages the use of foreign sales corporations, which have a tax rate advantage.

Another example may be seen in a principal owner's contribution of stock to a charity as of year-end, followed early in the next year by purchase of the stock from the charity by the corporation for its treasury. In legal form these two transactions are a personal contribution of securities and a purchase of treasury stock. Assuming, however, that the tax benefits are achieved by the stockholder, these transactions in substance also may be some or all of a cash dividend to the stockholder, a contribution to the corporation's capital by the stockholder, or a cash contribution by the corporation to the charity.

Interdependent and Reciprocal Transactions. In some situations two or more companies may engage reciprocally in material transactions. These relationships may arise out of an economic interdependence of the two parties or may be simply a means of exaggerating recorded worth on financial statements of both parties. For example, "if you'll buy my three cats, I'll buy your two dogs."

By a strict interpretation of SFAS 57, the reciprocal buy/sell transaction can be considered a related party transaction. When the parties have a history of reciprocal transactions, the auditor must decide whether a particular transaction, represented to be complete, is actually linked to prior or prospective buy/sell transactions. Where such reciprocal transactions are in substance nonmonetary exchanges, APB 29, *Accounting for Nonmonetary Transactions*, offers appropriate guidance. Usually, such transactions do not culminate an earning process (N35.108).

Accommodations. One party may participate in a transaction as an accommodation for another, sometimes receiving a fee or commission for the service. Such direct compensation is not always apparent, but in practice it is advisable to assume the existence of a quid pro quo. Accommodations can look very real on paper, but their usual substance is commonly summed up in such descriptives as *swap, sham, parking, laundering,* and *straw man.* The party being accommodated usually conceals the transaction. The need to record fee income makes concealment by the accommodator less likely.

Executive Compensation and Perquisites. Yachts, private jet airplanes, and hunting lodges are examples of items in the perquisite category. Although these transactions may have economic benefit to a recipient, they are usually a bigger boost to the person's ego than to his income. The SEC requires disclosure under Rule 402(c) of Regulation S-K of the personal benefits accruing to officers and directors from use of company assets.

A conflict of interest may exist in transactions covering the compensation and expense reimbursements of management. Ordinarily, sufficient controls can be established to assure arm's-lengthness (e.g., approval of significant salaries by the board of directors and review of expense reimbursements by management at a level senior to that being considered), and thus eliminate such transactions from the related party category. But difficult questions can arise when the management personnel basically sets its own compensation or other monetary rewards (e.g., by domination of the board of directors).

No-Charge Transactions. Especially in situations involving a component of a business enterprise, a related component, often the parent company, may provide products or perform valuable services without charge. In theory, the going price for (or perhaps the performer's cost of) the product or service should be imputed in the benefitting company's statements and the opposite effect imputed in the providing company's statements. Most often only disclosure of the situation is provided. However, in SEC filings allocations of expenses incurred by a parent on behalf of a subsidiary are required to be made in a subsidiary registrant's financial statements (SAB 55, Topic 1.B).

QUALITATIVE CHARACTERISTICS

Form vs. Substance

Many related party transactions have form/substance problems because substance depends so much on the intentions of the parties and it is most difficult to probe those intentions when the parties are not at arm's length.

Legal Form. Related party transactions can be described by their legal form, such as profit-sharing plan, stock bonus, or other fringe benefit; a purchase or sale of products or services or of property, securities, or receivables; a lease; a loan; a sale and leaseback; or a financing service, guarantee of debt, maintenance of a compensating balance, and so on. They can also be described by their economic substance, which may be different from their legal form. For example, what is legally a lease may in economic reality be a purchase; what is a sale in legal form may in economic reality be a borrowing. Just what the economic substance of a transaction is may also be subjective and controversial. To identify it usually depends on understanding the reasons for the transaction.

SFAC 2, *Qualitative Characteristics of Accounting Information*, (1980d) subsumes *substance over form* into the qualities of reliability (¶ 59) and representational faithfulness (¶ 63). SFAC 2 says (¶ 160):

> Substance over form is an idea that . . . is not included because it would be redundant. The quality of reliability and, in particular, of representational faithfulness leaves no room for accounting representations that subordinate substance to form. Substance over form is, in any case, a rather vague idea that defies precise definition.

Accounting Qualities. The accountant's basic concern is to achieve fair presentation in the financial statements. The information given in the statement cannot be fairly presented unless it reflects the substance and not just the form of the transactions underlying the information. Unless notified to the contrary, the reader of financial statements normally assumes that the economic activity of an entity is a result of transactions with nonrelated parties. In fact, it is a fundamental assumption that financial statements represent the results of arm's-length transactions between independent parties influenced by normal market conditions. Even when related party transactions are fully disclosed, therefore, they may cast some doubt on the financial statements; when these transactions are material or their purpose is questionable, users may well doubt both the existence and the amounts of the economic activity presented in the statements.

In addition to the need to recognize substance, financial statements need to be evaluated for freedom from bias and be verifiable.

Freedom from bias. To be useful, financial statements must be free of bias. In SFAC 2, the qualities of neutrality and fairness are included under the broad heading of *reliability* — the faithfulness with which a measure represents what it purports to represent (¶ 59). Further:

> Bias in measurement is the tendency of a measure to fall more often on one side than the other of what it represents instead of being equally likely to fall on either side. Bias in accounting measures means a tendency to be consistently too high or too low.[¶ 77]
>
> Accounting information may not represent faithfully what it purports to represent because it has one or both of two kinds of bias. The measurement method may be biased, so that the resulting measurement fails to represent what it purports to represent. Alternatively, or additionally, the measurer, through lack of skill or lack of integrity, or both, may misapply the measurement method chosen. In other words, there may be bias, not necessarily intended, on the part of the measurer. [¶ 78]
>
> Accounting information cannot avoid affecting behavior, nor should it. If it were otherwise, the information would be valueless — by definition, irrelevant — and the effort to produce it would be futile. It is, above all, the predetermination of a desired result, and the consequential selection of information to induce that result, that is the negation of neutrality in accounting. To be neutral, accounting information must report economic activity as faithfully as possible, without coloring the image it communicates for the purpose of influencing behavior in *some particular direction*. [¶ 100; emphasis in original.]

Related party transactions, by their very nature, cannot be free of bias. They present an obvious problem of measurement and further difficulties in deciding on the extent of adequate disclosure.

Verifiability. The verifiability of financial statements is the duplicability of their results from a given set of assumptions or facts by independent means using the same measurements (¶ 82). Information that is unverifiable and, therefore, unauditable generally justifies less confidence. With many related party transactions there may be no independent means of measurement, and so their verifiability is difficult at best.

Business Purpose. Practice has identified a number of related party transactions in which the business purpose or economic substance calls for different accounting from that suggested by the legal form of the transaction.

Third party benefit. A third party with management influence over both of the transacting parties is the actual beneficiary of the transaction. Examples of this kind of transaction have involved executives of reporting companies who also own all or a portion of other companies that transact with the reporting company. Additional compensation or contribution to capital seems to be involved here, but the appropriate accounting to follow in such cases is not settled in practice.

Accommodation and sham transactions. These transactions were mentioned previously in the section entitled "Accommodations." If an accommodation or sham can be identified, the accounting to follow is usually apparent.

Structured leases. Month-to-month leases of major facilities from related parties have been used to avoid capitalization.

Artificial pricing. For income tax or other reasons, two related entities may deal with each other at prices that cannot be supported in terms of economic substance. To change the accounting to acknowledge the artificial pricing often defeats the purpose of the transaction. The appropriate accounting to follow in such cases is not settled in practice. SFAS 57 (R36) does not speak to the issue, and segment reporting under SFAS 14 specifically requires use of the prices charged without qualification (S20.129).

Materiality

Materiality is a term connoting economic significance. Although the concept is essential to the preparation of financial statements, it is a highly subjective form of measurement, depending as much on the preparers' and auditors' viewpoints as it does on current practice and the facts of the specific situation. Authoritative bodies address the issue of materiality from time to time, but the only official concepts that have been produced are contained in SFAC 2 (¶¶ 123–132), summed up in paragraph 132 as follows:

The omission or misstatement of an item in a financial report is material if, in the light of surrounding circumstances, the magnitude of the item is such that it is probable that the judgment of a reasonable person relying upon the report would have been changed or influenced by inclusion or correction of the item.

Authoritative Guidance. Authoritative literature generally does not discuss the materiality of related party transactions. Disclosure of material related party transactions is required (R36.102), and an auditor's opinion may need to be modified to some extent, depending on materiality, if satisfaction is not obtained regarding management representations on the "equivalence" issue (AU 334.12) (discussed later). But materiality itself is not defined for these contexts.

The SEC has offered a general definition of materiality by stating that publicly held companies may limit their disclosure of information "to those matters about which an average prudent investor ought reasonably to be informed" (Regulation S-X, Rule 1-02(n)). This definition is nearly a tautology, however, and does not extend specifically to related party transactions.

Regulation S-K, Instruction 1 to Item 404(a), describes materiality in relation to disclosure of transactions with management:

The materiality of any interest is to be determined on the basis of the significance of the information to investors in light of all of the circumstances of the particular case. The importance of the interest to the person having the interest, the relationship of the parties to the transaction with each other and the amount involved in the transaction are among the factors to be considered in determining the significance of the information to investors.

The SEC extended its definition of materiality to include managerial integrity in a 1964 decision, *In re Franchard Corp.*[1] This position was underscored during later investigations in which the SEC enforcement staff stated that the size of disclosed illegal payments was irrelevant in comparison to the potential damage done to investors by doubts about the integrity of management.

Quantitative Materiality. In the absence of standards or workable guidelines, current practice occasionally provides some small assistance. In some areas of accounting and reporting, materiality is pegged to a given minimum percentage. For example, in reporting on dilution in earnings per share, any reduction of less than 3% can be ignored (E09.105, fn. 3). On the other hand, a business combination will fail to qualify for pooling-of-interests accounting if more than 10% of the stock of a combining company is acquired in exchange for consideration other than common stock (B50.105). About 10 years ago, when considering materiality in relation to the need for a comment in the auditor's report regarding lack of consistency, a range of up to 10% was considered material. Today that percentage would likely be much less.

For related party transactions, even a 3% test of materiality may be unsatisfactory. Authoritative literature does not support such a generalization, but the SEC has sometimes applied more rigid criteria for materiality than the 3% test. For example, amounts that would change an upward trend in earnings to a downward trend, even if less than 3% of earnings, might be considered material. The same has been true

---

[1] In re Franchard Corp., 42 Sec. and Exchange Commission 163 (1964).

when a questionable or illegal payment is being measured for purposes of disclosure. The SEC has also been observed to allow items of more than 3% to be considered immaterial, for example, the 10% test permitted in the definition of a significant subsidiary (Regulation S-X, Rule 1-02(v)). Because abuses have made related party transactions suspect, a prudent course to follow until additional standards are established would be to use a more rigid standard of materiality for disclosure, and for auditing and reporting, of such transactions.

Qualitative Materiality. Materiality does not depend entirely on relative size: the concept involves qualitative as well as quantitative judgments. The qualitative characteristics of materiality are discussed further in Chapter 2, but an example related to the components area can be seen in SAS 21, *Segment Information* (AU 435). The SEC, in FRR § 503, also on segment information, adopted the SAS 21 comments on materiality and stated that a company should take into account such qualitative factors as the significance of the matter to the company (e.g., whether a matter with a relatively minor impact on the company's business is represented by management to be important to its future profitability), the pervasiveness of the matter (e.g., whether it affects or may affect numerous items in the segment information), and the impact of the matter (e.g., whether it distorts the trends reflected in the segment information). When qualitative materiality significantly alters the apparent immateriality of a matter, the pertinent information must be disclosed.

Equivalence

When the goods or services rendered in a related party transaction are commonplace or easily replicated, the standard of equivalency may be met without difficulty because the values can easily be determined in a nonrelated environment. But when the goods or services are more nearly unique, comparisons to transactions in an arm's-length environment become more difficult and the recording will therefore be more subjective and less verifiable.

Equivalence is a problem primarily with transactions beyond the normal course of business. Essentially, it requires asking whether the related party transaction would have taken place had the parties not been related and, if so, what the terms and manner of settlement would have been in the equivalent arm's-length transaction. The AICPA, the SEC, and auditors have divergent views on how to deal with the question.

Authoritative Guidance. The only authoritative direct references to equivalence are found in SAS 6 (AU 334.12) and SFAS 57 (R36.103). The essence of this guidance is that, except for routine transactions, it is generally impossible to judge whether an arm's-length transaction would have taken place or what the terms and manner of settlement would have been. Accordingly, if the financial statements include a representation to the effect that terms are no less favorable than terms for an unrelated party and the auditor cannot find any substantiation for that remark, the auditor should include a comment to that effect in his report, along with a qualified or adverse opinion, depending on materiality.

SAS 6 does not describe audit procedures for resolving the equivalence issue, lead-ing some auditors to conclude that no judgment on the issue is required. Such an interpretation would seem at variance with the expectations of the SEC. In AAER 1 (ASR 227) the Commission contended that the auditors had failed to conduct suffi-cient tests to establish the value of an inventory repurchase between related parties. In AAER 1 (ASR 241) the SEC also pointed out that a footnote failed to disclose charges for management fees by a related company that bore no necessary relation-ship to the value of the services provided, the auditor having determined previously that such charges were practically impossible to verify.

Nonequivalent Transactions. SAS 6 (AU 334.08f) mentions two cases known to be nonequivalent: receiving or providing accounting, management, or other services at no charge; and a major stockholder absorbing corporate expenses. SFAS 57 (R36.101) briefly acknowledges that "an enterprise may receive services from a related party without charge and not record the receipt of services." Other examples would include:

• Guarantee of debt without charge;
• Agreement with third parties to support the operations of a related company or to maintain that company's income at specified levels through product purchases or otherwise, usually without charge;
• Income tax concessions, such as payment for use of investment tax credits that the related party is unable to use or failure to charge a component its share of consolidated income taxes; and
• Cash advances with nominal or no interest charges.

In these situations the state of the art is unsettled for private companies. The transaction itself is often disclosed as a related party transaction, but the disclosure seldom deals with the lack of equivalence and the auditor seldom modifies his report with respect to this nonequivalence. For publicly held companies some imputation generally is required.

AUDITING CONSIDERATIONS

In this chapter the usual sequence, accounting before auditing, is reversed. The chal-lenge of identifying and evaluating transactions that may be related party transac-tions is necessary before the proper accounting or disclosure can be determined.

Audit Approach

The guidance given in SAS 6 (AU 334)[2] regarding identifying, auditing, and report-ing on related party transactions should serve as a sound basis for the audit

---

[2] While this chapter usually refers to SAS 6 (AU 334) as if it were the complete auditing authority on related party transactions, the auditing literature in AU 334 is a combination of SAS 6 as amended by SAS 45. The latter pronouncement was issued to delete the financial disclosure guidance in SAS 6 after the

approach. Because the procedures set out are not all-inclusive (AU 334.01), auditors should consider whether additional procedures are necessary.

For example, SAS 6 advises auditors that if they do not fully understand a particular transaction they should consider confirming the amount, terms, guarantees, and other significant data with the other party (AU 334.10). One might add that the auditor ought also to be alert for any further written agreements or oral understandings that might modify the terms outlined in the agreements and documents at hand.

Of course, if both related parties intend to deceive the auditor, no confirmation, regardless of what points are covered, is likely to produce reliable information on which he can base his opinion. Therefore, a confirmation reply from a related party is in some cases more akin to a representation by management than to an outside confirmation.

Preliminary Evaluations. At the outset of the audit the auditor should evalaute the extent of known relationships and related party transactions to decide whether his client is an auditable entity. An auditability assessment requires cautious judgment; auditability cannot simply be assumed. Related party involvements may be too pervasive or nonsubstantive to allow a valid audit. Inevitably, the auditor will need to weigh the integrity of management. The Commission on Auditors' Responsibilities pointed out in their *Report, Conclusions and Recommendations* (1978): ". . . when management is untrustworthy, there is a significant chance that a valid independent audit cannot be performed" (p. 38). "Significant chance" seems a rather soft choice of words; seasoned auditors would substitute "probability." In this regard the National Commission on Fraudulent Financial Reporting (NCFFR 1987) observed:

> Because the Commission has found that the majority of fraudulent financial reporting cases involve top management, the auditor should not assume management integrity but should apply professional skepticism to this determination.

Since related party involvements can present significant problems, the auditor must consider whether he is capable of taking special action to resolve these problems. He may conclude, for example, that uncertainties can be diminished to an acceptable level by extraordinary audit procedures designed to provide sufficient audit evidence for that purpose. (A number of Accounting and Auditing Enforcement Releases suggest, however, that sufficient procedural safeguards are elusive.)

Should the auditor conclude that he will proceed, a number of further preliminary evaluations are called for. These are summarized in SAS 6 and include: an examination of management responsibilities and the relationship and business purpose of each component, an evaluation of internal control over management's activities, and an examination of other factors (AU 334.05). If the client still appears trustworthy and auditable, the auditor must then determine the scope of the audit and choose appropriate procedures for identifying and auditing the related party transactions. Additionally, SAS 53 (AU 316), issued in 1988, requires the auditor to assess the risk

---

FASB essentially incorporated it into accounting standards via SFAS 57 (R36). Accordingly, references are made herein to SAS 6 when discussing auditing aspects, and to SAS 57 when discussing accounting aspects.

that material errors and irregularities exist. After this assessment the auditor is required to design his audit to provide reasonable assurance that material errors and irregularities are detected. SAS 53 further instructs the auditor to plan and perform his audit with an attitude of professional skepticism, and neither assume that management is dishonest nor that management is totally forthright.

Identifying Related Party Situations

SAS 6 gives audit procedures for determining the existence of related parties (AU 334.07) and for identifying transactions with those related parties (AU 334.08). However, these procedures may not uncover every situation the auditor wishes to examine. Because of the relative informality with which related parties can make agreements, the ensuing transactions may be poorly recorded or even overlooked by management. Worse, they may be deliberately concealed. At some point the auditor will need to draw on his own practical experience and judgment in deciding how to proceed.

Concealment of related party relationships and transactions has resulted in several lawsuits against auditors, alleging that an auditor is expected to be consummately thorough in his attempt to identify concealed related party transactions or management involvement that has a material effect on the financial statements. Though the procedures in the auditor's power cannot guarantee the discovery of all concealed management involvement, the auditor must not resign himself to nondiscovery for that reason. SAS 6 recognizes that an examination made in accordance with GAAS cannot be expected to assure that all related party transactions will be discovered (AU 334.04); thus the SAS develops an *awareness* responsibility for the auditor and sets forth specific procedures for related party transactions.

Conducive economic factors often lead to the concealment of related party transactions. SAS 6 lists some of these (AU 334.06), summarized below:

1. Insufficient working capital or credit
2. Favorable earnings needed to support stock price
3. Overly optimistic forecasts
4. Dependence on few products, customers, or transactions
5. Many failures in the industry
6. Excess capacity
7. Significant litigation
8. Technological obsolescence dangers

Other factors would include overexpansion, indigestible acquisitions (particularly into areas that are new to the company), and a long-term operating cycle. Figure 25.1 summarizes SAS 6 procedures for identifying related parties and transactions with them; in reading each separate point, it should be assumed that the step is directed toward the auditor's attempt to locate related parties and related party transactions. Comments on certain of these procedures follow.

Deliberate Concealment. Attempts to deliberately conceal relationships or transactions with related parties will influence, if not change, the auditing, accounting, and possibly the disclosures. Deliberate concealment, which may amount to fraud if done with an intent to mislead, may also affect the auditor-client relationship, for the auditor must now decide whether to continue his professional relationship with the company.

The auditor's legal counsel should be consulted in concealment situations. Auditor-client relationships can be continued despite the concealment *if* the client takes satisfactory action, such as firing the involved officials or transferring them to less sensitive positions. SAS 54, *Illegal Acts by Clients* (AU 317), discussed further in Chapter 5, provides additional guidance to the auditor in such circumstances. It is reasonable for an auditor to expect such action, for it is consistent with measures taken by the SEC. For example, the SEC has said that officers involved in fraud or concealment could not serve as chief executive or chief financial officers of SEC-reporting companies, at least for a period of time.

Information Normally in Auditor's Files. In continuing engagements, the auditor's permanent files, audit programs, the preceding year's working papers, and (if he is auditing a recently accepted publicly held client) his documentation of a new-client investigation may contain applicable information. To the extent they do, the matter should be extracted for the current year's audit working papers, to ensure appropriate consideration. The existence in the past of nonrecurring, material related party transactions may, in some instances, be indicative of current opportunities or propensities.

With respect to new clients, the auditor will be amassing his information foundation, and thus, apart from the predecessor auditor's working papers (discussed later in this chapter), there may not be a great deal of prior information to review. However, if the client is publicly held there may be a substantial amount of information gathered as part of the new-client investigation procedure.

In most audits, clients engage the services of the audit firm's tax personnel to prepare, or advise in connection with the preparation of, income tax returns. Also, client executives often engage the audit firm's tax department to prepare their personal income tax returns. Accordingly, a direct inquiry should be made of the partner responsible for tax services to the client and its executives (or other tax personnel he designates as being knowledgeable with respect thereto) as to whether they have found any evidence (not already known) concerning material related party transactions. Recognizing that tax return preparation almost invariably postdates the audit completion, tax personnel should be asked to bring to the audit partner's attention relevant information arising after completion of the audit. This interchange of information is permitted under IRS Reg. § 7216.

If the audit firm also provides management consulting services to the client, the partner responsible for such services (or others he designates as being knowledgeable with respect to those consulting engagements) should be asked whether, during the course of the consulting engagement, any information came to their attention concerning material related party transactions that may not already be known to the auditor.

Information Available From External Sources. It is a recognized audit procedure that minutes of meetings of the board of directors and its important committees be

Determining Existence

a. Evaluate the company's procedures for identification and proper accounting.
b. Inquire of management as to the names of all related parties and whether there were any transactions with them.
c. Review SEC and other regulatory agency filings for the identification of possibly related parties.
d. Determine the names of all employee pension and other trusts and their officers and trustees.
e. Review stockholder listings of closely held companies to identify principal stockholders.
f. Review prior years' audit working papers for the names of known related parties.
g. Inquire of predecessor, principal, or other auditors of related entities.
h. Review material investment transactions to determine whether these may have created related parties.

Identifying Transactions

a. Provide all audit personnel with the names of known related parties so that they may become aware of transactions.
b. Review the minutes of meetings of the board of directors and executive or operating committees.
c. Review proxy and other material filed with the SEC and other regulatory agencies.
d. Review conflict-of-interest statements obtained by the company from its management.
e. Review business transacted with major customers, suppliers, borrowers, and lenders for indications of previously undisclosed relationships.
f. Consider whether transactions are occurring but not being given accounting recognition, such as receiving or providing services at no charge.
g. Review accounting records for large, unusual, or nonrecurring items with emphasis on items near the end of the reporting period.
h. Review confirmations of compensating balance arrangements.
i. Review invoices from law firms.
j. Review confirmations of loans receivable and payable for indications of guarantees.

FIG. 25.1   Procedures for Identifying Related Parties and Transactions With Them
Source: AU 334.07-.08 (abridged).

reviewed. In performing this review, the auditor should be alert to indications of material related party transactions.

If the company has recently had a first SEC registration (or a registration has recently occurred after several years during which no registrations were filed) the company's counsel (special SEC counsel, if engaged) will have performed a circularization of management for purposes of disclosures that had to be made in the registration statement. Where these circumstances exist, the auditor should obtain, with the authorization of his client, access to the counsel's circularization files.

Also, recurring registration statements, proxy statements, stock exchange listing applications, and the nonfinancial portions of Forms 10-K, 10-Q, and 8-K may contain information concerning related party transactions. It is generally understood that the auditor reviews the complete text of all such documents somewhere during the course of the audit engagement. There may be instances, however, where voluminous exhibits accompany some of these filings. Accordingly, the auditor should consider whether there is a need to peruse the exhibits.

A rather obvious source of external information is represented by trade newspaper and magazine articles about the client. Occasionally, such publicity will describe operating practices or innovations that may point to possible related party transactions.

Timing of Material Transactions. Material transactions entered into at or near year-end or quarter-end are often designed to bolster the earnings of the company. The auditor should pay special attention to any transactions timed toward the end of a reporting period, questioning whether there is related party involvement, as might be suggested by transactions closed in haste or documents that may have been backdated.

In a business involving a large volume of small transactions, the auditor expects to see a relatively level, seasonally adjusted transaction volume. In instances where the business consists of a small number of large transactions, it may be credible that the closing of transactions clusters near year-end or quarter-end. However, such circumstances require more thorough audit certainty to establish the appropriateness of the timing of transactions—certainly a problem not unique to related party transactions.

It may also be determined by the auditor that documentation was executed subsequent to the period-end but intended by the parties to be effective as of the period-end. In these cases, legal advice may be required as to whether the transaction is binding on (thus economically affecting the assets and liabilities of) the company on the "as of" date. Enforceable agreements-in-principle or oral agreements are sometimes considered acceptable, pending "completion of the paper work," but should be approached with skepticism.

Conflict of Interest Programs. If a client has a policy of performing a circularization of its management group for conflicts of interest, the auditor should review the results.

Many major corporations have such procedures, but it is relatively uncommon in small organizations. In those instances where it is used, the auditor is often engaged to receive the completed questionnaires and decide which should be brought to the attention of the board of directors or designated individual in the client's organization. When the auditor is involved in the client's circularization program, he may be aware of possible related party transactions from screening the answers. A major drawback of such a program is that it does not, of course, have any means of assuring that the respondents answer truthfully. Further, such questionnaires are not likely to cover all related parties as defined earlier (e.g., principal stockholders).

Management Representations. Where the auditor perceives the existence of conditions that afford the opportunity for related party involvement in a material transaction, he should obtain specific representations from the parties that (if such is the case) they have no direct or indirect involvement in the transaction. Further, such a letter might well repeat representations made to the auditor concerning the identity of the parties to the transaction, the purpose of the transaction (if not evident), and its terms. The importance of obtaining such representations is highlighted in a related auditing standards interpretation (AU 9334.20–.21).

Management personnel could, of course, have personal reasons for diverting further inquiries if they should be asked to provide specific representations concerning a material transaction. However, the mere fact that representations are not satisfactory evidence per se in such situations does not eliminate their usefulness as a starting point and as documentation of what the auditor was told.

There may be significant client relations problems created if the auditor indiscriminately adopts an "affidavit" of sorts, even on a fairly limited basis. For example, it would be rare for the auditor to ask for representation from individual family members of the management individual; where there is a concern of this nature, he would ordinarily have the management party make such representation for his family members.

Oral representations as to the absence of related party transactions, when conditions are conducive to them, should be acceptable only if the auditor is fully satisfied through his other audit procedures.

Consultation With Company Attorneys. The auditor may find consultation with company legal counsel useful in identifying related parties. In theory at least, legal counsel of the client should be the auditor's staunchest ally. Both should have as their objective the presentation of financial statements of a quality that will keep their mutual client out of difficulty—both operating and legal. In a few cases, however, some attorneys may have supported their client to the detriment of the auditor.

Auditors often need to rely on the expertise of legal counsel in related party matters, usually doing so with attorneys' letters called for by SAS 12 (AU 337). An attorney might state that the existence of material related party transactions represents a contingency on which he does not wish to report because of possible breach of the attorney-client privilege. The auditor should assume as a matter of course that an attorney's refusal to discuss an acknowledged transaction is indicative of the attorney's serious concern. (See Chapter 26 for a discussion of attorneys' letters.)

In at least two instances the disciplinary arm of the SEC has taken a position that the auditor must substantiate legal counsel's opinion regarding the date of a transaction (ASRs 173 and 241, now in AAER 1). Authoritative auditing literature has not supported this position. However, the prudent auditor should have his own counsel study a legal opinion on which his client has based the accounting for and disclosure of a material related party transaction, where there is any question about the persuasiveness of the legal opinion.

Change of Auditors. Clients sometimes change auditors because of disagreements over the treatment of related party transactions. A change of auditors where nonordinary related party transactions are prevalent can indicate unauditable or nonsubstantive related party transactions. Strong disagreements will be made public if they come within SEC regulations (FRR § 603, incorporated in Form 8-K rules and in Regulation S-K) and requirements of the SEC Practice Section of the AICPA. Additionally SAS 61, *Communication with Audit Committees* (AU 380), requires such matters to be brought to the attention of the client's audit committee. But the issue may never come to light if it never reaches the disagreement stage (as defined by the SEC) or involves a privately held company. For this reason, a succeeding auditor in an environment of material and complex related party transactions should attempt to determine any disagreements through consultation with the previous auditor (see SAS 7; AU 315).

Basic

a. Obtain an understanding of the business purpose of the transaction. (Until the auditor understands the business sense of material transactions, he cannot complete his examination. If he lacks sufficient specialized knowledge to understand a particular transaction, he should consult with persons who do have the requisite knowledge.)

b. Examine invoices, executed copies of agreements, contracts, and other pertinent documents.

c. Determine whether the transaction has been approved at the appropriate level.

d. Test for reasonableness the compilation of amounts to be disclosed, or considered for disclosure.

e. Arrange for intercompany account balances to be audited as of concurrent dates, and for the examination of specified, important, and representative related party transactions by the auditors for each of the parties.

f. Inspect or confirm and obtain satisfaction as to the transferability and value of collateral.

Extended

a. Confirm transaction amount and terms, including guarantees, with the other party.

b. Inspect evidence in possession of the other party.

c. Confirm or discuss significant information with intermediaries, such as banks, guarantors, agents, or attorneys, to obtain a better understanding.

d. Refer to financial publications, trade journals, credit agencies, and other information sources when there is a concern about unfamiliar customers, suppliers, or other major counterparties.

e. With respect to material uncollected balances, guarantees, and other obligations, obtain information as to the financial capability of the other party. The auditor should decide on the degree of assurance required and the extent to which available information provides such assurance.

FIG. 25.2   Procedures for Examining Related Party Transactions
Source: AU 334.09-.10 (abridged).

Examining Related Party Transactions

Once he has determined that some kind of related party transaction has taken place, the auditor's next concern is a practical one. He must judge whether the transaction will make enough of a difference on the client's financial statements to merit the time and attention of detailed audit procedures. Closely intertwined with this question of materiality is the determination of economic substance. (The *qualitative* characteristics of materiality and substance were described earlier in this chapter.) The auditor looks at the bare economic facts of the transaction and asks: What kind of agreement was this—a sale, a lease, a fair exchange of assets, or perhaps something else?

To help determine substance, the auditor can try to compare the available facts to what they would have been in an equivalent transaction between nonrelated parties. For obvious reasons, the nature of the related party relationship itself often invalidates the comparison. Nevertheless, the concept of equivalence (discussed in an earlier section) can be a useful guide in helping the auditor determine the proper method of accounting for a transaction. It can also cue the auditor to the possibility that his client has not recorded certain facts that may need to be disclosed in the financial statements.

Figure 25.2 summarizes SAS 6 procedures for examining related party transactions, separated into basic procedures (those to be considered as normal) and extended procedures (those to be considered when necessary to fully understand a particular transaction). Note that SAS 6 (AU 334.09–.10) does not *mandate* these procedures, it suggests them. In particular, AU 334.10 points out that the extended procedures are not normally called for by GAAS and that advance arrangements for performing them may need to be made with the client.

An AICPA Auditing Interpretation (AU 9334.17-.19) provides additional guidance for examining related party transactions. This Interpretation states in part that:

> As in examining any other material account balance or class of transactions, the auditor needs to consider audit risk and design and apply appropriate substantive tests to evaluate management's assertions. . . . The higher the auditor's assessment of risk regarding related party transactions, the more extensive or effective the audit tests should be. . . . In assessing the risk of the related party transactions the auditor obtains an understanding of the business purpose of the transactions. Until the auditor understands the business sense of material transactions, he cannot complete his examination. If he lacks sufficient specialized knowledge to obtain that understanding for a particular transaction, he should consult with persons who do have the requisite knowledge. In addition, to understand the transaction, or obtain evidence regarding it, the auditor may have to refer to audited or unaudited financial statements of the related party, apply procedures at the related party, or in some cases audit the financial statements of the related party.

Challenging Substance. There are no assured methods for determining the substance of a related party transaction. Not only do informed practitioners disagree among themselves on the substance of a given transaction, but the auditor can find himself in complete disagreement with management on the question of substance. Present auditing standards require auditors to obtain certain written representations from management (AU 333.01). Ordinarily, these would include information concerning related party transactions and related amounts receivable or payable (AU 333.04(e)). Of course, the auditor cannot rely solely on these representations but must also perform whatever inquiries, confirmations, and other procedures are appropriate under the circumstances. All too often, however, there is not much conclusive evidence available about the intentions of the parties.

The flexibility and informality inherent in the related party relationship thus place a considerable burden on the auditor seeking to determine a transaction's substance. The pricing and terms of related party transactions are readily changeable under circumstances that seldom arise in arm's-length dealings. Sometimes a related party agreement that seems to convey the substance of a transaction is quickly revised or revoked when an auditor points out that it would produce undesired financial results or reporting requirements. Such an abrupt about-face makes it doubtful that the planned transaction had an auditable substance. Clearly, such an arrangement is only tentative.

Also, transactions that would otherwise require extensive description of terms and conditions are often reduced to a page or two when the contracting parties are related. Simple agreements covering complex related party transactions may be appropriate in some circumstances, but auditors should always consider the need for extended audit effort to ascertain substance in such cases.

When an auditor has unresolved doubts about the substance of a material related party transaction or about management's representations regarding it, he would be expected to modify his report accordingly.

Audit of All Parties. When related parties are dealing among themselves, the auditor should try to audit, or at least review, the records of all the parties. Authoritative literature does not address the problems of an auditor engaged for only one or a few of the entities involved. Yet some managements controlling several companies may engage a different auditor for each company. Since an auditor in that position has a reduced chance of understanding any related party transactions, such a practice should warn him of the possibility that transactions may not be what they appear.

Suppose, for example, that the company under audit makes a material cash advance to another company whose accounts are not audited. How the other company uses the money will be impossible to determine. An executive could represent that the advance was for working capital when in fact he used it to cover margin calls on his own commodities trading. Even if the auditor reviewed, but did not audit, the accounts of the other company, the true use of the money could be obscured.

This example illustrates the point that in situations where material transactions occur with related companies or parties that are not audited, the auditor should recognize that he may be confronted with an "unauditable entity." This may be true even if the related company is audited by another firm. Depending on his analysis of the situation, he can try to persuade the client to use only one audit firm for all related parties, or he can insist on reviewing the work of the other auditors in accordance with AU 543.12–.13. If the client refuses, the auditor must decide whether he can obtain sufficient evidence through review and inquiry procedures. He may even decide to resign if he concludes that a single entity in such a situation is an unauditable entity.

The situation is exacerbated when material transactions involve individuals such as stockholders or officers, for the financial affairs of individuals are seldom subject to audit or open to review and the other side of a transaction may forever remain obscured from the auditor.

Approval by Directors. It is common practice that a known material related party transaction is a subject of resolution at the board of directors' level. Of course, discovery of concealed management involvement is unlikely to gain board approval, but rather precipitate some other action by the board or its representatives.

It is also a common audit procedure for an auditor having doubts about whether a company's business purpose has been furthered, or at least not hampered, by a material related party transaction to obtain the board of directors' approval of such transaction. A discussion with the company's legal counsel as to the nature of the auditor's concern may be helpful so that legal counsel could then advise the board as to the need for approval. In any event, where the auditor believes such approval is required and it is not forthcoming, he will have to consider the material transaction as unauthorized, and therefore unacceptable, for financial reporting purposes.

Care must be taken not to demand the board of directors' attention to insignificant items—for example, a question concerning the amplitude of an executive's expense allowance that in and of itself is not a material figure in the financial statements. (Such matters, of course, may be brought to the attention of the appropriate level of management, including the board, but the auditor should not insist on formal resolution except in cases that have a material impact on the financial statements.)

In some privately held organizations the board of directors may substantially or completely consist of officers of the company. Thus, approval of a material transaction in which there was management involvement may not really be substantive. In the case of publicly held companies there will at least be some number of outside directors. In major publicly held companies there will be a substantial proportion of outside directors, who will clearly bring a strong measure of independence to the board. If the company is a NYSE company, it will have an all-outsider audit committee that can be responsive in these situations. (See Chapter 6.)

If a material related party transaction occurs in a segment of a larger entity, it will often be more appropriate to ask for approval of the board of directors of the parent company.

Confirmation of Material Transactions. Material transactions and balances (especially those suspected of being, or known to be, related party transactions) should be considered for confirmation with the other parties to the transactions. The inquiry should specify the documents involved in the transaction and ask whether there are any other documents or understandings. Admittedly, such a procedure is unlikely to detect deliberately collusive practices between the parties to a transaction, but it could disclose a "side deal" or perhaps a guarantee by a member of management.

In some cases, components of a business enterprise for example, the auditor knows in advance that a balance confirmed by a component would rarely constitute independent evidence. When the confirmation would be sent to a component of the entity and the auditor is auditing both components, he may be able to obtain the needed information by direct reference to the component's records. When the auditor is the principal auditor but does not audit the component, he usually has the right to look into the component's records and may want to do so (AU 543.13).

It is important to keep in mind that there may be industry practices (such as a small group of buyers and sellers) that defeat successful confirmation efforts.

Equivalence. Although the SEC and parties suing auditors would assert otherwise, it is not possible to determine whether a transaction would have taken place if the parties had not been related; usually, what the terms would have been in an arm's-length transaction cannot be determined either (AU 334.12). Therefore, when considering equivalence the auditor is often concerned with finding the substance of a transaction rather than disclosing arm's-length equivalence in the financial statements.

Some material transactions with related party involvement can easily be compared with arm's-length transactions (e.g., the sale of readily marketable securities). In most instances, however, this comparison is not easily attainable. For example, an auditor may obtain independent appraisals of the fair value of the property or services involved in a transaction. Such appraisals establish neither an arm's-length price nor whether the transaction would have taken place, but they help to indicate whether the transaction differs in substance from an arm's-length exchange.

The auditor should ask the client whether a comparison has been made and what the results were. Although generally the auditor is not required to make a comparison when the company has not done so, he may decide that a significant portion of the evidence he requires in connection with the transaction can only be provided by making or attempting such comparison. In those situations, he will pursue the matter.

Further, because disclosure of a material transaction in which there is related party involvement will usually be required or otherwise may be given in the client's financial statements, management may wish to state therein that (if a comparison were feasible) the terms of the transaction were substantially equivalent (or were not substantially equivalent and the reasons therefor) to what would have been arrived at as a result of arm's-length negotiation between independent parties. If the client does not make such a representation in the financial statements, the auditor must be satisfied that the comparison, if it were actually made by the client, resulted in a conclusion of substantial equivalence; in any event, the auditor must not otherwise hold the opinion that substantial equivalence does not exist where a comparison was not made even though it may have been feasible.

ACCOUNTING CONSIDERATIONS

For the most part, the accounting treatment to be given to related party transactions is the same as that for unrelated parties. SAS 6 states (AU 334.02):

> Certain accounting pronouncements prescribe the accounting treatment when related parties are involved; however, established accounting principles ordinarily do not require transactions with related parties to be accounted for on a basis different from that which would be appropriate if the parties were not related. The auditor should view related party transactions within the framework of existing pronouncements, placing primary emphasis on the adequacy of disclosure. In addition, the auditor should be aware that the substance of a particular transaction could be significantly different from its form and that financial statements should recognize the substance of particular transactions rather than merely their legal form.

While these words from the Auditing Standards Board may seem comforting to the auditor worried about whether he has dug to the bottom of some complex related party transaction, the SEC is not nearly so convinced about this accounting prescript. In many cases the SEC requires deferral of profit, or carryover of seller's cost, in related party transactions included in registrants' financial statements (see e.g., SAB 48, Topic 5.G). AAERs involving proceedings against auditors have often taken a similar position, when such matters were found after the fact.

Evidence of the complexity of the problem can be found in EITF Issue 84-39, *Transfers of Monetary and Nonmonetary Assets Among Individuals and Entities Under Common Control*, in which the Task Force was unable to reach a consensus.

Related Party Sales and Purchases

Of all the issues pertaining to related party transactions, perhaps the most crucial are those involving sales and purchases between the parties. Since authoritative literature is limited, custom and usage must serve as a guide. The key issues are discussed in the sections that follow.

Price Structure. Setting a sale or transfer price is not the function of financial accounting; the contracting parties are expected to arrive at the price. (Of course, accounting requirements have been influential in determining transfer price.) If profit cannot be recognized for accounting purposes, or valuations in excess of seller cost cannot be recorded by the buyer, cost rather than fair value is often used. But when fair value is the price intended to be used, the parties must try to determine what the fair value would be in an equivalent arm's-length relationship.

Minority Interests. The presence of a minority or public interest in either of the related parties raises questions about fair and equitable treatment of those other interests. To the extent that public or minority interests are not identical in each entity in a related party transaction, a sale at any price other than fair value will either disadvantage or advantage those interests.

Profit Recognition/Deferral. Neither professional literature nor Regulation S-X prohibits the recognition of profit in sales transactions between related parties. However, deferral of profit recognition has become the principal approach used, because of SEC administrative actions in reviewing filings, especially for companies having an initial public offering. The prevailing attitude seems to be that it is too difficult to convince the SEC staff of the arm's-lengthness of related party transactions, so it is just as well to defer profit recognition to the future, when it can be "proved up" in an unrelated party transaction. Once resigned to this treatment, the optimistic view is that there are profits "reserved" for future periods, when they might be needed. Sometimes this is true, other times not. Conservatism seems to play the overriding role.

One situation transcends profit recognition: Where the sale price is at fair value and the seller is not justified in recording a profit, the selling entity will on occasion record the "profit" as a contribution to capital. This accounting is most often confined to situations in which the buyer has direct ownership interest in the seller.

Asset Valuation. On the buyer's side, when fair value is used for the price, at least three methods of asset accounting have been observed in practice. In some instances the acquired property has been recorded at the price paid. In other instances the difference between the seller's cost and the price paid has been accounted for as a so-called *dangling debit*, deducted from the total of stockholders' equity, or as a constructive dividend. Constructive dividend accounting seems to be confined to situations in which the buyer has a direct ownership interest in the seller.

Authoritative guidelines do not exist that would aid in arriving at uniform accounting solutions for either the buyer or seller in such situations. Thus a variety of solutions might occur in practice for similar related party transactions.

Accounting After the Transaction. If the seller appropriately recognized profit and the buyer appropriately recorded the purchased asset at his cost, these amounts are simply carried over into subsequent periods. Otherwise, further accounting may be necessary.

Consider a situation in which the seller has sold at fair value and deferred the profit or credited contributed capital. The buyer has accounted for the difference between his own purchase price and the seller's historic cost as a constructive dividend or as a dangling debit. Deferred income and the dangling debit will presumably be adjusted at resale or some other time. But accounts probably will not be adjusted for an item carried as a contribution to capital or a constructive dividend.

A further complication will arise if the buyer and seller record differently. For example, the buyer may record the purchased property at the price paid while the seller credits contribution to capital. Or the buyer may charge a constructive dividend while the seller defers income. Either way, one party may have subsequent gain or loss while the other will not.

Resales. If property is sold at seller's cost that is less than fair value, the buyer may realize a profit upon subsequent sale. This happens occasionally in practice, and sometimes is even planned, perhaps to bolster sagging earnings by buying appreciated property from a related party at less than fair value and then selling it to an unrelated party. Is profit recognition by the middleman appropriate, or does it belong to the initial seller? If the middleman can recognize profit, is a minimum holding period required? Or can a company buy property from a related party one day at that party's cost and sell it at a fair value and record a sizable gain the next day? These and other questions on subsequent accounting remain unanswered, and the accounting treatment used should attempt to best reflect the substance of the series of transactions. The SEC staff can be expected to exercise vigilance in this area.

Stock Issuances

Transactions involving issuance of stock (or other ownership interests) in exchange for nonmonetary assets or services are numerous and often involve material amounts. The question of the appropriate accounting to follow is pertinent to both the company involved and to the stockholder or owner. APB 29, *Accounting for Non-monetary Transactions* (N35), gives some guidance on certain transactions with stockholders and owners, but consideration of accounting for stock issuance transactions was deferred at the time (1973) APB 29 was issued.

This matter has yet to be satisfactorily concluded. As recently as late 1986, the EITF, in issue 86-29, discussed nonmonetary transactions involving boot, in some cases with one of the transacting parties acquiring an ownership interest greater than 20% in the other. While acquired interests greater than 50% were deemed to fall under APB 16 as business combinations, the 20% to 50% related party category is still in limbo, pending further EITF discussion.

As to services received and paid for in stock, some accountants would prefer to record services at their fair value, thereby permitting the provider to record profit to the extent that there are outside interests. The more common practice, and the one required by the SEC, is to record such transactions in the receiving company at the owner-seller's cost. The SEC has often required the deferral of profit or carryover of seller's cost in related party transactions. SAB 48 (Topic 5.G) reflects this SEC position and requires that assets acquired from promoters or shareholders in exchange for stock prior to or at the time of a registrant's initial public offering be recorded at the historical cost to the promoter or shareholder. Deviations from this policy have been rare, generally applicable to situations where the fair value of the stock issued or assets acquired is objectively determinable, and the promoter's or shareholder's ownership following the transaction is not so significant that a substantial indirect interest exists in the assets. Estimating the fair value of the stock is not appropriate if the stock is privately held or seldom traded.

In addition, the SEC staff states in SAB Topic 4.E that deferred compensation arising from capital stock issued or to be issued to officers or employees at prices below market value should be presented in the balance sheet as a deduction from stockholders' equity. The staff indicates that this treatment is consistent with its position that receivables arising from transactions involving a registrant's stock should be presented as deductions from equity and not as assets. The staff does not suggest that a receivable from an officer or director is to be deducted from stockholders' equity if the receivable is paid in cash prior to the publication of the financial statements and the payment date is stated in a note to the financial statements. However, the staff would consider the subsequent return of such cash to the officer or director to be part of a scheme to evade the reporting requirements of securities laws.

Stock issuances for other than cash are discussed more fully in Chapter 20.

DISCLOSURE

Some managements seems reluctant to disclose much information about related party transactions, though the degree of reluctance is somewhat dependent on the nature of parties to the transaction. Some accountants intuitively follow the belief that the stronger the objection of management to disclosure, the greater the need for disclosure, though this is perhaps too facile an approach.

SFAS 57 Requirements

SFAS 57, *Related Party Disclosures* (R36), establishes disclosure standards for related party relationships and transactions. The requirements are generally consistent with those originally contained in SAS 6, *Related Party Transactions* (AU 334), prior to its amendment by SAS 45. Until the issuance of SFAS 57 in 1982, the SAS 6 disclosure requirements were one of the few instances in which auditing standards dispensed accounting guidance because of a void in GAAP, which until then contained only a few requirements—for example, to disclose the nature and extent of related party leases (L10.125), or to adjust the reporting of transactions between companies under common control (N35).

Unfortunately, inclusion of disclosure rules in auditing standards via SAS 6 had no binding effect on preparers of financial statements. And even though the SEC included SAS 6 disclosures in its own rules during 1980 (since rescinded in recognition of SFAS 57), this failed to cover companies that were not SEC registrants. Thus, SFAS 57 is housekeeping, in a sense, although some subtle changes in the words may have later interpretive effects.

SFAS 57 provides definitions of such key terms as "affiliate," "control," "immediate family," "management," "principal owners," and "related parties," and identifies several common types of related party transactions, such as sales, purchases, transfers of real and personal property, borrowings and lendings, and services (e.g., accounting, management, legal). In addition to those between a parent and a subsidiary, related party transactions encompass transactions between an entity and its principal owners, management, or members of their immediate families; between affiliates; or between an entity and its pension plan.

SFAS 57 emphasizes that related party transactions cannot be presumed to have been carried out at arm's length, nor can an arm's-length relationship in a transaction necessarily be implied by management representations.

Except for compensation arrangements, expense allowances, and other similar items in the ordinary course of business, SFAS 57 requires disclosure of the following (R36.102):

1. The nature of the relationship(s) involved.
2. A description of the transactions, including transactions to which no amounts or nominal amounts were ascribed, for each of the periods for which income statements are presented, and such other information deemed necessary to an understanding of the effects of the transactions on the financial statements.
3. The dollar amounts of transactions for each of the periods for which income statements are presented and the effects of any change in the method of establishing the terms from that used in the preceding period.
4. Amounts due from or to related parties as of the date of each balance sheet presented and, if not otherwise apparent, the terms and manner of settlement.

For entities under common control and for which such common control relationships could significantly affect their operations, disclosure is also required of the existence and nature of the control relationships, even if there are no transactions between the commonly controlled entities (R36.104). SFAS 57 also allows management to represent that related party transactions were consummated on terms equivalent to those that prevail on an arm's-length basis, if the assertion can be substantiated.

Despite the continuing progress, a number of issues remain unresolved, as discussed below.

Profit or Loss Disclosure. Neither SFAS 57 nor SAS 6 states any requirement for disclosure of profit or loss to the selling related party. In practice, the profit or loss is often disclosed by the seller, but this information is infrequently disclosed in the financial statements of the buying related party. It would seem that such information is equally important to the users of both sets of financial statements.

Duration of Disclosure. When balance sheet amounts of the purchasing party include capitalized profits of the selling party, the amount of profit may have been disclosed by the purchaser in the year of purchase, as previously noted. Continuing disclosure would seem to depend on the general principle of making the financial statements meaningful. In practice, however, an initial disclosure is typically abandoned in subsequent years.

Recognizing Substance. SFAS 57 places emphasis on disclosure of transactions between related parties. When such transactions have been recorded in the accounting records by form that differs materially from substance, the transactions must be restated in the financial statements to comply with GAAP, and the profit or loss effect must be deferred until the involved asset has either been sold to an unrelated party or otherwise consumed. Often the fact that the substance differs from form should be disclosed even where the substance has been reflected in the financial statements.

There may be occasions when disclosure is not enough even if the profit has been deferred; the auditor may need to address the matter in his report.

Equivalence. SFAS 57 cautions against representing the terms of a transaction to be no less favorable than those that would have been obtained from an unrelated interest (R36.103). This position is understandable since it is generally impossible to determine whether the transaction would have taken place at all had the parties not been related or, assuming that it had taken place, what the terms and manner of settlement would have been.

However, the frequent practice of remaining silent on the issue may not be supportable. Users of the financial statements may find that lack of disclosure hampers their understanding.

Examples of related party disclosures abound, though many of them do not use the words "related party." A current selection of examples may be found in *Updated Illustrations of the Disclosure of Related Party Transactions, Financial Report Survey (FRS) 30* (AICPA, 1985e). This update covers SFAS 57 disclosures and augments FRS 8, issued in 1975 to illustrate compliance with the then-current SAS 6.

SEC Requirements

SEC financial statement disclosure requirements are contained in Rule 4-08(k) of Regulation S-X and are substantially similar to those of SFAS 57, described above. In addition, the SEC definition of "related party" in Rule 1-02(t) of S-X, is cross-referenced to that in SFAS 57.

Item 404 of Regulation S-K, *Certain Relationships and Related Transactions*, describes other disclosures required in the nonfinancial portion of SEC filings.

Components of a Business Enterprise

One of the most frequent types of related party disclosures concerns entities bound together by complete or partial ownership—either ownership of one entity by another or ownership of entities by a third party. Such transactions as those between a subsidiary and its parent, between two companies under common control, or between a company and its shareholders all fall into this category. As the following subsections indicate, the need for additional disclosure guidelines is apparent.

GAAP Disclosure. Disclosures required in separate financial statements of a component generally should closely follow SFAS 57 disclosure requirements for related party transactions. Additional disclosures for components have been seen in practice, primarily because of the interdependence of the component. Such additional disclosures often include the basis of intercompany transactions and any material amount of unrealized intercompany profit remaining in inventories or in property, plant, and equipment.

Where the intercomponent relationships are significant, disclosures may flow from one component to another. For example, a contingent liability or a major lawsuit against one component may have to be disclosed in the separate statements of another related component; or use of proceeds of a significant intercompany advance for extraordinary purposes (e.g., loan to an officer) may have to be disclosed in the statements of the component making the initial advance.

When going concern problems of one component are alleviated by the parent's or another component's guarantee of debt, the separate statements of the component should disclose all relevant terms of the guarantee. A firm, legally enforceable guarantee usually is necessary to satisfy the auditor that a going concern paragraph in his report is unnecessary.

Nothing is inherent in a component that requires an exception to the standard audit report. An unmodified opinion should be appropriate on a component statement, provided intercomponent transactions are "not unreasonable." However, if intercomponent transactions have been recorded at unreasonable prices, some auditors believe that the auditor's report should describe the circumstances in a separate paragraph and that a qualified or adverse opinion should be expressed.

SEC Requirements. In 1983, the SEC issued SAB 53, *Financial Statement Requirements in Filings Involving the Guarantee of Securities by a Parent or Subsidiary*, which expressed the SEC staff's view on the necessary disclosures, or the necessary separate financial statements to be furnished, relating to intercompany guarantees (now contained in SAB Topics 1.G and 1.H). Further, in 1983, the SEC issued SAB 54, *Push Down Basis of Accounting Required in Certain Limited Circumstances* (Topic 5.J), and SAB 55, *Allocation of Expenses and Related Disclosure in Financial Statements of Subsidiaries* (Topic 1.B). These SABs express the SEC staff's views on these topics in relation to a component's financial statements. These SABs are discussed in Chapters 23 and 24.

INTERNATIONAL ACCOUNTING STANDARD

In July 1984, the International Accounting Standards Executive Committee issued IAS 24, *Related Party Disclosures*. This Standard generally conforms to the disclosure requirements of SFAS 57.

26

Uncertainties

UNCERTAINTIES IN BUSINESS

Final results do not necessarily match original expectations. Uncertain outcomes clearly apply to economics, and that fact should be understood in reading reports on economic activities such as published financial statements. The issue of uncertainties is raised in numerous other chapters; this chapter provides a foundation for understanding accounting and auditing uncertainties.

Types of Uncertainties

Changing Environment. A business, to a great extent, is a function of the environment in which it operates. It can be significantly affected by changing social, political, and economic factors over which it may have no control, as exemplified by:

1. The litigiousness of our society on the part of individuals in the form of liability claims or by corporations such as the Pennzoil-Texaco litigation.
2. The nationalization or seizure of businesses by foreign government.
3. The large number of businesses seeking the protection of the courts against their creditors.

Remote Uncertainties. Benjamin Franklin said that nothing in the world is certain but death and taxes. However, for a business enterprise, not even death and taxes are certain. Corporate entities do not necessarily have the limited lives of individuals. The financial accounting framework includes a basic feature called the *going concern* concept, which assumes more or less indefinite continuation of operations in the absence of intent or evidence to the contrary. Still, abrupt cessation caused by major and remote uncertainties does threaten the existence of many going concerns, as was dramatized by the nuclear accident at Three Mile Island, the earthquakes in California, and the tragic incident in Bhopal, India.

Tax Liabilities. The IRS's aggressive interpretation of the Internal Revenue Code and the regulations (see Chapter 48) has made it clear that even though the existence of a system of taxation is certain, no taxpayer can determine tax liability with precision. The IRS challenges, interprets, and changes tax liabilities through an active program of examinations and issuance of rulings. Although payment of taxes may be certain for a profitable enterprise, the amount due is often not certain.

Macroeconomic Issues. SFAC 1 recognizes that "the outcome of economic activity in a dynamic economy is uncertain and results from combinations of many factors" (¶ 20). Events beyond the control of the enterprise that affect the world and the economy as a whole create uncertainties about the future environment in which the enterprise will operate. Such macroeconomic matters include war, an oil embargo, inflation, recession, high interest rates, tight credit, the unavailability of capital funds, and a myriad of other events.

Industry Uncertainties. Every enterprise is also subject to uncertain future events that may affect only the enterprise or the industry as a whole. The value of an inventory may be significantly reduced or even rendered worthless by a new product that operates more effectively and less expensively (e.g., electronic calculators, computers and software). Other major business uncertainties may include litigation and governmental regulation. Although a business may be very successful, its nature or management structure may be severely affected if key management personnel leave unexpectedly.

Control Over Uncertainty

An enterprise usually has some control over routine uncertainties. For example, collectibility of receivables cannot be a concern if there are no credit sales. If credit sales are made, the enterprise can control its type of customer, such as selecting only AAA-rated companies in an effort to limit bad-debt losses. An enterprise that wants to minimize the chance of interruption in fuel or other supplies can arrange for alternate sources of supply.

Business is concerned with profits, however, and minimizing risks and uncertainties is not always good business policy and will not necessarily maximize profits.

Implications for Financial Accounting and Reporting

Financial accounting and reporting attempt to interpret economic operating events such as sales, production, purchasing, and collections. Some operating events are quite easy to account for because the transaction is completed in a short time and has few uncertainties. For example, a purchase and sale for cash, all in one day, is easily measurable and does not require estimates. But most operating events are not so clear-cut. As a result, two of the basic features of financial accounting are estimation and judgment. Financial statements prepared under GAAP must reflect many factors. As the operations of an enterprise become more complex, the need to make estimates increases. The present accounting model permits only a single-valued approach to the presentation of a probabilistic reality, so the alternative of presenting a range of measurements reflecting alternate possible outcomes, rather than a single point estimate, does not exist. Uncertainties therefore must be dealt with by footnote or other supplemental disclosure rather than by direct incorporation into financial statements.

FINANCIAL ACCOUNTING AND REPORTING

Definitions

Three overlapping terms frequently used in this chapter are uncertainty, contingency, and estimate.

1. An *uncertainty* is any matter that may affect the financial statements or the disclosures required therein whose outcome is not susceptible of reasonable estimation.
2. A *contingency* is an existing condition, situation, or set of circumstances involving uncertainty that will ultimately be resolved when future events occur or fail to occur.
3. An *estimate* is a nonexact measurement used to assign an amount to the effects of business transactions and events (APB Statement 4, Chapter 2, ¶ 35). "Estimates resting on expectations of the future are often needed, but their major use, especially of those formally incorporated in financial statements, is to measure financial effects of past transactions or events or the present status of an asset or liability" (SFAC 1, ¶ 21 (FASB, 1978)).

Thus, uncertainties include all contingencies and some estimates. A contingency is always an uncertainty, but some uncertainties are not narrowly defined as contingencies (e.g., general business risks). An estimate made of a future outcome is an uncertainty, but an estimate made to approximate amounts that could be determined nearly exactly if inordinate effort were expended is not an uncertainty.

Objectives

To be consistent with the overall objectives of financial accounting and reporting, information on uncertainties reported in financial statements should be useful to the reader who is considering making, retaining, or disposing of an equity investment in, or a loan to, an enterprise. Thus, for uncertainties that probably will have a material effect on financial position or results of operations, an estimate of the effect of the uncertainty should be recorded in the current financial statements, or, in cases where reasonable estimates cannot be made, their existence should be disclosed.

When estimates are routine, such as expected future warranty costs for normal adjustments to a product, current operations are charged based on prior experience (factual data), and details could confuse rather than enlighten the reader. However, when management is not able to reasonably estimate the effect of a material uncertainty, it may be more useful to disclose the circumstances – and perhaps the inapplicability of past experience or other factual data. This might be the case, for example, when an unusual lawsuit is brought against an enterprise. With proper disclosure the user of the financial statements can then factor the potential effect into his own perception of financial condition and prospects and, depending on his purpose, decide on the extent, if any, to which the uncertainty should affect his business decision.

A brief chronology of the profession's recent considerations of risks and uncertainties is outlined in the following subsections.

Trueblood Committee. The *Report of the Study Group on the Objectives of Financial Statements* (the Trueblood Committee) concluded that full factual disclosure is important to a user because the user can then make his own assessment. The Trueblood Committee also concluded that it would be useful to state assumptions, interpretations, and predictions and to estimate both a single value and a range of possible results. Classification of information by relative risk based on the assessment of uncertainties would permit the user to compare the information and make decisions based on his own risk preferences (AICPA, 1973d, pp. 33–34). The Commission on Auditors' Responsibilities supported these conclusions (1978, pp. 23–30).

FASB Concepts. The FASB's Conceptual Framework Project (see Chapter 2) parallels the recommendations of the Trueblood Committee; financial information should be useful to investors and lenders, should be classified on a range from most factual to most interpretive, should disclose assumptions, and should consider changing values. SFAC 1, *Objectives of Financial Reporting by Business Enterprises*, concludes that users are aided in evaluating estimates and judgmental information by explanations of underlying assumptions and methods used (¶ 54).

The profession must be concerned with whether there are detrimental effects of disclosure – such as litigation whose disclosure might cause damage, or proprietary information whose disclosure might affect competitive position. In some cases disclosure detriments may outweigh user benefits, but this argument is becoming less and less compelling as disclosure requirements proliferate.

Cohen Commission. Following a recommendation of the Commission on Auditors' Responsibilities (CAR, 1978, p. 29), the accounting profession has been considering, without resolution, whether to require the placement of all information on uncertainties in a single note to the financial statements, as contrasted with the current practice of dispersing such information throughout the notes to the financial statements.

AICPA Task Force on Risks and Uncertainties. In the early and mid-1980s, both the accounting profession and Congress were significantly concerned with the adequacy of financial reporting. Numerous industries—including banking, savings and loans, energy, and major organizations within those industries—were experiencing the fallout from substantial changes in national and international economies. Businesses that had received unqualified audit reports were suddenly declaring bankruptcy, being declared statutorily insolvent, or revealing major financial difficulties.

For example, for many years, savings and loan associations had issued mortgages with fixed interest rates. During the period of very high interest rates, many S&Ls needed to borrow at high rates but were earning at very low fixed rates. The result was a significant working capital drain and insolvency for many S&Ls, although they had received unqualified audit opinions. If investors and other users of financial reports had been aware of the concentrations that some S&Ls had in fixed, low rate mortgages, they may have been better able to assess the risks faced by the S&L and their own concomitant investment risk. (See Chapter 41 for a further discussion regarding S&Ls.)

The Risks and Uncertainties Task Force was established by AcSEC to explore approaches for providing improved disclosures that would assist users in better assessing the existence of significant risks and uncertainties. In July 1987, this Task Force issued its report (AICPA, 1987l) that included recommendations regarding disclosures on certain significant risks and uncertainties. Specifically, it recommended that a company disclose information regarding risks and uncertainties existing at the balance sheet date that relate to:

• The nature of the company's operations.

• Estimates necessary in the preparation of the financial statements that are particularly susceptible to change could result in a material adjustment, and may occur in the near term. For example, the carrying value of inventory may be impaired due to the impending release of a competitive product that would make the inventory obsolete.

• Current vulnerability of the company due to a concentration in terms of assets, customers, or suppliers other than those common to the industry in which the entity operates. This would be disclosed only if the potential impact is at least reasonably possible in the near future and the impact would be severe.

The Report included disclosure examples, many of which are based on actual disclosures, for each of the conditions under which disclosures were recommended.

FASB Agenda Item. The FASB has not yet dealt with the issue of risks and uncertainties as a formal agenda item since the release of SFAS 5. However, it has noted that certain disclosures suggested in the AICPA Task Force Report may coincide with certain disclosures proposed in the Board's Exposure Draft, *Disclosures about Financial Instruments* (FASB, 1987a). Accordingly, the Board may further consider the specific issues raised in the AICPA Report as the financial instruments project progresses. See Chapter 21 for an in-depth discussion of this FASB project.

SEC. A proposed release from the SEC (33-6711) dealing with MD&A presented the Commission's expectation regarding coverage of significant risks and uncertainties. The SEC had under consideration the necessity for expanding the disclosures required in MD&A with greater emphasis on risks known by management that could affect the company in the future. In March 1988, the SEC staff, without withdrawing the concept release, stated its decision that changes to the MD&A rules were not needed at this time. The staff noted that in reviewing disclosure made by more than 200 companies in 12 industries. deficiencies were noted in about 90% of the cases. The staff plans to review more compaines' disclosures and eventually publish an interpretive release about frequently observed deficiencies.

Auditing Standards Board. The ASB issued an exposure draft of a proposed Statement on Standards for Attestation Engagements (SSAE), *Examination of Management's Discussion and Analysis* (AICPA, 1987i). The final statement, if issued, would provide guidance regarding the auditor's involvement with MD&A when engaged by the client to do so. This proposal had been tabled to await the results of the above SEC proposal. In view of the SEC action mentioned in the preceding paragraph, the ASB has now placed its proposal in abeyance.

Measurement and Disclosure Standards

One of the FASB's early projects resulted in SFAS 5, *Accounting for Contingencies* (C59), which contains accounting and disclosure requirements for loss contingencies. It also incorporates the guidance of ARB 50 that precludes recognition of gain contingencies but does require disclosure; it also precludes the accrual by charges against income of any reserves for general contingencies, self-insurance, and catastrophe losses for insurance companies.

SFAS 5 defines a contingency as "an existing condition, situation, or set of circumstances involving uncertainty as to possible gain . . . or loss . . . to an enterprise that will ultimately be resolved when one or more future events occur or fail to occur" (C59.101). The future event or nonevent will establish the actual amount of the asset or liability. Because the amount is not known when earlier financial statements are issued, an estimate is recorded if sufficient evidence is available to set an amount. For example, a suit for $1 million against an enterprise for a breach of contract (existing condition) may result in an ultimate liability of $250,000 determined by adjudication or settlement (future events) with the plaintiff. If this is deemed to be the probable result, $250,000 will be accrued currently.

Uncertainties, because they include the broad area of accounting estimates, are not always contingencies as contemplated by SFAS 5. For example, amounts owed to others for services rendered but not yet billed may require an estimate in the accounting process, but a contingency is not involved; the cost does not depend on a future confirming event. An obligation has been incurred, although the amount of the obligation requires estimation.

Accrual. Accrual of an estimated loss contingency by a charge against earnings is required if, and only if, two conditions are met: (1) it is probable an asset has been impaired or a liability has been incurred, and (2) the loss can be reasonably estimated (C59.105). FASB Interpretation 14 requires accrual of the most likely estimate of the loss if it is possible to determine a range of loss, and it requires recording at least the lowest point in that range when no amount within the range is a better estimate than any other amount. Ability to estimate a range of loss when the loss is probable indicates that a reasonable estimate can be made; therefore, accrual is required.

In order to apply the SFAS 5 approach, the FASB provided the following definitions of three points on the range of probability:

1. *Probable.* The future event or events are likely to occur.
2. *Reasonably possible.* The chance of the future event or events occurring is more than remote (slight) but less than likely (probable).
3. *Remote.* The chance of the future event or events occurring is slight.

Although the FASB provided these definitions, SFAS 5 did not include specific quantitative probabilities. Therefore, a great deal of judgment is necessary in applying them.

Disclosure. The *nature of an accrual* made for a loss contingency must be disclosed, but the amount of the accrual sometimes need not be disclosed. When to disclose the amount accrued is open to judgment; however, it seems prudent to make such disclosure whenever the accrual is unusual or material to current earnings or materially affects the trend of earnings. Many enterprises make no disclosure regarding litigation or other contingencies if the amounts involved are not material and an unfavorable outcome is less than reasonably possible.

Disclosure of the existence of a material *unaccrued loss contingency* is required when a reasonable possibility exists that a loss may have been incurred. If a reasonable estimate of the amount or range of loss can be made, disclosure of the amount is necessary; otherwise, inability to estimate should be disclosed.

Unasserted Claims. Unasserted claims or assessments are given special consideration in SFAS 5. An unasserted claim or assessment is one in which the injured party or potential claimant has not yet notified the reporting entity of a possible claim or assessment. For example, suppose X claimed that Z used sales practices that were in restraint of trade and damaging to X. The court awarded damages to X, which Z has recorded as a charge against earnings. Z believes Y might win a similar damage award, but since Y has been silent, Y's potential claim against Z is an unasserted claim.

Another example of an unasserted claim could be a situation in which a patient died in a hospital operating room because of negligence by the medical staff. The

Loss can / Loss is	Probable	Reasonably possible	Remote
Be estimated	Accrue and disclose nature	Disclose nature ①	No accrual or disclosure
Not be estimated	Disclose nature	Disclose nature	No accrual or disclosure

① Disclosure of amount or range is also required or a statement that an estimate of the amount cannot be made

FIG. 26.1 SFAS 5—Accrual and Disclosure Requirements for Loss Contingencies and Unasserted Claims That are Probable of Assertion

distraught family of the patient may not even think about potential legal action against the hospital for months. The hospital's fiscal year may end, and financial statements may be released for the period in which the event occurred. Because the injured parties (the family members) have not mentioned or threatened litigation, this is an unasserted claim at the financial statement date.

Disclosure of an unasserted claim or assessment is not required unless it is probable that the claim will be asserted and there is a *reasonable possibility* that the outcome will be unfavorable. If it is probable that the assertion will be made and *probable* that the outcome will be unfavorable, accrual is necessary if the amount can be estimated reasonably, just as with an asserted claim.

Unasserted claims have been given this special treatment because disclosure could cause the injured party to recognize the injury and assert the claim; in other words, the disclosure tends to be self-fulfilling. Attorneys were also concerned with the loss of attorney-client privilege if certain disclosures were made regarding unasserted claims. These problems and the compromise worked out between accountants and attorneys are discussed later in the "Attorneys' Letters'" section of this chapter.

A matrix summarizing accrual and disclosure requirements is presented in Figure 26.1.

Subsequent Events. Information becoming available after the balance sheet date but before issuance of the financial statements may indicate that an asset became impaired or a liability was incurred *after* the date of the financial statements. Disclosure of such losses or loss contingencies may be necessary to keep the financial statements from being misleading. SFAS 5 (C59.112) gives some guidance, although not very specific, as to what would make such disclosure necessary. It seems prudent to disclose any matter that could have a material effect on financial position or operations or could materially affect the trend of operations.

If disclosure is deemed necessary, the nature of the loss or contingency and the amount or range of the possible loss should be disclosed. If the effect on financial position is extremely material, supplemental pro forma financial data giving effect to the loss as if it had occurred at the date of the financial statements may be useful. Of course, if the material loss contingency existed at the date of the balance sheet, accrual is necessary when the loss is probable and the amount can be reasonably estimated.

The auditing literature deals specifically with subsequent events and categorizes them into two types with differing requirements (AU 560), distinguished by whether the condition giving rise to the event existed prior to or subsequent to the balance sheet date.

If the conditions existed prior to the year end, the financial statements should be adjusted for the impact of the event. This is known as a Type 1 subsequent event. An example would be the settlement of litigation where no liability had previously been recognized.

A Type 2 subsequent event may simply be disclosed in the notes to the financial statements. Such disclosure should clearly present the facts related to the event, and if material, should present pro forma financial data giving effect to the impact of the event as if it had occurred at the balance sheet date. An example of a Type 2 event is a casualty loss such as destruction of a plant after year end but prior to issuance of the financial statements.

Gain Contingencies. An element of conservatism was reflected in ARB 50, which specified that gain contingencies, unlike loss contingencies, usually are not to be reflected in the accounts. The FASB incorporated this approach into SFAS 5 (C59.118) without passing judgment on the continued usefulness of conservatism as a principle. Thus gain contingencies are not to be recognized prior to realization, but adequate disclosure of potential material gain contingencies is required under SFAS 5. This disclosure should not lead to overly optimistic estimates of the likelihood of realizing a gain. Some accountants question the inconsistency of only disclosing, rather than accruing, gain contingencies whose realization may be as predictable as recorded loss contingencies.

Guarantees. Disclosure of guarantees of indebtedness of others, obligations of commercial banks under standby letters of credit, and guarantees to repurchase receivables or property sold or otherwise assigned is required even though the probability of loss may be remote. Disclosure should include the nature and amount of the guarantee and might also state, or be net of, the value of any expected recovery from an outside party (C59.113). To clarify that the terminology "guarantees of indebtedness of others" includes indirect guarantees, the FASB issued FIN 34, *Disclosure of Indirect Guarantees of Indebtedness of Others.* The Interpretation states that

> an indirect guarantee of the indebtedness of another arises under an agreement that obligates one entity to transfer funds to a second entity upon the occurrence of specified

events, under conditions whereby (1) the funds are legally available to creditors of the second entity and (2) those creditors may enforce the second entity's claims against the first entity under the agreement. Examples of indirect guarantees include agreements to advance funds if a second entity's income, coverage of fixed charges, or working capital falls below a specified minimum. (C59.114)

Oral guarantees. On December 12, 1985, the SEC issued FRR 23 (§ 104). This Release is significant in that it describes the SEC's belief that certain oral guarantees are contingent liabilities that require disclosure. The Release directs auditors to ensure that their procedures address oral guarantees.

The incident causing the issuance of this Release involved the sale of assets to a third party by a company (the seller). A significant factor in the sale was an oral guarantee by certain senior financial executives of the seller made to the bank providing the financing to the third party for its purchase of the assets. The bank, however, did not report the existence of the guarantee to the seller's auditors in response to a confirmation request. The Release states that "the false and misleading response [by the bank] contributed to the [seller's] failure to properly account for this transaction [i.e., not as a sale, as the risks of ownership never passed], the failure of the [seller's] independent auditor to discover the improprieties in the [seller's] financial statements, and therefore to the [seller's] filing with the Commission materially false and misleading financial statements."

Additionally, the Release states:

> The Commission believes that it is critical that financial institutions and other entities which receive audit confirmation requests maintain a system by which information of material significance concerning guarantees and other contingent liabilities is available to those persons responding to audit confirmation requests and employ reasonable procedures to keep such information current, accurate and complete. Failure to maintain such a system may prevent auditors from receiving all information of material significance to the audit of the issuer's financial statements.

Subsequently, the Planning Subcommittee of the ASB stated that it had reviewed the literature and concluded that the existing guidance was appropriate and covered both oral and written guarantees. There may be situations, however, where the auditor will wish to supplement the wording of the standard bank confirmation inquiry form, to make appropriate inquiries of the lending officer, and to consider additional wording in the client representation letter making explicit reference to oral and written guarantees.

The ASB has formed a task force to consider the subject of oral guarantees and the standard bank confirmation form because bankers frequently do not respond to some of the questions on the confirmation form and have been charging a fee for responding. It has also discussed revisions to the bank confirmation and directed its task force to prepare an auditing interpretation on making inquiries of, and confirming transactions with, an entity's financial institution (banker) as well as on the use and form of the standard bank confirmation. As of mid-1988, the task force is still at work.

Self-Insurance. Before SFAS 5, many enterprises that did not carry insurance against certain risks, such as property damage from fire or explosion, charged earnings in a systematic fashion (e.g., as if an insurance premium were being expensed) to set up an insurance reserve against which actual losses could then be charged. Charges in lieu of insurance are no longer permitted. Lack of insurance may be considered a loss contingency, because a future event, if it occurs, will confirm the fact and amount of loss (C59.133–134).

Charges against earnings for unspecified business risks, sometimes known as *general contingency reserves*, also are prohibited. An appropriation of retained earnings for such contingencies and for uninsured risks remains permissible (C59.117). This involves segregating retained earnings, but not by a charge to earnings. When losses occur, they cannot be charged against the appropriated retained earnings, but must be charged against current earnings. Disclosure of uninsured or underinsured risks is not required (C59.116), because of the difficulties in developing criteria; however, when the risk of loss appears reasonably possible, disclosure seems called for.

Insurance Coverage. Rapidly increasing costs of insurance coverage and the problem of availability of coverage for certain types of risk (e.g., professional malpractice, product liability, director's and officer's liability, and pollution liability) are significantly affecting many companies. To keep premium costs under control or to meet the requests (insistence) of their insurers, some companies are rewriting the terms of their coverage, for example, increasing the amounts of deductibles, reducing the coverage, or both; others are self-insuring or forming captive insurance companies, which may be either wholly or jointly owned.

In addition, general liability policies are being revised from an occurrence basis to a claims-made basis. An occurrence basis policy covers liabilities for accidents that take place during the policy year, regardless of when the claim is brought. A claims-made policy, on the other hand, only covers liabilities for accidents that take place during the policy period with the condition that the claim is brought during that period. If a claim is brought after the period covered, there is no coverage.

These changes can leave companies with gaps in coverage, especially if they change insurers or if an insurer cancels coverage. There is often a substantial time delay between the occurrence of an accident and the filing of a claim. If the claim is not brought within the policy period and there is a change in insurers or the type of insurance, there might be no coverage.

The new claims-made format has provisions for "tail coverage." The incumbent insurer is required to provide a policy that will cover the time period between a policy's cancellation or nonrenewal and the inception of a new policy. Basically, this policy extends the retroactive feature to match the new retroactive date on another policy and therefore would eliminate gaps in coverage. However, tail coverage is very expensive in relation to the expiring policy.

Financing, debt covenants, and compliance with laws and regulations. Reductions in the amounts of insurance coverage or the inability to obtain certain types of insurance coverage can restrict an entity's borrowing ability or cause an entity to violate covenants of debt agreements requiring such coverage. An entity may also be required by statute or by order of a regulatory agency to maintain certain types and levels of insurance. Additionally, if an entity is unable to obtain adequate amounts of director's and officer's liability insurance, the entity may be significantly affected by resignations of some or all of its directors, which in turn could cause violation of a debt covenant, state law, or regulation.

Obviously, the present insurance situation could have a significant impact on both for-profit and not-for-profit entities. An evaluation of the effects of this situation should be made, and if material, the entity's accounting for insurance should be challenged for appropriateness and a determination should be made as to whether adequate disclosures (see following subsection) have been made in the circumstances.

Additionally, if material liabilities covered by insurance have been incurred by an entity, consideration should be given to the ability of the insurer to meet its obligations under the policy. Situations have occurred, especially in reinsured excess layers, indicating potential problems in this area.

Disclosure of insurance coverage. In early 1987, the AICPA published a report on *Disclosure of Insurance Coverage* (AICPA, 1987h). The impetus for this report was the significant increase in insurance premiums and deductibles, and decreases in or elimination of certain types of previously available insurance coverage taking place at that time. As a result, companies reduced, dropped, or were even denied certain types of coverage, resulting in a concomitant rise in uninsured risk.

The scope of the report includes publicly held companies and entities with public accountability (e.g., municipalities and charitable organizations). The report encourages disclosure of

* Exposure to risks of future material loss related to torts; theft of, damage to, expropriation of, or destruction of assets; business interruption; errors or omissions; injuries to employees; or acts of God; and those risks that have not been transferred to unrelated third parties through insurance.

* The actual and potential effects of losses from these risks on the company's historical or planned operations, including exposure to losses from claims, curtailment of research and development or manufacturing, or contraction or cessation of other activities, such as discontinuance of a product line.

* Comparison of current insurance coverage by major categories of risk to coverage in prior periods, without necessarily quantifying such coverage or changes in coverages.

* Recent claims experience.

* A description of the reporting entity's risk management programs without giving a misleading impression about their effectiveness.

The GASB has issued a Discussion Memorandum, *Accounting and Financial Reporting for Risk Management Activities* (GASB, 1987b), that, in part, discusses the issue of inadequate insurance coverage for certain risks. See Chapter 31 of this *Handbook* for additional discussion.

Claims-made insurance policies. The EITF has also delved into the insurance coverage area. In Issue 86-12, last considered in July 1986, the task force addressed the *Accounting by Insureds for Claims-Made Insurance Policies.* According to the EITF Issues Summary, this issue involves "the need for the enterprise to recognize a liability for the probable losses from incurred but not reported (IBNR) claims that will be reported after the expiration of the claims-made policy."

The Issue is complex and has been addressed by the EITF four times. The Task Force consensus is that SFAS 5, *Accounting for Contingencies* (C59), requires a company to record a liability for probable and reasonably estimable losses from IBNR claims and incidents. The estimated cost of purchasing "tail" coverage is generally not relevant in determining the loss to be accrued if the company has not purchased such coverage. When the fiscal year and policy year do coincide, expense equal to the annual premium plus the anticipated normal adjustment of the year-end IBNR liability could be accrued on a pro rata basis over the year. Any unusual claims or incidents not insured under the current policy would be recognized in the interim period in which they become known. When fiscal and policy year do not coincide, accrual in interim periods could be based on the estimated premium of the claims-made coverage that the company expects to acquire.

Litigation and Government Action. One of the major uncertainties facing every business is the risk of litigation. Class actions, shareholders' derivative actions, individual suits, and actions brought by government agencies are not uncommon. And the effect—the possible outcome—may require current accounting or disclosure of the contingent liability, that is, the potential future obligation of an uncertain amount resulting from past activities. There are many different types of litigation in which an enterprise may become involved, and it seems that new ones are constantly invented.

Figure 26.2 lists a few types of litigation an enterprise may face. (See C59.139–.140 for a more complete discussion.) This sample list illustrates the wide range of matters that may be the subject of litigation. Consequences to the business enterprise could include payment of damages, payment of fines and penalties, repayment of revenue previously received, and even discontinuation of certain operations. The entire nature of the entity may change as a result of the uncertainty. For example, the Texaco–Pennzoil litigation related to the acquisition of Getty Oil caused Texaco to incur millions of dollars in litigation costs and to file for bankruptcy.

Because the cost of defending against a private lawsuit or one brought by the government can be prohibitive, an enterprise may agree to a settlement despite its belief in its innocence. Of course, not all actions are harmful to an enterprise; for a plaintiff in litigation, the outcome could be beneficial.

Catastrophe Losses. One of the most controversial prohibitions in SFAS 5 relates to catastrophe losses of property and casualty insurance companies. When an insurance company issues a policy, it assumes a risk that a catastrophe (e.g., a hurricane) might occur within the policy coverage period. It has been argued that insurance companies are able to predict the occurrence rate of catastrophes, and amounts of losses from them, using actuarial methods based on past occurrences. Insurance companies use such methods for rate-setting purposes; therefore, such reasonably estimated losses should be accrued.

The FASB concluded that catastrophe reserves fail to satisfy SFAS 5's conditions for accrual because losses over the relatively short periods of time covered by policies in force cannot be estimated reasonably. Therefore, unless the catastrophe occurs within the policy period, no asset is impaired and no liability is incurred at the balance sheet date, so no accrual for a catastrophe loss should be made (C59.146–.148).

Private actions

- Antitrust
- Restraint of trade
- Breach of contract
- Patent infringement
- Product liability
- Violation of federal securities laws

Government actions

- Discrimination — racial, sex, age, and so forth
- Environmental protection
- Antitrust
- Restraint of trade
- Violation of federal securities laws
- Violation of wage and price guidelines or controls
- Renegotiation of government contracts
- Income tax disputes
- Violation of other laws and regulations, for example, Foreign Corrupt Practices Act

FIG. 26.2   Examples of Types of Litigation

However, a property and casualty insurer is required to accrue losses from catastrophes that occurred before the date of the financial statements but have not yet been claimed by the policyholders if it is probable that claims will be made and if a reasonable estimate of the loss can be made (C59.149).

Interim Financial Statements. Interim financial statements usually contain more estimates than annual financial statements and thus may be less reliable. For example, claims or assessments against the enterprise may be given careful consideration by inside and outside counsel at year end but not at an interim date. APB 28, *Interim Financial Reporting* (I73.125), briefly covers the reporting of contingencies and other uncertainties in interim financial reports. It says they are to be disclosed in the same manner as in annual financial statements; however, materiality is to be judged in relationship to the annual financial statements, not to the interim figures. Required disclosures are to be repeated in each interim report until the contingency has been removed, resolved, or determined to be immaterial.

Estimates

Nearly all financial statement amounts require some degree of estimation. Collectibility of current accounts receivable must be evaluated to present the accounts at estimated net realizable value; inventories stated at cost must be measured against estimated market value less an estimate for disposal costs; various accrued liabilities require estimation of services received or amounts due; even accounts payable are subject to future adjustment due to such possibilities as improper billing or inadequate product performance. Cash is possibly the only asset recorded with no uncertainties surrounding it, and then only if denominated in the currency of the country in which the reporting entity resides. Perhaps the only liabilities with no uncertainties surrounding them are notes and loans payable based on amounts previously borrowed (as opposed to payment for goods or services), and again, only if denominated in the currency of the country in which the reporting entity resides.

In some cases, the impact of estimates on financial statements is significant and special kinds of disclosure may be required. For example, in the notes to the 1986 financial statements of Manville Corp. it was disclosed that in 1985 the company recorded a provision for losses of $27.1 million from claims related to asbestosis. This amount represented an estimate of the present value of *anticipated* claims.

The AICPA Auditing Standards Board, in SAS 57, *Auditing Accounting Estimates* (AU 342), included a list of the various accounting estimates commonly made in preparing financial statements. Figure 26.3 presents that list.

In dealing with the many estimates required in preparing financial statements, the auditor must judge in each case whether amounts have been or can be estimated reasonably. Neither SFAS 5 nor any other authoritative literature contains definitive guidelines on measuring the difference between uncertainties that can and cannot be estimated reasonably. Although estimates are always uncertainties, they are not necessarily loss contingencies. Thus estimates regarding events in the normal course of business are generally included in the financial statements without specific disclosure, unless a reasonable estimate cannot be made and the effect could be material.

Asset Realization. Assets are generally valued on a balance sheet at historical cost amounts; however, they may be written down if future utility clearly does not warrant a recovery of the cost through future utilization or realization of revenues. Future events affecting asset values include collectibility of specific receivables, salability of inventories, recovery of deferred costs (including start-up and preopening costs), recovery of investments, and threat of expropriation by foreign governments.

Liability Determination. Liabilities may also be affected by future events that determine their amount. Although prior experience or other factors may allow a reasonable estimate for financial statement purposes, future events may prove the estimate to be inaccurate. For example, in one case, government intervention forced a tire manufacturer to "voluntarily" recall tires of a certain model and replace them with new tires because of what the government said was a faulty product. Although the company may not have believed its warranty covered such alleged defects, government action created an "implied warranty."

An enterprise theoretically should accrue all future costs, including product recall cost, in the period of sale to obtain a proper matching of revenues and expenses. The cost of the recall would be accrued in the period of sale if the company could foresee all costs that would be incurred. However, since a company cannot, almost by definition, be aware of a recall at the time of sale, the actual costs are charged in the period or periods in which they become known.

Other examples where future events may change an estimated liability include costs to complete a long-term contract, ultimate determination of tax liability, policy

Receivables:
Uncollectible receivables
Allowance for loan losses
Uncollectible pledges

Inventories:
Obsolete inventory
Net realizable value of inventories where future selling prices and future costs are involved
Losses on purchase commitments

Financial Instruments:
Valuation of securities
Trading versus investment security classification
Probability of high correlation of a hedge
Sales of securities with puts and calls

Productive facilities, natural resources and intangibles:
Useful lives and residual values
Depreciation and amortization methods
Recoverability of costs
Recoverable reserves

Accruals:
Property and casualty insurance company loss reserves
Compensation in stock option plans and deferred plans
Warranty claims
Taxes on real and personal property
Renegotiation refunds
Actuarial assumptions in pension costs

Revenues:
Airline passenger revenue
Subscription income
Freight and cargo revenue
Dues income
Losses on sales contracts

Contracts:
Revenue to be earned
Cost to be incurred
Percent of completion

Leases:
Initial direct costs
Executory costs
Residual values

Litigation:
Probability of loss
Amount of loss

Rates:
Annual effective tax rate in interim reporting
Imputed interest rates on receivables and payables
Gross profit rates under program method of accounting

Other:
Losses and net realizable value on disposal of segment or restructuring of a business
Fair values in nonmonetary exchanges
Interim period costs in interim reporting
Current values in personal financial statements

FIG. 26.3 Examples of Accounting Estimates
Source: Appendix to SAS 57, (AU 342.16).

reserves of a life insurance company if the mortality rates and other assumptions change from those used to estimate the liability, and costs required to restore strip-mined property to original condition.

Other Estimates. Many other cases exist where amounts may be estimated based on reasonably reliable data. Although it is recognized that estimates can and probably will be changed based on actual results, they are considered sufficiently reliable to record in the financial statements. Examples include depreciation based on estimated service lives of assets, collectibility in total as opposed to specific receivable collectibility, and write-off of costs based on geological estimates of proved oil and gas reserves.

Estimates and contingencies such as endorsements, guarantees of debt, and assignment of receivables with recourse may require disclosure only, not accrual, because of the remoteness that future events will cause a liability to accrue. On the other hand, most lawsuits that may create material liability are not recorded; they are disclosed, not because of the uncertainty of the confirming future event, but because of the inability to make a reasonable estimate of the outcome.

Incongruities

GAAP is not consistent as to treatment of the various types of estimates and uncertainties in financial accounting and reporting. For example, the FASB has decided that it is inappropriate to allow financial statement preparers to estimate general research and development recoverability. Since any such estimates are considered too subjective, all such costs must be expensed. However, estimates as to the future utility of other assets, including those that appear to be very similar to research and development expenditures (e.g., preoperating expenses and start-up costs), may still be deferred based on estimates of future utility. The FASB simply has not followed through on this final phase of R&D-type costs, hence the incongruity. (See Chapter 39 for further discussion.)

AUDITING

Objectives

Management must estimate the outcome of future events to determine the appropriate amounts and disclosures to include in the financial statements. Estimates that tend to recur over the normal business cycle may be based on prior experience (e.g., useful lives of depreciable assets and collectibility of customer accounts). For the unusual estimates, management may rely on outside experts for advice on the outcome of contingencies such as litigation.

The auditor's objective is to be satisfied (if possible) that management's estimates are reasonable. In reaching this overall conclusion, the auditor obtains and evaluates evidential matter relevant to the existence of the contingency or estimate and the appropriateness of financial accounting, reporting, and disclosure. The auditor must distinguish between uncertainties that can be reasonably estimated and therefore should be accrued and uncertainties that are inestimable in amount and thus should not be accrued. As to the latter, the auditor may modify his opinion for material uncertainties where a reasonable estimate of amount cannot be made. (See Chapter 11.)

SAS 57

Management is responsible for determining accounting estimates, such as allowances for loan losses, warranty expense, and obsolete inventory; auditors are responsible for assessing the reasonableness of such estimates. Although professional standards provide guidance for the auditing of some specific accounting estimates, no general guidance has ever been established. In SAS 57, *Auditing Accounting Estimates* (AU 342), issued in 1988, the ASB provides guidance to auditors to assist in evaluating the reasonableness of accounting estimates from a generic viewpoint. The Standard defines an accounting estimate as

> an approximation of a financial statement element, item, or account in the absence of exact measurement. Accounting estimates in historical financial statements measure the effects of past business transactions or events or the present status of an asset or liability.

In developing accounting estimates, management normally follows this process:

- Identify situations for which accounting estimates are required.
- Gather relevant, sufficient, and reliable data on which to base the estimate.
- Identify the relevant factors that may affect the accounting estimate.
- Develop assumptions that represent management's judgment of the most likely circumstances and events with respect to the relevant factors.
- Determine the estimated amount based on the assumptions and other relevant factors.
- Determine that the accounting estimate is presented in conformity with applicable accounting principles and that disclosure is adequate.

The risk of misstatement of the amount of an estimate is significant because estimates are subjectively determined using varying assumptions. To reduce the risk of misstatement, management should establish a control structure that includes:

- Accumulation of sufficient and reliable data on which to base an accounting estimate.
- Preparation of the accounting estimate by qualified personnel.
- Adequate review and approval of the accounting estimates by appropriate levels of authority, including:
  - Review of sources of relevant factors.
  - Review of development of assumptions.
  - Review of reasonableness of assumptions and resulting estimates.
  - Consideration of the need to use the work of specialists.
- Comparison of prior accounting estimates with subsequent results to assess the reliability of the process used to develop estimates.
- Consideration by management of whether the resulting accounting estimate is consistent with the plans of the entity.

An auditor should obtain sufficient evidence to assure that

1. All necessary accounting estimates have been developed,
2. The accounting estimates are reasonable in the circumstances, and
3. The accounting estimates are presented in conformity with applicable accounting principles and are properly disclosed.

That assurance presumes that management has identified all material accounting estimates. An auditor can evaluate this by applying the following procedures:

- Consider assertions embodied in the financial statements to determine the need for estimates.
- Evaluate information obtained in performing other procedures, including:
  - Information about changes made or planned in the entity's business, including changes in operating strategy and the industry in which the entity operates, that may indicate the need to make an accounting estimate.
  - Changes in the methods of accumulating information.
  - Information concerning identified litigation, claims, and assessments and other contingencies.
  - Information obtained from reading available minutes of meetings of stockholders, directors, and appropriate committees.
- Inquire of management regarding the existence of circumstances that may indicate the need to make an accounting estimate.

In addition, the company's historical experience in making correct estimates is an important consideration.

In testing the reasonableness of an accounting estimate, an auditor should consider the following audit procedures:

- Obtain an understanding of the process established by management to develop accounting estimates and determine whether the process is appropriate in the circumstances.
- Study and evaluate controls over the process and the supporting data.
- Identify the sources of information that management used in forming the assumptions and consider whether the information is reliable and sufficient for the purpose based on information gathered in other audit tests.
- Consider whether there are additional key factors or alternative assumptions about the factors.
- Evaluate whether the assumptions are consistent with one another, the supporting data, and relevant historical data.
- Analyze historical data used in developing the assumptions to assess whether it is comparable and consistent with data of the period under audit, and determine whether it is sufficiently reliable for the purpose.
- Consider whether changes in the business or industry may cause other factors to become significant to the assumptions.
- Review available documentation of the assumptions used in developing the accounting estimates, inquire about any other plans, goals, and objectives of the entity, and consider their relationship to the assumptions.
- Test the calculations used to translate the assumptions into the accounting estimate.
- Consider whether there are more appropriate ways to translate assumptions into estimates.
- Consider obtaining the opinion of a specialist regarding certain assumptions.

An appendix to SAS 57 identifies a large number of examples of accounting estimates.

Audit Procedures

When dealing with estimates, the auditor is assessing "soft" data that cannot be measured until a future event occurs or fails to occur. Accordingly a substantive approach to auditing, rather than a reliance-on-systems approach, is usually followed. In auditing the reasonableness of management's estimates for normal recurring items, the auditor may be able to rely somewhat on past experience of the enterprise or the industry. However, for nonrecurring contingencies each matter may be unique, so past experience is not useful. The auditor often must place a great deal of reliance on management representations (AU 333) and must form an opinion that management is capable of making informed estimates and has the requisite integrity to report them objectively.

In performing all auditing procedures, the auditor should remain alert to evidence that may indicate an uncertainty or contingency that requires specific attention. Procedures such as confirming cash balances, accounts and notes receivable, and accounts and notes payable and reviewing contracts may disclose specific uncertainties or contingencies.

SAS 57 covers auditors' procedures generically. Listed below are substantive procedures specifically designed to bring to the auditor's attention those areas requiring estimates that may need to be reflected in the financial statements or disclosed as a contingency.

1. Obtaining oral representations (through discussion with upper and middle level management) and written representations (as part of the overall audit letter of representations) indicating that management has disclosed all known contingent liabilities and has, to the best of its knowledge, appropriately accounted for the contingencies and adequately disclosed them in the financial statements. (See AU 333.)

2. Reviewing minutes of meetings: board of directors, committees of the board, and shareholders. Important obligations, contracts, lawsuits, and related matters are likely to be discussed at these meetings.

3. Reviewing income tax liability status, tax returns, and IRS agents' reports. Income tax liability is determined through filing of tax returns for the current liability and by accruing deferred taxes. The Internal Revenue Service has the option, very often exercised for business enterprises, to subject the tax return to an examination. The revenue agent's report gives the auditor information on whether there are additional tax accruals that should be considered. (See Chapter 48.)

4. For clients operating in a regulated industry, the auditor should be reviewing correspondence with, and reports prepared for, regulatory agencies – for example, the Federal Reserve Board, Federal Deposit Insurance Corporation, and the Office of the Comptroller of the Currency in the case of banks.

5. Obtaining information on guarantees and letters of credit at balance sheet date and confirming these with the outside party.

6. Reading contracts, loan agreements, leases, and correspondence from government agencies to determine what commitments the enterprise may have.

Other substantive procedures include inquiring of responsible company officials as to whether the client has complied with applicable laws, controls, and regulations imposed by various government agencies. Specific areas of concern should include the Foreign Corrupt Practices Act, wage and price controls, employee safety regulations, environmental regulations, and filing requirements of the SEC and other government agencies. The auditor should discuss these potent liabilities with company officials and ascertain the details of any contingent liabilities, including an estimate of the maximum potential liability, whether any security has been pledged to secure payment, and the likelihood of a contingency becoming an actual liability.

The opinion and advice of the company's legal counsel will be necessary to evaluate whether there has been noncompliance with laws and regulations and to estimate the potential effects of noncompliance. Legal expense should be analyzed and lawyers' invoices reviewed for an indication of areas of professional services suggesting possible contingent liabilities. As billings from attorneys often are itemized, matters not previously known to the auditor may bring to his attention contingencies that could become actual liabilities. A key audit procedure has the auditor inquire of and obtain a written response from the company's lawyers as discussed in the "Attorneys' Letters" section of this chapter.

Estimates and Uncertainty. Once the auditor is aware of the existence of uncertainties, he must then evaluate their effect on the financial statements. In addition to the auditing procedures and evidential matter considered above, the auditor must utilize his general knowledge of business conditions and specific knowledge of the entity being audited. In determining whether a reasonable estimate can be made or whether an uncertainty exists, the auditor uses inductive reasoning to reach conclusions. Certain matters, for example, collectibility of normal customer receivables and useful lives of assets, are within management and auditor expertise and should be subject to reasonable estimation and evaluation.

In evaluating evidence to determine the appropriateness of management's estimates, the auditor must consider the objectivity of such evidence. Can the potential effect truly be measured within reasonable limits? How imminent is the possibility of the contingent future confirming event? How material is the potential effect on the financial statements? What independent expert advice has been used in arriving at the conclusion?

For instance, in the familiar situation of determining whether the allowance for doubtful receivables is appropriate, consideration is given to the entity's prior history of collection. Also important, however, is knowledge as to whether the company has changed its method of doing business with customers. Has there been a change in the type of customer? A change in customer base, for example, from major Fortune 500 companies with high credit ratings to many small, fledgling businesses that have a higher degree of business failures indicates that an increase in the allowance might be necessary. Even if the company being audited has no prior experience with a particular type of customer, reasonable estimates can usually be made by referring to external information, such as statistics from other companies doing business with comparable customers, and by obtaining credit information on nonestablished customers.

The potential effect of other far less common uncertainties may be exceedingly difficult to estimate. For example, consider an enterprise operating in a country where threat of expropriation may endanger both the assets and the continuation of business in that country. Useful information would include whether the country has openly indicated its intention to expropriate property of the enterprise or other enterprises and what the country has done in the past. It may be known that, although the country has a recent history of expropriation, payments have equaled or exceeded the carrying amounts of assets taken; therefore, the potential effect on the enterprise may be only the loss of continuing business in that country. All other factors being equal, disclosure would be the only requirement in such a case. However, if it appears that expropriation is imminent and sufficient payment by the country is not likely, a current provision charged against income for asset impairment may be necessary.

Attorneys' Letters

Background. When dealing with uncertainties, especially contingent liabilities resulting from litigation, potential litigation, and government regulation, the auditor must communicate with the entity's outside counsel and, where applicable, house counsel. Although attorneys are experts at law, many factors limit their ability to opine accurately on the outcome of litigation, including proliferation of litigation, the increasing impact of current judgments and settlements in similar cases, and an inclination to settle. Attorneys are the first to admit they cannot accurately predict the outcome of unasserted claims. In a world where manufacturers may be deemed liable for defects in material or workmanship long beyond the express warranty period and the amount of the ultimate liability may extend beyond previously imagined proportions (Ford Motor Company's alleged failure to correct safety deficiencies in gasoline tanks in certain Pinto automobiles is just one example), no one can be expected to foresee the future and accurately predict the ultimate liability. Consider the judgments against pharmaceutical manufacturers for effects of drugs taken decades ago where the specific manufacturer is not even known, or the use of asbestos as insulation when the fact that it causes lung cancer was not known.

Crowded court dockets, delaying tactics by both plaintiff and defendant, and other factors also increase the difficulties in trying to estimate potential outcome. Much litigation ends in settlement between the opposing parties for amounts well below damages originally sought. Countersuits by a defendant may result in damages being assessed against the original plaintiff. Even in cases where legal arguments and common sense may indicate a particular outcome, jury perceptions may differ. A change in the social environment may occur over the lengthy period of the litigation, and the appeal process adds to uncertainty of outcome.

Evidential Matter. Auditors seek opinions of outside experts such as geologists, actuaries, and appraisers to support information supplied by management. The auditor views outside legal counsel as an expert in legal matters and seeks his expertise and knowledge of the company to help him reach a conclusion as to the appropriateness of accounting for and disclosure of litigation and other contingent liabilities. A standard auditing procedure requires that company management write to outside legal counsel requesting counsel's opinion on the status and the potential outcome of litigation and other contingent liabilities.

Before 1976, auditors requested that management ask their counsel to provide information on any pending litigation and any other contingent liabilities, such as unasserted claims, of which counsel had knowledge. Although attorneys responded to client requests, many were silent as to unasserted claims. Auditors were generally satisfied with replies being received from outside counsel and generally were unaware of limitations being put on such responses. Many attorneys who previously responded to auditors' requests became reluctant to respond to general requests, because they were aware of the increasing amount of litigation and believed that the less information available to outsiders, including auditors, from whom information could be "discovered" by a potential plaintiff, the better they could protect their clients from adverse consequences of litigation.

The attorney-client privilege does not extend to information disclosed to an auditor; because an auditor's communication with his clients is not legally privileged, attorneys were concerned that disclosing an evaluation of potential effects of a claim might be viewed in court as an admission of guilt, and they were adamant about not giving potentially damaging information to auditors that could then be caught by "fishing" plaintiffs. Attorneys were also concerned with their own exposure to litigation if they were held responsible for damages arising from an inaccurate estimate of a client's potential liability.

SAS 12. The problem between auditors and attorneys centered around the auditors using the attorneys' letters to *discover* unasserted claims and the attorneys' reluctance to jeopardize privilege.

In late 1975 a compromise was agreed to by the American Bar Association (ABA) and the AICPA. From the auditor's point of view, SAS 12 (AU 337) contains the essence of the compromise—guidance to the auditor on procedures to follow to identify and satisfy himself as to the accounting and reporting for litigation, claims, and assessments.

Under SAS 12 (337.02–.05), management has the responsibility to adopt policies and procedures to identify, evaluate, and account for litigation, claims, and assessments. The auditor assesses whether all required estimates and disclosures related to management's identified litigation, claims, and assessment have been made, including the period in which the underlying cause occurred, the probability of an unfavorable outcome, and the amount and range of potential loss. Since management is the primary source of information on contingent liabilities, the auditor's procedures should include:

1. Discussing with management their policies and procedures for identifying, evaluating, and accounting for litigation, claims and assessments.

2. Obtaining from management a description and evaluation of the contingent liabilities existing at the date of the balance sheet and subsequent thereto, including identification of matters referred to legal counsel.

3. Obtaining assurances from management that all matters required to be disclosed by SFAS 5 (C59) have been disclosed.

4. Examining documentation in the client's possession, including correspondence and invoices from attorneys.

5. Obtaining management's assurance that it has disclosed all unasserted claims the lawyer has advised the client are probable of assertion and required to be disclosed in accordance with SFAS 5. (The attorney should be informed that the auditor has received such assurance.)

A difficulty facing the auditor in the area of unasserted claims is that the ABA Statement of Policy and the ABA Code of Professional Responsibility call for an attorney to resign an engagement when a client does not follow the attorney's advice to disclose material unasserted claims. SAS 12 restates this responsibility as a reminder that the auditor should consider the need for inquiries as to the reasons the attorney is no longer associating himself with the enterprise (AU 337.11). This solution, worked out between auditors and lawyers, and approved by the SEC, attempts to give the auditor assurances from the enterprise, corroborated by its attorney, that all disclosures required under SFAS 5 have been made; at the same time the attorney-client privilege has not been breached.

However, the legal profession's policy statement is not binding on a lawyer. The auditor should therefore determine whether the attorney understands and follows the ABA Statement of Policy. Some attorneys may specifically disassociate themselves from the ABA statement, making the gathering of evidential matter by the auditor much more difficult. In such cases, the auditor must assure himself that he has obtained sufficient information to be able to determine that management and counsel are not aware of material matters that should be but are not disclosed in the financial statements. Perhaps the attorney will agree to another procedure; discussion will be necessary if the auditor is to become satisfied that he has received the necessary information.

Inquiry of Attorney. The audit inquiry letter to outside counsel is the auditor's primary means of corroborating information on contingencies furnished by management. SAS 12 (AU 337.09) lists specific matters to be covered in an audit inquiry letter, including information regarding unasserted claims as agreed to in the compromise between auditors and attorneys, as follows:

• A listing of pending and threatened litigation.

• A listing of unasserted claims and assessments considered by management to be probable of assertion with unfavorable outcome reasonably possible.

• A request that the attorney describe and evaluate the outcome of each pending or threatened matter listed, including a request for additions to the list.

• A request that the attorney comment on unasserted claims where his views differ from management's evaluation.

• A statement by client's management acknowledging an understanding of the lawyer's professional responsibility involving unasserted claims or assessments.

• A request that the attorney confirm whether the client's understanding of the attorney's professional responsibility is correct.

• A request that the attorney indicate whether his response has been limited and the reasons for such limitation.

• A description of materiality levels agreed upon for purposes of the inquiry and response.

Sample Inquiry Letter. An example of an inquiry letter to an attorney is presented in Figure 26.4. Some of the matters it mentions could be elaborated on:

1. *Judgments rendered or settlements made.* Include in this listing the following information with respect to any material judgment or settlement involving the company: the nature of the judgment or settlement, the amount incurred, and the implications, if any, for the company and its financial statements.

2. *Pending or threatened litigation.* Include in this listing the nature of the litigation, how management is responding or intends to respond (e.g., to contest the case vigorously or to seek an out-of-court settlement), the progress of the case or negotiations to date, an indication of the likelihood of an unfavorable (favorable) outcome, and an estimate (if one can be made) of the amount or range of potential loss (gain).

3. *Unasserted claims and assessments.* Include in this listing the following information with respect to those matters considered by management to be probable of assertion and that, if asserted, would have at least a reasonable possibility of an unfavorable outcome: the nature of the matter, how management intends to respond if the claim is asserted, an indication of the likelihood of an unfavorable outcome, and an estimate (if one can be made) of the amount of range of potential loss.

4. *Other matters.* The auditor may request the enterprise to inquire about other matters, for example, specified information on certain contractually assumed obligations of the company such as debt guarantees of others. Requests pertaining to unpaid legal fees should be covered in a separate statement.

Materiality Guidelines. It may be appropriate for management to limit the letter of inquiry to contingencies that are considered to be material. It is important that such a materiality judgment be agreed to by the enterprise, the auditor, and the attorney.

In a few instances, suits can be classified as clearly immaterial by any aspect: the amount, the nature, and the anticipated impact on the financial statement. However, in today's litigious climate, most suits are instituted for amounts far in excess of the damages incurred and are clearly material to the financial statements if settled for the amount of the action. The enterprise may believe certain of these suits to be without merit, having no material impact on the financial statements, and accordingly omit them from the listing sent to their attorney. It may be difficult for the auditors to obtain the necessary "other" corroborative evidence to agree to the omission of these actions as immaterial. If there is a particular reason to be concerned in this regard, the auditor should request management to prepare a listing of pending or threatened litigation that it feels will have no material impact on the financial statements and include that listing with the standard letter of inquiry. This procedure is recommended not only to assure the validity of management's evaluations but to assist the attorney in responding. The attorney would be responsible for corroborating the completeness of the listing.

Attorney's Response. As part of the compromise between attorneys and auditors, in December 1975 the American Bar Association issued *Statement of Policy Regarding Lawyers' Responses to Auditors' Requests for Information* (reprinted in AU 337C). This paper contains a standard, approved by the ABA board of gover-

ABC Manufacturing Company
1211 Avenue of the Americas
New York, NY 10036

January 15, 19XX

Fulback & Wolsky
9904 M Street NW
Washington, DC 20599

Gentlemen:

Our auditors, Touche Ross & Co., 1633 Broadway, New York, NY 10019, are making an examination of our financial statements for the fiscal year ended December 31, 19XX. In connection
with their examination, we have prepared and furnished to them the attached description and
evaluation of judgments rendered and settlements made, and of certain contingencies involving
matters with respect to which you have been engaged and to which you have devoted substantive attention on behalf of the Company in the form of legal consultation or representation.

For the purpose of your response to this letter, we believe that as to each contingency an amount
in excess of $50,000 would be material, and in total, $250,000. However, determination of materiality with respect to the overall financial statements cannot be made until our auditors complete
their examination. Your response should include matters that existed at December 31, 19XX and
during the period from that date to the date of completion of their examination, which is anticipated to be on or about February 12, 19XX.

Please provide our auditors with the following information:

1. Such explanation, if any, that you consider necessary to supplement the listed judgments
   rendered or settlements made involving the Company from the beginning of this fiscal year
   through the date of your reply.
2. Such explanation, if any, that you consider necessary to supplement the listing of pending or
   threatened litigation, including an explanation of those matters in which your views may differ
   from those stated; and an identification of the omission of any pending or threatened litigation,
   claim, and assessment; or provide a statement that the list of such matters is complete.
3. Such explanation, if any, that you consider necessary to supplement the attached information
   concerning unasserted claims and assessments, including an explanation of those matters in
   which your views may differ from those stated.

We understand that whenever, in the course of performing legal services for us with respect to a
matter recognized to involve an unasserted possible claim or assessment that may call for financial statement disclosure, you have formed a professional conclusion that we should disclose or
consider disclosure concerning such possible claim or assessment, as a matter of professional
responsibility to us, you will so advise us and will consult with us concerning the question of such
disclosure and the applicable requirements of Statement of Financial Accounting Standards No.
5. Please specifically confirm to our auditors that our understanding is correct.

Please specifically identify the nature of and reasons for any limitation on your response.

Very truly yours,

President

**FIG. 26.4 Sample Inquiry Letter to Attorney (See also AU 337A for a general form of inquiry
letter.)**

nors, for lawyers' responses to auditors' inquiries and represents some modifications of positions traditionally held by lawyers. The statement was developed for the guidance of attorneys in responding to auditors' requests, but does not represent conduct required of lawyers. Annex A of the ABA statement provides illustrative forms of response letters for both outside and inside counsel.

The Statement of Policy discusses lawyers' concerns about protecting the confidentiality of lawyer-client communications and protecting open communication between a client and his attorney. Attorneys agree they are the best source of information on asserted claims, and they will respond to normal requests for information from the client.

The Statement of Policy also indicates that an attorney should disclose any limitation on his response. Limitations on an attorney's response might include those dealt with in the following subsections.

Special counsel. A lawyer may respond that he has been engaged not as general counsel, but to work on specific engagements referred to him by the client. This limitation is particularly prevalent with companies that, because of either their specialization or geographic location, retain a variety of attorneys. It is sometimes difficult to distinguish the general counsel for the company from among the many firms. The auditor may view a *general counsel* as one who is knowledgeable about, and responsible for, all legal activities of the client.

Inside general counsel. An enterprise may employ an inside general counsel or *house counsel.* This could be the company's internal legal staff or an outside firm that derives substantially all its business from the enterprise. The inside counsel is as fully bound by the ABA Code of Professional Responsibility as outside counsel. Accordingly, the auditor should obtain the corroborative evidence from this source. However, a response from outside counsel is usually superior audit evidence to that received from inside counsel. If outside counsel has devoted substantive attention to a client's legal matters and refuses to respond to the inquiry, inside general counsel's opinion cannot be substituted (AU 337.08). Whether substantive attention has been given is a matter of the attorney's judgment which the auditor must evaluate. (See the section entitled "Auditing Interpretations" later herein.)

Inability to evaluate litigation. Management or its representatives are responsible for evaluating the degree of probability of an unfavorable outcome as well as the amount or range of potential loss for financial statement purposes. The letter of inquiry to the lawyer requests corroboration of management's estimate. The lawyer may decline to corroborate management's estimate for one reason or another, for example: "The matter is in discovery stage" or "The issues are not yet sufficiently defined." Further, a lawyer may respond with statements that are clearly not acceptable for the auditor's purposes, such as: "The litigation is being defended vigorously and the client has meritorious defenses"; "From what we presently know, it appears that the company has a good chance of prevailing"; "We believe the claim is grossly exaggerated from the evidence available"; or "We are unable to express an opinion but the company believes . . ." These statements do not corroborate the probability of outcome or the amount or range of loss. An auditor receiving such a response may review the matter with the attorney and the client and attempt to obtain a more complete and acceptable response.

If the attorney persists, management and the auditor may obtain other corroborating evidential matter by reviewing with management their procedures and documentation, scanning related files, reviewing results of similar actions, and discussing the matter with inside counsel and, in certain circumstances, other outside counsel who gave substantive attention to the matter. If the auditor cannot obtain satisfaction from the attorney and there is insufficient other corroborating evidential matter to support management's estimate, a qualified opinion, with an explanatory paragraph discussing the reasons for the qualification, should be rendered.

Refusal to furnish information. The lawyer may refuse to furnish the information requested, may refuse to evaluate litigation, or may respond in a manner that can only be interpreted as a refusal. In these instances, the auditor is faced with a limitation of scope and should render an "except for" qualified opinion.

If the lawyer refuses to respond to the request, the auditor may attempt to hold a conference with the attorney and the client to review the matter of the attorney's refusal and to probe his reason for refusing to respond. An attempt to obtain oral confirmation may also be made. If an oral response is received, the auditor should write a letter of understanding of the meeting and send it to the attorney. It may also be desirable to furnish the client a copy of this letter.

If the attorney refuses to attend a conference and refuses to respond, there are no practical ways to obtain the necessary corroborative evidential matter or enough satisfaction to render an unqualified report.

Lawyer as a director/officer. The ABA statement (AU 337C, commentary on ¶ 2) advises that

a lawyer who is also a director or officer of the client would not include information which he received as a director or officer unless the information was also received (or, absent the dual role, would in the normal course be received) in his capacity as legal counsel in the context of his professional engagement. Where the auditor's request for information is addressed to a law firm as a firm, the law firm may properly assume that its response is not expected to include any information which may have been communicated to the particular individual by reason of his serving in the capacity of director or officer of the client.

A reply limiting the response in this manner is acceptable if it does not exclude the lawyer/director entirely. The ABA position was meant to exclude only knowledge the individual might have obtained outside of his professional engagement. The law firm is responsible for including in its response any knowledge the director might have learned in his professional capacity as attorney.

Lawyer's professional responsibility. Before discussing information that would disclose a confidence or require evaluation of a claim, the attorney must discuss with his client the consequences of disclosure, recognizing that an adverse party may assert that any evaluation is an admission of liability. The client should request attorney responses regarding unasserted claims only if the client believes that such claims are probable of assertion and a material loss is reasonably possible. In this regard, the ABA's Statement of Policy (AU 337C, ¶ 6) provides:

> The auditor may properly assume that whenever, in the course of performing legal services for the client with respect to a matter recognized to involve an unasserted possible claim or assessment which may call for a financial statement disclosure, the lawyer has formed a professional conclusion that the client must disclose or consider disclosure concerning such possible claim or assessment, the lawyer, as a matter of professional responsibility to the client, will so advise the client and will consult with the client concerning the question of such disclosure and the applicable requirements of SFAS 5.

The auditor should recognize that this undertaking does not require an attorney to go out of his way to obtain information regarding unasserted possible claims unless they are apparent to him in the performance of legal work for which he is retained and is engaged by a client. The lawyer's responsibilities are to consider an unasserted possible claim if he realizes one exists and to recognize that there may be a requirement for financial statement disclosure; he does not commit to devoting substantive attention to searching for such claims.

Because a lawyer is not considered an expert as to detailed disclosure requirements under SFAS 5, he should notify a responsible officer or employee of the client of an unasserted possible claim that he has concluded must be considered for disclosure to the auditor and should satisfy himself that the officer or employee understands the requirements of SFAS 5. Having done this, the lawyer has fulfilled his commitments unless he has concluded that the unasserted possible claim is probable of assertion; such a claim, if material, must be disclosed in the financial statements.

The ABA Statement of Policy, in referring to disclosure, applies to whether or not the unasserted claim or assessment must be brought to the auditor's attention, and does not refer to the requirements of disclosure under SFAS 5. It is the client's responsibility to evaluate whether financial statement disclosure is required, and it is the auditor's responsibility to evaluate the appropriateness of that disclosure.

Documentation. Responses from attorneys should be retained in the audit working papers. They should be annotated to indicate disposition of significant matters, for example, an item of litigation may be indicated as having been disclosed in the notes to the financial statements, as not material enough to consider for disclosure, or as the cause of a "subject to" opinion. Where conversations with attorneys either supplement or substitute for an attorney's letter, a memorandum documenting the conversations should be prepared and included in the working papers, and a copy should be sent to the attorney for his confirmation. The standard audit letter of representations (AU 333) should include assurances from management that disclosure has been made to the auditor of contingent or other possible liabilities that are probable of assertion (and that must therefore be disclosed in the financial statements in accordance with SFAS 5), or that counsel otherwise has advised should be disclosed.

Auditing Interpretations. Some problems have been encountered in applying the standard attorney's letter. Subsequent to SAS 12, the AICPA issued the following interpretations:

Alternative wording of the illustrative audit inquiry letter to a client's attorney. This interpretation provides an example of a modified Illustrative Letter. This modification is based on a typical situation where management requests the attorney to prepare the list that describes and evaluates pending or threatened litigation, claims, and assessments and also represents that there are no unasserted claims or assessments that are probable of assertion and that, if asserted, would have a reasonable possibility of an unfavorable outcome as specified by SFAS 5, *Accounting for Contingencies.* It also includes a separate "response" section with language that clarifies the auditor's expectations regarding the timing of the attorney's response.

Client has not consulted an attorney. This interpretation provides guidance to the auditor and an example of a representation to be received from the client in circumstances where management has not consulted an attorney.

Use of the client's inside counsel in the evaluation of litigation, claims, and assessments. This interpretation provides guidance to the auditor in circumstances where the client's inside counsel is handling litigation, claims, and assessments either exclusively or in conjunction with outside lawyers.

Assessment of an attorney's evaluation of the outcome of litigation. The ASB has issued an interpretation (AU 9337) providing some examples of attorneys' evaluations concerning litigation that may be considered to provide sufficient clarity that the likelihood of an unfavorable outcome is "remote," even though the attorney does not use that term.

In addition, the interpretation provides examples of attorneys' evaluations that are unclear as to the likelihood of an unfavorable outcome.

AUDITORS' REPORTING ON UNCERTAINTIES

The auditor must evaluate evidence concerning management's accounting and reporting of the uncertainties to determine the appropriate type and form of opinion. If an uncertainty is not appropriately disclosed, an exception may be required in the auditor's report. If the disclosure is in conformity with GAAP, the auditor must still determine whether the effect of the uncertainty is sufficiently material to financial position to require a modified opinion or, in extreme cases, a disclaimer of opinion. The types and forms of auditor's reports are described in Chapter 11.

Materiality

Although specific materiality measurements are not discussed in SFAS 5, the base against which to measure materiality is a factor in determining the type of report to be issued by the auditor. SAS 58 provides that

> Some uncertainties are unusual in nature or infrequent in occurrence and thus more closely related to financial position than to normal recurring operations . . . In such instances, the auditor should consider the possible loss in relation to shareholders' equity and other rele-

vant balance sheet components such as total assets, total liabilities, current assets and current liabilities. [AU 508.29]

However, when an uncertainty is closely related to normal recurring activities, such as in the case of public utility revenues collected but subject to refund, materiality may be measured in relation to the potential effect on both income and financial position. Because future resolution of the uncertainty will not result in a retroactive adjustment of the income being currently reported (A35.102), current income is not exposed to adjustment; net worth is exposed to the future charge against future earnings. Assuming appropriate footnote disclosure is given, the auditor's opinion on the financial statements is usually modified when the effect on net worth may be material (AU 508.31).

If the effect of the contingency may be pervasive as opposed to being isolated and measurable, the auditor may disclaim an opinion on the financial statements. SAS 58 permits such disclaimer, but makes it clear that appropriate disclosure and a modified opinion are enough to adequately inform financial statements users (AU 508.16, fn. 11).

Disclosure criteria are likewise stringent because the financial statements should inform the user of a potentially material charge to future earnings. Thus, for footnote disclosure, the appropriate materiality base may be income from continuing operations or net income. If disclosure is insufficient, an exception for failure to follow GAAP should be taken in the auditors' report.

Going Concern

Underlying financial accounting and reporting is the *going concern* concept. Unless otherwise stated, it is assumed that the reporting entity will continue for a sufficient time to realize its assets and discharge its liabilities in the normal course of business; therefore, use of liquidation values is not appropriate. However, businesses do fail, expecially in recessionary times. Perhaps the most fundamental uncertainty the auditor must evaluate is whether an entity has the ability to continue. Factors usually leading to failure are continuing operating losses and inability to obtain adequate financing. Operating problems may manifest themselves as continued losses, doubt as to future revenues, impairment of operating ability (possibly through legal proceedings or unavailability of essential materials), or seriously ineffective management control over operations. Financing problems may be reflected by a deficiency in working capital, a deficiency in assets, or debt defaults.

The auditor uses the enterprise's earnings and financing history as predictors, with other evidence, to gauge the potential success of future operations and financings. Other evidence includes the liquidity of assets, the prior reliability of budgets and forecasts, and whether the enterprise's current situation will affect its access to credit or equity markets. How long a company might be able to hold out in the face of adversity is also crucial.

Although the auditing literature (AU 508.23–.32) provides that a modified opinion could be issued in every case of a material uncertainty, no matter how extreme, there are situations where an auditor may decide that a disclaimer of opinion is warranted; this may depend on the risk that the financial statements and his relationship thereto may be misunderstood if he issues a less categorical report.

For example, the auditor may conclude that a disclaimer of opinion should be issued when failure may be so imminent, the effect of failure on the financial statements would be pervasive, or the uncertainties are numerous.

The imminence of the uncertainty, as the auditor sees it, is one of the important factors in determining the type of opinion to issue. For example, when it is evident that the entity cannot operate indefinitely if the losses of the past continue, but it can withstand another year of such losses without going out of business, the auditor may determine that a going concern paragraph in his report is not necessary.

Auditor Guidance. The ASB has been studying the auditing and reporting issues related to the going concern assumption. In early 1988, the ASB issued SAS 59, *The Auditor's Consideration of an Entity's Ability to Continue in Existence* (AU 341). This Statement supersedes SAS 34 which covered the same general area and discusses:

1. The time horizon of concern to the auditor,
2. The manner in which an auditor considers continued existence during the audit process,
3. The circumstances that cause an audit report to be modified, and
4. The form of the report modification.

SAS 59 states that the auditor should consider a time horizon not longer than the next year-end reporting date. The prior guidance in SAS 34 was unspecific, and many auditors thought that the horizon should be the date the next annual report would ordinarily be issued, stated perhaps as one year following the date of the auditors' report. In deciding it had to be specific, the ASB chose a normal company closing date, presumably to ease the difficulty of preparing internal forecasts and focusing other considerations on a date at which confirmatory data would normally be prepared. In any event, "surprise failures" may be somewhat lessened in the nine or ten months following the issuance of the annual financial statements.

The SAS indicates that an auditor has a responsibility during an audit to consider conditions and events that might affect a company's continued existence. Some of the audit procedures that might be employed to test a concern about continued existence include:

1. Applying analytical procedures;
2. Reviewing subsequent events;
3. Reviewing compliance with the terms of debt and loan agreements;
4. Reading the minutes of meeting of stockholders, board of directors, and other important committees;
5. Inquiring of an entity's legal counsel about litigation, claims, and assessment;
6. Confirming with related and third parties details of arrangements to provide or maintain financial support to those parties; and
7. Obtaining written representations from management.

Many conditions and events could cause concern about a company's ability to continue operations; these may vary widely in importance and, at times, may be interrelated. Examples include factors that relate to solvency (e.g., negative trends, negative cash flows, or adverse financial ratios) and to indications such as loan defaults, dividend arrears, or debt restructurings. In addition, factors not relating directly to solvency might include loss of key management personnel, labor difficulties, uneconomic long-term commitments, legal proceedings, or legislation. If conditions or events raise questions, the auditor should:

- Gather evidence about potentially mitigating or aggravating factors. The condition of assets, liabilities, and equity may be a signal. Can assets be sold without disrupting operations, factored, or subjected to sale-leaseback arrangements? As to liabilities, are there unused lines of credit available, can loan due dates be extended, or is debt-restructuring feasible? In addition, can poor operations be discarded or can maintenance or other expenditures be delayed? Regarding equity, can dividends be passed, or can more equity capital be secured? Positive responses to some of these questions may lessen the auditor's concern about a company's ability to continue in operation.

- Evaluate management's plans for dealing with conditions or events that raise questions. If it appears to the auditor that adverse circumstances exist, he should consider management's plans, if any, to put into effect any of the steps previously described. If prospective financial information is available and considered relevant, the auditor should also review and evaluate such information.

- Assess whether substantial doubt exists about a company's ability to continue. If, after he has considered management's plans to mitigate the adverse conditions, the auditor believes that substantial doubt remains about the entity's ability to continue, he should consider the financial statement effects. There may be a concern about the recoverability and classification of particular assets or the amounts and classification of particular liabilities.

- Consider the adequacy of disclosure about possible discontinuance. Some of the information that might be disclosed includes:
  - Pertinent conditions giving rise to the assessment of substantial doubt about continued existence,
  - The possible effects of such conditions,
  - Management's evaluation of the significance of those conditions,
  - Other factors, and
  - Management's plans (including relevant prospective financial information).

- Consider the need to modify the audit report. If the auditor concludes that there is substantial doubt about the entity's ability to continue in existence, the audit report should be modified with an additional paragraph to reflect that conclusion. (If the circumstances warrant, the auditor may disclaim an opinion.) If appropriate, the modification should indicate the uncertainty about the recoverability and classification of recorded asset amounts and the amounts and classification of liabilities. A sample report follows:

> The accompanying financial statements have been prepared assuming that Y Company will continue as a going concern. As discussed in Note X to the financial statements, substantial doubt exists at December 31, 1989 as to the ability of Y Company to do so. The financial statements do not include any adjustments to reflect the possible future effects on the recoverability and classification of recorded asset amounts and the amounts and classification of liabilities that might result from the possible inability of Y Company to continue in existence.

AUDITORS' COMMUNICATIONS WITH AUDIT COMMITTEES

As discussed in detail in Chapter 6, a membership rule of the AICPA's SEC Practice Section that took effect on June 30, 1987 requires the auditor to bring significant uncertainties (among other matters) to the attention of the audit committee of an SEC client's board of directors. In so doing, the auditor is to include an assessment of the reasonableness of management's assumptions and estimates related to such uncertainties.

In early 1988, the ASB issued SAS 61, *Communication with Audit Committees* (AU 380). Unlike the SEC Practice Section rule, this SAS is aimed at all audit clients, not only public companies. SAS 61 requires communication of numerous items, including

> estimates that are particularly sensitive because of their significance to the financial statements and because of the possibility that future events affecting them may differ markedly from management's judgements.

Elevating the issue of adequacy of estimates to the audit committee level is clear evidence of the emphasis that will be placed on auditor performance in this area.

27

Prospective and Pro Forma Financial Information

FUTURE-ORIENTED INFORMATION – OVERVIEW

The conduct of business and investing activities in pursuit of future economic benefits has always been the goal of the free market. The achievement of this goal has necessarily required predictions, however informally developed, of customer preferences, changes in costs, shifts in the economy, changes in interest rates, and numerous other factors, all of which are difficult to make.

"When life was simpler," the businessman was closer to his customer and the money markets were much less complex. Many changes in the way business is conducted, including the internationalization of economies, have made it more difficult to plan strategically, and to assess the likelihood that an investment made today will yield acceptable future returns. However, changes in information technology, specifically the dramatic improvements in the ability of smaller and inexpensive computers to rapidly handle voluminous amounts of data, greatly assist managements and investors in dealing with these complexities. Additionally, managements and investors are demanding more soft information; although less reliable than historical cost information, it is often more relevant in making today's investment decisions.

Availability

Some future-oriented information in the form of forecasts commonly is included in information provided to potential investors. For example, it is standard practice to include prospective financial information (PFI) in offerings of limited partnership equity investments and debt offerings of hospitals, sports arenas, and other quasi-governmental entities. In addition, the high level of leveraged buyout activity, with the attendant problem of whether the company incurring a huge debt load can service it, has been the cause of many high-yield bond offering documents containing projections of future operations and cash flows. Even when PFI is not required, including it has become so widespread in these specialized offerings that promoters and underwriters seem to insist on it.

Most companies today routinely develop estimates of their expected future operations and prospects, but only for internal use. Companies that publicly disclose future estimates give only very limited information. The disclosures range from nods or remarks like "That's in the ball park," signifying concurrence with a statement made by an analyst, to comprehensive presentations in the form of financial statements, including a statement of the principal underlying assumptions. Even in this superficial mode, PFI has become a tool in defending against hostile takeovers; a target company may announce its future earnings expectations in the hope of either fending off the attacker or inducing a higher bid.

Future-oriented information about publicly held companies is available today, although much of it must reach investors through professional analysts who evaluate the potential return on investment of particular securities and the related levels of risk. In preparing their analyses, analysts obtain forecasts from management presentations both in public meetings and in private sessions.

Usefulness

The three most important factors affecting the usefulness of future-oriented financial information are (1) the purpose for which the information is intended, (2) the degree of uncertainty inherent in the information, and (3) the extent of disclosure provided. These factors are interrelated. For example, the reader's ability to evaluate the likelihood that predicted results will be achieved (degree of uncertainty) may depend on the extent of disclosure of pertinent information.

Intended Purpose. Some estimates are attempts to predict the impact of expected transactions and events, while others are intended only to facilitate an assessment of the effect of particular events that may or may not happen. In either case, estimates may deal only with some, not all, of the factors that bear on the company's future economic performance. For example, an estimate could be made of the impact of specified raw material cost levels on selling prices, sales volume, and profitability.

The most useful type of future-oriented financial information is that which directly meets the user's particular needs. When these needs are not specified, however, a future operations estimate made by a publicly held company is generally expected to show how the most likely events will affect the company's financial statements.

Degree of Uncertainty. Any prognostication is inherently uncertain, and the degree of uncertainty can vary widely. In some cases, it may be possible to express uncertainty mathematically, but in other cases such precision is beyond reach. In fact, it is usually impossible to identify all the factors that will influence the outcome in question. In such cases, the best way to convey the degree of uncertainty may be simply to disclose the assumptions that underlie the predicted results, and let the reader judge for himself.

Extent of Disclosure. Traditionally, the extent of disclosure of PFI has varied over a broad range, from general statements of factors expected to affect future operations and summaries of management's plans and objectives, to estimates of the dollar amounts of one or more key financial indicators, and even to condensed statements of future operating results and financial position. Each of these kinds of disclosures may be accompanied by a description of the underlying assumptions and other useful evaluative information; then again, there may be no evaluative information.

The PFI disclosed may be of a general nature, but often it concerns only certain factors bearing on a special purpose. Privately held companies, for example, often provide bankers and other creditors with their estimates of future performance and the related rationale. As mentioned earlier, hospitals, sports stadiums, and other public service-oriented projects frequently provide comprehensive estimates of their future prospects when they seek financing through state financing authorities.

Public companies sometimes provide additional, more specific prospective information to professional financial analysts, who use it to develop their views of the merits of investments in the company. Analysts' predictions, frequently widely disseminated, are based in part on opinion and estimates beyond the analysts' control, and may not have been subjected to the discipline and full-disclosure conventions applied to the information that companies formally publish. As a result, the ultimate user has no way to evaluate the quality of the analyst's predictions and assessments available to him.

Generally, the more limited a company's disclosure, the more difficult it is to assess the quality of the information, and hence its reliability. The information may represent no more than the pro forma effect of a hypothetical condition on actual results reported for a past period, for example, disclosure of what the effect of a one percent variation in the prime rate would have been in last year's financial statements. In other cases where limited information is disclosed, it may have been extracted from a comprehensive estimate of expected future results, for example, the effect of a one percent variation in the assumed prime rate on expected operating results for next year.

SEC Position

Traditional Prohibitions. In 1969, an internal study group headed by SEC Commissioner Francis Wheat set out to review the operation of the disclosure provisions of the Securities Act of 1933 and the Securities Exchange Act of 1934, as well as the Commission rules and regulations. The group concluded that no change was called for in the Commission's prohibitive policy on projections, because the information is too uncertain and an unsophisticated person could be misled. Thus the SEC's longstanding policy generally not to permit projections in filings with the Commission remained firmly entrenched.

Subsequently, reconsideration of this policy was signaled in speeches by the late William Casey, who was appointed SEC chairman in December 1971. In late 1972, the SEC's Division of Corporate Finance Division conducted extensive public hearings on the use of estimates, forecasts, or projections of economic performance by publicly held companies. In 1973, the Commission concluded that its policy of prohibiting projections in filings did not prevent their being widely sought by, disclosed to, or relied on by investors; and the Commission expressed concern that not all investors had equal access to material projection information.

SEC Actions. In 1976, the Commission amended its rules to delete the reference to earnings predictions as possibly misleading. Still remaining neutral, however, the SEC did not encourage or discourage the provision of projections. The SEC said it would not object to disclosure in filings of projections made in good faith and having a reasonable basis, if presented in an appropriate format and accompanied by information adequate for investors to make their own judgments.

In typical SEC fashion, issuers were reminded of their responsibilities to make full and prompt disclosure of material facts, and noted that mangement's assessments of the company's future performance may frequently be a material fact.

Advisory Committee Recommendations. The Advisory Committee on Corporate Disclosure, chaired by former commissioner A. A. Sommer, in its final report in November 1977, recommended that the Commission encourage voluntary disclosure of management projections and permit companies considerable latitude on specific disclosures (SEC, 1977). The Commission subsequently adopted this recommendation, but at the same time admonished issuers to make full and prompt disclosure of material facts concerning previously disclosed projections that no longer had a reasonable basis.

Safe Harbor Rule. In 1979, the Commission issued a safe harbor rule covering only projections included in SEC filings or in the annual report to shareholders. Accordingly, only companies that disclose their future performance estimates broadly rather than selectively are legally protected. The Commission thus allows registrants to disclose, in a straightforward manner, estimates of future economic performance, to provide investors with information they would not otherwise have. That the Commission would offer legal protection to companies under these conditions seems totally consistent with its regulatory role of assuring adequate and full disclosure.

The safe harbor rule applies to more than just projections of financial items and disclosed underlying assumptions. It also applies to statements of management plans and objectives, and to MD&A of future performance prospects and the related assumptions.

Safe harbor protection is available to noninvestment company registrants, new registrants that include forward-looking disclosures in an initial registration statement, and third parties retained to review projections. Management, or the third party, is protected so long as the plaintiff does not succeed in showing that the covered statement had no reasonable basis, or was made or reaffirmed in bad faith.

A summary of SEC releases dealing with disclosure of future eonomic performance is shown in Figure 27.1.

Industry Concerns. The publication of future-oriented information by industry in response to the SEC's recommendations continues to be limited. From the point of view of businesses, forward-looking disclosures entail a number of problems:

1. Projections may convey an unwarranted impression of accuracy.
2. Projections are virtually certain to become outdated very quickly. Therefore, to be useful and to avoid misleading the public, they would almost inevitably require frequent updating.
3. Forecasts and projections may be used by competitors to the detriment of the reporting entity.
4. Management may feel compelled to meet published forecasts to the point of making short-run decisions that are not in the shareholders' best interests.
5. Failure of the enterprise to meet its indicated projections could generate stockholder dissatisfaction and possibly litigation.

In view of these concerns, it is not surprising that instances of voluntary forward-looking disclosure have not been significant. This reflects the fact that to most businesses the unresolved practical problems are seen to outweigh the intangible benefits attributable to this type of disclosure.

Management's Discussion and Analysis. Under existing requirements as of mid-1988, the SEC encourages registrants to present forward-looking information on a

Release No.	Date	Summary
33-5362	February 1973	Announcement of a policy change to allow (but not encourage) companies that so choose to disclose their future performance estimates in filings with the commission.
33-5581	April 1975	Issuance for public comment of rule and form proposals for implementing the policy change announced in 1973. Under the proposals, disclosure of future economic performance estimates would not have been made mandatory, but once disclosed, extensive reporting requirements would have been triggered.
33-5699	April 1976	Proposal of Guides 4 and 62 on disclosure of projections of future economic performance, deletion of Rule 14a-9 reference to projections as possibly misleading, and withdrawal of other 1975 rule and form proposals relating to future performance estimates.
33-5992 and 33-5993	November 1978	Issuance of final Guides 5 and 62 on disclosure of projections of future economic performance, and proposal for public comment of a safe harbor rule for projections that would have placed the burden of proof on the defendant. In these releases, the commission first adopted the recommendation of the Advisory Committee on Corporate Disclosure to encourage rather than merely permit the disclosure of future economic performance estimates.
33-6084	June 1979	Adoption of a safe harbor rule for reasonably based projections issued in good faith. The burden of proof is on the plaintiff.

FIG. 27.1 Summary of SEC Releases on Disclosure of Future Economic Performance

voluntary basis. The requirements for MD&A disclosures in general call for discussion of trends that are not expected to continue, and events expected to have a significant impact on cash flow and liquidity—obviously incorporating a large dose of prognostication by management. As more fully discussed in Chapter 4, the information provided in MD&A in reponse to these requirements is quite circumscribed, but nevertheless more than might be obtained in the absence of SEC rules.

An SEC release (33-6711) outstanding since early 1987 asks for comments on, among other matters, the adequacy of current MD&A requirements for forward-looking information, and what effect changes therein might have on litigation involving and liability of auditors, board members, and management.

PROFESSIONAL GUIDELINES

AICPA Guide

For many years, the AICPA has been wrestling with the difficult issue of whether and how CPAs should become associated with their clients' published PFI. When

AICPA committees could not reach a consensus on the entire issue, the subject was segmented into separate aspects. In 1975, the AICPA Management Advisory Services Division issued MAS 3, *Guidelines for Systems for the Preparation of Financial Forecasts*. Also in 1975, the Accounting Standards Division published SOP 75-4, *Presentation and Disclosure of Financial Forecasts*. And in 1980 the AICPA Auditing Standards Division issued a guide entitled *Review of a Financial Forecast*.

However, because of the wide variety of reporting practices followed by CPAs reporting on engagements involving PFI, the AICPA decided to develop guidelines that would apply to types of PFI other than financial forecasts and to engagements other than reviews. A joint effort by the ASB and AcSEC resulted in the issuance of the *Guide for Prospective Financial Statements* (AICPA, 1986j), referred to in this chapter simply as the Guide. This document presents guidelines for the preparation and presentation of financial forecasts and projections, and for accountants' reports thereon.

The Guide supersedes the previously published guidelines, and incorporates the *Statement on Standards for Accountants' Services on Prospective Financial Information* (AU 2100). This standard, issued by the ASB in 1985, established the authoritative guidance for the accountants' role and responsibilities when associated with the issuance of prospective financial information. An accountant complying with the rules in the Guide automatically will comply with the ASB requirements, which are not superseded.

The primary emphasis of the remainder of the PFI portion of this chapter is on these recent guidelines provided by the AICPA. Given the highly judgmental nature of PFI and the many uncertainties inherent in its development and in possible future outcomes, it is critical that the preparer of and accountant involved with PFI be fully conversant with the Guide and adhere to its guidelines as closely as possible.

Types of Prospective Financial Information

There are two types of PFI recognized in the Guide: forecasts and projections. Pro forma financial information is not considered prospective financial information, but rather is a presentation designed to demonstrate the effects of specific future or hypothetical transactions or events on historical financial statements as if the transactions or events had been consummated at an earlier date. Pro forma financial information is discussed at the end of this chapter.

The Guide recognizes that PFI is referred to by a number of different names (i.e., forecasts, projections, feasibility studies, break-even analyses, and budgets); however designated, if the information meets the definitions in the Guide, then the Guide applies and should be followed. The Guide states one major exception: it does not normally apply to engagements involving PFI to be used solely in connection with litigation support services (see Chapter 49).

Forecasts. Financial forecasts are defined as prospective financial statements that are based on a responsible party's assumptions regarding the future conditions and actions that are likely to occur in the period covered. The statements would, therefore, reflect the responsible party's expectations about the future financial position, performance, and cash flows of the entity.

A financial forecast may be expressed as a single point estimate of forecasted results, or as a range. If expressed as a range, the responsible party determines the key assumptions to form the range within which the item or items subject to the assumptions are reasonably expected to fall. The range should be objectively determined and not biased, so that there is a probability of the future outcome falling at or near the limits of the range.

Projections. Financial projections are defined as prospective financial statements that are based on the existence of one or more hypothetical assumptions. A financial projection is generally prepared to evaluate the impact of one or more possible courses of action. In essence it attempts to respond to the question "What if . . . ?" A financial projection relies on the responsible party's assumptions reflecting conditions it expects would exist in the future and courses of action it expects to take, given the hypothetical assumptions. A projection, like a forecast, may contain a range.

The main distinction of a projection from a forecast is the term "hypothetical" – an assumption designed to present a condition or course of action that may not necessarily occur, but which is consistent with the purpose of the projection. An example of a hypothetical is an assumption that a company will receive debt financing; and such an assumption is appropriate if the PFI is being prepared for presentation to a financial institution to assist the company in obtaining that debt financing.

Responsible Party

A responsible party is defined as the person(s) having the responsibility for determining the assumptions necessary for preparation of the prospective financial statement. Generally, this party is management; however, certain outside interested parties such as a potential acquirer may play an instrumental role in the process. An accountant performing PFI services in accordance with professional standards *cannot* be the responsible party without impairing his independence.

Uses

Prospective financial statements are designed either for general or limited use. The intended use of the information dictates the appropriateness of the type of PFI that can be presented.

General Use. Statements intended for general use are defined as prospective financial statements to be distributed broadly to unidentified recipients who do not have access to the responsible party directly, and therefore can neither ask questions about the presentation nor affect the assumptions. For such general purposes, the most useful statements are those that portray the responsible party's expected results.

The *only* prospective financial information applicable in a general use situation is a financial forecast. Because of the high degree of uncertainty regarding the outcome of any hypothetical transaction or event and the inability of the users of the PFI to gather whatever additional information they may consider necessary, projections are *not* considered appropriate for general use.

Limited Use. Statements intended for limited use are defined as prospective financial statements that are distributed to recipients who have the ability to ask questions or negotiate directly with the responsible party. The recipient will generally have the opportunity to play an active role in developing the assumptions. Therefore, both forecasts and projections are appropriate for limited use.

Preparation

Given the difference in the nature of PFI compared to the other types of services provided by accountants, the Guide includes an extensive discussion of the factors that should be considered in providing the appropriate level of professional service. Among these factors are that PFI should be prepared

- In good faith,
- With appropriate care by qualified personnel,
- Using appropriate accounting principles.

The process for preparation should:

- Be based on seeking the best information reasonably available at that time.
- Use information consistent with the plans of the entity.
- Identify the key factors to be used as a basis for assumptions.
- Determine that the assumptions used are appropriate.
- Provide the means to determine the relative effect of variations in the major underlying assumptions.
- Include, where appropriate, the regular, periodic comparison of the PFI with attained results.
- Include adequate review and approval by the responsible party at the appropriate levels of authority.

Presentation

Although different in significant respects, financial forecasts and projections are similar in presentation. The discussion in the following sections presumes that forecasts and projections should be presented similarly, except as otherwise noted.

Format. It is generally preferable to put PFI in the same format as the historical financial statements that would be issued for the periods covered. This eases comparisons by the users of the PFI with historical information during the covered period and with historical information for prior periods. PFI can take one of three forms:

1. It can be prepared in the form of a complete basic set of financial statements, with the normal footnotes replaced by a summary of significant accounting policies and assumptions.

2. The full financial statements may be summarized or condensed (again replacing the footnotes with significant accounting policies and assumptions).

3. It may be limited to significant items if those items would also be presented in the historical financial statements for the period covered by the PFI. The significant items (or equivalent items based on industry practices) are (Guide, § 400.06):

   a. Sales or gross revenues

   b. Gross profit or cost of sales

   c. Unusual or infrequently occurring items

   d. Provisions for income taxes

   e. Discontinued operations or extraordinary items

   f. Income from continuing operations

   g. Net income

   h. Primary and fully diluted earnings per share

   i. Significant changes in financial position (cash flows)

   j. A brief discussion by the responsible party of:

      • What the PFI is intended to present

      • The fact that the assumptions are based on that party's judgment at the date of preparation

      • An indication that the PFI may not necessarily be achieved

   k. Summary of significant assumptions

   l. Summary of significant accounting principles and policies

The first nine items (a through i) in the third format approach represent the minimum ingredients necessary in a forecast. A presentation that eliminates any one of these items from the PFI, when it would be included in historical financial statements, would be considered a partial presentation. In that situation, the PFI is *not* appropriate for general use. However, if any of the excluded items can be derived from the information included, the PFI would not be considered a partial presentation. The last three items (j, k, and l) must accompany all prospective financial statements. The exclusion of any of these items would make the presentation deficient because of inadequate disclosure.

In addition, every page of the forecast should include a statement referring the reader to the summary of significant accounting policies and assumptions.

Figures 27.2 and 27.3 present examples from the Guide of significant assumptions for a financial forecast and a financial projection, respectively.

Accounting Principles and Policies. A summary of significant accounting principles and policies must be included as a disclosure item. Generally, PFI should be prepared on a basis that is consistent with the accounting policies expected to be used in the historical financial statements for the period covered by the PFI. It occasionally may be appropriate, however, to use a different basis of accounting in the PFI; for example, PFI prepared on a cash basis may be used if cash flow is considered more relevant to the user. In situations where the prospective basis of accounting differs from the historical basis, this fact should be disclosed, including the fact that the PFI basis is not in conformity with GAAP.

XYZ COMPANY, INC.
Summary of Significant Forecast Assumptions and Accounting Policies
Year Ending December 31, 19X3

This financial forecast presents, to the best of management's knowledge and belief, the Company's expected financial position, results of operations, and changes in financial position (cash flows), for the forecast period. Accordingly, the forecast reflects its judgment as of February 17, 19X3, the date of this forecast, of the expected conditions and its expected course of action. The assumptions disclosed herein are those that management believes are significant to the forecast. There will usually be differences between forecasted and actual results, because events and circumstances frequently do not occur as expected, and those differences may be material. The comparative historical information for 19X1 and 19X2 is extracted from the Company's financial statements for those years. Those financial statements should be read for additional information.

a. **Summary of Significant Accounting Policies.** (not illustrated)

b. **Sales.** The overall market for the Company's products has grown over the past five years at an average rate of 2 percent above the actual increase in gross national product, and the Company's market share has remained steady at 14 to 16 percent. Based on a recent market study of demand for the Company's products, sales are forecasted to increase 11 percent from 19X2 (which is 2 percent above the Department of Commerce Bureau of Economic Analysis estimate of the rise in gross national product in the forecast period), with a market share of 15 percent and unit price increased to cover a significant portion of forecasted increases in cost of manufacturing.

c. **Cost of Sales**

   Materials. Materials used by the Company are expected to be readily available, and the Company has generally used producer associations' estimates of prices in the forecast period to forecast material costs. The price for copper, a major raw material in the Company's products, recently has been disrupted by political events in certain principal producer countries. As a result, industry estimates of copper prices in the forecast period range from 15 to 30 percent above 19X2 prices. The Company expects to be able to assure sufficient supplies and estimates that the cost of copper will increase by 22 percent over 19X2. However, due to the uncertainties noted above, the realization of the forecast is particularly sensitive to the actual price increase. A variation of five percentage points in the actual increase above or below the assumed increase would affect forecasted net earnings by approximately $485,000.

   Labor. The Company's labor union contract, which covers substantially all manufacturing personnel, was negotiated in 19X2 for a three-year period. Labor costs are forecasted based upon the terms of that contract.

d. **Plant and Equipment and Depreciation Expense.** Forecasted additions to plant and equipment, $4.4 million, comprise principally the regular periodic replacement of manufacturing plant and vehicles at suppliers' quoted estimated prices and do not involve a significant change in manufacturing capacity or processes. Depreciation is forecasted on an item-by-item basis.

e. **Selling, General, and Administrative Expenses.** The principal types of expense within this category are salaries, transportation costs, and sales promotion. Salaries are forecasted on an individual-by-individual basis, using expected salary rates in the forecast period. Transportation costs comprise principally the use of contract carriers; volume is forecasted based

(continued)

FIG. 27.2 Sample Summary of Significant Forecast Assumptions
Source: AICPA, 1986j. Guide for Prospective Financial Statements, § 410.05.

upon the sales and inventory forecasts (including forecasts by sales outlet), and rates are forecasted to rise by 16 percent over 19X2, based upon trucking industry forecasts. Sales promotion costs are expected to increase by approximately 14 percent above the level of 19X2 in order to meet increased competition and maintain market share. The level of other expenses is expected to remain the same as in 19X2, adjusted for expected increases in line with the consumer price index (assumed to rise 9 percent on the mean of [*several widely used estimates*]).

f. **Miscellaneous Income.** The forecast assumes royalty income of $950,000 will be received based on an agreement under which the Company is to receive a minimum of $950,000 for the first 10,000,000 units produced under its patented die casting process and $.05/unit above that level. Management believes it is unlikely that production will exceed 10,000,000 units. The balance of miscellaneous income is assumed to come from investment of excess cash and other sources.

g. **Bank Borrowings and Interest Expenses.** The forecast assumes that the Company will obtain an extension of existing short-term lines of credit at terms comparable to those in effect in 19X2 (2 percent over prime rate). The Company used the arithmetic mean of [*three widely used estimates*] of bank prime rate during the forecast period (ranging from 12 percent to 14 percent) to estimate prime rate at 13 percent. However, because of recent volatility in the financial markets, short-term interest rates have been very unstable, ranging from 12 percent to 17 percent during 19X2.

The Company has forecasted additional long-term borrowings of $6 million and has entered into preliminary negotiations with its bankers for this financing. The borrowings are principally to fund purchases of plant and equipment and additions to other long-term assets and will be secured by such additions. Based upon the preliminary negotiations, the Company has assumed that the additional long-term financing will bear interest at 14 percent.

h. **Income Taxes.** The provision for income taxes is computed using the statutory rates in effect during 19X2, which are not expected to change, and assuming investment tax credit on qualifying investments at rates in effect in 19X2.

i. **Dividend.** The Company's normal dividend policy is to pay out the previous year's dividend increased to the extent of at least one-third of any increase in profits over the previous year, provided the board of directors considers that the Company's cash and working capital position will not be adversely affected. The dividend has been forecasted at $1.50 per share, assuming an increased payout over 19X2 of one-third of the excess of forecasted net earnings for the year ending December 31, 19X3, above those of 19X2.

FIG. 27.2 (continued)

Where a different basis of accounting would cause a difference in the results of operations, it may be useful to reconcile the results of operations on the different basis. Also, if an accounting change is expected during the period covered by the PFI, the change should be reflected in the PFI in the same fashion as it would be shown in historical financial statements.

Presentation of Amounts. Most PFI may normally be expressed in a specific monetary amount as a single point estimate of prospective results; but information

ABC COMPANY, INC.

Summary of Significant Assumptions Employed in Preparation of the Statement of Projected Results of Operations and Cash Flow Assuming Construction of an Additional Plant

For the Five Years Ending December 31, 19X7

This financial projection of operations and cash flow assuming construction of an additional plant present, to the best of management's knowledge and belief, the expected results of operations, changes in financial position, and cash flow for the projection period if such a plant were constructed to increase production capacity by approximately 20 percent. Accordingly, the projection reflects its judgment as of October 24, 19X2, the date of this projection, of the expected conditions and its expected course of action if such plant were constructed. The presentation is designed to provide information for potential bank financing of the construction of the additional plant and cannot be considered to be a presentation of expected future results. Accordingly, this projection may not be useful for other purposes. The assumptions disclosed herein are those that management believes are significant to the projection; however, management has not decided that it will construct such a plant. Even if the plant were constructed, there will usually be differences between projected and actual results, because events and circumstances frequently do not occur as expected, and those differences may be material.

a. **Summary of Significant Accounting Policies.** (not illustrated)

b. **Hypothetical Assumption—Increase in Production Capacity by Construction of a New Plant.** The projection is based on the assumption that production capacity will be increased by approximately 20 percent by the construction of a 160,000 square foot production facility in Richmond, Virginia.

   Construction on the new plant is projected to begin in February 19X3 and be completed by June 30, 19X4, at a total cost of $10,000,000 including construction-period interest of $1,300,000. Production cost estimates and the projected completion date have been estimated based on competitive bids received.

   The decision to proceed with the project and awarding of contracts will depend on the completion of financing arrangements.

c. **Sales.** The overall market for the Company's products has grown over the past five years at an average rate of 2 percent above the actual increase in gross national product, and the Company's market share has remained steady at 14 to 16 percent. Based upon a recent market study of demand for the Company's products, sales are projected to increase 11 percent per annum from 19X2 to 19X4 (which is consistent with a rate 2 percent above the Department of Commerce Bureau of Economic Analysis' estimate of the rise in gross national product in the projection period), with a market share of 15 percent and unit prices increased to cover projected increases in cost of maufacturing. Based upon the study, an additional 15 percent increase in sales is projected to occur beginning in 19X5 and will be met by the added capacity resulting from the plant expansion.

d. **Cost of Sales**

   Materials. Materials used by the Company are expected to be readily available, and the Company has generally used producer associations' estimates of prices in the projection period to project material costs. The Company expects to be able to assure a sufficient supply of materials and estimates that the cost of materials will increase by 12 percent per annum.

(continued)

FIG. 27.3   Sample Summary of Significant Projection Assumptions
Source: AICPA, 1986j. Guide for Prospective Financial Statements, § 410.05.

Labor. The Company's labor union contract, which covers substantially all manufacturing personnel, will be subject to renegotiation in 19X6. Labor costs until that time are projected based on the existing contract. For 19X7, labor costs, including fringe benefits, are projected to increase 19 percent per year above the 19X6 level. The outcome of the projection is particularly sensitive to variances in such labor costs. For each percentage point variance from the projected increase, net income and cash will vary by approximately $380,000.

e. **Plant and Equipment and Depreciation Expense.** Projected additions to plant and equipment, other than the assumed plant expansion, are principally the regular periodic replacement of manufacturing plant and vehicles at suppliers' quoted estimated prices and do not involve any significant changes in manufacturing capacity or processes. Depreciation is projected on an item-by-item basis. Depreciation on the new facility is projected on a straight-line basis over twenty years.

f. **Selling, General, and Administrative Expense.** The principal types of expense within this category are salaries, transportation costs, and sales promotion. Salaries are projected on an individual-by-individual basis, using expected salary rates in the projection period. Transportation costs are principally for contract carriers; volume is projected based upon the sales and inventory projections, and rates are forecasted to rise by 16 percent per year based upon trucking industry forecasts. Sales promotion costs are expected to increase in line with the consumer price index, as is the level of other expenses.

g. **Bank Borrowings and Interest Expense.** The projection assumes that the Company will obtain an extension of existing short-term lines of credit at terms comparable to those in effect in 19X2 (2 percent over prime rate). The Company used the arithmetic mean of [*three widely used estimates*] of bank prime rate during the projection period (ranging from 12 percent to 14 percent) to estimate prime rate at 13 percent. The Company projects additional long-term borrowing of $10 million to finance the planned plant expansion (including $1,300,000 of construction-period capitalized interest) and has entered into preliminary negotiations with its bankers for this financing. Based upon the preliminary negotiations, the Company has assumed that the additional long-term financing will bear interest at 14 percent.

h. **Miscellaneous Income.** The projection assumes that royalty income of $950,000 will be received annually based on an agreement under which the Company is to receive a minimum of $950,000 for the first 10,000,000 units produced under its patented die casting process and $.05/unit above that level. Management believes it is unlikely that production will exceed 10,000,000 units in any of the projection periods.

i. **Income Taxes.** The provision for income taxes is computed using the statutory rates in effect during 19X2, which are not expected to change. The Company anticipates that it will take investment tax credits on the machinery and equipment to be installed in the new plant when the plant is placed in service in 19X4.

j. **Dividend.** The Company's normal dividend policy is to pay out the previous year's dividend increased to the extent of at least one-third of any increase in profits over the previous year, provided the board of directors considers that the Company's cash flow and working-capital position will not be adversely affected.

FIG. 27.3 *(continued)*

may also be expressed as a range within which the affected items are expected to fall. If a range is given, the outcome should not have a bias toward either limit.

If forecasts and projections are included in the same presentation each should be clearly labeled to highlight the inherent differences that exist between the two.

Sensitivity of Assumptions. Disclosure of the sensitivity of the prospective results to significant assumptions (e.g., interest rates or occupancy rates) may be included with the PFI, but it is not required. A sensitivity analysis could be used to demonstrate the expected effect of a change in a key assumption on the forecasted or projected results.

The primary concern relates to those assumptions that are particularly subject to large variations over time, or that would have a significant impact on the PFI even though variations may be small. If there is a reasonable possibility that such variability or impact may occur, these assumption attributes should be disclosed.

In addition, forecasts can be supplemented with schedules of projections that show, for the same period, differences in operating results and financial position resulting from assumptions other than those expected to materialize. If the use of the statement is general, presentations of projections, as a supplement to forecasts, are only allowed for the period for which the forecasts are shown. In limited use presentations, projections can be shown as a supplement to forecasts for additional periods beyond the forecasted period.

If any hypotheticals are included in the forecast assumptions, they should also be disclosed.

Period to Be Covered. PFI reliability decreases as the prospective time period increases. The Guide suggests that the PFI should cover at least one year of "normal" operations to be useful.

In presenting PFI, both the industry in which the entity operates and the potential use of the prospective information should be considered in determining the period to be presented. In other words, industry operating cycles as well as industry practice should be a consideration. In addition, the user's evaluation criteria, such as return on investment, should be considered.

It may not always be practical to present prospective financial information for a sufficient number of periods to demonstrate achievability of anticipated results. In such situations, the presentation should, at a minimum, include a discussion of such later results. For example, if the PFI does not extend to the period in which the disposition of a significant asset would occur, either supplemental information or a discussion of the disposition normally would be presented.

Dating and Updating. The date of the completion of the prospective financial information should be disclosed to assist users in determining its currentness.

Prospective financial information is not usually expected to be updated. In fact, the responsible party generally should state that it does not intend to update the information. However, if the responsible party determines that updated PFI is required, there should be a discussion in the assumptions section describing the reasons for updating. In addition, if the responsible party discovers that previously issued PFI is potentially misleading or is erroneous, users who are known to be relying on it should be notified and, where possible, new information should be issued.

Historical or Pro Forma Financial Statements. For purposes of comparison, it is often useful to present either historical or pro forma financial information along with the PFI. However, prospective financial information should be clearly labeled to preclude a reader from confusing it with either historical or pro forma financial information.

Materiality. The concept of materiality is applied to PFI in the same manner as it is applied to historical information. However, materiality must be assessed in relation to the level of uncertainty and precision of the PFI, which obviously will not have the same degree of precision as historical information.

Guide Amendments

As of August 1988, the AICPA was working on an amendment to the AICPA *Guide for Prospective Financial Statements* to be released in the form of an SOP. The amendment would address questions that have arisen in practice, tentatively including the following:

• Reporting on financial forecasts which include a projected sale of an entity's real estate investment.
• Sales prices assumed in a projection of the sale of an entity's real estate investment.
• Reporting on information accompanying a financial forecast in an accountant-submitted document.
• Financial projections included in general use documents.
• Support for tax assumptions.
• Periods covered by an accountant's report on prospective financial information.

THE ACCOUNTANT'S ROLE

The services an accountant may perform for PFI engagements and guidance concerning those services are described in the AICPA Guide (§§ 500–1000). These services include compilations, examinations, and agreed-upon procedures. An accountant may also perform procedures that exceed those described in the guide, for example, as part of a financial feasibility study. The Guide, however, applies only to those services performed in compiling or examining the prospective financial statements included in the financial feasibility study and to the resulting report. An illustration of a report on an examination of a financial forecast expanded to describe a feasibility study is presented in Section 720.20 of the Guide.

Compilations

The AICPA Guide describes a compilation as a professional service that involves (§ 600.01):

a. Assembling, to the extent necessary, the financial forecast [or projection] based on the responsible party's assumptions.

b. Performing the required compilation procedures, including reading the financial forecast [or projection] with its summaries of significant assumptions and accounting policies, and considering whether they appear to be (i) presented in conformity with AICPA guidelines, and (ii) not obviously inappropriate.

c. Issuing a compilation report.

Required Procedures. A compilation is not designed to provide any assurance on the PFI, or on the reasonableness of the underlying assumptions. In fact, the brevity of the compilation procedures generally cannot assure that the accountant would discover significant issues that might be found in an examination rather than a compilation.

In performing a compilation of prospective financial information, an accountant should:

1. Determine the accounting principles used in the preparation of the PFI and whether they differ from those applied in the historical statements.

2. Determine the manner in which the responsible party has identified the key factors and developed its assumptions.

3. Determine the significant assumptions used as the basis for the information.

4. Determine whether there are any obvious internal inconsistencies among the assumptions.

5. Test clerical accuracy and recompute on a test basis the translation of the assumptions into the PFI.

6. Read the PFI and determine:

  • Whether it is presented in conformity with the AICPA presentation guidelines; and

  • Whether it appears to be appropriate in relation to his knowledge of the entity, the industry and the expected future conditions and actions.

7. If a significant part of the prospective period has passed, determine (and evaluate) the actual results of operations and cash flows in relation to the PFI.

8. Obtain written representations from the responsible party regarding the assumptions relied on and the basis and support for the approach and expectations used in preparing the PFI.

9. Upon the completion of the above procedures, consider whether the information received, including representations, is appropriate, complete, and not misleading. If concern exists, additional or revised information should be obtained.

Optional Procedures. Because the required procedures for compilation of a forecast or projection are quite limited, the accountant may want to perform additional procedures that go beyond the Guide to develop a greater level of comfort. These might include some or all of the procedures discussed in the following sections.

Understanding the process. To aid in his understanding of the entire process used by the responsible party in preparing the prospective financial information, the accountant performing a compilation could:

1. Determine whether the responsible party's process for developing the prospective financial information is consistent with the AICPA guidelines.
2. Identify and document the client's preparation process through inquiry, observation, review of manuals, memoranda, instructions, and forms used (if any), analysis of models and statistical techniques (if used), and review of documentation. (How were key factors identified and assumptions developed?)
3. Determine and document the responsible party's review and approval procedures (i.e., how are errors prevented or detected?).
4. Assess whether assumptions have been approved by the appropriate person(s) and whether they address and are consistent with the key factors.
5. Determine if the accounting principles used to prepare the prospective information are consistent with previous historical financial statements (if any) and those expected to be used in historical statements to be prepared for the prospective period, and are comparable with those typically used in the industry.
6. Determine whether prior period financial information is taken into consideration. Compare prospective information to the prior period and obtain explanations of differences.
7. Evaluate risks inherent in the business and the sensitivity of the prospective information to variations in particular assumptions.

Evaluating assumptions. In evaluating the assumptions used in the preparation of the PFI, the accountant performing a compilation could:

1. Identify key factors and evaluate the completeness of the assumptions used to quantify the factors.

   a. Read appropriate documents such as board of directors minutes, budgets, contracts, and policy statements, noting consistency of the entity's plans and related decisions with assumptions.
   b. Compare the factors used in preparing PFI to factors that influenced historical financial results.
   c. Compare the factors used in the PFI to those used in available financial forecasts of other entities in the same industry.

2. Determine if there are any additional factors or changes in assumptions about factors that should have been considered. Determine that the assumptions used adequately address these factors.
3. Relying on knowledge of the entity and its business, consider any particularly risky or sensitive aspects of the business (such as market, competition, lease terms, and length of time of forecast or projection period).
4. In the case of projections, evaluate all hypotheticals for appropriateness, determining whether all relevant and critical internal/external sources of information (support) have been considered (e.g., existing agreements, historical information, market studies and appraisals).

5. Compare historical financial statements prepared for an expired part of the period to the prospective information, noting any deviations and their potential effect on the PFI.

6. Perform a review of the tax provision in the forecast or projection or obtain a tax opinion from the entity's tax counsel.

Evaluating preparation and presentation. The accountant performing a compilation could evaluate the preparation and presentation of the prospective information as follows:

1. Determine that prospective information is internally consistent and reflects the effect of each assumption on all related prospective amounts.

2. Determine that prospective information is consistent with the content of the offering memorandum (if applicable).

3. Determine that the assumptions discussed were used in the prospective information and are adequately described.

4. Determine that the presentation is in conformity with the AICPA guidelines.

5. Compare with results of operations for any significant part of the prospective period that has expired.

6. Determine and document range variables. Is the relative impact of a variation disclosed for each material, sensitive assumption?

Reporting. The accountant's standard report on a compilation of prospective financial information should include:

1. An identification of the PFI presented.

2. A statement that the accountant has compiled the PFI in accordance with AICPA standards.

3. A statement that a compilation is limited in scope and does not allow the accountant to express an opinion or any other form of assurance on the PFI.

4. A caveat that the PFI results may not be achieved.

5. A statement that the accountant assumes no responsibility to update his report for subsequent events.

The standard report is to be modified if presentation deficiencies exist or required disclosures are omitted.

Presented in Figure 27.4 and 27.5 are sample standard reports appearing in the Guide on the compilation of a forecast and the compilation of a projection.

Examinations

The objective of an examination is to provide the accountant with a basis for reporting whether the prospective financial statements were properly prepared relying on the stated assumptions, whether those assumptions are reasonable and have adequate support, and whether the presentation conforms with AICPA standards. The AICPA Guide describes an examination of a financial forecast or projection as a professional service that involves (§ 500.06):

We have compiled the accompanying forecasted balance sheet, statements of income, retained earnings, and [cash flows] of XYZ Company as of December 31, 19XX, and for the year then ending, in accordance with standards established by the American Institute of Certified Public Accountants.

A compilation is limited to presenting in the form of a forecast information that is the representation of management and does not include evaluation of the support for the assumptions underlying the forecast. We have not examined the forecast and, accordingly, do not express an opinion or any other form of assurance on the accompanying statements or assumptions. Furthermore, there will usually be differences between the forecasted and actual results, because events and circumstances frequently do not occur as expected, and those differences may be material. We have no responsibility to update this report for events and circumstances occurring after the date of this report.

FIG. 27.4   Standard Compilation Report on a Forecast
Source: AICPA, 1986j. Guide for Prospective Financial Statements, *§ 620.02.*

a. Evaluating the preparation of the financial forecast [or projection].

b. Evaluating the support underlying the assumptions.

c. Evaluating the presentation of the financial forecast [or projection] for conformity with AICPA presentation guidelines.

d. Issuing an examination report.

In contrast to a compilation it is essential that the accountant, in the performance of an examination of prospective financial statements, carefully challenge the reasonableness and appropriateness of the underlying assumptions. The following is a summarization of the procedures for the conduct of an examination as discussed in the Guide.

Procedures. In planning the examination, the accountant should consider and document the following:

1. The accounting principles to be applied and the type of presentation to use.
2. The expected level of attestation risk related to the prospective financial statements, that is, the risk that the accountant unknowingly relies on an assertion that is materially misstated.
3. Initial judgments about materiality thresholds.
4. Specific items within the prospective financial statements that may require revision or adjustment.
5. Situations that may require extending or modifying the examination procedures.
6. Knowledge of the client's business and industry.
7. The responsible party's level of experience in preparing PFI.
8. The time period covered by the prospective financial statements.
9. The process by which the responsible party develops its PFI.

The accountant should perform appropriate procedures to provide reasonable assurance that the:

We have compiled the accompanying projected balance sheet, statements of income, retained earnings, and [cash flows] of XYZ Company as of December 31, 19XX, and for the year then ending, in accordance with standards established by the American Institute of Certified Public Accountants.

The accompanying projection and this report were prepared *for* [state special purpose, for example, "the DEF National Bank for the purpose of negotiating a loan to expand XYZ Company's plant"] and should not be used for any other purpose.

A compilation is limited to presenting in the form of a projection information that is the representation of management and does not include evaluation of the support for the assumptions underlying the projection. We have not examined the projection and, accordingly, do not express an opinion or any other form of assurance on the accompanying statements or assumptions. Furthermore, even if [describe hypothetical assumption, for example, "the loan is granted and the plant is expanded"] there will usually be differences between the projected and actual results, because events and circumstances frequently do not occur as expected, and those differences may be material. We have no responsibility to update this report for events and circumstances occurring after the date of this report.

FIG. 27.5 Standard Compilation Report on a Projection
Source: AICPA, 1987j. Guide for Prospective Financial Statements, § 620.02.

1. Presentation is properly based on the identified assumptions.
2. Computations made are mathematically accurate.
3. Assumptions are internally consistent.
4. Accounting principles used in the PFI and the accounting principles expected to be used in the historical financial statements for the same time period are consistent with those used in the most recent historical financial statements. If they differ it must be determined that they are consistent with the purpose of the presentation.
5. The appropriate AICPA guidelines have been applied to the PFI.
6. Assumptions have been adequately disclosed.

If reasonable assurance cannot be achieved by the foregoing procedures the accountant must determine and implement an appropriate course of action to eliminate the problem.

Understanding the Process. In performing an examination of PFI the accountant should review and understand the process used by the responsible party in preparing the PFI and in so doing perform the related procedures for a compilation engagement. In addition, he must identify and test controls incorporated into the process to prevent or detect errors.

Evaluating Assumptions and Presentation. In evaluating assumptions used in the preparation of the PFI, the accountant should perform the related procedures for a compilation engagement and, in addition:

We have examined the accompanying forecasted balance sheet, statements of income, retained earnings, and [cash flows] of XYZ Company as of December 31, 19XX, and for the year then ending. Our examination was made in accordance with standards for an examination of a forecast established by the American Institute of Certified Public Accountants and, accordingly, included such procedures as we considered necessary to evaluate both the assumptions used by management and the preparation and presentation of the forecast.

In our opinion, the accompanying forecast is presented in conformity with guidelines for presentation of a forecast established by the American Institute of Certified Public Accountants, and the underlying assumptions provide a reasonable basis for management's forecast. However, there will usually be differences between the forecasted and actual results, because events and circumstances frequently do not occur as expected, and those differences may be material. We have no responsibility to update this report for events and circumstances occurring after the date of this report.

FIG. 27.6 Standard Examination Report on a Forecast
Source: AICPA, 1986j. Guide for Prospective Financial Statements, *§ 720.02.*

We have examined the accompanying projected balance sheet, statements of income, retained earnings, and [cash flows] of XYZ Company as of December 31, 19XX, and for the year then ending. Our examination was made in accordance with standards for an examination of a projection established by the American Institute of Certified Public Accountants and, accordingly, included such procedures as we considered necessary to evaluate both the assumptions used by management and the preparation and presentation of the projection.

The accompanying projection and this report were prepared for [state special purpose, for example, "the DEF National Bank for the purpose of negotiating a loan to expand XYZ Company's plant"] and should not be used for any other purpose.

In our opinion, the accompanying projection is presented in conformity with guidelines for presentation of a projection established by the American Institute of Certified Public Accountants, and the underlying assumptions provide a reasonable basis for management's projection [describe the hypothetical assumption, for example, "assuming the granting of the requested loan for the purpose of expanding XYZ Company's plant as described in the summary of significant assumptions"]. However, even if [describe hypothetical assumption, for example, "the loan is granted and the plant is expanded"], there will usually be differences between the projected and actual results, because events and circumstances frequently do not occur as expected, and those differences may be material. We have no responsibility to update this report for events and circumstances occurring after the date of this report.

FIG. 27.7 Standard Examination Report on a Projection
Source: AICPA, 1986j. Guide for Prospective Financial Statements, *§ 720.02P.*

1. Trace support for key factors to sources to determine if those sources of information were actually used. Evaluate appropriateness of support and test support, especially if developed internally.
2. Evaluate whether the assumptions are adequately supported. In the case of projections, hypotheticals should be critically evaluated for appropriateness because of their inherently higher level of uncertainty.

3. Determine whether sufficient and appropriate internal and external sources of information (support) have been considered (e.g., existing agreements, historical information, market studies, and appraisals). Investigate alternative sources of support.

4. Consider alternative approaches to developing assumptions to corroborate the appropriateness of the assumptions and the results of applying them.

5. Evaluate whether there is a reasonable basis for the PFI over the entire time period covered.

6. Confirm the information supporting key assumptions with external sources.

7. Inquire as to the professional standing of experts who supply support for key assumptions. As necessary, use another expert to corroborate findings. Data submitted to the expert should be reviewed for consistency with the PFI.

8. Obtain a letter from client's legal counsel, if appropriate.

The accountant should evaluate the preparation and presentation of the PFI by performing the related procedures for a compilation engagement and, in addition, compare amounts with source documents, tracing the aggregate information to the amounts in the PFI.

Review of Offering Document. If the PFI is to be included in an offering document for the sale or exchange of securities, the accountant should read the offering memorandum or document and:

1. Determine that it is consistent with the prospective information and notes thereto.

2. Obtain, if available, a recent certified balance sheet for the general partner(s), a partnership, or corporation, (applicable to limited partnership offerings).

3. Obtain, if available, certified financial statements showing at least one year's operating history of the entity.

4. Determine whether the prospective information is distinguished from historical financial statements in the presentation.

Reporting. The accountant's standard report on an examination of prospective financial information should include:

1. A discussion of the type of PFI presented.

2. A statement that the examination was made in accordance with AICPA standards, and a brief description of those standards.

3. The accountant's opinion that the presentation of the PFI is in conformity with AICPA guidelines and that the assumptions used provide a reasonable basis for the forecast, or for the projection given the hypotheticals.

4. A caveat that the PFI results may not be achieved.

5. A statement that the accountant has no continuing responsibility for updates to reflect events that occur subsequent to the issuance of the report.

If the accountant believes the PFI departs from AICPA presentation guidelines, a qualified opinion or an adverse opinion should be issued. An adverse opinion should be issued if a significant assumption is not disclosed or any underlying key assumption that materially affects the PFI does not provide a reasonable basis for the forecast (or for a projection, if the assumptions do not provide a reasonable basis for the presentation, given the hypotheticals). A disclaimer is appropriate if the accountant is precluded from applying necessary procedures.

Presented in Figures 27.6 and 27.7 are samples of standard reports provided in the AICPA Guide on an examination of a forecast and projection, respectively.

Agreed-Upon Procedures

In general terms, the procedures to be performed by the accountant are clearly defined and are limited to those that have been agreed upon by the accountant and a *user* of the information. This agreement establishes the scope of the accountant's involvement and the degree of his association with the resulting information.

The AICPA Guide describes an engagement to apply agreed-upon procedures specifically applicable to a financial forecast or projection as a professional service that involves (§ 500.08):

a. Having the specified users participate in establishing the nature and scope of the engagement and take responsibility for the adequacy of the procedures to be performed by the accountant.

b. Applying the agreed-upon procedures.

c. Issuing a report that indicates it is limited in use and intended solely for the specified users, enumerates the procedures performed, states the accountant's findings, and refers to conformity with the arrangements made with the specified users.

A financial forecast or projection to which agreed-upon procedures are applied must include a summary of significant assumptions.

Presented in Figure 27.8 is an example of an accountant's report on applying agreed-upon procedures to a financial forecast.

Preparation Assistance

Accountants may assist clients in preparing prospective financial statements. In fact, they may and should provide such assistance if the participation in the preparation process does not affect their objectivity and independence. To assure that objectivity and independence are not compromised, management must accept responsibility for defining the rationale employed and for selecting the assumptions to be used. In other words, accountants can and should make recommendations, but not decisions. Generally, reports on compilations or examinations should not refer to preparation assistance rendered by the accountant to management. In certain "limited use" situations such a reference can be made, but it should not be done in a way that implies additional responsibility on the part of the accountant.

SEC Engagements

In a "No Action" letter dated May 26, 1987, the SEC staff stated that an accounting firm's independence would be impaired if it assisted in the preparation of a client's

---

Board of Directors—XYZ Corporation
Board of Directors—ABC Company

At your request, we have performed certain agreed-upon procedures, as enumerated below, with respect to the forecasted balance sheet, statements of income, retained earnings, and [cash flows] of DEF Company, a subsidiary of ABC Company, as of December 31, 19XX, and for the year then ending. These procedures, which were specified by the Boards of Directors of XYZ Corporation and ABC Company, were performed solely to assist you in connection with the proposed sale of DEF Company to XYZ Corporation. It is understood that this report is solely for your information and should not be used by those who did not participate in determining the procedures.

a. With respect to forecasted rental income, we compared the assumptions about expected demand for rental of the housing units to demand for similar housing units at similar rental prices in the city area in which DEF Company's housing units are located.

b. We tested the forecast for mathematical accuracy.

Because the procedures described above do not constitute an examination of prospective financial statements in accordance with standards established by the American Institute of Certified Public Accountants, we do not express an opinion on whether the prospective financial statements are presented in conformity with AICPA presentation guidelines or on whether the underlying assumptions provide a reasonable basis for the presentation.

In connection with the procedures referred to above, no matters came to our attention that caused us to believe that rental income should be adjusted or that the forecast is mathematically inaccurate. Had we performed additional procedures or had we made an examination of the forecast in accordance with standards established by the American Institute of Certified Public Accountants, matters might have come to our attention that would have been reported to you. Furthermore, there will usually be differences between the forecasted and actual results, because events and circumstances frequently do not occur as expected, and those differences may be material. We have no responsibility to update this report for events and circumstances occurring after the date of this report.

FIG. 27.8 Accountant's Report on the Application of Agreed Upon Procedures
Source: AICPA, 1986j. Guide for Prospective Financial Statements, *§ 820.04, Sample Report 1.*

financial projection for the specific limited use of obtaining a bank loan. The example used by the SEC was as follows: The accounting firm proposed to use its staff to assemble projections on the accountant's computer, using a model developed by the accountant. All assumptions on which the projections would be constructed would be provided by the client. The client would approve and accept responsibility for all the material presented, and the final projection would be issued with the accountant's compilation report.

The SEC Chief Accountant's Office has stated the following position with respect to the preparation of PFI for SEC companies:

If an accountant prepares prospective financial information (forecasts or projections) for a client, the accountant's independence with respect to historical periods encompassed by the prospective information will ordinarily be deemed to be impaired (regardless of whether or not (1) the accountant "reports" on the prospective information, or (2) the prospective information is restricted to the client's internal use only).

This SEC position treats the preparation, or assistance in the preparation, of prospective financial information as analogous to bookkeeping services. The SEC does not permit bookkeeping services because they are considered a violation of an accountant's independence. The accounting profession believes that this interpretation of preparation assistance is very narrow. A Task Force of the AICPA's Professional Ethics Executive Committee has been created to deal with this issue and is currently conducting discussions with the SEC.

PRO FORMA FINANCIAL INFORMATION

Overview

Pro forma financial information is used to depict the effect of certain significant transactions or events that have occurred or will probably occur after the date of historical financial statements, but before their issuance; or that have occurred during a year but are not fully reflected in the historical financial statements. Examples of such transactions are business combinations, changes in accounting principles, loss contingencies, and certain capital transactions. The purpose of pro forma financial information is to increase the relevance and usefulness of historical financial statements and facilitate the understanding of the effects of such transactions on them.

Professional Requirements

Pro forma financial information requirements can be found in the professional literature for the types of transactions discussed in the following sections.

Business Combinations. APB 16 requires pro forma financial information for the effects of a purchase business combination by an acquiring enterprise (other than a nonpublic enterprise, exempted by SFAS 79) for the period in which the purchase occurred. The pro forma financial information is to be provided in the notes to the financial statements as supplemental information and is to include (B50.165):

a. Results of operations for the current period as though the enterprises had combined at the beginning of the period, unless the acquisition was at or near the beginning of the period

b. Results of operations for the immediately preceding period as though the enterprises had combined at the beginning of that period, if comparative financial statements are presented

The pro forma financial information at a minimum is to disclose revenue, income before extraordinary items, net income, and earnings per share.

Additionally, APB 16 requires the presentation of supplemental information in the notes to the financial statements for business combinations occurring subsequent to the date of the historical financial statements but prior to their issuance (B50.120–.124).

Changes in Accounting Principles. APB 20 requires that income before extraordinary items and net income be computed on a pro forma basis and disclosed in the income statement for all periods presented as if the newly adopted accounting principle had been applied during all periods affected (A06.115). The pro forma amounts are to include both (1) the direct effects of the change and (2) nondiscretionary adjustments such as profit sharing expense and certain royalties that would have been recognized if the newly adopted accounting principle had been followed in prior periods. (A06.115, fn. 2). Similar requirements apply to interim financial reports (I73.137(c)).

Further, pro forma information is often provided in situations where a new statement has been issued by the FASB or GASB that will cause a change in accounting principle but is not yet effective. Disclosure of the impact that the new standard will have on the historical financial statements upon adoption is appropriate if reasonably estimable.

Loss Contingencies. SFAS 5, *Accounting for Contingencies* (C59.112), states that in the case of a loss arising after the date of the financial statements but before their issuance, disclosure may best be made by supplementing the historical financial statements with pro forma financial data giving effect to the loss as if it had occurred at the date of the financial statements. SAS 1 (AU 560), although an auditing standard, provides similar guidance for subsequent events that do not require adjustment of the historical financial statements.

Earnings per Share. APB 15, *Earnings per Share* (E09), requires the presentation of supplementary earnings per share data for the effect of certain conversions that occurred during a period or subsequent to the close of a period but before issuance of the historical financial statements. The supplementary EPS data should present the primary EPS as it would have been if the conversion(s) had taken place at the beginning of the period (E09.113).

APB 15 similarly requires the presentation of supplementary EPS data for certain recapitalizations that occurred during a period or after the close of a period but prior to issuance of the historical financial statements (E09.114).

SEC Requirements

SEC requirements for the presentation of pro forma financial information is contained in a number of SEC forms, rules, and administrative staff positions. Article 11, "Pro Forma Financial Information," of Regulation S-X prescribes the presentation (Rule 11-01) and preparation (Rule 11-02) requirements for this financial information.

The applicability of Article 11 to a particular filing is governed by the form used in the filing (e.g., Form S-1, S-2, S-3, S-4, 8-K, or Schedule 14A). Rule 11-03 allows the filing of a financial forecast in lieu of the pro forma earnings statement described in Rule 11-02. If such a forecast is used, it should cover a period of at least 12 months from the later of the date of the most recent balance sheet filed or the consummation date of the transaction, and is to be presented in accordance with AICPA standards (discussed in the preceding portion of this chapter).

Further guidance on SEC administrative practices regarding pro forma information is given in FRR 2 (§ 506), SAB 45 (Topic 2.C), SAB 55 (Topic 1.B), and SAB 74 (Topic 11.M).

Presentation. Rule 11-01 of Regulation S-X states that pro forma financial information is to be provided when any of the following conditions exist:

(1) During the most recent fiscal year or subsequent interim period for which a balance sheet is required by Rule 3-01, a significant business combination accounted for as a purchase has occurred (for purposes of these rules, the term "purchase" encompasses the purchase of an interest in a business accounted for by the equity method);

(2) After the date of the most recent balance sheet filed pursuant to Rule 3-01, consummation of a significant business combination to be accounted for by either the purchase method or pooling-of-interests method of accounting has occurred or is probable;

(3) Securities being registered by the registrant are to be offered to the security holders of a significant business to be acquired or the proceeds from the offered securities will be applied directly or indirectly to the purchase of a specific significant business;

(4) The disposition of a significant portion of a business either by sale, abandonment or distribution to shareholders by means of a spin-off, split-up, or split-off has occurred or is probable and such disposition is not fully reflected in the financial statements of the registrant included in the filing;

(5) During the most recent fiscal year or subsequent interim period for which a balance sheet is required by Rule 3-01, the registrant has acquired one or more real estate operations or properties which in the aggregate are significant, or since the date of the most recent balance sheet filed pursuant to that section the registrant has acquired or proposes to acquire one or more operations or properties which in the aggregate are significant;

(6) The registrant previously was a part of another entity and such presentation is necessary to reflect operations and financial position of the registrant as an autonomous entity; or

(7) Consummation of other events or transactions has occurred or is probable for which disclosure of pro forma financial information would be material to investors.

Preparation. Rule 11-02 states that the objective of pro forma financial information is to provide investors

with information about the continuing impact of a particular transaction by showing how it might have affected historical financial statements if the transaction had been consummated at an earlier time. Such statements should assist investors in analyzing the future prospects of the registrant because they illustrate the possible scope of the change in the registrant's historical financial position and results of operations caused by the transaction.

The pro forma financial information is to consist of a pro forma condensed balance sheet and income statement and explanatory notes. The pro forma statements are ordinarily presented in columnar form showing the condensed historical financial statements, pro forma adjustments, and the pro forma amounts. FRR 2 (§ 506.02.a.ii) states that the requirements for the preparation of the pro forma condensed income statement are designed to "elicit disclosures that clearly distinguish between the one-time impact and the on-going impact of a transaction. . .". Accordingly, the rule requires the pro forma condensed income statement to depict the effects of the transaction on income from continuing operations and before nonrecurring charges or credits directly attributable to the transaction. Therefore, discontinued operations, extraordinary items, and the cumulative effect of accounting changes would not be reflected in the pro forma income statement.

The pro forma adjustments related to the income statement are computed assuming the transaction took place at the beginning of the period presented and include only those adjustments that are directly attributable to the transaction, are expected to have a continuing effect on the enterprise, and are factually supportable.

The pro forma adjustments related to the balance sheet are computed as if the transaction took place at the end of the most recent period for which the balance sheet is required. The pro forma adjustments for the balance sheet, however, include all adjustments that are directly attributable to the transaction and factually supportable, regardless of whether the impact is expected to have a continuing effect on the enterprise.

Reporting on Pro Forma Financial Information

Audited Financial Statements. Pro forma financial information included in audited financial statements is typically marked "unaudited" and not referred to in the auditor's report on the financial statements.

SEC Filings. Pro forma financial information is required by various SEC forms in a variety of circumstances, and the auditor is often called upon to state an opinion on the pro forma adjustments to be applied to the historical financial statements of an enterprise.

The SEC has taken the position that an auditor reporting on the pro forma adjustments must have audited the historical financial statements of the enterprise. For a business combination in which two or more entities are involved, an auditor may issue a "compilation only" report, but only if he has audited one of the entities and the other entity or entities have either been audited by him or another CPA. Thus, auditors are precluded by the SEC from expressing any kind of assurance on pro forma financial information based on unaudited historical financial statements.

An illustration of a report on pro forma adjustments is presented below. This report may be issued separately or by adding a paragraph to the standard auditor's report.

We have also reviewed the application of the proposed transactions to which effect has been given in the preparation of the pro forma balance sheet of the XYZ Corporation as of August 31, 19— as stated in the notes thereto. In our opinion, such proposed transactions have been properly applied. [Poloway, 1988, ¶ 5222]

Note that the report addresses the pro forma transactions and their application to the historical financial statements rather than the fairness of presentation of the pro forma financial statements. Standards for this type of reporting have not been developed by the profession as yet, although they are coming soon, as discussed in the next section.

An illustration of a "compilation only" report for pro forma financial information reflecting a business combination in which the entities involved were audited by one or more CPAs is presented in the following illustration. An auditor would not normally issue this type of report unless he has audited all or a major part of the financial statements comprising the pro forma financial statements.

We have also reviewed as to compilation only, the pro forma combined balance sheet of XYZ Company and MNO company as of December 31, 19—, and the related pro forma combined statement of earnings of the companies for the five years then ended. The financial statements of MNO Company have been examined by other independent public accountants whose report thereon has been furnished to us and is included elsewhere in this Prospectus (or Proxy Statement). In our opinion, which as to MNO Company is based upon the aforementioned report of other independent public accountants, such pro forma statements have been properly compiled on the basis stated therein. [Poloway, 1988, ¶ 5223]

Proposed Standard on Reporting. The Auditing Standards Division of the AICPA is in process of developing a *Statement on Standards for Attestation Engagements* (AICPA, 1987n) to provide guidance on auditing and reporting on pro forma adjustments. The standard, expected to be issued late in 1988, will specify that an accountant may agree to report on an examination of pro forma adjustments only if the following conditions are met:

1. The document that contains the pro forma financial information includes (or incorporates by reference) the complete historical financial statements of the entity and, in the case of a business combination, contains the appropriate historical financial information for the entities or parts comprising the combined entity.
2. The historical financial statements of the entity or entities on which the pro forma financial information is based have been audited or reviewed.
3. The accountant reporting on the pro forma adjustments must have an appropriate level of knowledge of the entity's accounting and financial reporting practices. This level of knowledge is normally obtained by the accountant auditing or reviewing the entity's most recent historical financial statements.

The accountant's report on pro forma adjustments would include:

1. An identification of the pro forma financial information.
2. A reference to the financial statements from which the historical financial information is derived and a statement as to whether such financial statements were audited or reviewed.

We have examined the pro forma adjustments reflecting the transaction (or event) described in Note 1 and the application of those adjustments to the historical amounts in [the assembly of] the accompanying pro forma condensed balance sheet of X Company as of December 31, 19X1, and the pro forma condensed statement of income for the year then ended. The historical condensed financial statements are derived from the historical financial statements of X Company, audited by us, and of Y Company, audited by other accountants, appearing elsewhere herein (or incorporated by reference). Such pro forma adjustments are based upon management's assumptions described in Note 2. Our examination was made in accordance with standards established by the American Institute of Certified Public Accountants and, accordingly, included such procedures as we considered necessary in the circumstances.

The objective of this pro forma financial information is to show what the significant effects on the historical financial information might have been had the transaction (or event) occurred at an earlier date. However, the pro forma condensed financial statements are not necessarily indicative of the results or related effects on financial position that would have been attained had the above-mentioned transaction (or event) actually occurred earlier.

[Additional paragraph(s) may be added to emphasize certain matters relating to the attest engagement.]

In our opinion, management's assumptions provide a reasonable basis for presenting the significant effects of the above-mentioned transaction (or event) described in Note 1, and the related pro forma adjustments give appropriate effect to those assumptions and are properly applied to the historical financial statement amounts in the pro forma condensed financial statements.

FIG. 27.9 Proposed Accountant's Report on Pro Forma Adjustments
Source: AICPA, 1987n. Proposed Statement on Standards for Attestation Engagements — Reporting on Examination of Pro Forma Adjustments.

The report on pro forma adjustments should refer to any modification in the accountant's report on the historical financial statements.

3. A statement that the examination of the pro forma adjustments was made in accordance with standards established by the AICPA.

4. A separate paragraph explaining the objective of pro forma financial information and its limitations.

5. The accountant's opinion as to whether management's assumptions provide a reasonable basis for presenting the significant effects of the transaction or event and whether the related pro forma adjustments give appropriate effect to those assumptions and are properly applied to the historical financial statement amounts in the pro forma financial information.

An example of a report, taken from the proposed standard on the examination of pro forma adjustments is shown in Figure 27.9.

28

Bankruptcy, Reorganization, and Restructuring

TROUBLED COMPANY ENVIRONMENT

Fickle markets, seesawing energy costs, fluctuating exchange rates, rapid technological changes, increasing competition, and other such factors sometimes combine with improvident management actions, deteriorating liquidity, and increased financial leverage to create the economic maelstrom from which troubled companies must extricate themselves to survive. Whatever the initial cause of their economic distress, most troubled companies are simultaneously buffeted by operational, legal, and financial problems. It is the interaction of multiple survival-threatening factors as opposed to a discrete problem that usually distinguishes a troubled company from a company with trouble.

Typically, troubled companies experience a history of operating losses, emanating from failing operations or oppressive commitments or litigation, and culminating in their inability to obtain needed financing. As losses mount, cash shortages develop, necessitating the draw down of available credit lines and deferral of payments due. Creditors respond: vendors curtail trade credit and lenders demand collateral or impose other onerous requirements.

As cash shortages become more severe, less is invested in inventories and needed capital improvements, leading to reduced customer service and erosion of customer goodwill. Employee morale also erodes, and turnover increases as concerned employees are more susceptible to enticements from aggressive competitors. These factors tend to exacerbate the situation, decreasing competitiveness and accelerating the pace of operational decline and concomitant working capital deficiencies.

Rehabilitating the Troubled Business

Rehabilitating a troubled business entails eliminating the foregoing problems so that it can operate normally and compete effectively in its industry. Operating losses must be eliminated and profitable operations restored, and liabilities must be settled at affordable amounts. In other words, the business must be made viable; it must adjust its cost/profit and capital structures to be aligned with other companies competing in its industry if it is to have satisfactory long-term economic performance prospects.

The *rehabiliatation process* is an arduous undertaking involving continuation of the regular day-to-day business activities while simultaneously restructuring operations and capitalization. This dynamic process consists of the following phrases, as illustrated in Figure 28.1:

* Stabilizing the business
* Assessing future performance prospects
* Developing rehabilitation strategies and a business plan
* Implementing the business plan

Stabilizing the Business. Initial attention must be devoted to the urgent activities necessary to reverse the "death spiral" in which a business is consuming its working

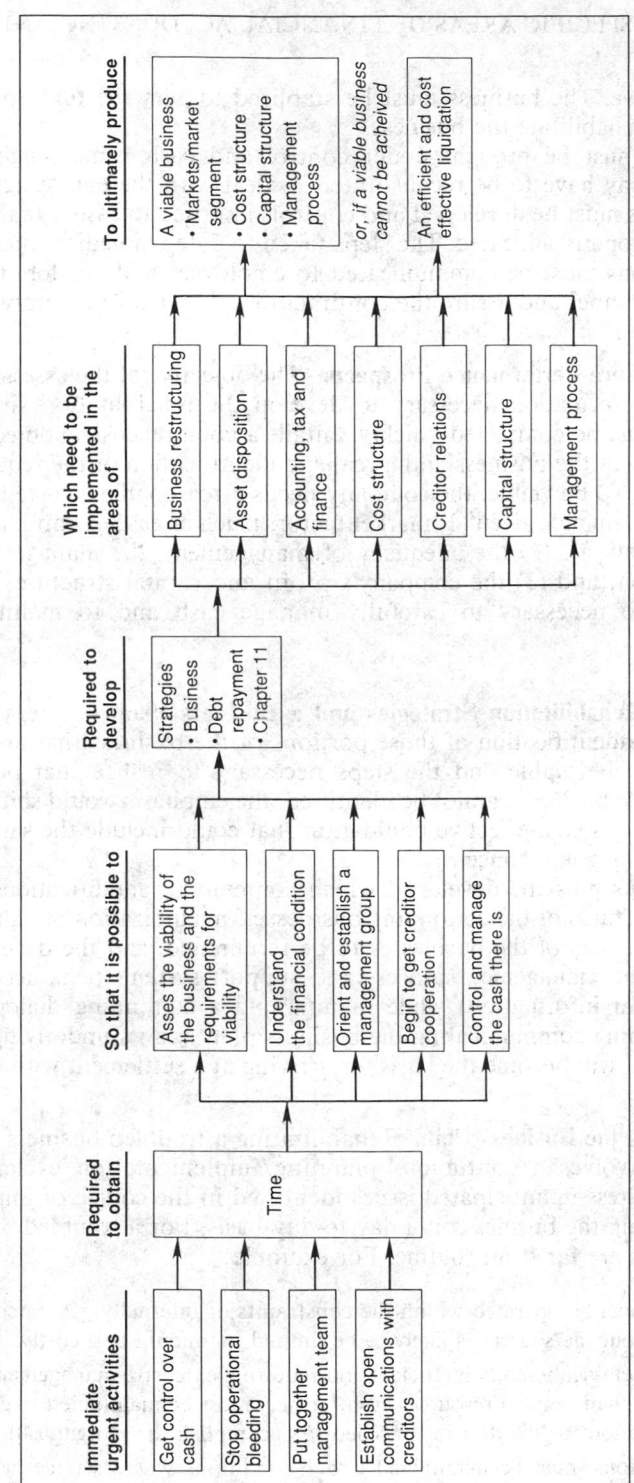

Immediate urgent activities

- Get control over cash
- Stop operational bleeding
- Put together management team
- Establish open communications with creditors

Required to obtain

Time

So that it is possible to

- Asses the viability of the business and the requirements for viability
- Understand the financial condition
- Orient and establish a management group
- Begin to get creditor cooperation
- Control and manage the cash there is

Required to develop

Strategies
- Business
- Debt repayment
- Chapter 11

Which need to be implemented in the areas of

- Business restructuring
- Asset disposition
- Accounting, tax and finance
- Cost structure
- Creditor relations
- Capital structure
- Management process

To ultimately produce

A viable business
- Markets/market segment
- Cost structure
- Capital structure
- Management process

or, if a viable business cannot be achieved

An efficient and cost effective liquidation

FIG. 28.1 Overview of a Typical Rehabilitation Process

capital to survive. The business must be stablized to gain the time to assemble its resources and rehabilitate the business.

Operations must be brought under control and cash hemorrhaging stanched. Management may have to be reconstituted to deal with the emergency. Near-term cash projections must be developed and controls imposed to assure that limited cash resources are properly allocated. The steps taken to date, immediate plans, and near-term expectations must be communicated to employees and vendors to curtail the loss of key personnel and assure the continuation of sources of supply.

Assessing Future Performance Prospects. The objective of the assessment stage is to obtain the information necessary to develop the rehabilitation strategies. This stage, which must be completed quickly, entails a comprehensive, objective analysis of the condition of the business and a realistic identification of the requirements for future viability. To be viable, the company needs a reasonable chance to participate in industry performance given (1) market factors (such as ease of entry, market share, company reputation); (2) the adequacy of management, the management process, and organization; and (3) the company's profit and capital structures. During this stage, it is also necessary to carefully manage cash and to maintain creditor cooperation.

Developing Rehabilitation Strategies and a Business Plan. Strategy formulation begins with the identification of those portions of the business that appear to have the potential to be viable and the steps necessary to realize that potential. If a potentially viable business cannot be identified, the emphasis would shift to planning for an efficient and cost-effective liquidation that could include the sale of portions of the business as going concerns.

Detailed plans must be developed which contemplate modifications to the cost and capital structures of the continuing businesses, maximization of values from disposition of the assets of the businesses to be terminated, and the development and refinement of the management process and support systems (e.g., accounting, tax, and management information) while maintaining a continuing dialogue with the creditors, including communicating the business plan and its underlying basis. Ultimately, this plan will become the basis for arriving at a settlement with the creditors.

Implementing the Business Plan. Rehabilitating a troubled business is a dialectic process that involves a continuous planning/implementation cycle, with plans modified to address unanticipated issues identified in the course of implementation while maintaining the business on a day-to-day basis. For a troubled business, day-to-day activities are far from routine. For example:

* The business must be operated within the constraints of internally generated cash; capital available from outside sources is likely to be limited in amount and costly.
* Temporary systems (inherently inefficient and requiring extensive management involvement which stretches management resources even farther) must be maintained to garner the supporting information for the decisions needed to accomplish the reorganization goals.
* Customer relations must be maintained under conditions where service has deteriorated because of employee turnover and reduced working capital.

* Special arrangements must be made to assure the continued availability of goods and services from creditors no longer willing to extend trade credit. Such creditors usually insist on cash on delivery, or even on order for products manufactured to the company's specifications.

* Programs must be implemented to retain key employees who may be asked to defer pay increases or even to agree to pay cuts in view of the limited cash resources. Inevitably, the employees must work harder and for longer hours to meet the unusual demands of a troubled environment. They are also more likely to be approached by competitors who are aware of the company's plight.

Selecting the Forum for Reorganization

Usually all of the interested parties benefit if a troubled business can be successfully reorganized since reorganization preserves valuable going concern attributes. The alternative is to liquidate the business and abandon many of its intangible assets. Some reorganizations are accomplished through formal *Chapter 11 reorganization proceedings* under the supervision of a federal bankruptcy judge; others are accomplished by agreement of the parties in an *out-of-court restructuring*.

In either forum, the same fundamental business problems must be resolved. Theoretically, if a company can be reorganized in court, it can also be reorganized out of court. Major companies have been sucessfully reorganized out-of-court, notably Chrysler Corporation and International Harvester, and others have restructured their finances through debt and equity exchange offers. Out-of-court restructurings tend to reflect the legal rights and obligations of the various parties; however, disputes are compromised rather than adjudicated. Generally, practical considerations govern the selection of the reoganization forum.

Cost vs. Discipline. Chapter 11 reorganization proceedings are generally more costly than out-of-court proceedings. The court process imposes formal documentation requirements and a time schedule designed to afford all affected parties the opportunity to excercise their legal rights. In addition to specific required information, various parties are entitled to professional representation at the expense of the *debtor estate*; the court must approve all matters outside of the normal course of business and only after a "noticed" hearing (one held with advance notice) upon formal motion. While the formality entails costs, it also provides a disciplined mechanism for the equitable resolution of disputes. For an out-of-court restructuring to succeed, the parties must be able to compromise their differences without court intervention.

Creditor Group Demography. Situations in which creditor claims are relatively concentrated (i.e., most of the claims are held by a few claimants) lend themselves well to out-of-court restructurings. Fewer parties need to be involved in the negotiations. Large claimholders are often willing to permit smaller claimholders to be paid in full in order to retain "control" of the case even though their recovery is diluted. By virtue of their greater interest, large claimholders are generally more willing to invest the time necessary to achieve a successful reoganization. In an out-of-court restructuring, it may be possible to obtain an earlier resolution that might be achievable in formal proceedings. The prospect of a higher or faster recovery can justify the cost of participation for the large claimholder.

Impact on Customers. Companies whose products are sold subject to warranties of parts and service or under long-term contracts might normally prefer to reorganize out-of-court because a bankruptcy filing might engender a loss of customer confidence in their ability to honor product warranties or perform their contract obligations. Warranty claims arising from sales made prior to the petition are prepetition unsecured claims and may not be honored without court approval. Also, most debtors experience a loss of business following a Chapter 11 filing. It is reasonable to expect a greater loss of business where there is doubt about the future availability of replacement parts and trained service personnel or a contractor's ability to complete his obligations under a contract.

Involuntary Petitions. The choice of reorganization forum might be taken out of the hands of the management of the troubled business by three or more creditors with $5,000 in claims who file an *involuntary petition*. A debtor can consent to an involuntary *Chapter 11 reorganization petition* and thereby convert it to a voluntary one. Similarly an involuntary *Chapter 7 liquidation petition* can be converted to a voluntary Chapter 11 petition. On the other hand, the debtor could seek to have the involuntary petition dismissed.

The only prerequisite for an involuntary petition is that the debtor is generally not paying its debts as they become due. The bankruptcy court could also dismiss or suspend an involuntary petition if it appears that a pending out-of-court workout could better serve the interests of the parties.

FORMAL REORGANIZATION PROCEEDINGS

The *U.S. Bankruptcy Code* delineates the rights and obligations of the various parties in Chapter 11 reorganization cases. It also shapes out-of-court restructurings as the parties to such a restructuring strive to arrive at an agreement without recourse to the courts. Out-of-court restructuring plans tend to be designed to reflect the rights of the parties so that no party needs to petition the court to protect his rights. Therefore, a general understanding of the provisions of the Bankruptcy Code is fundamental to understanding the issues financial accounting must address in both reorganizations and restructurings. As a comprehensive analysis of bankruptcy law is beyond the scope of this chapter, the discussion that follows is intended to highlight the usually significant issues.

Bankruptcy Code Overview

Throughout most of history, bankrupts (those adjudged insolvent) were objects of public disgrace. Having no means to secure legal forgiveness of indebtedness they could not repay, bankrupts were incarcerated in debtors' prisons. Early laws governing business bankruptcies, in this country as elsewhere, provided only for the liquidation of the assets of debtor estates and governed the distribution of the proceeds to creditors. As the bankruptcy laws and practices in this country evolved, reorganization rather than liquidation of the debtor business received greater emphasis. The current Bankruptcy Code, created by The Bankruptcy Reform Act of 1978, as amended, completely replaced the 1898 Bankruptcy Act.

Objectives. The Bankruptcy Reform Act, as its name implies, created the Bankruptcy Code to reduce perceived inequities and inefficiencies in the old law. The Code has three principal objectives:

1. Rehabilitation of the debtor.
2. Protection of the rights of parties in interest.
3. Efficiency.

Rehabilitation of the debtor. Creditor interests are paramount under the Code. At the heart of the Code is the *best interests* rule, the requirement that unless there is 100% acceptance of the *plan of reorganization* by a class of creditors, each member of that class must receive at least as much as it would receive in Chapter 7 (liquidation). Through the provisions of Chapter 11 (reorganization), the Code facilitates the rehabilitation of the debtor business where it appears possible to preserve going concern values, thereby enhancing creditors' recoveries. The Code contains specific provisions discussed briefly below, such as the automatic stay and the exclusivity period, that tangibly aid in the rehabilitation of the business.

Protection of the rights of parties in interest. The Code delineates the rights of the various parties in interest, and provides mechanisms to protect those rights. One or more committees may be appointed as *fiduciaries* for those they represent to assure adequate representation of disparate interests, for example, those of unsecured creditors, secured creditors, and equity security holders. Committees are empowered to retain professionals and request the appointment of a trustee or examiner, and they are specifically charged with a duty to investigate and monitor the debtor's affairs.

In addition, parties in interest may petition the court to redress specific grievances. For instance, a secured creditor may seek to be compensated for the use of its collateral during the pendency of the proceeding, and a creditor who believes that the business cannot be successfully reorganized may petition the court to convert a Chapter 11 case to a Chapter 7 liquidation.

Efficiency. Through the establishment of the U.S. Trustee system, the Reform Act separated the supervision and jurisprudence functions, to enable the bankruptcy judges to concentrate their attention on matters requiring judicial determination. Other changes adopted in the Code are intended to minimize litigation and encourage consensual reorganization plans. In addition, judges have a great deal of discretion in overseeing the appointment of committees and in the conduct of litigation and, accordingly, frequently encourage the parties to compromise their differences.

Plan of Reorganization/Liquidation. A Chapter 11 proceeding contemplates the reorganization of the debtor pursuant to a plan of reorganization. After a plan is formally proposed to the bankruptcy court, a copy of the plan and a ballot, with a disclosure statement approved by the bankruptcy court as containing adequate information for informed consent, is sent to each class of impaired creditors and security holders for acceptance or rejection. A plan will be accepted by a class of creditors if two thirds in amount and one half in number of the *allowed claims* (those authenticated by the court) in the class actually voting accepts the plan in writing. The equity security holders' class accepts a plan if accepted in writing by holders of at least two thirds of the allowed securities who actually vote.

The bankruptcy court will then consider, at a noticed hearing, whether to confirm the plan. In order to confirm the plan, the court must find, among other things, that: (1) each holder of a claim or an interest in each class of creditors and equity security holders will receive under the plan at least as much value as such creditors or security holders would receive in a liquidation; (2) each impaired class of creditors and equity security holders has accepted the plan by the requisite vote; and (3) the plan is feasible, that is, confirmation of the plan is not likely to be followed by a liquidation or any further financial reorganization of the debtor or its successors unless the plan proposes such liquidation or reorganization.

If any impaired class of creditors or equity security holders does not accept the plan, assuming at least one impaired creditor class accepted the plan and all other Bankruptcy Code requirements are met, the proponent of the plan may invoke the *cram-down provision* of the code. Under this provision, the court may confirm a plan without regard to its non-acceptance by an impaired class of creditors or equity security holders if certain requirements of the Bankruptcy Code are met. Where the cram-down provision is invoked, no junior class of creditors or security holders may receive a distribution under the plan unless any dissenting senior class is paid in full. For instance, the interests of equity security holders would be eliminated if any impaired class of creditors fails to accept the plan and is not otherwise paid in full.

Rights of the Debtor and Trustee

Operation of the business. The Code prescribes the rights and obligations of a trustee;[1] however, a trustee is usually not appointed. Normally, the debtor's management operates the business as debtor-in-possession, with full power to manage the business affairs of the debtor in the ordinary course, subject to bankruptcy court approval of certain actions. The appointment of the debtor-in-possession is automatic; no special court order is necessary. Unless circumscribed by the court, the debtor-in-possession has all of the rights and powers and is responsible for the performance of all trustee functions except certain investigatory responsibilities relating to the conduct of the debtor-in-possession.

---

[1] In addition to being accountable for all property received, a Trustee is required to: (1) examine claims and object to the allowance of those he believes are improper; (2) file reports with the court and tax authorities; (3) furnish information requested by parties in interest; (4) investigate the acts and conduct of the debtor and the financial and operational aspects of the business and report his findings; and (5) as soon as practicable file a plan or recommend conversion of the case to a Chapter 7 proceeding.

Exclusivity period. Under the Bankruptcy Code, the debtor has the exclusive right to file a plan with the court for an initial period of 120 days, and solicit acceptance of any such plan for an initial period of 180 days after the filing of its Chapter 11 petition. Upon application by the debtor, these periods may be extended by the court, and in large cases they invariably are. If requested extensions are not granted or if a debtor fails to file or secure acceptances of a plan within the respective exclusivity periods, any party in interest may file a plan. Further, if the bankruptcy court were to appoint a trustee, the debtor's period of plan exclusivity would be terminated.

Automatic stay. In general, during the pendency of the reorganization proceedings, actions in respect of prepetition matters by creditors and other claimants (including default remedies and enforcement of other contractual obligations) are automatically stayed, and the debtor is prohibited from paying obligations that arose before the petition was filed, unless the requisite approval is obtained from the court.

Executory contracts. Under the Code, a debtor may assume or reject lease obligations and other executory contracts. Executory contracts are generally defined as contracts that have not been completely performed by *both* contracting parties. Examples include leases, employment contracts, and purchase commitments. Contracts performed except for payment by the debtor are not executory contracts. Parties whose executory contracts are rejected may file claims with the court. These claims are treated as prepetition unsecured claims. Certain types of long-term contract claims are specifically limited in amount.

Debtors may continue to perform executory contracts until they are assumed or rejected. Upon assumption, the debtor must cure all defaults, including paying past-due prepetition amounts. Debtors usually delay assuming most executory contracts until the reorganization plan is confirmed, as this also postpones the need to cure defaults. Further, claims arising on subsequent rejection of assumed executory contracts become *administrative expenses* (essentially obligations of the estate incurred after the petition date) that would have to be satisfied in full before prepetition unsecured creditors could receive a distribution under the reorganization plan.

The Bankruptcy Code permits debtors to assign assumed executory contracts to third parties even where contract language prohibits assignment. The ability to assign bargain long-term leases, for example, has provided substantial value to debtor estates.

Recoupment of preferential payments and protection from set-off. A fundamental precept underlying the Code is that prepetition creditors are entitled to share in plan proceeds on a pro rata basis but are not permitted to improve their positions to the detriment of other similarly situated creditors. Consequently, the Code enables a debtor estate to recover preferential transfers and fraudulent conveyances, and limits creditors' set-off rights.

A payment by an insolvent debtor on account of antecedent debt that enables a creditor to receive more than it would have received in a Chapter 7 liquidation (assuming the payment had not been made) is a voidable preferential transfer unless the creditor can prove that an exception applies. The exceptions are intended to preclude recoveries by the estate for transactions pursuant to normal financial relationships. Similarly, the Code permits the debtor to void transactions intended to defraud creditors and certain non-arm's length transactions.

The Code also constrains creditors from setting off mutual prepetition debts without the court's permission. The creditor is treated as a secured creditor to the extent of the potential setoff involving prepetition receivables and payables, however, and the creditor's consent is required for the debtor to use certain types of collateral. A creditor is not permitted to set off a post-petition liability against a prepetition receivable from the debtor.

Other. The Code also provides other protections and rights that enhance the debtor's chances to reorganize. Public utilities are prohibited from discontinuing service to a debtor because of an unpaid prepetition obligation. The debtor is offered a 20-day grace period in which to work out a means of protecting the utility for future service, usually through security deposits.

The Code permits debtors to incur unsecured obligations in the ordinary course of business as administrative expenses. In other words, post-petition creditors are senior to prepetition creditors. Where, as is usually the case, debtors cannot obtain sufficient unsecured credit, the court may approve granting post-petition creditors a super-priority over other post-petition creditors, a lien on "free" assets, and even a lien equal or senior to a prior lien providing that the prior lienholder is adequately protected.

Rights of Parties in Interest

Absolute priorities of claims. The Bankruptcy Code specifies the priorities of the different types of claims that might be filed in a proceeding. Under the absolute priority doctrine, more senior claims must be paid in full before a less senior claim is entitled to receive anything. Creditors can elect to receive less than that to which they are probably legally entitled, and usually do so to avoid delays associated with protracted litigation.

The Code protects the interests of secured creditors to the extent of the value of the collateral in which they have a security interest, subject to reduction for administrative expenses incurred to protect or realize such property. The other assets of the estate are available to the other parties in interest, and to secured creditors to the extent that the secured claims exceed the value of the collateral. Administrative expenses of the proceeding rank first among the absolute priorities, followed by certain specified priority claims (e.g., tax claims of governmental agencies and certain types of employee claims in limited amounts). General unsecured claims are next, followed by the claims of preferred and then common shareholders.

Right to file claims. Creditors have the right to file *proof of claim* to establish the amounts owed them by the debtor. However, they need not file proofs of claim to preserve their rights if they agree with the amount of their claims scheduled by the debtor unless the debtor has characterized their claims as contingent, disputed, or unliquidated. In a Chapter 7 case, a creditor must file a proof of claim to preserve its rights in any event.

Reclamation claims. In order to avail itself of its rights to reclaim goods sold to a debtor while the debtor was insolvent, a creditor must demand reclamation in writing within 10 days after the goods are received by the debtor. Since valid reclamation demands also may be satisfied in cash, it is not unusual for creditors who sold goods to a debtor within 10 days of a petition to file reclamation claims in the hope of receiving payment rather than return of the goods.

Reclamation claims often involve many complications. Goods which have been sold by the debtor to a third party and those that cannot be specifically identified cannot be reclaimed. Secured creditors may contend that, upon receipt, the goods become collateral for their debt. Reclamation demands must also meet technical requirements, for example, as to form and timeliness. Notwithstanding the complexities, creditors who can improve their overall recoveries by exercising their reclamation rights will usually attempt to do so.

Adequate protection of secured creditors. A secured creditor may request *adequate protection* where property in which it has a collateral interest is used by the debtor. Under the adequate protection doctrine, the secured creditor is entitled to protection against a decrease in the value of its interest in the property through periodic cash payments, replacement liens, or other relief. By demonstrating that it is not adequately protected, the secured creditor could be granted relief from the automatic stay that prevents repossession of the property. A secured creditor can also obtain relief from the stay by demonstrating that the debtor does not have an equity in property, and that the property is not required for an effective reorganization.

Committees and information. Various parties in interest may be entitled to representation by committees consisting of persons willing to serve in the capacity of fiduciaries for the interests they represent. Disparate interests are recognized in establishing the composition and number of committees. The court must appoint at least one *Official Creditor's Committee.* Applications may be made seeking the appointment of additional committees.

The principal role of committees in a proceeding is to consult with the company concerning the administration of the reorganization and to participate in the formulation of a plan of reorganization. Committees also are empowered to raise issues with the bankruptcy court relating to the business of the debtor or the conduct of the proceedings. A debtor estate must pay the expenses of the committee, including the fees and expenses of counsel, accountants, and other professionals the court authorizes the committee to engage.

Committees, generally working through their retained professionals, are entitled to access to the information needed to perform their functions.

Debtor Financial Information

As part of any formal reorganization proceeding, a debtor is required to file specific financial information with the court. In addition, a debtor files pertinent financial information in conjunction with its motions seeking court approval for certain undertakings and adversary proceedings. Debtors also provide financial information to the official committees. They must continue to prepare and furnish financial information pursuant to federal securities law requirements as well.

Financial Information Required with Petition. In asking the court for relief, a debtor is required to file a petition. In some jurisdictions, the debtor also must state the reasons for the filing and provide other information in an affidavit, including the following financial information:

- The amount due each of the twenty largest unsecured creditors, indicating whether such claims are contingent, unliquidated, disputed, or partially secured.
- A summary of the debtor's assets and liabilities.
- The number and classes of publicly held securities, including the number of holders of each class.
- The nature and status of pending and threatened actions or proceedings.
- A listing of owned and leased premises.
- A listing of property held by others.
- Estimates of receipts and disbursements, including the separate payroll amounts for employees and officers.

It is often not practicable for troubled debtors to provide all of this financial information at the time the petition is filed, and the court will waive the requirements except for the information concerning the twenty largest creditors which is needed to form the Official Unsecured Creditors' Committee.

Statement of Financial Affairs and Schedules. Along with the petition, the debtor is required to file a completed *Statement of Financial Affairs*, related schedules, and historical financial statements covering the past several years. The statement of financial affairs contains 21 questions concerning the nature and history of the debtor's business, the nature and locations of assets and records, litigation, management, ownership, and other matters. The schedules consist of detailed listings of the debtor's assets and liabilities, segregated by type. Figure 28.2 lists the required schedules.

As with the debtor's affidavit, many debtors are not able to complete the statement of financial affairs and asset and liability schedules in time to include them with the petition. The court will allow additional time for the information to be filed. Also, it is important to note that the schedules are not filed and forgotten. They should be prepared using the best available information and they may be amended or updated as often as necessary throughout the pendency of the case.

Monthly Operating Reports. Court-required monthly operating reports generally emphasize cash transactions and balances in working capital accounts, with pre- and post-petition data separated where possible. The information is usually required for the current month and on a cumulative basis from the date the petition was filed. Some courts require that detailed supporting schedules (e.g., a copy of the check register) accompany the reports.

Generally, the required information is such that most debtors will not have difficulty in complying. Arrangements can normally be made to accommodate special problems of a particular debtor or to modify the normal reporting format to better reflect the nature of the debtor's business. While consolidated monthly financial

Schedule A — Statement of All Liabilities of Debtor
   Schedule A-1 — Creditors Having Priority
   Schedule A-2 — Creditors Holding Security
   Schedule A-3 — Creditors Having Unsecured Claims without Priority

Schedule B — Statement of All Property of Debtor
   Schedule B-1 — Real Property
   Schedule B-2 — Personal Property
   Schedule B-3 — Property Not Otherwise Scheduled
   Schedule B-4 — Property Claimed as Exempt

Summary of Debts and Property
Schedule of Current Income and Current Expenditures
Statement of Executory Contracts
Lists of Creditors
List of Equity Security Holders

FIG. 28.2 Schedules Accompanying the Statement of Financial Affairs

statements in conventional GAAP format may also be filed, they do not supplant the requirement for the cash-oriented monthly operating reports.

Normal Financial Reporting. Filing a Chapter 11 petition does not modify in any way a company's obligation to file financial statements with the Securities and Exchange Commission. In addition to the normal distribution, annual reports, quarterly reports, and other filed financial statements would also be provided to persons who requested documents filed with the court.

Special considerations applicable to the preparation of GAAP financial statements of a company in reorganization proceedings are discussed later in this chapter under "Special Considerations During a Proceeding."

Supplemental Reports for Creditors' Committees. The monthly operating reports (and perhaps regular GAAP financial statements) do not provide all of the information needed by a creditors' committee to adequately monitor the debtor's operations. In the interest of efficiency, most debtors will arrange to regularly prepare and furnish more detailed information and analyses to the committees and their professional representatives. The nature of the supplemental reports, however, will vary with the case. They will commonly include:

- Consolidating financial statements
- Aged accounts receivable trial balances
- Product line or divisional profit and loss information
- Details of operating expenses by natural expense category
- Operating and cash flow projections and reconciliations of prior projections with actual results
- Analyses of inventory, including advance payments for goods not yet received
- Analyses of postpetition credit

- Analyses of actual performance in relation to plans
- Analyses of intercompany transactions and balances
- Details of proposed capital expenditures

Motions and Adversary Proceedings. A debtor must obtain court approval prior to undertaking activities outside the ordinary course of business (e.g., sale of subsidiary). In a Chapter 11 case, most motions are initiated by the debtor. In making a motion, a debtor will set forth in an affidavit the principal justifications for his proposed course of action. Conversely, a debtor will need to justify his position in an adversary proceeding initiated by a creditor (e.g., use of cash collateral, i.e., cash and equivalents and proceeds of accounts receivable and inventory in which both the debtor and a secured party have an interest). The financial impact of the matter will usually carry a great deal of weight with the judge. A few examples illustrate the point:

- Early in a case, a debtor might apply to assume an executory contract for the repair of major equipment used in its manufacturing process. Assumption could involve paying substantial past due prepetition balances as well as the costs of continuing repairs. Typically, the debtor would prepare analyses demonstrating the advantages to the estate of assuming the contract and demonstrating that the estate could afford the cash expenditures required. The debtor would also show why there is no better way to have the repairs completed.
- In seeking authorization to use cash collateral in its reorganization efforts, a debtor would provide operating and cash flow projections to demonstrate the beneficial impact on the estate and in particular on the secured creditor.
- In its efforts to recoup preferential payments, a debtor might offer financial information to controvert the creditor's claim that the debtor was not insolvent at the time of the transfer.

A debtor also would develop the same type of financial information when attempting to obtain the consent of parties in interest to its position; such information would also be provided to the court in conjunction with a motion to which the parties have consented—just as it would if the matter were being litigated.

Best Interests Analysis. The court, to confirm a plan of reorganization, must find that each member of each class of creditors and security holders will receive at least as much under the proposed plan as it would if there were a liquidation. Accordingly, the debtor's financial condition might be set forth in a *statement of affairs* (also called a *report of financial condition*) prepared by the proponent of the reorganization plan to reflect the results of a liquidation analysis. This information would be provided in some form in the *disclosure statement* but not necessarily in the form of a report of financial condition. (Note that this statement of affairs differs from the statement of financial affairs, described previously.)

Income Tax Considerations

Although the issuance of an order for relief creates a separate debtor estate under the Bankruptcy Code, it does not create a new taxable entity. Accordingly, the debtor must file its tax returns when normally due, in the same manner and form and using the same tax accounting methods previously employed, subject to otherwise available elections. Moreover, the estate retains its tax attributes, for example, carryovers of net operating losses (NOLs), investment tax credits, foreign tax credits, and capital losses. For most Chapter 11 companies, accumulated NOL carryovers for both regular and alternative minimum tax (AMT) purposes (and perhaps other carryforward benefits) are substantial and represent a significant contingent asset of the estate.

A general discussion of the impact of certain bankruptcy-related transactions and conditions that affect preservation of tax attributes for federal income tax purposes—major considerations in many Chapter 11 reorganizations in view of the magnitude of the potential benefits—is included in the following subsections. A comprehensive review of all the exceedingly complex federal income tax factors affecting Chapter 11 companies is beyond the scope of this chapter. State income tax treatments, also potentially significant, are not covered herein; they do not necessarily conform to federal treatments and vary from state to state.

Discharge of Indebtedness. Forgiveness of debt ordinarily generates cancellation-of-indebtedness taxable income. However, the Internal Revenue Code provides that the amount that would otherwise be reported as discharge of indebtedness income will instead reduce tax attributes. If the debtor so elects, it may first reduce the basis of certain depreciable property; if not, net operating loss carryovers would be reduced first, followed as necessary by other favorable tax attributes in the order specified in the Internal Revenue Code.

Generally, issuance of debtor's stock to its creditors (with or without cash, notes, or other property) in satisfaction of their claims eliminates the attribute reduction requirement. The *stock-for-debt exception* does not apply if only a nominal or token amount of stock is issued or where certain safe harbor proportionality rules are not met. What constitutes a nominal or token amount is not statutorily defined. Tax attributes must be reduced to the extent of the cancellation of the indebtedness of each unsecured creditor who receives stock, the value of which in relation to that creditor's claim is less than 50% of the value of all stock issued to unsecured creditors in relation to their aggregate claims, to the extent that the claims are not satisfied with cash or other property.

Ownership Changes. Certain changes in ownership of a loss corporation can reduce or eliminate NOL carryovers under § 382 of the Internal Revenue Code. The specific provisions applicable to ownership changes resulting from a proceeding depend on the date the petition for relief was filed. The petition date is not relevant for post-confirmation ownership changes.

Petitions filed prior to August 14, 1986. Certain changes in control of a corporation resulting from a proceeding that commenced prior to August 14, 1986 would result in elimination of all NOL carryovers unless the corporation continues substantially the same business after confirmation of its reorganization plan. Generally, a control change resulting from a taxable acquisition of the corporation over a two year period by fewer than 11 owners, resulting in an ownership change of 50% or more of the corporation's stock, results in the loss of the company's NOLs unless the company's current business is maintained.

On the other hand, if, as part of the control change, the former shareholders and creditors receive ownership of at least 20% (in fair market value) of the stock through a tax-free *G Reorganization*, all of the NOLs would be preserved. The amount of NOLs preserved is reduced proportionately to the extent that former creditors and shareholders receive less than 20% of the stock.

Petitions filed after August 13, 1986. Under a special *bankruptcy rule*, a one-time lump sum reduction of the NOL is permitted following certain changes in ownership resulting from a reorganization proceeding if stock representing at least 50% of the value of the reorganized corporation is owned by former shareholders and trade creditors whose debt predated the inception of the proceeding by at least 18 months. Under this rule, the NOL is reduced by an amount equal to the sum of unpaid interest related to the cancelled debt accrued within approximately three years prior to the ownership change and 50% of the cancellation of indebtedness income not recognized due to the stock-for-debt exception.

As an alternative, a corporation qualifying for the bankruptcy rule could elect to be subject to an annual limitation on NOL utilization instead of the lump sum NOL reduction. The maximum amount of NOL that may be utilized annually is the product of the fair market value of the company multiplied by the *long-term federal tax-exempt rate* published monthly by the Treasury Department.

A greater than 50% aggregate ownership change as to any 5% or greater shareholder over a three-year test period triggers the above considerations. In any case, failure to maintain business continuity for two years after a change in ownership results in elimination of the NOL.

Post-confirmation ownership changes. A second greater than 50% change in ownership within two years of a previous ownership change resulting from a bankruptcy proceeding would eliminate any of the remaining NOLs of a corporation covered under the bankruptcy rule. If a company did not initially qualify or elect the bankruptcy rule, a second ownership change following a bankruptcy proceeding would result in adjustment of the annual limit on the use of NOLs based on an updated valuation and interest rate at the time of the second change. In any event, restrictions on the marketability of stock issued pursuant to a reorganization plan, while possibly adversely affecting the value of the stock, could protect valuable tax attributes.

Alternative Minimum Tax. If greater than the regular tax otherwise due, a corporation is required to pay a 20% AMT. The AMT base is taxable income adjusted for certain items of preference, including 50% of any excess of financial statement income over taxable income, subject to a maximum 90% reduction in any year through the use of available NOL (as specifically defined for AMT purposes).

Book-to-tax differences frequently arise in reorganization proceedings because of matters such as:

- Discharge of indebtedness.
- Timing differences in the recognition of liabilities and valuation provisions.

• Differences in the carrying value and tax basis of assets and liabilities occasioned by a change in the basis of accountability used for financial statement purposes.

As these differences could be substantial, a corporation could use up all of its NOL for AMT purposes long before its regular NOLs have been used, and thus have to pay alternative minimum taxes until the regular NOLs are used up or expire. At that point, the regular tax in excess of the 20% AMT rate would be subject to a reduction for a portion of previously paid AMT tax. (AMT is covered in greater detail in Chapter 17.)

As of August, 1988 Congress is considering a technical correction that would eliminate certain bankruptcy-related book-to-tax differences for AMT purposes.

Role of the Accountant

The Bankruptcy Reform Act of 1978 significantly changed the administration of bankruptcy cases, expanding and enhancing the importance of the accountant's role. In addition to shifting much of the administrative burden of the proceedings from the court to the U.S. trustee system, the Act established the role of an examiner[2] and limited the SEC's involvement. (Under the prior Bankruptcy Act, the SEC was required to issue an advisory report to the court in each Chapter X case and had certain rights of appeal of bankruptcy court decisions).

Retention. To be assured that they will be paid for their work, professionals must be formally retained to serve in court proceedings. To retain a professional accountant, the retaining party (typically a debtor, trustee, examiner, or official committee) would make application to the court setting forth the need for the accountant, the terms of his engagement, including a retainer, if any, and outlining the scope of his work.

The accountant would submit an affidavit stating that he is a disinterested person as defined in the Code, that he has neither received nor made commitments for compensation other than as provided in the Code and that he is eligible for employment pursuant to the Code and applicable bankruptcy rules. Many accountants also include a detailed listing of services to be provided, hourly rates to be charged, and terms of payment. Since any party in interest could object to the amount of fees or the necessity of the work to be performed, it is often in the accountant's best interests to have his retention order be as specific as possible.

Following a hearing, at which any party in interest could object, the court would issue an order approving the accountant's retention and specifying payment terms and any restrictions the court imposes. The court might limit aggregate charges or specify a time period governing the accountant's retention.

---

[2] An examiner is an official who may be appointed upon the request of a party in interest after notice and a hearing, to investigate the acts, conduct, and financial condition of the debtor and the operation of the debtor's business, sometimes in lieu of appointment of a trustee. (Ordinarily, a trustee would be appointed where there is clear evidence of mismanagement or fraud.) The courts have exercised wide discretion in appointing examiners, determining the scope of their duties, and permitting them to employ professionals to assist them in their role. Accountants may also serve as examiners or trustees; however, the discussion herein is limited to the accountant's role as an independent accountant for the trustee, examiner, or an official committee.

Normally, accountants and other professionals may apply to the court for interim compensation and reimbursement of expenses once every 120 days; however, the court could hold hearings more frequently or permit special payment arrangements between hearings. At the conclusion of the case, final fee hearings are held. The court could award greater or lesser amounts depending on the circumstances. Judges consider many factors in determining fees. Typically, along with details of the services rendered, the time required, and the expenses incurred, applications for compensation describe the degree of skill required, difficulties encountered, time constraints, efficiency of the accountant's efforts, results obtained, extent to which other employment was precluded, customary charges, and other matters.

Normal Accounting Services. The filing of a reorganization petition does not diminish the need for accounting and auditing services of the types ordinarily provided to companies not involved in such proceedings. SEC registrants must continue to file regular annual and quarterly reports and current reports of significant developments. Financial statements are an important part of information flow in reorganization proceedings. Debtors must continue to prepare and file tax returns. As a result, the role of the debtor's independent accountant typically would include normal audit and compliance services. In fact, it is not unusual for accountants to provide more extensive than normal services because debtor management's credibility is often tainted, especially in the early stages of a proceeding. Further, because of extraordinary demands placed on the debtor's accounting personnel as a result of the proceeding, the outside accountant may provide services in areas ordinarily covered by company personnel.

The circumstances of a reorganization proceeding may complicate the provision of normal services. Frequently, the quality of the debtor's internal control structure and record-keeping are strained, and "band-aid systems" are hastily created to handle unusual types of transactions and segregated pre- and postpetition balances. Management priorities shift, and transactions arising from the proceeding must be given accounting recognition.

Special Assistance. Accountants provide a wide variety of special services in proceedings. Accountants may be retained by debtors, official committees, unofficial committees, trustees, examiners, potential acquirors, and individual creditors or shareholders.

The accountant's role varies somewhat with the party served; however, it ordinarily encompasses special services in one or more of the following areas:

* Preparation of reports/monitoring
* Expert testimony
* Investigatory services
* Consultation

Preparation of reports/monitoring. Accountants engaged by committees and other parties in interest perform an important function in assisting their client to monitor the debtor's progress and in formulating positions on pending motions. Accountants engaged by the debtor perform an equally important complementary function in providing credible financial information and analyses to facilitate monitoring. The reporting/monitoring services performed often involve preparation assistance by the debtors' accountants and review or challenge by the committee's accountants of monthly operating reports and financial statements and supplemental reports and analyses (e.g., those listed in the earlier section entitled "Supplemental Reports for Creditors' Committees" or otherwise prepared in support of debtor motions).

It should be noted that depending on the nature and scope of the accountant's efforts, the accountant might not issue a formal report describing his work and conclusions. Frequently, his role will be limited to informal comments. Where formal reports are called for, they should conform to applicable professional standards regarding attestation engagements or special reports, as discussed in Chapter 11.

Expert testimony. In bankruptcy litigation, accountants are frequently called on to provide expert testimony as a logical extension of their other services. The scope of an accountant's testimony can be quite broad, certainly beyond traditional financial accounting and tax matters. For example, an accountant might be asked to offer testimony concerning valuations, financial forecasts or projections, the impact of a proposed course of action, tabulations of the creditors' votes on a proposed reorganization plan, and other matters. The accountant's qualifications to serve as an expert witness will be established during his *voir dire* examination (i.e., establishment of expertise). Nonetheless, a litigant might challenge whether particular matters fall within his realm of expertise.

Careful advance preparation is required for providing expert testimony. Such preparation includes planning and performing investigative activities, developing exhibits to summarize pertinent findings, and assisting counsel in formulating questions for direct examination and in anticipating questions that might be asked upon cross examination. It is essential that the accountant work closely with counsel in all of these areas to assure that his testimony will address the legally pertinent facts.

Time constraints, the state of available records, the nature of the subject matter, or other circumstances may be such that the accountant will not be able to perform all of the procedures he would deem necessary to issue a professional opinion on financial data which is the subject matter of his expert testimony. In such circumstances, the accountant should clearly state in the record the scope of his work and the degree of responsibility he is taking. As an expert witness, the court will normally afford him some latitude in responding to questions calling for a simple "yes" or "no" answer.

Investigatory services. Under the Code, a trustee, an examiner, and official committees have explicit investigative responsibilities. Accountants can make substantial contributions to conducting such investigations in an efficient and effective manner. Accountants are commonly involved in investigations of preferential transfers, fraudulent conveyances, fraudulent accounting practices, and analyses of potential causes of action the estate might pursue.

Consultation. While an accountant's role in providing assistance in a reorganization proceeding includes attest functions, it is primarily consultative in nature, and covers a broad range of business as well as accounting advice. In reorganization proceedings, complex decisions often must be made based on partially verified information that is available—even if it is incomplete—and often under significant time and operational constraints. In such circumstances the accountant's judgment and analytical approach are of paramount importance. The accountant must recognize the risks entailed in these conditions.

FINANCIAL ACCOUNTING AND REPORTING CONSIDERATIONS

A reorganizing company must consider its changing circumstances in preparing financial statements in conformity with generally accepted accounting principles. Some changes may require recognition in the accounts, others only disclosure in the financial statements.

Changes in business conditions due to exogenous factors (e.g., marketplace conditions) and explicit management programs to restructure operations can affect fundamentally healthy companies as well as troubled companies. For the most part, the same accounting and disclosure considerations pertain whether the company is involved in a formal bankruptcy proceeding or an out-of-court negotiation. For example, accounting for a recapitalization plan would be the same whether it results from an out-of-court debt restructuring or confirmation of a plan of reorganization. The terms of the plan, not the forum in which it was formulated, have accounting significance. However, certain additional considerations derive from events and conditions during the pendency of formal bankruptcy proceedings and affect only companies involved in formal proceedings.

Changes in Business Conditions

All businesses must realign their operations to address changes in the economic environment. Most such realignments (e.g., ongoing programs to close unprofitable stores of multilocation retailers and to close out unprofitable product lines of manufacturers) occur regularly and do not unusually affect reported financial position and operating results. However, almost all troubled company operational restructurings and some healthy company restructurings, do affect comparisons of periodic financial performance. While the following discussion pertains to significant restructuring efforts of troubled companies, it is equally applicable in nontroubled situations.

Restructuring Charges. Restructurings include programs such as closing down, consolidating, relocating, selling, or abandoning operations; providing early retirement, severance, relocation, or transfer benefits to employees; and liquidation of slow-moving inventories and overdue receivables. Restructuring charges include the costs of developing and administering such programs, the costs of the programs themselves, and program-related asset valuation and liability provisions. Thus restructuring charges include provisions associated with normal business operations as well as those directly associated with a decision to sell, abandon, spin off, or otherwise dispose of a portion of a business. The operating statement classification of restructuring charges depends on the nature of items involved.

Discontinued Operations. APB 30 requires reporting as separate elements of discontinued operations the results of operations of a discrete segment of a business prior to the date of adoption (the measurement date) of a formal disposal plan and any gain or loss from disposal, including anticipated operating losses (or gains up to the amount of disposal losses recognized) between the measurement and disposal dates. Net disposal losses should be anticipated as of the measurement date, but net gains should not be recognized until realized. Only costs and expenses directly assocoiated with the disposal decisions (e.g., severance pay, additional pension costs, interest, and corporate overhead which will be eliminated) are includable in gain or loss from the disposal of a segment of a business. APB 30 (I13.102) expressly prohibits including in gain or loss from the disposal of a segment of the business costs and expenses associated with normal business activities, such as adjustments of accruals on long-term contracts, and asset writedowns and writeoffs. Discontinued operations are required to be reported as a separate component of income before the cumulative effect of accounting changes and extraordinary items with each element shown, net of applicable income taxes for the current and prior periods. Disclosure of revenues applicable to discontinued operations is required, and disclosure of per share data relating to discontinued operations is permitted.

The Emerging Issues Task Force concluded in Issue 87-24 that only interest directly identifiable with operations to be disposed of may be allocated to discontinued operations. Such interest includes interest on debt to be assumed contractually by the buyer and interest allocated to the net assets to be disposed of based on a uniform debt-to-equity ratio. Alternative allocation techniques (e.g., based on total assets or assumed repayment of debt with sale proceeds) should not be used. The allocation of interest will affect the disposal loss (for operations up to the disposal date) as well as results of operations up to the measurement date.

Closed Operations. On the other hand, the termination of operations constituting only a portion of a continuing segment should be reported separately within results of continuing operations. As with discontinued operations, anticipated losses from operations after the date of the decision to terminate (the measurement date) and any anticipated loss on sale or abandonment of the business or its assets would be reported as part of the disposal gain or loss. However, operating results prior to the measurement date would not be segregated on the face of the income statement, but could be disclosed in the notes. The tax effect of the loss from partially terminating continuing operations would not be netted against the loss; it would be included in the income tax provision or credit. Also, the per share impact of the closed operations disposal may not be disclosed on the face of the income statement.

Unusual Items. APB 30 states: "A material event or transaction that is unusual in nature or occurs infrequently but not both, and therefore does not meet both criteria for classification as an extraordinary item, should be reported as a separate component of income from continuing operations" (I22.101). In addition to losses on disposition of closed operations, troubled companies commonly report restructuring charges associated with normal business operations, bankruptcy administration expenses, provisions for creditors claims, and other unusual or nonrecurring charges as unusual items. SAB 67 (Topic 5P) requires publicly held companies to deduct

	In Thousands	
	1979	1978
		Restated
		(Notes 3 and 7)
Loss from continuing operations before unusual items and income tax credit	$ (90,751)	$(43,487)
Unusual Items:		
Disposal of properties and termination expenses, including net loss from closed supermarket operations after February 10, 1979 (Note 3)	(35,636)	
Adjustment for self-insurance, a significant portion of which applies to prior years (Note 2)	(14,523)	
Bankruptcy administration costs, less interest income of $2,107 on restricted cash	(5,628)	
Loss from continuing operations before income tax credit	(146,538)	(43,487)
Income tax credit (Note 14)		8,776
Loss from continuing operations	(146,538)	(34,711)
Loss from discontinued J.M. Fields operations (Notes 2 and 3):		
From operations, including provision for creditor's claims of $10,096 in 1979	(47,659)	(19,840)
From disposal of properties and termination expenses, including net loss from operations after February 10, 1979	(11,319)	
Loss from operations, before cumulative effect of accounting changes	(205,516)	(54,551)
Cumulative effect of accounting changes (Note 7)	(5,563)	(37,672)
Net Loss	$(211,079)	$(92,223)

FIG. 28.3   Debtor Statement of Operations Showing Bankruptcy Elements (Footnotes omitted)
Source: Excerpt From Food Fair, Inc. (Debtor In Possession) Statements of Consolidation Operations. July 28, 1979.

restructuring charges not classified in discontinued operations in determining income from continuing operations (where income from continuing operations is shown) and generally prohibits the use of subtotals such as "income before restructuring charges." The Emerging Issues Task Force nevertheless concluded that nonpublic companies should not be precluded from classifying restructuring charges as a nonoperating item as long as the footnotes contain adequate disclosure (EITF Issue 87-4).

Figure 28.3 illustrates many of the above considerations. In this pre-SAB 67 case, the debtor also classified as unusual items certain charges that appeared as if they might have belonged, at least in part, in operations of prior years. However, material weaknesses in internal control, employee turnover, and record keeping deficiencies — common conditions for many troubled companies — made it impracticable to reasonably allocate the charges among the current and prior years.

Classification of Assets Held for Disposition. Assets held for disposition should be segregated on the balance sheet and classified among current assets on classified balance sheets if they are expected to be realized within one year. If the realization period is uncertain, they should be classified among noncurrent investments. It is appropriate to reduce the carrying amounts of the assets held for disposition by related liabilities (e.g., mortgage loans payable, capital lease obligations, and deposits received on sales). Full disclosure should be made of the composition of the net assets held for disposition.

Impairment of Long-Lived Assets. Where a company has shut down long-lived productive assets and is holding them for disposal as part of an operational restructuring effort, GAAP clearly requires a write-down, if necessary, to reduce the carrying amount of the assets to net realizable value. GAAP is less clear where there is an indication that the company may be unable to recover the carrying amount of long-lived productive assets continued in use.

Normally, provision is made for permanent impairment in value of operating assets, providing the amount of loss can be reasonably measured. This highly subjective concept is difficult to apply in practice and is inherently manipulable as it usually necessitates estimating future revenues, allocating them to particular asset groups, and possibly discounting those revenues at an appropriate rate. Nonetheless, recognition of impairment in value of long-lived assets in use appears to be becoming more prevalent, and the FASB is considering placing this topic on its formal agenda. (Impairment is considered more fully in Chapter 15.)

Special Considerations During a Proceeding

The Bankruptcy Code alters the legal conditions under which a debtor operates, thereby giving rise to special financial accounting considerations during the pendency of the case.

Consolidated Financial Statements. Ordinarily, the accounting presumption that consolidated financial statements are more meaningful than the separate financial statements of the companies comprising a consolidated group still pertains in a Chapter 11 reorganization. However, if the companies do not remain under common control, consolidated financial statements might no longer be appropriate. For example, if a trustee is appointed to operate a particular subsidiary, it should not be consolidated.

Where consolidated financial statements continue to be prepared it may be appropriate to include special disclosures to enable creditors and shareholders of component entities to interpret the pertinent financial statements. For example, the notes to the financial statements might include a condensed consolidating balance sheet or disclose the assets and liabilities of "filed" and "non-filed" entities separately. (See Figure 28.4.) However, the financial statements need not be redesigned so that each creditor of each filed subsidiary can evaluate what he is likely to receive for his claim; information of that type is distributed as a part of the reorganization process.

Classification of Prepetition Liabilities. Because payment of prepetition liabilities generally is prohibited during the pendency of the reorganization proceedings, most are combined under a caption such as "Liabilities Deferred Pursuant to Chapter 11 Reorganization Proceedings" and included in the non-current section of a classified balance sheet. Prepetition liabilities permitted to be paid earlier are classified in the

Summarized financial information as of July 31, 1982 and for the year then ended for the operations subject to reorganization proceedings and those excluded from such proceedings is as follows.

(Dollars in Thousands)

	Subject to reorganization proceedings		Not subject to reorganization proceedings		
	U.S.	Canada	Other foreign*	Eliminations	Consolidated
Assets					
Current assets	$190,112	$13,021	$107,126	$(30,239)	$280,020
Other assets	113,910	5,431	18,654	(28,927)	109,068
Total	$304,022	$18,452	$125,780	$(59,166)	$389,088
Liabilities and Shareholders' Equity					
Prepetition liabilities	$251,028	$11,795	$ —	$ —	$262,823
All other liabilities	136,965	5,332	99,806	(31,867)	210,236
Shareholder's equity (deficit)	(83,971)	1,325	25,974	(27,299)	(83,971)
Total	$304,022	$18,452	$125,780	$(59,166)	$389,088
Net Revenues	$430,988	$29,635	$198,760	$(45,848)	$613,535
Income from continuing operations before income taxes and extraordinary credit	$(40,414)	$(2,093)	$(6,547)	$8,640	$(40,414)

* The Parent Company has guaranteed indebtedness of its foreign subsidiaries totaling $15.2 million, including $10.3 million in Canada, which guarantees are subject to the Reorganization Proceedings.

FIG. 28.4   Sample Disclosure of Summarized Financial Information of Filed and Nonfiled Companies
Source: Excerpt from AM International, July 31, 1982 Annual Report.

normal manner. These include items such as reclamation claims, amounts related to capital leases that have been or are expected to be affirmed and are being performed, mortgage or other secured loans being paid in accordance with their terms, and other obligations approved for payment by the court.

Classification of Assets Pledged as Collateral. Classification and disclosure of assets pledged as collateral for secured loans are much the same as for a company not involved in reorganization proceedings. However, if the court has granted a secured creditor relief from the automatic stay and thus permitted repossession of the collateral, the affected assets should be segregated in the balance sheet or netted against the related debt and the circumstances disclosed.

If litigation is pending concerning the repossession of pledged assets, the notes to the financial statements should contain full disclosure of the relevant issues, including the potential impact of an unfavorable outcome (e.g., repossession of assets essential to the reorganization of the business could necessitate the liquidation of the debtor).

Timing of Accounting Recognition. Although there are no special rules for companies in Chapter 11, there are special conditions in which GAAP must be applied. Usual timing considerations relate to provisions associated with discontinued and closed operations, provisions for restructuring expenses, accruals of administrative expenses of a proceeding, and creditor claims.

Provisions for discontinued or closed operations should be recorded as of the measurement date, as described earlier. Creditor claims provisions and most restructuring charges should be recognized as soon as they can be estimated. Bankruptcy administrative expenses and certain types of restructuring charges (e.g., costs of administering restructuring programs) are usually recognized as incurred; however, it is also acceptable to provide for them as early as reasonable estimates can be made.

As a part of a formal proceeding, creditors seeking to establish the amounts due them may file proofs of claim. Claimed amounts frequently differ from the amounts recorded on the debtor's books, and the differences can be substantial. Differences may be due to a number of factors such as timing differences in the shipment and receipt of goods, disputes, contingencies appropriately not recorded by the debtor, and debtor record-keeping deficiencies.

Adjustments to recorded liabilities arising from the claims reconciliation process should be recorded as the amounts are established, without reduction for any anticipated discharge of indebtedness pursuant to the reorganization plan. Material unreconciled differences should be disclosed. Where differences appear to arise from deficiencies in the debtor's records, it may be proper to record them promptly.

Interest on Prepetition Indebtedness. Generally, interest ceases to accrue during the pendency of a proceeding on all prepetition debt, except for secured debt where the value of the underlying collateral exceeds the amount of the debt and for interest charges related to capital leases which are being performed. However, there could be circumstances (e.g., where the debtor is solvent) where postpetition interest will be allowed on all debt, whether secured or unsecured. Accordingly, postpetition interest on prepetition indebtedness should be recorded to the extent it is expected to be allowed by the court.

Recapitalization/Liquidation Plan Issues

Basis of Accountability. A key issue in accounting for a confirmed plan of reorganization or an out-of-court restructuring plan is whether the historical cost basis of accounting for assets and liabilities should be continued or a new basis of accounting established. Although Chapter 7A of ARB 43 (Q15) describes an elective procedure by which a new basis of accounting is to be implemented to reflect a quasi-reorganization (also called corporate readjustment) as if a court-approved reorganization had occurred, there is no explicit mandate for its use.

Reorganization Accounting. A reorganization entails a major change in the financial structure of a corporation or a group of associated corporations that results in alterations in the rights and interests of security holders and the creation of new legal entities. It might also entail a realignment of or change in management, business policy, production, or trading methods.

Basis of accountability	Ownership or control	Business continuity	Management continuity
New	Old shareholder interests are eliminated	Major changes unique to company	Senior and operating management changes
	Creditors receive majority of equity interests		
	Creditors receive securities convertible to majority interests in new equity		
	Creditors' representatives dominate Board		
	Liabilities restructured generally		
	Restrictive covenants effectively invalidate old shareholder interests	Some changes unique to company	
	Creditors receive a minority equity position	Changes not unique to company	
	Creditors receive rights to convert to minority equity position		
	Creditors granted minority board representation		
	Covenants not unduly restrictive		
Historic	Old shareholder interests remain intact	No changes	No changes

FIG. 28.5 Determination of Basis of Accountability (The most persuasive factors are those most distant from the two intersecting lines.)

These same types of changes often are brought about when a company is acquired. It is logical, therefore, that the accounting for a reorganization should parallel the accounting for an acquisition that has similar key attributes. Accordingly, the valuation guidance in APB 16 (B50) should be applied in accounting for a reorganization. Figure 28.5 illustrates the relative importance of the major factors in determining the appropriateness of using reorganization accounting.

Quasi-Reorganizations. The concept of an accounting "fresh start" provides the justification for permitting a corporation that is not required to adopt a new basis of accountability to elect to do so. Accordingly, GAAP provides:

An enterprise [that] elects to restate its assets, capital stock, additional paid-in capital and retained earnings through a readjustment and thus avails itself of permission to relieve its future income account or retained earnings of charges that would otherwise be made against it shall make a clear report to its shareholders of the restatements proposed to be made, and obtain their formal consent. It shall present a fair balance sheet as at the date of the readjustment, in which the adjustment of carrying amounts is reasonably complete, in order that there may be no continuation of the circumstances that justify charges to additional paid-in capital. [Q15.104; taken from ARB 43, Chapter 7A, ¶ 3]

A quasi-reorganization was never intended to provide a discretionary means by which a corporation could avoid recognizing losses required under GAAP. Accordingly, quasi-reorganization accounting should not be used by a company having a history of operating losses and a deficit in retained earnings unless the facts demonstrate a high probability that it will be profitable in the future. Losses required to be recognized under GAAP should be recorded prior to effecting a quasi-organization, not as a result thereof. For example, while the write-down of property and equipment to fair values is a quasi-reorganization adjustment, the write-off of an uncollectible receivable should be shown in the statement of operations covering the period immediately preceding the effective date of the quasi-reorganization.

Accounting procedure. In a reorganization or quasi-reorganization, the plan of reorganization is accounted for as if the parties in interest purchased the business and its net assets from the debtor estate in exchange for their claims. Thus the assets of the reorganized company are restated to their fair values and the liabilities to present values, with the net amount of those adjustments added to or deducted from the deficit. The balance in the retained earnings or deficit account is then closed to other capital accounts so that the new entity has a zero balance in beginning retained earnings. The new retained earnings account is dated to disclose the elimination of the deficit. (See Figure 28.6.)

In SAB 78, *Quasi-Reorganization* (Topic 5.S), issued August 25, 1988, the SEC staff states that write-ups of assets or reductions of liabilities to fair values in a quasi-reorganization are limited to an amount sufficient to offset decreases in other assets or increases in other liabilities to their fair values. Therefore, there should be no net asset write-up in a quasi-reorganization. The SEC staff confirmed that this SAB does not apply to formal reorganization proceedings.

Additionally, SAB 78 takes the position that if a company is planning to make a discretionary accounting change (to a preferable method) which will result in income due to recording of its cumulative effect, such a change must be made as part of the quasi-reorganization, and factored into the deficit elimination; the change is not to be allowed to result in an increase in net assets, either at the time of recording the quasi-reorganization or thereafter.

Finally, the SAB notes that a FASB statement with a required implementation date within 12 months after the quasi-reorganization must be adopted as part of the quasi-reorganization; and that consideration should be given to concurrent adoption of a FASB statement with an effective date beyond 12 months.

Deficit reclassifications. A company that accounts for its reorganization or restructuring plan by maintaining its historical cost basis of accountability may wish to eliminate its deficit against other capital accounts to satisfy legal requirements for payment of dividends or for other reasons. The accounting literature does not define the circumstances under which a deficit reclassification allowed under applicable law is permissible; thus the procedure is theoretically discretionary. SAB 78 states that a reclassification of a deficit is not permitted unless all the other requisite actions involved in a quasi-reorganization are also effected.

1. Accounting Policies

   a. *Reorganization Proceedings.* Penn-Dixie, Inc., ("Penn-Dixie Industries") and its then wholly-owned subsidiary, Penn-Dixie Steel Corporation ("Penn-Dixie Steel" or "Steel") filed petitions for reorganization under Chapter 11 of the Federal Bankruptcy Code ("Petitions for Reorganization") in April of 1980. Callanan Industries, Inc., a then wholly-owned subsidiary of Industries, and Callanan's subsidiaries, ("Callanan") did not file a petition under the Bankruptcy Code. On March 15, 1982, following acceptance by the requisite vote of each class of creditors and interests entitled to vote on the plans, the reorganization plans of Industries and Steel became final and the companies emerged from bankruptcy proceedings. In accordance with the terms of the reorganization plans, Penn-Dixie Steel was merged into Penn-Dixie Industries and the Company's name was changed to Continental Steel Corporation ("Continental" or the "Company"). Distributions of cash, Common Stock and a $4,200,000 10% Convertible Subordinated Income Debenture were effected in March of 1982 in payment of liabilities which had been deferred pursuant to the reorganization proceedings. The retained deficit of the Company was eliminated, as called for in the reorganization plans and as approved by the Company's Board of Directors, by the transfer of the capital in excess of par value account of an amount equal to said retained deficit as of March 31, 1982. As a result of the Company's emergence from Chapter 11, former creditors acquired approximately 51% of the outstanding stock of the Company and the ability upon conversion of the 10% Debenture to acquire additional Common Stock that would increase their ownership to approximately 63%.

   b. *Quasi-Reorganization.* In recognition of the change in ownership of the Company as brought by the emergence from Chapter 11, the Company believed it to be appropriate to adjust the carrying value of assets and liabilities to their fair market value as of March 31, 1982. The Board of Directors of the Company directed that management consider obtaining regulatory approval for adjusting the carrying value of assets and liabilities to a fair value. Following extensive research and consultations with legal counsel, independent accountants and the Securities Exchange Commission, management recommended and the Company's Board of Directors approved a quasi-reorganization to be effective as of March 31, 1982. Accordingly, all assets and liabilities of the Company have been retroactively restated as of March 31, 1982, to their fair value determined as follows:

   • Inventories – market value reduced by selling costs and a reasonable profit allowance.

   • Property, plant and equipment – recent appraisal values.

   • Assets of previously discontinued operations (including investments in Callanan Industries) – estimated amount to be received upon sale of the assets (actual amount received has been used for those properties sold prior to the date of this report).

   • Debt due beyond one year – principal and interest payments due beyond one year have been discounted at 15%.

   • 10% Convertible Subordinated Income Debenture – appraisal from an investment banker.

   • Liability for pension plans – amounts have been discounted at 15%.

   • Federal income taxes – the installment obligation to pay prior year taxes is subject to a market rate of interest and has been recognized at face value. No asset was established to reflect the value of the Company's net operating loss carryforwards. Where the foregoing valuation methods resulted in an asset or liability's assigned value being different than the related tax basis, the Company will incur taxable income or deduction when the account is

FIG. 28.6   Illustrative Quasi-Reorganization Accounting Policy Disclosure
Source: Continental Steel Corporation, 1982 Annual Report.

realized at its assigned value. The potential income tax related to that income or deduction, discounted at 15% to the estimated date of realization, has been reflected in the assigned value. In the cases of land and inventory carried at LIFO (except for the LIFO decrement that occurred in 1982) it is expected that the company will continue to hold the assets indefinitely so that no future taxable income will result; therefore, no tax adjustment was made to the fair value of the asset. The net effect of adjusting values for potential income taxes was to decrease net assets by approximately $3,460,000, of which approximately $1,500,000 relating to LIFO inventory was transferred to income in 1982 when the LIFO inventory decrement occurred.

Troubled Debt Restructuring. A troubled debt restructuring is defined in SFAS 15 as one in which "the creditor for economic or legal reasons related to the debtor's financial difficulties grants a concession to the debtor that it would not otherwise consider. That concession either stems from an agreement between the creditor and the debtor or is imposed by law or a court" (D22.104). Changes in lease or employment-related agreements (e.g., pensions), and situations in which creditors merely delay taking legal actions to enforce their rights are not covered. Nor does SFAS 15 necessarily apply to all debt restructurings of financially troubled debtors. For example, a troubled debt restructuring is not involved

- For a debtor who transfers (or for a creditor who receives) property having a fair market value at least equal to the pre-restructuring carrying amount of the debt, or
- If the restructuring effectively represents a refinancing to reflect current market interest rates and maturity dates (D22.107).

SFAS 15 applies to troubled debt restructurings consummated under federal bankruptcy law unless (pursuant to the federal statutes or in a quasi-reorganization with which the troubled debt restructuring coincides) the debtor restates its liabilities generally. FASB TB 81-6 suggests by way of example that:

enterprises involved with Chapter XI bankruptcy proceedings frequently reduce all or most of their indebtedness with the approval of their creditors and the court in order to provide an opportunity for the company to have a fresh start. Such reductions are usually by a stated percentage so that, for example, the debtor owes only 60 cents on the dollar. Because the debtor would be restating its liabilities generally, Statement 15 would not apply to the debtor's accounting for such reduction of liabilities. [D22.512]

When a restructuring to which SFAS 15 does not apply results in the early extinguishment of debt (e.g., when the debtor restates its liabilities generally in a bankruptcy law restructuring), any resulting gains and losses are measured pursuant to APB 26 provisions (D14). In cases in which the company records a quasi-reorganization at the same time as (or not too long after) it accomplishes a reorganization under federal bankruptcy law (as shown in Figure 28.6), practice has been diverse with respect to the accounting treatment for the debt extinguishment gain or loss. A few companies that have adopted quasi-reorganization accounting within the year of emergence from bankruptcy have recorded the debt restructuring gains or losses as extraordinary items in the statement of operations, although most have adjusted equity accounts as part of recording the quasi-reorganization.

The SEC's issuance of SAB 78 in late August 1988 may be partly in response to prior mixed practice. SAB 78 (Topic 5.S), discussed in the two preceding sections, takes the position that there cannot be a net write-up of assets in a quasi-reorganization.

Measuring debtors' restructuring gains. The amount of gain or loss, if any, to be recognized by a debtor could vary depending on whether SFAS 15 or APB 26 applies to the transaction. Under SFAS 15, no gain is recognized by the debtor unless the recorded liability exceeds the total of the fair values of assets and equity interests transferred to the creditor plus the sum of future cash payments (including contingent amounts and amounts designated as interest) specified by the terms of the restructured debt. Under SFAS 15 (D22.109–.115), gains would be determined as follows:

- If the debtor transfers assets (including transfers by foreclosure or repossession) to fully settle a payable, the difference between fair and carrying values of the assets transferred is a gain or loss on the disposition of assets, and the excess of the carrying amount of the payable over the fair market value of the assets transferred is a gain on restructuring.

- If the debtor issues an equity interest to fully settle a payable, the debtor should account for the equity interest at its fair value. The excess of the carrying amount of the payable over the equity at fair value (less legal fees and other direct issuance costs) is a gain on restructuring.

- If a restructuring involves a modification of terms, the debtor should account for it prospectively. Where the future cash payments (principal and interest excluding contingent amounts) exceed the carrying amount of the payable, no gain or loss is recorded. The interest expense for future periods is computed using the *interest method*, by which a constant effective interest rate is applied to the payable at the beginning of each period between the restructuring and maturity dates. The effective rate is the discount rate that equates the present value of the future cash payments required by the modified agreement, excluding amounts contingently payable, with the carrying amount of the payable.

- If the payable exceeds the total future cash payments based on the new terms, a gain is recognized on the restructuring equal to the excess of the carrying amount of the payable over the future cash payments. (Gains should not be recognized to the extent that the maximum future cash payments *including contingent amounts* exceeds the carrying amount of the liability.) Since the cash payments are less than the carrying amount of the payable, there is no interest expense recognized in the future. Each payment is considered to be principal.

- If the debt is restructured by partial settlements (transferring assets and/or granting an equity interest) and modified terms, the debtor must first account for the asset and/or equity issuance as described above, and then account for the modified terms.

- Direct costs of a debt restructuring reduce the gain recorded, or if there is no gain are expenses of the period.

If SFAS 15 does not apply the gain is determined under APB 26 (D14) by comparing the recorded liability with the sum of the fair values of assets and equity interests transferred to the creditor plus the present value of specified future payment obligations discounted at a current fair market rate of interest.

Operations statement classification. Material gains arising from debt restructurings, determined under either SFAS 15 or APB 26, are classified by debtors as extraordinary items regardless of whether they result from confirmation of a plan of reorganization, an exchange of securities, a negotiated out-of-court restructuring of indebtedness, or in any other manner.

Disclosures by debtor. Disclosures required by the debtor for the period in which the restructuring occurs include (1) a description of the principal changes in terms and/or the major features of the settlement; (2) the gain (aggregate and per share) on restructuring of payables less tax effect; and (3) aggregate net gain or loss on transfers of assets (D22.121). In financial statements for periods after restructuring, the extent to which amounts contingently payable are included in the carrying amount of restructured payables should also be disclosed (D22.122).

Creditors' accounting. In most matters, the accounting for troubled debt restructuring by creditors under SFAS 15 (D22.123–.135) is symmetrical with that for debtors. However, there are a few important exceptions, including the following:

- The required operating statement classifications are different, that is, the debtor considers gains recognized at the time of restructuring as extraordinary, but the creditor treats its losses as ordinary. In this regard TB 79-6 (D22.502) states that the assessment of the collectibility of a receivable with modified terms continues to be necessary.
- The debtor includes contingent cash payments in the total future cash payments specified by modified terms to the extent necessary to prevent recognizing a gain at the time of restructuring that may be offset by future interest expense, but the creditor excludes contingent receipts from the total future cash receivable unless subsequent realization is probable and the amount can be reasonably estimated. Contingent cash payments not included in the total future cash payments at the time of the restructuring are recorded as interest when the contingency is removed. (This same principle also applies to other future cash receipts which may have to be estimated. For example, if the number of interest payments is flexible because the face amount and accrued interest is collectible on demand or becomes collectible on demand at a certain point in time, estimates of total future cash receipts should be based on the minimum number of periods possible under the terms of the restructuring.) TB 79-7 (D22.504) states in this regard that future cash receipts in excess of the recorded investment in a receivable should be accounted for as interest income even if a previous writedown results in an unusually high effective interest rate.
- If the future interest rate may fluctuate, estimates of the total future cash payments are based on the interest rate in effect at the time of the restructuring. For example, if the terms of the restructuring specify that interest will be paid at the prime rate, the prime rate at the restructuring date is used to calculate the total future cash payments. Increases in the rate are accounted for as changes in estimate, when realized. However, if the interest rate decreases below the initial interest rate, a loss is recognized for the difference between the total future cash payments based on the lower current interest rate and the recorded amount of the receivable.
- A debt restructuring can be a troubled debt restructuring for the debtor, but not for the creditor. As described in FASB TB 80-2, such a situation could occur if a debtor is granted a

concession by a creditor who purchased the loan from the original creditor for less than the restructured amount of the loan (D22.507–.508).

Any allowances for uncollectible amounts at the time of the restructuring should be offset against the losses determined under SFAS 15 provisions.

Disclosures by creditors. At each balance sheet date, a creditor must disclose, for each receivable whose terms have been modified, the aggregate recorded receivable, the interest income which would have been recorded if the restructuring had not taken place, and the amount of interest income recorded for the period. These disclosures do not have to be made if the creditor would have been willing to accept a new receivable with comparable risk for an interest rate equal to or less than the effective rate of the restructured receivable. A creditor must also disclose the amount of commitments to lend additional money to debtors whose receivables have been restructured (D22.136–.137).

Voluntary and Bankruptcy Liquidations. Although the liquidation of an entity ordinarily is associated with bankruptcy where the creditors would receive a higher distribution than if the company were to be reorganized, companies are also liquidated voluntarily. Whatever the reason for the decision to liquidate, the fundamental financial accounting assumption that the entity will continue in existence as a going concern is no longer appropriate. "The objectives of financial reporting do not necessarily change if an enterprise shifts from expected operation to expected liquidation, but the information that is relevant to those objectives, including measures of elements of financial statements, may change" (SFAC 1, ¶ 42, fn. 10).

Whenever an entity is to be liquidated pursuant to a plan of liquidation, its historical costs are no longer pertinent to users' needs and a new basis of accountability applies. "A liquidation basis of accounting may be considered generally accepted accounting principles for entities in liquidation or for which liquidation appears imminent" (AU 9509.33–.36).

The assets and liabilities of the liquidating entity or trust formed to carry out the plan of liquidation should be presented in a *statement of net assets in liquidation* at estimated realizable amounts, reduced by estimated costs of liquidation. It should be accompanied by a *statement of changes in net assets in liquidation* as well as notes describing the plan of liquidation, the basis of presentation, and additional applicable disclosures normally required under generally accepted accounting principles. Depending on the extent and significance of operations, the results of operations might be included in a separate statement or summarized in the footnotes. Figure 28.7 shows a statement of net assets in liquidation and the footnote describing the basis of presentation.

Additional Disclosures

In addition to the customary disclosures required by GAAP and disclosures applicable to specific accounting considerations discussed above, a reorganizing company must make disclosures related to its peculiar circumstances. The special disclosures,

	December 31, 1982	January 5, 1983
		(Note B)
Assets		
Cash and short-term investments	$28,837,000	$961,000
Participation rentals and other receivables, net of allowance for possible loss of $57,000	886,000	886,000
Notes receivable	4,397,000	4,397,000
Real estate investments	7,449,000	7,449,000
TOTAL ASSETS	41,569,000	13,693,000
Less Liabilities		
Notes payable	2,694,000	2,075,000
Accounts payable and other liabilities	1,270,000	1,270,000
Liquidation distribution payable	27,257,000	-0-
	31,221,000	3,345,000
5¾ Convertible Subordinated Debentures	6,906,000	-0-
Less cash escrowed for purchase of Debentures	6,906,000	-0-
	-0-	-0-
TOTAL LIABILITIES	31,221,000	3,345,000
NET ASSETS IN LIQUIDATION	$10,348,000	$10,348,000
Number of shares of beneficial interest outstanding (units of interest in liquidating trust)	2,725,707	2,725,707
Net assets in liquidation per outstanding share	$3.80	$3.80

NOTE B – BASIS OF PRESENTATION

The accompanying Statement of Net Assets in Liquidation as of December 31, 1982 and January 5, 1983 reflects the transactions of the Trust utilizing liquidation accounting concepts as required by generally accepted accounting principles. Under this method of accounting, assets are recorded at their estimated realizable values and recorded liabilities reflect estimated remaining obligations. Liquidation accounting methods have been adopted as of December 31, 1982. Prior to that date the Trust recorded the results of operations using accounting principles applicable to going concern entities.

The accompanying Statement of Net Assets in Liquidation as of January 5, 1983 reflects the assets and liabilities of the Trust immediately before the transfer to the Liquidating Trust. Certain assets and liabilities (not significant) relating to the period from January 1, 1983 to January 5, 1983 have been recorded as of December 31, 1982.

Because of the adoption of the liquidation basis of accounting as of December 31, 1982, the presentation of comparable prior years' financial data is not considered meaningful and has been omitted.

FIG. 28.7   Statement of Net Assets in Liquidation
Source: U.S. Realty Investments (liquidated January 5, 1983).

some of which might not necessarily apply in a particular case, may be categorized as description of the proceedings, financial statement comparability, uncertainties, investigatory findings, and incomplete information.

Description of the Proceedings. The notes to the financial statements should disclose that the company and some or all of its subsidiaries have petitioned the court for relief under Chapter 11 of the Bankruptcy Code, or is otherwise attempting to restructure its finances. For companies in formal proceedings, the notes should contain a general description of Code provisions and state whether the business is being operated by management as a debtor-in-possession or by a court-appointed trustee. In addition, important developments in the proceeding and their impact on the financial statements should be included, for instance, special charges resulting from rejection of executory contracts and the provisions of a proposed reorganization plan.

Financial Statement Comparability. It may not be meaningful to provide comparative financial statements along with the first financial statements issued reflecting a change in the basis of accountability (i.e., a change to a reorganization, or liquidation basis of accounting). In such circumstances, the reasons for omitting comparative statements should be described. Where comparative financial statements are provided, the notes should contain sufficient disclosure to enable the financial statement user to understand the reported results and make meaningful comparisons of current financial results with those of past and future periods. Accordingly, provisions for administrative expenses, creditor claims, executory contract rejection charges, and other unusual items should be disclosed along with the extent to which interest has not been accrued. Also, the notes should disclose the composition of deferred prepetition liabilities.

Uncertainties. Troubled companies face uncertainties related to the business as a going concern, to measurement of claims, and to the potential impact of reorganization efforts.

Going concern uncertainties. When an entity's ability to continue in existence is in doubt, the notes to the financial statements should describe the existence of and basis for the uncertainty, the steps being taken to resolve the uncertainty, and the potential effects on the financial statements if the company is not able to continue in existence. In this regard, for SEC filings, a careful determination must be made as to whether the financial statements should be prepared on a going concern or on a liquidation basis of accounting. FRR 16 (Section 607.02) states that financial statements will be considered false and misleading if prepared on an inappropriate basis of accounting. Figure 28.8 illustrates a going concern uncertainty disclosure.

Measurement of claims. Material unreconciled differences between claims filed and recorded balances should be disclosed in the notes to the financial statements. As indicated in the earlier section entitled "Timing of Accounting Recognition," creditor claims filed normally exceed recorded liabilities, frequently by substantial amounts. The processing of claims is a long and arduous undertaking that usually entails obtaining detailed supporting information from vendors, comparing it with company records, and conducting negotiations with individual creditors to resolve differences. The process may continue well after the plan of reorganization has been confirmed by the court.

Potential impact of reorganization efforts. The number and degree of uncertainties deriving from a debtor's reorganization efforts decrease as the case progresses, but

Note 2. Economic Environment of the Industry

The depressed economic conditions which currently exist within the petroleum industry have had a negative impact on the Company's operations since March 1982. As a result of these depressed conditions, an unprecedented number of drilling rigs are idle and their collateral value has substantially eroded. All of these factors, as long as they exist, will continue to affect adversely the Company's future profit margins and cash flow.

On December 8, 1982, the Company was informed by the bank providing the Company's current line of credit that borrowings thereunder will be limited to amounts advanced through November 30, 1982 ($13,500,000) pending further discussions regarding collateral values and other matters.

If the current depressed economic conditions continue to exist, the continuation of the Company as a going concern will depend upon its ability to attain satisfactory levels of future cash flows either from profitable operations or from additional debt financing, debt modification or additional capital financing. The accompanying consolidated financial statements have been prepared on a going concern basis and do not include any adjustments relating to the recoverability and classification of the recorded asset amounts or the amounts and classification of liabilities that might be necessary should the Company be unable to continue in existence.

FIG. 28.8 Illustrative Disclosure by a Company of Going Concern Uncertainty
Source: Astro Drilling Company, 1982 Annual Report.

some usually survive the confirmation of the plan of reorganization. Uncertainties originating with a debtor's reorganization efforts often include those relating to:

- Changes in operations, including the impact of the proceeding itself on operations and the extent to which operations will be terminated.
- Amounts to be realized from disposal of businesses or assets, the timing of the disposals, and the costs of disposition.
- The extent to which executory contracts will be rejected and the amounts of related claims.
- The outcome of litigation or compromises among the parties in interest of legal issues such as those relating to valuation of assets (This may affect the postpetition interest allowed on prepetition obligations.), the treatment of claims and interests of related debtors (Will they be equitably subordinated, or will the debtors be substantively consolidated?), petitions for relief from the automatic stay (Will secured creditors be permitted to repossess assets of the estate?), the amounts of voidable transfers, the amounts and status of claims against the estate, and other matters.

The notes to the financial statements should disclose the nature of the material uncertainties, the anticipated manner and timing of their resolution, and their potential impact on the financial statements.

Investigatory Findings. Frequently, one or more regulatory agencies or a trustee, examiner, or official committee initiate investigations into aspects of the case. Regulatory investigations commonly focus on matters such as fraud, the adequacy or accuracy of financial reporting, and insider trading. The investigations conducted under the auspices of the bankruptcy court might center on causes of the bankruptcy, fraud allegations, related party transactions, and preferential transfers. Full disclosure of pending investigations should be made in the notes to financial statements.

Incomplete Information. Many troubled companies experience deterioration in their internal control structures and record-keeping. The unusual steps that must be undertaken to stabilize a failing business (e.g., shifting management priorities and satisfying demands for information not routinely generated, changing the business and accounting systems, reducing workforce, and increasing management and employee turnover) interfere with organizational discipline and exacerbate internal control weaknesses. As a result, customarily available information may not exist, and there may be unusual doubts concerning the reliability of recorded balances. It may not be possible to provide some of the disclosures required by GAAP, and it may be necessary to make adjustments based extensively on estimates.

The notes to the financial statements should characterize uncertainties surrounding recorded balances, describe estimation techniques employed, and mention which disclosures have been omitted.

AUDITING CONSIDERATIONS

This section deals with the considerations faced by an auditor in performing an audit of the financial statements of a troubled company in accordance with generally accepted auditing standards. In addition, this section covers auditors' reports and unusual management representations and independence issues. Not covered are the more extensive procedures that might be required in a special investigation or other assignment possibly performed concurrently with the audit.

The scope of an audit of a troubled company's financial statements inevitably is more extensive than would be required in normal circumstances. The audit scope is influenced by considerations relating to uncertainties and the propriety of recording of transactions.

Determination of Audit Scope

An auditor must exercise careful judgment in balancing his desire to obtain the "right" answer against the practicalities of the situation. It simply may not be practicable for him to perform sufficient work to resolve material uncertainties or to satisfy himself as to the propriety of the recording of transactions.

Uncertainties. Conditions of the types discussed at the outset of this chapter raise substantial doubts about an entity's ability to continue in existence. Troubled situations can sometimes be identified at an earlier stage through the use of financial statement ratios, risk scoring techniques, and questionnaires.

Bankruptcy predictors. There have been a number of articles written about using financial statement liquidity ratios in predicting bankruptcies. Many widely used ratios for depicting financial health (e.g., the current ratio and debt-to-equity ratio) are effective only as very short-range indicators. The so-called *long-term liquidity* and *short-term liquidity* trend ratios have been developed to indicate whether a company may have financial problems within the next five years.

The long-term liquidity trend ratio uses the *gambler's ruin* prediction technique to determine the probability that future negative trends could render a company illiquid based on prior year-to-year liquidity changes and assumptions as to the liquidation values of the various assets. The ratio is expressed as a decimal fraction; the closer the value is to one, the greater the likelihood of illiquidity.

The short-term liquidity trend ratio uses the *discriminant analysis* technique to combine five key ratios mathematically in order to produce a score value (commonly known as a *Z Score*) that can be compared to empirically developed indicators of short-term illiquidity.

The predictive value of ratio analysis is somewhat limited because it is based primarily on financial statement data and financial statements are lagging indicators (reflecting existing conditions and past transactions). Other scoring techniques have been developed which designate subjectively determined values for particular non-financial characteristics that empirically have been associated with business failures. For example, high risk attributes of management structure (e.g., autocratic CEO with passive board), information systems (e.g., no budget) and other factors are each assigned a value. The values for all risk factors present are added together to obtain the total score, which is then compared to a standard. (See Chapter 7 for a further discussion.)

Questionnaires can also be used. Figure 28.9 contains a questionnaire designed to identify mature and developing troubled situations using readily available information not commonly found in financial statements.

Procedures to address going concern uncertainties. Under SAS 59, *The Auditor's Consideration of an Entity's Ability to Continue as a Going Concern* (see Chapter 11), the examination of the financial statements of a company should include an evaluation of whether there is substantial doubt about the entity's ability to continue as a going concern for at least a year beyond the financial statement date, as is assumed for financial accounting purposes in the absence of information to the contrary. As part of the reorganization or restructuring process, the entity will prepare information pertinent to the auditor's considerations. Such information includes business plans, liquidation analyses, and information prepared for the creditors. In formal proceedings, information used in the legal process also will be available. The auditor's consideration of such information should include verification of data to underlying documentation, and evaluation of assumptions on which prospective financial information is based. (See Chapter 27.) Ultimately, the auditor of a troubled company will have to rely on his judgment; accordingly, he need not extend the scope of his procedures into areas which do not appear likely to prove fruitful.

Proper Recording of Transactions. Deterioration in internal controls and in the quality and availability of accounting records in some troubled company cases is extensive enough to raise serious questions concerning whether transactions have been properly recorded. In some cases, the auditor will conclude that he will be able to satisfy himself by performing additional substantive procedures. In other cases, he will decide to the contrary, and it will then be necessary for him to issue either a qualified opinion (or disclaimer of opinion) due to a scope limitation.

This questionnaire is intended to facilitate the identification of troubled companies. The questionnaire is designed to be completed in only a few minutes. If there is a *yes* answer to a question in Section I, Mature Troubled Situations, or Section II, Developing Troubled Situations, the client's situation should be analyzed more thoroughly. Section II need not be completed if there is a yes answer to a Section I question.

	Yes	No
Mature Troubled Situations		
1. Is the client currently in default (or concerned about defaulting within the next 18 months) with respect to one or more loan covenants for which the client has not obtained a waiver that will not expire until after 18 months?	□	□
If yes, as a result of such default, is the lender entitled to accelerate the due date of the debt?	□	□
2. Has the client pledged all or substantially all of its assets as collateral for loans of a type not customary in its industry?	□	□
3. Has the client consulted with or engaged or contemplated consulting with or engaging any of the following specialists:		
• Bankruptcy counsel or other special counsel	□	□
• Investment bankers or consultants to assist in balance sheet restructuring	□	□
• Turnaround experts or consultants to assist in operations restructuring	□	□
4. Is the client negotiating or contemplating negotiating a debt restructuring, or has the client announced the need for a debt restructuring?	□	□
5. Is the client experiencing deteriorating relationships with its creditors:		
• Have creditors agreed to renew long-standing financing arrangements only upon significant modifications to customary terms and conditions?	□	□
• Have the creditors taken unusual actions to improve their positions (e.g., setting off cash balances)?	□	□
• Has the client transferred its bank balances, lock boxes, etc. to a bank(s) from which it has no borrowings?	□	□
• Have the client's creditors met informally or formed a committee in order to foster cooperation in resolving the client's financing needs?	□	□
• Has the client experienced difficulty in obtaining normal trade credit or issued trade notes as a substitute for customary open account financing?	□	□
• Other (specify)	□	□
6. Has the client failed to make payroll tax deposits or other payments as they mature on a regular basis?	□	□
7. Has the client inquired about or sought to change accounting methods to improve financial position or operating results?	□	□
Developing Troubled Situation		
1. Does the client have outstanding forward purchase commitments in excess of anticipated requirements?	□	□
2. Is the client's inventory mix out of balance in relation to what is selling, considering lead times, potential vendor strikes, or other disruptions and other relevant considerations?	□	□
3. Is the client's fixed asset capacity utilization (e.g., sales per square foot in retail, capacity utilization in manufacturing, or idle rigs in energy) significantly below normal for the client or the industry?	□	□

FIG. 28.9　Troubled Company Questionnaire

---

4. Is the client considering divestitures or asset dispositions as a result of its operating or financial problems? ☐ ☐
5. Do the company's projections indicate potential problems? ☐ ☐
6. Are substantially all of the client's obligations guaranteed?
   * Parent guarantees of subsidiary debt ☐ ☐
   * Personal guarantees of debt ☐ ☐
7. Does the client have significant exposure for pending litigation? ☐ ☐
8. Has the client failed to take advantage of favorable prompt payment discounts on a regular basis? ☐ ☐
9. Is the client or are its customers in a severely troubled industry? ☐ ☐

For example, when financial statements are to be issued in the early stages of a reorganization case, it is rarely possible for management to complete its claims reconciliation process prior to issuance. In such circumstances, it would not be practicable for the auditor to reconcile the claims. The auditor would consider the nature of differences between reconciled claimed and recorded amounts, his evaluation of the internal control structure, the amount of unreconciled claims, the amount of recorded liabilities, and the amount of income (or, more likely, loss) from operations in determining whether to modify his report.

On the the other hand, pervasive inadequacies in accounting records and internal controls would preclude an auditor from satisfying himself as to the propriety of the recording of transactions. Under such conditions, it would be fruitless for an auditor to extend his procedures.

Auditor's Reports

Usually, prior to the completion of a reorganization, the auditor will conclude that he must modify his report or disclaim an opinion because of significant going concern uncertainties, or possibly because of information deficiencies. The issues should be set forth in the auditor's report in an explanatory paragraph, referenced to pertinent footnote disclosures. The report should contain the reasons for the modification or denial of opinion. Figure 28.10 contains an auditor's report (a disclaimer) that will illustrate many of the issues discussed above.

Subsequent to confirmation of the reorganization plan, the auditor may be able to issue a standard report on the financial statements of the reorganized entity. If the matters that caused the auditor to modify his opinion on the financial statements of an earlier period are now resolved, the auditor should no longer modify a currently issued opinion with respect to the earlier period. All of the substantive reasons for the different opinion should be included in a separate explanatory paragraph of the report (AU 508.78).

There could be circumstances where the reasons for a modified auditor's report might survive a successful reorganization for a period of time, for example, where there are inadequate fixed asset records and the historical basis of accountability is

Board of Directors and Shareholders
Food Fair, Inc. (Debtor in Possession)
Fort Lauderdale, FL

We have examined the consolidated balance sheet of Food Fair, Inc. and subsidiaries (debtor in possession) as of July 28, 1979, and the related statements of operations (deficit), retained earnings and changes in financial position and the additional information listed in the accompanying index of financial statements and schedules for the year then ended. With significant exceptions, as described in the following paragraph, our examination was made in accordance with generally accepted auditing standards and, accordingly, included such tests of the accounting records and such other auditing procedures as we considered necessary in the circumstances. The consolidated financial statements for the year ended July 29, 1978, were examined by other auditors whose report thereon, dated March 9, 1979, contained a disclaimer of opinion because of the significance of restrictions on their examination scope for 1978 and uncertainties affecting the consolidated financial statements. As set forth in Note 7, the 1978 consolidated financial statements have been restated to reflect the capitalization of certain leases as required by Statement of Financial Accounting Standards No. 13, and reclassifications have been made to reflect the subsequent discontinuance of the J.M. Fields department store segment. We have reviewed such restatements and reclassifications, and we believe they have been properly applied.

Material weaknesses in the Company's and its subsidiaries' systems of internal control and deficiencies in record-keeping practices and other conditions described in Note 2 were such that, in a number of instances, present Company employees, many of whom had only recently assumed their current positions, were unable to locate adequate documentation in support of and provide satisfactory explanations for recorded transactions and balances. These conditions precluded us from obtaining sufficient competent evidential matter to satisfy ourselves on the extent to which 1979 operations reflect certain revenues and expenses which relate to prior or future periods and as to whether there are incorrect classifications within the statements of operations and changes in financial position. The Company has initiated programs, not yet fully developed or implemented, to correct material deficiencies in internal control and record-keeping practices to enable it in the future to regularly prepare reliable operating results and external financial reports on a timely basis.

As more fully described in Note 1, the Company and certain of its subsidiaries sustained substantial operating losses and developed a severe working capital shortage in the fiscal year ended July 29, 1978, and filed petitions under Chapter XI of the Bankruptcy Act, seeking an arrangement of their unsecured indebtedness. On October 2, 1978, the Bankruptcy Court entered an order authorizing the Company to continue as a debtor in possession. On April 28, 1980, the Official Creditors Committees approved by a majority vote the elements of a proposed Plan of Arrangement. In order for the Plan to become effective, the shareholders must approve certain corporate changes described in Note 4, and the Plan must be approved by a majority vote, in number and amount, of each class of eligible creditors and confirmed by the Court. The Plan will not be confirmed unless, among other things, the Court finds the Plan to be feasible and in the best interests of the creditors within the meaning of the Bankruptcy Act. In order to generate sufficient cash to effectuate the Proposed Plan of Arrangement, the Company must, in some combination, realize net proceeds from its disposition program in excess of the carrying amounts reflected in the balance sheet, settle claims that have been or may be filed with the Court at amounts below the liabilities deferred in the balance sheet, and/or operate profitably enough and obtain additional funds from programs presently under consideration. If the Chapter XI proceed-

FIG. 28.10   Report of Independent Accountants on a Debtor in Possession
Source: Food Fair, Inc., 1979 Form 10-K. (Wording not modified to reflect audit reporting standards of SAS 58 and SAS 59 issued in 1988 (see Chapter 11).)

ings are not concluded by confirmation of a plan of arrangement, we are advised that it is possible that the proceedings will be transferred to the Corporate reorganization provisions of Chapter X of the Act and a Trustee appointed, or the Company may be adjudicated a bankrupt and its assets liquidated.

As described in Notes 5 and 6, the Company is defendant in a number of lawsuits, is the subject of ongoing investigations by the Securities and Exchange Commission and a Federal grand jury, and has other significant contingencies. Further, since October 2, 1978, the Company has: 1) sustained significant losses prior to and in connection with discontinuance of its J.M. Fields discount department store segment and closing of more than half of its supermarket operations, and has entered into a program to dispose of the related assets; 2) sustained significant losses in the year ended July 28, 1979, from the ongoing supermarket operations; and 3) been notified that upon termination of the Chapter XI proceedings, the U.S. Department of Agriculture intends to terminate its license under the Perishable Agriculture Commodities Act (PACA), and it is unable to predict with certainty whether such license, which it believes is essential to its business, can be renewed on terms within its financial resources.

The accompanying consolidated financial statements have been prepared on the basis of accounting principles applicable to a going concern which contemplate the realization of assets and liquidation of liabilities in the normal course of business and at the amounts stated in the accompanying consolidated balance sheet. The Company's ability to continue as a going concern is dependent on:

— Obtaining the approval of the shareholders for prerequisite corporate changes and the approval of the creditors and the confirmation by the Court of a plan of arrangement.

— Achieving profitable operations and generating cash sufficient to comply with terms of a confirmed plan of arrangement and then reestablishing and sustaining normal trade credit terms with suppliers.

— Obtaining adequate financing for the future needs of the Company, including that needed to complete its Capital Improvements Program;

— Completing the development of and implementing satisfactory systems of internal control and recordkeeping practices so that it is able to prepare reliable operating and external financial reports on a timely basis;

— Favorably resolve pending litigation, Federal grand jury and SEC investigations, and other contingencies referred to in Notes 5 and 6; and

— Renewing its PACA license.

Should the Company be unable to satisfactorily resolve the material uncertainties listed above, it would likely be unable to continue as a going concern and/or be adjudicated a bankrupt, and it would be required to realize its assets and liquidate its liabilities in other than the normal course of business and possibly at amounts materially different from those included in the accompanying consolidated balance sheet.

In 1979, as described in Note 7, the Company adopted new methods of accounting with which we concur, as a result of which the Company now charges warehousing costs and payroll taxes to operations as incurred.

Material weaknesses in the Company's and its subsidiaries' systems of internal control and deficiencies in the recordkeeping practices prevented the Company, and therefore us, from obtaining sufficient evidence to provide the disclosures required by generally accepted accounting principles that have been omitted as described in Note 2.4 and to ascertain the extent

(continued)

to which 1979 results of operations reflect incorrect classifications and include revenues and expenses which relate to prior or future periods, including:

1. The portion, which would be significant, of the $14,500,000 adjustment for self-insurance described in Note 2.3, which applies to years prior to 1979, and

2. The extent, if any, to which the provision for creditor's claims, as described in Note 2.1, applies to years prior to 1979.

Also, it is not possible to determine the effect on all of the accompanying 1979 consolidated financial statements of such adjustments as might have been required had the outcome of the material uncertainties relating to the Company's continuation as a going concern been known. Accordingly, we are unable to and do not express an opinion on the accompanying consolidated financial statements referred to in the first paragraph of this report.

FIG. 28.10 (continued)

continued. In such circumstances, the modification would be removed when the impact on the financial statements would no longer be deemed material.

Chapter 11 of this *Handbook* contained additional information on Auditors' Reports.

Management Representations

Typically, troubled companies, particularly those in formal proceedings, experience turnover at senior management levels. Newly arrived officers may be reluctant to provide the standard management representation letters requested by auditors. They are properly concerned that they may not be aware of significant past transactions or current conditions not disclosed to the auditors that could affect the auditor's opinion on the financial statements.

Because the representations requested are limited to the knowledge and belief of the responding officers, the new managers' concerns ordinarily can be resolved by permitting them to disclose in the representation letter the dates of their employment. Where there has been significant senior management turnover, the auditor might want to expand the list of signatories to include additional managers whose tenure includes the period covered by the financial statements.

If he is unable to obtain satisfactory management representations, the auditor will disclaim an opinion on the financial statements.

Independence

In evaluating his independence in relation to a troubled client, an auditor must consider unpaid fees and the extent of his work. If independence has been impaired, the auditor should state in his report that he is not independent and disclaim an opinion on the financial statements.

An auditor's independence is not impaired solely because his client is prohibited by law from paying fees for services rendered prior to the date of its petitioning the court for protection. If, however, the client fails to pay the fees for some other reason or objects to the auditor's claim for fees for prepetition services, the auditor must carefully evaluate the impact of his independence. If the unpaid amount for prior services is clearly significant to both the auditor and the client, the auditor would ordinarily conclude that his independence is impaired.

Where the client lacks qualified accounting personnel and adequate financial records, the auditor often will assist in the preparation of the financial statements. The auditor must be alert to the possibility that his involvement in the preparation of the financial statements could become so extensive that his independence becomes impaired.

PART **IV**

Industries Other Than Financial Services

29

Retail Industry

OVERVIEW

Definition of Retailing

Retailing is the business of selling goods to the consumer, most commonly conducted by a retailer who owns or operates a store. In some instances the business is conducted without a store, through operations such as door-to-door selling, mail order, or electronic selling. Others besides traditional retailers may also take part in selling, such as manufacturers, importers, and wholesalers who sell directly to the consumer.

Retailing is one of the largest industries in the U.S. and necessarily adapts to the changes in and demands of society. Consequently, retailing is a highly diversified business, with various forms of ownership and strategy mix.

Ownership Classification. Retail ownership classifications vary and may include independents, chains, franchises, and licensed departments.

The *independent* retailer owns, and generally operates, one retail unit. Such retailers are plentiful in the United States, mainly because of the ease of entry into the business. Independents are generally smaller enterprises.

A *chain* is a multiple of retail units under common ownership. The chain often takes advantage of centralization, with a single organization supplying management, purchasing, and other forms of support for all of the units. Ideally the advantages that come with the size of a chain include greater resources, more bargaining power with manufacturers, and increased efficiency in store operations, administration, and advertising. A chain may have more than one division, enabling it to sell different kinds or qualities of merchandise in different store formats, such as a general merchandise store and a home center. A store in a chain is generally operated by a hired manager who executes policy set down by someone else, such as the owners.

A *franchise* is operated and generally owned by a franchisee (often an individual) conducting business under the name and pattern of a multi-unit, chain-type organization (the franchisor). The franchisee generally pays an initial fee and a percentage of operations for the right to sell specified merchandise in a specific location under clearly defined conditions. The franchisee often receives assistance from the franchisor in the form of training, promotions, and administrative support.

A *licensed department* is an area of a retail store rented by an outside party for the purpose of selling a specified type of merchandise under conditions stipulated by the store. The licensed department operator benefits from the consumer traffic generated by the larger retailer; the retailer benefits by supplementing his own merchandise categories with those of the licensed operator. The merchandise techniques of the licensed department operator usually blend with those of the store, so that the licensed department appears to the customer as part of the store's operations.

Strategy Mix. Retailing shows even greater diversity when considered from the standpoint of retail strategy mix – product, price, service, promotion, and location.

The *department store* operates under a strategy that offers a wide assortment of merchandise of above-average quality at competitive prices. Product lines are generally segmented into departments such as apparel and related accessories, health and beauty aids, and furniture and other home accessories, each with its own space and staff. The department store offers customer service, promotes itself heavily in newspapers and through direct mail, and is usually located in a downtown business center or major shopping mall.

The *discount store* has a fairly wide assortment of merchandise, usually concentrated in the apparel and home accessory lines, but may also include drug store merchandise, auto parts, and recreational and other types of merchandise of somewhat lower quality and considerably lower price than that of the department store. Discount stores may be found in the same locations as department stores and may promote as heavily, but offer a lower level of service. The discount retailer is sometimes known as a "mass merchandiser."

The *variety store* is a vestige of what was known as the "5 and 10¢ store" selling a wide assortment of low-priced merchandise. These stores offer little in the way of service, and can be found in downtown districts, shopping centers, and more isolated sites.

The *specialty store* concentrates in a narrow category of merchandise, such as apparel, jewelry, hardware, auto supplies, toys, or electronics. The specialty store often tries to stock its category of merchandise to great depth and offer a high level of customer service. These stores are generally located in business districts and malls.

The *retail catalog showroom* generally displays one of each item sold. Items selected for purchase are then retrieved from the stock room by sales personnel or placed on order to be delivered from a warehouse or other location. Catalog showrooms generally offer a limited range of merchandise at prices similar to a discount store. The primary advertising done by these retailers is in the form of catalogs mailed to homes. These showrooms can be located at malls, in business districts, and more isolated sites.

The *membership store* (including warehouse clubs) caters to select groups of consumers such as members of unions, clubs, and organizations based on occupation, military affiliation, and so on. Membership is required to make purchases and may include small retailers as well as consumers. Direct mail is the primary means of advertising, since the target audience is clearly identified. Merchandise available can vary from a wide assortment to a fairly limited range of goods. Prices are low and services are few. Membership clubs may operate in warehouse settings, often in rather isolated locations.

The *supermarket* carries an extensive assortment of foods sold at competitive prices and is usually part of a large chain. Supermarkets are usually neighborhood stores that promote heavily in newspapers, often offering discount coupons. Except for specialty areas within the store, such as the drug store, bakery and delicatessen, the supermarket is largely self-service.

The *convenience store* offers a limited assortment of food products, generally basics such as milk and bread, as well as other merchandise such as newspapers and cigarettes. These are neighborhood stores frequently located on major roads, and are open daily for many hours, offering convenience to customers. Prices are above average and services relatively few.

Non-store retailing includes mail order, door-to-door, television, electronic, and party selling (e.g., Tupperware). Shoppers are introduced to merchandise through catalogs, television, or a computer monitor, either in a public access location or in the home. Purchases can be made by mail, over the telephone, or through an interactive computer network. Merchandise available varies, and prices are generally lower because of the retailer's reduced operating costs. Electronic shopping, however, is still in its infancy; and its costs may be higher, resulting in higher prices to consumers. Non-store retailing accounts for a significant portion of retail sales.

Evolution of the Industry

Prior to World War II, retailing was dominated by the large downtown department stores and independent retailers, generally local "Mom and Pop" operations. The only major chains were enterprises such as Sears Roebuck, J.C. Penney, and Montgomery Ward, and variety chains such as S.S. Kresge and F.W. Woolworth. In the food industry, A&P was one of few major grocery store chains. Large scale general merchandise retailing was limited to the downtown department store. There was no discount store as we know it today and specialty stores played a relatively minor role in retailing.

After World War II, as Americans began to buy automobiles in large numbers and settle in the suburbs, retailers saw the need to bring stores to their customers.

Land was plentiful and relatively inexpensive, and erecting a store with a large parking lot accessible to shoppers from the cities as well as the suburbs was a sensible business idea. Clustering a variety of stores in a single location was a logical next step, resulting in the creation of the shopping center.

With the economy booming and couples starting families after the war, retailing was a robust industry. Entrepreneurs saw the opportunity to offer an alternative to the traditional department store while concentrating on brand name, hard goods lines. The resulting discount store was large and offered as full a line of merchandise as the department store, but because of its free-standing and out-of-the-way location and its no-frills atmosphere, it offered consumers similar merchandise at a lower price. Some of the variety stores saw a serious threat in the discounters and modified their formats. For example, S.S. Kresge formed its own discount store division – K Mart. Discounting also took market share away from the traditional supermarket and drug store, differentiating the product in each case by price.

The growth and expansion of retail stores was relatively easy through the 1950s and 1960s. But by the 1970s choice locations were fewer and competitors numerous in most regions of the country. Customers could get the same merchandise for the same price at any number of stores within a short distance from home. Retailers had to work harder to penetrate a market and to keep their hard-won customers. They did so with sharper merchandising – paying greater attention to merchandise quality, fashion appeal, service, and in-stock conditions. They also installed controls that kept their costs down and prices competitive.

This need to merchandise more sharply influenced the tremendous growth in specialty stores in the 1970s and early 1980s. Much smaller than the traditional department or discount store, the specialty retailer could carve out a niche more readily, target customers more accurately, and adapt more quickly to changing lifestyles, fashions, and attitudes. A specialty store strategy could be implemented and managed much more easily than that of a larger organization. In addition, smaller stores often meant less overhead and greater sales per square foot and per employee.

Besides the growth of specialty stores, the 1970s brought a major increase in mail order and catalog showroom retailing, and in membership clubs. The 1980s saw the advent of television shopping, with a great variety of merchandise displayed on television that could be ordered by telephone. The spread of the computer also reached retailing at this time. Shoppers could "tune into" merchandise categories of their own choosing and see still or animated displays of merchandise; they could compare brands, features, and prices through a simple interaction with the computer; and they could then order items in the same way.

Diversification, Consolidation, and Acquisitions

The look of retailing changed dramatically in the 1980s. A number of new names appeared on the scene and became serious contenders for market share. Traditional retail companies reacted to these challengers and to the specialty wave by diversifying into different segments. Companies merged or were acquired by others. More than a few of the old names in retailing closed their doors for the last time. Companies opened wide ranges of specialty stores selling apparel, computers, books, and other merchandise. While some companies diversified, others were consolidating, selling off unprofitable units and even divisions.

A sampling of those gone from the list of active retailers includes once successful companies such as Korvettes, Gimbel's (previously acquired by Batus), City Stores, and W.T. Grant. Associated Dry Goods was acquired by May Department Stores, which thus achieved a significant measure of diversification in a single acquisition. Allied Stores and Federated Department Stores were acquired by a Canadian real estate developer, which then sold off a number of divisions in each. Macy's and Hills were the objects of leveraged buy-outs by management.

The terms *buying* and *selling* now had new meaning for retailers—referring not to the sale of merchandise, but of stores, divisions, and companies.

Environmental Factors

Retailing is directly or indirectly affected by numerous factors, the most influential of which are economic, demographic, social, competitive, and technological.

The primary *economic* factor is the condition of the country's economy or the economy of the area in which the retailer operates. The ability of consumers to buy naturally affect the potential for retailers to succeed. At issue is not only the level of personal income enjoyed by the retailer's customer base but also the level of discretionary income and consumer confidence in the future. As family discretionary income rises—for example, with the added income of a housewife returned to the labor force—the potential for increased sales rises. As that income falls—for example, because of a down-turning economy or widespread layoffs—the retailer's potential for short-term success declines.

A related economic factor is the use of credit. Although credit was once frowned upon by many Americans, it has become a major means of purchasing for millions. A recent study of a number of representative retailers found that approximately 58% of retail sales involved extensions of credit by retailers (Touche Ross, 1986). Retail credit has also expanded through the explosion of third party credit, such as bank and travel and entertainment credit cards.

Retailers are also affected by *demographics,* the population changes and shifts in a retailer's market. Shifts from rural to urban to suburban areas have influenced the location and success of retail stores. Shifts from one region to another, such as from the rustbelt to the sunbelt, can have similar effects. Retailers are also affected by shifts in the age structure of the population. For example, in the 1950s children made up a large percentage of the population and represented a certain mix of merchandise opportunities for retailers. In the 1980s that group was in the thirty- to forty-five-year-old bracket, representing different kinds of opportunities. In addition to shopper demographics, retailers are affected by the type and numbers of people making up the labor force in the areas of their stores. One of the major challenges facing retailers in the 1980s has been the shortage of qualified workers willing to work in retailing.

Social factors such as lifestyle preferences affect what retailers sell, and where, when, and in what atmosphere. For example, two-income families often produce more discretionary income and thus a more demanding consumer in terms of quality of merchandise and service. The demand for convenience in the form of location, ease of purchase, and the products themselves varies with the lifestyle of the retailer's clientele. Since attitudes can change—as the attitude toward credit did—retailers must be able to adapt.

Competition is always a major influence on retailers. As competition increases, retailers become more vigilant about the issues that most concern their own customers, whether price, style, quality, or convenience. Competition provides a major incentive for operating more efficiently and for devising new ways to differentiate one's stores from the competition.

Technological changes also affect retailing. As a people-intensive industry involving an unusually large number of small transactions and a continuous flow of related data, retailing is always striving to find simpler, more efficient systems for its operations. With the advance of technology and its adaptation to retailing, the industry has worked to reduce the amount of required labor and the margin for human error. Retailing has also increased its capacity to capture data about its merchandise process from planning through distribution and selling, and to use that data for operating and strategy decisions. The point of sale (POS) terminal and its related computer network have been a boon to the information capabilities of the technologically sophisticated retailer.

Future Trends

For the immediate future, retailing will function according to the dictates of a zero-sum reality. The industry as a whole is not taking a larger share of consumers' discretionary income than it has in past years. Any gains individual retailers make will come at the expense of other retailers. At a time when the industry seems "overstored," retailers must venture out of their normal markets and maximize the efficiency and responsiveness of their operations.

As successful retailers grow across the country, the overstored condition in the industry will intensify. Towns of 30,000 to 50,000 people, once seen as too small to support a major retail store, are now the sites for prototypes. Retailers will use existing store space more creatively for new retail classifications or services, or for other commercial ventures.

Changes in society will also force changes in retailing. Retailers will be able to reach customers in their homes, workplaces, and other public places as technology increasingly enters retail transactions. Consumers will demand these options and retailers will respond.

The store itself will remain the dominant format for shopping, however, but may concentrate its in-store merchandise in inventory classifications where "feeling the merchandise" is critical. Many stores also will differentiate themselves through services matched to their target groups. Productivity will change, with improved technology being used for more functions. Electronic communication between retailer and vendor, for instance, will reduce lead times in ordering merchandise, improve in-stock conditions, and improve overall profit.

The future will also see more manufacturers taking market share from retailers by direct selling. Some retailers will react to this intrusion by establishing joint ventures with manufacturers.

SIGNIFICANT RETAIL ACCOUNTING ISSUES

Inventory Methods

There are two basic methods of placing a cost value on inventory in the retail environment: (1) the cost method and (2) the retail method, preferred by most retailers. The *cost method* uses the actual or average cost of merchandise as the basis for determining inventory value. The *retail method* uses the relationship of retail price to cost for purchases to determine the cost of inventory. As the number of items and transactions increases, the cost method becomes increasingly cumbersome and expensive to apply. The retail method is an averaging method and is more convenient for most types of merchandise, as it enables the retailer to determine profits without taking frequent physical inventories. To function properly, merchandise having like cost-to-retail relationships must be grouped together.

In computing book and taxable income, retailers have traditionally used either the FIFO (first-in, first-out) or LIFO (last-in, first-out) method of accounting. The impact of inflation on inventory costs has caused many retailers to switch to LIFO because it reduces taxable income in periods of rising prices. Retailers invest heavily in merchandise and must know at all times the value and quantity of their inventory to make day-to-day merchandising decisions. For example, current retail and cost values of inventory must be known to rationally modify actions called for in merchandising plans.

The accounting and EDP departments are responsible for providing this information. Merchandise information used to assist management in the operation of the business is frequently provided by an off-line process not integrated with the inventory accounting system. With profits based on inventory costs and merchants and management measured according to profits, inventory cost is of vital concern to many people in the organization.

Cost Method. The cost method provides valuation of inventory using only cost figures. This means that all inventory records provide the cost of the merchandise, either by specific identification or by some averaging technique. Other retail statistics, such as initial markup and subsequent price changes, are maintained in supplementary records and are not necessarily a part of the accounting system. A physical inventory is taken, and unit counts are then extended at cost values.

Cost of sales is determined in one of two ways: by assigning a cost to all individual units sold, or by starting with the beginning inventory at cost, adding purchases at cost, and subtracting the ending physical inventory extended at cost. For interim periods between physical inventories, cost of sales is determined by applying estimated gross margin percentages to sales. Shortage is automatically included in the cost of sales because the ending physical inventory will be reduced for shortages. Under the cost method, an additional computation must be performed to determine lower-of-cost-or-market value, as required in GAAP basis financial statements.

The cost method is well-suited to departments and stores with high unit-value items, where it is important to maintain unit control. These items generally are easier to track as they move through inventory, as there are fewer units and fewer transactions.

Retail Method. As companies grow, it becomes impractical to track each inventory unit and its cost. Thus most retail organizations use the retail method to keep track of the amounts invested in inventory, especially where the number of items is large.

The retail inventory method is an averaging method that assumes the cost complement (the percentage relationship of cost to retail for merchandise purchases) of actual items in ending inventory is represented by the cost complement of purchases. The retail method provides a means for reasonably estimating the cost value of an inventory extended at retail selling prices. This method expresses all percentages, such as initial markup and gross profit, relative to the retail price, rather than to the cost price, of the merchandise.

A simple example will explain the principal difference between the cost and retail inventory methods. A dress is purchased for $50, and retails for $105. The markup is $55, or 110% of the cost price. Under the retail method, the $55 markup is expressed as 52.4% of the retail price. In applying the retail method, the total cost of merchandise on hand is determined by first calculating the sum of current retail prices. The dress will be listed at its selling price of $105 and reduced to cost value by multiplying the selling price by the cost complement of 47.6% (the reciprocal of the markup percentage). This produces a cost of $50 (47.6% × $105). Under the cost method, by comparison, the dress would be valued by direct reference to the $50 cost. Although this is a simplified example, it illustrates that when many items are involved, it is easier to use the cost complement percentage (retail inventory method) than the cost method.

If the retail price of the dress is marked down by $25, the cost complement of 47.6% under the retail method would be applied to this new retail selling price. This produces a cost of $38 (($105 − $25) × 47.6%). The retail markdown of $25 therefore produces a cost write-down of $12 ($50 − $38 = $12). Thus this step also automatically values inventory at lower of cost or market, as required for GAAP basis financial statements. Under the retail method, the cost associated with taking a markdown affects income immediately. Under the cost method, this differential is effectively deferred until the merchandise is sold, or is specifically reflected in lower-of-cost-or-market adjustments at a financial reporting date.

There are many benefits to the retail inventory method including:

1. It is the most efficient method of keeping track of many items, since all transactions, such as sales and markdowns, are accomplished in terms of retail values and specific costs are not needed for individual items sold.

2. Periodic determination of inventory cost and gross profits can be made without taking physical inventories, because perpetual inventory records are maintained at retail selling prices. However, physical inventories (at retail) are generally taken twice a year to check the accuracy of the perpetual inventory.

3. Physical inventory taking is simplified because the count can be taken at the readily available retail prices and compared to corresponding book amounts.

4. All merchant-oriented inventory information is expressed in terms of retail dollars so that the buyer can plan sales, stock levels, gross margins, markdowns, desired merchandise turnover, and open-to-buy in a consistent manner.

5. The retail method permits a determination of inventory shortage by referring to retail values without having to compare unit counts to unit records.

6. The retail method automatically produces an inventory at the lower of cost or market, provided appropriate markdowns are taken on a timely basis. This method records the reduction in gross profit when the price reduction is taken, rather than waiting until the sale is made.

The retail method is not without its disadvantages; these include:

1. A large volume of record-keeping is required to accumulate price changes, markups, and markdowns.
2. As an averaging method that assumes a homogeneous markup percentage for purchases, it smooths extremely high or low relationships of cost to retail for individual purchases. It also assumes that ending inventory is representative of total purchases throughout the period.
3. It is subject to some amount of distortion. For example, deferred markdowns will cause an overstatement of inventory.

Applying the retail inventory method. The retail inventory method is applied in a step-by-step fashion. The steps are, for each department:

1. Calculate total inventory available for sale at retail and cost (opening inventory plus purchases).
2. Calculate the cumulative markup percentage and cost complement.
3. Calculate the total retail reductions (sales, markdowns, employee discounts, and shortage provisions) from inventory.
4. Determine the ending inventory at cost and retail.
5. Calculate the cost of goods sold.
6. Determine the gross margin.

The procedure may seem complicated, but it can be learned easily if viewed as a series of six steps, each one building on and using the information gathered in the previous steps. Facilitating the retail inventory method is the retail stock ledger, represented in Figure 29.1. This accounting report, usually closed out at the end of each semiannual season for FIFO purposes, but kept open for the entire fiscal year for tax LIFO purposes (as discussed under "Tax Impact of LIFO"), details the book inventory dollar totals for each merchandise grouping. The six steps are illustrated with sample figures:

1. Total inventory available for sale. Beginning inventory plus purchases represents the inventory to be accounted for in the period, at both cost and retail. The elements that constitute merchandise received are: vendor invoice cost less discounts and returns to vendors, freight-in charges at cost only, assigned retail for all purchases, and additional markups at retail only. In Figure 29.1, total inventory available for sale is calculated to be $160,800 at cost and $333,000 at retail.
2. Cumulative markup and cost complement. Cumulative markup is the difference between the retail selling price and the total cost of merchandise. In Figure 29.1 the amount is $172,200. Cumulative markup percentage is the total markup in dollars divided by the total retail price. Knowing the cumulative markup as a percentage of retail is very useful in comparing actual and planned figures and the current period's performance against the

	Cost	Retail	Cumulative markup percent	Cumulative cost percent
Beginning inventory	$100,000	$208,000	51.9%	48.1%
Add:				
Purchases, net of returns	60,000	120,000		
Freight in	2,000			
Less cash discount (2%)	(1,200)			
Additional markups		5,000		
Net additions	60,800	125,000		
Total inventory available for sale	160,800	333,000	51.7%	48.3%
Less:				
Net sales		100,000		
Net markdowns		20,000		
Shortage		2,000		
Employee discounts		1,000		
Total retail reductions		123,000		
Ending inventory	101,430	$210,000		
Cost of goods sold	$ 59,370			
Gross margin:				
Net sales		$100,000		
Less cost of goods sold		59,370		
Gross margin		$ 40,630		

FIG. 29.1   Retail Stock Ledger

prior period. In the example, cumulative markup percentage is 51.7%, or $172,200 ÷ $333,000. The cumulative cost complement is cost divided by retail (or 100% minus the cumulative markup percentage). In Figure 29.1 this is 48.3%.

3. Total retail reductions from inventory. Total reductions represent the cumulative retail value of net sales, net markdowns, shortages, and employee discounts. Each of these elements is defined later herein.

   Net sales consist of customer purchases less customer returns.

   Net markdowns are markdowns less markdown cancellations. Markdowns reduce merchandise from its original marked and recorded retail price to a reduced retail price at which it is marked and finally sold. After merchandise value has been reduced at retail (marked down), the retailer may want to restore it to its original retail price or some intermediate higher price. This action to restore the item to a higher retail price would be a markdown cancellation.

   Shortage is the difference between the actual physical inventory at retail and the retail amount in the stock ledger. A provision for estimated shortage is usually made as a percentage of sales for the periods between physical inventories. The provision is adjusted to actual when a physical inventory is taken.

   Employee discounts are the differences between recorded retail price and the price at which merchandise is sold to employees.

In Figure 29.1, total retail reductions are calculated to be $123,000.

4. Ending inventory at cost and retail. Ending inventory at retail is calculated first, by subtracting total retail reductions from the retail value of the merchandise available for sale during the period. In Figure 29.1, the ending inventory at retail is $210,000. Ending inventory at cost is determined by multiplying ending inventory at retail by the cumulative cost complement percentage. In Figure 29.1, the cumulative cost percentage of 48.3% multiplied against ending retail inventory results in a cost of $101,430.

5. Cost of goods sold. The merchandise cost of goods sold is calculated by subtracting ending inventory at cost from total merchandise available for sale at cost. In Figure 29.1, the cost of goods sold is $59,370.

6. Gross margin and gross margin percentage are statistics that measure the profitability of merchandise grouped together for accounting purposes. To calculate gross margin, total cost of goods sold is subtracted from net sales. To calculate gross margin percentage, gross margin is divided by net sales. In Figure 29.1, the gross margin is $40,630, and the gross margin percentage is 40.6%.

Applying the retail inventory method requires discipline and consistency. Nevertheless, retailers have found it to be the best available method for controlling the elements of gross margin.

Inventory Valuation

A major objective in accounting for inventories is to determine income by properly matching appropriate costs against revenues. The principal methods used in that computation under GAAP are FIFO and LIFO. FIFO matches the oldest cost of items purchased with revenue from current sales. LIFO matches the most recent cost of items purchased with the revenue from current sales. Since many retailers expect that inflation is here to stay, LIFO rather than FIFO is generally used.

As discussed in the following section, a reduction in income tax payments is the most tangible advantage of using LIFO. In effect, the tax impact of the cumulative difference between the FIFO and LIFO inventory is an interest-free loan from the government. This benefit, however, accrues only with continuing inflation. The anticipated tax advantage is reduced, or even reversed, if there is a drop in price levels below those at which the base inventory is priced.

Tax Impact of LIFO. The LIFO method of inventory valuation saves tax dollars in periods of inflation. Since LIFO enables a retailer to match most recent, and higher, inventory costs with current sales, it reduces taxable income and consequently the company's tax liabilities. Conversely, in using FIFO during an inflationary period, the retailer is matching current sales against older and lower costs. The result is generally greater taxable income and higher tax payments than under LIFO.

This effect is illustrated in Figure 29.2; the data in each column is discussed in the following subsections.

Column 1—Retail inventory. The initial data required is identical to that used in converting to cost under the retail method, namely, the retail inventory value as

Year ended	(1) Retail Inventory	(2) Index (base=100)	(3) Retail Inventory at base year prices (1)/(2)	(4) Retail layer Increase (decrease)	(5) Retail layer at base year prices	(6) Retail layer at end of period prices (2)×(5)	(7) LIFO cost complement	(8) LIFO cost at end of period (6)×(7)
1st Year								
1/31/X0	$25,000	100.0	$25,000	$25,000	$25,000	$25,000	66.4	$16,600
1/31/X1	36,000	108.4	33,210	8,210	8,210	8,900	65.3	5,812
					$33,210	$33,900		$22,412
2nd Year								
1/31/X0	$25,000	100.0	$25,000	$25,000	$25,000	$25,000	66.4	$16,600
1/31/X1	36,000	108.4	33,210	8,210	8,210	8,900	65.3	5,812
1/31/X2	40,000	110.0	36,364	3,154	3,154	3,469	66.0	2,290
					$36,364	$37,369		$24,702
3rd Year								
1/31/X0	$25,000	100.0	$25,000	$25,000	$25,000	$25,000	66.4	$16,600
1/31/X1	36,000	108.4	33,210	8,210	6,304	6,834	65.3	4,463
1/31/X2	40,000	110.0	36,364	3,154			66.0	
1/31/X3	36,000	115.0	31,304	(5,060)			65.8	
					$31,304	$31,834		$21,063

FIG. 29.2   Computation of LIFO Inventory

indicated by the balance in the inventory records. Note that in the first year, the values for the opening and closing inventories are listed. The reason is that the price levels at the beginning of the first year in which the LIFO election for tax purposes is made acts as the base level and all future years are measured against this level.

In subsequent years' computations, each year's retail inventory valuation, from the base year on, is listed separately. This is necessary to determine the inventory layers composing the year-end LIFO valuation. Each year's inventory represents a layer or level of inventory valuation that is used as a segment of the total LIFO valuation. This segmentation is necessary because each layer's current valuation must be calculated by the same factors involved in its origination. If the inventory level decreases at year end (as shown in year 3), the decrease is taken from the immediately preceding inventory layer.

Column 2—Index. This column indicates the level of price change that occurred from the beginning of the year in which use of the LIFO method commenced. Thus, in the illustration, 1/31/X0 bears the index of 100.00, against which all future years will be measured.

An appropriate index must be used and is subject to challenge by the IRS. In Figure 29.2, the index shown for each year is hypothetical. In practice, however, department stores generally use the Bureau of Labor Statistics (BLS) LIFO index, which has express IRS approval. This index was first published in 1948 with price level data from 1941; it is now published monthly.

The BLS index is presently classified into 23 groups. Because the computation of LIFO is made on a departmental grouping basis for department stores, the BLS groupings must be correlated with a listing of appropriate departments by each retailer.

Column 3—Retail inventory at base year prices. Dividing the inventory at retail at each year end by the appropriate index factor eliminates the influence of the price level change and restates the various retail valuations in commmon base year dollars.

Column 4—Retail layer increase or decrease. By subtracting each year's inventory at base year dollars from the preceding year's inventory at the same base year dollars, the yearly retail increase (incremental layer) or decrease (liquidation of layer) starting from the base year total is established. Column 3 eliminates differences attributable to price level, and thus the amounts in Column 4 represent quantity changes for each year.

Column 5—Retail layer at base year prices. The amounts for each year in Column 5 are derived from those in Column 4 and project the various layers of inventory sufficient to cover the base dollar valuation indicated in Column 3, plus each year's increase. Decreases (as shown in Column 4) are eliminated by applying them against increases in the immediately preceding year or years until fully eliminated.

At the end of the first year there was an increase in quantities; this increase and the base layer at the beginning of the year are listed in Column 5 at base year dollars. The layers for each period are then priced out individually by use of the index identified with the period during which each layer was created (Column 6).

The second year shows a similar increase in physical quantities and, again, a layer at base year prices is added to the inventory valuation. During the third year, however, a decrease in quantities occurred. This decrease, therefore, has to be offset against the inventory layers built to that point, the latest one being used first. As the term LIFO implies, the liquidation of layers is started with the last layer and proceeds to each immediately preceding layer as needed. Using this procedure, the 1/31/X2 layer is completely eliminated and a portion of the 1/31/X1 layer is also liquidated to absorb the 1/31/X3 decrease. Once an inventory layer has been depleted in this manner, it cannot be reinstated for future years' computations.

Column 6—Retail layer at end of period prices. Here the retail layers at base year prices, as obtained in Column 5, representing the quantitative composition of the LIFO valuation, are restored to the price levels existing at the time each layer was created. This is done by multiplying the retail increment in base year dollars by the price index that is denominated as a factor of the base year index. This step supplies the LIFO valuation at retail, which must now be converted to cost.

Column 7—LIFO cost complement. The procedure for converting the LIFO valuation at retail to cost is substantially the same as the basic retail inventory cost conversion described earlier. If FIFO cost were being determined, the cost complement is based on gross markup (without including markdowns). However, tax regulations applicable to retail LIFO require the use of a cost complement based on a net markup (i.e., markups net of markdowns). The lower cost complement used in the FIFO retail method results in a lower-of-cost-or-market valuation, but for tax purposes LIFO is strictly a cost method regardless of market. The use of the net markup percentages thus eliminates the lower-of-cost-or-market effect.[1]

Column 8—LIFO inventory at cost. By use of the LIFO cost complement (Column 7) in conjunction with the retail layers at their respective period prices (Column 6), a LIFO cost valuation is now obtained.

Earnings Impact of LIFO. The Internal Revenue Code requires that a taxpayer electing the LIFO method for tax purposes must also use it for financial reporting purposes. This regulation is known as the *LIFO conformity rule.* Strict conformity in the application of the method, however, is not required by the IRS, and disclosure of non-LIFO information is permitted and often given. (See Chapter 14.) With lower taxable income and the resulting lower tax payments, LIFO virtually always results in lower reported earnings. This will not concern a retailer's stockholders or credit grantors, as knowledgeable business people are familiar with LIFO and applaud the cash savings through lower taxes, despite its effect on earnings.

Markup Cancellations. Initial markup represents the relationship between cost and retail at the time of purchase. In an effort to obtain higher initial markups, many retailers employ markup cancellations—price reductions included in the calculation of the cumulative markup percentage. Misuse of markup cancellations increases the cost complement and thus the cost value assigned to inventory. For example, assume that the markdowns in Figure 29.1 instead were markup cancellations. Total inventory available for sale would then be $313,000 because the markup cancellations would reduce the initial markup. The revised cumulative markup percent would become 48.6%, and cumulative cost percent accordingly would be 51.4%. Ending inventory would increase by $6,510 to $107,940.

The foregoing example illustrates the extreme sensitivity of the retail method to the proper classification of price reductions. Accordingly, care should be taken to ensure that markup cancellations are used only to correct identifiable errors in original markups or to reduce unusually high initial markups to normal department percentages. Failure to so limit markup cancellations will result in overstatement of ending inventory and the understatement of cost of goods sold.

Dissimilar Markup Percentages. For effective use of the retail method, it is essential that only inventory with similar markups be grouped together. The example shown in Figure 29.3 follows the calculation methodology in Figure 29.1. With one of the two dissimilar items sold, the remaining item in inventory is valued significantly below its actual cost of $25 because of the retail inventory method

---

[1] In some cases LIFO cost may be higher than market. When this occurs, reserves not deductible for tax purposes are established to reduce LIFO cost to market. Retailers with high levels of markdowns, such as off-price retailers, generally do not use LIFO. Because gross markups must be employed for LIFO, companies in a high markdown environment may have a LIFO cost valuation higher than FIFO. This cancels one of the retail method's primary advantages, in that the LIFO cost valuation would not necessarily produce an inventory at the lower of cost or market.

	Cost	Retail	Cumulative markup percentage	Cumulative cost percentage
Purchase—Item 1	$50.00	$100	50.0%	50.0%
Purchase—Item 2	25.00	30	16.7%	83.3%
Merchandise available for sale	75.00	130	42.3%	57.7%
Less: Net Sales—Item 1		100		
Ending Inventory—Item 2	17.31	$ 30		
Cost of Goods Sold	$57.69			

FIG. 29.3 Effect of Dissimilar Markup Percentages

averaging effect. To avoid this problem, retailers combine like merchandise with similar markup percentages into accounting groups referred to as *departments*.

Internal Loading. Another possible means of aiming for increased initial markups involves adding internal loads to inventory cost. An *internal load* represents a fictitious addition to inventory cost, increasing initial markup dollars when a department's normal markup percentage is added to the inflated cost. A common addition is an *advertising load.* This effectively capitalizes advertising cost into the cost of merchandise. Actual advertising expense is offset against the credit set up in conjunction with the advertising load.

Although loading practices may be acceptable merchandise management techniques, they can result in an inventory valuation not in compliance with GAAP. Accordingly, all loads should be monitored and removed from the calculation of ending inventory.

Purchase Discounts. Retailers frequently earn discounts for prompt cash payments in accordance with invoice terms, raising a question as to whether purchases should be recorded gross or net of discounts. Predominant practice within the industry is to record purchase gross; however, discount retailers usually record the invoices net.

If purchases are recorded gross, discount earned during the period is classified as a reduction of cost of goods sold and a reserve is set up against inventory at the end of the period to eliminate the estimated amount of discount taken on the end of period inventory but still included in its cost valuation.

Merchandise In Transit. Merchandise is frequently purchased by retailers freight on board (FOB) shipping point. At period end, an accrual should be made for all such merchandise shipped by the vendor but not received by the retailer.

Capitalization of Costs Under TRA 1986. Traditionally under GAAP and for tax purposes, all direct costs associated with obtaining goods for resale were included in the valuation of inventory. The direct costs included the invoice price less any discount, plus transportation costs. Generally, buying, storage, and other indirect costs incurred by retailers while the goods were in their possession were not considered inventoriable costs and were expensed as incurred.

The Tax Reform Act of 1986 (TRA 1986) provides that all costs of acquiring goods are to be expensed only when the related goods are sold. Under TRA's *uniform capitalization rules,* retailers can elect one of two methods of capitalizing costs incurred in acquiring goods.

The first method is *full absorption,* used by manufacturers. Most retailers, though, will probably utilize the *simplified method.* Under the simplified method, the costs to be capitalized into inventory are included in four broad categories:

1. Offsite storage or warehousing
2. Purchasing
3. Handling, processing, assembly, and repackaging
4. General and administrative expenses

Offsite storage or warehousing. Costs attributable to offsite storage or warehousing facilities are required to be capitalized. Costs attributable to onsite storage facilities are not required to be capitalized. A storage facility is considered onsite if the facility is physically attached to, and an integral part of, a retail sales facility where the taxpayer sells merchandise stored at the facility to customers physically present at the facility.

The costs attributable to an offsite storage facility include direct and indirect labor; occupancy expenses (including rent, depreciation, utilities and maintenance, insurance, security, and taxes); materials and supplies; tools and equipment; and general and administrative costs that directly benefit or are incurred by reason of the offsite storage activities.

Purchasing. Costs attributable to purchasing activities are required to be capitalized. Purchasing activities include functions associated with a purchasing department: direct and indirect labor; office machines; supplies; telephone; travel; and general and administrative expenses that directly benefit or are incurred by reason of the purchase activities.

Handling, processing, assembly, and repackaging. Costs attributable to handling, processing, assembly, repackaging, and other similar costs, are required to be capitalized. Costs incurred in transporting goods from the place of purchase to the storage facility, to another storage facility, and to the retail establishment must be capitalized. The costs that must be capitalized include direct and indirect labor (including pension and other fringe benefits; tools; vehicles and equipment (maintenance, rent, depreciation, and insurance); materials and supplies; and attributable general and administrative expenses.

General and administrative expenses. A portion of the direct and indirect costs incurred by an administrative, service, or support function that directly benefits from or is incurred by reason of offsite storage, purchasing, or handling contracts must likewise be capitalized. Certain costs may be excluded if they benefit only the overall management or policy guidance functions.

Costs incurred by the following types of functions or departments ordinarily are required to be allocated among production or resale activities:

1. The administration and coordination of resale activities (wherever performed in the business organization).
2. Personnel operations, including the cost of recruiting, hiring, relocating, assigning, and maintaining personnel records of employees.
3. Materials handling and warehousing and storage operations.
4. Accounting and data services operations, including cost accounting, accounts payable, disbursements, billing, accounts receivable and payroll.
5. Data processing.
6. Security services.
7. Legal departments.

Costs incurred by the following types of functions or departments ordinarily are not required to be allocated to particular activities:

1. Functions or departments responsible for overall management or for setting overall policy for all activities or trades or businesses, such as the board of directors (including their immediate staff), and the chief executive, financial, accounting, and legal officers (including their immediate staffs), provided that no substantial part of the cost of such departments or functions directly benefits a resale activity.
2. General business planning.
3. Financial accounting (including the accounting services required to prepare consolidated reports, but not including any accounting for particular production or resale activities).
4. General financial planning (including general budgeting) and financial management (including bank relations and cash management).
5. General economic analysis and forecasting.
6. Internal audit.
7. Shareholder, public, and industrial relations.
8. Tax department.
9. Other departments or functions that are not responsible for day-to-day operations but are instead responsible for setting policy and establishing procedures to be used with respect to all activities, trades, or businesses.

Retailers may also develop their own method for applying the capitalization rules, as it is likely that detailed analyses of inventory management costs will result in reducing the amount of costs to be capitalized. For example, buyers typically perform more than purchasing functions, such as marketing, advertising, display, and selling activities.

Accordingly, these costs should be separated from purchasing costs. Also, in analyzing distribution and warehousing costs, those activities that do not relate to processing merchandise purchases may not need to be capitalized.

Financial accounting treatment. Before the enactment of TRA 1986, a small segment of retailers had included some or all of the TRA 1986-mandated costs in inventory values; a greater proportion did not. While compliance for tax purposes is required, several options for financial reporting purposes appear to exist: (1) conform financial statements cost components to TRA 1986; (2) include only certain TRA costs for financial statement purposes; and (3) do not change financial statement cost components.

For those retailers that do not change the financial statement costs to fully conform to TRA 1986, a temporary difference between book and tax will result. When a retailer chooses to conform to TRA 1986 for financial statement purposes, this represents a change in accounting. Care should be taken because not all costs required to be capitalized under TRA 1986 are considered capitalizable under GAAP (e.g., depreciation calculated under ACRS).

Inventory capitalization rules and current practice regarding preferability justification are discussed fully in Chapter 14. FIN 1 states that any change in the elements of cost included in inventory is an accounting change under APB 20 requiring cumulative effect accounting treatment in the period of change (A06.108). In addition, assuming material amounts or prospectively material amounts, APB 20 requires that the change must be justified as a preferable one (A06.112).

Business Combinations

Most of the usual business combination accounting considerations (see Chapter 23) apply to retailers generally. However, special attention in purchase business combinations must be focused on merchandise inventories, property and equipment, and identifiable intangible assets.

Merchandise Inventories. APB 16, *Business Combinations*, requires that inventory acquired in a business combination accounted for by the purchase method be recorded at its fair value as of the date of the combination (B50.146c). Fair value is further defined as being equal to selling price less disposal costs and a reasonable profit. Most retailers employ the retail method of accounting, with the cost complement being stated at either FIFO or LIFO. This raises unique issues regarding the application of purchase accounting to inventories. The following paragraphs describe the methodology utilized by many retailers to calculate the fair value of inventory in a purchase acquisition.

If a retailer using the retail method of accounting follows FIFO, inventories will be stated at the lower of cost or market. Buying, warehousing, and shelving costs (essentially those costs necessary to place inventory on the shelf in a salable state) should be added. This cost basis is then evaluated to determine that the retail sales price yields an adequate margin to allow for selling costs as well as reasonable profit. Accordingly, assuming the acquirer does not normally include buying, warehousing, and shelving cost in the inventory valuation, the gross margin obtained after the acquisition from the sale of acquired inventories (having had a one-time addition for buying, warehousing, and shelving costs) will be lower than that realized on an ongoing basis. However, with the capitalization of such costs now required under TRA

1986, many retailers will conform book and tax; and in these cases there may be a less pronounced effect after acquisition.

If the retail method of accounting follows LIFO, inventories are also stated at a lower of cost or market. However, depending on when the retailer adopted LIFO and the effects of inflation since that time, inventory stated at cost may be significantly less than market. Typically, a retailer in this situation will calculate the fair value of the inventory in the manner discussed in the previous paragraph for FIFO inventories. The LIFO reserve will be added back and buying, warehousing, and shelving costs will be included. However, if the acquired company does not step up the tax basis, SFAS 96 (I25) provides that, in valuing these assets, the estimated future tax effect of a difference between the tax basis and the amount otherwise appropriate to assign to the inventory is a temporary difference as to which deferred taxes should be provided (see Chapter 17).

If inventory of an entity acquired in a purchase business combination is treated as a separate business unit or a separate LIFO pool, the fair value of the acquired inventory should be considered the LIFO-base inventory for financial accounting purposes. If, however, the acquired inventory is combined into an existing pool of the acquirer, the fair value of the inventory should be considered as part of the current year's purchases.

When the tax basis of the acquired company's assets and liabilities is not stepped up to the purchase price, the LIFO inventory amount for tax purposes will differ from the new LIFO amount established for book purposes. From that point forward, two LIFO computations will have to be made: (1) the old amounts for tax, and (2) the new starting amounts for financial reporting. This results in nonconformity of book and tax but is permitted under LIFO tax regulations.

Property and Leaseholds. Although some retailers may own a substantial number of their stores and distribution centers, others lease both their stores and distribution centers. In the latter instance, a purchaser frequently obtains operating leaseholds having below-market rental rates. The intangible asset to be recorded in this situation represents the present value of the differential between the market rental rate and the current rental rate. In calculating the value of this asset, consideration should be given to lease renewal periods, if renewal is probable. This favorable portion of the lease (sometimes referred to as leasehold values) is included in property and equipment and is amortized (usually straight-line) over the remaining life of the lease.

Capital leases should remain capitalized after the acquisition unless the lease terms have been modified in connection with the acquisition. Assuming no change in terms, the fair value of the capital lease obligation should be calculated as the present value of future payments at appropriate current interest rates. If modified, a *de novo* determination should be made as to whether the lease is an operating lease or a capital lease.

Where an acquired retailer owns a substantial portion of its real estate, the purchaser may decide to sell some of these real estate holdings to finance a portion of the acquisition. As a result, these assets should be classified as "assets held for sale," and valued at net realizable value.

Identifiable Intangible Assets. Identifiable intangible assets should not be included as part of goodwill but should be recorded separately at their fair values and amortized over their estimated useful lives. In this classification are certain long-lived legal rights and competitive advantages developed or acquired by a business enterprise.

For a retailer, the most frequently identifiable acquired intangibles are the favorable portion of operating leases mentioned above, customer lists or credit card customers, the corporate buying function, an assembled workforce, and private labels. The fair value of intangible assets acquired in a purchase business combination is usually determined by an independent valuation firm.

The value of an acquired customer list or credit card customers represents the cost of replacing this list or base of customers. This asset is amortized ratably over the average life of an active customer.

Many retailers purchase at least a portion of their inventory through a central buying function, especially when a significant amount is imported. The portion of purchase price to be allocated to the corporate buying function is the estimated cost of replacing it, either through the employment of an external group or by rebuilding the group internally. This asset is typically amortized over the estimated period that the entity expects to receive benefits – normally a lengthy period.

The value of an assembled workforce relates specifically to the costs to hire and train the current base of employees. This asset should be amortized based on employee turnover statistics. Both the costs and related amortization periods may be determined separately for executives, management, and clerical employees.

Today, more and more retailers are developing their own private label merchandise to build customer loyalty and to reduce promotional pressures from brand-name vendors. Although the value of the incremental revenues that result from offering this merchandise for sale cannot be measured easily, the cost to replace the design and production effort elements can be determined. The amortization period for this asset also would be lengthy, similar to that used for trademarks and tradenames.

Deferred Payment Account Sales

Retailers who offer their own credit frequently allow the customer to schedule payments over an extended period of time (e.g., four to twenty-four months). Examples are revolving credit and sales of major appliances and furniture.

Under industry practice, the financing activity is separated from the sale, and the income (gross profit) from the deferred payment sale is reported in full when the sale is made. Payment installments maturing beyond one year from the date of the financial statements are included in current assets. Although most retailers choose not to do so because of the extra effort involved for a relatively minor amount, the finance charge revenue earned between the last cycle billing date and the close of the period may be accrued, as it has been earned under GAAP.

Classification of Deferred Taxes. Prior to TRA 1986, retailers who sold property under revolving credit plans were able to treat part of the receivables from sales on such plans as installment receivables. They could therefore report the resultant

	Companies reporting
Expense costs in year incurred	51
Expense costs in fiscal year store opens	15
Amortize costs over a twelve to twenty-four month period after store opens	11
Other	2

FIG. 29.4 Treatment of Preopening Expenses
Source: Touche Ross & Co., unpublished research.

income on the installment method for tax purposes. The related tax liability was classified as current deferred to parallel the current classification of the related asset.

Under TRA 1986, retailers no longer are able to use the installment method for revolving credit plans, although it continues to be permitted for true installment sales. Deferred taxes previously provided on installment sales become payable, per TRA, over four years: 15% in the year of change; 25% in the second year, and 30% in the third and fourth years. Accordingly, the deferred taxes payable after one year as a result of this provision of TRA 1986 are classified as long-term in accordance with SFAS 96 (I25.123).

Preopening Expenses

Retailers incur preparatory costs of a noncapital nature prior to opening a store. These costs may include payroll, occupancy, training, advertising, and similar items. As determined in a 1987 database search of the financial statements of 79 publicly held retailers, most companies expense the costs as incurred or expense the costs in the year the store opens. Deferral, if any, of such costs is for a short term. The survey results are shown in Figure 29.4.

Leases

There has been significant growth over the last twenty years in the number of stores and the rate of new store openings. Most store premises are leased, not owned. Lease accounting is covered in detail in Chapter 19; however, a recent FASB pronouncement particularly affects retailers.

Many operating leases include scheduled rent increases. TB 85-3 (L10.526) requires that rent expense on an operating lease be recognized on a straight-line basis over the lease term, regardless of the rental step-ups. This view is based on the concept that operating leases convey only an occupancy right, and therefore should be expensed uniformly over the duration of usage of the leased property.

Contingent rental payments, that is, those that depend on future events such as sales volume, inflation, and future property taxes, are not included in scheduled minimum lease payments and thus are exempt from the straight-lining procedure.

SIGNIFICANT AUDITING ISSUES

The retail business environment does not lend itself to the audit verification of significant account balances at year end. Since the transactions are relatively small in amount, voluminous in number, and aggregate to large balances, an audit approach should be designed to understand, test, and evaluate the systems for recording these transactions, rather than to verify the existence of the resulting balances at a point in time. No internal control system can prevent all errors because of the prohibitive costs that would be incurred. Retail systems, therefore, are designed generally to prevent significant errors and irregularities from occurring and/or going undetected. Audit procedures are similarly designed to provide reasonable assurance that no material errors exist in the accounts in the aggregate rather than in individual accounts, and in the resulting financial statements.

Three principal items in a retailer's balance sheet have significant audit implications, principally as to existence and valuation:

1. Accounts receivable
2. Merchandise inventories
3. Accounts payable

Numerous transactions are processed which in turn affect these reported balances; therefore, the safeguarding of cash receipts, cash disbursements, and merchandise inventories are also significant issues for the retail auditor.

Sophisticated EDP systems process this multitude of transactions, resulting in aggregate large balances that are not easily verifiable by applying substantive audit procedures. The most efficient audit plan to test a retail system is based on the study and evaluation of the significant controls within the system, and tests of compliance of these controls to ensure that they are functioning properly. A key audit procedure is the review of the systems flow for adequate checks and balances and an appropriate level of segregation of duties.

An important year-end test is to review key statistics and analyses. This analytical review aids in the further verification of large recorded account balances. The nature of the retail environment requires an audit approach that allows an auditor to be reasonably assured that the inherent audit risks and issues are addressed and that no material errors exist in the accounts in the aggregate.

Chapters 7 through 10 discuss audit performance concepts, internal controls, sampling, and EDP auditing. In the following sections, additional guidance is given on auditing in the three principal retail audit areas.

Accounts Receivable

A retailer offering its own credit generally has thousands of customer accounts receivable balances. Therefore, a well-defined audit plan is required to consider these potential audit issues:

- The validity of these transactions and their resulting balances.
- The collectibility of the recorded balances.
- The proper safeguarding of cash receipts and accounts receivable collections.

A review of the system that records cash and charge sales, returns, and payments will include performing sampling tests of such transactions. Additionally, a review of the safeguarding of recorded transactions enables an auditor to further substantiate the validity of a recorded balance.

To ensure the *validity of a transaction,* the auditor reviews statistics indicating the nature of customer complaints and the resulting adjustments made to the recorded balances. This review provides the auditor with a barometer to measure the effectiveness of a company's systems. Unusual trends and significant adjustments reflected in these statistics may indicate that a system lacks certain controls. The pervasiveness of any indicated control weaknesses will be further gauged by mailing confirmations to customers on a test basis.

With many small dollar balances constituting the aggregate balance, the circularization of customer accounts receivable balances (a required procedure under GAAS – AU 331) is usually done on a negative basis. The negative method is preferred because retail customers are likely to respond if they believe the balance is in error (AU 331.05). Additionally, if material weaknesses in a system existed and were not reported by the company in its statistical analysis of adjustments, these weaknesses are likely to be highlighted by customers responding to a written confirmation.

The complexity and sophistication of retail companies' accounts receivable systems vary throughout the industry. Most companies utilize comprehensive EDP systems to process sales transactions. Computer audit software is available or can be specially developed to test the validity of recorded transactions and balances. Examples of tests to be performed by such software include clerical tests of the accounts receivable files and resulting general ledger balances. Through stratification of account attributes, audit software may be used to identify potential irregular and unusual accounts for investigation. These attributes can include account characteristics such as over-credit-limit, do-not-dun status; closed, high-balance, and past-due employee accounts; and large dollar transactions.

Audit procedures that assist an auditor in obtaining reasonable assurance of an account's validity are analytical reviews of statistical comparisons. Such statistics can include percentage of increase over the previous comparable period in total sales, credit sales, and accounts receivable balances. Understanding the reasons for unusual fluctuations will enable the auditor to be reasonably assured of their validity.

The collectibility of a recorded balance and its related value at any given date can be audited by performing a thorough review of a system for granting credit to a new customer and authorizing credit to an established customer. A breakdown in either system can result in unnecessary account write-offs.

The aging of a retail accounts receivable balance is an excellent indicator of collectibility. The auditor should develop tests to ensure that a company's accounts receivable balances have been properly aged and reported. Computer audit software can be of great assistance to an auditor in evaluating the accuracy of a company's aging.

A company's procedure for writing off accounts can also affect the aging and the ultimate collectibility of an account. An auditor should review and test the system for write-offs to ensure that only accounts deemed uncollectible are written off, and that approval is granted at proper levels of authority.

To be assured that a recorded balance is properly valued, the auditor conducts a thorough review of accounts receivable statistics. Included are statistics such as the number of days of credit sales in accounts receivable, accounts receivable turnover, accounts receivable agings, write-offs as a percentage of credit sales, recoveries on written-off accounts, and bad debt expense between comparative periods. Additionally, the number of months' write-offs in the reserve should be compared to historical trends and the retailer's write-off policies. A situation in which these statistics divulge unexpected relationships should be carefully investigated and evaluated.

The proper *safeguarding of cash receipts and accounts receivable collections* requires segregation of duties between the recording and processing functions of accounts receivable. Many retailers use outside services or lockboxes to safeguard these tangible assets, possibly mitigating the risk of pilferage and manipulation. Reviewing the systems that process customer account remittances is an essential audit step.

Chapter 13 covers receivables generally, and contains an extensive discussion of auditing receivables.

Merchandise Inventories

Inventory is one of the most difficult retail audit areas because of the many types of system interfaces that can affect recorded inventory balances, including purchases and sales of merchandise and retail price changes. These three primary system interfaces are tracked by the retailer using the retail FIFO method in each individual department's retail stock ledger.[2]

Areas of potential inventory audit risks, and the key issues include:

- Pricing
- Cutoff
- Physical existence
- Retail value
- Inventory cost valuation

As to *pricing*, if the prices recorded in the purchase journal are not the prices actually marked on the merchandise, or if the costs reflected in the purchase journal are not the vendor's invoice costs, the retail stock ledger will not reflect a valid cost or price of goods available for sale. Auditors must understand the retailer's pricing policies and procedures for recording markups and markdowns. He should review the systems that process the initial pricing and price changes of merchandise and test an appropriate sample of paperwork, to achieve reasonable assurance that these policies and procedures are being followed and are proper.

An auditor also must understand the procedures for recording purchases in the purchase journal. As goods are recorded at both cost and retail, the auditor should review and test an appropriate sample of purchase journal transactions to ensure that these purchases are recorded at invoice cost for the number of items or units received, and that the retail price initially recorded was the authorized price.

Retail inventories are highly susceptible to pilferage and theft. Merchandise inventories are subject to shortage from the point of leaving the manufacturer's plant

---

[2] The FIFO method is invariably used in the retail stock ledger even if LIFO is used for tax and financial reporting purposes.

to the point of sale. The retailer should have strong controls in place to safeguard goods in the areas of ordering, receiving, marking, and distribution as well as on the sales floor. The observation of the taking of physical inventory and testing of its compilation are essential audit procedures. (As further discussed in Chapter 14, observation by the auditor of the inventory count is a required procedure under GAAS–AU 331.)

The *cutoff* on recording of sales and purchase transactions in an accounting period directly affects the recorded balance of merchandise inventories. If the accounting does not match the physical movement of goods, both earnings and inventory balances will be misstated. The auditor must understand the retailer's policies for recording sales and purchases and perform cutoff tests to evaluate compliance with these policies.

The proper valuation of merchandise inventories at the lower of cost or market is an audit risk in all industries. Because of the complexity of the retail method, inventory can be misstated if goods are not properly marked or if the related paperwork is not processed on a timely basis.

In checking on *physical existence* through inventory taking, most retailers perform an aging of their inventories as of the same date. Based upon the results of the aging, the auditor should be able to assess the ultimate salability of inventory at recorded prices, and hence its related valuation. For example, high-fashion items in the soft goods area generally have a selling life of no more than six months, while most staple goods can be sold at their original marked prices for as long as the items are in good condition.

If goods are improperly priced or markdowns have not been recorded on a timely basis, inventory will be misstated at *retail value*. The auditor should review the systems for pricing approval and thoroughly understand the markdown policies and systems, to be reasonably assured that inventories at retail are properly stated.

An accurate valuation of retail inventories is dependent on the recording of price changes in the proper period. Gross margin can be artificially supported in one period by taking required markdowns in a subsequent period. An auditor should therefore review the activity and level of markdowns taken in a subsequent period to evaluate whether markdowns have been properly recorded in the period under audit.

To obtain reasonable assurance of the reasonableness of *inventory cost valuation*, the auditor conducts a thorough analytical review and comparison with prior periods of merchandise inventory statistics, such as gross margin, markdowns, markups, inventory agings, inventory as a percentage of sales, inventory turnover, and inventory shortage, as a percentage of sales on both an aggregate and departmental basis.

Inventory auditing is discussed in detail in Chapter 14.

Accounts Payable

A large retailer has numerous vendors for merchandise and expense items. The amounts owed to these vendors generally constitute a retailer's largest current liability. Because of the interrelationships of inventory and accounts payable, a substantial portion of accounts payable audit work should be performed in conjunction with the audit of merchandise inventories. An auditor should develop an audit plan that reasonably ensures:

- The multitude of transactions and resulting balances are valid.
- All liabilities are recorded in the proper period.
- Only valid liabilities can be paid.

The *validity* of accounts payable transactions and balances can be reasonably assured by thoroughly reviewing the systems for recording the transactions, testing the related systems and transactions, and reviewing and testing the procedures for authorization to incur and record these liabilities.

Account validity will also be addressed by reviewing vendor correspondence statistics on a sample basis for potential irregularities and unusual conditions. A negative trend in certain of these correspondence statistics could point to potential system breakdowns.

An additional corroborative test of balance validity can include a substantive test of clerical accuracy of the trial balance and general ledger balance using computer audit software. Such software can also be used to highlight potential unusual accounts for investigation based on attributes such as large debit balances, hold-for-payments, and vendors with more than one vendor number.

Returns to vendors may be caused by overstocks attributable to poor quality of merchandise, unsalable styles, and large seasonal purchases that did not meet planned sales levels. Retailers also have receivables from vendors for the vendors' share of cooperative advertising. The collectibility of these balances often is a function of continued purchases from the vendor; or direct payments may be made by the vendor to the retailer. The auditor should obtain an aging of these debit balances to evaluate their ultimate collectibility. Considerations should also be given to confirmation of these balances.

The validity of an accounts payable balance will also be corroborated by performing overall analytical review techniques (such as the aging of accounts payable and the number of days purchases are in accounts payable). This technique, coupled with the above procedures, is superior to attempting to verify the existence of a balance through circularization, as response rates tend to be very low and thus provide little overall coverage.

A *search for unrecorded liabilities* is an essential audit step to test that all liabilities are recorded in the proper period. Both merchandise and expense payables should be tested to ensure that transactions are recorded in the appropriate period. Merchandise purchases will comprise the majority of transactions to be tested in a search for unrecorded liabilities. As the number of these purchase transactions is voluminous, computer audit software can be utilized to stratify a merchandise purchase file into listings of transactions for testing, for example, goods received prior to the end of a period but journalized subsequent thereto. Through review of this listing and the underlying paperwork, the auditor can evaluate whether goods have been properly accrued at the end of the reporting period.

A retailer pays a multitude of vendors. These disbursements should be only for *valid and authorized liabilities*. Because of the large number of transactions involved, an auditor should review the controls over the vendor master file to be reasonably assured that adequate controls are in place to prevent and detect possible unauthorized vendors and payments. Retailers' systems for cash disbursements should also include controls to detect and prevent a duplicate payment to a vendor.

30

Health Care

THE HEALTH CARE ENVIRONMENT

Health care represents one of the largest businesses in the United States. Annual expenditures are approaching $500 billion, nearly 11% of the gross national product. In 1986, this represented an average expenditure of $1,837 per person. As seen in Figure 30.1, nearly 82% of these expenditures were directly related to the delivery of health care services, such as that provided by hospitals, nursing homes, and doctors. The level of spending on health care services in the United States is significantly greater than in any other country.

The health care industry is complex and diverse. Although it encompasses many characteristics of any service industry, it also combines service delivery with a complicated financing system and extensive regulatory requirements. The development of health care as an industry has paralleled advances in medical technology and in social awareness of health care. Traditionally viewed as a not-for-profit, community based service, the industry has undergone dramatic changes in recent years. Its organization and composition have matured to the point of being highly specialized in terms of service delivery and management.

Industry Trends

Restrictive spending policies on the part of government, commercial insurers and private industry have increased competition for financial resources. Regulation, imposed through governmentally funded programs and licensure requirements, has had a significant influence on the delivery of, and payment for, service. The industry can best be described as operating under regulated competition.

There are many positive aspects to these changes. The industry had become inefficient and undermanaged with the nearly uncontrolled growth of the past two decades. Emphasis on improving the delivery of service has also brought increased attention to financial management. The change in the nature of health care as a business also demands greater accountability, with creditor and other commercial entities (rather than the donor) becoming the principal user of financial statements. The combination of more sophisticated business activities and an increasing need for health service creates an environment in which health care will continue to be one of the largest business segments in the United States.

Health Care Segments

Health care providers have adopted settings to best utilize their expertise, as well as to respond to the regulatory and payment environment. Of the resulting distinct segments, each has unique business and management issues. The discussion in this chapter deals primarily with corporate entities.

Hospitals. Hospitals make up the largest segment of the health care delivery system. There are approximately 6,800 hospitals in the United States, of which nearly 85% are community based institutions providing short-term general and specialty care services. The remaining hospital classifications include psychiatric, rehabilitative, and respiratory institutions, and federal facilities.

Hospitals typically provide both inpatient and outpatient services. *Inpatient* ser-

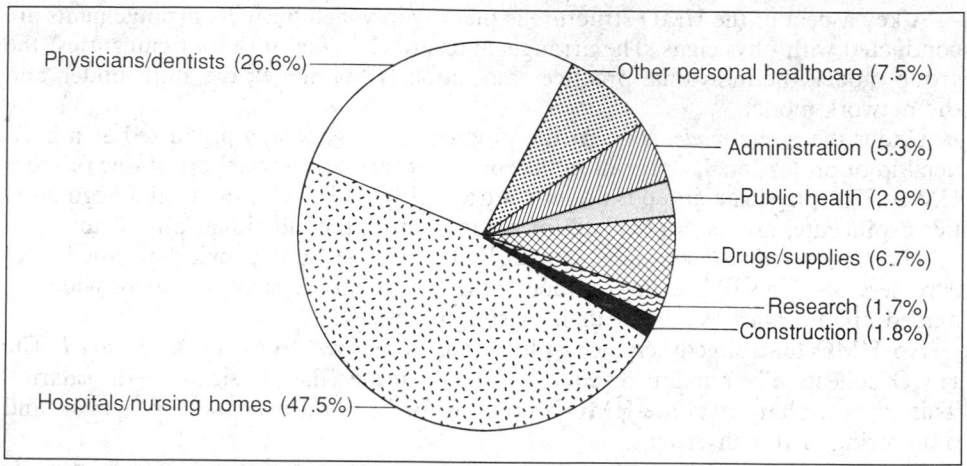

FIG. 30.1   Health Care Expenditures by Service Type
Source: Office of the Actuary, Health Care Financial Administration, June 1987

vices represent room and board as well as continuous nursing care while the patient is in the hospital. *Outpatient* services are those which do not require the patient to be admitted to the hospital overnight. These may include emergency, clinical, laboratory, or radiology services. In recent years, improved medical technology and changes in physician practices have resulted in increasing use of outpatient settings for many treatments and procedures that had previously been limited to inpatient service.

Hospitals are also classified by the level of inpatient care provided. These classifications distinguish between *acute care* (the provision of general health care services) and *tertiary care* (special personnel and equipment available for treatment of complex cases). An acute or tertiary care hospital may be a *general* hospital, or a *specialty* hospital with a majority of patients in a specific category, such as a children's hospital or a respiratory therapy hospital.

Hospitals where the average length of stay does not exceed 30 days are considered *short-term* care facilities. *Long-term* care hospitals usually are specialty facilities that treat cases requiring extended treatment periods, such as rehabilitation therapy. Over 92% of hospitals in the United States are short-term care facilities.

Health Maintenance Organizations. One of the fastest growing segments of the health care industry in recent years has been the health maintenance organization (HMO). There are currently over 500 HMO plans in the United States with total membership in excess of 25 million. HMOs often act merely as brokers between patients and providers, dealing with the financing aspect of health care services.

HMOs arrange the availability of health care services for members who pay monthly premiums. The plans usually offer members a wider range of service at lower out-of-pocket costs accomplished through measures to control the delivery of service. Accordingly, members must receive health care services from providers designated by the HMO. These providers are in turn under contract with the HMO to provide services at agreed upon rates.

A key aspect of the HMO structure is the way in which business arrangements are conducted with physicians. The arrangements are classified into four categories: the group model, the individual practice association (IPA) model, the staff model, and the network model.

Under the *group model* concept the physicians are generally organized as a partnership or professional corporation that provides services to members of one or more HMOs. The physician group is under contract with the HMO, usually at a negotiated per capita rate, and is responsible for compensating the individual physicians.

The *IPA model* also contracts with an HMO but does so to provide specific health care services. The IPA then contracts with individual physicians who provide the agreed upon service as part of their existing practices.

An HMO that directly employs physicians is referred to as the *staff model*. The HMO collects all premium revenue and compensates the physicians with salaries. This type of plan offers the HMO a great deal of control over the deployment and monitoring of the physicians.

Physicians in specialty group practices may contract with the HMO to provide their specialty services. This approach is referred to as the *network model*, that in practice is very similar to the group model structure.

It is important to distinguish between HMOs and other health care entities. From an accounting and financial reporting perspective HMOs are very different. The organizational structure and business practices are more akin to an insurance company than to a hospital. Accordingly, this chapter separately addresses the unique accounting practices and financial statement reporting policies of HMOs.

Long-Term Care Facilities. Entities that provide care with an average length-of-stay of more than 30 days are described as long-term care facilities. This can include hospitals, but most often refers to nursing homes that generally provide nonacute care for the purpose of recuperation, maintenance of chronic conditions, or delivery of health services to the elderly and other patients not capable of living independently. The level of care provided varies with the patients' requirements and is a significant determinant in the operations of the facility.

Long-term care services are classified in three categories: *skilled nursing facilities* (SNF), *intermediate care facilities* (ICF), and *custodial care services*. SNFs provide continuous inpatient services ordered by and provided under the direction of a physician, and thus require the use of skilled professional personnel. ICFs provide care, pursuant to physicians' orders, for patients who require more than basic room and board but do not need continuous service. Custodial care is prescribed by a physician and includes basic accommodations and minimal medical care under the supervision of a registered nurse.

Continuing Care Retirement Communities. These communities (CCRCs) make up a rapidly growing segment of the health care industry. CCRCs provide accommodations, medical care, and certain other social services under a contract between the CCRC and the resident.

The basis for charging fees to residents varies. CCRCs commonly accepted a one-time fee to provide all services to a resident over the remainder of his life. Such arrangements created financial difficulties because of inaccuracies in projecting life expectancies, need for medical services, and operating costs. Fee arrangements now typically include an advance fee with adjustable periodic fees. Even so, this does not eliminate the risk-sharing concept under which most CCRCs operate, as individual contract terms and limitations on fee adjustments make financial management difficult.

Home Health Agencies. In 1987, there were about 6,000 home health agencies (HHAs) in the United States, nearly three times the number of 10 years ago. HHAs are intended primarily for the elderly, chronically ill, disabled, or as a follow-up to hospitalization, with services provided to patients in their residences, thus avoiding the use of institutional care.

HHA medical services are provided under the orders of a doctor and include nursing service, rehabilitation therapy, health education, and medical social services. Support services, primarily homemaker assistance, are designed to help patients regain their health while remaining at home.

HHA services are provided by a variety of entities; a common one is the visiting nurses associations (VNAs). These organizations arrange home visits by qualified health care professionals, who bill on a unit of time basis at rates varying with the type of service.

The growth in HHAs has resulted largely from pressures to control the cost of health care services. Providing care at home is much less expensive than in an institutional setting. Conversely, the economics of the home care business have not been favorable because of regulatory limits on payments for services.

Health Care Organization Forms

The following discussion of the manner in which health care entities are organized—legally, from a management perspective, and for delivery of service—focuses on hospitals, the largest and most complex health care segment. Most other health care segments (except HMOs, addressed separately) are similar, and perhaps simpler.

Organization Structure. Hospitals are organized legally as either for-profit investor-owned corporations (14%), government entities (27%), or voluntary not-for-profit corporations (59%). *Investor-owned hospitals* are similar to any proprietary business in that they are owned by stockholders, exist primarily to provide a return to the investors, and are subject to income taxes. *Government hospitals* can be federal, state, or local governmental units and typically receive some form of funding or assistance through a taxing authority.

Not-for-profit hospitals are tax-exempt corporations formed under state law, having as their primary purpose a charitable mission to benefit those in need of health care. Although not aimed at earning a profit in the commercial sense, they must still generate funds to maintain capital and invest in new services and technology. These entities are exempt from most taxes because of their charitable mission and the restriction that income cannot inure to the benefit of private individuals.

Not-for-profit hospitals are governed by a board of directors or a board of trustees. The board has ultimate authority in managing the assets and operations of the hospital, and also has a fiduciary responsibility to the community served by the hospital. This responsibility and its associated legal implications have become an important concern in recent years because of malpractice lawsuit exposure and an increasing incidence of failed operations.

Similar to private enterprise, top management of a health care entity typically comprises a chief executive officer, a chief operating officer, and a chief financial officer. Traditionally, the chief executive of a hospital has been called the administrator, and the financial officer has been called the controller. The chief executive officer is responsible for implementing the policies of the board, and the other officers report to him.

Below top management, the organization structure varies significantly, and there is no single structure common to all hospitals. Hospitals are highly departmentalized to conform to the types of services provided. The major classifications of service are routine, ancillary, and general. *Routine service* refers to basic room and board and includes nursing care. *Ancillary services* are diagnostic or therapeutic services performed by specific departments, such as laboratory and radiology. *General services* are those that support general patient care and the operation of the hospital, such as dietary and housekeeping. Each of the major service areas generally has a manager, supported by department heads or their equivalent. In addition, hospitals have a general and administrative area that includes accounting, data processing, patient billing, and other similar functions. This area is usually the responsibility of the chief financial officer and will also have a department head.

Horizontal and Vertical Integration. In the past, health care was delivered through the hospital as a stand-alone entity. As the system grew, so did the size and complexity of hospitals. With this growth, health care as a business became more sophisticated, competition increased, and alternative structures developed to diversify operations and expand services.

The first major change in health care delivery came through the formation of chains and systems. This horizontal integration was most apparent with investor-owned corporations as they acquired facilities and developed networks. Not-for-profit hospitals also became active in horizontal integration, forming their own systems and alliances. Presently there are local, regional, and national health care systems of investor-owned and not-for-profit hospitals.

A more recent activity involves vertical integration. For example, hospitals have acquired or opened nursing homes, clinics, and home health agencies. Health care organizations are also becoming involved in activities not directly related to providing health care, such as day care centers, wellness programs, and joint ventures with physicians. Some organizations are even entering the financing aspect of health care by forming HMOs.

The integration of health care organizations has in many cases improved services, increased efficiencies, and resulted in better availability of health care. But it also often has created more complex organizations, more competition, and a need for more sophisticated financial accounting and reporting.

Third-Party Payment

A unique characteristic of the health care industry is that the consumer (patient) is often not responsible for payment. This responsibility is assumed by or contracted to a third party, such as Medicare, Medicaid, and commercial insurance.

Principles of Payment. Third parties pay for services under several methodologies. These include payments based on

- Charges
- Costs
- Per diems
- Fixed-rate-per-case
- Capitation

Charges. Third-party payments based on charges are made in direct relationship to patient billing. Most often the payment is a stipulated percentage of the charges, regardless of the total amount. This method of payment is simple to determine and assures the health care provider of a certain level of payment.

Costs. Under this method the provider must go through an agreed-upon cost determination process. The payment arrangement generally defines allowable costs and establishes the methodology for computing the costs and allocating overhead. Although still significant, cost based reimbursement is becoming less common.

Per diems. A per diem payment is an agreed-upon amount per day of care. For example, the total payment for a stay in a hospital would be computed by multiplying the rate by the number of days; the actual charges do not affect the payment. The advantage of this method is its simplicity. However, it creates risk for both parties as the per diem rate may not closely correspond to the actual cost of services.

Fixed rate per case. A fixed-rate-per-case payment will differ only as to the specific illness, but it is not affected by the actual charges. This method requires an illness classification system based on quantified or coded medical record information. The provider will benefit or be penalized depending on how closely the use of services correlates with the norm for a particular case.

Capitation. Capitation payments usually relate to HMO agreements. They represent a fixed amount per member for providing health care services during a period. For example, a hospital may receive $50 per member per month from an HMO for agreeing to provide all hospital care services to those members. Capitation arrangements sometimes include risk-sharing provisions if utilization rises above or falls below predetermined levels. The agreements can become quite complex, requiring special accounting treatment.

Third-party payors use various forms of these payment methods. Commercial insurance companies usually pay on the basis of charges. Medicaid payment methods will vary from state to state, but the cost and per diem methods are most common. Medicare uses the fixed-rate-per-case method for all inpatient services and the costs method for most outpatient services.

Prospective and Retrospective Settlement. Third-party payments determinable in advance are generally known as prospective settlement systems. The rates of payment can be computed prior to providing the service, such as under per diem and fixed-rate-per-case methods. Retrospective settlements require that actual financial and service data be analyzed for a period to determine final payment, as is the case of cost-based methods.

Both systems pay for services based on estimates, and therefore require settlements at the end of each period. The prospective system settlement need only match units of service to the payment rate, whereas the retrospective system requires final determination on the basis of actual costs as well as units of service.

Medicare Prospective Payment System. Prior to 1966, the federal government did not play a significant role in the health care delivery system. Government funding was available for construction of facilities through the Hill-Burton program and for certain welfare programs, but direct involvement was limited. Hospitals received payment for services directly from patients or from commercial insurance companies. Health care insurance and employee benefits programs were not widely available.

On July 1, 1966, Title XVIII of the Social Security Act created the Medicare program, intended to pay for and assure delivery of health care service to the elderly. It provided hospital insurance to all qualified individuals under Part A and offered optional supplementary medical insurance under Part B. Part A is funded primarily through FICA taxes while Part B is funded through insurance premiums. Title XIX of the Social Security Act created the Medicaid program, which provides health care services for the indigent and is administered at the state level with partial federal funding.

From 1966 to 1983, Medicare paid hospitals the allowable costs of providing care to program beneficiaries. Effective October 1, 1983 (but not fully implemented until October 1, 1987, as discussed in EITF Issue 86-2), the Medicare Prospective Payment System (PPS) was adopted for all hospitals, excepting children's, rehabilitative, and psychiatric hospitals. Under PPS, outpatient services continue to be paid on the basis of costs; but inpatient services are now paid at predetermined rates for each patient discharged. The rates vary depending on each illness, classified into approximately 470 *diagnosis related groups* (DRGs).

DRGs are assigned to cases through the use of medical record clinical codes based upon the International Classification of Diseases—Ninth Edition (*ICD-9 Codes*). The ICD-9 codes are combined with specific personal data on the patient (age, sex, preexisting conditions, etc.) and processed through a "grouper" software program that assigns a DRG. Each DRG has a relative weight representing the theoretical use of service above or below the norm of 1.00. The weight is then multiplied by a standard rate to determine payment for that particular case.

During the initial transition years of PPS, hospitals were paid using standard rates that blended the hospital's actual cost with a federal standard rate. Effective during hospital fiscal years beginning on or after October 1, 1987, the blending discontinued and now only the federal standard rate is used. However, variations still exist in rates; urban and rural hospitals have separate rates, and each hospital uses its metropolitan statistical area (MSA) wage index to adjust the standard rate. The federal rates are revised annually on October 1 for inflation and other factors. PPS also allows for additional payments to hospitals with qualified medical education programs or that serve a high percentage of indigent patients.

PPS provides that Medicare will pay its share of cetain actual costs on a pass-through basis. This applies mostly to capital costs (depreciation, interest, lease payments, etc.), that Congress intends to eventually incorporate into the DRG payments.

The DRG concept has had a significant influence on hospital operations, encouraging efficiency and control of costs. It has also been criticized as being too restrictive, forcing hospitals to lower the quality of care—although there is some evidence that many hospitals have improved their profitability under PPS. One certainty of PPS is that it controls the level of consumption of resources in providing health care, a major consideration in its adoption by the federal government.

HEALTH CARE PROVIDERS—ACCOUNTING AND REPORTING

Financial statements for health care providers encompass both not-for-profit and investor-owned entities. Investor-owned providers will follow basic financial reporting concepts, discussed in Chapter 3. This section is directed primarily toward not-for-profit health care providers, with differences relating mostly to use of fund accounting and income tax related matters. A sample balance sheet, statement of revenues and expenses, and statement of changes in fund balances for a not-for-profit hospital are shown in Figures 30.2, 30.3, and 30.4, respectively.[1]

Overview

Before Medicare, there was little need for extensive financial information. Operations were relatively simple, complex third-party payment arrangements did not exist, and major expenditures were funded through philanthropic sources rather than financed.

With the advent of the Medicare program, accurate and auditable records became critical. Revenues and expenses now had to be segregated by department and type of service. Detailed statistics on patient volume, numbers of procedures, and use of services now were required for accurate cost determination. Billings for services and accounting for payments now caused complex record-keeping. Most third-party payors, particularly Medicare, conducted audits to determine proper settlements and could deny payment if data were not adequately documented. The health care industry was forced to develop sophisticated recordkeeping systems.

---

[1] FASB 95, *Statement of Cash Flows* (C25), applies to investor-owned (proprietary) health care entities, but not to not-for-profit entities. Although necessary for a complete presentation of financial position and results of operations, a sample statement of cash flows is not presented here, because an AICPA Task Force is in the process (as of August 1988) of developing a paper on financial statement display for not-for-profit organizations, which would encompass reporting of cash flows.

GENERAL FUNDS

ASSETS

	December 31	
	1987	1986
Current assets:		
Cash and short-term investments	$ 1,703,000	$ 3,875,000
Assets whose use is limited and that are required for current liabilities	970,000	1,300,000
Patient accounts receivable, net of estimated uncollectibles of $2,500,000 in 1987 and $2,400,000 in 1986	15,100,000	14,194,000
Estimated third-party payor settlements –		
Medicare	441,000	600,000
Supplies	1,163,000	938,000
Other current assets	406,000	438,000
Due from donor restricted funds, net	–	500,000
Total current assets	19,783,000	21,845,000
Assets whose use is limited:		
By board for capital improvements	11,000,000	10,000,000
By agreements with third-party payors for funded depreciation	9,234,000	6,151,000
Under malpractice funding arrangement – held by trustee	3,007,000	2,682,000
Under indenture agreement – held by trustee	11,708,000	11,008,000
	34,949,000	29,841,000
Less assets whose use is limited and that are required for current liabilities	970,000	1,300,000
	33,979,000	28,541,000
Property and equipment, net	51,038,000	50,492,000
Other assets:		
Deferred financing costs	693,000	759,000
Investment in affiliated company	917,000	576,000
Total other assets	1,610,000	1,335,000
	$106,410,000	$102,213,000

LIABILITIES AND FUND BALANCE

	December 31	
	1987	1986
Current liabilities:		
Current installments of long-term debt	$ 1,470,000	$ 1,750,000
Accounts payable	2,217,000	2,085,000
Accrued expenses	3,396,000	3,225,000
Retainage and construction accounts payable	955,000	772,000
Estimated third-party payor settlements –		
Medicaid	2,143,000	1,942,000
Deferred third-party reimbursement	200,000	210,000
Advances from third-party payors	122,000	632,000
Due to donor restricted funds, net	300,000	–
Total current liabilities	10,303,000	10,616,000
Deferred third-party reimbursement	746,000	984,000
Estimated malpractice costs	3,807,000	2,682,000
Long-term debt, excluding current installments	23,144,000	24,014,000
Fund balance	67,910,000	63,917,000
Commitments and contingent liabilities	–	–
	$106,410,000	$102,213,000

DONOR RESTRICTED FUNDS

ASSETS	December 31 1987	December 31 1986
Specific purpose funds:		
Cash	$ 48,000	$ 75,000
Investments, at cost which approximates market	728,000	455,000
Grants receivable	100,000	67,000
	$ 876,000	$ 597,000
Plant replacement and expansion funds:		
Cash	$ 24,000	$ 321,000
Investments, at cost which approximates market	252,000	165,000
Pledges receivable, net of estimated uncollectibles of $60,000 in 1987 and $120,000 in 1986	132,000	—
Due from general funds	150,000	380,000
	$ 558,000	$ 866,000
Endowment funds:		
Cash and cash equivalent investments	$ 1,253,000	$ 1,303,000
Investments, net of $175,000 valuation allowance in 1987, market value $5,198,000 in 1987 and $5,013,000 in 1986	5,256,000	5,320,000
Due from general funds	150,000	100,000
	$ 6,659,000	$ 6,723,000
Student loan funds:		
Cash and cash equivalent investments	$ 330,000	$ 303,000
Loans receivable, net of estimated uncollectibles of $90,000 in 1987 and 1986	513,000	468,000
	$ 843,000	$ 771,000

LIABILITIES AND FUND BALANCES	December 31 1987	December 31 1986
Specific purpose funds:		
Accounts payable	$ 205,000	$ 63,000
Deferred grant revenue	50,000	—
Due to general funds	—	255,000
Fund balances	621,000	279,000
	$ 876,000	$ 597,000
Plant replacement and expansion funds:		
Due to general funds	—	345,000
Fund balance	558,000	521,000
	$ 558,000	$ 866,000
Endowment funds:		
Fund balances	$ 6,659,000	$ 6,723,000
	$ 6,659,000	$ 6,723,000
Student loan funds:		
Accounts payable	$ —	$ 9,000
Advance from U.S. Government	42,000	—
Fund balance	801,000	762,000
	$ 843,000	$ 771,000

FIG. 30.2 Sample Hospital Balance Sheets

Source: Adapted from AICPA 1988 Exposure Draft, Audits of Providers of Health Care Services (AICPA, 1988c). Appendix A.

	Year ended December 31	
	1987	1986
Net patient service revenue	$91,646,000	$87,839,000
Other operating revenue	5,680,000	4,994,000
Total operating revenues	97,326,000	92,833,000
Operating expenses:		
Wages, salaries and benefits	65,891,000	60,091,000
Supplies and other	15,112,000	13,573,000
Purchased services	8,383,000	8,218,000
Medical malpractice costs	1,125,000	200,000
Depreciation and amortization	4,782,000	4,280,000
Interest expense	1,422,000	1,439,000
Total operating expenses	96,715,000	87,801,000
Income from operations	611,000	5,032,000
Nonoperating revenue (expense):		
Unrestricted gifts and bequests	1,122,000	1,136,000
Loss on investment in affiliated company	(53,000)	–
Income on investments:		
Use limited by board for capital improvements	1,120,000	1,050,000
Use limited under indenture agreement	100,000	90,000
Use limited by agreements with third-party payors for funded depreciation	850,000	675,000
Nonoperating revenue, net	3,139,000	2,951,000
Excess of revenues over expenses	$ 3,750,000	$ 7,983,000

FIG. 30.3   Sample Hospital Statement of Revenues and Expenses of General Fund
Source: Adapted from AICPA 1988 Exposure Draft, Audits of Providers of Health Care Services (AICPA, 1988c), Appendix A.

Financial statement users also began to multiply, as health care entities started to borrow through public and private financing sources. The fiduciary responsibilities of board members became more extensive. These changes, plus the significant expansion in the health care delivery system, created a demand for audited financial statements. Presently, substantially all larger health care enterprises engage independent public accountants to perform annual financial statement audits.

Accounting characteristics of hospitals, the largest component of the health care industry, include sophisticated data-processing applications, a high volume of small transactions, very labor-intensive operations, and extensive management-oriented reporting capabilities. These factors require special consideration in the preparation and audit of financial statements.

The accounting practices of health care providers have evolved over time to be responsive to both financial and managerial information requirements. The evolution of health care accounting practices has generally paralleled the overall evolution of accounting practices. However, the recent dynamic changes in the health care industry have accelerated this process.

Financial Accounting.   The FASB conceptual framework project (see Chapter 2) resulted in the issuance of SFAC 1, *Objectives of Financial Reporting by Business*

FIG. 30.4 Sample Hospital Statement of Changes in Fund Balances

| | Year ended December 31, 1987 | | | | | Year ended December 31, 1986 | | | | |
| | | Donor-Restricted Funds | | | | | Donor-Restricted Funds | | | |
	General Funds	Specific Purpose Funds	Plant Replacement and Expansion Funds	Endowment Funds	Student Loan Funds	General Funds	Specific Purpose Funds	Plant Replacement and Expansion Funds	Endowment Funds	Student Loan Funds
Balances at beginning of year	$63,917,000	$279,000	$521,000	$6,723,000	$762,000	$56,679,000	$221,000	$501,000	$5,973,000	$712,000
Additions:										
Excess of revenues over expenses	3,750,000	—	—	—	—	7,983,000	—	—	—	—
Gifts, grants and bequests	—	842,000	220,000	—	—	—	518,000	290,000	—	40,000
Investment income	—	50,000	20,000	750,000	27,000	—	40,000	15,000	650,000	10,000
Gain on sale of investments	—	—	100,000	20,000	12,000	—	—	20,000	100,000	—
Transfer to finance property and equipment additions	243,000	—	(243,000)	—	—	255,000	—	(255,000)	—	—
	3,993,000	892,000	97,000	770,000	39,000	8,238,000	558,000	70,000	750,000	50,000
Deductions:										
Provision for uncollectible pledges	—	—	(60,000)	—	—	—	—	—	—	—
Transfer to Sample Health Systems	—	—	—	—	—	(1,000,000)	—	—	—	—
Realized loss on sale of investments	—	—	—	(659,000)	—	—	—	—	—	—
Unrealized loss on marketable equity securities	—	—	—	(175,000)	—	—	—	—	—	—
Transfer to other operating revenue	—	(550,000)	—	—	—	—	(500,000)	(50,000)	—	—
	—	(550,000)	(60,000)	(834,000)	—	(1,000,000)	(500,000)	(50,000)	—	—
Balances at end of year	$67,910,000	$621,000	$558,000	$6,659,000	$801,000	$63,917,000	$279,000	$521,000	$6,723,000	$762,000

Source: Adapted from AICPA 1988 Exposure Draft, Audits of Providers of Health Care Services, (AICPA, 1988c). Appendix A.

SOP Number	
78-1	ACCOUNTING BY HOSPITALS FOR CERTAIN MARKETABLE EQUITY SECURITIES
78-7	FINANCIAL ACCOUNTING AND REPORTING BY HOSPITALS OPERATED BY A GOVERNMENTAL UNIT (Superseded by AICPA Audit and Accounting Guide, *Audits of State and Local Governmental Units*, 1986g)
81-2	REPORTING PRACTICES CONCERNING HOSPITAL-RELATED ORGANIZATIONS
85-1	FINANCIAL REPORTING BY NOT-FOR-PROFIT HEALTH CARE ENTITIES FOR TAX-EXEMPT DEBT AND CERTAIN FUNDS WHOSE USE IS LIMITED
87-1	ACCOUNTING FOR ASSERTED AND UNASSERTED MEDICAL MALPRACTICE CLAIMS OF HEALTH CARE PROVIDERS AND RELATED ISSUES

FIG. 30.5   AICPA Statements of Position of the Accounting Standards Division Related to Health Care Entities

Enterprises (FASB, 1978c), and SFAC 4, *Objectives of Financial Reporting by Non-business Organizations* (FASB, 1980c). These concept statements serve as the foundation for health care accounting and reporting. Health care providers normally prepare financial information in conformity with GAAP, and accordingly use accrual basis accounting.

The AICPA has been a major source of accounting guidance for the health care industry. The *Hospital Audit Guide* (AICPA, 1985c), prepared by the AICPA Health Care Committee to provide guidance in auditing and reporting on hospitals, was first published in 1972. Although other forms of health care entities are mentioned in the Guide, it specifically limits its application to hospitals. The Guide describes proper accounting and reporting treatment for hospitals under GAAP. Subsequent editions have been released with appendices containing AICPA SOPs related to hospitals with the latest (fifth edition) containing SOPs issued through January 1, 1985 (see Figure 30.5 for a current list of these SOPs).

In 1988, the AICPA released an exposure draft of a new Audit and Accounting Guide, *Audits of Providers of Health Care Services* (AICPA, 1988c). This proposed guide reflects the current business and regulatory environment and incorporates all current technical pronouncements that apply to hospitals, HMOs, long-term care facilities, continuing care retirement communities, and home health agencies.

The GASB (see Chapter 31) has recognized the merit and need for consistency in accounting and reporting by health care providers and has recognized the AICPA *Hospital Audit Guide* and related SOPs as being applicable for governmental providers.

Two professional bodies are widely recognized in the industry for expertise in health care accounting and reporting matters. These are AICPA Health Care Subcommittee and the Healthcare Financial Management Association Principles and Practices Board.

AICPA Health Care Subcommittee. This subcommittee consists of expert accountants who address issues related to health care accounting and reporting. It

Statement	
1	UNIFORM ACCOUNTING AND REPORTING IN HOSPITALS
2	DEFINING CHARITY SERVICE AS CONTRASTED TO BAD DEBTS
3	SUPPLEMENTARY REPORTING OF HOSPITAL FINANCIAL REQUIREMENTS
4	REPORTING OF CERTAIN TRANSACTIONS ARISING IN CONNECTION WITH THE ISSUANCE OF DEBT
5	ACCOUNTING AND REPORTING FOR AGENCY RELATIONSHIPS
6	HOW TO MEASURE WORKING CAPITAL; CLASSIFICATION AND DEFINITION ISSUES
7	THE PRESENTATION OF PATIENT SERVICES REVENUE AND RELATED ISSUES
8	THE USE OF FUND ACCOUNTING AND THE NEED FOR SINGLE FUND REPORTING BY INSTITUTIONAL HEALTH CARE PROVIDERS
9	ACCOUNTING AND REPORTING ISSUES RELATED TO CONTINUING CARE RETIREMENT COMMUNITIES

FIG 30.6   HFMA Principles and Practices Board Statements

follows a due process procedure in issuing statements by exposing proposed statements for public comment. The Health Care Subcommittee was responsible for the SOPs noted in Figure 30.5 and preparation of the forthcoming health care entities audit guide.

HFMA Principles and Practices Board. The Healthcare Financial Management Association (HFMA) Principles and Practices (P&P) Board is similar to the AICPA Subcommittee in several respects. It consists of expert health care accountants and financial managers with representation from the accounting profession and industry. Members are appointed by the Board of Directors of HFMA, the largest financial trade association in the industry, comprising over 25,000 health care financial professionals throughout the United States. The P&P Board exposes proposed statements for public comment and issues final statements as guidance to health care entities. A list of P&P Board statements is included in Figure 30.6.

The P&P Board is generally more narrowly focused than the AICPA Subcommittee, responds relatively quickly to current issues, and addresses more controversial topics. At times it has appeared more as an interpretive body, but in recent years has been directed primarily toward participating in the establishment of accounting principles.

Managerial Accounting. The reporting requirements of third-party payors have been a constant driving force behind health care industry accounting systems. Providers are generally required to file an annual "cost report" as a condition of their participation in the Medicare program. These reports accumulate revenues and expenses in a prescribed format in accordance with *The Provider Reimbursement Manual,* which is issued by the U.S. Department of Health and Human Services and incorporates the legislative and regulatory provisions of the Medicare program.

Other third-party payors, and in some cases state regulatory agencies, often require completion of cost reports or similar documents.

Industry dynamics have had an even more pronounced impact on managerial accounting systems. The change from traditional third-party reimbursement of costs or charges to the present myriad of payor arrangements has dramatically increased the information needs of health care management. Numerous commerical and proprietary software programs have been developed to meet these needs.

Fund Accounting

Because eleemosynary health care providers often receive resources that are externally restricted, most incorporate fund accounting procedures into their systems. AICPA SOP 85-1, *Financial Reporting by Not-for-Profit Health Care Entities for Tax-Exempt Debt and Certain Funds Whose Use is Limited* (TP 10,370), concluded that funds of such entities can be grouped into two major categories: general funds and donor-restricted funds. Operations controlled by and under the authority of the board of directors or trustees, and contributions and donations not specifically restricted by the donor, are reflected in the general funds. SOP 85-1 requires simply that the funds be segregated, that activity in the general and donor-restricted funds be adequately disclosed in the statement of changes in fund balances, and that the nature of donor-restricted funds be disclosed.

General Fund. The general fund has been defined as all assets and liabilities of a health care provider that are not restricted for an identified purpose by donors or grantors. The general fund will thus include assets whose use is limited by the board of directors or under agreement with an outside party other than a donor or grantor. SOP 85-1 defines assets whose use is limited to include (TP 10,370.07):

- Assets set aside by the governing board for identified purposes and over which the board retains control and may, at its discretion, subsequently use for other purposes.
- Proceeds of debt issues and funds of the health care entity deposited with a trustee and limited to use in accordance with the requirements of an indenture or similar document.
- Other assets limited to use for identified purposes through an agreement with an outside party other than a donor or grantor.

As its name implies, the accounting systems and transactions in the general fund are comparable to those ordinarily found in other organizations, tailored to meet the specific information needs of the industry.

Donor-Restricted Funds. To limit potential confusion of financial statement readers, SOP 85-1 concluded that only assets restricted by a donor or by a grantor should be reported as donor-restricted funds (TP 10,370.23b). Typically, donors or grantors may restrict funds for specific operating purposes, for acquisition of property and equipment, and for endowments. Detailed records are normally maintained for each donation or grant, or for each identified purpose, to assure that resources are utilized in accordance with their respective restrictions. The accounting presentation of donor-restricted funds varies depending on the type of restriction or purpose of such funds. If donor funds are restricted for a specific operating purpose, they are recorded as additions to fund balance. When expenditures are made for the intended purpose they are recorded as transfers to other operating revenue. When donor-restricted funds are used to acquire property and equipment, a transfer is made from the donor-restricted fund balance to the general fund balance. When endowment funds become available for general purposes the available amount is normally recorded as nonoperating revenue in the general fund.

Single Fund Reporting. The single fund reporting concept involves eliminating the separate balance sheets for general funds and donor-restricted funds, such as are shown in Figure 30.2. Instead, donor-restricted assets would be included in the single balance sheet, appropriately labeled within the classification of assets whose use is limited. Liabilities, deferred revenues, and fund balances of donor-restricted funds would also be separately identified, with appropriate disclosure of any limitations. The traditional fund balance classification would be relabeled as equity, separated between donor-restricted funds and unrestricted equity.

Single fund reporting is advocated by HFMA P&P Board Statement No. 8, *The Use of Fund Accounting and the Need for Single Fund Reporting by Institutional Healthcare Providers.* However, the practice is not widely accepted in the health care industry. Proponents argue that it presents the financial statements of a health care entity on a basis comparable to other business entities, consistent with trends in the nature of health care operations. Opponents state that single fund reporting is not in conformity with the *Hospital Audit Guide* or SOP 85-1, and is therefore a violation of GAAP.

The exposure draft of *Audits of Providers of Health Care Services* (AICPA, 1988c) somewhat sanctions single fund reporting by specifically not requiring separate fund reporting. The nature of restrictions on donor-restricted resources would *generally* be disclosed, however. While the exposure draft still deals extensively with the concept of fund accounting, and presents sample financial statements accordingly, the change in emphasis is obvious. It is likely that the use of single fund reporting will become more widely practiced following finalization of the new audit guide.

Revenue Cycle

Revenue Recognition. Patient service revenue is recognized when the goods or services are provided to the patient. Customary charges are normally applied to the service rendered based on a per day, per service, or per unit rate structure. Accountability is established for each individual patient based on inpatient admission or outpatient registration. Accounting systems are designed to capture all goods and services provided to a patient, apply customary charges, and summarize the individual transactions. Bills are prepared for payment by individual patients or by third-party payors (Medicare, Medicaid, Blue Cross, and so forth).

Revenue Reporting. A health care provider's primary source of revenue obviously is delivery of patient care; and the principal revenue classification in the statement of revenues and expenses is labeled patient service revenue.

Patient service revenue is usually further classified into routine service, other nursing service, and ancillary service; this subclassification is disclosed either on the face of the statement or in a note. Some entities also separately classify outpatient service revenue.

Nonhospital health care providers classify service revenue based on the care provided. Long-term care facilities use classifications similar to hospitals, and may also separate routine care by the level of service (e.g., skilled nursing, intermediate care, and so forth). Continuing care retirement communities generally use captions such as resident service revenue or resident care fees. Home health agencies may use descriptors such as nursing care, therapy, and homemaker services.

Note that the patient, not the third-party payor, is deemed to be the customer. Therefore, the SFAS 14 requirement to report the amount of revenues from a customer accounting for 10% or more of total revenues does not apply (TB 79-5; S20.503-.504).

Revenue Deductions. Deductions from patient service revenue, to arrive at net patient service revenue, include uncollectible accounts, contractual discounts to third-party payors, courtesy discounts, and charity care. Uncollectible accounts may be classified as an operating expense if it is possible to distinguish charity (indigent patients) from bad debts (nonindigent nonpayers).

Until recently, deductions from revenue had been shown as a line item on the face of the statement of revenues and expenses. Reporting only net patient service revenue, with disclosure of deductions in a footnote or parenthetically, has now become widely accepted. This change is the result of significant third-party payor arrangements such as the Medicare PPS, based on some method other than charges incurred by patients. Thus, information on gross revenue may be of little significance to the financial statement user. (The example of a statement of revenues and expenses in Figure 30.3 follows the net revenue method.)

The establishment of allowances (revenue deductions) under agreements with third-party payors is one of the most critical accounting areas for health care providers. The estimation process requires an understanding of the settlement methodology utilized by the third party and accumulation of relevant underlying service statistics and other factors. As a result, providers usually record accounts receivable and contractual allowances in specific third-party payor categories to facilitate analysis.

Differences between estimates and settlements are recorded in the period of final determination as part of that period's revenue deductions. Differences are not treated as prior-period adjustments unless the adjustment involves a corrrection of an error (as defined in SFAS 16, *Prior Period Adjustments* (A35)).

The exposure draft of the new audit guide states that contractual discounts should be disclosed if deemed necessary, presumably if such amounts are material in relation to revenues. Uncompensated services such as uncollectible accounts and charity care also should be disclosed if material.

Patient Accounts Receivable. Accounts receivable are initially recorded based on gross patient service revenue. The party responsible for payment is then billed in full or at a predetermined rate.

Along with the revenue deduction that reduces gross patient service revenue to net patient revenue, allowances are recorded to reduce accounts receivable to the actual amount expected to be received. These allowances include contractual allowances or third-party rate adjustments, as well as an estimated provision for uncollectible accounts, based on receivables aging and historical collection patterns.

Third-Party Payor Arrangements

Settlement Accounts. Included in settlement accounts are actual current-period activity and changes in accounting estimates for previously recorded settlements under third-party payor arrangements. Effectively, the settlement accounts represent the net amount due to (or from) the provider as of the balance sheet date for all fiscal periods not yet closed out by the third parties.

Most third-party payor agreements require that all data related to beneficiary services during a given fiscal period must be accumulated prior to computing final settlements. This typically includes both statistical information (discharges, patient days, outpatient visits, etc.) and financial information (charges, costs, and payments received). On an interim basis, payments for services are made at agreed-upon or estimated rates. Providers maintain separate accounting records to distinguish interim payment activity from settlement transactions. As settlement amounts are recognized, the general ledger accounts are adjusted to reflect the balance due to or from each third-party payor. Because settlement computations necessarily contain estimates and certain third-party payors will later audit the computations, subsequent adjustments may be required.

Timing Differences. Agreements with third-party payors may specify a payment basis that differs from accrual accounting. As a result, interperiod allocations arising from deferred credits and charges, similar in nature to those found in income tax accounting for temporary differences, are required.

The most common timing differences involve:

- Depreciation methods
- Contributions to self-insurance funds
- Capitalized interest
- Accruals for sick pay and pension plans
- Gains and losses on debt extinguishment

Timing differences may become permanent differences due to changes in regulations or provisions of third-party payment programs, for example, adoption of a fixed-rate payment system. Health care providers must regularly challenge all recorded deferred debits and credits and determine that the current manner of reimbursement from third-party payors and the provider's projected operating results will allow for their future realization. If not, the effect of eliminating the deferral should be recognized in the current period. This is discussed in detail in a proposed Practice Bulletin, *Accounting for Third-Party Reimbursement by Health Care Entities*, currently under review by AcSEC and expected to be finalized later in 1988.

Other Operating Revenue

Other operating revenue relates to ongoing activities not directly related to patient service. Included are cafeteria and pharmacy sales, education program revenues, health care facility rentals, gift shop sales, and similar items. Research, education, and other types of grant proceeds should also be included in other operating revenue to the extent that related expenses are included in operations. Subclassifications of other operating revenue should be disclosed if individually material.

Operating Expenses

Expenses may be classified on a functional basis or by the nature of expense. The *Hospital Audit Guide (AICPA, 1985c) recommends the following formats:*

Functional classification:
   Nursing services
   Other professional services
   General services
   Fiscal services
   Administrative services
   Depreciation
   Interest

Natural classification:
   Salaries and wages
   Employee benefits
   Fees to individuals and organizations
   Supplies
   Purchased services
   Depreciation
   Interest
   Other expenses

Financial statements often do not include as much detail as recommended. The specific classification will depend on management preference and the sophistication of accounting systems and personnel.

Nonoperating Revenues and Expense

Revenues and expenses peripheral and incidental to the patient service operations of the health care entity are classified as nonoperating. Typical classifications include investment income, unrestricted contributions, and unrestricted income from endowment funds. Nonoperating revenues and expenses are reported below income from operations.

Related Organizations

Health care entities are often affiliated with other organizations involved in health service, or with entities such as foundations whose express purpose is to raise, hold, and dispense funds only for the benefit of the affiliated health care entity. Separate organizations initially arose in an effort to maximize payments under third-party payor arrangements by excluding contributions from operating results. Currently they are established primarily for legal and reporting considerations.

The legal separation between affiliated organizations and the health care entity does not overcome the accounting issue of whether the entities should be consolidated or combined for financial reporting purposes. SOP 81-2, *Reporting Practices Concerning Hospital-Related Organizations* (TP 10,340), was issued to clarify reporting on related organizations. The SOP builds on ARB 51, *Consolidated Financial Statements* (C51), stating that if a related organization is not consolidated or combined (because the requirements in ARB 51 are not met), the health care entity should present summarized financial information in the notes to the financial statements and clearly describe the nature of the relationship.

Under the SOP, a separate organization is considered to be related if:

1. The health care entity controls the separate organization through contracts or other legal documents that provide the authority to direct the organization's activities, management, and policies; or
2. The health care entity is for all practical purposes the sole beneficiary of the organization. The entity should be considered the organization's sole beneficiary if *any one* of the three following circumstances exists:

   a. The organization has solicited funds in the name of the entity, with the express or implied approval of the entity, and substantially all the funds solicited by the organization were intended by the contributor, or are otherwise required, to be transferred to the entity or used at its discretion or direction.

   b. The entity has transferred some of its resources to the organization and substantially all of the organization's resources are held for the benefit of the entity.

   c. The entity has assigned certain of its functions to the organization, which is operating primarily for the benefit of the entity.

The example in Figure 30.7 is extracted from SOP 81-2, and illustrates the disclosure that might be made by a not-for-profit hospital that is considered to be related to a separate not-for-profit organization because the hospital controls it and is deemed to be its sole beneficiary.

Occasionally a separate organization will fail to meet the criteria for consolidation, combination, or presentation of summarized financial information, yet still hold material amounts of funds for the health care entity's benefit. In these circumstances the entity is nonetheless required to disclose the existence of these resources as well as the nature of the relationship. If there have been any material transactions during the periods covered by the financial statements, these should be disclosed.

The FASB in SFAS 56 (He4) has designated the provisions of SOP 81-2 as being preferable for purposes of justifying accounting changes made regarding related organizations.

Note—Sample Hospital Foundation

Sample Hospital Foundation (the foundation) was established to raise funds to support the operation of Sample Hospital. The foundation's bylaws provide that all funds raised, except for funds required for operation of the foundation, be distributed to or be held for the benefit of the hospital. The foundation's bylaws also provide the hospital with the authority to direct its activities, management, and policies. The foundation's general funds, which represent the foundation's unrestricted resources, are distributed to the hospital in amounts and in periods determined by the foundation's board of trustees, who may also restrict the use of general funds for hospital plant replacement or expansion or other specific purposes. Plant replacement and expansion funds, specific-purpose funds, and assets obtained from income from endowment funds of the foundation are distributed to the hospital as required to comply with the purposes specified by donors. A summary of the foundation's assets, liabilities, and fund balances, results of operations, and changes in fund balances follows [omitted].

FIG. 30.7   Note Disclosure of a Hospital Foundation
Source: SOP 81-2 (TP 10,340.14).

Investments in Marketable Equity Securities

Financial statement reporting of investments deals primarily with classification and disclosure of values. Investments should be classified as current or noncurrent depending on the purpose held and marketability, and should be segregated between general fund assets and donor-restricted assets. If maintained on a pooled basis, the nature of participation and method of allocating income should be disclosed.

Marketable equity securities require additional disclosures. For both general funds and donor-restricted funds, aggregate cost and market values as of each balance sheet date should be presented with gross unrealized gains and gross unrealized losses as of the most recent date. The net realized gain or loss, if material, along with the method of computation (e.g., specific cost or average cost) should also be disclosed. Significant post-balance-sheet changes in the value of marketable equity securities should be disclosed.

SFAS 12, *Accounting for Certain Marketable Securities* (I89), and related interpretations apply to investor-owned hospitals. AICPA SOP 78-1, *Accounting by Hospitals for Certain Marketable Equity Securities* (TP 10,160), specifies the requirements for not-for-profit providers specifically excluded by SFAS 12. The SOP amended the *Hospital Audit Guide* so that it substantially conforms to SFAS 12, insuring that essentially the same reporting principles would be used by both not-for-profit and investor-owned hospitals.

Both SFAS 12 and SOP 78-1 require that a marketable equity security portfolio be carried at the lower of its aggregate cost or market value. SOP 78-1 further specifies that for the purpose of determining carrying amount, "marketable equity securities owned by a not-for-profit hospital should be grouped into separate portfolios . . ." (TP 10,160.05). Funds are grouped for purposes of the lower of cost or market determination in essentially the same groupings used for financial reporting purposes. While groupings will vary, typically they include:

- General funds – noncurrent
- General funds – current
- Donor-restricted funds – specific purpose
- Donor-restricted funds – endowment

Investments are recorded at cost when acquired. If investments are received as a donation or gift they are recorded at their then fair market value, which becomes "cost" for future accounting determinations. If at a balance sheet date the aggregate cost of a portfolio exceeds the aggregate market value, this excess is accounted for as a valuation allowance. The accounting for changes in valuation allowances depends on the classification of the portfolio, as is the usual practice under SFAS 12. For example, changes in a valuation allowance for general funds – current will be recorded as nonoperating revenue (expense) or as a component in fund balance if the investments are in general funds – noncurrent or in a donor-restricted fund (TP 10,160.07).

The accounting for realized gains and losses and for income from investments also depends on the classification and character of the underlying investment. This is especially true for investments of donor-restricted funds. However, investment income or realized gains and losses of general funds are recorded as nonoperating revenue (expense) in the period they are earned or realized (TP 10,160.09-.10).

For transactions between funds, SOP 78-1 specifies that "gains or losses on investment trading between unrestricted [general] and [donor] restricted funds and between various categories of [donor] restricted funds should be recognized as realized gains and losses . . ." (TP 10,160.11). For investment trading between general and board-designated funds no such amounts should be recognized.

Advance Fees and Continuing Care Obligations

The distinguishing feature of a CCRC is the availability of health care services as a complement to basic housing for the elderly. HFMA P&P Statement 9, *Accounting and Reporting Issues Related to Continuing Care Retirement Communities*, was issued in 1986 to promote consistency in financial reporting, especially as to the recognition of revenue and obligations to provide future services.

Fee arrangements of a CCRC can be classified as advance fee only, periodic fee only, or a combination of periodic fee with advance fee. Advance fee arrangements require a single fee upon admission, entitling the resident to all contractual services for the duration of his life. Such arrangements are now obsolete due to the difficulty encountered in adequately pricing all variables at inception. Periodic fee arrangements are substantially normal rental agreements that may be adjusted as required by current CCRC financial considerations. The combination of periodic fee with advance fee is now the most prevalent.

Revenue Recognition. Periodic fees represent a charge for current services and accommodations and thus should be recognized as revenue when due. Advance fees generally represent prepayment for future services and often include amounts which are refundable. Revenue for receipt of advance fees should be deferred and recognized over future periods.

A deferred revenue account should be established to account for advance fees not subject to refund. The estimated future service period (remaining lives) is then used as a basis for amortization of the advance fees. HFMA P&P Statement 9 states that "an amortization methodology that properly matches revenues with related costs should consider the increasing costs of providing care later in the resident's lives, and the extent that anticipated related revenues from periodic fees or investment income, if any, will cover those costs" (p.4).

The refundable portion, if any, of advance fees should be recorded as a liability. If some or all of the fees become no longer subject to refund, the nonrefundable amount is thereupon transferred to deferred revenue.

Liability for Future Services. If the present value of obligations to provide future service exceeds the present value of future deferred revenue, the excess obligation must be recorded as a liability for future services. Future costs should consider all components of housing expense, health care services, and the general impact of inflation. Future revenues should also consider future fees to be received, amortization of advance fees, recoveries from third-party payors, and other income or contributions expected to be realized.

The AICPA Health Care Committee has prepared a draft SOP on *Accounting and Reporting by Continuing-Care Retirement Communities for Fees and the Obligation to Provide Future Services and the Use of Facilities, and for the Initial Direct Costs of Acquiring Continuing-Care Contracts.* The draft has been sent to the FASB for approval to release as an exposure draft. The proposed SOP is similar to HFMA Statement 9. It specifically provides that preoccupancy proceeds which will result in future revenues should be deferred, and that initial direct costs of acquiring continuing-care contracts should be capitalized and amortized on a straight-line basis over the average expected remaining lives of the residents under contracts.

Long-Term Debt

Tax-Exempt Debt. Health care entities use tax-exempt debt extensively to finance capital projects, with debt often taking the form of revenue bonds issued through a state financing authority. Recent tax legislation has constricted the availability of tax-exempt funding, but it remains the most prevalent form of financing.

Prior to issuance of SOP 85-1, reporting practices for tax-exempt debt were not consistent, treated variously as obligations of both restricted and general funds. Under the SOP, if the debt was issued for the benefit of the entity and is to be repaid by the entity, is is to be reported as a liability of the general fund (TP 10,370.23).

Capitalization of Interest. SFAS 62, *Capitalization of Interest Cost in Situations Involving Certain Tax-Exempt Borrowings and Certain Gifts and Grants* (I67.116A-C), discusses the unique characteristics of such transactions.

SFAS 62 requires the capitalization of interest cost of restricted tax-exempt borrowings less any interest earned on related interest-bearing investments acquired with the proceeds, from the date of borrowing until the specified qualifying assets acquired with the borrowed funds are ready for their intended use (I67.116B). The stated intent of SFAS 62 is to recognize the overall *net* cost of financing as the cost of the qualifying assets. However, interest earned from temporary investment of donor-restricted funds shall be considered an addition to the gift or grant, rather than capitalized (I67.116A).

Funds on Deposit With Trustees. Most hospitals cannot legally issue tax-exempt bonds directly. Consequently, states have enacted laws allowing finance authorities to issue bonds on behalf of health care providers. In such transactions, it is common for the finance authorities to require the deposit of bond proceeds with trustees.

AICPA SOP 85-1, *Financial Reporting by Not-for-Profit Health Care Entities for Tax-Exempt Debt and Certain Funds Whose Use is Limited* (TP 10,370), specifies the reporting requirements for trusteed funds. Such funds are recorded as assets whose use is limited, and are classified as current if they will be used to pay (in accordance with limits on their use) for current liabilities. Income on trusteed funds, to the extent not capitalized, should either be reported as other operating revenue, or netted against related interest expense with appropriate parenthetical disclosure (TP 10,370.23). Income from use-limited assets (see next section) should be reported as nonoperating revenue.

Assets Whose Use Is Limited

Under SOP 85-1, assets whose use is limited should be reported separately. This applies to both internal and external limitations, such as under debt indentures, trust agreements, third-party payor arrangements, and board designation. In practice, this classification is most often used to report funds held by trustees under bond indentures and investments identified for specific purposes, such as for the replacement of fixed assets (funded depreciation).

Assets whose use is limited to the payment of items reported as current liabilities should be reported as current assets. In most other cases the amounts are classified as noncurrent. Figure 30.8 contains an example of the financial statement format for assets whose use is limited, with general fund amounts included in both current and noncurrent classifications. Assets whose use is limited may include a portion of borrowed funds held by a trustee, as discussed in the previous section.

At-Risk Payment Arrangements

The desire to control health care costs has contributed to the increasing number of arrangements under which health care providers are at financial risk under contracts with third-party payors. In the simplest form, a hospital or physician will contract to provide services to a patient population for a capitation fee (fixed amount per patient). Such arrangements are popular with HMOs, employers, and other organizations responsible for providing covered members with access to health care services. Providers are at risk to the extent the cost of providing health care services exceeds capitation revenue. Conversely, they stand to profit if costs are less than capitation revenue.

Payments received under at-risk contracts are generally recorded in a deferred revenue account. Deferred revenues are then applied to patient receivables on the basis of the provider's assumed contractual payment rate and contractual allowances

	General Fund	
	1987	1986
Assets Whose Use is Limited:		
By board for capital improvements	$ 300,000	$ 100,000
By agreements with third-party payors	700,000	400,000
Under bond indenture agreement — held by trustee	3,000,000	2,000,000
Total assets whose use is limited	4,000,000	2,500,000
Less assets whose use is limited and that are required for current liabilities*	(500,000)	(500,000)
Noncurrent assets whose use is limited	$3,500,000	$2,000,000

* Contra account reflected as a current asset of the general fund.

FIG. 30.8   Financial Statement Disclosure of Assets Whose Use is Limited
Source: SOP 85-1, Exhibit 1.

are recognized. The contract must be analyzed periodically to determine if the provider has an additional receivable or liability, requiring recognition of additional income or loss. Some providers may view at-risk adjustments as not related to patient care and would thus classify such adjustments as other operating revenue or operating expense.

SFAS 5, *Accounting for Contingencies* (C59), and FIN 14, *Reasonable Estimation of the Amount of a Loss* (C59.124–.127), provide guidance for the assessment of possible losses with respect to risk contracts. Providers who enter into at-risk contracts must recognize a loss when it is probable that expected future costs will exceed expected capitation revenue and recoveries. This requires providers to analyze historical experience, related utilization trends, and other factors that may influence future services to be provided under the contract.

Medical Malpractice Insurance

The rapidly increasing cost and decreasing availability of commercial policies providing professional liability (malpractice) insurance have resulted in dramatic changes in the health care industry. Accounting for coverage has been as diverse as the programs themselves. AICPA SOP 87-1, *Accounting for Asserted and Unasserted Medical Malpractice Claims of Health Care Providers and Related Issues* (TP 10,410), has been issued to address the diversity in accounting practice.

The key conclusion of SOP 87-1 (based on SFAS 5, *Accounting for Contingencies (C59)*) is:

The ultimate costs of malpractice claims, which include costs associated with litigating or settling claims, should be accrued when the incidents occur that give rise to the claims, if it can be determined that it is probable that liabilities have been incurred and if the amounts of the losses can be reasonably estimated. [TP 10,410.21]

SFAS 60, *Accounting and Reporting by Insurance Enterprises* (In6), provides the basis for many of the detailed conclusions of SOP 87-1. The diversity of malpractice insurance programs and the requirement to accrue the ultimate costs of claims require the segregation of expected losses into several categories: (1) asserted claims, (2) unasserted claims from reported incidents, and (3) unasserted incidents. The estimate of loss for each of these categories should be based on assessment of individual claims or a group of similar claims, should consider hospital-specific data and experience, and also should consider industry data to the extent relevant. Providers insured by a claims-made policy (covering only claims reported to the insurer during the policy term) may accordingly need to estimate the ultimate costs associated with both categories (2) and (3) previously mentioned.

Although a commercial insurance policy for medical malpractice is similar to liability insurance policies generally, many malpractice policies are retrospectively rated, and some are issued by captive insurance companies. If ultimate premiums are determined by a retrospective rating based on experience, the minimum premium plus an estimate of additional premiums to be paid for the coverage period is recorded as expense. If a provider purchases insurance from a wholly-owned captive, the captive must accrue the ultimate cost of losses and these must be reflected in the financial statements of the provider either directly or through consolidation. If the insurance is purchased from a multiprovider captive, the policy premium is expensed along with an estimate of losses from asserted and unasserted claims in excess of the premium. If the estimate of losses cannot be made, the provider should disclose the contingency.

Similarly, providers who accrue for malpractice claims through self-insurance trusts must look beyond the amount funded, or recommended to be funded, to such trusts, because self-insurance is not considered to be insurance under GAAP (C59.136). Rather, the estimated ultimate costs of malpractice claims should be recognized as expense in the year incurred regardless of when such amounts are funded. Trusteed assets set aside for malpractice claims are normally recorded as general fund assets whose use is limited.

Many providers discount estimated ultimate malpractice claims and related costs payable in the future to the current date, to recognize the time value of money for the period that normally precedes payment. This approach is currently considered an acceptable practice for self-insured malpractice claims of health care providers, but may change depending on the outcome of an AICPA project on discounting generally.

HMO ACCOUNTING AND REPORTING

Overview

HMOs, which began more than 50 years ago, have become one of the fastest growing segments of the health care market. Their acceptance is a viable alternative to the traditional health care delivery system has provided them with the opportunity to realize significant growth in membership and number of plans since the early 1980s.

As with many young businesses, the operating systems of HMOs are continually being developed and refined to better support financial management and reporting.

Although most HMOs must process a high volume of small transactions, the level of sophistication and the capability of operating systems vary widely.

Regulation. An HMO is regulated by the insurance commission of the domiciliary state. These state regulatory agencies have not specified statutory accounting principles for HMOs, although they do require an annual statement of condition and require the filing of premium rates with which HMOs must comply. The states prescribe reserve requirements in the form of minimum net worth, insolvency insurance, restricted cash balances, and other similar conditions.

An HMO may apply for *federal qualification* to help expand its market penetration using the U.S. government's *dual choice* requirements. Under the dual choice rule, employers are required to offer their employees an HMO if they offer another form of health insurance from an independent carrier, such as Blue Cross. Once federally qualified, the HMO is required to charge the same premium to all members of the plan in a defined community; this is known as *community rating*. There is some latitude available in the community rating approach to the HMO, but this is not as flexible as the experience rating approach used by casualty insurance companies. A nonfederally qualified HMO may, however, use experience rating to establish its premiums.

State Insurance Department Questionnaire. Most states have adopted a uniform statement for reporting by an HMO. This statement includes a balance sheet, a statement of revenue and expenses, a statement of changes in financial position and net worth, various enrollment and utilization data, and supporting schedules of cash, restricted assets, investments, premiums, and other receivables. The uniform statement also includes generalized interrogatories helpful to an understanding of the HMO's business. A sample questionnaire is shown in Figure 30.9.

Organization Models. The HMO is a hybrid of an insurance company and a provider of a health care service. The organization model adopted by the HMO has a significant bearing on operations and structure. For example, the *staff model* employs its own doctors, constructs its own health centers and occasionally hospitals, and operates in a fully integrated fashion. In this environment, an HMO generally retains the primary insurance risk and provides the delivery of health care services at the physician level (or hospital level if applicable).

The *group model* HMO contracts with physician groups who may serve more than one HMO. The HMO owns very little in the way of health care capital (bricks and mortar), but and makes a substantial investment in computer hardware and software. In this environment the HMO generally retains the risk of loss in delivery of health care services at the hospital level, but passes the risk of loss for outpatient and physician services to the participating physician groups. The physicians are compensated by the group.

The *IPA model* operates similarly to the group model, except that its contracts for provision of health care services are with an IPA or with individual physicians. In the IPA environment each physician works independently, and the HMO monitors the physician's management of services as they affect the total delivery of health care to the members.

1. Has any change been made since the last reporting date in the charter, articles of incorporation, by-laws, or contracts with physicians or hospitals or subscribers?

2. Is the HMO authorized to conduct business in other states? Which ones?

3. Is the HMO directly or indirectly owned or controlled by any other company corporation, group of companies, partnership, or individual?

4. List the following capital stock information for the HMO:

	Common	Preferred
Number of shares authorized	_____	_____
Number of shares outstanding	_____	_____
Par or stated value per share	_____	_____
Dividend rate	_____	_____
Are dividends cumulative?	_____	_____

   If preferred stock is participating, attach note(s) disclosing terms of such participating rights.

5. Attach a schedule showing individual stockholdings in excess of 10% of the HMO's capital stock outstanding.

6. Has the HMO an established procedure for annual disclosure to its Board of Directors of any material interest or affiliation on the part of any of its officers, directors, or responsible employees which is in, or is likely to, conflict with the official duties of such person?

7. Did any officer or salaried employee of the HMO receive, directly or indirectly, any commission on the business transactions of the HMO?

8. Was money loaned during the period covered by this report to any officer or director?

9. Are officers and employees of the HMO covered by a fidelity bond?

10. Were all stocks, bonds, and other securities owned as of the end of the reporting period in the actual possession of the HMO?

11. Is the purchase or sale of the investments of the HMO approved by either the Board of Directors or a subordinate committee thereof?

12. Has any present or former officer, director, or any other person or firm filed any claim of any nature whatsoever against the HMO which is not included in the statement of liabilities?

13. Have damage claims for medical injury been initiated against the HMO during the reporting year?

14. Has the HMO been subject to any administrative orders, cease and desist orders, fines, or suspensions during the reporting year?

15. Have any other legal actions been taken against the HMO during the reporting year?

16. Does the HMO have direct professional liability coverage (commonly known as "malpractice insurance")?

   If the HMO has such insurance, provide the following information:

   a. Name of Carrier: _____

   b. Limits of Coverage: _____

   c. Expiration Date: _____

   (continued)

FIG. 30.9   Sample State Insurance Department HMO Questionaire
Source: Brandon Insurance Service Company, Nashville, Tennessee.

17. Are providers of the HMO contractually obligated to maintain professional liability coverage?

18. Provide the following information on the HMO's general liability insurance coverage:

    a. Name of Carrier: _____

    b. Limits of Coverage: _____

    c. Expiration Date: _____

If the HMO does not have this coverage, explain: _____

19. Provide the following information on the HMO's reinsurance (stop-loss) coverage:

    a. Name of Carrier: _____

    b. Limits of Coverage: _____

    c. Expiration Date: _____

If the HMO does not have this coverage, please explain: _____

20. Describe arrangements, if any, which the HMO may have to protect subscribers and their dependents against the risk of insolvency, including conversion privileges with other carriers, agreements with providers to continue rendering services, and any other similar arrangements:

21. Does the HMO set up its claim liability for the other medical services on an invoice date basis or service date basis? If both explain. If other than an invoice date basis or service date basis, describe basis used:

22. Provide the following information regarding number of HMO participating physicians:

    a. At start of reporting year: _____

    b. Added during reporting year: _____

    c. Terminated during reporting year: _____

    d. End of reporting year: _____

23. List the number of formal grievances heard by the HMO grievance committee during the reporting year: _____

24. Provide the following information for accounts that are ten percent (10%) or more of total HMO enrollment:

    a. *Type of account.* In the table below please describe the account using one of the following terms:

        • Federal Employees

        • County and Municipal Employees

        • State Employees

        • Corporate Nonpublic-Service Sector

        • Corporate Nonpublic-Manufacturing

        • Union and Trust Funds (Account contract should be with a union or trust fund; do not include accounts for contracts with above categories even if these are unionized.)

        • Medicaid

        • Medicare

        • Other

    b. *Percentage of Total Enrollment.* Please provide the percentage of total enrollment represented by this account.

    c. *Renewal Date.* Please provide the renewal date (month/day/year) for this account's contract.

FIG. 30.9 *(continued)*

Under the *network model*, physicians in single- and multispecialty group practices will contract with an HMO to provide specific services. This model is not recognized for purposes of federal qualification.

Becoming more prominent in the marketplace are *preferred provider organizations* (PPOs). These organizations construct a delivery system with specific "preferred" providers, that is, physicians and hospitals. The PPO differs from an HMO in the benefit package provided to subscribers. PPOs also frequently have affiliations or joint ventures with insurance companies.

Management companies are often established to provide all accounting and administrative functions for the HMO, and are prevalent in start-up plans. Generally the manager enters into a long-term contract that specifies the services to be provided, charging a fixed percentage of the member premiums. Management companies may service independent plans, or plans in which they invest or own.

Systems

The core of the HMO's operating system is the *enrollment data base*. Individual members of the HMO are classified within the system by subscriber group (i.e., employer), primary care physician, type of coverage, and numerous other categories. This file is critical as it serves as the nucleus for billing subscriber groups, paying valid claims, and in IPA and group plans, for establishing and settling physician *retentions* and *withholds*. The retentions and withholds represent amounts held back from payment to the physician and eventually paid over to the extent the physician achieves targeted cost levels for medical services. The enrollment data base may also be used to perform utilization review functions and to evaluate physicians.

Revenue System. Because HMOs are prepaid health care plans, they collect premiums in advance of the coverage period. The HMO bills its subscriber groups based on membership information as of the billing date, usually one month prior to the month of coverage. The sponsoring organization is billed by the HMO for either an aggregate fixed sum or an amount per enrollee. Many employer groups do not pay the exact amounts billed because their records will reflect unreported membership changes. In paying a revised amount, the employer may also submit the changes to the membership data. This results in retroactive billing adjustments requiring the HMO to adjust its revenue recognition for current enrollee additions, deletions, and other changes.

The enrollment and billing information should be linked with the other systems, particularly claims. A major reason is the need to accumulate claims experience by age, sex, and other categories to arrive at responsive premium setting policies.

Receivables System. Theoretically, a prepaid health care plan should not have any subscriber receivables. However, payments are not always timely received, and some subscriber groups may experience operating problems that will delay payments. Bad debts are not a significant problem for the HMO, because their contract with the employer provides for termination if premiums are not paid promptly.

Claims Disbursement System. Generally, HMOs will pay for medical claims under the following forms of payment:

• Charges or discounted charges
• Capitation arrangements
• All-inclusive per diems

Capitation arrangement are primarily used in compensating physicians. The HMO pays a predetermined amount to the physician or other provider based on the number of members. In many HMOs, such as IPA models, the HMO will also be required to capture data regarding the actual claim that the doctor would have submitted had he not been under a capitation arrangement. This data is used to settle physician retentions and withholds (i.e., risk sharing pools) based on the doctors' ability to control health care costs.

All-inclusive per diems represent a fixed rate for all the services rendered by a provider. These arrangements are primarily used with hospitals. The HMO will also monitor the actual claims experience under per diem arrangements to evaluate the appropriateness of the rates used and the performance of physicians.

The claims disbursement system should be integrated with the eligible enrollment and other operating systems of the HMO to assure that valid claims are only paid for current members.

Referral System—Utilization Review. Many HMOs have established preauthorization or referral system procedures to prevent unnecessary utilization of health care services. The referral system requires preapproval of all hospital admissions, with projected length of stay, and of all medical services outside the HMO's provider unit. This system is very useful to an HMO in projecting its medical expenses.

The utilization review function acts as a concurrent review of hospitalization and physician services. The utilization review department will monitor a patient's progress while in the hospital and evaluate the number of hospital days per thousand members, the average length of stay, and other key medical factors that provide statistical guidance to the HMO in managing its business.

Financial Statement Reporting

So far, little guidance has been provided to the industry in the form of specific accounting requirements. A proposed SOP, *Accounting by Prepaid Health Care Plans* (AICPA 1986a), addresses the issues facing the growing HMO market and proposes standards to enhance consistency in HMO accounting principles.[2]

The proposed SOP, expected to be published in 1988, provides guidance on accounting for health care costs, contract losses, stop-loss insurance, and acquisition costs of prepaid health care plans. The SOP recommends:

---

[2] The proposed Audit and Accounting Guide, *Audits of Providers of Health Care Services* (AICPA, 1988c), also discusses HMOs, and when finalized will incorporate the proposed SOP.

1. Prepaid health care plans should accrue health care costs as services are rendered, including estimates of costs incurred but not yet reported to the plan. When it is determined that a contract with a sponsoring employer or other group will be terminated, and a provider of prepaid health care services is obligated to render services to specific members beyond the current period (because of contract or regulatory requirements), the subsequent costs to be incurred net of any related anticipated revenues, should be accrued at that time. Amounts payable to hospitals, physicians, or other health care providers under risk retention, bonus, or similar programs should be accrued during the contract period based on relevant factors such as experience to date.

2. A loss should be recognized when it is probable that expected future health care costs and maintenance costs during the unexpired term of a group of existing contracts will exceed anticipated future premiums and stop-loss insurance recoveries on those contracts.

3. Stop-loss premiums should be reported as health care costs with recoveries reported as a reduction of the related health care costs.

4. Acquisition costs (marketing costs to acquire subscriber contracts) of prepaid health care plans should be expensed as incurred.

The sample balance sheet in Figure 30.10 shows the differences in the usual elements of financial condition and in their presentation for staff, group, and IPA HMO models (the network model is similar to the group model and is thus not presented). The presentation of an HMO's operating results highlights operating revenues, medically related operating expenses, and administrative expenses. An example of an HMO statement of revenue and expenses is shown in Figure 30.11.

Health Care Costs. Existing practices in HMO accounting for costs are varied. Among the approaches in use are:

* Cash basis;
* Accrual of health care costs as the costs are reported to the plan;
* Accrual for services rendered including an estimate of costs incurred but not yet reported; and
* Accrual of the estimated cost to complete the hospital services to be provided to hospitalized members if the hospitals is compensated on a fee-for-service basis.

The proposed SOP (AICPA, 1986a) recommends that prepaid health care plans should accrue health care costs as services are rendered, including estimates of cost incurred but not yet reported to the plan. The SOP further indicates that when a contract with a sponsoring employer is terminated, the estimated costs to be incurred after the contract period – offset by any anticipated revenue – should be accrued.

Risk retention and bonus arrangements are generally subject to periodic settlements based on actual claims experience during the period. Therefore, past experience should indicate whether a payment or reduction in expense is reasonably assured. Such amounts payable to hospitals, physicians, or other health care providers should be accrued during the contract period based on prior experience.

Incurred but Not Reported Liabilities. Claims incurred but not reported (IBNR) represent costs associated with the delivery of health care services that have been

	Staff	Group	IPA
Assets			
Cash and equivalents	$ 46,141,000	$11,204,000	$15,496,000
Investments	16,521,000	–	–
Subscriptions and premiums receivable	3,835,000	2,256,000	3,077,000
Accounts receivable – medical group/ affiliates	727,000	1,175,000	1,289,000
Prepaid expenses and inventories	2,582,000	595,000	332,000
Other receivables	5,991,000	38,000	301,000
	75,797,000	15,268,000	20,495,000
Property, plant, and equipment	84,162,000	896,000	1,895,000
Long-term receivables – medical groups/ affiliates	–	249,000	–
Funds held by trustees for construction	28,467,000	–	–
Restricted funds		599,000	63,000
Other	6,851,000	–	87,000
	$195,277,000	$17,012,000	$22,540,000
Liabilities and Fund Balances			
Accounts payable and accrued expenses	$ 17,335,000	$ 1,616,000	$ 1,131,000
Accounts payable – affiliates and medical groups	–	3,300,00	17,914,000
Accrued claims payable – hospitals and physicians	21,818,000	4,350,000	
Unearned premium revenue	3,099,000	1,712,000	1,682,000
Current maturities of long-term debt	1,459,000	19,000	195,000
Risk incentive payable	–	–	19,000
Retention fund payable	–	–	987,000
	43,711,000	10,997,000	21,928,000
Long-term debt and capital lease obligations	114,741,000	78,000	1,150,000
Fund Balance	36,825,000	5,937,000	(538,000)
	$195,277,000	$17,012,000	$22,540,000

FIG. 30.10 Sample Balance Sheet Comparing Three HMO Models

incurred during a period but are not reported to the HMO before the close of the period. The IBNR accrual is the most sensitive element in the financial statements of an HMO; it is influenced by factors over which the HMO often has little control, making projections difficult. Some of the variables are:

• Physician admission patterns
• Hospital/physician billing habits
• Member misunderstanding of the benefit package

The IBNR liability is generally determined from actuarially based *lag analyses*. These analyses project the lapse of time between the incurrence of a claim and its receipt by the HMO. With a seasoned base, the HMO will have the ability to project IBNR based upon the lag factor. The lag analyses can be adjusted for changes in membership, changes in population, and other relevant factors.

Revenues:	
Member premiums	$207,808,879
Other health center revenues	12,930,586
Other	8,709,524
Total Revenues	229,448,989
Operating Expenses:	
Ambulatory health services	122,823,742
Hospital services	61,688,058
Noncovered services	6,244,380
Research, teaching, and community service expenses	1,326,520
TOTAL MEDICAL COSTS	192,091,700
Health plan administration and other	29,098,924
Total Expenses	221,190,624
Excess of Revenue Over Expenses	$ 8,258,365

FIG. 30.11   Sample Statement of HMO Revenues and Expenses (functional basis)

In addition to lag analyses, an HMO with a strong referral system will be able to project its IBNR liability using the referral system data. A referral system has a preauthorized listing of all hospital admissions or other medical services. When extended with average cost projections by type of service, a reasonable IBNR estimate can be made.

Losses on Existing Group Contracts. HMOs usually receive a fixed monthly payment for a contract period of one year to cover premiums for the provision of health care services to members. If calculation of the premium is based on a community rating or a community rating by class, the premium charged by the HMO is generally a fixed amount with almost no fluctuation based on actual experience. If premiums are based on an experience rating, however, an estimate of the actual costs to be incurred under the contract is made to set the premium rate. Under most of these arrangements the premium, once set, will not change for the duration of the contract. A major consideration in pricing the contract is the ability to control medical costs, thereby reducing the employer's costs as well as enhancing the HMO's profitability.

The proposed SOP on prepaid health care plans suggests that when future health care costs and maintenance expenses during the unexpired term of a group of existing contracts are expected to exceed anticipated future premiums and stop-loss recoveries on these contracts, a loss should be recognized. Contracts should be grouped consistent with the HMO's practices for establishing premium rates (e.g., by community-rating practices, geographical area, or statutory requirements) to determine if an anticipated loss exists.

Stop-Loss Arrangements. HMOs often use stop-loss insurance to transfer a portion of their risk to another company. That is, a plan may insure a portion of health care costs incurred on behalf of a member during a contract period in excess of a stipulated amount. A plan generally purchases stop-loss insurance to limit the plan's total losses during a contract period.

The proposed SOP recommends that stop-loss premiums be reported as a health care cost and stop-loss recoveries be reported as revenue. Accrued stop-loss recoveries should be classified as assets, reduced by appropriate valuation allowances.

Member Acquisition Costs. For insurance companies, the cost associated with acquiring business that increases premium revenue is deferred and amortized as the related revenues are earned. An HMO's costs relating to obtaining subscriber contracts and member enrollment are commissions paid to brokers, brochures, and advertising. The proposed SOP recommends that costs relating to acquisition of membership for prepaid health care plans be expensed as incurred.

Risk Sharing Arrangements. An HMO's contractual arrangement with physicians, groups, IPAs, or hospitals determines which entity bears the risk of adverse experience. An HMO may fix its costs and thus limit its risk by compensating health care providers on a capitation basis rather than on a fee-for-service basis. Physicians or health care providers compensated in this manner thus have incentives to keep total costs below the fees received. Contracts may also provide for bonuses if use of hospitals and outpatient services are lower than expected.

Likewise, an IPA may limit its risk by contracting with the physicians or hospitals on a capitation basis. In the IPA model, the physician usually receives a percentage of a fee; the remaining amount is held by the IPA for distribution at a later date based on actual costs and other incentive measures. In the staff and group models the cost of physician and outpatient services are relatively fixed because the physicians and support personnel are salaried employees of the HMO.

Accordingly, in many situations, substantial portions of an HMO's total costs are relatively fixed and do not vary with the volume of services provided. Incremental costs consist mostly of services purchased on a fee basis, primarily specialized services from nonparticipating providers.

Under many risk sharing arrangements, the settlement amounts with the physician or hospital include an estimate of IBNR.

Unearned Premium Revenue. In many HMOs, premiums are received from the subscriber group prior to the date of eligibility for coverage, and are recorded as unearned premium revenue. A plan may bill for its enrollment on a cycle basis throughout the month, necessitating calculation of the unearned portion at period end. This portion is recorded as an unearned premium by the plan; but some HMOs do not recognize a receivable for unearned premium, eliminating both amounts from the plan's financial statements.

Long-Term Debt. Many nonprofit HMOs borrow under arrangements similar to those of nonprofit hospitals. They can utilize Health and Education Facilities Authority bonds, as well as other tax-exempt issue types. HMOs should follow hospital reporting and accounting practices for these debt arrangements.

Related Party Transactions. In many cases the physicians and the hospitals will have representation on the board of directors of the HMO, resulting in related party transactions. Consideration should be given to the appropriate disclosure requirements stated in SFAS 57, *Related Party Disclosures* (R36).

Restricted Funds. Many HMOs have restricted funds as a result of state insurance department requirements for statutory reserve purposes or because of long-term debt agreements. These restricted funds should be adequately disclosed and appropriately classified as current or long-term, depending on their expected utilization.

The HMO's statement of financial condition filed annually with the state department of insurance requires separate reporting for all restricted funds and restricted assets.

Marketable Securities. Most HMOs have excess cash invested in a variety of marketable securities. The HMO will generally invest in government securities and cash equivalents, and avoid the equity markets. SFAS 12 does not apply to nonprofit HMOs, but it is applicable to for-profit HMOs.

AUDITING CONSIDERATIONS

Accounting Systems

Health care entities generally, and hospitals in particular, have complex and sophisticated accounting systems. The systems process large volumes of data, classify information into departmental and other categories, and produce extensive management accounting and reporting information. The major accounting systems include the revenue system (enrollment patient revenues, billing, accounts receivable, and cash receipts), claims disbursement system, payroll system, and general ledger system. Subsystems – such as those for medical records, fixed assets, and materials management – are often integrated with the major systems.

Most health care entities rely on electronic data processing (EDP) systems to generate and maintain accounting records. The auditor must have an adequate understanding of the EDP applications to develop the appropriate audit approach. The majority of data processing software is developed and sold by independent vendors. Large, established vendors often have internal control functions built into the software, to provide system documentation, special reports, and possibly certain audit capabilities. This will provide some level of audit assurance, but the auditor must still perform adequate documentation and testing procedures to assess the reliability of the data processing information. General data processing controls related to hardware and users should also be assessed. (See Chapter 10.)

Audit Approach – Other Than HMOs

The audit of a health care entity must be performed in accordance with GAAS. The AICPA's *Hospital Audit Guide* (1985c) and exposure draft of the new Audit and Accounting Guide, *Audits of Providers of Health Care Services* (AICPA, 1988c), contain extensive discussion of audit objectives and procedures. Certain key components of health care entity financial statements have a significant influence on audit procedures. These include revenue recognition, patient accounts receivable, and third-party payor arrangements.

Revenue Systems. Audit procedures in this area relate primarily to testing revenue recognition and the basis for payment from certain third-party payors.

Revenue is recognized on an accrual basis as determined by charges for services. As part of the overall assessment of the revenue system, detailed procedures will be performed, on a test basis, of documentation of services provided to patients. In most cases, a number of specific internal control attributes are identified through system flowcharting and walkthrough. Statistical sampling methods (see Chapter 9) can then be used to select inpatient stays or outpatient visits for testing of selected attributes.

The patient's medical record is the primary source of documentation for services performed, which in turn should agree to charges based on standard rates at the time of service. The amount of charges are usually detailed in the patient accounting (business office) file. The medical record is the source for clinical and demographic information, whereas the patient accounting file contains the financial information.

In addition, the auditor must develop methods to test the information on payor responsibility. This is particularly important in cases where payment is based on the nature of the patient's illness. For example, under Medicare PPS payments for inpatient service are based on a predetermined rate multiplied by a weighting factor identified as a result of the patient's DRG. The DRG thus determines net patient service revenue.

The auditor can test the accuracy of DRG coding in several ways. Medical record information and DRG coding under the Medicare program are required to be reviewed on an ongoing basis by an independent peer review organization (PRO). The results of this testing can be reviewed by the auditor. Also, the ICD-9 codes from selected medical records could be recoded to test DRG assignment in the patient accounting file. The auditor must recognize the limitations on his expertise in medical record coding in performing this type of test. The medical records could also be reviewed by an independent medical records technician employed by the auditor.

Patient Accounts Receivable. Patient accounts receivable often represent the second largest asset of health care entities, exceeded only by fixed assets. Receivables are an area of relatively high risk for an auditor primarily because of the significance of contractual adjustments and allowances for uncollectible accounts. Audit procedures related to patient accounts receivable must be designed to provide assurance both that they exist and that they are reported net of all revenue deductions.

A major consideration for the auditor involves understanding the methods and timing for recognition of contractual adjustments. These adjustments should be recognized at the time of determining the responsible payor; for all practical purposes, this is at the time of billing. The receivables should be reduced to the anticipated payment amounts through direct writedown or creation of contra-accounts (treatment may vary depending on whether the account has been billed or is unbilled).

Fixed-rate payments methods, such as Medicare PPS, require additional procedures. Payments are dependent on the DRG at the time of discharge. At the end of a reporting period certain cases will be in-house, meaning they are not discharged until the following reporting period. Contractual allowances must be provided to reflect the best estimate of the pro rata share of the anticipated payment as of the end of the reporting period. This is usually determined by allocating the payment between periods based on either the percentage of charges or patient days in each period. The allocation method should be applied consistently.

Audit procedures related to the allowance for uncollectible accounts should consider the basis on which bad debts occur for health care entities. Analysis of receivables should segregate accounts between third-party payors and those not under a contractual arrangement. Consideration should also be given to the collectibility of deductible and coinsurance amounts related to contractual arrangements.

Third-Party Payor Arrangements. More than any other issue, the understanding of third-party payor arrangements has distinguished health care as a specialized industry. Settlement acounts for third-party payors are generally material to the financial statements and involve a complex computation process.

Two types of settlement accounts exist. The substantial majority of settlement accounts relate to a regulatory payment program, such as Medicare or Medicaid. The other type is a contractual agreement with a specific payor, which is generally less complex than regulatory programs but may be driven off the same basic process. Audit procedures should be designed to assess both the settlement process (i.e., compliance with regulations) and the underlying financial and statistical data.

Audit Approach—HMOs

Knowledge of the Organization. To perform an audit in conformity with GAAS, there is an obvious need to become familiar with the operating structure, accounting practices, and activities of the HMO. In the HMO environment, the auditor should be aware of the peculiarities and differences among the different models of HMO. Each model portrays a different financial condition, and therefore represents different risks for the auditor to consider. The auditor should also be knowledgeable about:

1. The 1988 exposure draft of the AICPA Audit and Accounting Guide, *Audits of Providers of Health Care Services.*
2. Applicable laws or regulations of the state insurance commission.
3. Provisions of documents restricting the use of resources received by the organization.
4. The articles of incorporation and by-laws of the HMO.
5. The income tax status (not-for-profit or investor-owned) and related accounting and reporting implications.

Internal Control Structure. Many HMOs have a high level of automation, but some of these systems are still relatively unseasoned. Therefore, the auditor must obtain a thorough understanding of the HMO's data processing environment. (See Chapters 8 and 10.)

The most significant areas of the internal control structure that the auditor must evaluate are the enrollment file, the claims disbursement area, and the adjudication process. The enrollment file must be evaluated as to its ability to generate timely and reliable data about the plan's membership and to provide accurate data to the HMO's other operating systems.

The claims approval process and the adjudication system are important because the governing board of the HMO will be particularly attentive to the ability of the HMO to pay its claims and the timeliness of payment. The system of internal control over approval and payment of claims is also critical in the calculation of the IBNR accrual and settlements with physicians in the risk sharing arrangements.

Incurred but Not Reported Liabilities. The IBNR liability is the most sensitive element in the financial statements of an HMO. The auditor should have a thorough understanding of the plan's methodology fortified by an understanding of the operating results and medical utilization for the year. To determine the reasonableness of the IBNR accrual, the auditor should perform analytical review procedures on the data generated in the utilization review function. The auditor may consider performing systems testing on the summarization and posting of payments through the claims systems. In addition, the auditor may wish to utilize the services of an actuary to review the development and adequacy of the IBNR accrual.

The IBNR claims liability should be tested for mechanical accuracy, and its adequacy should be evaluated by using ratios such as number of days of hospital costs in the ending accrual and evaluation of hospital days per thousand members. In addition, the auditor should be aware of the cost accounting techniques employed in settlements with hospitals and physicians.

31

Governmental Units

THE GOVERNMENT ENVIRONMENT

Governmental accounting and financial reporting have changed drastically since the mid-1970s as the result of a number of major municipal financial crises. These changes can be categorized as:

* Changes in GAAP for state and local government. Many changes and new principles have been implemented in the last two decades, and further significant changes are on the way.
* Changes in the authority for establishing GAAP for governments. The GASB was established as an equal of the FASB to bring sufficient resources to the process of establishing GAAP for governments.
* Attitudes have changed. Today more governmetal officials, users of financial information, and auditors support GAAP financial reporting and independent audits for governments. Most governments are making exerted efforts to develop financial statements that conform to GAAP.
* Legislation. The Single Audit Act was passed in 1984, significantly expanding the need for and scope of government audits.

Levels of Government

Federal Government. The federal government is, of course, the largest governmental entity with annual budget outlays in excess of $1 trillion. This amounts to almost one fourth of the gross national product.

Despite its size and significance, a number of financial management problems plague the federal government, in part because it is not subject to the balanced budget requirements applicable to most state and local governments.

Also, unlike most state and local governments, the federal government does not prepare general purpose financial statements; consequently, there is nothing to subject to an indepedent audit. The Secretary of the Treasury (with the help of the Comptroller General and General Accounting Office) has issued prototype financial statements for the U.S. government annually since 1975. A number of conceptual and methodological issues need to be resolved before it can be claimed that these financial statements are presented in conformity with GAAP and be subjected to independent audits.

The lack of a Chief Financial Officer is also identified as a problem of federal financial management. A bill (H.R. 3142) proposed by Congressman Joseph J. DioGuardi (R-N.Y.) would create a chief financial officer with oversight responsibility for all financial management in federal departments and agencies. The bill would also create assistant secretaries for financial management in each agency, require preparation of annual financial statements on a GAAP basis for each agency, and call for annual audits of those statements by the independent Comptroller General.

Federal financial assistance to state and local governments has increased substantially over the past few decades. These funds are administered by multiple federal agencies and departments, each with individual compliance and reporting requirements. Audit coverage of these programs very often overlapped. In part, to remedy this situation, Congress passed the Single Audit Act of 1984 to

- Improve the financial management of state and local governments with respect to federal financial asistance.
- Establish uniform requirements for audits of programs obtaining federal financial assistance.
- Promote the efficient and effective use of audit resources.
- Ensure that federal departments and agencies rely upon and use the audit work done pursuant to the Act.

State Government. Like the federal government, most states are comprised of a wide variety of departments, commissions, boards, and agencies. Gathering all the financial data from these agencies and presenting them on a comparable basis is a complex task. Until recently, state financial data was gathered only for the budget process, not necessarily in the form required to prepare financial statements in conformity with GAAP. Further, the number and variety of organizations that must be combined to produce GAAP financial statements has increased as the definition of the reporting entity has changed, reflecting recent new accounting principles.

Many state governments have met the challenge and by the late 1980s have made significant progress in developing new accounting systems that gather information for both budget and GAAP reporting. Many have issued GAAP financial statements that have received unqualified opinions from independent auditors.

Local Government. Local governments include counties and municipalities (cities, towns, townships, villages) and similar governments. These units are creatures of the state and subject to statutes that sometimes dictate rules on accounting for and reporting of financial information. However, most local governments are preparing GAAP-based financial statements that are audited by independent CPAs.

Special Purpose Units. Special purpose governments are organizations established to provide a single or limited number of functions (as distinguished from general purpose governments such as states, counties, or cities). Special purpose governments are known by many names, such as authorities, enterprises, commissions, or districts. They may be statewide, include portions of a state, two or more states, or may be local only.

In some cases, special purpose units are merely segregated funds or discrete functions of a single governmental unit. In other cases they are partly or fully independent. They may be the creation of two or more governmental units subject to an agreement between them, or they may be established by specific state legislation, either with or without the involvement of local governments. Examples of special purpose government units are port authorities, airports, industrial development districts, libraries, sanitation districts, and mosquito abatement districts.

To the extent these special districts, authorities, or commissions charge users for the basic value of their service, their accounting will usually be on an accrual basis, like that of a commercial enterprise. Otherwise the unit will follow governmental accounting principles. When the unit is the creation of an individual state or local government, its financial statements are usually included with the other financial statements of the state or local government, in addition to its separately issued financial statements.

School Districts. In some states, school districts are independent governmental units with many of the same taxing powers as municipalities. In other states, the school district is effectively an arm of the local unit and must look to that unit for its resources. In almost all cases, the financial statements of the school district follow the same principles as other governmental units, although variations in financial reporting terminology are common.

ESTABLISHING GAAP FOR GOVERNMENTS

Governmental Accounting Standards Board

Until 1984, one of the most difficult questions facing preparers and auditors of state and local government financial statements was determining what constitutes GAAP. The creation of the GASB that year resolved this issue.

Prior to that time, pronouncements of the National Council of Governmental Accounting (NCGA) were generally acknowledged as the primary authoritative source of GAAP. GAAS, defining the hierarchy of GAAP for independent auditors, did not specifically recognize NCGA pronouncements as the authoritative source of GAAP. However, GAAS did recognize pronouncements of bodies composed of expert accountants that followed a due process procedure providing for broad distribution of proposed pronouncements to the public for comment. NCGA pronouncements were certainly considered GAAP under this definition; and the failure by an independent auditor to follow those pronouncements was usually deemed a violation of GAAS under the AICPA's *Rules of the Code of Professional Conduct*.

The organizations participating in the creation of GASB agreed on a hierarchy for determining GAAP for state and local governmental entities. The resulting *Structural Agreement* provides that "the GASB will establish standards for activities and transactions of state and local governmental entities and the FASB will establish standards for activities and transactions of all other entities" (FAF, 1984).

AICPA Code of Professional Conduct—Rule 203

Rule 203 of the AICPA's *Code of Professional Conduct* states that

> A member shall not (1) express an opinion or state affirmatively that the financial statements or other financial data of any entity are presented in conformity with generally accepted accounting principles or (2) state that he or she is not aware of any material modifications that should be made to such statements or data in order for them to be in conformity with generally accepted accounting principles, if such statements or data contain any departure from an accounting principle promulgated by bodies designated by Council to establish such principles that has a material effect on the statements or data taken as a whole. If, however, the statements or data contain such a departure and the member can demonstrate that due to unusual circumstances the financial statements or data would otherwise have been misleading, the member can comply with the rule by describing the departure, its approximate effects, if practicable, and the reasons why compliance with the principle would result in a misleading statement.

In 1986, the Council of the AICPA passed a resolution designating GASB as the authoritative body for establishing GAAP for state and local governments. This gave GASB the same status for state and local government entities as FASB has for private sector entities.

In addition, the Governmental Accounting Standards Advisory Council (GASAC) has developed model legislation that recognizes the GASB as the authoritative body for establishing GAAP for state and local governments. Such legislation would require state and local governments to follow GAAP for reporting purposes. GASAC is currently working with various interested parties to have this legislation introduced in the state legislatures across the country.

Hierarchy of GAAP

The *Structural Agreement* provides a hierarchy of GAAP for state and local government entities as follows:

1. Pronouncements of GASB.
2. Pronouncements of FASB.
3. Pronouncements of bodies composed of expert accountants that follow a due process procedure, including broad distribution of proposed accounting principles for public comment, for the intended purpose of establishing accounting principles or describing existing practices that are generally accepted.
4. Practices or prouncements that are widely recognized as being generally accepted because they represent prevalent practice in a particular industry or the knowledgeable application to specific circumstances of pronouncements that are generally accepted.
5. Other accounting literature.

Shortly after its formation, the GASB issued its first Statement of Governmental Accounting Standards, *Authoritative Status of NCGA Pronouncements and AICPA Industry Audit Guide* (SGAS 1). This statement recognized the existing NCGA pronouncements and the audit guide as authoritative until and if superseded by subsequent standards issued by the GASB. Therefore, GASB pronouncements and those recognized by GASB, such as NCGA pronouncements and the AICPA Industry Audit Guide, *Audits of State and Local Governmental Units* (AICPA, 1986g), are considered the primary sources of GAAP. Pronouncements of FASB are applicable if the accounting treatment of a transaction or event is not addressed by pronouncements of GASB or those acknowledged by GASB as authoritative. If both GASB and FASB pronouncements are silent regarding a particular transaction or event, preparers and auditors should look to the other sources of GAAP referred to in the hierarchy.

The *Structural Agreement* also addresses the question of separately issued financial statements of certain public sector entities such as colleges and universities, utilities, hospitals, and pension plans. It provides that GAAP for separately issued general purpose financial statements of these entities should be guided by FASB standards except in those circumstances in which GASB has issued an applicable pronouncement. It also states that GASB pronouncements are applicable to these entities when they are included in the combined general purpose financial statements issued by a state or local governmental entity.

The first step in the process of identifying appropriate GAAP is to determine if an entity is a state or local governmental unit. For general purpose governments the determination is usually obvious. For many other government-related organizations, such as utilities and enterprise funds, it is necessary to review the legislation, ordinances, or charters that created the entities to determine if the entity is a state or local governmental unit subject to GASB pronouncements.

The difficulty in determining the correct source of accounting principles usually occurs with government enterprise funds and certain components that separately issue financial statements such as enterprise-type activities or government-owned colleges and universities. GASB has not issued pronouncements specifically addressing the accounting and financial reporting for them.

Often the current accounting pronouncements issued or recognized by GASB acknowledge the FASB as the authoritative source of GAAP. However, GASB has issued pronouncements addressing disclosure requirements for various types of transactions that are common to enterprise-type activities and colleges and universities (e.g., retirement plans, demand bonds, investments, deposits, repurchase and reverse repurchase agreements, and Internal Revenue Code (IRC) § 457 deferred compensation plans). While the accounting *measurement* for these transactions is determined by the applicable FASB pronouncements, the *disclosure* requirements established by GASB are also applicable.

Where multiple government units have pooled resources to provide services or self-insurance, the determination of whether those entities are a state and local government unit or a private not-for-profit entity may be difficult. In those circumstances it may be necessary to either check with the office of the Secretary of State in the respective state to determine whether those entities have been chartered as nonprofit or to determine whether the entity has applied for exempt status with the IRS. In addition, an opinion of general counsel should be obtained.

The Question of Jurisdiction

Certain groups representing organizations that have counterparts in the private sector, such as hospitals, utilities, and colleges and universities, have questioned the jurisdictional arrangement established by the *Structural Agreement*. They argue that the hierarchy of GAAP could result in a lack of comparable financial statements among similar types of entities. For instance, a private university that follows FASB principles may report a specific transaction differently than a public university that follows GASB principles (e.g., pension disclosures).

These organizations contend that they compete for the same pool of resources from charitable contributions, government contracts and grants, as well as in the public debt market and, therefore, have the same users of financial statements. They believe that the goal of financial reporting should be to provide the users of financial statements with comparable reporting between similar types of activities regardless of whether the entities exist in the public or private sector.

This question was presented to the Financial Accounting Foundation (FAF), the parent organization of both the FASB and the GASB, for its review. The FAF Structure Committee decided that a review of the jurisdictional division between GASB and FASB would occur as a part of the sunset review provisions provided for in the *Structural Agreement*. That review will commence in January 1989. The Structure Committee also recommended that:

* Each Board and its staff should give more emphasis to communicating with the other about current and planned projects.
* Each Board should, where possible, avoid duplication of efforts and research.
* The chairpersons and directors of research of both Boards should establish mechanisms for communicating between Boards and staff on current and planned projects as well as for sharing or performing joint research on topics of mutual interest.
* New agenda items that could result in one Board reaching a different conclusion than the other should be reported to the FAF Board of Trustees.
* Each Board should explicitly state its justifications for coming to a conclusion that differs from a conclusion already published by the other Board.

While the jurisdictional division between GASB and FASB creates the potential for conflicting standards, the differences to date are few. The majority of standards issued by GASB on subjects that affect both public and private sector activities deal with issues of disclosure, rather than recognition and measurement. If a conflict arises it may be necessary for GASB to take action. For example, GASB issued SGAS 4, *Applicability of FASB Statement No. 87, "Employers' Accounting for Pensions," to State and Local Governmental Employers*, instructing state and local governmental units not to adopt the FASB requirements for pension accounting. GASB has also issued SGAS 8 barring certain state and local governmental entities from adopting the requirements of SFAS 93, *Recognition of Depreciation by Not-For-Profit Organizations*.

GASB Pronouncements

Since its creation GASB has issued the following final pronouncements (through mid-1988):

* *Authoritative Status of NCGA Pronouncements and AICPA Industry Audit Guide* (SGAS 1)
* *Financial Reporting of Deferred Compensation Plans Adopted Under the Provisions of Internal Revenue Code Section 457* (SGAS 2)
* *Deposits With Financial Institutions, Investments (including Repurchase Agreements), and Reverse Repurchase Agreements* (SGAS 3 and GASBTB 87-1)
* *Applicability of FASB Statement No. 87, "Employers' Accounting for Pensions," to State and Local Governmental Employers* (SGAS 4)
* *Disclosure of Pension Information by Public Employee Retirement Systems and State and Local Governmental Employers* (SGAS 5)
* *Accounting and Financial Reporting for Special Assessments* (SGAS 6)
* *Advance Refundings Resulting in Defeasance of Debt* (SGAS 7)
* *Applicability of FASB Statement No. 93, "Recognition of Depreciation by Not-For-Profit Organizations," to Certain State and Local Governmental Entities* (SGAS 8)
* *Objectives of Financial Reporting* (Concepts Statement 1)
* *Demand Bonds Issued by State and Local Governmental Entities* (Interpretation 1)

GASB has also codified the pronouncements of the NCGA, AICPA and its own pronouncements. The *Codification of Governmental Accounting and Financial Reporting Standards as of June 15, 1987* is an integration of currently effective accounting and reporting standards for state and local governments. It is organized into five parts: concepts, general principles, financial reporting, specific balance sheet and operating statement items, and stand-alone reporting—specialized units and activities. All GASB pronouncements listed above except for SGAS 8 are incorporated in the Codification. The Codification was reviewed and approved for publication by the GASB and is considered authoritative.

The Role of Other Organizations

Government Finance Officers Association. Several important publications on governmental accounting have been issued by the Government Finance Officers Association (GFOA). Its members are government officials (predominantly in the financial area), independent CPAs, and management consultants active in government finance. The NCGA, one of GFOA's ancillary organizations, was the standard-setting predecessor to the GASB.

The GFOA established widely recognized standards for preparation of the comprehensive annual financial report (CAFR). As shown in Figure 31.1, the CAFR is divided into three major sections—introductory, financial (including the general purpose financial statements), and statistical.

Two independent reviewers, who are members of the GFOA's Special Review Committee, evaluate a government's CAFR against a checklist of approximately 300 separate criteria. The Committee then votes on whether the CAFR substantially conforms to the GFOA program standards. A government unit whose CAFR is judged by the GFOA to conform may be awarded a Certificate of Achievement for Excellence in Financial Reporting. The significance of this achievement is evidenced by the fact that only about a thousand governments have received this award.

In 1979, to update, clarify, amplify, and reorder then-existing government GAAP, the NCGA issued *Statement 1—Governmental Accounting and Financial Reporting Principles* and *Statement 2—Grant, Entitlement, and Shared Revenue Accounting and Reporting by State and Local Governments*. Statements 1 and 2 bacame the basis of *Government Accounting, Auditing and Financial Reporting* (GAAFR), issued by the GFOA. Known as the *Blue Book*, it provides a major enunciation of governmental GAAP. The NCGA also issued a series of statements and interpretations prior to the creation of GASB. The *Blue Book* was revised and republished in June 1988.

American Institute of CPAs. The AICPA Audit and Accounting Guide, *Audits of State and Local Governmental Units* (1986g), deals with auditing of governmental units. This industry audit guide is the authoritative source of guidance, and it acknowledges that GASB is the authoritative source of accounting principles. Other industry audit guides may provide guidance applicable to certain government organizations.

General Accounting Office. The U.S. General Accounting Office (GAO), under the Comptroller General of the United States, is the auditing arm of Congress. In

1. **Introductory Section**
   a. Title Page
   b. Table of Contents
   c. Letter of Transmittal
   d. Certificate of Achievement for Excellence in Financial Reporting
   e. Listing of Principal Officers
   f. Organizational Chart
   g. Other Material Deemed Appropriate by Management

2. **Financial Section**
   a. Financial Reporting Pyramid (Levels)
      - General Purpose (Combined) Financial Statements
      - Combining Statements – By Fund Type
      - Individual Fund and Account Group Statements
      - Schedules
   b. Components
      - Auditor's Report
      - Combined Balance Sheet
      - Combined Statement of Revenues, Expenditures and Changes in Fund Balances
      - Combined Statement of Changes in Financial Position
      - Notes to the Financial Statements

3. **Statistical Section**
   - Ten Year Trend Data

FIG. 31.1   Comprehensive Annual Financial Report Content
Source: Governmental Accounting, Auditing, and Financial Reporting (GFOA, 1980).

addition to its primary responsibility with respect to the federal government, the GAO has involved itself with audits of federal grants to state and local governmental units. Its significant influence on state and local government has come from recommendations of audit standards for federal grants and from its sponsorship of cooperative auditing programs among government agencies.

The GAO published *Standards For Audit of Governmental Organizations, Programs, Activities and Functions* (1988), known as the *Yellow Book*. This publication requires adherence to GAAP and provides guidance for the audits of federally funded programs, including financial and compliance audits, program results audits, and efficiency and economy audits. The *Yellow Book*, discussed in greater detail in the "Auditing Standards" section of this chapter, last published in 1981, was revised by the GAO in July 1988.

Office of Management and Budget. In 1984, the U.S Congress passed the Single Audit Act. This Act requires audits of grants-in-aid provided by the federal goverment to state and local governments. The Single Audit Act requires state and local governments to issue entity-wide audited financial statements in addition to statements of federally assisted programs. The Office of Management and Budget

(OMB) oversees the implementation of the Act and has issued appropriate guidelines. The OMB, GAO, and Inspectors General of federal agencies that provide grants-in-aid cooperate in this effort.

GAAP FOR STATE AND LOCAL GOVERNMENTS

Fund Accounting

Most qualitative characteristics of accounting information for nongovernmental entities (discussed in Chapter 2) equally apply to governmental units. However, major differences caused by the governmental environment arise in the objectives of financial reporting, resulting in some differences in governmental accounting. The major difference between business enterprise accounting and governmental accounting is the use of funds. In a governmental unit, the basic accounting entity is not the entire governmental unit; rather, it is the individual fund. Governments set up separate funds to record different kinds of activity, and while their general purpose financial statements traditionally aggregate similar type funds, they do not eliminate interfund transactions.

A governmental unit's funds usually fall into three classes: governmental funds, proprietary funds, and trust and agency funds. In a limited number of cases a fund type known as a *discrete presentation* may be used.

Governmental funds record activities that are unique to governmental units—those units supported by taxation, grants, and similar revenues. Proprietary funds record activities that are self-supporting and resemble commercial activities. Trust and agency funds record amounts the government is holding as trustee or agent. In addition to these classes of funds, there are two *account groups*, one for fixed assets and another for long-term debt.

Separate fund accounting is prescribed in a variety of ways. For local governments, a requirement is often written into state law. Governmental units often pass their own resolutions that specifically provide for the establishment of separate funds. Special tax levies for specific purposes such as public safety services are frequent examples. In addition, bond ordinances often provide for the maintenance of separate funds designated for specific purposes.

The laws, ordinances, and documents that provide for the establishment of separate funds may be either mandatory or permissive. GAAP for governments suggests that only the minimum number of funds necessary to meet legal specifications and operational or management requirements should be established.

Separate funds for accounting purposes do not mean that there must be separate bank accounts. Current automated accounting systems allow for separate accounting units but permit the pooling of cash resources, as long as the portion attributable to each pooled activity is properly identified and maintained.

Governmental Funds

The category of governmental funds includes the four fund types discussed below.

General Fund. The general fund is the accounting entity that is used for the general operations of the government. It includes the financial transactions for all activities not required to be accounted for in separate funds.

Special Revenue Funds. Special revenue funds ordinarily are used to account for revenue sources restricted for specific purposes, and the related expenditures. In some cases the expenditures are recorded in other funds, necessitating transfers. In practice, the legal restriction is often broadly interpreted. Thus, if a government levies a special tax to provide for public safety, that levy and related expenditures may be accounted for in a special revenue fund even though there is no legislation or regulation requiring its establishment.

Consequently, many governmental units will report expenditures for general governmental operations in several funds when all of these activites could have been reported in the general fund. This discretionary designation of funds is not unique to special revenue funds. Many of the other fund types have permissive uses. Therefore, when analyzing the general purpose financial statements of a given governmenal unit, or when trying to make comparisons with other units, activities that have been discretionarily segregated into various funds must be identified.

Debt Service Funds. Debt service funds are used to account for the receipt of monies (usually specifically designated tax revenue) restricted for the payment of general long-term debt, most often general obligation bonds. Somctimes general obligation debt is accounted for in enterprise funds, and conversely some long-term debt service may be accounted for in the general fund. This could happen when items are acquired on an installment purchase or capital lease basis, or when there is no legal requirement to establish a debt service fund.

Some jurisdictions have a separate debt service fund for each general obligation long-term debt outstanding. In other jurisdictions it is considered sufficient to have one all-inclusive debt service accounting entity. Use of a debt service fund is required when specified by law, bond resolution, or covenant.

Capital Projects Funds. These funds are used for the acquisition or construction of major capital projects, especially if there is a restricted revenue source (e.g., a bond issue designated for construciton of a new city hall or a new school). An individual project is sometimes considered a separate fund, but often the projects are regarded as separate accounts within a single fund. In some cases capital projects are accounted for in the general fund.

Special Assessment Funds. GASB Statement 6, *Accounting and Financial Reporting for Special Assessments* (SGAS 6), establishes accounting and financial reporting standards for capital improvements and services financed by special assessments. The special assessment fund type as defined in NCGA Statement 1, *Governmental Accounting and Financial Reporting Principles*, was eliminated for financial reporting purposes.

Special assessment transactions will be accounted for in other funds and account groups, depending on whether (1) the assessment is a service-type or capital-type and

(2) the government is obligated in some manner to assume payments on the special assessment debt.

SGAS 6 also provides guidance on reporting capital improvement assessment projects for which (1) initial financing is provided by existing resources; (2) no debt is issued; (3) the assets constructed or acquired will benefit an enterprise fund; and (4) the government is not obligated in any manner for the related debt.

The provisions of SGAS 6 were effective for periods beginning after June 15, 1987, with earlier application encouraged. Accounting changes made to adopt this statement were to be applied retroactively, if practicable.

Proprietary Funds

The class of proprietary funds includes two fund types, enterprise funds and internal service funds.

Enterprise Funds. An enterprise fund is similar in purpose to a commercial entity, and it follows accrual accounting principles. An enterprise fund is used when the cost of particular services is to be paid through usage charges designed to recover such cost, including depreciation. Examples are water supply and sewage disposal systems.

When the governmental unit does not intend to recover its service costs through specific user charges, the activity is often accounted for in special revenue funds. The main distinction here lies in the accounting for fixed assets and long-term liabilities. Enterprise funds record fixed assets and related depreciation and all liabilities of the fund, while special revenue funds do not.

Even though a service is not funded primarily by user charges, an enterprise fund can be established whenever the governing body has decided that periodic determination of net income is appropriate for such reasons as capital maintenance, public policy, management control, and accountability.

Internal Service Funds. Internal service funds are used to account for goods or services provided on a cost reimbursement basis by one department or agency of a governmental unit to other departments, agencies, or governmental units. The cost of goods or services provided should include all costs, including depreciation.

Trust and Agency Funds

Trust and agency funds generally are used to account for those assets held in trust by a governmental unit for other governmental units or private individuals. Such funds can be classified as *expendable, nonexpendable, pension,* or *agency* funds. When monies held in trust are to be used for a particular purpose, they are classified as either expendable (if the principal can be spent) or nonexpendable (if only income earned on the principal can be spent).

In an agency fund, the governmental unit serves only as custodian, for example, one governmental unit acts as the tax collecting agent for another. Such monies are placed in the fund as collected and periodically are paid over to the other governmental unit.

Account Groups

General Fixed Asset Account Group. This group comprises the governmental unit's fixed assets, excluding those employed in enterprise or internal service funds. The inclusion of infrastructure fixed assets such as streets and bridges is optional. Fixed assets are recorded either at cost or, if actual cost is unknown, at estimated historical cost. Some governmental units compute and show an allowance for depreciation, but no depreciation expense is charged to any fund. The asset is balanced, for double-entry bookkeeping purposes, with a credit to "Investment in Fixed Assets" and may reflect the source of funding for the asset.

General Long-Term Debt Account Group. This group is comprised of the long-term debt not included as a liability in any other fund of the governmental entity. This debt is balanced, for double-entry bookkeeping purposes, by an "asset" reflecting the commitment of future taxing power to repay the debt. The general long-term debt of the government includes bonds, notes, capital leases, claims and judgments, unfunded pension obligations, and liability for compensated absences.

Discrete Presentation

When a component unit (such as a college or university) included in the reporting entity uses accounting principles not in conformity with governmental GAAP but that otherwise are generally accepted, a discrete presentation of the unit may be used if inclusion of the unit would distort a fund-type of the reporting entity. In such a case, the reporting entity's notes to the financial statements should clearly disclose the accounting principles used by the component unit.

In this case, the financial statements of the component unit should be shown in the general purpose financial statements of the government as a discrete presentation.

FINANCIAL REPORTING

Objectives

In its *Codification of Governmental Accounting and Financial Reporting Standards* (GASB Codification), GASB has incorporated objectives established in NCGA Statement No. 1 for general purpose external financial reporting by state and local governmental entities, applicable to both government-type and business-type activities. The financial reporting objectives set forth by GASB are

- Financial reporting should assist in fulfilling government's duty to be publicly accountable and should enable users to assess that accountability by
  - Providing informaton to determine whether current-year revenues were sufficient to pay for current-year services;
  - Demonstrating whether resources were obtained and used in accordance with the entity's legally adopted budget, and demonstrating compliance with other finance-related legal or contractual requirements; and

– Providing information to assist users in assessing the service efforts, costs, and accomplishments of the general entity.

• Financial reporting should assist users in evaluating the operating results of the governmental entity for the year by

– Providing information about sources and uses of financial resources;

– Providing information about how it financed its activities and met its cash requirements; and

– Providing information necessary to determine whether its financial position improved or deteriorated as a result of the year's operations.

• Financial reporting should assist users in assessing the level of services that can be provided by the governmental entity and its ability to meet its obligations as they become due by

– Providing information about its financial position and condition;

– Providing information about its physical and other nonfinancial resources having useful lives that extend beyond the current year, including information that can be used to assess the service potential of these resources; and

– Disclosing legal or contractual restrictions on resources and the risk of potential loss of resources.

General Purpose Financial Statements

Government financial reports consist of combined or general purpose financial statements, including notes to these financial statements, plus combining and individual fund financial statements as appropriate. This is graphically illustrated in Figure 31.2. A governmental unit's combined financial statements comprise a separate column for each of the seven fund types, two account groups, and discrete presentations (if appropriate). Under current practice, if there is a column showing a total of all the other columns, it is labeled "Memorandum Only," and there are no eliminations of interfund balances and transactions.

Financial statements necessary to fairly present financial position and operating results in conformity with GAAP are referred to as general purpose financial statements. These are generally the minimum used in official statements for securities offerings. The general purpose statements consist of: .

1. A combined balance sheet for all fund types and account groups (Figure 31.3).

2. A combined statement of revenues, expenditures, and changes in fund balances for all four types of governmental funds (Figure 31.4).

3. A combined statement of revenues, expenditures, and changes in fund balances, budget and actual, for all general and special revenue funds, and similar fund types for which annual budgets have been legally adopted (Figure 31.5).

4. A combined statement of revenues, expenses, and changes in retained earnings (or equity) for all proprietary funds.

5. A combined statement of changes in financial position for all proprietary funds.

6. Notes to the financial statements.

Figures 31.3, 31.4, and 31.5 have been extracted from GASB's Codification to illustrate the format of the basic financial statements; the complete examples, along

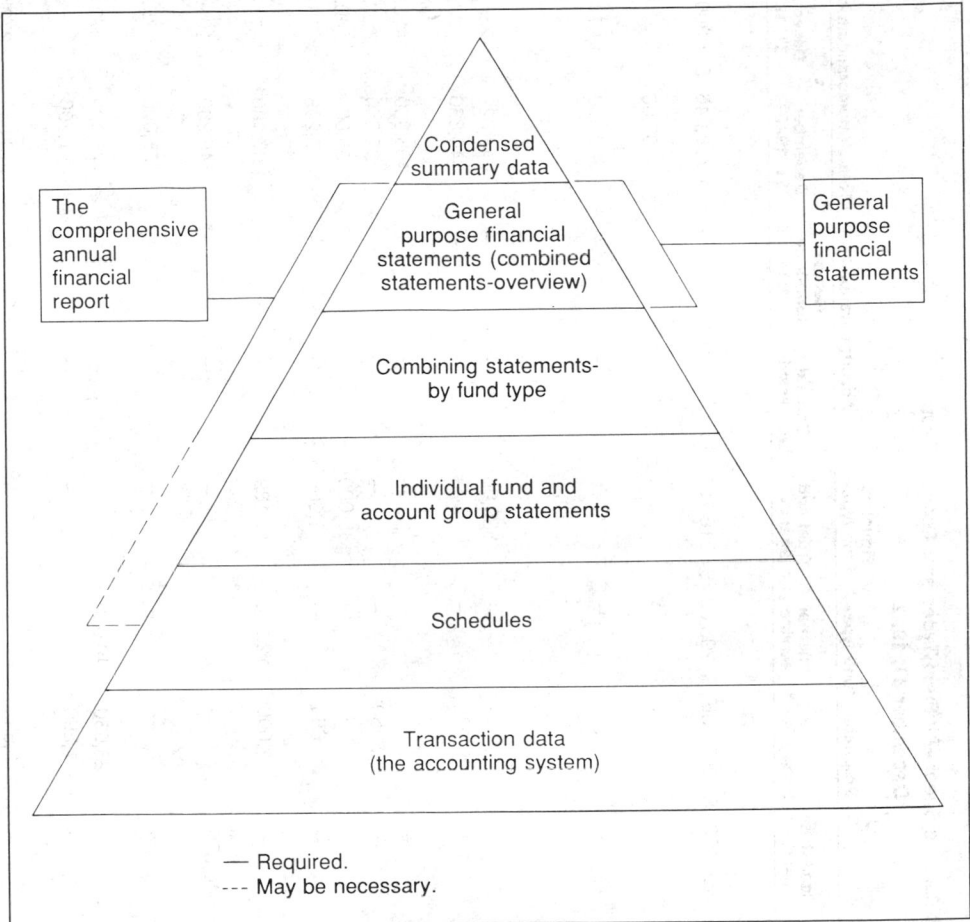

FIG. 31.2   The Financial Reporting Pyramid for a Governmental Unit

Source: Governmental Accounting Standards Board, 1987. Codification of Governmental Accounting and Financial Reporting Standards, *p. 97.*

with those applicable to proprietary funds, are found on pages 149 to 164 of the 1987 GASB Codification. When reviewing matters that follow in this chapter, it will be helpful to refer to Figures 31.3, 31.4, and 31.5 for the proper context.

Other Principles

Measurement Focus/Basis of Accounting. The GASB Codification (Section 1600) sets forth accounting and reporting standards relative to the basis of accounting used by state and local governmental entities. The GASB Codification provides that the modified accrual basis of accounting should be used in measuring financial position

(continued on page 31-25)

Combined Balance Sheet—All Fund Types and Account Groups
December 31, 19X2

	Governmental fund types				Proprietary fund types		Fiduciary fund types	Account groups		Totals (memorandum only)	
	General	Special revenue	Debt service	Capital Projects	Enterprise	Internal service	Trust and agency	General fixed assets	General long-term debt	December 31, 19X2	December 31, 19X1
Assets											
Cash	$258,500	$101,385	$235,624	$659,100	$257,036	$29,700	$216,701	—	$ —	$1,758,046	$1,300,944
Cash with fiscal agent	—	—	102,00	—	—	—	—	—	—	102,00	—
Investments, at cost or amortized cost	65,000	37,200	160,990	—	—	—	1,239,260	—	—	1,502,450	1,974,354
Receivables (net of allowances for uncollectibles):											
Taxes	58,300	2,500	3,829	—	—	—	580,00	—	—	644,629	255,400
Accounts	8,300	3,300	—	100	29,130	—	—	—	—	40,830	32,600
Special assessments	—	—	458,930	—	—	—	—	—	—	458,930	420,000
Notes	—	—	—	—	2,350	—	—	—	—	2,350	1,250
Loans	—	—	—	—	—	—	35,000	—	—	35,000	40,000
Accrued Interest	50	25	1,907	—	650	—	2,666	—	—	5,298	3,340
Due from other funds	2,000	—	—	—	2,000	12,000	11,189	—	—	27,189	17,499
Due from other governments	30,000	75,260	—	640,000	—	—	—	—	—	745,260	101,400
Advances to Internal service funds	65,000	—	—	—	—	—	—	—	—	65,000	75,000
Inventory of supplies, at cost	7,200	5,190	—	—	23,030	40,000	—	—	—	75,420	70,900
Prepaid expenses	—	—	—	—	1,200	—	—	—	—	1,200	900
Restricted assets:											
Cash	—	—	—	—	113,559	—	—	—	—	113,559	272,968

Investments, at cost or amortized cost	—	—	—	—	176,800	—	—	—	—	176,800	143,800
Land	—	—	—	—	211,100	20,000	—	1,259,500	—	1,490,600	1,456,100
Buildings	—	—	—	—	447,700	60,000	—	2,855,500	—	3,363,200	2,836,700
Accumulated depreciation	—	—	—	—	(90,718)	(4,500)	—	—	—	(95,218)	(83,500)
Improvements other than buildings	—	—	—	—	3,887,901	15,000	—	1,036,750	—	4,939,651	3,922,200
Accumulated depreciation	—	—	—	—	(348,944)	(3,000)	—	—	—	(351,944)	(283,750)
Machinery and equipment	—	—	—	—	1,841,145	25,000	—	452,500	—	2,318,645	1,924,100
Accumulated depreciation	—	—	—	—	(201,138)	(9,400)	—	—	—	(210,538)	(141,900)
Construction in progress	—	—	—	—	22,713	—	—	1,722,250	—	1,744,963	1,359,606
Amount available in debt service funds	—	—	—	—	—	—	—	—	306,280	306,280	284,813
Amount to be provided for retirement of general long-term debt	—	—	—	—	—	—	—	—	1,889,790	1,889,790	1,075,187
Amount to be provided from special assessments	—	—	—	—	—	—	—	—	458,930	458,930	420,000
Total Assets	$494,350	$224,860	$963,280	$1,299,200	$6,375,514	$184,800	$2,084,816	$7,326,500	$2,655,000	$21,608,320	$17,479,911

(continued)

FIG. 31.3 Example of a Governmental Unit Combined Balance Sheet for All Fund Types and Account Groups

Source: Governmental Accounting Standards Board, 1987. Codification of Governmental Accounting and Financial Reporting Standards, pp. 149–152.

Liabilities and Fund Equity

	Governmental fund types				Proprietary fund types		Fiduciary fund types	Account groups		Totals (memorandum only)	
	General	Special revenue	Debt service	Capital Projects	Enterprise	Internal service	Trust and agency	General fixed assets	General long-term debt	December 31, 19X2	December 31, 19X1
Liabilities:											
Vouchers payable	$118,261	$33,850	$ —	$ 49,600	$131,071	$15,000	$3,350	$ —	$ —	$ 351,132	$ 223,412
Contracts payable	57,600	18,300	—	119,000	8,347	—	—	—	—	203,247	1,326,511
Judgments payable	—	2,000	—	33,800	—	—	—	—	—	35,800	32,400
Accrued liabilities	—	—	—	10,700	16,870	—	4,700	—	—	32,270	27,417
Payable from restricted assets:											
Construction contracts	—	—	—	—	17,760	—	—	—	—	17,760	—
Fiscal agent	—	—	—	—	139	—	—	—	—	139	—
Accrued Interest	—	—	—	—	32,305	—	—	—	—	32,305	67,150
Revenue bonds	—	—	—	—	48,000	—	—	—	—	48,000	52,000
Deposits	—	—	—	—	63,000	—	—	—	—	63,000	55,000
Due to other taxing units	—	—	—	—	—	—	680,800	—	—	680,800	200,000
Due to other funds	24,189	2,000	—	1,000	—	—	—	—	—	27,189	17,499
Due to student groups	—	—	—	—	—	—	1,850	—	—	1,850	1,600
Deferred revenue	15,000	—	555,000	—	—	—	—	—	—	570,000	423,000
Advance from general fund	—	—	—	—	—	65,000	—	—	—	65,000	75,000
Matured bonds payable	—	—	100,000	—	—	—	—	—	—	100,000	—

Matured interest payable	—	—	2,000	—	—	—	—	—	—	2,000	—
General obligation bonds payable	—	—	—	—	700,000	—	—	—	2,100,000	2,800,000	2,110,000
Special assessment debt with governmental commitment	—	—	—	—	—	—	—	—	555,000	555,000	420,000
Revenue bonds payable	—	—	—	—	1,798,000	—	—	—	—	1,798,000	1,846,000
Total Liabilities	215,050	56,150	657,000	214,100	2,815,492	80,000	690,700	—	2,655,000	7,383,492	6,876,989
Fund Equity:											
Contributed capital	—	—	—	—	1,392,666	95,000	—	—	—	1,487,666	815,000
Investment in general fixed assets	—	—	—	—	—	—	—	7,326,500	—	7,326,500	5,299,600
Retained earnings:											
Reserved for revenue bond retirement	—	—	—	—	129,155	—	—	—	—	129,155	96,975
Unreserved	—	—	—	—	2,038,201	9,800	—	—	—	2,048,001	1,998,119
Fund Balances:											
Reserved for encumbrances	38,000	46,500	—	1,076,500	—	—	—	—	—	1,161,000	410,050
Reserved for inventory of supplies	7,200	5,190	—	—	—	—	—	—	—	12,390	10,890

(continued)

FIG. 31.3 *(continued)*

	Governmental fund types				Proprietary fund types		Fiduciary fund types	Account groups		Totals (memorandum only)	
	General	Special revenue	Debt service	Capital Projects	Enterprise	Internal service	Trust and agency	General fixed assets	General long-term debt	December 31, 19X2	December 31, 19X1
Reserved for advance to internal service funds	65,000	—	—	—	—	—	—	—	—	65,000	75,000
Reserved for loans	—	—	—	—	—	—	50,050	—	—	50,050	45,100
Reserved for endowments	—	—	—	—	—	—	134,000	—	—	134,000	94,000
Reserved for employees' retirement system	—	—	—	—	—	—	1,426,201	—	—	1,426,201	1,276,150
Unreserved:											
Designated for debt service	—	—	306,280	—	—	—	—	—	—	306,280	325,888
Designated for subsequent years' expenditures	50,000	—	—	—	—	—	—	—	—	50,000	50,000
Undesignated	119,100	117,020	—	8,600	—	—	(216,135)	—	—	28,585	106,150
Total Fund Equity	279,300	168,710	306,280	1,085,100	3,560,022	104,800	1,394,116	7,326,500	—	14,224,828	10,602,922
Total Liabilities and Fund Equity	$494,350	$224,860	$963,280	$1,299,200	$6,375,514	$184,800	$2,084,816	$7,326,500	$2,100,000	$21,608,320	$17,479,911

FIG. 31.3 (continued)

**Combined Statement of Revenues, Expenditures, and Changes in Fund Balances
All Governmental Fund Types and Expendable Trust Funds
For the Fiscal Year Ended December 31, 19X2**

	Governmental fund types				Fiduciary fund type	Totals (memorandum only) Year ended	
	General	Special revenue	Debt service	Capital projects	Expendable trust	December 31, 19X2	December 31, 19X1
Revenues:							
Taxes	$ 881,300	$ 189,300	$ 79,177	$ —	$ —	$1,149,777	$1,137,900
Special assessments	—	—	55,500	—	—	55,500	250,400
Licenses and permits	103,000	—	—	—	—	103,000	96,500
Intergovernmental revenues	186,500	831,100	41,500	1,250,000	—	2,309,100	1,258,800
Charges for services	91,000	79,100	—	—	—	170,100	160,400
Fines and forfeits	33,200	—	—	—	—	33,200	26,300
Miscellaneous revenues	19,500	71,625	36,235	3,750	200	131,310	111,500
Total Revenues	1,314,500	1,171,125	212,412	1,253,750	200	3,951,987	3,041,800
Expenditures:							
Current:							
General government	121,805	—	—	—	—	121,805	134,200
Public safety	258,395	480,000	—	—	—	738,395	671,300
Highways and streets	85,400	417,000	—	—	—	502,400	408,700
Sanitation	56,250	—	—	—	—	56,250	44,100
Health	44,500	—	—	—	—	44,500	36,600
Welfare	46,800	—	—	—	—	46,800	41,400
Culture and recreation	40,900	256,450	—	—	—	297,350	286,400
Education	509,150	—	—	—	2,420	511,570	512,000
Capital outlay	—	—	—	1,939,100	—	1,939,100	803,000

(continued)

FIG. 31.4 Example of a Governmental Unit Combined Statement of Revenues, Expenditures, and Changes in Fund Balances—All Governmental Fund Types and Expendable Trust Funds

Source: Governmental Accounting Standards Board, 1987. Codification of Governmental Accounting and Financial Reporting Standards, pp. 154–155.

	Governmental fund types				Fiduciary fund type	Totals (memorandum only) Year ended	
	General	Special revenue	Debt service	Capital projects	Expendable trust	December 31, 19X2	December 31, 19X1
Debt service:							
Principal retirement	–	–	115,500	–	–	115,500	52,100
Interest and fiscal charges	–	–	68,420	–	–	68,420	50,000
Total Expenditures	1,163,200	1,153,450	183,920	1,939,100	2,420	4,442,090	3,039,800
Excess of revenues over (under) expenditures	151,300	17,675	28,492	(685,350)	(2,220)	(490,103)	2,000
Other financing sources (Uses):							
Proceeds of general obligation bonds	–	–	–	900,000	–	900,000	–
Proceeds of special assessment debt	–	–	–	190,500	–	190,500	–
Operating transfers in	–	–	–	74,500	2,530	77,030	89,120
Operating transfers out	(74,500)	–	–	–	–	(74,500)	(87,000)
Total Other financing sources (uses)	(74,500)	–	–	1,165,000	2,530	1,093,030	2,120
Excess of revenues and other sources over (under) expenditures and other uses	76,800	17,675	28,492	479,650	310	602,927	4,120
Fund Balances—January 1	202,500	151,035	227,788	605,450	26,555	1,213,328	1,209,208
Fund Balances—December 31	$ 279,300	$ 168,710	$256,280	$1,085,100	$26,865	$1,816,255	$1,213,328

FIG. 31.4 (continued)

Combined Statement of Revenues, Expenditures, and Changes in Fund Balances
Budget and Actual—General and Special Revenue Fund Types
For the Fiscal Year Ended December 31, 19X2

	General fund			Special revenue funds			Totals (memorandum only)		
	Budget	Actual	Variance—favorable (unfavorable)	Budget	Actual	Variance—favorable (unfavorable)	Budget	Actual	Variance—favorable (unfavorable)
Revenues:									
Taxes	$ 882,500	$ 881,300	$(1,200)	$ 189,500	$ 189,300	$ (200)	$1,072,000	$1,070,600	$ (1,400)
Licenses and permits	125,500	103,000	(22,500)	–	–	–	125,500	103,000	(22,500)
Intergovernmental revenues	200,000	186,500	(13,500)	837,600	831,100	(6,500)	1,037,600	10,017,600	(20,000)
Charges for services	90,000	91,000	1,000	78,000	79,100	1,100	168,000	170,100	2,100
Fines and forfeits	32,500	33,200	700	–	–	–	32,500	33,200	700
Miscellaneous revenues	19,500	19,500	–	81,475	71,625	(9,850)	100,975	91,125	(9,850)
Total Revenues	1,350,000	1,314,500	(35,500)	1,186,575	1,171,125	(15,450)	2,536,575	2,485,625	(50,950)
Expenditures									
Current:									
General government	129,000	121,805	7,195	–	–	–	129,000	121,805	7,195
Public safety	277,300	258,395	18,905	494,500	480,000	14,500	771,800	738,395	33,405
Highways and streets	84,500	85,400	(900)	436,000	417,000	19,000	520,500	502,400	18,100
Sanitation	50,000	56,250	(6,250)	–	–	–	50,000	56,250	(6,250)
Health	47,750	44,500	3,250	–	–	–	47,750	44,500	3,250
Welfare	51,000	46,800	4,200	–	–	–	51,000	46,800	4,200

(continued)

FIG. 31.5 Example of a Governmental Unit Combined Statement of Revenues, Expenditures, and Changes in Fund Balances—Budget and Actual for All General and Special Revenue Fund Types

Source: Governmental Accounting Standards Board, 1987. Codification of Governmental Accounting and Financial Reporting Standards, pp. 157–158.

	General fund			Special revenue funds			Totals (memorandum only)		
	Budget	Actual	Variance—favorable (unfavorable)	Budget	Actual	Variance—favorable (unfavorable)	Budget	Actual	Variance—favorable (unfavorable)
Culture and recreation	44,500	40,900	3,600	272,000	256,450	15,550	316,500	297,350	19,150
Education	541,450	509,150	32,300	—	—	—	541,450	509,150	32,300
Total Expenditures	1,225,500	1,163,200	62,300	1,202,500	1,153,450	49,050	2,428,000	2,316,650	111,350
Excess of revenues over (under) expenditures	124,500	151,300	26,800	(15,925)	17,675	33,600	108,575	168,975	60,400
Other Financing Sources (Uses): Operating transfers out	(74,500)	(74,500)	—	—	—	—	(74,500)	(74,500)	—
Excess of revenues over (under) expenditures and other uses	50,000	76,800	26,800	(15,925)	17,675	33,600	34,075	94,475	60,400
Fund Balances—January 1	202,500	202,500	—	151,035	151,035	—	353,535	353,535	—
Fund Balances—December 31	$ 252,500	$ 279,300	$26,800	$ 135,110	$ 168,710	$33,600	$ 387,610	$ 448,010	$ 60,400

FIG. 31.5 (continued)

and results of operations of governmental and similar funds and that the full accrual basis should be used by proprietary and similar funds to recognize revenues and expenses.

The modified accrual basis of accounting reflects the concept that a governmental fund is a means of providing accountability and is not concerned with the determination of net income, but only with the measurement of increases and decreases in available, spendable financial resources. In addition, most budgetary practices in government are also primarily concerned with spendable resources.

Revenue Recognition. The GASB Codification provides that revenues and other governmental fund financial resources are recognized in the accounting period when they become both measurable and available to finance expenditures of the fiscal period. "Available" is defined as being collectible within the current period or soon enough thereafter to be used to pay liabilities of the current period. Treatment of some specific revenue sources is summarized in the following subsections.

Property taxes. GASB Codification § P70 provides that property taxes should be recognized in the fiscal year for which the taxes have been levied provided that they are expected to be collected within 60 days of year end (apart from unusual circumstances). Property taxes collected in advance of the year for which they are levied should be recorded as deferred revenue and should be recognized as revenue in the year for which they are levied.

Sales taxes. GASB Codification § S10 provides that sales taxes collected by merchants but not required to be remitted to the taxing authority at the end of the fiscal year should not be accrued. However, taxes collected and held by one government agency for another at year end should be accrued if they are to be remitted in time to be used to liquidate obligations of the fiscal year.

Taxpayer-assessed revenues. GASB Codification § 1600 states that it is not practical to attempt to accrue taxpayer-assessed income and gross receipts taxes; therefore, such items are best recognized when cash is received. The Codification also provides that refunds should be recorded as a liability and a reduction of revenues when the claims are filed.

Grants. GASB Codification § G60 requires that grant revenues should be recognized in accordance with the measureable-and-available criteria applicable to governmental funds. The GASB Codification also notes that some resources such as entitlements or shared revenues are more restricted in form than in substance. These should be recorded at the time of receipt, but may be recorded earlier if they are to be received soon enough after year end to liquidate year-end obligations. The GASB Codification provides that the revenues from expenditure-driven grants should be recognized at the time the expenditure is incurred.

Other revenues. GASB Codification § 1600 provides that fines and forfeits, golf and swimming fees, inspection charges, parking fees and meter receipts, and various other miscellaneous revenues should be recognized when cash is received.

Expenditure Recognition. The GASB Codification (§ 1600) states that the focus of governmental fund accounting is on decreases in net financial resources (expenditures) rather than on expenses. Most expenditures and transfers out are measurable and should be recorded when the related liability is incurred. However, the GASB Codification allows for modifications to accrual accounting as follows:

• The treatment of unmatured principal and interest on general long-term debt are recognized in the period of payment unless resources to meet future payment have been provided in the Debt Service Fund during the current year, in which case the expenditures *may* be recognized in the current year.

• Inventory items may be considered expenditures either when purchased or when used.

• Expenditures for insurance and similar services extending over more than one accounting period either may be allocated among periods or may be accounted for as expenditures in the year of acquisition.

Other exceptions to recording expenditures when the liability is incurred, such as compensated absences and claims and judgments, are discussed in this chapter.

In 1987, GASB issued an Exposure Draft, *Measurement Focus and Basis of Accounting-Governmental Funds* (1987c), which if adopted would significantly modify the manner in which revenues and expenditures are recognized by moving closer to a full accrual basis of accounting.

Budgetary Accounting

Most governmental units adopt an annual budget for general fund expenditures, and some also have budgets for special revenue funds, debt service funds, and other funds. Some governments also adopt long-term (e.g., three-year) capital budgets. Budgeting is the method used by legislative bodies to control the expenditures of a governmental unit. Budgets normally cover revenues as well as expenditures, but the revenue is only an estimate used to determine the amount that will be available for spending.

For financial reporting purposes, GAAP requires presenting a comparison between amounts budgeted and actual amounts received and spent for the General Fund, Special Revenue Fund, and Other Governmental Funds for which annual budgets are legally enacted. This comparison gives the user of the financial statements information about how successfully the administration of the governmental unit has adhered to budget limitations and how closely actual spending has approximated the original plan. To use budget information as an evaluative tool, however, it is necessary to understand the level at which budget control operates. In the budget preparation process, a great amount of detail is usually developed, but the official budget document will contain only a portion, the remainder being relegated to background data. The level of detail remaining in the official budget largely determines the extent of authority the administration has in deviating from the projections. Amounts considered part of the official budget can be changed only by the legislative body, whereas the administration normally has authority to change the amounts presented as background data.

It is also necessary to understand the basis for budget preparation. Some governmental units prepare cash basis budgets, which of course are not comparable to accrual basis financial statements. A cash basis budget can meaningfully be compared only with a statement of cash receipts and disbursements. Thus the general purpose financial statements compare actual to budget using the basis of accounting on which the budget was prepared, even if that basis is not GAAP.

Reporting Entity

GASB Codification § 2100 establishes the criteria for determining what organizations, activities, and functions should be included in the financial statements of a specific governmental unit with a separately elected legislative body. This is referred to as the *reporting entity*.

The criteria assume that all functions of government are considered to be the responsibility of elected officials and should be reported at the lowest level of legislative authority. However, because there are certain exceptions to the assumption that all governmental functions are responsible to an elected official, § 2100 (¶ 113) of the GASB Codification indicates that certain potential component units may be excluded from the reporting entity even though a degree of oversight may be exercised or financial interdependency may exist. The decision to include or exclude a unit is often highly judgmental and there is diversity in practice.

The GASB Codification provides that *oversight responsibility* is the threshold criterion for determining what constitutes the reporting entity, with the most significant manifestation of oversight being financial interdependency. *Financial interdependency* is described as a relationship that either produces a financial benefit for or imposes a financial burden on a unit of government, such as entitlements to surplus, responsibility for deficits, or guarantees of or moral responsibility for debt.

Other manifestations of oversight that normally accompany financial interdependency include selection of governing authority, designation of management, ability to significantly influence operations, and accountability for fiscal matters.

If any of the manifestations of oversight criteria exist, the GASB Codification indicates that the unit should be included in the reporting entity. However, professional judgment should be applied to the individual facts to determine if a particular organization should be included in the reporting entity, as rigid application of the criteria could lead to inappropriate reporting practices.

Where oversight exists at several levels of government, the official with authority over the various levels of government should resolve the issue. The GASB Codification provides that a possible solution might be to include the component in one reporting entity's financial statements and provide for disclosure in the other's financial statements.

The standards require that the criteria used in determining the reporting entity should be disclosed in the notes to the financial statements, including instances where the criteria are met but the component is excluded.

During 1988, the GASB was in the process of reexamining the definition of the reporting entity that may result in clarification of the criteria for including or excluding a component unit from the general purpose financial statements. In this regard, a Discussion Memorandum, *An Analysis of Issues Relating to the Financial Reporting Entity* (GASB, 1988), was issued in June 1988.

Deferred Compensation Plans

Deferred compensation programs have become common in state and local governments. GAAP requires that, for employers using governmental fund accounting, Internal Revenue Code (IRC) § 457 deferred compensation plan balances should be displayed in an agency fund of the governmental employer that has legal access to the resources. Also to be disclosed is whether the assets are held by the employer, a public employee retirement system (PERS), a nongovernmental third party, or another governmental entity under a multijurisdiction plan. Governmental public utilities and public authorities should report both the liability and the corresponding designated asset in the balance sheet.

Note disclosure must be made of (1) the requirement of IRC § 457 that the assets in the plan remain the property of the employer until paid or made available to participants, subject only to the claims of the government's general creditors, and (2) the government's fiduciary responsibilities under the plan.

Deposits, Investments, and Reverse Repos

SGAS 3, *Deposits With Financial Institutions, Investments (Including Repurchase Agreements), and Reverse Repurchase Agreements*, requires certain note disclosures regarding those items. The required disclosures should generally be made for the entity as a whole, but additional or separate disclosures for component units, pension trust funds, or other funds or fund types should be made in certain circumstances.

Disclosure is required of the types of investments authorized by legal or contractual provisions, as well as disclosure for the financial reporting period, of significant violations, if any, of legal or contractual provisions related to deposits and investments.

Required disclosures related to the deposit and investment portfolio as of the balance sheet date will provide users with information about credit and market risks. These disclosures include the carrying amounts and market values of investments by investment type and in total, as well as information about the level of credit risk associated with deposits and investments. Credit risk is affected by insurance coverage and registration of securities in the name of the governmental entity and, in the absence of insurance coverage or registration, by the custodial arrangements for investments, securities underlying repurchase agreements, and collateral on deposits. Entities are also required to disclose situations that resulted in significantly greater credit risk during the period even though such risk no longer exists as of the balance sheet date.

For reverse repurchase agreements, SGAS 3 requires disclosure of the authorization source permitting their use, significant violations, if any, of legal or contractual provisions of the agreements during the period, and summary information about the credit risk associated with the agreements as of the balance sheet date.

Liabilities resulting from reverse repurchase and fixed-coupon reverse repurchase agreements are required to be shown as "obligations under reverse repurchase agreements" and should not be netted against the related assets on the balance sheet. Interest costs associated with these agreements are required to be shown as interest expenditures or expense and should not be netted against the interest income from the related investments, shown separately. Yield maintenance repurchase and reverse repurchase agreements are required to be accounted for as purchases and sales of investments, with gains or losses on those investments recognized at the time of the purchase or sale.

Repurchase agreements are further discussed in Chapter 21.

Demand Bonds

Demand bonds are long-term debt issuances with demand (put) provisions that require the issuer to repurchase the bonds, upon notice from the bondholder, at a price equal to the principal plus accrued interest. To assure its ability to redeem the bonds, issuers of demand bonds frequently enter into short-term stand-by liquidity agreements and long-term takeout agreements. Interpretation No. 1, *Demand Bonds Issued by State and Local Governmental Entities,* which interprets NCGA Statement 1 and NCGA Interpretation 9, states that demand bonds should be reported by state and local governmental entities as general long-term debt, or excluded from current liabilities of proprietary funds, provided that the issuer has entered into a valid financing agreement to convert bonds that have been put but cannot be resold into some other form of long-term obligation. In the absence of such an agreement, demand bonds should be classified as governmental fund liabilities, or as current liabilities of proprietary funds. Note disclsoure of the details of demand bond agreements is also required.

Claims, Judgments, and Compensated Absences

When determining the accounting and financial reporting treatment of claims, judgments, and compensated absences, consideration must be given to the accounting distinctions between proprietary fund types and governmental fund types.

For proprietary fund types the expense and related liabilities are recorded in the fund. Changes in these liabilities are charges or credits to operations in the current period.

General government liabilities are recorded in either the General Long-Term Debt Account Group or in a governmental fund. The liability should be reported in a governmental fund if it is to be liquidated with expendable, available financial resources. Those liabilities that will not consume such resources should be recorded in the account group. Changes in these liabilities are charges to operations of the current period only if funded by available resources.

Pension Disclosures

SGAS 5, *Disclosure of Pension Information by Public Employee Retirement Systems and State and Local Governmental Employers,* establishes standards for disclosure, in notes to financial statements and as required supplementary information, by a PERS and state and local governmental employers. Disclosures are required both in financial reports issued by the PERS and in financial reports issued by employers, including those that do not fund their pension obligations. This statement describes the computation of the pension benefit obligation and requires disclosure of the computation method, plan provisions, actuarially determined contribution requirements, contributions actually made, and significant actuarial assumptions. An actuarial valuation to recalculate this information should be made at least biannually, with an update in the intervening year.

Supplementary 10-year trend information is also required, including comparisons of:

• Net assets available for benefits to the pension benefit obligation.

• Unfunded pension benefit obligation to annual covered payroll.

• Revenues by source to expenses by type.

Employers may make reference to the availability, in publicly available PERS reports or in their own comprehensive annual financial reports, of 10-year trend information, rather than include it in their general purpose financial statements.

Advance Refunding

SGAS 7, *Advance Refundings Resulting in Defeasance of Debt*, provides guidance on accounting for advance refundings accomplished through issuance of new debt that results in defeasance of debt carried in the general long-term debt account group. The proceeds of the new debt should be reported as an "other financing source— proceeds of refunding bonds" in the fund receiving the proceeds. Payments to the escrow agent from resources provided by the new debt should be reported as an "other financing uses—payment to refunded-bond escrow agent." Payments to the escrow agent made by using other resources of the entity should be reported as debt-service expenditures.

SGAS 7 also provides guidance on disclosures about advance refundings for all governmental entities regardless of where the debt is reported. Among the required disclosures is the economic gain or loss on the refunding—the difference between the present value of the old debt-service requirements and the present value of the new debt-service requirements, discounted at the effective interest rate (as defined by this statement) of the new debt and adjusted for additonal cash paid.

AUDITING STANDARDS

Single Audit Act

The Single Audit Act of 1984 substantially expanded the need for audit services by governments. More than 17,000 governments filed single-audit reports in the first year of the Act. This compares to fewer than 14,000 corporate entities that must file annual reports with the SEC. The Act requires an annual audit "by independent auditors in accordance with generally accepted government auditing standards" for each state and local government that receives federal financial assistance of $100,000 or more. These audits "shall cover the entire state or local government operations" but "may exclude public hospitals and public colleges and universities."

The OMB, responsible for regulating the implementation of the Act, issued Circular A-128 to provide specific guidance for single audits. OMB designated a Federal

Inspector General as a "cognizant agent" for each audited government unit. *Cognizant agents* ensure that audits are timely and that both the reports and corrective action plans are properly transmitted to appropriate government authorities.

The Act and OMB Circular A-128 require the auditor to issue for the entity:

* A report on an examination of the general purpose or basic financial statements of the entity as a whole, or the department, agency, or establishment covered by the audit.
* A report on internal accounting control based solely on a study and evaluation made as a part of the audit of the general purpose or basic financial statements.
* A report on compliance with laws and regulations that may have a material effect on the financial statements.

For federal financial assistance programs:

* A report (on a supplementary schedule) of the entity's federal financial assistance programs, showing total expenditures for each program.
* A report on compliance with laws and regulations, identifying all findings of noncompliance and questioned costs.
* A report on internal controls used in administering federal financial assistance programs.
* A report on fraud, abuse, or an illegal act, or indications of such acts, when discovered (a written report is required).

The requirements of the Act will, in practice, also affect nongovernmental entities. *Subrecipients* are defined as any organizations that receive federal financial assistance through a state or local government. It includes many not-for-profit entities. State and local governments are required to include subrecipients within their efforts to comply with the Act.

AICPA Industry Audit Guide

The AICPA Audit and Accounting Guide, *Audits of State and Local Governmental Units* (1986g), provides assistance to auditors of nonfederal government units. It revises an earlier 1974 edition and reflects changes in accounting and auditing since that time. Existing guidance is codified and significant new requirements are dealt with, such as:

* Requirements for serving as the principal auditor. The auditor must (1) be engaged by the oversight entity as principal auditor for the reporting entity and (2) be responsible for examining at least the general fund or principal operating fund of the oversight entity.
* The auditor's opinion on the general purpose financial statements. This deals with a number of problem areas. For example, the materiality level must be established at the level of fund types and account groups, rather than for the reporting entity in total.
* The auditor's report when a budget has not been legally adopted.
* Joint audit reports.
* Consideration of compliance with laws, regulations, and budgets.

The audit guide also contains several chapters and a sample Single Audit auditor's report.

GAO Yellow Book

The GAO released a revision of the 1981 edition of the *Yellow Book* in July 1988. This document establishes generally accepted government auditing standards for all audits of all governmental organizations and federal financial assistance including single audits. All AICPA auditing standards are incorporated in the *Yellow Book*, and additional guidance is given on and requirements established for financial and compliance audits of federal assistance programs, economy and efficiency audits, and program audits. In addition to the coverage of the AICPA audit guide standards, the 1988 version of the *Yellow Book* states:

• Audit planning should include consideration of the requirements of all levels of government.
• A test should be made of compliance with applicable laws and regulations.
• Auditors should design audit steps and procedures to provide reasonable assurance of detecting errors, irregularities, and illegal acts.
• Auditors should be alert to situations or transactions that may indicate fraud, abuse or illegal acts.
• Written reports should be submitted to appropriate officials of the audited organizations as well as to those officials arranging for the audit.
• The audit report should state that the examination was made in accordance with generally accepted government auditing standards.
• A report should be prepared on tests of compliance with applicable laws and regulations, including a statement providing positive assurance for those items tested and negative assurance on those items not tested.
• A report should be prepared on the auditor's understanding of the entity's internal control structure and his assessment of the control risk.

The 1988 revisions include expanded requirements for continuing professional education, the necessity of an internal quality control system, and participation in an external quality control review program. The *Yellow Book* revisions also incorporate references to the Single Audit Act, expand the discussion of audit risk and materiality in governmental auditing, and clarify the auditor's responsibility for follow-up on findings and recommendations.

The 1988 version is applicable to audits of periods beginning January 1, 1989.

Other Relevant Documents

Other standards documents that may be relevant to auditors of governmental (and not-for-profit entities) subject to Single Audit requirements include:

• *Compliance Supplement for Single Audits of State and Local Governments.* This document identifies the compliance requirements of 62 programs representing more than 90% of federal aid to state and local governments. It provides a safe harbor for compliance audit work.

- *OMB Circular A-102.* This document establishes uniform financial and administrative requirements for state and local governments receiving federal assistance and covers topics such as cash depositories, records retention, program income, and grantee financial systems standards.
- *OMB Circular A-87.* This document provides uniform rules for determining costs applicable to grants and contracts with state and local governments, and defines allowable costs.

CURRENT DEVELOPMENTS

Accounting Issues

Soon after its creation, GASB held a series of public hearings with various constituent groups representing a broad spectrum of users, preparers, and attestors of financial statements of state and local governments to determine what projects needed to be addressed. Subsequently, GASB established its agenda comprising eight projects: financial reporting, measurement focus/basis of accounting, pension accounting, deferred compensation, special assessment accounting, fixed assets, codification of governmental GAAP, and public authority financing reporting. It is the policy of the GASB to hold annual public hearings addressing its agenda. These hearings and other concerns within the industry have resulted in additional projects, including risk management activities and recognition of depreciation.

Certain topics currently under consideration by the GASB are discussed in the following subsections.

Measurement Focus/Basis of Accounting. The purpose of this project is to reexamine the revenue and expenditure recognition criteria of governmental fund types. The project is designed to examine the appropriateness of the concepts of "measureable" and "available" and to review the lack of consistency in the revenue recognition criteria in existing standards. Also, the project is examining the expenditure recognition criteria for such items as compensated absences, claims and judgments, inventories, debt service, prepaid expenses, and transfers.

In February 1985, the GASB issued a Discussion Memorandum, *Measurement Focus and Basis of Accounting—Governmental Funds* (GASB, 1985) addressing three possible measurement focuses: flow of economic resources, flow of total financial resources, and flow of current financial resources. The discussion memorandum also provided an analysis and discussion of the advantages and disadvantags of each.

The flow-of-economic-resources approach would require governmental funds to measure the sources, uses, and balances of economic resources regardless of when cash is received or disbursed and would require the amortization (depreciation) of the costs of fixed assets within the fund. The flow of economic resources is essentially the same as the accrual accounting model used in business enterprises.

The flow-of-total-financial-resources approach would require governmental funds to measure sources, uses, and balances of resources regardless of when cash is received or disbursed; but amortization of the costs of fixed assets in the fund would not be required.

The flow-of-current-financial-resources approach would require governmental funds to measure sources that are cash or will be converted to cash within a specified period of time after the end of the fiscal year. This flow is similar to the existing modified accrual basis of accounting currently used for governmental funds.

The responses to the discussion memorandum were almost equally divided in their preference: 29% favored the flow of economic resources, 30% favored the flow of total financial resources, 36% favored the flow of current financial resources, and 5% expressed preference for some other basis. However, a clear majority favored a change from modified accrual to some method closer to a full accrual method that is consistent with either the flow of total financial resources or with the flow of economic resources.

After completing the analysis of the responses to the Discussion Memorandum, the GASB field-tested criteria based on the flow of total financial resources to determine its impact on governmental entities: the field test included thirty-six entities. This test ascertained that the accrual of compensated absences had the most significant impact on the fund balance of the entities, with tax refunds (state governments only), claims and judgments, other miscellaneous adjustments, workers' compensation claims, and underfunded pension liability also having a major impact.

In 1987, GASB issued an Exposure Draft, titled *Measurement Focus and Basis of Accounting—Governmental Funds* (GASB, 1987c) based on the flow-of-total-financial-resources measurement focus. This proposal essentially would require the use of an accrual basis of accounting. Recognition of revenues would take place as follows: real estate taxes in the year *for* which it was levied; sales tax in the period the taxable event occurs; and income taxes over the period the taxable income is earned. Prepayments would be expensed when consumed.

One of the most significant changes would be the movement of all noncapital debt from the general long-term debt account group to the governmental funds. Compensated absences, for example, would become a governmental fund liability and increases in its amount from year to year would become fund operating charges. Judgments and claims liabilities are not specifically addressed in this exposure draft but are dealt with in the "Insurance" section later in this chapter. It is expected that the final pronouncement on insurance will follow a financial-resources-measurement focus (on the accrual basis of accounting) and require that judgments and claims liabilities be recorded in the governmental funds. Governmental fund balances for many governments will reflect cumulative deficits as a result of these changes.

The governmental fund balance would also be subclassified to include three components: GAAP fund balance, budgetary fund balance, and unbudgeted funds.

Fixed Assets. The current accounting and financial reporting standards for the governmental-fund types requires that fixed assets such as land, buildings, and equipment be reported in the General Fixed Asset Account Group. Existing literature permits, but does not require, reporting of infrastructure fixed assets, such as roads and bridges, in that account group. Because in many circumstances these assets represent a significant investment, many have advocated that infrastructure assets be reported. Others have argued that since infrastructure fixed assets do not generally represent financial resources to a government, they should not be reported. In addition, many believe that the requirement for reporting fixed assets at historical cost is misleading and that some other basis such as replacement cost would be more meaningful.

In August 1987, in response to these questions and various other concerns, GASB issued a discussion memorandum addressing these and other issues. The Discussion Memorandum, *Accounting and Financial Reporting for Capital Assets of Governmental Entities* (GASB, 1987a), covers the reporting of

* Infrastructure and general capital assets
* Valuation basis for capital assets
* Using-up of general capital assets
* Accumulated depreciation for general capital assets
* Costs of deferred maintenance for capital assets
* Budgeted versus actual data for capital projects
* Capital projects plans for capital assets
* Age, condition, and capacity of capital assets

Pension Accounting and Reporting. This project addresses the alternative pension reporting methods permitted by existing standards, under which governmental entities are permitted to follow alternative methods of reporting as established by NCGA Statement 1, NCGA Statement 6, and SFAS 35.

This project was divided into two subprojects: (1) pension disclosures and (2) pension accounting and reporting. The subproject dealing with disclosures, aimed at providing interim guidance pending an analysis of the accounting and financial reporting issues, has been completed; the result is SGAS 5, *Disclosure of Pension Information by Public Employee Retirement Systems and State and Local Governmental Employers.*

The accounting and reporting subproject encompasses the accounting and reporting issues for pension plans and state and local governmental entities from both the plan and employer perspectives. Differences among the alternative accounting treatments currently permitted and the display of the pension benefit obligation on the employer's balance sheet will be addressed.

Insurance. As a result of the insurability crisis facing many state and local governmental entities and the various insuring mechanisms developed (e.g., insurance funds and public entity risk pools, and the various accounting treatments being used to report them), the GASB established a project on "Accounting and Financial Reporting for Risk Management Activities."

In September 1987, the GASB issued a Discussion Memorandum, *Accounting and Financial Reporting for Risk Management Activities*, (GASB, 1987b). The discussion memorandum provides an analysis of risk retention and risk transfer activities of governmental entities to elict responses concerning the appropriate recognition and measurement criteria for related assets, liabilities, revenues, and expenditues/ expenses. The discussion memorandum considers the various accounting treatments permitted by both the FASB and governmental accounting literature, the fund type for reporting these activities, and disclosures.

Auditing Issues

Recently the auditing profession has come under significant criticism concerning the quality of audits of governmental entities, particularly in relation to the audits of federal financial assistance programs. These criticisms, and the actions being taken, are described in the following subsection.

Quality Concerns. In 1985, at the request of the chairman of the Legislation and National Security Committee of the U.S. House of Representatives Committee on Government Operations, the GAO undertook a study of the quality of audits of federal financial assistance programs performed by nonfederal auditors. The GAO reported that 25% of audit reports that were desk-reviewed by federal Inspectors General required correction. The GAO also reported that 45% of audits that had working paper reviews were deficient. Deficiencies noted related to an absence of adequate planning and supervision, little or no testing of compliance with laws and regulations, inadequate or nonexistent evidence of a study and evaluation of internal controls, and insufficient documentation of work performed or conclusions reached. In a subsequent review, the GAO's previous findings were sustained. Based on the review of a sample of 120 audits, the GAO found that 34% did not adequately comply with GAAS or with the *Yellow Book*.

In response, the AICPA appointed a task force to develop an action plan for improving the quality of audits of governmental units. The task force issued its recommendations in the *Report of the Task Force on the Quality of Audits of Governmental Units* (AICPA, 1987m).

The report contains 25 recommendations divided into five subject areas: education, engagement, evaluation, enforcement and exchange. The recommendations include the following:

* Auditors should complete relevant continuing professional education programs.
* A mechanism should be created to monitor and evaluate the quality of training programs and instructors.
* Auditing and reporting on compliance with applicable laws and regulations should be covered by an SAS.
* AICPA and government staffs should improve their capabilities to provide timely technical advice.
* OMB's *Compliance Supplement of Single Audits of State and Local Governments* and the question and answer booklet should be updated annually.
* A study of the audit services procurement process should be undertaken with creation and dissemination of a model request for proposal.
* Agency implementation regulations for the single audit should be standardized.
* All audit quality activities should come under the responsibility of knowledgeable officials, such as the Inspector General, state auditor's office, or independent local auditor's office.
* The agency that oversees the audit process should have an improved system for referring substandard audits to licensing authorities and professional organizations.

The AICPA organized an Implementation Task Force to follow up and report on the status of implementation of these recommendations. By mid-1988, significant progress had been made with most of the recommendations fully or nearly implemented.

32

Not-For-Profit Organizations

OVERVIEW

Not-for-profit organizations constitute a unique grouping of a broad variety of entities. They are unique in their purpose, terminology, financial statement presentation, and accounting policies.

Not-for-profit enterprises are sometimes called nonprofit or nonbusiness organizations. Their one common characteristic is that they are not organized to realize a profit on the goods or services they provide as their basic activity. Some believe that using the term *nonprofit* for those not having a profit motive is inappropriate. The FASB in its earlier statements had been using the term *nonbusiness.* However, a nonprofit hospital, for example *is* a business. Although unwieldy, perhaps the correct terminology should be *businesses not organized for a profit.* The FASB subsequently selected the term *not-for-profit* to describe those organizations not organized to generate a profit, and this term is used throughout the rest of this chapter.

Not-for-profit organizations are also referred to as tax-exempt organizations. In fact, it is common for such organizations to refer to themselves according to the Internal Revenue Code section under which they receive exempt status, for example, a "501(c)(3) organization." However, despite the common misconception that these organizations are completely tax-exempt, they do pay taxes on income (less expenses) from any activity unrelated to their basic purpose; and exemption from federal income taxes does not automatically exempt an organization from state income taxes. Additionally, although an entity may be organized as a not-for-profit entity, it may not meet the requirements necessary to qualify as a tax-exempt organization.

In response to charges of unfair competition, the House Ways and Means Committee has formed an Oversight Subcommittee to conduct hearings on the income-producing activities of not-for-profit organizations. The hearings specifically address charges that not-for-profit organizations have an unfair advantage because of their preferred tax status and thus compete unfairly with taxable businesses.

In addition, the IRS is currently conducting studies of the income of not-for-profit entities. While the results will not be available until 1990, the study will be relevant in deciding whether to tax these entities, and how any tax, if established, should be applied.

Types of Not-For-Profit Organizations

This chapter focuses on nongovernmental not-for-profit enterprises, which include some of the most prominent and socially visible organizations in the United States. A recent report by the IRS (based on exemption data) indicates that there are over a million such organizations, representing revenues in excess of $300 billion. The IRS report does not consider the countless chapters of many national organizations that may be counted as a single entity in the IRS list. Although not exhaustive, the following list illustrates the broad range of not-for-profit organizations:

* Botanical societies
* Cemetery organizations
* Child care organizations
* Civic organizations

- Condominium and residential management associations
- Eleemosynary organizations
- Fraternal organizations
- Health care organizations
- Hospitals
- Labor unions
- Libraries
- Museums
- Performing arts organizations
- Philanthropic organizations
- Political parties
- Private and community foundations
- Private elementary and secondary schools
- Professional associations
- Public broadcasting stations
- Religious organizations
- Research and scientific organizations
- Schools, colleges, and universities
- Social, recreational, and country clubs
- Trade associations
- Voluntary health and welfare organizations
- Zoological societies

Appendix 32A contains a listing of the various tax exemption categories.

Accounting for Not-For-Profit Organizations

Not-for-profit organizations tend to have specialized accounting and reporting practices, often differing significantly from those of profit oriented enterprises. Also, some types of organizations follow practices not used by any other type of not-for-profit organizations. The most obvious contrast with business organizations is reflected in financial statements. Typically, the statements of not-for-profit organizations are not widely distributed, generally going only to a limited number of governing bodies, creditors, resource providers, and oversight agencies. Furthermore, the statements are often designed as special purpose reports to meet the informational needs of those users and thus may not be especially informative to the general user of financial statements.

Among the reasons that minimal attention has been given to the widespread diversities in accounting and reporting for not-for-profit enterprises has been the orientation of the standard-setting organizations themselves. The FASB and its predecessor organizations have had to concentrate on accounting principles and practices applicable to business enterprises. ARB 43, issued in 1953, included the following:

The committee has not directed its attention to accounting problems or procedures of religious, charitable, scientific, educational, and similar not-for-profit institutions, municipalities, professional firms, and the like. Accordingly, except where there is a specific statement of a different intent by the committee, its opinions and recommendations are directed primarily to business enterprises organized for profit. [Introduction, ¶ 5].

Accounting and reporting by not-for-profit enterprises evolved gradually over the years, influenced significantly by interested industry groups. In the 1970s, the AICPA became active in the area, publishing pronouncements such as SOP 78-10, *Accounting Principles and Reporting Practices for Certain Nonprofit Organizations* (TP 10,250), and audit guides for several types of not-for-profit organizations. In 1979, the FASB issued SFAS 32, *Specialized Accounting and Reporting Principles and Practices in AICPA Statements of Position and Guides on Accounting and Auditing Matters* (No5), which states that the AICPA audit guides for not-for-profit organizations contain preferable accounting principles for purposes of justifying a change in accounting principles. Finally, in December 1980, the FASB issued SFAC 4, *Objectives of Financial Reporting by Nonbusiness Organizations*, to provide some guidance on the overall objectives of the financial statements of not-for-profit organizations. In addition, both the AICPA and the FASB have begun to issue guidance on not-for-profit financial reporting, including SOP 87-2 (an amendment of SOP 78-10), *Accounting for Joint Costs of Informational Materials and Activities of Not-For-Profit Organizations That Include a Fund-Raising Appeal* (TP 10,420), and SFAS 93, *Recognition of Depreciation of Not-for-Profit Organizations* (D40 and No5), to improve consistency in accounting and financial reporting practices. These statements and audit guides are discussed later in this chapter. Appendix 32-B provides a summary of accounting principles and existing guidance related to not-for-profit entities.

Differentiation From Business Enterprises. The unique characteristic of the numerous and varied not-for-profit organizations is that they are *not organized for profit*. This clearly distinguishes these organizations from typical business entities. SFAC 4, *Objectives of Financial Reporting by Nonbusiness Organizations,* focuses on organizations whose predominantly nonbusiness characteristics heavily influence their operations. The major distinguishing characteristics of not-for-profit organizations as outlined in SFAC 4 are described in the following subsections.

Receipts of significant amounts of resources from providers who do not expect repayment or economic benefits proportionate to the resources provided. In a business enterprise, the prices charged for goods or services are meant to cover costs and allow a profit. Investors or owners of a business enterprise expect this return (a profit) on their investment. However, not-for-profit enterprises have no owners with an interest similar to equity shareholders in a business enterprise. Dues-paying members, contributors, and grantors provide needed capital without necessarily receiving or even expecting commensurate benefits. Providers may expect *some* return on their "investment," but not a *proportionate* return. It often happens that the benefit received is disproportionately small (e.g., Christmas seals) or disproportionately large (e.g. education at a college or university where the tuition charge covers only a portion of the actual costs).

Operating purposes that are primarily other than providing goods or services at a profit or profit equivalents. Most notably, the not-for-profit enterprise's financial statement shows no counterpart to earnings or profits as found in a business enterprise. In fact, many do not earn revenue on exchange transactions. Instead of a statement of earnings, information is generally provided on revenues received and expenses incurred in a *Statement of Revenues and Expenses* or a *Statement of Activity*. Further, the typical financial statement classification of expenses by object (e.g., salaries, general and administrative expenses) is less meaningful for most not-for-profit organizations; thus a different categorization of expenses – by activity or service – is often provided.

Absence of defined ownership interests that can be sold, transferred, or redeemed, or that convey entitlement to a share of a residual distribution of resources in the event of liquidation of the organization. A typical business enterprise is owned by one or more individuals or entities; ownership is generally evidenced by shares of stock or another form of equity interest. This form of equity interest has a value that can be sold or transferred. Not-for-profit organizations are not owned by an individual or any entity. They are formed for the benefit of their members or the general public and thus have no salable value based on an ability to generate a future profit. Upon dissolution, the assets of a not-for-profit generally are transferred to another similar not-for-profit organization.

Similarity to Business Enterprises. On the other hand, a not-for-profit organization does have some attributes in common with business enterprises, as described in the following subsections.

Both provide goods or services to segments of the economy. Although the nature of the goods and services provided may (but need not) be different, it is the public or some specific sector of the economy that ultimately receives the goods or services. For example, some hospitals may be operated for profit, but a not-for-profit hospital provides the same service – health care.

Both obtain resources from external sources. For a business enterprise, the external sources include equity capital from owners. For a not-for-profit enterprise, the external sources may include donations or dues from members. Both may obtain resources from trade creditors, bank loans, or debt securities.

Both are accountable to the resource providers. The stockholders and other resource providers of a business enterprise are interested in the company's profitability and future cash flow prospects (among other matters). Resource providers of a not-for-profit enterprise are interested in the organization's performance – how well the resources provided were spent. One way to account for the use of resources is, of course, to prepare financial statements and to distribute them to the resource providers.

Both must obey applicable laws and regulations. This includes paying all taxes for which they are liable, filing annual returns with the IRS and state agencies to

Nonbusiness organization	Business enterprises
Resource providers	Investors
Constituents	Lenders
Governing and oversight bodies	Suppliers
Managers	Employees
	Customers
	Managers

FIG. 32.1   Users of Financial Information

maintain their exempt status, and observing limits, where applicable, as to the amount that may be spent for fund raising or for noncharitable purposes.

Both must be financially viable. A business enterprise must generate profits to remain viable. Similarly, in the long run, a not-for-profit entity must receive adequate resources to achieve its objectives. While not organized for profit, an objective of a not-for-profit entity is to continue in existence and render its services.

Financial Reporting Concepts

To understand financial reporting by not-for-profit organizations, it is important to differentiate among the varied users of financial statements. SFAC 4 discusses the types of users of externally reported financial information. A comparison of not-for-profit statement users (from SFAC 4) with those identified for business enterprises (from SFAC 1) is shown in Figure 32.1. These lists appear different partly because the users have been grouped differently, but in actuality the users are quite similar.

For nonbusiness organizations, users are defined (in SFAC 4, ¶ 29) as follows:

* *Resource providers*: ". . . those who are directly compensated for providing resources – lenders, suppliers, and employees – and those who are not directly and proportionately compensated – members, contributors, and taxpayers."

* *Constituents*: ". . . those who use and benefit from the services rendered by the organization." Sometimes resource providers are also constituents.

* *Governing and oversight bodies*: ". . . those responsible for setting policies and for overseeing and appraising managers of nonbusiness organizations. Governing bodies may include boards of trustees, boards of overseers and regents, legislatures, councils" and other similar groups. Their responsibilities include reviewing the organization's activities for conformance with laws, restrictions, or guidelines. Oversight bodies include oversight committees of legislatures, governmental regulatory agencies, national headquarters of organizations with local chapters, accrediting agencies, and agencies acting on behalf of contributors and constituents. In membership organizations, governing bodies are commonly the elected representatives of a constituency that is largely composed of resource providers. In organizations such

as charities, hospitals, and private colleges, governing bodies may be self-perpetuating through the election of their own successors.
* *Managers*: those ". . . responsible for carrying out the policy mandates of governing bodies and managing the day-to-day operations of an organization."

Resource providers need information to make decisions about allocating resources to not-for-profit organizations. They are especially interested in whether the organization has efficiently and effectively met its objectives. This information is critical to their decision whether to continue supporting the organization. Resource providers and other users also need information to assess the ability of the organization to continue providing services. Past performance, as well as expectations about future performance, are used to evaluate an organization's ability to continue in existence.

Financial reporting should provide information to users of financial statements that is useful in the assessment of management's performance. Management is responsible for ensuring that resources have been used as directed, have been used efficiently and effectively, and that the custodial and safekeeping functions of the resources have been maintained.

The organization's fiscal performance should be reflected in financial reporting. Information about its service efforts, its accomplishments, and its net resources (and their adequacy for continued existence) should be provided to users of not-for-profit financial statements to assist them in making informed decisions about the entity. Financial reporting should therefore provide information about the types and amounts of inflows and outflows of resources, by activity. The information should indicate whether the inflows and outflows relate to general operations or a specific restricted fund activity. Restricted fund, endowment fund, and plant fund activities should be separately identified and described.

Information about the financial performance of each activity is also important. For example, it is just as important to know how salary expenses were allocated to the organization's activities as it is to know how much was spent on salaries.

Finally, information about the ways in which an organization obtains and spends cash and borrows and repays its debts enables users of financial information to better understand the entity's operations, evaluate its finances, and assess its liquidity.

FUND ACCOUNTING

Fund accounting is the most distinctive difference between not-for-profit organizations and business enterprises. It is also perhaps the most widely misunderstood. Fund accounting is a *separate* accounting for restricted resources that are either *legally* restricted by a donor or another outside party or *designated* by the board for a specific purpose or use. When such resources (together with the related liabilities) are accounted for separately, the separate set of accounts constitutes a *fund,* and the *net assets* in the fund are called the *fund balance*. Some resources, of course, are not restricted, and these are included in *unrestricted funds*. A single not-for-profit organization, therefore, may have several separate funds.

To use a simple example, assume that a newly formed not-for-profit organization receives two cash donations on December 31 – $100,000 that the donor specifies is

Example 1—Layered Format

A. Unrestricted Funds

Assets		Liabilities and fund balances	
Cash	$ 10,000	Fund Balance	$ 10,000

B. Restricted Funds

Building fund:			
Cash	$100,000	Fund Balance	$100,000

Example 2—Multicolumn Format

	Unrestricted fund	Building fund	Total
Assets			
Cash	$10,000	$100,000	$110,000
Liabilities and Fund Balances			
Fund balances:			
Unrestricted	$10,000	$ —	$ 10,000
Restricted	—	100,000	100,000
	$10,000	$100,000	$110,000

Example 3—Restricted Assets Identified

Assets	
Current assets:	
Cash	$ 10,000
Noncurrent assets:	
Cash held for building fund	100,000
	$110,000
Liabilities and Fund Balances	
Fund Balances:	
Unrestricted	$ 10,000
Restricted	100,000
	$110,000

FIG.32.2 Example of Restricted Asset Presentations

only to be used to purchase a headquarters building and $10,000 that may be used for the general operations of the organization. In the organization's balance sheet as of December 31, there are three presentation possibilities, shown in Figure 32.2:

1. Separate funds in a layered format (Example 1).
2. Separate funds in a multicolumn format (Example 2).
3. A single balance sheet with the restricted assets identified (Example 3).

All three formats are used in actual practice depending on the type of organization or the nature of the restrictions on an organization's assets.

The *layered format* does not provide for an aggregation of the various assets, liabilities, and fund balances to display the financial position of the whole organization. Thus, the balance sheet could be quite lengthy if the organization has many restricted funds. Common criticisms of this presentation are that: (1) the financial statements become very complex and nearly incomprehensible unless it is made crystal clear exactly what the various restricted funds represent; and (2) it is quite a challenge to determine the financial position of the organization as a whole, especially if the numerous funds have receivables and payables from and to each other.

In *multicolumn format* statements there often is no total column, since many preparers of financial statements believe that presenting a total column is like "mixing apples and oranges." For example, showing total cash may give the false impression that the organization can use all that cash in its operations. Thus, a common criticism shared with the layered format is that it can be difficult to determine the financial position of the organization as a whole. However, the multicolumn format is most often used when an organization has more than two types of restricted funds since it easily presents all the activities of an organization in a single, easy-to-read format.

The *restricted asset identification format* is most like that used for a business enterprise and is used by many not-for-profit organizations that classify assets as current or noncurrent. With this classification, the format also can be cumbersome. Some relief may be provided by classifying assets and liabilities as restricted or unrestricted by type of fund, but this presentation does not work well when there are numerous funds.

Appendix 32C contains excerpts from the 1987 financial statements for the African-American Institute. Reference to those statements will enhance the usefulness of the discussion that follows in this chapter.

Elements of Financial Statements

In 1985 the FASB issued SFAC 6, *Elements of Financial Statements* (replacing SFAC 3, which had covered only business enterprises). SFAC 6 defines 10 elements of financial statements. Seven of these elements apply to both business enterprises and not-for-profit organizations: assets, liabilities, equity (business enterprises) or net assets (not-for-profit organizations), revenues, expenses, gains, and losses. Three elements apply to business enterprises only: investments by owners, distributions to owners, and comprehensive income. SFAC 6 also defines three classes of net assets of not-for-profit organizations and the changes in those classes of net assets during a period. If an entity were to use fund accounting, it would generally have to use these three groupings of net assets within each fund, as applicable. These classes are discussed in the following sections.

Permanently Restricted Net Assets. These assets represent contributions or other inflows of assets whose use is limited by the donor, and whose benefits do not expire with the passage of time or by actions of the organization.

An example of a type of fund which would be classified as a permanently restricted net asset is an endowment fund. These funds represent gifts and bequests accepted with donor stipulations such as:

* Principal must be held in perpetuity, using only the income earned upon investment of the principal.
* Principal must be maintained until the occurrence of a specific event or after a specified period of time.
* Income is to be used for general purposes, or for a specific purpose, as designated by the donor.

Technically, the fund is an *endowment fund* only if the principal amount is to be maintained intact in perpetuity. If the principal is to be maintained until the occurrence of a specified event or only for a specified period, the fund is a *term endowment fund,* and therefore may be better classified as temporarily restricted.

If the governing board of an organization determines that certain resources are to be retained and invested, the fund is a *quasiendowment fund.* This type of fund is actually a board-designated fund, and should be classified as a temporarily restricted fund. Some other organizations, principally colleges and universities, include quasiendowment funds with other endowment funds under the caption "endowment and similar funds."

Temporarily Restricted Net Assets. These assets represent contributions or other inflows of assets whose use is limited by the donor, but whose benefits expire with the passage of time or through the actions of the organization.

There are several different types of funds that could be classified as temporarily restricted. These are as follows:

* Current restricted fund
* Plant fund (or land, building, and equipment fund)
* Agency fund
* Other funds, (e.g. loan funds and annuity fund)

Current restricted fund. Also called the *donor-restricted fund* or *fund for specified purposes,* this category consists of operating funds restricted by donors and grantors who specify the permitted use. For example, $1,000 given to a local hospital to be used for reading materials for patients would be included in the current restricted fund. Usually, the unexpended balances in the fund are relatively small, since these gifts and grants are generally used shortly after receipt. When the amounts are not to be used currently for a normal activity of the organization, they are usually included in another fund. A list of restricted donations, including the name of the donor or the activity for which the donations are restricted, is sometimes provided with the financial statements.

Plant fund. Sometimes referred to as the *land, building, and equipment fund, capital assets fund,* or *fixed asset fund;* this fund is used to segregate investments in, and contributions specifically designated for, the acquisition of land, buildings, and equipment. Its purpose is to segregate capital assets not expendable for current operations. Generally, there is no need for such a fund, and these investments may be included in the unrestricted fund balance; doing so will communicate the fact that

(1) the fixed assets are not legally restricted and (2) they are used in the day-to-day activities of the organization.

Agency fund. Sometimes called a *custodian fund, philanthropic fund,* or *funds held in trust for others;* this fund simply represents resources received by an organization to be held or disbursed only on instructions of the person or organization from whom they were received. For example, a college or university may hold funds belonging to the student government association to be disbursed only on the association's instructions.

Other funds. These include *loan funds, annuity funds,* and *life income funds* and are most often associated with colleges and universities. A *loan fund,* as its name implies, represents resources restricted for loans (to students, faculty, or staff). An *annuity fund* represents gifts of money or other property with the restriction that the organization make periodic payments to the donors or other specified individuals for a specified period of time. A *life income fund* represents gifts of money or other property with the restriction that the organization periodically pay out the income earned by the donated assets. Such payments may be made to the donors (or other specified individuals) for the lifetime of the income beneficiary. The primary difference between an annuity fund and a life income fund is that the principal amount of the life income fund will remain intact, whereas annuity payments might also use the principal.

Unrestricted Net Assets. These are net assets that are neither temporarily nor permanently restricted, and essentially represent operating funds.

For financial reporting purposes, the type of net assets would be grouped according to the type of restriction. An example of this presentation is shown in Appendix 32-C; note that restricted funds are categorized into three types—undesignated, board-designated, and invested in capital assets (with capital assets shown among noncurrent assets). The assets of the single restricted fund grouping—endowment funds—are included in noncurrent assets.

Merits of Separate Fund Presentation

Knowledgeable accountants differ regarding the merits of fund accounting and presentation. The differences of opinion are a symptom of the evolution of accounting for not-for-profit organizations, which has occurred more slowly than it has for business enterprises.

Recent years have seen increasing discussion of the need for fund accounting and individual fund presentation as opposed to a single set of financial statements presenting the assets and obligations of the entire organization. The following discussion presents the arguments for and against fund accounting and reporting, based on the FASB research report, *Financial Accounting in Nonbusiness Organizations* (Anthony, 1978, pp. 104–112).

Arguments for Separate Fund Presentation. Proponents of fund accounting primarily emphasize four points:

1. Because there are legal restrictions on resources, it is necessary to report compliance with those restrictions; fund accounting is a convenient way do so.

2. An aggregated statement is misleading because restricted resources are not interchangeable with unrestricted resources.

3. Aggregated statements are not adequate to represent what really is a complex situation. Because of restrictions on resources or spending, statements prepared as if the organization were a business enterprise are inappropriate.

4. Although there may be abuses of fund accounting in some organizations, these abuses are not inherent attributes of fund accounting.

Arguments for a Single Set of Financial Statements. Opponents of fund accounting primarily emphasize five points:

1. Separate financial statements for each fund group fragment the overall organization instead of presenting the activities and financial position of the organization as a whole.

2. Separate accounting by different funds is difficult to understand and tends to confuse the reader. Therefore, a single set of financial statements is more understandable; also, readers familiar with financial statements of business enterprises are accustomed to that format.

3. It is possible for management to manipulate the financial statements by using its discretion as to the fund or funds in which costs should be included.

4. Because there are transfers and reimbursements among funds, it can appear that revenues are being counted twice.

5. The existence of restrictions on resources and whether these restrictions have been complied with can be disclosed in footnotes to financial statements.

EFFECTIVE INTERNAL ACCOUNTING

External financial reports of not-for-profit organizations assist the governing board, constituents, creditors, and other outside interested parties in assessing the performance of upper-level managers. Within the organization, the accounting system should be designed to provide appropriate feedback regarding the performance of the various operating activities. The relationships of upper-level managers to externally interested parties and to subordinates is illustrated in Figure 32.3.

In monitoring and controlling the activities of subordinates, upper-level managers should expect the accounting system to be supported by an effective internal control structure, and to provide the following:

1. An effective departmental budgeting program.

2. Measurement of departmental contributions toward the operating objectives of the organization, including the disclosure of information for evaluating departmental performance.

3. A system of allocation that can be used in establishing prices for services that will recover costs from user fees (either fully or partially, as appropriate).

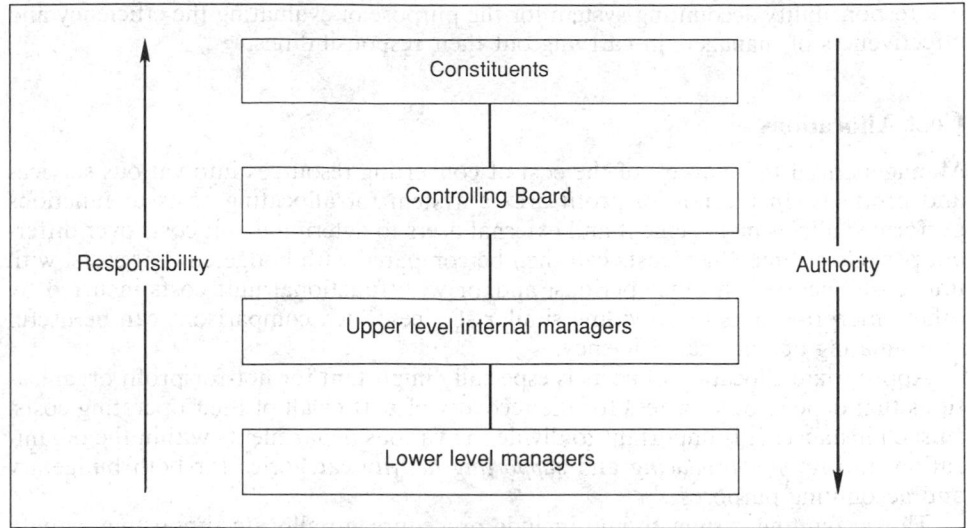

FIG. 32.3   Responsibility/Authority Flow in a Nonprofit Organization

Effective Budgeting

The budget expresses the operating plans of the organization in financial terms. Most budgets involve a combination of amounts appropriated for specific purposes and for ongoing activities. Appropriation-type budgets are used by organizations that rely on taxes and/or contributions for resource inflows and that provide services on the basis of need. On the other hand, the budgets of profit enterprises are established in relationshp to anticipated volume of operations. Between these two limits are organizations that depend on user fees for some of their operating revenues and whose outflow budgets typically include both appropriation- and activity-based items.

Internally, not-for-profit organizations usually have supervisory responsibility divided along the lines of departments or the service functions provided by the organization. Therefore, it is important that the overall budget be subdivided according to subordinate manager responsibilities. Such an arrangement has the effect of establishing budgeted standards for each of these individual managers and, in that way, of holding each manager accountable for his segment of operations.

Contribution to Operating Objectives

To evaluate the effectiveness of departmental managers, the accounting system must be organized in a way that aligns actual outflows to the specific areas of responsibilities that are used in the budgetary system. This allows assessment of managers' adherence to budgetary allocations and of the units of service provided by their departments. Functional unit costs or expenditures per unit of service provided can be developed and compared with the budget on a departmental basis. In effect, this is a responsibility accounting system for the purpose of evaluating the efficiency and effectiveness of managers in carrying out their responsibilities.

Cost Allocations

Managers need to be aware of the cost of converting resources into various services and products. In the not-for-profit area a system for allocating costs to functions performed allows management and external users to determine unit costs over different periods of time. Such costs can then be compared with budgeted unit costs, with unit costs incurred in other periods, and/or with functional unit costs incurred by other enterprise units in providing similar services. Such comparisons can be useful in evaluating operational efficiency.

Appropriate allocation of costs is especially important for not-for-profit organizations that depend on user fees for the recovery of part or all of their operating costs. In such instances it is important to divide the various departments within the organization into *revenue-producing* and *supporting activity* categories for both budgetary and accounting purposes.

The accounting system should include procedures to allocate supporting activity costs to revenue-producing departments. After such allocations have been completed as part of the budgeting process, the anticipated cost per unit of billable service can be determined by dividing total cost by the anticipated number of units of services to be provided. Such cost allocation procedures have been used for many years by hospitals in arriving at service billing rates (as discussed in Chapter 30). Logically, a similar system of cost allocation could be used in establishing college and university tuition and fee schedules.

Internal Controls

Dependable internal control procedures are based on an accounting system, organization chart, and procedures manual that include these characteristics:

1. A work assignment arrangement that provides for an appropriate separation of custodial and record-keeping responsibilities.
2. An organization chart and procedures manual that places specific operational responsibilities on specific persons within the organization.
3. Adequate records, forms, and authorization procedures.
4. A personnel policy ensuring that all personnel are appropriately qualified for the responsibilities assigned to them.
5. Provision for a periodic check of actual procedures being followed against those prescribed in the procedures manual.
6. Appropriate provisions for the physical protection of assets such as cash and securities.

In the process of assuring compliance (point five in the preceding list) it is important to employ an internal auditor or group when an organization becomes large enough to preclude the top-level manager from personally checking compliance. Internal audit has the responsibility for determining that lower-level supervisors and employees comply with managerial directives and the procedures spelled out in the

---

Colleges and Universities

- Industry Audit Guide, *Audit of Colleges and Universities* (1975)
- SOP 74-8, *Financial Accounting and Reporting by Colleges and Universities*

Voluntary Health and Welfare Organizations

- Industry Audit Guide, *Audit of Voluntary Health and Welfare Organizations* (1974)

Other Not-For-Profit Organizations

- SOP 78-10, *Accounting and Reporting Practices for Certain Nonprofit Organizations*

FIG. 32.4 AICPA Not-For-Profit SOPs and Guides Given Authority Under SFAS 32

procedures manual. (See Chapter 7 for a discussion on the relationship of internal and external auditors).

ACCOUNTING AND REPORTING

Not that long ago, a common misconception about accounting by not-for-profit organizations was that GAAP did not apply and, therefore, such organizations did not have to follow any authoritative accounting pronouncements. This idea is, of course, incorrect; possibly it results from the 1953 statement in ARB 43, cited earlier: "... except where there is a specific statement of a different intent by the committee, its opinions and recommendations are directed primarily to business enterprises organized for profit."

Authoritative Literature

A very significant pronouncement affecting not-for-profit organizations was issued in 1979 as SFAS 32, *Specialized Accounting and Reporting Principles and Practices in AICPA Statements of Position and Guides on Accounting and Auditing Matters* (A06.112). It amends APB 20, *Accounting Changes*, by adding the following provision:

The specialized accounting and reporting principles and practices contained in the AICPA Statements of Position and Guides on accounting and auditing matters listed in Appendix A of FASB Statement No. 32 [now in A06, Exhibit 112A] are preferable accounting principles for purposes of justifying a change in accounting principle.

APB 20 provides that a change in accounting principle does not conform with GAAP unless the enterprise justifies the new alternative principle as preferable. SFAS 32 now grants authority to many of the SOPs and guides issued by the AICPA in the past. Several of these publications deal specifically with nongovernmental nonprofit entities, as listed in Figure 32.4. This means that

- There is no requirement for an organization to change accounting practices to comply with the SOPs and guides if it is currently using other acceptable accounting and reporting practices.
- If an organization does change, the principles in the SOPs or guides are the preferable accounting principles.
- If an organization changes to an accounting principle other than one specified in the applicable SOP or guide, the organization has the burden of proof to demonstrate that the new principle is preferable. In this case, the auditor reporting on the financial statements with the objective of rendering an unqualified opinion ' ould also have to be satisfied that the organization has demonstrated the preferability of the new principle before he renders an opinion that the financial statements are prepared in conformity with GAAP. As a practical matter, therefore, it is likely that, when changing accounting principles, the organization will adopt the principles and practices included in the SOPs and guides.

FASB Activity

SFAS 32 is viewed only as an interim solution. Definitive authoritative pronouncements for many accounting and reporting practices of not-for-profit organizations are still needed. Since the release of SFAS 32 in 1979, the FASB has issued SFAC 4, *Objectives of Financial Reporting by Nonbusiness Organizations* (discussed earlier), and SFAC 6, *Elements of Financial Statements* (modifying SFAC 3 to incorporate not-for-profit enterprises.) SFAS 93 was also issued requiring not-for-profit enterprises to recognize depreciation (but the effective date has been delayed, as discussed in "Fixed Assets".

The FASB staff has expressed the view that the most pervasive problems in which there is the greatest diversity in practice among various not-for-profit entities include:

- *Depreciation*, intended to be resolved with the issuance of SFAS 93.
- *Contributions*, discussed later in this chapter.
- *Investments*, which to some extent may be dealt with in the FASB Financial Instruments project (Chapter 21).
- *Reporting entity*, to be dealt with in the FASB long-term project dealing with reporting entity issues for all enterprises (Chapter 24).
- *Financial statement display*, being considered by the AICPA's Task Force on Not-For-Profit Organization Display Issues, which is preparing a paper for the FASB's consideration.

Also in process is an FASB project dealing with recognition and measurement issues related to contributions of cash or other donated goods and services, or pledges for future contributions. Although existing guidance supports the recognition of pledges receivable, guidance on the timing of recognition is not clear and practice is diverse.

Accounting Basis

Until the FASB deals with unresolved issues in accounting for not-for-profit entities, the guidance given in AICPA guides and SOPs forms the basis for much of current practice.

In general, SOP 78-10, *Accounting Principles and Reporting Practices for Certain Nonprofit Organizations* (TP 10,250), provides that the accrual basis should be used in the financial statements of all not-for-profit organizations.[1] Although the accrual basis of accounting underlies GAAP for business enterprises, the cash receipts and disbursements method of accounting is frequently used by not-for-profit organizations. There is also a hybrid of the cash basis and the accrual basis – the modified cash (or modified accrual) basis. Under the modified cash basis, some transactions are recorded on a cash basis and others on an accrual basis, although different organizations do not necessarily account for the same transactions in the same way. Many organizations record transactions on a cash basis during the year and convert to the accrual basis at year-end for reporting purposes. The main advantage of the cash basis lies in its simple record-keeping requirements, similar to maintaining a checkbook. In many voluntary not-for-profit organizations, simplicity is important because of the lack of a sufficiently large accounting staff. Additionally, the cash method is selected by many organizations if no significant difference will result from using the cash method versus the accrual method.

Accounting Practices – General

Financial Statements. The three basic financial statements required for a typical not-for-profit organization are a balance sheet, a statement of activity, and a statement of cash flows. The statement of activity includes information regarding the support, revenue, capital or nonexpendable additions, and expenses classified into functional categories. This statement may have a different title, such as any of the following: support, revenue, expense, capital additions, or changes in fund balances. SOP 78-10 presents examples of financial statements, including representative footnote disclosures, for the following 13 types of organizations (TP 10,250.129–.141):

1. Independent school
2. Cemetery organization
3. Country club
4. Library
5. Museum
6. Performing arts organization
7. Private foundation
8. Public broadcasting system
9. Religious organization
10. Research and scientific organization
11. Trade association

---

[1] Professional pronouncements regarding not-for-profit entities, including SOP 78-10 and the AICPA industry audit guides for colleges and universities (AICPA, 1975) and for voluntary health and welfare organizations (AICPA, 1974) were augmented by issuance in 1981 of the AICPA's Audit and Accounting Guide, *Audits of Certain Nonprofit Organizations* (AICPA, 1981c). This Guide does not supersede the earlier guides, but does add accounting (and auditing) specification for other not-for-profit organizations, based essentially on SOP 78-10 (which is bound into the 1981 Guide).

12. Union

13. Zoological and botanical society

A summary of the more significant accounting practices commonly followed by not-for-profit organizations (named in SOP 78-10 [TP 10,250.005]) is provided. Appendix 32-C includes selected financial statements of the African-American Institute.

Investments. Investments may be carried either at amortized cost, lower of cost or market, or fair market value (TP 10,250.077–.083). If carried at cost, investments are written down to market when market values have declined substantially and the decline is considered other than temporary. If the investments are carried in a current portfolio, any adjustment to write down the assets is reflected in the current period statement of activity. If the investments are carried in a noncurrent portfolio, the adjustment is reflected as a direct reduction in the fund balance account. The financial statements of investments carried at cost should disclose the fair market value of the investments either parenthetically or in a footnote.

When investments are carried at the lower of cost or market, a decline below cost in the aggregate market value of a portfolio (by fund group) is charged directly to the fund balance; recoveries in aggregate market up to original cost are also restored through direct credit to the fund balance.

For investments carried at market, the carrying amount of the investments should be adjusted each year for any change in the fair market value, with the increase or decrease being reported in the current statement of activites if the investments are in the current fund, or as an element of the changes in fund balance, if carried in noncurrent funds.

Financial statements should disclose total realized and unrealized gains and losses and investment income earned during the period.

Pledges. Pledges generally are not enforceable and should only be recognized when an organization has a history of collecting its pledges and is aware of the credit standing of its donors.

Pledges are recognized as support in the period to which the donor has designated the pledge or the period in which the pledged funds have been solicited for use.

Fixed Assets. Fixed assets are capitalized at cost. Donated fixed assets are recorded at their fair market value, if determinable, or at a nominal value if a fair market value cannot be readily ascertained.

Works of art and historical treasures owned by not-for-profit organizations, including museums, libraries, and art galleries, are generally not capitalized because of the difficulty in determining a value. However, if information is available to support values (e.g., cost records if acquired, or fair market values if donated), then the assets are generally recorded, although not subsequently depreciated. If not capitalized, the balance sheet should contain a caption entitled "works of art" or "collections" with no dollar amount; appropriate footnote disclosure is required.

In August 1987, the FASB issued SFAS 93, *Recognition of Depreciation by Not-For-Profit Organizations*. It requires all not-for-profit organizations to depreciate long-lived tangible assets and to make the disclosures currently required for business entities (D40.105). There has been much diversity in past practices of not-for-profit organizations (including the policy of not recognizing depreciation on some or all assets). SFAS 93 should result in consistency in the future. This Statement is effective for fiscal years beginning after May 15, 1988. However, in June 1988 as a result of jurisdictional questions by the GASB, the FASB issued an exposure draft of a proposed Statement (FASB, 1988a) to defer the effective date to fiscal years beginning on or after January 1, 1990.

Restricted Funds. Restricted funds represent gifts, grants, bequests, or other income restricted by the donor for a specific purpose or activity or for use at a specific time. Restricted gifts should be supported by a written document stipulating the conditions.

When received, restricted funds are initially deferred and recognized as support income only to the extent that expenses related to the restricted gift have been incurred. For example, if a donor contributed cash of $10,000 to be used for scholarships, the $10,000 would be credited to deferred revenues until funds were actually expended for scholarships. The deferred revenue would be reduced dollar for dollar as scholarships were incurred. Both the revenue and the related expenses would be reflected in the statement of activity as restricted fund transactions.

Membership Dues. Dues paid for membership in a trade, membership, or similar organization ordinarily are recognized as revenue over the period of membership. However, a specific determination needs to be made as to whether the dues represent fees paid for future services or are in fact contributions. If the dues represent fees for future services, they should be amortized over the term of the membership. If, however, the member is receiving no benefit from the membership, the dues generally are treated as contributions and recognized when received. There are situations where dues represent both contributions and fees for future services, and the dues accordingly should be allocated between both.

Trade and membership organizations typically bill their members in advance of the membership year; consequently, dues received in advance are recognized as deferred revenue until the membership period begins, at which time amortization over the year begins.

Presently, there are some differences in accounting for the initial billing of dues and the recording of a receivable for those dues. A receivable is generally recorded when an exchange of goods or services has taken place and there is a contractual obligation on the part of the recipient to pay. With respect to services, the exchange is considered to have taken place when the service has been performed. In both these instances, the recipient of the goods or services has an obligation to pay and a receivable may be recorded at that time by the provider of the goods or service.

Membership dues could be treated similarly. However, the provider organization generally has no indication that an individual or an organization wants to be a member until the member has paid. Consequently, the exchange of goods or services takes place after money has been collected. The obligation then rests with the provider to supply the goods or service. Members are under no obligation to continue their membership. Thus, the realization of the dues income related to membership renewals does not occur until the dues have been collected. As a result, revenue is generally not recorded for membership dues until they are collected.

Contributions and Donations. Unrestricted contributions are recognized as revenue in the period in which they are received. Restricted contributions are recognized when the related expense has been incurred or other conditions have been met.

Donated materials are recorded at their fair market value if determinable, or at a nominal value if no fair market value can be readily ascertained. If donated materials pass through the organization (acting as agent) to the beneficiaries, no values should be recorded (TP 10,250.071).

Donated services are difficult to value and vary significantly among not-for-profit organizations. SOP 78-10 indicates that donated services should not be recorded as an expense, with an equivalent amount recorded as a contribution or support, unless all of the following circumstances exist (TP 10,250.067):

a. The services performed are significant and form an integral part of the efforts of the organization as it is presently constituted; the services would be performed by salaried personnel if donated or contributed services were not available for the organization to accomplish its purpose; and the organization would continue this program or activity.

b. The organization controls the employment and duties of the service donors. The organization is able to influence their activities in a way comparable to the control it would exercise over employees with similar responsibilities. This includes control over time, location, nature, and performance of donated or contributed services.

c. The organization has a clearly measurable basis for the amount to be recorded.

d. The services of the reporting organization are not principally intended for the benefit of its members. Accordingly, donated and contributed services would not normally be recorded by organizations such as religious communities, professional and trade associations, labor unions, political parties, fraternal organizations, and social and country clubs.

Services that generally are not recorded as contributions, even though the services may constitute a significant factor in the operation of the organization, include supplementary efforts of volunteer workers provided directly to beneficiaries (e.g., auxiliary activities that would not otherwise be provided) and periodic services of volunteers in concentrated fund-raising drives (TP 10,250.069). If donated services are recorded, the methods used to value them should be disclosed in the footnotes.

Grants. Many not-for-profit organizations receive grants as a form of revenue from both governmental and nongovernmental entities. These grants usually specify (1) that the grantee organization perform a service or produce a product (generally in the form of a publication) in exchange for the grant funds; and (2) a period of coverage, for example, the product or service must be completed within a defined time interval. Most grants also specify a fixed dollar amount that may include a provision for overhead.

Grants are recognized as revenue when expenses directly related to the grant plus overhead (as specified in the contract) are incurred. Grants earned but not received are recorded as receivables. Grants received but not yet earned are deferred.

Not-for-profit organizations that receive federal grants are expected to comply with OMB Circular A-110, *Grants and Agreements With Institutions of Higher Educations, Hospitals and Other Nonprofit Organizations*. Circular A-110 sets forth standards for obtaining consistency and uniformity among federal agencies in the administration of grants and is to be applied to recipients of federal grants. The standards encompass the following:

* Cash depositories
* Bonding and insurance
* Retention and custodial requirements for records
* Program income
* Cost sharing and matching
* Standards for financial management systems
* Financial reporting requirements
* Monitoring and reporting program performance
* Payment requirements
* Revision of financial plans
* Closeout procedures
* Suspensions and termination procedures
* Standard form for applying for federal assistance
* Property management standards
* Procurement standards

Any not-for-profit organization with federal funding should be aware of these standards and should adopt appropriate internal policies and procedures to comply with them. Many federal agencies reserve the right to audit each grantee organization, thus compliance with A-110 becomes an integral part of each organization's accounting procedures. (See "Audits of Grants" later in this chapter.)

Whether or not the organization receives federal funding, a not-for-profit organization with significant grant activity must develop a cost system to monitor and track costs by grant. Many nongovernmental grantor organizations reserve the right to review a grantee's books and records and the methodology used to arrive at an overhead rate.

A not-for-profit organization may also make grants to other organizations, including other not-for-profit entities. In these circumstances, the grantor should record the grant as an expense when the recipient is entitled to the funds; normally this will occur at the time of board or other appropriate approval.

Program Activities. Most not-for-profit organizations present expenses in the Statement of Activity by program or function rather than by natural expense classifications (e.g., salaries, travel, rent, and so forth). It is generally more informative to users of the financial statements to know the function or activity on which money was spent rather than the type of expense.

The type of program or functional activity presented will vary according to the type of organization and its services. A matrix format can provide both functional and natural classifications as shown in Appendix 32-C.

Fund-Raising Costs. Fund-raising costs incurred to induce others to contribute funds are a significant element in the financial statements of most not-for-profit entities. Fund-raising costs should be expensed as incurred unless the costs can be specifically identified with a future event (which is unlikely, because these costs are generally incurred on an overall organizational basis).

SOP 87-2, *Accounting for Joint Costs of Informational Materials and Activities of Not-For-Profit Organizations That Include a Fund-Raising Appeal* (TP 10,420), recommends that such costs be allocated between fund-raising and program activities or management and general functions if it can be shown that a bona fide non-fund-raising activity has been conducted in connection with the appeal. In determining what is bona fide, consideration should be given to the content of the materials or activities, the reasons for distribution, and the intended recipients. Costs that relate primarily to the entity (e.g., an annual report) should be allocated to management and general expense.

Income Taxes. A not-for-profit organization is exempt from taxes on income that is directly related to its purpose. Conversely, unrelated business income is taxable to the extent that revenues exceed expenses for that particular unrelated business activity.

Types of unrelated business income include rentals, advertising, trade show or convention exhibit income, insurance programs, mailing list or label sales, and consulting.

To be exempt from income taxes, each not-for-profit organization must apply for exemption from the federal government and, in some cases, from the state government as well. The type of exemption that the organization receives will determine the appropriate rules and regulations that it must follow.

Most trade and membership organizations will be classified as either a *Section 501 (c)(3)* or *Section 501(c)(6)*, which the IRS defines as follows.

A 501(c)(3) organization is a corporation, community chest, fund, or foundation that is organized and operated exclusively (i.e., substantially) for one or more of the following purposes: charitable, religious, educational, scientific, literary, testing for public safety, fostering amateur sports competition, or the prevention of cruelty to children or animals. No part of its net earnings may benefit any private shareholder or individual. Contributions to 501(c)(3) organizations are tax-deductible by the contributor.

A 501(c)(3) organization may lose its exemption if a "substantial part of its activities" consists of attempting to influence legislation. In addition, a 501(c)(3) organization may not be involved in any political campaign on behalf of any candidate for public office. A public charity may make an election to replace the "substantial part of activities" test with a limit defined in terms of expenditures for influencing legislation.

Every 501(c)(3) organization is treated as a private foundation (subject to excise tax on net investment income and restrictions on its activities) unless it qualifies as a public charity under IRC § 509(a)(1), (2), (3), or (4).

In general, to be classified as a public charity, one-third of its support must be public (grants, contributions, etc.); however, there is a limit on each corporate or individual contribution of 2% of total support (over a four year period). All 501(c)(3) organizations are required to annually assess their "public charity" status to determine whether they continue to qualify.

Organizations exempt under 501(c)(6) are associations of persons having some common business interest. Its purpose is to promote that interest but not to engage in a business whose purpose is to earn a profit. As with a 501(c)(3) organization, no part of its net earnings may benefit any private shareholder or individual. 501(c)(6) organizations may engage in legislative activity relevant to the common business interest of its members and may participate in political campaigns on behalf of candidates for public office. Contributions to 501(c)(6) organizations are *not* tax-deductible.

College and University Issues

Colleges and universities can be subdivided into state-supported and private.[2] Both receive a major portion of their revenues from user charges. State-supported institutions receive most of their fees from state allocations based on some measure of enrollment, but they usually require some direct payment by the student in the form of tuition and fees. The private university receives all of its user-based fees directly from students, parents of students, alumni, or scholarship funds. Both types of institutions also typically receive significant amounts in the form of gifts, contributions, and grants.

Financial Statements. Colleges and universities present three basic statements: (1) a balance sheet, (2) statement of changes in fund balances, and (3) statement of current fund revenues, expenditures, and other changes.

The statement of changes in fund balances is essentially a statement of changes in financial position and presents each fund's revenues and other additions, expenditures and other deductions, and the transfers among funds.

The statement of current fund revenues, expenditures, and other changes is a statement unique to colleges and universities. Essentially, it is a statement of the financial activities of only the current funds, both unrestricted and restricted. The amounts of revenues and expenditures reflected in this statement are identical to those presented in the statement of changes in fund balances for the current fund

---

[2] Under FASB/GASB *Structural Agreement* (described in Chapter 31), public-sector colleges and universities are to follow GAAP in the same manner as not-for-profit colleges and universities, unless GASB has issued a specific pronouncement to the contrary. SGAS 8, *Applicability of FASB Statement No. 93, Recognition of Depreciation by Not-For-Profit Organizations, to Certain State and Local Governmental Entities*, instructs public-sector colleges and universities to not follow the named SFAS.

activity except that the statement of current fund revenues, expenditures, and other changes is presented in more detail; and it does not purport to show the results of operations as in a typical statement of revenues and expenditures.

The objectives of the statement of current fund revenues, expenditures, and other changes include:

* Providing the reader with adequate information concerning the details of the sources and uses of current funds.
* Enabling the institution to report the total of unrestricted and restricted current funds expended for each of the functional categories, so that the total level of financial activity for each function is disclosed.
* Facilitating the presentation of a comparison with prior years.

In addition, supporting schedules may be presented to show the financial position and activities of various auxiliary enterprises (such as intercollegiate athletics, student health services, dormitories and housing system, and the college bookstore), and the various individual fund entities.

In accounting for resource inflows, colleges and universities distinguish between *operating revenues* and *nonoperating revenues*. All operating revenues, such as tuition and fees, unrestricted gifts, and endowment income, flow through the operating statement. Resource inflows that are externally restricted to specified nonoperating uses (such as endowment or the acquisition of fixed assets) are recorded in designated fund groups (such as endowment and similar funds, or plant funds).

Accounting Practices. The AICPA Audit Guide, *Audits of Colleges and Universities* (AICPA, 1975),[3] states that the accounts of colleges and universities should be maintained on the accrual basis of accounting, except that depreciation is not recognized as an element of expense in the statement of activity. SFAS 93, *Recognition of Depreciation by Not-For-Profit Organizations* (D40), requires recording depreciation for fiscal years beginning after May 15, 1988; and it has resulted in a great deal of controversy. Many private colleges and universities are resisting the change and have indicated that they may accept a qualified auditor's opinion rather than make the change.[4] However, in June 1988 the FASB issued an exposure draft of a proposed Statement (FASB, 1988a) to defer the effective date of SFAS 93 to fiscal years beginning on or after January 1, 1990.

Many of the accounting practices followed by not-for-profit organizations generally are also followed by colleges and universities. These include the accounting for:

* Investments
* Pledges
* Restricted funds
* Contributions and donations
* Grants

---

[3] See note 1.
[4] See note 2.

* Program activities
* Fund-raising

Colleges and universities use fund accounting extensively. The following fund groups are typical:

* Current funds
* Loan funds
* Endowment and similar funds
* Annuity and life income funds
* Plant funds
* Agency funds

Because of the number of funds typically presented and the detail of accounts within each fund, the balance sheet of a college or university is usually quite lengthy. Examples may be found in Exhibit A in the Audit Guide (adapted in Exhibit 1 of SOP 74-8, *Financial Accounting and Reporting by Colleges and Universities* (TP 10,020)).

Current Funds. Current funds include spendable resources—those available to be used directly in operating the institution; the current obligations required to be satisfied with those resources are also included. Current funds are divided into two subcategories: *unrestricted current funds* include those resources that (within the limits of budgetary constraints) may be used at the discretion of management; *restricted current funds* include spendable resources restricted to specified operating uses by donors or other outside agencies.

The current fund balance sheet is similar to a balance sheet of any other not-for-profit organization. Typical accounts are cash, investments, receivables, inventories, prepaid expenses, and accounts payable and accrued expenses.

Current fund revenues are somewhat distinctive, and comprise the following:

* *Student tuition and fees.* Tuition and fees for educational purposes are recognized in the period in which the related education is taking place. If the academic term straddles a fiscal year end, the entire tuition is generally reported within the fiscal year in which the program is predominantly conducted.
* *Government appropriations.* These amounts represent unrestricted and restricted amounts received from the government.
* *Grants and contracts.* Revenue from governmental and nongovernmental grants and contracts is recognized to the extent of direct costs incurred plus overhead. Revenues related to direct costs are reported as restricted revenues; revenues related to indirect costs are reported as unrestricted revenues.
* *Endowment income.* Amount represents income earned by endowment funds that is available for current operations. These amounts may be restricted or unrestricted.
* *Sales and services of educational departments.* Revenue recognized from activities carried on primarily for the training of students, such as dairy creameries, is recognized in this category. Otherwise, the revenue is included in sales and services of auxiliary enterprises.

- *Sales and services of auxiliary enterprises.* Auxiliary enterprises are conducted to provide service to the students and faculty and include such activities as residence halls, food service, and college stores.

Current fund expenditures and transfers include all operating expenses incurred in accordance with GAAP, expenditures from current funds for equipment renewals and replacements, and amounts transferred to plant funds for debt service.

As with other not-for-profit organizations, expenditures should be reported on a functional basis. The categories outlined below are typically used by colleges and universities:

- Educational and general expenditures
  - Instruction and departmental research
  - Organized activities related to educational departments
  - Sponsored research
  - Other sponsored programs
  - Extension and public service
  - Libraries
  - Student services
  - Operation and maintenance of plant
  - General administration
  - Student aid
- Educational and general mandatory transfers
  - Provision for debt service
  - Loan funds matching grants
- Auxiliary enterprise expenditures and mandatory transfers
- Other transfers

Loan Funds. These include loans to faculty, students, or staff. The agreements under which these funds operate usually specify the loan-granting restrictions. Cash not committed for loans is invested.

Endowment and Similar Funds. These funds include resources invested for the purpose of producing operating revenue. *Regular endowment funds* are externally restricted from use for any purpose other than investment purposes (i.e., the principal must remain intact), and the revenue is used for general operating purposes. The revenues from *designated endowment funds* generally can be used only for the purposes specified in the endowment agreement, such as scholarships or individual schools within the university.

Term endowment funds are similar to regular endowment funds except that after the passage of a stated period of time or the occurrence of a particular event, all or part of the principal may be expended.

Quasiendowment funds represent resources designated by the governing board of the institution for use as endowment. Since they are internally designated, the governing board has the right to rescind its action and allow the principal to be expended.

Annuity and Life Income Funds. Most colleges and universities accept contributions subject to donor claims, such as the right of the donor to receive an annuity for a specified period of time (or for life) or the right of the donor to receive the income from the contribution for the remainder of the donor's life. Upon termination of these annuity or life income agreements, the assets remaining in the fund become the property of the college or university. The accounts of an annuity fund will include an actuarially determined liability for annuities payable.

Plant Funds. Plant funds are used to carry the acquisition costs of fixed assets and the renewal and replacement of instrumental properties. Obligations (such as bonds payable) relating to those assets, plus resources restricted to debt retirement or capital expenditures, are also included in the plant fund.

Plant funds are usually reflected in the financial statements in four categories:

* *Unexpended plant funds* represent amounts unspent at the reporting date and consist of cash, investments, receivables, and accounts payable, as well as notes and mortgages payable to the extent that proceeds have not yet been spent. Additions to unexpended plant funds include contributions, restricted fund appropriations, investment income, and transfers from other funds. Deductions include investment losses and disbursements for plant purposes.

* *Renewals and replacement funds* include resources not yet expended for plant renewal and replacement. Usually a separate account within the general ledger is maintained for each project. Assets and liabilities of the fund are similar to unexpended plant funds. Additions include investment income and transfers from other funds. Deductions consist of expenditures for renewals and replacements, some of which may be capitalized as investment in plant (see the last item in this list). Other deductions include investment losses and transfers to other funds.

* *Funds for retirement of indebtedness* represent funds held strictly for the retirement of debt. Assets are similar to those in other funds. Additions to the fund include transfers from other funds, investment income, and governmental appropriations. Deductions include the payment of principal and interest and investment losses.

* *Investment in plant* consists of the physical assets of the college or university and the related debt. The accounting for fixed assets is similar to that for not-for-profit organizations generally. Additions include capital expenditures made from unexpended plant funds and funds for renewals and replacement, from payment of indebtedness made by other funds, and from gifts of fixed assets. Reductions include sales, disposals, and abandonment of plant assets (and depreciation, based on SFAS 93).

Agency Funds. These are used to account for resources held by the college or university as custodian or fiscal agent for others, such as student organizations, faculty organizations, or perhaps even individual students or faculty members. In the financial statements the total of the agency funds may be grouped under "deposits held in custody for others."

Voluntary Health and Welfare Organization Issues

The AICPA industry audit guide, *Audits of Voluntary Health and Welfare Organizations* (1974),[5] defines voluntary health and welfare organizations as entities that "derive their revenue primarily from voluntary contributions from the general public to be used for general or specific purposes connected with health, welfare, or community services." Note that this definition has two parts: the revenue must be derived primarily from voluntary contributions from the general public, and it must be used for purposes connected with health, welfare, or community services. There are many organizations that meet one part of this definition but not the other.

Financial Statements. Three financial reports are usually prepared for health and welfare organizations, presented in such a way that comparisons can be made with prior periods. The *balance sheet* should be subdivided by fund entities. The statement of support, revenue and expenses, and changes in fund balances is the basic operating statement, which should separately report the amount of resource inflows realized from public support and revenue realized from items such as membership dues and investment income. It is also important that expenses be subdivided by services performed and that expenses for support services be separated from those for program services.

The *statement of functional expenses* identifies the various expense items with the related service categories. This statement serves primarily as a supporting schedule for the operating statement. The expense side of this statement should be classified into the following categories:

- Program services – vary widely from one organization to another. Each program should adequately describe its purpose and should include all costs applicable to the program.
- Management and general – should include expenditures made to support the overall objectives of the organization, that is, those not associated with a specific program.
- Fundraising – namely, the costs of soliciting contributions.

Expenses usually will need to be allocated among the various functions. The allocations should be calculated on a reasonable and consistent basis.

Accounting Practices. Accounting practices of health and welfare organizations have varied significantly in the past because the industry had no generally accepted publication defining those procedures. In 1964, the National Health Council published *Standards of Accounting and Financial Reporting for Voluntary Health and Welfare Organizations*. That publication (sometimes referred to as the *Black Book*) was subsequently revised in 1974 to incorporate most of the procedures set out in the 1974 AICPA Audit Guide. Those two publications now constitute the best available descriptions of GAAP for voluntary health and welfare organizations.

Most of the accounting practices now followed by voluntary health and welfare organizations are those applicable to not-for-profit organizations generally, as dis-

---

[5] See note 1.

cussed earlier in this chapter. In particular, the accrual basis of accounting, with capitalization of assets and recognition of depreciation, is followed.

Typical Funds. Health and welfare organizations often receive restricted contributions for the creation of endowment funds, purchase of fixed assets, and other specified uses. Therefore, fund accounting procedures are often used to demonstrate compliance with those externally imposed constraints. These organizations will always have a current unrestricted fund and may have one or more of five restricted-type funds. These include current restricted funds; land, building, and equipment fund; endowment funds; custodian funds; and loan and annuity funds.

The *current unrestricted fund* is used to account for all resources over which the governing board has discretionary control in carrying on the operations of the organization, except for amounts invested in land, buildings, and equipment. It is the operating fund of the organization, obtaining its resources from contributions, bequests, program service fees, dues, investment income, and, in some cases, the sale of goods and services.

The board of trustees of a health and welfare organization may designate current unrestricted fund resources for specific purpose projects, or it may choose to invest some of the resources to earn investment income. These designated assets should not be included with donor-restricted funds. Instead, they are reflected as part of the unrestricted fund balance.

Current restricted funds, as in other organizations, are used to account for resources that are expendable only for externally specified operating purposes.

The *land, building, and equipment fund* is used to account for resources externally designated for acquiring or replacing land, buildings, and equipment. It includes, of course, currently owned land, buildings, and equipment. Liabilities associated with the assets in this fund, such as mortgages payable, are also included. Depreciation is recognized on depreciable assets, and accumulated depreciation is shown as a reduction of the fixed assets in this fund.

Endowment funds are used to account for resources externally restricted for a specific purpose. Revenues earned from investing such funds are expended either for general purposes or as specified by the donor of the endowment.

Custodian funds are used to account for assets received by the organization with the stipulation that they be held or disbursed on instructions from the person or organization providing them.

Other funds include resources restricted to making loans for specified purposes of the organization, and annuity funds representing gifts having the restriction that periodic payments are to be made to the donors or other specified individuals for a specified period of time.

AUDITING CONSIDERATIONS

GAAS applies to examinations made for the purpose of expressing an opinion on the fairness of presentation of financial statements in conformity with GAAP. In addition, the auditor may be engaged to:

1. Review or compile (rather than audit) the financial statements (covered by SSARs); or
2. Issue special reports in connection with:

   a. Financial statements that are prepared in accordance with a comprehensive basis of accounting other than GAAP;
   b. Specified elements, accounts, or items in a financial statement;
   c. Compliance with contractual agreements or regulatory requirements; or
   d. Financial information presented in prescribed forms or schedules that may require a prescribed form of auditor's report.

In these cases, SAS 14 (AU 621) provides guidance on the appropriate wording of the auditor's report. If an organization prepares its financial statements using the cash basis or modified accrual basis, for example, the auditor should refer to SAS 14. (See also Chapter 11.)

If the special report is to be audited, GAAS applies; if unaudited, SSARS apply. The purpose of this section of the chapter is to discuss some auditing considerations peculiar to not-for-profit organizations, many of which will also be applicable to special reports of not-for-profit organizations.

GAO Yellow Book

In 1972, the U.S. General Accounting Office (GAO) first issued *Standards for Audit of Governmental Organizations, Programs, Activities and Functions*, generally called the *Yellow Book*. Although its title does not indicate applicability to not-for-profit organizations, the *Yellow Book's* requirements do apply to all not-for-profit organizations that receive federal financial assistance. In this regard, in mid-1988 the AICPA issued an exposure draft of a proposed SAS, *Compliance Auditing: The Auditor's Responsibility for Testing Compliance with Laws, Regulations, and Contractual Terms Governing Financial Assistance Certain Entities Receive From Government*. This exposure draft explains that the auditor's responsibility for *testing* compliance with laws and regulations in an audit of financial statements performed in accordance with the *Yellow Book* is the *same* as that under GAAS.

The current version of the *Yellow Book*, issued in July, 1988, incorporates all of the AICPA auditing standards and added guidance pertinent to the specific types of organizations. The requirements of the *Yellow Book* are discussed in greater detail in Chapter 31 ("Governmental Units").

Audits of Grants

As a result of concerns about deficiencies in audits, the GAO, at the request of Congressman Jack Brooks, chairman of the Legislation and National Security Subcommittee of the House Committee on Government Operations (the Brooks Committee), undertook a study of the quality of audits of federal grants performed by nonfederal auditors. The study was aimed at determining (1) the extent to which CPAs comply with professional auditing standards during their audits of recipients of federal assistance and (2) the overall quality of their audits.

The first report on the study, issued in November 1985, was based on a study of 46 Regional Inspector General (RIG) offices representing six federal departments and one agency that administered 95% of all federal assistance in 1984.

In general, the GAO found that one out of every five of the audits was not accepted until the auditor (1) performed more audit work, (2) clarified work performed, or (3) provided more support for work performed. A few reports were never accepted because the auditor did not obtain and document sufficient, competent evidential matter to support conclusions and opinions.

In March 1986, the GAO issued its second report. This report concluded that 34% of the governmental audits performed by CPAs did not satisfactorily comply with "Yellow Book" (governmental audit) standards. Based on the sample surveyed, the GAO estimates that 2,200 of 6,420 audits of grants in fiscal year 1984 were unsatisfactory. More than half of the unsatisfactory audits had "severe standards violations." The two biggest problems encountered in reviewing the governmental audits were insufficient audit work in testing compliance with governmental laws and regulations and in evaluating internal controls, including controls over federal expenditures. The findings in this report appear to be consistent with those of the previous study.

As a result, the GAO suggested that the accounting profession take the following actions:

• Strengthen enforcement efforts through positive enforcement programs and referral of substandard audits to disciplinary bodies that should act promptly and decisively;
• Broaden requirements for continuing professional education to include a specified level of governmental accounting and auditing for CPAs performing governmental audits;
• Require governmental audits to be included in peer reviews;
• Place greater emphasis on governmental accounting and auditing in the uniform CPA examination;
• Include governmental audits in CPA firms' internal reviews of their audit quality; and
• Seek expansion of college curricula to include greater attention to the nature and performance of governmental accounting and auditing.

A spokesman for the AICPA, testifying at a hearing of the Brooks Committee in March 1986, presented three recommendations approved by the AICPA board of directors and reviewed some of the AICPA's activities designed to improve audit quality.

In presenting the AICPA's recommendations, the spokesman indicated that they involve requirements that would be implemented through the process of engaging auditors and would involve education, evaluation, and enforcement. Therefore, as a condition of accepting an engagement to audit a recipient of federal financial assistance, auditors should be required to:

• Complete continuing education courses in the unique aspects of auditing and reporting of federal financial assistance programs;
• Agree to have the AICPA report the status and disposition of an investigation triggered by an inspector general; and

- Participate in an approved peer review program, similar to the requirement in the program recently adopted by the Rural Electrification Administration.

Some of the actions taken by the AICPA in the areas of education of auditors, evaluation of audit quality, and enforcement of standards include publication of an audit guide on audits of state and local governmental units; presentation of training programs throughout the country on the Single Audit Act; circulation to the members of the findings of the GAO study; and expansion of the peer review program of the Division for CPA firms to include examination of governmental audits.

Another initiative of the AICPA in response to the GAO findings was the appointment of a Task Force to develop a comprehensive action plan for improving the quality of audits of governmental units and restoring confidence in the audit process in the governmental arena. The Task Force issued its recommendations in February 1987 in *Report of the Task Force on the Quality of Audits of Governmental Units* (AICPA, 1987q).

The Report contains twenty-five recommendations divided into five major subject areas: education, engagement, evaluation, enforcement, and exchange. The recommendations must be implemented by auditors, the governmental unit being audited, or the agency that oversees the audit relationship, either individually, or in concert in some cases.

The more important recommendations include:

- Requiring auditors to complete training programs in relevant continuing professional education areas.
- Creating a mechanism to monitor and evaluate the quality of training programs and instructors.
- Developing a statement of auditing standards that deals with auditing for the reporting on compliance with applicable laws and regulations. (See discussion in preceding section.)
- Improving the AICPA and government staff capability to provide timely technical advice.
- Updating annually the Office of Management and Budget (OMB) publication, *Compliance Supplement for Single Audits of State and Local Governments*.
- Updating the OMB publication, *Questions and Answers—The Single Audit Process*, to reflect the issuance of OMB Circular A-128.
- Requesting that a study of the audit procurement process be undertaken.
- Creating and disseminating a model request for proposal.
- Standardizing agency implementation regulations for the single audit.
- Placing all audit quality activities under the responsibility of knowledgeable officials, such as the Inspector General, state auditor's office, or independent local auditor's office.
- Requiring auditors to participate in a peer review program.
- Improving the system used by the agency that oversees the audit process for referring substandard audits.

Knowledge of the Organization

Beyond the obvious need to be familiar with the operating structure, accounting practices, and the activities of the specific organization, the auditor should be familiar with the industry in which the organization operates. For example, the auditor should be knowledgeable about:

1. Applicable industry audit guides and SOPs.
2. Tax laws that may apply to the organization.
3. Applicable laws or regulations that affect specific activities of the organization, such as regulations relating to grants received from the federal government or other sources.
4. Provisions of documents restricting the use of resources received by the organization.

Internal Controls and Audit Procedures

Internal controls for not-for-profit organizations may not be as strong as those of a business enterprise because:

1. The governing body (e.g., board of trustees) may be fairly large, made up of volunteers who are relatively inactive in the day-to-day affairs of the organization.
2. There may be a limited availability of resources to strengthen controls.
3. The accounting function may receive relatively little attention either because of a lack of staff or because the organization places most of its emphasis upon its operating activities or programs.
4. There may be a small staff, so that a desired segregation of duties is difficult to attain.

For many organizations, the budget is a key element of internal control when it is frequently compared to actual results, and deviations are challenged. The budget is usually prepared by the staff and approved by the governing body.

Specific issues and areas of concern regarding internal controls and audit procedures are discussed in the following sections. (For a complete general discussion of these audit areas, see Chapters 8 and 7, respectively. See also the two audit guides discussed in this chapter for more details regarding not-for-profit organizations.)

Audit Committees. Many organizations have audit committees made up of board members not involved in the day-to-day activities. The committee may meet with the auditors prior to the audit to discuss the audit scope, internal controls, or particular areas or activities that the committee believes should be stressed during the audit. After the audit is complete, the auditors may again meet with the committee to discuss the results of the audit and areas where internal controls or operating procedures may be improved. (See Chapter 6.)

Cash Receipts. Not-for-profit organizations receive cash from many sources — direct mail campaigns, door-to-door solicitation, radio and television solicitation, special events, and contributions from unrelated organizations and groups. It is of great concern, of course, that all reported contributions are in fact received by the organization. Although control over cash contributions can never be absolute, it should be sufficient to reasonably assure the auditor that contributions are not materially misstated.

Investments. The audit of investments for a not-for-profit organization is similar to the audit of investments in a business enterprise. The auditor must be satisfied, through written confirmation or physical examination, that the investments owned by the organization actually exist. Determination of the basis of carrying the investment (cost or market) should be made and the values assigned to each security must be corroborated. Purchases and sales of investments should be verified by examining brokers' advices and other supporting documentation. The auditor should also be satisfied that the transaction was appropriately authorized.

Audit procedures should be employed to test the reasonableness of investment income and gains (or losses). The auditor should also be satisfied that the income has been recorded in the appropriate fund (current operating, restricted, or endowment).

Some organizations have investment pools, in which several funds are joined for investment diversification and administrative ease. The auditor should ascertain whether there are any restrictions (inside or outside the organization) that would prohibit the pooling of investments. The calculation of the allocation of investment income and gains (or losses) should be tested and the appropriateness of the methodology used to allocate the amounts must be ascertained.

Pledges. In many instances pledges made to a not-for-profit organization are not legally binding on the donor. Thus the auditor must evaluate whether the pledgor is likely to pay a pledge recorded as a receivable. Some of the audit procedures that an auditor may wish to employ include the review of the aging and estimated collectibility of the pledges and a review of the allowance for uncollectible pledges. Factors to be considered include the organization's past collection experience, its policy on follow-up and enforcement, and the credit standing of the donors. The auditor may also wish to confirm unpaid pledges.

Fixed Assets. Typical audit procedures employed for business enterprises will also be utilized by auditors of not-for-profit organizations. Specialized audit procedures include the examination of the provisions of gifts and bequests to ascertain whether there are any donor restrictions on the use or disposition of fixed assets. The appropriateness of the valuation of donated fixed assets should be challenged. In some cases, it may be necessary to use the work of a specialist to appraise these assets (see AU 336).

If the organization is undergoing a building fund campaign, the auditor should review and test the transactions of the campaign. Finally, the provisions of any long-term debt agreements should be reviewed to ascertain that there is compliance with all restrictive covenants related to fixed assets.

Grants. An organization may receive grants from outside organizations, such as the federal and state governments or private foundations, requiring a determination that the resources are being used in accordance with the grant provisions. Federal agency grantors publish audit guides that govern the accounting for supported programs. Organizations receiving federal grants should follow the procedures prescribed by the guide as well as those specified in the grant agreement. The auditor should familiarize himself with the provisions of the audit guide of the particular agency (or agencies) involved and consider the agency's reporting requirements in establishing the scope of his examination.

The auditor should be concerned that the grant may be used or accounted for improperly, since the grantor may disallow certain costs and require the organization to make refunds. Many grants, especially from federal or state agencies, specify that the accounting records of the grantee organization are subject to audit by the grantor or a designated party.

The auditor of a not-for-profit organization that receives federal grants should familiarize himself with the Office of Management and Budget's Circular A-110 (discussed earlier) to ensure that the organization is complying with applicable government standards. In addition, when performing an audit of a particular government grant, the auditor should incorporate the audit standards found in the GAO's *Yellow Book* (see Chapter 31).

Some general procedures that the auditor may wish to consider include the confirmation of the grant with the granting agency. Information to be confirmed includes the amount of the grant, funds expended to date, the period of the grant, and specific requirements.

The auditor should satisfy himself as to the adequacy of the organization's cost system and its ability to accumulate costs by each grant.

Restricted Gifts. Auditing considerations for restricted gifts are similar to those for grants. The auditor should read the original documents relating to the gifts, examine evidence supporting the amounts spent and the unexpended balance, and review reports sent to the donors. Because it is sometimes difficult to determine that the funds have been used for their restricted purpose, the auditor in those cases may need to obtain an opinion from the organization's legal counsel. Also, the auditor should be aware that restricted gifts are often refundable to the grantor if not essentially usable for the purpose intended or if the purpose of the gift has been achieved without spending the entire gift.

Membership Dues. In a membership organization, dues usually are paid for a period of one year or longer that may not coincide with the organization's fiscal year. Thus, part of the revenue from dues may be deferred until earned. In addition, some organizations have several membership levels, each requiring different dues amounts. All of this can create a formidable accounting task, particularly if the amount of deferred dues is material.

In smaller organizations, the accounting may be accomplished by using a lapse schedule based on the period over which the dues are to be recorded as revenue. In large organizations, the accounting may be done by computer, and the calculations can be tested by using statistical sampling techniques (see Chapter 9). This typically will require reviewing the documents supporting the amount paid and the membership period and testing either the amount deferred or the amount recorded as revenue.

As mentioned previously, accounts receivable are generally not recorded for membership dues since the member has no obligation to pay. Consequently, if an organization does record a receivable, audit procedures similar to those used for pledges should be employed. Factors to consider include the economic and political environment of the organization, members' ability to pay and willingness to join for another year, and the organization's history of dues collections.

Finally, some organizations allocate dues revenue between fees and contributions. The auditor should ascertain the reasonableness of the methodology used and employ procedures to test the allocations of revenue.

Donated Services. If the value of donated services is recorded in the financial statements, it can alter such key indicators as the ratio of support services (general management expenses) to total contributions. However, the professional pronouncements discussed earlier in this chapter restrict the circumstances in which the value of these donations may be recorded. The auditor will want to review the nature and valuation of the donated services and perhaps confirm significant amounts with donors.

Interfund Borrowings. Borrowings between funds, especially from a restricted fund to an unrestricted fund, can create auditing problems. If, for example, a borrowing violates legal prohibitions against interfund loans, the auditor may need to modify his report. The auditor should verify that all interfund borrowings are disclosed and have been approved by the governing board.

Sometimes the collectibility of interfund loans is in doubt. For example, funds may have been "loaned" to a plant fund that has no ability to repay (except by disposing of the assets in the fund). The auditor might also question why a separate plant fund was created in these circumstances.

Tuition and Other Service Fees. Most of the audit procedures employed for tuition and other service fees will be analytical in nature. Among the auditor's tests might be comparisons of each major revenue account with prior periods and budgets, and with statistical reports including enrollment, occupancy, and meals served. The auditor will also review gross margins of auxiliary units.

Programmatic or Functional Expenses. The audit guides and SOP 78-10 generally require or encourage the presentation of expenses on a functional basis. For this purpose, the organization's cost accounting techniques should be sufficient to satisfy the auditor that the expenses have been reasonably allocated to the proper program. However, the auditor should be aware that definitive guidelines for allocation procedures by not-for-profit organizations are not included in the audit guides or SOP 78-10, and therefore a variety of allocation procedures will be encountered in practice.

Income Taxes. Because not-for-profit organizations may be subject to taxes on certain types of income, receiving tax-exempt status from the IRS does not automatically exempt the organization from state income taxes. The organization must file periodic returns with regulatory authorities, and the organization's returns filed with the IRS are subject to audit. The auditor should be alert to possible tax exposures. Procedures the auditor may wish to consider include:

- Examining both the federal and state income tax exemption letters.
- Ensuring that all applicable returns have been filed.
- Identifying any unrelated business income and the related expense and evaluating the adequacy of the provision for taxes (identifying the unrelated business income can be accomplished by reviewing prior years' returns and reviewing changes in the operations of the organization to ascertain whether the change results in any unrelated business income, and by monitoring changes in the tax laws related to not-for-profit organizations).
- Reviewing the lobbying activities of the organization.
- Reviewing the private foundation status of the organization if it is so classified (the auditor should consider the adequacy of the tax provision and ensure that the organization has complied with the provisions of the tax code).
- If the organization has been classified as a public charity, the auditor should be aware that the organization, on an annual basis, must qualify for this preferred status. (The auditor should review the appropriate computation to be satisfied as to the organization's continued status as a public charity. If it does not qualify, the organization may be treated as a private foundation and thus be subject to certain excise taxes.)

Appendix 32A
INCOME TAX EXEMPTIONS

There are currently 27 Internal Revenue Code classifications of organizations that *may* qualify for exemption from federal income taxation. These classifications, and the types of organizations included, are shown in this appendix. It should be remembered that

1. *Tax-exempt status is not automatic.* For most organizations, a form must be filed with the Internal Revenue Service, and each category has its own set of rules governing how the organization must operate. Also, as stated earlier, federal exempt status does not automatically exempt the organization from state taxes, for which a separate application is ordinarily required.

2. *There are likely to be restrictions on the activities of the organization.* For example, there may be restrictions on (a) providing services at reduced rates to an individual when the reduced rates are not available to others receiving the service, (b) lobbying activities, or (c) participating in political campaigns.

3. *Taxes may be payable by a tax-exempt organization.* Although this may seem contradictory, a tax-exempt organization must pay taxes on income derived from activities not related to the organization's exempt purpose. Based on the type of organization, taxes *may* be payable for such *unrelated business income* as investment income, net advertising revenues, or income derived from debt-financed property.

4. *Most tax-exempt organizations are required to file annual returns with the Internal Revenue Service and state agencies.* For example, returns are required to be filed with the IRS on Form 990 for most organizations, Form 990-C for a farmers' cooperative, Form 990-PF for a private foundation, or Form 990-BL for Black Lung Benefit Trusts. Also, Form 990-T is used for exempt organizations with unrelated business income.

In addition to tax exemption, organizations *may* also qualify for low postal rates or for exemption from paying local sales taxes, and contributions received by the organization *may* be tax deductible by the contributor. However, these factors do indicate the obvious need for competent legal and tax advice by nonprofit organizations, and both accountants and auditors should be aware of these factors.

Federal Tax Exemption Classifications[*]

Code	Section	Type of Organization
501	(c)(1)	Corporation organized under act of Congress as a U.S. instrumentality
501	(c)(2)	Corporation organized for the exclusive purpose of holding property, with its net income turned over to an exempt organization
501	(c)(3)	Corporation and any community chest fund or foundation organized and operated exclusively for religious, charitable, scientific, testing for public safety, literary, or educational purposes; to foster national or international amateur sports competition (if none of its activities involve the providing of athletic facilities or equipment); or for the prevention of cruelty to children or animals.
501	(c)(4)	Civic league, an organization not organized for profit but operated exclusively for the promotion of social welfare, or a local association of employees whose members are employees of a particular municipality
501	(c)(5)	Labor, agricultural, or horticultural organization
501	(c)(6)	Business league, chamber of commerce, real estate board, board of trade, or professional football league
501	(c)(7)	Club organized for pleasure, recreation, and other nonprofit purposes

[*] Reproduced with modification and permission from Chapter 6 of the 1988 U.S. Master Tax Guide, published and copyrighted by Commerce Clearinghouse, Inc., Chicago.

Code	Section	Type of Organization
501	(c)(8)	Fraternal beneficiary society, order, or association
501	(c)(9)	Voluntary employees' beneficiary association
501	(c)(10)	Domestic fraternal society or association
501	(c)(11)	Teachers' retirement fund association
501	(c)(12)	Benevolent life insurance association, mutual ditch or irrigation company, or mutual or cooperative telephone company
501	(c)(13)	Cemetery company
501	(c)(14)	Credit union without capital stock
501	(c)(15)	Insurance company or association other than life
501	(c)(16)	Corporation organized by an association under Code Section 521 for the purpose of financing the ordinary crop operations
501	(c)(17)	A trust or trusts forming part of a nondiscriminatory plan providing for the payment of supplemental unemployment compensation benefits
501	(c)(18)	Nondiscriminatory employee pension trust or trusts created before June 25, 1959
501	(c)(19)	War veterans' organization or post
501	(c)(20)	Organization or trust forming part of a qualified group legal services plan under Code Section 140
501	(c)(21)	A trust established by coal operators for claims of compensation under the black lung acts
501	(d)	Religious or apostolic association if it has a common or community treasury
501	(e)	Cooperative hospital service organization
501	(f)	Cooperative service organization for the collective investment of funds of operating educational organizations
521		Farmers' or fruit growers' cooperative
527		Political action committees
528		Exempt function income of condominium and residential real estate management associations

Appendix 32B

SUMMARY OF NOT-FOR-PROFIT ACCOUNTING PRINCIPLES

Entire books have been devoted to the accounting practices of particular types of non-profit organizations, as well as to the practices of nonprofit organizations as a group. Although such detailed discussion is not possible here, it may be useful to summarize the accounting principles specified in AICPA SOP 78-10, which currently is the most comprehensive document dealing with accounting principles for nonprofit organizations.

This appendix presents the SOP content, contrasted with that of the two other audit guides discussed in this chapter, as well as with the Hospital Audit Guide (AICPA, 1972), discussed in Chapter 30 but also included here because of the similarity of not-for-profit hospital issues with issues affecting not-for-profit organizations generally. The presentation is made in the following categories, and therefore the paragraph references do not always follow consecutively:

1. Financial statements
   a. General
   b. Comparative
   c. Combined

2. Assets
   a. Fixed assets
   b. Pledges
   c. Investments

3. Liabilities

4. Fund accounting
   a. General

   b. Interfund borrowings
   c. Annuity and life income funds
   d. Agency funds
   e. Funds held in trust by others

5. Revenues
   a. General
   b. Donated services, materials, and facilities
   c. Investment income

6. Expenses
   a. General
   b. Fund-raising costs
   c. Grants

SOP 78-10 does not alter the principles stated in the AICPA audit guides for hospitals, colleges and universities, and voluntary health and welfare organizations (or those for state and local governmental units covered in Chapter 31). In many respects the accounting in the guides and the SOP is the same, but in some important respects there are differences—the treatment of investments, fixed assets, and current restricted resources for example—requiring that the earlier guides be consulted for those kinds of organizations.

Many topics in SOP 78-10 are not discussed in the three other audit guides discussed in this chapter; for other topics, SOP 78-10 and one or more of the audit guides differ. While certain variations might be expected because of the nature of the organization, it is possible that the FASB, as it extracts the accounting and principles from the various pronouncements for issuance as Statements of Financial Accounting Standards, will decide the appropriate practice to follow, so that standards will be uniform where there are no substantive differences.

In addition to the above guides and SOP 78-10, other SOPs deal with nongovernmental nonprofit organizations:

• SOP 74-8, *Financial Accounting and Reporting by Colleges and Universities (TP 10,020),*

• SOP 78-1, *Accounting by Hospitals for Certain Marketable Equity Securities (TP 10,160),*

• SOP 85-1, *Financial Reporting by Not-for-Profit Health Care Entities for Tax-Exempt Debt and Certain Funds Whose Use Is Limited* (TP 10,370)

• SOP 87-2, *Accounting for Joint Costs of Informational Materials and Activities of Not-for-Profit Organizations That Include a Fund-Raising Appeal* (TP 10,420).

These should be consulted in their specific topical areas.

SOP 78-10's Accounting Principles and Reporting Practices for Certain Not-For-Profit Organizations *

Topic	SOP 78-10 Par. No.	Key to Audit Guides
Financial Statements-General		
Accrual basis of accounting required for GAAP financial statements.	11	
Use cash basis statements for special purpose; report accordingly.	13	2, 3
Basic financial statements:	16, 25	5, 6, 7
1. Balance sheet		
2. Statement of activity		
3. Statement of changes in financial position		
4. Separate statement of changes in fund balance acceptable.	25	
Flexible format allowed.	18	
Use classified balance sheet if not otherwise indicated.	24	1
Totals of all fund groups is preferable, but not required.	40	5, 6, 7
Comparative Financial Statements		
Comparative statements encouraged, but not required. If information summarized, sufficient disclosure is required.	41	1
Combined Financial Statements		
Combined financial statements required for financially interrelated organizations if *control* and any of the following exist:	44	5, 6, 7
1. Separate entities solicit funds in the name of and with the approval of the reporting organization, and funds are intended for the reporting organization.		
2. Reporting organization transfers some of its resources to another separate entity whose resources are held for the benefit of the reporting organization.		
3. The reporting organization assigns functions to a controlled entity whose funding is primarily derived from sources other than public contributions.		
Disclose basis for combining and describe interrelationship of organization.	44	4
If related organizations hold unrestricted resources that are restricted to the reporting organization, it may be appropriate to present the resources as restricted in combined financial statements.	45	1
If affiliated organizations are not combined, disclosure should be made by the reporting organization of affiliation and relationships.	46	

---

* The numbers in the Key to Audit Guides column represent the following:

1 – This topic is not discussed in any of the three industry audit guides.

This topic is not discussed in the

2 – Hospital Audit Guide
3 – Colleges and Universities Audit Guide
4 – Voluntary Health and Welfare Organizations Audit Guide

This topic is treated differently in the

5 – Hospital Audit Guide
6 – Colleges and Universities Audit Guide
7 – Voluntary Health and Welfare Organizations Audit Guide
8 – SOP 87-2, Joint Costs of Informational Materials

If no reference is made to the audit guides, the guides and SOP 78-10 are substantially in agreement.

Topic	SOP 78-10 Par. No.	Key to Audit Guides
If a religious organization concludes that meaningful financial information would not result from combined financial statements, they need not combine.	48	2, 4
Fixed Assets		
Capitalize purchased fixed assets at cost; donated fixed assets at fair value at date of gift.	105	
Retroactively capitalize fixed assets at historical costs.	105	
Depreciate exhaustible fixed assets over estimated useful lives and disclose depreciation.	107, 110	6
Depreciation need not necessarily be included in basis for grants, allocations, or reimbursements.	109	2, 3
Disclose the cost, or contributed value, of current additions and disposals.	114	1
Collections that have a limited life should be capitalized and amortized over life.	115	1
Pledges		
Record legally enforceable pleddges as assets at their estimated realizable value, and recognize as "support" in period designated by donor and as "deferred support" if period extends past balance sheet date.	64, 65	5, 6, 7
Record pledges and restricted contributions and specifically related costs as deferred if related to succeeding periods.	95	3
Investments		
Investments should be reported as follows:	116	5, 6, 7
1. Marketable debt securities (if ability and intention to hold to maturity) at amortized cost, market value, or lower of amortized cost or market value.		
2. Marketable equity securities and marketable debt securities not expected to be held to maturity at either market value or lower of cost or market.		
3. Other investments at fair value, or lower of cost or fair value.		
4. Investment pools should equitably allocate realized and unrealized gains and losses on investments using market value unit method.		
If investments are carried at other than market, disclosure should be made of market value.	79	2, 3
Recognize adjustments due to unrealized gains or losses of a noncurrent investment account as a direct addition or deduction to fund balance if account is carried at lower of cost or market.	80	6, 7
Reflect adjustments to current investment account due to unrealized gains and losses in the statement of activity if account is carried at lower of cost or market.	80	6
Reflect increases or decreases in investments carried at market in the period in which they occur.	81	3
Record interfund sales or exchanges involving restricted funds at fair value and the difference between the carrying amount and fair value as realized gains and losses.	82	
Disclose in notes a summary of total realized and unrealized gains and losses and income from investments by all funds, except life income and custodial funds.	83	

Topic	SOP 78-10 Par. No.	Key to Audit Guides
Liabilities		
Encumbrances are not liabilities.	12	2, 4
Significant commitments should be disclosed.	12	2, 4
Fund Accounting-General		
Fund basis of accounting acceptable to segregate restricted and unrestricted resources. If not fund basis, disclose restricted resources.	15	5, 6, 7
Board-designated amounts should be included in the unrestricted fund balance. Total of all unrestricted fund balances required.	20	
Plant fund may be reported separately or combined with *either* unrestricted or restricted fund as appropriate.	22	5, 6, 7
Current restricted resources and resources restricted for acquisition of fixed assets should be reported as "deferred revenue" until the restrictions are met.	21	5, 6, 7
Reflect other restricted resources (endowments) separately in fund balance. If significant, disclose nature of restriction on fund balances and deferred revenues.	22	
Changes in fund balance should include	25	4, 6
1. Excess or deficiency of revenue and support over expenses after capital additions.		
2. Adjustments in carrying amounts of noncurrent marketable securities and other investments.		
3. Interfund transfers.		
Noncurrent restricted gifts, grants, and bequests (including restricted investment income and gains and losses on investments) to endowment, plant, and loan funds should be recorded as "capital additions" or "nonexpendable additions."	28, 29	5, 6, 7
Interfund Borrowings		
Interfund transfers should be considered permanent, recorded as transfers, and disclosed when evident that repayment is not likely.	118	4,5
Disclose material interfund borrowings when restricted funds have been loaned or if there is a liquidity problem.	119	2,4
Interfund borrowings may be legally prohibited.	118	2,4
Annuity and Life Income Funds		
Record annuity gifts as	121	2,6,7
1. Asset — not stated.		
2. Liability — present value of actuarially determined liability at date of gift.		
3. Difference — if expendable, support in year of gift: if not expendable, deferred revenue.		
The principal of life income gifts should be recorded as deferred support in the balance sheet when received.	121	4,5,6
Record annuity or life income gifts as support or capital additions when specified terms are met.	121	4,5,6
Agency Funds		
Separate or combined disclosure of agency funds.	123	4,5,6

Topic	SOP 78-10 Par. No.	Key to Audit Guides
Funds Held in Trust by Others		
Funds held in trust by others, not controlled by the organization, and for which the organization is not the remainderman, should not be included in the balance sheet even though income is derived from the funds. Disclosure should be made of the funds and any significant income derived from them.	122	4,6
Revenue-General		
Statement of activity should have an "excess (deficiency) of revenues and support over expenses" line. If presenting "capital additions," use two "excess" lines, one before and one after.	30	5,6,7
Record unrestricted gifts, grants, and bequests in the statement of activity above "excess" line before capital additions.	63	5,6,7
Separate disclosure not necessary of contributions to organizations by governing board members, officers, or employees if contributor receives no reciprocal economic benefit.	49	1
Current restricted gifts, grants, bequests, and other income should be recognized based on the following concepts:	59	
1. Economic events.		
2. Donor restrictions are complied with when organization incurs an expense in the manner specified in donative instrument.		
3. Unexpended restricted funds should be reported in a manner reflecting restrictions.		
Current restricted gifts, grants, bequests, and other income should be accounted for as revenue and support to the extent that expenses have been incurred for donor-specified purpose. Present "deferred revenue or support" in the balance sheet, outside the fund balance section, until restrictions are met.	62	5,6,7
Recognize subscriptions and revenues from services and sales of goods in period provided.	84	
Recognize membership dues in period to which dues relate.	84	1
Recognize nonrefundable initiation and life membership dues as revenue in period it is receivable, *if* future fees will cover future services. If not, amortize fees to future periods based on average membership duration, life expectancy or other appropriate method.	84	1
Donated Services, Material, and Facilities		
Donated or contributed services should not be recorded as contribution and expense unless	63	
1. The services are a significant, integral part of the organization that would otherwise be performed by salaried personnel.		
2. The organization controls and influences duties of the service donors.		
3. There is a clearly measurable basis for the recorded amount.		
4. The services are not intended principally for the benefit of members.		
Disclosure is required of methods used in valuing, recording, and reporting donated services and of those donated services not recorded or reported.	70	5
Record, at fair value, only significant donated materials and facilities that are clearly measurable and that are not passed on to another group.	71	

Topic	SOP 78-10 Par. No.	Key to Audit Guides
Investment Income		
Report investment income as follows:		
1. Unrestricted – revenue when earned.	72	
2. Restricted – deferred in balance sheet.	73	5,6,7
3. Endowment – if required to be added to principal, capital addition; if expendable, deferred amounts.	73	5,6,7
Report investment gains and losses as follows:		
1. Unrestricted and current restricted – in statement of activity before "capital additions."	72	5,6,7
2. Endowments – as "capital additions" or "deductions" if required to be added to principal; if utilized, record as transfer from endowments to other.	73,76	5,6,7
3. Other restricted – as deferred amounts in balance sheet.	72	5,6,7
If endowment gains or losses are transferred to a restricted fund to which investment income is reported as deferred revenue, gain should be transferred to deferred revenue.	76	5,6,7
Account for net gains on investments in quasi-endowment funds the same as for current funds.	76	2,4,6
Expenses-General		
A summary of the cost of providing services on a functional basis in the statement of activity is required when the public contributes; if services are not presented on functional basis, notes should describe programs.	85	
Functional classification should include program services describing activities and supporting services.	86	2,3
Costs should be presented separately for each significant program and supporting activity.	87	
Local organizations that are collecting agents for a state or national organization should report the remittance as a deduction from support and revenue; otherwise, such remittances are program expenses.	90	2,3
Costs pertaining to various functions should be allocated if applicable.	98	2
Interperiod allocation of taxes should be made if timing differences exist between the income base for tax and financial reporting purposes.	103	3,4
Fund-Raising Costs		
Fund-raising costs, including cost of merchandise sold, should be disclosed; if paid directly by a contributor, report as support and expense.	92	2,5
Special fund-raising events should be reported net of direct benefit costs, with disclosure of costs.	93	3,5
Total of all fund-raising activities should be disclosed; fund-raising costs should be expensed when incurred.	94	6
Joint costs of informational materials or activites that include a fund-raising appeal should be allocated between fund raising and the appropriate program or management function only if it can be demonstrated that a bona fide program or management and general function has been conducted in conjunction with the fund-raising appeal.	97	8
Grants		
Costs incurred in solicitation of grants from foundations or governments and cost of membership development should be shown in separate categories of supporting expense.	96	4,6

Topic	SOP 78-10 Par. No.	Key to Audit Guides
Grants made to others should be recorded as expenses and liabilities when recipient is entitled to it.	101	1
Grants subject to periodic renewal should be recorded when renewed.	102	1
If the grantor reserves the right to revoke the grant regardless of the performance of the grantee, unpaid grants should not be recorded as an expense and liability.	102	1

Appendix 32C   The African-American Institute, Excerpted Financial Statements

THE AFRICAN-AMERICAN INSTITUTE

BALANCE SHEETS

September 30, 1987 with Comparative Totals for 1986

| | Operating funds | | | | Fixed asset fund | Total all funds | |
| | Unrestricted | | | Restricted funds | | 1987 | 1986 |
	General fund	Board designated investment fund	Total unrestricted				
ASSETS							
Cash	$348,973	$ 174,269	$ 523,242	$302,252	$ —	$ 825,494	$1,123,274
Investments (Notes 1 and 2)	—	9,541,906	9,541,906	—	—	9,541,906	5,582,493
Accounts receivable							
U.S. government agencies	—	—	—	134,614	—	134,614	—
Other (net of allowance for uncollectible amounts of $5,000 in 1987 and 1986	94,236	—	94,236	—	—	94,236	173,442
Prepaid expenses	71,762	—	71,762	—	—	71,762	42,014
Fixed assets, net (Notes 1 and 3)	—	—	—	—	165,793	165,793	104,777
TOTAL ASSETS	$514,971	$9,716,175	$10,231,146	$436,866	$165,793	$10,833,805	$7,026,000
LIABILITIES AND FUND BALANCES							
Accounts payable and accrued expenses	$344,217	$ —	$ 344,217	$ —	$ 77,161	$ 421,378	$ 240,759
Accrued vacation payable	158,493	—	158,493	—	—	158,493	182,664
Deferred revenue and support (Note 1)							
U.S. government agencies	—	—	—	68,564	—	68,564	574,856
Nongovernmental contributions	—	—	—	368,302	—	368,302	236,858
TOTAL LIABILITES	502,710	—	502,710	436,866	77,161	1,016,737	1,235,137
Commitments and contingencies (Notes 4, 6, and 7)							
Fund Balances	12,261	9,716,175	9,728,436	—	88,632	9,817,068	5,790,863
TOTAL LIABILITES AND FUND BALANCES	$514,971	$9,716,175	$10,231,146	$436,866	$165,793	$10,833,805	$7,026,000

THE AFRICAN-AMERICAN INSTITUTE

STATEMENT OF SUPPORT, REVENUE AND EXPENSES AND CHANGES IN FUND BALANCES

Year Ended September 30, 1987 with Comparative Totals for Year Ended September 30, 1986

	Operating funds				Fixed asset fund	Total all funds	
	Unrestricted			Restricted funds		1987	1986
	General fund	Board designated investment fund	Total unrestricted				
SUPPORT AND REVENUE							
Support							
United States Government agencies (including joint venture) (Note 4)	$ —	$ —	$ —	$14,665,447	$ —	$14,665,447	$14,977,275
Individual, corporate and foundation contributions	153,095	—	153,095	683,034	—	836,129	652,971
Special events (net of expenses of $97,413 in 1987 and $79,573 in 1986)	111,051	—	111,051	—	—	111,051	139,754
	264,146	—	264,146	15,348,481	—	15,612,627	15,770,000
Revenue							
Programs	—	—	—	185,379	—	185,379	207,499
Investment income	14,680	430,240	444,920	—	—	444,920	387,985
Gain on sale and reinvestment of securities	—	4,211,983	4,211,983	—	—	4,211,983	604,194
Net unrealized investment losses	—	(91,839)	(91,839)	—	—	(91,839)	—
Miscellaneous income	12,025	—	12,025	—	—	12,025	9,914
Total revenue	26,705	4,550,384	4,577,089	185,379	—	4,762,468	1,209,592
Total support and revenue	290,851	4,550,384	4,841,235	15,533,860	—	20,375,095	16,979,592
Less net adjustments and disallowances of United States Government agencies (Note 4)	—	—	—	(737)	—	(737)	(3,684)
NET SUPPORT AND REVENUE	290,851	4,550,384	4,841,235	15,533,123	—	20,374,358	16,975,908

EXPENSES						
Program services						
Assisting African development	36,563	36,563	11,495,970	—	11,532,533	10,758,192
Refugee training and assistance	—	—	1,197,917	—	1,197,917	1,028,726
Strengthening African-American relations	231,702	231,702	1,635,914	—	1,867,616	2,961,635
Total program services	268,265	268,265	14,329,801	—	14,598,066	14,748,553
Supporting services						
Management and general	475,698	475,698	1,204,059	44,948	1,724,705	1,673,281
Fund raising	25,382	25,382	—	—	25,384	56,857
Total supporting services	501,080	501,080	1,204,059	44,948	1,750,087	1,730,138
TOTAL EXPENSES	769,345	769,345	15,533,860	44,948	16,348,153	16,478,691
EXCESS (DEFICIENCY) OF SUPPORT AND REVENUE OVER EXPENSES	(478,494)	4,071,890	(737)	(44,948)	4,026,205	497,217
FUND BALANCES (DEFICIT), beginning of year	(71,105)	5,686,086	—	104,777	5,790,863	5,293,646
TRANSFERS						
For the purchase of fixed assets	(28,803)	(28,803)	—	28,803	—	—
Income transferred from Investment Fund to Operating Fund (Note 5)	591,400	—	—	—	—	—
To cover audit disallowances by United States Government agencies (Note 4)	(737)	(737)	737	—	—	—
FUND BALANCES, end of year	$12,261	$9,728,436	$ —	$ 88,632	$ 9,817,068	$ 5,790,863

THE AFRICAN-AMERICAN INSTITUTE
STATEMENT OF FUNCTIONAL EXPENDITURES
Year Ended September 30, 1987 with Comparative Totals for Year Ended September 30, 1986

	Program services				Supporting services			Total expenditures	
	Assisting African development	Refugee training and assistance	Strengthening African-American relations	Total	Management and general	Fund raising	Total	1987	1986
PROGRAM COSTS									
Human resources development	$ 9,464,526	$ 636,466	$ 41,450	$10,142,442	$ —	$ —	$ —	$10,142,442	$ 9,806,470
Rural development	25,434			25,434				25,434	459
International visitor			983,469	983,469				963,469	1,723,966
Conferences, information activities			210,388	210,388				210,388	137,634
Research, publications	3,343	2,029	193,178	198,550				198,550	196,233
Exhibitions, cultural activities	1,176		21,478	22,654				22,654	52,208
TOTAL PROGRAM COSTS	9,494,479	638,495	1,449,963	11,582,937				11,582,937	11,916,970
OTHER INSTITUTE EXPENSES									
Salaries and related benefits	1,304,573	471,307	323,316	2,099,196	694,471	22,666	717,137	2,816,333	2,926,702
Professional fees and other outside services	71,893			71,893	101,774		101,774	173,667	108,686
Supplies and materials	20,428	7,547	2,978	30,953	20,640	82	20,722	51,675	69,425
Duplication and printing	14,860	19,647	2,922	37,429	6,266	82	6,348	43,777	44,001
Telephone and cablegrams	167,581	32,388	23,109	223,078	17,854	372	18,226	241,304	279,563
Postage and shipping	36,613	12,981	9,245	58,839	6,758	515	7,273	66,112	75,154
Occupancy	108,912			108,912	595,033		595,033	703,945	678,720
Rental and maintenance of equipment	94,614			94,614	26,198		26,198	120,812	50,767
Travel	217,883	15,552	55,986	289,421	17,444	10	17,454	306,875	193,877
Board and staff meetings					19,482		19,482	19,482	21,204
Membership and subscriptions			97	97	8,035	1,655	9,690	9,787	8,630
Insurance	500			500	44,348		44,348	44,848	16,456
Other	197			197	121,454		121,454	121,651	40,835
	2,038,054	559,422	417,653	3,015,129	1,679,757	25,382	1,705,139	4,720,268	4,514,020
Total expenses before depreciation and amortization	11,532,533	1,197,917	1,867,616	14,598,066	1,679,757	25,382	1,705,139	16,303,205	16,430,990
Depreciation and amortization					44,948		44,948	44,948	47,701
TOTAL EXPENDITURES	$11,532,533	$1,197,917	$1,867,616	$14,598,066	$1,724,705	$25,382	$1,750,087	$16,348,153	$16,478,691

(Notes omitted)
Reprinted with permission

33

Telecommunications, Utilities, and Transportation

REGULATORY ENVIRONMENT OVERVIEW

This chapter covers nonfinancial regulated industries, namely telecommunications, electric and gas utilities, gas pipelines, and various transportation businesses. Space limitations prevent discussing certain businesses in these categories such as water and sewer utilities, and maritime and specialized carriers.

It must be acknowledged that, in a sense, virtually every business is regulated in some fashion, and it is mostly a matter of degree. For example, all publicly held companies, and the accounting firms that serve them, are subject to SEC regulation in a very pervasive way. Other actively regulated industries are financial institutions, covered in Section V of the *Handbook*; oil and gas production, discussed in Chapter 34; and health care, discussed in Chapter 30.

In recent years, extensive deregulation of certain industries has occurred. For example, under the Airline Deregulation Act of 1978, the function of the Civil Aeronautics Board (CAB) was changed; although the CAB continues to exercise strong control over airline safety standards, its former mission restricting competition is reduced. This has resulted in greater ease of market entry and exit and in setting fares, and less control over assuring service to smaller communities. Although the regulatory atmosphere has diminished over time, many industries still are affected to a significant degree by federal, state, and local regulatory processes.

Most regulation is justified on one of two grounds: to alleviate the effects of market failure or to meet social policy objectives. Natural monopoly, destructive competition, and inadequate information in the marketplace are examples of market failure. Providing airline, bus, or public utility services to small communities is a typical social policy objective.

To carry out their mission, many regulatory agencies have been given the authority to require specific accounting or financial reporting practices by the industries they regulate.

TELECOMMUNICATIONS

Characteristics and Environment

Evolution From Monopoly Status. Until recently, the U.S. telecommunications industry was relatively monolithic. A small number of carriers were given monopoly franchises to complete the extension of affordable telephone service throughout the country, with regulation substituting for competition to assure that rates and service quality were satisfactory. American Telephone & Telegraph Company (AT&T) and its Bell Operating Companies (BOCs) provided a limited range of services within major metropolitan areas and maintained the national intercity network. AT&T's Western Electric unit manufactured most of the equipment used in the network and on customer premises. "Independent" telephone companies provided service in many small towns and rural areas.

The telecommunications industry today is characterized by an array of services, equipment, and vendors and by a more varied and lenient regulatory environment. Distinctions among services, equipment, and user applications have been removed to a large extent, resulting in the "information age" as contrasted with the traditional telecommunications services of two decades ago. The force behind this change is a virtual explosion in new technology. Innovations such as microwave, satellites, digitalization, and optical fiber have made multiple networks economically feasible and greatly expanded the range of potential services and products. Integrated services digital network (ISDN) technology is being introduced that permits one wire to carry multiple services such as data transmission, video, and facsimile in addition to voice.

Telecommunications users—especially large industrial, commercial, and governmental customers—want the freedom to choose products and services responsive to their needs. Consequently, public policy has shifted away from the preference for a single public utility provider and has increasingly sought to foster a multivendor, competitive marketplace.

Multijurisdictional regulation. Telecommunications is regulated at both the federal and state levels. The Federal Communications Commission (FCC) has jurisdiction over interstate and international telecommunications, as specified in the Communications Act of 1934 and the Communications Satellite Act of 1962, while state public utility commissions (PUCs) regulate the intrastate sphere.

The regulatory framework is complicated by several factors:

1. The dividing line between the federal and state jurisdictions is a source of continuing debate.
2. The confluence of telecommunications and computer technology has made statutory terms such as "telecommunications" and "telephone and telegraph service" obsolete. Generally regulators have retained authority over "basic" telecommunications (i.e., the simple transmission of voice or data signals through public networks), while suspending or avoiding regulation of "enhanced" or "information" services that involve the computerized manipulation, storage, or transformation of the information being transported (e.g., electronic mail, voicemail, videotex).
3. Different degrees of regulation have been applied to different activities and providers, typically keyed to the amount of competition in particular markets.

In addition to regulatory rules, this industry is heavily influenced by antitrust policy. The U.S. Department of Justice and the federal courts have become prominent players since the settlement of the Department's antitrust suit against AT&T in 1982. The Modification of Final Judgment (MFJ) entered in that case required AT&T to divest its local exchange operations and imposed various constraints on the severed BOCs. For example, they are prohibited from providing long distance or enhanced services and from manufacturing telecommunications equipment. The Justice Department and the U.S. District Court for the District of Columbia continue to administer these MFJ provisions. In some areas, antitrust law enforcement conflicts with regulatory policy.

Although the major changes associated with deregulation and divestiture are past, the new rules are by no means completely settled. Regulatory jurisdiction and policy continues to change:

1. A number of states have enacted new statutes that call for more streamlined and flexible regulatory procedures; others have delegated to their PUCs the power to relax or remove regulatory restrictions when specified conditions are met.
2. In some states, regulatory policies remain on the books but their enforcement has been modified by the implementation of a "moratorium" or "social contract" in which the PUC and telephone companies (telcos) agree to freeze local rates in exchange for allowing telcos to enter certain markets on an unregulated basis.
3. Both the states and the FCC are considering whether to modify or abandon the traditional focus on rates of return in favor of regulating prices.

4. The MFJ was liberalized by the District Court in 1987 and is scheduled for further reviews at three-year intervals.

Proliferation of unregulated providers. Technological innovations have made it possible to offer existing products and services more cheaply and with a greater range of features and functions. They have also led to the creation of entirely new offerings. Public policy has been to encourage the entry of numerous vendors into the marketplace, to develop and refine new technological applications through the competitive process. In some cases new entrants vie with AT&T, the BOCs, and other regulated traditional providers by selling facilities and services that "bypass" the traditional networks. In other instances, the traditional providers have been excluded from the markets and the unregulated entities have the field to themselves.

For example, as alternate long distance networks became feasible, other common carriers gained entry to the intercity markets formerly reserved to AT&T. In the equipment area, the FCC repealed the traditional rules under which customers leased their phone sets, switchboards, and wiring from telcos; today an array of such equipment is available not only from unregulated AT&T and telco subsidiaries but also from a variety of competing "interconnect" contractors and retail outlets. In the field of computer-related telecommunications, scores of new vendors have moved into businesses such as protocol conversion, packet switching, electronic mail, and electronic publishing.

Diversification. Seeing their monopoly markets invaded by newcomers and barred from entering some of the new electronic information service businesses, the traditional carriers have complained that they are being asked to compete with one hand tied behind their backs. Rivals contend that traditional carriers should be constrained so that new competitive ventures are not cross-subsidized with profits from regulated activities and control of essential network facilities (e.g., by giving their affiliates preferential access to information about network changes and customer usage patterns) is not abused. Regulators, courts, and legislators have responded by fashioning new regulatory policies that give traditional carriers some freedom to diversify while subjecting them to controls that address the concerns about unfair competition.

Although there is continuing controversy over the need for and effectiveness of the safeguards, the new regulatory flexibility has enabled the traditional carriers to embark upon a wide variety of new endeavors that include cellular radio, paging, equipment sales, computer retailing, real estate development, printing and publishing, financial services, and international ventures. As this diversification has progressed, AT&T, the BOCs, and the independent telcos have become varied organizations in which unregulated or lightly regulated enterprises are increasingly prominent alongside their regulated core business.

Economic Conditions. The introduction of widespread competition and deregulation during the 1980s has occurred in a relatively benign economic setting. Should the picture change, the viability of many telecommunications companies could become decidedly less assured and policymakers could come under very strong pressure to reexamine the assumption that reliance on free markets is beneficial for this industry. Nevertheless, telecommunications seems better positioned than most sectors. Accordingly, the prospect is for a continuation of the recent trend toward a more varied business environment in which a bigger role is played by unregulated or lightly regulated ventures.

Types of Enterprises

Traditional telecommunications carriers. The traditional carriers include AT&T, the BOCs, independent telcos, and several others. Virtually all of the major companies have diversified into a variety of businesses. Most of these activities are not regulated directly although both the FCC and the PUCs scrutinize the relationships and transactions between the other units and the regulated operations.

American Telephone & Telegraph remains the largest of the traditional carriers. Although facing strong competition, it is still the leading long distance provider and telecommunications equipment vendor. It has moved into computers and office equipment and is active in numerous foreign markets. AT&T has negotiated a number of joint ventures and other cooperative arrangements both here and abroad. All of AT&T's communications-related activities — services, manufacturing, and equipment sales — have been merged into a single entity for reporting purposes, although intrastate toll services are provided through a different subsidiary for each state.

The 22 *Bell operating companies* are now owned by the seven Bell regional holding companies: Ameritech, Bell Atlantic, BellSouth, NYNEX, Pacific Telesis, Southwestern Bell, and US West. In addition to the BOCs, each holding company typically has a variety of subsidiary companies engaged in unregulated businesses.

The largest *independent telephone companies*, such as General Telephone & Electronics (GTE), Continental Telecom (Contel), and Centel, have similar corporate profiles. There are another 1,400 smaller independent telephone companies, most of which do not operate with a holding company parent.

Western Union is another major traditional carrier. Due to technological and regulatory changes affecting its basic telegraph and telex businesses, Western Union has experienced severe financial difficulties that have necessitated cutbacks, asset sales, and restructuring.

Communications Satellite Corporation (Comsat) is the company Congress created in 1962 to be the sole U.S. marketing agent for the International Telecommunications Satellite Organization (Intelsat) and a similar entity that furnishes satellite capacity for maritime navigation services. Consistent with the general deregulatory trend in public policy, Comsat's protected status has been diminished and it faces growing competition. Comsat has diversified into various unregulated fields in response to these developments.

Radiotelephone common carriers (RCCs) is the other major form of traditional carrier. RCCs provide conventional mobile radio telephone service. Many have diversified into businesses such as paging and cellular radio.

Nontraditional providers. The industry that previously consisted of the Bell System and independent telcos is now populated by thousands of diverse entities. None of these is subject to the degree of regulation typical of local exchange service, and many are not regulated at all.

More than 400 *other common carriers* now compete with AT&T in the long-distance business. Designated as OCCs by the FCC, these include both facilities-based carriers which have their own networks, and resellers who lease capacity in bulk from AT&T or others and then resell it to their customers. Even facilities-based carriers typically augment their networks by purchasing and reselling capacity on the ubiquitous AT&T network.

MCI, US Sprint, and some other OCCs compete with AT&T nationally for both residential and business customers, but many others are more specialized, attempting to establish themselves as niche suppliers serving specific regions or segments of the commercial and governmental markets. Others are "carriers' carriers" primarily leasing capacity on their networks to fellow OCCs. Some specialize in a particular technology, such as satellite or optical fiber transmission, while others have assembled networks offering a combination.

OCCs are required to obtain radio licenses and construction permits from the FCC but otherwise federal regulation of this industry segment has been suspended; and about half the states have reduced or eliminated their regulation of interexchange services.

The FCC's regulation of telco interstate access charges and AT&T's toll rates does exert a significant indirect influence upon the OCCs. Until the early 1980s, OCCs enjoyed a substantial discount compared to AT&T in the access charges they paid local telcos for originating and terminating long distance traffic. Now that the MFJ and FCC regulations require telcos to furnish OCCs with network access that is equal to AT&T's, the FCC has been restructuring access tariffs so that telcos charge AT&T less and the OCCs more. The resulting drop in AT&T's rates and corresponding rise in OCC access costs has severely tested the OCCs, causing many to change business strategies, cut back expenditures, combine, or cease operations.

Interconnect contractors vendors provide equipment ranging from discrete terminals or switches to entire networks through direct sale or under lease contracts, frequently through third party lessors. Many also help customers design, install, and maintain facilities.

The interconnect industry flourished when traditional carriers provided customer premises equipment (CPE) under tariff. Interconnects took advantage of price subsidies and tariff inflexibility to underprice the regulated carriers and, in many instances, were able to respond more effectively to user needs through superior equipment and more flexible installation practices. However, when the FCC detariffed CPE and the MFJ permitted BOCs to provide CPE, these advantages disappeared. Fierce competition now characterizes the interconnect industry, with shrinking profit margins and numerous business failures. In a number of cases, manufacturers have acquired or established distribution networks, cutting off some vendors from access to certain lines of equipment.

Value-added networks (VANs) facilitate telecommunications linkups among computers by providing the protocol conversion needed to allow incompatible machines to communicate and the packet switching that allows multiple transmissions on a single circuit.

Mobile telephone services include conventional radio telephone service, cellular radio, and paging. Numerous independent vendors have entered this market to offer mobile services in competition with those furnished by telcos and RCCs. When cellular technology emerged in the early 1980s, the FCC elected to award two licenses in each market: a "wireline" franchise to the local telcos, and a "nonwireline" franchise going to someone other than the utility. Hundreds of large and small entities entered the competition for the nonwireline cellular franchises, and numerous partnerships were formed to decide the award through settlement rather than continued competition. Cellular franchises have also been traded among companies seeking to consolidate their holdings. Once it was clarified that a telephone company could hold cellular franchises outside its own service territory, several of the Bell regional companies purchased nonwireline franchises in a number of major metropolitan markets.

The intense interest in cellular franchises illustrates the enthusiasm over the prospects for mobile services generally. As is true of many other segments of the telecommunications industry, however, the near-term picture is dominated by heavy capital investments, high marketing expenses, and financial turmoil among providers who lack staying power.

Customer-owned, coin-operated telephone (COCOT) providers have sprung up in competition with telcos to provide *public telephone* service in airports, restaurants, truck stops, parking garages, and so forth. In some cases the phone belongs to the owner of the premises. Many companies have entered the business of owning multiple payphones, paying each location owner a share of the revenues to use the premises. Still others develop "turnkey" payphone businesses in various cities, offering investors a ready-made package of equipment and locations and various management services as well. Most states have now taken advantage of a 1984 ruling that said PUCs could permit private payphones; typically the service is tariffed but not otherwise regulated. The situation varies from state to state and there will probably be frequent revisiting of regulatory policies relating to COCOTs.

Accounting Considerations

Impact of Environmental Changes. Virtually all services provided by regulated entities (except for basic services required by residences and small businesses) are subject to some degree of competition, necessitating precise information on the costs and revenue streams for specific products, lines of business, and markets. Likewise, there is a need to address the accounting and disclosure issues that accompany situations such as obsolescence caused by technological changes, new marketing strategies, and competition.

This presents special issues for traditional carriers. Despite the fact that many of their core markets are contested and an increasing share of their business is in new, unregulated ventures, regulatory accounting remains significant to their financial management. Federal and state regulators continue to prescribe charts of accounts, accounting policies, and reporting requirements for those areas of their business that remain tariffed. The orientation of regulatory accounting is unresponsive to the new competitive business environment because

1. Costs and revenues are accounted for according to a monopoly perception of services.
2. Cost identification is by broad pools and aggregates not necessarily useful for management decision-making in competitive markets.
3. The evolution of accounting policies and procedures is under the control of a variety of regulatory agencies, which tends to retard the pace of change due to their differing approaches and protracted proceedings.

4. Accounting improvements generally lag well behind the evolution of products and services in the marketplace.
5. Adapting regulatory accounting systems to measure the profitability of specific services is very difficult and requires significant extra resources.

In the traditional, regulated environment, accounting was comparatively simple and static; carriers were primarily concerned with applying established, familiar procedures prescribed by regulatory agencies. Compliance was the principal objective and there was minimal need for management information beyond that required for regulatory purposes. Now that the telecommunications field is more dynamic, diverse, and demanding, there is a corresponding need for more sophisticated accounting expertise.

Conflicting governmental directives. Because a variety of governmental jurisdictions and agencies are involved in making and interpreting public policy concerning the telecommunications industry, there are instances of conflict and inconsistency involving accounting and financial management issues. For example, the FCC recently attempted to preempt state jurisdiction over depreciation policy, since a number of states resisted federal rules that increased depreciation expense and therefore rates. The FCC approach involves the use of equal-life-group and remaining-life procedures for determining depreciation rates and amortization of the embedded investment in station connection costs. In 1986, the U.S. Supreme Court ruled in favor of states protesting the FCC's assertion of authority. In some states this means switches and other facilities are now subject to two different sets of rules on depreciation accounting; FCC regulations apply to the portion allocated to the interstate jurisdiction while PUC rules apply to the portion deemed intrastate.

Similarly, the FCC is prepared to permit BOCs to furnish enhanced services if certain cost accounting and competitive safeguards are observed, whereas the District Court administering the MFJ views the FCC-prescribed safeguards as ineffectual and has only grudgingly relaxed the MFJ ban that prohibits the companies from providing such services.

Uniform System of Accounts. The FCC prescribes a Uniform System of Accounts (USOA) and Financial Reporting Requirements for Telephone Companies. Although states have the power to prescribe accounting independent from that of the FCC, in practice the large majority closely follow FCC requirements.

Effective January 1, 1988, all carriers providing interstate services under FCC regulation were required to account for the interstate activities in conformity with a new USOA (47 C.F.R. § 32). This replaces the system of accounts that had been in effect since 1934. In developing the new USOA, the FCC substantially reorganized the chart of accounts, disaggregated several categories of accounts, and provided for the incorporation of GAAP. Basic characteristics of the new USOA are as follows:

1. Reorientation of the structure of the chart of accounts to be more consistent with that used by unregulated firms.
2. Asset accounts numbered and listed in an order based on decreasing liquidity rather than having plant accounts listed first.

3. Liabilities oriented in the same manner as assets.
4. An account numbering scheme that generally aligns specific expenses and related assets.

Account organization is functional for plant, expenses, and revenue accounting:

1. Plant accounts are classified according to function performed in providing services (e.g., switching, transmission).
2. Expense accounts supporting assets such as computers, buildings, and motor vehicles contain a matrix to collect costs by type, such as depreciation, labor, or engineering.
3. Overheads are grouped together (e.g., marketing, engineering, accounting).
4. Revenues are classified by types of services rendered (e.g., interstate toll, private line, local service).
5. Plant accounts are disaggregated by type of technology as part of the accounts rather than in subsidiary records.

Revisions in the USOA were designed to update regulatory accounting to that appropriate for today. However, in the 10 years since the revision began, evolution in telecommunications technology and markets has been so significant that the industry technology remains well ahead of the rules.

The accounting requirements stipulate the basis for reporting, minimum levels of aggregation, and procedures to be followed by subject carriers; however, the carriers are free to follow internally determined procedures and practices, disaggregate the accounts either as subaccounts or memo records, or otherwise adopt individualized approaches, provided the minimums set forth in the new USOA are satisfied.

GAAP Conformity. Because of the slow administrative process in revising systems of accounts, both the FCC and the industry have perceived the value of developing accounting procedures on a more timely basis in view of the rapid evolution of industry competition. In the FCC's view, the use of GAAP rather than RAP (Regulatory Accounting Practices) would more accurately portray current operations, thus conforming with the needs of the investment community as well as regulators. As a result, GAAP has been adopted as the basis for the FCC's prescribed accounting.

Changes in accounting brought about by GAAP pronouncements can be implemented by the carriers after giving notice to the FCC, provided the FCC does not prohibit the change. This provides the FCC with oversight without the cumbersome procedures inherent in the rule-making required previously. State responses to carriers' adoption of GAAP are likely to vary considerably, ranging from close conformity with FCC policy to the development of unique requirements by individual states.

Cost Allocations and Cost Accounting. Two inherent characteristics of traditional telecommunications services bear significantly on accounting for cost of services. First, most services are not dependent on specific types of technology used to provide the services. The actual physical media used to make a long distance call may be a combination of several different types. Furthermore, calls between the two same numbers may well involve routes that are entirely different from one call to the next. Second, price regulation practiced by the states and FCC starts with the profit margins to be allowed as a percentage of investment and works backward to assign other costs to specific types of services. These costs (and profit margins) are assigned to services and/or jurisdictions based largely on regulatory determinations, which may or may not correspond to the actual costs of providing the services. This occurs because of the difficulty of identifying many costs for specific services and the long PUC tradition of subsidizing specific services.

Although state procedures vary considerably, the procedures followed by the FCC provide a good model for typifying cost assignment and allocation procedures. Major categories of allocations include:

1. *Jurisdictional separations.* Used to assign costs to the interstate jurisdiction; affects all rate-regulated carriers. The federal jurisdiction takes a portion of costs from the states, leaving the residue to be recovered from intrastate services.

2. *Access charges.* Used to recover exchange carrier non-traffic sensitive (NTS) costs assigned to interstate jurisdiction for call origination and termination services provided to inter-exchange carriers. A flat subscriber line charge has been added to monthly local telephone bills to recover a portion of NTS costs directly from end users.

3. *Interim cost allocation manual (ICAM).* Used to allocate AT&T costs assigned to the inter-state jurisdiction among MTS/WATS and private line services. The development of the manual involved protracted negotiations within the FCC and between the agency and AT&T; this process began in 1965 and culminated in "interim" approval of the plan in 1981.

4. *Joint and common costs.* FCC costing rules govern the assignment and allocation of joint and common costs of regulated and unregulated services provided by AT&T, BOCs, and other telcos. AT&T and the BOCs have the option of providing certain types of unregulated services through either separate subsidiaries or within the regulated entity. If such services are provided through the regulated entity, the regulated entity cost of facilities and person-nel shared between regulated and unregulated service are segregated based on specified principles. AT&T, the BOCs, and about 30 independent telcos have filed and obtained approval of a manual to implement this policy. Smaller carriers must develop and use a manual, but do not need FCC approval. In addition, the larger carriers must obtain annual attestation audits by independent public accounting firms, certifying to compliance with the manual.

The FCC proceeding (Docket 86-111) that produced the joint and common cost accounting rules in 1986 was a landmark endeavor. From a regulatory perspective, it was significant because the FCC reversed its earlier position and decided that accounting separation could be as effective as separate subsidiaries in segregating unregulated from regulated costs. The agency's order has been criticized because it allowed AT&T and the BOCs to come up with their own individual cost manuals rather than imposing a single set of detailed cost assignment and allocation proce-dures. Critics also contend that cost accounting in general and the FCC's rules in particular are too elastic to provide needed protection against cross-subsidies, and that the provision for independent audits and FCC reviews of cost manuals are insuf-ficient to provide meaningful scrutiny.

From a management perspective, the FCC order was significant because it made direct assignment and causation the key principles in the prescribed allocation process. This brings FCC cost accounting policy closer to that typical of the private sector. However, the methodology uses fully distributed costing and incorporates other features with a regulatory orientation; critics charge that the FCC approach therefore does not fully meet the current and future information needs of telephone company managers.

Competition and Technological Obsolescence. In a regulated monopoly context, accountants do not have to address issues arising from the rigors of competition or the specter of technological obsolescence. This has changed with the transformation of the telecommunications industry.

Financial viability. Going concern issues arise from the fact that many new telecommunications markets require substantial capital investments, and achieving the market penetration needed to break even is often hindered by competition, lack of name recognition, customer unfamiliarity with new products and services, and problems in meeting service and delivery commitments. Changes in regulatory policy can also threaten financial viability by abruptly altering factors such as costs included in pricing, allowed rates of return, and barriers to market entry. Industry developments such as mergers, takeovers, and changes in distribution arrangements are another source of rapid and sometimes adverse changes.

Asset values. Valuation, depreciation, and other matters linked to assets are increasingly affected by both competitive and technological developments. The commercialization of new technologies and applications that enhance performance, add new capabilities, or otherwise improve the current state of the art are occurring at a much more rapid rate than before. Introducing innovative new facilities, products, and services can improve a company's competitive position and/or lower its operating costs. However, the introduction of new technology, by a company or its competitors, can diminish or eliminate the usefulness of existing plant, equipment, and inventory. Likewise, new regulatory policies or decisions can strand certain types of facilities or cripple certain product offerings. In these cases, it is economic value that is impaired; the assets involved may have many remaining years of physical useful life. Accounting issues thus arise as to the timing and treatment of such developments in the financial statements.

For example, rapid advancements in technology and the development of competition in many markets have caused a significant deficiency in telephone plant accumulated depreciation. The FCC and a number of PUCs have recently adopted policies that will accelerate the recovery of depreciable costs. Nevertheless, some carriers may be unable to recover the deficiency because of PUC opposition, or because the competitive nature of markets precludes passing on the costs to users. In these circumstances the implications of SFAS 71, *Accounting for the Effects of Certain Types of Regulation* (Re6) and SFAS 90, *Regulated Enterprises—Accounting for Abandonments and Disallowances of Plant Costs* (Re6), should be carefully considered.

Other Issues. Current issues with the potential for having a material effect on the financial statements of regulated entities include pension costs and the 1986 tax law changes.

Adoption of GAAP by the FCC and the requirements of SFAS 87, *Employers' Accounting for Pensions* (P16), have had the effect of recording a major over-funding for pensions. Because these costs have been imposed on ratepayers in prior periods, regulators are looking for recovery of the excess costs. The dollar amount for many carriers is very large.

The reduction of corporate tax rates in the 1986 tax law revisions resulted in a significant excess of previously recorded deferred taxes. Although the companies have 30 years to repay the excess, consumer groups and PUCs are looking for immediate rate reductions reflecting the lower tax rates. Several of the more prominent aspects of the interplay of the tax law changes with the new and complex SFAS 96, *Accounting for Income Taxes* (I25), are discussed under "Income Taxes" in the Electric and Gas Utilities portion of this chapter.

Auditing Considerations

Auditing telephone utilities is a complex undertaking, with emphasis on plant, revenues, and rate-regulation. The cycle approach described in Chapter 8 is an efficient means for audit planning. Because of the large volumes of data processed, utility audits will employ a number of statistical sampling applications (Chapter 9) and computer-assisted audit techniques (Chapter 10). The transaction characteristics in utilities also are readily susceptible to analytical procedures, discussed in detail in Chapter 7.

Audits of unregulated and noncommunications portions of telecommunication companies do not present unique issues, except as allocations between regulated and other businesses may be involved. A few matters of special significance to telephone utilities are mentioned below.

Complex Computer Environment. Two important characteristics of the traditional carriers (and many of the newer entrants) having important implications for auditing are the massive investment in items of property and the enormous number of small-value transactions involved in the provision of services. The carriers have extensively mechanized the record-keeping for property, plant, and equipment, as well as the billing and collection procedures. Although not part of the day-to-day operations, cost allocations and assignments have been extensively mechanized as well. This results in an industry that is one of the largest users of computers. Audit risk centers on the processing environment.

In telephone service revenue systems, manual processes occur only at the service order input stage and in the preparation of journals. Accumulating, editing, rating, and updating customer accounts as well as billing are all internal computer processes, including interfacing between the various subsystems.

Telco property and cost systems provide the controls over additions to and deletions from telephone property, as well as maintaining the detailed continuing property record for certain classes of assets. The proper allocation of costs between capital and expense affects regulatory rate determinations and the speed with which the company can recover its investment. A further area of potentially high audit risk is the appropriateness of the depreciation rates applied to the telephone property accounts.

In both of these areas, control risk derives from the possibility of a material error occurring due to the presence of repetitive type errors, hardware malfunctions, system failures, and unauthorized changes to programs and/or master file information. (See Chapter 10.)

Attesting to Cost Separations. Audit issues were created by the FCC's provision for independent audits of carrier cost manuals in its joint and common cost order (and by similar PUC directives). The FCC mandated that larger carriers obtain an annual report by an independent public accounting firm attesting that the cost system in place accurately reflects the carrier's approved cost allocation manual, and that the allocations reported to the FCC were performed accurately in accordance with the system. The rules require that each attestation report provide a "positive" level of assurance.

The FCC's Accounting and Audits Division is to approve the manuals and assure compliance both by conducting its own reviews and by evaluating the CPA reports. FCC rules require that engagement letters with independent public accountants include a provision allowing FCC access to audit workpapers and other documentation relating to the attestation examination.

The cost manuals were approved in 1988 and the first annual attestation reports will be completed in 1989. Although only limited guidelines are yet available on the scope and methodology of such reviews, it is apparent there are issues revolving around the inherent subjectivity of some allocation decisions. As noted in the AICPA's *Statement on Standards for Attestation Engagements:*

> Competent persons will not always reach the same conclusion because (a) such estimates and measurements often require the exercise of considerable professional judgment and (b) a slightly different evaluation of the facts could yield a significant difference in the presentation of a particular assertion. [AU 2010.17]

Moreover, the statement also requires CPAs to consider "materiality," a point on which there also can be differences of opinion. This raises the possibility of difficult judgments by auditors as to the reasonableness of client decisions in applying cost allocation policies, as well as the potential for differences between independent auditors and FCC staff auditors.

It is also significant that the FCC rules call for an audit of compliance with the allocation plan contained in the manual approved by the FCC, as opposed to a review concerning the validity of the plan itself. Strictly read, this separates the CPA's attestation from questions as to the overall sufficiency of the accounting separation strategy the FCC has adopted or the effectiveness of a specific carrier's approved plan. There is nevertheless the possibility of attestation reports becoming an issue in debates over the success of the new policy in safeguarding competitors and ratepayers from cross-subsidies.

ELECTRIC AND GAS UTILITIES

Characteristics and Environment

Investor-Owned Utilities. The predominant pattern in the U.S. utility industry is that of investor ownership and public regulation. The electric power needs of almost all major metropolitan areas are served by about 200 investor-owned utilities (IOUs). They operate about 90% of the nation's total generating capacity and serve approximately 80% of the total retail customers. These major IOUs are vertically integrated, combining the generation, transmission, and distribution functions. A number of them are in other utility and nonutility lines of business as well. Equity and debt securities of these companies are traded on the major U.S. stock exchanges and are a significant factor in the U.S. capital markets. Although IOUs are nongovernmental entities, they enjoy monopoly status conferred through governmental franchises, and accordingly they are subject to government regulation.

Public Power. There are some exceptions to the nongovernmental ownership pattern. There are over 2,000 municipal and public utility district power systems, and about 800 rural electric cooperatives. Generally they are quite small, although Los Angeles, Sacramento, and Memphis are examples of large cities served by government-owned utilities rather than IOUs.

A small number of federal government agencies involved in power generation and wholesaling also constitute an exception to the general rule. The chief power generators are the Army Corps of Engineers and the Bureau of Reclamation (part of the Interior Department), which operate power plants at dams throughout the South and West. The Western Area Power Administration and three considerably smaller power marketing administrations (PMAs) market federal hydropower to utilities and to other bulk users such as irrigation districts, military bases, and federal laboratories. The largest PMA, the Bonneville Power Administration (BPA), has a somewhat broader mandate in that it is responsible not simply for selling the power output of federal dams but for meeting the energy needs of the Pacific Northwest; it has therefore developed thermal generating plants to augment its power supply. The Tennessee Valley Authority has an even broader statutory scope; it is charged with aiding the economic development of its region and thus engages in a variety of developmental, environmental, and reseach activities in addition to supplying power from hydroelectric, coal, and nuclear facilities.

Coordinating Mechanisms. The fact that the U.S. power grid is a conglomeration of many individual systems presents special coordination problems. Three mechanisms have been developed to provide needed coordination:

1. *Regional reliability councils.* In the aftermath of blackouts in the 1960s, major utilities united into nine regional reliability councils to coordinate planning, design, construction, and operation of generating and transmission facilities. The National Electric Reliability Council functions as a forum for dealing with interregional and national issues, and sets standards for interconnection.

2. *Interconnections.* Three large networks link numerous systems that in turn are tied together by interconnections. These networks encompass virtually all of the generating plants in the

United States and most in Canada, reducing peak loads for constituent systems and mini-mizing generating capacity needed for North American industry as a whole.

3. *Power pools.* These are voluntary organizations of utilities that enter into different types of cooperative planning, standard-setting, and operation. They run the gamut from informal groupings to formal arrangements complete with enforcement mechanisms and penalty provisions. There are about 20 major formal power pools in the United States.

Monopoly Status. Public utilities are unique. They are usually considered to be "natural" monopolies. This characterization is based on the notion that electric power and gas (for general public usage) is most efficiently produced and distributed by only one entity for any homogenous population group. It would be highly inefficient, for example, to permit several electric companies to compete and perhaps provide duplicate services for a large city such as New York. Concentration in one company minimizes the need for capital equipment (which is enormous in utilities), provides for averaging varying customer demands, and avoids the need for duplicate transmission lines.

Utilities provide a product that is inelastic and noninventoriable. The inelasticity relates to the demand for power. Utilities cannot change their product or customer mix based on projected profitability. Power availability is essential to all classes of customers regardless of the profitability of those classes. Further, electricity must be used when it is produced. It cannot be stored. Gas may be stored but only in very limited quantities. Therefore, to meet the maximum projected demand in any period, excess fixed plant capacity must be maintained at all times, and utilities must be permitted to charge rates to recover that excess.

Rate Regulation. The basic thrust of rate regulation in the public utilities industry is to provide fair, nondiscriminatory prices to customers while providing investors a fair return on their investment. There are normally three methods of rate-making:

1. *Cost-of-service.* This approach attempts to balance revenue needs with total operating expenses, depreciation, income taxes, and a provision for a return on investment (both equity and debt).
2. *Operating ratio.* This approach equates total estimated revenue requirements with estimated operating expenses. The ratio is expenses to revenues. The calculation should provide the dollars required to meet total expenses and cost of capital.
3. *Debt service.* This method approaches the estimated revenue requirements by measuring the need against total operating expenses plus a multiple of interest expense on long-term debt (called the times-interest-earned ratio).

The cost-of-service approach is the method most generally used in the industry.

The United States has a two-tier regulatory system. Basically the Federal Energy Regulatory Commission (FERC) regulates wholesale power sales while the state PUCs regulate retail sales.

Federal Energy Regulatory Commission. The FERC is an independent agency (succeeding the Federal Power Commission) that is nominally affiliated with the Department of Energy (DOE). With respect to electric power, the Commission's jurisdiction focuses on setting rates and charges for the transmission and sale of wholesale power by IOUs. The FERC requires regulated electric utilities to use a USOA and has established accounting and reporting requirements. It also issues licenses for smaller hydroelectric projects. (The federal government has reserved to itself the authority to develop and operate the larger projects.) The FERC oversees planning and coordination and the activities of the industry interconnection and pooling organizations. It has statutory authority to require the filing of contingency plans to deal with anticipated power shortages.

The FERC's role is limited with respect to rates charged by PMAs. Basically it ratifies rates already approved on an interim basis by the PMA administrator and a DOE official; ratification is withheld only if the rates are insufficiently justified and/ or appear to be inconsistent with statutory requirements. The Commission has indicated that its role in this area is more like that of an appeals court than a regulatory agency. However, the FERC does have direct authority for both interim and final rate approval in the case of the BPA.

The Public Utility Regulatory Policies Act of 1978 (PURPA) introduced several regulatory innovations. PURPA contains provisions designed to promote the development of nonutility power suppliers in the hope that they would provide electricity more cheaply than through the construction of new central station power plants. The law encourages two types of entities: (1) industrial-end users who as a by-product of their industrial processes produce waste heat that can be employed to generate electricity and (2) small power producers using methods employing power sources such as windmills, wood chips, and municipal waste to make electricity. Cogenerators and small power producers designated as qualifying facilities (QFs) are entitled to sell their output to utilities at rates equal to the utilities' "avoided cost." QFs are exempted from regulation; the FERC administers the process of awarding QF status, and the states define the rules for computing avoided cost.

Department of Energy units. Several components of the DOE have ancillary authority concerning electric power. The Economic Regulatory Administration has responsibilities stemming from the energy crisis of the 1970s. For example, it administers import programs, oversees energy conservation initiatives, and plays a role in the supervision of industry planning and coordination. The Energy Information Administration collects and publishes data on reserves, production, demand, consumption, distribution, and technology.

Nuclear Regulatory Commission. The NRC is an independent federal agency that regulates the construction and operation of nuclear power plants.

PUCs. State public utility or public services commissions regulate the retail distribution segment of electric and gas utility service. In most states, the commissioners are appointed by the governor, but in a few they are elected. PUCs regulate entry, service territory, rate level and rate design, and various financial affairs. They also have the authority to approve the construction and siting of new facilities.

Municipalities. Generally, municipally owned power systems are regulated by the local government involved rather than by the state PUC. For example, rates for the Memphis Light, Gas, and Water Division are set by the Memphis City Council.

Regulatory functions. U.S. regulatory bodies perform three major functions. They (1) set rates through periodic case proceedings; (2) exercise continuous review over matters such as facility planning, service quality, and financing; and (3) conduct special studies dealing with overall approaches and issues. A description of those functions follows:

1. *Rate cases.* Rate-making is accomplished at irregular intervals depending on factors such as inflation rates, changes in tax policy, and utility construction needs. The major elements of a rate case are (a) determining revenue requirements including the amount of gross revenues required by the utility and the appropriate costs to include in cost-of-services rates (used and useful plant, construction in progress, and amortization of other unique expenses), and (b) determining the rate structure including the appropriate price to charge each customer class and establishing appropriate economic and social criteria.

2. *Continuous review.* Major examples of matters regulatory bodies address on an ongoing basis are (a) facilities planning approval including issuing certificates of convenience and necessity for construction of new facilities, (b) depreciation certification including the determination of appropriate depreciation expense levels to include in cost of service, (c) merger and acquisition approval including reviews and authorizations of mergers and acquisitions and the determination of benefits for ratepayers, (d) determination of service area changes including reviews and authorizations of franchises, (e) issuance of debt and equity securities and capital structure approval, and (f) service complaint processing including reviews of complaints from ratepayers regarding service problems (i.e., quality and timeliness).

3. *Special studies.* Regulatory bodies undertake special studies to examine topics such as (a) determination of special rate-making approaches including topics such as fuel adjustment clauses, marginal cost rates, and time-of-day rates, and (b) determination of future policy goals concerning conservation and "least cost" planning.

SEC Jurisdiction. The abuses of the power trusts in the 1920s and 1930s led to the enactment of the Public Utility Holding Company Act of 1935 (PUHCA). This statute is one of the principal reasons for the small number of IOU combinations despite the incentives to obtain economies of scale because of competition and technological advances.

The SEC is the federal agency with primary responsibility for administering PUHCA, which subjects electric holding companies to two basic types of regulation. First, it requires that the corporate and capital structures of the holding companies be sufficiently simple so that they are readily susceptible to state and local regulation; basically they are limited to owning contiguous electric power systems in one state and can diversify into other businesses and geographical areas only with SEC permission. Second, it empowered the SEC to veto holding company financings, mergers, and acquisitions.

The level of regulatory activity under PUHCA has dwindled in recent years, particularly during the 1980–1988 presidential administration. Only 12 companies remain subject to the Act. In the early 1980s the SEC unsuccessfully tried to get Congress to repeal the legislation, contending that in today's world its objectives are adequately met through other regulatory authority exercised by the SEC, the FERC, and the PUCs. There are now some indications that legislative or regulatory solutions may be found for achieving significant combinations without subjecting the merger/acquisition transactions and the resulting entities to undue regulatory restrictions.

Environmental Factors and Power Usage. The U.S. public utility industry is currently plagued by two serious problems: the environmental aspects of the development of nuclear power and the present excess capacity of electric generating plants in many regions.

Nuclear power development. The development of nuclear power as a source of energy has virtually come to a halt. Although there were over 100 nuclear powered generating plants in operation by mid-1988 (which, with the exception of Three Mile Island, have been relatively trouble-free), further development and start-up, even for plants presently ready for operation, are difficult to predict. There is some possibility that the facilities now completed or near completion will never be permitted to start operations, at least not using nuclear power. One example is an agreement reached in mid-1988 to abandon the Shoreham facility on Long Island, New York even though it is completed but has never been utilized beyond the preliminary test stage.

Environmental groups opposing the development of nuclear power have escalated their opposition following the 1979 accident at Three Mile Island Unit No. 2 in Pennsylvania. Although that accident resulted in the complete closure and containment of a large generating plant for which estimated clean-up costs were a billion dollars at the end of 1986 ($731 million had been expended to that time), it was not especially physically damaging. But the psychological impact was severe, and was exacerbated by the 1986 accident at the Chernobyl (Russia) generating plant, which resulted in severe physical damage and loss of life, with an effect on many neighboring countries.

The NRC is responsible for determining that nuclear power plants are (1) strictly controlled (including adequate provision for nuclear waste disposal), (2) designed to be accident-free, and (3) have workable emergency plans for containment and evacuation in the event of accidents. In promulgating these requirements the NRC rigorously controls the construction and operation of nuclear power plants. That rigor slows construction and delays commencement of operations, resulting in increased cost of construction and operation.

Initially, electricity produced by nuclear means was projected to cost a fraction of electricity produced by conventional means; but this is currently not true in many cases. Earlier estimates were based on oil prices almost double their mid-1988 levels and may not have adequately considered the high cost of safety inspection, waste disposal, and emergency plans—partly caused by regulatory intervention in the construction and operation process and the resulting extraordinary delays.

Notes to the financial statements of many investor-owned public utilities are replete with descriptions of large cost overruns and regulatory disallowances for nuclear generating units. Figure 33.1 provides statistics on estimated cost overruns, abandonments, or disallowances for assessing the impact on rate-making at nuclear

Nuclear project	Estimated (in billions)	
	Cost of project	Cost overrun, abandonment, or regulatory disallowance
Clinton	$3.8	$1.1
Comanche Peak 1 and 2	6.7	?[1]
Fermi 2	4.2	.3
Midland	3.7	2.1[2]
Nine Mile Point 2	5.9	2.0
Palo Verde 1, 2 and 3	1.5	.1
Perry 2	.4	?[3]
San Onofre 2 and 3	4.5	.3
Seabrook 1	5.7	1.0[4]
Shoreham	4.9	1.4[4],[6]
Zimmer Station	4.5	.9[5]

(1) Only $1.3 billion allowed in rate base as of December 31, 1986.
(2) Planned for conversion to natural gas. $2.1 billion is cost of abandoned facilities.
(3) Construction suspended. Project may be abandoned.
(4) Certain government parties are seeking abandonment (or mothballing) of facility.
(5) Planned for conversion to coal.
(6) Abandonment agreement reached in 1988.

FIG. 33.1   Nuclear Project Costs and Projected Disallowances—Selected Utilities
Source: 1986 annual reports, various utilities (except as to note 6).

projects of selected utilities. In most cases, the amounts presented are before the effects of income tax reductions on any final recorded losses and could be affected by current, protracted litigation in state courts challenging the amounts for rate base inclusion purposes. The eventual losses recognized may be greater or less than the amounts presented; but in any event, the amounts of the final losses will be massive.

Regardless of the actual amounts of final rate base disallowances, the projection is of such magnitude that the future ability of investor-owned public utilities to secure capital in the marketplace is in some jeopardy. Figure 33.2 presents an extract from the notes to the 1986 annual report of the Cincinnati Gas and Electric Company that discusses some of the uncertainties surrounding the Zimmer Station conversion to a coal-fired process. Because of the uncertainty that exists concerning the ability of utilities to place completed nuclear facilities in operation, notes to the financial statements of utilities increasingly are being expanded to disclose such unusual exposures.

Alternate sources. Alternate methods of producing energy are proliferating. The QFs sanctioned by the 1978 PURPA legislation were the major source of new generating capacity during the 1980s. This may suggest appropriate exploitation of the efficiencies available from decentralized production, filling the gap created by the reluctance of utilities to undertake major new construction projects. However, critics contend that the need for QF capacity is exaggerated, and that the PURPA program is not economically efficient and compromises system reliability.

CG&E cannot presently predict when, if ever, the Plant will be completed and placed in operation as a coal-fired plant; whether all approvals and permits necessary to convert and operate Zimmer Station can be obtained; the ultimate cost of Zimmer Station; or, to the extent Zimmer costs are not disallowed pursuant to the Stipulation, whether the PUCO will allow CG&E to earn a return on its entire investment in Zimmer Station or to recover all or part of the portion of its investment on which a return may not be allowed. Currently, none of the costs of Zimmer Station are included in CG&E's rate base. If resolved adversely to CG&E, these uncertainties could have a material adverse effect upon CG&E's ability to finance the cost of the Zimmer conversion, its financial position, results of operations, and dividends.

FIG. 33.2   Uncertainties Regarding the Zimmer Station
Source: Cincinnati Gas and Electric Company, 1986 Annual Report.

In 1988, the FERC launched a series of rulemakings designed to remedy problems in administering PURPA and to encourage further evolution of alternative supply options. FERC proposed to recognize a new class of alternative wholesale suppliers known as independent power producers (IPPs). IPPs might be formed by industrial end-users, architectural, engineering, and construction firms, or (under certain conditions) electric utilities themselves. The FERC also is proposing the establishment of federal guidelines for state-supervised competitive bidding (as a means of determining how to meet future needs for new capacity), and is working on proposals involving transmission access and bulk power markets.

Although the outcome of these proposals is uncertain, it appears that regulatory policy is following a path similar to that in the telecommunications and natural gas areas. If so, the industry will likely experience a degree of deregulation with respect to generation, increased "unbundling" of the generation, transmission, and distribution functions, and growing competition from nontraditional players.

Accounting Considerations

The development of nuclear power, the political climate, and the significant investment in facilities have dictated most of the accounting developments in the utilities industry in recent years. Understanding the major events in the industry therefore provides a background to understanding the actions of the FASB.

Companies subject to rate regulation account for certain transactions differently than unregulated companies. Most of those differences can be attributed directly to the peculiarities of the rate-making process, in which government agencies have the authority to permit, defer, or deny the recognition of revenues and costs in establishing rates.

The statutes authorizing the establishment of Uniform Systems of Accounts by regulatory agencies usually do not refer to GAAP, but accounting prescribed by the USOAs conforms, for the most part, to the financial accounting standards issued by the FASB. The FERC and most other federal agencies go through rule-making procedures before modifying their USOAs to incorporate new accounting pronouncements.

Early Standards. Differences in the application of GAAP between regulated and nonregulated enterprises, although relatively few in number and generally relating to the timing of recognition of certain elements of revenues and costs, often have a material impact on the financial statements of regulated companies. The unique aspects of applying accounting principles to companies whose rates are established by government agencies were first recognized by the accounting profession in 1954. In ARB 44 (Revised), *Declining Balance Depreciation*, now superseded, the AICPA's Committee on Accounting Procedures dealt with the narrow issue of the nonrecognition of deferred income taxes for rate-making purposes arising from the use of the declining balance method of depreciation for income tax purposes while some other method of depreciation was used for financial reporting purposes. The Committee indicated that in the rare situations in which the accounting for deferred income taxes was not considered appropriate, disclosure was required of the amount of deferred income taxes not recorded for financial reporting purposes.

In 1962, the APB issued "Accounting Principles for Regulated Industries," an Addendum to APB 2, *Accounting for the "Investment Credit"* (now superseded). The Addendum provided that

- GAAP pertains to business enterprises in general, including "public utilities, common carriers, insurance companies, financial institutions and the like," that are subject to government regulation.
- Differences may arise in the application of GAAP because of the rate-making process. "Such differences usually concern mainly the time at which various items enter into the determination of net income in accordance with the principle of matching costs and revenues."
- To reflect the results of a rate-making process, a cost "may be deferred in the balance sheet [but] only when it is clear that the cost will be recoverable out of future revenues, and it is not appropriate when there is doubt, because of economic conditions or for other reasons, that the cost will be so recoverable."
- The imposition by regulatory agencies of accounting requirements not directly related to the rate-making process does not necessarily mean that those requirements conform to GAAP.
- "The financial statements of regulated businesses other than those prepared for filing with the government for regulatory purposes preferably should be based on generally accepted accounting principles (with appropriate recognition of rate-making considerations . . .)."
- "In reporting on the financial statements of regulated businesses, the independent auditor should . . . deal with material variances from generally accepted accounting principles (with appropriate recognition of rate-making considerations . . .), if the financial statements reflect any such variances, in the same manner as in his reports on nonregulated businesses."

Those broad guidelines were interpreted in different ways, leading to confusion in their application. A source of concern was the vagueness regarding the specific industries to which they applied. Also, a difference of opinion existed as to the appropriate accounting principles to be followed in presenting general purpose financial statements for external use, namely, (1) did financial statements prepared in conformity with accounting principles prescribed by regulatory agencies (that differ in material respects from those followed by nonregulated enterprises) provide sufficient information for external users (e.g., financial analysts and investors) who lack the authority to require specific financial information? or (2) should GAAP have been followed in all instances in financial statements intended for use by the public?

General Effects of Rate Regulation. The problems mentioned in the preceding section led the FASB to begin study. The first comprehensive review of the accounting for rate-regulated companies and how their unique features affected their operations and financial statements was conducted in the late 1970s and resulted in the FASB issuing a Discussion Memorandum, *Effects of Rate Regulation on Accounting for Regulated Enterprises* (FASB, 1979). That Discussion Memorandum was designed to

- Determine whether there are circumstances that would support a different application of GAAP by regulated enterprises in general purpose financial statements.
- Identify any such circumstances, principally those resulting from rate-making, and determine any impact they should have on the identification and measurement of assets, liabilities, revenues, and expenses.
- Establish criteria for recognizing circumstances that should be reflected in the application of GAAP by regulated enterprises.

After considering the issues in and public responses to the Discussion Memorandum, the FASB reaffirmed that accounting prescribed by regulators is not GAAP per se. Rather, GAAP should be established in the regulatory environment giving cognizance to the special effects of regulation on general-purpose financial reporting.

In 1982, the FASB issued SFAS 71, *Accounting for the Effects of Certain Types of Regulation* (Re6), amending the operative paragraphs of ARB 44 (Revised) and superseding the Addendum to APB 2. In broad terms, SFAS 71 requires costs that do not qualify as assets under GAAP to be capitalized if recovery is reasonably assured through the regulatory rate-making process.

Asset capitalization criteria. Rate-making actions by regulators can provide reasonable assurance that an asset exists even though GAAP might otherwise preclude recognition of an asset. For example, a regulatory commission might authorize a utility to incur a major research and development cost that could benefit future customers and also direct the utility to capitalize and amortize that cost (as part of allowable costs) over the future period expected to benefit from the results of that cost. If the following criteria are met the utility would capitalize the research and development cost for financial reporting purposes even though SFAS 2, *Accounting for Research and Development Costs* (R50), would otherwise require such costs to be charged to expense as incurred:

1. It is probable that future revenue in an amount at least equal to the capitalized cost will result from inclusion of that cost in allowable costs for rate-making purposes (Re6.119(a)). In this context, probable means that the future event or events are likely to occur (Re6.119, fn. 10).
2. Based on available evidence, the future revenue will be provided to permit recovery of the previously incurred cost rather than to provide for expected levels of similar future costs. If the revenue will be provided through an automatic rate-adjustment clause, this criterion

requires that the regulator's intent should be to permit recovery of the previously incurred cost (Re6.119(b)).

Impairment of value. Sometimes actions of regulators can increase or decrease the value of an asset. If a regulatory commission determines that certain costs are not part of allowable costs, for example, part of the cost of current nuclear generating plants, the value of those plants is impaired. Some of those costs are considered by rate commissions to result from improper or inefficient management, and some commissions have placed cost caps on facilities under construction. Costs in excess of the cost caps are not recoverable in future periods, and consequently the carrying amounts of the facilities to which those excess costs relate must be reduced to reflect the asset value impairment. Later in this chapter segment, SFAS 90, *Regulated Enterprises—Accounting for Abandonments and Disallowances of Plant Costs* (Re6), and SFAS 92, *Regulated Enterprises—Accounting for Phase-In Plans* (Re6), are discussed. These two standards are aimed primarily at the problems currently being encountered by utilities relating to significant cost overruns, disallowances, and abandonments in nuclear facilities.

Regulatory-created liabilities. Actions by regulators can create or increase liabilities for utilities, usually obligations to customers. Those events include the following:

1. A regulator may require refunds to customers. Refunds that meet the criteria of SFAS 5, *Accounting for Contingencies* (C59), shall be recorded as liabilities and as reductions of revenue or as expenses of the regulated enterprise. [Re6.121(a)]

2. A regulator can provide current rates intended to recover costs that are expected to be incurred in the future with the understanding that if those costs are not incurred future rates will be reduced by corresponding amounts. If current rates are intended to recover such costs and the regulator requires the enterprise to remain accountable for any amounts charged pursuant to such rates and not yet expended for the intended purpose, the enterprise shall not recognize as revenues amounts charged pursuant to such rates. Those amounts shall be recognized as liabilities and taken to income only when the associated costs are incurred. [Re6.121(b)]

3. A regulator can require that a gain or other reduction of net allowable costs be given to customers over future periods. That would be accomplished, for rate-making purposes, by amortizing the gain or other reduction of net allowable costs over those future periods and reducing rates to reduce revenues in approximately the amount of the amortization. If a gain or other reduction of net allowable cost is to be amortized over future periods for rate-making purposes, the regulated enterprise shall not recognize that gain or other reduction of net allowable costs in income of the current period. Instead, it shall record it as a liability for future reductions of charges to customers that are expected to result. [Re6.121(c)].

Specific Issues Affected by Regulation. SFAS 71 requires rate-regulated companies to recognize two kinds of costs not generally recognized by nonregulated companies. First, if rates are based on costs that include an allowance for equity funds used during construction, the company will capitalize and increase net income by the allowance used for rate-making. Second, if the rates are based on costs that include reasonable intercompany profits, the company will not eliminate such profits in its GAAP financial statements.

CWIP and AFUDC. For many years regulatory authorities have held that utility customers should not pay for costs of financing construction that will benefit only future users. A basic regulatory principle is that current customers should pay a return only on assets that are currently performing a useful service. As a result, many regulators have withheld major plant construction costs from the rate base until the new plants are "used" or "useful." To offset the loss of return on their investment, utilities have been allowed to recover the cost of construction funds from future users by capitalizing an allowance for funds used during construction (AFUDC), also known as interest during construction, as part of construction work in progress (CWIP). AFUDC is subsequently recovered through depreciation and affects the utility's return on investment through its inclusion in the determination of future rates.

Although there is general agreement among the regulatory agencies that AFUDC is an appropriate regulatory accounting concept, there are considerable differences in its application. The agencies agree that costs of debt funds should be capitalized, but differ on whether imputed interest on equity funds should be included as part of AFUDC. The agencies also differ on other matters, such as the determination of the appropriate AFUDC rate and the capitalization period.

Considerable concern has been expressed in recent years over the quality of a utility's earnings in view of the sizable increase in the amount of the AFUDC in relation to net income. Generally, utility companies have substantial funds tied up in CWIP. Because property is by far the largest item in most utilities' balance sheets and because the utilities do much of their own construction, the effect of capitalizing a return on equity funds used in construction (in addition to capitalizing interest on debt funds so used) is frequently material to both the balance sheet and the income statement. In some cases AFUDC has exceeded 50% of net income.

This concern has prompted many regulatory authorities to reconsider their practice of disallowing CWIP costs in the rate base. They have noted the frequent increases in construction programs, the long construction periods, and the consequent drain on utilities' cash flow. Nuclear generating stations cost billions of dollars and may take ten or more years to build. Some contend that current customers would benefit from placing CWIP costs into the rate base, even though CWIP may not be "used" or "useful" in the traditional sense. The benefits to current customers, it is claimed, would include: (1) assurance that their future energy needs will be met; (2) achievement of air-pollution, water-pollution, and safety standards; and (3) reduction in revenue requirements over the plant's life, since the rate base on which customers pay a rate of return would be lower (because of absence or minimization of AFUDC).

The application of FASB standards to AFUDC matters is as follows:

1. *Allowance on equity funds.* The practice of capitalizing an allowance on equity funds is generally accepted in regulated industries but is not permitted in nonregulated industries. SFAS 71 requires that the amount of cost capitalized for rate-making purposes, generally the cost of debt and equity capital, also should be capitalized for financial reporting pur-

poses. Thus the requirements for nonregulated industries in SFAS 34, *Capitalization of Interest Cost* (I67), do *not* apply. SFAS 90, *Regulated Enterprises—Accounting for Abandonments and Disallowances of Plant Costs*, indicates that the cost of equity capital should be capitalized only if it is probable that such cost will be included in allowable costs for rate-making purposes. (Re6.125)

2. *AFUDC rate determination.* In SFAS 34, the FASB stipulates that "The amount of interest cost to be capitalized for qualifying assets is intended to be that portion of the interest cost incurred during the assets' acquisition periods that theoretically could have been avoided . . . if expenditures for the assets had not been made" (I67.109). Regulatory agencies' determinations of an AFUDC rate can be contrasted with SFAS 34. The FERC prescribes formulas for determining AFUDC rates, thus providing a uniform method that gives recognition to the interrelationship between capital utilized for rate-base purposes and the capital components of AFUDC. These formulas permit a utility to achieve a rate of return on its total utility operations, including its construction program, at about the rate that would be allowed in a rate base.

3. *Other AFUDC application problems.* SFAS 34 states: "If the enterprise suspends substantially all activities related to acquisition of the asset, interest capitalization shall cease until activities are resumed" (I67.114). Most regulatory agencies have adopted similar rules. Some, however, are more specific. The FERC, for example, has stated that "interest during construction may be capitalized starting from the date that construction costs are continuously incurred on a planning progressive basis" and that the "capitalization of interest stops when the facilities have been tested and are placed in or ready for service."

   Interest may not be capitalized during periods of intentional delay or interrupted construction if the interruption is deemed unreasonable. Labor strikes, for example, have been deemed unreasonable by the FERC. In the case of multiunit generating plants, an average in-service date or offset method can be used. Under that method, the days of nonproduction attributable to construction are offset against the days of production in the period to arrive at an average in-service date. The AFUDC on all common plant facilities ceases when the first unit of a multiunit generating plant goes into operation.

4. *AFUDC tax treatment.* A separate issue involving AFUDC is that of the federal income tax effect of the debt component of AFUDC. Interest on debt will, of course, be deducted for income tax purposes, though capitalized for accounting purposes. Capitalized interest is often a major element in the origination of deferred taxes.

Many state regulatory authorities have determined that current utility customers should not benefit from the related income tax reduction, that is, that the taxes should be "normalized" rather than "flowed-through." Prior to issuance of SFAS 96 (see "Income Taxes" later herein), two methods had been used to normalize the tax effects: a net-of-tax method and a deferral method. Both methods require a charge to cost of service to restore the tax benefit already removed. Under the net-of-tax method, AFUDC is reduced and other income is increased. Under the deferral method, AFUDC remains the same and defered tax is increased. The FERC prescribes the deferral method for utilities whose state regulatory authorities have not ruled on treatment of the tax benefits of the debt component of AFUDC.

Intercompany Profits. In the unregulated industry environment, intercompany profits are required to be eliminated in consolidation. However, for regulated industries, SFAS 71 provides that

---

Consolidation Policy

The accompanying consolidated financial statements include the accounts of Consumers Power Company (the Company) and its subsidiary companies, which are all wholly owned . . . . These statements exclude all intercompany amounts, except intercompany profits in gas inventory, which are allowed by the rate-making policies of the Michigan Public Service Commission (MPSC).

FIG. 33.3 Disclosure of Intercompany Profits Not Eliminated
Source: Consumers Power Company, 1986 Annual Report.

- Profit on sales to regulated affiliates shall not be eliminated in general-purpose financial statements if both of the following criteria are met:
  a. The sales price is reasonable.
  b. It is probable that, through the rate-making process, future revenue approximately equal to the sales price will result from the regulated affiliate's use of the products. [Re6.126]
- The sales price usually shall be considered reasonable if the price is accepted or not challenged by the regulator that governs the regulated affiliate. Otherwise, reasonableness shall be considered in light of the circumstances. For example, reasonableness might be judged by the return on investment earned by the manufacturing or construction operations or by a comparison of the transfer prices with prices available from other sources. [Re6.127]

In the usual case, intercompany sales to affiliates are not material. However, depending on the extent and type of affiliations and purchasing practice, the effect on the consolidated financial statements of companies following this practice can be significant. Figure 33.3 presents the footnote disclosure of Consumers Power Company related to intercompany gas sales.

Fuel cost adjustment clauses. Electric and gas utility rates may include adjustment clauses allowing companies to modify customer rates to reflect changes in the cost of fuels used to produce electricity and of purchased gas needed for natural gas pipelines and gas distribution. Those utilities will often establish a deferred charge in their financial statements for increased costs not currently recovered through customer rates, and later match the increased costs with additional revenue collected through surcharges on customer bills. In nonregulated industries, costs of this type would ordinarily be charged to expense as incurred, since the physical items or assets have been consumed and the service rendered to customers. However, regulated industries may defer fuel adjustment costs if they meet the general standard in SFAS 71 that provides for recording an asset when recovery from future revenues is probable (Re6.119).

During periods of rapidly rising fuel prices, adjustment clauses help prevent earnings erosion. Conversely, they could result in reductions in customer bills if fuel costs should decrease. Administratively, adjustment clauses reduce the need for iterative proceedings, thereby decreasing the burden on the commissions and diminishing the cost of regulation to consumers.

The FERC allows regulated utilities to maintain the deferred charge resulting from unrecovered fuel adjustments cost on their financial statements as long as the state PUC allows it. However, the value of uncollected fuel and gas costs recorded as deferred charges can be undermined by utility company action (e.g., applying for a rate increase); by state commission decision (e.g., subsequently ruling that deferred charges are not allowed); or by audit (e.g., detection of improper items included in the adjustment determination).

Rate increases subject to refund. A rate increase, once granted, may be challenged in court. Often in such cases, the rates may be placed into effect, with a notification to customers that some or all of the increase may be subject to refund depending on the outcome of court proceedings. SFAS 71 indicates that when a utility increases rates prior to regulatory approval, it is similar to a warranty obligation on goods sold; therefore, a loss contingency to cover possible refunds may be required. The provisions of SFAS 5, *Accounting for Contingencies* (C59.105), apply to both approved and pending rate applications, and generally require recognition of a loss if it is probable and can be reasonably estimated.

Leases. Leasing (see Chapter 19) is an important tool for financing capital expenditures in regulated industries. Interest costs are frequently lower in a lease than with a utility's own debt financing. Moreover, lease costs can be lowered through the depreciation available to and currently usable by the lessor. Examples of commonly leased items in utilities are generating stations and nuclear fuel.

The FERC does not provide for capitalization of leases in its USOA. Each lease payment is charged entirely as rental expense, resulting in a constant expense and cost-of-service charge over the life of the lease. This treatment creates a smoothing effect on utility rates and allows FERC-regulated utilities to finance capital expenditures without increasing the rate base for long-term debt. The effect on long-term debt is particularly important for utilities whose ratio of debt to capital structure is limited by law or regulation.

SFAS 71 indicates that the classification of a lease is not affected by a regulator's actions. For financial reporting purposes, a regulatory agency cannot eliminate a liability that it did not impose previously. As a result, utilities are required to follow the provisions of SFAS 13, *Accounting for Leases* (L10), regardless of regulatory edict. SFAS 71 states:

> The nature of the expense elements related to a capitalized lease (amortization of the leased asset and interest on the lease obligation) is not changed by the regulator's action; however, the timing of expense recognition related to the lease would be modified to conform to the rate treatment. Thus, amortization of the leased asset would be modified so that the total of interest on the lease obligation and amortization of the leased asset would equal the rental expense that was allowed for rate-making purposes. [Re6.147]

Reacquired long-term debt. Gains and losses on reacquired long-term debt are currently recognized in income under APB 26, *Early Extinguishment of Debt* (D14). However, the FERC allows companies to amortize such gains and losses under certain conditions, with different accounting requirements depending on whether the extinguishment involves refunding.

For reacquisitions without refunding, utilities amortize, in equal monthly amounts over what would have been the remaining life of the debt issue reacquired, the difference between the amount paid and the net carrying amount (face value adjusted for unamortized premium or discount, debt expense, and reacquisition costs) if the regulatory authority allows such amortization in computing the allowed rate of return. Otherwise, the utility will recognize currently the gain or loss on reacquiring long-term debt without refunding.

For reacquisitions with refunding, the difference between the amount paid and the net carrying amount may be amortized in equal monthly amounts over either what would have been the remaining life of the debt reacquired or the life of the new issue.

For financial reporting purposes, SFAS 71 requires that a difference between a utility's carrying amount and reacquisition price of an extinguished debt required for regulatory purposes to be amortized over future periods be treated as an adjustment of interest expense (Re6.140–.142). If the reacquisition price exceeds the carrying amount (a loss), and recovery of the excess is reasonably assured as a result of a regulator's approval of increased rates to cover the excess, the excess should be capitalized as an asset. That asset is then amortized over the period in which it is allowed as part of the rate base. Conversely, if the carrying amount exceeds the reacquisition price (a gain) and a regulator decides to reduce rates as a result of the gain, that action requires the utility to record a liability to be amortized over the period that the rate base is reduced.

Compensated absences. SFAS 43, *Accounting for Compensated Absences* (C44), generally requires accrual of a liability for the amount of currently earned compensation payable for future absences. For regulatory purposes, those amounts are permitted as allowable costs only when paid. For financial reporting purposes, utilities are required by SFAS 71 to ignore the regulatory approach since regulation cannot eliminate an obligation that was not originally imposed by regulation. In such cases, utilities are required to record presently an asset representing the amount of increased revenue that results from the regulators allowing the inclusion of compensated absence costs in allowable costs when future payments are made.

Original costs and acquisition adjustments. Public utilities regulated by the FERC and most PUCs are generally required to report plant assets in their accounts at *original cost*—the cost to the *first* organization putting the plant assets into public service. Public utility holding companies regulated by the SEC will also record plant assets at original cost if the companies held are subject to the regulations of another regulatory agency, such as the FERC. An excess of purchase price over depreciated original cost is reported as an acquisition adjustment.

The original-cost concept has had great significance since the Federal Power Commission (FPC, now the FERC) instituted the first USOA for electric utilities in the 1930s and required companies to restate their plant accounts at original cost. The excess of bona fide cost over original cost was recorded as an acquisition adjustment, and the remaining amounts, which consisted of write-ups and other improper charges, were written-off. Acquisition adjustments often resulted because the purchase price for a plant was related to gross earnings of the facility rather than to the value of the property or because the price included amounts for territorial rights (FPC, 1950).

Because of such abuses of capitalized plant costs, the value of utility plants were greatly overstated and the rate base was increased. The restatement and review procedures of the 1930s resulted in acquisition adjustments and write-offs totalling about $1.6 billion, which represented nearly 25% of the reported cost. The FPC authorized the amortization of acquisition adjustments over periods not to exceed 15 years. The states generally followed the FPC's action.

The original-cost concept poses no problem for utility companies that build or contract for their facilities, since original cost and historical cost are identical, assuming prudent construction costs. However, original cost and historical cost ordinarily will be different for the purchasing companies.

A utility that purchases plant assets from another utility will record the assets at the selling company's original cost less accumulated depreciation. Purchase cost may be used for original cost if plant assets are acquired from a nonutility and such acquisition constitutes the *first* use of the asset in public service.

The disposition of excess over original cost when utility assets are purchased depends on whether the transaction benefits the purchasing company's customers. The FERC will allow the company to amortize the acquisition adjustment to expenses recovered through the cost of service if the utility can demonstrate an economic benefit to its customers, such as reduced rates or improved service.

When the purchase price is less than the seller's depreciated original cost, the FERC requires the purchasing utility to record the original cost in the plant account and credit the excess of depreciated original cost over acquisition cost to accumulated depreciation.

APB 16, *Business Combinations* (B50), and APB 17, *Intangible Assets* (I60), require (1) the recording of goodwill (or negative goodwill) in a purchase business combination in which the fair value of the consideration given exceeds (is less than) the fair value of the net assets required; and (2) the amortization of that goodwill (or negative goodwill) over the period benefited but not to exceed 40 years. Neither goodwill nor negative goodwill may be written off at consummation of a business combination. However, SFAS 71 states that if a regulator permits "goodwill to be amortized over a specific period as an allowable cost for rate-making purposes, the regulator's action provides reasonable assurance of the existence of an asset" (Re6.135). With the above situation, goodwill would be amortized for financial reporting purposes over the period permitted for rate-making purposes, and not in accordance with APB 17. Conversely:

> If [a] regulator excludes amortization of goodwill from allowable costs for rate-making purposes, either by not permitting amortization or by directing the [utility] to write off the goodwill, the value of the goodwill may be reduced or eliminated. If there is no indication that the amortization will be allowed in a subsequent period, the goodwill would be amortized for financial reporting purposes and continually evaluated to determine whether the unamortized costs should be reduced significantly by a charge to income in accordance with [APB 17]. [Re6.135]

Research and development costs. The FERC allows amortization of significant and nonrecurring research and development (R&D) expenditures over a period not to exceed five years if they would otherwise distort charges for the period. SFAS 2, *Accounting for Research and Development Costs* (R50), requires R&D expenditures to be expensed as incurred, because of the uncertain relationship between current expenditures and future benefits.

The FERC definition of R&D includes expenditures incurred by or on behalf of public utilities for experimental, design, installation, construction, or operational activities reasonably related to existing or future utility business. Those activities include costs for the design, development, implementation, or improvement of a facility, plant process, product, formula, or invention, and the development of proposed alternative sources of electricity or substitute gas supplies.

The rate of return allowed by the FERC during the previous three-year period is used to determine the rate base effect of R&D. Eligible amounts are reduced by revenue received due to R&D ventures. If amounts received exceed 5% of net income before including such revenue, then the revenue is also amortized for rate-base purposes over a period not to exceed five years.

Pension costs. The determination of the amount of pension cost allowable for rate-making purposes may differ from net periodic pension cost computed by following the provisions of SFAS 87, *Employers' Accounting for Pensions* (P16). SFAS 87 indicates that such a difference may be required to be recorded as an asset or liability by reason of the action of a regulatory commission (Re6.155). That action changes the timing of the recognition of pension costs as an expense but does not alter the total pension cost that would be recognized over time.

Accounting changes. A utility may change accounting methods under GAAP that do not result in changing allowable costs for rate-making purposes. SFAS 71 indicates that in such a situation the utility should follow APB 20, *Accounting Changes* (A06). For example, a change that results in a lease being capitalized with no resulting income statement effect (and no allowable cost effect) would be accounted for following APB 20. However, if a utility institutes an accounting change that affects allowable costs for rate-making purposes, that change would be treated the same for financial reporting purposes as it is for regulatory purposes.

Decommissioning costs. Electric utilities with nuclear power plants face the responsibility of ultimately shutting down and dismantling (decommissioning) those plants. The cost of removing other retired assets generally has not been considered a major expense, particularly when compared with expected salvage values. However, the cost of decommissioning nuclear plants is likely to be significantly larger than removal costs for other assets. For a large power plant complex, this could amount to billions of dollars.

Several alternatives exist for assuring the availability of funds for decommissioning. One method is the use of an accounting technique known as *negative net salvage*; that is, straight-line depreciation expense is determined by dividing original cost plus estimated decommissioning costs, net of salvage, by estimated operating life. This method would satisfy the equity argument by helping to insure that decommissioning costs are included in rate determination and therefore are paid for by those who benefit from the asset. This alternative would also include reducing the rate base by depreciation charges that include an element for decommissioning, thus providing a

---

Nuclear Plant Decommissioning Costs

Since 1980 the Company has not been recovering nuclear plant decommissioning costs in its retail electric rates. Beginning January 1, 1987, the Company has been authorized by the MPSC to collect decommissioning costs through a monthly surcharge on customers' bills. These funds will be deposited in trust as required by the MPSC order authorizing the surcharge. The surcharge is based upon estimated decommissioning costs in 1987 dollars of $50 million and $100 million for the Big Rock Point and Palisades plants, respectively, and is based upon certain assumptions as to remaining plant life, inflation and fund earnings.

A Nuclear Regulatory Commission proposal would require a utility to accumulate a decommissioning fund either within five years or one-third of a plant's remaining operating license period, whichever is greater, to the level that would have been attained if the accumulation of funds had started at the beginning of the plant's life. The Company believes that any additional, unfunded decommissioning costs, which could be significant, would be recoverable through adjustments of rates charged to its customers.

FIG. 33.4 Disclosure of Approach to Nuclear Plant Decommissioning Costs
Source: Consumers Power Company, 1986 Annual Report.

return on customers' money. It is important to recognize that this procedure is only an accounting technique. It does not necessarily provide a separate fund for decommissioning costs. A utility conceivably could avail itself of funds collected through negative net salvage for other uses, such as debt repayment, plant construction, and operating expenses. The utility of course would still be responsible for financing the decommissioning.

Other alternatives for assuring the availability of funds for decommissioning include: (1) prepayment of cash or other liquid assets, invested so that principal plus accumulated interest over the life of the plant are sufficient to cover decommissioning costs; (2) a sinking fund approach; (3) the purchase of surety bonds by the utility; (4) the purchase of decommissioning insurance in case of premature reactor shutdown; and (5) the use of general tax revenues. Figure 33.4 presents the footnote disclosure of Consumers Power Company describing the amount and method of providing for nuclear plant decommissioning costs.

Abandonments and Disallowances. Because of the serious implications of potential major asset write-offs in this industry, the AICPA published an Issues Paper, *Application of Concepts in FASB Statement of Financial Accounting Standards No. 71 to Emerging Issues in the Public Utility Industry* (AICPA, 1984b). The principal matters discussed in that paper include

1. Appropriate accounting for various types of phase-in plans that have been proposed for recovery of the cost of new electric generating facilities.
2. Circumstances that warrant loss recognition when major amounts of incurred costs of new plants are disallowed for rate-making purposes.
3. Appropriate accounting for abandonments of incomplete plants.

The Issues Paper was presented to the FASB for consideration, and in January 1985, the Board added to its agenda a project to revise SFAS 71.

In December 1986, the FASB issued SFAS 90, *Regulated Enterprises—Accounting for Abandonments and Disallowances of Plant Costs* (Re6). SFAS 90 applies to (1) the recorded costs of previously abandoned assets, (2) the recorded costs of assets for which future abandonment is probable or becomes probable in the future, (3) previously disallowed plant costs, and (4) disallowances of plant costs that are likely to occur in the future. (Additionally, the FASB staff issued TB 87-2, *Computation of a Loss on Abandonment* (Re6.501–.521), to correct the example given in SFAS 90 (Re6.157–.166).)

SFAS 90 concludes that when partial or no return on investment is likely to be provided, the incremental future revenue expected to result from a regulator's inclusion of the cost of an abandoned plant in allowable costs for rate-making purposes is to be reported as an asset at its present value (using the utility's incremental borrowing rate) when the abandonment becomes probable. If the carrying amount of the abandoned plant exceeds that present value, a loss should be recognized. SFAS 71 previously had required that asset to be reported at the lesser of the cost of the abandoned plant or the probable gross revenue.

As to disallowances, SFAS 71 previously had required asset impairments to be recognized but did not specify what constitutes an impairment or provide specific guidance about how impairments should be measured. SFAS 90 rectified this:

> When it becomes probable that part of the cost of a recently completed plant will be disallowed for rate-making purposes and a reasonable estimate of the amount of the disallowance can be made, the estimated amount of the probable disallowance [must] be deducted from the reported cost of the plant and recognized as a loss. If part of the cost is explicitly, but indirectly, disallowed (for example, by an explicit disallowance of return on investment on a portion of the plant), an equivalent amount of cost shall be deducted from the reported cost of the plant and recognized as a loss. [Re6.127E]

Most larger utilities mentioned the issuance of SFAS 90 in their 1986 annual reports. Although the statement generally is not effective for calendar-year companies until January 1, 1988, some utilities provided an estimate of the effect of applying the statement to abandoned facilities and disallowed costs. Figure 33.5 presents a footnote disclosure of the possible effects of adopting SFAS 90.

SFAS 90 does not specify how abandonment and disallowance charges are to be classified—against operating income or as extraordinary. Under SFAS 71, some utilities had treated unrecoverable costs written off as extraordinary. The SEC staff stated, in SAB 72, *Classification of Charges for Abandonments and Disallowances* (Topic 10.E), that registrants should not use extraordinary treatment for SFAS 90 writeoffs, because SFAS 90 does not specifically sanction this. Further, if SFAS 90 is being retroactively adopted (as permitted), charges that were extraordinary items under SFAS 71 will have to be reclassified against restated operating income.

Phase-In Plans. Some portion of the costs of nuclear facilities has been and will continue to be disallowed for rate-making purposes either by regulatory commissions or court adjudication. Those costs will be accounted for generally as losses following the provisions of SFAS 90. However, not all of the remaining costs will automatically

Applying SFAS 90 to the Company in 1988, and assuming full recovery of the Company's abandoned portion of its Midland investment over 15 years and a return on this investment at the weighted cost rate for debt and preferred and preference stock, the Company estimates its loss, after tax, would be $190 million. Making the same assumptions except that no return is allowed the Company estimates its loss, after tax, would be $480 million.

Additional losses, when probable and reasonably estimable, would be recognized if either disallowances of portions of the abandoned Midland investment occur and/or portions of the Midland investment transferred to the MCV are not placed in commercial operation. However, if the Company is successful in recovering portions of its investment from contractors involved in the Midland project, the losses could be reduced.

If significant portions of the Midland investment are not recovered through the rate-making process, through the MCV or otherwise, the adverse effect on the Company's financial position and results of operations could be significant. . . .

FIG. 33.5   Disclosure of the Projected Loss From Applying SFAS 90
Source: Consumers Power Company, 1986 Annual Report.

become immediately allowable for rate-making purposes because they are so large they would cause a "rate spike." A rate spike is a significant, one-time increase in utility rates and generally is unacceptable to the users of electric power, and therefore also unacceptable to PUCs. As a result, regulators and utilities have developed plans to moderate the effect of large, one-time increases in rates. Those plans include spreading the allowable costs over an extended period; such an approach is called a phase-in plan.

The adoption of phase-in plans raised accounting questions that were not answered by SFAS 71. Those questions include (1) whether future rates will be sufficient to recover the phase-in costs, (2) whether phase-in plans represent a rejection of the basic premise that rates in any given period are based on the cost of service to customers during that period, and (3) whether capitalization of an allowance on equity after operations commence is appropriate.

Although the exposure draft for SFAS 90 addressed the accounting for phase-in plans, after considering public comments received in letters and during the public hearing, the FASB decided that additional effort would be needed to resolve the phase-in issue. As a result, the accounting for phase-in plans was dropped from SFAS 90. In 1987, the FASB issued SFAS 92, *Regulated Enterprises—Accounting for Phase-In Plans* (Re6). The statement generally is effective for fiscal years beginning after December 15, 1987, so calendar-year companies are affected beginning with interim reporting during 1988.

Capitalization criteria. If a phase-in plan is required by a regulatory commission for a facility completed or substantially constructed before January 1, 1988, the following criteria must be met for all allowable costs (those permitted to be deferred by the regulatory commission) to be capitalized for financial reporting purposes (Re6.125C):

1. The allowable costs in question are deferred pursuant to a formal plan that has been agreed to by the regulator.
2. The plan specifies the timing of recovery of all allowable costs that will be deferred under the plan.
3. All allowable costs deferred under the plan are scheduled for recovery within 10 years of the date when defcrrals begin.
4. The percentage increase in rates scheduled under the plan for each future year is not greater than the percentage increase in rates scheduled under the plan for each immediately preceding year. That is, the scheduled percentage increase in year two is no greater than the percentage increase granted in year one, the scheduled percentage increase in year three is no greater than the scheduled percentage increase in year two, and so forth.

Modifications and supplements. If an existing phase-in plan is altered by action of the management of a utility, or a regulator issues an order directing that a previous plan be replaced or modified, the capitalization criteria discussed above must be applied to the combination of the original and altered plans. Deferral would be considered to have commenced at the date of the earliest deferral under either plan, and final recovery would be considered to have occurred when all the amounts deferred are recovered.

Plans in existence for years prior to the first year covered by the effective date of SFAS 92 that are modified to meet (1) the capitalization requirements relating to the 10-year recovery period and (2) the annual percentage increase in rates permitted, are considered to meet the capitalization requirements. In those cases, measurement starts at the date of amendment rather than the date of the first deferral under the original plan.

Allowance for shareholder earnings. Normally regulators permit an allowance for the cost of equity funds to be capitalized for rate-making purposes for plants under construction. SFAS 92 further clarifies the circumstances under which the cost of equity funds may be capitalized. Assuming a phase-in plan meets the capitalization criteria discussed previously, allowable costs to be capitalized may include a cost for equity funds or earnings on shareholders' investment. If a provision for capitalization of earnings on shareholders' investment is permitted by a regulatory commission for some purpose other than a phase-in plan during construction, that provision *cannot* be capitalized for financial reporting purposes.

Classification of capitalized amounts. The cumulative amounts of costs capitalized pursuant to a phase-in plan are to be reported as an asset and shown separately in the balance sheet. For income statement presentation, the amount of capitalized cost that is recovered is to be reported as a separate item in other income and expense, not as a reduction of expenses.

Disclosure. The following disclosures are required by SFAS 92:

1. The terms and conditions of phase-in plans placed in effect during the year or ordered by a regulatory commission for future years.

2. The net amount deferred for rate-making purposes at year end and the net change in any deferrals for rate-making purposes during the year.

3. The nature and amount of an allowance for earnings on shareholders' investment capitalized for rate-making purposes but not for financial reporting purposes.

Discontinuance of Application of SFAS 71. In 1986, the FASB added to its agenda a project to specify the accounting required when an enterprise discontinues application of SFAS 71. The FASB has tentatively concluded that the result of discontinuing application should be a balance sheet that reflects assets, liabilities, and shareholders' equity as they would be if SFAS 71 had never been applied. The Board tentatively has agreed that the net effect of the change, as of the date it took place, should be included in net income as an extraordinary item in the period of change. The Board also tentatively agreed to require that the proposed statement be applied by enterprises that have previously discontinued application of SFAS 71. In mid-1988, the FASB released an Exposure Draft, *Regulated Enterprises—Accounting for the Discontinuation of Application of FASB Statement No. 71* (1988e) that reflects the foregoing conclusions. It is expected to be finalized late in 1988, and be effective immediately, (i.e., for fiscal years ending after December 15, 1988).

Income Taxes. Although Chapter 17 of the *Handbook* covers the generic impact of SFAS 96, *Accounting for Income Taxes* (I25), issues directly related to regulated industries are discussed in this chapter. SFAS 96 provides specific guidance in some areas, but there also are implementation issues raised and not yet resolved.

SFAS 96 reaffirms that companies meeting the criteria for applying SFAS 71 are not exempt from the requirements on accounting for income taxes; the statement (Re6.128A):

a. Prohibits net-of-tax accounting and reporting.

b. Requires recognition of a deferred tax liability (1) for tax benefits that are flowed through to customers when temporary differences originate and (2) for the equity component of the allowance for funds used during construction.

c. Requires adjustment of a deferred tax liability or asset for an enacted change in tax laws or rates.

These requirements affect the deferred tax accounting in the regulated industry environment, in particular the recognition of regulatory assets and liabilities and the AFUDC. Prior to SFAS 96, net-of-tax accounting was common in the utility industry; accordingly, there will be significant adjustments to gross-up previously netted items, in addition to reflecting the extensive changes made by the Tax Reform Act of 1986.

Regulatory assets and liabilities. It is common for the regulatory rate-setting body to adjust the rates charged to customers for increases or decreases in the taxes payable by a regulated enterprise. To the extent it is probable that the effect of those tax changes are included in the rate base, a regulatory asset or liability is to be recognized in accordance with SFAS 71. SFAS 96 takes the position that the asset or liability represents a temporary difference and therefore a related deferred tax asset or liability should also be recognized.

The FASB has discussed, but not yet resolved, the question of whether the accumulated balances of all regulatory assets and liabilities required by SFAS 71 should be disclosed, including the timing of their expected recovery or repayment through the rates charged to customers. Obviously, given the materiality of many of these assets and liabilities, the information would be useful because of their impact (through SFAS 96 "scheduling") on the deferred tax computation.

AFUDC. This item in particular is significantly affected by the requirements of SFAS 96, which necessitates grossing-up the AFUDC and concomitantly increasing the deferred tax liability. The AFUDC borrowed-funds component of construction work in progress must be grossed-up with the adjustment being recorded as a construction cost. The gross-up on the equity component of AFUDC in CWIP should be recorded as a regulatory asset, presented separately. The AFUDC component of plant already in service for both borrowed funds and equity should not be adjusted. However, a deferred tax liability must be recognized for the temporary difference between the carrying amount of the asset and its tax basis. If future rates will be adjusted to recover these taxes a regulatory asset should be recognized (see Figures 33.6 and 33.7).

As to the equity component of AFUDC, these figures explain the mechanics of applying SFAS 96 to CWIP when AFUDC contains an equity component and (1) future revenues will recover the cost component or (2) the revenue already has been collected from customers.

Carry-backs and carry-forwards. One of the major requirements of SFAS 96 is the use of carry-backs and carry-forwards in scheduling and therefore in computation of any deferred tax amounts. The FERC, however, historically has taken the position that carry-backs and carry-forwards could not be used to reduce a deferred tax liability. Given that the use of carry-back and carry-forward assumptions are so fundamental to the liability approach in SFAS 96, the FERC is in the process of reconsidering its prohibition.

Scheduling and regulatory assets. One of the issues raised with the FASB staff is: If in the scheduling process there are tax benefits that cannot be recorded as an offset against the tax liability, would it still be appropriate to recognize the related regulatory assets? For example, a net deductible amount may not be usable to offset an earlier year's liability due to scheduling limitations. If the deduction were related to an item that is recoverable in future rates the issue is whether the regulatory asset that would normally be recognized in accordance with SFAS 71 should in fact be recorded since the related deductible amount will not affect the deferred tax liability.

CWIP. In the case of items still under construction there is the question of what temporary differences should be considered in scheduling, and when. For example, assume that a net temporary difference of $100 exists representing capitalized interest, and it is the only difference between the book and tax bases of the assets. The asset is expected to go into service in two years and will have a life of 10 years.

Recognition of an Asset for the Probable Future Revenue to Recover Future Income Taxes Related to the Deferred Tax Liability for the Equity Component of AFUDC

Assumptions:

a. During year 1, the first year of operations, total construction costs for financial reporting and tax purposes are $400,000 (exclusive of AFUDC).

b. The enacted tax rate is 34% for all future years.

c. AFUDC (consisting entirely of the equity component) is $26,000.

The asset for probable future revenue to recover the related income taxes is calculated as follows:

   34 percent of ($26,000 + A) = A (where A equals the asset for probable future revenue)
   A = $13,394

At the end of year 1, the related accounts are as follows:

Construction in progress	$426,000
Probable future revenue	$ 13,394
Deferred tax liability [34% of ($26,000 + $13,394)]	$ 13,394

Adjustment of a Deferred Tax Liability for an Enacted Change in Tax Rates

Assumptions:

a. Same as for the example above, except that

b. A change in the tax rate from 34% to 30% is enacted on the first day of year 2.

As of the first day of year 2, the related accounts are adjusted so that the balances are as follows:

Construction in progress	$426,000
Probable future revenue	$ 11,143
Deferred tax liability [30% of ($26,000 + $11,143)]	$ 11,143

FIG. 33.6   Tax Effects of Equity Component in AFUDC—Probable Future Revenue
Source: Adapted from SFAS 96, (I25.157).

The cost of construction incurred to date is $1,000, therefore the tax basis is $900. One approach to scheduling would be to allocate the $100 difference using the book depreciation method over the expected service period of the asset. Another approach would be to spread each of the bases over that period, which would have a different effect assuming the depreciation method used for tax purposes differed from that used for book purposes.

The FASB staff has expressed a tentative conclusion that using the net deductible or taxable amount (i.e., the first approach above) is appropriate because the asset is not yet in service.

Auditing Considerations

Utilities have a large volume of small transactions with customers and accordingly the larger utilities make extensive use of computers. To obtain supplies of gas or

---

Adjustment of a Deferred Tax Liability for an Enacted Change in Tax Rates When That Deferred Tax Liability Represents Amounts Already Collected From Customers for the Future Payment of Income Taxes

Assumptions:

a. Amounts at the end of year 1, the current year, are as follows:

Construction in progress for financial reporting	$400,000
Tax basis of construction in progress	$300,000
Deferred tax liability (34% of $100,000)	$ 34,000

b. A change in the tax rate from 34% to 30% is enacted on the first day of year 2. As a result of the reduction in tax rates, it is probable that $4,000 of the $34,000 (previously collected from customers for the future payment of income taxes) will be refunded to customers, together with the tax benefit of that refund, through a future rate reduction.

The liability for the future rate reduction to refund a portion of the deferred taxes previously collected from customers is calculated as follows:

$4,000 + 30% of L = L (where L equals the probable future reduction in revenue)
L = $5,714

As of the first day of year 2, the related accounts are adjusted so that the balances are as follows:

Construction in progress	$400,000
Probable reduction in future revenue	$ 5,714
Deferred tax liability [30% of ($100,000 − $5,714)]	$ 28,286

FIG. 33.7 Tax Effects of Equity Component in AFUDC—Revenue Collected From Customers
Source: Adapted from SFAS 96 (I25.157).

power for distribution to customers, utilities will incur significant costs either in purchases from pipelines (for gas) or power grids (for electricity); or they will generate a large proportion of their own power, and perhaps sell any excess when available. In addition, utilities have a very significant investment in plant and are almost always in the process of constructing plant additions or betterments, which raises the issue of proper accounting for AFUDC. The various other regulatory constraints also raise substantive audit questions. Utilities other than electric and gas will have analogous situations. Accordingly, the auditor will focus principally on these areas as he plans and executes the audit.

Chapters 7 and 8 discuss the essential aspects of performing the audit and of internal controls. In particular, the cycle approach described in Chapter 8 will be most useful in planning the audit of a utility; and analytical procedures (described in Chapter 7) will provide indications of out-of-pattern areas that require the application of further auditing procedures. The large volumes of transactions processed by computer require computer-assisted audit techniques (see Chapter 10) and are also readily testable using statistical sampling techniques (Chapter 9).

Matters mentioned earlier under "Telecommunications Auditing Considerations" are also applicable to electric and gas utilities, in that the plant investment and the nature of the customer base are comparable.

Concerns About Contingencies. As discussed in the preceding accounting sections, electric utilities are experiencing severe problems in completing nuclear plants and placing them in operation. The attitudes of many PUCs is that the shareholders will have to absorb a large part of these costs because it is not fair (or politic) to make users pay for the entire cost of nuclear plants, especially if (1) the cost is higher than electricity generated by other means, and (2) the plant will not, or may not be, placed into operation. Any auditor of an entity involved with an uncompleted nuclear plant needs no reminder of the difficulties faced in making an assessment of recoverability of costs; and even the FASB has been moved to pronounce on abandonments and disallowances because of their prevalence.

The ultimate exercise may come for auditors in attesting to financial statements of companies that cease applying principles for regulated industries under SFAS 71 because they conclude that the regulatory environment of cost-based rate-setting no longer exists; the FASB's tentative decision to require restoring the accounts to what they would have been had SFAS 71 never been applied will exacerbate management's (as well as the auditor's) evaluation of plant asset recovery.

This type of concern also affects the natural gas industry for a different (but similar) reason: take-or-pay contracts (discussed later) made uneconomical to utility buyers and pipelines because of falling prices.

In this environment, auditors' reports frequently will contain an explanatory paragraph regarding contingencies and perhaps going concern status. It is no longer unthinkable that monopoly utilities may become bankrupt. This presents the auditor with the likelihood of litigation – although one would think that with all the publicity given to the industry's plight, it would be somewhat presumptive to sue the auditors.

NATURAL GAS PIPELINE COMPANIES

Natural gas pipeline companies provide a vital link in the natural gas industry. A pipeline gathers natural gas from producers' wells and facilities, including its own, and transports it to customer facilities (either its own or another supplier's) or to other pipelines. The operations of pipeline companies include all aspects of the natural gas industry including production, purchasing, gathering, storage, transportation, and the sale of natural gas (primarily to public utilities). Natural gas pipelines compete not only with other pipelines in the sale and delivery of natural gas but also with alternative sources of energy such as coal and fuel oil.

Regulation

The natural gas industry is regulated principally under the Natural Gas Act of 1938 (NGA) and the Natural Gas Policy Act of 1978 (NGPA). The FERC has been granted the regulatory authority to administer the NGA and accordingly has power over interstate transportation of natural gas and interstate sales of natural gas for resale.

The NGPA significantly revised federal regulation under NGA by effectively ending price controls over natural gas discovered after 1977. Additionally, subsequent orders of the FERC have attempted to make the industry more competitive and market-driven. NGA rate regulation continues, nevertheless, for interstate pipeline transportation and sales for resale by interstate pipelines.

Pipeline rates are set by determining the total cost of providing service during a test period and dividing that cost by the total units of sales or service. The basic elements of an interstate pipeline's cost of service are return on rate base plus expenses, including depreciation, depletion, amortization, and taxes. To establish "just and reasonable" rates, the FERC attempts to establish a rate that will enable the pipeline to recover its operating expenses while earning a reasonable return on invested capital.

A pipeline's rate base consists principally of its net investment in plant and property that provide service to the public. To the rate base is applied an appropriate rate of return consisting of an embedded cost of debt, preferred dividends for preferred securities, and earnings for common stockholders. The derived return is then included along with a working capital allowance in the cost of service calculation.

Pipelines, however, are permitted to flow through purchased gas adjustments (i.e., changes in their costs of gas) in their rates without the lengthy and expensive filing of a major rate case. Base tariff rates are then restated periodically for these purchased gas adjustments.

Business Environment

Natural gas accounts for almost 50% of all energy consumed in U.S. households and commercial facilities, compared with under 20% for oil. The abundance of natural gas, its clean-burning aspects, competitive price, and efficient million-mile underground pipeline system have made it very attractive to energy users.

The natural gas industry is in a period of transition from a price-controlled, highly regulated industry to an industry in which competition is fostered and market forces are allowed to operate. While in the past the pipeline business had been a "cash cow" for its owners, the industry is changing into a merchant/seller and a transportation company. The FERC has been requesting some experimentation involving buyers of natural gas (e.g., utilities or major industrial customers) being permitted to make their own purchase arrangements with gas producers (e.g., buying spot gas when it is inexpensive). Under an "open access" policy, a pipeline would then be required to transport it from the source to the user for a transportation fee. Although this approach might forestall major natural gas users from switching to other sources of energy, the issue is controversial in the industry.

In addition, natural gas producers and pipeline companies had entered into various contractual arrangements in the heavily regulated period of the late 1970s to insure the pipelines of adequate supplies of natural gas in a period of shortages; these shortages were caused to a great extent by the regulatory maintenance of artificially low prices for interstate sales of natural gas for resale. The pipeline companies want some relief from onerous take-or-pay arrangements before embracing "open access."

Take-or-Pay Arrangements

Take-or-pay contracts committed the pipelines to purchase quantities of natural gas for many future periods at prices that often turned out to be in excess of market prices when the time of the purchase arrived. These contracts continue to represent

---

3. Take-or-Pay Obligations

Approximately $11,400,000 and $14,500,000 were included in "Current portion of gas stored underground and prepaid expenses" at December 31, 1987 and 1986, respectively, relating to take-or-pay provisions of gas purchase contracts with producers. In general, when the Company has paid for gas not taken, its gas purchase contracts provide the right to make up the gas at later dates, generally limited to five years. At present, FERC regulations allow the inclusion of the financial cost of carrying such take-or-pay payments and, a portion of take-or-pay settlements, in the Company's cost-of-service to be recovered in its rates. The potential exists that future take-or-pay settlements or payments may be substantially in excess of those made to date.

A number of gas producers have instituted litigation arising out of take-or-pay claims against the Company, where these claims were not resolved by negotiation or other means. Additional claims have been and may be asserted and litigation has been or may be commenced during 1988, the amounts of which, when aggregated with existing amounts claimed or in litigation, could be very substantial.

The Company believes that meritorious defenses have been and will be asserted in pending and potential litigation, and intends to continue active litigation of take-or-pay claims, including appeals where necessary. The Company also intends to continue active pursuit of negotiations and other alternatives to eliminate or mitigate the adverse impacts, if any, of these claims and obligations, and believes the outcome of such litigation will not have a material adverse effect on the Company's consolidated financial position.

FIG. 33.8   Disclosure of Take-Or-Pay Obligations
Source: Colorado Interstate Gas Company, 1987 Form 10-K.

major current and future obligations for pipeline companies, and many companies are attempting to renegotiate their terms as well as pass on some or all of the renegotiation costs to their customers.

These attempts naturally have met with some opposition from the producers who are party to these arrangements. In addition, a satisfactory means of passing on renegotiation costs has not been satisfactorily resolved with the FERC. Whatever the final arrangements, producers, pipelines, and the FERC must find an equitable solution.

SFAS 47, *Disclosure of Long-Term Obligations* (C32), addresses the disclosure of commitments under unconditional purchase obligations such as take-or-pay contracts. An example of disclosure of take-or-pay obligations for natural gas pipeline companies is presented in Figure 33.8. SFAS 47 is also discussed in Chapter 21.

TRANSPORTATION

Environment

The transportation industry is regulated federally in varying degrees primarily by the Interstate Commerce Commission (ICC) and the Department of Transportation (DOT). In addition, all states and some local governments regulate the intrastate or local aspects of the industry.

In the early 1980s, a significant reduction in the authority of the federal regulatory agencies occurred in the form of the Airline Deregulation Act of 1978, the Motor Carrier Act of 1980, and the Staggers Rail Act of 1980 (SRA). These acts greatly increased the autonomy of the carriers by granting them considerable freedom in entry, rate-setting, and route selection.

The motor carrier industry is highly competitive with carriers offering a multitude of rates and service options. Many of the new entrants have been able to operate at significantly lower costs primarily because of more favorable nonunion labor costs, more efficient operations, and a better mix of routes and services. As a result, these new carriers have been able to slash rates and put severe economic pressure on not only older established motor carriers but also on the railroads.

The economic climate of the early 1980s has caused significant consolidations of the airline and railroad components of the industry. These merged operations have been able to eliminate costly duplicate facilities and significantly reduce labor costs. As a result, the newly structured railroads have been able to compete more favorably with motor carriers, especially in long haul shipments and intermodal (piggyback) operations.

Also of concern to enterprises in the transportation industry is the continuation of relatively low-cost and ample supplies of diesel, jet, and other fuels.

Railroads

Specialized Accounting Principles. A key concept in the regulation of railroad rates by the ICC is that of revenue adequacy. Railroads whose revenues are considered inadequate have greater flexibility in rate-setting and in rate disputes. The ICC has determined that a railroad has adequate revenues when its return on investment (ROI) equals or exceeds the cost-of-capital rate. In computing ROI, the investment base of a railroad is reduced by deferred tax liabilities, as this source of funding is provided interest-free by the government. The cost of capital rate is an industry-wide weighted average computed using the industry's proportions of debt and equity as determined by current market values and interest rates.

In applying the above concept and for other ICC regulatory determinations, uniform railroad accounting principles and costing systems are needed. Thus, the Railroad Accounting Principles Board (RAPB) was established by SRA to (1) establish a body of cost accounting principles to serve as the framework for implementing the regulatory provisions in which cost determination plays a vital role, and (2) make the administrative and legislative recommendations it deems necessary to integrate the principles into the regulatory process.

According to the SRA, the ICC must implement and enforce the RAPB's principles through the rule-making process, which affords interested parties an opportunity to participate. Because the ICC is ultimately responsible for cost principles, it must review the principles in light of rule-making comments from interested parties and reasonably explain the rules it adopts. However, as part of the rule-making process, the ICC must accord substantial deference to the RAPB's principles and to the rationale underlying those principles.

In 1988 the RAPB issued eight railroad accounting principles (four general and four specific) that will serve as the basis for determining costs in railroad regulatory matters. These principles are summarized as follows:

General Principles

- Causality. Costs shall only be attributed to cost objectives when a causal relationship exists (the cost would not have been incurred but for the requirements of the cost objectives).
- Homogeneity. Cost information shall be organized in homogeneous cost pools.
- Practicality. Cost and related information shall be feasible to obtain, efficiently determined, and material in amount.
- Data integrity. Cost and related information shall be valid, accurate, and verifiable.

Specific Principles

- Entity. The railroad entity shall comprise the activities of affiliated railroads and their railroad-related affiliates.
- Cost of capital. The cost-of-capital rate shall be a weighted-average rate computed using the proportions of debt and equity as determined by their market values and their current market rates.
- Asset valuation and related expense. Assets shall be valued at either the value of resources foregone by the entity to acquire the assets (GAAP cost) or at the current market value, depending on the regulatory application.
- Productivity. To measure cost changes accurately, indices used for railroad regulatory purposes shall incorporate changes in productivity as well as changes in input prices.

Track Structures. Retirement-replacement-betterment (betterment) accounting was the method railroads were required to use for track structures in reports to the ICC through 1983. Under betterment accounting, the initial cost of track structures was capitalized and no systematic depreciation was taken. The cost of equal-quality replacements was charged to expense as incurred. "Betterments" occurred when improved quality components were installed. An amount equal to the current cost of the component replaced was expensed, and the excess amount, which represents the betterment portion, was capitalized. Capitalized amounts were recovered when the asset was retired.

Historically, betterment accounting was the subject of much debate. Proponents argued that betterment accounting accurately reflects economic reality, particularly during periods of inflation, because income is charged with current replacement costs rather than with depreciation based on understated historical costs. Critics of betterment accounting contended that it fails to recognize properly the cost of capital used or consumed in operations, particularly during periods when maintenance is postponed or accelerated. Income is overstated during periods of postponed or deferred maintenance because operating expense is inadequately charged for the costs of capital consumed. In addition, the decline in the service value of assets is not recognized through depreciation charges to operations. The opposite is true during periods of accelerated maintenance; income is understated because operating expense is charged with the full cost of replacements that will benefit future periods.

In 1983, the ICC ruled that railroads must use depreciation accounting rather than betterment accounting for regulatory reporting purposes. In this regard the FASB issued SFAS 73, *Reporting a Change in Accounting for Railroad Track Structures* (A06.123), which amended APB 20 to require a change from betterment accounting to depreciation accounting to be reported by restating financial statements of prior periods.

Motor Carriers

Operating Rights. Motor carriers regulated by the ICC must obtain *operating rights*—certificates or permits authorizing transportation of commodities over defined routes or areas—before they can engage in interstate or foreign commerce. Carriers can either obtain operating rights directly from the ICC or purchase another carrier's rights. The cost of operating rights includes either regulatory agency fees and related legal fees or the purchase price, if acquired separately from other carriers.

Enactment of the Motor Carrier Act of 1980 significantly decreased the value of intangible operating rights. The Act makes it easier for carriers to enter a market because it requires the ICC to grant certificates unless "the transportation to be authorized by the certificate is inconsistent with the public convenience and necessity." Diversion of revenue on traffic from an existing carrier is not in and of itself justification for denying a certificate.

In response to the Motor Carrier Act of 1980, the FASB issued SFAS 44, *Accounting for Intangible Assets of Motor Carriers* (I60). SFAS 44 requires that the costs of a motor carrier's intangible assets, if not separately allocated in the past, now had to be assigned to (1) interstate operating rights, (2) other identifiable intangible assets (including intrastate operating rights), and (3) goodwill, by applying the criteria in APB 16 (B50.146) and APB 17 (I60.105–60.107), based on the circumstances existing when the assets were acquired. All unamortized costs related to interstate operating rights should be expensed and, if material, reported as an extraordinary item. Any subsequent write-off of other identifiable intangible assets or goodwill should not be reported as an extraordinary item.

If a motor carrier cannot separately identify and assign costs to interstate operating rights, other identifiable intangible assets, and goodwill, or finds it is impracticable to do so, it should presume that the entire excess of purchase cost over identifiable net assets acquired relates to interstate operating rights.

Airlines

AICPA Guide. The Airline Deregulation Act of 1978 was a legislative milestone, substantially reducing the amount of government regulation of air carriers and their activities. With the amount and cost of regulation reduced, a number of smaller carriers have entered the industry, primarily commuter service and regional airlines. Given these changes, the AICPA issued an Industry Audit Guide, *Audits of Airlines* (AICPA, 1981b), to assist both new entrants to the business and independent accountants in gaining an understanding of the unique accounting practices and auditing considerations in the industry.

The Guide describes the organization and operations of airlines, the regulatory environment, general accounting and auditing practices, and specific applications of accounting principles and auditing procedures. The Guide, however, is not intended to codify preferable accounting practices, but rather aims to summarize the practices being followed in the industry. The sections that follow contain a synopsis of the important accounting and auditing provisions of the Guide.

Uniform System of Accounts and Reports. Reporting of accounting information by airlines is governed by a Uniform System of Accounts and Reports (USAR), issued by the CAB. The USAR consists of standard accounts and related instructions covering their use. The CAB's policy is to conform its accounting requirements to GAAP, with the result that most airlines' published annual reports follow the wording and captions of the USAR accounts.

Revenues are divided into three categories—transport (air transportation revenues); public service (federal subsidies); and transport-related (liquor sales, sublease income, and revenues from maintenance performed for other airlines). The functional classifications for operating expenses are based on the type of activity or service rendered and are highlighted in Figure 33.9.

Accounting Considerations. Each technical section of the AICPA Guide describes in some detail the accounting practices common in the industry, along with a corresponding list of suggested audit procedures. Specific areas covered include revenues, maintenance, personnel and payroll, insurance, depreciation, developmental and pre-operating costs (for new routes), inventories, and the effects of governmental regulation. Finally, the Guide includes illustrative financial statements and a glossary of airline industry terms.

Separate sections of the Guide are devoted to internal accounting control, analytical procedures, and segment information, which is required in more detail by the DOT than by SFAS 14 (S20).

The unusual accounting practices of the industry arise from the nature of its operations: decentralized sales, mobility of the bulk of its assets, continuous interairline transactions, dispersed accounting controls, and the constant need for huge capital investment. However, for many airlines most accounting functions (recording of revenues, disbursements, inventories, etc.) are centralized at one location.

The following sections briefly highlight the significant accounting issues.

Revenues. The Guide comments that the most unusual characteristic of the airline industry is its revenue cycle. The factors contributing to the complexity of revenue recognition in the industry include the following:

• Sales are made at numerous locations.

• Third parties may handle a substantial portion of ticket transactions.

• Tickets are generally refundable up to one year following their issuance.

• Multiple fare types are available for similar service.

• A single ticket may comprise multiple flight segments on different carriers, requiring proration of the total ticket fare.

• Since most tickets are sold in advance of the flight date, unearned revenue is a major item for virtually all carriers.

Generally, revenue is recognized upon use of a ticket by a passenger, either on the basis of matching used coupons with those issued and reflected as unearned revenue (exclusive of other airlines' shares) or through a sampling of used coupons if issued tickets are not separately accounted for.

Classification	Expenses Included	Major Items
Flying operations	In-flight operations and holding of aircraft (except depreciation) and operational personnel in readiness for assignment to an in-flight status.	Fuel, flight personnel (except flight attendants) payroll, and employee benefits.
Maintenance	Direct and indirect expenditures for repair and maintenance.	Labor, material, outside services, and general or overhead expense allocations.
Passenger services	Expenditures relating to comfort, safety, and convenience in flight and during delays.	Personnel and flight attendant's payroll and passenger food and supplies.
Aircraft and traffic servicing	Compensation to ground personnel and other expenses incidental to the protection and control of in-flight aircraft movement; handling and servicing while in operation; scheduling and preparation of operational flight crews for assignment; and handling of ground property and equipment.	Payroll costs and employee benefits; general services purchases; and servicing supplies, landing fees and facility rentals.
Reservations, sales, and advertising	Outlays to create a public preference for an air carrier; to stimulate the development of an air transportation market; or to develop air transportation in general.	Passenger handling and traffic solicitations payroll and benefits; travel agent commissions; and advertising.
General and administrative	Expenditures of benefit to more than one operating function.	Record-keeping and statistical personnel; federal excise and state taxes; stationery supplies, etc.
Depreciation and amortization	Depreciation of operating property and equipment and amortization of intangible assets.	Depreciation of flight equipment, maintenance equipment, and ground property; amortization of developmental and preoperating costs; and capitalized leases.
Transport-related	Costs relating to generation of transport-related revenues.	Liquor; maintenance for other carriers; and cost of subleases.

FIG. 33.9   Airline Operating Expense Classifications
Source: AICPA, 1981b. Industry Audit Guide, Audits of Airlines, New York, pp. 91–92.

Inventories. In an airline operation, inventories (e.g., spare parts, materials, and supplies) are for internal consumption, not for external sale. They are valued at cost, less an allowance for obsolescence that corresponds to the useful lives of the carrier's fleet.

Fixed assets. Fixed assets generally consist of flight equipment, ground property and equipment, and capital leases. Rotable parts and assemblies (spare parts which are used on airplanes for a period, removed, repaired, and reinstalled) and work-in-progress accounts used to accumulate costs to be capitalized are also classified as fixed assets. Some airlines include progress payments on flight equipment purchase contracts made to aircraft manufacturers as fixed assets. Other carriers include these in other noncurrent asset captions.

Flight equipment, consisting of airframes, engines, and improvements to owned or leased aircraft, is classified as operating or nonoperating in accordance with CAB regulations. Operating property and equipment include all items in use in air transport or related services. In addition, property and equipment undergoing overhaul, modification, or repair, and property and equipment held for standby use (ready for immediate use as backup) remain in the operating accounts.

The Guide states that ground property and equipment include "land, buildings, leasehold improvements (such as those made in passenger and cargo terminals) and equipment (including that used to service aircraft and traffic loads on airport grounds and in terminals, to prepare and service food, to maintain flight and ground properties, and to conduct sales, training, and other office functions)" (p. 55). Capital leases include leases meeting SFAS 13 criteria (L10) and are used to acquire both flight equipment and ground property and equipment.

Depreciation. Because the industry is capital-intensive, a carrier's accounting policy for depreciation is important. Most companies in the industry apply the straight-line method for financial reporting purposes.

Depreciation may be applied to a single asset (unit depreciation) or to a group of assets that are similar in nature. An airline may use unit or group depreciation methods on different groups of assets. Group depreciation usually is applied where there is a significant number of assets having relatively small unit values. Unit depreciation is generally applied to aircraft and engines that have large unit costs and are comparatively few in number.

The expected useful life of an asset and its estimated residual value will vary, based on several factors. Airplanes are maintained in relatively the same condition throughout their service lives; therefore, replacement of property and equipment is generally due to (1) market growth, (2) technological developments, (3) perceived operating cost efficiencies, and (4) perceived revenue-generating capabilities. These factors affect individual airlines in different ways. Thus the determination of aircraft lives and residuals hinges on the company's projections of when an aircraft will be replaced, the ability to finance replacements, and other factors, such as length of flights and number of takeoffs and landings which affect the cost of maintaining aircraft in flying condition.

Purchase incentives. Purchase incentives are frequently negotiated with aircraft manufacturers under which the manufacturer will issue credits that can be used for the purchase of spare parts, but may not be applied as part of the purchase price of aircraft (this is, of course, an inducement to purchase a particular manufacturer's aircraft). Other incentives include guaranteed trade-in values and purchase credits for flight crew training equipment (flight simulators). For accounting purposes, the credit may be treated as a reduction of the purchase price of the aircraft or recorded as a deferred credit and accreted over the life of the related aircraft; in either event, the net result is the same.

Auditing Considerations. Among the key factors that may be presented and affect the independent auditor's examination of an airline's financial statements are:

* Effective organizational structure.
* Clearly defined management responsibilities.
* Detailed procedural manuals.
* Comprehensive budgeting process with close monitoring.
* Effective internal auditing.

The Guide provides considerable detail regarding the audit approach and likely procedures, and should be consulted for in-depth consideration as needed. (See also Chapter 7 regarding audit performance (including analytical review) and Chapter 8 regarding internal controls.) A brief mention of a few incisive areas of the Guide is given in the sections that follow.

Potential problems. Several audit areas present special problems that the audit plan should anticipate (Guide, pp. 15–16):

* Unreported ticket sales, that can result from delays or from lack of controls surrounding the matching of tickets lifted with tickets sold.
* Expenses incurred at the local level in the pursuit of passenger service, including meals, transportation, and accommodations of various kinds for both scheduled and delayed passengers.
* Commissions, authorized or unauthorized, on sales of aircraft in foreign countries.
* Improper commissions or unauthorized payments to travel agents.
* The risk of ticket exchange transactions, whether authorized or unauthorized, and similar arrangements that are inherent in a business devoted to the sale of an attractive but perishable commodity.
* The failure to act properly or promptly on audit findings, including those of internal auditors and regulatory agency auditors.

Analytical procedures. SAS 56, *Analytical Procedures* (AU 329), should be used in designing and performing such procedures, to which the airline industry lends itself very readily. Specifically, the auditor will normally review the "relationship of financial and nonfinancial data, focusing on operational statistics developed independently of the accounting process and their relationship to current accounting data." These statistics include such key operating data and statistics as yield, load factor, break-even load factor, and fuel consumption. By comparing the various data of the airline being audited with those of other airlines, the auditor may identify out-of-pattern situations that may require further investigation.

AICPA Project in Process. The AICPA has issued an Exposure Draft of a proposed SOP, *Accounting for Frequent Travel Award Programs, Developmental and Preoperating Costs, Purchases and Exchanges of Take-Off and Landing Slots, and Airframe Modifications* (AICPA, 1987a). Accounting for frequent travel award programs developed into a more controversial issue than originally anticipated, resulting in its split-off into a separate proposed SOP in August 1988. The conclusions of the two proposed SOPs are

- Frequent travel award programs. An amount based on the allocated revenue value to the airline of a free travel award (rather than its incremental cost) should be deferred in the unearned transportation liability account. Such deferral should occur as mileage is accumulated, rather than when free award levels are reached (as is presently practiced by the airlines).

- Developmental and preoperating costs. Because of the current deregulated environment and the uncertainty regarding the recoverability of route developmental costs, developmental costs and preoperating costs related to preparation of operations of new routes should not be capitalized as previously permitted under the Guide. Preoperating costs related to the integration of new types of aircraft or services would continue to be eligible to be capitalized, as permitted in the Guide.

- Take-off and landing slots. When airlines buy or exchange slots, the recorded asset is an identifiable intangible asset that should be accounted for in conformity with APB 17, *Intangible Assets* (I60), and APB 29, *Accounting for Nonmonetary Transactions* (N35). (Generally, when similar productive assets are exchanged, such as one slot exchanged for another slot, the transaction would not result in the culmination of an earnings process and should be based on recorded amounts.)

- Airframe modifications. These modifications enhance the usefulness of aircraft; therefore the costs associated with the changes should be capitalized and depreciated over the lesser of the estimated useful lives of the aircraft or the modifications. The cost of the replaced asset net of accumulated depreciation and anticipated recovery value should be charged to income in the current period.

The exposure period for the initial proposed SOP ended in mid-1987. A final SOP is expected in late 1988, covering all issues except frequent travel awards. The exposure period for the second SOP ends in late 1988.

34

Natural Resources

OVERVIEW

Throughout history, the progress of man has been dependent on the development of natural resources. Industrialized society would be unable to exist in its present form without exploitation of nature's products, many of which have been created over long periods of time and cannot be replaced readily through the technological capabilities of man.

Oil and gas, hard minerals, and timber are discussed in this chapter. Each of these forms of natural resources has its own distinct characteristics, and from an economic standpoint the expenditures required to convert them to a form suitable for industrial use vary in nature and capital intensity.

Oil and gas resources include all forms of hydrocarbon deposits that are extracted in a liquid or gaseous state. The accounting for oil and gas resources differs from the accounting for other natural resources primarily because of the substantial investment required before the presence of commercially recoverable quantities of oil or gas can be determined. Exploration for oil and gas also involves many risks; it is common for no oil or gas at all to be recovered from a particular exploration investment.

Hard minerals include all other resources extracted from the earth, such as coal, uranium, precious metals, sand, gravel, and other mineral deposits. Although prediscovery costs for hard minerals are generally significant, they are not as great as they are with oil and gas. Costs of extraction after discovery, however, are usually more substantial than in the case of oil and gas. In some cases, for example, discovered deposits may be so enormous that the entire deposit is unlikely to be extracted and marketed in any reasonably estimable time frame. Price volatility is frequently great, and can affect the recoverability of any investment. In such cases, the proper basis for allocation of costs over production is difficult to determine. In some cases, environmental regulations require large outlays to reclaim the land from which the minerals were extracted, and although these costs may not be accurately estimated until late in the productive life of the project, it is necessary to anticipate them for both planning and accounting purposes during the entire production period.

Timber has traditionally been considered a natural resource rather than an agricultural product. It requires a long growing cycle and, historically, after a forest was clear-cut it was allowed to grow back without human assistance. Today, however, much timber is harvested on a sustained-yield basis through carefully managed reforestation programs, which makes accounting for timber resources more like accounting for agricultural products than accounting for oil and gas or hard minerals. However, timber resource accounting is discussed in this chapter both because of tradition and because the time over which timber is replaced is so much longer than the replacement cycle for most agricultural products.

FOCUSING ON RESERVES

A company's *reserves* are its unextracted oil and gas or mineral deposits or, in the forest products industry, its standing timber. In this section, hydrocarbons and hard minerals are the focus; later in the chapter, standing timber is considered.

Because most deposits of hydrocarbons and minerals are located beneath the surface of the earth, direct observation of their exact quantity and quality is impossible. Both the characteristics of the deposit and the rate at which it can be extracted must be estimated by an evaluation of geological and geophysical data or, in oil and gas exploration, if drilling has begun, by analysis of samples from the drilling. These early estimates of a deposit may prove quite inaccurate. Only after there has been sufficient production to provide a reliable history of the operating characteristics of the deposit can a reasonably reliable estimate be made, and it may take several years to accumulate such a history.

Reserve Categories

Proved Reserves. Those reserves that are reasonably certain to be recoverable using existing technology and under current economic conditions are classified as *proved reserves*. Proved reserves are used as a basis for amortization of cost under historical cost accounting methods. Detailed definitions of proved reserves for oil and gas appear in ASR 257 (FRR § 406.01a.i.), and these definitions have been adopted by the FASB (Oi5.405).

Proved Developed Reserves. When equipment is in place to permit extraction of proved reserves, the reserves are classified as *proved developed reserves*; otherwise, they are proved undeveloped reserves. In general, development costs are amortized on the basis of proved developed reserves. Hydrocarbons or other minerals that cannot be extracted using conventional extraction methods are not considered proved until the advanced recovery equipment is installed and shown to be operational on the specific deposit, field, or geological structure.

Other Reserve Categories. Other categories of reserves have been defined by engineers and geologists to indicate the probability of commercially recoverable resources even though additional testing is necessary to classify the reserves as proved. Resources in such categories as *inferred reserves, probable reserves*, or *possible reserves* may be of potential future benefit to a company, but are generally considered so uncertain that they are not used as a basis for historical cost amortization or revenue recognition or for formal supplemental disclosure purposes.

Reserve Accounting

Despite the inescapable vulnerability of reserves to misevaluation, management must make decisions on property acquisition and exploration and development activities; and investors and lenders must make decisions on their involvement with the company and its primary financial resources – its reserves. Management's responsibility is to supply financial information to these decision makers.

The traditional accounting approach has been to capitalize those costs that are expected to result in future benefits (i.e., costs associated with reserves) and to expense all other costs. But the question of which costs should be capitalized and which should be expensed is difficult to answer when the cost objective cannot be observed or measured with an acceptable level of precision. With little conclusive evidence to support many capitalization or expense decisions, the accountant must rely on reserve estimates to reach an essentially subjective judgment as to whether the capitalized costs can or cannot be realized through related future revenues.

Another difficulty is that the discovery of significant reserves is not reflected in the accounts, even though it enhances the value of the company. It is only as reserves are produced and sold that financial statements eventually reflect the income from discoveries. In some cases, the reserves are not utilized until many years after discovery; the company then reports income that reflects in part a realization of the value of reserves discovered many years before.

A great deal of controversy has arisen over the use of traditional sales-realization-based accounting in the oil and gas producing industries. Two primary historical cost approaches – full cost and successful efforts – evolved in oil and gas accounting, with numerous variations in detail. As a result, comparability has been impaired, even between companies using the same primary accounting method.

This lack of comparability has been the cause of extensive professional and SEC effort to change the accounting methodologies. Although improvements have occurred, much of the effort has been unavailing.

OIL AND GAS PRODUCING INDUSTRY

The development of the petroleum industry began in 1859 when the first commercially successful wildcat oil well was completed in Pennsylvania. Shortly thereafter, in 1870, the Standard Oil group was formed, dominating all aspects of the country's oil and gas refining, marketing, and transportation activities for 40 years. Following the dissolution of the group and the oil demands brought about by World War I, the industry entered a period of rapid, competitive growth. Then, with the 1930s came the Depression – and the beginning of governmental regulation of production. A new upsurge in demand was felt as a result of World War II, followed by expansion of U.S. investment overseas (particularly in the Middle East and North Africa), mammoth natural gas pipeline projects, and the development of the petrochemical industry.

In the early 1970s, yet another phenomenon faced the oil and gas industry. Massive oil shortages occurred in the industrialized nations. As a result of those shortages, there was a concerted effort by many nations to conserve the use of oil. As one example, the production and sale of more fuel-efficient automobiles increased dramatically. In addition, in some cases, industry shifted to other forms of fuel or developed more efficient uses of oil. Those changes dramatically reduced the consumption of oil, and only currently, after more than 10 years, is there an increase in the use of oil.

Another facet of the 1970s oil shortage was the large amount of petrodollars accumulated by the oil producing nations. Those dollars were recycled into significant investments by the oil producing nations in Europe and the United States.

In the 1980s, the supply of oil became so plentiful that there is now an oversupply. This flip-flop from the 1970s has resulted primarily from the industrialized nations' conservation measures and dissension in the Middle East oil cartel. Although oil use is again increasing, oil prices as of mid-1988 are still depressed at least relative to the high prices of the early 1970s. However, some industry experts predict that by 1992 there is a distinct possibility that the world will face yet another shortage similar to the one that occurred in the 1970s.

Hydrocarbon Reserves

The petroleum industry's purpose is to find reserves, or hydrocarbon deposits, that can be extracted in liquid or gaseous states under existing operating technology and economic conditions. Finding reserves depends on complex engineering approaches and is subject to a high degree of uncertainty. Exploratory methods include analysis of geological structures and development of surface and subsurface maps, the latter by seismic testing, analysis of core samples obtained through the drilling of stratigraphic test wells, and other techniques. As accumulated data provides evidence of the probability that a favorable structure has been identified, further tests are performed to gather information suggestive of quantities and quality of oil and gas in the reservoir, of the most effective way to develop the area, and of the boundaries of the field and each reservoir within the field. Even the application of such expensive, sophisticated techniques as these provides no guarantee that economically recoverable quantities of oil and gas are present in the reservoir identified.

Numerous technical terms are used in this chapter. The interested reader may refer to the FASB Discussion Memorandum, *Financial Accounting and Reporting in the Extractive Industries* (FASB 1976), and to the glossary of terms contained in the U.S. Department of Energy's *Financial Reporting System*.

Accounting Methods

Traditional accounting methods are based on historical cost, emphasizing measurement and classification of costs incurred in finding and developing reserves. Those costs are generally associated with four phases of activity:

1. Preacquisition (or prospecting)
2. Acquisition and exploration
3. Development
4. Production

(Comprehensive definitions of those costs and the assets to which they relate are provided in SFAS 19, *Financial Accounting and Reporting by Oil and Gas Producing Companies* (Oi5.106–.115).

Phases of Activity—Related Costs. The various costs incurred in the oil and gas industry are categorized by the activity to which they relate. The activities and costs are discussed in the following subsections.

Preacquistion costs are incurred to identify possible areas of oil or gas deposits and to gain preliminary indications of the nature of those deposits. Included are the costs of geological and geophysical studies (G&G costs), specific outlays to obtain rights to conduct these studies (shooting rights), costs of contracted geological and geophysical services, salaries of a company's own geologic and geophysical crews, and related overhead items.

Acquisition and exploration costs are incurred to acquire and retain mineral interests in properties, whether by purchase, lease, or other means, and to conduct further
geological and geophysical studies and to drill exploratory wells. Initial acquisition
costs include lease bonus payments, legal costs, and options. Costs associated with
carrying and retaining undeveloped properties, such as delay rentals, property taxes,
property maintenance costs, and shut-in royalties, are often considered as costs of
delay in exploration and are usually included in this category. Exploratory costs
include drilling and equipping wells on unproved acreage, licenses and permits to
drill, and drilling of exploratory-type stratigraphic test wells.

Development costs are incurred to obtain access to the discovered reserves and to
provide facilities necessary to extract the resources and prepare them for transportation from the field. Development costs include costs to prepare the development
drilling site; costs to drill and equip development wells, including development-type
stratigraphic wells and service wells; and costs of offshore platforms, down-hole
equipment, and the wellhead assembly. In addition, development costs also include
leased production facilities such as pumps, compressors, flow-lines, separators, and
tankage; gas cycling plants; gathering systems to the point of custody transfer in the
field; and costs of improved recovery equipment. If support facilities (such as living
quarters or field power plants) or processing facilities (such as natural gas processing
plants) have value that is primarily dependent on the value of the reserves in the
field, the cost of these facilities is also considered a development cost.

Production costs are incurred in lifting oil and gas from subsurface reservoirs, gathering, treating, field processing, field storage, and operating and maintaining field
equipment. These costs may include severance taxes and other taxes on the assets in
the field; costs to repair field equipment; labor costs incurred in maintenance, operation, and inspection of production facilities; insurance; and any necessary equipment, materials, supplies, fuel, or other items required for production. Production
activities are usually regarded as terminating at the point at which product is delivered from a production storage tank into a refining or main transporting facility,
known as the *point of custody transfer* in the field.

In the past, several approaches existed in the presentation of periodic results of
operations and financial statement classification of costs arising from the activities
of oil and gas producing enterprises. The greatest diversity in practice appears in
the accounting for preacquisition, acquisition, and exploration costs. Two distinguishable accounting methods have evolved as generally accepted, the *full cost* and
the *successful efforts* method. These were developed based on differing views of the
circumstances that should result in the capitalization (or deferral) of costs
incurred.es

Full Cost Method. Under the broadest form of the full cost concept (not
acceptable for SEC companies), all costs incurred in prospecting, acquisition,
exploration, and development activities – generally including those portions of
general and administrative costs that are associated with these activities – are
capitalized. Cost centers are usually not defined by the existence of contiguous oil
and gas bearing geological formations. In the broadest application of this method, a
single company-wide cost center may be established, regardless of the location of an
enterprise's properties. Traditionally, it has been more common for individual
continents, countries, or large geographic regions within countries to be adopted as

cost centers. Offshore properties are normally included with onshore properties in a cost center.

Capitalized costs are amortized as production occurs from the reserves in a cost center. If no recoverable reserves are discovered in a cost center within a reasonable period of time after expenditures have been made, capitalized costs in that center are written off as a loss. If capitalized costs exceed the estimated present value of net revenues from future production of reserves in a cost center, the costs are written down to that estimated value, that is, to their allowable ceiling.

There are two areas in full cost accounting that have been subject to modification in practice. One is the selection of the cost center, as previously described. The other is the timing of transfer of preproduction costs into a producing cost center. Some companies assign preproduction costs to the cost center as they are incurred, whereas others defer the transfer until a determination is made whether the related undeveloped properties will be productive or nonproductive. This affects the timing of amortization.

The major premise underlying the full cost concept is that the value of reserves discovered should be related to the total of all direct and indirect costs incurred in their discovery and development. Exploration costs, including the drilling of dry holes, are considered prerequisites for production from developed reserves and, therefore, are capitalized.

Successful Efforts Method. Under the successful efforts concept the only costs capitalized are those acquisition, exploration, and development costs directly associated with properties at which commercially recoverable reserves are discovered. In accordance with this concept, cost centers generally have been established on the basis of specifically identified reserves. The *field* is the predominant cost center used in practice, although some companies using the successful efforts method have accounted on a lease, district, or division basis.

In general, the costs of geological and geophysical studies, the costs of carrying undeveloped properties, and general and administrative costs are charged to expense as incurred. All acquisition, exploration, and development costs associated with properties where commercially recoverable reserves are not discovered are written off at the time the property is determined to be nonproductive. Capitalized costs are amortized as production occurs from reserves within a cost center.

Prior to standardization through SFAS 19 (Oi5.118–.132), variations occurred in the application of the successful efforts method in practice. Some companies amortized the costs associated with nonproductive properties based on an experience factor rather than recording a loss when the properties were determined to be worthless. Some capitalized a portion of geological and geophysical costs instead of expensing them as incurred. Nonproductive development costs, such as development of dry holes, were expensed as incurred by some and capitalized to the productive cost center by others. And, as mentioned previously, there have been variations in the cost centers selected.

The successful efforts concept rests largely on the premise that only costs directly identifiable with future benefits should be recorded as assets. Thus, discovery costs, other than the cost of acquiring the property, should be capitalized only if associated with the reserves toward which exploratory and development efforts are specifically directed.

Department of Energy Requirements

The Energy Policy and Conservation Act of 1975 (EPCA) provided the initial impetus for the development of uniform accounting practices. One of its purposes was to provide a means for developing a comprehensive energy database. In accordance with this objective, the Department of Energy (DOE) developed its *Financial Reporting System* (FRS), with which certain major companies must comply. The requirements of FRS will be extended to most major producers and a sample of smaller companies in coming years. The DOE has the authority to require reporting by virtually all companies in the industry.

The DOE has not prescribed an accounting method and has indicated that it does not advocate any particular method, although a preference for development of a form of reserve value accounting has been expressed. The FRS does include numerous definitions, including those of proved reserves, that have been adopted by the SEC and conformed to by the FASB. FRS also requires separate reporting, not required under GAAP or SEC rules, for individual segments of integrated operations.

FASB Action and SEC Reaction

EPCA mandated the development of uniform accounting policies within the oil and gas industry. When the EPCA was introduced in 1975 most oil and gas producers had long used a form of either successful efforts or full cost accounting. During the years 1975–1977, the FASB concluded that, of the two methods, successful efforts was preferable, and in 1977 issued SFAS 19, *Financial Accounting and Reporting by Oil and Gas Producing Companies* (Oi5), that mandated only one accounting method, a form of successful efforts.

However, the SEC did not agree with the FASB conclusions and instead determined that none of the currently followed accounting and reporting practices based on historical cost, including the SFAS 19 approach, provided sufficient useful information about the *value* of a company's oil and gas resources to represent a preferable method. In ASR 253 (FRR § 406), the SEC adopted the disclosure requirements of SFAS 19, yet rejected the imposition of the successful efforts method on the entire oil and gas industry.

Reserve Recognition Approach. The SEC also proposed an alternative approach, termed reserve recognition accounting (RRA), a form of current value accounting, that would present the value of proved reserves as assets, and increases therein as income.

Until RRA could be fully developed, the SEC decided to permit use of either the successful efforts method under SFAS 19 or the full cost method (under ASR 258, as amended by FRR 14 (FRR § 406.01.c)). The SEC proposed, moreover, that this financial information would be supplemented by audited disclosures pertaining to oil and gas reserves and the estimated future net revenues therefrom.

The FASB accepted the SEC's decision regarding the SFAS 19 successful efforts method and issued SFAS 25, *Suspension of Certain Accounting Requirements for Oil and Gas Producing Companies* (Oi5.102). Although suspension of SFAS 19 made its requirements optional, the FASB nevertheless prescribed SFAS 19 as preferable for purposes of accounting changes under APB 20, *Accounting Changes* (Oi5.102). The FASB also made a number of other revisions to the earlier standard to bring it into conformity with ASR 257 (FRR § 406.01.a.i–ii).

In ASR 269 (now rescinded), the SEC added requirements for two supplementary disclosures based on RRA. The first was an RRA summary of the past year's results of oil and gas producing activities, while the second was a schedule of annual changes in the estimated present value of future net revenues from proved oil and gas reserves. However, the age of RRA was destined to be short-lived.

Withdrawal of Reserve Recognition Project. In ASR 289, issued in 1981, the SEC announced that "it no longer considers Reserve Recognition Accounting to be a potential method of accounting in the primary financial statements of oil and gas producers." While ASR 289 did not change the Regulation S-X requirements for RRA-based supplemental disclosures, it did express the SEC's support of an FASB project to develop a comprehensive package of disclosures for oil and gas producers. The SEC noted that, although it had decided against full implementation of RRA, it remained committed to some sort of value-based disclosure of reserves.

Required Disclosures—SFAS 69

Shortly after the SEC abandoned RRA as a potential method of accounting in the primary financial statements of oil and gas producers, the FASB added a project to its agenda to formulate a comprehensive set of disclosures for oil and gas producing activities. The result of the project was the release in 1982 of SFAS 69, *Disclosures About Oil and Gas Producing Activities* (Oi5), that amends SFAS 19 and SFAS 25.

General Disclosure Approach. SFAS 69 continues the requirement that enterprises engaged in oil and gas producing activities must disclose the method of accounting for costs incurred and the manner of amortizing capitalized costs. Also, publicly traded enterprises that have significant oil and gas producing activities are required to include the following disclosures as supplementary information:

• Proved oil and gas reserve quantities.
• Capitalized costs relating to oil and gas producing activities.
• Costs incurred in oil and gas producing activities.
• Results of operations for oil and gas producing activities.
• A standardized measure of discounted future net cash flows relating to proved oil and gas reserves.

These disclosures are required only when a complete set of annual financial statements is presented, but are not required in interim financial reports.

Oil and gas producing activities are deemed significant if one or more of the following tests is met (Oi5.158):

1. Revenues from oil and gas producing activities (as defined) are 10% or more of the enterprise's combined revenues of all industry segments.

2. Results of operations for oil and gas producing activities, excluding the effect of income taxes, are 10% or more of the greater of:

   a. The combined operating profit of all industry segments that did not incur a loss, or

   b. The combined operating loss of all industry segments that did incur a loss.

3. Identifiable assets relating to oil and gas producing activities are 10% or more of combined identifiable assets of all industry segments.

These tests conform to those used in SFAS 14, *Financial Reporting for Segments of a Business Enterprise* (S20), to determine significant industry segments.

Proved Oil and Gas Reserve Quantities. An enterprise's disclosures of proved reserves and proved developed reserves must include net quantities at the beginning and end of the year and changes in net quantities of proved reserves for the year. Changes resulting from the following should be shown separately with appropriate explanation of significant changes (Oi5.161):

• Revisions of previous estimates
• Improved recovery
• Purchases of minerals in place
• Extensions and discoveries
• Production
• Sales of minerals in place

These disclosures must be separately presented for the enterprise's home country (if significant reserves are located there) and for each foreign geographic area in which significant reserves are located.

The reserve quantities disclosed must include 100% of the net reserve quantities of the parent and its consolidated subsidiaries (whether or not wholly owned) and the company's proportionate share of reserves of proportionately consolidated enterprises. (If a significant portion of the reserve quantities relate to a significant minority interest of a consolidated subsidiary, that fact and the approximate portion is to be disclosed.) Net reserve quantities of an entity accounted for by the equity method must *not* be included in the enterprise's disclosures of net reserve quantities. However, the investor's share of the investee's net reserve quantities must be separately disclosed as of the end of the year (Oi5.164).

Capitalized Costs. An enterprise must disclose the aggregate capitalized costs relating to its oil and gas producing activities and the aggregate related accumulated depreciation, depletion, amortization, and valuation allowances as of the end of the year.

The enterprise also must separately disclose capitalized costs of unproved properties, if significant, and the enterprise's share of capitalized costs of an investee accounted for by the equity method (Oi5.168–.170).

Acquisition, Exploration, and Development. Property acquisition costs, exploration costs, and development costs for the year must be disclosed (whether capitalized or expensed as incurred). Costs incurred in foreign countries must be separately disclosed for each geographic area for which reserve quantities are disclosed, and costs incurred to acquire mineral interests with proved reserves must be separately disclosed from costs of acquiring unproved properties.

As with disclosures of capitalized costs and reserve quantities, the enterprise must disclose separately its share of an equity method investee's costs in the aggregate and for each geographical area (Oi5.171–.173).

Results of Operations. The result of operations of oil and gas producing activities must be disclosed in the aggregate and for each geographic area for which reserve quantities are disclosed and must present the following (Oi5.174–.179).

* Revenues (separately disclosing sales to unaffiliated enterprises and sales for transfers to an enterprise's other operations);
* Production (lifting) costs;
* Exploration costs;
* Depreciation, depletion, and amortization, and valuation provision;
* Income tax expense (based on the statutory rate adjusted for deductions, credits, and allowances relating to oil and gas producing activities reflected in consolidated income tax expense); and
* Results of operations for oil and gas producing activities (excluding corporate overhead and interest costs).

If the company's financial statements include investments accounted for using the equity method, the investee's results of operations for oil and gas producing activities must not be included in the disclosure of the enterprise's results of operations as discussed above; rather, those results must be separately disclosed in the aggregate and for each geographic area for which reserve quantities are disclosed.

Discounted Future Net Cash Flows. An enterprise is required to present a standardized measure of discounted future net cash flows provided by its oil and gas producing activities (Oi5.180–.184). The following disclosures are required as of the end of the year, in the aggregate and for each geographic area for which reserve quantities are disclosed:

1. Future cash inflows, computed by applying year-end prices of oil and gas to year-end quantities of proved reserves;
2. Estimated future development and production costs;
3. Future income tax expenses, based on the above items;
4. Future net cash flows
5. Discount, at 10%; and
6. The resulting standardized measure.

If the financial statements include investments accounted for by the equity method, the enterprise's share of the investee's standardized measure of discounted future net cash flows must not be included in the enterprise's disclosure of the standardized measure required in the preceding list, but must be separately disclosed in the aggregate and for each geographic area for which reserve quantities are disclosed.

The aggregate change for the year in the standardized measure of discounted future net cash flows must be disclosed, and, if individually significant, the components of the change should be separately presented. These include changes in (Oi5.183):

1. Sales and transfer prices and future production costs;
2. Future development costs;
3. Sales and transfers of product during the period;
4. Extensions, discoveries, and improved recovery;
5. Purchases and sales of minerals in place;
6. Revisions in quantity estimates;
7. Development costs incurred; and
8. Income taxes and discount accretion.

Figures 34.1, 34.2, and 34.3 present examples of the various required supplemental disclosures.

Comparison With SEC Requirements. In FRR 9 (§ 406.02), the SEC announced its conclusion that the disclosure requirements of SFAS 69 provide adequate information about oil and gas producing activities, particularly because they include a presentation of the standardized measure of discounted future net cash flows. In general, the SEC's disclosure requirements in Rule 4-10(k) of Regulation S-X and in Item 302(b) of Regulation S-K (as amended by FRR 9) coincide with SFAS 69. Certain differences, discussed in FRR § 406.02, are as follows:

• The SEC requires that disclosures related to annual periods be presented for each such annual period for which an income statement is required (typically three years), whereas SFAS 69 limits such disclosure to years with complete sets of annual financial statements. Under SFAS 69, the disclosures for the second preceding year technically could be omitted as, typically, only two balance sheets are given, and thus only two complete sets of financial statements are presented. In practice, the SEC requirements ordinarily should be met.

• The criteria and the time frame for determining the "significance" of oil and gas activities and thus the applicability of the disclosure requirements to various enterprises have been conformed between FASB and SEC. However, in those circumstances in which the discounted present value of a registrant's reserves is significantly in excess of 10% of consolidated total assets, the SEC expects that the general requirements for disclosure of material amounts will require some disclosure of reserves and future net revenue even if the stated tests in SFAS 69 are not met.

• The SEC rules require the disclosures whenever required by applicable federal securities forms regardless of the FASB definition of covered companies. The SFAS requires disclosure based on a "publicly traded" concept. Companies could be subject to the disclosures under one rule and not the other. In practice, the disclosures ordinarily should be made if the criteria of either rule are met.

Company-owned reserves	Natural gas systems Developed	Exploration and production		Total
		Developed	Undeveloped	
Natural gas-proved (000 Mcf)				
1987	355,416	71,941	8,422	435,779
1986	365,612	76,502	9,303	451,417
1985	400,183	73,606	10,905	484,694
Oil, condensate and NGL-proved (000 barrels)				
1987	133	492	17	642
1986	158	518	17	693
1985	249	572	16	837

Changes in proved reserves reported annually since the end of 1984 are shown in the following table:

Total proved reserves	Natural gas (million cubic feet)		Oil, condensate and NGL (thousands of barrels)	
	Natural gas systems	Exploration and production	Natural gas systems	Exploration and production
Total, end of 1984	572,072	89,810	251	619
Production during 1985	(36,186)	(8,925)	(49)	(98)
Extensions and discoveries	7,789	575	–	–
Revisions of previous estimates	(143,492)	3,051	47	67
Total, end of 1985	400,183	84,511	249	588
Production during 1986	(26,839)	(4,773)	(53)	(43)
Extensions and discoveries	–	1,003	–	–
Revisions of previous estimates	(7,732)	5,064	(38)	(10)
Total, end of 1986	365,612	85,805	158	535
Production during 1987	(28,062)	(4,709)	(56)	(62)
Extensions and discoveries	–	1,157	–	47
Revisions of previous estimates	17,866	(1,890)	31	(11)
Total, end of 1987	355,416	80,363	133	509

All reserves are located in the United States. Most of the company-owned gas reserves are dedicated to the Colorado system. All volumes presented on this page are stated at a pressure base of 14.65 psia.

FIG. 34.1 Supplemental Information on Oil and Gas Producing Activities, Reserves
Source: Colorado Interstate Gas Company, 1987 Annual Report on Form 10-K.

Results of Operations for Oil and Gas Producing Activities	Year ended December 31,		
(thousands of dollars)	1987	1986	1985
Revenues			
Sales	$ 2,939	$ 3,070	$ 8,857
Transfers	9,416	12,779	23,420
Total	12,355	15,849	32,277
Production costs	(3,262)	(4,153)	(4,518)
Operating expenses	(312)	(1,653)	(1,885)
Depreciation, depletion, and amortization	(5,014)	(5,235)	(8,439)
	3,767	4,808	17,435
Income tax expense	(1,507)	(2,212)	(8,020)
Results of operations for producing activities (excluding corporate overhead and interest costs)	$ 2,260	$ 2,596	$ 9,415

The average amortization rate per equivalent Mcf was $0.99 in 1987, $1.04 in 1986 and $0.90 in 1985.

FIG. 34.2 Supplemental Information on Oil and Gas Producing Activities, Results of Operations

Source: Colorado Interstate Gas Company, 1987 Annual Report on Form 10-K.

- Certain value-based disclosures may be omitted under SEC rules for limited partnerships under certain circumstances, in accordance with the previous SEC staff administrative practice discussed in SAB Topic 12.A.3.

SEC-Mandated Full Cost Rules

The SEC-mandated full cost accounting rules were prescribed in ASR 258, as amended by FRR 14 (FRR § 406.01.c), for the express purpose of conforming "existing practice to a relatively standardized method that, in the Commission's view, is generally consistent with the conceptual basis of full cost accounting." The SEC rules are to be applied to all oil and gas producing operations of a registrant and its subsidiaries. However, the requirements do not apply to investees accounted for under the equity method, unless they too are directly subject to SEC requirements.

Basis for Capitalization. Cost centers are to be established on a country-by-country basis only. All costs associated with acquisition, exploration, and development activities, including preacquisition costs, are to be capitalized within each cost center. Internal costs directly identified with those activities may be capitalized.

Production (lifting and workover) costs, general and administrative costs (such as corporate overhead), all costs reimbursed by other persons, and all costs related to drilling arrangements on which income is recognized are to be charged to expense.

Standardized Measure of Discounted Future Net Cash Flows Relating to Proved Oil and Gas Reserve Quantities:

Future cash inflows from the sale of proved reserves and estimated production and development costs as calculated by the Company's independent engineers are discounted at 10% after they are reduced by the Company's estimate for future income taxes.

The calculations are based on year-end prices and costs, and statutory tax rates that relate to existing proved oil and gas reserves in which the Company has mineral interests.

The standardized measure is not intended to represent the market value of reserves and, in view of the uncertainties involved in the reserve estimation process, including the instability of energy markets, may be subject to future material revisions (thousands of dollars):

| | At December 31, | | | | | |
| | 1987 | | 1986 | | 1985 | |
	Natural gas systems	Exploration and production	Natural gas systems	Exploration and production	Natural gas systems	Exploration and production
Future cash inflows	$110,430	$197,335	$164,993	$224,047	$273,684	$239,267
Future production and development costs	(11,654)	(57,303)	(22,218)	(59,785)	(36,614)	(66,569)
Future income tax expenses	(32,009)	(43,270)	(45,419)	(48,052)	(108,577)	(72,668)
Future net cash flows	66,767	96,762	97,356	116,210	128,493	100,030
10% annual discount for estimated timing of cash flows	(22,808)	(46,984)	(30,146)	(52,522)	(45,062)	(40,651)
Standardized measure of discounted future net cash flows	$ 43,959	$ 49,778	$ 67,210	$ 63,688	$ 83,431	$ 59,379

Principal sources of change in the standardized measure of discounted future net cash flows during each year are as follows (thousands of dollars):

| | 1987 | | 1986 | | 1985 | |
	Natural gas systems	Exploration and production	Natural gas systems	Exploration and production	Natural gas systems	Exploration and production
Sales and transfers, net of production costs	$(24,090)	$ (9,119)	$(26,071)	$(11,696)	$(28,100)	$(27,759)
Net changes in prices and production costs	(21,546)	(4,348)	(38,399)	(12,718)	5,844	(78,025)
Extensions and discoveries	—	1,906	—	854	12,388	447
Development costs incurred during the period that reduced estimated future development costs	—	233	—	1,600	—	42
Revisions of previous quantity estimates	4,720	(13,862)	(2,236)	3,875	(16,548)	4,776
Accretion of discount	6,692	7,011	12,396	5,148	6,904	7,668
Net change in income taxes	10,973	4,269	38,089	17,246	12,151	46,239
Net change	$(23,251)	$(13,910)	$(16,221)	$ 4,309	$ (7,361)	$(46,612)

None of the amounts include any value for storage gas which was approximately 66 billion cubic feet at the end of 1987.

FIG. 34.3 Supplemental Information on Oil and Gas Producing Activities, Standardized Measure of Discounted Future Net Cash Flows

Source: Colorado Interstate Gas Company, 1987 Annual Report on Form-10K.

Costs to Be Amortized. All capitalized costs included in a country's pool, including those that are unevaluated and in the process of being evaluated, must be depleted based on proved reserves. The costs to be amortized should also include estimated future expenditures to be incurred in developing proved reserves and estimated dismantlement and abandonment costs, net of estimated salvage values.

Unusually significant investments in unevaluated properties and major development projects may be excluded from the amortization computation until proved reserves can be attributed to the properties. (Examples of such costs are the acquisition of major offshore leases, installation of offshore drilling platforms, and improved recovery projects.) Such properties are subject, however, to impairment evaluations (described in the later section entitled "Successful Efforts Accounting"); and, if impairment is indicated, the amount of impairment should be added to the costs to be amortized.

Amortization Method. Amortization is computed by the unit-of-production method over the proved reserves attributable to each cost center. Oil and gas are to be converted to a common unit of measure (equivalent units) based on physical units, unless computation on the basis of monetary units of current gross revenues is more appropriate. As a practical matter, conversion to equivalent units based on physical measures of energy content is usually computed at the rate of 6,000 cubic feet (six Mcf) of gas to one barrel of oil. Amortization computations are to be made on a consolidated basis, with investees accounted for on the equity method treated separately.

Limitation on Capitalized Costs. For each cost center, aggregate capitalized costs less accumulated amortization and related deferred taxes may not exceed a defined ceiling. The ceiling is equal to the sum of (1) the present value of future net revenues from production of proved reserves in the center plus (2) the cost of properties not being amortized plus (3) the lower of cost or fair value of unproved properties included in costs being amortized less (4) income tax effects related to book/tax basis differences of the properties involved. Any amounts in excess of the computed ceiling should be written off and not reinstated for any subsequent ceiling increases.

In 1986, the SEC Commissioners, to the surprise and consternation of many oil and gas producers, rejected a proposal by the Chief Accountant to soften the application of the "ceiling test." As a result, many energy companies were required to take substantial write-downs because of the depressed value of their reserves in the first quarter of 1986. The Chief Accountant had agreed at the outset that the proposed suspension was a concession to the needs of the industry. Under the proposal, companies that used the full cost accounting method would still have had to take writedowns, but the amount would have been determined on a "best judgment" basis by management as to whether the decline in oil prices would be temporary.

The SEC Office of the Chief Economist (OCE) argued against the proposal as a major deviation from the reason the rule originally was devised, that is, reliance on the current value of oil. In rejecting the proposal, the Commission explained that it would consider a proposal that would revise the accounting for the full cost method, instead of moderating a portion of the rule.

Property Conveyances. The accounting rules for mineral property conveyances (including oil and gas properties) were established by SFAS 19 (Oi5.133–.138) as adopted by the SEC, and are discussed in greater detail in the later section, "Successful Efforts Accounting." In the SEC version of full cost accounting, discussed in Regulation S-X, 4-10(i)(6), there are some exceptions to those rules:

1. No gains or losses are recognized on sales or abandonments of properties unless treatment as an adjustment of capitalized costs would significantly alter the relationship between those costs and proved reserves in a cost center. A significant alteration would not be expected for sales involving less than 25% of the reserve quantities of a cost center.

2. If cash consideration received from the sale of unproved properties or drilling arrangements either exceeds total cost of the properties plus exploration and development costs to be incurred subsequently, or represents reimbursement for amounts currently charged to expense, then income should be recognized.

3. Significant purchases of properties with lives substantially shorter than the composite life of the cost center should be accounted for separately.

Interest Capitalization. Capitalization of interest by oil and gas companies following the full cost method must conform with SFAS 34, *Capitalization of Interest Cost*, (I67), and FASB Interpretation 33, *Applying FASB Statement No. 34 to Oil and Gas Producing Operations Accounted for by the Full Cost Method* (I67.108). Interest must be capitalized on unusually significant investments in unproved properties and major development projects that are not being depreciated, depleted, or amortized currently, and on significant properties and projects in cost centers with no production, provided that exploration or development activities on such assets are in progress.

Gain or Loss on Property Transfers. In 1984, the SEC issued FRR 17 (FRR § 406.01.c.iv) on gain or loss recognition of property transfers by full cost companies. Generally, the rules prohibit income recognition in connection with sales or other conveyances of oil and gas properties, and they describe the specific circumstances in which income may be recognized for management fees and compensation relating to contract services. The more important features of the amended rules are as follows:

1. Management fees received in connection with partnership income funds may be recognized as income, provided any estimated development expenditures required to produce the exisiting proved reserves are less than 10% of the partnership's cost of the properties.

2. No income may be recognized for contractual services (e.g., drilling, well service, and equipment supply services) performed on behalf of investors in oil and gas producing activities managed by the company or an affiliate.

3. No income may be recognized for contractual services to the extent that the consideration received represents an interest in the underlying property.

4. In other instances, income recognition for drilling and contractual services on properties in which the producer has an economic interest is permissible under the following conditions:

   a. For properties held for more than a year before the date of the performance of service, income may be recognized with the elimination of intercompany profit following GAAP as long as the interest in the properties was acquired in "transactions unrelated to the service contracts."

b. For properties acquired within a year of the related service, income may be recognized only to the extent that cash consideration exceeds the producer's share of all costs, including property acquisition cost, the cost of performing the service, and other costs incurred and expected to be incurred in connection with the property.

5. Income may be recognized for amounts that represent reimbursement of organization, offering, general and administrative expenses and that are a direct result of a transaction, if such amounts are also currently incurred and charged to expense in the current period.

Exclusions From Amortization Base. In 1982, the SEC noted that it had observed a significant lack of consistency in the application of the full cost accounting rules that permit companies to exclude certain costs from the amortization base. Accordingly, the SEC provided two alternative approaches to determining excluded costs, with the first alternative permitting exclusion from the amortization base of all unevaluated costs under the following conditions:

1. Impairment must be assessed at least annually and the amount of impairment added to the costs to be amortized.

2. The cost of drilling an exploratory dry hole must be included in the amortization base as soon as it is determined that the well is dry.

3. Geological and geophysical costs not associated with specific unevaluated properties must be included in the amortization base as incurred.

The rules also address the nature and amount of costs of major development projects that may be excluded. Furthermore, the rules codify the SEC staff's previous policy that once proved reserves are established, the related costs must be included in the amortization base, even if other factors prevent immediate production or marketing. Similarly, once costs are put into the full cost amortization base, they cannot later be transferred out. ASR 258 (FRR § 406.01.c.i) also requires new disclosures by full cost companies of costs excluded from amortization. The aggregate amount of unproved properties and major development projects excluded from amortization must be shown separately on the face of the producer's balance sheet. A new table is also required, which presents, by category of costs:

1. The total costs of unproved properties and major development projects that are excluded from amortization as of the most recent fiscal year end.

2. The amounts of such excluded costs incurred in each of the three most recent fiscal years and the aggregate for any earlier fiscal years in which costs were incurred.

The categories of cost to be disclosed are acquistion, exploration and development costs (for significant development projects), and capitalized interest.

Successful Efforts Accounting

Successful efforts accounting requirements prescribed by the SEC in ASR 257 (FRR § 406.01.b) are identical to those stated in SFAS 19 (Oi5).

Asset Classification. Under successful efforts accounting, the assets involved in oil and gas producing activities are broadly classified into four categories. The first, *mineral interests in properties*, consists of the rights to extract oil and gas, and is subdivided into *unproved properties* and *proved properties*. The other three categories are *wells and related equipment and facilities*; *support facilities and equipment*; and *uncompleted wells, equipment, and facilities*. The costs of assets included in the four categories are to be capitalized as incurred.

Basis for Capitalization. Under successful efforts accounting, cost centers are to be established on a field basis. In general, only those costs directly related to the acquisition, exploration, and development of proved reserves in an individual field may be capitalized.

Preacquisition G&G costs are expensed as incurred, as are the costs of carrying undeveloped properties. Certain contingent exploratory costs, such as dry-hole contributions and bottom-hole contributions, are also treated in this manner.

Property acquisition costs and postacquisition exploratory costs are initially capitalized to the appropriate unproved property and uncompleted well accounts, pending evaluation of the property. If proved reserves are discovered in the field, the costs are transferred to proved properties and to wells and related equipment and facilities. If proved reserves are not found, the costs are charged to expense. This determination can be made in two ways. First, if an exploratory well is completed as a dry hole, all costs accumulated for that field should usually be written off. Second, if a conclusive determination has not been made as a result of drilling, costs related to unproved properties are annually subjected to an impairment test, as discussed in a separate section later in this chapter.

Development costs are capitalized as incurred, even if a specific development well is unsuccessful. All development costs are included in the category of wells and related equipment and facilities.

Production costs are charged to operations when incurred, and include the direct overhead that can be traced to production activity. Costs such as maintenance of production office facilities, record-keeping, and similar overhead items are to be charged to period expense as incurred. The depreciation, depletion, and amortization of proved property costs and related equipment are considered production costs.

Exploratory Dry Holes. The successful efforts method as discussed in SFAS 19 provides no guidance on the accounting for exploratory holes that are still in progress at the end of a financial statement period and that, prior to the publication of financial statements, turn out *not* to hold proved oil and gas reserves in commercially recoverable quantities.

In response to this matter the FASB issued FIN 36, *Accounting for Exploratory Wells in Progress at the End of a Period* (Oi5.130), which requires that such a dry hole be charged to expense, just as if it had been found to be dry as of the balance sheet date. That is, the costs incurred through the end of the period, net of any salvage value, shall be charged to expense for that period.

Amortization Method. Amortization is computed on the unit-of-production method. Conversion to equivalent units is made on the basis of physical units of energy content (usually six Mcf of gas to one barrel of oil).

Capitalized acquisition costs of proved properties are to be amortized on the basis of proved reserves, whereas capitalized development costs and the costs of exploratory wells and exploratory-type stratigraphic test wells that have found proved reserves are amortized on the basis of proved developed reserves. Costs of development wells in progress are carried without amortization until the development well is completed. Costs of large capital investment programs associated with several development wells, such as offshore platforms, should be assigned to completed or uncompleted wells on some reasonable basis such as the number of wells expected to be completed in the program. Those proved developed reserves that will be produced only after significant future expenditures are made should also be excluded from amortization computations.

Amortization may be computed on a property-by-property basis or on the basis of a reasonable grouping of properties with a common geological structure, such as a field or reservoir. As a practical matter, amortization is usually computed on a field basis, because costs are aggregated within cost center in that manner.

Estimated salvage values and anticipated future dismantlement, restoration, and abandonment costs are to be provided for in determining amortization rates.

Impairment of Unproved Properties. Unproved properties must be assessed periodically to determine if they have suffered an impairment in value. If so, a valuation allowance is to be provided. In general, impairment occurs when it becomes doubtful that the carrying value of the property will be recovered.

Impairment would be indicated if a dry hole is drilled on an unproved property and there are no firm plans for further drilling, or if an unproved property has been held for a major portion of the initial lease term without commencement of drilling activity. The assessment for impairment should be done on a property-by-property basis if the acquisition costs are individually significant. If they are not, the allowance may be determined, in the aggregate or by groups, on the basis of experience factors such as exploratory well success rates on similar types of properties and average holding periods of unproved properties.

The impairment test is also relevant when an exploratory well is completed and has located reserves, but a substantial capital expenditure, such as installation of a trunk pipeline, is required before production can begin. Here, classification of the reserves depends on whether the expenditure can be justified. This often requires drilling more exploratory wells to better assess the economic benefit of the additional expenditures. In this situation, capitalized costs may be retained if the discovered reserves are sufficient to justify the expenditures and additional exploratory drilling is in progress or firmly planned. If both conditions are not met, the costs of the exploratory well are to be expensed. As a general rule, exploratory drilling costs may not be carried for longer than one year after well completion without a determination that proved reserves have been found.

The requirement for an impairment assessment related to unproved properties does not change the current practice of using realization tests for impairment of proved properties.

Surrender or Abandonment. Capitalized acquisition costs related to the surrender or abandonment of unproved properties should be charged against the allowance for impairment to the extent that such an allowance has been provided, with a loss being recognized for any excess. If only a portion of a proved property is abandoned or retired, such as an individual well or item of equipment, no loss shall be recognized. Rather, the asset being abandoned or retired shall be deemed fully amortized and charged to accumulated depreciation, depletion and amortization (DD&A), unless the abandoment or retirement was the result of a catastrophic event or other major abnormality.

When the last well of the proved property ceases to produce and the entire proved property or proved property group is abandoned, a loss should be recognized if the carrying value of the property differs from the salvage value net of any reclamation costs.

Property Conveyances. Oil and gas financing and conveyance arrangements take on a wide variety of complex forms. The following discussion deals with the general concepts embodied in SFAS 19 (Oi5.133–.138), which do not intend to address every special situation that might occur. A careful reading of the rules adopted by the SEC in ASR 257 (FRR § 406.01.c.iv) is required when considering a specific conveyance transaction.

The rules governing the accounting for mineral property conveyances and related transactions focus on the substance of the arrangement: Is it a transfer of rights and responsibilities of operating a property or is it a financing arrangement? If a transaction is in substance a borrowing repayable in cash or its equivalent, it is to be accounted for as a borrowing, with no recognition of gain or loss.

For example, if cash advances are made to an operator to finance exploration in return for the right to purchase oil or gas discovered, and if the advances are repayable in cash should insufficient oil or gas be discovered to offset them, the transaction should be accounted for as a receivable by the lender and a borrowing by the operator. This treatment must also be used if the funds advanced are repayable in cash from the proceeds of a specified share of future production until the advance, plus interest, is repaid in full.

When a transaction results in a true conveyance, the key considerations in determining whether gain or loss recognition is appropriate relate to liquidity of proceeds, certainty of cost recovery, obligation for future performance, and the nature of the property. No gain or loss may be recognized at the time of conveyance when there is a transfer of assets used in oil and gas producing activities for other assets used in those activities, such as in a carried interest, free well, or overriding royalty transaction, or in a pooling of assets under a joint venture or unitization.

A loss (but not a gain) may need to be recognized if part of an interest in a property is sold, but recovery of costs applicable to the retained interest is highly uncertain if the seller has a substantial obligation for the future performance.

A gain may usually be recognized on the sale of all or part of a property if the proceeds are in cash or its equivalent, collectibility is reasonably assured, and the seller has no obligation for substantial future performance. Otherwise, proceeds are generally considered a recovery of cost.

Accounting Requirements—Nonpublic Companies

The FASB's decision in SFAS 25 to indefinitely suspend the requirements of SFAS 19, virtually unavoidable with the SEC permitting both full cost and successful efforts, resulted in a large number of alternatives for nonpublic companies compared with those for SEC registrants. Although there is no specified form of either full cost or successful efforts accounting that nonpublic companies must follow, they must apply SFAS 25. Therefore, they must use the same definitions of proved reserves adopted by the SEC, disclose their method of accounting in the financial statements, and provide the same disclosures of reserve quantities, costs incurred, and capitalized costs as SEC companies.

Certain of the mineral conveyance and related transaction provisions of SFAS 19 were also adopted by the SEC for full cost companies and thus affect all public companies. Since the SEC adopted these provisions, it is reasonable to expect that even those conveyance rules not imposed on private companies will be extended to all companies, public and private.

Interest capitalization for full cost companies applies to public and nonpublic companies alike, since there is an FASB standard (SFAS 34 (I67)). Finally, the income tax allocation requirements of SFAS 19 (Oi5.139–.141), as amended by SFAS 96, *Accounting for Income Taxes*, discussed in the next section, have been retained, and thus also apply to nonpublic companies.

Income Taxes

Provisions in the income tax law permit treatments for many of the costs of oil and gas exploration and development that differ from the accounting methods specified for financial reporting. Under SFAS 19 (Oi5.139–.141) and FRR § 406, the need for comprehensive interperiod tax allocation for differences in timing between tax and financial income has been firmly established. Income tax accounting procedures are discussed at length in Chapter 17; aspects applicable to the oil and gas producing industry are discussed briefly here.

Timing differences for oil and gas exploration and development activities arise from two primary sources: (1) *intangible drilling costs,* and (2) *amortization of tangible equipment* when cost depletion is used. Under tax regulations, expenditures for intangible drilling costs (IDC) may be deducted in the year incurred, or capitalized and amortized over the productive life of the property. If capitalized, IDC on wells in progress may be deducted when the well is found to be nonproductive.

Tangible property employed in producing oil and gas may be tax-depreciated under the same rules used for similar property employed in other kinds of activities. For example, costs of machinery, tools, equipment, pipes, and related installation costs not deducted as IDC may be capitalized and depreciated over the useful life of the equipment using acceptable tax methods, rather than the unit-of-production method required for financial reporting under either full cost or successful efforts accounting. Interperiod tax allocation must, of course, be followed for these temporary differences.

For tax purposes, certain small producing companies may be permitted to use percentage depletion rather than cost depletion on their oil and gas properties. The primary benefit of percentage depletion is that a taxpayer may, over the life of the property, deduct an amount greater than the capitalized cost of the property. The lower the capitalized cost (e.g., through immediate deduction of IDC), the greater the potential tax savings through the use of percentage depletion. However, the annual amount of percentage depletion allowable is limited to the lesser of 50% of the taxable income from the property to which it has been applied or 65% of the taxpayer's taxable income from all sources before the percentage depletion deduction and certain other items. Percentage depletion in excess of the 65% limit may be carried over to the next year.

In SFAS 96, *Accounting for Income Taxes* (I25), the FASB has changed the financial statement approach to accounting for the income tax effects of the interaction of temporary differences and the excess of statutory depletion.

For purposes of comprehensive interperiod income tax allocations, the possibility that statutory depletion in future periods will decrease or eliminate income taxes that might be due should be considered, but only to the extent that such depletion results from revenues that are exactly equal to the amounts of the assets that are subject to such depletion, and subject to any tax law limitation. "The tax benefit of any additional excess of statutory depletion over cost depletion for tax purposes shall be recognized," when deducted for tax purposes. The effects of interaction cannot be used to anticipate any such tax benefit (Oi5.141).

Accounting Changes

After shelving plans for RRA, the SEC issued ASR 300 (FRR § 406.01.d), abolishing its prior rule that virtually forbade changes from one SEC-approved accounting method to another.

ASR 300 simplifies matters considerably by stating that oil and gas producers should rely on existing GAAP when changing accounting methods. Therefore, since GAAP (SFAS 19 and SFAS 25) state that the successful efforts method is preferable, changes to the successful efforts method may be made without a preferability letter from the registrant's independent accountant. If, however, a registrant's particular circumstances support full cost as preferable to successful efforts, that change has to be justified by the registrant, and a preferability letter from the registrant's independent accountant must be submitted to the SEC.

SEC Staff Interpretations

The SEC staff has issued several interpretations regarding accounting by oil and gas producers. SAB 47, *Financial Statements of Oil and Gas Exchange Offers* (Topic 2.D), presents the staff's views concerning the financial statements of oil and gas exchange offers (also referred to as "roll-ups" or "put-togethers"), and whether a swap of shares in a corporation for interests in oil and gas properties should be accounted for as a purchase or as a pooling.

Under SAB 47 if a roll-up transaction occurs in which there is a "high-degree of common ownership or common control" between the issuer and the offerees, a nonpublic company (i.e., a company that was not public prior to the exchange) should account for the transaction as a reorganization of entities under common control.

APB 16, *Business Combinations* (B50), excludes from its coverage "a transfer of net assets or exchange of shares between companies under common control." "Like-a-pooling" accounting is generally applied to such transactions. If the equity of the

---

Master Limited Partnership

Effective as of December 1, 1985, Sun conveyed to Sun Energy Partners, L.P. (Partnership), a Delaware limited partnership, all of its domestic oil and gas properties, certain related assets and cash in exchange for approximately 97.3 percent general partnership interest in the Partnership in the form of units of partnership interest (Units). In addition, the Partnership assumed, with certain exceptions, the liabilities of Sun's domestic oil and gas business. The remaining 2.7 percent of the Units were sold in a public offering resulting in net proceeds to the Partnership of approximately $190 million. The Units sold in the public offering are listed on the New York Stock Exchange, Inc.

Sun presently intends to conduct all of its domestic oil and gas activities through the Partnership. Sun controls the Partnership through wholly owned subsidiaries which are the sole general partners with the public unitholders holding limited partnership interests. Eighty-five percent of the Board of Directors of Sun Company, Inc. (Company) must approve any additional issuance, sale or transfer of Units which would result in Sun and its affiliates holding less than eighty-five percent of the then outstanding Units. The information pertaining to Sun's domestic oil and gas activities found in Supplemental Financial and Operating Information – Oil and Gas Data reflects the size and scope of the business now conducted through the Partnership.

* * * * *

The Partnership operates through Sun Operating Limited Partnership, a Delaware limited partnership, and several other operating partnerships (collectively the Operating Partnerships). In all of the partnerships which comprise the Operating Partnerships, the Partnership holds a 99 percent interest as the sole limited partner and Sun, in exchange for a cash contribution, holds a 1 percent interest through wholly owned subsidiaries which act as the sole general partners.

The $5,713 million of assets and the $2,694 million of liabilities assumed from Sun have been recorded by the Partnership and the Operating Partnerships (collectively Sun Energy Partners) at Sun's historical carrying values. As a result of the initial public offering of limited partnership Units, Sun's share of the equity of Sun Energy Partners increased by $104 million. This resulted in the recognition of a gain, of $74 million (after related income taxes of $30 million) or $.67 per share of common stock in 1985.

FIG. 34.4   Accounting for Formation of an Oil and Gas Master Limited Partnership
Source: Sun Company Inc. 1986 Annual Report.

"parent" in commonly controlled companies changes as a result of the issuance of stock, then the provisions of SAB 51, *Accounting for Sales of Stock by a Subsidiary* (Topic 5.H) and TB 85-5, *Issues Relating to Accounting for Business Combinations, Including ... Stock Transactions between Companies under Common Control ...* (B50.596A–.596C), apply. These circumstances are illustrated in Figure 34.4.

In this figure, an oil and gas producing company conveyed its domestic oil and gas properties to a master limited partnership (MLP) in exchange for a 97.3% interest, with the remaining 2.7% interest sold by the MLP to the public. The price paid by the public was greater by $104 million than the applicable share of net assets, and this dilution was recorded as a gain by the transferor.

In addition, SAB Topic 12, *Oil and Gas Producing Activities* (comprising ASR 257, SAB 41, and SAB 47), discusses various oil and gas accounting and disclosure matters, including the computation of future net revenues, the presentation of reserve quantity disclosures, and various full cost accounting matters.

Auditing Considerations

The auditor must gain a thorough understanding of industry practices, accounting and reporting requirements, and the nature of the client's systems and transactions. Then, because of the complexity, volume, and variety of transactions that usually occur in the operations of oil and gas producing companies, the auditor must subject pertinent systems of accounting and internal control to appropriate testing.

Compliance with contractual agreements is a particularly significant audit issue, since seemingly minor differences in the terms of operating or other agreements may have significant effects on how a transaction should be recorded.

The functions of the land, geological, and operating departments must also be understood, and adequacy and reliability of their records should be tested. In general, test points must be established for every phase of information flow in which the generation or approval of data or its ultimate entry into the accounting system takes place. As the foregoing discussion of current accounting requirements implies, classification of costs is a matter of substantial concern.

Reserve Value Disclosures. Originally, the AICPA issued SAS 33, *Supplementary Oil and Gas Reserve Information* (AU 555), to be applied in conjunction with SAS 27, *Supplementary Information Required by the Financial Accounting Standards Board* (superseded by SAS 52, AU 551).

Subsequently, SAS 33 was superseded by SAS 45, *Omnibus Statement on Auditing Standards—1983*, to address the supplementary information required by SFAS 69. The portion of SAS 45 dealing with this supplementary information is presently contained in AU 557 and describes those procedures the auditor should follow in applying SAS 52. (SAS 45 has been withdrawn by SAS 52, effective when an auditing interpretation is issued to replace SAS 45.)

The auditor's association with the supplemental reserve value disclosures has the objective of determining whether the information contained in the disclosures complies with the SEC's requirements in FRR § 406 in relation to the financial statements taken as a whole. Since the process of reserve estimation and valuation is complex and beyond the expertise of auditors, who are not trained reservoir engineers, the auditor should obtain either a consulting engineer's *opinion* on the enterprises reserve information or a consulting engineer's *reserve estimates* for substantially all the company's reserves.

A consultant's opinion would normally be sufficient if a company has adequate records and an internal staff of reservoir engineers; otherwise, an engineer's reserve estimates would probably be required. In either event, the auditor must be satisfied that the engineer is independent of the entity and that the engineer's work covers all properties with significant potential for material adjustment.

If a consulting engineer's opinion is used, the auditor must ascertain that the engineer has surveyed a representative cross-section of the company's properties. The auditor is responsible for testing the data submitted to the engineer on which the engineer's opinion will be based. Tests of the listing of properties, production, cost, price, and discount factors, and ownership interest proportions should be made by the auditor.

The auditor may find it useful to integrate the consulting engineer's report in assessment of both the adequacy of allowances for impairments and the base of costs related to proved properties used for DD&A.

Neither the SEC nor the FASB require these reserve value disclosures as part of the financial statements (they are unaudited supplementary information, for public companies), so lesser tests may suffice to determine that reported book values do not exceed the appropriate limits (i.e., the net present value ceiling) and that amortization rates are proper. At a minimum, an auditor should test the information supplied to the company's engineers to determine whether sufficient evidence exists to support the reported book values and amortization. Although the reserve value information requirement applies only to public companies, the reserve *quantity* data is required for all companies.

Industry Audit and Accounting Guide. In 1986, The AICPA issued an Audit and Accounting Guide, *Audits of Entities with Oil and Gas Producing Activities* (AICPA, 1986f). The Guide deals with the unique aspects of the oil and gas industry that are important to an auditor in examining and reporting on the financial statements of companies in this industry. Specific areas covered include:

• Statutory rules and regulations applicable to this industry.

• Illustrations of the form and content of financial statements.

• Suggested auditing approach addressing audit focus, audit planning (e.g., assessing risk, nature of operations, use of specialists, and geographical considerations), and audit considerations for important balance sheet and income statement items.

• Internal control considerations including subjects such as lease records, division-of-interest file maintenance, property accounting, physical security, joint interest billing, and nonoperated interests.

• Accounting principles limited to the successful efforts method (SFAS 19) and the full cost method specified by the SEC.

Windfall Profit Tax

In 1979, the President elected to phase out the domestic crude oil price controls established in the early 1970s, but at the cost of what many have described as the largest tax ever imposed on a single industry. The so-called windfall profit tax is an excise, or severance, tax levied on the first sale of domestic crude oil. Producers, defined as holders of the economic interest in the oil, are the taxpayers under the law. Certain royalty owners (state and local governments, and interests owned by charitable institiutions before January 22, 1980 and by Indian tribes) are exempt from the tax.

The tax is levied on excess revenues from sales at a price above a statutory base price, and is withheld from gross receipts by either the first purchaser of the oil or the operator of the property. The excess revenues (i.e., the windfall profit) from a barrel of oil which is subject to tax cannot exceed 90% of the net income attributable to the barrel of oil.

The tax structure is correlated with the price control program, from which it has adopted the tier system for classification of oil. There are, however, some significant differences between the two programs. One example is the definition of a property which is treated in the DOE sense for pricing and tax calculations, but which follows the Internal Revenue Code (IRC) definition for determining the net income limitation and calculation of percentage depletion.

There are numerous considerations and variables that come into play in calculating the tax and determining record-keeping requirements. An in-depth reading of the regulations is necessary to gain a complete understanding of all requirements, which are not covered here.

Although this tax was significant when initially imposed, the low level of oil prices in recent years has essentially negated its impact. There is significant sentiment in Congress to repeal this tax. If the repeal does not take place, the tax is scheduled to be phased out over a period of years with total elimination by 1993.

THE HARD MINERALS INDUSTRY

Accounting for hard mineral extraction has been less complex and less subject to public review than has oil and gas accounting. Nevertheless, similar issues arise in the application of accounting rules to the hard minerals industry.

Mineral Reserves

The principal asset of a mining company is generally the rights it holds to extract natural resources. In some cases, those rights arc valuable because of the intrinsic value of the resource. In other cases, notably sand and gravel operations, the value of the rights derives from permission obtained by the company to extract the resources in an area where they can be marketed at a profit. In either case, the commercially recoverable reserves are the focus of operations and of the accounting system.

Because there are wide variations in geologic structures, marketability, costs, and other economic determinants of the value of hard minerals, the accounting principles and related definitions must be viewed as general guides, and must be adapted to the circumstances existing for each specific type of resource. Definitions of reserves vary, but they are generally considered to be those resources that are commercially recoverable under current economic conditions. Although the former GAAP requirements related to disclosures of changing prices information are now voluntary, SFAS 89, *Financial Reporting and Changing Prices* (C28), provides guidance by defining proved mineral reserves as follows:

> In extractive industries other than oil and gas, the estimated quantities of commercially recoverable reserves that, on the basis of geological, geophysical, and engineering data, can be demonstrated with a reasonably high degree of certainty to be recoverable in the future from known mineral deposits by either primary or improved recovery methods. [C28.413]

When mineral prices vary widely, the use of current prices and costs for reserve definition purposes can result in wide period-to-period variations in estimated reserves. This occurs, for example, when marginal ore deposits (*gangue*) become sufficiently valuable to be recovered in times of high prices but their recovery becomes uneconomic as prices fall. For example, the recent increase in the price of copper has resulted in the reopening of several large mines that had been closed for years.

If reserve quantities are used as a basis for amortization of capitalized costs, a large base results in smaller amortization charges during periods of high prices, because more reserves are considered economically recoverable; the reverse occurs in periods of low prices. To minimize this problem, and to relate amortization of costs of reserves to the generally long-run nature of mining operations, it is probably more reasonable to use an estimate of longer-term economic conditions for reserve estimates. Reference to past price and cost behavior in the specific mineral may be used as a basis for assessment of future conditions in the absence of major shifts that would require separate consideration. Disclosure of the economic basis used for reserve determination is generally necessary to enable a reader to evaluate the company's operations.

In certain circumstances, reserve quantities may be so large relative to annual production that exhaustion of reserve may not occur until long after the benefits of the rights acquired are exhausted. In such cases, reserves may be limited to those quantities estimated to be recovered over some reasonable period (e.g., 40 years). Reserves recoverable after that time may be treated separately for amortization and disclosure purposes.

Cost Classifications

The four types of costs likely to arise in the hard minerals extractive industry are (1) exploration, (2) acquisition, (3) development, and (4) production. These classifications are similar to those used in the oil and gas industry.

Exploration. Exploration costs are normally incurred prior to acquisition of the right to extract resources. For most hardrock mining activity, exploration costs consist of the relatively fixed costs of the company's exploration and scouting department. They include salaries of geologists, incidental expenditures for mapping, and the cost of studies of geologic structures, together with the direct overhead for those activities. Costs incurred to obtain *shooting rights* on properties are also a part of exploration costs. Shooting rights cover those procedures necessary to test the underlying geologic structure for the actual presence of potentially recoverable minerals.

Because these costs are usually ongoing and tend to be low relative to the total costs of any particular extractive operation, it has been predominant practice to expense them as incurred, This treatment is also consistent with the approach usually taken for tax reporting purposes.

Some companies, however, believe that the practice of expensing exploration costs as incurred understates the balance sheet costs of mineral properties and may understate current income while overstating future income through smaller amortization charges during the productive cycle. Those companies, therefore, capitalize exploration costs identified wih successful prospects.

Because of the wide variety of minerals and related geologic structures, of success probabilities, and of exploration costs relative to total costs of the mine or other facilities, support may be found for each method of recording exploration costs. To minimize the likelihood of misunderstanding, disclosure of the method used for recording exploration costs is necessary when such costs are material. Disclosure of balances of capitalized exploration costs would also be helpful for comparisons between companies.

Acquisition. Acquisition costs may be incurred either as fee interests or as leasehold interests. Contrary to the practice in the oil and gas industry, acquisition costs are usually incurred only if there is a high degree of certainty about the existence of natural resources on the property. It is common practice to capitalize property acquisition costs under either fee or leasehold interests. Capitalizable costs would include the purchase price of fee interests; lease bonus costs; surveying, legal, and recording fees; and other related costs of acquistion. Costs of in-house legal and surveying staff that are directly related to the acquisition, together with associated overhead, may also be capitalized. Typically, though, in-house costs are expensed, whereas the costs for identical sevices from outside suppliers are capitalized. (In theory, the treatment of similar costs should be the same, whether the services are obtained from within or from outside the company.) Time records or other source documents may be used to provide an allocation basis for salaries, out-of-pocket costs, and related overhead.

Capitalized acquisition costs may be written off if the property is found not to be commercially productive. Technological or governmental restrictions are more likely to be the cause of nonproductivity than is the nonexistence of ores or other minerals on the property.

Development. Development costs include site access and preparation, removal of overburden, mining equipment, support facilities, and the installation of those facilities. Many mining companies classify postacquisition costs as development costs. Those costs are normally subdivided into *intangible development costs* (IDCs) and the *costs of tangible (depreciable) property* at the site of extractive operations, since tax provisions make separate accounting for those two types of costs necessary. In most cases, following tax practice, IDCs are expensed as incurred, but in a few cases they are capitalized. The costs of tangible equipment, buildings, and other related depreciable property items are capitalized. Normally, disclosure is made of the accounting method employed for IDCs.

Production. Production costs include costs to operate the mine and the costs that arise from the extraction of minerals or other natural resources. In many cases, once a mine has started producing, all further development costs are regarded as production costs rather than as capitalizable along with preproduction development costs. Production costs are inventoried as the products are extracted and charged to cost of goods sold as the products are sold. The depreciation, depletion, and amortization of exploration, acquisition, and development costs are also considered part of the inventoriable costs of the extracted product.

Impairment

Because typical practice in the mining industry is to immediately expense exploration costs and IDCs, there is little likelihood that the capitalized cost balance for

mining properties will be more than the net realizable value of the property. However, in those few cases in which accounts include capitalized exploration and intangible development costs, a net realizable value limitation is a distinct possibility. If
the balance in the property account exceeds the net realizable value of the properties,
a valuation allowance should be provided.

The value limitation may be determined either on a property basis or on the basis
of each country in which the company holds mining interests. In some instances, it
may be appropriate to aggregate company-wide costs and net realizable values in
determining whether impairment has taken place, although the separate-country
basis is probably the most common.

The value of mining properties may be determined either through the use of data
on sales of similar properties and equipment or by the use of discounted cash-flow
techniques. If mineral prices fluctuate widely, an expectation of future average prices
may give more consistent valuation results than the use of current (spot) prices. Once
a property has been written down for valuation purposes, subsequent write-ups,
although occasionally found in practice, may result in inconsistent reporting results.
The FASB recommended against such subsequent write-ups for oil and gas properties, thus setting a precedent that may be considered applicable to other extractive
operations.

In the now-abandoned changing prices disclosure experiment, the FASB had concluded that a requirement for disclosure of the fair value of mineral resources was
inappropriate because of the unreliability of the measurements that could be used.
That unreliability exists partly because the measurement of the fair value of mineral
reserves depends "on estimates of the physical quantities of the reserves, the rate of
extraction, future selling prices, future development and extraction costs, and the
discount rate" (SFAS 39, ¶ 51). As a result of FASB-sponsored research, observers
indicated that they believed that the estimation of physical quantities of mineral
resources are frequently materially affected over time. At any given time, the subjectivity that is inherent in the estimation process results in wide differences among
independent appraisers. Further, the reliability of any data is low because the estimation process requires forecasts of future events, especially price changes, that have
been subject to extreme variability due to economic and political changes. However,
until rescission by SFAS 89, the Board did require disclosure of data about mineral
resource quantities.

Amortization

The capitalized cost balances for a particular property are usually amortized over the
expected production from the property on a unit-of-production basis. Some variations arise because of the different types of extractive operations and different philo-
sophical approaches to the amortization question.

Tangible equipment costs may be depreciated over production from the mine or
over the life of the equipment, whichever is shorter. A unit-of-production method
may be employed, or, consistent with tax regulations, these assets may be depreciated on a time basis.

Acquisition costs and capitalized exploration and development costs are generally
amortized on a unit-of-production basis over the total production from the property.
When properties are acquired in fee, it is necessary to ascertain the portion of the

acquisition cost that derives from extractive rights and the portion that derives from the land itself. Land costs are, of course, not amortized.

Indefinite Life. In the past it was common practice not to amortize any of the capitalized acquisition or intangible costs. That treatment was supported on the basis that mine lives were generally indefinite and more similar to land than to amortizable assets. Support for no amortization was also provided by the frequency with which book value equaled the salvage value of a property. Contemporary practice and literature suggest, however, that those costs should be amortized. In part, this may be because of changes in technology and regulation and other factors that tend to limit the economic life of an extractive operation. Moreover, regulations calling for the restoration of properties at the end of extractive operations may result in a negative salvage value.

Still, the indefinite life of many mining properties causes some problems in the determination of amortization rates. When the productive life of the property is indefinite or so long as to be irrelevant for amortization purposes, an arbitrary time limit is usually set for amortization. Although no standard time limit has been established either in practice or in specific recommendations for mining operations, the amortization of goodwill bears many similarities to that of some mining properties. Thus, the 40-year maximum for goodwill provided in APB 17, *Intangible Assets* (I60), although somewhat arbitrary for tangible minerals, may provide a useful benchmark. In practice, many companies amortize those costs over the lesser of the productive life of the property or some set time period.

Restoration Costs. In many cases, environmental regulations call for extensive restoration of properties on completion of extractive operations. Those future costs are associated with all production from the property. Thus, a liability may be assumed to arise that should be provided for over the production period, yet practice varies. The FASB has held that for oil and gas operations those expected future costs must be considered in determining the depreciation and amortization rates (Oi5.128), but no such rules have been established for the hard minerals extractive industry. In fact, when the productive life of a property is indefinite in theory, the present value of any restoration liability may be immaterial. An assessment of the facts and circumstances for each extractive operation is necessary to support the chosen treatment of those costs. When a performance bond has been established to provide for restoration costs, the portion of the bond that is expected to offset restoration costs may be used as a basis for recognizing the current portion of those costs. This may be acomplished through a valuation allowance against the performance deposits, through establishment of a liability account, or through expensing current performance bond payments as may be appropriate in the circumstances.

Amortization Basis. Separate amortization bases may be called for when an acquired property has been only partially developed. Capitalized acquisition costs and capitalized exploration costs may be assumed related to all the minerals on the property, whether developed or undeveloped. The appropriate amortization basis for acquisition costs would, therefore, be the total reserves on the property. Development costs may be associated only with those reserves that are developed.

For this reason, it is common practice to amortize development costs over the related proved developed reserves.

Joint Products

In many extractive processes, several products may be derived from the same extracted ore. When that occurs, the accounting may be based on either a by-product or a joint product approach. With the by-product method, a primary product is identified. The primary product is charged with all the production and amortization costs less the net realizable values of the by-products. The by-products are carried at their net realizable value. Under the joint costing approach, the production and amortization costs are prorated to each of the jointly produced items on some reasonable equivalence basis. In most cases, the relative sales value of the products is used as a basis. Thus, for example, if one product accounts for 60% of the net revenues to be received from sale of the products from a specific quantity of ore, the cost assigned to that product would equal 60% of the total costs of the extracted ore. Other bases for allocation include weight and energy content. Except for the oil and gas industry, in which relative energy content has been specified as the basis for proration, the preference is for equivalent market values. This preference arises because market value may be the only common element for diverse products and use of market values provides identical gross margins at the point of product separation for each of the joint products.

Income Taxes

Accounting for the effects of provisions in the tax law gives rise to a number of analyses that must be conducted to minimize the effective tax levels and to provide for appropriate interperiod tax allocation in the financial statements. Tax law permits the use of percentage depletion for virtually all natural resources without the production restrictions imposed on oil and natural gas (unless cost depletion results in a larger amount). Rates are specified in the IRC and, depending on the mineral, range from 5% to 22%. Rates are applied to "gross income from mining." This gross income is computed at the point of sale, generally after processes that are considered mining in nature (as opposed to manufacturing), and may include the price received at plants or mills where such processing takes place, provided such mills are within 50 miles of the property. Particularly in the case of an integrated mining and manufacturing company, an analysis of income must be made to determine the portion related to mining versus manufacturing.

Tax law permits certain aggregations of mines that may enable a mine owner to obtain a greater allowance than would be obtained if each property were treated separately, but the depletion allowance generally is limited to 50% of the taxable income from a property. Percentage depletion may be taken even if accumulated allowances exceed the tax basis of the property. However, depletion in excess of the basis may be subject to minimum tax provisions.

Tax regulations also permit the immediate write-off of most exploration expenditures, subject to recapture when the property commences production or is sold. IDC and certain costs of tangible equipment necessary to maintain production may be deducted as incurred subject to a recovery test. Because percentage depletion is computed regardless of recorded cost, and may be taken in excess of cost, maximum tax benefits are usually obtained by deducting exploration and IDC as incurred and employing percentage depletion. Tangible equipment may be depreciated using acceptable methods for nonmining equipment.

Except for the benefits of percentage depletion, differences between tax income and income for financial reporting purposes are considered temporary differences. In accordance with SFAS 96, *Accounting for Income Taxes* (I25), interperiod tax allocation is required for those differences computed using tax rates in the enacted tax law and changed as a current period charge or credit if the tax law changes. It has been pointed out that when percentage depletion exceeds the financial reporting basis for the property, the benefits of percentage depletion may serve to offset taxes that would otherwise be payable. This *interaction* between percentage depletion and financial income has been discussed by a number of authorities. Some feel the interaction should be anticipated when computing the deferred tax provision on the grounds that, because of these tax provisions, the ultimate amount of tax payable will be reduced. Others suggest that the interaction benefits are subject to substantial uncertainty, and therefore should only be recognized as realized. The latter position was adopted by the FASB and the SEC in their oil and gas industry rules. Practice varies in the hard minerals extractive industry.

Disclosures

It is common practice to disclose quantities of minerals produced, subdivided by types of mineral or other natural resource. In addition, when there are significant operations in a particular mine or nation, companies often make disclosure of the production and, in some cases, the revenues for those mines or nations.

Disclosure of quantities of coal reserves held is usually made for companies with significant coal operations. Practice is mixed with respect to the disclosures of estimated reserves of other hard rock minerals. The portions of financial statements that are unique to the hard minerals industry and the related disclosure and explanatory notes are illustrated in Figure 34.5.

Many mining companies enter into long-term purchase agreements with buyers of the mine output. Often these agreements are required if the company is to obtain financing for development costs at a particular mine site. The contract assures the extractive operator that there will be a sufficient market for the production to make mine development an economically viable project. If purchases under such contracts are necessary to make the mining operation economically viable, disclosure of the contract and related details may be necessary for assessment of the risks involved in company operations. In some cases the contract prices, increased-cost recovery provisions, minimum purchases, cancelation terms, and even the names of the other party to any substantial contract are disclosed.

Auditing Considerations

Although auditing the hard minerals industry has many similarities to auditing the oil and gas producing industry, the auditor needs to develop an understanding of the unique practices and accounting and reporting in hard minerals, and of the internal accounting controls and systems his client has established. In addition, he must evaluate those controls and systems through review and testing.

Portion of Balance Sheet

Receivables		
Mineral sales		$2,000
Inventories		
Mine supplies		100
Mineral product		10
Property, plant, and equipment		
Land and mineral rights		500
Plant and equipment		5,000
		5,500
Less accumulated depreciation and depletion		1,500
		$4,000

Portion of Statement of Income

Mineral sales		$10,000
Costs and expenses		
Cost of minerals produced	$7,500	
Depreciation and depletion	800	
Selling, administrative and general	700	9,000
Earnings before taxes (etc.)		$ 1,000

PORTION OF NOTES TO FINANCIAL STATEMENTS
Summary of Accounting Policies
Property, Plant, and Equipment

Property, plant, and equipment carried at cost includes expenditures for new facilities and expenditures that substantially increase the productive lives of existing plant and equipment. Maintenance and repair costs are expensed as incurred. Mineral rights are depleted at a rate based on the cost of the mineral properties and estimated recoverable tonnage. Depreciation of plant and equipment is determined by the straight-line and accelerated methods over the estimated useful lives of the assets. Exploration and development costs are capitalized during the construction and preoperating stage. These costs are amortized against production after commercial operations are commenced.

Income Taxes

Deferred taxes are provided for the income tax effect resulting from temporary differences between financial statement pretax income and taxable income. The investment tax credit, to the extent allowable, is applied as a reduction of the provision for income taxes. Deferred taxes related to mineral resource activities are provided on the excess of tax deductions for development and exploration costs over the amount of such costs charged to income in the financial statements.

FIG. 34.5   Example of Financial Statement Elements and Related Notes to Financial Statements Unique to the Hard Minerals Industry

As discussed previously, one of the unique problems in this industry relates to mineral reserves, which must be estimated to determine the cost of minerals produced. The auditor will need to understand the work of mineral engineers, and he may need to use the work of a specialist in accomplishing this assessment. SAS 11 *Using the Work of a Specialist* (AU 336), provides professional guidance for the auditor under those circumstances.

It is also necessary to review the details of the mineral properties to see that mineral rights are included in the ownership rights of the land, that options for rights have not expired or been forfeited, and that advance royalty payments are expected to be recoverable from future operations based on existing economic conditions. In addition, if changing prices disclosures are voluntarily presented by a mineral resource company, the auditor should apply the provisions of SAS 8, *Other Information in Documents Containing Audited Financial Statements* (AU 550), in the review for that data.

TIMBER RESOURCES

One characteristic of the forest products industry is unique: the raw material, timber, used in the manufacture and processing of forest products is renewable. Oil, gas, and hard minerals, once extracted, are gone forever. Admittedly, agricultural products are also renewable, but the short plant-to-harvest cycle allows reasonably accurate projections of yield quantities. This is not true with timber. The shortest timber cycle from planting to harvest is about 20 years, and the longer cycles are commonly 50 to 80 years. Return on investment is not at all certain, because of potential loss of timber resources through natural disaster, fire, insect infestation, and disease. Further, prediction of market conditions so many years into the future is impossible.

Accounting for and auditing of the timber segment of the forest products industry presents some unusual problems discussed in this section. Once lumber and pulp have been produced, traditional accounting methods are applicable.

Accounting Considerations

Cost Capitalization. Timber and timberland are acquired through (1) purchase of the land and timber thereon, (2) lease of the land with assumption of timber-cutting rights, or (3) purchase of timber-cutting rights only on land owned by private interests or the federal government. In addition, cut timber is often purchased on the open market.

When the forest products company maintains an economic interest in the land as well as in the timber on that land, that interest is called fee timber and is classified as a fixed asset. The economic interest applies both to purchased and leased land and timber, even though the lease agreement may provide that the deforested land reverts to the original landholder upon termination of the lease rights (i.e., upon completion of the logging operation). Timber leases generally meet the capitalization criteria and are, likewise, classified as fixed assets.

Fee timber acquisition costs, such as surveys, purchase price, brokerage costs, and legal fees, are also capitalized. Additionally, development costs such as road construction, temporary lodging facilities, and land-clearing activities are also capitalized, generally as land improvements. Carrying costs such as interest and taxes on the timberland and overhead costs related to the development period may be capitalized, but only if incurred prior to the start of harvesting operations. However, most companies treat interest, taxes, and overhead as current period operating expenses. Similar acquisition and development costs related to timber-cutting rights on leased land are capitalized.

Even after cutting has begun, it is proper to capitalize costs attributable to future harvests (e.g., land clearing, reseeding or planting, and forest management). Costs associated with research and development related to new growing techniques or improving trees genetically are expensed.

Often, timber-cutting rights are purchased from land owners under long-term contracts. The deposits required under such contracts are capitalized and depleted as timber is harvested from the land. Costs related to purchase of timber on the open market are treated the same as the purchase of raw materials in any industry, that is, capitalized as raw material inventory and expensed as used.

Depletion. Just as oil, gas, and hard mineral reserves are depleted over time, so too are timber resources. Thus, some portion of the total cost of the fee timber should be depleted based on the proportion of timber harvested during the year to total timber available for cutting. Many companies adjust depletion rates on an annual basis.

Generally, small- and medium-sized firms use a single average depletion rate for all the timber, regardless of its geographic location or grade. Larger companies frequently break down the rate by track (i.e., geographically) or by species and grade of timber, which results in a more precise depletion calculation.

The actual method used to calculate depletion is disclosed in notes to the financial statements, and the depletion charge itself is separately disclosed only when it is material. If timber harvesting is a significant part of a company's operations, timber assets are shown on the balance sheet as a separate line item, typically "Timber and timberlands at cost, less cost of timber harvested."

Modern forest products companies subscribe to sustained-yield forestry, that is, replacement of the amount of timber cut by an equal or greater amount of timber growth. The effect is that total timber available for harvest remains about the same or is increased. In certain hardwood areas, natural regeneration occurs on the former sites of standing timber. Seeds that have dropped to the forest floor over time and remained dormant are later exposed to adequate sunlight and water. These seedlings naturally grow to maturity with little actual forest management expenses warranted. Softwoods, for example, southern pine, do not naturally regenerate as easily. Extensive forest management efforts must be expended in cutting seed stock from mature trees, growing and planting the seedlings, and managing the growth process. The cost of naturally regenerated stands of timber on owned or leased land permitting more than one rotation cutting may be small compared to original acquisition costs.

Inventories. Due to the nature of this type of asset the physical measurement of the amount of inventory and its valuation are complex. Both of these issues are discussed in the following subsections.

Physical measurement. It would be very difficult to measure accurately the quantity, species, and grades of standing timber. Therefore, the determination of quantities must depend on estimation formulas developed by the forestry industry and sampling surveys performed by foresters. Standard volume tables have been developed over the years, and the forester uses them to measure volumes of available timber. Aerial surveys may be used to verify generally the acreage and the quantities of the various species carried on the company's books.

Measurement of harvested wood (in log or chip form for use in pulp production and in log or finished lumber form at sawmills) also requires the services of an expert. Generally, the auditor would observe the estimation process conducted by the expert. Standard scales are used to measure quantities, and frequently an experienced auditor can ascertain species and grades. Pulpmill wood is generally measured in terms of cords and converted to tons or vice versa. Sawmill inventories of raw logs are counted at the boom ponds or cold decks of mills in terms of cords and are converted to board feet. Finished lumber may be measured and counted, and board feet determined therefrom.

Valuation. Standing timber constitutes the reserves of the forest products industry, and it is in this area that the accounting practices peculiar to the industry are most evident. Unlike oil and gas reserves or hard mineral deposits, timber supplies can be replenished. But unlike agricultural products, the growth cycle occurs over extended periods of time, from 20 years to as long as 80 years. The problem then becomes one of valuing a resource that is simultaneously being depleted and regenerated.

Valuation of many forms of harvested timber is made in conjunction with the estimation of physical inventories. Most companies use lower of cost (determined by the LIFO method) or market, but it is rare that market value of timber is lower than cost. Periodical publications of the industry and industry associations provide up-to-date market values.

Cost Accounting. One of the difficulties in determining actual costs is the matching of logs processed to the cost of the standing timber. Ordinarily, as mentioned, acreages of timberland are purchased and depletion rates established based on estimates of cords or board feet contained thereon, regardless of species or grade. Yet when the timber is cut into finished boards or plywood at sawmills or processed into pulp, cost is assigned to the timber by quality. For example, the unit purchase price for the timber in a given tract may turn out on average to be $20 per cord. However, the more valuable species may have a unit cost substantially higher.

Overall, however, gross costs do tend to average out; thus, average costs generally are reflected in the accounting records. Few companies attempt to determine unit costs per species or grade in the felling, transporting, milling, and processing operations. If a company replenishes its standing timber on a sustained-yield basis without natural regeneration, cost per unit may be more accurately determined, since companies predetermine species to be harvested eventually and maintain continuing records of site preparation, seeding, planting, pruning and thinning, spraying, and similar costs.

Income Taxes

Under IRC § 1231, timber is considered an asset used in a trade or business, and under Section 631, gains on timber harvested are treated as capital gains (under the tax law in 1988, however, the capital gains rate and ordinary income rate are the same), whereas losses are treated as ordinary deductions. However, the taxpayer must elect the advantages of Section 631, and once made, the IRS only rarely permits reversal.

The provisions of Section 631 apply only to companies that have an economic interest in the timberland, and that interest must have been held for a specified period of time before the timber is harvested.

One of the provisions of Section 631 involves companies that harvest timber for use in their own mills. The fair market value of the timber harvested is added to cost of sales of the mill and is an ordinary deduction. The fair market value then also becomes a theoretical sales price—in that the timber itself has not been sold—which is netted against the historical cost basis; the resultant amount is taxed at capital gain rates.

Another provision of Section 631 deals with entities that sell timber to others. Assuming the timber has been owned for the statutory time period and at the time of sale the seller retains an economic interest in the timber, any gain on the sale would be treated as a capital gain. The buyer who mills and then sells the lumber, however, may not treat gains as capital gains.

Inflation-Adjusted Disclosures

Inflation-adjusted disclosures (under SFAS 40) became optional for all companies with the issuance of SFAS 89 (C28). However, for forest products companies wishing to provide these disclosures, valuation of the current cost of timber resources is an area requiring additional judgment. The FASB concluded that timberlands and growing timber, among other specialized assets, have certain special features that distinguish them from current cost measurement methods used for other assets. Thus, they concluded that historical costs may be adjusted by using an externally generated index of a broad-based measure of general purchasing power such as the consumer price index, to determine current costs for timber resources.

Further, the historical cost base may either (1) be limited to these costs capitalized in the primary financial statements, or (2) include all costs of developing timber resources (the reforestation approach) including forest management, planting, fertilization, fire protection, property taxes and nursery stock, whether or not those costs are capitalized in the primary financial statements. (Of course, any current cost adjustment would need to be measured in relation to the recoverable amount criteria in SFAS 89 if the recoverable amount is judged to be materially and permanently lower than the current cost amount. If this concern exists, current cost would be adjusted downward to the recoverable amount.)

Because of the wide diversity permitted between these two current cost valuation approaches, voluntary current cost disclosures may not be comparable among forest products companies if different methods are elected.

Auditing Considerations

The auditor needs to develop an understanding of industry practices, accounting, and reporting, and of the internal accounting controls and systems that his client has established. He should evaluate the controls and systems through review and testing.

One of the significant specialized problems in this industry relates to estimating the amount of timber resources to determine the cost of timber harvested. When other costs such as road construction and reforestation costs are capitalized, the cost pool encompasses not only acquisition costs but also these other capitalized costs. Generally, the cost amortizable for harvested timber is determined in relation to total investment in timber and estimated total standing timber.

The auditor will need to understand and use the work of foresters and others to assess the estimates of timber based on sampling surveys, aerial surveys, and standard volume tables. The auditor may need to use the work of a specialist in accomplishing this assessment. SAS 11 (AU 336) provides professional guidance for the auditor under these circumstances.

It is also necessary to review the details of the timberland properties to see that timber rights are included among the client's rights, that options for rights have not expired or been forfeited, and that advance royalty payments are expected to be recoverable from future operations based on existing economic conditions.

35

Real Estate

INDUSTRY ACCOUNTING OVERVIEW

The real estate industry encompasses many individual activities covered by several separate accounting standards. This chapter has four major accounting sections that do not precisely follow the organization of the existing standards; therefore it is important at the outset to establish which activities are discussed in the chapter's various sections.

The lead-off section on income-producing property covers all real estate transactions other than retail land sales and syndications of real estate ventures, each covered in a following section. A separate section also covers aspects of the single-family homebuilding industry not discussed under the "Income-Producing Property" section — essentially those accounting matters relating to construction contracting.[1]

FASB Releases

Two FASB standards directly apply to the real estate industry and to real estate transactions in general. These are SFAS 66, *Accounting for Sales of Real Estate* (Re1), and SFAS 67, *Accounting for Costs and Initial Rental Operations of Real Estate Projects* (Re2).[2]

SFAS 66 adopted the specialized accounting principles from two AICPA Industry Accounting Guides, *Accounting for Profit Recognition on Sales of Real Estate* (1973b) and *Accounting for Retail Land Sales* (1973c). SFAS 66 also incorporates SOP 75-6, *Questions Concerning Profit Recognition on Sales of Real Estate* (TP 10,100) and SOP 78-4, *Application of the Deposit, Installment, and Cost Recovery Methods in Accounting for Sales of Real Estate* (TP 10,190).

SFAS 67 incorporates SOP 80-3, *Accounting for Real Estate Acquisition, Development, and Construction Costs* (TP 10,320), and SOP 78-3, *Accounting for Costs to Sell and Rent and Initial Rental Operations of Real Estate Projects* (TP 10,180). SFAS 67 also encompasses those portions of the prior guide on *Accounting for Retail Land Sales* that deal with real estate projects.

SFAS 66 (nonretail land sales portion) and SFAS 67 are discussed principally in the section "Income-Producing Properties." In addition, the EITF has discussed numerous real estate accounting issues, discussed in relevant sections.

In mid-1988, the FASB issued SFAS 98, *Accounting for Leases: Sale-Leaseback Transactions Involving Real Estate; Sales-Type Leases of Real Estate; Definition of the Lease Term; [and] Initial Direct Costs of Direct Financing Leases*. This statement avers that in all real estate transactions, SFAS 66 is the controlling document, and

---

[1] This chapter does not cover Common Interest Realty Associations (CIRAs), which include condominium and homeowners' associations. An exposure draft of an audit and accounting guide was issued on August 31, 1988, with the principal issue relating to whether common areas are to be recorded as assets of the CIRA. Accountants involved in financial reporting and auditing for CIRAs should refer to the exposure draft for guidance.

[2] In the FASB General Accounting Standards codification, SFAS 66 and SFAS 67 are classified in section R10, aimed at companies that enter into occasional real estate transactions. Section R10 thus omits the more complex matters found in real estate businesses. However, the entire contents of SFAS 66 and SFAS 67 are included in the FASB Industry Standards codification under sections Re1 and Re2; these Industry Standards references will be used in this chapter.

that *all* real estate sale-leaseback transactions must meet the requirements of SFAS 66 for sales recognition by the seller-lessee. This is further discussed in Chapter 19.

AICPA Releases

In addition to the four SOPs that were incorporated into SFAS 66 and SFAS 67, two additional SOPs are relevant in the real estate industry:

* SOP 78-9, *Accounting for Investments in Real Estate Ventures* (TP 10,240), discusses the accounting for investments in and transactions with real estate ventures (whether in corporate, partnership, or undivided interest form). This SOP is covered in the section entitled "Income Producing Properties."

* SOP 81-1, *Accounting for Performance of Construction-Type and Certain Production-Type Contracts* (TP 10,330), discusses the use of the completed contract and percentage-of-completion methods of accounting for long- and short-term construction contracts. Although this SOP is principally discussed in Chapter 36, several aspects bear emphasis with respect to single-family homebuilders.

The AICPA also releases Practice Bulletins through AcSEC; Practice Bulletin No. 1 incorporates prior Notices to Practioners still having relevance. One such notice deals with accounting by lenders for acquisition, development, and construction loans (ADC loans), and describes conditions under which a transaction is deemed to be an equity investment in real estate (e.g., a joint venture) rather than a loan. ADC loans are discussed in Chapter 41.

SEC Requirements

The SEC has dealt with real estate companies and transactions in numerous releases. Indeed, the SEC had a release on real estate transactions well before the AICPA took any action (ASR 95, *Accounting for Real Estate Transactions Where Circumstances Indicate That Profits Were not Earned at the Time the Transactions Were Recorded* (1962, now rescinded)). The SEC's 1962 release contained a number of examples which at the time appeared rather complex, were difficult to apply, and necessarily were subjectively applied by the SEC staff. Today, these examples would appear somewhat elementary.

Apart from general requirements applicable to all registrants, Regulation S-X requires schedules to be filed by certain real estate companies regarding real estate holdings and accumulated depreciation (Rule 12-28) and mortgage loans on real estate (Rule 12-29). In SAB Topic 7.C, the staff points out that the information contained in these schedules is of such significance that it should also be given in financial statements included in shareholder reports. Regulation S-K contains Industry Guide 5, *Preparation of Registration Statements Relating to Interests in Real Estate Limited Partnerships,* discussed in the section entitled "Real Estate Syndications."

Additionally, relevant matters are covered in SABs, as discussed in the applicable sections of this chapter.

Industry Structure

The legal form taken by a real estate entity, or created for a real estate transaction, is determined in large part by the tax motivations of the investors, the initial capital outlay required (and the means by which it will be financed), and the risks involved in acquiring, developing, operating, and selling a project. The most common forms of equity ownership are:

• Corporation.
• Corporate joint venture. A corporation owned and operated by a small group of venturers to accomplish a mutually beneficial venture or project.
• General partnership. An association in which each partner has unlimited liability.
• Limited partnership. An association in which one or more general partners have unlimited liability and one or more limited partners have limited liability. A limited partnership is usually managed by the general partner or partners, subject to restrictions, if any, imposed by the partnership agreement.
• Undivided interest. A form of joint venture ownership in which two or more parties jointly own property, and title is held individually to the extent of each party's interest.
• Sole proprietorship. Ownership by one person.

Debt structures related to real estate transactions vary in form with payment terms that may be fixed or variable, and the following attributes may be present in varying degrees. The debt may

• Be secured by real estate.
• Provide for equity participation in the operating cash flow and appreciation in value.
• Have conversion features.

A partnership or joint venture structure is commonly used as a vehicle to spread the equity risk among the companies or individuals who are active, working partners in the project. In other instances, the joint venture form may be adopted as a financing arrangement in which the sponsoring partner will develop, manage, and operate the project while a number of passive partners simply contribute capital in exchange for a return on equity.

Income-producing property businesses and homebuilders will use all the forms described, while retail land sales companies will ordinarily be corporations. Real estate syndications are often in limited partnership form, including a number of publicly traded master limited partnerships; however, recent tax law changes have made limited partnerships less attractive, and the trend is toward the use of real estate investment trusts (REITs).

INCOME-PRODUCING PROPERTY

Property Development

Income-producing properties developed for sale or operation by commercial developers include:

- Apartment houses
- Office buildings
- Industrial buildings
- Shopping centers
- Mobile home parks
- Hotels/motels/parking lots
- Congregate care facilities
- Mixed-use development

The commercial developer may be building the facility to hold for his own account as an investment or building to order for a third-party user, or he may develop and sell the facility to a prospective investor or real estate syndicate. Each of these separate products has distinctive features and problems, but all require land. As a result, most developers restrict themselves to small geographic areas.

Development of income-producing property is seasonal and sensitive to the availability of funds. Periods of "tight money," result in increased interest rates on both short- and long-term loans, and have a negative impact on the prospective buyer. This fluctuating rate of development generally causes all but the largest real estate enterprises to keep overhead to a minimum, thus discouraging capital investment and the assembly of large central staffs.

SFAS 67, Accounting for Costs and Initial Rental Operations of Real Estate Projects (Re2), deals with all aspects of income-producing properties except sales recognition criteria. It covers: (1) acquisition costs, (2) holding costs, (3) project costs, (4) amenities, (5) incidental operations, (6) allocation of costs to components, (7) revisions of estimates, (8) abandonments and changes in use, (9) selling costs, (10) rent-up costs, (11) initial rental operations, and (11) net realizable value. These matters are discussed in the following sections.

Acquisition Costs. Acquisition costs are generally classified as preacquisition costs, direct acquisition costs, and indirect acquisition costs.

Preacquisition costs are all costs related to deciding whether to acquire the property and to the actual acquisition process. Some of these costs include

- Appraisal, research, and consulting fees.
- Market feasibility and environmental studies.
- Architectural and engineering services.
- Legal and other professional services.
- Zoning approvals.
- Finders' fees, good-faith deposits, and standby fees.

Preacquisition costs, including payment to obtain a purchase option, should be capitalized provided that all of the following conditions are met (Re2.104):

- Costs are directly identifiable with the specific property.
- Costs would be properly capitalizable if the property were already acquired.

- Acquisition of the property or acquisition of an option to acquire the property is "probable" (i.e., likely to occur).
- Total capitalized costs do not exceed net realizable value.

Direct acquisition costs are those costs directly associated with the acquisition of the property and should be capitalized (Re2.107). Generally they include:

- Purchase price of the property;
- Escrow, title guarantee, title search, and recording fees; and
- Brokers' fees and commissions.

Indirect acquisition costs are those indirectly associated with the acquisition of property, such as overhead and other qualifying general and administrative costs. Overhead costs, such as those incurred by planning and development departments, may be capitalized under SFAS 67 (Re2.107) as part of the cost of land improvements. Such costs may be provided by outside contractors or may be identifiable internal costs.

General and administrative expenses ordinarily should be charged to expense as period costs. However, there may be situations where capitalization of these costs is proper because they can be closely identified with the property.

Holding Costs. Holding costs are incurred after the property has been acquired and while the developer is obtaining the necessary architectural plans, zoning approvals, permits, construction financing arrangements, and permanent loan commitments. In other situations, some developers hold inventories of property for future development. Holding costs usually include property tax, insurance payments, and interest costs associated with the financing of the property.

As a general rule, holding costs should be capitalized as part of the cost of the property during the periods in which the property is being developed (Re2.107). Costs incurred for such items after the property is substantially complete and ready for its intended use, or during periods when no development is in progress, should be charged to expense as incurred.

Property held for future development requires continual evaluation as to recoverability of the accumulated capitalized costs.

Development and Construction Costs. After the predevelopment process is complete, the development and construction stages begin. As a general rule, all incurred costs directly related to the property should be capitalized during the development and construction periods, provided there are no net realizable value limitations. Costs incurred for periods after the project is substantially complete and ready for its intended use should be expensed (Re2.106).

Complex accounting problems can arise, since the development and construction process usually covers several accounting periods and may involve multiple purchase and sale transactions that require special cost accumulation and cost allocation techniques. Development and construction costs that need to be accounted for include direct and indirect project costs, amenities, and interest costs; additional issues involve component allocations, revision of estimates, and incidental operations.

Direct costs (i.e., costs specifically identified with a property) should be capitalized as a cost of the project. Such costs consist of:

• Building plans, architects' fees, permits, surveys, cost of zoning changes, and so forth.
• On-site and off-site improvements consisting of roads, sewers, utilities, grading, sidewalks, landscaping, parking areas, traffic controls, and common-area recreation facilities.

Indirect costs that are specifically related to the project should be capitalized as a cost of the project (Re2.409). Indirect project costs generally consist of construction administration and legal and accounting fees. Indirect costs may relate to several projects and should be allocated to each project in a rational manner based on the nature of the activity (Re2.409). This allocation process may be based on determining the percentages of time spent on each development effort, as well as time spent on other activities. General and administrative costs as well as costs not clearly related to a specific project or projects should be expensed as incurred. If management is actively involved in the development process, it may be appropriate to allocate a portion of the payroll expense to the project as a capitalizable cost.

Amenities are installed to make a particular development more attractive. They can include golf courses, clubhouses, lakes, parks, and marinas. These amenities may or may not be income-producing, and may be sold or transferred in connection with the sale of individual units, sold separately, or operated by the developer (Re2.108).

In the first situation, the cost of the amenity, including the allocated land cost and any net operating costs to be subsidized by the developer, should be allocated as a cost applicable to each individual unit because the cost of the amenity is associated with the project's sale. In the second situation, an amenity may have a cost greater than what it could be sold for on the market, because it may not be attractive to an outside investor given its integration with the main facilities. Accordingly, the actual development cost of the amenity in excess of its estimated fair value (established as of the substantial completion date) should be capitalized and allocated as a common cost. Future operating results are to be included in income; and a sale subsequent to substantial completion should result in a gain or loss based on the differences between selling price and cost (i.e., fair value at date of substantial completion) less accumulated depreciation.

Interest costs incurred over a period of time to construct an asset or carry out other activities necessary to bring it to usable condition should be capitalized as a part of the historical cost of that asset. The objective of interest capitalization is to obtain a measure that reflects the total investment in the property and to match the interest cost against revenue generated from the property in future periods. The accounting rules regarding interest capitalization are contained in SFAS 34 (I67).

Allocation of capitalized costs to components is necessary when portions of a development or project are completed in stages or phases and sold before all development and construction work is completed. To properly match costs with revenues, costs must be assigned to the individual components of the project being sold based on specific identification. The matching process is a significant problem in a development company because of the length of time a project may be in progress and nonhomogeneity in the value of units within a development. It can be further complicated by the assignment of land parcels to amenities that have varying revenue potential.

SFAS 67 states that if specific identification is not practicable, the capitalized costs are allocated as follows (Re2.111):

* Costs incurred prior to construction (e.g., land costs and other common costs) are allocated to each land parcel benefited, based on the relative fair market values before construction as determined at the date of allocation.
* Construction costs are allocated to individual units (lots) in the phase or project on the basis of relative sales value of each unit (lot).

Revisions of cost allocation estimates that relate to only the current period are accounted for in the period of change (Re2.112). Revisions of estimates relating to cost allocations that affect both current and future periods are accounted for prospectively in current and future periods. Such estimates must be reviewed at least annually until the project is substantially complete and ready for its intended use.

Incidental operations arise from such activities as leasing land that is not intended to be developed until a later date, renting facilities (intended to be leased, occupied, or sold at a later date), or operating temporary parking lot facilities. Net operating income should be accounted for as a reduction of capitalized development costs, whereas net operating losses should be charged to current operations (Re2.110).

Abandonments and Changes in Use. If real estate is abandoned, capitalized assets should be written off as current expenses or, if appropriate, to allowances established for that purpose (Re2.113–.115). The costs of these abandoned projects should not be allocated to other components of those projects or to other projects. Property donated to governmental agencies for uses that will benefit a project are not abandonments.

Changes in the use of a real estate project or a portion of the project may occur after significant development or construction costs have been incurred. In general, development and construction costs incurred before the change should be written off to the extent they have no continuing value in the changed project.

Selling Costs. Regardless of what method of profit recognition (discussed in the "Real Estate Sales" section later) is being used, it is permissible to capitalize certain costs incurred in selling real estate projects if they are expected to be recovered from the sales proceeds or from incidental operations. Such costs must be for tangible assets used in the sales process (e.g., model units) or for obtaining regulatory approvals.

Other costs directly related to (and expected to be recoverable from) sale of the property may be deferred if a profit recognition method other than full accrual is being used.

Valuation Issues. Land and buildings held for sale, or being developed for sale, represent the inventory of a commercial developer. ARB 43 (I78.109–.113) notes that inventory should be carried at the lower of cost or market, with market not to exceed net realizable value (NRV). NRV is generally the fair market value reduced by the costs of completion and disposition (Re2.410).[3] In most cases, the NRV criteria should be based on a project-by-project analysis. An individual project, for this purpose, consists of components that are relatively homogeneous, integral parts of the whole.

In determining the cost of a particular project for purposes of applying the lower-of-cost-or-market criteria, all project costs, including costs to complete, must be considered.

When the capitalized costs of a real estate project held for sale, or for development and sale, exceed estimated NRV, an allowance should be provided to reduce the carrying amount of the asset to NRV. The use of an allowance account allows the accumulation of the total project costs while still valuing the asset at the lower of cost or market for financial statement purposes (I78.114; Re2.124). Rental properties may also have an impairment in value through insufficient rental demand. If deemed other than temporary, an allowance for losses should be provided (Re2.125).

Joint Ventures. Because of the risks involved in large projects and the frequent needs for substantial financing and a variety of expertise, developers will often team up with other industry entities on a project. Further, it is common that a party owning an ingredient critical to the development (such as raw land or air rights) will participate as a joint venture partner. In other situations, a transaction involving an income-producing property (perhaps uncompleted) and structured as a joint venture may in fact be a sale in economic substance, and should be measured under the rules of SFAS 66, discussed in the later section "Real Estate Sales." Conversely, transactions structured as loans may in fact be joint venture investments (e.g., ADC loans, discussed in Chapter 41, with one specific aspect covered in the next subsection).

Investors may make capital contributions to the joint venture in the form of cash, property, or services rendered. Noncash investments in a joint venture should be recorded at the venturer's cost of the assets contributed; as a general rule, a venturer should not recognize a profit as a result of a capital contribution. An investor contributing property to a venture may obtain a disproportionately small interest in the venture based on a comparison of the carrying amount of the property with the cash contributed by the other investors. Such a situation may indicate that the investor has suffered a loss that should be recognized. If no loss is indicated and the venturer's contribution is greater than his equity in the joint venture's net assets, the excess should be accounted for like goodwill (I82.109n).

There are three general methods for reporting an investment in a joint venture: the cost method, the equity method, and the consolidation method. A fourth method, pro rata (or proportionate) consolidation, may also be appropriate in certain circumstances. (These methods are discussed in Chapter 24.) Whatever method is used, it should be identified; and footnote disclosure should contain separate financial data for material joint ventures. Frequently, full financial statements will be presented for

---

[3] In 1988, the AICPA established a task force on costs of capital. This group plans to resolve the issue of whether interest should be included as a holding cost in determining NRV for purposes of establishing loan loss allowances, as this aspect is not treated uniformly in the financial service industries. The planned SOP might have an effect on how NRV is calculated in the income-producing real estate industry.

significant joint ventures, and condensed or combined financial statements may be shown for others.

Other accounting matters are discussed in SOP 78-9, *Accounting for Investments in Real Estate Ventures* (TP 10,240), as follows:

1. Investor accounting for losses in a venture. Losses in excess of investments and advances are to be recorded by the investor if the investor will be required directly or indirectly to provide additional financial support.

2. Treatment of equity method adjustments. Intercompany profit should be eliminated based on the investor's ownership percentage; 100% should be eliminated if the venture is controlled. Further, if the venture uses other than GAAP, the financial statements should be adjusted prior to applying the equity method.

3. Transactions with the venture. All sales of real estate to the venture by a venturer are governed by SFAS 66. Profit may be recognized for services performed by a venturer to the extent of outside interests, provided there are no substantial uncertainties about the investors' ability to perform the services, and their total cost is known. If the investor buys real estate or services from the venture, the buyer's share of the venture's profit should be treated as a reduction of purchase price.

4. Sale of investment in a venture. Such a sale is to be evaluated under SFAS 66 criteria.

ADC loans on operating properties. In Issue 86-21, *Application of the AICPA Notice to Practitioners Regarding Acquisition, Development, and Construction Arrangements to Acquisition of an Operating Property,* the EITF considered whether loans made for the acquisition of *operating* properties that grant the lender a right to participate in expected residual profit from the sale or refinancing of the property are subject to the AICPA's Notice to Practitioners regarding ADC loans (Practice Bulletin No. 1).

The EITF reached a consensus that, although that Notice was aimed at ADC loans made by financial institutions, it equally applies to shared appreciation mortgages, loans on operating real estate, and ADC arrangements entered into by nonfinancial institutions. Depending on the nature of the expected profit, the transaction might be a joint venture in substance, to be accounted for accordingly.

The SEC Observer indicated that *all* registrants must follow the guidance in the Notice, and followed this up with SAB 71, *Financial Statements of Properties Securing Mortgage Loans* (Topic 1.I), which requires filing of financial statements of properties securing mortgage loans in circumstances under which the loan may be deemed to be an investment in real estate or a joint venture, rather than a loan. SAB 71 provided a measurement basis more stringent than the AICPA's ADC loan criteria (now contained in Practice Bulletin No. 1), by stating that loan accounting would be appropriate only if the initial and continuing investment criteria in SFAS 66 were met by the buyer (Rel.111–.112). This caused an outcry from affected registrants and resulted in slight modifications in SAB 71A, which moderated the stringent criteria by stating that the ADC guidelines could still be used instead of the SFAS 66 criteria. The SAB emphasized that if the borrower's equity (used in deciding if the obligor on the "loan" had sufficient equity in the property) consisted of contributed property that was recently acquired, it should be valued at cost rather than at appraised values.

Rental Operations

Rent-Up Costs. Costs to rent real estate projects under operating leases should be deferred and charged to expense in future periods if their recovery is reasonably expected from future rental operations. Examples of such costs include brokerage commissions, costs of model units and their furnishings, rental facilities, semi-permanent signs, and unused rental brochures (RE2.120).

Deferred rental costs directly related to revenue from a specific operating lease should be amortized over the lease term, commencing with the beginning of the rental period (Re2.121). Deferred rental costs that are not directly related to revenue from a specific lease should be amortized over the period of expected benefit, commencing when the project is substantially completed and available for occupancy. Unamortized costs associated with a lease should be charged to expense when it becomes probable that recovery will not occur (e.g., the lease will be terminated).

Initial Rental Operations. Once major construction activity is completed and the project is capable of producing revenue, a rental project should be considered "substantially complete and held available for occupancy." SFAS 67 notes that the accounting for costs and revenues should reflect this change in the status of the project as follows (Re2.122):

- Rental revenues and operating costs are recognized in income and expense as they accrue.
- Carrying costs are charged to expense when incurred.
- Depreciation commences based on the cost of the project.
- Amortization of rent-up costs commences.

It is important to note that a single parcel of land or a building may represent more than one project. Accordingly, each portion should be accounted for as a separate project (Re2.123).

Rental Revenues. Rental revenues are derived from commercial properties (e.g., shopping centers, office buildings, and marinas) and from residential rentals. In addition to fixed minimum rentals, it is common for lessees to pay to the lessor an amount to cover the various costs of operating the property, and, for retail leases, an additional monthly rent based on sales volume; all such amounts are included in the lessor's rental income. (Under net leases in which the tenant pays these costs directly, the amounts of course are not included in the lessor's revenue.) For financial reporting purposes, rent received in advance is treated as revenue of the period in which it is earned.

Operating Expenses. Significant direct rental operating expenses include depreciation, insurance, repairs and maintenance, property taxes, custodial and security expenses, utilities, interest, and property management (either by employees or by contract with third parties). Such costs are generally classified as current period expenses, but if they cover more than the current period they are classified as prepaid expenses, to be allocated to future periods in a systematic and rational manner.

Costs to rent real estate projects that do not meet the criteria for deferral should be accounted for as period costs and charged to expense as incurred. Examples of such costs include media advertising costs, rental salaries, and overhead.

Rental Concessions. In Issue 83-3, *Rental Concessions Provided by Landlord*, the EITF discussed the situation in which a landlord may offer incentives or concessions to a prospective tenant, such as paying the tenant's moving expenses, reimbursing the tenant for unamortized leasehold improvements in his present space, or assuming the tenant's obligation to make payments under the old lease.

Although no consensus was reached, Task Force members generally supported the following accounting positions:

* Concessions should be recognized by the tenant as adjustments to rental expense on a straight-line basis over the term of the new lease.
* Moving expenses paid directly or reimbursed by the new landlord, or reimbursements for unamortized leasehold improvements that have no continuing value are concessions and should be recognized currently.
* If the new landlord assumed the tenant's obligation under the old lease, any concession should be measured as the estimated loss to be incurred by the landlord in assuming the old lease. Views differed about whether any loss on the assumption of the tenant's old lease should be recognized immediately or deferred over the term of the new lease.
* If a tenant is unable to either terminate the old lease or sublease the old space, the tenant should accrue the loss currently for the remaining lease payments under the old lease. Similar accounting should apply if the tenant subleases the old space at a loss.

This matter is comprehensively dealt with by the FASB staff in proposed TB 88-b, which takes the position that all concessions are adjustments of rentals and should be spread over the new lease, answering the first three points in the preceding list. The TB is silent as to the fourth point, but the EITF's general view would govern. This matter is further discussed in Chapter 19.

Real Estate Sales

The complexity of income-producing real estate sales transactions often causes major accounting difficulties. Accounting cannot be based solely on legal form, because in many cases the form (often designed to establish a desired tax basis) may obscure the economic substance. As a result, GAAP requires a transaction to be accounted for in accordance with its economic substance, and each transaction must be carefully evaluated to determine the appropriate accounting and reporting treatment under SFAS 66 (Re1). An example of a form/substance difference that has been dealt with in FASB pronouncements is a sales-type lease of real estate, in which the requirements of SFAS 66 rather than SFAS 13 (Accounting for Leases, L10) govern. (See Chapter 19.)

In accounting for the sale of real estate, two basic criteria must be met for the earnings process to be complete and for full accrual profit to be recognized: (1) the collectibility of the sales price must be reasonably assured, and the amount of profit determinable; and (2) the seller should not be obligated to perform significant activities after the sale to earn the profit.

Recognition of all of the profit at the time of sale (or at some later date when both conditions are met) is referred to as the full accrual method (Re1.103). If the full accrual method is not applicable because all of the criteria are not fully met, SFAS 66 provides for several other methods that range from no profit recognition to some profit recognition. These methods are the deposit, cost recovery, installment, and reduced profit methods, discussed in the later section "Other Profit Recognition Methods." In addition, if a seller's continuing involvement causes the transaction to be deemed not a sale, none of these methods is applicable and the transaction is treated as a financing, leasing, or profit-sharing arrangement.

In all sales methods other than the deposit method, a receivable from the buyer is established, net of property-related debt previously owed by the seller but now assumed by the buyer. Under the deposit method, and in nonsale treatment as a financing, leasing, or profit-sharing agreement, the property and the related debt will stay on the "seller's" balance sheet.

A graphic representation of the factors and criteria that must be considered in determining the proper method of profit recognition is provided in a decision tree in Figure 35.1.

Full Accrual Method. SFAS 66 states that profit on real estate sales transactions (including partial sales) should not be recognized by the full accrual method until *all* the following criteria are met (Re1.105):

- A sale is consummated.
- The buyer's initial and continuing investments are adequate to demonstrate a commitment to pay for the property.
- The seller has transferred to the buyer the usual risks and rewards of ownership in a transaction that is in substance a sale.
- The seller does not have a substantial continuing involvement with the property.
- Any receivable from the buyer is not subject to future subordination.

These criteria are necessary to demonstrate that the buyer's risk of loss through default will motivate him to complete the transaction; they are examined in the sections that follow.

Consummation of Sale. A sale is considered consummated and eligible for full accrual accounting when: "(1) the parties are bound by the terms of a contract, (2) all consideration has been exchanged, (3) any permanent financing for which the seller is responsible has been arranged, and (4) all conditions precedent to closing have been performed" (Re1.106).

If it is determined that a sale has not been consummated according to the four criteria, full accrual profit recognition is not appropriate and the deposit method of accounting described in the later section "Other Profit Recognition Methods" should be used until the sale is consummated. If the net carrying amount of the property exceeds the sum of the deposit and the fair value of other consideration received, the seller should recognize a loss at the date of the transaction (Re1.120–121).

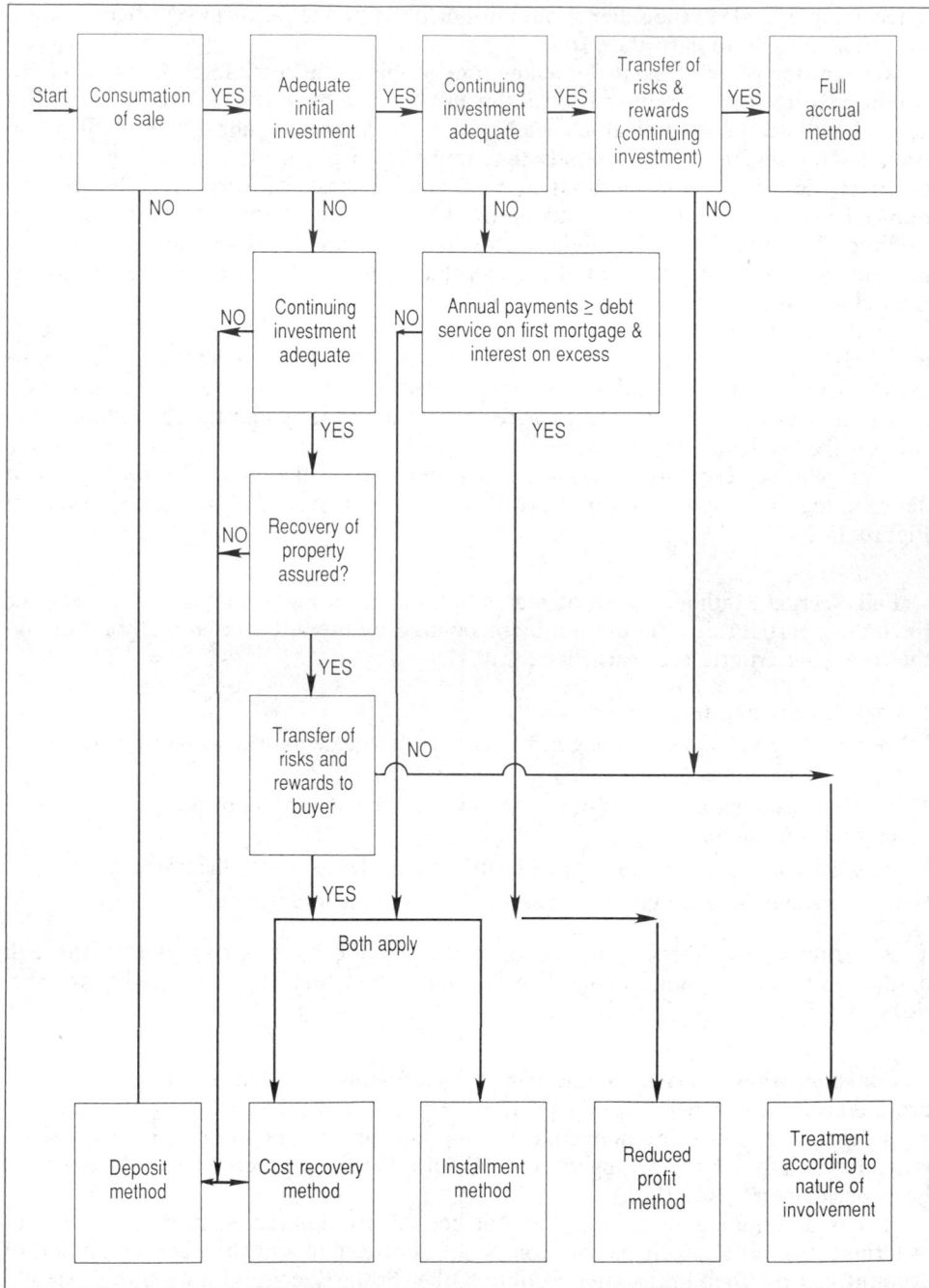

FIG. 35.1   Decision Tree for Profit Recognition on Sales of Real Estate

Source: Benedetto Bongiorno and Robert Garland. Real Estate Accounting and Reporting Manual. *Boston: Warren, Gorham & Lamont, Inc., 1983, p. 2-49.*

If the consummation of sales criteria are met and a sale has been consummated, the transaction should be further examined to see whether it meets the other full accrual criteria: adequacy of initial and continuing investment and transfer of seller's risk and rewards of ownership.

Buyer's Initial Investment. In accounting for sales of real estate, collectibility of the sales price is generally demonstrated by the buyer's commitment to pay. This is evidenced by substantial investments that give the buyer a sufficient stake in the property. Once the amount of the sale's value and the initial investment have been determined, the adequacy of the initial investment can be measured.

The buyer's initial investment is defined as: (1) cash paid by the buyer as a down payment, (2) a buyer's note backed by irrevocable letters of credit from an independent lending institution, (3) payments made by the buyer to third parties to reduce existing indebtedness on the property, and (4) other amounts paid by the buyer that are part of the sales value (Rel.109). The following items should be excluded from the calculation of the buyer's initial investment (Rel.110):

• Amounts paid by the buyer to outside parties for improvements to the property (these payments benefit the buyer and not the seller).
• Any funds that will be provided either directly or indirectly by the seller.
• A permanent commitment by an independent third party to replace a loan made by the seller.

The sales value, for the purpose of determining the adequacy of a buyer's initial investment in a real estate transaction, is defined as: (1) the stated selling price increased by all amounts that are, in substance, additional sales proceeds (e.g., funds paid to the seller for the exercise of a real estate option); and (2) the stated selling price decreased by (a) the amount of any discount required to reduce a receivable to its present value (e.g., receivables with below-market interest rates) and (b) the net present value of any services provided by the seller without stated compensation or at less than prevailing rates (Rel.107).

If the sales contract or accompanying agreements require the seller to provide services at no charge or at less than prevailing rates, the sales price should be reduced to allow for reasonable compensation for such services, to be recognized in the future as they are performed (Rel.131).

A buyer's initial investment is generally considered adequate if the investment in the property is large enough to give the buyer a sufficient stake in the property so that the risk of loss through default motivates the buyer to honor his obligations to the seller (Rel.108). The adequacy of a buyer's initial investment is measured by comparing it to the sales value of the property. To qualify, the initial investment should be at least equal to a major part of the difference between usual loan limits and the sales value. Figure 35.2 provides a listing of minimum initial investment requirements for real estate sales. Minimum initial investment by the buyer should be the greater of (1) the amount shown in Figure 35.2; or (2) whichever is the lesser of (a) the sales value of the property in excess of 115% of the amount of a newly placed permanent loan (or commitment therefor), or (b) 25% of sales value.

Thus, for example, an initial investment of $22,000 on a hotel that has a sales value of $100,000, a cash flow sufficient to service all indebtedness, and a newly

	Minimum initial investment expressed as a percentage of sales value
Land	
Held for commercial, industrial, or residential development to commence within two years after sale	20%
Held for commercial, industrial, or residential development to commence after two years	25
Commercial and Industrial Property	
Office and industrial buildings, shopping centers, and so forth:	
Properties subject to lease on a long-term lease basis to parties with satisfactory credit rating; cash flow currently sufficient to service all indebtedness	10
Single-tenancy properties sold to a buyer with a satisfactory credit rating	15
All other	20
Other income-producing properties (hotels, motels, marinas, mobile home parks, and so forth):	
Cash flow currently sufficient to service all indebtedness	15
Start-up situations or current deficiencies in cash flow	25
Multifamily Residential Property	
Primary residence:	
Cash flow currently sufficient to service all indebtedness	10
Start-up situations or current deficiences in cash flow	15
Secondary or recreational residence:	
Cash flow currently sufficient to service all indebtedness	15
Start-up situations or current deficiences in cash flow	25
Single-Family Residential Property (including condominium or cooperative housing)	
Primary residence of the buyer	5*
Secondary or recreational residence	10*

* If collectibility of the remaining portion of the sales price cannot be supported by reliable evidence of collection experience, the minimum initial investment shall be at least 60 percent of the difference between the sales value and the financing available from loans guaranteed by regulatory bodies such as the Federal Housing Authority (FHA) or the Veterans Administration (VA), or from independent, established lending institutions. This 60-percent test applies when independent first-mortgage financing is not utilized and the seller takes a receivable from the buyer for the difference between the sales value and the initial investment. If independent first mortgage financing is utilized, the adequacy of the initial investment on sale of single-family residential property should be determined in accordance with [Re1.151].

FIG. 35.2   Minimum Down Payment Requirements for Profit Recognition on Real Estate Sales
Source: Re1.152.

placed permanent loan against the property of $60,000, will have initial investment reckoned as follows:

Sales value	$100,000
115% of newly placed loan	69,000
1. Excess of sale value (a above)	$ 31,000
2. 25% of sales value (b above)	$ 25,000
3. Lesser of a or b	$ 25,000
4. Table requirements	$ 15,000
5. Required initial investment: greater of 3 or 4	$ 25,000

The foregoing example was created to depict what SFAS 66 says. However, in practice, the leverage is almost always higher, and almost invariably the 25%-of-sales-value requirement is operative.

The installment method can be used if it is determined that the buyer's initial investment is not adequate but the other criteria for full accrual profit recognition have been met and recovery of the property is reasonably assured if the buyer defaults (Rel.122). The cost method can be used in any event; but it must be used if recovery of the property is *not* reasonably assured.

Buyer's Continuing Investment. The next step in evaluating the buyer's degree of commitment to the property is to determine if the balance of the purchase price is financed through standard financing arrangements. Unusual financing arrangements might raise questions as to the substance of the transaction and whether the buyer will feel impelled to pay his full debt to the seller. Guidelines determining the adequacy of the buyer's continuing investment are as follows (Rel.112 and .117):

1. A buyer's continuing investment is not considered adequate unless the buyer is contractually obligated to make annual debt service payments in an amount at least equal to the level annual payment needed to pay that debt and interest on the unpaid balance over the duration of a loan normally available from a financial institution (for commercial buildings, generally 25 to 30 years).

2. The seller's receivable should not be subject to future subordination except (a) to a first mortgage on the property existing at the time of sale, or (b) to a future loan provided for by the terms of the sale, if the proceeds of that loan will be applied first to the payment of the seller's receivable.

Sales contracts may provide for release of part or all of the property from liens when specified conditions, such as payment of a stated release price, are met. Also, payments from the buyer to the seller are frequently specified by terms of the agreement to apply first to the released property. If any of these release provisions are present, SFAS 66 (Rel.113) states that a calculation must be made at the time of closing to ascertain that the buyer's investment is adequate at both the closing date in relation to the entire property and at the scheduled release dates in relation to the property not released or not subject to release.

If the initial and continuing investment criteria are not met, profit should be recognized on each portion released when it meets all other full accrual criteria as if each release were a separate sale (Re1.115). The requirements for a buyer's initial and continuing investment are cumulative and must be applied at the closing date and annually thereafter. If the initial investment exceeds the minimum prescribed, the excess should be applied toward the required annual increases in the buyer's continuing investment (Re1.116).

If the buyer's continuing investment criterion is not met, but the other full accrual criteria are met, and the recovery of the property sold is reasonably assured if the buyer defaults, then the installment method should be used. If recovery of the property is not reasonably assured, the cost recovery method should be used. However, if annual payments by the buyer will cover at least the sum of (1) the amortization on the maximum first mortgage loans that could be obtained on the property and (2) appropriate interest on the excess of the actual debt over the hypothetical first mortgage, then the reduced profit method should be used.

Seller's Continuing Involvement. If a seller continues to be involved in the property in any way that results in retention of substantial risks and rewards of ownership, full profit recognition is not appropriate (Re1.118). In these instances, profit is recognized by a method determined by the nature and extent of the seller's continuing involvement. As a general rule, profit can be recognized at the time of sale if the amount of the potential loss of profit resulting from the continuing involvement by the seller can be reasonably determined. The profit then recognized is reduced by the *maximum* exposure to loss (Re1.125).

Several of the continuing involvement situations mentioned in SFAS 66 are (Re1.126–.143):

• The seller has an obligation or an option to repurchase the property.

• The seller guarantees return of the buyer's investment or a return on that investment for a limited or extended period.

• The seller is involved in initiating or supporting operations and support is required or presumed to be required for a limited or extended period of time.

If a transaction has one or more of these characteristics, in substance it is probably not a sale but rather a financing, leasing, or profit-sharing arrangement. SFAS 66 does not describe any methodology for the forms of accounting.

Frequently, sales contracts provide that the seller will participate in future profits with no risk of loss, and with no significant performance required after the date of sale in order to earn the contract price. This does not preclude profit recognition.

If the seller is obligated to arrange for permanent financing as a condition precedent to closing, a sale for accounting purposes does not occur until such financing is available to the buyer.

Some forms of real estate transactions involve the sale of property accompanied by an agreement requiring the seller to develop the property, construct facilities, or provide off-site improvements. Profit should be allocated to the remaining development and construction services by the percentage-of-completion method (Re1.141).

Frequently, a seller may agree to deliver to the buyer an income-producing property when it is operating at a level sufficient to cover operating expenses, debt service, and all other obligations. In such cases, the seller often constructs facilities and operates the property at his own risk until the property has reached a specified level of operations. If a seller is required to support the property for an extended time period the transaction is accounted for as a financing, leasing, or profit-sharing arrangement. (There is no specific authoritative guidance on how such accounting methods might be applied.) If the time frame is limited (i.e., less than five years), profit should be recognized when there is reasonable assurance that future operations will be sufficient to pay all expenses including the seller's debt (Rel.129).

If a seller sells a partial interest (Rel.133) in a property (such as an undivided interest in an apartment house), full accrual profit (sales value less the proportionate cost of the partial interest sold) may be recognized at the time of sale, provided all criteria for treatment as a sale are met and the seller is not required to support the property to an extent greater than its remaining interest.

Other Profit Recognition Methods. The methods of profit recognition mentioned in this section should be used when a sale has been consummated but the full accrual method is not appropriate. If after adoption of any of these methods the transaction meets the requirements for the full accrual method, the seller may change to the full accrual method. The remaining unrecognized profit is thereupon recognized in income. SFAS 66 does not describe the balance sheet treatment for those other methods.

The *installment method* apportions each cash payment made by the buyer between cost recovered and profit as provided under SFAS 66 (Rel.154–.159). The apportionment is in the same ratio as total cost and total profit bear to the sales value.

Under the *deposit method*, the seller does not recognize any profit and does not record notes receivable. The seller continues to report in its financial statements the property and the related existing debt, even if it has been assumed by the buyer, and discloses that those items are subject to a sales contract. The seller continues to charge depreciation to expense as a period cost for the property for which deposits have been received. Cash received from the buyer, including the initial investment and subsequent collections of principal and interest, is reported as a deposit on the contract (Rel.163–.165).

A *reduced profit* is determined by discounting the receivable from the buyer to the present value of the lowest level of annual payments required by the sales contract (Rel.166–.167). This method permits profit to be recognized from level payments on the buyer's debt over the established term and postpones recognition of other profits until lump sum or other payments are made.

The *cost recovery* method should be used when there is sufficient uncertainty that the seller will recover his cost upon default by the buyer (Rel.160). In such a case, it would be inappropriate to recognize any profit on the transaction until such uncertainty has been resolved.

EITF Issues. The EITF has dealt with several issues relating to real estate sales, as briefly mentioned in the sections that follow.

Exchange of real estate involving boot. In Issue 87-29, *Interrelationship Between EITF Issue No. 86-29 and FASB Statement No. 66*, the EITF questioned whether the consensus achieved in Issue 86-29, *Accounting for Certain Nonmonetary Transactions*, has resulted in a "loop" in professional guidance. SFAS 66 indicates that exchanges of real estate are covered by APB 29, which addresses nonmonetary transactions. However, in Issue 86-29, *Nonmonetary Transactions: Magnitude of Boot and the Exceptions to the Use of Fair Value*, the EITF reached a consensus that an exchange of nonmonetary assets that involves a significant boot (25% or more) should be considered a monetary (rather than nonmonetary) transaction and accordingly is not covered by APB 29.

The issues are whether SFAS 66 covers an exchange of real estate that is not covered by Opinion 29 because the exchange is considered to be a monetary transaction under the consensus for Issue 86-29, and, if so, how SFAS 66 should be applied.

The EITF reached a consensus that exchanges of real estate that are considered monetary under Issue 86-29 should be split into two transactions based on relative fair values. For the party receiving boot, the monetary part would be treated as a sale of an interest in real estate governed by SFAS 66; and the nonmonetary portion of the exchange would be accounted for under APB 29 (N35.108). For the party paying boot, the monetary portion is treated as the acquisition of real estate, and the nonmonetary portion is also based on APB 29 (N35.108). It should be noted that the SEC staff will take a case-by-case approach to accounting for exchanges of real estate involving boot.

Profit Recognition on Sales of Real Estate With Insured Mortgages or Surety Bonds (Issue 87-9). Some real estate sellers and lenders may require mortgage insurance on a portion of the financing provided to the buyer by the seller, particularly in transactions involving residential property; or surety bonds may be accepted by sellers as support for the buyers' notes in lieu of irrevocable letters of credit.

SFAS 66 provides that "the buyer's notes supported by an irrevocable letter of credit from an established independent institution" may be included as part of the buyer's initial and continuing investment in determining whether to recognize profit under the full accrual method (Rel.109).

The accounting issue is whether a financial instrument from an independent insuring institution may be considered the equivalent of an irrevocable letter of credit for purposes of determining whether to recognize profit under the full accrual method. The EITF reached a consensus that mortgage insurance was not acceptable, but agreed to accept a surety bond issued by an established independent insuring institution if the bond has all the rights and obligations of an irrevocable letter of credit. Since surety bonds rarely would have such features, the practical answer from the EITF is "no" on this item as well.

The EITF subsequently discussed whether the consensus on insured mortgages applied only to fully insured mortgages or also to partially insured mortgages. A consensus was reached that if a mortgage is fully insured by a governmental agency, the small downpayment required under FHA or VA programs could be substituted for the criteria in SFAS 66 (Rel.153–.154) because all of the credit risk has been transferred to the government. In partially insured situations or with respect to private mortgage insurance, the minimum requirements in Rel.153–.154 must be followed. This matter is still open because other similar situations were raised by EITF members.

Transfer of Ownership Interest as Part of Down Payment Under FASB Statement No. 66 (Issue 88-12). In this issue, the EITF considered whether a note given by a buyer (who had previously owned 25% of the property) and secured by the property sold could be used to indicate a reasonable likelihood that the seller (who had owned the other 75%) will collect the note. The buyer had additionally paid 10% down, whereas the SFAS 66 guidelines would require 15%. The Task Force concluded that cash is cash, and the note did not count for initial investment purposes. Therefore, the EITF reached a consensus that, the security for the note notwithstanding, the note does not meet the SFAS 66 criteria for initial investment, and thus this transaction does not merit the full accrual method.

Antispeculation Clauses in Real Estate Sales Contracts (Issue 86-6). Land sale agreements sometimes contain clauses that require the buyer to develop the land in a specified manner within a given period of time and that prohibit certain uses of the property. If the buyer fails to comply with the provisions of the sales contract, the seller has the right, but not the obligation, to reacquire the property. The accounting issue is whether SFAS 66 precludes the seller from accounting for the transaction as a sale because of the seller's continuing involvement through the antispeculation clause.

The EITF consensus held that if the probability of the buyer not complying with the contract is remote, then the contingent option would not preclude sales recognition. Factors that would lead to a conclusion that buyer noncompliance is remote include economic loss to the buyer from repurchases and the buyer's perceived ability to comply with the provisions of the sales contract.

Profit Recognition on Sales of Real Estate With Graduated Payment Mortgages or Insured Mortgages (Issue 84-17). This issue addressed whether the profit recognition criteria in SFAS 66 should be strictly applied to sales of real estate involving graduated payment mortgages or mortgages that are partially or fully insured. The EITF reached a consensus that if such sales do not meet the continuing investment tests in SFAS 66 (Re1.112) because of the negative loan amortization, they should not result in full immediate profit recognition. The issue of partially or fully insured mortgages was addressed separately in Issue 87-9 (discussed in a preceding subsection).

RETAIL LAND SALES

The principal activity of retail land sales companies is the retail marketing of numerous undeveloped lots subdivided from a larger parcel of land. Purchasers may buy lots for use as primary or secondary homesites or as recreational property. Some projects may be fully or substantially complete and ready for ultimate use, while others may be so remote or lacking in significant improvements that ultimate use for any purpose except speculation is doubtful. Additional improvements, or "amenities," are usually included in the promotional sales package, but they may not be built until most or all of the lots have been sold.

Retail land sales usually have down payments so small that banks and savings and loan associations would not lend at market rates, or would buy the resulting paper only if there were a substantial discount. Generally, the sales contract is cancelable within a stipulated period, and the seller's normal recourse in the event of default is to reclaim the land parcel (Re1.101, fn. 1).

Federal Regulation

The Interstate Land Sales Full Disclosure Act, effective in 1969, has as its purpose the protection of consumers from fraudulent activities that occasionally have taken place in the retail land development area. The Act makes it unlawful, except where exempted, for any developer with 25 or more lots or parcels of subdivided land to sell or lease (by use of the mail or by any means of interstate commerce) any such land offered as part of a common promotional plan, unless the land is registered with the Office of Interstate Land Sales Registration (OILSR) of the U.S. Department of Housing and Urban Development, and a printed *Property Report* is furnished to the purchaser or lessee in advance of the signing of an agreement for lease or sale. Even when registered under the Act, all land sales or leases are voidable within seven days if the purchaser is supplied with a printed property report; if no report is furnished, the contracts are voidable for two years.

In addition, as a result of not registering sales, contracts may be voidable at the election of the purchaser, and the developer may be required to refund the purchase price of the lot plus the reasonable costs of all improvements by the purchaser. The potential financial impact on an unregistered developer of such refunds and reimbursements obviously could be quite severe.

Nature of the Business

The life cycle of a retail land sales project has four phases: development, sales, collection, and improvement.

The first and sometimes easiest part of the life cycle of a project is the development effort. In the development effort, the retail land sales company: (1) acquires the land; (2) prepares a master plan for the subdivision; and (3) obtains required local, state, or federal government approvals for sales of individual lots. All costs during the development effort are capitalized.

Once the development effort is complete, a sales strategy to sell the lots is implemented. The sales strategy may include certain sales promotion techniques and an offer to arrange for purchasers' financing.

After a lot has been sold, the receivables from the sale, if any, must be collected. Because a sale cannot be recognized unless there is a reasonable expectation that the receivable will be collected, and because there is no personal recourse to the buyer in most retail land company sales, the choice of accounting method may be dictated by the collection experience of the company.

It is common to construct some improvements during the sales effort. Most of the

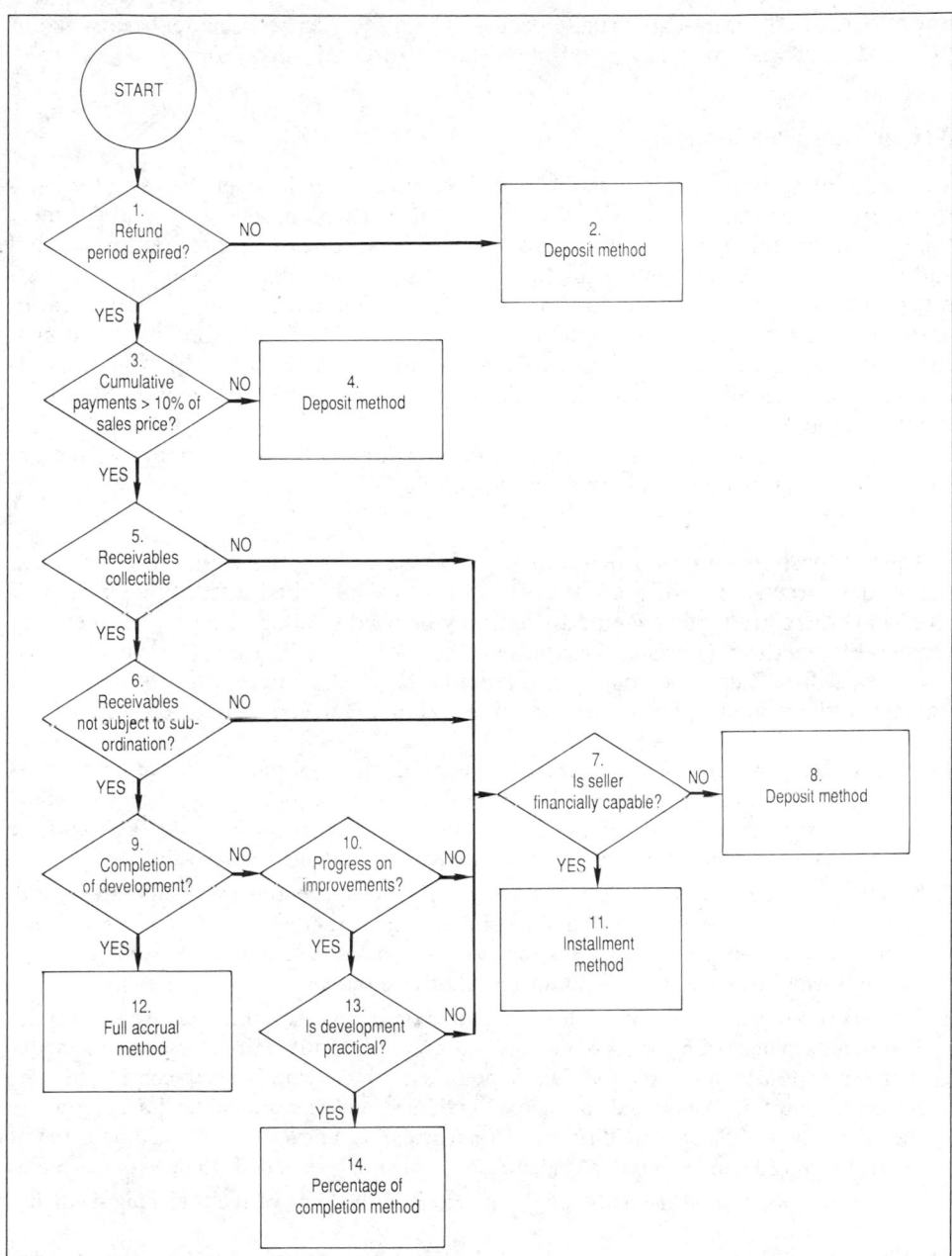

FIG. 35.3   Profit Recognition for Retail Land Sales
Source: Re1.196.

improvement effort, though, usually occurs after a sale has been made, because companies do not wish to spend cash unless sales efforts are successful.

Accounting Requirements

The accounting objective of a retail land developer is to (1) meet the tests for sales recognition (moving the buyer's transaction out of the deposit stage), and (2) meet the criteria for full accrual method profit recognition. Prior to achieving full accrual status for a sale, the installment method may also be applicable. Switch over is permitted when and if the criteria for the full accrual method are eventually attained. In addition, the percentage-of-completion method is overlaid on profit recognition if the seller is obligated to make improvements applicable to the lots sold. The accounting requirements discussed in the following sections are contained in SFAS 66 (beginning at Re1.144).

Figure 35.3 illustrates the process for determining which accounting method should be used for retail land sales transactions.

Cost Allocations. Once a determination of the costs to be capitalized has been made, it is necessary to allocate these costs to the individual lots. Under SFAS 67 (Re2.111) there are various methods that may be used to allocate costs. Further, any reasonable method consistently applied that fairly matches costs with related revenues will suffice. The four general methods of allocation of costs to specific parcels sold are area, specific identification, relative value, and hybrid methods.

1. *Area method.* The area method allocates costs on the basis of the number of lots or sites within a development, different size of lots in square footage, or acreage. The area method is usually appropriate for rather small developments (or parts of large developments) or other situations where the individual parcels have substantially similar values.
2. *Specific identification method.* Costs that can be specifically identified with an individual lot or specific subdivision are allocated to it. SFAS 67 indicates that the specific identification method is preferable, but recognizes that this method is generally not feasible for large tracts of land involving substantial amenities, diverse purposes, or varying values.
3. *Relative value method.* Costs are allocated to lots on the basis of their relative fair values; that is, anticipated selling prices of the lots may establish relative fair values. This method is more appropriate when more than one type of use for the land is being considered (e.g., residential units, industrial and commercial buildings, and recreational facilities), or where the sales values of the lots are different. Of particular significance in this method is that it takes into consideration unusable land, amenities such as lakes, and high density situations.
4. *Hybrid methods.* Hybrid methods simply utilize more than one of the foregoing methods.

When determining which costs should be allocated, the raw land cost associated with unusable land should generally be allocated to other lots on as reasonable a basis as possible. In addition, if the land is purchased in several separate parcels that have been combined into a single unit for development purposes, it is generally more reasonable to aggregate the costs for allocation purposes. Finally, off-site improvements such as main and access roads, bridges, main utility lines, parks, golf courses, artificial lakes, and tennis courts are usually nonrevenue-producing items. Their costs should be allocated on some reasonable basis over the lots to be sold.

Land and its development costs represent inventory and the retail lot developer therefore must concern himself with lower-of-cost-or-market valuation. A write-down or reserve is needed when the cost of sales (land, improvement costs, and future development costs) and selling expenses exceed the sales amount (less existing valuation and collection allowances).

Changes in estimates relating to both current and future periods are accounted for prospectively, even though this results in lower profit margins in those periods than in prior periods. If the change in estimate affects only the current period, it is accounted for in the current period.

If a project or a phase of a project is abandoned, all capitalized costs of that property or phase should be expensed.

Sales Effort. Generally, full accrual profit recognition in the retail land sales industry does not take place at the time of sale because: (1) realization is not reasonably certain, and/or (2) performance by the seller is not complete. The earnings process usually consists of several factors, including the sales effort, collection effort, and improvement effort.

Selling costs that are identifiable with a project (and with obtaining sales contracts) are direct costs of a business activity producing identifiable revenue, and are a substantial portion of the total cost of sales. Such costs differ from general selling expenses, which are identifiable with the business as a whole. For these reasons, selling costs directly identified with lot sales and specific project promotion are deemed to be the same as the costs of land and improvements for purposes of allocating revenue and, accordingly, are deferrable until a sale is recognized (Re1.172). Deferred selling costs should be limited to those closely associated with obtaining sales and limited to amounts expected to be recovered from collectible contracts. Accordingly, excess selling costs attributable either to decreases in sales volume or unproductive sales programs should be charged to expense currently, or otherwise provided for by an adjustment of the allowance for losses on cancellation.

Advertising expenses and general selling expenses not deferrable include:

- Cost of sales brochures.
- Mass media advertising.
- Billboards.
- Salesmen's base salaries, if not offset against commissions earned.
- Depreciation and maintenance of sales facilities.
- Costs of obtaining lists of prospective purchasers.
- Costs of contacting prospective purchasers by mail or phone.

Current trends in deferring expenses indicate that only direct incremental costs should be deferred. Thus the following items, which may have been deferred in the past, are in a gray area and probably should be expensed:

- Mass selling programs such as group dinners and free weekends.
- Gifts given to those attending mass selling programs or to on-site visitors.

- Salaries directly identifiable with a promotion program.
- Facilities used exclusively for prospective buyers.

Sales Recognition. Technically, a sale occurs at the time a customer becomes contractually obligated to buy and makes a down payment. However, until a contract qualifies for sales recognition, all collections (including interest) should be recorded as deposits (Re1.163). From an accounting standpoint, a sale should not be recognized and profit should be deferred until (1) the customer has demonstrated a serious intent to complete his part of the contract, and (2) the company has demonstrated that it is capable of fulfilling its obligations under the contract.

Retail land sales should be recognized by the *full accrual method* when and if *all* of the following criteria have been met (Re1.145):

1. *Expiration of refund period.* The buyer has made the down payment and all required subsequent payments until the period of cancellation with refund expires.
2. *Sufficient cumulative payments.* The cumulative payments of principal and interest must equal or exceed 10% of the contract sales price.
3. *Collectibility of receivables.* Collection experience for the project indicates that at least 90% of the contracts in force will be collected in full.[4] In any event, a down payment of 20% is an acceptable indication of collectibility.
4. *Nonsubordination of receivables.* The receivable from the sale is not subject to subordination to new loans on the property, except that subordination by an individual lot buyer for home construction purposes is permissible.
5. *Completion of development.* The seller is not obligated to complete improvements of lots sold or to construct amenities or other facilities applicable to lots sold. (In other words, the seller has nothing left to do.)

The *percentage-of-completion method* is to be used if all of the criteria for the full accrual method have been met except for completion of development, with two additional provisos (Re1.146):

1. *Progress on improvements.* The project's improvements must have progressed beyond preliminary stages, and there are no indications that the work will not be completed according to plan.
2. *Development is practicable.* There is a reasonable expectation that the land can be developed for the purposes represented and that the properties will be useful for those purposes at the end of the normal payment period.

The percentage-of-completion method recognizes the fact that the earnings process is *not* complete, because the seller is obligated to complete improvements or other facilities (i.e., amenities) applicable to lots sold. Accordingly, the revenue at the time of sale is measured by the relationship of costs already incurred to total esti-

---

[4] The fulfillment of this condition is based on contracts in force for a duration of six months after specified criteria have been met (Re1.145, fn. 21, and Re1.146). In addition, a seller's prior project, rather than the project under consideration, may be used as evidence in specified circumstances.

mated costs, and the remaining revenue is recognized in proportion to additional costs incurred.

The *installment method* should be used if a project does not meet the criteria prescribed for either the accrual method or percentage-of-completion method. The criteria for the use of the installment method under SFAS 66 are (Rel.147):

1. The period of cancellation with refund has expired.
2. Cumulative payments equal or exceed 10% of contract price.
3. The seller is clearly financially capable of providing the promised land improvements and off-site facilities, and can meet all other representations it has made.

Under the installment method (Rel.154–.159), the buyer's cash payments are split between cost recovered and profit. The entire contract price is recorded as revenue and a receivable (net of principal payments received) at the time of sale. Cost of sales therefore includes all costs related to the lot, including a provision for future improvements. All deferred selling costs are expensed at the time of sale. The remaining profit is deferred to the extent that the contract is not yet paid and is presented as a separate deduction on the income statement.

The unamortized deferred income is netted against receivables on the balance sheet. Interest income is recorded as earned in the future based on the rate stated in the contract, unless it is greater than an appropriate rate (in which case the contract is appropriately revalued). An illustration of profit recognition under the installment method, with debt assumed by the buyer, is shown in Rel.188–.195. This very lengthy example should be referred to for comprehensive coverage of numerous retail land sales accounting issues.

Cancellations. If a contract accounted for under any of the methods discussed in the preceding section is canceled (with or without refund), unrecoverable deferred selling costs should be charged to expense and forfeited deposits credited to income. Projects that have qualified for the full accrual or percentage-of-completion methods normally provide sufficient experience to demonstrate that the write-off of deferred selling costs on cancellation would be minimal and would be more than offset by the income derived from forfeitures and from contracts that do not cancel.

If the installment method is used, it may be necessary, however, to provide an allowance for unrecoverable deferred selling costs on contracts that may be canceled. A cancellation of a contract on the installment method reduces contract receivables, deferred income, and the liability for future improvements. The land is returned to inventory, restoring recoverable costs to land and improvements. An excess of the cost of the canceled contract over recoverable costs and deferred revenue should be recognized as a loss (in essence, unrecovered selling costs).

Changes in Methods. When a transaction is accounted for as a deposit, it may later achieve sales recognition status under the installment, percentage-of-completion, or full accrual methods. When this occurs, the sale is recorded as prescribed under such other method, and all applicable selling costs are charged to expense. If a project accounted for on the installment method later qualifies for percentage-of-completion method treatment, the entire project is cumulatively adjusted to the new method and the effect is accounted for as a change in estimate (Re1.149). For projects on the percentage-of-completion method, achievement of full accrual profit recognition incrementally occurs, in relation to completion of improvements. When exiting the deposit method, all applicable deferred selling costs should be charged to expense in accordance with the accounting method then in use, and the interest portion of deposits credited to income.

Valuing Receivables. If a project meets all the criteria required for reporting income under the full accrual method or under the percentage-of-completion method, an additional determination must be made as to the value of the receivable that represents the balance of the sales price.

In determining an appropriate discount rate for present valuing, the receivable resulting from the retail land sale must be evaluated based on the stated interest rate compared to the market interest rate for a similar receivable. Because a fully comparable lending situation ordinarily does not exist, the stated interest rate must be compared to an alternative lending situation. All discount calculations should be by individual project. Where there is a large volume of reasonable small sales, it is generally advisable to compute a discount factor that can be applied to the total net receivables added during the reporting period.

Financial Reporting

SFAS 66 specifically requires the following disclosures for retail land sales companies, in addition to any other disclosures generally required under GAAP (Re1.150):

* Accounts receivable maturities for each of the five succeeding years.
* Amount of delinquent accounts receivable and methods for determining delinquency.
* The weighted average and range of stated interest rates on receivables.
* Estimated total costs and estimated dates of expenditures for improvements for major areas from which sales are being made, for the five succeeding years.
* Amount of recorded obligations for improvements.

Financial statement presentation for retail land sales companies is illustrated in SFAS 66, with examples given for the full accrual, percentage-of-completion, and installment methods (Re1.193–.195).

SINGLE-FAMILY RESIDENCES

The development of lots and the construction of single-family dwellings for sale, whether for primary or secondary (leisure) residences, is referred to as the homebuilding industry. Single-family dwellings include individual detached houses, cooperatives, and condominium units. In terms of gross sales, the homebuilding industry is the largest single segment of the real estate industry, and is particularly sensitive to the overall economy and especially to interest rate fluctuations. The homebuilder, therefore, must be innovative in his methods of construction, financing, and marketing. Because of the housing market's economic sensitivity, the financial position and operating results of the homebuilder can change drastically in a relatively short time.

As a result of unpredictable interest rates, the increasing costs of single-family homes, and, in many large cities, restrictive rent control and stabilization laws, the conversion of relatively inexpensive residential rental units (apartments) to expensive owner-occupied cooperatives and condominiums has increased significantly; these conversions do not present unusual or unique accounting problems for the converter.

Nature of the Business

Essentially, the homebuilder is a producer of inventories for sale. These inventories include:

* Raw land
* Land under development and construction-in-progress
* Finished dwellings

The finished products discussed in this section are houses, condominiums, cooperative apartments, and time-sharing units. Different accounting treatments can apply depending on individual circumstances.

The *acquisition activities* of the single-family residential developer are segregated into preacquisition and land acquisition and planning. The preacquisition phase involves the selection of a geographic area, identification of available tracts of land suitable for a general development concept (e.g., subdivisions, condominiums, leisure homes, time-sharing intervals), and preliminary market research.

Land acquisition is a critical phase. The company must be cognizant of zoning, environmental protection, community growth, and other government regulations concerning development in the area chosen. Once a tract of land has been identified, the developer either acquires an option on the tract or enters into a contract to acquire the land contingent on the satisfactory resolution of such items as zoning or approval of site plans. Some of the more common steps a developer goes through from conception of the project to the start of developing the site are:

* *Zoning.* The zoning of a tract of land determines how the land may be used. If the existing zoning is in conflict with the builder's plans, the land must be rezoned.
* *Options to purchase.* Options are used to acquire rights to land for future use.
* *Development suitability.* Prior to acquisition, geological and topographical information is obtained, either from available governmental sources or through studies made on the property.
* *Profit-potential studies.* When the land tract has been optioned or acquired, a feasibility study is undertaken to determine the profit potential available through development.
* *Construction planning.* The formal design by engineers and architects must often be submitted to the authorities for approval, and changes in the approved plan must be cleared through these authorities.

Land development includes site preparation, installation of streets, curbs, gutters, storm drains, sewers, and utilities, and preparation of the lot to the point where the building foundation can be laid. This phase may also include construction of off-site facilities such as reservoirs, power substations, approach streets, and community recreational facilities.

The *construction* phase encompasses all activities from laying the foundation through the completion of the unit. Generally, the homebuilder provides construction supervision, but the actual work is performed by various subcontractors.

The *marketing and sales activities* of a large homebuilder usually include a marketing department or an affiliate of the company performing the marketing activities. For smaller companies, independent realtors often perform the marketing activities.

The *financing function* is a critical factor from the time of land acquisition through the ultimate sale of the finished dwelling. Homebuilders are usually highly leveraged, and interest and other financing costs are significant expense elements.

Accounting Requirements

Accounting for residential construction under contract for the buyer is covered by ARB 45 (Co4), SOP 81-1 *Accounting for Performance of Construction-Type and Certain Production-Type Contracts* (TP 10,330), and the companion Audit and Accounting Guide, *Audits of Construction Contractors* (AICPA, 1981d), all discussed in Chapter 36. Residential construction undertaken "on spec" is governed by SFAS 67 (Re2), and profit recognition on sales is addressed by SFAS 66 (Re1); both of these topics are discussed earlier in this chapter in the "Income-Producing Property" section. The foregoing sources should be referenced when considering homebuilder accounting. Three matters especially applicable to homebuilders are mentioned in the following sections.

Construction Contractor Accounting. The economic activity of a contract homebuilder is made up of a number of individual profit centers of different durations – one for each discrete contract. The two generally accepted methods of accounting for such contracts are the percentage-of-completion method and the completed contract method.

If the *percentage-of-completion method* is used, income or economic activity is recognized throughout the life of the contract based on a periodic measurement of progress. That method is preferable to the completed contract method when the following conditions are present (Co4.103–.105):

• Estimates of the final outcome for costs and revenues are reasonably accurate and dependable.
• The contract is enforceable by both parties.
• The owner can be expected to satisfy his obligations.
• The homebuilder can be expected to perform his obligations.

Percentage-of-completion accounting should not be used where the outcome of a contract or the ability of the parties to perform is questionable due to circumstances such as pending legislation or litigation, the possibility of severe economic disruptions, or unpredictable weather or subsurface conditions. If any of these conditions are present, then the completed contract method should be used.

The basic principle behind the percentage-of-completion method is that income recognized as work is performed on the contract. In brief, a ratio (usually cost incurred to date versus total expected cost) is determined and applied to the expected gross profit on the contract to determine the profit to be recognized in the financial statements. The gross profit earned to date is added to the cost incurred to date to arrive at revenue to be recognized. If a loss is expected on the contract, the entire loss must be reflected when its existence is known.

Under the *completed contract method*, income is recognized only when a contract is completed or is considered substantially complete. All cost and progress billings against a contract are accumulated in balance sheet accounts until the period in which the contract is completed.

Condominiums, Co-ops, and Time-shares. Accounting for the sale of condominiums, cooperative apartments, and time-sharing interests is similar to that for houses. Even though the entire project is not completed, the percentage-of-completion method may be used on the sale of individual units or time-sharing interests if the following criteria are met (Rel.137):

- There must be a binding sales contract; the buyer must be unable to request a refund and financing for the buyer must be available (or committed if outside financing is to be used).
- Down payment requirements must have been met.
- All conditions precedent to closing must be met.
- Costs yet to be incurred and aggregate sales proceeds must be reasonably estimable.
- Sufficient units must have been sold to assure that the property will not revert to a rental complex.
- Construction must be beyond a preliminary stage.

The percentage-of-completion method may be used even though a certificate of occupancy, which is a condition precedent to closing, has not yet been obtained.

If it is determined that a sale has not been consummated, the deposit method of accounting is to be used. If a contract is canceled without a refund to the buyer, deposits that are forfeited are recognized as income by the seller.

The criteria for the recognition of profit by homebuilders under the full accrual method are generally applicable to fee-simple time-sharers (absolute ownership without limitations). In general, time-sharing developers use the full accrual method in a successful, established project. The cost recovery (Rel.160) or deposit methods (Rel.163) should be used when a time-sharing project does not have a sufficient history to estimate all costs and collectibility of receivables. These methods should be continued until the history has been established.

Combined Land and Construction Sale. In Issue 86-7, *Recognition by Homebuilders of Profit From Sales of Land and Related Construction Contracts*, the EITF discussed a specific application of SFAS 66 involving the revenue recognition pattern for contract sales in which a homebuilder builds a single-family home on the homebuilder's lot. This type of contract does not distinguish between the sale of the lot and the construction of the house, and the homebuilder does not relinquish title to the lot until closing. The accounting issue is how the homebuilder should recognize earnings from a contract that provides for a lot sale and construction of the home.

The EITF reached a consensus that profit recognition is not appropriate until the rigorous initial and continuing investment conditions in SFAS 66 (Re1.105) are met. Usually this will result in deposit method accounting being used.

REAL ESTATE SYNDICATION

Nature of the Business

In a real estate syndication activity, an entity raises equity funds from investors to acquire an interest in real estate.

Real estate is syndicated by a variety of enterprises, such as real estate companies, securities broker/dealers, commercial banks, savings and loan associations, insurance companies, finance companies, and companies organized exclusively to syndicate real estate. The syndicator receives various fees, some cash and some noncash as discussed later herein, as compensation for the variety of activities involved in syndication.

Real estate syndications may be organized as limited partnerships, trusts, or joint ventures, but in this section they will be generally referred to as partnerships or syndicates. The partnership's interests in real estate may be represented by direct ownership, mortgages, master leases, sale-leasebacks, or options to acquire real estate. Although investors may pay their total capital contributions to the partnership at the inception of the syndication, investors often make initial cash payments and issue promissory notes (investor notes) requiring payment of specific installments, with recourse to their personal assets. Investor notes may be collateralized by irrevocable letters of credit or by surety bonds.

Investors in real estate syndication expect to:

- Earn operating income
- Receive distributions of cash
- Receive tax benefits from investments
- Realize appreciation of investment
- Receive a combination of the above

Prior to the Tax Reform Act of 1986 (TRA 1986), one of the major goals of syndications was to maximize the accelerated tax deductions available from investing in a real estate project and to use these benefits to attract investor capital. This eventually led to the proliferation of syndications that were profitable for their tax attributes rather than their economics and accordingly were viewed as tax-shelter-abusive by the IRS. Due to the changes enacted in TRA 1986, today's syndications are no longer driven by accelerated tax deductions.

The process of syndicating (and operating) real estate is complicated, time consuming, and expensive. Typical steps in this process are:

- *Identification phase.* This phase involves locating the desirable property and working with realtors and various agents and negotiating for control of the property for the period required to raise adequate funds to close the transaction.
- *Development phase.* The development phase involves structuring the investment in terms of the timing of various payments; preparing the offering document; evaluating regulatory requirements; and planning and implementing an announcement of the availability of the offering.
- *Marketing phase.* The marketing phase includes presenting the program to the internal sales staff as well as to outside selling groups; selling the syndication interests to investors; and implementing a control system for investor funds, documents, and signatures and depositing funds in a trustee account.
- *Legal closing phase.* This phase involves closing the escrow and acquiring the property, recording the certificate of limited partnership and mailing a copy of it with the certificates of interest to the limited partners.
- *Operating phase.* The operating phase involves managing and maintaining a start-up property, operating the property, managing the partnership, and distributing any cash proceeds from operations or from sale.

Investor Considerations. Through the group ownership concept of real estate limited partnerships, the investor realizes several economic advantages. Perhaps the most important advantage is that, by combining with others, the investor improves his relative buying position as there are fewer large buyers than small buyers. Thus the partnership can consider both small and large properties, and it is probable that it can acquire a better property than the individual investor could have acquired on his own.

Generally, the yields are greater on the larger properties since buyer competition for the smaller properties drives up the prices. For large properties, further advantages are achieved through professional property management, which may not be economical for small properties. Because the cost of using experts is spread over a number of limited partners, the syndicate is in a position to hire more talented people. The cost of hiring such people to do similar work for a private investor would be prohibitive.

In evaluating an investment, the potential investor must examine:

- The disclosures in the offering document.
- The track record and reputation of the syndicator/general partner.
- The investment property with the help of a professional advisor who has the appropriate background, education, and experience.
- Financial projections, if available, relative to such factors as tax deductions and cash flows.
- The risk factors involved.
- The federal tax consequences to the limited partners with respect to such factors as the classification of the partnership as such, the tax preference items, the basis of the property, and the disposition of the property.

Suitability standards are generally imposed by regulatory agencies and by the syndicator to help avoid having an investor make a purchase he cannot afford to use.

These standards generally require that the investor have specified minimum net worth and a specified minimum income before being allowed to invest.

Apartment projects have been the most frequently syndicated real estate ventures, but syndications include other properties such as raw land, motels, warehouses, fast-food restaurants, mobile home parks, campgrounds, recreational developments, modular housing projects, and hotels.

The principal reasons for the failure of real estate syndications include the following:

- Excessive front-end compensation and other promotional interests received by the syndicator and its affiliates.
- Excessive purchase price paid for the property.
- Insufficient down payment with large balloon payments.
- Poor management of the properties.
- Failure by the limited partners to contribute necessary additional assessments.
- Lack of expertise or experience of the syndicator, resulting in inability to select suitable properties and to arrange sound financial structuring.
- Construction cost overruns or increases in operating costs, requiring additional cash contributions from the partners.

Offering Materials. Generally, accounting matters and accounting disclosures in an offering of a real estate syndicate are limited to prospective financial information (see Chapter 27), financial statements, and tax opinions. These represent only a part of the information needed by prospective investors in the real estate syndicate. In all instances, if investments are being offered, the offeror is subject to various regulatory bodies. These are the SEC, state blue sky commissions, and, in some instances, state financing authorities.

Generally, the following types of specific disclosures are necessary:

- Description and history of the project and its locale, and biographical data on principal parties involved.
- Description of risk factors.
- Description of past and expected future arrangements involving related parties or conflicts of interest.
- Summary of material pending legal proceedings.
- Comprehensive but brief description of the securities or interests being offered.
- Financial information concerning the project, the general partners, the promoters, and possibly other parties involved.
- Summary of legal considerations, regulatory restrictions, tax matters, and related pertinent data.
- Disclosure of the terms and amounts of fees paid to the promoters, general partners, and other parties to the contemplated transactions.
- Description of the intended use of the proceeds of the offering.
- Historical financial statements of existing entities.

The Securities Act of 1933 (§ 5), as amended, requires registration with the SEC of every offer to sell a security, sale or delivery of a security, and of a prospectus relating to a security, unless an exemption under the Act is available. In real estate syndicates, the limited partnership interests purchased by the limited partners should always be considered a security (SEC Release 33-4877). The SEC has issued Guide 5, *Preparation of Registration Statements Relating to Interests in Real Estate Limited Partnerships*, as a comprehensive reference; this guide should be followed in a public offering. It is intended to assist issuers, accountants, and attorneys in the preparation of filings, and to minimize SEC delay in their review.

Limited Offering Exemption. Transactions exempted from registration requirements of the 1933 Act are not exempt from antifraud, civil liability, or other provisions of the federal securities laws. Since most offerings of limited partner interests in real estate syndicates are conducted under an exemption from registration with the SEC, a general understanding of the various exemptions is needed. For a detailed discussion and listing of the rules, refer to *Accountants SEC Practice Manual* (Poloway, 1988).

Accounting by the Syndicate

Marketing Costs. Costs attributable to the marketing aspects of selling investment interests should be capitalized (Re2.117 .118). These costs are directly attributable to an activity involving the sale of a real estate project and therefore should not be accounted for as a period cost.

Costs incurred by the real estate syndicate or its affiliate for commissions and/or remuneration to broker/dealers for selling investor interests are incurred for purposes of raising capital and therefore are applied as a reduction of the amounts raised by the partnership.

Generally, costs expended by the syndicate for the services of a syndicator, acting as liaison to the broker/dealer community, and professional fees incurred during the process of compiling the offering document and related professional opinions, are part of the cost of syndicating the real estate entity. These costs also are applied as a reduction of the amounts raised by the partnership.

Financing Costs. The cost of borrowing funds generally includes, in addition to interest, all forms of charges and discounts attributed to the borrowing process. Financing and commitment fees payable to a general partner should be capitalized and amortized over the life of the loan period, except for debt costs incurred during the construction period, which are part of the cost of the real estate. The total cost of borrowing should be evaluated in light of marketplace comparables to determine the reasonableness of such charges. SFAS 34 states that capitalization ends and amortization begins when the real estate asset is ready for its intended use (I67.115).

Many times, financial arrangements made with a permanent lender provide for a portion of the interest on the debt to be paid upon occurrence of an economic event; this is often known as an "equity kicker." The contingent part of the unpaid amount is considered either interest cost being incurred or contingent accumulated equity inuring to the lender.[5] Each individual fact pattern and the resulting economic effects determine the accounting treatment. In instances where (1) the lender is not an affiliate of the real estate syndicate entity, (2) the terms can be compared favorably to marketplace terms, and (3) there is value in the asset to cover debt and unpaid interest, the accounting treatment will generally result in interest cost being accrued currently.

If substantially all or part of the activity related to the transaction is of a contingent nature, the interest is likely to be tax deductible only when paid, as opposed to when it might be accruable.

Development Costs. Typically, in most real estate syndicates, numerous fees are paid or are payable to the general partner and its affiliates, sponsor and its affiliates, or third parties. Funds to pay these obligations frequently come from the limited partners' equity contributions. The general treatment of costs related to acquisition of real estate for development, and to initial rental operations, are discussed earlier in this chapter.

Development fees in such forms as acquisition fees, construction supervisory fees, and general partner origination fees should be capitalized (Re2.103–.107) when all of the following conditions are met:

• The costs are directly identifiable with specific assets.
• The costs incurred provide discernable future benefits.
• Market values are used as a limiting factor for recording the cost.

Made-Up Rental Shortfalls. In Issue 85-27, *Recognition of Receipts From Made-Up Rental Shortfalls*, the EITF considered the sale of property still in the rent-up stage to a recently formed real estate limited partnership. The general partner of the syndicate agrees to buy the property on behalf of the partnership only if the seller agrees to a leaseback of the premises on a master lease for two years. The syndicate pays a fee to the seller to induce him to enter into the master leaseback; this fee is held in escrow as if it were a portion of the purchase price. The seller then subleases the vacant premises at the best rates obtainable, and if any of the subleases meet certain criteria, the syndicate relieves the seller of his lease payment obligation for that space. To the extent the seller does not write subleases meeting these criteria, or is unable to sublease all the vacant space, the rental payments made to the syndicate would substantially exceed the fee paid by the syndicate. At issue is the accounting treatment to be used by the syndicate for the fee it pays the seller and the rent it receives from the seller (the seller's accounting is not being addressed).

A consensus was reached that the syndicate's receipts from and payments to the seller should be treated as adjustments to the basis of the property, thus affecting future depreciation, rather than as current income and expense.

---

[5] As of mid-1988, the AICPA Real Estate Committee was working on an issues paper regarding participating mortgages, which is intended to deal with contingent payments to lenders.

Accounting by the Syndicator

Forms of Income. The AICPA Real Estate Committee has prepared a draft paper on income from syndication activities,[6] which lists the following common sources of syndication income:

- Fees for organizing partnerships (syndication fees).
- Fees for providing services as a broker or dealer on sales of investment units.
- Fees for selling properties already owned by the syndicator to partnerships or arranging for the acquisition of properties by the partnerships (brokerage or property acquisition fees).
- Fees for guaranteeing cash flows, arranging financing, property management, construction supervision, development, and property lease-up.
- Profit on the sale of real estate.

Consideration paid to a syndicator may consist of cash, notes, or other receivables, an interest in the partnership, or the right to share in proceeds of the sale or refinancing of the property. At the time of syndication, the syndicator generally is paid cash from partnership funds received as initial payments from investors or from proceeds of borrowings secured by investor notes. Subsequent payments may be made to the syndicator by the partnership based on the availability of cash from additional installments on investor notes, partnership operations, proceeds of mortgage refinancing, or proceeds from the sale of the properties. The notes given to the syndicator (partnership notes) may be collateralized by investor notes or mortgages or other liens against the properties. Some or all of the notes may have long-term maturities and may pay portions of the interest currently.

Income Recognition. In late 1985, the EITF considered Issue 85-37, *Recognition of Note Received for Real Estate Syndication Activities.* This discussion, though very brief, opened a widescale reassessment of syndicator accounting, which is not resolved as of mid-1988.

EITF discussion. Issue 85-37 posed a complex set of facts, replete with exhibits illustrating the problem. This issue is described here in abridged form, leaving out many of the details. The essential features of the transaction are:

1. A syndicator acting as 1% general partner forms and markets a limited partnership to acquire income-producing property from a third party. The partnership provides certain tax advantages to the partners related to the holding of real estate; it is projected to break even on cash flow for a period of years (ending when the tax advantages have been consumed), at which time disposition by sale is planned to a third party or to another syndicate formed to "recycyle" the property.
2. The syndicator advances to the partnership 10% of the purchase price necessary to acquire the property and the balance is paid by a 90% first mortgage amortizable over 40 years.

---

[6] The AICPA Real Estate Committee had developed an Issues Paper on syndicator accounting, based on EITF Issue 85-37, discussed in the next section; in May 1988, AcSEC asked the committee to draft the subject in the form of an SOP.

3. The limited partners pay in 10% of the equity subscription to the partnership at the outset and execute non-interest-bearing, full-recourse promissory notes (called investor notes) payable in nine annual 10% installments. The initial partners' funds are paid to the syndicator as its syndication fee.

4. The partnership issues a note payable to the syndicator (called the partnership note) in an amount that equals 25% of the total limited partners' subscription, in consideration of various services, and for the funds advanced as the property down payment. The partnership note is payable in 10 years or upon earlier sale of the property. It bears interest payable annually, at an amount that is exactly equal to the 10% annual installments paid in by the limited partners. To secure collection of the interest, the syndicator requires that the investor notes be pledged by the partnership as collateral.

5. At the time of sale, the proceeds (net of the first mortgage balance) are to be first applied to the payment of the partnership note, and excess proceeds are to be shared in some predetermined manner.

Although many issues could be raised about various accounting aspects of the foregoing transaction, the question addressed to the EITF was what value, if any, could be ascribed by the syndicator to the partnership note; this amount would be treated as income by the syndicator for its syndication efforts, in addition to the cash fee received and less expenses incurred.

The Issues Summary suggested several possible methods, recapped as follows:[7]

1. *Earned income method.* The syndicator would discount the sum of the partnership note and the collateralized annual interest payments thereon at an appropriate rate and record the present value as current income. In subsequent periods, the accretion would be credited to income and the annual cash payments received would reduce the accreted receivable balance.

   The main support for the earned income method came from the AICPA Issues Paper on *Accounting by Lease Brokers* (1980a). A principal element in lease broker accounting has been the recognition in income, at lease inception, of the present value of the expected residual and its accretion over the life of the transaction.

   The earned income method drew additional support from the fact that income-producing property has rarely lost its value over time and thus could be relied on to generate adequate funds to pay the partnership note. The general partner could avoid market dips by judicious timing of the eventual sale, within a range of several years.

2. *Mortgage method.* The syndicator would account for the partnership note like a second mortgage. Assuming the annual cash interest is at a market rate, this method records the face amount of the partnership note as a receivable, and the cash interest payments in subsequent periods are credited to income as they accrue.

   This method relies on the fact that the partnership note is a monetary asset received in exchange for services rendered and therefore should be recorded as income subject to an evaluation of its collectibility.

---

[7] The purchased residual method is omitted here, as there is no indication that anyone is or had been using it.

3. *Cash method.* The syndicator would assign no value to the partnership note but would discount the collateralized interest payments due via the investor notes and record the present value as income. In subsequent periods accretion would be credited to income.

The cash method is based on the premise that it is not possible to know whether the property could be sold for any amount in the future, much less the amount necessary to pay off the partnership note. Accordingly, only the "guaranteed" future cash flows may be considered income and any other income must await the actual receipt of sales proceeds.

In each case, the purchase money advanced to the partnership and all other expenses incurred by the syndicator would be charged off concurrent with the initial income recognition. The mortgage method would result in the greatest amount of initial income recognition, and the cash method, the least.

The EITF did not try to reach a consensus on an issue this complicated, because a variety of approaches were in use at privately held syndicators. The SEC Observer made it clear at the meeting (and at two subsequent EITF meetings) that the SEC staff would accept only the cash method for syndicators whose financial statements were included in syndication public offerings, unless and until the matter was formally considered and a professional promulgation released. The AICPA Real Estate Committee was therefore requested to study the matter.

AICPA Real Estate Committee activities. Over the course of more than two years, the Committee (and a specific task force thereof) considered the various issues. The threshold issue was identified early: Should SFAS 66 apply to syndicators that do not sell real estate to the syndicate? A variation on this issue was whether SFAS 66 should be applied to "flips" in which the syndicator buys and promptly resells the property to the syndicate. The Committee eventually concluded that SFAS 66 should be applied.

The decision to apply SFAS 66 spawned several additional questions discussed in the AICPA draft:

1. Should sales value include (a) all fees, (b) certain fees, (c) all fees except syndication fees, or (d) no fees paid or to be paid to the syndicator, except for fees clearly identified with future services?

2. For the purpose of calculating sales value and the buyer's investment under SFAS 66, should the amount of fees excluded from sales value be adjusted if such fees are not (a) within the range of fees that are justifiable based on fees charged by others in similar transactions or (b) in amounts otherwise justifiable based on commissions and fees paid by the syndicator to independent and related brokers and other independent third parties?

3. Should cash received by the syndicator be allocated first to fees excluded from sales value regardless of contractual provisions?

4. If the underlying real estate transaction does not qualify for full accrual profit recognition, should income be required to be deferred on fees that are excluded from sales value (a) always, (b) never, or (c) under certain circumstances?

5. Should a syndicator recognize income on nonrefundable fees before the property has been acquired by the partnership?

6. In a syndication transaction, should the carried interest in the partnership received or retained by the syndicator be valued for the purpose of income recognition (a) at fair value,

(b) at cost based on accounting for the transaction as a partial sale, (c) at zero, (d) based on the measurement of a residual interest in the partnership, or (e) at the amount of cost incurred?

The reason for focusing on sales value in the first two questions above is subtle, but most incisive: By adding many fees into sales value, the required initial and continuing investments by the buyer rise, because they are defined in terms of sales value. This leads to the third question: how should the cash received be applied? If it is applied first to syndicator fees that are not part of sales value, then there is less (if any) remaining to apply as the buyer's initial investment. In discussing these issues, the preference of AcSEC seemed to be that the requirements for profit recognition by syndicators should be made as rigorous as possible.

Future action. The Real Estate Committee brought this topic to AcSEC for a brief discussion in 1988. It was decided that the draft issues paper should be redrafted as an SOP containing AcSEC's conclusions, at which time it would be considered by the FASB; and a decision would then be made by the FASB as to whether to encourage AcSEC to issue it. This process will take some time.

Apart from illustrating the complexities of the syndication business, this case also shows how long it can take for a complex issue to be resolved (and therefore how long an unofficial SEC ruling can be kept in effect). It is unclear exactly what the final SOP will say, but the answer to the threshold issue mentioned in the preceding section is unlikely to be revised. It should also be noted that application of SFAS 66 will not necessarily result in an answer as conservative as the SEC-preferred cash method, and could in some cases (depending on structuring) result in higher income recognition than the other methods discussed in the EITF Issues Summary No. 85-37. For these reasons it would be premature to predict approval by the SEC and FASB.

Partnership Roll-Ups. In Issue 88-14, *Settlement of Fees With Extra Units to a General Partner in an MLP*, the EITF considered the accounting treatment to be applied by a general partner to a transaction in which a number of existing real estate limited partnerships were rolled-up into a new master limited partnership (MLP) with partnership units traded on the New York Stock Exchange. In consideration of relinquishing all rights to collect fees from the prior partnerships, the general partner of the old partnerships was given a number of units in the MLP, and also became the general partner of the MLP. The general partner was not required to perform any substantive uncompensated services for the MLP after the roll-up.

The issue focused on how the MLP units received by the general partner should be valued. Some task force members felt that, because the units were marketable and there were no future services required, the earnings process was complete and revenue should be recognized based on the market value of the additional interest received. A consensus was not reached, as several members felt that given the related party nature of the roll-up, the general partner had not yet "earned" the income and might not until it ceased being the general partner. These members might also hold that even if the MLP units were sold for cash, revenue was not earned and would have to be accounted for as a deferred credit unless the general partnership status was terminated. In addition, some members focused on the applicability of the equity method of accounting for general partners, and would consider the units received as a reduction of the equity under APB 18 to be amortized into the general partner's income over time. (I82.109n).

The FASB staff will consider this matter further in its work-in-progress relating to MLPs. The SEC Observer indicated that registrants would no longer be permitted (after June 2, 1988) to record income in transactions of the type discussed in this EITF issue.

AUDITING CONSIDERATIONS

General Auditing Matters

Auditing for real estate developers and homebuilders is essentially the same as that applied to construction contractors as described in the following chapter. It should be noted that although normal internal control review and reliability considerations apply, a control reliance audit approach is improbable in the real estate industry when considering individually large transactions. Thus retail land sales company audits will tend more toward control reliance, and auditing of individually large real estate transactions will be substantive. (See Chapters 7 and 8.)

Real estate transactions, including syndications, are evidenced by a proliferation of legal forms and documents. The auditor's main objective is to attest to the substance of the transactions. Understanding and recognizing the substance of each transaction has been and continues to be the auditor's primary problem.

In today's sophisticated transactions, the areas most difficult for auditors to assess are:

- Revenue recognition.
- Debt financing versus equity financing.
- Earnings process for debt financing.
- Underlying value of the real estate supporting the debt.

The guides prepared in the early 1970s and incorporated into SFAS 66 and SFAS 67 covered only accounting matters. This was understandable because most of the professional difficulties at the time that resulted from real estate auditing involved the application of fluid accounting practices. With the expanding complexity of transactions, however, there is an even greater need for the auditor to understand how to get the needed information and what to watch for. Accordingly, the AICPA Real Estate Committee has been considering the preparation of a real estate audit guide, as none exists for this industry. This project is deferred as of mid-1988. With almost endless variation in real estate transactions, the industry's problem issues will continue to be the source of FASB and EITF pronouncements. The sections that follow deal with a few of the more complex areas of concern to auditors.

Real Estate Sales

The auditor must look at the environment in which the client operates and the client's methods of doing business, to determine the inherent risks created by both. He must evaluate these risks and the client's internal control structure to ascertain the degree to which the client is susceptible to management involvement in material transactions.

Examining Documentation. The auditor should obtain and study the documents related to the real estate transaction and corroborate their authenticity. Because of the complexity usually encountered in this area, other experts—especially lawyers—may be called on to assist in reducing the voluminous contracts having a variety of legal names down to a statement of essential ingredients.

The existence of SFAS 66, SFAS 67, and EITF issues should also cause the auditor to focus on certain aspects critical to meeting the requirements of those pronouncements.

Substantially all transactions involving the transfer of land and buildings are financed by notes, mortgages, or contracts because of the large·dollar amounts involved. These financial instruments usually provide a relatively small portion of the total value of the transferred property to be paid in cash, either at execution of the agreement or upon the occurrence of some event that transfers title to or possession of the property.

In addition to the standard terms for principal and interest payments, these instruments may contain options for the lender or seller to buy or repurchase portions of the property at fixed prices or at appraised amounts. Other provisions may require the payment of additional sums to the lender or seller if net income or cash flow exceeds specified levels, or if the resale price of the property exceeds specified levels.

An agreement might also contain restrictive covenants with respect to use or resale of the property, amount of debt the buyer is permitted to incur, parties to whom the property may be resold, and restrictions on various other activities of the buyer. Other agreements may specify additional obligations of the seller, such as agreements to provide funds for future operations, to provide improvements not available at time of transfer, to buy the property back upon the occurrence of certain events or completion of certain items, guarantees of specific return on amounts invested, or other items of continued involvement. There may also be side agreements containing various commitments by a buyer or seller; these agreements may contain any of these items described or any other item the buyer and seller agree upon.

The auditor should obtain copies of purchase or sale agreements for all major transactions and review the documents, including all related side agreements, to determine whether there are any commitments by the buyer or seller that might have continued impact on the financial statements. These documents must be carefully evaluated to be sure there are no unrecognized financial aspects of the transactions. The rules with respect to recognition of profit must be considered in this review. Option agreements also must be carefully evaluated to determine if the asset and liability must be recorded (e.g., are circumstances such that the company in substance *must* exercise the option?).

The potential for liability for improvements of property sold also must be carefully considered. The auditor should be alert for any indication of seller participation in the buyer's financing and for any other indication that the transfer of property was not an arm's-length transaction.

In light of the potential for revision of the original terms of these agreements or of various side agreements, the auditor must ascertain whether there have been any changes in the documents from year to year and must evaluate the impact of such changes. Also, each agreement should be reviewed each year to determine that all terms and covenants have been complied with. To accomplish this continued review process, the auditor should obtain and retain a file of all documents relating to each major transaction. Each year the auditor should review major transactions that were open at the previous year end to determine that the accounting for disposition or changes in status was proper.

Receivables. Notes, mortgages, and contract receivables often represent a significant portion of the assets of a real estate development company. In many instances, these documents are readily convertible into cash through discounting or other sales. The auditor must recognize this characteristic of these assets and determine that they are actually valid assets of the client by applying procedures comparable to those applied to marketable securities, including physical inspection or other verification of the existence and safekeeping of the original receivable documents.

Subordination. In some circumstances, a buyer may use his newly acquired property as collateral for loans from third parties. The proceeds from these loans may help the buyer in maintaining cash flow sufficient to pay his debt to the seller.

The auditor should satisfy himself that no agreements, understandings, commitments, or other side agreements exist which would permit the future subordination of the seller's receivable. He should do this by obtaining confirmations from the buyer and from other parties who might have knowledge of such agreements or understandings. The audit letter of representations should contain representations to this effect.

Real Estate Appraisals. The AICPA recently issued an Audit and Accounting Guide, *Guide for the Use of Real Estate Appraisal Information* (1987j). This guide presents recommendations of the Real Estate Committee for the application of GAAS to audits of financial statements of entities that use real estate appraisals. The guide has been prepared to assist independent auditors in:

- Understanding the real estate appraisal process, its valuation concepts, and principles.
- Using real estate appraisal information in examinations of financial statements.
- Applying SAS 11, *Using the Work of a Specialist* (AU 336), to the work of a real estate appraiser.

The guide discusses circumstances in which an appraisal may be needed as audit evidence and reviews valuation concepts and the appraisal process. It also explains factors to be considered in the selection and evaluation of a real estate appraiser. Appendices to the guide include:

• Contents of an appraisal report.
• Illustration of the calculation of net realizable value.
• Certain real estate terms common to appraisal information.

Retail Land Sales

Land development has been regulated principally by local governments, which impose a battery of building and mechanical codes, zoning ordinances, and subdivision regulations – although more recently there has been some trend toward regional, state, and federal control of real estate development. The emphasis on environmental concerns in many cases has resulted in requirements for the filing of environmental impact statements and related increases in regulation by the various governmental agencies. The auditor must obtain an understanding of these industry features to recognize problems in the course of his audit.

Provision for Losses. Frequently, the receivable resulting from real estate transactions is disproportionately large when compared to the other assets of the company. Therefore, careful consideration should be given in evaluating the internal control over this area. The auditor should be concerned with the amount provided for expected losses and satisfy himself that it adequately covers probable losses.

The audit of the allowance should include confirmation of significant portions of transactions, along with the effects that the client's credit granting policies and economic conditions might have on each resulting receivable.

It is not unusual for a developer to have sold his position, with the buyer maintaining a right of recourse. Therefore the developer also must continue to fully analyze and maintain an adequate reserve on accounts sold with recourse.

Because retail land sales buyers may cancel their contracts within a specified time period, the amounts received are carried as deposits. In addition, transactions that have passed the unilateral cancellation cutoff date may still be treated as deposits because of failure of the project to qualify for one of the sales accounting treatments. The auditor should evaluate the company's controls over deposits, confirm them on a test basis, and assess that they are properly classified in the financial statements. The auditor should also evaluate the reserve for cancellations on transactions that have been recorded as sales.

Audit efforts in the cancellations area are usually directed at the statistical data available from the client regarding historical incidence of cancellations; the auditor should consider the integrity of the data, whether it is usable for the project under consideration, and whether other factors (e.g., changes in selling methods) would make this data nonrepresentative.

Future Performance Costs. Normal construction risks such as environmental problems, zoning, local and state ordinances, personnel requirements, and equipment and material shortages make the auditor's evaluation of anticipated costs difficult. The most credible means of determining future improvement costs is through engineering studies provided by a qualified outside consultant. If this is not available, thorough management estimates should suffice. In analyzing either outside engineering studies or management estimates, the auditor should consider use of outside experts (AU 336).

36

Construction Contractors

OVERVIEW

Nature of the Industry

The construction industry is an amazingly diverse industry in terms of the number of contracting specialties. The scope ranges from strictly serving a local economy to significant project involvement on an international basis. An indication of the significance of the construction industry is the fact that it consistently contributes approximately 5% to the gross national product of the United States.

Many contractors, especially building contractors, are local businessmen building for the local residential and commercial markets. Certain categories of contractors with specialties such as highway and petroleum pipeline construction generally do

36-1

not limit their area of operations. The size of contracting businesses also has a broad range, from a sole proprietorship with only a few employees to a major, international corporation with thousands of employees.

Economic Impact

The fortunes of the construction industry are affected substantially by demographic and economic trends. After World War II and into the late 1970s, building contractors were in a boom period. However, this ended abruptly in 1979 when the United States entered a period of rapidly rising interest rates, peaking at a prime rate close to 20%. The result was a deeply depressed demand for housing and construction generally. Mortgage rates of 16% literally drove the cost of housing out of the reach of most families. However, the demand for commercial construction, which is more significantly affected by tax incentives, only faltered. After 1980, as interest rates dropped, the demand for residential and commercial construction jumped. Simultaneously, the western and southwestern areas of the United States were growing rapidly as people and companies moved in from the economically depressed "Rust Belt." Construction contractors were speeding to catch up with the tremendous growth in demand.

The severe drop in oil prices in 1985 had major negative repercussions in the Southwest, with the result that construction in that area has significantly exceeded demand. Additionally, at least in part due to tax incentives, there has been substantial overbuilding of commercial properties in most urban areas of the United States. Consequently, there has been a general decline in construction, and numerous contractors have failed. Of course, there are numerous reasons for any business, including construction, to fail in troubled times. Too rapid a growth by diversifying into other construction specialties without adequate expertise, geographic expansion, poor management, and weak financial controls all have contributed to the failure of many construction companies in the past few years.

The unpredictability of economic and demographic swings, weather conditions that affect progress on a project, and escalating material and labor costs all represent significant risks to the financial success of a contractor. Obviously, these also represent risks to those who invest in and lend to contractors as well as to those who audit them.

Significant Definitions

Like most industries, the construction industry has its unique terminology. This section briefly identifies several terms used throughout the chapter.

- *Over- and underbillings.* Contracts are typically overbilled or underbilled at any given point in time. Very seldom is a contractor able to bill his exact percentage of completion to the customer. Underbillings, which are assets akin to receivables, represent costs and earnings that are calculated under the percentage-of-completion method that have not yet been billed to the customer. Conversely, overbillings, carried on the liability side of the balance sheet, represent billings in excess of costs and calculated earnings on contracts in progress.

- *Backcharges.* Amounts that a general contractor will bill a subcontractor for labor and other costs incurred to complete or clean up the subcontractor's portion of the project are called backcharges. These charges are very often subject to dispute.
- *Fixed price contracts.* Also known as a lump sum contract, these contracts specify a single amount due for completion of a project. Under this type of a contract, the price risk lies entirely with the contractor.
- *Unit price contracts.* These contracts provide that a contractor will perform the work for a specified price per unit of production. This type of contract is commonly used in highway construction (where the units are miles).
- *Cost-plus contracts.* The contractor will be paid an amount equal to costs, as defined in the contract, plus specified overhead and profit rates, in a cost-plus contract. The fee or profit element may be specified as a lump sum rather than a percentage of the cost. Often a cost-plus contract will specify a maximum price that the contractor cannot exceed. This type of contract is also called a *top max* contract. Some contracts can also provide for a sharing arrangement with the owner in which the contractor, if completing the contract below a targeted cost, will share the savings, based on some specified ratio, with the owner.
- *Time and materials contracts.* These are very similar to a cost-plus contract and typically provide for payments to the contractor on the basis of labor hours at a specified hourly rate plus payment for materials and other costs allowable under the contract.

Types of Contractors

The *general contractor* is responsible for the entire construction project and is the one at risk for any costs incurred in excess of the total contract amount. The general contractor typically enters into subcontracts with other contractors for any portion of the work he does not feel qualified to perform, and he is fully responsible for performance by the subcontractor. He is also referred to as the *prime contractor*, which means he has the direct relationship with the property owner.

A *subcontractor* is typically a contractor with special expertise, such as electrical, mechanical, excavation, or steel erection. The subcontractor's performance responsibility is to the general contractor; he reports to and is paid under contract by the general contractor.

On larger contracts, there may also be a *construction manager* (who may be a general contractor) who also provides oversight services. This individual will be responsible for the overall interface between all contractors and the owner and will typically be the owner's representative in the field. His responsibilities include approving budgets, billings, and change orders.

Credit Grantors

The construction industry is served principally by two credit institutions – commercial banks and bonding companies. *Banks* provide traditional secured and unsecured loans. Typically they will require either reviewed or audited financial statements in deciding whether to grant credit to a contractor. Savings and loan associations have also become more involved in construction financing in recent years.

Bonding companies, generally insurance companies, provide assurance of creditworthiness for contractors in the form of surety bonds. The bonding process is not an insurance process, but is rather a prequalification process. The bonding company is giving assurance to an owner that the contractor has the financial ability to perform on the contract. Most large projects are bonded at least at the general contractor level, but it is also becoming commonplace for owners and general contractors to require bonds on subcontractors.

Bonding companies rely heavily on financial statements of contractors, and most require either reviewed or audited financial statements when the bond lines are significant. Bonding companies have incurred significant losses over the last few years, and obtaining underwriting has become much more difficult. It is not unusual for bond lines to be terminated even for financially sound contractors when the surety company reevaluates this line of business.

For an in-depth look at financing aspects of the construction industry, see the *Touche Ross Guide to Granting Credit to Contractors* (1984).

ACCOUNTING AND FINANCIAL REPORTING

Accounting for contractors was first codified in ARB 45 (Co4), issued in 1955. In 1965, an AICPA Industry Audit Guide, *Construction Contractors*, was published; and it was superseded in 1981 by an AICPA Audit and Accounting Guide, *Construction Contractors* (1981d). The 1981 Guide includes SOP 81-1, *Accounting for Performance of Construction-Type and Certain Production-Type Contracts* (TP 10,330). The SOP sets forth in detail the acceptable accounting methods for construction contractors.[1]

Accounting Methods

There are two acceptable methods of accounting for contracts: percentage-of-completion and completed contract. Prior to SOP 81-1, the accounting literature freely allowed the use of either method, although percentage-of-completion was the predominant method. In SOP 81-1, percentage-of-completion accounting was given preference over completed contract accounting. SFAS 56, issued in 1982, designated both the Guide and SOP as preferable for purposes of justifying accounting changes under APB 20 (Co4.114).

Percentage-of-Completion Method. Under this method, periodic recognition is given to income and expense as progress is completed on contracts. This method is consistent with the nature of a contractor's business. Ownership of the phases of a project is typically transferred to the property owner as they are completed. In other words, as materials and the labor necessary to convert those materials are utilized, they become the property of the owner. Because of the estimation process used in determining the percentage completed, financial statements prepared under this

---

[1] Most of the accounting practices discussed herein are based on SOP 81-1, and therefore numerous TP 10,330 citations appear. In addition, because certain aspects of government contracting (discussed in Chapter 37) have general applicability to contractors, references to a 1987 exposure draft of an AICPA Audit and Accounting Guide, *Audits of Government Contractors*, will also be found herein; these citations are designated AICPA, 1987c.

method have a greater degree of uncertainty than would statements prepared under completed contract accounting. Nonetheless, percentage-of-completion accounting ordinarily is a more meaningful method of revenue recognition because it better reflects the timing of completion of the earnings process, and closely parallels cash flows. For these reasons, credit grantors can readily understand a contractor's financial status under percentage-of-completion accounting.

It bears mention that percentage-of-completion accounting and the related revenue recognition pattern do not necessarily correspond with billings. Most contractors attempt to include in their cost estimates and billing schedules significant front-end billings. Billings are not an acceptable method for contact revenue recognition, except by coincidence.

Underlying the ability to use the percentage-of-completion method is the contractor's ability to make reasonable estimates. There is a rule-of-thumb in the construction industry that a successful contractor has the ability to properly estimate his contracts; therefore, he should also have the ability to make the estimates necessary to employ percentage-of-completion accounting.

Figures 36.1 and 36.2 are examples of a sample balance sheet and related notes for a construction contractor using the percentage-of-completion method.

Completed Contract Method. Under this method, all contract revenue and expense on jobs in progress is deferred, with recognition in the income statement only when the contract is completed. The result is the recording of both income and expense in periods after the work is done. When using this method, contracts that are substantially complete can be considered complete for financial statement purposes prior to being complete for tax purposes, even when the tax method is completed contract accounting. In this case, the remaining revenue and expense are accrued as of the balance sheet date. For tax purposes, contracts usually will be reported as closed when they are finally completed and accepted. Under GAAP, contract losses nevertheless must be accrued when known, even though these losses may not yet be tax-deductible under the completed contract method.

There are only two instances when completed contract accounting is acceptable under SOP 81-1:

1. When financial position and results of operations would not differ significantly from those that would result from using percentage-of-completion accounting (TP 10,330.31). This could occur in the case of a contractor with short duration contracts; use of the completed contract method is unlikely to distort the results. (The SOP does not define short duration and long duration contracts.)
2. When there are inherent hazards relating to contract conditions or general factors that would raise questions about a company's ability to accurately estimate a contract (TP 10,330.32).

If a company uses completed contract accounting, it is difficult for a credit grantor to understand the contractor's volume and relative profitability, because this method distorts the relationship between cash flows and revenue recognition.

PERCENTAGE CONTRACTORS, INC.
Consolidated Balance Sheets
December 31, 19X8 and 19X7

Assets	19X8	19X7
Cash	$ 264,100	$ 221,300
Certificates of deposit	40,300	
Contract receivables (Note 2)	3,789,200	3,334,100
Costs and estimated earnings in excess of billings on uncompleted contracts (Note 3)	80,200	100,600
Inventory, at lower of cost, on a first-in, first-out basis, or market	89,700	99,100
Prepaid charges and other assets	118,400	83,200
Advances to and equity in joint venture (Note 4)	205,600	130,700
Note receivable, related company (Note 5)	175,000	150,000
Property and equipment, net of accumulated depreciation and amortization (Note 6)	976,400	1,019,200
	$5,738,900	$5,138,200

Liabilities and shareholders' equity	19X8	19X7
Notes payable (Note 8)	$ 468,100	$ 578,400
Lease obligations payable (Note 9)	197,600	251,300
Accounts payable (Note 7)	2,543,100	2,588,500
Billings in excess of costs and estimated earnings on uncompleted contracts (Note 3)	242,000	221,700
Accrued income taxes payable	52,000	78,600
Other accrued liabilities	36,600	36,000
Due to consolidated joint venture minority interests	154,200	26,200
Deferred income taxes (Note 13)	619,200	408,000
	4,312,800	4,188,700
Contingent liability (Note 10)		
Shareholders' equity		
Common stock — $1 par value, 500,000 authorized shares, 300,000 issued and outstanding shares	300,000	300,000
Retained earnings	1,126,100	649,500
Total shareholders' equity	1,426,100	949,500
	$5,738,900	$5,138,200

FIG. 36.1   Balance Sheet—Percentage-of-Completion Method
Source: Construction Contractors (AICPA, 1981d) (notes 2 and 3 shown in Fig. 36.2).

Figures 36.3 and 36.4 provide a sample balance sheet and related notes for a construction contractor using the completed contract method.

Selection of Method. Because the percentage-of-completion and completed contract methods are not acceptable alternatives for the same circumstances, the determination of which is preferable should be based on an evaluation of the specific circumstances (TP 10,330.21). Generally, the use of the percentage-of-completion

2. Contract Receivables

	December 31, 19X8	December 31, 19X7
Contract receivables		
Billed		
Completed contracts	$ 621,100	$ 500,600
Contracts in progress	2,146,100	1,931,500
Retained	976,300	866,200
Unbilled	121,600	105,400
	3,865,100	3,403,700
Less: Allowances for doubtful collections	75,900	69,600
	$3,789,200	$3,334,100

3. Costs and Estimated Earnings on Uncompleted Contracts

	December 31, 19X8	December 31, 19X7
Costs incurred on uncompleted contracts	$15,771,500	$12,165,400
Estimated earnings	1,685,900	1,246,800
	17,457,400	13,412,200
Less: Billings to date	17,619,200	13,533,300
	$ (161,800)	$ (121,100)
Included in accompanying balance sheets under the following captions:		
Costs and estimated earnings in excess of billings on uncompleted contracts	$ 80,200	$ 100,600
Billings in excess of costs and estimated earnings on uncompleted contracts	(242,000)	(221,700)
	$ (161,800)	$ (121,100)

FIG. 36.2 Contract Notes—Pecentage-of-Completion Method
Source: Construction Contractors (AICPA, 1981d).

method depends on management's ability to make reasonably dependable estimates of contract revenues, costs, and the extent of progress toward completion. SOP 81-1 states that the percentage-of-completion method is *preferable* if reasonably dependable estimates can be made and if all of the following conditions exist (TP 10,330.23):

• The contract includes provisions that clearly specify the enforceable rights of the parties as to goods or services to be provided and received, the consideration to be exchanged, and the manner and terms of settlement.
• It is expected that the buyer can satisfy his obligations under the contract.
• It is expected that the contractor can perform his contractual obligations.

It is presumed that sufficiently dependable estimates can be made by entities that engage continuously in long-term contractual arrangements, and for whom such contracts represent a significant part of their operations.

COMPLETED CONTRACTORS, INC.
Balance Sheets
December 31, 19X8 and 19X7

Assets	19X8	19X7
Current assets		
Cash	$ 242,700	$ 185,300
Contract receivables (less allowance for doubtful		
accounts of $10,000 and $8,000) (Note 2)	893,900	723,600
Costs in excess of billings on uncompleted contracts (Note 3)	418,700	437,100
Inventories, at lower of cost or realizable value on first-in,		
first-out basis (Note 4)	463,600	491,300
Prepaid expenses	89,900	53,900
Total current assets	2,108,800	1,891,200
Cash value of life insurance	35,800	32,900
Property and equipment, at cost		
Building	110,000	110,000
Equipment	178,000	163,000
Trucks and autos	220,000	200,000
	508,000	473,000
Less: Accumulated depreciation	218,000	203,200
	290,000	269,800
Land	21,500	21,500
	311,500	291,300
	$2,456,100	$2,215,400

Liabilities and stockholders' equity	19X8	19X7
Current liabilities		
Current maturities, long-term debt (Note 5)	$ 37,000	$ 30,600
Accounts payable	904,900	821,200
Accrued salaries and wages	138,300	155,100
Accrued income taxes	53,000	36,200
Accrued and other liabilities	116,400	55,550
Billings in excess of costs on uncompleted contracts (Note 3)	34,500	43,700
Total current liabilities	1,284,100	1,142,350
Long-term debt, less current maturities (Note 5)	245,000	241,000
	1,529,100	1,383,350
Stockholders' equity		
Common stock – $10 par value, 50,000 authorized shares,		
23,500 issued and outstanding shares	235,000	235,000
Additional paid-in capital	65,000	65,000
Retained earnings	627,000	532,050
	927,000	832,050
	$2,456,100	$2,215,400

FIG. 36.3   Balance Sheet—Completed Contract Method
Source: Construction Contractors (AICPA, 1981d) (notes 2 and 3 shown in Fig. 36.4).

The completed contract method is preferable only in circumstances in which reasonably dependable estimates cannot be made, or in which there are other inherent hazards that make estimates doubtful (TP 10,330.25). Examples are contracts whose validity is seriously in question or whose completion may be subject to the outcome of pending legislation or litigation.

2. Contract Receivables

	December 31, 19X8	December 31, 19X7
Completed contracts, including retentions	$438,300	$408,600
Contracts in progress		
Current accounts	386,900	276,400
Retentions	78,700	46,600
	903,900	731,600
Less: Allowance for doubtful accounts	10,000	8,000
	$893,900	$723,600

Retentions include $10,300 in 19X8, which are expected to be collected after 12 months.

3. Costs and Billings on Uncompleted Contracts

	December 31, 19X8	December 31, 19X7
Costs incurred on uncompleted contracts	$2,140,400	$1,966,900
Billings on uncompleted contracts	1,756,200	1,573,500
	$ 384,200	$ 393,400
Included in accompanying balance sheets under the following captions:		
Costs in excess of billings on uncompleted contracts	$ 418,700	$ 437,100
Billings in excess of costs on uncompleted contracts	(34,500)	(43,700)
	$ 384,200	$ 393,400

FIG. 36.4　Contract Notes—Completed Contract Method
Source: Construction Contractors (AICPA, 1981d).

Profit Center Determination

The basic assumption for revenue recognition, cost accumulation, and profit measurement is that each contract is, in itself, a profit center. This assumption can be overcome, however, if a contract or series of contracts meets the criteria discussed in the following sections for segmenting and combining contracts. If a group of contracts (for combining) or a phase of a single contract (for segmenting) meet all the requisite conditions, a profit center other than the individual contract may be appropriate for accounting purposes.

Whether to combine or segment a contract may also depend on matters beyond the contract level, such as change orders, options, or additional provisions. For example, some contracts may have follow-on provisions in the form of options. In such cases, the decision whether to combine contract addendums for profit recognition purposes should be based on an analysis of the criteria in SOP 81-1 (TP 10,330.61–.64). If an option does not provide an adequate basis for establishing an estimated profit because the price and specifications are not adequately defined, it may not be appropriate to combine it with the basic contract.

Combining Contracts. At times a contractor may sign multiple contracts relating to the same project. SOP 81-1 generally requires that multiple contracts be combined in determining revenue recognition and costs. There are several criteria that must be met for contracts to be combined for accounting purposes (TP 10,331.37). The contracts:

1. Must have been negotiated as a package, with an overall profit margin objective. Contracts not executed simultaneously may be considered to have been negotiated as a package only if the time interval is short. The longer the interval, the more likely it is that the economic circumstances have changed.
2. Essentially are an agreement to do a single project, for example, interrelated phases.
3. Require closely interrelated activities that have substantial common costs (i.e., they cannot be specifically identified with or allocated to the phases of the project).
4. Are performed concurrently or sequentially under the same project management, either at the same location, or in the same general vicinity.
5. Are in substance an agreement with one customer.

Segmenting Contracts. An individual contract (or a group of contracts) may have characteristics that would indicate they should be segmented, because different phases or elements have different margin rates. A project may be segmented if certain steps are taken, are adequately documented, and can be verified (TP 10,330.40):

a. The contractor had submitted bona fide proposals on the separate components of the project and on the entire project.
b. The customer had the right to accept the proposals on either basis.
c. The aggregate amount of the proposals on the separate components approximated the amount of the proposal on the entire project.

If the project does not meet these criteria, it may still be segmented, but only if the terms and scope call for separable phases. These phases are often bid or negotiated separately; and different gross profit rates apply to the segments because there are differences in risk or in the relationship of the supply and demand for the services provided in different segments. Further, all of the following conditions must be met (TP 10,330.41):

1. For each segment having a profit margin higher than the overall project profit margin, the contractor is able to demonstrate that similar services frequently have been provided to other customers under separate contracts.
2. The prior sales that demonstrate the contractor's success in earning higher margins on certain services have been substantial (e.g., the evidence is not based on sales during a period of shortage, or on sales to related parties).
3. It can be clearly demonstrated that there are significant cost savings to the contractor because of joint supervision, overhead, and/or equipment mobilization applicable to the segments.
4. The prices assigned to the separate segments are verifiable by reference to sales to other customers, and this is documented.

If all these conditions are met, then contract segmentation in which the sum of the segments is greater than the total contract price will require allocation of the excess to each of the segments. This allocation is performed by allocating the excess in the same proportions as the prices assigned to each segment bear to the total of all segment prices. Upon completion of all segments, the prices will then aggregate the contract total.

The rules are quite stringent in this area simply because there might be a natural tendency by a contractor to be overly optimistic about the cost savings that will occur in a project, resulting in accruing too much income in the earlier segments and then having to report no profits, or even losses, in later stages.

Progress Measurement

There are several methods for determining the percentage of the contract completed; SOP 81-1 groups them into input and output types of measurement. Input measures are based on some measure of effort devoted to the contract, and include principally the cost ratio method and the labor hours or dollars method. Output measures are based on results achieved, such as units-of-work or actual work completed as certified by a qualified professional.

The *cost ratio method* relies on the ratio of costs incurred to date to the total estimated cost of the contract. This method typically follows the flow of costs, but at times may not reflect reality because the incidence of cost incurrence (e.g., acquiring most of the materials early on, but having significant delays in their installation) deviates from observable results. Nevertheless, if this method is used because it is the contractor's consistently applied method or it is the appropriate choice for the project in comparison with other approaches, the cost of uninstalled materials specifically produced, fabricated, or constructed for the project are included in the cost ratio (TP 10,330.50, fn. 9). Note that this does not include the cost of materials not unique to the project even though they have been purchased or accumulated at the job site.

In using the cost ratio method, care should be exercised that significant items purchased for use on a number of projects are excluded. Because of costs of materials not unique to a project are excluded from the measurement of progress, they should not be allowed to affect the timing of profit recognition. The preferable treatment is to classify these stock items as materials inventory, and to charge them against current operations as they are used.

Under the *labor hours or dollars method*, the ratio used is equal to the amount of hours or labor dollars incurred throughout the reporting period divided by the total estimated amount of hours or labor dollars. This is an effective measurement approach when materials are a large percentage of the total cost, but the risk related to completion of the project hinges on the labor element.

The *units of work method* is another commonly used method that will often produce the best results—if it is feasible given the nature of the project, for example, in the highway construction business. It requires the determination of the number of units that are to be produced under the contract (e.g., miles of concrete laid), and generally recognizes revenue at a uniform amount per unit.

From the viewpoint of a financial statement user, some measure of actual work completed is a desirable method because revenue recognition is based on the estimates of an independent party, usually an architect or engineer. It is important when relying on this method that the criteria used to establish the amount completed is objective and measurable, and reviewed by the contractor's management.

Whatever method is selected, it should be consistently applied to avoid significant distortions in reported revenue that could result by changing from one method to another. It is possible for a contractor to have a policy of using the cost-to-cost relationship, but because of circumstances use a different method in a particular contract. In such cases, disclosure in the financial statements is required if the contract is material.

Cost Estimates. Estimates of contract costs will change as a result of contract modifications, experience, and additional information acquired. Accounting estimates should therefore be reviewed and adjusted regularly over the term of a contract. How frequently estimates are reviewed and updated, and in what depth, depends on the entity's financial, contractual, or other reporting requirements.

If the percentage-of-completion method is used, changes in estimates of total contract costs may result in changes in the accrual rates of fees for cost-type contracts or changes in the accrual rates of profit for fixed price contracts. The cumulative effect of a change in estimate should be reported in the accounting period in which the change is made by adjusting the total amount of fees or profit recorded to date, so that the result is the same as the amount that would have been accrued if the newly determined fee or profit rate had been applied in all earlier accounting periods (TP 10,330.82). As a result, the amount of accrued fees or profit at any point in time will agree with the current cost estimate for that contract.

In estimating total costs to be incurred in completion of a contract, all available data must be evaluated. The AICPA exposure draft, *Audits of Government Contractors* (1987c, ¶ 182), provides guidance that also is useful for construction contractors in evaluating relevant factors, which include the following:

* Changes in cost of materials to be purchased in the future, which are not covered by firm purchase orders.
* Changes in future labor costs, including fringe benefits.
* Changes in indirect costs, such as manufacturing and engineering overhead and general and administrative expenses.
* Fluctuations in total production activity and their effects on allocation bases for various indirect costs.
* Specific contract provisions relating to performance requirements, warranties, and damages.
* Changes in costs of subcontracts.
* Technical problems encountered in performance of the contract.
* Contract changes.

Computing Income Earned. SOP 81-1 offers two alternatives for the computation of income earned during a reporting period using the percentage-of-completion method. The SOP refers to them as Alternatives A and B. The basic difference between them is that under Alternative A the gross profit on the contract is assumed to be earned evenly throughout the contract period. Therefore, balance sheet accounts are established to level the gross profit. Under Alternative B, the gross profit percentages can fluctuate from period to period.

Contract average gross profit. Under Alternative A, earned revenue, cost of earned revenue, and gross profit should be determined as follows (TP 10,330.80):

a. *Earned Revenue* to date should be computed by multiplying total estimated contract revenue by the percentage of completion (as determined by one of the acceptable methods of measuring the extent of progress towards completion). The excess of the amount over the earned revenue reported in prior periods is the earned revenue that should be recognized in the income statement for the current period.

b. *Cost of Earned Revenue* for the period should be computed in a similar manner. Cost of earned revenue to date should be computed by multiplying total estimated contract costs by the percentage of completion on the contract. The excess of that amount over the cost of earned revenue reported in prior periods is the cost of earned revenue that should be recognized in the income statement for the current period. The difference between total cost incurred to date and cost of earned revenue to date should be reported on the balance sheet.

c. *Gross Profit* on a contract for a period is the excess of earned revenue over the cost of earned revenue.

Periodic gross profit. Under Alternative B, earned revenue, cost of earned revenue, and gross profit are determined as follows (TP 10,330.81):

a. *Earned Revenue* is the amount of gross profit earned on a contract for a period plus the costs incurred on that contract during the period.

b. *Cost of Earned Revenue* is the cost incurred during the period excluding the cost of materials not unique to a contract that have not been used for the contract and costs incurred for subcontract work that is still to be performed.

c. *Gross Profit* earned on a contract should be computed by multiplying the total estimated gross profit on the contract by the percentage of completion (as determined by one of the acceptable methods of measuring extent of progress towards completion). The excess of that amount over the amount of gross profit reported in prior periods is the earned gross profit that should be recognized in the income statement for the current period.

If the cost ratio method is used, there is typically no difference in gross profit reported under either of the alternatives. When the cost ratio method is not used, Alternative B is the most frequently used method.

Contract Incentives. Revenue on contracts containing provisions for incentives and award fees should be recognized in conformity with the criteria in SOP 81-1, provided the contractor can make reasonably dependable estimates. Further, as noted in the proposed guide, *Audits of Government Contractors*, all components of contract revenue – the basic contract price, contract options, change orders, claims, and incentives payments such as award fees and performance incentives – should be considered in determining total estimated revenue (AICPA, 1987c, ¶ 155). However, such incentives should not be automatically included in determining total estimated revenue merely because a contract makes provision for them. Sometimes a contractor may not be able to reliably predict whether performance targets will be met, and consequently will be unable to reasonably estimate amounts to be received under incentive or award provisions. In such cases, they should be excluded in determining total estimated revenue.

For *cost incentives*, the contractor's ability to make reasonably dependable estimates of costs to complete is used to assess whether actual costs will meet targeted cost objectives. For *performance incentives*, substantial qualitative judgment and experience with the types of activities covered by the contract may be necessary to assess whether actual performance will produce results that meet targeted performance objectives. Estimating projected performance versus targeted performance is similar to the process used to estimate percentage of completion, and therefore is consistent with the concept of accounting for contracts under the percentage-of-completion method.

Contract Losses. Under either the completed contract method or the percentage-of-completion method, anticipated losses on contracts (TP 10,330.85-.89) should be:

1. Accrued when the losses become evident.
2. Computed based on the total estimated cost to complete the contract.
3. Presented separately as a liability on the balance sheet or deducted from related accumulated costs.
4. Included in the income statement as an element of contract costs rather than as a reduction of contract revenue.

Losses on contracts should not be allocated to future periods by spreading them to the remaining contract years, or by deferring them in expectation of receiving future or follow-on contract awards or the purchaser's exercise of options.

Construction Costs

Prior to SOP 81-1 some contractors charged only direct costs to cost of construction, while others made an attempt to allocate indirect expenses to contracts. A well-managed construction company must have adequate systems to accumulate all costs directly identifiable with specific contracts; in addition, indirect costs incurred in completing construction projects should be allocated on some rational basis to each contract. The sum of the direct and allocated indirect costs, matched against contract revenue, allows management to properly assess the profitability of each contract.

The general accounting principles for construction costs outlined in SOP 81-1 are (TP 10,330.72):

1. All direct costs such as material, labor, and subcontracting costs should be included.
2. Indirect costs that are incurred generally to complete projects are allocable to contracts.
3. Methods of allocating indirect costs should be systematic and rational.
4. Selling, general, and administrative costs should be charged to expense as incurred.
5. Costs under cost-type contracts should be included as contract costs in the same manner as costs under other types of contracts.
6. Estimates of gross profit or losses on contracts should be based on costs to complete that reflect all costs generally included in contract costs.
7. Inventoriable costs should never be greater than the estimated realizable value of the related contracts.

8. Interest costs may be capitalizable, or may be charged to expense, depending on the criteria in SFAS 34, *Capitalization of Interest Cost* (I67).

Costs are to be classified as period expenses if they are not readily identified as direct costs or as allocable indirect costs. All allocable indirect costs, once identified, are assigned to an appropriate overhead pool. Determining which items properly belong in which pool is often the most difficult part of the process. After the pools are determined, an allocation basis must be established to allocate the pools of costs to each contract.

Under the Tax Reform Act of 1986 (TRA 1986), certain types of general and administrative expenses and interest costs must now be allocated to contracts. These "extended period contract rules" were devised to allocate as many types of costs to contracts as possible, thereby reducing current tax deductions for costs perceived by Congress as still applicable to contracts for which taxable profits have not yet been reported. This change in tax law, however, should not necessarily affect what is allocated to contracts within the financial statements, if it is clear that the tax allocations are not in conformity with GAAP. If, however, material changes are made in capitalization policies either to more closely (or exactly) follow tax requirements (because this is justifiable under GAAP), an accounting change is involved. (See Chapter 14 for a discussion of how this type of change is presented in financial statements). It is clear in the Guide that general and administrative expenses are not allocable to contracts and should, therefore, be considered period expenses.

Customer-Provided Materials. If the customer furnishes the materials to be used on the job, as is often the case when a contractor is working for a not-for-profit organization, the accounting for these materials depends on the risk assumed by the contractor. Under SOP 81-1:

> If the contractor is responsible for the nature, type, characteristics, or specifications of material that the customer furnishes or that the contractor purchases as an agent of the customer, or if the contractor is responsible for the ultimate acceptability of performance of the project based on such material, the value of those items should be included as contract price and reflected as revenue and costs in periodic reporting of operations. [TP 10,330.60]

The deciding point is whether the contractor has any risk related to the adequacy of the furnished materials. If he does not, the amounts should be excluded from both costs and revenues.

Contract Price

Contract price is the amount the contractor has the right to receive for performance in accordance with the contract. For lump-sum or fixed-price contracts the contractor agrees to complete a project for a specified price. A cost-plus contract specifies the price as the reimbursement of direct and indirect cost, as defined, plus a fee, for performance of the contract. The contract should clearly define the amount that the contractor has the right to receive or the basis for computing the amount.

Routinely, contracts are modified based on circumstances that arise during the construction process, as discussed in the two sections that follow.

Change Orders. Modifications to contracts are typically documented on change orders. At any given point, they can be either approved or not approved, and priced or unpriced. Each change order needs to contain a clear statement as to the surrounding circumstances. Approved and priced change orders are the easiest to deal with, and are simply additions to or subtractions from the contract amount. Unpriced change orders are those for which performance is defined but the adjustment to the contract price is open. Unpriced change orders can be considered collectible only if the contractor believes it is probable that the costs will be recovered from contract revenues. Several factors to consider when evaluating the ability of the contractor to collect approved but unpriced change orders are (TP 10,330.62):

1. The customer has furnished written approval of the scope of the change order.
2. Separate documentation exists for identifiable and reasonable change order costs.
3. The contractor has been successful in the past in negotiating change orders for these types of contracts and change orders. Also, the contractor's relationship and history of negotiating change orders with the customer involved in the claim at hand should be considered.

Accounting for unpriced change orders when using the percentage-of-completion method should conform with the following guidelines (TP 10,330.62):

a. Costs attributable to unpriced change orders should be treated as costs of contract performance in the period in which the costs are incurred if it is not probable that the costs will be recovered through a change in the contract price.

b. If it is probable that the cost will be recovered through a change in the contract price, the cost should be deferred (excluded from the cost of contract performance) until the parties have agreed on the change in contract price, or, alternatively, they should be treated as costs of contract performance in the period in which they are incurred, and contract revenue should be recognized to the extent of the costs incurred.

c. If it is probable that the contract price will be adjusted by an amount that exceeds the costs attributable to the change order and the amount of the excess can be reliably estimated, the original contract price should also be adjusted for that amount when the costs are recognized as costs of contract performance if its realization is probable. However, since the substantiation of the amount of future revenue is difficult, revenue in excess of the costs attributable to unpriced change orders should only be recorded in circumstances in which realization is assured beyond a reasonable doubt.

If change orders exist that are both unapproved and unpriced, they should be evaluated as claims (discussed in the next section). If approved but unpriced change orders exist and the completed contract method of accounting is used, costs are to be deferred as part of contract costs.

Claims. Claims represent amounts in excess of the agreed contract price that a contractor believes is owed by its customer. Change orders that are both unapproved and unpriced (see previous section) are treated the same as claims.

Claims arise for a variety of reasons. There can be delays due to bad weather that were not anticipated in the contract, inefficiencies induced by owner conditions, and many other unexpected conditions and events that will cause a contractor to incur costs in excess of estimated costs. When such events occur and the contractor (or subcontractor) believes that the owner (or the general contractor) caused the occurrence of the overruns, the contractor will attempt to recover the excess costs through claims. Claims are becoming an increasingly prevalent part of the construction process as more owners are forcing contractors to resort to formal arbitration and litigation to collect on claims. Because claim amounts are often significant, they represent a high risk area in the financial statements.

Specific requirements must be met before a claim can be recognized as revenue. It must be probable that the claim will result in a change in contract price, and the amount must be reasonably estimable. In addition, four more conditions must exist to justify revenue recognition (TP 10,330.65):

1. Either a legal basis exists for the claim or a legal opinion has been otained indicating there is a reasonable basis for the claim.
2. The additional costs were caused by unanticipated circumstances and are not the result of performance deficiencies by the contractor.
3. Costs related to the claim are identifiable or determinable and are reasonable considering the work performed.
4. Evidence supporting the claim is both objective and verifiable.

If those conditions are met, the contractor may record the claim as a receivable and as revenue in its financial statements. The revenue from the claim should be equal to the net realizable value of the costs incurred under that claim. Costs attributable to the work performed should be treated as contract costs in the period incurred.

This method of claim accounting is intended to properly match revenues and costs, but because of the highly subjective nature of claims and the difficulty in determining their probable outcome, industry practice generally is to record claims when received or awarded, as a conservative approach.

Financial Reporting and Disclosure

A checklist for determining whether a contractor's financial statements and related disclosures are reasonably complete is presented in Appendix 36. Specific issues are covered in the following sections.

Balance Sheet Classification. Industry practice allows a construction company to classify contract-related assets and liabilities as current assets and current liabilities based on an operating cycle that conforms to the typical contract cycle of that entity. For example, if a contractor typically has an 18-month contract cycle, its contract-related items would be classified as current if they reasonably approximated that time frame. If the contractor used a traditional 12-month cycle, then certain of those contract related assets and liabilities would be classified as noncurrent. The AICPA Audit Guide, *Construction Contractors* (1981d), indicates that it is preferable for an entity that has an operating cycle of one year or less to use a classified balance sheet; if the entity has an operating cycle in excess of one year, an unclassified balance sheet should be used.

The typical contractor has an operating cycle that exceeds one year. However, in practice most of these companies elect to use classified balance sheets because credit grantors are accustomed to them, and because published industry statistics are based on classified balance sheet formats.

Deferred Income Taxes. Prior to TRA 1986, most contractors used the percentage-of-completion method for financial reporting purposes and the completed contract method for tax purposes. Accordingly, construction contractors recognized deferred income taxes in their financial statements as a result of these different methods.

TRA 1986 however, placed severe restrictions on the use of the completed contract method. Beginning with contracts entered into after February 28, 1986, TRA 1986 requires that construction contractors use either the percentage-of-completion method or the percentage-of-completion-capitalization-cost method (PCCCM) that limits the amount of tax-deferred income. While the percentage-of-completion method is based on the ratio of gross profit earned during the year to total expected gross profit, PCCCM is based on a combination of the percentage-of-completion method and the taxpayer's normal tax method of accounting (e.g., the completed contract method). The tax law allows small businesses with gross annual receipts of $10 million or less to use the completed contract method for tax purposes, provided their long-term contracts will be completed within two years.

For those companies that continue to use different methods of contract revenue recognition for financial reporting and tax purposes, SFAS 96, *Accounting for Income Taxes* (I25) states that the resulting temporary differences between the tax and financial reporting basis of assets and liabilities should be combined with all other temporary differences to determine any deferred tax that should be recognized at the balance sheet date. As more fully discussed in Chapter 17, deferred taxes are measured using the enacted tax law and rates in effect for the future years in which temporary differences are expected to reverse.

SFAS 37, *Balance Sheet Classification of Deferred Income Taxes* (superseded by SFAS 96), required classifying deferred taxes based on the current or noncurrent status of the item that gave rise to the timing difference. In the typical case of a contractor using an operating-cycle concept longer than 12 months for balance sheet classification, under SFAS 37 deferred taxes resulting from contract-related assets and liabilities were classified as current even though they would turn around beyond 12 months. This was also true for book/tax differences that had no related asset or liability. (For example, under percentage-of-completion accounting used for book purposes and completed contract method used for tax purposes, there will be untaxed income related to contract, not completed for tax purposes, even though all amounts due from the customer may have been paid and the contract closed out for financial reporting purposes.) SFAS 37 had required these deferred taxes to be classified as current if they were expected to turn around within the operating cycle used for balance sheet classification purposes.

SFAS 96 requires that deferred income taxes be classified as either current or noncurrent depending on the expected reversal date of the temporary difference. Classified as current are deferred taxes relating to:

1. Temporary differences related to an asset or liability classified as current because of an operating cycle longer than one year.
2. Temporary differences for which there is no related asset or liability, whenever other related assets and liabilities are classified as current because of an operating cycle longer than one year.

Inventories and Partial Payments. Inventories related to contracts are generally the result of costs accumulated under fixed price-type contracts accounted for under the completed contract method, and certain *output* measures for contracts accounted for under the percentage-of-completion method. Costs under cost-type contracts or fixed price-type contracts, which use *input* measures (such as cost-to-cost) to compute the percentage of completion, are generally displayed as unbilled receivables even though they are accumulated in inventory-type accounts.

Most contractors bill on contracts as promptly as practicable. Costs incurred under cost-type contracts are usually reimbursable, and therefore are billed as incurred. As work progresses, contractors often receive some payments on fixed price-type contracts in the form of progress payments, payments based on partial completion, or advance payments. The specific balance sheet description for accumulated costs and payments under fixed price-type contracts depends on the method of accounting used by the contractor.

Progress payments received on fixed price-type contracts should be applied first to amounts on individual contracts that are carried in unbilled receivables and then to accumulated costs of contracts in progress (inventory). Advance payments not related to work progress on a contract are reported similar to progress payments; however, if these advance payments exceed unbilled receivables and accumulated costs, the excess is classified as a liability.

Receivables. Receivables (both billed and unbilled) are generally segregated into amounts due on contracts in progress, amounts due on completed contracts, and retentions receivable. (Retentions or retainages are amounts withheld by a customer until certain conditions are met, as specified by the terms of the contract.) Unbilled amounts occur if sales or revenues, although appropriately recorded, cannot yet be billed under contractual terms, or if the price for work completed has not been determined.

Receivables on contracts are usually shown in the balance sheet separately from other receivables, or the separation is disclosed in a note. Unbilled amounts (net of progress payments) are stated separately if the amounts constitute a significant portion of receivables from contracts. The amount of progress payments offset against unbilled receivables should also be disclosed. This information gives the reader an idea of the relative liquidity of the contractor's receivables.

Over- and Underbillings. Amounts shown as overbillings (i.e., billings in excess of costs and estimated earnings on contracts in progress) should be reported as liabilities. Amounts recorded as underbillings (e.g., costs and estimated earnings in excess of related billings on contracts in progress) should be reported as assets.

Joint Ventures. Joint venturing in the construction industry is a typical way of bringing two contractors together for mutual benefit in the performance of a single project. Ventures are formed for a number of reasons; examples include a contractor who has the operational capacity to perform the job but needs bonding capacity to obtain a contract award, or a contractor moving to a new location to perform a job who needs a local contractor to provide the labor force and subcontractors.

Prior to issuance of the construction contractors audit guide in 1981, corporate joint ventures had been accounted for by contractors in several ways. A common practice was a hybrid accounting method in which the investment in the joint venture was accounted for as a single line item on the balance sheet, either current or noncurrent depending on the underlying contract terms. The joint venture revenues and expenses, however, were proportionately consolidated in the contractor's income statement; that is, if a contractor was a 50% partner, 50% of each line item amount in the joint venture's income statement was added to the related amount in the contractor's income statement. The Guide indicates that there have been at least five other methods also used in practice:

1. Full consolidation with the other venturer's interest shown as minority interest.
2. Partial or proportionate consolidation in which the contractor records its proportionate interest in the joint venture's assets, liabilities, revenues, and expenses on a line-by-line basis without distinguishing between the amounts related to the venture and those held directly by the venturer.
3. Expanded equity method in which the contractor presents its proportionate share of the venture's total assets and total liabilities segregated only by current and noncurrent portions.
4. Traditional equity method under APB 18 (I82).
5. Cost.

The Guide points out that corporate joint ventures are required, under APB 18 (I82), to be accounted for using the equity method. However, if the venture is both majority-owned and controlled, it is actually a subsidiary and should be treated like any other subsidiary. (Under SFAS 94 (C51), effective for 1988, as discussed in Chapter 24, majority-owned subsidiaries must be consolidated.)

It is very difficult in most construction joint ventures to determine which party is the controlling partner, particularly in 50/50 joint ventures. Such factors as the identification of the administrative partner, who is performing the bookkeeping, and who has the rights to incur debt on behalf of the joint venture, should be considered. For joint ventures in the form of general partnerships, the equity method is also the correct approach. However, for a bona fide undivided interest in an unincorporated joint venture, the proportionate consolidation method may be used in lieu of the equity method.

Note Disclosures. Typical note disclosures in the financial statements of contractors are discussed in the next two subsections.

Accounting policies. Contractors generally include a description of the following accounting practices in the disclosure of significant acccounting policies:

- Basis on which costs related to contracts in progress are stated (including accounting practice for indirect costs).
- Methods used to determine revenues and related costs (incuding policies for combining and segmenting contracts and the recognition of contract incentives).
- Methods used to measure progress toward completion on the percentage-of-completion method, or criteria specifically used to determine when a contract is substantially complete on the completed-contract method.
- Method of measurement (e.g., cost ratio method or the units of work method).
- Accounting policy for loss contracts.
- Operating cycle used in preparing the financial statements.
- Method of accounting for construction joint ventures, for example, proportionate consolidation, full consolidation, or equity method.
- Method of accounting for claims.

If an accrual method is used to account for claims, the audit guide recommends disclosure of the amount recorded and the gross amount. However, many contractors prefer not to disclose this information because they believe disclosure can jeopardize the likelihood of recovering their claims. If claims are accounted for on the cash basis, the amount of claims outstanding should be disclosed.

Other note disclosures. The following disclosures should also be included in the notes to the financial statements:

- Condensed financial statements of significant joint ventures, if any.
- Components of over- and underbillings on uncompleted contracts at the balance sheet date (typically, this includes billings to date, costs incurred, and estimated earnings, with a reconciliation to the net balance sheet impact of over- and underbillings).
- Backlog of contracts open at year end. (See Figure 36.5 for sample notes regarding backlog under the completed contract and percentage-of-completion methods.)

SEC requirements. Under Regulation S-X (Rule 5-02.3(c)), as augmented by ASR 164 (FRR § 206.02), contractors that are SEC registrants are required to disclose the following supplementary note explanation:

- Total amount retained by customers and the amount expected to be collected beyond one year. The SEC encourages registrants to disclose estimated collections by year if they are able to do so with reasonable accuracy based on experience or other factors. ASR 164 states that material amounts of retainage should be disclosed no matter when collection is expected.
- Receivables not billed or billable, and the amount to be collected beyond one year.
- Claim amounts included in billed or unbilled receivables, the collection of which is uncertain. Contractors that classify unbilled amounts as inventories should disclose the nature and status of such amounts, if material.
- ASR 164 requires registrants to provide reasonable estimates of costs, such as general and administrative, that are included in inventories.

PERCENTAGE-OF-COMPLETION METHOD

14. Backlog

The following schedule shows a reconciliation of backlog representing signed contracts, excluding fees from management contracts, in existence at December 31, 19X7 and 19X8:

Balance, December 31, 19X7	$24,142,600
Contract adjustments	1,067,100
New contracts, 19X8	3,690,600
	28,900,300
Less: Contract revenue earned, 19X8	22,432,500
Balance, December 31, 19X8	$ 6,467,800

In addition, between January 1, 19X9 and February 18, 19X9, the company entered into additional construction contracts with revenues of $5,332,800.

COMPLETED CONTRACT METHOD

7. Backlog

The estimated gross revenue on work to be performed on signed contracts was $4,691,000 at December 31, 19X8, and $3,617,400 at December 31, 19X7. In addition to the backlog of work to be performed, there was gross revenue, to be reported in future periods under the completed-contract method used by the company, of $2,460,000 at December 31, 19X8, and $2,170,000 at December 31, 19X7.

FIG. 36.5   Backlog Notes
Source: Construction Contractors (AICPA, 1981d).

Supplementary Information. It is also common to include as supplementary information certain analyses that credit grantors find useful. Such information may include an analysis of contracts open at year end and closed during the year, and a reconciliation to the income statement or earnings on those contracts. Also included may be an indication of the backlog of contracts not begun at year end. See Figures 36.6 and 36.7 for samples of supplementary disclosures frequently provided by construction contractors.

AUDIT CONSIDERATIONS

The initial focus of any audit engagement includes achieving an understanding of the client and its business, and the degree of professional risk associated with the engagement. The environment in which a contractor operates and the nature and duration of the contracts are significant determinants of audit risk.

In performing an audit of a construction contractor, the guidance contained in the AICPA Audit and Accounting Guides, *Construction Contractors* (1981d) and *Audits of Government Contractors* (exposure draft, 1987c) should be studied. Both guides contain useful information on contemporary audit issues in both segments.

PERCENTAGE CONTRACTORS INC.
Sechedule 1
Earnings from Contracts
Year Ended December 31, 19X8

	Revenues earned	Cost of revenues earned	Gross profit (loss)	Gross profit (loss)
Contracts completed during the year	$ 6,290,800	$ 5,334,000	$ 956,800	$ 415,300
Contracts in progress at year end	16,141,700	14,636,900	1,504,800	921,400
Management contract fees earned	121,600	51,800	69,800	1,700
Unallocated indirect and warranty costs		46,700	(46,700)	(38,100)
Minority interest in joint venture		128,000	(128,000)	(26,200)
Charges on prior year contracts		162,000	(162,000)	
	$22,554,100	$20,359,400	$2,194,700	$1,274,100

FIG. 36.6 Supplementary Information—Earnings From Contracts
Source: Construction Contractors (AICPA, 1981d).

The sections that follow merely highlight some of the more significant issues; in particular, there are many situations in which the auditor should obtain confirmations and make physical inspections, which should be determined by reference to the guides.

Audit Risk

As discussed earlier, the construction industry is typified by a high degree of risk. It is quite common for a significant portion of a contractor's equity to be "on the come," that is, arising from projects in progress. It also follows that if a contractor has more jobs closed and gross profit realized than jobs open with gross profit yet to come, the degree of risk associated with the financial statements is reduced, and therefore the audit will be easier.

The auditor's analysis focuses on the components of construction revenue and cost (on both open and closed contracts), on the estimating capabilities of the contractor, and on existing backlog, and relates these various components to the financial statements taken as a whole. All important contracts and related documents should be read to assure an understanding of the rights and obligations of each party.

Revenue Recognition

The audit of revenue recognition is a key element of the audit. The auditor must understand the measurement methods (e.g., cost-to-cost, units of work) and account

PERCENTAGE CONTRACTORS, INC.

Schedule 2: Contracts Completed, Year Ended December 31, 19X8

Contract Number	Type	Contract totals Revenues earned	Cost of revenues	Gross profit (loss)	Before January 1, 19X8 Revenues earned	Cost of revenues	Gross profit (loss)	During the year ended December 31, 19X8 Revenues earned	Cost of revenues	Gross profit (loss)
1511	B	$5,475,300	$4,802,500	$ 672,800	$3,223,400	$2,932,700	$290,700	$2,251,900	$1,869,800	$382,100
1605	A	695,000	880,900	(185,900)	596,100	558,100	38,000	98,900	322,800	(223,900)
1624	A	140,700	150,700	(10,000)	29,600	31,800	(2,200)	111,100	118,900	(7,800)
1711	A	2,725,100	2,391,700	333,400	1,654,100	1,510,000	144,100	1,071,000	881,700	169,300
1791	B	4,770,100	4,288,900	481,200	3,028,500	2,929,600	98,900	1,741,600	1,359,300	382,300
1792	A	635,000	457,900	177,100				635,000	457,900	177,100
Small contracts		413,400	349,500	63,900	32,100	25,900	6,200	381,300	323,600	57,700
		$14,854,600	$13,322,100	$1,532,500	$8,563,800	$7,988,100	$575,700	$6,290,800	$5,334,000	$956,800

Schedule 3: Contracts In Progress, December 31, 19X8

Contract Number	Type	Total contract Revenues	Estimated gross profit (loss)	From Inception to December 31, 19X8 Revenues earned	Total costs incurred	Cost of revenues	Gross profit (loss)	Billed to date	Estimated cost to complete	At December 31, 19X8 Costs and estimated earnings in excess of billings	Billings in excess of costs and estimated earnings	For the year ended December 31, 19X8 Revenues earned	Cost of revenues	Gross profit (loss)
1845	A	$6,750,200	$877,000	$5,890,500	$5,244,500	$5,143,900	$746,600	$5,976,000	$628,700	$15,100		$5,664,200	$4,984,500	$679,700
1847	B	1,471,800	127,100	1,250,400	1,139,800	1,139,800	110,600	1,195,800	204,900	54,600		962,800	899,000	63,800
1912	A	451,800	(130,100)	108,600	238,700	238,700	(130,100)	98,100	343,200	10,500		98,600	191,500	(92,900)
1937	B	11,125,000	847,900	7,337,900	7,045,500	6,721,100	616,800	7,808,000	3,231,600		$145,700	6,981,900	6,469,900	512,000
1945	A	3,650,100	497,000	2,395,200	2,061,300	2,061,300	333,900	2,491,500	1,091,800		96,300	2,395,200	2,061,300	333,900
Small contracts		51,300	8,400	49,800	41,700	41,700	8,100	49,800	1,200			39,000	30,700	8,300
		$23,500,200	$2,227,300	$17,032,400	$15,771,500	$15,346,500	$1,685,900	$17,619,200	$5,501,400	$80,200	$242,000	$16,141,700	$14,636,900	$1,504,800

Contract types
A – Fixed-price.   B – Cost-plus-fee.

FIG. 36.7   Supplementary Information—Contracts Completed and in Progress
Source: Construction Contractors (AICPA, 1981d)

ing methods (i.e., percentage-of-completion or completed contract) utilized by the contractor, and design tests of these methods. Tests of original contract amounts and the amounts of change orders are important elements in the audit of contract revenues.

Method of Accounting. Because the percentage-of-completion method and the completed contract method of accounting are not free-choice alternatives, the auditor needs to carefuly consider the specific circumstances in determining the appropriateness of the contractor's determinations.

In examining contracts accounted for by the percentage-of-completion method, the auditor's primary objective is to determine that income recognized during the current period is based on the total profit projected for the contract at completion and on work performed to date. Each component of total profit on a contract – final contract price, incentive fees and similar provisions, contract costs to date, and estimated cost to complete – should be tested.

The auditor should be satisfied that the methods used by the contractor to measure progress produces a reasonable measurement as to each different type of contract, and that contracts are properly combined by type for profit recognition purposes. In reviewing costs incurred to date when the cost-to-cost method is used, information obtained from contract cost records or correspondence files should be considered, as it may indicate that certain costs (e.g., advance billings by subcontractors or costs of undelivered or uninstalled materials) should be disregarded to accurately measure work performed to date. Contract billings to customers should generally approximate the physical percentage of completion, if the provisions of the contract require billings to correspond to progress on the contract.

The auditor's primary objective in examining contracts accounted for by the completed contract method is to determine that:

1. The amount and timing of profit recognition for completed contracts is proper.
2. The anticipated losses on uncompleted contracts are recognized in the current period.
3. The decision as to when a contract is considered to be complete is consistent.

Profit Center. Generally, each contract is a profit center for revenue recognition, cost accumulation, and income measurement, unless the contract or series of contracts meets the conditions for combining or segmenting contracts. Because combining or segmenting contracts may significantly affect periodic income recognition, the auditor should consider the circumstances, contract terms, and management intent in assessing compliance with the provisions in SOP 81-1 (TP 10,330.39–.41).

Internal Controls. A contractor's internal control structure should provide reliable information on the amount and timing of revenue recognition on contracts. Contract revenues are based on the terms of the contract and generally are related, at least indirectly, to contract costs. The following guidance on internal control objectives, included in the AICPA exposure draft, *Audits of Government Contractors* (1987c, ¶ 274) is also useful in evaluating the internal controls of construction contractors. The draft guide states that internal control should provide reasonable assurance that:

* Estimates of contract revenues and costs are periodically updated and reported to the appropriate levels of management.

* Revenue recognition is based on current estimates of progress in terms of cost incurred, physical completion, or other appropriate measure.

* Recorded contract revenues are periodically compared with contract terms for compliance.

* Change order and claim revenues are recognized in conformity with GAAP.

* Adjustments to recognized contract profits resulting from management decisions are thoroughly documented.

* The method used to estimate progress toward completion is reasonable, or reasonably reflects actual progress under the contract.

* Revenues recognized on all contracts during the period are reconciled to the total revenues reflected in the financial statements.

* Management reporting of estimate updates provides sufficient information to allow for the determination of whether a contract loss reserve is required.

Contract Costs

Cost information is used to control costs, to evaluate the status and profitability of contracts, and to prepare customer billings; therefore it must be accurate. For the auditor to become satisfied with the amount of revenue recognized, contract costs must also be subjected to detailed audit tests in most situations. Contract costs are therefore an element of revenue recognition calculations, because costs incurred to date are often part of the calculation.

Contract cost records should be designed so that actual costs can be compared with estimated costs. Costs should be classified and summarized by categories that are consistent with the contract cost or price estimate, such as materials, subcontract charges, labor, labor-related costs, equipment costs, and overhead.

Percentage-of-Completion Cost Components. In a job cost system, contractors typically accumulate costs by contract. If the contractor's job cost system, including subsystems that generate information affecting job costs (payroll, materials procurement, equipment, etc.), has adequate internal controls and such control procedures can be relied on, then a compliance-testing approach to costs incurred is appropriate. Otherwise, substantive tests would have to be performed to satisfy the auditor as to the accumulation of costs by contract. Adequate controls assure that:

* Distribution of costs to the contract for which they are incurred is accurate.
* Costs charged to a contract are reasonable and in accordance with its specific provisions.
* Cost accumulation is consistent with the manner in which the costs were estimated.
* The contractor's memorandum cost records, if any, are periodically reconciled to the formal accounting records.
* Costs incurred on all projects or contracts during the period are reconciled to costs presented in the financial statements.

Estimated Costs to Complete. The testing of estimated costs to complete, which by their very nature involve expectations of future performance, is often a complex, highly subjective aspect of the audit and involves representations of management. Further, the data available to test those representations may often be limited.

The auditor should first assess the relative risk factors, including performance risk and risk associated with the contract terms. For example, the financial exposure from an inaccurate estimate to complete is typically greater for fixed-price-type contracts than cost-reimbursement contracts. Also, there is generally greater exposure on fixed-price contracts for new, sophisticated projects because of uncertainty about their technological feasibility. Therefore, the auditor should understand estimation procedures, including:

1. The cost data available to the contractor when the bid was inititally prepared.
2. The development of cost data.
3. Whether estimates were updated to include changes based on actual experience as to cost, labor productivity, and scrap factors.
4. Whether the contractor assigns project managers to monitor specific contracts.

The auditor should also consider the level of involvement of management in the estimating process and the adequacy of follow-up procedures. The contractor should periodically review and revise, as appropriate, estimates of cost to complete throughout the year to the extent new information becomes available.

The auditor should perform analytical procedures as to the performance history of a contractor's estimating department and should determine whether previous years' estimates are close to or differ significantly from actual results.

General tests of the project's status at a point in time should also be performed. Such procedures typically include inquiries of project managers and engineers about product design and the status of contract performance. Additionally, current performance should be compared to anticipated future performance. Although the approach contractors take to estimating cost-to-complete may vary, the auditor must become satisfied that the approach used provides a result that:

1. Is systematic and consistent with the cost accumulation method, so that actual and estimated costs are comparable across periods.
2. Includes all significant elements of costs (i.e., quantities and prices utilized in the estimates associated with the project). The elements of cost that comprise the estimated costs to complete should include those same elements of cost that have actually been incurred to date.
3. Considers past experience and future prospects as to escalation in labor, material price, and indirect cost, particularly when the duration of the contract is over an extended period.

Progress Payments

Progress payments are the customer's way of financing work performed under fixed price-type contracts. Audit procedures in this area normally include reviewing subsequent cash receipts, obtaining reasonable assurance that costs included in billings were actually expended by the contractor, and reviewing activity in the progress payment accounts, including analysis of progress billings, progress payments received, and liquidation of the progress payment account.

Retentions

Contract provisions may permit the customer to withhold a defined amount or percentage of a contract price until certain conditions have been met. Sometimes, amounts are retained for long periods of time. To determine whether the contractor is making sufficient progress in satisfying the conditions necessary to ensure ultimate realization of retained amounts, the auditor should understand the basis for significant retentions and identify the conditions causing amounts to remain unpaid.

Change Orders and Claims

When a contractor recognizes revenue on unapproved change orders or claims, the auditor must evaluate the propriety of such recognition through discussions with the company's attorneys, job site personnel, and management. Further, if an approved change order or claim is recognized in the financial statements, it is imperative that the auditor be satisfied that the four criteria set forth in the construction contractors audit guide (TP 10,330.65) are met.

Substantial judgment by both contractors and auditors is required in accounting for and auditing a contractor's claims against a customer (or a subcontractor's claim against a prime contractor) resulting from unapproved change orders. Factors that affect the realization of claimed amounts recorded by a contractor are often very complex, and several years may be needed to resolve disputed matters. During that time, management may make decisions about such matters as settlement and litigation strategy. As a result, amounts recovered may differ substantially from amounts originally anticipated and recorded by the contractor.

The audit procedures to be performed will vary, depending on the circumstances. However, the auditor should consider the following procedures:

- Review and understand contract terms.
- Read and understand the claim document, and evaluate its overall validity.
- Obtain an opinion of the contractor's legal counsel.
- Determine what stage the dispute is in.
- Review and evaluate claim pricing methodology, including a challenge of the primary assumptions and underlying data, if practicable.
- Test the underlying cost data.

It is not unusual for a contractor to include in the claimed amount costs that ordinarily are not accumulated in the job cost system. Accordingly, it will be necessary for the auditor to be satisfied that the inclusion of such amounts is appropriate in the circumstances. Obviously, it is also important to evaluate the collectibility of any claim, because validity of the claim notwithstanding, if the customer is unable to pay or it is not feasible to otherwise pursue collection, it would be erroneous to recognize it.

Job Site Visits

A critical audit procedure in assessing the realizability of the contractor's estimates of cost to complete is a visit to all significant job sites. In a site visit it is important that the auditor discuss with the contractor's on-site personnel their understanding of the accounting and cost accumulation procedures. These discussions should also include a detailed review of those line items appearing on the job cost report that are used to assess progress.

The job-site manager's understanding of progress to date and remaining work are likely to provide significant insight into potential disputes. Existing disputes represent an automatic element of risk, because they may require the contractor to expend resources beyond those originally anticipated to complete performance under the contract; alternatively, disputes could impair the contractor's ability to collect for work completed and in progress.

The job-site manager can also identify unplaced subcontracts that could be material to the job. Subcontracts that have not yet been placed represent an additional risk if they cannot be contracted for at a price equal to or less than the estimate included in cost to complete.

Additionally, while at the job site, the auditor should be alert to its physical conditions and the quality of the accounting records. The job site manager's attention to accounting detail and organization of the work may allow the auditor to infer whether the job manager's estimates of cost to complete are reasonable.

Appendix 36
CONTRACTOR FINANCIAL STATEMENT CHECKLIST

BALANCE SHEET

Contracts

1. Are billed amounts on completed contracts shown separately from receivables and disclosed in a note if material?
2. Are costs and estimated earnings on contracts in progress in excess of billings shown separately and summarized in a separate note?
3. Are billings in excess of costs and estimated earnings on contracts in progress shown separately under current liabilities and summarized in a separate note?
4. Are over- and underbilling amounts shown gross rather than offset against each other?
5. Is there a separate detailed schedule of contracts in progress that reconciles to the amounts on the balance sheet for over- and underbillings?

Claims and Items in Dispute

1. Are amounts shown separately?
2. Is basis of accounting for items disclosed in the notes (including legal opinions and pass-through amounts to subcontractors)?

STATEMENT OF EARNINGS AND RETAINED EARNINGS

1. Are the components of revenue earned and cost of construction disclosed in a note and in the supplementary information?
2. Does this disclosure include a separation of revenue earned, cost, and gross earnings, on contracts closed and in progress? Are separate line items shown for unallocated indirect costs, and callbacks and adjustments?

NOTES TO FINANCIAL STATEMENTS

1. Does the accounting policies note include:
   a. Method of accounting for long-term contracts?
   - Revenue recognition method
   - Contract cost components
   - Revisions in estimates
   - Loss on contracts
   - Claims
   - Construction management contracts
   b. Definition of operating cycle?
   c. Allocation of indirect construction costs?
2. Is there a separate note detailing contracts in progress? This should include contract amounts, accumulated costs, estimated earnings and the related billing to date. Over-and underbillings should be shown separately in the note.
3. Is there a backlog reconciliation for the year? (Beginning balance plus new contracts and change orders less revenue earned for the year should equal the current backlog at year end.) Is the total of new contracts entered into after year end, but before the date of the accountant's report, disclosed in this note?

SUPPLEMENTARY INFORMATION

1. Is there a schedule of *Earnings from Contracts* (see, e.g., Figure 36.6) that shows the following detail as applicable?

   a. Contracts completed:
      Revenue earned, cost, gross earnings

   b. Contracts in progress:
      Revenue earned, cost, gross earnings

   c. Construction management contract fees earned:
      Revenue earned, cost, gross earnings

   d. Unallocated indirect costs

   e. Callbacks and adjustments

   f. Totals of revenue earned, cost, gross earnings

2. Is there a *Schedule of Contracts Completed* (see, e.g., Figure 36.7) that reconciles to the financial statements and provides the following details?

   a. Contract number and type

   b. Contract totals:
      - Revenue earned
      - Cost of construction
      - Gross earnings

   c. Prior to the current year:
      - Revenue earned
      - Cost of construction
      - Gross earnings

   d. During the current year:
      - Revenue earned
      - Cost of construction
      - Gross earnings

   Do the totals agree to the *Earnings from Contracts* schedule and the *Contracts in Progress* note?

3. Is there a schedule of *Contracts in Progress* (see, e.g., Figure 36.7) with the following details?

   a. Contract number, type, and current contract amount?

   b. Contract totals to date:
      - Revenue earned
      - Cost of construction
      - Gross earnings
      - Progress billings
      - Under (over) billings

   c. During the current year:
      - Revenue earned
      - Cost of construction
      - Gross earnings

      Do the totals agree to the *Earnings from Contracts* schedule and *Contracts in Progress* footnote?

4. Is future workload (backlog) disclosed in the following detail?
   - Backlog remaining
   - Estimated cost to complete

- Estimated gross earnings
- Work contracted for after year end but before date of accountant's report

5. Is there a schedule of *Indirect Construction Cost?*

If so, does the schedule separate costs by category, such as shop and yard, equipment, vehicles, benefits?

Does the allocation policy disclosed in the footnotes correspond with the disclosure in the schedule?

6. Is there a separate schedule of *Selling, General, and Administrative Expenses?*

37

Government Contracting

OVERVIEW

The U.S. government procures a wide variety of products and services ranging from mundane items such as clothing to esoteric items such as supercomputers. Thus government contractors are not restricted to defense procurement activities, but represent many businesses in many industries.

The extensive regulatory and cost accounting requirements placed on government contractors result in unique business risks and constraints. Many are caused by congressional oversight of the funding and review process. Contractors therefore must understand the legislative and regulatory requirements to operate effectively.

Environment

Fraud, Waste, and Mismanagement. Newspaper headlines draw attention to mischarges for labor, kickbacks, product substitution, false claims, and inflated spare parts prices. No company, large or small, is immune. As long as the defense budget is comparatively high, such publicity is not likely to abate.

Government agencies responsible for audits and investigations seem very busy in attacking procurement fraud, if measured by statistics. A recent report by the Government Accounting Office (GAO) reflects a significant increase in fraud investigations between 1983 (870 investigations) and 1986 (1,919 investigations). During GAO's review, 55 of the top defense contractors were being investigated in 274 cases of alleged procurement fraud. Most of the cases involved cost mischarging (133 cases), defective pricing (57 cases), and product substitution (25 cases). Additionally, GAO reports that suspensions and debarments nearly tripled from 1983 (280) to 1987 (898) (Federal Contracts Report). Even if no additional procurement fraud cases were to be initiated, the courts would be busy for years with the existing cases.

In addition to the increased activity by investigative agencies, noninvestigative organizations such as the Defense Contract Audit Agency (DCAA), which have extensive day-to-day dealings with contractors, have increased their efforts to identify possible cases of wrongdoing.

Public opinion polls show that 70% of the taxpayers believe the government is commonly being overcharged by contractors. Almost 60% of those polled believe that the culprits should be barred from additional contracts or have current contracts cancelled. Congressional hearings highlighting charges for public relations and other "questionable" expenditures have only added to the "rip off" perception.

The Major Fraud Act of 1988 (HR 3911) was passed by the House of Representatives in May and is expected to pass the Senate before the 1988 presidential election. The provisions of the bill include

* Payment of up to $250,000 to persons supplying information that leads to criminal convictions.
* Job protection for informants.
* Mandatory minimum two-year prison sentence if the violation involves a "foreseeable and substantial risk of personal injury" (as might be the case with items substituted for contracted products).
* Extension of the statute of limitations for procurement fraud from 5 to 7 years.

Any chance of significantly moderating the severe provisions of HR 3911 are dim as the result of developments during mid-1988. A "scandal" was uncovered allegedly involving overpayments to contractors based on improper data submitted to and knowingly approved by government procurement officers. The ongoing investigation could affect many contractors; and this has prompted the SEC to issue FRR 32, *Statement of the Commission Regarding Disclosure Obligations of Companies Affected by the Government's Defense Contract Procurement Inquiry and Related Issues*. This FRR does not actually say anything that is not already in SEC disclosure requirements: it admonishes registrants to disclose the possible or anticipated effects, if they could be material. However, the fact that FRR 32 was released is evidence that the present investigation is a very serious one.

The number of dishonest contractors is probably minor in relation to the many thousands of companies doing work for the government. Most cases considered to be wrongdoing may not be deliberate acts of fraud, but may be the result of mistakes, carelessness, sloppy bookkeeping, lax controls, and well-intended deeds gone astray.

What changes from time to time are the criteria for deciding which activities will be prosecuted as criminal acts rather than settled administratively. Accordingly, government contractors should be fully aware of practices that may be considered improper — or merely appearances of wrongdoing—and the potential penalties involved. Contractors also should be familiar with government review techniques so that self-reviews can be performed and a prevention program established.

Investment Requirements. Federal budget pressures are causing Congress to require increased investment by contractors and to forestall additional cash outlays by the government. Most prime contractors, to varying degrees, have the capacity to invest and risk their capital to obtain potentially large production contracts that will "pay off" over 10 to 20 years. However, these pressures may reduce the participation of smaller government contractors that may not be willing or able to risk their companies based on long-term prospects. As a result, two major changes are evolving in the government contracting business: (1) more joint ventures among prime contractors to spread the investment risk; and (2) subcontractors stepping up to the investment challenge to keep prime contractors from assuming all the work. If these changes do not mature there could be an erosion of the strong contractor and subcontractor base that historically has been an important source of technology and innovation for the government.

Regulatory Changes. Increased regulation by governmental agencies has been a side effect of the large buildup of defense spending in the 1980s. The government's emphasis on fraud, waste, and mismanagement over the past several years has created an environment in which the integrity of many contractors is routinely questioned by the government and the media. Some contractors may deserve to be criticized. However, many companies doing business with the government are caught in the backlash of adverse publicity, and face increased regulatory oversight from government agencies and Congress.

In the usual commercial environment, contract negotiations focus on price, not on cost or profit. Several competing proposals from Congress, the DoD, and the private sector are likely to result in legislation that will ultimately limit contractors' profits. Past profit studies sponsored by the DoD have, in the analysis of many interested parties, produced inconclusive results as to the "right" amount of profit, because profits from doing business with the government are being compared to commercial profits.

In addition, vigorous pursuit of violations of the Truth in Negotiations Act, which requires contractors to submit to the government details about costs to be incurred during performance of a negotiated contract, remains an important government device to guard against alleged profiteering by some contractors.

Private Sector Initiatives. The most notable private sector initiative was the work of the Packard Commission, whose report was finalized in 1986. Besides recommending numerous changes in procurement policy, the Commission recommended that the industry be responsive to criticism of its business practices. The result was the Defense Industry Initiatives (Aerospace Industries Association, 1986), under which companies voluntarily agreed to have their ethics programs reviewed by CPAs and reported on to a third party. As of late 1987, approximately 40 companies had signed up for an annual review for a three-year period. In the future, either more companies will have to voluntarily sign up for the program or it may become mandatory.

Export Sales. Many government contractors are well positioned to export products to a worldwide customer base and have, in fact, been major contributors in moderating the large U.S. trade deficit. Competition from developing countries, however, is pressuring contractors into finding new markets for export sales. To the extent trade protection legislation is enacted, the task becomes even more difficult. Joining with non-U.S. partners in manufacturing products for foreign markets is one approach that is increasingly being used.

Technology transfer is also a major issue in the exporting of high-tech products, and national security concerns must be weighed against the need to export.

Procurement Process

The U.S. government is one of the largest purchasers of goods and services in the world. Companies contracting with the federal government encounter situations not common in commercial contracting. As a customer, the federal government is different; it conducts its procurement activities under a specific group of laws and regulations.

The government purchases many standard commercial items sold in large quantities to the general public. However, the majority of procured goods and services are items required only by the government. Prices for those items are generally not available and must be determined by other factors, such as the estimated cost to produce the product or provide the service, plus a profit for the supplier. Most regulations for pricing government contracts focus on measurement of factors involved in the pricing determination.

Competition is an important factor used to control federal procurement costs. The two most commonly used methods of procurement are sealed bidding and competitive proposals. Sealed bidding consists of the issuance of an Invitation for Bids, which specifies the product or service needed. Contractors respond with sealed bids, which are opened publicly. The contract is generally awarded to the lowest price bidder. Competitive proposals are submitted in response to a Request for Proposal or Request for Quote. The government then negotiates with individual respondents. Noncompetitive proposals may be utilized if

- There is only one responsible source of goods or services;
- There is an urgent need to obtain the goods or services;
- The services are by nature experimental or developmental;
- There are international agreements to provide the services;
- The procurements are authorized or required by statute;

- It is a matter of national security; or
- It is in the "public interest."

The government uses several types of contracts, discussed in the next section. The type of contract used has a direct effect on the extent of the government's financial review and surveillance. The government generally has little interest in the contractor's accounting practices if the contract has been awarded under sealed bid procedures and if the final contract price will be unaffected by the cost of performance. However, if costs incurred are a factor in establishing how much the government will pay, the contract generally gives the buyer the right to review the contractor's books and records.

When a contractor responds to a procurement notice, the buying agency evaluates the proposal for its responsiveness to the request and reviews the contractor's background. A contractor should address all important terms in its proposal. The contractor selected is not necessarily the one offering the lowest price, because the compelling factors discussed above often weigh heavily in the procurement decision.

To prepare for negotiations, the contracting officer requests an evaluation of the cost and pricing data submitted by the contractor. All relevant facts that can be reasonably expected to contribute to assessing the soundness of estimates of future costs are included in the proposal evaluations. The evaluations are generally performed by the government's contract audit personnel, and involve verifying historical or forecasted cost data and evaluating the cost estimating techniques. The contract auditor also determines whether the methods used to estimate costs and actual practices used to accumulate costs differ significantly. Consistency in estimating and accounting procedures is a requirement of the procurement regulations.

Negotiating pricing arrangements is a critical step in the procurement process. The contract type determines the amount of risk each party assumes. A fixed-price contract without definite specifications for what is to be delivered may result in significant financial exposure to a contractor. The federal procurement system is based on the premise that the greater the risk assumed by the contractor, the greater the earnings potential. Therefore, the appropriate contract type for a given procurement is intended to achieve a proper balance between risk and profit.

Contract Types. Numerous types of contracts are found in the government procurement process. The most frequently used types are described below.

Contracts based on cost. The following contracts are tied to costs incurred by the contractor:

- Cost sharing. The contractor is reimbursed only for an agreed-upon portion of costs incurred without a provision for a fee.
- Cost-without-fee. The contractor is reimbursed for costs without a fee.
- Cost-plus-fixed-fee. The contractor is reimbursed for costs plus a fixed fee.
- Cost-plus-award-fee. The contractor is reimbursed for costs plus a fee, which usually consists of two parts: a fixed amount that does not vary based on performance, and an amount based on performance measures of quality, timeliness, ingenuity, and cost-effectiveness.
- Cost-plus-incentive-fee. The contractor is reimbursed for costs plus a fee that is adjusted by a formula based on the ratio of total allowable costs to target costs.

Fixed-price contracts.

• Firm fixed-price. The price is not subject to adjustments based on cost experience.

• Fixed-price incentive. An initial firm target cost and profit, a price ceiling (but not a profit ceiling or floor), and a formula for determining final profit and price, are established based on the relationship between the final negotiated total cost and the total target cost.

• Fixed-price, providing for performance incentives. This type incorporates incentives to the contractor to surpass stated product performance targets; it provides for increases in profit to the extent that such targets are surpassed and for decreases to the extent that such targets are not met.

• Fixed-price level-of-effort. The contractor is obligated to devote a specified level of effort, usually calling for investigation or study in a specific research and development area over a stated period of time, for a fixed dollar amount.

Other types of contracts. Some government contracts may be based on the following arrangements:

• Time and material. The contractor is paid a fixed hourly rate for direct-labor hours expended. The rate includes direct labor, indirect expenses, and profit. The actual cost of materials or other specified items is usually added.

• Letter contract. This approach may be used to authorize the contractor to start work before the final contract has been awarded. The final contract must be negotiated as soon as possible.

• Basic ordering agreement. This agreement describes the supplies or services the contractor will provide and the method by which the price will be determined. The agreement sets forth the terms and conditions of delivery and the activities for which purchase orders may be issued pursuant to the basic agreement.

Evolution in Procurement Approaches. The vast differences in the missions and needs of the various government departments and agencies, the large number of federal employees engaged in contracting activities, and the myriad of regulations, all contribute to the difficulties encountered in contracting with the federal government. As a result, there is no typical government contract.

Many goods and services can be, and are, acquired through formal advertising or negotiation on a competitive basis, and most government contracts are competitively awarded. However, a major portion of procurements for large contracts, especially in the DoD, historically have been awarded under limited competition or to sole source vendors.

The growing federal deficit and defense budget have increased pressures on the government to award contracts competitively and reduce costs. The federal government has responded by increasing competition, reducing the number of sole source contracts, and implementing new and revised regulations (such as the 1987 changes in the *Weighted Guidelines Method* for profit calculations). Regulations that require contractors to assume more risks and absorb more costs have been promulgated. Examples are the requirements for contractors to finance up to 50% of all special tooling and test equipment and to absorb a sizable portion of costs in a development contract on the gamble of being awarded a large production contract. Additionally, many types of contracts, including R&D contracts, which had been awarded on a cost reimbursement basis, are now awarded under fixed price arrangements.

   Profit limitations. Profit generally is a proportionately small but significant component of negotiated prices. The *Weighted Guidelines Method* was promulgated in 1963 in an effort to offer contractors opportunities for higher profits as a motivation for better performance and lower costs charged to the government. Since 1963, the government has been fine-tuning its profit policy and experimenting with various methods to move the emphasis from costs incurred to capital invested.

   The latest experiment went into effect in mid-1987, applicable to all contracts valued at $500,000 or more. It is a process under which the government evaluates a contractor and a proposal against specific criteria stated in the regulation and assigns percentage weights and values to the following categories: contract performance risk, contract type risk, and facilities investment. The government and the contractor agree on a profit percentage based on those weights and percentages. The guideline does not apply to

* Nonnegotiated contracts
* Architectural and engineering contracts
* Construction contracts
* Termination settlements
* Cost-plus-award-fee contracts
* Not-for-profit organizations
* Preexisting contracts

The major change in the 1987 profit policy is the emphasis on facilities capital and the elimination of profit on general and administrative expenses (G&A), bid and proposal costs, and R&D.

   Advance Payments. The government generally considers advance payments to be the least preferable method of contract financing. However, advance payments may be considered useful and appropriate for the following types of contracts:

* Contracts for experimental, research, or development work with not-for-profit educational or research institutions.
* Contracts for managing and operating government-owned plants.
* Contracts for acquisition of facilities for government ownership.
* Highly classified contracts under which assignment of claims would be undesirable for national security reasons.
* Contracts entered into with financially weak contractors whose technical ability is essential.

   Progress Payments. Progress payments are the most common type of government financing. Progress payments are intended to help finance a contractor's performance and reduce the contractor's investment in work-in-process inventory. As a result, the government benefits by obtaining lower competitive prices from contractors that do not incur high commercial financing rates. For civilian agencies, the rates of progress payments are 80% for large businesses and 85% for small businesses.

Contractors may request progress payments monthly through the life of the contract until the maximum allowable percentage has been reached, as long as the payments represent progress made under the contract. The government's interest is protected by having vested title to the inventory related to progress payments. Contractors must certify that they have not encumbered that property.

Contractors begin repaying (liquidating) their obligation to the government as soon as deliveries and invoicing begin. The liquidation rate is usually the same as the progress payment rate.

Flexible progress payments, unique to DoD, were designed to allow the rate of progress payments to be tailored to the contractor's cash flow requirements. For the purpose of flexible progress payments, cash needs are measured and projected in relation to the contractor's investment in the underlying work-in-process inventory over the life of the contract. The total investment is measured by a weighted average of total costs to be incurred by the contractor to complete performance of the contract, and the contractor's investment (set at 25%) in the weighted-average amount not yet paid by the government. Flexible progress payments are available on negotiated fixed price contracts exceeding $1 million that will be performed in the United States and for which contractors have submitted certified cost or pricing data.

The government may also guarantee a loan made by a private financial institution to a defense contractor. The guarantee will usually call for sharing the lender's loss (if this should occur) rather than covering it fully.

Regulation

Federal Acquisition Regulation. On April 1, 1984, the Federal Acquisition Regulation (FAR) replaced the Federal Procurement Regulation, the Defense Acquisition Regulation, and the NASA Procurement Regulation. FAR established a single regulation for use by all executive agencies in their acquisition of supplies and services with appropriated funds.

FAR states that all contracts and contract modifications for supplies and services or experimental, developmental, or research work, which are negotiated with commercial organizations based on incurred costs, must adhere to the FAR cost principles and procedures. Those cost principles must be used to: (1) price negotiated contracts for supplies, services, experimentation, development, and research; and (2) modify contracts with commercial organizations whenever cost analysis is performed in the procurement process. In addition, the use of FAR is mandatory when:

- Determining reimbursable costs under cost-reimbursement contracts and subcontracts, and the cost-reimbursement portion of time-and-material contracts;
- Negotiating overhead rates;
- Claiming, negotiating, or determining costs under terminated fixed-price and cost reimbursement contracts;
- Establishing the final price of fixed price incentive contracts;
- Redetermining prices of prospective and retroactive price redetermination contracts; and
- Pricing changes in other contract modifications.

Under FAR, the total cost of a contract is the sum of the allowable direct and indirect costs allocable to the contract, incurred or to be incurred, less allocable credits, if any, and any allocable cost of money. In ascertaining what constitutes a cost, any generally accepted method of determining or estimating costs that is equitable and is consistently applied may be used, including standard costs properly adjusted for applicable variances.

A uniform accounting system or method of determining total cost is neither suggested nor mandated by FAR. That is, contractors are free to develop and use the type of accounting system they deem appropriate to properly reflect the financial results of their operations, including methods of differentiating direct and indirect costs, the number and content of overhead cost pools, and the method of allocating such overhead costs to cost objectives. A contractor's freedom to develop its own accounting system to determine total cost is, however, limited by Cost Accounting Standards Board (CASB) promulgations, as well as the concepts presently appearing in FAR.

Cost Accounting Standards. The Defense Production Act amendments of 1970 included provisions for the establishment of the CASB. The Board was created to promulgate uniform cost accounting standards[1] for negotiated defense contracts, in response to

- Inconsistent accounting practices used by contractors;
- Too much flexibility in cost accounting under GAAP and Armed Services Procurement Regulations; and
- High volume of negotiated contracts and defense spending.

The CASB went out of existence in 1980, but 19 Cost Accounting Standards (CAS) remain in effect. They are listed in Figure 37.1, grouped according to their basic purposes.

Coverage. Unless exempt, a contractor's first negotiated defense contract or subcontract of over $500,000 is subject to all of the standards. Additional defense contracts of $100,000 or more will also be covered.

There are two types of CAS-covered contracts, full coverage and modified coverage. Full coverage means that a business unit must comply with all 19 standards listed in Figure 37.1. Contracts with foreign companies are only subject to CAS 401 and 402. Contracts awarded to business units that received less than $10 million in covered contracts in the preceding cost accounting period and the amount of which is less than 10% of the business unit's total sales during that period, are subject to modified coverage and therefore must comply only with Standards 401 and 402.

---

[1] Under CAS § 331.20(k), a cost accounting practice is "any disclosed or established accounting method or technique which is used for measurement of cost, assignment of cost to cost accounting periods, or allocation of cost to cost objectives."

System constraints

CAS 401   Consistency in Estimating, Accumulating, and Reporting Costs

CAS 402   Consistency in Allocating Costs Incurred for the Same Purpose

CAS 405   Accounting for Unallowable Costs

CAS 406   Cost Accounting Period

Assigning costs to accounting periods

CAS 404   Capitalization of Tangible Assets

CAS 408   Accounting for Costs of Compensated Personal Absence

CAS 409   Depreciation of Tangible Capital Assets

CAS 412   Composition and Measurement of Pension Cost

CAS 413   Adjustment and Allocation of Pension Cost

CAS 414   Cost of Money as an Element of the Cost of Facilities Capital

CAS 415   Accounting for the Costs of Deferred Personal Compensation

CAS 416   Accounting for Insurance Costs

CAS 417   Cost of Money as an Element of the Cost of Capital Assets Under
            Construction

Assigning costs to cost objectives within a period

CAS 403   Allocation of Home Office Expenses to Segments

CAS 407   Use of Standard Costs for Direct Materials and Direct Labor

CAS 410   Allocation of Business Unit General and Administrative Expenses to Final
            Cost Objectives

CAS 411   Acquisition Costs of Material

CAS 418   Allocation of Direct and Indirect Costs

CAS 420   Accounting for Independent Research and Development and Bid and
            Proposal Costs

FIG. 37.1   Current Cost Accounting Standards

CAS 401 requires the contractor to accumulate and report costs on the same basis it uses in preparing cost estimates for contract-bidding purposes. In flexibly priced contracts, this prevents the contractor from bidding low on the basis of one cost accounting practice and then charging higher amounts to the government on the basis of some other practice. CAS 401 also requires the contractor to prepare cost estimates on the same basis it expects to use in accumulating costs. For fixed-price contracts, this prevents the contractor from preparing a cost estimate based on one practice when it expects to account for its costs through some other practice that would allocate fewer costs to that contract. An example of a cost accounting practice that is inconsistent with CAS 401 is the estimation of labor costs by function (e.g., assembly, machining) when such costs will be accumulated in a single account without distinguishing between functions.

CAS 402 forbids double counting:

> each type of cost is [to be] allocated only once and on only one basis to any contract or other cost objective. . . . All costs incurred for the same purposes, in like circumstances, are either direct costs only or indirect costs only with respect to final cost objectives.

An example of double counting is the charging of any kind of cost such as travel, supervision, or quality control directly to a contract when other travel, supervision, or quality control costs incurred in like circumstances are treated as indirect costs.

Nondefense contracts subject to CAS must have the same type of CAS coverage as the most recently awarded national defense contract currently being performed by the same business unit.

Exemptions. Prime contractors and subcontractors are exempt under the law if the price negotiated is based on established catalog or market prices of commercial items sold in substantial quantities to the general public or on prices set by law or regulation. While adequate price competition is not a criterion for an exemption for prime contracts, it is a criterion for firm fixed-price subcontracts if the following four conditions are met: (1) all competing firms are solicited identically, (2) a minimum of two offers are received from unaffiliated firms, (3) price is the only consideration in selecting the successful contractor, and (4) the lowest offer is accepted.

Some types of contracts are specifically exempted from CAS. The most significant include:

* Firm fixed-price contracts or subcontracts awarded without submission of cost data (as long as that omission is not attributable to a waiver of the requirement for certified cost or pricing data).
* Contracts with businesses that qualify as small business concerns under the Small Business Administration regulations.
* Contracts with U.K. contractors for performance substantially in the U.K. as long as the contractors have filed completed disclosure statements with the U.K. Ministry of Defence, which are in accord with U.K. government accounting conventions.
* Contracts with foreign governments.
* Certain contracts with educational institutions.

Disclosure statement. A disclosure statement is a written description of a contractor's established cost accounting practices and procedures, which must be used in determining costs under affected government contracts.

A company seeking the award of a defense prime contract or subcontract greater than $10 million but that has not previously submitted a CAS disclosure statement must submit such a statement with its cost proposal or, with the approval of the contracting officer, within 90 days after the contract has been awarded. In addition, if the company has received CAS-covered negotiated defense (but not nondefense) prime contracts or subcontracts exceeding $10 million during its most recently completed cost accounting period, it is required to file a disclosure statement within 90 days of the close of the fiscal year.

The disclosure statement contains a great deal of detail and covers general information about certification, direct costs, indirect costs, direct versus indirect costs, depreciation and capitalization practices, other costs and credits, pension costs, deferred compensation and insurance costs, and corporate/group expenses.

Disclosure statements must be revised to reflect requirements of new standards, to correct noncompliant practices, and to reflect "changes in cost accounting practices" agreed to by the contracting parties.

The responsible Administrative Contracting Officer reviews and approves all disclosure statements and revisions based on the advice of the DCAA.

Truth in Negotiations Act. The Truth in Negotiations Act was enacted into law by Congress in 1962. The Act and its provisions on defective pricing, which have been strengthened over the years, are an important means of guarding against alleged profiteering by contractors. Its objective is to put government negotiators on a par with contractors by requiring contractors to disclose cost or pricing information.

The Act requires contractors involved in negotiated procurements to submit details about costs expected to be incurred while performing on contracts, and to certify that the data is current, accurate, and complete on the date of the certification. To the extent that the certification is erroneous, and the use of such data causes the contract price to be greater than it would otherwise be, the government gets a lower contract price under a price reduction clause. It should be noted that contractors are not required to use the disclosed information in developing prices. Contractors can exercise their best judgment in establishing costs and developing prices. Not using the data in developing a price *is not* defective pricing. However, not disclosing the fact that such data was available, even if the contractor decided it was not useful in pricing, *is* defective pricing.

Applicability. The defective pricing provisions of the Truth in Negotiations Act that apply to government agencies and their contractors cover

• Negotiated prime contracts over $100,000;
• Prime contract modifications or changes over $100,000;
• Negotiated subcontracts over $100,000 at any tier, if the prime contract and any upper-tier subcontract provided for submission of cost and pricing data; and
• Subcontract modifications or changes over $100,000 at any tier, if the prime contract and all upper-tier subcontracts provided for cost and pricing data.

The defective pricing provisions for modifications or changes in contracts or subcontracts can also reach contracts that were initially the result of sealed-bid procedures. This reflects the government's overall concern that competition does not necessarily result in a reasonable price. When a contractor modifies a contract, there is no "real" competition, leading the government to seek the assurances provided by disclosure of data.

Exemptions. The Act exempts contracts and subcontracts from disclosure even for awards over $100,000 if the price is based on one of the following conditions:

• Adequate price competition.
• Established catalog market prices of commercial items sold in substantial quantities to the general public.
• Prices set by law or regulations.
• Exceptional cases in which the head of an agency determines that the requirements may be waived and the reasons are stated in writing.

Price Reductions. To enforce the obligations of contractors to disclose cost or pricing data, the Truth in Negotiations Act provides for a price reduction for defective pricing if cost or pricing data was inaccurate, incomplete, or noncurrent.

This statutory provision and its regulatory implementation have been the subject of many decisions from the U.S. Claims Court and the Board of Contract Appeals. Those decisions must be considered to understand the full magnitude of a contractor's responsibility for disclosure.

Subcontract considerations. The government's right to lower the prime contract price extends to situations in which the price was greater because a subcontractor provided defective cost or pricing data. FAR rules governing submission of data require the prime contractor to submit cost or pricing data for (1) proposed subcontracts of $1 million or more and (2) proposed subcontracts of $100,000 or more if they are also greater than 10% of the prime contract price. The same exemptions that apply to prime contractors apply also to prospective and actual subcontractors for each component, as long as the prime contractor's subcontract estimate is based on that subcontractor's data. Those requirements flow down to all tiers, that is, the data of a first-tier prospective subcontractor must include data from the most likely second-tier subcontract, which is (1) over $1 million or (2) over $100,000 and greater than 10% of the price of the first-tier subcontract.

The prime contractor and the higher-tier subcontractors all have a responsibility to review and evaluate cost or pricing data of prospective and actual subcontractors, which is included as part of the prime contractor's cost or pricing submission to the government.

FAR requires the prime contractor to "flow down" this standard contract clause in its subcontracts to obtain cost or pricing data from actual subcontractors (1) before any subcontract expected to exceed $100,000 is awarded and (2) before the pricing of any subcontract modification involving aggregate increases or decreases in costs (plus applicable profits) that are expected to exceed $100,000, except if the standard exemptions apply.

Under the FAR, the prime contractor is responsible for defective data submitted by a subcontractor. To protect itself, a prime contractor may negotiate the inclusion of an indemnification clause for defective pricing in its subcontracts.

Government's burden of proof. The government bears the burden of proof to show entitlement to a price cut under the price reduction clause of the contract. Basically, the government must prove the following:

• An executed "Certificate of Current Cost Pricing Data" exists.
• The information provided by the contractor fits the definition of cost or pricing data and existed before the price agreement.
• Current, accurate, and complete data was reasonably available to the contractor before the price agreement.
• Current, accurate, and complete data was not submitted to the contracting officer or an authorized representative and the government did not have actual knowledge of the data.
• The government relied on the defective data in its negotiations with the contractor.

• The government's reliance on the defective data caused the contract price to be greater than it otherwise would have been.

Each of the burden-of-proof criteria has evolved over time, primarily from case law interpretation.

Defense Contract Audit Agency Reviews. The DCAA acts as financial adviser to the contracting officer. Organizationally, DCAA was placed outside the procurement organizations to make it independent from the influence of contract decision-makers. DoD internal audit agencies review procurement files to ensure that DCAA advice is properly considered in contract dealings. This arrangement is intended to provide a system of checks and balances. DCAA is not expected or encouraged to criticize contracting officer actions.

In 1978, most federal agencies were required by law to establish an Office of the Inspector General (IG). For non-DoD agencies, this meant that existing internal audit, contract audit, and investigative organizations were merged. The IG has reporting responsibilities to both the department head and Congress. This dual reporting approach raises an obvious concern for contractors audited by a non-DoD IG: Are the reviewers performing a routine audit, or an investigation?

Pressure to change the DCAA's role has come from all sides. Congress considered including the DCAA in the IG organization and has drafted legislation on numerous occasions. The non-DoD IGs who used DCAA services pressed for an audit scope beyond the routine contract audit function. When the Justice Department used DCAA auditors to perform services on key and complex accounting fraud cases, it discovered that DCAA was an excellent resource. These forces have created subtle shifts in the DCAA organization, reflected in DCAA's ability to use subpoena powers, its influence on the modification of audit programs, a closer cooperation with investigative organizations, and a change in referrals of potential acts of wrongdoing.

Although the DCAA's continuing official position is that it does not look for wrongdoing, this is not necessarily the case. In areas with the highest visibility—defective pricing, for example—DCAA has added specific steps to its audit programs to determine if any wrongdoing might have occurred. Although only changes in the defective pricing audit program have received publicity, it may be assumed that other key audit areas have also been affected.

Closer DCAA cooperation with investigative organizations and other elements within the DoD IG office is obvious. High-level DCAA personnel are assigned as full-time liaison to the Defense Procurement Fraud Unit; and DCAA participates in joint reviews with non-DoD IGs and internal audit organizations.

For many years, DCAA never forwarded reports of potential wrongdoing to an investigative agency without a review by DCAA headquarters' general counsel. The Justice Department and other investigative officials objected to this practice as a delay tactic in initiating investigations. As a result, DCAA local auditors have been authorized to notify investigative organizations of possible fraudulent activities, referring to suspicious situations simply as "possible irregular activity." Field auditors' referrals are processed through the chain of command to DCAA headquarters, including the DCAA general counsel. In the late 1970s, about 25 referrals were made annually; by 1987 a level of more than 10 times that number had been reached.

To avoid the accusation of being "contractor friendly," as Congress has claimed, DCAA started several programs, such as the following, to improve its image as the defense-dollar "watchdog":

• Defective pricing guidelines and audit frequency have been expanded.

• DCAA has submitted numerous proposed cost principles to the FAR Committee to address areas that DCAA believes contractors tend to abuse.

• Making agreements with contractors for access to specific records has been cast aside in favor of a policy aimed at total access.

Selection of Contracts for Audit. All contracts and subcontracts over a specific dollar amount and a judgmental sample below that level are reviewed. The sample selection criteria are complex, and include whether the contractor is considered a major contractor, how much confidence DCAA has in the contractor's estimating system, and the DCAA's annual office quotas. Other influencing factors include higher than proposed profits, costs from operations proposed but never begun, and vendor refunds. DCAA also responds to requests for defective pricing reviews from contracting officers regardless of these criteria.

ACCOUNTING AND FINANCIAL REPORTING ISSUES

Industry Audit Guide

The AICPA Audit and Accounting Guide, *Audits of Government Contractors* (current edition 1983d, initially issued in 1975), is under revision. The exposure draft (AICPA, 1987) addresses the many changes that have occurred in the government contracting environment in the intervening 12 years.

The objectives of the Guide are to provide general background on the industry and to assist independent accountants in dealing with accounting, auditing, and financial reporting issues related to government contractors. The revised Guide is expected to be finalized near the end of 1988. A significant portion of the discussion that follows in this chapter is based on the draft guide.[2]

Basic Accounting Issues in Contracting

Defense contracts tend to be long-term in nature, requiring management to evaluate relatively long-term activities and allocate the anticipated outcome to intervening accounting periods. The process is complicated by the use of significant management estimates for total contract revenues and costs, and by the measurement of actual progress made toward completion of each contract. Accordingly, in accounting for contracts, a basic accounting policy decision must be made as to which generally

---

[2] All references to the exposure draft are cited by paragraph number only. Contractor accounting principles are also found in SOP 81-1, *Accounting for the Performance of Construction-Type and Certain Production-Type Contracts* (TP 10,330). This SOP for the most part is covered in Chapter 36. "Construction Contractors," which should be referred to for additional details.

accepted method is applicable: the percentage-of-completion method or the completed contract method.

SOP 81-1, *Accounting for Performance of Construction-Type and Certain Production-Type Contracts* (TP 10,330), deals with the principal accounting issues facing contractors generally and provides guidance on the application of GAAP to contracts for which specifications are provided by the customer. The major issues covered by the SOP, which are also relevant to accounting by government contractors, are discussed in Chapter 36. In particular, the following sections of that chapter should be consulted on matters of common interest to both construction and government contracting:

* Accounting methods
  - Percentage-of-completion method[3]
  - Completed contract method
  - Selection of method
* Profit center determination
  - Combining contracts
  - Segmenting contracts
* Progress measurement
  - Cost estimates
  - Computing income earned
  - Contract incentives
  - Contract losses
* Construction costs
* Contract price
  - Change orders
  - Claims

Program Method. The program method, rather than the percentage-of-completion method, sometimes has been used with production-type contracts. Under the program method, the contractor believes reasonably dependable estimates of the total number of units to be delivered can be made. Thus, even though the contracts in hand specify a smaller number of units that the customer is committed to purchase, the contractor will accumulate costs for the "program" rather than for the contract (i.e., the program is designated as the profit center). The allocation of costs to products delivered is then done on the basis of the estimated number of units to be produced overall.

---

[3] The initial coverage of the percentage-of-completion method is found in ARB 19, *Accounting Under Cost-Plus-Fixed-Fee Contracts*, issued during World War II along with other ARBs regarding government contracting issues topical at the time. ARB 19 was codified in ARB 43, Chapter 11, "Government Contracts" (Co5), and the requirements for its use have not changed substantially since issuance in 1953. ARB 45, *Long-Term Construction-Type Contracts* (Co4), issued in 1955, also covers the percentage-of-completion method. The information contained in the draft Audit Guide, augmented by SOP 81-1, incorporates and expands on the principles from ARBs 43 and 45.

There has been little use of this method in government contracting because of the inherent uncertainties involved in how many units can be sold, how long it will take to produce and sell them, and what the final actual costs will be. Further, if the government owns the design and tooling, it may not be possible to sell the product to anyone else. Finally, regardless of the desirability of the product or the dependability of estimates, future contracts may not be funded by Congress. The program method has essentially been limited to major commercial aircraft production.

The draft Audit Guide concludes that the program method is not acceptable for government contracts or subcontracts (¶¶ 209–212).

Specific Government Contracting Issues

Costs of Production. The costs of production of inventory in excess of contract requirements should be allocated between the contract and other inventory costs. The recoverability of the inventory costs should be assessed in determining whether they should be classified as assets.

Contract Incentives. Government contracts often provide for certain incentives to contractors that may increase or decrease fees for cost-type contracts or target profits for fixed-price-type contracts (¶¶ 179–181).

Frequently, there is a basis for reasonably predicting performance in relation to established targets. If so, the effect of the resulting upward or downward adjustment should be recorded in a manner consistent with the accounting method used for the contract. Situations in which performance may not be reasonably predictable may involve either a single opportunity to accomplish a test or a demonstration in accordance with established performance criteria, or the awarding of fees that may be determined solely by the government and that are subject to retroactive adjustment after the contractor's performance has been evaluated.

Shared R&D Arrangements. Research and development is defined in SFAS 2, *Accounting for Research and Development Costs*, as follows (R50.104):

a. *Research* is planned search or critical investigation aimed at discovery of new knowledge with the hope that such knowledge will be useful in developing a new product or service . . . or a new process or technique . . . or in bringing about a significant improvement to an existing product or process.

b. *Development* is the translation of research findings or other knowledge into a plan or design for a new product or process or for a significant improvement to an existing product or process whether intended for sale or use. It includes the conceptual formulation, design, and testing of product alternatives, construction of prototypes and operation of pilot plants. It does not include routine or periodic alterations to existing products, production lines, manufacturing process, and other ongoing operations even though those alterations may represent improvements, and it does not include market research or market-testing activities.

Government contractors may incur costs for research and development of products that may be sold both commercially and under government contracts. Under

SFAS 2, R&D costs not directly reimbursed by others or indirectly reimbursable under the terms of a contract (e.g., an allowable amount of R&D costs) are required to be charged to expense when incurred. Contractors should, therefore, determine whether R&D costs for government products are allowable under the terms of a contract. Those costs may not be allowable by FAR unless they are specifically provided for in the government contract or another agreement (¶ 189).

SFAS 2 does not discuss how to account for costs of R&D activities conducted for others under contract. Contractors sometimes enter into contracts in which the government agrees to share the estimated costs of certain R&D activities (e.g., the development of a prototype for new or advanced weapons systems). Under such contracts, the contractor may be obligated to perform only on a *best-efforts* basis, that is, the contract does not require delivery of a product (or service) meeting certain defined specifications. Further, the parties to the contract expect the total costs of the R&D activity specified in the agreement to exceed the amounts funded by the government.

Both parties may benefit from such agreements. The contractor benefits by having lower net R&D costs and the right to retain the results of the R&D efforts. Additionally, the contractor benefits from the knowledge gained from such R&D activities that may be used in future production, including "follow-on contracts" for full-scale production of products based on the prototypes or models developed during the R&D phase. The government, on the other hand, benefits from the agreement by receiving nonexclusive rights to the results of the R&D effort. Consequently, the government can encourage contractors to focus their R&D efforts on activities that are relevant to its long-range, strategic objectives in areas such as national defense.

The types of activities (and contractual agreements) discussed above are not performed for the purpose of designing, engineering, fabricating, constructing, and manufacturing tangible assets (product), which would permit the cost thereof to qualify for deferral. Instead, such activities are undertaken with the expectation that the results of those efforts may be used in future, not current, production. The draft guide therefore states (¶¶ 201–208) that R&D sharing differs from production-type contracts as covered in SOP 81-1 (TP 10,330) and that such activities accordingly are treated like R & D and charged to expense as incurred.

To summarize, R&D expensing treatment, not contract accounting treatment, applies to situations that meet all of the following conditions:

1. The activities qualify as R&D as defined by SFAS 2 and are performed in connection with the contract.

2. The contractor retains a right to the data and the results of the research and development activities.

3. The contractor is obligated under the contract to perform only on a best-efforts basis, not to deliver a product or service meeting stated specifications.

4. The contractor and the customer enter into the agreement at the inception of the contract expecting costs incurred to exceed amounts to be funded. (This condition is met if the contract or other documentation specifically acknowledges that both the contractor and the customer have this expectation). It is implicit in this condition that at the outset there is significant uncertainty as to the likelihood that the contractor will receive follow-on contracts related to the R&D activity.

5. The R&D contract is not combined with other contracts nor segmented in accordance with SOP 81-1 (TP 10,330.35–.42).

Amounts funded by the customer as a result of the cost-sharing feature of a best-efforts R&D agreement should be offset against the contractor's total R&D expense, rather than recognized as contract revenues.

Contract Terminations for Convenience. Accounting for terminations for convenience of the government (¶¶ 191–193) is based on the rights established in contracts and in procedural rules for such terminations. The effects on income of terminations for convenience should be recognized when the amounts associated with the contract can be reasonably determined. Allowable and unallowable costs should be charged to expense. Because unallowable costs should not be included in the total costs of a flexible-price or cost reimbursement contract, revenue from claims should be recognized on the basis of allowable costs only.

Claims of subcontractors and other vendors should be recorded as liabilities at the estimated amounts payable. To the extent that such amounts may be recovered by the prime contractor, they should be included as part of the claim.

Contract Terminations for Default. In addition to normal contract liabilities, a contractor should record liabilities resulting from a termination caused by its default (¶ 194), including damages, excess reprocurement costs, and progress payments to be repaid. Previously recorded earnings may be reduced as a result of termination for default. In such cases, prior period amounts should not be adjusted; instead, the income effect should be included in the loss resulting from the termination of the contract in the current period.

Financial Reporting and Disclosure

Reporting and disclosure practices for companies in which sales or revenues under government contracts and subcontracts constitute a large portion of operations are discussed in this section.

In most respects, financial reporting and disclosure requirements for companies that perform government contracting do not differ from those for other business enterprises. In addition to authoritative AICPA and FASB pronouncements, ASR 138 (FRR § 216) and ASR 164 (FRR § 206) provide specific guidance to publicly held companies on SEC disclosure requirements for (1) long-term contracts and programs, (2) extraordinary or material, unusual charges and credits to income, and (3) material provisions for losses. Further, FRR 32, released August 1, 1988, admonishes contractors to disclose the possible or anticipated effects of fraud investigations (as discussed in the earlier section on "Fraud, Waste and Mismanagement").

Note Disclosures. Government contracts that require complex systems or involve significant technological advances may present significant problems in performance and in estimating costs, profits, and losses. The following matters may affect income statement comparability and, therefore, may indicate a need for disclosure in the notes to the financial statements (¶ 230):

- Unusual or infrequent contract price adjustments
- Substantial provisions for loss
- Material changes in contract estimates
- Substantial incentive income
- Significant claims revenues
- Significant problems encountered in the performance of contracts materially affecting operations

Defective Pricing. The Truth in Negotiations Act permits the government to reduce contract prices if a contractor does not submit accurate, current, and complete information about costs or pricing before certain negotiated contracts or contract amendments are awarded. If it is determined that there is defective pricing, contract prices including profit or fees may be adjusted; the circumstances should be disclosed if the amounts are material.

Defective pricing alleged by the government is frequently disputed by the contractor. If so, consideration of the circumstances and the materiality of the amounts potentially involved (including consultation with legal counsel) is required in deciding whether disclosure should be made in the notes to the financial statements.

Contract Claims. Contract claims, either against the contractor or the government, usually are a normal part of doing business and do not require disclosure, unless the amounts are significant in the context of the overall financial statements. The accounting and reporting for claims are discussed in SOP 81-1 (TP 10,330.65–.67).

Contract Terminations. Contractors should generally disclose the effects of contract terminations in their financial statements in the period in which the termination occurs. If sufficient information is not available to predict the effect of a very recent termination, the best information available should be given. If there are indications of a possible contract termination, such as notice of a possible termination, performance problems, or procurement cutbacks, and if the termination would be material to the contractor's operations, the circumstances and their potential effects should be discussed in the notes to the financial statements (¶¶ 196, 216, and 233).

Deferred Taxes. Most contractors will use a method of contract accounting for financial reporting purposes that differs from the method used for tax purposes, with the objective of deferring taxable income for as long as possible. Changes in tax laws in 1982, 1986, and 1987 have significantly restricted contractors' abilities in this area, by limiting the use of the completed contract method for tax purposes to situations where the contract spans two tax years and the contract items are unique (i.e., not normal inventory production). Otherwise, contractors that had been using completed contract accounting for tax purposes are required to change to the percentage-of-completion-capitalization-cost (PCCCM) method for new contracts after February 28, 1986 (¶¶ 241–244).

In addition, costing rules have changed significantly for tax reporting, in that many costs previously tax-deducted as current expenses must now be deferred until completion of the contract, so as to coincide with the timing of income taxability. Some of these additional costs may also be deferrable under GAAP but not all (¶¶ 245–248).

Both the income recognition and the cost capitalization matters described above will give rise to temporary differences between book and tax, requiring the provision of deferred taxes under SFAS 96, *Accounting for Income Taxes* (I25). (Also see Chapter 36 for classification of the resulting deferred taxes in the balance sheet.)

AUDITING CONSIDERATIONS

Audit Planning

In planning and performing the audit, the auditor should refer to the guidance contained in the exposure draft, *Audits of Government Contractors* (AICPA, 1987c). The discussion in this chapter is limited to an auditing overview.

Auditors performing audits of government contractors often must deal with complex issues and problems, primarily because of the environment in which contractors operate, and because contractors may use complicated accounting methods that require significant judgments by management.

An important element in planning the audit engagement is the auditor's understanding of the contractor's business. To understand a contractor's business the auditor must be knowledgeable about:

* The contractor's products and the proportion of the work that is government work.
* Competition in the industries in which the contractor operates.
* Types of contracts and customers and information on methods used in bidding for new business.
* Contractor accounting policies, CAS, the contractor's Disclosure Statement, and FAR and FAR Supplements.

Audits of government contractors focus primarily on individual contracts that are used as profit centers to record cost and recognize revenue. Because the government contracting business is highly regulated, a critical audit consideration is the extent to which the contractor is complying with applicable regulations. The auditor must therefore focus on whether the contractor's internal control structure and related policies and practices have been designed to ensure compliance with regulations.

Compliance With Regulations. Government contractors should have controls that assure compliance with applicable regulations and enable the company to identify and respond to changes in those regulations.

FAR governs almost all aspects of the acquisition process, including a detailed set of *cost principles*, which must be understood by the contractor to properly (and knowledgeably) account for contract costs and pricing contracts. Because government regulations have a pervasive effect on the contractor's operations, accounting practices, and cost recoverability, it is important for the auditor to consider whether controls in this area are effective (¶¶ 259–263).

Estimating and Proposal Systems. Because inaccurate estimates may increase the risk of a defective pricing assertion by the government, controls over estimating systems and the preparation of proposals are necessary to ensure that cost and pricing data included in proposals are accurate, complete, and current. Management's risk in signing a certification of contract cost or pricing data may be substantially increased if controls are inadequate.

Project Administration. Project administration includes project reporting, maintenance of cost and price estimates, identification and control of change orders and other contract modifications, monitoring of project schedules, and maintenance of contract documentation. Whether a contract is profitable is often determined by the quality, effectiveness, and efficiency of project administration. To evaluate the status and profitability of each project, management needs timely and reliable cost and status reports on each contract.

To estimate profit or loss to date, management should regularly review and evaluate the status of contracts in progress. This procedure is an integral part of an effective system of internal control because management can use the information to take appropriate corrective actions to improve performance on specific contracts.

Quality Assurance. Problems in the quality assurance area can directly affect the contractor's financial statements because they may cause progress payments to be withheld or contracts to be terminated. Further, the contractor may have to incur additional and unexpected costs to correct excessive quality problems, thus adversely affecting financial results. In contrast, quality assurance problems may be caused by poorly stated government specifications that would entitle the contractor to an equitable adjustment in the contract price as compensation for the company's additional costs.

Contract Revenues and Costs. Controls over contract revenues are much the same as those applicable to contracting in general, and are covered in Chapter 36 in the section entitled "Revenue Recognition."

In establishing controls over the recognition, distribution, and accumulation of contract costs of government contractors, the unique features of the government environment should be considered. Adequate controls will ensure that (¶ 272):

- Costs are accurately distributed to the contract for which they are incurred.
- Costs are reasonable and in accordance with the specific contract provisions.
- Costs charged to each project or contract are based on actual costs and are in accordance with the applicable government cost principles.
- The cost accounting system segregates unallowable costs or has the capability of providing sufficient detail to do so.
- Cost allocation practices used to charge costs to contracts are reasonable, reflect the beneficial or causal relationship between costs and cost objectives, and are in conformity

with applicable cost accounting standards and the contractor's disclosure statement, if applicable.

• Costs are accumulated in a manner consistent with the way they were estimated.

• Memorandum records, if any, used by the contractor are periodically reconciled to the contractor's formal accounting records.

• Costs incurred on all projects or contracts during the period are reconciled to the costs reflected in the financial statements.

• Costs associated with contracts that have not been formally funded by the government are evaluated for recoverability. (A contractor's prior experience with work on unfunded contracts is an important consideration in this evaluation.)

Government-Furnished Property. Many contractors use property furnished by the government (e.g., equipment used for operations and materials to be used in the final product) and must therefore follow specific regulations for control over and accountability for such property. The controls should ensure compliance with regulations, and also ensure that government-furnished property is not charged to contracts or included in the contractor's assets for financial reporting purposes.

Interorganization Transfers. Controls over transfers within the enterprise should be designed to ensure that such transactions are identified and accounted for appropriately. Transfers of government contract-related property and purchases and sales of materials and services between divisions, subsidiaries, and affiliates of the contractor should generally be recorded at the transferor's cost for both financial reporting and government contract costing purposes (¶ 285).

Major Audit Areas

Contract Costs and Revenues. The principal emphasis of an examination of the financial statements of a government contractor relates to the profit centers (generally individual contracts) for recognizing costs, revenues, and income. The financial information developed by companies to recognize profit on contracts at a point in time normally includes actual costs incurred to date and estimated costs to complete.

Cost estimates involve significant management judgments. Audit personnel assigned responsibility for contract reviews must be sufficiently knowledgeable about government contracting to challenge the reasonableness of management's estimates and the underlying assumptions.

The determination of income on a contract requires aggregating, for each profit center, the accumulated costs to date, estimated costs to complete, estimated revenues at completion, and revenues earned to date. The auditor should consider the effect of CAS and FAR rules in evaluating the allocation and allowability of costs charged to contracts.

Procedures aimed at determining that costs incurred to date have been properly recorded should be performed. Additionally, the auditor should be satisfied that accumulated costs include identifiable direct and indirect costs and that overhead and G&A costs have been allocated in an acceptable and consistent manner.

Classified Contracts. Because some government contracts involve classified government programs, some level of security clearance from the government is generally required for access to certain financial and other data. Consequently, in auditing the financial statements of government contractors that perform significant classified contracts, the independent auditor must seek appropriate security clearance. Obtaining such clearance requires from as little as 3 months to as many as 12 or 18 months. It is therefore advisable to arrange for clearance as early in the engagement as possible.

If clearance cannot be obtained in time to perform the examination or clearance is denied, it is likely that audit procedures will be limited to inquiry of management about classified contracts. The independent auditor should evaluate whether that limitation may require a nonstandard auditor's report. The auditor's decision about the effect of that scope limitation on the report depends on the accountant's assessment of the materiality of, and audit risk associated with, classified contracts.

If the independent auditor concludes that management's responses to the inquiries are not sufficient for assessing the materiality of classified contracts or the audit risk associated with them, the report will be modified (¶¶ 403–405).

Accounts Receivable. A government contractor's accounts receivable may include billed receivables, unbilled receivables, progress payments, retentions, and change orders.

Billing. Government contractors' billing procedures may differ substantially from those of other business enterprises. During the course of long-term contracts, contractors generally submit progress billings based on either costs incurred or on a predetermined schedule (milestone billing). Contractors may also submit billings before performance to request advance payments.

Contractor personnel responsible for government billings should be adequately trained in the applicable regulations and should receive timely and accurate billing-related information for each contract. Control procedures should ensure that the method of billing is in accordance with the specific contract terms.

Billed receivables. Billed receivables differ from commercial receivables because the customer's ability to pay is normally not questioned in a government contracting environment. The auditor generally performs procedures to determine whether the amount included in accounts receivable represents the amount billed to the government according to the terms of the contract, and that billed receivables include only allowable and allocable costs under FAR and CAS.

Unbilled receivables. Unbilled receivables occur when sales or revenues have been recorded but have not been billed currently. The receivables may consist of (1) unbilled amounts resulting from the use of the percentage-of-completion or another method of revenue recognition that differs in timing from the contractual billing terms, (2) costs incurred that will be billed under cost reimbursement-type contracts, and (3) differences between provisional overhead billing rates and actual allowable overhead rates.

Collectibility review. Direct confirmation of billed receivables addressed to the procurement office should be attempted; however, replies are rare and it is likely that alternative procedures will need to be performed. Direct confirmation of unbilled receivables generally is not possible. Alternative audit procedures, including an examination of subsequent billings and cash collections and an evaluation of billing information on the basis of accumulated cost data, should be performed. Possible unallowable costs should be considered. The auditor may also discuss with the appropriate contracting officer and DCAA representatives the status of the determination of overhead costs and other matters that may affect the contractor's ability to realize unbilled receivables. The length of time that receivables have remained unbilled should be reviewed because it may indicate whether there are disputed costs, contract modifications, or other matters that may affect ultimate collectibility.

Change Orders. Change orders are categorized into two broad types. A formal change order is a written document issued by the government stating that specific changes to the contract are being made. Because the government acknowledges that a change is being made, it is likely that only the amount of the equitable adjustment in terms of contract price or delivery is disputed. To evaluate a contractor's estimate of the effect of formal change orders on both the costs to complete the contract and the amount of profit or loss to be recognized during the period, the auditor should:

- Ensure that estimated contract revenue and costs are adjusted to reflect approved change orders.
- Evaluate the reasonableness of the estimated costs of performing the change order in the same manner as the evaluation of other contract costs. (This is often difficult because change order costs are not always easily segregated from the contract costs.)
- Examine the signed change order document for terms and conditions that may affect the contractor's recovery of costs under the change order and for approval of the change by all affected parties.

Constructive change orders represent an informal action, failure to act, or omission on the part of the government and may be either written or oral. They are often subtle and difficult to identify, document, and quantify. Nevertheless, their force and effect are the same as formal change orders. Constructive change orders frequently result in disputes about the contractor's right or entitlement to equitable adjustments because the government and the contractor often disagree about whether an informal act or omission is a valid contract change.

For such unpriced change orders, the appropriate accounting depends primarily on the probability of cost recovery based on some measure of the likely occurrence of future events. Factors that should be considered in evaluating the probability of recovery are (1) whether the customer has approved the scope of the change in writing, (2) whether there is separate documentation for identifiable and reasonable change order costs, and (3) the extent of the contractor's historical experience in negotiating change orders.

Although the government has officially recognized that contractors are entitled to additional funds through change orders, revenue recognition and cost recovery on constructive change orders generally present problems to contractors and their auditors. It is therefore important for a contractor to have a system in place that provides adequate controls over identifying, negotiating, and processing changes in contracts as well as updated information on constructive changes, so that their effects can be adequately assessed and recognized in the financial statements.

Because the eventual recovery of unpriced change orders depends on the facts and circumstances, there are significant judgments involved. The auditor should perform procedures necessary to satisfy himself that the contractor's assertions are reasonable. Those procedures may include discussion with customers, obtaining opinions from legal counsel, and reviewing correspondence between the customer and the contractor (¶¶ 328–334).

Inventories. A government contractor's inventories may include contract related costs, costs for tooling and spare parts, or other deferred costs. In reviewing inventory, the auditor should determine that the types of deferred contract costs and the circumstances under which they are recorded in inventory are in accordance with the contractor's guidelines, and that they are realizable. Physical inventories, such as spare parts, can be tested using methods similar to those used for commerical enterprises.

Government contractors see realization as the principal risk involved in inventories. Because government contractors typically produce inventory for specific customers under specific contracts, evaluating the realizability of inventory remaining after the contract is complete should be straightforward.

Transferring inventory between contracts by using a borrow/payback system may result in transfers at an incorrect price or in credits for transfers not applied to the proper contracts. Therefore, the auditor must be especially alert in auditing inventory if such a system exists.

Contractor Claims. Claims are frequently disputes resulting from constructive change orders. Like change orders, revenues from claims and costs may be the determining factor as to whether a contract will ultimately be profitable. Consequently, contractors need controls that (¶ 280):

- Identify potential claim conditions.
- Begin communications with the government.
- Fully document the basis for entitlement and the costs relating to the changed conditions.
- Accurately recognize the impact of the claims on reported contract revenues and costs.
- Segregate costs associated with the claim.

Chapter 36 contains a general discussion about contractor claims and the four recognition criteria stated in SOP 81-1 (TP 10,330.65) that must be met to recognize revenue on claims. The proposed government contractors audit guide (¶ 342) presents and elaborates on those criteria as follows:

- *The contract or other evidence provides a legal basis for the claim; or a legal opinion has been obtained, stating that under the circumstances there is a reasonable basis to support the claim.* An effective means of obtaining evidence about management's compliance with this criterion is to obtain from the contractor's legal counsel an opinion on both the legal basis of the claim and the probability of recovery. The existence of a changes clause in the contract does not provide an absolute legal basis for a claim.

- *Additional costs are caused by circumstances that were unforeseen at the contract date and are not the result of deficiencies in the contractor's performance.* The contractor is generally considered responsible for cost increases caused simply by underestimating the original work, contractor inefficiencies, and similar factors that are not the government's responsibility and, therefore, generally do not provide a basis for a claim against the government. The additional costs mentioned in this condition are generally costs incurred because of constructive or formal change orders issued by the government.

- *Costs associated with the claim are identifiable or otherwise determinable and are reasonable in view of the work performed.* Although circumstances may vary, contractors should generally segregate the costs associated with changes in contract scope or method of performance once those changes are recognized. If the formal accounting system does not permit this segregation, memorandum records should be used. In some cases, however, the basic nature of the change may be identified, but its impact may be so pervasive that easy identification of the related increased costs is very difficult. This is particularly true in the case of certain constructive changes, including defective government specifications, which often require the contractor to remove or alter work previously performed or change the sequence in which work is to be performed.

- *The evidence supporting the claim is objective and verifiable, not based on management's "feel" for the situation or on unsupported representations.* The specificity of the information contained in the claim document and the adequacy and completeness of the working papers and other documentation underlying the claim are critical to this process. The contractor's performance history with respect to contracts of this type is among the additional factors to be considered.

Government Claims. Government claims against a contractor generally involve one of three issues: unallowable costs, mischarged costs, or defective pricing.

The allowability of costs is governed by procurement regulations. Interpretation of those regulations is a significant source of disputes between contractors and the government. Costs are mischarged if they are not allocated to cost objectives in accordance with CAS and contract terms. Defective pricing claims occur if the contractor does not comply with the Truth in Negotiations Act (¶ 353).

The auditor should evaluate each of those issues (which may be in the form of asserted or unasserted claims) and their potential effects on the financial statements. Procedures normally involve an evaluation of controls over cost and estimating systems and substantive procedures performed on the disputed amounts, including comparisons with historical data and other tests.

38

Media and Entertainment

OVERVIEW

This chapter discusses print media (magazines, books, and newspapers) and nonprint media (broadcasting and cable television). It also covers several aspects of the entertainment industry (motion pictures, video tapes and disks, production and distribution of records, and music publishing) that have been dealt with in FASB pronouncements. In addition, two other kinds of businesses that might be called entertainment, depending on one's perspective, are briefly described in this chapter: professional sports teams and casinos.

Probably the most salient feature nonprint media and entertainment businesses have in common is their heavy investment in intangible assets. Notwithstanding the costs of studios, transmitters, satellites, record-pressing plants, and the like, the essential investments are in such items as licenses, operating rights, and affiliation agreements. A particular characteristic of the entertainment industry is its speculative nature. There is often a significant risk involved in providing the financial backing for a new motion picture or recording artist or in buying the broadcast rights to an entertainment production.

Because of the variety of types of businesses involved in media and entertainment, the chapter coverage is restricted to significant accounting and auditing matters, and operating characteristics related thereto. In particular, reference should be made to Chapters 7 through 10 for a discussion of audit performance and methodologies.

MAGAZINE PUBLISHING

Industry Environment

New magazines are continually introduced to focus on specific segments of the consumer and business market. For example, because the percentage of the U.S. population over age forty is rapidly increasing, some new magazines cater to the interests of those from forty to sixty years old, and other new magazines address senior citizens. Additionally, the middle-income segment of the population, which has a greater tendency to travel for vacations, is increasing, resulting in a proliferation of travel magazines in recent years.

As with any industry that experiences a period of rapid expansion, there is generally a subsequent shakeout, and some entrants fail. Financial reporting should reflect those risks, and auditing approaches should be designed to assess their impact.

In general, magazines can be classified as either consumer publications or business publications. Consumer publications satisfy the interests of the general public or the special interest groups that make up the general public, whereas business publications satisfy the interests of business, professional, or technical people.

The nature of a magazine depends on its editorial policy and distribution channels; these in turn determine many of the specific characteristics of the magazine. The characteristics that define the nature of a magazine include:

• Subject matter
• Geographical area covered
• Circulation size (paid or controlled)

- Physical size
- Number of pages (folio)
- Subscription price
- Importance and amount of advertising

Operations. A magazine's success depends on an appropriate balance in meeting the needs of the two groups that are the major sources of its revenue: readers and advertisers. The relative importance of each as a revenue source depends on the magazine's policies and priorities.

To a significant extent, the "product" of a magazine is service, that is, fulfilling the informational needs of readers and providing a medium for advertisers. The needs of the reader may range from informational requirements to entertainment; and advertisers want to reach those that are most likely to buy their product. The publisher's task is to establish a policy regarding editorial content and distribution that will best match the needs of readers and advertisers.

Editorial. Editorial activities include planning future issues, personnel assignment, review of material submitted, design of an individual issue, and copy-editing. The cover design, artwork, and page layouts help create an image, often a key marketing tool.

Advertising. Advertising sales continue to be the largest source of revenues for all but a few magazine publishers. However, in recent years the share of revenues derived from circulation has been increasing, in part because publishers have increased efforts to make single-copy sales. The advantage to the publisher of single-copy sales is that the cost of postage is avoided, but the disadvantage is that the reader must make a separate decision to buy each issue.

Several independent, nonprofit groups supported by publishers, advertisers, and agencies have been organized to audit magazine circulation. The largest organizations are the Audit Bureau of Circulation (ABC) and Business Publications Audit (BPA). Because advertising rates are based on circulation (preferably audited), most magazines with significant advertising content belong to one of these groups.

Advertising rates are generally determined on the basis of a cost-per-thousand (CPM) of circulation. Rates are standardized on rate cards (or schedules). Premiums are charged for extra colors and special locations, and volume discounts are given for frequency, amount of space, or dollar amount.

Most consumer and business magazines sell advertising through their own sales force, which may be organized by geographic area or by industry. Space salespeople often work on a salary-plus-commission basis.

Circulation. The circulation of magazines is classified into three general types:

- *Free (or controlled).* Publishers distribute their magazines to decision makers without charge (or at a very low subscription price), and advertising sales are made based on the known circulation. Business publications typically use this type of circulation, often audited by BPA.

- *Paid.* Readers pay a share of the cost of publication, and paid space advertising is based on the paid circulation. The level of circulation may be audited (principally by the ABC) and the nature of the readership is determined from sophisticated market and demographics research.
- *Passalong.* The readership consists of individuals other than those who initially received the magazine.

The methods of obtaining subscriptions are classified by their source—direct from the publisher or through outside sources. Because of the high cost of obtaining new subscriptions, publishers seek subscriptions that will be renewed.

The quality of circulation is important to advertisers. In general, the more "voluntary" the purchase (as in response to direct mail or insert cards) the more attractive the reader is to the advertiser and the publisher; the more direct solicitation applied (as with school plans and telephone sales), the less attractive the subscriber.

Included in paid circulation are single-copy sales. The distribution network delivers almost 3,000 magazines to about 130,000 retail outlets. The system consists of three levels: national distributors (there are about 13) allocate copies to regional wholesalers (there are about 450), who in turn allocate copies to retailers. Wholesalers normally process returns from the retailers and accordingly are the source of information as to actual sales.

Other functions. Magazines are almost always mailed under a second-class postage permit. Even second-class postage is expensive and continual increases seem inevitable. Other costs are increasing, although less dramatically. Furthermore, increases in costs of production and distribution have outstripped increases in advertising rates. To cut costs, the magazine publishers have reduced the size (smaller dimensions and fewer pages) and weight (lighter-weight paper) of magazines. To increase revenues, publishers have increased newsstand prices, give fewer and less extensive discount subscriptions, and are promoting single-copy sales.

Many magazines are printed by major printers specializing in magazine work. The composition (typesetting) of magazines has been computerized, saving costs in relation to hot-metal typesetting. Most printing is done by the offset process, more economical than the letterpress process. Except in the case of the largest publishers, magazine paper is purchased in bulk by large printers direct from the mills.

Generally, outside computer service bureaus handle the fulfillment of subscriptions for magazine publishers. *Fulfillment* includes processing of subscriptions, handling cash (caging), maintaining subscriber records, printing mailing labels, and sending out billing and renewal notices. The specialization of the fulfillment functions by a few large service bureaus has resulted in economies of scale, measurably reducing the cost per subscription.

Accounting Considerations

Accounting and control systems other than those related to subscription fulfillment are not significantly different from those of other commercial enterprises. Although the editorial, circulation, and distribution operations have not changed substantially over time, the related systems for managing and reporting have become increasingly sophisticated. This has been especially true in the area of subscription fulfillment, for

---

Book and Magazine Revenue

Book sales, less provisions for estimated returns, are recorded at the time of shipment. Magazine subscription sales are deferred as unearned income at the time of sale. As magazines are delivered to subscribers, the proportionate share of the subscription price is taken into revenue. Subscription selling expenses are deferred and charged to expense as the related subscription income is earned.

FIG. 38.1   Example of Magazine and Book Revenue Recognition Policies
Source: The Times Mirror Company, 1986 Annual Report.

which electronic data processing (EDP) systems have enabled publishers (or their computer service bureaus) to record a myriad of information on a specific subscription and publication basis.

In general, publishers are organized by product (magazine). For each magazine, the editorial, circulation, and distribution functions are normally separate. Subscription fulfillment, production, accounting, and other support functions are normally centralized. The costs of these shared functions are allocated to each magazine's operating statement for internal management analysis and control purposes. Each magazine will normally have all of its dedicated activities (except regional advertising sales representatives) at one location.

The key accounting areas are highlighted in the following sections.

Revenues

Net advertising revenue. Net advertising revenue is defined as the revenue received from the sale of advertising space in a magazine after agency commissions and cash discounts have been deducted.

For accounting control purposes, it is desirable to use separate accounts to distinguish the original billing from the various classes of subsequent adjustments. Some companies use separate categories of accounts for national and regional advertising, and for four-color and black-and-white advertising.

Subscription revenue. Gross subscription revenue is the amount earned by the publisher after the deduction of (1) refunds on cancellations and (2) charge orders not collected. Net subscription revenue is gross subscription revenue less commissions paid to subscription agencies. When subscriber copies are delivered, a proportionate amount of subscription income is transferred from deferred subscription revenue to the income statement. Figure 38.1 shows an example of revenue recognition policies of a magazine and book publisher.

At the end of each reporting period, the estimated reserve for cancellations or nonpayment of credit subscriptions is charged to operations for that portion of the subscription already served. The portion related to unserved subscriptions is charged against the deferred liability.

Single-copy revenue. Single-copy revenue includes sales of issues that have been closed out as well as copies shipped, less estimated returns, of issues not yet closed.

The income account is credited with gross sales as each issue is distributed. Concurrently, the single-copy returns account is charged for the total price of the estimated number of copies to be returned, with the offsetting credit made to the reserve for returns (a contra-receivable account). As returns are reported, a credit is transferred from the reserve to distributor accounts receivable. During the month an issue is closed out, the net difference remaining in the reserve for that issue is transferred to single-copy sales.

Other income. Specific items included in other income are:

- Plates. Miscellaneous typesetting and mechanical preparation costs charged to advertisers, net of direct costs of producing them.
- Reprints and royalties. Income from reprints and royalties on publisher's material, net of any portion of royalties paid to the author.
- Financial income. Interest and dividend income from investments.
- List rentals. Income from rental of names and addresses of subscribers to other organizations.
- Scrap. Income from sale of scrap paper and silver (from used films).
- Seminars. Income from seminars, schools, conferences, expositions, and symposia related to the magazine's market, net of related costs.

Costs and Expenses

Manufacturing. Manufacturing cost represents the charges related to the physical production of the magazine and the costs of supplies. Paper is purchased through a printer or a broker, or directly from a mill. Transportation to the printer is included in the total cost of paper. Paper costs also include charges for storage, handling, and shipping of returnable cores and skids, local hauling, and insurance.

Printing cost is related to the number of copies in the press run, the number of pages in each copy, and the various types of equipment used. Elements included as printing costs are:

- Composition. All the work on editorial and advertising copy from receipt of copy by the printer until the pages are ready for printing. The elements include typesetting, proofreading, receiving, handling, return shipping, additions, authors' alterations, killed matter, and page makeup.
- Makeready. Preparatory operations, such as color separations and other camera work, stripping, and platemaking.
- Presswork. All printer's charges from completion of composition until the printed sheets have come off the press, including makeready and ink costs.
- Binding. The entire cost of cutting, folding, gathering, binding, trimming, affixing address labels, and related operations.

When the art director has the final responsibility for typesetting and/or engraving, a publisher may choose to charge these expenses to the editorial department.

Overtime can be an important variable in printing costs and requires careful monitoring. Larger magazines usually have at least two accounts in which they monitor overtime: composition and presswork.

The production department includes all employees who control the manufacture and physical quality of the magazine, supervise technical and production matters with the printer, handle mechanicals and all other material going to the printer, maintain production control at the printing plant, purchase paper, and perform the technical work on production cost control and budgets.

Distribution. This category includes all the costs of physically distributing the copies, whether by subscription or through single-copy sales outlets, including postage, transportation, wrapping, and handling. The distribution department includes all employees who perform traffic work, schedule shipments, deal with the transportation companies, handle transportation claims, and so forth.

Subscription fulfillment. Subscription fulfillment expenses include all costs of processing subscription orders and payments; maintaining subscriber lists; addressing wrappers, labels, or envelopes; addressing invoices, renewal notices, and promotions; maintaining records for the audit of circulation; and answering subscriber complaints. A major responsibility of subscription fulfillment is to generate statistical reports for the accounting and circulation departments.

Many publishers retain outside firms to handle all fulfillment functions, with charges based on the number of subscriber names maintained. If performed in-house, expenses include salaries and the rental, depreciation, and maintenance of equipment.

The cost of subscription fulfillment for each publication varies according to the volume of work performed. The volume of work depends on a number of factors, the most important of which are frequency of publication, number of subscribers, copies serviced, changes to the subscription list, and the volume of charge business. Although subscription fulfillment is a shared service, it is ordinarily not practical to allocate fulfillment costs on the basis of the preceding factors. Among publications issued with the same frequency, it is usually adequate to allocate total fulfillment cost on the basis of the number of subscribers.

Promotion. Subscription promotion expenses include all costs of obtaining new and renewal subscriptions. The amount of detail needed varies by magazine, according to circulation methods. At a minimum, a distinction should be made between direct mail costs and subscription agency costs.

Included in single-copy promotion are costs of planning and directing single-copy sales, coordination with national distributors' marketing activities, and coordination with wholesalers and retailers.

Advertising costs. Advertising includes the cost of all efforts directed toward maintaining and increasing sales of advertising space, other than the cost of the sales force itself. Cost of market and readership surveys initiated by the advertising department, as well as audience and other studies used to support advertising sales efforts, are also included.

Advertising sales costs include the sales department, both personnel who solicit advertising in the field and those handling the contracts in the office.

Editorial. All costs directly and indirectly related to the editorial content of the magazine are considered editorial expenses. These include:

1. Manuscripts. Articles, stories, and other editorial material purchased from freelance writers and other outside sources. A separate subclassification may be established for material that is not used (kill fees).
2. Art. Artwork, sketches, illustrations, art supplies, photographic equipment, and photographs. A separate subclassification may be established for work that is not used.
3. Surveys. Readership studies and other special or continuing projects initiated by the editorial department that are intended to develop information about the magazine's market, public taste, trends, reader preferences, and so forth.
4. Compensation. All employees performing editorial and art services, including:
   * Editorial executives, chief editors, and art director.
   * Writers and editors.
   * Artists and photographers.
   * Editorial assistants and researchers.

Administration. In a multipublication company, each magazine will have a publisher distinct from general company executives. The salary and related expenses of the publisher and other administrative personnel working directly for the publisher are not part of the company overhead; they are direct charges to the specific publication.

Overall general and administrative costs include joint-service departments that serve two or more publications. Allocation methods to assign these costs to magazines should be applied on a consistent basis. Inability of any publication to bear its share of costs should not influence the method of allocation.

Auditing Considerations

Audit Approach. When designing an overall audit approach to a magazine publishing engagement, certain factors should be considered.

The financial success of a magazine publisher is fundamentally dependent on circulation, either as a direct source of revenue from magazine sales or as an indirect source of revenue from advertising sales. Because many magazines do not succeed after an initial development period, the auditor must assess the probabilities for continued existence, considering the circulation level and trend. These must be evaluated against management's budgeted levels which in turn must be evaluated for reasonableness. The auditor's evaluation is especially critical for single-publication publishers and new magazine ventures.

Specific Areas

Subscription fulfillment. The subscription sales system (subscription fulfillment) is an area for which a cycle audit approach is especially applicable. The entire cycle from the credit sale (or cash receipt) to fulfilling the obligation (delivery of copies under a subscription) should be audited in its entirety (rather than as separate audits of each affected account).

The distribution system, for both single-copy and subscription sales, triggers the revenue-earning process when issues are shipped or mailed. Risk exposures in this area relate to single-copy sales returned and the credit subscription *burn rate* (or frequency of initial and renewal subscription sales for which there are no subsequent cash receipts). Controls include a review of the provision for both single-copy returns and burn rate on credit sales. Reserves for returns and nonpayment are estimated based on past experience and future projections.

The control of cash receipts on subscription sales is especially sensitive, and the relevant controls are part of subscription fulfillment. When subscription fulfillment is performed by an outside service bureau, a third party review should be arranged, if cost-effective; otherwise the auditor should devise and implement procedures to audit revenues and cash receipts.

A key area of concern is the control over cash collected on subscription receivables. If fulfillment is performed by the publisher, the auditor should perform an evaluation of the EDP activity as a basis for reliance on the system of internal controls.

Costs of acquiring subscriptions. Internal control over the accumulation and deferral of marketing costs is a key area of concern. Usually, certain subscription acquisition costs may be deferred and amortized over the life of the subscription (see Figure 38.1). The system of internal control should ensure the propriety of the accounting treatment for the various costs and the auditor should test those controls.

Editorial material. Acquired editorial material is inventoried as a cost of future issues of the magazine. A well-managed function needs controls over the acquisition, authorization, inventory, aging, and write off of this editorial material. An audit of the system should ensure that an effective and efficient allocation of editorial costs is made and that the balance is reviewed periodically for recoverability.

Printing costs. The publisher will record the printer's bill by its components (paper, printing, binding, warehousing, shipping or mailing, and so forth). The reasonableness of production costs can be assessed through an analysis of the relationships between the various cost components of the print bill, with special attention to paper usage and spoilage.

Income Taxes

The timing of reporting of revenue and expenses for income tax purposes may differ somewhat from the timing used in the recognition of revenue and expenses for accounting and financial reporting purposes. Items that may give rise to those temporary differences include subscription income, subscription agency commissions, and other subscription acquisition costs; start-up costs for new publications; returns on single-copy sales; reserves for advertising rebates and other discounts; and transactions involving the acquisition and sale of publications.

Under an IRS ruling (Rev. Rul. 57–86), publishers can elect recognition of expenses for circulation promotion and acquisition on the cash basis for tax purposes, while recognizing the related subscription income on the accrual basis over the life of the subscription. This election is made for each individual magazine, not by the corporate entity. To the extent that taxes are deferred, this procedure is, in effect, a source of financing.

For example, sales of subscriptions through agencies often entail substantial discounts and agency commissions. Industry practice is to record the agency sales net of discount with the aggregate agency commission recorded as a cost of circulation acquisition. This commission is currently deductible for tax purposes, while the related revenues are recognized on the accrual basis.

BOOK PUBLISHING

Industry Environment

Although unit and dollar sales are concentrated in a few large publishing houses, there are approximately 1,750 book publishers, most of them publishing fewer than five new titles annually. The industry is characterized by labor intensiveness, easy entry, and regionalization (largely concentrated in the eastern United States).

Classification of Book Types. The industry classifies books by subject matter, market, and method of distribution. The Association of American Publishers defines the main classifications in its annual statistics questionnaire as follows:

1. *Trade* books include adult and juvenile books, and hardbound and paperbound books created predominantly for the general consumer and marketed primarily through wholesalers and jobbers. Paperbound books such as those published and distributed by mass-market paperback publishers are excluded.

2. *Professional* books are those not created primarily as texts and deal with technical, scientific, and business subjects, including (1) the physical, biological, and social sciences, (2) technology, (3) engineering, and (4) other professions. These books are created primarily for the professional audience consisting of practicing and research scientists, engineers, architects, technicians, mechanics, and teachers. Business and other professional books are addressed to businessmen, managers, accountants, and other professional persons.

3. *Medical* books include primarily medical reference books. Nursing textbooks and other medical and health science texts published by medical publishers are included here but all such textbooks published by nonmedical publishers are considered educational publications.

4. *Mass-market paperback* books are soft-cover works of adult or juvenile fiction and nonfiction distributed predominantly to mass-market outlets such as newsstands, drug stores, chain stores, and supermarkets. For the most part, mass-market paperbacks consist of reprints of trade books, although the number of paperback originals has been constantly increasing.

5. *Religious* books include bibles, hymnals, prayer books, and other works. These may be fiction or nonfiction, adult or juvenile, hardbound or paperback works. Because it is

becoming increasingly difficult to distinguish between certain religious and trade books, books with only peripheral religious content are now classified as trade even when they are published by a religious publisher.

6. *Mail-order* publications are created specifically for offer and delivery by mail directly to the general consumer.

7. *Book club* books are usually special editions of books published by others. They are made available by book clubs serving either consumer or professional audiences.

8. *University press* books are published by nonprofit adjuncts to universities, museums, or research institutions. Titles are similar in subject matter and distribution to trade or professional books but generally concentrate on scholarly topics.

9. *Subscription reference* books consist principally of multivolume sets of encyclopedias marketed to the consumer primarily door-to-door or by direct mail.

10. *Educational* publications include elementary, secondary, and college texts, sold on a contract basis to schools or school systems. College texts are often selected by faculty members but are sold directly to students through college or private bookstores.

Operations. Book publishers can be organized either by function or by product. A business organized by function assigns persons and allocates costs to specific functional areas (editorial, marketing, etc.) rather than to individual product (titles). In a business organized by product, those functions and the associated costs are separately identified and allocated to each product, that is, to individual books.

In practice, most publishers use a combination of those two organizational structures. Hardbound publishers and, to a lesser extent, paperback publishers maintain sales and cost accounting data by title although they tend to centralize their editorial and marketing functions. The advantage of a product organization is that information is obtained with respect to each title's profitability.

Book publishing is a seasonal business, especially for those dealing in trade books, textbooks, and mail order. Short-term lines of credit are the most often used method of financing operations during off-season periods. Because a publisher's customers are generally slow payers and in many cases have an unlimited right of return, accounts receivable include a higher percentage of older accounts.

Allowing the customer an unlimited right of return affects the amount and timing of revenue recognition. SFAS 48, *Revenue Recognition When Right of Return Exists*, requires sales and costs of sales reported in the income statement to be reduced to reflect estimated returns (R75.108).

Determining the size of the initial press run is a crucial step in the publishing process. In the past, trade publishers overprinted a book to reduce the per-copy cost, with the result that many unsold copies were written down or *remaindered,* that is, deeply discounted. Advances in printing technology have made short print runs more economical; thus a publisher is less tempted to overprint. Also, overprinting has become more expensive because of tax considerations (see the section entitled "Income Taxes" below).

Editorial. This process covers the selection and acceptance of manuscripts and their preparation for publication, including determining the publishing schedule, format and size, method of manufacturing, number of pages, type size, and so forth. The role of a copy editor varies from publisher to publisher: some are given free rein to make major modifications to manuscripts while others, usually in relation to works by established authors, are limited to correction of typographical errors and errors in grammar and punctuation. The process of selection and acceptance involves the following steps:

- Discovery. Generally, over 70% of new trade titles published each year come from previously published authors or are solicited by editors. The remainder come from literary agents, foreign publishers, or employees. Only a negligible percentage comes from unsolicited sources. Literary agents serve as middlemen between publisher and author, receiving roughly 10% of an author's total income from a published property as commission.
- Screening. This is the filtering process, usually involving hundreds of unsolicited manuscripts. In addition, it involves an editor's working with authors to improve and polish early manuscript drafts and to develop authors' outlines.
- Negotiating Contracts. If a manuscript or well-developed idea is accepted by the publisher, a contract is negotiated with the author. Most contracts provide for:
  - Royalties to the author. From 10% to 15% of the suggested retail price is normal for hardcover trade books. Lower rates are customary for mass-market books, textbooks, and so forth.
  - Author's advances against royalties. These are generally nonrefundable to the publisher in the event sales are insufficient or the book is not published.
  - Subsidiary rights income. Sales to a mass-market paperback publisher, a film company, or a television producer are examples of such income. Generally 50% or more goes to the author.
  - Manuscript delivery timetable.
  - Title to the copyright.
  - Indemnification of the publisher against plagiarism or invasion of privacy.

Production. The production department is responsible for coordinating the production planning process, from estimating production and manufacturing costs to the shipment of finished books. Most book publishers contract printing and binding to third parties.

Marketing. Marketing planning is done in two ways: (1) on an overall basis, encompassing all aspects of the publishing process, and (2) by publication, establishing a marketing strategy for each new title or edition. The marketing of an individual book varies depending on its type and price. Generally, new titles are advertised in the print media related to the book's field of interest. Publicity is generated through profiling and interviewing authors, often on television talk shows. Marketing policies generally encompass the following factors:

1. *Pricing* is based on a markup factor, which is approximately four to six times the manufacturing cost.
2. *Marketing costs* vary by type of publication, running from 10% to 35% of the net sales of a publishing house.
3. *Discount* percentages are not uniform within the industry, but they are commonly based on the total number of copies of a single book purchased or the quantities of each type of book ordered.

4. *Return* policies are also not uniform within the industry. For example, one publisher's return policy may provide for a 100% credit of the net invoice amount within a stipulated period such as 90 to 180 days, while another may allow no returns for credit but offer a higher initial discount percentage.

5. *Cooperative advertising and allowances* encompass the splitting of advertising and promotion costs between publishers and retailers and the granting of credits to retailers for shipping charges. Generally, these matters are covered by contract for each title. Advertising and publicity expenditures, autographing parties, television appearances by an author, and the like might be split under a cooperative advertising agreement.

6. *Sales organizations* in publishing houses are paid a salary plus commission. Many smaller firms, however, use sales representatives who carry more than one line of books and are paid on a commission basis.

Distribution. The processing of orders and warehousing of books—called *fulfillment*—is a significant expense for most publishers. The warehousing decision, that is, whether a publisher should warehouse books internally or use external, third party facilities, can have a significant bearing on overall distribution costs.

Subsidiary rights. The sale of subsidiary rights is a significant revenue enhancer for publishers, even though authors generally receive between 50% and 75% of the income from such sales. The income generated varies widely among types of books, with hardbound titles garnering the highest amounts. Certain categories of books are unprofitable prior to sale of subsidiary rights; trade books, for example, generally only break even prior to sale of subsidiary rights.

Accounting Considerations

Inventory. Although most publishers engage third-party printers and binders, they inventory materials necessary for performing these jobs. The publishers' in-house inventory consists of:

- Books in process (cost of preparing a book for publication, including author's expenses, artwork, editing, and legal expenses, but excluding prepublication promotion expenses and authors' advances and royalties)
- Folded and gathered sheets (printed)
- Bound books (finished goods)

Valuation of inventories of a book publisher involves consideration of the following factors:

1. *Reserve for returns,* generally determined on a title-by-title basis, is perhaps the most subjective valuation made in book publishing operations. There is no "right" method of calculating this reserve; instead, industry and internal statistics on past returns are compiled and percentages are determined by type of book. The percentage is then applied against gross sales. Two factors must be considered to evaluate these statistics properly: (1) the average return period (the length of time subsequent to publication before retailers start to return titles); and (2) the effect of a bestseller on the overall pattern of returns. Generally, the

bestseller should be evaluated separately because its active sale period is likely to be longer, its return pattern different, and its percentage of returns lower than the average.

2. *Obsolescence* must also be considered, although books are rarely ever considered obsolete in the normal context of a manufacturing operation (i.e., they will always have some level of future sales).

3. *Salability* can generally be evaluated in a straightforward manner. Over 75% of sales of trade titles occurs within 90 days of publication, and a relatively narrow range of a book's sales potential can be determined soon after its publication. This is not necessarily the case for other types of books; the publisher of educational textbooks generally agrees to inventory a single printing of a given textbook for a period of up to seven years.

Deferred Costs. Deferred costs include authors' advances against royalties, prepaid expenses, and miscellaneous deferred amounts. Advances are made to authors upon acceptance of a manuscript or proposal (usually including a detailed outline and sample chapter). These advances are generally nonrefundable, except for nondelivery of the final manuscript. The company must determine periodically if sales will generate sufficient royalties to *earn out,* or sell sufficient copies to cover the advance; if not, unrecoverable amounts should be written off.

Plant Costs. Plant costs are nonrecurring manufacturing costs. They include:

- Manuscript development
- Permission to use copyrighted art, photographs, or text excerpts
- Outside editorial services
- Art, photographs, or design
- Composition (typesetting)
- Process camerawork and stripping

The type of book usually dictates the method of accounting for plant costs. For a book with a relatively short expected life, such as a novel, plant costs would be expensed on publication or charged to the inventory of the first printing; for a book with a longer life, such as a textbook, plant costs are capitalized and amortized over the expected life of the book. Publishers may also write off these costs as incurred.

Accrued Royalties. Arrangements between authors and publishers are a matter of contract specifying the advance against royalties to be paid prior to publication and the royalty rate to be paid. Royalties are generally accrued when earned and paid by publishers semiannually. Accrued royalties are a current liability unless payment to the author is contractually deferred for a period in excess of one year.

Sales. Gross sales consist of actual billings to customers for sales of *current titles* (released for sale within the last 12 months) at standard trade discounts or net prices; *backlist titles* (released for sale in any year prior to the publisher's current fiscal year) at standard trade discount or net prices; and remainder sales (sales of books at or below production cost or those sold in the remainder market).

Returns and allowances represent credits issued to customers for the return of books as new. Exchange allowances on displayed textbooks, allowances made to customers for disputed charges, and proceeds from the sale of books of other publishers taken in exchange are also included.

Subsidiary Rights. For accounting purposes, subsidiary rights income is recorded net of the authors' portion, and includes all amounts received from the following:

* Hardbound reprints.
* Paperbound reprints.
* Book club editions.
* Permissions.
* Foreign editions and translations (income from leasing of English language publication rights abroad or from translation into foreign languages).
* Serial publication, digests, and syndication.
* Television, radio, motion picture and recording adaptation; also, use of titles or characters from books in advertising.

Generally, payments by the purchaser of the rights are made in stages (for example, one-third each on signing, delivery, and use or publication). Because the manuscript is generally delivered to or usable by the buyer when the agreement is reached, the publisher has generally "performed" under the normal terms of a subsidiary rights contract, and the income from sale is accruable upon signing.

Fulfillment Expenses. These expenses represent the cost of processing and physically distributing a customer's order after it has been placed. Some companies segregate from general accounting activities the billing, accounts receivable, and attendant record-keeping functions pertaining to fulfillment. Many small companies use the services of contract fulfillment agents who perform both the record-keeping and physical handling functions attendant to fulfillment.

Increasingly, sales orders placed by retailers for books are being handled on a tape-to-tape basis with the publisher. The retailer will submit a computer tape to the publisher containing all relevant order information. The tape will then be processed by the publisher directly against the company's computerized inventory files and the order will be filled by the warehouse. This eliminates a hard-copy purchase order as supporting evidence for the transaction; but the invoicing of the retailer is still done using hard copy.

Auditing Considerations

Audit Approach. In designing an overall approach to the audit of a book publisher, there are several factors that must be considered.

Operations. The operating results of publishers, especially those publishing trade books, are directly tied to the introduction of successful new titles each year. This differs from many other industries in which a product has a longer life. Two basic strategies used by book publishers are: (a) publish several titles with moderate short and long-term sales potential, creating a type of "annuity" to offset years when no bestseller emerges; or (b) rely on publishing a bestseller annually. The latter strategy can be very risky and is not followed by many publishers. A best seller is difficult to predict; and most trade books earn little profit, if any, before the sale of subsidiary rights. The auditor must evaluate the degree of risk associated with the publisher's strategy.

Adequacy of reserves. Several accounts require subjective evaluation by the auditor. These include inventory valuation (on a title-by-title or category basis), reserve for returns, and deferred authors' advances. For example, evaluating the adequacy of the reserve for returns is difficult because it must be determined by trended statistics rather than by strict application of historical percentages. In addition, when a reserve for a prior period is considered to have been erroneous, determining whether the variance was caused by factors prior or subsequent to the valuation date (i.e., whether it was an error or a change in circumstances) is virtually always inconclusive. Accordingly, a revised reserve estimate is accounted for as a change in estimate (A06.109).

Revenue recognition. A sale can occur when a book is available for shipping, not when it is physically shipped. Generally, there is a one or two day tolerance. For example, if there is evidence that shipment could have been made (i.e., the order is filled and simply waiting to be picked up) a sale may be recordable by the publisher even if shipment is delayed for a short period. The auditor must ascertain that cut-off is properly accomplished.

Review of contracts. Virtually all arrangements between publishers and authors are covered by a contract. Most publishers' processing systems are integrated, so that there is a connection between the recording of sales and returns and the accrual and payment of authors' advances and royalties. In addition, arrangements with printers or binders are covered by either a master contract or by individual project contracts. Contracts also cover significant third-party arrangements, sales commissions, and retailers' discounts.

The auditor should identify and read significant contracts to evaluate that appropriate recognition is given in the financial statements.

Income Taxes

Until 1980, the IRS effectively subsidized publishing operations through tax policy, principally in the area of inventories: a publisher could write down inventory (to zero in many cases) after a title's active sales life (for trade books, 90 to 180 days). However, in 1980 the U.S. Supreme Court handed down a decision that had far-reaching implications for book publishers. The case, *Thor Power Tool Co. v. Commissioner*[1] dealt with the tax-deductibility of inventory write-downs. As applied to book pub-

---

[1] Thor Power Tool Co. v. Commissioner, 439 US 522 (1979); Revenue Procedure 80-5, as amended by Internal Revenue News Release 80-48 (4/8/80); and Revenue Ruling 80-6.

lishers, inventory write-downs are not tax deductible until or unless (1) an effort has been made to resell a book returned by the customer and that effort results in a sales price in the secondary market lower than the carrying value of the book; (2) a book is actually sold; or (3) a book is destroyed. In most cases, the result is that tax-deductibility is deferred until the *Thor* conditions are met. For financial statement purposes, write-downs are required based on lower-of-cost-or-market considerations, and accordingly will occur earlier than the *Thor* conditions are met. Thus, a temporary difference is created that will provide future tax benefits, which may or may not be recognized currently depending on the application of SFAS 96 (see Chapter 17).

Mass-market paperback publishers had difficulty for years in supporting estimated returns as an exclusion from gross sales for tax purposes. IRC § 458 partially alleviates this problem by permitting publishers to exclude from gross income the sale of paperbacks that are returned within four months and fifteen days after the end of the taxable year.

However, the reserve for returns used for financial reporting purposes, based on estimated total returns that may run out as long as a year after sale, is generally much larger than the amount of adjustment to gross income allowed under IRC § 458. Therefore temporary differences that are often significant will result.

NEWSPAPER PUBLISHING

Industry Environment

Although most newspapers are local and privately owned by individuals or families, a significant trend has been the appearance of large, publicly owned newspaper chains. These chains are continually growing through the acquisition of smaller or medium-sized daily papers that often are monopolies in their communities and are, therefore, attractive prospects. This trend has brought professional management and increased sources of capital to those papers. Acquisitions of smaller papers have not posed antitrust problems because of the localized nature of the newspaper markets.

The competition from all other media for the advertising dollar is a significant factor in this industry. Although the advertising share held by newspapers is larger than any other individual media segment, the competition increases each year. New competition is generated by such publications as free shopper newspapers, city magazines with extensive cultural and entertainment coverage, and specialized publications. In addition, the nonprint media – television, radio, and cable – divert potential advertising dollars from newspapers. Some newspapers and chains have therefore diversified into other segments of the media industry such as magazine and book publishing, and television and radio broadcasting. The Federal Communications Commission (FCC) currently denies daily newspapers the right to buy television stations in their own cities.

The advent of the electronic newspaper, which displays up-to-the-minute information on home video terminals, with all the related advertising potential, could also adversely affect newspaper publishing. Whether large-scale developments of this new medium prove feasible, either legally or economically, remains to be seen.

Figure 38.2 presents an example of an income statement for a newspaper enterprise.

Consolidated Statements of Income

| | Fiscal year ended | | |
	December 27, 1987	December 28, 1986	December 29, 1985
Net operating revenues			
Newspaper advertising	$1,787,077,000	$1,588,985,000	$1,213,577,000
Newspaper circulation	645,356,000	575,806,000	464,976,000
Broadcasting	356,815,000	351,133,000	265,480,000
Outdoor advertising	201,771,000	210,572,000	207,572,000
Other	88,428,000	75,001,000	57,816,000
Total	3,079,447,000	2,801,497,000	2,209,421,000
Operating expenses			
Cost of sales and operating expenses, exclusive of depreciation	1,717,478,000	1,564,545,000	1,231,209,000
Selling, general and administrative expenses, exclusive of depreciation	539,826,000	497,244,000	370,163,000
Depreciation	124,485,000	111,229,000	85,512,000
Amortization of intangible assets	36,595,000	31,980,000	18,017,000
Total	2,418,384,000	2,204,998,000	1,704,901,000
Operating income	661,063,000	596,499,000	504,520,000
Non-operating income (expense)			
Interest expense	(85,681,000)	(79,371,000)	(25,926,000)
Interest income	2,504,000	6,044,000	2,590,000
Other	12,509,000	17,032,000	3,593,000
Total	(70,668,000)	(56,295,000)	(19,743,000)
Income before income taxes	590,395,000	540,204,000	484,777,000
Provision for income taxes (note 7)	271,000,000	263,800,000	231,500,000
Net income	$319,395,000	$276,404,000	$253,277,000
Net income per share	$1.98	$1.71	$1.58

FIG. 38.2 Example of Newspaper Enterprise Income Statement
Source: Gannett Co. Inc., 1987 Annual Report.

Operations. Newspaper publishing is protected from prior restraint by the First Amendment to the U.S. Constitution. The most celebrated test of this protection is the publication by the *New York Times* of the Pentagon Papers. The greatest risk of legal liability rests in libel suits. Most newspapers' libel insurance coverage is substantial.

Other litigation relates to shield laws that protect reporters from being forced to reveal confidential sources of information. Such litigation, although highly publicized, does not have a significant impact on a newspaper's financial condition.

The ABC is a cooperative organization that is supported by newspapers, magazines, and advertising agencies; it establishes methods and classifications for reporting circulation, and audits and certifies such circulation. Accounting firms with knowledge of the circulation function are sometimes called on to provide special services in this area.

Editorial. A newspaper is normally bought by the reader for its editorial content. Editorial policy will therefore shape the market segments reached and the circulation achieved. The editorial process includes the following:

• Obtaining the news. From either direct or indirect sources. Direct sources include local news reporters; staff reporters at the paper's regional, national, or international bureaus; and feature writers for special news categories such as social and cultural news, entertainment, and fashion. Indirect sources include wire services and freelance correspondents.

• Writing and editing.

• Layout. All aspects of the physical presentation of the news, including the size and location of headlines, articles, pictures, and captions. Editorial policy will determine the nature and extent of treatment of individual events and the allocation of space of the various departments and between news and advertising.

Advertising. A newspaper's advertising is divided into three categories; retail (or local), classified, and national (or general). Advertising is the most significant portion of a newspaper's revenue (as much as 80%). In terms of dollar volume, retail advertising is the largest, followed by classified advertising.

Accounting Considerations

Advertising Revenues. Advertising revenues are determined by the volume of advertising linage available and rates charged for that linage. Linage in classified advertising (primarily real estate, automobile, and help-wanted ads) is the most sensitive to cyclical downturns. Retail advertising is less cyclical because competition among retailers to maintain market share forestalls significant reductions. If a newspaper has a monopoly in an area, advertising rates are more easily increased without risk of linage loss.

Advertising rates are typically based on the size of a paper's circulation, and accordingly there is a continuous effort to attract readers from other newspapers and other media. Marketing tools to increase circulation have become quite sophisticated. For example, more emphasis has been placed on articles featuring "soft news" topics such as medicine, participation sports, fashion, food preparation, home design, and similar subjects. To offer local advertisers more focused advertising, papers have developed special sections or editions targeted at readers in specific geographic areas.

Premiums are charged to advertisers for color and for choice locations. In *trade-out advertising*, the newspaper *barters* its advertising space for other services (e.g., from a local car dealer). The revenues and expenses represented by such exchanges should be recorded gross.

Costs and Expenses. Production consists of the steps necessary to produce the finished newspaper mechanically and includes page makeup, camera process (or platemaking), and press operation. Page makeup consists of "cutting and pasting" into photographic galley proof pages the news that comes from the computer banks, along with the advertising copy, and then assembling the pages. The makeup pages are then photographed, and the film is exposed to an aluminum sheet (offset process) or a sensitized plastic sheet (letterpress process), which is etched to make the printing impression. The metal or plastic plate is then positioned on the printing cylinder and readied for the press run.

Newsprint and labor are the most significant production cost categories. To reduce newsprint costs, newspapers have instituted efficiencies such as altering typefaces to allow more characters per inch, reducing space between lines, and using lighter-weight or recycled paper. Purchase contracts for paper are generally long-term, and result in fixed obligations and costs. Some larger newspapers vertically integrate by investing in newsprint mills to gain a captive supply for at least part of their requirements.

In addition to cost reduction efforts, a newspaper will often use its excess printing capacity to generate additional revenue, by selling printing services to others.

Subscription and newsstand prices have been gradually increased, to the extent feasible in the market, to reflect the increased costs of production. A limiting factor is that high levels of circulation must be maintained to attract advertising revenues.

Auditing Considerations

Systems other than the subscription fulfillment transaction cycle are not significantly different from those of other commercial enterprises. In general, multinewspaper publishers are organized by product (newspaper) for each of which the editorial, circulation, distribution, subscription fulfillment, and production functions are normally separate, dedicated activities. Accounting and other support functions are usually centralized with portions of their costs allocated to each newpaper's profit and loss statement for internal management analysis and control purposes. Each newpaper will normally have all of its dedicated activities (except regional advertising sales representatives) at one location.

Audit Approach. A reliance approach is generally adopted in engagements with the largest newpapers, and a substantive approach is adopted in most other cases.

Specific Areas

Circulation revenue recognition. Distribution triggers the revenue and earnings process. Risk exposure in this area relates to (1) newspapers returned from newsstands or other retail sales points and (2) credit subscription sales for which no cash is subsequently received. Controls include a review of and provision for both newsstand returns and losses on credit sales. From an audit perspective the risks are not great since the time lag between the date of sale and the actual information on returns is brief and the losses from bad debts on credit sales are readily predictable.

Cash and receivables. Many of the receivables are due from local retailers and classified advertising customers. Controls in this area include credit checks of customers. Areas of audit concern include the aging of the receivables and the general economic condition in the local geographic area (as most of the accounts relate to small, local customers).

Subscription liability. This liability represents the future obligation to deliver issues to subscribers. Auditing consideration of the appropriateness and adequacy of controls over the entire subscription fulfillment cycle is similar to that for magazine publishers, discussed earlier.

Costs of obtaining subscriptions often are deferred and amortized over the subscription term; accordingly, the auditor must evaluate that costs are classified correctly.

Income Taxes

In general, newspaper publishers do not generate any unusual temporary differences. The IRS has held that the publication date of an advertisement is the date on which the earnings cycle is completed, and the related revenue must be reported at that point. Accordingly, for tax purposes, accruals must be made for any unbilled advertising. The employment status (as employees or independent contractors) of carriers, correspondents, and stringers must be based on the individual circumstances. The status designated determines whether any payroll tax payments and related withholdings need to be made.

BROADCASTING

Industry Environment

Television broadcast networks compete for advertising revenues with newspaper groups having national and regional coverage, cable TV, magazines, outdoor advertising, direct mail, and independent TV stations. Although the 30-second commercial still dominates, all networks also offer advertisers 15-second commercial spots. This innovation burdens the networks by requiring them to sell double the units to fill the same time slots.

The number of viewers has diminished as a result of changing lifestyles and a significant increase in dual career families. Although the hours devoted to TV viewing have increased, the three major networks' combined audience share has diminished because viewers now have more choices on cable TV and independent stations. VCR ownership is also having a significant effect on viewing habits.

Independent stations and the networks are feeling the effects of increasing programming costs. An emphasis on cost containment has manifested itself through network efforts to negotiate more favorable broadcast rights and license fees, ordering fewer episodes of a series, increasing off-shore production, accepting fewer miniseries and specials that tend to be expensive, and exerting pressure on suppliers to reduce the use of extravagant special effects and shooting sites.

In 1987, the traditional diary method of audience measurement was phased out by A.C. Nielsen and AGB Television Research, Inc. Introduced in their place were "people meters"—hand-held instruments used by viewers to record what they are viewing at a particular time, thus providing audience size and demographic data. The meter-rating methods have indicated wide discrepancies for a significant number of shows versus what had been obtained from diaries. Further, the meter-rating results provided by each of these two companies have conflicted, raising questions about their accuracy and casting doubt on the reliability of both the new and the old data. Although these conditions suggest continuing confusion for broadcasters and advertisers, people meters probably will eventually provide more detailed, timely, and accurate information.

Regulation

The FCC has primary jurisdiction over broadcasting. There are three phases of regulation:

1. Allocation of space in the radio or TV frequency spectrum.
2. Assignment of stations in each service area within the allocated frequency bands.
3. Regulation of existing stations.

During the term of their license, broadcast stations serve the public interest, convenience, and necessity. Broadcast licenses must meet certain legal, technical, and financial qualifications; and license violators can incur penalties ranging from reprimands, fines, and short-term probationary licenses to non-renewal or revocation of licenses.

In 1985, the FCC liberalized its decades old multiple-ownership rules, raising from seven to twelve the number of television stations a single entity can own. An entity may own twelve television stations provided that total audience does not exceed 25% of the total national television audience. The rule restricting television ownership to five VHF stations was also lifted. For computational purposes, UHF stations, which carry a weaker signal than VHFs, are allowed to reduce the market's television audience by one half when determining audience-reach percentages. In addition, group owners with interests in stations that are more than 50%-owned by minorities are permitted to own up to fourteen stations and reach 30% of the national television audience, as long as two of those fourteen stations are controlled by minorities.

The rule that prohibits any entity from owning more than one station of the same service within the same market continues. Newspaper owners may not purchase broadcast properties in the same market in which their papers are published, although there is some indication that this proscription may be reconsidered.

Accounting and Auditing Considerations

SFAS 63, *Financial Reporting by Broadcasters* (Br5), provides standards of financial accounting and reporting for broadcast entities that transmit radio or television program material. This SFAS was extracted from (and supersedes) the specialized accounting principles and practices in AICPA SOP 75-5, *Accounting Practices in the Broadcasting Industry*. SFAS 63 deals with three specific accounting issues unique to this industry: (1) license agreements for program material, (2) barter transactions and, (3) network affiliation agreements.

Program License Agreements. A license agreement for program material is a contract entered into between a broadcaster ("licensee") and a production company

Program Rights — Program rights represent license agreements for the right to broadcast programs and are stated at cost less amortization. Program rights are amortized using a method designed to match costs with estimated revenues. Prior to 1986 program rights were amortized primarily using accelerated methods based on program usage. Because the Company's program library value includes a substantial investment in programs for which viewership of repeat broadcasts declines relatively little, in 1986 the Company increased its estimate of the aggregate revenues to be derived from repeat broadcasts. To match costs with the changed estimate of revenues, the Company began amortizing program rights using the straight-line method based on the license period or based on usage, whichever yields the greater accumulated amortization. In 1986 management determined the value of certain program rights was less than book value. The resultant write-down reduced income from operations and net income by $5,100 and $2,700 ($ .26 per share), respectively.

The portion of the unamortized balance expected to be amortized within one year is classified as a current asset. The liability for program rights fees is not discounted for imputed interest.

FIG. 38.3 Example of Policies Related to Programs Acquired for Broadcasting
Source: Scripps-Howard Broadcasting Company, 1986 Annual Report.

or syndicator (the "licensor") that gives the licensee, in exchange for a license fee, the right to broadcast program material either a specified or unlimited number of times over the license period. SFAS 63 requires that a licensee account for a license agreement as a purchase of rights, and accordingly report an asset and a liability for the rights acquired and obligations incurred when the license period begins and certain other conditions are met, as follows (Br5.104):

a. The cost of each program is known or reasonably determinable.

b. The program material has been accepted by the licensee in accordance with the conditions of the license agreement.

c. The program is available for its first showing or telecast. Except when a conflicting license prevents usage by the licensee, restrictions under the same license agreement or another license agreement with the same licensor on the timing of subsequent showings shall not affect this availability condition.

If any of these conditions is not met, the transaction is not recorded in the financial statements. For example, the right to air a future live sporting event does not meet the third condition. If the license agreement is not recorded in the financial statements but is significant, the licensee must disclose the agreement as a commitment. Figure 38.3 shows a policy footnote excerpt relating to programs acquired for broadcasting.

SOP 75-5 had required that assets and liabilities related to a license agreement be reported at their present values; SFAS 63 provides an option that allows the gross amounts to be recorded (Br5.105). A review of the financial statements of the major broadcast entities indicates that the gross cost option is preferred, as shown in Figure 38.3. For those selecting the present value option, the discounting must be performed in accordance with APB 21, *Interest on Receivables and Payables* (I69).

The prepaid program costs should be appropriately amortized as discussed in the following subsections.

Cost to be amortized. If the cost of a license agreement is payment for a group of programs it should be allocated to individual programs within the package based on the relative value of each program (Br5.106). This valuation is often specified in the agreement; if it is not, the licensee will determine value allocations on some reasonable basis.

Amortization period. Generally, prepaid program costs are to be amortized over the estimated number of future showings expected to occur. However, if an agreement allows for unlimited showings during the license period and the number of future showings cannot be estimated, the cost is generally amortized over the license period.

Amortization approach. Conceptually, the prepaid program costs should be amortized in relation to the program's contribution to periodic revenues. However, it is often difficult to determine the timing and amount of an individual program contribution.

Feature programs are generally amortized on a program-by-program basis, whereas a program series or syndicated products are amortized as a series. The cost of feature programs that have no repeat value should be attributed entirely to the first showing and be written off when first aired. If a program is expected to air more than once and generate a larger amount of revenue from the first airing than from the succeeding airings, the licensee must attribute more of the cost and thus higher amortization expense to the earliest airing. If, however, the revenue stream from a program is expected to be constant, the straight-line method of amortization may be used (Br5.107).

Balance sheet classification. License agreements typically have a term longer than one year. As a result, the prepaid program cost must be segregated between current and noncurrent classifications according to the projected broadcast date for a single-run program or estimated usage for a group of programs. The liability for fees also should be segregated between current and noncurrent classifications based on the payment terms specified in the agreement.

Periodic valuation. Prepaid program costs are to be reported at the lower of unamortized cost or estimated net realizable value. The determination of value may be made on a program by program, series, package, or time-of-day (e.g., prime time) basis. Periodically, the licensee's management must review its existing program inventory and outstanding commitments to determine whether:

• There is excess program inventory; or
• Based upon previous experience, viewer preference or a change in market conditions, there is evidence that a series, package, or time of day will be unprofitable.

In such an instance, a write down to net realizable value will be necessary (Br5.108).

Barter Transactions. Barter, as defined in SFAS 63, represents the exchange of available advertising time for products or services. The items a broadcaster will typically barter for include merchandise, travel, hotel and restaurant services, other media advertising privileges (e.g., barters with a publisher), fixed assets, and program material. Although barter transactions are entered into by both radio and television broadcasters, they are more prevalent in radio.

Nonmedia barter transactions are governed by APB 29, *Accounting for Nonmonetary Transactions* (N35), which specifies that nonmonetary transactions should be recorded at the fair value of either the consideration surrendered or received, whichever is more readily determinable. However, SFAS 63 concludes that it is the value of the product or service *received* that dictates the valuation of the transactions (Br5.109).

The only exception to this requirement is that network affiliated stations do not record any costs for those programs furnished to them by the network in exchange for the advertising time available within those programs. In these circumstances, the station would record cash compensation received from the network for advertising time as "affiliate compensation revenue."

Barter revenue is recognized when the commercial is broadcast (thus completing the earnings process for the broadcaster), but the products or services received are charged to operations on receipt or when used. If a commercial is broadcast before the product or service is received, a receivable is recorded; on the other hand, if the product or service is received or used in advance of the commercial being aired, the broadcaster must reflect a liability to the advertiser. Therefore, it is imperative for the broadcaster to keep accurate records related to each barter agreement.

Many barter transactions are entered into for commercial air time on a specific date in the very near future. As a result, the advertiser will often limit the time in which specific services can be utilized. It is important to periodically review barter contracts to ensure that they have not expired and the unused services still represent a valid asset of the broadcaster.

Bartering of program licenses. In Issue 87-10, *Revenue Recognition by Television "Barter" Syndicators*, the EITF dealt with accounting for a barter transaction in which a television program director or producer grants a program license to a local station in exchange for a fee and advertising time. The advertising time is then generally sold to a third-party national advertiser. Thus the transaction is part sale and part barter. The question raised in this case was the timing of revenue recognition for the advertising portion of the transaction.

The EITF concluded that if the criteria in SFAS 53 dealing with licensing agreements (Mo6.105; discussed in the section, on "Motion Picture Films") were met and noncancelable contracts existed with both the station and the third-party advertiser, the earnings process should be considered complete and the barter revenue can be recognized. If such contracts do not exist revenue cannot be recognized until the advertising airs.

Network Affiliation Agreements. A network affiliation agreement provides for a station to receive network programming (which includes advertising already sold by the network) at no cost. In addition, the station receives cash compensation based on the number of network programs aired by the station in a given week.

Network affiliation agreements (Br5.110) are presented on a broadcaster's balance sheet as an intangible asset. If a station terminates a network affiliation agreement and does not immediately enter into another one, it should recognize a loss equal to the unamortized balance related to the terminated agreement. If the station immediately enters into another affiliation agreement with a fair value lower than the amount of the unamortized balance applicable to the old agreement, the difference should be recognized as a loss. However, a gain would not be recognized if the fair value of the new affiliation agreement exceeds the unamortized balance applicable to the old agreement.

CABLE TELEVISION

Industry Environment

Cable TV (or CATV) was developed in the 1940s to provide small communities with the ability to receive conventional TV signals that would otherwise be inhibited because of difficult terrain or physical distance from TV stations. The original service, in essence, provided a collective antenna for regions with poor or nonexistent reception.

Basic cable service today includes signals of national television networks, local and distant independent, specialty and educational television stations, satellite-delivered nonbroadcast channels, locally originated entertainment programs, educational programs, public service announcements, and continuous time, news, and weather information. In addition, for an extra monthly charge, systems also offer one or more special services ("pay cable") that generally consist of motion pictures, live and taped sports events, concerts, and other features presented usually without commercial interruption.

Cable systems are generally constructed and operated under nonexclusive franchises granted by state and local governmental authorities. Those franchises contain many conditions, some of which are subject to renegotiation during their term, such as time limits on commencement or completion of construction, and conditions of service (including the number of channels, types of programming and free service to schools and other public institutions, and the maintenance of insurance and indemnity bonds).

Regulation

The provisions of a CATV franchise are subject to the Cable Communications Policy Act of 1984 (the Cable Act). An important recent change in the Cable Act was the deregulation of basic cable rates effective in 1987. System operators are now able to raise monthly subscription rates on basic cable service at their own discretion, rather than being limited to a 5% annual rate increase cap.

The Cable Act affects many aspects of the cable communications business including:

• Granting, modification, and renewal of franchises.
• Regulation of rates and services.

- Payment of franchise fees.
- Dedication of cable channels for public, educational, governmental and commercial purposes.
- Protection of subscriber privacy and consumer interests.

The Cable Act also restricts common ownership or control of cable systems with co-located broadcast stations or local telephone companies. The principal responsibility for implementing the Cable Act's policies is allocated between the FCC and state or local franchising authorities.

The Cable Act provides for FCC jurisdiction over certain technical and programming aspects of cable communications. For example, the FCC recently issued rules reinstituting mandatory cable carriage for local television stations. The new rules, which attempt to overcome constitutional concerns raised by a 1985 federal court decision invalidating similar regulations, will require cable systems with more than 20 channels to devote up to 25% of their channel capacity to carriage of local TV stations through 1993. In addition, cable operators will be required to offer each subscriber an input selector ("A/B Switch") enabling conversion from signal receipt via the cable system to use of the subscriber's own antenna. The FCC also has statutory authority to regulate rates and conditions imposed by telephone and power companies for cable systems' use of utility pole and conduit space, in states where such rates are not regulated. The U.S. Supreme Court recently upheld the FCC's authority in the area of pole access.

Regulatory responsibility for essentially local aspects of the cable business such as franchisee selection, billing practices, system design and construction, safety, and consumer services, remains with either state or local offices, and in some jurisdictions with both. State and local franchising jurisdiction is not unlimited, however, and must be exercised in a manner consistent with Cable Act provisions. Although the Cable Act also establishes renewal procedures designed to protect incumbent franchisees against arbitrary denials of renewal, renewal is by no means assured because the franchisee must continue to meet stringent standards to qualify.

Cable communications systems are subject to federal copyright licensing covering carriage of television broadcast signals. In exchange for filing certain reports and contributing a percentage of their revenues to a federal copyright royalty pool, cable operators can obtain blanket permission to rebroadcast copyrighted material.

Accounting and Auditing Considerations

In 1981, the FASB issued SFAS 51, *Financial Reporting by Cable Television Companies* (Ca4). This statement extracts (and supersedes) the specialized principles and practices from AICPA SOP 79-2, *Accounting by Cable Television Companies*, and establishes financial accounting and reporting standards for certain costs, expenses, and revenues related to cable television systems. SOP 79-2 was originally developed to clarify and standardize the diverse accounting practices being followed in the cable television industry.

Prematurity Period. The prematurity period is the period during which the cable television system is partially under construction and partially in service. The

Prior to receiving the first revenues from subscribers of a cable television system constructed by the Company, all construction costs, operating expenses and interest related to the system are capitalized. From the time of such receipt until completion of construction, but no longer than two years (defined as the "prematurity period"), portions of certain fixed operating expenses and interest are capitalized in addition to direct construction costs. The portions capitalized are decreased as progress is made toward obtaining the subscriber level expected at the end of the prematurity period, after which no further expenses are capitalized. Expenses, other than interest, capitalized during the two years ended May 31, 1986 and 1985 were $183,200 and $174,200, respectively. No such amounts were capitalized during the year ended May 31, 1987. In addition, costs (including labor, overhead and other costs of completion) associated with installation in homes not previously served by cable television are capitalized and included as "distributed systems."

FIG. 38.4   Example of Disclosures of Cable Television Capitalized Plant Costs
Source: Jones Intercable Inc., 1987 Annual Report.

prematurity period is determined before, and begins with, the point at which revenue is earned from the first subscriber. Although the length of the prematurity period will vary depending on the development and construction plans and may exceed two years in the case of major urban markets, there is a presumption that the prematurity period will not exceed two years. The end of the prematurity period is based on either plans for completion of the first major construction period or achievement of a specified predetermined subscriber level (Ca4.403). See Figure 38.4 for a sample disclosure of capitalized costs.

During the prematurity period, costs and expenses are categorized in three ways:

1. *Costs that are entirely capitalized.* This includes cost of cable television facilities, including materials, direct labor, and construction overhead (Ca4.104a). Costs incurred prior to the prematurity period are generally capitalized. Interest related to the construction of the facilities is capitalized in accordance with SFAS 34, *Capitalization of Interest Cost* (I67).

2. *Costs that are entirely expensed.* This includes subscriber-related costs and general and administrative expenses. Subscriber-related costs are costs incurred to obtain and retain subscribers, such as costs of billing and collection, bad debts, mailings, repairs and maintenance, franchise fees related to revenues or number of subscribers, management salaries, and office rent (Ca4.104b).

3. *Costs that are partially capitalized and partially expensed.* This includes programming costs and other system costs that are incurred in anticipation of servicing a fully operational system and do not vary with the volume of subscribers. The portion of those costs attributable to current operations should be expensed currently with the remainder capitalized (Ca4.104c).

The proportion of costs in the last category that are to be expensed currently is generally calculated by use of a fraction based on the relationship between the average number of actual or anticipated subscribers and the total number of subscribers expected at the end of the prematurity period (Ca4.105). Costs that have been capitalized should be amortized over the same period used to depreciate the main cable television facility. During the prematurity period, both depreciation and amortization expense are determined by multiplying monthly depreciation and amortization of total costs expected to be capitalized prior to completion of the prematurity period by the fraction previously described. The depreciation method used during the prematurity period should be the same method that will be applied by the company after the prematurity period.

The principal impact of SFAS 51 is to prescribe an accounting treatment in which the capitalized cost declines (as a percentage of total system costs) each month of the prematurity period, while the expensed cost increases. As a result, at the start of the prematurity period most system costs are capitalized; toward the end, most are expensed.

Hookup Revenue and Costs. Initial hookup revenue is recognized as revenue only to the extent of direct selling costs incurred in obtaining the subscriber. Direct selling costs include commissions, advertising, and costs of document processing. The remainder of hookup revenue is deferred and amortized over the estimated average period that subscribers are expected to remain connected to the system (Ca4.109).

Subscriber Installations. Cable TV is a capital intensive business. The largest asset component of cable television companies is generally property and equipment, recorded at cost including labor, interest, and other costs of construction and completion.

Initial subscriber installation costs, including material, labor, and overhead costs of the drop (the cable that brings the signal from the main cable to the subscriber's television set) are capitalized and depreciated over a period no longer than the depreciation period used for the cable television facilities. Installations are generally capitalized at a standard rate based on the net increase in the number of subscribers receiving service. The costs of subsequently disconnecting and reconnecting subscribers are charged to expense (Ca4.110).

Franchise Costs. Costs of a successful franchise application should be capitalized and amortized in accordance with the provisions of APB 17, *Intangible Assets* (I60). Costs of unsuccessful franchise applications and abandoned franchises are charged to expense.

MOTION PICTURE FILMS

Industry Environment

The motion picture industry once consisted of a relatively small number of film companies that stood apart from other segments of the entertainment industry. With the onset of television, followed by VCRs and cable TV, the desires and expectations of the viewing public have changed substantially. These dynamics have resulted in dramatic changes in the distribution and licensing of rights to use motion pictures. Movie companies now sell the film rights at a relatively early stage to videotape distributors, television networks, and cable TV companies.

To some extent the industry has lost its glamour as the primary provider of entertainment, but the changes have enhanced the industry's ability to market its products more broadly. The viewer now has the opportunity to attend a movie theatre, rent the movie on a videotape, or subscribe to a cable network and view a relatively recent movie release at no additional cost. Additionally, the introduction of pay cable (in which a viewer may reserve a movie to be played over the cable at a requested time) provides a convenience not previously available. Given the high costs of movie production, all of these new distribution methods offer the opportunity to generate more revenues.

Accounting and Auditing Considerations

In 1982, the FASB finalized its guidance in this area, releasing SFAS 53, *Financial Reporting by Producers of Motion Picture Films* (Mo6). SFAS 53 extracted (and superseded) the specialized accounting principles and practices from the AICPA Industry Accounting Guide, *Accounting for Motion Picture Films*, and SOP 79-4, *Accounting for Motion Picture Films.*

Licensing Agreements. Upon completion of a film, the producers earn their revenues by the sale of rights granting others permission to use the film. Typically, the producer enters into a licensing agreement with a theatre, television station, or cable TV system allowing exhibition of the film. The agreement specifies the conditions of exhibition such as the date on which exhibition may begin, the length of the exhibition period or the number of exhibitions allowed, and the basis on which the producer will be compensated for the right to use the film. The conditions of these agreements vary according to whether they are with a theatre or a TV station. The major accounting issues relate to the timing of revenue recognition, which in part is affected by the conditions in the agreement and the costs of producing the film.

Figure 38.5 shows a sample disclosure of motion picture revenue recognition policies.

Television stations. These licenses are assumed to be outright sales on which revenue can be recognized at the beginning of the licensing period if all of the following conditions for each film are met (Mo6.105):

- The license fee is known.
- Cost is known or reasonably determinable.
- Collectibility of the fee is reasonably assured.
- The film has been accepted by the licensee.
- The film is available for its first showing.

The sales price of each film should equal the present value of the amount of the license fee specified in the contract (Mo6.108). The computation should be based on the provisions contained in APB 21, *Interest on Receivables and Payables* (I69).

Revenues from theatrical distribution of films in the United States and Canada are recognized as the films are exhibited. Distribution of the Company's films to theatres in foreign countries and to the home video markets is effected through subdistributors who control various aspects of distribution. When the terms of sale to such subdistributors include the receipt of non-refundable guaranteed amounts by the Company, revenue is recognized when the film is available to the subdistributors for exhibition or exploitation and other conditions of sale are met. When the arrangements with such subdistributors call for distribution of the Company's product without a minimum amount guaranteed to the Company, such sales are recognized when the Company's share of the income from exhibition or exploitation is earned. Revenues from network, pay cable and syndication television licensing agreements are recognized when the films are available for broadcast.

FIG. 38.5 Example of Policies Regarding Motion Picture Revenue Recognition
Source: Orion Pictures Corporation, 1987 Annual Report.

Movie theatres. Unlike licenses to television stations, movie theatres generally agree to pay a percentage of box office receipts in exchange for the right to show the movie. Given uncertainties that often exist regarding future box office receipts, SFAS 53 delays recognition of revenue until the movie is actually exhibited (Mo6.102 and .103). However, if nonrefundable guarantees are paid by the licensee such that the agreement is the equivalent of an outright sale, revenue recognition could take place earlier if the conditions for recognition specified for licenses to television stations are met, as discussed earlier.

Costs of Production. The cost of producing most movies has increased significantly over the years. Costs include compensation to the actors and actresses, which may be contractually fixed or may have a variable element, cost of filming crews, costumes, sets, and transportation, to mention only a few. Most of these costs are capitalized and amortized over the revenue generating life of the film. The following sections discuss some of the special types of capitalized costs and related amortization approaches.

Participations. This cost is the variable portion of compensation paid to those involved in the production, such as actors and directors. Generally, the participation is expressed in terms of a percentage of future revenues on profits expected on the film from all or specified licensing agreements with exhibitors (Mo6.411).

Exploitation costs. These costs include all expenditures made to promote a film and to make it available to exhibitors. Such costs include advertising, copying of the film, and any other costs that are incurred to enhance future revenues (Mo6.402).

Story costs. The basis for a film may be a book or a stage play. Significant costs are often incurred to obtain the rights to the original material and adapt it for the production of a film; these costs should be capitalized. However, if the acquired right has been held for three years with no current prospect for use, the capitalized cost should be charged to earnings (Mo6.116).

Amortization approaches. There are two commonly used methods of amortization, both of which attempt to amortize costs in relation to revenue patterns:

1. *Individual-film-forecast-computation.* This method relies on the ratio of the current period's gross revenue to the projected or total gross revenue over a particular film's life. The estimated revenue from all sources should be included. In some instances, there are non-interest-bearing licensing agreements that should be discounted before inclusion in the projected total gross revenues (Mo6.110).

2. *Periodic-table-computation.* This approach relies on tables that reflect the historic revenue patterns for a large group of films. This method is permitted only if it would approximate the result of using the individual-film-forecast-computation (Mo6.112).

Inventory Valuation. A periodic assessment of the net realizable value of the unamortized balance of production and exploitation costs should be made for each film (Mo6.115). If recovery of the balance is not assured based on current estimates of future gross revenues, the balance should be written down. Costs written down may be written back up only if the recovery takes place in the same year. Occasionally, it is necessary to write down the capitalized costs before a film is released; this can be the result of a reassessment of budgeted gross revenues, or because of substantial cost overruns in comparison with the original budget.

Balance Sheet Classification. License agreements should not be reflected as assets in the balance sheet until revenue recognition is appropriate (Mo6.118). At that point, film costs should be separated between current and noncurrent assets. Costs of completed films to be released shortly should be shown as current assets.

SEC Disclosures. In 1984, the SEC staff expressed concern regarding the adequacy of disclosures by motion picture film companies regarding unamortized film costs and recoverability. An AcSEC Task Force studied the matter, and the resulting guidance was published in the "News Report" section of the April 1986 *Journal of Accountancy* (pp. 18–20). The SEC staff has stated that the following disclosures (listed in the article) are required for registrants.

1. *Earnings process.* Information regarding the types of films produced, the markets served (e.g., movie theaters and television), the order in which the markets are exploited (i.e., movie theatres first, then television and then videotape distributors, or some other order); the length of the revenue cycle, and revenue recognition policies. Additionally, the types of capitalized costs should be described.

2. *Unamortized costs.* The percentage of unamortized film costs expected to be amortized in the next three years. If that percentage is expected to be less than 60% of the unamortized cost the registrant should provide additional discussion, such as the time period over which 60% would be amortized.

3. *Additions to film costs.* Gross additions to film costs and the amount of amortization should be reflected in a statement of cash flows. (This recommendation as written refers to a funds statement, now superseded by SFAS 95.)

4. *Individual-film-forecast method.* This method requires a projection of future revenues and amortizes the cost on the basis of the relationship between estimated total revenue and actual revenue for the year. A description of the calculation of amortization and any significant changes in revenue estimates should be discussed, and should describe the policies regarding:
   * Amortization of cost of released productions;
   * Accounting policies regarding profit participations;
   * The fact that estimated future revenues are reviewed periodically; and
   * The fact that revisions may be made to amortization rates or write-downs made to net realizable value.

RECORDS AND MUSIC

Industry Environment

A recording company enters an agreement with an artist to produce a musical work; or the artist may offer a work already produced. The company's role is to develop a finished, salable product. As in the motion picture industry, the methods of conveying the music to the public have changed significantly over the years from phonograph records to reel-to-reel tapes, to eight track tapes, to cassettes, to compact disks, and currently to digital tapes. The progression in mode has been one of tremendous increases in the quality and clarity of the sound. Although these technological advances have affected the industry in many ways, the basic business of bringing music to the consumer to enjoy in the privacy of the home or automobile remains unchanged.

In many respects the accounting issues in the records and music industry are similar to those in film production. The owner of the music copyright or record master enters license agreements with a licensee permitting the use of the music, and the copying and sole use of the record. Generally, the licensor incurs costs in the form of payments to composers, artists, studios, and recording engineers.

Accounting and Auditing Considerations

In 1981, the FASB released SFAS 50, *Financial Reporting in the Record and Music Industry* (Re4). This SFAS was extracted from (and supersedes) SOP 76-1, *Accounting Practices in the Record and Music Industry,* and constitutes the current accounting guidance for this industry.

Revenues. The licensor enters licensing agreements related to either a copyright on a particular musical composition or for an existing record master. These agreements generally call for a fixed fee or a fee based on actual sales.

Some agreements are noncancelable and may, in substance, constitute an outright sale for which revenues may be recognizable currently. Certain conditions must exist for the agreement to be treated as an outright sale, as follows (Re4.102):

* The agreement must be clearly noncancelable;
* The fee is fixed;
* The licensee has possession of the rights with no limitation on their exercise; and
* There are no remaining obligations to deliver music or a record master.

If all these conditions are met the earnings process is considered complete and revenue recognition occurs. Of course, collectibility of the fee must be reasonably assured.

If a minimum guarantee is received by the licensor in advance of sales of the music or records, the licensor should report it as a liability. Revenue is then recognized as the terms of the agreement are met, and the liability is reduced accordingly. If it is not possible to determine the amount of periodic license fee earned, it may be allocated to periods on a straight-line basis over the term of the agreement (Re4.103).

Costs. The most significant costs are production costs and artist compensation. All costs incurred in the development of the record master generally are capitalized and shown as an asset. The recoverability of this cost must be periodically assessed by comparing the balance to the estimated future revenues. Amortization should be done on a systematic approach in relation to the stream of future revenues.

Artists are generally compensated with royalties based on individual record sales. Advance royalties often are paid, and are offset by future royalties earned. Advances should be recorded as an asset and charged to expense as revenues are generated by sales. Again, recoverability must be periodically assessed (Re4.105).

Disclosures. Because of the significance of the amounts, the following items should be appropriately disclosed (Re4.108–.109):

* Commitments for advances to be paid in future periods.
* Future royalty guarantees.
* Balance of the capitalized cost of record masters.

PROFESSIONAL SPORTS

Industry Environment

One of the most important leisure activities of the American public is attending sports events, listening to them on the radio, or viewing them on television. As an indication of the importance of electronic media to sports teams, the Boston Celtics for the year ended June 30, 1987, reported that almost 40% of combined revenues of $20.3 million (excluding advertising and playoffs) was derived from television and radio contracts.

Financial information on sports clubs is limited because the majority are privately held. However, from articles in the general press it is clear that: (1) player compensation, both annual and deferred, is a material part of total expenditures and annual expenses; (2) although sports teams generally have a healthy cash flow, they also have significant contractual obligations for the payment of future compensation; and (3) in most cases, television contracts are lucrative. In addition, post-season playoff games for qualifying teams add significantly to their gross revenues; in the case of the Celtics, playoff games added almost 20% of revenues for the year ended June 30, 1987.

The major professional sports in the United States – football, basketball, baseball, and ice hockey – have become big business to the owners, the players, and the unions. Early in the history of professional sports, highly publicized football players were paid $200 or $300 per game. Even allowing for the change in the value of the dollar, salaries in professional sports have since grown to astronomical sums, with many annual player contracts for amounts in excess of $1 million. Obviously, these substantial increases in compensation are, in the end, added to charges for tickets or TV rights, both of which have increased significantly in recent years.

Additionally, player strikes have occurred with increasing frequency, disrupting normal operations and significantly affecting the financial well-being of some teams. However, the common perception is that sports teams are very prosperous, and as a result, union demands escalate from contract to contract.

Types of Entities. Most professional sports clubs are either closely held corporations, wholly owned subsidiaries of other corporations, or partnerships. As a result, public financial disclosure is limited. In many cases, the organizations tend to be small, at least in number of full-time nonplayer personnel employed. In addition, a number of part-time employees are hired as statisticians and press attendants. Of course, the principal employees of sports teams are the coaches and players. Each sport's league limits the number of players that may be included on the team roster both off-season and during the season.

Sports teams compete in both home and away games. The arenas or stadiums in which they compete are either self-owned, owned by a public municipal agency that leases the facilities, or owned by another sports organization that also uses the facility.

Major Issues. There are three major issues with which sports organizations must contend:

1. *Free choice.* To a degree, players must be restricted in the amount of freedom they enjoy in selecting teams with which to play. As with most careers, employees (players) do not have an absolute choice of employers based on taste or monetary considerations. Without some restrictions, players would move frequently from team to team based on a sports team's field success, monetary reward, or both. Permitting absolute freedom of movement would likely result in the better players gravitating to the teams with the best performance, creating a permanent performance imbalance, that is, one team winning continuously or an explosion in players' compensation. In recent years, more flexibility in player movement has been permitted in most professional sports, and one result has been significant increases in player compensation.

2. *Long-term player contracts.* Expensive, long-term contracts have become prevalent in recent years. Such contracts may be a considerable burden for sports teams, especially when the career of a player with this type of contract is ended due to injury or his performance deteriorates.

3. *Seasonality of business.* Every professional sport is a seasonal activity. In a considerable part of each year, little or no revenue is earned although general business expenses continue.

Accounting Considerations

Player Contracts. Long-term player contracts have become prevalent, often extending for 10 or more years. Occasionally, those contracts cover periods of a player's declining abilities or even extend beyond a player's retirement. A sports club faced with a situation in which the player is not active, but carrying a deferred cost relating to an unexpired period in a long-term contract, should expense the remaining deferred cost as a current period charge.

It is difficult to determine how most sports teams treat such costs; but it seems necessary under GAAP that deferral and amortization be discontinued when an asset (the active player) no longer has value. Figure 38.6 presents the Celtics' accounting policy relative to long-term player contracts. Figure 38.7 is an extract from the related Form 10-K that demonstrates the dollar magnitude of current and long-term player contracts for both present and former players.

Roster Cost. In cases where a team has been sold, its economic assets (the services of players under contract) are recorded in the allocation of purchase price by the buyer as identifiable, intangible assets, based on the fair value of the player contracts. Therefore, as that asset is amortized over the useful lives of the respective contracts, a team that has been sold will present higher operating expenses than a team that has not been sold.

This phenomenon was commented on at some length in "Accounting for Baseball" (Sorter, 1986), in which the author describes his engagement to determine the profitability of the major league clubs for 1984 on behalf of the club owners, who were in negotiations with the Players Association. Although clearly in conformity with APB 16 purchase price allocation guidelines, the fair values placed on player contracts were criticized as resulting in amortization charges that were inappropriate for purposes of computing profitability. The effect was significant; for 1984 combined operations, the expense charge was $12 million out of a total baseball loss of $43 million (before interest expense).

Sorter suggests that perhaps the player roster cost in a purchase business combination should be associated with ownership and excluded from operating results. This of course would contravene APB 16, and undoubtedly would lead to other entities rationalizing the same treatment for similar purchased intangibles, especially if their goal is to report higher profits. This problem illustrates that GAAP is not useful for all things, in particular for player contract negotiations.

Seasonality. Professional sports operation is seasonal. Generally, little or no revenue is earned during at least one quarter of the year, and in each sport full operation occurs in at least one quarter. However, seasonal adjustments are not a

Deferred player acquisition costs ascribed to contracts acquired by BCI in 1983 are being amortized on the straight-line method over an average contract life of five years. The costs of player contracts acquired from other teams are amortized over the term of the respective players' contracts. Upon termination of a player's services, any applicable unamortized deferred player acquisition costs, net of sale proceeds if any, are charged to expense.

FIG. 38.6 Accounting Policy for Long-Term Player Contracts
Source: Boston Celtics Limited Partnership, 1987 Annual Report on Form 10-K.

The By-laws of the NBA require each member team to enter into a uniform player contract with each of its players. As of June 30, 1987, the Boston Celtics' contracts with its present players and 18 past players provided for the payment of current compensation and deferred compensation as follows:

Fiscal year	Current compensation payments	Deferred compensation payments	
		Unearned	Earned
1988	$6,992,500	—	$ 687,863
1989	6,085,000	$ 200,000	942,315
1990	5,110,000	305,000	635,434
1991	3,445,000	305,000	635,434
1992 and thereafter	2,145,000	3,100,000	3,243,802

Substantially all of the payments shown above are guaranteed and must be paid during the balance of the term of the player's contract even if the player is released or, in some cases, injured. A small portion of such payments are not guaranteed under certain conditions, such as the release of the player prior to a specified date or the player's failure to comply with prohibitions on certain activities. As of September 15, 1987, the Boston Celtics had outstanding loans to players aggregating $1,069,000.

FIG. 38.7 Disclosure of Current and Deferred Player Contracts
Source: Boston Celtics Limited Partnership, 1987 Annual Report on Form 10-K.

serious problem, at least from a public reporting perspective, since so few of these enterprises are publicly held.

In the case of the Celtics, the seasonal nature of revenues and expenses as discussed in MD&A is presented in Figure 38.8.

CASINOS

Industry Environment

Although forms of gambling have existed since primitive times, the present form of gaming originated in sixteenth-century Europe. In the United States, gambling became a significant industry after World War II. Presently, open gambling is a big

The operations and financial results of the Boston Celtics are seasonal. On a cash flow basis, the Boston Celtics receive a substantial portion of their receipts from the advance sale of season tickets during the months of July, August and September, prior to commencement of the NBA regular season. Most cash receipts from Playoff ticket sales are received in March of each year. Most of the Boston Celtics' operating expenses are incurred and paid during the regular season, which extends from late October through Mid-April, and during the Playoffs, which follow the regular season and extend into June.

For financial reporting purposes, the Partnership recognizes its revenues and expense on a game-by-game basis. Because the NBA regular season begins in October, the first quarter which ends on September 30 will generally include limited or no revenue and will reflect a loss attributable to general and administrative expense incurred in the quarter. Based on the present NBA game schedule, the Partnership will generally recognize approximately one-third of its annual regular season revenue in the second quarter, approximately one-half of such revenue in the third quarter, and the remainder in the fourth quarter, and it will recognize all of its Playoff revenue in the fourth quarter.

FIG. 38.8   Disclosure of Seasonal Nature of Professional Basketball Operations
Source: Boston Celtics Limited Partnership, 1987 Annual Report on Form 10-K.

business in Reno, Las Vegas, and Lake Tahoe, Nevada, and in Atlantic City, New Jersey. Other forms of gambling, such as lotteries, are conducted by many states.

Casinos operate a variety of gambling forms depending on state law and the rules of state gaming commissions. The forms of gambling include blackjack, roulette, poker, slot machines, keno, bingo, and race and sports betting. Of course, gambling is also permitted at many race tracks throughout the United States, including the racing of horses, trotters, or dogs (not discussed in the *Handbook*). In addition, gambling is permitted for specialized sports such as jai alai. Gambling is generally a high volume cash business although provision is made on a selective basis for granting credit to regular customers.

Regulation

Gambling in the United States is closely controlled by state and local authorities under numerous laws, regulations, and ordinances. These controls deal with the responsibility, financial stability, and character of casino owners and operators. Casino ownership must be approved by a gaming commission.

A casino operates pursuant to a renewable, nontransferable license. The gaming commissions have broad powers to require a casino to:

(a) suspend or dismiss officers, directors, or other key employees or (b) sever relationships with other persons who refuse to file appropriate applications or whom the authorities find unsuitable to act in such capacities. [AICPA, 1984d]

In addition, gaming commissions may require that certain procedures be followed in specified areas, including:

1. Employment practices, security standards, management control procedures, accounting and cash control methods, advertising procedures, entertainment standards, alcoholic beverage distribution procedures and gaming equipment purchasing procedures.
2. Specified gaming rules, and the manner of granting credit.
3. Reports on casino operations.

If gaming laws are determined to have been violated, a license can be limited, conditioned, suspended, or revoked. Fines can also be assessed.

Accounting Considerations

The AICPA Audit and Accounting Guide, *Audits of Casinos* (AICPA, 1984d), provides limited accounting guidance and focuses primarily on the unique audit issues.
While casinos are similar in many respects to other industries, some accounting facets are unique. These areas include:

1. Gross revenue includes net gaming wins and losses.
2. Promotional allowances are goods and services given to customers to induce gambling. The normal selling price of these items is either disclosed in a note or added to gross revenue and shown as a deduction therefrom.
3. Base jackpots generally are allocated to expense over the estimated period of play prior to payout. Any unallocated portion of the base jackpot remaining when the jackpot is paid is expensed at that time.
4. Gaming chips are accounted for as soon as the casino receives them regardless of whether they were issued immediately. When cash is exchanged for gaming chips, a liability exists as long as those chips are not exchanged for cash or won by the house. The liability is computed by determining the difference between the total chips placed in service and the actual inventory of chips in the hands of the casino. This liability is adjusted periodically based on an estimate of chips that will never be redeemed.
5. Some casinos accept wagers on horse races and professional or amateur sporting events. The amount received by the casino is a liability until the outcome of the event is known.

In SAB 69 (Topic 11.L), *Income Statement Presentation of Casino-Hotels,* the SEC staff states that the amounts of revenue and expense for casino, hotel, and restaurant operations should be presented separately.

Auditing Considerations

Audit Approach. Auditing of casino operations is complex. With the number of employees handling money and the large volume of cash involved, control is a difficult problem. Most of the auditor's interest is accordingly directed toward controls over the cash cycle. The auditor should emphasize internal control reviews to establish that proper controls are in place and are functioning. Specifically, the auditor should:

1. Be familiar with the gaming commission's rules and regulations.

2. Read any recent communication from the gaming commission and be aware of the status of investigations, if any, into matters affecting the casino.
3. Be aware of and review the work of internal auditors. (Some gaming commissions require casinos to have internal audit staffs.)

Compliance tests of accountability and casino revenue should normally be performed periodically during the year. Those tests include observation of:

1. Collection of drop boxes and buckets, which are locked containers at table and slot machines for the purpose of collecting cash, chips and coins.
2. Procedures in the cashiers' cage and the count room where the cashiers operate and the casino bankroll is stored.
3. Fill slips, credit slips, and other credit instrument accountability procedures. (Fill slips evidence the transfer of a supply of chips, coins, or tokens from the casino's bankroll to a table or slot machine. Credit slips are used to record the return of chips, IOUs, markers, and negotiable checks from a table to the bankroll.)

The primary substantive test, observation of the cash count, is normally performed at the balance sheet date. If it is performed at another time, the auditor should be in a position to rely on the system of internal control and should perform other substantive tests sufficient for him to extend any conclusions about the interim tests of cash to the balance sheet date.

Internal Control Structure. It is impossible to record all gaming table transactions without disrupting play. As a result, gaming operations are subject to considerable risk of customer or employee dishonesty. Controls to discourage such dishonesety include:

1. Paper safeguards that cover authorization and accountability controls. Those safeguards include the use of forms and other documentation that are monitored through the gambling process and the analysis of certain statistical yardsticks that are used to compare results and trends.
2. Physical safeguards that include electronic surveillance (including overhead booth areas and closed circuit TV), table drop boxes, safes, count room equipment, gaming equipment access controls, slot machine meters, and so on.
3. Human safeguards that include continued personal supervision of and accountability for transactions and the proper segregation of duties.

Because there is a lack of physical evidence that supports the reported gaming revenues, the auditor usually relies on the system of internal control. If such reliance is not justified, the auditor may face a scope limitation.

Reliance on the system of internal control entails a significant amount of on-line compliance testing, far more than would normally be applied, because there is little or no trail of documentary evidence. In a casino, the evidence is based on the existence and observation of people-to-people checks. The auditor should make numerous corroborative inquiries and actual observations of routine operations.

Observations of casino floor operations, cage, and count room should be on a surprise basis and should be repeated throughout the time period being examined. Access to restricted areas should be precleared and promptly obtained.

Analytical Review Procedures. Analytical review procedures are vitally important in testing casino operations. Statistics and trends that should be reviewed closely by the auditor are listed in Figure 38.9. Those factors generally represent such items as probable win ratios, physical factors affecting casino attendance, and general demographic data such as economic conditions, gaming commission betting limits and changes in clientele.

Although the factors displayed in Figure 38.9 are useful, they are not invariable. Statistics in the gaming industry fluctuate in the short run primarily because the games are based on chance. However, variations over the long run should be minimal, unless a casino changes its method of operations.

Cash and Revenue Cutoff. Cash on hand usually includes (AICPA, 1984d, pp. 25–26):

1. Currency and coins.
2. House chips, including reserve chips.
3. Personal checks, cashier's checks, and traveler's checks for deposit.
4. Customer deposits, often called customer or front money (the related cash is usually comingled with the casino's cash, and the customer deposit total is treated as a liability).
5. Chips of other casinos. (Regulations normally prohibit acceptance of foreign chips; nevertheless, they may be present in the casino cage in small amounts and, in effect, represent receivables from the issuing casinos.)
6. Chips on tables.
7. Gaming device loads (coins put into machines when they are placed in service).
8. Fills and credits. (These documents are treated as assets and liabilities, respectively, of the casino cage during a business day because they evidence the transfer, in or out, of assets. When win or loss is recorded at the end of the business day, they are removed from accountabilty.)

From an auditing standpoint, the most crucial procedure is to assure that all of these cash sources are counted simultaneously, usually at the balance sheet date. A large staff and prior planning are essential. The count is usually performed while the casino is in operation, normally at a shift change, except for reserve chips. The count is time consuming and if the inventory can be controlled by the auditor, the count can be made at a less busy time.

Regarding revenue cut-off procedures, most casinos operate on a 24 hour basis and play is essentially continuous. Therefore it is not often possible to establish the same cutoff points for the casino cage count and for all games and machines. It often requires several hours to remove the cash from all gaming devices and the drop boxes at table games. The important consideration is that there be reasonable assurance that revenue is recorded properly. The auditor must ascertain that the cutoff plan is adequate and applied consistently from year to year.

Factors to be Considered	Causes of Variations
TABLE GAMES	
• Win-to-drop percentage • Win per table • Drop per table • Comparison to statistical probability curves (regression analysis)	• Change in rules of the game • Use of more decks or dealing devices • Change in volume of credit play
SLOT MACHINES	
• Win-to-handle percent • Comparison of theoretical win to actual win • Handle per machine	• Large jackpots • Reliability of meters and readings taken • Changes in machines or theoretical percentages • Mechanical failures
KENO	
• Win-to-write percent	• Changes in payout schedules • Large payouts
RACE AND SPORTS BOOK	
• Win-to-write percent	• Layoff of bets • Adjustment of point spreads • Limits on odds
* * * * * *	

Relationships with other departments
• Hotel
• Conventions
• Special events
	Overall factors that may affect comparisons
	• Economic conditions
	• Variations from industry statistics
	   — Types of clientele
	   — Size of operations
	   — Wager limits
	• Seasonality of operations
	• Lack of sufficient volume
	• Promotional programs
	• Turnover of personnel
	• Changes in competition
	• Change in clientele

Relationships with outside conditions • Traffic flow • Weather • Special events	

FIG. 38.9   Casino Operations—Analytical Review Factors
Source: Adapted from AICPA, 1984. Audit and Accounting Guide, Audits of Casinos, pp. 21–23.

Receivables From Patrons. The auditor should verify that either (1) a record of accountability has been established when credit is first extended to customers or (2) sufficient documentation of the extension of credit is established by use of an appropriate prenumbered form.

For recording receivables, the following controls are relevant (AICPA, 1984d, pp. 33–34):

• Accountability for receivables should be established at the time chips are advanced to patrons or as soon thereafter as is practical.

- Responsibility for the custody of instruments evidencing casino receivables, the accountability for them, and the receipt of collections should be separated as soon as practical.
- Tabulation of the receivable amount should be performed at either the end of each shift or the end of each day, and it should be compared to recorded accountability.
- Periodic examination of the instruments, preferably on a surprise basis, should be made by someone independent of the custodial function.
- Accounts submitted for write-off should be investigated by an employee independent of credit granting, custodial functions, and collection through contact with the patron. Approvals of write-offs will generally be made by the credit manager, the casino manager, the controller, and the chief operating officer, although this may vary depending on the amounts involved.

39

Smaller and Emerging Businesses

OVERVIEW

This chapter covers smaller privately held businesses, which can exist in several forms: corporations, partnerships, or proprietorships. Corporations and partnerships also have several possible variations. Some issues related to high technology companies are covered, because most high-tech companies start out as small businesses. In addition, some commentary is given regarding going public — exiting the unique environment of the smaller and emerging business.

The environment for small businesses is complex and would take volumes to cover with any hope of completeness. The space limitations of this chapter necessarily restrict the discussion to highlights, with a focus on the accounting and financial reporting issues commonly encountered.

CHARACTERISTICS OF SMALLER BUSINESSES

Environment

Small business has been a major creator of jobs and a driving force in developing new and innovative products and services. Much of the booming technology and service sector is dominated by these businesses, which can react and innovate more quickly than large businesses.

Small businesses typically have limited resources, are owner-managed, and constantly face changing stages of development. The major advantage of small businesses is that they quickly tend to find their specific market niches and adapt to changes in the market place. But in being small, these businesses must rely heavily on accountants and other outsiders for specific problem solving and advice.

Small businesses and high technology businesses face many of the same problems in their start-up stages: limited resources and limited ability to manage growth. But the goals of each generally are different, with small business tending to be benefits-driven and high technology earnings-driven.

While there is a level at which a company can be profitable and elect to stop growing, most small companies want to grow to increase earnings and the owner's wealth. Because small businesses are often directed by their entrepreneurial founders who are unlikely to be financially oriented, administrative problems can appear when the founder fails to realize that he is no longer managing a handful of knowledgeable employees involved in every facet of the business.

Small businesses are very sensitive to keeping income taxes to a minimum. When faced with problems pitting GAAP versus IRS regulations, small businessmen tend toward the latter. It is often impossible to segregate tax strategies and decisions of small businesses from those that affect the owner.

Ownership Forms

Smaller businesses can vary considerably in how they are structured. They can range from proprietorships to private partnerships to solely owned or family owned corporations, under several IRS classifications. Beyond this stage of closely held and relatively simple ownership, private corporations can spread out into multiple-subsidiary enterprises, some with minority interests, or into a series of corporations affiliated through common ownership by one or more natural persons rather than through corporate parent-subsidiary relationships. And for some, more commonly for high-tech companies, there will be the eventual public offering and the need to cope with a long list of SEC rules and regulations.

The more common forms of small business ownership are discussed in the following sections.

Proprietorship. An individual can enter business as a proprietor at any time, with almost no legal formality, except for licenses and permits that may be called for by applicable regulations. Small retail merchants are commonly proprietors, and so are the sole-practitioner physician and the employed individual who concurrently operate a separate business. For federal tax purposes, a proprietor files on Schedule C of Form 1040, and in thus declaring in-business status, he is required to keep adequate books and records according to IRS requirements.

As proprietorships grow, their needs in the financial planning, accounting, and taxation areas expand. Frequently, the proprietor will shift into a corporate form to insulate personal assets from business risks.

Partnership. The Uniform Partnership Act is a model statute that has been adopted by most states to govern the creation and operation of partnerships. A partnership is defined in the Act as "an association of two or more persons to carry on as co-owners of a business for profit." A "person" may be an individual, a business corporation, or any other entity having the same rights, privileges, and responsibilities as an individual.

Partnership advantages differ from corporate advantages. A corporation is recognized as a legal entity apart from its owners. Thus, shareholders are, with rare exceptions, liable only to the extent of their investment, a feature important to the public investor. In contrast, a partnership generally does not limit liability for the partners. However, an advantage is that a partnership is easy to create. A written or even oral agreement is all that is necessary; no special approval is required by any governmental unit. In addition, a partnership can be formed with a specified limited existence and can provide tax advantages when, in certain circumstances, the partners reflect on their income tax returns ordinary and capital losses in excess of their cash investments in the partnership.

The typical partnership is organized by individuals to operate a private business.[1] Partnerships formed for a specific limited objective usually have a limited term of existence, while those formed to operate an ongoing business or profession are likely to be of indefinite duration. Typically, the number of partners is small; but there is no legal limitation, and some professional partnerships – accounting firms and legal firms, for example – have hundreds.

The unincorporated *joint venture* is a form of partnership composed of a limited number of parties with a specific business purpose. Most joint ventures are of short duration, although when they are formed to handle a large project that will take

---

[1] Many investment vehicles are structured as partnerships, and often are publicly traded. This chapter does not discuss investment partnerships. See Chapters 21, 35, and 44.

years (such as building a dam or port), or to exploit a natural resource deposit, they remain in existence until their purpose is achieved.

A partnership may be a *general partnership* or a *limited partnership*. In a general partnership each partner may be held personally responsible for all the partnership's debts, while in a limited partnership the liability of the limited partners is limited to their respective contributions to the capital of the partnership.

The limited partnership is composed of one or more general partners plus one or more limited partners. A general partner typically is active in the management of the company and is recognized as a principal agent of the company; a limited partner cannot take part in the management. In most instances, the transfer of limited partnership interests is permitted without a termination of the partnership.

A partnership is not considered a separate taxable entity. Each member of a partnership includes his distributive share of various partnership items on his individual tax return. Thus, the Form 1065 tax return required to be filed by a partnership serves only to provide information necessary in determining the character and amount of each partner's distributive share of various partnership items, such as income, expense, and tax credits.

Since the cash aspects of the businesses are of prime interest, it is common for private partnerships to maintain their books essentially on a cash basis, with some modification to recognize noncash expenses such as depreciation and amortization. Such an approach facilitates the preparation of the income tax return and the determination of the individual partners' taxable income or losses. As a partnership grows in size and in the number of partners, however, the need for additional financial data for operations and planning purposes also increases; a transition to the accrual basis of accounting for other than income tax purposes may fulfill this need.

Professional Corporation. The professional corporation (PC) or professional association (PA) is used by doctors, lawyers, CPAs, and other professionals to operate as an association providing all the features of a corporation except for limited liability. These associations are recognized as a corporate entity for income tax purposes.

Privately Held Corporation. Probably the most prevalent form used by small businesses, the privately held corporation, is any corporation (including S corporations, mentioned later in this section) that has not distributed its stock ownership through a public offering, and that does not have more than 500 shareholders (the attainment of which would require filing with the SEC).

Corporations are sanctioned by the laws of each of the states, and there are numerous variations in these laws. Except for PCs and PAs, corporations are limited in responsibility for their liabilities to the extent of corporate assets; the personal assets of owners are therefore insulated assuming that creditors, or persons obtaining judgments against the corporation, do not successfully assert improper removal of assets.

Subchapter S corporation. Under the Internal Revenue Code (IRC), certain corporations electing to be treated as partnerships for income tax purposes are known as S corporations. The tax regulations for S corporations limit the number of shareholders to no more than 35. Also, no more than one class of stock may exist; all shareholders must be individuals or estates; and no more than 20% of the corporation's income can come from nonoperational sources such as interest, dividends, rents, or royalties. In all respects other than for tax purposes, the company operates as a corporation.

External Financing and Going Public

Earnings Motivations. Companies with hopes of becoming publicly held or bought out by a larger concern usually are earnings-driven. The principals running the businesses may by now be accountable to a small group of outside shareholders (e.g., venture capitalists). After some holding period, these investors are looking for an exit vehicle, whether through a public offering or sale to a larger entity. They realize that, to attract potential public investors or facilitate a private sale, the company must demonstrate the ability to generate profits. Therefore, companies grooming for public offering or sale frequently take aggressive accounting positions that enhance reported earnings; and tax concerns generally apparent in small businesses become less relevant.

Venture Capital. The venture capital community in the United States is quite extensive. When a company receives venture capital funding, it may come from several firms simultaneously and be injected into the company in several rounds of financing. Each round is scheduled to meet the company's needs and is not committed unless progressive objectives are being achieved. The venture capital firms ordinarily like to take an active role in the top management of the company through the board of directors. Since these firms are generally looking for high investment returns within five to seven years, it is common for them to jettison a founder who they believe is not satisfactorily performing.

Various development-financing organizations exist in the United States for high technology businesses. They are often funded by state or local programs and function like venture capital firms, although they typically do not take as active a role in managing the companies in which they invest.

A projection is required in any standard business plan provided to venture capitalists. Institutions or individuals providing debt financing also utilize projections to observe that a company has the capacity to service a contemplated debt. Projections serve as benchmarks against which future performance may be measured, assisting financiers in monitoring their investments and owners in staying closely attuned to future cash flow needs.

Valuing the Business. The most important concept in the valuation of a high technology business is that it is based on evaluating the future earnings potential, not on the balance sheet. Investors/buyers do not focus on the balance sheet to see what assets exist, because it is not their intention to liquidate the business. The investors will be seeking a future exit vehicle to realize their rate-of-return goals. The exit vehicle usually takes the form of grooming the company to become an acquisition candidate, or taking the company public. The pricing in such an exit will hinge on the earnings stream, as discussed in the following subsection.

Valuation factors. Numerous factors need to be considered in valuing a small company. These have been categorized into three groups: product risk, market risk, and management risk, all interrelated. Each group must be evaluated qualitatively and quantitatively. An investor will evaluate the feasibility of the technology involved in the product. He will also focus on the ultimate product potential in the marketplace and the ability of the management team to bring it to market and keep it there. An individual buying out a family owned business must focus on these same factors, but weigh them slightly differently. For instance, the break-up of a family run business may lead to management changes that could significantly affect the earnings potential of a company.

One simplified pricing model is described later herein. It requires that earnings growth estimates be made, and that rate-of-return expectations be specified. The rate-of-return factor is needed so that the return an investor expects to earn is commensurate with the risk he bears. Venture capitalists, when investing in high technology companies, seek returns of 25% or greater because of frequent business failures. On the other hand, the rate of return a buyer of a well-established small business would require should be less because of the relatively risk-free nature of the investment.

Price/earnings factors will be gathered from publicly held companies similar to the company, especially competitors, and from other sources. The projected earnings figure (not the current earnings figure) is multiplied by the price/earnings factor and discounted back over the investors' desired return period.

As an example, an investor having a return threshold of 25% compounded annually is considering an investment of $500,000 for a period of five years. At such time he will expect $1,526,000 (the original investment plus the compound return). The investor reviews the potential investee company's projections and other corroborative data, concluding that the company will earn $1 million in the fifth year. The price/earnings multiple in the investee's industry is 12 times, indicating a fifth-year value of $12 million. Thus, he needs an approximately 13% equity interest ($1,526,000/$12,000,000) for $500,000 today.

SEC Small Business Provisions. Although the SEC is normally thought of as the public control mechanism for high volume securities transactions of very large U.S. corporations and foreign entities that sell securities in the United States, the Commission also has small business capital formation as an important objective. The securities laws are complex and filing requirements for large securities transactions are voluminous. For a discussion of those requirements, see Chapter 47.

The SEC has recognized that the complexity and magnitude of filing requirements for normal securities transactions, if not altered, would discourage small companies from entering the public capital markets. As a result, several regulations provide somewhat more simplified filing and disclosure requirements for smaller public offerings and offerings made under special circumstances. Those small company regulations include registration on Form S-18, intrastate public offerings, private offerings, Regulation A offerings, and the accredited investment exemption. In addition, Regulation D coordinates most of the requirements for the limited offering exemptions and has streamlined the requirements for the private offer and sales of securities.

Form S-18 registration. As an alternative to filing on Form S-1, the full and most complex registration statement required for the sale of securities, the SEC permits a simplified approach using Form S-18. That form is available for the registration of securities to be sold for up to $7.5 million in cash. However, Form S-18 is not available to issuers that are already subject to the continuous reporting requirements of the 1934 Exchange Act.

Form S-18 is less expensive and extensive than other forms of registration. The form permits the issuer to:

• Provide audited financial statements, prepared in accordance with generally accepted accounting principles, for two fiscal years (Form S-1 requires the issuer to provide audited financial statements, prepared in accordance with more detailed SEC regulations, for three fiscal years);

• Include less extensive narrative disclosure, particularly in the areas of the description of business, than that required by Form S-1; and

• File with either the SEC Regional Office nearest to where the company conducts its principal business operations or with the SEC Division of Corporation Finance in Washington DC. The primary advantage of regional filing is that regional office personnel may be more familiar with local economic conditions, the business community, the financial environment, and, in some cases, the background and history of the company.

Intrastate offering exemption. To finance local business operations, an intrastate offering exemption is permitted. The exemption is available only if a company:

• Is incorporated in the state in which the offering is made;

• Conducts a significant amount of business in that state; and

• Offers and sells the securities only to residents of that state.

There is no limit on the size of the offering but the company must secure evidence that all purchasers of the security sold are residents of the state. In addition, the initial purchasers may not resell the security to persons outside the state within nine months. These requirements are vigorously enforced.

Private offering exemption. A special exemption is provided for transactions that do not involve any public offering. Although some uncertainty exists about the meaning of what constitutes a private offering, generally the requirement has been interpreted to mean sales to persons who are "sophisticated investors," that is, persons who have access to information about a company, are capable of interpreting the information, and are sufficiently expert to know the meaning of the data provided. Members of management of a company are examples.

The exemption requires that purchasers:

• Have sufficient knowledge and experience in financial and business matters that they are capable of evaluating the risks and merits of the investment (the "sophisticated investor"), or are able to bear the economic risk of the investment;

• Have access to the type of information normally provided in a prospectus; and

• Agree not to resell or distribute the securities

No public solicitation or advertising of an issue subject to this exemption may be made. Further, if the security is sold to only one person who is not a sophisticated investor, the entire offering may violate the 1933 Securities Act.

Regulation A. If an offering does not exceed $1.5 million (in any 12 month period), the SEC has the authority to exempt the offering from registration. Such an offering, frequently referred to as a "short form" registration, requires the filing of a notification, an offering circular (similar to a prospectus), and exhibits. The advantages of this short form registration are that required financial statements need not be audited; and unless the issuer has total assets of more than $5 million and more than 500 shareholders, there are no periodic SEC financial reporting requirements.

Regulation D. Three rules under Regulation D coordinate and streamline the requirements for private offers and sales of securities – Rules 504, 505, and 506.

Under Rule 504, any number of persons can purchase up to a total of $1 million of securities in a 12 month period. However, at least $500,000 of the securities must be registered under a state's securities laws. All that is required by the SEC is the filing of a Form D notice within 15 days after the first sale.

Under Rule 505, any number of accredited investors and not more than 35 nonaccredited investors may purchase (for investment and not for resale) an issue of securities of not more than $5 million. The securities are "restricted" in that they may not be resold for at least two years. The SEC requires the filing of a Form D notice within 15 days after the first sale, and is empowered to ask for the text of the information given to nonaccredited purchasers.

An *accredited investor* is defined in the SEC regulations; in general various institutional investors qualify, as well as natural persons with net worth, individually or jointly with spouse, of at least $1 million or income of $200,000 ($300,000 jointly with spouse) for each of the two most recent years and has a reasonable expectation of reaching that income level in the current year.

If only accredited investors are included in the offering, there is no specific information required to be given to them under Rule 505. If nonaccredited investors are offerees, certain financial data, depending on the size of the offering, must be provided to all purchasers during the course of the offering and prior to the sale. The issuer must be available to answer questions about itself and the offering.

Rule 506 is similar to Rule 505, except that there is no ceiling on the amount of money that can be raised, and any nonaccredited investor offerees must be sophisticated investors, (i.e., have sufficient knowledge and experience in financial and business matters to be able to evaluate the offering). Like Rule 505, if securities are sold to nonaccredited investors, certain financial information must be furnished to all purchasers.

ACCOUNTING CONSIDERATIONS

The typical external reader of the financial statements of a privately held company is likely to be a financing institution, such as a bank, vendor, or a leasing company.

Depending on the type and amount of financing provided, the private company is subjected to varying levels of reporting requirements. Generally, some form of internally prepared financial data must be submitted throughout the year, and annual financial statements often will need to be audited. Although this might appear to be reasonably standard, in fact the environment of smaller business accounting is different than what is found in larger publicly held companies, as discussed in the sections that follow.

Regulatory and Standards Overload

There is a pervasive feeling among small businesses that there is far too much government regulation and required reporting. "Standards overload" comes from many sources including the IRS, FASB, AICPA, and a host of government agencies. This data deluge puts pressure on all companies, of course, but the burden is particularly great for small companies, which often do not have the necessary personnel or expertise.

Small business as a constituency probably gets less than its due from legislators, because it is difficult for persons who are essentially independent and entrepreneurial to collaborate into lobbying forces. Therefore, small businesses ask for relief from accounting standards overload through their accountants, who are present and have to listen in support of their own livelihood. Small businesses argue that adherence to all GAAP requirements is not relevant for them, as it was designed for large public companies, and that it is very costly to apply.

AICPA Actions. Several groups have addressed the issue of GAAP for small businesses. In 1981, the Derieux Committee released *The Report of the Special Committee on Small and Medium Sized Firms* (AICPA, 1981e), which addressed part of the issue. The report recommended that the AICPA form a Special Committee on Accounting Standards Overload to review whether smaller companies could be exempt from applying GAAP requirements that are deemed irrelevant or costly. This committee was formed, studied the issues, and concluded in its report (AICPA, 1983f) that accounting standards overload is a serious problem for privately held, small companies. The committee urged that the FASB investigate simplifying GAAP for all entities, allowing differential disclosure for small, nonpublic companies based on the needs of the users and on cost-benefit considerations.

FASB Actions. Although the FASB and the accounting profession have resisted creating a less complex level of GAAP for privately held companies, a few steps have been taken in this regard.

In 1978, the FASB released SFAS 21, *Suspension of Reporting Earnings per Share and Segment Information by Nonpublic Enterprises* (E09.101 and S20.101). This was the first official differentiation between public and nonpublic companies.

In 1981, the FASB released an Invitation to Comment, *Financial Reporting by Private and Small Companies* (1981b). The comment letters indicated that CPAs' perceptions of the information needs of users of private company financial statements differed from the needs reported by those users; this was reported in *Financial*

Reporting by Privately Owned Companies; Summary of Responses to FASB Invitation to Comment (1983c).

A subsequent FASB-sponsored research report, *Financial Reporting by Private Companies: Analysis and Diagnosis* (Abdel-khalik, 1983) was based on a nonrandom sample of 667 responding business managers, bankers, and practicing CPAs, and provided some interesting conclusions:

1. Only 20% of fee increases by CPAs were attributed to increases in accounting standards, the rest to inflation.
2. Departures from GAAP often occur in small company financial reports, to reduce costs and because the departure is not deemed relevant by owners.
3. GAAP financial statements are quite important to bankers, who tend to equate GAAP reporting with the involvement of outside CPAs. Bankers are reluctant to accept a "small-GAAP" set of rules because they feel that this would dilute the credibility of reporting. They would prefer to continue receiving reports with GAAP departures, in which the matter is at least highlighted, allowing its relevance to be assessed.
4. Complaints about GAAP involve some element of politicking, which cannot be resolved by standard setters. In any event, evaluating costs and benefits of standards for small businesses is a matter for the attention of both the FASB and the AICPA.

The result of all this effort was a commitment by the FASB to pay closer attention to the needs of small businesses and their CPAs; but the FASB admonished that there are no quick solutions, and that the special circumstances of small businesses will need to be addressed on an issue by issue basis.

Curiously, only two matters have been dealt with since the research report was issued (through mid-1988): (1) SFAS 79, *Elimination of Certain Disclosures for Business Combinations by Nonpublic Enterprises* (B50.165), relieved private companies of the burden of reporting pro forma results of operations following a purchase combination; and (2) SFAS 87, *Employers' Accounting for Pensions* (P16), may be delayed in implementation by nonpublic companies (but otherwise, no modifications were made). It would appear that, for now, the FASB feels there are few opportunities to modify GAAP for small businesses, and perhaps feels the 1983 research report justifies this attitude.

Capital Structure

Stock Incentives. Professional managers capable of moving companies through their emerging growth stages are accustomed to being well compensated. The traditional profit-sharing and retirement plans seen in many large companies cannot be used, because of minimal profits, if any. A cash bonus system is usually viewed as a misallocation of the company's resources; cash is in short supply and is primarily needed for vital research and development (R&D). A compensation package that will entice these executives usually allows key employees to share in the growth in the value of the company through stock ownership. While in the early years the stock awarded has very little value, it will grow in value as the company develops, sells its product, and grows. Eventually, the company may be taken public or sold to a larger concern. In these instances, these key executives will have an opportunity to sell their holdings and realize their compensation, which simply will have been deferred.

The award of stock options is the compensation method of choice for many high-technology companies. Both tax and accounting guidelines generally indicate that, if these options allow an individual to purchase shares at the then fair market value at date of grant, no compensation expense need be recognized on the corporation's part (or income on the employee's part) at the time of grant.

From a tax perspective, qualified and nonqualified plans should be distinguished. Qualified plans allow an employee to tax-defer profits he derives from options exercised until he actually sells his shares; and the company receives no tax benefit. In a nonqualified plan, an employee is taxable for the difference between the exercise price and the fair market value on the date of exercise; however, the corporation is entitled to a tax deduction in the same amount.

APB 25, *Accounting for Stock Issued to Employees* (C47), sets forth guidelines for determining whether stock option plans result in compensation costs to the sponsor, and if so, how the sponsor should measure them. Further clarification has been provided in two interpretations: FIN 28, *Accounting for Stock Appreciation Rights and Other Variable Stock Option or Award Plans* (C47.119–.122); and FIN 38, *Determining the Measurement Date for Stock Option, Purchase, and Award Plans Involving Junior Stock* (C47.135A–.135E).[2]

These guidelines specify that compensation expense, if any, is calculated based on the difference between the quoted market price and the option price of the stock on the measurement date. The *measurement date* of a stock option is the date that both the number of shares and the exercise price of the option are known.

Stock option plans are grouped into two categories—fixed and variable. Under a fixed plan, the number of shares and the exercise price are determined on the date the option is granted. The company only recognizes compensation expense for the difference between the quoted market price and the exercise price on that date.

A variable plan can be differentiated from a fixed plan because the number of shares or the exercise price is not determinable on the date of grant; thus the measurement date is not triggered. Also included in the definition of a variable plan are those plans that entitle an employee to receive cash in lieu of stock upon exercise of a stock option. For example, in a plan that provides stock appreciation rights (SARs) the right to receive cash for the difference between the exercise price and the quoted market price of the stock causes the plan to be a variable plan, because the employee is entitled to cash in lieu of the options.

Under either a fixed or a variable plan, a company must recognize compensation expense for the difference between the quoted market price and the exercise price on

---

[2] In 1983, the SEC and the FASB began to come to grips with the accounting for junior common stock plans. Such plans were becoming increasingly popular among the many new "high tech" companies which were a significant factor in the hot new issues market on Wall Street during that year.

These plans were extremely useful to such companies in that they provided a defense against competing start-up companies in retaining key talent. Important employees were offered the junior common stock at a price significantly less than the company's regular common stock. If certain performance goals were met (i.e., in levels of sales or earnings), the stock was immediately exchangeable for the company's regular common stock, which presumably had appreciated greatly in value.

The SEC took the position that a junior common stock plan would have to be accounted for in a way similar to that of stock appreciation rights. The amount of compensation expense to be recognized would not be determined at the inception of the plan, but rather, it would be measured at the date the junior common stock was convertible to full common stock. In 1984, the FASB issued FIN 38, which prescribed the accounting supported by the SEC.

the measurement date. Over the vesting period between date of grant and date exercise is first permitted, an employee performs services to which stock compensation expense is applicable. If the quoted price of the stock increases or decreases during the course of the service period, or during the period up to the measurement date under a variable plan, compensation expense is adjusted accordingly.

Tandem or *combination* plans may also be used. These plans offer an employee the opportunity to exercise either a fixed stock option or a variable SAR. Compensation expense should be measured according to the terms an employee is most likely to elect for a given period. However, there is a rebuttable presumption that the SAR is what will be chosen.

The FASB added a project on stock-based compensation plans to its agenda in March, 1984. The ongoing discussions have centered on how to measure compensation cost (developing a valuation method) and from what date it is appropriate to measure this cost. The valuation methods, to one degree or another, are based on the "minimum value" method (which uses discounted values) while grant, vesting, and service expiration dates have received equal attention as measurement dates. So far, the FASB has reaffirmed its support of a position that would require compensation expense to be measured using a "fair value" over the vesting period.

A great deal of discussion has taken place in the profession on whether a plan is fixed or variable, and the EITF has confronted a variety of specific queries. Considerable additional discussion on stock compensation plans and on the EITF issues is contained in Chapter 20.

Stock Issued for Services. Smaller businesses, often short on cash, may pay for services by issuing stock, which almost invariably will not have a quoted market price. APB 29, *Accounting for Nonmonetary Transactions* (N35), states that it does not apply to the acquisition of nonmonetary assets or services on issuance of capital stock. In practice, however, the concepts laid out in APB 29 are used. Therefore, the value of the transaction will be based on what is more readily ascertainable: the value of the common stock given up or the value of the services rendered. Unless there has been a recent cash-based equity transaction, it is difficult to assign a fair value to the stock. If the goods or services received are standard commercial items (e.g., inventory) there should be little problem in valuation. However, in most instances, consulting services are involved and their value is not clearly evident. If an external and objective value is not available, the board of directors or management will have to declare a fair value for the shares. See Chapter 20 for a further discussion.

Related parties (officers, directors, or employees) are often involved in this situation, further complicating the matter. Chapter 25 discusses related parties and the necessary additional considerations.

Rights and Warrants. The instrument most frequently used by high-tech companies to raise additional capital is the issuance of rights to existing shareholders to enable them to purchase common stock at a stipulated price for a stated time period. These rights are issued for cash consideration, which is credited to additional paid-in capital.

Warrants essentially are identical to rights except that warrants are often given by the company to purchasers of debt securities and to underwriters in exchange for their services during private placements or initial public offerings.

Rights and warrants may also be issued for services, and if there is no quoted market value for the company's common shares, it is even less likely that there is a readily ascertainable fair value for the rights on warrants. Whatever value is assigned will be charged to operations. The credit will be to equity, and these rights and warrants will thus have no impact on the net worth of the company. Because high-tech companies are earnings-driven, a charge to operations is usually not desired by the board or management; therefore, auditors must pay close attention to this valuation process.

Multiple Entities and Related Parties

The smaller privately held company can evolve into a complex corporate entity as its products and services diversify. This structure might take the form of a parent corporation with numerous wholly owned subsidiaries or a series of brother-sister corporations, all owned by the same stockholders. Special consideration must be given to two areas in which such multiple entities are frequently involved.

The first involves transactions between members of the consolidated or combined group. Invariably there are numerous intercompany transactions, including product sales, inventory transfers, management fee allocations, and so forth. These must be identified and properly eliminated in the preparation of financial statements.

The second concern centers on transactions with related parties. This involves transactions with corporations or individuals not included in the consolidated or combined financial statements, but which have some form of affiliation. A typical related party situation might involve corporate stockholders owning land and a building through a trust (established for personal tax and financial planning reasons) and leasing the property to the corporation.

Each entity in a related party group can be involved in activities that are part of the "whole" enterprise, including manufacturing, leasing of real estate, wholesaling of the manufactured product, and so forth. Questions often asked by management in these circumstances are: What entities should we be reporting on? What form of financial statements should management be supplying to its readers?

Management should carefully consider its audience in determining which entities to include in the financial statements. It may be very important for a banker to see the real estate owned by the family trust in combined financial statements, as this significant asset could affect a lending decision. Conversely, at an annual management/owner meeting, the financial statement users would probably focus on the performance of the operating company or companies, and not on the value of the real estate owned by the trust.

In a parent-subsidiary situation, the reporting entity is defined by GAAP for consolidations (C51). Reporting latitude exists, however, in the brother-sister or combined corporation situation. Management may determine that different kinds of financial statements should be developed, each targeted to a specific audience, to provide the most meaningful financial data for decision-making purposes.

Development Stage Enterprises

In SFAS 7, *Accounting and Reporting by Development Stage Enterprises*, the FASB established special standards of financial reporting for development stage enterprises, defined as those devoting substantially all of their efforts to establishing a new business, and in which either (1) planned principal operations have not commenced or (2) there have been no significant revenues therefrom (De 4.102). If a long development process is required for the company's intended product, process or service, the company could remain in the development stage for many years. SFAS 7 requires the same GAAP for development stage enterprises as is applied to established operating enterprises. This means that costs not meeting the usual definition of assets must be expensed as incurred, a practice that had not been followed uniformly before SFAS 7.

The financial statements for a development stage enterprise are required to include specified information (De4.107):

1. A balance sheet, including any cumulative net losses reported with a descriptive caption such as "deficit accumulated during the development stage" in the stockholders' equity section.

2. An income statement, showing amounts of revenue and expenses for each period covered by the income statement and, in addition, cumulative amounts from the enterprise's inception.

3. A statement of changes in financial position, showing the sources and uses of financial resources for each period for which an income statement is presented and, in addition, cumulative amounts from the enterprise's inception. [This becomes a statement of cash flows in keeping with SFAS 95.]

4. A statement of stockholders' equity showing, from the enterprise's inception:

   a. For each issuance, the date and number of shares of stock, warrants, rights, or other equity securities issued for cash and for other consideration.

   b. For each isssuance, the dollar amounts (per share or other equity unit and in total) assigned to the consideration received for shares of stock, warrants, rights, or other equity securities. Dollar amounts shall be assigned to any noncash consideration received.

   c. For each issuance involving noncash consideration, the nature of the noncash consideration and the basis for assigning amounts.

An example of an operating statement of a development stage enterprise is included in Figure 39.1. Note the disclosure of cumulative amounts as required in the preceding list. The other statements, not shown, carry similar cumulative information. Numerous additional examples of financial statements and footnote disclosures can be observed in AICPA Financial Report Survey 27, *Illustrations of Accounting and Reporting by Development Stage Enterprises* (AICPA, 1984g).

In the first year in which an enterprise is no longer considered to be in the development stage, the notes to the financial statements must disclose that in prior years the enterprise had been in the development stage. Even if comparative financial statements are presented, all cumulative data and related disclosures may be omitted.

ADVANCED NMR SYSTEMS, INC.
(A company in the development stage)
STATEMENTS OF OPERATIONS

	Year ended December 31			Cumulative from June 1,1983 (Date of Inception) to December 31, 1986
	1986	1985	1984	
Operating Expenses				
Research and development	$1,289,761	$1,273,630	$ 796,647	$3,360,038
General and administrative	503,357	568,491	450,165	1,774,000
Loss From Operations	1,793,118	1,842,121	1,246,812	5,134,038
Interest Income	237,307	408,207	560,737	1,396,606
Net Loss and Deficit Accumulated During the Development Stage	$1,555,811	$1,433,914	$ 686,075	$3,737,432
Net Loss per Share	$.14	$.13	$.06	$.35
Weighted Average Number of Shares Outstanding	11,091,835	11,013,510	10,949,800	10,774,753

FIG. 39.1   Development Stage Company Operating Statement
Source: Advanced NMR Systems, Inc. 1986 Annual Report on Form 10-K.

Research and Development Costs

SFAS 2, *Accounting for Research and Development Costs* (R50), requires that all R&D costs are to be charged to expense when incurred. This includes materials, equipment, and facilities; personnel engaged in R&D activities; purchased intangibles; contract services; and indirect costs (overhead). Exceptions to this rule are:

1. Accounting for costs of *Computer Software to be Sold, Leased or Otherwise Marketed*, SFAS 86 (Co2) are not covered by SFAS 2.
2. Direct and indirect cost incurred under contractual arrangements reimbursable by others is covered by contractor accounting promulgations (Co4 and Co5).
3. Intangibles purchased from others (R50.107c) and materials, equipment and facilities (R50.107a) acquired or constructed for R&D activities and that have alternative future uses (in R&D projects or otherwise) are to be capitalized and amortized to research and development over their expected period of utility.

To assist in identifying what costs should be classified as research and development, SFAS 2 provides the following definition (R50.104):

a. *Research* is planned search or critical investigation aimed at discovery of new knowledge with the hope that such knowledge will be useful in developing a new product or service ... or a new process or technique ... or in bringing about a significant improvement to an exisiting product or process.

b. *Development* is the translation of research findings or other knowledge into a plan or design for a new product or process or for a significant improvement to an existing product or process whether intended for sale or use. It includes the conceptual formulation, design, and testing of product alternatives, construction of prototypes, and operation of pilot plants. It does not include routine or periodic alterations to existing products, production lines, manufacturing processes, and other ongoing operations even though those alterations may represent improvements, and it does not include market research or market testing activities.

As simplified as it is, the foregoing definition is nonetheless quite abstract; thus the FASB provided lists (R50.111–.112) of what qualifies for R&D treatment and what does not, as shown in Figures 39.2 and 39.3.

SFAS 2 (R50.109) requires disclosure in the financial statements of the total R&D costs charged to expense in each period for which an income statement is presented.

Costs Reimbursable by Others. SFAS 2 (R50.102) excludes from its scope of coverage the accounting for R&D conducted for others, stipulating that this question is a part of accounting for contracts in general. Thus, in a contract that provides for reimbursements by the customer of all direct costs and specific indirect costs, such costs, along with profit increments determined in accordance with contract provisions, are receivables (whether billed or unbilled). However, in a fixed-price contract that requires the achievement of a specific result, the cost accumulations are akin to inventories, until relieved through cost of sales upon billing. As with all such contracts, a periodic assessment is necessary to evaluate whether costs upon completion will exceed revenues, thus requiring an anticipatory charge against operations.

Some problems arise in accounting for partial reimbursement situations. For example, a company may be researching a scientific problem for its own proprietary purposes, but to obtain necessary funds it may contract to sell to a third party certain rights in whatever commercially feasible results are achieved. Ordinarily such arrangements must be deemed to be R&D activities, with the amounts received from the third party recognized as income when earned in accordance with the terms of the contract and with all the R&D costs charged to expense as incurred. However, it is often difficult to discern the substance of these transactions, and considering the variety of the kinds of partial interests that can be sold, each such transaction requires careful analysis to achieve the proper accounting.

R&D in a Business Combination. The cost of a purchase business combination allocated to identifiable assets to be used in R&D activities and having no alternative future uses must be charged to expense by the acquiring company at consummation. This is the substantive point in FIN 4, *Applicability of FASB Statement No. 2 to Business Combinations Accounted for by the Purchase Method* (B50.151–.152).

Identifiable R&D assets include developed assets such as patents, blueprints, and formulas, and also assets used in R&D such as equipment and materials. Such assets obtained in a purchase business combination and having an alternative future use in R&D or otherwise should be capitalized at their fair values (B50.146) and amortized

- Laboratory research aimed at discovery of new knowledge.
- Searching for applications of new research findings or other knowledge.
- Conceptual formulation and design of possible product or process alternatives.
- Testing in search of or evaluation of product or process alternatives.
- Modification of the formulation or design of a product or process.
- Design, construction, and testing of preproduction prototypes and models.
- Design of tools, jigs, molds, and dies involving new technology.
- Design, construction, and operation of a pilot plant that is not of a scale economically feasible to the enterprise for commercial production.
- Engineering activity required to advance the design of a product to the point that it meets specific functional and economic requirements and is ready for manufacture.

FIG. 39.2 Examples of Research and Development Activities
Source: SFAS 2 (R50.111).

- Engineering follow-through in an early phase of commercial production.
- Quality control during commercial production, including routine testing of products.
- Troubleshooting in connection with breakdowns during commercial production.
- Routine, ongoing efforts to refine, enrich, or otherwise improve the qualities of an existing product.
- Adaptation of an existing capability to a particular requirement or customer's need as part of a continuing commercial activity.
- Seasonal or other periodic design changes to existing products.
- Routine design of tools, jigs, molds, and dies.
- Activity, including design and construction engineering, related to the construction, relocation, rearrangement, or start-up of facilities or equipment other than (1) pilot plants and (2) facilities or equipment whose sole use is for a particular research and development project.
- Legal work in connection with patent applications or litigation, and the sale or licensing of patents.

FIG. 39.3 Examples of Activities That Are Not Research and Development
Source: SFAS 2 (R50.112).

over their useful lives. The amortization is an R&D expense. Examples of assets having alternative future uses include multiple use buildings, machinery, and salable patents on products or processes.

This interpretation seems to contain inherent contradictions. It directs that in a purchase business combination, values be ascribed to assets to be used in R&D activities even if they have no alternative future use. Yet SFAS 2 denies the accounting existence of a "no-alternative-future-use asset." Companies are therefore literally required to ascribe value when, by definition, no value exists; and then they are required to write it off. This phenomenon is further discussed in Chapter 23.

R&D Partnerships. High technology businesses typically invest enormous amounts of capital in R&D. Financing of expenditures is often done through a limited partnership with the following pattern (which has many possible variations):

- A corporation and its owners establish the new entity, usually a limited partnership. Officers, directors, or shareholders of the sponsor firm sometimes are partners (limited or general); however, the corporation itself is the general partner.
- Under the partnership agreement, the general partner controls the partnership. Limited partners have certain rights of approval and usually provide substantially all of the partnership's funds. The sponsoring corporation pays for its general partnership interest by putting up some of its preliminary development rights.
- The partnership engages the corporation to do R&D work. The corporation then agrees to perform the work on a best-efforts basis, with the understanding that the partnership will provide sufficient funds for research and own the rights to any resulting product.
- All or substantially all of the losses will be allocated to the limited partners to provide them with income tax deductions (less attractive since passage of the Tax Reform Act of 1986 designating such losses as passive losses having significant deductibility restrictions).
- After the R&D work is completed, the limited partnership then licenses its product rights to the sponsoring corporation in exchange for royalties.
- Royalties are distributed among the limited partners according to the terms of the partnership agreement. After the limited partners have received a specified return on their original investments, the general partners begin to receive a major portion of the royalties.

Occasionally, the sponsor-partnership agreement is complicated by provisions that require the sponsor to buy all rights or that permit the sponsor to acquire the limited partners' interests for a specified amount. Other provisions written into these agreements sometimes limit financial return to the limited partners or guarantee minimum royalty payments to the partnership.

SFAS 68, *Research and Development Arrangements* (R55), states that when a company's R&D activities are funded by other parties, such as partnerships or joint ventures, the nature of the obligation incurred by the company would determine whether those activities would be accounted for as a liability or as a contract. If repayment of the funds provided to the company does not depend *solely* on the success of the R&D activities, the company would record a liability and charge the costs of performing the R&D to expense as incurred.

There is a presumption that an R&D arrangement is a borrowing if there is any significant indication that the company will repay any of the funds provided to it, even though the activities are unsuccessful. If a borrowing, the cash or other assets received by the company are reported as debt, and the R&D costs are expensed for financial reporting purposes.

R&D arrangements are tantamount to executory contracts if (1) the financial risk has been transferred from the company, (2) the results of the project belong to the partnership or joint venture, and (3) the company is not obligated to acquire the results or the partnership's interest in the project. When these factors are present, the company recognizes a liability at the present value of amounts to be paid (B50.125b) only if and when it exercises an option to acquire the results of the R&D project; it also recognizes a tangible or intangible asset in an equal amount.

Some R&D arrangements provide an opportunity for the enterprise to purchase the partnership's interest in or otherwise obtain the exclusive rights to the results of the R&D effort in return for the enterprise's stock. As the first of these R&D arrangements matured, questions arose as to whether it was possible to have a pooling-of-interests with an R&D limited partnership or, if such an acquisition had to be a purchase, what date to use to value the stock (i.e., the original agreement date or the date the option was exercised).

TB 84-1, *Accounting for Stock Issued to Acquire the Results of a Research and Development Arrangement* (R55.501–.504), explains that if a sponsoring company issues stock to acquire successful R&D results, the stock issued and the assets acquired should be recorded at the fair value of the stock or the assets, whichever is more clearly evident, as of the date the research results are acquired; such a transaction is not a business combination and thus pooling accounting is not appropriate.

In SAB 63, *Views on Application of SFAS 68, "Research and Development Arrangements"* (Topic 5.O), the SEC staff states its position on the SFAS 68 provisions regarding unwritten conditions that may create a presumption a company will repay funds provided by other parties under an R&D arrangement (R55.105). One of those conditions is:

> A significant related party relationship between the enterprise and the parties funding the research and development exists at the time the enterprise enters into the arrangements. [R55.106(c)]

The SEC staff interprets "a significant related party relationship" to mean a 10% or greater ownership of the company providing the R&D funds by related parties (defined in SFAS 57 (R36.405)). In some circumstances, the SEC staff might apply a test of less than 10%.

SFAS 68 also states that the presumption of repayment can be overcome only by substantial evidence to the contrary (R55.105). The SEC staff believes that the apparent or projected inability by the sponsor company to repay the R&D funds in cash (or debt) is not a persuasive demonstration that the funding parties are accepting all the risks of the R&D activities. Other means of payment, including stock issuance, are often plausible.

Computer Software

Software Development. Many high technology businesses operate in software development, a subject given only slight coverage in SFAS 2. To deal with many issues that were arising, the FASB issued FIN 6, *Applicability of FASB Statement No. 2 to Computer Software* (R50.115–.119), in 1975. This interpretation states that purchased software that has alternative future uses apart from its use in R&D may be capitalized, while purchased software used exclusively in R&D (and development costs of internally developed computer software) must be charged to expense as incurred.

SFAS 86, *Accounting for the Costs of Computer Software To Be Sold, Leased, or Otherwise Marketed* (Co2), reversed some of the conclusions reached in SFAS 2 and

FIN 6, especially those pertaining to internally developed computer software. Also, FRR 12 (§ 218), under which the SEC imposed a moratorium effective April 14, 1983 precluding registrants from adopting a practice of capitalization (but not prohibiting it where it already had been the practice), became no longer applicable. SFAS 86 specifies that development costs incurred subsequent to the time a product reaches technological feasibility should be capitalized rather than expensed as incurred. *Technological feasibility* occurs when a detailed program design has been completed. If the program design itself is not in existence, the presence of a working model can be used as proof of technological feasibility.

Once the software development costs have been capitalized, SFAS 86 specifies that these costs are to be amortized over the anticipated revenue stream of the product. The minimum amortization amount is straight line over the anticipated economic life. The unamortized portion of the capitalized software development costs must also be consistently evaluated to ensure that it is stated at the lower of cost or market.

Subsequent to achievement of technological feasibility, the company will incur coding and testing costs related to the software. The FASB terms these the "costs of producing product masters." Costs that may be capitalized include both those that are direct (e.g., engineering personnel) and those that are indirect (e.g., indirect labor, and depreciation on equipment). If these standards are applied to the typical software development process, the initial version of any computer software package will probably have very few costs that qualify for software capitalization. However, enhancements to that program (since the product has already achieved technological feasibility) will very often qualify, as discussed in EITF Issue 85-35. These costs must be distinguished from maintenance costs that must be expensed as incurred. And, obviously, normal inventory production costs should be added to inventory.

A company often will develop interdependent hardware and software. SFAS 86 is categorical in stating that all components of the product or process must have attained technological feasibility before costs qualify for capitalization as software development costs.

Purchased computer software is accounted for in much the same manner as that developed internally. It is evident that the purchased software itself is technologically feasible if it has been marketed by the selling company. However, this software may become part of an integrated package that has not yet crossed the technological feasibility line, in which case the purchased software cannot be capitalized. The criteria in SFAS 86 allows considerable room for interpretation.

The required disclosures for capitalized computer software are straightforward. The unamortized amount of the costs must be disclosed as of the end of each of the periods presented, in addition to the amount of amortization (or write-down to market) for each period.

In 1987, ADAPSO released a report on *Software Capitalization—A Technical Approach*, containing a series of papers by computer software and services industry executives aimed at establishing "consistency and realism" in the software capitalization process. The report was released because ADAPSO perceived a wide range of practices developing under SFAS 86, from very aggressive to very conservative, and was concerned that either extreme would result in the financial community becoming "skittish" about software industry stocks.

SFAS 86 is also discussed in Chapter 15.

Revenue Recognition. The recognition of revenue on software products is another issue that has recently required the attention of standard setters. There are no specific authoritative pronouncements, although there is some guidance in SFAC 5 and SFAC 6, and in SFAS 48, *Revenue Recognition When Right of Return Exists* (R75). This guidance, however, has been interpreted differently, leading to diverse practices.

In 1987, the AICPA prepared Issues Paper 87-1 on *Software Revenue Recognition* (1987o). This issues paper (IP) analyzes the primary issues and makes recommendations for solutions by the FASB. In mid-1988, the FASB asked the AICPA to process the IP into an SOP.

The IP enumerates several different ways in which companies market their computer software. These include:

1. Licensing to end users for internal use.
2. Licensing to others to market to end users.
3. Selling all rights developed.
4. Specific development contracts to develop software for end users.
5. Use by service bureaus.

The IP notes that a software product is unique in that revenue is being recognized on granting of a license rather than on the sale of a tangible product, and it discusses a number of basic issues in considerable detail. The conclusions reached are that:

1. Revenue for software licenses with no other obligation on the part of the vendor may be recognized on delivery if (a) collectibility is reasonably assured, and (b) the software licensee is the end user.
2. Revenue on the sale of a license to reproduce and distribute software that is unlimited as to time and quantity should be recognized on delivery of the software master if (a) the license fee is fixed and (b) the license fee has been paid.
3. If collectibility is reasonably assured, revenue on a license to reproduce and distribute copies in limited quantities or for a limited period of time for a nonrefundable fixed fee should be recognized on delivery of the software master or first copy.
4. Revenue for nonrefundable fixed fees on software licenses should be recognized on delivery of the software master or first copy if a contract also provides for variable fees beginning with the licensee's use of the software product.
5. Revenue for nonrefundable fixed fees on software licenses should be recognized on delivery of the software master or first copy if the contract also provides for variable fees that begin after the license has been in effect for a specified amount of time or a specified volume of usage has been achieved.
6. Revenue from licenses that are cancelable should be recognized over the license term.
7. The percentage-of-completion method should be used to recognize revenue in situations in which: (a) the contract requires a vendor to customize its software to meet the customer's specifications and also provides for other significant vendor obligations; (b) the vendor, through experience, can estimate the extent of progress toward completion, contract revenues, and contract costs; and (c) the contract states the enforceable rights of each party, the price, and the manner and terms of settlement.

8. The cost of software used in a contract but developed before the contract and not capitalized should not be included in measuring progress to completion.

9. Revenue from postdelivery customer support services contracts should be recognized over time.

10. Nonrefundable subscription fees from data services contracts should be recognized over the period of the service.

11. Revenue attributable to the unused portion of minimum usage fees should be recognized at the expiration of the carryforward period.

Simplified LIFO

Problems involving costing and manual computations of inventories are multiplied when companies use last-in, first-out (LIFO). Many companies do not understand the concept, and simply take for granted that LIFO generally saves the company tax dollars. Management therefore often looks to its CPAs to deal with LIFO and overhead capitalization issues.

To alleviate the record-keeping burden on companies using dollar-value LIFO, the IRS had allowed businesses with less than $2 million in annual gross receipts (in each of the three tax years ending with the current tax year) to use only one LIFO pool. The Tax Reform Act of 1986 created new rules applying to businesses with less than $5 million in annual gross receipts, requiring the use of multiple pools. However, if a business has a valid election under the prior tax laws and continues to meet the old requirements, the prior law may continue to be applied.

All companies using the dollar-value LIFO method are also allowed to utilize published government indexes on price changes to simplify LIFO calculations. If, however, a company has more than $2 million in receipts, it may use only 80% of the index change. These techniques eliminate many of the calculations otherwise required.

These LIFO simplifications have made it practical for nearly every small business to elect dollar-value LIFO, but there are some caveats: For small businesses using 100% of the index change, AcSEC had informally supported the acceptability of simplified LIFO for GAAP purposes, assuming that the types of items included in the government's index are representative of the types of items included in the company's inventory. AcSEC would not accept the 80% approach for GAAP purposes, but in such a case the company could use the 100% approach for financial reporting, and the 80% approach for tax purposes, considering the effect of the 20% to be a temporary difference accounted for under SFAS 96. (These and other LIFO matters are discussed in Chapter 14.)

Key-Person Life Insurance

In small businesses, most frequently the services of partners or owners often are critical to the continued operation of the business. Death of a principal owner can be catastrophic, perhaps causing the business to fail. Accordingly, insurance policies are purchased on the lives of key operating persons, with other owners or the business as beneficiaries.

The cash surrender value method is required to account for such policies and is discussed in Chapter 15.

SPECIFIC PARTNERSHIP MATTERS

Partnership Formation

Although a partnership can be created by either oral or written agreement, the latter is obviously preferred in a businesss undertaking. The partnership agreement should be signed, and a copy retained by each partner. It is also desirable that the agreement be filed with the recorder or other appropriate official in the county in which the partnership has its principal place of business. In the case of a *limited partnership* such filing is imperative.

The following matters should be covered by the partnership agreement:

1. Names of partners and the firm name.
2. Kind of business to be conducted.
3. Capital contribution of each partner.
4. Duration of the partnership contract.
5. The time to be devoted to the business by each, and any limitation on outside business interests.
6. Method of dividing profits and losses.
7. Restrictions on the agency powers of the partners.
8. Salaries to be paid partners, or limitations on the withdrawal of profits.
9. Method of admitting new partners.
10. Provision for insurance on lives of partners for benefit of the firm.
11. Procedure to be followed in voluntary dissolution.
12. Procedure on death or withdrawal of partner, including method of valuation of tangible assets and goodwill, and provision for continuation of the business by the remaining partners.

The accounting basis of assets other than cash contributed to a partnership are valued at amounts mutually agreeable to the partners. Valuing these assets at the book value to the contributing partner may be inadequate and an appraisal might be appropriate to obtain the proper value.

If contributions of assets other than cash are made to a new partnership, the agreement should cover the matter of income tax treatment in the event that such assets are subsequently disposed of. In general, such assets retain the tax basis of the previous owner. This results in the taxable gain or loss to all the partners on disposal if the income tax basis to the partnership is different than the partnership's carrying amount.

Sharing Profits and Losses

A major advantage of a partnership is the unlimited variation it allows in the sharing of profits and losses. The partners may share on any basis or method on which they agree, such as:

1. Sharing all profit or loss in proportion to each partner's capital at the beginning of the year.

2. Sharing all profit or loss in proportion to the average capital balance maintained by each partner during the year.
3. Sharing all profit or loss in proportion to each partner's capital at year end.
4. Paying agreed upon salaries to the partners and dividing the remainder on one of the bases above.
5. Paying salaries and interest on capital to the partners and then dividing the remainder on one of the preceding bases.

Another method is simply to divide net income and losses equally. If the partnership agreement is silent regarding sharing profit or loss, the law assumes it is the intention of the partners to share it equally. The method of sharing income or loss should be disclosed in the financial statements.

Interest on Capital. With regard to interest on invested capital, the partnership agreement should cover at least four points:

1. A specific interest rate or directions for determining the rate.
2. The procedure to be followed if the partnership net income before interest is insufficient to meet the interest requirement.
3. The procedure to be followed in the event the partnership has net a loss.
4. The capital balance on which interest is to be allowed; beginning, average, or ending capital may be used. If average capital is used, the agreement should also state the procedure to determine average capital.

Partners' Salaries. Each working partner should be entitled to a salary as compensation for his services. Legally, partners are not entitled to compensation for their services in carrying on partnership business, other than their share in the profits, unless compensation is specifically authorized in the partnership agreement. The agreement should specify the amounts of compensation to be paid to partners, or state the procedure to determine the amounts. Similar to interest on invested capital, the partnership agreement should also state the procedure to be followed if the partnership has insufficient net income to meet the salary requirement or has a net loss.

Cash Distributions. Generally there is less need for cash accumulation in a partnership than in a corporation, since most partnerships are service organizations, thus having a greater emphasis on labor than on capital. Also, although partnerships are not subject to federal income taxes, the individual partner is taxed on his share of the partnership taxable income, and he needs cash to meet his tax obligaions. Thus, the partnership tends to distribute cash to the partners as soon as it is available.

Division of Profits. The fictitious partnership of Adams and Baker will be used to illustrate the division of profits. The articles of copartnership include the following provisions as to the distribution of profits:

Partners' loans. Loans made by partners to the partnership shall bear interest at the rate of 10% per annum. Interest shall be charged regardless of whether the revenue and expense account balance is sufficient to cover the interest.

Partners' salaries. On December 31 of each year, salaries at the following amounts per annum shall be allowed by a charge to the revenue and expense summary account and credits to the respective drawing accounts of the partners: Adams, $17,200; Baker, $11,800. Partners' salaries are to be allowed whether or not the revenue and expense account balance is sufficient to cover the salaries.

Interest on partners' invested capital. Each partner is to be allowed interest at the rate of 10% per annum on the balance of his capital account at the beginning of each year. Such interest is to be allowed whether or not earned, and is to be allowed regardless of whether the revenue and expense account balance is sufficient to cover the interest.

Remainder of revenue and expense account balance. The balance of the revenue and expense account, after provision for salaries, interest on loans, and interest on invested capital, is to be divided equally.

On December 31, the books of the partnership show the following balances before recognition of interest on partners' loans and before salary and interest on partners' capital allowances:

	Debit	Credit
Sundry assets	$ 500,000	$ –
Sundry liabilities	–	100,000
Adams, capital	–	190,000
Adams, drawings	23,000	–
Baker, capital	–	123,000
Baker, drawings	14,000	–
Adams, loan	–	20,000
Revenue and expense	–	104,000
	$ 537,000	$ 537,000

Balances of the capital accounts on January 1 were: Adams, $140,000; Baker, $100,000. The loan from Adams was made on July 1. The division of profits is as shown in Figure 39.4.

Formal presentation of the activity of the partners' capital accounts is often made through the statement of changes in partners' equity as discussed under "Realization and Liquidation."

Partners' Loans

At times, a partner may want to invest assets in the partnership on a temporary basis, or the partnership may need the extra funds for a limited period; in such cases, the partner may make an advance that is treated as a loan rather than as an increase

Adams and Baker, Partnership Schedule of Division of Profits

For the Year Ended December 31, 19XX

	Total	Adams	Baker
Interest on loan	$ 1,000	$ 1,000	$ —
Interest on capital	24,000	14,000	10,000
Salaries allowed	29,000	17,200	11,800
Remainder — equally	50,000	25,000	25,000
Profit earned	$104,000	$57,200	$46,800

FIG. 39.4   Schedule of Division of Net Income

in capital. Interest on the loan should be treated as a partnership expense, and the loan should be disclosed as a liability of the partnership.

A partner's withdrawal of assets from the partnership should be treated as a loan to the partner or as a capital withdrawal, depending on the circumstances. Some factors to consider are whether the amount is material relative to the partner's personal net assets, whether repayment terms are stipulated, and whether the loan will be long outstanding. The presence of these factors would indicate that the loan is, in substance, a withdrawal. However, if the partner has the intent and ability to repay the loan, it should be recorded as a note receivable.

Receivables and payables arising from transactions between a partner and the partnership should be classified on the balance sheet between current and noncurrent in the same manner as similar transactions with nonpartners. Such amounts should be separately stated and not combined with other receivables and payables.

Changing Partners.

There are several ways of accounting for the sale of a part or all of the interest in a partnership, or for the admission or withdrawal of partners. Legally, any such event constitutes a termination of the existing partnership and the inauguration of a new partnership, unless the partnership agreement provides for continuation, with or without a special accounting, beyond the date of the event.

Admission.

The *goodwill method* of accounting for the admission of a new partner requires a revaluation of the partnership at fair market value. The current partners are allocated their shares of the increase or decrease in value, and the new partner is then admitted to the partnership either by purchase of a proportion of the rights of another partner or by joining the partnership through a cash capital contribution. By this accounting approach, the newly organized partnership will begin with net assets stated at fair market value, thereby averting a future "windfall" profit (or detriment) to the new partner from realization of fair value excesses (or deficiencies) otherwise unrecorded at the date of his admission. This approach may be useful for internal purposes, but does not comply with GAAP.

An alternative approach that complies with GAAP, often referred to as the *bonus method*, is to retain preadmission net assets at historical cost and simply record the new partner's cash contribution as his capital. To the extent there are unrecorded excess values, it may be specified that the newly admitted partner will not share in them upon realization; or more commonly, the capital contribution required will be disproportionately high in relation to the new partner's income-sharing percentage. Even when the cash basis method of accounting is used, the above approach may be followed to block the new partner from sharing in unrecorded assets such as accounts receivable.

As stated earlier, the partners can agree on any method of sharing among themselves so long as it can be computed objectively. If the agreed-upon method is based on something other than GAAP, the financial statements can still be presented using GAAP.

When a person is admitted as a partner into an existing partnership, that person becomes liable for all the obligations of the partnership that existed at the time of his admission as though he had been a partner when such obligations were incurred. However, this prior liability can be satisfied only out of partnership property.

If there is a sale by a partner of his interest to a third party acceptable to the remaining partners, this does not affect the carrying amounts of assets or liabilities, because the transaction is made outside the partnership. Thus, the price may be influenced by many factors other than the financial position or results of operations of the partnership.

It is possible for a party to acquire the interest of a partner without actually becoming a partner. When a partner sells or assigns his interest in the partnership to a party who is not a member of the partnership but has not received the unanimous approval of the other partners (assuming such an action is not precluded by the partnership agreement), the purchaser does not become a partner. One partner cannot force his copartners into partnership with an outsider. Under the Uniform Partnership Act, the purchaser in such a case only acquires the seller's interest in the profits and losses of the partnership and, upon dissolution, the interest to which the original partner would have been entitled. The purchaser has no voice in management and may not obtain an accounting except in the case of dissolution. Also, the purchaser cannot ordinarily make capital withdrawals without the consent of the partners.

Withdrawal

Similar considerations arise when a partner withdraws from the partnership. If the retiring partner's distribution is predicated on the fair market value of the partnership's assets and liabilities rather than on historical cost, he will receive a payment that may be either greater or less than the amount shown as his current invested capital. One way of recording such a transaction is to revalue the entire partnership at fair market value (the goodwill method) and then to allocate the new valuation to the capital accounts of the remaining partners according to their participation.

Another approach is to recognize in the accounts only the proportionate excess amount applicable to the retiring partner, the *partial goodwill method* or the *pushdown method*. Some favor the latter method as a conservative one that essentially maintains the records at historical cost; others criticize it as being piecemeal. When a retiring partner is paid more than his stated capital and no revaluation in whole or in part is made (the bonus method), the excess payment is ordinarily allocated to the remaining partners according to their profit and loss ratios and regarded as essentially a bonus payment to the withdrawing partner.

During a discussion of Issue 85-46, *Partnership's Purchase of Withdrawing Partner's Equity*, in which a withdrawing partner sells his interest back to the partnership, several EITF members indicated the pushdown method was widely used when there was a substantial change in ownership. Some members indicated that the goodwill method was infrequently used in these circumstances, and questioned its validity. They expressed support for the pushdown method by indicating that withdrawals from a partnership should not be accounted for differently than similar transactions involving corportions.

A withdrawing partner may continue to be liable for the partnership's obligations incurred prior to his withdrawal. The withdrawing partner can be released from his obligations if the settlement includes specific release therefrom by the continuing partners and by the creditors.

The effects of partners' admissions and withdrawals on the capital accounts, including the method of accounting used, should be disclosed as part of the statement of changes in partners' capital.

Realization and Liquidation

A partnership may be disposed of either by selling the business as a unit or by the sale (realization) of the individual assets and liquidation of the liabilities followed by the final distribution of the remaining assets (usually cash) to the partners. As the assets are realized, resulting losses (or gains) are apportioned among the partners in the agreed upon ratio. When the realization process is complete, if outside creditors have been paid in full or if cash has been reserved for that purpose, payments may be made to the partners according to the remaining capital balances.

The following is the order of distribution upon realization and liquidation: (1) payment of creditors in full, (2) payment of partners' loans, and (3) payment of partners' capital accounts.

Distribution of cash to partners may take place upon completion of the realization and liquidation process; or cash may be distributed as the process is taking place. The latter method, which is called installment liquidation, is often used when the realization process stretches over a considerable period of time.

Financial Statements

The financial statements of a partnership presented in conformity with GAAP are essentially the same as those prepared for a corporation, except for the equity section of the balance sheet and the absence of income taxes.

Because of partners' interest in cash flow, and because the cash basis is usually used for income tax purposes, it is common to find the financial statements of partnerships presented on a cash basis. SAS 14, *Special Reports*, recognizes that "in some circumstances . . . a comprehensive basis of accounting other than generally accepted accounting principles may be used" (AU 621.03). Such a basis may be the "cash

Adams and Baker, Partnership Statement of Changes in Partners' Equity			
For the Year Ended December 31, 19XX			
	Total	Adams	Baker
Balance, January 1, 19XX	$240,000	$140,000	$100,000
Contributions	73,000	50,000	23,000
Net income	104,000	57,200	46,800
Distributions	(37,000)	(23,000)	(14,000)
Balance, December 31, 19XX	$380,000	$224,200	$155,800

FIG. 39.5   Example of Statement of Changes in Partners' Equity

receipts and disbursements basis of accounting, and modifications of the cash basis having substantial support, such as recording depreciation on fixed assets . . ." (AU 621.04(c)). Also recognized as a comprehensive basis of accounting is the basis used by the reporting entity to file its income tax return for the period covered by the financial statements (AU 621.04(b)).

Financial statements presented on a basis of accounting other than GAAP do not purport to present financial position and results of operations. Thus the statements should not be described in terms generally associated with accrual basis statements. For example, "statement of assets and liabilities arising from cash transactions" might be used instead of "balance sheet" (AU 621.07). SFAS 95, which requires a statement of cash flows, is not applicable to financial statements presented on a basis of accounting other than GAAP, since the statements do not purport to present financial position and results of operations.

Changes in partners' equity during the period should be disclosed in the financial statements. If there has been little change, the details may be incorporated on the face of the balance sheet rather than in a separate schedule. Ordinarily, however, a statement of changes in partners' equity will be presented. See Figure 39.5 for an example.

The income statement of a partnership does not include a provision for income taxes. Income taxes are the responsibility of the individual partners, not of the partnership. The notes to a partnership's financial statements ordinarily disclose the omission of a provision for income taxes to emphasize that the net earnings figure is not comparable to that of a taxable enterprise.

Pro Forma Statements

In a business combination in which a partnership is the acquired company, certain pro forma adjustments are needed to place the partnership on a corporate basis. For example, a pro forma adjustment is made for income taxes that would have been paid if the company had been a corporation rather than a partnership.

The need for other pro forma adjustments depends on the circumstances and the accounting methods used by the partnership. Reasonable salaries and interest paid to the partners may be presented as expenses in the pro forma financial statements. And, in some instances, expense accounts of the partners may be shown on a pro forma basis as participation in net income or loss rather than as company expenses.

Investments in Partnerships

The accounting for an investment by one corporation in another corporation has received considerable attention in the accounting literature, whereas the treatment of a corporation's investment in a partnership has not been extensively discussed.

The investor's percentage of ownership is the principal determinant of the accounting method to be used. ARB 51 (C51.101) states that consolidated financial statements are generally considered more meaningful when an entity has a controlling financial interest (more than 50% of the voting interest).

Ownership of 20% to 50% of an entity's common stock ordinarily presumes that the owner is able to exercise significant influence over that entity; and this, according to APB 18 (I82.104), requires the use of the equity method of accounting. APB 18 also requires the use of the equity method for investments in corporate joint ventures. An AICPA interpretation, *Investments in Partnerships and Ventures* (I82.508), generally recommends the equity method of accounting for investments in partnerships and unincorporated joint ventures, in accordance with APB 18.

Many corporations have significant interests in publicly held partnerships or unincorporated joint ventures, particularly in real estate construction or oil and gas exploration. Original cost is not an acceptable method of accounting for such an investment, but three other basic methods are in use: the equity method, full consolidation, and proportional consolidation. Income accounting results for the investor are the same under all three methods, but individual financial statement amounts will vary significantly depending on which method is used. These methods are discussed in Chapter 24.

Tax Consequences of Retaining a Fiscal Year

The Revenue Act of 1987 provides that partnerships and Subchapter S corporations may elect to retain their fiscal year ends despite the provisions of the Tax Reform Act of 1986 that require adoption of a calendar year end.

If such an election is made, a payment must be made each year that approximates the income tax that would have been paid had the partners or owners of such entities filed a short-period income tax return as an adjunct to adopting a calendar year end.

In EITF Issue 88-4, *Classification of Payment Made to IRS to Retain Fiscal Year*, the Task Force reached a consensus that such a tax payment should be accounted for as an asset by the partnership or S Corporation, as the payment is viewed as an annually adjusted deposit and is identified with the entity, not with individual partners or owners.

AUDITING AND OTHER CPA SERVICES

Serving Small Business Needs

Smaller and emerging businesses encounter a plethora of reporting and legal compliance requirements. A considerable portion of the practice of many CPAs serving small business consists of providing services other than auditing. Compilation and review services, often referred to as unaudited statement and writeup work, are a major element of such nonaudit services; other frequent services are tax matters, management advisory services, record-keeping assistance, data processing, and projections (discussed in Chapter 27).

Audit Engagements

Systems. Depending on the contacts of the founding group, personnel with specialized strengths in marketing, finance, and operations management may be present in the organization. Commonly, a technical engineer and marketing individuals will start a high technology company, bringing in financial expertise when funding is needed and operations expertise when the company is changing from a start-up to an emerging business.

Founders of high technology companies generally do not like a complex internal control structure and thus use a hands-on management style. This typically produces a free-wheeling operation that overlooks detail and documentation, often completing the task at hand via an unorthodox method.

Segregation of duties becomes an issue for small companies when the same person performs cross-functional activities. This can increase the possibility of errors and improprieties that could become large financial losses for the company. Limited personnel can undermine whatever internal controls exist if employees perform several duties. The CPA must take these factors into account when performing an audit or other accounting services for the smaller and emerging business. If the CPA is engaged to perform an audit, these control structure characteristics will almost invariably dictate that a substantive approach be taken, rather than one that places a degree of reliance on internal controls. (These audit approaches are discussed in Chapter 7.)

R&D and Computer Software. Auditing of R&D costs involves most of the usual audit procedures. There is, however, the very difficult differentiation to be made between R&D costs, which must be expensed as incurred, and inventory-type costs, which may be deferred until matched with future sales. The nature of the costs is the same, but a distinction must be found in the purpose of the cost and must be based to an extent on the persuasive representation of the management. The auditor can analytically compare specific costs with like costs in the past, with budgeted amounts, and with bills of materials for salable products; and he can discuss the costs with responsible management to satisfy himself that costs are properly classified.

In the area of costs reimbursable by others, the usual audit concerns exist. Is the contract being accounted for appropriately? Depending on the facts, the completed-contract method may be a better fit than the percentage-of-completion method. Is there a loss inherent in the project? How can this be evaluated by the auditor? These questions are applicable to most contracts, and can be understood better by reference to the contractor auditing discussions in Chapters 36 and 37.

The auditor must apply his industry expertise in conjunction with appropriate consultants in high technology areas. For example, he may consult with a colleague who has extensive experience in computer software development when considering a capitalized asset in this area. He must use his business judgment, common sense, and auditor's skepticism to ask questions and make comparisons with past experience and budgeted results in corroborating management's representations. The work of an outside specialist (AU 336) may need to be incorporated as an audit procedure to produce sufficient competent evidential matter and achieve audit satisfaction.

Partnership Auditing and Reporting. The independent auditor of the financial statements of a private partnership faces the same kind of auditing problems he would encounter if the entity were operating as a corporation. Furthermore, the disclosure requirements under GAAP are essentially the same.

The partnership agreement is the basic document under which the partnership has been organized and is operated. The independent auditor must read this document carefully to understand the partnership's organization and to identify the aspects of the agreement that bear on financial and accounting matters.

In reporting to the company, any material omissions or deviations from the agreement should be brought to the attention of management for review and possibly for revision and adjustment. Typically, contentious items may be found in the payment of salaries and interest on capital, the accounting for admission and retirement of partners, the distribution of earnings, minimum capital accounts, and withdrawal limitations. The auditor should also be alert to partnership agreement requirements that are not in conformity with GAAP (or another comprehensive basis of accounting) so that necessary adjustments can be made.

When the basis of accounting used in reporting by the partnership is not GAAP but another comprehensive basis of accounting the independent auditor ordinarily includes a middle paragraph describing the basis of accounting. An example of such a middle paragraph is as follows:

As described in Note X, the Partnership's policy is to prepare its financial statements on the accounting basis used for income tax purposes; consequently, certain revenue and related assets are recognized when received rather than when earned, and certain expenses are recognized when paid rather than when the obligation is incurred. Accordingly, the accompanying financial statements are not intended to present financial position or results of operations in conformity with generally accepted accounting principles. [AU 621.08]

Once the audit report has clearly established the basis of accounting, the opinion then reads the same as a standard opinion except that alternative wording is used for the phrase "in conformity with generally accepted accounting principles." An example of such wording is:

In our opinion, the financial statements referred to above present fairly the assets, liabilities, and capital of ABC Partnership as of December 31, 19XX and its revenue and expenses and changes in its partners' capital accounts for the year then ended, on the basis of accounting described in Note X. [AU 621.08]

In reporting on partnership financial statements prepared on a cash or income tax accounting basis, the auditor must be alert that the financial statements do not obscure significant matters. If they do, the auditor should consider the need to modify his opinion concerning adequate disclosure, or should recommend that the statements be prepared on an accrual basis if that would solve the problem.

Special Reports

The smaller business often has unique reporting requirements that will fall into the category of special reports, covered in SAS 14 (AU 621). Special reports may deal with the following items (AU 621.01).

a. Financial statements prepared on a basis of accounting other than generally accepted accounting principles;

b. Specified elements, accounts or items of a financial statement;

c. Compliance with aspects of contractual agreements or regulatory requirements related to audited financial statements; and

d. Financial information presented in prescribed forms or schedules that require a prescribed form of auditors' report.

Allowable bases of accounting, other than GAAP consist of income tax basis, cash or modified cash basis, a basis used to comply with government reporting requirements, or a definitive set of criteria applied to financial statements, such as price-level accounting. The AICPA has issued a booklet on *Other Comprehensive Bases of Accounting* (1986l), as part of its Technical Information for Practitioners Series (TIPS). This booklet deals with cash basis and tax basis presentations, and gives extensive examples of financial statements and footnote disclosures.

Often, the smaller business chooses to report under the federal income tax basis of accounting. If no requirement for GAAP financial statements exists, the cost of preparing them may not be beneficial in relation to the needs of the financial statement users. There are several alternative income tax bases on which a taxpayer may report, from the strict cash basis to full accrual. This is determined by the nature of the entity's operations and the related IRS regulations. Disclosure requirements are similar to those for GAAP financial statements but also require that each financial statement should prominently indicate that it is prepared on the income tax basis of accounting.

Reports on specified elements of financial statements typically address financial statement components that affect other transactions. Examples include a report on gross sales required by a leasing agreement that provides for percentage rental payments or a report on payments required by a royalty agreement.

A debt agreement may require an independent public accountant to issue a report regarding the company's compliance with certain debt covenants. The auditor is confined to addressing those items that are financial in nature and within the scope of his auditing procedures. A disclaimer is specified as to those covenants that are outside of this area. The independent auditors' report normally gives negative assurance regarding the applicable covenants and cannot be issued unless the auditor has examined the financial statements to which the agreement relates.

In 1986, the AICPA issued its first Statement of Standards on Attestation Engagements. This provides a framework for increasingly demanded attest services in which accountants are asked to provide assurances as to other than historical financial statements, and in forms other than the auditor's standard report. Typical attest services include reports on compliance with statutory or contractual obligations, supplements to financial statements, investment performance, pro forma historical financial statements, and description of internal accounting controls. (See Chapter 5.)

Compilation and Review Services

Many privately held companies that do not need an audit desire the services of accountants to assist in the preparation of unaudited statements and to provide other services. Thus a large portion of the practice of many CPAs consists of providing services other than auditing, including tax services, management consulting or advisory services, and recordkeeping or data processing. Accounting and review services, often referred to as unaudited statement and writeup work, are a major element.

In 1978, the AICPA Accounting and Review Services Committee began publishing Statements on Standards for Accounting and Review Services (SSARS). This committee is the senior technical committee with authority to issue pronouncements in connection with unaudited financial statements or other unaudited financial information of a nonpublic entity.

SSARS 1, *Compilation and Review of Financial Statements*, (AR 100), divides the accountant's association with unaudited financial statements into compilations and reviews. *Compilations* are defined as "presenting in the form of financial statements information that is the representation of management (owners) without undertaking to express any assurance on the statements." *Reviews* are defined as "performing inquiry and analytical procedures that provide the accountant with a reasonable basis for expressing limited assurance that there are no material modifications that should be made to the statements in order for them to be in conformity with generally accepted accounting principles, or if applicable, with another comprehensive basis of accounting." SSARS 2, *Reporting on Comparative Financial Statements* (AR 200), discusses how the accountant deals with situations in which a different level of work was performed in each of the years, or a different accountant performed the work in an earlier period.

Intent of the Engagement. The client's intent when engaging the accountant is important in determining the nature and scope of his report. If an accountant engaged to render accounting and review services also performs some audit procedures, he has not audited the financial statements. Conversely, once an auditor is engaged to perform an audit, clients cannot switch to a compilation or review engagement once the auditor has discovered matters adversely affecting the financial statements. The client can disengage the auditor, but an auditor should be wary of midstream shifts by clients, since these may signal problems regarding his association as accountant with the unaudited statements. (See SSARS 4, AR 400.)

When a client requests a change from an audit to an unaudited engagement, the reasons may include new circumstances affecting the requirements for an audit, a misunderstanding of the nature of an audit, or restrictions on the scope of the audit whether or not client-imposed. The accountant should pay particular attention to the implications of a scope restriction, as this may signal that the information affected by the scope restriction may be incorrect. The accountant may have to issue an audit report disclosing the scope limitation and its effect on the auditor's opinion. Whenever the scope restriction is a prohibition from corresponding with the client's legal counsel or a refusal to sign a letter of representations, or both, an audit report must be issued stating a disclaimer of opinion.

Conversely, the accountant engaged to render accounting and review services may be requested to upgrade to an audit. Such a request may usually be complied with, because it involves an expansion of the accountant's work.

Additional Responsibilities. When engaged to either compile or review financial statements, if the accountant becomes aware of a departure from GAAP, he must evaluate whether this requires mention in his report. Lack of consistency in the application of GAAP and uncertainties do not have to be mentioned in the accountant's report unless appropriate disclosure regarding such matters is not included in the financial statements. Several examples of modifications of reports are given in AR 100.40. In a compilation engagement, sometimes the client may omit substantially all disclosures required by GAAP or another comprehensive basis of accounting. In this case, the accountant should add a third paragraph to his compilation report as follows (AR 100.21):

> Management has elected to omit substantially all of the disclosures . . . required by generally accepted accounting principles. If the omitted disclosures were included in the financial statements, they might influence the user's conclusions about the company's financial position, results of operations, and cash flows. Accordingly, these financial statements are not designed for those who are not informed about such matters.

Although this form of report is appropriate in a compilation, for which the accountant expresses no assurance, it is not permissible in a review in which the accountant's objective is to express limited assurance. The omission of substantially all disclosures required by GAAP is pervasive and certainly inconsistent with the idea of limited assurance. This form of accountant's review report cannot be issued even if the statements are marked "for internal use only."

Compilation. Compilations require that the accountant fulfill three basic requirements:

1. He must have knowledge of the accounting principles and practices in the client's industry.
2. He must have general understanding of the entity's business transactions and accounting records and of the qualifications of the entity's accounting personnel, as well as an understanding of the accounting basis and form and content of the financial statements.
3. He is not required to make inquiries, obtain verifications or corroborations, or review any information in connection with his engagement. However, if the accountant obtains any information that causes him to believe certain matters are incorrect, incomplete, or unsatisfactory, he must either perform a follow-up to obtain a satisfactory resolution, or, if the client refuses to provide additional or revised information, he must withdraw from the engagement.

The accountant's compilation report has three elements (AR 100.14):

We have compiled the accompanying balance sheet of XYZ Company as of December 31, 19XX, and the related statements of income, retained earnings, and cash flows for the year then ended in accordance with standards established by the American Institute of Certified Public Accountants.

A compilation is limited to presenting in the form of financial statements information that is the representation of management. We have not audited or reviewed the accompanying financial statements and, accordingly, do not express an opinion or any other form of assurance on them.

FIG. 39.6   Standard Compilation Report
Source: AR 100.17 (as amended by SSARS 5 (AR 500)).

1. A compilation has been performed.
2. A compilation is limited to presenting management's representations in financial statement format.
3. No audit or review has been performed, and accordingly, no opinion or assurances whatever are expressed.

The standard form of a compilation report is shown in Figure 39.6.

Although an accountant who is not independent cannot perform an audit, and although SSARS 1 also precludes the accountant who is not independent from issuing a review report, he may issue a compilation report disclosing that he is not independent. He cannot, however, state the specific reasons for nonindependence, since disclosing these may confuse the reader. When the accountant is not independent, he should add as the last paragraph of the above report (AR 100.22): "We are not independent with respect to XYZ Company."

Review. When performing a review, the accountant must fulfill the same requirements as when performing a compilation. In addition, he must have knowledge of the entity's production, distribution, and compensation methods; types of products and services; operating locations; and material transactions with related parties. The accountant must also perform inquiry and analytical procedures, which would ordinarily consist of the following (detailed in AR 100.27):

1. Inquiries concerning the entity's accounting principles and practices and the methods followed in applying them.
2. Inquiries concerning the entity's procedures for recording, classifying, and summarizing transactions and accumulating information for disclosure in the financial statements.
3. Analytical procedures designed to identify relationships and individual items that appear to be unusual:
   a. Comparison of the financial statements with statements for comparable prior period(s).
   b. Comparison of the financial statements with anticipated results, if available (e.g., budgets and forecasts).

c. Study of the relationships of the elements of the financial statements that would be expected to conform to a predictable pattern based on the entity's experience.

4. Inquiries concerning actions taken at meetings of stockholders, board of directors, committees of the board of directors, or comparable groups.

5. Reading the financial statements to consider whether they appear to conform with GAAP.

6. Obtaining reports from other accountants, if any, who have been engaged to audit or review the financial statements of significant components of the reporting entity, its subsidiaries, and other investees.

7. Inquiries concerning:
   a. Whether the financial statements have been prepared in conformity with GAAP consistently applied.
   b. Changes in the entity's business activities or accounting principles and practices.
   c. Questions arising in the review work.
   d. Material subsequent events.

The accountant's report on reviewed financial statements has five elements (AR 100.32):

1. A review has been performed.
2. The financial statements are management's representations.
3. A review consists of inquiries and analytical procedures.
4. A review is less than an audit and therefore no audit opinion is expressed.
5. The accountant is not aware of material modifications that should be made to the financial statements except as disclosed.

The standard form of a review report is shown in Figure 39.7.

Personal Financial Statements

Just as companies require financial statements, sometimes the owners require *personal financial statements* for estate planning, financing, or other purposes.

Personal financial statements utilize current value information because the data is more relevant to the reader than historical cost information. Also, because financial records of individuals are often informal, current value information may be more reliable than historical cost records. Current value information can often be obtained through independent measures that can be verified, generally resulting in a high degree of reliability.

Personal financial statements consist of:

1. *A statement of financial condition.* This is the basic personal financial statement which presents the estimated current values of assets, the estimated current amounts of liabilities, the estimated income taxes on the differences between the estimated current values of assets and the estimated current amounts of liabilities and their tax bases, and net worth at a specified date. The term "net worth" is the difference between total assets and total liabilities, after deducting estimated income taxes on the differences between the estimated current values of assets and the estimated current amounts of liabilities and their tax bases.

We have reviewed the accompanying balance sheet of XYZ Manufacturing Company as of Decemer 31, 198X, and the related statements of income, retained earnings, and cash flows for the year then ended, in accordance with standards established by the American Institute of Certified Public Accountants. All information included in these financial statements is the representation of the management of XYZ Manufacturing Company.

A review consists principally of inquiries of company personnel and analytical procedures applied to financial data. It is substantially less in scope than an examination in accordance with generally accepted auditing standards, the objective of which is the expression of an opinion regarding the financial statements taken as a whole. Accordingly, we do not express such an opinion.

Based on our review, we are not aware of any material modifications that should be made to the acompanying financial statements in order for them to be in conformity with generally accepted accounting principles.

FIG. 39.7   Standard Review Report
Source: AR 100.35.

2. *A statement of changes in net worth.* This optional statement presents the major sources of increases and decreases in net worth, such as income, expenses, changes in the estimated current values of assets, estimated current amounts of liabilities, and estimated income taxes on the differences between these amounts and their tax bases. One statement combining income and other changes is desirable because of the mix of business and personal items in personal financial statements.

3. *Comparative financial statements.* The presentation of comparative financial statements of the current period and one or more prior periods is optional; however, such a presentation is more informative than the presentation of financial statements for only one period.

Illustrative financial statements are shown in Appendix A of SOP 82-1, *Accounting and Financial Reporting for Personal Financial Statements* (TP 10,350). This SOP, included as an Appendix to the revised *Personal Financial Statements Guide* (AICPA, 1983e), originally was sanctioned by the FASB as preferable (SFAS 32) but was deleted from the "approved list" by SFAS 83 because the FASB decided that its jurisdiction should not include personal financial statements. In addition, SFAS 83 superseded FIN 10, which applied to marketable securities in personal financial statements.

Disclosures.   Personal financial statements should include sufficient disclosures to make the statements adequately informative. The disclosures may be made in the body of the financial statements or in the notes. SOP 82-1 contains a listing (not all-inclusive) of matters designed to be indicative of the nature and type of information that ordinarily should be disclosed. These include a clear indication of the individuals covered, the methods used in determining the estimated current values of major categories of assets and the estimated current amounts of major categories of liabilities, and changes in methods from one period to the next, and so forth. The notes to the illustrative financial statements in Appendix A of SOP 82-1 give an example of some disclosures.

Estimating Current Values. Current value is the approximate price at which an item would be exchanged in an arm's-length transaction between buyer and seller. This kind of exchange is relatively easier to value where tradeable assets such as marketable securities are concerned. It is not so easy to gauge current value for restricted securities or for those of privately owned enterprises.

The AICPA Guide suggests the following methods as possibly useful in estimating current values when recent sales information is not available:

* Capitalization of past or prospective earnings.
* Use of liquidation values.
* Adjustment of historical cost based on changes in a specific index.
* Use of appraisals.
* Use of present value (discounted amount) of projected cash receipts. (This is usually the most expedient method of estimating the current values of monetary assets.)

Further guidance as to the detailed procedures to follow when using these methods is contained in the Guide. The Guide also suggests consulting a specialist when necessary for valuation of art works, jewelry, real estate, and certain other assets.

Under SOP 82-1, payables and other liabilities in personal financial statements should be presented at the discounted amount of cash to be paid. The audit tests of those amounts do not ordinarily differ from those performed in examinations of other financial statements.

Estimating Income Taxes. Under SOP 82-1, the tax provision should include an amount for estimated income taxes on the differences between estimated current values of assets and estimated current amounts of liabilities and their tax bases, including consideration of negative tax bases of tax shelters, if any. The estimated income taxes should be presented between liabilities and net worth in the statement of financial condition. The methods and assumptions used should be fully disclosed. An examination of the provision should consider the appropriateness of the tax bases, tax rates, and calculation methods used. Appendix D of SOP 82-1 gives an example of computing the excess of estimated current values of assets over their tax bases and the provision for estimated income taxes thereon.

Investments in Closely Held Businesses. Under SOP 82-1, only the net investment in a closely held business should be presented in the statement of financial condition, and summarized financial information about assets, liabilities, and operations of the business should be disclosed in the footnotes.

Personal Financial Planning

Personal financial planning is a systematic process for organizing personal finances, intended to assist in achieving a person's financial goals and objectives. It includes, but is not limited to, tax planning and projections and cash flow analysis. Personal financial planning focuses on financial control so that objectives such as providing resources for a home, education, travel, personal business needs, or retirement can be met.

The CPA's Role. CPAs are uniquely qualified to perform engagements involving comprehensive financial planning for small businessmen and entrepreneurs. The various levels of planning include:

1. Providing personal financial planning as a service incidental to other areas of accounting practice.
2. Providing single-issue planning services for income tax, estate tax, retirement, or other areas.
3. Providing personal financial planning services as the coordinator of a group of specialists.
4. Providing comprehensive financial planning services by offering a variety of interrelated services to individuals or family groups.

Financial Planning Elements. The financial planning process starts with an assessment of a client's objectives and goals, preferably in dollar terms. After this assessment, a plan must be developed, and usually comprises six elements:

- Income taxes
- Cash flow
- Investments
- Insurance
- Retirement
- Estate planning

In addition, special areas such as education funding, business analysis, or an action checklist may be included.

Once the plan has been developed it may be executed by the client usually with the advice of the CPA, and actual results should be compared with plan periodically.

SSARS 6, *Reporting on Personal Financial Statements Included in Written Personal Financial Plans* (AR 600), exempts such financial statements from the review and compilation standards, provided that a special report form is used (as specified in AR 600.05).

Legal Concerns. The Investment Advisers Act of 1940 (§ 202(a)(11)) requires that:

Any person who, for compensation, engages in the business of advising others, either directly or through publications or writings, as to the value of securities or as to the advisability of investing in, purchasing, or selling securities, or who, for compensation and as part of a regular business, issues or promulgates analyses or reports concerning securities ... [must register with the SEC].

A financial planner who recommends the purchase of a specific security or group of securities as part of a financial plan thus seems to be subject to the provisions of the Act.

The requirement to register under the Act should not be taken lightly. According to the AICPA's Personal Financial Planning Practice Aid 1, *Issues Involving Registration Under the Investment Advisers Act of 1940*, (1986k), some of the concerns are:

1. Investment advisers registered under the Act are required to keep various books and records, which may be examined by the SEC.

2. Investment advisers registered under the Act must provide their clients with a disclosure document that may prove to be difficult and expensive for a CPA firm or a CPA to produce.

3. Certain state securities authorities have promulgated investment adviser registration requirements that are different from and more extensive than the requirements that must be met under the Act. Some states, for example, require investment advisers registered in the state to file audited balance sheets with the state.

Some activities by personal financial planners are considered to be of very significant legal risk (Goldwasser, 1986). Those activities include:

1. Recommending specific investments. A high degree of investment expertise is required (not usually the forte of a CPA). Such recommendations most likely trigger application of the Investment Advisers Act of 1940.

2. Recommending utilization of a specific individual for investment adviser, insurance, legal matters, and so forth. Such advice is risky even if the CPA is thoroughly satisfied as to the competence of the individual to whom referral is made.

3. Conflicts of interest. At a minimum, the CPA's relationships with others on whom a client relies should be completely disclosed to the client.

PART V

Financial Service Industries

40

Commercial Banking

BANKING ENVIRONMENT

Competition

Prior to 1970, commercial banks enjoyed a near monopoly in the financial services sector because they alone offered demand deposits. Established banks were protected from competition, in that applicants for new bank charters were required to show that existing banks in the market would not be adversely affected by their entry. Additionally, incorporators had to prove the new bank would be financially successful within a short time. These restraints have been relaxed and major competition abounds from other banks (domestic and foreign), thrifts, and nondepository financial institutions such as money market funds, finance companies, brokerage firms, and insurance companies. Commercial banks are still distinguished by their ability to accept demand deposits, but restraints over other institutions' ability to offer competitive deposit-like services are disappearing.

Depository institutions traditionally obtained charters based on their lending specialization, and the characteristics of an institution's liabilities determined the types of loans offered. Commercial banks, which had relied on demand deposits, were expected to provide short-term loans. Thus real estate lending by banks was prohibited for many years. By contrast, the principal liabilities of thrift institutions had been savings deposits, which were thought to be longer-term; thus their loan portfolio could be long-term.

Currently, large thrifts are competitive in both attracting and employing funds. They are permitted to engage in most banking activities and are still able to provide some services prohibited for banks; for example, the Competitive Equality Banking Act of 1987 allows thrift holding companies (but not banks) to have charters in multiple states.[1]

Nondepository financial organizations such as consumer finance companies use their competitive edge of fewer restrictions, lower reserve or capital requirements, and less regulation to offer bank-like services. Broker/dealers compete by offering diversified and deposit-like products, such as money market accounts, investment trusts, and loan products. Competition has intensified for several reasons:

* Lack of product differentiation for some services
* Elimination of interest rate restrictions on deposits
* Lessening of constraints restricting interstate banking
* Greater use of advanced technology
* Industry deregulation

The elimination of maximum interest rates on savings deposits and of the prohibition on interest rate competition for deposits probably has been the most important deregulating factor.

---

[1] The Competitive Equality Banking Act of 1987 is covered in detail in Chapter 41.

Other Factors

Interest rate volatility has altered the financial services market. In the past, when market rates exceeded what banks were permitted to pay, depositors withdrew their funds from bank deposit accounts and invested them in higher-yielding assets. Money market funds and direct investments in money market instruments were the chief beneficiaries when this so-called disintermediation occurred.

Large population movements also changed customers' habits. Convenience and location have become the key factors in selecting services; personal loyalty has been replaced by shopping for highest interest rates paid on deposits and the lowest rates charged on loans.

Communications technology and computer systems are available to almost every institution, permitting easy and inexpensive gathering, storing, analyzing, and retrieval of data. Communications technology has changed the delivery system for banking services, permitting convenient access to broad customer populations. Most transactions are now processed by electronic impulse, for example, automated clearinghouses, direct payroll deposits, direct bill disbursements, debit cards, and POS (point-of-sale) terminals. Automated teller machines (ATMs), a very popular way of offering banking services, can be located economically in shopping centers, airports, and recreation facilities. Credit cards are another way of transferring funds and securing credit. Any bank (as well as most bank competitors) can participate in a credit card program through a licensing arrangement.

Banking activities have been influenced by a series of laws and regulations, including:

- The McFadden Act of 1927, prohibiting branching across state lines.
- The Glass-Steagall Act of 1933, which prohibited interest payments in excess of established ceilings (Regulation Q) and restricts banks from underwriting and dealing in securities (except U.S. government securities and general obligation bonds of state and local governments).
- The Douglas Amendment of 1956 to the Bank Holding Company Act, which bans bank holding companies from purchasing a bank in another state.
- The Depository Institutions Deregulation and Monetary Control Act of 1980, which relaxed interest rate regulations (Regulation Q) and requires all depository institutions to adhere to the reserve requirements of the Federal Reserve Board.

Banking Structures

Banks wishing to engage in commercial banking must secure a corporate charter or license from the appropriate state or federal agency. The major reason for requiring incorporation is to provide for closer, more efficient control of banking activities to assure higher safety and liquidity standards. In many states, it is not necessary to receive a charter to engage in banking. Those banks established without a charter or license are referred to as private banks.

There are two basic types of commercial banking activities, wholesale and retail,[2] with differences in operations, services, and clients. Retail banking is oriented

---

[2] This chapter mentions but does not discuss bank trust departments or common trust funds. For guidance on trust departments, refer to Chapter 18 of the AICPA Industry Audit Guide (1984c).

toward attracting individual savings deposits as a source of funds and making numerous small loans to individuals. Wholesale banking relies on large corporate loans, capital market products, and funding from large corporate demand deposits, and borrowings from money markets.

Unit, Branch, and Group Banking. Banks may be classified as unit, branch, or group banks. *Unit banking* exists when services are provided by a single-office institution. Unit banking is giving way to *branch banking* in most states; a single bank's branch offices may be located nearby, as well as sometimes across state lines and national borders. The extent and variety of banking services performed at the branch level vary; the affairs of the branches are directed by their managers in accordance with policies established by the head office.

Group banking exists when two or more banks are controlled or owned by a corporation, individual, or group of individuals. Group banks do not have the same financial flexibility as branches (mobility of funds, larger lending limits, and availability of funds in excess of local deposits). *Chain banking* is a form of group banking in which two or more commercial banks are controlled by the same individual or group of individuals. Control may be accomplished through stock ownership, common directors, or any other manner permitted by law. Each bank member within the chain maintains its own identity and has a separate board of directors. This type of organization is similar to but less regulated than a *bank holding company*.

The Bank Holding Company Act defines a holding company as one that controls one or more banks by the direct or indirect ownership of 25% or more of the voting shares, or exercises a controlling influence over the management or policies, of one or more banks. Each subsidiary bank retains its own board of directors, responsible to the stockholders and regulatory authorities for proper operations.

A bank holding company offers economic advantages such as diversification and increased revenue opportunities, because it may engage in an extended list of activities, often with more flexibility than a bank directly performing these activities. Regulatory rulings permit banks to perform financial services closely related to banking as long as they do not impair the bank's solvency and liquidity.

The Board of Governors of the Federal Reserve System is charged with the responsibility of administering the Bank Holding Company Act and in so doing supervises the formation and expansion of bank holding companies. Organizers of a holding company are required to have Board approval before a holding company is formed, before a company can acquire over 5% of the voting stock of any bank, and/ or before bank holding companies can merge.

Correspondent Banking. Correspondent banking is an arrangement whereby one bank carries deposits with another bank in exchange for services; smaller banks often find it more economical to purchase certain services rather than produce them, and a shift is occurring toward the use of a specific service charge.

The major service performed by the "upstream" correspondent bank has been the clearing of checks. Additionally, a loan in excess of a smaller bank's legal lending limit can be purchased by a correspondent bank, or the larger bank may sell a portion of its loan portfolio to the smaller bank if the latter needs an increased loan portfolio. In addition, the correspondent bank may serve as an investment advisor and purchase, sell, and hold securities for the smaller bank.

Banks lend to other banks to enable them to increase their reserves. Upstream correspondent banks, located in the large money centers, assemble and make federal funds available to their correspondents during tight money periods, and when small banks have excess reserves, stand ready to purchase their federal funds.

Multinational Banking. U.S. national banks and some state banks may form federally chartered Edge Act corporations to conduct business in other countries. Edge Act corporations are exempt from many of the regulations that apply to domestic banking activities. Banks also operate through international subsidiaries that receive both domestic and foreign regulatory attention, and through branches located in foreign cities.

The number of foreign banks in the United States is substantial. Foreign banks are concentrated in about a dozen states; approximately 90% of their assets are located in California, Illinois, and New York.

A U.S. branch of a foreign bank performs the usual banking services such as accepting deposits, making loans, and financing international trade. A U.S. subsidiary of a foreign bank is a separate entity and may be owned in whole or in part by a foreign bank holding company. A U.S. agency differs from a branch or subsidiary in that it may finance international trade and make loans, but it cannot accept deposits. The funds a U.S. agency employs in the performance of its functions are derived from the home country.

A U.S. representative office of a foreign bank cannot originate or consummate banking transactions, and usually provides a public relations function; thus it is subject to limited state regulation with no federal oversight. A U.S. affiliate is not owned by a foreign bank, but the foreign bank and its affiliate may have common ownership by a holding company. An affiliate may perform broad or limited banking services, depending on the permission granted by the state in which it operates.

The International Banking Act of 1978, codified under Regulation K of the Board of Governors of the Federal Reserve System, regulates foreign banks. A foreign bank must select one home state of operation and can establish a new branch or agency outside the home state only with that state's permission. Additionally, foreign banks are subject to reserve requirements imposed by the Federal Reserve System if the parent bank has worldwide assets of $1 billion or more. Although foreign banks operating in the United States are not required to be members of the Federal Reserve System, they may enjoy their services on comparable terms.

Regulation

Regulators. The regulatory authorities administer the banking laws, promulgate and interpret regulations, and supervise bank policies to further the public interest. Regulators use the review of bank regulatory reports and the examination process to keep informed of both the legality and the soundness of an individual bank's operations.

Federal regulators of banks include the Office of the Comptroller of the Currency (OCC), the Federal Reserve Board (FRB), and the Federal Deposit Insurance Corporation (FDIC). At the state level, banks may be regulated by one of fifty state banking departments (SBDs). The Federal Financial Institutions Examination Council (FFIEC) is an interagency body empowered to prescribe uniform principles, standards, and report forms for federal examinations and to make recommendations to promote uniformity in supervision. In addition to representation from the three federal banking regulators, the FFIEC is composed of members from the Federal Home Loan Bank Board (FHLBB) and the National Credit Union Administration (NCUA). Some banking activities come under the purview of other federal agencies, such as the Department of Justice, the SEC, and the Federal Trade Commission.

Bank regulation by the OCC, FRB, FDIC, and SBDs collectively encompasses the following activities:

* Issuance of charters
* Review and analysis of reports of condition and income
* Periodic examination
* Issuance and enforcement of regulations
* Rendering counsel and advice on operating problems
* Approval of proposed changes in the scope of corporate functions and capital structures
* Authorization of branches and trust departments
* Approval of mergers and consolidations
* Organization and regulation of bank holding companies
* Regulation of service corporations
* Liquidation of banks

Figure 40.1 summarizes regulatory bodies and supervisory requirements for commercial banks.

Office of the Comptroller of the Currency. The major regulatory responsibilities of the OCC are approving national bank charters and branch office applications (where permitted by state law); evaluating applications for merger where the surviving bank is a national bank; enforcing operating regulations in and examining national banks; and declaring failing national banks insolvent.

Federal Reserve System. Besides conducting monetary policy of the United States, the Federal Reserve has wide regulatory and supervisory powers over member banks. The FRB is responsible for granting permission for mergers and new branches and for conducting bank examinations. It has the sole responsibility for approving the formation of, or acquisitions by, bank holding companies. To reduce overlap with the OCC, the FRB has primary supervisory responsibility for state chartered member banks and for all bank holding companies. With most of the largest U.S. banks having established holding companies, the Federal Reserve Board exercises significant influence over the banking system.

Federal Deposit Insurance Corporation. The FDIC's regulatory responsibilities cover insured banks. To avoid excessive duplication with the OCC and the FRB, the FDIC is primarily concerned with insured state chartered banks that are not

Bank	Bank holding company	State Banks and Trusts				Foreign agency and representative
		National bank	FRB member	FDIC-insured nonmember	Non-insured nonmember	
Chartered by		OCC	SBD	SBD	SBD	SBD FRB
Examined by	FRB	OCC FRB FDIC	FRB FDIC SBD	FDIC SBD	SBD	SBD FRB
Submit report to	SEC FRB	OCC FRB FDIC	FRB FDIC	FDIC	SBD	SBD FRB
Reserves required by		FRB	FRB	SBD	SBD	SBD FRB
Subject to regulations of	SEC FRB	OCC FRB FDIC	SBD FRB FDIC	SBD FDIC	SBD FRB	SBD FRB
Mergers and branches authorized by	FRB	OCC FRB	SBD FRB	SBD FDIC	SBD FRB	SBD FRB

OCC = Comptroller of the Currency   FDIC = Federal Deposit Insurance Corporation
FRB = Federal Reserve Board   SBD = State Banking Department
SEC = Securities and Exchange Commission

FIG. 40.1   Examination and Supervisory Requirements for Commercial Banks

members of the Federal Reserve System. The FDIC examines insured banks that are not FRB members, and declares failing banks insolvent. Although the FDIC does not directly charter banks, it affects the chartering through its approval of a bank's application for deposit insurance, which is a competitive necessity.

The FDIC has the authority to assist a troubled bank or assume its assets. When the FDIC takes over a bank that has failed, it either allows the bank to go into receivership and reimburses the depositors through a payoff method, or arranges for a merger with another bank under an assumption method. The FDIC can also establish a newly organized bank to assume the assets and liabilities of a failed bank.

The FDIC Insurance Fund would be insufficient to pay all deposits of up to $100,000 per individual deposit account in the event of a collapse of the banking system; however, there is the implied guarantee of the federal government if the fund becomes exhausted.

State banking departments and agencies. Although their responsibilities vary from one state to another, state banking authorities normally approve the charters for new state banks, open and close branch offices (if the state permits branching), determine the scope of bank holding company operations within the state, and examine financial institutions chartered by the state. SBDs also have powers to protect the public interest by regulating the activities of finance companies and enforcing various consumer regulations, such as credit disclosure and usury laws.

Generally, SBDs are more permissive in the types of banking practices they allow. As a result, a large number of banks prefer state charters. Most large New York City banks whose operations are global in scope are state-chartered banks.

Securities and Exchange Commission. The Securities Act of 1933 generally exempts from registration any security issued or guaranteed by a national or state bank and any security issued by or representing an interest in or direct obligation of a Federal Reserve Bank. The Securities Exchange Act of 1934 also exempts banks from supervision and regulation by the SEC and grants the regulatory powers to the other federal banking agencies. The Act, however, requires these agencies to substantially conform their disclosure requirements with those of the SEC. Most large banks report to the SEC because they are owned by a publicly held holding company.

Regulations. Commercial bank regulations may be classified according to their principal objective: (1) bank safety, (2) banking structure, and (3) protection of the interest of consumers. A summary of major banking regulations is shown in Figure 40.2.

Safety regulations. Bank safety regulations are directed toward preventing failures, and in many cases are anticompetitive because a reduction of competition reduces the risk of bank failures.

To ensure safety of both new and existing institutions and to serve the public's interests, regulators require a new bank applicant to demonstrate that (1) it will meet the "convenience and needs" of the community, (2) it will not unduly jeopardize other banks in the area, (3) it has the ability to generate earnings sufficient to cover the expenses of bank operations, (4) it has adequate management talent, and (5) it can meet minimum capital requirements.

Banks are required to have adequate capital at the time of organization and to maintain satisfactory amounts of capital throughout their life. A national bank cannot extend a loan to a borrower exceeding 15% of its capital; state-chartered banks have similar lending limits. Most investments must be in corporate or municipal bonds that are investment grade quality. Finally, banks must maintain adequate liquid assets in the event of sudden or large deposit withdrawals.

Banks are prohibited from investing in corporate equity securities. However, they are permitted to trade in equity securities through their trust departments in a trustee or fiduciary capacity. Banks are allowed to enter the retail brokerage business and buy and sell securities for their customers.

Underwriting and trading activities are restricted by the Glass-Steagall Act, which separated investment banking from commercial banking because some banks placed securities they were unable to sell into their investment portfolio or into the portfolios of trust department clients. Banks are, however, allowed to underwrite and deal in securities of the federal government and selected securities of state and local governments.

Structure regulations. Bank structure regulations are directed toward the size and distribution of banks in the system. Increased competition may lower loan rates,

---

Regulation

Monetary Policy-Related Regulations

A	Loans to depositories
D	Reserve requirements
G, X	Credit by banks, broker/dealers, and others
U, T	Credit for margin borrowers
Q	Interest rate ceilings on various types of deposits

Bank Safety and Soundness

F	Financial disclosure to stockholders and others
L	Interlocking directorates in banking
O	Loans to officers, directors, and stockholders
P	Security devices and procedures
R	Interlocking relationships between banks and the securities industry

International and Holding Company Activities of Banks

K	International banking
Y	Bank holding company activities

Activities of the Federal Reserve Banks

H	Membership in the Federal Reserve System
I	Stock ownership in Federal Reserve Banks
J	Federal Reserve check processing rules and procedures
N	Reserve Banks' relations with foreign banks and governments
V	Loan guarantees

Consumer Protection

AA	Unfair and deceptive acts or practices
B	Equal credit opportunity
BB	Community reinvestment
C	Home mortgage disclosure
CC	Expedited funds availability
E	Electronic fund transfers
M	Consumer leasing
R	Flood insurance
S	Financial privacy
Z	Truth-in-lending and fair credit reporting

FIG. 40.2 Summary of Major Banking Regulations

increase deposit rates, and lower fees charged for other services; however, increased competition may also increase the probability of bank failures.

Each state establishes its own policies on branching for banks headquartered in that state, and federally chartered banks are subject to state laws on branching. Recently, some states have allowed interstate branch banking on a reciprocal basis. Other states allow regional interstate branching to protect its banks from being acquired by larger banks.

Banks planning to merge must receive the approval of one of the three federal banking agencies. The agency with primary jurisdiction must seek the nonbinding opinions of the remaining two agencies. In addition, all bank mergers are subject to review by the Department of Justice under antitrust legislation, and will not be approved if they substantially reduce competition or will result in a monopoly. There is one exemption from the competition criteria in bank merger cases—a bank declared failing by the FDIC.

Consumer protection regulations. A final class of regulations are those designed to protect consumers. The regulatory philosophy is that: (1) consumers as a class have unequal market power relative to credit and other market participants; and (2) consumer markets, when left to their own devices, may not allocate credit in the most socially desirable manner. The major consumer lending regulations, by and large, apply to all consumer credit grantors.

Examinations and Reporting. Banks are examined regularly by one or more of the regulatory agencies. The primary objective is to determine the soundness of the bank. Bank examinations have helped stabilize the banking system by insuring that banks comply with regulations and sound management practices. Examinations also help regulators identify problem banks so that corrective action can be taken. A regulatory examination is not equivalent to an audit by an independent accounting firm.

Accounting system. The FFIEC has established a uniform report system for all federally supervised depository institutions, holding companies, and their subsidiaries. Many state regulators have adopted this same reporting format. The quarterly Consolidated Report of Condition and Income is the basic regulatory report, containing a balance sheet, an income statement, and other schedules. It is usually referred to as the Call Report, a name derived from the earlier regulatory practice of telephoning banks to obtain financial statements on a specified date near the end of a calendar quarter. All banks are required by regulation to have a calendar fiscal year.

Director's examination. A directors' examination is an examination of a bank caused by its board of directors. Examinations are generally performed by internal auditors or by an independent auditor. The bylaws of national banks, and some state laws, call for periodic directors' examinations to be performed by or under the supervision of the board of directors, and certain of the bank supervisory agencies require submission of reports on these examinations. Directors' examinations are further discussed in the "Auditing Considerations" portion of this chapter.

On-site regulatory authority examinations. Regulatory examinations are geared toward depositor rather than investor interests, and are directed toward determining the bank's solvency, the degree of competence of management, and compliance with the laws under which a bank operates. Supervisory examinations are usually scheduled to occur on an 18- to 24- month cycle. More frequent examinations can be expected for troubled banks and banks that have filed registration statements, change of ownership notifications, or other special notices.
The part of the examination to which the most time is devoted is the evaluation of the creditworthiness of the bank's loan portfolio. Another important part is an evalu-

Composite rating	Rating description
1	Banks in this group are sound in every respect. They can withstand vagaries in the business cycle more ably than banks with lower composite ratings. No cause for supervisory concern.
2	Banks in this group are fundamentally sound, but minor weaknesses are detected which can be corrected in the normal course of business. Supervisory response is limited to the extent that minor deficiencies are resolved.
3	Banks in this group exhibit financial, operational, or compliance weaknesses ranging from moderately severe to unsatisfactory. Such institutions are vulnerable to adverse business conditions, but the possibility of failure is low.
4	Banks in this group have serious financial weaknesses or other conditions that are unsatisfactory. Unless effective action is taken to correct the banks' problems, they could develop into situations that could lead to failure. Though the potential for failure. Though the potential for failure is present, it is not pronounced; close supervision is required.
5	Banks in this group have extremely high probability of failure. The problems are so severe that immediate corrective action and financial assistance is required. Constant supervisory attention is required.

FIG. 40.3 Uniform Composite Bank Examination Ratings

ation of the quality of the bank's operations and management. A summary of the bank examination report is presented and discussed with the bank's management and is made available to the independent public accountants. If the bank's operations are in violation of the law, poor operating procedures are detected, or the bank's capital is below regulatory requirements, management is requested to correct the violation over a period of time, and the bank's progress is closely monitored.

Federal regulators have adopted a uniform supervisory rating system called CAMEL. Under CAMEL, bank examiners focus on five perfomance dimensions:

- Capital adequacy
- Asset quality
- Management competency
- Earnings
- Liquidity

Each category is assigned a rating of 1 (best) to 5 (worst), and a composite rating for the bank is computed. An interpretation of the composite ratings is presented in Figure 40.3.

ACCOUNTING AND FINANCIAL REPORTING

Financial institution regulation developed more rapidly than GAAP and GAAS, and audited financial statements of banks were generally unavailable to the public prior to 1964. Thus, regulation has usually been designed to serve the agencies, not other financial statement users. In 1971, ASR 121 eliminated SEC certification exemptions for banks owned by publicly held bank holding companies. Thus, only within the last two decades have many financial institutions, under pressures from investors and analysts, begun to prepare financial statements in accordance with GAAP.

RAP/GAAP Differences

Bank holding companies are required to comply with GAAP under Regulation S-X. Any adjustments to the financial statements because of differences in Regulatory Accounting Practices (RAP) are made in consolidation, and there is no need for further disclosure. The following is a listing of the more important differences between RAP and GAAP:

1. *Sale of Receivables.* SFAS 77, *Reporting by Transferors for Transfers of Receivables with Recourse* (R20), permits sale treatment under GAAP if specified conditions are met. RAP requires such loan sales to be recorded as a collateralized borrowing by the selling bank and as a loan by the purchasing bank.

   If a loan portfolio is sold without recourse but an escrow account is established to absorb losses arising within the loan portfolio, regulators will permit its treatment as a sale, as long as the bank cannot be required to absorb losses in excess of the escrow balance. This recent modification of regulatory accounting was made to facilitate securitization of loan portfolios.

2. *Trading Account Securities.* The AICPA Audit Guide, *Audits of Banks* (1984c), requires trading account securities to be accounted for at current market value. Regulators allow banks to carry trading securities at either market value or lower of cost or market.

3. *Sale/Leasebacks.* Regulatory authorities apply GAAP to transactions involving the sale and leaseback of bank premises. However, instead of the GAAP amortization of gains over the leaseback term, the FDIC and FRB require deferral and amortization over a period of not less than 10 years, while the OCC requires amortization over the remaining life of the assets. If a bank can justify a shorter period by providing evidence that an alternative facility has been acquired, it will be permitted to recognize the gain sooner.

4. *Futures Contracts and Forwards.* Under SFAS 80, *Accounting for Futures Contracts* (F80), gains and losses on hedged transactions are deferred and recognized as an adjustment to the carrying amount of the hedged item. RAP does not permit hedge accounting; futures must be valued at either market or lower of cost or market. Gains and losses are recognized in the period the changes in valuation occur and are reported for RAP purposes as other noninterest income or expense.

5. *In-Substance Defeasance.* According to SFAS 76, Extinguishment of Debt (D14), a debtor considers debt to be extinguished, and related gains or losses recognizable, for financial reporting purposes if the debtor establishes and funds an irrevocable trust to be used solely for satisfying scheduled payments of both interest and principal and if additional contributions by the debtor are considered remote. RAP requires this debt to be reported as a liability and the trust shown separately as an asset.

6. *Assets Acquired by Foreclosure.* Under RAP, certain bank assets, primarily real estate and stock acquired as a result of foreclosure, cannot be carried indefinitely by a bank at cost or at market value, but must be written down as prescribed. If a material amount of assets is,

in effect, not reflected in the financial statements, those statements will not be in conformity with GAAP.

7. *Loan Loss Allowances.* In Issue 85-44, *Differences Between Loan Loss Allowances for GAAP and RAP*, the EITF reached a consensus that differences could exist between loan loss allowances on a GAAP and RAP basis because of the subjectivity involved in estimating the amount of loss or the use of arbitrary factors by regulators. The proceedings summary in *EITF Abstracts* comments that "auditors should be particularly skeptical in the case of GAAP/RAP differences and must justify them based on the particular facts and circumstances."

Reference Sources

AICPA Guidance. The AICPA Industry Audit Guide, *Audits of Banks* (AICPA, 1984c), describes both accounting and auditing matters unique to banking. It is often referred to in this chapter simply as the Bank Audit Guide.

SFAS 83 (Bt7.101) designates the accounting principles in this Guide as preferable for the purposes of justifying a change in accounting principles. Several issues were left unresolved in the guide because AICPA felt they were also significant to other industries and institutions. Most have subsequently received attention from either the AICPA or FASB.

Guide Open Issue	Dealt With In
Allocation of purchase price in a bank acquisition and related amortization of goodwill	SFAS 72 (Bt7)
Accounting (financing vs. sales) for transactions involving securities, loans, and other earning assets (for example coupon and principal stripping of securities and transfers of assets with recourse)	SFAS 77 (R20)
Definition of "substantially the same" as it applies to securities and other assets exchanged or swapped	SOP Exposure Draft (AICPA, 1988e)
Loan and other fee recognition	SFAS 91 (L20)
Whether interest cost-to-carry should be a factor in determining the net realizable value of restructured real estate loans and other real estate owned	SOP Project (underway)
Possible modification of the statement of changes in financial position	SFAS 95 (C25)
Accounting for futures and forwards	SFAS 80 (F80)
Accounting and financial statement presentation of bankers' acceptances	EITF Issue 85-34

An AICPA Auditing Procedure Study, *Auditing the Allowance for Credit Losses of Banks* (1986c), provides guidance on the lending process, internal control structure, and other matters that will assist the auditor when planning the audit approach to the allowance for credit losses. The AICPA *Disclosure Checklist for Banks* (1986h) is a technical practice aid to assist auditors in preparing bank financial statements. The

Report of the Special Task Force on Audits of Repurchase Securities Transactions (AICPA, 1985r) provides audit guidance for repurchase transactions.

In 1987 AcSEC began to issue Practice Bulletins to disseminate its views on certain financial accounting and reporting issues. Practice Bulletins provide guidance on several issues of particular interest to banks:

* Mortgage banking activities
* Interest as a holding cost
* Bank loan disclosures
* Deposit float
* Accounting for foreign loan swaps
* Acquisition, development, and construction loans
* Accounting for foreign debt/equity swaps
* Income recognition on loans to financially troubled countries

Regulatory Agencies

Federal Financial Institutions Examination Council. The regulators' interpretation of GAAP and RAP are contained in the instructions to the Call Reports. Although these interpretations are not GAAP, an auditor may find it helpful to understand how bank regulators view GAAP. Most accounting issues are discussed in a detailed glossary provided with the instructions.

Office of the Comptroller of the Currency. Reporting requirements for national banks are located in 12 CFR §§ 11, 16, and 18. Additional guidance as to the OCC's interpretation of regulatory reporting is provided in *Examining Issuances* and *Banking Issuances*. The OCC also publishes the *Comptroller's Manual for National Bank Examiners* and the *Comptroller's Handbook for National Bank Examiners*.

Federal Reserve Bank. Regulation F prescribes the registration requirements and submission of annual and quarterly reports of state member banks of the FRB. The FRB publishes a *Federal Reserve Regulatory Service* that includes statutes administered by the Board as well as regulations, interpretations, rulings, and opinions. "Board Interpretations" are also published in response to questions that have significant policy implications.

Federal Deposit Insurance Corporation. The FDIC's requirements for reporting by insured state nonmember banks can be found in *Part 335, Rules and Regulations of the FDIC*. Additional published guidance as to the rules, regulations, interpretations, and policy statements is also available from the FDIC.

Securities and Exchange Commission. Article 9 of Regulation S-X governs the form and content of financial statements of bank holding companies and banks included in filings with the SEC. Industry Guide 3, *Statistical Disclosure by Bank Holding Companies*, specifies the required disclosure of data directly related to items on the financial statements as well as other statistical data. Although Guide 3 disclosures are not required in financial statements, most bank holding companies include such information in annual reports.

Several SAB's are of particular importance to bank reporting:

SAB No.	Topic	Content
40	6.H	Compensating balances and short-term debt
46	6.G	Quarterly financial data
49-49A, 56, 66, 75	11.H	Loans and related alllowances for loan losses to borrowers in foreign countries with liquidity problems
50	1.F	Financial statements and disclosures necessary in the formation of a one bank holding company
60	11.J	Disclosures of financial guarantees
71-71A	1.I	Financial statement requirements of properties securing mortgage loans
70	5.R	Nonrecourse debt collateralized by lease receivables

In addition, the SEC has issued FRR 28, *Accounting for Loan Losses by Registrants Engaged in Lending Activities* (§ 401.09); and FRRs 11, 13 and 27 (§ 401) deal with financial statement presentation and disclosure by banks.

Bank Assets

Presented in Figure 40.4 is the asset section of the balance sheet of a sample bank. Most bank assets (except troubled loans) are highly marketable and can be quickly liquidated. The classification of the balance sheet into current and noncurrent is not considered useful.

Cash and Due From Banks

Cash items. Cash items include currency, deposit balances held directly or indirectly at the Federal Reserve Banks, and cash items in the process of collection (CIPC).

Currency meets the cash needs of customers and is included as part of legal reserves, as are deposits held at the Federal Reserve Bank (usually the largest item of cash). Legal reserves are those items that may be counted as reserves required under Regulation D, in proportion to actual customer deposits held. Check clearing and collection of funds from other banks is usually processed through the cash items account.

CIPC, often called deposit float, represents the value of checks drawn on other banks deposited by customers but not yet collected, and therefore not available for investment. When collected, the amounts are transferred to the bank's Federal Reserve account.

In their financial statements, banks have traditionally reported customer deposits of checks drawn on other banks as liabilities to the customers and as assets to the bank (cash). However, some banks believe that deposit float should be netted. AcSEC Practice Bulletin 1 (TP 12,010) concluded that netting of deposit float is

Assets	December 31	
	19X2	19X1
Cash and due from banks	$ 559,100	$ 542,500
Interest-bearing deposits in banks	100,000	50,000
Federal funds sold and securities purchased under resale agreements	160,000	50,000
Trading account assets	238,000	266,300
Investment securities	3,769,500	4,352,800
Loans and lease finance receivables	5,131,500	4,571,000
Less: allowance for credit losses	93,000	82,300
Net loans and lease finance receivables	5,038,500	4,488,700
Premises and equipment, net	197,800	181,700
Due from customers on acceptances	23,700	37,900
Accrued interest receivable	40,800	39,400
Other assets	100,000	40,000
Total assets	$10,228,200	$10,049,300

FIG. 40.4   Asset Section of Sample Bank Balance Sheet

inappropriate. The EITF also supported that conclusion (Issue 84-9, *Deposit Float of Banks*).

Demand deposits balance at other banks.   Banks hold demand deposits balances at other banks for a number of reasons. Small banks that are not members of the Federal Reserve System can usually meet their reserve requirements by holding pass-through accounts at member banks. Many small banks also use their deposits at larger banks to process correspondent transactions performed on their behalf. Both the due-from-banks asset (balances with other commercial banks), and the due-to-banks liability (interbank deposits), are important results of correspondent banking relationships. If material, these correspondent balances are disclosed separately from other cash balances because they represent restricted cash.

Reciprocal due to/from balances should be offset if legally permissible in the process of collection or payment. After reciprocal adjustments are made, due-to debit balances should be disclosed as loans receivable while due-from credit balances are reclassified as short-term borrowings.

Banks also hold demand deposits at nonaffiliated foreign banks to obtain foreign currency. Foreign currency deposits are called *nostro* (our) accounts. *Vostro* (their) accounts exist when foreign banks maintain dollar or foreign currency deposits in U.S. banks.

Interest-Bearing Deposits.   Interest-bearing time deposits held with other domestic and foreign banks and overseas branches of U.S. banks are often referred to as placements, interbank deposits, or redeposits. Maturities of these instruments may range from overnight to several months or years. Eurodollar placements make up a substantial portion of interest-bearing time deposits. If material, interest-bearing deposits should be presented in a separate caption on the balance sheet; otherwise they should be combined with cash and due from banks.

Federal Funds. Federal funds are a unique product of the U.S. banking system. A bank with Federal Reserve deposits in excess of its reserve requirements can lend (sell) the excess, at an agreed rate of interest, to a second bank needing additional funds to meet its reserve requirements. Federal funds transfers redistribute the total banking system reserves, thus facilitating their efficient use. Ordinarily, purchases and sales are for one day.

Banks that sell federal funds acquire assets (Federal Funds Sold) and lose a corresponding amount of reserves on the balance sheet. Banks that purchase (borrow) federal funds gain reserves but acquire a liability (Federal Funds Purchased).

Federal funds may be sold for purposes other than to meet reserve requirements. The lending of immediately available funds for one day or under a continuing contract are referred to as Fed Funds transactions. Immediately available funds are those that the purchaser does not have to collect through the Fed and therefore can either invest or dispose of on the same day that the transaction occurs. A continuing contract has no specified maturity and does not require advance notice of either party to terminate. Such contracts may also be known as rollovers or as open-ended agreements.

Banks often operate on both sides of the market on the same day. If the federal funds purchase and sale transactions are undertaken with different banks, no right of offset exists and the balances should not be netted on the balance sheet. Federal funds sold overnight should be recorded separately as an asset or combined with securities purchased under resale agreements (reverse repurchase agreements); if sold with maturities greater than one day, they should be classified as a loan. Federal funds purchased overnight should be shown separately or combined with securities sold under repurchase agreements; if purchased with maturities extending beyond one day, they should be included with other borrowings.

Repurchase Agreements. A bank may invest excess funds by buying U.S. government securities from a borrowing bank or a U.S. government securities dealer for immediate delivery. On the agreed date, often the following day, the borrower repurchases the securities at the same price plus interest at a predetermined rate. These transactions are referred to as securities sold under agreements to repurchase (repos) by the borrowing bank and as securities purchased under reverse repurchase agreements by the lending bank (reverse repos). See Chapter 21 and *Report of the Special Task Force on Audits of Repurchase Securities Transactions* (AICPA, 1985d) for special accounting and audit considerations.

Trading Account Securities. Banks involved in underwriting and dealing in certain permitted securities seek to earn a profit by trading for their own account or selling the securities to customers. A markup in price, known as a spread, represents compensation to the bank for distributing and making a market in the securities. Large banks are the principal underwriters of U.S. Treasury securities and municipal general obligation securities. The Federal Reserve now permits banks and bank holding companies to underwrite limited types of other securities (e.g., money market instruments and commercial paper).

At the date of acquisition, securities should be designated as either trading or investment, and that designation should be documented. Trading account assets are exempt from most requirements of SFAS 12 (I89), as they come under the rules for industries having specialized accounting practices (I89.108–.111). Instead, the accounting treatment follows the AICPA Audit and Accounting Guide, *Audits of Brokers and Dealers in Securities* (AICPA, 1985a). In general, the guide recommends the market value concept for all securities (including short positions).

Short positions represent the bank's obligation to purchase the related security. They should be presented as a liability if material. The broker/dealer audit guide recommends that material long and short positions in the same security should not be netted. Borrowed securities should not be shown on the balance sheet, but disclosed. In addition, the major categories of securities in the trading portfolio should be disclosed in the notes to the financial statements.

The Bank Audit Guide recommends that transfers of securities from the trading account to the investment account should be at market value, with gain or loss recognized. Transfers of investment securities to the trading account should also be at market value, but gains should be deferred until final disposition.

Regulators permit banks to carry trading securities either at market value or lower of cost or market. Most banks comply with GAAP and use market.

Investment Securities. Generally, banks (but not bank holding companies) are prohibited by regulatory agencies from investing in equity securities, although there are minor exceptions generally relating to investments in subsidiaries engaged in bank-related activities, repossessed collateral, and investments in specified government corporations. Also, banks that are members of the Federal Reserve System are required under Regulation I to own stock in their regional Federal Reserve Bank.

Banks occasionally become owners of corporate stocks pledged as collateral on loans that became uncollectible. These stocks must be disposed of within a reasonable time, generally no more than five years. The FRB has allowed an exception to this rule for debt/equity swaps with lesser developed countries (LDCs).

Determination of quality. Bank examiners look closely at the investment account to determine quality and value. For this purpose, securities are placed in three categories: investment securities that meet the standards of quality, doubtful securities, and loss. Classification as doubtful securities indicates a credit problem exists, and a portion of their book value is deducted by the examiner in computing the bank's capital. Securities in the loss classification must be written off.

Investment securities cannot include predominantly speculative securities. While marketability has been emphasized by regulatory agencies, they also recognize that a large number of issues of small localities that are less marketable than rated issues are nevertheless of high quality and eligible for a bank's portfolio.

Under OCC guidelines, national banks may purchase and hold investment company shares without limitation, if the investment company's portfolio consists of investments in which the bank could invest directly without limitation.

Some instruments may be considered loans. The financial statement classification should be determined by the nature of the item and not solely by its form.

Objective of bank investment portfolio. Liquidity is a principal consideration in an investment portfolio; thus bank securities portfolios contain short-term, highly marketable securities held in lieu of non-interest-bearing reserves.

Commercial banks hold U.S. Treasury obligations because they are highly marketable and are safe from default; however, yields on Treasury obligations are not as high as on securities of similar maturity. Agency securities are issued by federal agencies that administer selected federal lending programs. There is a minor default risk in agency securities, because most are not direct obligations of the U.S. government. Municipal securities are sold by city, state, and other local governments to finance education, water, electricity, recreation, and other community services. The default risk, while low overall, varies widely among issuers.

Accounting for investment securities. Marketable equity securities held for investment are accounted for under the provisions of SFAS 12 (I89); ordinarily these securities are not significant to a bank. Accounting policies for investment securities not covered by SFAS 12 (typically bonds) are:

1. Investment securities are recorded at cost. Premium or discount should be amortized using the interest method over a period extending from the purchase date to the earliest call date or to the maturity date if there is no call date.

2. For GNMA modified pass-through securities and similar instruments, estimated average life of the contract should be used for the discount or premium amortization period.

3. Investment security gains and losses should be recognized on the completed-transaction basis in the income statement.

4. Investment securities should be written down to market value when the bank cannot demonstrate an intent or ability to hold the obligations to maturity; when there is evidence of impairment in value that is other than temporary, a write-down is also required. Once such a write-down is made, no reinstatement is allowed. Investment securities subject to troubled debt restructuring should follow SFAS 15 (D22).

SOP 83-3, *Reporting by Banks of Investment Gains and Losses* (TP 10,360), requires that banks display such gains and losses on a separate line in the income statement, on a pretax basis. SOP 83-3 was issued after the SEC mandated this presentation under FRR 11 (§ 401). Previously, such gains were shown net of tax, below "income from securities gains (losses)."

Wash sales. Wash sales occur when securities are "sold" with the intent to acquire the same or substantially similar securities in a short period of time. If a commercial bank "sells" a security and acquires the "same" or "substantially similar" securities in a reasonably short period of time, no sale should be recognized.

What constitutes a reasonably short period of time is a matter of judgment. AcSEC has issued an SOP exposure draft, *Definition of "Substantially the Same" for Debt Instruments* (AICPA, 1988e), which would require that all of the following criteria be met to conclude that securities are substantially the same:

1. The debt instrument must have the same primary obligor, except for debt instruments guaranteed by a sovereign government, central bank, or agency thereof, in which case the guarantor must be the same.

2. The debt instrument must be identical in form and type; for example, the exchange of Government National Mortgage Association (GNMA) I securities for GNMA II securities would not meet this criterion. Similarly, the exchange of loans made to foreign debtors that are otherwise the same except for different U.S. foreign tax credit benefits would not meet this criterion.

3. The debt instruments must bear the identical contractual interest rate.

4. The debt instruments must have the same maturity, and must have the same aggregate unpaid principal amounts.

5. In the case of mortgage-backed pass-through securities: (a) the mortgages collateralizing the securities must be similar with respect to maturities (i.e., expected remaining lives) resulting in approximately the same market yield; (b) the securities must be collateralized by a similar pool of mortgages, such as single-family residential mortgages; (c) the aggregate principal amounts of the securities given up and reacquired must be within the accepted "good delivery" standard for the type of security involved; and (d) the breakage must be within the accepted "good delivery" standards for the type of security involved. (Under SOP 85-2, *Accounting for Dollar Repurchase—Dollar Reverse Repurchase Agreements by Sellers-Borrowers* (TP 10,380.25), breakage (difference in principal amounts) of up to 2.5% is allowed without affecting "good delivery." Under the proposed SOP, the breakage allowance would be modified as indicated.)

Cash securities used to hedge interest rate risks. Banks exposed to interest rate risk in their interest rate swap portfolios or other interest rate sensitive assets or liabilities might hedge by purchasing or short-selling a cash security (e.g., a U.S. Treasury bond). A cash security is often selected because it provides a more efficient hedge than other hedge instruments. The hedge is terminated when the cash security is sold. When the security is sold an accounting issue arises as to the recognition or deferral of the gain or loss upon disposition. In Issue 87-1, *Deferral Accounting for Cash Securities That Are Used to Hedge Rate or Price Risk,* the EITF was unable to reach a consensus; however, the majority of members believed that hedge accounting should not be used.

Perpetual preferred stock redemption agreements. In Issue 85-23, *Effect of a Redemption Agreement on Carrying Value of a Security,* the EITF considered the accounting by a bank holding company (BHC) for underwater preferred stock investments that had been carried at lower of cost or market in accordance with SFAS 12 (I89), resulting in a valuation allowance deducted from equity. The BHC entered into an agreement with a third party whereby that party would purchase the stocks at par in 26 years. In the interim, the BHC would pay a quarterly fee. Contending that these stocks no longer had an underwater value because of the purchase agreement, the BHC reversed the valuation allowance in equity and treated the interim fees as an adjustment of yield on the preferred stocks.

The EITF disagreed with this accounting, although no consensus was reached on what the correct accounting should be. The FASB staff position was that the SFAS 12 accounting should not change, and that the fee should be expensed as paid. The EITF proceedings signalled the end of this manuever to eliminate some portion of the valuation allowance debit from equity by payment of a small fee; this result also gratified representatives of the FRB present at the meeting, who were concerned about possible ramifications for similar situations.

Loans. Loans are the primary business activity of a commercial bank, accounting for approximately 60% of all assets. They generate the majority of a bank's profits and help attract deposits.

Loans consist of promissory notes, which are the borrowers' unconditional written promises to pay the lender a specific amount of money, usually at some specified future date. Repayments can be due (1) in installments, (2) in total on a single date, or (3) upon demand. Loans can have either a fixed or a variable (floating) rate of interest.

Loans may be secured or unsecured.[3] Security, or collateral, reduces the financial injury to the lender if the borrower defaults. The value of an asset as collateral depends on its expected resale value. Banks often establish loan to collateral value ratios. For example, bank policy may limit a loan to 75% of collateral value to protect it from market deterioration or disposal expenses.

Different types of loan commitments may be agreed upon by borrowers and commercial banks, such as line of credit, term loan, and revolving credit. The purpose of the loan commitment is to (1) provide some assurance to the borrower that funds will be available when and if they are needed, and (2) provide the lender with a basic format to structure the customer's loan request properly.

A line of credit is an agreement under which a lender can borrow up to a predetermined limit on a short-term basis (less than one year); however, if a customer's circumstances change, a bank may cancel or change the amount of the limit at any time. A customer does not have to use a line of credit and incurs a liability only for the amount borrowed. With a line of credit, it is customary for a bank to require an annual cleanup period (usually one month) to ensure that the funds are not being used as a source of permanent working capital by the borrower.

A term loan is an agreement under which the bank lends the customer a certain dollar amount for a period exceeding one year. These loans may be amortized over the life of the loan or paid in a lump sum at maturity.

Revolving credit is an agreement under which the bank lends up to a certain limit for a period in excess of one year. A customer has the flexibility to borrow, repay, or reborrow as he sees fit during the revolving credit period. At the end of the period, all outstanding loan balances are payable, or, if stipulated, may be converted into a term loan.

Bank loans may also be classified according to risk category such as (1) commercial and industrial, (2) real estate, (3) consumer, (4) agricultural, (5) securities, (6) loans to financial institutions, or (7) other. A more detailed description of these groups can be found in the Bank Audit Guide.

---

[3] The accounting for mortgage loans is the same as that required for thrift institutions. See Chapter 41.

Accounting for loans. Loans should be presented on the balance sheet in an aggregate amount. Note disclosures should include an analysis of loans by major types of lending activities and other information, such as maturities of significant categories of loans and the amounts of loans at fixed and variable rates of interest.

Unearned discount, the allowance for loan losses, and unamortized loan fees (net of direct loan origination costs), should be deducted from related loan balances. Loan fee income and direct loan origination costs represent an adjustment of yield that should be included with interest and fees on loans as described in SFAS 91, *Accounting for Nonrefundable Fees and Costs Associated with Originating or Acquiring Loans and Initial Direct Costs of Leases* (L20).

A Practice Bulletin is expected to be issued in late 1988 regarding *Amortization of Discounts on Acquired Loans.* This PB deals with loans acquired in a purchase business combination or otherwise purchased at a discount from face amount, and loans transferred to a subsidiary intended to be spun-off to the parent's shareholders. In brief, the PB requires that the discount to be amortized as part of loan yield should not be greater than the amount expected to be collected in cash, and then only if the timing of future receipts is reasonably predictable. A particular aim of the PB is LDC debt on which the seller is not accruing income because of realization concerns. The draft PB contains illustrations of when it is and is not proper to amortize discount.

The amount of loans on a nonaccrual basis (including loans accruing at a reduced rate) and the income effect of nonaccrual loans should be disclosed if they are material. Disclosure requirements for loans involved in troubled debt restructurings are presented in SFAS 15, *Accounting for Debtors and Creditors for Troubled Debt Restructurings* (D22).

Loans to related parties are subject to compliance with applicable regulations. Accordingly, loans made by banks to officers, directors, employees, and principal holders of equity securities (and entities with which they are affiliated) in the normal course of business should be disclosed if they represent a material portion of the loan portfolio or if their amount is material in relation to stockholders' equity. Also, disclosure should be made if evidence indicates that significant amount of related party loans were made at other than ordinary terms. (See SFAS 57, *Related Party Disclosures,* (R36).)

The summary of significant accounting policies included in the notes to financial statements should describe:

• Methods of recognizing loan income (including nonaccrual policy) and loan fees, and
• The method used in determining the allowance for loan losses.

Lease-Finance Receivables. Leasing is a significant area of lending for commercial banks, particularly large banks. They have three primary motives to enter into lease agreements. First, the rate of return on leasing activities is comparable (after risk adjustment) to that earned on bank lending. Second, leasing complements the commercial lending function of banks by offering customers an alternative form of intermediate-term financing. Finally, the bank can acquire the tax benefits of owning the leased property. Accounting and disclosure requirements for lease-financing are covered in SFAS 13 (L10) and Chapter 19.

Allowance for Credit Losses. The allowance for credit losses is the estimated amount of losses in a bank's loan and lease portfolio and is maintained by charges against operating expenses. In the event the allowance for credit losses is deemed to be less than losses currently anticipated, the necessary increase should be recognized as a current period charge to operating expenses. The notes to the financial statements should include a summary of the activity in the allowance for loan losses account for each period for which financial statements are presented.

FRR 28, *Accounting for Loan Losses by Registrants Engaged in Lending Activities* (§ 401.09), prescribes certain requirements for documentation by lenders to support their loan loss provisions. The release requires lenders to have adequate documentation that a systematic methodology has been applied to determine the amount of loan losses reported, and to be prepared to demonstrate the existence of a rationale that supports each reporting period's determination that the amounts are adequate.[4]

The SEC is especially concerned that adequate documentation of procedures exists for:

1. Performing periodic detailed reviews to identify risks inherent in loan portfolios (e.g., problem loans, potential problem loans, loans to be charged off) and assessing the overall quality (i.e., collectibility) of loan portfolios, and

2. Determining amounts of allowances and provisions for loan losses to be reported based on the results of the detailed reviews.

The AICPA issued an auditing procedures study, *Auditing the Allowance for Credit Losses of Banks* (AICPA, 1986c), which listed the following factors as important in determining the adequacy of a bank's allowance for credit losses:

- Composition of the loan portfolio
- Identified potential problem loans, including loans classified by bank regulatory agencies
- Trends in loan volume by major categories, especially categories experiencing rapid growth, and trends in delinquencies, nonaccrual, and restructured loans
- Previous loss and recovery experience, including timeliness of charge-offs
- Concentrations of loans to individuals and their related interests, to industries, and in geographic regions
- Size of individual credit exposures (a few large loans versus numerous small loans)
- Degree of reliance placed on internal loan review and internal audit functions
- Total amount of loans and problem loans, including delinquent and nonaccrual loans, by officer
- Lending, charge-off, collection, and recovery policies and procedures
- Local, national, and international economic and environmental conditions

---

[4] As of mid-1988, the AICPA had in process an SOP on *The Use of Discounting in Determining Loan Loss Allowances*, aimed at rectifying the diversity of practice among various financial institutions. The SOP, if finalized as drafted on July 22, 1988, would require that, in determining loan loss allowances, financial institutions (including banks) should not discount future cash payments expected to be received on loans that are not *collateral-dependent*. Collateral-dependent loans—those whose repayment is expected to come only from the operation, development, and/or sale of the collateral—should be evaluated as in-substance forclosures under SFAS 15 (D22).

- Experience, competence, and depth of lending management and staff
- Results of regulatory examinations
- Related party lending

There are additional factors to be considered in LDC loans. See the section entitled "Lesser Developed Country Debt" later in this chapter for a further discussion.

Regulatory classification of loans. Loans examined by regulators are classified in one of five categories: loss, doubtful, substandard, other loans especially mentioned (OLEM), or satisfactory. Loans classified as loss are thought to be uncollectible and the bank is required to write them off. Doubtful loans are expected to result in some losses, although the exact amount is not precisely determinable. Loans classified as substandard have some element of risk and, if not watched closely, may result in losses to the bank. OLEM are considered currently protected but potentially weak as to the paying capacity of the obligor; and OLEM constitute an undue and unwarranted credit risk but not to the point of justifying classification as substandard. Satisfactory loans are those that meet the standards of prudent banking practice and appear to be in no danger of defaulting.

OCC policy does not classify or require charge-offs or reserves on performing real estate loans simply because newly appraised values have diminished. However, if performance of the primary loan is dependent on the bank advancing new loans to make payments, then all or part of the total debt may appropriately be classified, depending on the borrower's creditworthiness and the value of all collateral pledged.

Classifications are to be applied prospectively and are not to be used as a basis for adjusting any amount previously charged off.

Loan sales and securitizations. Loan sales are sales, transfers, or assignments of loans or loan participations to third parties with or without the knowledge of the borrower. Banks sell loans to and buy loans from other banks to improve liquidity, to gain an operational advantage, and for other reasons such as diversification of the portfolio or to broaden their client base.

The major accounting consideration is whether such a transaction is in substance a borrowing or a sale. For example, repurchase agreements and "sale" of only a small percentage of the loans tend to make the transaction a borrowing that does not result in immediate recognition of gain or loss. Also, many permutations are possible in sales of loans with servicing rights (discussed in Chapter 41).

Participation in a loan should be classified according to the same classifications as other loans. If the originating bank retains the risk, the entire loan should be reported as an asset of that bank, and considered in establishing loan loss allowances; and the participation proceeds should be reported as borrowings. SFAS 77, *Reporting by Transferors for Transfers of Receivables With Recourse* (R20), addresses the reporting for loan and participation sales.

Distributing loans to shareholders. In Issue 87-17, *Spin-Offs or Other Distributions of Loans Receivable to Shareholders,* the EITF considered the proper accounting for a transaction in which a bank holding company placed loan receivables into a newly formed subsidiary, which it then spun off to its shareholders. The issue raised was whether the loans should be transferred at carrying amounts, or at fair value if lower.

The EITF consensus held that fair value was applicable, as this was a dividend-in-kind, and not a spin-off of an operating company. If spin-off at higher carrying amounts was permitted, the company would have been able to avoid allocating a portion of its loss reserve to these loans, making such portion available for other loans reserves. Given the EITF consensus, the transaction is not likely to be replicated. However, a spin-off might occur of a subsidiary that holds loans already written down by its parent before transfer. In a proposed Practice Bulletin (discussed under "Accounting for Loans" in the preceding main section), AcSEC is expected to release guidance on the appropriateness of accreting discount on such spun-off loans.

Sales of loans written off. In Issue 86-8, *Sale of Bad Debt Recovery Rights*, the EITF considered the accounting for a sale to a third party of the right to any recoveries made on loans previously written off by the seller. Does this result, from the seller's perspective, in a gain, a credit to the loan loss reserve, a secured borrowing, or an effective restoration of some of the written off loan? The Task Force concluded that this is a secured borrowing, but did not reach a consensus regarding the effect on the loan loss reserve.

Loans sold to special-purpose entities. After the issuance of SFAS 77 (R20) regarding transfers of receivables, some banks devised an apparently conforming methodology for selling loans to thinly capitalized special-purpose corporations (or to charities) that would pay for the loans using funds borrowed from third parties. The objective inferred by the FASB staff was that SFAS 77 was being used to justify off-balance sheet financing, and that this result was not intended.

The EITF considered this topic in Issue 84-30, *Sales of Loans to Special-Purpose Entities,* but did not reach a consensus. The OCC representative present at the meeting pointed out that under RAP no recourse is permitted in transactions to be accounted for as sales (slightly modified since that time; see the section on "RAP/ GAAP Differences" earlier in this chapter); hence this type of transaction would not be a sale under RAP. Ultimate resolution is expected to come in later phases of the FASB's consolidations project (see Chapter 24), in which consideration will be given to consolidation of this type of buyer-entity. In the interim, these sales continue under various formats designed to comply with SFAS 77.

Troubled Debt Restructurings. Under SFAS 15, *Auditing by Debtors and Creditors for Troubled Debt Restructurings* (D22), a creditor does not record a loss, if, among other matters, it will still receive the preexisting principal amount of a restructured troubled debt via future cash payments (whether denominated as principal or interest). SFAS 15 in many respects was the result of the banking community interacting with the FASB to emphasize that the lending business operated on an overall basis, and that individual loans were expected to go bad now and then. The alternative would have been to discount restructured debt so as to yield a market rate of interest.

SFAS 15 applies to all troubled debt restructurings, not only those done by banks (which may be the majority of them), and is discussed in Chapter 28.

Premises and Equipment. Bank premises include land, buildings, furniture, fixtures, equipment, and leasehold improvements used for banking purposes or purchased for potential use in banking operations. The amount of a bank's investment in fixed assets is limited by regulation. Bank supervisory authorities require the capitalization and depreciation of bank premises and equipment according to GAAP.

The FDIC has issued guidelines for the appropriate treatment of sale-leaseback transactions, sometimes used as a means of increasing net income and capital accounts. In general, GAAP should be followed for presentation of these transactions in Call Reports. However:

1. In short-term leasebacks, the allocation of profit on the sale between the portion eligible to be recognized immediately and the deferred portion must be based on an assumed minimum lease term of at least 10 years, regardless of the actual minimum lease term. The FDIC will allow an exception to this only if bank management can provide sufficient evidence to support that the substance of the lease is less than 10 years.
2. If the bank, as seller-lessee, finances the purchaser's acquisition in a sale-leaseback transaction and the term of the note exceeds the lease term, the bank should recognize profit based over the term of the note, unless bank management has sufficient substantive evidence to indicate that the lease is of a shorter-term nature than the note.

Due From Customers on Acceptances. Customers' acceptance liability represents a receivable from customers on outstanding drafts and bills of exchange that have been drawn on and accepted (guaranteed) by a banking institution (the "accepting bank") or its agent for payment at a future date (usually within six months) that is specified in the instrument. Drafts accepted by a banking institution are referred to as "acceptances executed" or "bankers acceptances" and in effect, add the bank's own credit standing to that of its customer. The customer named in the draft as responsible for payment to the accepting bank is referred to as the account party. Most bankers' acceptances arise in foreign trade transactions. Export and import firms find it less risky to deal in drafts guaranteed by well-known banks than those drawn against the bank accounts of unfamiliar commercial companies.

Bankers' acceptances can be held by the bank, discounted, or sold in the secondary market as a source of funds. When an accepted draft is held by the bank, it should be reported as a loan. The accepted draft is negotiable and may be sold and resold subsequent to its original discounting. The accepting bank has an unconditional obligation to pay the holder of the acceptance the face amount of the draft upon presentation at the specified maturity date; the account party has an unconditional obligation to pay the accepting bank at or before the maturity date.

In Issue 85-34, *Banker's Acceptances and Risk Participations,* the EITF addressed the issue of whether a sale of a risk participation in banker's acceptances should be considered a proportionate extinguishment of the obligations. A risk participation is a contract between the accepting bank and a participating bank that agrees to reimburse the accepting bank in the event that the account party fails to honor its obligation. Although the EITF was unable to reach a consensus, the majority agreed that, based on SFAS 76 (D14), the liability has not been extinguished.

Other Assets. The following accounts are among those frequently grouped under other assets:

* Investments in subsidiaries that have not been consolidated (pre-SFAS 94)
* Investments in companies owned 50% or less
* Other nonmarketable investments
* Other real estate owned (OREO)
* Accrued interest receivable
* Accrued income receivable
* Accounts receivable (deposits for special purposes, advances to trusts, etc.)
* Prepaid expenses and deferred charges (insurance, taxes,[5] FDIC assessments, and such)
* Suspense accounts (items recorded and held subject to clarification and transfer to the proper account, such as loan account and branch clearing transactions)

These accounts may be presented in the balance sheet in one or more categories, depending on the materiality of the amounts, and they are usually presented as the last asset item(s).

Accounting for these items is similar to that for other business enterprises, with the exception of OREO, discussed in the next section.

Other Real Estate Owned. Real estate acquired through foreclosure and held pending disposition should be valued at the lower of its fair value or the recorded investment in the related loan. Fair value is the amount a seller currently can reasonably expect to receive in an exchange with a willing seller (but not in a forced or liquidation sale). It should be measured by market value if an active market exists. If no active market exists for the assets, the market price for similar assets may be helpful in estimating the fair value of the assets acquired. Alternatively, if no market price is available, a derived fair value may be determined by discounting the expected future cash flows at a rate commensurate with the risk involved.

A derived value is based on the assumption that the collateral will be held as inventory until prices increase. The SEC has rejected this notion in most circumstances. FRR 28 (§ 401.09) concludes:

> The Commission will presume that active markets reflect objective measures of current fair values, determined by the beliefs of reasonably informed persons regarding the present and future economic utility of the items being traded and the risks associated therewith. Thus, without independent and objective support for derived valuations that can be demonstrated to more appropriately reflect fair value in particular sets of circumstances, derived valuations exceeding current values in active market should not be used in cases where fair value accounting is required by GAAP.

---

[5] A related topic arose at the EITF in Issue 85-31, *Comptroller of the Currency's Rule on Deferred Tax Debits.* The OCC limits deferred tax charges for RAP purposes to the amount that would be recoverable by loss carrybacks. The EITF concluded that this rule does not affect GAAP presentations (now governed by SFAS 96).

If at foreclosure the fair value of the real estate acquired is less than the bank's recorded loan, a write-down should be recognized through a charge to allowance for loan losses. If at a later date it is determined that the carrying amount (plus completion and holding costs) cannot be recovered through sale or use, the additional loss should be recognized at that date by a charge to other expense and not through a charge to the allowance account.

Some lenders have contended that no loss recognition is required by SFAS 15 (D22.126–D22.127) on the premise that if collateral is not formally repossessed, there is no requirement to recognize losses based on its fair value. However, the SEC believes that many loan modifications are in-substance repossessions of collateral, that SFAS 15 (D22.130) applies, and that loss recognition is required if the carrying amounts of the loans exceed the fair value of the collateral.

Under FRR 28, the following criteria are to be applied to determine whether loan collateral has been repossessed in substance:

1. The debtor has little or no equity in the collateral, considering its current fair value.

2. Proceeds for repayment of the loan can be expected to come only from the operation or sale of the collateral.

3. Either:

   a. The debtor has formally or effectively abandoned control of the collateral to the creditor, or

   b. The debtor has retained control of the collateral but, because of the current financial condition of the debtor, or the economic prospects for the debtor and/or the collateral in the foreseeable future, it is doubtful that the debtor will be able to rebuild equity in the collateral or otherwise repay the loan in the foreseeable future.

If the property is in a usable or saleable condition at the time of foreclosure, subsequent holding costs should be expensed as incurred; otherwise, completion and holding costs, including such items as real estate taxes, maintenance, and insurance, should be capitalized as incurred, up to the recoverable amount for the property. Legal fees and other direct costs incurred by the bank in a foreclosure should be expensed when incurred. SFAS 15, *Accounting by Debtors and Creditors for Troubled Debt Restructurings* (D22), and SFAS 66, *Accounting for Sales and Real Estate* (Rel), provide guidance on accounting for receipt and sale of OREO, respectively.

Bank Liabilities

Presented in Figure 40.5 is the liability section of a sample bank balance sheet. The principal liabilities of a bank include: (1) deposits, both interest- and non-interest-bearing, domestic and foreign; (2) federal funds purchased and securities sold under agreements to repurchase; (3) other borrowed funds; (4) bankers acceptances outstanding; (5) other liabilities; (6) long-term debt; and (7) commitments and contingencies. Categories (2) and (4) are discussed under "Assets," where counterpart items are classified.

Non-Interest-Bearing Deposits. These include demand deposits, demand certificates of deposit, bank checks, and escrow deposits. Overdrawn customer

Liabilities	December 31	
	19X2	19X1
Deposits		
Non-interest-bearing:		
Domestic offices	$1,080,000	$1,193,400
Overseas offices	360,200	464,100
Interest-bearing:		
Domestic offices	4,571,800	4,173,600
Overseas offices	2,461,800	2,558,000
Total deposits	8,474,300	8,389,100
Federal funds purchased and securities sold under repurchase agreements	126,900	227,800
Other borrowed funds	101,000	28,000
Acceptances outstanding	23,700	37,900
Other liabilities	186,500	206,200
Long-term debt	600,000	600,000
Long-term subordinated debt constituting primary regulatory capital	100,000	100,000
Total liabilities	$9,612,400	$9,589,000
Commitments and contingencies	–	–

FIG. 40.5   Liabilities Section of Sample Bank Balance Sheet

accounts, however, are loans and should be classified as assets, subject to evaluation for collectibility.

U.S. Treasury deposits are called tax and loan accounts and are held by most commercial banks. Large banks also receive substantial correspondent deposits from small banks.

Banks draw checks on themselves for purposes of paying expenses, disbursing loan amounts, paying dividends, withdrawing account balances, and in exchange for cash from customers. Bank checks are often termed official, cashier's, treasurer's, expense, and loan disbursement checks, and include money orders.

Also included in non-interest-bearing deposits are deposits collateralizing loans, deposits subject to escrow or other withdrawal restrictions, and deposits representing funds withdrawable only on presentation of drafts drawn under commercial or travelers' letters of credit.

Interest-Bearing Deposits. Savings deposits generally consist of savings accounts, negotiable orders of withdrawal (NOW) accounts, and club accounts. Savings deposits that bear interest are becoming less important as a source of funds for all banks as consumers switch to higher-yielding time deposits and more convenient checking-type accounts.

Banks can issue money market deposit accounts that have no interest ceiling but require a minimum deposit balance and are limited as to the number of third-party transfers made each month. SuperNOW accounts require a minimum balance but have no interest rate ceiling, and allow depositors to write an unlimited number of checks.

Time deposits have become the largest source of funds for commercial banks, accounting for nearly one-third of total bank funds. Unlike demand deposits, time deposits are legally due as of a maturity date and funds normally cannot be transferred to another party by a written check. They can be owned by both consumers and corporations, and their characteristics vary widely with respect to maturity, minimum amount, early withdrawal penalties, negotiability, and renewability. The principal types of bank time deposits are savings certificates, 91-day money market certificates, and term certificates of deposit (CDs), which are unsecured liabilities issued in denominations of $100,000 or more by large, well-known commercial banks; and they are traded actively on a well-organized secondary market. CDs have a fixed maturity date and pay an explicit rate of interest.

Eurodollars are short-term time deposits denominated in U.S. dollars, maintained at foreign banks or foreign branches of U.S. banks. Eurodollar deposits have been widely used by U.S. banks when domestic borrowing sources have been restricted by interest rate ceilings. The market is similar to the Fed Funds market except that interbank loans may be obtained for as long as six months. The base rate in this market is the London Interbank Offered Rate (LIBOR).

Most banks disclose deposit liabilities in separate captions on the balance sheet. The principal components of deposit liabilities are usually presented separately and include: non-interest-bearing domestic and overseas deposits and interest-bearing domestic and overseas deposits, CDs of $100,000 or more and, if material, NOW accounts. Regulation F of the Board of Governors of the Federal Reserve System sets forth guidelines for required disclosures on deposits.

Under Federal Reserve Regulation D, transaction accounts and time deposit accounts in banks and in all other deposit-type financial institutions are subject to reserve requirements. Transactions accounts are those from which account holders can regularly make withdrawals, transfers, or payments. The bank's reserve position, often referred to as its money position, is reported weekly by large banks.

Borrowed Funds. Borrowed funds are typically short-term borrowings by commercial banks from the wholesale money markets or the Federal Reserve Bank. They are similar to deposits but are not insured by the FDIC.

Banks have two methods of short-term borrowing available to them from their district Federal Reserve Bank: discounting and advancing. In discounting, the Federal Reserve rediscounts, with recourse, a bank's eligible loans. In advancing, a bank executes a promissory note payable to the Federal Reserve Bank, collateralized by government securities. The interest rate charged on these loans is set by the individual reserve bank.

Borrowing from the Federal Reserve is used to cover short-term deficiencies in required reserves. The traditional term of a discount loan is 15 days, although these loans may be renewed. Borrowing from the discount window requires the bank to apply to and receive the approval of the Federal Reserve district bank, which exercises close administrative control. The amount of borrowing at the discount window is quite small.

Bank holding companies or their nonbank subsidiaries, like other business enterprises, regularly issue commercial paper. Commercial paper is generally short-term, negotiable, and not subordinated. Other forms of short-term borrowing include unsecured notes and borrowings under lines of credit.

GAAP presentation is an adaptation of Regulation F: all short-term borrowings, other than federal funds purchased and securities sold under agreements to repurchase are grouped together and classified as other borrowed funds.

Long-Term Debt. Unsecured debt securities or debentures are the most commonly issued long-term debt. Debentures may be subordinated to other specified debt and may be convertible into shares of common stock. Debenture maturities generally range from seven to 40 years. Banks or their subsidiaries also acquire premises using traditional real estate mortgages. Long-term debt subordinated to the rights of depositors provides further protection to insulate depositors and other creditors from financial loss. This debt is often called borrowed capital or capital notes, because it assumes part of the protection function ordinarily associated with equity capital. If specified criteria are met, a portion of this debt can be treated as bank capital for lending limit computations and other regulatory purposes. Capital notes account for only a small percentage of the liabilities of banks.

Debentures, mortgage notes, and capital notes are normally classified together as long-term debt for financial statement presentation purposes. For both regulatory and financial reporting, capital notes must be presented in the liability section of the balance sheet. The notes to the financial statements should provide details as to the significant components of long-term debt and, when appropriate, maturity dates, interest rates, pledged property, and significant restrictive covenants.

Many large bank holding companies have issued fixed or floating rate securities that require either: (1) their conversion into common stock, perpetual preferred stock, or other primary capital at maturity (mandatory convertible notes); and (2) obtaining the cash used to repay the obligation through issuances of common stock or other primary capital securities (equity commitment notes). The notes mature in 12 years; but either type of note may be redeemed after approximately four years by payment of cash generated from the issuance of primary capital securities. In addition, after four years, mandatory convertible notes may be exchanged for capital securities at the bank's option.

A careful review of the terms of both these types of notes is necessary to determine whether they should be treated as debt (usually the case) or equity and whether the periodic payments should be treated as interest or dividends.

The EITF discussed the issue of whether these contingently issuable shares should be included in computing primary and fully diluted earnings per share. In Issue 85-18, *Earnings-per-Share Effect of Equity Commitment Notes*, the EITF concluded that they should not be included in either of the earnings per share calculations, unless the bank could issue only common stock to repay the notes. The SEC Observer at the EITF meeting also felt that supplemental EPS might be needed, using the current market price to determine the number of shares issuable.

Other Liabilities. Other liabilities include commonly observed accruals and deferrals, as well as suspense accounts (items recorded and held subject to clarification and transfer to the proper account, such as unapplied deposit account transactions and branch clearing transactions).

Commitments and Contingencies. In the normal course of business, banks will have various outstanding commitments and contingent liabilities. SFAS 5, *Accounting for Contingencies* (C59), provides guidance as to the appropriate disclosure. Although banks have always provided commitments to extend credit, they have recently increased their fee-based activities. Generally these transactions do not involve recording assets or taking deposits. Examples of these off-balance sheet items include:

- Direct credit substitutes
- Trade and performance-related contingencies
- Securitization of loans
- Other commitments

Direct credit substitutes. Financial guarantees are usually extended as letters of credit, because U.S. banks are prohibited from providing direct guarantees. A bank may guarantee a loan, however, if a sponsor provides the bank with a guarantee against any loss. Fees charged for this type of transaction are a function of the administrative costs and the net loan spread the bank would expect to realize from directly lending to the sponsor. The bank acts merely as a conduit for the sponsor who has chosen not to provide a direct guarantee.

Standby letters of credit might require the bank to redeem an issue of debt securities upon the default of the borrower. Banks often extend such standby letters of credit to back securities issued by tax-exempt borrowers or to back a company's commercial paper. Under a direct-pay letter of credit, the bank pays all maturing obligations and obtains reimbursement from the borrower.

Trade- and performance-related contingencies. Documentary letters of credit are obligations on the part of a bank to a third party to redeem a customer's maturing obligation if the customer cannot perform. Documentary letters of credit often facilitate international trade transactions.

Banks may provide performance guarantees or bonds to assure completion under construction contracts. These include:

- Bid bonds
- Performance bonds
- Advance payment guarantees or bonds
- Retention money guarantees or bonds
- Maintenance bonds

Bid bonds are usually required of bidders on contracts, to assure that they will accept the contract if offered, and will proceed with the execution of the contract. Performance bonds are demanded to provide funds if the contractor fails to perform for any reason.

Advance payment guarantees assist contractors in purchasing and assembling the necessary materials, equipment, and personnel to get the construction started, so as to meet the requirements for receipt of progress payments under the contract.

Often the buyer of a project retains a portion of the progress payments otherwise due, to cover possible contractor's construction mistakes. Because most contractors prefer to receive the progress payments as quickly as possible, they will often substitute a retention money guarantee or bond in place of the retention.

Maintenance bonds provide funds for correcting defects in the construction discovered after completion of the actual construction.

Securitization of loans. Securitization is the process of converting an institution's loans or mortgages into negotiable securities that may be purchased by other financial institutions or by private investors. Specific arrangements to provide recourse can take many forms, including: (1) an explicit guarantee that credit losses will be reimbursed or that the assets will be replaced by assets of similar quality; (2) an agreement to repurchase assets before maturity; or (3) indemnification by a third party guarantor for losses. (See Chapter 21 for a discussion of securitization.)

Other commitments. Revolving credit agreements and overdraft facilities are commitments by banks to lend to customers under predefined terms. The commitments generally contain covenants allowing the bank to refuse to lend if there has been an adverse change (as defined) in the borrower's financial condition.

Banks that make short-term loans under long-term credit arrangements to borrowers (revolving credit arrangements) will sometimes sell these loans without recourse (a strip participation) to another financial institution (the purchaser). At maturity of the loan, if certain loan covenants are not met, the bank may refuse to relend to the borrower. Accordingly, the purchaser has the risk of loss if the borrower defaults. At issue is whether the bank may record strip participation transactions as sales. In Issue 87-30, *Sale of a Short-Term Loan Made Under a Long-Term Credit Commitment*, the EITF concluded that the lender may record strip participations as sales if the revolving credit agreement contains substantive relending covenants. If the covenants are nonsubstantive (i.e., the borrower virtually cannot fail to meet them), the transferor bank has not sold the strip because it has an obligation to relend.

A Note Issuance Facility (NIF) is a medium-term arrangement enabling borrowers to issue short-term paper, typically of three or six months' maturity, in their own names. Usually a group of underwriting banks guarantees the availability of funds to the borrower by purchasing any unsold notes at each rollover date, or by providing a standby credit. Facilities offered by competing banks are variously called standby note issuance facilities (SNIFs), revolving underwriting facilities (RUFs), transferable revolving underwriting facilities (TRUFs), note purchase facilities (NPFs), and Euronote facilities.

Other commitments include futures, forwards, options, swaps, and forward rate agreements, which are discussed in Chapter 21.

A bank that has entered into significant transactions not reflected on its balance sheet should disclose the type, amounts, and risks associated with these contracts. SFAS 5, *Accounting for Contingencies* (C59), provides guidance as to the appropriate financial statement disclosures for these items. The FASB has released an exposure draft of a proposed SFAS on *Disclosures About Financial Instruments* (1987a). The exposure draft considers additional disclosures for these contingencies as well as other financial assets and liabilities (see Chapter 21).

Under SAB 60, *Financial Guarantees* (Topic 11.J), the SEC requires bank holding companies to make certain disclosures, including:

* A general description of the type of obligations guaranteed, the relative amount and range of maturity dates of each, and the degree of risk involved
* The amount of exposure with respect to the debts of others guaranteed
* The manner in which the registrant recognizes guarantee revenue
* The amount of unearned premiums
* Whether the registrant provides a reserve for losses by charges against income and, if so, the basis for the reserve and its amount
* Any other information that may be necessary to adequately describe the obligations guaranteed

SAB 60 followed an EITF discussion in Issue 85-20 of *Recognition of Fees for Guaranteeing a Loan*. Suggestions for a solution included relating the fee earned to risk reductions, and spreading it over the life of the underlying loan, even though the guarantor was not a lender. The Task Force reached a consensus that fee income should be recognized over the guarantee period, with direct costs recognized relative to fee income. Also released subsequent to the EITF discussion, SFAS 91 (L20) specifies accounting for commitment fees, which share some attributes with guarantees; if SFAS 91 were to be followed, the interest method would be used to spread the guarantee fee and related direct costs over the term of the guarantee.

Bank Stockholders' Equity

The stockholders' equity section of a bank balance sheet typically includes capital stock, both preferred and common, paid-in capital in excess of par or stated value (usually referred to as capital surplus), and retained earnings (often referred to as undivided profits). An example of the stockholders' equity section of a bank balance sheet is shown in Figure 40.6.

Special reserve accounts may also be set up for anticipated losses on loans and investments. Reserve accounts involve no transfers of funds or setting aside of cash, but are merely an appropriation of retained earnings (C59.117). Actual loan losses are, of course, charged to operations. The greater the ratio of stockholders' equity to deposits, the stronger the protection to depositors. Banks maintain much lower stockholders' equity accounts than other businesses, often less than 10% of total assets.

Several aspects of a bank's equity structure that are unique to the banking industry are discussed in the following sections.

Treasury Stock. Banking law generally forbids banks to hold treasury stock although bank holding companies may do so. However, banks can acquire their own stock if it is collateral for a defaulted loan. Such shares must be sold or otherwise disposed of within six months.

Capital Surplus. Capital surplus includes amounts paid in excess of par or stated value on the sale of the bank's capital stock, and transfers from undivided profits.

	December 31	
Stockholders' Equity	19X2	19X1
Preferred stock, no par value (authorized: 5,000,000 shares; issued and outstanding: 500,000 shares in 19X2)	$ 50,000	$ —
Common stock, par value $5; 15,000,000 shares authorized, issued and outstanding	75,000	75,000
Capital surplus	200,000	200,000
Retained earnings	302,000	192,400
Cumulative translation adjustments	(11,200)	(7,100)
Total stockholders' equity	615,800	460,300
Total liabilities and stockholders' equity	$10,228,200	$10,049,300

FIG. 40.6 Stockholders' Equity Section of Sample Bank Balance Sheet

Lending limits are based on permanent capitalization, and supervisory agencies will occasionally approve transfers to increase the lending limits.

Bank supervisory authorities generally require newly organized banks to allocate part of the paid-in surplus to undivided profits. Such amounts are used to avoid creating a deficit during the initial (and usually unprofitable) periods of operations. The paid-in surplus amount allocated to undivided profits should be clearly identified by an appropriate explanatory caption or a footnote, as it is not available for dividend payments; it should be restored as quickly as profitable operations and regulations permit.

Dividends. The regulatory authorities have established various restrictions on the payment of cash dividends, to protect depositors against dissipation of a bank's permanent capital. National banking law (12 USC § 60) allows directors to declare dividends up to the amount of net profits, not to exceed the bank's common capital. While this seems very generous, it should be noted that the regulators' concept of net profits differs substantially from GAAP net income. To obtain regulatory net profits the provision for loan losses must be added back to net income, which is reduced by net charge-offs (gross charge-offs minus recoveries). A dividend may not be declared unless at least 10% of the bank's net profits, as so defined, during the preceding two half-year periods (in the case of annual dividends) has been transferred to the capital surplus.

OCC approval is required if the total of all dividends declared by a bank in any calendar year exceeds the total of its net profits for that year combined with its retained net profits of the preceding two years, less any required transfers to surplus or to a sinking fund for the retirement of preferred stock.

Bank Income Statement

Interest revenue on a bank's earning assets is the primary source of bank revenue; interest expense on the funds employed by the bank is usually the primary cost category. Other revenue items, such as service charges, fees, and net trust income, are important revenue sources for most banks. Other expenses, most notably the costs associated with the bank's employees and its premises and equipment, are also significant. A bank's income statement should be presented in accordance with the interest margin concept; that is, interest expense accounts should be deducted from interest revenue accounts to derive net interest income (interest margin). A sample bank income statement is shown in Figure 40.7.

	Years ended December 31	
	19X2	**19X1**
Interest revenue		
Interest and fees on loans and lease receivables	$6,859,000	$5,527,000
Interest on investment securities		
U.S. Treasury securities	741,000	836,000
Obligations of other U.S. government agencies and		
corporations	186,000	268,000
Obligations of states and political subdivisions	1,248,000	1,256,000
Other securities	58,000	42,000
Interest on trading securities	221,000	241,000
Interest on federal funds sold and securities purchased under		
reverse repurchase agreements	332,000	105,000
Interest on deposits in banks	86,000	72,000
Total interest revenue	9,731,000	8,347,000
Interest expense		
Interest on deposits	6,446,000	5,340,000
Interest on federal funds purchased and securities sold under		
repurchase agreements	253,000	78,000
Interest on subordinated debentures	80,000	80,000
Total interest expense	6,779,000	5,498,000
Net interest income	2,952,000	2,849,000
Provision for credit losses	60,000	68,000
Net interest income after provision for credit losses	2,892,000	2,781,000
Other income		
Trust department income	187,000	166,000
Service fees	106,000	103,000
Trading profits and commissions	174,000	67,000
Securities gains (losses)	131,000	(30,000)
Other operating income	74,000	77,000
Total other income	672,000	383,000
Other expense		
Salaries and wages	727,000	718,000
Pensions and other employee benefits	153,000	130,000
Occupancy expenses, net	356,000	304,000
Other operating expenses	747,000	648,000
Total other expense	1,983,000	1,800,000
Income before income taxes	1,581,000	1,364,000
Income taxes	146,000	33,000
Net income	$1,435,000	$1,331,000
Net income per share of common stock	$9.57	$8.87

FIG. 40.7   Sample Bank Income Statement
Source: Derived from AICPA Industry Audit Guide, Audits of Banks, *1984c, p. 143.*

Interest and Fees. Lending is the single most important source of interest revenue for commercial banks. The profit in a lending relationship is derived from the difference (spread) between the interest received on the loan and the cost of the related funding.

The lending cycle also produces loan commitment and origination fees. Banks commonly charge fees related to commitments by the bank to lend money to a specific customer at the customer's demand based on need, or on the occurrence of particular events. To keep committed funds available may mean holding a higher proportion of assets in liquid form than would otherwise be necessary. Because liquid assets usually produce lower returns, the commitment fee is charged to offset the income lost as a result of the commitment. Commitment fees and loan origination fees are combined with interest revenue from loans.

SFAS 91, *Accounting for Nonrefundable Fees and Costs Associated with Originating or Acquiring Loans and Initial Direct Costs of Leases* (L20), prescribes the accounting for nonrefundable fees and costs associated with lending, committing to lend, or purchasing a loan or group of loans. The provisions of SFAS 91 apply to all types of loans (including debt securities) as well as to all types of lenders (including nonfinancial institutions). The statement also specifies the accounting for fees and initial direct costs associated with leasing activities. In summary, SFAS 91 requires that:

1. Loan origination fees must be recognized over the life of the related loan as an adjustment of yield.

2. Certain direct loan origination costs must be recognized over the life of the related loan as a reduction of the yield. Costs eligible for deferral may not include any solicitation costs, and include only:

   a. Incremental direct costs of loan origination incurred with third parties.

   b. Certain costs directly associated with activities performed to originate a loan. (Those activities include evaluating the prospective borrower's financial condition; evaluating and recording guarantees, collateral and other security arrangements; negotiating terms; preparing and processing loan documents; and closing the transaction).

3. All loan commitment fees must be deferred (except for certain retrospectively determined fees) and recognized over the loan commitment period; all other commitment fees must be recognized as an adjustment of yield over the related loan life or, if the commitment expires unexercised, recognized in income upon its expiration.

4. Loan fees, certain direct loan origination costs, and purchase premiums and discounts on loans must be recognized as an adjustment of yield generally by the interest method. Prepayments may be anticipated in certain circumstances.

5. Generally, when a loan is refinanced or restructured at terms at least as favorable to the lender as comparable loans to comparable customers who are not refinancing a loan, the fees and costs associated with the old loan should be recognized in income when the loan is refinanced. Otherwise, they are carried forward as an adjustment of the basis of the new loan (and recognized as an adjustment of yield).

6. Credit card and charge card fees should be recognized over the period the cardholder is entitled to use the card.

Implementation guidance has also been issued for SAFS 91 in the form of a special report (FASB, 1987c). Additional questions regularly arise, however; the EITF is scheduled to discuss *Fees and Costs Associated With Loan Syndications and Loan Participations* (Issue 88-17).

Interest on deposits in banks. Interest earned on balances with banks comes primarily from Eurodollar redeposits and is most significant to large banks that have foreign operations. Interest on balances with banks is essentially interest on loans receivable, although many banks refer to such time deposits in other banks as placements.

Interest on federal funds sold and repurchase agreements. Although the terms "buy" and "sell" are often used when discussing federal funds transactions and repurchase agreements, these are, in fact, loans. A bank earns interest when it lends (sells) some of its excess balances in a Federal Reserve bank to another bank. It also earns interest by buying securities from another bank or bond dealer with the agreement that the seller will buy back the securities at the same price plus interest for the period. Since none of the usual risks of investment apply to either transaction, both are technically loans.

Interest from investment and trading account securities. The amount of revenue from this source depends on the size and composition of the investment and trading portfolios. See the discussion under the earlier section entitled "Bank Assets."

Interest Expense. Interest expense is incurred on NOW and SuperNOW deposit accounts, passbook savings, savings certificates, money market accounts, CDs of $100,000 and over, other time deposits, short-term borrowings (including federal funds purchased and repurchase agreements), other borrowed funds, and long-term debt.

Provision for Credit Losses. This provision is the amount charged against earnings to establish a reserve sufficient to absorb expected loan and lease losses. (See the discussion in the earlier section entitled "Allowance for Credit Losses.")

Other Income and Expense. Other (non-interest) income includes the net income from the bank's trust department, service charges on deposit accounts, trading account profits and commissions, securities gains and losses, and other operating income.

Other operating income includes: other commissions; charges for the collection of domestic checks, notes, and bills of exchange; the sale of bank drafts; the acceptance of bills of exchange in domestic trade; servicing real estate mortgages or other loans owned by others; data processing services; gross rentals from other real estate; rentals of safe deposit boxes; and recoveries on securities previously charged off.

Other expenses are the same as would be found in any commercial enterprise, principally employee compensation and fringe benefits, and occupancy costs.

Income Taxes. Banks are subject to the standard corporate income tax rates, but several special tax rules apply.

Increase (Decrease) in Cash and Cash Equivalents

Cash flows from operating activities

Interest received on loans and investments	$ 5,350	
Fees and commissions received	1,320	
Financing revenue received under leases	60	
Interest paid	(3,925)	
Cash paid to suppliers and employees	(795)	
Income taxes paid	(471)	
Net cash provided by operating activities		$1,539

Cash flows from investing activities

Proceeds from sales of trading and investment securities	22,700	
Purchase of trading and investment securities	(25,000)	
Net increase in credit card receivables	(1,300)	
Net decrease in customer loans with maturities of 3 months or less	2,250	
Principal collected on longer term loans	26,550	
Longer term loans made to customers	(36,300)	
Purchase of assets to be leased	(1,500)	
Principal payments received under leases	107	
Capital expenditures	(450)	
Proceeds from sale of bank premises	260	
Net cash used in investing activities		(12,683)

Cash flows from financing activities

Net increase in demand deposits, NOW accounts, and savings accounts	3,000	
Proceeds from sales of certificates of deposit	63,000	
Payments for maturing certificates of deposit	(61,000)	
Net increase in federal funds purchased	4,500	
Net increase in 90-day borrowings	50	
Proceeds from issuance of nonrecourse debt	600	
Principal payment on nonrecourse debt	(20)	
Proceeds from issuance of 6-month note	100	
Proceeds from issuance of long-term debt	1,000	
Payments to acquire treasury stock	(175)	
Repayment of long-term debt	(200)	
Proceeds from issuance of common stock	350	
Dividends paid	(240)	
Net cash provided by financing activities		10,965
Net decrease in cash and cash equivalents		(179)
Cash and cash equivalents at beginning of year		6,700
Cash and cash equivalents at end of year		$ 6,521

FIG. 40.8 Sample Bank Statement of Cash Flows—Direct Method
Source: SFAS 95 (C25.153).

Under the Tax Reform Act of 1986, the loan loss deduction is to be based on the actual charge-off experience. Banks with over $500 million in assets must eliminate prior tax deductions for loan loss reserves by recapturing those deductions over a four-year period beginning in 1987. Other special rules provide opportunities for extensive tax savings through proper planning. The highly technical nature of these

Net income	$1,056
Adjustments to reconcile net income to net cash provided by operating activities	
Depreciation	$ 100
Provision for probable credit losses	300
Provision for deferred taxes	58
Gain on sale or trading and investment securities	(100)
Gain on sale of equipment	(50)
Increase in taxes payable	175
Increases in interest receivable	(150)
Increase in interest payable	75
Decrease in fees and commissions receivable	20
Increase in accrued expense	55
Total adjustments	483
Net cash provided by operating activities	$ 1,539

Disclosure of accounting policy:

For purposes of reporting cash flows, cash and cash equivalents include cash on hand, amounts due from banks, and federal funds sold. Generally, federal funds are purchased and sold for one-day periods.

FIG. 40.9   Reconciliation of Earnings to Net Cash Flow Provided by Operating Activities
Source: SFAS 95, (C25.153).

rules puts the subject beyond the scope of this *Handbook*, but tax accountants should be alert to the potential for savings.

Bank Statement of Cash Flows

SFAS 95 (C25) requires that a statement of cash flows be presented by all business entities, including banks. Figure 40.8 illustrates the FASB's recommended reporting format using the direct method. Gross cash receipts and payments from operating activities are reported on the face of the statement. Additionally, a reconciliation of net income to cash flows from operating activities is presented in a separate schedule in Figure 40.9. Under the indirect method (not shown), the reconciliation portion in Figure 40.9 is given instead of the related segment in Figure 40.8; and the other two categories (investing and financing activities) are essentially the same as in the direct method.

Loans made with maturities beyond three months are presented gross, as both loans made and principal collected. Revolving credit lines and changes in bankers acceptances also must be presented gross. Credit card receivables are considered loans with original maturities of three months or less; therefore, the net change may be presented. Cash flows related to leveraged leases are presented separately as investing and financing activities.

Transactions involving trading and investment securities are combined and presented gross because original maturities of the investments themselves are longer than three months. Gains and losses on securities (both realized amounts related to sales and unrealized amounts primarily related to trading securities) are presented as reconciling items when using the indirect method.

The gross proceeds from issuance of and the payments for maturing CDs with terms of more than three months are to be shown. For transaction and savings accounts, only the net change should be presented. Interest credited directly to deposit accounts having the general characteristics of demand deposit accounts are treated as cash receipts; the related interest expense is treated like other cash expenses under operating activities. The net change in the deposit accounts during a period, part of which was caused by interest credit, is reported under financing activities.

SFAS 95 does not specifically address the presentation of interest credited to deposit accounts not having the general characteristics of demand deposit accounts, such as interest on CDs. Because cash receipts and payments related to CDs with terms of more than three months must be presented separately, the change resulting from interest credits should be included under financing activities combined with proceeds from sales of CDs.

Changes in accrued interest receivable or payable must be reflected as a reconciling item between net income and net cash flow from operating activities, regardless of whether the accrued amount is classified with loans or deposits on the balance sheet.

Banks may roll over commercial loans and CDs at maturity. Rollovers should not be reported in the statement because there is no cash receipt by or payment to the bank (other than interest).

Other fee-based services may have cash flow implications beyond the fee received. For example, a bank that services mortgage loans for others accepts cash from the debtors and remits that cash, less a servicing fee, to the investor. Only the fee received from these transactions should be presented because the bank is holding, receiving, or disbursing cash as the agent for its customer.

OTHER ACCOUNTING AND REPORTING ISSUES

Acquisition Accounting

Business combinations involving banking and thrift institutions follow the basic rules contained in APB 16 (B50) and APB 17 (I60); in addition, they must adhere to special rules prescribed by SFAS 72, *Accounting for Certain Acquisitions of Banking or Thrift Institutions* (Bt7), and FIN 9, *Applying APB Opinions No. 16 and 17 When a Savings and Loan Association or a Similar Institution Is Acquired in a Business Combination Accounted for by the Purchase Method* (Bt7). The principal effect of these pronouncements on bank mergers is that the amortization of a discount on an acquired loan portfolio will be offset by amortization of goodwill attributable to any excess of liabilities assumed over assets acquired, both at fair values.

The details of SFAS 72 and FIN 9 are described in Chapter 41. Several matters specific to banks are mentioned in the sections that follow.

It should be noted that the SEC has generally allowed FDIC cash contributions in regulatory assisted mergers of troubled banks to be recorded as additions to additional paid-in capital. Under SFAS 72, regulatory agency contributions would be applied to reduce general goodwill arising in the acquisition; however, such goodwill ordinarily does not arise in troubled bank acquisitions. In these instances, SFAS 72 specifies that the credit should be made to income (Bt7.113). The SEC permission for inclusion directly in paid-in capital recognizes that undesirable tax consequences could arise if the amounts were credited to income.

Amortization of Intangibles. Regulatory authorities and the SEC require banks to write off identified intangible assets over a period not in excess of 10 to 15 years. The FRB and the SEC allow bank holding companies to write off goodwill over a period of up to 25 years. Although APB 17 permits the amortization of goodwill and other intangible assets up to the maximum of 40 years, banks have adopted the shorter regulatory guidelines for both regulatory reporting and financial statement presentation purposes.

In Issue 85-33, *Disallowance of Income Tax Deduction for Core Deposit Intangibles,* the EITF considered the accounting treatment of a possible disallowance by the IRS of deductions for amortization of a core deposit intangible (CDI) set up in a purchase business combination to reflect the value to the buyer of the acquiree's customer relationships. Under APB 16 these amounts would have been recorded in the purchase net of tax consequences. The Task Force concluded that, absent a misuse of facts, the IRS disallowance, if sustained, represents a change in estimate to be accounted for currently; and the carrying amount of the CDI should be evaluated for impairment (but not written up to restore the taxes netted).

Under SFAS 96, net-of-tax accounting has been abolished, and prior business combinations are to be restated if retroactive adoption of SFAS 96 is elected. However, if prospective adoption is chosen, the EITF's consensus in Issue 85-33 essentially holds true. (See Chapter 17.)

Pushdown Accounting. Bank regulators and the SEC have diverse views as to the application by banking institutions of pushdown accounting—the revision of an acquiree's assets and liabilities to the fair value amounts assigned by the acquirer, including goodwill. The SEC requires the application of pushdown accounting in all acquisitions involving a substantial change in ownership, that is, when more than 90% of a bank's voting stock has been acquired (SAB 54, Topic 5.J). The FDIC permits its use at 90% or above, but does not require it. Conversely, the FRB and OCC prohibit the application of pushdown accounting; however, the OCC in certain instances requires accounting policies that produce an identical result. For example, when a bank holding company uses a shell bank as an acquirer to facilitate a statutory merger, the shell bank must record the assets and liabilities at fair market value in accordance with APB 16 (B50.145-.146).

Loan Loss Allowances in a Purchase. SAB 61, *Adjustments to Allowances for Loan Losses in Connection With Business Combinations* (Topic 2A.5), provides that changes in the allowance for loan losses should be made through income statement provisions for loan losses rather than through purchase accounting adjustments, unless the acquiring institution can justify that its estimate is based on following a different course of action for the asset than previous management had followed.[6]

---

[6] Although written to apply to bank loan portfolios, the question has arisen as to the applicability of the concept in SAB 61 to other types of acquired assets. The EITF is scheduled to discuss this in Issue 88-13, *Application of SEC Staff Accounting Bulletin No. 61 to Other Than Loan Losses.*

Lesser Developed Country Debt

Many banks extended loans to private companies and governments of LDCs. Subsequent declines in the primary commodities markets (oil, metals) have resulted in adverse shifts in the exchange rates of LDC currencies relative to the U.S. dollar (the currency in which repayment of principal and interest is required). This has caused severe liquidity problems within the LDCs, often necessitating government intervention. In addition, some loans to private sector borrowers have been assumed by their governments, permitting the central bank to negotiate directly with the lenders.

Banks must assess the probability that the LDC central bank will be able or will intend to service its debts. Some LDC central banks have renegotiated their debts, extending payment terms to gain time to implement appropriate economic policies and to earn the required foreign exchange to service the debt. Other LDCs have obtained additional loans to assist in meeting their financing needs. In a few cases, LDCs have chosen to interrupt the servicing of their debts.

Allowance for Loan Losses. A bank's loan portfolio should be carried at historical cost, less loan writeoffs and the allowance for loan losses. The portion of a bank's allowance associated with the LDC loans may be determined by reference to individual LDC countries, or by total LDC exposure, or by some combination of both methods.

The allowance related to LDC loans is available to absorb losses on any LDC loan. SFAS 5, *Accounting for Contingencies* (C59), recognizes the need to establish an allowance for groups of similar loans in certain circumstances. In practice, the allowance is not actually allocated to a specific country unless an "Allocated Transfer Risk Reserve" (discussed later) has been established by order of bank regulatory authorities. Consequently, many banks have established "basket allowances" to value their LDC loans in the aggregate.

Loans Swapped for Debt or Equity. The AICPA has considered the accounting treatment by banks for exchanges of their public and/or private sector loans to debtors in financially troubled LDCs for (1) other loans to financially troubled LDCs (foreign loans swaps), and (2) equity investments in companies in the same countries (debt/equity swaps). In May 1985, the AICPA released a Notice to Practitioners (currently Appendix H of Practice Bulletin 1 (TP 12,010.09)) outlining accounting for foreign loan swaps. The notice specifies that loan swaps should be accounted for at current fair value; however, it recognizes that the establishment of fair values for LDC loans is difficult because of the major uncertainties about timing and amount of future cash flows. When the notice was issued, the secondary market for LDC loans was in its infancy, and an objective market valuation was not available. Thus, values used in early swaps have been most subjective.

Practice Bulletin 4, *Accounting for Foreign Debt/Equity Swaps* (TP 12,040), issued in May 1988, furnishes guidance on the accounting for debt/equity swap programs recently established by several financially troubled LDCs. Although these programs vary, their principal characteristics are as follows. The U.S. dollar-denominated LDC debt held by a bank can be converted into an approved local equity investment. The bank is credited with local currency approximately equal at the official exchange rate. A discount from the official exchange rate is usually imposed as a transaction fee. The local currency that is credited to the bank can only be used for the approved equity investment. Restrictions are placed on the annual dividends paid and the repatriation of capital or the proceeds from a sale.

As with loan swaps, debt/equity swaps should be recorded at current fair value determined at the date of exchange. With the secondary market for LDC debt considerably more developed but still considered thin, Practice Bulletin 4 concludes that both the secondary market price of the loan given up and the fair value of the equity investment or net assets received should be considered in arriving at the fair value of a debt/equity swap.

To assist in determining the current fair value of loan swaps and debt/equity swaps AICPA Practice Bulletin 1 recommends that the following factors be considered:

• Similar cash transactions
• Market value, if any, of similar financial instruments
• Credit standing of the debtor and/or guarantor, including prospects for reentry into the voluntary lending markets in the forseeable future
• Prevailing interest rates
• Pricing options available (e.g., prime-based vs. LIBOR-based loans)
• Anticipated delays in receipt of payments
• Tax consequences, including the effect of foreign withholding taxes on after-tax yields

When determining the current fair value of debt/equity swaps, the AICPA recommends management also consider:

• Estimated cash flows from the equity investment or net assets received
• Currency restrictions, if any, affecting dividends, the sale of the investment, or repatriation of capital.

All major banks have now established large allowances for LDC debts. Because of the existence of the allowances, if the fair values of the swap proceeds received (loan, equity investment, or net assets) is less than the recorded loan investment and other considerations, the loss should be charged to the allowance for loan losses. The swap loss should include any discounts from the official exchange rate that were imposed as a transaction fee. All other fees and transaction costs of the swap should be expensed as incurred.

In July, 1988 the AICPA released Practice Bulletin 5, *Income Recognition on Loans to Financially Troubled Countries.* This bulletin provides guidance to creditors as to the accounting for interest payments received from debtors that had previously suspended loan payments. The bulletin concludes that if an adequate allowance for loan losses exists, a creditor may recognize receipts as income when the debtor country has become current as to principal and interest and has normalized its relations within the international community.

SEC-Required Disclosure of Foreign Assets. In view of the large exposure that many bank holding companies have to foreign loans and other revenue producing assets, the SEC requires separate information about these activities. The information must be provided if either (1) assets, or (2) revenues, or (3) income (loss) before income expense, or net income (loss), associated with these activities exceeds 10% of the corresponding amount in the financial statements. The disclosures include the amount of foreign loan revenue, income (loss) before taxes, net income (loss), and identifiable assets, (net of allowances). Outstanding foreign country amounts include loans, accrued interest, acceptances, interest-bearing deposits or investments, and other monetary assets denominated in U.S. dollars or other nonlocal currency (or in local currency if not hedged or funded by local borrowings).

Countries experiencing liquidity problems. Liquidity problems are defined as the inability to raise sufficient currency to meet principal or interest repayment obligations. Companies engaged in lending activities to countries with these problems must furnish further information. Disclosures required if the aggregate outstandings exceed 1% of total assets include the following:

* Identification of countries with these conditions
* Disclosure of the amount outstanding together with the percentage relationship to total amounts
* Discussion of material adverse effects on the financial condition or results of operations

The disclosures should be updated by subsequent developments and presented in tabular format. Updates should include amounts of new outstandings, collections of principal and interest, interest income accrued, and other changes. Gross changes should be presented except for short-term trade credits and interbank deposits, and the analysis should set forth both long- and short-term end-of-period balances.

Interest income and interest expense collected should be disclosed when the outstandings are on nonaccrual status.

Restructurings. If outstandings are restructured, or if an agreement in principle for restructuring has been reached, disclosure should be made of pre- and post-restructuring maturities and interest rates on the restructured amounts, future commitments arising in connection with the restructurings, and amounts removed or expected to be removed from nonaccrual status. Disclosures of weighted-average or actual maturities and interest rates on outstandings are also required.

Deposit/relending arrangements. SAB 66, *Disclosures by Bank Holding Companies Regarding Certain Foreign Loans* (Topic 11.H), discusses arrangements whereby borrowers in the foreign country remit local currency to the foreign country's central bank, in return for the central bank's assumption of the borrower's nonlocal currency obligations. The local currency is held on deposit at the central bank, for the account of the lender banks, and may be subject to relending to other borrowers in the country. Such arrangements should be carefully analyzed to determine whether the local currency payments to the foreign central bank represent collections of outstandings for financial reporting purposes, or whether such outstandings should be classified as nonaccrual, past due or restructured loans.

Allowance for loan losses. An analysis of the allowance related to LDC debts should include:

1. The amount of allowances
2. The amounts and percentages of outstandings, clearly defined (e.g., whether the amounts of prior charge-offs or trade-related outstandings are included or excluded)
3. The amounts of charge-offs, recoveries, and additional provisions, swaps, or sales
4. The valuation of swaps and the rationale for determining such valuations
5. The accounting policies for any 20% or greater investments obtained in swaps, considering restrictions on sales, dividends, and currency exchange.

Allocated transfer risk reserves. The International Lending Supervision Act of 1983 requires banks to establish reserves against transfer risk (the possibility that an asset cannot be serviced in the currency of payment because of a lack of foreign exchange in the country of the obligor) unless the banking institution has already appropriately written down the assets. Allocated transfer risk reserves (ATRRs) represent the minimum reserves necessary in the view of the regulators.

SAB 56, *Reporting of an Allocated Transfer Risk Reserve in Filings Under the Federal Securities Laws* (Topic 11.I), outlines the SEC requirements as follows:

• ATRRs not written off should be disclosed as part of the discussion of loan loss experience; the ATRR should be shown and discussed separately in the reconciliation of the allowance.
• Disclosure of the ATRR in the footnotes may also provide a more complete explanation of charge-offs and provisions for loan losses. Exclusion of the ATRR from regulatory capital and surplus does not address the broader issue of the adequacy of allowances. It is the responsibility of each registrant to determine whether GAAP requires an additional provision for losses in excess of the amount required in an ATRR.

Mexican debt exchange program. In early 1988, the SEC released SAB 75, *Accounting and Disclosures by Bank Holding Companies for a "Mexican Debt Exchange" Transaction* (Topic 11.H.2). Under this program, the Mexican government has created U.S. dollar-denominated bonds with a LIBOR-based rate maturing in 20 years; and it has accepted certain bids from holders to exchange preexisting debt for the new bonds (which are fully secured as to principal only by U.S. Treasury securities).

SAB 75 requires that tenderers of existing debt must either (1) write down the existing loans to the bid price or increase the loan loss allowance commensurately; or (2) evaluate that existing loan loss allowances are sufficient to cover the decrease in carrying amount to bid price, even if the bid was too low to be accepted by Mexico. Once accepted for exchange by Mexico, the old debt is removed as an asset and the new debt is recorded as an asset. The allowance for loan losses, adjusted as described in the preceding sentence, is reduced for the excess of the old debt asset over the new debt asset.

The SAB is crammed with detailed disclosure requirements. Few major U.S. banks participated because they concluded that the exchange was not advantageous.

Regulatory Issues. FRB and OCC policy with respect to interest accruals on LDC problem loans is as follows:

• Banks may not accrue interest on any loan when principal or interest is due and has remained unpaid for 90 days or more unless the loan is both well secured and in the process of collection.

• Loans that reach nonaccrual status may not be restored to accruing status until all delinquent principal and/or interest has been brought current, or the loan becomes both well secured and in the process of collection.

• The date on which a loan reaches nonaccrual status is determined by the contractual terms of the loan, not official reporting dates.

The OCC's policy on loan swaps parallels the AICPA's Practice Bulletin. However, their circular states that "the principles set forth are equally applicable to swaps of domestic loans in which the borrower is financially troubled."

As a result of debt/equity swap programs, the FRB amended Regulation K to allow banks to acquire ownership of foreign companies engaged in nonfinancial activities in exchange for foreign government debt obligations held by the banks. Banks may acquire as much as 100% of the shares of the foreign nonfinancial company under the following circumstances: the nonfinancial company must be in the process of being transferred from public to private ownership; the country in which the company is located must be a heavily indebted developing country; the shares must be acquired through debt/equity swaps; and the shares must be held by the bank holding company or its subsidiary.

Bank Capital Regulatory Requirements

When examining a bank, federal and state regulators use the concept of bank capital when examining a bank capital: primary capital and total capital. Both types are computed by adding to stockholders' equity the following items:

• Contingency and other capital reserves
• Minority interests in consolidated subsidiaries
• Allowance for loan and lease losses
• Mandatory convertible instruments and perpetual debt (allowable up to 20% of primary capital)

Total capital consists of primary capital plus limited-life preferred stock and subordinated notes and debentures that qualify by having a weighted average life of seven or more years and that do not exceed 50% of primary capital.

Minimum Capital. Adequate bank capital is required by regulators before granting a charter to a bank. During the ongoing examination process a bank's capital is the focus of the examiner's attention, as failure to meet minimum regulatory standards can result in closing of the bank.

The current federal regulatory guidelines for adequate bank capital are, as a percentage of total assets:

* Primary capital—5.5%
* Total capital
  —Acceptable—Above 7%
  —Possibly Undercapitalized—6 to 7%
  —Undercapitalized—Below 6%

The minimum capital requirements assume adequate liquidity and a moderate amount of risk in the loan and investment portfolios and in off-balance sheet activities. Each of the regulatory agencies reserves the right to require a higher capital ratio if warranted by a bank's liquidity and overall degree of risk, including standby letters of credit and other off-balance sheet risks.

Proposed Capital Adequacy Guidelines. In 1987 the regulators proposed a new definition and measurement of capital adequacy. The guidelines would chart a bank's risk profile by establishing a relationship between assets and five general risk categories (weighted at 0, 10, 25, 50, or 100%). Off-balance sheet assets are converted into balance sheet equivalents before being placed into risk categories. Assets are then assigned to categories depending on credit risk, which is based mainly on the type of borrower. Also, primary capital as a regulatory measurement would be superseded by common tangible equity (stockholders' common equity less intangible assets, minority interest in consolidated subsidiaries, and certain preferred stock).

AUDITING CONSIDERATIONS

Planning the Audit

Banks have custody of large amounts of monetary items, which makes them highly vulnerable to misappropriation and fraud. The processing of large volumes (both in terms of number and value) of differing transactions requires complex accounting and internal control systems and widespread computer processing. Banks operate under greater decentralization of authority; consequently, there are difficulties in maintaining uniform operating practices and accounting systems. Banks often assume significant off-balance sheet commitments, which do not initially involve general ledger accounting entries. Formal operating procedures, well-defined limits for individual discretion, and rigorous internal control procedures are required to control these conditions. Finally, government regulations often influence generally accepted accounting and auditing practices within the industry.

These characteristics create special matters for auditors to understand. Those include: (1) the nature of the risks associated with the transactions or groups of transactions undertaken by banks; (2) the scale of banking operations and the exposures that can arise within short periods of time; (3) the complexity of systems utilized to process transactions; and (4) the effects of regulations. Those performing a bank audit should have:

- Expertise in banking products, services, and operations
- Appropriate EDP expertise in the context of the bank's EDP operations
- Resources to perform the necessary work at the dispersed locations, if required

Engagement Scope. Typically, an auditor may be engaged to:

- Report on the financial statements of a bank or holding company
- Assist the board of directors in performing a directors' examination
- Report on the internal controls of the bank
- Report on the internal controls of trust department activities
- Report on the financial statements of common trust funds managed by the trust department

Bank financial statements. In determining the scope of an audit of the financial statements of the bank, the auditor should consider the bank's use of specialized accounting principles. In an audit of a bank known to be in financial difficulty, the auditor must also consider the nature of any special reporting relationships that might need to exist between the auditor and banking regulators, so that there is mutual nonsurprise.

The auditor's standard report on the financial statements is the same as that used for other business enterprises and should comply with SAS 58, *Reports on Audited Financial Statements* (AU 508).

Director's examinations. The bylaws of national banks and most state banking laws and regulations require periodic directors' examinations. Directors examinations generally emphasize asset quality (the review and classification of loans), liquidity, capital adequacy, management ability, and future earnings ability. The examinations are conducted under the supervision of the directors or a committee of the board of directors. In addition, the directors' report may contain additional comments and observations of the directors. These reports must be made available to the appropriate regulators.

Where the directors have engaged an independent auditor to make all or a part of the required examination, the report of the directors or a committee thereof may take any one of several forms. The conventional independent auditor's report may be a part of the directors' examination results, but because the directors have the ultimate responsibility for setting the scope of the examination, the outside auditor may be requested to perform only certain procedures. This activity usually falls within SAS 14, *Reports Relating to the Results of Applying Agreed-Upon Procedures to Specified Elements, Accounts, or Items of a Financial Statement* (AU 621), and the related SAS 35 (AU 622). Expected to be finalized in late 1988 is the AICPA exposure draft of a proposed SOP, *Directors' Examinations of Banks* (AICPA, 1988f). This SOP would amend Appendix C of the Bank Audit Guide (in which the 1980 "Suggested Guidelines" are reproduced) by focusing on the scope that may be requested by directors in relation to normal GAAS audit procedures, particularly in the area of higher-risk accounts (e.g., certain loans). An illustrative engagement letter and auditor's report reflecting such omissions is provided.

For further information on directors' examinations, see *Duties and Liabilities of Directors of National Banks* (OCC, 1972) and *Suggested Guidelines for CPA Participa-*

tion in Bank Directors' Examinations (AICPA, 1980d). Appendix C of the Bank Audit Guide also provides guidance.

   Reports on internal control structure. Banks often request auditors to report on their study and evaluation of the bank's system of internal control structure, either in conjunction with the audit or in addition to it. (See Chapter 8.)

   Trust department reports. An auditor may report on the application of agreed-upon procedures to specified areas of a trust department in accordance with SAS 35, *Special Reports—Applying Agreed-upon Procedures to Specified Elements, Accounts, or Items of a Financial Statement* (AU 622). A report on a study and evaluation of the internal accounting control system of a bank's trust or other department that controls nonbank assets held for others in trust, investment advisory, and custody accounts should also conform with the requirements of SAS 30, *Reporting on Internal Accounting Control* (AU 642), or SAS 60, *Communication of Internal Control Structure Related Matters Noted in an Audit* (AU 325). An audit interpretation, *Reports on Internal Accounting Control of Trust Departments of Banks* (AU 9642.14–.17), provides further guidance. The Bank Audit Guide also discusses the audit of a trust department, and in Appendix B illustrates the format of a common trust fund report.

   Audit Timing. The auditor's opinion on a bank's financial statements generally cannot be based solely on the results of substantive tests. The high volume of transactions, the manner in which transactions are executed, and the decentralization of operations usually requires the auditor to place significant reliance on the bank's systems of internal control. Therefore the auditor may perform a significant amount of the audit procedures during interim periods and limit substantive procedures to analytical procedures, the investigation of unusual transactions, and limited detailed tests of income statement and financial condition items, as deemed necessary. Extensive analytical information is usually available from external sources for banks for both planning and substantive procedure purposes.

   Inherent Risks. There are several inherent risks peculiar to financial institutions in general, and therefore to banks. They can be broadly grouped into those relating to: (1) product and service; (2) operations; and (3) organizational structure.

   Product and service risks. The major types of risks related to product and service are:

• Credit and transfer
• Interest rate
• Currency
• Market
• Liquidity
• Theft, fraud, and error
• Fiduciary

Credit risk is the risk of being unable to collect amounts due from customers and counter-parties due to factors such as a deterioration in their financial condition or unwillingness to pay. Credit risk is significant to most banks. Loans may develop credit risk problems because of the following factors:

• Poor credit policies
• Weak credit extension or monitoring procedures
• Deterioration in the financial condition of borrowers
• Changes in the general economy, the condition of a particular industry, or the economy of a geographic area in which the bank extends credit

Transfer risk is the risk of non-repayment of a loan in local currency by a foreign borrower due to factors such as insufficient foreign exchange reserves of the borrower's country. Transfer risk results from economic conditions of a foreign economy and a decision by the government of the foreign country. Credit and transfer risks are the principal factors in considering the adequacy of the allowance for loan losses. SAS 57, *Auditing Accounting Estimates* (AU 342), and *Auditing the Allowances for Credit Losses of Banks* (AICPA, 1986c) provide guidelines for determining the adequacy of the allowance for loan losses.

Interest rate risk is the risk of loss due to mismatches between interest rates earned on the lending of funds to customers and paid to creditors on the financing of such funds. For example, a bank with intermediate- or long-term fixed rate assets that are financed with short-term liabilities would be adversely affected by a rise in interest rates. If the rates rise substantially, the bank must refinance the short-term borrowings at higher rates, which may result in lower overall profit margins or negative margins.

Currency risk is the risk of loss due to movements in the exchange rates applicable to foreign currency assets, liabilities, rights, and obligations. Market risk is the risk of loss due to movements in market prices of assets which are not held to maturity.

Banks are exposed to liquidity risk when they invest disproportionately in long-term assets. For example, if a bank is required to sell these assets to generate cash when their market value has decreased, large losses may be incurred. In addition, a bank can acquire its assets through short-term borrowed funds. Since the acquisition and maintenance of these funds are market sensitive, considerable liquidity risk is present. If the bank's liquidity is not sufficient to meet prospective needs and there is evidence that the bank may have to dispose of certain assets to obtain liquidity, the auditor should consider the propriety of the accounting basis for any assets that the bank may have to sell. In more serious situations of illiquidity, the auditor may need to refer to SAS 59, *Auditor's Consideration of an Entity's Ability to Continue as a Going-Concern* (AU 341).

Theft, fraud, and error risk is the risk of loss due to theft and fraud by employees and other parties, and errors by employees. Since banks possess highly marketable monetary items there is a great risk of theft and fraud.

Finally, because banks operate in a fiduciary role, they have a risk of loss due to factors such as failure to maintain safe custody or to properly manage assets on behalf of their customers.

Operations risk. Operating risks primarily arise out of the need to process large volumes of transactions accurately within short time frames. This almost always requires the use of complex computer systems. A high degree of discipline must exist to protect against: (1) failure to process executed transactions within the required time frames, causing an inability to receive or make payments for those transactions; (2) wide-scale error due to breakdown in processing internal controls; (3) loss of data due to system failure; and (4) exposure to market risks due to lack of accurate and timely financial information.

Because banks usually need to conduct operations in a number of locations, the dispersion of transactions, processing, and internal controls may result in control breakdowns which can occur and remain undetected because of the physical separation between management and those who process the transactions.

Finally, banks must monitor and manage significant, short-term exposures. These exposures can arise from transactions with customers and counter-parties and can include credit, interest rate, currency, and market risks. The process of clearing transactions may cause a significant build-up of receivables and payables during a day, most of which are closed out by the end of the day. This is usually referred to as intra-day payment risk.

Organizational structure risks. The structural risks primarily arise out of a bank's need to achieve profitability through the use of high financial leverage. The use of leverage results in exposure to: (1) the risk of erosion of capital resources as a result of a relatively small percentage loss in asset value; and (2) the risk of being unable to obtain the funds required to maintain operations at a reasonable cost as a result of a loss of market confidence. Other structural risks arise out of a bank's required adherence to regulatory rules and guidelines which may result in fines or operating restrictions. The need to maintain an adequate capital base pursuant to regulatory requirements also amplifies the need for a system of internal control that provides reasonable assurance of proper maintenance and disclosure of required capital.

Materiality. The auditor should consider the levels of financial leverage since it can cause a relatively small error (in percentage terms) on the balance sheet to have a significant effect on the income statement. Errors relating only to the balance sheet may therefore be permitted to have a much higher level of materiality than those that could also affect the income statement. Finally, regulatory requirements for maintaining a certain minimum capital level may necessitate the establishment of a materiality level that would identify errors of a size that could result in a breach of the minimum capital requirements.

Audit Evidence. Banks undertake transactions having complex underlying features that may not be apparent from the level of processing and recording. This results in the possibility that all aspects of a transaction may not be fully or correctly recorded, with the resultant risk of:

* Loss due to failure to take timely corrective action.
* Failure to record adequate provisions for loss on a timely basis.
* Inadequate or improper disclosure in the financial statements and other reports.

Accordingly, the auditor needs to acquire a good understanding of the nature of the transactions and the types of documentation to be examined.

Banks also typically engage in transactions having a low revenue or profit element as a percentage of the principal exposure. Many of these transactions may not be recorded on the balance sheet. Examples of such transactions include financial guarantees, letters of credit, agreements to purchase and sell foreign exchange, and interest rate or currency swaps.

EDP Considerations

Banks typically address the volume and time frame control issues through the use of computerized systems. They have traditionally been leaders in the purchase or development of distributed processing, data base systems, security software, and telecommunications systems. Much of this technology is also found in small institutions and in institutions using a service bureau to process their transactions.

The use of public and private communication links, the increasing use and reliance on electronic funds transfer systems, and the use of shared automatic teller machine networks, while increasing the services to customers, have also created an exposure for banks that requires constant monitoring and reliance on strict access controls. Typical banking systems also incorporate applications that can automatically generate transactions based on predetermined criteria, such as interest rate calculation, accrual rate calculation, late payment notification, and so forth. Consequently, it will usually be necessary for the auditor to utilize computer assisted audit techniques to efficiently evaluate systems and controls within these systems (i.e., in sufficient depth and within a satisfactory time frame).

Special skills may be needed to describe or test the characteristics of computer processing that affect the internal accounting structure control. Thus, in many banking environments it often becomes necessary to consider using the special skills of an EDP auditor. Because of the increasing cost of software and the amount of time and resources required to modify a sustem after implementation, the EDP auditor should be a prominent figure in the development and acquisition of EDP systems. Chapter 10 extensively discusses auditing in an EDP environment.

Related Party Transactions

Related party transactions are a troublesome issue for auditors of banks. Many transactions appear to be connected as banks often lend to and borrow from the same customer. The auditor should be particularly aware of the added risk of transactions with related party implications. Management must ensure that normal measures of banking prudence, such as credit assessment and the receipt of collateral, are appropriately exercised. The auditor therefore needs to perform procedures sufficient to identify all significant related or connected parties and related party transactions, as well as to carefully assess the reasonableness of the terms and amounts of such transactions and their collectibility. The auditor should also be aware of regulatory guidance or restrictions on related party transactions.

Reliance on Internal Control

SAS 55, *Consideration of the Internal Control Structure in a Financial Statement Audit* (AU 319), identifies five objectives of internal controls:

1. Transactions and activities have been properly authorized
2. Duties are appropriately segregated to reduce the opportunities for an employee to both perpetrate and conceal errors or irregularities
3. Records and documents are designed to be adequate to ensure proper recording of transactions and events
4. Adequate safeguards exist over access to and use of assets and records
5. Independent checks are made on performance and proper valuation of recorded amounts, including comparison of assets with recorded accountabilities.

   SAS 55 (Appendix D) refers to objectives management should consider in establishing specific internal control policies and procedures, as previously discussed in SAS 1. These are not explicitly discussed in the body of SAS 55, but they are implicit in an internal control structure. These objectives are:

- Transactions are executed in accordance with management's general or specific authorization.
- Transactions are recorded as necessary:
  - To permit preparation of financial statements in conformity with GAAP or any other criteria applicable to such statements, and
  - To maintain accountability for assets.
- Access to assets is permitted only in accordance with management's authorization.
- The recorded accountability for assets is compared with the existing assets at reasonable intervals and appropriate action is taken with respect to any differences.

   In addition, banks have the further objective of ensuring that they adequately fulfill their fiduciary responsibilities. These five objectives are discussed in the sections that follow.

   Management's Authorization. A bank's operations are generally large and dispersed in relation to commercial companies of comparable size. Decision-making functions therefore are usually decentralized and the authority to commit the bank to material transactions is delegated among the various levels of management and staff. Such delegation will almost always be found in the lending, investing, and funds transfer functions. Accordingly, a structured system is required to formally identify and document: (1) employees who can authorize specific transactions; (2) procedures to be followed in granting authorizations; (3) limitations on the amounts that can be authorized by individual employee and/or by staff level; and (4) any requirements that may exist for concurring authorization. Banks also need procedures for monitoring the aggregate level of exposures that occur across the different activities, departments, and offices of the bank.

   The proper functioning of a bank's authorization controls will be particularly important to the auditor for transactions entered into near the date of the financial statements, where some aspects of the transaction have not yet been fulfilled, or where insufficient evidence is available to assess the value of the assets acquired or liabilities incurred.

Recording of Transactions. Because banks process large volumes and values of transactions, reconciliation of procedures for control accounts to subledgers must operate within a time frame that ensures the ability to detect and correct errors with a minimal risk of loss. End-of-day balances may not be indicative of the volume of transactions processed through the systems or of the maximum exposure to loss during the course of a business day. This is particularly true in executing and processing money market instruments or securities transactions. Assessment of controls in these areas must take into account the ability to maintain control during the period of maximum volumes or financial exposure. Such control reconciliations may be conducted hourly, daily, weekly, or monthly depending on the volume, nature of the transactions, level of risk, and transaction settlement time frames.

Many banking transactions are subject to specialized accounting rules, and control procedures are needed to ensure compliance by employees (frequently located outside the accounting department) initiating accounting entries. Employees may also enter into transactions not recorded on the general ledger. Accordingly, control procedures must be in place to ensure that such transactions are recorded and monitored in a manner that (1) provides management with the required degree of control, and (2) allows for the prompt determination of any change in their status that results in a profit or loss (e.g., foreign exchange purchase and sale commitments, where changes in exchange rates will result in changes in unrealized profits or losses).

Finally, most banking transactions must be recorded in a level of detail susceptible of verification both internally and by the bank's customers and counterparties.

Authorized Access to Assets. The assets of a bank are generally negotiable, of high value, and in a form that cannot be safeguarded solely by physical procedures. To ensure that access is permitted only in accordance with management's authorization, a bank usually uses controls such as: (1) passwords that restrict computer access to authorized employees; (2) segregation of the record-keeping and access functions (including the use of computer generated transaction confirmation reports available immediately and only to the employee in charge of the record-keeping functions); (3) joint access arrangements (e.g., whereby the passwords of two employees are required to obtain access to the computerized records on which the assets are maintained); and (4) frequent third party confirmation and reconciliation of asset positions by an employee independent of transaction origination.

Comparison of Records With Assets. The large amounts of assets handled by banks, the transaction volumes, the potential for change in the value of those assets due to fluctuations in market prices, and the importance of confirming the continuous operation of access and authorization controls, will necessitate the frequent operation of reconciliation controls. This will have particular importance for: (1) assets whose values are determined by reference to external market prices, such as securities and foreign exchange contracts; and (2) assets in negotiable form, such as cash, bearer securities, and deposit and security positions with other institutions. As to assets in negotiable form, failure to detect errors and discrepancies on a timely basis (which may be daily where money market transactions are involved) could lead to irretrievable loss.

The reconciliation procedures used to achieve this control objective will normally be based on physical counts and third party confirmation. Given the scale and the frequency with which these procedures are normally conducted, internal audit will play an important role in ensuring that the procedures are continuously performed in an effective manner.

In designing an audit strategy to assess the effectiveness of a bank's reconciliation controls, the auditor should consider the number of accounts requiring reconciliation and the frequency with which these reconciliations need to be performed. A large portion of the audit effort will need to be directed to the documentation, testing, and evaluation of the reconciliation controls, and to the work of the internal auditor. External auditors typically place extensive reliance on internal auditors as an internal control, and on internal audit procedures in support of external audit workpapers. The auditor needs to evaluate the internal audit function to determine the extent to which the work of the internal auditor is useful in his examination of the financial statements. This has particular relevance for banks with decentralized operations. Specific guidance on such evaluation is contained in SAS 9, *The Effect of Internal Audit Function on the Scope of the Independent Auditor's Examination* (AU 322), which is discussed in the Appendix to Chapter 7.

In addition, because reconciliations are cumulative in their effect, most can be satisfactorily audited at the year-end date, assuming that they are promptly prepared as of that date, if the auditor is satisfied that the reconciliation control procedures are effective. The auditor also needs assurance in examining a reconciliation that items have not been improperly transferred to other accounts not subject to reconciliation and investigation at the same time.

Fiduciary Duties. The main objective of internal controls with regard to the fiduciary activities is to ensure that (1) all duties arising from fiduciary relationships are adequately performed, and (2) all assets in the bank's custody arising from fiduciary relationships are adequately safeguarded. An essential feature of the system is the proper segregation of fiduciary assets from the bank's own assets and the discharge of fiduciary responsibility by a separate department or by a subsidiary of the bank.

Substantive Procedures

After evaluating the system of internal control, the auditor must determine the nature, timing, and extent of the substantive tests to be performed on individual account balances and other information contained in the bank's financial statements. The risks that shape the bank's internal control structure should be considered. Based on the Bank Audit Guide, the Audit considerations affecting *product and service risks* include the need to:

1. Physically examine, confirm, and reconcile negotiable items
2. Specifically test individually significant balances with emphasis on examination of underlying documentation and third-party confirmations

3. Examine the post year-end transactions and events for evidence of impairment of value at the year-end date.

The audit considerations affecting *operations risk* include the need to:

1. Complete internal control tests prior to the year-end so that the audit can be completed on a timely basis.
2. Use computer audit techniques, such as the use of interrogation software, to achieve the desired extent of EDP control testing in the limited available time.
3. Use analytical review procedures to detect conditions of audit concern where the number of accounts or transactions precludes the testing of a satisfactory sample of items.
4. Consider the use of statistical sampling techniques where there are a large number of homogenous accounts or transactions and the auditor wishes to examine a representative sample.
5. Be satisfied as to the appropriate reconciliation of asset and liability accounts with counter-parties to provide assurance as to the propriety and accuracy of completed transactions.
6. Establish a basis for reliance on the work of the internal auditors as a means of obtaining satisfactory coverage both geographically and in terms of the extent of transactions and coverage of account balances.
7. Ensure that audit staff and representatives conducting examinations at other locations of the bank are properly instructed and that the results of their work are properly reviewed.

The audit considerations affecting *organizational structure risks* include the need to:

1. Ensure that all significant principal positions and related unrealized profits and losses have been recorded.
2. Consider the viability of the bank by assessing evidence of factors such as funding difficulties.
3. Consider the implications of noncompliance with regulatory rules and guidelines.

To achieve the audit objectives, the auditor will find that certain substantive procedures are particularly relevant to the examination of a bank's accounts, as discussed in the following sections.

Inspection. Inspection consists of examining records, documents, or tangible assets. The auditor needs to inspect such items to be satisfied as to the physical existence of negotiable assets, and to ensure an understanding of the terms and conditions of significant agreements (individually or in the aggregate) supporting enforceability and accounting treatment. The auditor might inspect such items as securities, loan agreements, commitment agreements, asset sale agreements, and compliance with regulatory requirements and instructions.

In carrying out inspection procedures, the auditor should be particularly vigilant regarding the existence of assets held in a fiduciary capacity and should ensure that adequate procedures exist to properly segregate them from the bank's operating assets.

Confirmation. Confirmation consists of the response to an inquiry to corroborate information contained in the accounting records. Auditors often confirm to obtain evidence of recognition by the bank's customers and counter-parties of amounts, terms, and conditions of important transactions. Audit confirmations are also regularly utilized to test internal controls, and in this usage they may be dual-purpose procedures, not only substantive tests.

Because of the existence of significant amounts of monetary assets, liabilities, and off-balance sheet commitments, confirmation of balances often proves to be relatively the safest and most practical method of determining the existence and completeness of the amounts of assets and liabilities disclosed in the financial statements. Examples of areas for which the auditor may use confirmation, as a compliance and/or a substantive audit procedure, are: (1) collateral security positions on specific loans; and (2) asset, liability, and forward purchase and sale positions with customers and counter-parties (such as nostro and vostro accounts, book-based security position, loan accounts, deposit accounts, guarantees, and letters of credit).

Analytical Procedures. Analytical review procedures, discussed in detail in Chapter 7, consist of studying significant ratios and trends and investigating unusual fluctuations. Analytical review is not applicable to items of such a large size that the auditor will need to examine them individually.

The two most important elements in the determination of a bank's earnings are interest income and interest expense. These have direct relationships to interest-bearing assets and interest-bearing liabilities, respectively. To establish the reasonableness of these relationships, the auditor can examine the degree to which the reported income and expense vary from the amounts calculated on the basis of average balances outstanding and the bank's stated rates during the year. This analysis should also highlight the existence of significant amounts of nonperforming loans. In addition, the auditor may wish to assess the reasonableness of the stated rates in comparison to those prevailing in the market during the year for similar classes of loans and deposits. Evidence of rates charged or paid above market rates may indicate, in the case of loan assets, the existence of excessive risk, or in the case of deposit liabilities, liquidity or funding difficulties.

By applying analytical procedures to account composition, the auditor may detect certain conditions of audit concern, such as undue concentration of risk in particular industries or geographic areas, and potential exposure to interest rate, currency, and maturity mismatches.

Most banks develop extensive statistical and financial information. While specifics will vary among banks, their basic purpose tends to remain the same, that is, to provide measures of performance in relation to prior years, to budget, and to other banks. The auditor can use this data to conduct an in-depth analytical review of trends and peer group analyses. In addition, several private companies provide extensive financial statement analysis data for most banks.

Those ratios the auditor is most likely to encounter and to find useful are listed in Figure 40.10.

Representation Letters

Client representations are particularly important in the context of a bank audit in providing additional assurance that the information and evidence provided by man-

---

Asset quality ratios

- Loan losses to total loans
- Nonperforming loans to total loans
- Loan loss reserves to nonperforming loans
- Earnings coverage to loan losses
- Increase in loan loss reserves to gross income

Liquidity ratios

- Cash and liquid securities (e.g., those due within 30 days) to total assets
- Interbank and money market deposit liabilities to total assets

Earnings ratios

- Return on average total assets
- Return on average total equity
- Net interest margin as a percentage of average total assets and average earning assets
- Interest income as a percentage of average earning assets
- Interest expense as a percentage of average interest bearing liabilities
- Noninterest income as a percentage of average commitments
- Noninterest income as a percentage of average total assets
- Noninterest expense as a percentage of average total assets

Capital adequacy ratios

- Equity capital as a percentage of total assets
- Equity capital as a percentage of risk assets

FIG. 40.10   Bank Financial Ratios Useful in Analytical Review

agement is complete. This is especially true of bank transactions that normally are not reflected in the accounts. Special items in representation letters for banks include communications with regulatory agencies (including oral communication), allowances for credit losses, commitments to purchase or sell securities under forward-placement financial futures contracts, standby commitments, and other significant written and oral commitments such as line and/or letters of credit, loan commitments, agreements to repurchase or sell loans and investment securities, and guarantees of obligations of others.

41

Thrift Industry

THRIFT AND MORTGAGE BANKING ENVIRONMENT

Savings and Loans

The term "thrift" refers to both savings and loan associations and savings banks. However, in practice and in this chapter the terms "thrift," "savings and loan" (S&L), "savings bank," and "association" are used interchangeably. The type of thrifts existing today originated in the 1930s with the creation of the Federal Savings and Loan Insurance Corporation (FSLIC) to insure depositor accounts. In periods of relatively stable interest rates, which the United States experienced until about 1978, there was no unusual failure rate of thrifts. S&Ls performed their traditional role of lending on residential properties and holding mortgages for the long term. The principal sources of funds were depositors' passbook accounts, receiving interest at low, regulated rates. Earning only a modest rate was, in theory, the "price" to depositors of government insurance. Stable rates permitted a positive "spread" between the cost of these deposits and the earnings on long-term fixed rate mortgages. In the latter 1970s, the government deregulated the interest rates that S&Ls could pay depositors. At the same time interest rates increased. The system began to strain.

Since interest-bearing liabilities of most S&Ls reprice more quickly than interest-bearing assets, the net interest spread decreased, or even turned negative. This new economic environment of volatile interest rates and shrinking spreads forced many S&Ls to change their business. They entered into a wide range of new product lines such as real estate development, insurance, mortgage banking, and credit guarantees. In addition, some associations began to use new financial instruments to reduce interest rate risk, such as financial futures contracts and interest rate swaps.

These actions, against the backdrop of a changing financial services environment, altered the competitive nature of the industry. Previously, S&Ls had primarily competed with each other, and out-of-state branches were rare. S&Ls now had to compete directly with banks, mortgage bankers, insurance companies, mutual funds, broker/dealers, and others. The competition had changed from local to national: the competition might be a super-regional bank, a mutual fund that collected deposits by mail throughout the country, or a national insurance company.

The regulators were not idle during this time; they issued a large number of regulations. Some provided regulatory assistance to associations, while others tried to prevent transactions that in the regulators' eyes were unduly risky.

A number of S&Ls, particularly those in Texas and Oklahoma, suffered large decreases in their net worth. The dwindling reserves of FSLIC, combined with the deficiency in assets of financially troubled associations, caused the U.S. General Accounting Office (GAO) to issue a report in 1987 that deemed the FSLIC to be bankrupt.

The Competitive Equality Banking Act (CEBA) was subsequently passed in 1987 by Congress. CEBA permits the district banks of the Federal Home Loan Bank Board (FHLBB) to issue bonds. The proceeds from the bonds will be used by FSLIC to close or merge some of the troubled associations. There is a concern that the amount of funds to become available through the bonds will not be sufficient to take care of the large number of problem S&Ls. (CEBA also set certain regulatory accounting requirements, discussed later.)

The convergence of these events has forced the industry to change dramatically. The search for new profits has resulted in a continuous stream of complex transactions for which the accounting is often unclear. While accountants struggle to account for these transactions under the framework of GAAP, regulatory accounting principles (RAP) have become extremely difficult to apply.

Mortgage Bankers

The line that distinguishes mortgage bankers – or mortgage companies, as they are often called – from savings and loans is becoming increasingly fuzzy. Many S&Ls have created mortgage banking subsidiaries. Other S&Ls have realigned their basic activities so that they operate much like a mortgage banker. Mortgage banking thus can be defined better as certain transaction types rather than as a unique industry. Accordingly the accounting and auditing sections of this chapter will not differentiate between S&Ls and mortgage bankers, because the transactions discussed often apply to both.

Mortgage banks are engaged primarily in originating, marketing, and servicing real estate mortgage loans. A mortgage bank finances its portfolio (inventory) with short-term bank borrowings collateralized by the loans.

The major functions of a mortgage bank are:

* Originating loans – locating borrowers, underwriting, processing loan documents, and distributing funds.
* Selling mortgages – finding permanent investors to purchase long-term mortgages.
* Servicing loans – collecting monthly payments, maintaining escrow accounts for taxes and insurance, monitoring delinquencies, and performing bookkeeping.

Generally, the mortgage banker is either originating or purchasing loans to fill a commitment to a permanent investor for a specific package of loans at a guaranteed yield, or is investing in a portfolio while negotiating with potential investors seeking such a package. Mortgage bankers originate (or purchase) two types of loans – residential and commercial. Since a residential loan is relatively small, mortgage bankers will generally originate these without a specific commitment from a permanent investor. Rather, they will seek block commitments from investors for a large dollar amount of residential loans meeting broad criteria. While these loans are being held for resale, the mortgage banker assumes the primary risk for collectibility of the loans and fluctuations in interest rates. In the case of commercial loan originations (shopping centers, office buildings, etc.), there is usually a commitment from a permanent investor to finance the project after construction is completed.

Mortgages are normally sold to various permanent investors, such as insurance companies, savings banks, commercial banks, S&Ls, FHLMC (Federal Home Loan Mortgage Corporation), FNMA (Federal National Mortgage Association), and GNMA (Government National Mortgage Association) (described later). They can also be swapped into FHLMC, FNMA, or GNMA mortgage-backed securities and sold to the same kinds of investors.

Mortgage origination usually does not result in substantial profits because the costs associated with the process (applications, appraisals, and so forth) do not significantly exceed the fees received from the mortgagor. In a competitive market the mortgage banker may even absorb those fees. Instead, income is primarily derived from servicing the loans and from related businesses (e.g., insurance, property management, and appraisal services). Loan servicing generates revenues at a fixed percentage of the outstanding principal balance of the mortgage. The mortgage banker also uses the escrow funds from loans in its inventory and servicing portfolios as compensating balances for its warehouse borrowing, thereby reducing its interest expense.

GOVERNMENT REGULATION

Regulatory Structure and Ownership

The primary governmental and quasi-governmental agencies affecting savings institutions are:

- *Federal Home Loan Bank Board.* FHLBB is an independent agency governed by three members appointed by the President of the United States. The Board supervises the Federal Home Loan Bank System which provides a credit reserve for savings institutions comparable to what the Federal Reserve System does for banks. The System comprises 12 district Federal Home Loan Banks, whose capital stock is completely owned by the member institutions. FHLBB also supervises the Federal Savings and Loan System which charters and supervises federal S&Ls.

- *Federal Savings and Loan Insurance Corporation.* FSLIC insures each investor's account at member associations up to $100,000. The board members of the FHLBB make up the board of trustees of FSLIC. FSLIC must insure all federally-chartered S&Ls and may insure other S&Ls, cooperative banks, and homestead associations. It has broad sanctioning power over an association's operations, directors, and personnel if FSLIC net worth regulations are not met.

- *Federal Reserve System.* The "Fed" carries out monetary policy, supervises banking in the United States, and provides various central banking services.

- *Federal Deposit Insurance Corporation.* FDIC insures each investor's account up to $100,000 for member banks. It can act as a receiver for closed banks, and purchase assets from or extend deposits to troubled or closed banks.

- *State banking departments.* These perform functions similar to the FHLBB for member institutions. There is a supervision overlap between the state and federal government if an institution is state chartered but federally insured.

- *Federal Home Loan Mortgage Corporation.* FHLMC, or Freddie Mac, is a quasi-governmental secondary market agency that was formed in 1970. Its purpose is to increase the availability of funds flowing into the housing market by developing a secondary market for conventional, FHA and VA mortgages. FHLMC finances its purchases with debt and mortgage-backed securities (FHLMC pass-through certificates, or PCs).

- *Federal National Mortgage Association.* FNMA, or Fannie Mae, is a government agency formed in 1938 to create a secondary market for FHA mortgages. Converted to a private corporation by sale of common stock to the public in 1968, most of its recent purchases are nongovernmental fixed and adjustable rate loans, though it also purchases FHA and VA loans. FNMA also finances its purchases with debt and mortgage-backed securities (FNMA PCs).[1]

---

[1] "Mortgage participation certificates" and "pay-through bonds" are sometimes also referred to as PCs. The acronym "PC" thus has been expanded into a generic reference for most varieties of MBS,

• *Government National Mortgage Association.* GNMA, or Ginnie Mae, is a government agency created in 1968 to replace FNMA when the latter was privatized. GNMA supports government housing programs by buying FHA and VA loans, financing its purchases with debt and mortgage-backed securities (GNMA PCs).

The SEC also has regulatory and supervisory authority, but has delegated such authority to the FHLBB as to stock S&Ls' initial and ongoing filings. FHLBB regulations covering the form and content of financial statements of stock associations are essentially the same as SEC regulations. All filings are made with the FHLBB except for S&L holding corporations that must file with the SEC under the SEC bank holding company regulations.

Savings and loans are chartered by either the FHLBB or by a state banking department. An S&L that is chartered by the FHLBB will have the word "federal" in its corporate name; all others are state-chartered. S&Ls are usually insured by FSLIC, though some states once had S&L insurance funds. However, several state funds went bankrupt in the mid-1980s, and state insurance was eliminated. Associations can also elect to be "uninsured," that is, the savings accounts of their depositors are not insured.

A federally chartered S&L is regulated by the FHLBB and FSLIC. A state chartered and FSLIC-insured association is regulated by the state banking department and FSLIC. State chartered uninsured associations are regulated by the state banking department.

The ownership form of an S&L can be stock or mutual. Prior to 1980, almost all were mutual associations owned by depositors. A stock association is owned by its stockholders.

Savings banks, a cross between an S&L and a commercial bank, are similar to S&Ls but are regulated by banking industry regulators. Savings banks, mostly located in the Northeast section of the country, can be chartered by either the state or FHLBB (most are state chartered). A savings bank can be insured by the Federal Deposit Insurance Corporation (FDIC) (state or federal charter), or by FHLBB (federal charter only); or it can be uninsured. State-chartered savings banks are regulated by the state regulators, FDIC (if insured), and the Federal Reserve (if they are a member). Federally chartered savings banks are regulated by the FHLBB and either FSLIC or FDIC. Like an S&L, the ownership form of a savings bank can be either mutual or stock.

Regulatory Intent

The focus and intent of regulation has changed several times during the 1980s. Early in the decade, when Richard Pratt was the chairman of the FHLBB, associations were given financial relief through regulatory accounting principles (e.g., losses on sales of certain mortgage assets could be deferred). Then during the mid 1980s, the FHLBB issued regulations under chairman Edwin Gray that focused on reducing the

---

including those that do not exactly pass through an undivided interest in the cash flows. For example, a pay-through instrument may divide cash flows into several series, with each series having a different priority and/or timing of receipt of cash flows. CMOs and Real Estate Mortgage Investment Conduits (REMICs), discussed in Chapter 21, are examples of cash flows segregated by series.

types and magnitude of permissible transactions. The FHLBB's present chairman, Danny Wall, will undoubtedly issue regulations reflecting his priorities.

Key Regulations

Competitive Equality Banking Act. During 1987, Congress passed CEBA, authorizing the creation of a financing corporation to issue bonds whose proceeds will be used to bolster the FSLIC's insurance fund. The district banks will contribute cash to the financing corporation, which will use the cash to purchase zero coupon Treasury securities to collateralize the bonds.

At the end of 1987 the FHLBB issued the following seven primary regulations in response to CEBA:

* Uniform accounting standards
* Troubled debt restructuring
* Classification of assets
* Appraisal policies and practices
* Individual capital requirements
* Qualified thrift lender test
* Capital forbearance

Uniform accounting standards. CEBA mandates that thrift institutions use either commercial bank regulatory accounting, or GAAP applicable to S&Ls. The FHLBB chose the latter with some transition rules regarding the calculation of regulatory capital. CEBA requires thrifts to follow GAAP for transactions that occur on or after January 1, 1989. However, for the sole purpose of computing regulatory capital, certain items need not be in compliance with GAAP as specified later herein.

Until January 1, 1993, investments in mutual funds invested in liquid assets may be accounted for on a cost basis instead of at the lower of cost or market as required under GAAP. Further, deferred gains and losses on sales of mortgage assets may continue to be amortized over the respective remaining lives of the mortgage assets (i.e., beyond January 1, 1993).

The cumulative RAP/GAAP differences as of January 1, 1989 for the following items must be eliminated from regulatory capital at that date:

* Lower-of-cost-or-market write-downs on marketable equity securities.
* Gains and losses on option contracts.
* Interest that cannot be accrued under regulatory standards because the loan is delinquent.
* Difference in allowances for loan losses between GAAP and RAP.

Certain other RAP/GAAP differences were grandfathered (also for the sole purpose of calculating regulatory capital) and will be phased out from January 1, 1989 through December 31, 1993:

* Gains and losses on financial futures transactions.
* Gains on sales of real estate developed by the association or its subsidiaries.

- Unamortized balance of premiums and discounts on mortgage assets (resulting from RAP/GAAP differences in amortization method and life).
- Loan origination and commitment fees (resulting from higher income recognition amounts allowed under RAP).
- Appraised equity capital.

Associations can elect whether to "amortize" these differences into RAP-based income from 1989 through 1993 or to eliminate the cumulative differences as they exist at January 1, 1989. Associations can also elect to eliminate RAP/GAAP differences before January 1, 1989. Finally, institutions that feel they cannot meet the requirements of the rule can apply for delayed compliance.

Thus, except for delayed compliance, regulatory capital as defined by FSLIC regulations will continue after December 31, 1993 to include: general loss allowances; net worth certificates; income capital certificates; some types of subordinated debt and other instruments that FHLBB may authorize; and the unamortized balance of deferred gains and losses on sales of mortgage assets.

Troubled debt restructuring. Associations must account for troubled debt restructurings in accordance with SFAS 15, *Accounting by Debtors and Creditors for Troubled Debt Restructurings* (D22). CEBA recognizes that there is a difference between net realizable value of collateral as calculated for S&Ls and net realizable value as calculated for banks, in that banks do not have to consider interest as a holding cost. Under CEBA, a loan that results from a troubled debt restructuring will not be automatically classified; nor is it exempt from classification (see following subsection). Rather, the credit standing of the new loan will be evaluated on its own merits.

Classification of assets. All assets, including real estate owned and securities, can be classified as *substandard, doubtful,* or *loss.* Effective December 31, 1987, the association must have sufficient general allowances provided for substandard and doubtful assets. (General loss reserves can be included as regulatory capital, following the same treatment used by commercial banks.) For assets classified in the loss category, a specific allowance of 100% must be set up or the asset must be written off.

On an interim basis, an association must continue to include in its calculation of regulatory capital a contingency component of 20% of *scheduled items* (primarily loans over ninety days delinquent and real estate owned by foreclosure) existing at September 30, 1987.

Appraisal policies and practices. An S&L's board of directors and management is responsible for establishing appraisal policies, hiring appraisers, and reviewing the work of appraisers. All appraisals must be based on "market value" as defined in the regulation, but no longer must conform to R-Memorandum 41c (appraisal standards).

Individual capital requirements. Under this regulation, the FHLBB may tailor the minimum capital requirements for an individual association. This authority is delegated through the district banks specifically to an association's principal supervisory agent, who must notify the institution of its minimum capital requirement, and explain why the requirement was set at that level. For the present, the principal supervisory agent must obtain the concurrence of the Office of Regulatory Policy Oversight and Supervision (ORPOS) before requiring additional regulatory capital. The concurrence requirement may be dropped after guidelines for setting individual minimum capital requirements have been developed by ORPOS.

Qualified thrift lender test. An association must meet a qualified thrift lender test in which the association has qualified thrift investments that equal or exceed 60% of its tangible assets for three out of four quarters in two out of three years beginning January 1, 1988. Qualified thrift investments generally are most housing-related investments, purchased servicing rights, and excess servicing fee receivables. Preconstruction loans, commercial loans, and consumer loans do not count as qualified thrift assets. An institution that loses it status as a qualified thrift lender cannot requalify for five years. While nonqualified, access to FHLBB advances is restricted, as are the activities of subsidiaries of thrift holding companies.

Capital forbearance. An institution with regulatory capital of not less than 0.5% of its regulatory capital base can obtain forbearance if it demonstrates that its capital position is the result of losses on loans backed by collateral diminished in value due to adverse economic conditions. An association with regulatory capital of less than 0.5% is eligible for forbearance if the association can demonstrate that it has reasonable prospects of returning to a satisfactory level of regulatory capital by January 1, 1995. The regulation also states that forbearance can be terminated if the assumptions upon which it was granted are not fulfilled.

Net Worth. Under FHLBB regulations, insured institution capital requirements must rise to 6% of total liabilities over a transition period. There is a credit for achieving a reduction in interest rate risk, and an incremental capital requirement if certain types of assets are held. A primary intent of this regulation is to create a risk-based capital requirement for existing S&Ls. (Special rules apply to newly chartered institutions.)

These FHLBB regulations require all insured institutions to conform with a "standard group" of insured institutions having a base factor as it relates to total liabilities at December 31, 1986 of 3% (*base ratio*). (The 1986 base factor is adjusted for growth and amortization, as defined in prior regulations.) Institutions having a base ratio of less than 3% will have their base ratio increased by 90% of the greater of (1) the industry's return on assets or (2) the institution's own return on assets. S&Ls with a base ratio greater than 3% remain at base ratio level until the ratio for the standard group exceeds their ratio. Thereafter, their base ratio shall be the ratio of the standard group. The phase-in of the ratio will increase each July 1 and January 1 by one half of the most recent April calculation until group base ratios reach 6% of total liabilities.

Each insured institution also must have regulatory capital at lease equal to 6% of its total liabilities in excess of its base liabilities. Base liabilities are the lesser of total liabilities at December 31, 1986 or total liabilities at the end of the quarter for which regulatory capital is being computed.

Every insured institution must also have additional regulatory capital, called the *contingency component,* equal to the sum of: (1) 20% of scheduled items, (2) 2% of recourse liabilities, (3) 2% of standby letters of credit, and (4) 10% of equity risk investments.

The required capital for an insured institution is reduced if the association's one-year or three-year assets and liabilities reprice within ranges set by the regulation. This maturity matching credit will not, however, reduce an institution's capital requirement below 4% of total liabilities on or after January 1, 1990.

Equity Risk Investments. The FHLBB made several revisions during 1987 to Regulation 563.9–8 relating to equity risk investments (formerly called direct investments). These are investments in equity securities, real estate, service corporations, and operating subsidiaries, and include land loans and nonresidential construction loans with loan-to-value ratios greater than 80%. Associations that meet their specific minimum capital requirements and have tangible capital of less than 6% of total liabilities are permitted to have equity risk investments that are the greater of 3% of assets or 2.5 times tangible capital.[2] Associations meeting minimum capital requirements with tangible net worth of at least 6% are permitted to invest up to three times tangible capital. If an association does not meet minimum regulatory capital requirements, supervisory approval must be received before any equity risk investments can be made.

The regulation also limits the investment an S&L may make in any single real estate project to the amount of the association's aggregate loans-to-one-borrower limitation.

Regulatory Capital Assistance

The regulators created several methods to increase the net worth of S&Ls, primarily those programs discussed in the following subsections. The FHLBB also issued several accounting regulations during the early 1980s that improved regulatory (RAP-basis) earnings and net worth; these regulations created RAP/GAAP differences, discussed specifically later.

Subordinated Debt. Regulations 561.13c and 563.8–1 permit subordinated debt to be counted as net worth, if the following criteria are met. The debt

1. Cannot be insured by FSLIC.
2. Cannot be used as collateral.
3. Must be unsecured.
4. Must be approved as regulatory capital by the FHLBB.

The portion of the debt that matures not earlier than seven years (from the current reporting date) is fully includible in net worth. For debt maturing in whole or in part

---

[2] "Tangible capital" is equity capital as defined by GAAP less goodwill and other intangible assets plus qualifying subordinated debt and qualifying nonpermanent preferred stock.

in less than seven years, one-seventh of the subordinated debt must be excluded from net worth for each year the maturity is less than seven.

Regulatory-Assisted Mergers. FSLIC sometimes provides incentives to an association, or an investor group, to acquire an ailing association. The incentives can vary, but are often one or more of the following:

* Forbearance of a portion of regulatory net worth. For instance, if an association has actual net worth of $25 million and the FHLB has granted forbearance of $1 million, the association's regulatory net worth is $26 million.
* Subsidization of losses on some of the acquired association's loan portfolio.
* Guarantee of a net spread between the acquired association's interest bearing assets and liabilities.
* Issuance of an income capital certificate to the acquiring association.
* Cash infusion.

SFAS 72, *Accounting for Certain Acquisitions of Banking and Thrift Institutions* (Bt7), discussed later, addresses how to account for regulatory assistance.

Appraised Equity Capital. Regulation 563.13 permits associations to include in net worth the unrealized appreciation on an association's leased or owned fixed assets. Appraised equity capital is the difference between the carrying value and the fair market value of office land, buildings, and improvements. The main features of this regulation include:

* The appraisal must be performed by an independent appraiser.
* The appraisal must include all eligible properties with a carrying value that is 20% or more of the association's total carrying value of eligible properties.
* Ineligible properties are land held for future development, real estate owned (REO) through foreclosure, and idle facilities that are not currently being used as offices.
* The amount is determined at only one point in time; there is no updating.

If an association has not included appraised equity capital in net worth by December 31, 1986, it can no longer avail itself of this form as capital assistance.

Net Worth Certificates. To be eligible to issue net worth certificates, savings banks and S&Ls must have net worth below 3% of total liabilities. Purchases of net worth certificates by FSLIC and FDIC are designed to cover a percentage of the losses experienced by the institution over the previous six months. The regulations permit these agencies to purchase certificates to cover 50% of the operating loss of institutions with net worth between 1% and 2%, and 70% of the loss for institutions with net worth between 0.5% and 1%. Both agencies require, among other things, that the institution prepare and submit a business plan for each request.

Under the FSLIC version of this program, FSLIC issues its interest-bearing note payable to the association; and the association issues a net worth certificate that pays

FSLIC a return. The level of return depends on the association's level of earnings and net worth.

The FHLBB intended the FSLIC note to be recorded as an asset of the S&L and the net worth certificate as equity under both RAP and GAAP. However, the FASB determined that, under GAAP, the transaction cannot be recorded on the balance sheet, as the FSLIC note and the net worth certificate offset.

Net worth certificates issued by the FDIC to mutual savings banks not only fail to comply with GAAP, but also should not be reflected on the bank's regulatory balance sheet. This "no GAAP/no RAP" treatment results from the form of the transaction, in which the FDIC simply provides for bookkeeping entries rather than the actual issuance of notes and payment of interest and dividends.

Income Capital Certificates. These instruments were also designed to increase GAAP and RAP net worth of troubled S&Ls. An income capital certificate is issued by the S&L to FSLIC in exchange for cash or, more likely, an interest-bearing negotiable FSLIC note. *Annual income payments* are required to be paid by the S&L to FSLIC. The annual interest receivable on the FSLIC note usually equals the annual income payment.

Income capital certificates that allow the association to call the certificate at its option are referred to as *permanent* income capital certificates. The holder (i.e., FSLIC) of the permanent income capital certificate has no right to cause the certificate to be redeemed. In some cases, the permanent income capital certificate may not be callable for a period of time that may coincide with the term of the FSLIC promissory note.

In 1986, the FASB endorsed a conclusion that the issuer of an income capital certificate should present it in the liability or equity section of the balance sheet, depending on its characteristics, and present the FSLIC promissory note as an offset. A net increase in liabilities or equity would be reported only if and when the FSLIC note was sold.

ACCOUNTING AND FINANCIAL REPORTING

Accounting Model

The historical cost basis model is GAAP for thrift institutions. It has been prescribed by industry regulators, primarily the FHLBB, since the inception of regulatory institutions during the 1930s, and was probably adopted with little thought as to its appropriateness for financial institutions. Because S&Ls were not considered to be traders, they did not adopt a market value accounting basis, as did securities broker/dealers during the 1930s.

For a long time the use of the historical cost accounting model for thrift institutions did not cause excessive problems. This was because interest rates paid by borrowers and received by depositors were largely fixed at levels that provided S&Ls with an adequate margin, or *spread*.

In the last decade, problems resulting from use of the historical cost accounting model for thrift institutions have become more apparent, primarily because of two

Consolidated Statements of Operations *(In Thousands Except for per Share Amounts)*

Year Ended December 31,	1986	1985	1984
Interest Income			
Loans	$299,124	$316,571	$310,346
Investment securities	104,091	70,484	58,589
Time deposits and funds sold	4,414	9,962	31,566
Total interest income	407,629	397,017	400,501
Interest Expenses			
Due depositors	247,939	279,135	321,933
Funds borrowed	61,175	46,911	36,090
Total interest expense	309,114	326,046	358,023
Net interest income	98,515	70,971	42,478
Provision for loan losses	13,652	7,819	13,014
Other Income:			
Service fees	29,460	21,366	17,715
Loan servicing fees	5,103	5,347	5,441
Loan organization fees	9,245	5,322	7,606
Other	6,046	5,097	6,296
Total other income	49,854	37,132	37,058
Other Expense:			
Salaries and employee benefits	47,452	39,356	32,846
Occupancy and equipment	14,485	12,882	11,845
Other	33,177	28,328	28,068
Total other expense	95,114	80,566	72,759
Gain (loss) on sale or revaluation of assets, net	68,919	8,444	(10,116)
Income (loss) before federal income taxes (benefits) and extraordinary items	108,522	28,162	(16,353)
Federal income taxes (benefits)	36,700	8,568	(5,573)
Income (loss) before extraordinary items	71,822	19,594	(10,780)
Extraordinary items, net of federal income tax effect	(1,168)	(739)	1,135
Net income (loss)	$ 70,654	$ 18,855	$ (9,645)
Earnings (Loss) per Share			
Income (loss) before extraordinary items	$7.22	$2.01	$(1.17)
Extraordinary items, net of federal income tax effect	(.11)	(.08)	.12
Net income (loss)	$7.11	$1.93	$(1.05)

FIG. 41.1   Sample Savings and Loan Association Statement of Operations
Source: Washington Mutual Savings Bank, 1986 Annual Report.

factors: (1) deregulation and highly volatile interest rates; and (2) engagement in nontraditional investing activities by the managements of many thrifts.

There was scant attention by the FASB to S&L accounting issues during the 1970s and early 1980s. The FASB began to focus on the industry's accounting problems in 1983, with the issuance of SFAS 72 (Bt7). Also, the EITF has devoted a significant amount of its effort to accounting issues that involve financial instruments and transactions, many of which are included in the later discussion of significant accounting issues. (Other EITF issues that pertain to S&Ls but are narrower in focus or occur infrequently are also mentioned at the end of this accounting section.)

The FASB has a major project in process on financial instruments and off-balance sheet financing. (See Chapter 21.) The accounting standards resulting from this project will probably have a major effect on S&L financial statements.

Financial Reporting

The AICPA Savings and Loan Committee is in the process of completely redrafting the Audit and Accounting Guide, *Audits of Savings and Loan Associations* (AICPA, 1987f), aiming to issue an exposure draft for comment in 1989. The Guide, revised several times since its initial release in 1973, is important since it covers most of the GAAP applicable to S&Ls.

The Audit Guide provides examples of financial statements for savings and loans. The following subsections briefly sketch the unique financial statement classifications and disclosures.

Balance Sheet. The balance sheet is unclassified, with assets listed more-or-less in their level of liquidity. Under SOP 86-1, *Reporting Repurchase—Reverse Repurchase Agreements and Mortgage-Backed Certificates by Savings and Loan Associations* (TP 10,400), which amends the S&L Audit Guide, mortgage-backed securities (MBS) are a separate line item, because they are more liquid than loans receivable and usually have less credit risk.

Variations will be found in the placement of and captions used for many of the newer financial investments, such as "interest only/principal only" mortgage-backed security strips (IO/POs) and residuals relating to collateralized mortgage obligations (CMOs).

Income Statement. Many S&Ls are not following the format in the Audit Guide (all income first, less interest expense, less general and administrative and other expenses). Instead, associations often disclose the components of interest income and interest expense, arriving at a net spread, or margin, This *net spread* is critical to outside analysts because it represents the more stable portion of the association's earnings (ignoring changes in the level of interest rates).

Figure 41.1 illustrates the format of a consolidated statement of operations used by many associations.

Statement of Cash Flows. Savings and loans are required to implement SFAS 95, *Statement of Cash Flows* (C25) in fiscal years beginning after July 15, 1988. This

| | | At June 30, | | | |
| | | 1987 | | 1986 | |
	Stated Rate	Amount	Percent	Amount	Percent
Balance by interest rate:					
Transaction accounts:					
NOW checking accounts	5.25	$ 28,507	1		
NOW checking accounts	5.70			$ 30,911	2
Statement savings accounts	5.50	17,464	1	6,558	
Money market accounts	6.70 - 7.15	445,434	21	300,575	22
Total transaction accounts		491,405	23	338,044	24
Certificate accounts:					
	5.25 - 6.25	154,864	7	180	
	6.26 - 8.25	1,044,041	48	494,792	36
	8.26 - 10.25	75,380	4	126,947	9
	10.26 - 12.25	238,939	11	242,672	18
	12.26 - 14.25	131,945	6	138,059	10
	14.26 - 16.25	46,116	2	48,821	4
	16.26 - 16.55	6,375		6,847	
Total certificate accounts		1,697,660	78	1,058,318	77
Net deferred losses on financial futures (see Note 5)		(11,298)	(1)	(10,968)	(1)
Commissions on brokered deposits (attributable to brokered deposits of $996,627 and $375,213 at June 30, 1987 and 1986, respectively)		(5,273)		(4,857)	
Total		1,681,089	77	1,042,493	76
Total savings deposits		$2,174,494	100	$1,380,537	100
Weighted average annual interest rate on total savings deposits		8.78%	(I)	9.55%	(I)
Remaining contractual maturity of certificate accounts:					
Under one year		$1,150,272	68	$ 530,800	50
One to three years		169,459	10	185,902	18
Three to five years		126,703	7	52,200	5
Five to seven years		86,022	5	105,085	10
Seven to ten years		121,963	7	128,294	12
Over ten years		43,241	3	56,037	5
Total		$1,697,660	100	$1,058,318	100
Interest expense on savings deposits consists of the following:					
NOW checking accounts		$ 1,800		$ 952	
Statement savings accounts		1,096		365	
Money market accounts		21,743		17,108	
Certificates		144,899		92,429	
Total		$ 169,538		$ 110,854	

(I) Included in the weighted average interest rate is the amortization of the net deferred losses on financial futures (see Note 5), amortization of commissions on brokered deposits and the effect of interest rate swap agreements (see Note 6).

At June 30, 1987 and 1986, pass-through certificates guaranteed by U.S. Government or instrumentalities with an aggregate market value of approximately $39,000 and $15,600, respectively, were pledged as collateral for certain certificate accounts.

FIG. 41.2   Sample Disclosure of Savings Deposits
Source: Franklin Savings Association, 1987 Annual Report.

should not be difficult for S&Ls, which traditionally have reported cash flows in a manner approximating the SFAS 95 format.

Footnotes. The significant accounting policies note should discuss:

* The carrying basis for debt investment securities (cost for long-term investments, or lower of cost or market for trading securities or those that the S&L will be unable to hold to maturity).
* Income recognition policy for loan origination fees, commitment fees, premiums, and discounts (essentially as prescribed by SFAS 91 (L20)).
* Method for determining the allowance for loan losses.
* Carrying basis for REO by foreclosure and real estate owned for development.
* Method of accounting for financial futures, various kinds of interest rate swaps, and similar financial instruments.
* Accounting for troubled debt restructurings.

The footnote disclosures for assets, liabilities, and commitments are relatively uncomplicated. Loans and mortgage-backed securities are often pledged as collateral for CDs and other borrowings, and the carrying amount of these pledged assets must be disclosed.

The maturity by year of savings deposits must also be disclosed. Savings deposits are often stratified by range of interest rate, as shown in the example in Figure 41.2.

For S&Ls that use repurchase and reverse repurchase agreements, the disclosure requirements of SOP 86-1, *Reporting Repurchase—Reverse Repurchase Agreements and Mortgage-Backed Certificates by Savings and Loan Associations* (TP 10,400), must be followed. (See Chapter 21).

The footnotes must also disclose the nature and amount of differences between GAAP net worth and regulatory capital as reported to the FHLBB.

RAP/GAAP Differences

The differences between regulatory accounting practices (RAP) and GAAP through the 1970s usually were not material to the financial statements. As discussed earlier, the deteriorating financial condition of many S&Ls in the early 1980s impelled the FHLBB to issue several accounting regulations that enhanced the financial position of an association as measured under RAP. As a result, the RAP basis financial statements often were materially different than GAAP basis financial statements.

One of the objectives of the CEBA regulations is to eliminate RAP elements that Congress believed reduced the credibility of S&L financial statements. CEBA is discussed in the earlier section entitled "Key Regulations."

Accounting Issues (Except for Business Combinations)

Valuation of Loans and Real Estate Owned. Since 1980, valuation issues regarding loans and REO have become significant, particularly as to properties that are located in economically distressed regions. Compounding the problem are S&Ls that make high-risk loans in an attempt to improve shrinking net interest spreads; these loans often become troubled loans or REO by foreclosure.

The S&L Audit Guide requires the allowance for losses on troubled or doubtful loans to be based on net realizable value. Net realizable value is the estimated sales price less: (1) costs to sell (such as sales commissions); (2) costs to complete; and (3) holding costs, such as taxes, insurance, and the cost of the association's equity and debt capital. Projected cash flows from a loan must be scheduled on a time line and then present-valued using the association's average cost of capital. The cost-of-capital portion of a loan loss allowance, while required for S&Ls, is not required for commercial banks.[3]

If it is probable, as defined by SFAS 5, *Accounting for Contingencies* (C59), that the association will foreclose on the loan, the allowance must be based on the loan's fair market value. Fair market value is defined by SFAS 15, *Accounting by Debtors and Creditors for Troubled Debt Restructurings* (D22), discussed in Chapter 28. Real estate acquired through foreclosure or through a troubled debt restructuring must be recorded at its fair market value, which becomes the association's new cost basis. Future evaluations of carrying value of the property are performed by using the net realizable method discussed above.

FRR 28, *Accounting for Loan Losses by Registrants Engaged in Lending Activities* (§ 401.09), provides the SEC's interpretation of SFAS 5 and SFAS 15. The FRR challenges whether loans or real estate acquired through foreclosure might be overvalued. FRR 28 requires the following:

1. A systematic methodology in determining the amount of loan losses to be reported, with adequate documentation.

2. Accounting for loan collateral as if repossessed, whether it is repossessed formally or substantively. The SEC is concerned that certain loans are actually "in-substance foreclosures" because

   a. The debtor has little or no equity in the collateral, considering its current fair value; *and*

   b. Proceeds for repayment of the loan can be expected to come only from the operation or sale of the collateral; *and*

   c. The debtor has either

      (1) Formally or effectively abandoned control of the collateral to the creditor, *or*

      (2) Retained control of the collateral but, because of the current financial condition of the debtor, or the economic prospects for the debtor and/or the collateral in the foreseeable future, it is doubtful that the debtor will be able to rebuild equity in the collateral or otherwise repay the loan.

3. The valuation of foreclosed (actual or in-substance) property is based on price quotes from an *active market*. According to the SEC, an active market does not have to mean that there is a willing buyer *and* a willing seller. An active market simply means that similar property

---

[3] As of mid-1988, the AICPA had in process an SOP on *The Use of Discounting in Determining Loan Loss Allowances*, aimed at rectifying the diversity of practice among various financial institutions. The SOP, if finalized as drafted at July 22, 1988, would require that in determining loan loss allowances, financial institutions (including S&Ls) should *not* discount future cash payments expected to be received on loans that are not *collateral-dependent*. Collateral-dependent loans – those whose repayment is expected to come only from the operation, development and/or sale of the collateral – should be evaluated as in-substance foreclosures under SFAS 15 (D22).

is being sold, even if the sales are distress sales. If there is not an active market, FRR 28 permits fair value to be derived based on discounted cash flows. However, the discount rate must be a risk-based rate of return, and the projected cash flows cannot be based on optimistic forecasts as to market improvement.

In Issue 87-5, *Troubled Debt Restructurings: Interrelationship between FASB Statement No. 15 and the AICPA Savings and Loan Guide*, the EITF debated whether the loans that went through a troubled debt restructuring in which the interest rate was reduced below the cost of funds should be valued under SFAS 15 (with no loss necessary) or the S&L Audit Guide's net realizable value requirement, which would indicate a loss. The consensus was reached that once a loan becomes troubled, its net realizable value must be evaluated continuously (theoretically, daily). The reasoning process would seem to indicate there is no conflict between SFAS 15 and the Audit Guide because: (1) a loan that went through a troubled debt restructuring had to have been a troubled loan; (2) the net realizable value test should have been performed prior to the restructuring; and (3) if any allowance was needed to reduce the carrying value of the loan to its net realizable value, that allowance should have been set up prior to the restructuring. Thereafter, the SFAS 15 evaluation can be made.

Creative transactions have evolved in an attempt to remove troubled loans or REO from a S&L's books with little or no loss recognized. In EITF Issue 87-18, *Use of Zero Coupon Bonds in a Troubled Debt Restructuring*, the following facts were assumed:

* Debtor's outstanding loan is $339,000.
* Debtor enters into a troubled debt restructuring with the creditor.
* Under the terms of the restructuring,
  – Debtor liquidates a portion of the collateral for $139,000 and remits the proceeds to the creditor.
  – The remaining debt of $200,000 is restructured to provide "principal" of $160,000 due in 10 years. Interest is due annually at 2.5% over the 10 years. Total interest paid will be $40,000.
  – The debtor sells some of the remaining collateral and buys $100,000 of zero coupon bonds that will mature at a value equal to each year's debt service requirement.
  – The zero coupon bonds are held by the savings and loan and are the sole collateral for the new $200,000 debt.

The acounting question is whether the zero coupon bonds have effectively been received in exchange for the loan receivable. If so, SFAS 15 requires the asset received to be carried at its fair market value ($100,000) which would require the creditor to recognize a loss of $100,000 ($200,000 loan receivable less $100,000 of zero coupon bonds received in exchange).

The EITF reached a consensus that the creditor should write off the loan receivable, set up the zero coupon bonds at their fair market value, and recognize a loss on the transaction of $100,000.

In issue 87-19, *Substituted Debtors in a Troubled Debt Restructuring*, the EITF addressed a topic similar to Issue 87-18. Issue 87-19 uses the following facts:

- Creditor and debtor agree to a troubled debt restructuring of a debtor's home mortgage loan receivable of $208,864.

- Debtor will pay creditor $575 per month for 30 years. Total payments will be $207,000 (approximating $208,864).

- The debtor sells the house for $70,000 on a contract for deed. The seller (debtor) retains legal title to the house.

- New homeowner's payments are $575 per month for 30 years; his payments are made directly to the creditor.

The issue is whether the creditor has a new loan (from the new homeowner) in settlement of the old loan, or whether debtors have been substituted. If the creditor has a new loan, the excess of the mortgage loan receivable over the market value of the new receivable must be recognized as a loss. However, if debtors on the $208,684 loan have simply been substituted, then a loss would not need to be recognized.

The EITF reached a consensus that the creditor must recognize a loss on the disposition of the original loan and record the new receivable at its fair value. SFAS 15 requires the difference between the carrying value of the original loan receivable and the fair value of the new loan receivable to be recognized as a loss (D22.124). Some EITF members also believed that the loss must be recognized because there was an in-substance foreclosure under D22.130 as well as under the FRR 28.

Loans Held for Sale. Mortgage bankers, or mortgage banking operations of S&Ls, originate loans with the intent of selling them as quickly as possible. These loans should be carried at the lower of cost or market until they are sold. If the association subsequently decides to hold the loans as long-term investments, the loans are transferred to a long-term investment category at the then lower of cost or market.

Sometimes an association will decide to sell certain loans that were classified as long-term investments. When this decision is made, the loans should be carried at the lower of cost or market after the decision date.

Not exactly a loan held for sale but in the same genre are *Equity Certificates of Deposit*, discussed in EITF Issue 84-31. These CDs provide the investor with a basic return plus an amount that is contingent on the performance of specific assets (e.g., a specified loan or group of loans) held by the S&L. The EITF concluded that the contingent interest should be recorded as expense during the same period that the increased value of the related asset is recorded. If the expense accrual were made earlier, the asset would effectively be subjected to a writedown. By the same token, the asset value should not be increased without reflecting the CD holder's share.

Sale of Loans and Mortgage-Backed Securities. Although intuitively it would seem easy to decide if a loan (or MBS) had been sold, the determination is often quite complex. SFAS 77, *Reporting by Transferors for Transfers of Receivables with Recourse* (R20), is the primary authoritative guidance for sale transactions including participation agreements (i.e., transfers of specified interests in a group of receivables). Although SFAS 77 is limited to transfers with recourse, accountants often look to it for guidance on transfers without recourse.

Face amount of loans sold	$10,000,000
Weighted average maturity	360 months
Weighted average coupon — received by seller from mortgagors	10.75%
Weighted average coupon — received by buyer from seller	10.10%
Stated servicing fee	None
Normal servicing fee	.30%
Prepayments assumed*	None
Monthly cash flows to seller, net of normal servicing (10.45% interest)	$ 91,100
Monthly cash flows to buyer	(88,497)
Monthly excess cash flows	$ 2,603
Excess servicing fee receivable to be capitalized (present value of 360 monthly cash flows of $2,603, discounted at 10.10% (buyer's implicit yield))	$294,134

* Refer to SFAS 91 (L20) for discussion of prepayment treatment options.

FIG. 41.3   Calculation of Excess Mortgage Servicing Fee

SFAS 77 applies to transfers that *purport* to be sales of receivables. In other words, if the transaction is not in the form of a sale, SFAS 77 does not apply. Only transferors, not transferees, are covered.

A transfer is recognized as a sale if all of the following criteria are met (R20.105):

- The transferor surrenders control of the future economic benefits of the receivables.
- The transferor's obligation, under the recourse provisions of the sales agreement, can be reasonably estimated. Generally, the transferor must have past experience with the recourse provisions so that a reasonable estimate can be made. Also, the current transferred receivables should have characteristics similar to prior transferred receivables so that the transferor has relevant prior experience.
- The transferee cannot require the transferor to repurchase the receivables, except for the recourse provisions of the agreement.

If the transfer meets the above criteria, the transaction must be accounted for as a sale. The sales price must be adjusted for all probable adjustments (as defined by SFAS 5, *Accounting for Contingencies* (C59)).

Mortgage servicing rights retained. SFAS 65, *Accounting for Certain Mortgage Banking Activities* (Mo4), also requires the sales price to be adjusted for the difference between the present value of the actual servicing fee and the present value of the *normal servicing fee* over the life of the loans. This difference is capitalized and is amortized over the life of the loans as an adjustment to servicing income. This results in future servicing income approximating the servicing income that would have been earned under a normal servicing fee. An example of how to calculate excess servicing is shown in Figure 41.3.

The normal service fee requirement of SFAS 65 resulted in many practice problems during 1985–1987. Most have been resolved by the FASB and the EITF, although the challenge of properly estimating future prepayments continues. After the question was debated in EITF Issue 85-26, the FASB resolved the definition of normal service fee by issuing TB 87-3, *Accounting for Mortgage Servicing Fees and Rights* (effective for transactions entered into on or after December 31, 1987). The TB defines a normal service fee for loans sold to GNMA, FHLMC, or FNMA as the minimum servicing fee used by GNMA, FHLMC, and FNMA for similar loans. In addition, if the normal service fees are expected to be less than the estimated servicing costs, the expected loss should be recognized at the time the loans are sold.

If loans are sold directly to private sector investors, the seller retains the servicing of the loan, and the loans and servicing arrangements are comparable with loans and servicing arrangements of the secondary market-makers, the seller should use the same normal servicing fee rate that would have been used if the loans had been sold or securitized by one of the secondary market makers.

TB 87-3 also discusses how to account for the capitalized cost of a purchased servicing right when a mortgage loan is refinanced. The TB concludes that the enterprise should not consider estimated future net servicing income (servicing revenue in excess of servicing costs) from the refinanced (new) loan for the purpose of amortizing any capitalized cost related to acquisition of the mortgage service rights for the loans that were refinanced. In other words, the remaining capitalized purchased servicing that relates to the refinanced loan should be written off. The rationale for this conclusion is that the mortgage servicing right represents a contractual relationship between the servicer and the investor in the loan, not between the servicer and the borrower. The mortgage service right cost is amortized in proportion to, and over the period of, the net servicing income from the loans whose sale (with servicing retained) created the service asset.

In Issue 86-38, *Implications of Mortgage Prepayments on Amortization of Servicing Rights,* the EITF addressed how to adjust the excess servicing fee receivable for changes in prepayment assumptions. The consensus holds that if actual prepayments are greater than assumed prepayments, the excess service fee receivable must be reduced to the present value of the currently projected cash flows, discounted however at the original discount rate.

If prepayments decrease, a new (higher) discount rate should be calculated that results in the present value of the currently projected excess cash flows being equal to the recorded excess service fee receivable. (See Figure 41.3 for an example of the calculation of the excess service fee receivable.) The favorable change is recognized prospectively over the remaining life of the loans using this higher discount rate.

There have been several EITF Issues that have addressed whether a "sale" of loans has actually occurred. Some of the more significant issues are discussed in the following subsections.

Convertible mortgages. Issue 87-25, *Sale of Convertible, Adjustable-Rate Mortgages With Contingent Repayment Agreement* deals with mortgages that allow the mortgagor to convert the Convertible Adjustable Rate Mortgages (CARM) to a fixed-rate loan during a specified period, if the mortgagor meets certain conditions and pays a conversion fee. The new fixed-rate loan will bear a slightly higher interest rate than similar nonconvertible loans available at the time of conversion. The conversion fee paid by the CARM mortgagor will be less than the origination fees charged on a standard new mortgage. If the CARMs are transferred from the originating S&L to an investor with an agreement that the originating association will repurchase them if converted, a question arises as to whether the transfer is a sale.

The EITF was unable to reach a consensus on whether the transfer to the investor is a sale or borrowing. The FASB staff believes that the transfer should be accounted for as a borrowing; the SEC observer believes that if sale treatment is applied and the CARMs are originated and sold simultaneously, any gains should be deferred and amortized as a commitment fee under the provisions as SFAS 91 (L20.107).

Partial participations. EITF Issue 84-21, *Sale of a Loan With a Partial Participation Retained,* addressed transactions in which all principal payments but only some of the interest payments on a loan were sold with the seller retaining the remainder. For example, the loans might have a weighted average coupon of 14% but the buyer will only receive the current market rate of 12%. The 2% differential is the partial participation retained by the seller.

The EITF considered whether the present value of the retained interest payments should be included in the gain computation and recognized immediately, or whether the interest income should be recognized as it is received over the remaining life of the loan. The consensus reached was that the S&L Audit Guide requires the retained interest income to be included in the gain computation. (See Figure 41.3 to observe how the retained interest affects the gain computation.)

EITF Issue 85-13, *Sale of Mortgage Service Rights on Mortgages Owned By Others,* questions how to account for the subsequent sale of the partial interest participation (i.e., in the future interest income stream) retained by the seller. In the facts given, the subsequent sale occurred soon after the original sale. The EITF questioned whether the gain should be computed in the same manner as the gain on the original sale of the related loans, and whether this gain plus the original gain should be limited to the gain that would be recognized if the servicing rights were to be sold outright.

The EITF reached a consensus that

* Gain recognition is appropriate at the sale date.
* There are difficulties in measuring the amount of the gain.
* Accounting rules do not specify an upper limit on the computed sales price. However, all information should be considered when computing the sales price, including the amount of the gain that would be recognized if the servicing rights were to be sold outright for a fixed cash price.

Senior/subordinated first-out loan participations. In sales of senior/subordinated first-out loan participations, the association's right to cash flows based on its participation is subordinated to a third party's interest. Therefore, all cash receipts go to the third party until the third party's receivable is satisfied. Thereafter, cash receipts are retained by the association. The accounting issue is whether the recourse obligations of the transferor can be reasonably estimated under SFAS 77 (R20.105b) so that sales treatment is applicable. The senior/subordinated structure increases the difficulty of estimating the recourse obligations.

Generally, most accountants would conclude that the recourse obligations of a senior/subordinated structure can be reasonably estimated when the transfer involves single family loans; but this is not necessarily so for commercial loans, resulting in varying treatments.

Transfers collateralized by commercial properties. During 1988, the AICPA Savings and Loan Associations Committee began consideration of whether it is appropriate to permit the transfer of commercial mortgages (and securitized forms thereof) to be eligible for sale treatment, given the greater difficulty of reasonably determining obligations under recourse provisions. While the committee's draft did not preclude sale treatment under stipulated conditions, the matter has not yet been resolved by AcSEC.

Sale of Mortgage Servicing Rights. When an S&L sells loan servicing rights on loans it does not own, a gain (or loss) is recognized. AcSEC concluded in 1982, however, that if the S&L owns the loans, no gain should be recorded. Instead, the proceeds are to be deferred and the gain amortized into income over the life of the loans.

Loan portfolio servicing may be sold with a fractional equity participation (e.g., 10%) retained. Although the sale of servicing cannot result in a gain if the entire ownership in the loans is retained, income may be recognized if the equity retention is small.

Often there is a time lag between the date the sales agreement is signed and the closing date when payment is made and title to the servicing rights is passed. This time lag might be required to notify the borrowers of a change in servicers, to obtain approval from guarantors (e.g., FNMA, FHLMC, GNMA), and to transfer the loan documents and servicing files from the seller to the buyer. The accounting issue is whether the sale can be recognized on the contract date, or whether sale recognition must be deferred until the closing date.

The sale can be recognized on the contract date if the earnings process is complete as of the contract date. The substance of the transaction will govern, using the following guidelines:

- The loans to which the servicing relates are specifically identified.
- The buyer demonstrates a commitment to make the purchase as of the contract date. The downpayment should be at least 10% of the sales price. There must be reasonable assurance the buyer has the financial capacity to pay the remaining amount at closing.
- The buyer is already approved as a servicer by the guarantor for the kind of servicing involved in the transaction. If the buyer has not previously been approved as a servicer, there can be no assurance that such approval will be obtained. Therefore, recognizing a sale before the closing date is inappropriate.
- The time interval between the contract date and the closing date is reasonable. The interval should be no greater than needed to accomplish the necessary closing steps; generally, it should not exceed six months.
- All the risks and rewards relating to the servicing rights must be transferred to the buyer as of the contract date. These include the risks and costs related to delinquency, foreclosure, and prepayment as well as the benefits including service fees, ancillary fees (such as late charge penalties), and the benefits from collecting and holding escrow funds.

- No repurchase options should exist. The seller's replacement of a loan that prepays within a stipulated time period, or that has subsequently become delinquent, is prohibited.
- The earnings process must be virtually complete. The seller cannot be obligated to perform significant activities after the contract date to earn the profit. The seller's obligations beyond the contract date should be limited to assisting in the physical transfer of records, notifying the various parties affected, and continuing under a subservicing agreement to collect monthly mortgagor payments, forward payments and related accounting reports to the buyer, collect escrow deposits, and pay taxes and insurance from escrow during the transitional period. Any compensation received by the seller for this subservicing activity should be based on a fee per loan to cover incremental costs, and should *not* be a percentage of the principal balance outstanding.

If the sale cannot be recognized until the closing date, the cash received at the contract date should be accounted for as a deposit until the closing date.

Allocation of purchased servicing rights to loans later sold. EITF Issue 86-39, *Gains From the Sale of Mortgage Loans With Servicing Rights Retained,* deals with the purchase of mortgage loans with the intent to subsequently sell the loans but retain the servicing rights.

SFAS 65 (Mo4) requires allocation of a portion of the purchase price to the mortgage servicing right under certain conditions. If the related loan is sold at a gain, however, the gain must first be offset against the cost of the servicing rights. While some EITF members questioned the logic of this offset in light of changes in the mortgage servicing market since SFAS 65 was issued, the consensus was that SFAS 65 requires it regardless of the reason for the gain.

Implications of mortgage prepayments. EITF Issue 86-38, *Implications of Mortgage Prepayments on Amortization of Servicing Rights,* addressed how unanticipated prepayments should affect the carrying value of purchased servicing rights. A consensus was reached that if projected future net servicing income is less than the capitalized cost of servicing rights, the asset must be written down. The future amortization rate is changed prospectively, consistent with the change in expected future net servicing income.

The projected servicing revenue is based on future cash flows and can be either undiscounted or discounted, consistent with the method used to evaluate the entity's other intangible assets.

Subservicing agreements. A servicer may decide to sell its servicing rights to an unrelated party which may not wish to actually service the accounts, and which therefore must arrange for subservicing, that is, having another party perform the necessary processing. This transaction may be done because the purchaser concludes that even with payment for subservicing, there is a satisfactory return on the "investment" in the servicing rights.

In Issue 87–34, *Sale of Mortgage Servicing Rights With a Subservicing Agreement,* the EITF considered a situation in which the seller agreed to do the subservicing for the buyer, and the seller-subservicer's cost of performance would be less than the fee received. The EITF consensus held that this transaction is not a sale of servicing, but rather is a financing, with the "sale" proceeds deemed a borrowing. The EITF further concluded that if the fees to be received were less than subservicing costs, a loss should be recognized at the time of the "sale."

Trading Accounts. Historically, S&Ls held investment securities to maturity. Thus there was no question as to whether a security was being held for investment purposes or for trading purposes. Since trading of securities was rare, the AICPA S&L Audit Guide did not address it.

Beginning in the 1980s, several factors caused a change in the holding philosophy. Large movements in interest rates sometimes resulted in significant unrealized gains, and some associations realized these gains to strengthen regulatory net worth. Also, evolution of the industry away from traditional product lines resulted in some associations instituting treasury or capital markets departments, often designated as profit centers, that actively managed the investment portfolio.

Although S&Ls sometimes will choose to realize gains on investment securities, they usually have a policy of not selling at a loss. Since most S&Ls have adequate liquidity to hold onto below-market securities, they are able to meet the accounting requirements for cost basis accounting: they have the intent and the ability to hold securities which if presently sold would result in a loss.

Notwithstanding an S&L's intent and ability to hold, some accountants and regulatory agencies believe that a significant volume of security sales demonstrates that at least some securities should be classified as trading securities, to be carried at market or at the lower of cost or market. To date, no definitive guidelines have been issued on such classification for S&Ls.

If an association is deemed to be trading securities, the AICPA 1984 Accounting and Audit Guide, *Audits of Banks* (AICPA, 1984c) is often followed. The Bank Audit Guide states that trading securities are to be carried at market value, and the unrealized appreciation or depreciation is recognized in income in the current period. The Bank Audit Guide states:

> When securities are purchased, a bank should determine whether they are intended for its trading or its investment account. A bank should not record newly purchased securities in a suspense account and later determine the category. Recording the securities in either the trading or investment account should be documented with management approvals. [p. 40]

Concerning transfers between the investment and trading accounts, the Bank Audit Guide states:

> A bank may also transfer securities from its investment securities account to its trading account, although that also should be unusual. The securities should be recorded at market value at the date of transfer and thereafter should be treated as trading securities. A writedown from cost to estimated market value should be charged to investment security losses at the time of transfer. Recognition of a gain from write-up of cost to estimated market value should be deferred until final disposition of the securities, since the particular securities were not designated as part of the trading account at the original acquisition date. Such gains, when recognized, should be reported as investment security gains. [p. 41]

In mid-1988, the AICPA Savings and Loan Associations Committee completed drafting of a practice bulletin that would provide extensive guidance on distinguishing between trading and investment activities of S&Ls. While the draft would allow application of the guidance on an individual transaction basis, its intent is to comprehend the overall objectives of the S&L and the strategies followed by the S&L in their attainment. Thus, there will be no categorical distinctions made. In early August 1988, AcSEC asked the committee to redraft the paper into the form of an SOP.

Investments in Mutual Funds. EITF Issue 86-40, *Investments in Open-End Mutual Funds That Invest in U.S. Government Securities,* addresses the accounting for thrifts' investments in mutual funds. To meet liquidity requirements, thrifts may invest in certain open-end mutual funds that invest only in short-to-medium term obligations of the U.S. government or its agencies or in government-guaranteed obligations. The accounting issue is the appropriate basis at which the financial institution should report its investment in this type of mutual fund. Under SFAS 12, *Accounting for Certain Marketable Securities* (I89), an investment in a marketable equity security, which includes such mutual fund shares, is reported at the lower of cost or market. But if the underlying government securities were instead owned directly by a financial institution having the ability and intent to hold the securities to maturity, the assets would be carried at amortized cost.

The Task Force reached a consensus that the financial institution should follow SFAS 12. The reasoning is that the financial institution does not have the ability to control whether the underlying securities in the fund are held to maturity, as this decision is made by the fund's management.

Acquisition, Development, and Construction Activities. Some financial institutions have entered into real estate acquisition, development, and construction (ADC) loans in which they have virtually the same risk and potential rewards as those of owners or joint venturers, and therefore accounting for such arrangements as loans is not appropriate. To address this issue, AcSEC issued a series of Notices to Practitioners (NTPs). The third notice was published in *The CPA Letter* (February 10, 1986 and since incorporated into AcSEC Practice Bulletin 1, Section 1; TP 12,010.09). The primary content of the NTP, which applies if the lender participates in expected residual profit in ADC loans, is discussed in the following subsections.[4]

General. Expected residual profit is the amount of profit above a reasonable amount of interest and fees earned by the lender for the use of funds. The extent of profit participations and their forms vary. For example, assume that the contractual interest on a condominium project is a fair market rate and the expected sales prices are sufficient to cover at least principal and accrued interest. If the lender shares in an agreed proportion (e.g., 20%, 50%, or 90%) of any profit on sale of the units, this is a direct form of profit participation.

A slightly different form of arrangement, however, may produce approximately the same result. For example, the interest rate may be set at a level higher than in the preceding case, and the lender may receive a smaller percentage of any profit on sales of units. Thus, a greater portion of the expected sales price is required to cover the

---

[4] ADC loans have also been discussed extensively by the EITF in Issues 84-4 and 86-21.

contractual accrued interest, leaving a smaller amount to be allocated between the lender and the owner. In those circumstances, the lender's share of expected residual profits may be approximately the same as in the preceding case. The same result may also occur if the interest rate is set at even a higher level and the lender does not share at all in a proportion of profit on sale of the units. A fourth variation might be one in which the lender shares in gross rents or net cash flow from a commercial project, such as an office building or an apartment complex.

Equity-type ADC arrangement. In addition to the lender's direct or indirect participation in expected residual profits, these ownership-type ADC arrangements usually have most of the following characteristics (paraphrased from the NTP):

- The financial institution agrees to provide all or substantially all necessary funds to acquire, develop, or construct the property. The borrower has title to but little or no equity in the underlying property.
- The financial institution funds the commitment or origination fees, or both, by including them in the amount of the loan.
- The financial institution funds all or substantially all interest and fees during the term of the loan by adding them to the loan balance.
- The financial institution's only security is the ADC project. The institution has no recourse to other assets of the borrower, and the borrower does not guarantee the debt.
- The financial institution's recovery of its investment in the project is dependent on: (1) the sale of the property to independent third parties; (2) refinancing by the borrower with another source; or (3) the property being placed in service and generating sufficient net cash flow to service principal and interest on the debt.
- Foreclosure during the project development as a result of delinquency is unlikely because the borrower usually is not required to make any payments until completion. Therefore, the loan normally cannot become delinquent.

Loan-type ADC arrangements. Even though the lender participates in expected residual profit, the following characteristics suggest that the risks and rewards of an ADC arrangement are more like those associated with a loan (paraphrased from the NTP):

- The lender participates in less than a majority of the expected residual profit.
- The borrower has an equity investment substantial to the project that is not funded by the lender. The investment may be in the form of cash payments by the borrower or contribution by the borrower of land or other assets. The value attributed to the land or other assets should be net of any encumbrances, and should exclude value expected to be added to the land by future development or construction. Recently acquired property contributed by the borrower generally should be valued at no higher than cost.
- Either (1) the lender has recourse to substantial tangible, salable assets (with a determinable sales value) of the borrower (other than the ADC project) that are not pledged as collateral under other loans; or (2) the borrower has provided to the lender an irrevocable letter of credit from a creditworthy, independent third party for a substantial amount of the loan over the entire term of the loan.

- A take-out commitment for the full amount of the financial institution's loans has been obtained from a creditworthy, independent third party. If the take-out commitment is conditional, the conditions should be reasonable and their attainment probable.

- Noncancellable sales contracts or lease commitments from creditworthy, independent third parties are currently in effect that should provide sufficient net cash flow on completion of the project to service normal loan amortization. Any associated conditions should be probable of attainment.

Personal guarantees. Some ADC arrangements include personal guarantees of the borrower and/or a third party. AcSEC believes that the existence of a personal guarantee alone rarely provides a sufficient basis for concluding that an ADC arrangement should be accounted for as a loan. Where the substance of the personal guarantee and the ability of the guarantor cover a substantial proportion of the loan, accounting treatment for the ADC arrangement as a loan may be justified. The substance of a personal guarantee depends on (1) the ability of the guarantor to perform under the guarantee, (2) the practicality of enforcing the guarantee in the applicable jurisdiction, and (3) a demonstrable intent to enforce the guarantee.

Examples of personal guarantees that have a likelihood of being honored include those supported by liquid assets placed in escrow, pledged marketable securities, or irrevocable letters of credit from a creditworthy, independent third party or parties in amounts sufficient to provide the necessary equity support for an ADC arrangement to be considered a loan. In the absence of such support, financial statements of and other information from the guarantor may be considered to determine the guarantor's ability to perform. Because of the high-risk nature of many ADC arrangements, AcSEC believes financial statements that are current and complete, include appropriate disclosures, and are reviewed or audited by independent CPAs, are the most helpful.

Particular emphasis should be placed on the following factors in evaluating a guarantor's financial statements:

- There should be evidence of sufficient liquidity to perform under the guarantee. There may be little substance to a personal guarantee if the guarantor's net worth consists primarily of assets pledged to secure other debt.

- If the financial statements do not disclose and quantify guarantees provided by the guarantor to other projects, inquiries should be made as to their existence. Also, it may be appropriate to obtain written representation from the guarantor regarding other contingent liabilities.

The enforceability of the guarantee in the applicable jurisdiction should also be determined. Even if the guarantee is legally enforceable, business reasons that might preclude the financial institution from using the guarantee should be assessed. Those business reasons could include: (1) the length of time required to enforce a personal guarantee; (2) whether it is normal business practice in that jurisdiction to enforce guarantees on similar transactions; and (3) whether the lender must choose between pursuing the guarantee or the project's assets. Written representations from management of the S&L regarding its intent to enforce personal guarantees may be advisable.

Sweat equity. Some ADC arrangements recognize value for the builder's efforts after inception of the arrangement. This is sometimes referred to as "sweat equity." AcSEC believes that sweat equity is not at risk by the borrower at the inception of an ADC project, and therefore it should not be considered a substantial equity investment on the part of the borrower in determining whether the ADC arrangement should be treated as a loan.

Accounting guidance. In the interest of more uniformity in accounting for ADC arrangements, AcSEC recommends the following:

- If the lender is expected to receive over 50% of the expected residual profit (as previously defined) from the project, the lender should account for income or loss from the arrangement as a real estate investment as specified by SFAS 67, *Accounting for Costs and Initial Rental Operation of Real Estate Projects* (Re2), and SFAS 66, *Accounting for Sales of Real Estate* (Re1).

- If the lender is expected to receive 50% or less of the expected residual profit, the entire arrangement should be accounted for either as a loan or as a real estate joint venture, depending on the circumstances. At least one of the four characteristics (see "Loan-type ADC arrangements," above) that suggest the risks and rewards are similar to a loan, or a qualifying personal guarantee, should be present for the arrangement to be accounted for as a loan. Otherwise, real estate joint venture accounting would be appropriate.

- In the case of a loan, interest and fees may be recognized in accordance with SFAS 91 (L20) subject to recoverability. SOP 75-2, *Accounting Practices of Real Estate Investment Trusts* (TP 10,060), and the AICPA S&L Audit Guide provide guidance that may be relevant in assessing the recoverability of loan amounts and accrued interest.

- In the case of a real estate joint venture, the provisions of SOP 78-9, *Accounting for Investments in Real Estate Ventures* (TP 10,240), and SFAS 34, *Capitalization of Interest Cost* (I69), as amended by SFAS 58, *Capitalization of Interest Cost in Financial Statements That Include Investments Accounted for by the Equity Method,* provide guidance for such accounting. In particular, SOP 78-9 (TP 10,240.34) provides guidance on the circumstances under which interest income should not be recognized.

ADC arrangements accounted for as investments in real estate or joint ventures should be combined and reported in the balance sheet separately from those ADC arrangements accounted for as loans.

Some accountants believe that in those instances where the lender is expected to receive a nominal portion of the expected residual profits, the arrangement should qualify for loan treatment without having to meet any of the four loan-type qualifying characteristics or a qualifying personal guarantee.

Other considerations. The lender may transfer its share of the expected residual profit in a project to the borrower or a third party for cash or other consideration. If there is a sale of the expected residual profit in an ADC arrangement accounted for as a loan, AcSEC believes that the proceeds from the sale should be recognized prospectively as additional interest over the remaining term of the loan. The expected residual profit is considered additional compensation to the lender, and the sale results in a quantification of the profit. If there is a sale of the expected residual profit in an ADC arrangement accounted for as an investment in real estate or a joint venture, gain recognition, if any, is appropriate only if the criteria of SFAS 66 (Rel) are met. (For example, if the financial institution was the seller of the property at the initiation of the project, gain recognition, if any, should be determined by reference to SFAS 66.) Consideration must be given to the entire ADC arrangement, including continuing relationships between the financial institution and the project (such as recourse to the S&L for properties that fail to operate satisfactorily).

The terms of an ADC arrangement may subsequently change as a result of renegotiation of the terms; consequently, the accounting treatment should be periodically reassessed. An ADC arrangement originally classified as an investment or a joint venture could subsequently become treated as a loan if the risk to the lender were to diminish significantly and the lender was not to receive over 50% of the expected residual profit in the project. The lender would have to demonstrate a change in the facts, not merely the eventual absence of, or reduced participation in, the expected residual profit. For instance, risk may be reduced if a valid take-out commitment from a qualified lender is obtained and all of its conditions are met, thus assuring the primary lender recovery of its funds.

If the lender, on the other hand, assumes further risks and/or rewards in an ADC arrangement, for example, by releasing collateral that had supported a guarantee of over 50% of the loan, the lender's position may change to that of an investor in real estate. However, neither improvement nor deterioration in the economic prospects for the project by itself justifies a change in the initial classification of an ADC arrangement. A change in classification of an ADC arrangement should be evaluated based on the guidance in the Notice to Practitioners, should be accounted for prospectively, and should be supported by appropriate documentation.

If an ADC arrangement accounted for as a real estate joint venture continues into a permanent phase with the project generating a positive cash flow and paying debt service currently, income should be recognized in accordance with SOP 78-9 (TP 10,240).

Participation in ADC loans. Many participations in loans are bought and sold by other financial institutions. The accounting treatment for a purchase that involves ADC arrangements should be based on a review of the transaction at the time of purchase in accordance with the guidance in the third Notice to Practitioners. A participant therefore would look to its individual percentage of expected residual profit; for example, a participant who will not share, directly or indirectly, in any of the expected residual profit will not look to the classification criteria in the NTP. Any reciprocal transactions between institutions, including multiparty transactions, should be viewed together and accounted for in accordance with their combined substance.

Regulatory ADC requirements. In 1985, FSLIC issued a regulation entitled *Accounting for Acquisition, Development and Construction Loans* (Regulation 571.17). This regulation follows the guidance given in the first Notice to Practitioners. As such, the regulation is not as comprehensive and stringent as the accounting guidance set forth in the AICPA's third notice.

In 1987, the FHLBB issued a proposed rule in which it commented that insured institutions are expected to follow the guidance of the accounting profession in determining when an ADC transaction is deemed to be a loan and when it is a real estate investment or a joint venture. This proposal has been effectively enacted by the application of CEBA requirements, discussed at the outset of this chapter.

SEC views on ADC loans. Although the third notice was acceptable to the SEC, the SEC Observer at the February 1986 EITF meeting did not believe that the notice should be applied only to new arrangements. He stated that if application of the third notice would result in a different balance sheet classification of ADC arrangements held at December 31, 1985, the financial statements issued for periods after December 31, 1985 should use the revised classification, without restating prior years.

Mortgage Loan Modifications. In 1982 AcSEC addressed how to account for a modification of a mortgage loan receivable. In the situation reviewed, the remaining future payments were altered by agreement between the mortgagor and mortgagee. A common modification involved the S&L reducing the interest rate by half if the mortgagor would double his monthly payment.

AcSEC decided that such a modification would require a loss to be recognized if the present value of the new (modified) future cash flows is less than the present value of the old (original) future cash flows, both discounted at market rate as of the modification date.

The EITF also addressed this subject in Issue 84-19, *Mortgage Loan Payment Modifications.* The facts here were that the mortgagor would increase his periodic loan payments by 50% and, in exchange, the mortgagee would reduce the principal balance of the loan by 1% after each 12 consecutive increased payments.

The EITF reached a consensus that if it is probable the mortgagor will continue to make the increased payments, the mortgagee should accrue the forgiveness expense over the period in which the increased payments are made.

Pass-Through Certificates. In the early 1970s, GNMA, FNMA, and FHLMC developed pass-through and mortgage participation certificates (PCs).[5] With a PC, the certificate holder owns an undivided equity interest in the pool of loans that underlie the mortgage-backed security (MBS). Each certificate holder receives a proportionate share of cash flows from the underlying loans. The PC program has been very successful in creating a secondary market with tremendous liquidity.

The pass-through securities were developed to allow S&Ls to package their loans into mortgage-backed securities easily convertible to cash. The accounting issue faced was whether a sale had occurred when the loans were exchanged for mortgage-backed securities, with gain or loss recognition required. The AICPA Savings and Loan Committee and major accounting firms agreed that the exchange should be accounted for as a sale unless the loans and the MBS have certain uniform character- istics, as defined by FHLBB R-Memorandum 49-1, *FHLMC Swap Transactions Which Qualify as "Reciprocal Sales of Mortgage Loans."* These characteristics are:

- Both the sale of the mortgage loans and the sale of the PCs must be at par.

---

[5] See note 1.

- After establishing the original pool of mortgage loans, neither the mortgage loan sellers nor FHLMC (unless exercising its rights under warranty requirements) may make any substitution for loans constituting the original pool.

- When purchasing a pool of mortgages from a group of institutions, that is, a multiple-seller swap transaction, a minimum of 80% of the number of loans constituting the pool must bear interest rates with a range no greater than 200 basis points (2%) between the lowest rate and the highest rate in the pool.

Organization Expenses. Start-up thrift institutions generally spend up to two years in an organization stage. During this time, they file applications with regulatory bodies, sell stock, issue debt, and obtain FSLIC insurance. The costs incurred may be grouped into the following categories:

1. Traditional organization costs, such as legal fees, printing fees, and application fees that are required to establish the thrift's legal structure.
2. Preopening costs that include rent, salaries, utilities, supplies, and hiring and training of personnel to establish a facility and to be ready to open for business.
3. Legal, accounting, printing, and commission costs incurred in raising equity capital or debt.

Although there are no specific authoritative pronouncements in this area, practice is reasonably well developed. Expenses incurrred for the first two categories are usually deferred and amortized over not more than five years. Costs incurred in raising equity are charged against the net proceeds of the related offering. Similar costs of raising debt are classified as deferred charges and amortized by the interest method over the term of the related debt.

Guarantee Fees. Some S&Ls use their mortgage-backed assets to guarantee debt obligations of others. A common example is an association's guarantee of the principal and interest payments on revenue bonds issued by a municipality. The association pledges some of its loans as collateral for the guarantee. As compensation, the municipality pays the association an initial fee plus an annual fee for the duration of the guarantee.

Accounting for the guarantee fees is based on the same principles that govern recognition of loan origination fees. Therefore, SFAS 91 (L20) should be followed. The initial fee, and related direct costs, are deferred and recognized over the life of the agreement. The annual fee is prorated monthly. The guarantee is not recorded as a liability in the thrift's financial statements.

Accounting Issues for Business Combinations

The principal areas of accounting concern in a business combination of savings and loan associations are:

- Nature of the transaction—pooling or purchase.
- Valuing the acquired loan portfolio and accreting the discount.
- Identification, valuation, and amortization of intangibles.

* Subsidy of below-market portfolio yield.
* Postacquisition restatement, referred to as push down accounting.
* Adjusting deferred taxes for tax-basis differentials.

Summary of Professional Pronouncements. Accounting standards for business combinations in general are discussed in Chapter 23. The primary concept of APB 16 (B50) is that if a business combination meets certain specified criteria it must be accounted for as a pooling of interests. If it does not meet these criteria, it must be accounted for as a purchase. In negotiating, the parties may agree on conditions deliberately aimed at meeting (or failing to meet) the pooling criteria, but once the conditions are set, the result is either a pooling or a purchase; it is not a matter of choice. APB 17 (I60) requires that goodwill resulting from a purchase business combination be amortized over its estimated life, but not in excess of forty years. SFAS 72 (Bt7) amends and interprets APB 16 and 17 for combinations of banking or thrift institutions.

On September 1, 1981 the FHLBB issued R-Memorandum 31b directing that goodwill be accounted for in accordance with GAAP as set forth in APB 16 and APB 17. The FHLBB rule quotes liberally from FIN 9 (Bt7), which states that in a purchase acquisition of a savings and loan association its assets (including identifiable assets, such as income and business generation capacities of existing assets, core deposits, and the nature of territory served) and liabilities must be fair valued individually as in any other type of acquisition.

The SEC, the FHLBB, the AICPA, and the FASB all have issued releases concerning accounting for S&L business combinations:

1. On December 23, 1981, the SEC issued SAB 42 (Topic 2A.3) to discuss the application of existing financial accounting standards to financial institution business combinations accounted for by the purchase method. SAB 42 expresses the SEC's concern that although adequate overall guidance is provided in APBs 16 and 17 and FIN 9, the applicable accounting standards may not have been properly considered in all cases, and the allocation of the purchase price to all identifiable intangible assets acquired may not have received adequate consideration. The SEC also encourages accelerated goodwill amortization in some situations.

2. On December 29, 1981, the FHLBB issued (to its supervisory agents) Memorandum SP-24, *Determining an Appropriate Accounting Technique for Mergers of S&L Associations.* The Memorandum reconfirms SAB 42 in stating that GAAP is appropriate for savings and loan association mergers, and provides more detailed guidance in:

   * The determination of whether the purchase or pooling method is appropriate in a given case.

   * How to apply the purchase method.

   Memorandum SP-24 notes that the tests in APB 16 are difficult to apply to mutual S&Ls. Because many of those tests are inapplicable or inadequate, especially in distinguishing the transfer of controlling interests, the FHLBB expressed a concern that some business combinations involving mutual associations are too readily structured to achieve purchase accounting, when perhaps the pooling-of-interests method is the proper approach in substance.

Thus the FHLBB expanded on the APB 16 criteria to distinguish for its purposes the circumstances in which either pooling or purchase accounting is to be applied. These expanded criteria are not a part of APB 16, and therefore are not officially sanctioned as interpretations of GAAP.

3. In December 1981, AcSEC approved a Notice to Practitioners published in the January 11, 1982 *CPA Letter*. The guidance in this notice is generally consistent with the SEC and FHLBB releases.

4. In July 1982, AcSEC requested the FASB to address the accounting for business combinations of mutual thrift institutions, because guidance was needed to reduce diversity in practice. On August 11, 1982, the FASB added to its agenda a project to address the amortization of the unidentifiable intangible asset recognized in purchase acquisitions. In February 1983, SFAS 72, *Accounting for Certain Acquisitions of Banking or Thrift Institutions* (Bt7), was issued. (See the subsection "Intangibles" later in this section for a discussion of SFAS 72.)

5. On December 31, 1985, the SEC released SAB 42A (Topic 2A.3) to indicate that the staff did not believe there would be any justification for an amortization period in excess of 25 years for goodwill arising from an acquisition of one financial institution by another. The SAB is referring to goodwill arising when the acquisition price is in excess of the fair value of the net assets acquired (which otherwise could be amortized over 40 years under APB 17). The intangible arising when the liabilities of the acquired institution exceed the fair value of the tangible and identifiable intangible assets would continue to be amortized in accordance with SFAS 72 (Bt7). The rationale for this departure from the maximum 40-year amortization period is based on the deregulation environment and its impact on financial institutions.

Pooling vs. Purchase. In business combinations involving S&Ls that are bargaining in their own interests (without pressure from or intervention by regulators), the criteria in APB 16 should be applied in the conventional way. This can be done readily in a stock-for-stock transaction but becomes more difficult when one or both of the associations are mutuals. Although APB 16 does not deal directly with this matter, it is clear that mutuals are not excluded and that appropriate adjustment should be made for differences in the nature of ownership interests. In a mutual, the savings depositors are the shareholders (although most often they grant a proxy to management to permit the ongoing governance of the association). Accordingly, it is possible to meet the pooling criteria in a combination of two mutuals. For example, Mutual A can combine with Mutual B by issuance of the savings accounts of Mutual A to the savings account holders of Mutual B (all other conditions being met).

In deciding whether all pooling criteria are met in a merger of mutuals, other factors may need to be considered. For example, evaluating the criterion relating to the combination of preexisting voting interests may be difficult where the management control group of each association effectively constitutes the ownership (even though technically by proxy). Indeed, FHLBB Memorandum SP-24 considers mutual association depositors more akin to creditors, and management as the ownership interests. If the terms of the transaction were to provide that the proxies (representing the voting rights) were to transfer from the controlling group of one institution to the controlling group of the other institution, this could contribute to a decision to reject pooling treatment.

As another example, evaluating a planned disposition of a significant part of one of the S&L's assets, such as a block of loans, would depend on whether that would be deemed to be within, or not within, the ordinary course of business. The FHLBB memo seems to urge the conclusion that the loan sale transaction should not upset pooling accounting.

Standing alone, no single judgmental factor such as the two examples given above is conclusive, but a combination of factors may add up to a decision that the transaction is to be accounted for as a purchase.

Some accountants believe that all mergers of a weaker association with a stronger one, through regulatory pressure or intervention, must be accounted for as purchases. Such "arranged" or "FSLIC-assisted" mergers, regardless of form, are seen as failing the pooling criteria because the major impetus is being provided by a regulatory agency that is not directly a party to the transaction, but which has assumed operating control.

Valuation of the Acquired Loan Portfolio. The valuation process is simple at a theoretical level. Cash flows from the loans are projected over future periods and are discounted to their present value. As a practical matter, however, this can be a difficult and time-consuming task. An expert may be used by the S&L to make the necessary estimates and calculations.

To simplify the calculation, loans are often grouped in pools that have similar prepayment characteristics. Factors that are usually considered are the geographic location of the mortgaged property, the age of the loan, the interest rate, and the outstanding balance. Based on these factors, a prepayment rate is determined for each pool, future cash flows are projected, and the cash flows are then discounted to arrive at their present value. Some of the methods used to derive the appropriate discount rate can be complex. However, the basic objective is to use a rate that makes sense based on the credit risk inherent in the loans and the timing of the cash flows (six months out, two years out, ten years out, etc.).

The discount arising from the revaluation of an acquired loan portfolio is amortized by the level yield method as described by SFAS 91 (L20). If prepayment assumptions are used, the statement requires a constant reevaluation of prepayment history and the related effect on the yield of the loan portfolio. (Use of prepayment assumptions is optional. See Chapter 21 and Appendix B to SFAS 91.)

Intangibles. Under APB 16 (B50) and APB 17 (I60), the excess of consideration given over the fair value of tangible and identifiable intangible net assets received represents goodwill. Frequently, the only consideration given by an acquiring association is the assumption of liabilities that exceed the fair value of tangible assets received. SFAS 72 modifies certain provisions of APBs 16 and 17 and FIN 9 (Bt7), and specifies the accounting when the fair value of liabilities assumed exceeds the fair value of tangible and intangible assets acquired. The principal provisions of SFAS 72 (B50 and Bt7) are:

1. Intangible assets that are acquired in a business combination and can be separately identified are called identifiable intangible assets (e.g., existing core deposits and branch locations). They are assigned a portion of the acquired enterprise's total cost, provided fair values can be reliably determined. Fair values of intangibles that relate to borrower or depositor relationships shall be based on the estimated benefits attributable to the relationships that exist at the date of the acquisition. New borrowers or depositors cannot be considered. Identified intangible assets are amortized over the estimated lives of those existing relationships.

2. If the fair value of liabilities assumed exceeds the fair value of tangible and identified intangible assets acquired, that excess constitutes an unidentifiable intangible asset (goodwill). This type of goodwill is amortized over a period no greater than the estimated remaining life of long-term interest-bearing assets acquired (those with a maturity of more than one year). Goodwill must be written off in direct relationship to the scheduled liquidation of the association's long-term interest-bearing assets. If no significant long-term interest-bearing assets were acquired, amortization should be over a period not exceeding the average remaining life of the acquired customer (deposit) base.

3. Any remaining excess of purchase price over the fair value of net assets acquired (i.e., goodwill as traditionally contemplated in business combinations) shall be amortized in accordance with APB 17.

4. If a large disposition of the acquired institution's operating assets (such as branches) occurs, the portion of the unidentifiable intangible assets discussed above that is attributable to these operating assets must be included in the cost of assets sold. A write-off of a portion of the unidentifiable intangible asset must be considered (but is not necessarily required) if there is a large disposition of the interest-bearing assets of the acquired institution.

In Issue 85-8, *Amortization of Thrift Intangibles,* the EITF considered amortization of unidentifiable intangible assets resulting from the acquisition of banking or thrift institutions. In the facts of this case, the combination resulted in the total amount of the unidentifiable intangible asset arising from the acquisition being in excess of the discount amount on the acquired long-term interest-bearing assets (generally due to the payment of some cash in the acquisition or the precombination existence of a deficit in the acquired bank or thrift). Application of APB 17, *Intangible Assets* (I60), to the net amount (unidentifiable intangible asset minus the discount amount) was considered, but the EITF reached a consensus that SFAS 72 "goodwill" (the amount by which the fair value of liabilities assumed exceeds the fair value of the tangible and identifiable intangible assets acquired) should be amortized to expense as specified in SFAS 72 (B50.158A, Bt7.108, and I60.133), generally over a period no greater than the estimated remaining life of the long-term interest-bearing assets acquired. Any remaining goodwill is to be amortized in accordance with APB 17.

In Issue 85-42, (similar in some respects to Issue 85-8), the EITF addressed *Amortization of Goodwill Resulting From Recording Time Savings Deposits at Fair Values* in a purchase acquisition. Such goodwill can arise because the time deposits bear interest rates in excess of rates prevailing at the acquisition date. In fair valuing the liabilities assumed, a premium is therefore assigned to the time deposits. In the acquisition under EITF consideration, the fair value of liabilities assumed also exceeds the fair value of the tangible and identifiable intangible assets acquired, resulting in the type of unidentifiable intangible asset addressed by SFAS 72. Further, the unidentifiable intangible asset exceeds the discount on the long-term interest-bearing assets acquired.

The Task Force reached a consensus that the SFAS 72 type of goodwill should be amortized to expense over a period no greater than the estimated remaining life of the long-term interest-bearing assets acquired, in conformity with SFAS 72. Any remaining goodwill would be amortized in accordance with APB 17.

Regulatory Assistance Subsidies. Regulatory assistance that effectively assures the recovery of a specified spread on the acquired long-term interest-bearing assets must be reflected in establishing the fair value of these assets. Actual assistance amounts are included in income when earned. Other forms of financial assistance should be recorded as acquired assets if receipt is probable and the amount is reasonably determinable. Otherwise, when such assistance later becomes due, it is first credited to the unidentifiable intangible representing the excess of the fair value of liabilities assumed over the fair value of tangible and identifiable intangibles acquired, and then against any remaining goodwill. If regulatory assistance is to be later repaid based on achievement of specified future operating results, such amounts are charged to those future operations and do not affect the accounting for assistance earned as described above.

Since the release of SFAS 72 in early 1983, regulatory assistance forms have become much more complex and the amounts very large, as the FSLIC moves to resolve some of the more intractable S&L problems. Consequently, the EITF is scheduled to discuss *FSLIC Assisted Acquisitions of Thrifts* (Issue 88-19). The SEC has also stated that a SAB is in process on this subject as of mid-1988.

Push Down Accounting. Under this accounting methodology, the new parent's cost basis is "pushed down" in the separate financial statements of the acquired S&L in place of the acquiree's historical, preacquisition amounts. Thus, the beginning "cost basis" of the acquired association's assets and liabilities is their fair market value as of the acquisition date. Also pushed down would be the intangibles arising on consolidation.

The SEC has commented on push down accounting in SAB 54 (Topic 5.J). In addition SAB 73, issued in 1987, specifies conditions under which push down accounting must be applied in the separate financial statements of a subsidiary. The SEC staff's view is that when the form of ownership is within the control of the parent, the basis of accounting for purchased assets and liabilities should be the same regardless of whether the entity continues to exist or is merged into the parent's operations. Therefore, the parent's cost of acquiring the subsidiary should be pushed down.

Where push down accounting is not applied, footnote disclosure of the parent's basis for the separate reporting unit's loan portfolio and depositor accounts, and a description of any subsidy arrangement with the FSLIC, should be made, whether a balance sheet only, or a full set of financial statements, is presented.

In 1986, the FHLBB issued R-Memorandum 55a permitting push down accounting as long as it is applied in conformity with GAAP. This requirement can be met either by the auditor issuing: (1) an opinion letter to management stating that establishment of a new cost basis at the time of acquisition and the current use of push down accounting are in conformity with GAAP; or (2) an auditor's report on the association's financial statements that is not qualified with respect to the use of push down accounting.

Deferred Taxes in a Purchase Combination. Prior to the 1987 passage of SFAS 96, *Accounting for Income Taxes* (I25), APB 16 had required that differences between the tax basis of acquired assets and assumed liabilities had to be given effect in the valuation of those assets and liabilities individually. Thus, a loan portfolio having a pre-tax-effected value of $50 and a tax basis of $100 would be presented at $65 (using a 30% tax rate), because the presumed later deduction for a greater tax basis would result in a tax benefit of $15. (Some accountants would also have discounted the $15 back from the time at which it was estimated that the benefits would be realized.) This is referred to as tax-effecting, or stating assets or liabilities net of tax.

The above example is very simplified, of course. Many times the benefit was not recorded because there was little assurance that the benefit would ever be realized, given poor operating history of the acquirer (and perhaps of the acquiree). This requirement of APB 16 has been completely changed by SFAS 96, which must be adopted no later than fiscal years beginning after December 15, 1988, and need not be adopted retroactively. Thus, some S&Ls that hold off until 1989 to adopt SFAS 96 might continue to have tax-effected assets and liabilities.

Under SFAS 96, the acquirer will view tax basis differentials the same as any other temporary difference between book and tax. Thus for a purchase occurring after SFAS 96 has been adopted, the type of benefit illustrated in the example above would be a debit temporary difference, which could be assigned value by the acquirer only if there were credit temporary differences that offset it and that would cumulatively reverse in the same future tax years. In short, SFAS 96 does not permit net deferred tax debits. If in an S&L acquisition no value is assigned to the debit temporary difference, and it later is realized, the benefit would be credited to goodwill.[6]

Special transition provisions are stated in SFAS 96 for entities that choose not to adopt retroactively. The net-of-tax balances of assets and liabilities remaining from prior purchase combinations are not to be grossed-up to their pretax amounts; instead the net balance less the tax basis is considered the temporary difference to be recorded in connection with the prospective adoption of SFAS 96.

S&Ls are permitted tax deductions for estimated bad debts in amounts that often are greater than amounts needed for GAAP financial reporting purposes. These excess amounts are considered part of the GAAP net worth. Under APB 11, deferred taxes were not applied to these excess tax deductions because their reversal was indefinite. This special treatment has been continued under SFAS 96, but the excess deduction has been made into a tax preference item for alternative minimum tax (AMT) purposes.

For an extended discussion of the effect of SFAS 96 in general, refer to Chapter 17. For its overall effect on business combinations, refer to Chapter 23.

---

[6] Prior to SFAS 96, practice had been mixed. In EITF Issue 85-3, the Task Force decided that a previously unrecognized tax benefit realized within approximately one year after the business combination should be credited to goodwill.

Other Issues

EPS in a Mutual Conversion. Occasionally, a mutual S&L will convert to a stock association by offering stock subscriptions to its depositors (not many of whom will subscribe), simultaneous with offering the unsubscribed shares to the general public for cash. Also as part of the same series of transactions, the mutual-cum-stock association is a party to a pooling with another stock S&L, whose stock will be issued to the subscribers of the mutual's stock (both depositors and nondepositors). There have been moderate arguments about whether this transaction is a pooling, but uniform treatment as a pooling has developed in practice.

EITF Issue 84-22, *Prior Years' Earnings Per Share Following a Savings and Loan Association Conversion and Pooling,* explored how to calculate earnings per share (EPS) for an S&L that acquired another S&L in a combination accounted for as a pooling immediately after the acquiree had converted from a mutual association to a stock association. Although APB 15 requires restatement of the combined enterprise EPS for all prior periods, applying this standard is problematic because the acquired S&L, as a mutual, did not have any stock (or EPS).

The EITF reached a consensus that the acquired S&L should not be included in the restated historical EPS of the combined association for years prior to its conversion. This EPS presentation should be adequately disclosed in the financial statements.

FSLIC Management Consignment Program. In EITF Issue 85-41, *Accounting for Savings and Loan Associations under FSLIC Management Consignment Program* (MCP), a financial institution is closed and most of its assets and liabilities are transferred to a newly-chartered federal mutual association. Another association's management is contracted by FSLIC to run the new savings and loan until it either becomes profitable or is liquidated.

The EITF reached a consensus on the following accounting issues:

- The accounting treatment would be the same whether the former financial institution was a stock association or a mutual association.
- The transfer of assets and liabilities to the newly chartered institution does not constitute a business combination as defined by APB 16.
- FCLIC's actions constitute a significant event that warrants a revaluation of the assets and liabilities transferred to the new thrift; carry-over of the historical cost basis of the assets and liabilities is inappropriate.
- In valuing the assets and liabilities of the new thrift, the fair valuation guidelines of APB 16 should be followed.
- The new thrift should recognize the fair value of those identifiable intangibles that can be reliably measured (for example, servicing rights on loans owned by others).
- Any amount resulting from liabilities in excess of identified assets should not be classified as goodwill, but is to be shown as deficit equity presented separately from subsequent retained earnings.
- The new values assigned would become the new cost basis, and subsequent accounting should follow GAAP; assets would not be marked to market on a continuing basis.

• Accounting for the ultimate disposition of the institution (sale, liquidation, or emergence as a viable enterprise outside FSLIC control) would be consistent with the current accounting for similar events.

Taxes in a Bank/S&L Pooling. An S&L must change its legal entity form before it can merge with a non-S&L financial institution, such as a bank or insurance company. When the S&L converts to a different legal entity, taxes may become payable on its existing bad debt reserves, which have been partially tax-advantaged because of S&L status. Deferred taxes are not provided on these reserves in accordance with APB 23 and SFAS 96. In Issue 86-31 *Reporting the Tax Implications of a Pooling of a Bank and a Savings and Loan Association*, the EITF considered how to account for the income tax that results from the merger assuming that pooling accounting is applicable.

The Task Force consensus was that any income taxes arising from the merger should be accounted for as a charge to current expense in the combined financial statements, as would be the case with any other pooling expenses.

FSLIC Secondary Reserve Prepayments. Many S&Ls carried as an asset a prepayment to the secondary reserve of the FSLIC. This asset was created by insurance premiums prepaid since 1961 as required by law, plus interest earned on the prepayments, less both the amounts used to pay the institution's regular annual FSLIC insurance premiums and the amounts refunded in cash directly to the institution.

In 1987, the GAO released a report on FSLIC that showed FSLIC's liabilities exceeded its assets. As a result, the secondary reserve was absorbed into FSLIC's primary reserve, and S&Ls had to write off the asset. Later in 1987, Congress enacted CEBA, incorporating a provision that would allow associations, under certain circumstances, to "recover" a portion of their secondary reserve; this would be done by reducing the FSLIC insurance premiums the association would have to pay in future years. The question raised in EITF issues 87-22, *Prepayment to the Secondary Reserve of the Federal Savings and Loan Insurance Corporation,* was whether the CEBA provision eliminates the need to write off the secondary reserve. Also discussed was whether the write-off should be classified as ordinary or extraordinary if the secondary reserve nevertheless should be written off.

The EITF reached a consensus that the secondary reserve should be written off, and that the write-off should be classified as ordinary expense. In November 1987, the AICPA issued Practice Bulletin 3 (TP 12,030) addressing this issue. The conclusions reached in PB 3 are consistent with those reached by the EITF.

Freddie Mac Preferred Stock. In TB 85-1, *Accounting for the Receipt of Federal Home Loan Mortgage Corporation Participating Preferred Stock* (Bt7.501–.505), the FASB staff settled a debate that had first been discussed by the EITF in Issue 85–7 and had not been intended to reach the level of an FASB pronouncement. Freddie Mac, all of whose stock is owned by the 12 district Federal Home Loan Banks, distributed preferred stock to the district banks with the proviso that the banks would distribute it to their own stockholder institutions, namely, the S&Ls in the district.

Some CPAs felt strongly that this distribution was like a stock dividend, and should not give rise to income at the S&L level. The FHLBB argued that income was generated because the S&Ls now had a tradeable security that differed from the common stock held in the district banks, which was redeemable only at par. TB 85-1 agreed with the FHLBB, and extraordinary income was recognized by the S&Ls.

The initial distribution restricted ownership of the preferred stock to S&Ls that are common stockholders in the district banks. In mid-1988, the FHLBB approved transferability of the shares to outside investors by creating a class of unrestricted stock that could be exchanged for the prior stock upon payment by owners of $7 per share. Shares not exchanged would remain restricted.

Bank Holding Company Disclosures. In 1987 the SEC issued SAB 69 (Topic 11.k) to provide the staff's views regarding disclosure for registrants engaged in lending and deposit activities. The SAB notes that while Article 9 of Regulation S-X and Industry Guide 3 of Regulation S-K (statistical disclosure by bank holding companies) apply to bank holding companies, the SEC staff also believes that other registrants, including S&L holding companies, should make the same disclosures.

Article 9 of Regulation S-X specifies the form and content of, and the requirements for, financial statements of bank holding companies filing with the SEC. Similarly, bank holding companies disclose supplemental statistical disclosures in filing, pursuant to Guide 3.

The SEC staff had been considering the need for more specific guidance in the area, but believes that the FASB's project on financial instruments, which is expected to result in expanded disclosures, may make SEC action in this area unnecessary.

Many of the Industry Guide 3 disclosures were already required by FSLIC regulation 563b and 563c. The Guide requires additional disclosures for investment securities, nonaccruing assets, rate-volume tables, and other items. Although the SEC does not regulate savings and loans other than holding corporations, the FHLBB will adjust their disclosure requirements to conform with Article 9 and Guide 3.

SEC-Required Financial Statements of Borrowers. SAB 71 (Topic 1.I) concerning the requirements for financial statements of properties securing mortgage loans, was issued in 1987 to clarify that when a registrant has mortgage loans whose economic substance is an investment in real estate or a joint venture (e.g., ADC loans), Rule 3-14 of Regulation S-X must be followed. This rule requires audited income statements, disclosure of material factors, and other information regarding these real estate investments.

The AICPA's third Notice to Practitioners on ADC loans (TP 12,010.09) set the criteria for determining whether a transaction is a loan or is in substance an investment or joint venture. SAB 71 provides additional guidance for making this determination. Specifically, the SEC staff believes that if the borrowers's equity in the property meets the criteria in paragraphs 11 and 12 of SFAS 66 (Re 1.111–.112), the lender's transaction can be accounted for as a loan.

SAB 71 is not meant to extend the third notice. Rather, the SEC is permitting certain parts of SFAS 66 (which actually pertains to the sale of real estate) to be used in determining whether Rule 3-14 disclosures are necessary.

AUDITING CONSIDERATIONS

Auditing a savings and loan association once was straightforward. Loan and savings accounts were confirmed, key regulations were reviewed for compliance, and the remaining asset and liability accounts were reviewed and tested for reasonableness. However, recent factors such as an increasing number S&L failures, a related increase in lawsuits in which the auditors are named, and substantial increase in the complexity of the S&L business environment, have resulted in these audits becoming riskier and much more complex.

The auditor's risk can be mitigated in several ways, most significantly by staffing the audit engagement with personnel well-versed in industry accounting and regulatory aspects. Additionally, the auditor should identify the significant and complex audit areas early in the audit process, and focus the audit effort on those areas.

Audit Approach

Reliance on Internal Controls. S&Ls process an extremely large volume of transactions; and some balance sheet accounts, such as loans and savings, are comprised of numerous individual balances. Therefore, auditors usually test and rely on the association's internal control structure. A complete discussion of internal controls and their relation to the audit is provided in Chapter 8.

The auditor will typically test the following internal control systems in an S&L audit:

- Teller operations (processing and balancing)
- General ledger
- Loans (origination and payments received)
- Savings (origination and withdrawals)
- Payroll
- Cash disbursements

Other internal control systems also might be tested depending on the business and operations of the S&L. For example, many savings and loans are selling originated loans but retaining the servicing. In this situation, the auditor will usually test the loan servicing system.

Substantive Tests. The substantive audit procedures for savings and loans do not vary greatly from the audit procedures used for nonfinancial companies, described in Chapter 7. A combination of positive and negative confirmations are sent on individual loans receivable and savings accounts. Loan participations purchased by the S&Ls are confirmed with respect to outstanding balance, unpaid escrow (taxes and insurance), and delinquent loans.

Analytical Tests. Analytical tests are often used to ascertain the reasonableness of the following balances:

- Loan interest income (by type of loan)

- Investment interest income (by type of investments)
- Savings interest expense
- Long-term debt interest expense
- Accrued interest on loans receivable and savings

Many other analytical tests not unique to the S&L industry can be performed, as discussed in Chapter 7.

Problem Audit Areas

The audit areas presenting the greatest risk will vary based upon the particular S&L's product line, the geographic location of the loans in its portfolio, management's skills, and other factors. In general, the following matters are high on the list of audit problem areas:

- Valuation of real estate owned and troubled loans
- Cutoff and ownership in MBS transactions
- Gain or loss on sales of loans
- Effect of prepayments on carrying values
- Financial instruments and transactions

The audit issues that pertain to these areas are discussed in the following sections.

Valuation of Real Estate Owned and Troubled Loans. An important audit objective is to evaluate the carrying value of troubled loans and REO. Satisfying this objective has become increasingly difficult because of the significant decrease in value of commercial and residential properties in some parts of the United States. These declines have persisted despite expectations of a near-term recovery. The auditing profession has also become more sensitive to the valuation issue because of the SEC's release of FRR 28, in which the SEC expresses its concern that audited carrying values of REO and of troubled loans are sometimes overstated.

The AICPA S&L Audit Guide requires troubled loans receivable to be carried at net realizable value. The auditor, through discussions with management and review of loan delinquency reports, should ascertain which loans are troubled. While most troubled loans are identified through delinquency reports, there may be loans that management believes will require foreclosure or a troubled debt restructuring, even though only one or two months delinquent.

After the troubled loans are identified, the expected disposition of the problem (foreclosure, catch-up payments, or loan restructuring) needs to be determined. If the loan receivable will be a nonearning asset for a substantial duration, the valuation allowance must be discounted to reflect the cost-of-money holding cost.[7]

The focal point of this analysis is expected cash flows. The projected amount and timing of future cash inflows to the S&L are dependent on several factors:

---

[7] See Note 3.

1. Association management should provide their best estimate of the timing and amount of cash flows.
2. The auditor can refer to appraisals on the property as support for the amount of the cash flows. However, appraisals must be used carefully, particularly for properties in economically distressed areas. In these situations, the assumptions underlying the appraisal should be carefully reviewed, and appraisals more than a year old should be used with care; or perhaps the auditor should call for a new appraisal. Further, the appraiser will sometime use a discount rate, or a *capitalization rate,* that the auditor may believe is not appropriate. The auditor should also be aware that appraisers do not have a uniform methodology. The AICPA's *Guide for the Use of Real Estate Appraisal Information* (AICPA, 1987j) is a necessary reference source for auditors.
3. The auditor may be able to look at past history to observe how long similar properties were held before resale, and the portion of the appraised value that the association was actually able to obtain. Sales commmissions and marketing costs, which are sometimes not considered by the appraiser, must also be included in this analysis. Moreover, if the association expects to finance the resale of the property, and the loan rate is expected to be below the market rate for similar loans, a market rate must be imputed.

During the review of loans the auditor must be alert for troubled loans that are actually in-substance foreclosures, as described in FRR 28. If so, the loan is to be carried at its fair market value, defined by SFAS 15 (D22).

In addition to FRR 28, EITF Issue 87-19 (discussed earlier in "Accounting Issues") provides a specific example of an in-substance foreclosure. The auditor also must be alert to transactions that may appear to be restructurings of the receivable but are actually extinguishments of old receivables and the receipt of new assets. EITF Issues 87-18 (also discussed earlier) gives an example based on the use of zero coupon bonds.

The auditor should use the same basic audit procedures for REO that he uses for troubled loans. In the end, the valuation process is highly subjective. The process calls for the auditor to challenge the judgments of both management and appraisal experts involving numerous critical factors such as projected cash flows, a market rate of return, estimated costs to complete, and the length of the holding period. In some cases, it may be extremely difficult, or perhaps impossible, to determine the probable loss. Accordingly, if troubled loans or REO are significant to the association's net worth, and the probable loss cannot be determined, the auditor should consider the need to modify or even disclaim an opinion on the association's financial statements.

Cutoff and Ownership in Loan Sales and MBS Transactions. Purchases and sales of loans receivable and mortgage-backed securities as well as loan servicing operations require special internal controls that many S&Ls lack. As a result, cutoff errors, sometimes significant, can occur. The following paragraphs describe the basic transaction types that may be prone to error, and list some of the responsive audit procedures.

Mortgage-backed security transactions. Three agencies are the primary issuers of pass-through certificates: FHLMC, FNMA, and GNMA. The different characteristics of each are summarized in Figure 41.4. The time lag between an agency's receipt of homeowner payments and their remittance to the MBS owner varies among the three. For example, GNMA's number of days to first payment is 45 days. Thus, there should be approximately 45 days accrued interest on GNMA PCs at the end of a month.

The purchase of MBS is recorded in the same way as the purchase of any other interest-bearing security; that is, the premium or discount and purchased interest must be computed and recorded.

The sophistication of an MBS accounting system is usually dependent on the level of MBS activity. For example, S&Ls that extensively trade mortgage-backed securities are likely to have a precise system for tracking the related principal and interest accruals and receipts.

Usual audit procedures include:

1. Determining that the basis for accrued interest on mortgage-backed securities, if not exact, is based on reasonable parameters given the provisions of the three agency programs for pass-through certificates.
2. To test for proper cutoff on mortgage-backed securities sold prior to year-end, reviewing the principal and interest receipts the association has forwarded to the purchaser of the MBS.
3. Testing the accounting for additions and disposals of mortgage-backed securities, paying particular attention to purchased interest and gain or loss recognition.

Loan sales. To determine if the sale and subsequent activity are being properly recorded, the auditor must understand the terms of the sale agreement with respect to such matters as interest yield to the purchaser, servicing fees, cutoff dates, principal and interest remittance schedules, and recourse provisions.

The currently recognized gain or loss (to the seller) and the premium or discount (to the buyer) on the loan sale is determined based on selling price and the carrying value of loans sold. If loan servicing is retained by the seller, also to be considered are the yield on the loans sold, effective yield to the purchaser, and the level of service fees.

In computing gain or loss, the sales price must be adjusted for excess service fees. If there are excess (or insufficient) service fees, an excess service fee receivable (or payable) must be recorded and amortized over the actual life of the security. A provision also must be made for the cutoff of principal and interest payments on the loans sold.

After reviewing the loan sale agreement, the auditor might find that the investor and the association have agreed upon a variation of the pure pass-through of principal and interest on loans sold. For example, the association may have to remit total scheduled payments (based on amortization schedules for each loan) and payoffs. As a result, the association may have to set up a special asset account for delinqencies and other underpayments.

Usual audit procedures include:

1. Determining that the liability for collections on loans sold reconciles to the subsequent month's remittance to the investor. Consider timing differences between the cutoff date and the remittance date (e.g., principal and interest receipts for the period through the 25th of

	GNMA I	GNMA II	FHLMC	FNMA
Issuer	FHA-approved lender	FHA-approved lender(s) (single-issuer and multiple issuer pools)	FHLMC	FNMA
Underlying Mortgages	FHA/VA	FHA/VA	Conventional or FHA/VA	Conventional or FHA/VA
Guarantee	Full and timely payment of principal and interest	Full and timely payment of principal and interest	Full and timely payment of interest and eventual full payment of principal, or full and timely payment of principal and interest (separate programs)	Full and timely payment of principal and interest
Guarantor	GNMA (full faith and credit of U.S. Government)	GNMA (full faith and credit of U.S. Government)	FHLMC	FNMA
Monthly Payment	Multiple checks, one for each certificate	One check per investor of all holdings	Federal funds	Federal funds
Delivery	Physical (definitive) certificate settlement in Federal funds, changing to book entry	Physical (definitive) certificate settlement in Federal funds, changing to book entry	Book-entry through Federal Reserve banks, settlement in Federal funds	Book-entry through Federal Reserve banks, settlement in Federal funds
Days to First Payment (Approximates No. of Days Accrued Interest)	45	50	75	55
Denomination	$25,000 minimum $5,000 increment	$25,000 minimum $5,000 increment	$25,000 minimum $5,000 increment	$25,000 minimum

FIG. 41.4 Governmental Agency Mortgage Pass-Through Programs

the month are remitted on the 15th of the following month). The liability account must be adjusted for any receipts after the cutoff date.

2. Determining that the investor trial balance agrees with the general ledger.

3. Using the terms stated in the loan sale agreement, testing the accuracy of the service fee income that is deducted from the interest receipts.

4. Testing the initial recording and cutoff of significant loan sales during the year. The test should include a review of the gain or loss and the interest sold.

Participation purchases. Participation purchase agreements can vary markedly. Thus, it is important that the auditor understand the key terms of each agreement: receipts of principal and interest (scheduled or actual receipts), the cutoff period, the number of days' lag between receipt of payment and due dates, the interest rate, and servicing fees, if any.

Some associations rely solely on the reports received from the servicer in accounting for participations purchased. Other associations keep track by subsidiary ledger of participations on a loan-by-loan basis.

Usual audit procedures include:

1. Understanding the reporting and maintenance of the loans by the servicer, including remittance of principal and interest and adjustable rate mortgage (ARM) adjustments. (To some extent the auditor relies on the servicer auditor's statement that the sevicer is properly recording loan transactions and servicing the loans. However, the auditor can still ascertain that the association is monitoring the ARM adjustments being made by the servicer.)

2. Testing initial recording and cutoff of significant participations purchased during the year. Pay particular attention to the inclusion of purchased interest.

3. Determining that the investor's servicing report for the month subsequent to year end reconciles with the general ledger account for participations purchased as of the audit date.

4. Testing accrued interest on participations purchased using key terms detailed in the participation agreements.

Gain or Loss on Sales of Loans. Loan sales in which servicing is retained by the selling association must be reviewed to determine that a *normal service fee* has been properly included in the gain/loss computation. TB 87-3, *Accounting for Mortgage Servicing Fees and Rights*, defines a normal service fee; nonetheless, the auditor still must challenge the associations's prepayment estimate and the manner in which it is applied, because of its significant effect on servicing estimates. In the past, S&Ls had often used a balloon prepayment assumption under which there would be no prepayments for 12 years, and the outstanding balance would then be fully prepaid. Today, most S&Ls recognize that this prepayment assumption is not valid and calculate a prepayment amount as a part of each month's payment.

The auditor must also determine that the transfer meets the requirements of SFAS 77, *Reporting by Transferors for Transfers of Receivables With Recourse* (R20), for sale treatments, as discussed earlier herein.

Effect of Prepayments on Carrying Values. Recent significant interest rate fluctuations and the existence of a large pool of MBS have sensitized the marketplace to the potential volatility of prepayments on MBS. A significant change in the level of prepayments can have a substantial effect on both the market value of mortgage assets and on the GAAP carrying value of several categories of assets. Examples are:

- Excess servicing fee receivables
- Capitalized loan servicing costs
- Loans receivables, or MBS, that have significant premiums or discounts
- Interest-only or principal-only mortgage-backed security strips (IO/POs)
- Deferred hedging gains or losses associated with mortgage-backed assets

Prepayments do not affect the carrying value of the above assets in a uniform manner, because some accounting rules are contradictory. For example, the carrying value of excess servicing fee receivables and the capitalized loan servicing costs should be adjusted based on the consensus reached in EITF Issue 86-38, *Implications of Mortgage Prepayments on Servicing Rights*. However, the consensus requires that a different methodology be used to adjust each of these two elements. Premiums and discounts on loans and mortgage-backed securities, IO/PO strips, and deferred hedging gains and losses related to mortgage-backed assets are required to be amortized by the level yield method as described in SFAS 91 (L20); use of this method when prepayments are assumed is illustrated in Case 4, Appendix B (L20.130–.132). The calculations are complex, requiring constant reestimation of future project prepayments, and usually are performed on a computer.

Financial Instruments and Transactions. Many S&Ls, not only the "high-tech" ones, are investing in complex financial instruments and transactions. IO/PO strips, CMOs and Real Estate Mortgage Investment Conduit (REMIC) bonds, and their related residuals are becoming common at many smaller S&Ls. Further refinement in these innovative instruments seems to be constant. No sooner had PO strips been initiated than certain S&Ls began carving up the PO pool into subpools, some of which do and some of which do not pay interest, and selling these subpools to other investors.

There is no standard set of procedures that can be employed in auditing these types of transactions. In general, the outstanding balance and significant terms of the transaction should be confirmed with an outside party. Also, any agreement should be thoroughly read and understood. To clearly understand the substance of these transactions, it is often important to talk with treasury or capital markets personnel of the S&L, as the association's accounting personnel may not have the details or the type of knowledge necessary to understand these transactions (see Chapter 21).

ADC Loans. In an ADC loan, the provision for residual profit participation by the lender may be contained in the loan, or in a participation or other agreement. Management has the responsibility to insure that the agreement provisions are stated clearly, provide for objective measurement, and are considered enforceable. The auditor should review agreement provisions in that light and review management's process to become satisfied regarding enforceability.

Regardless of the accounting treatment for an ADC arrangement, management has a continuing responsibility to review the collectibility of uncollected principal, accrued interest, and fees, and to provide for appropriate allowances. The auditor should determine whether the allowances provided by management are adequate. In connection with this determination, the auditor should review relevant evidential matter, including feasibility studies, appraisals, forecasts, noncancellable sales contracts or lease commitments, and information concerning the track record of the developer. In addition, ADC arrangements may involve related parties, and the auditor should be aware of such a possibility and should design procedures accordingly. Progress information may be less than desirable for the auditor's purpose and may require supplemental procedures. Additional procedures might include on-site appraisers or construction consultants, to assist in the assessment of the collateral value.

AUDIT REPORTING

Guidelines for Auditors' Reports

There have been numerous instances of regulatory action requiring merger, reorganization, or liquidation of specific institutions; and the survival of some existing associations also continues to be uncertain because they have substantial nonearning assets, such as delinquent loans and troubled real estate investments. These nonearning assets cause the interest paid on liabilities to exceed interest earned on assets, resulting in negative spreads and negative cash flows.

Actions taken by FSLIC with respect to institutions that fail to meet regulatory capital requirements range from leaving current management in place with little or no restrictions, to seizure and full liquidation in the most aggravated situations. Another action used by regulators is seizure with immediate reopening as a mutual S&L having a FSLIC-appointed new management team. This may be a permanent solution, or may be a holding action while orderly liquidation or a search for a merger partner is taking place.

The net worth (both GAAP- and RAP-basis) and the liquidity of an association are the most crucial factors in evaluating the status of a troubled S&L. However, expected future cash flows are also important in projecting future net worth or liquidity problems. Institutions usually do not have serious near-term liquidity problems because they generally have significant cash flows from principal repayments on loans; and these may be used to fund losses from operations. Also, loans may be sold in secondary markets or used as collateral for borrowings.

If losses from operations represent cash losses, covering them with recapture of principal could seriously impair the ability of the institution to continue to service its liabilities. Cash losses from operations may be mitigated through sale or other conversion of nonearning assets to earning, and presumably cash-producing, assets.

When an S&L manifests cash flow or operating problems, it is important that the auditor critically evaluate an institution's business plan for at least the following year. If the business plan is critical to the auditor in arriving at the form of his report, he should consider evaluating the business plan forecast following the guidance in the AICPA's *Statement on Standards for Accountants' Services on Prospective Financial Information* (AU 2100).

Figure 41.5 provides guidance on the form of the auditor's opinion and related disclosures. As with any guidelines, there may be factors in a specific situation that are overriding and indicate a different answer.

The footnote disclosure should explain current and projected compliance with regulatory capital requirements. In addition, if the projected regulatory capital is negative, the reasons and future prospects should be discussed.

The premise underlying the opinion formats and disclosures recommended in Figure 41.5 is that current liquidity and net worth, as well as projected cash flows and management's ability to persevere in a difficult situation, are the most critical factors. Present experience shows that FSLIC is not inclined to sanction an association unless liquidity, cash flow, or management's abilities are in question, or regulatory net worth is too low for the regulators to tolerate. However, failure to meet regulatory capital standards is a serious matter that generally requires a nonstandard opinion.

Going-Concern Commentary. Financial statements are prepared assuming that a business will continue as a going concern, in the absence of evidence to the contrary. This assumption is the basis for depreciating long-term assets over their lives, for carrying deferred charges over to subsequent years, and for carrying mortgages and other nonequity investments at cost. Ordinarily, the validity of the continued existence assumption can be taken for granted when a company is operating profitably and is adequately financed. In these situations, a standard, or unmodified, auditor's report (see Chapter 11) is warranted.

In some cases, however, the validity of the continued existence assumption may come into question. SAS 59, *The Auditor's Consideration of an Entity's Ability to Continue as a Going Concern* (AU 341), issued in 1988, now requires the auditor to evaluate whether there is a substantial doubt about an entity's ability to continue for at least one year from the date of the financial statements. This new rule differs from prior rules that required the auditor to react only if relevant matters came to his attention.

In performing an audit of an S&L, the auditor should be alert to and investigate matters such as the following:

1. Information that may indicate liquidity problems, such as:
   a. Negative trends in interest rate spreads, recurring operating losses, negative cash flows, or adverse key financial ratios (return on average assets, net worth, etc.).
   b. Other indications (e.g., noncompliance with debt agreement convenants, or the necessity for new sources of financing).
2. Information that might jeopardize an association's ability to continue to operate, without necessarily indicating potential solvency problems:
   a. Internal matters (e.g., loss of key management or operating personnel, substantial dependence on the success of certain projects, or uneconomic long-term commitments).
   b. External matters (e.g., legal proceedings, legislation, or inability to meet regulatory capital requirements and satisfy regulatory concerns).

Case[a] Required	Regulatory Capital Requirement		Projected Cash Flow Operations[c]	Auditor's Opinion	Disclosure Required
	Current Y/E	Projected[b]			
1	Complies	Complies	Positive	Unmodified	No
2[f]	Complies	Fails/positive	Positive	Modified[d]	Yes
3	Fails/positive	Complies	Positive	Modified	Yes
4[f]	Complies	Fails/positive	Negative	Modified	Yes
5[f]	Fails/positive	Fails/positive or negative	Positive or negative	Modified Modified	Yes Yes
6[f]	Negative	Negative	Negative	Modified[e]	Yes

(a) All cases assume that the institution has adequate sources of liquidity. If liquidity is a problem, a modified opinion or a disclaimer is necessary along with footnote explanation.

(b) Projected as of the end of next year.

(c) Cash flow from operations is net earnings (loss) adjusted for noncash charges to earnings, such as deferred taxes and depreciation.

(d) The presumption is that a modification is required, but this could be overcome under special circumstances. The following factors should be considered when deciding if a modified opinion is necessary. The number and relative importance of these factors will vary in each situation.

   1. *Quality of earnings*. Quality earnings are comprised of economically sound transactions, not transactions that are entered into because they receive favorable accounting or reporting treatment. Also, there is high assurance that accrual earnings will be realized in the future (unlike, for example, loans in which fee or interest income is recognized but is not collected).

   2. *Trend of earnings*. Earnings are improving.

   3. *Examiner's reports*. The examiners do not have an adversarial relationship with management. The report does not indicate significant concerns about asset quality, management or the association's ability to continue to operate.

   4. *Management*.
      a. *Quality*. Management possesses the skills to manage the association in the current environment.
      b. *Positive steps taken*. Management recognizes the association's problems and is taking steps to solve them. Common steps are:
         (1) Focusing on markets and products of greatest promise
         (2) Reducing interest rate risk
         (3) Reducing general and administrative expenses
         (4) Reducing non-income generating assets (e.g., facilities)
         (5) Improving quality of loans if necessary
      c. *Support by regulators*. The regulators appear to have confidence that management can capably operate the association.

   To overcome the modification assumption, the projections must extend at least one year from the date of the financial statements under SAS 59.

(e) A disclaimer of opinion should also be considered.

(f) In all of these cases, the auditor should contact the regulators to determine if the District Bank's Director of Examinations plans any action as a result of the failure to comply with net worth requirements.

FIG. 41.5   Guidelines for Auditors' Reports on Savings and Loan Associations

When a significant uncertainty exists regarding the continuation of the entity as a going concern, the auditor's report should include one or more midparagraphs describing the going concern uncertainty.

SAS 58, *Reports on Audited Financial Statements*, effective for reports issued on and after Jaunary 1, 1989, eliminates the auditor's option of issuing a qualified opinion in cases of material uncertainties. The only choices now available are: (1) a standard auditor's report modified by an additional paragraph(s) describing the uncertainties; and (2) a disclaimer of opinion. The same care that had been taken in the past in deciding whether to qualify an opinion for uncertainties should continue to be applied in determining whether the client's situation warrants the addition of the extra paragraph(s).

The following is an example of an explanatory paragraph of an auditor's report for an association with adequate liquidity sources that fails to meet the regulatory net worth requirements and has negative GAAP net worth:

The accompanying financial statements have been prepared assuming that the Association will continue as a going concern. As discussed more fully in Note A, the Association's continued existence is dependent on a return to profitable operations and forbearance by regulatory authorities as to actions that could be taken by them that would impair or preclude the Association's ability to attain the objective of profitable operations. Management's estimates of amounts to be realized on nonperforming assets, particularly troubled loans and real estate owned or in judgment, are based on an assumption that an orderly disposition thereof will occur. The financial statements do not include any adjustments relating to the recoverability of recorded asset amounts or the amounts and maturities of liabilities that might be necessary should the Association be unable to continue in existence or be otherwise precluded from the orderly conduct of its affairs.

The footnote disclosure accompanying the foregoing auditor's report is as follows:

Note A: *Continued Existence Considerations*
The Association's operations were adversely affected in 1989 and 1988 because of nonperforming loans and real estate owned or in judgment. The approximate net carrying amount of each of these categories of non-performing assets at September 30 of each year was as follows:

	September 30	
	1989	*1988*
Nonperforming:		
Loans, net	$50,000,000	$10,000,000
Real estate owned or in judgment, net	20,000,000	5,000,000
	$70,000,000	$15,000,000

In addition, operations were significantly affected in 1989 through charges to earnings of approximately $14,000,000 for loss reserves associated with these nonperforming assets.

As a result of these and other factors, the Association has incurred net losses of $12,000,000 and $1,000,000 for the years ended September 30, 1989 and 1988, respectively, and has an accumulated deficit of $6,000,000 at September 30, 1989.

Consequently, the Association fails to meet minimum net worth requirements imposed by the Federal Savings and Loan Insurance Corporation (FSLIC) at September 30, 1989. (Regulatory accumulated deficit was $2,000,000 as compared with a regulatory capital requirement of $18,000,000.) As such, the Association is subject to legal or administrative actions that could be taken by regulatory authorities which might

include, among others, operating restrictions or restrictions on additional Federal Home
Loan Bank borrowings.

As a result of the above matters, the Association's continuing existence as a going concern is dependent on a return to profitability (principally through conversion of
nonperforming assets to performing assets) and through forbearance by the Federal Home
Loan Bank Board with respect to the imposition of operating restrictions that might impair
or preclude the attainment of profitable operations and with respect to restrictions on the
maintenance of existing or additional borrowings.

Disclaimer of Opinion. Professional standards permit, but do not require, the
auditor to disclaim an opinion if there are serious uncertainties. However, a modified
standard report is used in most situations.

A disclaimer may be appropriate if an S&L has signed (or will shortly sign) a
consent-to-merge agreement with the FHLBB. Such an agreement requires the S&L
to merge with any partner that the FHLBB directs. The agreement also requires association management to clear all significant (and many trivial) decisions with the
FHLBB prior to implementation. The auditor might also issue a disclaimer if it is
known or apparent that the regulators have lost faith in the management of the association or are actively interested in closing the association. The following is an example of a disclaimer (final two paragraphs of the opinion).

> The financial statements referred to above have been prepared on a going concern basis
> that contemplates continuity of operations, realization of assets, and liquidation of liabili-
> ties in the ordinary course of business. The Association has incurred losses from operations
> for the year ended September 30, 1989 and as of September 30, 1989, and 1988, had a
> deficiency in assets of $10,000,000 and $6,000,000 under generally accepted accounting
> principles (Note L). Unaudited interim financial information reflects continuing losses sub-
> sequent to September 30, 1989. As discussed in Note A, the Association did not meet the
> minimum net worth requirement of the Federal Savings and Loan Insurance Corporation
> (FSLIC) at September 30, 1989 and has entered into a supervisory agreement with FSLIC.
> If the Association continues to incur losses and regulatory net worth becomes minimal, it is
> probable that the Association will be required to enter into a Consent Resolution that
> authorizes the FSLIC to negotiate a plan of merger, consolidation, reorganization, or trans-
> fer of assets and liabilities. The consolidated financial statements do not include any
> adjustments relating to the recoverability of recorded assets or liabilities that might be
> necessary should the Association be unable to continue in existence or be otherwise pre-
> cluded from the orderly conduct of its affairs.

> Due to the uncertainties regarding the Association's ability to attain profitable opera-
> tions and continued forbearance by regulatory authorities, we are unable to express and do
> not express an opinion on the accompanying consolidated financial statements for the
> years ended September 30, 1989 and 1988.

Basis of Reporting—RAP/GAAP

Beginning January 1, 1989, audited financial statements must be prepared in accordance with GAAP, with no deviations. The footnotes to the financial statements
must include a reconciliation of equity capital on a GAAP basis to regulatory capital
based on FSLIC regulations.

Footnotes to the financial statements typically disclose that the association has met minimum regulatory capital requirements. The dollar amount of required regulatory capital does not have to be disclosed. However, if the association's financial statements are included as part of (1) a conversion application/proxy; (2) a filing with the SEC; or (3) any offering circular, then FSLIC regulation 563c.102, paragraph 24(a) requires a statement as to:

whether or not the institution is in compliance with the Federal regulatory capital requirements (and state requirements where applicable). Also include the dollar amount of those regulatory capital requirements and the amount by which the institution exceeds or fails to meet those requirements.

The FHLBB issued several net worth enhancing regulations in the early 1980s, notably permitting associations to defer losses on the sale of mortgage-backed assets and to include in net worth the excess of the appraised value over the book value of office buildings. These regulations created the first significant differences between RAP and GAAP net worth.

To accommodate S&Ls wishing to issue their financial statements under these net worth enhancement regulations, the Auditing Standards Board issued *Reports in Filings Other Than With the Regulatory Agency on Financial Statements Prepared Using FHLBB Accounting Practices—Savings and Loan Associations* (AU 9544.10–.14). The interpretation states that if an S&L uses FHLBB accounting principles in financial statements that are filed with other than the FHLBB, the auditor should issue a qualified (modified, under SAS 58) or adverse opinion. The interpretation also describes an additional paragraph that can be included in the auditor's report to explain that the financial statements are prepared in accordance with FHLBB regulations.

Currency and Foreign Transactions Reporting Act

FHLBB Bulletin PA-7a-3 requires auditors to issue a special purpose report addressing that: (1) an association has established operating procedures and guidelines to comply with FHLBB T–Memorandum 53-7; (2) compliance tests have been performed by the auditor to ensure the association's operating procedures and compliance guidelines are being applied as described; and (3) the association's operating procedures and compliance guidelines have been updated for any amendments to the Act.

Memorandum 53-7 explains the requirements to comply with the Currency and Foreign Transactions Reporting Act, which contains recordkeeping and reporting provisions regarding domestic and foreign financial transactions. The financial institution must file a Currency Transaction Report (CTR) with the U.S. Department of the Treasury within 15 days after a customer deposits, withdraws, or transfers currency in excess of $10,000 (or its equivalent in foreign currency). Multiple transactions by, or for, any person which in any one day total more than $10,000 should be treated as a single transaction, if the financial institution is aware of them. Financial institutions record the transaction on Treasury Form 4789. The form shows the identity of the person who made the transaction, the identity of the person for whom the transaction was made, and the description of the transaction (deposit, withdrawal, cashed check, exchange of currency, loan payment, purchase of official check, or any other cash transaction).

Financial institutions are required to verify the identity of the person conducting the transaction. This may be done by examining any document normally accceptable as a means of identification when cashing checks, such as a driver's license or credit card. Financial institutions do not have to file CTRs for currency transactions with Federal Reserve Banks, Federal Home Loan Banks, or other domestic financial institutions. However, a list of such entities with which otherwise reportable transactions have occurred must be maintained. Currency transactions over $10,000 with foreign banks (including Canadian and Mexican banks) must be reported.

Financial institutions may exempt certain transactions from the reporting requirements, such as currency deposits or withdrawals by an established depositor who operates a retail business. However, financial institutions must maintain documentation, in a centralized location, of customers exempt from the currency transaction reporting requirements. The documentation should include identifying information (name, address, business, taxpayer identification number, and account number), the basis for the exemption (i.e., primarily a cash business such as a restaurant, church, carwash, etc.), and whether the exemption covers withdrawals, deposits, or both, as well as the dollar limit of the exemption. The Department of the Treasury can require an institution to provide a report that lists the institution's exempt customers.

The second major recordkeeping and reporting provision covers transportation of money into and out of the United States. Unlike the domestic reporting provisions, this section requires reporting of both currency and monetary instruments. A Currency and Monetary Instrument Report Form 4790 (CMIR) must be filed with the U.S. Customs Service within 30 days after transportation occurs, when any person, including a financial institution, physically transports, mails, or ships (or causes or attempts to do so) currency or monetary instruments in excess of $10,000 (or its equivalent in foreign currency) out of the United States. Also, any person, including a financial institution, receiving currency or monetary instruments in excess of $5,000 from outside the United States, on which no CMIR has been filed by the sender, must file a CMIR with the U.S. Customs Service.

Change in Accountants

FHLBB Bulletin PA-7a-4 requires association management to notify the Director of Examinations in writing within 15 days after the services of an external auditor have been terminated. The notification must discuss the reasons for the termination. It must also state whether within the past 24 months there had been any unresolved issues, scope restrictions, unanswered questions, or disagreements with the terminated external auditor on any matter of accounting principles, practices, audit procedures, financial statement disclosure, and/or auditing procedure which, if not resolved to the satisfaction of the terminated external auditor, would have caused (or will cause) the accountant to refer to the matter in his opinion.

The terminated external auditor must submit a letter to the Director of Examinations as to whether he agrees with the statements contained in the association's letter. The terminated auditor's letter must be sent within 10 days after he has been notified of his termination.

The association cannot appoint a new external auditor until it has received written approval from the Director of Examinations. The new external auditor must submit an engagement letter (as defined by Bulletin PA-7a) to the Director of Examinations prior to beginning any new audit work.

Extensions of Time to File Audit Reports

FHLBB Bulletin PA-7a-5 requires the auditor to request an extension of time if he will not be able to issue his audit report within 90 calendar days after the association's fiscal year end. This request will result in an extension of 30 days. If an extension of more than 30 days is needed, the association's board of directors must send a resolution authorizing the request for extension to the Supervisory Agent's Director of Examinations.

Verification of Mortgage Collateral for FHLBB Advances

The FHLBB district banks require the auditor to submit a letter verifying that the association has sufficient collateral for the bank's advances and complies with applicable regulations. Each district bank sets its own collateral requirements; accordingly, the auditor's letter will vary by FHLBB district. Regulation 525.7(b) defines eligible collateral as:

1. Fully disbursed whole first mortgages on improved residential property that are not more than 90 days delinquent.
2. Securities issued, insured, or guaranteed by the U.S. government or any of its agencies. This includes (but is not limited to) securities issued or guaranteed by FHLMC, FNMA, and GNMA.
3. Bank deposits.
4. Property that is acceptable to the district bank.

42

Securities and Commodities Broker/Dealers

BROKER/DEALER ENVIRONMENT

The securities fulfills three basic functions through a variety of financial products, services, and institutions. The functions and services include:

- *Capital formation.* Supplying capital to users is accomplished through services such as corporate finance consultation, public offerings, private placements, asset securitization, and merchant banking.
- *Market liquidity.* Market liquidity is maintained by bringing together buyers and sellers of investments. Services involve acting as agents (brokers) for customers, trading and arbitrage activities as principal, formation of investment funds or pools, market-making, and specialist activities.
- *Transfer of risk.* Investor exposure to market volatility is reduced through a variety of products such as futures, fowards, swaps, and options.

A variety of securities industry institutions facilitate the processing of these products and services, and each institution has a significant impact on the accounting and auditing requirements of a securities and comodities broker/dealer. In this chapter, securities broker/dealers and futures commission merchants are identified as SBDs and FCMs, respectively. It should be noted that most of the large SBDs are also FCMs; accordingly, many of the practices and systems used by SBDs in these cases are also applicable to the FCM business. In addition, there are numerous technical terms used in this chapter with necessarily brief definition; for further information, the reader is directed to the Audit and Accounting Guide, *Audits of Brokers and Dealers in Securities* (AICPA, 1985a). Some of the key types of institutions are:

- *Brokers.* Agents for customers.
- *Dealers.* Principals (for their own account).
- *Exchanges.* Central meeting places for buyers and sellers of listed securities.
- *Clearing organizations.* Trade processing and settlement facilitators.
- *Over-the-counter market.* Market where unlisted securities are bought and sold.
- *Depositories.* Facilities where securities are safekept.
- *Transfer agents.* Shareholder record keepers that oversee issuance and cancellation of certificates.
- *Regulatory agencies.* Regulators of the markets primarily for the protection of customers.

Overview

The environment in which an SBD operates may be described by the following seven general characteristics:

1. *Velocity.* Transaction turnaround is rapid.
2. *Volume.* Large numbers of transactions have to be managed and processed.
3. *Volatility.* Constant (sometimes extreme) change results from many external factors.
4. *Liquidity.* Assets are primarily cash and securities, and physical security has high priority.

5. *Regulation.* The industry is highly regulated by the SEC, Commodity Futures Trading Commission (CFTC), New York Stock Exchange (NYSE), various states, and so forth.

6. *Leverage.* Transactions, especially in commodity futures accounts, are entered into with the deposit of margin.

7. *Dynamics.* It is an industry in transition, in which new products and services are frequently developed.

These characteristics create significant operational and business risk, including the areas of concern described in the following sections.

Internal Control Structure. SBDs and FCMs have numerous accounting systems and subsystems (general ledger, trading, cage management, securities, margin, order entry, and so forth) processing a multitude of transactions. To accomplish this processing, the industry relies significantly on electronic data processing (EDP) and communications equipment. Controls over the capacity and efficiency of EDP systems can have a major impact on the day-to-day operations of the firm and its ability to react to change. Although it may be possible to utilize an outside computer service bureau or a correspondent, doing so does not diminish management's responsibility for adequate internal controls in this critical area.

A weak internal control structure is the predominant reason for securities firm failures. Therefore, it is essential that a firm's accounting and operational systems and controls be strong. The importance of controls is underscored by the requirement that independent auditors must issue to the SEC and/or CFTC a letter on internal control in connection with their examination of the financial statements.

Extension of Credit. Granting credit to customers and other institutions is another major risk for SBDs and FCMs. Clearing firms, as guarantors of trades, must continually monitor their correspondents for collateral sufficiency, nature, and location and must be able to liquidate the collateral quickly if that is necessary to fully recover the amount of the loan or receivable. A firm must have an adequate system to monitor margin or other credit granted and to obtain timely management reports. The credit system must monitor the status of:

• Concentrations in security positions and futures contracts that serve as collateral for loans.
• Established restrictions and limits.
• Outstanding margin calls.
• Mark-to-market customer long and short positions.
• Unsecured debit balances.
• Location of all collateral.

A firms's policy should also require periodic credit reviews of customer and institutional accounts, account executives' knowledge of their customers, accountability for losses suffered, and the establishment and monitoring of approved credit lines. The policy should provide for loan requirements that are not less than minimum regulatory requirements.

Commitments, Inventory, and Investment Positions. Commitments and firm inventory and investment positions, which are generally made in connection with underwriting, market-making, trading, and merchant banking activities, are areas of significant exposure. Close surveillance is essential to proper risk management because of market velocity, volatility, and leverage. A case in point are commitments; these typically are not recorded in the accounting records until a trade is ultimately executed, yet the dollar amounts of open commitments, inventory, and investment positions at risk can be substantial. It is imperative, therefore, that clear policies and methodologies exist within the firm as to limits, valuation, concentrations, and strategy approval.

Legal and Regulatory Compliance. As a result of operating in a highly regulated environment where compliance with all regulations is strictly enforced, a firm is always susceptible to penalties restricting its activities and to fines for noncompliance. Management typically assigns responsibility for monitoring regulatory compliance to either a compliance department, an internal audit department, or a combination of the two. In addition, independent auditors are engaged to monitor certain regulations regarding the adequacy of internal controls, the safeguarding of customer and firm assets, capital requirements, custody and control requirements, commodity customer segregated funds requirements, and the prompt payment for securities by customers. Complicated compliance requirements make it imperative that management understand the activities of the compliance and internal audit departments, and ensure that all employees understand their personal compliance responsibilities. Because management often is not aware of compliance problems until a complaint arrives, a regulatory examination is completed, or a lawsuit is filed, it is essential, for effective compliance, that there be well-defined policies, good training, competent people supervising revenue-generating and back-office activities, and individual accountability and reporting.

Financial Risks. The dynamic nature of the securities industry increases the potential for financial risks. Of specific interest to outside auditors and financial management of an SBD are:

* Control over and accounting for complex products such as asset-backed securities, interest rate and foreign currency swaps, and principal positions taken in merchant banking activities.
* Management of and regulatory reporting requirements for operations located overseas.
* Impact of tax law changes on product offerings and tax accounts.
* Impact of new regulations.

Globalization. Continued relative strength and stability of the U.S. economy have increasingly drawn foreign investors into U.S. markets. Conversely, sophisticated U.S. investors and corporations have increasingly sought to reduce risk by diversifying and arbitraging among all available markets and currencies, and to capitalize on trading opportunities created by imbalances among them. Exchanges have participated in this globalization through expanded trading hours, electronic linkages, and computerized trading activity.

Rapidly evolving communications technology has induced a radical change in traditional markets and facilitated the globalization process. Principal domestic markets are now linked through the Intermarket Trading System, National Association of Securities Dealers Automated Quotations (NASDAQ), and the Small Order Execution System.

Domestic exchanges are being electronically interconnected with foreign exchanges. Linkages now exist between the American, Midwest, and Toronto stock exchanges; the Chicago Mercantile and the Singapore Metals exchanges; the Comex and the New Zealand exchanges; the Boston and Montreal stock exchanges; and others. Consequently, a 24-hour, electronically integrated, international market is rapidly becoming a reality.

The complexity of a global market presents new challenges to industry management and independent auditors in the areas discussed thus far – internal controls, credit extension, commitments and positions, legal compliance, and financial risks.

Regulation

The Securities Exchange Act of 1934 (the 1934 Act) was adopted in response to the unrestrained speculation and manipulative schemes that characterized the U.S. securities markets in the 1920s and culminated with the market crash in 1929. The 1934 Act established a comprehensive system to regulate and control transactions in securities. Originally covering exchanges, members of exchanges, and securities listed on exchanges, the 1934 Act has been expanded over the years to cover virtually all participants in the securities markets and to an ever-increasing range of activities. Thus the 1934 Act today provides a comprehensive scheme of regulation for virtually all brokers and dealers in securities, the exchanges, over-the-counter facilities, and the mechanisms for clearing and settling transactions among SBDs, depositories, and transfer agents.

Under the 1934 Act, all aspects of an SBD's activities are comprehensively regulated. However, the discussion in this chapter focuses on the *financial responsibility rules* with which they must comply. A summary of significant financial responsibility rules applicable to SBDs is shown in Figure 42.1; these rules are discussed in the sections that follow.

Self-Regulatory Organizations.

Self-regulatory organizations (SROs) are membership organizations authorized under the securities laws to regulate their members. The 1934 Act defines self-regulatory organizations to include the registered national securities exchanges, registered associations of securities dealers, the Municipal Securities Rule-Making Board, and the registered clearing agencies. The National Association of Securities Dealers (NASD) is the premier registered association of securities dealers.

Clearing agencies are clearing houses that settle securities transactions between SBDs and depositories, hold certificates in bulk for members, and facilitate book entry transfer of securities.

SEC Rule	Description
8c-1 and 15c2-1	Fraudulent practices and hypothecation of customers' securities
15c3-1	Uniform Net Capital Rule
15c3-3	Reserve formula and possession or control of customers' fully paid and excess margin securities
17a-3	Maintenance of records
17a-4	Retention of records
17a-5	Financial reporting and audit requirements
17a-11	Notification concerning violations of SEC rules
17a-13	Quarterly security counts, comparisons, and verifications

FIG. 42.1   Summary of Significant SEC Rules for Financial Responsibility of Brokers and Dealers in Securities

SROs with the broadest impact on SBDs are the NYSE and the NASD, which have an obligation under the 1934 Act to enforce the securities laws. These organizations establish standards for conduct among members and for fair business practices. They conduct examinations of members and also provide arbitration services to settle disputes between members and with customers.

Securities Investor Protection Act. The back-office crisis of the late 1960s motivated Congress to enact the Securities Investor Protection Act (SIPA) in 1970. The Act created the Securities Investor Protection Corporation (SIPC), a government-chartered corporation designed to provide specific, limited protection to customers of securities firms that are forced to liquidate. Although SIPC is not a government agency, five of its directors are appointed by the President, subject to Senate approval. Membership in SIPC is mandatory for all SBDs.

SIPA is considered an amendment to the 1934 Act and modifies the bankruptcy laws with respect to the liquidation of SBDs. When notified by the SEC and the SROs that an SBD is in or approaching financial difficulty and that customers' funds or securities are threatened, SIPC will seek the appointment of a trustee by the federal court to take control and commence a liquidation. Once a trustee is appointed the result is inevitable: the SBD will be dissolved. Self-liquidation under the supervision of an SRO without the appointment of a trustee is also permitted if SIPC believes that such liquidation will not result in customer losses.

Customers effecting securities transactions with the failed SBD receive protection under SIPA, but creditors do not. Customer securities that can be identified are returned; otherwise the customer will receive cash to cover his losses up to $100,000 for credit balances and $500,000 for unreturned securities. Customer claims exceeding these limits are treated as general creditor claims.

Regulation of Securities Broker/Dealers

Focus report (Rule 17a-5). The financial reporting requirements for SBDs are the key elements of an "early warning" system, designed to promptly identify financial and operational problems. The current system includes a specially designed report, Form X-17A-5, known as the FOCUS report (the acronym for Financial and Operational Combined Uniform Single Report); periodic examination by the regulatory authorities; and notification requirements when certain adverse conditions exist. Rule 17a-5 has several main components. It requires:

- Filing of unaudited monthly and quarterly FOCUS reports and an annual audited report.
- Engagement of an independent auditor and selection of a fiscal year.
- Notification by the SBD of the replacement of the independent auditor.
- Providing customers with a balance sheet, one of them audited twice a year.
- Specifically for the independent auditor:
  - Performance of specified minimum audit procedures, including several requirements that go beyond GAAS, to accomplish specific regulatory goals.
  - A statement by the auditor on "material inadequacies" in the SBD's internal controls.
  - Verification by the auditor of SIPC assessments.

Generally, SBDs who do a public business and carry customer accounts must file the Part I FOCUS report monthly and a complete set of unaudited financial and operational data quarterly in Part II.

Extensions to file beyond 30 days are discouraged as regulators are extremely concerned with timely and accurate information regarding the financial and operational condition of the SBD. The system tries to force prompt disclosure of information. Indeed, the last unaudited FOCUS report filed with the regulators is usually compared with the audited report for the same date (received later) to test the integrity of the unaudited reports as filed. For this purpose, the audited report must include a reconciliation of differences between the audited report and the unaudited filing. The rule sets forth minimum auditing requirements including:

- Verifying compliance with certain important financial responsibility requirements.
- Reviewing the system of internal accounting control to determine the existence of any "material inadequacies," as defined in the rule, and, if any exist, indicating any corrective action taken.

Net capital rule (Rule 15c3-1). The object of the net capital rule is to assure that SBDs maintain sufficient liquid assets to satisfy their current indebtedness, particularly customer claims. Actually a liquidity and leverage test at a point in time, the rule attempts to convert a going concern balance sheet into an analysis akin to a realization and liquidation statement. In its operation the rule has three components:

1. *Net capital.* The amount of an SBD's unencumbered liquid assets.
2. *Required net capital.* The amount of net capital required to be in compliance with the rule. Required net capital is a function of the SBD's business and is affected by the volume and type of business conducted; it is measured in proportion to its liabilities (primarily to customers).
3. *Minimum net capital.* A stated minimum dollar amount of net capital that an SBD must have regardless of the amount determined to be otherwise required under the rule.

The net capital test is a moment-to-moment test; the SBD may not effect a transaction in securities at any time net capital is not sufficient to meet the requirements under the rule.

The formula for determining the amount of net capital an SBD must have is generally as follows:

* Net worth, as defined under GAAP,
* Plus subordinated liabilities,
* Less (1) assets defined in the rule as not readily marketable, (2) assets not readily convertible into cash, (3) deductions for certain operational inefficiencies, and (4) discounts (also known as haircuts) from the market value of marketable securities and open contractual commitments.

The rule is very conservative in its view of what is readily convertible into cash. Assets that have intrinsic value may be zero-valued under the rule because their value cannot be determined by a market quotation or their collectibility is not secured with readily salable assets.

The regulatory requirements represent minimum compliance levels. Regulators monitor the net capital carefully and SBDs must maintain an adequate cushion to avoid an inadvertent violation and to avoid the early warning levels that would trigger increased reporting and scrutiny.

Customer securities control and reserves (Rule 15c3-3). This rule was created in response to the severe operational problems of the late 1960s and the concern that customer funds and securities might be used inappropriately by SBDs to finance their own speculative activities, thereby exposing their customers to unwarranted risk of loss. The rule permits the use of customers monies only to finance other customer transactions.

The rule has two main parts, the first of which requires SBDs to have physical possession or control of all fully paid and excess margin securities carried for the accounts of customers. An SBD must determine daily that it complies with this segment of the rule. The second part requires the SBD to make a weekly computation (as of the close of business each Friday) of the formula for the determination of reserve requirements for brokers and dealers (the "reserve formula"). The reserve formula determines "credits," that is, the amount of customer monies or monies obtained from the use of customer securities. Subtracted from that figure are "debits," or the amount of money owed by customers or by other SBDs relating to customer transactions. If the credits exceed the debits, the broker/dealer must deposit the excess by the morning of the second business day following the computation in a Special Bank Account for the Exclusive Benefit of Customers (the "reserve bank account"). If the debits exceed the credits no deposit is made.

Books and records (Rules 17a-3 and 17a-4). Rule 17a-3 requires that specified records be kept current, including:

* A complete set of financial accounting records
* General ledger
* Subsidiary ledgers

- Summary journals
- A stock record

It also specifies that the SBD prepare certain records regarding transactions, employees, and customers as well as a periodic trial balance and the net capital computation.

The stock record is a self-balancing, double entry perpetual inventory system used to account for shares of stock or principal amount of debt, buy security issue. The "long" side of the ledger indicates to whom securities are owed, and the "short" side indicates where the certificates for those securities are actually located. To be in balance, there must be enough securities on the short side to meet all of the long positions.

Rule 17a-4 specifies the required duration that certain records are to be maintained. SBDs are permitted to preserve the firm's records on microfilm or utilize a service bureau whose records by agreement are available to the SEC and the SROs.

Securities count (Rule 17a-13). Rule 17a-13 requires the SBD to count all securities quarterly, or cyclically within the quarter.

Extension of credit (Regulation T). Under the authority of the 1934 Act, Regulation T was adopted by the Board of Governors of the Federal Reserve System (FRB) to control the extension of credit by SBDs to customers for the purpose of purchasing securities. The objective of the regulation is to (1) control the amount of the nation's credit extended to speculate in the securities market and (2) dampen leverage securities speculation.

All securities transactions with an SBD are covered by Regulation T, although margin is not required for certain transactions. The rule also covers same day substitutions, day trading, stock borrows, market function accounts, and other very specific provisions.

Securities purchased in a cash account must be paid for in full within seven days; margin calls must also be paid within seven days. Generally payment may not be made by the sale of the same securities purchased (a "free ride"). If the customer fails to pay and no extension has been received, the SBD must liquidate the account and not effect a transaction for the account for 90 days (a "frozen account") unless the money is in the account to cover a purchase. An order to sell securities for a cash account should not be accepted unless the customer owns the securities and will promptly deliver the certificate. Otherwise the sale is classified as a short sale and should be effected in a margin account, with a margin deposit.

Securities purchased on margin require an "initial margin" of 50% as a "down payment" of the purchase price. The margin need not be maintained at this level; however, a subsequent transaction will trigger the requirement that the entire account be remargined.

Margin rules. The FRB establishes the initial margin or down payment required to purchase margin securities. However, the exchanges and the NASD have established the maintenance rules regarding the minimum equity required in SBD margin accounts. In general, the customer is required to maintain equity in the margin account equal to 25% of the market value of long positions in the account and 30% of the market value of short positions in the account.

In addition, most SBDs have "house rules" that generally provide for a higher maintenance margin requirement, particularly with respect to specific individual securities or specified classes of securities.

Rules of fair practice. The SROs have adopted rules for the "business conduct of members" that are based on what the NASD describes as just and equitable principles of trade. They cover a range of conduct with customers from execution of trades, mark-ups on principal trades, delivery of securities, corporate financing, free-riding, withholding publication of transactions and quotations, fair dealing with customers, and a host of other areas.

Customer securities hypothecation (Rules 8c-1 and 15c2-1. Most margin account agreements generally provide that customer's securities pledged with the SBD to secure the customer's debit balance can be repledged or hypothecated to banks to finance the debit balance.

Notification of rule violations (Rule 17a-11). As part of the early warning system employed by the SEC and the SROs, SBDs who are in or approaching financial difficulty are required under certain circumstances to give prompt notice of such difficulties by telegram, and under certain circumstances to provide more frequent and comprehensive financial data to the regulators.

Early warning reporting. If the net capital of an SBD exceeds certain warning parameters, the more comprehensive Part II or IIA FOCUS Report must be filed on a monthly basis until the net capital is below the early warning level for three consecutive months.

The SBD must also give prompt notice to the regulators if subordinated debt scheduled to mature within six months would result in net capital levels that would trigger the early warning parameters.

Regulation of Futures Commission Merchants. The CFTC, established in 1975 after an extensive rulemaking procedure, had adopted minimum financial and related reporting requirements for futures commission merchants.

Similar to the rules for SBDs, the minimum financial and reporting requirements for FCMs are divided into the following areas:

• Financial reporting
• Early warning requirements
• Net capital requirements
• Segregation regulations
• Record-keeping regulations

Filing requirements. Each FCM must file Form 1-FR with the CFTC quarterly and with certain SROs for each fiscal year. Forms must be filed no later than 45 days after the date for which the report is made (except for the fourth quarter which must be filed no later than 90 days after the close of the fiscal year) and must be certified by an independent public accountant. Each Form 1-FR which is not as of the year end must contain a:

* Statement of financial condition
* Statement of changes in ownership equity
* Computation of the minimum capital requirements
* Schedule of segregation requirements and funds on deposit in segregation

In addition, the annual Form 1-FR must contain a statement of income, a statement of changes in financial position (cash flows under SFAS 95), and a statement of changes in liabilities subordinated to claims of general creditors. The certified statements need not be filed in 1-FR format as long as they are presented in conformity with GAAP.

Net capital rule. All FCMs are subject to an early warning system that requires notices to be sent to the CFTC and SRO whenever adjusted net capital drops below specified levels. Generally these levels are approximately 150% of the minimum capital requirements. An FCM must also notify the CFTC and the SROs if (1) at any time its books and records are not current, (2) it has been notified by an independent public accountant of the existence of a material inadequacy, or (3) it determines that a position it carries for another FCM, normally referred to as an omnibus account, must be liquidated because the other FCM has failed to meet a margin call.

As to accountant's qualifications and reports, the audit must be conducted in accordance with GAAS and must also include a review and appropriate tests of the accounting system, the internal control procedures, and the procedures for safeguarding customer and firm assets.

To continue in business an FCM must maintain adjusted net capital equal to or in excess of a calculated amount not less than $50,000.

Adjusted net capital means the amount of by which current assets exceed liabilities adjusted by certain percentage deductions of those assets (haircuts). Generally, current assets include those assets readily convertible into cash, while liabilities generally encompass all liabilities except those subordinated to the claims of general creditors. For FCMs involved only in commission and trading businesses, the computation of adjusted net capital should be identical to the computation of net capital for SBDs as contained in the SEC Rule 15c3-1 (discussed earlier).

Segregation of customer funds. All funds received by an FCM to margin or secure a futures or options transaction must be separately accounted for and segregated as the property of the customer. To compute the segregated amount, the firm must aggregate the net payable to each customer. This amount must be segregated and on deposit with a bank, trust company, clearing organization, or another FCM.

Books and records. The CFTC's record-keeping regulations generally require that all books and records used and generated by the FCM in its business be kept for a period of five years and should be readily accessible for the first two years of this period.

Internal Control Reporting Requirements

SEC rules. Under Rule 17a-5, the SEC requires the independent accountant to review and report on internal control. The objective is to obtain disclosure of material inadequacies at the date of the examination in the accounting system, internal controls, and procedures for safeguarding securities. Four specific areas of review are listed in the rule:

1. Periodic computations of aggregate indebtedness and net capital.
2. Quarterly securities examinations, counts, verifications and comparisons, and the recording of differences.
3. Compliance with the prompt payment requirements for securities.
4. Physical possession or control of all fully paid and excess margin securities of customers.

The AICPA Audit and Accounting Guide, *Audits of Brokers and Dealers in Securities* (1985a; generally referred to in this chapter as the SBD Guide), states that the accountant's report should (p. 52):

1. express an opinion on the adequacy of the practices and procedures listed above in relation to the definition of a material inadequacy as stated in Rule 17a-5(g)(3); and
2. disclose material weaknesses in internal control (including procedures for safeguarding securities) that are revealed through a study and evaluation conducted to determine the scope of auditing procedures.

Rule 17a-5(g)(3) defines a material inadequacy as any condition that does or would:

- Inhibit an SBD from promptly completing securities transactions or promptly discharging his responsibilities to customers, other SBDs, or creditors.
- Result in material financial loss.
- Result in material misstatements of the SBD's financial statements.
- Result in violations of the SEC's record-keeping or financial responsibility rules.

SAS 30, *Reporting on Internal Accounting Control* (AU 642), states that an agency may publish specific criteria for evaluating the adequacy of internal control for its purposes. SAS 30 also gives guidance on reports on internal control based solely on a study for the use of management, specific regulatory agencies, and other specified third parties. A *material weakness* in internal accounting control is narrowly defined as a condition that results "in more than a relatively low risk of errors or irregularities in amounts that would be material in relation to financial statements" (AU 642.30). In contrast, the term *material inadequacy* as used in the SEC rule is broad and encompasses both a material weakness in internal accounting control and other material inadequacies.[1]

---

[1] SAS 60, *Communication of Internal Control Structure Related Matters Noted in an Audit* (AU 325), was released in 1988, superseding SAS 30 requirements applicable to internal control reporting based only on an audit (AU 642.47–.53). SAS 60 replaces the concept of *material weaknesses* with the concept of *reportable conditions* when reporting on internal control as part of a financial statement audit. SAS 60 does not affect the SEC or CFTC definitions of material inadequacy.

The auditor's responsibility with respect to a material inadequacy is to call it to the attention of the chief financial officer (or financial principal) of the broker or dealer, who shall have a responsibility to inform the SEC and the designated examination authority (i.e., the SRO) by telegraphic notice within 24 hours thereafter. A material inadequacy that has been corrected still constitutes a material inadequacy for the auditor's purposes if it was not reported by management to the SEC and the broker's designated examining authority.

The SBD Guide contains examples of the required SEC reports on internal control.

CFTC rules. The CFTC requirements for internal control reporting are similar to those of the SEC, except that the notification requirements under the CFTC rules for reporting a material inadequacy are three business days rather than the 24 hours allowed under SEC rules. Furthermore, the CFTC requires a written report to be filed within five business days, describing the corrective action taken.

The SBD Guide contains examples of the required CFTC reports on internal control.

ACCOUNTING AND FINANCIAL REPORTING

AICPA Audit and Accounting Guide

The AICPA Audit and Accounting Guide, *Audits of Brokers and Dealers in Securities* (1985a), constitutes most of the authoritative literature on accounting for and auditing of SBDs and FCMs. It presents recommendations of the AICPA Stockbrokerage and Investment Banking Committee regarding the application of GAAS to audits of SBD financial statements. It also includes descriptions of and recommendations on specialized accounting and reporting principles and practices. A separate guide for futures commission merchants is in process at the AICPA as of mid-1988.

SFAS 32 (as amended by SFAS 83) specifies that the specialized accounting and reporting principles and practices contained in the SBD Guide are preferable accounting principles for purposes of justifying a change in accounting principles (St4.101).

Broker/Dealer Balance Sheet

The balance sheet ordinarily does not present current and noncurrent classifications, as the majority of the significant assets and liabilities are recorded at fair value and are converted to cash in a normal operating cycle. The significant accounts that normally are found on an SBD's balance sheet include:

Assets
- Securities purchased under agreements to resell
- Firm inventory accounts
- Receivables from brokers and dealers
- Receivables from customers

- Secured demand notes
- Exchange memberships

Liabilities

- Bank loans
- Securities sold under agreement to repurchase
- Payables to brokers and dealers
- Securities sold, not yet purchased
- Payables to customers
- Subordinated liabilities

These accounts are discussed in the sections that follow.

Repurchase and Resale Agreements. Securities purchased/sold under agreements to resell/repurchase are called repurchase transactions, or repos, and are security sales with an agreement by the seller to repurchase the same or a substantially identical security at a stated price. The time interval between origination and reversal of a repo varies depending on the terms of the agreement. Examples include:

- *Overnight repo.* Repurchase date is the following day.
- *Term repo.* Repurchase date is a specified date in the future, normally within six months.
- *Open repo.* Indefinite repurchase date, in which the borrower or lender typically has the option to close at any time.
- *Repo to maturity.* Term extends to the maturity date of the underlying security.

Although repo and reverse repo transactions are documented as security sales, they are in fact loans and borrowings, and are to be so accounted for. In a repo, securities owned by the SBD are "sold," but since the same (or substantially identical) securities must be "bought" back, the "sales proceeds" are a borrowing by the SBD, with the securities representing the collateral for the debt. The buyer is not entitled to collect the interest on the collateral; instead this belongs to the seller, who pays a negotiated rate of interest to the buyer on the temporary sales proceeds. The securities sold are not removed from the SBD's trading or investment account, but the proceeds are credited to a payable account.

In a reverse repo, the opposite occurs. The buyer agrees to sell the securities back to the seller; the cash paid out is classified with receivables. In each transaction one party has a repurchase agreement and the counterparty has a reverse repurchase agreement.

If an SBD buys a reverse repo and at about the same time matches it with a repo, this is called a matched repurchase agreement. In this form of trading, the SBD earns a profit or incurs a loss based on the difference between interest earned on the repo and interest paid on the reverse repo. In some cases the principal amounts of the two transactions are not the same. Because there is no legal right of offset, matched repos are shown broad—as both receivables (along with other reverse repos) and payables (along with other repos).

Footnote disclosure is often given of the amount of matched repo included in the balance sheet. Collateral (i.e., the securities) related to repos and reverse repos is also often disclosed.

Repos are further discussed in Chapter 21.

Inventory and Short Sales. Securities purchased for the account of the SBD for trading or investment purposes are included in firm inventory. Trading securities include readily marketable securities and result in the firm's recognition of ordinary gains or losses from marking them to market, recorded in the current period's profit or loss. Investment securities include both readily marketable and not readily marketable securities (i.e., venture capital investments, oil leases, and so forth) purchased with the expectation of being held for longer durations. For investment accounts, marketable and not readily marketable securities are recorded at market value or fair value, respectively. Not readily marketable investments may include securities that (1) represent a large block of a security with limited liquidity, (2) have no market on a securities exchange or no independent publicly quoted market, or (3) cannot be publicly offered or sold because registration has not taken place under the Securities Act of 1933.

Valuation of not readily marketable securities and other investments as firm inventory at fair value measures the trading and investment decisions of the SBD's management. Appreciation or depreciation in the value of securities is directly reflected in the firm's income statement. Not readily marketable securities should be separately disclosed in the statement of financial condition if material.

Trading in securities for the firm's own account sometimes leads to a liability for securities sold, not yet purchased. The amount of such liability is the market value of the securities sold "short." These "shorts" must be recorded as liabilities and are marked to market.

The general categories of firm inventory (i.e., U.S. government obligations, corporate stocks, and so forth) along with any restrictions on issues that are pledged, should be disclosed in the notes to the financial statements.

Receivables and Payables—Broker/Dealers. Assets and liabilities arising from security transactions between brokers are generally significant accounts in the financial statements of an SBD. The major categories of receivables and payables include:

Asset Accounts

- Failed-to-deliver
- Securities borrowed
- Receivable from clearing corporation

Liability Accounts

- Failed-to-receive
- Securities loaned
- Payable to clearing corporation

Failed-to-deliver. An SBD that does not deliver the securities sold on the settlement date is said to have failed to deliver the securities to the purchasing broker. In this case, the selling broker records the selling price as an asset in the receivable account "due from brokers or dealers"; this asset will be collected upon eventual delivery of the securities. The firm is obliged to deliver the securities when they are available in deliverable form or may borrow the securities from other brokers to make delivery.

The related credit entry is the firm trading account if the securities sold belonged to the firm, or a customer's account if the securities sold belonged to a customer.

Securities borrowed. The firm may borrow securities from another broker/dealer to make delivery when a security sold is not in a deliverable form. The situation usually arises when:

1. A customer or the firm is selling short; that is, the customer or firm is selling securities it does not own.
2. A customer sells securities but has not yet delivered them to the broker.
3. The firm has received the securities but, because they are not properly endorsed, they cannot be delivered.

When a firm borrows a security, it advances cash as collateral to the lending broker equal to the market value of the securities borrowed. This amount is recorded as the receivable due from the lending broker. If the market value of the borrowed security increases, the lender of the security may call upon the borrower to remit additional cash representing such increase. Conversely, if the market value declines, the borrowing broker may call for a return of part of his cash collateral. This marking to market results in an increase or decrease in the receivable balance. It should be noted that the borrowing broker normally charges interest (called a rebate), which is recorded on the borrowing broker's books as interest income.

When the securities become deliverable, the borrowed securities are returned to the lending broker and all cash advanced to the lending broker representing market value and subsequent mark-to-market calls for securities borrowed are returned to the borrowing broker.

Failed-to-receive. A purchasing SBD is said to have failed to receive the securities from the selling broker if on settlement date the securities purchased are not received. In this case, the SBD must record the purchase price of the securities as a liability to the selling SBD and include the amount in "payable to brokers or dealers." Upon delivery of the securities, the liability account is eliminated as payment is made to the selling broker. Delivery by the selling broker is usually made a short time after the settlement date, normally not exceeding one month.

When the firm is buying the securities for its own account, a corresponding debit entry is recorded in the firm trading account; when the firm is purchasing the securities for the account of a customer, the corresponding debit is made in a customer account (accounts receivable—customer name).

Securities loaned. Securities loaned are financing arrangements in which securities are lent, with interest charged for the funds advanced. Customers' fully paid and excess margin securities may not be used for lending purposes. The lending broker receives as collateral cash equal to the securities' market value, which is recorded as payable to the borrowing broker and repaid upon return of the securities.

If the market value of the collateral increases while the loan is outstanding, the lending broker may call upon the borrower to put up additional collateral.

Clearing corporation balances. Clearing corporations provide efficient and orderly trade clearance and settlement services, affording participants better control by allowing securities to be moved through book entry procedures, rather than physically. The clearing corporation performs post-trade processing and trade comparisons among the numerous brokers, and acts as a settlement vehicle between the buying and selling broker.

The large volume of daily trade settlements is processed under a system known as the Continuous Net Settlement (CNS) System involving both the clearing corporation and a securities depository. On a daily basis, a firm's trades of a given security are netted to a single receive or deliver position, through the use of sophisticated EDP apparatus. The net selling broker (one who sells more of a particular security than he buys) would then "deliver" the securities to the receiving firm via the depository's records, by a participant computer terminal system located in the SBD's offices. If there are not sufficient quantities of the needed security at the depository, the firm can either deposit additional securities in the depository or borrow the securities to cover delivery.

All CNS transactions are also netted to one money settlement position daily, and if the value of the securities received (purchased) is greater than that delivered (sold), the SBD must pay the clearing corporation the net value. If the value delivered is greater than that received, the converse occurs.

The clearing corporation prepares daily reports for participants showing activity by security, the related money balances, and the net settlement amount for the broker's clearance. This report also describes the projected trades that will clear on the following day. This helps the cashier's department to maintain adequate quantities of securities that will be needed for clearance in the coming days.

A small proportion of trades for which the clearing corporation cannot match the selling broker with the buying broker are listed, and the brokers are notified of the unmatched status for further investigation. Upon resolution, the trades are then put back into the system for clearance through the normal channels.

An example of a well-known clearing corporation is the National Securities Clearing Corporation (NSCC), which operates in tandem with the Depository Trust Company (DTC).

Receivables and Payables—Customers. A primary function of an SBD is to buy and sell securities on behalf of its customers. Customer purchase transactions are entered into the "receivable from customers" account, and the customer sale transactions into the "payable to customers" account. The transactions are recorded either in the customer's cash account or his margin account, as applicable. A customer may have both a cash and a margin account; although maintained separately, both should be combined in financial statement presentations.

A customer who opens a cash account agrees to pay the full price of each security purchased by the settlement date. When a customer purchases securities, a debit entry is made into his cash account for the purchase price. The purchase is executed on the trade date, and the customer must pay for the securities on the fifth business day thereafter (settlement date). The firm can liquidate an account by selling the security if it is not paid for by the seventh business day. The customer may order that the certificate be delivered to him, or he may leave it with the broker for safekeeping. All net customer debit balances are included in the "receivable from customers" category appearing in the statement of financial condition.

When a customer sells securities, a credit balance develops in his cash account if he has not been paid the sale proceeds, or elects to keep money on deposit. Some brokers pay interest on customers' credit balances, but they are not required to do so. All net customer credit balances are included in the "payable to customers" category appearing in the statement of financial condition.

A customer's margin account is used to record transactions that involve borrowing from the SBD. The amount lent by the broker to the customer purchasing on margin is the customer's margin account debit balance, which will not change because of any increase or decrease in the market value of the security purchased. A margin account credit balance is the amount of cash left in a customer's account after he has fully paid for the securities.

Customer statements that detail all transactions (e.g., security purchases, sales, interest income and expense, dividends) are prepared and mailed monthly by the SBD. The statements also show the money balance and the details of the customer's security position.

Subordinated Cash Loans and Demand Notes. Two sources of regulatory net capital available to SBDs are subordinated cash loans and secured demand notes, often made by persons associated with the SBD (often a partner, shareholder, officer, employee, or their relatives). If the subordinated cash loan is subject to a qualified subordination agreement, and the collateral securing the secured demand note is subject to a collateral agreement (as defined in Appendix D of Rule 15c3-1 of the 1934 Act), the principal amount of the loan or note qualifies as capital for purposes of computing the SBD's net capital. However, subordinated debt cannot represent more than 70% of the total of net worth and subordinated debt.

Cash loans. In a typical subordinated cash loan agreement, the lender lends cash to the SBD and in return receives a written promise in the form of a note, which sets forth the repayment terms, the interest rate, and an agreement by the lender to subordinate his claim to other general creditors of the SBD.

Secured demand notes. A secured demand note is an interest-bearing promissory note (not always at market) executed by the lender, payable upon demand of the SBD to which it is granted. The SBD records the note as an asset and sets up a subordinated liability account. The demand note receivable is collateralized by securities, and the right to demand payment may be conditioned on the occurrence of certain events.

If the securities pledged as collateral are subject to qualified subordination agreement (referred to as a secured demand note collateral agreement), their market value must be reduced by the net capital haircut percentages in determining the adequacy of the collateral. The adjusted value (i.e., market value less haircut) of the securities must be equal to or greater than the principal amount of the secured demand note to adequately collateralize it, thus permitting the principal amount of the note to qualify as SBD capital. The lender actually retains ownership of the collateral, and has the benefit of any increase but also bears the risk of any decrease in its value.

Securities pledged as collateral must be fully paid for and must be in bearer form or registered in the name of the SBD or custodian. This allows for transferability of the securities in the event they are required to be liquidated. The lender may withdraw any excess collateral, or substitute cash or other securities as collateral.

The securities received as collateral and cash, if any, are recorded in a manner similar to the recording of customer accounts.

Financial statement presentation. For financial reporting purposes:

• A separate statement of changes in liabilities subordinated to claims of general creditors is required as part of the audited financial statements. This statement describes the balance at the beginning of the year and all additions, dispositions, and maturities affecting each category of the subordination agreement held.

• The components of subordinated liabilities, with interest rates and maturity dates specified, should be disclosed in the notes to the financial statements.

• Subordinated liabilities and stockholders' equity should not be combined in a single amount. However, it is permissible to include both categories under the heading "Subordinated Liabilities and Stockholders' Equity" provided there are separate subtotals for each component.

Exchange Memberships. An exchange membership represents the right to transact business on a specific exchange. SBDs often have multiple memberships on a single exchange, with the memberships usually registered in the names of individuals affiliated with the firm. A membership is considered to be an asset of the brokerage concern if it is held by the broker under an "A-B-C agreement" or if its use has been contributed to the broker under a subordination agreement.

Under an A-B-C agreement, the member agrees that upon dissolution of the member organization or his ceasing to be a participant therein (or upon his death or other contigencies), he or his legal representatives will comply with the terms of one of the following options:

1. Retain his membership and pay to the member organization the amount necessary to purchase another membership.
2. Sell his membership and pay the proceeds over to the member organization.
3. Transfer his membership for a nominal consideration to a person designated by the member organization and satisfactory to the exchange.

The propriety of considering exchange memberships as assets of the brokerage concern should be ascertained by reference to partnership agreements or other applicable documents of the firm.

Exchange memberships should be valued at cost or at a lesser amount when there is an indication of a permanent impairment in value of a significant amount. Exchange memberships that are contributed for use by the broker and subordinated to the claims of general creditors should be carried at market value, with an offsetting amount shown as part of subordinated liabilities in the statement of financial condition.

Bank Loans. Bank borrowings represent obligations incurred by a broker to:

* Finance securities purchases by customers on margin.
* Satisfy amounts owed as a result of the securities settlement process.
* Finance the firm's securities inventories.
* General corporate purposes.

These borrowings are generally collateralized by securities measured at market value. The amount of the borrowings (and the value of securities in collateral status) may vary daily as a result of market fluctuations and trading volume. Therefore, when the market value of the collateral increases, the SBD may request the bank to release securities in excess of the amount required to fully secure the loan. Conversely, if the market value of the collateral declines, the lender may request the deposits of additional collateral.

Bank loans are either classified as firm loans or customer loans, depending on the type of collateral. Customer-owned securities can collateralize only customer loans; securities belonging to the firm, subordinated lenders, and partners (or principal officers or directors) of the firm are used as collateral for firm loans. Once a customer's securities are fully paid for or constitute excess margin, there must be prompt removal of such securities used as collateral (Rule 15c3-3). When used as collateral, ownership of the securities does not change, but their location is moved to the lending bank.

Broker/Dealer Income Statement

The significant accounts specific to an SBD and normally found on an SBD income statement include:

* Commission income (expense)
* Interest income (expense)
* Trading gain (loss)
* Underwriting income
* Management and investment advisory income
* Floor brokerage and exchange fees

Commission Income and Expense. The SBD's fee for executing a trade is called a commission, and is charged for both purchases and sales of securities. Commission income often represents the largest source of revenue. It is directly correlated with customer trading volume and the total dollar amount of the trades. A portion of the revenue received by the SBD is paid to the registered representative and is recorded as commission expense.

Interest Income. Interest is earned primarily on debit balances in customer margin accounts. A reverse repurchase agreement, which is a collateralized loan, also generates interest income. In the purchase of securities with a simultaneous agreement to resell the same or substantially identical securities, interest is earned on the cash paid on purchase of the security, for the period of time until resale. A similar result occurs in securities borrowed transactions, in which the borrowing SBD has deposited cash with the other broker, who will pay interest thereon. Interest-bearing corporate, municipal, and government securities held for firm trading and investment purposes also earn applicable interest for the period held.

Interest Expense. Interest charges typically arise in four types of transactions:

1. Bank loans to finance payment for securities purchased for the firm's own account or to finance customer margin purchases.
2. Repurchase agreements with financial institutions to finance payment for securities purchased. The repurchase price is higher than the original purchase price, with the difference representing interest.
3. Securities loaned to other SBDs, with interest paid on the cash received.
4. Subordinated cash loans and demand note loans.

Trading. A securities dealer may buy and sell securities for its own account. Inventories of securities are valued at market, and market adjustments (the difference between carrying value and market value) are reflected in income along with realized gains and losses.

Underwriting. Corporate and governmental issuers of securities normally engage an SBD to underwrite the security being offered. The underwriter contracts to buy the issue on a firm commitment or on a best efforts basis.

When the SBD sells the securities to the public, the difference between the purchase price paid by the public and the contract price paid by the broker to the issuer represents underwriting income or loss, which may also include related corporate finance fees.

It should be noted that even if the entire contracted amount is not sold during the reporting period, an unrealized gain (loss) may be reflected in the broker/dealer's income statement when the inventory account is marked to market.

Because the dollar amount of most new securities issues is very large and the potential losses through unsuccessful marketing are normally too great for any single SBD to assume, group accounts or syndicates may be formed to spread the risk (see the later section entitled "Investment Banking Cycle").

Material underwriting commitments open at a reporting date are typically disclosed in the notes to the SBD's financial statements. Like trading positions, these commitments are marked to market and unrealized gain or losses are recorded in income.

Advisory Income. Fees are received by SBDs providing investment advice, research, and administrative services for customers. In many cases, the customer is a pension fund with a large investment portfolio. The fee is usually based on the net assets of the fund if the portfolio is managed by the SBD.

Floor Brokerage and Exchange Fees. When an SBD wishes to trade on an exchange at which it is not a member, it must trade through another member broker who will charge a floor brokerage fee. Payments are made periodically either directly to the member broker or through a clearing organization.

Exchange fees represent amounts assessed by each of the exchanges for the privilege of conducting business, based on a monthly report of net commissions earned on transactions executed on the exchange. The expenses are proportional to the volume of trading carried out by the SBD on the exchanges.

Other Financial Statements and Disclosures

In addition to the statement of financial condition (balance sheet), statement of operations (income statement), and statement of cash flows,[2] Rule 17a-5 requires that the annual audited financial statements also include a statement of changes in stockholders' (partners') equity and a statement of changes in liabilities subordinated to claims of general creditors.

The following supporting schedules must also be filed with the audited report:

1. Computation of net capital.
2. Computation of reserve requirements.
3. Schedule of segregation requirements and funds in segregation.
4. Information relating to possession or control requirements.
5. A reconciliation, including appropriate explanations, of material differences, if any, between the SBD computation of the first three items and computations by the independent accountant. If there are no material differences, a statement indicating this fact must be made.

The audited financial statement must be filed (received by the SEC) within 60 days after the date of the financial statements.

If exemptions from compliance with certain rules of the SEC have been granted, the independent accountant should ascertain that the conditions of the exemptions are met as of the examination date; further, no facts should have come to his attention to indicate that the exemptions had not been complied with since his previous examination.

Other Broker/Dealer Issues

Settlement Date vs. Trade Date. Most securities transactions are recorded on a settlement date basis to facilitate:

---

[2] See Figures 40.8 and 40.9 which show a sample statement of cash flows for a commercial bank, following the rules in SFAS 95, *Statement of Cash Flows* (C25), effective for annual financial statements for year ended after July 15, 1988. These figures are derived from SFAS 95 (C25.153), and are applicable to any diversified financial institution, which would include the larger broker/dealers.

- Orderly settlement of transactions with customers and other dealers.
- Continuous net settlement with various clearing organizations.
- Compliance with many of the minimum financial responsibility and record-keeping requirements of the SEC.

However, as indicated in the SBD Guide,

> generally accepted accounting principles normally require that financial effect be given to transactions at the time an event takes place – that is, the time an entity acquires a resource from or incurs an obligation to others – which would make the use of the trade date accounting appropriate. [p.36]

Brokers and dealers using settlement date accounting are not considered in violation of GAAP if the difference between trade date and settlement date accounting is not material. Agency and principal transactions should both be reported in the income statement on a trade date basis. However, only principal transactions need be reflected in the balance sheet.

The SEC requires the FOCUS report and net capital computation to be prepared on the same basis as the SBD's financial statements. Accordingly, if a broker or dealer uses settlement date accounting because it immaterially differs from trade date accounting as contemplated by the SBD Guide, it must also compute its net capital (including haircuts) on a settlement date basis.

Distribution Fees Under Rule 12b-1. Within the last several years a new form of collecting distribution fees from mutual funds has arisen; these mutual funds are often referred to by the SEC rule number as Rule 12b-1 funds. Instead of the SBD collecting a sales charge initially (a front-end load), the charge is collected over time and is paid by either the fund or the customer as a redemption charge. For example, a fund might be charged a 1% distribution fee per year by the SBD and the customer might pay the SBD a redemption charge that declines based on the number of years the investor remains in the fund, such as 5% the first year, 4% the second year, and so forth. The details are discussed in the section in Chapter 44 entitled "Distribution Under Rule 12b-1."

A question has arisen whether the distributor could accrue as income at the time of the sale the related fees expected to be received either through the distribution payments from the fund or from the customer redemption charges. This matter was discussed by the EITF in Issue 85-24, *Distribution Fees by Distributors of Mutual Funds That Do Not Have a Front-End Sales Charge.* A consensus was reached that the income accrual method was not appropriate, and that prior accounting methods should not be changed.

Half-Turn Commissions. When a customer buys a commodity futures contract, he is not charged a commission until that contract is closed, normally through the sale of that futures contract. As the FCM has performed all the required services and incurred the cost of earning one half of the commission when the customer enters into the transaction, he is entitled to and should accrue half of the round-turn commission. Similarly the FCM should recognize half of any costs that will be charged to him on the round turn.

Presentation of Margin Deposits. FCMs require their futures and option customers to deposit cash or marketable securities (generally U.S. obligations) as margin for their futures and options transactions. An issue has developed whether the cash and marketable securities should be shown on the FCM's balance sheet. Presently there are two methods accepted in practice.

The first method is to include cash on deposit and the cash payable to customers on the balance sheet; this approach excludes the marketable security deposits. This approach is analogous to treatment by SBDs and commercial banks, which do not include securities held in trust on the balance sheet.

The second method is to include both the cash and the marketable securities on the balance sheet. The argument for full inclusion is that it clearly shows the total payable to customers and the related assets available to meet these obligations. Moreover, laws applicable to FCMs specifically provide that, in the event of bankruptcy, the cash and marketable securities on deposit from customers will be treated as fungible items; in the event of a shortfall they will be distributed to all customers ratably. The draft AICPA industry audit guide for FCMs (not issued for comment as of mid-1988) currently would require that only cash deposits be included on the balance sheet; this topic is under discussion at the AICPA.

Hedging. It is common practice for SBDs and FCMs to trade in futures, options, swaps, forwards, and other similar products normally used as hedging vehicles. Sometimes these trades are made in a speculative mode, and at other times are done for hedging purposes. It is industry practice to mark to market these instruments and the items hedged to market. Thus the normal problems associated with hedging transactions are not an issue for SBDs.

AUDITING CONSIDERATIONS

Independent auditors in the securities and commodities industries are retained to perform standard audit services including financial statement audits and internal control reviews, as well as diverse business consultation services.

Audit Engagements

Financial statements audits are the prevalent type of engagement. All SBDs are required by Rule 17a-5 of the 1934 Act to file audited financial statements with the SEC and designated self-regulatory organizations within 60 days after the end of each fiscal year. All futures commission merchants are required to file audited financial statements with the CFTC and designated self-regulatory organizations within 90 days after the end of each fiscal year. An extension to these deadlines can be arranged under certain circumstances, but is discouraged by the regulators.

In addition to issuing an opinion on the financial statements, the auditor is required to include certain supplementary schedules in his report for SBD and FCMs. SBDs require:

- Computation of net capital under Rule 15c3-1.
- Computation of reserve requirements under Rule 15c3-3.
- Information relating to possession and control requirements under Rule 15c3-3.
- Report on internal control.

FCMs require:

- Computation of minimum capital requirements under Rule 1.17 (Commodity Exchange Act).
- Schedule of segregation requirements and funds on deposit in segregation.
- Report on internal control.

Developing the Audit Strategy

The most critical component of the audit, given the high degree of risk associated with SBDs and FCMs, is planning the audit strategy. Because of the industry's cyclical nature and the fact that securities markets are affected by many external factors, auditors must be cognizant of general economic trends, share trading volume, market volatility data, and general financial news that could affect clients. It is imperative that engagement staff be knowledgeable in the specialized business aspects of their assignment areas.

The auditors should be conversant with business, accounting, and auditing issues in the industry, and be able to identify material transactions and potential errors. They should remain alert to qualitative information that appears in the news with respect to the SBD audit client.

Reliance on internal controls. After the SBD is found to be auditable and the auditor deems his professional risk to be acceptable, the auditor needs to determine the extent to which he will rely on internal controls to deal with some potential error types. In making this decision, two key questions must be answered:

- What is the most effective and efficient way to complete the audit engagement?
- What amount of error would be material to the financial statements?

Except for the larger SBDs, a substantive audit approach is usually more cost-effective than reliance on controls. Thus, in most audits, extensive substantive testing of account balances at interim dates and at year end is the audit approach employed. This choice is reinforced by the fact that changes in significant balance sheet amounts result from frequent inventory turnover and collection of receivables (daily or weekly).

If the auditor chooses a reliance approach, the extent of such reliance will be affected by his evaluation of the strength of the controls. Some of the key controls on which the auditor should focus his evaluation efforts are:

- *Risk.* Controls over potential error types and opportunities for loss should exist for significant products and transactions. These controls should address open or unpaid transactions, as well as contractual and contingent commitments (including delayed delivery); underwriting; when-issued securities; repurchase agreements; standby agreements; and commodity spot, futures, and forward contracts.
- *Trading limits.* Limits should be established and monitored for each trader, department, and the organization as a whole.
- *Capital commitments.* It should be clearly understood who in the organization can commit capital, how much may be committed, and what the approval process is.
- *Concentrations.* Parameters should be established to detect, monitor, and evaluate risks of potential accumulations of large positions in inventory and in accounts of customers and noncustomers (i.e., partners, principal officers, brokers, and employees).
- *Credit.* Procedures should be established to:
  - Specify which customers will be accepted and the amounts of their approved credit lines.
  - Monitor limits and types of credit extended in customer, noncustomer, and other credit accounts.
  - Formulate house margin requirements.
  - Review the need for additional margin, mark-to-market, and collateral deposits for all accounts.
- *MIS Systems.* Management information systems should be in place to monitor exceptions (such as security or commodity concentrations and credit-over-lines) on a daily basis.

Senior management should be actively involved in the control process for it to be effective. The establishment of formal groups such as new product, capital commitment, and credit committees to determine, approve, and assess the limits of credit and market risk is one method for top management to be actively involved in the control structure.

For larger SBDs it is common for the auditor to place some degree of reliance on the internal control structure. For many retail-oriented firms, where transaction volume is high but dollar volume low, it makes sense to place the maximum warranted reliance on controls. For trading-oriented SBDs, the auditor will usually blend a reliance approach with a moderate amount of substantive testing of account balances.[3] For specialty-type SBDs whose business results in a relatively small number of large, complex transactions, such as investment banking or merchant banking firms, substantive auditing procedures ordinarily would be most appropriate. For full-line SBDs, the audit plan usually involves all of the preceding approaches, applied appropriately to each segment.

Regulatory authorities are one of the primary users of SBD financial statements; accordingly, regulatory net capital is a key criterion for developing materiality guidelines. In the audit of small, closely held SBDs, it is not uncommon to see 5% of regulatory capital defined as material for audit planning purposes. Where the auditor has appraised the professional risk as high, this would lead to the establishment of more stringent materiality guidelines.

---

[3] See Chapters 7 and 8 for a discussion of reliance and substantive approaches.

Computer systems. Another focus of the audit strategy is the use of computer-assisted audit techniques, specially designed brokerage audit software packages, and time scheduling for the auditor's use of the SBD's computer facilities (or of the outside service bureau's, if applicable). Given the pervasiveness of computers in the securities industry, audit staff should be skilled in auditing data processing facilities and related activities. In addition, computer audit specialists may be needed in complex areas. (See Chapter 10.)

Other matters. The auditor should also consider the need for in-house or outside specialists to appraise or assess particular types of inventory, such as precious metals. The use of the SBD's internal audit department to assist in performing the outside audit is also a major consideration (see Chapter 7 Appendix). As a practical matter, other than the largest firms, most SBDs have small internal audit departments with limited resources available for assistance.

Securities Clearance Cycle

The securities clearance cycle, also known as the "back office" function, encompasses the processing and recording of trades and the movement of cash and securities relating to trades. The back office consists of several departments that clear transactions for their customers. These are:

- Order department
- Purchase and sales department
- Margin department
- Cashier's department
  - Vault
  - Receipt and delivery
  - Transfer
  - Reorganization
- Proxy department
- Dividend department
- Stock record department

The *order department* receives orders from the account executive for the purchase or sale of securities (transmitted to the floor of a securities exchange) and orders for over-the-counter securities (transmitted to the trading desk). Notices received of the executed trades are compared with the customer order and an order ticket is then prepared and sent to the purchase and sales department.

For each trade, the *purchase and sales department* (P&S) must accurately record, compute commissions, compare and reconcile, and confirm. Each trade is assigned a CUSIP,[4] or in-house, number that identifies the issuer and issue. In addition, to handle the clearing of many trades, the trade tickets are assigned a code that designates the type of transaction, point of execution, and any other details needed

---

[4] Acronym for Committee on Uniform Security Identification Procedures.

for proper processing. Every trade processed must undergo a series of computations, including the money amount

- Involved in the transaction,
- To be received by the selling and buying firms, and
- To be paid to or received from the customer.

Mistakes in these computations can cause many problems, resulting in poor service to the customer and unnecessary expense to the SBD.

The details of the trade are confirmed with the other (or contra) broker, who must agree in all respects. In the P&S department, each trade is grouped with all other trades of the same origin on the "blotter" (an original-entry record that covers purchases, sales, cash receipts and disbursements, and securities received and delivered). Comparisons with contra brokers are primarily performed via clearing organizations that match the compared trades, list uncompared trades, and send a daily report to the brokers involved. Uncompared trades are researched either with the clearing corporation or the contra broker. When differences are resolved, each broker must resubmit an exchange ticket to the clearing corporation for comparison.

For securities that are not clearing house-eligible, these comparisons must be effected by broker-to-broker verification, whereby each party to the trade sends a comparison to the other.

In addition to a conversational notice of execution from the stockbroker, the customer receives a written confirmation from the SBD. Among other information, this confirmation contains a description of the trade (quantity, price, commission, and so forth), trade date, settlement date, branch, and customer account number.

The *margin department* is responsible for monitoring all customer accounts and complying with regulations concerning the extension of credit and certain possession and control aspects of Rule 15c3-3. Money or securities may not be paid or delivered to a customer unless authorized by the margin department.

With the principal function of checking the credit status of customers, the margin department is responsible for initial and maintenance margin calls, granting extensions of time for cash account customers to pay for securities purchased, and issuing instructions for moving securities to or from safekeeping or segregation.

The *cashier's department*, or cage, is responsible for moving all securities and funds within the firm. The work of this department is divided among four major sections:

1. *Vault section.* Acts as custodian for securities entering or leaving safekeeping, segregation, or the "active box." Safekeeping securities fully paid for and registered in the name of the customer are held in custody for the accounts of customers. Segregation securities are those set aside for customers who have fully paid for them, and securities of margin customers in excess of margin requirements, that are registered in the name of the SBD. The active box contains securities used by the SBD to carry out its daily business, such as stock loans or deliveries.

2. *Receive and deliver section.* Keeps records of all securities that enter or leave the SBD's premises. Although most security deliveries and receipts are handled through a clearing corporation, significant business is also transacted in the cage. Before a security is accepted or delivered, it must be verified against settlement date records (e.g., blotters) for security

name and number of shares. The certificate must be examined to make sure that it is in "good deliverable form" (containing necessary endorsements, proof of ownership, and so forth). A firm failing to deliver a security by settlement date sends a fail-to-deliver notice to the receiving firm. Conversely, the receiving firm will send a fail-to-receive notice to the delivering firm.

3. *Transfer section.* Sends registered securities to the transfer agents to be re-registered in the new owner's name. This section acts on instructions received from the margin department. Before securities are sent to a transfer agent, they are checked for necessary endorsements, and a record is made of certificate numbers. When new certificates are returned, they are checked to verify that they have been properly transferred and are given to vault section personnel (if the broker is to hold the securities) or are delivered to the customers. Securities that are not in negotiable form because legal documents (such as those necessary to qualify an executor, administrator, or guardian) are not available are said to be in legal transfer.

4. *Reorganization section.* Keeps track of the reorganization changes among issuers and makes appropriate changes in customer accounts. Such changes may result from corporate mergers or spin-offs.

The main function of the *proxy department* is to act as an intermediary between corporations and their stockholders. Corporations issue proxy statements enabling stockholders to vote on key issues. However, when stockholders keep their shares in the name of an SBD, the issuing corporation will send the proxy to the proxy department, which will in turn send the information to the customer-stockholder. Proxies signed by customers are returned to the proxy department, which completes a blank proxy in accordance with the customer's instructions, signs it in the name of the SBD, and sends it to the corporation.

The *dividend department* normally has three responsibilities:

1. Monitoring dividends declared by corporations;
2. Collecting and recording interest and cash or stock dividends on securities owned by the firm or its customers; and
3. Crediting customers' accounts with dividends and interest.

The *stock record department* is responsible for keeping track of the movement of all securities into, out of, and within the firm. A stock record "break" occurs when the total long and total short positions are out of balance.

Inherent risks and related controls. The risks inherent in the securities clearance cycle are numerous but can generally be classified into three categories: business, financial, and regulatory.

Risks and Controls. The SBD faces the *business risk* that customers, account executives, or both in collusion will fraudulently execute trades or otherwise seek to divert assets from the firm. Additionally, account executives may grant commission discounts to customers to such an extent that the SBD is unable to recover the cost of trading. Other business risks include market price declines, granting of credit in excess of customers' ability to pay, unauthorized or erroneous trading that leads to claims (and/or litigation) by customers, loss or theft of physical securities, improper distributions of dividends or interest, and untimely fail-to-receive buy-ins.

Controls include branch manager approval on major trades and discounts, margin department review of unusual trading practices and of establishment of credit limits by senior management, and charging of losses due to errors against departmental or branch profits. Additional controls are physical security over cage conditions (such as timelocks, guards, bonding of employees), reconciliation of positions in securities on dividend record date with physical securities, and aging of fails and transfers on a daily basis.

Financial risks include those resulting from improper accounting for transactions that have been processed through the securities clearance cycle. Commission income, customer receivables and payables, fail to deliver or receive, suspense accounts, and dividends and interest receivable, are several of the more significant accounts affected by transactions processed through this cycle.

To diminish financial risks, the internal control structure should be continually monitored and tested for effectiveness and updated for any changes in the processing system. An example of such a control is the daily procedure of reconciling reports from clearing organizations, to detect misrecorded or unrecorded transactions.

Because SBDs are highly regulated and constantly monitored for compliance with various rules pertaining to such matters as operations and sufficiency of capital, there also is a significant *regulatory risk*.

Adequate controls should exist within the securities clearance cycle to ensure that the SBD properly complies with regulations and that there is proper reporting in the case of noncompliance.

Auditing Procedures. Auditing procedures applied to the securities clearance activities include tests of the controls, tests of year-end financial statement account balances, and tests of regulatory compliance. Key procedures, noted in Figure 42.2, should be implemented to various degrees depending on the number of transactions, the reliability of the internal controls, and materiality of account balances.

Agency Trading Cycle

Agency trades are all stock and bond trades executed on an exchange by the SBD acting as an agent for his customer. The accounts affected by an agency trade include many balance sheet and income statement accounts and stock record categories:

- Initiation of the trade results in a customer receivable with ensuing commission revenue and expenses.
- Cash settlement of the trade affects the cash account and customer account.
- Margin settlement affects the customer account and interest revenue.
- A default trade affects an error expense account.
- Nonpayment of a trade could result in a bad debt expense.
- An unauthorized trade affects the legal reserve account.

The SBD passes his customer's order by wire to the firm's representative on the exchange, who then takes the order to the particular stock specialist on the floor. The

---

- Tests of controls (with respect to financial statement balances)
  - Compliance testing of trade processing system (Order, P&S, and Margin departments)
  - Regulation T and margin compliance tests (Margin Department)
  - Review internal audit branch reports for material weaknesses at branch levels
- Tests of financial statement balances
  - Direct confirmation of customer accounts, transfer and fail items, depositories, and clearing organizations
  - Review of clearing organization reconciliations
  - Physical security count
  - Analytical review of balances
  - Detailed analysis of suspense items
- Tests of regulatory compliance
  - Regulation T and margin compliance tests
  - Physical security count in accordance with Rule 17a-13
  - Review of aged fails to deliver, aged transfers, aged short security differences, and aged dividends
  - Review of compliance with possession or control provisions of Rule 15c3-3

FIG. 42.2   Key Auditing Procedures—Securities Clearance

specialist acts as auctioneer in the process, maintains an orderly market, and executes orders for the exchange. After execution the firm's representative on the floor wires the price back to the SBD. The customer receives a confirmation from the SBD which shows the per-share execution price, the firm's commission charge, and the total cost or proceeds.

SBDs who are members of the New York and American stock exchanges agree to execute all trades in stocks of these exchanges "on the floor" unless special permission from the board of the exchange is granted to execute trades in listed stocks "off-the-floor" (but still under the supervision of the exchange). Often these are block trades, or trades of a large number of shares of a stock, which might disrupt the regular market auction price.

Not all security markets are as liquid as the listed stock markets. The corporate bond market in particular is less active with the majority of issues not even listed on an exchange, but traded in the over-the-counter market.

Over-the-counter markets also exist for stocks not listed on the exchanges. To become listed on an exchange, a company must meet certain capitalization and other requirements (see Chapter 20). Many companies, especially new start-up companies, cannot or do not wish to meet these requirements, and thus are members of NASDAQ. NASDAQ is not an auction market like the NYSE but is a computerized system that keeps track of the "bids and asks" on stocks listed by its members. Members contact each other to initiate trades.

Risks and Controls.   The risks attached to agency trades include those generally associated with granting credit to customers, and other risks, as follows:

1. The customer DKs (doesn't know) the trade.
2. The customer does not pay for the trade.
3. The firm does not fill the customer's order.
4. The account executive performs unauthorized trades on behalf of the customer.
5. The commission charged the customer is incorrect.
6. The commission payout to the account executive is incorrect.

The key controls related to agency trades are:

1. *Open order confirmations and trade confirmations.* Any activity in the form of an order, whether or not filled, should be confirmed by mail to the customer, thereby permitting feedback if an erroneous or unauthorized trade was made.
2. *Customer account statements mailed monthly.* The customer should receive a statement detailing all activity during the month.
3. *Reconciliations of trades with clearing houses.* All trades need to be reconciled prior to settlement date, to ensure that all are recorded. This reconciliation enables the SBD to promptly identify unmatched trades and resolve them.
4. *Standard credit controls.* Opening an account should entail a review of customer creditworthiness. Additionally, the margin department should continuously review any receivables and follow up with the account executive and the branch manager.
5. *Customer complaints.* A broker dealer usually has a compliance department to handle customer complaints. This helps to identify problem account executives (those who have many complaints) or problem customers that may warrant special handling.
6. *Standard commissions.* A deviation from a standard commission charge to a customer should be authorized by the local or regional branch manager.
7. *Payouts.* A payroll authorization form should be completed by the employee and the branch manager detailing payouts related to commissions earned. The payroll authorization form should be maintained by both the payroll department and the branch.

Auditing Procedures. The key auditing procedures for agency transactions include both tests of compliance with established procedures and substantive tests of account balances. The compliance procedures should be integrated so that they flow through all aspects of agency trading, beginning with the selection of agency trades from a blotter. Each trade should then be agreed to the following:

- Daily stock record
- Clearing house reconciliation
- Customer confirmation
- Customer statement
- Cash received or margin applied
- Daily commission revenue
- Commission payroll expense

This compliance test should also ensure that the totals of the various daily reports are the basis for monthly accumulations of revenue, expense, customer balances, firm balances, cash, and other affected accounts.

Substantive tests should include both reviews of client reconciliations for cash and with security depositories, and the confirmation of customer accounts and bank accounts.

Another audit procedure involves a review of regulatory and compliance department correspondence to ensure that the risk of potential litigation is properly evaluated. Outside attorney confirmations are necessary to review the adequacy of legal reserves established to cover inappropriate investments or unauthorized trades by an account executive on behalf of a customer.

The auditor also needs to evaluate that proper supervision is exercised over account executives, through the branch manager reviewing either all daily trades or unusual volumes for a specific account executive.

Principal Trading Cycle

In principal trading (or firm trading), the SBD operates for its own trading or investment purposes, and not on behalf of its customers. Security positions held either in firm inventory accounts or firm investment accounts are usually financed by bank loans, securities loaned, and repurchase agreements. Investment securities include marketable and not readily marketable securities carried as inventory in the expectation of being held for longer periods of time. Both trading and investment securities are valued at current market or realizable value, and any unrealized gains or losses are currently recognized in income. The key accounts affected include securities owned, securities sold but not yet purchased, trading gains and losses, and interest revenue and expense.

Risks, Controls, and Auditing Procedures. The following sections discuss the major areas of inherent risk within principal trading. Within each major risk area, the key internal controls that should be utilized are noted, followed by the key auditing procedures.

Credit risk. The SBD must consider the creditworthiness of any third parties involved in the principal trade. In financing or settlement of principal positions, the SBD may grant an initial line of credit in excess of the contra broker's ability to pay. In addition, there is the risk of trading with unauthorized customers and brokers. Credit risk is increased by concentration of positions in one issuer or with one contra SBD, and by failure to collect or maintain adequate collateral.

The key controls include: (1) programming the trade processing system to reject any trade not executed with an approved customer or SBD; and (2) instituting a rigorous credit-check function to monitor and evaluate credit lines for customers and SBDs.

Key auditing procedures should include:

1. Examining and verifying evidence of compliance with the key controls in processing trades with approved parties.

2. Reviewing the exception report for noncompliance with credit limits as established by senior management.

3. Reviewing established procedures to assure that the proper amount of collateral is being maintained and that marks to market are made on a timely basis.

Market risk. Unfavorable price moves can occur in the SBD's trading position due to changes in the market or economy or in the company's own conditions. Market risks can be mitigated by using various hedging strategies and by quickly turning over positions.

The key control over market risks is the establishment of a system for daily monitoring of the value and duration of the firm's trading positions; this system should accurately mark the trading positions to current market values based on data from outside, independent sources. In addition, the SBD should establish appropriate hedging strategies through the use of options and forward and futures contracts.

The key auditing procedures should include:

1. Testing trades for compliance with the daily trading system.

2. Reviewing the trading policies and their compliance with approved strategies.

3. Testing the accuracy of the mark-to-market system and period-end pricing.

Concentration risk. Concentration risk increases due to adverse price movements in the securities of a single issuer or product. There is also the possibility of a contra broker going out of business. The key control for concentration risks is the establishment of a trade processing system for daily monitoring of individual positions and counterparty position limits. The key auditing procedure involves reviewing the SBD's exception reports for noncompliance with position limits established by senior management.

Processing risk. Transactions in firm trading accounts might be performed by unauthorized personnel, or traders might exceed authorized trading limits or execute transactions in unauthorized securities. Some trading transactions might not be recorded, and trading department records might not agree with other firm records. The key controls over processing risks include:

1. Authorization from senior management on the various trading limits, accomplished by establishing overall dollar limitations on total trading activity for each trader and trading account, and limitations on the types of instruments traded, strategies employed, and concentration of positions within a security or with a particular broker, institution, or bank.

2. Daily inventory reports (monitored daily by both trading and accounting management) summarizing activity with unauthorized customers, trading in excess of limits, trading in unauthorized products, employing unauthorized trading strategies, concentrations of security positions, trading by unauthorized personnel, and excessive or unusual inter-account trading.

3. Confirmation of all trades with contra SBDs, and systems that identify all matched trades and highlight any unmatched trades.

4. An approved customer list, regularly updated and circulated to the traders.

The key auditing procedures include (1) monitoring compliance with limits and reviewing daily inventory reports; (2) examining and testing the reconciliation of the trading department inventory records to securities stock and financial accounting records; and (3) reviewing inventory reconciliation positions and valuations.

Regulatory risk. There is the risk that material inadequacies might exist in the internal control structure and record-keeping, and that incorrect calculations and improper classifications might have been used in computing net capital requirements.

The key control for regulatory risk is the establishment of a system that monitors the adequacy of internal controls and compliance with specific regulatory rules, and that accurately calculates the deductions on firm trading accounts for inclusion in the net capital requirements computation.

The key auditing procedures will address the adequacy of the internal control structure. In addition, the auditor will examine and test the minimum financial responsibility (net capital) calculations.

Financial risk. Proper pricing of firm trading and inventory accounts is critical in obtaining accurate amounts for trading gains and losses and interest income and expense. There is a risk that the market for securities maintained in firm trading and inventory accounts might become less liquid. Further, the difference between trade date inventory and settlement date inventory could become material.

The key controls for these risks include:

1. Use of outside pricing services to value securities in the firm trading and inventory accounts.
2. Establishment of a system that uses the SBD's computer system in conjunction with the outside pricing service to mark positions to market on a daily basis and to calculate the amount of interest income and expense to be recognized.
3. Sufficient detail in the system to distinguish between trade date and settlement date positions.

The key auditing procedures include examining and verifying evidence of compliance with the company's mark-to-market system to assure that securities are being properly priced. A judgmental selection of various security positions within firm trading and inventory accounts should be made for this purpose.

Investment Banking Cycle

This cycle includes all activities conducted to raise capital for corporations and governmental entities through securities offerings that vary significantly in size and in type of security offered. Investment banking activities, which generate significant revenues but also create exposure to significant risks, are dominated by several large firms with significant capital and expertise. However, several smaller firms have also been successful by specializing in specific products or industries. Revenues earned from these activities are extremely variable because the number and type of investment banking transactions is highly dependent on market conditions.

Investment banking, also called corporate finance in some firms, usually encompasses numerous activities other than underwriting security issues, as discussed here. For example, investment bankers will design securitized asset transactions and interest rate swaps for clients, along with other specialized financial instruments and transactions. (These topics are discussed throughout the *Handbook* from the perspective of the company involved in issuing the product. An extended discussion is provided in Chapter 21.)

Syndicate Offerings. In a syndicated underwriting, groups of firms are typically formed into a syndicate to spread the risk of underwriting an issue among the members. The syndicate typically includes a manager, syndicate participants, and a selling group. The manager is ordinarily the investment banker who initially advises the securities issuer. The manager forms the syndicate, maintains the syndicate records (including the commitments for each syndicate member and an accumulation of expenses incurred, such as legal fees and printing costs), and negotiates the selling price with the issuer.

The manager decides whether the syndicate will purchase the securities from the issuer on a "firm commitment" or "best efforts" basis. Most offerings are made under a firm commitment, in which the syndicate purchases the securities at a fixed price and then attempts to sell these securities to the public at a higher price. Any securities not sold to the public then become the property of the syndicate. A "best efforts" underwriting reduces the risk because securities that cannot be sold to the public are not required to be purchased by the syndicate.

The manager also coordinates the due diligence obligations for the syndicate, and maintains an after market for the securities when necessary. For its efforts, the manager receives a manager's fee and often also receives rights or warrants from the issuer (which can be a significant additional source of future revenue).

Each of the syndicate participants agrees to underwrite, or take down, a specific portion of the issue in a "firm commitment" underwriting and consequently has an obligation to purchase these securities from the issuer. This obligation can be either divided or undivided. In a divided account, a syndicate member who commits to 20% of the account has a maximum liability of 20% of the issue. In an undivided account, a participant assumes additional risk because the syndicate as a whole assumes responsibility for the entire issue. Consequently, a participant in an undivided account who had planned to purchase only 20% of the issue may have to purchase additional securities because the other participants were not able to sell their assigned portions of the issue. A nonsyndicate member of the selling group assumes less risk; he is not committed to purchase a portion of the issue but earns a selling concession based on the amount of securities sold.

The manager, syndicate participants, and selling group members all share in the "spread," which represents the difference between the amount paid to the issuer for the securities and the amount to be received from the public on the sale of the securities. The components of underwriting revenue are summarized in Figure 42.3.

In marketing the issue, the manager may receive orders for securities exceeding the amount of securities in the issue. Typically there is an overallotment option (or "green shoe") that allows the manager to purchase additional shares from the issuer for a period of 30 days after the effective date of the issue, at the same price as the original purchase price.

Assumptions	
Public offering price	$100,000,000
Proceeds to issuer	90,000,000
Spread	$ 10,000,000
Allocation of spread:	
Manager's fee	$ 2,000,000
Underwriters' discount	2,500,000
Selling concession	5,000,000
Expenses	500,000
Total spread	$ 10,000,000
Syndicate participation:	
Manager	40%
Firm A	25
Firm B	20
Firm C	15
	100%
Division of Spread	
Manager's share	
Manager's fee	$ 2,000,000
40% of underwriter's discount	1,000,000
	$ 3,000,000
Syndicate members' shares	
Firm A – 25% of underwriter's discount	$ 625,000
Firm B – 20% of underwriter's discount	500,000
Firm C – 15% of underwriter's discount	375,000

Note: In addition, each syndicate member (as well as nonsyndicate selling brokers) will receive a portion of the selling concession based on amounts sold.

FIG. 42.3 Illustration of Division of Spread in an Underwriting Syndicate

The manager typically must maintain a market in the security, and in this capacity may be required to purchase and sell the security in the after market. Significant losses can be incurred if the security falls in price shortly after issuance.

Risks and Controls. Investment banking functions and activities expose underwriters to a variety of risks including:

• Litigation
• Losses on unsold positions
• Losses on unprofitable spreads
• Net capital violations

Although the syndicate manager has the greatest risk of litigation, syndicate participants and members of selling groups could also incur substantial losses if a determination is made that sufficient diligence was not used in connection with the offering; in such a case they may be held liable for losses incurred by investors. To minimize this risk, firms often require each significant underwriting transaction to be approved in advance by a capital commitments committee consisting of a group of senior executives.

Underwriters also require the completion of standard "due diligence" procedures before capital is committed, and may restrict the types of underwritings to those industries in which the firm has specific expertise. In addition, the underwriter may limit its involvement as a syndicate participant to those underwritings where the manager is well known.

There is also a significant risk of loss on unsold positions. If an underwriter is unable to sell its portion of a firm commitment underwriting, it will become inventory exposed to market price fluctuations. This risk can be reduced by having all underwriting transactions approved by a capital commitments committee and by participating only in firm commitment underwritings with divided accounts or in "best efforts" underwritings.

Risk of financial loss is caused by entering into investment banking transactions with unprofitable spreads. This risk is monitored by completing a thorough profitability analysis before any significant transaction is executed.

An underwriter incurs regulatory risk primarily related to the net capital charges, or haircuts, on securities positions. These charges are a percentage of the market value of the security, varying by type of security. An underwriter also is required to take these charges on firm commitments not yet sold to customers. Consequently, before entering into any "firm commitment" underwritings, the underwriter must be sure there is sufficient net capital to absorb the haircuts on unsold commitments.

Auditing Procedures. Auditing procedures for investment banking activities are concentrated in the identified risk areas, and can include both tests of controls and tests of year-end account balances. The amount and type of procedures performed varies significantly from one engagement to another because they are dependent on the number of transactions, the client's internal control structure, and the materiality of the investment banking activities to the SBD's activities as a whole. Typical key audit procedures in the investment banking cycle are:

1. *Litigation test.* The auditor identifies litigation related to investment banking activities by sending standard confirmation requests to attorneys regarding pending litigation, legal settlements, and unasserted claims. Based on the confirmation responses and discussions with attorneys and management, the auditor must evaluate whether any reserve for litigation is required.

2. *Underwriting revenue recognition test.* This test typically includes making a selection of underwriting transactions and testing the recorded revenue by reviewing supporting documentation such as cash receipts, prospectuses, and underwriting agreements.

3. *Net capital test.* Net capital charges are tested by reviewing the capital charges taken on underwriting positions and commitments and comparing the charges taken to those required by SEC Rule 15c3-1.

4. *Syndicate receivable test.* Significant receivables from and payables to syndicate members should be confirmed with the other party or audited by reviewing cash receipts and cash disbursements subsequent to the audit date.

5. *Deferred expense test.* Deferred expenses are often recorded as an asset on the books and records of a syndicate manager for items such as printing costs and legal fees incurred in connection with an underwriting to be offered to the public in a subsequent period. If material, the auditor should examine supporting documentation and challenge whether these items should be expensed currently.

Financing Cycle

SBDs are contractually obligated to pay for or deliver securities on the settlement date, and accordingly usually finance transactions by pledging the underlying securities as collateral. When the SBD's business consists principally of financing large numbers of small dollar agency transactions, a centralized treasury system using sophisticated money management techniques will often be employed to control available cash throughout the branch network. Cash needs will be supplemented by banks with whom the SBD has an established relationship. Zero balance checking accounts and frequent use of drafts are common cash management techniques for most retail-oriented brokerage firms.[5]

It is important to have systems that accurately segregate customers' fully paid securities from those available for loan. Given the fungible nature of securities, the requirements to protect customer funds and securities, and the dynamic operating environment, an SBD needs to accurately process daily transactions and update key files that provide information as to the status of securities available for loan and securities hypothecated.

Risks and Controls. Financing activities and related functions such as loan origination, loan documentation, interest accruals, collateral management, loan substitution and recall, and financial and regulatory reporting, involve a variety of risks including the following:

• Improper accounting for interest
• Overpayment of interest
• Inadequate use of cash or securities
• Unsuitable execution of approved trading strategies
• Inaccurate collateral management
• Potential regulatory violations

Auditing Procedures. The major auditing procedures in the financing cycle are relatively straightforward:

• Confirm loan balances, key terms, collateral, and location of collateral.
• Review and analyze mark-to-market exposure on the collateral.
• Determine whether customers' fully paid securities are securing loans for more than the time frames allowed under Rule 15c3-3.

---

[5] The SBD should guard against excessive zeal in managing branch cash networks. This type of activity contributed to the eventual demise of E.F. Hutton & Co.

- Review and test the allocations of customer and proprietary collateral used in the 15c3-3 reserve formula calculation.
- Analyze and test interest calculations.
- Review compliance with Rule 17a-13 (quarterly count rule).

Auditing Futures Commission Merchants

The regulations of the CFTC outline the audit objectives of the independent accountant in conducting an audit. The auditor must have a good knowledge of FCM business functions and the rules regulating those functions. In addition to providing an opinion on the FCM's financial statements, the accountant is required to issue:

- An opinion on the regulatory-required schedules of the computation of net capital, the computation of funds required to be segregated, and funds on deposit in segregation.
- A letter on any material inadequacies found to exist during the audit.

   The primary business of an FCM is acting in an agency capacity for customers who wish to trade futures contracts. A futures contract is an agreement to make or take delivery of a standardized amount of a commodity with standardized minimum quality grades, during a specified month under the terms and conditions established by the contract market (exchange) upon which trading is conducted, at a price established in the trading pit. Commodity futures contracts are traded in such items as wheat, corn, gold, crude oil, treasury bonds, foreign currencies, and stock indexes. An FCM receives a commission for its services.

   Flow of Futures Transactions. The account executive accepts the order and communicates it to the FCM's order department. The order department communicates it to the floor of the appropriate exchange, where a floor broker executes the order by open and competitive outcry with another floor broker who is willing to accept for himself, or for a customer, the opposite side of the order. Once the order is executed it is communicated back through the FCM to the customer. The FCM will notify the customer of the execution of the trade, normally conversationally and then in writing through a purchase or sale confirmation. It is also communicated to the clearinghouse of the exchange, which steps into the middle of each contract and becomes the buyer to every seller and the seller to every buyer.

   Recording Transactions. The FCM opens a futures transaction by memo entry. The FCM is required by exchange regulations to collect original margin from the customer; this is normally deposited in the form of cash or treasury instruments. The FCM in turn must deposit with the clearinghouse of the exchange an original margin deposit for this futures contract, which is based on the rules of the exchange and may differ from the customer deposit amount.

   Settlement. As of the daily close of business, the clearinghouse will establish and mark each open futures contract to a settlement price, paying the unrealized gain to or collecting the unrealized loss from the FCM. This marking to market is also reflected in each customer's open trade equity. The futures commission merchant will not, however, pay or collect the unrealized gain or loss each day to or from its customer. The FCM must collect more margin when unrealized losses in a customer's account fall below so-called maintenance margin requirements – generally around 70% to 75% of original margin requirements. If unrealized losses fall below this set amount, the customer must bring his deposit up to the original margin requirement.

This description is an oversimplification because the FCM will have more than one futures contract and one customer open with each exchange. Most U.S. clearing organizations clear futures transactions on a net basis; the payment and collection of original margin and variation margin is based upon the net open contracts by commodity. A reconciliation is therefore necessary between the net positions shown by the clearinghouse and the open positions shown by the FCM. This is commonly called point balancing, which reconciles the customer's cash balances and open trade equity for each commodity futures contract by month of contract maturity (along with the market value and resultant gain or loss related to each contract) to the clearinghouse's cash balances and open trade equity.

The trading cycle generates receivables from and payables to customers and clearing organizations, and commission revenue and floor brokerage expenses; these items tend to be the major components in an FCM's financial statements.

Margining of Customers' Accounts. Minimum margin requirements set by commodity futures exchanges may be raised by the FCM. The auditor should evaluate the sufficiency of margin, not only to compute the FCM's net capital, but also to test the credit risk involved in particular accounts. It is important to take into consideration not only the cash and open trade equity of each customer, but also the securities or letters of credit that are on deposit with the futures commission merchant for the customer.

Deficits are the most significant credit risk to the FCM. An account may be under-margined but not in a deficit, which would arise if the liquidation of a customer's account would result in the customer owing money to the FCM. An account can be and typically is under-margined well before it goes into deficit.

Other Transaction Forms. A futures option is similar to a futures contract. It provides the right to assume a futures contract for a fixed price at any time during the specified period, and (except for dealer options) is traded on an exchange or board of trade. The transaction cycle for options is similar to the commodity cycle previously described.

A spot or cash transaction in a given security or physical commodity takes place directly between the buyer and the seller. Even when an FCM is acting in an agency capacity it must deal directly with the buyer and seller; there are no organized exchanges or clearing mechanisms involved. The contracts entered into by the two parties usually will specify the quantity, grade, location, and delivery time of the securities or the commodities to be traded.

A cash market transaction in which two parties agree to the purchase and sale of an instrument at some future date is commonly called a forward contract. In contrast to futures contracts, forward contracts are not standardized or transferable, usually can be canceled only with the consent of the other party, and are not traded on federally designated contract markets. The most common example of forward contracts are foreign exchange contracts.

The auditing of both forward and spot transactions generally is not difficult in that it involves simply the verification of the existence of the spot commodity or forward contract and its current market price. Because forward contracts are not traded on organized exchanges there is also a credit risk involved in each of these contracts, generally limited to any unrealized gain receivable from the counterparty.

Engagements Other Than Audits

Independent auditors may also be engaged to perform services other than financial statement audits and internal control reviews. Some examples of these other services are

- Special reviews
- Regulatory consulting
- Liquidation services
- Acquisition reviews
- Litigation support services
- Business start-ups

Special Reviews. Auditors may be requested by an SBD to review internal controls and provide recommendations in product areas where transaction volume has grown significantly. In numerous cases, existing systems are not designed to handle the complexities of the newly created products. This type of review may include detailed reconciliation procedures and the reconstruction of account balances, in addition to the identification of control weaknesses.

Independent auditors can also be requested by internal compliance personnel, legal counsel, or regulatory authorities to perform special investigations and full internal control reviews, in which areas for review concentration may be specifically identified. Examples include insider trading investigations, compliance procedures, and sales practices. The form of the auditor's report and the underlying procedures performed differ depending on the circumstances. The auditor's report may be one of the following:

- A special report on performance of agreed-upon procedures.
- A report on all or part of the internal control structure for the restricted use of management or regulatory agencies, based on pre-established criteria.
- An opinion on the complete internal control structure.

Independent auditors must comply with a plethora of applicable auditing standards in performing and reporting under these various circumstances.

Regulatory Consulting. Regulatory consulting engagements are frequently related to Rules 15c3-1 (net capital rule) and Rule 15c3-3 (customer reserve formula), which are based on financial information contained in the accounting records. These rules are very complex and subject to interpretation, and can have a significant impact on an SBD's operations. In some cases, the regulatory authorities may require that an independent auditor perform agreed-upon procedures related to these computations. In other cases, independent auditors may assist in structuring transactions to ensure compliance with these rules; or the SBD may request detailed reviews aimed at streamlining the preparation process for these periodic computations.

SIPC Liquidations. Auditors are often called upon by SIPC in connection with the liquidation of SBDs that cannot maintain the minimum capital as required by Rule 15c3-1. Liquidations have increased in recent years as the financial markets have become more volatile. As part of its responsibility to protect customers, SIPC may need independent auditors to verify customer claims, assist in selling off the assets in an orderly manner, and allocate the sales proceeds to customers and other creditors on an equitable basis. In these engagements, the auditor may actually be processing transactions; consequently, he may incur some risk beyond that associated with his usual role. Such engagements ought to be discussed with legal counsel prior to acceptance.

Acquisition Reviews. There has been a marked increase in the need for "due diligence" reviews as major consolidations have occurred in the securities industry. An acquirer will often engage independent accountants to review an acquiree SBD's activities and identify risks, and to assist in performing the acquirer's due diligence review in determining whether to proceed with the acquisition. If a decision is made to proceed, the review will also provide information to be used in negotiating the purchase price.

The accountant typically will perform agreed-upon procedures in these engagements and issue a report which complies with SAS 35, *Special Reports—Applying Agreed-Upon Procedures to Specified Elements, Accounts, or Items of a Financial Statement* (AU 622). The accountant's risk on due diligence reviews primarily relates to the failure to identify and quantify business issues that are material to the acquisition.

Litigation Support. Independent accountants are often called on to provide expert witness testimony regarding the accounting and regulatory treatment for specific securities transactions. In addition, accountants often play a key role in fraud investigations and determinations of insurance claims. In these engagements, the accountants review significant amounts of data in an attempt to quantify the amount of losses incurred.

Business Start-Up. Independent accountants are also frequently engaged to assist companies entering the securities business. In many cases, these are foreign entities not knowledgeable in the U.S. securities industry, or U.S. companies that do not have the required industry expertise. These engagements involve developing business plans, assisting in regulatory filings, designing and implementing accounting systems, and developing financial models.

43

Insurance Companies

PURPOSE AND FUNCTION OF INSURANCE

Insurance spreads losses over many persons or objects exposed to similar risks. The principles of probability and the law of large numbers serve as the foundation on which the concept of insurance is based.

For a particular risk to be insurable, it must possess several distinctive characteristics. It must be common to a large number of persons or objects having homogeneous characteristics. A loss must be accidental or of an uncertain nature; thus, property and liability losses that are a certainty are generally not insurable (e.g., decline in value as the result of depreciation). To be insurable, an object must have a financially measurable value; thus, intangibles and articles possessing intrinsic value are generally not insurable. It must not be likely that a loss will affect the majority within a defined population. Losses may be severe for a few, but generally must not be cataclysmic, such as losses resulting from wars, which are excluded from typical insurance policies.

Insurance risks are generally classified into two major categories: personal or property. The forms of insurance relating to these risks are frequently referred to as life, property, and liability. Other less common forms of insurance are title and guaranty insurance. Although all are termed insurance, the underlying risks differ substantially. Examples of personal risks that may be insured include losses from death, illness, or disability. Examples of property risks include loss of assets from fire or theft, or liability arising from damages or injuries to others.

Life Insurance Companies

Life insurance companies market several types of products relating primarily to personal risk:

1. *Life insurance* is distinguished from other forms of insurance by the long period of risk coverage and by risk that increases with age. There are three customary types of life insurance products:

   a. *Whole life* insurance provides coverage over the insured's entire life and is paid only upon the death of the policyholder. The premiums are usually level and are either payable over a certain period of time (e.g., 20 years) or over the life of the insured.

   b. *Endowment* insurance provides coverage over the term of contract and is paid either to the beneficiary or, if still living at the maturity date, to the owner of the policy (usually the insured).

   c. *Term* life insurance provides death-benefit coverage for only a specified period of time. This is usually the least expensive form of life insurance and the policyholder often has the option to renew this policy for an additional period (at increased premiums) up to a stipulated maximum age.

2. *Pension contracts* typically provide retirement benefits for a company's employees. There are a wide array of pension contracts, including defined benefit and defined contribution products, that may be tailored for groups and for individuals.

3. *Interest-sensitive policies* encompass many of the above forms of traditional life insurance policies and pension contracts, with the addition of: (a) features that allow benefits to fluc-

tuate based on investment options available to the policyholder, and (b) flexible premium payments. Examples of the types of policies that are categorized as interest sensitive are:

- Single premium deferred annuity
- Flexible premium deferred annuity
- Variable annuity
- Universal life insurance
- Variable life insurance
- Single pay life insurance

4. *Health and accident insurance*, which is offered by both life insurance and property and liability insurance companies, is primarily marketed through group plans. There are two basic types: protection against loss of income when disabled, and reimbursement for medical expenses when ill.

Property and Liability Companies

Property insurance indemnifies against the loss of or damage to insured property. Liability insurance indemnifies the insured against damages caused by the insured to others. Property insurance and liability insurance are often written under one policy because of the usual necessity for the insured to obtain both forms of coverage.

There are several types of property and liability coverages, referred to as *lines of business*. Lines of business are generally classified as personal lines or commercial lines, with the classification dependent on the type of customer. *Personal lines* insurance represents coverages sold to individuals. The most common types of personal lines policies are private passenger automobile insurance and homeowners' insurance, including coverage for both damage to the insured's car or home and liability for damages to others. *Commercial lines* insurance represents coverages sold to various business entities. Some of the more significant lines are business property, including coverage for fire, windstorm, hail, and water damage; workers' compensation for injuries sustained by employees in the course of their employment; and commercial automobile. Commercial lines policies also include other liability coverages, such as professional liability, medical malpractice, and product liability.

Many specialty insurers also provide *surplus lines* insurance. This includes coverage for risks that do not fit traditional underwriting guidelines, risks not measurable with standard premium rates, or risks not written by standard carriers due to conditions in the insurance marketplace. Surplus line insurers are not licensed in the state where the risk is located and, as such, are not subject to the same restrictions as licensed insurers.

Other Insurance Products

Title insurance indemnifies against loss arising from defects in title of real estate or from liens or encumbrances on property. This is a unique kind of insurance, because it represents a policy with an indefinite term and because the risks, if any, pertaining to title policies exist at the time the policies are issued.

Mortgage guaranty insurance insures lenders against nonpayment by borrowers. Policies are written for a specified time period and are commonly required by lenders who finance greater than 80% of property value. Mortgage guaranty insurance is the same as that offered by the federal government under the FHA or VA.

Financial guaranty insurance, a concept that has been applied to a wide array of financial risks, is intended to ensure that a specific financial obligation created by a business transaction will be fulfilled. In general, a writer of this line of business does not grant a conventional or typical form of coverage. In effect, the "insurer" lends the debtor its own credit rating. In other words, this type of insurance is commonly used as a means of credit enhancement to raise the investment community's perception of a borrower's creditworthiness, providing the borrower with a broader access to credit. However, in the event the debtor defaults, the guarantor is liable.

Organization of Insurance Companies

Insurance companies are organized as either stock or mutual companies. A *stock* company operates like any other corporation in that it is organized to generate a profit for its shareholders. The shareholders elect a board of directors, who, in turn, elect or appoint the officers of the corporation. Any person or group possessing the required capital and complying with the laws and regulations set forth in the state statutes may organize a stock insurance company. Although the statutes vary from state to state, the underlying objectives are essentially the same. For example, the statutes frequently stipulate that the company charter must contain provisions limiting the business of the companies to the activities incidental to operating either a property and liability or a life insurance business. In addition, the organizers must obtain a license to do business, which is issued only after the required capital and surplus funds are paid in. Subject to certain limitations, earnings of the corporation may be paid out to its shareholders in the form of dividends.

A *mutual* insurance company is a nonproprietary entity. Control, or ownership, of the company rests with the policyholders currently possessing an in-force insurance policy issued by the company. The policyholders annually elect a board of directors who elect or appoint officers to manage the company on a day-to-day basis for the benefit of the policyholders. With respect to voting rights, some mutual companies incorporate their proxies into the insurance applications themselves.

In principle, mutual companies are formed to provide insurance for their members. Since a mutual company has no paid-in capital, a reserve must be built up against the possibility of excessive losses. These additions to surplus are regarded as one of the costs of a mutual company's operations. Remaining profits are returned to the policyholders in the form of policy dividends.

Other Entities

Captive insurance companies historically provided popular tax advantages for industrial companies that had both a need for risk management and significant insurance costs. With a captive company, a company can pay premiums to its own insurance subsidiary and either retain or reinsure its risks. Another approach is to insure with an unrelated insurance company and reinsure (i.e., take back) a portion of the risk through its captive. While there are obvious tax advantages if the company can effectively be self-insured and still get tax deductions for the "premiums," recent tax rulings have severely limited the tax advantages of captives.

Pools, syndicates, and associations are made up of insurers or reinsurers through which risks are underwritten, with premiums, losses, and expenses shared in agreed-upon amounts. Pools represent an additional means by which a company may obtain diversification through a sharing of knowledge and underwriting expertise. Syndicates, similar in many respects to pools, are generally organized to participate in certain classes and lines of business, for example, Lloyd's of London.

Associations are frequently referred to as shared market mechanisms used to make insurance available to persons or entities unable to obtain necessary insurance in the regular market. The most common form of association, joint underwriting association, ensures the availability of automobile insurance to those drivers who are unable to obtain insurance in the voluntary market. Joint underwriting associations have also been created in some states to help alleviate insurance availability problems in the fields of medical malpractice and workers' compensation insurance.

Fraternal life insurance companies may be incorporated societies, orders, or lodges, without capital stock, formed solely for the benefit of their members and their beneficiaries. These insurers are organized as not-for-profit entities, similar to mutual insurance companies.

Risk retention groups developed as a result of the difficulty of many professionals (e.g., accountants, doctors, and lawyers) to obtain appropriate amounts of liability insurance protection during the 1980s. These organizations, in several respects are similar to captive insurance companies. Rather than self-insure, several professions have sought to share the burden of loss among their peers by establishing these risk-sharing mechanisms.

Reinsurance

Reinsurance is an insurance contract between two insurance companies. Reinsurance enables an insurance company, referred to as the ceding company or reinsured, to transfer all or a portion of the risk borne under an insurance policy (or group of policies) to another insurance company, referred to as the assuming company or reinsurer. The process of reinsurance may continue with the assuming company electing to further transfer all or a part of the risk originally reinsured to one or more other companies. This further transfer of risk is referred to as a retrocession.

Almost without exception, the policyholder is unaware of the reinsurance transaction since the relationship between the insurer and insured continues unchanged. Despite the contractual transfer of all or part of a risk between companies, the original insurer remains liable to the insured. In other words, to the extent that an assuming company might be unable to meet its obligations, the ceding company remains liable.

From the perspective of the insurance company, reinsurance serves several very significant purposes. Reinsurance functions to limit a company's exposure on particular risks or classes of risk. Reinsurance may also be used as a means of protecting against accumulation of an unanticipated number of losses. In addition, an insurer can maintain appropriate capital levels and operating ratios, as well as diversify its risks, by utilizing a strategic approach toward reinsurance.

Forms of Reinsurance. The two forms, or methods, of transacting reinsurance are on a pro rata or excess-of-loss basis. The *pro rata* form is a sharing concept whereby the insurance company shares premiums, as well as losses, in some predetermined percentage with the reinsurance company. In the London insurance market, pro rata reinsurance is commonly referred to as *proportional* reinsurance. Pro rata reinsurance is said to take the form of a partnership relationship because of the sharing nature of the transaction. It is used more often in property lines of business than in liability lines. Life insurance companies frequently use a similar form of reinsurance commonly referred to as coinsurance.

The *excess-of-loss* form of reinsurance provides that, for a stated premium, the insurance company will be reimbursed by the reinsurer for all losses in excess of a predetermined amount. This predetermined amount is commonly referred to as the insurance company's *retention*. The emphasis in excess-of-loss reinsurance agreements is on limiting the amount of loss, as opposed to sharing.

Types of Reinsurance. Within the two conceptual forms of reinsurance there are two types of reinsurance agreements: facultative reinsurance and treaty reinsurance. *Facultative* reinsurance involves the reinsurance of individual risks by offer and acceptance. The ceding company (cedant) has the option to offer the risk and the reinsurer has the option to accept or refuse it. Each facultative agreement, or cession, is a separate contract for all, or any part, of a risk that the cedant wishes to reinsure. The reinsurer underwrites each facultative cession on individual merit, accepting it formally by issuing a reinsurance certificate. The certificate is a contract that describes the risk and spells out the terms. Facultative reinsurance has particular functions and advantages in that it:

- Reduces the cedant's commitment in a specific risk exposure category and/or line of business.
- Reduces the share of liability ceded to treaty reinsurers in specific risks.
- Allows the insured to write hazardous and unusual risks that may be excluded under its normal treaty arrangements.
- Enables the primary underwriter to obtain counsel from the reinsuring underwriter on risk of questionable or uncertain nature.

Facultative reinsurance involves individual exposure, whereby risk is transferred only when a particular cession offered by the ceding company is accepted by the reinsurer at mutually agreed-upon terms. Facultative reinsurance can be entered into on either a pro rata or excess-of-loss basis.

Treaty reinsurance, in contrast, involves a comprehensive contract which generally covers a book or entire class of insurance business. In a pro rata treaty, the reinsurer agrees to accept a specified proportion of the cedant's premiums and losses on a specific portion of the cedant's future business. The reinsurer is liable for a specified proportion of every loss and expense incurred under the contract. The reinsurer also pays a ceding commission to reimburse the cedant for a portion of acquisition and overhead costs. The net result is that the reinsurer's loss experience, as it relates to the business being ceded in the pro rata treaty, is in direct proportion to the loss experience of the cedant. Like facultative reinsurance, treaty reinsurance has particular functions and advantages in that it:

• Reduces surplus strain on a relatively small or new company with steadily increasing premium volume.

• Enables a company to participate as a reinsurer in a particular category and/or line of business in which it may not have underwriting expertise.

In an excess treaty, the reinsurer agrees in advance to reimburse the cedant for all losses, or a large portion of the losses, over the cedant's net retention. In return, the reinsurer typically receives a percentage of the cedant's net premium income. With excess treaty reinsurance, the reinsurer becomes involved in a loss only after the loss has exceeded the cedant's net retention. At that point, the reinsurer pays the excess amount of loss up to its limit of liability; the balance of the loss then reverts back to the cedant.

REGULATION OF INSURANCE COMPANIES

Origin and Nature of Regulation

Insurance companies organized during the formative years of our country were chartered by individual states, not unlike current practices. Even during the early years, states imposed certain limitations on specific activities and investments and required periodic reports of financial condition. While for the most part regulation has been provided by state insurance departments, the question of jurisdiction of regulation has arisen often. By passing the McCarran-Ferguson Bill in 1945, Congress affirmed that regulation of insurance by the states was in the best interests of the public. The regulation of the insurance industry was thus left to the states so long as Congress considered state regulation adequate.

Although varying from state to state, the primary objectives of the statutes as they currently exist are to provide for (1) monitoring and promoting insurance companies' solvency to ensure payment of claims, (2) enforcing fair dealings with policyholders, (3) developing uniform financial reporting to ensure the correct monitoring of each company, and (4) determining the propriety of premium rates that insurance companies may charge to policyholders. In addition, each state's statutes contain provisions as to minimum capitalization, margins of solvency, and dividend restrictions. These provisions commonly vary depending on the type of company and/or lines of business.

Formation and Role of the NAIC

Despite the many common goals of the state insurance departments, the need to overcome the diversity and inconsistencies of regulation by individual states, especially for companies conducting business in several states, was identified. As a result, the National Convention of Insurance Commissioners was formed in the early 1870s. This organization now is known as the National Association of Insurance Commissioners (NAIC). While the recommendations and findings of the NAIC are not binding, they are highly regarded and usually are adopted by the states. One result is that each insurance company files uniform financial statements as prescribed by the NAIC. Another major NAIC accomplishment is the development of uniform examination procedures for insurance companies. Under these procedures, the country is divided into six zones. Insurance company examinations are performed every three to five years, and representatives from each zone (insurance examiners employed by the state insurance departments) may participate. The NAIC procedures contain two key elements:

1. An *early warning system*, also known as the Insurance Regulatory Information System (IRIS), which applies a series of tests to the published financial statements and provides a warning to the state insurance department that a company may be in financial difficulty.
2. An *Examiners Handbook* (NAIC, 1976) which contains the *Financial Condition Examiner's Handbook* as well as the *Market Conduct Examination Handbook* and provides guidance for scheduling, planning, and conducting an examination of an insurance company.

There has been a continued trend toward CPA annual audits in place of, or supplemental to, the NAIC zone examinations. Several states already require CPA-audited statements for insurance companies conducting business, or domiciled, in their domain, and others are proposing similar requirements. To achieve uniformity among the states that have not yet adopted audit rules, the NAIC has developed a *model rule* for the requirement of annual audited financial statements. Many of the provisions contained therein have been extracted from the various state CPA rules already in existence.

Accomplishing Regulatory Intent

The state insurance departments monitor and promote insurance companies' solvency by enforcing a variety of laws and regulations. For example, insurance companies are restricted as to the quality and type of investments they may make: the investment portfolio may be limited to a certain percentage of common stock and restrictions may be placed on the grade or rating of bonds that may be purchased and held as investments. To assure that securities are valued uniformly by all insurers, the NAIC annually publishes a manual *(Valuation of Securities)* to be used by insurance companies in valuing securities included in financial statements conforming to statutory accounting principles. Additionally, the statutes define those assets not permitted to be reported as assets (i.e., *nonadmitted assets)* in annual statements filed with insurance departments.

To promote fair dealings with policyholders, there are requirements for the inclusion of standard provisions in policies, and for state insurance departments to review and approve the various forms of policies. To ensure propriety of premium rates charged to policyholders, most insurance company rate filings must be approved by the insurance commissioners.

Regulatory Reality

Insurance company failures in the 1980s have placed the regulatory system under scrutiny and have raised questions about the ability of state insurance departments to protect the public against insolvencies. Two of the most noteworthy insolvencies were the Mission Insurance Company and its four subsidiaries, and the Baldwin-United Group.

The Mission companies, ordered into liquidation in February 1987, have been estimated to be insolvent by a very substantial amount. During its operations, Mission participated as both an insurer and reinsurer of commercial liability coverages. Apparently one of the primary causes of the Mission companies' insolvency was excessive losses on reinsurance underwriting. Extensive effort was put into the formulation of a rehabilitation plan that would have saved the company from liquidation, but the plan failed when a number of Mission's reinsurers themselves became insolvent or simply stopped paying reinsurance claims.

Baldwin's failure, on the other hand, was considered to be primarily the result of selling single premium deferred annuities with high interest rates guaranteed for long periods. When interest rates fell from their highs of the early 1980s, Baldwin's return on its investment portfolio became less than the amounts it had guaranteed on its annuity contracts. Additionally, many of Baldwin's subsidiaries were heavily invested in stocks of Baldwin affiliates, causing a chain reaction when Baldwin began to experience difficulties.

Although most states require triennial financial examinations, the absence of a more timely and extensive monitoring system has been cited as a potential weakness in regulating the industry. Some critics have also indicated that the states are not adequately staffed to monitor the large number of companies under their respective jurisdictions.

Despite the efforts of the state insurance departments and the NAIC to effectively and uniformly regulate insurance companies, the limited antitrust exemption provided by the McCarran-Ferguson Act has been periodically challenged, particularly during periods when affordability and availability of insurance are prominent issues. As in the past, those opposed to regulation of the industry by state insurance departments suggest federal regulation as an alternative.

ACCOUNTING AND FINANCIAL REPORTING

There are several major groups of users of financial statements of insurance companies—policyholders, regulators, and stockholders. The policyholders and regulators are primarily concerned with the solvency of the insurer, whereas the stockholders are primarily concerned with the value of their existing or potential investment. Statutory and GAAP financial statements are intended to meet the diverse needs of these users.

Statutory Accounting

Statutory accounting practices, differing from those of normal commercial accounting, are primarily concerned with serving and protecting the needs of the policyholders, and consequently emphasize financial strength, liquidating value, and solvency of the insurance company. Operating results are less important. Statutory accounting practices are prescribed or permitted by state insurance authorities and are codified by the NAIC in *Accounting Practices and Procedures for Life and Accident and Health Insurance Companies* (NAIC, 1979), and *Accounting Practices and Procedures for Fire and Casualty Insurance Companies* (NAIC, 1980).

Some financial rules are unique to statutory insurance accounting:

1. Acquisition costs such as commissions, premium taxes, and related items are charged to current operations as incurred, whereas premium income is taken into earnings over the period covered by the policy.
2. Certain assets (furniture and equipment, and certain receivables) are not permitted to be reported on the balance sheet in the annual statement and are referred to as *nonadmitted assets* based on the theory that they are not sufficiently liquid.
3. There is no provision for deferred taxes.
4. The mortality and interest assumptions for life insurance reserves are dictated by the domiciliary (home) state insurance department and are generally conservative.

GAAP Accounting

In June 1982, the FASB issued SFAS 60, *Accounting and Reporting by Insurance Enterprises* (In6), which comprises the specialized accounting and reporting principles and practices relating to insurance enterprises contained in the two Industry Audit Guides, *Audits of Stock Life Insurance Companies* (AICPA, 1985b) and *Audits of Fire and Casualty Insurance Companies* (AICPA, 1982b); SOP 78-6b, *Accounting for Property and Liability Insurance Companies;* SOP 79-3, *Accounting for Investments of Stock Life Insurance Companies;* and the relevant part of APB 23, *Accounting for Income Taxes—Special Areas* (I25.182). A proposed revision to the fire and casualty audit guide, retitled *Audits of Property and Liability Insurance Companies* (AICPA, 1987e), has been exposed for comment and should become finalized in 1988.

In December 1987, the FASB issued SFAS 97, *Accounting and Reporting by Insurance Enterprises for Certain Long-Duration Contracts and for Realized Gains and Losses From the Sale of Investments* (In6). This statement addresses the accounting for universal life-type contracts, limited-payment long-duration insurance contracts, and investment contracts. It also amends SFAS 60 with respect to the reporting of realized gains and losses.

SFAS 60

Scope. SFAS 60 applies to the general purpose financial statements of stock life insurance enterprises, property and liability insurance enterprises, and title insurance enterprises.[1] Certain sections of the statement do not apply to mortgage guaranty insurance enterprises (namely, premium revenue, claim cost recognition, and acquisition costs). Mutual life insurance enterprises are also excluded from the scope of the statement. As with the AICPA Guides and SOPs, SFAS 60 is silent as to its applicability to wholly-owned stock life insurance subsidiaries of mutual life insurance enterprises. With the FASB apparently having chosen to take no position

---

[1] In addition to SFAS 60 applicability, title insurance companies are also covered by SFAS 61, *Accounting for Title Plant* (Ti7).

on this subject, current practice will continue to govern the accounting and reporting by these entities. Statutory accounting principles are regarded as GAAP for mutual life insurance companies and their stock life subsidiaries.

General Principles. SFAS 60 focuses on the *type of contract* being issued (e.g., short-duration or long-duration) rather than on the type of insurance company issuing the contract. This focus reflects the simple dictum that "like events should be accounted for similarly under similar circumstances." As a practical matter, short-duration contracts cover most property/liability insurance products and long-duration contracts cover most life insurance products.

The distinction between short-duration and long-duration contracts also considers the nature of the insurance enterprise's obligations and the policyholder's rights under the provisions of the contract. SFAS 60 contains the following guidance (In6.107):

> Insurance contracts ... shall be classified as short-duration or long-duration contracts depending on whether the contracts are expected to remain in force for an extended period. The factors that shall be considered in determining whether a particular contract can be expected to remain in force for an extended period are:
>
> a. *Short-duration contract.* The contract provides insurance protection for a fixed period of short duration and enables the insurer to cancel the contract or to adjust the provisions of the contract at the end of any contract period, such as adjusting the amount of the premiums charged or coverage provided.
>
> b. *Long-duration contract.* The contract generally is not subject to unilateral changes in its provisions, such as noncancellable or guaranteed renewable contracts, and requires the performance of various functions and services (including insurance protection) for an extended period.

Although the Statement provides examples of the classification of various types of insurance products, the general discussion provided in the introductory paragraphs may ultimately prove to be the best guidance. The general principles for insurance enterprises are:

1. For short-duration contracts, premiums are recognized as revenue over the period of the contract in proportion to the amount of insurance protection provided (In6.109). To properly match revenues and expenses, acquisition costs incurred in selling the policy are deferred and amortized in proportion to the recognition of premium revenue. In addition, a liability for unpaid claims and claim adjustment expenses is accrued for all insured claims having occurred as of the balance sheet date.

2. The general principle for long-duration contracts is to recognize profit related to the contracts over the duration of the contract. This is accomplished by recognizing premium as revenue when due from the policyholders and recognizing expenses and the benefits expected to be paid over the expected period of the contract. The liability for expected benefits and expenses is established as the excess of the present value of the future benefits and expenses over the present value of the future net premiums (the portion of the premium required to provide for benefits and expenses) to be collected (In6.110).

3. The general principle for accounting for investments by insurance enterprises presumes that they have the ability and intent to hold long-term fixed maturity investments to maturity and that there are no declines in the market value of such investments other than temporary declines. Therefore, such investments are recorded at amortized cost. Equity securities are carried at market, and real estate is carried at depreciated cost (In6.112).

Premium Revenue Recognition. As noted in the preceding section, premiums from short-duration contracts generally are recognized as revenue in proportion to the amount of insurance protection provided. This generally results in a straight-line recognition of premium over the insurance policy period (In6.113).

For certain types of contracts, premiums are subject to adjustment after the contract period, generally based on either experience or exposure. Policies adjusted for experience, such as retrospectively rated policies, finalize their premiums when the amount of the losses that occurred can be estimated. Many commercial property and casualty policies are retrospectively rated. An example of a retrospectively rated policy is one which provides workers' compensation coverage. If the insured is able to maintain a safe work environment and reduce the amount of accidents, then a portion of the premium may be returned. In contrast, if the number of work-related accidents increases substantially, then an additional premium may be charged.

Workers' compensation policies are also an excellent example of policies whose premiums are adjusted for exposure. The premium for any contract will generally be adjusted based on the number of people actually employed during the contract period. The greater the number of employees, the greater the exposure that an injury will occur.

Premium revenue recognition for contracts subject to adjustment shall include an estimate of the later adjustment so that the ultimate premium is recorded as revenue over the period of the contract. For those policies for which the ultimate premium cannot be reasonably estimated, the cost recovery method or deposit method may be used until the ultimate premium becomes reasonably estimable (In6.114).

Premium revenue for long-duration contracts, such as whole-life contracts, guaranteed renewable term life contracts, endowment contracts, and annuity contracts is recognized when premiums are due from policyholders (In6.115).

Claim Cost Recognition. For both short- and long-duration insurance contracts, the expense related to claim costs should be recognized when the insured event occurs. This requires establishing a liability for those insured events that have occurred for which claim payments have not been made. This liability includes an estimate of costs related to claims that have not been reported to the insurance enterprise (In6.117). The process of estimating these costs is extremely judgmental. (See "Establishing Reserves" later in this chapter.)

"The liability for unpaid claims shall be based on the estimated ultimate cost of settling the claims . . . (In6.118)." This principle implies that the time value of money (i.e., discounting) should not be considered in establishing reserves. However, a footnote to this section of SFAS 60 and the specified financial statement disclosures (In6.166d) require certain information if discounting is used in establishing the liability for short-duration contracts. These disclosure requirements imply that discounting is acceptable, if disclosed. In practice, enterprises follow an SEC position that setting the liability at ultimate value is considered preferable except for the liability related to certain types of long-term fixed workers' compensation periodic payments.

The liability for unpaid claims may, however, be reduced by the amount of estimated recoveries for salvage (sale of damaged property on which claims have been paid (In6.430)) or subrogation (right to obtain repayment of claims from a third party who is liable for costs related to the insured event (In6.432)).

The liability for unpaid claims shall include the direct and indirect costs expected to be paid in connection with the settlement of the claims (In6.120).

Liability for Future Policy Benefits. The liability for future policy benefits represents the present value of future benefits less the present value of future net premiums. The effect of this liability is to accrue the expenses related to a contract over the life of the contract. Without this liability, long-duration contracts would record large profits over the life of the contract, and then, when the benefit is paid at the end of the contract, a large loss would be recorded.

The use of present-value concepts requires estimates of the rate of return that will be earned on funds received as well as estimates of the future cash flows related to the contracts. Assumptions as to cash flows and rates of return are made at the time insurance contracts are issued. The assumptions can be categorized as follows:

1. *Investment yields (rate of return).* "Interest assumptions ... shall be based on estimates of investment yields (net of related investment expenses) expected at the time insurance contracts are made. The interest assumption for each block of new insurance contracts (a group of insurance contracts that may be limited to contracts issued under the same plan in a particular year) shall be consistent with circumstances, such as actual yields, trends in yields, portfolio mix and maturities, and the entreprise's general investment experience." (In6.128).

2. *Terminations.* Most contracts allow the policyholder to end the contract and receive a reduced benefit or cash surrender value. Assumptions are made as to how many contracts will terminate before the occurrence of the insured event and what the benefit, if any, will be.

3. *Mortality and morbidity.* For those contracts that do not terminate prior to the insured event, assumptions are made as to when the insured event will occur and as to the amount of the benefit. Mortality assumptions represent assumptions as to when the insured will die. The related benefit is generally fixed as the amount of the insurance policy. Morbidity assumptions are related to disability insurance and are based on the incidence of disability and the related claim costs. Therefore, assumptions must be made as to how many insureds will be disabled, the length of the disability, and the amount of benefit to be paid.

4. *Expense Assumptions.* The final category of cash flows requiring assumptions are the "expected nonlevel costs, such as termination or settlement costs ..." (In6.132).

Once these assumptions are established in the year a contract is made, the assumptions are used to account for the contract in all future years (In6.127). However, if actual experience with respect to these assumptions indicates that existing liabilities, together with the present value of future premiums, will not be sufficient to cover the present value of future benefits and expenses and the remaining amortization of acquisition costs, then a *premium deficiency* exists and the assumptions must be revised (In6.141).

Acquisition and Other Costs. All costs not related to claims, and policy benefits that do not vary with and are not primarily related to the acquisition of insurance contracts, are charged to expense as incurred (In6.133).

Acquisition costs are those costs that vary with and are primarily related to the acquisition of new and renewal insurance contracts. Examples of these costs are commissions, salaries of employees involved in underwriting and issuing policies, and medical or inspection fees. Acquisition costs are capitalized and charged to expense in proportion to the related premium revenue. To properly associate the expense with related revenue it is necessary to group expenses by type of contract issued, consistently with the enterprise's manner of acquiring, servicing, and measuring the profitability of its insurance contracts. Unamortized acquisition costs, frequently referred to as *deferred policy acquisition costs* (DPAC) or *deferred acquisition costs* (DAC) are classified as an asset (In6.134–.135).

The method for computing DPAC for short-duration contracts differs from the method used for long-duration contracts. For short-duration contracts, the common method is to determine the percentage relationship of acquisition costs to written premium, and to multiply that percentage by the related unearned premiums, resulting in the DPAC. In contrast, the calculation for long-duration contracts requires the use of present value techniques, using the same assumptions as those used in computing the liability for future policy benefits.

If the aggregate of expected claim costs, claim adjustment expenses, dividends to participating policyholders, and other expenses plus the remaining DPAC exceeds the related unearned premiums on short-duration contracts, then a premium deficiency exists. The concept of premium deficiency essentially follows the general concept of "loss recognition" that requires current recognition of losses related to contractual obligations to perform future services. To the extent a premium deficiency exists on a short duration contract the DPAC must be expensed. If the deficiency is greater than the DPAC, the DPAC is expensed and a liability is established for the remainder (In6.140).

Reinsurance. Companies that assume reinsurance will account for the contracts in the same manner as contracts written directly with insureds. Enterprises ceding reinsurance account for the contracts by netting most balances. Income statement balances for premium revenues and claim or benefit expenses are reduced for amounts of premiums, claims, or benefits ceded. Balance sheet accounts for unearned premiums and the liability for unpaid claims or benefits are also reduced for ceded activity. Receivables from reinsurers for reimbursement of paid claims, and payables to reinsurers for their share of premium revenues, are netted on a reinsurer-by-reinsurer basis. Proceeds from reinsurance transactions that represent recovery of acquisition costs proportionally reduce the DPAC (In6.145).

Investments. Underlying the accounting for insurance enterprise investments is the concept that such investments are long-term. Therefore, investments with stated principal, such as bonds and mortgage loans, are carried at amortized cost, and real estate is carried at cost less accumulated depreciation. Common and nonredeemable preferred stocks are carried at market value.

If an insurance company's bond investments have a decline in market value that is other than temporary, or if the enterprise does not have the ability or intent to hold the bonds to maturity, then the bonds are carried at current market value.

SFAS 60 had required that realized gains and losses on all investments be reported in the income statement below operating income, net of income taxes. This requirement was amended by SFAS 97 to require that realized gains and losses be reported on a pretax basis as a component of other income. Unrealized gains and losses, primarily the difference between cost and current market value of common and nonredeemable preferred stocks, are reported, net of applicable deferred taxes, as a separate component of equity, with the change each year charged or credited directly thereto (In6.156).

Separate Accounts. Separate accounts represent assets and liabilities maintained by life insurance enterprises to fund fixed benefit or variable annuity contracts, variable life insurance contracts, pension plans, and similar activities. The contract holder generally assumes the investment risk with the insurance company receiving a fee for investment management, certain administrative expenses, and mortality and expense risks assumed (In6.159).

Investments in separate accounts related to variable contracts are reported at market value. Separate account assets and liabilities are generally reported as summary totals in the balance sheet of the insurance company.

Disclosures. SFAS 60 includes specific financial statement disclosure requirements. These disclosures include:

1. Accounting policies regarding liabilities for unpaid claims and future policy benefits, and DPAC.
2. Discounting information, if the liability for unpaid claims is discounted or if anticipated investment income is used in assessing premium deficiencies on short-duration contracts.
3. The impact of reinsurance contracts on the financial statements.
4. The impact of participating insurance on the financial statements.
5. Certain statutory accounting information, including any restrictions on dividend payments.
6. Certain tax disclosures relative to life insurance companies.

SFAS 97

Background. In December 1987, the FASB issued SFAS 97, *Accounting and Reporting by Insurance Enterprises for Certain Long-Duration Contracts and for Realized Gains and Losses From the Sale of Investments* (In6), which will be effective for fiscal years starting after December 15, 1988. The need for SFAS 97 arose as a result of significant changes in life insurance products over the last several years and the recent popularity of the single premium deferred annuity (SPDA) product. The AICPA audit guide, *Audits of Stock Life Insurance Companies,* established the accounting model for life insurance, and was incorporated into SFAS 60. However, it did not deal with universal life-type products, nor did it contemplate the significance of annuities as an investment product.

Many believe that the forms of universal life contracts, which lack the fixed and guaranteed terms that are typical for the long-duration contracts contemplated by SFAS 60, should require a different accounting method. The terms of these contracts generally grant significant discretion to policyholders over the amount and timing of premium payments, and to insurers over the amounts credited or charged to the policyholder (In6.104A).

While evaluating the accounting for universal life contracts, the FASB decided to review the accounting for some long-duration contracts with terms that are fixed and guaranteed but do not have level premiums or the insurance protection characteristics contemplated by SFAS 60.

Scope. SFAS 97 applies to three classes of long-duration contracts: investment contracts, limited-payment contracts, and universal life-type contracts.

Investment contracts are defined as long-duration "contracts that do not subject the insurance enterprise to risks arising from policyholder mortality or morbidity . . ." (In6.107A).

Limited-payment contracts are long-duration "insurance contracts with terms that are fixed and guaranteed, and for which premiums are paid over a period shorter than the period over which benefits are provided . . ." (In6.108A).

Universal life-type contracts are long-duration insurance contracts with terms that are neither fixed nor guaranteed, including contracts that provide death or annuity benefits, and that are characterized by any one of the following features (In6.108B):

a. One or more of the amounts assessed by the insurer against the policyholder – including amounts assessed for mortality coverage, contract administration, initiation, or surrender – are not fixed and guaranteed by the terms of the contract.

b. Amounts that accrue to the benefit of the policyholder – including interest accrued to policyholder balances – are not fixed and guaranteed by the terms of the contract.

c. Premiums may be varied by the policyholder within contract limits and without consent of the insurer.

The statement excludes conventional forms of participating and nonguaranteed-premium contracts unless the substance of such contracts is that they are universal life-type contracts.

Investment Contracts. Investment contracts, as defined, are not to be accounted for as insurance contracts. Payments received are recorded as liabilities, not revenues, and are accounted for in a manner consistent with the accounting for interest-bearing or other financial instruments (In6.107C).

The type of contract most signficantly affected by this principle is commonly referred to as a *guaranteed investment contract* (GIC), frequently sold as a pension product. The customer pays a premium for the GIC and receives a benefit based on a guaranteed rate of return. SPDAs, in which premiums received by the insurance company accumulate prior to the commencement of annuity benefits, are also affected. The FASB believes that such contracts are more like financial instruments (e.g., savings accounts) issued by other financial institutions and should be accounted for in a similar manner. Many GICs allow the contractholder to purchase an annuity at a guaranteed price at the end of the contract. While such contracts expose the insurance company to a risk that the guaranteed rate will not be adequate to cover the cost of the annuity, the statement does not recognize the risk as a mortality risk and considers the annuity purchase option, if exercised, as a separate transaction.

Limited Payment Contracts. The liability for policy benefits established in accordance with SFAS 60 is the present value of future benefits less the present value of future net premiums. However, any gross premium in excess of net premium shall be recognized over the period during which benefits are provided. This excess represents the anticipated profits on the contract.

SFAS 60 generally recognizes profits in proportion to premium revenue. This concept evolved from the fact that premiums on traditional whole-life insurance policies are paid over the entire period of coverage and represent an even base to recognize profit.

With the popularity of single premium life insurance, some companies were using the SFAS 60 concept and recognizing a significant portion of the anticipated profit over the "premium period," that is, at the time of receipt of the single premium. The SFAS 97 method recognizes profit over the entire period that service is provided.

While such revenue accounting for single premium products was considered to be the biggest abuse of SFAS 60, the FASB decided to apply this new method to all limited-payment contracts, including many traditional products that have premium paying periods as long as 30 years.

Universal Life-Type Contracts. The liability to be established for policy benefits for universal life-type contracts is based on the *retrospective deposit method.* This method essentially records the contract value at the balance sheet date as the liability, along with any other amounts that have been assessed for future services (unearned revenues) and additional amounts refundable on termination (In6.132B).

Premiums collected on universal life-type contracts are not reported a revenue, but instead are credited directly to the liability for policy benefits. Revenues are recorded when amounts are assessed against the contract value; and if such assessments are intended to cover more than one period, the revenues are allocated accordingly.

These provisions are based on the FASB's view that the flexibility in these contracts, as compared with long-duration contracts whose terms are fixed and guaranteed, justifies different accounting treatment. Many insurance enterprises disagree, believing that they assume the same risks when issuing these contracts as they do in other long-duration contracts.

Acquisition costs are to be "amortized over the life of a book of universal life-type contracts at a constant rate based on the present value of the estimated gross profit amounts expected to be realized over the life of the book of contracts" (In6.137A). Although this method differs from the SFAS 60 method of amortizing acquisition costs based on expected premium revenues, it does maintain the use of present value concepts.

Other Provisions. Other provisions include:

1. *Internal replacement transactions,* under which a policyholder uses the cash surrender value of a previous policy to make an initial premium payment on a new, universal life-type policy, are to be treated as separate transactions, with the policy being replaced accounted for as a termination.
2. Provisions of SFAS 60 regarding premium deficiency, reinsurance, and financial statement disclosure equally apply to limited-payment and universal life-type contracts.
3. Realized investment gains and losses are to be reported as a component of operating income on a pretax basis.

SEC Reporting and Disclosure

Insurance enterprises registered with the SEC are required to disclose additional information as required by Regulations S-X and S-K. Article 7 of Regulation S-X requires certain disclosures in the financial statements, including the alternate value of investments (e.g., cost for common stock and market value for bonds), gross realized and unrealized gains and losses, and specified details related to income taxes. Other disclosures are required to be made in schedules and exhibits. Article 7 also has been modified to reflect FRR 20, *Rules and Guide for Disclosures Concerning Reserves for Unpaid Claims and Claim Adjustment Expenses of Property-Casualty Underwriters* (§ 403), issued in late 1984.

Schedules. Article 7 is also the source for the schedule requirements. Significant requirements include:

• Summary of investments. Breakdown of investments by type and disclosure of related costs, market value, and carrying value.
• Supplementary insurance information. Segmented detail of certain balance sheet and income statement accounts.
• Reinsurance. Detailed information of ceded and assumed reinsurance.
• Supplemental information concerning property-casualty operations. Detailed information regarding the liability for unpaid claims, including the amount of expense in the current year that represents a change in the prior year's estimate.

The last schedule became a requirement in reaction to significant losses reported in years subsequent to the initial establishment of the liabilities.

Exhibits and Industry Guides. Regulation S-K requires an exhibit disclosing information from Annual Statement Schedules O and P filed with state insurance regulatory authorities. This information provides further detail as to the adequacy of loss reserves from year to year.

Regulation S-K, in Industry Guide 6, requires discussion in the "description of business" portion of registration statements about various matters related to loss reserves and disclosures regarding loss reserve developments, discounting, and differences from reserves filed with statutory authorities.

Variable Products. Many separate accounts used to fund variable annuity and life insurance products are registered with the SEC under the 1933 and 1940 Acts as *management investment companies* or *unit investment trusts.* Prior to 1986, registration of these products took place on the same forms used by mutual funds. In 1986 the SEC adopted forms specifically designed for variable annuity products. Variable life products continue to be registered on general forms.

The specific form of the registration depends on the type of insurance product and the form of investment vehicle used. Variable annuities funded through management investment companies, where the fund contains its own portfolio of investments, register on Form N-3. Variable annuities funded through unit investment trusts, where the fund's investments represent purchases of a series of mutual fund shares, register on Form N-4. Forms N-3 and N-4 are amended annually to update the registration.

Variable life insurance separate accounts register on Form N-8b-2 and are updated annually on form S-6.

Staff Accounting Bulletins. In addition to the requirements of Regulations S-X and S-K, the SEC staff has issued two SABs specifically related to property-casualty insurance companies.

Discounting by property-casualty insurance companies. SAB 62 (Topic 5.N) concludes that claim reserves related to short-duration contracts may be discounted at the same rate that is used for statutory reporting purposes. In addition, settled claims may be discounted if the terms are fixed and determinable on an individual claim basis and the discount rate is reasonable.

However, in addressing a question regarding a change in discount rate, the SAB indicates that such a change would be considered a change in accounting and would require a preferability letter from the independent accountant.

Financial guarantees. SAB 60 (Topic 11.J) requires specific disclosures related to financial guarantee insurance, including the amount of exposure with respect to debts guaranteed.

Other Significant Areas

Establishing Reserves. Actuaries are an integral part of the insurance industry, particularly in the life insurance industry, in which the largest liability is the actuarially calculated policy reserve. Actuaries also have significant involvement in the development, and particularly in the pricing, of products marketed by life insurance companies.

Property and liability companies establish loss reserves for the estimated amount of reported claims and *incurred but not reported* claims (IBNR). The estimation may be very subjective, and depending on the type of insurance, many years may elapse before settlement is made. Property and liability insurance companies attempt to establish an accurate data base of loss development and other experience statistics; yet even with a reliable data base, many unknowns remain—such as inflation, economic conditions, and litigation. The degree of difficulty in establishing loss reserves is dependent on the nature of the loss. For example, it is much easier to estimate the loss on an automobile collision claim than to estimate the ultimate damages relating to product liability or medical malpractice. That there are many unknowns is evident from the footnotes of many property and casualty insurance companies: reserves are described as estimates, and if those estimates vary from actual, differences will be charged to operations in the period in which they are resolved.

Many states require insurance enterprises to certify that their provision for reserves is adequate. The form of the certificate and the requirement as to who may sign it vary, ranging from experienced loss reserve specialists to designated Fellows of the Casualty Actuarial Society.

Reinsurance Transactions. Several insurance company financial failures to a large extent have been attributable to inadequate accounting and reporting controls over reinsurance transactions and, in some cases, to poorly defined or poorly executed audit procedures. The SEC, in a July 1979 letter to the AICPA, set forth its view that there was a lack of authoritative literature on the nature and extent of audit procedures applicable to reinsurance transactions. In response, the AICPA formed the Reinsurance Task Force to develop issues papers on auditing of reinsurance transactions and on related accounting and reporting issues. The task force issued two auditing SOPs: *Auditing Property and Liability Reinsurance* (AUD § 11,060), which supplements *Audits of Fire and Casualty Insurance Companies* (AICPA, 1982b); and *Auditing Life Reinsurance* (AUD § 11,070), which supplements *Audits of Stock Life Insurance Companies* (AICPA, 1985b). The SOPs provide guidance on certain significant aspects of internal accounting controls for property and liability reinsurance and life reinsurance. They do not, however, address accounting for and reporting of reinsurance transactions and related issues.

Reinsurance Accounting and Reporting Issues. The Reinsurance Task Force is in the process of drafting Issues Papers on reinsurance accounting and reporting conventions. Among the topics currently being evaluated in discussion papers are the following:

- Transfer of risk in reinsurance transactions
- Foreign property and liability reinsurance
- Fronting arrangements
- Loss portfolio transfers

These papers are in varying stages of completion. Issues papers approved by the AICPA Insurance Companies Committee and by AcSEC have been completed on foreign reinsurance and loss portfolio transfers.

The FASB declined to consider the loss portfolio transfer (reinsurance) issues paper pending further work by the task force related to the transfer of risk. That paper requires that certain conditions be met in order to account for a transaction as relieving the ceding company of its recorded obligation.

The foreign reinsurance issues paper is being rewritten as a proposed SOP. It provides accounting guidance for transactions that typically involve delayed reporting patterns, limited data, and foreign currency exchange gains and losses.

The fronting issues paper provides guidance for disclosing and accounting for fronting arrangements. The timing of income recognition is based on several factors, including whether the arrangement involves only policy issuance or both policy issuance and administration. AcSEC has rejected the advisory conclusions of the paper, taking the position that fronting is no more than a form of reinsurance and should be accounted for like other reinsurance contracts.

Discounting Claims. In connection with the revision of the industry audit guide, *Audits of Fire and Casualty Insurance Companies* (AICPA, 1982b) by the AICPA Insurance Companies Committee, one major issue is yet unresolved. The issue is whether incurred claims should be discounted (i.e., reduced to present value).

The Committee prepared a draft issues paper on discounting claims reserves, which concluded that incurred claims *should be* recorded at the present value of the anticipated net cash payments when the payment pattern and ultimate cost are fixed and reasonably determinable, and should be discounted using a rate based on estimates of investment yields (net of related investment expense) at the time the claims are incurred. However, AcSEC decided to postpone further consideration of the paper pending completion of its major project on discounting in general.

Computation of Premium Deficiencies. In 1984, AcSEC sent to the FASB an issues paper on calculating premium deficiencies under short-duration contracts (AICPA, 1984e). This issue, along with discounting loss reserves, was not addressed by SFAS 60. A premium deficiency on short-duration contracts is the amount by which anticipated claims, claim adjustment expenses, policyholder dividends, unamortized acquisition costs, and maintenance expenses exceed related income. After reviewing the issues paper, the FASB decided to set it aside; further consideration awaits the outcome of additional work by the AICPA.

TAXATION AND TAX ACCOUNTING

Overview

Stock and mutual life insurance companies are taxed under the provisions of Subchapter L (Part I) of the Internal Revenue Code of 1986. The complex three-phase taxation system of the 1959 Life Insurance Income Tax Act was replaced by a single phase taxation system in 1984. While simplified in comparison with prior law, there are many facets of life insurance company taxation requiring special analysis.

Property and liability companies (referred to in this taxation section as property and casualty – P&C – companies), both stock and mutual, are taxed under Part II of Subchapter L of the 1986 Internal Revenue Code. In general, P&C companies are taxed in a manner similar to the taxation of regular corporations for federal purposes. The predominant distinguishing characteristics of these companies relate to the nature and relative significance of certain book-tax temporary differences. While P&C companies historically had differed from regular corporations primarily due to the ability of P&C companies to deduct reserves for losses, the Tax Reform Act of 1986 has added several other unique features, mentioned later in this chapter in the

"Property and Liability Insurance Companies" section, to P&C taxation. With certain very limited exceptions, insurance companies must have calendar year ends.

Life Insurance Companies

For federal tax purposes, a company will not be taxed as a life insurance company unless certain criteria are met: more than half the business of the company during the taxable year must be comprised of issuing insurance or annuity contracts or reinsuring of risks underwritten by insurance companies. Also, a company's life insurance reserves must be at least 50% of total reserves. Failure to satisfy the 50% test will result in the company being taxed as a regular corporation, not eligible for any special tax benefits available to life insurance companies.

The taxable income of a life insurance company is subject to tax at regular corporate rates. In practice, many life insurance companies are subject to effective tax rates substantially lower than the top corporate rates, due to special tax deductions unique to the life insurance industry. For example, "small" life insurance companies are eligible for a special tax deduction up to 60% of their life insurance company taxable income. Additionally, life insurance companies may fully deduct from taxable income dividends paid to policyholders, subject to certain restrictions.

Under SFAS 96, life insurance companies that prepare GAAP financial statements must provide deferred taxes on differences between GAAP pretax income and taxable income to the extent such differences are deemed temporary. Common temporary differences for life companies are policy acquisition costs and loss reserve differentials.

SFAS 96 requires that deferred taxes for all enterprises be continually adjusted to reflect the tax rates and rules scheduled to be in effect when the turnaround of temporary differences is expected to occur. Thus it would seem that insurance companies have been treated equally, but this is not the case: insurance enterprises carry marketable equity securities at market value, with the increase or decrease (net of deferred taxes) classified in the equity section of the balance sheet. SFAS 96 provides, however, that (as an intended "simplification") if there is a change in rates or rules, the adjustment to deferred taxes relating to elements of comprehensive income not included in current operations (such as the insurance companies' market versus cost differential on marketable equity securities) should be charged to tax expense related to continuing operations. This "misclassification" effect, when a change in rates or rules occurs, may be minor for most commercial enterprises, but could be substantial for insurance companies.

Single-Phase Taxation System. The complex three-phase life insurance company tax system of prior law was replaced in 1984 by a single-phase system that more closely resembles the corporate tax imposed on regular corporations. Stock and mutual life insurance companies are now taxed on their life insurance company taxable income (LICTI), comprised of both underwriting and investment income (excluding tax-exempt income). Numerous special deductions are allowable in arriving at LICTI, including deductions for:

• Benefits (claims) paid
• Increases in loss reserves

- Policyholder dividends
- Certain small life insurance companies
- Consideration paid for reinsurance

Additionally, general corporate deductions are allowable for life insurance companies. Because of large investment portfolios, the most beneficial general corporate deduction is often the domestic dividends-received deduction. Also, a current deduction for 100% of policy acquisition costs is allowed, even though these are deferred for financial reporting purposes.

Methods of Accounting. For federal tax purposes, life insurance companies are generally required to use the accrual method of accounting. This is somewhat theoretical, however, because the Internal Revenue Code requires a life insurance company to rely on the company's annual statement approved by the NAIC in determining taxable income or allowable deductions. The annual statement, prepared primarily on a cash basis, is the normal starting point for computing a life insurance company's taxable income. In contrast, GAAP reporting more clearly reflects the full use of the accrual method of accounting, resulting in GAAP-tax differences relating to income recognition, policy acquisition costs, salvage and subrogation, and so forth.

Loss Reserves. Consistent with GAAP, an increase or decrease in tax loss reserves results in a negative or positive adjustment to income, respectively. For tax purposes, life insurance reserves must be computed or estimated on the basis of recognized mortality or morbidity tables. Reserves vary depending on the type of contract involved. While not entirely clear, the use of claims experience and payment patterns satisfactory for state insurance authorities should usually be satisfactory for determining tax basis reserves. However, in practice there will frequently be a difference between tax (statutory) loss reserves and GAAP reserves, due to differences in interest rate assumptions, payment patterns, and premium deficiency reserves.

Policyholder Dividends. Life companies are allowed a deduction for policyholder dividends paid or accrued during the taxable year. Policyholder dividends are defined broadly, and include experience-related refunds, excess interest paid or credited to policyholders over and above that required by state law, and any adjustments that reduce the premium otherwise payable under the contract.

Mutual life insurance companies must reduce their policyholder dividends-paid deduction by a "differential earnings amount" (intended to reflect the portion of policyholder dividends that represents a return of equity to policyholders in their capacity as owners of the company). Since this reduction, computed on the company's asset base, could exceed the actual policyholder dividends, it becomes in effect a separate – and often significant – item of taxable income to mutual companies.

Tax-Exempt Income. Tax-exempt income and income eligible for the dividends-received deduction must be allocated between the company and policyholders. A life company may only exclude or deduct its share of such income. The policyholders' share of such income is theoretically used to partially fund the company's loss reserves. Since the company is allowed a deduction for increases in loss reserves, the allocation between company and policyholder is intended to prevent what would otherwise be a double tax benefit to the corporation.

Small Company Exclusion. Certain "small" life insurance companies may permanently exclude up to 60% of their life insurance company taxable income (LICTI) from taxation. Any life company that has LICTI of under $15 million in a year is eligible for the special deduction (unless the company has assets in excess of $500 million). The effective tax rate for these eligible small companies thus may be substantially less than the normal statutory tax rate.

Consolidated Returns. Two or more life insurance companies may elect to file consolidated federal income tax returns if they constitute an "affiliated group of includible corporations." An affiliated group for tax purposes requires a parent-subsidiary relationship. The parent company must own 80% or more of the life subsidiary to be eligible for tax consolidation. Once an election is made, the group must continue to file consolidated returns unless permission is obtained to deconsolidate.

There are severe restrictions on the ability of life insurance companies to consolidate for tax purposes with nonlife companies. Even if eligible to consolidate, there are limits placed on the ability to use the losses of one group to offset the income of the other group. Special rules apply for loss carry-backs and carry-forwards.

Property and Liability Insurance Companies

Although P&C companies are taxed in a manner similar to regular corporations, several special rules regarding income recognition and tax deductions apply.

In general, all items of underwriting and investment income are includible in taxable income. The principal differentiating feature of a P&C company is its ability to deduct increases in reserves for losses, in contrast to the strict hurdles of the "all events test" and economic performance applicable to accrual basis taxpayers generally. This long-standing difference continues under TRA 1986 limited however in its full benefit by loss reserve discounting and other miscellaneous tax accounting provisions.

Loss Reserve Discounting. P&C companies must discount their loss reserves to take into account the time value of money. If the loss reserves have been discounted for any other purposes, the tax law requires that such reserves first be grossed up before being discounted in accordance with specific federal tax discounting rules.

Discounting of loss reserves for tax purposes is based on industry-wide loss payment patterns and assumed federal interest rates. In some cases, a company may be eligible to use its own historical loss payment patterns when discounting its reserves. Regardless of the methodology used, it is likely that discounted tax reserves will be noticeably less than GAAP basis reserves, thereby resulting in annual temporary differences.

The federal tax requirement to discount loss reserves became effective January 1, 1987. As a result of the one-time required adjustment, Congress provided "fresh-start" relief: the decrease in loss reserves caused by discounting did not cause a P&C company to recognize income, as would otherwise be required under general insurance company taxation principles.

The loss reserve fresh start resulting from congressional action effectively produces a special tax benefit for all P&C companies. Over time, a company receives a double deduction for the amount of the fresh start. This double deduction is recognized over a term of years, determined by reference to the payment period for claims represented by loss reserves on January 1, 1987. Considered a permanent difference under APB 11 (as verified by TB 84-3 and EITF Issue 86-37), the fresh-start amortization effectively reduced the federal tax rate of a P&C company. Under SFAS 96, however, this item becomes a temporary difference, to be taken into account in establishing the liability for future taxes.

Policy Acquisition Costs and Unearned Premiums. For tax purposes, a P&C company is allowed to fully deduct policy acquisition costs such as agents' commissions. For financial reporting purposes, such costs must be capitalized and amortized. A temporary difference thus results under SFAS 96.

Even though policy acquisition costs are immediately deductible for tax purposes, premiums received but not yet earned are not reportable. This represents a significant departure from normal tax accounting rules. Starting in 1987, only 80% of the increase in a company's unearned premiums can be excluded from taxable income. A temporary difference will result from the taxation of 80% of unearned premium increases, because such increases are not income under GAAP.

Tax-Exempt Income. The tax deduction for increases in loss reserves must be reduced by 15% of tax-exempt interest income and 15% of dividends eligible for the dividends-received deduction. However, only interest or dividends on exempt obligations or on stock purchased or acquired after August 7, 1986 are subject to this provision.

Small Company Exemption. Stock and mutual P&C companies with net written premiums or direct written premiums (whichever is greater) of under $350,000 for a taxable year are exempt from federal income taxation. Companies with net written premiums or direct written premiums (whichever is greater) between $350,000 and $1,200,000 for the year may elect to be taxed only on their investment income. All members of the same controlled group of corporations must be considered as one for purposes of determining the amount of direct or net written premiums.

Alternative Minimum Tax. P&C companies may be subject to a flat 20% alternative minimum tax (AMT), beginning in 1987. The AMT is a separate tax system parallel to the regular corporate tax. A company must pay the higher of the regular tax or the AMT. Very few P&C companies will avoid paying federal tax as a result of the AMT provisions.

The mechanics of the AMT system are complex, and are fully described in Chapter 17. Essentially, a company starts with taxable income and adds back certain "preference" items to arrive at alternative minimum taxable income (AMTI). The most notable preference is one half the difference between pretax book income and taxable income. P&C companies, which traditionally report boot income substantially in excess of taxable income (due to favorable tax treatment for such items as exempt income, dividends received, policy acquisition cost write-offs, etc.), are likely to be particularly hard hit by the AMT.

In measuring the book-tax income preference, companies that issue GAAP financial statements must determine pre-tax book income according to such statements. If GAAP statements are not issued, tax regulations specify the hierarchy of financial statements that must be used.

AUDITS OF INSURANCE COMPANIES

The primary objective of an independent public accountant's annual examination of any company is to determine whether, in the accountant's opinion, the company's financial statements present fairly the financial position of the company at the examination date and the results of its operations and cash flows for the period then ended, in conformity with GAAP applied on a basis consistent with that of the preceding period. The independent public accountant's report on an insurance company's financial statments may contain an opinion as to whether such statements are in conformity with accounting practices prescribed or permitted by regulatory authorities.

One of the first steps in conducting an examination is to obtain the requisite knowledge of the company's business and the industry in which it operates. In the planning phase of an examination, the independent public accountant should become aware of the various economic, financial, and organizational conditions that create or contribute to business risks faced by companies in the industry. This knowledge is essential to the appropriate assessment of audit risks that may be associated with an examination. Invariably, situations will differ among companies; however, conditions specific to the insurance industry that should be considered include:

* Extensive rate and product competition.
* Social climate (increasing damage awards and environmental claims) as well as economic inflation.
* Regulatory environment.
* Reliance on third parties for accounting and reporting information.
* Need to meet surplus requirements set by regulatory authorities.
* Need for liquidity and adequate funds to pay policyholder/beneficiary claims.

Additionally, there are several factors more commonly associated with property and liability insurance companies that merit consideration, such as:

- Extensive use of estimates, primarily in the determination of loss reserves.
- Cyclical nature of underwriting, caused mostly by economic conditions.
- Long-tail nature of liability insurance, which is defined as the lag between occurrence, reporting, and settlement of a loss.

The most common approach to auditing an insurance company is on a transaction cycle basis. The type or number of transaction cycles will vary among the different types of insurance companies. The major transaction cycles of a property and liability insurance company are as follows:

1. *Premium cycle.* This cycle is comprised of transactions that occur in the basic revenue generating process. The more common activities encountered include:

   - Underwriting and policy issuance
   - Agency/branch accounting
   - Billing and cash receipts
   - Maintenance of policy records
   - Determination of unearned premium reserves

2. *Loss cycle.* This cycle is comprised of transactions that occur in the payment of claims to policyholders. Activities associated with this cycle include:

   - Receiving notice of and recording losses
   - Establishment of reserves for unpaid losses
   - Adjustment and settlement of losses

The major transaction cycles peculiar to a life insurance company are as follows:

1. *Premium cycle.* Typical activities associated with the transactions that occur in the generation of premium revenue and establishment of policy reserves include:

   - Underwriting and policy issuance
   - Agency/branch accounting
   - Maintenance of policy records
   - Billing and cash receipts

2. *Policy benefit cycle.* This cycle is characterized by transactions that occur in the payment of benefits to policyholders. Typical activities include:

   - Determination of policy benefit reserves
   - Recording of benefits claimed
   - Establishment of applicable reserves for unpaid benefits
   - Settlement of benefits claimed

Another major transaction cycle common to both property/liability and life insurance companies is the investment cycle. This cycle includes the purchase and sale of investments and receipt of investment income.

Property and Liability Insurance Companies

In July 1987 the AICPA issued an Exposure Draft of a proposed audit and accounting guide, *Audits of Property and Liability Insurance Companies* (AICPA, 1987e). This guide, which will supersede the 1966 AICPA Industry Audit Guide, *Fire and Casualty Insurance Companies* and the statements of position that amended that guide, has been prepared to assist the independent auditor in examining and reporting on financial statements of property and liability insurance companies, pools, syndicates, and other organizations such as governmental insurance pools. Significant areas discussed in this guide include:

- Audit considerations, including a discussion of the study and evaulation of internal control and electronic data processing (EDP).
- The premium cycle, which includes a discussion of rating, transactions, accounting principles, and special risk considerations.
- The claim cycle, which includes a discussion of accounting practices and special risk considerations.
- The investment cycle, which includes a discussion of regulation, various investment alternatives, accounting practices, and special risk considerations.
- Reinsurance, which includes a discussion of the types of reinsurance, accounting practices, ceded reinsurance, and assumed reinsurance.
- Taxes, which includes both federal and state taxation.
- Differences between statutory accounting practices and GAAP.
- The auditor's report, which includes a discussion of the various types of reports and illustrations of those reports.

In addition, appendices discuss internal accounting controls and auditing objectives and procedures.

Premium Cycle. One of the initial processes in the premium cycle (also referred to as the underwriting cycle) is the evaulation and acceptance of risks. The objectives within this function are: (1) to evaluate the acceptability of the risk; (2) to determine the premium; and (3) to evaluate the company's capacity to retain the entire risk (i.e., need for reinsurance).

Cycle operations. To initiate new business, an agent, or broker, will submit an application for insurance to the insurance company. This application is usually accompanied by a deposit from the customer for a portion of the estimated premium.

Pending issuance of the policy, the agent or broker provides the insured a binder, which is a temporary contract that may be oral or written. The period covered by the binder is usually short, often limited to 30 days or less. A written binder is evidence of an understanding by both parties of what the insurance covers, the amount of insurance, the premium charged, and the company writing the insurance. The cash is recorded in a clearing or suspense account and deposited, and the application is forwarded to the company's underwriting department for evaluation. The risks are investigated in accordance with company procedures; these may include a review of exposure and potential loss based on the applications, changes, or endorsements to existing policies submitted by the agent or broker. For example, applications for automobile insurance may be checked by requesting motor vehicle reports issued by a state department of motor vehicles. Applications for certain property coverages may require engineering surveys or fire hazard surveys.

If the underwriter determines that the applicant falls within the company's underwriting guidelines and is an acceptable risk, an underwriting report is prepared.

Accounting entries are made for accepted applications by crediting premiums written, clearing the premium-cash suspense account for the deposits, and recording the balances due as premiums receivable. The combinations of the various rating codes entered on the underwriting report becomes the basis for the premium rates charged. A portion of the premiums is deferred because the billed premiums are for services to be performed by the insurance company over the term of the policy. At the end of each reporting period, unearned premiums are calculated, and the change in unearned premiums is recorded as a charge or credit to premium income.

A renewal of a policy is a new contract, but unless otherwise stated, the terms are those of the original policy. The risk insured under the original policy expires when the policy expires, and each renewal must be considered as an application for a new risk. When a policy is renewed, the premium is determined in the same manner as for new business.

Finally, after a risk has been accepted and the premium has been calculated, the underwriter must determine whether the entire risk should be retained or whether all or part of it should be reinsured.

After applications and endorsements have been accepted, they are submitted, along with an underwriting report, to a coding unit for verification of various items on the underwriting report. Verified applications are then coded for entry of data into the statistical system. In high transaction volume processing, coded applications are batched and input control totals are established before delivery to the data processing department for entry. Alternatively, many companies have the capacity to submit applications on-line. After coded applications and endorsements have been entered into the system, batch control totals generated by the computer are compared to the input control totals. Processing the information typically generates a premium register and documents that include information such as terms of the policy, lines of coverage, premiums, insurance identification card, agent information, and the billing statement. The policy, including any endorsements, is prepared and assigned a sequential policy number and sent directly to the insured or to the agent or broker for distribution.

The next set of activities includes the billing and collection of premiums. The two basic methods used are agency billing and direct billing, with some companies using both. Under *direct billing*, the company bills the insureds directly via periodic statements for premiums due and, on collection, remits commissions to the agents.

Agency billing is done on what is called an account current basis. Under one variation of this method, the agent maintains a detailed listing of individual policies, bills the insureds, collects the premium, and remits the proceeds to the company net of commissions. This is referred to as the *item basis* or *rendering basis*. Under a second variation, referred to as the *billing basis*, the company sends the agent a statement, based on the agent's detailed reporting to the company, that shows all activity during the month. The statement reflects the net account due to or from the agent.

Audit approach—premium cycle. The primary audit objectives associated with the premium cycle are to ascertain:

* Adequacy of controls over policy forms and policy issuance.
* Proper performance of the underwriting function.
* Proper recording of premiums.
* Appropriateness of accounting policy used for revenue recognition and consistency of application.
* Proper matching of premiums earned with related policy acquisition costs.
* Application of premium receipts to the related receivables.
* Proper accounting for reinsurance assumed and ceded.

Policy copies and policy extracts, commonly referred to as "dailies," are the basic records from which transactions are recorded. For this reason, auditing procedures related to (1) premium income, (2) commissions and expense allowances to agents and brokers, (3) reinsurance assumed and ceded and related commissions, (4) uncollected premiums, (5) funds held by or deposited with ceded reinsurers, (6) unearned premiums, and (7) premiums in force must be coordinated. Where a numerical policy form control is maintained, tests should be made to see that policy forms supplied to agents are entered on the policy control records. Skipped policy numbers should be investigated in accordance with company procedures, and a test should be made to determine that such procedures are followed. Tests of policies entered on the policy control records determine that the policies were actually issued and copies were received from agents. A determination that policies are recorded as premium income is made by test examination of source documents in the files for an indication of data processing entry, for example.

All premium transactions shown on selected policies, including reinsurance ceded, should be traced to premium registers to ascertain that premium transactions have been properly recorded.

If underwriting files indicate reinsurance ceded, the computation of reinsurance premiums and commissions should be tested. When policies are cancelled, return premiums on ceded reinsurance should be checked to see that they are being received and processed. The auditor should review the reinsurance contracts or treaties and make a test of payments of commissions on reinsurance assumed and ceded, to ascertain compliance with contract provisions. There are frequently greater delays in the recording of reinsurance ceded or assumed than in the recording of direct business. The company's policies and practices on these premium transactions should be determined, and tests should be made to measure the effects on financial statements.

Unearned premium reserves are usually verified, as the calculation is readily performed using EDP equipment. Individual transactions could be printed out, and the determination of unearned premiums can be verified for small segments of a line of business. Companies normally maintain control records showing premiums added to the "in-force" premiums in the current month and the original premiums thereon. Included also is a summary, by line, of expirations removed from the current in-force premiums. Control reports of this nature normally summarize and record the totals that may be verified to a reconciliation of beginning and ending in-force premiums, thereby accounting for all changes made during the month.

Loss Cycle. Losses, also called claims, and loss adjustment expenses are the major costs incurred by property and liability insurance companies; the liabilities for unpaid claims and claim adjustment expenses, also called reserves, are the major liabilities reported on the balance sheet. Because of the difficulty and subjectivity of estimating these costs and because of their significance to the financial statements, the determination of the adequacy of the claims and claim adjustment expense liabilities is a primary concern in the audit of a property and liability insurance company.

The major types of claims are property, liability, and workers' compensation, discussed in the following subsections.

Cycle operations. Property claims generally are reported and settled quickly, often within one year. They usually are first-party claims (i.e., the claimant is the policyholder), and thus they are direct obligations of the insurer to pay the insured. In addition, the occurrence and extent of loss are ascertainable with relative ease because the claims relate to tangible property. The processing of property claims is often expedited by means of "bulk reserving" or small-claim procedures, under which many small claims are summarized and aggregated.

Liability claims are reported more slowly than property claims and settlement is often a lengthy process, especially if litigation is involved. Liability claims are third-party claims in which the insurer has agreed to pay, defend, or settle claims made by third parties against the insured.

Workers' compensation claims are reported quickly and settled slowly. The amount of most claim payments is set by law and may change during the life of a claim. A claim settlement is characterized by numerous payments to the claimants or survivors for medical expenses and loss of earnings, possibly over extended periods of time.

The first activity in the loss cycle occurs when notice of a loss or accident is received at the home or branch office directly from the insured or through agents. A file number serving as the basis for all future reference is assigned to the claim, usually in numerical sequence, and a loss file and abstract are prepared. Policy applications or other records of insurance coverage are examined to determine if the loss is covered by the insurance policy and if the policy was in force at the time the loss occurred.

One of the next functions, claims adjusting, may involve a field investigation, an appraisal and negotiation of the claim, and approval of the company's claim department. Through an investigation the adjuster determines, among other things, whether the claimed loss actually occurred, his estimate of the amount of the loss, whether the loss may be excludable under the terms of the policy, and whether the company has a right to recover part or all of the loss through salvage, subrogration, or reinsurance.

Insurance companies use several different methods to adjust claims. Companies may use home or branch office adjusters, who are salaried employees of the company, or independent adjusters, who are professionals who charge fees for their investigation and adjustment service.

Recent unexpectedly high jury awards, the growth of malpractice and environmental claims, and the introduction of structured settlements have severely complicated the claim estimation process. Structured settlements involve the purchase of an annuity to pay settlements to claimants over future periods, thereby reducing the ultimate amount paid out on claims. The trend in jury awards has defied any logical means of projection; economic value does not appear to be the only basis for award. Clearly, social values have also entered into this process.

In the claim settlement process, claim and claim expense payments originate with signed proofs of loss, medical bills, repair bills, or statements of fees for services rendered by independent adjusters or lawyers. When these documents are received. They are reviewed and compared with the claim files before payment is authorized.

Methods in which claims are paid vary among insurance companies. Authority may fall within the treasurer's department, or possibly the claims department. In many companies, authority to issue drafts may be given to field offices, adjusters, and sometimes agents; in those cases, copies of the drafts and related supporting documents are forwarded to the claims department.

Companies settle claims by means of checks or drafts. Some companies record claims paid when the checks or drafts are issued. Other insurance companies record claims paid when the drafts clear the bank.

To understand the process of estimating loss reserves, it is essential to understand that the cost of claims is incurred when the insured events occur. As a result, property and liability insurance companies must estimate the amount of unpaid claims well in advance of payment. The process of estimating claims requires the exercise of sound judgment and prudence. Since the estimation of claims is based principally on an analysis of historical experience, insurance companies are greatly concerned with the compilation of claims data and the development of analysis of related experience statistics.

Property and liability insurance companies have two kinds of unpaid claims: reported claims, and incurred but not reported (IBNR) claims. Estimates of unpaid claims are reported on the company's financial statements as liabilities. Various methods are used by companies to determine the amount of unpaid claims, but in general, estimated liabilities are established for claims that have been reported; additional estimates are made for claims that are likely to have been incurred but have not yet been reported to the company. Estimates of claims that are paid over a period of years reflect anticipated information and other social and economic factors, using information based on historical and reasonably foreseeable events and trends.

Audit approach—loss cycle. The primary audit objectives associated with the loss cycle are to ascertain that:

- Claims are processed timely, accurately, and in a consistent manner, including the propriety of statistical data.
- Adjustment and settlement of claims are in accordance with company guidelines.
- Claim costs have been properly accumulated, classified, and accounted for.
- Reserves for losses and loss adjustment expenses are sufficient.
- There has been a proper accounting for reinsurance assumed and ceded.

In the course of performing audit procedures in the loss cycle, the auditor should evaluate the effectiveness of the loss department's supervision of claim processing by verifying (from detailed records) paid losses, loss expenses paid, and the set up of reserves, both on a direct basis and on a net basis after reinsurance recoverable. Claim files should be examined on a test basis for paid losses and allocated loss adjustment expenses. Policy files shold be examined in a test number of cases to determine that coverage was within the policy limits and that losses were within the period of the policy. Inspections should be made of correspondence from adjusters, company claim examiners' approvals, proofs of loss, and loss expense invoices. This review should include an examination of the related paid drafts or checks for the propriety of amounts and names of payees and endorsers.

When examining claim files on which reinsurance is applicable, the losses and loss adjustment expense recoverable should be traced to reinsurance records. If applicable, salvage and subrogation should be noted, and a review should be made of the controls and procedures in effect for these items. At year-end, the auditor should obtain listings of losses reported and still unpaid, along with the related reinsurance recoverable where reserves are established on a case basis. These should be tested for arithmetical accuracy, and totals should be traced to financial statements. On a test basis, open claim files should be examined to support listed amounts.

If loss reserves are based on average costs, reviews should be made of the methods used to establish such costs. Factors to be reviewed are the logic used, trends over a period of years, and whether the volume of losses is great enough to establish reserves that are credible. Comparison of loss figures with the industry and review of the company's loss experience figures for a period of years should be made, using a period long enough to provide an adequate level of assurance that the actual settlement costs used in the reserving process are appropriate.

Statutory requirements relative to setting minimum reserves should be reviewed to ascertain compliance. In this regard, statistical information is schedules that support the amount of minimum reserves should be checked.

Life Insurance Companies

Premium Cycle. The underwriting cycle for life insurance companies is similar in many respects to the underwriting cycle of a property and liability insurance company.

Cycle operations. The underwriting process involves the selection (evaluation and acceptance) of risks. Applicants for life insurance fall within one of the following categories:

- Standard risks at standard rates
- Substandard risks at special rates
- Uninsurable risks

The majority of all applicants for life insurance are classified as risks that are insurable at standard rates. Uninsurable risks are those applicants who are rejected for coverage.

An application for life insurance generally requires very specific information, for example, the applicant's age, sex, occupation, and marital status. It also includes other basic information, most of which relates to historical information about the applicant. The application may also contain comments by the agent that could have an effect on the insurability of the applicant or the class in which he or she may fall for insurance rating purposes.

In some instances, a medical report may be completed before the risk is submitted to the life insurance company for review. This report is usually comprised of two parts. The first contains questions related to medical history. If the medical history does not appear routine, the insurer's medical director will probably request additional information from the applicant's physician. The second part of the medical report is a summary of the examining physician's findings. A medical examination may or may not be required depending on the amount of insurance applied for, the age of the applicant, or other factors; each company has its own guidelines in this regard. (One of the most significant factors to be dealt with by life insurers in decades has been the alarming increase in the incidence of the acquired immune deficiency syndrome (AIDS) virus. The nature of this disease has had a direct impact on the underwriting guidelines of life insurance companies.)

Based on the information contained in the application, the medical report, and the inspection report, the applicant is rated as a standard or substandard risk, or as uninsurable.

If an applicant is an insurable risk, a policy or contract is prepared for issuance. This is generally done at the company's home office where a policy number is assigned to each policy and where overall numerical control of policies is maintained. After a policy is prepared and a policy number assigned, the policy is sent to the agent or branch office for delivery to the policyholder. The initial premium is collected at this time unless it was received with the application. Close control must be exercised over policies delivered but not paid for by the policyholders. Generally, the agent must remit the collected premium or return the prepared policy to the company within a specified period of time.

The manner in which premiums charged by life insurance companies are determined differs in some respects from that of property and liability insurers. In a life insurance company, the term *gross premium* refers to the premium charged to the policyholder. It is an amount that must reflect the competitiveness of the industry, and yet be sufficient to accumulate a fund (coupled with earnings thereon) that will yield a sum adequate to provide for all policy benefits, acquisition costs and other expenses, margins for contingencies, and a desired profit margin.

The *net premium* associated with a policy represents a calculation of the statutory reserve liability and is based on stipulated assumptions as to mortality and interest rates. These assumptions must be within limits prescribed by state insurance laws and thus do not necessarily bear a logical relationship to the mortality and interest rates assumed in computing the gross premium. As mentioned earlier, the statutory assumptions tend to be quite conservative.

Conceptually, the difference between the gross premium and the net premium is referred to as *loading*. This term may be misleading since this difference is a hypothetical figure and does not necessarily represent an allowance for expenses and profit. In actuality, some companies have gross premiums for some plans that are equal to, or less than, the net premium, thus producing zero or negative loadings.

Audit approach—premium cycle. The primary audit objectives in the premium cycle include the need to ascertain, by selecting and examining a sample of policy files, that:

• Controls over underwriting and issuance of policies are adequate.

- Premiums are properly recorded and billed.
- Premiums are collected and accurately applied.
- There is a proper accounting for commissions.

As part of the audit procedures involving tests of the underwriting cycle, the auditor should satisfy himself that there are appropriate safeguards with respect to the issuance of policies. In most life insurance companies, policies are not prenumbered, but they are assigned policy numbers at the home office. Accordingly, other controls must be established for policies; for example, the auditor should determine that policies delivered to agents but not issued to policyholders have been accounted for by the company. Some companies control this by billing the agent upon delivery of the policy.

In addition, the auditor should test premium billing and accounting for both renewal premiums as well as first-year premiums. For selected policies in force, the auditor should check the calculation of the related premiums to the appropriate premium rate tables. He should also determine that appropriate premium amounts are billed, accounted for, and subsequently collected.

Premiums received but not yet applied are usually maintained in a suspense account. The auditor's test should be designed to determine that the company is properly clearing these items from suspense on a timely basis. Tests of premiums can be correlated with audit tests of (1) premiums paid in advance, (2) premium deposit accounts, (3) policy loans, (4) dividends, (5) commissions, (6) surrenders, (7) claims, and (8) reserves.

Policy Benefit Cycle. Forms of benefits are death benefits, endowments, annuity payments, surrender payments, policyholder dividends, and disability benefits. Payments are made to the insured or to someone that the policyowner has designated.

Cycle operations. Death benefits under life insurance contracts are paid in a lump sum or under other elective arrangements. Once the company has determined that the claim is proper, payment of the death benefit is made. In addition to the face amount of the benefit, life insurance companies pay interest on the proceeds from date of death to the date the amount is disbursed.

If the insured lives to the maturity of an endowment insurance contract, the stipulated proceeds are paid at maturity. If the insured dies before the endowment matures, the company will pay a death claim to a named beneficiary. Annuity payments are made by the life insurance company to the designated person in accordance with the terms of the annuity contract. Surrender or loan values usually accrue under whole life or endowment contracts and are paid, or are available, on surrender of, or borrowing on, the policy. Disability benefits include waiver of premium during the disability period, and also loss-of-income benefits. Health insurance policies, offered by many life insurance companies, may provide hospital, surgical, medical, or loss-of-income coverage.

The processing of benefits generally involves a determination that the contract is in force and that the payments to be made are in accordance with the contract. In the case of disability payments, there is a medical question as to whether the insured has in fact been disabled. In this regard, life insurance companies generally obtain statements from physicians and/or hospitals to satisfy themselves that the person has been disabled.

When death claims are presented, they should be entered in the claim register. A claim number is usually assigned sequentially to each claim as it is registered and a claim file is initiated. If the policy was in force at the time of death, the company obtains proof of death. Documents used to substantiate the insured's death usually consist of a certificate of death and a statement from a physician.

After determining that the policy has been in force and the death of the insured has occurred, the next step is to determine that provisions of the contract have not excluded the risk which caused the death. For example, the policy may have stipulated that the contract did not provide coverage in the event the insured died while piloting a private plane.

The company then determines the amount to be paid to the beneficiary. If a policy loan is outstanding on the contract, the amount of the loan will be deducted from the proceeds. Conversely, items such as advance premiums on deposit and additional insurance purchased by dividends are usually added to the face amount together with interest on the proceeds.

If the policy under which the death claim has been submitted involves reinsurance, information regarding the policy will be supplied to the reinsurance department so that proper reimbursement will be received from the reinsurer.

Audit approach—policy benefit cycle. The primary audit objectives associated with the benefit cycle include the auditor's evaluation of:

• Proper establishment of policy benefit reserves
• Timely claims processing
• Proper recordng of claims
• Adequacy of claim reserves
• Proper adjustment and payment of claims
• Accuracy of statistical records

Policy benefit reserves are established by applying reserve factors to the policies in force. The reserve factors are actuarially determined based on appropriate mortality, morbidity, interest, and expense assumptions. The testing of the policy benefit reserves should include testing that the policy in force includes all outstanding policies, and should be coordinated with the testing of new policies issued and policies deleted for payment of benefits. The testing of reserve factors requires the use of actuaries to assess the appropriateness of the assumptions used and that the factors have been properly calculated.

Death claims should be tested by reference to the related claim files. Each file selected should be reviewed to determine that it contains the proper support. The file should also indicate that the company has determined that premiums on the policy were paid through date of death, whether there were any policy loans, whether the risk which caused death was covered, and whether there was recoverable reinsurance. In addition, the auditor should test whether policies that have matured, were surrendered, or terminated by death have been deleted from the listing of policies used in calculating reserves, to ensure that the liability is not overstated by having both a policy benefit and claim reserve established.

Matured endowments should be tested to determine that payment is subject to a precontrol of all endowments maturing within the year. The tests should determine that all such payments are in accordance with the contract and have been properly approved. Cash surrenders should be tested to determine that the amount paid is in accordance with policy terms and that the policy has been surrendered and cancelled. Benefits paid under accident and health contracts should be tested to determine that the policy was in force, that proper support exists for the payment, that the benefits paid are in accordance with the terms of the contract, and that the claim data is properly recorded.

The aggregate amount of dividends that may be paid to policyholders should be compared with the amount approved by the board of directors. The auditor should determine that benefits are properly allocated and applied to participating policies. Consideration should also be given to direct confirmation of benefit payments with policyholders or beneficiaries, especially where payments are made to agents for delivery.

Investment Cycle.

The audit of investments in an insurance company in many respects involves the same objectives and procedures as would be considered in any other enterprise, as discussed in Chapter 12. The principal objectives in auditing investments are to verify the existence and carrying value of the investments, to determine ownership, and to assess the propriety of accounting for related income and for gains and losses from the sale of investments. Two additional objectives peculiar to insurance companies are the verification of the legality of investments (in accordance with guidelines set forth in the state's insurance code) and the appropriate basis of valuation.

Specific Auditing Problems

Estimation of Loss Reserves. As indicated previously, the estimation of loss reserves by a property and liability insurance company involves a series of complex tasks. Likewise, the process of assessing the adequacy of these reserves is one of the most difficult areas encountered in the examination of an insurance company. Frequently, the analysis of loss reserves in a small insurance or reinsurance company is complicated further by a low volume of claims and lack of sufficient comprehensive historical data. As a result, the method used to establish loss reserves in companies of this nature should receive thorough attention. One of the most common approaches is the use of industry statistics to both estimate and analyze loss reserves, where other possibly more accurate means are not feasible due to lack of adequate historical data for the company.

Analysis of casualty loss reserves is another area of audit concern. Unexpected periods of inflation or recession, changes in social concerns and jury awards, and the period of time over which liability claims are settled, all greatly influence the estimation of reserves.

Reinsurance. Property and liability reinsurance warrants special consideration in assessing audit risk. A company ceding reinsurance does not have its legal obligations to the insureds relieved through reinsurance. The ceding company only obtains the right of reimbursement from the assuming company. Hence, should the assuming company not have financial stability or sufficient capacity to meet its obligations as they come due, the ceding company remains liable.

On the other hand, assumed reinsurance requires a thorough assessment as to the accuracy and reliability of the data received from the ceding company. Often this data is not received in a timely enough manner to facilitate a meaningful analysis, nor is it in sufficient detail or classified in a manner consistent with that used by the assuming company.

Furthermore, SFAS 60 attempts to address the issue of risk transfer and states the following:

> To the extent that a reinsurance contract does not, despite its form, provide for indemnification of the ceding enterprise by the reinsurer against loss or liability, the premium paid less the premium to be retained by the reinsurer shall be accounted for as a deposit by the ceding enterprise. Those contracts may be structured in various ways, but if, regardless of form, their substance is that all or part of the premium paid by the ceding enterprise is a deposit, the amount paid shall be accounted for as such. A net credit resulting from the contract shall be reported as a liability by the ceding enterprise. A net charge resulting from the contract shall be reported as an asset by the reinsurer. [In6.146]

In other words, for a transaction to be treated as reinsurance, the risk of loss must transfer to the assuming company. The problem herein lies with the absence of a clear definition as to what constitutes risk transfer. This may be quite a difficult conclusion to reach and is a topic that is constantly debated.

44

Other Financial Institutions

INVESTMENT COMPANIES

Investment companies provide professional investment management for pools of funds obtained from shareholders or other equity participants. Investment companies can be classified into three distinct categories. An investment company is either a face-amount certificate company, a unit investment trust, or a management company. A *face-amount certificate* company is an investment company engaged or proposing to engage in the business of issuing installment-type face-amount certificates. A *unit investment trust* (UIT) is an investment company other than a voting trust, organized under a trust indenture or similar instrument, that issues only redeemable securities representing an undivided interest in a unit of a specified securities portfolio. If an investment company is not a face-amount certificate company or a UIT, then it is a *management company.*

Investment companies are organized in various ways: as corporations, grantor or other common law trusts, limited partnerships, or other special purpose entities such as the so-called separate accounts of insurance companies (which are not, in fact, separate entities in any sense other than at law). Whatever the form, all fall under the definitions and regulatory scheme of the Investment Company Act of 1940 (the 1940 Act). The basic definition of an investment company under the 1940 Act (§ 3(a)(1)) is any issuer that is or holds itself out as being engaged primarily, or proposes to engage primarily, in the business of investing, reinvesting, or trading in securities. The accounting principles and auditing procedures developed by the AICPA and included in the revised edition of the Audit and Accounting Guide, *Audits of Investment Companies* (1987d), are intended to apply to all investment companies except real estate investment trusts (REITs).

Structure

Management Companies. Management companies are either open-end or closed-end. An open-end company, typically referred to as a *mutual fund,* offers for sale, or has outstanding, an ownership interest that is redeemable. All other management companies are closed-end, that is, shares therein may be traded on the market, but they are not redeemable upon presentation to the issuer (or a designee). A redeemable security is any security other than short-term paper for which the holder is entitled to receive his proportionate share of the issuer's current net assets, or the cash equivalent thereof.

Management companies are further classified as diversified or nondiversified companies. A diversified company has at least 75% of its total assets represented by cash, cash items, government securities, securities of other investment companies, and other securities (limited for any one other security to an amount not greater than 5% of the value of total assets). A nondiversified company is, of course, one that fails these tests.

Unit Investment Trusts. UITs are organized under a trust agreement and indenture among the sponsors, the trustee, and an evaluator. This form is used primarily to hold a portfolio of tax-exempt bonds, or other bonds or equities; it is also used to accumulate the shares of a particular mutual fund under a contractual plan, permitting investors to pay in regular installments over a fixed period. It has no board of directors or other management, and issues only redeemable units representing an undivided interest in the trust's portfolio (usually securities or other readily marketable investments such as gold bullion or diamonds). Units remain outstanding until a unitholder tenders them to the trustee for redemption or until the trust is terminated.

UITs are generally organized as either grantor trusts or regulated investment companies (RICs), a decision made by the sponsor based on the character and tax treatment accorded to the income from the trust's investments. Trust agreements usually call for distribution of income on a monthly, quarterly, or semi-annual basis; RICs must distribute their income, under provisions of the Internal Revenue Code (IRC). The proceeds of redemptions, maturities, or sales of the investments held by the trust are usually distributed to unitholders unless needed to pay for redemption of units tendered to the trustee. Even when proceeds of principal transactions are not remitted to unitholders, as holders of undivided interests, they are deemed to have participated in them. This aspect of the IRC has had a profound impact on the UIT market, as it significantly increases the probability of taxable income with no cash distribution.

The form and content of financial statements of UITs are prescribed by Article 6 of Regulation S-X and are discussed in Chapters 6 and 7 of the Audit Guide.

Investment Advisor Companies. The 1940 Act requires persons in the business of advising others about securities to register with the SEC. The registration application must describe the investment advisor's background and business associations, authority with respect to clients' funds and accounts, and basis for compensation (which cannot provide for a sharing of gains or appreciation).

The law prohibits fraudulent practices by advisors, and specifies the books, records, papers, and memoranda that must be maintained and preserved. If an investment advisor has custody of any funds or securities in which a client has a beneficial interest, such funds or securities must be properly segregated and verified by unannounced actual examination at least once each calendar year by an independent accountant. The independent accountant's statement that he has made such an examination must be filed promptly with the SEC. In addition, any "material inadequacy" in the books and records and safekeeping facilities must be identified, and corrective action taken or proposed must be indicated.

Regulation and Supervision

Investment Companies. Investment companies are subject to both state and federal regulation. The 1940 Act (§ 3) provides generally for SEC registration of any investment company with the following characteristics:

1. It has outstanding securities beneficially owned by more than 100 persons.
2. It is offering or (proposing to offer) its securities to the public.

Unregistered companies may not conduct interstate business and are denied the use of the mails for purchases or sales of securities. Intrastate sales of shares also require registration with state securities commissions. State "blue sky" laws generally regulate the sale and distribution of securities to residents of a state, but do not regulate the operations and/or management of investment companies.

The SEC Division of Investment Managements is responsible for review and regulation of investment companies. After initial registration with the SEC under the 1940 Act, an investment company must report periodically to its shareholders and the SEC. Companies offering shares to the public are subject to the Securities Act of 1933 (the 1933 Act), and closed-end companies with publicly traded securities must comply with the Securities Exchange Act of 1934 (the 1934 Act).

Investment Company Act. Several major provisions of the 1940 Act, along with other related important SEC requirements, are as follows:

1. The initial registration filed with the SEC must describe officers' backgrounds, the terms of management advisory contracts, and the company's intended investment policies and mode of operations. This information must be kept current by periodic revision.

2. No investment company or principal underwriter thereof may make a public offering of the company's securities unless the company has a net worth of at least $100,000 or the SEC is given adequate assurance that firm agreements exist with fewer than 25 persons to purchase securities that will bring the net worth up to $100,000. These subscriptions must be paid in prior to any additional offerings.

3. Closed-end investment companies may issue debt securities or incur a bank loan only if the amount issued is covered three times by assets; preferred stock must be covered twice. Only one class of bonds and one class of preferred stock may be issued and preferred stock must have voting rights. Open-end companies may not issue senior securities, and any bank loans must be covered three times by assets. Unit investment trusts may have only one class of securities. Face-amount certificate companies must have minimum capital of $250,000 and may not issue preferred stock.

4. Annual reports must be issued to shareholders, including financial statements accompanied by a CPA's verification. Except for UITs, a mid-year report is also required, and is frequently audited.

5. Dividends to shareholders from sources other than undistributed net income must be accompanied by a notice disclosing the source, so that shareholders may distinguish income from captial gains distributions. This requirement is considerably less than what such entities must report under the IRC, which mandates extensive Form 1099 reporting for payments to shareholders for interest, dividends, original issue discount, gross proceeds, and capital gains. Additionally, after 1988, mutual funds are required to add back management fees to distributed income, and report such fees separately as an item shareholders may deduct on their own returns (subject to limitations).

6. Sales practices, largely self-regulated, must follow the rules of fair practice of the National Association of Securities Dealers (NASD). At least 40% of the directors must be persons who are not officers or employees of the investment company, its investment advisor, or principal underwriter.

Other key provisions of the 1940 Act cover standards of operating conduct, including intercompany investments, self-trading, dealings with sponsors, and custody of assets.

Regulations governing the sales practices, financing and operations of fixed trusts, installment plans, and face-amount certificate companies are also included in the 1940 Act.

Open-end companies must reissue prospectuses regularly because they continuously offer new shares for sale to the public; however, closed-end companies need do so only when offering new securities. In addition to the required financial statements, the prospectus must contain information about the history, functions, investment policies, capitalization, management, provisions for the purchase and redemption of shares, pricing of shares, and dividend record of the company. A complete listing of the portfolio of investments, shown at both cost and market values, also must be presented.

A brief summary of some of the Act's sections of interest to accountants is shown in Figure 44.1.

Reporting and Record-Keeping Requirements

Financial Statements. The registration statements and annual reports of regulated investment companies contain detailed financial statements that must be audited by an independent CPA. Whether the investment company's securities are in the custody of the company or of a member of a national securities exchange, the independent accountant must periodically examine the securities, occasionally without advance notice to the custodian, and must report his findings to the SEC.

Financial statements included in reports filed with the SEC are generally required to conform to Article 6 of Regulation S-X. Financial statements included in reports to shareholders should generally conform with those in reports filed with the SEC and should include: a statement of assets and liabilities (or a statement of net assets) and a detailed statement of investments; a statement of operations; a statement of changes in net assets; and schedule of selected per share data.

In addition, the aggregate purchases and sales of security investments during the periods covered and the remuneration paid to officers, directors, and advisors must be reported. UIT annual reports sent to unitholders are generally prepared by the trustee and do not conform to those filed with the SEC; as a matter of industry practice, such reports are prepared on a cash basis. Proposed requirements under Form N-7 (see "Registration and Reporting" later in this chapter), if adopted, will significantly change the form and content of trustee reports to unitholders. While they will not fully conform to Regulation S-X, they will be much more comparable, and will be identical with those required by the SEC for maintenance of an effective registration statement on Form S-6.

Record-Keeping. Rules under the 1940 Act (§ 31(a)) prescribe the accounting records that must be maintained by an investment company. These records may be examined periodically by SEC representatives (§ 31(b)).

The 1934 Act specifies the records that must be maintained by the principal underwriter of the company, the period for which records must be preserved, and the reports that must be filed with the SEC (§ 15(b)). These records also are subject to periodic examination by SEC representatives.

§ 2	General definitions.
§ 2(a)(41)	Definition of "value" with respect to assets of registered investment companies.
§ 3	Definition of investment company.
§ 3(b)	Exceptions and exemptions under the Act.
§§ 4 and 5	Classification and subclassification of management companies.
§ 8	Registration guidelines.
§ 12	Guidelines for functions and activities and restrictions placed upon investment companies.
§ 15	Requirements for written investment advisory and underwriting contracts.
§ 17	Guidelines for transactions of certain affiliated persons and underwriters. This section prohibits self-dealing and prescribes under § 17(f) the requirements for custodian relationships and verification by an accountant of assets under custody.
§ 18	Guidelines for capital structure of investment companies.
§ 19	Requirements for written disclosures to shareholders of the source of any distribution when not solely from accumulated undistributed earnings. This section also makes it unlawful for any investment company to distribute long-term capital gains more than once every twelve months. Because of new distribution requirements under the Tax Reform Act of 1986, the SEC permitted companies to make more than one distribution during 1986 and 1987.
§ 20	Proxy preparation and filing requirements for an investment company, including the requirement for a balance sheet of the investment advisor, certified by an independent accountant.
§ 30	Periodic and other reports that must be filed, and the timing of such filings. The major requirements are for the filing of semiannual and annual reports within 60 days on Form N-SAR. An independent accountant's report on internal controls must be included in the year-end Form N-SAR. At least semiannually, financial statements must be given to stockholders and the annual statement must be accompanied by a certificate of independent accountant's verification.
§ 32	Annual selection of an independent accountant by a majority of disinterested directors; ratified at the next annual meeting of shareholders.

FIG. 44.1 Investment Company Act of 1940—Sections of Interest to Accountants

Registration and Reporting. The registration of fund securities to be offered under the Securities Act of 1933 is filed on Form N-1A for open-end funds, on Form N-2 for closed-end funds, and on Form S-6 for UITs. Each SEC form consists principally of the prospectus describing the fund's objectives, policies, management, and investment restrictions, and includes audited financial statements.

The 1940 Act (§ 30(d)) and SEC rules require RICs and UITs to send reports either annually or semiannually to shareholders. The fiscal year-end report must cover the entire year and, in the case of companies other than unit trusts, must contain audited financial statements that conform to Regulation S-X. Under current law, audited financial statements must be included in any registration statement or prospectus filed for UITs whose units are traded in secondary markets.

Prior to 1985, different types of investment companies used different forms for annual reports to the SEC. In response to the changes made in SEC procedures for reviewing disclosure documents of investment companies, for performing routine inspections of those companies, and to aid in developing a computerized data base of information for the industry, the SEC adopted Form N-SAR for investment company *annual reports*, effective April 30, 1985. This form contains separate sections for different types of investment companies, replacing five separate annual reporting forms.

The key registration forms used in the investment company industry in complying with the 1933, 1934, and 1940 Acts are discussed in the following subsections.

Form N-8a. Used for notification of registration under the 1940 Act, Form N-8a includes the name, address, and other pertinent data relating to the company. The filing of this unaudited form registers the investment company under the 1940 Act.

Form N-1A. This form replaced Form N-1 for use by open-end management investment companies to register under the 1933 and 1940 Acts. It provides a detailed description of the company, its practices, policies, objectives, management, and so forth. The initial filing of this form requires audited financial statements (an opening balance sheet in the case of mutual funds, a balance sheet and portfolio of investments in the case of a unit trust).

Information in currently effective registration statements and prospectuses must be updated for significant events occurring subsequent to the effective date. Prospectuses for mutual funds are generally updated annually with audited financial statements. Post-effective registration statement amendments on Form N-1A must be filed (and be accepted by the SEC) to permit a fund to continue to offer its shares for sale under the 1933 and 1940 Acts. Financial statements included in such posteffective amendments must be audited; and the date of the financial statements must be within 16 months of the date of the previous audited financial statements.

Forms N-1, N-3, and N-4. These forms are used by insurance company variable annuity separate accounts registered under the 1933 and 1940 Acts. The specific form depends on the legal form of the company and its expected market.

Form N-7. Form N-7 was proposed by the SEC in 1985; the proposal has been redrafted once, and as of mid-1988 it is still awaiting further SEC actions. If adopted, it will be used for the registration of UITs and would substantially eliminate the requirement for audited financial statements in posteffective registration statements. This form will establish a two-part format for disclosure to investors, consisting of: (1) a simplified prospectus that would satisfy prospectus delivery requirements and (2) a statement of additional information that would be available to investors on request.

Expense Tables and Standardized Yield Disclosures. The SEC has taken two regulatory actions that affect mutual funds effective May 1, 1988:

1. Form N-1A has been amended to require a tabular presentation of fees and expenses.
2. Several rules and forms under the 1933 and 1940 Acts affecting the advertising of mutual funds and insurance company separate accounts have been revised so that investors can have consistent data for comparison of different funds.

Foreign Custodial Arrangements. Rule 17f-5 provides an exemption from the custody requirements of the 1940 Act in that U.S. registered management investment companies may place and maintain their foreign securities, cash, and cash equivalents with eligible foreign custodians. The foreign custody arrangements may involve: (1) U.S. investment companies and foreign banking institutions, trust companies, securities depositories, and clearing agencies; and (2) Canadian investment companies and overseas branches of qualified U.S. banks. Under Rule 17f-5:

1. A minimum equity of $200 million for foreign banks and trust companies, and $100 million for foreign subsidiaries of U.S. banks and bank holding companies, is required.
2. Although a fund's board of directors may use an expert or intermediary to select a foreign custodian and to oversee performance, the board of directors must approve the choice of country or custodian before the arrangement is implemented.
3. The board of directors must establish a system to annually monitor foreign custodial arrangements.
4. Only the amounts of cash or cash equivalents reasonably necessary to effect foreign securities transactions may be maintained in a foreign bank or securities depository.
5. Only the central system (i.e., a securities clearing agency using a book entry system for transfers) may be used for handling securities in any given country.

Distribution Under Rule 12b-1. Rule 12b-1, which governs the distribution of shares by registered open-end management investment companies (mutual funds), states that a company may not act as distributor of securities for which it is the issuer, except through an underwriter. A mutual fund is deemed to be acting as distributor if it engages directly or indirectly in financing any activity that is primarily intended to result in the sale of its shares, including but not necessarily limited to: (1) advertising; (2) compensation of underwriters, dealers, and sales personnel; (3) printing and mailing of prospectuses to other than current shareholders; and (4) printing and mailing of sales literature.

A mutual fund may act as a distributor of securities of which it is the issuer provided that any payments made by it in connection with the distribution are made under a written plan that describes all material aspects of the proposed distribution financing, and that all agreements relating to the implementation of the plan are in writing. Further, the plan of distribution and any related agreements must:

1. Be approved by holders of a majority of the company's outstanding voting securities.
2. Be approved by the board of directors, and unanimously by the directors who are not "interested persons" and have no direct or indirect financial interest in the operation of the plan. (The directors' votes must be cast in person at a meeting called for this specific purpose.)

3. Provide, in substance that:
   a. It shall continue in effect for a period of more than one year from the date of its execution or adoption only so long as such continuance is specifically approved at least annually, as in item 2.
   b. Any person authorized to direct the disposition of moneys paid or payable by the company under the plan or related agreements shall provide to the board of directors, and the directors shall review, at least quarterly, a written report of the expenditures and the purposes for which they were made.
   c. The plan may be terminated at any time by vote of a majority of the disinterested members of the board or by vote of a majority of the outstanding voting securities of the company.
   d. An agreement related to the plan may be terminated at any time, without the payment of any penalty, by a majority of the disinterested board members or by a vote of a majority of the outstanding voting securities, on not more than 60 days' written notice to any other party to the agreement.
   e. The agreement will automatically terminate if it is assigned.
4. Provide that unless shareholder approval is obtained, the plan may not be amended to materially increase the amount to be spent for distribution. Material amendments of the plan must be approved in the manner described in item 2.

A company may implement or continue a plan only if the directors who vote to approve such implementation or continuation conclude, in the exercise of reasonable business judgment and in light of their fiduciary duties (under state law and under §§ 36(a) and (b) of the 1940 Act), that there is a reasonable likelihood that the plan of distribution will benefit the company and its shareholders.

Accounting by distributors for 12b-1 fees was discussed by the EITF in Issue 85-24, *Distribution Fees by Distributors of Mutual Funds That Do Not Have a Front-End Sales Charge*. Distributors were concerned that income recognition of fees was being unduly delayed for 12b-1 funds, in comparison with fee recognition for other funds.

Most mutual funds have a front-end sales charge, called a "load," whereby the investor's funds are immediately reduced. This charge is picked up as income by the distributor. In 12b-1 funds, also called "no-load" funds, all of the investor's funds are invested immediately, and if the investor maintains his investment in the fund for a stipulated period (usually five years), there is no charge on withdrawal; otherwise, a charge is assessed and paid over to the distributor, with the rate of charge decreasing annually. Throughout this five-year period, the distributor is paid a fee, authorized annually by the disinterested members of the board (as previously described), and eventually receives as much as (or more than) would have been obtained through a front-end load.

Because the 12b-1 fund product had only recently been promoted, some mutual fund distributors questioned the appropriateness of the traditional practice of deferring costs and amortizing them over the period during which the investor may be assessed. In their view, the fees should be accrued at the time of distribution, because they are assured either through payment of expenses, as approved annually by the board, or by the exit fees charged to investors.

The EITF reached a consensus that prior practice should not be changed. The matter was taken to the Stockbrokerage and Investment Banking Subcommittee, which agreed with the distributors; however, when the matter reached AcSEC (which is required to clear subcommittee matters), AcSEC sided with the initial EITF consensus, and the matter was put to rest. The fundamental decision point was that the disinterested members of the fund's board of directors had to vote annually to continue the plan of distribution, and it was therefore conceivable (though it has not happened) that continuation might not occur.

Financial Reporting Considerations

SEC Requirements. FRR 8 (§ 404.06) covers financial statements filed by registered investment companies. Important provisions of the release include:

1. Registered investment companies other than issuers of face-amount investment certificates are required to present an all-inclusive statement of operations. That is, both realized and unrealized gains and losses are included in the determination of the net increase or decrease in net assets resulting from operations.
2. The reporting format for the presentation of the balance sheet or a substitute statement of net assets is prescribed. A statement-of-net-assets format may not be used unless the investment in securities of unaffiliated issuers is 95% or more of total assets.
3. Investments must be stated at market value.
4. Changes in net assets resulting from share transactions are presented net on the face of the statement, with details as to sales and redemptions in a footnote.
5. Cash should include only cash on hand and demand deposits; time deposits are considered an investment.

Other provisions of FRR 8 deal with disclosure of restricted securities, timing of recognition of interest income, information regarding income tax consequences, and contingencies arising from intercompany relationships.

Additionally, in FRR 29, *Accounting for Distribution Expenses*, the SEC ruled that all 12b-1 funds must deduct distribution charges as expenses. A few funds had been treating these as a reduction of capital.

AICPA Guide. In 1987, the AICPA issued a revision of the 1973 version of the Audit and Accounting Guide, *Audits of Investment Companies* (1987d), making significant changes in accounting and financial reporting standards and practices. The Guide incorporates several SOPs,[1] several amendments to the Internal Revenue Code, revised SEC rules, and changes in industry practices. Sample financial statements have been modified to reflect the requirements of FRR 8, and new chapters on unit trusts and variable annuities were added. The Guide is extensive, and should be referred to for detailed accounting and auditing information on the various types of investment companies. The summary discussions in this section conform to the Guide.

---

[1] SOP 74-11, *Financial Accounting and Reporting by Face-Amount Certificate Companies* (TP 10,030); SOP 77-1, *Financial Accounting and Reporting by Investment Companies* (TP 10,140); and SOP 79-1, *Accounting for Municipal Bond Funds* (TP 10,260).

Valuation of Securities. Investment companies should generally report security investments at market value. The methodology utilized to value fund investments is described, typically in detail, in each fund prospectus.

For listed securities, the last or closing sales price is usually appropriate. If traded on more than one exchange, the closing price on the exchange on which the security is principally traded should be used. If there is no exchange transaction on the valuation date, the valuation should be within the range of the closing bid and asked prices, if available.

For over-the-counter securities there are several possible sources of market prices. A company may use the mean of the bid prices or bid and asked prices from several transactions, or an average from within a range of transactions that is best considered to represent value in the circumstances. Any of these conventions is acceptable if consistently applied.

If market quotations appear to be unusual, if the number of quotations indicates a thin market, or if the securities are restricted, the securities should be fair valued by the board of directors considering all the relevant factors.

The SEC has specified in ASR 118 (FRR § 404.03) the factors that should be considered in valuing a security. They include: (1) the fundamental analytical data relating to the investment, (2) the nature and duraton of restrictions on dispositions of the securities, and (3) an evaluation of the forces influencing the market in which the securities are traded. Information considered by the directors and judgmental factors applied should be documented in the board minutes, and the supporting data should be retained for examination by the independent auditor.

In auditing securities valuations made by the board, the auditor should review the information considered, ascertain the procedures followed by the board, and read relevant minutes. If the auditor is unable to express an unqualified opinion because of inherent uncertainty in valuations based on the board's subjective judgment, the auditor should nevertheless state in his certificate whether the procedures were reasonable and whether the underlying documentation was appropriate.

Auditing Considerations

The primary objective in auditing a management investment company (mutual fund) is to form an opinion that its financial statements present fairly the net assets, results of operations, and changes in net assets for the period under audit, in conformity with GAAP applied on a consistent basis.

The examination should be performed in accordance with GAAS and should include a review of the internal control structure, including that of the custodian, to determine whether the controls are sufficient to safeguard the assets of the fund.

General audit objectives and corresponding audit techniques are discussed in the sections that follow.

Investment Securities. The investment accounts require audit emphasis because portfolio securities represent substantially all of the fund's assets. Interest, realized gains and losses on disposition of investments, and changes in unrealized investment appreciation and depreciation constitute most of the corresponding operations.

The audit approach to the investment account of a fund should begin with a review and evaluation of the internal control environment and structure. This approach should consider the record-keeping and other compliance requirements under the 1940 Act.

Audit objectives should include ascertaining whether:

* The fund has proper ownership and accounting control over portfolio investments.
* The values of portfolio investments are reasonable, and costs thereof for book and tax purposes are properly recorded.
* Income from investments, and realized gains and losses from security transactions, are properly accounted for.
* The fund has complied with restrictions under its stated investment objectives and policies.

These audit objectives should be satisfied through various audit techniques that could include, but are not limited to:

* Verification of physical existence through confirmation with the custodian, or by physical inspection (confirmation with brokers should be made for any investments purchased/sold but not yet received/delivered, i.e., unsettled transactions).
* Verification of portfolio valuations through confirmation with a third party pricing service; all confirmed prices should be compared to those used by the fund and other-than-minor differences (individually or in the aggregate) should be investigated.
* Recalculation tests (throughout the period) of investment income recorded by the fund, to determine whether interest income is being accurately recorded.
* Examination of selected security transactions for proper authorization, timely execution, and accurate calculation of realized gain or loss.

Shareholder Accounts. Shareholder account balances and transactions usually are a significant audit area. A reliable total of the fund's shares outstanding is essential to the correct presentation of net asset value and dividends. The accuracy of the recording of share sales and repurchases depends primarily on the adequacy of the distributor's and the transfer agent's controls over order information.

The audit objectives pertaining to shareholders' accounts encompass ascertaining whether:

* Orders are executed at amounts authorized.
* Processing of cash settlements of transactions is timely, with proper cutoffs.
* Processing of transactions is accurate and well documented.
* The fund's procedures properly determine the number of outstanding shares that are used to compute daily net asset value per share and the fund's dividend declaration.
* The number of outstanding shares of capital stock at the balance sheet date is correct and agrees to the records of the fund's transfer agent.
* Receivables for fund shares sold and payables for fund shares redeemed are properly stated.
* The fund maintains adequate control over the record-keeping of shareholder accounts.

- Dividends from investment income and distributions to shareholders from realized gains are properly computed and recorded.
- Procedures are satisfactory for processing shareholder "as of" transactions.

Many of the auditing procedures that will be used by the auditor to accomplish the foregoing objectives will involve detailed analysis of controls and testing of specific transactions.

Selected fund share balances may be confirmed at various times during the period under examination. The auditor should also consider performing a review of the transfer agent controls, in accordance with guidelines provided in the *Investment Company Audit Guide* (AICPA, 1987d, pp. 69–71).

Other Auditing Issues. Distribution and management fees should be tested for accuracy and propriety for selected days throughout the period. This test work, when combined with analytical procedures, helps to provide assurance that the fund is being properly assessed for fees.

Tests should be made to determine that dividend accruals have been properly computed; for example, the total dividend distribution could be recomputed and compared to notification and payment (less shareholder reinvestments) to the dividend disbursing agent.

Financial Reports. In addition to reviewing all shareholder reports and financial statements, the auditor should conduct compliance tests to ascertain that each report is in conformity with the accounting requirements of the 1940 Act, Article 6 of Regulation S-X, and GAAP.

The auditor should consider performing a general review of the fund's practice with regard to state blue sky regulations to determine that the fund has an adequate number of shares registered in each state in which shares are being marketed.

Income Taxes

A principal audit objective is to achieve satisfaction that the fund maintains its status as a RIC if that is its stated intention.

Under Subchapter M of the IRC, an investment company registered under the 1940 Act can elect RIC status and be relieved of income taxes on distributed investment income and realized gains. To qualify, the company must (1) distribute as taxable dividends not less than 90% of its net investment income for any taxable year; (2) derive at least 90% of gross income from dividends, interest, and gains from sales of securities; and (3) comply with other percentage limitations regarding both gains on securities held less than three months and composition of investment assets.

If realized security gains are retained, the investment company may elect to pay the federal income tax on such gains for the account of its shareholders. Such taxes would then be deemed to be distributed to the shareholders and the basis of their holdings would be adjusted as if the net after-tax gain had been distributed and reinvested.

Nonregulated investment companies are required to pay normal corporate taxes on net income and realized gains. For all investment companies subject to income taxes, the financial statements should show the provision for federal, state, and foreign taxes applicable to net investment income and gains or losses on investments, including deferred taxes on unrealized gains or losses.

In addition to the requirement to maintain its status under subchapter M, a fund must also meet distribution requirements under IRC § 4982 to avoid assessment of an excise tax on certain undistributed RIC income. This tax, added by the Tax Reform Act of 1986 and amended by the Revenue Act of 1987, imposes an excise tax on a calendar year basis equal to 4% of the excess of the required distribution over the distributed amount. To avoid this excise tax the investment company must distribute at least 97% of its taxable income (under § 852(b)(2)) for the calendar year plus 98% of its capital gain net income (under § 4982(e)(2)) for the 12 months ending October 31.

VENTURE CAPITAL INVESTMENT COMPANIES

Background

Venture capital investment companies provide early-stage development funding and expansion financing to companies that require additional capital for growth but that do not yet have access to conventional funding sources. They differ from other investment companies primarily in their ability to leverage their investments and to carry significant amounts of debt on their financial statements. Further, such companies often contend with a different regulatory scheme than UITs or management companies; for example, publicly traded SBICs report under Article 5 of Regulation S-X rather than Article 6.

Such companies may be organized in corporate form, as partnerships, proprietorships, or trusts. Venture capital investment companies include Small Business Investment Companies (SBICs) and Business Development Companies (BDCs). They may be publicly traded or privately held; and they can be subsidiaries of financial institutions and operating companies.

Venture capital investment companies often invest in companies in the early stages of business development when the risks as well as the opportunities for future returns are the greatest. Venture capital investment companies try to moderate investment risk by diversifying their portfolios based on the number of investments, the variety of the kinds of securities (such as notes, options, convertible debentures, preferred stocks, or common stocks), and the stage of development and financing of the entities.

The business purpose of most venture capital investment companies is to hold their investments, generally for less than five years, and then earn high returns by selling all or parts of their portfolio investments when and if they have appreciated sufficiently. Their purpose is not to maintain portfolios of long-term investments, even though some investments may be held for long periods. Profits earned on investments that have appreciated compensate the venturer for losses on unsuccessful investments.

The portfolios of venture capital investment companies may be illiquid because of the nature of the investments, which usually are securities with no public market. Gains on disposition of those investments are often realized over an extended holding period. The nature of the investments therefore requires valuation procedures that differ markedly from those used by typical investment companies.

Investments are generally disposed of by offering shares to the public, selling the shares to the management of a portfolio company based on the terms of the original investment, selling shares to third parties, or distributing shares to the venture capital investment company's investors.

Special income tax provisions applying to SBICs are the availability of a 100% deduction on qualifying dividends received and ordinary loss rather than capital loss treatment on the sale or exchange of investments in convertible securities or on stocks acquired under conversion privileges.

Stages of Financing. The following are the types of financing provided during different stages of an investee's development:

* Early stage financing.
  - Seed Financing – a relatively small amount of funding is provided to prove a concept.
  - Start-up Financing – funding for product development and initial marketing.
  - First Stage Financing – funding to start production and sales.
* Expansion financing or second-stage-or-later financing – for working capital needs, major expansion, or to provide cash until an investee offers its securities to the public or is acquired by another entity.

Venture capital investment companies also provide financing for leveraged buyouts, mergers and acquisitions, and in turnaround situations. If an SBIC registers with the SEC, it will use Form N-5, with information requirements identical to Form N1-A (discussed earlier in "Registration and Reporting").

Unique Characteristics. Although the investments of venture capital investment companies are intended to be passive investments, venture capitalists are often more actively involved with their portfolio companies than typical passive investors. Their involvement may consist of serving on a portfolio company's board of directors or providing formal or informal technical advice.

Under certain circumstances, a venture capitalist may: (1) require registration of unregistered or restricted securities initially received as part of the financing transaction; (2) receive debt securities having conversion provisions that are directly related to the results of operations; or (3) maintain a higher-than-usual percentage of ownership in a portfolio company through direct ownership of common stock or stock convertible to common stock.

Small Business Investment Companies

SBICs are venture capital investment companies that provide equity capital or long-term loans to eligible small businesses for growth, expansion, and modernization. SBICs are regulated by the Small Business Administration (SBA) and are licensed under Section 301 of Title III of the Small Business Investment Act of 1958. Most SBICs are corporations, but the SBA Act also allows SBICs to operate as limited partnerships. Further, some SBICs are registered as closed-end investment companies under the 1940 Act, and may choose favorable tax treatment as regulated investment companies.

Section 301(d) Licensees. Certain SBICs are known as Section 301(d) licensees, also referred to as Minority Enterprise Small Business Investment Companies (MESBICs). They are often subsidiaries or affiliates of other SBICs and are licensed to finance small businesses that are at least 51% owned by members of socially or economically disadvantaged groups as defined by the SBA. MESBICs can obtain additional leverage by selling to the SBA preferred stock that carries a 3% cumulative dividend. Although the preferred stock is considered to be equity for accounting purposes, it is considered debt for regulatory purposes. The SEC has traditionally accepted such preferred stock as not violating the one-class-of-securities requirement of the 1940 Act. MESBICs registered under the 1940 Act also may choose favorable tax treatment as regulated investment companies.

Leveraging Opportunities. By statute, SBICs may borrow from the SBA up to three times the original investment of the SBIC's investors, often at advantageous rates. SBICs that meet the SBA's requirements for classification as investment companies may borrow up to four times their private capital. To qualify for that classification, most licensees must have at least $1 million in unencumbered private paid-in capital and must invest or commit to invest 65% of their total funds in small business ventures. The SBA limits the amount of financing an SBIC can extend to a single concern to 20% of its private capital (30% of the private capital for MESBICs).

Currently, an SBIC may borrow up to $35 million from the SBA. An SBIC's subsidiary that performs management consulting services is required by SBA regulations to be wholly owned by the SBIC and to be consolidated in the SBIC's financial statements.

Significant Regulations. It is important that the independent auditor of an SBIC or MESBIC be aware of the following significant regulations (selected from 13 CFR § 107). SBICs must:

* Participate actively in providing financing to eligible small business concerns (as defined in 13 CFR § 121) and in the case of MESBICs, to entities that are socially or economically disadvantaged in their ability to participate in the free enterprise system.
* Deposit excess funds or funds not used for current operations in short-term interest bearing accounts (13 CFR § 107.708).
* Have a minimum unencumbered private capital of $1 million.
* Receive SBA approval to transfer control or ownership in the SBIC or MESBIC.
* Avoid conflicts of interest with self-dealing in, or obtaining any personal benefits from financing, a small business.
* Avoid charging small business concerns more than the permitted interest rate, or imposing prohibited costs, such as finder's fees or consulting fees.
* Avoid exceeding the lending limit to one small business concern without written SBA approval.

- Avoid exercising control of operations of portfolio investees (although licensees may take temporary control to protect their investments by filing a plan with the SBA providing for relinquishment of control in no more than seven years).
- Avoid providing funds to small business concerns for the following purposes:
  - Investments in and loans to real estate concerns (those classified in SIC code group 65).
  - Relending or reinvesting, except to certain disadvantaged entities.
  - Use outside the United States.
  - Purchase of stock in, or for other financing of, the SBIC.
  - Use in a passive business.
- Generally provide long-term financing for a minimum of five years.

The SBA considers a licensee to be in default and its capital to be impaired if its net realized deficit exceeds 50% of its private capital (75% for MESBICs). The regulations (13 CFR § 107.203(d)) require realized but undistributed net earnings to be reduced by net unrealized losses, if any (investment depreciation less investment appreciation). The regulations also require MESBICs to pay to the SBA all dividends on its 3% cumulative preferred stock before declaring dividends to others.

Business Development Companies

BDCs are closed-end investment companies that invest in companies referred to as *eligible portfolio companies*, which are entities that are not able to receive financing through conventional channels. In addition, BDCs provide significant managerial assistance to most portfolio companies in their operations, or in formulating business objectives and policies, by exercising control or by acting through the directors, officers, or employees of the portfolio companies.

BDCs may invest additional funds, referred to as *follow on investments*, in former eligible portfolio companies and may also invest in certain bankrupt or insolvent companies.

At least 70% of the assets of BDCs must be in liquid assets or invested in small, developing, or financially troubled businesses to which the BDC must give significant managerial assistance.

Although BDCs register under the 1934 Act and must meet its periodic reporting requirements, they may choose to be regulated by the SEC as if they came under the 1940 Act. As amended, the 1940 Act allows a BDC to sell common stock at amounts below its net asset value and to issue senior securities representing indebtedness, including preferred stock, with warrants and options.

BDCs can offer forms of incentive compensation to their managements not always available to the managements of registered investment companies. For example, BDCs can issue warrants, options, or rights to purchase voting securities to officers and directors, and can finance their exercise through loans. They can sometimes adopt profit sharing arrangements or pay performance fees to external advisors.

A BDC may be the parent of an SBIC. However, because BDCs are not actually registered under the 1940 Act, they are ineligible for favorable tax treatment as registered investment companies.

Accounting Practices

The assets of a venture capital investment company may be in the form of portfolio securities, assets acquired in the liquidation of portfolio companies, cash and temporary investments, fixed assets, unamortized organization expenses, and prepaid expenses. Portfolio securities may be in the form of equity securities, including options and warrants, other rights, debt securities with or without conversion privileges, or detachable warrants, loans, and limited partnership interests.

A venture capital investment company presents its investment portfolio and temporary investments at market value for freely traded securities or at an estimate of values determined by the board of directors or its equivalent for securities for which market prices are unavailable.

A venture capital investment company that is a taxable entity provides for income taxes, including deferred taxes on unrealized appreciation or depreciation and other temporary differences. Those that qualify and elect to be taxed as regulated investment companies under Subchapter M of the IRC and that distribute all of their taxable income to their shareholders do not provide for income taxes.

Valuation of Securities. Methods used by investment companies generally to value various kinds of securities, such as listed securities, over-the-counter securities, and securities for which market quotations are unavailable are discussed earlier in the "Investment Companies" section of this chapter. Those methods also apply to the valuation of securities held by venture capital investment companies. Nevertheless, even in the valuation of marketable securities, the valuation process should consider the effects of factors such as whether: (1) a limited number of securities are available for trading, (2) the venture capital investment company holds such a large number of shares that the market price would be adversely affected if they were traded, or (3) the securities are restricted.

Venture capital investment companies typically invest in companies whose securities are not publicly traded, have an unproven track record, and may have liquidity problems. They often acquire a package of an investee's securities, including combinations of debt, convertible securities, warrants, and common shares, sometimes over an extended period of time. Packages of securities are frequently valued as a whole, considering relevant factors such as the cost of the investment, an evaluation of the entity's earnings prospects, performance and sales expectations for its products or services, and the availability and likelihood of exercise of conversion features.

The SBA considers cost to be an important indication of value and states in *Accounting Standards and Financial Requirements of Small Business Investment Companies*, that "cost may be the most appropriate measure of value of venture-type securities until sufficient evidential matter is available to the licensee's Board of Directors ... to form a basis for valuing the securities at other than cost" (13 CFR § 107). SBA Policy and Procedural Release No. 2006 provides guidelines to assist directors in valuing portfolio securities. Auditors should be satisfied that those guidelines or other reasonable methods are used to value securities.

In its proposed SOP, *Accounting for Venture Capital Investment Companies*, the AICPA Investment Companies Committee states that startup investments should be reported at value because "value is usually assumed to be the same as cost during the early stages of such investments unless there is persuasive evidence of a quantifiable increase or decrease in the value of the investment" (AICPA, 1988a, ¶ 57). The SOP states further that an investment in a closely held entity is usually reduced if its performance has deteriorated significantly from expected levels and its ability to earn profits has been permanently impaired. The carrying amount of the investment may also be reduced if the investee issues securities similar to those held by the venture capital investor, but at a lower price.

Conversely, carrying amounts of investments in closely held companies may be increased if a public market is established for the investor's securities, if securities similar to those held by the venture capital investment company are issued at an amount higher than the investor's carrying amount, or if the company's performance is significantly better than expected.

Venture capital investment companies may receive debt securities without conversion features as part of a package or as a result of subsequent financing extended to an investee in which it already has an equity interest. Such debt securities may be due on demand or on specified maturity dates and may have fixed or floating interest rates. Debt securities having specified maturity dates are generally held to maturity. Because such securities are generally a part of a package and are usually issued by startup or early stage companies, most often they are not at market interest rates and it is not possible to find an equivalent rate. As a result, many venture capital investment companies value straight debt securities intended to be held to maturity (even if not part of a package) at amortized cost, which is reduced if collectibility is in doubt. If they will not be held to maturity, they should be reported at market values based on available market quotations, or valued at fair value by the board of directors using applicable market discount factors.

Financial Reporting

For regulatory purposes, SBICs must follow the reporting requirements of the SBA and present their reports on SBA Form 468. SBICs not registered under the 1940 Act or the 1934 Act also use the SBA format for nonregulatory financial reporting purposes.

SBA Requirements. SBICs are required to file semiannual reports of financial condition with the SBA. The SBA requires the annual report to be audited and to be submitted no later than three months after a licensee's year end. The auditor is required to report defalcations (if any came to his attention during the audit) to the SBIC and to the SBA's Deputy Associate Administrator for Investment. In addition, the auditor is also required to report other financial or regulatory irregularities to the SBIC, which is required to report them to the SBA within 30 days. Within 60 days of submitting his report, the auditor must request a confirmation from the SBA that the report had been received from the SBIC. Any reports sent to the SEC (for SBICs that are SEC registrants) must also be submitted to the SBA's investment division.

SBICs prepare a statement of financial position in balance sheet form rather than as a statement of net assets or statement of assets and liabilities, as is done for investment companies. Loans and investments are presented before current or other assets because of their significance in the financial statements of SBICs. Further, long-term debt is presented before current or other liabilities. Loans and investments are presented at cost and adjusted to value by recognizing unrealized appreciation or depreciation.

A corporate or limited partnership SBIC may invest in a MESBIC or have a wholly owned management consulting subsidiary. Such investments are considered to be held for the long-term and for operating purposes. Therefore, they are not reported at value, but on the equity method.

The SBA requires consolidated statements only if a corporate SBIC has a management consulting subsidiary (limited partnerships that invest in such a company should present combined financial statements). If an SBIC temporarily owns more than 50% of a financed concern, it should continue classifying it as a loan or investment and should present it at value rather than consolidating it.

Accounting for capital accounts of SBICs organized as partnerships differs from that normally used by other entities. The regulations require partners' capital accounts to be divided into the following four subsections:

1. Partners' permanent capital contribution.
2. Partners' unrealized gain on securities held.
3. Partners' non-cash gain/income (restricted capital).
4. Partners' undistributed net realized earnings (earned capital).

SBICs are required to present a *Statement of Undistributed Realized Earnings*, segregating amounts attributable to noncash gains/income and to undistributed net earnings realized. The *Statement of Operations Realized* measures separately on an accrual basis net investment income (loss) and realized gain (loss) on the sale of securities.

Investment companies have been required under GAAP to present a statement of changes in net assets, which includes an amount for changes in unrealized appreciation. However, the SBA has required SBICs to file a statement of changes in financial position that excludes changes in unrealized gains (losses) on securities, to show the extent to which the SBIC has generated cash and used idle funds. As of early 1988, it is not known whether the SBA will change its requirement to a statement of cash flows, as required by SFAS 95. The AICPA Investment Companies Committee is currently developing guidance on the application of SFAS 95 to financial reporting by investment companies generally.

Additional statements unique to reporting requirements for SBICs are discussed in *Accounting Standards and Financial Reporting Requirements for Small Business Investment Companies* (13 CFR 107).

Current Accounting Issues

The AICPA Investment Companies Committee has developed a proposed SOP, *Accounting for Venture Capital Investment Companies* (1988a), to deal with two issues: (1) whether all venture capital investment companies should report their investments at value; and (2) whether the investments of a venture capital investment company that is the subsidiary of an operating company should be reported at value in consolidation. The FASB has reviewed the proposed SOP and has taken exception to the notion that all venture capital investment companies, whether or not they are registered with the SEC or are SBA licensees, should report their investments at value. The FASB also has difficulty with the definition of a venture capital investment company, even though the proposed SOP provides criteria for differentiating such companies from operating companies.

The valuation-in-consolidation issue first arose in Issue 85-12, *Retention of Specialized Accounting for Investments in Consolidation.* The EITF reached a consensus that, assuming the specialized accounting treatment is appropriate at the subsidiary level, it should not be changed in consolidation. The particular case discussed related to an SBIC's or venture capital company's investments carried at fair value. There was much concern expressed, however, by the FASB staff and the SEC Observer, because of the opportunity for abuse by designating a subsidiary as special purpose when in fact it was not (for example, research and development operation "disguised" as an SBIC subsidiary's fair-valued investment performing research and development that would be charged to expense if performed at the top company level).

As of early 1988, the FASB staff has agreed with the conclusion in the SOP that specialized industry practices should be retained in consolidation and therefore that the investments of venture capital investment company subsidiaries should be reported at value in the consolidated financial statements of the parent.

The FASB has raised one additional issue dealing with the consolidation of majority-owned subsidiaries, as required by SFAS 94 (C 51). The FASB believes that venture capital investment companies should consolidate investments in which they hold a majority of the shares. The Investment Companies Committee objects to that view of the exemption in ARB 51 (continued in SFAS 94) for temporary investments. The FASB has difficulty in accepting the Committee's view that such investments are temporary in nature if they are to be held for extended periods and the date of disposition is unknown.

Because the foregoing issues remain unresolved at the FASB, the proposed SOP had not been officially exposed as of mid-1988, and may in fact be abandoned.

REAL ESTATE INVESTMENT TRUSTS

A REIT obtains funds by issuing shares to obtain equity capital and by borrowing from financial institutions and other lenders. It then invests the funds in real estate, either as an equity owner or as a lender. Generally owned by passive owners and not operators, REITs began to grow when the IRC was amended in 1961 to give small investors better real estate investment opportunities.

Few other financial intermediaries have experienced the heady growth that the REITs had in the 14 years between 1961 and 1975. In 1961, total industry assets were estimated at $300 million; by year end 1974, assets totaled about $21 billion (according to *REIT Fact Book, 1986*, published in 1987 by the National Association of Real Estate Investment Trusts (NAREIT), the source of all industry data not otherwise referenced in this section).

In 1975, the trend dramatically reversed. That year, industry assets declined to $12 billion as a result of a national recession that severely affected the value of real estate. Not only did the REITs' difficulties shake the nation's financial system, they pointed out the need for improved accounting practices by the industry.

Beginning in 1984, REITs again began to grow at a respectable rate. By year end 1986, REIT assets totaled $24 billion.

Equity Structure

By meeting certain requirements of the IRC a REIT is exempt from most state and federal income taxes. It acts as a conduit, passing its earnings along to shareholders. In this regard an REIT is like a mutual fund; however, its capital structure is better likened to that of a closed-end investment company. A REIT does not redeem shares on demand. An investor must sell his shares in the marketplace, where the price is only coincidentally equal to net asset value per share (if known). Since most REITs are publicly held entities, they must meet the registration and filing requirements of the SEC.

A REIT's shareholders elect directors or trustees, who determine its broad investment strategy and act much like a corporation's board of directors. The day-to-day operations of many REITs are administered by an external advisor (often a subsidiary of another financial institution such as a commercial bank, mortgage banker, or insurance company), that also advises the trustees on investment opportunities and alternatives. Because the advisor charges for its services and because there is no legal or regulatory requirement for external management, many REITs have dispensed with the services of a separate advisor.

Income Taxes

The impetus for the expansion of REITs was an amendment to the IRC (§§ 856–859) effective January 1, 1961, subsequently amended, most recently in the Tax Reform Act of 1986. Prior to 1961, the illiquid nature of traditional real estate investments and sizable cash requirements precluded small investor participation. The 1961 amendment was designed to distinguish REITs from other financial intermediaries and forestall real estate developers and other types of companies from converting to REITs for their own tax advantages.

An enterprise that elects to receive tax treatment as a REIT must meet IRS requirements, outlined as follows:

- It must be a corporation (other than a bank or an insurance company), trust, or association, and meet requirements for a minimum number of shareholders with a limitation on the concentration of ownership.
- It must meet specified quantitative income tests designed to ensure that income is derived mostly from real estate related assets held for investment.
- Its assets must consist mostly of real estate related assets, cash, cash items, and government securities, with limitations on ownership of the securities of any one issuer.
- It must distribute at least 95% of its taxable income excluding capital gains.

Types of REIT Investments

A REIT can be categorized by the type of investment it makes: an equity REIT owns income-producing properties and derives its earnings mostly from rents; a mortgage REIT finances real estate projects owned by others and derives its earnings mostly from interest; a hybrid REIT combines both types of investments. A "finite-life" REIT is designed to self-liquidate after a specified time period, such as 10 to 20 years; by having a stated term, the market value of its shares should more closely track the fair value of its net assets, making it attractive to short-term investors.

Equity REITs. Equity REITs, which dominated the industry in its early years, offer the small investor the advantages associated with sound real estate investments, including:

- Increase in economic value of assets that are indestructible (land) or durable (buildings).
- Benefits of leverage, because real estate investments are often financed largely by borrowings, and as long as the project's assets are earning in excess of its cost of money the equity holder with a proportionately small investment receives a higher rate of return.
- Protection against inflation.
- Availability of accelerated depriciation and other tax shelter benefits (prior to the Tax Reform Act of 1986).

Equity REITs invest in industrial, commercial, and residential properties, including hotels, shopping centers, apartment buildings, office buildings, and warehouses. They lease their properties to others (usually on a long-term net lease basis), or they hire an independent property manager.

Mortgage REITs. Mortgage REIT assets span the spectrum of real estate lending and include long-term senior debt, junior mortgages, and (less frequently) short-term construction and development loans. In addition to contractual interest, long-term loans often provide the REIT with some of the benefits normally associated with property ownership, and allow the REIT a share of the cash flow generated by the property or a share of the property's appreciation in value.

Some REITs—often those sponsored by mortgage banking firms—have assumed an important role in the secondary home mortgage market. These REITs acquire pools of single family home mortgages with proceeds raised by issuing collateralized mortgage obligations (discussed in Chapter 21).

Accounting and Reporting Issues

1974 Recession and Aftermath. REITs were major victims of the 1974 economic recession. According to *Fortune*, of the 20 stocks showing the greatest percentage decline on the New York Stock Exchange in 1974, 18 were REITs and included the industry's five largest trusts (Robertson, 1975, p. 113).

Hardest hit were the mortgage REITs specializing in construction and development loans. The 1974 recession was characterized by tight money markets; as interest rates climbed, mortgage REITs incurred losses because many had previously committed themselves to lending funds at fixed rates below their increasing cost of money. The recession struck at property developers too: increasing costs of construction and falling demand for completed projects forced many to default on their obligations to REITs. As the risk of default increased, REITs found that an important source of funds, the commercial paper market, dried up; REITs were forced to rely on bank lines of credit.

Equity trusts generally fared better during the 1974 recession, although the value of their publicly traded shares also declined sharply. Profits were reduced or eliminated as inflation drove up property operating costs and deteriorating economic conditions caused higher vacancy rates.

The REIT crisis inevitably affected commercial banks. To prevent wholesale bankruptcy of REITs, which would have strained the nation's financial system, commercial banks and trusts renegotiated their loan terms in a variety of ways, including the following:

* Commercial banks extended large unsecured lines of credit to many REITs;
* Interest rates were reduced, interest payments suspended and maturity dates extended; and
* Banks swapped their loans for assets owned by REITs or acquired those assets through foreclosure.

As discussed in the next section, these events caused accountants to focus on the accounting practices of REITs and contributed to the development of accounting for troubled debt restructurings.

Professional Pronouncements. REIT accounting practices are covered by a variety of professional pronouncements. SOP 75-2, *Accounting Practices of Real Estate Investment Trusts* (TP 10,060), as amended by SOP 78-2 (same title, TP 10,170), is of particular importance. SFAS 32 established the preferability of these SOPs for purposes of justifying a change in accounting principles under APB 20 (Re3.101). Even before the release of SFAS 32, the guidance of the SOPs had found general acceptance in the REIT industry.

Depending on the type of REIT and the nature of its transactions, accounting literature covering leasing (Chapter 19), sales and operations of real estate (Chapter 35), and real estate acquisition, development, or construction arrangements (Chapter 41) also may apply.

Rule 3-15 of Regulation S-X covers special disclosure requirements of REITs that are SEC registrants.

Losses From Loans. Since the release of SOP 75-2, REITs use a single approach "when it appears that an original borrower will be unable to make the payments required by the terms of his loan agreements" (TP 10,060.10). In this approach:

* The allowance for losses should be based on an evaluation of *individual* loans rather than on an overall, "systematic" provision such as a percentage of net income.
* The carrying amount of individual loans (including accrued interest) should be compared to the *estimated net realizable value* of the property collateralizing the loan.
* Individual loans should be evaluated at annual and interim reporting dates.

The estimated net realizable value of the collateral property, rather than the credit standing of the borrower, determines the amount to be allowed for loan losses; this is realistic because only rarely would a borrower from an REIT be able (or willing) to repay a loan from other sources (TP 10,060.12).

Net realizable value is defined as the sales price a property could command on the open market, allowing a reasonable time to find a purchaser and reduced by estimated costs to (1) place the property in saleable condition, (2) dispose of the property, and (3) hold the property to the point of sale, including interest, property taxes, and other cash requirements.

The requirement to include holding costs, especially interest, in the determination of net realizable value was and remains controversial. Interest has traditionally been accounted for as a period cost, but AcSEC concluded that "the principle of providing for all losses when they become evident" (TP 10,060.18) requires that estimated future interest costs be anticipated when losses on loans appear likely. SOP 75-2 also discusses factors to be considered in determining a property's estimated net realizable value, stipulates the method for determining the rate for interest costs during the holding period, and concludes that the following items should be separately disclosed on the balance sheet of a REIT: loans, earning; loans, nonearning; foreclosed properties held for resale; and allowance for losses (TP 10,060.28).

If a REIT, for liquidity or other reasons, does not expect to be able to hold a foreclosed property for a reasonable time, it should use the property's estimated selling price at immediate liquidation value (rather than estimated net realizable value) as the basis for determining the loan loss provision.

Foreclosed Properties. SOP 75-2 requires a REIT to provide for losses on foreclosed properties in the same manner it provides for losses on loans, with the following exception: when an REIT elects to hold a property as a long-term investment, the net realizable value at that time becomes the asset's new accounting basis; it should not be adjusted upward until a third-party exchange transaction takes place (TP 10,060.27).

Troubled Debt Restructurings. SFAS 15 requires that assets exchanged in a troubled debt restructuring be recorded at fair value (D22.109,.124), which may differ significantly from net realizable value as defined in SOP 75-2. SOP 78-2 (TP 10,170) amends SOP 75-2 by stipulating that properties acquired by REITs in a troubled debt restructuring should be recorded at fair value. After the restructuring, the REIT must provide an allowance for losses based on the property's net realizable value as described in the preceding section. Under SOP 78-2, a REIT should also provide for losses when a troubled debt restructuring with a debtor is probable.

If a troubled debt restructuring by the REIT with a *creditor* is probable, the REIT determines the amount that the expected loss under SFAS 15 exceeds the loss based on the net realizable value of assets to be transferred. Against this amount, the REIT nets (offsets) any related gain on reduction of the debt that will result from the asset transfer, although such gain must be reasonably determinable and cannot exceed the expected loss on the transfer of assets. The REIT then provides for the excess of the net amount over the loss allowance that was based on the asset's estimated net realizable value (TP 10,170.06).

SOP 78-2 specifies the income statement classification for charges and credits arising from the troubled debt restructurings and stipulates that certain information be disclosed in the notes to the REIT's financial statements. (See Chapter 28 for a discussion of troubled debt restructurings.)

Other Accounting Issues. SOP 75-2 (TP 10,060) also discusses several other accounting matters applicable to REITs:

* Recognition of interest revenue is presumed to be discontinued when certain conditions exist, such as past due payments of principal or interest.
* Commitment fees (fees paid by a borrower to a lender for a promise of a future loan), while covered in the SOP, should now be accounted for according to SFAS 91 (L20); generally, they should be deferred and recognized over the life of the loan as a yield adjustment.
* When a REIT obtains support from its advisor, such as the purchase of loans or property in excess of market value, the property should be transferred at market value. Operating support should be reflected as income or a reduction of fees, and reported separately if material. The relationship of the REIT and its advisor, and the amount and nature of the transaction, should be fully disclosed.

FINANCE COMPANIES

Finance companies provide a variety of financing to consumers and business enterprises. In addition, many businesses provide financing, through captive finance entities, to purchasers of their products and services.

Consumer Lending

Consumer loans are usually payable in installments and collateralized by real estate, household goods, or other property. Obviously, the creditworthiness of the borrower and the value of the collateral (if any) are paramount in the lending decision.

In addition, sales of a variety of consumer goods and services are financed through retail sales contracts, subsequently sold (usually at a discount) by the retailer to independent or captive finance companies.

Commercial Lending

Commercial lending activities of finance enterprises include factoring arrangements, revolving loans, floor plan loans, and other lending and leasing arrangements. Commercial loans are usually collateralized by accounts receivable, inventory, or property, plant, and equipment.

Factoring is the purchase, usually without recourse, of trade accounts receivable by a financing enterprise, commonly called a factor. The customers of the factor's clients send their payments directly to the factor. The factor also provides clients with other services including credit review, bookkeeping, and collection.

Revolving loans are usually collateralized by the accounts receivable of borrowers. Outstandings under revolving loan arrangements are limited to agreed-upon percentages of the accounts receivable. Collections on the receivables are remitted (usually on a daily basis) to the finance enterprise.

Floor plan loans, also called *wholesale loans,* are made to businesses to finance specific inventory purchases such as automobiles, recreational vehicles, and watercraft. The inventory serves as collateral.

Accounting Considerations

Accounting guidance for finance enterprises is provided in the AICPA's Audit and Accounting Guide, *Audits of Finance Companies (Including Independent and Captive Financing Activities of Other Companies)* (AICPA, 1988b). This guide updates the 1973 guide, which had allowed the "rule of 78s," the "combination method," and the "cash method" as revenue recognition methods. Under the 1988 Guide, these methods are no longer considered to be acceptable. The 1988 Guide requires:

• Recognition of interest income on finance receivables using the interest method.

• Use of the accrual-with-suspension basis for recording interest income.

• Inclusion of interest as a holding cost in determining the carrying amount of repossessed collateral expected to be held for more than a brief period.

Finance Receivables. Finance receivables include both interest-bearing and discount loans. The face amount of an interest-bearing loan equals the amount of cash loaned. For a discount loan, the face amount of the loan differs from the amount of cash loaned, and the difference is the unearned interest income to be earned by the lender over the loan's life.

Finance companies that act as factors may advance cash to clients under various factoring arrangements. Advances are usually limited to specified percentages of unpaid amounts of factored receivables. As such, finance companies look for repayment of advances from collections of the factored receivables rather than by direct payments from clients. Accordingly, advances are customarily netted against amounts owed to clients for the purchase of the receivables rather than treated as receivables in the financial statements. Overadvances to clients, however, are treated as receivables, segregated in the balance sheet from the receivables under the factoring arrangements.

A finance company may sell a portfolio of receivables to another finance company or lending institution. If recourse provisions are part of the sales transaction, SFAS 77, *Reporting by Transferors for Transfers of Receivables With Recourse* (R20), applies (see Chapters 13 and 21).

Repossessed Assets. When finance companies foreclose on uncollectible loans, assets collateralizing the loans may be repossessed. Repossessed assets are to be carried at the lower of unpaid loan balance or the fair value of the assets at the time of repossession or foreclosure, and classified as "other assets" in the balance sheet.

If the repossessed assets are held or are likely to be held for more than a brief period prior to sale, their carrying values should be evaluated periodically for recoverability, and if appropriate, a separate additional valuation allowance should be provided based on "net realizable value," determined as follows:

• Estimated future sales price plus proceeds from use during the expected holding period, reduced by

• Estimated costs of disposition, and further reduced by

• Estimated holding costs, such as taxes and maintenance, including the cost of funds dedicated to holding such assets. The cost of funds should be based on the enterprise's combined cost of debt and equity.

Differences between the carrying amounts of the repossessed assets and the amounts at which they are subsequently sold are to be recognized as gains or losses. Accordingly, such differences are not to be charged or credited to the allowance for credit losses.

Allowance for Credit Losses. A finance company should provide an allowance for credit losses adequate to cover estimated losses in its receivable portfolio. In this regard SFAS 5, *Accounting for Contingencies* (C59), requires that this allowance be established by charges to the provision for credit losses in periods when it is probable that an asset has been impaired, provided the amounts can be reasonably estimated.

SFAS 5, however, precludes the recognition of losses if events causing the losses have not yet occurred. Accordingly, losses should not be anticipated and recognized at the date of loan origination unless unusual circumstances exist.

Many *consumer* finance companies determine their allowance for credit losses on an overall portfolio approach based on historical relationships, because making an account-by-account analysis is impractical where there are many small and homogeneous loans. However, commercial and other finance companies normally evaluate their outstanding loans individually because of the diversity of borrowing arrangements and circumstances.

Regardless of the method used to estimate the allowance for credit losses, conditions existing at the estimation date – such as the amount of delinquent receivables and the number of days past due, economic trends, credit policies and procedures, and the mix and industry concentration of receivables – should all be considered in evaluating the adequacy of the allowance.

Interest Income. The difference between interest bearing and discount loans has no economic or accounting significance. In this regard APB 21, *Interest on Receivables and Payables* (I69.108) requires that a discount on a receivable be amortized to income so as to result in a constant effective yield on the net receivable over its term. This is the *interest method* and that method should be used by finance companies to account for interest income.

Interest income on receivables should be accrued over time in accordance with the terms of the contracts. If collection of a receivable becomes improbable, however, accrual of the interest income should be suspended. Interest previously accrued on such a receivable should not be reversed but should be taken into consideration in evaluating the adequacy of the allowance for credit losses.

The accrual of interest income should generally not be resumed until future collectibility of the receivable (including the accrued interest thereon) becomes probable. This determination is a matter requiring judgment and the consideration of many factors, including whether:

• The customer has resumed making regular payments for a certain number of installments.

• The reason for the customer's delinquency has been eliminated (such as reemployment of a consumer borrower or an improved economic outlook for a commercial borrower) or was an isolated circumstance unlikely to recur.

- An increase in the ratio of collateral values to loan amounts has occurred.
- There are any other substantive indications of the customer's regaining the ability to repay the loan.

Nonrefundable Loan Fees. Finance companies often charge various types of fees, including loan origination and commitment fees, in connection with lending transactions. These fees are to be accounted for in accordance with SFAS 91, *Accounting for Nonrefundable Fees and Costs Associated With Originating or Acquiring Loans and Initial Direct Costs of Leases* (L20). SFAS 91 generally requires such fees to be deferred and recognized as yield adjustments over the life of related receivables using the interest method (L20.117).

Financial Reporting Considerations

Finance Receivables. Discount loans and interest bearing loans should be presented similarly on the balance sheet with discount loans presented net of unearned interest. Accrued interest receivable, however, may be presented separately on the balance sheet. Unamortized loan fees that are being recognized as an adjustment to yield should be classified on the balance sheet as part of the related loan balance. The allowance for credit losses should be deducted from finance receivables and an analysis of the changes in the allowance provided in the notes to the financial statements.

The composition of finance receivables should be disclosed either on the balance sheet or in the notes to the financial statements in a manner that addresses the various risks and liquidity of the loans. In addition, disclosure should be provided concerning the terms and maturities of the finance receivables. See Figure 44.2 for an example of a footnote containing such disclosures.

Income Statement. With respect to the income statement of a finance company, the 1988 AICPA Guide states:

The banking industry has adopted an income statement format that emphasizes presentation of net interest income. Because of the similarity between many banking activities and finance company activities, the Finance Companies Special Committee believes that such a presentation is of increasing relevance for the finance industry. Nevertheless, certain factors may limit the usefulness of the net income presentation. An income statement that does not emphasize net interest income may be more appropriate for companies that engage primarily or solely in factoring operations or that otherwise derive a substantial portion of their income from commissions for services rather than from interest earned on loans. [p.81]

The interest and finance income of a finance company should be presented separately from other kinds of income. In addition, the provision for credit losses should be presented separately as an expense item.

B. Finance Receivables and Allowance for Credit Losses

Finance receivables as of December 31 consisted of the following (in thousands of dollars):

	19X5	19X4
Consumer		
Real estate secured	$131,961	$104,078
Other	119,135	97,857
Accrued interest	3,175	2,550
	254,271	204,485
Commercial		
Accounts receivable loans	32,002	27,440
Factored accounts		
Receivables	21,404	18,594
Inventory loans to clients	2,965	2,876
Overadvances to clients	2,947	2,260
Floor plan loans	5,441	5,763
Other	29,962	23,620
Accrued Interest	1,200	1,013
	95,921	81,566
Total finance receivables	350,192	286,051
Allowance for credit losses	(9,506)	(7,839)
Unearned credit insurance premiums and claim reserves	(7,037)	(6,046)
Finance receivables, net	$333,649	$272,166

On December 31, 19X5, the accrual of interest income was suspended on $4,086,000 and $2,107,000 of consumer and commercial loans, respectively.

Changes in the allowance for credit losses were as follows (in thousands of dollars):

	Consumer		Commercial				
	Real estate secured	Other	Accounts receivable loans	Factored accounts	Floor plan loans	Other	Total
Balance as of December 31, 19X3	$ 762	$3,885	$628	$556	$112	$620	$6,563
Provision for credit losses	597	1,564	627	534	129	172	3,623
Loans charged off	(376)	(1,357)	(749)	(639)	(154)	(156)	(3,431)
Recoveries	58	490	225	192	46	73	1,084
Balance as of December 31, 19X4	1,041	4,582	731	643	133	709	7,839
Provision for credit losses	651	2,090	664	583	121	175	4,284
Loans charged off	(448)	(1,601)	(808)	(710)	(147)	(178)	(3,892)
Recoveries	76	601	243	213	44	98	1,275
Balance as of December 31, 19X5	$1,320	$5,672	$830	$729	$151	$804	$9,506

FIG. 44.2 Example of Finance Receivables Disclosures
Source: Audit and Accounting Guide, Audits of Finance Companies (*AICPA, 1988b*).

On December 31, 19X5, contractual maturities of finance receivables were as follows (in thousands of dollars):

	19X6	19X7	19X8	19X9	19Y0	There after	Total
Consumer							
Real estate secured	$20,963	$10,785	$10,474	$8,480	$8,917	$72,342	$131,961
Other	51,325	29,374	20,164	9,507	2,423	6,342	119,135
Commercial							
Accounts receivable loans	32,002						32,002
Factored accounts	27,316						27,316
Floor plan loans	4,686	755					5,441
Other	6,140	8,243	5,192	4,934	5,453		29,962
Accrued interest	4,375						4,375
Total finance receivables	$146,807	$49,157	$35,830	$22,921	$16,793	$78,684	$350,192

It is the Company's experience that a substantial portion of the consumer loan portfolio generally is renewed or repaid before contractual maturity dates. The above tabulation, therefore, is not to be regarded as a forecast of future cash collections. During the years ended December 31, 19X5 and 19X4, cash collections of principal amounts of consumer loans totaled $57,670,000 and $40,719,000 respectively, and the ratios of these cash collections to average principal balances were 25% and 29%, respectively.

FIG. 44.2 (continued)

Income Recognition

Interest income from finance receivables is recognized using the interest (actuarial) method. Accrual of interest income on finance receivables is suspended when a loan is contractually delinquent for ninety days or more. The accrual is resumed when the loan becomes contractually current, and past-due interest income is recognized at that time. In addition, a detailed review of commercial loans will cause earlier suspension if collection is doubtful. Premiums and commissions for credit life insurance are recognized as revenue using the interest method. Premiums and commissions for credit accident and health insurance are recognized over the terms of the contracts based on the mean of the straight-line and interest methods.

Credit Losses

Provisions for credit losses are charged to income in amounts sufficient to maintain the allowance at a level considered adequate to cover the losses of principal and interest in the existing portfolio. The Company's charge off policy is based on a loan-by-loan review for all receivables except consumer loans and factored receivables, which are charged off when they are 180 days and 90 days contractually past due, respectively.

FIG. 44.3 Example of Recognition and Credit Disclosures
Source: Audit and Accounting Guide, Audits of Finance Companies (AICPA, 1988b).

Amounts of loan fees recognized as adjustments to yield should be classified in interest income while other fees that are being recognized on a straight-line basis should be included with service fee income.

Other Disclosures. The summary of significant accounting policies should disclose the method of income recognition being used by the finance company. The notes to the financial statements should also include disclosures of policies for suspending and resuming interest income accruals on delinquent loans, and policies for charging off uncollectible loans. See Figure 44.3 for an example of such footnote disclosures.

Auditing Finance Receivables and Income

An audit of finance receivables and income should be designed to provide reasonable assurance that:

* Loans and receivables are valid obligations owed to the entity at the date of the financial statements.
* The allowance for related credit losses is adequate to provide for estimated losses in the loan portfolio at the date of the financial statements.
* Accrued interest revenues for the period on both interest-bearing and discount loans have been properly recorded.
* Provisions for credit losses have been properly recorded.
* Adequate disclosures, including proper disclosure of any pledged or assigned receivables, are included in the financial statements.
* Deferred loan origination costs are properly stated and amortization is properly computed.

Loan Files. Loan files are an important source of legal documentation supporting a finance company's rights and claims. These files should also contain documentation concerning the basis for originally granting the loan and for renewals and extensions, as well as providing information concerning the current status of the loan and the borrower. In this regard the files should contain, where applicable, recent financial statements of the borrower, credit reports, Uniform Commercial Code (UCC) filings, appraisal reports, and evidence of existing insurance coverage.

Credit Approval Policies. The auditor should understand the finance company's credit approval policies and be especially alert for changes in those policies to less conservative requirements. The auditor should also evaluate whether the company challenges and appropriately modifies its credit policies in response to important changes in the economic and business environment.

Allowance for Credit Losses. The evaluation of the adequacy of the allowance for credit losses is the most important and difficult area of a finance company's audit. Accordingly, the evaluation should be performed by experienced auditors with specialized knowledge of industries in which the finance company's loans are concentrated.

For consumer loans (that usually consist of large volumes of relatively small balances), ratio analysis, historical statistics, current aging conditions, and other general trends are particularly useful in evaluating collectibility.

For commercial loans, less emphasis is placed on statistical data and historical trends because of the uniqueness of the individual loans and the diversity of loan balances and circumstances. Audit procedures performed in evaluating the collectibility of commercial loans thus focus on the financial condition of the borrowers, industry concentrations and the current economic conditions in those industries, and current values of underlying collateral such as accounts receivable, inventory, real estate, and other property.

CREDIT UNIONS

Credit unions are cooperative financial institutions, owned and operated by members of an affiliated group. This common bond may be a geographical location, a common employer, a professional affiliation, or a social membership.

Originating in the United States in the early 1900s, the primary purpose of the credit union was to satisfy the credit needs of the smaller saver and borrower who had often been ignored or rejected by other financial institutions. As a group, credit unions have grown more rapidly than any other type of financial institution in recent years due in part to offering an ever expanding menu of financial services coupled with the economic advantages of being tax exempt. In 1988, there were over 16,000 credit unions with 58 million members and total assets exceeding $187 billion.

Equity Structure

The credit union is owned by its members, each of whom has one vote. The members elect the board of directors and a supervisory committee (similar to a corporation's audit committee) from its membership. The board sets policy and direction for the credit union while the supervisory committee is responsible for assuring the financial well-being of the credit union through oversight of the internal control structure and audit surveillance of its activities.

Regulation and Supervision

A credit union is chartered either through a federal charter under the Federal Credit Union Act or by state charter in the state in which it operates. Federally chartered credit unions are subject to the rules and regulations of the National Credit Union Administration (NCUA), an agency reporting to the Department of the Treasury. State chartered institutions are subject to the rules and regulations of their respective states' supervisory agencies.

Federal rules and regulations are quite sophisticated and specific, and compliance is monitored by federal examiners, who report formally at the end of their annual examinations and require written replies by the credit union to all their recommendations. State rules and regulations vary significantly, as do state supervisory authorities, but most require annual examinations and follow-up on the findings. The supervisory agency examination is concentrated in such areas as regulatory compliance, liquidity, quality of loans, and the adequacy of reserves. At present, although there is no requirement for an annual audit by an independent certified public accountant, such an audit may often be substituted for a state examination at the discretion of the responsible agency.

The bylaws of federally chartered and most state chartered credit unions call for an "annual audit" of the books and records of the institution by the supervisory committee. This "audit" is typically smaller in scope than a full audit performed under GAAS and may specifically require performance of only certain procedures. An independent CPA may be hired to assist in performing these limited procedures and report on their results. This activity falls within the purview of SAS 35, *Special Reports—Applying Agreed-Upon Procedures to Specified Elements, Accounts or Items of a Financial Statement* (AU 622).

Accounting and Auditing Considerations

Independent audits of credit unions, other than very large institutions, were uncommon before the 1970s. Since then an increasing number of credit union boards of directors have elected to provide audited statements to their membership. In 1986, the AICPA issued an Audit and Accounting Guide, *Audits of Credit Unions* (1986e). This document provides guidance to the auditor by establishing both GAAP and GAAS, and should be consulted for a detailed discussion. Areas of particular concern are covered in the sections that follow.

Internal Control Environment. A credit union typically originates in the shop, with the shop foreman maintaining the cash box on a part-time basis; it eventually grows large enough to move to a separate facility with the custodial and record-keeping functions becoming a full time job for the same individual. This process creates the likelihood that the sophistication of internal controls will lag behind the growth of the credit union. Nevertheless, there is an inherent trust by the membership that must be maintained.

The effectiveness of internal controls is paramount in any financial institution due in part to the high volume of transactions. Significant reliance must be placed on controls because each transaction cannot be reviewed for propriety. The auditor must therefore study the internal control structure to the degree necessary to plan his examination, even if he chooses to use a substantive approach rather than an approach that relies on the adequate functioning of the internal control structure.

In addition to potential weaknesses in internal control, there are several risks associated with the credit union's lending and investment policies, and in the economic environment in which the credit union operates.

Loan underwriting policies must work in concert with the economic environment to minimize the risk of loss. A deterioration in the national or local economy, or a downturn in the health of a particular industry, will expose the credit union to increased risk if lending policies are too lenient or if loans are mostly of a single type or concentrated in a single geographic area.

Another risk to the credit union is the imbalance or improper matching of rate and term on its own borrowings with the interest rate and term of loans made. Rapid changes in short-term borrowings used to finance loans at fixed rates can cause a shrinking or negative spread. Further, liquid funds must be available at reasonable rates to meet withdrawal requests. Absence of forethought in making investments could result in the need to sell at a loss in order to fund the withdrawals.

Finally, there is the risk of violation of regulations, which could have a direct (penalty) impact on the financial statements. The auditor must familiarize himself with the regulations that have such an effect and review for compliance accordingly. Such issues vary between federal and state credit unions, and may include maintenance of reserve levels, legality of investments, loan interest rates, investments in fixed assets as a percentage of total assets, liquidity ratios, and compliance with by-laws.

Data Processing. Most credit unions of any size utilize an electronic data processing system to process members' transactions. This system may be batch processing or on-line; it can be an in-house system, or part of a large service bureau run independently or shared with other credit unions on a cooperative basis. The software utilized may be internally developed or developed and maintained by a software house. Typical applications include processing loans, shares, payroll deductions, payroll, general ledger functions, automated teller transactions, credit cards, and so forth.

The internal controls over in-house operations may have little discipline; and software developed in-house may not have the degree of formal documentation customarily found in a software house. The auditor must consider the impact these circumstances may have on his procedures. In addition, if the responsibility for development and maintenance of software is the responsibility of a third party, the auditor must be cognizant of the strength of controls, because a significant degree of reliance will be placed on this process. Consideration should be given to a review of controls in place at the third party's location.

If the data processing is performed by an outside service bureau, the auditor should consider the need for performance of a third party audit as discussed in the AICPA Audit Guide, *Audits of Service Center-Produced Records* (1987g).

Investments. Credit unions are restricted by law from making investments in securities other than U.S. Treasury obligations, U.S. governmental agency obligations, certificates of deposit in federally insured financial institutions, investments in central credit unions, and certain other instruments. Investments should be accounted for following the lower-of-cost-or-market principles of SFAS 12, *Accounting for Certain Marketable Securities* (I89), with reductions to market offset against equity.

Because investments are commonly made with only temporarily idle funds, care should be taken to ascertain the likelihood of early disposition of such securities. If the credit union cannot demonstrate, through its present liquidity position and historic investment management, the ability to hold the investment until maturity, the allowance, ordinarily reported in equity for declines in market value, should be charged to current earnings.

Loans. Loans are made by a credit union only to its members, and are primarily consumer loans (both secured and unsecured), real estate loans, and a few other types. There are certain regulatory constraints on lending to members, including maximum loan amounts, maximum term, maximum proportion of real estate loans, and so forth.

The credit union may charge the member for loan fees at the time of loan origination. These fees (and direct costs incurred) must be accounted for in accordance with SFAS 91, *Accounting for Nonrefundable Fees and Costs Associated With Originating or Acquiring Loans and Initial Direct Costs of Loans* (L20).

In addition to the risk of ultimate collectibility, loan risk can result from inadequacy of documentation supporting the right of collection. The quality of documentation is typically verified by the auditor through tests of the individual loan files and controls over loan file generation, coupled with confirmation by the member of the existence of the loan and its terms and outstanding balance.

Collectibility of the loan portfolio must be assessed and an appropriate allowance for estimated uncollectible loans provided through periodic charges to operations. Loans should be written off when they are deemed uncollectible. Determination of the adequacy of the allowance for loan losses should be made considering many factors, including prior collection history, aging of the existing loan trial balance, concentration of loans, economic conditions of the region, collection procedures utilized by the credit union, adequacy of collateral, and so forth.

Share Accounts. Credit unions offer a variety of savings vehicles to its members. These include regular share accounts, share drafts (checking accounts), and various certificates of deposit. Deposits in the members' regular savings accounts are known as *shares,* since the members are the owners of the credit union. Consequently, the interest paid on those deposits or shares are termed dividends.

For regulatory purposes credit unions have treated share accounts as equity and dividends as a reduction in retained earnings. Under GAAP, to be consistent with other mutually owned financial institutions, share accounts are shown as liabilities, and dividends are charged to operations as the cost of investable funds.

Equity. The equity of a credit union includes accumulated undistributed earnings, both specifically appropriated and unappropriated. Credit unions are required, by both federal and state regulations, to create and maintain a regular reserve for loan and other losses taken out of gross income, up to a specified limit (based on outstanding loans). The remainder of the undistributed earnings are available for payment of dividends to its members or for other specific reserves as determined by the board of directors. Under GAAP, necessary reserve requirements are classified as an allowance for loan losses against the loans receiveable, and thus only the excess of the regulatory reserve over the needed allowance is classified as part of equity for GAAP. Further, directors' appropriations of retained earnings (e.g., for loss contingencies) must be restored to retained earnings when no longer needed; under SFAS 5, *Accounting for Contingencies* (C59), actual losses must be charged to operations.

Income Taxes. Credit unions are currently exempt from federal income taxes, though from time to time Congress considers removing or significantly limiting their tax-exempt status. Certain income unrelated to the operations of the credit union, however, is taxable, and care should be taken to identify such income and its tax consequences.

RAP/GAAP Differences. Credit union operations are governed by regulations promulgated by the NCUA[2] and the various state supervisory agencies. These institutions require or permit certain regulatory accounting practices (RAP) that differ from GAAP to be used when reporting financial position and the results of operations. In addition to the classification of shares as equity and dividends as a charge to retained earnings previously mentioned, the most frequent differences are accounting for the current provision for loan losses as a charge to reserves in retained earnings rather than to current earnings, and the use of a modified accrual basis of accounting for financial statement presentation.

---

[2] National Credit Union Administration, *Accounting Manual for Federal Credit Unions, Supervisory Committee Manual for Federal Credit Unions, National Credit Union Administration Rules and Regulations, The Federal Credit Union Act, Federal Credit Union Bylaws*. Washington D.C.: U.S. Government Printing Office. These publications spell out the rules and regulations for federally chartered credit unions and are a necessary reference when auditing these institutions.

PART **VI**

The Profession

45

The Accounting Profession

EVOLUTION OF U.S. PUBLIC ACCOUNTING

"Accountant" can refer to a number of occupations: bookkeeper, auditor, preparer of financial statements and tax returns, financial and tax consultant, controller or other financial executive, researcher, and teacher. An accountant may be engaged in public practice, doing work for other companies as clients; in private practice, on the internal accounting, financial, or audit staff of a corporation or organization; or as an educator in accounting at a business school or university.

The focus of this chapter is the public practice of accounting. The most important function performed for society by the practicing CPA is the independent audit of financial statements, a function essential to the operation of the nation's economic system. And it is the public accountant's ability to perform this function that has been the subject of almost continuous controversy.

Early Factors

During the years following the Civil War, the American economy expanded rapidly. European investors, especially the British, saw the opportunity and began to invest heavily in this country.

In the late 1800s an accounting profession as such did not exist in the United States – there was no professional organization to standardize procedures or enforce ethical behavior. Many English and Scottish accountants were sent to the United States to examine the financial condition of British-owned companies. These early accountants were part of a well-disciplined and organized profession. Not only did they establish accounting firms here (many of the present U.S. firms trace their beginnings to English and Scottish accountants in the late 1880s), but they helped the American accountants establish, in 1887, the first national professional organization, the American Association of Public Accountants. The association grew slowly. Starting with only 31 members, by 1896 it had grown to only 45, most of whom were in the New York City area (Chatfield, 1977, p. 151).

Accountants were first licensed as professionals in this country in 1896, when the state of New York passed a law that permitted the issuance of a license to practice as a "certified public accountant" to qualified persons (those who passed an examination) and prohibited the use of the title by others. Licensing laws were soon adopted in other states; however, the statutes passed were not uniform, and this lack of uniformity continues to exist today.

Changing Roles

Besides European investors, U.S. commercial banks were also among the early clients of public accountants. At the turn of the century, companies financed operations mostly through short-term loans, and bankers hired accountants to check their customers' records. Companies rarely needed what today would be recognized as an audit of their financial statements. Instead, companies hired accountants to perform a variety of other services – for example, setting up books, advising on recording transactions and closings, and consulting on general business matters. Accountants also spent a great deal of time verifying the clerical accuracy of the books; they pored over the details of transactions searching for misappropriations of cash and other employee irregularities.

A milestone was reached in 1902 when the United States Steel Corporation became the first American company to publish financial statements accompanied by an auditor's report, and a number of large corporations followed suit. Other developments affected the profession's future during the first third of the twentieth century:

1. *Developing governmental involvement* came with the concentration of certain industries into monopolies and trusts. This led President Theodore Roosevelt to enforce the *Sherman Anti-*

Trust Act of 1890, to establish the Department of Commerce and Labor, and to expand the authority of the Interstate Commerce Commission. Early on, government executives recognized the need for improved reporting by companies of their business affairs.

2. *Corporate income taxes* were levied under laws passed in 1909 and 1913, and companies needed the help of accountants to prepare returns. An interesting side note is that the 1909 law mandated that companies base their taxes on calendar-year (rather than fiscal-year) results. Although the 1913 law lifted this requirement, many companies had already adopted the calendar fiscal year, the taproot of the accountant's hectic busy season.

3. *Public equity financing* was used by more and more businesses in the 1920s. Companies believed that permanent capital, rather than bank debt, made them less vulnerable to cyclical vagaries. Consequently, auditors had to face the problem of attesting to financial data for distribution to stockholders who generally had little accounting knowledge.

4. *Promulgation of the Securities Acts in 1933 and 1934* and the creation of the SEC followed the Stock Market Crash of 1929. These Acts prescribed disclosures that had to be made to investors in connection with the sales of securities, and created the SEC to oversee the securities markets and prescribe principles of accounting and reporting (see Chapter 47 for an in-depth discussion of the SEC).

Accounting and Auditing Standards

Public accountants faced these early challenges largely without the benefit of professional guidelines. Not only were examinations of corporate accountants conducted without a set of uniform standards, but also the variety of corporate accounting and reporting practices was virtually unrestricted. Bankruptcies of widely known concerns and other signs of financial abuse compounded the problems. The profession's early leaders recognized that unless accountants took an active role in solving these problems, further federal regulation was inevitable.

The American Institute of Accountants, predecessor of today's AICPA, became the focal point for the profession's reform efforts. Itself a combination of several professional organizations, including the American Association of Public Accountants, the institute began efforts to evaluate and explain accounting practices and to establish appropriate standards for the conduct of audit examinations. In fact, the AICPA functioned as the standard setter in the accounting principles area until 1973, when this responsibility was transferred to the FASB (see Chapter 46); auditing standard-setting (GAAS) continues to be very much in the AICPA's bailiwick (see Chapter 5).

Professional Principles

The AICPA also provided the profession with a Code of Professional Conduct to guide accountants in serving their clients, the public, and their fellow practitioners. The Code, which was significantly restructured in early 1988, is built on the following basic principles:

* Independence, integrity, and objectivity.
* Observance of professional and technical standards.
* Recognition of responsibilities to the public, to clients, and to colleagues.

LICENSING PROCESS

Accountants are licensed by state or territorial boards of accountancy. To receive a license, an applicant must pass the four-part uniform CPA examination developed by the AICPA and adopted by all 54 licensing jurisdictions. Nearly all jurisdictions participate in a system of reciprocity; a CPA in good standing in one jurisdiction will be certified, upon application, by most other jurisdictions. An applicant who has passed parts of the examination in one jurisdiction is often not required to pass them again in another.

There is, unfortunately, a lack of uniformity in education and experience requirements. Most jurisdictions require a bachelor's degree, but some require only two years of college study; a very few require none at all. There is even greater variety in experience requirements. Many jurisdictions require two to four years of public accounting experience, but some accept other accounting experience, and a few accept advanced education as a substitute for all or part of the experience requirement.

Beamer Committee

The AICPA has long sought to establish uniformity in the licensing requirements of all jurisdictions, and in 1969 a special AICPA committee (the Beamer Committee) recommended that a minimum of five years of study should be required in all jurisdictions, along with no qualifying experience (AICPA, 1969b, p. 6). Even though the AICPA endorsed the Beamer Committee's recommendations, the five-year requirement has not yet been adopted by the vast majority of state boards. However, the profession's Code of Professional Conduct adopted in 1988 requires, starting in the year 2000, 150 credit hours of college education in certain areas of study as a condition for membership in the AICPA.

The AICPA has had greater success, however, with a different approach, namely, urging that the states require CPAs to demonstrate they are continuing their professional education as a condition for continued licensing. The AICPA council adopted a resolution to that effect in 1971 with the support of the National Association of State Boards of Accountancy (NASBA). As a result, by the end of 1987, 48 out of 54 jurisdictions have instituted a requirement for some form of continuing professional education. The AICPA's Code of Professional Conduct also requires the completion of continuing professional education as a condition for membership in the AICPA.

THE PRACTICE OF PUBLIC ACCOUNTING

Forms of Practice

Public accounting firms take three basic forms: the sole proprietorship, the partnership, and the professional corporation. The CPA sole proprietor, though he may or may not hire others, is the sole owner of the practice. His exposure to liability for debts and professional performance extends to all personal assets.

Two or more persons may join together to form a partnership; in fact the larger public accounting firms number their U.S. partners in the high hundreds, with some well over 1,000. All partners are jointly liable for debts and professional performance of the partnership. Partnerships are governed in most states under the Uniform Partnership Act, and the few states that have not adopted this Act have similar laws.

Some accounting firms have elected to organize as professional corporations. Even though professional corporations do not afford their owners a limitation on liability for professional performance, there are advantages of incorporation that are useful to some practitioners, for example, the ease of transfer of ownership and the deductibility of premiums for most insurance programs covering owner-employees.

Types of Firms

Accounting firms vary considerably in their size and the types of services they offer. The largest *international firms* having their major operations in the United States form a group known as the Big Eight: Arthur Andersen & Co.; Coopers & Lybrand; Deloitte Haskins & Sells; Ernest & Whinney; Peat, Marwick, Main & Co.; Price Waterhouse & Co.; Touche Ross & Co.; and Arthur Young & Company. The Big Eight accounting firms offer extensive services, and they all maintain offices throughout the world.

Approximately the next 25 largest accounting firms are characterized as *national firms*. Though less widespread than the Big Eight, national firms have offices throughout the United States and many have offices or affiliates in other countries as well. There are also about 30 *regional firms*, concentrated in specific sections of the country and having few offices outside those areas. The thousands of *local firms* in the United States generally have offices within a limited area—in a single state, in neighboring cities—or may have only one office.

Scope and Nature of Services

Depending on the size and resources of the firm and the needs of its clients, an accounting firm's services fall into three general categories: accounting and auditing, tax, and management consulting. This classification could further be refined by industry, for example, banking, health care, insurance, retailing, manufacturing, and so on.

Accounting and Auditing. Accounting and auditing services include such activities as designing reliable record-keeping systems, assisting in the preparation of financial statements, and auditing financial statements to report whether they have been prepared in conformity with GAAP.

Companies also frequently need expert accounting advice on complex transactions. For example, a company interested in acquiring another business may ask its accounting firm to help evaluate the financial aspects of the proposed merger and to explain the financial statement effects of the combination. Similar advice is sought when companies contemplate a public offering of their securities, decide to expand into new industries or markets, or engage in activities such as leasing or real estate development, where accounting standards are constantly evolving.

While firms of all sizes can provide a limited or a full range of services depending on the technical resources they decide to gather, the larger accounting firms generally serve the more complex businesses—diversified companies with widespread operations, heavily regulated companies, and public companies monitored by the SEC.

The type of accounting and auditing services provided may also vary depending on the type of accounting firm. Sole practitioners and smaller local firms may only rarely be engaged to audit their clients' financial statements. But they may frequently provide bookkeeping assistance, help compile or perform limited reviews of their client's business and personal financial statements, and advise on installing or improving accounting systems. Perhaps the most valuable service offered by a smaller CPA firm is providing accounting and financial expertise that less sophisticated clients cannot afford to maintain internally. At the other end of the spectrum, the largest accounting firms derive a substantial portion of their revenues from audits of financial statements.

But the largest and the smallest firms are alike in that they offer their expertise whenever a client, large or small, encounters financial and accounting challenges. Regardless of the size of the accounting firm or the client, the relationship all CPAs hope to cultivate is exemplified when a businessman boasts that he never makes a major business decision without consulting his CPA.

Tax. Accounting firms offer tax services in varying degrees to the individual as well as the corporation. For the individual, tax services include the preparation of returns, and may include estate planning and executive financial counseling. For the corporation, the accounting firm can prepare or review tax returns, but a more significant contribution is tax planning – the legitimate avoidance or deferral of taxes. CPAs may also become qualified to represent their clients before the Internal Revenue Service or in Tax Court. (See Chapter 48 for a discussion of this phase of practice.)

Management Consulting. The management consulting services offered by major accounting firms cover a wide range of activities, and some of these activities are indeed the same as those involving advice and counsel to clients in connection with accounting and auditing services. Often the distinction lies in the complexity of the project, not in its nature. Of course, there are numerous management consulting services requiring special expertise, and firms providing those services must have appropriately qualified personnel.

Although this *Handbook* expressly deals with accounting and auditing, a general listing of the kinds of management consulting services available (in varying degrees) from CPA firms may provide a useful perspective of the environment in which firms practice:

- *Management Information Systems Services:*
  - Assistance in planning, design, and implementation of management information systems
  - Evaluation of data processing equipment and software
  - Review of data processing operations and controls
  - Assistance in implementing changes and improvements in existing systems
- *Financial Services:*
  - Evaluation and assistance in improvement of general accounting, financial planning, budgeting, capital expenditure, cash management, cost accounting, and related systems and procedures
  - Assistance in preparing financial projections for managements' planning purposes

—Review of financial forecasts and reporting on the reasonableness and appropriateness of the underlying assumptions

—Assistance in the analysis and financial evaluations of specific business practices or operations

—Assistance in the analysis and evaluation of alternate financing sources

• *Merger and Acquisition Services:*

—Assistance in developing growth and acquisition strategy

—Assistance in reviewing and evaluating target companies

—Transaction evaluation and assistance in negotiation

• *Valuation and Appraisal Services:*

—Performance of preacquisition merger and acquisition appraisals

—Performance of postacquisition allocation of purchase price appraisals

—Performance of real estate appraisals

—Performance of appraisals for litigation or insurance purposes

• *Operations Services:*

—Assistance in developing and improving production planning, scheduling, and inventory management policies and procedures

—Assistance in developing and implementing changes for improving the control and efficiency of operations

—Assistance in developing and implementing changes for improved transportation and distribution methods

• *Marketing Services:*

—Assistance in the analysis of marketing plans and programs, product profitability, pricing, and performance measurement

—Evaluation and improvement of marketing controls and procedures

• *Human Resource Services:*

—Assistance in management development and training programs

—Assistance in the analysis and development of executive compensation programs

—Assistance in review and development of personnel practices and procedures

• *General Services:*

—Review and analysis of policies, objectives and goals, profit opportunities, and business plans

—Development of procedures for strategic planning and control

—Assistance in the analysis and development of organization plans and structure

—Assistance in government contracting matters

Consulting Services and Auditor Independence

Most consulting services may be performed for nonaudit clients as well as audit clients, and the major accounting firms compete on a broad front with large and well-known management consulting firms. The SEC, various congressional committees, the accounting profession itself, and, of course, competing consulting firms, have shown a great interest in whether the performance of such services for publicly held audit clients might affect the audit firm's independence, in appearance if not in fact.

In 1969, an AICPA ad hoc committee on independence reported that, among the 34 state boards of accountancy responding to its inquiry as to whether there had ever been disciplinary action regarding a lack of independence in cases involving consulting services, none had ever reported such a case. In addition, the independent Commission on Auditors' Responsibilities, formed in the 1970s to consider the changing role of the CPA in society, sought evidence of a conflict between the performance of attest and consulting services and concluded that management consulting did not in fact compromise an auditor's independence (CAR, 1978, pp. 1–17).

By the mid-1970s, however, criticism of CPA activity in the consulting area – in particular, criticism directed by potential competitors – increased. During the congressional hearings of the late 1970s the issue of scope of services continued to appear as a principal oversight concern of government agencies and congressional panels. As a result, in 1978 the SEC the issued ASR 250, requiring public companies to make certain disclosures in proxy materials about fees for nonaudit services. The requirement was withdrawn in 1982, after over three years of experimenting with such disclosure, because, in the words of the SEC, of "the absence of evidence that investors want or use the disclosure, or that performance of nonaudit services impairs accountants' independence."

In 1979, the Public Oversight Board (POB) issued *Scope of Services by CPA Firms* (POB, 1979), primarily dealing with the issue of whether to limit the scope of services that may be furnished to SEC audit clients. The POB concluded that "there are many potential benefits to be realized by permitting auditors to perform MAS [management advisory services] for audit clients that should not be denied to such clients without a strong showing of actual or potential detriment."

In its 1979 report, the POB concluded that restraints on scope of services should be predicated only on the determination that certain services would impair a member's independence in rendering an opinion on a client's financial statements.

Since the POB's 1979 report, consulting and other nonattest services have continued to diversify and grow, and the need for guidance by the AICPA has become more apparent. In providing these other services or products, auditors may be confronted with circumstances of real or apparent conflicts of interest. For example, if nonattest services place auditors in a position where they are viewed as a part of management, they will lose their appearance of independence, or independence could be impaired when the results of a consulting engagement have a direct and material effect on the financial statements on which the auditor expresses an opinion.

This concern was demonstrated in another report issued by the POB in November 1986 entitled *Public Perceptions of Management Advisory Services Performed by CPA Firms for Audit Clients* (POB, 1986). In preparation for the survey, the POB obtained promotional materials, advertisements, and other information from firms, and identified the types of services being offered. The survey responses indicated key public groups perceive that certain types of MAS are likely to impair auditor objectivity and independence. About one half or more of the respondents in each of the key public groups surveyed indicated that the following engagements, when performed for an audit client, could cause a "great deal of" or "some" impairment:

- Negotiating mergers, acquisitions, and divestitures (76%)
- Performing actuarial services which directly affect amounts involved on the balance sheet (64%)
- Implementing a strategic plan (63%)
- Identifying merger and acquisition candidates (62%)
- Valuing assets acquired in a business combination (61%)
- Executive search for senior management personnel (56%)
- Renegotiations or redetermining price under procurement contracts (50%)
- Developing a strategic plan (49%)
- Developing an executive compensation plan (47%)

In response to a survey question, audit committee chairmen indicated that their committees review MAS engagements performed by their auditors for impairment of auditor independence and, for the most part, conduct such review before the services are performed. The POB published this report without comment and indicated that the results of the survey may be useful to the SEC Practice Section of the AICPA (SECPS) as well as to individual firms in deciding what action, if any, should be taken.

Under present rules, members of the AICPA's Division for CPA Firms—SECPS are required annually to report to the division the gross fees for both consulting and tax services performed for SEC audit clients expressed as a percentage of total fees charged to all SEC audit clients, and to refrain from performing the following types of consulting services that may impair auditor independence:

1. Psychological testing.
2. Public opinion polls.
3. Merger and acquisition assistance for a finder's fee.
4. Executive recruitment for managerial, executive, or director positions with audit clients, and specified related services.
5. Actuarial services to insurance companies where the client does not have, or does not obtain from third parties, the primary actuarial capability.
6. Any other service inconsistent with the firm's responsibilities to the public.

Additionally, the auditor is required to report annually to the SEC client's audit committee the total fees received from the client for consulting services and a description of the consulting services rendered. The data supplied on MAS fees indicates that almost 80% of the SEC registrants audited by SECPS member firms obtain no MAS services from their auditor.

PROFESSIONAL STANDARDS AND ORGANIZATIONS

Within the accounting profession, six institutions are responsible for establishing standards and for regulating and disciplining practitioners: the AICPA, the FASB (discussed in Chapter 46), the GASB (discussed in Chapter 31), the SEC (discussed in Chapter 47), state societies of certified public accountants, and the state boards of accountancy as represented by their organization, the NASBA.

American Institute of Certified Public Accountants

The AICPA's objectives, as stated in its bylaws, are to: unite certified public accountants in the United States; to promote and maintain high professional standards of practice; to assist in the maintainance of standards for entry to the profession; to promote the interests of CPAs; to develop and improve accounting education; and to encourage cordial relations between CPAs and professional accountants in other countries. [BL 101.01]

Membership in the institute is open to "those who are in possession of valid and unrevoked certified public accountant certificates issued by the legally constituted state authorities" (BL 220.01).

Accounting Pronouncements and Guidance. AICPA accounting guidance is issued by AcSEC. Unlike those of the FASB and GASB, AcSEC's views are not enforceable standards under the Institute's Code of Professional Conduct (unless those views have been approved by the FASB). One objective of AcSEC, however, is to provide guidance to members to influence their judgments on accounting issues not otherwise covered in authoritative literature. Another objective is to provide input on the form and content of pronouncements of the FASB, the GASB, and other bodies having authority over accounting standards. In this regard, accounting and reporting recommendations included in AcSEC publications are subject to disposition by the FASB and GASB.
    The various publications issued by AcSEC will be briefly described in the following subsections.

Audit and accounting guides. Various components of the AICPA may issue audit and accounting guides, after approval of proffered accounting guidance by AcSEC; these may deal with particular circumstances that require special attention (i.e., audits of pension plans) or with specialized industries, (i.e., the construction industry). The sections of an audit and accounting guide that deal with auditing procedures and auditors' reports must be approved by the Chairman of the ASB. AICPA members may be called on to justify departures from recommendations concerned with auditing procedures and auditors' reports. All audit and accounting guides are exposed for public comment prior to finalization.

Statements of position. Statements of position are issued primarily to revise or clarify audit and accounting guides so as to influence the development of accounting and reporting practices in directions the AICPA believes are in the public interest. They may be prepared by a committee, subcommittee, or task force, and must be approved by a majority of AcSEC after an exposure period and consideration of comments received.

Practice bulletins. AcSEC may issue practice bulletins to disseminate its views on accounting issues and to provide guidance to AICPA members on emerging accounting and financial reporting issues that have not been considered by the FASB or the GASB. They provide AcSEC with a form of communication that can reach practitioners and can be readily retrieved after publication. AcSEC may also use practice bulletins to extract advisory conclusions or portions of issues papers for publication as interim guidance until the FASB or GASB addresses the topics of the papers.

Issues papers. Issues papers may be prepared:

- As a prelude to revising an existing AICPA industry audit and accounting guide.
- To discuss accounting problems in an industry not covered by an existing guide.
- To discuss other accounting problems not covered by existing GAAP.
- To discuss other accounting problems for which guidance is insufficient or unclear, resulting in alternative accounting treatments; or to reconsider prior topics due to changes in the business environment.

Issues papers present more or less neutral discussions of the subject, including definitions of relevant terms and an overview of current practice. Past issues papers have presented advisory conclusions approved by a majority of AcSEC; but in late 1987 AcSEC reluctantly acceded to FASB's request that advisory conclusions be omitted from issues papers. The FASB had expressed concern about the AcSEC advice being implemented prematurely, and would like the issues papers to be more like research papers.

Auditing Pronouncements and Guidance. The ASB issues auditing standards and guidance in the form of SASs and interpretations thereof. Rule 202 of the Institute's Code of Professional Conduct requires compliance with SASs. (See Chapter 5 for an in-depth discussion of auditing standards.)

Ethical Pronouncements and Guidance. The AICPA's Code of Professional Conduct (discussed later in this chapter) provides ethical rules and guidance to the practitioner.

State Societies of Certified Public Accountants

Each state and territory of the United States (and the District of Columbia) has a CPA society. Major activities of state societies are providing members with continuing professional education courses, and establishing and conducting a quality review program for member firms.

State societies are also active in lobbying on state legislative bills affecting the licensing of CPAs, and members of state societies are frequently active on their state boards of accountancy.

State Boards of Accountancy

All states and territories, and the District of Columbia, have boards of accountancy, charged with the responsibility for administering the public accountancy laws. The state boards award the license to practice to each person who successfully completes the uniform CPA examination and meets the education and experience requirements imposed by the state statutes. State boards also have been very active in establishing and enforcing continuing professional education requirements.

Other Professional Organizations

Many other professional organizations have had a pronounced effect on the profession and on the development of accounting and auditing standards. Often these organizations conduct related research, and they interact heavily with standard-setting and other rule-making bodies. Notable among these organizations are the American Accounting Association (AAA), National Association of Accountants (NAA), Financial Analysts Federation (FAF), Financial Executives Institute (FEI), the Institute of Internal Auditors (IIA), and several governmental associations relevant to GASB.

The AAA is the national organization of academic accountants. Its Committee on Financial Accounting Standards presents an academic point of view before the FASB, AICPA, and other decision-making bodies, although its responses are not deemed to be the view of the AAA, but only of the members participating in the response. The AAA is one of the sponsors of the Financial Accounting Foundation (see Chapter 46), the parent body of the FASB. The association works closely with the American Assembly of Collegiate Schools of Business (AACSB) in establishing accreditation standards for programs and professional schools of accounting.

The NAA, also a sponsor of the Financial Accounting Foundation, primarily represents accountants working in corporations as controllers, financial executives, and internal accountants. Its Management Accounting Practice Committee frequently comments on developing standards. The NAA awards a credential comparable in many ways to the CPA certificate. The Certificate in Management Accounting (CMA) requires that an individual pass a five-part examination as well as satisfy specific education and experience requirements.

The FAF is the national organization for financial analysts and is also a sponsor of the Financial Accounting Foundation. The FAF makes annual awards for excellence in corporate financial reporting.

Members of the FEI have major financial responsibilities in their companies — they are vice-presidents of finance, chief financial officers, treasurers, controllers, and the like. The FEI's Committee on Corporate Reporting responds to proposals from the FASB, the SEC, the AICPA, and Congress. The FEI is also a sponsor of the Financial Accounting Foundation. The Financial Executives Research Foundation supports research relevant to reporting practices and accounting principles.

The IIA develops standards for internal audit practice, and represents auditors directly employed by businesses to review and improve their own internal controls and operating efficiency.

PROFESSIONAL CONDUCT

In early 1988, the membership of the AICPA approved a set of proposals to restructure professional standards. These proposals were based on a 1986 report by a special committee of the AICPA (the Anderson Committee). The report, entitled *Restructuring Professional Standards to Achieve Professional Excellence in a Changing Environment* (AICPA, 1986n), called on the profession to adopt a new approach to ethical and technical standards governing the performance of CPAs. A summary of the approved proposals follows:

1. Update of the existing Rules of Ethics with a Code of Professional Conduct. The new Code consists of a Principles section and a Rules section. The Rules section is enforceable, making it necessary for AICPA members to conform with them to retain membership. The Rules apply to *all* AICPA members (i.e., members in public practice, in industry, in government, and in education).
2. Establishment of a Quality Review Program and implementation of a practice-monitoring membership requirement. Members in public practice may retain their AICPA membership only if they practice in firms that participate in an AICPA approved practice-monitoring (quality review and peer review) program.
3. Revision of procedures for complaints in the Ethics Division and restructuring of the Joint Trial Board.
4. Adoption of continuing professional education requirement. This membership requirement necessitates that all members in public practice complete 120 hours of CPE for each three-year reporting period (60 hours initially increasing to 90 hours for members not in public practice).
5. Adoption of postbaccalaureate education requirement. This requirement establishes a membership admission provision that requires that those entering the profession after the year 2000 have at least 150 collegiate-level semester hours including a bachelor's degree or its equivalent. This Rule thus requires 30 hours of postbaccalaureate education.

Code of Conduct

The AICPA's Code of Professional Conduct consists of two sections, the Principles and the Rules. The Principles provide the framework for the Rules, which govern the performance of professional services by members. The Council of the AICPA is authorized to designate bodies to promulgate technical standards under the Rules, and the bylaws require adherence to those Rules and standards.

The Principles of the Code are as follows:

1. *Responsibilities.* "In carrying out their responsibilities as professionals, members should exercise sensitive professional and moral judgments in all their activities." Members have responsibilities to all those who use their professional services and to each other in cooperating to improve the art of accounting and maintain the public's confidence.
2. *The Public Interest.* "Members should accept the obligation to act in a way that will serve the public interest, honor the public trust, and demonstrate commitment to professional-

ism." The profession's public consists of clients, credit grantors, governments, employers, investors, the business and financial community, and others who rely on the objectivity and integrity of certified public accountants.

3. *Integrity.* "To maintain and broaden public confidence, members should perform all professional responsibilities with the highest sense of integrity." Integrity requires a member to be honest and candid and not to subordinate the public trust to personal gain.

4. *Objectivity and Independence.* "A member should maintain objectivity and be free of conflicts of interest in discharging professional responsibilities. A member in public practice should be independent in fact and appearance when providing audit and other attestation services." Objectivity is a distinguishing feature of the profession that requires the member to be impartial, intellectually honest and free of conflicts of interest. Independence precludes relationships that may appear to impair a member's objectivity in performing attestation services.

5. *Due Care.* "A member should observe the profession's technical and ethical standards, strive continually to improve competence and the quality of services, and discharge professional responsibility to the best of the member's abililty." Due care requires competence and diligence in the performance of services and a commitment to learning and professional improvment.

6. *Scope and Nature of Services.* "A member in public practice should observe the Principles of the Code of Professional Conduct in determining the scope and nature of services to be provided." Services should not create a conflict of interest in the performance of an audit nor be inconsistent with the CPA's role as a professional.

Evolving Ethics

In the past decade the AICPA membership also voted to repeal the prohibition against advertising and also two controversial Rules of Conduct: Rule 401 (encroachment), which prohibited members from soliciting business from an enterprise already served by another accountant; and a section of Rule 502 that prohibited members from "a direct, uninvited solicitation of a specific potential client." Consistent with the approach taken as to other professions, the Antitrust Division of the United States Department of Justice had challenged the legality of both rules on the grounds that they inhibit competition among accounting firms. The end result is that there are no longer any rulings or interpretations underlying the basic principle dealing with responsibilities to colleagues.

However, in 1987 the AICPA dug in its heels against a proposal by the Federal Trade Commission (FTC). The FTC has concluded that several provisions of the AICPA rules violate certain provisions of the Federal Trade Commission Act, and asked the Institute to sign a consent order agreeing to substantial changes in the rules.

The proposed consent order would have required amendments of the AICPA Rules of Conduct to permit members to accept commissions, accept contingent fees for nonattest engagements, use trade names, pay for referrals, engage in unrestricted advertising, and vouch for the achievability of forecasts, all presently prohibited activities. The FTC also proposed to permit accounting firms to practice as commercial corporations with non-CPA ownership of shares, which is presently prohibited.

The AICPA Board concluded that the proposed consent order is contrary to the best interests of the public at large, the profession generally, and institute members specifically, and is therefore inconsistent with the Principles of the Code of Professional Conduct. As a result, the AICPA Board agreed to take all appropriate legal steps to resist any action the FTC may take against the AICPA. In August 1988, recognizing the improbability of prevailing over the FTC in all of the contested issues, the Council of the AICPA voted to enter into an agreement with the FTC, under which the AICPA will retain its right to prohibit members from accepting commissions from or charging contingent fees to clients for which the CPA performs audit, review, compilation and PFI examination services; however, these practices would not be prohibited where the CPA does not perform such services. If a referral fee or commission is received by the CPA for recommending products or services of others to a client, that fact would have to be disclosed to the client. Additionally, the advertising rules would be made less stringent.

Now that contingent fees are to be permitted, the question arises as to when, if ever, the consultant-CPA can perform audit, review, compilation, or PFI examination services for a client that previously had been charged a contingent fee or commission. Perhaps this will be clarified in a final agreement yet to be prepared and signed by the FTC and AICPA, and then subjected to public comment for 60 days.

Disciplinary Process

AICPA and State Societies. The AICPA and most state CPA societies enforce the institute's Code of Professional Conduct through the Joint Trial Board. The joint trial board consists of AICPA members elected for three-year terms by Council. The trial board hears and adjudicates charges involving alleged violations of a state CPA society's bylaws or code of professional conduct. Punishment, when decided, ranges from a private letter of criticism to expulsion from membership in both the institute and the state society, accompanied by a published announcement to the entire membership of the member's expulsion and the reasons for it. Such disciplinary action is obviously damaging to the reputation of the offending CPA, and frequently results in revocation of his license to practice by the state board of accountancy.

State Boards of Accountancy. Ultimate responsibility for discipline in the accounting profession rests with the various state boards of accountancy, charged with licensing and disciplining accountants practicing in their jurisdictions. They have the power to revoke a CPA's certificate and/or his license to practice.

SEC Enforcement. The SEC has exercised disciplinary authority over the accounting profession (and others, primarily lawyers, who routinely practice before the SEC) under its Rule of Practice 2(e)(1), which the SEC believes empowers it to temporarily or permanently disqualify an accountant or a firm from practicing before it. "Practice" includes the rendering of opinions on financial statements of public companies. Thus, the authority claimed by the SEC under Rule 2(e) provides, in effect, ultimate control over the right of a firm, no matter how large, and its individual members, to engage in their professional pursuit, even though the disciplinary issue may relate to only a single audit engagement.

Through seeking injunctions or obtaining consent decrees, which may be and often are litigated, the SEC has at its disposal the use of powerful sanctions: it can restrict the growth of the firm by limiting the amount of new business taken on and by prohibiting it from merging with other firms; it can require of both an individual and a firm that they become involved in continuing professional education programs and in other quality improvement activities; and finally, it can prohibit both an individual and a firm from practicing before it. (Refer to Chapter 47 for a more extensive discussion of the SEC's enforcement powers, and Chapter 49 for a discussion of Rule 2(e) and litigation involving SEC challenges.)

SELF-REGULATORY PROGRAM

In response to concerns about the quality of auditing services expressed during the course of Congressional hearings on SEC oversight of the accounting profession in 1977 and 1978, the AICPA created a self-regulatory organization, the Division for CPA Firms, with two sections—an SECPS and a Private Companies Practice Section (PCPS). As of June 30, 1987, 1,710 firms were members of the Division for CPA Firms, with 395 firms members of the SECPS. SECPS member firms, according to an analysis by the POB, audit approximately 89% of all publicly traded companies. The sales volume of these companies account for 99% of the aggregate sales volume of all publicly traded companies (POB 1987).

The two sections have similar membership requirements, including a triennial peer review of each member firm to determine whether it has an effective system of quality control that meets established standards and provides reasonable assurance of professional quality in the performance of accounting and audit services. The SECPS has additional requirements that apply to audits of SEC registrants and other specified entities in which there is a public interest. For example, such audits must be subjected to review by a second partner in addition to the review by the partner with primary responsibility for the engagement. Member firms must also rotate partners in charge of such audits at least every seven years.

The POB oversees and reviews the activities of the SECPS in the public interest. The Board consists of five members not engaged in public accounting who represent a broad spectrum of experience.

As stated earlier under "Professional Conduct" the membership of the AICPA approved in early 1988 a membership requirement that members in the practice of public accounting must practice in firms enrolled in AICPA-approved practice-monitoring programs. In this regard, a firm that is a member of the AICPA Division for CPA Firms in deemed to be enrolled in such a program.

SEC Practice Section

The SECPS provides the structure and processes for the self-regulatory program. The functions of the section are conducted through three major committees: the Execu-

- The firm's quality controls over its accounting and auditing practice are to be subjected to peer review every three years, and at any other time as may be imposed as part of a disciplinary action.
- All partners and members of the professional staff resident in the USA must complete at least 120 hours of continuing professional education over three years, but not less than 20 hours in any given year.
- The audit partner in charge of an SEC engagement can serve in that capacity for a maximum of seven consecutive years.
- A preissuance concurring review of an audit report for an SEC client must be made by a partner other than the audit partner in charge.
- Report annually to the audit committee or board of SEC clients the following matters:
  - Material errors and irregularities
  - Material weaknesses in internal control
  - "Opinion shopping" situations
  - Disagreements with management on material financial and reporting matters
  - Material contingencies and their accounting and reporting
  - Material/unusual transactions and their accounting and reporting
  - Material changes in accounting principles
  - Total fees for management advisory services and description of those services
- The firm must provide specified information annually about its operations for inclusion in files open to the public.
- A firm must promptly report to the Special Investigations Committee any litigation against it or its personnel, or publicly announced investigations by regulatory agencies, where these matters allege deficiencies in auditing and reporting on present or former SEC clients.

FIG. 45.1   Summary of Major Membership Requirements for SEC Practice Section Membership
Source: AICPA, Division for CPA Firms SEC Practice Section SECPS Manual, 1986i.

tive Committee, the Peer Review Committee, and the Special Investigations Committee.

The overall requirements for membership in the SECPS, selected and paraphrased from the SECPS Manual (AICPA, 1986i), Section IV.3, pp. 1-6 through 1-11, are shown in Figure 45.1. The manual also describes the organization of the SECPS, standards for performing and reporting on Peer Reviews, procedures for the Peer Review Committee, organization and operations of the Special Investigations Committee, continuing professional education requirements, and minimum liability insurance requirements.

Executive Committee. The SECPS is governed by an Executive Committee that has the status of a senior committee of the AICPA, and it is composed of representatives from twenty-one member firms. The Executive Committee establishes general policies for the section and has the authority to amend its membership requirements, to establish budgets and dues to finance the operations of the section, to deal with complaints against members, to impose sanctions on member firms, to appoint committees and task forces, to interact with other AICPA boards and committees, and to consult with the POB.

Peer Review Committee. The Peer Review Committee, consisting of 15 members appointed by the Executive Committee, establishes standards for peer reviews, administers the peer review program, and reviews each report.

Special Investigations Committee. The Special Investigations Committee (SIC) responds to concerns raised by alleged audit failures. The functions assigned to the SIC are the following:

1. Assist in providing reasonable assurance to the public and to the profession that member firms are complying with professional standards in the conduct of their practice before the SEC by identifying corrective measures, if any, that should be taken by a member firm involved in a specific alleged audit failure.
2. Assist in improving the quality of practice by member firms before the SEC by determining whether facts relating to specific alleged audit failures indicate that changes in GAAS or quality control standards need to be considered.
3. Recommend to the Executive Committee, when deemed necessary, appropriate sanctions with respect to the member firms involved.

Member firms are required to report promptly to the SIC certain litigation, proceedings, or investigations involving the firm or its personnel. Generally speaking, reportable cases are those alleging audit deficiencies in connection with filings made by a firm's SEC clients under the federal securities laws.

The committee conducts its activities in four modes described as screening, monitoring, investigating a firm, and investigating a case—all on a confidential basis. However, in keeping with its oversight and public reporting roles, the POB has complete access to the process.

According to a report of the SIC issued in 1986 (AICPA, 1986m), 160 instances of alleged audit failure had been added to its agenda in the past 6 years. The SIC had closed its files on 128 of those cases as of December 31, 1985.

In 17 cases, firms took corrective actions, such as reassigning personnel, strengthening internal procedures, and requiring additional professional education. Special reviews of a firm's quality controls were performed in 11 cases. Eight cases were referred to the Institute's Professional Ethics Division for an investigation into the work of specific individuals.

Peer Review

As described earlier in this chapter, one of the SECPS membership requirements is that a firm undergo a peer review of its accounting and auditing function every three years. A peer review is intended to evaluate whether a firm's system of quality control for its accounting and auditing practice meets the objectives of quality control standards established by the AICPA in its Statement on Quality Control Standards, and is being complied with.

A system of quality control for a CPA firm should cover the following activities and elements:

* Independence
* Acceptance and continuance of clients
* Hiring
* Assigning personnel to engagements
* Supervision
* Consultation
* Professional development
* Advancement
* Inspection

Upon completion of the peer review, the review team communicates its findings to the reviewed firm and prepares a publicly available written report in accordance with the standards for reporting on peer reviews. The review team also prepares a letter of comments when applicable.

Public Oversight Board

The POB was established to represent the public interest by providing continuing independent overview of SECPS activities. It consists of five individuals of recognized integrity and high reputation and is structured to assure independence. It has the authority to appoint, remove, and set the terms of compensation of its members and to select its chairman; the only limitation on its authority is that appointment of its members must have the concurrence of the AICPA Board of Directors. The SECPS has no authority over the POB.

The POB monitors all of the activities of the SECPS, with special emphasis on the effectiveness of the peer review program and the special investigations process. It also recommends to the Executive Committee whenever it sees fit, improvements in the section's membership requirements, standards, policies, and procedures. It publishes an annual report on its evaluation of the activities of the section and has the authority to issue other reports as appropriate.

POB representatives have monitored each peer review since inception of the program. Three types of monitoring programs are used by the POB staff to assess peer reviewers' adherence to standards. These programs have been modified over time to incorporate refinements resulting from experience and from discussion with SEC staff members.

* The *visitation-observation program* consists of a review of workpapers prepared and reports issued, including letters of comments and related responses ("reports") and visits to offices of the reviewed firm during the performance of the review.
* The *workpaper review program* consists of a review of workpapers and reports, without visitations.
* The *report review program* consists of a review of reports issued and the reviewer's summary review memorandum.

The POB staff workpapers document the reasons for POB's concurrence or non-concurrence with the reviewers' judgments. Because they are available for SEC review, the workpapers mask the identity of clients, the reviewed firm's offices, and personnel involved.

In 1987, the POB issued its ninth annual report (POB, 1987). The report indicates that in calendar year 1985, 127 member firms were required to undergo a peer review; of these, 113 were firms that had previously been reviewed by peers and 14 were firms that submitted their quality control system to peer review for the first time. Six of the 113 firms were required to undergo a full-scope review prior to expiration of the normal three-year cycle because the previous review had disclosed quality control system deficiencies requiring extensive or significant corrective action by the firm.

As of June 30, 1987, 111 peer review reports had been accepted by the POB. Reports of the remaining 16 firms were held open pending resolution of certain matters, either by the reviewed firm or by the review team.

Of the firms reviewed in 1986, 115, or 91%, received unqualified opinions. The vast majority of these opinions (105) were accompanied by letters of comment. The balance of the reviewed firms received qualified opinions. No firms received adverse opinions. Since inception of the peer review program, about 950 SECPS peer reviews have been performed with 88% of the reports issued unqualified, 10% qualified, and 2% adverse. Although difficult to measure quantitatively, it appears that the peer review process continues to improve the quality of accounting and auditing practice by member firms because: (1) review teams become more experienced year by year, are more proficient at identifying quality control deficiencies, and are holding the reviewed firms to higher and higher standards; and (2) comparisons of letters of comment issued in 1986 with those previously issued to the same firms indicate that the deficiencies that do exist tend to diminish from review to review.

SEC Oversight

The SEC staff oversees the activities of the SECPS through frequent contact with the POB and members of the executive and peer review committees of the SECPS. In addition, the staff reviews POB files and selected working papers of the peer reviewers. The SEC has stated that it believes the peer review process contributes significantly to improving quality controls of members and thus should enhance the consistency and quality of practice before the SEC.

The SEC, however, has stated that it has no basis for reaching any conclusions about the special investigation process or the POB's oversight of that process as it does not have sufficient access to the process.

To address this concern, the SECPS has entered into an access arrangement concerning SIC activity with the Chief Accountant's office of the SEC. This arrangement, which is being evaluated on a trial basis by both the SECPS and the SEC, provides the Chief Accountant's office, through the POB, with certain information on cases reported to the SIC after March 31, 1985, and subsequently closed by the Committee. Under the agreement, the SEC's staff has access to a case summary developed by the SIC and is able to discuss the summary with the staff of the POB.

Mandatory Peer Review Proposal. In April 1987, the SEC proposed (in Release 33-6695) that public accounting firms auditing the financial statements of publicly held companies should be subject to a peer review at least once every three years as a condition for practicing before the SEC. The peer reviews would have to be performed in accordance with SEC standards by a peer review organization that also meets SEC criteria. (Presumably the SECPS would continue to qualify.) If a public accounting firm decided not to join a peer review organization, the firm would have the option of having a peer review performed by another public accounting firm under the supervision of the SEC staff, which would also evaluate the review. (Of course, this alternative presumes that the firm to be reviewed could find another firm willing to conduct a review under the supervision of the SEC.)

The comment period for the proposal ended in July 1987. The SEC is currently reviewing the comment letters that have been received and evaluating the proposal in light of the recommendations of the Treadway Commission (as discussed later in this chapter) and the AICPA's new Code of Professional Conduct, which requires firm membership in an approved practice-monitoring program.

CURRENT ENVIRONMENT

The profession of accounting has indeed changed from its origins in the United States 100 years ago. To understand these changes is to comprehend the evolution of an industrial society that has prospered and grown, but not without trauma. With each evolutionary step the accounting profession has accepted, or been forced to accept, increased risks and responsibilities in the performance of its services. As President Reagan wrote on the 100th anniversary of the accounting profession in 1987:

> Your organization and the CPA profession have played a paramount role in establishing and maintaining the integrity of our capital markets. Independent auditors give credibility to the financial statements of business enterprises and governmental agencies. Without that credibility, creditors and investors could scarcely make the kind of responsible decisions that give our economy stability and vitality. Our financial markets would shrivel up without you.

These words from the President of the United States attribute to the independent accountant a great responsibility that carries with it enormous risks. These risks have manifested themselves in ever-increasing litigation, an upward spiral in jury awards and out-of-court settlements, and skyrocketing premiums for professional liability insurance that provides reduced coverage. Chapter 49 provides more insight into this current phenomenon.

What are the responsibilities of the independent accountant? What should they be? How should the accounting profession be regulated? Are professional standards adequate for these times? What changes should be made, if any? These are the important questions of the day and are at the heart of recent actions by the accounting profession and the subject of various congressional investigations and professional studies currently in process.

In 1984 and 1985, the accounting profession was in a state of disruption caused by a number of events including the failures of several large banks and government securities dealers without apparent warning. These failures, which appeared to threaten the very financial structure of the United States, occurred at a time when the Subcommittee on Oversight and Investigation of the Committee on Energy and Commerce of the U.S. House of Representatives (the Dingell Committee) was in the process of holding hearings to investigate the profession. Chairman Dingell had introduced these hearings by quoting from a U.S. Supreme Court opinion[1] that described the accounting profession as the "public watchdog." These hearings have continued into 1988. Their purpose has been to investigate the accounting profession and to specifically evaluate: (1) the effectiveness of the present auditing system, auditor independence, and the implications of certain audit failures (i.e., where "clean" opinions were rendered just prior to a financial collapse); (2) the extent and adequacy of the SEC's oversight of the accounting profession; (3) the appropriateness (in terms of the public interest) of a standards-setting process significantly influenced by preparers and their CPAs; and (4) the effectiveness of the profession's self-regulatory programs. The hearings included testimony from representatives of the AICPA, POB, FASB, SEC, General Accounting Office (GAO), academia, and selected accounting firms.

In addition to this governmental activity, the GAO, at the request of Congressman Jack Brooks, chairman of the Legislation and National Security Subcommittee of the House Committee on Government Operations (the Brooks Committee), undertook a study of the quality of audits of federal grants performed by nonfederal auditors. The study (discussed further in Chapter 32) was aimed at determining the extent to which CPAs comply with professional auditing standards during their audits of recipients of federal assistance and the overall quality of CPAs' audits.

These governmental hearings and studies sparked a number of other actions by the federal government in the form of proposed legislation, and by the AICPA, and others to address the concerns of the governmental committees and the public and to take appropriate measures to improve audit quality, auditors' communications, and financial reporting.

These actions are discussed in the following sections.

Dingell Hearings (The Wyden Bill)

In May 1986, Congressman Ron Wyden introduced in the House of Representatives the Financial Fraud Detection and Disclosure Act of 1986. The bill (HR 4886) was cosponsored by six other Democratic members of the Dingell Committee, including John D. Dingell, the committee chairman. If enacted in the form introduced, the Act would have required auditors of public companies to:

• Detect, without regard to materiality, *any* actual or suspected illegal or irregular activity by any director, officer, employee, agent, or other person associated with the audited entity.

• Report publicly and to applicable federal, state, or local regulatory or enforcement agencies all instances of actual or suspected illegal or irregular activities.

• Evaluate and report publicly on the audited entity's system of internal administrative and accounting control.

---

[1] United States v. Arthur Young & Co. 465 US 805 (1984).

• Sign the audit report as individuals, rather than using just the firm name.

The bill would protect auditors who act in good faith from liability for any public or other report on actual suspected illegal or irregular activities.

At a June 1986 hearing of the Dingell Committee, the AICPA strongly opposed the bill, indicating that the primary responsibility for dealing with fraud and illegal acts, including the responsibility to report such matters to the appropriate regulators, rests with the companies' boards of directors and audit committees. The AICPA stressed the independent auditor's responsibility to report reservations in the auditor's opinion and to consider resigning from an engagement in specified circumstances.

Shortly thereafter, the SEC stated its intention to oppose this bill. The Commissioners were concerned that the bill would make fundamental changes in auditors' relationships with clients and regulators and effectively turn independent professionals into state-regulated examiners.

In August 1986, a revised version of the Wyden bill was introduced in Congress that reflected two major changes. The first change introduced the concept of materiality although in a much broader fashion than is normally applied to financial statements. The second change placed the primary burden for reporting irregularities and illegal acts to enforcement and regulatory agencies on the company itself, not on the auditor.

This legislation on financial fraud detection and reporting has not yet been reintroduced in Congress because the Subcommittee is considering the final recommendations of the National Commission on Fraudulent Financial Reporting (the Treadway Commission, described later) and recent actions by the profession and the SEC in addressing these matters. These actions include the adoption by the profession of a new Code of Professional Conduct (described earlier in this chapter), the issuance by the AICPA of the "expectation gap" auditing standards, and the release by the SEC of new rules that address certain "opinion shopping" concerns and disclosure when a company changes its accountants.

Treadway Commission

The Treadway Commission was established in 1985 by the AICPA to study management-related fraud and was chaired by former SEC Commissioner James Treadway. The Treadway Commission was a private-sector initiative, jointly sponsored and funded by the AICPA, AAA, FEI, IIA, and NAA. The Treadway Commission had three major objectives (NCFFR, 1987, p. 2):

1. Consider the extent to which acts of fraudulent financial reporting undermine the integrity of financial reporting; the forces and the opportunities, environmental, institutional, or individual, that may contribute to these acts; the extent to which fraudulent financial reporting can be prevented or deterred and to which it can be detected sooner after occurrence; the extent, if any, to which incidents of this type of fraud may be the product of a decline in professionalism of corporate financial officers and internal auditors; and the extent, if any, to which the regulatory and law enforcement environment unwittingly may have tolerated or contributed to the occurrence of this type of fraud.

2. Examine the role of the independent public accountant in detecting fraud, focusing particularly on whether the detection of fraudulent financial reporting has been neglected or insufficiently focused on and whether the ability of the independent public accountant to detect such fraud can be enhanced, and consider whether changes in auditing standards or procedures—internal and external—would reduce the extent of fraudulent financial reporting.

3. Identify attributes of corporate structure that may contribute to acts of fraudulent financial reporting or to the failure to detect such acts promptly.

The Treadway Commission's study, issued in October 1987 and entitled *Report of the National Commission on Fraudulent Financial Reporting* (NCFFR, 1987), states that fraudulent financial reporting is the result of various forces—environmental, institutional, and opportunistic—that are present to some degree in all companies. Common situations include a desire to inflate the value of a company's stock and to defer facing up to financial difficulties. Direct or indirect personal gain or self-preservation is usually the motivator. Examples of these situational pressures include (pp. 23–24):

- Sudden decreases in revenue or market share. A single company or an entire industry can experience these decreases.
- Unrealistic budget pressures, particularly for short-term results. These pressures may occur when headquarters arbitrarily determines profit objectives and budgets without taking actual conditions into account.
- Financial pressure resulting from bonus plans that depend on short-term economic performance. This pressure is particularly acute when the bonus is a significant component of the individual's total compensation.

The Treadway Commission's report examines the factors within a company that are conducive to fraudulent reporting, which include an inattentive board and audit committee, weak internal controls, unusual or complex transactions, extreme sensitivity of reported amounts to management estimates, absence of specified GAAP for major transactions, ineffective internal auditing, and an effete ethical climate.

With respect to independent accountants, the Treadway Commission's report points out that the most common SEC allegations against auditors in fraudulent reporting cases are the failure to obtain sufficient evidence and a lack of proper skepticism about "red flags."

The Treadway Commission's report contains numerous recommendations for public companies, independent accountants, the SEC and other regulators, and educators. Forty-nine specific recommendations are summarized in the Appendix.

AICPA "Expectation Gap" Project

In late 1985, the ASB initiated several projects to respond to changing public expectations and concerns (described earlier in this chapter) by members of Congress, the media, the judicial system, and the accounting profession. Many of these concerns revolve around what has been described as an "expectation gap"—the gap between what the public expects from accountants and what accountants believe they are actually responsible for.

In February 1987, the ASB issued 10 responsive exposure drafts, 9 of which would affect auditing standards. The tenth is a proposed Attestation Standard, *Examination of Management's Discussion and Analysis* (see Chapter 4). The proposed auditing standards were finalized in 1988. A summary listing of these new SASs from the perspective of the independent auditor follows, giving the chapter in the *Handbook* in which further discussion is contained.

1. *Errors and Irregularities*—SAS 53. The auditor's responsibility to detect and report on errors and irregularities is expanded. This SAS provides guidance to improve his ability to meet that responsibility. (Chapter 5)

2. *Illegal Acts*—SAS 54. The auditor's responsibility for detecting and communicating information about illegal acts is clarified. (Chapter 5)

3. *Auditor's Report*—SAS 58. Periodically, the profession reexamines the content of the auditor's report. However, no changes have been made since 1948. This SAS attempts to help users better understand the auditor's role by eliminating some technical language from the report and making it more explicit. (Chapter 11)

4. *Evaluating Continued Existence*—SAS 59. The auditor is required to evaluate the ability of each audit client to continue in business. The SAS comments that substantial doubt about continuance may exist even though asset recoverability and liability classification are not a problem. (Chapters 11 and 26)

5. *Risk Assessment*—SAS 55. This SAS broadens the concept of a control structure of a company, to consist of the control environment, accounting system, and specific control procedures. In addition, the auditor's responsibility to study and evaluate internal control during audit planning is expanded. (Chapter 8)

6. *Analytical Procedures*—SAS 56. Public expectations of the degree of responsibility an auditor should assume for detecting fraudulent financial reporting are increasing. This SAS attempts to respond to those expectations by requiring the use of analytical procedures in all audit engagements. (Chapter 7)

7. *Auditing Accounting Estimates*—SAS 57. Accounting estimates involve uncertainty and subjectivity and, as a result, are more susceptible to misstatement than factual data. This SAS requires an auditor to determine that all necessary accounting estimates have been prepared, are reasonable, and are properly accounted for. (Chapter 26)

8. *Communication With Audit Committees*—SAS 61. This SAS requires an auditor to communicate with a company's audit committee or an owner of an owner-managed enterprise about certain substantive matters, for example, the implications of audit adjustments, disagreements with management, and difficulties encountered in performing the audit. (Communications of this type are already required annually as a membership requirement of the SECPS.) (Chapter 6)

9. *Communication About Internal Control Matters*—SAS 60. This SAS clarifies the internal control reporting language and replaces the concept of material weakness with the concept of reportable condition. (Chapter 8)

SEC Rules for Reporting Changes in Accountants

In April 1988, the SEC issued FRR-31 (§ 603) amending Form 8-K, Regulation S-K, and Schedule 14A for changes in accountants and potential opinion shopping situations.

The adopted rules are designed to clarify the circumstances in which public companies are deemed to have had disagreements with their former auditors, and provide for more complete disclosure concerning the circumstances surrounding the change in accountants. They also call for enhanced disclosure of potential opinion shopping situations in connection with a change of auditors, by requiring disclosure of certain issues discussed with the newly engaged auditor during the registrant's two most recent fiscal years and any subsequent interim period prior to the new accountant's engagement.

The SEC also issued a proposed release for public comment that would reduce the time period for reporting changes in accountants. The proposal, expected to be adopted, would reduce from 15 to 5 calendar days the time allowed for filing a Form 8-K disclosing a change in accountants. Additionally, the time allowed for filing the former accountant's letter (as an exhibit to the Form 8-K or a registration statement) would be reduced from 30 to 10 calendar days. The accountant may provide an interim letter, to be followed by the final letter within the allotted ten day period. Notwithstanding these maximum time limits, the accountant's letter (whether interim or final) must be filed within two days of its receipt.

CONCLUSION

The accounting profession faces many problems, challenges, and difficult decisions over the next several years. The "expectation gap" auditing standards and Code of Professional Conduct must be applied effectively, the Treadway Commission Report recommendations addressed appropriately, and further congressional as well as SEC actions, dealt with judiciously. The results of these activities, of course, cannot be predicted but needless to say they are of extreme importance to the future of the accounting profession.

Appendix 45

SUMMARY OF RECOMMENDATIONS OF THE NATIONAL COMMISSION ON FRAUDULENT FINANCIAL REPORTING

The NCFFR Report (1987) includes 49 specific recommendations aimed at reducing the opportunity for fraudulent financial reporting. The numbering included below is intended to facilitate reference to this abbreviated recital of recommendations, and is not shown in the original. The order of presentation also varies slightly from that contained in the Report.

Recommendations for Management of Public Companies

1. Oversee the financial reporting process; identify, understand, and assess the factors that may cause the company's financial statements to be fraudulently misstated.
2. Maintain internal controls to provide reasonable assurance that fraudulent financial reporting will be prevented or subject to early detection.
3. Develop and enforce written codes of corporate conduct.
4. Maintain accounting functions that are designed to meet the company's financial reporting obligations.

Recommendations for Internal Auditors of Public Companies

5. Maintain an effective internal audit function staffed with an adequate number of qualified personnel appropriate to the size and the nature of the company.
6. Ensure that internal audit functions are objective.
7. Consider the implications of their nonfinancial audit findings for the company's financial statements.
8. Be involved in the audit of the entire financial reporting process and properly coordinated with the independent public accountant.

Recommendations for Audit Committees of Public Companies

9. Be required by SEC rule to exist and be comprised solely of independent directors.
10. Be informed, vigilant, and effective overseers of the financial reporting process and the company's internal controls.
11. Develop a written charter setting forth the duties and responsibilities of the committee.
12. Have adequate resources and authority to discharge the committee's responsibilities.
13. Review management's evaluation of factors related to the independence of the company's public accountant.
14. Before the beginning of each year, review management's plans for engaging the company's auditor to perform management advisory services during the coming year, considering both the types of services that may be rendered and the projected fees.
15. Be required by SEC rule to include in the annual reports to stockholders a letter signed by the chairman of the committee describing the committee's responsibilities and activities during the year.
16. Be advised when management seeks a second opinion on a significant accounting issue.
17. Oversee the quarterly reporting process, including approving financial results prior to public release.

Other Recommendations for Public Companies

18. Be required by SEC rule to include in annual reports to stockholders management reports signed by the chief executive officer and the chief accounting officer and/or the chief financial officer. The management report should acknowledge management's responsibilities for the financial statements

and internal control, discuss how these responsibilities were fulfilled, and provide management's assessment of the effectiveness of the company's internal controls.

19. Be required by SEC rule to disclose publicly the nature of any material accounting or auditing issue discussed with its old and new auditor during the three-year period preceding a change in auditors.

20. The Commission's sponsoring organizations should cooperate in developing additional, integrated guidance on internal control.

Recommendations for Independent Public Accountants

21. Be required by the SEC to review quarterly financial data of public companies before release to the public.

22. Recognize and control the organizational and individual pressures that potentially reduce audit quality.

Recommendations for the Auditing Standards Board

23. Revise standards to restate the independent public accountant's responsibility for detection of fraudulent financial reporting, requiring the independent public accountant to (a) take affirmative steps in each audit to assess the potential for such reporting and (b) design tests to provide reasonable assurance of detection. Revised standards should include guidance for assessing risks and pursuing detection when risks are identified.

24. Establish standards to require independent public accountants to perform analytical review procedures in all audit engagements and provide improved guidance on the appropriate use of these procedures.

25. Revise the auditor's standard report to state that the audit provides reasonable but not absolute assurance that the audited financial statements are free from material misstatements as a result of fraud or error.

26. Revise the auditor's standard report to describe the extent to which the independent public accountant has reviewed and evaluated the system of internal accounting control; also, provide explicit guidance to address the situation where, as a result of his knowledge of the company's internal accounting controls, the independent public accountant disagrees with management's assessment as stated in the proposed management's report.

27. Reorganize to afford a full participatory role in the standard-setting process to knowledgeable persons who are affected by and interested in auditing standards but who either are not CPAs or are CPAs no longer in public practice.

Recommendations for the AICPA's SEC Practice Section

28. Strengthen the peer review program by increasing review of audit engagements involving public company clients new to a firm. For each office selected for peer review, the first audit of all such new clients should be reviewed.

29. Revise standards for the concurring partner review to include, among other things: (a) involvement in the planning stage of the audit in addition to the final review stage; (b) a requirement for prior experience by the concurring partner with audits of SEC registrants and familiarity with the client's industry; and (c) have the concurring partner consider himself a peer of the engagement partner for purposes of the review.

Recommendations for the Securities and Exchange Commission

30. Be authorized to impose civil money penalties in administrative proceedings [including Rule 2(e) proceedings] and to seek civil money penalties from a court directly in an injunctive proceeding.

31. Be authorized to issue a cease and desist order when it finds a securities law violation.

32. Seek explicit statutory authority to bar or suspend corporate officers and directors involved in fraudulent financial reporting from future service in that capacity in a public company.

33. Conduct an affirmative program to promote increased criminal prosecution of fraudulent financial reporting cases by educating and assisting government officials having criminal prosecution powers.

34. Require all public accounting firms that audit public companies to be members of a professional organization that has peer review and independent oversight functions and is approved by the SEC.

35. Take enforcement action when a public accounting firm fails to remedy deficiencies cited in the public accounting profession's quality assurance program.

36. Be given adequate resources to perform existing and additional functions that help prevent, detect, and deter fraudulent financial reporting.

37. Reconsider its long-standing position, insofar as it applies to independent directors, that the corporate indemnification of officers and directors for liabilities that arise under the Securities Act of 1933 is against public policy and therefore unenforceable.

Recommendations for Regulators Other Than the SEC

38. The Office of the Comptroller of the Currency, the Federal Reserve Board, the Federal Deposit Insurance Corporation, and the Federal Home Loan Bank Board (including the Federal Savings and Loan Insurance Corporation) should adopt measures patterned on the Commission's recommendations directed to the SEC to carry out their own regulatory responsibility relating to financial reporting under the federal securities laws.

39. The financial institution regulatory agencies and the public accounting profession should provide for the regulatory examiner and the independent public accountant to have mutual access to information they develop about examined financial institutions.

40. State boards of accountancy should implement positive enforcement programs that periodically would review the quality of services that the independent public accountants they license render.

41. Parties charged with responding to various tort reform initiatives should consider the implications that the perceived liability crisis holds for long-term audit quality and the independent public accountant's detection of fraudulent financial reporting.

Recommendations for Business and Accounting Curricula

42. Foster knowledge and understanding of the factors that may cause fraudulent financial reporting and the strategies that can lead to a reduction in its incidence.

43. Promote a better understanding of the function and the importance of internal controls, including the control environment.

44. Inform students about the regulation and enforcement activities by which government and private bodies safeguard the financial reporting system and thereby protect the public interest.

45. Help students develop stronger analytical, problem solving, and judgment skills.

46. Emphasize ethical values by integrating their development with the acquisition of knowledge and skills.

47. Encourage business and accounting faculty to develop their own personal competence as well as classroom materials for conveying information, skills, and ethical values.

48. Test students for professional certification on the information, skills, and ethical values that further the understanding of fraudulent financial reporting and that promote its reduction.

49. As part of their continuing professional education, independent public accountants, internal auditors, and corporate accountants should study the forces and opportunities that contribute to fraudulent financial reporting, the risk factors that may indicate its occurrence, and the relevant ethical and technical standards.

46

Financial Accounting Standards Board

HISTORY OF STANDARD SETTERS

Correspondence With the New York Stock Exchange

The phrase *generally accepted accounting principles* (GAAP), used throughout this *Handbook*, is part of the standard lexicon of today's financial community. Its origin is found in early correspondence between the American Institute of Accountants (now the AICPA – see Chapter 45 for a discussion of this major professional organization) and the New York Stock Exchange. Prior to this correspondence, enforceable rules of accounting simply did not exist. Leading accountants and others in the business community grew increasingly uneasy with deficiencies in financial reporting practices observed during the boom economy of the mid-1920s. A joint effort by the AICPA and the New York Stock Exchange to remedy accounting abuses and better define the role of the auditor was first proposed in 1926, although the dialogue did not begin until 1930, following the stock market crash of 1929.

The result of the joint effort was a pamphlet, *Audits of Corporate Accounts,* published by the AICPA in 1934 and distributed to all members.

The SEC

The significance of *Audits of Corporate Accounts* was overshadowed by the Securities Act of 1933 and the Securities Exchange Act of 1934. As discussed in Chapter 47, the latter act created the SEC, which was given the authority to

> prescribe, in regard to reports made pursuant to this title, . . . the methods to be followed in the preparation of reports, in the appraisal or valuation of assets and liabilities, in the determination of depreciation and depletion, in the differentiation of investment and operating accounts, and in the preparation . . . of separate and/or consolidated balance sheets or income accounts. [§ 13(b)]

With the passage of those acts, some thought that the debate over the creation of enforceable standards appeared to be resolved. Why, then, has the search for an appropriate method of standard setting continued? In 1938, the Commission voted (three to two) to accept, in filings, financial statements prepared according to accounting principles for which there was "substantial authoritative support" (ASR 4, FRR § 101). In effect, the SEC turned to the accounting profession to provide leadership in establishing accounting standards. Without this decision, today's accounting standards (for publicly held companies at any rate) would likely be a set of rules established by an agency of the federal government. Although some prefer the clarity of rules – you either follow them or violate them – others see significant dangers in the fact that too often the rules established by many government agencies are arbitrary and the result of political pressure. The 1938 decision of the SEC was both a watershed and a challenge for the accounting profession. The SEC did not abdicate its authority, since at any time it can recast itself as the standard setter, but chose instead to oversee accounting standards as they developed.

The Committeee on Accounting Procedure

The AICPA's Committee on Accounting Procedure (CAP), revitalized and enlarged in 1938, issued pronouncements entitled Accounting Research Bulletins (ARBs). The committee examined specific accounting topics, a procedure criticized as the *piecemeal approach*. Given the economic and social crises of the 1930s, it is doubtful whether the CAP could have developed a broad conceptual framework.

Begining with the fourth ARB, each ARB contained a proviso that it represented "the considered opinion of at least two-thirds of the committee. . . . Except in cases in which formal adoption by the Institute membership has been . . . secured, the authority of the bulletins rests upon the general acceptability of opinions so reached." What little teeth the proviso contained was in these phrases: "It is recognized also that any general rules may be subject to exception; it is felt, however, that the burden of justifying departure from accepted procedures must be assumed by those who adopt other treatment" (ARB 4, p. 36).

Fifty-one ARBs were issued by the committee before its 1959 demise, including ARB 43, which restated and revised those previously issued. In spite of their ambiguous authority, the bulletins did achieve general acceptability.

The Accounting Principles Board

Formation. By the mid-1950s, it was becoming increasingly clear that the process of standard setting needed change. Alvin Jennings, as president of the AICPA, summarized the criticism of the profession as follows:

> We are told that the public finds reports inadequate and insufficent; that stockholders have need for more quality and less quantity; and that it is our reponsibility that it is not possible to compare operating results of companies within a given industry or one industry with another because of the wide choices in accounting methods which are available. [1958, p. 28]

To the extent that Jennings believed such criticisms were valid, he felt that they should be aimed at financial statement preparers as well as attestors. Nonetheless, he did believe that improvements could be made. Thus, a special committee, called the *Powell Committee,* was formed, and it proposed and obtained the creation in 1959 of the APB and an accounting research staff.

Evolving Authority of the APB. Problems beset the APB and the research function from the beginning, and unfortunately, a conceptual framework was not forthcoming. The pronouncement coming closest to being the elusive accounting framework, APB Statement 4, *Basic Concepts and Accounting Principles Underlying Financial Statements of Business Enterprises,* was not issued until October 1970. As the one dissenting board member assessed it, the statement "fails to provide what purports to be a 'basis for guiding the future development of financial accounting.' . . . The Accounting Principles Board is looking backward to what has occurred rather than forward to what is needed" (APB Statement 4, ¶ 105).

In 1964, the AICPA council adopted recommendations that departures from promulgated accounting principles should not only be justified, but should also be *disclosed* in the financial statements or in the auditor's opinion thereon. Three other recommendations also adopted by the council were:

1. "Generally accepted accounting principles" are those principles which have substantial authoritative support.
2. Opinions of the Accounting Principles Board constitute "substantial authoritative support."
3. "Substantial authoritative support" can exist for accounting principles that differ from Opinions of the Accounting Principles Board. [APB 6, Appendix A]

However, it remained unclear what constituted principles having "substantial authoritative support" but which were not set forth in APB opinions.

Suggested as an interim solution at the time (Armstrong, 1969) was a two-level hierarchy: class one consisted of APB opinions, ARBs, SEC rules, AICPA industry audit guides, and, in the absence of these other items, industry practice; class two items (not all of equal weight) ran the gamut from industry regulatory authorities to speeches of prominent spokesmen. Nothing in class two was alone sufficient evidence of authoritative support, but these items could help an accountant make a case.

Rule 203. In 1973, to complete the 1964 council resolutions by making adherence to the disclosure requirements an ethical standard, the AICPA adopted Rule 203 of the Code of Professional Conduct:

> A member shall not express an opinion that financial statements are presented in conformity with generally accepted accounting principles if such statements contain any departure from an accounting principle promulgated by the body designated by Council to establish such principles which has a material effect on the statements taken as a whole, unless the member can demonstrate that due to unusual circumstances the financial statements would otherwise have been misleading. In such cases his report must describe the departure, the approximate effects thereof, if practicable, and the reasons why compliance with the principle would result in a misleading statement. [ET 203.01]

Thus, substantial authoritative support, which had never been successfully pinned down, was removed from the profession's official literature as a basis for departure from authoritative pronouncements. Since Rule 203 has taken effect, rarely has an auditor issued an unqualified report stating that adherence to an authoritative pronouncement would have resulted in misleading financial statements.

SEC Reaffirmation of the Private Sector Role. When Rule 203 was adopted in 1973, standard setting was in the process of passing from the hands of the APB to the FASB, the subject of the next section. In reaffirming the profession's role originally encouraged by ASR 4 in 1938, the Commission said: " . . . principles, standards and practices promulgated by the FASB in its Statements and Interpretations . . . will be considered by the Commission as having substantial authoritative support, and those contrary to such FASB promulgations will be considered . . . to have no such support" (ASR 150, FRR § 101). Oddly enough, just when the profession expunged "substantial authoritative support," the SEC chose to preserve it, because of its fundamental importance as the Commission's rationale for private-sector standard setting.

THE CONCEPT OF THE FASB – STUDY ON ESTABLISHMENT OF ACCOUNTING PRINCIPLES

In March 1971, the AICPA appointed a distinguished group of seven to "find ways for the American Institute of Certified Public Accountants to improve its function of establishing accounting standards" (AICPA, 1972b, p. 87). The group, chaired by Francis M. Wheat, a former Securities and Exchange Commissioner, investigated the accounting standard-setting process then in effect and concluded that the AICPA could best improve its role by relinquishing it. Thus was born the FASB, which began operations in 1973, charged with promulgating and maintaining the standards governing financial accounting and reporting.

Composition and Methodology of the Study Group

The Study on Establishment of Accounting Principles, initiated by the AICPA in 1971, was undertaken to examine the standard-setting process and determine "what changes are necessary to attain better results faster." No holds were barred; the study group was asked to evaluate then-existing suggestions for improvement but also to consider "entirely new approaches," always keeping in mind "the public interest . . . [because] the function of setting accounting principles affects the public" (AICPA, 1972b, p. 87).

In addition to the chairman, Francis Wheat, the study group consisted of three CPAs, an investment banker, an accounting professor, and a financial executive.

The study group met with numerous individuals and organizations and held public hearings. Participants in the hearings were asked to consider the major questions, which had been included in the notice of public hearings. (These questions are listed in Figure 46.1.)

Recommendations for a New Standard-Setting Structure

The study group's final report, *Establishing Financial Accounting Standards,* proposed the structure for standard setting that is in effect today: the FASB. The FASB is actually one arm of the Financial Accounting Foundation, a nonprofit corporation independent of other business and professional organizations. The other arm is the Financial Accounting Standards Advisory Council (FASAC). The foundation is governed by a board of trustees, who appoint members of the FASB and raise funds for its operations. The FASB has full responsibility for the establishment of standards of financial accounting and reporting. FASAC members, also appointed by the trustees, perform a number of advisory functions, including consulting with the FASB to establish priorities.

The shortcomings of the standard-setting process under the APB led the study group to identify criteria essential for the new structure's success. First, the standard-setting body would have to be independent and objective, both in fact and in appearance. As a result, FASB members sever their previous business affiliations, work full time at salaries commensurate with their positions, and observe stringent conflict-of-interest policies.

The study group's second criterion was that the standard-setting process should have broad-based participation. The FASB was launched with the active cooperation

1. **Establishing Accounting Principles: Scope of the Task.**
   What is meant by the term "accounting principles?" Would it be more accurate and useful to refer to "financial accounting and reporting standards?" Should the body with primary responsibility for formulating such standards limit itself to fundamentals, should it develop detailed standards, or should it undertake to do both?

2. **Should The Primary Responsibility for Establishing Accounting Standards Reside in a Governmental Body or a Nongovernmental Body?**
   Should the SEC or another government agency take over the basic task? Or should it remain with a nongovernmental body, such as the Accounting Principles Board? If a nongovernmental body, what should be its relationship to the AICPA? To the SEC? What is the nature of its authority and by what means can its pronouncements be enforced?

3. **Composition of a Nongovernmental Standards Board.**
   Who should serve on the board? Should they all be CPAs? Members of the AICPA? What is the optimum size? In lieu of the present volunteer board, would it be preferable if the chairman, or chairman and some members, or all of the members were paid and served full time? If so, what should be their term of office? What needs to be done about staffing? How should the board be financed?

4. **Methods of Operation of a Nongovernmental Standards Board.**
   The procedures of the Accounting Principles Board have evolved to the point where the board now holds public hearings on subjects for proposed opinions. Are these proceedings satisfactory? How could they be improved? By what vote of its members should a nongovernmental standards board act? Majority? Two thirds? Other? What procedures would enable such a board to take swift action on developing problems? Is the present procedure for obtaining unofficial interpretations of APB opinions satisfactory? If not, how should it be changed? Should there be an appeal procedure? To whom?

5. **Accounting Research Support for a Nongovernmental Standards Board.**
   What sort of research is necessary as a prelude to the establishing of financial accounting standards? Who should conduct it? What guidelines for research studies would improve their quality and shorten the time for their completion? How should accounting research be financed?

FIG. 46.1 Study on Establishment of Accounting Principles: Memorandum of Pertinent Questions
Source: AICPA, Establishing Financial Accounting Standards, Report of the Study Group on Establishment of Accounting Principles, New York, 1972b, pp. 95–96.

of the AICPA, the American Accounting Association, the Financial Executives Institute (FEI), the National Association of Accountants (NAA), and the Financial Analysts Federation. The sponsoring organizations (later expanded to include the Securities Industry Association) not only assist in raising funds for the FASB's operations but also participate in the selection of trustees. Other elements of the structure that help meet this goal of broad-based participation are that

- Members of FASAC represent those interested in financial accounting and reporting matters;
- The number of trustees drawn from the ranks of practicing accountants is limited by quota (four of sixteen, according to the bylaws); and
- Due-process procedures for proposed standards promote widespread involvement.

The third criterion established by the study group was that a small, full-time board would be most efficient. The FASB consists of seven full-time members, in contrast to the APB's eighteen part-time members. The study group viewed the FASB as "small enough to be efficient and large enough to provide for a variety of backgrounds" (AICPA, 1972b, p. 72). A full-time board is also better able to monitor and supervise an expanded research function.

The fourth criterion was that the accounting profession support the new standards board. In May 1973, the council of the AICPA designated the FASB "as the body to establish accounting principles pursuant to Rule 203 of the Rules of the Code of Professional Conduct . . ." (ET Appendix B).

Other Findings of the Study

Before reaching these conclusions, the study group considered whether it was appropriate to leave standard setting in the hands of the private sector. It concluded that four disadvantages of governmental standard setting outweighed its possible advantages: (1) susceptibility to political pressure, (2) inflexibility and lack of responsiveness, (3) damage to the profession's vitality, and (4) extension of government's power over privately held companies and organizations (or, alternatively, two competing sets of accounting standards).

The study group also considered suggestions that a multi-tier structure was needed. Some believed an appeal process for Board decisions was required; others wanted two boards dealing with, respectively, broad concepts and the applications of concepts in practice. The study group, in the belief that these suggestions would "introduce confusion and uncertainty in the system," said that "continuous review of its past pronouncements is a proper function of the Standards Board itself" (AICPA, 1972b, p. 64).

In summary, the study group was satisfied that a standard-setting organization structured according to its recommendations would fulfill the ultimate objective for success: "acceptance of its standards by the business community, practicing accountants, the SEC and the public" (p. 23).

PRESENT ORGANIZATION

An overview of the organization consisting of the Financial Accounting Foundation (FAF), the FASB, the FASAC, the GASB, and the GASAC is shown in Figure 46.2.

Financial Accounting Foundation

The FAF, a nonprofit corporation, is managed by a 16-member board of trustees, which appoints the members of the FASB, GASB, FASAC, and GASAC, arranges for financing, and reviews all operating and project plans. The bylaws of the FAF prohibit the trustees, in the exercise of their oversight duties, from influencing the standard-setting process of the FASB and GASB. (See Chapter 31 for a discussion of GASB.)

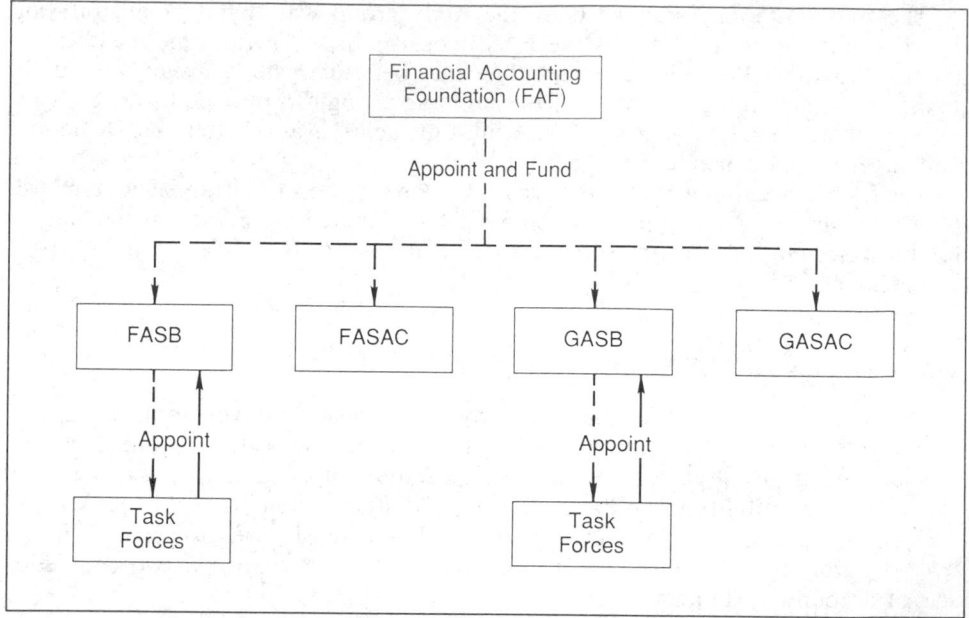

FIG. 46.2 Organization of Financial Accounting Foundation

Trustees are appointed by the various sponsoring organizations of the FAF. Figure 46.3 shows the stipulated composition of the board of trustees.

The FAF (comprising FASB and GASB) requires substantial funding (its 1987 expenses were $12.9 million), which is provided mainly by contributions and sales of publications. The accounting profession provides about one half of the funds contributed, and the balance comes from industry and the financial community.

Financial Accounting Standards Board

The stated mission of the FASB is to establish and improve standards of financial accounting and reporting for the guidance and education of the public, including issuers, auditors, and users of financial information (FASB, 1987b).

To accomplish its mission, the FASB acts to

1. Improve the usefulness of financial reporting by focusing on the primary characteristics of relevance and reliability and on the qualities of comparability and consistency.
2. Keep standards current to reflect changes in methods of doing business and changes in the economic environment.
3. Consider promptly any significant areas of deficiency in financial reporting that might be improved through the standard-setting process.
4. Improve the common understanding of the nature and purposes of information contained in financial reports.

No. of trustees	Required background	Sponsoring organization making the nomination
4	CPAs in public practice when elected	AICPA
2	Financial executives	Financial Executives Institute
1	Financial executive	National Association of Accountants
1	Financial analyst	Financial Analysts Federation
1	Accounting educator	American Accounting Association
1	Investment banker	Securities Industries Association
3	Governmental executives	National governmental associations
3	At large	One selected by principal national association in the banking industry
16		

FIG. 46.3 Trustees of the Financial Accounting Foundation
Adapted from: Financial Accounting Standards Board. Facts About FASB, 1987. *Stamford, CT, 1987b, p. 2.*

The Board follows certain precepts in the conduct of its activities. They are:

- To be objective in its decision making and to ensure, insofar as possible, the neutrality of information resulting from its standards.
- To weigh carefully the views of its constituents in developing concepts and standards.
- To promulgate standards only when the expected benefits exceed the perceived costs.
- To bring about needed changes in ways that minimize disruption to the continuity of reporting practice.
- To review the effects of past decisions and interpret, amend, or replace standards in a timely fashion when such action is indicated.

The Board consists of seven members who come from diverse employment backgrounds, but who are required to have knowledge of accounting, finance, and business and a concern for the public interest in matters of financial accounting and reporting among other attributes. Members serve staggered five-year terms and are eligible for reappointment for one additional consecutive term.

The Board generally deliberates as a group in its Norwalk, Connecticut headquarters in meetings open to the public. (It had been located in Stamford until mid-1988.) Meeting dates and agendas are announced in *Action Alert*, available through subscription, which also contains a brief summary of matters decided at the previous meeting. The Board approves new standards and interpretations by majority vote.

The trustees appoint a member of the FASB as chairman with special responsibilities. The chairman presides at Board meetings and is responsible for preparing the Board's budget and operating and project plans. The chairman has personnel responsibilities too: appointing task force members and hiring technical people for the research and program functions. He also serves as the principal spokesman for the Board.

The research and technical staff reports to the Director of Research and Technical Activities, who in turn reports to the FASB chairman. The staff consists of approximately 40 technical specialists who conduct research, analyze comments received by the Board, lead discussions at Board meetings, and make recommendations to the Board, as well as draft and edit discussion memoranda, exposure drafts, statements, interpretations, technical bulletins, and other FASB documents.

As this *Handbook* goes to press, the present Board members and the expiraton of their terms of service are as follows:

Member	Term Expires December 31
Dennis R. Beresford (Chairman)	1991
Victor H. Brown	1992
Raymond C. Lauver	1993
James J. Leisenring	1989
C. Arthur Northrop	1990
A. Clarence Sampson, Jr.	1992
Robert J. Swieringa	1990

Dennis R. Beresford (Chairman)

Before becoming chairman of the FASB on January 1, 1987, Dennis R. Beresford was national director of accounting standards at Ernst & Whinney. He was a member of AcSEC for six years and served as its chairman for three years. Mr. Beresford also was a member of the EITF and FASAC.

Victor H. Brown

Victor H. Brown joined the FASB in 1983. He was executive vice-president, chief financial officer, and director of The Firestone Tire & Rubber Company. Previously, he was vice-president and controller of Standard Oil Company (Indiana), National Director of Operations of Touche Ross & Co., and chairman of the accounting department at the University of Buffalo.

Raymond C. Lauver

Raymond C. Lauver joined the FASB in 1984. He was national director of accounting services for Price Waterhouse. Mr. Lauver has served as a member and chairman of AcSEC and as a member of the AICPA board of directors.

James J. Leisenring

James J. Leisenring joined the FASB in 1987. He was director of research and technical activities, a position considered equal to that of a Board member although without a vote. Prior to his appointment to that position in 1982, he was partner and director of accounting and auditing in the firm of Bristol, Leisenring, Herkner & Co. Mr. Leisenring was chairman of the ASB for three years.

C. Arthur Northrup

C. Arthur Northrup became a member of the FASB at the beginning of 1986 after serving as controller and then treasurer of IBM Corporation.

A. Clarence Sampson, Jr.

A. Clarence Sampson became a member of the FASB after 28 years with the SEC. He was Chief Accountant of the SEC for nine years prior to joining the FASB.

Robert J. Swieringa

Robert J. Swieringa became a member of the FASB effective January 1, 1986. He was professor of accounting at the Johnson Graduate School of Management at Cornell University and previously was a member of the faculty of the Stanford University Graduate School of Business. He received his Ph.D. from the University of Illinois.

Financial Accounting Standards Advisory Council

The Council consists of no fewer than 20 members appointed by the trustees (currently it has 31 members). The members represent varied professional and occupational backgrounds so as to be broadly representative of preparers, auditors, and users of financial information. Council members customarily serve four years without pay. The chairman is employed by the FAF, and other members serve pro bono.

The council generally meets four times a year and serves several functions:

* *Advisory.* The council advises the FASB on the priorities of competing agenda projects. Individual council members are expected to provide their views on major technical matters and FASB operations. The council, as a body, does not take positions on accounting issues.
* *Communications.* Since council members are usually well-placed within their professions, they are often exposed to a diversity of views held by the various sectors of the Board's constituency. The communication flow works in reverse too; council members keep other influential leaders informed of the Board's progress and its positions on accounting issues.
* *Task force involvement.* Council members advise the FASB on the selection of *task forces*, groups of professional specialists appointed to research major agenda issues. From time to time, council members serve directly on task forces.

The Structure Committee

The bylaws of the FAF require that the "trustees shall ... review periodically the Bylaws of the Foundation and the basic structure of establishing and improving standards of financial accounting and reporting" (FASB, 1987b). During 1982 the Structure Committee of the FAF reviewed the operating efficiency of the FASB and published its findings and recommendations (FAF, 1982). This was the third structure review performed at the FASB; other reviews were conducted in 1977 and 1979. The review focused primarily on the operating efficiency of the Board, including the effectiveness of the Board's due process procedures, the FASB's workload and output, and cost-saving opportunities. The review consisted of both an internal review of the organizational structure and operating procedures of the FASB, and an external review that involved soliciting views of individuals familiar with the operations of the FASB.

The principal conclusion of the Structure Committee's review was that the FASB is operating efficiently and effectively. The committee concluded that the due process procedures followed by the FASB in issuing pronouncements are appropriate. They also concluded that the Board is dealing with the appropriate issues, but there is an additional need for timely guidance on implementation questions and emerging issues that have important financial-reporting implications.

Timely Guidance

In response to the Structure Committee's suggestion, a seven-member task force was appointed to advise the FASB on development of a plan to provide timely guidance for implementation of accounting standards, and on emerging issues that have important financial-reporting implications. That task force was headed by Robert C. Thompson, vice-president of finance of the Shell Oil Company and former chairman of the FEI and the FEI's Committee on Corporate Reporting. The task force was charged with assessing the need for more timely guidance and recommending the best method of furnishing that guidance or solving the problem without diluting the authority of the FASB.

The task force issued its report to the FASB in July 1983 (FASB, 1983b), with two specific recommendations to enhance the Board's ability to deliver timely guidance: (1) expansion of the use of FASB TBs and (2) establishment of an advisory group to assist the Board and its staff in identifying and responding to issues requiring prompt guidance.

In June 1984, the FASB issued TB 79-1 (revised), which modified the scope, purposes, and procedures for issuing TBs (more fully described later under "Technical Bulletins"). The modifications reflected the Board's willingness to follow the Structure Committee's recommendation to expand the scope of TBs and to modify the procedures for issuing them. The modifications included greater involvement of the Board (i.e., considering all proposed TBs and related comments at a public meeting). A TB would not be issued if a majority of the Board disagreed with the guidance provided therein.

The Board also voted to establish, on an experimental basis, an advisory task force to assist the Board in identifying implementation issues and emerging problems. The Board subsequently established the EITF, which consists of representatives from all major public accounting firms plus representatives from the FEI and the NAA. The Chief Accountant of the SEC participates as an observer. The group held its first meeting in July 1984. (More information on the EITF is presented later in this Chapter.)

Size of the Board and Voting

One major issue left open by the Structure Review Committee in its 1982 report was the size of the Board, that is, whether reducing the number of Board members from seven to five would be an appropriate means of improving efficiency and reducing costs. The trustees of the FAF subsequently voted unanimously to retain the seven-member Board and the simple majority voting procedure.

A five-to-two vote was required when the FASB was organized in 1973, but was changed to a simple majority as a result of a review of FASB operations by the FAF Structure Committee in 1977.

Review and Special Committee Reports

A special Review Committee of Trustees of the FAF was appointed in January 1985 to:

1. Commission and administer an independent opinion survey of the attitudes of constituents of the FASB.
2. Review all previous considerations and conduct such additional research as might be deemed necessary regarding the composition of the FASB and backgrounds and qualifications for Board members.
3. Make recommendations regarding any actions to be taken on the criticisms by constituents suggested by information obtained as a result of the Committee's review.
4. Recommend whether a broad study of the standards-setting structure by the Structure Committee of the Board of Trustees or others was needed prior to the comprehensive review the Trustees are committed to undertake in 1988-1989.

The Harris Survey. Louis Harris and Associates conducted the survey of constituents' attitudes about the FASB. In the Survey Report, Harris commented: "At a time when any positive overall rating between 50% and 60% is viewed as unusual and a real measure of success, the rise for the FASB from 73% to 87% positive over the past five years must be considered close to *one of a kind*" (Louis Harris, 1985).

Although he gave the FASB high praise for its overall rating, Harris warned that (1) There is a need to maintain a reasonable balance in standard setting that meets the varied needs and interests of the constituency; (2) the Board must be attentive to those criticisms that are proffered (although admittedly based on minority commentary); and (3) the critics want the Board to do a better job of acting more promptly to correct deficiencies in financial reporting, justifying standards on a cost/benefit notion, and reviewing the effects of past decisions.

Board Composition, Qualifications, and Selection. After its evaluation, the Review Committee commented that for Board members, background experience is a secondary consideration to technical proficiency, and that although a reasonable mix of backgrounds is important (from public accounting, industry, user groups, and academe), experience in public accounting is preferable to experience in business or industry.

Board members should have the following qualifications (as recommended by the Review Committee and adopted by the Trustees):

* *Knowledge of financial accounting and reporting.*
  At least a reasonable level of knowledge and technical competence in financial accounting and reporting, regardless of background.
* *High level of intellect applied with integrity and discipline.*
  Ability to absorb complex information, analyze it objectively, and make lucid decisions about it.
* *Judicial temperament.*
  Ability to consider impartially the evidence on all the many sides of the issues and then to reach a decision.
* *Ability to work in a collegial atmosphere.*
  Participate in group decision-making, which requires give-and-take among the decision makers in order to arrive at timely, workable solutions to problems.

- *Communication skills.*
  Ability to communicate effectively in both oral and written form, including discussion in Board meetings, dialogue with fellow Board members and the technical staff, speeches, and contacts with persons outside the FASB.
- *Awareness of the financial reporting environment.*
  The FASB deals with technical accounting issues, but its decisions must be made in the context of trends and events in the economic community as a whole.
- *Commitment to the FASB's mission.*
  A candidate for membership on the FASB should be committed to the Board's mission as a private-sector, self-regulatory organization and to the hard work required to fulfill it. [FAF, 1986]

The Board member selection process recommended by the Review Committee and adopted by the FAF Trustees is more formalized than in the past. It requires more participation by constituent groups and includes early public announcement of vacancies, a calendar of action steps or events, submission of names for consideration, and identified Selection Committee procedures to be followed.

Other Concerns. The Review Committee identified a number of other constituent concerns that the Committee believed should be addressed. As a result, in December 1985, a Special Committee of FAF Trustees was again appointed. That Committee considered the following criticisms.

Due process and the "sunshine rule" are cumbersome and an impediment to decision-making. After evaluation, it was determined that the Board's due process procedures should *not* be changed. Some believed that criticisms stemmed from a lack of knowledge about the Board's process. As a result, the Board has undertaken to provide more communication to constituents about the process.

A low level of participation by users and corporate chief executive officers in the FASB process. The Board's plan to increase users' participation includes: (1) expanding the speechmaking process, (2) permitting "unreimbursed" (i.e., no fees charged) speaking engagements by Board members, and (3) increasing liaison group contacts. For chief executive officers (CEOs) the plan includes: (1) increasing the circulation of the FASB's Status Report, (2) greater use of "personalized" letters, (3) attempting to use regional and industry CEO groups, and (4) encouraging the Trustees to elect CEOs to the FAF Board of Trustees and FASAC.

Small business problems with GAAP (standards overload). The Board has considered small businesses in establishing accounting standards, and will continue to do so. Different treatment of small businesses will depend on:

1. Whether the different treatment would alleviate "standards overload" or contribute to it by providing two solutions instead of one.
2. Whether a proposed solution would enhance or diminish the credibility of financial reporting.

3. Whether there is persuasive evidence that user needs are different for different entities or that the costs outweigh the benefits.

4. Whether there is a difference in the economic basis of a transaction for different entities. [FAF, 1986]

The danger of the EITF establishing de facto accounting standards. The Trustees apparently do not believe that the EITF establishes de facto accounting standards. The EITF's role is described as identifying and suggesting solutions to problems. However, some believe that establishing EITF "consensus" positions that the SEC staff has stated will be enforced by the SEC is indeed establishment of de facto GAAP by the EITF. On balance, the EITF has helped to solve a vexing problem concerning speed of solutions to emerging accounting problems, and the system appears to be working.

The Board doesn't seem to adequately address cost vs. benefit considerations. The Board will continue to attempt to better articulate its views on the costs and benefits of standards. However, some believe that this criticism can never be completely answered. Measuring the benefits of accounting standards is almost an intuitive process. There is no practical way to measure benefit, and the problem has been exacerbated by the lack of user responses to all Board proposals. There are simply few, if any, user groups that are sufficiently organized or technically well versed to provide the Board with any meaningful data about the benefits of proposed standards.

The Report also discusses the need to continue to attract technically competent people for the Board's staff, the structure and role of FASAC, and the structure and role of the FAF.

Conclusion. The Special Review Committee concluded that it believes the FASB structure is working satisfactorily and that there is no need for any further review of FASB activities until the required comprehensive review in 1988–1989.

THE STANDARD-SETTING PROCESS

The FASB's innovative structure is underscored by extensive due-process procedures set forth in the Rules of Procedure.

Identification of Issues

Accounting issues and problems are brought to the Board's attention from virtually every segment of its constituency: public accounting firms, the SEC, business and nonprofit organizations, the AICPA, other trade and professional associations, governmental units, academicians, and occasionally, the U.S. Congress. Some matters are pervasive; Board decisions in these areas might ultimately affect the accounting and reporting practices of a significant segment of the economy. Most are narrower; a company might question the applicability of a particular standard (or guideline within a standard) to a single transaction. Occasionally, fresh issues evolve from innovative methods of financing or conducting trade. Others involve long-standing problems such as consolidation practices or accounting for financial instruments. Paradoxically, even solutions generate new issues as evidenced by SFAS 13, *Accounting for Leases* (L10), and the subsequent implementation questions that were raised by financial statement preparers and attestors (see Chapter 19).

No rules can be set out for determining whether a problem requires Board attention. Usually issues have many elements, and even a narrow question can point out an inadvertent omission or flaw in a standard that requires correction. Further, the Board itself actively seeks to identify accounting issues; it does so by maintaining liaisons with other organizations (e.g., the SEC, GASB, AICPA) and by monitoring the application of its standards in practice.

Agenda Setting

The Board's agenda consists of projects that the Board has approved for further development and consideration. In selecting major projects, the Board will consult with its own technical staff, the FASAC, the EITF, and other organizations.

Selecting agenda projects is a critical step in the process. In addition to weighing the demand on its own resources, the Board considers a number of factors in selecting a project for its agenda. The issue's perceived urgency and the pervasiveness of the problem are obviously important, but so is its interrelationship with other projects under consideration. There are practical aspects to a proper mesh: Does the estimated timing for the proposed project conflict with higher-priority issues? Is qualified staff available? There are also theoretical aspects to a proper mesh: Does the proposed project complement, amplify, or otherwise relate to existing agenda topics?

Task Forces

Early in the life of major Board projects, an advisory task force of outside experts is usually appointed.

Task forces represent the diversity of views surrounding issues. Specifically, a task force will advise and consult with the Board on

- Definition of the problem and scope of the project
- Additional research needed
- Preparation of a discussion memorandum
- Preparation of an exposure draft
- Ways in which an exposure draft might be revised
- Other matters on which the Board seeks guidance

The task force exists until a final standard is issued or a decision is made to drop the project or include it in another project. It may be reconvened if the standard is subsequently reviewed or implementation problems arise.

Discussion Memoranda and Research Projects

Under the Rules of Procedure, the Board generally issues a *discussion memorandum* for major projects. A discussion memorandum defines the problem and the scope of the project, presents alternative solutions and their implications, and solicits written comments from interested parties. The document is neutral—no single solution is favored over others. (An *invitation to comment* may also be used; the responses may assist the Board in deciding whether to proceed with a project.)

Normally, respondents are asked to consider and evaluate all the issues outlined in discussion memoranda and to consider the potential economic consequences and the implementation costs of the solutions advocated. Discussion memoranda contain a bibliography and often a less technical summary of the issues to help readers explore the problem.

The Board sometimes commissions agenda-related research projects conducted by the Board's technical staff or outside consultants, usually academics. If a research project is conducted at this point in the process, its results are incorporated in the discussion memorandum. The Board also commissions research projects to evaluate the consequences of its own standards following their release.

Public Hearings on Financial Accounting Standards

At public hearings the project issues receive an open airing. Like discussion memoranda, these hearings are not mandatory, although the Board has always held them in connection with important projects. The Board listens to oral presentations and will often explore a participant's view through questions. These sessions are announced well in advance in the Board's newsletter, *Status Report*, and the financial press. Anyone can make a presentation, but written summaries of presentations are required in advance.

Comment Letters

Although public hearings provide for a direct interchange between the Board (and its staff) and interested parties, most of the input to the Board on a project is received in comment letters. They are considered individually by Board members (even when many virtually identical letters are received because an affected association urges its members to "cast their votes") and are carefully analyzed by the staff.

Deliberations

After accumulating information through staff research, task force investigation, responses to discussion memoranda, and presentations at public hearings, the Board begins to digest it. The volume of data can be staggering; for example, in response to the discussion memorandum that culminated in SFAS 15, *Accounting by Debtors and Creditors for Troubled Debt Restructurings*, the Board received 895 comment letters. Further, the technical staff, the task force, and the FASAC all respond to the Board's requests for further facts and viewpoints as deliberations continue.

The goal of the deliberation step is to produce a proposed standard known as an *exposure draft*. The staff responds to Board suggestions and modifies successive (or alternative) drafts of a proposed statement as deliberations continue. Until approved as an exposure draft, drafts are not available to the general public. However, meetings of the Board (with rare exception) are public, as are task force and FASAC meetings. In addition, a brief summary of matters discussed at FASB meetings is reported in the FASB publication, *Action Alert*. Attendees at these meetings do not have floor privileges unless specifically granted by the chairman.

The deliberation process can be lengthy, since viewpoints of individual Board members may change based on new facts and perceptions; changes in Board membership can also affect the direction of a project in process.

Exposure Drafts

An exposure draft is intended to be a nearly final standard, but, as a proposal, it is often modified before becoming a binding requirement. Both exposure drafts and final standards are required by the bylaws to contain a statement of the standard, an effective date, background information, and the basis for the Board's conclusions. The basis for conclusions includes the reasons behind the Board's choice of certain alternatives; it is an extremely valuable tool in understanding the standard itself. (It also helps accountants explain to reluctant clients or superiors the reason for the proposed or final standard.) The bylaws require proposed statements to be exposed for public comment—normally for at least 60 days, but that may be shortened to not less than a 30-day period if the Board decides a shorter period is necessary. Often there is the mistaken impression that the Board's position is solidified by the time an exposure draft is released and that the exposure process is merely a formality. This is rarely true. The Board will reevaluate its conclusions in further deliberations as members respond to new facts and arguments that surface in the wide range of comments received.

An exposure draft may be issued without any prior discussion memoranda or hearings, if the Board considers the matter urgent.

Statements of Financial Accounting Standards

After further deliberation, the Board approves a final SFAS by majority vote. Besides whatever modifications are made to the exposure draft, a final statement differs from it in two respects:

1. The standard becomes part of GAAP whenever the standard's stipulated effective date is reached. If the standard is pervasive, the Board will allow sufficient time between the issue and effective dates so that companies can prepare for adoption.
2. A final standard identifies dissenting members and summarizes their arguments. The complexity of major Board projects virtually assures that one or more of the seven members will dissent.

Postenactment Review

Just as business adapts to changing conditions, the rules of financial accounting and reporting must also be refined or reconsidered. To this end, SFASs are reviewed by the Board in response to requests from constitutents or at the Board's own initiative. In May 1978, as a formal agenda project, the Board invited the public to comment on FASB statements that had been in effect for at least two years (SFASs 1–12). This exercise has not been repeated. It appears that problems have had a way of making themselves known without taking a census. The EITF is very instrumental in identifying new problems with prior statements.

As a result of the previously mentioned project, SFAS 8, *Accounting for the Translation of Foreign Currency Transactions and Foreign Currency Financial Statements*, received a barrage of criticism. The Board decided to reconsider it and, as a result, in December 1981, issued SFAS 52, *Foreign Currency Translation* (F60).

Thus, the standard-setting process is actually circular. It does not end when a standard is released; instead, as envisioned by the Wheat Committee, the final standard itself becomes eligible for consideration as an accounting issue and the process begins anew.

Other Pronouncements

The Board issues pronouncements other than SFASs, and the extent of the due-process procedures used varies depending on the significance of the matter.

Statements of Financial Accounting Concepts. SFACs do not establish new standards or require any change in the application of existing accounting principles, but are intended to provide guidance in solving problems. Because of their long-range importance, SFACs are developed under the same extensive due-process procedures the FASB must follow in developing SFASs on major topics. (See Chapter 2.)

Amendments. Amendments are actually SFASs, not a separate class of pronouncements, and thus are equally binding. Most amendments are not the result of major Board projects; usually they expand the original pronouncement to cover situations omitted, or they resolve unforeseen conflicts between two pronouncments. Due-process procedures applied to amendments are usually more expeditious.

Interpretations. Interpretations explain, clarify, or elaborate on existing pronouncements. They are usually issued when clarification is needed as to how the original statement's conclusions apply to a specific type of transaction. Most interpretations are issued using abbreviated due-process procedures, and have the same authority as statements.

Technical Bulletins. TBs issued by the FASB staff may address issues not directly covered by existing standards and may provide guidance that differs, for particular situations, from the general application required by existing pronouncements. Generally, guidance can be provided in a TB if it is not expected to cause a major change in practice for a significant number of companies, if the cost of implementation is not expected to be significant, and if the guidance does not conflict with a broad fundamental accounting principle or create a novel accounting practice. Proposed TBs must be discussed by the Board in a public meeting prior to distribution for public comment. The comments received on proposed Bulletins must also be discussed by the Board in a public meeting prior to the issuance of a final TB. A TB may not be issued if a majority of the Board members object to the guidance in it or object to communicating that guidance by means of a TB.

Because they can be issued with the least due process, TBs appear to have become the medium of choice for miscellaneous matters, in preference to interpretations and amendments. The Board has concluded that TBs may be used to correct unintended consequences of requirements shown in SFASs, even if this requires rewriting some passages in the original. A good example is TB 84-4, dealing with in-substance defeasance of debt (D14.507–.510).

Expanding the Process

As the discussion of standard setting makes clear, the Board is constantly faced with the question of which issues deserve its attention and resources. The Board is inclined to deal with pervasive topics, rather than to delve into accounting problems of particular industries or other issues of more limited scope. This gap in standard setting has created problems: companies in the same industry sometimes account for similar transactions in diverse ways, and they and their auditors cannot state that one method above others constitutes *the* GAAP.

AICPA Pronouncements and Documents. To help bridge the gap between pervasive and narrower issues, the Accounting Standards Division of the AICPA issues various pronouncements and guidance including Audit and Accounting Guides, Statements of Position, Practice Bulletins, and Issues Papers. The views expressed in these documents are not enforceable standards to be adhered to by members under Rule 203 of the AICPA's Code of Professional Conduct, although they do constitute recognized sources of GAAP when there is nothing available in authoritative pronouncements (see AU 411.05–.08). One objective, however, is to provide guidance to influence judgments on accounting issues not otherwise covered in authoritative literature. Another objective is to influence the form and content of pronouncements of the FASB, the GASB, and other bodies having authority over accounting standards. In this regard, accounting and reporting recommendations included in the AICPA publications mentioned above are subject to disposition by the FASB and the GASB. AICPA issues papers are usually outstanding for years before FASB action is taken. In 1987, the FASB requested that AcSEC refrain from including tentative conclusions in issues papers, as such conclusions tend to become implemented in practice and present difficulties when the FASB ultimately decides to address the matter. AcSEC has acceded, reluctantly, to this request. (See Chapter 45 for more information on AICPA pronouncements.)

The Emerging Issues Task Force. The EITF, as discussed previously in the "Timely Guidance" section of this chapter, also helps bridge the gap between the pervasive and narrow issues. The EITF not only helps identify implementation issues and emerging problems, it also attempts to reach a consensus of the group regarding the proper accounting treatment for each of them.

Issues Grouped by Type	
Income taxes	23
Financial institutions	29
Financial instruments	47
Off-balance-sheet financing	12
Pensions/employee benefits	13
Business combinations	20
Inventory/fixed assets/leases	12
Real estate	7
Other	19
Total	182

Issues have been classified on a broad basis in one category; however, an issue may involve matters relevant to several categories.

FIG. 46.4 EITF Issues Grouped by Type

Disposition of Issues	
Resolved by the FASB	23
Resolved by the SEC	4
Resolved by the AICPA	2
FASB staff work in progress	3
AICPA committee work in progress	1
Issue to be addressed within an existing FASB major project	6
Consensus was reached on the accounting	110
No resolution	22
Further discussion by the Task Force is pending	11
Total	182

FIG. 46.5 Disposition of EITF Issues

The EITF has been prolific during its relatively short life. It has dealt with 182 issues of diverse nature through mid-1988. A summary of the types and disposition of these issues are presented in Figures 46.4 and 46.5.

In areas of diverse accounting practice or areas in which practice has not been previously established, an EITF consensus has been looked upon as preferable practice. There is concern that EITF consensus positions that are not intended to be formal standards nevertheless become de facto standards. The SEC has made it clear that it considers these consensus positions to be preferable accounting practice. Many people believe that the EITF has led to a narrowing of diversity in practice and that it therefore performs a beneficial role in the profession.

In a number of instances, the FASB staff has issued TBs on issues raised by the EITF. In addition, in a few instances, the Board has covered issues in SFASs. Discussion of significant EITF issues are included in the *Handbook* chapters to which the issues relate.

CURRENT DEVELOPMENTS

The FASB is in its second decade of standards-setting activities. During the 14 years since its inception in 1973, the FASB has issued 95 SFASs, 6 SFACs, 38 Interpretations, and 44 TBs. A complete listing of these releases is included in the Major Accounting and Auditing Pronouncements section at the end of this *Handbook*.

The Board's production appears staggering. Considering the numbers of documents produced, it is not surprising that the cry of "standards overload" has intensified. But numbers are deceiving. Among the 98 SFASs are 16 that have been superseded by subsequent FASB statements. In addition, 11 statements have been issued that extract the substance of prior AICPA SOPs and industry guides with little or no change. These statements simply formalized guidance that had previously existed in practice. Besides these 27 statements, 2 statements make the provisions of certain AICPA industry guides and SOPs preferable for purposes of making an accounting change, and 11 statements, 6 interpretations, and 9 TBs relate to leasing standards. In other cases, a number of Board pronouncements amend or interpret previous literature (ARBs, APBs, and SFASs).

In summary, it appears that perhaps half of the pronouncements the Board has produced provide significant substance concerning matters changed from, or previously not considered in, earlier Board pronouncements. It is interesting that the FASB Current Text contains material on 45 general subjects and 26 special industry subjects and some of these subjects are governed by accounting standards issued long before anyone even thought of an FASB.

In the view of some observers, the standards overload lament is an emotional reaction to a phenomenon that is a product of our business world as it becomes more complex day by day. Unless all parties interested in financial reporting are willing to rationally apply broad general accounting principles (and the evidence of such willingness is sparse), numerous and detailed accounting standards will continue to be promulgated by the FASB.

Continuing Major Projects

Consolidation and the Equity Method. This project has three phases. The first phase will develop a concept of reporting entity and deal with related conceptual matters and apply those concepts, together with those in the Board's concept statements (SFACs 1–6), to reach conclusions on the broad issue of consolidation policy. Also covered will be consolidation technique. While continuing to consider the concept of a reporting entity, the Board concluded that enough progress had been made to proceed with the latter part of the first phase. As a result, in October 1987, the Board issued SFAS 94, *Consolidation of All Majority-Owned Subsidiaries (C51)* amending ARB 51, *Consolidated Financial Statements* (C51). The statement requires consolidation of *all* majority-owned subsidiaries, and is effective for fiscal years ending after December 15, 1988. A discussion document on the concept of reporting entity is expected in 1988. (See Chapter 24.)

Stock Compensation Plans. In March 1984, the Board added a reconsideration of APB 25, *Accounting for Stock Issued to Employees* (C47), to its agenda. An Invitation to Comment, *Accounting for Compensation Plans Involving Certain Rights Granted to Employees* (FASB, 1984a) was issued in May 1984. The Board is currently addressing the issues in the Invitation to Comment. Although the Board has reached some tentative conclusions about measurement date and methods of valuation, the staff continues to perform research on the project. When that research is completed, the Board will address the timetable for an exposure draft, public hearing, and the final statement. (See Chapter 20.)

Financial Instruments. In May 1986 the FASB added to its agenda a project on financial instruments and off-balance-sheet financing. An initial and interim objective will be to improve disclosures about financial instruments and transactions, both for market prices and other information about items now carried in balance sheets, and for obligations, commitments, and guarantees not now recognized in balance sheets. An exposure draft was issued in late 1987 (FASB, 1987a) with a final statement due late in 1988 (but expected to be postponed). The FASB decided that recognition and measurement problems should be approached through several separate, although related, questions to be considered later in the project. One or more discussion documents will be issued commencing in 1988 about recognition, hedging, and other transfers of market and credit risk, and measurement of financial assets and liabilities and transactions. (See Chapter 21.)

Postemployment Benefits Other Than Pensions. From 1981 through 1983, employers' accounting for postemployment benefits other than pensions was considered by the Board as part of the project on employers' accounting for pensions and other postemployment benefits. Two discussion memorandums and a preliminary views document were issued during that period. In February 1984, the Board decided to consider postemployment benefits other than pensions in a project separate from the pensions project. Research indicated that the cost of other postemployment benefits is significant for some companies and that very few companies were disclosing information about those costs in their financial statements. Accordingly, in November 1984 the Board issued SFAS 81, *Disclosure of Postretirement Health Care and Life Insurance Benefits* (P50), requiring certain disclosures about postretirement life insurance and health care benefits in notes to employers' financial statements. Requiring those disclosures is viewed as an interim step pending completion of the Board's study of the measurement and recognition issues and issuance of a final statement on accounting for the cost of postretirement benefits other than pensions.

The Board has tentatively concluded that postretirement health care benefits represent a form of deferred compensation and that an obligation should be recognized based on services rendered.

An exposure draft is scheduled for late 1988, and a public hearing is planned for early 1989 with issuance of a final Statement expected late in 1989. (See Chapter 16.)

Not-For-Profit Organizations. In March 1986, the Board added a project to its agenda addressing two standards issues: the recognition of depreciation by all not-for-profit organizations and accounting for contributions. The project is considering the specialized accounting principles and practices included in the AICPA Industry Audit and Accounting Guides, *Audits of Certain Nonprofit Organizations* (including SOP 78-10, *Accounting Principles and Reporting Practices for Certain Nonprofit Organizations*), *Audits of Colleges and Universities, Audits of Voluntary Health and Welfare Organizations,* and *Hospital Audit Guide.*

The project addressing the applicability of depreciation accounting to all not-for-profit organizations was completed in August 1987 when the Board issued SFAS 93, *Recognition of Depreciation by Not-For-Profit Organizations.*

Subsequently the FASB decided that the effective date for SFAS 93 should be deferred until fiscal years beginning on or after January 1, 1990 (extended from May 15, 1988). An exposure draft of an amendment to SFAS 93 was released in mid-1988 (FASB, 1988a). The decision was taken in light of the current efforts of the FAF to establish an acceptable jurisdictional arrangement (i.e. FASB versus GASB) for the separately issued financial statements of colleges and universities and other similarly affected entities. (See Chapter 32.)

The part of the project addressing contributions involves studying recognition and measurement issues associated with receiving or making contributions (restricted or unrestricted) or pledges for future contributions of cash or other goods or services. Currently, most of the Audit Guides suggest that pledges receivable be recognized as assets; however, the Guides and practice differ regarding the timing for recognition of pledges and of the related revenues. This project is considering those specialized principles, measurement of donated nonmonetary assets and services, and recognition of a liability by the grantor of a pledge.

An exposure draft addressing accounting for contributions is expected to be issued late in 1988.

47

Securities and Exchange Commission

ORIGIN

In over 50 years of existence, the SEC has been an integral part of the financial reporting environment in the United States. While there are widely diverse views regarding its effectiveness, and while its level of activity has varied considerably, there is no doubt that its aggregate impact on accounting and auditing since it was created in 1934 has been greater than any other single institution.

The Commission emerged from legislation enacted in the first years of the New Deal and was designed to provide protection to investors and to prevent abuses that were widely felt to have led to the stock market boom and speculative excesses of the late 1920s and the stock market crash of 1929 that followed.

1933 and 1934 Acts

The first major legislation to emerge from this effort was the *Securities Act of 1933* (1933 Act). The 1933 Act prescribed the disclosures that had to be made to investors in connection with sales of new securities by corporations. It also dramatically increased the legal obligation of those who sold securities and of accountants and underwriters who performed services in connection with the sale. The 1933 Act placed reponsibility for its administration on the Federal Trade Commission (FTC).

New issue disclosure was only a small part of the perceived problem, however, and in 1934, Congress and the administration focused on the capital markets by passing the Securities Exchange Act of 1934 (1934 Act). The 1934 Act created the SEC to oversee the securities markets and vested the Commission with broad authority to make rules regulating broker-dealers, stock exchanges, and disclosures by listed companies. At the same time, the 1933 Act was amended to give the SEC the powers previously assigned to the FTC.

These two acts represent the basic securities legislation in effect in the United States today. They have been amended on several occasions, but the basic regulatory framework remains intact. In 1964, the securities of companies traded in the over-the-counter market were made subject to the provisions of the 1934 Act. In addition, the Foreign Corrupt Practices Act of 1977 amended the 1934 Act to:

1. Require that issuers keep books and records that accurately reflect company transactions and asset dispositions;
2. Require that issuers maintain a system of internal accounting control that:
    a. Assures proper execution of authorized transactions,
    b. Permits preparation of financial statements in accordance with GAAP and maintains accountability for assets,
    c. Assures that access to assets occurs only with management authorization, and
    d. Assures that the recorded accountability for assets is compared to existing assets at reasonable intervals; and
3. Prohibit falsification of accounting records.

Other Acts

During the 1920s, interlocking holding companies controlled a large part of the country's utility investment through complex pyramidal structures. The economic depression of the 1930s resulted in chaos in utility financing, and the pyramidal structures accentuated the impact. Thus, in 1935, the Public Utility Holding Company Act gave the Commission the authority to oversee the reorganization and simplification of public utility holding companies.

In 1939, the Trust Indenture Act was passed, which established certain requirements for trustees under indenture agreements between security issuers and holders of the securities; the Commission was given authority to administer this statute.

In 1940, the Commission's authority was extended to include investment companies and investment advisers. The Investment Company Act of 1940 gave the Commission direct regulatory authority over all investment companies, including their organization, business practices, and financial reporting. At the same time, the Investment Advisers Act gave the Commission power to require the registration of investment advisers and a certain, very limited regulatory authority over such advisers.

In addition to the responsibilities set forth in the securities laws, the Commission is given certain responsibilities and authority under federal bankruptcy laws. The SEC may enter bankruptcy proceedings to protect public investors and may advise the court on the fairness of reorganization plans in major bankruptcies.

ORGANIZATION OF THE COMMISSION

Commissioners and Staff

The Commission is made up of five commissioners appointed by the President of the United States and confirmed by the Senate. Each commissioner is appointed for a five-year term, and one term expires on June 5 each year. If a commissioner does not serve out his term, his successor is appointed to complete the unfinished term. No more than three commissioners may be members of the same political party at any time.

One of the commissioners is designated as chairman by the President and serves as chairman at the President's pleasure. His term as commissioner, however, is not subject to termination by the President. Thus when there is a change of administrations from one major party to the other, it is common for there to be a change in the chairman, but not a complete turnover of commissioners.

All commissioners have an equal vote on matters before the Commission but the chairman exercises a disproportionate influence in most cases both through his control of the Commission's agenda and by the power he has as presiding officer at meetings. In addition, the chairman serves as chief executive officer of the Commission and hence maintains control over budgets and staff appointments. An overwhelming majority of commissioners have been lawyers by training, while a much smaller number have been accountants.

The regulatory activities of the Commission are carried on through four operating divisions, four staff offices, nine regional offices, and two offices concerned with the Commission's judicial activities. These groups are collectively known as the SEC staff.

Operating Divisions

Corporation Finance. The Division of Corporation Finance has the basic responsibility for administering the disclosure policy of the Commission. It is responsible for maintaining the files of registration statements and 1934 Act reports (e.g., Form

10-K), which are the basic raw materials of the Commission's responsibility to assure adequate disclosure.

There are a few groups in the division that handle specialized projects and problems, for example, disclosure for oil and gas industries and disclosure problems of small business (reflecting the Commission's concern that its requirements not represent a major detriment to small business in raising capital in the public markets).

Enforcement. The Division of Enforcement has responsibility for surveillance over the capital markets and the investigation of possible violations of law. When the Division, based on a preliminary investigation, believes that a violation has occurred, it may obtain from the Commission an order of investigation, which permits it to subpoena records and take testimony under oath. After completing its investigation, the Enforcement Division reports to the Commission with a recommendation as to what action if any should be taken, and the Commission determines the next step.

In its enforcement actions in court, the Commission normally seeks an injunction prohibiting the continuation of violative behavior or a similar violation in the future. Such an injunction, if granted, exposes violators to both civil and criminal contempt actions if they continue their behavior. In addition, the Commission may obtain, as part of a settlement, other forms of "ancillary relief" to assure that the public will be protected from future violations and that violators will not profit from their activities.

Although the Commission frequently prosecutes civil actions to their conclusion, far more commonly the defendants seek a settlement with the Commission. In such cases, the Commission enters into *consent decrees*, under which those accused, without admitting or denying the violation, agree not to engage in proscribed activities and frequently also agree to specific sanctions. These may include the refund of profits made in connection with the activity in question, the agreement to surrender control of an enterprise, the secession from practice before the Commission by independent public accountants, and other remedies as appropriate in particular cases.

The Commission does not have the power to bring criminal actions under the law. When investigations suggest that there are violations of law sufficiently serious to warrant a criminal action, the Commission normally refers the case to the Department of Justice for prosecution. Staff of the Enforcement Division commonly work with U.S. attorneys when the Department of Justice decides to prosecute.

Market Regulation. The Division of Market Regulation is responsible for regulating the securities trading markets, including the national market system brought into operation in 1975.

Investment Management. The Division of Investment Management has the responsibility for regulating the mutual fund industry and investment advisers. It processes filings by companies that operate in these areas, and it establishes rules covering business practices in this industry.

Staff Offices

Chief Accountant. The Chief Accountant of the SEC has the basic responsibility of advising the Commission on all accounting matters and has direct responsibility for Regulation S-X, which describes the form and content of financial statements filed with the Commission. He also has primary responsibility for FRRs and for maintaining liaison with the accounting profession (including designation as observer at meetings of the EITF and with the FASB. He advises the Commission on enforcement matters relating to professional accountants and accounting and reporting matters, and he also serves as a spokesman for the Commission's accounting policies in public forums.

The Chief Accountant serves as a consultative resource on specific questions relating to registrants' accounting and auditing problems referred to his office by the Divisions of Corporation Finance and Enforcement; he often meets with registrants and their independent accountants to discuss significant issues affecting the registrant's financial statements.

In addition, the Chief Accountant is an invited observer at EITF meetings, and almost always attends; if he is unable to attend an SEC staff member will take his place. The Chief Accountant sometimes refers issues to the EITF; and he takes the opportunity to state SEC staff views at EITF meetings. In this forum, he is able to uniformly communicate with senior technical partners of the Big Eight accounting firms as well as other influential parties.

General Counsel. The General Counsel is the SEC's chief legal officer and adviser and is deeply involved with virtually all of the Commission's rule-making initiatives that have legal implications. The General Counsel provides legal advice to other divisions and offices, is the principal litigator of the Commission, and is responsible for developing statements of the SEC's legal position that are filed by the Commission as *amicus curiae.*

Economic and Policy Research. The Directorate of Economic and Policy Research is directed by the Chief Economist of the Commission. His role is to advise the Commission on economic policy matters. The Directorate gathers and regularly publishes economic data about the marketplace, and it has participated in numerous studies of the Commission's policies.

Regional Offices

The SEC has nine regional offices, located in New York, Boston, Atlanta, Chicago, Fort Worth, Denver, Los Angeles, Philadelphia, and Seattle. There are branch offices in Detroit, Houston, San Francisco, Miami, and Salt Lake City. The regional offices play an important role in surveillance over securities activities in their areas. Their largest function is to decentralize enforcement. They conduct investigations, bring injunctive actions, and generally undertake the same activities as the Division of Enforcement does on a national basis.

Judicial Offices

Opinions and Review. The Office of Opinions and Review drafts the Commission's formal opinions in the cases brought before it. This office also must explain the Commission's reasoning and relate current decisions to previously established precedents.

Administrative Law Judges. The Office of Administrative Law Judges hears cases presented by the Division of Enforcement and other divisions. The administrative law judge is the first level of judicial review for most cases, and he makes the initial findings of fact and decisions on legal issues. The judges' decisions may be appealed to the Commission and subsequently to the Federal Court of Appeals.

SEC POLICY ON ACCOUNTING MATTERS

Specific Accounting Authority

The 1933 Act gives the Commission specific statutory authority to prescribe principles of accounting and reporting. Section 19 of the Act provides:

> Among other things, the Commission shall have authority . . . to prescribe the items or details to be shown in the balance sheet and earning statement, and the methods to be followed in the preparation of accounts, in the appraisal or valuation of assets and liabilities, in the determination of depreciation and depletion, in the differentiation of recurring and non-recurring income . . . and in the preparation . . . of consolidated balance sheets or income accounts.

In addition, the Commission has been given authority in Section 13 of the 1934 Act to prescribe procedures for periodic accounting and reporting to the Commission.

Responsibility in the Private Sector

While the Commission has virtually unlimited statutory authority to set accounting principles, as a matter of policy it has used this authority sparingly. The SEC's basic policy decision not to undertake the establishment of accounting principles was made in 1938 with the issuance of ASR 4 (FRR § 101). That release provided that financial statements filed with the Commission that were prepared in accordance with accounting principles for which there was no *substantial authoritative support* would be presumed to be misleading. The concept of substantial authoritative support was used to encourage the accounting profession to establish standards narrowing the areas of difference in accounting practices. The American Institute of Accountants (later renamed the AICPA) created the Committee on Accounting Procedure in response to this initiative, followed in turn by the Accounting Principles Board in 1958 and the FASB in 1972. (See Chapter 46 for discussion of the history and activities of those standard-setting bodies.)

In 1972, the Commission reiterated its policy of reliance on the private sector, in ASR 150 (FRR § 101). Noting its long-standing policy of looking to bodies designated by the accounting profession to provide leadership in establishing and improving accounting principles, the SEC endorsed the establishment of the FASB "in the belief that the Board would provide an institutional framework which will permit prompt and responsible actions flowing from research and consideration of varying viewpoints." FRR § 101 acknowledges the experience and expertise of the members of the FASB and the commitment of resources to it as "impressive evidence of the willingness and intention of the private sector to support the FASB in accomplishing its task" and notes that the SEC intends to "continue its policy of looking to the private sector for leadership in establishing and improving accounting principles and standards through the FASB with the expectation that the body's conclusions will promote the interests of investors."

The conclusions of FRR § 101 express the SEC's policy that "principles, standards and practices promulgated by the FASB in its statements and interpretations will be considered by the Commission as having substantial authoritative support and those contrary to such FASB promulgations will be considered to have no such support."

This policy was challenged in court by Arthur Andersen & Co. on the grounds that the policy constituted an illegal delegation of authority to the FASB. The court rejected Andersen's request for a temporary injunction, noting that the plaintiff had little likelihood of succeeding on the merits of the case. Subsequently the case was dismissed for lack of standing. While this is less than a complete judicial endorsement of the Commission's policy, one court certainly was not convinced that the Commission's policy was illegal.

Subsequent to the issuance of ASR 150, substantial questions were raised as to the desirability of the policy in hearings before the Metcalf and other subcommittees of Congress. These committees in the end did not formally criticize the Commission's judgment, and in its annual reports to Congress on its oversight role, the SEC has reiterated its policy as being responsive to the interests of investors.

Oversight and Occasional Overruling

The Commission has steadfastly maintained its general policy of reliance on the private sector for accounting standards setting; nevertheless, it has not adopted a totally passive role. The Commission's oversight responsibilities necessitate a close working relationship with standard-setting bodies so that each is fully aware of the views of the other. Both organizations seek to avoid confrontation that could result in the deterioration of the relationship, a policy frequently referred to as "mutual nonsurprise."

The degree of cooperation between the bodies has varied substantially over time. On occasion, the standard-setting body has worked virtually as a partner with the Commission staff in drafting opinions, so that the input of the SEC staff was direct and substantial. At other times, the private-sector standard-setting body has kept the SEC at a distance, discussing pronouncements with the staff only in general terms prior to their issuance. However, friction between the two bodies has been rare.

On a few occasions, the Commission has expressed itself strongly on what accounting principles it would consider acceptable in certain areas, and in most of those cases, the standard-setter has accepted that judgment. In addition, on a few occasions, the SEC has requested a solution to a particular problem, both parties knowing that the Commission would be compelled to act if the standard-setter did not.

There have also been a few occasions in which the Commission overruled the actions of the standard-setting body. The first of these occurred when the SEC declined to support the APB's 1962 decision (APB 2) on how to account for investment credit.

In addition, the Commission overruled SFAS 19 (Oi5) on accounting in the oil and gas industry. In 1975, when Congress directed the SEC to determine the best method of accounting in the oil and gas producing industry, the Commission asked the FASB to develop its conclusions on the matter. These were issued in 1977 in SFAS 19 in which the FASB opted for the successful efforts method of historical cost accounting for oil and gas properties. The Commission concluded that it could not support this approach, and it proposed a solution called reserve recognition accounting, intended to reflect revenues when oil and gas reserves became proven rather than when their sale took place. (See Chapter 34 for further discussion.)

Although the FASB recognizes that it cannot sustain positions that are directly contrary to the expressed judgments of the SEC, at the same time the Commission recognizes that if it attempts to overrule the Board regularly, this would destroy the standard-setting mechanism it believes to be the most effective. Accordingly, both parties seem to see the benefit of working together rather than at cross-purposes.

Meetings With Registrants and Their Auditors

While the Commission's formal authority in the area of accounting principles and practices is considerable, in many ways this is eclipsed by its informal influence, for it also has substantial impact through its interaction with registrants and independent public accountants in particular cases. Ultimately, it is the Commission that must decide whether the accounting treatment used by registrants (either in filings or in prefiling conferences with registrants and their auditors) is in conformity with its rules and regulations. While evaluation of conformity with GAAP is primarily the responsibility of the independent accountant, the Commission will on some occasions disagree with him when it comes to appropriate accounting for a particular set of facts. In such circumstances, there normally are meetings between the registrant, the SEC staff, and the independent accountant to discuss and resolve the issue.

If the registrant and the staff cannot reach agreement, the issue may be referred to the Commission for its consideration. The Commission usually has the last word in such cases, since its potential authority over registrants is enormous. For example, it can refuse to accelerate the effectiveness of a registration statement, issue a stop order, bar trading in a security, or bring an enforcement action.

Despite this substantial authority, the Commission and its staff do not often impose their judgment on registrants and their independent accountants. In most cases, the staff will raise questions about the accounting treatment of a particular event, the registrant will fully explain its basis for choosing the accounting used, and the staff will accept it. This policy properly places on the registrant and its independent accountant the responsibility for achieving a fair presentation. Thus the comment letters, or so-called deficiency letters, issued by the staff with regard to a preliminary 1933 Act or a 1934 Act report filing are usually resolved by explanation rather than confrontation.

Integrated Disclosure System

In a series of releases issued from September 1980 through March 1982, the SEC proffered a major revision to the reporting and disclosure process for substantially all filings pursuant to the 1933 and 1934 Acts. Uniformity has also been achieved for nonfinancial disclosures under the 1934 Act and for a major portion of those under the 1933 Act. From time to time, further changes continue to be made. Regulations S-X and S-K are the primary regulations that are covered by the integrated disclosure system.

Under the integrated disclosure system, substantially identical disclosures are included in filings with the SEC and distributed to security holders in prospectuses, proxy statements, and annual reports. For example, the audited primary financial statements that are included in annual reports to shareholders for commercial and industrial companies largely conform to the requirements of Regulation S-X, and as a result, are substantially identical with those required to be in prospectuses and in all documents filed with the SEC. The primary financial statements include only the disclosures required under GAAP as set forth in pronouncements of the FASB (and similar pronouncements of predecessor bodies), plus a few disclosures not required under GAAP that the Commission insists are necessary. Also, under the integrated disclosure system, substantial uniformity of disclosures outside the primary financial statements is achieved for the various SEC filings through Regulation S-K.

Regulation S-X. The basic accounting regulation of the Commission is Regulation S-X, which prescribes rules for the form and content of financial statements filed with the Commission. Figure 47.1 lists the major sections of this regulation. Article 5 relates to commercial and industrial companies and is the most frequently used provision.

Regulation S-K. Regulation S-K specifies the SEC's requirements covering the content of nonfinancial statement portions of registration statements and certain periodic filings under the 1934 Act. Generally, Regulation S-K functions as a guideline. Unless a form or schedule governing a particular filing requirement specifies that information prescribed by an item of Regulation S-K must be presented, no information is required.

A description of the content of Regulation S-K is contained in Figure 47.2.

Registration Forms. As part of the simplification process attempted by the SEC through the integrated disclosure system, the filing forms also were revised. As a result, the more significant 1933 Act filing forms now used include:

1. *Form S-1.* Requires complete disclosure to be set forth in the prospectus and permits no incorporation by reference. The form is to be used by registrants required to file under the 1934 Act for less than three years, and may be used by registrants voluntarily, or is to be used by those for whom no other form is available. (Form F-1 is required for foreign private issuers.)

2. *Form S-2.* This is the second tier of registration form. Unlike Form S-1, it provides for incorporation by reference of 1934 Act reports and has streamlined disclosure and report-

Rules of General Application

Article 1   Definition of terms used in Regulation S-X

Article 2   Qualifications of accountants and the form and content of accountants' reports

Article 3   Uniform requirements for financial statements and periods to be covered in essentially all filings

Article 3A   Consolidated and combined financial statements and principles of consolidation

Article 4   Rules of general application to all financial statements, including required general notes thereto

Specialized Rules Applicable to Financial Statements

Article 5   Various financial statement categories for commercial and industrial companies

Article 6   Registered investment companies

Article 6A   Employee stock purchase, savings, and similar plans

Article 7   Insurance companies

Article 9   Banks and bank holding companies

Article 10   Interim financial statements

Article 11   Pro forma financial information

Schedules

Article 12   Form and content of various detailed schedules to be filed as supplements to the financial statements

FIG. 47.1   Major Sections of Regulation S-X

ing requirements. This form may be used by companies that have been subject to 1934 Act reporting for at least three years. (Form F-2 is required for foreign private issuers.)

3. *Form S-3.* This form affords maximum use of incorporation by reference of 1934 Act reports and requires the least disclosure in the prospectus. Eligibility for Form S-3 depends upon a designated minimum value of stock being held by nonaffiliates (the "float"), currently pegged at $150 million, or, alternatively, $100 million of float coupled with an annual trading volume of three million shares. (Form F-3 is required for foreign private issuers.)

4. *Form S-4.* The S-4 prospectus requirements are divided into four sections. The first section calls for information about the transaction and the expanded summary. The next two sections specify the information about the companies involved and also dictate the different levels of prospectus presentation and incorporation by reference that must be used. The degree of incorporation by reference depends on which form (S-1, S-2, or S-3) the companies would use in making a primary offering of their securities. The fourth section gives the requirements for voting and management information; all voting information must appear in the prospectus. The amount of management information that must appear in the prospectus, similar to company information, again depends on which registration may be used in primary offering. (Form F-4 is required for foreign private issuers.)

5. *Form S-8.* Registration statement for a company's shares to be offered to its employees pursuant to an employee benefit plan.

6. *Form S-11.* Registration form for certain real estate companies.

Regulation S-K

Subject	Item Number
Business	
Description of business	101
Description of property	102
Legal proceedings	103
Securities of the registrant	
Market price of and dividends on the registrant's common equity and	
related stockholder matters	201
Description of registrant's securities	202
Financial information	
Selected financial data	301
Supplementary financial information	302
Management's discussion and analysis of financial condition and results of	
operations	303
Changes in and disagreements with accountants on accounting and	
financial disclosure	304
Management and certain security holders	
Directors and executive officers	401
Executive compensation	402
Security ownership of certain beneficial owners and management	403
Certain relationships and related transactions	404
Registration statement and prospectus provisions	
Forepart of registration statement and outside front cover page of	
prospectus	501
Inside front and outside back cover pages of prospectus	502
Summary information, risk factors, and ratio of earnings to fixed charges	503
Use of proceeds	504
Determination of offering price	505
Dilution	506
Selling security holders	507
Plan of distribution	508
Interest of named experts and counsel	509
Disclosure of Commission position on indemnification for 1933 Act liabilities	510
Other expenses of issuance and distribution	511
Undertakings	512
Exhibits	601
Miscellaneous	
Recent sales of unregistered securities	701
Indemnification of directors and officers	702
List of industry guides	
1933 Act industry guides	801
1934 Act industry guides	802

FIG. 47.2 Content of Regulation S-K

7. *Form S-18.* Optional form for registration of securities with an aggregate cash price of $7,500,000 or less.

8. *Form S-20.* Optional form for registration of standardized options.

Forms S-1, S-2, and S-3 are used primarily to offer securities to the public. Form S-4 is used principally in business combinations.

The 1934 Act includes a general form for registration of securities (Form 10) and several continuous reporting forms:

1. *Form 8-K.* Filing form covering current transactions required to be disclosed promptly.

2. *Form 10-K.* General form for annual reports filed with the Commission by registrants.

3. *Form 10-Q.* General form for quarterly reports.

Form 20F is prescribed for use by foreign private issuers in lieu of Forms 10 and 10-K.

Electronic Data Gathering, Analysis and Retrieval (EDGAR)

In September 1984, the Commission began accepting electronic filings from registrants in its pilot EDGAR system. Participation in the project was on a voluntary basis, and as of the end of August 1986, the pilot project was closed to new participants.

The pilot project was designed to assist the Commission in the creation of an operational electronic filing, processing, and dissemination system. In a recent status report to Congress on the EDGAR project, the Commission concluded that the ongoing pilot project demonstrates the feasibility of electronic filing. The Commission has issued a Request for Proposal for the operational system of an electronic filing system.

The SEC anticipates that all documents processed by the Divisions of Corporation Finance and Investment Management under the 1933 Act, the 1934 Act, the Public Utility Holding Company Act of 1935, the Trust Indenture Act of 1939, and the Investment Company Act of 1940 will be required to be filed electronically once the operational EDGAR system is in place.

Financial Reporting Releases

The SEC frequently issues accounting and disclosure regulations to supplement the guidance provided by the FASB and the AICPA. These regulations take the form of official Commission releases, which are issued under the jurisdiction of the Office of the Chief Accountant. Except for those dealing with enforcement matters, the policies detailed in these Financial Reporting Releases (FRRs) have been incorporated into Regulations S-X and S-K and the related Industry Guides included in Items 801 and 802 of Regulation S-K.

Staff Accounting Bulletins (SABs) supplement the formal accounting regulations of the Commission. The SABs represent informal interpretations by the SEC staff on various matters contained in GAAP and Regulation S-X.

In May 1982, the SEC codified the existing, relevant accounting-related releases which were called ASRs into a single document by issuing FRR 1. Enforcement releases were codified separately. (See text later in this chapter.) Now, statements of accounting policy by the Commission are made through these new releases, rather than through Accounting Series Releases (ASRs). The contents and codification of FRRs issued to date are contained at ¶¶ 2501 through 3951 of *SEC Accounting Rules* (CCH).

Codification. FRR 1 (Release 33-6395) is organized by topic and is intended to stand on its own, obviating the need to refer to specific ASRs or FRRs. Appendix B of the codification, "Disposition of Accounting Series Releases" (CCH Fed. Sec. L. Rep. ¶ 73,351), states whether each former ASR was:

1. Omitted as obsolete or no longer necessary,
2. Carried forward as an enforcement release, or
3. Incorporated in one of the major topical sections of the codification below.

The major topical sections of the codification are the following:

- 100 General
- 200 Annual financial statements
- 300 Interim reporting
- 400 Specialized industries
- 500 Information outside of financial statements
- 600 Matters relating to independent accountants

Staff Accounting Bulletins

For many years, the staff followed the procedure of offering informal interpretations to registrants and their independent accountants concerning both the rules of the Commission and the accounting principles and practices the staff considered acceptable in filings with the Commission. Since only a relatively small number of accountants represent substantial numbers of SEC registrants, an informal information system grew up that communicated these interpretations and allowed registrants to be aware of the policies being followed.

In 1975, the Commission decided it would be desirable to put in writing the more significant of these informal interpretations and practices followed by the staff in administering the securities laws, so that all registrants could be aware of them without relying on a totally informal system. Accordingly, it authorized the creation of a series of SABs. These bulletins are issued jointly by the Office of the Chief Accountant and the Division of Corporation Finance without the Commission's official approval; thus they are not official rules or interpretations of the Commission. Occasionally, controversial bulletins are shown to the Commission on an informal basis before publication.

Codification. In January 1981, the SEC issued SAB 40, which codified SABs 1 through 38. (SAB 39 was rescinded.) The codification was intended to revise the material in the SABs to conform to current GAAP and to eliminate material that was duplicative of GAAP. For example, the SAB material on interest capitalization was deleted, recognizing the issuance of SFAS 34 (I67) on interest capitalization. In addition, certain interpretive material on accounting for leases, prior-period adjustments, and involuntary conversions were deleted due to FASB actions. Other changes reflect the adoption of the integrated disclosure system in 1980.

The codification, for which an updated index was issued in SAB 46, classifies the SABs into twelve topics:

1. Financial Statements
2. Business Combinations
3. Senior Securities
4. Equity Accounts
5. Miscellaneous Accounting
6. Interpretations of Accounting Series Releases
7. Real Estate Companies
8. Retail Companies
9. Finance Companies
10. Utility Companies
11. Miscellaneous Disclosure
12. Oil and Gas Producing Activities

The bulletins issued since SAB 40 deal with a variety of topics, for example, termination of pension plans, sales of stock by subsidiaries and related financial statement presentation requirements, accounting and disclosure by banks, accounting for oil and gas activities, and the SEC staff's position that the AICPA Issues Paper on last-in, first-out (LIFO) should be considered authoritative. (See Chapter 14.) The codification of SABs issued to date is contained at ¶¶ 7003 through 7891 of *SEC Accounting Rules* (CCH).

SHELF REGISTRATION

Rule 415

Rule 415, adopted in 1982, governs the so-called shelf registration, that is, registration of securities that are to be offered and sold on a delayed or continuous basis in the future. The Rule contains detailed eligibility requirements for its use.

Using Shelf Registrations

Once a shelf registration has been filed and becomes effective, changes in data can be accomplished in any one of three ways: (1) sticker (prospectus supplement), (2) incorporation by reference of a subsequently filed 1934 Act document, or (3) posteffective amendment.

Form S-3 (Item 12) requires that certain documents filed after the effective date of the registration statement be incorporated by reference into the prospectus. This includes any subsequent Form 10-K or other reports filed under 1933 Act Sections 13(a) or 15(d) primarily on Forms 10-Q and 8-K. Forms 10-Q and 8-K, which are automatically incorporated by reference into a Form S-3, do not update the effective date of the registration.

Posteffective amendments are also required for significant acquisitions or dispositions and restatements of financial statements. These too are considered "fundamental changes" in later periodic reports (Forms 10-K, 10-Q, and 8-K) and may be incorporated by reference into the registration statement, rather than as posteffective amendments. When this option is used, a new effective date is established.

Auditor's Role

The ongoing nature of a shelf registration has created some uncertainty and concern among independent accountants as to their responsibilities under Section 11 of the 1933 Act to perform subsequent-events reviews sufficient to give them reasonable basis to believe that the financial statements and any related financial information were not misleading as of the effective date of the registration statement. In May 1983, the AICPA published an interpretation of SAS 37, *Filings Under Federal Securities Statutes* (AU 711); this publication addresses those issues.

Comfort Letters to Underwriters

Although sales of securities under S-3 Shelf Registrations do not require the use of underwriters, almost invariably they will be employed and will request the customary comfort letters. Because the sales of securities will be subsequent to the effective date of the registration, by as much as a year, it is essential that auditors have an advance understanding with their client and the potential underwriters on the timing and contents of the desired comfort letter. While numerous underwriters may be listed, only one underwriting agreement will be used, and sometimes a single underwriter's legal counsel will be identified, who is presumably acceptable to any underwriter participating in the offering. Accordingly, it may be possible for the auditor to agree with the designated counsel on the comfort letter requirements.

Assuming the auditor is required to deliver a comfort letter at the closing date, which is ordinarily five business days after the sale date, the auditor would have no more than seven calendar days to complete the procedures needed to issue the comfort letter. To be in a position to issue a comfort letter on such a tight schedule, the auditor should be engaged by the client to perform timely reviews of interim financial statements and all reports filed on form 10-Q based on the standards in SAS 36 (AU 722). The client should also supply the auditor with all Form 8-K filings, preferably before they are finalized so that changes needed to avoid an exception in the comfort letter can be made. SAS 49, *Letters for Underwriters* (AU 634) issued in September 1984, addresses the content and wording of comfort letters related to shelf registration statements and an appropriate draft comfort letter that may be furnished in connection with shelf registrations when an underwriter has not been selected. (For further discussion of comfort letters, see Chapter 20.)

PROXY REVIEW PROGRAM

The integrated disclosure system attempts to simplify the disclosure requirements for the registration of securities under the 1933 Act and for continuous reporting under the 1934 Act. The SEC also has a seven-part program in process to simplify its third major disclosure system, relating to proxy solicitations.

To date, six of the seven proxy review projects have been completed and final rules adopted:

1. Adoption of a uniform Item 404 of Regulation S-K concerning disclosure of management transactions and relationships (Release 33-6441, December 1982);
2. Changes in the process for communications with beneficial owners (Release 34-20021, July 1983);
3. Amendments to the shareholder proposal rules (Release 34-20021, August 1983);
4. Simplification of the Executive Compensation disclosures in Item 402 of Regulation S-K (Release 33-6486, September 1983);
5. Adoption of the Form S-4 to simplify the registration form for business combinations, as discussed previously, under "Registration Forms"; and
6. Adoption of amendments to the proxy rules to bring to the proxy context the benefits of the integrated disclosure system (Releases 34-23789, November 1986, and 34-24514, May 1987).

The remaining project, a review of proxy contest rules, is still on the SEC's agenda and will be addressed in the future.

SEC OVERSIGHT OF AUDITING AND THE PROFESSION

General Auditing Authority

The 1933 Act provides that financial statements filed with the Commission shall be audited by independent public accountants and that the Commission may prescribe the form and content of the auditor's report. The 1934 Act does not prescribe an auditor's report, but Section 13(a) (2) gives the Commission the authority to require auditor's reports for filed statements, and it has done this. At the time the securities laws were enacted, Congress considered the possibility of government auditors, but ultimately accepted the counsel of a number of witnesses from the profession that audits by independent public accountants would achieve the same result more efficiently and effectively.

The degree of SEC authority over auditing standards and procedures, and for that matter, the organization of the accounting profession, has been a subject of dispute in recent years. The Commission's view is that its authority to prescribe the form and content of the auditor's report gives it sufficient authority to prescribe auditing standards, since it may indicate what the auditor says about what he does. In addition, the SEC has devoted substantial attention to a broad definition of what constitutes auditor independence and believes that it thus has substantial influence over the way an auditing firm may operate. Finally, the Commission has enforcement powers to investigate accounting firms and issue staff reports on their practices when it feels them to be deficient or to commence enforcement actions.

This combination of powers gives the SEC substantial de facto authority over the accounting profession, and to date the profession has not chosen to litigate the Commission's authority in most of these areas. One attempt was made to question the Commission's authority to discipline accountants under Rule 2(e); in this circumstance, the Court of Appeals for the Second Circuit generally upheld the Commission's authority. This case (Touche Ross & Co. v. SEC, CCH Fed. Sec. L. Rep. ¶ 96,854 (2d. Cir. 1979)) was not appealed to the Supreme Court.

The Commission has used its influence in this regard to encourage the auditing standard-setting bodies to adopt standards consistent with the SEC's view of auditor responsibility. While there have been disputes about the extent of SEC authority, in large part the profession and the Commission have reached accommodation on most of the crucial issues.

Auditors' Independence. A second major dimension has been the establishment of guidelines regarding the independence of auditors. FRR § 600 deals with matters relating to independent public accountants and addresses their independence. In general, the Commission's policies in this regard were issued earlier than those issued by the accounting profession itself, although in substantive respects the accounting profession has gradually incorporated the Commission's independence requirements in its own rules of conduct.

In practice, the Commission has fostered the independence of accountants, both by supporting them in individual circumstances when a client seeks to have the auditor's judgment overruled by the SEC staff and by imposing general requirements that make it difficult for clients to obtain more palatable answers to accounting issues by changing auditors. In 1971, the Commission imposed a requirement for disclosure on Form 8-K whenever an auditor change took place, including the filing of information by the registrant and a letter by the displaced auditor giving a description of any disagreements on matters of accounting and disclosure that preceded the change. This requirement was extended to first-time registrants in 1986; disclosure must be given in the offering prospectus, with required letters, if any, filed as exhibits.

In April 1988, the SEC issued FRR 31 (§ 603) revising Form 8-K. The SEC revised Form 8-K because of an increased concern about "opinion shopping," that is, seeking the advice of independent public accountants beyond that of the accountant who performs the audit in an attempt to secure an accounting decision more amenable to the company's wishes. In this regard, the SEC staff is explicitly reviewing all reports of changes in auditors for evidence of shopping, and one enforcement case (AAER 54) resulted in a consent decree against an accounting firm that had allegedly allowed itself to be shopped.

FRR 31 amended the disclosure requirements for changes in and disagreements with accountants to:

- Better explain the meaning of the term "disagreements" and provide examples of situations that should be reported as disagreements.
- Require disclosure of the fact that the company's board of directors (or its audit committee) did (or did not) discuss any disagreements with the former accountant.
- Require disclosure about limitations that the company has imposed on discussions between the new and former accountants concerning any disagreement.
- Require disclosure of whether the former accountant resigned, declined to stand for reelection, or was dismissed.

The release also addresses the SEC's concerns about potential opinion shopping situations. The release also requires disclosure of

- Any issue that is or may be material to the company's financial statements that has been discussed with the new accountants during the company's two most recent fiscal years or in any subsequent interim period prior to their engagement.
- A brief discussion of the new and former accountants' views on those issues.

Investigation and Enforcement. The Commission has also taken an active role in the auditing area through its investigatory and enforcement powers. Over the years, it has frequently issued releases that detail the results of its investigation of auditing performance that it considered deficient, and has expressed its views on the practices about which it was concerned and on what those practices should be. In addition, in some of the enforcement actions resulting from these investigations, the Commission has obtained as part of a settlement agreement an undertaking from the accounting firm involved to perform research activities of various sorts, which have contributed to the development of auditing standards. A later section of this chapter explores the enforcement philosophy in more depth.

Index of Enforcement Proceedings. Originally, enforcement proceedings were published in ASRs. All ASRs related to enforcement proceedings issued prior to May 1982 have been transferred to Accounting and Auditing Enforcement releases (AAERs); these are indexed alphabetically and topically. Subsequent enforcement proceedings have been released in AAERs.

While AAERs have been largely directed toward public accountants or public accounting firms, recent cases and statements by SEC officials indicate that the SEC, in cases involving accounting irregularities, is also expanding its scope beyond public accountants and their firms to include companies or the companies' officers, directors, or employees.

The areas of major concern are "cooked books," "cute accounting" or "loopholing," and "shopping" for accounting principles (discussed previously). During 1984, the number of enforcement actions based on accounting irregularities was estimated as four times the number of insider trading cases. Former Commissioner James Treadway has spoken out against cooked books consistently. He emphasized that cooked books undermine the entire disclosure process, even when personal gain is not the objective. The liability for false financial reports can involve managers, officers, directors, and even outside auditors, as well as third parties, such as customers and suppliers. In fact, at least one SEC case has charged a third-party supplier with collusion to misstate the financial results of a registrant.

A number of federal securities law violations may result from cooked books, including violations of 1934 Act reporting and antifraud provisions by distributing false financial statements, or 1933 Act violations by using false financial information in a stock or debt offering. Also, such financial fraud may indicate a potential violation of the Foreign Corrupt Practices Act.

The issue of fraudulent financial reporting obviously affects independent public accountants because of the potential accounting and auditing risks. The auditor's liability will depend on whether he failed to conduct his audit in accordance with GAAS. The auditor should be alert for red flags, such as premature recognition of revenue and padding inventories.

By "cute accounting," the SEC staff refers to the misapplication of accounting principles or pushing standards past the point of acceptability to achieve results that may be misleading. Similarly, "loopholing" involves exploiting a weakness in GAAP or creating a transaction not clearly covered by any existing rule. The SEC is concerned about the use of such practices in initial public offerings as well as in ongoing filings, and the staff has publicly stated that such cases, when noted in the review process, will be sent directly to the Enforcement Division without any request for explanation by the registrant.

AAERs are too numerous to list here. A summary description may be secured by reference to *SEC Accounting Rules* ¶¶ 4051 et seq. (CCH).

Organization of the Profession

Early Congressional Initiatives. The Commission has at various times exerted substantial pressure on the profession to make changes in its approach and organization. The most noteworthy example is the Commission's action in urging the creation of a new section of the AICPA made up of firms in SEC practice and the development of an extensive program of peer review within that section.

The establishment of the SEC Practice Section of the AICPA Division for Firms arose in part through the initiatives of Congress, whose hearings conducted by Senator Metcalf, Congressman Moss, and Senator Eagleton foreshadowed a significant threat of greater government involvement. As a result of these hearings, the Commission undertook the preparation of an annual report to Congress on its oversight of the accounting profession. Those reports have been submitted annually since 1978.

Dingell Hearings. The SEC's campaign against accounting irregularities and financial fraud has been highlighted and perhaps stepped up as a result of the congressional hearings begun in 1985, investigating the SEC and the accounting profession. The hearings were chaired by John Dingell (D-Mich.). Among other matters, the hearings investigated

1. The effectiveness (in terms of the public interest) of a standards-setting process that is significantly influenced by preparers and their CPAs,
2. The accounting profession, and

3. The present auditing system, auditor independence, and the implications of certain recent audit failures.

The hearings continued into 1986 and involved testimony by CPAs, the SEC, the FASB, the General Accounting Office, various academics, and others.

In May 1986, legislation was introduced by seven members of Congress that would require auditors to report immediately to government authorities suspicions of fraud or other illegalities raised during an audit. The legislation is on hold pending completion of initiatives by the AICPA and others. At present, auditors are required to inform only corporate directors and management. (See Chapter 45 for further discussion.)

Insider Trading. Comments by John Shad, former Chairman of the SEC, and others indicate that enforcement efforts continue to be directed at violations of insider trading rules. The number of insider trading cases on the current docket, and under active investigation, has increased dramatically in the last several years. One of the major concerns is that there seems to be a lack of sensitivity, sometimes perhaps inadvertent, to protecting confidential information. As a result, the SEC sought, and Congress enacted, legislation (Insider Trading Sanctions Act of 1984) that significantly increased the penalties for insider trading by providing for a maximum fine equal to triple the profits from such trading.

SEC ENFORCEMENT PROGRAM AND PHILOSOPHY

The primary aim of the SEC enforcement program is to maintain the integrity of the marketplace and deter fraud. While its statutory authority is clear and its authorizations broad, the Commission has limited resources and finds it impossible to investigate and prosecute every possible violation. Consequently, the Commission has sought in recent years to focus its enforcement efforts at key points where maximum impact can be achieved. For this reason, enforcement efforts involving professionals, such as accountants and lawyers, have been important, even though the number of cases in which professionals were involved has not been large.

The reasoning of the Commission is simple: These professionals are an essential element in providing access to the marketplace, since the sale of securities cannot take place without their involvement. It is hoped that holding the professional responsible at these points of access can prevent many questionable activities before they occur. By insisting on high standards of performance by accountants and increasing them where the Commission deems it necessary, more reliable and meaningful financial information for the investing public should be assured.

Quality Control in CPA Firms

The Commission's enforcement program deters substandard performance by increasing the risk to an accounting firm of a Commission injunctive action and of private actions for money damages. As a result, it becomes desirable for individuals and firms to devote greater resources and more care to the avoidance of such performance. Although professionals in general have a desire to do a good job, excellence is costly, and in a world of competing claims and equities, a program that raises the cost of deficient work should have the impact of improving performance, although the equation between these is not crystal clear. The threat of an enforcement action and the costs of an adverse determination by a court—unfavorable publicity, possible civil judgments, the financial burden of litigation, and perhaps ultimately a loss of professional stature with a consequent decline in business—all combine to reduce the likelihood of substandard professional performance.

In response to Commission actions, actions by private litigants, and some public concern about the adequacy of audits, accounting firms have been substantially increasing their commitment of resources to more extensive quality controls. This should result in better auditing judgments and perhaps minimize the frequency of future enforcement actions. In those cases in which erroneous judgments occur, quality control procedures should lessen the likelihood that they will go undetected and result in the auditor's acceptance of financial statements that are not fairly presented. While quality review procedures are important, they should not be overemphasized. It is not productive to load a mountain of review on a pinhead of audit field work. The qualified and alert auditor in the field is still the first line of defense.

Highlighting Problem Areas

In addition to encouraging better quality controls, enforcement actions may be beneficial in directing attention to areas in which auditing standards may be more effectively articulated and applied. Although Commission actions are based on the facts of particular cases, in some situations the facts may be typical of general problem areas; Commission opinions, orders, and complaints may therefore emphasize matters that require professionwide attention.

Decision to Take Enforcement Action

In deciding whether to institute an enforcement action, the Commission considers each case in light of several major factors, including the seriousness of the perceived professional deficiency and the extent to which the auditor had knowledge of what was happening. The Commission also considers the degree to which the auditor appeared to be an active participant in a scheme to mislead the public through artful or incomplete disclosure or through the creative selection of accounting principles designed to present a picture inconsistent with reality.

There are many enforcement actions brought by the Commission involving deficient financial reporting in which auditors are not named as defendants. The Commission does not have a policy of pursuing every possible professional deficiency it can find simply for the joy of the hunt. Selectivity in the use of resources and attention to the more serious cases are keys to an effective program.

It is, of course, important that the SEC's enforcement program be a fair one to specific firms and individuals affected in each separate case. Safeguards to ensure fairness do exist in the procedures followed by the staff and the Commission, and although various parties may disagree with conclusions reached, the judgments made are based on a full consideration of the facts, including any written presentations from the proposed defendant, known as Wells submissions (after the name of the advisory committee that recommended this procedure).

Before a case involving an accountant is sent to the Commission, it is submitted to the Chief Accountant for review on the merits. The Assistant Chief Accountant for enforcement matters in the Office of the Chief Accountant generally reviews the testimony and other evidence and reports his conclusion to the Chief Accountant. In many cases, the proposed defendant will request a meeting with the Chief Accountant to discuss the case, and this meeting is generally held before any recommendation is forwarded to the Commission. After careful review of the evidence, the Chief Accountant then makes his recommendation, which is submitted to the Commission along with the recommendation of the Division of Enforcement. Cases against accountants rarely have been brought without the concurrence of both the Chief Accountant and the Division of Enforcement. If the case involves novel or particularly difficult questions, the Commission's Office of General Counsel will also review the recommendations.

After recommendations have been sent to the Commission together with Wells submissions by proposed defendants, the commissioners and their legal assistants review the case with great care, frequently asking questions of the staff about details in the case. Then the case is discussed at the Commission table before any decision is reached, and these discussions are substantive in nature. The staff is subjected to vigorous questioning, and the principles and objectives underlying the proposed action are considered in depth.

All of these procedures normally occur prior to an action being brought by the Commission; it is recognized that such an action against a professional has a substantial impact on his reputation even before any judicial determination is made. After the action is brought and Rule 2(e) proceedings, if any, are concluded, the normal due process of the legal system is, of course, still available to provide protection against unjust actions.

While virtually all Commission cases are civil in character, on rare occasions it is concluded that a case is sufficiently serious to be referred to the Department of Justice for consideration of criminal prosecution. Referrals in regard to accountants have only been made when the Commission and the staff believed that the evidence indicated a professional accountant certified financial statements that he knew to be false when he reported on them. The Commission does not make criminal references in cases that it believes are matters of professional judgment, even if the judgments appear to be bad ones.

Enforcement Remedies

In most cases, the sanctions imposed in Commission proceedings serve the remedial purpose of improving the quality of an accounting firm's work. In other cases, the performance of particular individuals or firms is found to be so deficient that their continued practice before the Commission in the public marketplace carries too great a risk and hence is unacceptable. While small firms have more commonly been involved in such cases, a consistent pattern of deficient work by a large firm might lead to a similar conclusion. Three forms of sanctions have been used with some frequency:

1. *Temporary or permanent suspension of right to practice before the Commission.* In cases involving unacceptable performance, the Commission has the authority under Rule 2(e) of its Rules of Practice to bar an individual or a firm from practice before the Commission. It may also suspend the professional or the firm from Commission practice until there is an appropriate showing of fitness to resume. The ultimate sanction of a permanent bar is not frequently used, since the Commission usually believes that a professional firm can take actions to bring its performance up to an acceptable level and can provide the Commission with assurance that such a level is being maintained. Even when an accountant has been barred from practice before the Commission, his right to practice may be reinstated after the passage of time, upon a proper showing of fitness.

2. *Quality control review and inspection.* Over the years, the Commission has attempted to use sanctions that will meet the needs presented in each particular case. New sanctions have been developed in consent situations that the Commission believes hold some promise. When cases raise questions concerning the adequacy of an accounting firm's quality control procedures, the Commission may require the firm to submit its procedures for review by the Commission's staff or by a group of outside professionals. As a result of this review, the firm and the Commission may agree on certain additional quality control and audit procedures to be followed. Such procedures may emphasize particular areas of practice that relate to the specific enforcement action, but they are generally not limited to such areas. If the peer review report is not satisfactory to the SEC, further action will be required. In recent years, the SEC has been relying on the peer review program, established as a requirement for membership in the SEC Practice Section of the AICPA Division for Firms (in which membership is voluntary) to accomplish SEC-sanctioned reviews. In those particular instances where the AICPA peer review is performed as a "firm on firm" review, the SEC delegates to the AICPA's appointed panel (which the SEC refers to as "The Committee for the [XYZ] Review") the additional responsibility to act as a review committee for the SEC. The panel accordingly is responsible to report not only to the AICPA but also to the SEC on the results of the review. Even in those instances, the SEC will occasionally request the panel to review certain areas of a firm's practice that are beyond the scope of the peer review program, and report to the SEC on those specific areas. In Release 33-6695 (April 1987, still pending), the SEC has proposed to require a mandatory peer review system for all independent public accountants that audit publicly held companies. Such a review would have to be performed once in each three-year-period. Subsequently the membership of the AICPA approved a new Code of Professional Conduct that mandated peer review as a requirement for membership. (For further discussion, see Chapter 45.)

3. *Limiting the firm's new business.* In some cases, the Commission has imposed a partial or complete limitation on new SEC business for a firm, either for a prescribed period or until such time as a peer review group is able to inspect a practice and report to the Commission. In this way, the Commission is able to obtain outside evidence that the program has been effectively implemented before the firm is allowed to grow, either in the aggregate or in the areas that are affected most.

48

Internal Revenue Service

TAX ORIGINS

Accountants are involved in virtually all tax matters for their clients, including income, estate and gift, excise, payroll, property, franchise taxes, and so forth. However, taxes directly and indirectly based on income are by far the most significant. The accounting profession may have its origins in the attest function, but income taxes have been a major factor in the professions's growth. Income-type taxes are imposed by countries other than the United States, as well as by many states and even cities. Life is even more complicated than it appears because of these foreign, state, and local income taxes; but because this chapter focuses on how the IRS affects the profession's environment, the discussion is limited to the U.S. federal income tax.

It is difficult to realize that the income tax has not always been a significant part of our government's revenue. For almost all of its first 100 years as an agricultural economy, this country relied almost completely on external revenue in the form of customs duties. There were at times some internal taxes, principally excise and stamp, and an income tax was even considered to help finance the War of 1812. But it was not until the Civil War that excise taxes grew in importance to become the principal source of revenue. An income tax was used for a few years in the late 19th century, but efforts to retain it met with considerable opposition and ultimately judicial disapproval as a violation of the U.S. Constitution[1]. The country's growing need for revenue led to the ratification of the Sixteenth Amendment in 1913 and the income tax was born.

It did not take long for the tax to be recognized as extraordinarily complex. One of our greatest jurists, Learned Hand, has described the law:

> The words merely dance before my eyes in a meaningless procession: cross-reference to cross-reference, exception upon exception – couched in abstract terms that offer no handle to seize hold of – leave in my mind only a confused sense of some vitally important, but successfully concealed, purport, which it is my duty to extract, but which is within my power, if at all, only after the most inordinate expenditure of time ... these monsters are the result of fabulous industry and ingenuity, plugging up this hole and casting out the net, against all possible evasion. [Hand, 1947, p. 167].

SOURCES OF TAX RULES – OVERVIEW

As is to be expected under our tripartite system of government, tax rules are developed by all three branches – the Congress, the executive, and the judiciary. Most of the tax law is not new. Until 1939, there were a series of Revenue Acts, each self-contained and setting out a complete set of rules, even though in many instances the rules were the same as those in earlier Acts. In 1939, an Internal Revenue Code was enacted and later legislation would amend only selected provisions of it. The Internal Revenue Code of 1954 was a substantial restructuring of the rules and it replaced the 1939 Code. Most recently, the Tax Reform Act of 1986 replaced the 1954 Code with

---

[1] Pollock v. Farmers' Loan & Trust, 158 US 691 (1895).

the Internal Revenue Code of 1986. It must be realized that earlier tax law has more than mere historical significance. Apart from the need today to defend tax returns filed in earlier years, the determination of taxable income realized from an asset transaction today may depend on the tax law in force many years ago when the asset was acquired.

Many provisions of today's tax law can be traced to the rules of earlier years but this does not make them any easier to understand. The problem is even greater when one realizes there have been more than 400 separate public laws since 1954 alone, all changing the tax law, some making limited change, others extensive change. To make matters worse, even the changes require change; for example, before the ink was dry on the 1986 Tax Reform Act (TRA 1986), a Technical Corrections Act was drafted, itself running several hundred pages. The need for additional revenue as part of the deficit reduction process, mandated by budget reconciliation, undoubtedly will add hundreds more pages. Even where the statute itself has never changed, an endless process of interpretation has adapted it to the changing circumstances of our society. As it might have been said, age cannot wither nor custom stale the infinite variety of our tax laws.

Once a law is enacted, the Treasury Department issues regulations and procedures to interpret the law. These are first announced as proposed regulations by publication in the *Federal Register*. As a rule, the public is invited to comment on the proposed regulations and to appear at the hearings if these are held. After consideration of the comments, the regulations are issued in final form by publication in the *Federal Register*. Regulations, generally, are effective as of the same date as the statute they interpret. In some instances, the effective date is different, such as the date of publication of the final regulation or after a period of time such as 60 days subsequent to publication.

Some laws contain a provision directing the issuance of regulations to establish the detailed rules of a broad statutory framework. For example, consolidated returns may be filed by corporations connected by degrees of stock ownership specified in the law, but the details of how such returns are to be filed is to be the subject of regulations. Such regulations are referred to as "legislative" regulations and generally are more authoritative than "interpretive" regulations issued to give the Treasury's explanation of the statute.

In its primary role of collecting taxes, the IRS designs forms and develops procedures that by their nature are interpretations of the law. The IRS also will provide taxpayers with formal opinions on the tax consequences of transactions, all of which are more interpretations of the law. In the audit of tax returns and review of refund claims, there is more interpretation of the law as issues are resolved.

Taxpayers and the IRS may disagree, in which case the courts have to resolve the issue. Court decisions are another interpretation of the law. All of these sources— legislative, executive, and judicial—are discussed in greater detail below.

HOW TAX LAWS ARE ENACTED

Under the Constitution, tax legislation must begin with the House of Representatives, which in effect means the Ways and Means Committee. Major legislation generally is a response to a request from the President, although Congress itself may take the initiative. Typically, there are public hearings conducted first by the Ways and Means Committee at which the Administration presents its views, followed by representatives of affected taxpayers. Out of these hearings, decisions are reached by the Committee and formal legislation is then drafted. A Committee Report is prepared to explain the bill which then goes to the floor of the House for vote, possibly after floor debate. Once approved, the bill goes to the Senate where the process is repeated. Hearings are held by the Senate Finance Committee; amendments are considered; a decision is reached on the bill and a Committee Report prepared to explain it; and the bill goes to the Senate for vote, again after possible debate. In many instances, particularly in the case of major legislation, the House and Senate versions will differ in material respects. A Committee of Conference, appointed by the Senate and House, then meets to reconcile the differing versions. A Conference Report is prepared and the legislation is sent back to the House and Senate for approval which generally is forthcoming. The bill, now approved by both Houses of Congress, goes to the President for signature.

The date of signing becomes the date of enactment, which, unless otherwise stated in the new law, is its effective date. In many instances, different provisions of a new law have different effective dates. A provision may be enacted to be effective as of the date on which it was first announced that Congress was considering the change, or as of the date of an announcement of a congressional committee decision. The possibility of an earlier effective date requires practitioners to be aware of pending legislation so that in advising clients they can warn them not only of the current law but of what it may become, permitting clients to plan business and personal affairs accordingly.

Once a law is enacted, it becomes the responsibility of the Treasury Department to issue regulations, a process described earlier in this chapter.

REVENUE RULINGS AND PROCEDURES

Private Rulings

The United States has a program of advice on tax consequences more extensive than that available in other countries. A taxpayer planning to engage in a significant transaction can request, and frequently receive, a letter from the National Office of the IRS, known as a ruling, on the tax treatment of the transaction. In some situations, a ruling is required as matter of law, for example, when a taxpayer wishes to change a tax accounting method, enter into certain transactions with foreign corporations, obtain tax-exempt status, change from consolidated returns to separate returns, or qualify a pension or profit-sharing plan.

Rulings are not binding on the IRS in a formal sense, but in the absence of misrepresentation as to the facts, or fraud, they give a high degree of certainty to the taxpayer to whom the ruling is issued. In fact, a ruling is the closest thing to insurance a taxpayer can obtain. However, other taxpayers who may be similarly situated cannot rely on that ruling. Although rulings generally take several months to obtain, in a complex transaction involving substantial sums and potential tax consequences, a ruling may be a "must" before taxpayers proceed.

Rulings will not be issued on all questions, and the IRS has a list of subjects on which it will not rule. Also, the IRS has announced criteria for rulings on certain transactions, and taxpayers who cannot meet these criteria cannot obtain a ruling.

When a ruling is not required by law, the inability to obtain it is not fatal. A ruling is no more than an opinion of the IRS on a transaction. While a favorable ruling usually forestalls any future challenge by the IRS, the inability to obtain a ruling does not mean the courts would reject the transaction, nor does it even mean that the IRS will challenge the transaction. However, if a ruling, which is not required under the law, cannot be obtained or timely obtained (and it must be noted that sometimes taxpayers planning a transaction do not have the luxury of waiting the months usually required for the ruling), then the prudent taxpayer will at least obtain an opinion of its lawyers or accountants that the desired tax consequences will be achieved.

Ruling requests may be submitted by the taxpayer or by its duly appointed representative. Law firms and accounting firms frequently handle such requests for their clients. Many such firms maintain an office in Washington, D.C. to processs such requests for their clients and also for the clients of other firms, usually on a referral basis. Conferences with IRS personnel may be needed; the taxpayer may attend the conference or let his representative completely handle the matter. Most ruling requests are described in a letter to the IRS, but some require the submission of an IRS form designed specifically for that purpose. All requests require the submission of considerable information, including the names of the taxpayer and all other interested parties, details of the transaction, and copies of contracts, if any. Financial information also may be appropriate. The request should include a statement of the position desired by the taxpayer as supported by the Code, regulations, other IRS rulings, and court decisions.

Revenue Procedures

The IRS uses revenue procedures (Rev. Proc.) to announce guidelines on a wide range of subjects, such as reorganizations, depreciation, changes of accounting method or period, or the use of magnetic tape. Some procedures list criteria for a ruling on particular transactions and if these are not met, a ruling will not be issued.

Technical Advice Memorandums

The National Office of the IRS provides to its field offices a technical advice process in connection with audits of tax returns. The process is similar to private rulings for taxpayers on planned transactions. When an issue raised in the audit of a return cannot be resolved, an alternative to the appeals office (described in the "Resolution of Disputes" section below) is to submit the issue to the National Office for technical advice. Either the taxpayer or the agent may request this, although the issue is actually submitted by the IRS district office. The taxpayer cannot veto a decision by the agent to seek technical advice. The agent can deny the taxpayer's request, but the taxpayer can appeal this decision.

Published Rulings

Each week in the *Internal Revenue Bulletin,* the IRS publishes revenue rulings and revenue procedures. The revenue rulings usually are based on previously issued private rulings or technical advice memorandums. These have been reviewed extensively and rewritten within the National Office and may be used as authority for positions in returns or ruling requests by any taxpayer. These rulings and procedures are republished for storage and retrieval in semiannual Cumulative Bulletins. While the number varies from year to year, several hundred revenue rulings are published every year.

Publishing Private Rulings

The original text of private rulings and technical advice memorandums also are released by the IRS approximately three months after they are issued. Identifying data is deleted and taxpayers who request rulings usually indicate to the IRS what information besides names should be deleted. More than 100 rulings and technical advice memorandums are released each week. There is no system for retrieval of such rulings except through a computer data base. Even though the text is available, as a matter of law these rulings may not be relied on by other taxpayers. However, the ruling indication of IRS views is most helpful to taxpayers planning similar transactions. Also, the release of a private ruling may suggest planning opportunities to other taxpayers, leading to submission of their own ruling requests.

RETURN FILING AND EXAMINATION PROCEDURES

In contrast to property taxes, where typically the tax authorities determine the value of the property, calculate a tax, assess it, and send a bill, the taxpayer prepares its income tax return with more and more professional assistance as the law increases in complexity. The return is filed by the taxpayer. The balance due is paid when the return is filed although much of the tax has been paid already by a system of withholding in the case of wages and salaries for individuals, and by way of estimated taxes for other income of individuals and for corporations.

The income tax usually is referred to as self-assessed. Its success depends on the integrity and attitude of taxpayers who believe that the system is evenhanded and fair. Taxpayers have to believe not only that they can be caught and penalized for their noncompliance but that the system has the mechanism for seeing to it that everybody follows the rules. This calls for a system to select and examine returns—the audit process. The following sections elaborate on this process.

Internal Revenue Service

The Internal Revenue Service has the day-to-day responsibility for administration of the tax law. Its head is the Commissioner of Internal Revenue, appointed by the President. Its National Office is in Washington, D.C. There are seven regional offices and 61 district offices throughout the country. Each state has at least one district office and larger states have more. It is the district offices with whom taxpayers and their representatives deal most. Taxes are collected by ten Internal Revenue Service Centers. Returns are filed there also and the activities of the Service Centers are coordinated with those of the District Directors.

Returns are reviewed at the Service Centers for mathematical errors; bills are sent for underpayments and refunds made for overpayments. Through a process of visual inspection and a sophisticated, closely guarded data-processing program, returns are selected to be reviewed by the district offices and forwarded there for that purpose. There is an elaborate, but efficient, administrative system for the audit of returns and the resolution of disputes arising in that process. If this system cannot resolve the dispute, the taxpayer's recourse is to the courts.

Office Audits

Audits of individual returns (other than those related to business returns under audit), are normally handled through the *office audit* procedure. The taxpayer receives a letter from an IRS office inviting him to appear at the IRS office on a specified date and at a particular time. The taxpayer can go alone, may be accompanied by a representative (typically the accountant who prepared the return), or may send the representative in his stead. This representative must be authorized in writing to appear on behalf of the taxpayer.

IRS office auditors tend to have less training and experience than field auditors. They handle a relatively large workload of returns, but these returns involve few complex tax issues.

Field Audits

Audits of business returns, as well as of returns of individuals related to the business, are conducted outside IRS offices, usually at the taxpayer's place of business. As with office audits, taxpayers may handle the examination themselves, may be assisted by an authorized representative, or may have the representative handle the examination completely. Typically, the accountant who prepared the return handles the examination, but it is also common for accountants to assist a taxpayer in the examination even though the return was prepared by the taxpayer.

Revenue agents engaged in field audits view themselves as professionals engaged in an activity comparable to the work of the audit professional in a CPA firm. They tend to focus their work on areas of the tax return that offer the most potential for additional tax revenue.

RESOLUTION OF DISPUTES

Agent Level

Disagreement with the office auditor or the revenue agent conducting a field audit is not unusual. The taxpayer or representative who can document a version of the facts that is favorable to the taxpayer's case can often persuade the IRS people involved

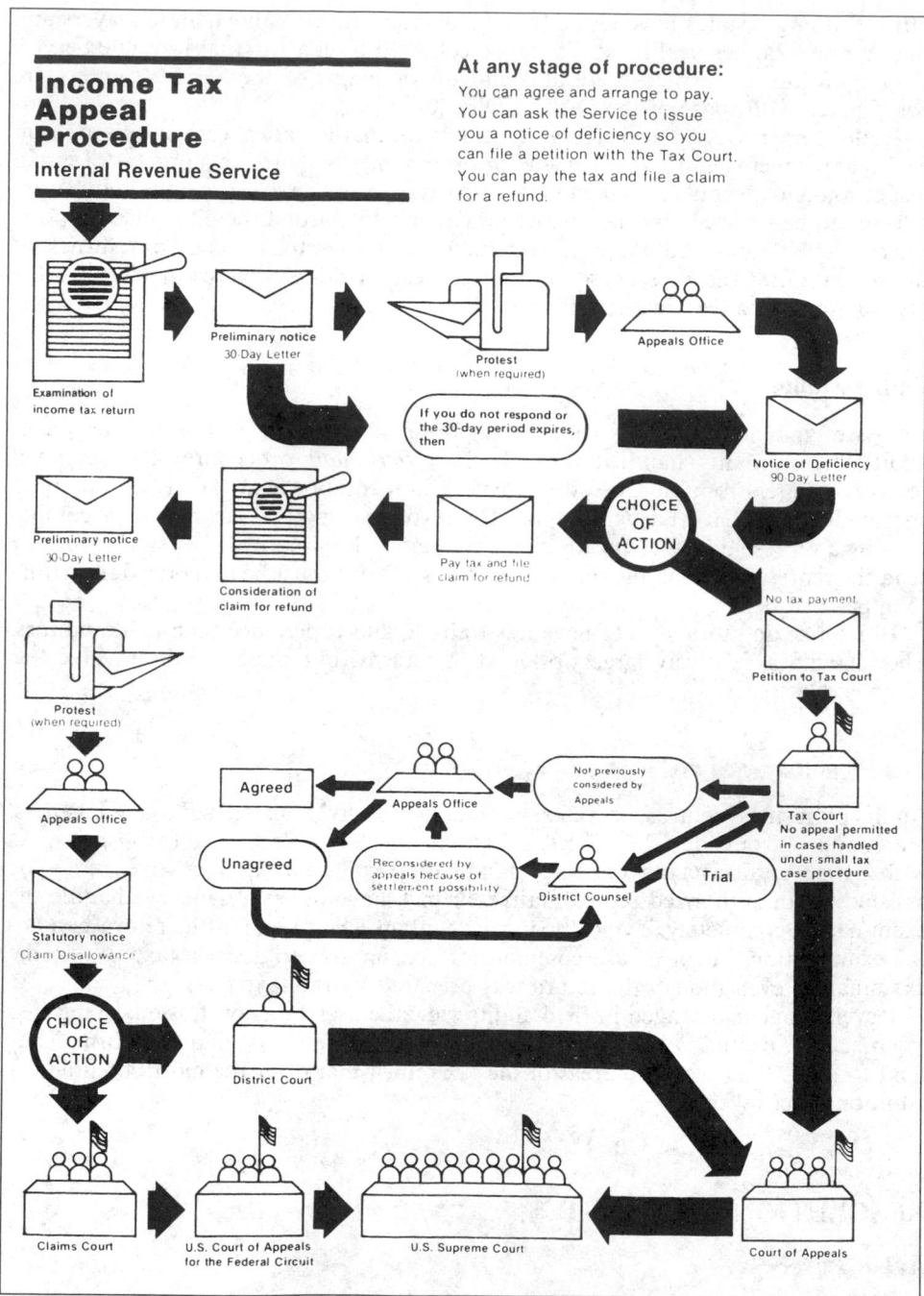

FIG. 48.1   Income Tax Appeal Procedure

Source: Internal Revenue Service, Publication 556, Examination of Returns, Appeal Rights, and Claims for Refund *(1987).*

that the version is "true." Similarly, well-reasoned arguments reflecting a grasp of the tax law and dealing with questions of interpretation raised by the revenue agent often succeed in persuading the agent to change his position.

However, the agent is not the only person who must be convinced. IRS procedures include a review within the district office. If the agent is to agree to the taxpayer's position, there may have to be sufficient documentation and supporting memoranda to help the agent write a report that will be accepted by the reviewer.

The agent may accept an issue that is part of a case, particularly when it is a judgment question such as reasonable compensation, accumulation of earnings, travel and entertainment, capitalization versus expensing of repairs, and so forth. These are matters in which the agent has a fair amount of discretion in deciding the adequacy of support. But this agreement on an issue should not be confused with settling a whole case. Agents are not permitted to settle cases by making compromises. That authority belongs to the appeals officer, discussed in the next section.

If as a result of the audit the IRS agent feels an additional tax is due, the taxpayer will usually be asked to agree to the assessment. He does so by signing a Form 870, which states the *amount* of additional tax (usually called a deficiency), but not the *basis* for it. The effect of signing Form 870 is to waive the taxpayer's statutory right to receive a "90-day letter" before the tax can actually be billed. If the taxpayer does not plan to contest the issue futher, the advantage of signing Form 870 is to limit the period for which interest will be charged on the deficiency. This can be substantial, as discussed in the later section entitled "Interest and Penalties." While Form 870 contains language indicating that the taxpayer agrees the deficiency is correct, this does not prevent filing a claim for refund and even bringing a suit in court to receive it.

Appeals Office

If the taxpayer does not sign a Form 870, the IRS sends a "30-day letter" setting forth the details of the proposed deficiency and offering an opportunity to protest that proposed deficiency to the appeals office within 30 days. The "30-day letter" is the starting point of the appeal procedure shown in Figure 48.1.

The appeals office is part of the regional structure of the IRS, but it includes additional branch offices scattered throughout each region. As with the agent-level examination of the returns, taxpayers may represent themselves; but it is far more usual for an accountant or lawyer to appear on behalf of the taxpayer at this level. If the amount in dispute does not exceed $2,500 for any single year involved, a case can be brought to the appeals office through a simple letter requesting that it be forwarded from the district office to the appeals office and that a hearing with an appeals officer be granted. A written protest is optional if the amount in dispute for any year is more than $2,500 but does not exceed $10,000. A brief written statement of the issues is required.

If the amount in dispute for any year is over $10,000, a written protest must be filed. The protest must set forth the facts, the IRS position, the taxpayer's position, and such supporting arguments and citations as seem appropriate, and should end with a request for an appeals office conference on the matter.

The function of appeals officers is to settle cases. They have the authority to compromise issues on the basis of the probable outcome should the issues be taken to court. They are usually receptive to an offer of settlement submitted for the taxpayer that seems to reflect realistically the relative strengths of the taxpayer's and the IRS's positions. The appeals office conference is expected to be a quasi-judicial hearing in terms of the attitude of the appeals officer, but it is conducted informally, with no formal record of the exact words said by either side.

Appeals officers are more experienced revenue agents, by and large, than those engaged in field audits. As a result, the appeals officer is frequently more willing than the revenue agent to see the taxpayer's side when the taxpayer has a meritorious case. On the other hand, it is not unknown for an appeals officer to identify issues that may have escaped the notice of the field agent. While the appeals officer's instructions are not to raise new issues unless they are substantial in nature, the possibility of new issues being raised is one of the risks to consider when bringing a matter to the appeals officer level. The accountant representing the taxpayer at this level needs technical ability and advocacy skill.

If the taxpayer fails to file a protest, or if the protest and conference do not resolve the issue, a "90-day letter" ultimately will be issued by the IRS. This informs the taxpayer that unless a petition is filed with the Tax Court within 90 days, the IRS will proceed to assess the tax and take whatever actions may be necessary to collect it.

THE COURTS AND TAXPAYER DISPUTES

Tax Court

If the taxpayer is unable to reach a satisfactory resolution of the controversy with the appeals office, but does not want to pay the tax before seeking further settlement opportunities or ultimate judicial review, the next step is to file a petition with the U.S. Tax Court. Cases are tried before the Tax Court in cities throughout the United States. Individual Tax Court judges travel from city to city to hear cases. At the time of filing a petition, the taxpayer indicates the city in which he would like to have the case tried. The case will be heard in either that city or one close to it where the court plans to hold sessions.

The taxpayer may still represent himself before the Tax Court, but it is much more usual to be represented by a lawyer or a CPA. Lawyers, generally, can be admitted upon application and practice before the Tax Court, but accountants who are not also lawyers must take a special examination to perform this function.

Cases submitted to (docketed in) the Tax Court are handled for the government by IRS lawyers who are part of the regional counsel's office. If an appeals office conference was not held before the taxpayer docketed the case, such a conference will probably be scheduled at this point. If the appeals office has considered the case already, the management of the case will normally be in the hands of regional counsel's office, and the appeals officer involved may work closely with regional counsel.

Through discussions and negotiations with either the appeals officer or regional counsel, the majority of Tax Court cases are settled without any trial. Even those that go to trial will have most of the facts stipulated (agreed to by the government and the taxpayer) in advance, so that the actual trial before the Tax Court may take no more than a few hours. After the hearing, the taxpayer and the government file briefs setting out their separate views of the facts and the applicable law.

The decision of the court is appealable, either by the taxpayer or by the government, to the U.S. Circuit Court of Appeals, but if there is no appeal, the Tax Court's decision is a complete and final determination of the issues.

The Tax Court also has a relatively informal (and frequently speedier) procedure for handling cases in which the amount at issue is not over $10,000 for any one year. Under this procedure there is no right of appeal from the Tax Court's decision, nor can the decision be used as a precedent in any other cases. The trial judges who handle these small cases generally give the taxpayer's case equitable consideration.

Other Courts

In the procedure noted above, an issue is presented to the Tax Court without the taxpayer first paying the deficiency. But if the taxpayer prefers to have his case heard by some other court, he must first pay the deficiency and then go either to the U.S. district court, where a jury trial may determine the facts, or to the U.S. Claims Court. The taxpayer may represent himself in these courts, but is not likely to do so. If he wishes to be represented, it must be by a lawyer admitted to practice before the specific court. In these courts, the government is represented by the tax division of the Department of Justice.

The Tax Court, the district court, and the Claims Court may follow different precedents in deciding tax issues that have not been reviewed by the Supreme Court. A decision in the Tax Court or the district court is appealable to the judicial circuit in which the taxpayer resides; an opinion of the Claims Court is appealable only to the U.S. Court of Appeals for the Federal Circuit. Decisions of the courts of appeals may be reviewed by the Supreme Court but that Court will only accept a case for review where there is a conflict between circuits or the issue is unusually important. Only a few tax cases are reviewed by the Supreme Court each year. Because of these complications, and because the tax must be paid before going to the district court or the Claims Court, any decision to litigate in court requires the active participation of legal counsel.

COLLECTIONS AND REFUNDS

Collection Enforcement

Taxpayers who ignore IRS notices of tax due will normally have their salaries garnisheed, liens filed against their bank accounts, or their property seized. The taxpayer or his representative can discuss notices of tax due with the IRS collection personnel to correct errors and, in legitimate hardship situations, to arrange for payment terms or even some compromise of the amount due. The IRS has extraordinary power to seize property and collect taxes. Taxpayers who do not take that power seriously can be severely damaged.

Refund Procedures

A taxpayer may file a return which shows payments of withholding or estimated tax which are more than the tax. In that case, the return itself is a claim for refund or a request that the overpayment be credited against the next year's tax. When the over-payment is identified after the return is filed, a refund claim must be filed. A tax-payer who has filed a tax return normally has three years from the due date of the return or the date filed, whichever is later, to file a claim for refund of the tax involved in that return. After the taxpayer has paid a deficiency, a refund claim for the amount paid can be filed during the two years following the date of payment. As with a return, a refund claim may be prepared by the taxpayer alone or with the assistance of a professional. The IRS typically either honors the claim or may decide to examine the claim before making a decision. A refund of more than $200,000 cannot be made until 30 days after the IRS submits a report on the claim to the Joint Committee on Taxation.

When a revenue agent contacts the taxpayer in connection with a refund claim, the procedure is somewhat similar to the audit of a tax return. This audit focuses mainly on the refund claim, but agents may also find other issues to offset the amount claimed as a refund and may even discover additional tax due. Because of this risk, taxpayers generally seek professional assistance with refund claims. If the claim is disallowed, the taxpayer can bring a refund suit in either a district court or the Claims Court.

As noted previously, a taxpayer who has agreed to a deficiency by signing Form 870 may still bring suit to recover the tax paid. Thus, an action in a district court or the Claims Court after denial of a refund claim is an alternative route to the Tax Court in the examination and settlement process.

INTEREST AND PENALTIES

Taxpayers pay interest on tax deficiencies from the due date of the return to the date of payment. The interest rate is changed every quarter and is compounded daily. The rate is three percentage points higher than the short-term federal rate. Tax disputes frequently take several years to resolve and by the time of resolution, the interest sometimes will exceed the tax. The interest will be deductible by corporations, but in the case of individuals it may be "personal interest," the deduction for which is being eliminated and by 1990 will not be available at all. The IRS does pay interest on refunds but at a rate two percentage points higher than the short-term federal rate. This too is compounded daily and is taxable income for the taxpayer.

If interest costs are not enough to prove how serious Congress is about the tax, the Code provides for various nondeductible penalties. A penalty equal to 5% per month or any part of a month, not to exceed 25% of the balance due, is imposed for late filing of a return. This can be avoided by obtaining an extension of the due date from the IRS, usually a simple procedure. Interest is charged on any balance due. There are penalties, calculated much like interest, for underpayment of estimated tax.

If a tax deficiency is more than 10% of the correct tax (but at least $5,000 for individuals or $10,000 for corporations), a 25% penalty for substantial understate-ment of tax is imposed unless the taxpayer can show substantial authority for the position on its return. The penalty also does not apply if the taxpayer includes in its return a special statement (Form 8725 may be used) disclosing its position. Such statements will not prevent imposition of a penalty where tax shelters are involved unless the taxpayer can show a reasonable relief that its position was more likely than not correct.

If *any* part of a deficiency (regardless of amount) is attributable to negligence or intentional disregard of tax rules by the taxpayer, there is a penalty of 5% of the *entire* deficiency plus one half the interest on the part of the deficiency attributable to the negligence. (See the later section entitled "Regulations for Preparers and Representatives" for a discussion of penalties for negligence on the part of tax return preparers.) If *any* part of a deficiency (regardless of amount) is attributable to fraud, there is a civil penalty of 75% of the *entire* deficiency, plus one-half the interest on the part of the deficiency attributable to the fraud. Basing negligence and fraud penalties on the entire deficiency easily can cause the penalty to be substantially greater than the tax "saved." The item, for example, may be $1,000, with a tax of $350. But other issues in the return lead to a deficiency of $50,000. The negligence penalty before the interest factor is $2,500; the fraud penalty would be $37,500. A pretty steep price!

In the case of fraud, criminal monetary penalties and jail terms may be imposed as well.

PROFESSIONAL TAX PRACTICE

Law Firms

Large law firms provide a wide range of legal services, including those of a sizable tax department; some small firms express no knowledge of or interest in tax practice. There are also firms of various sizes that do practically nothing but tax work. Law firms tend to be less involved with compliance work than accounting firms, although many law firms do prepare individual, partnership, fiduciary, and small corporation returns, commonly using accountants or paralegal personnel to handle most of the work involved.

Law firms compete directly with many accounting firms in tax planning and in handling tax controversies, including revenue agent examinations and, more frequently, conferences at the appeals office level. Whether or not they represent clients at the administrative levels, lawyers in tax practice do handle tax litigation in the Tax Court, the Claims Court, the district courts, courts of appeals, and the Supreme Court. Accountants, on the other hand, unless qualified to represent taxpayers in Tax Court, would not be involved at all at the judicial level except in assisting the lawyers.

Return Preparers

As returns have become more complicated, more and more taxpayers have turned to preparers. Returns are prepared by a wide range of people, including not only lawyers and CPAs, but also people licensed by the states as public accountants, former IRS employees, and employees of commercial tax return preparation organizations. Banks, insurance companies, and brokerage houses also prepare returns, sometimes using their own personnel and sometimes in association with a commercial preparer. Commercial tax return preparation organizations usually do only individual returns.

Some of these return preparers can come to the taxpayer's aid when the IRS examines a return they have prepared, while others can do very little. Commercial return preparers may accompany the taxpayer on his visit to the IRS and explain items in the return, but they are rarely well-equipped—and frequently not permitted under IRS rules—to argue the taxpayer's case on his behalf before the IRS agent. They cannot represent the taxpayer above the agent level. CPAs, lawyers, former IRS employees, and practitioners who have passed a special examination enrolling them to practice before the IRS can represent a taxpayer at all levels within the IRS. Many of them can also offer tax planning services.

The IRS does not regulate the preparation of tax returns. Rather, it regulates the conduct of all tax return preparers. This is not a play on words, since anybody can prepare any federal tax return for a fee. However, preparers must comply with several rules. Some of these govern mechanical matters; for example, the taxpayer must be given a copy of the return before he signs the original. Other rules impose a penalty on the preparer whose negligence in preparing a return results in an understatement of tax liability. The IRS can obtain injunctions against further tax return preparation practice if a preparer is guilty of negligent preparation, misrepresentation of experience or education, or guaranteeing refunds to taxpayers. These rules and penalties are described further under the later section entitled "Regulations for Preparers and Representatives."

Some states license preparers who are not CPAs, attorneys, or persons enrolled to practice before the IRS. The purpose of this licensing is to provide the public with assurance of some level of professional and financial responsibility on the part of the preparer in the event of error, not to establish technical qualifications for the persons licensed.

Accounting Firms

A limited number of smaller accounting firms specialize in tax practice. They offer tax planning advice and represent taxpayers in tax disputes through the level of the Tax Court. In most smaller firms, however, tax practice is handled by each person along with all the other services provided by the firm. Everyone is more or less a jack of all trades.

As firms grow, they tend to departmentalize. A tax department is usually the first to be set apart. Before long, the senior tax people have developed their own relationships with clients, and the tax department has begun to operate somewhat autonomously, though in close cooperation with the audit people. This is as much a reflection of the growing complexity of professional practice as it is of the firm's size or the number of its offices. The range and level of knowledge required for competence in any one of the disciplines that make up the practice of an accounting firm today are such that it is a rare audit partner who feels comfortable in dealing with the specifics of a complex tax problem. Similarly, tax partners are reluctant to deal with accounting issues.

With the establishment of a separate tax department, the need for coordination of tax work with accounting and auditing services becomes apparent. At one time, the staff people who provided accounting and auditing services to the client prepared the client's tax returns, and the tax department reviewed them. Today, it is more likely that returns are prepared in the tax department (frequently by paraprofessionals and usually with the assistance of outside computer service organizations) and reviewed by others in the tax department.

The tax department also handles questions raised by the accounting and auditing people. It takes the initiative in pointing out, both to the auditors and the client, any tax planning opportunities that may advance the client's interests.

The tax provision and liability disclosed in the financial statements are reviewed by both audit and tax people. The auditor prepares or reviews the client's calculations, including identification of book-tax differences and how the taxes shall be reported in the financial statements. The tax department also reviews the calculations, but it is concerned with technical tax issues including not only whether book-tax differences have been identified properly but also the existence of possible areas of IRS controversy that could lead to greater tax expense and liability. For example: Was there in fact a tax-free exchange? Is the interest paid to stockholders a disguised dividend? Is the company a personal holding company? (The relationship between audit and tax functions is described in the section on "Relationships With the CPA's Audit Function.")

TAX ENGAGEMENTS

Advocacy in Tax Practice

When a tax practitioner requests a private ruling on behalf of a taxpayer, he presents the facts and reasons for granting a ruling, not as an impartial observer, but as an advocate for the taxpayer's cause. Similarly, a tax return should present the results of a taxpayer's affairs in the light most favorable to the taxpayer. The preparation of a return can be viewed as the first step to the courts although, of course, a dispute actually does not begin unless the revenue agent raises issues or suggests deficiencies. Then the practitioner who prepared the return customarily handles the examination of it by the IRS. (To do this he must be authorized in writing to represent the taxpayer.)

Initially, the practitioner may only explain how figures were combined or reclassified for the return. But when he starts to explain why the figures were treated as they were, argues the taxpayer's cause with the agent, and continues with the protest to the IRS appeals office, he is forthrightly advocating his client's cause.

Although the CPA acts as an advocate throughout the engagement, in tax practice he is nevertheless an objective professional. That is, he does not substitute the client's judgment of what is proper for his own. Under standards generally followed as this is written, he will assist the client in taking a position, and will advance an argument on behalf of the client, only if there is *reasonable support* for it. Reasonable support has been found in relevant case law, in the published writings of recognized tax authorities, in informed concurring opinion of legal counsel, and, for partners of larger accounting firms, in the concurring opinion of another tax partner.

The reasonable support standard may not be appropriate in the future. The IRS has proposed regulations under which tax practitioners authorized to practice before it must exercise due diligence in preparing returns or advising on return positions to be satisfied that there is substantial authority for the return or the advice. The "substantial authority" standard was selected by Congress as the basis for a dollar penalty on taxpayers for a relatively large deficiency. (See the earlier section on "Interest and Penalties.") If the proposed IRS regulation were adopted, the penalty for the practitioner would be suspension of the right to practice before the IRS. Serious questions as to the propriety of so drastic an action may be raised, including the possible creation of a conflict of interest between the practitioner and the client. Thus far, Congress has enacted only the provision dealing with penalties for the preparer of returns, described in later sections entitled "Penalties for Rule Infractions and Qualitative Penalties".

The AICPA and the American Bar Association have suggested that if "reasonable support" is not to be the test, the standard should be whether the practitioner "has a good faith belief that the position has a realistic possibility of being sustained administratively or judicially on its merits if challenged." Until there is a change in the regulations, "reasonable support" is an acceptable standard.

This area must be watched. Professional practice does not countenance lying or misrepresentation, but neither does it require the CPA to volunteer information detrimental to his client or to point out the weaknesses of his client's position. The client's value system must be given consideration. The CPA must make sure that the client understands the positions taken on his behalf and the available alternative positions, and fully acquiesces in what is being done. The client must understand the tax controversy potential of the return. This includes the possible additional tax, the possibility of the substantial understatement penalty, and the interest cost.

Tax Planning

Sometimes tax planning takes the form of an answer to a question raised by the taxpayer: the taxpayer first identifies his problem and then asks the tax practitioner a question. For example, a question about a specific charitable contribution and the limits on deduction may simply be answered yes or no, but a discussion of related aspects may prompt the practitioner to suggest a review of the feasibility of a tax-exempt foundation to be used by the corporation and to study the estate plans of its principal shareholders. Sometimes the tax practitioner takes the initiative, suggesting a tax-saving possibility based on knowledge of the client's affairs.

In tax planning, the practitioner frequently answers inquiries about the tax consequences of a proposed transaction, and even about how to structure a transaction so as to solve not only the client's tax problem but that of the other party as well. Tax planning requires research to support recommendations. In many instances it is desirable (and sometimes necessary) to obtain advance assurance in the form of a ruling from the IRS that the desired tax consequences will be achieved. CPAs can and do represent clients in obtaining such rulings from the IRS.

Tax planning also includes writing letters to clients explaining new tax legislation, directing attention to specific administrative rulings or court decisions, and explaining how these may help the client. There may be oral presentations to a group at a client meeting, or seminars to which many clients are invited.

Tax Returns

Accounting firms prepare tax returns for corporations, partnerships, and individuals, often as a service incidental to other engagements, such as the annual audit, the review of unaudited financial statements, or a compilation (write-up) of financial statements. The preparation of a business tax return requires access to detailed information, and because this is facilitated by a thorough understanding of the client's business, the preparation is often done by the auditors. If they and the tax people work together on the planning of the audit or other engagement, tax people are available to answer questions that arise during the engagement, not just when the return is prepared. The auditor-prepared return can then be reviewed by qualified tax people familiar with the client's situation. Alternatively, it may be preferable because of the complexity of even the mechanical aspects of tax returns for them to be prepared by the tax department. As indicated earlier, many firms use paraprofessionals who are skilled in return preparation. They work under the supervision of the tax department, which can resolve any technical questions in the return preparation.

The accounting firm typically prepares the tax returns of smaller clients, but larger clients often maintain tax departments of their own, thus reducing the firm's involvement in return preparation and other compliance work. For such clients, the firm is used primarily in tax planning. When the firm prepares tax returns for an individual, this quite often involves returns such as trust returns, partnership returns for investment activities, and returns for other members of the individual's family.

Accounting firms also prepare returns for individuals in the community who have no other client relationship with the firm. Corporate executives, lawyers, bankers, doctors, brokers, other professionals, and government officials all need professional tax service. By serving them well, the firm hopes to be kept in mind when these individuals become aware of others, whether businesses or individuals, who need the professional services of a CPA firm.

Tax return engagements do not require an audit of the information furnished by the client, but they do require sufficient contact with the taxpayer to satisfy the preparer that the return will be prepared in accordance with the tax law. For example, a CPA preparing a return does not have to see receipts or canceled checks for charitable contributions, but he should believe, either from his knowledge of the taxpayer or by asking him, that the amounts can be substantiated if the IRS challenges the return. Nor does the CPA have to ascertain that each donee is qualified for deductible contributions, but if an organization's name indicates it might not be qualified, he should verify its status. Other aspects of the need to consider the reasonableness of the return data are discussed under the later section entitled "Qualitative Penalties."

Tax Fraud

In the process of a tax return examination, the revenue agent may introduce another IRS representative as a special agent from the Criminal Investigation Division. At this point the CPA should stop work in connection with the examination of the return, advise the client to obtain legal counsel, and then proceed only with the authorization or at the direction of legal counsel. In fraud cases, the government first resolves the criminal issue, that is, will the taxpayer go to jail? It can be most dangerous for anyone who is not thoroughly familiar with the taxpayer's rights to assist the client at this stage, and this requires an experienced lawyer, preferably one with expertise in tax fraud matters. The problem is that information learned by the CPA is not privileged. Thus, unless the CPA is acting under the direction of counsel, his involvement may well result in his having to give evidence against the taxpayer that otherwise might not be obtainable by the IRS.

It is not uncommon for an attorney who is defending a taxpayer on tax fraud charges to engage a CPA to assist in the development of information necessary to the defense. Even if the fraud charge itself cannot be refuted, the CPA can help in the defense of issues that are not related to the fraud, since the 75% civil fraud penalty applies to the entire deficiency.

The experience of the CPA, even one who devotes all his time to tax matters for business clients, may not be helpful if he is acting alone in a criminal fraud situation. In a typical tax examination, the aim is to determine the tax liability. From the viewpoint of the CPA and the client, the less tax the better, allowing for recognition of the need to compromise and settle issues. In a fraud examination, on the other hand, the IRS's first goal is to determine whether or not to prosecute the taxpayer criminally. Only after this has been resolved will the IRS turn its attention to the amount of tax due. The attitudes of the parties in a criminal tax investigation are totally different, and the adversary atmosphere is very clearly present. Relatively trivial items could be the basis for criminal prosecution. The leadership and advice of an attorney is necessary if the taxpayer is to have the benefit of the rights available under the Constitution.

It must be emphasized that the instigation of a criminal investigation does not mean that the taxpayer is guilty. Of the many criminal investigations begun, only a small fraction actually proceed to indictment, trial, and conviction. Nevertheless, the risks for the taxpayer (and his advisers) are far too great to permit using any but the most skilled and knowledgeable practitioners in this uncertain area.

Some accounting firms regularly work under the direction of an attorney in criminal tax fraud matters and render outstanding service in that capacity. These firms usually have continuing relationships with attorneys who specialize in criminal tax fraud, and the attorney rather than the taxpayer is the accounting firm's client. Other firms will not accept tax fraud engagements except when the taxpayer being investigated is already a client of the firm. Under the best of circumstances, a tax fraud investigation is a difficult assignment that occupies a disproportionate amount of partner's and managers' time, including possible courtroom appearances.

Tax Research Materials

In comparison to other fields of accounting practice, research on tax matters is relatively easy. In addition to loose-leaf tax services with weekly updating, there are numerous treatises, periodicals, and other published materials that are well organized and easily accessible to all practitioners. Computer data bases are also available and allow searches of millions of pages of material to be conducted in a short period of time. (See Chapter 50.)

CLIENT RELATIONSHIPS

Investigation of Clients

Typically, an accounting firm will receive requests for services, particularly the preparation of individual returns, from many people. It is thus necessary to decide whether to accept each opportunity presented. The problem is not much different from deciding whether to accept an audit engagement, although fees and available personnel are less likely to be a problem with a tax return than an audit. If these considerations are no obstacle, the firm must decide whether it wants to be associated with the new client.

There is no requirement that a firm must provide services to anyone with whom it does not want to be associated. Accepting a disreputable person as a tax client can cause image problems, fee problems, and even problems in the relationship between the firm and the IRS. Thus, every prospective tax client should be investigated as appropriate to ascertain whether the client will meet the firm's acceptance standards. Most firms do not want clients who have criminal records or engage in unethical business or financial operations. To some extent, a client may be evaluated on the basis of his professional advisers, and thus may seek to be associated with a reputable accounting firm. By the same token, the firm can be evaluated on the basis of its clients. It should not, for a mere fee, lend its name or reputation to those who do not warrant it.

Engagement Letters

Engagement letters or memoranda are used to ensure a meeting of the minds on what services the firm will render, how it will charge for these services, when bills for these services will be paid, and any other matters that have been or should be agreed on between the client and the firm. They should be worded with some care. For example, it might not be advisable to undertake to "prepare all required tax returns" for a multistate business when, in fact, what is intended is the preparation of only the federal income tax returns and certain state returns. The returns for other states may be prepared by the client's personnel or may not be prepared at all because the client believes it is not taxable there. These matters can be included in an engagement letter covering all services in the case of audit clients, or they can be stated in a separate letter.

Fee Policies

The subject of fees should also be cautiously drafted in engagement letters. When tax work is intended to produce beneficial results that can be objectively measured, the fee arrangement should normally be described in such a way that the minimum charge will be time at standard billing rates, with the door open for additional amounts to be charged on the achievement of specified results.

Although auditing services of CPAs may not be offered on the basis of a fee that is contingent on the results of the servies, in tax work this type of fee is permissible if it is based on the results of court action or the findings of government agencies. Thus, in an engagement to represent the taxpayer in a specific tax controversy, it would be proper either to make the amount of the fee entirely dependent on the results or to base the fee on time with provision for an additional amount to be paid when results beyond a certain minimum are achieved. The Professional Ethics Division of the AICPA has held, however, that basing a fee for *preparing* a tax return on the amount saved in taxes would violate the rules against contingent fees (ET 391.023–.024). If this were viewed as guaranteeing the client a refund, the IRS could use it as grounds for enjoining a preparer from engaging in the preparation of tax returns.

Liability to Clients

The accountant may be liable to his client for negligent tax work. As it is true of the dollars-and-cents value of good results, the dollars-and-cents cost of negligent work can very easily be demonstrated. The liability to the client will normally be the amount of loss actually sustained by the client, which may include an allowance both for interest and for the fees and expenses of other professionals incurred as a result of the accountant's negligence.

It may be instructive to describe some situations in which an accountant's negligence in tax services could result in a loss to the taxpayer. Many taxpayers are required to make payments of estimated taxes and are subject to penalties if these payments are not made in accordance with the law. The taxpayer may allege that the accountant was instructed to prepare a "safe" estimate, but the IRS may assert that not enough was paid and assess a penalty. The taxpayer likely would expect the accountant to reimburse him for the penalty.

It is unlikely that an accountant will be held liable for suggesting a course of action to a client if the risks as well as the benefits of that course of action, and the available alternative approaches, have been explained to the client and the client acquiesces in the position taken. On the other hand, suppose an accountant incorrectly advises a client that the sale of stock of one of his controlled corporations to another of his controlled corporations will produce capital gain results, which will not be taxable because the taxpayer can use capital losses that otherwise are not deductible. Upon examination of the return, IRS treats the transaction as a dividend to be taxed as ordinary income. In this case the taxpayer may seek to hold the accountant liable for the difference in tax and for the related expenses incurred.

Meticulous attention to the details of tax return preparation and filing will normally eliminate most, if not all, of the mistakes that can result in amounts being owed the client by the accountant – even small amounts. Such occurrences can damage the accountant's credibility and affect his reputation with the client and possibly in the business community at large. The best method of controlling liabilities resulting from tax practice may be to evaluate routinely the risk to the client of wrong advice and, when that risk is large, to double-check the conclusions reached.

It goes without saying that whether or not the accountant will be found liable for the taxpayer's deficiency or penalty, he will first make every effort to reduce, if not eliminate, the amount involved. For example, there are a number of ways to calculate estimated tax payments, and one of the exceptions may apply. The dividend issue described earlier might be attacked from several angles. Perhaps it can be demonstrated that the requisite control was not present, or perhaps a review of the corporation's earnings and profits will show they were not enough to support the dividend treatment. The presumption that IRS findings are correct is by no means conclusive. Frequently, they can be rebutted with careful work. Of course, it is always better to make these efforts at the time the service is first provided to the taxpayer, not later after the IRS mounts an attack.

Liability to Third Parties

Except for the preparer penalties discussed in the following section, the accountant has no liability to the IRS or to third parties who are not affected by the return for negligence in preparation of the return. However, third parties who *are* affected by a return can claim that the accountant is liable to them. Such parties would include stockholders of certain corporations, partners in partnerships, and beneficiaries of trusts or estates, among others.

Liability to third parties may also be alleged where no return is prepared. For example, suppose the accountant gives a categorical opinion that a partnership's activity will result in passive income for its partners, which is desirable for those who have otherwise nondeductible passive losses for other investments. The opinion is made available to prospective investors and the described tax results are not achieved. The investors, whether or not they are the accountant's clients, may seek restitution. In some instances, the SEC or a state regulatory authority may consider action against the accountant, either because of the tax opinion itself or because of an alleged failure to comment on the uncertainty of the tax problems when giving an opinion on the financial statements of the partnership. As with other possible liability matters, the best defense is careful work before a position is recommended or an opinion given.

RELATIONSHIPS WITH THE IRS

Regulations for Preparers and Representatives

In general, income tax return preparers are persons who prepare returns for a fee or who hire persons to prepare returns for others. The term preparer includes not only the person who signs the return, but also anyone who prepares a substantial part of it or decides how it is to be prepared. Further, the preparer of a Subchapter S return or a partnership return can be deemed also responsible for certain items in a stockholder's or partner's return.

Penalties for Rule Infractions

Penalties are imposed on preparers and their employers for a variety of acts or failures to act. The penalties vary in amount, depending on the offense. For example, the failure to give a taxpayer a copy of the return brings a $25 penalty, and so does the failure to sign a return or include the preparer's social security number. These penalties are largely mechanical in operation and application. The IRS probably recognizes that an occasional omission of a social security number or an inadvertent failure to give a taxpayer a copy of his tax return is not an act requiring a penalty.

Qualitative Penalties

There are also penalties relevant to the quality of the prepared return. A penalty of $100 is imposed if any part of an understatement of liability in a return is due to the preparer's negligent or intentional disregard of rules and regulations. If there is a willful attempt to understate the tax, the penalty is $500.

These penalties mean that the return preparer is responsible for the *reasonableness* of tax information. Although a preparer may rely on information furnished by the taxpayer, he may not ignore its implications. The preparer is expected to make reasonable inquiries if the information furnished appears to be incorrect or incomplete. He may also be required to make inquiries of the taxpayer to determine the existence of facts and circumstances that may be necessary for the claiming of deductions.

The regulations illustrate the need for inquiry with an example of a tax return preparer who used the amounts of medical expense and travel and entertainment expenses furnished by a taxpayer. Although the taxpayer had, in fact, paid smaller amounts, the preparer calculated the deductions using the information supplied, which resulted in an understatement of liability. The preparer had no reason to believe that the information given was incorrect or incomplete. He asked for no documentation of medical expenses, but did inquire about the records to support the travel and entertainment expenses. The representations made to him by the taxpayer were satisfactory. In this example, the IRS concluded that the understatement of liability was not due to the preparer's negligence or willful attempt to understate liability and, accordingly, no penalty applied (Reg. § 1.6694-1(b)(2)).

In any situation where the examination of a return results in the assessment of a deficiency, it is likely that the examining agent will consider whether the understatement of liability was due either to the preparer's negligence or to willful intent. Such preparer penalties should be resisted even though it may seem that it is a nuisance to spend much time to save $100 or even $500. Preparer penalties for negligence or a willful attempt to understate tax are referred to the Director of Practice and could lead that IRS official to suggest more serious sanctions such as a suspension of the preparer's right to practice before IRS. At the administrative level, all that can be done is to persuade the agent not to impose the penalty, as the administrative procedures available in defending against tax deficiencies are not available as to preparer penalties. Once the penalty is imposed, the preparer who wants to continue resistance has no alternative but to pay at least 15% of the penalty and then bring a refund action in district court. Unfortunately, this guarantees a maximum amount of damaging publicity.

The $100 and $500 penalties are not the IRS's sole weapons; it also has the right to go to court to obtain an injunction against specific actions, including the preparation of tax returns. The best defense against assertion of penalties is to document the support for a position taken in a return.

Circular No. 230

A substantial part of a CPA's tax practice is the representation of taxpayers before the tax authorities. The rules governing this service are set forth in the Treasury Department's *Circular No. 230 (Revised 9/85) Regulations Governing the Practice of Attorneys, Certified Public Accountants, Enrolled Agents, and Enrolled Actuaries Before the Internal Revenue Service.* This circular covers just about all activities connected with any presentation to the IRS on behalf of a client and its tax affairs, except tax returns. As discussed earlier (see the section entitled "Advocacy in Tax

Practice"), amendments have been proposed as to a standard for positions taken or advised in tax returns.

If a charge is made that a practitioner has behaved improperly, there are appeal procedures. The bulk of the actions to reprimand, suspend, or permanently disbar practitioners tend to be connected with complicity in tax fraud or the practitioner's failure to file his own returns or pay his own tax.

Working Paper Availability

Since 1981, IRS official policy as described in the *Internal Revenue Manual* (IRM 4024) is that tax reconciliation workpapers should be available to an examining agent. These are workpapers used to assemble and compile financial data for a tax return. Typically these will include final trial balances and/or a schedule of consolidating and adjusting entries. They include information used to trace financial information to the tax return. The IRS view is that the agent needs these workpapers since they tie the tax return to the general ledger. As a practical matter, such papers can readily be made available.

Audit and tax accrual workpapers are another matter and are treated differently by the IRS. Audit papers are viewed by the IRS as those prepared in the course of an examination of financial statements to support the CPA's opinion as to the fairness of the presentation of the financial statements in conformity with GAAP and to demonstrate compliance with GAAS. Tax accrual papers are those prepared to estimate a company's contingent tax liability. They can include not only analyses of tax accounts and a tax computation, but also a memorandum discussing items reflected in the financial statements as income or expense where the tax treatment is not clear. (The nature of these is discussed in greater detail under the later section entitled "Tax Accrual Workpapers.") As to these papers, the IRS agent who is not involved in a fraud examination should seek access only in unusual circumstances. Agents are expected to:

> keep in mind that the taxpayer's records are the primary source of factual data to support the tax return. Accountants' audit or tax accrual workpapers should normally be used only when such factual data cannot be obtained from the taxpayer's records and then only as a collateral source for factual data, access to which should be requested with discretion and not as a matter of standard examining procedure.

The Manual prescribes these steps before workpapers are sought:

1. The schedule (M-1), which provides a reconciliation between income reported in the financial statements and that reported in the income tax return, must be completed.
2. The tax examination must be substantially complete.
3. Specific issues involving unresolved questions must be identified.
4. Factual information must have been requested from the taxpayer relating to the unresolved questions, and analyses of the same information must have been requested from the taxpayer's independent accountant.

If these steps have been completed and the agent still believes that the independent accountant's workpapers are required, a request may be made for them, but it must first be approved by the chief of the examination division of the IRS district office. The request must also be limited to the unresolved questions previously identified.

Supreme Court View

The U.S. Supreme Court unanimously decided in *Arthur Young & Company*[2] that the independent auditor's workpapers are not privileged. The IRS summons authority is subject only to traditional privileges and limitations:

* There must be a legitimate purpose for the inquiry;
* The information sought must not be in the possession of the IRS already; and
* The IRS must follow its prescribed administrative rules.

Unless Congress wishes to legislate an immunity for the tax accrual workpapers, there are no other restrictions. In its decision, the Supreme Court considered the possibility that if the IRS had access to the accountant's workpapers, this would interfere with the integrity and candor of the audit process. The Court said that the accountant could refuse to certify financial reports or could footnote or otherwise qualify an opinion if the client had failed to make sufficient disclosure to the accountant regarding tax accrual matters. The Court also believed that the SEC or a private litigant would be able to obtain information and that there was no reason to limit the IRS to a lesser authority.

The court approved the above procedures from the *Internal Revenue Manual,* which expressed an intention not to seek the tax accrual workpapers as a matter of course. Eight days after the Supreme Court decision in *Arthur Young,* the IRS announced that it did not plan to change those procedures for requesting tax-accrual workpapers (IRS News Release, IR 84-45, March 29, 1984).

RELATIONSHIPS WITH THE CPA'S AUDIT FUNCTION

Preparation of Returns

Most CPA firms prepare more individual returns than business returns. Since most individual taxpayers file their returns on the basis of the calendar year, this preparation is concentrated in the early months of the year, and even with extensions and the use of computers, this concentration presents a scheduling problem. Individual returns are usually prepared in the tax department and paraprofessionals may be used.

Business returns, that is, returns for corporations or partnerships, are fewer in number but are more likely to present complex preparation problems. Much of the audit work done in connection with financial statements is closely related to the work necessary for preparing business tax returns. Thus it is helpful for audit personnel to participate in the preparation of these returns. If time schedules permit, it is

---

[2] United States v. Arthur Young & Co. 465 US 805 (1984).

usually more efficient for the business return to be prepared at the time of the audit than at a later date. Simpler returns may be handled entirely by audit personnel, with specific questions or problems referred to the tax department. A review of such a return could be done by an audit manager or the audit partner in charge of the engagement who is familiar with the client. Even with simple returns, however, it is probably wise to have a tax person review the return.

Time schedules, complexities of the law, and other forces have resulted in less audit participation in return preparation. Even when tax people prepare the returns, some assistance from the auditors is usually necessary. Clients with their own tax departments will prepare their own returns, but may ask the CPA firm's tax people to review them. (See the section on "Tax Provision and Accrual Review.")

As indicated earlier, tax return preparers must sign the returns or pay a penalty. The preparer signs as an individual although firm affiliation can be indicated. In the typical accounting firm, several people are involved in the preparation of the return, but only one signs it. For many years, before the adoption of stricter tax return preparer rules, it was not unusual for auditors to sign tax returns. Now the regulations clearly state that when more than one person prepares a return, it should be signed by the one who has the ultimate responsibility for its accuracy. This probably results in more returns being signed by tax partners and managers.

Finding Tax Problems

A tax problem can be a tax opportunity in disguise. In reviewing the details of a client's operations, an auditor can identify problems in completed and contemplated transactions that will have tax implications. He should therefore be familiar enough with tax matters to recognize these problems, even though his knowledge may be insufficient to solve them.

Many firms assign a tax person to each client to work with the audit people as the audit is being planned, answering questions, solving problems, and indentifying opportunities for service. This tax person is also responsible for reviewing the tax provision, tax liability, and tax return.

Accounting and Auditing Problems

Conversely, a review of a company's affairs from a tax point of view frequently raises accounting questions. For example, a company may be assuming that a contemplated change in financial accounting will be used for tax accounting as well. The tax person reviewing the change, however, will consider whether it requires permission, and even whether it is advantageous for tax purposes at all. A change in the accounting period may result in a net operating loss carry-over, and this consequence, overlooked at first, will involve an unexpected cost affecting the financial statements. The tax person's review may also uncover situations with audit implications, such as payments made but not deductible for tax purposes, that the auditor must consider.

Recommendations made to the company for tax planning may also have accounting or auditing implications. For example, a recommendation that the company adopt the last-in, first-out (LIFO) method of inventory valuation has significant accounting implications. (See Chapter 14 for a further discussion of LIFO as well as other changes in inventory accounting, for example, changes in the allocation of indirect costs to inventory.) Other changes that could produce tax savings may depend on using a different accounting method from that used for financial reporting purposes, and this in turn may require a calculation of deferred taxes. Again, when a company acquires another business, it is most important that both the tax people and the auditors consider the differences between the tax rules governing tax-free acquisitions and the accounting rules governing the treatment of a transaction as a purchase or pooling. An aggressive position taken in a tax return provides yet another example. Tax personnel and auditors must consider such an action within the framework both of the tax rules and of the accounting rules governing the treatment of a contingency, as set forth in SFAS 5 (C59).

Tax Provision and Accrual Review

The government remains a significant partner in business operations even after TRA 1986 rate reductions. The calculations of its share, taking into account temporary differences, has a substantial impact on the financial statements. This calculation, whether done by the company or by the auditors, should be reviewed by the tax people from at least two points of view.

First, the potential for tax controversy must be assessed, with regard both to the year being reviewed and to any prior years that are open under the statute of limitations, even if the returns are not being examined by the IRS. Exposure to tax deficiencies will range from "probable" to "remote." Based on the auditor's findings as to the facts of transactions, tax personnel can consider the issues that may be raised and the likely outcome if raised. The proper application of SFAS 5 to this evaluation of possible issues is done by auditors, but they need the assistance of tax personnel to understand the issues.

Second, the tax calculation must be reviewed for compliance with tax regulations. In an opinion on financial statements, the auditor may determine that the effect of an error is not material and therefore may not insist on its correction. In tax matters, however, immateriality is not grounds for treating an item of income or deduction in any manner other than that prescribed by law. In addition to reviewing tax calculations, the tax department should examine financial statement footnotes that describe or explain the company's tax expense or liability.

The involvement of the tax department does not mean that the audit partner has delegated his responsibility for the treatment of the tax accounts in the financial statements. The tax department's participation in the audit – to review the tax provision and related deferred charge or deferred credit accounts – provides the audit partner with the benefit of the tax department's expertise, but the audit partner still decides how the tax consequences of the year's events will be presented in the financial statements.

Some companies, particularly large corporations, have sought protection against any IRS access to workpapers (discussed earlier) by using legal counsel to review the tax accrual and give an opinion to the auditor. The AICPA Auditing Standards Division released an interpretation (AU 9326.06–.17) in 1981 that essentially states:

1. Limitations on access to any information considered by the auditor to be necessary to substantiate the tax accrual will affect the ability of the auditor to issue an unqualified opinion on the financial statements. The auditor must consider whether the failure of a company to

prepare and maintain adequate records on tax matters, and/or the restriction of access to such information, constitutes a scope limitation. Consideration should also be given to the adequacy of working paper documents when a company imposes restrictions as to the content of the auditor's working papers on the tax accrual.

2. Legal counsel is not considered a "specialist" under GAAS. Therefore, while an opinion of legal counsel on specific tax issues, to which substantive legal attention has been given, can be useful to the auditor in forming an opinion as to the tax accrual, sole reliance on such an opinion is not appropriate.

Tax Accrual Workpapers

Under GAAS, adequate evidence in support of transactions and balances must be gathered and documented in the workpapers. In the matter of tax provisions and accruals, facts are necessary, but descriptions of remote contingencies or gratuitous comments contribute nothing and should not be included in the audit papers. The form and content of the tax provision and accrual workpapers will vary but they should show that taxes have been audited in conformity with GAAS. In general, they will include:

1. Calculation of the tax provision.
2. Analysis of the current and deferred tax liability accounts, including identification and evaluation of material contingencies; and, for SEC clients, data needed for Regulation S-X disclosures.
3. Analysis of temporary differences.
4. Reconciliation of the prior year provision to the return as filed.

Documentation of tax contingencies should be tailored to these major components:

1. *Material contingencies* (or several related contingencies which in the aggregate are material) *for which accrual is or may be required.* Such items should be documented just as any other material balances and transactions examined during the audit. If a decision is made that accrual is not required, satisfactory documentation of that decision is needed.
2. *Material contingencies* (or several related contingencies which in the aggregate are material) *for which disclosure may be required.* Disclosure is required when there is a reasonable possibility that a material loss is not probable and/or its amount (or the range of loss) cannot be reasonably estimated. Such disclosure is part of the audited financial statements and suitable workpaper documentation is needed.
3. *Contingencies that are not individually material, for which accrual is or may not be appropriate.* The manner in which these items are documented in the workpapers could create the potential for questions from an IRS agent in the event access is granted to the agent. Items which are separately immaterial do not require documentation. However, if the sum of these types of items is material, documentation of the composition of the total is required, with written commentary as appropriate for each accrual.
4. *Nonspecific accruals (i.e., "cushions") or those which can be identified but for which no accrual need have been made.* Such accruals must be, by definition, not material. Workpapers should contain sufficient data to maintain continuity of identification from year to year. Other than an indication of immateriality, no evaluative comments are needed.

AICPA PRONOUNCEMENTS AND OTHER GUIDES

In addition to the rules they must follow under Treasury Department Circular 230 and the tax return preparer regulations, members of the AICPA are bound by their organization's Code of Professional Conduct. However, the AICPA does not extend to tax practice those rules that clearly apply only to the examination of financial statements.

In tax practice, a member or associate must observe the same standards of truthfulness and integrity he is required to observe in any other professional work. This does not mean, however, that a member or associate may not resolve doubt in favor of his client, as long as there is reasonable support for his position (ET 102.01). This is consistent with the advocacy role of the CPA in tax practice. As discussed in the earlier section entitled "Advocacy in Tax Practice," proposed changes in Treasury Department Circular 230 could impose a narrower standard of permissible advocacy which practitioners would have to follow.

Statements on Responsibilities in Tax Practice

The AICPA Federal Tax Division has issued Statements on Responsibilities in Tax Practice. The primary effect of these statements is educational. They do not have the authority of Circular 230 and they do not establish a separate code of conduct for tax practice. The statements cover the need for answering questions on returns; whether to sign a return if it treats an item differently from the manner agreed to in an earlier year's revenue agent's examination; the extent to which items in a return may be estimated; what the CPA should do when he learns of an error in an earlier return; advising clients on tax consequences; how much verification is needed of data to be used in return preparation; and the need for disclosure of positions taken in returns.

Disclosure. Disclosure of a position in a tax return may be advisable even when a regulation or standard of practice does not require it. Sometimes disclosure of relevant information improves and protects the taxpayer's position. For example, if a taxpayer has omitted from gross income an amount that exceeds 25% of the gross income shown on the return, the statute of limitations for assessing additional tax is six years from the date of filing the return instead of the usual three years. However, if there is a statement in the return disclosing the amounts omitted, these amounts are not included in measuring the 25% omission.

It is reasonably clear that adequate disclosure generally will prevent the imposition of fraud penalties. While it is not so clear that disclosure will prevent the imposition of a negligence penalty, it could certainly be a factor in determining whether there were reasonable grounds for the position taken in the return.

At one time, it could be argued that merely reporting a transaction in a return could constitute disclosure, but that seems less likely today. As a general matter, disclosure must be in sufficient detail to alert the IRS as to the nature of the transaction so that a reasonably informed decision can be made as to whether to audit the return. Thus, when an individual reported a gain from a sale of stock, with no indication that the transaction was the receipt of property to redeem shares in a closely held corporation, the Tax Court held there was not enough disclosure.[3] The failure to show the redemption as such in the return permitted the IRS more than three years later to find a 25% understatement of income caused by undervaluation of the property received.

If disclosure is relied on to avoid imposition of the substantial understatement penalty, the regulations require a clearly identified statement as to the nature of the item, its amount, and the specific facts or the position taken. Rev. Proc. 87-48 lists certain items which need not have the separate statement but the return itself still should have enough detail to alert the IRS to possible issues.

SOME PHILOSOPHICAL ISSUES

Conformity

Tax accounting's dependence on (not subservience to) financial accounting is a logical consequence of any tax based on or measured by income. Different tax accounting methods have been developed to meet special needs without seriously interfering with the improvement of financial accounting. While these different accounting methods usually result in a figure for taxable income that is lower than that for financial income, deferred tax accounting prevents this discrepancy from distorting the financial statement. (See Chapter 17.)

It has been suggested from time to time that the tax laws could be simplified, and their administration facilitated, if tax accounting were to conform to GAAP. For some years, in fact, the IRS has permitted a change in tax accounting only on the condition that the same change be reflected in the taxpayer's books and financial statements. This provides the IRS some additional procedures for deciding whether to allow the change. The determination that the new methods are acceptable for financial accounting purposes is based on an independent review, and apparently this simplifies the processing of requests by the IRS. Unfortunately, however, this approach discriminates in favor of companies that do not need to have a CPA participate in the preparation of their financial statements, because they usually can make any change in book accounting and financial reporting that would permit the use of a different (and more advantageous) tax method.

A policy of strict conformity as a condition for the use of a tax accounting method would inhibit improvements in financial reporting. As new tax concepts developed that offered more favorable treatment, there would probably be considerable pressure on the accounting profession to approve the new methods for financial statement purposes. This could hinder efforts toward sounder accounting and weaken the profession's ability to develop principles governing appropriate financial reporting.

The Tax Reform Act of 1986 marked a change from the long-standing practice of using the tax laws as an incentive for economic investment and activity. This may reduce one source of pressure on financial accounting. However, as discussed in the later section entitled "Alternative Minimum Tax," a policy of conformity may be with us now. Its effect on the development of accounting principles remains to be seen.

---

[3] Estate of Fry v. Commissioner, 88 TC No. 55 (1987).

LIFO

The problems that would be raised by enforced conformity are illustrated by the LIFO method of inventory valuation. This is probably the only situation in which the statute requires that the taxpayer using one accounting method for tax purposes may not use any other method to ascertain income "for the purpose of a report or statement . . . (1) to shareholders, partners, or other proprietors, or to beneficiaries, or (2) for credit purposes" (IRC § 472(c)). Some obvious problems with respect to this sweeping requirement were resolved by regulations, but other, perhaps not so obvious, problems continued to arise, causing considerable confusion and uncertainty about the right to use or continue to use the LIFO method.

For tax purposes, LIFO is strictly a cost method. (An accounting discussion of LIFO is contained in Chapter 14.) When this flow-of-cost assumption is used for tax purposes, inventories must be valued at cost only, not at the lower of cost or market. This is squarely in conflict with GAAP, which requires the use of the lower of cost or market in financial statements. The conflict was resolved only by a clear statement in the income tax regulations that the use of the lower of LIFO cost or market in a company's financial statements would not be considered a violation of the LIFO conformity requirement (Reg. § 1.472-2(e)).

Less obvious problems came to light as the SEC, APB, and FASB issued pronouncements on particular accounting issues. To the extent that any of these pronouncements required that inventories be restated, or that the effect of accounting changes be described in detail, they created a conflict with the statutory requirement that no method other than LIFO be used in financial reporting. For example, the financial accounting for the purchase of a business requires that its assets be valued at the purchase price; but for tax purposes, such a purchase may qualify as a nontaxable exchange, in which event inventories may not be restated. If these inventories had been valued at LIFO, would the difference in values between the financial statements and the tax returns mean that the taxpayer had violated the conformity requirement? After much debate, the IRS decided that it would not (Rev. Proc. 72-29).

For another example, a company that changes to LIFO must in the year of the change indicate the effect on earnings. This disclosure of results under an accounting method other than LIFO may be a literal violation of the conformity requirement; but once again, the IRS agreed that since it was the result of accounting pronouncements, it would not be regarded as a violation that called for termination of the LIFO election (Rev. Proc. 76-3).

To appreciate the seriousness of these episodes, it is necessary to understand that the IRS did not promptly advise affected taxpayers of the consequences of the conformity requirement. On the contrary, it was with considerable reluctance and delay that the IRS agreed not to press the conformity requirement, provided the "violation" resulted from compliance with an official pronouncement of the SEC, FASB, APB, or some equivalent authority. And then this allowance was applied quite literally. Late in 1978, for example, the IRS announced that there would be a violation of the LIFO conformity requirement if a taxpayer that was not subject to SEC jurisdiction decided to disclose information on replacement cost of inventories.

The LIFO conformity issue could have grave effects on a company. A violation of the rule could result in a substantial additional tax cost on the difference between

LIFO and first-in, first-out (FIFO) cost. While a company may not be permitted to explain specifically what its earnings would have been on FIFO, it is allowed to explain what its inventories would have been, and a reasonably knowledgeable reader of the financial statement could quickly calculate FIFO earnings. It is also interesting to note that the IRS, except for statements in rulings, does not seem inclined to take action to assess a deficiency because of a violation of the conformity rule.

As concern grew in recent years about paper profits in inventory, and more and more companies began to use LIFO, the straitjacket effect of the conformity rule became apparent. Finally, during the summer of 1979, the IRS issued regulations to permit the use of LIFO with an explanation in supplementary information of its effect on the financial statements (Reg. § 1.472-2(e)). This was 25 years after the enactment of the 1954 Code. Any conformity rule for other tax provisions should not have to wait that long before it is made workable.

Alternative Minimum Tax

By comparison with TRA 1986 version of an alternative minimum tax (AMT), the preceding discussions of conformity and LIFO are abstract philosophy. AMT is a live problem, the full impact of which will be appreciated as more financial statements and tax returns are prepared.

In reality, AMT is a separate parallel tax system for the determination of corporate income tax. The determination of the AMT begins with corporate taxable income computed under the "regular" system. Added to or subtracted from this amount are numerous tax preference items. Then a $40,000 exemption is deducted and the resulting adjusted alternative minimum taxable income (AMTI) is multiplied by a flat 20% rate. The final step is to compare this result (the AMT) to the "regular" tax. The corporation pays the greater of the two taxes. It sounds fairly straightforward but in reality it is quite complex.

Aside from the added complexity of calculating the AMT, accounting for its effects will present a multitude of problems, especially for the unwary. The difficulty really hits home when you realize that differences between pretax accounting income and pretax taxable income must now be tracked on four bases:

Financial Reporting

1. Regular tax provision or benefit

2. AMT provision or benefit

Tax Return

3. Regular tax payable

4. AMT tax payable

If this is not complicated enough, foreign tax credits, investment credits (some still linger on), and loss carry-overs and carry-backs are calculated differently for regular tax and AMT. Also, there is a system of credits against regular tax of later years for AMT paid on deferral-type preferences.

Book Tax Preference. Prior to TRA 1986, corporations could be subject to a simple add-on minimum tax, measured by certain tax preference items. In a political reaction to the perception that too many corporations report high earnings but pay little or no federal income tax, the new Act repealed the corporate add-on minimum tax for taxable years beginning in 1987 and replaced it with a new 20% flat rate alternative minimum tax (AMT) that is designed to ensure that a corporation will pay a tax of at least 10% of its economic (book) income.

This is accomplished by imposing the AMT not only on an expanded list of preference items but also on a newly created book income preference for 1987, 1988, and 1989 based on 50% of the difference between pretax financial statement income and regular taxable income adjusted by all other preference items. After 1990, the tax concept of "earnings and profits" will be used.[4] The book income preference is an item that all corporations will have to consider in determining whether AMT is applicable. The tax law now links income as reported in the financial statements with taxable income. This is conformity with a vengeance! All differences between pretax accounting income reported to shareholders, creditors, or others and taxable income as determined by the tax law will enter into the AMT calculation. This includes not only such temporary differences as depreciation but also items for which special tax deductions are allowed, such as dividends and even exempt items such as municipal bond interest.

Pretax accounting income for AMT purposes is obtained from a number of sources in a strict order established by the law. Companies must always use the highest priority source:

1. Financial statements filed with the SEC.
2. Financial statements audited and certified by a CPA that have been used as a report or statement for credit purposes, issued to shareholders, or used for any other substantial nontax purposes.
3. Financial statements provided to the federal government or its agencies.
4. Financial statements provided to a state government or its agencies (or a political subdivision).
5. A noncertified report or financial statement actually used for credit purposes, sent to shareholders, or used for any other substantial nontax purpose.

If a corporation has none of the above or only has a report or financial statement listed in the fifth category, an election can be made to treat the earnings and profits as pretax financial income for AMT.

Conflict of Interest

When an accountant is auditing a corporation as well as doing tax work for shareholders and executives, there is a possibility that he will become aware of information in his tax consultant capacity that he may want to use as an auditor. For example, he may be preparing a tax return for the purchasing vice-president of an

---

[4] At the risk of oversimplification, "earnings and profits" could be viewed as retained earnings computed on a tax basis, recognizing that there are numerous exceptions and adjustments.

audit client and learn that this individual is a stockholder of a Subchapter S corporation that is selling services or materials to the audit client. This is important information which he should immediately disclose to those in his firm responsible for the audit.

The Internal Revenue Code imposes significant sanctions, including penalties and jail sentences, for the unauthorized disclosure of tax return information (IRC § 7216). However, an accountant who prepares a tax return for a taxpayer is permitted by the regulations under Section 7216 to disclose the tax return information to others in his firm in connection with their audit or tax work. Tax clients should be informed that there may be such disclosures. Otherwise the CPA firm is breaching its implied promise of confidentiality inherent in the tax client relationship in order to carry out its responsibilities in an audit capacity. As a practical matter, therefore, when any tax work is done for an employee of a company that is an audit client, the practitioner should always ask in advance for permission to disclose any information learned in the process of preparing the return that might be relevant to the firm's work for the audit client. When the purpose of this request is explained to the employee, objections are unlikely. After all, the accountant has no intention of advising the employer about the individual's financial standing, but only wants to ensure that the employer is protected against the possibility of improprieties or conflicts of interest between the employee and his company.

It is most important that the employee feel fully assured that, unless there is some evidence of impropriety or conflict of interest, his tax return information will never be disclosed. Any reluctance on the part of the employee to give his accountant all the information necessary for the preparation of his tax return will affect the accountant's ability to be effective as a tax consultant, and may raise questions for the auditor as well.

A PROPER BALANCE

The CPA, like any other tax practitioner, works for the taxpayer. His goals are to help the taxpayer comply with the law and to minimize his tax burden. There is no doubt that these two goals are perfectly compatible. In these concluding comments, we can look again to jurist Learned Hand. In an oft-quoted comment, he said:

> Over and over again courts have said there's nothing sinister in so arranging one's affairs as to keep taxes as low as possible. Everybody does so rich or poor; and all do right, for nobody owes any public duty to pay more than the law demands: taxes are enforced exactions, not voluntary contributions. To demand more in the name of morals is mere cant.[5]

Our tax laws are extremely complex and grow more so every day. A bare list of tax laws enacted since 1954 would fill many pages, and we can confidently expect more legislation in the future. Legislation, in turn, begets regulations, administrative pro-

---

[5] Commissioner of Internal Revenue v. Newman, 159 F2d 848 (2d Cir. 1947).

nouncements, judicial decisions, and professional articles. The taxpayer faces an increasingly awesome and mysterious tax system. No matter how intelligent he may be, he most assuredly needs professional help in dealing with it. And in providing that help, the CPA in tax practice helps make the system work, for without the assistance of knowledgeable practitioners, it would probably collapse of its own weight.

49

Accounting, Auditing, and the Law

OVERVIEW

Providing any kind of professional service carries the risk that its adequacy may be challenged by affected parties. The professional accountant in public practice[1] is a principal participant in the legal arena, because the service offerings of accounting firms are broad—and constantly expanding.

Some accounting firms may limit their exposures by declining to offer certain services. For example, a firm may decide that it will not perform audits of public companies, thereby avoiding most of the reach of the federal securities laws. Many small firms will also decline to perform auditing work, preferring to serve clients with review, compilation, and tax work. Although risk exposure may be reduced, these services too will garner their share of challenge.

It is not possible for a firm of any size to significantly limit its exposures, other than through careful client acceptance, through maintaining proper expertise to perform the services offered, and through diligent performance of the work. The regional, national, and international firms offer essentially a full range of services, and by their very size have more than enough complexity in assuring that clients are honest and not unduly risk-generating, that the partners and staff maintain the measure of competence required by their assignments, and that all the rules are followed.[2]

Throughout this *Handbook*, most chapters identify risks associated with audit performance, in specific areas of the financial statements, in specific industries, and in recurrent problem areas such as related party transactions. Auditing has been emphasized in this chapter because auditing is a major segment of the *Handbook*, and auditing generates most of accountants' litigation. But certainly many other professional services provided by accounting firms are the subject of challenge.

A legal perspective could be written on the topic of most of the *Handbook*'s chapters, but of course this is not feasible in a limited space. Accordingly, this chapter outlines the judicial and regulatory systems, the legal theories by which accountants become embroiled, and what happens to them in the litigation process. In addition, a few major risk areas are briefly described at the conclusion.

Public Responsibility

Many courts emphasize that with professional liability insurance and the substantial revenues of the top eight accounting firms, the accounting profession is in a sufficiently strong position to bear the risk of financial loss. Other courts emphasize the "public" responsibility "assumed" by the accounting profession.

Indeed, the Supreme Court, in *United States v. Arthur Young & Co.,*[3] commented:

By certifying the public reports that collectively depict a corporation's financial status, the independent auditor assumes a public responsibility transcending any employment rela-

---

[1] The generic term "accountant" is used in various contexts in this chapter. In performing a particular service, the accountant may be an auditor, consultant, tax advisor, actuary, and so on.

[2] The AICPA has issued Statements on Quality Control Standards to assist in this effort; for discussion, see Chapter 5.

[3] United States v. Arthur Young & Co., 465 US 805 (1984).

tionship with the client. The independent public accountant performing this special function owes ultimate allegiance to the corporation's creditors and stockholders, as well as to the investing public.

The courts have thus reflected the same divergence of opinion which exists between the profession and many financial statement users. Although the profession still promulgates its own standards, they are constantly being redefined by the courts, government agencies, and, in some instances, legislative bodies. The practitioner's risk of liability in connection with routine engagements is growing and the exposure of both the professional and the profession should not be underestimated.

In this environment, it is not surprising that the accounting profession has encountered increasing damage awards. For example, a jury in New York recently rendered a damage award in excess of $80,000,000 against an accounting firm. Settlements of such litigation frequently involve the payment of tens of millions of dollars.

Common Law

Until recently, the scope of accountants' liability at common law for negligent misrepresentation was still restricted. The old common law rule of "privity" remained in place for decades. Under this rule, absent a contractual or fiduciary relationship, the accountant did not owe a duty of care to an injured party. Accountants were thus shielded against liability to third parties for simple negligence.

In 1983, certain courts began to question the continuing validity of the privity doctrine. The New Jersey Supreme Court held that an accounting firm was potentially liable at common law to certain reasonably foreseeable third parties who detrimentally relied on allegedly negligently audited financial statements.[4] Less than one month later, the Wisconsin Supreme Court, with some policy limitations, followed New Jersey's lead.[5] More recently, a California Court of Appeals and the Mississippi Supreme Court reached similar conclusions.[6]

A number of state courts still endorse the strict privity rule, precluding anyone except the client from suing accountants for negligence.[7] However, the majority of state courts, following the Restatement of Torts 2d, Section 552, allow actually known or specifically intended third-party users or classes of users of financial statements to sue accountants for negligent auditing.

Securities Law

The Securities Act of 1933 and the Securities Exchange Act of 1934 are among the progenitors of the modern development of the law of accountants' liability. As interpreted by the courts, these statutes create liability on the part of independent certi-

---

[4] H. Rosenblum Inc. v. Adler, 93 NJ 324 (1983).

[5] Citizens State Bank v. Timm, Schmidt & Co., 335 NW2d 361 (1983).

[6] International Mortgage Co. v. John P. Butler Accountancy Corp., 177 Cal. App. 3d 806 (4th D. 1986); Touche Ross & Co. v. Commercial Union Ins. Co., 514 So2d 315 (Miss. 1987).

[7] See, e.g., Investors' Tax Sheltered Real Estate Ltd. v. Laventhol, Krekstein, Horwath & Horwath, 370 So2d 815 (Fla. 1979), cert. denied, 381 So2d 767 (Fla. 1980); Credit Alliance Corp. v. Arthur Andersen & Co., 68 NY2d 536 (1985).

fied public accountants to third-party purchasers of securities, where offering materials contain false financial statements certified by the auditor. They also subject accountants to liability in connection with the purchase or sale of unregistered securities, particularly where the accountant has acted with "scienter," or intent to defraud. Since scienter is defined by the courts to include not only knowing but reckless conduct, the scope of accountants' potential liability is broader than that recognized by the common law. Indeed, with the successful importation into civil law of the criminal law concepts of aiding and abetting and conspiracy, accountants were made answerable under the federal securities laws for the fraud of others, for example, management fraud.

Criminal Law

The exposure of accountants to criminal penalties is also expanding. Criminal liability against accountants under the Securities Act, the Securities Exchange Act, and the federal mail fraud statute can now be established without any showing of specific intent on the part of the defendant to violate any law. Recklessness has been held to suffice to establish criminal liability.[8] Moreover, proof of compliance with generally accepted practices in the profession is only persuasive, but not conclusive, evidence of good faith as a defense to criminal liability under the federal securities laws.[9]

GOVERNMENT REGULATION

All three branches of government – judicial, executive, and legislative – regulate or otherwise affect the accounting profession.

The Judicial System

The U.S. judicial system divides authority to resolve civil disputes and determine allegations of criminality between state and federal courts.

Federal Courts. Article III, Section 1 of the Constitution grants Congress power to create the federal court system and to define the jurisdiction of the federal courts. Federal jurisdiction extends to (1) cases involving the Constitution and federal laws (federal-question cases) and (2) cases involving controversies between citizens of different states (diversity cases). The Constitution gives the Supreme Court original jurisdiction in a very limited number of cases.

---

[8] See United States v. Benjamin, 328 F2d 854 (2d Cir.), cert. denied, 377 US 953 (1964) (accountants "should not be able to escape criminal liability on a plea of ignorance when they have shut their eyes to what was plainly to be seen or have represented a knowledge they knew they did not possess.")

[9] See United States v. Simon, 425 F2d 796 (2d Cir. 1969), cert. denied, 397 US 1006 (1970).

The federal court of first resort is generally the District Court.[10] Matters requiring a trial, whether before a jury or a judge, must be heard in a District Court. The country is divided into 88 judicial districts.

To minimize conflicts, the 88 judicial districts are grouped into 11 regional judicial circuits, each having one court of appeals with jurisdiction to review the decisions of the district courts within its territory. The jurisdiction of each regional circuit court spans several states, with the exception of the Court of Appeals for the District of Columbia Circuit; that court reviews only the decisions of a single district court and of a number of federal agencies. In addition, Congress in 1982 created the Court of Appeals for the Federal Circuit, which has most of the jurisdiction of the former Court of Customs and Patent Appeals and the appellate branch of the Court of Claims, together with exclusive jurisdiction over patent appeals from the district courts. Three judges normally preside over each case heard by a federal appellate court.

The jurisdiction of the courts of appeals is limited, by statute, to final decisions of the district courts,[11] and a very few interlocutory, or nonfinal, decisions.[12] Thus, a court of appeals may review interlocutory orders granting or denying an injunction, and certain other orders that have a direct and immediate effect on the litigants. In addition, a district judge may certify a "controlling question of law" for immediate appellate review, if that procedure will "materially advance the ultimate termination of the litigation."[13] The circuit court has broad discretion whether to accept a certified question for review. In addition, the circuit courts have jurisdiction to hear appeals from the decisions of various federal regulatory agencies.

A circuit court's interpretation of a federal statute or agency regulation is binding on the district courts within that circuit, but not on courts within the other circuits. Indeed, conflicts often occur among the courts of appeal. To resolve these conflicts, the Supreme Court may review a case. Alternatively, Congress may revise the statute in question in order to clarify the law.

Congress has conferred discretionary jurisdiction on the Supreme Court (referred to as certiorari jurisdiction) to review decisions of the federal appellate courts,[14] and decisions of state courts involving an interpretation of the federal Constitution.[15] If the Supreme Court declines to review a case, its refusal constitutes neither approval nor disapproval of the result or reasoning of the decision it has declined to review.

State Courts. Each state maintains a system of courts, with jurisdiction to determine all disputes except those subject to federal jurisdiction. Absent a federal constitutional question or a conflict with federal law, decisions of state courts as to

---

[10] Certain specialized courts, such as the Claims Court and the Tax Court, may be courts of first resort for disputes within their jurisdiction. Bankruptcy courts present a special problem. Pursuant to 28 USC Section 151, enacted as part of the bankruptcy amendments of 1984, the district courts may refer their jurisdiction over bankruptcy cases to bankruptcy judges, who constitute a unit within the district court known as the bankruptcy court.

[11] 28 USC § 1291.

[12] 28 USC § 1292.

[13] 28 USC § 1292(b).

[14] 28 USC § 1254.

[15] 28 USC § 1257.

common law or state statutes are binding and conclusive. The Supreme Court cannot review a state court decision that does not involve federal constitutional or statutory interests.

Courts and Professional Standards. Accounting principles that are generally accepted and have substantial authoritative support—such as Opinions of the APB, Statements of the FASB, and ARBs—may have persuasive influence on accounting matters that approaches the force of law. For example, in ASR 150 (FRR § 101) the SEC declared that, for its purposes, financial statements prepared in accordance with accounting practices for which there was no substantial authoritative support were presumed to be misleading. The SEC regards the principles, standards, and practices promulgated by the FASB in its statements and interpretations as having substantial authoritative support.

Similarly, state regulations may accord quasi-legal status to GAAP. For example, the New York Securities Takeover Disclosure Rules provide that required financial statements must be prepared in accordance with GAAP, which must be consistently applied.[16] Nor has there been any case in recent years that effectively outlaws a generally accepted accounting principle formally adopted by the profession's rule-making body.

Nevertheless, courts are not bound by standards of the accounting profession. Even if an accountant has fully complied with those standards, a trial court may find an accountant liable. In *Fund of Funds, Ltd. v. Arthur Andersen & Co.*,[17] for example, the judge charged the jury, in part, as follows:

> You have heard considerable testimony from witnesses concerning generally accepted accounting principles and generally accepted auditing standards, including the duty of confidentiality. These principles and standards are relevant, but not determinative of the standards of care that may be required of an auditor under the Federal Securities Laws. You alone must determine whether the plaintiff proved the elements of each claim according to these instructions.[18]

The Executive Branch

Many federal agencies regulate the accounting profession. The most important are discussed in the following sections.

Securities and Exchange Commission. Since its creation in 1934, the SEC has constructed an awesome machinery for enforcement of its rules and regulations against professionals. This mechanism consists of informal and formal investigations, suits for injunction, disciplinary proceedings, and criminal references.

---

[16] Reg. § 12.5, 2 CCH Blue Sky L. Rep. ¶ 35,655.

[17] 545 F. Supp. 1314 (SDNY 1982).

[18] See also United States v. Simon, 425 F2d 796 (2d Cir. 1969), cert. denied, 397 US 1006 (1970) (disclosure in accordance with GAAP does not absolve accountants from liability unless financial statements as a whole "fairly present" financial position and "accurately report" operations.)

Investigations. SEC enforcement personnel may make a "preliminary investigation" of a possible violation without specific commission authorization, but with no subpoena power. The response to informal investigation is voluntary. However, the auditor must carefully avoid giving any knowingly false or inaccurate information, either oral or written, to personnel of the SEC – a federal crime under the federal false statement statute.[19]

The SEC is authorized formally to investigate "whether any person has violated, is violating, or is about to violate" federal securities laws, to decide whether to take enforcement action, and to obtain evidence for the action. A witness or other interested person has no appeal, because an SEC investigation is considered a nonadversary fact-finding inquiry in which there are no parties, that is, no accused, no penalties, and no (stated) issues. A formal order of investigation identifies statutes and rules that may have been violated; the areas of inquiry, however, are typically stated very broadly.

A person subpoenaed to testify at a formal SEC investigation is entitled to be represented by counsel. However, due process does not require that SEC investigations be conducted like trials. For example, evidence inadmissible in a court may be admissible at the hearing. The SEC has discretion to furnish information obtained in its investigations to other government agencies, state securities and accountancy authorities, the AICPA and state professional societies, and private litigants.

The SEC will entertain Offers of Settlement submitted by accountants in response to its investigations. For example, the SEC accepted an Offer of Settlement submitted by Arthur Andersen & Co. (AA) in response to an SEC investigation which resulted in the issuance in 1981 of ASR 292. As part of its Offer of Settlement, in which AA agreed to be censured by the SEC, AA represented that it had taken steps to prevent the recurrence of problems in its audits of Mattel, Inc. and Geon Industries. These steps included formalization of policies on intrafirm consulting; adoption of a policy requiring rotation of audit partners; requirement of a second partner review of audit reports; expanded personnel training programs; updating of practice and procedure manuals; and the establishment of a Public Review Board. In addition, AA represented that it had undergone two peer reviews of its audit work and quality control procedures by an outside accounting firm.[20]

Disciplinary proceedings. Virtually since its creation, the SEC has professed the need to discipline the professionals who practice before it. SEC Rule of Practice 2(e) (1) accordingly provides that the SEC may temporarily or permanently disqualify from practicing before it any person found by the SEC after a hearing

- Not to possess the requisite qualifications to represent others.
- To be lacking in character or integrity, or to have engaged in unethical or improper professional conduct.
- To have willfully violated, or willfully aided and abetted the violation of any provision of the federal securities laws, or the rules and regulations thereunder.

---

[19] 18 USC § 1001.

[20] In the Matter of Arthur Andersen & Co., (Accounting Series Releases Transfer Binder) Fed. Sec. L. Rep. (CCH) ¶ 72,314.

The proceeding is governed by the SEC Rules of Practice, and is prosecuted by the SEC Division of Enforcement before an administrative law judge.

The SEC has justified its use of Rule 2(e) by invoking the important role accountants and attorneys play in commercial transactions,[21] and by invoking its limited resources and its need for the assistance of professionals in preventing abuses of the marketplace. Courts have upheld the SEC's authority to commence disciplinary proceedings under Rule 2(e).[22]

In some circumstances, the SEC may, without a hearing, suspend the right of a professional to practice before it. Such a suspension may occur if the professional's license to practice has been revoked or suspended in some other jurisdiction, or if the professional has been convicted of a felony or misdemeanor involving moral turpitude. The commission can also temporarily suspend, without a preliminary hearing, any professional who, in an action for misconduct brought by the commission, has been permanently enjoined from violating or aiding and abetting the violation of the federal securities laws and related rules and regulations. Similar authority exists with respect to findings entered in administrative proceedings, unless the violation is found not to have been willful. Finally, the SEC may censure an individual or firm after an administrative finding of violation.

Notwithstanding the limited choice of sanctions apparently available under Rule 2(e), the SEC since 1973 has negotiated various affirmative or "mandatory" sanctions, including:

1. Peer reviews and inspections of a firm's auditing standards and procedures.
2. Restrictions for specified periods against mergers with other firms.
3. Prohibitions for specified periods against undertaking new engagements likely to result in filings with the SEC.
4. Requirements to develop and implement auditing procedures for certain types of transactions.
5. Censure of firms, other than following permanent injunctions or criminal convictions.
6. Imposition of continuing education programs.
7. Requirements to give notice of the commission's findings to potential new SEC clients.

A Rule 2(e) disciplinary proceeding against the firm of Lester Witte and one of its partners, John P. Shea, provides an example of such affirmative sanctions. After being charged by the SEC with numerous deficiencies in an audit of Lippincott, a publishing corporation, the firm and its engagement partner consented in 1981 to the following sanctions:

1. Censure for Lester Witte.
2. One-year suspension for Shea as to any and all publicly held clients of Lester Witte.
3. Additional quality controls for the firm.

---

[21] United States v. Benjamin, 328 F2d 854 (2d Cir.), cert. denied sub nom. Howard v. United States, 377 US 953 (1964).

[22] Touche Ross & Co. v. SEC, 609 F2d 870 (2d Cir. 1979).

4. Peer review within one year under the AICPA's SEC Practice Section standards, and prompt implementation in the audit practice of all reasonable peer review recommendations.

5. A second peer review, within three years.

6. Continuation of the proceedings and Commission jurisdiction during this three-year interval.[23]

Injunctions. The Commission may also begin injunctive proceedings against alleged violators of the federal securities laws, including accountants. The objective of such proceedings is to prevent recurring or future violations.

Courts have usually been unwilling to enjoin violations of the securities laws without persuasive proof of an inclination to commit future violations.[24] In *SEC v. Geotek*,[25] for example, the court refused to grant an injunction against Arthur Young (AY), concluding that the SEC had failed to show a reasonable likelihood that AY would commit future violations. Nevertheless, since 1970 the SEC has named auditors as codefendants with management in a number of major injunction suits.[26]

The SEC may refer cases it believes merit criminal prosecution to the Department of Justice. Such references are usually made only when the SEC believes that an accountant certified financial statements that he knew were false when he reported on them, not simply in matters of professional judgment.

Foreign Corrupt Practices Act. The SEC also enforces the Foreign Corrupt Practices Act of 1977 (FCPA),[27] codified as an amendment to the Securities Exchange Act of 1934,[28] which imposes record-keeping and internal control requirements on public companies. An accountant or other person who falsifies accounting records, circumvents internal accounting controls, or commits other irregularities within the meaning of the FCPA may be subject to the penalties imposed by Section 32(a) of the Securities Exchange Act of 1934, including administrative proceedings, civil liability, and criminal penalties.

Although proceedings against accountants alleging violations of the FCPA have been rare, the case of *SEC v. World-Wide Coin Investments, Ltd.*[29] shows that possible violations of the FCPA may lead an auditor to disclaim an opinion on a company's financial statements contained in a 10-K report. The auditor in *World-Wide* cited deficiencies in the company's internal controls, including lack of detailed records and the unavailability of supporting data for the firm's examination, as reasons for its decision.

---

[23] In the Matter of Lester Witte & Co., John P. Shea, Release No. AS-285, (Accounting Series Releases Transfer Binder) Fed. Sec. L. Rep. (CCH) ¶ 72,307.

[24] SEC v. Bangor Punta Corp., 331 F. Supp. 1154, 1163 (SDNY 1971), aff'd in part and rev'd in part, 480 F2d 341 (2d Cir.), cert. denied, 414 US 924 (1973).

[25] 426 F. Supp. 715 (ND Cal. 1976), aff'd sub nom. SEC v. Arthur Young & Co., 590 F2d 785 (9th Cir. 1979).

[26] See, e.g., SEC v. Price Waterhouse, Civ. No. 85-CIV-4787 (SDNY 1985), Release No. AAER-62, (Enforcement Releases Transfer Binder) Fed. Sec. L. Rep. (CCH) ¶ 73,462.

[27] Pub. L. No. 95-213.

[28] 15 USC § 78q(b).

[29] 567 F. Supp. 724 (ND Ga. 1983).

Federal Trade Commission and Antitrust Actions. During the late 1970s, the Federal Trade Commission (FTC) conducted an extensive investigation of both the business and professional aspects of accounting firms. While the antitrust laws have been enforced with less vigor in recent years, the Commission continues to demonstrate an interest in applying the antitrust laws to the accounting profession.

In 1987, the FTC announced its intention to file a complaint against the AICPA, alleging that AICPA rules prohibiting, among other things, acceptance of engagements on a commission or contingency fee basis, use of trade names by CPA firms, and payment to other persons for referrals, violate Section 5 of the Federal Trade Commission Act.

The Antitrust Division of the Justice Department may also challenge professional rules of conduct which it believes unreasonably restrain competition. In *United States v. State Bd. of Certified Pub. Accountants of La.*,[30] for example, the Justice Department alleged that the Louisiana State Board conspired unreasonably to restrict advertising and solicitation of business by accountants.

Internal Revenue Service. The IRS has an enormous impact on the accounting profession. Accountants prepare income tax returns, determine the tax provisions of financial statements, and render tax opinions.

Under federal regulation,[31] the Secretary of the Treasury may suspend or disbar from practice before the IRS any accountant who is found after a hearing to be "incompetent" or "disreputable," who violates regulations governing practice before the IRS, or who, with intent to defraud, misleads or threatens a client. The Director of Practice in the Treasury Department may file an administrative complaint against an accountant, alleging such violations.[32] An example of a case in which an accountant was disbarred from practice before the IRS is *Harary v. Blumenthal*[33] (attempt to influence IRS agent in conduct of audit demonstrated unfitness). In addition, regulations governing practice before the IRS include detailed requirements for the preparation of tax shelter opinions.[34] The IRS has also expressed the belief that accountants have an obligation to promote responsible tax reporting and to advise against abusive tax shelters.

State Enforcement Proceedings. Traditionally, state agencies and licensing authorities commenced enforcement proceedings only in response to public inquiries. Recently, however, state agencies have rejected the idea of a totally complaint-based enforcement process. Such states have passed statutes that require state or municipal bodies using certified public accountants for attest-type functions to submit random samples of such work to the licensing agency for review. Such reviews are conducted either by agency members on ad hoc panels or by licensed certified public accountants. If apparent violations of technical professional standards are found, the agency institutes a complaint on its own motion.

---

[30] Civ. No. 83-1947 (ED La. 1983).

[31] 31 USC § 330.

[32] 31 CFR § 10.54.

[33] 555 F2d 1113 (2d Cir. 1977).

[34] 31 CFR § 10.33.

The Legislative Branch

Oversight Committees. Congressional oversight of the accounting profession is conducted by several committees of Congress, including the House Committee on Energy and Commerce, Subcommittee on Oversight and Investigations. The Subcommittee has studied the role of the accounting profession in light of scandals involving several government securities dealers and other public companies whose financial statements were audited by prominent firms shortly before the companies collapsed.

In 1988, Congress held hearings on the role of two prominent accounting firms in the collapse of ZZZZ Best, a publicly traded carpet-cleaning company. The company and its founder were charged with violations of the Racketeer Influenced and Corrupt Organizations act (RICO)[35] and federal securities and tax laws. Congress studied how the company was able to engage a new auditor less than a week after its former auditor withdrew from its engagement because it suspected fraud, and why the auditor that withdrew took months to notify the SEC about its suspicions.

Legislative Initiatives. Congress and various state legislatures in recent years have proposed legislation that would significantly affect accountants. Some of this proposed legislation has grown out of hearings conducted by the House Subcommittee on Oversight and Investigations into recent financial frauds perpetrated by government securities dealers and other public companies.

In 1986, Representative Wyden (D-Ore.) introduced the Financial Fraud Detection and Disclosure Act. The bill would have imposed important and controversial new responsibilities on public companies and their auditors. Although Congress did not pass the bill and it was not reintroduced in 1987, similar legislation may yet be introduced and passed.

If passed, the Financial Fraud Detection and Disclosure Act would have required every issuer of securities under the federal securities laws to devise and periodically evaluate a system of administrative and internal accounting controls, and include such evaluation in the issuer's annual report. Each audit required by the securities laws would have to be conducted so as to reasonably ensure the detection and reporting of any material illegality or financial irregularity, and would have to undertake to evaluate the client's administrative and accounting controls. If the auditor became aware of any information indicating the occurrence of an illegality or irregularity – whether or not material – the auditor would be required to extend the audit procedures to verify whether the illegality or irregularity occurred. The auditor would be required to inform the client's management of any such occurrence, and would then have to review management's response. Unless the auditor was satisfied that the client had taken appropriate steps to correct and prevent the recurrence of the illegality or irregularity and had reported same to the appropriate authorities, the auditor would be required to report the illegality or irregularity on his own.

Congressional subcommittees have also been studying ways to revise RICO. Although RICO was intended to attack the infiltration of legitimate business by

---

[35] Although RICO is commonly referred to as an "act," it is in fact part of an act: Title IX, "Racketeer Influenced and Corrupt Organizations," of the Organized Crime Control Act of 1970, P.L. 91-452 (18 USC §§ 1961 et seq.).

organized crime, it has been used more extensively in civil lawsuits against banks, investment bankers, insurance companies, and accountants who have no connection with organized crime. Legislative proposals to amend RICO are discussed later in this chapter.

Various states have adopted other laws that directly affect accountants. For example, 17 states recognize an accountant-client privilege, which protects certain communications between accountants and their clients from disclosure. Other states have enacted statutes that limit the potential liability of accountants to third parties.

Professional Self-Regulation

Since 1975, the AICPA and state societies of certified public accountants have worked together to regulate the profession, by means of the so-called Joint Ethics Enforcement Plan, or JEEP. Under JEEP, the ethics committees of the AICPA and the state societies act as each other's agents to investigate ethics complaints and present those complaints, if deemed appropriate, to a joint adjudicatory body known as the Joint Trial Board.

In 1987, the membership of the AICPA approved by referendum a significant change from the former complaint-based structure. Members of the AICPA, in cooperation with state CPA societies, must now participate in practice review programs (peer reviews), in which peer accountants and firms would periodically monitor each other's compliance with professional standards in practice situations. The adoption of this system by the AICPA now makes peer review the primary mechanism for professional self-regulation. (See Chapter 45.)

THEORIES OF LIABILITY

The efforts of the legal system to define the scope of an accountant's professional responsibility emanate from the common law. In addition, a number of statutes, most importantly the federal securities laws, govern an accountant's potential liability for negligent or intentionally fraudulent acts.

Common Law

While the common law does not require the auditor to insure or guarantee the infallibility of his work product, it clearly mandates that the auditor perform his professional services with due care; that is, with the same degree of skill, judgment, and knowledge possessed by other members of his profession. To prove an auditor's lack of due care, litigants must persuade the trier of fact, often through the testimony of accounting and auditing experts, that the auditor has deviated from professional accounting and auditing standards.

In choosing among various legal theories, plaintiffs' counsel must consider procedural and substantive rules governing such matters as jurisdiction, venue, statutes of limitation, burdens of proof, and damages. Perhaps the most significant consideration affecting the choice of legal theory, however, is whether the plaintiff is a client or nonclient of the auditor.

The term *client* is not restricted to the entity or person by whom the auditor may originally be engaged. The term also extends to others who may "stand in the shoes" of the client. These persons may raise any claim of the original client against the auditor, subject always to any defenses the auditor may have asserted against that client. Such persons and entities include sureties that pay clients' losses under fidelity bonds, trustees in bankruptcy, shareholders who bring derivative actions for the benefit of corporate clients, government agencies such as the Federal Deposit Insurance Corporation and the Federal Savings and Loan Insurance Corporation (when functioning as receivers for insolvent financial institutions), and, in the case of partnership-clients, general, but not limited, partners. The term *client* does not include corporate officers and directors, employees, depositors, or policyholders.

Actions in Contract. An auditor may be liable to a client for breach of contract when the auditor fails to use due care in performing the audit. The contract that provides the basis for this kind of action comes into existence when the auditor and his client mutually agree to an engagement for professional accounting or auditing services. This contract may be oral or written. It is usually evidenced by an engagement letter.

An engagement contract sets forth the rights and obligations of each party. The accountant's obligation is to perform the audit by examining the client's financial statements and by expressing an appropriate opinion in accordance with professional standards. The client's obligations include payment of a fee of a set amount or at an agreed rate. If the contract is silent about a fee, the auditor is entitled to a reasonable fee that reflects the value of the work performed. The client must also provide draft financial statements or their equivalent (e.g., trial balances) with supporting data. In addition, the client must grant the auditor complete access to all client books and records and must not otherwise hinder the auditor's performance.

A client who materially breaches his obligations under the engagement contract excuses the auditor from completing his contractual obligations. An auditor who suspends or discontinues an audit without excuse may be liable for the economic injury his client suffers, due to loss of confidence among existing and potential lenders and investors, or failure to meet the requirements of public filings or loan undertakings.

The engagement contract imposes a continuing obligation on the auditor to reaffirm his opinion, at his client's request, in the absence of any information that would undermine the basis for his opinion. Before reaffirming, the auditor is entitled to receive from his client and from a successor auditor, if any, certain current assurances as to subsequent events. The client is also obliged to pay the auditor a reasonable fee for any additional work the auditor performs in reaffirming his original opinion.

A nonclient may bring an action against an auditor premised on a claim that it is a third-party beneficiary of the engagement contract between the auditor and his client. Although few courts have actually imposed liability on auditors under this theory, in the recent case of *Raritan River Steel Co. v. Cherry, Bekaert & Holland*,[36] the court allowed a trade creditor to maintain an action against accountants, premised

---

[36] 79 N.C. App. 81, 339 SE2d 62 (N.C. App. 1986), rev'd on other grounds 322 N.C. 200, 367 SE2d 609 (N.C. 1988).

on the theory that the creditor had been a third-party beneficiary of the audit report provided to the client. The creditor alleged that the audit engagement had been entered into for the creditor's direct — not merely incidental — benefit.

Fraud. If the auditor has acted with an intent to deceive the reader of his reports, both clients and nonclients may sue for fraud. The elements of fraud which a plaintiff must prove are (1) a false representation by the auditor, (2) scienter, (3) the auditor's intent to induce plaintiff's reliance on the false representation, (4) the plaintiff's reliance on the false representation, and (5) resulting damage suffered by the plaintiff. In suits brought against auditors, courts have held that fraudulent intent may be established by proving that the auditor acted either with conscious knowledge of the falsity of the representation (actual knowledge), or without belief in its truth, or in reckless disregard of its truth.[37]

The possibility of a fraud claim becomes especially problematic for the auditor when his conduct is alleged to rise to the level of gross negligence, that is, an extreme or flagrant deviation from professional standards of due care. In such cases, courts have found that gross negligence may be evidence from which the trier of fact may draw an inference of fraud.

In *State Street Trust Co. v. Ernst*,[38] a bank sued defendant auditors, alleging that it had made a loan to a finance company in reliance on the company's financial statements as certified by the auditors. The auditors had supplied 10 copies of their report to the company, knowing that the financial statements were to be relied on by creditors. One month after supplying these copies, the auditors sent a letter to the company, containing facts known to the auditors when they prepared their original report, which in effect severely qualified it. The court held that this conduct "was itself gross negligence and an important piece of evidence raising an inference of fraud":

> A representation certified as true to the knowledge of the accountants when knowledge there is none, a reckless misstatement, or an opinion based on grounds so flimsy as to lead to the conclusion that there was no genuine belief in its truth, are all sufficient upon which to base liability. A refusal to see the obvious, a failure to investigate the doubtful, if sufficiently gross, may furnish evidence leading to an inference of fraud so as to impose liability for losses suffered by those who rely on the balance sheet.

In other words, heedlessness and reckless disregard of consequences may take the place of deliberate intention. The difficulty posed by these cases is in determining the kind or number of instances of gross negligence sufficient to infer fraud. In *William Iselin & Co. v. Muhlstock, Elowitz & Co.*,[39] for example, the court upheld a jury verdict in favor of an accounting firm that had audited financial statements on which plaintiff lenders allegedly relied. The dissent argued that numerous instances of the accounting firm's gross negligence, including failure to verify independently the cash account, failure to confirm the amount due from factors by direct correspondence,

---

[37] See, e.g., O'Connor v. Ludlam, 92 F2d 50 (2d Cir.), cert. denied, 302 US 758 (1937) (pre-federal securities laws action).

[38] 278 NY 104 (1938).

[39] 52 AD2d 540 (1st Dept.), appeal dismissed, 40 NY2d 989 (1976).

failure to confirm inventory, and failure properly to confirm accounts payable and receivable, should have led a reasonable jury to infer fraud.

Negligence. If an auditor fails to perform an engagement with due care, he may be sued for negligence. To prevail in a suit alleging negligence, a plaintiff must prove (1) that the auditor had a duty to the plaintiff to exercise due care, (2) that the auditor breached that duty by failing to perform in accordance with professional standards, (3) that the auditor's breach was a proximate cause of plaintiff's injury, and (4) that the plaintiff suffered actual loss or damage as a result of his injury.

Suits by clients against auditors often allege negligent failure by the auditor to detect management fraud. In such cases, clients can readily prove the existence of a duty of care on the part of the auditor by reason of the engagement contract. However, auditors have often successfully argued that any negligence on their part could not have been the proximate cause of the client's injury, because of management's defalcations. For this defense to prevail, the auditors must show that management's fraud benefited the company and did not allow management merely "to line its own pockets."[40] Where the client can show that its former management acted "adversely" to the company's interests, management fraud may not be a defense to the claim.[41]

The main obstacle to negligence suits by nonclients against accountants is the proof of the existence of a duty of care running from accountant to the nonclient plaintiff. Three distinct standards have emerged defining the extent of an auditor's duty to nonclients. These standards, which vary according to jurisdiction, are as follows:

Privity or near-privity. The landmark decision of *Ultramares Corp. v. Touche*[42] absolves the auditor of negligence in the absence of a relationship of privity, that is, a direct contractual relationship. Under this theory, nonclients who relied on a negligently prepared audit report have no remedy at common law.

The rationale for the standard of privity is rooted in Judge Cardozo's observation in *Ultramares* that "a thoughtless slip or blunder . . . may expose accountants to a liability in an indeterminate amount for an indeterminate time to an indeterminate class." The auditor typically has no control over the identity or number of nonclients who rely on his report or over the magnitude of the risk these nonclients may take in reliance on his report. Absent some limitation, the auditor's liability is therefore likely to be disproportionate to the size of his fee and the degree of his culpability.

Ultramares and its requirement of strict privity remained the dominant standard for a generation. Starting in the 1960s, however, judges and legal scholars sharply criticized the *Ultramares* decision so that its influence began to wane. Nevertheless, in the mid-1980s, the New York Court of Appeals renewed its commitment to *Ultramares* by holding that nonclients cannot maintain an action against an accountant for negligence without alleging a relationship of privity or one "sufficiently intimate to be equated with privity."[43] According to the court in *Credit Alliance*, a

---

[40] See, e.g., Cenco, Inc. v. Seidman & Seidman, 686 F2d 449 (7th Cir.), cert. denied, 459 US 880 (1982).

[41] In the Matter of Investors Funding Corp. Sec. Litigation, 523 F. Supp. 533 (SDNY 1980).

[42] 255 NY 170 (1931).

[43] Credit Alliance Corp. v. Arthur Andersen & Co., 65 NY2d 536, modified, 66 NY2d 812 (1985).

nonclient who relies to his detriment on erroneous financial reports must satisfy three tests to hold the auditor of these reports liable:

1. The accountant must have been aware that the financial reports were to be used for a particular purpose or purposes,
2. In the furtherance of which a known party or parties was intended to rely, and
3. Some conduct on the part of the accountant linking him to that party or parties, which evinces the accountant's understanding of that party or party's reliance.

On the basis of these tests, the court dismissed a plaintiff's claims because plaintiff failed to allege that the defendant auditors had issued their report for plaintiff's use and reliance, or that there had been any dealings between plaintiffs and the auditors. In contrast, in a companion appeal in the same opinion, the court upheld a third-party lender's claim on the basis of allegations that "a primary, if not the exclusive, end and aim" of the audit was to provide the lender with reliable financial information prior to extending credit, and that there had been direct communication between the lender and the auditors regarding the client's financial condition.

Eight states, other than New York, have endorsed the privity or near-privity standard in case law: Arkansas, Colorado, Delaware, Florida, Illinois, Indiana, Kansas, and Pennsylvania.[44] In addition, the AICPA has drafted and circulated a model statute containing a "privity of contract" limitation on negligence suits against CPAs, as modified by *Credit Alliance*.[45] Arkansas, Illinois, and Kansas have passed legislation based on this model statute.

Specifically foreseen persons and class. An intermediate standard is expressed in Section 552 of the Restatement of Torts 2d (1977), which limits the liability of a professional for negligent misrepresentation to loss suffered

(a) by the person or one of a limited group of persons for whose benefit and guidance he intends to supply the information or knows that the recipient intends to supply it; and
(b) through reliance upon it in a transaction that he intends the information to influence or knows that the recipient so intends or in a substantially similar transaction.

Properly applied, the Restatement narrows an auditor's liability to a comparatively small group of persons and classes whose reliance on the allegedly negligent misrepresentation is (or should be) specifically foreseen by the accountant. However, the language of the Restatement is general and susceptible of different interpretations.

An early case applying Section 552 of the Restatement was *Rhode Island Hospital Trust Nat'l Bank v. Swartz, Bresenoff, Yavner & Jacobs,* [46] which upheld the complaint of a bank against a defendant-auditor who knew and acknowledged that the bank required annual financial statements of the audit client-borrower under a loan

---

[44] See, e.g., Investors Tax Sheltered Real Estate Ltd. v. Laventhol, Krekstein, Horwath & Horwath, 370 So2d 815 (Fla. 1979), cert. denied, 381 So2d 767 (1980); Toro Co. v. Krouse, Kern & Co., 827 F2d 188 (7th Cir. 1987) (Indiana); Landell v. Lybrand, 264 Pa. 406 (1919).

[45] 65 NY2d 536 (1985).

[46] 455 F2d 847 (4th Cir. 1972).

agreement. More recently, the Georgia Supreme Court interpreted Section 552 of the Restatement to mean that the "liability of accountants, extends to those persons, or the limited class of persons who the professional is actually aware will rely upon the information. . . ." [47]

The courts of 13 states have endorsed the Restatement standard of liability in common law negligence actions by third parties against accountants. As reasons for abandoning the "privity" standard, these courts have emphasized the increased scope of liability of other professionals to nonprivity users of their services; the questionable fairness of imposing the burden of economic loss on "innocent" financial statement users rather than on the auditor; the incentive that expanded liability would give auditors to improve auditing procedures and obtain insurance against increased risks; and the ability of the accounting profession to pass added audit costs and increased insurance premiums to clients through higher fees.

Both those opposing and those favoring expanded liability have criticized the Restatement. Opponents have argued that auditors require special protection because more persons and entities are affected by auditing services than by the services of other professionals. Those in favor of widening the scope of auditors' liability have criticized the Restatement because it arbitrarily favors larger and more sophisticated lenders, creditors, or purchasers who will take definitive steps to protect themselves as members of a specifically foreseen class. They further contend that the Restatement offers few guidelines to assist in its application, thereby leading to court decisions that are inconsistent and confusing. Because of the criticism directed at the Restatement, the trend toward its adoption has been slowed.

Foreseeability. New Jersey became the first state to adopt this standard, by far the most expansive of the three existing standards affecting the liability of auditors to nonclients. In *H. Rosenblum, Inc. v. Adler*,[48] New Jersey's Supreme Court held that the auditor has "a duty to all those whom that auditor should reasonably foresee as recipients from the company of the statements for its proper business purposes, provided that the recipients rely on the statements pursuant to those business purposes." Since then, courts in four other states, including an appellate court in California, have followed suit, although these states have not uniformly adopted *Rosenblum*'s limitation that the statement be received "from the company." Two other states appear to be leaning in the direction of recognizing the foreseeability standard.

In cases such as *International Mortgage Co. v. John P. Butler Accountancy Corp.*,[49] *Citizens State Bank v. Timm, Schmidt & Co.*,[50] *Touche Ross & Co. v. Commercial Union Insurance Co.*,[51] and *Rosenblum*, courts have invoked the greater ability of the audit firm to pass a loss to its customers, the availability of insurance, the incentives for improved audits, the objective of similar treatment for all professionals, the availability of disclaimers to limit reliance on the auditor's report, and the possibility of seeking contribution or indemnification from the client and its blameworthy officers

---

[47] Badische Corp. v. Caylor, 386 SE2d 198, 200 (Ga. 1987).

[48] 93 NJ 324 (1983).

[49] 177 Cal. App.3d 806 (4th D. 1986).

[50] 335 NW2d 361 (Wis. 1983).

[51] 514 So2d 315 (Miss. 1987).

and employees, as reasons for adopting the foreseeability standard of accountants' liability. The court in *John P. Butler* also cited the Supreme Court's description of the auditor as a "public watchdog" upon whom all financial statement users rely.[52]

In opposition to the "reasonably foreseeable" standard, accountants have argued that they do not control their clients' records, and that this lack of control distinguishes them from other professionals. Accountants also argue that both competition in auditing and pressure from clients make the use of disclaimers commercially impossible, and that courts are likely to scrutinize, if not prohibit, general or widespread use of disclaimers; that an auditor who tries to contract with a client for a right of indemnification or even contribution may jeopardize his professional independence; and that the right of indemnification from an entity that may prove insolvent or from individuals who may be judgment-proof would yield little or no recompense.

Accountants have also argued that increased risks for auditors could make the cost of insurance prohibitive and eventually might cause coverage to be unavailable, a result that would particularly disadvantage small accounting firms and might curtail the availability of accounting services to small businesses. Similarly they have argued that increased auditors' liability and an unstable insurance market could also jeopardize the accounting profession's ability to attract and retain high-caliber auditors, which may in turn have a long-term adverse impact on audit quality.

The debate between proponents and critics of the foreseeability standard is bound to intensify, especially in light of the new vitality that the *Credit Alliance* decision has given to the standard of privity and near-privity. None of the three standards of accountants' liability to nonclients for negligence is now clearly dominant.

Breach of Warranty. Clients and nonclients may seek recovery against an auditor on theories of breach of express or implied warranty. Under these theories plaintiffs would argue that when the auditor issues his opinion in accordance with professional standards, he expressly or implicitly warrants that the financial statements are fit to be used for the ordinary purpose of aiding plaintiffs' business decisions. In support of their arguments, plaintiffs often draw analogies to principles of product liability law which hold a manufacturer strictly liable for goods that prove unfit for the ordinary purposes for which they are to be used.

Thus far, most judges and legal commentators have recognized just how unsuited warranty principles are to the work product of auditors. The auditor's task is not to guarantee accuracy but to issue an opinion on the fairness of his client's financial statements. Because an auditor limits his tests to selected samples and does not exhaustively review each and every transaction, the auditor may not uncover misstatements and irregularities. Accounting decisions are also matters of judgment. Alternatives in GAAP allow a client to make qualitative choices that might result in wide variations in the financial statements.

Breach of Fiduciary Duty. A lawsuit filed by a client or a nonclient may also charge that an auditor's lapse in professional performance constitutes a breach of his fiduciary duty to the plaintiff. In most professional engagements, an auditor is not a

---

[52] United States v. Arthur Young & Co., 465 US 805 (1984).

fiduciary; the auditor's obligation to attest requires an attitude of objective independence that precludes such a relationship.

Statutory Liability

Statutes affecting the liability of accountants have developed in the broad context of legislative responses to perceived misfeasance in the marketplace. Accordingly, these statutes are not specifically directed at the practitioner or his work product.

Securities Laws. Provisions of the federal securities laws impose standards of responsibility more stringent than those of the common law on persons associated with securities transactions, including secondary defendants such as accountants and auditors. In public offerings of securities registered under the Securities Act of 1933, Section 11 imposes liability—for purchasers' losses resulting from a material misstatement or omission—on issuers and associated persons, including auditors, unless they can prove that they exercised due care, that is, that they were not negligent. Under the Securities Exchange Act of 1934, Section 18(a) imposes liability on issuers and secondary persons, including associated auditors, for losses by reliant purchasers or sellers of securities due to a materially false or misleading statement, unless a defendant can prove good faith and no knowledge of the deficiency. Section 10(b) of the 1934 Act, in connection with Rule 10b-5 promulgated thereunder, prohibits misrepresentations, omissions, and fraud in connection with purchases or sales of securities. Further, state "blue sky" or securities laws contain liability provisions generally similar to those in the federal acts.

Securities Act of 1933—Section 11. Section 11(a) gives purchasers of registered securities a right of recovery against the issuer and other specified persons for resulting losses if the registration statement contains any misstatement or any omission of a material fact necessary to make the statement not misleading. In particular, a purchaser may sue an auditor who has examined and expressed his opinion on financial statements in a registration statement, and has consented to the use of his opinion in the registration statement, if the financial statements contain a material misrepresentation or omission. A claim under Section 11 must be made within one year after discovery of the untrue statement or omission, or one year after such discovery should have been made, but in no event later than three years from the date the securities were offered to the public.

Under Section 11(a), in contrast to suits at common law, a plaintiff need *not* prove

1. Negligence or fraud by the auditor in auditing the financial statements.
2. Reliance on the auditor's opinion (unless plaintiff acquired his securities after the registrant made generally available an earnings statement for a period of at least twelve months beginning after the effective date of the registration statement).
3. A causal relationship between the omission or misstatement and plaintiff's loss.
4. Any contractual relationship between plaintiff and the auditor, issuer, sellers, or underwriters.

In order to recover against an auditor, plaintiff must prove only that he has suffered a loss by investing in a security registered under the Act and that the audited financial statements contain a material omission or misstatement.

The auditor may escape liability by proving that:

1. After making reasonable investigation (i.e., exercising "due diligence"), he had reasonable ground to believe, and did believe, that the statements in the audit opinion were true, that is, that he was not negligent; or
2. There was no causal relationship between the false audit opinion and plaintiff's loss; or
3. Plaintiff knew the audit opinion was false when he acquired the security.

Thus Section 11(a) is a more favorable legal theory for plaintiffs than common law negligence, for under Section 11(a), the auditor must affirmatively prove that he was not negligent; at common law, a plaintiff must prove that the auditor *was* negligent.

The leading case of *Escott v. Barchris Construction Corp.*[53] contains an important description of an auditor's responsibilities, where a plaintiff claims under Section 11 that the auditor certified materially misleading financial statements. In *Barchris*, the court held that the issuer's auditor failed to sustain a defense of "due diligence" under the statute in connection with, among other things, its review of events subsequent to the date of the certified balance sheet (S-1 Review). Although the senior accountant performing the review was not obligated to make a complete audit, he ignored certain "danger signals" in the materials he did examine which required further investigation under the circumstances.

The court's opinion in *Barchris* also contains a discussion of "materiality" under Section 11. The court cited a definition of "material fact" as one "which if it had been currently stated or disclosed would have deterred or tended to deter the average prudent investor from purchasing the securities in question." In the circumstances of the case, the court concluded that an overstatement of approximately 14% in operating income was a "comparatively minor error," but held that an overstatement of a current ratio by less than 15% was material.

Securities Act of 1933—Section 12(2). Section 12(2) is similar to § 11(a) in that it provides an express cause of action to a purchaser of a security who has been injured by reason of a material misrepresentation or omission. Like the § 11(a) claim, a plaintiff need only prove the misrepresentation or omission and the burden shifts to the defendant to prove due diligence and a reasonable belief in the truth of the statement made. However, unlike a § 11(a) claim, (a) the security need not be publicly offered, (b) the misrepresentation or omission may be oral or contained in a "prospectus" which is not the subject of a registration statement, and (c) the relief granted is rescission rather than money damages based upon the decline in the price of the security. Finally, the defendants that can be sued are limited to the seller or offeror of the securities and, according to certain courts, those persons who were a "substantial factor" causing the securities transaction to occur.[54]

[53] 283 F. Supp. 643 (SDNY 1968).

[54] See, e.g., In re Gas Reclamation, Inc. Sec. Litigation, 659 F. Supp. 493, 508 (SDNY 1987). In the recent case of Pinter v. Dahl, 56 USLW 4579 (1988), the U.S. Supreme Court was presented with substantially the same issue under Section 12(1) of the Securities Act, which provides rescissionary relief

Securities Exchange Act of 1934—Section 18(a). Section 18(a) of the 1934 Act imposes liability on any person who makes a materially false or misleading statement in any document filed with the SEC. The section expressly creates a private right of action for damages.[55] It has been held, however, that Section 18(a) does not impose liability for unaudited interim financial statements or for reports sent directly to shareholders but not filed.[56]

At first glance, Section 18(a) liability appears to resemble Section 11 liability for 1933 Act registration statements. However, under Section 18(a) a plaintiff must prove the following elements:

1. That he actually knew of and relied on the allegedly false or misleading statement in making his investment decision, and that at the time of his action he was not aware that the information was false or misleading.
2. That his damages were caused by his reliance on the false or misleading statement.
3. That the purchase or sale price was affected by the false or misleading statement.

Further, Section 18(a) absolves a defendant who can prove that he acted in good faith and had not known at the time of the filing that his opinion was false or misleading, that is, that he had not acted with scienter. Because of these limitations, the remedy created by Section 18(a) "has rarely been invoked."[57]

Exchange Act—Section 10(b). As interpreted by the courts, Section 10(b) of the 1934 Act, together with SEC Rule 10b-5 promulgated thereunder, have become formidable legal hazards to accountants and others. Rule 10b-5 makes it unlawful "in connection with the purchase or sale of any security," for any person

1. To employ any device, scheme, or artifice to defraud.
2. To make any untrue statement of a material fact or to omit to state a material fact necessary in order to make the statements made, in the light of the circumstances under which they were made, not misleading.
3. To engage in any act, practice, or course of business which operates or would operate as a fraud or deceit upon any person.

Unlike the civil liability provisions contained in the 1933 Act (or, in the case of Section 18(a), the 1934 Act), neither Section 10(b) nor Rule 10b-5 provides an express private remedy for damages. However, courts have consistently held that investors injured by violations of Rule 10b-5 have an implied private right of action

---

against sellers who have unlawfully failed to register securities. The Court restricted liability under Section 12(1) to those who parted with title to the securities in question and those who actually "solicit" the sale of such securities. The Court's reasoning in *Pinter,* if applied to liability under Section 12(2), would appear to reject the "substantial factor" test as a basis for imposing liability on non-sellers, and would limit accountants' liability under Section 12(2) to those rare circumstances where the accountant actually solicits the sale of a security.

[55] Ross v. A.H. Robins Co., 607 F2d 545 (2d Cir. 1979), cert. denied, 446 US 946 (1980).

[56] Rich v. Touche Ross & Co., 415 F. Supp. 95 (SDNY 1976).

[57] Ross v. A.H. Robins Co., 607 F2d 545, 552.

for damages, despite the lack of an express provision creating such a private right.[58] Also, in *Herman & MacLean v. Huddleston*,[59] the Supreme Court ruled that auditors and others may be sued under the antifraud provisions of Section 10(b), even though an express remedy is available under another provision of law (such as Section 11 of the 1933 Act).

The threshold requirement for the maintenance of an action under Rule 10b-5 is that the plaintiff must have bought or sold a "security." The term "security" is defined in Section 3(a) of the 1934 Act. The definition includes, among other things, an "investment contract." The Supreme Court has repeatedly endorsed a broad construction of the term.[60]

In *Exchange Nat'l Bank of Chicago v. Touche Ross & Co.*,[61] for example, the bank sued an accounting firm in connection with the bank's purchase of unsecured subordinated notes. The bank alleged that, in purchasing the notes, it had relied on the accounting firm's opinions as to the financial position of its borrower-client. The court held that the accounting firm could be liable under Section 10(b) because the notes were "securities" within the meaning of the Act, after a detailed analysis of the notes in which the court contrasted them to "commercial" loans.[62]

Another requirement for the maintenance of an action under Rule 10b-5 is that a plaintiff must be either a "purchaser" or "seller" of securities.[63] As a consequence, holders of a security who were merely dissuaded from selling or buying it on the basis of an alleged misstatement or omission cannot maintain an action under Rule 10b-5. Again, however, the courts have interpreted the terms "purchase" and "sale" broadly to allow suit by holders of puts, calls, options, and other contractual rights or duties to purchase or sell securities.[64] In addition, stockholders of a corporation that purchased or sold securities in an allegedly fraudulent transaction may maintain derivative actions on behalf of the corporation, even if they were not themselves purchasers or sellers.[65]

A third requirement for the maintenance of an action under Rule 10b-5 is that the misstatement or omission alleged by the plaintiff must have occurred "in connection with" the purchase or sale of a security. The case of *SEC v. Texas Gulf Sulphur Co.*[66] established an exceedingly broad meaning for the phrase "in connection with" the purchase or sale of a security. In *Texas Gulf Sulphur*, a company that had issued a materially misleading press release was not then engaged in issuing or otherwise dealing in its securities. Nevertheless, the court interpreted the "in connection with"

---

[58] Superintendent of Ins. v. Bankers Life & Casualty Co., 404 US 6 (1971).

[59] 459 US 375 (1983).

[60] Landreth Timber Co. v. Landreth, 471 US 681, 686 (1985).

[61] 544 F2d 1126 (2d Cir. 1976).

[62] Courts' construction of the term "security" is not limitless, however. See Matter of Hawaii Corp., 567 F. Supp. 609 (D. Haw. 1983) (claims by trustee of corporation under Rule 10b-5 against accountants dismissed because shares of stock transferred to corporation pursuant to reorganization were not "securities").

[63] Birnbaum v. Newport Steel Corp., 193 F2d 461 (2d Cir.), cert. denied, 343 US 956 (1952); Blue Chip Stamps v. Manor Drug Stores, 421 US 723 (1975).

[64] Blue Chip Stamps v. Manor Drug Stores, 421 US 723 (1975).

[65] Herpich v. Wallace, 430 F2d 792 (5th Cir. 1970).

[66] 401 F2d 833 (2d Cir. 1968) (en banc), cert. denied, 394 US 976 (1969).

phrase as requiring only that misrepresentations by defendants be likely to cause reasonable investors to purchase or sell the company's securities in reliance on the misrepresentations. Since 1968, therefore, audit opinions and audited or unaudited financial statements with which auditors become associated are considered statements "in connection with" purchases and sales of securities for purposes of an action under Section 10(b).

Once a plaintiff has established that he has standing to sue under Rule 10b-5, he must prove the substantive elements of a cause of action under Section 10(b). These elements are (1) a factual misrepresentation or omission, (2) materiality, (3) scienter, (4) reliance, and (5) causation of injury.[67]

The concept of a misstatement or omission is the same under Rule 10b-5 as under other provisions of the federal securities laws. It may be limitlessly varied in different circumstances.[68]

The standard of materiality is likewise the same under Rule 10b-5 as under other provisions of the federal securities laws.[69] It has been held that the basic test of materiality is whether a "reasonable man" would attach importance to a misrepresented fact in determining whether to purchase or sell a security.[70] Again, however, it is impossible to derive a rule that would determine what constitutes a material fact in every case. Materiality is a mixed question of law and fact, involving the application of a legal standard to a particular set of facts.[71]

The leading case of *Ernst & Ernst v. Hochfelder*[72] established that scienter, or intent to defraud, is an element of a private action under Section 10(b).

In *Hochfelder*, the president-majority shareholder of a small brokerage firm had induced customers to invest in high-yield escrow accounts. Investment checks were made payable to the president or to a designated bank for his account. The escrow accounts were fictitious, and the president converted the money to his own use. He concealed this scheme by insisting that he alone personally open mail addressed to him or to his attention. The auditors were accused by plaintiffs of "inexcusable negligence" in failing to discover the lapse of internal accounting controls that would have revealed the fraud.

The court held that a private cause of action under Section 10(b) may not be maintained by showing only that a defendant was negligent. Rather, plaintiff must allege and prove that a defendant acted with scienter, that is, *intent* to deceive, manipulate, or defraud. The court explicitly avoided deciding, however, "whether, in some circumstances, reckless behavior is sufficient for civil liability under § 10(b) and Rule 10b-5."

Lower court decisions after *Hochfelder* have, however, approved a standard of "recklessness" in determining whether a private action may be maintained against an

---

[67] Fund of Funds, Ltd. v. Arthur Andersen & Co., 545 F. Supp. 1314 (SDNY 1982).

[68] See, e.g., Oleck v. Fischer, (1979 Transfer Binder), Fed. Sec. L. Rep. (CCH) ¶ 96,898 (SDNY 1979), aff'd, 623 F2d 791 (2d Cir. 1980) (allegation that audited balance sheet failed to disclose risks incurred by company in investment in another company).

[69] See, e.g., Austin v. Loftsgaarden, 675 F2d 168, 179 (8th Cir. 1982).

[70] See, e.g., List v. Fashion Park, Inc., 340 F2d 457, 462 (2d Cir.), cert. denied sub nom. List v. Lerner, 382 US 811 (1965).

[71] T.S.C. Indus., Inc. v. Northway, Inc., 426 US 438, 450 (1976).

[72] 425 US 185 (1976).

accountant under Section 10(b),[73] and have held that this standard is the same one required by the landmark common law case of *Ultramares*: whether the accountant lacked a genuine belief, even if unreasonable, in the truth of the statements made.[74]

Recent decisions interpreting Section 10(b) frequently have held that proof of the materiality of a misstatement or omission gives rise to a rebuttable presumption of reliance.[75]

For example, in *Affiliated Ute Citizens of Utah v. United States*,[76] the Supreme Court held that a plaintiff who can establish materiality in an omission case under Rule 10b-5 need not prove reliance. In *Affiliated Ute*, the plaintiffs were former shareholders of a corporation who had not been told by officers of the defendant bank appointed as stock transfer agent that a secondary market existed in which the price exceeded that paid by the bank for the sellers' shares. The Supreme Court held:

> Under the circumstances of this case, involving primarily a failure to disclose, positive proof of reliance is not a prerequisite to recovery. All that is necessary is that the facts withheld be material in the sense that a reasonable investor might have considered them important in the making of this decision. . . . This obligation to disclose and this withholding of a material fact establish the requisite element of causation.

More recently, in *Basic, Inc. v. Levinson*,[77] the Supreme Court upheld the "fraud on the market" theory of reliance by investors who sell or buy shares of stock in impersonal market transactions. The court established a rebuttable presumption that persons who trade in a company's securities do so in reliance on the integrity of the market price. The court further held that in an open and developed market, the integrity of the market price will be compromised by any material misstatements made by a company in connection with its securities.

The element of causation in a Rule 10b-5 case has two prongs, sometimes called "transaction causation" and "loss causation."[78] Often, proof that a plaintiff relied on a defendant's misstatements or omissions is sufficient to establish "transaction causation," that is, that those misstatements or omissions caused plaintiff to purchase or sell the security in question.[79] Plaintiff must also prove that the alleged misstatement or omission proximately caused his pecuniary loss.[80]

The risk of liability in securities litigation has been magnified by the development of two types of collective adjudications of controversies involving large numbers of persons: the class action and the derivative action. Plaintiffs generally favor a class action over a derivative action, because any recovery is paid directly to the members

---

[73] Admiralty Fund v. Hugh Johnson & Co., 677 F2d 1301 (9th Cir. 1982).

[74] Seiffer v. Topsy's Int'l, Inc., 487 F. Supp. 653 (D. Kan. 1980); McLean v. Alexander, 599 F2d 1190 (3d Cir. 1979).

[75] Seiffer v. Topsy's Int'l, Inc., 487 F. Supp. 653 (D. Kan. 1980).

[76] 406 US 128 (1972).

[77] 108 S.Ct. 978 (1988).

[78] See, e.g., Bennett v. United States Trust Co., 770 F2d 308, 313 (2d Cir. 1986), cert. denied, 106 S.Ct. 800 (1987).

[79] Basic Inc. v. Levinson, 108 S.Ct. 978 (1988).

[80] See, e.g., Bastian v. Petren Resources Corp., No. 86 C. 2006 (ND Ill. 1988) (claims under Section 10(b) dismissed because plaintiff failed to allege that omissions in offering memorandum caused decline in value of limited partnership interests).

of the class; in a derivative action, the recovery is paid to the company in which the shareholders own stock, not to the shareholders themselves. Some suits are maintainable as either class or derivative actions, or both at once.[81]

As applied to securities law cases, the federal class action rule requires not only that there be questions of law or fact common to the class, but that such common questions predominate over individual questions. In practice, federal courts have been receptive to class actions, both to reduce duplicative litigation and to support the interests of multitudes of small investors who could not sue individually. Further, recent cases such as *Basic, Inc. v. Levinson*[82] have made it much easier for plaintiffs to prove that common questions predominate over individual ones.

Although courts have allowed plaintiffs to maintain private actions under Section 10(b), they have not found implied private rights in other sections of the federal securities laws that do not expressly provide for them. In *Touche Ross & Co. v. Redington*,[83] for example, the trustee in liquidation of a brokerage firm sought to impose liability on the defendant, by reason of its allegedly improper audit of the brokerage firm's financial statements, which were required to be filed with the SEC by Section 17(a) of the 1934 Act. The Supreme Court dismissed the case after deciding that Section 17(a) does not confer a private remedy for damages. In *Transamerica Mortgage Advisors, Inc. v. Lewis*,[84] the Supreme Court also held that a private action is not sustainable under Section 206 of the Investment Advisers Act (similar to Rule 10b-5), although lower courts had previously upheld suits that charged defendant accountants with aiding and abetting violations of the section.

There is conflicting authority concerning the availability of a private right of action under Section 17(a) of the 1933 Act, the language of which is similar to, but possibly narrower than,[85] the language of Section 10(b) of the 1934 Act.[86] Further, although most courts that allow a private right under Section 17(a) of the 1933 Act have held that the section requires allegations of scienter,[87] plaintiffs often argue that actions under Section 17(a) (2) and (3) may be predicated on the basis of mere negligence.[88] Many actions brought against accountants alleging violations of the securities laws contain a claim under this section.

Racketeer Influenced and Corrupt Organization. Although the RICO statute was originally intended to combat the infiltration of organized crime into legitimate

---

[81] Ernst & Ernst v. United States District Court, 439 F2d 1288 (5th Cir. 1971).

[82] 108 S.Ct. 978 (1988).

[83] 442 US 560 (1979).

[84] 444 US 11 (1979).

[85] Section 17(a) of the 1933 Act prohibits fraud in the *"offer* or sale" of securities, rather than in connection with the *purchase* or sale of securities, as required by Section 10(b). For this reason, one court has held that any private right of action under Section 17(a) must be limited to sellers. Frymire v. Peat, Marwick, Mitchell & Co. [Current Binder] Fed. Sec. L. Rep. ¶ 93,682 (CCH) (ND Ill. 1987).

[86] See, e.g., Landry v. All American Assurance Co., 688 F2d 381 (5th Cir. 1982) (no private right); Newman v. Prior, 518 F2d 97 (4th Cir. 1975) (private right exists).

[87] See, e.g., In re Diasonics Sec. Litigation, 599 F Supp. 447 (ND Cal. 1984).

[88] See Manufacturers Hanover Trust Co. v. Drysdale Sec. Corp., 801 F2d 13 (2d Cir. 1986), cert. denied, 107 S. Ct. 952 (1987) (declining to decide whether a private right of action exists under Section 17(a) of the 1933 Act, or whether liability under that section may be predicated on mere negligence).

business, it has instead become a tool for private litigants to recover treble damages for what are in essence "garden variety" fraud claims. Almost all cases that have addressed the issue have held that one need not prove a nexus to organized crime in order to recover under the RICO statute.[89]

The RICO statute proscribes four types of activities[90] (a) using or investing income derived from a pattern of racketeering activity in the acquisition, establishment, or operation of an enterprise; (b) acquiring or maintaining an interest in or control of an enterprise through a pattern of racketeering activity; (c) conducting or participating in the conduct of an enterprise's affairs through a pattern of racketeering activity; and (d) conspiring to violate any of the above prohibitions.

The term "racketeering activity," as defined by the RICO statute, encompasses a long list of federal and state crimes, including mail fraud and wire fraud. A person can violate the mail and wire fraud statutes by simply using the United States mails or wires in furtherance of a fraudulent scheme. In fact, a defendant does not personally have to use the mails or wires in order to violate the mail or wire fraud statutes; it is enough if it is reasonably foreseeable that his activities will result in the use of the mails or wires.[91] Since fraudulent schemes often involve the use of the mails or wires, most such frauds, including fraud in the issuance of financial statements, can be phrased as RICO violations.

A single instance of racketeering activity does not constitute a RICO violation; one must engage in a "pattern of racketeering activity" to violate the RICO statute. According to the RICO statute, a pattern of racketeering activity requires at least two acts of racketeering activity. In the now famous footnote 14 in *Saedima, S.P.R.L. v. Imrex Co.*,[92] the U.S. Supreme Court noted that while two acts of racketeering activity are necessary to form a pattern, they may not be sufficient. The Court went on to point out that RICO is not targeted against sporadic activity; therefore, in determining whether instances of racketeering activity constitute a pattern, the court must measure their *continuity plus relatedness*.

In *Eastern Corporate Credit Union v. Peat, Marwick, Mitchell & Co.*,[93] the court held that an auditor who was alleged to have committed three acts of mail or wire fraud over a five-week period in connection with a single audit did not engage in a pattern of racketeering activity, since the allegations amounted to no more than a single, isolated fraudulent episode.

In *Professional Assets Management, Inc. v. Penn Square Bank, N.A.*,[94] the court also found that the pattern requirement was not satisfied because all instances of mail and wire fraud by the accountant arose out of one engagement to perform one audit. But in *First Federal Savings and Loan Association of Pittsburgh v. Oppenheim, Appel, Dixon & Co.*,[95] the court held that the mailing of three audit confirmation

---

[89] See, e.g., Bunker Ramo Corp. v. United Business Forms, Inc., 713 F2d 1272, 1287 n.6 (7th Cir. 1983) ("It is well established that RICO does not require proof that the defendent or the enterprise are connected with organized crime.")

[90] 18 USC § 1962(a)–(d).

[91] United States v. Georgalis, 631 F2d 1199, 1206 (5th Cir. 1980).

[92] 473 US 479 (1985).

[93] 639 F. Supp. 1532 (D. Mass. 1986).

[94] 616 F. Supp. 1418 (WD Okla. 1985).

[95] 629 F. Supp. 427 (SDNY 1986).

letters (relating to a single audit) on three different days to three different plaintiffs relating to different securities holdings constituted a pattern, even though the mailings were in furtherance of a single scheme.

In *Bank of America National Trust & Savings Association v. Touche Ross & Co.*,[96] five plaintiff banks alleged that they were induced to extend credit to a corporation in reliance on financial statements prepared by Touche Ross & Co. The court held that the complaint satisfied the pattern requirement in that plaintiffs alleged nine separate acts of wire and mail fraud, involving the same parties over a period of three years. The court specifically held that racketeering acts which are part of the same scheme or transaction may qualify as distinct acts for purposes of the pattern requirement.

In sum, in any specific case it may be difficult to predict whether the allegations against the accountants will be held to constitute a pattern of racketeering activity.

Plaintiffs most often allege that the accountant violated section 1962(c) of the RICO statute. This section prohibits a person from conducting or participating in the conduct of an enterprise's affairs through a pattern of racketeering activity. In section 1962(c) claims involving auditors, the question arises as to whether auditing a client should be considered participation in the conduct of the client's affairs. The few cases that have directly addressed this issue have answered it in the affirmative.

The most extensive discussion of this issue is found in *Bank of America*,[97] in which the court found that plaintiffs had alleged sufficient participation by the accountants in the affairs of their client and therefore denied the auditors' motion to dismiss. The court held that it is not necessary that a RICO defendant participate in the management or operation of the enterprise. The court emphasized that participation may be direct or indirect. It interpreted the word "conduct" simply to mean the performance of activities necessary or helpful to the enterprise, and held that the preparation of financial statements falls under this definition. In *Bennett v. Berg*,[98] however, the court held that participation in the conduct of the affairs of an enterprise "ordinarily will require some participation in the operation or management of the enterprise itself."

It is noteworthy that in *Bank of America*, the court left open the factual question as to whether independent auditors could participate in the affairs of their client. In *Ahern v. Gaussoin*,[99] however, the court denied the defendant auditors' summary judgment motion on the ground that plaintiffs came forward with evidence raising an issue of fact as to whether the auditors had a "substantial connection" with the enterprise, their client. The court pointed out that in addition to conducting annual audits for the client, the accountants prepared interim financial statements, and assisted in the client's SEC registration and in the preparation of quarterly aging reports. The court held that it is not necessary to show that the defendant had control over the conduct of the enterprise's affairs under 1962(c). In contrast, in *Robertson v. White*,[100] the court held that plaintiffs had sufficiently alleged control by the defendant accountants over the enterprise, even though plaintiffs had simply alleged that the accountants had issued fraudulent audit reports.

---

[96] 782 F2d 966 (11th Cir. 1986).

[97] *Ibid.*

[98] 710 F2d 1361 (8th Cir.), cert. denied, 464 US 1008 (1983).

[99] 611 F. Supp. 1465 (D. Ore. 1985).

[100] 633 F. Supp. 954 (WD Ark. 1986).

Although the effect of much recent RICO jurisprudence has been to make it easier for plaintiffs to assert RICO claims against accountants and others, many of the legal issues relating to RICO have still not been settled, and it is too soon to predict whether RICO will retain its status as a means for recovering treble damages for run of the mill frauds.

Bills have been introduced in the House and Senate, the effect of which would be to make it more difficult and less profitable for plaintiffs to assert RICO claims. One proposed bill would eliminate recovery of treble damages if state or federal securities laws provide a remedy for the wrongs alleged by plaintiff, unless defendants have also engaged in unlawful insider trading. The AICPA has indicated its opposition to a proposed exception to this provision, under which treble damages would still be recoverable by plaintiffs with securities portfolios of less than $12,000.

Proposed legislation to amend RICO has also contained one or more of the following provisions: a RICO action by a private plaintiff may be brought only against someone who was convicted of two acts of racketeering activity; treble damages are recoverable only if the plaintiffs had retained the accountants to provide financial statements that the plaintiff alleges are false, or if the accounting firm accepted a bribe in exchange for agreeing to falsify financial statements; no damages are recoverable for pain and suffering; punitive damages are permitted but are limited to twice the actual damages and are recoverable only in consumer cases; and evidence as to punitive damages may be introduced only after a finding of liability.

Tax Laws. An accountant or any other person who prepares a tax return and understates the taxpayer's liability may be liable for certain penalties under the Internal Revenue Code. If an income tax preparer negligently understates a taxpayer's liability, there is a $100 penalty; if the preparer willfully attempts to understate liability, there is a $500 penalty.[101] Moreover, one who aids or assists in the preparation of a tax return which he knows will result in an understatement can be assessed a penalty of $1,000 (if the tax return is for an individual) or $10,000 (if the tax return is for a corporation).[102]

The Code also provides stiff penalties for promoters of abusive tax shelters. A person who promotes a tax shelter and makes a statement relating to the shelter's tax effects that he knows or has reason to know to be false or fraudulent is subject to a penalty of "the greater of $1,000 or 20% of the gross income derived or to be derived by such person from such activity."[103]

Secondary Liability

In certain circumstances, an accountant may be civilly liable for his client's unlawful activities based on various theories of secondary liability. An accountant may also be liable for the unlawful activities of his employees.

---

[101] IRC § 6694.

[102] IRC § 6701.

[103] IRC § 6700.

Aiding and Abetting. Charges of aiding and abetting are very often alleged in connection with violations of the federal securities laws. Accountants may be found liable for aiding and abetting violations of Section 10(b) of the 1934 Act, in connection with misstatements by their clients. Courts have also found accountants liable for aiding and abetting violations of section 14(a) of the 1934 Act, which imposes liability on solicitors of proxies that contain material misstatements or omissions. [104]

An accountant may be liable for aiding and abetting the performance of an unlawful act if the plaintiff proves:

1. The existence of a violation of law by the primary (as opposed to the aiding and abetting) party;

2. "Knowledge" of this violation on the part of the aider and abettor; and

3. "Substantial assistance" by the aider and abettor in the achievement of the primary violation. [105]

The standard of knowledge required to prove the second element of aiding and abetting liability varies, depending on the duty the accountant is deemed to owe the plaintiff. Although the plaintiff must generally prove that an alleged aider-abettor had actual knowledge of a securities law violation, [106] under certain circumstances, proof that an accountant recklessly disregarded the possibility of a violation is sufficient to show knowledge. Thus, where the accountant knows or can reasonably foresee that third parties will rely on an audit or opinion letter, some courts have held that recklessness may establish aiding and abetting liability. [107]

The kind of "assistance" that a plaintiff must prove to establish the third element of aider and abettor liability also varies according to the duty the accountant is held to owe the plaintiff. For example, even inaction may suffice where the accountant owes a duty of disclosure.

Control Person. Under Section 15 of the 1933 Act and Section 20 of the 1934 Act, a person who controls another person will be liable for the securities laws violations of that person. An outside auditor is generally not considered to be a controlling person with respect to his client. [108] On the other hand, an accounting firm is considered to be in control of its nonpartner employees and thus, under certain circumstances, can be liable for their wrongdoing even if it did not directly participate in those acts. The accounting firm can avoid liability if it can show that it acted in good faith and did not induce the securities law violation (Section 20 of the

---

[104] There is a split of authority concerning accountants' liability for aiding and abetting violations of Section 12(2) of the 1933 Act, which imposes liability on sellers of securities for misstatements made in a propectus or oral communication that contains a material misstatement or omission. Liability for aiding and abetting may be affected by the recent decision in Pinter v. Dahl; cf. Note 54.

[105] International Inv. Trust v. Cornfeld, 619 F2d 909, 922 (2d Cir. 1980).

[106] Landy v. FDIC, 486 F2d 139, 162-163 (3rd Cir. 1973), cert. denied, 416 US 960 (1974).

[107] See, e.g., Oleck v. Fischer (1979 Transfer Binder) Fed. Sec. L. Rep. (CCH) ¶ 96,898 (SDNY 1979), aff'd, 623 F2d 791 (2d Cir. 1980).

[108] In re Commonwealth Oil/Tesoro Petroleum Sec. Litigation, 484 F. Supp. 253, 268-69 (WD Tex. 1979).

1934 Act) or that it had no knowledge of or reasonable ground to believe in the existence of the facts underlying the violation.

Conspiracy. A conspiracy is an agreement to commit an unlawful act. Conspiracy is sometimes used to create secondary liability under the securities laws. It is important to note that a defendant can be held liable for aiding and abetting the violation of a law only if the law was actually violated, but a person can be held liable for conspiring to violate a law even if ultimately the law was not actually violated.

Vicarious Liability. An employer is generally liable for the torts committed by an employee in the course of his employment. Similarly, a principal is liable for torts committed by his agent while acting within the scope of his agency. In a partnership, every partner is both principal and agent to every other partner. Thus when an accounting firm is set up as a partnership, the firm and each partner in the firm is liable for all torts committed by any partner or any employee of the firm in the course of their employment, that is, while performing professional work for the firm. The firm and the partners are vicariously liable regardless of whether they participated, authorized, or ratified the wrongful act.[109]

Generally, punitive damages will not be awarded against someone who is vicariously liable in situations where such damages may be appropriate for imposition upon those who are directly liable.

Joint and Several Liability

A defendant who is found liable for securities laws violations or under common law principles occasionally may be able to shift all or part of the damages assessed against him to another party who contributed to the plaintiff's injuries. There are three separate legal bases for distributing plaintiff's losses in such a manner: indemnification and contribution, both of which seek compensation from a third party, and comparative negligence, which allows the reduction or elimination of plaintiff's damages where plaintiff himself was responsible for all or part of his loss.

Indemnification. The principle of indemnification permits a defendant to shift the entire loss to a third party, so that the original defendant ultimately may be relieved from his obligation to compensate the plaintiff. However, the existence of a claim for indemnity does not mean that plaintiff will not recover from the initial defendant; the latter party remains fully responsible for plaintiff's losses whether his indemnification claim is successful or not.

The duty can arise either by the existence of a contractual relationship, such as an insurance policy, or by virtue of an implied common law duty. For example, an

---

[109] See, e.g., Sharp v. Coopers & Lybrand, 457 F. Supp. 879 (ED Pa. 1978), aff'd, 648 F2d 175 (3d Cir.), cert. denied, 455 US 938 (1981) (accounting firm liable under common law doctrine of respondeat superior for recklessness of tax supervisor in preparation of tax shelter opinion letter signed by partner of firm).

employer who is found vicariously liable for the acts of his employees may be able to seek indemnity from the employee who actually caused plaintiff's injuries.

Contribution. Contribution is similar to indemnification procedurally in that the action is commenced in the same manner by the same parties. However, whereas indemnification involves the shifting of plaintiff's *entire* loss to a third party, contribution principles permit the original defendant to shift only a portion of the loss to the other party.

The federal securities laws expressly provide for contribution where the claim arises under Sections 9 and 18 of the Securities Exchange Act. Under Section 11(f) of the Securities Act of 1933, furthermore, a defendant liable for false statements in a registration statement "may recover contribution . . . from any person who, if sued separately, would have been liable to make the same payment, unless the person who has become liable was, and the other was not, guilty of fraudulent misrepresentation."[110]

Although neither Section 10(b) nor Rule 10b-5 of the Securities Act of 1934 contains a contribution provision, many federal courts have found a common law right to the remedy. The Second Circuit Court of Appeals, for example, has held that "under the securities laws, a person who has defrauded the plaintiff in violation of those laws may be liable for contribution to another person who has similarly defrauded the plaintiff."[111]

Comparative Negligence. Comparative negligence differs significantly from contribution and indemnification. The latter two theories effectively provide only for a more equitable apportionment of plaintiff's injuries among those parties who might have caused or contributed to the claimant's harm. Under the doctrine of comparative negligence, however, plaintiff's recovery may be limited or even precluded, based on plaintiff's own culpability for the injury suffered. Although the doctrine is known generally as "comparative negligence," the term actually encompasses three separate theories: contributory negligence, comparative negligence, and pure comparative negligence.

Contributory negligence, a somewhat outmoded theory which today exists only in a handful of states, acts as a general bar to plaintiff's recovery if that individual can be shown by defendant to have contributed even partially to his own injuries. That theory has been widely displaced by the less draconian comparative negligence standard, which itself has two branches. In many of the states which have adopted comparative negligence, a plaintiff who is found to be "more liable" than a defendant will be entirely barred from recovery; if plaintiff is "less liable" but still at fault, his damages will be reduced accordingly.

A number of states, including New York, have adopted a modified or "pure" comparative negligence standard, whereby damages are adjusted to reflect plaintiff's contribution to his own injuries even if the plaintiff is found to have been more negligent than the defendant. For example, an apportionment of liability reflecting

---

[110] 15 USC § 77.

[111] Tucker v. Arthur Andersen & Co., 646 F2d 721, 727, 727 n.7 (2d Cir. 1981); see also Sirota v. Solitron Devices, Inc., 673 F2d 566, 578 (2d Cir.), cert. denied, 459 US 838 (1982).

that the plaintiff was 60% negligent while the defendant was 40% liable will result in a damages award to the plaintiff of 40% of the total injury.

Criminal Liability

The federal statutes under which accountants are most likely to be criminally prosecuted are

- *The general mail fraud statute,*[112] and the *wire fraud statute,*[113] which prohibit use of the United States mail and the transmission of interstate or foreign communications by wire, radio, or television, in any scheme to defraud or to obtain money or property by false or fraudulent representations.
- *A securities fraud and false filing statute,* Section 24 of the 1933 Act, prohibiting willful violation of any provision of the 1933 Act or SEC rules under it, and the willful making of a material misstatement or omission in a registration statement filed under the Act.
- *A second securities fraud and false filing statute,* Section 32(a) of the 1934 Act, prohibiting willful violation of any provision of the 1934 Act or SEC rules under it, and the willful and knowing making of a false or misleading statement of any material fact in any application, report, or document required to be filed with the SEC or a securities exchange under the Act or related SEC rule.
- *The general false statement statute,*[114] prohibiting knowing and willful falsification or concealment of any material fact, or the making of a "false, fictitious or fraudulent" statement or representation, orally or by use of a false writing or document, with knowledge of the falsehood, to government personnel in any matter within the jurisdiction of any department or agency of the United States.
- *The false statement to bank statute,*[115] which prohibits any person from intentionally making any false statement or overvaluation of any property, for the purpose of influencing in any way the action of a wide variety of banking and other financial institutions on any application for a loan or other extension of credit.

An accountant may also be (1) prosecuted for aiding and abetting or conspiracy in the commission of crimes described above; and (2) charged with state crimes, such as violations of Section 409 of the Uniform Securities Act, state criminal fraud statutes, and unauthorized-practice laws.

In 1986, for example, the audit partner of a national accounting firm pled guilty to an indictment charging him, among others, with mail and wire fraud, fraud in connection with loan and credit applications, and conspiracy.[116] The partner admitted that he intentionally created fictitious journal entries to conceal massive losses incurred by E.S.M. Government Securities, Inc., in return for bribes by officers of the company.

---

[112] 18 USC § 1341.

[113] 18 USC § 1343.

[114] 18 USC § 1001.

[115] 18 USC § 1014.

[116] See In re Alexander Grant & Co. Litigation, 110 FRD 528 (SD Fla. 1986).

The concept of *mens rea* or criminal intent is essential to criminal prosecutions. Where accountants are alleged to have participated in wrongful financial falsifications by corporate managements, one typical issue is whether the evidence established beyond a reasonable doubt that the accountant knew he was participating in a crime and therefore was acting willfully.

United States v. Benjamin[117] affirmed the conviction of an accountant on securities fraud charges. In describing the standard of culpability applicable to the prosecution of accountants for criminal fraud, the court held: "the Government can meet its burden by proving that a defendant deliberately closed his eyes to facts he had a duty to see . . . or recklessly stated as facts things of which he was ignorant." This case also illustrates the use of circumstantial evidence to create an inference of criminal intent. In *United States v. Weiner*,[118] which involved the fraudulent overstatement of the net income and assets of Equity Funding Corp. of America, the principal audit personnel were convicted of willful and knowing violation of the false filing provisions of the securities laws, in connection with their audit opinions on financial statements filed with the SEC.

In another criminal case, referred to in *United States v. Clark*,[119] the government failed to prove that the auditors knew of alleged management falsifications. The indictment alleged that the auditors acquired knowledge of, and accepted, "false, fictitious and non-existent construction costs" for a particular fiscal year, which resulted in an overstatement of earnings for that year. The auditors successfully denied knowledge of any false construction costs, and defended their audit examination by citing their rejection of management's proposed percentage-of-physical-completion test, which would have yielded higher earnings than the cost percentage test. The auditors successfully asserted that, although percentage-of-completion accounting for construction contracts is recognized in GAAP, the audit evaluation of results for any fiscal year during the construction period is necessarily uncertain.

An auditor who obtains knowledge of a client's illegal acts in the regular performance of professional services may become criminally implicated if he does not take appropriate steps to disassociate himself from the illegality.

United States v. Simon[120] appears to hold that an auditor has an obligation in issuing his opinion to require that the financial statements adequately disclose known management irregularities that significantly affect the financial condition and operating results of the company.

In *United States v. Natelli*,[121] the court of appeals affirmed a criminal conviction of the audit partner under the false filing provision of the 1934 Act. In connection with a merger proxy statement,

1. The auditor prepared and proposed to the client retroactive adjustments that had the effect of concealing a currently discovered prior-period discrepancy and that failed to conform to professional accounting standards of adequate disclosure of prior-period adjustments to income; and

---

[117] 328 F2d 854 (2d Cir.), cert. denied, 377 US 953 (1964).
[118] 578 F2d 757 (9th Cir.), cert. denied, 439 US 981 (1978).
[119] 360 F. Supp. 936 (SDNY) 1973).
[120] 425 F2d 796 (2d Cir. 1969), cert. denied, 397 US 1006 (1970).
[121] 527 F2d 311 (2d Cir. 1975), cert. denied, 425 US 934 (1976).

2. The auditor acquiesced, without proof, to a contract sale by management that increased net income (and later proved to be fictitious).

The court said that "circumstantial evidence, particularly with proof of motive, where available, is often sufficient to convince a reasonable man of criminal intent beyond a reasonable doubt." The case is a stark warning to auditors that although an accounting error may (or may not) be an act of negligence, a failure to take appropriate action upon its discovery may be interpreted as an act of willfulness within the meaning of the criminal law.

There is no existing precedent that determines whether an accounting partnership could be indicted for alleged felony under the federal securities laws or, if it could, whether it could be convicted if fewer than all of the partners were indicted and convicted. Accounting partnerships have been charged as unindicted coconspirators in criminal proceedings in which individual partners have been indicted.

PRELIMINARIES TO LITIGATION

Litigation Warnings

Typically, an accountant or auditor who is a defendant in a lawsuit will have had strong suspicions that he will be sued. Indeed, the absence of any forewarning is more likely the result of ignoring the signs. Although it is highly doubtful that the events triggering potential litigation can be changed by the time warning signs appear, contacting counsel about potential litigation before it is formally commenced may enable steps to be taken to control or reduce potential exposure.

Risk Identification. The warning signs of litigation are varied and frequently ambiguous; they may range from the patent (e.g., overt threats to sue), to the subtle (e.g., a casual telephone call seeking facts). There is no litmus test. At best, approximate rules-of-thumb are an accountant's only guide.

Typically, lawsuits against accountants arise where the financial condition of an accountant's client (or former client) suddenly and seriously deteriorates. The more sudden and the greater the financial deterioration, the more likely the accountant will be sued.

Many lawsuits against accountants are commenced by third parties who have extended credit to an accountant's client based on its financial condition. At first blush, an accountant may conclude that there is no litigation risk because he did not guarantee his client's financial condition. However, courts are frequently receptive to the argument that a substantial deterioration in the client's financial condition could not have occurred "overnight," and that potential warning signs, now more obvious with the benefit of hindsight, should have alerted the auditor to problem areas or caused the auditor to expand the scope of his work at an earlier date.

Another common type of lawsuit asserted against accountants involves securities claims by a client's shareholders. Often, when market price of the client's stock drops significantly because of adverse changes in the client's financial condition, shareholders allege that the accountants knew or should have known of the adverse situation long beforehand but failed to require appropriate disclosures. More recently, clients have attempted to hold their former accountants responsible for their own insolvency or bankruptcy.

Thus, whenever an accountant's client suffers a material adverse change in its financial condition, the accountant should be on notice of a potential litigation problem. This is especially true when the client becomes insolvent or bankrupt. In those situations, a lawsuit—even one of very dubious merit—against the accountant may represent a third party's only hope to recover his losses.

Accordingly, an accountant should advise his counsel of situations in which potential or actual losses to third parties can be traced to adverse changes in the financial condition of his client. At an early stage, counsel can assess the situation and determine whether steps need to be taken. Action can range from monitoring events to developing a factual record to demonstrate in a later proceeding that losses suffered by the putative plaintiff are due entirely to conduct other than the accountant's.

Subpoenas and Investigations. A common precursor to litigation against an accountant is an investigation by a governmental authority or agency, such as a grand jury, prosecutor, insurance regulator, the SEC, or the IRS. Litigation against the accountant may ultimately be brought by the investigatory body, private parties, or both.

Fact finding in governmental investigations, as well as in private civil litigation, is commonly accomplished by issuing a subpoena. A properly issued subpoena requires the subpoenaed party to provide testimony or documents under penalty of contempt. Alternatively, a governmental authority or private litigant may informally request information or documents in lieu of serving a subpoena. Formal subpoenas and informal requests should be treated with equal seriousness.

Whenever an accountant is served with a subpoena or is requested to provide information by an investigatory body or a private litigant, counsel should be consulted immediately. Nor should the accountant volunteer any information or make any commitments in the initial contact, since the accountant may be the incipient target of litigation or a governmental proceeding.

Pre-Litigation Issues

Once the accountant learns that the possibility of litigation exists, a number of matters should be addressed with counsel, as discussed in the following sections.

Privileges. An accountant-client privilege is not uniformly accepted. Indeed, it is not accepted in the federal courts. Varying forms of the accountant-client privilege are accepted in the courts of fewer than 20 states. New York, for example, does not recognize the accountant-client privilege.

The accountant-client privilege, as is true with most privileges, belongs to, and is for the benefit of, the client, not the professional. The most common features of an accountant-client privilege are the following: (1) the privilege is limited to communications made in the course of the accountant's professional employment; (2) the privilege may be waived by consent of the client; and (3) the privilege can be waived when the information is material to the accountant's defense of an action brought against it by the client.

If the accountant practices in a state in which the accountant-client privilege is recognized, the accountant or his attorney should carefully consider the scope of the privilege and also consider applicable case law construing the privilege.

If available, and when properly utilized, the accountant-client privilege can effectively thwart unwarranted invasion of the accountant's work product, yet permit the accountant to defend himself.

Finally, underlying all privileges is the concept of confidentiality. Consequently, if the communication between client and accountant is disclosed to third parties, there is a substantial risk that any privilege will be waived.

Legal Counsel Review. A legal review is generally undertaken in larger accounting firms when there is a "whiff of trouble," that is, the risk of a lawsuit involving the firm or the possibility of a client seeking protection under the federal bankruptcy laws. Legal reviews provide early warning of potential accounting and auditing issues and enable the accountant and his attorneys to develop lines of defense for use in pleadings and depositions.

It is a common practice for an "independent partner" — a partner with no connection with the accounting work performed for the client — to focus on the accounting issues likely to be raised and to review and report to counsel on the quality of the accounting workpapers and files maintained by the office that performed the work. The independent partner doing the investigative work should not communicate with the engagement personnel.

Standstill and Tolling Agreements. The mere passage of time may compel the bringing of a lawsuit to avoid a defense that it is untimely or has been unreasonably and improperly delayed. To meet the problems posed by time limitations, attorneys have developed standstill or tolling agreements. In these agreements, potential parties to a litigation agree to limit or waive the defense of the statute of limitations or laches (an equitable doctrine similar to the statute of limitations).

A standstill agreement allows potential adversaries to delay and possibly avoid the assertion of claims against each other and, potentially, to pursue a joint defense against a common adversary in a lawsuit. For example, codefendants may agree to a standstill of potential cross-claims while preparing a joint defense to a plaintiff's claim.

A standstill agreement may give the accountant an opportunity to prepare a defense or to dissuade a prospective plaintiff from bringing suit. The party with the potential claim may decide not to assert its claim for a variety of reasons, including the gradual recognition that the claim has problems of proof.

Ownership and Security of Workpapers. Workpapers are written documentation prepared or assembled by an accountant to support his audit conclusions and opinion. Workpapers are the property of the accountant who prepares them. The accounting records of a client and the financial statements with respect to which an accountant may render an opinion are the property of the client. An accountant's workpapers may be produced to others for their review in a lawsuit or administrative hearing conducted by the SEC or other administrative agency.

Because the workpapers are the primary, if not the sole, evidence that the accountant has properly performed his work, it is critical that the workpapers be properly maintained. An original workpaper should never be permanently removed from the workpapers' files, nor should documentation be added to the original workpapers after the completion of the services rendered to the client.

When litigation is anticipated, audit workpapers should be segregated, carefully indexed, and secured. Pre-litigation reproduction must be carefully monitored by the accountant or his attorney to assure that workpapers are not lost, damaged, destroyed, or sequentially altered.

Client Relations. In anticipation of a lawsuit, an accountant must make careful assessments of the present and likely future relationship with his client. In many securities laws actions, both the client and accounting firm are named as defendants by a shareholder, or class of shareholders. In such litigation, the accounting firm must determine whether to conduct a joint defense with its client or whether cross-claims will be asserted between the client and the accountant. In making such an assessment, the accountant should consider the client's solvency and the prospect for future business, measured against potential exposure to damages. He must also consider the potential effect on his independence as an auditor.

Former Employees. When the accounting firm anticipates that it may be sued, it should determine which individuals at the firm worked on the engagement that will be the subject of the litigation. Given the large turnover of individuals at accounting firms, there is a likelihood that at least some of the individuals who performed the accounting work on the engagement are no longer employed by the firm.

An early effort should be made to determine where these former employees work, and, more importantly, under what circumstances they left the accounting firm. This inquiry is particularly important since the former employee may be asked to give testimony by a private plaintiff, or in enforcement procedures by the SEC or other regulatory agencies. It may be helpful for an individual still working at the accounting firm who had a good relationship with the former employee to contact that former employee and explain the circumstances under which he may be contacted. It also may be helpful for the attorney representing the accounting firm to represent the former employee at the accounting firm's expense.

Damage Exposure Analysis. In anticipation of a lawsuit, the accounting firm should make at least a preliminary assessment of the amount of damages the firm may be required to pay either in settlement of the lawsuit or to satisfy any potential judgment. If the firm has audited the financial statements of a public company and is being sued in connection with such audit, it should determine the scope of its liability to the company's public shareholders through analysis of trading prices, volume, and trends. Also, the accounting firm should determine its exposure, if any, to lending institutions and trade creditors that may have relied on the firm's work product in providing credit to the client.

THE LITIGATION PROCESS

Initiation of Litigation

The manner in which a lawsuit is commenced differs from state to state, and between state and federal forums. The common element in all forums, however, is service of process.

In New York State, for example, a lawsuit against an accountant is commenced by serving the accountant with either a summons or a summons and complaint ("process"). In federal court, a lawsuit is commenced by filing a complaint with the court and thereafter serving a summons and complaint on the accountant. Generally, an accountant will be personally served with process. However, in many forums, other procedures are available if personal service cannot be effected.

Discovery

The longest and often the most important stage of a lawsuit is known as "discovery." In discovery, the plaintiff attempts to gather, both from the accountant and others, evidence that will support his case. Likewise, the defendant attempts to discover evidence from the plaintiff and from others that will undermine the plaintiff's case and support the defendant's case.

As with service of process, various discovery mechanisms may be available in different forums, including depositions, document requests, interrogatories, and requests to admit.

In depositions, attorneys for each party question witnesses under oath. Those witnesses are represented by their own attorneys during the questioning, regardless of whether they are parties to the litigation. Each party to the litigation may also make written requests of any other party for different types of documents, and may direct written questions ("interrogatories") at any other party, which must be answered in writing under oath (normally with the assistance of the answering party's attorney). Further, each party may request the other to admit certain matters. The responses to these requests, if any, are also answered in writing under oath (with the help of the answering party's attorney).

Although the purpose of discovery is to create open access to relevant information, discovery mechanisms may be abused. For this reason, the discovery stage of a litigation often generates motion practice before the court, which has the power to issue protective orders limiting or restricting the manner, scope, and timing of discovery. As might be expected, there are substantial variations among jurisdictions and judges as to the latitude, permissible burdens, and speed of the discovery process.

Settlement

Most lawsuits are resolved by settlement between the parties before, during, or even after trial. Evaluation of the wisdom of a settlement is an ongoing process that changes during the stages of a lawsuit, and involves a constant reassessment of the accountant's exposure to liability. That assessment must be objective. An accountant should never rely solely on his own judgment of the legal sufficiency of his accounting or auditing work. The accountant should seek additional and impartial input, whether from other partners in the firm or from outside experts.

Factors which should be taken into account in negotiating a settlement are the accountant's likelihood of an adverse decision or verdict, the amount of damages for which he may be held liable, whether his exposure is for compensatory damages or for a combination of compensatory and punitive damges, and the costs of defending the action.

Trial

At trial, each side has the opportunity to present evidence in support of its position. Usually, the plaintiff has the burden of presenting proof to establish a prima facie case. The defendant then has the opportunity to present evidence to refute the plaintiff's case and to establish his defenses.

The trier of fact determines whether a particular fact has been established. In certain circumstances, the judge may be the trier of fact. In accounting cases, the jury will usually perform this function. A jury trial presents a particular challenge in an accounting case because juries are not composed of accounting experts nor of peers of the accountant. Rather, a jury is likely to be composed of individuals who have little or no understanding of even the fundamentals of accounting and auditing.

Near the end of the trial, after each side has finished presenting evidence, the judge will instruct the jury how to arrive at a decision. These instructions will be based on the applicable legal principles in the case. Within the guidelines of these instructions, the jury will make its decision.

Appeals

In some forums, appeals may be taken from rulings made by the judge prior to trial. In other forums, such as in the federal courts, appeals must usually await the completion of trial.

An appeal after a determination at trial is generally made with respect to legal issues rather than factual issues. For example, the party taking the appeal may argue that an improper instruction was given to the jury or that the judge made an incorrect ruling with respect to the admission or exclusion of certain evidence.

It is extremely difficult to appeal from the determination of a factual issue. It is not enough that an appellate court might disagree with the factual determination made at trial. In order to prevail, an appellant must convince the appellate court that there was no credible evidence to support the factual determination made by the lower court.

THE BUSINESS OF LITIGATION

The profession has been somewhat slow to respond to the risks of practice created by the increased perceptions of the accountant's public function. One exception, however, is the marketing of services to assist lawyers and litigants in prosecuting and defending claims of professional misfeasance.

Although professionals, particularly large accounting firms, once hesitated to "take sides" in the wars fought in courtrooms, client pressure and the lucrative nature of such work have made expert testimony and litigation support accepted business practices.

Expert Witness

The admission of expert testimony is governed by the Federal Rules of Evidence and state evidentiary codes. Rule 702, the basic federal rule regarding expert testimony, provides that if "scientific, technical, or other specialized knowledge will assist the trier of fact to understand the evidence or to determine a fact in issue," a witness who is "qualified as an expert by knowledge, skill, experience, training, or education" may testify as to his specialized knowledge "in the form of an opinion or otherwise." Under this rule, a judge must resolve two questions in the affirmative before he will permit a purported expert to testify: (1) will expert testimony assist the trier of fact (the judge or jury) to determine a fact in issue; and (2) does the witness qualify as an expert?

Since technical knowledge of accounting issues is not normally possessed by a juror, courts usually sustain the admission of expert testimony to explain such issues. However, courts frequently limit the testimony of accounting experts to technical problems and may not permit the expert to express an opinion on such ultimate facts as negligence or fraud.

For example, in *Fineburg v. United States*,[122] the defendant offered the expert testimony of an accountant to rebut evidence of his intent to defraud. The accountant was prepared to testify, based on his examination of the defendant's financial records, that the defendant's business could have improved so that he could have repaid his debts. Since intent to defraud is an issue that juries are normally expected to evaluate, however, the court excluded the accountant's testimony.[123]

The second question pertaining to the admissibility of expert testimony is whether the witness offered as an expert qualifies as such. The trial judge has wide latitude in determining the expert's qualification. In sophisticated litigation, it is extremely difficult to prevent qualification. However, questions about an expert's "limits" or biases and prejudices frequently affect the weight or significance a judge or jury will give to the expert's opinions. Indeed, the trier of fact has the right to reject or disregard entirely an expert's testimony.

An accounting expert may be permitted to testify as to the generally accepted auditing standards at a particular time or the proper standards for the presentation of financial information. Although courts generally allow the expert to testify as to whether, in his opinion, the defendant's conduct met those standards, the trier of fact is free to apply the stated principles to the facts and to arrive at conclusions other than those expressed by the expert.

---

[122] 393 F2d 417 (9th Cir. 1968).

[123] See Barry v. United States, 501 F2d 578, 584 (6th Cir. 1974), cert. denied, 420 US 925 (1975) (testimony of expert witness may be disregarded if it conflicts with sound judgment of the trier of fact based on his evaluation of all the evidence).

In the matter of Ernst & Ernst [124] illustrates the difference in weight between expert testimony as to proper accounting standards and issues of ultimate fact. In this case, the SEC considered expert testimony from professors of accounting, a former president of the AICPA, a former chief accountant of the SEC, and the chief accountant at the time of the hearing, concerning generally accepted accounting principles at the time of the suit. With respect to this issue, the SEC held that the accountants' testimony should have been given "considerable" weight. With respect to the question whether the respondents had conducted a sufficient audit, however, the SEC gave but "relatively little" weight to the experts' testimony.

The same distinction is implicit in *United States v. Simon.* [125] Rejecting the defendant's argument that the jury was bound to accept the uncontradicted expert testimony of several accountants, the court stated:

> We think the judge was right in refusing to make the accountants' testimony so nearly a complete defense. The critical test according to the charge was the same as that which the accountants testified was crucial. We do not think the jury was also required to accept the accountants' evaluation whether a given fact was material to overall fair presentation, at least not when the accountants' testimony was not based on specific rules or prohibitions to which they could point, but only on the need for the auditor to make an honest judgment and their conclusion that nothing in the financial statements themselves negated the ... (facts).

Rule 706 of the Federal Rules of Evidence and the rules of some state courts permit the court to appoint its own experts. This frequently occurs in complex estate matters and bankruptcy proceedings. Although attacks on an expert's qualifications are permitted under such circumstances, they are rarely successful and the expert's opinions are usually given great weight by the factfinder.

Litigation Support

In addition to or as an alternative to offering testimony, accountants often function as expert advisors to attorneys in prosecuting or defending complex litigation. Many accounting firms have developed large practice areas to provide such services. This assistance may consist of analysis of another professional's work product, the preparation of complaints and discovery requests, or attendance at depositions of accountants appearing as fact witnesses.

Since accounting firms have increasingly developed computer capabilities as a business tool, lawyers have sought accountants' support in cases involving large volumes of documents or statistical data. Accountants assist in the administration of creditor claims in bankruptcy proceedings, the settlement of class actions in product liability and securities cases, and the valuation of assets. Accountants also frequently work with investment bankers, securities analysts, claims adjusters, and scientists in helping lawyers and litigants.

---

[124] (1937-1982 Accounting Series Releases Transfer Binder) Fed. Sec. L. Rep. (CCH) ¶ 72,270 (1978) (ASR 248).

[125] 425 F2d 796, 806 (2d Cir. 1969), cert. denied, 397 US 1006 (1970).

In assisting one litigant against another, the accountant-as-expert must not only ascertain that there are no conflicts of interest but also that positions he may take are not contrary to those adopted by clients of his own firm. Such inquiries are not limited to accounting or tax matters, but may extend to economic, social, or even political matters.

SPECIFIC RISK AREAS

Management Fraud

Management fraud is usually more dangerous than nonmanagement employee fraud, and the exposure of auditors to charges of professional dereliction in connection with management fraud is severe. Management fraud less often involves embezzlement or its equivalent, on a quantitatively material scale, than it does willful deception concerning the financial position and operating results of a business. In these cases, management's objective is to deceive the security holders and the public as well as the auditors.

The court in *Lincoln Grain, Inc. v. Coopers & Lybrand*[126] upheld the following jury instruction, which describes an auditor's duty to detect management fraud:

> Under the engagement agreement between the parties, and under Generally Accepted Auditing Standards, the defendant did not undertake to do a detailed fraud audit, or to disclose fraud or defalcations. The defendant must be aware of the possibility that fraud may exist in the plaintiff company. However, an ordinary audit cannot be relied upon to assure that fraud or deliberate misrepresentations by plaintiff's management will be discovered. The defendant is not an insurer or guarantor if it turns out that fraud occurred and the defendant did not discover it. The defendant does have a responsibility for failing to detect fraud when such failure clearly results from the defendant's failure to comply with Generally Accepted Auditing Standards. The subsequent discovery of fraud does not of itself mean that the defendant's examination was negligently done.

The profession has been busy in the area of detection of management fraud. The National Commission on Fraudulent Financial Reporting (sponsored by the AICPA and other professional associations of accountants) released its final report in 1987, with numerous recommendations for auditors, management, audit committees, educators, and legislators. A complete discussion of the report, which could influence federal legislation regarding auditors' responsibilities, is contained in Chapter 45.

In 1988, the AICPA's Auditing Standards Board issued SAS 53, *The Auditor's Responsibility to Detect Errors and Irregularities* (AU 316). This standard requires the auditor to design his audit to provide reasonable assurance that material errors and irregularities will be detected. (See Chapters 5 and 7.)

---

[126] 216 Neb. 433 (Neb. 1984).

Illegal and Questionable Acts

Financial statements were traditionally conceived of as presentations of economic and financial data, not as critiques of business morality. In those circumstances, an auditor becoming aware of illegal or questionable payments or other dubious behavior within the audited entity had an understandable responsibility of defined and limited scope. First, had the payments or activities been approved, if necessary at the board level, on behalf of the enterprise? Second, were the payments or activities material for any reason (not limited to quantitative measures) in relation to financial position or result of operations? If the answers to these questions were satisfactory, the audit inquiry could be concluded.

During the mid-1970s, investigations by the SEC and others revealed evidence of illegal political contributions, bribery of foreign government officials, and other illegal and questionable payments by businesses. In many instances such misbehavior was compounded by deliberate falsifications of accounting records (e.g., off-book slush funds) or other accounting deficiencies (e.g., misleading or inadequate description or documentation). The SEC ascribed a qualitative materiality, regardless of amount, to these irregularities, because of their implications for the credibility of financial data and accounting controls and the integrity of management.

This series of events gave rise to the promulgation by the profession of SAS 17, *Illegal Acts by Clients*, in 1977. This has now been updated by SAS 54 (same title), issued in 1988. The latest revision makes the auditor responsible for detecting illegal acts that could have a material effect on the financial statements the same as his responsibility for detecting errors and irregularities (see preceding section).

Auditor Disagreements and Changes

The termination of an audit engagement may be a signal to the successor auditor that the predecessor and the client disagreed about accounting principles, auditing procedures, or other matters. Such termination may also be a sign that the client is engaged in so-called opinion shopping. SEC rules mandating disclosure of auditor-client disagreements and changes of auditors are intended to protect the accountant's independence and to discourage changing of accountants to obtain more favorable accounting treatment.[127]

Regulation S-K[128] provides detailed instructions for disclosure of certain disagreements or events that took place prior to an accountant's resignation or dismissal. Among other things, the Regulation mandates disclosure of

[1] any disagreements with the former accountant [2] on any matter of [a] accounting principles or practice, [b] financial statement disclosure, or [c] auditing scope or procedure, [3] which disagreements if not resolved to the satisfaction of the former accountant would have caused him to make reference in connection with his report to the subject matter of the disagreement(s).

---

[127] See ASR 165, (Accounting Series Releases Transfer Binder) Fed. Sec. L. Rep. (CCH) ¶ 72,187.

[128] 17 CFR 229.304. The SEC recently moved the substance of the disclosure requirements for changes in accountants from Form 8-K (required to be filed by companies whose securities are registered under the 1934 Act), 17 CFR 249.308, to Item 304 of Regulation S-K. See 53 FR 12924 (April 20, 1988).

Disclosure of such disagreements is required regardless of whether or not they were resolved to the accountant's satisfaction.[129] ASR 165 (FRR § 603.02.c) states that the term "disagreements" is to be interpreted broadly. However, recent amendments to the disclosure item clarify that preliminary differences of opinion based on incomplete facts are not considered "disagreements" if those differences are later resolved by obtaining more complete factual information. Regulation S-K also requires a statement as to whether the termination was recommended or approved by an audit committee or, if none, by the board.

The SEC recently codified, in Item 304 of Regulation S-K, the positions taken in ASR 165 concerning certain reportable events that may not have resulted in an expressed "disagreement" between the auditor and management. Such reportable events occur if the auditor resigned or was dismissed after informing his client that internal controls necessary to develop reliable statements did not exist; that the auditor had discovered facts which led him no longer to be able to rely on management representations; or that information has come to the auditor's attention that made him unwilling to be associated with statements prepared by management. In addition, Regulation S-K requires disclosure of situations in which the former accountant has advised the client that the auditor must significantly expand the scope of his audit, and the auditor resigns or is dismissed before the expanded audit has been performed. The former accountant must also disclose all instances during the past two years in which information has come to his attention that would materially affect the client's financial statements, if the matter was not resolved to the former accountant's satisfaction prior to his dismissal.

Regulation S-K requires disclosure of reportable disagreements or events that took place within the client's two most recent fiscal years, or in any subsequent interim period preceding the former accountant's resignation or dismissal. Item 9 of Schedule 14A, relating to disclosure in proxy statements, requires a registrant to provide the same information required to be disclosed by Regulation S-K.

Finally, the SEC's latest revisions include provisions aimed at opinion shopping: The registrant must disclose instances in which the newly engaged auditor was consulted, during the time frame mentioned in the preceding paragraph, on matters of accounting principles or auditor reporting, if (1) such consultations met the requirements of SAS 50, *Reports on the Application of Accounting Principles* (AU 625; see Chapter 11), or (2) the consultation issues were the subject of a reportable event or disagreement with the former auditor.

Purchase Audits and Reviews

Purchase audits and reviews encompass a broad variety of professional accounting and auditing services performed in connection with some substantial change or proposed change in the ownership, control, or management of a business, such as a sale of all or a substantial part of its securities or assets, a statutory merger, or a recapitalization, reorganization, or "spin-off."

A purchaser may sometimes claim that he has been misled by inadequate or controversial accounting (and occasionally misrepresentation) by the officers or princi-

---

[129] CFR 240.14a-101.

pals of the acquired business, or by inadequate performance by an independent auditor in a purchase audit or review. The purchaser may claim that the accounting principles and methods employed by the seller, as applied to such items as doubtful receivables, excess or obsolete inventory, and unprofitable contracts, have been unsatisfactory.

In assigning blame for a disappointing acquisition, a purchaser may overlook his own errors of judgment. Courts sometimes conclude that the seller has defrauded both the purchaser and the co-defendant accountant, or that the demise of the business subsequent to its purchase has been caused by the purchaser's own mismanagement.

In *McLean v. Alexander*,[130] for example, a sophisticated investor purchased all the outstanding stock of a company specializing in the manufacture of laser-beam devices for use in construction. The company retained a local accounting firm to perform an audit, explaining that it was needed quickly in order to help the company attract investment capital. The audit report showed that the company possessed very limited assets and had negative earnings for the 11-month period covered. Nevertheless, the investor agreed to purchase the company for many times the value of the assets listed on the balance sheet. He did so on the basis of the company's sales projections that indicated increasing sales and high potential for further increases.

After the purchase was completed, the investor learned he had been defrauded. What had been represented to him to be actual sales were in fact only consignments or sales conditioned on resales. The investor sued the seller's management, an investment banker, and the auditors who had examined the balance sheet.

Only one item on the balance sheet, accounts receivable, was found at trial to be misleading. This item, however, represented accounts supposed to be due and owing as a result of sales on which the investor had relied in deciding to purchase the company. The issue before the court was whether the accountants could be held to have acted with the requisite scienter in certifying the figure for accounts receivable; that is, whether the auditors knew at the time they certified the figure that they lacked the knowledge required to form an opinion as to its accuracy.

The trial judge found the auditors liable. The appeals court reversed, after analyzing in detail the efforts made by auditors to verify that the accounts comprising the figure for accounts receivable were genuine sales. The court concluded that although the auditors may have been negligent in not pursuing further certain inconsistencies in the documentation of the sales, they had not engaged in fraud within the meaning of the securities laws. In this case, the sellers had defrauded both the purchaser and the sellers' auditors.

Among the riskiest of all purchase audits for accountants are those in which the purchase price of a transaction is linked by formula to net worth or earnings, represented by audited financial statements of the acquired business. The "soft" numbers in financial statements—for example, allowances for doubtful receivables, excess and obsolete inventory, and unprofitable contracts, as to which there may be reasonable difference of opinion—in these transactions become hard money, transferable between pockets of buyer and seller.

The most common type of lawsuit against accountants arising from a purchase audit is grounded in allegations that the seller's regular auditor issued a false or mis-

---

[130] 599 F2d 1190 (3d Cir. 1979).

leading audit or review opinion. Auditors of acquired businesses also have occasionally been charged by purchasers with misrepresenting the viability of the purchased business.

In *CBS, Inc. v. Ziff-Davis Publishing Co.*,[131] a purchaser of a magazine business claimed that it had overpaid for the magazines in reliance on an audit that contained various misrepresentations, resulting from failure to properly allocate certain costs to the acquired business, overstatement of revenues, failure to establish adequate allowances for doubtful accounts receivable, and other errors. The purchaser had, however, engaged its own outside auditors to investigate the seller's business, and had concluded before the closing of the purchase that there were material misrepresentations in the financial statements. Under these circumstances, the court held that the purchaser could not have relied on the audit, and dismissed the purchaser's claims against the seller's accountants.

The seller, too, may charge an auditor with liability either for negligence or fraud, and may claim indemnification for the cost of having warranted the financial statements audited or reviewed by the accountants, even though the seller's warranties were much broader than a standard audit opinion, or the auditor had made a review without audit. In *Coleco Industries, Inc. v. Berman*,[132] for example, the accountants had made errors in unaudited interim financial statements that had been warranted by officers of the seller. The court held the accountants liable to the officers for the amount of their liability to the purchaser because of the breach of the warranty contained in the purchase agreement. The amount of such liability, however, was offset by the previous settlement that the accountants had made with the purchaser.

When a purchaser's regular auditor audits a business to be bought, and the audit is to be relied on by the purchaser in completing the purchase, the auditor exposes himself to significant potential risks both as to purchaser and to seller. Such an engagement has all the problems encountered by an auditor in a first audit—familiarization with the system, policies, procedures, and business of the acquired business. Under those conditions, and possibly with less than normal cooperation from the seller, the hazard of a misunderstanding or of deception by the seller is increased.

The seller may believe that the purchaser's auditor, who has had no previous professional relation with the acquired business, is overly critical of the seller's accounting, and perhaps is biased in favor of his regular client, the purchaser.

The acquired business is entitled to an auditor's opinion that supports such client's financial statements within the limits of GAAP. However, the auditor's regular client—the purchaser—may expect, and the auditor may believe that he should furnish, information on details of accounting valuations and other applications of accounting methods by the acquired business. Yet the furnishing of such information to the purchaser cannot be unconditionally justified, except as may be expressly authorized by the seller.

The result may be a genuine conflict of interest on the part of the auditor, which may expose him to charges that he neglected or otherwise prejudiced one interest in favor of another. For this reason, accountants should consider declining purchase

---

[131] Index No. 13965/85 (Sup. Ct. NY Co.), aff'd, 125 AD 2d 1015 (1st Dept. 1986).

[132] 432 F. Supp. 275 (ED Pa. 1976), aff'd and rem'd in part, 567 F2d 569 (3d Cir. 1977), cert. denied, 439 US 830 (1978).

audit and review engagements in which there are substantial inherent conflicts of interest, even though there is no lack of independence.

Purchase audits undertaken for both purchaser and the acquired business expose the auditor somewhat differently, and even more broadly. The auditor owes a duty of care to both, and may be held liable for negligence to either (or both). Such an engagement involves an inherent conflict of interest. In *Matter of Hawaii Corp.* [133] the trustee of a company in bankruptcy claimed that the company's former auditors had been negligent and reckless in performing accounting services in connection with the company's reorganization. The company's board of directors had engaged the auditors to provide pro forma financial statements reflecting the combination of the company with a controlling (but financially weaker) shareholder-company, and to express opinions as to the most advantageous means of effecting the combination. The trustee's principal claims were that the accountants should not have accounted for the reorganization by considering the controlling shareholder as the "acquired" company and should have used the "purchase" method of accounting for the transaction; and that the accountants failed to inform the directors of material adverse changes in the controlling shareholder-company's financial position that occurred during the period covered by a comfort letter. The trustee claimed that, had the accountants not failed in these respects, the board of directors (a majority of which were members of the board of the controlling shareholder-company) never would have approved the reorganization.

The court found for the accountants in all respects. The court was convinced that, in economic substance, the reorganization involved the assumption by the surviving company of the assets and liabilities of the controlling shareholder; that the accountants properly treated the surviving company as the acquirer; that the accountants properly declined to use the purchase method of accounting for the transaction; and that the accountants' review and analysis of the comfort period were consistent with their commitment and with good accounting practices. The court further found that the board would have proceeded with the reorganization irrespective of the accountants' conduct, and that the ultimate failure of the business was due not to the reorganization but to extraneous factors, including a possibly unwise course of expansion that the directors embarked on after the reorganization.

Franklin Supply Co. v. Tolman [134] also involved accounting services undertaken for both buyer and seller. The U.S. purchaser of a Venezuelan oil well supply company, despite its negotiation from the seller of a reduction in the purchase price of the business, sued the audit firm that had been engaged (and whose fee had been shared equally) by both buyer and seller. The court found that the auditor owed a duty of care to both purchaser and seller, and had committed negligence, though not fraud, by not disclosing that (1) the oil well equipment inventory had been valued by regular prices of normal suppliers (ruled by the court on expert testimony to be an acceptable method of valuation), rather than by lower prices of surplus suppliers; and (2) defendant's Venezuelan auditor was an alternate director of the seller and during the audit period had been a director of the seller (without ruling on the effect on independence of defendant).

---

[133] 567 F. Supp. 609 (D. Hawaii 1983).
[134] 454 F2d 1059 (9th Cir. 1971).

When audits are performed in connection with a specific transaction such as a merger or other business acquisition, the contracting parties frequently take a special interest in particular data or accounts because of their comparative importance, unresolved questions, or other information. Auditors have had rather poor success in maintaining their contention that their audit opinion relates only to the financial statements as a whole, not to individual elements, and they have no hope of maintaining that proposition as to a matter in which they accept an instruction to give special attention to particular accounts (such as accounts payable or accounts receivable), or other designated matters. Moreover, a special instruction of *inattention* to particular accounts may also be a source of trouble.

Audit firms should consider creating special forms of engagement letters for purchase audits and reviews that attempt to anticipate abnormal problems and risks in such engagements and that are designed to override purchase contract provisions that, if read literally, make a professional engagement impossible. Ideally, such a letter would disclaim any undertakings not contained within the engagement letter and would specifically disclaim any undertakings contained in the purchase-sale agreement. The letter should identify the auditors' client as the acquired business (regardless of who is to pay the audit fee), and should specify that the presale management of the acquired business should be the sole determiner of the financial statements or data that the auditor is obliged to recognize. Any special provisions in the engagement letter, including any variations from GAAP and GAAS, should be examined carefully in advance, and suitable disclaimers included concerning the possible effect on fairness of presentation.

The selection and application of accounting principles and valuation decisions may involve matters of judgment and discretion for which the engagement by the contracting parties of an accountant-as-arbitrator may be appropriate.

If an auditor cannot avoid assuming professional responsibility to both the purchaser and the acquired business, he should attempt to stipulate that as to all claims that might be made by either the purchaser or the acquired business relating to the exercise of professional judgment and discretion, he is entitled to the immunities of an arbitrator (i.e., with no liability for acts performed in good faith even though negligently). However, in engagements relating to public companies, the auditor cannot avoid assuming professional responsibility to other users, such as shareholders and creditors, of the audited financial statements.

50

Professional Research

PURPOSE AND OBJECTIVES

When the term *research* is used in the context of accounting or auditing, the image of a scholarly paper often comes to mind. However, academicians are not the sole source of accounting and auditing research.

This chapter highlights the needs for research within the practicing part of the accounting profession, discusses some of the products of the research effort, and examines research tools and methods currently used.

Some accounting and auditing research efforts are published and distributed, frequently as monographs or booklets. Other research consists of gathering factual background to reach an informed conclusion on a practice issue. This research is not always formally published, although its findings may result in the issuance of a professional standard or other authoritative document. Research of this kind may be performed or sponsored by the organization charged with the dissemination of the standard, or it may be performed by a group obviously interested in the development of a standard in a certain direction. Background information is increasingly being made public, as a result of the movement toward open rule making.

Some research, seldom available to the public, is directed toward problem resolution in a professional environment. Performed by individual companies or CPA firms, this research attempts to solve specific accounting or auditing problems related to the company or a client. Although the findings themselves are kept private, they often result in new or revised firm policies or guidelines. They may also be included in communications to standard-setting bodies describing practice problems resulting from new types of transactions or implementation problems arising from the application of existing authoritative literature. Additionally, this kind of research may enable a practice firm to comment effectively on a proposed standard.

In addition to performing their own research, companies, organizations, and CPA firms encourage research by funding or sponsoring academic research.

Most of the major accounting firms have established foundations to fund research projects in accounting and auditing theory and practice. Generally, the sponsoring firm agrees to contribute a certain amount each year to the foundation, to be used for research projects. The foundation's board must then select appropriate proposals for research projects that appear to have potential for expansion of knowledge about a particular aspect of accounting or auditing.

Many professional organizations also provide funds to support academic accounting and auditing research. The AICPA has long been an active sponsor, funding the Accounting Research Studies and, subsequently, the Auditing Research Monographs. The Planning Executives Institute and the Financial Executives Institute have also been active in sponsoring accounting, financial, and business-planning research and in publishing the results of that research. The National Association of Accountants has sponsored extensive research, concentrating on management accounting.

ACCOUNTING STANDARD SETTING—THE FASB

By its very nature, the FASB is a research organization. The FASB needs and depends on its own research activities as well as those of outsiders, and much of this research culminates in useful input for the development of authoritative pronouncements.

A formal research group within the staff acts as a focal point for the development of standards. As projects arise, a project manager and team are assigned to develop a proposal for consideration by the Board. In conceiving and designing the proposal, the project team draws on its fundamental knowledge and the results of both prior research and research conducted for that particular project.

If the Board accepts the proposal, the project team carries on with its research efforts throughout the due-process procedures for developing a new standard (see Chapter 46). The drafting of a discussion memorandum requires a detailed analysis of existing relevant literature. The project team may need to research existing practice or schedule discussions with individuals experienced in the project area. Other important research information may be uncovered in response to the discussion memorandum or in documents and comments obtained in the public hearing.

Two members of the Board's staff advise the project team throughout their research. The first is a project consultant, whose primary assignments are other FASB projects; he can thus bring an outside perspective to the project development. The other is the in-house research specialist. Like an internal auditor, the research specialist draws on his technical knowledge to review the project approach and suggest improvements. The in-house research specialist reports periodically to the Board on the quality of the ongoing projects and recommends ways of making the research program more effective.

The research specialist also edits the *FASB Research Report* series and advises the Board on results of studies and their implications for FASB policy decisions. The research specialist may suggest new investigations into topics discussed in research reports.

Influencing Standard Setting

To provide the standard-setting group with input and to protect the interests of their memberships, some professional organizations have established a formal mechanism to respond to proposals issued by the FASB and other groups.

Professional Organizations. Between 1959 and 1973 the APB functioned as the primary accounting standard-setting group. Its technical research arm, the Accounting Research Division of the AICPA, was created in the hope that its studies would be adopted by the APB. Although this did not happen directly, the research activities proved to be useful in the formulation of APB pronouncements. The Accounting Research Division ultimately issued 15 Accounting Research Studies.

Currently the AICPA's Accounting Standards Executive Committee (AcSEC) carries on accounting research, issuing statements of position (SOPs), practice bulletins (PBs), and issues papers on accounting topics that usually are related to specific industries or issues.

These statements are recommendations to the FASB and do not have the authority of an FASB pronouncement. However, under SFAS 32 (A06) most SOPs issued prior to the statement and all subsequent SOPs are deemed to establish preferability for purposes of making accounting changes.

The National Association of Accountants (NAA) has designated their Management Accounting Practices (MAP) Committee as the mechanism for communications with the FASB. The MAP Committee periodically meets with the FASB to discuss the standard-setting process and how the NAA can contribute more directly to the process, beyond its role of providing research data through responses to proposed pronouncements. The MAP Committee also comments on proposals by the SEC and the AICPA.

The Financial Executives Institute's comments to the FASB are developed by its Committee on Corporate Reporting. Similarly, the Financial Analysts Federation has designated its Financial Accounting Policy Committee to comment on FASB proposals and the proposals of other bodies.

These and many other organizations also influence standard setting by alerting their members to proposed standards. This stimulates direct commentary to the standard-setting group by those whose accounting or reporting may be directly affected.

CPA Firms. CPA firms are vitally concerned with the standard-setting process. Since the CPA firm ultimately will be the initial interpreter of any new standard (and perhaps the only one if the standard deals with auditing), the firm will want the new standard to be as clear as possible and will therefore comment on proposals.

Once standards have been issued, the CPA firm becomes involved with implementation. Generally, firms issue internal policies and guidelines concerning new standards, and these necessarily require a degree of research. Later, as both clients and the firm become more familiar with the standard and have had experience applying it, the firm may wish to modify the initial policies and guidelines. Research efforts will again play an important role in the formulation of the revisions. All along, the firm may be commenting to the FASB about the need for standards revisions or formal interpretations.

Industry. A number of large industrial corporations also maintain research staffs to respond to standard-setting and regulatory initiatives and to test the impact of new accounting proposals on their operations.

AUDITING STANDARD SETTING

During the past decade, disclosures of massive fraud, which often led to the collapse of an entity, have made the public more aware of auditing issues. Congress and the SEC specifically have taken an intense interest in the development of auditing standards. Further, the proliferation of professional accounting pronouncements during the last few years has required the development of additional auditing procedures and new auditor reporting standards.

The establishment of auditing standards (discussed in Chapter 5) has traditionally been vested in the AICPA. Since these standards apply only to those who practice in the auditing profession, interest by those outside the profession arose only infrequently in the past. In recent years greater concern has been expressed by those not directly affected, partly because of increased audit fees that have accompanied the implementation of new audit standards. Some concern also stems from the belief held by some members of Congress that business failures ought to be predictable if an adequate audit has been performed and the auditors' report has properly reflected any concerns about the company's ability to continue in existence.

AICPA

Although the promulgation of auditing standards is one of the most important functions of the AICPA, the amount of effort devoted to auditing research has not been significant. In 1978 the AICPA formalized its auditing research function by creating the position of Director of Auditing Research. The function of this position is to provide research to support the activities of the group promulgating auditing standards, the ASB. The auditing research function has published six monographs on a variety of auditing issues.

Other Groups

Additional auditing standards research has been provided by accounting firms, both through participation in the ASB and its predecessors, and through responses to auditing standards proposals. The firms' contribution to auditing standard setting is described in a subsequent section.

The Commission on Auditors' Responsibilities (CAR), popularly known as the Cohen Commission, evaluated the auditing standard-setting process and recommended improvements (CAR, 1978). The commission drew from many different sources, including a number of research projects that it commissioned. Some of these projects were never completed (e.g., the project to study the effectiveness of auditor reporting on uncertainties). Others were only analytical approaches, designed to highlight areas of future study.

In 1987, the National Commission on Fraudulent Financial Reporting (NCFFR) issued its recommendations to reduce the incidence of such reporting (see Chapter 45 for an in-depth discussion). Its recommendations were directed not only to independent accountants, but to public companies, the SEC, and others involved in the regulatory process, and educational institutions as well. Significant research was performed by the staff of the NCFFR in identifying factors that lead to fraudulent reporting, and in developing recommendations for improving audit effectiveness, internal controls, regulatory oversight, and so forth to prevent and detect its occurrence.

AREAS OF RESEARCH

Perhaps the most complex research task is the resolution of accounting, auditing, and reporting problems that are not specifically dealt with in authoritative pronouncements. These issues may be specific to a given company or common among many companies, and can arise from many different sources. For example, a new professional pronouncement invariably generates application questions and problems. Changes in business practices and shifts in the general economic environment may also bring about a new emphasis in the reporting area and cause new accounting problems. All of these issues must be dealt with initially by the reporting enterprise and its CPA firm.

Changing Economic Environment

Over the past few years, significant changes in the political and economic environment in the United States have resulted in increased government controls and regulations in some areas or deregulation in others, which in turn have precipitated challenges to financial accounting and reporting and the role of the auditor in society.

The surging rate of inflation in the late 1970s and early 1980s was one of the most significant developments, pointing to the inadequacies of the historical cost basis of financial accounting. In response to criticism of the historical cost model the FASB issued SFAS 33, *Financial Reporting and Changing Prices*, which specified that the standard was an experiment and would be evaluated at a later date.

Subsequently, the FASB commissioned a number of research studies related to SFAS 33. Some of those studies were conducted by academics while others were conducted by public accounting firms and other professional organizations. The purpose of the research was to assess the usefulness of information reported in accordance with SFAS 33 and the problems related to generating it. The results of the studies were presented at a research conference sponsored by the FASB in December 1982.

Laws and Regulations

The proposal or enactment of laws by Congress and regulation by government agencies such as the SEC frequently generate activities that broadly can be categorized as research. When the laws and regulations are vaguely written, there may be serious implementation problems; the researcher thus tries to devise methods of coping or complying with them.

A classic example of a law that has commanded extensive and continuing research efforts is the Foreign Corrupt Practices Act of 1977. Many articles have been written attempting to explain the law and analyze its effect on business. Publicly held corporations began clamoring for guidance on how to evaluate whether their systems and procedures were adequate to comply with the accounting standards provisions of the act. These provisions used language drawn from professional auditing literature, so it was only natural for corporate management to turn to their auditors for assistance. As a result, nearly all the major accounting firms undertook significant responsive research projects. The difficulties of compliance were exacerbated by the lack of definitions in the act; further, the professional language included in the act has a special meaning for the external auditor, and was not intended to be directly applied in the context of management's own responsibility for devising and maintaining an "adequate" system of internal accounting control.

Accounting Principles Problems

Many accounting firms, particularly the larger ones, have devoted significant resources to the assistance of and consultation with firm members in resolving accounting problems encountered while conducting audits or while counseling clients in planning a transaction. This assistance usually takes several forms, and the firms differ somewhat in their methods of providing it. Interpretations of existing professional literature, expressions of preference in accounting areas on which authoritative literature is silent, and guidance in resolving specific problems all require the application of research and problem-solving techniques.

Professional Literature Interpretation. Authoritative accounting literature consists of certain pronouncements issued by the FASB and GASB (standards and interpretations), and its predecessors, the APB and the CAP. For companies required to file with the SEC, Financial Reporting Releases constitute additional requirements. Further, the following are considered semiauthoritative literature:

• FASB and GASB TBs
• Statements of Position of AcSEC
• AICPA Audit and Accounting Guides
• AICPA Practice Bulletins
• Interpretations of APB opinions
• Staff Accounting Bulletins of the SEC, for SEC reporting companies
• Emerging Issues Task Force Consensuses
• FASB and GASB Concept Statements

The usefulness of these pronouncements varies from topic to topic. Some pronouncements are written as broad standards and are highly conceptual, for example SFAS 5, *Accounting for Contingencies* (C59). Others are written very much like a rule book, for example SFAS 13, *Accounting for Leases* (L10).

Because these pronouncements are subject to differing interpretations, many CPA firms prepare material to help their staffs and clients apply them. Preparing interpretive material always requires a degree of research. Initially, the preparers may study background material that was used by the standard-setting body. Comments by the members of the standard-setting group may also aid in explaining the application or intent of a particular part of the standard; and comments to the standards group can alert researchers to problems that may have to be dealt with formally. Finally, the firm can confer with its own members, particularly specialists in an industry that the standard directly affects.

Standards change, and professional practice firms consequently have to update their interpretive materials. In doing so they will rely heavily on the firm's experience in applying the standard. Thus the firm's own past decisions regarding its clients, as well as precedents derived from public financial statements, will be drawn on. The firm may very well choose to discuss these internal decisions with other major firms to assure a degree of interfirm consistency or to resolve an intramural debate.

Lack of Authoritative Literature. Many areas in accounting are not directly discussed in authoritative or semiauthoritative literature. The professional practice firm must study these areas to provide timely guidance to its staff. Often the firm expresses only a preference, and may acknowledge that other accounting methods are acceptable; but sometimes a treatment is mandated, with no alternative.

In formulating its position, the firm must study current practice to analyze alternative treatments and distinguish among fact patterns that call for dissimilar accounting. Analogies may also be drawn between the issue under consideration and similar transactions already encompassed by authoritative literature. Discussions of the issue appearing in professional journals and other firms' position papers may be used in reaching a conclusion.

The maintenance of these internal positions on an ongoing basis is important to a CPA firm. Where no specified GAAP requirements exist, practice tends to change more readily and therefore should be monitored closely.

Especially in the area of financial instruments and transactions (see Chapter 21), authoritative guidance has been sparse. Currently the FASB is studying this area, in a project expected to take several years. In the meantime, accounting firms are issuing opinion letters as to the proper accounting in these circumstances, following the guidance in SAS 50, *Reports on the Application of Accounting Principles* (AU 625). The SAS acknowledges the need for these letters in the absence of specification in areas of GAAP. Specifically required is an adequate amount of research prior to issuing the SAS 50 response (AU 625.06).

Consultation. Where the professional practice firm has been able to maintain an up-to-date reference system, engagement management can often resolve a specific client question or problem by combining the materials prepared by their firm with their own knowledge and experience. Sometimes, however, the engagement management will consult with others in accordance with their firm's established consultation policies, especially if the transaction is unusual, if they cannot locate any relevant material, or where the accounting principle is rapidly evolving. This last situation is exemplified in accounting for financial instruments. The FASB has not issued any standard on accounting for security options, although AcSEC has released an issues paper (AICPA, 1986b) to which the FASB has expressed some objection. The FASB intends to cover options in the broad financial instruments project. Meanwhile many financial transactions involve options, and the accountant must account for them somehow.

To fill this need, CPA firms have established groups and designated individuals devoted solely or primarily to research and consultation. The large firms have some type of centralized (or regionalized) research group, although the responsibilities and functions of the groups vary. In some firms, the research group itself only provides examples on request—other firm members work with engagement management in finding a solution to the accounting or reporting problem. In other firms, the research group participates coequally with engagement management to the extent that in designated matters neither can mandate a solution without the concurrence of the other. The types of research tools utilized by these groups are described in the section on "Research Tools."

Auditing Procedures Problems

Generally, the research effort in specific audits on the proper application of audit procedures is kept internal, and the client may not even be aware that an auditing problem is under discussion. However, there is no reason clients cannot involve themselves in the audit research if they wish.

Industry Audit Approach Consultation. When first engaged by a client, particularly one in an industry with unusual characteristics, the engagement management may not be familiar with the peculiarities of the industry and therefore may first have to research both the industry and the client. For background material, engagement management can examine relevant books and other reference materials. If this material contains detailed audit procedures specifically tailored to the industry, these procedures can provide a foundation on which to build the audit approach appropriate to the new client. If additional guidance is necessary, engagement management usually finds it useful to obtain the help of a firm member who has experience with similar clients in the industry.

Central research groups also can be of some assistance in developing an approach to a specific audit, but the need for continual on-site consultation during the first audit tends to argue against the use of a central research group member in such a situation. When members of the central research group do not have a depth of current experience in the specific industry being considered, they may call on the services of an otherwise uninvolved practice office partner or manager to work with the engagement personnel. Alternatively, the central research group may consult several experienced practice office partners or managers, and then synthesize their ideas and suggestions for use by the engagement management.

Specific Audit Consultation. Problems may arise in the application of specific audit steps because of conditions in the client's records, client reluctance to have certain procedures performed, or the need to issue a special report. These situations frequently require consultation outside the practice office.

In some firms, auditing and accounting consultation occurs within the same central group. In other firms, a specialized group may be established to deal exclusively with various auditing issues. Regardless of the structuring of the firm, the discussions tend to move rapidly away from the generalities of GAAS and focus on the specifics of the audit situation. In such cases, the application of mature judgment and experience becomes of paramount importance.

In establishing unified audit procedures and practices, some firms have mandated the application of certain procedures that are not specifically detailed by GAAS. When a client objects to the performance of such proprietary procedures, firm policies often require consultation with a designated group, usually the central technical group. This central group will usually have sufficient experience and authority to consider the problem in light of previous decisions and, if warranted, to modify the prescribed procedure. Such mandatory consultation has the advantage of facilitating communication of alternative approaches that have proved effective in parallel situations. It also makes possible the maintenance of a consistent audit approach should the firm decide to modify its current audit procedure requirements.

Application of Sophisticated Audit Tools. Encompassed in this category are statistical sampling procedures (Chapter 9), audit procedures in a computer environment, and utilization of computer software to perform certain audit procedures (Chapter 10). Firms generally have a department devoted to the development of sophisticated audit tools. In some firms, problems in applying these tools in a specific audit situation are directed to the firm units responsible for their development; in others, such questions may be directed to designated individuals in the central research group. Research consultants most likely will be practice office personnel experienced in the application of such tools. Because of the specialized problems that can arise during an audit in a computer environment, it is imperative that the individuals consulted be more than computer technicians understanding only the hardware and software; the techniques and objectives of the audit itself must be understood.

Two other documents that provide guidance in the application of statistical methods in auditing are SAS 39, *Audit Sampling* (AU 350), and an audit and accounting guide by the same name (AICPA, 1983b).

Accounting Theory Research

Research into the theory of accounting has traditionally been considered the province of academics. This conclusion is probably due to the lack of publicity about accounting firms' efforts in the area. Actually, there is a great deal of theoretical and a priori research being conducted by accounting firms.

Theoretical Research. Theoretical research by accounting firms has been spurred to some extent by a general inquiry into the objectives of financial statements and the conceptual framework for accounting and reporting (see Chapter 2). Galvanized by a significant increase in the rate of inflation, and recognizing that the historical cost model may no longer be valid in an inflationary era and may in fact produce misleading results, several firms tried to devise alternative accounting and reporting models that would realistically portray the financial condition and results of management decisions. Some firms also sought to encompass a new information model that would be more predictive than the historical cost model. Although the stimulus for the research arose from a common source, there was a lack of unanimity in the conclusions.

Some firms espoused forms of current value accounting and reporting. Others, reacting to inflationary conditions, advocated a price-level adjustment form of accounting. Significant experimentation by accounting firms was conducted in the attempt to design a workable supplemental or alternative accounting model, and the results were provided to the FASB, which was, at that time, in the process of developing a conceptual framework.

In recent years, theoretical research by accounting firms has dwindled, as the FASB agenda has incorporated more major issues that had previously motivated the firms. In addition, the FASB has moved more forcefully into the research area (although mostly empirical rather than theoretical) through projects commissioned for the academic community. Twenty of such FASB Research Reports have been issued through the end of 1987, as listed in Figure 50.1.

Other Research. Professional practice firms also undertake research projects in order to prepare responses to FASB discussion memoranda and exposure drafts. These commentaries provide the firms' current working experience for the FASB's consideration of the issues. The responses necessarily reflect a bias because they are

Topic	Author	Published in
Usefulness to Investors and Creditors of Information Provided by Financial Reporting	Griffin	1987
Accounting for the Translation of Foreign Currencies: The Effects of Statement 52 on Equity Analysts	Griffin and Castanias	1987
Foreign Exchange Risk Management Under Statement 52	Evans and Doupnik	1986
Determining the Functional Currency Under Statement 52	Evans and Doupnik	1986
Incremental Information Content of Statement 33 Disclosures	Beaver and Landsman	1983
Financial Reporting by Private Companies: Analysis and Diagnosis	Abdel-khalik	1983
Accounting for Income Taxes: A Review of Alternatives	Beresford, Best, Craig and Weber	1983
Recognition in Financial Statements: Underlying Concepts and Practical Conventions	Johnson and Storey	1982
Usefulness to Investors and Creditors of Information Provided by Financial Reporting: A Review of Empirical Accounting Research	Griffin	1982
Financial Reporting and Changing Prices: A Review of Empirical Research	Frishkoff	1982
Reporting of Summary Indicators: An Investigation of Research and Practice	Frishkoff	1981
Survey of Present Practices in Recognizing Revenues, Expenses, Gains, and Losses	Jaenicke	1981
Recognition of Contractual Rights and Obligations: An Exploratory Study of Conceptual Issues	Ijiri	1980
Reporting of Service Efforts and Accomplishments (Nonbusiness Organizations)	Brace, Elkin, Robinson and Steinberg	1980
The Effects of the Issuance of the Exposure Draft and FASB Statement No. 19 on the Security Returns of Oil and Gas Producing Companies	Dyckman	1979
An Empirical Investigation of the Effects of Statement of Financial Accounting Standards No. 8 on Security Return Behavior	Dukes	1978
The Impact of Statement of Financial Accounting Standards No. 8 on the Foreign Exchange Risk Management Practices of American Multinationals: An Economic Impact Study	Evans, Folks and Jilling	1978
Statement of Financial Accounting Standards No. 5: Impact on Corporate Risk and Insurance Management	Goshay	1978
Economic Consequences of Financial Accounting Standards: Selected Papers	FASB	1978
Financial Accounting in Nonbusiness Organizations: An Exploratory Study of Conceptual Issues	Anthony	1978

FIG. 50.1   FASB Research Reports

based on decisions previously made by the firm in its practice regarding situations similar to those addressed in the discussion memorandum. However, because the responding firm has experienced such issues it is able to describe specific implementation problems foreseen in the suggested approach. Thus, the research efforts in writing such papers necessarily focus on determining the current state of accounting in the particular area and commenting on the appropriateness of one or more of the suggested alternatives proposed by the discussion memorandum. The firm may also want to assess the reasonableness of the proposed accounting treatments by determining what effect they would have on the financial statements of clients—the does-it-make-sense approach.

The professional practice firm may also need to prepare position papers when the accounting methods used in a client's financial statements are challenged by an outside body such as the SEC or the AICPA's SEC Practice Section, or when a client asks to have an accounting treatment explained. These situations almost invariably arise because the accounting literature is not specific or because alternative treatments seem to be available. In such cases, it is frequently necessary to draw analogies and to describe the probable results of alternative approaches, demonstrating that the firm's conclusion is the appropriate one.

Auditing Theory Research

Professional practice firms conduct significant research in the area of audit techniques. Yet, because much of this research is directed toward improved audit techniques for internal use, the results are not widely publicized.

Audit Approaches. It has been said that the primary output of an audit—the auditor's report on the financial statements—has a relatively low level of utility to the client. Audits are frequently conducted because of government (principally SEC) mandates or because of outside demands from creditors and potential creditors. When the audit is perceived simply as an expedient regulatory obstacle, the professional practice firm is under pressure to reduce the cost of the audit and, hence, the fee.

In the late 1970s, recognizing that an evaluation of audit techniques and approach was overdue, several of the major firms undertook projects to reevaluate their audit approach and documentation requirements and to devise different methods of performing an audit. The mandates for accurate accounting and control contained in the Foreign Corrupt Practices Act stimulated the development of new audit approaches. In some instances, the reevaluation process resulted in the conclusion that one could audit more effectively by applying risk evaluation to the various elements of the financial statements. This research project eventually led to a redesigned overall audit approach and defined a revised audit process comprising a series of logical, sequential steps.

Of course, when a firm's research group decides to make significant changes in the audit approach, they must run rigorous field tests of their proposed methodology before attempting to implement it. Should they decide to implement the new approach, their next objective will be writing a set of guidelines so that firm members

Monograph Number	Topic	Author	Published in
6	Auditor Reviews of Changing Prices Disclosures	AICPA and FASB Staff	1984
5	Audit Problems Encountered in Small Business Engagements	Raiborn	1982
4	The Market for Compilation Review and Audit Services	Arnold and Diamond	1981
3	Internal Accounting Control Evaluation and Auditor Judgment	Mock and Turner	1981
2	Behavior of Major Statistical Estimators in Sampling Accounting Populations (effectively superseded by SAS 39)	Neter and Loebbecke	1975
1	The Auditor's Reporting Obligation	Carmichael	1978

FIG. 50.2 Auditing Research Monographs

will understand how to audit under the new system and why this new approach is better and more logical than the old one.

The AICPA's Auditing Standards Division has assisted in this area by commissioning audit research monographs, listed in Figure 50.2. The institutional research in auditing matters is sparse because researchers require access to "live" cases in firms, something not easily arranged on a timely basis. Accordingly, academic research is more prevalent. In any event, the firms do most of the needed research on their own for specific situations that require a prompt response.

Results of Audit Research Projects. The results of audit research projects can take many forms. As indicated above, one type of project may result in a significant change to the way in which the firm performs its audits and documents its results. More often, however, audit research projects are undertaken to explore certain aspects of the audit process in depth, reinvestigate the efficacy of certain procedures, or review past conclusions reached because a particular procedure was used.

Business Problems Research

In recent years, professional practice firms have conducted research projects or studies in areas of general business problems. In some respects the firms are uniquely qualified to perform such research: they have professional standing, a lack of ostensible bias, and an attitude of independence.

Many of these projects involve surveys to obtain and summarize factual information. To the extent that such information is not public, the practice firms may be able to obtain it more readily because of confidence by business that the information will be kept confidential. In addition, the firms' expertise in analyzing business and financial trends adds credibility to the conclusions drawn from the data and hence increases the willingness of business to provide needed data.

The types of problems included in such research projects are varied. For example, a project may measure the economic health of specific muncipalities and identify characteristics predictive of future financial problems, or survey corporate boards of directors to find out how board members view their responsibilities and how such responsibilities might be changed. These types of projects, focused as they tend to be on matters directly relevant to how businesses operate, also tend to improve the quality of audits in providing additional information to aid the auditor in understanding his clients and the environment in which they operate.

RESEARCH TOOLS

In the preceding sections there have been several references to the need for accountants to clearly understand and analyze appropriate professional literature and to utilize precedent. There are a number of tools, some of them created and developed recently, that have greatly enhanced the ability of an accounting researcher to locate examples and retrieve data. Computerized data bases are an innovation made possible by advances in electronics that bring a huge amount of information to the researcher's own computer screen. However, for an accountant's information needs to be satisfied, it is necessary to know where to look and how to use the information retrieval system.

Computerized Data Bases

The recent explosion in the quantity of accounting-related information has antiquated the traditional methods used by researchers to find answers to technical questions. For years, manual research techniques—reference to topical indices of codified texts of professional pronouncements, leafing through annual reports, and recall— were used. However, there are now too many sources of information and too much information for manual methods to be comprehensive or efficient.

Computerized information retrieval systems are expanding rapidly, multiplying the researcher's efficiency and enhancing the comprehensiveness and accuracy of research results. With a myriad of computerized business data bases now available, accountants can choose those most likely to provide the information they need. Moreover, these data bases can now be accessed by a personal computer using an appropriate modem to transmit and receive data over telephone lines.

Selecting an appropriate data base is no easy matter, however, because of the different types and sources of information and the forms of presentation. Some data bases contain statistics, others have abstracts or bibliographic citations or both, while still others present the full texts of the source documents. Certain data bases contain index terms, or descriptors, to facilitate retrieval of relevant records, and others have numeric codes for events, products, industries, or geographic locations.

Although overlapping of data sources is frequent, many documents or portions of documents are not included in certain data bases. Also, data base producers require different protocols to structure searches and different commands to print results. The following discussion explains the types of information useful to accountants and indicates and describes the data bases most likely to satisfy their needs.

Information Needs of Accountants

Accountants often need information that data bases can provide. The most commonly requested information enables accountants to:

* Determine preferred practice
* Compose footnotes
* Resolve client conflicts
* Locate prior firm decisions
* Find authoritative pronouncements
* Survey current practice
* Obtain statistics
* Collect industry information
* Evaluate prospective clients
* Collect information on a key person
* Write an article or a speech
* Identify firm policy or practice
* List companies by auditor

The Data Base Selection Guide shown in Figure 50.3 (Gale, 1985) relates accountants' information needs to appropriate data bases.

Mead Data Bases

The data bases of Mead Data Central (Mead) contain the full texts of materials rather than abstracts; they are free-text searchable (that is, the words appearing in the actual text—as opposed to controlled vocabulary or index terms from a thesaurus—can be searched); and they are user interactive (that is, searches may be modified continuously depending on previous results). Mead's data bases include NAARS, COMPNY, INFOBK, NEXIS, LEXIS, DISCLOSURE, and ABI/INFORM and may include an individual firm's private library.

DIALOG and ORBIT

DIALOG and ORBIT include periodical literature, books, news, statistics, and index data combined from almost 400 data bases covering business, science, technology, economics, social sciences, and humanities. These data bases are searchable by combinations of key words similar to LEXIS/NEXIS but using different protocols, with the output consisting of titles of articles, names of journals, index terms, authors, organizational sources, and abstracts (not full texts). DIALOG data bases are accessed using file numbers, whereas ORBIT uses file names.

The data bases from these systems most often used by accountants are DISCLOSURE, ABI/INFORM, Standard & Poor's News, Predicasts, Accountants' Index, Books in Print, and Marquis Who's Who.

Information Need	Mead					CPA Firm Private Library	DIALOG				Mead and DIALOG	
	NAARS Annual Reports	NAARS Literature	COMPNY	INFOBK	NEXIS	CPA Firm Private Library	Disclosure/Spectrum	Marquis Who's Who	Predicasts (PTS)	Standard & Poor's	ABI/INFORM	Disclosure
Determine preferred practice	X				X	X						
Compose footnotes	X	X				X						
Resolve client conflicts	X	X				X						
Locate prior firm decisions						X						
Find authoritative pronouncements	X				X	X						
Survey current practice	X											X
Obtain statistics	X	X							X			X
Collect industry information	X	X	X	X	X	X			X	X	X	X
Evaluate prospective clients	X	X	X	X	X	X		X	X	X	X	X
Collect information on a key person	X				X			X		X	X	X
Write an article or speech				X	X			X			X	X
Identify firm policy or practice						X						
List companies by auditor	X											X

FIG. 50.3 Data Base Selection Guide
Source: Gale, 1985.

Data Base Libraries

NAARS. For accountants, one of the most valuable research tools is the National Automated Accounting Research System, or NAARS. NAARS is the AICPA's accounting and auditing library of Mead's computer retrieval system known as LEXIS/NEXIS, which also has extensive legal and tax research information. NAARS became operational in 1972 through the joint efforts of the Information Retrieval Committee of the AICPA and Mead Data Central, Inc. and has become the mainstay of accounting research.

It contains the published financial statements of approximately 20,000 annual reports of over 4,200 companies and subsidiaries listed on the New York Stock Exchange, the American Stock Exchange, and over-the-counter companies indicated by the Federal Reserve to be on margin. The on-line annual reports are in six files, by date, going back to 1983, with an additional 10 years of earlier annual reports stored off-line that can be made available for searching at extra cost. The annual reports include financial statements, footnotes, and auditors' reports, plus other information, such as the company's *Fortune* number, Standard Industrial Classification (SIC) code, balance sheet date, and auditor. All annual reports have been divided into segments, for example, the balance sheet, the income statement, footnotes, the auditors' report, the current assets portion of the balance sheet, and the stockholders' equity section of the balance sheet. This increases accuracy and reduces cost by permitting the search to be performed in a specific portion of the annual report (i.e., a particular segment or groups of segments). NAARS can also perform certain arithmetic operations on dates, SIC codes, *Fortune* ranking, total assets, net worth, total sales, and net income or loss.

In addition, NAARS contains an accounting and auditing literature file of the full texts of updated authoritative and semiauthoritative pronouncements by the AICPA, the SEC, the FASB, the Cost Accounting Standards Board, the International Accounting Standards Committee, and the International Federation of Accountants (Auditing Guides). It also includes the minutes and issues summaries of the FASB's Emerging Issues Task Force. Superseded documents are also available; they may be searched separately or together with the current literature.

NAARS research does not depend on the use of an index in that the full text of the document is included in the database and is word searchable. In order to retrieve or locate a particular item, the researcher transmits the words or phrases that he expects would be used in the relevant documents. The computer then searches the database and provides the number of documents which satisfy the search. It can then produce a list of documents that contain those words or phrases and display the relevant portions. NAARS is interactive, that is, the researcher can review the results of the initial search. The text of the retrieved material is shown on the computer terminal screen in the subscriber's office, and the researcher can modify it, redoing the search as often as needed.

A search can be restricted to (or focused on) a portion, or segment, of an annual report. NAARS segments are shown in Figure 50.4.

NAARS results can be displayed or printed in the following formats:

1. FULL. The full text of the annual report is displayed on the screen. This option is seldom used, because it requires the researcher to review too much information—most of which will

Full Segment Name	NAARS Segment Code
General information	
Name of company	CO
SIC code	SIC
Stock Exchange	EXCH
Type of document	DOC
Date of balance sheet	DB/S
Auditor	AUD
Total assets	ASET
Net worth	N/W
Total sales	SALS
Net income or loss	N/I
Comments	COM
Type of financial statements	TYP
Fortune index	FORTN
Balance sheet	
Balance sheet	B/S
Title (balance sheet)	TITLE-B/S
Current assets	CURA
Noncurrent assets	NCURA
Unclassified assets	UNCLA
Total assets	TASET
Current liabilities	CURL
Noncurrent liabilities, credits, and minority interests	NCURL
Unclassified liabilities	UNCLL
Total liabilities	TLIAB
Stockholders' equity	EQUIT
Total liabilities and stockholders' equity	TLSE
Statement of Income	
Statement of income	I/S
Title (income)	TITLE-I/S
Income before extraordinary items	IBEI
Extraordinary items and accounting changes	EXTOR
Net income or loss	INC
Earnings per share	EPSH
Capital Changes	
Statement of capital changes	CAPCHG
Funds Statement	
Funds statement	F/S
Title (funds statement)	TITLE-F/S
Funds provided	PROV
Funds used	USD
Components of change	COMP
Footnotes	
Footnotes (Also, Note 1 through Note 40)	FTNT
Title of notes to financial statement or financial review	TITLE-FTNT
Auditor's report	REPRT
Management Responsibility Letter	MGT

FIG. 50.4   NAARS Annual Report Financial Statement Segments

be irrelevant. It is more economical to print a full report from microfiche than to print it from NAARS at two cents a line.

2. SEGMENTS. This directs NAARS to display a menu of segments of the annual report, enabling the researcher to select those of interest in full text. These are the same as the components of the annual reports that may be searched, as shown in Figure 50.4.

3. KWIC. This directs NAARS to display the key words in context from the report that satisfied the search request along with the 25 words before and after. KWIC can be expanded to include as many as 999 words before and after those satisfying the search request. KWIC is by far the most widely used of the NAARS options, because it enables the researcher to quickly review the relevant part of each report and the context in which each disclosure is made.

4. CITE. This output mode simply lists the documents retrieved.

NAARS is publicly available for specific research requests through the AICPA. Rates charged depend on the amount of computer and staff time expended and are reasonable, considering the vast volume of material available for searching and the expertise necessary to formulate complex searches.

COMPNY. COMPNY is the library in Mead's LEXIS financial information service that contains the company and industry research reports by analysts from investment banks, brokerage firms, and research institutes. COMPNY files include:

• CO – Company reports covering 3,000 companies.
• IND – Industry research reports on 95 industries.

The following U.S. and international reports are written by financial analysts from Merrill Lynch Pierce Fenner & Smith, Inc.; Paine Webber Mitchell Hutchins, Inc.; Piper Jaffray & Hopwood, Inc.; Rauscher Pierce Refsnes, Inc.; Robert W. Baird & Co., Inc.; J.C. Bradford & Co.; Cable Hawse & Ragen; Drexel Burnham Lambert Inc.; Cyrus J. Lawrence, Inc.; Fitch Investors Service, Inc.; and Yamaichi Research Institute.

• SECABS – Abstracts of SEC filings, including over 7000 8-Ks.
• FILING – Full text of selected 10-Ks and 10-Qs covering companies in the CO file, searchable separately as 10-K and 10-Q files.
• COLIST – Names and ticker symbols of companies covered in the research reports, FILING files and NAARS annual reports.
• INDLST – Industries covered in brokerage house reports.
• EARN – Consensus earnings projections provided by Zacks Investment Research, Inc.
• PARTNR – Information on U.S. limited partnerships registered with the SEC.
• TRICO; TRIEST – Data on publicly owned and privately held businesses. Both files are combined in TRINET.
• ENS – Evans Electronic News Service covering economic, financial, industrial, agricultural, and international developments.

The Information Bank Library. INFOBK, an improved version of the original New York Times Information Bank which first appeared in 1973, is now a library of Mead's NEXIS.

INFOBK is a free-text searchable data base, accessible using the same search protocol as the other Mead data bases. It contains the *New York Times* (NYT), Abstracts (ABS), and Advertising and Marketing Intelligence (AMI) files.

• The NYT contains complete (full-text) stories from the *New York Times* from June 1, 1980 to the present.
• The ABS file contains abstracts of current affairs, business, economic, social, and political information from selected articles in fifty newspapers and magazines from January 1969 to the present.
• The AMI file contains advertising and marketing information (abstracts) from January 1979 to the present, from over fifty trade and professional publications. These cover *Fortune* 500 industrials, consumer products manufacturers, major advertising agencies, public relations firms, and media organizations.

These files contain abstracts from general circulation newspapers such as the *Washington Post,* the *New York Times,* and the *Chicago Tribune*; business publications such as the *Wall Street Journal, Barron's, Business Week, Financial Times, Fortune,* and the *Journal of Commerce*; science publications such as *Aviation Week & Space Technology* and *Scientific American*; international affairs journals such as the *Economist, Foreign Affairs,* the *Japan Economic Journal, Latin America Weekly,* and *Middle East*; other periodicals such as *Consumer Reports, New Yorker, Newsweek, Time, Sports Illustrated,* and *U.S. News & World Report*; and advertising and marketing publications such as *Advertising Age, Adweek, Journal of Advertising, Marketing News, Merchandising,* and *Women's Wear Daily.*

NEXIS. The NEXIS library provides current (updated weekly) and recent news articles from over 100 magazines, newspapers, wire services, and newsletters. The magazines include *Newsweek, Forbes, Business Week, Dun's Review,* the *Economist, U.S. News & World Report, Congressional Quarterly, Weekly Report,* and *Editorial Research Reports.* Newspapers include *American Banker,* the *Washington Post, Christian Science Monitor,* the *Bond Buyer, Legal Times,* and the *Japan Economic Journal.* The wire services include United Press, PR Newswire, Reuters, Associated Press, Business Wire, Kyodo News Service, and Xinhua News Agency. Newsletters include *Platt's Oilgram News, Defense and Foreign Affairs, Securities Week, Wharton Economic News Perspectives,* and *World Financial Markets.*

CPA Firm Private Library. The private library of a CPA firm may contain the firm's major technical manuals and various other internal documents and releases of a technical nature. Because of the sensitivity of some of this information, access to the library invariably is limited to certain qualified users within the firm.

Disclosure/Spectrum Ownership. Disclosure/Spectrum Ownership details the common stock holdings of major institutions, corporate insiders, and 5% beneficial owners for approximately 5,000 Disclosure II companies. This information is derived from filings made with the SEC on a quarterly or as-required basis as the ownership of stock changes. The detailed data covers specific institutions and individuals, their relationship to the company, their holdings, and their most recent trades. Disclosure/Spectrum Ownership may be used to analyze the holdings of publicly traded companies as an indication of market strength.

Marquis Who's Who. Marquis Who's Who (DIALOG File 234) contains detailed biographies on 101,000 top professionals. It includes career history, education, publications, family background, political activities, and special achievements. It corresponds to the printed publication, *Marquis Who's Who in America.*

Predicasts. PTS Predicasts Overview of Markets and Technology (PROMT) (DIALOG File 16) abstracts all significant information appearing in thousands of newspapers, business magazines, government reports, trade journals, bank letters, and special reports throughout the world. The PROMT data base provides the following kinds of information: acquisitions, capacities, end uses, environment, international trade, market data, new products, production, regulations, and technology. This information covers products and services and includes the following industries: chemical, communications, computers, electronics, energy, fibers, food, instruments and equipment, metals, papers, plastics, and rubber.

PTS U.S. Forecasts (DIALOG File 81) contains abstracts of published forecasts for the United States from trade journals, business and financial publications, key newspapers, government reports, and special studies. Each record typically contains historical base period data, a short-term forecast, and a long-term forecast. Also included are 25,000 records from the Census of Manufacturers for the years 1967, 1972, and 1977. Coverage includes general economics, all industries, detailed products, and end-use data. PTS U.S. Forecasts is a good source for hard-to-find statistics on specific subjects.

PTS U.S. Time Series (DIALOG File 82) is composed of two subfiles, Predicasts Composites and Predicasts Basebook. Predicasts Composites contains about 500 time series on the United States, giving historical data since 1957 and a projected consensus of published forecasts through 1990. Coverage includes population, GNP, per capita income, employment, production or usage of major materials, products, energy, and vehicles, as well as detailed construction, industrial production, and price series. Predicasts Basebook contains annual data from 1957 to date for about 47,000 series on U.S. production, consumption, prices, foreign trade, agriculture, mining manufacturing, wages, and end-use distribution for many types of industries, products, and services.

Standard & Poor's News. Standard & Poor's News Online (DIALOG Files 132, 134) is provided by Standard & Poor's Corporation, New York, and contains information from 1979 to the present, with daily updates. This data base offers both textual descriptions and financial information on more than 10,000 publicly owned U.S. companies and subsidiaries, covering interim earnings, dividends, management changes, contract awards, mergers, acquisitions, bond descriptions, and litigation. It contains up-to-date and comprehensive financial information from SEC filings, interim earnings reports, and press releases, and is the equivalent of the printed *Standard & Poor's Corporation Records, Daily News and Cumulative News.*

Standard & Poor's Corporate Descriptions. Standard & Poor's Corporate Descriptions (DIALOG File 133) contains detailed business and financial information on about 11,000 publicly held corporations.

ABI/INFORM. ABI/INFORM (DIALOG File 15), prepared by UMI/Data Courier, contains abstracts and bibliographic citations of selected articles from about 800 publications in business-related fields from 1971 to the present. The records also contain carefully chosen index terms from a controlled vocabulary giving the user the option of supplementing the free-text search to improve the precision of the retrieved articles. Publications include the *Journal of Accountancy, Barron's Financial Executive, Forbes, Fortune, Journal of Accounting Research, Business Lawyer,* and the *CPA Journal.* ABI/INFORM is also in Mead's BUSABS library.

DISCLOSURE. The DISCLOSURE data base (DISCLO File in Mead's COMPNY library; DIALOG File 100), produced by Disclosure Information Group, Bethesda, Md., contains business and financial information, including the full management discussion and analysis, extracted from 10-Ks, 20-Fs, 10-Qs, 8-Ks, proxies, and registration statements of new registrants for over 10,000 publicly owned companies that file with the SEC. It does not include footnotes, which are in NAARS. Company records are continuously updated from these reports to reflect the current corporate "picture."

DISCLOSURE can be accessed on personal computers and on Mead's UBIQ terminals. DISCLOSURE may be searched with Dialog protocol (its numerous records are described in the Dialog "blue sheet") or with Mead's protocol.

One of the most useful segments of DISCLOSURE is its filing index which lists, for each company, all SEC filings for the most recent 18 months.

LEXIS. LEXIS consists of federal law libraries containing general law (United States Code, Federal Register, Code of Federal Regulations); tax law (Internal Revenue Code); securities law; trade regulations; patent, trademark, and copyright law; communications law; labor law; bankruptcy law; energy law; contracts law; state law libraries containing court decisions of all fifty states; United Kingdom law libraries; and French law libraries.

Lexis also includes Auto-Cite (which permits verification of case-law citations, provides parallel citations, and lists cases affecting a case's validity as precedent), *Shepard's Citations,* Matthew Bender publications, LEXPAT (containing every patent issue since 1975), and the *Encyclopaedia Britannica.*

Dow Jones News Retrieval. This data base has current news from the *Wall Street Journal, Barron's,* the *Washington Post,* and the Dow Jones News Service. It also has quotes and market averages, corporate earnings estimates, and detailed financial information on companies and industries. It is accessible through standard micro-computer terminals.

Books in Print. This file (DIALOG File 470) is the continuing record of forthcoming books, books in print, and books going out of print for all books published or distributed in the United States. The file, updated monthly, includes scientific, technical, medical, scholarly, children's, and popular books. The data base contains a listing of books produced by some 12,000 U.S. publishers going back to 1900. Forthcoming books are announced up to six months in advance of publication.

Books in Print records include basic bibliographic information (author, title, publisher, date) as well as U.S. Library of Congress subject headings and card numbers, International Standard Book Number, and price.

See Figure 50.5 for other on-line business data bases.

Drawbacks and Advantages of Computerized Research Systems

Among the ways computer research systems fall short of being ideal tools are the following:

• The need for an experienced searcher to develop and modify complex strategies to assure retrieval of relevant results. In NAARS searching, an accounting background is necessary to understand the concepts being searched and to evaluate the results.

• The lack of uniform searching protocol for different research systems.

• The lack of complete information (e.g., NAARS has annual report financial statements for only about 4,200 (40%) of companies filing with the SEC and includes a few 10-Ks, but not 10-Qs, 8-Ks, proxies, or prospectuses). Also, there can be up to a six-month lag between the time a document is filed and the time it appears on-line in NAARS. NAARS does not include management's discussion and analysis.

However, computerized research systems allow the researcher to obtain results with speed and accuracy that manual indexes cannot rival. These systems have an almost infinite index, allowing each word or phrase to be searched, whereas manual indexes have limited, incomplete, and subjectively selected terms. All documents satisfying the search request are available on the terminal screen within a few seconds, and they may be viewed and printed as desired. Also, a search may be modified to narrow or combine concepts or reformulated to retrieve more relevant results.

It seems certain that as the number and contents of data bases expand, accountants will have access to a greater variety and volume of information with their personal computers, if only they know where to look and how to find it. In this regard, data bases using the recently developed CD-ROM technology are now available and increasing in number. CD-ROM discs offer the advantage of reduced costs by eliminating on-line telecommunications charges, on-line time charges by data base vendors, and search costs. They are especially useful for universities, libraries, and individuals doing research who do not need current information. A disadvantage is their lack of up-to-date information. Also they may lack the SORT feature, which enables retrieved documents to be put in numerical or alphabetical order.

DIALOG File	Contents
CIS (File 101)	Index to publications of the U.S. Congress
Foreign Trade & Econ Abstracts (File 90)	The world's literature on markets, industries, economic data, and economic research
TRINET Company Database (File 532) TRINET Establishment Database (File 531)	Current information on public and private manufacturing and nonmanufacturing companies and establishments with twenty or more employees in all product areas and sectors of industry
Encyclopedia of Associations (File 114)	Information on trade associations, professional societies, labor unions, and other types of groups consisting of voluntary members
Foreign Traders Index (File 105)	Directory of manufacturers, service organizations, retailers, wholesalers, distributors, and cooperatives in 130 foreign countries
Magazine Index (File 47)	Index to over 435 popular magazines
National Newspaper Index (File 111)	Index of five major newspapers – the Wall Street Journal, the New York Times, the Christian Science Monitor, the Los Angeles Times, and the Washington Post
Newsearch (File 211)	Daily index to over 1,700 newspapers, magazines, and periodicals
Federal Register Abstracts (File 136)	Comprehensive coverage of federal regulatory agency action as published in the Federal Register
Federal Index (File 20)	Coverage of government activities from the Federal Register, Congressional Record, The Washington Post, and presidential documents
D&B-Dun's Financial Records (File 519)	Financial statements for over 700,000 private and public companies
Moody's Corporate News – U.S. (File 556)	Business news and financial information on approximately 13,000 publicly held U.S. corporations
Energyline (File 69)	Abstracted information on energy issues and problems
Congressional Record Abstracts (File 135)	Comprehensive abstracts covering each issue of the Congressional Record
PTS Annual Reports Abstracts (File 17)	Textual and statistical abstracts of annual reports of over 3,000 publicly held U.S. and international companies
PTS F&S Indexes (Funk & Scott) (Files 18, 98)	Company, product, and industry information covering mergers, new products, sales and profit forecasts, price changes, antitrust actions, and sales, licensing, and joint venture agreements, both domestic and international

FIG. 50.5 Other On-Line Data Bases

OTHER RESEARCH RESOURCES

Financial Report Surveys

The Technical Research Division of the AICPA publishes *Financial Report Surveys*, a series of reports primarily developed through use of the NAARS data base. These surveys, currently 36 in number, are a quick and handy source of reference in specific areas and might obviate the need for a complete NAARS search in resolving a problem. Topics covered include accounting for uncertainties, pension-related disclosures, and examples of reports by management on its responsibility for financial statements. These surveys may be purchased from the AICPA.

Accountants' Index

For many years, the *Accountants' Index* was the only good index to accounting literature, utilizing broad subject headings. Like all indexes, its usefulness depends to a great extent on the judgment of the indexer and the ability of the user to review large amounts of data in order to locate material of interest. The original index was published in 1920 and annual supplements continue to be issued. It is now available online as well as in hardcover form in business libraries.

The Accountants' Index File, designated ACCOUNTANTS, is available exclusively from Pergamon ORBIT Infoline. It is a computerized version of the hardcover *Accountants' Index* produced by the AICPA, and its period of coverage is from 1974 to the present, with quarterly updating. Since each record is an index, it does not include an abstract, such as in ABI/INFORM records. It provides extensive coverage of English-language literature in accounting and related business and financial areas, including accounting, auditing, data processing, financial reporting, financial management, investments and securities, management, taxation, and special business and industries. Source documents covered are primarily derived from over 300 U.S. and foreign periodicals. Approximately 20% of the file covers books, pamphlets, government documents, and other forms of nonperiodical literature.

AICPA Index

In 1977 the Information Retrieval Committee of the AICPA determined that an indexing system developed by a public accounting firm for internal use, encompassing all authoritative and semiauthoritative accounting literature, was the most useful system of its type in existence and selected it as the basis of the AICPA's *Index to Accounting and Auditing Technical Pronouncements*. Material is indexed under a string of terms and additional explanatory material can be added to the index string itself to further describe the contents of a particular item. A cross-referencing of index terms directs the user to other terms that are narrower or broader than the term with which he began.

A major advantage of this system is a software package to process the material prepared by the indexer and to explode entries so that a single indexing will result in several entries in the final index. The printed index can be conveniently carried in a briefcase to the client's office.

Some of the major CPA firms use this indexing system to combine their own internal literature with the external literature, including additional index terms as needed.

Most references in this *Handbook* to the codified literature of the AICPA *Professional Standards* and FASB *Accounting Standards* use AICPA and FASB codification numbers which are referenced in the *Index*. The *Index to Accounting and Auditing Technical Pronouncements* can be purchased from the AICPA.

Firm Manuals and Guides

The practice firm researcher often has at his disposal significant research material in the form of manuals and guides, research papers, position papers, and documentation of decisions reached by his firm's central research groups, but accessing it may be difficult. As previously noted, some firms have prepared an index to internal materials using the AICPA *Index*. Other firms, however, recognizing the power of Mead's full-text retrieval system, have stored their firm's own materials in a private library in the NEXIS/LEXIS system. Thus, the researcher can review not only public disclosures but also the proprietary material of his own firm using on-line searches.

Consultation With Other Firms

Another research tool, which may not be widely known, is the process of consultation with other firms. This process is often a necessity when one firm wishes to follow an accounting treatment that appears in financial statements examined by another practice firm.

Consultation can uncover data and audit peculiarities not appearing in the financial statements to help the firm decide whether the original case is sufficiently comparable to serve as precedent.

Consultation with other firms is also useful when a firm is developing guidance for its members in areas not clearly covered by authoritative accounting literature. Exploring alternative treatments may shed additional light on a particular treatment. In addition, certain firms are recognized within the profession as having a particular expertise in a specific area of accounting theory or in a particular industry, such as oil and gas and public utilities.

HOW ACCOUNTING RESEARCH USING DATA BASES IS PERFORMED IN A CPA FIRM

The primary accounting research function is carried out by a Research Associate.[1] An accountant working in a practice office may contact the Research Associate directly, or indirectly through a national office partner, if he needs information within the Research Associate's scope.

---

[1] The description given here is based on the approach used in Touche Ross & Co. Similar approaches are used in other firms.

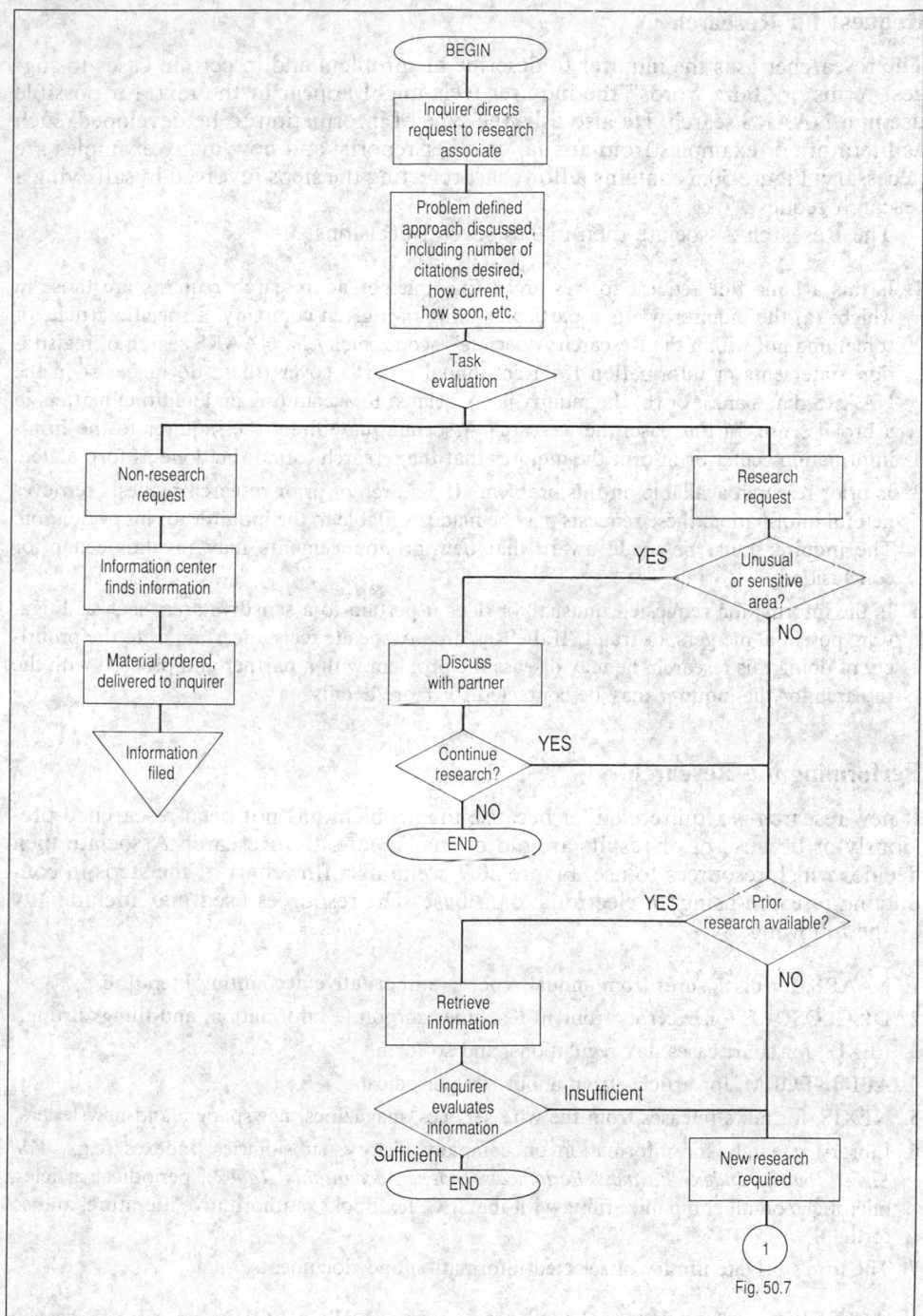

FIG. 50.6   Decision Chart—Initial Research Request

Request for Research

The researcher asks the inquirer to describe his problem and in certain cases to suggest terms or "buzz words" the inquirer feels might appear in the text, for possible use in a NAARS search. He also asks the type of information to be developed, such as literature or examples from annual or other reports, and how many examples are necessary. Figure 50.6 contains a flowchart refecting the steps involved in satisfying a research request.

The Research Associate then makes several decisions:

1. Is this a bona fide request for research? Examples of nonresearch requests are those in which: (a) the inquirer wants a particular filing of a given company, a specific article, or something not within the Research Associate's scope, such as a NAARS search of registration statements or information from an annual report's cover (these do not exist in the NAARS data bank); or (b) the inquiry is not related to accounting and auditing matters in a broad sense. In this case, the Research Associate may direct the inquirer to the firm's information center or inform the inquirer that the research cannot be done as formulated.
2. Is prior research available on this problem? If a search of prior research requests retrieves helpful information, these requests may be made available to the inquirer for his evaluation. The inquirer must be made aware that new pronouncements may invalidate a prior conclusion.
3. Is the information requested unusual, or does it pertain to a sensitive area, such as litigation, potential mergers, or fraud? If the Research Associate feels uncertain as to the propriety of doing this research, he may discuss the problem with a partner and proceed with the research, or the inquirer may be contacted for more details.

Performing the Research

If new research is required, either because the problem has not been researched previously or because prior results are old or inadequate, the Research Associate then decides which resources to use. Figure 50.7 contains a flowchart of the steps in conducting research using an electronic data base. The resources used may include any of the following:

1. NAARS, for disclosures from annual reports, authoritative accounting literature.
2. DISCLOSURE for excerpts from 10-Ks, other corporate information, and filings listing.
3. LEXIS, for court cases, tax regulations, and so forth.
4. ABI/INFORM, for articles from about 800 periodicals.
5. NEXIS, for news releases from the wire services, magazines, newspapers and newsletters.
6. Library research, for information on company history, subsidiaries, indexes (e.g., *Wall Street Journal Index, Business Periodicals Index, Accountants' Index*), periodical articles, microfiche on all companies filing with the SEC, textbooks, authoritative literature, and so forth.
7. The firm's private library of selected information and documents.

A LEXIS search of law and tax materials, an ABI/INFORM or NEXIS search may also be performed like a NAARS search, by connecting key words likely to

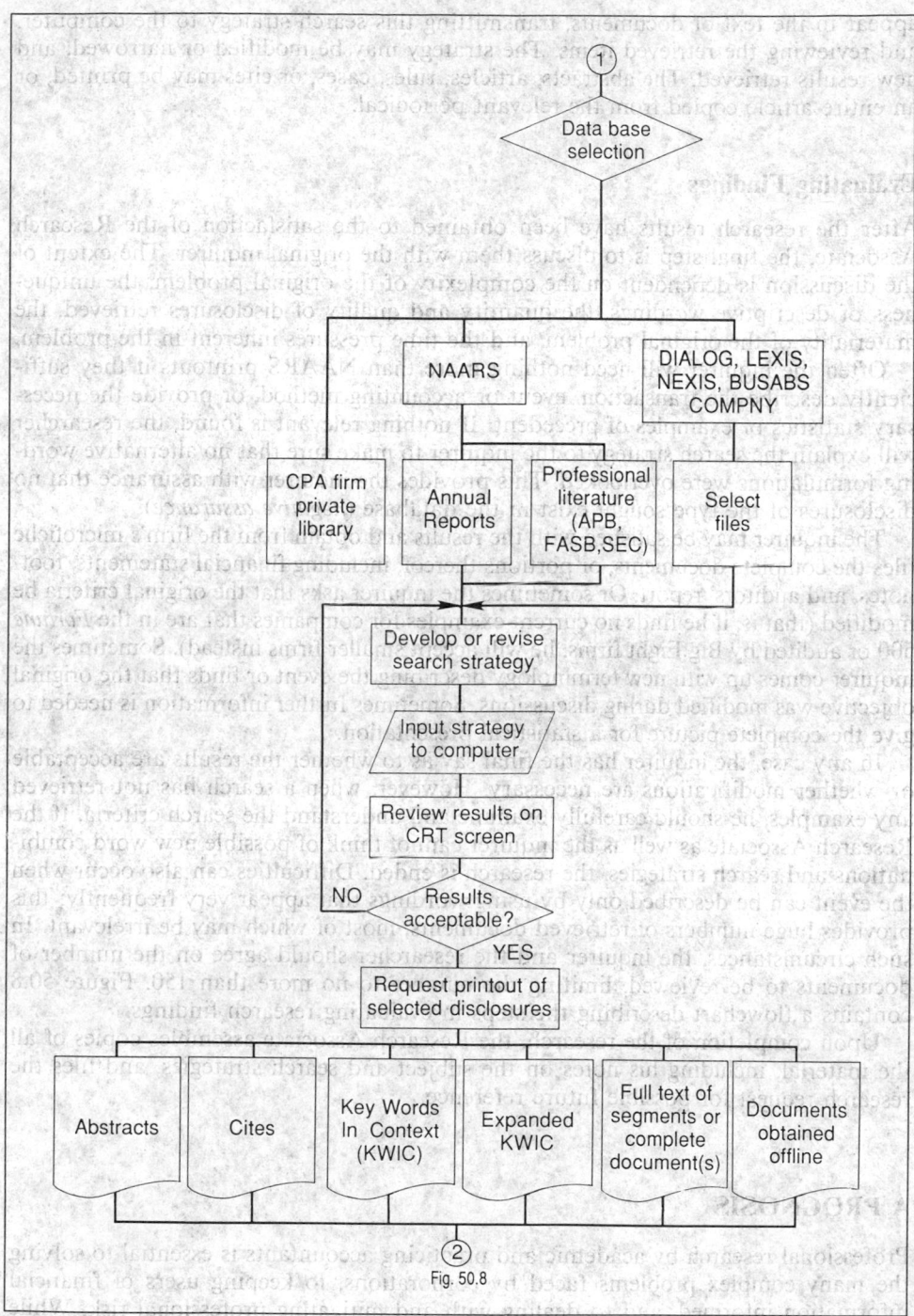

FIG. 50.7 Flowchart—Electronic Data Base Research

appear in the text of documents, transmitting this search strategy to the computer, and reviewing the retrieved items. The strategy may be modified or narrowed, and new results retrieved. The abstracts, articles, rules, cases, or cites may be printed, or an entire article copied from the relevant periodical.

Evaluating Findings

After the research results have been obtained to the satisfaction of the Research Associate, the final step is to discuss them with the original inquirer. The extent of the discussion is dependent on the complexity of the original problem, the uniqueness of descriptive wordings, the quantity and quality of disclosures retrieved, the materiality of the original problem, and the time pressures inherent in the problem.

Often the inquirer will need nothing more than NAARS printouts if they sufficiently describe the transaction, event or accounting method, or provide the necessary statistics or examples of precedent. If nothing relevant is found, the researcher will explain the search strategy to the inquirer to make sure that no alternative wording formulations were overlooked. This provides the inquirer with assurance that no disclosures of the type sought exist in the database (*negative assurance*).

The inquirer may be satisfied with the results and obtain from the firm's microfiche files the complete documents, or portions thereof, including financial statements, footnotes, and auditors' report. Or sometimes the inquirer asks that the original criteria be modified (that is, if he finds no current examples for companies that are in the *Fortune* 500 or audited by Big Eight firms, he will accept smaller firms instead). Sometimes the inquirer comes up with new terminology describing the event or finds that the original objective was modified during discussions. Sometimes further information is needed to give the complete picture for a statistical presentation.

In any case, the inquirer has the final say as to whether the results are acceptable or whether modifications are necessary. However, when a search has not retrieved any examples, he should carefully examine and understand the search criteria. If the Research Associate as well as the inquirer cannot think of possible new word combinations and search strategies, the research is ended. Difficulties can also occur when the event can be described only by using wordings that appear very frequently; this provides huge numbers of retrieved documents, most of which may be irrelevant. In such circumstances, the inquirer and the researcher should agree on the number of documents to be reviewed, limiting the number to no more than 150. Figure 50.8 contains a flowchart describing the steps in evaluating research findings.

Upon completion of the research, the Research Associate assembles copies of all the material, including his notes on the subject and search strategies, and files the research request for possible future reference.

A PROGNOSIS

Professional research by academic and practicing accountants is essential to solving the many complex problems faced by corporations, to keeping users of financial information informed, and to dealing with and mitigating professional risk. While the academic generally deals with the longer-range issues, the practicing professional

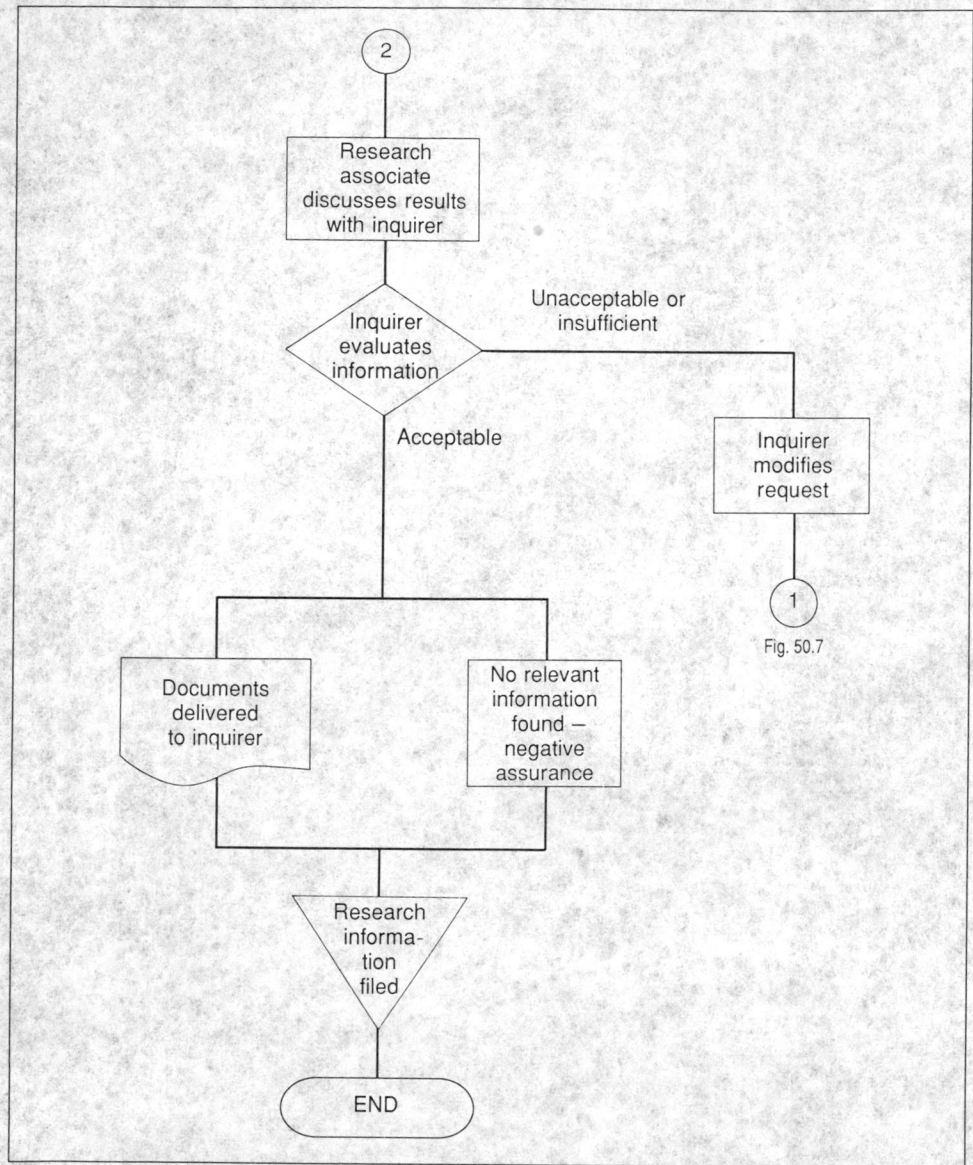

FIG. 50.8 Evaluating Research Results

focuses on solving client-related problems and on providing input to standard-setting bodies.

For both academic and practicing professionals, the information explosion will necessitate much more use of sophisticated research tools, data bases, and methodologies.

Major Professional Practice Pronouncements

Professional pronouncements listed in this section are discussed in those *Handbook* chapters indicated in brackets at the end of each title; if mentioned in more than one chapter, the principal coverage chapter(s) is indicated in **boldface type**. Some superseded (and some interpretive) pronouncements do not show chapter numbers; a reader interested in pursuing the subject is advised to locate in this listing the superseding (or amended) pronouncement and refer to the chapter(s) appearing there. Some subjects have, of course, simply disappeared.

The professional pronouncements are grouped as follows:

Accounting Research Bulletins (ARBs)

The ARBs have been superseded to a great extent or significantly amended by subsequent pronouncements. Therefore, only those ARBs specifically mentioned in the *Handbook* are listed below.

No.	Title
4	*Foreign Operations and Foreign Exchange* (included in ARB 43) [22, 46]
19	*Accounting Under Cost-Plus-Fixed-Fee Contracts* (included in ARB 43) [37]
23	*Accounting for Income Taxes* (included in ARB 43) [17]
38	*Disclosure of Long-Term Leases in Financial Statements of Lessees* (included in ARB 43) [19]
40	*Business Combinations* (included in ARB 43) [23]
43	*Restatement and Revision of Accounting Research Bulletins* (superseded in part by subsequent pronouncements) [**14**, 1, 4, 12, 13, 18, 19, 20, 22, 28, 32, 35, 37, 46]
44	*Declining-Balance Depreciation* (Rev.) (superseded by SFAS 96) [**17**, 33]
45	*Long-Term Construction-Type Contracts* [**36**, **37**, 13, 35]
48	*Business Combinations* (superseded by APB 16) [23]
50	*Contingencies* (superseded by SFAS 5) [26]
51	*Consolidated Financial Statements* (superseded in part by APB 16, APB 23, SFAS 94, and SFAS 96) [**24**, 14, 30, 39, 44, 46]

Accounting Principles Board Opinions (APBs)

No.	Title
*1	*New Depreciation Guidelines and Rules* (superseded by SFAS 96)
*2	*Accounting for the "Investment Credit"* [**17**, 33]
*3	*The Statement of Sources and Applications of Funds* (superseded by APB 19)
4	*Accounting for the "Investment Credit"—Amending APB 2* [17]
*5	*Reporting of Leases in Financial Statements of Lessee* (superseded by SFAS 13) [19]
*6	*Status of Accounting Research Bulletins* [22, 46]
*7	*Accounting for Leases in Financial Statements of Lessors* (superseded by SFAS 13) [19]
*8	*Accounting for the Cost of Pension Plans* (superseded by SFAS 87) [16]
*9	*Reporting the Results of Operations* [3]
*10	*Omnibus Opinion—1966* [13, 18, 19, 21, 24]
*11	*Accounting for Income Taxes* (superseded by SFAS 96) [**17**, 22, 23, 24, 41, 43]
12	*Omnibus Opinion—1967* [3, 12, 16, 18]
13	*Amending Paragraph 6 of APB Opinion 9, Application to Commercial Banks*
14	*Accounting for Convertible Debt and Debt Issued With Stock Purchase Warrants* [**18**, 20, 21]
15	*Earnings per Share* [**20**, 3, 27, 41]

---

*Extensively superseded or amended by subsequent pronouncements.

No.	Title
16	*Business Combinations* [**23**, 3, 13, 14, 15, 16, 17, 20, 24, 25, 27, 28, 29, 33, 34, 38, 40, 41]
17	*Intangible Assets* [**15**, **23**, 24, 33, 34, 38, 40, 41]
18	*The Equity Method of Accounting for Investments in Common Stock* (amended by SFAS 94) [**24**, 4, 18, 21, 25, 35, 36, 39]
*19	*Reporting Changes in Financial Position* (superseded by SFAS 95) [3]
20	*Accounting Changes* [**3**, 4, 11, 13, 14, 15, 24, 27, 29, 32, 33, 34, 36, 44]
21	*Interest on Receivables and Payables* [**18**, 12, 13, 15, 21, 38, 44]
22	*Disclosure of Accounting Policies* [**4**, 24]
23	*Accounting for Income Taxes—Special Areas* [**17**, **24**, 22, 23, 41, 43]
24	*Accounting for Income Taxes—Investments in Common Stock Accounted for by the Equity Method (Other Than Subsidiaries and Corporate Joint Ventures)* (superseded by SFAS 96) [17]
25	*Accounting for Stock Issued to Employees* [**20**, 23, 39, 46]
26	*Early Extinguishment Debt* [**18**, **28**, 19, 33]
*27	*Accounting for Lease Transactions by Manufacturer or Dealer Lessors* (superseded by SFAS 13)
28	*Interim Financial Reporting* [**3**, 4, 11, 17, 26]
29	*Accounting for Nonmonetary Transactions* [**13**, 18, 20, 25, 33, 35, 38, 39]
30	*Reporting the Results of Operations—Reporting the Effects of Disposal of a Segment of a Business, and Extraordinary, Unusual, and Infrequently Occurring Events and Transactions* [**3**, **28**, 4, 13, 14, 15, 24, 25]
*31	*Disclosure of Lease Commitments by Lessees* (superseded by SFAS 13)

FASB Statements of Financial Accounting Concepts (SFACs)

No.	Title
1	*Objectives of Financial Reporting by Business Enterprises* [**1**, **2**, 3, 4, 20, 26, 28, 30, 32]
2	*Qualitative Characteristics of Accounting Information* [**2**, 1, 8, 25]
3	*Elements of Financial Statements of Business Enterprises* (superseded by SFAC 6) [**2**, 3, 17, 32]
4	*Objectives of Financial Reporting by Nonbusiness Organizations* [**32**, 2, 30]
5	*Recognition and Measurement in Financial Statements of Business Enterprises* [**2**, **13**, 1, 3, 4, 39]
6	*Elements of Financial Statements* (a replacement of SFAS 3, incorporating an amendment of SFAS 2) [**2**, **3**, 1, 12, 13, 15, 16, 17, 18, 22, 32, 39]

---

*Extensively superseded or amended by subsequent pronouncements.

FASB Statements of Financial Accounting Standards (SFASs)

No.   Title

1   *Disclosure of Foreign Currency Translation Information* (superseded by SFAS 8) [22]

2   *Accounting for Research and Development Costs* [**15, 39**, 1, 2, 13, 23, 24, 33, 37]

3   *Reporting Accounting Changes in Interim Financial Statements* (an amendment to APB 28) [3]

4   *Reporting Gains and Losses From Extinguishment of Debt* (an amendment to APB 30) [**18**, 3]

5   *Accounting for Contingencies* [**26**, 2, 3, 4, 5, 12, 13, 14, 15, 19, 20, 21, 23, 27, 30, 33, 40, 41, 44, 48, 50]

6   *Classification of Short-Term Obligations Expected to Be Refinanced* (an amendment to ARB 43, Chapter 3A) [**18**, 3]

7   *Accounting and Reporting by Development State Enterprises* [**39**, 15]

8   *Accounting for the Translation of Foreign Currency Transactions and Foreign Currency Financial Statements* (superseded by SFAS 52) [**22**, 46]

9   *Accounting for Income Taxes—Oil and Gas Producing Companies* (an amendment to APBs 11 and 23) (superseded by SFAS 19)

10   *Extension of "Grandfather" Provisions for Business Combinations* (an amendment to APB 16) [23]

11   *Accounting for Contingencies—Transition Method* (an amendment to SFAS 5)

12   *Accounting for Certain Marketable Securities* [**12**, 1, 2, 16, 21, 30, 40, 41, 44]

13   *Accounting for Leases* (extensively superseded and amended by subsequent pronouncements) [**19**, 1, 2, 13, 17, 18, 24, 25, 28, 33, 35, 40, 46, 50]

14   *Financial Reporting for Segments of a Business Enterprise* [**4**, 3, 24, 25, 33, 34]

15   *Accounting by Debtors and Creditors for Troubled Debt Restructurings* [**28**, 18, 40, 41, 44, 46]

16   *Prior Period Adjustments* [**3**, 17, 23, 30]

17   *Accounting for Leases—Initial Direct Costs* (an amendment to SFAS 13) (superseded by SFAS 91) [**19**]

18   *Financial Reporting for Segments of a Business Enterprise—Interim Financial Statements* (an amendment to SFAS 14) [**4**, 3]

19   *Financial Accounting and Reporting by Oil and Gas Producing Companies* (superseded in part by SFAS 69 and other pronouncements) [34, 47]

20   *Accounting for Forward Exchange Contracts* (an amendment to SFAS 8) (superseded by SFAS 52)

21   *Suspension of the Reporting of Earnings per Share and Segment Information by Nonpublic Enterprises* (an amendment to APB 15 and SFAS 14) [**4**, 25, 39]

22   *Changes in the Provisions of Lease Agreements Resulting From Refunding of Tax-Exempt Debt* (an amendment to SFAS 13) [**18, 19**]

23   *Inception of the Lease* (an amendment to SFAS 13) [**19**]

24   *Reporting Segment Information in Financial Statements That Are Presented in Another Enterprise's Financial Report* (an amendment to SFAS 14) [**4**]

25   *Suspension of Certain Accounting Requirements for Oil and Gas Producing Companies* (an amendment to SFAS 19) [34]

26   *Profit Recognition on Sales-Type Leases of Real Estate* (an amendment to SFAS 13) (superseded by SFAS 98) [**19**]

No.	Title
27	*Classification of Renewals or Extensions of Existing Sales-Type or Direct Financing Leases* (an amendment to SFAS 13) [19]
28	*Accounting for Sales With Leasebacks* (an amendment to SFAS 13) (extensively amended by subsequent pronouncements) [19]
29	*Determining Contingent Rentals* (an amendment to SFAS 13) [19]
30	*Disclosure of Information About Major Customers* (an amendment to SFAS 4) [14]
31	*Accounting for Tax Benefits Related to U.K. Tax Legislation Concerning Stock Relief* (superseded by SFAS 96) [17]
32	*Specialized Accounting and Reporting Principles and Practices in AICPA Statements of Position and Guides on Accounting and Auditing Matters* (an amendment to APB 20) [32, 39, 42, 44, 50]
33	*Financial Reporting and Changing Prices* (superseded by SFAS 89) [**4**, 1, 3, 11, 14, 50]
34	*Capitalization if Interest Cost* (superseded and amended in part by subsequent pronouncements) [**18**, 14, 15, 33, 34, 35, 36, 38, 41, 47]
35	*Accounting and Reporting by Defined Benefit Pension Plans* [**16**, 31]
36	*Disclosure of Pension Information* (an amendment to APB 8) (superseded by SFAS 87) [16]
37	*Balance Sheet Classification of Deferred Income Taxes* (an amendment to APB 11) (superseded by SFAS 96) [36]
38	*Accounting for Preacquisition Contingencies of Purchased Enterprises* (an amendment to APB 16) [23]
39	*Financial Reporting and Changing Prices: Specialized Assets—Mining and Oil and Gas* (a supplement to SFAS 33) (superseded by SFAS 89) [34]
40	*Financial Reporting and Changing Prices: Specialized Areas—Timberlands and Growing Timber* (a supplement to SFAS 33) (superseded by SFAS 89)
41	*Financial Reporting and Changing Prices: Specialized Assets—Income-Producing Real Estate* (a supplement to SFAS 33) (superseded by SFAS 89)
42	*Determining Materiality for Capitalization of Interest Cost* (an amendment to SFAS 34) [18]
43	*Accounting for Compensated Absences* [**16**, 12, 33]
44	*Accounting for Intangible Assets of Motor Carriers* (an amendment to ARB 43, Chapter 5, and an interpretation of APBs 17 and 30) [**33**, 3]
45	*Accounting for Franchise Fee Revenue* [13]
46	*Financial Reporting and Changing Prices: Motion Picture Films* (a supplement to SFAS 33) (superseded by SFAS 89)
47	*Disclosure of Long Term Obligations* [**18**, 21, 33]
48	*Revenue Recognition When Right of Return Exists* [**13**, 38, 39]
49	*Accounting for Product Financing Agreements* [**14**, **21**]
50	*Financial Reporting in the Record and Music Industry* [38]
51	*Financial Reporting by Cable Television Companies* [38]
52	*Foreign Currency Translation* [**22**, 2, 4, 21, 46]
53	*Financial Reporting by Producers and Distributors of Motion Picture Films* [38]
54	*Financial Reporting and Changing Prices: Investment Companies* (an amendment to SFAS 33) (superseded by SFAS 89)

No.	Title
81	*Disclosure of Postretirement Health Care and Life Insurance Benefits* [16]
82	*Financial Reporting and Changing Prices: Elimination of Certain Disclosures* (an amendment to SFAS 33) (superseded by SFAS 89) [4]
83	*Designation of AICPA Guides and Statement of Position on Accounting by Brokers and Dealers in Securities, Employee Benefit Plans, and by Banks as Preferable for Purposes of Applying APB Opinion 20* (an amendment to SFAS 32 and APB 30 and a rescission of FIN 10) [39, 40, 42]
84	*Induced Conversions of Convertible Debt* (an amendment to APB 26) [18]
85	*Yield Test for Determining Whether a Convertible Security Is a Common Stock Equivalent* (an amendment to APB 15) [20]
86	*Accounting for the Costs of Computer Software to Be Sold, Leased, or Otherwise Marketed* [**15**, **39**, 13]
87	*Employers' Accounting for Pensions* [**16**, 23, 33, 39]
88	*Employers' Accounting for Settlements and Curtailments of Defined Benefit Pension Plans and for Termination Benefits* [**16**, 3]
89	*Financial Reporting and Changing Prices* [**4**, 1, 3, 11, 14, 15, 34]
90	*Regulated Enterprises—Accounting for Abandonments and Disallowances of Plant Costs* (an amendment to SFAS 71) [33]
91	*Accounting for Nonrefundable Fees and Costs Associated With Originating or Acquiring Loans and Initial Direct Costs of Leases* (an amendment to SFAS 13, 60, and 65 and a rescission of SFAS 17) [**21, 40, 41**, 13, 15, 19, 44]
92	*Regulated Enterprises—Accounting for Phase-in Plans* (an amendment to SFAS 71) [33]
93	*Recognition of Depreciation by Not-for-Profit Organization* [**32**, 2, 15, 31, 46]
94	*Consolidation of All Majority-Owned Subsidiaries* (an amendment to ARB 43, Chapter 12, ARB 51, and APB 18) [**24**, 13, 18, 20, 21, 36, 40, 44, 46]
95	*Statement of Cash Flows* [**3**, 4, 12, 38, 39, 40, 41, 42, 44]
96	*Accounting for Income Taxes* [**17**, **23**, 3, 4, 11, 12, 14, 15, 22, 24, 29, 33, 34, 36, 37, 38, 39, 40, 41, 43]
97	*Accounting and Reporting by Insurance Enterprises for Certain Long-Duration Contracts and for Realized Gains and Losses From the Sale of Investments* [43]
98	*Accounting for Leases* [**19**] • *Sale-Leaseback Transactions Involving Real Estate* • *Sales-Type Leases of Real Estate* • *Definition of the Lease* • *Initial Direct Costs of Direct Financial Leases*

FASB Interpretations (FINs)

No.	Title
1	*Accounting Changes Related to the Cost of Inventory (an Interpretation of APB Opinion No. 20)* [**14**, 29]
2	*Imputing Interest on Debt Arrangements Made Under the Federal Bankruptcy Act (an Interpretation of APB Opinion No. 21)* (superseded by SFAS 15)

No.	Title
25	*Accounting for an Unused Investment Tax Credit (an Interpretation of APB Opinion Nos. 2, 4, 11, and 16)* (superseded by SFAS 96)
26	*Accounting for Purchase of a Leased Asset by the Lessee During the Term of the Lease (an interpretation of FASB Statement No. 13)* [26]
27	*Accounting for a Loss on a Sublease (an Interpretation of FASB Statement No. 13 and APB Opinion No. 30)* [19]
28	*Accounting for Stock Appreciation Rights and Other Variable Stock Option or Award Plans (an Interpretation of APB Opinion Nos. 15 and 25)* [20, 39]
29	*Reporting Tax Benefits Realized on Disposition of Investments in Certain Subsidiaries and Other Investees (an Interpretation of APB Opinion Nos. 23 and 24)* (superseded by SFAS 96)
30	*Accounting for Involuntary Conversions of Nonmonetary Assets to Monetary Assets (an Interpretation of APB Opinion No. 29)* [13, 15]
31	*Treatment of Stock Compensation Plans in EPS Computations (an Interpretation of APB Opinion No. 15 and a Modification of FASB Interpretation No. 28)* [20]
32	*Application of Percentage Limitations in Recognizing Investment Tax Credit (an Interpretation of APB Opinion Nos. 2, 4, and 11)* (superseded by SFAS 96)
33	*Applying FASB Statement No. 34 to Oil and Gas Producing Operations Accounted for by the Full Cost Method (an Interpretation of FASB Statement No. 34)* [18, 34]
34	*Disclosure of Indirect Guarantees of Indebtedness of Others (an Interpretation of FASB Statement No. 5)* [21, 26]
35	*Criteria for Applying the Equity Method of Accounting for Investment in Common Stock (an Interpretation of APB Opinion No. 18)* [24]
36	*Accounting for Exploratory Wells in Progress at the End of a Period (an Interpretation of FASB Statement No. 19)* [34]
37	*Accounting for Translation Adjustments Upon Sale of Part of an Investment in a Foreign Entity (an Interpretation of FASB Statement No. 52)* [22]
38	*Determining the Measurement Date for Stock Option, Purchase, and Award Plans Involving Junior Stock (an Interpretation of APB Opinion No. 25)* [20, 39]

FASB Technical Bulletins (TBs)

No.	Title
79-1(R)	*Purpose and Scope of FASB Technical Bulletins and Procedures for Issuance* [46]
79-2	*Computer Software Costs* (superseded by SFAS 86)
79-3	*Subjective Acceleration Clauses in Long-Term Debt Agreements* [18]
79-4	*Segment Reporting of Puerto Rican Operations* [4]
79-5	*Meaning of the Term "Customer" as It Applies to Health Care Facilities Under FASB Statement No. 14* [30]
79-6	*Valuation Allowances Following Debt Restructuring* [28]
79-7	*Recoveries of a Previous Writedown Under a Troubled Debt Restructuring Involving a Modification of Terms* [28]
79-8	*Applicability of FASB Statements 21 and 33 to Certain Brokers and Dealers in Securities* (superseded and amended in part by SFAS 89)
79-9	*Accounting in Interim Periods for Changes in Income Tax Rates* [17]
79-10	*Fiscal Funding Clauses in Lease Agreements* [19]

FASB Emerging Issues Task Force (EITF Issues)

No.	Title
84-19	Mortgage Loan Payment Modifications [41]
84-20	GNMA Dollar Rolls [21]
84-21	Sale of a Loan With a Partial Participation Retained [41]
84-22	Prior Years' Earnings Per Share Following a Savings and Loan Association Conversion and Pooling [41]
84-23	Leveraged Buyout Holding Company Debt [23]
84-24	LIFO Accounting Issues [14]
84-25	Offsetting Nonrecourse Debt With Sales-Type or Direct Financing Lease Receivables [19]
84-26	Defeasance of Special-Purpose Borrowings [18]
84-27	Deferred Taxes on Subsidiary Stock Sales [24]
84-28	Impairment of Long-Lived Assets [15]
84-29	Gain and Loss Recognition on Exchanges of Productive Assets and the Effect of Boot [13]
84-30	Sales of Loans to Special-Purpose Entities [21, 40]
84-31	Equity Certificates of Deposit [41]
84-32	(Not used)
84-33	Acquisition of a Tax Loss Carryforward—Temporary Parent-Subsidiary Relationship [24]
84-34	Permanent Discount Restricted Stock Purchase Plans [20]
84-35	Business Combinations: Sale of Duplicate Facilities and Accrual of Liabilities [23]
84-36	Interest Rate Swap Transactions [21]
84-37	Sale-Leaseback Transaction With Repurchase Option [19]
84-38	Identical Common Shares for a Pooling of Interests [23]
84-39	Transfers of Monetary and Nonmonetary Assets Among Individuals and Entities Under Common Control [25]
84-40	Long-Term Debt Repayable by a Capital Stock Transaction [21]
84-41	Consolidation of Subsidiary After Instantaneous In-Substance Defeasance [18]
84-42	Push-Down of Parent Company Debt to a Subsidiary [23]
84-43	Income Tax Effects of Asset Revaluations in Certain Foreign Countries [22]
84-44	Partial Termination of a Defined Benefit Pension Plan [16]
85-1	Classifying Notes Received for Capital Stock [20]
85-2	Classification of Costs Incurred in a Takeover Defense [23]
85-3	Tax Benefits Relating to Asset Dispositions Following an Acquisition of a Financial Institution [41]
85-4	Downstream Mergers and Other Stock Transactions Between Companies Under Common Control [23]
85-5	Restoration of Deferred Taxes Previously Eliminated by Net Operating Loss Recognition
85-6	Futures Implementation Questions [21]
85-7	Federal Home Loan Mortgage Corporation Stock [41]
85-8	Amortization of Thrift Intangibles [41]
85-9	Revenue Recognition on Options to Purchase Stock of Another Entity [21]
85-10	Employee Stock Ownership Plan Contribution Funded by a Pension Plan Termination [16]

No.	Title
87-25	*Sale of Convertible, Adjustable-Rate Mortgages With Contingent Repayment Agreement* [41]
87-26	*Hedging of Foreign Currency Exposure With a Tandem Currency* [22]
87-27	*Poolings of Companies That Do Not Have a Controlling Class of Common Stock* [23]
87-28	*Provision for Deferred Taxes on Increases in Cash Surrender Value of Key-Person Life Insurance* [15]
87-29	*Exchange of Real Estate Involving Boot* [35]
87-30	*Sale of Short-Term Loan Made Under a Long-Term Credit Commitment* [40]
87-31	*Sale of Put Options on Issuer's Stock* [21]
87-32	*(Not used)*
87-33	*Stock Compensation Issues Related to Market Decline* [20]
87-34	*Sale of Mortgage Servicing Rights With a Subservicing Agreement* [41]
88-1	*Determination of Vested Benefit Obligation for a Defined Benefit Pension Plan* [16]
88-2	*(Not used)*
88-3	*Rental Concessions Provided by Landlord* [35]
88-4	*Classification of Payment Made to IRS to Retain Fiscal Year* [39]
88-5	*Recognition of Insurance Death Benefits* [15]
88-6	*Book Value Stock Plans in an Initial Public Offering* [20]
88-7	*Hedging Correlation Issues Under FASB Statement No. 80* [21]
88-8	*Mortage Swaps* [21]
88-9	*Put Warrants* [21]
88-10	*Costs Associated With Lease Modification or Termination* [15, 19]
88-11	*Sale of Interest-Only or Principal-Only Cash Flows From Loans Receivable* [21]
88-12	*Transfer of Ownership Interest as Part of Down Payment Under Statement 66* [35]
88-13	*Application of SAB 61 to Other Than Loan Losses* [40]
88-14	*Settlement of Fees With Extra Units to a General Partner in an MLP* [35]
88-15	*Classification of Subsidiary's Loan Payable in Consolidated Balance Sheet When Subsidiary's and Parent's Fiscal Years Differ* [24]
88-16	*Basis In Leveraged Buyout Transactions When the Previous Owner's Interest Declines* [23]
88-17	*Fees and Costs Associated With Loan Syndications and Loan Participations* [40]
88-18	*Sales of Future Revenues* [13]
88-19	*FSLIC—Assisted Acquisitions of Thrifts* [41]
88-20	*Difference Between Initial Investment and Principal Amount of Loans in a Purchased Credit Card Portfolio* [21]

GASB Statement of Governmental Accounting Concepts (SGAC)

No.	Title
1	*Objectives of Financial Reporting* [31]

GASB Statements of Governmental Accounting Standards (SGASs)

No.	Title
1	*Authoritative Status of NCGA Pronouncements and AICPA Industry Audit Guide* [**31**, 16]
2	*Financial Reporting of Deferred Compensation Plans Adopted Under the Provisions of Internal Revenue Code Section 457* [31]
3	*Deposits With Financial Institutions, Investments (Including Repurchase Agreements), and Reverse Repurchase Agreements* [31]
4	*Applicability of FASB Statement No. 87, "Employers' Accounting for Pension," to State and Local Governmental Employers* [31]
5	*Disclosure of Pension Informaion by Public Employee Retirement Systems and State and Local Governmental Employers* [**31**, 16]
6	*Accounting and Financial Reporting for Special Assessments* [31]
7	*Advance Refundings Resulting in Defeasance of Debt* [31]
8	*Appalicability of FASB Statement No. 93, "Recognition of Depreciation by Not-for-Profit Organizations," to Certain State and Local Governmental Entities* [**31**, 32]

GASB Interpretation (GASBI)

No.	Title
1	*Demand Bonds Issued by State and Local Governmental Entities* (an Interpretation of NCGA Statement 1 and NCGA Interpretation 9) [31]

GASB Technical Bulletins (GASBTBs)

No.	Title
84-1	*Purpose and Scope of GASB Technical Bulletins and Procedures for Issuance*
87-1	*Applying Paragraph 68 of GASB Statement 3* [31]

Statements of Position of the AICPA Accounting Standards Division (SOPs)

Many SOPs have been superseded, withdrawn, or incorporated into other pronouncements. Although some of the old SOPS are mentioned in the *Handbook*, only those that are currently available in the *AICPA Technical Practice Aids* (TP) codification are listed.

No.	Title
74-8	*Financial Accounting and Reporting by Colleges and Universities* [32]
74-11	*Financial Accounting and Reporting by Face-Amount Certificate Companies* [44]
75-2	*Accounting Practices of Real Estate Investment Trusts* [**44**, 41]
76-3	*Accounting Practices for Certain Employee Stock Ownership Plans* [20]
77-1	*Financial Accounting and Reporting by Investment Companies* [44]
78-1	*Accounting by Hospitals for Certain Marketable Equity Securities* [**30**, **32**]
78-2	*Accounting Practices of Real Estate Investment Trusts* [44]

No.	Title
78-9	*Accounting for Investments in Real Estate Ventures* [**35**, **41**, 24]
78-10	*Accounting Principles and Reporting Practices for Certain Nonprofit Organizations* [**32**, 46]
79-1	*Accounting for Municipal Bond Funds* [44]
81-1	*Accounting for Performance of Construction-Type and Certain Production-Type Contracts* [**36**, **37**, 35]
81-2	*Reporting Practices Concerning Hospital-Related Organizations* [30]
82-1	*Accounting and Financial Reporting for Personal Financial Statements* [39]
83-1	*Reporting by Banks of Investment Securities Gains or Losses* [40]
85-1	*Financial Reporting by Not-for-Profit Health Care Entities for Tax-Exempt Debt and Certain Funds Whose Use is Limited* [30]
85-2	*Accounting for Dollar Repurchase—Dollar Reverse Repurchase Agreements by Sellers-Borrowers* [**21**, 40]
85-3	*Accounting by Agricultural Producers and Agricultural Cooperatives*
86-1	*Reporting Repurchase—Reverse Repurchase Agreements and Mortgage-Backed Certificates by Savings and Loan Associations* [**21**, **41**]
87-1	*Accounting for Asserted and Unasserted Medical Malpractice Claims of Health Care Providers and Related Issues* [30]
87-2	*Accounting for Joint Costs of Informational Materials and Activities of Not-for-Profit Organizations That Include a Fund-Raising Appeal* [32]

AcSEC Practice Bulletins (PBs)

No.	Title
1	*Purpose and Scope of AcSEC Practice Bulletins and Procedures for Their Issuance* [35, 40, 41]
2	*Elimination of Profits Resulting From Intercompany Transfers of LIFO Inventories* [14]
3	*Prepayments Into the Secondary Reserve of the FSLIC and Contingencies Related to Other Obligations of the FSLIC* [41]
4	*Accounting for Foreign Debt/Equity Swaps* [22, 40]
5	*Income Recognition on Loans of Financially Troubled Countries* [40]

AICPA Audit and Accounting Guides

Audits of Airlines [33]
Audits of Agricultural Producers and Agricultural Cooperatives
Audits of Banks [**40**, 41]
Audits of Brokers and Dealers in Securities [**42**, 40]
Audits of Casinos [38]
Audits of Certain Nonprofit Organizations [32]
Audits of Colleges and Universities [32]
Audits of Construction Contractors [**36**, 35]
Audits of Credit Unions [44]
Audits of Employee Benefit Plans [16]

Audits of Entities With Oil and Gas Producing Activities [34]
Audits of Finance Companies [44]
Audits of Fire and Casualty Insurance Companies [43]
Audits of Government Contractors [**37**, 36]
Audits of Hospitals [30]
Audits of Investment Companies [**44**, 12]
Audits of Savings and Loan Associations [41]
Audits of Service-Center-Produced Records [**10**, 44]
Audits of State and Local Governmental Units [**31**, 30]
Audits of Stock Life Insurance Companies [43]
Audits of Voluntary Health & Welfare Organizations [32]
Audit Sampling [9]
Guide for Prospective Financial Statements [27]
Guide for the Use of Real Estate Appraisal Information [**35**, 15, 16]
Personal Financial Statement [39]

Statements on Auditing Standards (SASs)

No.	Title
1	*Codification of Auditing Standards and Procedures* (a codification of all previous Statements on Auditing Procedures that have been extensively superseded or amended by subsequent pronouncements) [**5**, 9, 10, 14, 23, 27, 40]
2	*Reports on Audited Financial Statements* (superseded by SAS 58) [26]
3	*The Effects of EDP on the Auditor's Study of Evaluation of Internal Control* (superseded by SAS 48) [10]
4	*Quality Control Considerations for a Firm of Independent Auditors* (superseded by SAS 25) [5]
5	*The Meaning of "Present Fairly in Conformity With Generally Accepted Accounting Principles" In The Independent Auditor's Report* (superseded by SAS 52) [5]
6	*Related Party Transactions* (superseded by SAS 45) [25]
7	*Communications Between Predecessor and Successor Auditors* [25]
8	*Other Information in Documents Containing Audited Financial Statements* [**4**, **11**, 8, 34]
9	*The Effect of an Internal Audit Function on the Scope of the Independent Auditor's Examination* [**7**, 5, 40]
10	*Limited Review of Interim Financial Information* (superseded by SAS 24)
11	*Using the Work of a Specialist* [**5**, **7**, 14, 15, 16, 34, 35]
12	*Inquiry of a Client's Lawyer Concerning Litigation, Claims, and Assessments* [**26**, 5, 25]
13	*Reports on a Limited Review of Interim Financial Information* (superseded by SAS 24)
14	*Special Reports* [**3**, **11**, 5, 18, 32, 39, 40]
15	*Reports on Comparative Financial Statements* (superseded by SAS 58)
16	*The Independent Auditor's Responsibility for the Detection of Errors or Irregularities* (superseded by SAS 53) [5]
17	*Illegal Acts by Clients* (superseded by SAS 54) [**5**, 49]

No.	Title
18	*Unaudited Replacement Cost Information* (withdrawn)
19	*Client Representations* [**5**, **7**]
20	*Required Communication of Material Weaknesses in Internal Accounting Control* (superseded by SAS 60) [5]
21	*Segment Information* [**4**, 25]
22	*Planning and Supervision* [**5**, 10]
23	*Analytical Review Procedures* (superseded by SAS 56) [**5**, 10]
24	*Review of Interim Financial Information* (superseded by SAS 36) [5]
25	*The Relationship of Generally Accepted Auditing Standards to Quality Control Standards* [5]
26	*Association With Financial Statements* [**5**, 23]
27	*Supplementary Information Required by the Financial Accounting Standards Board* (superseded by SAS 52) [**11**, **34**]
28	*Supplementary Information on the Effects of Changing Prices* (superseded by SAS 52)
29	*Reporting on Information Accompanying the Basic Financial Statements in Auditor-Submitted Documents* (superseded by SAS 52) [11]
30	*Reporting on Internal Accounting Control* (superseded in part by SAS 60) [**8**, 5, 40, 42]
31	*Evidential Matter* [**7**, 10]
32	*Adequacy of Disclosure in Financial Statements* [4]
33	*Supplementary Oil and Gas Reserve Information* (superseded by SAS 45) [34]
34	*The Auditor's Considerations When a Question Arises About an Entity's Continued Existence* (superseded by SAS 59) [**5**, **26**]
35	*Special Reports—Applying Agreed-Upon Procedures to Specified Elements, Accounts, or Items of a Financial Statement* [**11**, 40, 42, 44]
36	*Review of Interim Financial Information* [**11**, 3, 6, 20, 47]
37	*Filings Under Federal Securities Statutes* [**11**, 47]
38	*Letters for Underwriters* (superseded by SAS 49)
39	*Audit Sampling* [**9**, 50]
40	*Supplementary Mineral Reserve Information* (superseded by SAS 52)
41	*Working Papers* [7]
42	*Reporting on Condensed Financial Statements and Selected Financial Data* [11]
43	*Omnibus Statement on Auditing Standards* (integrated into various SASs)
44	*Special-Purpose Reports on Internal Accounting Control at Service Organizations* [**8**, **10**, 12]
45	*Omnibus Statement on Auditing Standards—1983* (superseded in part by SAS 52) [11, 18, 25, 34]
46	*Consideration of Omitted Procedures After the Report Date* [11]
47	*Audit Risk and Materiality in Conducting an Audit* [**7**, **8**]
48	*The Effects of Computer Processing on the Examination of Financial Statements* [10]
49	*Letters for Underwriters* [**20**, 11, 47]
50	*Reports on Application of Accounting Principles* [**11**, **21**, 49, 50]
51	*Reporting on Financial Statements Prepared for Use in Other Countries* [22]

No.	Title
52	*Omnibus Statement on Auditing Standards—1987* [**11**, 4, 15]
53	*The Auditor's Responsibility to Detect and Report Errors and Irregularities* [**5**, **7**, 11, 25, 45, 49]
54	*Illegal Acts by Clients* [**5**, 11, 13, 25, 45, 49]
55	*Consideration of the Internal Control Structure In a Financial Statement Audit* [**8**, 5, 40, 45]
56	*Analytical Procedures* [**7**, **8**, 5, 33, 45]
57	*Auditing Accounting Estimates* [**5**, **26**, 25, 40, 45]
58	*Reports on Audited Financial Statements* [**5**, **11**, 4, 7, 24, 28, 40, 41, 45]
59	*The Auditor's Consideration of an Entity's Ability to Continue as a Going Concern* [**26**, **28**, 5, 11, 40, 41, 45]
60	*Communication of Internal Control Structure Related Matters Noted in an Audit* [**6**, **8**, 5, 7, 40, 42, 45]
61	*Communication with Audit Committees* [**6**, **5**, 25, 26, 45]

Statement on Standards for Accountants' Services on Prospective Financial Information

Financial Forecasts and Projections [27]

Statements on Standards for Attestation Engagements

Attestation Standards [5]
Attest Services Related to MAS Engagements [5]

Statements on Standards For Accounting and Review Services (SSARs)

No.	Title
1	*Compilation and Review of Financial Statements* [**39**, 23]
2	*Reporting on Comparative Financial Statements* [39]
3	*Compilation Reports on Financial Statements Included in Certain Prescribed Forms* [11]
4	*Communications Between Predecessor and Successor Accountants* [39]
5	*Reporting on Compiled Financial Statements* [39]
6	*Reporting on Personal Financial Statements Included in Written Personal Financial Plans* [39]

SEC Financial Reporting Releases (FRRs)

No.	Title
1	*Codification of Financial Reporting Policies* [47]
2	*Instructions for the Presentation and Preparation of Pro Forma Financial Information and Requirements for Financial Statements of Business Acquired or to Be Acquired* [27]
4	*Public Availability of Correspondence About Accountants' Independence* [5]

No.	Title
5	*Accountants' Liability for Reports on Unaudited Supplementary Financial Information* [11]
6	*Interpretative Release About Disclosure Considerations Relating to Foreign Operations and Foreign Currency Translation Effects* [22, 4]
7	*Adoption of Foreign Issuer Integrated Disclosure System*
8	*Financial Statement Requirements for Registered Investment Companies* [44]
9	*Supplemental Disclosures of Oil and Gas Producing Activities* [34]
10	*Qualifications and Reports of Accountants; Amendment of Rules Regarding Accountants' Independence*
11	*Revision of Financial Statement Requirements and Industry Guide Disclosure for Bank Holding Companies* [40]
12	*Accounting for Cost of Internally Developing Computer Software for Sale or Lease to Others* [39]
13	*Revision of Industry Guide Disclosures for Bank Holding Companies* [40]
14	*Oil and Gas Producers—Full Cost Accounting Practices; Amendment of Rules* [34]
15	*Interpretive Release Relating to Accounting for Extinguishment of Debt* [18]
16	*Rescission of Interpretation Relating to Certification of Financial Statements* [11, 28]
17	*Oil and Gas Producers—Full Cost Accounting Practices* [34]
18	*Business Combination Transactions—Adoption of Registration Form*
19	*Business Combination Transactions—Adoption of Registration Form—Foreign Registrants*
20	*Rules and Guide for Disclosure Concerning Reserves for Unpaid Claims and Claim Adjustment Expenses of Property-Casualty Underwriters* [43]
21	*Technical Amendments to Rules and Forms*
22	*Technical Amendments to Rules and Forms*
23	*The Significance of Oral Guarantees to the Financial Reporting Process* [21, 26]
24	*Disclosure Amendments to Regulation S-X Regarding Repurchase and Reverse Repurchase Agreements* [21, 4]
25	*Technical Amendments to Rule* [24]
26	*Interpretive Release About Disclosure of the Effects of the Tax Reform Act of 1986* [4]
27	*Amendments to Industry Guide Disclosures by Bank Holding Companies*
28	*Accounting for Loan Losses by Registrants Engaged in Lending Activities* [40, 41]
29	*Accounting for Distribution Expenses* [44]
30	*Disclosure of the Effects of Inflation and Other Changes in Prices* [4]
31	*Disclosure Requirements Concerning Changes in Accountants* [11]
32	*Statement by the Commission Regarding Disclosure Obligations of Companies Affected by the Government's Defense Contract Procurement Inquiry and Related Issues*

SEC Staff Accounting Bulletins (SABs)

No.	Title
1–38	(Superseded by SAB No. 40)

No.	Title
39	(No longer pertinent)
40	Codification of SAB Nos. 1–38 [**47**, 3, 15, 24]
41	Application of Financial Accounting and Disclosure Rules for Oil and Gas Producers [34]
42	Acquisitions Involving Financial Institutions [41]
42A	Interpretation Relating to Goodwill Amortization by Financial Institutions on Becoming SEC Registrants [41]
43	Early Adoption of ASR No. 302 [24]
44	Interpretation Regarding Implementation of ASR No. 302 [24]
45	Presentation of Pro Forma Information [27]
46	Revision of Interpretations on Interim Financial Reporting [47]
47	Oil and Gas Accounting [34]
47A	Correction of SAB No. 47
48	Transfer of Assets by Promoters and Shareholders [**20**, 25]
49	Loans to Borrowers in Countries With Liquidity Problems [40]
49A	Addition to SAB No. 49 [40]
50	Financial Statements and Industry Guide Disclosures in Filings Involving Formation of One-Bank Holding Company [40]
51	Accounting for Sales of Stock by Subsidiary [**24**, 34]
52	Accounting for Terminations of Overfunded Defined Benefit Pension Plans [16]
53	Financial Statement Requirements Where Securities are Guaranteed by Parent or Subsidiary [**24**, 25]
54	Application of "Push Down" Basis of Accounting in Financial Statements of Subsidiaries Acquired by Purchase [**23**, **24**, 25, 40, 41]
55	Allocation of Expenses and Related Disclosure in Subsidiaries' Financial Statements [**24**, 25, 27]
56	Interpretation Regarding Disclosure of Allocated Transfer Risk Reserves Mandated by Federal Banking Agencies [40]
57	Views Concerning Accounting for Contingent Warrants in Connection With Sales Agreements With Certain Major Customers [20]
58	LIFO Inventory Accounting Practices [14]
59	Views on Accounting for Noncurrent Marketable Equity Securities [**12**, 24]
60	Views Regarding Accounting for and Disclosure of Certain Financial Guarantees [**40**, **43**]
61	Adjustments of Allowances for Business Combination Loan Losses—Purchase Method Accounting [**23**, **40**]
62	Interpretations Regarding Discounting by Property-Casualty Insurers [43]
63	Views on Application of SFAS No. 68, "Research and Development Arrangements" [39]
64	Views on SAB Applicability, Common Stock Reporting, Redeemable Preferred Stock Accounting, and Issuance of Shares Prior to Initial Public Offering [20]
65	Views on ASR Nos. 130 and 135 Regarding Risk Sharing in Business Combinations Accounted for as Pooling of Interests [23]
66	Interpretations Concerning Bank Holding Company Disclosures of Foreign Loans [40]

Consolidated Bibliography

Abdel-khalik, A. Rashad.
    1983.   *Financial Reporting by Private Companies: Analysis and Diagnosis.* Research Report. Stamford, Conn.: Financial Accounting Standards Board.
    1972.   "The Efficient Market Hypothesis and Accounting Data: A Point of View." *Accounting Review.* October, pp. 791–793.

Accounting Standards Committee. 1975. *The Corporate Report.* London: The Institute of Chartered Accountants in England and Wales.

Aerospace Industries Association. 1986. *Defense Industry Initiatives on Business Ethics and Conduct.* Washington, D.C.

Altman, Edward. 1983. *Corporate Financial Distress—A Complete Guide to Predicting, Avoiding, and Dealing With Bankruptcy.* New York: John Wiley & Sons.

American Institute of Accountants (AIA). New York.
    1934a.   *Audits of Corporate Accounts.*
    1934b.   *Yearbook.* pp. 196–197.

American Institute of Certified Public Accountants (AICPA). New York.
    1988a.   *Accounting for Venture Capital Investment Companies.* Staff draft of proposed Statement of Position.
    1988b.   *Audits of Finance Companies (Including Independent and Captive Financing Activities of Other Companies).* Audit and Accounting Guide.
    1988c.   *Audits of Providers of Health Care Services.* Exposure draft of proposed Audit and Accounting Guide.
    1988d.   *Compliance Auditing: The Auditor's Responsibility for Testing Compliance With Laws, Regulations, and Contractual Terms Governing Financial Assistance Certain Entities Receive From Government.* Exposure draft of proposed Statement on Auditing Standards.
    1988e.   *Definition of Substantially the Same for Holders of Debt Instruments.* Exposure Draft of proposed Statement of Position.
    1988f.   *Directors' Examinations of Banks.* Exposure draft of proposed Statement of Position.
    1987a.   *Accounting for Frequent Travel Award Programs, Developmental and Preoperating Costs, Purchases and Exchanges of Take-off and Landing Slots, and Airframe Modifications.* Exposure draft of proposed Statement of Position.
    1987b.   *Accounting Trends and Techniques.*
    1987c.   *Audits of Government Contractors.* Exposure draft of proposed Audit and Accounting Guide.
    1987d.   *Audits of Investment Companies.* Audit and Accounting Guide.
    1987e.   *Audits of Property and Liability Insurance Companies.* Exposure draft of proposed Accounting and Audit Guide.

1987f.   *Audits of Savings and Loan Associations.* Audit and Accounting Guide. 4th revised ed.

1987g.   *Audits of Service-Center-Produced Records.* Audit and Accounting Guide.

1987h.   *Disclosure of Insurance Coverage.*

1987i.   *Examination of Management's Discussion and Analysis.* Exposure draft of proposed Statement on Standards for Attestation Engagements.

1987j.   *Guide for the Use of Real Estate Appraisal Information.* Audit and Accounting Guide.

1987k.   *Illustrations of Accounting for the Inability to Fully Recover the Carrying Amounts of Long-Lived Assets.* Financial Report Survey.

1987l.   *Report of the Task Force on Risks and Uncertainties.*

1987m.   *Report of the Task Force on the Quality of Audits of Governmental Units.*

1987n.   *Reporting on Examination of Pro Forma Adjustments.* Proposed Statement on Standards for Attestation Engagements.

1987o.   *Software Revenue Recognition.* Issues Paper.

1987p.   *The Use of Discounting in Financial Reporting for Monetary Items With Uncertain Terms Other Than Those Covered by Existing Authoritative Literature.* Issues Paper.

1986a.   *Accounting by Prepaid Health Care Plans.* Exposure draft of proposed Statement of Position.

1986b.   *Accounting for Options.* Issues Paper.

1986c.   *Auditing the Allowance for Credit Losses of Banks.* Auditing Procedure Study.

1986d.   *Auditors' Use of Microcomputers.* Auditing Procedures Study.

1986e.   *Audits of Credit Unions.* Audit and Accounting Guide.

1986f.   *Audits of Entities with Oil and Gas Producing Activities.* Audit and Accounting Guide.

1986g.   *Audits of State and Local Governmental Units.* Audit and Accounting Guide.

1986h.   *Disclosure Checklists for Banks.*

1986i.   *Division for CPA Firms SEC Practice Section SECPS Manual.*

1986j.   *Guide for Prospective Financial Statements.*

1986k.   *Issues Involving Registration Under the Investment Advisers Act of 1940.* Personal Financial Planning Practice Aid 1.

1986l.   *Other Comprehensive Bases of Accounting.* Technical Information for Practitioners Series 1.

1986m.   *Report on the Activities of the Special Investigations Committee of the SECPS* (for the period from inception through December 31, 1985).

1986n.   *Restructuring Professional Standards to Achieve Professional Excellence in a Changing Environment.*

1985a.   *Audits of Brokers and Dealers in Securities.* Audit and Accounting Guide. Revised ed.

1985b.   *Audits of Stock Life Insurance Companies.* Industry Audit Guide. 4th ed.

1985c.   *Hospital Audit Guide.* Industry Audit Guide. 5th ed.

1985d.   *Report of the Special Task Force on Audits of Repurchase Securities Transactions.*

1985e.   *Updated Illustrations of the Disclosure of Related Party Transactions.* Financial Report Survey 30.

1984a.   *Accounting for Key-Person Life Insurance.* Issues Paper.

1984b.   *Application of Concepts in FASB Statement of Financial Accounting Standards No. 71 to Emerging Issues in the Public Utility Industry.* Issues Paper.

1984c.   *Audits of Banks.* Industry Audit Guide. 2d ed.

1984d.   *Audits of Casinos.* Audit and Accounting Guide.

1984e.   *Computation of Premium Deficiencies in Insurance Enterprises.* Issues Paper.

1984f.   *Identification and Discussion of Certain Financial Accounting and Reporting Issues Concerning LIFO Inventories.* Issues Paper.

1984g.   *Illustrations of Accounting and Reporting by Development Stage Enterprises.*
            Financial Report Survey.
1984h.   *Report on the Study of EDP-Related Fraud in the Banking and Insurance Industry.*
1983a.   *Audit and Control Considerations in an On-Line Environment.* Computer Services
            Guideline.
1983b.   *Audit Sampling.* Audit and Accounting Guide.
1983c.   *Audits of Employee Benefit Plans.* Audit and Accounting Guide.
1983d.   *Audits of Government Contractors.* Industry Audit Guide. 2d ed.
1983e.   *Personal Financial Statements Guide.*
1983f.   *Report of the Special Committee on Accounting Standards Overload.* New York.
1982a.   *Accounting for Employee Capital Accumulation Plans.* Issues Paper.
1982b.   *Audits of Fire and Casualty Insurance Companies.* Industry Audit Guide. 4th ed.
1982c.   *The Acceptability of Simplified LIFO for Financial Reporting Purposes.* Issues
            Paper.
1981a.   *Audit and Control Considerations in a Minicomputer Environment.* Computer
            Services Guidelines.
1981b.   *Audits of Airlines.* Industry Audit Guide.
1981c.   *Audits of Certain Nonprofit Organizations.* Audit and Accounting Guide.
1981d.   *Construction Contractors.* Audit and Accounting Guide.
1981e.   *The Report of the Special Committee on Small and Medium Sized Firms.*
1980a.   *Accounting by Lease Brokers.* Issues Paper.
1980b.   *Accounting for the Inability to Fully Recover the Carrying Amounts of Long Lived*
            Assets. Issues Paper.
1980c.   *Accounting in Consolidation for Issuances of a Subsidiary's Stock.* Issues Paper.
1980d.   *Suggested Guidelines for CPA Participation in Bank Directors' Examinations.*
1979a.   *Accounting for Grants Received From Governments.* Issues Paper.
1979b.   *Joint Venture Accounting.* Issues Paper.
1979c.   *Report of the Special Advisory Committee on Internal Accounting Control.*
1979d.   *Report of the Special Committee on Audit Committees.*
1976.   *Report of the Committee on Generally Accepted Accounting Principles for Smaller*
            and/or Closely Held Businesses (Werner Report).
1975.   *Audits of Colleges and Universities.* Industry Audit Guide. 2d ed.
1974.   *Audits of Voluntary Health and Welfare Organizations.* Industry Audit Guide.
1973a.   *Accounting for Franchise Fee Revenue.* Accounting Guide.
1973b.   *Accounting for Profit Recognition on Sales of Real Estate.* Industry Accounting
            Guide.
1973c.   *Accounting for Retail Land Sales.* Industry Accounting Guide.
1973d.   *Report of The Study Group on Objectives of Financial Statements* (Trueblood
            Report).
1972a.   *Audits of Employee Health and Welfare Benefit Funds.* Industry Audit Guide.
1972b.   *Establishing Financial Accounting Standards* (Wheat Study).
1970.   *Basic Concepts and Accounting Principles Underlying Financial Statements of*
            Business Enterprises. Accounting Principles Board Statement No. 4.
1969a.   *Financial Statements Restated for General Price-Level Changes.* Accounting
            Principles Board Statement No. 3.
1969b.   *Report of the Committee on Education and Experience Requirements for CPAs.*
1967a.   *Disclosure of Supplemental Information by Diversified Companies.* Accounting
            Principles Board Statement No. 2.
1967b.   *Statement on Audit Committees of Boards of Directors.*
1962.   *Statement by the Accounting Principles Board.* Accounting Principles Board
            Statement No. 1.
1953.   *Review and Resume. Accounting Terminology Bulletin Number 1.*

Anthony, Robert. 1978. *Financial Accounting in Nonbusiness Organizations.* FASB Research Report. Norwalk, Conn.: FASB.

Archibald, T. Ross.
1972. "Stock Market Reaction to the Depreciation Switch-Back." *Accounting Review.* January, pp. 22–30.
1967. "The Return to Straight-Line Depreciation: An Analysis of a Change in Accounting Methods." *Emperical Research in Accounting: Selected Studies 1967,* pp. 164–180. Chicago: Institute of Professional Accounting, University of Chicago.

Arens, Alvin & Loebbecke, James.
1984. *Auditing—An Integrated Approach.* 3d ed. Englewood Cliffs, New Jersey: Prentice-Hall.
1976. *Auditing—An Integrated Approach.* Englewood Cliffs, New Jersey: Prentice-Hall.

Arkin, Herbert. 1974. *Handbook of Sampling for Auditing and Accounting.* 2d ed. New York: McGraw Hill.

Armstrong, Marshall. 1969. "Some Thoughts on Substantial Authoritative Support." *Journal of Accountancy.* April, pp. 44–50.

Beaver, William & Landsman, Wayne. 1983. *Incremental Information Content of Statement 33 Disclosures.* Research Report. Norwalk, Conn.: FASB.

————— & Rappaport, Alfred. 1984. "Financial Reporting Needs More Than the Computer." *Business Week.* August 13, p. 16.

Blish, Eugene. 1978. "Computer Abuse: A Practical Use of the AICPA Guide." *EDPACS* ("The EDP Audit, Control and Security Newsletter"). September, pp. 6–12.

Canning, John. 1929. *The Economics of Accounting.* Reprint. New York: Arno Press, 1978.

Chatfield, Michael. 1977. *A History of Accounting Thought.* Huntington, NY: Robert E. Krieger Publishing Co.

Commerce Clearing House, Inc. *SEC Accounting Rules.* Updated continuously. Chicago.

Commission on Auditors' Responsibilities (CAR).
1978. *Report, Conclusions, and Recommendations.* New York: AICPA.
1977. *Report of Tentative Conclusions.* New York: AICPA.

Directors and Boards. 1984. "Profile of 50 Audit Committees." Fall, pp. 41–44.

Evans, Thomas & Doupnik, Timothy.
1986a. *Determining the Functional Currency Under Statement 52.* Research Report. Norwalk, Conn.: FASB.
1986b. *Foreign Exchange Risk Management Under Statement 52.* Research Report. Norwalk, Conn.: FASB.

—————; Taylor, Martin & Holzmann, Oscar. 1985. *International Accounting and Reporting.* New York: Macmillan Publishing Co.

Federal Contracts Report. 1988. Vol. 49, p. 849, April 25. Washington, D.C.: Bureau of National Affairs, Inc.

Financial Accounting Foundation (FAF). Norwalk, Conn.
1986. *Report of the Special Committee to the Board of Trustees Financial Accounting Foundation.*
1984. *Agreement Concerning the Structure for a Governmental Accounting Standards Board.*
1982. *Operating Efficiency of the FASB.*

CONSOLIDATED BIBLIOGRAPHY

B-5

Financial Accounting Standards Board (FASB). Norwalk, Conn.

1988a. *Deferral of the Effective Date of Recognition of Depreciation by Not-for-Profit Organizations.* Exposure draft of SFAS.

1988b. *Definition of a Right of Setoff.* Proposed Technical Bulletin 88-a.

1988c. *Guide to Implementation of Statement 88 on Employers' Accounting for Settlements and Curtailments of Defined Benefit Pension Plans.*

1988d. *Issues Relating to Accounting for Leases.* Proposed Technical Bulletin 88-b.

1988e. *Regulated Enterprises—Accounting for the Discontinuation of Application of FASB Statement No. 71.* Exposure draft of SFAS.

1987a. *Disclosures About Financial Instruments.* Exposure draft of SFAS.

1987b. *Facts About FASB, 1987.*

1987c. *Guide to Implementation of Statement 91 on Accounting for Nonrefundable Fees and Costs Associated With Originating or Acquiring Loans and Initial Direct Costs of Leases.*

1987d. *Illustrations of Accounting for Pensions and for Settlements and Curtailments of Defined Benefit Pension Plans.*

1987e. *Rules of Procedure.*

1986a. *Accounting for Income Taxes.* Exposure draft of SFAS.

1986b. *Guide to Implementation of Statement 87 on Employers' Accounting for Pensions.*

1985. *Elements of Financial Statements.* Statement of Financial Accounting Concepts No. 6.

1984a. *Accounting for Compensation Plans Involving Certain Rights Granted to Employees.* Invitation to Comment.

1984b. *Financial Reporting and Changing Prices: Current Cost Information.* Exposure Draft of SFAS.

1984c. *Recognition and Measurement in Financial Statements of Business Enterprises.* Statement of Financial Accounting Concepts No. 5.

1983a. *Accounting for Income Taxes.* Discussion Memorandum.

1983b. "Board Responds to Concerns About Standards Overload." *Status Report.* No. 150.

1983c. *Financial Reporting by Privately Owned Companies; Summary of Responses to FASB Invitation to Comment.*

1983d. *Supplementary Disclosures About the Effects of Changing Prices.* Invitation to Comment.

1982. *Accounting for the Sale or Purchase of Tax Benefits Through Tax Leases.* Exposure draft of SFAS (revised).

1981a. *Accounting for the Sale or Purchase of Tax Benefits Through Tax Leases.* Exposure draft of SFAS.

1981b. *Financial Reporting by Private and Small Public Companies.* Invitation to Comment.

1980a. *Elements of Financial Statements of Business Enterprises.* Statement of Financial Accounting Concepts No. 3.

1980b. *Financial Statements and Other Means of Financial Reporting.* Invitation to Comment.

1980c. *Objectives of Financial Reporting by Nonbusiness Organizations.* Statement of Financial Accounting Concepts No. 4.

1980d. *Qualitative Characteristics of Accounting Information.* Statement of Financial Accounting Concepts No. 2.

1979. *Effect of Rate Regulation on Accounting for Regulated Enterprises.* Discussion Memorandum.

1978a. *Accounting for Certain Service Transactions.* Invitation to Comment.

1978b. *An Analysis of Issues Related to Interim Financial Accounting and Reporting.* Discussion Memorandum.

1978c.   *Objectives of Financial Reporting by Business Enterprises.* Statement of Financial Accounting Concepts No. 1.

1977.   *Accounting for Interest Costs.* Discussion Memorandum.

1976.   *Financial Accounting and Reporting in the Extractive Industries.* Discussion Memorandum.

1973.   *Accounting for Research and Development and Similar Costs.* Discussion Memorandum.

Financial Executives Institute (FEI). 1986. *Survey on Unusual Charges.* Committee on Corporate Reporting Study. Morristown, New Jersey.

Financial Executives Research Foundation. 1984. *Funds Flow.* Morristown, New Jersey.

Gale, Andrew. 1985. "Data Bases: An Accountant's Choice." *Journal of Accountancy.* December, pp. 111–112.

Goodfellow, James; Loebbecke, James & Neter, John. 1974. "Some Perspectives on CAV Sampling Plans." *Canadian Chartered Accountant.* (Part I) October, pp. 22–30, (Part II) November pp. 46–53.

Gormley, R. James. 1980. "Professional Risks in Purchase Audits and Reviews." *Journal of Accounting, Auditing, and Finance.* Summer, pp. 293–312.

Governmental Accounting Standards Board (GASB). Norwalk, Conn.

1988.   *An Analysis of Issues Relating to the Financial Reporting Entity.* Discussion Memorandum.

1987a.   *Accounting and Financial Reporting for Capital Assets of Governmental Entities.* Discussion Memorandum.

1987b.   *Accounting and Financial Reporting for Risk Management Activities.* Discussion Memorandum.

1987c.   *Measurement Focus and Basis of Accounting—Governmental Funds.* Exposure draft of SGAS.

1985.   *Measurement Focus and Basis of Accounting—Governmental Funds.* Discussion Memorandum.

Glodwasser, Dan. 1986. "Liability Pitfalls in Personal Financial Planning Engagements." *Personal Financial Planning.* June, pp. 118–121.

Government Finance Officers Association (GFOA). 1988. *Governmental Accounting, Auditing, and Financial Reporting* (GAAFR). (Blue Book.) Chicago.

Grady, Paul. 1965. *Inventory of Generally Accepted Accounting Principles for Business Enterprises.* Accounting Research Study No. 7. New York: AICPA.

Griffin, Paul. 1987. *Usefulness to Investors and Creditors of Information Provided by Financial Reporting.* Research Report. 2d ed. Norwalk, Conn.: FASB.

_____ & Castanias, Richard. 1987. *Accounting for the Translation of Foreign Currencies: The Effects of Statement 52 on Equity Analysts.* Research Report. Norwalk, Conn.: FASB.

Hand, Learned. 1947. "Thomas Walter Swann." Vol. 57. *Yale Law Journal.* p.167.

Hays, William. 1973. *Statistics for the Social Sciences.* 2d ed. New York: Holt, Rinehart & Winston.

Hicks, John. 1946. *Value and Capital.* 2d ed. Fairlawn, New Jersey: Oxford University Press.

Ijiri, Yuri. 1980. *Recognition of Contractual Rights and Obligations: An Exploratory Study of Conceptual Issues.* Research Report. Norwalk, Conn.: FASB.

Institute of Internal Auditors (IIA). 1978. *Standards for the Professional Practice of Internal Auditing.* Altamonte Springs, Fla.

Internal Revenue Service. *Internal Revenue Manual*. Updated continuously. Chicago: Commerce Clearing House.

International Accounting Standards Committee (IASC). London.
1987.   *Consolidated Financial Statements and Accounting for Investments in Subsidiaries.* Exposure draft of proposed Statement.
1986.   *Accounting for Investments in Associates and Joint Ventures.* Exposure draft of proposed Statement.

Jaenicke, Henry. 1981. *Survey of Present Practices in Recognizing Revenues, Expenses, Gains, and Losses*. Research Report. Norwalk, Conn.: FASB.

Jennings, Alvin. 1958. "Present Day Challenges in Financial Reporting." *Journal of Accountancy*. January, pp. 28–34.

Johnson, L. Todd & Story, Reed. 1982. *Recognition in Financial Statements: Underlying Concepts and Practical Conventions*. Research Report. Norwalk, Conn.: FASB.

Kohler, Eric. 1983. *A Dictionary for Accountants*. 6th ed. Englewood Cliffs, New Jersey: Prentice-Hall.

Louis Harris and Associates, Inc. 1985. *A Study of the Attitudes Toward and an Assessment of the Financial Accounting Standards Board*. Norwalk, Conn.: Financial Accounting Foundation.

Mair, William; Wood, Donald & Davis, Keagle. 1976. *Computer Control and Audit*. 2d ed. Altamonte Springs, Fla.: The Institute of Internal Auditors.

Martin, James. 1973. *Security, Accuracy, and Privacy in Computer Systems*. Englewood Cliffs, New Jersey: Prentice-Hall.

Mautz, Robert & Neumann, Fred.
1977.   *Corporate Audit Committees:* Policies and Practices. Cleveland, Ohio: Ernst & Whinney.
1970.   *Corporate Audit Committees*. Urbana, Ill.: University of Illinois Press.
_____ & Sharaf, Hussein. 1961. *The Philosophy of Auditing*. American Accounting Association Monograph No. 6. Sarasota, Fla.: American Accounting Association.

McCallion, Anne. 1986. "Computer Software: Guidance on Applying Statement 86." *Highlights of Financial Reporting Issues*. February. Norwalk, Conn.: FASB.

Moonitz, Maurice. 1962. *The Basic Postulates of Accounting*. Accounting Research Study No. 1. New York: AICPA.

National Association of Insurance Commissioners (NAIC). Milwaukee, Wis.
1980.   *Accounting Practices and Procedures for Fire and Casualty Insurance Companies.*
1979.   *Accounting Practices and Procedures for Life and Accident and Health Insurance Companies.*
1976.   *Examiners Handbook.*

National Association of Real Estate Investment Trusts. 1987. *REIT Fact Book, 1986*. Washington, D.C.

National Commission on Fraudulent Financial Reporting (NCFFR). 1987. *Report of the National Commission on Fraudulent Financial Reporting*. New York: AICPA.

National Health Council, Inc. 1974. *Standards of Accounting and Financial Reporting for Voluntary Health and Welfare Organizations*. New York.

Neter, John & Loebbecke, James. 1975. *Behavior of Major Statistical Estimates on Sampling Accounting Populations*. Auditing Research Monograph No. 2. New York: AICPA.

New York Stock Exchange (NYSE). New York.
1987.   *Fact Book 1987.*

1973.   *Recommendations and Comments on Financial Reporting to Shareholders and Related Matters: A White Paper.*

1939.   *Report of Subcommittee on Independent Audits and Audit Procedures of Committee on Stock Lists.*

Office of Comptroller of the Currency (OCC). 1972. *Duties and Liabilities of Directors of National Banks.* Washington, D.C.: U.S. Government Printing Office.

Paton, William & Littleton, A.C. 1940. *An Introduction to Corporate Accounting Standards.* Sarasota, Fla.: American Accounting Association.

Poloway, Morton, 1988. *Accountants SEC Practice Manual.* Chicago: Commerce Clearing House, Inc.

President's Blue Ribbon Commission on Defense Management (Packard Commission). 1986. *Final Report by the President's Blue Ribbon Commission on Defense Management.* Washington, D.C.

Public Oversight Board (POB). New York: AICPA.

1987.   *Annual Report 1986-1987.*

1986.   *Public Perceptions of Management Advisory Services Performed by CPA Firms for Audit Clients.*

1979.   *Scope of Services by CPA Firms.*

Reagan, Ronald. 1987. *Journal of Accountancy.* May 1987, p.11.

Roberts, Donald. 1978. *Statistical Auditing.* New York: AICPA.

Robertson, Wynham. 1975. "How the Bankers Got Trapped in the REIT Disaster." *Fortune.* March, pp. 113–115f.

Ronen, Joshua & Sorter, George. 1972. "Relevant Accounting." *Journal of Business.* April, pp. 258–282.

Sanders, Thomas; Hatfield, Henry & Moore, Underhill. 1938. *A Statement of Accounting Principles.* New York: American Institute of Accountants.

Securities and Exchange Commission (SEC). Washington, D.C.: U.S. Government Printing Office.

1987.   *Q & A: Small Business and the SEC.*

1977.   Report of the Advisory Committee on Corporate Disclosure.

Sorter, George, 1986. "Accounting for Baseball." *Journal of Accountancy.* June, pp. 126–133.

Sprouse, Robert & Moonitz, Maurice. 1962. *A Tentative Set of Broad Accounting Principles For Business Enterprises.* Accounting Research Study No. 3. New York: AICPA.

Touche Ross & Co.

1986.   *Economics of Retail Store Credit—1986.* New York: National Retail Merchants Association.

1984.   *Touche Ross Guide to Granting Credit to Contractors.* Englewood Cliffs, New Jersey: Prentice-Hall.

U.S. Congress, Senate Subcommittee on Reports, Accounting and Management of the Committee on Government Operations. 1976. *The Accounting Establishment, A Staff Study.* Washington, D.C.: U.S. Government Printing Office.

U.S. Department of Health and Human Services—Health Care Financing Administration. *The Provider Reimbursement Manual* (HIM-15). Updated continuously. Chicago: Commerce Clearing House, Inc.

U.S. General Accounting Office (GAO). 1988. *Standards for Audit of Governmental Organizations, Programs, Activities, and Functions* (Revised). Washington, D.C.: U.S. Government Printing Office.

U.S. Treasury Department. *Regulations Governing the Practice of Attorneys, Certified Public Accountants, Enrolled Agents, and Enrolled Actuaries Before the Internal Revenue Service.* Circular No. 230 (Revised September, 1985). Washington, D.C.: U.S. Government Printing Office.

Wishon, Keith. 1985. "Futures Contracts: Guidance on Applying Statement 80. *Highlights of Financial Reporting Issues.* Norwalk, Conn.: FASB.

_____ & Chevalier, Lorin. 1985. "Interest Rate Swaps – Your Rate or Mine?" *Journal of Accountancy.* September, pp. 63–84.

Wyatt, Arthur. 1963. *A Critical Study of Accounting for Business Combinations.* Accounting Research Study No. 5. New York: AICPA.

Index

[Chapter numbers are boldface and are followed by a hyphen; lightface numbers after the hyphen refer to pages within the chapter.]